INTERNATIONAL ARBITRATION

ASPEN CASEBOOK SERIES

INTERNATIONAL ARBITRATION

Cases and Materials

Second Edition

Gary B. Born

Published by Wolters Kluwer in New York.

Wolters Kluwer serves customers worldwide with CCH, Aspen Publishers, and Kluwer Law International products. (www.wolterskluwerlb.com)

To contact Customer Service, e-mail customer.service@wolterskluwer.com, call 1-800-234-1660, fax 1-800-901-9075, or mail correspondence to:

> Wolters Kluwer
> Attn: Order Department
> PO Box 990
> Frederick, MD 21705

Printed in the United States of America.

3 4 5 6 7 8 9 0

ISBN 978-1-4548-3920-0 (Casebound)
ISBN 978-1-4548-4802-8 (Loose Leaf)

Library of Congress Cataloging-in-Publication Data

Born, Gary, 1955- author.
  International arbitration: cases and materials / Gary B. Born. — Second Edition.
     pages cm.—(Aspen casebook series)
  Includes bibliographical references and index.
  ISBN 978-1-4548-3920-0 (alk. paper)
1. International commercial arbitration. I. Title.
  K2400.B672 2015
  341.5'22—dc23
                                2014044833

About Wolters Kluwer Law & Business

Wolters Kluwer Law & Business is a leading global provider of intelligent information and digital solutions for legal and business professionals in key specialty areas, and respected educational resources for professors and law students. Wolters Kluwer Law & Business connects legal and business professionals as well as those in the education market with timely, specialized authoritative content and information-enabled solutions to support success through productivity, accuracy and mobility.

Serving customers worldwide, Wolters Kluwer Law & Business products include those under the Aspen Publishers, CCH, Kluwer Law International, Loislaw, ftwilliam.com and MediRegs family of products.

CCH products have been a trusted resource since 1913, and are highly regarded resources for legal, securities, antitrust and trade regulation, government contracting, banking, pension, payroll, employment and labor, and healthcare reimbursement and compliance professionals.

Aspen Publishers products provide essential information to attorneys, business professionals and law students. Written by preeminent authorities, the product line offers analytical and practical information in a range of specialty practice areas from securities law and intellectual property to mergers and acquisitions and pension/benefits. Aspen's trusted legal education resources provide professors and students with high-quality, up-to-date and effective resources for successful instruction and study in all areas of the law.

Kluwer Law International products provide the global business community with reliable international legal information in English. Legal practitioners, corporate counsel and business executives around the world rely on Kluwer Law journals, looseleafs, books, and electronic products for comprehensive information in many areas of international legal practice.

Loislaw is a comprehensive online legal research product providing legal content to law firm practitioners of various specializations. Loislaw provides attorneys with the ability to quickly and efficiently find the necessary legal information they need, when and where they need it, by facilitating access to primary law as well as state-specific law, records, forms and treatises.

ftwilliam.com offers employee benefits professionals the highest quality plan documents (retirement, welfare and non-qualified) and government forms (5500/PBGC, 1099 and IRS) software at highly competitive prices.

MediRegs products provide integrated health care compliance content and software solutions for professionals in healthcare, higher education and life sciences, including professionals in accounting, law and consulting.

Wolters Kluwer Law & Business, a division of Wolters Kluwer, is headquartered in New York. Wolters Kluwer is a market-leading global information services company focused on professionals.

ABOUT THE AUTHOR

Gary B. Born is the world's leading authority on international commercial arbitration and international litigation. He is the author of numerous works on these subjects, including *International Commercial Arbitration* (2d ed. 2014), *International Arbitration and Forum Selection Agreements: Drafting and Enforcing* (4th ed. 2013), *International Arbitration: Law and Practice* (2012), *International Civil Litigation in United States Courts* (5th ed. 2011) and *International Commercial Arbitration: Commentary and Materials* (2d ed. 2001). Mr. Born has been practicing for over thirty years in the fields of international arbitration and litigation in Europe, the United States, Asia and elsewhere.

Clyde Raymond and Eleanor Juan Born
In Memory

SUMMARY OF CONTENTS

TABLE OF CONTENTS

PART I

INTERNATIONAL ARBITRATION AGREEMENTS

PART II

INTERNATIONAL ARBITRATION PROCEEDINGS

CHAPTER 8
SELECTION, CHALLENGE AND REPLACEMENT OF ARBITRATORS IN INTERNATIONAL ARBITRATION **671**

PART III

INTERNATIONAL ARBITRAL AWARDS

CHAPTER 16

PREFACE TO SECOND EDITION

This casebook aspires to provide an introduction to the contemporary constitutional structure, law, practice and policy of international arbitration. It aims to do so from an international perspective, focusing on international instruments, authorities and solutions, rather than on materials drawn from any single jurisdiction. The casebook also endeavors to examine all forms of international arbitration—including the arbitration of international commercial disputes, on which it focuses, as well as investor-state and inter-state (or state-to-state) disputes.

The materials in the second edition of this casebook are drawn principally from the legal framework established for international commercial arbitration by contemporary international arbitration conventions, legislation and institutional rules. The book focuses in particular on the United Nations Convention on the Recognition and Enforcement of Foreign Arbitral Awards (the "New York Convention"), the UNCITRAL Model Law on International Commercial Arbitration (the "UNCITRAL Model Law") and leading institutional arbitration rules (including the UNCITRAL Arbitration Rules). The book also examines the Convention on the Settlement of Investment Disputes between States and Nationals of Other States (the "ICSID Convention"), the 1907 Hague Convention for the Pacific Settlement of International Disputes (the "1907 Hague Convention") and other materials addressing the use of international arbitration to resolve investment and inter-state disputes.

Why does international arbitration merit study? International arbitration warrants attention, if for nothing else, because of its historic, contemporary and future practical importance, particularly in business affairs. For centuries, businesses, states and individuals have used arbitration as a preferred mechanism for resolving their international disputes, a preference which has become even more pronounced in the past several decades as international trade and investment have burgeoned. As both international commerce and governmental activities have expanded and become more complex, so too has their primary dispute resolution mechanism—international arbitration.[1] The practical importance of international arbitration is one reason that the subject warrants study by companies, lawyers, arbitrators, judges, legislators and law students.

At a more fundamental level, international arbitration merits study because it illustrates the complexities and uncertainties of contemporary international society—legal, commercial and cultural—while providing a highly-sophisticated and effective means of dealing with those complexities in a predictable and uniform manner. Beyond its immediate practical importance, international arbitration is worthy of attention because it operates within a framework of international legal rules and institutions which—with remarkable and enduring success—provide a fair, neutral, expert and efficient means of resolving difficult and contentious transnational problems. This framework enables private and public actors from diverse jurisdictions to cooperatively resolve deep-seated and complex international disputes in a neutral, durable and satisfactory manner. At their best, the analyses and mechanisms which have been developed in the context of international arbitration offer models, insights and promise for other aspects of international affairs.

As the materials excerpted in this casebook illustrate, the legal rules and institutions relevant to international commercial arbitration have evolved over time, in multiple and diverse countries, legal systems and settings. As a rule, where totalitarian regimes or tyrants have held sway, arbitration—like other expressions of private autonomy and association—has been repressed or pro-

---

1. The popularity of international commercial arbitration as a means of dispute resolution is discussed below. *See infra* pp. 33-39, 44-67, 99-114.

hibited; where societies have been free, both politically and economically, arbitration has flourished.

Despite periodic episodes of political hostility, the past half-century has witnessed the progressive development and expansion of the legal framework for international commercial arbitration, almost always through the collaborative efforts of public and private actors. While the latter have supplied the driving and dominant force for the successful development and use of international commercial arbitration, governments and courts from leading trading nations have contributed materially, by ensuring the recognition and enforceability of private arbitration agreements and arbitral awards, and affirming principles of party autonomy and judicial non-interference in the arbitral process, and limited judicial support for the arbitral process (*i.e.*, in granting provisional measures and taking evidence in aid of arbitration).

In recent decades, the resulting legal framework for international arbitration has achieved progressively greater practical success and acceptance in all regions of the world and most political quarters. The striking success of international arbitration is reflected in part in the increasing number of international (and domestic) arbitrations conducted each year, under both institutional auspices and otherwise,[2] the growing use of arbitration clauses in almost all forms of international contracts,[3] the preferences of business users for arbitration as a mode of dispute resolution,[4] the widespread adoption of pro-arbitration international arbitration conventions and national arbitration statutes,[5] the refinement of institutional arbitration rules to correct deficiencies in the arbitral process[6] and the use of arbitral procedures to resolve new categories of disputes which were not previously subject to arbitration (*e.g.*, investor-state, competition, securities, intellectual property, corruption, human rights and taxation disputes).[7]

The success of international arbitration is also reflected in a comparison between the treatment of complex commercial disputes in international arbitration and in national courts, where disputes over service of process, jurisdiction, forum selection and *lis pendens*, taking of evidence, choice of law, state or sovereign immunity, neutrality of litigation procedures and decision-makers, and recognition of judgments are endemic and result in significant uncertainty and inefficiency.[8] Equally, the litigation procedures used in national courts are often ill-suited for both the resolution of international commercial disputes and the tailoring of procedures to particular parties and disputes. In all of these respects, international arbitration typically offers a simpler, more effective and more competent means of dispute resolution, tailored to the needs of business users and modern commercial communities—and thus, again, warrants careful study by students of international affairs.

This casebook begins with an Introduction, in Chapter 1, of the subject of international commercial arbitration. This introduction includes an historical summary, as well as an overview of the legal framework governing international arbitration agreements and the principal elements of such agreements. Chapter 1 also introduces the primary sources relevant to the study of international commercial arbitration. The remainder of the casebook is divided into three general Parts.

---

2. *See infra* p. 114.

3. *See infra* pp. 99-104, 106-108, 114.

4. *See infra* pp. 106-08.

5. *See infra* pp. 33-39, 46-67.

6. *See infra* pp. 75-84.

7. *See infra* pp. 475-516.

8. The persistence and complexity of such disputes are beyond the scope of this work. They are discussed in G. Born & P. Rutledge, *International Civil Litigation in United States Courts* (5th ed. 2011); L. Collins (ed.), *Dicey Morris & Collins on The Conflict of Laws* (15th ed. 2012); R. Geimer, *Internationales Zivilprozessrecht* (5th ed. 2005).

The first Part of the casebook deals with international arbitration agreements, which are addressed in Chapters 2 to 6. These chapters describe the legal framework applicable to such agreements (Chapter 2), the presumptive separability or autonomy of international arbitration agreements (Chapter 3), the law governing international arbitration agreements (Chapter 3), the competence-competence doctrine (Chapter 3), the substantive and formal rules of validity relating to such agreements (Chapter 4), the interpretation of arbitration agreements (Chapter 5) and the issues related to identifying the parties to international arbitration agreements (Chapter 6).

The second Part of the casebook deals with international arbitration proceedings, which are addressed in Chapters 7 to 13. These chapters consider the legal framework applicable to such proceedings (Chapter 7), the selection of the arbitral seat (Chapter 7), the selection and challenge of arbitrators (Chapter 8), the conduct of the arbitration and arbitral procedures (Chapter 9), disclosure or discovery (Chapter 9), confidentiality (Chapter 9), provisional measures (Chapter 10), consolidation and joinder (Chapter 11), the selection of substantive law (Chapter 12) and legal representation and ethics (Chapter 13).

The third and final Part of the casebook deals with international arbitral awards, which are addressed in Chapters 14 to 16. These chapters examine the legal framework for international arbitral awards (Chapter 14), the form and contents of such awards (Chapter 14), the correction and interpretation of arbitral awards (Chapter 14), actions to annul or vacate arbitral awards (Chapter 15) and the recognition and enforcement of international arbitral awards (Chapter 16).

The focus of this casebook, in all three parts, is on international standards and practices, rather than on a single national legal system. Particular attention is devoted to the leading international arbitration conventions and the foundation they establish for the contemporary international arbitral process. These conventions include the New York Convention, the ICSID Convention and, although of more limited contemporary relevance, the 1907 Hague Convention for the Pacific Settlement of International Disputes. Identifying and refining the limits imposed by the foundational framework they establish is a central aspiration of this casebook.

This casebook also devotes substantial attention to contemporary national arbitration legislation—including the UNCITRAL Model Law and the arbitration statutes enacted in leading arbitral centers (including the United States, France, Switzerland, England, Singapore, Hong Kong and elsewhere). Here again, the book's focus is expressly international, concentrating on how both developed and other jurisdictions around the world give effect to the New York Convention and to international arbitration agreements and arbitral awards.

This casebook also focuses on the most commonly-used institutional arbitration rules, particularly those adopted by the International Chamber of Commerce ("ICC"), the American Arbitration Association's International Centre for Dispute Resolution ("ICDR"), the London Court of International Arbitration ("LCIA"), the International Centre for Settlement of Investment Disputes ("ICSID"), the Singapore International Arbitration Centre ("SIAC"), as well as the UNCITRAL Rules. Together with the contractual terms of parties' individual arbitration agreements, these rules reflect the efforts of private parties and states to devise the most efficient, neutral and objective means for resolving international disputes in a final and binding manner. These various contractual mechanisms constitute the essence of the international arbitral process, which is then given effect by international arbitration conventions and national arbitration legislation.

This casebook's international and comparative focus rests on the premise that the treatments of international commercial arbitration in different national legal systems are not diverse, unrelated phenomena, but rather form a common corpus of international arbitration law which has global application and importance. From this perspective, the analysis and conclusions of a court in one jurisdiction (*e.g.*, France, the United States, Switzerland, India, Singapore, England, or Hong Kong) regarding international arbitration agreements, proceedings, or awards have direct and material relevance to similar issues in other jurisdictions.

That conclusion is true both descriptively and prescriptively. In practice, on issues ranging from the definition of arbitration, to the separability presumption, the competence-competence doctrine, the interpretation of arbitration agreements, choice-of-law analysis, nonarbitrability, the role of courts in supporting the arbitral process the principles of judicial non-interference in the arbitral process, the immunities of arbitrators and the recognition and enforcement of arbitral awards, decisions in individual national courts have drawn upon and developed a common body of international arbitration law. Guided by the constitutional principles of the New York Convention, legislatures and courts in Contracting States around the world have in practice looked to and relied upon one another's decisions, and commentary on international arbitration, formulating and progressively refining legal frameworks of national law with the objective of ensuring the effective enforcement of international arbitration agreements and awards.

More fundamentally, national courts not only have but should consider one another's decisions in resolving issues concerning international arbitration. By considering the treatment of international arbitration in other jurisdictions, and the policies which inspire that treatment, national legislatures and courts can draw guidance for resolving comparable problems. Indeed, only by taking into account how the various aspects of the international arbitral process are analyzed and regulated in different jurisdictions is it possible for courts in any particular state to play their optimal role in that process. This involves considerations of uniformity, where the harmonization of national laws in different jurisdictions can produce fairer and more efficient results. Equally, this involves the ongoing reform of the legal frameworks for international arbitration, where national courts and legislatures progressively and cooperatively develop superior solutions to the problems that arise in the arbitral process.

This casebook explores the resulting legal framework for international arbitration—in the context of commercial, as well as investment and inter-state, disputes. It endeavors to do so in the same manner that this legal framework has been developed—by examining both international instruments and legislation, rules, authorities, and critiques from all leading jurisdictions, without preference for any particular jurisdiction, and by considering how these different sources have contributed towards the development of the contemporary law and practice of international arbitration. At the same time, the book suggests prescriptive solutions to the challenges of international dispute resolution, again, without preference for the approach of any particular jurisdiction.

The two editions of this book would not have been possible without able assistance and comments from colleagues, friends and competitors from around the world. In particular, Elke Jenner's exceptional secretarial and organizational talents, as well as the able assistance of Barbara Bozward and Katrin Frach, were invaluable. Very helpful research and other assistance was provided by Suzanne Spears, Kenneth Beale and Dr. Maxi Scherer, as well as by Sarah Ganslein and Nausheen Rahman. Numerous invaluable contributions to the second edition were made by Marc Lee, assisted by Olga Besperstova. All mistakes are of course mine alone.

Like international arbitration itself, this casebook is a work in progress. It is the successor to two earlier editions, addressing a complex field that is continuously evolving in response to changing conditions and needs. The casebook inevitably contains errors, omissions and confusions, which will require correction, clarification and further development in future editions, to keep pace with the field. Corrections, comments and questions are encouraged, by email to gary.born@kluwerlaw.com.

Gary B. Born
London, England

December 2014

ACKNOWLEDGMENTS

Excerpts from the following materials appear with the kind permission of the copyright holders:

Books and Articles

Arnaldez, Jean-Jacques, Derains, Yves & Hascher, Dominique (eds.), COLLECTION OF ICC ARBITRAL AWARDS 1996-2000. Copyright © Kluwer Law International, 2003.

Berger, Klaus Peter, LAW AND PRACTICE OF ESCALATION CLAUSES, 22(1) Arbitration International 2006, pp. 1-17. Copyright © Kluwer Law International, 2010.

Berger, Klaus Peter, THE INTERNATIONAL ARBITRATORS' APPLICATION OF PRECEDENTS, 9(4) *Journal of International Arbitration* 1992, pp. 5-22. Copyright © Kluwer Law International, 2010.

Bernini, Giorgio, REPORT ON NEUTRALITY, IMPARTIALITY AND INDEPENDENCE, originally published in International Chamber of Commerce (ICC) (ed.), The Arbitral Process and the Independence of Arbitrators. Copyright © ICC, 1991. ICC publications are available from www.storeiccwbo.org. Key ICC dispute resolution titles are also available at www.iccdrl.com.

Born, Gary, INTERNATIONAL COMMERCIAL ARBITRATION. Copyright © Kluwer Law International, 2014.

Buehring-Uhle, Christian, A SURVEY ON ARBITRATION AND SETTLEMENT IN INTERNATIONAL BUSINESS DISPUTES, in Drahozal, Christopher & Naimark, Richard (eds.), *Towards A Science of International Arbitration: Collected Empirical Research.* Copyright © Kluwer Law International, 2005.

Carter, James H., THE RIGHTS AND DUTIES OF THE ARBITRATOR: SIX ASPECTS OF THE RULE OF REASONABLENESS, originally published in ICC (ed.), The Status of the Arbitrator 24, 31 ICC Ct. Bull. Spec. Supp. (1995). Copyright © ICC, 1995. ICC publications are available from www.storeiccwbo.org. Key ICC dispute resolution titles are also available at www.iccdrl.com.

Craig, William Laurence, USES AND ABUSES OF APPEAL FROM AWARDS, 4(3) *Arbitration International* 1988, pp. 174-227. Copyright © Kluwer Law International, 2010.

District of Columbia (D.C.) Bar, DISTRICT OF COLUMBIA BAR OPINION 79 (1979), Code of Professional Responsibility and Opinions of the D.C. Bar Legal Ethics Committee 138 (1991). Reprinted with the permission of the D.C. Bar.

Ehrenhaft, Peter, DISCOVERY IN INTERNATIONAL ARBITRATION PROCEEDINGS, 42 Private Investors Abroad 1 (2000). Copyright © Peter Ehrenhaft, 2000.

Gaillard, Emmanuel & Savage, John (eds.), FOUCHARD GAILLARD GOLDMAN ON INTERNATIONAL COMMERCIAL ARBITRATION. Copyright © Kluwer Law International, 1999.

Glosser, Ottoarndt, SOCIOLOGICAL ASPECTS OF INTERNATIONAL COMMERCIAL ARBITRATION, in Sanders, Pieter (ed.), *The Art of Arbitration: Essays on International Arbitration Liber Amicorum*, pp. 144-146. Copyright © Kluwer Law International, 1982.

Hascher, Dominique T., NOTE—SENTENCE ARBITRALE AD HOC RENDUE À LAUSANNE 18 NOVEMBRE 1983—BENTELER ET AUTRES V. ETAT BELGE, *Revue de l'Arbitrage*, Volume 1989 Issue 2 (Comité Français de l'Arbitrage), pp. 339-352. Copyright © Kluwer Law International, 2010.

Houtte, Hans van, COUNSEL—WITNESS RELATIONS AND PROFESSIONAL MISCONDUCT IN CIVIL LAW SYSTEMS, 19(4) *Arbitration International* 2003, pp. 457-463. Copyright © Kluwer Law International, 2010.

Jayakumar, S. (former Singapore Minister for Law), SECOND READING SPEECH ON LEGAL PROFESSION (AMENDMENT) BILL, Singapore Parliament Report, Volume No. 78, Column Nos. 96-97, Sitting Date: 15 June 2004. Copyright © Singapore Parliament, 2004.

Kerr, Michael, ARBITRATION AND THE COURTS: THE UNCITRAL MODEL LAW, 34(1) Int'l & Comp. L.Q. 1 (1985). Copyright © Cambridge University Press, 1985.

Transparency International, GLOBAL CORRUPTION BAROMETER 2013. © Transparency International. All Rights Reserved. For more information, visit http://www.transparency.org.

Le Monde, SEVERE SENTENCES FOR A BOGUS "ARBITRATION" (July 5, 1988). Copyright © Le Monde, 1988.

Lowenfeld, Andreas F., THE MITSUBISHI CASE: ANOTHER VIEW, 2(3) *Arbitration International* 1986, pp. 178-190. Copyright © Kluwer Law International, 2010.

Park, William W., JUDICIAL CONTROLS IN THE ARBITRAL PROCESS, 5(3) *Arbitration International* 1989, pp. 230-279. Copyright © Kluwer Law International, 2010.

Queen Mary, University of London, 2013 International Arbitration Survey: Corporate Choices in International Arbitration. Copyright © PwC, 2013

Schlosser, Peter, THE DECISION OF 27 FEBRUARY 1970 OF THE FEDERAL SUPREME COURT OF THE FEDERAL REPUBLIC OF GERMANY (BUNDESGERICHTSHOF), 6(1) *Arbitration International* 1990, pp. 79-88. Copyright © Kluwer Law International, 2010.

Werner, Jacques, A SWISS COMMENT ON MITSUBISHI, 3(4) *Journal of International Arbitration* 1986, pp. 81-84. Copyright © Kluwer Law International, 2010.

Arbitral Awards and Procedural Orders

AD HOC AWARD IN STATE OF KUWAIT V. AMERICAN INDEPENDENT OIL COMPANY, 21 I.L.M. 976 (1982). Copyright © American Society of International Law, 1982.

ADF GROUP INC. V. UNITED STATES OF AMERICA, Procedural Order No. 2 Concerning the Place of Arbitration (11 July 2001) of ICSID Case No. ARB(AF)/00/1. Reprinted with the permission of the World Bank.

AWARD IN ICC CASE NO. 4491, in Arnaldez, Jean-Jacques, Derains, Yves & Hascher, Dominique (eds.), *Collection of Procedural Decisions in ICC Arbitration 1974-1985*. Copyright © Kluwer Law International, 1990.

AWARD IN ICC CASE NO. 6618, in Grigera Naón, Horacio, CHOICE-OF-LAW PROBLEMS IN INTERNATIONAL COMMERCIAL ARBITRATION, 289 *Recueil des Cours* 9 (2001). Copyright © Martinus Nijhoff Publishers, 2001.

AWARD IN VIAC CASE NO. SCH-4366, 2 UNILEX, E. 199414, (1994). Reprinted with the permission of UNILEX.

AWARD NO. 2930 OF 1982, in Sanders, Pieter (ed.), IX *Yearbook of Commercial Arbitration* 1984, pp. 105-108. This is an International Council for Commercial Arbitration (ICCA) work and has been reproduced with its kind permission. Copyright © Kluwer Law International, 2010.

AWARD OF 31 OCTOBER 1980, in Sanders, Pieter (ed.), VII *Yearbook of Commercial Arbitration* 1982, p. 150. This is an ICCA work and has been reproduced with its kind permission. Copyright © Kluwer Law International, 2010.

AWARD OF 17 FEBRUARY 1984 IN CASE NO. 4237, in Sanders, Pieter (ed.), X *Yearbook of Commercial Arbitration* 1978, pp. 52-60. This is an ICCA work and has been reproduced with its kind permission. Copyright © Kluwer Law International, 2010.

AWARD OF 9 JULY 1984 IN CASE NO. 109/1980 in van den Berg, Albert Jan (ed.), XVIII *Yearbook of Commercial Arbitration* 1993, pp. 92-110. This is an ICCA work and has been reproduced with its kind permission. Copyright © Kluwer Law International, 2010.

AWARDS IN ICC CASE NOS. 10373 AND 10439, in Lalive, Pierre, THE TRANSFER OF SEAT IN INTERNATIONAL ARBITRATION, IN LAW AND JUSTICE, in Nafzinger, James A.R. & Symeonides, Symeon (eds.), *Law and Justice in A Multistate World: Essays in Honor of Arthur T. von Mehren*. Copyright © Martinus Nijhoff Publishers, 2002.

BIWATER GAUFF (TANZANIA) LIMITED V. UNITED REPUBLIC OF TANZANIA, Procedural Order No. 3 (29 September 2006), 22 ICSID Rev.—FILJ 181 (2007) of ICSID Case No. ARB/05/22. Reprinted with the permission of the World Bank.

DECISION OF THE GENEVA CHAMBER OF COMMERCE OF 25 SEPTEMBER 1997, 19(4) *ASA Bulletin* 2001, pp. 745-750. Copyright © Kluwer Law International, 2010.

FINAL AWARD IN ICC CASE NO. 5294 OF 22 FEBRUARY 1988, in van den Berg, Albert Jan (ed.), XIV *Yearbook of Commercial Arbitration* 1989, pp. 137-145. This is an ICCA work and has been reproduced with its kind permission. Copyright © Kluwer Law International, 2010.

FINAL AWARD IN ICC CASE NO. 5460 OF 1987, in van den Berg, Albert Jan (ed.), XIII *Yearbook of Commercial Arbitration* 1988, pp. 104-109. This is an ICCA work and has been reproduced with its kind permission. Copyright © Kluwer Law International, 2010.

FINAL AWARD IN ICC CASE NO. 5622 OF 1988, in van den Berg, Albert Jan (ed.), XIX *Yearbook of Commercial Arbitration* 1994, pp. 105-123. This is an ICCA work and has been reproduced with its kind permission. Copyright © Kluwer Law International, 2010.

FINAL AWARD IN ICC CASE NO. 5946 OF 1990, in van den Berg, Albert Jan (ed.), XVI *Yearbook of Commercial Arbitration* 1991, pp. 97-118. This is an ICCA work and has been reproduced with its kind permission. Copyright © Kluwer Law International, 2010.

FINAL AWARD IN ICC CASE NO. 6379 OF 1990, in van den Berg, Albert Jan (ed.), XVII *Yearbook of Commercial Arbitration* 1992, pp. 212-220. This is an ICCA work and has been reproduced with its kind permission. Copyright © Kluwer Law International, 2010.

FINAL AWARD IN ICC CASE NO. 7626 OF 1995, in van den Berg, Albert Jan (ed.), XXII *Yearbook of Commercial Arbitration* 1997, pp. 132-148. This is an ICCA work and has been reproduced with its kind permission. Copyright © Kluwer Law International, 2010.

FINAL AWARD IN ICC CASE NO. 8445 OF 1996, in van den Berg, Albert Jan (ed.), XXVI *Yearbook of Commercial Arbitration* 2001, pp. 167-180. This is an ICCA work and has been reproduced with its kind permission. Copyright © Kluwer Law International, 2010.

HRVATSKA ELEKTROPRIVREDA D.D. V. REPUBLIC OF SLOVENIA, Order Concerning the Participation of A Counsel (6 May 2008) of ICSID Case No. ARB/05/24. Reprinted with the permission of the World Bank.

ICS INSPECTION AND CONTROL SERVICES LTD. (U.K.) V. ARGENTINA, DECISION ON CHALLENGE TO ARBITRATOR, (17 DECEMBER 2009). Reprinted with the permission of Investment Treaty Arbitration.

INTERIM AWARD IN CASE NO. 4131 OF 23 SEPTEMBER 1982, in Sanders, Pieter (ed.), IX *Yearbook of Commercial Arbitration* 1984, pp. 131-137. This is an ICCA work and has been reproduced with its kind permission. Copyright © Kluwer Law International, 2010.

INTERIM AWARD IN ICC CASE NO. 5029 OF 16 JULY 1986, in van den Berg, Albert Jan (ed.), XII *Yearbook of Commercial Arbitration* 1987, pp. 113-123. This is an ICCA work and has been reproduced with its kind permission. Copyright © Kluwer Law International, 2010.

INTERIM AWARD IN ICC CASE NO. 6149 OF 1990, in van den Berg, Albert Jan (ed.), XX *Yearbook of Commercial Arbitration* 1995, pp. 41-57. This is an ICCA work and has been reproduced with its kind permission. Copyright © Kluwer Law International, 2010.

INTERIM AWARD IN ICC CASE NO. 8786, originally published in 11(1) ICC Ct. Bull. 81. Copyright © ICC, 2001. ICC publications are available from www.storeiccwbo.org. Key ICC dispute resolution titles are also available at www.iccdrl.com.

INTERIM AWARDS AND FINAL AWARD IN ICC CASE NO. 4145 OF 1983, 1984 AND 1986, in van den Berg, Albert Jan (ed.), XII *Yearbook of Commercial Arbitration* 1987, pp. 97-110. This is an ICCA work and has been reproduced with its kind permission. Copyright © Kluwer Law International, 2010.

PARTIAL AWARD IN ICC CASE NO. 5625, originally published in Multi-Party Arbitration Under the Rules of the ICC Court of Arbitration. Copyright © ICC, 1982. ICC publications are available from www.storeiccwbo.org. Key ICC dispute resolution titles are also available at www.iccdrl.com.

PARTIAL AWARD IN ICC CASE NO. 8879, paraphrased in Grigera Naón, Horacio, CHOICE-OF-LAW PROBLEMS IN INTERNATIONAL COMMERCIAL ARBITRATION, 289 *Recueil des Cours* 9 (2001). Copyright © Martinus Nijhoff Publishers, 2001.

PRELIMINARY AWARD IN ICC CASE NO. 5505 OF 1987, in van den Berg, Albert Jan (ed.), XIII *Yearbook of Commercial Arbitration* 1988, pp. 110-121. This is an ICCA work and has been reproduced with its kind permission. Copyright © Kluwer Law International, 2010.

PRELIMINARY AWARD OF 22 SEPTEMBER 1983 IN CASE NO. 4132, in Sanders, Pieter (ed.), X *Yearbook of Commercial Arbitration* 1985, pp. 49-51. This is an ICCA work and has been reproduced with its kind permission. Copyright © Kluwer Law International, 2010.

PROCEDURAL ORDER IN ICC CASE NO. 5542, in Arnaldez, Jean-Jacques, Derains, Yves & Hascher, Dominique (eds.), *Collection of Procedural Decisions in ICC Arbitration 1993-1996.* Copyright © Kluwer Law International, 1997.

PROCEDURAL ORDER IN ICC CASE NO. 7170, in Arnaldez, Jean-Jacques, Derains, Yves & Hascher, Dominique (eds.), *Collection of Procedural Decisions in ICC Arbitration 1993-1996.* Copyright © Kluwer Law International, 1997.

THE LOEWEN GROUP, INC. AND RAYMOND L. LOEWEN V. UNITED STATES OF AMERICA, ICSID Case No. ARB(AF)/98/3. Reprinted with the permission of the World Bank.

Court Decisions

CHANNEL TUNNEL GROUP LTD. V. BALFOUR BEATTY CONSTRUCTION LTD., [1993] A.C. 334, Reprinted with the permission of the Incorporated Council of Law Reporting for England and Wales (ICLR), 2010.

CHRISTOPHER BROWN LTD. V. GENOSSENSCHAFT OSTERREICHISHER ETC., [1954] 1 Q.B. 8. Reprinted with the permission of the ICLR, 2010.

CIVIL CASE NO. 320 OF 1981, High Court of Barbados, 22 August 1983. Copyright © Crown Copyright of the Barbados Ministry of the Attorney General, 1983.

COMPAGNIE D'ARMEMENT MARITIME S.A. V. COMPAGNIE TUNISIENNE DE NAVIGATION S.A., [1971] A.C. 572. Reprinted with the permission of the ICLR, 2010.

CORPORACION TRANSNACIONAL DE INVERSIONES, S.A. DE C.V. V. STET INTERNATIONAL, S.P.A., 49 O.R. (3d) 414 (Ontario Court of Appeal, 2000). Reprinted with the permission of the Ontario Court of Appeal.

DALIMPEX LTD V. JANICKI, 64 O.R. (3d) 737 (Ontario Court of Appeal, 2003). Reprinted with the permission of the Ontario Court of Appeal.

DEUTSCHE SCHACHTBAU- UND TIEFBOHRGESELLSCHAFT MBH V. RAS AL-KHAIMAH NATIONAL OIL CO., [1987] 2 Lloyd's Rep. 246. Reproduced with the kind permission of Informa Law, an informa business.

DUBAI ISLAMIC BANK PJSC V. PAYMENTECH MERCHANT SERVICES INC., [2001] 1 All E.R. (Comm) 514, Copyright © LexisNexis, 2010.

ECO SWISS CHINA TIME LTD. V. BENETTON INTernationaL N.V., [1999] E.C.R. I-3055 (E.C.J.). Copyright © European Union, http://eur-lex.europa.eu/, 1999.

HALKI SHIPPING CORP V. SOPEX OILS LTD (THE HALKI), [1998] 1 Lloyd's Rep. 49. Reproduced with the kind permission of Informa Law, an informa business.

HARBOUR ASSURANCE CO. (U.K.) LTD. V. KANSA GENERAL INTERNATIONAL INSURANCE CO. LTD., [1992] 1 Lloyd's Rep. 81 (Q.B.). Reproduced with the kind permission of Informa Law, an informa business.

HASSNEH INSURANCE CO. OF ISRAEL V. STUART J MEW, [1993] 2 Lloyd's Rep. 243. Reproduced with the kind permission of Informa Law, an informa business.

JUDGMENT OF 10 JULY 1843 (FRENCH COUR DE CASSATION), 2 *Revue de l'Arbitrage* 1992, (Comité Français de l'Arbitrage), pp. 399-404, Copyright © Kluwer Law International, 2010.

JUDGMENT OF 21 MAY 1976 (VENEZIA CORTE DI APPELLO), in Sanders, Pieter (ed.), III *Yearbook of Commercial Arbitration* 1978, p. 277. This is an ICCA work and has been reproduced with its kind permission. Copyright © Kluwer Law International, 2010.

JUDGMENT OF 8 FEBRUARY 1978 (SWISS FEDERAL TRIBUNAL), in van den Berg, Albert Jan (ed.), XI *Yearbook of Commercial Arbitration* 1986, pp. 538-542. This is an ICCA work and has been reproduced with its kind permission. Copyright © Kluwer Law International, 2010.

JUDGMENT OF 1 FEBRUARY 1979 (PARIS TRIBUNAL DE GRANDE INSTANCE), *Revue de l'Arbitrage* 1980, (Comité Français de l'Arbitrage), p. 97. This is an ICCA work and has been reproduced with its kind permission. Copyright © Kluwer Law International, 2010.

JUDGMENT OF 20 AUGUST 1984 (MAHKAMAH AGUNG), in van den Berg, Albert Jan (ed.), XI *Yearbook of Commercial Arbitration* 1986, pp. 508-509. This is an ICCA work and has been reproduced with its kind permission. Copyright © Kluwer Law International, 2010.

JUDGMENT OF 5 NOVEMBER 1985 (SWISS FEDERAL TRIBUNAL), in van den Berg, Albert Jan (ed.), XII *Yearbook of Commercial Arbitration* 1987, pp. 511-513. This is an ICCA work and has been reproduced with its kind permission. Copyright © Kluwer Law International, 2010.

JUDGMENT OF 3 APRIL 1987 IN CASE NO. 3221 (ITALIAN CORTE DI CASSAZIONE), in van den Berg, Albert Jan (ed.), XVII *Yearbook of Commercial Arbitration* 1992, pp. 529-533. This is an ICCA work and has been reproduced with its kind permission. Copyright © Kluwer Law International, 2010.

JUDGMENT OF 18 JULY 1987 (BOLOGNA TRIBUNALE), in van den Berg, Albert Jan (ed.), XVII *Yearbook of Commercial Arbitration* 1992, pp. 534-538. This is an ICCA work and has been reproduced with its kind permission. Copyright © Kluwer Law International, 2010.

JUDGMENT OF 30 MARCH 1988 (SINGAPORE HIGH COURT), 5(3) *Journal of International Arbitration* 1988, pp. 139 – 148, Copyright © Kluwer Law International, 2010.

JUDGMENT OF 21 DECEMBER 1988 (ENGLISH HIGH COURT OF JUSTICE, QUEENS'S BENCH DIVISION), in van den Berg, Albert Jan (ed.), XVII *Yearbook of Commercial Arbitration* 1992, pp. 587-593. This is an ICCA work and has been reproduced with its kind permission. Copyright © Kluwer Law International, 2010.

JUDGMENT OF 17 FEBRUARY 1989 (HAMBURG HANSEATISCHES OBERLANDESGERICHT), in van den Berg, Albert Jan (ed.), XV *Yearbook of Commercial Arbitration* 1990, pp. 455-464. This is an ICCA work and has been reproduced with its kind permission. Copyright © Kluwer Law International, 2010.

JUDGMENT OF 18 JANUARY 1990 iN CASE NO. III ZR 269/88 (GERMAN BUNDESGERICHTSHOF), in van den Berg, Albert Jan (ed.), XVII *Yearbook of Commercial Arbitration* 1992, pp. 503-509. This is an ICCA work and has been reproduced with its kind permission. Copyright © Kluwer Law International, 2010.

JUDGMENT OF 3 FEBRUARY 1990 (GENOA CORTE DI APPELLO), in van den Berg, Albert Jan (ed.), XVII *Yearbook of Commercial Arbitration* 1992, pp. 542-544. This is an ICCA work and has been reproduced with its kind permission. Copyright © Kluwer Law International, 2010.

JUDGMENT OF 2 MARCH 1991 (HONG KONG SUPREME COURT), in van den Berg, Albert Jan (ed.), XVIII *Yearbook of Commercial Arbitration* 1993, pp. 377-384. This is an ICCA work and has been reproduced with its kind permission. Copyright © Kluwer Law International, 2010.

JUDGMENT OF 7 JANUARY 1992, SOCIÉTÉS BKMI ET SIEMENS V. SOCIÉTÉ DUTCO (FRENCH COUR DE CASSATION) 119 *Journal du droit international (Clunet)* 707. Copyright © LexisNexis, 2010.

JUDGMENT OF 7 MAY 1992 (INDIAN SUPREME COURT), in van den Berg, Albert Jan (ed.), XVIII *Yearbook of Commercial Arbitration* 1993, pp. 403-414. This is an ICCA work and has been reproduced with its kind permission. Copyright © Kluwer Law International, 2010.

JUDGMENT OF 30 MARCH 1993 (VAUD CANTONAL TRIBUNAL), in van den Berg, Albert Jan (ed.), XXI *Yearbook of Commercial Arbitration* 1996, pp. 681-684. This is an ICCA work and has been reproduced with its kind permission. Copyright © Kluwer Law International, 2010.

JUDGMENT OF 10 NOVEMBER 1993 (FRENCH COUR DE CASSATION), in van den Berg, Albert Jan (ed.), XXIII *Yearbook of Commercial Arbitration* 1998, pp. 770-773. This is an ICCA work and has been reproduced with its kind permission. Copyright © Kluwer Law International, 2010.

JUDGMENT OF 24 NOVEMBER 1993 (LUXEMBOURG COUR SUPÉRIEURE DE JUSTICE), in van den Berg, Albert Jan (ed.), XXI *Yearbook of Commercial Arbitration* 1996, pp. 617-626. This is an ICCA work and has been reproduced with its kind permission. Copyright © Kluwer Law International, 2010.

JUDGMENT OF 20 DECEMBER 1993 (FRENCH COUR DE CASSATION), 1 *Revue de l'Arbitrage* 1994, (Comité Français de l'Arbitrage), pp. 116-117. Copyright © Kluwer Law International, 2010.

JUDGMENT OF 10 FEBRUARY 1994 (INDIAN SUPREME COURT), in van den Berg, Albert Jan (ed.), XXII *Yearbook of Commercial Arbitration* 1997, pp. 710-714. This is an ICCA work and has been reproduced with its kind permission. Copyright © Kluwer Law International, 2010.

JUDGMENT OF 24 FEBRUARY 1994 (PARIS COUR D'APPEL), in van den Berg, Albert Jan (ed.), XXII *Yearbook of Commercial Arbitration* 1997, pp. 682-690. This is an ICCA work and has been reproduced with its kind permission. Copyright © Kluwer Law International, 2010.

JUDGMENT OF 7 MAY 1994 (GENOA CORTE DI APPELLO), in van den Berg, Albert Jan (ed.), XXI *Yearbook of Commercial Arbitration* 1996, pp. 594-601. This is an ICCA work and has been reproduced with its kind permission. Copyright © Kluwer Law International, 2010.

JUDGMENT OF 30 MAY 1994 (TOKYO HIGH COURT), in van den Berg, Albert Jan (ed.), XX *Yearbook of Commercial Arbitration* 1995, pp. 745-749. This is an ICCA work and has been reproduced with its kind permission. Copyright © Kluwer Law International, 2010.

JUDGMENT OF 30 DECEMBER 1994 (SWISS FEDERAL TRIBUNAL), 13(2) *ASA Bulletin* 1995, pp. 217-226. Copyright © Kluwer Law International, 2010.

JUDGMENT OF 14 FEBRUARY 1995 IN CASE NO. 93DA53054 (KOREAN SUPREME COURT), in van den Berg, Albert Jan (ed.), XXI *Yearbook of Commercial Arbitration* 1996, pp. 612-616. This is an ICCA work and has been reproduced with its kind permission. Copyright © Kluwer Law International, 2010.

JUDGMENT OF 7 APRIL 1995 IN CASE NO. 95/014 (AUSTRALIAN HIGH COURT), in van den Berg, Albert Jan (ed.), XXI *Yearbook of Commercial Arbitration* 1996, pp. 137-171. This is an ICCA work and has been reproduced with its kind permission. Copyright © Kluwer Law International, 2010.

JUDGMENT OF 21 MAY 1997 (FRENCH COUR DE CASSATION), 4 *Revue de l'Arbitrage* 1994, (Comité Français de l'Arbitrage), pp. 537-537. Copyright © Kluwer Law International, 2010.

JUDGMENT OF 16 JANUARY 1998, CIVIL APPEAL NO. 116 OF 1997 (HONG KONG SPECIAL ADMINISTRATIVE REGION HIGH COURT, COURT OF APPEAL), in van den Berg, Albert Jan (ed.), XXIII *Yearbook of Commercial Arbitration* 1998, pp. 666-684. This is an ICCA work and has been reproduced with its kind permission. Copyright © Kluwer Law International, 2010.

JUDGMENT OF 9 FEBRUARY 1998 (SWISS FEDERAL TRIBUNAL), 16(3) *ASA Bulletin* 1998, pp. 634-652. Copyright © Kluwer Law International, 2010.

JUDGMENT OF 28 APRIL 1998 (THE HAGUE GERECHTSHOF AND ROTTERDAM ARRONDISSEMENTSRECHTBANK), in van den Berg, Albert Jan (ed.), XXIII *Yearbook of Commercial Arbitration* 1998, pp. 731-734. This is an ICCA work and has been reproduced with its kind permission. Copyright © Kluwer Law International, 2010.

JUDGMENT OF 18 OCTOBER 1999 IN CASE NO. 5 U 89/98 (STUTTGART OBERLANDESGERICHT), in van den Berg, Albert Jan (ed.), XXIX *Yearbook of Commercial Arbitration* 2004, pp. 700-714. This is an ICCA work and has been reproduced with its kind permission. Copyright © Kluwer Law International, 2010.

JUDGMENT OF 19 JULY 2000 (ALMELO ARRONDISSEMENTSRECHTBANK), in van den Berg, Albert Jan (ed.), XXVI *Yearbook of Commercial Arbitration* 2001, pp. 827-831. This is an ICCA work and has been reproduced with its kind permission. Copyright © Kluwer Law International, 2010.

JUDGMENT OF 23 APRIL 2004 CASE NO. 9 SCH 01-03 (COLOGNE OBERLANDESGERICHT), in van den Berg, Albert Jan (ed.), XXX *Yearbook of Commercial Arbitration* 2005, pp. 557-562. This is an ICCA work and has been reproduced with its kind permission. Copyright © Kluwer Law International, 2010.

JUDGMENT OF 23 SEPTEMBER 2004 CASE NO. 4Z SCH 005-04 (BAYERISCHES OBERSTES LANDESGERICHT), in van den Berg, Albert Jan (ed.), XXX *Yearbook of Commercial Arbitration*

2005, pp. 568-573. This is an ICCA work and has been reproduced with its kind permission. Copyright © Kluwer Law International, 2010.

JUDGMENT OF 23 NOVEMBER 2004 (JERUSALEM DISTRICT COURT), in van den Berg, Albert Jan (ed.), XXXI *Yearbook of Commercial Arbitration* 2006, pp. 786-790. This is an ICCA work and has been reproduced with its kind permission. Copyright © Kluwer Law International, 2010.

JUDGMENT OF 26 JANUARY 2005 IN CASE NO. 3OB221/04B (AUSTRIAN OBERSTER GERICHTSHOF), in van den Berg, Albert Jan (ed.), XXXI *Yearbook of Commercial Arbitration* 2006, pp. 421-436. This is an ICCA work and has been reproduced with its kind permission. Copyright © Kluwer Law International, 2010.

JUDGMENT OF 12 AUGUST 2005 (INDIAN SUPREME COURT), in van den Berg, Albert Jan (ed.), XXXI *Yearbook of Commercial Arbitration* 2006, pp. 747-785. This is an ICCA work and has been reproduced with its kind permission. Copyright © Kluwer Law International, 2010.

JUDGMENT OF 7 SEPTEMBER 2005 (ISRAELI SUPREME COURT), in van den Berg, Albert Jan (ed.), XXXI *Yearbook of Commercial Arbitration* 2006, pp. 791-797. This is an ICCA work and has been reproduced with its kind permission. Copyright © Kluwer Law International, 2010.

JUDGMENT OF 14 DECEMBER 2006 IN CASE NO. 8 SCH 14/05 (CELLE OBERLANDESGERICHT), in van den Berg, Albert Jan (ed.), XXXII *Yearbook of Commercial Arbitration* 2007, pp. 372-382. This is an ICCA work and has been reproduced with its kind permission. Copyright © Kluwer Law International, 2010.

JUDGMENT OF 17 FEBRUARY 2011, GOVERNMENT OF PAKISTAN, MINISTRY OF RELIGIOUS AFFAIRS V. DALLAH REAL ESTATE & TOURISM HOLDING CO. (Paris Cour d'appel), in van den Berg, Albert Jan (ed.), XXXVI *Yearbook of Commercial Arbitration* 2011, pp. 590-593 This is an ICCA work and has been reproduced with its kind permission. Copyright © Kluwer Law International, 2011.

LUCKY GOLDSTAR INTERNATIONAL (H.K.) LTD. V. NG MOO KEE ENG'G LTD., [1994] ADRLJ 49 (H.K. High Court), *Alternative Dispute Resolution Law Journal*. Reproduced with the kind permission of Informa Law, an informa business.

ORDER NO. 5 OF 2 APRIL 2002 REGARDING CLAIMANT'S REQUEST FOR INTERIM RELIEF, 21(4) *ASA Bulletin* 2003, pp. 810-821. Copyright © Kluwer Law International, 2010.

ORDER OF REFERENCE OF 15 FEBRUARY 1995 (PARIS TRIBUNAL DE GRANDE INSTANCE), 3 *Revue de l'Arbitrage* 1996, (Comité Français de l'Arbitrage), pp. 503-511. Copyright © Kluwer Law International, 2010.

PETERSON FARMS INC. V. C&M FARMING LTD., [2004] 1 Lloyd's Rep. 603 Q.B. Reproduced with the kind permission of Informa Law, an informa business.

ROOSE INDUSTRIES LTD. V. READY MIXED CONCRETE LTD., [1974] 2 N.Z.L.R. 246. Copyright © New Zealand Council of Law Reporting, 2010.

SOLEIMANY V. SOLEIMANY, [1998] 3 W.L.R. 811. Reprinted with the permission of the ICLR, 2010.

UNION OF INDIA V. MCDONNELL DOUGLAS CORP., [1993] 2 Lloyd's Rep. 48. Reproduced with the kind permission of Informa Law, an informa business.

VERITAS SHIPPING LTD. V. ANGLO-CANADIAN CEMENT LTD., [1966] Lloyd's Rep. 76, (Q.B. 1965). Reproduced with the kind permission of Informa Law, an informa business.

WALKINSHAW V DINIZ [2000] 2 All E.R. (Comm.) 237. Copyright © LexisNexis, 2010.
WESTACRE INVESTMENTS INC. V. JUGOIMPORT-SPDR HOLDING CO. LTD. AND OTHERS, [1998] 4 All E.R. 570. Copyright © LexisNexis, 2010.

XL INSURANCE LTD. V. OWENS CORNING CORP., [2000] 2 Lloyd's Rep. 500 (Q.B.). Reproduced with the kind permission of Informa Law, an informa business.

Arbitration Rules, Codes and Guidelines

UNITED NATIONS COMMISSION ON INTERNATIONAL TRADE LAW MODEL (UNCITRAL) ARBITRATION RULES, U.N. Doc. A/Res/38/91, 15 December 1976. Copyright © UNCITRAL, 1976.

UNCITRAL ARBITRATION RULES, adopted by UNCITRAL on 25 June 2010. Copyright ©
UNCITRAL, 2010.

AMERICAN ARBITRATION ASSOCIATION (AAA) ARBITRATION RULES, amended and effective October 1, 2013. Copyright © AAA, 2013.

AAA CODE OF ETHICS FOR ARBITRATORS IN COMMERCIAL DISPUTES, effective 1 March 2004. Copyright © AAA, 2007.

GRAIN AND FEED TRADE ASSOCIATION Arbitration Rules, effective April 1, 2012. Copyright GAFTA, 2012.

HONG KONG INTERNATIONAL ARBITRATION CENTRE ADMINISTERED ARBITRATION RULES, effective November 1, 2013. Copyright © Hong Kong International Arbitration Centre

ICC RULES OF ARBITRATION, in force from January 1, 2012. Copyright © ICC, 2011. Reproduced with permission of ICC. The text reproduced here is valid at the time of reproduction. As amendments may from time to time be made to the text, please refer to the website www.iccarbitration.org for the latest version and for more information on this ICC dispute resolution service. The text is also available in the ICC Dispute Resolution Library at www.iccdrl.com.

ICC ARBITRATOR STATEMENT OF ACCEPTANCE, AVAILABILITY, IMPARTIALITY AND INDEPENDENCE. Reproduced with permission of ICC. The text reproduced here is valid at the time of reproduction. As amendments may from time to time be made to the text, please refer to the website www.iccarbitration.org for the latest version and for more information on this ICC dispute resolution service. The text is also available in the ICC Dispute Resolution Library at www.iccdrl.com.

INTERNATIONAL CENTER FOR DISPUTE RESOLUTION (ICDR) ARBITRATION RULES, amended and effective June 1, 2014. Copyright © AAA, 2014.

INTERNATIONAL CENTRE FOR SETTLEMENT OF INVESTMENT DISPUTES (ICSID) ARBITRATION RULES. Reprinted with the permission of the World Bank.

LONDON COURT OF INTERNATIONAL ARBITRATION (LCIA) ARBITRATION RULES, effective October 1, 2014. Copyright © LCIA, 2014.

NETHERLANDS ARBITRATION INSTITUTE (NAI) ARBITRATION RULES, in force as of January 1, 2010. Copyright © NAI, 2010.

PERMANENT COURT OF ARBITRATION ARBITRATION RULES 2012, effective December 17, 2012. Copyright © Permanent Court of Arbitration (PCA), 2012.

IBA RULES ON THE TAKING OF EVIDENCE IN INTERNATIONAL ARBITRATION, adopted May 29, 2010. The IBA Rules on the Taking Evidence in International Arbitration are reproduced by kind permission of the International Bar Association, London, UK, and are available at: www.ibanet.org/Publications/publications_IBA_guides_and_free_materials.aspx. © International Bar Association, 2010.

SWISS RULES OF INTERNATIONAL ARBITRATION, effective June 2012. Copyright © Swiss Chambers' Arbitration Institution, 2012.

SINGAPORE INTERNATIONAL ARBITRATION CENTRE ARBITRATION RULES, effective April 1, 2013. The copyright of the SIAC Rules 2013 vests with the Singapore International Arbitration Centre and is reprinted here by kind permission of the Centre.

1996 NOTES ON ORGANIZING ARBITRAL PROCEEDINGS. Copyright © UNCITRAL, 1996.

IBA GUIDELINES ON CONFLICTS OF INTEREST IN INTERNATIONAL ARBITRATION, adopted October 23, 2014. The IBA Guidelines on Conflicts of Interest in International Arbitration are reproduced by kind permission of the International Bar Association, London, UK, and are available at: www.ibanet.org/Publications/publications_IBA_guides_and_free_materials.aspx. © International Bar Association, 2014.

IBA GUIDELINES ON PARTY REPRESENTATION IN INTERNATIONAL ARBITRATION, adopted May 25, 2013. The IBA Guidelines on Party Representation in International Arbitration are reproduced by kind permission of the International Bar Association, London, UK, and are available at: www.ibanet.org/Publications/publications_IBA_guides_and_free_materials.aspx. © International Bar Association, 2013.

Laws

Model Arbitration Clauses

INTERNATIONAL ARBITRATION

CHAPTER 1
INTRODUCTION TO INTERNATIONAL ARBITRATION

International arbitrations take place within a complex and vitally-important international legal framework. As summarized in this introductory chapter, contemporary international conventions, national arbitration legislation, and institutional arbitration rules provide a specialized and highly-supportive enforcement regime for most contemporary international commercial arbitrations and international investment arbitrations. A significantly less detailed legal framework exists for inter-state arbitrations, although international law instruments provide a workable enforcement regime even in this context.

The international legal regimes for international commercial and investment arbitrations have been established, and progressively refined, with the express goal of facilitating international trade and investment by providing a stable, predictable and effective legal framework in which these commercial activities may be conducted:

> The New York Convention and the Model Law deal with one of the most important aspects of international commerce—the resolution of disputes between commercial parties in an international or multinational context, where those parties, in the formation of their contract or legal relationship, have, by their own bargain, chosen arbitration as their agreed method of dispute resolution…. An ordered efficient dispute resolution mechanism leading to an enforceable award or judgment by the adjudicator, is an essential underpinning of commerce…. The recognition of the importance of international commercial arbitration to the smooth working of international commerce and of the importance of enforcement of the bilateral bargain of commercial parties in their agreement to submit their disputes to arbitration was reflected in both the New York Convention and the Model Law.[1]

This chapter summarizes the principal components of the contemporary international legal framework for international commercial, investment, and state-to-state arbitrations. First, the chapter provides an overview of leading international arbitration conventions, including particularly the New York Convention (with regard to international commercial arbitration) and the ICSID Convention (with regard to international investment arbitration). Second, the chapter briefly describes leading national arbitration statutes (including particularly the UNCITRAL Model Law). Third, the chapter summarizes the differences between *ad hoc* arbitration and institutional arbitration, particularly in the context of international commercial arbitration, including a summary of leading international arbitral institutions. Fourth, the chapter describes the principal elements that are typically found in contemporary international arbitration agreements. Fifth, the chapter summarizes the principal choice-of-law issues that arise in the international arbitration process (including the law governing the parties' underlying agreement, whether a contract or treaty, the law governing the arbitration agreement and the procedural law governing the arbitral pro-

---

1. *Comandate Marine Corp. v. Pan Australia Shipping Pty Ltd*, [2006] FCAFC 192, ¶¶192-193 (Australian Fed. Ct.).

ceedings). Finally, the chapter summarizes leading research tools and sources for international arbitration.

A. HISTORICAL OVERVIEW OF INTERNATIONAL ARBITRATION

A brief consideration of the history of arbitration in international matters is useful as an introduction to contemporary international arbitration. In particular, this review identifies some of the principal themes and objectives of international arbitration and places contemporary developments in context. An historical review also underscores the extent to which state-to-state and international commercial arbitration developed in parallel, with strikingly similar objectives, institutions and procedures.

1. Historical Development of Arbitration Between States

The origins of international arbitration are sometimes traced, if uncertainly, to ancient mythology. Early instances of dispute resolution among the Greek gods, in matters at least arguably international by then-prevailing standards, involved disputes between Poseidon and Helios over the ownership of Corinth (which was reportedly split between them by Briareus, a giant),[2] Athena and Poseidon over possession of Aegina (which was awarded to them in common by Zeus),[3] and Hera and Poseidon over ownership of Argolis (which was awarded entirely to Hera by Inachus, a mythical king of Argos).[4] Egyptian mythology offers similar accounts of divine arbitrations, including a dispute between Seth and Osiris, resolved by Thot ("he who decides without being partial").[5]

a. Inter-State Arbitration in Antiquity

Deities aside, international arbitration was a favored means for peacefully settling disputes between states and state-like entities in Antiquity: "arbitration is the oldest method for the peaceful settlement of international disputes."[6] Historical scholarship provides no clear conclusions regarding the first recorded instance of international arbitration between states (or state-like entities). In the state-to-state context, some cite what contemporary reporters would denominate as the case of *Lagash v. Umma*, apparently settled in 2550 B.C. by King Mesilim of Kish,[7] or the 2100 B.C. case of *Ur v. Lagash*, in which the King of Uruk ordered one city to return territory seized by force from another.[8] Others look to two disputes decided in the 8th century B.C. by Eriphyle, a noblewoman, over Argos's plans to wage war on Thebes,[9] a 650 B.C. dispute between Andros and Chalcis over pos-

---

2. J. Ralston, *International Arbitration From Athens to Locarno* 153 (1929).

3. C. Phillipson, II *The International Law and Custom of Ancient Greece and Rome* 129 (1911).

4. J. Ralston, *International Arbitration From Athens to Locarno* 153 (1929).

5. Mantica, *Arbitration in Ancient Egypt*, 12 Arb. J. 155 (1957).

6. A. Stuyt, *Survey of International Arbitrations 1794-1989* vii (3d ed. 1990).

7. L. Edmonson (ed.), *Domke on Commercial Arbitration* §2.1 (3d ed. 2010 & Update 2013).

8. Lafont, *L'arbitrage en Mésopotamie*, 2000 Rev. arb. 557, 568-69.

9. D. Roebuck, *Ancient Greek Arbitration* 71 (2001). Eriphyle, the sister of the King of Argos, also appears to have been one of the first recorded instances of a corrupt arbitrator, accepting bribes of a magic necklace and a magic robe to decide, *inter alia*, against her husband.

session of a deserted city,[10] or a controversy between Athens and Megara in 600 B.C. over the island of Salamis.[11]

In one authority's words, "arbitration was used throughout the Hellenic world for five hundred years." [12] This included the frequent inclusion of arbitration clauses in state-to-state treaties, providing for specified forms of arbitration to resolve future disputes that might arise under the treaty,[13] as well as submission agreements with regard to existing "inter-state" disputes.[14]

The procedures used in many ancient arbitrations between Greek city-states would not be unfamiliar to contemporary litigants. The parties were represented by agents, who acted as counsel (in a dispute between Athens and Megara, Solon represented the former),[15] the parties presented documentary evidence and witness testimony (or sworn witness statements), oral argument was presented through counsel, with time limits imposed on counsel's arguments, and the arbitrators rendered written, signed and reasoned awards.[16]

One aspect of ancient state-to-state arbitration that would strike contemporary observers as unusual was the number of arbitrators. Although most tribunals apparently consisted of three members, there were instances where tribunals consisted of large numbers (variously, 600 Milesians, 334 Larissaeans, and 204 Cnidians), which arguably reflect a quasi-legislative, rather than adjudicatory, function.[17] Other "arbitrations" appear to have been more in the nature of non-binding mediation, or political consultation, than true arbitration.[18]

Arbitration was also used to settle disputes between state-like entities during the Roman age. Although commentators observe that the use of arbitration declined from Hellenic practice,[19] it was by no means abandoned. Territorial units of Rome, as well as vassal states and allies, appealed to the Roman Senate, to Roman proconsuls, or to other Roman institutions for "arbitral" decisions or the appointment of arbitrators to resolve territorial and other disputes.[20] In general, however, the historical record indicates that Rome preferred political or military solutions, within the Empire, to inter-state arbitration or adjudication.

---

10. Fraser, *A Sketch of the History of International Arbitration*, 11 Cornell L.Q. 179 (1925-1926) (citing A. Raeder, *L'Arbitrage international chez les Hellènes* 16-17 (1912)).

11. Smith, *"Judicial Nationalism" in International Law: National Identity and Judicial Autonomy at the ICJ*, 40 Tex. Int'l L.J. 197, 203 n.30 (2004-2005).

12. Fraser, *A Sketch of the History of International Arbitration*, 11 Cornell L.Q. 179, 188 (1925-1926).

13. J. Ralston, *International Arbitration From Athens to Locarno* 156-58 (1929); M. Tod, *International Arbitration Amongst the Greeks* 65-69 (1913).

14. S. Ager, *Interstate Arbitrations in the Greek World, 337-90 B.C.* 8-9 (1996); Westermann, *Interstate Arbitration in Antiquity*, II Classical J. 197, 199-200 (1906-1907).

15. M. Bohacek, *Arbitration and State-Organized Tribunals in the Ancient Procedure of the Greeks and Romans* 197-204 (1952); J. Ralston, *International Arbitration From Athens to Locarno* 161-62 (1929); D. Roebuck, *Ancient Greek Arbitration* 46-47 (2001).

16. S. Ager, *Interstate Arbitrations in the Greek World, 337-90 B.C.* 15 (1996); J. Ralston, *International Arbitration From Athens to Locarno* 162-64 (1929).

17. J. Ralston, *International Arbitration From Athens to Locarno* 159 (1929).

18. S. Ager, *Interstate Arbitrations in the Greek World 337-90 B.C.* 264-66 (1996) (describing Rome's increasingly frequent role as "mediator and arbitrator" in disputes between Sparta and the Achaean League), 281 (describing "interven[tion]" and "mediation" by Megara in a dispute between Achaia and Boeotia).

19. Fraser, *A Sketch of the History of International Arbitration*, 11 Cornell L.Q. 179, 190 (1925-1926) ("The republic lost what Greece had gained, and the empire lost the little the republic had won.").

20. J. Ralston, *International Arbitration From Athens to Locarno* 171-72 (1929).

b. Inter-State Arbitration in the European Middle Ages

After an apparent decline in usage under late Roman practice, international arbitration between state-like entities in Europe experienced a revival during the Middle Ages. Although historical records are incomplete, scholars conclude that international arbitration "existed on a widespread scale" during the Middle Ages, that "the constant disputes that arose in those warlike days were very frequently terminated by some kind of arbitration," and that "it is surprising to learn of the great number of arbitral decisions, of their importance and of the prevalence of the '*clause compromissoire.*'"[21] The states of the Swiss Confederation[22] and the Hanseatic League,[23] as well as German and Italian principalities,[24] turned with particular frequency to arbitration to settle their differences, often pursuant to agreements to resolve all future disputes by arbitration.[25]

Determining the precise scope and extent of international arbitration between states or state-like entities during the Medieval era is difficult, in part because a distinction was not always drawn between judges, arbitrators, mediators and *amiables compositeurs.*[26] Indeed, one of the most famous "arbitrations" of the age—Pope Alexander VI's division of the discoveries of the New World—appears not to have been an arbitration at all, but rather a negotiation or mediation.[27] On the other hand, numerous treaties throughout this period drew quite clear distinctions between arbitration (in the sense of an adjudicative, binding process) and conciliation or mediation (in the sense of a non-binding procedure).[28]

The procedures used during arbitral proceedings in Medieval times bore important resemblances to those used today. Both parties presented arguments through counsel, evidence and testimony was received by the tribunal, the tribunal deliberated and a written award was made.[29] There is even evidence that written briefs were a standard element of

---

21. Fraser, *A Sketch of the History of International Arbitration*, 11 Cornell L.Q. 179, 190-91 (1925-1926). *See* J. Ralston, *International Arbitration From Athens to Locarno* 177-78 (1929) (citing 1235 treaty of alliance between Genoa and Venice providing for arbitration of future disputes; 1343 "arbitral convention" between Denmark and Sweden promising to arbitrate any serious future disputes; and 1516 treaty of "perpetual peace" between France and England).

22. J. Verzijl, VIII *International Law in Historical Perspective* 189-90 (1974) (citing historical authorities).

23. J. Ralston, *International Arbitration From Athens to Locarno* 176-77 (1929).

24. J. Verzijl, VIII *International Law in Historical Perspective* 189-90 (1974).

25. Fraser, *A Sketch of the History of International Arbitration*, 11 Cornell L.Q. 179, 192 (1925-1926); J. Ralston, *International Arbitration From Athens to Locarno* 176-77 (1929).

26. Fraser, *A Sketch of the History of International Arbitration*, 11 Cornell L.Q. 179, 195 (1925-1926); J. Ralston, *International Arbitration From Athens to Locarno* 179 (1929) ("By a quite universal practice it would appear that before proceeding to adjudge, the arbitrator acted in the capacity of what subsequently became known as *amiable compositeur*—in other words he sought to find a basis for the composition of difficulties before considering them from the standpoint of law.").

27. E. Bourne, *The Demarcation Line of Pope Alexander VI*, in *Essays in Historical Criticism* Chap. VII (1901).

28. See examples cited in J. Ralston, *International Arbitration From Athens to Locarno* 180 (1929).

29. Fraser, *A Sketch of the History of International Arbitration*, 11 Cornell L.Q. 179, 196 (1925-1926); J. Ralston, *International Arbitration From Athens to Locarno* 185-86 (1929) (describing four-member legal teams of Kings of Castile and Navarre in 1176).

inter-state arbitral procedures.[30] Parties appear to have placed importance on the prompt resolution of their disputes, including by imposing time limits in their agreements on the arbitrators' mandates.[31] And, if a losing party flouted the arbitrator's decision, the arbitrator or another authority was sometimes empowered to impose sanctions to enforce compliance.[32]

During the 16th, 17th and 18th centuries, the popularity of international arbitration as a means of resolving inter-state disputes apparently declined significantly. Although by no means entirely abandoned, the rising tide of nationalism apparently chilled historic reliance on arbitration: "nor is arbitration the immediate jewel of Tudor souls."[33] It was only at the end of the 18th century, with Jay's Treaty between the newly-founded United States and Great Britain (discussed below),[34] that international arbitration in the state-to-state context saw a new resurgence.

c. Inter-State Arbitration in the 18th and 19th Centuries

Great Britain's North American colonies appear to have embraced inter-state arbitration from at least the moment of their independence. The 1781 Articles of Confederation provided a mechanism for resolving inter-state disputes between different American states, through what can only be categorized as arbitral procedures.[35]

More significantly, "the modern era of arbitral or judicial settlement of international disputes, by common accord among all writers upon the subject, dates from the signing on 19 November 1794 of Jay's Treaty between Great Britain and the United States."[36] Among other things, in a determined effort to restore amicable relations between the United States and Great Britain, Jay's Treaty provided for the establishment of three different arbitral mechanisms, dealing with boundary disputes, claims by British merchants against U.S. nationals and claims by U.S. citizens against Great Britain.[37] This was a remarkable step, between recent combatants, which ushered in a new age of inter-state arbitration.

The United States continued its tradition of arbitrating international disputes throughout the 19th century. It included an arbitration clause (albeit an optional one) in the 1848 Treaty of Guadalupe Hidalgo, which provided for resolution of future disputes between the United States and Mexico "by the arbitration of commissioners appointed on each side, or by that

---

30. Fraser, *A Sketch of the History of International Arbitration*, 11 Cornell L.Q. 179, 197-98 (1925-1926) (case study of arbitration by Henry II of England between Castile and Navarre); Roebuck, *L'arbitrage en droit anglais avant 1558*, 2002 Rev. arb. 535, 538.

31. J. Ralston, *International Arbitration From Athens to Locarno* 186 (1929) (citing 1405 treaty requiring award to be rendered within six weeks and three days).

32. J. Ralston, *International Arbitration From Athens to Locarno* 187-88 (1929) (discussing penalty bonds, undertakings and possibility that violators of arbitral awards might be excommunicated by Pope).

33. Fraser, *A Sketch of the History of International Arbitration*, 11 Cornell L.Q. 179, 198 (1925-1926).

34. *See infra* pp. 5-6.

35. J. Ralston, *International Arbitration From Athens to Locarno* 190 (1929). The Articles of Confederation provided for states with inter-state disagreements to jointly appoint five "commissioners or judges" to resolve their disputes; failing agreement, a complex list system was prescribed, in which each party was entitled to strike names of unsuitable candidates. Articles of Confederation, Art. IX (1781).

36. J. Ralston, *International Arbitration From Athens to Locarno* 191 (1929).

37. Jay's Treaty, Arts. V-VII (1794).

of a friendly nation."[38] The United States did the same in the 1871 Treaty of Washington with Great Britain, excerpted in the Documentary Supplement at pp. 65-71, providing the basis for resolving a series of disputes provoked by the Civil War; the Treaty provided for arbitration of the disputes before a five-person tribunal, with one arbitrator nominated by each of the United States and Great Britain, and three arbitrators nominated by neutral states.[39] One product of the Treaty of Washington was the so-called "Alabama Arbitration," in which Great Britain was ordered to pay $15.5 million in gold (equivalent to roughly Great Britain's annual government budget) for having permitted the outfitting of a Confederate privateer that caused substantial damage to Union shipping.[40] The United States and Great Britain also repeatedly resorted to arbitration to settle various boundary and other disputes during the 19th and early 20th centuries.[41]

Agreements to arbitrate in the Americas were not confined to matters involving the United States. On the contrary, between 1800 and 1910, some 185 separate treaties among Latin American states included arbitration clauses, dealing with everything from pecuniary claims to boundaries and to general relations.[42] For example, an 1822 agreement between Colombia and Peru, which was intended to "draw more closely the bonds which should in future unite the two states," provides that "a general assembly of the American states shall be convened ... as an umpire and conciliator in their disputes and differences."[43] Moreover, many Latin American states engaged in inter-state arbitrations arising from contentious boundary disputes inherited from colonial periods, which the disputing parties submitted to a foreign sovereign or commission for resolution.[44] Arbitration of such matters was not always successful, especially when the disputed territory was rich in natural resources or minerals,[45] and boundary disputes at times required additional arbitrations to interpret an initial award.[46]

d. Arbitral Procedures in Inter-State Arbitrations

As outlined above, arbitral procedures have varied substantially, both over time and in different geographic and political settings. At least in part, that reflects the inherent flexi-

38. Treaty of Guadalupe Hidalgo, Art. XXI (1848). The United States and Mexico entered into a number of other treaty arrangements during the 19th century, to resolve various categories of disputes. J. Ralston, *International Arbitration From Athens to Locarno* 203-07 (1929).

39. Treaty of Washington, Art. 1 (1871).

40. *See infra* p. 104; Bingham, *The* Alabama Claims *Arbitration*, 54 Int'l & Comp. L.Q. 1 (2005); F. Hackett, *Reminiscences of the Geneva Tribunal of Arbitration* (1911).

41. J. Ralston, *International Arbitration From Athens to Locarno* 194-95 (1929).

42. W. Manning, *Arbitration Treaties Among the American Nations* (1978).

43. W. Manning, *Arbitration Treaties Among the American Nations* 1 n.1 (1978).

44. Woolsey, *Boundary Disputes in Latin-America*, 25 Am. J. Int'l L. 324, 325 nn.1, 2 (1931) (Argentine and Paraguayan territory dispute settled by 1878 arbitral award issued by U.S. President Hayes; Costa Rican and Nicaraguan territory dispute settled by 1888 arbitral award issued by U.S. President Cleveland; Argentine and Chilean territory dispute settled by 1902 arbitral award issued by King Edward VII of United Kingdom).

45. *See* Donovan, *Challenges to the Territorial Integrity of Guyana: A Legal Analysis*, 32 Ga. J. Int'l & Comp. L. 661, 675-78 (2004) (describing demise of arbitral ruling over Venezuela-British Guyana territory with gold deposits); Woolsey, *Boundary Disputes in Latin-America*, 25 Am. J. Int'l L. 330 (1931) (describing inconclusive nature of arbitration over Ecuador-Peru territory rich in tropical resources).

46. *See* Convention Between Costa Rica and Panama for the Settlement of the Boundary Controversy, 6 Am. J. Int'l L. 1, 1-4 (Supp. 1912); K. Carlston, *The Process of International Arbitration* 66-70 (1946).

bility of the arbitral process, which leaves the parties (and arbitrators) free to devise procedures tailored to a particular dispute and legal or cultural setting.

Despite this inherent flexibility, the procedures used in state-to-state arbitrations have also displayed, with remarkable consistency, certain enduring common characteristics. These have included an essentially adversarial procedure, with states being free—and required—to present their respective cases, often through counsel and/or agents; an adjudicative procedure, with decisions being based on the evidentiary and legal submissions of the parties; and continuing efforts to devise procedures that would provide a fair, efficient and expeditious arbitral process.[47] As already noted, historic approaches towards the inter-state arbitral process often produced procedures that were not dissimilar to those used in contemporary state-to-state arbitrations.

Arbitral procedures that evolved in state-to-state arbitrations during the 19th century bore even closer resemblance to contemporary proceedings, with international tribunals more systematically exercising their power to establish rules governing pleadings and proceedings.[48] Governments were generally represented by an agent, who represented the interests of the state, and a counsel, who provided advice, managed the case and appeared before the tribunal.[49] Cases were initiated by a written memorial, which asserted the basic legal claims and alleged sufficient facts to establish jurisdiction; the opposing party's response then could come in the form of an answer, a plea, a motion to dismiss, or an exception.[50]

Although rules for evidence varied, tribunals generally preferred documentary evidence to live witnesses and, rather than excluding certain types of evidence, would accept all evidence and weigh it at their discretion.[51] With the increased frequency of state-to-state arbitration over the course of the 19th century, practices of civil and common law countries converged, eventually giving way to the partial codification of these procedures in international instruments.[52] Again, the procedures outlined in these 19th century instruments bear striking similarities to contemporary procedural regimes in international arbitration.

One of the enduring features of international arbitration procedure in the state-to-state context, regardless of time or cultural setting, has been the nomination of members of the tribunal by the individual parties. From almost the beginning of recorded modern history—through every age until the present—party-nominated arbitrators have been an enduring, essential feature of the international arbitral process. Thus:

a. In a 1254 treaty of peace among various German states, future disputes were to be settled by mixed tribunals composed of judges of equal number of the two parties and

---

47. *See infra* pp. 6-10, 69-84.

48. *See* C. Bishop, *International Arbitral Procedure* (1930); K. Carlston, *The Process of International Arbitration* 3-33 (1946); Institut de Droit International, *Projet de règlement pour la procédure arbitrale internationale* (Session de La Haye, 1875).

49. J. Ralston, *International Arbitration From Athens to Locarno* 75-76 (1929).

50. J. Ralston, *International Arbitration From Athens to Locarno* 77-78 (1929). *See also* K. Carlston, *The Process of International Arbitration* 7 (1946).

51. J. Ralston, *International Arbitration From Athens to Locarno* 79-80 (1929). *See also* K. Carlston, *The Process of International Arbitration* 26-27 (1946); Pietrowski, *Evidence in International Arbitration*, 22 Arb. Int'l 373, 374-75 (2006).

52. *See* K. Carlston, *The Process of International Arbitration* 260-64 (1946); Institut de Droit International, *Projet de règlement pour la procédure arbitrale internationale* (Session de La Haye, 1875).

presided over by a "*gemeiner Mann*" (umpire).[53] Northern Italian states and Swiss cantons adopted the same approach during the 12th, 13th and 14th centuries, with the occasional variation that each party was required to select a national of the counter-party as co-arbitrator.[54]

b. In one of the earliest Medieval plans for institutional international arbitration of state-to-state disputes, in 1306, Pierre Dubois proposed a means of settling disputes among European principalities, involving each party nominating three arbitrators, to be joined by three additional ecclesiastics.[55]

c. The 1343 Arbitral Convention between King Waldemar of Denmark and King Magnus of Sweden provided for each state to select three bishops and three knights and, if the resulting tribunal was unable to resolve matters, to select two (one each) of its number to make a final decision.[56]

d. The 1516 Treaty of Perpetual Peace between the Swiss Cantons and Francis I provided for arbitration before "four men of substance, two named by each party," and "if their opinions are divided, the plaintiff may choose from the neighboring counties a *prud'homme* beyond suspicion and who will meet with the arbitrators to decide the difficulty."[57]

e. The 1655 Treaty of Westminster between France and England provided for resolution of future disputes by six arbitrators, three named by each side, with unresolved matters being referred to the Republic of Hamburg, which was charged with selecting a further tribunal.[58]

f. The 1781 Articles of Confederation, of the American colonies, provided for the arbitral resolution of disputes between states by an arbitral process, with the concerned states being involved in selection of the tribunal, either by agreement or through an innovative list system.[59]

g. Jay's Treaty of 1794, between the United States and Great Britain, provided for three arbitral mechanisms, with the tribunals consisting of either three arbitrators (one appointed by the United States and one by Great Britain, with the two party-nominated arbitrators selecting a third, either by agreement or a prescribed list system) or five

---

53. J. Ralston, *International Arbitration From Athens to Locarno* 180 (1929).

54. J. Verzijl, VIII *International Law in Historical Perspective* 192-93 (1974).

55. Fraser, *A Sketch of the History of International Arbitration*, 11 Cornell L.Q. 179, 179 n.3 (1925-1926) (citing authorities).

56. J. Ralston, *International Arbitration From Athens to Locarno* 178 (1929).

57. J. Ralston, *International Arbitration From Athens to Locarno* 178 (1929) (quoting A. Mergnhac, *Traité théorique et pratique de l'arbitrage international* 40 (1895)).

58. J. Ralston, *International Arbitration From Athens to Locarno* 185 (1929).

59. Articles of Confederation, Art. IX (1781) ("[The two disputing States] shall then be directed to appoint by joint consent, commissioners or judges to constitute a court for hearing and determining the matter in question: but if they cannot agree, Congress shall name three persons out of each of the United States, and from the list of such persons each party shall alternately strike out one, the petitioners beginning, until the number shall be reduced to thirteen; and from that number not less than seven, nor more than nine names as Congress shall direct, shall in the presence of Congress be drawn out by lot, and the persons whose names shall be so drawn or any five of them, shall be commissioners or judges, to hear and finally determine the controversy, so always as a major part of the judges who shall hear the cause shall agree in the determination.").

arbitrators (two appointed by the King of England, two by the President of the United States and the fifth by agreement or through the use of a prescribed list system).[60]

h. The Treaty of April 11, 1839, between the United States and Mexico provided for a tribunal of five, with two arbitrators appointed by each state and (absent agreement) the fifth arbitrator being selected by the King of Prussia.[61] A large number of other treaties between the United States and various Latin American states provided for party-nominated arbitrators on either three or five-person tribunals.[62]

i. The so-called Portendick claims, between Great Britain and France (concerning an allegedly unlawful French blockade of the Moroccan coast), were referred to the King of Prussia, who in turn referred implementation of his award to a tribunal consisting of one arbitrator nominated by each state and a third whom he selected.[63]

j. The 1871 Treaty of Washington provided (with regard to U.S. claims against Great Britain) for two party-nominated arbitrators on a tribunal of five, with the remaining three arbitrators being nominated by neutral states.[64] To resolve claims by private citizens against either of the two signatory nations, the treaty provided for three-person tribunals, with each state nominating one arbitrator and an umpire being selected by agreement or by a neutral third party.[65] Other arbitration provisions between the United States and Great Britain very frequently involved party-nominations of members of the tribunal.[66]

k. An 1897 reference to arbitration between Austria and Hungary, relating to territorial claims near Lake Meerauge, was referred to a tribunal consisting of two party-nominated arbitrators and an umpire.[67]

l. "Mixed" claims tribunals have been repeatedly used, in a wide variety of contexts, to resolve claims arising out of war, unrest, or similar circumstances. The invariable procedure for constituting a tribunal was for one arbitrator to be nominated by each side, and a presiding arbitrator or umpire to be selected by agreement or by a neutral power.[68]

m. The 1899 Hague Convention for the Pacific Settlement of International Disputes and the 1907 Hague Convention for the Pacific Settlement of International Disputes established rules for the constitution of arbitral tribunals, including provisions for each

---

60. Jay's Treaty, Arts. V-VII (1794); H. Miller, II *Treaties and Other International Acts of the United States of America* 1776-1863 245 (1931).

61. Treaty of 11 April, 1839, Arts. I, VII; H. Miller, IV *Treaties and Other International Acts of the United States of America* 1776-1863 189 (1931).

62. J. Ralston, *International Arbitration From Athens to Locarno* 205-26 (1929) (including Mexican pecuniary and boundary disputes, Chilean, Colombian, Ecuadorean, German, Peruvian, Spanish and other pecuniary disputes, Norwegian shipping claims, and a host of other matters).

63. J. Ralston, *International Arbitration From Athens to Locarno* 227-28 (1929).

64. Treaty of Washington, Art. I (1871), excerpted at p. 65 of the Documentary Supplement.

65. Treaty of Washington, Art. XII (1871), excerpted at p. 69 of the Documentary Supplement.

66. J. Ralston, *International Arbitration From Athens to Locarno* 194-96 (1929). A leading example of this involved disputes over the harvesting of fur seals on U.S. islands. *Ibid.*

67. J. Ralston, *International Arbitration From Athens to Locarno* 236 (1929).

68. J. Ralston, *International Arbitration From Athens to Locarno* 246-49 (1929).

party to nominate two co-arbitrators and for the co-arbitrators to select an umpire, failing which a neutral party would be chosen to make the selection.[69]

n.   Both the Permanent Court of International Justice and its eventual successor, the International Court of Justice, provided mechanisms for the constitution of the Court that included *ad hoc* judges nominated by each party.[70]

o.   Under the 2000 Eritrea-Ethiopia Boundary Commission Arbitration Agreement, each party appointed two commissioners and the president of the Commission was selected by the party-appointed commissioners, failing which the Secretary-General of the United Nations would have appointed the president in consultation with the parties.[71]

p.   The 2008 arbitration agreement between the Government of Sudan and the Sudan People's Liberation Movement/Army (the representatives of which would become the Republic of South Sudan in 2011) provided that each party would appoint two arbitrators and the party-appointed arbitrators would appoint a fifth arbitrator, or the Secretary-General of the Permanent Court of Arbitration would do so.[72]

A scholar of state-to-state arbitrations during the 19th century concluded his discussion of the procedural aspects of the subject by referring to:

> the very common idea that the sovereign power of the contestants should find representation on the court, an idea which finds illustration even in the Permanent Court of International Justice. The theory is that the representatives of the parties can speak with authority within the bosom of the court with regard to the law and contentions of their governments, an idea which would not be tolerated because of manifest evils within the bosom of a national court.[73]

As discussed below, this approach was also an enduring feature of international commercial arbitrations between private parties and in international investment arbitrations between private parties and states.[74]

2. Historical Development of Commercial Arbitration

Just as arbitration between states has an ancient, rich history, so arbitration of commercial disputes can be traced to the beginning of recorded human society. It is occasionally suggested that "as a technocratic mechanism of dispute settlement, with a particular set of rules and doctrines, international commercial arbitration is a product of this century [*i.e.*, the 20th century]."[75] Insofar as this implies that international commercial arbitration is a

---

69. 1899 Hague Convention, Art. 24; 1907 Hague Convention, Arts. 45, 54. *See* R. Caldwell, *A Study of the Code of Arbitral Procedure Adopted by the Hague Peace Conference of 1899 and 1907* (1921).

70. Statute of the PCIJ, Arts. 5, 6 (1920); Statute of the International Court of Justice, Arts. 5, 6 (1945). *See generally* S. Rosenne, III *The Law and Practice of the International Court 1920-2005* 1079-89 (4th ed. 2006).

71. Agreement Between the Government of the State of Eritrea and the Government of the Federal Democratic Republic of Ethiopia (the "Algiers Agreement") (2000).

72. Arbitration Agreement Between the Government of Sudan and the Sudan People's Liberation Movement/Army on Delimiting Abyei Area (2008).

73. J. Ralston, *International Arbitration From Athens to Locarno* 226 (1929).

74. *See infra* pp. 13, 696-702.

75. Shalakany, *Arbitration and the Third World: A Plea for Reassessing Bias Under the Specter of Neo-Liberalism*, 41 Harv. Int'l L.J. 419, 430 (2000). *See also* Sornarajah, *The Climate of International Arbitration*, 8(2) J. Int'l Arb. 47, 50-51 (1991) ("International commercial arbitration, particularly in the field of foreign investment contracts, developed principally in the latter part of the twentieth century....").

recent phenomenon, it is contradicted by a detailed historical record, which leaves no serious doubt as to the long tradition—stretching for many centuries—of arbitration and related forms of dispute resolution as a means for resolving international business disputes.

a. Commercial Arbitration in Antiquity

As in the state-to-state context, some of the earliest reports of commercial arbitration are from the Middle East. Archaeological research reports that clay tablets from contemporary Iraq recite a dispute between one Tulpunnaya and her neighbor, Killi, over water rights in a village near Kirkuk, which was resolved by arbitration (with Tulpunnaya being awarded ten silver shekels and an ox).[76] Arbitration was also apparently well known in ancient Egypt, with convincing examples of agreements to arbitrate future disputes (used alongside what amount to forum selection clauses) included in funerary trust arrangements in 2500 B.C. and 2300 B.C.[77]

Arbitration was no less common in ancient Greece for the resolution of commercial and other "private" disputes than for state-to-state disputes.[78] Homer describes an 8th century B.C. resolution of a blood debt through a public arbitral process, where the disputants appealed to a man "versed in the law," of their mutual choice, who presided over a tribunal of elders which publicly heard the parties' claims and rendered reasoned oral opinions.[79] The example suggests the use of arbitration to resolve disputes between private parties in Antiquity, but also indicates the lack of clear boundaries in some periods between governmental dispute resolution mechanisms and "private," consensual arbitration.

The reasons for resorting to arbitration in Antiquity appear to be remarkably modern. Historical research indicates that ancient Greek courts—like today's courts in many countries—suffered from congestion and back-logs, which led to the use of arbitrators, retained from other city states (rather like foreign engineers or mercenaries), to resolve pending cases.[80] Similarly, a summary of the basic legal rules governing commercial arbitration in ancient Greece is not far distant from contemporary legislation in the area:

> If any parties are in dispute concerning private contracts, and wish to choose any arbitrator, it shall be lawful for them to choose whomsoever they wish. But when they have chosen by mutual agreement, they shall abide by his decisions and shall not transfer the same charges

---

76. Burrows & Speiser, *One Hundred New Selected Nuzi Texts*, 16 Annual Am. Schools Oriental Research, 79, 95 (1936) (document 41), cited in L. Edmonson (ed.), *Domke on Commercial Arbitration* §2.1 (3d ed. 2010 & Update 2013).

77. Mantica, *Arbitration in Ancient Egypt*, 12 Arb. J. 155, 158-60 (1957) ("Records of very advanced procedures of arbitration survive from those [Greco-Roman] periods").

78. D. Roebuck, *Ancient Greek Arbitration* 45-46, 348-49, 358 (2001) ("Everywhere in the Ancient Greek world, including Ptolemaic Egypt, and at all times within our period, disputing parties considered arbitration to be a natural, perhaps the most natural, method of resolving the differences they could not settle themselves, even though they sometimes resorted to litigation (or in earlier times self-help) when they could not get their own way.").

79. Hammond, *Arbitration in Ancient Greece*, 1 Arb. Int'l 188 (1985) (citing Homer, *The Iliad* XVIII 497-508).

80. Bonner, *The Institution of Athenian Arbitrators*, 11 *Classical Philology* 191, 192 (1916); Hammond, *Arbitration in Ancient Greece*, 1 Arb. Int'l 188, 189 (1985); D. Roebuck, *Ancient Greek Arbitration* 348-49 (2001) ("Arbitration was the natural and regular process of choice for those who could not afford litigation, were afraid of its outcome, preferred privacy, or were manipulating the alternatives").

from him to another court, but the judgments of the arbitrator shall be final.[81]

Arbitral procedures in ancient Greece appear to have been largely subject to the parties' control, including with regard to the subject matter of the arbitration, the arbitrators, the choice of law and other matters.[82] Although sole arbitrators were not uncommon, parties frequently agreed to arbitrate before three or five arbitrators, with each party selecting one (or two) arbitrator(s) and the party-nominated arbitrators choosing a presiding arbitrator (a "*koinos*").[83]

Arbitration of commercial matters in ancient Roman times was more common than Roman state-to-state arbitrations, with compliance with arbitration agreements and awards enforceable in Roman courts, sometimes through a penalty mechanism or sanctions.[84] A leading scholar on Roman law summarizes the subject as follows:

> from the beginning of the empire, Roman law allowed citizens to opt out of the legal process by what they called *compromissum*. This was an agreement to refer a matter to an *arbiter*, as he was called, and at the same time the parties bound themselves to pay a penalty if the arbitrator's award was disobeyed. Payment of the penalty could be enforced by legal action.[85]

As in Greece, awards in Roman practice were reasoned, binding and apparently subject to little judicial review: "The award of the arbiter which he makes with reference to the matter in dispute should be complied with, whether it is just or unjust; because the party who accepted the arbitration had only himself to blame."[86] Parties could seek enforcement of arbitral awards in the courts (or other government forums), although the enforcement mechanisms that were available varied over time.[87]

It appears that arbitral procedures in Roman times were not dissimilar to those in more modern eras. In a parallel to modern arbitral practice, the arbitrator's jurisdiction was strictly limited to "the terms of the agreement for arbitration (*compromissum*), and, therefore, he cannot decide anything he pleases, nor with reference to any matter that he pleases, but only what was set forth in the agreement for arbitration, and in compliance

---

81. Demosthenes, *Against Meidias*, in Demos*thenes Against Meidias, Androtion, Aristocrates, Timocrates, Aristogeiton* 69, 94. *See also* Velissaropoulos-Karakostas, *L'arbitrage dans la Grèce antique: Epoques archaïque et classique*, 2000 Rev. arb. 9.

82. D. Roebuck, *Ancient Greek Arbitration* 347-48 (2001) ("If the parties chose to submit their disputes to private arbitration, then throughout the arbitration process they had almost unlimited freedom of choice. By their agreement they controlled the subject-matter in dispute, the selection of arbitrators, the limits of their jurisdiction, the rules of procedure and even whether they should decide the issue according to the law or should determine according to their sense of fairness.").

83. D. Roebuck, *Ancient Greek Arbitration* 349 (2001) (where tribunal consisted of more than one arbitrator, "each party would then appoint one, sometimes two, who would be identified with that party's interests either as a friend or member of the family. The parties' arbitrators would then appoint a *koinos*, someone common to both sides, who took his place as an equal with the others").

84. *See* D. Roebuck & B. de Fumichon, *Roman Arbitration* 94 (2004) ("The Romans probably began to make use of arbitration *ex compromisso*, a private arbitration created and controlled by the written agreement of the parties but supported by the *praetor*, at some time in the second century BC, at a time of great imperial and colonial expansion").

85. Stein, *Arbitration Under Roman Law*, 41 Arb. 203, 203-04 (1974).

86. *Digest*, 4, 8, 27, 2 (Ulpian), in S. Scott (ed.), III *The Civil Law* (1932).

87. M. Kaser & K. Hackl, *Das römische Zivilprozessrecht* 640 (2d ed. 1996); B. Matthias, *Die Entwicklung des römischen Schiedsgerichts*, in *Festschrift zum fünfzigjährigen Doktorjubiläum von Bernhard Windscheid* 102 (1888).

with the terms of the same."[88] Arbitrators in the Classical age reportedly remained entirely free in their decisions: "they were not bound by any rules of substantive law."[89] Parties enjoyed substantial autonomy with regard to the arbitral procedures.[90]

Among other things, and paralleling state-to-state practice, historical records reveal the widespread use of party-nominated arbitrators: "a common practice … [was] to refer the matter to two arbitrators and the praetor is bound to compel them, if they disagree, to choose a third person themselves and his authority can be obeyed."[91] If an arbitrator agreed to hear a dispute (*receptum arbitrum*), but subsequently refused to do so, local judicial officials could apparently compel him to fulfil his duties.[92]

Although few records of ordinary commercial disputes from this era have survived, historians nonetheless conclude that arbitration was widely used in ancient Rome.[93] There were few limits on the subjects of arbitration, and in practice a wide range of commercial and family matters were arbitrated.[94]

In the post-Classical period, arbitration became increasingly popular because of deficiencies in state court systems, which were characterized as unreliable, cumbersome and costly, and which faced particular difficulties in inter-state matters.[95] During this era, the enforceability of arbitration agreements was progressively recognized, even without a penalty mechanism.[96] This result was generally based on the principle of *pacta sunt servanda*, which was developed and applied by canonical jurists in the context of agreements to arbitrate.[97]

The Church began to play a leading role in the later Roman Empire, with arbitral jurisdiction frequently being exercised by Christian bishops (*episcopalis audentia*). Once parties had agreed to "Episcopal" arbitration, a subsequent award was enforceable without judicial review.[98] Simultaneously, arbitral tribunals established within Jewish congrega-

88. *Digest*, 4, 8, 32, 15 (Paulus); S. Scott (ed.), III *The Civil Law* (1932); Stein, *Labeo's Reasoning on Arbitration*, 91 S. African L.J. 135 (1974); R. Zimmerman, *The Law of Obligations* 513-14 (1996) ("the arbitrator can act only on the basis of a contractual relationship (*sui generis*) existing between himself and the parties to the dispute").

89. R. Zimmermann, *The Law of Obligations* 529 (1996). *See also* Coing, *Zur Entwicklung des Schiedsvertrages im Ius Commune* 36, in G. Baumgärtel *et al.* (eds.), *Festschrift für Heinz Hübner* (1984).

90. D. Roebuck & B. de Fumichon, *Roman Arbitration* 160 (2004) ("The parties controlled the scope of the arbiter's powers to dictate the form of the proceedings").

91. Stein, *Arbitration Under Roman Law*, 41 Arb. 203, 205 (1974).

92. M. Kaser & K. Hackl, *Das römische Zivilprozessrecht* 639 (2d ed. 1996); Matthias, *Die Entwicklung des römischen Schiedsgerichts*, in *Festschrift zum fünfzigjährigen Doctorjubiläum von Bernhard Windscheid* 102 (1888).

93. D. Roebuck, *Roman Arbitration* (2004); F. Sanborn, *Origins of the Early English Maritime and Commercial Law* 8-9 (1930); Stein, *Arbitration Under Roman Law*, 41 Arb. 203, 203-04 (1974).

94. D. Roebuck & B. de Fumichon, *Roman Arbitration* 105 (2004) ("With these few exceptions [for inheritance and status of slaves/citizens] … arbitration *ex compromisso* was used comprehensively to deal with all types of disputes, relating to land and goods and slaves, and breaches of contract of all kinds").

95. K.-H. Ziegler, *Das private Schiedsgericht im antiken römischen Recht* 199-201 (1971).

96. K.-H. Ziegler, *Das private Schiedsgericht im antiken römischen Recht* 182 (1971); R. Zimmermann, *The Law of Obligations* 527 (1996).

97. K.-H. Ziegler, *Geschichtliche und dogmatische Aspekte des Schiedsvertrages*, in R. Zimmermann (ed.), *Rechtsgeschichte und Privatrechtsdogmatik* 671 *et seq.* (1999).

98. M. Kaser & K. Hackl, *Das römische Zivilprozessrecht* 643 (2d ed. 1996).

tions were granted similar powers, enabling them to decide not only religious, but also commercial, disputes.[99]

Arbitration continued to play—so far as the historical record can be understood—an important role in commercial matters in the Byzantine period, in Egypt and elsewhere. Although the records and details of such arbitrations are uncertain, those materials that survived involve merchants, family feuds, inheritance disputes and other private law matters being submitted to binding arbitration, with the results being enforced through penalty mechanisms (as in Roman times).[100]

b. Commercial Arbitration in the European Middle Ages

A wide variety of regional and local forms of arbitration were used to resolve private law disputes throughout the Middle Ages in Europe. A recurrent theme of this development was the use of arbitration by merchants in connection with merchant guilds, trade fairs, or other forms of commercial or professional organizations. As in the state-to-state context,[101] arbitration was particularly common during Medieval times in the Swiss Confederation, Northern Italy, Germany and neighboring regions (the Hanseatic League, in particular), France and England. Indeed, it is "very common," if inaccurate, "to say that commercial arbitration had its beginning with the practices of the market and fair courts and in the merchant gilds."[102]

In Medieval England, the charters of numerous guilds—such as the Company of Clothworkers or the Gild of St. John of Beverley of the Hans House[103]—provided for mandatory arbitration of disputes among members. The guilds "entertain actions of debt and covenant and trespass, and hardly dare we call such assemblies mere courts of arbitration, for they can enforce their own decrees."[104] Where merchants did business with one another at trade fairs, outside the context of a guild, arbitration also played a role. Indeed, because fairs involved numerous itinerant or foreign merchants, this appears to have been a direct forbearer of more modern forms of international commercial arbitration.[105]

Arbitration of "international" disputes of this sort was preferred for reasons of expedition and commercial expertise, as well as, increasingly, the inadequacy of the local courts or other decision-makers to deal with the special jurisdictional and enforcement obstacles presented by foreign or "international" litigation. In Blackstone's words, which again might be uttered almost equally well today:

---

99. K.-H. Ziegler, *Das private Schiedsgericht im antiken römischen Recht* 175 (1971).

100. Mantica, *Arbitration in Ancient Egypt*, 12 Arb. J. 155, 161-62 (1957); Modrzejewski, *Private Arbitration in the Law of Greco-Roman Egypt*, 6 J. Juristic Papyrology 239 (1952).

101. *See supra* pp. 4-5.

102. Wolaver, *The Historical Background of Commercial Arbitration*, 83 U. Pa. L. Rev. 132, 133 (1934-1935).

103. J. Cohen, *Commercial Arbitration and the Law* 4 (1918).

104. F. Pollock & F. Maitland, *The History of English Law* 668 (2d ed. 1898). For a less expansive view, *see* A. Carter, *A History of English Legal Institutions* 258-59 (1902) ("Members of the same gild were bound to bring their disputes before the gilds before litigating the matter elsewhere.").

105. Arbitration was also relied on to resolve disputes in a wide range of substantive areas outside of commerce proper, including real estate, medical negligence, employment, determinations of feudal status, and even complaints of assault or arson. *See* Roebuck, *L'arbitrage en droit anglais avant 1558*, 2002 Rev. arb. 535, 567-76.

The reason of their original institution seems to have been, to do justice expeditiously among the variety of persons that resort from distant places to a fair or market; since it is probable that no inferior court might be able to serve its process, or execute its judgments, on both or either of the parties....[106]

The guilds and fairs developed their respective arbitral mechanisms with substantial independence from local court systems. That is reflected in the explanation provided by Gerard Malynes, a 17th century English authority on the law merchant:

The second meane or rather ordinarie course to end the questions and controversies arising between Merchants, is by way of Arbitrement, when both parties do make choice of honest men to end their causes, which is voluntarie and in their own power, and therefore called Arbitrium, or free will, whence the name Arbitrator is derived: and these men (by some called Good men) give their judgments by Awards, according to Equitie and Conscience, observing the Custome of Merchants, and ought to be void of all partialitie or affection more nor lesse to the one, than to the other, having onely care that right may take place according the truth, and that the difference may bee ended with brevitie and expedition....[107]

It also appears that English courts were quite prepared during this early period to give effect to arbitration agreements by enforcing penalty clauses associated with them, by barring litigation on claims within the scope of arbitration agreements and by a robust enforcement of arbitral awards.[108]

Arbitration appears to have been equally important to commercial affairs in Germany, Switzerland, Northern Italy and France. The Edict of 1560, promulgated by Francis II, made arbitration mandatory for the resolution of commercial disputes among merchants; at the same time, it declared arbitration agreements valid, even without a penalty clause, thereby moving beyond Roman law requirements for a *compromissum*.[109] Although successive French Parliaments apparently fought to restrict the binding character of commercial arbitration, the practice remained well-established until the French Revolution.[110]

Commercial arbitration was also prevalent in the Swiss cantons and German principalities.[111] In these areas of Europe, arbitration developed from two principal sources, which began to fuse in the 14th and 15th centuries. On the one hand, local traditions of arbitration

---

106. S. Tucker, III *Blackstone's* Commentaries 33 (1803) (quoted in Wolaver, *The Historical Background of Commercial Arbitration*, 83 U. Pa. L. Rev. 132, 136 (1934-1935)).

107. G. Malynes, *Lex Mercatoria, or The Ancient Law Merchant; Divided Into Three Parts: According to the 'Essentiall Parts of Trafficke: Necessarie for All Statesmen, Judges, Magistrates, Temporal and Civil Lawyers, Mint-men, Merchants, Mariners, and All others Negotiating in All Places of the World* Chapter XV (1622). *Id.* at Chapter XV (1685 ed.) ("[W]hen Merchants by their Letters or Commissions use these or the like words, Let All things be done as shall be thought most expedient or convenient, that the said Commissions or Directions are to be left to the interpretation of Arbitrators when any question ariseth, which is also in many more questions concerning Merchants.").

108. Simpson, *The Penal Bond with Conditional Defeasance*, 82 L.Q. Rev. 392 (1966).

109. R. David, *Arbitration in International Trade* 88-89 (1985).

110. D. Bell, *Lawyers and Citizens: The Making of A Political Elite in Old Regime France* 31 (1994); R. David, *Arbitration in International Trade* 88-89 (1985); Kessler, *Enforcing Virtue: Social Norms and Self-Interest in An Eighteenth-Century Merchant Court*, 22 Law & Hist. Rev. 71, 82-86 (2004).

111. Bader, *Arbiter, arbitrator seu amicabilis compositor*, 77 Zeitschrift für Rechtsgeschichte Kan. Abt. 239, 240 *et seq.* (1960); H. Krause, *Die geschichtliche Entwicklung des Schiedsgerichtswesens in Deutschland* 36 *et seq.*, 52 (1930).

were integrated into the feudal system; on the other, the Catholic Church offered arbitral mechanisms and practices which were developed under canonical law.[112]

Whatever its sources, it is clear that commercial arbitration was very widely used in these regions of Europe during the Middle Ages. Consistent with this, early codifications of procedural law dating from the 14th, 15th and 16th centuries provided for arbitration as a supplement to local court proceedings.[113] Research in Southern Germany, Switzerland and Austria also reveals thousands of "arbitration deeds" (*"Schiedsurkunde"*) evidencing a rich and varied arbitral practice in these regions during the Middle Ages.[114] A representative example was Bavaria, where there is substantial evidence of commercial arbitration in the 13th and 14th centuries.[115] Another anecdotal example is drawn from the archives of the principality of Fürstenberg, which contain more than 500 arbitral deeds for the period between 1275 and 1600 (compared to records for some 25 court proceedings).[116]

Despite its deep historical roots, commercial arbitration also encountered recurrent challenges, often in the form of political and judicial mistrust or jealousy. These challenges have sometimes been overstated, and they have almost always been overcome by the perceived benefits of the arbitral process in commercial settings and the (eventual) acceptance of these benefits by governmental bodies. Moreover, the enforceability of arbitration agreements appears frequently to have been achieved, in historical commercial settings, largely through non-legal sanctions, such as commercial, religious and other sanctions effectuated via guilds or similar bodies.[117] Nonetheless, the historical record is not complete without addressing some of the more significant challenges that have sporadically emerged to the legal enforcement of arbitration agreements and awards.

c. Commercial Arbitration in England

In the common law world, Lord Coke's 1609 decision in *Vynior's Case* enjoys the greatest notoriety for its treatment of agreements to arbitrate. The case involved a suit by Vynior against Wilde, seeking payment on a bond, which had secured the parties' promise to submit a dispute over a parish tax to arbitration.[118] Coke granted judgment for Vynior on the bond, but added the following reasoning:

> [A]lthough ... the defendant was bound in a bond to ... observe [the] arbitrament, yet he might countermand it; for a man cannot by his act make such authority ... not countermandable, which is by the law and of its own nature countermandable; as if I make a letter of attorney ... so if I make my testament and last will irrevocable[.] And therefore ... in both cases [*i.e.*, both where an arbitration agreement is supported by a bond and where the

---

112. H. Krause, *Die geschichtliche Entwicklung des Schiedsgerichtswesens in Deutschland* 2 *et seq.*, 40 *et seq.* (1930).

113. H. Krause, *Die geschichtliche Entwicklung des Schiedsgerichtswesens in Deutschland* 58 *et seq.* (1930).

114. *See* Bader, *Arbiter, arbitrator seu amicabilis compositor*, 77 Zeitschrift für Rechtsgeschichte Kan. Abt. 239, 240 *et seq.* (1960).

115. M. Kobler, *Das Schiedsgerichtswesen nach bayerischen Quellen des Mittelalters* 107-08 (1966).

116. *See* Bader, *Arbiter, arbitrator seu amicabilis compositor*, 77 Zeitschrift für Rechtsgeschichte Kan. Abt. 239, 240 *et seq.* (1960).

117. *See also infra* pp. 21-26; Benson, *An Exploration of the Impact of Modern Arbitration Statutes on the Development of Arbitration in the United States*, 11 J.L. Econ. & Org. 479, 480 n.2, *passim* (1995).

118. *Vynior v. Wilde* (1609) 77 ER 595 (English King's Bench).

agreement incorporates no bond] the authority of the arbitrator may be revoked; but then in the one case he shall forfeit his bond and in the other he shall lose nothing.[119]

As long as penalty bonds remained enforceable, Coke's dictum was of limited practical import; parties could, and routinely did, include penalty provisions in their agreements to arbitrate.[120]

The common law's treatment of such provisions was changed, however, in 1687, when Parliament enacted the Statute of Fines and Penalties, which disallowed recovery of penalties generally, limiting bond-holders to the recovery of actual damages.[121] Apparently to correct the effect of this statute on commercial arbitration, Parliament soon thereafter enacted one of the world's first arbitration statutes, adopting what is sometimes called the 1698 Arbitration Act.[122] Reflecting an objective of promoting commerce that would recur in later eras, the Act's objects were:

> *promoting trade*, and rendering the awards of arbitrators more effectual in all cases, for the final determination of controversies referred to them by *merchants and traders, or others, concerning matters of account or trade, or other matters.*[123]

These objects were realized by providing that parties could make their arbitration agreement "a rule of any of His Majesty's Courts of Record," which would permit enforcement by way of a judicial order that "the parties shall submit to, and finally be concluded by the arbitration and umpirage."[124] This legislation sought to remedy, at least in part, the damage effected by the combination of Coke's dicta in *Vynior's Case* and the Statute against Fines, allowing Blackstone to conclude:

> [I]t is now become the practice to enter into mutual bonds, with condition to stand to the award or arbitration of the arbitrators or umpire therein named. And experience having shown the great use of these peaceable and domestic tribunals, especially in settling matters of account, and other mercantile transactions, which are difficult and almost impossible to be adjusted on a trial at law; the legislature has now established the use of them.[125]

It nonetheless remained the case that, at English common law, an arbitration agreement was—on the authority of the dicta in *Vynior's Case*, which later hardened into solid precedent—"revocable" at will. Although damages were in theory recoverable when an arbitration agreement was revoked, damages could not readily be proven or recovered for breach of an arbitration agreement—rendering such agreements nearly unenforceable in cases where the 1698 Arbitration Act did not apply.[126]

Outside the statutory "safe haven" of the 1698 Arbitration Act, common law enforcement of arbitration agreements was made even more problematic by the decision in *Kill v. Hollister*. There, the court permitted an action on an insurance policy to proceed, not-

---

119. *Vynior v. Wilde* (1609) 77 ER 595, 598-600 (English King's Bench).

120. R. David, *Arbitration In International Trade* 109 (1985) (noting willingness of English courts to enforce penalty provisions); W. Holdsworth, 12 *A History of English Law* 519-20 (2d printing 1966); Roebuck, *The Myth of Judicial Jealousy*, 10 Arb. Int'l 395 (1994).

121. An Act for the Better Preventing Frivolous and Vexatious Suits, 1697, 8 & 9 Will. III, Ch. 11.

122. Samuel, *Arbitration Statutes in England and the USA*, 8 Arb. & Disp. Resol. L.J. 2, 4 (1999).

123. An Act for Determining Differences by Arbitration, 1698, 9 & 10 Will. III, Ch. 15 (emphasis added).

124. An Act for Determining Differences by Arbitration, 1698, 9 & 10 Will. III, Ch. 15.

125. S. Tucker, IV *Blackstone's Commentaries on the Laws of England* 16-17 (1803).

126. *See Doleman & Sons v. Ossett Corp.* [1912] 3 KB 257, 267-68 (Fletcher Moulton, L.J.).

withstanding an arbitration clause, on the grounds that "the agreement of the parties cannot oust this court."[127] In subsequent centuries, that doctrine—which appeared to raise a broad-based public policy objection to arbitration (and forum selection) agreements—provided ample support for both English and U.S. proponents of judicial hostility to arbitration.[128]

Nonetheless, subsequent legislative reforms in England gradually introduced greater support for commercial arbitration agreements and arbitral tribunals' powers. The 1833 Civil Procedure Act restated the rule that an arbitration agreement which was made a rule of court could not be revoked, while providing arbitrators with a mechanism to summon witnesses and the power to administer oaths.[129]

At the same time, in the middle of the 19th century, English courts revisited the analysis in *Kill v. Hollister*, arriving at a very different view. The leading authority is *Scott v. Avery*, where Lord Campbell said:

> Is there anything contrary to public policy in saying that the Company shall not be harassed by actions, the costs of which might be ruinous, but that any dispute that arises shall be referred to a domestic tribunal, which may speedily and economically determine the dispute? ... I can see not the slightest ill consequences that can flow from such an agreement, and I see great advantage that may arise from it.... Public policy, therefore, seems to me to require that effect should be given to the contract.[130]

He also disposed of the "ousting the court of jurisdiction" adage—proffered in *Kill v. Hollister*—by remarking dismissively that "it probably originated in the contests of the different courts in ancient times for extent of jurisdiction, all of them being opposed to anything that would altogether deprive every one of them of jurisdiction."[131] In a subsequent case, decided the same year, Lord Campbell declared:

> Somehow the Courts of law had, in former times, acquired a horror of arbitration; and it was even doubted if a clause for a general reference of prospective disputes was legal. I never could imagine for what reason parties should not be permitted to bind themselves to settle their disputes in any manner on which they agreed.[132]

While Lord Campbell's derisory description of the English courts' historical attitude towards commercial arbitration appears to have been overstated,[133] the more enduring

---

127. *Kill v. Hollister*, 19 Geo. II 1746, 1 Wils. KB 129.

128. *See infra* pp. 21-26.

129. English Civil Procedure Act, 1833, 3 & 4 Will. IV, Ch. 42, §§39-41.

130. *Scott v. Avery* (1856) 5 H.L. Cas. 809, 853 (House of Lords).

131. *Scott v. Avery* (1856) 5 H.L. Cas. 809, 853 (House of Lords).

132. *Russell v. Pellegrini* (1856) 6 E. & B. 1020, 1025 (English King's Bench). Lord Campbell also provided a famously cynical explanation for the alleged historic hostility of English common law judges to arbitration: "This doctrine had its origin in the interests of the judges. There was no disguising the fact that, as formerly, the emoluments of the Judges depended mainly, or almost entirely, on fees, and as they had no fixed salaries there was great competition to get as much as possible of litigation into Westminster Hall and there was a great scramble in Westminster Hall for the division of the spoil.... And they had great jealousy of arbitration whereby Westminster Hall was robbed of those cases." *Scott v. Avery* (1856) 25 L.J.Ex. 308, 313 (House of Lords).

133. Horowitz & Oldham, *John Locke, Lord Mansfield and Arbitration During the Eighteenth Century*, 36 (I) Hist. J. 137 (1993) (denying that common law hostility to arbitration was particularly marked or significant); Roebuck, *The Myth of Judicial Jealousy*, 10 Arb. Int'l 395, 403-04 (1994).

point is his own resounding endorsement of the arbitral process in commercial matters—a point of view that was formulated with increasing vigor by English courts and legislatures in succeeding decades.

This was confirmed in the 1854 Common Law Procedure Act, one of the first modern efforts at a comprehensive arbitration statute.[134] Among other things, the Act provided (albeit circuitously) for the irrevocability of any arbitration agreement, by permitting it to be made a rule of court, regardless whether the parties had so agreed.[135] At the same time, however, the statute introduced new limits on the arbitral process by providing for fairly extensive judicial review of the substance of arbitrators' awards, through a "case stated" procedure that permitted any party to obtain judicial resolution of points of law arising in the arbitral proceedings.[136]

At the end of the 19th century, England enacted the 1889 Arbitration Act, which was in turn widely adopted throughout the Commonwealth.[137] The Act confirmed the irrevocability of agreements to arbitrate future disputes,[138] while granting English courts discretion whether or not to stay litigations brought in breach of such agreements (effectively permitting specific performance of arbitration agreements to be ordered).[139] At the same time, the Act preserved previous features of English arbitration law, including the "case stated" procedure for judicial review and the powers of the English courts to appoint arbitrators and assist in taking evidence.[140]

d. Commercial Arbitration in France

A broadly similar set of historical developments occurred in France as in England. There, as discussed above, the Edict of 1560 and merchant practice led to widespread use of arbitration for resolving commercial disputes.

The French Revolution changed this, like much else. Consistent with more general notions of social contract and democratic choice, the arbitration agreement was initially afforded enhanced dignity. Arbitration was described as producing "pure, simple and pacific justice,"[141] which was legislatively declared to be "the most reasonable means for the

---

134. English Common Law Procedure Act, 1854, 17 & 18 Vict., Chapter 125.

135. English Common Law Procedure Act, 1854, 17 & 18 Vict., Chapter 125, §17 ("Every agreement for submission to arbitration by consent, whether by deed or instrument in writing not under seal may be made a rule of any one of the superior courts of law or equity at Westminster, on the application of any party thereto, unless such agreement or submission contain words purporting that the parties intend that it should not be made a rule of court.").

136. English Common Law Procedure Act, 1854, 17 & 18 Vict., §4. The Act also required arbitrators to issue their awards within three months of their appointment, unless the parties or a superior court judge agreed to extend the time limit. *Id.* at §15.

137. *See* Samuel, *Arbitration Statutes in England and the USA*, 8 Arb. & Disp. Resol. L.J. 2, 6 (1999) ("The 1889 Arbitration Act can be regarded as the first modern arbitration statute in the common law world.").

138. English Arbitration Act, 1889, 52 & 53 Vict., Chapter 49 (arbitration agreement is irrevocable, unless otherwise indicated).

139. English Arbitration Act, 1889, 52 & 53 Vict., §4.

140. English Arbitration Act, 1889, 52 & 53 Vict., §§5, 8, 10, 19.

141. M. de Boisséson, *Le droit français de l'arbitrage interne et international* ¶8 (2d ed. 1990) (quoting Thouret, Member of Constituent Assembly).

termination of disputes arising between citizens."[142] In due course, arbitration was elevated to constitutional status in the Constitution of 1793 (Year I) and the Constitution of 1795 (Year III).[143]

As with many other things, the French Revolution soon turned on these progeny, with arbitration eventually being considered (ironically) a threat to the rule of law and the authority of the revolutionary state.[144] With this hostility in the air, the 1806 Napoleonic Code of Civil Procedure imposed numerous procedural and technical restrictions on arbitration agreements and procedures. In particular, Article 2059 of the Civil Code and Article 1006 of the Code of Civil Procedure generally provided that agreements to arbitrate future disputes were unenforceable.[145] The Commercial Code permitted agreements to arbitrate future disputes only in limited circumstances, consisting of maritime insurance contracts and certain corporate and partnership contexts.[146] More generally, as one commentator observes:

> [A]ll the provisions of the [Napoleonic Code of Civil Procedure] do appear to reflect, so to speak, a hatred of arbitration agreements and provide evidence of a secret desire to eliminate their existence.[147]

This hostility towards the arbitral process was reflected in contemporaneous French legal commentary, which held that "arbitration is a rough draft of the institutions and the judicial guarantees"[148] and "[a] satire of judicial administration."[149]

French courts did little during the 19th century to ameliorate this hostility. An 1843 decision of the Cour de Cassation in *Cie l'Alliance v. Prunier*, excerpted below at pp. 178-79, held broadly that agreements to arbitrate future disputes were not binding unless they identified the particular dispute and specified the individuals who were to serve as arbitrators.[150] The stated rationale, which would recur in other historical and geographical settings, was that parties should be protected against the advance and abstract waiver of access to judicial protections and guarantees.[151] That was coupled with a parallel percep-

---

142. Law of 16-24 August 1790, Art. 1 ("As arbitration is the most reasonable means of terminating disputes between citizens, the legislators shall not make any provision that would diminish either the favor or the efficiency of an [arbitration] agreement.").

143. French Constitution of Year I, 1793, Art. 86 ("The right of the citizens to have their disputes settled by arbitrators of their choice shall not be violated in any way whatsoever."); French Constitution of Year III, 1795, Art. 210 ("The right to have disputes settled by arbitrators of the parties' choosing shall not be infringed in any way whatsoever.").

144. R. David, *Arbitration in International Trade* 90 (1985).

145. M. de Boisséson, *Le droit français de l'arbitrage interne et international* ¶¶8-11 (2d ed. 1990); R. David, *Arbitration in International Trade* 90 (1985); French Code of Civil Procedure, 1806, Art. 1006.

146. French Commercial Code, 1807, Arts. 51-63, 332; M. de Boisséson, *Le droit français de l'arbitrage interne et international* ¶10 (2d ed. 1990).

147. R. David, *Arbitration in International Trade* 90 (1985) (quoting Bellot).

148. B. Bourbeau, *Procédure civile*, Tome IV, Videcoq 1844, 422 (quoted in E. Loquin, *JurisClasseur Procédure civile, Fascicule 1010: Arbitrage—Aperçu historique—Aperçu de droit comparé* ¶25 (2013).

149. Mounier, *Rapport Rigaud sur le projet de loi relative à l'arbitrage forcé*, 1856 Dalloz Périodique 56, 113.

150. *Judgment of 10 July 1843, Cie L'Alliance v. Prunier*, 1843 Dalloz (I) 343, reprinted in 1992 Rev. arb. 399 (French Cour de cassation civ.). *See infra* pp. 178-79.

151. *Judgment of 10 July 1843, Cie L'Alliance v. Prunier*, 1843 Dalloz (I) 343, reprinted in 1992 Rev. arb. 399, 404 (French Cour de cassation civ.) ("Whereas the requirement for compulsory designation of the arbitrators by name at the time the arbitration agreement is entered into is aimed at avoiding disputes regarding

tion that "[o]ne does not find with an arbitrator the same qualities that it is assured to find with a magistrate: the probity, the impartiality, the skillfulness, [and] the sensitivity of feelings necessary to render a decision."[152] The judicial decisions that followed upon these observations significantly limited the practicality and usefulness of arbitration agreements in 19th (and early 20th) century France.

As discussed below, it took some eight decades before this judicial hostility was moderated by the French courts and legislature—first in international cases and later in domestic ones.[153] Indeed, it was only with France's ratification of the Geneva Protocol of 1923, discussed below, that agreements to arbitrate future international commercial disputes became fully enforceable in French courts.[154]

e. Commercial Arbitration in the United States of America

A broadly similar course to that in England and France was followed with regard to commercial arbitration in the United States during the 18th and 19th centuries. Consistent with America's role in the development of state-to-state arbitration in the 18th century, arbitration was widely used to resolve commercial (and other) disputes during Colonial times and the early years of the Republic.

Despite this, over the course of the 19th century, significant judicial (and legislative) hostility to arbitration agreements developed, as American courts developed a peculiarly radical interpretation of historic English common law authority. Importantly, the resulting judicial hostility to the arbitral process did not prevent the use of extra-judicial and commercial mechanisms for enforcing arbitration agreements and awards,[155] but it nonetheless undoubtedly obstructed use of arbitration in the 19th century United States. This hostility was only fully overcome in the early 20th century, when determined efforts by America's business community resulted in enactment of the Federal Arbitration Act ("FAA") and similar state arbitration legislation.

Difficulties in resolving private disputes existed from the earliest days of European settlement in North America—which was hardly surprising, in light of the lack of governmental administrative structures and trained lawyers in the colonies, coupled with the fluid, sometimes chaotic dynamism of colonial life. Equally unsurprising is the use of various forms of arbitration to address these difficulties. Early Dutch settlers in New York, frustrated with efforts to replicate wholesale European judicial institutions, turned to the election of a council of "arbitrators," which was in fact a form of judicial body whose jurisdiction appears in at least some cases to have been mandatory.[156]

---

the composition of arbitral tribunal, and especially protecting citizens against their own lack of reflection, that could lead them to agree to future arbitrations while lacking sufficient prudence, and without being sufficiently thorough as to their understanding of future circumstances, without being sure that the arbitrators who volunteered to hear the case would be able to deal with the matter and be trustworthy ..."); J.-L. Delvolvé, J. Rouche & G.H. Pointon, *French Arbitration Law and Practice* ¶8 (2d ed. 2009).

152. C. Tenella Sillani, *L'arbitrato di Equità: Modelli, Regole, Prassi* 162 (2006) (quoting *Judgment of 10 July 1843, Cie L'Alliance v. Prunier*, 1843 Dalloz (I) 561 (French Cour de cassation civ.)).

153. *See infra* pp. 61-64.

154. *See infra* pp. 30-33; French Commercial Code, 1925, Art. 631.

155. *See* Benson, *An Exploration of the Impact of Modern Arbitration Statutes on the Development of Arbitration in the United States*, 11 J.L. Econ. & Org. 479, 481-82 (1995).

156. J. Auerbach, *Justice Without Law?* 32 (1983); Jones, *Three Centuries of Commercial Arbitration in New York: A Brief Survey*, 1956 Wash. U. L.Q. 193, 195 (1956).

Nonetheless, from an early date, it was also common to refer disputes in New Amsterdam to truly consensual arbitration:

> [T]he arbitrators were left to the choice of the litigants, or appointed by the court.... These references were frequent upon every court day, and ... though the amount involved was frequently considerable, or the matter in dispute highly important, ... appeals to the court from the decision of the arbitrators were exceedingly rare.[157]

Some commentators conclude that, after the 1664 hand-over of administration in New York to the English, the use of arbitration in commercial matters was one of the enduring features of continuing Dutch influence.[158]

Arbitration of commercial matters was widespread in the American colonies during the 17th and 18th centuries. Drawing on English, as well as Dutch, practice, the colonists found the flexibility, practicality and speed of arbitral processes well-suited to their conditions: "From whatever source they derived the practice, the colonists engaged in extensive arbitration throughout the period of English rule."[159] Relying on court files (relatively sparse and terse), newspaper accounts (more fulsome), merchants books and chamber of commerce records, historians have sketched a picture of widespread, routine use of arbitration in Colonial commercial matters, including in transactions between businesses in different colonies, typically by agreement between the parties after disputes had arisen.[160]

Following the American Revolution, the routine use of arbitration to resolve commercial disputes did not diminish. On the contrary, as New York developed over the course of the 19th century from a small, closely-knit colonial town into a cosmopolitan center of commerce, the use of arbitration grew apace with the expansion of commercial affairs.[161] One commentator concludes:

> [I]t is clear that arbitration has been in constant use in New York from its beginnings to 1920. It did not suddenly come into being at that time because of the passage of a statute making agreements to arbitrate future disputes enforceable. Rather, it has existed with and without the benefit of statutes, and both separate from, and in connection with, court adjudication.[162]

The driving motivation for arbitration in commercial matters during this period continued to be the perception by businesses "that government courts of the period did not

---

157. Jones, *Three Centuries of Commercial Arbitration in New York: A Brief Survey*, 1956 Wash. U. L.Q. 193, 196 (1956) (quoting Daly, *History of the Court of Common Pleas*, 1 Smith xxix (N.Y.C.P. 1855)).

158. A. Flick (ed.), 3 *History of the State of New York* 14-16 (1933); Jones, *Three Centuries of Commercial Arbitration in New York: A Brief Survey*, 1956 Wash. U. L.Q. 193, 197-98 (1956).

159. Jones, *Three Centuries of Commercial Arbitration in New York: A Brief Survey*, 1956 Wash. U. L.Q. 193, 198 (1956).

160. Aiken, *New Netherlands Arbitration in the 17th Century*, 29 Arb. J. 145 (1974); Benson, *An Exploration of the Impact of Modern Arbitration Statutes on the Development of Arbitration in the United States*, 11 J.L. Econ. & Org. 479, 481-82 (1995).

161. Jones, *Three Centuries of Commercial Arbitration in New York: A Brief Survey*, 1956 Wash. U. L.Q. 193, 213-14 (1956).

162. Jones, *Three Centuries of Commercial Arbitration in New York: A Brief Survey*, 1956 Wash. U. L.Q. 193, 211-18 (1956). *See also* Benson, *An Exploration of the Impact of Modern Arbitration Statutes on the Development of Arbitration in the United States*, 11 J.L. Econ. & Org. 479, 481-85 (1995) ("Arbitration actually was in widespread use in the United States almost three centuries before modern arbitration statutes were passed in the 1920s; its history traces back to the colonial period.").

apply commercial law in what the merchant community considered to be a just and expeditious fashion."[163]

As its role as the dominant U.S. commercial and financial center would suggest, New York practice was representative of the country as a whole at the time. Research into specific jurisdictions, including New Jersey, Pennsylvania, Connecticut, Massachusetts, Delaware, Virginia and Ohio, reveals a history similar to that in New York.[164] As one early 19th century commentator noted, the commercial arbitration system established by New York merchants offered a lead that "has been taken by the merchants of [Philadelphia] and other cities."[165]

Some early legislative efforts were made to support the arbitral process in commercial matters. In 1791, the New York legislature enacted a statute virtually identical to England's 1698 Arbitration Act,[166] providing for the enforcement of agreements to arbitrate future disputes where they had been made a rule of court.[167] A 1793 American insurance policy contained an arbitration clause, making it clear that the legislation had a practical orientation.[168]

Nonetheless, it appears that the principal means by which arbitration agreements and arbitral awards were enforced during the Colonial era was through non-legal or extra-legal commercial, professional and other mechanisms.[169] That is in part because of the character of U.S. commercial affairs at the time, and in part because of the general lack of satisfactory legal or judicial enforcement mechanisms.

Despite the prevalence of commercial arbitration as a means of dispute resolution, and the existence of some early legislative and judicial support, many 19th century U.S. courts developed a puritanical version of English common law hostility to agreements to arbitrate future disputes. Indeed, for some decades, U.S. courts held flatly that agreements to arbitrate future disputes were contrary to public policy and revocable at will; unlike England,

163. Benson, *An Exploration of the Impact of Modern Arbitration Statutes on the Development of Arbitration in the United States*, 11 J.L. Econ. & Org. 479, 482 (1995).

164. L. Edmonson (ed.), *Domke on Commercial Arbitration* §§2.6 to 2.9 (3d ed. 2010 & Update 2013); Gwynne, *The Oldest American Tribunal*, 1 Arb. J. 117, 120 (1937); Odiorne, *Arbitration Under Early New Jersey Law*, 8 Arb. J. 117 (1953).

165. J. Higgins, *Sampson Against the Philistines, or the Reformation of Lawsuits* 32-32 (2d ed. 1805).

166. *See supra* p. 17.

167. 1791 N.Y. Laws 219-220.

168. "And it is agreed, that if any Dispute should arise relating to the Loss on this Policy; it shall be referred to two indifferent Persons, one to be chosen by the Assured, the other by the Assurer, who shall have full Power to adjust the same; but in case they cannot agree, then such two persons shall choose a third; and any two of them agreeing, shall be obligatory to both parties." *1793 Insurance Company of North American Insurance Policy*, quoted in Wimm & Davis, *Arbitration of Reinsurance Disputes: Is There A Better Way?*, Disp. Resol. J. (Oct. 2004).

169. J. Auerbach, *Justice Without Law?* 19-46 (1983); Benson, *An Exploration of the Impact of Modern Arbitration Statutes on the Development of Arbitration in the United States*, 11 J.L. Econ. & Org. 479, 488 (1995) ("[A]rbitration was being developed and expanded under the auspices of trade associations, mercantile exchanges, and other commercial organizations where nonlegal sanctions apparently were relatively strong.").

U.S. courts appear to have developed no alternative legal mechanisms, whether through the use of penalty clauses or rules of court, to make such agreements enforceable.[170]

Joseph Story, a preeminent U.S. authority in a wide range of legal fields, reflected 19th century judicial hostility to arbitration agreements in the United States. In 1845, he stated the common law position in the United States, inherited from England and elaborated with particular vigor:

> Now we all know that arbitrators, at the common law, possess no authority whatsoever, even to administer an oath, or to compel the attendance of witnesses. They cannot compel the production of documents and papers and books of account, or insist upon a discovery of facts from the parties under oath. They are not ordinarily well enough acquainted with the principles of law or equity, to administer either effectually, in complicated cases; and hence it has often been said, that the judgment of arbitrators is but rusticum judicium. Ought then a court of equity to compel a resort to such a tribunal, by which, however honest and intelligent, it can in no case be clear that the real legal or equitable rights of the parties can be fully ascertained or perfectly protected? ... [An arbitration agreement is not specifically enforceable because it] is essentially, in its very nature and character, an agreement which must rest in the good faith and honor of the parties, and like an agreement to paint a picture, to carve a statue, or to write a book ... must be left to the conscience of the parties, or to such remedy in damages for the breach thereof, as the law has provided.[171]

While this left open the possibility of recovering money damages for breach of an arbitration agreement,[172] this was virtually never an effective (or even very plausible) means of enforcement, since adequate proof of injury resulting from a refusal to arbitrate was virtually impossible.[173]

Relying on literal interpretations of the English common law in *Vynior's Case* and *Kill v. Hollister*, and evidencing a disdain for the arbitral process reminiscent of early 19th century French authors,[174] Story's influential academic commentaries adopted similar reasoning:

> [W]here the stipulation, though not against the policy of the law, yet is an effort to divest the ordinary jurisdiction of the common tribunals of justice, such as an agreement, in case of any

---

170. *Robert Lawrence Co. v. Devonshire Fabrics, Inc.*, 271 F.2d 402, 406 (2d Cir. 1959) (discussing American courts' hostility to arbitration); J. Cohen, *Commercial Arbitration and the Law* 226-52 (1918); Sayre, *Development of Commercial Arbitration Law*, 37 Yale L.J. 595, 595-97 (1927-1928).

171. *Tobey v. County of Bristol*, 23 F.Cas. 1313, 1321-22 (C.C.D. Mass. 1845). *See also Prince Steam-Shipping Co. v. Lehman*, 39 F. 704 (S.D.N.Y. 1889) ("Such agreements have repeatedly been held to be against public policy and void."); *Meacham v. Jamestown F. & C. R.R. Co.*, 105 N.E. 653, 656 (N.Y. 1914) (Cardozo, J., concurring) ("It is true that some judges have expressed the belief that parties ought to be free to contract about such matters as they please. In this state, the law has long been settled to the contrary.... The jurisdiction of our courts is established by law, and is not to be diminished, any more than it is to be increased, by the convention of the parties.").

172. *Finucane Co. v. Bd of Educ. of Rochester*, 82 N.E. 737 (N.Y. 1907).

173. *Aktieselskabet Korn-Og Foderstof v. Rederiaktiebolaget Atlanten*, 250 F. 935, 937 (2d Cir. 1918) (breach of contract yields only "nominal damages" unless arbitral expenses have actually been incurred); *Munson v. Straits of Dover S.S. Co.*, 99 F. 787, 789 (S.D.N.Y. 1900) ("[N]o case is to be found in which ... any other than nominal damages have ever been indicated to be recoverable, because too loose, indefinite and incapable of verification."), *aff'd* 100 F. 1005 (N.Y. 1900); Sayre, *Development of Commercial Arbitration Law*, 37 Yale L.J. 595, 604-05 (1927-1928).

174. *See supra* pp. 16-21.

disputes, to refer the same to arbitrators, Court of Equity will not, any more than Courts of Law, interfere to enforce that agreement, but they will leave the parties to their own good pleasure in regard to such agreements.... The regular administration of justice might be greatly impeded or interfered with by such stipulations if they were specifically enforced. And at all events courts of justice are presumed to be better capable of administering and enforcing the rights of the parties than any mere private arbitrators, as well from their superior knowledge as from their superior means of sifting the controversy to the very bottom.[175]

Citing this and other similar rationales, American courts applied an extreme interpretation of English common law precedents to withhold meaningful judicial enforcement of arbitration agreements throughout much of the 19th century.[176]

Moreover, U.S. courts and legislatures did not quickly follow the path of *Scott v. Avery* or the 1889 English Arbitration Act, which had taken steps to facilitate the enforcement of arbitration agreements in England.[177] As the Second Circuit once wrote, "[one] of the dark chapters in legal history concerns the validity, interpretation and enforceability of arbitration agreements" by U.S. courts in the 19th century.[178]

Importantly, even while many U.S. courts refused to enforce commercial arbitration agreements during the middle and late 19th century, arbitration remained both popular and effective in American commercial settings: "The use of commercial arbitration developed during the colonial and post-revolutionary periods in spite of this [judicial] hostility."[179] As already noted, it did so on the basis of non-legal commercial sanctions and enforcement mechanisms, including through membership in commercial guilds, societies, or religious groups, all of which proved sufficiently resilient to overcome judicial hostility.[180]

Moreover, even with regard to judicial enforcement, other movements were afoot in the United States by the late 19th century. Courts in a number of U.S. jurisdictions rejected the common law notion that arbitration agreements were either unenforceable or revocable, and instead upheld them,[181] while also enforcing arbitral awards with minimal judicial

---

175. J. Story, 1 *Commentaries on Equity Jurisprudence as Administered in England and America* §670 (13th ed. 1886).

176. *See Kulukundis Shipping Co. v. Amtorg Trading Corp.*, 126 F.2d 978, 982-86 (2d Cir. 1942), for a detailed (and influential) historical review of the enforceability of arbitration agreements at common law. *See also* S. Rep. No. 68-536, at 2-3 (1924) (citing "[judges'] jealousy of their rights as courts, coupled with the fear that if arbitration agreements were to prevail and be enforced, the courts would be ousted of much of their jurisdiction"); G. Born, *International Commercial Arbitration* 47 (2d ed. 2014).

177. *See supra* p. 18-19.

178. *Robert Lawrence Co. v. Devonshire Fabrics, Inc.*, 271 F.2d 402, 406 (2d Cir. 1959).

179. Benson, *An Exploration of the Impact of Modern Arbitration Statutes on the Development of Arbitration in the United States*, 11 J.L. Econ. & Org. 479, 483 (1995).

180. Benson, *An Exploration of the Impact of Modern Arbitration Statutes on the Development of Arbitration in the United States*, 11 J.L. Econ. & Org. 479, 484-85 (1995) (New York Stock Exchange; Quakers; New York Chamber of Commerce).

181. *Burchell v. Marsh*, 58 U.S. 344, 351-52 (1854); *Snodgrass v. Gavit*, 28 Pa. 221 (Pa. 1857) (dictum); *Condon v. Southside R.R. Co.*, 14 Gratt. 320 (Va. 1858); *Doolittle v. Malcom*, 8 Leigh 608 (Va. 1837). *See generally* Benson, *An Exploration of the Impact of Modern Arbitration Statutes on the Development of Arbitration in the United States*, 11 J.L. Econ. & Org. 479, 485-87 (1995) (discussing cases).

review.[182] Rejecting Story's doctrinal authority, an 1858 Virginian decision declared, in terms that could have been written 150 years later, that:

> The only ground on which [the arbitration agreement] can be said to be unlawful is, that in referring all disputes and difficulties arising under the contract to the engineer or inspector, it tends to oust the courts of law of their jurisdiction; and is therefore against the policy of the law and void.... I am certainly not disposed to extend the operation of a rule which appears to me to have been founded on very narrow grounds, directly contrary to the spirit of later times, which leaves parties at full liberty to refer their disputes at pleasure to public or private tribunals.[183]

Soon thereafter, the U.S. Congress enacted legislation encouraging efforts to use arbitration to resolve international commercial disputes, although it does not appear that the statute had significant practical effects.[184] What did continue to have practical effect, though, were commercial and professional associations, which ensured that arbitration remained a central part of commercial life, even during the "dark chapters in legal history," when U.S. courts were most hostile to arbitration and agreements to arbitrate.[185]

U.S. judicial and legislative hostility to commercial arbitration substantially eroded in the late 19th and early 20th centuries. Judicial opinions in the United States began increasingly to question the wisdom of Story's views,[186] while commercial pressure for legislative reform built.[187] This pressure eventually had its effect, and in 1920, New York enacted legislation providing for the validity and specific enforcement of arbitration agreements. That was followed in 1925 by similar provisions in the FAA (which are discussed in detail below), which paralleled negotiation and adoption of the 1923 Geneva Protocol (also discussed below).[188] While the New York arbitration legislation and the FAA allowed the annulment of awards for fraud, corruption and similar grounds, they enacted a sea change from the American common law by instituting a default rule that contracts to arbitrate should be enforced by the courts.[189]

---

182. *Ebert v. Ebert*, 5 Md. 353 (Md. 1854) ("[E]very reasonable intendment is now made in favor of [arbitral] awards ... and that all matters have been decided by them, unless the contrary shall appear on the face of the award."); *Doolittle v. Malcolm*, 8 Leigh 698 (Va. 1837).

183. *Condon v. Southside R.R. Co.*, 1858 WL 3945, at *6-7 (Va.).

184. 22 U.S.C.A. §161 (duty of foreign service officers to encourage use of arbitration and to facilitate arbitral processes).

185. Benson, *An Exploration of the Impact of Modern Arbitration Statutes on the Development of Arbitration in the United States*, 11 J.L. Econ. & Org. 479, 488 (1995) ("Arbitration was being developed and expanded under the auspices of trade associations, mercantile exchanges, and other commercial organizations where nonlegal sanctions apparently were relatively strong"). *See also* Bernstein, *Opting Out of the Legal System: Extra Legal Contractual Relations in the Diamond Industry*, 21 J. Legal Studies 115 (1992).

186. *Hamilton v. Liverpool, London & Globe Ins. Co.*, 136 U.S. 242 (1890) (recognizing arbitration award determining damages, where court decided general question of liability); *United States Asphalt Ref. Co. v. Trinidad Lake Petroleum Co.*, 222 F. 1006, 1008-11 (S.D.N.Y. 1915); *supra* p. 24.

187. *To Validate Certain Agreements for Arbitration*, H.R. Rep. No. 68-96 at 1 (1924); Chamber of the State of New York, *Report of the Committee on Arbitration* (1917); Sayre, *Development of Commercial Arbitration Law*, 37 Yale L.J. 595, 595 & n.2 (1927-1928).

188. *See infra* pp. 30-33, 53-54; U.S. FAA, 9 U.S.C. §§1 *et seq.*; Act of Apr. 19, 1920, Chapter 275, 1920 N.Y. Laws 803-07; Samuel, *Arbitration Statutes in England and the USA*, 8 Arb. & Disp. Resol. L.J. 2, 7-13 (1999).

189. Stone, *Rustic Justice: Community and Coercion Under the Federal Arbitration Act*, 77 N.C. L. Rev. 931, 982-87 (1999).

f. Commercial Arbitration in Other European Jurisdictions in the 18th and 19th Centuries

The history of commercial arbitration in other nations did not always involve the same degree of judicial or legislative hostility as occasionally demonstrated in 18th and 19th century England, France and the United States. Historically, commercial arbitration was commonly used by merchants in what is today Germany, perhaps particularly because of the lack of a centralized government (until comparatively recently) and the demands of inter-state commerce.[190] Thus, a German commentator at the beginning of the 20th century could observe, with regard to historic German experiences: "arbitral tribunals have at all times been regarded as an urgent necessity by the community of merchants and legislation has always granted them a place alongside the ordinary courts...."[191]

The role of arbitration in commercial matters was recognized, and given effect, in the civil codes of Baden (in 1864), Prussia (in 1864) and Bavaria (in 1869). All of these statutory codifications confirmed the role of arbitration in the resolution of commercial disputes, while granting arbitrators varying degrees of freedom from local procedural and substantive requirements and judicial control.[192] These various developments led to the treatment of arbitration in the first German Code of Civil Procedure of 1877 (which would remain the fundamental basis for Germany's legal regime for arbitration until 1998).

The 1877 German Code of Civil Procedure incorporated provisions that freed arbitrators from the obligation to apply strict legal rules (and, concurrently, from judicial review of the substance of awards). The drafters of the Code explained:

> By submitting themselves to arbitration the parties want to escape from the difficulties and complexities arising from the application of the law. They intend that the law as between them should be what the arbitrators, according to their conscientious conviction—*ex aequo et bono*—determine. They will therefore as a rule consider the arbitrators to be friendly mediators—*amiables compositeurs*, as the Belgian draft says—and it is obvious that they do so consider them whenever they appoint as arbitrators persons who are not learned in the law. As a rule therefore the goal of arbitration is attained only when the arbitrators are not bound to follow the ordinary rules of law when giving their awards.[193]

At the same time, at the end of the 19th and beginning of the 20th centuries, German courts gave active support to the arbitral process, including by pioneering the development of what would later be termed the separability doctrine, in order to facilitate the enforcement of arbitration agreements.[194]

By the turn of the 20th century, permanent arbitral tribunals, organized under the auspices of trade organizations, became a common feature of German business life. In 1909, 1,030 cases were pending before such arbitral tribunals in Berlin alone.[195] Contempora-

---

190. *See supra* pp. 14-16.

191. W. Haeger, *Schiedsgerichte für Rechtsstreitigkeiten der Handelswelt* 2 (1910) (quoted in Berger, *The New German Arbitration Law in International Perspective*, 26 Forum Int'l 1, 1 (2000)).

192. A. Lindheim, *Das Schiedsgericht im modernen Zivilprozeß* 17 (1891).

193. *Begründung des Entwurfs einer Zivilprozessordnung*, Deutscher Reichstag, II, Legislatur-Periode, I, session 1876, ad no. 6, p. 476 (quoted in Cohn, *Commercial Arbitration and the Rules of Law: A Comparative Study*, 4 U. Toronto L.J. 1, 16 (1942)).

194. *See infra* pp. 190-218.

195. W. Haeger, *Schiedsgerichte für Rechtsstreitigkeiten der Handelswelt* 21 (1910).

neous authors generally praised the arbitral process, highlighting its efficiency, trustworthiness and the commercial good sense of arbitrators with industry experience.[196]

Like some common law courts, however, the German courts came in the 1920s and 1930s to "guard[] their rights with extreme jealousy, and were only too inclined to set aside awards [on the basis of] even a slight failure to comply with the provisions of the Code."[197] The provisions of the German Code of Civil Procedure left considerable leeway to local courts to interfere with the arbitral process, which they not infrequently did, curtailing the practical value of arbitration.[198]

As already described, the Napoleonic Code of Civil Procedure (and Cour de Cassation, in an 1843 decision) had adopted a similarly anti-arbitration course in France, which persisted until the 1920s.[199] Belgian courts refused, unusually, to follow the approach of the French Cour de Cassation and gave effect to agreements to arbitrate future disputes.[200] The Netherlands took a similar approach, enacting an Arbitration Act as part of its Code of Civil Procedure in 1838 to provide a comprehensive legal framework for commercial arbitration.[201] The Dutch and Belgian approach reflected the Low Countries' historical fondness for arbitration,[202] which can be attributed in significant part to their mercantile cultures and the influence of Roman law.[203] Swiss cantonal legislation and constitutions were also generally supportive of arbitration during this era.[204]

B. CONTEMPORARY INTERNATIONAL ARBITRATION CONVENTIONS

With this historical background, the foundations for the contemporary legal regime for international arbitration were laid at the end of the 19th and beginning of the 20th centuries. As discussed below, the basic legal framework for international commercial arbitration was established in the first decades of the 20th century, with the 1923 Geneva Protocol and 1927 Geneva Convention, with the enactment of national arbitration legislation that

196. W. Haeger, *Schiedsgerichte für Rechtsstreitigkeiten der Handelswelt* 24 (1910).

197. Weiss, *Arbitration in Germany*, 43 Law Q. Rev. 205, 206 (1927). *But see* Kahn, *Arbitration in England and Germany*, 12 J. Comp. Legis. & Int'l L. 58, 76-77 (1930) (suggesting that Weiss's view of German courts is too bleak); Nussbaum, *Schiedsgerichtsschriftstellerei zwecks Störung internationaler Beziehungen* 384, 2 *Internationales Jahrbuch für Schiedsgerichtswesen* (1928) (arguing that Weiss misrepresents German law).

198. Nussbaum, *Schiedsgerichtswesen*, 42 Zeitschrift für Zivilprozessrecht 254, 259-60 (1912) (citing *Judgment of 28 January 1908*, 69 RGZ 52, 55 (German Reichsgericht)).

199. *See supra* pp. 20-21.

200. *Judgment of 17 December 1936*, Pas. 1936 I 457, 458 (Belgian Cour de cassation); R. David, *Arbitration in International Trade* 98 (1985); G. Keutgen & G. Dal, *L'arbitrage en droit belge et international* ¶42 (2d ed. 2006); Keutgen & Huys, *Chronique de Jurisprudence: L'arbitrage (1950-1975)*, Journal des Tribunaux 53, 54 (1976).

201. Rovine *et al.*, *Iran/United States Claims Tribunal*, 76 Am. Soc'y Int'l L. Proc. 1, 5 (1982) (remarks by Arthur Rovine, noting that under 1838 Act, arbitral awards were enforced "unless there [was] a gross fraud or the decision [was] without reason"); Sanders, *The Netherlands*, VI Y.B. Comm. Arb. 60 (1981) (describing Dutch arbitral procedure under 1838 law); A. van den Berg, R. van Delden & H. Snijders, *Netherlands Arbitration Law* §1.1 (1993).

202. van Bladel, *Arbitration in the Building Industry in the Netherlands*, 54 Disp. Resol. J. 42, 43 (May 1999).

203. Aiken, *New Netherlands Arbitration in the 17th Century*, 29 Arb. J. 145, 146-49 (1974).

204. R. David, *Arbitration in International Trade* 101-02 (1985).

paralleled these instruments and with the development of effective international arbitration rules.

Building on these foundations, the current legal regime for international commercial arbitration was developed in significant part during the second half of the 20th century, with countries from all parts of the globe entering into international arbitration conventions (particularly the New York Convention) and enacting national arbitration statutes designed specifically to facilitate the arbitral process; at the same time, national courts in most states gave robust effect to these legislative instruments, often extending or elaborating on their terms. As discussed below, this avowedly "pro-arbitration" regime ensures the enforceability of both international arbitration agreements and arbitral awards, gives effect to the parties' procedural autonomy and the arbitral tribunal's procedural discretion and seeks to insulate the arbitral process from interference by national courts or other governmental authorities.

At the same time, during the past several decades, the current legal regime for international investment arbitration was developed, particularly through the adoption of the ICSID Convention [205] and an extensive network of "bilateral investment treaties" ("BITs").[206] Similarly, if less extensively and comprehensively, the 1899 Hague Peace Conference adopted the Convention for the Pacific Settlement of International Disputes (which was subsequently amended in 1907),[207] followed by the 1929 General Act for the Pacific Settlement of International Disputes.[208] These instruments reflected a robust, "pro-arbitration" approach to the use of international arbitration to peacefully resolve inter-state disputes, while setting forth a basic legal framework in which international arbitrations could be conducted.

1. 1899 and 1907 Conventions for the Pacific Settlement of International Disputes

By the beginning of the 20th century, proposals for more universal state-to-state arbitration mechanisms became credible. Although seldom discussed in today's literature, an 1875 project of the Institut de Droit International produced a draft procedural code, based on existing inter-state arbitral practice and designed to provide basic procedural guidelines and mechanisms for future *ad hoc* arbitrations.[209] The project provides impressive testimony to both the frequency of inter-state arbitrations and the perceived desirability of more consistent, transparent and internationally-neutral procedures for such arbitrations.

In 1899, the Hague Peace Conference produced the Hague Convention of 1899 on the Pacific Settlement of Disputes, which included chapters on international arbitration and established a "Permanent Court of Arbitration" to administer state-to-state arbitration

---

205. *See* Convention on the Settlement of Investment Disputes Between States and Nationals of Other States, submitted on March 18, 1965, Washington, D.C., 575 U.N.T.S. 159, and entered into force on October 14, 1966; *infra* pp. 41-43.

206. *See infra* pp. 43-44.

207. *See* Convention for the Pacific Settlement of International Disputes (First Hague Conference, 1899), Arts. 15-29; Convention for the Pacific Settlement of International Disputes (Second Hague Conference, 1907); *infra* pp. 29-30.

208. *See* General Act for the Pacific Settlement of International Disputes, 93 L.N.T.S. 345; *infra* p. 30.

209. Institut de Droit International, *Projet de règlement pour la procédure arbitrale internationale* (Session de La Haye, 1875). *See* G. Born, *International Commercial Arbitration* 15 (2d ed. 2014).

under the Convention.[210] These provided the foundation for more formal inter-state adjudication, in the Permanent Court of International Justice and International Court of Justice,[211] as well as the founding of the Permanent Court of Arbitration ("PCA").[212] At the same time, arbitration remained a preferred method of resolving inter-state disputes, often selected by states during the 20th century in preference to standing international judicial bodies.[213]

Thus, Article 16 of the 1899 Convention recorded the Contracting States' recognition that "[i]n questions of a legal nature, and especially in the interpretation or application of International Conventions," international arbitration was the "most effective, and at the same time the most equitable, means of settling disputes which diplomacy has failed to settle." Articles 15 to 19 prescribed a set of rules regarding the constitution of inter-state arbitral tribunals and the conduct of inter-state arbitrations; among other things, the 1899 Convention established the PCA (seated in the Hague), for administering inter-state arbitrations.

The 1899 Convention was revised in 1907, with the new Convention for the Pacific Settlement of International Disputes including the addition or amendment of a number of provisions regarding international arbitral proceedings.[214] In 1929, a "General Act on Pacific Settlement of International Disputes" was negotiated (with a number of states, principally Western European, ultimately ratifying the Act).[215] As with the 1899 and 1907 Conventions, the Act sets forth a basic legal framework (subject to contrary agreement by the parties) for international arbitrations between state parties.

2. *Geneva Protocol and Geneva Convention*

During the first decades of the 20th century, businessmen and lawyers in developed states called for legislation to facilitate the use of arbitration in resolving domestic and, particularly, international commercial disputes.[216] These appeals emphasized the importance of reliable, effective and fair mechanisms for resolving international disputes to the expansion of international trade and investment.

---

210. 1899 Hague Convention, Arts. 15-29. *See also* Caron, *War and International Adjudication: Reflections on the 1899 Peace Conference*, 94 Am. J. Int'l L. 4 (2000); Werner, *Interstate Political Arbitration: What Lies Next?*, 9(1) J. Int'l Arb. 69, 71-72 (1992).

211. *See generally* S. Rosenne, I *The Law and Practice of the International Court, 1920-1996* 10-40, 99-106 (3d ed. 1997).

212. Caron, *War and International Adjudication: Reflections on the 1899 Peace Conference*, 94 Am. J. Int'l L. 4, 16-17 (2000).

213. Charney, *Third Party Dispute Settlement and International Law*, 36 Colum. J. Transnat'l L. 65, 68 (1997) ("While the establishment of the World Court was particularly significant, *ad hoc* arbitrations ... continue to be important" in twentieth century.); Merrills, *The Mosaic of International Dispute Settlement Procedures: Complementary or Contradictory*, 54 Neth. Int'l L. Rev. 361 (2007); A. Stuyt, *Survey of International Arbitrations 1794-1989* (3d ed. 1990).

214. 1907 Hague Convention. *See* S. Rosenne (ed.), T*he Hague Peace Conference of 1899 and 1907 and International Arbitration: Reports and Documents* (2001).

215. General Act on Pacific Settlement of International Disputes, concluded on September 26, 1928 in Geneva and entered into force on August 16, 1929, 93 L.N.T.S. 345.

216. Benson, *An Exploration of the Impact of Modern Arbitration Statutes on the Development of Arbitration in the United States*, 11 J.L. Econ. & Org. 479, 491-94 (1995) (emphasizing the role of lobbying from the legal profession); G. Born, *International Commercial Arbitration* 64 (2d ed. 2014); I. Macneil, *American Arbitration Law: Reformation, Nationalization, Internationalization* 25-26 (1992).

In 1923, initially under the auspices of the newly-founded International Chamber of Commerce ("ICC"), major trading nations negotiated the Geneva Protocol on Arbitration Clauses in Commercial Matters.[217] The Protocol was ultimately ratified by the United Kingdom, Germany, France, Japan, India, Brazil and about two dozen other nations.[218] Although the United States did not ratify the Protocol, the nations that did so represented a very significant portion of the international trading community at the time.

The Geneva Protocol played a critical—if often underappreciated—role in the development of the legal framework for international commercial arbitration. Among other things, Article I of the Geneva Protocol declared:

> Each of the Contracting States recognizes the validity of an agreement whether relating to existing or future differences between parties subject respectively to the jurisdiction of different Contracting States by which the parties to a contract agree to submit to arbitration all or any differences that may arise in connection with such contract relating to commercial matters or to any other matter capable of settlement by arbitration, whether or not the arbitration is to take place in a country to whose jurisdiction none of the parties is subject.[219]

This provision was complemented by Article IV, which provided:

> The tribunals of the Contracting Parties, on being seized of a dispute regarding a contract made between persons to whom Article 1 applies and including an arbitration agreement whether referring to present or future differences which is valid by virtue of the said article and capable of being carried into effect, shall refer the parties on the application of either of them to the decision of the arbitrators.[220]

In these two provisions, the Geneva Protocol planted the seeds for a number of principles of enormous future importance to the international arbitral process—including the presumptive validity of agreements to arbitrate future (as well as existing) disputes, the obligation of national courts to refer parties to arbitration, the concept of arbitrating "commercial" disputes and disputes "capable of settlement by arbitration" and the obligation to recognize international arbitration agreements on an equal footing with domestic arbitration agreements. As discussed below, all of these basic themes reappeared repeatedly in international conventions and national legislation over the next 90 years and remain the foundation of the contemporary legal framework for international commercial arbitration.[221] The Protocol also established standards which made international arbitration agreements *more* enforceable than domestic arbitration agreements had historically been in many nations,[222] reflecting a deliberate policy of promoting the use of arbitration to resolve international commercial disputes.

---

217. G. Born, *International Commercial Arbitration* 64-65 (2d ed. 2014); Lorenzen, *Commercial Arbitration—International and Interstate Aspects*, 43 Yale L.J. 716, 750 (1933-1934); A. van den Berg, *The New York Arbitration Convention of 1958* 6-7, 113-18 (1981).

218. 27 L.N.T.S. 158 (1924).

219. Geneva Protocol, Art. I. The Convention also permitted Contracting States to limit its scope to "contracts which are considered as commercial under its national law." *Ibid.*

220. Geneva Protocol, Art. IV.

221. *See infra* pp. 33-39 (New York Convention), 40-41 (European Convention), 47-51 (UNCITRAL Model Law).

222. *See supra* pp. 16-28 & *infra* pp. 177-90.

Additionally, Article III of the Geneva Protocol attempted to provide for the recognition of international arbitral awards. It declared:

> Each Contracting State undertakes to ensure the execution by its authorities and in accordance with the provisions of its national laws of arbitral awards made in its own territory....[223]

This provision was extremely limited, providing only for Contracting States to enforce awards made on their own territory (*i.e.*, not "foreign" awards, made in other countries). Even then, enforcement was required only in accordance with local law—effectively making the commitment dependent on each individual state's arbitration legislation. In contrast to the simple, but dramatic, provisions of the Geneva Protocol regarding arbitration *agreements*, Article III's treatment of arbitral *awards* was at best tentative and incomplete.

The Geneva Protocol was augmented by the Geneva Convention for the Execution of Foreign Arbitral Awards of 1927.[224] Recognizing the Protocol's deficiencies in dealing with this issue, the Geneva Convention expanded the enforceability of arbitral awards rendered pursuant to arbitration agreements subject to the Geneva Protocol. It did so by requiring the recognition and enforcement of such "foreign" awards within any Contracting State (rather than only within the state where they were made, as under the Protocol), and forbidding substantive judicial review of the merits of such awards in recognition proceedings.[225]

Regrettably, the Convention placed the burden of proof in recognition proceedings on the award-creditor, requiring the award-creditor to demonstrate both the existence of a valid arbitration agreement,[226] concerning an arbitrable subject matter,[227] and that the arbitral proceedings had been conducted in accordance with the parties' agreement.[228] The Convention also required the award-creditor to show that the arbitral award had become "final" in the place of arbitration[229] and was not contrary to the public policy of the recognizing state.[230] This requirement of finality led to the so-called "double *exequatur*" requirement—whereby an award could effectively only be recognized abroad under the Geneva Convention if it had been confirmed by the courts of the place of the arbitration.[231] This proved a major source of uncertainty regarding the finality of international arbitral awards.

Despite these shortcomings, the Geneva Protocol and Geneva Convention were major steps towards today's legal framework for international commercial arbitration. Most fundamentally, both instruments established, if only imperfectly, the basic principles of the

---

223. Geneva Protocol, Art. III.

224. Geneva Convention on the Execution of Foreign Arbitral Awards, 1927, 92 L.N.T.S. 302 (1929-1930). *See* G. Born, *International Commercial Arbitration* 67 (2d ed. 2014); A. van den Berg, *The New York Arbitration Convention of 1958* 6-7, 113-18 (1981).

225. Geneva Convention, Arts. 1-4.

226. Geneva Convention, Art. 1(a).

227. Geneva Convention, Art. 1(b).

228. Geneva Convention, Art. 1(c).

229. Geneva Convention, Art. 1(d).

230. Geneva Convention, Art. 1(e).

231. *See infra* pp. 1189-90, 1196-97; A. van den Berg, *The New York Arbitration Convention of 1958* 7 (1981).

presumptive validity of international arbitration agreements[232] and arbitral awards,[233] and the enforceability of arbitration agreements by specific performance,[234] as well as recognition of the parties' autonomy to select the substantive law governing their relations[235] and to determine the arbitration procedures.[236]

Further, the Geneva Protocol and Convention both inspired and paralleled national legislation and business initiatives to augment the legal regime governing international commercial arbitration agreements. In 1920, New York enacted arbitration legislation, largely paralleling the Protocol, to ensure the validity and enforceability of commercial arbitration agreements.[237] With an eye towards ratification of the Geneva Protocol, France adopted legislation in 1925 that made arbitration agreements valid in commercial transactions,[238] while similar legislation was enacted in England.[239]

Also in 1925, the United States enacted the Federal Arbitration Act—providing the first federal legislation in the United States governing domestic (and international) arbitration agreements. The centerpiece of the FAA was §2, which provided that arbitration agreements "shall be valid, irrevocable, and enforceable, save upon such grounds as exist at law or in equity for the revocation of any contract,"[240] while §§9 and 10 of the Act provided for the presumptive validity and enforceability of arbitral awards.[241] Much like the 1923 Geneva Protocol, the stated purpose of the FAA was to reverse decades of judicial mistrust in the United States of arbitration and render arbitration agreements enforceable on the same terms as other contracts.[242]

3. *New York Convention*

The Geneva Protocol and the Geneva Convention were succeeded by the United Nations Convention on the Recognition and Enforcement of Foreign Arbitral Awards.[243] Generally referred to as the "New York Convention," the treaty is by far the most significant contemporary legislative instrument relating to international commercial arbitration. It provides what amounts to a universal constitutional charter for the international arbitral process, and whose sweeping terms have enabled both national courts and arbitral tribunals to develop durable, effective means for enforcing international arbitration agreements and arbitral awards.

---

232. *See infra* pp. 177-90.

233. *See infra* pp. 1189-91, 1194-96.

234. *See infra* pp. 315-34.

235. *See infra* pp. 983-92.

236. *See infra* pp. 785-90.

237. *See* Act of Apr. 19, 1920, ch. 275, 1920 N.Y. Laws 803-807 (providing for validity of arbitration agreements); G. Born, *International Commercial Arbitration* 68 (2d ed. 2014).

238. French Commercial Code, 1925, Art. 631. *See also* von Mehren, *International Commercial Arbitration: The Contribution of the French Jurisprudence*, 46 La. L. Rev. 1045, 1049-51 (1985-1986) (discussing impact of 1925 amendment).

239. *See* G. Born, *International Commercial Arbitration* 68 (2d ed. 2014); Samuel, *Arbitration Statutes in England and the USA*, 8 Arb. & Disp. Resol. L.J. 2, 13 (1999).

240. U.S. FAA, 9 U.S.C. §2. For discussion of §2, *see infra* pp. 53-54.

241. U.S. FAA, 9 U.S.C. §§9, 10. For discussion of §§9, 10, *see infra* pp. 53-54, 1150-55, 1165-68, 1171-72.

242. *See supra* pp. 21-26 & *infra* pp. 189-90

243. 330 U.N.T.S., No. 4739; www.uncitral.org.

The Convention was adopted—like many national arbitration statutes—specifically to address the needs of the international business community, and in particular to improve the legal regime provided by the Geneva Protocol and Geneva Convention for the international arbitral process.[244] The first draft of what became the Convention was prepared by the International Chamber of Commerce in 1953. The ICC introduced the draft with the observation that "the 1927 Geneva Convention was a considerable step forward, but it no longer entirely meets modern economic requirements," and with the fairly radical objective of "obtaining the adoption of a new international system of enforcement of arbitral awards."[245]

Preliminary drafts of a revised Convention were prepared by the ICC and the United Nations' Economic and Social Council ("ECOSOC"), which then provided the basis for a three-week conference in New York—the United Nations Conference on Commercial Arbitration—attended by 45 states in the spring of 1958.[246] The New York Conference resulted in a document—the New York Convention—that was in many respects a radically innovative instrument, which created for the first time a comprehensive legal regime for the international arbitral process.

The original drafts of the New York Convention were focused entirely on the recognition and enforcement of arbitral *awards*, with no serious attention to the enforcement of international arbitration *agreements*.[247] This drafting approach paralleled that of the Geneva treaties (where the Geneva Protocol dealt with arbitration agreements and the Geneva Convention addressed awards).[248] It was only late in the Conference that the delegates recognized the limitations of this approach and considered a proposal from the Dutch delegation to extend the treaty from the recognition of awards to also address international arbitration agreements. That approach, which was eventually adopted, and the resulting provisions regarding the recognition and enforcement of international arbitration agreements form one of the central elements of the Convention.[249]

The text of the Convention was approved on June 10, 1958 by a unanimous vote of the Conference (with only the United States and three other countries abstaining).[250] The Convention is set forth in English, French, Spanish, Russian and Chinese texts, all of which are equally authentic.[251] The text of the Convention is only a few pages long, with the

244. A. van den Berg, *The New York Arbitration Convention* 7 (1981) ("although the Geneva Treaties were undoubtedly an improvement in comparison with the previous situation, they were still considered inadequate").

245. *Enforcement of International Arbitral Awards, Report and Preliminary Draft Convention* (ICC Publication No. 174 1953), reprinted in 9(1) ICC ICArb. Bull. 32, 32 (1998).

246. Sanders, *The History of the New York Convention*, in A. van den Berg (ed.), *Improving the Efficiency of Arbitration Agreements and Awards: 40 Years of Application of the New York Convention* 11, 12 (ICCA Congress Series No. 9 1999).

247. G. Born, *International Commercial Arbitration* 101 (2d ed. 2014); A. van den Berg, *The New York Arbitration Convention of 1958* 8-10, 56 (1981).

248. *See supra* pp. 30-33.

249. *See infra* pp. 34-35, 177-90.

250. For a brief summary of these negotiations, *see* A. van den Berg, *The New York Arbitration Convention of 1958* 1-10 (1981); Sanders, *The History of the New York Convention*, in A. van den Berg (ed.), *Improving the Efficiency of Arbitration Agreements and Awards: 40 Years of Application of the New York Convention* 11 (ICCA Congress Series No. 9 1999).

251. New York Convention, Art. XVI.

instrument's essential substance being contained in five concisely-drafted provisions (Articles I through V).

Despite its brevity, the Convention is now widely regarded as "the cornerstone of current international commercial arbitration."[252] In the apt words of Judge Stephen Schwebel, former President of the International Court of Justice: "It works."[253] Or, as the late Sir Michael Kerr put it, the New York Convention "is the foundation on which the whole of the edifice of international arbitration rests."[254]

It is often said that the Convention did not provide a detailed legislative regime for all aspects of international arbitrations (as, for example, the UNCITRAL Model Law would later do[255]). Rather, the Convention's provisions focused on the recognition and enforcement of arbitration agreements and arbitral awards, without specifically regulating the conduct of the arbitral proceedings or other aspects of the arbitral process. As one national court has observed, the Convention was designed to "encourage the recognition and enforcement of *commercial arbitration agreements* in international contracts and to unify the standards by which *agreements to arbitrate are observed and arbitral awards* are enforced in the signatory nations."[256]

Within these fields, an essential objective of the Convention was uniformity; the Convention's drafters sought to establish a single uniform set of international legal standards for the enforcement of arbitration agreements and arbitral awards.[257] In particular, the Convention's provisions prescribe uniform international rules that: (a) require national courts to recognize and enforce foreign arbitral awards (Articles III and IV), subject to a limited number of specified exceptions (Article V);[258] (b) require national courts to recognize the validity of arbitration agreements, subject to specified exceptions (Article II);[259] and (c) require national courts to refer parties to arbitration when they have entered into a valid agreement to arbitrate that is subject to the Convention (Article II(3)).[260] The Convention's exceptions to the obligation to recognize foreign arbitral awards are limited to issues of jurisdiction, procedural regularity and fundamental fairness, compliance with the parties' arbitration agreement and public policy; they do not include review by a recognition court of the merits of the arbitrators' substantive decision.[261]

---

252. A. van den Berg, *The New York Arbitration Convention of 1958* 1 (1981). *See also* G. Born, *International Commercial Arbitration* 103 (2d ed. 2014).

253. Schwebel, *A Celebration of the United Nations New York Convention on the Recognition and Enforcement of Foreign Arbitral Awards*, 12 Arb. Int'l 83, 85 (1996).

254. Kerr, *Concord and Conflict in International Arbitration*, 13 Arb. Int'l 121, 127 (1997).

255. *See infra* pp. 47-51.

256. *Scherk v. Alberto-Culver Co.*, 417 U.S. 506, 502 n.15 (1974) (emphasis added).

257. Patocchi & Jermini, in S. Berti *et al.* (eds.), *International Arbitration in Switzerland* Art. 194 ¶20 (2000) ("The provisions of the Convention … are to be interpreted and construed taking into account the need for a uniform interpretation of the Convention in all the contracting States."); A. van den Berg, *The New York Arbitration Convention of 1958* 1, 6, 54-55, 168-69, 262-63, 274, 357-58 (1981) ("the significance of the New York Convention for international commercial arbitration makes it even more important that the Convention is interpreted *uniformly* by the courts.") (emphasis in original).

258. New York Convention, Arts. III, V.

259. New York Convention, Art. II(1).

260. New York Convention, Art. II(3).

261. New York Convention, Arts. V(1), V(2); *infra* pp. 1198-99.

The New York Convention made a number of significant improvements in the regime of the Geneva Protocol and Geneva Convention for the enforcement of international arbitration agreements and arbitral awards. Particularly important were the New York Convention's shifting of the burden of proving the validity or invalidity of arbitral awards away from the party seeking enforcement to the party resisting enforcement,[262] its recognition of substantial party autonomy with respect to choice of arbitral procedures and law applicable to the arbitration agreement,[263] and its abolition of the previous "double *exequatur*" requirement (which had required that arbitral awards be confirmed in the arbitral seat before being recognized abroad).[264] The Convention's various improvements were summarized by the President of the U.N. Conference on the Convention as follows:

> [I]t was already apparent that the document represented an improvement on the Geneva Convention of 1927. It gave a wider definition of the awards to which the Convention applied; it reduced and simplified the requirements with which the party seeking recognition or enforcement of an award would have to comply; it placed the burden of proof on the party against whom recognition or enforcement was invoked; it gave the parties greater freedom in the choice of the arbitral authority and of the arbitration procedures; it gave the authority before which the award was sought to be relied upon the right to order the party opposing the enforcement to give suitable security.[265]

More generally, these provisions of the Convention were intended to promote the use of arbitration as a means of resolving international commercial disputes, in order to facilitate international trade and investment.[266]

Despite the Convention's brevity and focus on arbitration agreements and arbitral awards, the significance of its terms can scarcely be exaggerated. The Convention's provisions effected a fundamental restructuring of the international legal regime for international commercial arbitration, combining the separate subject matters of the Geneva Protocol and Geneva Convention into a single instrument which provided a legal framework that covered international arbitrations from their inception (the arbitration agreement) until their conclusion (recognition of the award). In so doing, the Convention established for the first time a comprehensive international legal framework for international arbitration agreements, arbitral proceedings and arbitral awards.

Moreover, the terms of this legal framework were important and remarkably innovative. Considering only the Convention's provisions mandating recognition of arbitral awards, subject to a limited, exclusive list of exceptions, one delegate to the New York Conference

---

262. *See* New York Convention, Arts. III-V; *supra* p. 32 & *infra* pp. 1195-96. The shift in the burden of proof was accomplished by Articles III and V, which required the award-creditor to present only minimal evidence in support of recognition of an award (in Article III), while specifying only limited grounds, which needed affirmatively to be proven, that could result in non-recognition (in Article V). *See infra* pp. 1195-96.

263. *See* New York Convention, Arts. V(1)(a), (d); *supra* pp. 32-33, 35 & *infra* p. 302.

264. *See supra* p. 32 & *infra* pp. 1196-97.

265. *Summary Record of the Twenty-Fifth Meeting of the United Nations Conference on International Commercial Arbitration*, U.N. Doc. E/CONF.26/SR.25, 2 (1958).

266. *Kaverit Steel & Crane Ltd v. Kone Corp.*, XIX Y.B. Comm. Arb. 643, 651 (1994) (Alberta Ct. App. 1992) ("it is common ground that the evident purpose of Alberta's acceptance of the [New York] Convention is to promote international trade and commerce by the certainty that comes from a scheme of international arbitration"); Park, *Neutrality, Predictability and Economic Cooperation*, 12(4) J. Int'l Arb. 99 (1995); A. van den Berg, *The New York Arbitration Convention of 1958* 17-19 (1981).

termed the Convention a "very bold innovation."[267] Equally, the Convention's introduction of uniform international legal standards mandatorily requiring the recognition and enforcement of international arbitration agreements, subject to only specified exceptions, was also a bold advance.[268] Taken together, the Convention's provisions regarding the recognition of arbitral awards and agreements also had the indirect, but nonetheless innovative, effect of providing an international legal framework within which the arbitral proceedings could be conducted largely in accordance with the parties' desires and the arbitrators' directions.

Despite its present significance, the New York Convention initially attracted relatively few signatories or ratifications. Only 26 of the 45 countries participating in the Conference signed the Convention prior to its entry into force on June 7, 1959. Many of the countries that did sign the Convention prior to June 1959, such as Belgium, the Netherlands, Sweden and Switzerland, did not ratify it for several years thereafter. Other nations, including the United Kingdom and most Latin American and African states, did not accede to the Convention until many years later.[269] The United States did not ratify the Convention until 1970.[270]

Over time, however, states from all regions of the globe reconsidered their position,[271] and as of 2014, some 153 nations had ratified the Convention.[272] The Convention's parties include virtually all major trading states and many Latin American, African, Asian, Middle Eastern and former socialist states. During the past decade, numerous states (including a number in the Middle East and Latin America) have departed from traditions of distrust of international arbitration and ratified the Convention.[273] The Convention has thus realized its drafters' original aspirations and come to serve as a global charter for international arbitration.

Article VII of the New York Convention provides that the Convention does not affect the validity of any bilateral or other multilateral arrangements concerning the recognition

267. *Summary Record of the Thirteenth Meeting of the United Nations Conference on International Commercial Arbitration*, U.N. Doc. E/Conf.26/SR.13, 3 (1958).

268. The effect of the Convention on the recognition and enforcement of international arbitration agreements is discussed below. *See infra* pp. 177-90, 375-92, 393-474.

269. For example, prior to 1980, the New York Convention had not been ratified by (among others) Algeria, Argentina, Bahrain, Bangladesh, Bolivia, Burkina Faso, Cameroon, China, Costa Rica, Guatemala, Guinea, Haiti, Indonesia, Kenya, Laos, Lebanon, Malaysia, Mali, Mauritania, Mozambique, Nepal, Panama, Paraguay, Peru, Saudi Arabia, Senegal, Singapore, Turkey, Uruguay, Venezuela, Vietnam and Zimbabwe. Between 1980 and the present, all of these states acceded to the Convention.

270. In the United States, historic distrust of arbitration and the domestic debate over the appropriate scope of the federal treaty power and the authority of the several states led to an initial recommendation from the U.S. delegation against ratifying the Convention. Czysak & Sullivan, *American Arbitration Law and the UN Convention*, 13 Arb. J. 197 (1958); Springer, *The United Nations Convention on the Recognition and Enforcement of Foreign Arbitral Awards*, 3 Int'l Law. 320 (1969).

271. In 1970, the United States reconsidered its position and acceded to the Convention. *See Message From the President on the Convention on the Recognition and Enforcement of Foreign Arbitral Awards*, S. Exec. Doc. E, 90th Cong., 2d Sess. 18 (1968); Quigley, *Accession by the United States to the United Nations Convention on the Recognition and Enforcement of Foreign Arbitral Awards*, 70 Yale L.J. 1049 (1961).

272. *See* www.uncitral.org for a list of states that have ratified the Convention.

273. In ratifying the Convention, many states have attached reservations that can have significant consequences in private disputes. These reservations frequently deal with reciprocity and limiting the Convention's applicability to disputes arising from "commercial" relations. *See infra* pp. 138-48, 169-75.

and enforcement of foreign arbitral awards (except the Geneva Protocol and Geneva Convention, which are terminated as between Contracting States to the New York Convention).[274] Article VII(1) of the Convention also provides that the Convention "shall not … deprive any interested party of any right he may have to avail himself of an arbitral award in the manner and to the extent allowed by the law or treaties of the country where such award is sought to be relied upon."[275] Article VII has been interpreted by many national courts in a "pro-enforcement" fashion, to permit agreements and awards to be enforced under either the Convention, as well as under another treaty (if that treaty is by its terms applicable), or under national law, provided that it is more favorable than the Convention.[276]

In virtually all Contracting States, the New York Convention has been implemented through national legislation. The practical effect of the Convention is therefore dependent on both the content of such national legislation and the interpretations given by national courts to the Convention and national implementing legislation.[277]

As noted above, an important aim of the Convention's drafters was uniformity.[278] The fulfillment of that aim is dependent upon the willingness of national legislatures and courts, in different Contracting States, to adopt uniform interpretations of the Convention. In general, national courts have risen to the challenge of adopting uniform interpretations of the Convention's provisions.[279] That process has accelerated in recent decades, as national court decisions have become increasingly available in foreign jurisdictions and national courts have increasingly cited authorities from foreign and international sources in interpreting the Convention.[280]

---

274. New York Convention, Arts. VII(1), (2). *See* G. Born, *International Commercial Arbitration* 3428-33 (2d ed. 2014).

275. New York Convention, Arts. VII(1), (2).

276. *See infra* pp. 381-82, 387-88, 1174-77.

277. *See infra* pp. 46-67.

278. *See supra* p. 35.

279. Early experience was more mixed. J. Lew, L. Mistelis & S. Kröll, *Comparative International Commercial Arbitration* 21, 729 (2003); P. Sanders, *Commentary*, I Y.B. Comm. Arb. 207 (1976), II Y.B. Comm. Arb. 254 (1977), IV Y.B. Comm. Arb. 231 (1979); A. van den Berg, *The New York Convention: Its Intended Effects, Its Interpretation, Salient Problem Areas* 26 (ASA Special Series No. 9 1996).

280. For representative examples, *see Mitsubishi Motors Corp. v. Soler Chrysler Plymouth, Inc.*, 473 U.S. 614, 660 (1985) (Stevens, J., dissenting) (citing Belgian and Italian decisions on nonarbitrability doctrine); *Europcar Italia, SpA v. Maiellano Tours, Inc.*, 156 F.3d 310, 314 (2d Cir. 1998) (reviewing Italian and German court decisions to determine if awards rendered under *"arbitrato irrituale"* were enforceable under Convention); *Ministry of Defense of Islamic Repub. of Iran v. Gould Inc.*, 887 F.2d 1357, 1364 (9th Cir. 1989) (citing English authority); *Lesotho Highlands Dev. Auth. v. Impregilo SpA* [2005] 2 All ER (Comm) 265, 280-81 (House of Lords) (citing U.S. authority); *Fiona Trust & Holding Corp. v. Privalov* [2007] EWCA Civ. 20 (English Ct. App.) (citing U.S. and German authority), *aff'd*, [2007] UKHL 40 (House of Lords); *Brostrom Tankers AB v. Factorias Vulcano SA*, XXX Y.B. Comm. Arb. 591, 596-97 (2005) (Dublin High Ct. 2004) (citing U.S. authority); *Karaha Bodas Co. v. Perusahaan Pertambangan Minyak Dan Gas Bumi Negara*, 364 F.3d 274 (5th Cir. 2004) (citing English, Hong Kong, Swedish, Swiss and other authorities); *TMR Energy Ltd v. State Prop. Fund of Ukraine*, XXIX Y.B. Comm. Arb. 607, 630 (2004) (Canadian Fed. Ct. 2003) (citing English authority); *Hebei Imp. & Exp. Corp. v. Polytek Eng'g Co.*, [1999] 2 HCK 205 (H.K. Ct. Fin. App.) (citing U.S. and Indian authorities); *Democratic Repub. of Congo v. FG Hemisphere Assocs. LLC*, [2011] HKEC 747, ¶¶152-155 (H.K. Ct. App.) (citing U.S., English and Canadian authority); *Bharat Aluminium Co. ("BALCO") v. Kaiser Aluminium Technical Service, Inc.*, C.A. No. 7019/2005, ¶¶94, 128, 142, 150 (Indian S.Ct. 2012) (citing U.S., English and Hong Kong authorities); *Gas Auth. of India, Ltd v.*

It also bears emphasis that the Convention is a "constitutional" instrument.[281] The Convention's text is drafted in broad and general terms, designed for application in a multitude of states and legal systems, over a period of decades. By necessity, as well as design, the interpretation of the Convention must evolve and develop over time, as national courts and arbitral tribunals confront new issues, develop more refined analyses and implement the treaty's underlying objectives.

The process of interpretation and application of the Convention can be uneven and slow, but it is very well-adapted to the evolving needs of the international arbitral process, which by its nature is characterized by changing commercial demands and conditions. It is also well-adapted to the nature of the Convention's constitutional structure, which leaves a substantial role for national law and national courts to play in the international arbitral process, but within the international framework and limitations imposed by the Convention's provisions.

4. *Inter-American Convention*

In the early years of the 20th century, much of South America effectively turned its back on international commercial arbitration. Only Brazil ratified the Geneva Protocol, and even it did not adopt the Geneva Convention. South American states were very reluctant to ratify the New York Convention, for the most part only beginning to do so in the 1980s.

Nevertheless, in 1975, the United States and most South American nations negotiated the Inter-American Convention on International Commercial Arbitration ("Inter-American Convention"), also known as the "Panama Convention."[282] The United States ratified the Convention in 1990; other parties include Mexico, Brazil, Argentina, Venezuela, Colombia, Chile, Ecuador, Peru, Costa Rica, El Salvador, Guatemala, Honduras, Panama, Paraguay, Uruguay, Dominican Republic, Nicaragua and Bolivia.[283]

The Inter-American Convention is similar to the New York Convention in many respects; indeed, the Convention's drafting history makes clear that it was intended to provide the same results as the New York Convention.[284] Among other things, the

---

SPIE-CAPAG SA, XXIII Y.B. Comm. Arb. 688, 694 (1998) (Delhi High Ct. 1993) (citing U.S. authority); *Attorney Gen. v. Mobil Oil N.Z., Ltd*, [1989] 2 NZLR 649, 668 (N.Z. High Ct.) (although U.S. judicial decisions reflect "United States judicial policy towards international investments and contracts ... such principles are appropriate even in this small country as international trade and commercial relationships are of critical importance").

281. *Cf.* Carbonneau, *The Reception of Arbitration in United States Law*, 40 Me. L. Rev. 262, 272 (1988) (New York Convention is "universal charter" of international commercial arbitration); Landau, *The Requirement of A Written Form for An Arbitration Agreement: When "Written" Means "Oral"* 19, 64 (ICCA Congress Series No. 11 2003) (New York Convention is a "living document").

282. Inter-American Convention on International Commercial Arbitration, signed in Panama on January 30, 1975. The Convention is available at www.sice.oas.org.

283. *See* www.sice.oas.org.

284. House Report No. 501, 101st Cong., 2d Sess. 4 (1990), reprinted in 1990 U.S.C.C.A.N. 675, 678 ("The New York Convention and the Inter-American Convention are intended to achieve the same results, and their key provisions adopt the same standards, phrased in the legal style appropriate for each organization. It is the Committee's expectation, in view of that fact and the parallel legislation under the Federal Arbitration Act that would be applied to the Conventions, that courts in the United States would achieve a general uniformity of results under the two conventions."); *Productos Mercantiles e Industriales, SA v. Faberge USA*, 23 F.3d 41, 45 (2d Cir. 1994) ("the legislative history of the Inter-American Convention's

Inter-American Convention provides for the presumptive validity and enforceability of arbitration agreements[285] and arbitral awards,[286] subject to specified exceptions similar to those in the New York Convention.[287]

The Inter-American Convention nonetheless introduces significant innovations, not present in the New York Convention. It does so by providing that, where the parties have not expressly agreed to any institutional or other arbitration rules, the rules of the Inter-American Commercial Arbitration Commission ("IACAC") will govern.[288] In turn, the Commission has adopted rules that are similar to the UNCITRAL Arbitration Rules.[289] The Convention has also introduced provisions regarding the constitution of the arbitral tribunal and the parties' freedom to appoint arbitrators of their choosing (regardless of nationality).[290] Less desirably, the Inter-American Convention departs from the New York Convention by omitting provisions dealing expressly with judicial proceedings brought in national courts in breach of an arbitration agreement.[291]

5. *European Convention*

The 1961 European Convention on International Commercial Arbitration[292] is one of the world's most important regional commercial arbitration treaties. Drafting of the European Convention began in 1954, aimed at producing a treaty that would improve upon the then-existing legal framework for international arbitration involving parties from European states and particularly East-West trade.[293] The drafting process was protracted (and delayed by the intervening New York Convention), but ultimately concluded with the signing of the Convention in Geneva on April 21, 1961.[294]

The European Convention entered into force in 1964, and as of 2014, 31 states were party to it. Most European states (but not the United Kingdom, the Netherlands, Norway, or Sweden) are party to the Convention, while some ten non-EU states are parties, including

---

implementing statute ... clearly demonstrates that Congress intended the Inter-American Convention to reach the same results as those reached under the New York Convention").

285. Inter-American Convention, Art. 1.

286. Inter-American Convention, Arts. 4, 5.

287. Inter-American Convention, Art. 5.

288. Inter-American Convention, Art. 3. The Inter-American Commercial Arbitration Commission is composed of national sections in about a dozen nations; the AAA is the U.S. national section. IACAC's administrative headquarters is located in OAS facilities in Washington, D.C., and is overseen on a day-to-day basis by a Director General.

289. IACAC Rules, available at www.sice.oas.org.

290. Inter-American Convention, Art. 2.

291. *Compare* New York Convention, Art. II(3); *infra* pp. 320-34. *See also* A. van den Berg, *The New York Arbitration Convention* 102 (1981) ("The Panama Convention shows a certain number of lacunae and obscurities in comparison with the New York Convention").

292. European Convention on International Commercial Arbitration, 21 April 1961, 484 U.N.T.S. 349. *See* G. Born, *International Commercial Arbitration* 117 (2d ed. 2014); A. van den Berg, *The New York Arbitration Convention* 92-98 (1981).

293. A. van den Berg, *The New York Arbitration Convention* 93 (1981) (European Convention's "main purpose is arbitration in East-West trade").

294. *See* Hascher, *European Convention on International Commercial Arbitration of 1961: Commentary*, XX Y.B. Comm. Arb. 1006 (1995).

Russia, Cuba and Burkina Faso.[295] The Convention consists of ten articles and a detailed annex (dealing with certain procedural matters).

The Convention addresses the three principal phases of the international arbitral process—arbitration agreements, arbitral procedure and arbitral awards. With regard to arbitration agreements, the Convention does not expressly provide for their presumptive validity, but instead provides for a specified, limited number of bases for the invalidity of such agreements in proceedings concerning recognition of awards.[296] The Convention also addresses the allocation of competence between arbitral tribunals and national courts over jurisdictional challenges, to the existence, validity, or scope of the arbitration agreement.[297] With regard to the arbitral procedure, the Convention limits the role of national courts and confirms the autonomy of the parties and the arbitrators (or arbitral institution) to conduct the arbitration proceedings.[298] With regard to arbitral awards, the Convention is designed to supplement the New York Convention, essentially dealing only with the effects of a judicial decision annulling an award in the arbitral seat in other jurisdictions (and not with other recognition obligations).[299]

The Convention's impact in actual litigation has not been substantial (owing to the limited number of Contracting States, all of whom are also party to the New York Convention). Nonetheless, the Convention's effects on international arbitration doctrine have been significant. This is particularly true with regard to the arbitrators' jurisdiction to consider challenges to their own jurisdiction (so-called "competence-competence")[300] and the parties' (and arbitrators') autonomy to determine the arbitral procedures.[301] The Convention is currently somewhat dated—reflecting its origins during the Cold War—and efforts have been proposed, thus far unsuccessfully, to revise its provisions.[302]

6. ICSID Convention

A central pillar of the international investment regime is the so-called "ICSID Convention" or "Washington Convention" of 1965. The Convention established the International Centre for Settlement of Investment Disputes ("ICSID"), a specialized arbitral institution, which administers arbitrations and conciliations, both pursuant to the Convention and otherwise.[303]

---

295. G. Born, *International Commercial Arbitration* 118 (2d ed. 2014).

296. European Convention, Art. V(1) ("either non-existent or null and void or had lapsed"). *See infra* pp. 177, 1199.

297. European Convention, Arts. III-VII, Annex.

298. European Convention, Arts. III-VII & Annex. *See infra* pp. 789-90.

299. European Convention, Art. IX. *See infra* pp. 1194; A. van den Berg, *The New York Arbitration Convention* 96 (1981) ("the European Convention cannot function without the New York Convention as the former is built upon the latter").

300. European Convention, Arts. V, VI. As discussed below, Article V confirms the arbitral tribunal's competence to consider challenges to its own jurisdiction, while Article VI provides in principle for national courts to permit initial resolution of jurisdictional objections by the arbitral tribunal. *See infra* pp. 283-85.

301. European Convention, Art. IV & Annex. *See infra* pp. 789-90.

302. United Nations Economic and Social Council, *Economic Commission for Europe*, U.N. Doc. No. TRADE/2000/7, ¶¶25-28; www.unece.org/ie/Wp5/eucon.htm (website of expert advisory group charged with reviewing European Convention for possible revisions).

303. ICSID Convention, Art. 1. *See* G. Born, *International Commercial Arbitration* 120-23 (2d ed. 2014).

The ICSID Convention was negotiated and opened for signature in 1965 and, as of 2014, has 150 Contracting States from every geographic region of the world.[304] The Convention is designed to facilitate the settlement of "investment disputes" (*i.e.*, "legal dispute[s] arising directly out of ... investment[s]") that the parties have agreed to submit to ICSID.[305] Investment disputes are defined as controversies that arise out of an "investment" and are between a Contracting State (or "host State") or a designated state-related entity from that state and a national of another Contracting State (or "investor"). The Convention does not apply to disputes not involving a Contracting State and an investor from another Contracting State or to disputes between private parties; it also does not apply to purely commercial disputes that do not involve an investment.

As to investment disputes that fall within its terms, the Convention provides both conciliation and arbitration procedures. The Convention does not provide an independent, stand-alone basis for arbitrating particular disputes under the Convention. Instead, an ICSID arbitration cannot be pursued without separate consent to ICSID arbitration by the foreign investor and host state, which usually takes the form of either an arbitration clause contained within an investment contract or consent provided in a foreign investment law, BIT (discussed below at pp. 511-16), or another treaty.[306]

If parties agree to submit a dispute to ICSID arbitration, the ICSID Convention (and related ICSID Arbitration Rules) provide a comprehensive, stand-alone regime, almost entirely detached from national law and national courts, for the conduct of ICSID arbitral proceedings. This regime differs materially from that applicable in international commercial arbitrations (under the New York Convention) and most other investment arbitration contexts.

Under the ICSID Convention regime, arbitral tribunals are granted exclusive competence to resolve jurisdictional challenges (subject to limited subsequent review by ICSID-appointed annulment committees (and not by national courts)).[307] This differs from international commercial arbitrations, where national courts play a significant role in considering and resolving jurisdictional disputes.

Likewise, ICSID awards are subject to immediate recognition and enforcement in the courts of Contracting States without setting aside proceedings or any other form of other review in national courts, either in the arbitral seat or elsewhere (but subject to local rules of state immunity of state assets).[308] Instead, ICSID awards are subject to a specialized internal annulment procedure, in which *ad hoc* committees selected by ICSID are mandated, in limited circumstances, to annul awards for jurisdictional or grave procedural violations;[309] if an award is annulled it may be resubmitted to a new ICSID arbitral tribunal.[310] This is a substantial difference from the New York Convention model, where awards are subject to annulment (in the national courts of the arbitral seat) and non-recognition (in national courts elsewhere).[311]

---

304. ICSID, *List of Contracting States and Other Signatories*, available at icsid.worldbank.org.
305. ICSID Convention, Art. 25(1).
306. *See infra* pp. 43-44, 511-16.
307. ICSID Convention, Arts. 41, 52, 53.
308. ICSID Convention, Arts. 53, 54.
309. ICSID Convention, Art. 52.
310. ICSID Convention, Art. 52.
311. *See infra* pp. 1113-87, 1189-266.

Moreover, ICSID (and not a national court) serves as the appointing authority in ICSID arbitrations, when necessary, selecting and replacing arbitrators from a list of individuals selected by individual Contracting States.[312] Again, this differs materially from appointment mechanisms in at least some non-ICSID settings (particularly *ad hoc* arbitrations, where national courts can be involved in the appointment and challenge process[313]).

Finally, the ICSID Convention provides that, absent agreement by the parties, ICSID arbitrations are governed by the law of the state that is party to the dispute (including its conflict of laws rules) "and such rules of international law as may be applicable."[314] In contrast, neither the New York nor Inter-American Convention contains comparable substantive choice-of-law provisions.

As of June 2014, ICSID had registered 473 cases (14 new cases in the first half of 2014), and ICSID tribunals had issued 180 awards.[315]

7. *Bilateral Investment Treaties and Other Investment Protection Agreements*

Bilateral Investment Treaties ("BITs") or Investment Protection Agreements ("IPAs") became common during the 1980s and 1990s as a means of encouraging capital investment in developing markets.[316] Capital-exporting states (including the United States, most Western European states and Japan) were the earliest and most vigorous proponents of the negotiation of BITs, principally with countries in developing regions. More recently, states from all regions of the world and in all stages of development have entered into BITs.[317] A recent study concluded that more than 2,800 BITs are presently operative.[318]

Most BITs provide significant substantive protections for investments made by foreign investors, including guarantees against expropriation and denials of fair and equitable treatment.[319] BITs also frequently contain provisions that permit foreign investors to require international arbitration (typically referred to as "investor-State arbitration") of specified categories of investment disputes with the host state—including in the absence of a traditional contractual arbitration agreement with the host state.[320] The possibility of "arbitration without privity" is an important option in some international disputes, and

---

312. ICSID Convention, Arts. 13(1), 38, 40(1).

313. *See infra* pp. 702-09, 758-76.

314. ICSID Convention, Art. 42.

315. *See* ICSID, *ICSID Caseload* 7 (July 2014).

316. In addition to the ICSID Convention, there are also multilateral conventions in particular regions or economic sectors. These include the Energy Charter Treaty, the North American Free Trade Agreement (NAFTA) and the Association of Southeast Asian Nations (ASEAN) Investment Agreement.

317. For example, 20 out of 58 BITs in 2010 were concluded between developing countries. UNCTAD, *World Investment Report 2011* (2011); UNCTAD, *Bilateral Investment Treaties 1995-2006: Trends in Investment Rulemaking* (2007). A few states, notably Brazil, have refused to conclude BITs, but most states, including the United States, China, all EU states, most Latin American, Asian states and many African states, have concluded substantial numbers of BITs.

318. *See* UNCTAD, *International Investment Agreements Navigator*, available at investmentpolicyhub.unctad.org/IIA.

319. For commentary, *see* C. McLachlan, L. Shore & M. Weiniger, *International Investment Arbitration* ¶¶1.24 to 1.30, ¶2.20 (2007); J. Paulsson, *Denial of Justice in International Law* (2005).

320. UNCTAD, *Bilateral Investment Treaties 1995-2006: Trends In Investment Rulemaking*, U.N. Doc. UNCTAD/ITE/IIA/2006/5 (2007).

represents a substantial development in the evolution of international arbitration.[321] In addition, many BITs contain provisions dealing with the finality and enforceability of international arbitral awards issued pursuant to the treaty.[322] A sample BIT (between the United Kingdom and Bosnia-Herzegovina) is included in the Documentary Supplement at pp. 73-78.

C. OVERVIEW OF NATIONAL ARBITRATION LEGISLATION

Many nations have enacted arbitration legislation, which implements the New York Convention (or other regional arbitration treaties) and provides a basic legal framework for international arbitration agreements, arbitral proceedings and arbitral awards. These statutory regimes are directed primarily at international commercial arbitration, but, in some instances, extend to international investment or inter-state arbitration. National arbitration statutes are of fundamental importance in giving effect to—or creating obstacles to—the functioning of the international arbitral process. Despite occasional rhetoric as to the "autonomy" of the international arbitral process,[323] it is essential to the efficient functioning of the arbitral process, and the realization of the parties' objectives in agreeing to arbitrate, that national courts give effect to such agreements and provide support for the arbitral process. The enactment of legislation accomplishing these ends has been a major objective—and achievement—of developed trading states during the last 50 years.[324]

Over the past several decades, most developed and less-developed states have enacted revised or improved legislation dealing with international commercial arbitration. The extent of these legislative revisions is striking, both in number and diversity. Important new enactments, or thorough revisions, have occurred in Algeria (1993, 2008), Argentina (1981, 2001), Australia (1974, 1989, 2010), Austria (2005, 2013), Azerbaijan (1999), Bahrain (1994), Bangladesh (2001), Belarus (1999), Belgium (2013), Bolivia (1997), Brazil (1996), Bulgaria (1993, 2007), Cambodia (2006), Canada (2014), Chile (2004), China (1982, 1991, 1994), Colombia (1996, 1998, 2012), Costa Rica (1997, 2011), Cyprus (1987), Czech Republic (1994, 2012), Denmark (2005), Djibouti (1984), Dominican Republic (2008), Ecuador (1997), Egypt (1994), El Salvador (2002), Estonia (2006), England (1996), Finland (1992), France (2011), Germany (1998), Greece (1999), Hong Kong (1997, 2011), India (1996), Indonesia (1999), Iran (1997), Ireland (1998, 2010), Israel (1968, 2008), Italy (1994, 2006), Japan (2004), Jordan (2001), Kazakhstan (2004), Kenya (1995, 2009), Kuwait (1995), Lebanon (1985, 2002), Libya (2010), Malaysia (2006, 2011),

---

321. *See infra* pp. 511-16; Paulsson, *Arbitration Without Privity*, 10 ICSID L. Rev. 232 (1995); C. Schreuer *et al.*, *The ICSID Convention: A Commentary* Art. 25 ¶¶378, 392-467 (2d ed. 2009).

322. For commentary on BITs, *see* UNCTAD, *Bilateral Investment Treaties 1995-2006: Trends In Investment Rulemaking*, U.N. Doc. UNCTAD/ITE/IIA/2006/5; R. Bishop *et al.*, *Foreign Investment Disputes—Cases, Materials and Commentary* (2005); A. Bjorklund *et al.*, *Investment Disputes Under NAFTA: An Annotated Guide to NAFTA Chapter 11* (2006); C. Dugan *et al.*, *Investor-State Arbitration* (2008); R. Dolzer & M. Stevens, *Bilateral Investment Treaties* (1995); L. Reed *et al.*, *A Guide to ICSID Arbitration* (2004); K. Vandevelde, *United States Bilateral Investment Treaties: Policy and Practice* (1992); Yackee, *Bilateral Investment Treaties, Credible Commitment, and the Rule of (International) Law: Do BITs Promote Foreign Direct Investment?*, 42 Law & Soc. Rev. 805 (2008).

323. *See* G. Born, *International Commercial Arbitration* 1583-89 (2d ed. 2014).

324. *See* Strong, *Research in International Commercial Arbitration: Special Skills, Special Sources*, 20 Am. Rev. Int'l Arb. 119 (2009).

Malta (1996), Mauritius (2008), Mexico (1989, 1993, 2011), Moldova (2008), Morocco (2008), Netherlands (1985, 2004, 2015), New Zealand (2007), Nigeria (1988), Norway (2004), Peru (1996, 2008), Philippines (2004), Poland (2005), Portugal (2012), Qatar (1990), Romania (2013), Russia (1993), Saudi Arabia (2012), Scotland (2010), Senegal (1998), Singapore (1994, 2010, 2012), South Africa (1965), South Korea (1999), Spain (2004, 2011), Sri Lanka (1995), Sweden (1999), Switzerland (1987, 2011), Syria (2008), Taiwan (2002), Tanzania (2002), Thailand (2002), Tunisia (1993), Turkey (2001), Ukraine (1994), United Arab Emirates (1992), Uruguay (1988, 2013), Venezuela (1998), Vietnam (2011) and Yemen (1992, 1997).

Particularly in civil law jurisdictions, early arbitration legislation was often a part or chapter within the national Code of Civil Procedure.[325] This continues to be the case in a number of jurisdictions even today.[326] In common law jurisdictions, the tendency was (and remains) to enact separate legislation dealing specifically with arbitration (or international arbitration).[327] The growing popularity of the UNCITRAL Model Law on International Commercial Arbitration[328] has made the latter approach of stand-alone arbitration legislation increasingly common.

As discussed below, in many, but not all,[329] cases, national arbitration statutes are applicable only to international (not domestic) arbitrations, or contain separate parts dealing differently with domestic and international arbitration. This approach has generally been adopted in order to permit the application of particularly "pro-arbitration" rules and procedures in the international context, which may not (for historical or other reasons) be appropriate for purely domestic matters.[330] Nevertheless, a number of countries have adopted the same legislation for both domestic and international arbitrations (even then, however, with specific provisions that treat the two fields differently with regard to particular subjects).[331]

Broadly speaking, there are two categories of national arbitration legislation: statutes which are supportive of the international arbitral process (increasingly, but not always, modeled on the UNCITRAL Model Law) and statutes which are not supportive of the arbitral process. Both of these types of legislation are discussed below.

---

325. M. de Boisséson, *Le droit français de l'arbitrage interne et international* ¶¶8-11 (2d ed. 1990); Weiss, *Arbitration in Germany*, 43 Law Q. Rev. 205, 206 (1927).

326. *See, e.g.,* French Code of Civil Procedure; German Code of Civil Procedure ("ZPO"); Netherlands Code of Civil Procedure; Belgian Judicial Code.

327. *See, e.g.,* U.S. FAA, 9 U.S.C. §§1-16; English Arbitration Act, 1996; Japanese Arbitration Law; Singapore International Arbitration Act; Indian Arbitration and Conciliation Act; Samuel, *Arbitration Statutes in England and the USA*, 8 Arb. & Disp. Resol. J. 1, 32 (1999).

328. *See infra* pp. 47-51.

329. *See infra* pp. 158-69.

330. The reasoning for distinguishing international matters from domestic ones rests on the greater jurisdictional, choice-of-law and enforcement uncertainties in the international context, and the need for predictability and certainty in international commerce. *See supra* pp. 14-15. These considerations have been relied on in some national court decisions. *See Mitsubishi Motors Corp. v. Soler Chrysler-Plymouth, Inc.*, 473 U.S. 614 (1985); *Scherk v. Alberto-Culver Co.*, 417 U.S. 506, 517 n.10 (1974); *Judgment of 3 June 1997*, 1998 Rev. arb. 537 (French Cour de cassation civ.).

331. *See infra* pp. 61-67. For example, England's, Spain's and Germany's enactment of the UNCITRAL Model Law deleted provisions limiting the legislation's application to "international" arbitrations, extending it to all arbitration. English Arbitration Act, 1996, §2; German ZPO, §1025; Spanish Arbitration Act, 2011, Art. 1(1).

1. Supportive National Arbitration Legislation

Most states in Europe, North America and Asia have adopted legislation that provides effective and stable support for the arbitral process. In many cases, developed jurisdictions have progressively refined their national arbitration statutes, adopting either amendments or new legislation to make their arbitration regimes maximally supportive for the international arbitral process and attractive to users. Thus, over the past 50 years, virtually every major developed country has substantially revised or entirely replaced its international arbitration legislation, in every case, to facilitate the arbitral process and promote the use of international arbitration.[332]

Paralleling the main features of the New York Convention, the pillars of modern arbitration statutes are provisions that affirm the capacity and freedom of parties to enter into valid and binding agreements to arbitrate future commercial disputes,[333] provide mechanisms for the enforcement of such agreements by national courts (through orders to stay litigation or to compel arbitration),[334] prescribe procedures for confirming or annulling arbitral awards[335] and require the recognition and enforcement of foreign arbitral awards.[336] In many cases, national arbitration statutes also authorize limited judicial assistance to the arbitral process; this assistance can include selecting arbitrators, enforcing a tribunal's orders with respect to evidence-taking or discovery and granting provisional relief in aid of arbitration.[337] In addition, most modern arbitration legislation affirms the parties' autonomy to agree upon arbitral procedures and, sometimes, the applicable substantive law governing the parties' dispute, while narrowly limiting the power of national courts to interfere in the arbitral process, either when arbitral proceedings are pending or in reviewing arbitral awards.[338]

As one distinguished authority put it:

> [One focus of national legislative developments over the past four decades] is found in the widening of the parties' autonomy in regulating qualifying aspects of the arbitration (number and manner of appointment of arbitrators; seat and language of the arbitration; rules applicable to the proceedings; rules applicable to the merits of the dispute; and waiver of means of recourse against the award).[339]

The central objective of these legislative enactments has been to facilitate international trade and investment by providing more secure means of dispute resolution. Recognizing that international transactions are subject to unique legal uncertainties and risks, developed and other states have sought to promote the use of arbitration expressly as a way of miti-

---

332. This includes legislation in France, Switzerland, Germany, Austria, Italy, Spain and all other Continental European states. It also includes England, Canada (and its provinces), Australia and New Zealand, as well as Singapore, Hong Kong, Japan, Korea, India and Malaysia.

The principal exception is the United States, where the FAA dates to 1925, while U.S. implementing legislation for the New York Convention dates to 1970. *See infra* pp. 51-56.

333. *See infra* pp. 177-90, 335-510.

334. *See infra* pp. 315-34.

335. *See infra* pp. 1113-73.

336. *See infra* pp. 1189-266.

337. *See infra* pp. 702-09, 830-38, 839-51, 905-32.

338. *See infra* pp. 788-90, 797-810, 983-90, 1134-73, 1199-266.

339. Bernardini, *The Role of the International Arbitrator*, 20 Arb. Int'l 113, 115 (2004).

gating such risks.[340] Among other things, they have done so through enacting modern arbitration statutes, giving effect to the constitutional principles of the New York Convention, ensuring the validity and enforceability of international arbitration agreements and awards, and facilitating the autonomy of the arbitral process.

a. UNCITRAL Model Law and 2006 Revisions

The United Nations Commission on International Trade Law ("UNCITRAL") Model Law on International Commercial Arbitration ("UNCITRAL Model Law") is the single most important legislative instrument in the field of international commercial arbitration. It has been adopted in a substantial (and growing) number of jurisdictions and has served as a model for legislation and judicial decisions in many others.[341] Revisions to the Model Law (in 2006) sought to improve its legislative framework,[342] introducing new features and providing a good representative example of ongoing legislative efforts aimed at improving the international arbitral process.

The Model Law was initiated by a proposal from the Asian African Legal Consultative Committee to supplement the New York Convention with a protocol regarding party-adopted arbitration rules.[343] The origins of the UNCITRAL Model Law are detailed in a Report by the U.N. Secretary-General, entitled *"Possible Features of A Model Law of International Commercial Arbitration."* Among other things, the *Report* declared:

> The ultimate goal of a Model Law would be to facilitate international commercial arbitration and to ensure its proper functioning and recognition.[344]

The Secretary-General's Report also identified a number of "defects" in national laws, which the New York Convention had sought to remedy, but which persisted in national legal systems:

> To give only a few examples, such provisions may relate to, and be deemed to unduly restrict, the freedom of parties to submit future disputes to arbitration, or the selection and appointment of arbitrators, or the competence of the arbitral tribunal to decide on its own competence or to conduct the proceedings as deemed appropriate taking into account the parties' wishes. Other such restrictions may relate to the choice of the applicable law, both the law governing the arbitral procedure and the one applicable to the substance of the dispute. Supervision and control by courts is another important feature not always welcomed by

---

340. *See supra* pp. 14-16, 36. *Konkan Railways Corp. v. Mehul Constr. Co.*, (2000) 7 SC 201 (Indian S.Ct.) ("To attract the confidence of the international mercantile community and the growing volume of India's trade and commercial relationship with the rest of the world after the new liberalisation policy of the Government, Indian Parliament was persuaded to enact the Arbitration and Conciliation Act of 1996 in UNCITRAL Model...."); S. Rep. No. 702, 91st Cong., 2d Sess. 1-2 (1970) ("In the committee's view, the provisions of S. 3274 [implementing the New York Convention] will serve the best interests of Americans doing business abroad by encouraging them to submit their commercial disputes to impartial arbitration for awards which can be enforced in both U.S. and foreign courts.").

341. *See infra* pp. 44-45, 50.

342. *See infra* p. 49; UNCITRAL Model Law, 2006 Revisions.

343. *Note to the Secretary General*, 8 UNCITRAL Y.B. 233 (1977).

344. *Report by the Secretary General, Possible Features of A Model Law of International Commercial Arbitration*, U.N. Doc. A/CN.9/207, ¶¶9-11 (1981).

parties especially if exerted on the merits of the case.[345]

The Report was the basis for extensive consultations and debates involving states, the business and international arbitration community (*e.g.*, International Council for Commercial Arbitration; ICC International Court of Arbitration), and regional organizations (*e.g.*, Asian-African Legal Consultative Committee).[346] These discussions ultimately produced the final draft of the Model Law, which UNCITRAL approved in a resolution adopted in 1985; the Model Law was approved by a U.N. General Assembly resolution later that year.[347]

The Model Law was designed to be implemented by national legislatures, with the objective of further harmonizing the treatment of international commercial arbitration in different countries. The Law consists of 36 articles, which deal comprehensively with the issues that arise in national courts in connection with international arbitration. Among other things, the law contains provisions concerning the enforcement of arbitration agreements (Articles 7-9), appointment of and challenges to arbitrators (Articles 10-15), jurisdiction of arbitrators (Article 16), provisional measures (Article 17), conduct of the arbitral proceedings, including language, seat (or place) of arbitration, procedures (Articles 18-26), evidence-taking and discovery (Article 27), applicable substantive law (Article 28), arbitral awards (Articles 29-33), setting aside or vacating awards (Article 34) and recognition and enforcement of foreign arbitral awards, including bases for non-recognition (Articles 35-36).

Under the Model Law, written international arbitration agreements are presumptively valid and enforceable, subject to limited, specified exceptions.[348] Article 8 of the Law provides for the enforcement of valid arbitration agreements, regardless of the arbitral seat, by way of a dismissal or stay of national court litigation.[349] The Model Law also adopts the separability doctrine,[350] and expressly grants arbitrators the authority (competence-competence) to consider their own jurisdiction.[351]

The Model Law prescribes a principle of judicial non-intervention in the arbitral proceeding.[352] It also affirms the parties' autonomy (subject to specified due process limits) with regard to the arbitral procedures[353] and, absent agreement between the parties, the tribunal's authority to prescribe such procedures.[354] The basic approach of the UNCITRAL Model Law to the arbitral proceedings is to define a basic set of procedural rules which—subject to a very limited number of fundamental, non-derogable principles of

---

345. *Report by the Secretary General, Possible Features of A Model Law of International Commercial Arbitration*, U.N. Doc. A/CN.9/207, ¶10 (1981).

346. H. Holtzmann & J. Neuhaus, *A Guide to the UNCITRAL Model Law on International Commercial Arbitration: Legislative History and Commentary* 12-13 (1989).

347. *Resolution No. 40/72 of the U.N. General Assembly, dated December 11, 1985*.

348. UNCITRAL Model Law, Arts. 7-8; *infra* pp. 189-90, 375-474. The original 1985 Model Law's "writing" requirement for arbitration agreements is broadly similar to, but somewhat less demanding than, Article II of the New York Convention. *See* UNCITRAL Model Law, Art. 7(2).

349. UNCITRAL Model Law, Art. 8(1); *infra* pp. 315-34.

350. UNCITRAL Model Law, Art. 16; *infra* pp. 190-218.

351. UNCITRAL Model Law, Art. 16; *infra* pp. 272-77, 284-85.

352. UNCITRAL Model Law, Art. 5; *infra* pp. 806-08.

353. UNCITRAL Model Law, Art. 19(1); *infra* pp. 788-89.

354. UNCITRAL Model Law, Arts. 19(2), 24(1); *infra* pp. 791-92.

fairness, due process and equality of treatment[355]—the parties are free to alter by agreement.[356] The Model Law also provides for judicial assistance to the arbitral process in prescribed respects, including provisional measures, constitution of a tribunal and evidence-taking.[357]

The Model Law mandates the presumptive validity of international arbitral awards, subject to a limited, exclusive list of grounds for annulment of arbitral awards in the arbitral seat; these grounds precisely parallel those available under the New York Convention for non-recognition of an award (*i.e.*, lack or excess of jurisdiction, non-compliance with arbitration agreement, due process violations, public policy, nonarbitrability).[358] The Model Law also requires the recognition and enforcement of foreign arbitral awards (made in arbitral seats located outside the recognizing state), again on terms identical to those prescribed in the New York Convention.[359]

During the 30 years since the UNCITRAL Model Law's adoption (in 1985), significant developments have occurred in the field of international commercial arbitration. As noted above, in 2006, UNCITRAL adopted a limited number of amendments to the Model Law aimed at reflecting those developments.[360] The principal revisions were made to Article 2 (the addition of general interpretative principles),[361] Article 7 (the definition and written form of an arbitration agreement),[362] Article 17 (the availability of and standards for provisional measures from international arbitral tribunals and national courts)[363] and Article 35 (procedures for recognition of awards).[364] The 2006 revisions of the Model Law made useful improvements (for the most part[365]). Nonetheless, one of the most important accomplishments of the revisions is their tangible evidence of the ongoing process by which states and business representatives seek to improve the international legal regime for the arbitral process.

The Model Law and its revisions represent a significant further step, beyond the New York Convention, towards the development of a predictable "pro-arbitration" legal framework for commercial arbitration. But the Model Law goes further than the Conven-

---

355. UNCITRAL Model Law, Art. 18 ("The parties shall be treated with equality and each party shall be given a full opportunity of presenting his case."), Art. 24(2) ("The parties shall be given sufficient advance notice of any hearing and of any meeting of the arbitral tribunal for the purposes of inspection of goods, other property or documents."); *infra* pp. 793-95.

356. This addressed concerns that national mandatory laws were unduly constraining arbitral procedures and that the definitions of mandatory and non-mandatory procedural laws were unclear. *Report by the Secretary General, Possible Features of A Model Law of International Commercial Arbitration*, U.N. Doc. A/CN.9/207, ¶¶12-13 (1981).

357. UNCITRAL Model Law, Arts. 9, 11-13, 27; *infra* pp. 705-09, 768-69, 832-33, 922.

358. UNCITRAL Model Law, Art. 34; *supra* pp. 34-35 & *infra* pp. 1159-63.

359. UNCITRAL Model Law, Arts. 35, 36; *infra* pp. 1194-1200.

360. UNCITRAL Model Law, 2006 Revisions; Menon & Chao, *Reforming the Model Law Provisions on Interim Measures of Protection*, 2 Asian Int'l Arb. J. 1 (2006); J. Paulsson & G. Petrochilos, *Revision of the UNCITRAL Arbitration Rules* (2006), available at www.uncitral.org; Sorieul, *UNCITRAL's Current Work in the Field of International Commercial Arbitration*, 22 J. Int'l Arb. 543 (2005).

361. UNCITRAL Model Law, 2006 Revisions, Art. 2A.

362. UNCITRAL Model Law, 2006 Revisions, Art. 7; *infra* pp. 390-91.

363. UNCITRAL Model Law, 2006 Revisions, Art. 17; *infra* pp. 873-76, 880-81, 902-03, 921-22.

364. UNCITRAL Model Law, 2006 Revisions, Art. 35; *infra* pp. 1190-91.

365. As discussed below, the 2006 Revisions authorization of *ex parte* provisional measures is of doubtful wisdom and has attracted substantial criticism. *See infra* pp. 895-96.

tion by prescribing in significantly greater detail the legal framework for international arbitration, by clarifying points of ambiguity or disagreement under the Convention,[366] and by establishing directly applicable national legislation.

Some 67 jurisdictions have adopted legislation based on the Model Law as of 2014, including Australia, Bermuda, Bulgaria, Canada, Cyprus, Germany, Hong Kong, India, Mexico, New Zealand, Nigeria, Norway, the Russian Federation, Scotland, Singapore, Spain, Tunisia and various U.S. states.[367] At least as important, the Model Law has set the agenda for reform of arbitration statutes, even in states (like England and Switzerland) where it has not been adopted. Moreover, decisions by courts in jurisdictions that have adopted the Model Law are beginning to produce a reasonably uniform international body of precedent concerning its meaning and application.[368]

The German Ministry of Justice explained some of the reasons for adopting the UNCITRAL Model Law during Germany's enactment of legislation derived predominantly from the Model Law:

> If we want to reach the goal that Germany will be selected more frequently as the seat of international arbitrations in the future, we have to provide foreign parties with a law that, by its outer appearance and by its contents, is in line with the framework of the Model Law that is so familiar all over the world. This is necessary, in particular, in view of the fact that in negotiating international contracts, usually not much time is spent on the drafting of the arbitration agreement. The purpose of the Model Law, to make a significant contribution to the unification of the law of international arbitration, can only be met if one is willing to prefer the goal of unification instead of a purely domestic approach when it comes to the question of the necessity and the scope as well as to the determination of the contents of individual rules.[369]

These objectives—accessibility, international uniformity, and a tested structure—have been cited in other jurisdictions.[370]

---

366. In particular, the Model Law makes clear the grounds for annulling international arbitral awards, defines the (limited) scope of national court interference in the arbitral process, and prescribes the types and extent of judicial support for international arbitrations.

367. For a list of jurisdictions adopting the Model Law, *see* www.uncitral.org. As of 2014, 21 jurisdictions had enacted legislation based on the text of the Model Law with amendments as adopted in 2006.

368. H. Alvarez, N. Kaplan & D. Rivkin, *Model Law Decisions: Cases Applying the UNCITRAL Model Law on International Commercial Arbitration* (2003); Case Law on UNCITRAL Texts ("CLOUT") UNCITRAL Model Law on International Commercial Arbitration, www.uncitral.org; UNCITRAL, *2012 Digest of Case Law on the Model Law on International Commercial Arbitration* (2012).

369. Bundestags Drucksache No. 13/5274 of 12 July 1996, reprinted in Berger, *The New German Arbitration Law* 140 (1998) (quoted in Berger, *The New German Arbitration Law in International Perspective*, 26 Forum Int'l 1, 4 (2000)).

370. *See* Law Reform Commission of Hong Kong, *Report on the Adoption of the UNCITRAL Model Law of Arbitration* 6, 11, (1987) ("the Model Law ... has the advantage of making [Hong Kong] law internationally recognisable and accessible;" "[The] primary reason for recommending the adoption of the Model Law ... is the need to make knowledge of our legal rules for international commercial arbitration more accessible to the international community.... We are convinced that it is much better [to avoid changes than] trying to improve what is already the result of many years work by an international group of experts"); Singapore Law Reform Committee, *Report of the Sub-Committee on Review of Arbitration Laws* 13 (1994) ("If Singapore aims to be an international arbitration centre it must adopt [the Model law expressing] a world view of international arbitration.").

That said, it is noteworthy that the world's leading international arbitration centers have generally not adopted the UNCITRAL Model Law. That is true, in particular, of France, Switzerland, England, the United States, the Netherlands, Belgium and Sweden.[371] In each of these jurisdictions, legislatures (and arbitration practitioners) have extensively debated the advisability of adopting the Model Law, but decided in favor of alternative solutions. Equally, at least some distinguished practitioners consider the Model Law to be a conservative, overly-detailed basis for national arbitration legislation.[372] Notwithstanding these criticisms, the UNCITRAL Model Law's contributions to the international arbitral process are enormous, and it remains, appropriately, the dominant "model" for national arbitration legislation.

b. United States of America

The United States is an important center for international arbitrations, and U.S. companies are even more important participants in the international arbitral process.[373] Despite general concerns about the U.S. legal system (focused on jury trials, discovery, punitive damages and delays), the United States has remained popular as an international arbitral seat over the past three decades.[374]

International arbitration in the United States is governed by an outwardly complex, but ultimately satisfactory, legal framework. Most important issues relating to international arbitration agreements and arbitral awards are governed primarily by U.S. federal (rather than state) law. In particular, the Federal Arbitration Act sets forth a basic statutory regime for arbitration, with separate chapters for both domestic arbitration (Chapter 1) and international arbitrations subject to the New York and Inter-American Conventions (Chapters 2 and 3).[375] The FAA has the distinction—and burden—of being the oldest surviving arbitration statute in any major jurisdiction. Additionally, although limited, the role of state law in the enforcement of international arbitration agreements is occasionally important.[376]

(1) Unenforceability of Arbitration Agreements Under U.S. Law in the 19th Century

As discussed above, many U.S. courts were hostile towards agreements to arbitrate future disputes for the better part of the 19th century. Even more so than English courts (where legislative reforms had intervened), some U.S. judges refused to grant specific

---

371. *See infra* pp. 51-67.

372. E. Gaillard & J. Savage (eds.), *Fouchard Gaillard Goldman on International Commercial Arbitration* ¶204 (1999).

373. The United States was the seat for 6.5% of ICC arbitrations commenced in 2013, 6.8% in 2008, 11.3% in 2003, 6.2% in 1998 and 4.1% in 1993. *1993-2013 ICC Statistical Reports* (1994-2014). More U.S. companies are parties to ICC arbitrations than any other nationality. In 2013, for instance, 8.2% of the parties to new ICC arbitrations were American, more than from any other nation. ICC, *2013 Statistical Report,* 25(1) ICC ICArb. Bull. 5, 12 (2014).

374. *See* G. Born, *International Commercial Arbitration* 152 (2d ed. 2014).

375. U.S. FAA, 9 U.S.C. §§1-15 (domestic and non-New York or Inter-American Convention international arbitrations), §§201-208 (New York Convention), §§301-307 (Inter-American Convention).

376. For a discussion of the respective roles of federal and state law in international arbitration in the United States, *see infra* pp. 56-59.

enforcement of arbitration agreements, and permitted their revocation at any time.[377] This grudging approach towards arbitration agreements reflected a variety of factors, including concern about private agreements "ousting" the courts of jurisdiction, skepticism about the adequacy and fairness of the arbitral process and suspicions that arbitration agreements were often the product of unequal bargaining power.[378]

These attitudes began to shift during the late 19th century, including in some U.S. state court decisions.[379] More importantly, following sustained lobbying from the business community, New York enacted an arbitration statute in 1920 designed to reverse common law hostility to arbitration and to render arbitration agreements enforceable in New York courts.[380] The New York statute provided a model for what became federal legislation dealing with arbitration—the Federal Arbitration Act (originally titled the "United States Arbitration Act").[381]

The FAA was strongly supported by the U.S. business community, which saw litigation as increasingly expensive, slow and unreliable: "The clogging of your courts is such that the delays amount to a virtual denial of justice,"[382] and the proposed FAA was intended to "enable business men to settle their disputes expeditiously and economically."[383] With virtually no opposition or amendment, the bill that became the FAA was unanimously adopted in 1925 by both the House of Representatives and the Senate.

The Act's stated purpose was to reverse the hostility that U.S. courts had developed towards arbitration agreements in commercial matters, and in particular the common law rules that arbitration agreements were revocable or unenforceable as contrary to public policy. According to the FAA's legislative history:

> The need for the law arises from an anachronism of our American law. Some centuries ago, because of the jealousy of the English courts for their own jurisdiction, they refused to enforce specific agreements to arbitrate upon the ground that the courts were thereby ousted from their jurisdiction. This jealousy survived for so long a period that the principle became firmly embedded in the English common law and was adopted with it by the American courts. The courts have felt that the precedent was too strongly fixed to be overturned without a legislative enactment.[384]

This historical description was not entirely accurate, omitting to note that English law had in fact developed reasonably effective mechanisms for enforcing arbitration agreements, while many U.S. courts (and legislatures) had failed to do so.[385] Nevertheless, this explanation captured one of the key statutory objectives of the FAA: "the fundamental

---

377. *See* G. Born, *International Commercial Arbitration* 41 *et seq.* (2d ed. 2014); *supra* pp. 21-26 & *infra* pp. 186-87; *Red Cross Line v. Atl. Fruit Co.*, 264 U.S. 109, 121-22 (1924); *Tobey v. County of Bristol*, 23 F.Cas. 1313 (C.C. D. Mass. 1845).

378. *See* G. Born, *International Commercial Arbitration* 41 *et seq.* (2d ed. 2014).

379. *See* G. Born, *International Commercial Arbitration* 41 *et seq.* (2d ed. 2014); *supra* pp. 25-26.

380. N.Y. Arbitration Law, L. 1920, c. 275, Consol. c. 72. *See supra* p. 26.

381. *See* G. Born, *International Commercial Arbitration* 41 *et seq.* (2d ed. 2014).

382. Hearings on S. 4213 and S. 4214 Before the Subcommittee of the Senate Committee on the Judiciary, 67th Cong., 4th Sess., at 14 (1923) (Letter from H. Hoover, Secretary of Commerce).

383. Hearings on S. 4213 and S. 4214 Before the Subcommittee of the Senate Committee on the Judiciary, 67th Cong., 4th Sess., at 14 (1923) (ABA Report).

384. 65 Cong. Rec. 1931 (1924).

385. *See* G. Born, *International Commercial Arbitration* 41 *et seq.* (2d ed. 2014).

conception underlying the law is to make arbitration agreements valid, irrevocable, and enforceable."[386]

(2) U.S. Federal Arbitration Act: Chapter One

As noted above, the FAA consists of three chapters: (a) the "domestic" FAA, 9 U.S.C. §§1-16, enacted in 1925 and applicable to agreements and awards affecting either inter-state or foreign commerce; (b) the New York Convention's implementing legislation, 9 U.S.C. §§201-210, enacted in 1970 and applicable only to awards and agreements falling within the New York Convention; and (c) the Inter-American Convention's implementing legislation, 9 U.S.C. §§301-07, enacted in 1990 and applicable only to awards and agreements falling under the Inter-American Convention.

The centerpiece of the domestic FAA is §2, which provides that arbitration agreements involving inter-state and foreign commerce[387] "shall be valid, irrevocable, and enforceable, save upon such grounds as exist at law or in equity for the revocation of any contract."[388] In turn, §§3 and 4 of the Act provide the principal mechanisms for enforcing §2's general rule that arbitration agreements are presumptively valid. Section 3 requires "any of the courts of the United States" to stay proceedings before it, if they involve issues that are "referable to arbitration," while §4 requires "United States district court[s]" to issue orders compelling arbitration of such issues.[389]

Other sections of the FAA address limited aspects of the arbitral process. Section 5 grants district courts the power to appoint arbitrators if the parties either have not done so or have agreed upon an appointment procedure which proves unworkable.[390] Section 7 of the Act authorizes the issuance of "subpoenas" (orders to provide evidence) by arbitral tribunals, and permits U.S. district courts to issue compulsory process to assist tribunals in taking evidence.[391] In turn, §§9-11 provide that arbitral awards may be confirmed as U.S. judgments, subject to only a limited number of enumerated exceptions.[392] These sections also set forth procedures for confirming, vacating, or correcting arbitral awards subject to the Act.[393]

The FAA is remarkably brief and, by contemporary standards, relatively skeletal. It is notable how many subjects are *not* directly addressed by the FAA. The statute does not expressly deal with such matters as the separability doctrine, the allocation of competence between U.S. courts and arbitrators to resolve disputes over arbitration agreements (competence-competence), challenging arbitrators, provisional relief, the conduct of arbitral proceedings, interlocutory judicial review, choice of law, form of the award, or costs.

---

386. Hearings on S. 4213 and S. 4214 Before the Subcommittee of the Senate Committee on the Judiciary, 67th Cong., 4th Sess. at 2 (1923).

387. The FAA applies to arbitration agreements and awards affecting either inter-state or foreign commerce. U.S. FAA, 9 U.S.C. §1; *infra* p. 138. These jurisdictional grants have been interpreted expansively. *See infra* pp. 167-68. The FAA's focus was principally domestic, although it also expressly applies to "foreign commerce." U.S. FAA, 9 U.S.C. §1.

388. U.S. FAA, 9 U.S.C. §2.

389. U.S. FAA, 9 U.S.C. §§3, 4. For a discussion of §§3 and 4, *see infra* pp. 315-34.

390. *See* U.S. FAA, 9 U.S.C. §5; *infra* pp. 705-09.

391. *See* U.S. FAA, 9 U.S.C. §7; *infra* pp. 833-35, 847-49.

392. *See* U.S. FAA, 9 U.S.C. §§9-11; *infra* pp. 1155-56.

393. *See infra* pp. 1134.

Notable also is the relative brevity of the FAA on most of the issues which it does address, such as the grounds and procedures for challenging either arbitration agreements or arbitral awards.[394]

(3) U.S. Federal Arbitration Act: Chapters Two and Three

After U.S. ratification of the New York Convention in 1970, Congress enacted amendments to the FAA, in a second chapter to the Act, implementing the Convention.[395] In ratifying the New York Convention, Congress was motivated (as with the domestic FAA in 1925) by a desire for more efficient dispute resolution:

> [I]t is important to note that arbitration is generally a less costly method of resolving disputes than is full-scale litigation in the courts. To the extent that arbitration agreements avoid litigation in the courts, they produce savings not only with the parties to the agreement but also for the taxpayers—who must bear the burden for maintaining our court system.[396]

In addition, Congress sought to facilitate the development of a stable and effective system of international commercial dispute-resolution, on which U.S. companies expanding into global markets could rely, in order to promote international trade and investment.[397]

Like the original domestic Act, the FAA's second chapter is remarkably brief. It provides that arbitration agreements shall be enforceable, and contains provisions authorizing U.S. courts to compel arbitration pursuant to such agreements (including in foreign arbitral seats).[398] The Act's second chapter also provides for the recognition and enforcement of awards that are subject to the Convention, simply by incorporating the Convention's terms.[399]

In 1990, the United States enacted implementing legislation for the Inter-American Convention, codified as a third chapter to the FAA.[400] The chapter incorporates much of the New York Convention's implementing legislation by reference,[401] adding provisions to deal with the Inter-American Commercial Arbitration Commission's rules[402] and the relationship between the New York and Inter-American Conventions.[403] Like the domestic FAA, at the heart of the third chapter are provisions requiring the enforcement of specified

---

394. The domestic FAA consists of only seventeen articles, a number of which are archaic or immaterial. This contrasts with the much lengthier English Arbitration Act and UNCITRAL Model Law, *supra* pp. 47-51 & *infra* pp. 64-67, while roughly paralleling French and Swiss legislative style, *supra* pp. 60-64.

395. U.S. FAA, 9 U.S.C. §§201-210.

396. 116 Cong. Rec. 22, 732-33 (daily ed. July 24, 1970) (Hamilton Fish). *See also id.* at 22, 731 (Andrew Jacobs).

397. S. Rep. No. 702, 91st Cong., 2d Sess. 1-2 (1970); Aksen, *American Arbitration Accession Arrives in the Age of Aquarius*, 3 Sw. U. L. Rev. 1 (1971).

398. U.S. FAA, 9 U.S.C. §206; *infra* pp. 189-90, 315-34, 654, 664-69. In addition, the amendments expand federal subject matter jurisdiction and removal authority in cases falling under the Convention. U.S. FAA, 9 U.S.C. §§203, 205.

399. U.S. FAA, 9 U.S.C. §§201, 207; *infra* pp. 1199-1266.

400. U.S. FAA, 9 U.S.C. §§301-308; *supra* pp. 39-40 & *infra* pp. 166, 174, 177, 320, 375-76, 684, 732, 797, 1023, 1060, 1072, 1085, 1098-99, 1111, 1118, 1189-1200.

401. U.S. FAA, 9 U.S.C. §302.

402. U.S. FAA, 9 U.S.C. §§303, 306; *infra* p. 797.

403. U.S. FAA, 9 U.S.C. §305; *supra* pp. 39-40.

arbitration agreements and awards, together with very briefly-described procedures for doing so.[404]

There is considerable "overlap" among the various sources of U.S. federal law affecting international arbitration agreements and awards. Arbitral awards and agreements falling under the New York Convention are of course governed by both the Convention and the second chapter of the FAA (which implements the Convention). In addition, however, these awards and agreements are potentially governed by the first, "domestic" chapter of the FAA, to the extent it is not "in conflict" with the Convention. [405] This potentially-confusing structure has the effect that domestic U.S. arbitration law (and judicial authority) serves as a "gap filler" of sorts, although the precise terms of this mechanism have not been definitively articulated by U.S. courts.

Despite the brevity of the FAA, in true common law fashion, U.S. courts have developed a fairly expansive body of "federal common law" of arbitration.[406] While not readily accessible to non-U.S. parties or practitioners, this case law provides a workable legal regime for international arbitrations.[407] This judicial authority also applies, indeed more broadly than in domestic matters, in the context of international arbitrations subject to the New York and Inter-American Conventions.[408] The federal common law of arbitration is of uncertain scope, but clearly extends to such subjects, discussed below, as the separability presumption, the competence-competence doctrine, the interpretation and validity of international arbitration agreements, the parties' autonomy with regard to arbitral procedures, the tribunal's procedural powers and the availability of provisional relief in connection with arbitrations.[409] Importantly, as also discussed below, the FAA and the federal common law rules derived from the FAA override (or "preempt") inconsistent state (and foreign) law rules governing the same subjects, particularly rules that seek to deny effect to agreements to arbitrate and arbitral awards.[410]

With respect to arbitration agreements, U.S. courts have repeatedly embraced the separability presumption,[411] have defined in considerable and influential detail the allocation of competence between courts and arbitrators to decide disputes over the formation, validity and interpretation of arbitration agreements,[412] have strongly affirmed the presump-

---

404. U.S. FAA, 9 U.S.C. §§202, 205, 207, 302-304; *infra* pp. 177, 315-34, 664, 1189-1200.

405. Section 208 of the FAA provides that the domestic FAA "applies to actions and proceedings brought under this chapter to the extent that [the domestic FAA] is not in conflict with this chapter or the Convention as ratified by the United States."

406. *Buckeye Check Cashing, Inc. v. Cardegna*, 546 U.S. 440, 447-48 (2006); *Southland Corp. v. Keating*, 465 U.S. 1 (1984); *Moses Cone Mem. Hosp. v. Mercury Constr. Corp.*, 460 U.S. 1 (1983); *Prima Paint Corp. v. Flood & Conklin Mfg Co.*, 388 U.S. 395 (1967).

407. *Cf.* Samuel, *Arbitration Statutes in England and the USA*, 8 Arb. & Disp. Resol. J. 1, 32 (1999) ("The [FAA] falls in the category of 'small but perfectly formed.' It is very resilient and loosely enough drafted in the right places to enable the court to do the right thing for the arbitral process.").

408. *See infra* pp. 55-57; *Mitsubishi Motors Corp. v. Soler Chrysler-Plymouth, Inc.*, 473 U.S. 614, 628 (1985).

409. *See infra* pp. 55-57.

410. *See supra* pp. 21-26 & *infra* pp. 56-57; *Scherk v. Alberto-Culver Co.*, 417 U.S. 506, 516-17 (1974).

411. *See Buckeye Check Cashing*, 546 U.S. at 445; *Prima Paint Co.*, 388 U.S. at 402; *infra* pp. 190-218.

412. *See PacifiCare Health Sys. v. Book*, 538 U.S. 401 (2003); *Howsam v. Dean Witter Reynolds*, 537 U.S. 79 (2002); *First Options of Chicago, Inc. v. Kaplan*, 514 U.S. 938 (1995); *infra* pp. 218-87, 371-73, 406-07, 416-20, 442-43, 469-70, 537-40, 549, 592-94.

tive validity of arbitration agreements (subject only to limited, internationally-neutral exceptions)[413] and have fashioned a decidedly "pro-arbitration" approach to the interpretation of arbitration agreements.[414]

With respect to the arbitral process, U.S. courts have emphasized the parties' freedom to agree upon arbitration rules and procedures,[415] the arbitrator's discretion in presiding over the arbitral process and adopting arbitral procedures[416] and the very limited scope for interlocutory judicial review of the arbitrator's decisions.[417] U.S. judicial decisions have also provided (with some exceptions) for court-ordered provisional measures[418] and disclosure,[419] as well as judicial support for constitution of arbitral tribunal.[420]

Finally, with respect to arbitral awards, U.S. courts have permitted vacatur (annulment) of awards made in the United States on limited grounds, generally paralleling those in the New York Convention,[421] but also permitting a limited degree of substantive judicial review of the merits of the arbitrators' award (under the so-called "manifest disregard" doctrine).[422] With regard to foreign arbitral awards, U.S. courts have held that such awards are presumptively valid and enforceable, subject only to the New York Convention's specified exceptions.[423]

(4) U.S. State Arbitration Laws

The role of the FAA within the U.S. legal system, and in particular in relation to the laws of the 50 states, can appear complex.[424] The basic principles can nonetheless be readily summarized.

In principle, a U.S. federal statute will override, or "preempt," inconsistent U.S. state law substantive rules addressing the same subjects.[425] Accordingly, insofar as the FAA was

---

413. *See Buckeye Check Cashing*, 546 U.S. 440; *Doctor's Assocs., Inc. v. Casarotto*, 517 U.S. 681 (1996); *Southland Corp.*, 465 U.S. 1; *infra* pp. 177-90.

414. *See First Options of Chicago*, 514 U.S. 938; *Mitsubishi Motors Corp.*, 473 U.S. at 628; *infra* pp. 189-90, 282, 364-67, 517-34.

415. *See Mitsubishi Motors Corp.*, 473 U.S. at 628 (party agreeing to arbitration "trades the procedures and opportunity for review of the courtroom for the simplicity, informality, and expedition of arbitration"); *McDonald v. City of W. Branch*, 466 U.S. 284, 292 (1984); *infra* pp. 786-89, 793-95.

416. *See infra* pp. 792-95.

417. *See infra* pp. 807-10.

418. *See infra* pp. 910-15, 921-23, 930-32.

419. *See infra* pp. 839-51.

420. *See infra* pp. 705-09.

421. *See BG Group PLC v. Repub. of Argentina*, 134 S.Ct. 1198 (2014).

422. *See infra* pp. 1165-68. This substantive review is referred to under the rubric of "manifest disregard of law." As discussed below, following a recent U.S. Supreme Court decision in *Hall Street Associates LLP v. Mattel, Inc.*, there is some uncertainty as to whether "manifest disregard" remains a basis for vacatur under the FAA. *See infra* p. 1168.

423. *See infra* pp. 1199-1266.

424. There has been a vigorous debate on the Supreme Court concerning the preemptive effect of the FAA. *Compare Southland Corp. v. Keating*, 465 U.S. 1 (1984) (Burger, C.J.) *with id.* at 25 (O'Connor, J., dissenting); *Allied-Bruce Terminix Co. v. Dobson*, 513 U.S. 265 (1995) (Breyer, J.) *with id.* at 285 (Scalia, J., dissenting). Academic debate has been just as robust. *Compare* Drahozal, *In Defense of Southland: Reexamining the Legislation History of the Federal Arbitration Act*, 78 Notre Dame L. Rev. 101 (2002) *with* I. MacNeil, *American Arbitration Law: Reformation, Nationalization and Internationalization* 83-147 (1992).

425. *American Ins. Ass'n v. Garamendi*, 539 U.S. 396 (2003); *Hines v. Davidowitz*, 312 U.S. 52 (1941).

intended to address particular substantive topics or general fields, it will preempt state law addressing those topics or fields.[426]

The U.S. Supreme Court has held that the domestic FAA "contains no express pre-emptive provision, nor does it reflect a congressional intent to occupy the entire field of arbitration."[427] At the same time, the Court has also repeatedly declared that the FAA creates a body of substantive federal rules relating to arbitration; in enacting the FAA, "Congress declared a national policy favoring arbitration and withdrew the power of the states to require a judicial forum for the resolution of claims which the contracting parties agreed to resolve by arbitration."[428] As a consequence, it is well-settled that U.S. state law rules that single out and purport to render inter-state and international arbitration agreements invalid, illegal, or revocable are preempted by the FAA.[429] As noted above, it is also settled, in both domestic and international contexts, that the FAA and federal law establish the presumptive separability of the arbitration agreement[430] and provide the exclusive standards for interpreting arbitration agreements[431] and for confirming and vacating arbitral awards.[432]

Nonetheless, in a purely domestic context, issues concerning the formation of arbitration agreements, as well as at least some issues of substantive and formal validity, are governed primarily by generally-applicable state contract law.[433] In contrast, there is substantial lower court and other authority holding that federal common law, derived from the New York Convention, governs the formation and validity of *international* (as distinguished from domestic) arbitration agreements.[434]

Apart from these complexities, U.S. state law is applicable to arbitration agreements and awards when—but only when—the Convention and FAA (and the federal common law derived from both sources) are inapplicable. That may be the case, for example, because

426. The U.S. Supreme Court has repeatedly held that the FAA preempts particular state law rules. *Allied-Bruce Terminix Co. v. Dobson*, 513 U.S. 265 (1995); *Perry v. Thomas*, 482 U.S. 483 (1987); *Southland Corp. v. Keating*, 465 U.S. 1 (1984); *infra* pp. 189-90, 310-12, 365-67.

427. *See Volt Info. Sciences, Inc. v. Bd of Trustees*, 489 U.S. 468, 477 (1989) ("The FAA contains no express pre-emptive provision, nor does it reflect a congressional intent to occupy the entire field of arbitration. But even when Congress has not completely displaced state regulation in an area, state law may nonetheless be preempted to the extent that it actually conflicts with federal law.").

428. *Southland Corp.*, 465 U.S. at 10. *See also Buckeye Check Cashing*, 546 U.S. at 444-48 ("Section 2 embodies the national policy favoring arbitration and places arbitration agreements on equal footing with all other contracts.").

429. *See infra* pp. 177-90, 310-12, 365-67, 393-510; *Doctors' Assocs.*, 517 U.S. 681; *Allied-Bruce Terminix Co.*, 513 U.S. 265; *Southland Corp.*, 465 U.S. at 10.

430. *See infra* pp. 190-218; *Buckeye Check Cashing, Inc.*, 546 U.S. 440; *Prima Paint Corp.*, 388 U.S. 395.

431. *See infra* pp. 517-34; *Mitsubishi Motors Corp.*, 473 U.S. at 628.

432. *See infra* pp. 1155-68, 1190-1266; *BG Group PLC v. Repub. of Argentina*, 134 S.Ct. 1198 (2014).

433. *First Options of Chicago*, 514 U.S. 938; *Allied-Bruce Terminix Co.*, 513 U.S. 265; *Perry*, 482 U.S. 483; *infra* p. 365 In contrast, state laws that are specifically directed towards the formation or validity of arbitration agreements (as distinguished from other types of agreements) are preempted by the FAA. *See Allied-Bruce Terminix Co.*, 513 U.S. 265; *Southland Corp.*, 465 U.S. 1; *infra* pp. 310-12, 365-67.

434. *See infra* pp. 310-12, 365-67; *Smith/Enron Cogeneration Ltd P'ship v. Smith Cogeneration Int'l, Inc.*, 198 F.3d 88 (2d Cir. 1999) ("When we exercise jurisdiction under Chapter Two of the FAA, we have compelling reasons to apply federal law, which is already well-developed, to the question of whether an agreement to arbitrate is enforceable"); *InterGen NV v. Grina*, 344 F.3d 134, 143 (1st Cir. 2003).

the agreement or award does not affect inter-state or foreign commerce (which is by definition virtually impossible in international commercial matters). State law may also be applicable to issues bearing on arbitration that federal statutory and common law do not directly or indirectly address. Although the issue is unsettled, that may include the availability of court-assisted discovery, provisional relief, or consolidation.[435]

Every U.S. state has adopted legislation dealing with commercial arbitration, and most states have enacted some version of the "Uniform Arbitration Act." First proposed in 1924 by the National Conference of Commissioners on Uniform State Laws (now known as the "Uniform Law Commission"), and adopted in 1955 (amended in 1956), the current, revised text of the Act was adopted by the Conference in 2000, making substantial changes to earlier versions.[436]

The 1955 Uniform Arbitration Act, which had been adopted (or substantially similar legislation had been adopted) by 49 jurisdictions,[437] was comparable to the FAA. Among other things, it required specific enforcement of arbitration agreements (as to both existing and future disputes)[438] and provided for the recognition and enforcement of arbitral awards with only limited judicial review.[439] The 2000 Revised Uniform Arbitration Act[440] usefully adds or modifies a number of provisions, including those concerning the constitution of the arbitral tribunal,[441] provisional measures,[442] the arbitral procedure,[443] the form of awards[444] and immunity of arbitrators.[445]

Nevertheless, a number of U.S. states have not adopted the Revised Uniform Arbitration Act, and a few have not yet followed its generally "pro-arbitration" lead. Several state statutes do not permit arbitration of various categories of claims, such as tort, real property, and insurance claims.[446] Other U.S. states have enacted legislation requiring that arbitration clauses be conspicuously identified (e.g., printed in capital letters, placed on the front of any contract, etc.).[447] And some state statutes do not provide for the same general rule of

---

435. *See infra* pp. 59, 839-51, 896-925, 944-50.

436. National Conference of Commissioners on Uniform State Laws, Revised Uniform Arbitration Act (2000). The drafters of the Act observe: "The Uniform Arbitration Act, promulgated in 1955, has been one of the most successful Acts of the National Conference of Commissioners on Uniform State Laws." Revised Uniform Arbitration Act, Prefatory Note (2000).

437. National Conference of Commissioners on Uniform State Laws, Revised Uniform Arbitration Act (2000), Prefatory Note.

438. Revised Uniform Arbitration Act, §§4, 6, 7.

439. Revised Uniform Arbitration Act, §§22-23.

440. As of 2014, the Revised Uniform Arbitration Act (2000) had been adopted by 18 jurisdictions (Alaska, Arizona, Arkansas, Colorado, District of Columbia, Florida, Hawaii, Michigan, Minnesota, Nevada, New Jersey, New Mexico, North Carolina, North Dakota, Oklahoma, Oregon, Utah and Washington). Of these, Alaska, Arizona, and Arkansas did not repeal the 1956 Act when they adopted the 2000 Act.

441. Revised Uniform Arbitration Act, §§11-12.

442. Revised Uniform Arbitration Act, §8.

443. Revised Uniform Arbitration Act, §§9, 15-17.

444. Revised Uniform Arbitration Act, §19.

445. Revised Uniform Arbitration Act, §14.

446. *See, e.g.*, Ark. Stat. Ann. §34-511 (1983) (tort claims); Ohio Rev. Code Ann. §2711.01 (1981) (real property disputes); Ky. Rev. Stat. §417.050 (1984) (insurance disputes). These state rules are preempted by the FAA in almost all circumstances. *See infra* pp. 177-90, 475-510, 531-32.

447. *See, e.g.*, Cal. Civ. Proc. Code §1295(b) (1999) (requiring special notice of arbitration clauses in medical services contracts); Cal. Civ. Proc. Code §1298 (1999) (requiring special notice of arbitration clauses

enforceability and limited judicial review of arbitral awards that the FAA and Uniform Arbitration Act require.[448]

In addition, especially in recent years, some U.S. states have enacted legislation designed to fill perceived gaps left in the U.S. federal framework for international arbitration.[449] In particular, California, Colorado, Connecticut, Florida, Georgia, Hawaii, Illinois, Maryland, North Carolina, Ohio, Oregon and Texas have adopted statutes purporting to deal comprehensively with the subject of international arbitration.[450] The extent to which these statutes are preempted by the FAA and federal common law principles remains unclear. To date, however, both these statutes and state law more generally have played a distinctly secondary role in the international arbitral process.[451]

One potential exception to this general rule was the Supreme Court's decision in *Volt Information Sciences, Inc. v. Board of Trustees of Leland Stanford Junior University*.[452] There, a California choice-of-law clause in the parties' purely domestic contract was interpreted, in vaguely-defined circumstances, to incorporate state procedural rules relating to arbitration, and the FAA was held not to preempt this result. Subsequent U.S. Supreme Court decisions,[453] and most lower court decisions,[454] have interpreted *Volt* narrowly, holding that general choice-of-law clauses ordinarily do not encompass state arbitration laws and that the FAA preempts state law rules that impede the enforcement of arbitration agreements.

in real property contracts); Mo. Ann. Stat. §435.400 (1999) (requiring notice of arbitration clause to appear in ten point capital letters before signature line); S.C. Code Ann. §15-48-10 (1999) (requiring front-page notice of arbitration clause in all but employment contracts, lawyer/client and doctor/patient pre-arrangements, and personal injury claims). These state law rules are also preempted by the FAA in almost all cases.

448. Ga. Code Ann. §7-111 (Supp. 1984); Neb. Rev. Stat. §25-2115 (1979); Pa. Cons. Stat. Ann. tit. 42, §7302(d)(2) (1982).

449. *See* Besson, *The Utility of State Laws Regulating International Commercial Arbitration and Their Compatibility with the FAA*, 11 Am. Rev. Int'l Arb. 211 (2000); Garvey & Heffelfinger, *Towards Federalizing U.S. International Commercial Arbitration Laws*, 25 Int'l Law. 209 (1991); McClendon, *State International Arbitration Laws: Are They Needed or Desirable*, 1 Am. Rev. Int'l Arb. 245, 250 (1990).

450. Cal. C.C.P. §1297.11 *et seq.*; Colorado International Dispute Resolution Act, Colo. Rev. Stat. §§13-22-501 to 13-22-507; UNCITRAL Model Law on International Commercial Arbitration, Conn. Gen. Stat. §§50a-100 to 50a-136; Florida International Arbitration Act, 39 Fla. Stat. Ann. §684; Ga. Code Ann. §§9-9-30 to 9-9-43; Hawaii International Arbitration, Mediation, and Conciliation Act, Haw. Rev. Stat. §§658D-1 to 658D-9; Maryland International Commercial Arbitration Act, Md. Cts. & Jud. Proc. Code Ann. §§3-2B-01 to 3-2B-09; North Carolina International Commercial Arbitration Act, N.C. Gen. Stat. §§1-567.30 to 1.567.68; International Commercial Arbitration Act, Ohio Rev. Code §§2712.01 to 2712.91; Oregon International Commercial Arbitration and Conciliation Act, Or. Rev. Stat. §§36.450 to 36.558; Texas General Arbitration Act, Tex. Rev. Civ. Stat. Ann., Arts. 249-1 to 249-43.

451. As discussed elsewhere, generally applicable state law provides most basic rules of contract law governing the formation of domestic arbitration agreements; federal common law principles appear to apply to the formation and validity of international arbitration agreements subject to the New York and Inter-American Conventions. *See supra* pp. 57-58 & *infra* pp. 365-67. State law can, of course, also provide the substantive rules governing the merits of the parties' dispute.

452. 489 U.S. 468 (1989).

453. *Mastrobuono v. Shearson Lehman Hutton, Inc.*, 514 U.S. 52 (1995); *Doctor's Assocs. Inc.*, 517 U.S. 681; *infra* p. 312.

454. *See infra* pp. 310-12.

c. Swiss Law on Private International Law

Like France, Switzerland is one of Europe's, and the world's, leading centers for international commercial arbitration.[455] Its arbitration legislation, and academic community, have also been at the forefront of developments in the field of international arbitration over the past century. International arbitration in Switzerland is governed primarily by a chapter of the federal Swiss Law on Private International Law, which entered into effect in 1989. Legislative proposals for revision of the Swiss arbitration legislation have been advanced, recently prompting a review of the legislation.[456] The arbitration chapter is noteworthy for its brevity, comprising only 19 articles, drafted in brief, declarative terms.[457]

The Swiss Law on Private International Law ("SLPIL") replaced, insofar as international arbitration is concerned, the Swiss Intercantonal Concordat.[458] Under the revised Swiss legislation, international arbitration agreements are readily and effectively enforced. The Law expressly recognizes the separability doctrine[459] and prescribes a specialized "pro-arbitration" choice-of-law regime, pursuant to which international arbitration agreements, providing for arbitration in Switzerland, are substantively valid provided they conform to either (a) the law chosen by the parties (where the parties have made a specific choice of law for the arbitration agreement); (b) the law applicable to the dispute (in particular, that applicable to the parties' underlying commercial contract); or (c) Swiss law.[460]

The Swiss Law on Private International Law also expressly confirms the arbitrators' competence-competence, while generally permitting arbitral tribunals to resolve jurisdictional challenges in the first instance.[461] Swiss law also provides for the arbitrability of a wide range of disputes[462] and the Swiss Federal Tribunal has adopted a relatively expansive "pro-arbitration" rule of interpretation of the scope of international arbitration agreements.[463] Where claims subject to an arbitration agreement are asserted in Swiss courts, the parties' arbitration agreement will be given effect by dismissing judicial proceedings.[464]

---

455. Switzerland was the seat for 16.0% of all ICC arbitrations filed in 2013, 16.5% in 2008, 15.8% in 2003, 20.4% in 1998 and 24.2% in 1993 (in each case, second behind France in the number of ICC arbitrations). *1993-2013 ICC Statistical Reports* (1994-2014).

456. Kommission für Rechtsfragen, *Bundesgesetz über das internationale Privatrecht: Die Attraktivität der Schweiz als internationalen Schiedsplatz erhalten* (Feb. 3, 2012), available at www.parlament.ch.

457. Chapter 12 of the SLPIL is translated in Wenger, in S. Berti *et al.* (eds.), *International Arbitration in Switzerland* (2000).

458. *See* Blessing, *Introduction to Arbitration—Swiss and International Perspectives*, in H. Honsell *et al.* (eds.), *International Arbitration in Switzerland* ¶414 (2000).

459. SLPIL, Art. 178(3); *infra* pp. 214-16.

460. SLPIL, Art. 178(2); *infra* pp. 306-07.

461. SLPIL, Art. 186; *infra* pp. 277-78.

462. SLPIL, Art. 177(1); *infra* pp. 475-510; G. Born, *International Commercial Arbitration* 960-61 (2d ed. 2014).

463. *See infra* pp. 517-34, 587-88.

464. SLPIL, Art. 7; *See infra* pp. 320-34; *Judgment of 6 August 2012*, DFT 4A_119/2012, ¶3.2 (Swiss Fed. Trib.) ("When a jurisdictional defense based on the arbitration agreement is raised before the state court and the arbitral tribunal has its seat in Switzerland, the state court's power of review is limited, according to the case law of the Federal Tribunal. The court must deny jurisdiction unless a summary review of the arbitration agreement leads to the conclusion that it is void, inoperative, or incapable of being performed."); *Judgment of 29 April 1996*, DFT 122 III 139 (Swiss Fed. Trib.) (where party challenges jurisdiction under arbitration agreement providing for seat in Switzerland, Swiss court must decline jurisdiction, unless it

Under the Swiss Law on Private International Law, the parties' freedom to agree upon the applicable procedural and substantive law is expressly recognized.[465] Judicial interference by Swiss courts in the arbitral process (other than regarding the availability of provisional measures and evidence-taking in aid of a tribunal) is narrowly limited.[466]

As to arbitral awards made in Switzerland, actions to annul are limited to grounds generally paralleling those in the New York Convention.[467] Parties can agree to exclude even this review of international arbitral awards, provided that none of the parties is domiciled in Switzerland.[468] Swiss courts will recognize and enforce foreign arbitral awards without substantial judicial review, subject only to the limits of the New York Convention.[469] Many judicial functions relating to international arbitration are centralized, with the Swiss Federal Tribunal generally having original jurisdiction in annulment actions.[470]

d. French Code of Civil Procedure

France is one of the leading centers for international commercial arbitration in Europe and, indeed, the world. More international arbitrations are reportedly seated in France than any other European jurisdiction,[471] and French arbitration legislation and judicial decisions have exceptional international importance.

International arbitration in France is governed by the French Code of Civil Procedure, principally as adopted in decrees promulgated on May 14, 1980, May 12, 1981 and January 13, 2011. The three decrees added (or revised) Articles 1442-1527 of the French Code of Civil Procedure.[472] Articles 1442-1503 of the Code of Civil Procedure apply to domestic arbitrations, while Articles 1504-1527 apply to "international" arbitrations.[473] Certain provisions applicable to domestic arbitration apply to international arbitrations, unless agreed otherwise by the parties (and subject to the specific rules applicable to international arbitrations set forth in Articles 1504-1527).[474]

---

concludes upon a *prima facie* examination that the arbitration agreement is null and void, inoperative or incapable of being performed); *Judgment of 16 January 1995*, DFT 121 III 38 (Swiss Fed. Trib.) (where party challenges jurisdiction under arbitration agreement providing for seat abroad, Swiss court must subject the question of validity and scope of the agreement to full judicial consideration).

465. SLPIL, Arts. 182, 187.

466. SLPIL, Arts. 179(2),(3), 180(3), 183(2), 184(2), 185.

467. SLPIL, Art. 190(2).

468. SLPIL, Art. 192; *infra* pp. 1170-71.

469. SLPIL, Art. 194.

470. SLPIL, Art. 191(1).

471. France was the seat for approximately 20.3% of all the ICC arbitrations filed in 2013, 17.3% in 2008, 24.3% in 2003, 23.8% in 1998 and 37.5% in 1993. *1993-2013 ICC Statistical Reports* (1994-2014). France has historically been the seat for more ICC arbitrations than any other state. G. Born, *International Commercial Arbitration* 141 *et seq.* (2d ed. 2014).

472. *See Code of Civil Procedure Book IV Arbitration*, in J. Paulsson (ed.), *International Handbook on Commercial Arbitration* (1984 & Update 2013), for English translations. The original version is available at www.legifrance.gouv.fr.

473. The term is defined to include matters involving cross-border transfers of goods or services. French Code of Civil Procedure, Art. 1504 ("An arbitration is international when international trade interests are at stake."). *See infra* pp. 158-69.

474. French Code of Civil Procedure, Art. 1506 ("Unless the parties have agreed otherwise, and subject to the provisions of the present Title, the following Articles shall apply to international arbitration....").

The provisions of the Code of Civil Procedure have produced a strongly pro-arbitration legal framework for international commercial arbitration. Both French courts and academics have interpreted French legislation, and developed non-statutory doctrine, in a manner which has been highly supportive of the international arbitral process.[475] This pro-arbitration approach was further enhanced by the recent revision of the French arbitration regime by the Decree dated January 13, 2011.

French law emphatically recognizes the autonomy of the arbitration agreement (or separability doctrine),[476] and provides for the presumptive validity and enforceability of arbitration agreements.[477] It also expressly grants arbitrators the power (competence-competence) to decide challenges to their jurisdiction.[478] Further, if claims which are allegedly subject to an arbitration agreement are brought in French courts, prior to constitution of the arbitral tribunal, the Code of Civil Procedure provides for dismissal of the judicial proceedings, except where the arbitration agreement is "manifestly void or manifestly not applicable";[479] if claims which are allegedly subject to arbitration are brought in French courts after the arbitral tribunal is constituted, then the court is required to dismiss them pending a jurisdictional decision by the arbitrators.[480]

With regard to the law applicable to the arbitration agreement, French courts have developed an innovative doctrine that arbitration agreements are autonomous from national law and instead are subject to specific principles of international law.[481] The nonarbitra-

475. E. Gaillard & J. Savage (eds.), *Fouchard Gaillard Goldman on International Commercial Arbitration* ¶¶148-151 (1999).

476. French Code of Civil Procedure, Art. 1447; *Judgment of 7 May 1963, Ets Raymond Gosset v. Frère Carapelli SpA,* 91 J.D.I. (Clunet) 82 (1964) (French Cour de cassation) ("In international arbitration, the arbitration agreement, whether concluded separately or included in the contract to which it relates, shall, save in exceptional circumstances …, have full legal autonomy and shall not be affected by the fact that the aforementioned contract may be invalid"); E. Gaillard & J. Savage (eds.), *Fouchard Gaillard Goldman on International Commercial Arbitration* ¶¶391 *et seq.* (1999).

477. *Judgment of 20 December 1993, Municipalité de Khoms El Mergeb v. Société Dalico,* 121 J.D.I. (Clunet) 432 (1994) (French Cour de cassation) ("by virtue of a substantive rule of international arbitration law, the arbitration agreement is legally independent of the main contract containing or referring to it, and the existence and effectiveness of the arbitration agreement are to be assessed, subject to the mandatory rules of French law and international public policy, on the basis of the parties' common intention, there being no need to refer to any national law"); *Judgment of 17 December 1991, Société Gatoil v. Nat'l Iranian Oil Co.,* 1993 Rev. arb. 281, 284-85 (Paris Cour d'appel) ("in the field of international arbitration, the principle of the autonomy of the arbitration agreement is of general application, as an international substantive rule upholding the legality of the arbitration agreement"); E. Gaillard & J. Savage (eds.), *Fouchard Gaillard Goldman on International Commercial Arbitration* ¶¶436-37 (1999).

478. French Code of Civil Procedure, Art. 1465; E. Gaillard & J. Savage (eds.), *Fouchard Gaillard Goldman on International Commercial Arbitration* ¶¶650-60 (1999).

479. French Code of Civil Procedure, Art. 1448; *infra* pp. 221-23, 274-75, 320-34.

480. French Code of Civil Procedure, Art. 1448, 1465; G. Born, *International Commercial Arbitration* 1110 *et seq.* (2d ed. 2014); E. Gaillard & J. Savage (eds.), *Fouchard Gaillard Goldman on International Commercial Arbitration* ¶¶668-82 (1999).

481. E. Gaillard & J. Savage (eds.), *Fouchard Gaillard Goldman on International Commercial Arbitration* ¶¶418-19, 436-37 (1999). *See Judgment of 4 July 1972, Hecht v. Buisman's,* 99 J.D.I. (Clunet) 843 (1972) (French Cour de cassation) ("…having drawn attention to the international nature of the contract between the parties and to the total autonomy of arbitration agreements in the field of international arbitration, the Court of Appeal rightly held the disputed clause to be applicable in the present case."); *Judgment of 20 December 1993, Municipalité de Khoms El Mergeb v. Société Dalico,* 121 J.D.I. (Clunet) 432 (1994) (French Cour de cassation). *See infra* pp. 182-83, 307-08.

bility doctrine has not been invoked to any significant extent by French courts, except in labor and consumer matters.[482] In contrast to a number of other leading jurisdictions, French courts do not appear to have developed "pro-arbitration" rules of interpretation of arbitration agreements.[483]

French law is liberal as to the form of international arbitration agreements. The 1981 Decree abolished all form requirements for international arbitration agreements. More recently, the 2011 revisions to the French arbitration legislation confirmed that "[t]he arbitration agreement shall not be subject to any requirement as to its form."[484]

French courts generally afford the parties to an arbitration agreement substantial autonomy with respect to choice of law, procedural rules, selection of arbitrators and the like.[485] In particular, French law expressly provides that arbitrators sitting in France are generally not bound by local rules of civil procedure applicable in French courts, and have very wide discretion in adopting arbitral procedures.[486] French law also confers the power to the arbitral tribunal—once it is constituted—to order any provisional or conservatory measures that it deems appropriate.[487]

The Code of Civil Procedure also grants French courts the power to assist in constituting an arbitral tribunal[488] and to issue certain court-ordered provisional measures in aid of arbitration.[489] The efficacy of France's arbitration legislation is materially advanced through its centralization of most arbitration-related judicial proceedings in the Tribunal de Grande Instance in Paris, which has developed very substantial expertise in the field.[490]

The Code of Civil Procedure permits actions in French courts to annul international arbitral awards made in France only on limited grounds (substantially similar to, and sometimes more liberal than, those in the New York Convention).[491] The Code of Civil

482. *See* E. Gaillard & J. Savage (eds.), *Fouchard Gaillard Goldman on International Commercial Arbitration* ¶574 (1999) (antitrust, intellectual property, bankruptcy and corporate law issues are arbitrable). *See also infra* pp. 446-60, G. Born, *International Commercial Arbitration* 962-64 (2d ed. 2014).

483. E. Gaillard & J. Savage (eds.), *Fouchard Gaillard Goldman on International Commercial Arbitration* ¶481 (1999); *infra* pp. 517-34.

484. French Code of Civil Procedure, Art. 1507.

485. French Code of Civil Procedure, Arts. 1508, 1509, 1511, 1512; E. Gaillard & J. Savage (eds.), *Fouchard Gaillard Goldman on International Commercial Arbitration* ¶¶753, 1171, 1200, 1427 (1999); *infra* pp. 683-88, 786-95, 988-89.

486. French Code of Civil Procedure, Arts. 1509; E. Gaillard & J. Savage (eds.), *Fouchard Gaillard Goldman on International Commercial Arbitration* ¶¶1200-02 (1999); *infra* pp. 633-34, 786-90.

487. French Code of Civil Procedure, Art. 1468. However, seizures of property and compulsory posting of security may only be ordered by the French courts.

488. French Code of Civil Procedure, Arts. 1452-1454.

489. French Code of Civil Procedure, Arts. 1449, 1468 (French courts may order provisional measures upon request before arbitral tribunal is constituted; following constitution of tribunal, the tribunal may issue such measures, except for seizures and security which may only be ordered by French courts); *infra* pp. 904-25.

490. Among other things, the Tribunal de Grande Instance de Paris is responsible for selecting arbitrators and dealing with other problems in constituting a tribunal, in cases where the parties have not agreed upon institutional or other mechanisms. *See* French Code of Civil Procedure, Arts. 1452-1454, 1505; *Judgment of 22 November 1989, Philipp Bros. v. Société Drexel Burham Lambert*, 1990 Rev. arb. 142 (French Cour de cassation Civ. 2e); *infra* pp. 702-09.

491. French Code of Civil Procedure, Art. 1520. Following the 2011 decree, French law allows the parties to waive (by special agreement) the right to seek annulment of an award made in France. *See* French Code of

Procedure also provides for the recognition and enforcement of international arbitral awards with the same exceptions.[492] Notably, Article 1526 provides that an action to set aside an award will not suspend enforcement of the award, while Article 1520 (referred to in Article 1525) does not include annulment of a foreign award as a ground for refusing recognition or enforcement.

e. English Arbitration Act, 1996

England is a significant center for international commercial arbitration, whose popularity has increased over the past two decades.[493] The continuing spread of English as the language of international business, and the development of London as an international financial and business center, promise continued growth in England's importance as an arbitral center.

Both international and domestic arbitrations seated in England, Wales, or Northern Ireland are governed by the English Arbitration Act, 1996, which provides a detailed (110 separate sections) statement of English arbitration law.[494] The Act is based roughly on the UNCITRAL Model Law, while introducing a number of formal and substantive innovations.[495] The Act departed from the historic common law approach towards arbitration legislation (*e.g.*, addressing isolated issues, often in response to judicial decisions[496]), in favor of greater codification (derived in part from the Model Law).[497] Indeed, the Act has produced the somewhat anomalous result that the cradle of common law jurisprudence now boasts a substantially longer, more detailed statutory statement of international arbitration law than any civil law jurisdiction (and, specifically, France and Switzerland, whose international arbitration statutes are exceptional for their brevity[498]).

Civil Procedure, Art. 1522 ("The parties may, by specific agreement, expressly waive at any time their right to challenge the award."); *infra* pp. 1159-65, 1169-72.

492. French Code of Civil Procedure, Arts. 1520, 1525; *infra* pp. 1199-1266.

493. The United Kingdom was the seat for 12.3% of all ICC arbitrations filed in 2013, 12.2% in 2008, 10.4% in 2003, 15.5% in 1998 and 8.9% in 1993. *1993-2013 ICC Statistical Reports* (1994-2014).

494. English Arbitration Act, 1996, §2(1) ("the provisions of this Part apply where the seat of the arbitration is in England and Wales or Northern Ireland"). In contrast, the previous English Arbitration Act, 1950, and the English Arbitration Act, 1979, did not define the arbitrations to which their provisions applied. The scope of application of these Acts was determined by common law principles of jurisdiction (which held that the English courts could generally only intervene in arbitrations held within the jurisdiction or subject to English law).

495. Goode, *The Role of the Lex Loci Arbitri in International Commercial Arbitration*, 17 Arb. Int'l 19, 19 (2001) ("the Arbitration Act 1996, unlike early versions of the draft Arbitration Bill prepared for the Departmental Advisory Committee on Arbitration, bears the strong impress of the Model Law"); Saville, *The Origin of the New English Arbitration Act 1996: Reconciling Speed with Justice in the Decision-Making Process*, 13 Arb. Int'l 237 (1997). The Act differs from the UNCITRAL Model Law in a number of respects. For a summary of the most important of these, *see* R. Merkin, *Arbitration Law* ¶1.22 (1991 & Update August 2013).

496. *See supra* pp. 16-19.

497. Samuel, *Arbitration Statutes in England and the USA*, 8 Arb. & Disp. Resol. L.J. 2, 24-32 (1999).

498. *Compare* the 19 (short) sections of the Swiss Law on Private International Law, the 24 (shorter) sections of the French Code of Civil Procedure and the 31 (short) sections of the FAA, including substantially duplicative implementing legislation for the Inter-American and New York Conventions.

The English Arbitration Act, 1996, was preceded in the 20th century by three other major pieces of arbitration legislation, enacted in 1950, 1975 and 1979.[499] The 1950 and 1975 Acts established a highly-regulated legal regime for arbitration in England, with substantial scope for judicial involvement in the arbitral process and review of arbitral awards.[500] In particular, English legislation prior to 1979 provided for a widely-criticized "case stated" procedure, which had granted parties to arbitrations seated in England a mandatory right of access to the English courts to review *de novo* issues of English law that arose in the course of arbitral proceedings (without the possibility of exclusion agreements to contract out of such review).[501] The Arbitration Act, 1979, revised this historic approach and established a more acceptable, if by no means ideal, regime for international arbitrations in England.[502]

Under the Arbitration Act, 1979, agreements to arbitrate were presumptively enforceable in England, including by means of a stay of national court litigation, and English courts imposed few "nonarbitrability" constraints. Moreover, although not formally accepting the "separability" doctrine, English courts did not in fact permit challenges to the parties' underlying contract to interfere unduly with the arbitral process.[503] The 1979 Act amended, but did not eliminate, the historic "case stated" procedure; the Act permitted parties to enter into exclusion agreements, which waived the right to judicial review of the merits of the arbitrators' award (save for cases involving shipping, commodities and insurance).[504] Where no such exclusion agreement existed, more demanding judicial review persisted, which was the cause for continuing criticism in many quarters.[505]

In response to these (and other) criticisms, the English Arbitration Act, 1996, was adopted, following an extensive consultation process with both English and foreign sources.[506] The Act was intended to—and did—significantly improve the legislative framework for international arbitration in England. The Act compiled all prior English legislative provisions relating to arbitration into a single statute, based in large part on the UNCITRAL Model Law, and sought to introduce a modern "pro-arbitration" legislative regime for international arbitration in England.[507]

499. *See* Hunter, *Arbitration Procedure in England: Past, Present and Future*, 1 Arb. Int'l 82 (1985); Samuel, *Arbitration Statutes in England and the USA*, 8 Arb. & Disp. Resol. L.J. 2, 14, 19 (1999).

500. Samuel, *Arbitration Statutes in England and the USA*, 8 Arb. & Disp. Resol. L.J. 2, 19 (1999).

501. English Arbitration Act, 1979, §§1(3)(a), 1(3)(b), 3; *Antaios Compania Naviera SA v. Salen Rederierna AB (The "Antaios")* [1985] AC 191 (House of Lords); *Pioneer Shipping v. B.T.P. Tioxide (The "Nema")* [1982] AC 724 (House of Lords); Macassey, *English Arbitration*, XV J. Institute Arb. 63 (1947).

502. For a critical overview, *see* Samuel, *Arbitration Statutes in England and the USA*, 8 Arb. & Disp. Resol. L.J. 2, 19 (1999) ("A great deal of ink has been spilt on this ill-conceived piece of compromise legislation.").

503. *Ashville Invs. Ltd v. Elmer Contractors Ltd* [1988] 3 WLR 867 (English Ct. App.); Samuel, *Separability in English Law*, 3(3) J. Int'l Arb. 95 (1986). The severability presumption was recognized in England in *Harbour Assur. Co. (UK) Ltd v. Kansa Gen. Int'l Ins, Co. Ltd* [1993] 1 Lloyd's Rep. 455 (English Ct. App.). *See infra* pp. 190-218.

504. *See* English Arbitration Act, 1979, §§3, 4; R. Merkin, *Arbitration Law* ¶22.5 (1991 & Update August 2014); *supra* pp. 19, 65.

505. Marriott, *The Politics of Arbitration Reform*, 14 C.L.Q. 125 (1995); *infra* pp. 65-67.

506. *See* U.K. Departmental Advisory Committee on Arbitration Law, *Report on the Arbitration Bill* (1997); *Supplement to the Departmental Advisory Committee on Arbitration Law of February 1996* (1997).

507. Chukwumerije, *Reform and Consolidation of English Arbitration Law*, 8 Am. Rev. Int'l Arb. 21 (1996); Mustill, *A New Arbitration Act for the United Kingdom? The Response of the Departmental Advisory*

The 1996 Act provides expressly for the validity of written (and some other) arbitration agreements (as to both existing and future disputes) and for the stay of English court proceedings concerning claims subject to valid arbitration agreements.[508] The Act also provides for the separability of arbitration agreements,[509] and for recognition of the arbitral tribunal's competence to rule on its own jurisdiction (competence-competence).[510] Recent English judicial decisions have interpreted the competence-competence doctrine broadly, and adopted a robust "pro-arbitration" approach to the interpretation of international arbitration clauses.[511] The Act does not address the subject of nonarbitrable disputes or claims, but English courts have adopted a narrow view of the doctrine.[512]

The 1996 Act contains a number of provisions granting arbitrators broad freedom in conducting arbitral proceedings, with a minimum of judicial interference.[513] This freedom includes wide authorization with respect to procedural and evidentiary matters,[514] appointment of experts,[515] ordering the payment of security for the costs of the arbitration[516] and granting conservatory or provisional measures.[517] Among other things, it is now clear that arbitrators conducting arbitral proceedings seated in England are not obliged to apply local rules of English civil procedure or evidence.[518] The Act also provides for English judicial assistance to arbitrations seated in England, including in taking evidence,[519] appointing or removing arbitrators[520] and granting provisional measures.[521]

With respect to awards made in England, the Act departs entirely from the historic "case stated" procedure and provides only limited grounds for annulling international arbitral

Committee to the UNCITRAL Model Law, 6 Arb. Int'l 3 (1990); Saville, *The Origin of the New English Arbitration Act 1996: Reconciling Speed with Justice in the Decision-Making Process*, 13 Arb. Int'l 237 (1997).

508. English Arbitration Act, 1996, §§5, 6, 9; *infra* pp. 320-34, 375-92.

509. English Arbitration Act, 1996, §7; *infra* pp. 190-218.

510. English Arbitration Act, 1996, §§30, 31, 67; Aeberli, *Jurisdictional Disputes Under the Arbitration Act 1996: A Procedural Route Map*, 21 Arb. Int'l 253, 260-65 (2005); *infra* pp. 218-87.

511. *See Fiona Trust & Holding Corp. v. Privalov* [2007] EWCA Civ. 200 (English Ct. App.), *aff'd*, [2007] UKHL 40 (House of Lords); *Film Fin. Inc. v. Royal Bank of Scotland* [2007] EWHC 195 (Comm) (English High Ct.); *Vee Networks v. Econet Wireless Int'l Ltd* [2004] EWHC 2909 (QB) (English High Ct.); *infra* pp. 218-87, 517-34.

512. *See* R. Merkin, *Arbitration Law* ¶3.17 (1991 & Update August 2013); *ET Plus SA v. Jean-Paul Weller & The Channel Tunnel Group Ltd* [2005] EWHC 2115 (QB) (English High Ct.); *infra* pp. 475-510.

513. The Act underscores the parties' autonomy and the arbitral tribunal's discretion to conduct the arbitral proceedings. English Arbitration Act, 1996, §§33, 34; *infra* pp. 777-78, 785-89, 806-10. Reflecting Article 5 of the UNCITRAL Model Law, the English Arbitration Act, 1996, provides that, in matters covered by Part I ("Arbitration Pursuant to an Arbitration Agreement") "the court should not intervene except as provided by this Part." English Arbitration Act, 1996, §1(c).

514. English Arbitration Act, 1996, §34(1) ("It shall be for the tribunal to decide all procedural and evidential matters, subject to the right of the parties to agree any matter"); *infra* pp. 785-96, 830-39.

515. English Arbitration Act, 1996, §37.

516. English Arbitration Act, 1996, §37; *infra* pp. 892-93

517. English Arbitration Act, 1996, §§38(4) & 39; *infra* pp. 871-77.

518. *See infra* pp. 634, 786, 831-32. This contrasts with the English Arbitration Act, 1950, which operated on the presumption that arbitrators were to act in accordance with the ordinary rules of evidence under applicable English law. *See Land Sec. plc v. Westminster City Council* [1994] 44 EG 153 (English High Ct.).

519. English Arbitration Act, 1996, §44; *infra* pp. 846-51.

520. English Arbitration Act, 1996, §§16, 18, 19, 24; *infra* pp. 702-09, 768-76.

521. English Arbitration Act, 1996, §44.

awards made in England. The Act's grounds for annulling awards are now limited to lack of substantive jurisdiction of the arbitral tribunal, limited categories of "serious irregularity" in procedural matters and limited appeals on points of law (which may only be brought with leave of the court and may be excluded by agreement between the parties).[522] The Act also provides for the recognition and enforcement of foreign arbitral awards, primarily by incorporating the provisions of the New York Convention.[523]

2. Less Supportive National Arbitration Legislation

Some nations regarded international commercial arbitration with a mixture of suspicion and hostility during much of the 20th century.[524] This hostility arose from a reluctance to compromise perceived principles of national sovereignty and from doubts concerning the fairness, neutrality and efficacy of contemporary international commercial arbitration. Although historic distrust for international arbitration has waned substantially in recent decades, it has not entirely disappeared and continues to influence legislation, judicial decisions and other actions in some countries.

Developing countries in many parts of the world refused for much of the 20th century to enforce agreements to arbitrate future disputes. This was particularly true in Latin America and much of the Middle East.[525] Some developing states took the position that international arbitration agreements were an unjustifiable infringement upon national sovereignty, which was to be vigorously resisted.[526] In many cases, arbitration agreements were valid

522. English Arbitration Act, 1996, §§67-69; *infra* pp. 1155-73. English courts have held that appeal for error of law is impliedly excluded where the parties have chosen a substantive applicable law other than English law or where the parties have chosen a set of institutional rules, such as the ICC Rules, which excludes the right of appeal to the extent possible. *Athletic Union of Constantinople v. Nat'l Basketball Ass'n* [2002] 1 Lloyd's Rep 305 (English Ct. App.); *Sanghi Polyesters Ltd (India) v. Int'l Inv. (KCFC) (Kuwait)* [2000] 1 Lloyd's Rep 480 (QB) (English High Ct.).

523. English Arbitration Act, 1996, §§100-104; *infra* pp. 1189-266.

524. *See, e.g.,* G. Born, *International Commercial Arbitration* 165 (2d ed. 2014); Kassis, *The Questionable Validity of Arbitration and Awards Under the Rules of the International Chamber of Commerce,* 6(2) J. Int'l Arb. 79 (1989); Shalakany, *Arbitration and the Third World: A Plea for Reassessing Bias Under the Specter of Neo-Liberalism,* 41 Harv. Int'l L.J. 419 (2000); Sornarajah, *The UNCITRAL Model Law: A Third World Viewpoint,* 6(4) J. Int'l Arb. 7 (1989); Sornarajah, *The Climate of International Arbitration,* 8(2) J. Int'l Arb. 47 (1991).

525. N. Blackaby, D. Lindsey & A. Spinillo, *International Arbitration in Latin America* 3-10 (2003); El-Ahdab, *Enforcement of Arbitral Awards in the Arab Countries,* 11 Arb. Int'l 169 (1995); Naón, *Arbitration in Latin America,* 5 Int'l Arb. 137 (1989); S. Saleh, *Commercial Arbitration in the Arab Middle East* 49-50 (1984).

526. Shalakany, *Arbitration and the Third World: A Plea for Reassessing Bias Under the Specter of Neo-Liberalism,* 41 Harv. Int'l L.J. 419, 427 *et seq.* (2000) ("national judicial sovereignty is the price of capitulation to a historically biased dispute settlement mechanism ... a 'system that is weighted in favor of the capital exporting states.'"); Sornarajah, *The UNCITRAL Model Law: A Third World Viewpoint,* 6(4) J. Int'l Arb. 7 (1989) ("there is a definite ambivalence in the attitudes of developing countries towards international commercial arbitration"); Afro-Asian Legal Consultative Committee, *Report of the Seventeenth, Eighteenth and Nineteenth Sessions Held in Kuala Lumpur (1976), Baghdad (1977) and Doha (1978)* 131 (institutional arbitration rules do "not work out particularly favourably for the developing countries in the matter of venue, choice of arbitrators, as also fees and charges leviable by the institutions concerned").

only if they concerned an existing (not a future) dispute, which was the subject of a submission agreement committing the parties to resolve the dispute by arbitration.[527]

In Latin America, the Calvo Doctrine (first articulated in 1896) declared, among other things, that foreign nationals were mandatorily subject to the jurisdiction of local courts, which could not be ousted by international arbitration agreements.[528] The doctrine was incorporated into national legislation and constitutional instruments, which not infrequently rendered international arbitration agreements invalid.[529] Political declarations from developing states also reflected the continuing hostility of many such states towards international arbitration, even well into the 20th century. A 1971 declaration of the Andean Commission reflected this position, declaring:

> [No agreement concerning foreign investment shall] withdraw possible ... controversies from the national jurisdiction of the recipient country.[530]

The same principles were later reflected in various declarations associated with the "New International Economic Order."[531]

Against this background, contemporary arbitration legislation in some developing states still does not provide effective enforcement of agreements to arbitrate future disputes; such provisions are sometimes either revocable at will or unenforceable in broad categories of disputes, or subject to idiosyncratic form or substantive requirements.[532] Similarly, in a number of states, international arbitral awards are subject to either *de novo* judicial review or to similarly rigorous scrutiny on other grounds.[533] Finally, some national courts have been prepared to interfere in the international arbitral process—for example, by purporting to remove arbitrators, to resolve "preliminary" issues, to bar foreign lawyers from appearing, or to enjoin arbitrations.[534]

---

527. Naón, *Argentine Law and the ICC Rules: A Comment on the ECOFISA Case*, 3 World Arb. & Med. Rep. 100 (1992); Brazilian Arbitration Law (Law 9307 of 1996), Arts. 6, 7 (arguably requiring post-dispute *compromis*).

528. C. Calvo, *Derecho Internacional Teórico y Práctico de Europa y América* (1868); C. Calvo, *Le droit international theorique et pratique* (4th ed. 1870-72). *See* Naón, *Arbitration and Latin America: Progress and Setbacks*, 21 Arb. Int'l 127, 134-37 (2005).

529. *See* Baker & Yoder, *ICSID and the Calvo Clause: Hindrance to Foreign Direct Investment in LDCs*, 5 Ohio St. J. Disp. Resol. 75, 91 (1989); Garcia-Amador, 2 *The Changing Law of International Claims* 481-82 (1984).

530. Decision 24 of the Andean Commission Concerning Treatment of Foreign Capital, Art. 51, 10 I.L.M. 15 (1971).

531. *Charter of Article 2(2) Economic Rights and Duties of States*, U.N. Resol. 3281 (XXIX), 29 U.N. GAOR Supp. (No. 31), U.N. Doc. A/9631 (1974); *Permanent Sovereignty Over Natural Resources*, G.A. Resol. 3171 (XXVII), 28 U.N. Doc. GOAR Supp. (No. 30), U.N. Doc. A/9030 (1973).

532. *See infra* pp. 177-90; Naón, *Argentine Law and the ICC Rules: A Comment on the ECOFISA Case*, 3 World Arb. & Med. Rep. 100 (1992); Brazilian Arbitration Law, Arts. 6, 7 (arguably requiring post-dispute *compromis*).

533. *See infra* pp. 186-90; *Judgment of 1 August 2002, Electrificadora del Atlántico SA ESP v. TermoRio SA ESP*, Expediente No. 11001-03-25-000-2001-004601 (21.041) (Colombian Consejo de Estado) ("As a consequence of the evidence given, the arbitration process and the award from the 21st of December of 2001 ... between the companies Electrificadora del Atlántico SA ESP and TermoRio ESP is annulled.").

534. For a detailed account of efforts made by some states to frustrate the arbitration of international disputes, *see* Kantor, *International Project Finance and Arbitration With Public Sector Entities: When Is Arbitrability A Fiction?*, 24 Fordham Int'l L.J. 1122, 1171-72 (2001) ("a substantial risk exists that courts in developing countries will intervene to halt arbitration of disputes between investors and public authorities of

Nonetheless, during the last two decades, a number of states that historically distrusted international arbitration have ratified the New York Convention and/or enacted legislation supportive of the arbitral process.[535] This includes India, China, Saudi Arabia, Argentina, Algeria, Bahrain, Brazil, Tunisia, Turkey, Nigeria, Peru and (at least for a time) Russia, Ecuador and Venezuela. Although there is often little practical experience with the application of arbitration legislation in such states, these statutes have the potential for providing a more stable, predictable framework for international arbitration.

Unfortunately, even where national law is superficially supportive of the international arbitral process, many national courts have displayed a readiness to hold arbitration agreements or awards invalid or to interfere with the arbitral process. That is particularly true when national courts are requested to do so by local companies, state entities, or individuals.[536] Moreover, the early years of the 21st century have witnessed a potential resurgence of historic ideological opposition to at least certain aspects of the international arbitral process, with developing states[537] and commentators[538] condemning the legitimacy and fairness of the process. It remains to be seen how substantial and long-lived this trend will be, although it has thus far attracted little interest outside a limited number of states.

D. OVERVIEW OF INSTITUTIONAL AND AD HOC ARBITRATION

International arbitrations may be either "institutional" or "*ad hoc.*" There are vitally important differences between these two forms of arbitration.

Institutional arbitrations are conducted pursuant to institutional arbitration rules, almost always overseen by an appointing authority with responsibility for various aspects relating to constituting the arbitral tribunal, fixing the arbitrators' compensation and similar mat-

---

that country, particularly in circumstances of pervasive economic and political turmoil and corruption"). *See also* G. Born, *International Commercial Arbitration* 1306-16 (2d ed. 2014).

535. Alfaro & Guimarey, *Who Should Determine Arbitrability? Arbitration in A Changing Economic and Political Environment*, 12 Arb. Int'l 415, 424-26 (1996); A. Asouzu, *International Commercial Arbitration and African States: Practice, Participation and Institutional Development* (2001); Asouzu, *The Adoption of the UNCITRAL Model Law in Nigeria: Implications on the Recognition and Enforcement of Arbitral Awards* 1999 J. Bus. Law. 185; Naón, *Arbitration in Latin America: Overcoming Traditional Hostility (An Update)*, 22 U. Miami Inter-Am. L. Rev. 203, 231-34 (1991); Naón, *Arbitration and Latin America: Progress and Setbacks*, 21 Arb. Int'l 127, 149-76 (2005).

536. Naón, *Arbitration and Latin America: Progress and Setbacks*, 21 Arb. Int'l 127, 150 (2005) ("despite the rosy landscape generally presented by the black letter law on arbitration in Latin America after its recent modernisation, its substance or spirit has not always been properly understood or applied. In certain cases, the Latin American courts have ignored express legal provisions aimed at facilitating arbitration or ensuring its efficacy, or advanced results notoriously incompatible with the policies favourable to arbitration underlying the new and updated legal arbitration framework"); Alfaro & Lorenti, *The Growing Opposition of Argentina to ICSID Arbitral Tribunals: A Conflict Between International and Domestic Law?*, 6 J. World Inv. & Trade 417 (2005).

537. *See* ICSID, *Venezuela Submits A Notice Under Article 71 of the ICSID Convention* (Jan. 26, 2012) (notification of Venezuela's denunciation of ICSID Convention), available at icsid.worldbank.org; ICSID, *Ecuador Submits A Notice Under Article 71 of the ICSID Convention* (June 9, 2009); ICSID, *Bolivia Submits A Notice Under Article 71 of the ICSID Convention* (May 16, 2007).

538. *See* Franck, *The Legitimacy Crisis in Investment Treaty Arbitration: Public International Law Through Inconsistent Decisions*, 73 Fordham L. Rev. 1521 (2005); Shalakany, *Arbitration and the Third World: A Plea for Reassessing Bias Under the Specter of Neo-Liberalism*, 41 Harv. Int'l L.J. 419, 430 (2000).

ters.[539] In contrast, *ad hoc* arbitrations are conducted without the benefit of an appointing and administrative authority or (generally) preexisting arbitration rules, subject only to the parties' arbitration agreement and applicable national arbitration legislation.

1. *Institutional Arbitration*

A number of organizations, located in different countries, provide institutional arbitration services, often tailored to particular commercial or other needs. As indicated above, the best-known international commercial arbitration institutions are the International Chamber of Commerce ("ICC"), the American Arbitration Association ("AAA") and its International Centre for Dispute Resolution ("ICDR"), and the London Court of International Arbitration ("LCIA"). These organizations, as well as the International Centre for Settlement of Investment Disputes ("ICSID"), Permanent Court of Arbitration ("PCA"), Singapore International Arbitration Centre ("SIAC"), Hong Kong International Arbitration Centre ("HKIAC") and Swiss Chambers of Commerce, are described below.

Also active in the field are the Stockholm Chamber of Commerce Arbitration Institute ("SCC"), World Intellectual Property Organization ("WIPO"), the German Institution of Arbitration ("DIS"), the International Arbitral Centre of the Austrian Economic Chamber ("VIAC" or "Vienna International Arbitral Centre"), the China International Economic and Trade Arbitration Commission ("CIETAC"), the Japan Commercial Arbitration Association ("JCAA"), the Dubai International Financial Centre ("DIFC"), the Cairo Regional Centre for International Commercial Arbitration ("CRCICA"), the Australian Centre for International Commercial Arbitration ("ACICA"), the Kuala Lumpur Regional Centre for Arbitration ("KLRCA") and the Indian Council of Arbitration ("ICI"). There are also a number of less widely-known regional or national arbitral institutions, often dealing with industry-specific matters (*e.g.*, insurance or commodities arbitrations).[540]

These (and other) arbitral institutions have promulgated sets of procedural rules that apply where parties have agreed to arbitration pursuant to such rules.[541] Among other things, institutional rules set out the basic procedural framework and timetable for the arbitral proceedings. Institutional rules also typically authorize the arbitral institution to select arbitrators in particular disputes (that is, to serve as "appointing authority"), to resolve challenges to arbitrators, to designate the place of arbitration, to fix or regulate the fees payable to the arbitrators and (sometimes) to review the arbitrator's awards to reduce

---

539. *See infra* pp. 70-84.

540. In a number of industries, specialized arbitral regimes provide well-established means of dispute resolution. Examples include maritime, commodities, construction, insurance and reinsurance and labor arbitration. *See infra* pp. 109-10; AAA, www.adr.org (providing descriptions and rules for construction, textile, apparel, labor, pension, consumer and insurance arbitrations); C. Ambrose & K. Maxwell, *London Maritime Arbitration* (2d ed. 2002); D. Johnson, *International Commodity Arbitration* (1991); F. Rose, *International Commercial and Maritime Arbitration* (1988). *See also* AAA Labor Arbitration Rules (labor disputes); AAA Rules for Impartial Determination of Union Fees (organized labor fees); ARIAS U.S. Rules for the Resolution of U.S. Insurance and Reinsurance Disputes (insurance and reinsurance); 2013 ARIAS Fast Track Arbitration Rules (insurance and reinsurance); 2013 German Maritime Arbitration Association Rules (maritime); 2012 London Maritime Arbitration Association Terms (maritime); 2013 Society of Maritime Arbitration Rules (maritime); 2014 National Grain and Feed Association Arbitration Rules (selected commodities); 2013 National Grain and Feed Association Rail Arbitration Rules (selected transport).

541. The incorporation of institutional arbitration rules is discussed below, *see infra* p. 87.

the risk of unenforceability on formal grounds. Each arbitral institution has a staff (with the size varying significantly from one institution to another) and a decision-making body.

It is fundamental that arbitral institutions do not themselves arbitrate the merits of the parties' dispute. This is the responsibility of the particular individuals selected as arbitrators.[542] Arbitrators are virtually never employees of the arbitral institution, but instead are private persons selected by the parties.[543] If parties cannot agree upon an arbitrator, most institutional rules provide that the host institution will act as an "appointing authority," which chooses the arbitrators in the absence of the parties' agreement.

2. Ad Hoc Arbitration

Ad hoc arbitrations are not conducted under the auspices or supervision of an arbitral institution. Instead, parties simply agree to arbitrate, without designating any institution to administer their arbitration. *Ad hoc* arbitration agreements will often choose an arbitrator (or arbitrators) who is (or are) to resolve the dispute without institutional supervision or assistance.[544] The parties will sometimes also select a preexisting set of procedural rules designed to govern *ad hoc* arbitrations. For international commercial and (increasingly) investment disputes, the United Nations Commission on International Trade Law ("UNCITRAL") has published a commonly-used set of such rules, the UNCITRAL Arbitration Rules.[545]

Where *ad hoc* arbitration is chosen, parties usually will (and certainly should) designate an appointing authority[546] that will select the arbitrator(s) if the parties cannot agree and consider any subsequent challenges to members of the tribunal. If the parties fail to select an appointing authority, then the national arbitration statutes of many states permit national courts to appoint arbitrators (but this is less desirable than selection of an experienced appointing authority).[547]

3. Relative Advantages and Disadvantages of Institutional and Ad Hoc Arbitration

Both institutional and *ad hoc* arbitration have strengths. Institutional arbitration is conducted according to a standing set of procedural rules and supervised, to a greater or lesser extent, by professional staff. This reduces the risks of procedural breakdowns, particularly at the beginning of the arbitral process, and of technical defects in the arbitration proceedings and arbitral award. The institution's involvement can be particularly constructive on issues relating to the appointment of arbitrators, the resolution of challenges to arbitrators, the selection of an arbitral seat and fixing the arbitrators' fees, where professional, specialized staff provide better service than *ad hoc* decisions by national courts with little, if any, experience or institutional resources for such matters.[548]

---

542. *See infra* pp. 694-95.

543. *See* G. Born, *International Commercial Arbitration* 1762 (2d ed. 2014).

544. *See infra* pp. 695.

545. For a discussion of the UNCITRAL Rules, *see infra* pp. 72-74.

546. *See infra* pp. 87-88. Most leading arbitration institutions (including the ICC, AAA and LCIA) will act as an appointing authority, for a fee, in *ad hoc* arbitrations.

547. *See infra* pp. 702-09.

548. As discussed below, national courts will generally have the power, under most developed arbitration statutes and where the parties have not otherwise agreed, to assist the arbitral process by appointing arbi-

Equally important, many institutional rules contain provisions that make the arbitral process more reliable and expeditious. This includes provisions concerning compe-tence-competence, separability, provisional measures, disclosure, arbitrator impartiality, corrections and challenges to awards, replacement of arbitrators and truncated tribunals, costs and the like.[549] Less directly, an arbitral institution lends its standing to any award that is rendered, which may enhance the likelihood of voluntary compliance and judicial enforcement.[550]

On the other hand, *ad hoc* arbitration is arguably more flexible, less expensive (since it can avoid sometimes substantial institutional fees) and more confidential than institutional arbitration. Moreover, the growing size and sophistication of the international arbitration bar, and the efficacy of international legislative frameworks for commercial arbitration, have partially reduced the relative advantages of institutional arbitration. Nonetheless, most experienced international practitioners decisively prefer the more structured, pre-dictable character of institutional arbitration, and the benefits of institutional rules and appointment mechanisms, at least in the absence of unusual circumstances arguing for an *ad hoc* approach.

4. *UNCITRAL Arbitration Rules*

The UNCITRAL Arbitration Rules occupy an important position, both historically and in contemporary arbitration practice. In 1973, UNCITRAL proposed the preparation of model arbitration rules.[551] The objective of the UNCITRAL Rules was to create a unified, predictable and stable procedural framework for international arbitrations without stifling the informal and flexible character of such dispute resolution mechanisms.[552] The Rules aimed to be acceptable to common law, civil law and other legal systems, as well as to capital-importing and capital-exporting interests.[553] The Rules were promulgated by Resolution 31/98, adopted by the General Assembly of the United Nations on December 15, 1976.[554]

UNCITRAL reviewed the usage of the Rules between 2000 and 2006 and, after exten-sive consultations and study, formally undertook a revision of the Rules.[555] On June 25,

---

trators, considering challenges to arbitrators and fixing compensation of arbitrators (where not otherwise agreed). *See infra* pp. 702-09, 758-76; G. Born, *International Commercial Arbitration* 1712 (2d ed. 2014).

549. *See infra* pp. 190-218, 218-87, 716-58, 772-76, 830-39, 877-83, 1125-34, 1169-72.

550. *See infra* pp. 1059-60.

551. *Report of the United Nations Commission on International Trade Law*, 6th Sess., U.N. Doc. A/9017, ¶85 (1973).

552. *Report of the Secretary-General on the Revised Draft Set of Arbitration Rules, UNCITRAL, 9th Session*, U.N. Doc. A/CN.9/112, Introduction ¶17 (1975). *See also U.N. Resolution 31/98 Adopted by the General Assembly on 15 December 1976* ("the establishment of rules for ad hoc arbitration that are ac-ceptable in countries with different legal, social and economic systems would significantly contribute to the development of harmonious international economic relations").

553. *Report of the Secretary-General on the Preliminary Draft Set of Arbitration Rules, UNCITRAL, 8th Session*, U.N. Doc. A/CN.9/97 (1975); D. Caron, L. Caplan & M. Pellonpää, *The UNCITRAL Arbitration Rules: A Commentary* 44-51, 565-79 (2006).

554. *Report of the United Nations Commission on International Trade Law on the Work of Its Eighteenth Session*, U.N. Doc. A/40/17 (1985). *See* D. Caron & L. Caplan, *The UNCITRAL Arbitration Rules: A Commentary* 2 *et seq.* (2d ed. 2013).

555. The UNCITRAL Working Group on International Arbitration and Conciliation began to study pos-sible revisions to the UNCITRAL Rules in 2006. *See Report of the Working Group on Arbitration and*

2010, UNCITRAL published extensive revisions of the original UNCITRAL Rules (the first revision since their adoption).[556]

The UNCITRAL Rules are designed for use in *ad hoc* international commercial arbitrations. When they were adopted in 1976, the Rules were the only set of rules available specifically for that purpose. Although alternatives now exist,[557] most states, which generally will have supported the Rules in the United Nations debates, and their state-owned entities, often find it difficult to object to their use in an arbitration agreement or arbitral proceeding.[558]

Like most institutional arbitration rules, the UNCITRAL Rules prescribe a basic procedural framework for the arbitration. This includes provisions for initiating an arbitration,[559] selection and challenge of arbitrators,[560] conduct of the arbitral proceedings,[561] choice of applicable law,[562] awards[563] and costs of the arbitration.[564] The Rules also contain provisions confirming the presumptive separability of the arbitration clause from the underlying contract, and the tribunal's power to consider jurisdictional objections (competence-competence).[565] Under the Rules, the Secretary-General of the Permanent Court of Arbitration serves a *sui generis* function, of designating a suitable appointing authority, unless the parties agree to a different appointment mechanism.[566]

The UNCITRAL Rules have contributed significantly to the harmonization of international arbitration procedures. That is reflected in part by the readiness of the AAA and the IACAC to have based the ICDR Rules and IACAC Rules substantially on the UNCITRAL

Conciliation on the Work of Its Forty-Seventh Session, U.N. Doc. A/CN.9/641 (2007); Paulsson & Petrochilos, *Report: Revision of the UNCITRAL Arbitration Rules (2006)*.

556. 2010 UNCITRAL Rules. By their terms, the revised Rules apply where the arbitration agreement was concluded after August 15, 2010. They also apply to arbitration agreements concluded earlier, where the parties agree to their application. 2010 UNCITRAL Rules, Art. 1(2). *See* G. Born, *International Commercial Arbitration* 1390-91 (2d ed. 2014).

557. The International Institute for Conflict Prevention and Resolution (formerly known as the CPR Institute for Dispute Resolution) has published, since 1989, a set of "Rules for Non-Administered Arbitration" (formerly called "Rules and Commentary for Non-Traditional Arbitration for Business Disputes"). The Permanent Court of Arbitration has promulgated sets of rules, based on the UNCITRAL Rules, applicable to disputes between private and public parties.

558. Experience with the UNCITRAL Rules has been positive. *See* PCA Optional Rules for Arbitrating Disputes Between Two States, Introduction ("Experience in arbitrations since 1981 suggests that the [1976] UNCITRAL Arbitration Rules provide fair and effective procedures for peaceful resolution of disputes between States concerning the interpretation, application and performance of treaties and other agreements, although they were originally designed for commercial arbitration"); D. Caron, L. Caplan & M. Pellonpää, *The UNCITRAL Arbitration Rules: A Commentary* 7 (2006) ("UNCITRAL Rules themselves are increasingly important").

559. 2010 UNCITRAL Rules, Arts. 3, 4.

560. 2010 UNCITRAL Rules, Arts. 6-15; *infra* pp. 694-702, 768-76.

561. 2010 UNCITRAL Rules, Arts. 17, 20-30; *infra* pp. 786-87, 791.

562. 2010 UNCITRAL Rules, Art. 35; *infra* pp. 969-70, 989.

563. 2010 UNCITRAL Rules, Arts. 33, 34, 36-39; *infra* pp. 1062-69, 1122, 1133.

564. 2010 UNCITRAL Rules, Arts. 40-43.

565. 2010 UNCITRAL Rules, Art. 23; *infra* pp. 213, 271.

566. 2010 UNCITRAL Rules, Art. 6. *See infra* pp. 684-85, 699-702. The parties can select an arbitral institution (like the ICC, AAA, or LCIA) as appointing authority without adopting that institution's rules. Alternatively, a designated individual or office-holder may be selected. *See infra* p. 672.

Rules.[567] A number of other arbitral institutions have either adopted the UNCITRAL Rules entirely, or have substantially adopted those rules in fashioning institutional rules.[568] Although designed principally for international trade disputes, the Rules are not limited to commercial matters and have been used successfully in both state-to-state and investor-state arbitrations.

5.   Leading International Arbitral Institutions

If institutional arbitration is desired, the parties must choose a particular arbitral institution and refer to it in their arbitration clause.[569] Parties ordinarily rely on one of a few established international arbitral institutions. This avoids the confusion and uncertainty that comes from inexperienced arbitrator appointments and administrative efforts.

All leading international arbitral institutions are prepared to, and routinely do, administer arbitrations seated almost anywhere in the world, and not merely in the place where the institution itself is located.[570] There is, therefore, no need to select an arbitral institution headquartered in the parties' desired arbitral seat (*e.g.*, the London Court of Arbitration or Vienna International Arbitral Centre can readily administer an arbitration seated in Paris or New York, while the American Arbitration Association can administer an arbitration seated in Vienna or London).

The services rendered by professional arbitration institutions come at a price, which is in addition to the fees and expenses of the arbitrators. Every arbitral institution has a fee schedule that specifies what that price is. The amounts charged by institutions for particular matters vary significantly, as does the basis for calculating such fees. For example, some institutions use hourly charges, while others charge based upon a percentage of the amount in dispute.

All leading arbitral institutions periodically revise their institutional arbitration rules. Like the rules themselves, these revisions are the product of extensive consultations among leading practitioners, academics, business users and arbitrators. These consultative processes are aimed at refining the institutional rules for the purpose of making arbitration agreements and awards more enforceable and arbitral proceedings more efficient. As with the refinement of national arbitration legislation, this is an example of the ongoing adaptation and improvement of the international arbitral process in response to criticisms, users' needs and changing conditions.

---

567. *See supra* p. 40 and *infra* pp. 77-79.

568. This includes the IACAC, ICDR, HKIAC, SIAC, CRCICA, KLRCA and Iran-U.S. Claims Tribunal.

569. Issues arising from arbitration agreements that incorporate institutional rules (sometimes defectively) are discussed below. *See infra* pp. 348-52.

570. *See infra* pp. 640-58. *See also* ICC, *ICC Rules of Arbitration* ("ICC Rules of Arbitration are used worldwide to resolve business disputes through arbitration…. [and] accommodate any preferences parties in dispute might have with respect to certain aspects of the proceedings, such as the choice of arbitrators, the place, and the language of arbitration."), available at www.iccwbo.org; 2014 ICDR Rules ("The ICDR provides dispute resolution services around the world in locations chosen by the parties. ICDR arbitrations and mediations may be conducted in any language chosen by the parties.").

a. International Chamber of Commerce ("ICC") International Court of Arbitration

The ICC International Court of Arbitration was established in Paris in 1923 (in parallel with efforts by the international business community to secure adoption of the Geneva Protocol and reforms of arbitration legislation in a number of developed states[571]). The ICC remains the world's leading international commercial arbitration institution, and has less of a national character than any other leading arbitral institution. [572]

The ICC's annual caseload was well above 300 cases filed per year during much of the 1990s, and, by 2011 had reached nearly 800 cases filed per year.[573] Most of these cases have been international disputes, many involving very substantial sums. The ICC's caseload includes disputes between parties from around the world, with parties from outside Western Europe involved in more than 50% of all ICC cases in recent years.[574] In 2013, as in other years, about 11% of the ICC's caseload involved states or state-related entities.[575]

The ICC has promulgated a set of ICC Rules of Arbitration (which are periodically revised, most recently in 2012[576]) as well as the ICC Mediation Rules, the ICC Rules for Expertise, the ICC Dispute Board Rules and the ICC Rules for A Pre-Arbitral Referee Procedure (Emergency Arbitrator Rules in the 2012 Rules of Arbitration).[577] Under the ICC Rules, the ICC (through the ICC International Court of Arbitration ("ICC Court")) is extensively involved in the administration of individual arbitrations. Among other things, the ICC Court and its Secretariat are responsible for service of the initial Request for Arbitration;[578] fixing and receiving payment of advances on costs of the arbitration by the parties;[579] confirming the parties' nominations of arbitrators;[580] appointing arbitrators if a party defaults or if the parties are unable to agree upon a presiding arbitrator or sole arbitrator;[581] considering challenges to the arbitrators including on the basis of lack of independence;[582] reviewing so-called "Terms of Reference," which define the issues and

---

571. *See supra* pp. 30-33.

572. The ICC model arbitration clause provides:

> "All disputes arising out of or in connection with the present contract shall be finally settled under the Rules of Arbitration of the International Chamber of Commerce by one or more arbitrators in accordance with the said Rules."

573. A total of 796 new cases were filed with the ICC International Court of Arbitration in 2011, 759 in 2012 and 767 in 2013. At the end of 2013, 1,511 cases were being administered by the Court. *2011-2013 ICC Statistical Reports* (2012-2014). These figures reflect a generally continual increase in the Court's active caseload, which has more than doubled in the last twenty years.

574. Parties to ICC arbitrations filed in 2013 were nationals of 138 different countries and independent territories. ICC, *2013 Statistical Report*, 25(1) ICC ICArb. Bull. 5, 6 (2014).

575. ICC, *2013 Statistical Report*, 25(1) ICC ICArb. Bull. 5, 10 (2014).

576. The revised Rules became effective as of January 1, 2012 and apply to any ICC arbitration commencing on or following that date, unless the parties agree otherwise. J. Fry, S. Greenberg & F. Mazza, *The Secretariat's Guide to ICC Arbitration* 64 (2012).

577. *See infra* pp. 882-83.

578. 2012 ICC Rules, Arts. 4(5), 5(4).

579. 2012 ICC Rules, Art. 36.

580. 2012 ICC Rules, Arts. 11-13.

581. 2012 ICC Rules, Art. 13.

582. 2012 ICC Rules, Art. 14.

procedures for the arbitration;[583] reviewing a tribunal's draft award for formal and other defects;[584] and fixing the arbitrators' compensation.[585]

The ICC Court is not, in fact, a "court," and does not itself decide disputes or act as an arbitrator. Rather, the ICC Court is an administrative body that acts in a supervisory and appointing capacity under the ICC Rules.[586] It maintains a sizeable legal and administrative staff of over 100 persons, from more than 30 nationalities, organized as a Secretariat.[587] Specialized teams of counsel and administrative staff are assigned to cases originating from particular geographic, linguistic and/or cultural regions. As detailed above, the Secretariat is substantially involved in the day-to-day supervision of arbitrations.

ICC arbitrations can be (and are) seated almost anywhere in the world. In 2013, ICC arbitrations were conducted in 63 different countries.[588] Over the last decade, an increasing number of ICC arbitrations have been seated outside of Europe, particularly in Asia and the Pacific, Brazil and the Middle East. Nonetheless, by far the most common seats for ICC arbitrations are France, Switzerland, England, other Western European states and the United States, as well as Singapore and Hong Kong.[589] In 2008, the ICC opened a regional office in Hong Kong, responsible for administration of ICC arbitrations seated in Asia.

The ICC Rules are broadly similar to the UNCITRAL Rules[590] (and many other leading institutional rules) in providing a broad procedural framework for the arbitral proceedings. This includes provisions for filing a request for arbitration and other initial written pleadings,[591] constituting an arbitral tribunal,[592] conducting the arbitration[593] and making an award.[594] As with most other institutional rules, only a skeletal procedural framework is provided, with the parties and arbitrators being accorded substantial freedom to adopt procedures tailored to particular disputes.

Unusually, the ICC Rules require both "Terms of Reference"[595] and a procedural timetable to be adopted by the Tribunal at the outset of proceedings[596] and that an award be

---

583. 2012 ICC Rules, Art. 23.

584. 2012 ICC Rules, Art. 33.

585. 2012 ICC Rules, Art. 37.

586. 2012 ICC Rules, Art. 1(2). The Court acts pursuant to internal rules governing its conduct. *See* Y. Derains & E. Schwartz, *A Guide to the ICC Rules of Arbitration* 1-8, 11-27 (2d ed. 2005); J. Fry, S. Greenberg & F. Mazza, *The Secretariat's Guide to ICC Arbitration* 17-19 (2012); ICC, *Internal Rules of the International Court of Arbitration*.

587. ICC, *2013 ICC Statistical Report*, 25(1) ICC ICArb. Bull. 5, 6 (2014).

588. ICC, *2013 ICC Statistical Report*, 25(1) ICC ICArb. Bull. 5, 12 (2014).

589. *See infra* p. 653; Verbist, *The Practice of the ICC International Court of Arbitration With Regard to the Fixing of the Place of Arbitration*, 12 Arb. Int'l 347 (1996); Jarvin, *The Place of Arbitration: A Review of the ICC Court's Guiding Principles and Practices When Fixing the Place of Arbitration*, 7 ICC ICArb. Bull. 55 (1996).

590. *See supra* pp. 72-74.

591. 2012 ICC Rules, Arts. 4, 5.

592. 2012 ICC Rules, Arts. 11-15.

593. 2012 ICC Rules, Arts. 16-29.

594. 2012 ICC Rules, Arts. 30-35.

595. 2012 ICC Rules, Art. 23; J. Fry, S. Greenberg & F. Mazza, *The Secretariat's Guide to ICC Arbitration* 9-10 (2012).

596. 2012 ICC Rules, Art. 24; J. Fry, S. Greenberg & F. Mazza, *The Secretariat's Guide to ICC Arbitration* 9 (2012).

rendered within six months (unless the Court fixes a different time limit based on the procedural timetable).[597] Also unusually, the ICC Rules provide for the ICC Court to review draft awards before they are finalized and executed by the arbitrators.[598] In addition, provisions were added to the ICC Rules in the 2012 amendments addressing multiple contracts and parties,[599] case management conferences[600] and emergency arbitrator procedures.[601]

With respect to arbitrators' fees, the ICC Rules fix both a minimum and a maximum amount that can be charged, based on the amount in dispute and other factors.[602] With respect to administrative expenses, the ICC Rules provide for a sliding scale of charges that is again based upon the amount in dispute between the parties and other factors. The ICC Rules require that the parties pay an advance on the costs of the arbitration calculated by the ICC Court.[603] The advance on costs is equally divided between the claimant and the respondent, although one party may pay the full amount in order to enable the arbitration to proceed if the other party defaults.[604]

The ICC's Rules have sometimes been criticized as expensive and cumbersome,[605] although the 1998 and 2012 amendments reflected a concerted effort to meet this criticism.[606] Despite criticism of its costs and delays, the ICC clearly remains the institution of preference for many sophisticated commercial users.

b. American Arbitration Association ("AAA") and International Centre for Dispute Resolution ("ICDR")

The AAA was founded in 1926, following the merger of two New York arbitration institutions (themselves founded in the early 1920s).[607] The AAA remains based in New York (with approximately 36 regional offices throughout the United States).[608] The AAA is

---

597. 2012 ICC Rules, Art. 30(1). This time limit is routinely extended. Y. Derains & E. Schwartz, *A Guide to the ICC Rules of Arbitration* 305 (2d ed. 2005).

598. 2012 ICC Rules, Art. 33; Y. Derains & E. Schwartz, *A Guide to the ICC Rules of Arbitration* 312-16 (2d ed. 2005).

599. 2012 ICC Rules, Arts. 7-10.

600. *See, e.g.*, 2012 ICC Rules, Art 24.

601. 2012 ICC Rules, Art. 29, Appx. V.

602. 2012 ICC Rules, Appx. III, Arts. 2, 4; Y. Derains & E. Schwartz, *A Guide to the ICC Rules of Arbitration* 330 (2d ed. 2005).

603. 2012 ICC Rules, Art. 36.

604. 2012 ICC Rules, Arts. 36(2), (5).

605. *See* Wetter, *The Present Status of the International Court of Arbitration of the ICC: An Appraisal*, 1 Am. Rev. Int'l Arb. 91 (1990); W. Craig, W. Park & J. Paulsson, *International Chamber of Commerce Arbitration* 35-36 (3d ed. 2000) (attempting to counter criticisms); Buehler, *Costs in ICC Arbitration: A Practitioner's View*, 3 Am. Rev. Int'l Arb. 116 (1992).

606. *See* W. Craig, W. Park & J. Paulsson, *International Chamber of Commerce Arbitration* 35-36 (3d ed. 2000); Y. Derains & E. Schwartz, *A Guide to the ICC Rules of Arbitration* 5 (2d ed. 2005).

A 2007 ICC task force studied ways to reduce costs and delay in ICC arbitrations. *See* ICC, *Techniques for Controlling Time and Costs in Arbitration* (2007).

607. I. MacNeil, *American Arbitration Law* 84-88 (1992).

608. Deye & Britton, *Arbitration by the American Arbitration Association*, 70 N.D. L. Rev. 281, 281 n.1 (1994).

the leading U.S. arbitral institution, and reportedly handles one of the largest numbers of arbitral disputes in the world.[609]

The primary arbitration rules administered by the AAA are the AAA Commercial Arbitration Rules.[610] These rules are used in a large majority of domestic U.S. arbitrations. Numerous other sets of AAA arbitration rules also exist, in particular for specialized types of disputes, and can be selected in the parties' arbitration agreement.[611]

Non-U.S. parties have sometimes been reluctant to agree to arbitration under AAA rules, fearing parochial predisposition and unfamiliarity with international practice. In recent years, the AAA has taken a number of steps aimed at overcoming this image and enhancing its position as an international institution.

In 1991, the AAA promulgated the AAA International Arbitration Rules, designed specifically for international arbitrations (which have since evolved into the current ICDR Rules).[612] In 1996, the AAA established an "International Centre for Dispute Resolution" ("ICDR"), with exclusive responsibility for administering the AAA's international arbitrations.[613] The ICDR has an administrative facility in New York and administers ICDR cases seated outside the United States with the support of a Senior Vice President located in Europe. The ICDR offers a worldwide list of more than 650 potential arbitrators and mediators.

The ICDR Rules provide the applicable set of AAA Rules in "international" disputes (except where the parties have otherwise agreed).[614] This alters the previous position, in which the primarily domestic AAA Commercial Arbitration Rules provided the fallback rules when parties to international agreements had agreed to AAA arbitration without designating a particular set of rules.

The ICDR Rules are based principally on the UNCITRAL Rules, and were intended to permit a maximum of flexibility and a minimum of administrative supervision. They are periodically revised, most recently in 2014.[615]

Under all versions of ICDR Rules, the AAA/ICDR administrative staff plays a less significant supervisory role than does the ICC Secretariat. Among other things, the AAA/ICDR does not receive or serve initial notices or requests for arbitration; does not require or review a Terms of Reference; and plays a less significant role in setting the ar-

---

609. The AAA reports that it has administered some 2.5 million arbitrations since its foundation.

610. *See* www.adr.org.

611. For example, these include specialized rules for construction, energy, health care, insurance, securities, labor and intellectual property disputes. *See* www.adr.org.

612. The AAA's International Rules were preceded by a set of "Supplementary Procedures for International Commercial Arbitration," adopted in 1982. The AAA Supplementary Procedures continue to be used in international cases in which the parties have selected rules other than the AAA International Rules. The Supplementary Procedures (as amended in 1999) provide: "Recognizing that international arbitration cases often present unique procedural problems, the AAA has created the following supplementary procedures to facilitate such cases when rules other than the International Arbitration Rules govern the proceedings. Unless the parties advise otherwise by the due date for the return of the first list, the AAA will assume that they are desired."

613. *See* 2014 ICDR International Dispute Resolution Procedures, Introduction.

614. 2014 ICDR Rules, Art. 1(3).

615. *See* www.adr.org. The 2014 Rules include, among other things, provisions on joinder, consolidation and expedited arbitration. 2014 ICDR Rules, Arts. 1(4), 7,8, E1-E10.

bitrators' fees.[616] The AAA/ICDR's administrative charges are based on the amount in dispute. With respect to the arbitrators' fees, arbitrators fix their own rates, which are published on their resumes for parties to consider when receiving a list of potential arbitrators. Compensation under the ICDR Rules is ultimately based on the "time spent by the arbitrators," their stated rates and the "size and complexity of the case."[617]

The ICDR Rules allow the parties to agree on any procedure for appointing arbitrators.[618] The 2014 Rules specifically provide that in the absence of such agreement, the list procedure shall apply, which has been so far used in practice in most AAA/ICDR appointments, whereby names drawn from the AAA/ICDR's rosters are presented to the parties for expressions of preference.[619] Although the AAA/ICDR's lists have historically been dominated by U.S. practitioners, the AAA/ICDR increasingly seeks to appoint arbitrators with international experience in appropriate international cases.[620] Nonetheless, some users have found the AAA/ICDR appointment procedures and selections patchy, with less involvement of experienced international practitioners than some other leading institutions.

c. London Court of International Arbitration ("LCIA")

Founded in 1892, the LCIA is, by many accounts, the second most popular European institution in the field of international commercial arbitration.[621] The LCIA's annual caseload, which is generally increasing, has exceeded 220 cases filed in recent years.[622] The LCIA has made a determined, and somewhat successful, effort in recent years to overcome perceptions that it is a predominantly English institution. Among other things, it has appointed five successive non-English presidents, and its vice-presidents include a number of non-English practitioners. In recent years, fewer than 20% of the LCIA's cases have involved a U.K. party.[623]

616. Unusually, the ICDR Rules also provide for a waiver of punitive damage claims (unless otherwise agreed). 2014 ICDR Rules, Art. 31(5).

617. 2014 ICDR Rules, Art. 35. Article 35(2) provides: "As soon as practicable after the commencement of the arbitration, the Administrator shall designate an appropriate daily or hourly rate of compensation in consultation with the parties and all arbitrators, taking into account the arbitrators' stated rate of compensation and the size and complexity of the case."

618. 2014 ICDR Rules, Art. 12(1); *infra* pp. 671-702.

619. *See* 2014 ICDR Rules, Art. 12(6). *See also* 2013 AAA Commercial Arbitration Rules, Rule 12 (providing, where the AAA's Commercial Arbitration Rules apply, specific procedures for appointments from the AAA's National Roster).

620. The ICDR maintains its own International Panel of Arbitrators.

621. The LCIA model arbitration clause provides:

"Any dispute arising out of or in connection with this contract, including any question regarding its existence, validity or termination, shall be referred to and finally resolved by arbitration under the Rules of the LCIA, which Rules are deemed to be incorporated by reference into this clause."

"The number of arbitrators shall be [one/three]. The place of arbitration shall be [City and/or Country]. The language to be used in the arbitral proceedings shall be _____. The governing law of the contract shall be the substantive law of _____."

622. The LCIA reports that 118 cases were referred to it in 2005, 133 in 2006, 137 in 2007, 215 in 2008, 272 in 2009, 246 in 2010, 224 in 2011 and 265 in 2012. *See* LCIA News, *Director General's Reviews* (2007-2012); LCIA, *Registrar's Report 2012* (2013). The number of disputes referred to the LCIA rose by 18.3% from 2011 to 2012. *See* LCIA, *Registrar's Report 2012* 4 (2013).

623. LCIA, *Registrar's Report 2012* (2013).

The LCIA administers a set of arbitration rules, the LCIA Arbitration Rules, which were extensively revised in 1998 and 2014. Although identifiably English in drafting style, and to a lesser extent in procedural approach, the LCIA Rules generally provide a sound basis for international dispute resolution, particularly for parties desiring common law procedures (*e.g.*, disclosure, security for costs). Broadly speaking, LCIA arbitrations are administered in a less comprehensive fashion than ICC cases. Among other things, the LCIA Rules contain no Terms of Reference procedure and do not provide for institutional review of draft awards.

In contrast to most other institutional rules, the LCIA Rules set out the powers of an LCIA arbitral tribunal in some detail.[624] The powers to order discovery[625] and security for legal costs (*i.e.*, a deposit or bank guarantee securing the estimated amounts that an unsuccessful claimant would be liable to reimburse to a successful respondent for its costs of legal representation)[626] are prominently included among the arbitrators' powers.

A particular procedural advantage of the LCIA Rules is their provision for expedited formation of the arbitral tribunal[627] and expedited appointment of replacement arbitrators.[628] Notably, the 2014 LCIA Rules introduced provisions for emergency arbitrators, similar to those in the 2012 ICC Rules.[629] The LCIA Rules also permit intervention of third parties in LCIA arbitrations (subject to prescribed conditions) and consolidation of arbitrations.[630] In 2011, the LCIA published abstracts of all 28 decisions (from 1996 to 2010) of the LCIA Court on challenges to arbitrators.[631]

Like the ICC, the LCIA does not maintain a standing list or panel of arbitrators. The LCIA's appointments of arbitrators have historically been drawn predominantly from the English bar and retired judiciary, in large part because many LCIA cases have involved contracts governed by English law. In cases not involving English law, the LCIA's selections of arbitrators are more international. The LCIA fixes the arbitrators' fees according to the time expended by the arbitrators at the hourly rates published by the LCIA and fixed by agreement between the arbitrators and the LCIA.[632]

Most LCIA arbitrations are seated in London. In the absence of agreement by the parties to the contrary, London will be the arbitral seat under Article 16(2) of the LCIA Rules, unless the arbitral tribunal decides that another arbitral seat is more appropriate.[633]

d. International Centre for Settlement of Investment Disputes ("ICSID")

In the field of investment arbitration, ICSID was established to deal with investment disputes under the ICSID Convention (discussed above).[634] It has adopted institutional arbitration rules for investment disputes (the ICSID Arbitration Rules).[635]

---

624. 2014 LCIA Rules, Arts. 14, 15, 18-22.
625. 2014 LCIA Rules, Arts. 22(1)(iv), (v).
626. 2014 LCIA Rules, Art. 25(1)(i)).
627. 2014 LCIA Rules, Art. 9A.
628. 2014 LCIA Rules, Art. 9C.
629. 2014 LCIA Rules, Art. 9B, *infra* pp. 882-83.
630. 2014 LCIA Rules, Arts. 22(1)(viii), (ix); *infra* p. 957.
631. Walsh & Teitelbaum, *The LCIA Court Decisions on Challenges to Arbitrators: An Introduction*, 27 Arb. Int'l 283 (2011).
632. 2014 LCIA Rules, Art. 28(1).
633. 2014 LCIA Rules, Art. 16(2).

Major international infrastructure and natural resource projects frequently include ICSID arbitration clauses, usually as a consequence of demands from host governments. ICSID has also frequently been included as an arbitral institution to administer arbitrations pursuant to bilateral investment treaties ("BITs"), which proliferated during the 1990s. As a consequence, ICSID has gained substantially greater experience in administering international arbitrations, and enhanced credibility as an arbitral institution during the past decade. That trend has continued in recent years, as ICSID has modernized the ICSID Rules, which led to some improvement in the institution's arbitral procedures.

ICSID's caseload has very significantly increased in the past 25 years, particularly as a consequence of arbitrations brought pursuant to BITs or investment protection legislation. As of June 30, 2014, the Centre had registered 464 ICSID arbitrations since its establishment, with 40 new ICSID arbitrations registered in 2013.[636] While only 13 ICSID awards were rendered between 1971 and 1990, 158 awards were rendered between 2001 and June 2014.[637]

e. Permanent Court of Arbitration ("PCA")

The PCA, established by the 1899 and 1907 Hague Conventions for the Pacific Settlement of International Disputes, is focused particularly on international arbitrations involving states and state-like entities.[638] As discussed above, the PCA was not established as a "court," with a standing panel of judges.[639] Rather, as originally established, the PCA was a registry for inter-state arbitrations conducted pursuant to the Hague Conventions, which provided a number of institutional administering services. In an often quoted phrase, the PCA has been described in its original form as "a permanent framework for temporary tribunals."[640]

Since the 1970s, the PCA has been called upon to act as a traditional appointing authority with increasing frequency and now routinely serves as an institutional administering body for arbitrations conducted under the PCA Arbitration Rules and *ad hoc* arbitration agreements. Additionally, and at least as important, the PCA serves as the default institution to select appointing authorities under the UNCITRAL Rules—a function that has assumed increasing importance in recent decades in both international commercial arbitrations and investment arbitrations.[641]

The Hague Conventions were negotiated with disputes between states in mind and the PCA's early activity was confined to this area. As discussed above, the PCA enjoyed very modest usage during its first 70 years of existence (when only 25 arbitrations and three

---

634. *See supra* pp. 41-44.

635. The ICSID Arbitration Rules are reproduced in the Documentary Supplement and are available at icsid.worldbank.org.

636. ICSID, *ICSID Caseload* 8 (July 2014).

637. ICSID, *ICSID Caseload* 17 (July 2014).

638. *See* G. Born, *International Commercial Arbitration* 185-89 (2d ed. 2014).

639. *See supra* pp. 29-30.

640. Daly, *Permanent Court of Arbitration*, in C. Giorgetti (ed.), *International Litigation in Practice: The Rules, Practice and Jurisprudence of International Courts and Tribunals* 39 (2012) (quoting Louis Renault, a leading participant at 1899 and 1907 Hague Conferences).

641. Levine, *Navigating the Parallel Universe of Investor-State Arbitrations Under the UNCITRAL Rules*, in C. Brown & K. Miles (eds.), *Evolution in Investment Treaty Law and Arbitration* 369 (2011).

conciliations were submitted to PCA tribunals).[642] By comparison, some 200 non-PCA inter-state arbitrations were conducted during the same time period (1900 to 1970), often pursuant to *ad hoc* submission agreements or compromissory clauses in bilateral treaties.

In a striking turn-around, the PCA's caseload has increased materially since 1995, in part because of the PCA's interpretation of Article 26 of the 1899 Convention (and Article 47 of the 1907 Convention), which permits the PCA to "place its premises and its staff at the disposal of the Signatory Powers for the operations of any special Board of Arbitration," as allowing the PCA to administer disputes between states and non-state actors.[643] The PCA's Administrative Council also expanded the PCA's remit to cover disputes involving international organizations, and disputes relating to natural resources and/or the environment.[644]

As a consequence, the PCA's caseload has significantly changed, both in size and composition. From 2000-2014 more than 150 arbitrations were brought to the PCA, in comparison to only 34 cases administered in the organization's first 100 years (1899-1999).[645] The substantial majority of these new filings were either international commercial or investment arbitrations, although there has also been growth in classic inter-state proceedings.[646] Out of 104 arbitrations administered in the course of 2013, eight were state-to-state disputes (the highest level in the PCA's history), while 62 were investor-state disputes under bilateral or multilateral investment treaties; 30 disputes arose under contracts or other agreements to which at least one party was a state, state-controlled entity, or intergovernmental organization.[647]

During the 1990s, the PCA promulgated four sets of procedural rules for various categories of arbitrations, all of which were based on the 1976 UNCITRAL Rules: Optional Rules for Arbitrating Disputes between Two States (1992); Optional Rules for Arbitrating Disputes between Two Parties of Which Only One Is a State (1993); Optional Rules for Arbitration Involving International Organizations and States (1996); and Optional Rules for Arbitration between International Organizations and Private Parties (1996). The PCA has also devised *ad hoc* procedural regimes, such as rules of procedure for arbitration pursuant to Annex VII of the United Nations Convention on the Law of the Sea ("UNCLOS"). All of these various rules have been used relatively infrequently (with most parties to PCA-administered arbitration instead electing to use the UNCITRAL Rules).[648]

In 2012, the PCA published a new set of Rules, which effectively consolidate and replace the PCA's existing four sets of rules (although the older rules were not withdrawn and technically remain in existence). The 2012 PCA Rules are similar to the 2010 UNCITRAL Rules, providing greater flexibility to the parties than the PCA's earlier rules, but are also

---

642. M. Hudson, *International Tribunals: Past and Future* 7 (1944). *See* Born, *A New Generation of International Adjudication*, 61 Duke L.J. 775, 796 (2012).

643. Daly, *Permanent Court of Arbitration*, in C. Giorgetti (ed.), *International Litigation in Practice: The Rules, Practice and Jurisprudence of International Courts and Tribunals* 40 (2012).

644. Daly, *Permanent Court of Arbitration*, in C. Giorgetti (ed.), *International Litigation in Practice: The Rules, Practice and Jurisprudence of International Courts and Tribunals* 40-41 (2012).

645. *See* www.pca-cpa.org.

646. Born, *A New Generation of International Adjudication*, 61 Duke L.J. 775, 779 (2012).

647. PCA, *113th Annual Report* 16 (2013).

648. Daly, *Permanent Court of Arbitration*, in C. Giorgetti (ed.), *International Litigation in Practice: The Rules, Practice and Jurisprudence of International Courts and Tribunals* 41 (2012).

specifically tailored to suit cases involving states, state-controlled entities and intergovernmental organizations.

One of the PCA's most significant functions is under the UNCITRAL Rules. As discussed below, the Secretary-General of the PCA serves a *sui generis* function under the UNCITRAL Rules, of designating a suitable appointing authority for the appointment of arbitrators when the parties to an agreement to arbitrate under the UNCITRAL Rules have not agreed upon the arbitrators or an appointing authority.[649] The 2010 UNCITRAL Rules also provide that the parties may designate the Secretary-General of the PCA directly as appointing authority.[650]

Under these provisions of the UNCITRAL Rules, the PCA has frequently designated appointing authorities in international commercial and investment disputes and, in a number of cases, acted directly as appointing authority itself. Among other things, the PCA has considered and resolved a substantial number of challenges to arbitrators, with its decisions frequently being made public.[651] In so doing, the PCA has played a significant and increasingly important role in the formulation of standards of independence and impartiality under the UNCITRAL Rules.

f. Swiss Chambers' Arbitration Institution

Most Swiss cantons have their own local Chamber of Commerce, many of which have administered institutional arbitrations, including international arbitrations.[652] On January 1, 2004, the leading Swiss Chambers of Commerce adopted a unified set of arbitration rules, the Swiss Rules of International Arbitration ("Swiss Rules" or "Swiss International Arbitration Rules"), and designated an Arbitration Committee to oversee arbitrations conducted under the Swiss Rules.[653] A June 1, 2012 revision of the Swiss Rules consolidated the administrative structure by replacing the Arbitration Committee oversight with the Swiss Chambers' Arbitration Institution, an independent association that, similar to the ICC, consists of a Court of Arbitration and Secretariat.[654]

---

649. 2010 UNCITRAL Rules, Art. 6(1).

650. 2010 UNCITRAL Rules, Art. 6.

651. *See Repub. of Mauritius v. U.K. of Great Britain & N. Ireland, Reasoned Decision on Challenge in PCA Case of 30 November 2011*, available at www.pca-cpa.org.

652. These included institutions in Basel, Bern, Geneva, Lausanne, Lugano and Zurich. *See* 2004 Swiss Rules, Introduction (b).

653. These Rules can be found at www.swissarbitration.org. *See also* Habegger, *The Revised Swiss Rules of International Arbitration—An Overview of the Major Changes*, 30(2) ASA Bull. 269 (2012); T. Zuberbühler, C. Müller & P. Habegger (eds.), *Swiss Rules of International Arbitration: Commentary* (2005).

The model Swiss Rules arbitration clause provides:

> "Any dispute, controversy or claim arising out of, or in relation to, this contract, including the validity, invalidity, breach or termination thereof, shall be settled by arbitration in accordance with the Swiss Rules of International Arbitration of the Swiss Chambers' Arbitration Institution in force on the date when the Notice of Arbitration is submitted in accordance with these Rules."

654. The Introduction (b) to the 2012 Swiss Rules describes the Institution as follows:

> "For the purpose of providing arbitration services, the Chambers founded the Swiss Chambers' Arbitration Institution. In order to administer arbitrations under the Swiss Rules, the Swiss Chambers' Arbitration Institution has established the Arbitration Court (hereinafter the 'Court'), which is comprised of experienced international arbitration practitioners. The Court shall render decisions as provided for under these Rules. It may delegate to one or more members or committees the power to take certain decisions pursuant to its Internal Rules. The Court is assisted in its work by the Secretariat of the Court (hereinafter the 'Secretariat')."

g. Singapore International Arbitration Centre ("SIAC")

The Singapore International Arbitration Centre ("SIAC") was established in 1991, initially for disputes arising out of construction, shipping, banking and insurance contracts. More recently, consistent with Singapore's increasing importance as an international commercial and financial center, SIAC has seen a wider range of disputes, including energy, financial, joint venture, sales and other matters.[655] In 2013, 259 new arbitrations were filed with SIAC, compared with 239 new filings in 2012 and 188 new cases in 2011.[656] Arbitrations filed in 2013 involved parties from 50 jurisdictions, with the largest number of non-Singaporean parties coming from India and China.[657] The SIAC Rules are based largely on the UNCITRAL Rules, and were recently revised in 2013.

h. Hong Kong International Arbitration Centre ("HKIAC")

The HKIAC was established in 1985 and had developed into Asia's leading international arbitration institution prior to hand-over of the British administration. On September 1, 2008, HKIAC adopted the HKIAC Administered Arbitration Rules, which are based on the UNCITRAL Rules (although parties are free to agree upon alternative procedural regimes).[658] The HKIAC Rules were revised in 2013, in response to users' comments and developments in other institutional rules.[659] The HKIAC enjoys a substantial caseload (260 cases filed in 2013, 293 in 2012 and 275 in 2011), although there are some debates regarding methodology.[660]

E. ELEMENTS OF INTERNATIONAL ARBITRATION AGREEMENTS

As already discussed, international commercial arbitration is almost always consensual;[661] arbitration generally occurs only pursuant to an arbitration agreement between the parties. There is a small, but important, category of cases in which international investment arbitrations may result without a consensual agreement, by virtue of provisions in international investment protection or other conventions or legislation.[662] This category of arbitrations

---

655. SIAC, *2013 Annual Report* 6 (2014).

656. SIAC, *2013 Annual Report* 6 (2014).

657. SIAC, *2013 Annual Report* 7-9 (2014).

658. The HKIAC's other arbitration rules include the Domestic Arbitration Rules, the Securities Arbitration Rules, the Electronic Transaction Arbitration Rules and the Short Form Arbitration Rules. *See* HKIAC, *Arbitration Rules & Guidelines*, available at www.hkiac.org. The 2008 HKIAC Rules were described as being inspired by the "light touch administered approach" of the Swiss International Rules of Arbitration.

659. *See* 2013 HKIAC Administered Arbitration Rules. The model arbitration provision for the HKIAC Rules provides:

> "Any dispute, controversy, difference or claim arising out of or relating to this contract, including the existence, validity, interpretation, performance, breach or termination thereof or any dispute regarding non-contractual obligations arising out of or relating to it shall be referred to and finally resolved by arbitration administered by the Hong Kong International Arbitration Centre under the Hong Kong International Arbitration Centre Administered Arbitration Rules in force when the Notice of Arbitration is submitted."

660. Of the 260 arbitrations, 75% were international and 25% were domestic; 81 arbitrations of the 260 arbitrations were fully administered by the HKIAC. HKIAC, *2013 Annual Report* 6 (2013).

661. *See supra* pp. 34-35; *United Steelworkers of Am. v. Warrior & Gulf Nav. Co.*, 363 U.S. 574, 582 (1960) ("arbitration is a matter of contract and a party cannot be required to submit to arbitration any dispute which he has not agreed to so submit").

662. *See infra* pp. 511-16.

(without "privity") is unusual, however, and underscores the essential requirement that international arbitration is consensual in character.

It is, of course, possible for parties to agree to submit an existing dispute to arbitration, pursuant to a "submission agreement" or "*compromis*." Typically, however, disputes are arbitrated as a consequence of preexisting arbitration clauses in the parties' underlying commercial contract. In the state-to-state context, agreements to arbitrate are encountered in bilateral and multilateral treaties,[663] as well as in submission agreements providing for the arbitration of disputes that have already arisen.[664]

Both private and state parties are largely free to draft their arbitration agreements in whatever terms they wish and in practice this freedom is liberally exercised. Like other contractual clauses, the terms of arbitration agreements are largely a product of the parties' interests, negotiations and drafting skills.[665]

International arbitration agreements ordinarily—and advisedly—address a number of critical issues. These are: (a) the agreement to arbitrate; (b) the scope of the disputes submitted to arbitration; (c) the use of an arbitral institution and its rules; (d) the seat of the arbitration; (e) the method of appointment, number and qualifications of the arbitrators; (f) the language of the arbitration; and (g) a choice-of-law clause. In particular cases, other provisions may be either vital to an effective international arbitration agreement or advantageous to one or both parties.[666]

1. Agreement to Arbitrate

It is tautological—but unfortunately not always the case in practice—that any arbitration clause must set forth the parties' agreement to arbitrate.[667] As a drafting matter, this means that arbitration agreements should (and usually do) expressly refer to "arbitration"—and not to expert determination, accounting, conciliation, mediation, settlement, "ADR," or some other form of non-judicial resolution.[668] As discussed in greater detail below, these other forms of alternative dispute resolution are not categorized as "arbitration" under many international treaties and national arbitration statutes, and will often not qualify for the "pro-enforcement" safeguards provided by these instruments.[669] Accordingly, a fundamental element of any international arbitration agreement is the parties' undertaking that "all disputes shall be finally resolved *by arbitration*...."

Similarly, most international arbitration agreements provide (and should provide) that disputes should be referred to arbitration for a "binding" or "final" disposition (and not to

---

663. For examples, see the bilateral and multilateral treaties discussed above at pp. 41-44.

664. For examples of submission agreements, *see, e.g.*, the *Alabama Arbitration* and the *Abyei Arbitration, infra* pp. 104-05.

665. There is a substantial body of commentary on drafting arbitration agreements, particularly in the commercial context. *See* Bernardini, *The Arbitration Clause of An International Commercial Contract*, 9(2) J. Int'l Arb. 45 (2002); R. Bishop, *A Practical Guide for Drafting International Arbitration Clauses* (2004); Bond, *How to Draft An Arbitration Clause Revisited*, 1 ICC ICArb. Bull. 14 (1990); G. Born, *International Arbitration and Forum Selection Agreements: Drafting and Enforcing* 37 *et seq.* (4th ed. 2013); P. Friedland, *Arbitration Clauses of International Contracts* (2d ed. 2007); J. Paulsson *et al.*, *The Freshfields Guide to Arbitration and ADR* (3d ed. 2011); Townsend, *Drafting Arbitration Clauses*, 58 Disp. Resol. J. 1 (2003).

666. *See infra* p. 90.

667. The definition of an "arbitration" agreement is discussed below. *See infra* pp. 115-37.

668. *See infra* pp. 132-34.

669. *See infra* pp. 116-37.

an advisory recommendation).[670] An arbitration clause also should not treat arbitration as a possible future option, applicable if the parties so agree after a dispute arises. Thus, arbitration clauses should (and usually do) provide that "all disputes *shall* be *finally resolved* by arbitration...."

2. Scope of Arbitration Agreement

Critical to any arbitration clause is its "scope"—that is, the categories of disputes or claims that will be subject to arbitration. For example, an agreement to arbitrate may provide that all disputes between the parties, bearing any conceivable connection to their contractual relations, are subject to arbitration. Alternatively, the parties may agree that only contract claims that clearly arise under the express terms of the parties' agreement (or particular provisions of that agreement) are to be arbitrated or that particular types of claims are to be excluded from an otherwise broad arbitration agreement.

There are a handful of formulae that are frequently used to define the scope of arbitration clauses.[671] These formulae include "any" or "all" disputes: (i) "arising under this Agreement"; (ii) "arising out of this Agreement"; (iii) "in connection with this Agreement"; and (iv) "relating to this Agreement." Alternative formulations are also used, including: (v) "all disputes relating to this Agreement, including any question regarding its existence, validity, breach or termination"; or (vi) "all disputes relating to this Agreement or the subject matter hereof."[672]

As a general rule, parties draft international arbitration clauses broadly, to cover all disputes having any connection with the parties' dealings. Doing so avoids the expense arising from parallel proceedings (where certain contractual disputes are arbitrated and other contractual, or non-contractual, disputes are litigated).[673] It also avoids the uncertainties resulting from potentially inconsistent judgments and jurisdictional disputes over the scope of the various proceedings.

Even where the parties have agreed in principle to a broad arbitration clause, there may be claims or disputes that one party does *not* want submitted to arbitration. This can include matters such as intellectual property rights or payment obligations, which are sometimes excluded or carved out of the scope of the arbitration clause.[674] Although these types of exclusions can serve legitimate objectives, most parties conclude that it is better to avoid efforts to exclude particular types of disputes from arbitration, except in unusual circumstances. Such exclusions often lead (undesirably) to parallel proceedings in both the arbitral forum and national courts, and to jurisdictional disputes over the application of a clause to particular claims.[675]

---

670. *See infra* pp. 132-33.

671. G. Born, *International Arbitration and Forum Selection Agreements: Drafting and Enforcing* 39 (4th ed. 2013).

672. The interpretation of these formulae is discussed below. *See infra* pp. 517-34.

673. *See infra* pp. 320-34, 528.

674. For examples of exclusions for particular types of issues, *see* G. Born, *International Arbitration and Forum Selection Agreements: Drafting and Enforcing* 42-44 (4th ed. 2013).

675. *See infra* pp. 517-34.

3. Institutional Versus Ad Hoc Arbitration

As discussed above, institutional arbitration is conducted pursuant to procedural rules promulgated by a particular arbitration institution, which generally also "administers" the arbitration.[676] If institutional arbitration is desired, the parties' arbitration agreement must select and refer to an arbitral institution and its rules. In general, every arbitral institution provides its own model arbitration clause; parties wishing to invoke the institution's rules should ordinarily use this clause as the basis for their agreement, departing from it only with care and for considered reasons.[677]

In cases where the parties do not wish to agree to institutional arbitration, they will sometimes select a preexisting set of procedural rules designed for *ad hoc* arbitrations (such as the UNCITRAL Rules).[678] Arbitration clauses frequently accomplish this result by references such as "all disputes shall be settled by arbitration in accordance with the UNCITRAL Arbitration Rules...."

4. Seat or Place of Arbitration

Another vital element of any international arbitration agreement is designation of the "seat" (or "place") of the arbitration.[679] This is the state where the arbitration has its formal legal or juridical seat, and where the arbitral award will formally be made.[680] It is also the place where many or all of the hearings in the arbitration will be conducted, although the tribunal may generally hold hearings elsewhere for reasons of convenience.[681] The text of contractual provisions selecting the arbitral seat is not complex, usually providing only "The seat of the arbitration shall be...."

As discussed below, there are a number of legal and practical consequences that follow from selection of an arbitral seat, making this one of the most important aspects of any international arbitration agreement.[682] These consequences include influencing the choice of law governing the arbitration agreement, the selection of the procedural law of the arbitration and the national courts responsible for applying that law, the selection of the national courts responsible for issues relating to constitution of the tribunal and the selection of the national courts responsible for (and arbitration law applicable to) annulment of arbitral awards.[683] All of these issues are of substantial importance to the arbitral process (which contrasts with domestic arbitration in many countries, where the selection of an arbitral seat is much less important).

5. Number, Method of Selection and Qualifications of Arbitrators

It is also common for international arbitration agreements to address the number, means of appointment and qualifications of the arbitrators. As discussed below, selection of the ar-

---

676. *See supra* pp. 70-72.

677. These model clauses are reproduced at G. Born, *International Arbitration and Forum Selection Agreements: Drafting and Enforcing* Appx. C (4th ed. 2013).

678. *See* G. Born, *International Arbitration and Forum Selection Agreements: Drafting and Enforcing* 60-61, 63-64 (4th ed. 2013); *infra* pp. 72-74.

679. *See infra* pp. 599-625 for a discussion of the concept of arbitral seat.

680. *See infra* pp. 599-600, 619-23.

681. *See infra* pp. 622-24.

682. *See infra* pp. 620-24.

683. *See infra* pp. 304-08, 619-24 for a discussion of these legal consequences.

bitrators is one of the most critical issues in any arbitration.[684] Addressing this issue in the arbitration agreement is a vitally-important precaution.

Arbitration clauses often specify the number of persons who will comprise an arbitral tribunal in the event of future disputes. If the parties do not agree upon the number of arbitrators, leading institutional arbitration rules generally grant the institution power to do so; otherwise, national courts will have the power to decide, pursuant to default rules in national arbitration legislation.[685] Nonetheless, relying on a judicial or institutional decision regarding the number of arbitrators can result in delays or jurisdictional disputes. As a consequence, parties often specify the number of arbitrators in their arbitration clause.

The text of provisions designating the number of arbitrators is not complex. For example, a typical clause would provide: "Any dispute shall be finally resolved under the [—Rules] by [three arbitrators][one arbitrator] appointed in accordance with the said Rules." An alternative provides: "The number of arbitrators shall be [three][one]."[686]

It is also essential for an arbitration agreement to include some method for selecting the arbitrator(s) if the parties cannot agree upon their identities. The most common such mechanism is designation of an "appointing authority," which will select a sole arbitrator or presiding arbitrator in the event that the parties (or party-nominated arbitrators) cannot do so, or if a party fails to select a party-nominated arbitrator.[687] All leading institutional arbitration rules provide for such a role by the sponsoring institution when the parties agree to arbitrate under an institution's rules,[688] and no special wording (aside from adopting the institution's rules) is necessary to select the institution as appointing authority.

Finally, international arbitration agreements can either directly specify or indirectly influence the qualifications and characteristics of the arbitrators.[689] For example, most leading institutional arbitration rules provide that a presiding or sole arbitrator shall not have the same nationality as that of any of the parties (unless otherwise agreed).[690] An arbitration agreement can also require (or prohibit) the appointment of persons with legal qualifications, or can require particular credentials or expertise (such as accounting degrees or engineering experience).[691]

---

684. *See infra* pp. 694-95; G. Born, *International Arbitration and Forum Selection Agreements: Drafting and Enforcing* 70 (4th ed. 2013).

685. *See infra* p. 688.

686. G. Born, *International Arbitration and Forum Selection Agreements: Drafting and Enforcing* 74 (4th ed. 2013).

687. *See infra* pp. 695-702.

688. *See infra* pp. 695-702; 2010 UNCITRAL Rules, Art. 6; 2012 ICC Rules, Arts. 8, 11-13; 2014 ICDR Rules, Art. 12. An institution will also appoint an arbitrator on behalf of a party that fails to exercise its right under the parties' arbitration agreement to do so. 2012 ICC Rules, Arts. 12(3)-(5), (8); 2014 ICDR Rules, Art. 12(6); 2014 LCIA Rules, Art. 7(2).

689. *See infra* pp. 709-16.

690. 2012 ICC Rules, Art. 13(5); 2014 LCIA Rules, Art. 6(1). *Compare* 2013 AAA Rules, Rule 15; 2014 ICDR Rules, Art. 12(4).

691. G. Born, *International Arbitration and Forum Selection Agreements: Drafting and Enforcing* 75 (4th ed. 2013). Such provisions are often *sui generis*, providing "each arbitrator shall be a Certified Public Accountant" or "the arbitrators shall be practicing lawyers." International arbitration clauses may also require particular language abilities, such as "each arbitrator shall be fluent in Spanish."

6. *Language of Arbitration*

Arbitration clauses in international agreements also frequently specify the language (or languages) of the arbitral proceedings and award.[692] Although sometimes overlooked, this is a point of vital importance, which can have a profound practical effect on the selection of the arbitrators and the character of the arbitral proceedings.

Absent the parties' agreement, institutional rules usually expressly authorize the arbitral tribunal to select the language(s) of the arbitration.[693] This will often be the language of the underlying contract or arbitration agreement. Even if institutional rules do not address the issue, national law will ordinarily give the tribunal authority to select a language for the arbitration.[694] Nonetheless, there is seldom any reason to leave this issue to chance, particularly given the simplicity of a provision to the effect that "the language of the arbitration shall be [English]."

7. *Choice-of-Law Clauses*

International arbitration can give rise to tortuous choice-of-law questions. As a consequence, many arbitration agreements are accompanied by a choice-of-law clause, specifying the substantive law applicable to the parties' underlying contract and related disputes.[695]

In addition to the substantive law governing the parties' underlying contract, other questions of applicable law frequently arise in connection with international arbitrations. Thus, as discussed in detail below, a different law may apply to the arbitration agreement (as distinguished from the parties' underlying contract); that is because an arbitration clause will be deemed a "separable" or "autonomous" contract in most legal systems, that may not be subject to the same substantive law as the underlying contract.[696] It is possible, and occasionally advisable, to adopt a choice-of-law clause that specifically addresses the law applicable to the arbitration agreement, as distinct from the parties' underlying contract.

It is also possible for a different law to apply to the procedural conduct of the arbitration itself, separate from that governing the arbitration agreement or underlying contract.[697] In most cases, the procedural law of the arbitration will be that of the arbitral seat, although there are rare exceptions.[698]

---

692. G. Born, *International Arbitration and Forum Selection Agreements: Drafting and Enforcing* 73-74 (4th ed. 2013).

693. 2010 UNCITRAL Rules, Art. 19; 2012 ICC Rules, Art. 20; 2014 ICDR Rules, Art. 18.

694. *See infra* p. 816.

695. For a discussion of the drafting of such choice-of-law clauses, *see* G. Born, *International Arbitration and Forum Selection Agreements: Drafting and Enforcing* 79-80 (4th ed. 2013).

696. *See infra* pp. 190-218.

697. *See infra* pp. 625-40.

698. *See infra* pp. 637-40. Parties sometimes include choice-of-law provisions that designate the procedural law applicable to arbitral proceedings. Significant complexities can arise from such provisions, and great care must be taken in utilizing them. *See infra* pp. 639-40; G. Born, *International Arbitration and Forum Selection Agreements: Drafting and Enforcing* 64-66 (4th ed. 2013).

8. Other Provisions of International Arbitration Agreements

Many international arbitration agreements contain other provisions in addition to the essential elements discussed above. The existence and nature of these provisions varies from case to case, depending on the parties' negotiations, drafting and interests. The most common additional elements include: (a) costs of legal representation; (b) interest and currency of an award; (c) disclosure or discovery powers of tribunal; (d) fast-track or other procedural rules, including so-called escalation clauses; (e) state/sovereign immunity waivers; and (f) confidentiality.[699]

F. OVERVIEW OF CHOICE OF LAW IN INTERNATIONAL COMMERCIAL ARBITRATION

Parties frequently agree to arbitration to avoid the jurisdictional and choice-of-law uncertainties that arise when international disputes are litigated in national courts. Unfortunately, international commercial arbitration can produce its own set of complex, often unpredictable choice-of-law issues. (Choice-of-law uncertainties tend to be less significant in inter-state and investment arbitrations, where international law at least nominally provides a single, uniform substantive legal regime governing the parties' dispute.)

Choice-of-law issues play an important role in international commercial arbitration. It is necessary to distinguish between four separate choice-of-law issues that can arise in connection with an international arbitration: (a) the substantive law governing the merits of the parties' underlying contract and other claims; (b) the substantive law governing the parties' arbitration agreement; (c) the law applicable to the arbitral proceedings (also called the "procedural law of the arbitration," the "curial law" or the "*lex arbitri*"); and (d) the conflict of laws rules applicable to select each of the foregoing laws.[700] Although not common, it is possible for each of these four issues to be governed by a different national (or other) law.

Each of the foregoing choice-of-law issues can have a vital influence on international arbitral proceedings. Different national laws provide different—sometimes dramatically different—rules applicable at different stages of the arbitral process. Understanding which national rules will potentially be applicable can therefore be critical.

1. Law Applicable to Substance of Parties' Dispute

The parties' underlying dispute will ordinarily[701] be resolved under the rules of substantive law of a particular national legal system. In the first instance, it will usually be the arbitrators who determine the substantive law applicable to the parties' dispute. As discussed in

---

699. G. Born, *International Arbitration and Forum Selection Agreements: Drafting and Enforcing* 82-110 (4th ed. 2013); *infra* pp. 109-10, 471-72, 544, 791, 830-39, 851-70.

700. For a more detailed discussion, *see infra* pp. 287-315, 619-22, 625-40, 961-1021. Additional sub-categories arise, for example, with regard to aspects of the law governing the arbitration agreement (*e.g.,* the law governing issues of formal validity, substantive validity, capacity, interpretation) or the arbitral proceedings (*e.g.,* the law governing the arbitrator's contract, the availability of provisional relief, privileges). *See infra* pp. 375-92, 393-474, 499-502, 517-34. 575-88, 828-29, 876, 888-89.

701. Parties sometimes agree to permit arbitrators to resolve their dispute without reference to law, that is, *ex aequo et bono* or as *amiable compositeur, see infra* pp. 1020-21, or by reference to a non-national legal system, *see infra* pp. 1018-20.

detail below, international arbitral awards typically give effect to the parties' agreements concerning applicable substantive law ("choice-of-law clauses").[702] The principal exception is where mandatory national laws or public policies purport to override private contractual arrangements.

Where the parties have not agreed upon the substantive law governing their dispute, the arbitral tribunal must select such a law. In so doing, the tribunal will sometimes (but not always) refer to some set of national or international conflict of laws rules. These varying approaches to the choice of substantive law in international arbitration are summarized here and examined in detail below.[703]

Although the historical practice was to apply the national conflict of laws rules of the arbitral seat, more recent practice is diverse. Some tribunals and commentators adhere to the traditional approach, while others look to the conflicts rules of all states having a connection with the dispute; additionally, some authorities adopt either international conflict of laws rules or validation principles.[704]

2. Law Applicable to Arbitration Agreement

As discussed elsewhere, arbitration agreements are universally regarded as presumptively "separable" from the underlying contract in which they appear.[705] One consequence of this is that the parties' arbitration agreement may be governed by a different national law than that applicable to the underlying contract. This can occur either by the parties' express choice of law or by the application of conflict of laws rules (which may select different substantive laws for the parties' arbitration agreement and their underlying contract).

As described below, four alternatives for the law governing an arbitration agreement are of particular importance: (a) the law chosen by the parties to govern the arbitration agreement itself; (b) the law of the arbitral seat; (c) the law governing the parties' underlying contract; and (d) international principles, either applied as a substantive body of contract law (as in France) or as rules of non-discrimination (as in most U.S. authority).[706]

3. Procedural Law Applicable to Arbitral Proceedings

The arbitral proceedings themselves are also subject to legal rules, governing both "internal" procedural matters and "external" relations between the arbitration and national courts. In most instances, the law governing the arbitral proceeding is the arbitration statute of the arbitral seat (*i.e.*, the location selected by the parties as the juridical place of arbitration).[707]

Among other things, the law of the arbitral seat typically deals with such issues as the appointment and qualifications of arbitrators, the qualifications and professional respon-

702. *See infra* pp. 983-92; UNCITRAL Model Law, Art. 28(1); 2010 UNCITRAL Rules, Art. 35(1).

703. *See infra* pp. 962-83.

704. *See infra* pp. 970-76. There is also authority supporting an arbitral tribunal's "direct" application of substantive rules of law, purportedly without prior recourse to any set of conflict of laws rules. *See infra* p. 976.

705. *See infra* pp. 190-218.

706. *See infra* pp. 287-315 for a discussion of the choice of law applicable to the arbitration agreement.

707. *See infra* pp. 619-21, 625-26, 637-38. Parties sometimes agree that hearings may be conducted somewhere other than the arbitral seat, for convenience, but this in principle is virtually never held to change the procedural law governing the arbitration. *See infra* pp. 624-38.

sibilities of parties' legal representatives, the extent of judicial intervention in the arbitral process, the availability of provisional relief, the procedural conduct of the arbitration, the form of any award and the standards for annulment of any award. Different national laws take significantly different approaches to these various issues. In some countries, national law imposes significant limits or requirements on the conduct of the arbitration[708] and local courts have broad powers to supervise arbitral proceedings.[709] Elsewhere, and in most developed jurisdictions, local law affords international arbitrators virtually unfettered freedom to conduct the arbitral process—subject only to basic requirements of procedural regularity ("due process" or "natural justice").[710]

In some jurisdictions, parties are free to select the law governing the arbitral proceedings.[711] This includes, in many cases, the freedom to agree to the application of a different procedural law than that of the arbitral seat. This seldom occurs in practice, and the effects of such an agreement are uncertain.[712]

4. Choice-of-Law Rules Applicable in International Arbitration

Selecting each of the bodies of law identified in the foregoing three sections—the laws applicable to the merits of the underlying contract or dispute, to the arbitration agreement and to the arbitral proceedings—ordinarily requires application of conflict of laws rules. In order to select the substantive law governing the parties' dispute, for example, the arbitral tribunal must ordinarily apply a conflict of laws system. And, just as different states have different rules of substantive law, they also have different conflict of laws rules. An international arbitral tribunal must therefore decide at the outset what set of conflicts rules to apply.

The actual practice of arbitral tribunals in selecting the law applicable to each of the foregoing issues varies significantly. Approaches include application of (a) the arbitral seat's conflict of laws rules; (b) "international" conflict of laws rules, either as a comprehensive choice-of-law system or as international principles of non-discrimination; (c) successive application of the conflict of laws rules of all interested states; and (d) "direct" application of substantive law (without any express conflicts analysis).[713]

The current state of conflict of laws analysis in international arbitration has not kept pace with the parties' aim of avoiding the peculiar jurisdictional, choice-of-law and enforcement difficulties that attend the litigation of international disputes in national courts. There is often uncertainty, and wasted time and expense, as a consequence of contemporary conflict of laws analysis. Nonetheless, as discussed in greater detail below, recent national court decisions and arbitral awards suggest the way towards development of in-

---

708. For example, foreign lawyers may not be permitted to appear in arbitrations conducted on national territory, *see infra* pp. 1029-35, arbitrators may be prohibited from ordering discovery, administering oaths, or granting provisional relief, *see infra* pp. 831-35, 873-75, 1035 or detailed procedural requirements or time schedules may be mandatorily applicable, *see infra* pp. 790-91.

709. *See infra* pp. 806-10.

710. The United States, England, Switzerland, France, Singapore and Hong Kong generally fall within this latter category.

711. *See infra* pp. 633-37 for a discussion of the choice of law applicable to the arbitral proceedings.

712. *See infra* pp. 637-40.

713. *See infra* pp. 969-76.

ternational principles of validation and non-discrimination that hold promise of realizing more fully the aspirations of the international arbitral process.[714]

G. OVERVIEW OF SOURCES OF INFORMATION ABOUT INTERNATIONAL ARBITRATION

One of the perceived benefits of international arbitration is its confidentiality or, at least, privacy.[715] Most international arbitral awards, and the submissions, hearings and deliberations in almost all international arbitrations, remain confidential. Although it has benefits, the confidentiality or privacy of the arbitral process is at the same time an obstacle to practitioners, decision-makers and academics, all of whom frequently desire precedent, authority or information about the arbitral process.

There are a wide variety of sources of information about international commercial arbitration that are useful for both practitioners and academics.[716] The number and detail of these sources has increased materially in recent years, and new projects are underway that would further expand the corpus of available information concerning the international arbitral process.

1. ICCA Yearbook of Commercial Arbitration and Handbooks

The *Yearbook of Commercial Arbitration* is published annually by the International Council for Commercial Arbitration. The *Yearbook* contains excerpts of arbitration awards (usually redacted), national arbitration legislation, judicial decisions and other materials relevant to international arbitration. The *Yearbook* is supplemented by handbooks on national arbitration legislation, containing international arbitration statutes from jurisdictions around the world.

2. Mealey's International Arbitration Reports

Since 1986, Mealey Publications has published a monthly summary of recent judicial decisions concerning international arbitration and arbitral awards. The *International Arbitration Report* is a source of timely information (including an email service) and provides full-text copies of significant awards and decisions. The Report's primary focus is U.S., but it increasingly includes authorities from other jurisdictions.

3. Journal du Droit International (Clunet)

Published in French, the *Journal du Droit International* reprints excerpts and summaries of arbitral awards and French judicial decisions concerning international arbitration and other private international law subjects. The *Journal* is a significant source of extracts of otherwise unavailable arbitral awards, often with comments by leading French practitioners or academics.

---

714. *See infra* pp. 306-08, 990.

715. *See infra* pp. 866-70.

716. There is extensive commentary on international arbitration. For bibliographies, *see, e.g.*, Hiramoto, *A Path to Resources on International Commercial Arbitration 1980-1986*, 4 Int'l Tax & Bus. Law. 297 (1986); Pechota, *Commercial Arbitration: An International Bibliography* (1992); S. Strong, *Research and Practice in International Commercial Arbitration: Sources and Strategies* (2009).

4. *Revue de l'Arbitrage*

Published four times a year, in French, the *Revue de l'Arbitrage* contains articles relating to international and domestic arbitration as well as commentary of French judicial decisions and arbitral awards. The *Revue* was founded in 1955 and was for many years directed by the late Professor Philippe Fouchard and Charles Jarrosson.

5. *Arbitration International*

Arbitration International is a journal, published quarterly since 1985 by the LCIA. It provides commentary on international commercial arbitration, with a particular focus on Europe and England.

6. *ASA Bulletin*

The *Bulletin* of the Swiss Arbitration Association ("ASA") is published quarterly. Available from Kluwer Law International, it contains excerpts of Swiss (and other) judicial decisions dealing with international arbitration, arbitral awards and commentary on recent developments.

7. *Collection of ICC Arbitral Awards*

Six volumes of ICC awards rendered between 1974 and 2011 have been published. The collections cover awards made between 1974-1985, 1986-1990, 1991-1995 1996-2000, 2001-2007 and 2008-2011.[717] In addition, the ICC has published a collection of procedural decisions in ICC arbitrations between 1993 and 1996.[718] Each collection includes excerpts or summaries of approximately 150 ICC arbitral awards, in both French and English. The excerpts are edited to avoid identifying the parties to the dispute. Many of the awards were previously published in the *Yearbook of Commercial Arbitration* or *Journal du Droit International (Clunet)*, but the collections are a convenient reference source. The ICC promises comparable collections in the future.

8. *International Legal Materials*

Sponsored by the American Society of International Law, the *International Legal Materials* are published six times each year. They contain a wide range of international legal documents, and do not focus specifically on arbitration. They are, however, a useful source of significant developments—legislative, judicial and otherwise—in the arbitration field.

9. *Born on International Commercial Arbitration*

A leading international commentary on international commercial arbitration published in 2009, with a second edition in 2014. *International Commercial Arbitration* is the work of the author of this casebook.

---

717. J.-J. Arnaldez, Y. Derains & D. Hascher (eds.), *Collection of ICC Arbitral Awards 2008-2011* (2013); J.-J. Arnaldez, Y. Derains & D. Hascher (eds.), *Collection of ICC Arbitral Awards 2001-2007* (2009); J. Arnaldez, Y. Derains & D. Hascher (eds.), *Collection of ICC Arbitral Awards 1996-2000* (2003); J. Arnaldez, Y. Derains & D. Hascher (eds.), *Collection of ICC Arbitral Awards 1990-1995* (1997); SS. Jarvin, Y. Derains & J. Arnaldez (eds.), *Collection of ICC Arbitral Awards 1986-1990* (1994); Jarvin & Y. Derains (eds.), *Collection of ICC Arbitral Awards 1974-1985* (1990).

718. D. Hascher (ed.), *Collection of Procedural Decisions in ICC Arbitration 1993-1996* (1997).

10. Fouchard Gaillard Goldman on International Commercial Arbitration

The leading French commentary on international commercial arbitration, published in 1999 in English, is authored by a distinguished French professor and practitioner, together with a very able colleague. In addition to providing encyclopedic discussions of French international arbitration law and practice, the work also offers insightful comment on more general developments.

11. Redfern and Hunter on International Arbitration

The leading English commentary on international commercial arbitration, *Law and Practice of International Commercial Arbitration*, is in its fifth edition. Authored by two respected English practitioners, now assisted by able co-authors, the book is required reading for any lawyer involved in international arbitration.

12. Commentary on International Chamber of Commerce Arbitration

International Chamber of Commerce Arbitration is authored by three experienced practitioners and commentators. The book is a comprehensive work on ICC arbitration, which was first published in 1984, and most recently revised and updated in 2000 to address the 1998 ICC Rules. The work is useful to any practitioner in an ICC arbitration, and contains commentary on the ICC rules, with shrewd practical observations.

Yves Derains and Eric Schwartz (both of whom held the office of Secretary General of the ICC International Court of Arbitration) have published *A Guide to the ICC Rules of Arbitration*, now in its second edition. The work is thoroughly researched and provides valuable practical guidance regarding the 1998 ICC Rules.

More recently, three former members of the Secretariat of the ICC International Court of Arbitration published *The Secretariat's Guide to ICC Arbitration*. The *Guide* provides a practical commentary on the 2012 ICC Rules and contains detailed and helpful guidance on the ICC Secretariat's and Court's application of the Rules. Other useful works on ICC arbitration have also recently been published.[719]

13. Commentary on New York Convention

Albert van den Berg's *The New York Arbitration Convention of 1958* is the leading work on the New York Convention. The author is a distinguished Dutch academic and practitioner, and his work assembles in a single source detailed commentary and materials relating to the New York Convention. Although the book's effort to annotate the Convention's various articles with judicial decisions is now dated (from 1981), it remains required reading on the subject. Several recent commentaries have also been published on the New York Convention, updating and expanding on Professor van den Berg's work.[720]

Giorgio Gaja's work on *The New York Convention* is an exhaustive compilation of the materials relevant to the negotiation and drafting of the Convention. Ideal for detailed research on particular aspects of the Convention, the book provides the successive drafts of

---

719. *See* M. Bühler & T. Webster, *Handbook of ICC Arbitration: Commentary, Precedents, Materials* (2d ed. 2008); E. Schäfer, H. Verbist & C. Imhoos, *ICC Arbitration in Practice* (2005).

720. H. Kronke *et al.*, *Recognition and Enforcement of Foreign Arbitral Awards: A Global Commentary on the New York Convention* (2010); R. Wolff (ed.), *New York Convention on the Recognition and Enforcement of Foreign Arbitral Awards: Commentary* (2012).

the Convention, the comments and questions of participating states, and various interim reports.

14. A Guide to the UNCITRAL Model Law on International Commercial Arbitration

Howard Holtzmann and Joseph Neuhaus have contributed a painstaking study of the UNCITRAL Model Law and its history. Particularly as the Model Law gains in adherents, the *Guide* will become a standard reference source for practitioners and courts.

15. International Arbitration Law Databases

There are several useful databases providing online access to both source materials and recent decisions under the New York Convention and/or UNCITRAL Model Law. UNCITRAL maintains a searchable, online database of publicly-available court decisions regarding the various instruments that have been produced by the Commission, including the New York Convention and the UNCITRAL Model Law on International Commercial Arbitration.[721] UNCITRAL also hosts an online "Guide" to the New York Convention that contains recent decisions by courts of Contracting States under the Convention, together with various basic documents relating to the Convention and its *travaux préparatoires*.[722] Other institutions have also recently launched online databases providing access to international arbitration materials and decisions.

16. KluwerArbitration and Kluwer Arbitration Blog

Released by Kluwer Law International, the KluwerArbitration online service contains an extensive, computer-searchable library of arbitral awards, judicial decisions and commentary. The Kluwer Arbitration Blog provides brief, topical articles and essays on international arbitration with online comments.

17. Global Arbitration Review

Billing itself as the "world's leading international arbitration journal," the *Global Arbitration Review* publishes (online and by email) five editions a week about topical developments in international commercial and investment arbitration. It also publishes periodic articles and commentary by arbitration practitioners and hosts live events at which international arbitration issues are debated.

18. Draft ALI Restatement of International Commercial Arbitration Law

The American Law Institute is preparing a *Restatement Third, The U.S. Law of International Commercial Arbitration*. The Reporters of the project are Professor George Bermann, Professor Jack Coe, Professor Chris Drahozal and Professor Catherine Rogers. The *Restatement* can be expected to have significant impact on U.S. international arbitration law.

---

721. *Case Law on UNCITRAL Texts: UNCITRAL Model Law on International Commercial Arbitration*, available at www.uncitral.org/uncitral/en/case_law.
722. *See* www.newyorkconvention1958.org.

PART I
INTERNATIONAL ARBITRATION AGREEMENTS

CHAPTER 2

LEGAL FRAMEWORK FOR INTERNATIONAL ARBITRATION AGREEMENTS

This chapter addresses the legal framework applicable to international arbitration agreements. First, the chapter examines the advantages and disadvantages of international arbitration, as compared with other modes of dispute resolution. Second, the chapter considers the various "jurisdictional requirements" of the New York Convention and leading national arbitration statutes (such as the UNCITRAL Model Law), as they apply to international arbitration agreements.[1] In particular, the chapter addresses the definitional issue of what constitutes an "arbitration agreement," an "international" arbitration agreement, a "commercial" relationship, and a "difference" or "dispute," as well as the New York Convention's reciprocity requirement.

A. REASONS FOR INTERNATIONAL ARBITRATION

Why is it that parties choose to resolve their international commercial (and other) disputes by "arbitration"? Nations and other political organizations provide courts, administrative tribunals and other forms of dispute resolution, sometimes specialized for commercial disputes. What aspects of the process of "arbitration" induce parties to forego use of these mechanisms of dispute resolution and instead to submit to decisions by international arbitral tribunals?[2] The materials excerpted below provide a variety of perspectives, from different historical periods, to these questions.

W. CRUM & G. STEINDORFF, *KOPTISCHE RECHTSURKUNDEN AUS DJEME*
pp. 835-37 (1912)

We fought each other before the most famous *comes, dioketes* [administrative tribunals] of the *castron* [district] of Jeme, about the house on Kuelol street…. After much altercation before the *dioketes*, he made a proposal on which we all agreed: we elected arbitrators from the *castron* and the *dioketes* sent them into the house and they made the division.

---

1. The jurisdictional requirements of the New York Convention (and other international conventions) and national arbitration statutes, as applied to arbitral awards, are discussed below. *See infra* pp. 1070-99. These requirements largely parallel those applicable to international arbitration agreements.

2. *See* G. Born, *International Commercial Arbitration* 73-93 (2d ed. 2014); C. Drahozal & R. Naimark (eds.), *Towards A Science of International Arbitration: Collected Empirical Research* (2005); Drahozal & Ware, *Why Do Businesses Use (and Not Use) Arbitration Clauses?*, 25 Ohio St. J. Disp. Resol. 433, 449 (2010); Queen Mary, University of London, *2013 International Arbitration Survey: Corporate Choices in International Arbitration* (2013).

M. BLOCH, *FEUDAL SOCIETY*
p. 359 (1961)

The most serious cases could be heard in many different courts exercising parallel juris-diction. Undoubtedly there were certain rules which, in theory, determined the limits of competence of the various courts; but in spite of them uncertainty persisted. The feudal records that have come down to us abound in charters relating to disputes between rival jurisdictions. Despairing of knowing before which authority to bring their suits, litigants often agreed to set up arbitrators of their own or else, instead of seeking a court judgment, they preferred to come to a private agreement.... Even if one had obtained a favourable decision there was often no other way to get it executed than to come to terms with a re-calcitrant opponent.

N.Y. WEEKLY POST-BOY
(May 20, 1751)

[L]et me tell you that after you have expended large Sums of Money, and squander'd away a deal of Time & Attendance on your lawyers, and Preparations for Hearings one Term after another, you will probably be of another Mind, and be glad *Seven Years* hence to leave it to that Arbitration which you now refuse.

TRANSPARENCY INTERNATIONAL, *GLOBAL CORRUPTION BAROMETER 2013*
pp. 3, 11, 17 (2014)

[Transparency International's *Global Corruption Barometer 2013*] examines how corrup-tion features in people's lives around the world. Drawing on the results of a Transparency International survey of more than 114,000 respondents in 107 countries, it addresses peo-ple's direct experiences with bribery and details their views on corruption in the main in-stitutions in their countries.... As the [Report] shows, corruption is seen to be running through the foundations of the democratic and legal process in many countries, affecting public trust in political parties, the judiciary and the police, among other key institutions.... Among the eight services evaluated, the police and the judiciary are seen as the two most bribery prone. For those interacting with the judiciary, ... 24% [report having paid a bribe]....

Bribery rates by service: Percentage of people who have paid a bribe to each service (average across 95 countries[3])
In the past 12 months, when you or anyone living in your household had a contact or contacts with one of eight services, have you paid a bribe in any form?

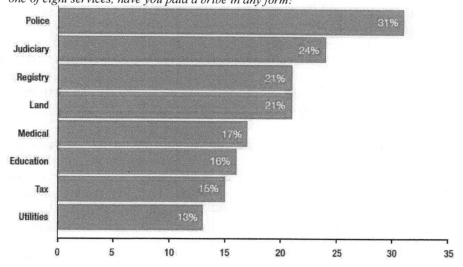

Reported bribes paid to the judiciary have increased significantly [compared with the 2010/2011 Report] in some parts of the world going up by more than 20% in Ghana, Indonesia, Mozambique, Solomon Islands and Taiwan.... In 20 countries [Afghanistan, Albania, Algeria, Armenia, Azerbaijan, Bulgaria, Cambodia, Croatia, Democratic Republic of the Congo, Georgia, Kosovo, Kyrgyzstan, Lithuania, Madagascar, Moldova, Peru, Serbia, Slovakia, Tanzania and Ukraine], people believe the judiciary to be the most corrupt institution. In these countries [where data was available], an average of 30% of people who came into contact with the judiciary report having paid a bribe.

LOEWEN GROUP v. UNITED STATES OF AMERICA
Award in ICSID Case No. ARB(AF)/98/3 (NAFTA) of 26 June 2003

This dispute arises out of litigation brought against first Claimant, the Loewen Group, Inc. ("TLGI") and the Loewen Group International, Inc. ("LGII") (collectively called "Loewen"), its principal United States subsidiary, in Mississippi State Court by Jeremiah O'Keefe Sr. (Jerry O'Keefe), his son and various companies owned by the O'Keefe family (collectively called "O'Keefe"). The litigation arose out of a commercial dispute between O'Keefe and Loewen which were competitors in the funeral home and funeral insurance business in Mississippi. The dispute concerned three contracts between O'Keefe and Loewen said to be valued by O'Keefe at $980,000 and an exchange of two O'Keefe funeral homes said to be worth $2.5 million for a Loewen insurance company worth $4 million approximately. The action was heard by Judge Graves (an African-American judge) and a jury. Of the twelve jurors, eight were African-American.

---

3. Data from the following countries was excluded due to validity concerns: Albania, Azerbaijan, Brazil, Burundi, Fiji, France, Germany, Lebanon, Luxembourg, Malawi, Russia and Zambia.

The Mississippi jury awarded O'Keefe $500 million damages, including $75 million damages for emotional distress and $400 million punitive damages. The verdict was the outcome of a seven-week trial in which, according to Claimants, the trial judge repeatedly allowed O'Keefe's attorneys to make extensive irrelevant and highly prejudicial references (i) to Claimants' foreign nationality (which was contrasted to O'Keefe's Mississippi roots); (ii) race-based distinctions between O'Keefe and Loewen; and (iii) class-based distinctions between Loewen (which O'Keefe counsel portrayed as large wealthy corporations) and O'Keefe (who was portrayed as running family-owned businesses). Further, according to Claimants, after permitting those references, the trial judge refused to give an instruction to the jury stating clearly that nationality-based, racial and class-based discrimination was impermissible....

Having read the transcript and having considered the submissions of the parties with respect to the conduct of the trial, we have reached the firm conclusion that the conduct of the trial by the trial judge was so flawed that it constituted a miscarriage of justice amounting to a manifest injustice as that expression is understood in international law....

O'Keefe's case at trial was conducted from beginning to end on the basis that Jerry O'Keefe, a war hero and "fighter for his country," who epitomised local business interests, was the victim of a ruthless foreign (Canadian) corporate predator. There were many references on the part of O'Keefe's counsel and witnesses to the Canadian nationality of Loewen ("Ray Loewen and his group from Canada"). Likewise, O'Keefe witnesses said that Loewen was financed by Asian money, these statements being based on the fact that Loewen was partly financed by the Hong Kong and Shanghai Bank, an English and Hong Kong bank which was erroneously described by Jerry O'Keefe in evidence as the "Shanghai Bank." Indeed, Jerry O'Keefe, endeavouring to justify an earlier advertising campaign in which O'Keefe had depicted its business under American and Mississippi flags and Loewen under Canadian and Japanese flags, stated that the Japanese may well control both the "Shanghai Bank" and Loewen but he did not know that. O'Keefe's strategy of presenting the case in this way was linked to Jerry O'Keefe's fighting for his country against the Japanese and the exhortation in the closing address of Mr Gary (lead counsel for O'Keefe) to the jury to do their duty as Americans and Mississippians. This strategy was calculated to appeal to the jury's sympathy for local home-town interests as against the wealthy and powerful foreign competitor.

Several additional examples will serve to illustrate this strategy. In the *voir dire* and opening statements, Mr Gary stated that he had "teamed up" with Mississippi lawyers "to represent one of your own, Jerry O'Keefe and his family." Mr Gary also stated: "The Loewen Group, Ray Loewen, Ray Loewen is not here to-day. The Loewen Group is from Canada. He's not here to-day. Do you think that every person should be responsible and should step up to the plate and face their own actions? Let me see a show of hands if you feel that everybody in America should have the responsibility to do that." Whilst the conduct of the *voir dire* may not in itself have been conspicuously out of line with practice in Mississippi State courts, the skilful use by counsel for Claimants of the opportunity to implant inflammatory and prejudicial materials in the minds of the jury set the tone for the trial when it actually began.

In the *voir dire* O'Keefe's counsel sought an assurance from potential jurors that they would be willing to award heavy damages. Once again, in their opening statements, O'Keefe's counsel urged the jury to exercise "the power of the people of Mississippi" to award massive damages. O'Keefe's counsel drew a contrast between O'Keefe's Mississippi antecedents and Loewen's "descent on the State of Mississippi."

Emphasis was constantly given to the Mississippi antecedents and connections of O'Keefe's witnesses. By way of contrast Mr Gary, in cross-examination of Raymond Loewen, repeatedly referred to his Canadian nationality, noted that he had not "spent time" in Mississippi and questioned him about foreign and local funeral home ownership. Jerry O'Keefe, in his evidence, pointed out that Loewen was a foreign corporation, its "payroll checks come out of Canada" and "their invoices are printed in Canada."

An extreme example of appeals to anti-Canadian prejudice was evidence given by Mr Espy, former United States Secretary of State for Agriculture who, called to give evidence of the good character of Jerry O'Keefe, spoke of his (Espy's) experience in protecting "the American market" from Canadian wheat farmers who exported low priced wheat into the American market with which American producers could not compete and later, having secured a market, then jacked up the price….

The strategy of emphasizing O'Keefe's American nationality as against Loewen's Canadian origins reached a peak in Mr Gary's closing address. He likened Jerry O'Keefe's struggle against Loewen with his war-time exploits against the Japanese, asserting that he was motivated by "pride in America" and "love for your country." By way of contrast, Mr Gary characterized Loewen's case as "Excuse me, I'm from Canada." Indeed, Mr Gary commenced his closing address by emphasizing nationalism: "[Y]our service on this case is higher than any honor that a citizen of this country can have, short of going to war and dying for your country." He described the American jury system as one that O'Keefe "fought for and some died for." Mr Gary said "they [Loewen] didn't know that this man didn't come home just as an ace who fought for his country—he's a fighter…. He'll stand up for America and he has."

Mr Gary returned to the same theme at the end of his closing address: "[O'Keefe] fought and some died for the laws of this nation, and they're [Loewen] going to put him down for being American." Mr Gary reminded the jury that many of O'Keefe's witnesses were Mississippians. On the other hand, Mr Gary characterized Loewen as a foreign invader who "came to town like gang busters. Ray came sweeping through…." Mr Gary even repeated the prejudicial evidence given by Mr Espy about the Canadian wheat farmers. Mr Gary likened Loewen to the Canadian wheat farmers. Loewen would "come in" and purchase a funeral home and "no sooner than they got it, they jacked up the prices down here in Mississippi." …

Claimants further complain that Mr Gary repeatedly portrayed Loewen as a large, wealthy foreign corporation and contrasted Jerry O'Keefe as a small, local, family businessman. There were a number of references by O'Keefe's counsel emphasizing this contrast. These references culminated in Mr Gary's closing address in which he incited the jury to put a stop to Loewen's activities. Speaking of Jerry O'Keefe, Mr Gary said:

> "He doesn't have the money that they have nor the power, but he has heart and character, and he refused to let them shoot him down." …
>
> "Ray comes down here, he's got his yacht up there, he can go to cocktail parties and all that, but do you know how he's financing that? By 80 and 90 year old people who go to get to a funeral, who go to pay their life savings, goes into this here, and it doesn't mean anything to him. Now, they've got to be stopped…. Do it, stop them so in years to come anybody should mention your service for some 50 odd days on this trial, you can say 'Yes, I was there,' and you can talk proud about it."

"1 billion dollars, ladies and gentlemen of the jury. You've got to put your foot down, and you may never get this chance again." ...

When the trial is viewed as a whole right through from the *voir dire* to counsel's closing address, it can be seen that the O'Keefe case was presented by counsel against an appeal to home-town sentiment, favouring the local party against an outsider. To that appeal was added the element of the powerful foreign multi-national corporation seeking to crush the small independent competitor who had fought for his country in World War II. Describing "Loewen" as a Canadian was simply to identify Loewen as an outsider. The fact that an investor from another state, say New York, would or might receive the same treatment in a Mississippi court as Loewen received is no answer to a claim that the O'Keefe case as presented invited the jury to discriminate against Loewen as an outsider....

TREATY OF WASHINGTON
Articles I-VI, X (1871)

[excerpted in Documentary Supplement at pp. 65-68]

[During the U.S. Civil War, the Confederacy contracted with English ship-builders to construct several warships in English shipyards. The United States protested to the United Kingdom, claiming that construction of the vessels was a violation of U.K. obligations of neutrality towards the United States. Despite the U.S. protests, the vessels left English ports and subsequently were manned by Confederate sailors, who inflicted substantial losses on U.S. shipping (sinking or capturing roughly 100 cargo ships). The most formidable of the Confederate vessels, named the Alabama, successfully attacked U.S. vessels in waters around the world, before finally being sunk, towards the end of the Civil War, by Union warships.

After the Civil War concluded, the United States demanded compensation from the United Kingdom, claiming that the U.K. acquiescence and tacit support for construction of the Alabama and other vessels resulted in massive damage to the United States, including the value of cargo vessels that were sunk or captured, the lost cargo (which was allegedly diverted from U.S. vessels to "safer" foreign vessels (primarily U.K. vessels)), and the costs of an allegedly prolonged war. The United Kingdom rejected the U.S. demands, provoking bitter diplomatic and political disputes. The two states eventually agreed, in the 1871 Treaty of Washington, to refer this dispute (and other disputes) to international arbitration. Pursuant to the Treaty, the United States and United Kingdom conducted the so-called "Alabama Arbitration" (seated in Geneva), which produced an award partially upholding the U.S. claims. The background of the Treaty of Washington and the ensuing arbitration are described in Bingham, *The Alabama Claims Arbitration*, 54 Int'l & Comp. L.Q. 1 (2005) and F. Hackett, *Reminiscences of the Geneva Tribunal of Arbitration* (1911).]

1907 HAGUE CONVENTION FOR THE PACIFIC SETTLEMENT OF INTERNATIONAL DISPUTES
Articles 37, 38, 40, 41

[excerpted in Documentary Supplement at p. 43]

ARBITRATION AGREEMENT BETWEEN THE GOVERNMENT OF SUDAN AND THE SUDAN PEOPLE'S LIBERATION MOVEMENT/ARMY ON DELIMITING THE ABYEI AREA

Articles 1-3 (2008) (also excerpted in Documentary Supplement at pp. 79-80)

[Since Sudan's independence in 1954, the country was engulfed by almost continuous civil war, generally pitting the largely Muslim, Arabic-speaking north against the primarily Christian and other non-Muslim south. In 2004, the Government of Sudan ("GoS") and the Sudan Peoples' Liberation Movement/Army ("SPLM/A"), the principal Sudanese resistance group, negotiated and signed a Comprehensive Peace Agreement ("CPA"). The CPA, concluded under United Nations auspices, aimed at ending the civil war and permitting a referendum in which southern Sudan could decide whether or not to form an independent state.

A central issue addressed by the CPA was the status of a territory located in south-central Sudan, called the Abyei Area, which lay on the border between southern and northern Sudan. Among other disputes, the GoS and SPLM/A disagreed about the territorial boundaries of the Abyei Area. The CPA provided for the Abyei Area to be delimited by a commission of experts (the Abyei Boundaries Commission ("ABC Experts")). After extensive submissions from the parties, the ABC Experts issued a report in July 2005 delimiting boundaries for the Abyei Area. Dissatisfied with the result, the GoS refused to accept the Report, leading to a prolonged stalemate with the SPLM/A, which threatened the broader peace process envisaged by the CPA.

The stalemate between the GoS and the SPLM/A was broken in July 2008, when the two parties agreed to arbitrate their disagreements regarding the ABC Experts Report and the boundaries of the Abyei Area. The parties' agreement is excerpted in the Documentary Supplement at pp. 79-84.

The Abyei Arbitration Agreement, and the resulting Abyei Arbitration, are described in materials on the website of the Permanent Court of Arbitration, under whose auspices the arbitration was conducted. Among these materials are the parties' written submissions, webcasts of the oral proceedings and the arbitral award made by the tribunal. *See* www.pca-cpa.org; www.wx4all.net/pca.]

RAINBOW WARRIOR AFFAIR
(1985)

[In July 1985, agents of the French Directorate General of External Security ("DGSE") planted mines on the "Rainbow Warrior," a protest vessel belonging to Greenpeace (an environmental advocacy group), when it was moored in Auckland Harbour, New Zealand. The vessel had been scheduled to sail to Mururoa Atoll, in French Polynesia, to protest against French nuclear testing; that voyage was prevented by the actions of the DGSE agents, which resulted in the vessel's sinking (and the death of one Greenpeace member). Criminal investigations by New Zealand police resulted in the arrests of two French DGSE agents (and their subsequent criminal convictions). France initially denied responsibility for the attack on the Rainbow Warrior and imposed economic sanctions on New Zealand in retaliation for the DGSE agents' arrest. Subsequently, however, France acknowledged responsibility for the sinking of the Rainbow Warrior and offered to pay reparations to both New Zealand and Greenpeace.

Despite negotiations between France and, respectively, New Zealand and Greenpeace, no agreement could be reached on reparations. As a consequence, France and New Zealand concluded an arbitration agreement, submitting disputes about reparations and treatment of the DGSE agents to the Secretary-General of the United Nations for resolution. After receiving written submissions from the parties, the Secretary-General rendered an award requiring France to formally apologize to New Zealand and to pay New Zealand $7 million (including for moral damage); he also ordered the transfer of the two DGSE agents to "an isolated island outside of Europe for a period of three years." *See United Nations Secretary General: Ruling on the Rainbow Warrior Affair Between France and New Zealand*, 26 I.L.M. 1346 (1987).

In parallel, France and Greenpeace concluded a separate arbitration agreement, submitting the question of France's financial liability for the sinking to an arbitral tribunal seated in Geneva, Switzerland. The tribunal was composed of Professor Claude Reymond, a Swiss law professor, Sir Owen Woodhouse, a retired New Zealand judge, and Professor Francois Terré, a French law professor. After receiving written submissions and conducting an evidentiary hearing, the tribunal rendered an award requiring France to pay Greenpeace $5 million in damages, $1.2 million for "aggravated damages," and $2 million in expenses, interest and legal fees. *See* Shabecoff, *France Must Pay Greenpeace $8 Million in Sinking of Ship*, N.Y. Times (Oct. 3, 1987). Following the award, the chairman of Greenpeace, David McTaggart, said that the decision "is a great victory for those who support the right of peaceful protest and abhor the use of violence." *Ibid*. The text of the arbitral award remains confidential.]

BÜHRING-UHLE, *A SURVEY ON ARBITRATION AND SETTLEMENT IN INTERNATIONAL BUSINESS DISPUTES*

in C. Drahozal & R. Naimark (eds.), *Towards A Science of International Arbitration* 25, 31-33 (2005)

Clearly the two most significant advantages and presumably the two most important reasons for choosing arbitration as a means of international commercial dispute resolution seem to be the *neutrality of the forum, i.e.*, the possibility to avoid being subjected to the jurisdiction of the home court of one of the parties, and the superiority of its legal framework, with treaties like the New York Convention guaranteeing the *international enforcements* of awards. Both attributes were thought to be "highly relevant" or "significant" by over 80% of the individuals responding, and in each case only 3 respondents (5%) thought that there really was no advantage.

On the scale from -1 ("advantage does not exist") to 3 ("highly relevant"), the aggregate of the answers with respect to the significance of both the neutrality of forum and the international enforceability of awards amounted to 2.4, which places both considerations on aggregate almost exactly halfway between "significant" and "highly relevant."

The next most important advantages were, by order of relevance, the *confidentiality* of the procedure, the *expertise* of the tribunal, the *absence of appeals*, and the *limited discovery* available in international commercial arbitration. Each of these four considerations was deemed "highly relevant" or "significant" by a clear majority (close to or over 60%) of the respondents. Within this group of arbitration advantages, the confidentiality of the procedure was the one least questioned (only 7% thought there was no advantage) and attained the highest average relevance, placing it close to "significant" (1.8). The other three considerations were doubted by about one fifth (between 10% and 23%) and produced average relevance values somewhere close to the midpoint between "one factor among many" and "significant": the possibility to choose a tribunal with special expertise "scored" 1.6, the absence of appeals 1.5, and the availability of limited discovery was placed at 1.3.

The aspect of limited discovery is slightly ambivalent in that some respondents tended to compare it to the extensive discovery practiced in American courts while for others the civil law practice, which does not know discovery in the common law sense, was the point of reference. So if a relatively high number of respondents (21%) thought that the practice of limited discovery was of no advantage their motivation might have been quite different. Also, the different legal traditions of the respondents led to significant "geographical" variations in the assessment of this aspect of arbitration practice. Another slightly ambivalent attribute of arbitration is the absence of appeals which by a large number of practitioners is crucial for the aim of obtaining a final decision within a reasonable time span but which, according to some of the practitioners interviewed, can also be seen as a disadvantage since the possibility to correct even grave errors of the arbitral tribunal is very restricted. Accordingly, this was the aspect that within this group of four arbitration advantages of some significance received the highest percentages both in the category "highly relevant" (37%) and "advantage does not exist" (23%).

Attributes of international commercial arbitration that, on aggregate were only regarded as slight advantages somewhere between "one factor among many" and "not relevant" were the *expedience* of the procedure, its *amicability* and the presumably greater degree of *voluntary compliance* with the results. In each case the number of respondents considering this attribute to be a "highly relevant" or "significant" advantage did not exceed 40% and was surpassed by the number of respondents who thought the advantage was non-existent. The average relevance was 0.7 for both the presumably greater speed and amicability of arbitration, and 0.5 for the supposedly higher degree of voluntary compliance with arbitral awards.

The two least significant of the 11 hypothetical advantages offered in the questionnaire were the presumably lower *costs* of the procedure, which on balance was regarded as irrelevant, and the *predictability* of its results which figured midway between irrelevant and non-existing. More than half (51%) of the respondents thought that the cost advantage did not exist and three quarters (75%) doubted that the results were more predictable. The aggregate significance amounted to 0.2 for the hypothetical cost advantage and -0.5, the lowest overall value of all the considerations discussed, for the supposedly greater *predictability* of results.

15 of the individuals responding specified a total of 8 "other" reasons why arbitration is chosen over litigation:

- the most frequently cited reason, which was mentioned five times, was the *possibility for the parties to select the members of the tribunal* themselves;
- next with four mentions was the perception that in international commercial disputes there really was *no alternative* to arbitration;
- then came with three mentions each the *greater flexibility* of the procedure and
- the possibility to choose the language of the procedure;
- attributes mentioned twice were the *preservation of business relationships* and
- the fact that arbitration constitutes a *"de luxe" form of litigation*;

- one mention each was given to the special *expertise* of the arbitrators *in* the applicable *foreign law* and
- the possibility to conduct a procedure less burdened by technicalities.

QUEEN MARY, UNIV. OF LONDON, *INTERNATIONAL ARBITRATION SURVEY: CORPORATE CHOICES IN INTERNATIONAL ARBITRATION*
pp. 6, 21, 22 (2013)

Earlier surveys by Queen Mary, University of London, had confirmed arbitration's overall popularity. In the 2008 survey, 86% of respondents said they were "satisfied" with arbitration. Likewise in 2006, 73% of participants identified international arbitration as their preferred mechanism for dispute resolution....

Arbitration ranked first more often than any of the other mechanisms (52% of respondents marked arbitration as most preferred). Arbitration was also ranked last less often than any other mechanism. Almost the same proportion of participants prefer arbitration when they are claimants (62%) as when they are respondents and have no counterclaim (60%)....

While, overall, arbitration remains the preferred dispute resolution mechanism for transnational disputes, many respondents and interviewees expressed concern over the related issues of costs and delays experienced in international arbitration proceedings....

Interviewees [also] expressed concern about their perception that the process of arbitration has become more sophisticated and more "regulated," with "control" over the process moving towards law firms—and away from the actual users of this process. Several interviewees linked concerns over increases in the costs of arbitration with this encroaching judicialisation.

Overall, however, both the survey and our interviews showed a continued support for arbitration, and an expectation that respondents will keep using this mechanism in the future.

UNITED KINGDOM/BOSNIA-HERZEGOVINA BIT
Articles 8, 9

[excerpted in Documentary Supplement at pp. 76-77]

NOTES

1. *Relative costs and speed of commercial arbitration and litigation.* The costs and efficiency of different dispute resolution mechanisms vary from time to time and place to place. Nonetheless, there have been recurrent complaints from commercial users, as well as individuals, about the delays and expenses imposed by many national court systems. Consider the complaints from the ancient Egyptian records, excerpted above from Crum and Steindorff. Compare them to the complaints from early colonial America.

   Is it possible to say that arbitration is necessarily quicker and cheaper than litigation in national courts? Doesn't that inevitably depend on how quickly each of the respective dispute resolution processes can proceed? Note that some commentators and users characterize arbitration as the slower, more expensive alternative. *Blue Tee Corp.*

v. Koehring Co., 999 F.2d 633 (2d Cir. 1993) ("this appeal ... makes one wonder about the alleged speed and economy of arbitration in resolving commercial disputes"); Lyons, *Arbitration: The Slower, More Expensive Alternative*, Am. Law. 107 (Jan./Feb. 1985); Queen Mary, University of London, *2013 International Arbitration Survey: Corporate Choices in International Arbitration* (2013). Compare the views of business users, reported by Bühring-Uhle.

In considering the relative cost and speed of international arbitration versus litigation, it is important to take into account the likelihood of jurisdictional disputes and parallel proceedings. Suppose a Japanese and a French company enter into a long-term sales agreement, which leads to disputes. Assuming there is no agreement to arbitrate such disputes, what is likely to occur after efforts to amicably settle the disputes fail? Where is the Japanese company likely to want the parties' disputes resolved? What about the French company? What happens if both companies pursue their favored means of dispute resolution? What happens if each company succeeds in obtaining a judgment in its favor from its local courts?

In considering the relative speed and cost of international arbitration, note also that parties are generally permitted to impose contractual time limits on the arbitral process (*e.g.*, by requiring an award to be made within a specified time period from the commencement of the arbitration). Is this ordinarily possible in national court proceedings?

2. *Absence of appellate review.* In addition to other factors affecting the costs and delays of different forms of dispute resolution, consider the possibility of appeals from first-instance judgments in national courts. In some jurisdictions, such appeals are essentially *de novo* re-litigations; in other jurisdictions, decisions of law are subject to *de novo* review, while reviews of factual finding are subject to more deferential appellate scrutiny. In contrast, in most developed jurisdictions, international arbitral awards are subject to only very limited judicial review (ordinarily only on issues of jurisdiction, procedural unfairness, or public policy), not extending to the merits of the arbitral tribunal's decision. Consider, in this regard, Article 34 of the UNCITRAL Model Law, excerpted at pp. 94-95 of the Documentary Supplement. Note that the possibility of *de novo* or otherwise extensive appellate review materially increases the possibility of delays and additional costs.

Is it desirable for there to be no or *de minimis* appellate review of an arbitrator's decisions? Does not appellate review provide an important check against arbitrary decision-making and erroneous conclusions? Is it worth giving up this check in order to obtain other benefits?

3. *Party autonomy with regard to arbitral procedures and selection of arbitrators.* One of the advantages of the arbitral process, both international and domestic, is the parties' autonomy to design their own dispute resolution procedures and to select their own arbitral tribunal. Parties can agree upon a "fast-track" arbitration, to be completed in a matter of weeks or months; they can agree to a "documents only" arbitration, which involves no oral testimony; or they can agree to an arbitral tribunal that includes technical experts. For the most part, such choices are not available in national courts.

In a number of national and international industries, specialized arbitral institutions and dispute resolution mechanisms have been designed by market players and trade associations. That is true, for example, in maritime, commodities, insurance and reinsurance, construction and other markets, where specialized arbitral institutions with specialized arbitration rules have developed. *See, e.g.*, AAA Labor Arbitration Rules; AAA Rules for Impartial Determination of Union Fees; 2014 National Grain and Feed Association Arbitration Rules (selected commodities disputes); 2012 London Maritime Arbitration Association Terms (maritime); ARIAS U.S. Rules for the Resolution of U.S. Insurance and Reinsurance Disputes.

How important is it for parties to be able to select their own procedural rules? Can parties do so in national courts? Why should they want to do so? Why should they be permitted to do so? Consider the following observations:

> "For a French party, the big advantage is that international commercial arbitration offers '*de luxe* justice.' ... Instead of having a $600 million dispute before the commercial court in Paris, where each party has only one hour for pleading and where you can't present witnesses and have no discovery; for a dispute of that importance it may well be worth the costs to get a type of justice that is more international and more 'luxurious'; what you get is more extensive and thorough examination of witness testimony—without the excesses of American court procedure." Bühring-Uhle, *A Survey on Arbitration and Settlement in International Business Disputes*, in C. Drahozal & R. Naimark (eds.), *Towards A Science of International Arbitration: Collected Empirical Research* 34 & n. 28 (2005).

Is it appropriate to permit parties to agree upon "*de luxe*" justice? On "rough" justice? On specialized procedures? Is it appropriate to forbid parties from doing so?

4. *Commercial or other expertise of arbitrators*. Related to the parties' autonomy to select "their" arbitral tribunal is the commercial (and other) expertise of arbitrators, as compared to national courts. Are parties permitted to select "their" judge in national court proceedings? Should they be?

Note also that many judges in national courts are generalists, hearing civil, criminal, domestic and other disputes and often having no commercial experience (either in business or as a practicing lawyer advising businesses). In contrast, parties often select arbitrators with specific and extensive experience in the subject-matter and/or law of their dispute (*e.g.*, arbitrators with experience in construction, joint ventures, insurance, or maritime disputes). This experience and expertise enhance the predictability and commercial reasonableness of the tribunal's ultimate decision. Compare the observations of the former president of the French Cour de cassation, explaining why he regarded arbitration as desirable: "[F]irst, what you do we don't have to do; ... [s]econd, in many fields you are more professional than we are." Lazareff, *International Arbitration: Towards A Common Procedural Approach*, in S. Frommel & B. Rider (eds.), *Conflicting Legal Cultures in Commercial Arbitration* 31, 33 (1999). Note also that parties can include contractual requirements in their arbitration agreement, specifying that the arbitrators have particular experience or qualifications. *See infra* pp. 710-16. For example, parties to an insurance or reinsurance policy can require that the arbitrator be an insurance practitioner, or a former insurance industry employee; parties to a telecommunications supply contract can require that the arbitrators have experience in that industry; parties to an oil and gas contract can require that the arbitrators have experience with oil and gas disputes. Alternatively, parties can agree to arbitrate under specialized institutional rules, tailored to particular industries (and having institutional lists of arbitrators with specialized expertise and experience). *See supra* pp. 70-71, 109-10.

5. *Neutrality of tribunal.* Recall the hypothetical above, where Japanese and French parties conclude a contract, which leads to disputes. Is it likely that the Japanese party would wish for disputes to be resolved in French courts? That the French party would be willing to have disputes resolved in Japanese courts? Why not? Consider the excerpts from the Transparency International report and the *Loewen* award. If you were a non-U.S. party, how comfortable would you be having your disputes resolved in U.S. courts? Are U.S. courts unusually bad, in terms of parochialism or "hometown" bias, compared to courts in other countries? How comfortable would you be having your own disputes resolved in one of the twenty countries identified in the Transparency International report?

One of the perceived advantages of international arbitration is that it permits parties to select a neutral decision-maker—which is not part of the governmental structure of either party's home state and which is not composed of nationals of either party's home jurisdiction. Alternatively, the parties can each select a co-arbitrator of their choice (including a co-arbitrator with the party's own nationality), while requiring the presiding arbitrator to have a neutral nationality. For example, in the hypothetical involving French and Japanese parties, the tribunal could be comprised of a French, a Japanese and a U.S. or Canadian (presiding) arbitrator. How important is the neutrality of the decision-maker in international disputes? Note the provisions regarding constitution of the tribunal in the Treaty of Washington and the Abyei Arbitration Agreement.

6. *Enforceability of international arbitration agreements.* Consider Article II of the New York Convention, excerpted at p. 1 of the Documentary Supplement. As noted above, as of 2014, some 153 countries are Contracting States to the Convention. *See supra* pp. 33-39, 44. Article II of the Convention obligates Contracting States to recognize international arbitration agreements and to enforce such agreements by referring their parties to arbitration. What is the practical importance of the obligation imposed by Article II of the Convention?

Consider the terms of the proposed Hague Convention on Choice of Court Agreements, excerpted at pp. 53-63 of the Documentary Supplement, which was drafted under the auspices of the Hague Conference on Private International Law. The Convention has not come into force yet, nor been implemented in the states which have ratified it. On January 30, 2014, the European Commission published a proposal for approval by the EU of the Hague Convention; if the proposal is adopted, the Convention will in due course enter into force between the EU and Mexico. *See* G. Born, *International Commercial Arbitration* 79 (2d ed. 2014). When the Convention does come into force, what effect will it have on the "enforceability premium" enjoyed by international arbitration agreements? Note the exceptions in Articles 2 and 9 of the proposed Convention.

7. *Enforceability of international arbitral awards.* Consider the excerpt from Bloch, regarding international dispute resolution in Europe during the Middle Ages. Similar issues arise today, in obtaining effective recognition of national court judgments in other states. Note that difficulties in enforcing national court judgments are particu-

larly likely where there have been parallel proceedings and jurisdictional disputes in different national courts.

Consider Articles III and V of the New York Convention, excerpted at pp. 1-2 of the Documentary Supplement. What do they provide, in general terms, with regard to the recognition and enforcement of foreign arbitral awards? Note that there is currently no comparable multilateral treaty providing for the recognition and enforcement of foreign court judgments. As a consequence, it is fair to say that international arbitral awards enjoy an "enforceability premium," as compared to national court judgments. How important is that consideration in determining whether or not to agree to an international arbitration agreement?

Consider again the proposed Hague Convention on Choice of Court Agreements, excerpted at pp. 53-63 of the Documentary Supplement. What does it provide with regard to the recognition of foreign judgments? To what extent would it affect the "enforceability premium" currently enjoyed by arbitral awards?

8. *Confidentiality.* As discussed in detail below, many international arbitrations are confidential. *See infra* pp. 851, 866-68. In most cases, the filings and hearings in an international commercial arbitration are not available to non-parties (or the press), and neither party is free to disclose such materials (or other information about the arbitration) to third parties. Consider the views of business users of arbitration, reported in the Bühring-Uhle study, regarding confidentiality. Why might it be important for commercial parties that their disputes remain confidential? To what extent may publicity of a dispute prevent its amicable resolution?

9. *International forum selection agreements.* A potential alternative to an international arbitration agreement is a forum selection clause. A forum selection clause specifies a national court for the resolution of the parties' disputes; the clause may be either exclusive (requiring resolution of all disputes exclusively in the specified contractual forum) or non-exclusive (permitting either party to pursue litigation in the specified contractual forum, but not precluding litigation in other forums). *See* G. Born & P. Rutledge, *International Civil Litigation in United States Courts* 462-63 (5th ed. 2011).

To what extent is a forum selection clause a satisfactory alternative to an arbitration agreement? Does a forum selection clause have the potential to impose contractual time limits on the length of a litigation? Can parties to a forum selection clause select the specific judge that they desire to decide their case? Can they insist that the judge have specified experience? Can the parties to a forum selection clause specify their own procedures and procedural timetable for "their" litigation? What is the relative enforceability of international arbitration agreements and international forum selection agreements? International arbitral awards and foreign court judgments?

Consider again the hypothetical concerning Japanese and French parties to a contract. Suppose the parties entertain the possibility of adopting a forum selection clause. What national courts should the parties choose? French? Japanese? If not the courts of either party, then what courts? What rationale is there for selecting, for example, an English, Swiss, Singaporean, or U.S. court? How do such courts compare to selecting an arbitral tribunal?

10. *Arbitration as means of resolving state-to-state disputes.* Consider Article 38 of the 1907 Hague Convention, excerpted at p. 43 of the Documentary Supplement. What aspects of arbitration led states to conclude that "international arbitration" is "recog-

nized by the signatory powers as the most effective, and at the same time the most equitable, means of settling disputes which diplomacy has failed to settle"? This is robust praise for the international arbitral process. What warrants it? Recall the discussion above of the use of international arbitration historically to resolve inter-state disputes. *See supra* pp. 2-10. Consider the limitations referred to in Article 38. Why are they included?

Consider the 1871 Treaty of Washington, which provided the basis for the *Alabama Arbitration*. Why did the United States and Great Britain decide to resolve their dispute by international arbitration? What were the alternatives? Consider the various procedural terms of the Treaty of Washington. What did the arbitral process permit the parties to accomplish? *See also* T. Balch, *The Alabama Arbitration* (1900); Bingham, *The Alabama Claims Arbitration*, 54 Int'l & Comp. L.Q. 1 (2005); F. Hackett, *Reminiscences of the Geneva Tribunal of Arbitration* (1911).

Consider the Abyei Arbitration Agreement. Why did the Government of Sudan and the Sudan Peoples' Liberation Movement/Army decide to resolve their disputes over Abyei by international arbitration? Again, what were the alternatives? Note the various procedural terms of the Abyei Arbitration Agreement, including the expedited timetable, the provisions for selection of the tribunal and provisions regarding publicity. What role did these provisions play in enabling the parties to resolve their dispute?

Consider the *Greenpeace* arbitration. Why do you think Greenpeace and France agreed to resolve their dispute by arbitration? Again, what were the alternatives? What advantages did arbitration offer to Greenpeace? To France?

11. *Arbitration as a means of resolving investment disputes.* Consider the facts in the *Loewen* case. Why is it that Canadian (or other foreign) investors in the United States might wish for their investment disputes to be resolved in a forum other than U.S. courts? Are U.S. courts uniquely inhospitable to foreign investors? Why might a U.S. investor in Canada want its investment disputes resolved in a forum other than Canadian courts? If a forum other than national courts is to resolve investment disputes, what forum might that be? Consider the U.K./Bosnia-Herzegovina BIT. What use does it make of international arbitration as a means of resolving investment disputes? Compare the ICSID Convention.

12. *Contemporary popularity of international arbitration.* International arbitration has demonstrated considerable popularity as a means of dispute resolution over the past century. Recall again Article 38 of the 1907 Hague Convention. Also recall the nearly global acceptance of the New York Convention and the ICSID Convention.

The popularity of international arbitration is reflected in steadily-increasing caseloads at leading arbitral institutions, with the number of reported cases increasing between two-fold and ten-fold in the past 20 years. Among other things, the International Chamber of Commerce's International Court of Arbitration received requests for 32 new arbitrations in 1956, 210 in 1976, 337 in 1992, 452 in 1997, 529 in 1999, 593 in 2006 and 767 in 2013—a roughly 24-fold increase over the past 60 years. Similarly, in 1980, the AAA/ICDR administered 101 international arbitrations; 207 in 1993, 453 in 1999, 586 in 2006 and 996 in 2012. Other institutions show similar growth in caseloads, as illustrated in the following table, which shows the number of new international arbitration cases filed with leading arbitral institutions between 1993-2013.[4]

	'93	'94	'95	'96	'97	'98	'99	'00	'01	'02	'03	'04	'05	'06	'07	'08	'09	'10	'11	'12	'13
AAA/ICDR	207	187	180	194	320	385	453	510	649	672	646	614	580	586	621	703	836	888	994	996	1165
BCICAC[567]	52	54	40	57	41	49	60	88	88	71	76	84	77	76	84	84	76	78	71	96	102
CIETAC[5]	486	829	902	778	723	645	609	543	731	684	709	850	979	981	1118	1230	1482	1352	1435	1060	1256
DIS	n/a	30	n/a	31	n/a	42	32	62	58	77	81	87	72	75	100	122	177	156	178	125	132
HKIAC[57]	139	150	184	197	218	240	257	298	307	320	287	280	281	394	448	602	746	624	502	456	463
ICC	352	384	427	433	452	466	529	541	566	593	580	561	521	593	599	663	817	793	796	759	767
ICSID	1	2	3	3	10	11	10	12	14	19	30	27	26	23	36	21	25	26	37	48	33
JCAA[5]	3	4	7	8	13	14	12	10	17	9	14	21	11	11	15	12	18	27	19	19	26
KCAB	n/a	33	18	36	51	59	40	40	65	47	38	46	53	47	59	47	78	52	77	85	77
KLRCA	3	n/a	n/a	6	n/a	n/a	10	n/a	n/a	2	4	3	6	1	2	8	7	2	3	17	28
LCIA[5]	29	39	49	37	52	70	60	87	71	88	104	87	118	133	137	215	272	246	224	265	290
LMAA[6]	n/a	n/a	n/a	3384	3191	3144	2574	2757	2852	2219	2618	2919	3027	2630	2673	3684	4445	3492	3555	3849	2966
NAI	24	22	20	17	32	43	31	27	46	53	33	39	32	29	28	45	44	32	50	32	49
PCA[6]	n/a	n/a	n/a	n/a	n/a	n/a	n/a	5	8	8	11	16	19	19	23	34	54	64	69	88	104
SCC	78	74	70	75	87	92	104	73	74	55	82	50	56	74	87	85	96	91	96	92	86
SIAC[5]	9	6	20	27	27	41	50	58	64	64	64	78	74	90	86	99	160	198	188	235	259
VIAC	48	64	44	47	47	46	37	65	63	33	45	50	54	36	40	51	60	68	75	70	56
TOTAL	1431	1878	1964	5330	5264	5347	4868	5176	5673	5014	5422	5812	5986	5798	6156	7705	9393	8189	8369	8292	7859

Cases Filed Annually with Leading Arbitral Institutions (1993-2013)

What explains the popularity of international arbitration as a means of dispute resolution? Is it because international arbitration is so good? Or that it is better than the alternatives? Something else?

---

4. G. Born, *International Commercial Arbitration* 94 (2d ed. 2014). Figures kindly provided by respective institutions.

5. Figures may include international and domestic cases.

6. Figures may include new and pending cases.

7. Figures may include other ADR cases (*e.g.*, conciliation, domain name disputes).

B. JURISDICTIONAL REQUIREMENTS FOR INTERNATIONAL ARBITRATION AGREEMENTS UNDER INTERNATIONAL ARBITRATION CONVENTIONS AND NATIONAL ARBITRATION LEGISLATION

As discussed elsewhere, the substantive terms of the New York Convention and most contemporary national arbitration statutes (again, such as the UNCITRAL Model Law) are "pro-arbitration," providing effective and robust mechanisms for enforcing international arbitration agreements and arbitral awards.[8] In particular, Article II of the Convention imposes obligations on Contracting States to recognize international arbitration agreements and to enforce them by referring the parties to arbitration;[9] similarly, Articles 7, 8 and 16 of the UNCITRAL Model Law provide parallel treatment of specified international arbitration agreements.[10] In addition, both international arbitration conventions and national arbitration statutes contain jurisdictional requirements that define what arbitration agreements and arbitral awards are (and are not) subject to those instruments' substantive rules. These requirements have important consequences, because they determine when the pro-enforcement regimes of the New York Convention and many national arbitration statutes are applicable—rather than other means of enforcement, which are sometimes archaic and often ineffective.

Despite the importance of the issue, defining precisely which international arbitration agreements are subject to the New York Convention is not always straightforward. As discussed in detail below, Article I of the Convention specifically defines those arbitral awards that are subject to the Convention.[11] In contrast, nothing in Article II of the Convention (or otherwise) expressly addresses which arbitration agreements are subject to Article II's "recognition" requirement. In the words of one commentator: "[T]he Convention does not give a definition as to which arbitration agreements fall under [Article II]."[12]

The jurisdictional requirements of the New York Convention impose non-trivial limitations on the scope of the Convention. There are numerous international arbitration agreements to which the New York Convention does *not* apply: "[T]here is a vast area not covered by the Convention."[13] In particular, five jurisdictional requirements of the New York Convention warrant attention.[14]

First, Article II(1) and II(2) limit the Convention's coverage to "arbitration agreement[s]" and "arbitral clause[s]," as distinguished from other types of agreements (*e.g.*, mediation or choice-of-court agreements). Second, where Contracting States have adopted a reservation to this effect, the Convention is generally applicable only to differences arising out of "commercial" relationships. Third, again pursuant to Article II(1), the parties' agreement must provide for arbitration of "differences which have arisen or which

---

8. *See supra* pp. 28-67 & *infra* pp. 177-90, 1189-99.

9. *See supra* p. 35 & *infra* pp. 177-90, 315-34.

10. *See supra* pp. 48-50 & *infra* pp. 177-78, 189-90, 317, 319, 330-31.

11. *See infra* pp. 1070-1093.

12. *See* van den Berg, *When Is An Arbitral Award Non-Domestic Under the New York Convention of 1958?*, 6 Pace L. Rev. 25, 51 (1985).

13. Comment, *International Commercial Arbitration Under the United Nations Convention and Amended Arbitration Statute*, 47 Wash. L. Rev. 441, 441 (1972).

14. The ICSID, Inter-American, 1961 European and other international arbitration Conventions also contain various jurisdictional requirements. *See supra* pp. 39-43 & *infra* pp. 146, 166.

may arise … in respect of a defined legal relationship, whether contractual or not." Fourth, the Convention is applicable in many national courts only on the basis of reciprocity (*i.e.*, *vis-à-vis* other nations that also have ratified the Convention). Finally, the Convention arguably applies only to agreements concerning "foreign" or "nondomestic" awards or, alternatively, to international arbitration agreements.

Like the New York Convention, contemporary international arbitration statutes in most states contain either express or implied jurisdictional limitations. As under the Convention, these jurisdictional requirements have substantial practical importance because they determine when the generally "pro-arbitration" substantive provisions of contemporary arbitration legislation apply, both to arbitration agreements and arbitral awards.

The jurisdictional requirements of national arbitration statutes vary from state to state. In general, however, these jurisdictional limits are broadly similar to those contained in the New York Convention: (a) requirements for an "arbitration agreement" (or "arbitral award"); (b) a "commercial relationship" requirement; (c) a "foreign" or "international" connection requirement; and (d) a "defined relationship" requirement. In addition, most arbitration statutes are generally (but not exclusively) applicable only to arbitrations seated in national territory. We examine each of these categories of jurisdictional requirements below, in conjunction with discussions of the parallel jurisdictional limitations under the New York Convention.

Finally, in the context of international investment arbitration, the ICSID Convention and BITs also contain significant jurisdictional limitations. In particular, both sets of instruments are addressed to the resolution of "investment" disputes, arising out of "investments" or "investment agreements" between a state and specified foreign nationals.[15] These jurisdictional requirements ensure that the specialized dispute resolution mechanisms of the ICSID Convention and BITs are available only in relatively limited, precisely-defined cases.

1. Definition of "Arbitration Agreement"

Most international commercial arbitration conventions and national arbitration statutes will apply only if the parties have putatively made an agreement to "arbitrate"—as opposed to an agreement to do something else; similar provisions exist in the case of investment and state-to-state arbitrations. This raises the definitional question of what constitutes an "arbitration agreement." For example, parties may agree to expert determination, conciliation, mediation, or other forms of alternative dispute resolution, or to a forum selection clause providing for litigation in a specified national court. Ordinarily, none of these forms of dispute resolution constitute "arbitration" within the meaning or scope of the New York Convention (or other international arbitration conventions) or national arbitration statutes.

Significant legal consequences follow under virtually all international conventions and national arbitration laws from characterization of a contractual provision as something *other than* an "arbitration agreement." In these instances, the "pro-arbitration" regimes of the New York Convention and national arbitration statutes do not necessarily apply to the agreement (or any resulting decision). Rather, ordinary domestic contract law rules or specialized legislation (*e.g.*, applicable to mediation or forum selection agreements) will

---

15. *See infra* pp. 169, 175, 511-16. *See also* ICSID Convention, Art. 25(1); C. Schreuer *et al.*, *The ICSID Convention: A Commentary* Art. 25 ¶¶3-4 (2d ed. 2009).

apply; in most cases, these other legal regimes will be materially less effective as means of enforcement than the New York Convention and parallel national arbitration statutes.[16] Given the importance of these consequences, there is a surprising lack of guidance under both international conventions and national legislation relevant to the question of what constitutes an "arbitration agreement." The materials excerpted below explore these issues.

UNITED NATIONS CHARTER
Article 33(1)

The parties to any dispute, the continuance of which is likely to endanger the maintenance of international peace and security, shall, first of all, seek a solution by negotiation, enquiry, mediation, conciliation, arbitration, judicial settlement, resort to regional agencies or arrangements, or other peaceful means of their own choice.

JIVRAJ v. HASHWANI
[2011] UKSC 40 (U.K. S.Ct.)

LORD CLARKE. On 29 January 1981 Mr Jivraj and Mr Hashwani entered into a joint venture agreement ("the JVA"), containing an arbitration clause which provided that, in the event of a dispute between them which they were unable to resolve, that dispute should be resolved by arbitration before three arbitrators, each of whom should be a respected member of the Ismaili community, of which they were both members. The principal question in this appeal is whether that arbitration agreement became void with effect from 2 December 2003 under the Employment Equality (Religion or Belief) Regulations 2003 ("the Regulations") on the ground that it constituted an unlawful arrangement to discriminate on grounds of religion when choosing between persons offering personal services.

The JVA was established to make investments in real estate around the world. By article 9 it is expressly governed by English law. Article 8 provides ...:

> "(1) If any dispute difference or question shall at any time hereafter arise between the investors with respect to the construction of this agreement or concerning anything herein contained or arising out of this agreement or as to the rights liabilities or duties of the investors or either of them or arising out of (without limitation) any of the businesses or activities of the joint venture herein agreed the same (subject to sub-clause 8(5) below) shall be referred to three arbitrators (acting by a majority) one to be appointed by each party and the third arbitrator to be the President of the HH Aga Khan National Council for the United Kingdom for the time being. All arbitrators shall be respected members of the Ismaili community and holders of high office within the community.
>
> (2) The arbitration shall take place in London and the arbitrators' award shall be final and binding on both parties."

The Ismaili community comprises Shia Imami Ismaili Muslims. It is led by the Aga Khan, whose title is the hereditary title of the Imam of the Ismaili community....

During the 1980s the joint venture came to comprise substantial business interests, first in Canada and later in the United States, Pakistan and the United Kingdom, with invest-

---

16. *See* G. Born, *International Commercial Arbitration* 240-41 (2d ed. 2014).

ments in properties, hotels and the oil industry. By late 1988 Mr Jivraj and Mr Hashwani had agreed to part company. On 30 October 1988 they entered into an agreement under which they appointed a three man conciliation panel ("the panel") for the purpose of the division of the joint venture assets. Each member of the panel was a respected member of the Ismaili community. The panel operated between October 1988 and February 1990 and many of the assets were divided between the parties in accordance with its directions. It was however unable to resolve all the issues between the parties. The parties then agreed to submit the remaining issues to arbitration or conciliation by a single member of the Ismaili community, namely Mr Zaher Ahamed. He issued a determination in December 1993, whereafter he had further exchanges with the parties until 1995, when he declared himself defeated....

[After further, lengthy negotiation, on] 31 July 2008, Messrs Zaiwalla & Co, acting on behalf of Mr Hashwani, wrote to Mr Jivraj asserting a claim for US$1,412,494, together with interest, compounded quarterly from 1994, making a total of US$4,403,817. The letter gave notice that Mr Hashwani had appointed Sir Anthony Colman[, a non-Ismaili,] as an arbitrator under article 8 of the JVA and that, if Mr Jivraj failed to appoint an arbitrator within seven days, steps would be taken to appoint Sir Anthony as sole arbitrator. The letter added that Mr Hashwani did not regard himself as bound by the provision that the arbitrators should be members of the Ismaili community because such a requirement "would now amount to religious discrimination which would violate the Human Rights Act 1998 and therefore must be regarded as void." It is common ground, on the one hand, that Sir Anthony Colman is not a member of the Ismaili community and, on the other hand, that he is a retired judge of the Commercial Court with substantial experience of the resolution of commercial disputes, both as a judge and as an arbitrator.

Mr Jivraj's response to the letter was to start proceedings in the Commercial Court seeking a declaration that the appointment of Sir Anthony was invalid because he is not a member of the Ismaili community. Mr Hashwani subsequently issued an arbitration claim form seeking an order that Sir Anthony be appointed sole arbitrator pursuant to §18(2) of the Arbitration Act 1996 ("the 1996 Act"). The application was made on the basis that the requirement that the arbitrators be members of the Ismaili community, although lawful when the agreement was made, had been rendered unlawful and was void because it contravened the Regulations.

The Regulations were made in the exercise of powers conferred by the European Communities Act 1972 following the making of the Council Framework Directive 2000/78/EC of 27 November 2000 ("the Directive") which, by article 1, was itself made for the purpose of establishing: "a general framework for combating discrimination on the grounds of religion or belief, disability, age or sexual orientation as regards employment and occupation, with a view to putting into effect in the member states the principle of equal treatment." The Regulations (as amended by §77(2) of the Equality Act 2006) provide, so far as material, as follows:

"2 Interpretation ... (3) In these Regulations ... references to 'employer', in their application to a person at any time seeking to employ another, include a person who has no employees at that time; 'employment' means employment under a contract of service or of apprenticeship or a contract personally to do any work, and related expressions shall be construed accordingly ...;

3 Discrimination on grounds of religion or belief (1) For the purposes of these Regulations, a

person ('A') discriminates against another person ('B') if—(a) on the grounds of the religion or belief of B or of any other person except A (whether or not it is also A's religion or belief), A treats B less favourably than he treats or would treat other persons; ...

6 Applicants and employees (1) It is unlawful for an employer, in relation to employment by him at an establishment in Great Britain, to discriminate against a person—(a) in the arrangements he makes for the purpose of determining to whom he should offer employment; (b) in the terms on which he offers that person employment; or (c) by refusing to offer, or deliberately not offering, him employment.

7 Exception for genuine occupational requirement
(1) In relation to discrimination falling within regulation 3 ...—(a) regulation 6(1)(a) or (c) does not apply to any employment ... where paragraph (2) or (3) applies....
(2) This paragraph applies where, having regard to the nature of the employment or the context in which it is carried out—(a) being of a particular religion or belief is a genuine and determining occupational requirement; (b) it is proportionate to apply that requirement in the particular case; and (c) either—(i) the person to whom that requirement is applied does not meet it, or (ii) the employer is not satisfied, and in all the circumstances it is reasonable for him not to be satisfied, that that person meets it, and this paragraph applies whether or not the employer has an ethos based on religion or belief.
(3) This paragraph applies where an employer has an ethos based on religion or belief and, having regard to that ethos and to the nature of the employment or the context in which it is carried out—(a) being of a particular religion or belief is a genuine occupational requirement for the job; (b) it is proportionate to apply that requirement in the particular case; and (c) either—(i) the person to whom that requirement is applied does not meet it, or (ii) the employer is not satisfied, and in all the circumstances it is reasonable for him not to be satisfied, that that person meets it." ...

It was submitted before the [trial] judge on behalf of Mr Hashwani that the term requiring arbitrators to be members of the Ismaili community was invalid by reason of one or more of the following: the Regulations, the Human Rights Act 1998 ("the HRA"), or public policy at common law. The judge held (i) that the term did not constitute unlawful discrimination on any of those bases and, specifically, that arbitrators were not "employed" within the meaning of the Regulations; (ii) that if, nonetheless, appointment of arbitrators fell within the scope of the Regulations, it was demonstrated that one of the more significant characteristics of the Ismaili sect was an enthusiasm for dispute resolution within the Ismaili community, that this was an "ethos based on religion" within the meaning of the Regulations and that the requirement for the arbitrators to be members of the Ismaili community constituted a genuine occupational requirement which it was proportionate to apply within regulation 7(3); and (iii) that, if that was also wrong, the requirement was not severable from the arbitration provision as a whole, so that the whole arbitration clause would be void....

The Court of Appeal reached a different conclusion from the [trial] judge on the principal points. It held that the appointment of an arbitrator involved a contract for the provision of services which constituted "a contract personally to do any work," and therefore satisfied the definition of "employment" in regulation 2(3). It followed that the appointor was an "employer" within the meaning of regulation 6(1) and that the restriction of eligibility for appointment as an arbitrator to members of the Ismaili community constituted unlawful discrimination on religious grounds, both in making "arrangements ... for the purpose of determining to whom he should offer employment" contrary to regulation

6(1)(a), and by "refusing to offer, or deliberately not offering" employment contrary to regulation 6(1)(c). The Court of Appeal further held that being a member of the Ismaili community was not "a genuine occupational requirement for the job" within the meaning of the exception in regulation 7(3)....

Finally the Court of Appeal held that, although there would be no difficulty in operating the agreement if the offending requirement was struck out, so doing would render the agreement substantially different from that originally intended, the term was void in its entirety under paragraph 1(1) of Schedule 4 to the Regulations and Mr Hashwani's nomination of an arbitrator was invalid. It is submitted on behalf of Mr Hashwani that both the judge and the Court of Appeal were wrong on this point, which I will call "the severance issue." ...

The reasoning of the Court of Appeal was straightforward. In short the Court of Appeal drew attention to the wide terms of articles 1 and 3 of the Directive. In particular it noted ... that the recitals to the Directive and the structure and language of article 3(1) as a whole indicate that it is concerned with discrimination affecting access to the means of economic activity, whether through employment, self-employment or some other basis of occupation, access to vocational guidance and training (which can be expected to provide a means of access to economic activity), conditions of employment (which affect those who have gained access to a means of economic activity) and membership of bodies whose purpose is to affect conditions of recruitment or employment or to regulate access to a particular form of economic activity, such as professional bodies that directly or indirectly control access to the profession or a significant means of obtaining work. The Court of Appeal then said:

> "The paradigm case of appointing an arbitrator involves obtaining the services of a particular person to determine a dispute in accordance with the agreement between the parties and the rules of law, including those to be found in the legislation governing arbitration. In that respect it is no different from instructing a solicitor to deal with a particular piece of legal business, such as drafting a will, or consulting a doctor about a particular ailment or an accountant about a tax return. Since an arbitrator (or any professional person) contracts to do work personally, the provision of his services falls within the definition of 'employment', and it follows that his appointor must be an employer within the meaning of regulation 6(1)....
>
> [Decisions holding that arbitrators' fees are subject to value added tax] confirm our view that the expression is apt to encompass the position of a person who provides services as an arbitrator, and why we think the judge was wrong to hold that the nature of the arbitrator's function takes his appointment outside the scope of the 2003 Regulations. Moreover, a contract of that kind, once made, is a contract of employment within the meaning of the 2003 Regulations. It follows, therefore, that for the purposes of the 2003 Regulations a person who has entered into a contract under which he is to obtain such services is an employer and the person engaged to provide them is an employee."

The critical question under this head is whether the Court of Appeal was correct to form a different view from the judge on this point. In my opinion it was not....

It is common ground ... that there is a contract between the parties and the arbitrator or arbitrators appointed under a contract and that his or their services are rendered pursuant to that contract. It is not suggested that such a contract provides for "employment under a contract of service or of apprenticeship." The question is whether it provides for "employment under ... a contract personally to do any work." There is in my opinion some significance in the fact that the definition does not simply refer to a contract to do work but to "employment under" such a contract. I would answer the question in the negative on the ground that the role of an arbitrator is not naturally described as employment under a contract personally to do work. That is because his role is not naturally described as one of employment at all. I appreciate that there is an element of circularity in that approach but the definition is of "employment" and this approach is consistent with the decided cases.

[The Court of Appeal cited the decision of the European Court of Justice in *Lawrie-Blum v Land Baden-Wurttemberg*, Case No. C-188/00, [1987] ICR 483, where the Court said:]

> "That concept (ie of 'worker') must be defined with objective criteria which distinguish the employment relationship by reference to the rights and duties of the persons concerned. The essential feature of an employment relationship, however, is that for a certain period of time a person performs services for and under the direction of another person in return for which he receives remuneration." ...

On the basis of those materials I would accept [the] submission that the [European] Court of Justice draws a clear distinction between those who are, in substance, employed and those who are "independent providers of services who are not in a relationship of subordination with the person who receives the services." I see no reason why the same distinction should not be drawn for the purposes of the Regulations between those who are employed and those who are not notionally but genuinely self-employed....

The essential questions in each case are ... whether, on the one hand, the person concerned performs services for and under the direction of another person in return for which he or she receives remuneration or, on the other hand, he or she is an independent provider of services who is not in a relationship of subordination with the person who receives the services. Those are broad questions which depend upon the circumstances of the particular case. They depend upon a detailed consideration of the relationship between the parties....

If [this] approach ... is applied to a contract between the parties to an arbitration and the arbitrator (or arbitrators), it is in my opinion plain that the arbitrators' role is not one of employment under a contract personally to do work. Although an arbitrator may be providing services for the purposes of [value added tax] and he of course receives fees for his work, and although he renders personal services which he cannot delegate, he does not perform those services or earn his fees for and under the direction of the parties.... He is rather in the category of an independent provider of services who is not in a relationship of subordination with the parties who receive his services....

The arbitrator is in critical respects independent of the parties. His functions and duties require him to rise above the partisan interests of the parties and not to act in, or so as to further, the particular interests of either party. [Instead,] he must determine how to resolve their competing interests. He is in no sense in a position of subordination to the parties; rather the contrary. He is in effect a "quasi-judicial adjudicator."

In England his role is spelled out in the 1996 [Arbitration] Act. By §33, he has a duty to act fairly and impartially as between the parties and to adopt procedures suitable to the circumstances of the particular case so as to provide a fair means of determination of the issues between the parties. Section 34 provides that, subject to the right of the parties to agree any matter, it is for the arbitrator to decide all procedural matters.... Once an arbitrator has been appointed, at any rate in the absence of agreement between them, the parties effectively have no control over him. Unless the parties agree, an arbitrator may only be removed in exceptional circumstances. The court was referred to many other statutory provisions in other parts of the world and indeed many other international codes, including the UNCITRAL Model Law on International Commercial Arbitration 1985, the ICC Rules and the LCIA Rules to similar effect....

In this regard an arbitrator is in a very different position from a judge.... [J]udges ... at every level are subject to terms of service of various kinds.... [A]lthough judges must enjoy independence of decision without direction from any source, they are in other respects not free agents to work as and when they choose, as are self-employed persons.

[In prior decisions suggesting that judges are employees,] the court was considering the relationship between the relevant department of state and the judges concerned. It was not considering the relationship between the judges and the litigants who appear before them. Here, by contrast, the court is considering the relationship between the parties to the arbitration on the one hand and the arbitrator or arbitrators on the other. As I see it, there is no basis upon which it could properly be held that the arbitrators agreed to work under the direction of the parties.... Further, in so far as dominant purpose is relevant, I would hold that the dominant purpose of appointing an arbitrator or arbitrators is the impartial resolution of the dispute between the parties in accordance with the terms of the agreement and, although the contract between the parties and the arbitrators would be a contract for the provision of personal services, they were not personal services under the direction of the parties....

For these reasons I prefer the conclusion of the [trial] judge to that of the Court of Appeal. I agree with the judge that the Regulations are not applicable to the selection, engagement or appointment of arbitrators. It follows that I would hold that no part of clause 8 of the JVA is invalid by reason of the Regulations and would allow the appeal on this ground.

[In the alternative, the Court of Appeal held that the requirement that the arbitration be an Ismaili was a "genuine occupational requirement."] It will be recalled that, by regulation 7(1), regulations 6(1)(a) and (c) do not apply where regulation 7(3) [quoted above] applies.... As I see it, the question is ... whether in all the circumstances of the case the requirement that the arbitrators should be respected members of the Ismaili community was, not only genuine, but legitimate and justified. I do not agree ... that the requirement that arbitrators be Ismailis cannot be objectively justified. [The argument] that an English law dispute in London under English curial law does not require an Ismaili arbitrator takes a very narrow view of the function of arbitration proceedings. This characterisation reduces arbitration to no more than the application of a given national law to a dispute.

One of the distinguishing features of arbitration that sets it apart from proceedings in national courts is the breadth of discretion left to the parties and the arbitrator to structure the process for resolution of the dispute. This is reflected in §1 of the 1996 [Arbitration] Act which provides that: "the parties should be free to agree how their disputes are resolved, subject only to such safeguards as are necessary in the public interest." The stipulation that an arbitrator be of a particular religion or belief can be relevant to this aspect of arbitration. [As an amicus submission of the ICC reasoned:]

> "The raison d'être of arbitration is that it provides for final and binding dispute resolution by a tribunal with a procedure that is acceptable to all parties, in circumstances where other fora (in particular national courts) are deemed inappropriate (eg because neither party will submit to the courts or their counterpart; or because the available courts are considered insuffi-

ciently expert for the particular dispute, or insufficiently sensitive to the parties' positions, culture, or perspectives)." ...

[The trial] judge held that the provision in the JVA which provided that the arbitrators should be respected members of the Ismaili community and holders of high office within the community was a [genuine occupational requirement] within regulation 7(3). He did so on the basis that the material set out above showed that ... one of the more significant and characteristic spirits of the Ismaili sect was an enthusiasm for dispute resolution contained within the Ismaili community. He said that he had no difficulty in determining this spirit to be an "ethos based on religion." He also relied upon the terms of the arbitration clause itself and the engagement by both sides of members of the Ismaili community to perform mediation and conciliation services from 1988 until 1994. In my opinion the judge was justified in concluding that the requirement of an Ismaili arbitrator can be regarded as a genuine occupational requirement on the basis that it was not only genuine but both legitimate and justified....

LORD MANCE.... I have read and agree entirely with the judgment of Lord Clarke on the first point: that is, whether the arbitrators contemplated by article 8 of the Joint Venture Agreement are persons who would be engaged in "employment under ... a contract personally to do work" within the meaning of regulation 2 of the Regulations....

The conclusion that they would not be is, I think, unsurprising for all the reasons that Lord Clarke gives. I note that as long ago as 1904 (RGZ 59, 247), the German Reichsgericht identified the particular nature of an arbitral contract, in terms which I think have a relevance to arbitration generally, when it said (in translation), that:

> "It does not seem permissible to treat the arbitrator as equivalent to a representative or an employee or an entrepreneur. His office has ... an entirely special character, which distinguishes him from other persons handling the affairs of third parties. He has to decide a legal dispute in the same way as and instead of a judge, identifying the law by matching the relevant facts to the relevant legal provisions. The performance expected from him is the award, which constitutes the goal and outcome of his activity. It is true that the extent of his powers depends on the arbitration agreement, which can to a greater or lesser extent prescribe the way to that goal for him. But, apart from this restriction, his position is entirely free, freer than that of an ordinary judge."

A more modern source, Gary B Born's authoritative work on *International Commercial Arbitration* [1607-09 (2009)], convincingly discusses the general international legal understanding of the nature of an arbitrator's engagement in the following passage:

> "There is also debate about how to characterize the arbitrator's contract, particularly in civil law jurisdictions where the characterization of contracts is often essential to determining their effects. Some commentators consider the arbitrator's contract to be an agency agreement, where the arbitrator serves as the parties' agent. Other authorities have suggested treating the arbitrator's contract as an agreement for the provision of services. A third approach has been to regard the arbitrator's contract as a *sui generis* or hybrid form of agreement, not being categorizable in conventional terms and instead giving rise to a unique set of right and duties.
>
> The proper analysis is to treat the arbitrator's contract as a *sui generis* agreement. That is in part because this characterization accords with the specialized and distinct nature of the arbitrator's mandate: as noted above, that mandate differs in fundamental ways from the provision of many other services and consists in the performance of a relatively *sui generis*

adjudicatory function. It is therefore appropriate, and in fact necessary, that the arbitrator's contract be regarded as *sui generis*.

At the same time, there are no other satisfactory characterizations of an arbitrator's contract. It makes no sense to treat the arbitrator's contract as an agency agreement. Under most legal systems, that characterization would require the arbitrator to follow the parties' directions and to provide the parties with information and an accounting—all of which can only with difficulty, if at all, be assimilated to the adjudicative role of an arbitrator.

Moreover, the role of an agent is inconsistent with the arbitrator's adjudicative function—which is precisely to be independent of the parties. This was underscored by a French appellate decision, which held that an agreement for the parties' 'representatives' to resolve their dispute could not be an arbitration agreement:

> 'A stipulation of that kind is incompatible with the actual concept of arbitration, since the arbitrators, though appointed by the parties, can under no circumstances become their representatives. That would imply, in particular, that they represent the parties and account for their functions. Such a role, and the obligations it entails, are alien to the functions of an arbitrator, which are judicial in nature.'

Equally, regarding the arbitrator as a service provider, like an accountant, investment banker, lawyer, or other professional, ignores the essential adjudicative character of his or her mandate. Arbitrators do not merely provide the parties with a service, but also serve a public, adjudicatory function that cannot be entirely equated with the provision of service in a commercial relationship. The proper analysis is therefore to regard the arbitrator's contract as a *sui generis* agreement specifying the terms on which this adjudicative function is to be exercised vis-à-vis particular parties and on particular terms."

Both these citations catch and support the essence of Lord Clarke's distinction between persons under the direction of another and arbitrators who perform an independent role, free of such control....

WALKINSHAW v. DINIZ
[2000] 2 All ER (Comm) 237 (QB) (English High Ct.)

THOMAS J. There is before the court an application by the defendant, Mr Diniz, to stay these proceedings brought against him by the Claimants ("Arrows") under §9 of the [English] Arbitration Act 1996 on the basis that the parties had agreed to refer the matters in dispute to arbitration under the contract between them.

On 24 October 1997 Arrows, owners and operators of the Arrows Formula One racing team, entered into a contract with Mr Diniz, a professional Formula One racing driver, under which Mr Diniz would drive for them during the 1998 and 1999 Formula One World Motor Racing Car Championships. [The] Championships are governed by the 1997 Concorde Agreement, ... to which all Formula One racing teams and the Fédération Internationale de l'Automobile ("FIA") are parties. The structure of the arrangements are such that agreements are also made between drivers and each team individually, and the agreement to which I have referred between Mr Diniz and Arrow was one such agreement.... Among the obligations of Arrows was the provision of a car, and a spare car, to a standard warranted under [clause] 7 of the agreement.... [T]he contract had to be registered by a body called "The Contract Recognition Board" (established under ... the 1997 Concorde Agreement) [CRB)]....

The Concorde Agreement also required each contract between the driver and his team to contain a provision for the resolution of conflicts by the [CRB]. This provision was incorporated into the contract between Mr Diniz and Arrows by the first part of [clause] 11:

"11.1 The Parties hereto expressly agree that this Agreement is (or as the case may be, forms a part of) a Contract as defined by clause 6(1) of Schedule 11 to the Concorde Agreement so that the Parties hereto hereby agree with each other to respect the terms of the said Schedule and in particular Clause 7 thereof which provides for the resolutions of conflicts by the Contract Recognition Board sitting in Geneva, Switzerland. Accordingly the Parties hereto expressly submit to the exclusive jurisdiction of any competent judicial or other body as regards interim or conservatory measures in that respect.

11.2 Subject to Clause 11.1 this Agreement shall be governed by English Law and shall be subject to the exclusive jurisdiction of the courts of England."

Clause 11.1 is the clause which was required to be inserted into the agreement by the terms of the Concorde Agreement. [Schedule 11, referred to in Clause 11.1, was a commercial contract between the parties.] ... I should record at this stage that it is the contention of Mr Diniz that the [CRB] is an arbitral body and not, as Arrows contend, merely a body to decide on the "rules of the game."

In accordance with those provisions, on 11 November 1997 the agreement between Mr Diniz and Arrows was registered by the [CRB]. [Disputes subsequently arose between Mr Diniz and Arrows, leading to (a) the termination of their agreement, (b) the convening of the [CRB], comprised of three well-known arbitration practitioners, and (c) related litigation in English courts. Mr Diniz sought to stay the English litigation under the English Arbitration Act, 1996, on the grounds that the proceedings before the [CRB] were an arbitration.]

It was the contention of Arrows that the [CRB] is not an arbitral body and a reference to it was not a reference to arbitration; the function of the [CRB] was merely to supervise the rules of the game or a sport.... As [Arrows] pointed out, there is no reference in [Schedule] 11 to the word "arbitrator" in connection with the [CRB] or to the [CRB] acting as "arbitrators." On the contrary, the reference is to the language of administration—"Contract Recognition Board," ["resolutions of conflicts"] and "decision." In contrast, [clause] 15.1 of [Schedule] 11 provided:

"15.1 All disputes arising in connection with this Schedule 11 (other than a dispute in respect of matters to be determined by the Board pursuant to Clause 7) shall be finally settled under the Rules of Conciliation and Arbitration of the International Chamber of Commerce in force at the date hereof, by one or more arbitrators appointed in accordance with the said Rules.
    15.2 Arbitration shall take place in Lausanne (Switzerland)."

These are powerful arguments, particularly as the schedule is a document which was clearly drafted with the greatest care by lawyers. But in my view, terminology, though a pointer, can be no more than that. It is necessary to examine the substance of whether the [CRB]'s function was an arbitral one or some other function.

Although an arbitral tribunal can, as a matter of the law of England and Wales, apply principles that are not strictly legal principles (§46 of the 1996 Act), it may be an indication of whether the process is an arbitral one if the decision-maker is free to make a decision on a non-legal basis. It is contended by Arrows that this was so, ... [under clause] 7.13 of [Schedule] 11.... However, this provision was merely setting out the simple rule to be applied if there were two valid contracts. In all other respects it is quite clear that the Contract Recognition Board was to apply the proper law of the contract.... The position is quite unlike that in *O'Callaghan v. Coral Racing Ltd* [[1998] EWCA Civ 1801] where the Court of Appeal held that in a gaming agreement, a reference of disputes to the editor of the Sporting Life was not an arbitration clause since ... "To my mind the hallmark of the arbitration process is that it is a procedure to determine the legal rights and obligations of the parties judicially, with binding effect, which is enforceable in law, thus reflecting in private proceedings the role of a civil court of law." In that case the procedure was devoid of legal consequence because the gaming transaction was null and void under the Gaming Act 1845. Therefore the editor of Sporting Life could not determine any matter which had legal consequences. Here, clearly, the [CRB] determined a matter that had legal consequences—which contract took precedence—and did so in accordance with the law and the specific rule (which I have set out) if all else failed....

In my view, it is a characteristic of arbitration that the parties should have a proper opportunity of presenting their case. Although there is nothing expressed in [Schedule] 11, it is quite clear from the procedure adopted by the [CRB] in this case that their procedures enable the parties to make proper representations and to have a full opportunity to present their case. I accept that that is a fundamental requirement of an arbitration, as it goes to the very integrity of the arbitrators and their impartiality.

In this case, when Arrows applied to the [CRB] on 29 January 1999 for copies of communications between the [CRB] and Sauber [(a representative of one of the parties)] and copies of the documents submitted by Sauber, a member of the staff of the Secretariat of the [CRB] replied: "The Secretariat is not prepared to send copies of any correspondence because it is confidential and because we consider it irrelevant to your purposes." In my view, there can be no doubt that a refusal by the [CRB] to provide communications between it and one of the parties would have been a strong indication that the process was not an arbitral one, as secret communications between one party and the tribunal are inimical to the arbitral process. However, the refusal to provide documents was made by a member of staff of the Secretariat. His letter made it clear that the request had to be addressed to the [CRB] members themselves. I have no doubt, given the procedures adopted in respect of other matters, and the high standing of the [CRB] members, that if an application had been made by Arrows to them, they would not have refused provision of these documents.

I accept again that the hallmarks of an arbitral process are the provision of proper and proportionate procedures for the provision and for the receipt of evidence. Arrows submitted that the procedures laid down in [Schedule] 11 and the decision of the [CRB] shows that there was no proper or proportionate procedure for the proper receipt of evidence. They pointed, in particular, to the fact that the [CRB] had said that it would hear the argument on jurisdiction and the merits of the dispute as to whether Arrows were in breach of [clause] 7 and the performance warranties within one day starting at noon, though they did indicate that it might be necessary for there to be further time. The secretary made it clear what his view was in his letter of 19 April 1999:

> "As to all such issues, it is a matter for each party to decide what written evidential material it seeks to adduce before the CRB within the confines of the CRB's orders; the CRB has of course power to extend the hearing if justice so required it; but at present the CRB considers it more than fair to TWR/Arrows that this second oral hearing should be limited to one day.

No previous oral hearings of the CRB, which have involved disputes much more complicated than this dispute, have ever lasted more than one day. This dispute has of course extended into two days as a result of TWR/Arrows' failure to attend the first hearing."

It was submitted, powerfully, by [Arrows] that this attitude of the secretary made it clear
that the procedure was a summary one wholly at variance with an arbitral process. For
example, there was no contemplation of the receipt of expert evidence or even the appointment of a tribunal-appointed expert, which is obviously necessary for the determination of the issue as to whether Arrows were in breach of the performance warranties and Mr
Diniz entitled to terminate [the contract, as he claimed the right to do].

Although the letter from the secretary is somewhat peremptory and surprising in its
tone, the [CRB] itself (as opposed to its secretary) does appear to have sought to give the
parties proper time in all other respects. For example, it adjourned its decision in February;
it sought submissions from the parties when an adjournment was requested. I am not
persuaded that this single and somewhat peremptory letter from the secretary, although
possibly indicating the adoption of a procedure inconsistent with a proper arbitral process,
enables the procedures to be characterised as those that did not have arbitral characteristics.
It is important that it was not the decision of the [CRB] itself....

[T]here is no evidence to suggest that the [CRB] itself considered that the resolution of
the dispute required the hearing to be completed in a day, or would refuse to hear expert
evidence, whether appointed by the parties or by the [CRB] itself. On the contrary, it seems
to me clear beyond doubt that if time was required the [CRB] would take the time and
arrange for the receipt of expert evidence. They clearly would have afforded proper and
proportionate means for the receipt of evidence.

It was submitted that the requirement that the [CRB] render its decision within three
days of the final conflicting contract meeting showed that it was a summary procedure
inconsistent with arbitration. I do not agree. There is no restriction on the number of conflicting contract meetings that can be called. If justice so requires, the [CRB] has to hold as
many meetings as is required, whatever the secretary may have said in his letter of 19 April
1999. All that is required is a speedy decision at the end of the final meeting. Such a requirement is plainly consistent with an arbitral or judicial process and not inconsistent with
it....

The [CRB] chosen to determine the issues must ... consist of three lawyers of international standing. In my view, this is a very important indication that the process is intended
to be an arbitral one. [T]he selection of the panel by the president of the Court of Arbitration of the [ICC] is a further factor pointing towards the fact that the process is intended to
be arbitral.

Clauses 2.4 and 2.5 of [Schedule] 11 excludes from participation in the [CRB] that is to
determine a matter referred to it those connected with the FIA or with Formula One Motor
Racing. This shows, again, an intention to make the tribunal impartial, consistent with the
arbitral process.

Finally, there are the considerations set out in [M. Mustill & S. Boyd,] *Law and Practice
of Commercial Arbitration in England* 41 (2d ed. 1989). They set out the following attributes which they consider must be present:

"(i) The agreement pursuant to which the process is, or is to be, carried on ('the procedural
agreement') must contemplate that the tribunal which carries on the process will make a
decision which is binding on the parties to the procedural agreement. (ii) The procedural

agreement must contemplate that the process will be carried on between those persons whose substantive rights are determined by the tribunal. (iii) The jurisdiction of the tribunal to carry on the process and to decide the rights of the parties must derive either from the consent of the parties, or from an order of the court or from a statute the terms of which make it clear that the process is to be an arbitration. (iv) The tribunal must be chosen, either by the parties, or by a method to which they have consented. (v) The procedural agreement must contemplate that the tribunal will determine the rights of the parties in an impartial manner, with the tribunal owing an equal obligation of fairness towards both sides. (vi) The agreement of the parties to refer their disputes to the decision of the tribunal must be intended to be enforceable in law. (vii) The procedural agreement must contemplate a process whereby the tribunal will make a decision upon a dispute which is already formulated at the time when the tribunal is appointed."

Each of those attributes was, in my view, present.... (i) It is clear that a decision reached by the [CRB] in respect of which the conflicting contracts had priority would be legally binding as between the parties to the decision. Paragraph 7.13 of [Schedule] 11 supports this view. (ii) The [CRB]'s procedure involves the tripartite determination of that question. (iii) Jurisdiction has been conferred by the parties by contracts signed by the Formula One racing teams with the FIA and the contracts between each driver and each team.... It is nothing to the point that these are contracts of adhesion and the parties have to assent thereto if they wish to participate in Formula One racing. (iv) The [CRB] is, as I have set out, chosen by a method to which the parties consented in the agreement. (v) For the reasons I have given I consider the agreement contemplates that the [CRB] will determine the matter impartially and owes equal obligations of fairness to both parties.... (vi) The agreements plainly contemplated that the agreement to have the [CRB] decide matters was intended to be enforceable. The parties, for example, expressly excluded their rights to resort to the courts for interim measures. (*See* [clause] 7.2 and 10.1 of [Schedule] 11). (vii) ... [The CRB] was appointed to try the issue which was formulated at the time the particular board of three was appointed, namely which of the contracts took precedence.

Having considered each of these detailed matters it is necessary to ask the general question: was the procedure intended by the agreements, looked at generally, an arbitral process or simply some other form of consensual dispute resolution to determine the rules of the game? Clearly many sporting events have procedures that are not arbitral. No general view can be taken and it is necessary to look at the features of the procedures in each case. In this case, standing back and looking at the arrangements as a whole, I am of the firm view that what was intended and contemplated was an arbitration confined to the question of conflicting contracts. Lawyers of distinction were to be chosen as members of the tribunal; evidence was to be received; procedures and hearings necessary for the fair determination of that issue were contemplated and a decision with reasons was required.

Although I have reached the view (both from detailed consideration of the matters I have set out, and by more general considerations) quite independently, I am very glad that it is also the view of the [CRB]. Although it could be said of the [CRB] that they were bound, in any event, to say that, I consider that the decision reached by lawyers of such considerable international standing and distinction is entitled to the highest respect.... I therefore conclude ... that the procedure was an arbitral one and the 1996 Act would have been applicable to it....

ELBERON BATHING CO. v. AMBASSADOR INSURANCE CO.
389 A.2d 439 (N.J. 1978)

CONFORD, J. The principal question on this appeal concerns the valuation methods to be used in ascertaining the "actual cash value" of a partial loss under Standard Form Fire Insurance Policy. We are also required to determine whether failure to apply the appropriate standard is sufficient cause to set aside an appraisal award. The appeal arises in the context of a judgment in the Law Division in favor of the insured plaintiffs in the amount of $52,000 for excess coverage based on a $77,000 appraisement minus $25,000 primary coverage (on another policy) for a loss due to fire....

Defendant, Ambassador Insurance Company, issued a fire insurance policy to plaintiffs, Elberon Bathing Co., Inc. and Elberon Bathing Club, to indemnify them against loss by fire to club facilities and contents situated in Long Branch. The $125,000 policy represented excess coverage over a $25,000 primary policy issued plaintiffs by Great Southwest Fire Insurance Company. On January 8, 1975, while the policy was in effect, plaintiffs' bathing club was damaged by fire to an amount "greatly in excess of $25,000." Great Southwest promptly paid Elberon the $25,000. However, plaintiffs and defendant were unable to adjust plaintiffs' covered loss under the excess policy. Pursuant to the terms of the policy and an "agreement for submission to appraisers," plaintiffs and defendant each appointed an appraiser. The appraisers were, in turn, to select a disinterested umpire. However, they were unable to reach agreement thereon. Plaintiffs then filed a complaint ... requesting the court to appoint an umpire pursuant to the terms of the policy.

Shortly thereafter the appraisers and umpire went to inspect the insured premises which had already been repaired. According to affidavits of the umpire and defendant's appraiser, the umpire and plaintiffs' appraiser believed that their role was merely to determine the replacement cost of the damaged property. The umpire and plaintiffs' appraiser determined the actual cash value of the entire property to be $180,000 and the amount of fire loss to the property to total $77,000. This consisted of $8,500 for damage to personal property and $68,500 for pure replacement cost of the realty destroyed. Defendant's appraiser refused to sign the award.

Plaintiffs sought entry of judgment on the appraisement. Defendant answered, denying the finality of the award on the basis of its contention that the umpire had not heard all the evidence nor considered all matters submitted to him. It further disclaimed liability because of Elberon's alleged fraud in submitting a claim which it knew was substantially in excess of the actual cost to it to repair the damage. Defendant demanded that the award be vacated, and requested a jury trial on all the issues. In addition, defendant separately sought discovery of various "loss estimates" prepared by plaintiffs' appraiser and gave notice, pursuant to the policy, of defendant's desire to examine plaintiffs' documents and representatives.

The trial judge ... [held] that the appraisers could properly determine that replacement cost was the appropriate measure of the actual loss, recoverable under the policy. He also found that there was no manifest mistake justifying setting aside the award. After deduction for the primary insurance coverage judgment was entered for plaintiff for $52,000. The Appellate Division, agreeing with the trial judge that under the appropriate narrow standard of review "the facts in the case do not dictate a basis for vacating the award," ... affirmed. We granted certification....

Defendant raises the question whether the trial court was required to proceed in this matter under and pursuant to the Arbitration Act, N.J.S.A. 2A-24-1 *et seq.* It asserts that if the Act was applicable, the award should be vacated because the procedures followed by the appraisers did not conform thereto. We have concluded that the Arbitration Act is not applicable.

A comparison of appraisal and arbitration will be helpful. The purposes of both are the same; to submit disputes to third parties and effect their speedy and efficient resolution without recourse to the courts. To assure minimum judicial intervention, the scope of judicial review of both types of recourse is narrow. The distinctions are significant. An agreement for arbitration ordinarily encompasses the disposition of the entire controversy between the parties, and judgment may be entered upon the award, whereas an appraisal establishes only the amount of loss and not liability. Arbitration is conducted as a quasi-judicial proceeding, with hearings, notice of hearings, oaths of arbitrators and oaths of witnesses. Appraisers act on their own skill and knowledge, need not be sworn and need hold no formal hearings so long as both sides are given an opportunity to state their positions.

The instant policy provision clearly called for an appraisal. That the procedures mandated by the Arbitration Act, *see, e.g.*, N.J.S.A. 2A:24-6, were not followed and that there was no finding with respect to liability tends to indicate that the fact-finders purported to conduct an appraisal. This was entirely proper. Nothing in the Arbitration Act requires that fire insurance appraisals comply with that statute. Indeed, the word "appraisal" is not found in the Act. *See In re Delmar Box Co.*, 127 N.E.2d 808, 810-811 (N.J. Ct. App. 1955), where the court noted the long-prevailing distinctions between appraisals and arbitration, and concluded that any determination that the formal requirements under the Arbitration Act should apply to fire loss appraisals should come from the Legislature.

Furthermore, since application of the broad evidence rule to appraisals will promote the interchange of information between the appraisers and the parties, one may expect enhancement of the fairness of the procedure without burdening the appraisal with the formalities of arbitration (*e.g.*, oaths, notice of hearings, etc.). Finally, since arbitrators are entrusted with the broader obligation to determine liability as well as the amount of the award, it is reasonable to require broader procedural safeguards in arbitration. The subject-matter responsibility of appraisers being less, the procedural safeguards attending an appraisal may be lower. However, the Court must correct any erroneous exercise of jurisdiction by an appraiser....

NOTES

1. *Definition of "arbitration agreement" under New York Convention.* Consider the definition of an arbitration agreement in Article II(1) of the New York Convention, excerpted at p. 1 of the Documentary Supplement. What, if anything, does that definition indicate about the characteristics of an agreement to arbitrate? Note that Article II(1) suggests that an arbitration agreement involves a contractual relationship between parties; that this agreement deals with disputes or differences, either future or existing; that these disputes will be submitted to and resolved by "arbitration"; and that the agreement may take the form of either an arbitration clause (in a broader commercial contract) or a separate contract (dealing only with arbitration). Note also, however, that the Convention does virtually nothing to explain what the process of

"arbitration," as contemplated by Article II(1) and the Convention generally, consists of.

How is the concept of "arbitration" to be defined for purposes of the Convention? Is it to be defined by national law or by a uniform international standard, derived from the Convention? If the latter, how would one go about attempting to derive such a definition?

2. *Definition of "arbitration agreement" under UNCITRAL Model Law.* Consider also the definition of "arbitration agreement" under Article 7 of the Model Law, excerpted at pp. 87-88 of the Documentary Supplement. Does this provision provide further elaboration, beyond that existing in the Convention, of the term "arbitration agreement"?

3. *Arbitration under 1907 Hague Convention for the Pacific Settlement of International Disputes.* Consider the treatment of international arbitration under Articles 37 to 90 of the 1907 Hague Convention, excerpted at pp. 43-50 of the Documentary Supplement. Contrast with the treatment of Good Offices and Mediation under Articles 2 to 8 and International Commissions of Inquiry under Articles 9 to 36 of the Convention. What appears to be the defining characteristics of arbitration under the Convention?

4. *Arbitration under ICSID Convention.* Consider the treatment of international arbitration under Articles 36 to 55 of the ICSID Convention, excerpted at pp. 21-25 of the Documentary Supplement. Contrast with the treatment of conciliation under Articles 28 to 35 of the Convention. Again, what appears to be the defining characteristics of "arbitration" under the Convention?

5. *What is "arbitration"?* How should the concept of an "arbitration" agreement be defined? Consider the definitions suggested in *Walkinshaw* and *Elberon*. How do these definitions differ from one another? How, if at all, do they differ from the process of inter-state arbitration detailed in the 1907 Hague Convention and of investment arbitration detailed in the ICSID Convention? Consider Article 37 of the 1907 Hague Convention, providing: "International arbitration has for its object the settlement of differences between States by Judges of their own choice, and on the basis of respect for law." What does this description include? Exclude? Note also Articles 40 and 41 of the 1907 Hague Convention, excerpted at p. 43 of the Documentary Supplement.

Consider the discussion of arbitration, and the role of the arbitrator, by the U.K. Supreme Court in *Jivraj*. What are the differences between an arbitrator and a judge? What are the similarities? Is an arbitrator really more independent than a judge? Who employs a judge? Do litigants employ "their" judge?

6. *Definitions of "arbitration."* Try and distill the essence of arbitration, and an arbitration agreement, from these various authorities. Compare your definition to the following efforts to define arbitration:

> "two or more parties, faced with a dispute which they cannot resolve for themselves, agreeing that some private individual will resolve it for them and if the arbitration runs its full course.... It will not be settled by a compromise, but by a decision." A. Redfern & M. Hunter, *Law and Practice of International Commercial Arbitration* ¶1-03 (4th ed. 2004).

> "a mode of resolving disputes by one or more persons who derive their power from the agreement of the parties and whose decision is binding upon them." de Vries, *International Commercial Arbitration: A Contractual Substitute for National Courts*, 57

Tulane L. Rev. 42, 42-43 (1982).

"a contractual method for the relatively private settlement of disputes." M. Reisman *et al.*, *International Commercial Arbitration: Cases, Materials and Notes on the Resolution of International Business Disputes* xxviii (1997).

"a device whereby the settlement of a question, which is of interest for two or more persons, is entrusted to one or more other persons—the arbitrator or arbitrators—who derive their powers from a private agreement, not from the authorities of a state, and who are to proceed and decide the case on the basis of such an agreement." R. David, *Arbitration in International Trade* 5 (1985).

"voluntary submission by parties to a special kind of private litigation which is accepted, tolerated and sanctioned by public international law and the laws of most civilized jurisdictions." Wetter, *The Legal Framework of International Arbitral Tribunals—Five Tentative Markings*, in H. Smit, N.M. Galston & S.L. Levitsky (eds.), *International Contracts* 271, 274 (1981).

"the voluntary submission by the parties of a dispute for decision by recognised and regular procedure other than litigation." Roebuck, *A Short History of Arbitration*, in N. Kaplan, J. Spruce & M. Moser (eds.), *Hong Kong and China Arbitration: Cases And Materials* xxxv (1994).

Which of these definitions is best? What are the flaws in each?

7. *What isn't arbitration?* One way to attempt to formulate a definition of arbitration is by determining what arbitration is not. Consider each of the following examples of dispute resolution processes that are related to, but distinguishable from, arbitration.

    (a) *Arbitration is not conciliation or mediation.* Consider the conciliation provisions of the ICSID Convention and the 1907 Hague Convention, excerpted at pp. 19-21 & 38-42 of the Documentary Supplement. Note Article 37 of the 1907 Hague Convention. *Compare* World Intellectual Property Organization, *Guide to WIPO Mediation* 4 (2004) ("What is mediation? Mediation is first and foremost a *non-binding* procedure. This means that, even though parties have agreed to submit a dispute to mediation, they are not obliged to continue with the mediation process after the first meeting. In this sense, the parties remain always in control of a mediation. The continuation of the process depends on their continuing acceptance. The non-binding nature of mediation means also that a decision cannot be imposed on the parties. In order for any settlement to be concluded, the parties must voluntarily agree to accept it. Unlike a judge or an arbitrator, therefore, the mediator is not a decision-maker. The role of the mediator is rather to assist the parties in reaching their own decision on a settlement of the dispute.").

    What dispute resolution process do the provisions cited above from the ICSID Convention and 1907 Hague Convention provide for? How do these processes differ from arbitration? Note that a basic objective of arbitration is to produce a binding award that not only finally decides the parties' dispute, but that is subject to only limited grounds for challenge in national courts. *See supra* pp. 46-51, 109 & *infra* pp. 1113-25, 1155-63. How is this comparable to mediation or conciliation?

    To what extent may mediation or conciliation involve the mediator or conciliator engaging in *ex parte* contact with each of the parties separately (in a form of shuttle diplomacy)? Would such *ex parte* contacts ordinarily be permitted in arbitration? *See infra* pp. 746-47. Consider how the decisions in *Walkinshaw* and *Elberon* regarded the possibility of *ex parte* contacts by arbitrators.

What "law" applies to the substance of the parties' dispute in a conciliation or mediation? Is the conciliator or mediator obliged to "apply" the applicable substantive law? What about an arbitrator? *See infra* pp. 1017-21. What is likely to be the reaction of the parties if a mediator or conciliator ignores the applicable law?

Note that the ICSID Convention and 1907 Hague Convention contain separate regimes for conciliation or mediation, on the one hand, and arbitration, on the other. In some jurisdictions, separate legislation has been adopted governing mediation, conciliation and related forms of alternative dispute resolution. *See, e.g., Adoption of the UNCITRAL Model Law on International Commercial Conciliation,* in *Report of the United Nations Commission on International Trade Law on Its Thirty-Fifth Session,* U.N. Doc. A/57/17, ¶141, Annex 1 (2002). In these instances, the different legal frameworks governing mediation or conciliation and arbitration will be apparent. In other jurisdictions, where there is no formal mediation or conciliation statute, these will be subject to a different legal regime than arbitration. *See* G. Born, *International Commercial Arbitration* 271 *et seq.* (2d ed. 2014).

Suppose that the parties' agreement provides: "All disputes under this contract shall be submitted to non-binding arbitration for the recommendation of a neutral arbitrator, made after hearing the parties' submissions." Is this an arbitration agreement?

(b) *Arbitration is not expert determination.* Just as arbitration is not conciliation or mediation, so too, arbitration is not expert determination, appraisal, or valuation. Commercial contracts often contain provisions for the resolution of certain categories of disputes by an expert, accountant, engineer, or other specialist selected (directly or indirectly) by the parties and authorized to render a binding decision on a specified issue. *See* ICC, *Arbitration and Expertise* (1994). Such provisions can involve accounting (or other financial) calculations by an accountant, quality determinations by an industry representative, oil and gas reserve estimates by an expert, engineering or construction judgments by an architect or engineer, or legal assessments by a lawyer. Are such provisions "arbitration agreements"—subject to international arbitration conventions and national arbitration legislation—or something else? In many national legal systems, these provisions are not "arbitration agreements"; rather, a distinction is drawn between "arbitration" and binding "expert determination," "appraisal," or "valuation." The latter categories are variously referred to as "*expertise-arbitrage*" (French), "*Schiedsgutachten*" (German) and "*bindend advies*" (Dutch). *See* G. Born, *International Commercial Arbitration* 259 (2d ed. 2014); J. Kendall, *Expert Determination* ¶1.1.1 *et seq.* (4th 2008). What exactly is the difference between "arbitration" and "expert determination"?

Consider the ICC Rules for Expertise, available at www.iccwbo.org. Note how they differ from the ICC Arbitration Rules. Consider the analysis in *Walkinshaw* and *Elberon*. What are the salient differences between expert determination and arbitration? How important are these differences? What are the reasons for not applying the New York Convention or UNCITRAL Model Law to agreements for expert determination, appraisal, or accounting? Is there an argument that such agreements are entitled to greater efficacy and deference than arbitration agreements? What would that argument be?

Consider the dispute resolution process that was at issue in *Elberon*. Is it arbitration or something else? How does the court distinguish the two? Is that persuasive? Compare the dispute resolution process that was at issue in *Walkinshaw*. Was it arbitration or something else? Was it more or less like arbitration than the process at issue in *Elberon*?

How did the standard articulated as a definition of arbitration in *Walkinshaw* compare with that in *Elberon*? Why exactly were the "Contract Recognition Board" proceedings held to be "arbitration" in *Walkinshaw*?

(c) *Arbitration is not litigation.* Consider the discussion of arbitration and arbitrators in *Jivraj*. How does arbitration, and arbitrators, differ from litigation, and national court judges?

It is elementary that arbitration is consensual. Simply put, absent an "agreement" to arbitrate, there is, by definition, no "arbitration agreement." Thus, although it hardly need be said, one thing that consensual arbitration is most obviously *not* is national court litigation pursuant to mandatory jurisdictional rules.

Litigation in national courts may also be conducted pursuant to consensual agreements, typically referred to as forum selection clauses (also variously termed "prorogation," "jurisdiction," or "choice-of-court" agreements). See G. Born, *International Arbitration and Forum Selection Clauses: Drafting and Enforcing* 17 *et seq.* (4th ed. 2013); G. Born & P. Rutledge, *International Civil Litigation in United States Courts* 461 *et seq.* (5th ed. 2011). It is very clear that a forum selection clause is not an arbitration agreement, and vice versa. Why is that? Who decides disputes in a national court? In an arbitration? What are the procedures in a national court? In an arbitration?

Consider again the Hague Convention on Choice of Court Agreements, excerpted at pp. 53-63 of the Documentary Supplement. Does it apply to arbitral awards? How does the Hague Convention differ from the New York Convention?

8. *Language of agreement not decisive in determining whether it is an "arbitration agreement."* Note that the language of the parties' dispute resolution provision is not necessarily decisive of the question whether or not it is an arbitration agreement. *See, e.g., Liberty Mut. Group, Inc. v. Wright*, 2012 WL 718857, at *5 (D. Md.) ("It is ... irrelevant that the contract language in question does not employ the word "arbitration" as such. Rather, what is important is whether the parties clearly intended to submit some disputes' to binding review by a third party.") (quoting *McDonnell Douglas Fin. Corp. v. Pa. Power & Light Co.*, 858 F.2d 825, 830-31 (2d Cir. 1988)); *Powderly v. Metrabyte Corp.*, 866 F.Supp. 39, 42 (D. Mass. 1994) ("use of the term 'arbitrate' is not a vital ingredient of an agreement to do so"); *Perceptics Corp. v. Société Electronique et Systèmes Trindel*, 907 F.Supp. 1139, 1142 (E.D. Tenn. 1992) ("no particular language is required to evidence an agreement to arbitrate"); *Gale Group, Inc. v. Westinghouse Elec. Corp.*, 683 So.2d 661, 663 (Fla. App. 1996) ("the words 'arbitrate' or 'arbitration' are not required to be expressly written in a contract to constitute a valid arbitration agreement"); *David Wilson Homes Ltd v. Survey Servs.*

Ltd [2001] BLR 267 (English Ct. App.) (absence of words "arbitration" and "arbitrator" from parties' agreement not decisive).

What do the foregoing authorities mean in practice? Suppose that the parties' contract includes a provision, titled "Arbitration," which provides: "All disputes shall be resolved exclusively by the courts of Saudi Arabia in accordance with Saudi law and Saudi Rules of Civil Procedure." Is that an agreement to arbitrate? Conversely, suppose that the parties agree to a provision titled "Disputes," which provides: "All disputes relating to this contract shall be finally decided by an individual, selected by the President of the International Court of Justice, who shall conduct proceedings in Washington D.C. permitting each party a fair opportunity to present its case." Is that an agreement to arbitrate?

Despite the foregoing, is the parties' use of the word "arbitration" not compelling evidence that they meant for their dispute resolution process to be treated as arbitration? In what circumstances should that agreement be disregarded? Is the parties' failure to use the word arbitration not an indication that they intended to agree to something other than arbitration? What if the procedures that the parties provide for are identical to those of an arbitration?

9. *Problematic "arbitration" clauses.* Consider the following clauses and explain whether or not they provide for arbitration:

> "All disputes under this contract will be submitted for *amicable compromise* to the Chief Executive Officers of the Buyer and the Seller."

> "All calculations of royalties under Article X of this contract which are not mutually agreed will be performed by PricewaterhouseCoopers."

> "All disputes under this contract shall be submitted for mediation, in utmost good faith, to a mediator selected by the Secretary General of the ICC. No party shall be free to commence any litigation before such mediator makes his or her decision."

> "All disputes under this contract shall be submitted for final decision by an individual mutually agreed by the parties or, failing agreement, selected by the president of the Chamber of Commerce of Singapore. Each party shall be permitted a fair opportunity to present its case to such individual, who shall make a binding award within 4 weeks of hearing the parties."

> "All disputes under this contract shall be finally resolved by international arbitration in the courts of the domicile of the party asserting claims hereunder."

In what respect is each of these provisions capable of being characterized as an arbitration agreement? In what respect is each of these provisions dissimilar from an arbitration agreement?

10. *Arbitral procedures.* To what extent does the definition of arbitration depend on the means of selecting the decision-maker and the nature of the dispute resolution procedures that are applied? Consider the discussion of these issues in *Walkinshaw* and (more briefly) in *Elberon*. Compare the provisions of Articles 36-54 of the ICSID Convention and Articles 41-90 of the 1907 Hague Convention, dealing with arbitral procedures and excerpted at pp. 21-25 & 43-50 of the Documentary Supplement. Why should the procedures that are used in a dispute resolution be relevant to whether or not the process is "arbitration"? Note that an "arbitration agreement" and an "arbitral award" have significant legal effects—that is, excluding the jurisdiction of national

courts and having final, binding legal effects like a national court judgment. Should these effects only be accorded to a process that has defined procedural characteristics?

There is a suggestion in *Walkinshaw* that an arbitration cannot be a "summary" procedure—that is, that it not be conducted so speedily as to prevent the parties from fully presenting their cases. *See supra* pp. 126-27. Does that mean that there cannot be "fast-track" arbitrations? *See* Davis *et al.*, *ICC Fast-Track Arbitration: Different Perspectives*, 3(2) ICC ICArb. Bull. 4 (1992); Smit, *Fast-Track Arbitration*, 2 Am. Rev. Int'l Arb. 138 (1991). Suppose that the parties agree that their arbitration shall be concluded within three months (or three weeks) from appointment of the arbitral tribunal. Consider the time-frame in the Abyei Arbitration Agreement. To what extent does the speediness of the dispute resolution proceeding affect its characterization as "arbitration"?

11. *"Baseball" arbitration.* There are a variety of forms of binding dispute resolution that have developed in particular commercial settings that resemble arbitration, but which also differ in significant ways from "normal" commercial arbitration. For example, so-called "baseball" arbitration (which originated in the United States) involves a process where, at the conclusion of the parties' submissions, each party provides the tribunal with its "best offer" in a sealed envelope. The tribunal is then charged with choosing one party's offer, or the other party's, rather than making an independent determination of the "correct" resolution under applicable law. *See* Borris, *Final Offer Arbitration From A Civil Law Perspective*, 24 J. Int'l Arb. 307 (2007); Gordon, *Final Offer Arbitration in the New Era of Major League Baseball*, 6 J. Am. Arb. 153 (2007).

Other forms of dispute resolution similarly limit the decision-maker's freedom to decide the parties' dispute in a characteristically adjudicative fashion, and instead prescribe a particular issue to be "answered" by the tribunal. In "high/low" or "bracketed" arbitration, for example, the parties agree on the minimum and maximum amounts that can be awarded. In some cases, the decision-maker is informed of the amounts designated by the parties, and in other cases, he or she is not. *See* G. Born, *International Commercial Arbitration* 282-83 (2d ed. 2014). Are these various forms of dispute resolution properly considered as "arbitration"? Why or why not? Consider the definitions of "arbitration" detailed above, and in *Walkinshaw* and *Jivraj*.

12. *Formal requirements for arbitration agreement.* Consider Article II(2) of the New York Convention and Article 7 of the UNCITRAL Model Law. Compare Article 25(1) of the ICSID Convention. These provisions impose formal requirements for the validity of an arbitration agreement, providing generally that such agreements must be in writing and with a signature or exchange of letters. These requirements are examined below. *See infra* pp. 375-92. For present purposes, consider whether these formal requirements are rules of validity or jurisdictional conditions for application of the Convention and/or Model Law. That is, if an agreement to arbitrate is not in writing, or is not signed, is that agreement (a) invalid, or (b) merely not subject to the Convention or Model Law, and therefore potentially subject to enforcement under generally-applicable contract law principles? Which approach is wiser? More consistent with the Convention and Model Law's objectives? Consider in this regard Article VII of the Convention.

13. *Ad hoc versus institutional arbitration.* What is the difference between "*ad hoc*" and "institutional" arbitration? Compare the provisions of the ICC Rules, which are among

the leading international commercial arbitration rules; note the significant involvement of the ICC at various stages in the arbitral proceedings. Identify these stages and the ICC's role. Compare the UNCITRAL Rules, which provide for very little involvement of any arbitral institution. Identify the stages at which an external institution is involved in arbitrations under the UNCITRAL Rules.

Contrast an arbitration clause that simply provides: "All disputes relating to this agreement shall be finally resolved by arbitration, before a sole arbitrator, in [London]." What are the benefits and costs of this *ad hoc* clause? As compared to a clause providing for arbitration under the ICC or UNCITRAL Rules? *See* Bond, *How to Draft An Arbitration Clause Revisited,* 1 ICC ICArb. Bull. 14 (1990); G. Born, *International Arbitration and Forum Selection Clauses: Drafting and Enforcing* 44-67 (4th ed. 2013); Townsend, *Drafting Arbitration Clauses*, 58 Disp. Resol. J. 1 (2003).

14. *"Future" and "existing" disputes.* Article II(1) of the New York Convention applies to agreements to arbitrate all disputes "which have arisen or may arise." The Convention was drafted in particular to apply to "future," as well as existing, disputes. As we have seen, agreements to arbitrate future disputes were often either invalid (as in 19th century France) or effectively unenforceable (as in 19th and early 20th century U.S. courts). Article II(1) reversed this historic treatment of agreements to arbitrate future disputes. At the same time, Article II(1) also gave presumptive effect to so-called "submission agreements," whereby parties agreed to arbitrate an existing dispute. (Note, for example, that this was the character of the agreements in the Treaty of Washington and the Abyei Arbitration Agreement.)

15. *Definition of "arbitral award."* Under leading international arbitration conventions and arbitration statutes, "arbitral awards" are afforded important legal effects: final, binding status, very limited judicial review and world-wide recognition. *See infra* pp. 1113-25, 1134-73, 1189-266. In contrast, expert determinations, conciliation reports, procedural decisions in an arbitration and other instruments that do not constitute arbitral awards are not subject to any such treatment. This parallels the limitation of international arbitration conventions and national arbitration legislation to "arbitration agreements." It is therefore essential to identify how to categorize a particular arbitral (or other) decision, and in particular to determine whether it is an "arbitral award" or something else. We return to this issue in Chapter 14, *infra* pp. 1059-69.

2. *Jurisdictional Requirements of International and National Arbitration Regimes*

As noted above, leading international and national arbitration regimes, directed principally at international commercial arbitration, contain a number of "jurisdictional requirements," which must be satisfied before the pro-arbitration terms of these regimes will apply.[17] These include: (1) the "commercial" relationship requirement; (2) the requirement for existing or future disputes; (3) the requirement for "foreign," "nondomestic," or "international" arbitration agreements; and (4) the reciprocity requirement. Separately, in the context of investment arbitration, the ICSID Convention and BITs set forth separate jurisdictional requirements. The requirements limit the application of these specialized enforcement regimes to specified categories of investment disputes. The following sections examine each of these sets of jurisdictional requirements.

17. *See supra* pp. 33-39; G. Born, *International Commercial Arbitration* 239-40 (2d ed. 2014).

a. "Commercial" Relationship Requirement

Both the New York Convention and many national arbitration statutes potentially apply only to "commercial" relationships. Thus, Article I(3) of the Convention provides that Member States may declare that the Convention applies only to "relationships ... which are considered as commercial under the national law of the state making [the] declaration." A number of nations, including the United States, have made declarations under Article I(3).[18]

Like the New York Convention, national arbitration statutes are frequently limited to "commercial" matters. Article 1(1) of the UNCITRAL Model Law expressly limits the law's application to "international *commercial* arbitration," while §2 of the FAA is limited to arbitration agreements in "transaction[s] involving *commerce*."[19] The materials excerpted below examine the application of the "commercial relationship" reservation under the New York Convention, and the related "commercial" requirement under some national arbitration legislation.

U.S. COMMERCIAL RELATIONSHIP RESERVATION TO NEW YORK CONVENTION

[The Convention will be applied] only to differences arising out of legal relationships, whether contractual or not, which are considered as commercial under the national law of the United States.

BAUTISTA v. STAR CRUISES, NORWEGIAN CRUISE LINE, LTD
396 F.3d 1289 (11th Cir. 2005) (also excerpted below at pp. 397-99)

RESTANI, Chief Judge. The S/S NORWAY's steam boiler exploded on May 25, 2003, while the cruise ship was in the Port of Miami. Six of the crewmembers represented in this action were killed and four were injured. Each crewmember's employment agreement with Defendant NCL [(Norwegian Cruise Line)] includes an arbitration clause, which the district court enforced pursuant to the [New York] Convention and its implementing legislation, 9 U.S.C. §§202-208 ("Convention Act"). Plaintiff's appeal presents an issue of first impression in this Circuit: whether the crewmembers' employment agreements were shielded from arbitration by the seamen employment contract exemption contained in §1 of the [FAA], 9 U.S.C. §§1-16. Because the FAA seamen exception does not apply and the district court had jurisdiction to compel arbitration, we affirm.

Following the explosion aboard the NORWAY, Plaintiffs filed separate but nearly identical suits in Florida circuit court against Defendant-Appellee NCL, owner of the NORWAY, and Defendant-Appellee Star Cruises, alleged by Plaintiffs to be the parent company of NCL. The complaints sought damages for negligence and unseaworthiness under the Jones Act, 46 U.S.C. App. §688, and for failure to provide maintenance, cure and unearned wages under the general maritime law of the United States. NCL removed the ten cases to federal district court pursuant to §205 of the [FAA], which permits removal before

---

18. *See* G. Born, *International Commercial Arbitration* 298 *et seq.* (2d ed. 2014).
19. UNCITRAL Model Law, Art. 1(1); U.S. FAA, 9 U.S.C. §2.

the start of trial when the dispute relates to an arbitration agreement or arbitral award covered by the Convention....

At the time of the explosion, each crewmember's employment was governed by the terms of a standard employment contract executed by the crewmembers and representatives of NCL in the Philippines between August 2002 and March 2003. The Philippine government regulated the form and content of such employment contracts ... through a program administered by the Philippine Overseas Employment Administration ("POEA"), a division of the Department of Labor and Employment of the Republic of the Philippines ("DOLE"). Each crewmember signed a one-page standard employment agreement created by the POEA, with some variations according to the position for which the crewmember was hired. Each agreement sets forth the basic terms and conditions of the crewmember's employment, including the duration of the contract, the position accepted, and the monthly salary and hours of work. Additional terms and conditions are incorporated by reference: Paragraph 2 provides that the contract's terms and conditions shall be observed in accordance with the POEA Department Order No. 4 and POEA Memorandum Circular No. 9. Department Order No. 4, in turn, incorporates the ... "Standard Terms and Conditions Governing the Employment of Filipino Seafarers On Board Ocean-Going Vessels" (the "Standard Terms"). Section 29 of the Standard Terms requires arbitration "in cases of claims and disputes arising from the [seaman's] employment," through submission of the claims to the National Labor Relations Commission ("NLRC"), voluntary arbitrators, or a panel of arbitrators.[20]

The POEA official verified and approved the execution of the employment contract by the crewmembers and NCL representatives. Although Plaintiffs dispute that the crewmembers saw the arbitration provision or had it explained to them, copies of the Standard Terms provided to the district court by NCL indicate the crewmembers initialed or signed the Standard Terms. NCL also provided affidavits from managers at various manning agencies licensed by the POEA to recruit seamen. In the affidavits, the managers attest that (1) they explained the employment documents to the seamen in their native language; (2) the seamen had an opportunity to review the documents; and (3) the seamen were required to attend a Pre-Departure Orientation Seminar for seamen ... which reviewed, among other subjects, the Standard Terms and dispute settlement procedures provided for in the employment contract....

[T]he district court granted NCL's motion to compel arbitration.... [T]he district court ordered that the parties submit to arbitration in the Philippines pursuant to §29 of the Standard Terms.... Plaintiffs appeal.

In deciding a motion to compel arbitration under the Convention Act, a court conducts "a very limited inquiry." *Francisco v. STOLT ACHIEVEMENT MT*, 293 F.3d 270, 273 (5th

---

20. The full text of §29 of the Standard Terms follows:

> "In cases of claims and disputes arising from this employment, the parties covered by a collective bargaining agreement shall submit the claim or dispute to the original and exclusive jurisdiction of the voluntary arbitrator or panel of arbitrators. If the parties are not covered by a collective bargaining agreement, the parties may at their option submit the claim or dispute to either the original and exclusive jurisdiction of the National Labor Relations Commission (NLRC), pursuant to Republic Act (RA) 8042 otherwise known as the Migrant Workers and Overseas Filipinos Act of 1995 or to the original and exclusive jurisdiction of the voluntary arbitrator or panel of arbitrators. If there is no provision as to the voluntary arbitrators to be appointed by the parties, the same shall be appointed from the accredited voluntary arbitrators of the National Conciliation and Mediation Board of the Department of Labor and Employment."

Cir. 2002). A district court must order arbitration unless (1) the four jurisdictional prerequisites are not met, *Std. Bent Glass Corp. v. Glassrobots Oy*, 333 F.3d 440, 449 (3d Cir. 2003);[21] or (2) one of the Convention's affirmative defenses applies. *Czarina, LLC v. W.F. Poe Syndicate*, 358 F.3d 1286, 1292 n.3 (11th Cir. 2004) ("jurisdictional prerequisites to an action confirming an award are different from the several affirmative defenses ...").

Two jurisdictional prerequisites are at issue here. First, we must determine whether the arbitration agreement arises out of a commercial legal relationship. Second, we ask whether there exists an "agreement in writing" to arbitrate the matter in dispute. Lastly, we consider Plaintiff's purported affirmative defenses that the arbitration provision is unconscionable under U.S. law and incapable of being arbitrated under the law of the Philippines. In analyzing these arguments, we are mindful that the Convention Act "generally establishes a strong presumption in favor of arbitration of international commercial disputes." *Indus. Risk Insurers v. M.A.N. Gutehoffnungshütte GmbH*, 141 F.3d 1434, 1440 (11th Cir. 1998) (citing *Mitsubishi*, 473 U.S. at 638-40....).

We have yet to determine whether the FAA exemption for seamen's employment contracts applies to arbitration agreements covered by the Convention Act.[22] The district court determined that it does not. This conclusion is consistent with that of the Fifth Circuit—the only court of appeals to decide the issue.... *Freudensprung v. Offshore Tech. Servs., Inc.*, 379 F.3d 327 (5th Cir. 2004)....

The Convention requires [in Article II(1)] that a Contracting State "shall recognize an agreement in writing under which the parties undertake to submit to arbitration all or any differences which have arisen ... between them in respect of a defined legal relationship, whether contractual or not, concerning a subject matter capable of settlement by arbitration." When the United States acceded to the Convention in 1970, it exercised its right to limit the Convention's application to commercial legal relationships as defined by the law of the United States....

Plaintiffs assert that the United States national law definition of "commercial" resides in §1 of the FAA, which defines "commerce" and provides that "nothing herein contained shall apply to contracts of employment of seamen." Although §1 clearly exempts seamen's employment contracts from the FAA, *see Circuit City Stores, Inc. v. Adams*, 532 U.S. 105, 109 (2001), the exemption's application outside the FAA is restricted by the second and third chapters of title 9. The three chapters of title 9 are closely interrelated, but, contrary to

---

21. These four require that (1) there is an agreement in writing within the meaning of the Convention; (2) the agreement provides for arbitration in the territory of a signatory of the Convention; (3) the agreement arises out of a legal relationship, whether contractual or not, which is considered commercial; and (4) a party to the agreement is not an American citizen, or that the commercial relationship has some reasonable relation with one or more foreign states. *Std. Bent Glass Corp.*, 333 F.3d at 449. It is beyond dispute that the second and fourth conditions are fulfilled in this case. The crewmembers' arbitration provisions provide for arbitration in the Philippines, a signatory of the Convention. The crewmembers are not American citizens, but are citizens of the Philippines.

22. The seamen employment contract exemption appears in §1 of the FAA:

§1. "Maritime transactions" and "commerce" defined; exceptions to operation of title ... "commerce," as herein defined, means commerce among the several States or with foreign nations, or in any Territory of the United States or in the District of Columbia, or between any such Territory and another, or between any such Territory and any State or foreign nation, or between the District of Columbia and any State or Territory or foreign nation, but *nothing herein contained shall apply to contracts of employment of seamen, railroad employees, or any other class of workers engaged in foreign or interstate commerce.*

Plaintiff's argument, they are not a seamless whole. As indicated, the FAA and the Convention Act compromise Chapter 1 and Chapter 2, respectively. Chapter 3 contains the legislation implementing the Inter-American Convention. Within the general field of arbitration, each act has a specific context and purpose. Congress, as it added the Convention Act and then the Inter-American Act to title 9, anticipated conflicts among these treaty-implementing statutes and the FAA. Congress addressed potential conflicts in two ways, each of which limits the degree to which title 9 may be considered a single statute.

The first is general in nature. The FAA applies residually to supplement the provisions of the Convention Act and the Inter-American Act. Rather than put the Convention Act and the Inter-American Act on equal footing with the FAA in the field of foreign arbitration, Congress gave the treaty-implementing statutes primacy in their fields, with FAA provisions applying only where they did not conflict. *See* 9 U.S.C. §208; 9 U.S.C. §307. This hierarchical structure accords with our understanding that, "[a]s an exercise of the Congress' treaty power and as federal law, 'the Convention must be enforced according to its terms over all prior inconsistent rules of law.'" *Indus. Risk Insurers*, 141 F.3d at 1440 (quoting *Sedco, Inc. v. Petroleos Mexicanos Mexican Nat'l Oil Co.*, 767 F.2d 1140, 1145 (5th Cir. 1985)).

The second technique for reconciling title 9's chapters is more specific. Certain provisions of the Convention Act and the Inter-American Act refer explicitly to specific sections of other chapters of title 9.... [In particular], §202 uses §2 as an illustration of the types of agreements covered by the Convention Act. In articulating the Convention's commercial scope under the laws of the United States, §202 of the Convention Act provides that an agreement falls under the Convention if it "aris[es] out of a legal relationship, whether contractual or not, which is considered as commercial, *including* a transaction, contract, or agreement described in §2 of this title [9 U.S.C. §2]." (emphasis added). Section 2 of the FAA makes valid and enforceable "[a] written provision in any maritime transaction to a *contract evidencing a transaction involving commerce* to settle by arbitration." 9 U.S.C. §2 (emphasis added).

The Convention Act's reference to §2 does not indicate an intent to limit the definition of "commercial" to those described in §2 of the FAA as modified by §1; the expansive term "including" would be superfluous if the FAA provided the full and complete definition. "Including" demonstrates that, at the very least, Congress meant for "commercial" legal relationships to consist of contracts evidencing a commercial transaction, as listed in §2, *as well as* similar agreements. We therefore understand the reference to §2 of the FAA to be generally illustrative of the commercial legal relationships covered by §202. The illustration rendered by §2 includes employment agreements and makes no mention of the §1 seamen exemption. Accordingly, the terms of the Convention Act do not provide that we read §1 into §202.

Plaintiffs cite committee testimony in the legislative history in the hope of demonstrating that Congress intended §202 of the Convention Act to incorporate the FAA seamen exception. Ambassador Richard Kearney, Chairman of the Secretary of State's Advisory Committee on Private International Law, testified before the Senate Foreign Relations Committee that "the definition of commerce contained in §1 of the original Arbitration Act is the national law definition for the purposes of the declaration. A specific reference, however, is made in §202 to §2 of title 9; which is the basic provision of the original Arbitration Act." S. Comm. on Foreign Relations, Foreign Arbitral Awards, S. Rep. No.

91-702, at 6 (1970). Although it is plausible to infer from Ambassador Kearney's comments that he believed the §1 exemptions should apply to the Convention Act, his views as a single State Department official are a relatively unreliable indicator of statutory intent.... Rather than directly incorporate an FAA provision that Congress did not, we adhere to the framework Congress provided and evaluate the applicability of an unmentioned FAA section according to the Convention Act's residual application provision.

As noted above, §208 of the Convention Act provides that non-conflicting provisions of the Arbitration Act apply residually to Convention Act cases: "Chapter 1 applies to actions and proceedings brought under this chapter *to the extent that chapter is not in conflict* with this chapter or the Convention as ratified by the United States." (emphasis added).... Under this residual provision, the issue is whether the FAA seamen exemption conflicts with the Convention Act or the Convention....

A conflict exists between the FAA seamen exemption, which is narrow and specific, and the language of the Convention and the Convention Act, which is broad and generic. Plaintiffs, under the impression that an FAA term may only be contradicted by name, argue that no conflict exists because §202 of the Convention Act is silent as to seamen's employment contracts. According to this logic, a statutory provision pertaining to persons above the age of eighteen would not conflict with a provision that exempts thirty year-olds. Because the Convention Act covers commercial legal relationships without exception, it conflicts with §1, an FAA provision that exempts certain employment agreements that—but for the exemption—would be commercial legal relationships....

Indeed to read industry-specific exceptions into the broad language of the Convention Act would be to hinder the Convention's purpose: "The goal of the Convention, and the principal purpose underlying American adoption and implementation of it, was *to encourage the recognition and enforcement of commercial arbitration agreements in international contracts* and *to unify the standards by which agreements to arbitrate are observed* and arbitral awards are enforced in the signatory countries." ... *Scherk v. Alberto-Culver Co.*, 417 U.S. 506, 520 n.15, (emphasis added).... In pursuing effective, unified arbitration standards, the Convention's framers understood that the benefits of the treaty would be undermined if domestic courts were to inject their "parochial" values into the regime: "In their discussion of [Article II(1)], the delegates to the Convention voided frequent concern that courts of signatory countries in which an agreement to arbitrate is sought to be enforced should not be permitted to decline enforcement of such agreements on the basis of parochial views of their desirability or in a manner that would diminish the mutually binding nature of the agreements." *Scherk*, 417 U.S. at 520 n.15. This concern is addressed by the broad language of §202 of the Convention Act. Considering the language of the Convention Act in the context of the framework of title 9 and the purposes of the Convention, we find no justification for removing from the Convention Act's scope a subset of commercial employment agreements. The crewmembers' arbitration provisions constitute commercial legal relationships within the meaning of the Convention Act. [The court went on to reject the crewmembers' objections to the validity of the arbitration agreements, based on claims of unconscionability and lack of notice, *infra* pp. 397-99.]

RM INVESTMENT & TRADING CO. PVT LTD v. BOEING CO.
XXII Y.B. Comm. Arb. 710 (1997) (Indian S.Ct. 1994)

RM Investment & Trading Co. Pvt Ltd ("RMI") and Boeing Co. ("Boeing") entered into a Consultant Services Agreement in 1986 whereby RMI agreed to provide Boeing with consultant services to promote the sale of Boeing aircraft in India. The agreement was originally intended to be operative until 31 December 1986, but ... was extended to 30 April 1987. In August 1987, Definitive Purchase Agreements for the purchase of two air-crafts were executed between Boeing and Air India. RMI claimed commission from Boeing but Boeing refused to pay. RMI initiated a lawsuit [in Indian courts] against Boeing seeking the recovery of US$ 17.5 million. The Consultant Services Agreement contained an arbitration clause providing for [AAA] arbitration. Boeing sought a stay of the proceedings, invoking the arbitration clause.... [T]he High Court dismissed Boeing's application to stay the suit, holding that the Consultant Services Agreement was not a "commercial" agreement. On appeal, this decision was reversed.... RMI appealed against the granting of the stay to the [Indian] Supreme Court.

We will first take up [the appeal] against the judgment ... whereby the application filed by Boeing under §3 of the [Indian Foreign Awards (Recognition & Enforcement) Act 1961][23] has been allowed and the proceedings in the suit filed by RMI have been stayed.... [T]he Division Bench of the High Court ... held that in view of the definition of the expression "foreign award" contained in §2 of the Act,[24] a suit cannot be stayed under §3 unless the Court is satisfied that the parties to the arbitration agreement stand in such legal relationship to each other which can be considered as "commercial." The learned Judges ... constructed the word "commercial" in the light of ... *Atiabari Tea Co. v. The State of Assam*, 1961 (1) SCR 809 [(Indian S.Ct.)], and *Fatehchand Himmatlal v. State of Maharashtra*, 1977 (2) SCR 828 [(Indian S.Ct.)], and the Model Law prepared by UNCITRAL and have held that "the transaction between RMI and Boeing is commercial and they do stand in commercial relationship." ...

[RMI] has urged that the learned Judges of the High Court have erred in holding that the Consultant Services Agreement ... is in the nature of a commercial contract. According to [RMI] a commercial contract is mercantile in nature involving sale and purchase of goods and a service agreement providing for rendering consultancy services cannot be treated as a commercial agreement.... Before we consider the meaning to be assigned to the word "commercial" in §2 of the Act, we would briefly refer to the terms of the agreement between RMI and Boeing.... [The Court cited provisions from the agreement and continued as follows:] From the terms of the Agreement ... it appears that RMI rendered consultancy services to Boeing as an independent contractor.... While RMI was entitled to payment of

23. Section 3 of the Foreign Awards (Recognition & Enforcement) Act 1961 reads in relevant part:

   "[I]f any party to an agreement to which Article II of the Convention ... applies ... commences any legal proceedings in any court against any other party to the agreement ... in respect of any matter agreed to be referred, any party to such legal proceedings may ... apply to the court to stay the proceedings and the court, unless satisfied that the agreement is null and void, inoperative or incapable of being performed or that there is not in fact any dispute between the parties with regard to the matter agreed to be referred, shall make an order staying the proceedings."

24. Section 2 of the Foreign Awards (Recognition & Enforcement) Act 1961 reads in relevant part:

   "In this Act ... 'foreign award' means an award on differences between persons arising out of legal relationships, whether contractual or not, considered as commercial under the law in force in India...."

compensation for such services, the costs, expenses and charges necessary or incidental to RMI's operations were to be borne by RMI.

It is not disputed that the sale of aircrafts by Boeing to customers in India was to be a commercial transaction. The question is whether rendering of consultancy services by RMI for promoting such commercial transaction as consultant under the Agreement is not a "commercial transaction." We are of the view that the High Court was right in holding that the agreement to render consultancy services by RMI to Boeing is commercial in nature and that RMI and Boeing do stand in commercial relationship with each other. While construing the expression "commercial" in §2 of the Act it has to be borne in mind that the "Act is calculated and designed to subserve the cause of facilitating international trade and promotion thereof by providing for speedy settlement of disputes arising in such trade through arbitration and any expression or phrase occurring therein should receive, consistent with its literal and grammatical sense, a liberal construction." The expression "commercial" should, therefore, be construed broadly having regard to the manifold activities which are integral part of international trade today....

While construing the expression "commercial relationship" in §2 of the Act, aid can also be taken from the Model Law prepared by UNCITRAL wherein relationships of a commercial nature include "commercial representation or agency" and "consulting." In *Micoperi SPA v. Sansouci Pvt Ltd*, 1 CLJ 511, ... the Calcutta High Court has construed the term "commercial" in the light of the provisions contained in Rule 1 of Chapter XII of the Rules of the Original Side of the Calcutta High Court which specifies the nature of suits covered by the expression "commercial suits." We do not find any reason for thus restricting the meaning of the term "commercial" in §2 of the Act on the basis of the provisions contained in the Rules of the High Court....

JUDGMENT OF 10 NOVEMBER 1993
XXIII Y.B. Comm. Arb. 770 (1998) (Tunisian Cour de cassation)

[Société d'Investissement Kal ("Kal") was a Tunisian company, 60% owned by Saudi nationals, engaged in construction. Kal retained Taieb Haddad (a Tunisian national) and Hans Barett (a non-Tunisian national and resident) (collectively, "the architects") to draw up an urbanization plan for the RafRaf Ghar El Melh resort in Tunisia. The contract contained a clause referring all disputes to ICC arbitration in Paris. A dispute arose concerning payment of fees and an ICC arbitration followed. The arbitral tribunal rendered an award in favor of the architects. When Kal refused to pay, the architects sought enforcement of the award in Tunisia. The Tunisian lower courts denied enforcement, finding that Tunisia had made a commercial reservation under the New York Convention and that architectural and urbanization works are not commercial under Tunisian law. The Supreme Court affirmed in the opinion excerpted below.]

Tunisia made the commercial reservation when adhering to the New York Convention. Thus, it will apply the Convention only with respect to disputes which are commercial according to Tunisian law. The subject matter of this dispute is a contract concerning architectural plans drawn by architects, which do not fall under the definition of Arts. 1-4 of the Commercial Code; [the contract] is not by its nature commercial according to Tunisian law. Since the contract between the parties is [not commercial], the New York Convention does not apply to it and the arbitral clause cannot be contained therein according to Art. I(3) of the Convention.

The parties have submitted the contract to Tunisian law (Art. 14). According to Art. 258 [of the Tunisian Code of Civil and Commercial Procedure] ("CCCP"),[25] arbitral clauses are allowed only for disputes concerning a commercial relationship. This contract is not commercial and does not concern a commercial relationship, thus it does not fall within the ambit of the jurisdiction of arbitrators, independent of its being international or not, since the international aspect is linked to the commercial nature: the two co-exist and if one is absent the other loses its second essential component. Hence, the referral to arbitration is not allowed; this conclusion is drawn from Arts. 277 and 318 CCCP. [Art. 277 of the pre-1993 Tunisian CCCP reads: "Arbitral awards must be made within Tunisian territory, otherwise, they are subject to the rules applicable to judgments made abroad."]

Also, contrary to what petitioners allege, Art. V of the Convention allows the enforcement court to deny enforcement if there are defects in the award; the court, therefore, is not limited to a formal review of the award. Since [Kal] has proven that the arbitral clause is not valid according to Tunisian law, which governs the contract, for lack of compliance with Art. 258 CCCP, because the contract is [not commercial] according to Art. I of the Convention, the enforcement court decided correctly, as it is allowed to do under Art. V of the Convention....

NORTH AMERICAN FREE TRADE AGREEMENT
Article 1136(7)

A claim that is submitted to arbitration under this [§B: "Settlement of Disputes Between A Party and An Investor of Another Party"] shall be considered to arise out of a commercial relationship or transaction for purposes of Article I of the New York Convention and Article I of the Inter-American Convention.

NOTES

1. *Definition of "commercial" under New York Convention.* What does the term "commercial," as used in Article I(3) of the New York Convention, mean? Does Article I(3) establish a uniform international definition of what matters are "commercial" and what matters are "non-commercial"? Or does Article I(3) leave it to individual contracting parties to define "commercial" under national law, without imposing any express external limits on national definitions? Compare the interpretation by the U.S. court in *Bautista* with that in the Tunisian Cour de cassation's *Judgment of 10 November 1993*. What role do domestic, national law definitions of "commercial" play in each case? Which interpretation is more consistent with the language of Article I(3)? With the Convention's purposes?

   How does the U.S. commercial relationship reservation define "commercial"? With reference to national or international law? Consider the analysis in *Bautista*.

   If the Convention were interpreted to impose a uniform international definition of "commercial" and "non-commercial" relationships, how would these terms be de-

---

25. Art. 258 of the [pre-1993] Tunisian Code of Civil and Commercial Procedure (CCCP) reads:

   "One may agree to arbitrate any dispute which has already arisen. One may also provide in an arbitration clause that all disputes which might arise out of commercial transactions and contracts, as well as between partners concerning their company, can be referred to arbitration."

fined? Where would one look, in the Convention or otherwise, for guidance in defining these terms?

2. *International limits under New York Convention on national definitions of "commercial" relationships.* Suppose a Contracting State defines "commercial" relationship extremely narrowly (*e.g.*, only contracts for the export or import of goods which were registered with national customs authorities). Is there anything in the New York Convention that would preclude a Contracting State from adopting such a definition and utilizing it in a commercial relationship reservation under Article I(3)? Consider the definition of "commercial" adopted in the *Judgment of 10 November 1993*. Is that definition consistent with Tunisia's obligations under the Convention?

Can one argue that, while Article I(3) of the Convention leaves contracting parties free to exclude non-commercial matters (or some non-commercial matters) from its commitments under the Convention, it does not permit Contracting States to exclude matters defined as "commercial" by the Convention from its obligations under the Convention? Can this interpretation be reconciled with the text of the Convention? *See also* G. Born, *International Commercial Arbitration* 299 (2d ed. 2014).

3. *"Commercial" relationship under 1961 European Convention.* Consider the title of the European Convention ("European Convention on International *Commercial* Arbitration") and Article I(a), which provides: "This Convention shall apply: (a) to arbitration agreements concluded for the purpose of settling disputes arising from international trade between physical or legal persons having, when concluding the agreement, their habitual place of residence or their seat in different Contracting States." Does the Convention adopt a uniform international definition of "commercial"? How else could Article I(a) be interpreted?

Consider the analysis of Article I(a) in *Benteler v. State of Belgium*, excerpted below at pp. 465-68. What reasons does the *Benteler* decision give for adopting a uniform international interpretation of Article I(a)? What exactly is the definition of "commercial" in *Benteler*? How does it compare to the definitions in the UNCITRAL Model Law and the FAA?

4. *National court definitions of "commercial" under New York Convention.* The Convention's "commercial" requirement has produced few difficulties in most national courts. In interpreting the "commercial" relationship requirement of the Convention and §202, most national courts have construed the requirement broadly. *See Faberge Int'l Inc. v. Di Pino*, 491 N.Y.S.2d 345 (N.Y. App. Div. 1985) (employment agreement is commercial, notwithstanding existence of fiduciary duties); *Canada Packers Inc. v. Terra Nova Tankers Inc.*, XXII Y.B. Comm. Arb. 669 (1997) (Ontario Super. Ct. 1992) (tort claims relating to relationship "that can fairly be described as 'commercial'" encompassed by Article I(3)'s "commercial"); *European Grain & Shipping Ltd v. Bombay Extractions Ltd*, VIII Y.B. Comm. Arb. 371 (1983) (Bombay High Ct. 1981) ("we have no doubt that the contract in the instant case, which was for the sale and purchase of a commodity, was clearly a contract which brought about a legal relationship which was commercial in nature under Indian law.").

Consider the court's decision in *Bautista*. Would seamen's disputes have been regarded as falling within the scope of the domestic U.S. arbitration act (Chapter 1 of the FAA)? Were seamen's disputes regarded as falling within the New York Convention and its U.S. implementing legislation (the "Convention Act," more frequently referred to as the second chapter of the FAA)? Why the difference in treatment? Compare the analysis in *RMI*. What weight does the Indian court attach to definitions of "commercial" under domestic court rules? To the purposes of the Convention and the definition of "commercial" under the UNCITRAL Model Law?

    For an exceptional contrary decision, *see Judgment of 10 November 1993*, XXIII Y.B. Comm. Arb. 770 (1998) (Tunisian Cour de cassation), excerpted above. *See also India Organic Chems., Ltd v. Chemtex Fibres Inc.*, [1978] All India Rep. 106 (Bombay High Ct.) (technology transfer agreement not "commercial"). What exactly did the Tunisian court hold? Is that decision defensible? Compare the analysis in *Judgment of 10 November 1993* with that in *Bautista* and *RMI*. Which is to be preferred? Which is more in keeping with the objectives of the Convention? What are the consequences of concluding that a relationship is not "commercial" for purposes of the Convention?

5.   *U.S. commercial relationship reservation under New York Convention.* Like a number of other Contracting States (such as Tunisia), the United States has made a commercial reservation pursuant to Article I(3) of the Convention. *See supra* p. 138. The U.S. reservation is codified in §202 of the FAA, which provides, among other things, that "[a]n arbitration agreement ... arising out of a legal relationship, whether contractual or not, which is considered as commercial ... falls under the Convention." As the *Bautista* court explains, §202 also provides that "commercial" relations include those that fall within the definition contained in §2 of the domestic FAA of arbitration agreements affecting inter-state and foreign commerce.

    Consider the analysis of the "commercial" relationship requirement under the FAA in *Bautista*. Does the court's analysis give proper weight to U.S. legislation safeguarding the interests of seamen? Is that legislation applicable to international seamen? Would international seamen be better or worse off if their agreements to arbitrate were not subject to the Convention? Are there mechanisms under the Convention in which the protective legislation of a Contracting State (*e.g.*, protecting seamen) can be given effect even if the Convention applies generally? Consider Articles II(1) and V(2) of the Convention.

    Is it wise for the United States to have adopted a commercial reservation? Note that a number of Contracting States have not done so. G. Born, *International Commercial Arbitration* 298 (2d ed. 2014). What purposes does adopting a commercial reservation serve? Note that, apart from the commercial reservation, Contracting States may still invoke "nonarbitrability" exceptions (Articles II(3), V(2)(a)) and "public policy" exceptions (Article V(2)(b)) under the Convention. In these circumstances, what purpose does the commercial reservation serve?

    Was *Bautista* correctly decided? What law did the *Bautista* court apply in reaching its conclusion: U.S. legislation (specifically, the second chapter of the FAA) or the Convention itself? Which law should the *Bautista* court have applied? Is it correct to conclude that a dispute between a seaman and his or her employer is "commercial"? Or, is such a dispute an "employment" dispute, which should be categorized as non-commercial? Doesn't an employment relationship involve the exchange of services for compensation? Isn't that a classic commercial activity?

6.   *Definition of "commercial" under UNCITRAL Model Law.* Consider the definition of "commercial" under Article 1(1) of the UNCITRAL Model Law, excerpted at p. 86 of the Documentary Supplement. Also consider the non-exclusive list of relationships or

activities that are categorized as "commercial" by note 2 to the Model Law. How would the Tunisian Cour de cassation's *Judgment of 10 November 1993* have been decided under the Model Law?

Consider the list of activities or relationships included in note 2. What types of relationships or contracts are not included in note 2? What about consumer transactions? Employee-employer disputes? Is there any doubt that consumer transactions and employee-employer disputes involve commercial relationships? How would *Bautista* have been decided under the Model Law?

7. *Application of New York Convention to investment arbitrations.* Is an agreement to arbitrate an "investment" dispute subject to the New York Convention? What if a Contracting State has made a commercial reservation (like the United States has done)? Or are investment arbitration agreements a subset of commercial relationships? Consider Article 1136(7) of the North American Free Trade Agreement. What does it suggest?

8. *Application of New York Convention to inter-state arbitrations.* Does the Convention apply to agreements to arbitrate between two states? Does it depend on what type of relationship the agreements concern?

Suppose Eritrea and Yemen agree to arbitrate territorial sovereignty over disputed islands located in the Red Sea, and the related maritime delimitation of Red Sea waters. Would that arbitration agreement be subject to the New York Convention? Assume that the Contracting State in question has made a commercial relationship reservation. Would the resulting award be subject to the Convention? What if Venezuela agreed to sell Cuba $2 billion in petroleum per year. Would an arbitration agreement, included in the oil delivery contract, be subject to the Convention?

Why shouldn't the Convention apply to all of these various agreements to arbitrate (and resulting awards)? Should states adopt commercial reservations? If they have, should they withdraw them?

b. "Existing or Future Disputes" and "Defined Legal Relationship"

The New York Convention and many national arbitration statutes also contain "requirements" concerning existing or future disputes and defined legal relationships.[26] The materials excerpted below explore the application of these requirements. In fact, as discussed below, these provisions are more in the nature of extensions or clarifications of the Convention and national legislation, designed to overcome historic obstacles to commercial arbitration, than limitations upon their reach.

It has also been suggested that there is an implied requirement under Articles I(1) and I(3) of the Convention that a "difference" exists between the parties. Similar interpretations have been adopted under national arbitration statutes, with some national courts holding that no obligation to arbitrate existed (or could be enforced) because no genuine "dispute" had arisen; particularly in recent years, these requirements have generally been rejected.[27]

Finally, Article II(3) of the Convention requires that an arbitration agreement be "in respect of a defined legal relationship, whether contractual or not." In virtually all com-

---

26. *See* G. Born, *International Commercial Arbitration* 294-96 (2d ed. 2014).
27. *See infra* pp. 148-54, 156-58; G. Born, *International Commercial Arbitration* 338-41 (2d ed. 2014).

mercial arbitrations, there is an arbitration agreement that relates to a written contract between the parties, and Article II(3)'s requirement is readily satisfied. As discussed below, the "defined legal relationship" requirement is more relevant in confirming that international arbitral tribunals may consider and decide non-contractual disputes.[28]

ROOSE INDUSTRIES LTD v. READY MIXED CONCRETE LTD
[1974] 2 NZLR 246 (Wellington Ct. App.)

MCCARTHY P. The appellant is a quarry operator ... and supplies for use by the respondent in its concrete mixing supply plant at Hamilton metal chips and what is called "all-in" materials. The contract is embodied in a formal agreement and covers a period of 10 years from 8 July 1967. Several clauses refer to "metal chips and all-in materials" but the clause relating to quality mentions metal chips only as being required to confirm to a particular standard specification. It does not say that the "all-in" materials shall also conform to the same standard specification.

A dispute arose between the parties regarding the quality of the "all-in" material delivered. The respondent contended that it was the intention of the parties, even though not expressly stated in the agreement, that those materials would conform to the same specification as that expressly applied to metal chips. The appellant denied that. The respondent then issued a writ claiming a declaration that the "all-in" materials are subject to the specification provision and, alternatively, that the agreement be rectified to provide for that and specific performance of the rectified agreement. The appellant moved for a stay relying on the arbitration clause contained in the agreement. That clause reads thus:

> "Any dispute which may arise between the parties to this agreement shall be settled by arbitration in accordance with the Arbitration Act 1908 and any subsequent amendments."

There can be little doubt that where there is an arbitration clause covering a dispute between parties, there is a *prima facie* right to a stay. Whether the dispute is within the purview of the clause is the important question in many cases. Parties to a contract may agree to submit almost anything to arbitration, including questions of law.

The learned Judge in the Supreme Court, Mahon J, refused a stay, generally on the ground that the arbitrator would have no jurisdiction to order rectification, for that was "clearly outside the arbitration clause." He thought that *Printing Mach. Co. v. Linotype and Mach. Co.* [1912] 1 Ch 566 where rectification was sought and a stay was refused was directly in point. The appellant now contends that Mahon J took too narrow a view of the arbitration clause, and failed to perceive that the *Printing Mach.* case was based on its own facts, especially the wording of its particular arbitration clause.

The clause we are concerned with is drawn in very wide terms. It covers "Any dispute which may arise between the parties." It is not, in terms, confined to disputes which arise out of the particular business arrangement. *Ex facie* it would cover any dispute whatever its character, but obviously some limitation has to be placed on it. The courts will in circumstances such as this limit the operation of a clause to conform with what seems to it to have been the intention of the parties. *In re Hohenzollern Actien Gesellschaft etc.* (1886) 54 LT 596, the pivotal words in the arbitration clause were "all disputes." Lord Esher MR said "I

---

28. *See infra* p. 154; G. Born, *International Commercial Arbitration* 294-96 (2d ed. 2014).

think that those words are to be read as if they were 'all disputes that may arise between the parties in consequence of this contract having been entered into.'" Lopes LJH read the words in this way: "all disputes in respect of the contract or its construction." In *Woolf v. Collis Removal Service* [1947] 2 All ER 260, the Court of Appeal had to construe an arbitration clause which was also in the widest possible terms. Lord Justice Asquith delivering the judgment of the Court said:

> "The arbitration clause in the present case is, as to the subject matter of claims within its ambit, in the widest possible terms. That clause is not, in terms, limited to claims arising 'under' the contract. It speaks simply of 'claims.' This, of course, does not mean that the term applies to claims of every imaginable kind. Claims which are entirely unrelated to the transaction covered by the contract would no doubt be excluded; but we are of opinion that, even if the claim in negligence is not a claim 'under the contract,' yet there is a sufficiently close connection between that claim and that transaction to bring the claim within the arbitration clause, even though framed technically in tort."

The clause in the present case could really not be wider. If the limitation to be imposed on the language restricts the disputes to those arising out of the written document, then the *Printing Mach.* case appears to be in point, and the observations of Warrington J that the claim for rectification is not a claim arising under the particular written document but a claim for another document altogether, would be pertinent.... It is true that in [the *Printing Mach.* case] the specific clause [was] of a wide character but it so happened that ...the Court construed the express words in a way which limited the disputes to those arising out of the written document. If we were so to restrict the arbitration clause in this case, then *Printing Mach.* would doubtless be good authority for reaching the same conclusion as did the Judge in the Supreme Court. But why should it be so limited? In our view the Court should restrict the operation of such a wide clause no further than necessary, and on that reasoning should exclude, in the words of Asquith LJ in *Woolf v. Collis Removal Service* [1947] 2 All ER 260, 263, only claims which are entirely unrelated to the commercial transaction covered by the contract. Here, the essential question in dispute is whether the parties intended that the "all-in" materials should be required to conform to the standard specification. That seems to be very much a question arising out of that commercial transaction. With great respect to Mahon J, we cannot agree that the particular dispute is not within the arbitration clause....

HALKI SHIPPING CORP. v. SOPEX OILS LTD
[1998] 1 Lloyd's Rep. 49 (QB) (English High Ct.)

MR JUSTICE CLARKE. [This was an application by the defendant charterers Sopex Oils Ltd to stay proceedings brought by the plaintiff owners Halki Shipping Corp. for demurrage pursuant to the Arbitration Act, 1996, §9.] The plaintiffs are the owners of the motor tanker *Halki* which was chartered to the defendants under a tanker voyage charter-party dated June 20, 1005 for the carriage of palm oil and coconut oil from various Far Eastern port to various ports in Europe.... Additional clause 9 of the charter-party provides:

> "9. General Average and Arbitration to be London, English law to apply. For Arbitration following clause to apply: Any dispute arising from or in connection with this Charter Party shall be referred to Arbitration in London. The Owners and Charterers shall each appoint an Arbitrator experienced in the shipping business. English Law governs this Charter Party and

all aspects of the Arbitration."

[Notwithstanding the arbitration clause, the plaintiffs sought damages in English court, claiming that the defendants failed to load and discharge the vessel within the laytime provided in the charter-party. As a result, they claimed demurrage in the amount of U.S. $517,473.96. The defendants did not admit liability but advanced defenses only as to a portion of the claim, which did not address some U.S. $416,175 of the claim.]

The defendants seek an order staying that action under §9 of the Arbitration Act, 1996 … [which provides]:

> "(1) A party to an arbitration agreement against whom legal proceedings are brought (whether by way of a claim or counterclaim) in respect of a matter which under the agreement is to be referred to arbitration may (upon notice to the other parties to the proceedings) apply to the court in which the proceedings have been brought to stay the proceedings so far as they concern that matter…. (4) On an application under this section the court shall grant a stay unless satisfied that the arbitration agreement is null and void, inoperative or incapable of being performed."

The plaintiffs say that the defendants have no arguable defence to their claim. Alternatively they say that they have no arguable defence to more than a very small part of the demurrage claimed, which they say is otherwise indisputable….

[The court first considered] whether the action brought by the plaintiffs is in respect of a matter which under the charter-party is to be referred to arbitration, since only in such a case may an application for a stay be made under §9 of the 1996 Act. The answer to that question depends upon whether on the true construction of the arbitration clause in the charter-party there is any relevant dispute between the parties….

The defendants say that there is a dispute between the parties within the meaning of the arbitration clause. They rely upon these facts. The plaintiffs claimed demurrage. The defendants have refused to pay the amount of demurrage claimed or any demurrage to the plaintiffs. They do not admit that they are liable for the amount of demurrage claimed or indeed any demurrage. In these circumstances they say that there is in ordinary language a dispute between the parties as to whether any and if so what demurrage is due. The plaintiffs say on the other hand that there is no dispute within the meaning of the clause because the vast majority of the demurrage claimed is indisputably due. By indisputably due they mean (as I understand it) that the defendants' defence is obviously unsustainable in fact or law or alternatively that the defendants have no arguable defence to their claim….

[The respondent] submits that the purpose of the arbitration clause was to submit to arbitration all disputes arising from or in connection with the charter-party. He submits that those will include any claim by one party which the other party refuses to admit or does not pay. Thus, for example, the owners might make a claim for freight which the charterers refused to pay only because they wished to make a cross-claim for damage to cargo but to which they had no defence. The parties contemplated that the arbitrators would have jurisdiction to make an award for freight. The parties cannot (he submits) have intended that the arbitrators would have no jurisdiction to make an award for freight in those circumstances. Indeed arbitrators have been making awards for freight in such circumstances over many years.

Unassisted by authority I would accept [the respondent's] submissions. It appears to me that there is indeed here a dispute relating to demurrage, just as there would be a dispute relating to freight in the above example. It seems to me to make no commercial sense to hold that the parties intended that the arbitrators should have jurisdiction over those parts of either party's claim in respect of which the other party has an arguable defence but not otherwise. It makes more sense to hold that the parties intended that the arbitrators should have jurisdiction over all claims which either party has refused to pay. Thus it was contemplated that all such claims should be determined by private arbitration before commercial men and not by the Courts.

[The claimant] recognizes the logic of his argument is that the arbitrators have no jurisdiction to make an award in respect of an indisputable part of the claim. He also accepts that they have often made such awards in similar circumstances in the past, but he says that the problem does not arise and will not arise in practice because parties do not take the point that the arbitrators have no jurisdiction on the ground that their defence is hopeless. In my judgment, that is or would not be a satisfactory state of affairs. It seems to me to be almost inconceivable that the parties to a contract of this kind intended to confer the kind of limited jurisdiction upon the arbitrators which [the claimant's] submissions would involve, if they were right.

I am not persuaded that parties might not take the point in the future. A respondent who had no defence to a claim might well sit back and do nothing while a claimant obtained an award and then resist enforcement proceedings on the basis that the arbitrators had no jurisdiction, by which time the claimant might be out of time to bring Court proceedings....

There is, as I see it, no commercial or legal reason to reach any other conclusion, especially in the light of the Arbitration Act, 1996. The arbitrators have power to make interim awards under §47 and, with the consent of the parties, provisional awards under §39 of the Act. There is no reason why the arbitral process should be any slower or less effective than legal process in the Courts.

[The claimant] submits that those conclusions are wrong and that the parties cannot have intended to submit to arbitration claims which were not disputable in the sense of claims to which the respondents obviously have no answer in fact or law. He says that in those circumstances, which are really cases of mere debt collecting, it is much more likely that the parties contemplated that the party entitled to payment would obtain judgment in the Courts in the ordinary way. For the reasons which I have tried to give I do not accept that that is so, although it is indeed true that there are a number of cases in which the Courts have said that the practice of permitting a party to obtain judgment [in court] in such a case is a useful one. I turn therefore to the authorities.

There is a strong body of authority in support of [the claimant's] submissions. Those cases include the following: *Ellerine Brothers (Pty) Ltd v. Klinger*, [1982] 1 WLR 1375 [(English Ct. App.)]; *Hayter v. Nelson and Home Ins. Co.*, [1990] 2 Lloyd's Rep. 265 ([English High Ct.)]; ... [T]he respondent argues that these cases are wrongly decided ... [I]t is convenient to refer first to ... *Hayter v. Nelson*.... In that case Mr Justice Saville was considering an application for a stay under §1 of the Arbitration Act, 1975. The relevant clause provided that any differences should be referred to arbitration. However he proceeded on the assumption that the word "differences" and the word "disputes" in an arbitration clause bore the same meaning. On that assumption he considered first what that meaning was. He referred ... to the decision of the Court of Appeal in *Ellerine v. Klinger*, where Lord Justice Templeman said (at p. 1383): "There is a dispute until the defendant admits that the sum is due and payable." Mr Justice Saville [reasoned]:

"In my judgment in this context neither the word 'disputes' nor the word 'differences' is confined to cases where it cannot then and there be determined whether one party is right or wrong…. The fact that it can be easily and immediately demonstrated beyond any doubt that the one [party] is right and the other is wrong does not and cannot mean that that dispute did not in fact exist. Because one man can be said to be indisputably right and the other indisputably wrong does not, in my view, entail that there was therefore never any dispute between them." …

He then made three general points, which are I think of some importance …: The first was that it is wrong to say that arbitration is necessarily a slow process. Arbitrators can proceed as quickly as the Courts, notably by making interim awards in appropriate cases. Thus if the claim is indeed indisputable there is no reason why the arbitrators should not make an interim award. I agree. It is, moreover, an important point in considering the submission made by [the claimant] that the Courts have regarded the power to give [summary] judgment under [English procedural rules] as useful. It has no doubt had its uses, but … there is no reason why arbitrators should not make interim awards just as quickly as the Courts can give [summary] judgment…. Indeed I suspect that if the plaintiffs had taken that route in this case, they might have had an interim award by now. The second point was that even if arbitration would be slower, that is the bargain which the parties made. The third point was that if the Courts are to decide whether or not a claim is disputable, they are doing precisely what the parties have agreed should be done by the private tribunal….

In the second part of his judgment Mr Justice Saville considered the true construction of the concluding part of §1(1) of the Arbitration Act, 1975 which provided that where proceedings were commenced in respect of any matter agreed to be referred to arbitration the Court was bound to grant a stay "… unless satisfied that the arbitration agreement is inoperative or incapable of being performed *or that there is not in fact any dispute between the parties with regard to the matter agreed to be referred.*" The words which I have italicized were not re-enacted in §9 of the 1996 Act. In my judgment, that is a key difference because it radically alters the position as it was before and, save in very limited circumstances, leaves all disputes within the arbitration clause to be determined by the agreed tribunal. In *Hayter v. Nelson* Mr Justice Saville held that the words "there is not in fact any dispute" meant "there is not in fact anything disputable" so that is such a case the Court could refuse a stay and give [summary] judgment. That may have been a useful provision … but it has now been removed leaving all questions within the jurisdiction or the arbitrators to be determined by them.

[The court also reasoned] that if there is no dispute when the plaintiff's claim is obviously good, it is difficult to see why there should be a dispute where it is obviously bad. It is, in my judgment, almost inconceivable that the parties intended to exclude the jurisdiction of the arbitrators in either such case. Whether the claim of either party was good or bad, whether obviously or otherwise, was the very thing which they agreed that the arbitrators should decide.

[The court referred to a statement in earlier decisions in *The Fuohsan Maru* [1978] 1 Lloyd's Rep. 24 (English Ct. App.) and *Ellis Mech. Serv. Ltd v. Wates Constr. Ltd*, [1978] 1 Lloyd's Rep. 33 (English Ct. App.):]

"… The question to be asked is: is it established beyond reasonable doubt by the evidence before the Court that at least £x is presently due from the defendant to the plaintiff? If it is, then judgment should be given for the plaintiff for that sum, whatever x may be, and in a case where, as here there is an arbitration clause, the remainder in dispute should go to arbitration. The reason why arbitration should not be extended to cover the area of £x is indeed because there is no issue, or difference, referable to arbitration in respect of that amount."

[The court refused to accept this rationale, citing the reasons noted above.] It is ... an approach that is no longer possible because the key words in §1(1) have been re-enacted in §9(4) of the 1996 Act....

In *Ellerine v. Klinger* the Court ... consider[ed] a question of construction of an arbitration agreement, in which it was agreed that all disputes or differences whatsoever should be referred to arbitration. The plaintiffs claimed an account. The defendants had simply done nothing. The Court of Appeal ... held that silence did not mean consent and that ... until the defendant admits that a sum is due and payable there is a dispute within the meaning of the arbitration clause. Even in such a case I can see an argument for saying that a claimant would be entitled to an award if the respondent then refused to pay. But, however that might be, *Ellerine v. Klinger* is authority for the proposition that where a party simply does nothing there is a dispute which the claimant is both entitled and bound to refer to arbitration....

For the reasons which I have tried to give I am firmly of the opinion that, however indisputable the plaintiffs' claim, there remains a dispute between the parties which they agreed to refer to arbitration. It follows both that the defendants are entitled to a stay of this action under §9(4) of the Arbitration Act, 1996 and that the plaintiffs are not entitled to [summary] judgment [from an English court] ... for any part of their claim....

NOTES

1. *"Defined legal relationship" requirement under New York Convention.* What does Article II(1) of the Convention mean when it refers to an agreement to arbitrate "differences ... in respect of a defined legal relationship, whether contractual or not"? Why is Article II(1) limited in scope to disputes concerning a "defined legal relationship"?

2. *"Defined legal relationship" requirement under UNCITRAL Model Law and other national arbitration legislation.* Consider Article 7(1) of the Model Law, excerpted at pp. 87-88 of the Documentary Supplement. Note that it contains a parallel "defined legal relationship" requirement, mirroring the New York Convention. Article 7(1) (and Article II(1) of the Convention) arguably exclude entirely open-ended arbitration agreements (*e.g.*, A and B agree to arbitrate any dispute which may ever arise between them). Consider the court's analysis in *Roose.* Does the court hold that an agreement to arbitrate all future disputes would be invalid? Or does it instead only attempt to ascertain the parties' intentions regarding the scope of their agreement? *Compare Judgment of 7 April 1933*, 12 GH (1934) (Austrian Oberster Gerichtshof) ("an arbitral tribunal can only decide disputes arising from defined legal relationships and not from undefined legal relationships").

   Suppose that the parties in *Roose* had agreed to arbitrate all future disputes between them, of any character, and that their dispute involved a transaction completely unrelated to the contract containing their arbitration agreement. Would that agreement be enforceable? Why is it that parties might not be permitted to agree to arbitrate any dispute that might ever arise between them in the future? Is there a concern about unwitting waivers of civil rights and access to judicial remedies? What if only sophisticated commercial parties were permitted to enter into such agreements? What if all global Fortune 100 companies entered into an agreement to submit all disputes between any of them, or their affiliates, to arbitration, rather than to national courts or administrative tribunals. Would that compromise public interests? Would it achieve legitimate commercial objectives?

3.   *"Differences which have arisen or may arise" under New York Convention.* Article II(1) of the New York Convention provides for the recognition of agreements to arbitrate "differences which have arisen or may arise." There has long been (and still is) a distinction between agreements to arbitrate *existing* disputes and those to arbitrate *future* disputes. At common law, the latter were effectively unenforceable, owing to the unwillingness of courts to order specific performance. *See, e.g., Tobey v. County of Bristol,* 23 F.Cas. 1313 (C.C.D. Mass. 1845), discussed below at pp. 186-87. *See also supra* pp. 16-19, 21-26. In some countries, agreements to arbitrate remain unenforceable unless they concern preexisting disputes or are confirmed after a dispute arises. This was historically true in parts of the Middle East and Latin America. *See* G. Born, *International Commercial Arbitration* 166 (2d ed. 2014); Naón, *Arbitration in Latin America,* 5 Int'l Arb. 137 (1989); S. Saleh, *Commercial Arbitration in the Arab Middle East* 39-40 (2d ed. 2006).

   The New York Convention and its predecessors attempted to overcome historic national biases against agreements to arbitrate future disputes. The Geneva Protocol obliged signatories to recognize arbitration agreements "whether relating to existing or future differences." Geneva Protocol, Art. I. *See supra* pp. 30-33. Article II(2) of the New York Convention and Article 1 of the Inter-American Convention contain language to the same effect.

4.   *"Differences which have arisen or may arise" under UNCITRAL Model Law and other national arbitration legislation.* Like the New York Convention, most national arbitration statutes confirm that both existing and future disputes may be arbitrated. Thus, Article 7(1) of the UNCITRAL Model Law provides for the enforceability of arbitration agreements concerning "disputes which have arisen or which may arise." Likewise, §2 of the FAA applies to both "written provision[s]" in contracts concerning "controvers[ies] thereafter arising out of such contract[s]" and to "agreement[s] in writing to submit to arbitration an existing controversy." Why is it important that agreements to arbitrate future, as well as existing, disputes be enforceable? After an international commercial dispute has arisen, how likely is it that parties will agree on a neutral forum for dispute resolution? Why not?

   Would the New York Convention permit a Contracting State to enact legislation providing that all agreements to arbitrate future disputes are null and void (and therefore not subject to recognition under Article II(1) of the Convention)? Wouldn't this contradict the Convention's basic structure and most important terms? What if a Contracting State provided that, as a matter of national public policy, all future disputes were nonarbitrable. Would this be permitted under the Convention?

   Compare the language of Article 39 of the 1907 Hague Convention, excerpted at p. 43 of the Documentary Supplement. Is there any reason that future disputes should be less capable of submission, in advance, to arbitration in the state-to-state context than in the commercial context?

5. *Differences "whether contractual or not" under New York Convention.* Note the reference to relationships "whether contractual or not" in Article II(1) of the Convention. This reference makes clear that non-contractual claims (such as tort, competition and other public law claims) may be arbitrated, and that arbitration agreements and awards relating to such claims are in principle enforceable under the Convention. *See infra* pp. 475-510, 530-32, for a discussion of the application of arbitration agreements to non-contractual claims. Would the Convention permit a Contracting State to enact legislation providing that all agreements to arbitrate non-contractual disputes were invalid? Or contrary to national public policy? Would these provisions not violate the Convention's structure and purposes? Construct the best argument that you can that such legislation is inconsistent with a Contracting State's obligations under the Convention.

6. *Differences "whether contractual or not" under UNCITRAL Model Law and other arbitration legislation.* Again paralleling the New York Convention, the UNCITRAL Model Law and arbitration legislation in other developed jurisdictions apply to agreements to arbitrate disputes "whether contractual or not." How important is it that arbitration agreements be valid and effective with regard to non-contractual, as well as contractual, disputes? What would be the practical effect of a rule providing that non-contractual disputes could not be arbitrated? What would happen if a dispute raised both contractual and non-contractual claims (as many disputes do)?

7. *"Disputes" or "differences" under New York Convention and national arbitration legislation.* As the decision in *Halki* illustrates, some national courts have held that arbitration agreements will only be enforced, by the granting of a stay or dismissal of litigation, with regard to "genuine" disputes or differences. Under these authorities, if a national court concluded that there was no credible basis for the respondent's position, then there would be no genuine "dispute" and, therefore, no grounds for requiring arbitration; in these circumstances, national courts would be free to hear the parties' dispute and grant relief (typically, summary relief on an expedited basis). Decisions adopting this analysis were referred to (but rejected) in *Halki*. In addition to the authorities cited in *Halki, see, e.g., Methanex N.Z. Ltd v. Fontaine Nav. SA*, [1998] 2 FC 583 (Canadian Fed. Ct.); *Fai Tak Eng'g Co. Ltd v. Sui Chong Constr. & Eng'g Co. Ltd*, [2009] HKDC 141 (H.K. Dist. Ct.); *Joong & Shipping Co. v. Choi Chong-sick*, XX Y.B. Comm. Arb. 284 (1995) (H.K. High Ct. 1994); *Fletcher Constr. N.Z. & S. Pac. Ltd v. Kiwi Co-operative Dairies Ltd*, CP 7/98, 13 (N.Z. High Ct. 1998) ("the test of whether there is a dispute between the parties for the purpose of [determining whether to stay proceedings and refer the parties to arbitration under Article 8(1) of the New Zealand Arbitration Act 1996] is not whether the party disputing liability is *bona fide* but whether it has arguable grounds for disputing liability").

    Consider the rationale in *The Fuohsan Maru* [1978] 1 Lloyd's Rep. 24, and *Ellis Mech. Servs. Ltd v. Wates Constr. Ltd* [1978] 1 Lloyd's Rep. 33, which was quoted in *Halki*, for permitting national courts to give summary judgment in cases where there was no "genuine" defense to a claim. Is that rationale persuasive? Note the view that it is "useful" to permit national courts to grant summary relief on an expedited basis where there is no genuine defense to a claim. Is that a sound basis for concluding that no genuine "dispute" exists? Note the *Halki* court's observation that a conclusion that no "dispute" exists means that the arbitral tribunal has no jurisdiction to consider the dispute. Is the court correct that this conclusion makes no sense?

What risks does the view, rejected in *Halki*, that there is no "dispute" in the absence of a credible defense to a claim pose to the arbitral process, particularly in international cases? Consider the court's treatment of this approach in *Halki*. What does the *Halki* court hold with regard to the requirement for a "dispute" or "difference"? Suppose one party advances a patently spurious defense; is there a "dispute" under *Halki*? Suppose one party does and says nothing in response to a statement that it has breached the parties' agreement and owes X to its counterparty; is there a "dispute" under *Halki*? Suppose one party affirmatively acknowledges liability for X, but does not pay; is there a "dispute" under *Halki*? How should each of these cases be treated? Note the court's conclusion in *Halki* that parties would not intend to limit the jurisdiction of arbitrators in any of these cases. Why not?

Would it, in general, be more efficient to permit national courts to grant relief in cases where liability is not disputed or is affirmatively admitted by the respondent? Consider the analysis of this issue in *Halki*. Note the court's view that an arbitral tribunal would have the power to grant relief no less quickly than a national court. Is that correct? What about the fact that the constitution of an arbitral tribunal can often take some weeks (or longer)? *See infra* pp. 671-709. What about the fact that arbitrators may be unwilling to grant relief without affording the parties a full opportunity to be heard? *See infra* pp. 793-95.

If relief could be obtained more efficiently in national courts, is that a sufficient reason for concluding that the parties' arbitration agreement does not encompass claims in such cases? Or for concluding that the New York Convention and national arbitration legislation do not apply in such cases? What language in Articles II(1) and (3) of the Convention would permit a court to deny effect to an arbitration clause where it concluded that there was no credible defense to the claimant's claim? Note the reference to "differences" in Article II(1). Compare the language of Article II(3). Does anything in either provision suggest that an arbitration clause need not be recognized if one party's defense is spurious? If one party concedes liability, but refuses to pay or otherwise perform? Would non-recognition of an agreement to arbitrate in such circumstances be consistent with the Convention's objectives?

Suppose that legislation in a Contracting State to the New York Convention permitted parties to seek a summary ruling, from national courts, in all cases, as to whether or not there was a "legitimate" or "genuine" dispute between the parties. Suppose also that arbitration would only be required if local courts concluded that such a dispute existed. Would this approach be consistent with the language and purposes of Article II(1) of the Convention? What risks would this approach create for the international arbitral process?

Consider Article 8(1) of the UNCITRAL Model Law, excerpted at p. 88 of the Documentary Supplement. Does anything in Article 8(1) suggest that the parties need not be referred to arbitration if one party concedes liability or advances a spurious defense?

Suppose that a party has a claim, which its counterparty admits but does not pay. Suppose further that the claimant will suffer irreparable injury if payment is not made promptly. How would the *Halki* court respond to this scenario? Assuming that a party would suffer irreparable injury if not granted immediate relief, does this argue for limiting the arbitrators' jurisdiction (by holding that no "dispute" exists)? Or does it argue for permitting concurrent jurisdiction in national courts to grant provisional measures in aid of an arbitration? *See infra* pp. 903-04, 923-25. For example, wouldn't the claimant be protected, in this hypothetical, by a national court order requiring the respondent to post security for the claimant's claim? *See infra* p. 896.

8.   *"Disputes" under ICSID Convention.* Consider the language of Article 25(1) of the ICSID Convention, excerpted at p. 18 of the Documentary Supplement. What category of disputes does the Convention extend to? What is meant by "any legal dispute arising directly out of an investment, between a Contracting State ... and a national of another Contracting State"? How is a "legal dispute" different from other kinds of disputes?

What is meant by an "investment" dispute? What constitutes an investment? What about the contracts at issue in *RMI* and the Tunisian Cour de cassation's *Judgment of 10 November 1993*. Why wouldn't they be investments? There is substantial authority and commentary on what constitutes an "investment" under the ICSID Convention and various BITs. *See* C. Dugan *et al., Investor-State Arbitration* 247 *et seq.* (2008); C. Schreuer *et al., The ICSID Convention: A Commentary* Art. 25 ¶¶113 *et seq.* (2d ed. 2009).

9.   *"Disputes" under 1907 Hague Convention.* Consider the title of the 1907 Hague Convention ("Convention for the Pacific Settlement of International Disputes"). Consider also Articles 39 and 40, excerpted at p. 43 of the Documentary Supplement. What is meant by "disputes" in the context of the Convention? Should the term have any different meaning in the inter-state context than in the commercial or investment context?

c. "Foreign" or "International" Arbitration Agreements

The New York Convention and most contemporary national arbitration statutes that regulate international arbitration apply only to arbitration agreements that have some sort of "foreign" or "international" connection.[29] This requirement is consistent with the purpose of both types of instruments, which is to facilitate the *international* arbitral process, without disturbing local legal rules for domestic arbitration matters.

Article I(1) of the New York Convention provides a definition of the arbitral awards to which the Convention applies. Under that definition, the Convention is applicable only to awards that: (i) are "made" in a state other than the Contracting State where recognition or enforcement is sought, or (ii) are "not considered as domestic awards" under the law of the enforcing state.[30] In contrast, as noted above, the Convention does not provide any equivalent definition of those arbitration agreements that are subject to the Convention. Different authorities have adopted different approaches to defining the scope of the

---

29. *See* G. Born, *International Commercial Arbitration* 313 (2d ed. 2014).

30. Article I(1) provides: "This Convention shall apply to the recognition and enforcement of arbitral awards made in the territory of the State other than the State where the recognition and enforcement of such awards are sought, and arising out of differences between persons, whether physical or legal. It shall also apply to arbitral awards not considered as domestic awards in the State where their recognition and enforcement are sought."

Convention as applied to international arbitration agreements; as discussed below, some authorities have applied Article I(1) by analogy to arbitration agreements (as well as awards),[31] while other authorities have extended the Convention more broadly to any "international" arbitration agreement.[32]

The limitation of the New York Convention to international arbitration agreements is similar to jurisdictional requirements in many national arbitration statutes. For example, Article 1(1) of the UNCITRAL Model Law provides that the Law applies only to "international commercial arbitration," as defined in Article 1(3) of the Law. These jurisdictional limits serve the general purpose of permitting separate legal regimes for international and domestic arbitration agreements (in light of the differing policies implicated in each case).[33]

The materials excerpted below illustrate the requirement for a "foreign" or "international" connection under the New York Convention and selected national arbitration legislation, particularly the UNCITRAL Model Law. Note that these materials generally apply to both arbitration agreements and arbitral awards, although the focus here is on arbitration agreements.

BERGESEN v. JOSEPH MULLER CORP.
710 F.2d 928 (2d Cir. 1983)

CARDAMONE, Circuit Judge. The question before us on this appeal is whether the [New York] Convention is applicable to an award arising from an arbitration held in New York between two foreign entities.... Sigval Bergesen, a Norwegian shipowner, and Joseph Muller Corporation, a Swiss company, entered into three charter parties in 1969, 1970 and 1971. The 1969 and 1970 charters provided for the transportation of chemicals from the United States to Europe. The 1971 charter concerned the transportation of propylene from the Netherlands to Puerto Rico. Each charter party contained an arbitration clause providing for arbitration in New York, and the Chairman of the [AAA] was given authority to resolve disputes in connection with the appointment of arbitrators.

In 1972, after disputes had arisen during the course of performing the 1970 and 1971 charters, Bergesen made a demand for arbitration of its claims for demurrage and shifting and port expenses. Muller denied liability and asserted counterclaims. The initial panel of arbitrators chosen by the parties was dissolved because of Muller's objections and a second panel was selected through the offices of the AAA. This panel held hearings in 1976 and 1977 and rendered a written decision ... in favor of Bergesen, rejecting all of Muller's counterclaims save one. The net award to Bergesen was $61,406.09 with interest.

Bergesen then sought enforcement of its award in Switzerland where Muller was based. For over two years Muller successfully resisted enforcement. On December 10, 1981, shortly before the expiration of the three-year limitations period provided in 9 U.S.C. §207, Bergesen filed a petition in the U.S. District Court for the Southern District of New York to

---

31. *See infra* pp. 164-66.

32. *See infra* pp. 164-66; G. Born, *International Commercial Arbitration* 314 *et seq.* (2d ed. 2014). In a broadly comparable fashion, the Inter-American Convention is applicable (according to its title and preamble) to "international commercial arbitration." *See infra* p. 166.

33. *See* G. Born, *International Commercial Arbitration* 233 *et seq.* (2d ed. 2014).

confirm the arbitration award.... District Judge Charles S. Haight, Jr. confirmed Bergesen's award, holding that the Convention applied to arbitration awards rendered in the United States involving foreign interests. Judgment was entered awarding Bergesen $61,406.09, plus interest of $18,762.01....

On appeal from this ... judgment, Muller contends that the Convention does not cover enforcement of the arbitration award made in the United States because it was neither territorially a "foreign" award nor an award "not considered as domestic" within the meaning of the Convention. Muller also claims that the reservations adopted by the United States in its accession to the Convention narrowed the scope of its application so as to exclude enforcement of this award in U.S. courts, [and] that the statute implementing the treaty was not intended to cover awards rendered within the United States.... Whether the Convention applies to a commercial arbitration award rendered in the United States is a question previously posed but left unresolved in this Court....

A proposed draft of the Convention which was to govern the enforcement of foreign arbitral awards stated that it was to apply to arbitration awards rendered in a country other than the state where enforcement was sought.... This proposal was controversial because the delegates were divided on whether it defined adequately what constituted a foreign award. On one side were ranged the countries of western Europe accustomed to civil law concepts; on the other side were the eastern European states and the common law nations. For example, several countries, including France, Italy and West Germany, objected to the proposal on the ground that a territorial criterion was not adequate to establish whether an award was foreign or domestic. These nations believed that the nationality of the parties, the subject of the dispute and the rules of arbitral procedure were factors to be taken into account in determining whether an award was foreign. In both France and West Germany, for example, the nationality of an award was determined by the law governing the procedure. Thus, an award rendered in London under German law was considered domestic when enforcement was attempted in Germany, and an award rendered in Paris under foreign law was considered foreign when enforcement was sought in France.

As an alternative to the territorial concept, eight European nations proposed that the Convention "apply to the recognition and enforcement of arbitral awards other than those considered as domestic in the country in which they are relied upon." Eight other countries, including the United States, objected to this proposal, arguing that common law nations would not understand the distinction between foreign and domestic awards. These latter countries urged the delegates to adopt only the territorial criterion. A working party composed of representatives from ten states to which the matter was referred recommended that both criteria be included. Thus, the Convention was to apply to awards made in a country other than the state where enforcement was sought as well as to awards not considered domestic in that state. The members of the Working Party representing the western European group agreed to this recommendation, provided that each nation would be allowed to exclude certain categories of awards rendered abroad. At the conclusion of the conference this exclusion was omitted, so that the text originally proposed by the Working Party was adopted as Article I of the Convention.... [T]he Working Party's intent was to find a compromise formula which would restrict the territorial concept. The final action taken by the Convention appears to have had the opposite result, *i.e.*, except as provided in paragraph 3, the first paragraph of Article 1 means that the Convention applies to all arbitral awards rendered in a country other than the state of enforcement, whether or not such awards may be regarded as domestic in that state; "it also applies to all awards not considered as domestic in the state of enforcement, whether or not any of such awards may have been rendered in the territory of that state." ...

With this background in mind, we turn to Muller's contentions regarding the scope of the Convention. The relevant portion of the Convention, Article I, is set forth [above.] The territorial concept expressed in the first sentence of Article I(1) presents little difficulty. Muller correctly urges that since the arbitral award in this case was made in New York and enforcement was sought in the United States, the award does not meet the territorial criterion. Simply put, it is not a foreign award as defined in Article I(1) because it was not rendered outside the nation where enforcement is sought.

Muller next contends that the award may not be considered a foreign award within the purview of the second sentence of Article I(1) because it fails to qualify as an award "not considered as domestic." Muller claims that the purpose of the "not considered as domestic" test was to provide for the enforcement of what it terms "stateless awards," *i.e.*, those rendered in the territory where enforcement is sought but considered unenforceable because of some foreign component. This argument is unpersuasive since some countries favoring the provision desired it so as to preclude the enforcement of certain awards rendered abroad, not to enhance enforcement of awards rendered domestically.

Additionally, Muller urges a narrow reading of the Convention contrary to its intended purpose. The Convention did not define non-domestic awards. The definition appears to have been left out deliberately in order to cover as wide a variety of eligible awards as possible, while permitting the enforcing authority to supply its own definition of "non-domestic" in conformity with its own national law. Omitting the definition made it easier for those states championing the territorial concept to ratify the Convention while at the same time making the Convention more palatable in those states which espoused the view that the nationality of the award was to be determined by the law governing the arbitral procedure. We adopt the view that awards "not considered as domestic" denotes awards which are subject to the Convention not because made abroad, but because made within the legal framework of another country, *e.g.*, pronounced in accordance with foreign law or involving parties domiciled or having their principal place of business outside the enforcing jurisdiction. We prefer this broader construction because it is more in line with the intended purpose of the treaty, which was entered into to encourage the recognition and enforcement of international arbitration awards. Applying that purpose to this case involving two foreign entities leads to the conclusion that this award is not domestic....

We now turn to the argument that the implementing statute was not intended to cover awards rendered within the United States. Section 202 of [the FAA,] which is entitled "Agreement or award falling under the Convention," provides in relevant part:

> "An agreement or award arising out of such a relationship which is entirely between citizens of the United States shall be deemed not to fall under the Convention unless that relationship involves property located abroad, envisages performance or enforcement abroad, or has some other reasonable relation with one or more foreign states."

The legislative history of this provision indicates that it was intended to ensure that "an agreement or award arising out of a legal relationship exclusively between citizens of the United States is not enforceable under the Convention in [United States] courts unless it has a reasonable relation with a foreign state." H.R. Rep. No. 91-1181, 91st Cong., 2d Sess. 2, *reprinted in*, 1970 U.S. Code, Cong. & Ad. News 3601, 3602. Inasmuch as it was apparently left to each state to define which awards were to be considered non-domestic, Congress spelled out its definition of that concept in §202. Had Congress desired to exclude arbitral awards involving two foreign parties rendered within the United States from enforcement by our courts it could readily have done so. It did not....

Muller's further contention that it could not have been the aim of Congress to apply the Convention to this transaction because it would remove too broad a class of awards from enforcement under the [FAA] is unpersuasive. That this particular award might also have been enforced under the [FAA] is not significant. There is no reason to assume that Congress did not intend to provide overlapping coverage between the Convention and the [FAA].... The judgment is affirmed.

BRIER v. NORTHSTAR MARINE INC.
1992 WL 350292 (D.N.J.)

ROSEN, United States Magistrate.... On or about October 21, 1990, plaintiff John H. Brier, Jr., the owner of the vessel and three other individuals were travelling from Connecticut to Maryland aboard a fifty-three (53) foot yacht titled the M/Y Joanie Bee.... As plaintiff was entering the Hereford Inlet in New Jersey, the vessel ran aground.... Plaintiff [contacted defendant] Northstar Marine, Inc. to ascertain whether the company could provide the necessary assistance to plaintiff in refloating his vessel. Captain Risko, the owner and operator of Northstar Marine, Inc. informed plaintiff that he could provide the necessary assistance.... Captain Risko informed Mr Brier that he would be conducting a salvage operation. He then read from a document known as the "Miranda Act for Salvors"[34] which basically states that the Lloyd's of London Form will be used. This form also states that the terms are "No Cure, No Pay," which allows the company to conduct the salvage operation without a prearranged price and at the completion of the operation the company will submit a claim. If the master or his insured do not agree with the claim, it must be arbitrated by the Lloyd's of London Arbitration Panel.

Somewhere between 8:25 a.m. and 9:00 a.m. on October 22, 1990, Mr Cassidy, the owner and operator of the Cape May Marine Services, arrived at plaintiff's motel room with an initial set of documents for plaintiff to sign prior to defendants attempting to refloat the boat. Among the documents was the Lloyd's Standard Form of Salvage Agreement (hereinafter, "LOF Agreement") which was approximately three pages long. Mr Cassidy then proceeded to scan the document with the plaintiff, highlighting each paragraph. The document provided that all disputes between the parties be arbitrated at Lloyd's of London in England and that English law will govern the resolution of the dispute. Plaintiff signed the documentation including the LOF Agreement and his vessel was thereafter refloated and towed to the Canyon Club Marina in New Jersey.... [The] plaintiff was [later] in-

---

34. Defendants allege that the exact wording of the Miranda Act of Salvagers is as follows:

"The Lloyds of London Salvage Agreement is a no cure, no pay agreement which permits us to assist you immediately without lengthy negotiations. After we have completed the job, if we are successful in salving your boat, we will make a salvage claim based upon the value of what we have saved. If we are not successful we will claim nothing. If you or your insurer believe that our claim is too high, you may request Lloyd's to appoint an arbitrator to determine how much we should be paid. Whatever amount the arbitrator awards us, we will accept. This agreement is published and approved by Lloyd's of London for use in salvage situations. Do you accept?"

formed that the costs of the refloating and towing his vessel amounted to $38,250.00. Plaintiff refused to pay this amount and on February 11, 1991 instituted the instant action [for a declaratory judgment that the LOF Agreement was an invalid adhesion contract. The defendants invoked the arbitration clause and the New York Convention. Plaintiff replied that the Convention did not apply.] …

It is plaintiff's contention that the provisions of the Lloyd's Standard Form of Salvage Agreement requiring the contractor and the owner to arbitrate their dispute concerning compensation in London pursuant to English law, when both are U.S. citizens and their relationship is not reasonably related to England, falls outside the [New York] Convention as enacted in the United States and therefore this court is precluded from requiring arbitration in accordance with the agreement.

In the present case the parties are in agreement that all are citizens of the United States…. However, my inquiry cannot end here since §202 … carves out certain exceptions even where all parties to the relationship are citizens of United States…. The legislative history of §202 makes it clear that where the matter is solely between citizens of the United States it will fall outside the Convention unless there is a reasonable relation with a foreign state…. Therefore, unless the facts allow this case to fit within one of the four jurisdictional requirements noted above, it will fall outside the Convention and render the arbitral agreement between these parties unenforceable.

Is the property located abroad? The only property involved in the case at bar is the vessel, the M/Y Joanie Bee, which is registered in the State of Connecticut and at all times material hereto has been located off the Coast of New Jersey. Does the agreement envisage performance abroad? The performance in the instant case involved the refloating of the vessel and the towing of it to Canyon Club Marina, in New Jersey. All performance which occurred in this case occurred within the coastal waters of New Jersey.

Does the agreement envisage enforcement abroad? Defendants argue that the LOF Agreement clearly satisfies the third condition in that the language of the contract envisions that English law would apply to the arbitration, and more importantly, the arbitration and any appeal therefrom, would be before the Committee of Lloyd's in London, England. Defendants rely on *Fuller Co. v. Compagnie des Bauxites de Guinea*, 421 F.Supp. 938 (W.D. Pa. 1976) to support their assertion that the present case is the type of enforcement Congress envisioned when it carved out the exceptions found in 9 U.S.C. §202.

However, *Fuller* is easily distinguishable from the case at bar. While it is true that both parties were considered United States citizens in *Fuller*, the court in *Fuller* found the "reasonable relationship" to exist under the performance exception not the enforcement exception. In *Fuller*, the contract envisaged that plaintiff would provide extensive technical services in Guinea. An affidavit submitted to the court stated that the total cost of Fuller's technical representatives in Guinea was $269,562.08. Consequently, the court held that the case fell within the exception due to the "substantial amount of performance of this contract in Guinea." As stated above performance of the contract in dispute was performed solely in New Jersey.

In contrast, plaintiff asserts that the enforcement of this agreement bears no reasonable relation to London, England. The fact that the parties are currently before this court to determine the enforceability of the arbitration agreement is of itself significant. Moreover, plaintiff asserts that the vessel upon which the contractor claimed a maritime lien was located in New Jersey and therefore the security posted to obtain the release of the vessel would have remained in this district subject to enforcement of a subsequent arbitration award. I agree. Accordingly, I find this district to be the proper place to enforce an arbitral award, not London, England....

Does the agreement have some other reasonable relation with one or more foreign states? Defendants argue that the current facts set forth a reasonable relation with the foreign nation. Their contention is that the parties willingly entered into the LOF Agreement which clearly compelled arbitration in London, England and that the Committee of Lloyd's is the only internationally recognized body which deals with salvage arbitrations and no other body is so recognized.[35] Furthermore, defendants assert that it is undisputed that Lloyd's sits in London, England and that English law controls their arbitrations and any appeal thereof. Consequently, defendants contend that the situs and law found in the LOF Agreement was selected with care and that of itself encompasses the reasonable relation with London, England.

Defendants' argument however, is circular. If I were to agree with defendants analysis that the reasonable relation with the foreign forum is created by the document itself, I would be allowing "the exception to swallow the rule." The only avenue which would bring this particular issue before the court is where a document has been signed by the parties, compelling foreign arbitration, and all the parties are U.S. citizens. Consequently, following defendants reasoning, in every case the parties would fall within the fourth jurisdictional exception, since the document itself would always name a foreign nation for arbitration.... Taking into consideration the purpose of the agreement and the motivation for the exception created by Congress[36] I find based on the narrow facts before me, that this case falls outside the Convention....

NOTES

1. *Uncertainty about scope of application of New York Convention to international arbitration agreements.* Consider the text of Article II of the New York Convention, excerpted at p. 1 of the Documentary Supplement. What categories of such agreements does Article II govern? Does Article II clearly address this issue? Does any other provision of the Convention do so?

2. *Possible limitation of New York Convention to "foreign" or "nondomestic" arbitration agreements.* Consider Article I(1) of the New York Convention, excerpted at p. 1 of the Documentary Supplement. As noted above, Article I(1) the Convention is applicable only to arbitral awards that: (i) are "made" in a state other than the Contracting State where recognition or enforcement is sought, or (ii) are "not considered as domestic awards" under the law of the enforcing state. Should the Convention's "foreign" or "nondomestic" award requirement apply to arbitration agreements? Under this theory, the Convention would only apply to arbitration agreements that would produce "foreign" or "nondomestic" awards subject to the Convention. Most

35. This court takes judicial notice of the fact that the Committee of Lloyd's has a long and admirable history and tradition of being particularly suited to arbitrate these type of matters. However, this alone does not establish the "reasonable relationship" required by 9 U.S.C. §202.

36. I find that Congress did not intend to expand jurisdiction to include local disputes between citizens of the United States since these matters were better left to the judiciary in the district where the incident occurred.

importantly, under this theory, if an arbitration agreement provided for arbitration in State A, under the arbitration laws of State A, then that agreement would ordinarily not be subject to the Convention in State A—because the award that would be produced pursuant to the arbitration agreement would not be "foreign" or "nondomestic" in State A. *See* G. Born, *International Commercial Arbitration* 315-19 (2d ed. 2014); van den Berg, *When Is An Arbitral Award Non-Domestic Under the New York Convention of 1958?*, 6 Pace L. Rev. 25, 51-54 (1985).

Why should Article I(1)'s provisions regarding awards be extended to arbitration agreements? Does anything in Article I(1)'s language, or the language of other provisions of the Convention, require such a result? Consider the text of Article II. Does it not apply generally to all arbitration agreements? Regardless of whether they produce "foreign" or "nondomestic" awards?

3. *Possible extension of New York Convention to "international" arbitration agreements.* Alternatively, the Convention can be read as not limited to arbitration agreements that produce "foreign" or "nondomestic" awards. How might this wider category of agreements be defined? Where would one look in the Convention for a definition of these agreements? Does it make sense to apply the Convention to all arbitration agreements, including agreements between two nationals of the same state, involving a transaction that is wholly localized within that state? Why not?

Can the Convention be interpreted as applying to all "international" arbitration agreements? How would "international" be defined for such purposes? What text in the Convention would support such a definition? Would a definition of the Convention as applying to all "international" arbitration agreements advance the purposes of the Convention? How?

4. *Application of New York Convention to arbitration agreements between local parties specifying foreign arbitral seat.* Consider the facts in *Northstar*. Does the Convention apply whenever a court in one Contracting State is presented with an arbitration clause specifying an arbitral seat in another Contracting State? Specifically, the arbitration clause in *Northstar* provided for arbitration in London, between U.S. parties; why wasn't this agreement subject to the Convention? Consider the text of Article I(1).

A number of U.S. courts other than *Northstar* have considered whether the Convention applies to arbitration agreements between U.S. nationals specifying a foreign arbitral seat. In *Wilson v. Lignotock U.S.A., Inc.*, 709 F.Supp. 797 (E.D. Mich. 1989), for example, the court held that, under §202, the Convention was not applicable to an agreement to arbitrate in Switzerland between a U.S. company and its U.S. employee, where the parties' underlying contract was to be entirely performed in the United States. *See also* G. Born, *International Commercial Arbitration* 316-17 (2d ed. 2014). If the Convention is interpreted as applying to all arbitration agreements that produce "foreign" awards, then wouldn't the Convention apply to the agreement at issue in *Northstar*? Does it in fact make sense to apply the Convention to any arbitration agreement (and only to an arbitration agreement) that produces a "foreign" or "nondomestic" award? How might *Northstar* be decided if the Convention were held applicable to "international" arbitration agreements?

5. *Application of New York Convention to arbitration agreement between foreign parties specifying arbitral seat within forum state.* Suppose two English entities, parties to an entirely domestic English transaction, agreed to arbitrate disputes relating to the

transaction in New York. If the validity of the agreement were at issue in a U.S. court, would the New York Convention apply? (Note that, in the United States, the resulting award would not be "foreign.") Conversely, how would *Northstar* have been resolved if it had arisen in English courts? Should the case have been resolved any differently than in U.S. courts?

Suppose a French entity and a German entity, parties to an international transaction, agreed to arbitrate disputes relating to the transaction in New York. If the validity of the arbitration clause were at issue in a U.S. court, would the Convention apply? What about in a French or German court?

6. *Limitation of Inter-American Convention to "international commercial arbitration."* Consider the title ("Inter-American Convention on International Commercial Arbitration") and the preamble of the Inter-American Convention, excerpted at p. 9 of the Documentary Supplement. Both appear, at least impliedly, to limit the Convention's scope to "international commercial arbitration." Is this term defined anywhere in the Convention? What meaning should be given to "international commercial arbitration" as used in the Inter-American Convention? What is the purpose of limiting the Convention to "international" matters?

Consider the following: (a) two U.S. citizens contract in the United States concerning a purely U.S. matter and agree to arbitrate in the United States; (b) two U.S. citizens contract in the United States concerning acts to be performed in State A and agree to arbitrate in the United States; (c) same as (a), but one contracting party is a State A national; (d) same as (b), but one contracting party is a State A national; (e) same as (a), but the arbitral seat is in State A. Which of the foregoing are "international"? Why?

7. *Limitation of 1961 European Convention to "international" arbitrations.* Consider the definition of the scope of the European Convention in Article 1, excerpted at p. 29 of the Documentary Supplement. What are the components of this definition? Consider the hypotheticals in the previous note. How would Article 1 of the Convention apply to each? Compare Article 1 to the New York and Inter-American Conventions. Which approach is preferable? Consider the analysis of Article I of the European Convention in *Benteler v. State of Belgium*, excerpted below at pp. 465-68. Why was the agreement there "international"?

8. *Rationale for limiting New York Convention, Inter-American Convention and European Convention to "international" arbitration agreements.* Consider the express and implied limitations in the New York Convention, the Inter-American Convention and the European Convention regarding "international" arbitration agreements. Broadly speaking, and with significantly different wording, all three instruments are limited to "international" or "foreign/nondomestic" arbitration agreements. What is the reason for this limitation? What benefits and costs does it produce? What would be wrong with adopting the Conventions' rules for domestic arbitrations?

9. *"International" relationship requirement under UNCITRAL Model Law and other national arbitration legislation.* Many contemporary national arbitration statutes apply only to "international" arbitration or, alternatively, contain specialized regimes for both "international" and "domestic" arbitrations.

(a) *Limitation of UNCITRAL Model Law to "international" arbitration agreements.* Consider the text of Article 1 of the Model Law, excerpted at p. 86 of the Documentary Supplement, which limits the Model Law's applicability to "international commercial arbitration," and then provides a definition of "international" arbitration. Compare Article 1(3)'s definition of "international" arbitration with the definition of "foreign" and "nondomestic" under the New York Convention. Compare Article 1(3) with §202 of the FAA and, in particular, with the *Northstar* decision.

Is the definition of "international" arbitration in the Model Law appropriate? Note that parties can effectively "opt in" to the Model Law by agreeing that their transaction and arbitration agreement are "international." Is that appropriate? Why or why not? *See* G. Born, *International Commercial Arbitration* 322-26 (2d ed. 2014).

(b) *Limitation of Swiss Law on Private International Law to "international" arbitration agreements.* Consider the text of Article 176(1) of the SLPIL, excerpted at p. 157 of the Documentary Supplement. How does Article 176(1)'s formulation compare with that of the Model Law and §202 of the FAA? Which approach is preferable? See also Article 1504 of the French Code of Civil Procedure.

10. *Effect of §202 of FAA on application of New York Convention.* Consider the text of §202 of the FAA, excerpted at p. 107 of the Documentary Supplement. How does §202 clarify the applicability of the New York Convention to international arbitration agreements? Is §202 an affirmative statement of the Convention's scope? Or is it rather a negative statement as to when the Convention will be "deemed" inapplicable? Consider both the first and second sentences of §202.

As *Northstar* illustrates, lower U.S. courts have interpreted §202 as adopting a "reasonable relationship" requirement for determining what arbitration agreements—as well as what arbitral awards—are subject to the Convention. That requirement is derived principally from the legislative history of the section. *See, e.g., Best Concrete Mix Corp. v. Lloyd's of London Underwriters*, 413 F.Supp.2d 182, 188 (E.D.N.Y. 2006); *Coastal States Trading, Inc. v. Zenith Nav. SA*, 446 F.Supp. 330, 341 (S.D.N.Y. 1977) (applying §202, incorrectly, to hold that arbitration agreement between U.S. and Panamanian company for shipment of oil from England to United States was not nondomestic); *Fuller Co. v. Compagnie des Bauxites de Guinée*, 421 F.Supp. 938, 941 (W.D. Pa. 1976); G. Born, *International Commercial Arbitration* 326-27 (2d ed. 2014).

11. *Rationale for §202.* What precisely is the legislative purpose of §202? Is there a U.S. public policy in precluding U.S. citizens from resolving disputes abroad? Recall the frequency of public statements of concern about overloaded U.S. dockets, delays in trials and appeals, and the high cost of the legal system. Is it wise to force U.S. parties to contribute to the back-log? Whatever the answer, the stated legislative purpose of §202's exclusion was to avoid application of the Convention to at least some categories of local disputes between Americans. Foreign Arbitral Awards, S. Rep. No. 91-702, 91st Cong., 2d Sess. 6 (1970) (Appx.; Statement of Richard D. Kearney) ("it was necessary to modify the definition of commerce to make it quite clear that arbitration arising out of relationships in inter-state commerce remains under the original Arbitration Act and is excluded from the operation of the proposed Chapter 2"). In the words of the House Report:

"[T]he second sentence of §202 is intended to make it clear that an agreement or award arising out of a legal relationship exclusively between citizens of the United States is not enforceable under the Convention in U.S. courts unless it has a reasonable relation with a foreign state." H.R. Rep. No. 91-1181, 91st Cong., 2d Sess. 2, reprinted in [1970] U.S. Code Cong. & Ad. News 3601, 3602.

Does this language justify the result in *Northstar*? Cannot one appropriately conclude that the *Northstar* agreement had a reasonable relationship to England, by selecting an English arbitral seat? Particularly where the (foreign) arbitral seat was selected because of its expertise, experience and (less clearly) neutrality?

12. *Application of New York Convention to transactions between U.S. nationals involving property or performance abroad.* U.S. nationals frequently enter into agreements with one another with respect to property located, or performance occurring, outside the United States. Section 202 seeks to make it clear that these agreements are subject to the Convention, even though they involve only U.S. nationals. *See Fuller Co. v. Compagnie des Bauxites de Guinea*, 421 F.Supp. 938 (W.D. Pa. 1976). What exactly is required to satisfy §202's requirement for property or performance located abroad?

13. *Application of New York Convention to transactions between U.S. nationals having a "reasonable relationship" to a foreign state.* Even if a transaction does not involve property or performance abroad, §202 also applies the Convention to agreements between U.S. nationals having a "reasonable relationship" to a foreign state. What would satisfy §202's "reasonable relationship" requirement? As a matter of statutory interpretation, doesn't a "reasonable relationship" necessarily involve things *other* than property or performance abroad (which are separately mentioned in §202)? Note that London was selected in *Northstar* for historical and legal reasons relating to the salvage industry. Why wasn't this sufficient to satisfy the reasonable relationship requirement?

Section 202's "reasonable relationship" standard was based on §1-105 of the U.S. Uniform Commercial Code, dealing with choice-of-law clauses. *See infra* pp. 990-91, 1090. As discussed elsewhere, §1-105 generally permits parties to a transaction to select a neutral foreign law that has no connection to the place where the parties' transaction was negotiated or will be performed; a "reasonable relationship" can be found in cases where the parties agree to the application of a neutral, predictable foreign legal system. *See infra* pp. 990-91. Why shouldn't §202 be interpreted as permitting selection of a neutral arbitral seat (especially where the seat has particular expertise or historical experience)? Should this be permitted even where a transaction only involves local nationals and is purely domestic in scope?

14. *Application of §202 outside consumer/employee context.* Suppose two sophisticated U.S. companies, from different parts of the United States, agree to arbitrate in Montreal, Canada (or London). What U.S. public policy would forbid this? Suppose that the arbitration agreement in *Northstar* had been carefully negotiated, with the advice of counsel. Isn't the real concern in *Northstar* that of a one-sided adhesion contract with unsophisticated consumers? If so, are there not mechanisms under the Convention for dealing with this concern? Note Article II's provision that Contracting States are not obligated to enforce agreements that are "null and void"; wouldn't that provision include defenses based on unconscionability? *See infra* pp. 393-412. Note the provisions in Articles II(1) and V(2)(a) regarding disputes that are nonarbitrable. *See infra* pp. 475-510.

15. *Consequences of concluding that §202 does not apply to arbitration agreement.* Assume, as the *Northstar* court held, that an arbitration agreement between two U.S. nationals is not subject to the Convention (and that the domestic FAA does not require enforcement). Then what? Is the entire arbitration agreement void? What does *Northstar* hold? Is the offending term, selecting a foreign arbitral seat, to be severed, leaving an arbitration agreement without a selection of an arbitral seat? Could a U.S. court then select, or could the arbitral tribunal select, a U.S. arbitral seat? *See also infra* pp. 658-69.

16. *Scope of 1907 Hague Convention.* Consider what category of disputes is encompassed by the arbitration provisions of the 1907 Hague Convention. Note that the Convention is directed towards "disputes between states." Is there any reason that the same provisions could not apply to disputes between a state and a non-state actor? Consider Article 38 of the Convention, excerpted at p. 43 of the Documentary Supplement. Does it limit the types of inter-state disputes that are subject to the Convention? Does it suggest that some disputes are better suited for arbitration than others? What disputes? What is meant by a dispute of a "legal matter"?

17. *Scope of ICSID Convention.* Consider the disputes that may be submitted to ICSID jurisdiction under Article 25 of the Convention, excerpted at pp. 18-19 of the Documentary Supplement. Note that the disputes must involve a Contracting State and the national of another Contracting State. Why is that? What would be wrong with a French investor proceeding against France in an ICSID arbitration?

d. Reciprocity Requirements Under International Conventions and National Arbitration Legislation

The concept of reciprocity plays a significant role in many private international law contexts. For example, the availability of international judicial assistance and the enforceability of foreign judicial judgments often depend on principles of reciprocity.[37] Reciprocity can also be relevant to the enforceability of international arbitral awards and arbitration agreements, under both international conventions and national arbitration legislation. The decision excerpted below examines the role of reciprocity in both contexts.

As discussed below, Article I(3) of the New York Convention provides Contracting States with the possibility of making a "reciprocity reservation"; additionally, Article XIV of the Convention also contains a general reciprocity provision (although its meaning is disputed).[38] In contrast, most contemporary national arbitration statutes do not contain express reciprocity requirements. Moreover, national courts have generally not considered whether such requirements should or may be implied. The materials excerpted and discussed below examine the role of reciprocity as applied to arbitration agreements under the New York and Inter-American Conventions and leading arbitration statutes, including the UNCITRAL Model Law.

---

37. *See* G. Born & P. Rutledge, *International Civil Litigation in United States Courts* 1094 *et seq.* (5th ed. 2011).

38. *See* G. Born, *International Commercial Arbitration* 343-44 (2d ed. 2014).

NATIONAL IRANIAN OIL CO. v. ASHLAND OIL, INC.
817 F.2d 326 (5th Cir. 1987) (also excerpted below at pp. 427-29)

GOLDBERG, Circuit Judge.... According to the [parties'] allegations, two Ashland Oil Company ("Ashland") subsidiaries, Ashland Overseas Trading Limited ("AOTL") and Ashland Bermuda Limited [entered into oil supply contracts with] the National Iranian Oil Company ("NIOC"), an instrumentality of the Islamic Republic of Iran.... [D]uring the Islamic Revolution in Iran, NIOC allegedly repudiated then renegotiated its contracts with Ashland's two subsidiaries on several occasions in 1978 and 1979.... On April 11, [1979], the parties allegedly executed a new contract....

On November 12, 1979, following the takeover of the American Embassy in Tehran ... President Carter banned the importation of all oil from Iran not already in transit. Several cargoes of crude, however, were then en route to AOTL. AOTL received and refined the oil, worth nearly $283,000,000. Despite NIOC's demand, neither Ashland nor its subsidiaries have rendered payment. Ashland, in essence, contends that it is not responsible for the alleged breaches of its subsidiaries and that NIOC itself breached the March and April agreements.

In accord with the terms of the arbitration clause of the parties' April contract, NIOC appointed an arbitrator to resolve the dispute.... Ashland refuses to participate in an arbitral proceeding in Iran because of the danger to Americans. Nor has Ashland agreed to participate in an arbitration elsewhere. NIOC thus brought suit against Ashland in federal district court, and alleged breach of contract in the first three counts of its complaint. In count four of its complaint, NIOC sought to compel arbitration in Mississippi, to have the court appoint an arbitrator and to stay litigation pursuant to the [FAA].

Ashland then filed a counterclaim, alleging tortious interference with and breach of contract by NIOC. NIOC responded to the counterclaim by filing an application that also sought to appoint an arbitrator, to compel arbitration, and to stay litigation. Because the terms of the agreement expressly provided for arbitration in Tehran, the district court found that it lacked the power to order arbitration in Mississippi under §4 of the Act, and thus it denied NIOC's motion. NIOC appeals from that order....

Section 4 ... facially mandates that two conditions must be met before a district court may compel arbitration: (1) that the arbitration be held in the district in which the court sits; and (2) that the arbitration be held in accordance with the agreement of the parties. In this case the forum selection clause, found in Article X of the April contract, provides that "the seat of arbitration shall be in Tehran, unless otherwise agreed by the parties." Relying on *Snyder v. Smith*, 736 F.2d 409 (7th Cir. 1984), the district court reasoned that the language of §4 deprived it of the power to compel arbitration in Mississippi, because to order arbitration in Mississippi would violate the forum selection clause and thus would not be "in accordance with the terms of the agreement." ...

[A]s NIOC now concedes, it has no right to an order compelling arbitration in Tehran. When the United States adhered to the [New York] Convention, U.S. courts were granted the power to compel arbitration in signatory countries. *See* 9 U.S.C. §206. But Iran is not one of the 65 nations [153 as of 2014] that have adhered to the Convention, and thus no American court may order arbitration in Iran. Consequently, NIOC has no right that is recognized under U.S. law to compel an arbitration in Iran....

When the United States adhered to the Convention, it expressly chose the option available in Article I(3), to "apply the Convention, *on the basis of reciprocity*, to the recognition and enforcement of *only* those awards made in the territory of another Contracting State." Declaration (emphasis added). While the House and Senate Committee reports do not inform us as to the purpose of adopting this reservation, its purpose seems obvious. Concerned with reciprocity, Congress must have meant only to allow signatories to partake of the Convention's benefits in U.S. courts and thus to give further incentives to non-signatory nations to adhere to the Convention. Were we now to order arbitration in Mississippi, despite the forum selection clause designating Tehran … we would do great violence to this obvious congressional purpose. Were we to order arbitration in the U.S. in the face of a forum selection clause designating a non-signatory forum, which was unenforceable *ab initio*, the non-signatory would have little reason to leave the Hobbesian jungle of international chaos for the ordered and more predictable world of international commercial law….

NOTES

1. *Reciprocity provisions in New York Convention.* Consider the text of Articles I(3) and XIV of the Convention, excerpted at pp. 1 & 4 of the Documentary Supplement. How are they similar? How do they differ? What do you think their purposes are?
2. *Reciprocity reservations under Article I(3) of the Convention.* Most Convention signatories, including the United States, have deposited reciprocity reservations. The U.S. reservation to the Convention provides, in relevant part: "The United States of America will apply the Convention, on the basis of reciprocity, to the recognition and enforcement of only those awards made in the territory of another Contracting State." Many other signatories to the Convention have adopted similar "reciprocity" reservations. *See* 9 U.S.C.A. §201, reproducing excerpts of such reservations.
3. *Meaning of Article I(3) reciprocity reservation.* What is the meaning of Article I(3) and reciprocity reservations made thereunder? Do these reservations focus on the nationality of the parties? The location of the arbitral seat? Something else? Suppose a company based in State A (which has not ratified the Convention) arbitrates with a company based in State B (which has ratified the Convention) in State C (which also has ratified the Convention, with a reciprocity reservation). In this case, would an award in favor of the State A company ordinarily be enforceable in accordance with the Convention in State C? Would an award in favor of the State B company ordinarily be enforceable in other Contracting States against the State A company? Would an award in favor of any company, rendered in State A, be enforceable under the Convention (except where a state had not made a reciprocity reservation)?
4. *Application of Article I(3)'s reciprocity limitation to arbitration agreements.* Consider the text of Article I(3) of the Convention and the reservations made thereunder again. Does Article I(3)'s reciprocity requirement apply to arbitration agreements, as distinguished from arbitral awards?
   (a) *Text of Article I(3)'s reciprocity limitation.* Consider the text of Article I(3) and its reference to reciprocity. Article I(3) is limited to "awards" and makes no reference to "agreements." Consider the text of the U.S. reservation pursuant to Article I(3); that reservation, tracking the Convention's text, is also limited to "awards" and makes no reference to "agreements." Given this, does Article I(3) create any exception to Article II's provisions regarding the enforceability of arbitration agreements?

(b) *Divergent U.S. authorities on application of Article I(3)'s reciprocity limitation to arbitration agreements.* Lower U.S. courts have reached divergent results on the question whether Article I(3)'s reciprocity limitation applies to arbitration agreements. According to one court, Article I(3)'s reciprocity "limitation clearly applies only to the recognition and enforcement of arbitral awards; it has no relevance to the problem pending before this court—whether to order arbitration under the terms of the Convention." *Fuller Co. v. Compagnie des Bauxites de Guinée*, 421 F.Supp. 938, 941 n.3 (W.D. Pa. 1976). Equally plausible, however, is an implied exception to Article II, for agreements that would produce unenforceable awards because of the reciprocity reservation. That is apparently the conclusion adopted in *NIOC. See also Ledee v. Ceramiche Ragno*, 684 F.2d 184, 185-86 (1st Cir. 1982); *Tolaram Fibers, Inc. v. Deutsche Eng'g der Voest-Alpine Industrieanlagenbau GmbH*, 1991 U.S. Dist. LEXIS 3565 (M.D.N.C.). How *should* Article I(3)'s reciprocity limitation be applied (if at all) to arbitration agreements?

5. *Application of Article XIV's reciprocity rule to arbitration agreements.* Article XIV of the Convention provides broadly that a "Contracting State shall not be entitled to avail itself of the present Convention against other Contracting States except to the extent that it is bound to apply the Convention." How does Article XIV apply to the enforcement of international arbitration agreements?

(a) *Who can invoke Article XIV?* Can private parties invoke Article XIV in private litigation? Or is Article XIV directed solely to state-to-state dealings? Note that Article XIV's language appears to be directed to the rights of "Contracting States" between themselves, and not to the rights of private litigants. That is also consistent with the Article's location in the overall structure of the Convention, in the final part of the Convention where other inter-state provisions are located. A few courts and commentators have nonetheless apparently interpreted Article XIV as granting rights to private litigants. *See Fertilizer Corp. of India v. IDI Mgt, Inc.*, 517 F.Supp. 948 (S.D. Ohio 1981); A. van den Berg, *The New York Convention of 1958* 13-15 (1981); *infra* pp. 1097-98. *But see Restatement (Third) U.S. Law of International Commercial Arbitration* §4-5 comment b (Tent. Draft No. 2 2012) ("Some commentators have argued that this provision creates an additional reciprocity requirement for awards subject to the New York Convention (neither the Panama Convention nor the reservations that the U.S. made in ratifying the Panama Convention contain a comparable provision). By its terms, however, Article XIV addresses only the rights of one Contracting State vis-à-vis another under the Convention, and does not purport to apply to private-party actions to enforce awards brought in national courts. Accordingly, the Restatement takes the position that Article XIV does not impose a reciprocity requirement in addition to that stated in paragraph (a).").

If Article XIV applies in private litigation, then what is the point of Article I(3), permitting reciprocity reservations? Would it make sense to have a provision allowing for reciprocity reservations when another provision of the Convention made reciprocity a generally-applicable right? On the other hand, what purpose does Article XIV have if it is not applicable in private litigation? When would a Contracting State itself use Article XIV?

      (b) *Does Article XIV apply to arbitration agreements?* Consider again the language of Article XIV. Does this language provide a sound basis for concluding that Article XIV does not apply to arbitration agreements specifying arbitral seats in non-Convention States?

6. *Can the U.S. reservation to the Convention be judicially extended?* Recall that the U.S. reservation to the Convention is limited to awards. Even if Article XIV permits Contracting States to make reciprocity reservations extending beyond Article I(3), has the United States done so? If not, then should a U.S. court do so? Would this involve judicial interference in the task of treaty negotiations, which is confided to the Executive Branch?

7. *How might a reciprocity limitation apply to arbitration agreements?* Assuming that either Article I(3) or Article XIV allows a reciprocity limitation to be placed on arbitration agreements under Article II, what precisely would that limitation say? Suppose a U.S. party and a Taiwanese party agree to arbitrate in Switzerland (Taiwan is not a party to the Convention, while Switzerland is). Would the reciprocity limitation relieve U.S. courts of an obligation to recognize the arbitration agreement? Suppose a U.S. party and a Swiss party agree to arbitrate in Taiwan.

      (a) *Reciprocity limitation does not relieve nationals of Convention States of obligations to arbitrate against nationals of non-Convention States.* Some U.S. courts have held that U.S. (and other) parties from Contracting States are required by the Convention to arbitrate against parties from non-Convention States, provided the arbitration agreement specifies an arbitral seat in a Contracting State. *See E.A.S.T. Inc. of Stamford, Conn. v. M/V Alaia*, 876 F.2d 1168 (5th Cir. 1989).

      (b) *Authorities concluding that reciprocity limitation relieves parties of obligations to arbitrate in non-Convention States.* Consider again the hypothetical where a U.S. and a Swiss party agree to arbitrate in Taiwan. Would a reciprocity limitation under Article I(3) or Article XIV relieve U.S. (or Swiss) courts of an obligation to recognize the arbitration agreement? How exactly would the language of Article I(3) and Article XIV apply in such circumstances? What purposes would be served by denying recognition of the arbitration agreement in these circumstances?

      Suppose (paralleling *NIOC*) a U.S. party and a Taiwanese party agree to arbitrate in Taiwan. Would a U.S. court be required to recognize the arbitration agreement? *NIOC* held that the Convention is not applicable to agreements to arbitrate in non-Convention States. For other decisions adopting this result, *see Ledee v. Ceramiche Ragno*, 684 F.2d 184, 185-86 (1st Cir. 1982); *Tolaram Fibers, Inc. v. Deutsche Eng'g der Voest-Alpine Industrieanlagenbau GmbH*, 1991 U.S. Dist. LEXIS 3565 (M.D.N.C.). *Compare Fuller Co. v. Compagnie des Bauxites de Guinée*, 421 F.Supp. 938, 941 n.3 (W.D. Pa. 1976).

8. *Wisdom of NIOC's interpretation of reciprocity limitation.* Suppose that Iran had ratified the New York Convention (which it did in 2001) and the *Ashland v. NIOC* arbitration were to proceed in Tehran. Would Ashland be better off after the Convention had been ratified by Iran? Or worse off? Consider the following: (a) the Convention would not limit the power of Iranian courts to annul awards made in Iran, *see infra* pp. 1059-61, 1110-11; (b) the Convention would greatly facilitate the ability of NIOC to enforce an award made in Iran against Ashland in the United States (where its assets are primarily situated) and other Contracting States, *see infra* pp. 1189-90, 1194-97;

(c) the Convention would not, as a practical matter, facilitate meaningfully the ability of Ashland to enforce an award against NIOC in Iran (where its assets are primarily situated); and (d) the Convention would facilitate Ashland's ability to enforce an award against NIOC in Convention States other than Iran, provided NIOC left assets in those jurisdictions.

Consider the *NIOC* court's explanation for its application of a reciprocity requirement: "Congress must have meant only to allow signatories to partake of the Convention's benefits in U.S. courts and thus to give further incentives to non-signatory nations to adhere to the Convention." How is this rationale applicable to the various factual scenarios outlined above? Does the court's decision and rationale help or harm U.S. parties?

9. *Effect of §3 of FAA on claims, asserted in U.S. courts, which are subject to arbitration in non-Convention seat*. Suppose that a party commences litigation in U.S. courts, in derogation of an arbitration agreement specifying a non-Convention arbitral seat. Does §3 of the FAA require that the litigation be stayed? Is it not clear that a valid arbitration agreement, within the meaning of §3, exists? Note that Article VII of the New York Convention provides a savings clause, which preserves for parties their otherwise available rights outside of the Convention. What basis is there for implying the Convention's reciprocity limitation into §3?

10. *Absence of express reciprocity requirement from leading national arbitration statutes*. Consider the texts of the UNCITRAL Model Law, FAA and SLPIL, excerpted at pp. 85-96, 103-09 & 157-60 of the Documentary Supplement. Do any of these statutes impose a reciprocity requirement for the enforcement of an international arbitration agreement?

Should the Model Law, FAA, SLPIL, or other arbitration legislation be interpreted as imposing an implied reciprocity requirement as a condition for enforcement of an international arbitration agreement? Suppose, for example, an Iranian company wishes to require a German company to arbitrate in Iran (although, let us assume, Iranian courts would not require an Iranian company to arbitrate in Germany). Should German courts uphold the parties' arbitration agreement and require the German company to arbitrate in Iran?

11. *Absence of provision for reciprocity reservation from Inter-American Convention*. Note that there is no provision in the Inter-American Convention for a reciprocity reservation. Consider, however, §304 of the FAA, excerpted at p. 109 of the Documentary Supplement, which introduces a reciprocity reservation with respect to the enforcement of arbitral awards. *See also infra* pp. 1098-99. Should the same reciprocity limitation be extended by U.S. courts to arbitration agreements? Does the Convention permit either such reciprocity requirement?

12. *Possible approaches to arbitration agreements after invalidating choice of non-Convention arbitral seat*. Suppose that either Article I(3) or Article XIV does permit states to impose reciprocity limitations on the recognition of arbitration agreements under the Convention, and that a state imposes such a limitation. What, precisely, is the effect upon an agreement, like that in *NIOC*, specifying an arbitral seat in a non-Convention State? Specifically, consider the following options: (a) the arbitration agreement is entirely void; (b) only the offending selection of a non-Convention arbitral seat is void, and the arbitral tribunal is permitted to select a

new seat; (c) only the offending selection of a non-Convention arbitral seat is void, and the court will select a new arbitral seat. What did the *NIOC* court hold? What is the correct result? What law governs this issue? The Convention? National law? If so, which national law?

Suppose a court refuses to enforce a choice of a non-Convention arbitral seat but concludes that the parties' basic agreement to arbitrate should still be enforced. What should it then do? Should it (as the *NIOC* court considered) order arbitration locally subject to its own judicial control? Note that, in *NIOC*, this would have resulted in rewriting the Ashland-NIOC agreement, changing the arbitral seat from one party's home forum to that of the other party. What would justify this? Note that the *NIOC* court refused to do this. *Compare infra* pp. 435, 656-57, 658-69.

Should a court order arbitration in a "neutral" arbitral seat, located in a Convention State? Should a court seek to replace the selection of a non-Convention arbitral seat with a Convention seat most nearly approximating the parties' original choice? For example, in *NIOC*, could the arbitral seat have been moved to neighboring Turkmenistan or Syria? Additionally, would it be appropriate for the arbitration to continue to be subject to the procedural law of Iran, and to actions to annul the award in Iranian courts? Or, should national courts leave the selection of an arbitral seat to the arbitral tribunal itself?

13. *Reciprocity in investment arbitration.* Consider the role of reciprocity in investment arbitration. Note the fundamental structure of BIT arbitrations. How does it involve reciprocity? Consider the U.K./Bosnia-Herzegovina BIT, excerpted at pp. 73-78 of the Documentary Supplement. If the United Kingdom is prepared to arbitrate against Bosnian investors, why not against U.S. investors? How, if at all, does investment arbitration under the ICSID Convention differ?

CHAPTER 3

INTERNATIONAL ARBITRATION AGREEMENTS: BASIC ISSUES

It is elementary that international arbitration is consensual: without an agreement to arbitrate, of some sort, there can be no arbitration.[1] At the same time, the terms of the parties' arbitration agreement play a central role in defining the character of any arbitration, including the arbitral proceedings, and in producing a valid, enforceable arbitral award. For these reasons, it is essential to understand clearly the nature and effects of international arbitration agreements. Although often brief, and superficially simple, these agreements raise complex legal issues. This chapter provides an introduction to five issues that are central to the enforcement and interpretation of international arbitration agreements.

First, the chapter considers the presumptive validity of international arbitration agreements under the New York Convention and modern national arbitration statutes. Second, the chapter examines the separability presumption, which provides that arbitration clauses are presumptively "separable" from the underlying commercial agreements in which they appear. Third, the chapter considers the competence and respective roles of arbitral tribunals and national courts in enforcing and interpreting international arbitration agreements. Fourth, the chapter explores the choice-of-law issues raised by international arbitration agreements. Finally, the chapter examines the effects, both positive and negative, of international arbitration agreements.

A. PRESUMPTIVE VALIDITY OF INTERNATIONAL ARBITRATION AGREEMENTS

One of the primary objectives of the New York, Inter-American and European Conventions was to overturn historic mistrust of arbitration in some jurisdictions and render international arbitration agreements more readily enforceable.[2] In furtherance of these objectives, Article II of the New York Convention, Article 1 of the Inter-American Convention and Articles II(1), IV and V of the European Convention all provide that international arbitration agreements are presumptively valid and enforceable. As discussed below, this basic rule is subject to an exclusive and limited number of bases for invalidity, where agreements are "null and void," "inoperative," or "incapable of being performed."[3]

At the same time, virtually all developed states (and many other nations) have enacted arbitration legislation which parallels the New York Convention's rule that international arbitration agreements are presumptively enforceable. Like Article II of the Convention, this legislation typically provides that arbitration agreements are valid and enforceable, subject only to defined grounds for challenging the validity of such agreements.[4] Leading

---

1. *See* G. Born, *International Commercial Arbitration* 97 (2d ed. 2014).
2. *See supra* pp. 33-41 & *infra* pp. 186-89.
3. *See infra* pp. 333-34, 375-474; G. Born, *International Commercial Arbitration* 838 (2d ed. 2014).
4. *See infra* pp. 189-90; G. Born, *International Commercial Arbitration* 108 (2d ed. 2014).

examples of such legislation include Article 8 of the UNCITRAL Model Law and §2 of the FAA.

The materials excerpted below explore the presumptive validity of international arbitration agreements under leading international and national instruments. They also address historic and lingering hostility to the arbitral process, which was (and, to an extent, still is) reflected in various rules of substantive invalidity of arbitration agreements.

JUDGMENT OF 10 JULY 1843, CIE L'ALLIANCE v. PRUNIER
1843 Dalloz (I) 343 (French Cour de cassation civ.)

Whereas, the jurisdiction of French courts is recognized under general principles of law; there is no exception to this principle of public policy other than the one regarding corporations, and cases where arbitration was agreed to on a voluntary basis;

Whereas the premium insurance policy, dated 28 September 1837, between l'Alliance and Prunier did not create any commercial relations between them, so that, Article 51 of the Commercial Code, regarding mandatory arbitration, cannot be applied in the present case;

Whereas Article 332 of the Commercial Code,[5] granting parties the right to submit their dispute to arbitrators, also could not be applied in this case, because it only applies to marine insurance; those insurance policies, deemed to constitute commercial transactions pursuant to Article 663 of the Commercial Code, are subject to a specific and special legislation, whose rules could not be extended by the judge, without obviously constituting an abuse of judicial powers, to terrestrial fire insurances, which constitute a purely non-commercial transaction for the insured party;

Whereas voluntary arbitrations are governed by the unique title of Book 3 of the Civil Procedure Code [including Articles 1003 ("All persons may enter arbitration agreements for the enforcement of rights of which they have free disposal.") and 1006 ("In order to be valid, the arbitration agreement shall designate the subject of the dispute and the arbitrators' names."), discussed below];

Whereas by agreeing to Article 15 of the September 28 insurance policy, l'Alliance and Prunier have provided that any dispute regarding fire damages, experts' operations and assessments, and the execution of the insurance policy, would be submitted to three arbitrators in Paris for a final and binding decision; but they have not named said three arbitrators, as required by Article 1006 of the Civil Procedure Code;

Whereas Article 1003 of the Civil Procedure Code, which allows any person to enforce its freely disposable rights through arbitration, shall not be separately relied on, as proclaiming a general principle exempt from any condition; on the contrary, this article shall

---

5. Article 332 provided:

"The insurance contract shall be written. Its date shall be the date it is entered into. It shall be stated whether it is before or after midday. It can be entered into as a private agreement. It shall not contain any blank. It shall provide:

The name and place of residence of the insured; his capacity as owner or commission agent; the name and designation of the vessel; the name of the captain; the name of the place where the goods have been or should be unloaded; the name of the port from which the vessel left or will leave; the ports or harbors in which it shall load or unload; those it shall enter; the nature and the value or estimate of the merchandise or goods being insured; the times at which the risks covered must start and end; the sum insured; the premium or the cost of insurance; *the submission of the parties to arbitrators, in case of a dispute, if it has been agreed upon*; and as a whole, any other condition that parties have agreed upon."

be interpreted in conjunction with subsequent articles, especially Article 1006; thus an arbitration agreement cannot be valid or, what amounts to the same, be validly entered into when the subject matter of the dispute and the names of the arbitrators are not set out therein; the distinction between an arbitration agreement and a compromise is not established by any provision of the law, and this distinction cannot be admitted without failing to understand the true spirit of the Civil Procedure Code regarding arbitrations; ...

Whereas the common practice of inserting into fire insurance policies a provision similar to article 15 of the 28 September 1837 insurance policy shall not prevail over Article 1006 of the Civil Procedure Code, whose provisions must be satisfied for an agreement to be valid ...;

Whereas if one considered as valid a simple arbitration agreement or arbitration clause in the case of fire insurances, one would have to acknowledge and recognize its validity in every contract where it would have been agreed that disputes regarding non-performance or performance issues would be submitted to unnamed arbitrators; this disposition will become routine and standard; the exception would become the rule, and one would be deprived of the guarantees offered by courts;

Whereas the requirement for compulsory designation of the arbitrators by name at the time the arbitration agreement is entered into is aimed at avoiding disputes regarding the composition of arbitral tribunal, and especially protecting citizens against their own lack of reflection, that could lead them to agree to future arbitrations while lacking sufficient prudence and without being sufficiently thorough as to their understanding of future circumstances, without being sure that the arbitrators who volunteered to hear the case would be able to deal with the matter and be trustworthy; in the present case, the importance and necessity of the provisions of Article 1006 are clearly underlined by the way the insurers want their clients to agree to resolve any dispute; l'Alliance, headquartered in Paris, and whose operations extend all over the French territory, wants, by means of article 15 of the policy, to compel its insured clients, wherever their domicile may be, whatever the extent of the damages suffered, into establishing a sovereign arbitral tribunal that would judge them in Paris, a place where a vast majority of the insured parties do not have any ongoing business and no acquaintances, located far from the place where the claim would have arisen, and where the prejudice caused could only be ascertained and assessed;

Whereas as a consequence, by establishing that the arbitration agreement contained in the 28 September 1837 policy was null and void for it failed to name the arbitrators, the challenged decision [did] not breach any law.... The Court ... dismisses the appeal.

DECISION 24 OF THE ANDEAN COMMISSION CONCERNING TREATMENT OF FOREIGN CAPITAL
Article 51, 10 I.L.M. 152 (1971)

[No agreement concerning foreign investment shall contain provisions] which withdraw possible ... controversies from the national jurisdiction of the recipient country....

SAUDI ARABIAN ARBITRATION LAW, 2012
Article 10(2)

It is permissible for governmental authorities to agree on arbitration only after the approval of the Prime Minister, unless there is a special provision of law that allows it.

ARKANSAS CODE, 2010
§16-108-201

(a) A written agreement to submit any existing controversy to arbitration arising between the parties bound by the terms of the writing is valid, enforceable, and irrevocable, save upon such grounds as exist at law or in equity for the revocation of any contract.

(b)(1) A written provision to submit to arbitration any controversy thereafter arising between the parties bound by the terms of the writing is valid, enforceable, and irrevocable, save upon such grounds as exist at law or in equity for the revocation of any contract.

(2) This subsection shall have no application to personal injury or tort matters, employer-employee disputes, nor to any insured or beneficiary under any insurance policy or annuity contract.

BRAZILIAN LAW NO. 9,307 OF 23 SEPTEMBER 1996
Articles 3, 7

3. The interested parties may submit the settlement of their disputes to an arbitral tribunal by virtue of an arbitration agreement, which may be in the form of either an arbitration clause or a submission to arbitration (*acte de compromis*).

7. If there is an arbitration clause but resistance as to the commencement of the arbitral proceedings, the interested party may request the Court to summon the other party to appear in Court so that the submission to arbitration may be drafted; the Judge shall order a special hearing for this purpose.

7(1). The plaintiff shall specify, in detail, the subject matter of the arbitration, attaching to its motion the document containing the arbitration clause.

7(2). If the parties attend the hearing, the Judge shall first try to conciliate their dispute. If he does not succeed, the Judge shall try to persuade them to sign, by mutual agreement, the submission to arbitration.

7(3). If the parties disagree on the terms of the submission to arbitration, the Judge, after hearing the defendant, shall decide on the contents thereof, either at the same hearing or within ten days, in accordance with the provisions of the arbitration clause, and taking account of the provisions of Articles 10 and 21(2) of this Law.

7(4). If the arbitration clause fails to provide for the appointment of arbitrators, the Judge, after hearing the parties, shall rule thereon, being allowed to appoint a sole arbitrator to decide the dispute.

7(5). If the plaintiff, without good cause, fails to attend the hearing designated for the drafting of the submission to arbitration, the case will be terminated without judgment on the merits.

7(6). If the defendant fails to attend the hearing, the Judge shall have the authority, after hearing the plaintiff, to establish the contents of the submission to arbitration, and to appoint a sole arbitrator.

7(7). The judgment granting the motion shall have the force of a submission to arbitration.

LEDEE v. CERAMICHE RAGNO
684 F.2d 184 (1st Cir. 1982)

COFFIN, Chief Judge.... The defendants-appellees are Italian corporations that make and market ceramic tiles. The plaintiffs-appellants are two Puerto Rico corporations and an individual citizen of the Commonwealth. In 1964 the parties entered into a distributorship agreement giving the appellants exclusive rights to sell and distribute the appellees' ceramic tiles in the Antilles. The agreement ... contained the following paragraph 9:

> "Any dispute related to the interpretation and application of this contract will be submitted to an Arbiter selected by the President of the Tribunal of Modena, [Italy,] who will judge as last resort and without procedural formalities."

In March, 1981, the appellants brought suit in the Superior Court of Puerto Rico, alleging that the appellees had breached the contract by unjustifiably terminating their distributorship. The complaint sought damages in accord with the provisions of the Puerto Rico Dealers Act, 292 10 L.P.R.A. §§278 *et seq.* The appellees removed the case to the U.S. District Court for the District of Puerto Rico. The district court ordered arbitration in accord with paragraph 9 and dismissed the complaint. This appeal ensued.

Appellants contend first that, under the laws of the Commonwealth of Puerto Rico, paragraph 9 is void and unenforceable. They invoke the general principle that contracting parties may not agree to clauses or conditions "in contravention of law, morals, or public order." 31 L.P.R.A. §3372. And to show that paragraph 9 is contrary to the public order, they direct our attention to the Dealers Act. The Dealers Act was enacted to help protect Puerto Rico distributors from the allegedly exploitative practices of certain foreign suppliers.[6] Substantively, it prohibited termination of dealership contracts except "for just cause." 10 L.P.R.A. §278a. Moreover, it declared that its provisions were of a public order and that the dealers' rights under it could not be waived....[It] reads:

> "Any stipulation that obligates a dealer to adjust, arbitrate or litigate any controversy that comes up regarding his dealer's contract outside of Puerto Rico, or under foreign law or rule of law, shall be likewise considered as violating the public policy set forth by this chapter and is therefore null and void." 10 L.P.R.A. §278b-2.

Appellants continue their argument by suggesting that, given the arbitration clause's unenforceability under Puerto Rico Law, the federal district court could not enforce it. They observe that Chapter One of the [FAA] is limited, in that it makes arbitration clauses enforceable "save upon such grounds as exist at law or in equity for the revocation of any contract." 9 U.S.C. §2. They contend that the Dealers Act provides grounds "at law or in equity" for revocation of paragraph 9. We need not, however, consider to what extent the phrase "grounds as exist at law or in equity" incorporates Commonwealth law.... In par-

---

6. The Act's statement of motives reads, in part:

> "The Commonwealth of Puerto Rico cannot remain indifferent to the growing number of cases in which domestic and foreign enterprises, without just cause, eliminate their dealers, concessionaires or agents, as soon as these have created a favorable market and without taking into account their legitimate interests. The Legislative Assembly of Puerto Rico declares that the reasonable stability in the dealer's relationship in Puerto Rico is vital to the general economy of the country, to the public interest and to the general welfare, and in the exercise of its police power, it deems it necessary to regulate, insofar as pertinent the field of said relationship, so as to avoid the abuse caused by certain practices." Laws of Puerto Rico, 1964, p. 231.

ticular, we need not consider whether the phrase incorporates the Dealers Act. The simple reason is that the district court did not purport to exercise authority under Chapter One of the [FAA]; rather, it acted under Chapter Two of the Act, 9 U.S.C. §201 *et seq.*, which implemented the [New York] Convention. If [an arbitration agreement falls within the Convention, as in this case, then a U.S. court] must order arbitration unless it finds the agreement "null and void, inoperative or incapable of being performed." Convention, Article II(3).

Appellants argue that the Dealers Act renders paragraph 9 of the contract "null and void, inoperative or incapable of being performed." They contend that the "null and void" clause was intended to incorporate the Dealers Act as an expression of Puerto Rico public policy. We disagree. Such an expansive interpretation of the clause would be antithetical to the goals of the Convention. In *Scherk v. Alberto-Culver Co.*, 417 U.S. 506, 517 n.10 (1974), the Supreme Court observed:

> "The goal of the Convention, and the principal purpose underlying American adoption and implementation of it, was to encourage the recognition and enforcement of commercial arbitration agreements in international contracts and to unify the standards by which agreements to arbitrate are observed and arbitral awards are enforced in the signatory countries."

The parochial interests of the Commonwealth, or of any state, cannot be the measure of how the "null and void" clause is interpreted. Indeed, by acceding to and implementing the treaty, the federal government has insisted that not even the parochial interests of the nation may be the measure of interpretation. Rather, the clause must be interpreted to encompass only those situations—such as fraud, mistake, duress, and waiver—that can be applied neutrally on an international scale. *I.T.A.D. Associates, Inc. v. Podar Bros.*, 636 F.2d 75 (4th Cir. 1981).[7] Nothing in the record suggests that the arbitration agreement was "null and void, inoperative or incapable of being performed" within the terms of Article II(3) of the Convention....

JUDGMENT OF 20 DECEMBER 1993, MUNICIPALITÉ DE KHOMS EL MERGEB v. SOCIÉTÉ DALICO

1994 Rev. arb. 116 (French Cour de cassation)

[The municipal council of Khoms El Mergeb (near Tripoli, Libya) entered into a contract dated June 15, 1981, ("Contract") with Dalico Contractors, a Danish company ("Dalico"). The Contract granted Dalico responsibility to conduct sewage disposal work. The Contract referred to standard conditions, "amplified and amended in the annex," as an integral part of the agreement, in addition to documents contained in the tender offers. Article 32 of the standard conditions (which were also signed on June 15, 1981), provided not only for the application of Libyan law to the Contract but also for the exclusive jurisdiction of the Libyan courts.

---

7. Our conclusion accords with the general mode by which appellate courts have construed the Convention and Chapter Two of the [FAA]. *See Parsons & Whittemore Overseas Co., Inc. v. Société Générale de l'Industrie du Papier (RAKTA)*, 508 F.2d 969, 973-74 (2d Cir. 1974) (construing narrowly the "public policy" defense to enforcement of awards under Article V(2)(b)); *McCreary Tire & Rubber Co. v. CEAT*, 501 F.2d 1032 (3rd Cir. 1974) (observing that there is "nothing discretionary" about Article II(3))....

Disputes arose between the parties. Despite the forum selection clause, Dalico initiated an ICC arbitration in Paris pursuant to an arbitration clause in one of the tender offer documents, and specified in the annex under the standard conditions as modifying Article 32 (referred to above). The municipal council objected to the ICC proceedings, claiming that the document referred to as the annex under the standard conditions was not signed and was invalid under Libyan law, which it argued applied the contract under Article 32. The arbitral tribunal rejected this claim in an award, which the municipal council challenged in French courts. The Paris Cour d'appel dismissed the action to annul the award in which the arbitrators upheld the existence and validity of the arbitration clause. The Cour de cassation affirmed.]

But whereas according to a substantive rule of international arbitration law, an arbitration clause is legally independent from the main contract in which it is directly contained or referred to, and its existence and efficiency are assessed according to the parties' common intent, and without necessarily referring to a national provision, provided that mandatory provisions of French law and international public policy are not violated; that in the present case, the Cour d'appel correctly explained its decision by establishing the existence of the arbitration clause regardless of the Libyan laws [that apply to] the contract, and upheld, by analysis and interpretation of the exhibits, that the object of the invoked annex was to substitute the original arbitration clause for the clause giving jurisdiction to the Libyan courts, and the integration of this clause within the entire contractual [provisions] proved that, although the document was not signed, it was the parties' common intent to be subject to the clause at issue....

JUDGMENT OF 7 SEPTEMBER 2005, HOTELS.COM v. ZUZ TOURISM LTD
XXXI Y.B. Comm. Arb. 791 (2006) (Israeli S.Ct.)

Zuz Tourism Ltd had entered into an exclusive distributorship agreement with hotels.com providing for arbitration in Texas under [AAA] rules. Upon discovering that hotels.com allegedly breached this agreement by engaging another Israeli representative, Hotels Online Ltd, which was not a party to any arbitration agreement, Zuz sued both hotels.com and Hotels Online Ltd in the Jerusalem District Court. In response, hotels.com applied for a stay of proceedings on the basis of the existence of an arbitration clause in the agreement and subsequently filed a request for arbitration with the AAA. The District Court, applying domestic rules, decided that it would not grant a stay, notwithstanding the arbitration clause, because of the injustice that would be caused to Zuz if it had to seek its remedies against hotels.com and Hotels Online Ltd in two different jurisdictions. [The District Court's judgment was appealed to the Israeli Supreme Court.]

It is a general rule that the agreement to hand over a certain matter to arbitration cannot dislodge the court's subject matter jurisdiction over the matter.... However, when a suit is brought before the court on a matter regarding which an arbitration agreement has been entered into, the court is authorized to stay the proceedings. In this manner the breach of the arbitration agreement is avoided. The main provision of the law that resolves the question of staying proceedings is §5 of the [Israeli] Arbitration Law.

> "5(a) When an action is brought in court in a dispute which it had been agreed to refer to arbitration, and a party to the action who is a party to the arbitration agreement applies for a stay of proceedings in the action, the court shall stay the proceedings between the parties to

the agreement, provided that the applicant has been and still is prepared to do everything required for the institution and continuation of the arbitration.... (c) The court may refrain from staying proceedings if it sees a *special reason* why the dispute should not be dealt with by arbitration."

We can see that when the conditions specified in the section are met, the court will as a rule stay the proceedings between the parties to the arbitration agreement, unless it finds that there exists a special reason that the dispute not be settled in arbitration....

An additional provision concerned with staying proceedings as a result of the existence of any arbitration clause can be found in §6 of the Arbitration Law:

"6. When an action is brought in court in a dispute which it had been agreed to refer to arbitration, and an international convention to which Israel is a party applies to the arbitration, and such *convention lays down provisions* for a stay of proceedings, the court shall exercise its power under §5 *in accordance with and subject to the those provisions.*"

It is apparent from the phrasing of the above-mentioned section that it is not applicable in every case a stay of proceedings is requested based on the existence of an arbitration clause. Its application is limited just to those cases where the arbitration is subject to an international convention to which Israel is party and which includes provisions regarding the stay of proceedings. In these cases, the section instructs that the court's discretion on the question of staying proceedings specified in §5 shall be used in accordance with the Convention's provisions and subject thereto. Therefore, §6 of the Law refers to the provisions of the conventions regarding the stay of proceedings and even gives them priority over the provisions of §5 of the Arbitration Law.

In the case before us there is no dispute between the parties that the [New York Convention] applies to the arbitration clause.... [T]he relevant provision in our case is Art. II of the Convention.... From the way Art. II(3) has been phrased, it emerges that the court is required to refer the parties to the process of arbitration, unless one of the three exception exists: the arbitration agreement is null and void, inoperative or incapable of being performed." We are prepared to assume ... that the District Court was correct in finding that there are both procedural and substantive needs for adding Hotels Online to Zuz's suit. If the only relevant provision of the law was the one in §5 of the Law, then on the above basis and based on Israeli precedents in cases involving a third party causing breach of an exclusive distribution arrangement, it would appear that the conclusion that there were no grounds to stay the proceedings against hotels.com would have been inescapable. However, in the matter before us the provision of §6 of the Law and Art. II(3) of the Convention apply. As a result, in accordance with §6 of the Law the court is required to determine the question of staying proceedings in accordance with the provisions of the Convention. The question that arises in ... our case, therefore, is the following: whether in cases to which §6 of the Law and Art. II(3) of the Convention apply, the court is authorized to avoid staying proceedings when a defendant who is not party to the arbitration agreement is added on.

In order to determine the matter, we must discuss two related subsidiary questions: the first, do the three exceptions included in Art. II(3) constitute a closed list, *i.e.*, whether in every case where the above-mentioned three exceptions are not present the court is required to stay proceedings; and the second, does the presence of a defendant who is not a party to the arbitration agreement constitute one of the three exceptions in Art. II(3).... In order to determine the extent of the court's discretion based on §6 of the Law when combined with Art. II(3) of the Convention, we must turn to the language of these provisions.

Section 6 of the Law instructs that the court's authority according to §5 of the Law—which is concerned with stay of proceedings—shall be used in accordance with and subject to the provisions of the convention applicable to the arbitration. Art. II(3) of the Convention states in mandatory language that the court 'shall ... refer' the parties to arbitration, unless one of the exceptions listed in the section is present. It appears that the manner in which both provisions were drafted leads to a single conclusion: that if one of the three exceptions mentioned in Art. II(3) does not appear, the court is as a rule required to order a stay of the proceedings....

It appears based on the language of the two above-mentioned provisions that the situation of a defendant who is not a party to the arbitration agreement is not included within the three exceptions listed in Art. II(3) of the Convention. As shall be clarified below, I believe that the rationale behind §6 of the Arbitration Law and Section II(3) lead to a similar conclusion. One of the main purposes of the Convention is the efficient enforcement of international arbitration agreements by determining uniform standards pursuant to which such agreements are to be enforced.... [T]he concern expressed in this respect is that the courts of the acceding states will avoid sending local defendants to arbitral proceedings in a foreign state and will, therefore, shy away from respecting international arbitration agreements.... It appears that there is a real similarity in the manner in which Art. II(3) has been interpreted in many of the common law countries. The rule determined in this respect is that the section has a mandatory character. If one of the exceptions mentioned in the section is not established, the court is required to stay the proceedings and refer the parties to arbitration proceedings, without having any discretion in the matter....

In addition, alongside the rule that Art. II(3) is of a mandatory nature, it has been determined, in the common law system, that a situation in which one or more of the defendants are not party to the arbitration agreement is not included in the ambit of any of the three exceptions of Art. II(3). In other words, the existence of a party who is not a party to the arbitration agreement does not make the existing arbitration agreement between the other parties, whether in whole or in part, null and void, inoperative or an agreement incapable of being performed. Therefore, in such a situation the court must order the stay of proceedings in respect of those parties who are party to the arbitration agreement....

We can see that the interest of certainty and the concern that international arbitration agreements will not be respected in order to prefer the interests of local litigants, have led foreign courts to adopt an interpretive position that limits discretion in terms of staying proceedings following the existence of international arbitration agreements....

[N]ot staying proceedings in spite of the existence of any international arbitration agreement because one or another of the sides is not a party to the arbitration agreement may cause an additional difficulty.... [A]s a result of not staying the proceedings, [the proceedings] will not be split up insofar as the suit of the plaintiff against the defendant who is party to the arbitration agreement—which should have been heard in arbitration—as this claim will be settled together with his suit against the defendant who is not party to that agreement. However, this cannot prevent the defendant who is a party to the arbitration agreement to act in accordance with the agreement and file an action on precisely the same matter with the arbitration in the foreign jurisdiction. This is indeed what hotel.com did in the case before us. As a result, disputes between parties to the arbitration agreement will be split and heard before two different tribunals: one party's claim will be heard by the Israeli courts, while the other party's claim will be determined by the arbitrator abroad. Thus the outcome of avoiding the stay of proceedings was, in fact, to prevent the splitting of hearings on one plane, but caused a split on the other.... In order to prevent this new split, the Israeli courts will be required to issue a preventive order against the litigant who is a party to the arbitration agreement preventing him from continuing to conduct his dispute with the arbitration tribunal and forcing him to litigate as a claimant in the Israeli courts. This will cause a further substantial deviation from the contractual agreement between the parties to the arbitration agreement....

I believe that all the above-mentioned considerations lead to the conclusion that the court's maneuverability on the basis of §6 of the Law together with Art. II(3) is significantly limited in comparison with the range of maneuver allowed by §5.... This result is consistent with the language of the Law and the language of the Convention. It is also consistent with one of the main purposes of Art. II(3): furthering legal certainty in relation to international arbitral agreements by balancing the concern that the courts of other jurisdictions will tend to prefer the interests of the local litigant and will therefore keep from honoring international arbitration agreements that dictate arbitration in a foreign state. I am prepared to assume that there may be exceptional cases in which the courts may avoid staying proceedings even if none of the three above-mentioned exceptions exist. However, these cases will be rare.

NOTES

1. *Historic unenforceability of arbitration agreements at common law.* As discussed above, it is often said that arbitration agreements were historically disfavored at common law in both England and the United States. *See supra* pp. 16-19, 21-26. Joseph Story stated the historic common law position in the United States, inherited from England, as follows:

   "Now we all know, that arbitrators, at the common law, possess no authority whatsoever, even to administer an oath, or to compel the attendance of witnesses. They cannot compel the production of documents, and papers and books of account, or insist upon a discovery of facts from the parties under oath. They are not ordinarily well enough acquainted with the principles of law or equity, to administer either effectually, in complicated cases; and hence it has often been said, that the judgment of arbitrators is but *rusticum judicium*. Ought then a court of equity to compel a resort to such a tribunal, by which, however honest and intelligent, it can in no case be clear that the real legal or equitable rights of the parties can be fully ascertained or perfectly protected? ... [An arbitration agreement is not specifically enforceable because it] is essentially, in its very nature and character, an agreement which must rest in the good faith and honor of the parties, and like an agreement to paint a picture, or to carve a statue, or to write a book ... must be left to the conscience of the parties, or to such remedy in damages for the breach thereof, as the law has provided." *Tobey v. County of Bristol*, 23 F.Cas. 1313, 1321-23, (C.C.D. Mass. 1845).

   Although Story's analysis reflected a substantial mistrust for the arbitral process, arbitration was popular and effective in American commercial settings: "The use of commercial arbitration developed during the colonial and post-revolutionary periods in spite of this [judicial] hostility." Benson, *An Exploration of the Impact of Modern Arbitration Statutes on the Development of Arbitration in the United States*, 11 J. L. Econ. & Org. 479, 483 (1995). It did so on the basis of non-legal commercial sanctions and enforcement mechanisms, including through membership in commercial guilds, societies, or religious groups, all of which proved sufficiently resilient to overcome judicial hostility. *Ibid*. Moreover, even with regard to judicial enforcement, courts in a number of American states rejected the common law notion that arbitration agreements were either unenforceable or revocable, and instead upheld them, while also enforcing arbitral awards with minimal judicial review. For example, an 1858 decision by the Supreme Court of Virginia held:

> "The only ground on which [the arbitration agreement] can be said to be unlawful is, that in referring all disputes and difficulties arising under the contract to the engineer or inspector, it tends to oust the courts of law of their jurisdiction; and is therefore against the policy of the law and void.... I am certainly not disposed to extend the operation of a rule which appears to me to have been founded on very narrow grounds, directly contrary to the spirit of later times, which leaves parties at full liberty to refer their disputes at pleasure to public or private tribunals." *Condon v. Southside R.R. Co.*, 1858 WL 3945, at *6-7 (Va.).

Consider Story's reasoning. Is it persuasive? Why should arbitration agreements be recognized as valid and enforced? What rationale does the Virginia Supreme Court adopt?

2. *Historic unenforceability of arbitration agreements in some civil law jurisdictions*. Arbitration agreements were also regarded with disfavor in a number of civil law jurisdictions during the 19th century.

(a) *France*. As discussed above, in the immediate aftermath of the French Revolution, arbitration was embraced in France as "the most reasonable means for the termination of disputes arising between citizens." Law of 16-24 August 1790, Art. 1. *See supra* pp. 19-21. In due course, arbitration was elevated to constitutional status. French Constitution of Year I, 1793, Art. 86 ("The right of the citizens to have their disputes settled by arbitrators of their choice shall not be violated in any way whatsoever."); French Constitution of Year III, 1795, Art. 210 ("The right to choose arbitrators in any dispute shall not be violated in any way whatsoever.").

Despite this, the Napoleonic Code of Civil Procedure adopted a staunchly anti-arbitration attitude. Among other things, Article 1006 of the Code of Civil Procedure, quoted *supra* p. 178, was interpreted as providing that agreements to arbitrate future disputes were unenforceable. Consider the Cour de cassation's decision in *Prunier*. What reasons does the Court provide for refusing to enforce agreements to submit future disputes to arbitration? Compare these to those advanced by Story.

Note the Cour de cassation's comment that if parties were able validly to agree to arbitration, then arbitration agreements and arbitration would become commonplace. Why does that suggest that arbitration agreements should be unenforceable? If large numbers of French citizens want to resolve their disputes by arbitration, shouldn't that argue for, not against, upholding the validity of agreements to arbitrate?

Consider the agreement to arbitrate at issue in *Prunier*. Note that the agreement was between an insurance company and an individual. Is it clear from the *Prunier* opinion whether the individual was a consumer? Note the Cour de cassation's concerns about the procedural fairness of the arbitration agreement. How one-sided was the agreement? Note the obstacles to transportation and communication in mid-19th century France. Could the *Prunier* case have been decided on unconscionability grounds?

Note that not all agreements to arbitrate future disputes were invalid under Article 1006 of the French Civil Procedure Code. How does the Cour de cassation justify the requirement that an agreement to arbitrate name the arbitrators in advance? Is that persuasive? *See infra* p. 695.

(b) *Germany*. A deep mistrust for arbitration developed in Germany between the two World Wars, becoming especially pronounced after the rise of the National Socialists in 1933. According to the *"Guidelines of the Reich Regarding Arbitral Tribunals,"* published in December 1933, "from a state-political point of view a further spread of arbitration would shatter confidence in state jurisdiction and the State itself." *Richtlinien des Reiches über Schiedsgerichte*, 95 Deutsche Justiz 52, 821 (1933). How is it that arbitration shatters confidence in the state? What vision of the state underlies this comment? Is a democratic state, guaranteeing its citizens substantial economic and political freedoms, threatened by arbitration? Compare the concerns about arbitration becoming commonplace in *Prunier*.

3. *Historic hostility of some developing states to international arbitration*. During the 20th century, some states treated international arbitration with antipathy. Numerous public pronouncements and academic commentaries condemned international arbitration as an unacceptable, unjustifiable infringement upon the sovereignty of developing (and other) states, which was to be vigorously resisted. Decision 24 of the Andean Commission reflects this attitude. Why were some developing states historically mistrustful of international arbitration? What are the benefits to a state from treating international arbitration agreements as unenforceable? What are the costs?

Consider Brazilian Law 9,307 of 23 September 1996. Note the distinction between an "arbitration agreement" and a "submission to arbitration." Until the 1996 legislation, only "submissions to arbitration," which were entered into after a dispute arose, were valid; pre-dispute arbitration clauses were not. Why would such an approach be adopted?

4. *Abandonment of historic hostility of developing countries to international arbitration*. The historic hostility of developing countries to international arbitration has substantially eroded over the past two decades. Prior to 1980, the New York Convention had not been ratified by (among others) Afghanistan, Algeria, Argentina, Bahrain, Bangladesh, Bolivia, Burkina Faso, Cameroon, China, Costa Rica, Guatemala, Guinea, Haiti, Indonesia, Kenya, Laos, Lebanon, Malaysia, Mali, Mauritania, Mozambique, Myanmar, Nepal, Pakistan, Panama, Paraguay, Peru, Saudi Arabia, Senegal, Turkey, Uruguay, Venezuela, Vietnam and Zimbabwe. Between 1980 and the present, all of these states acceded to the Convention. Similar numbers of states acceded to the ICSID Convention.

Consider again Brazilian Law 9,307. Note that it provides a mechanism for enforcing pre-dispute arbitration agreements. Despite the defects in the approach of Article 7 of Law 9,307, it is a step towards enforceability of arbitration agreements.

What explains the abandonment of hostility by developing states towards international arbitration? Consider briefly the structure and enforceability of international commercial arbitration agreements and awards. If a company based in a developing state wishes to avail itself of contractual (or other) rights against a foreign investor, in an enforceable fashion, is international arbitration a reasonably good remedy? What can a national of a developing state do with a judgment it obtains from its own courts against a foreign investor who badly performs a contract within the foreign country? What can a company based in a developing state do with an arbitral award it obtains against a foreign investor? What can a company from a foreign state do to resist an arbitral award made against it? Where will that award likely have to be enforced?

Do different considerations apply to accession to the ICSID Convention? To adoption of BITs with a state's principal sources of foreign capital?

5. *Presumptive validity of international arbitration agreements under New York Convention.* Consider Article II of the New York Convention, excerpted at p. 1 of the Documentary Supplement. What exactly does Article II provide with respect to the validity of international arbitration agreements? Are such agreements *always* valid under Article II? If not, when are arbitration agreements valid? What does it mean for an arbitration agreement to be "null and void"? What exactly does Article II accomplish? Note the discussion of Article II in *Hotels.com*.

6. *"Pro-enforcement" bias of Article II.* Both *Hotels.com* and *Ledee* interpret Article II of the Convention to establish a strong presumption favoring the validity of international arbitration agreements. Other courts have endorsed the same pro-enforcement bias. *See Rhone Mediterranee Compagnia Francese di Assicurazioni e Riassicurazioni v. Lauro*, 712 F.2d 50, 53-54 (3d Cir. 1983) ("The policy of the Convention is best served by an approach which leads to upholding agreements to arbitrate.").

For example, *Ledee* and other lower U.S. courts have said that the Convention prescribes weightier pro-enforcement policies than the domestic FAA. According to one court, "the liberal federal arbitration policy 'applies with special force in the field of international commerce.'" *David L. Threlkeld & Co. v. Metallgesellschaft Ltd*, 923 F.2d 245, 248 (2d Cir. 1991) (quoting *Mitsubishi Motors Corp. v. Soler Chrysler-Plymouth Inc.*, 473 U.S. 614, 631 (1985)). *See also Pepsico Inc. v. Oficina Central de Asesoria y Ayuda Tecmica, CA*, 945 F.Supp. 69 (S.D.N.Y. 1996) ("strong policy favoring prompt arbitration expressed in the U.N. Convention"); *Samson Res. Co. v. Int'l Bus. Partners, Inc.*, 906 F.Supp. 624 (N.D. Okla. 1995) ("the policy favoring arbitration is 'even stronger in the context of international business transactions'") (quoting *David L. Threlkeld & Co.*, 923 F.2d at 248). Note the similar approach of the court in *Hotels.com*.

What does it mean to say that the Convention is "pro-arbitration" or "pro-enforcement"? Consider the issues to which a "pro-arbitration" policy might apply: (a) doubts will be resolved in favor of the existence of an arbitration agreement; (b) doubts will be resolved in favor of the validity and legality of an arbitration agreement; and (c) doubts will be resolved in favor of interpreting the scope of an arbitration clause to cover borderline disputes. Is it appropriate for a "pro-arbitration" policy to be applied to any of these questions? To all? Would it not be more appropriate to enforce and interpret arbitration agreements "neutrally," like other contracts, without any bias?

7. *Presumptive validity of international arbitration agreements under contemporary arbitration statutes.* Consider Article 8(1) of the UNCITRAL Model Law, Article 178 of the Swiss Law on Private International Law ("SLPIL") and §2 of the FAA, excerpted at pp. 88, 157 & 103 of the Documentary Supplement. What does each provide

regarding the validity of arbitration agreements? What are the differences between the three provisions? How does each compare with Article II of the New York Convention?

Are *all* arbitration agreements valid under Article 8, Article 178 and §2? What arbitration agreements are invalid?

8. *Grounds for invalidity of international arbitration agreements.* What are the possible grounds for challenging the validity of international arbitration agreements under the New York Convention and contemporary arbitration legislation? What are the usual bases for disputing the existence or validity of other types of contracts? Is there any reason that generally-applicable contract law rules should not provide the grounds for challenging the validity and existence of arbitration agreements? The substantive grounds for challenging the validity or existence of international commercial arbitration agreements are detailed below. *See infra* pp. 333-34, 375-510.

Consider the choice-of-law analyses in *Ledee* and *Dalico*. Note how the U.S. and French courts adopt choice-of-law rules that apply some form of international principles, which give effect to international arbitration agreements, rather than national law rules, which would deny effect to such agreements. Compare the similar approach of Article 178 of the SLPIL.

9. *Representative examples of national laws disfavoring arbitration.* Consider the Saudi legislation excerpted above, requiring government approval of arbitration agreements entered into by "Government Agencies." Compare the Arkansas legislation. Are valid public policies served by these statutes? Is such legislation consistent with Article II of the New York Convention? Suppose a Contracting State invalidated all pre-dispute arbitration agreements? Required that prior government approval be obtained of all arbitration agreements? Would these requirements be consistent with Article II? What types of invalidity did Article II contemplate?

B. SEPARABILITY OF INTERNATIONAL ARBITRATION AGREEMENTS

In the international context, arbitration clauses are generally deemed to be presumptively "separable" or "severable" from the underlying contract within which they are found.[8] The "separability presumption" is specifically provided for by national arbitration legislation or judicial decisions from virtually all jurisdictions around the world, and by leading institutional arbitration rules.[9] The presumption is equally recognized in inter-state, as well as in commercial and investment, arbitration authorities.[10]

The separability presumption provides that an arbitration agreement, even though included in and related closely to an underlying commercial contract, is presumptively a separate and autonomous agreement. According to a leading international arbitral award: "it is now generally accepted, in the law and practice of international commercial arbitration, that an arbitration clause in a contract constitutes a separate and autonomous agreement between the parties, which is distinct from their substantive agreement."[11] The

---

8. *See* G. Born, *International Commercial Arbitration* 350-51 (2d ed. 2014).

9. *See* G. Born, *International Commercial Arbitration* 360 *et seq.* (2d ed. 2014).

10. *See* G. Born, *International Commercial Arbitration* 350-51 (2d ed. 2014).

11. *Award in ICC Case No. 9480*, discussed in Grigera Naón, *Choice-of-Law Problems in International Commercial Arbitration*, 289 Recueil des Cours 9, 55 (2001).

analytical rationale for the separability presumption is that the parties' agreement to arbitrate consists of promises that are distinct and independent from the underlying contract: "the mutual promises to arbitrate [generally] form the quid pro quo of one another and constitute a separable and enforceable part of the agreement."[12]

For reasons explored below, the separability presumption is generally (and correctly) seen as having vital consequences for the arbitral process: "Acceptance of [the] autonomy of the international arbitration clause is a conceptual cornerstone of international arbitration."[13] Among other things, the separability presumption is understood as implying the continued validity of an arbitration clause (notwithstanding defects in the parties' underlying contract), and as permitting the application of different substantive laws to the parties' arbitration agreement and underlying contract.[14] The following materials introduce the separability presumption and explore the role that it plays in the arbitral process.

KULUKUNDIS SHIPPING CO., SA v. AMTORG TRADING CORP.
126 F.2d 978 (2d Cir. 1942)

FRANK, Circuit Judge. The libel alleged that appellant (respondent) had, through its authorized representatives, agreed to a charter party with appellee (libellant). Appellant's answer in effect denied that anyone authorized to act for it has so agreed. After a trial, the district court made the following [factual findings]:

"1. Libellant, Kulukundis Shipping Co. SA, employed Blidberg Rothchild Co. Inc. as a broker and the respondent, Amtorg Trading Corporation employed Potter & Gordon, Inc. as its broker in the negotiations for the chartering of the ship 'Mount Helmos' for a trip to Japan.... Rothchild, of the firm of Blidberg Rothchild Co. Inc., and Gordon, acting on behalf of Potter & Gordon, Inc., agreed upon a charter and closed by Gordon executing and delivering to Rothchild a fixture Slip which is the usual trade practice, indicating the conclusion of charter negotiations in the trade of ship brokerage. All the material terms of the bargain are set forth in a fixture slip excepting demurrage, dispatch, and the date of the commencement of the charter term which all had been agreed on but were omitted by an oversight. A number of the terms, including the War Risks Clause of 1937, were fixed by the incorporation of a reference to an earlier charter of the steamer 'Norbryn.' Gordon acted with authority.

"2. Thereafter, respondent refused to sign the charter but instead repudiated it."

[The district court reached the following conclusion:] "1. Respondent has breached a valid contract and is liable in damages to the libellant." Pursuant to the foregoing, the court entered an order that appellee recover from appellant the damages sustained, and referred to a named commissioner the ascertainment of the damages....

[The respondent relied upon an arbitration clause in the charter.] The arbitration clause reads as follows:

"24. Demurrage or dispatch is to be settled at loading and discharging ports separately, except as per Clause 9. Owners and Charterers agree, in case of any dispute or claim, to settle

---

12. *Robert Lawrence Co. v. Devonshire Fabrics, Inc.*, 271 F.2d 402, 409 (2d Cir. 1959).

13. *See* W. Craig, W. Park & J. Paulsson, *International Chamber of Commerce Arbitration* §5.04 (3d ed. 2000).

14. *See* G. Born, *International Commercial Arbitration* 464 (2d ed. 2014).

same by arbitration in New York. Also, in case of a dispute of any nature whatsoever, same is to be settled by arbitration in New York. In both cases arbitrators are to be commercial men." ...

Appellant admits—as it must—that the district court had jurisdiction to determine whether the parties had made an agreement to arbitrate. Appellant contends, however, that, once the court determined in this suit that there was such an arbitration agreement, the court lost all power over the suit beyond that of staying further proceedings until there had been an arbitration as agreed to; in that arbitration, argues appellant, the arbitrators will have jurisdiction to determine all issues except the existence of the arbitration clause. This jurisdiction, it is urged, is broad enough to permit an independent determination, by the arbitrator, that the contract itself is not valid or binding. Appellee asserts that the defendant had repudiated the charter-party, and that, therefore, the arbitration clause must be wholly disregarded....

[Two issues are presented]: (a) Does the arbitration provision here have the sweeping effect ascribed to it by appellant? (b) Is it, as appellee contends, wholly without efficacy because appellant asserted that there never was an agreement for a charter party? ...

(a) Appellant ... concedes that, in such a case as this, before sending any issue to arbitrators, the court must determine whether an arbitration provision exists. As the arbitration clause here is an integral part of the charter party, the court, in determining that the parties agreed to that clause, must necessarily first have found that the charter party exists.[15] If the court here, having so found, were now to direct the arbitrators to consider that same issue, they would be traversing ground already covered in the court trial. There would thus result precisely that needless expenditure of time and money (the "costliness and delays of litigation") which Congress sought to avoid in enacting the [FAA]. In the light of that fact, a reasonable interpretation of the Act compels a repudiation of appellant's sweeping contention.

(b) If the issue of the existence of the charter party were left to the arbitrators and they found that it was never made, they would, unavoidably (unless they were insane), be obliged to conclude that the arbitration agreement had never been made. Such a conclusion would (1) negate the court's prior contrary decision on a subject which ... the Act commits to the court, and (2) would destroy the arbitrators' authority to decide anything and thus make their decision a nullity.

(c) The [FAA] does not cover an arbitration agreement sufficiently broad to include a controversy as to the existence of the very contract which embodies the arbitration agreement. Section 2 of the Act describes only three types of agreement covered by the Act: One type is "an agreement ... to submit to arbitration an existing controversy arising out of ... a contract, transaction," etc.; thus the parties here, after a dispute had arisen as to the existence of the charter party, might have made an agreement to submit to arbitration that "existing" controversy. But that is not this case. Section 2 also includes a "provision in ... a contract evidencing a transaction ... to settle by arbitration a controversy thereafter arising out of such contract or transaction...." Plainly such a provision does not include a provision in a contract to arbitrate the issue whether the minds of the parties ever met so as to bring about the very contract of which that arbitration clause is a part; a controversy

---

15. The situation would be different if a separate arbitration agreement had been made.

relating to the denial that the parties ever made a contract is not a controversy arising out of that contract. Nor is it a controversy "arising out of a transaction evidenced by a contract," for if no contract existed then there was no such transaction evidenced by a contract, therefore, no controversy arising out of that transaction. The third type of arbitration agreement described in §2 of the Act is a provision in a contract to settle by arbitration "a controversy thereafter arising out of … the refusal to perform the whole or any part thereof." This is familiar language; it refers to a controversy, which parties to a contract may easily contemplate, arising when a party to the contract, without denying that he made it, refuses performance; it does not mean a controversy arising out of the denial by one of the parties that he ever made any contract whatsoever.

It is clear then that, even assuming *arguendo*, that a contract could be drawn containing an arbitration clause sufficiently broad to include a controversy as to whether the minds of the parties had ever met concerning the making of the very contract which embodies the arbitration clause, such a clause would not be within the [FAA]. Accordingly, it perhaps would not be immunized from the prestatutory rules inimical to arbitration, *i.e.*, would not serve as the basis of a stay of the suit on the contract, leaving the parties to the arbitration called for by their agreement. Were the arbitration clause here sufficiently broad to call for arbitration of the dispute as to the existence of the charter party, it would, therefore, perhaps be arguable that it was entirely outside the Act, accordingly, irrelevant in the case before us; we need not consider that question, as we hold that the breadth of the arbitration clause is not so great and it is within the terms of §2 of the Act. We conclude that it would be improper to submit to the arbitrators the issue of the making of the charter party….

JUDGMENT OF 7 OCTOBER 1933, TOBLER v. JUSTIZKOMMISSION DES KANTONS SCHWYZ
DFT 59 I 177 (Swiss Fed. Trib.)

The appellant ("Tobler") assigned his invention-patents to the respondent ("Blaser") in a contract dated 13 April 1926. The contract contained the clause: "For the settlement of all disputes arising out of this contract the parties submit themselves to the judgment of an arbitrator, elected by common agreement, that is, the respective canton court president will be elected. Schwyz is expressly stipulated as seat of arbitration, where the arbitration proceedings are to be held." … Tobler asserted claims to the patents and other rights in proceedings before the District Court Schwyz. The District Court Schwyz held that it lacked jurisdiction due to the arbitration clause…. [Blaser appealed and the Swiss Federal Tribunal dismissed:] …

[T]he arbitrator himself (and not the federal judge) shall decide on his competence if challenged by a party…. [D]ue to the external unity (contained in the same document) of the arbitration agreement with the underlying contract to which it refers, the arbitration agreement shares the legal nature of [the underlying contract]…. [T]herefore the dispute about the arbitration agreement's binding nature (the competence of the arbitrator, insofar as dependent thereon) also appears as a dispute of substance and not as a dispute of procedure…. [T]he general subjugation to arbitration for the settlement of "disputes" arising from a contract, as agreed upon by the parties, also encompasses the dispute about the validity of the conclusion of this contract, that is [a dispute about] the existence of defects making the contract non-binding. The nullity of the underlying contract can therefore not result in the nullity of the arbitration agreement as well, but rather shall be only relevant for the substantive assessment of the claim by the arbitrator, [that is, only for] the claim's consequences that the arbitrator shall decide....

Pursuant to the applicable jurisprudence of the Federal Court, the arbitration agreement is not a contract of substantive but of procedural content. Even if it [the arbitration agreement] is combined in one document with the underlying contract, governed by civil law, to which it refers and thereby appears as component of the latter, it is nevertheless not to be considered as a provision within [the underlying contract], but rather as an individual agreement of a special nature. Accordingly, the nullity of the main contract, assessed correctly, may not readily result in the nullity of the arbitration agreement without further considerations, but rather only under the condition that the grounds for nullity simultaneously affect the main contract and the arbitration agreement (as for example if one party signed the contract in the state of mental incapacity or was forced to sign). In the present case the objection that the contract dated 13 April 1926 is only a simulated transaction can only affect the main contract; [the same is true of other challenges to the underlying contract, because] they as well ... only refer to defects that would adhere to the underlying contract (concerning assignment of patents). Furthermore, [there is no reason to reject the reasoning of] the District Court Schwyz ... that the clause "for the settlement of all disputes arising out of this contract submit themselves to the judgment of an arbitrator ..." encompasses the dispute about the validity of the main contract.... If even the dispute about the validity of the main contract is to be considered as within the competence of the arbitrator, then all the more this has to be assumed for the other objection of fraud, as it is raised by the applicant, that is, that the assignment of full entitlement to the patents in the contract dated 13 April 1926 concealed a mere trust relationship.

JUDGMENT OF 27 FEBRUARY 1970
6 Arb. Int'l 79 (German Bundesgerichtshof)

Under a contract made between 9 and 17 January 1952 the Plaintiff leased to the Defendant an area ... for the mining of quartzite and other fire-proofing material. Under the contract the Defendant was (*inter alia*) to pay to the Plaintiff a "material levy" of DM 1.80 per tonne of quartzite rock and quartzite sand recovered. The contract contained the following clause: "The material levy shall be based on the standard wage of a quarry worker, shall rise and fall percentage-wise with the latter, but not below 1.80 DM per tonne." The Defendant was also required to a certain extent to re-level the worked areas. On 26 May and 29 November 1955 respectively the parties signed an arbitration agreement, the beginning of which read: "Arbitration agreement to the contract of 9/17.1.1952 on the lease of land containing quartzite.... Differences of opinion or disputes arising from the above contract shall not be the subject of legal proceedings. Matters of dispute shall be decided by an arbitration procedure as defined in Article 1025 ff. of the Code of Civil Procedure."[16]

---

16. Article 1025 of the German Zivilprozessordnung (ZPO) provided:

> "(1) The agreement by which the settlement of a dispute is submitted to one or more arbitrators is legally valid when the parties have the right to enter into a settlement of the subject matter of the dispute. (2) The arbitration agreement is not valid if one of the parties has used any superiority it possesses by virtue of economic or social position in order to constrain the other party to make this agreement or to accept conditions therein, resulting in the one party having an advantage over the other in the procedure, and more especially in regard to the nomination or the non-acceptance of the arbitrator."

When the Plaintiff in 1958 had doubts over the effectiveness of the material levy clause, he requested information on the matter from the Landeszentralbank M. The Landeszentralbank M. informed him that a value guarantee clause was involved which required approval pursuant to Paragraph 3 phrase 2 of the Currency Law.[17] [Subsequently, a second Landeszentralbank rendered the same opinion.] ...

After further discussions, the Plaintiff lodged a claim for the levelling and filling in of the leased areas. The Defendant pleaded the arbitration agreement and pleaded further that the Plaintiff had no claim to the levelling and filling in of the land because the lease was a nullity. The Regional Court allowed the Plaintiff's claim. The Regional Appeal Court dismissed the Defendant's appeal.... The Regional Appeal Court considered the arbitration agreement a nullity and stated in this connection: The term in the contract on the material levy represented a non-approvable value guarantee clause covered by Paragraph 3 phrase 2 of the Currency Law. With the refusal of approval by the Landeszentralbank the clause had become conclusively ineffective. Under Article 139 of the Civil Code this meant that the whole lease was a nullity. [Article 139 BGB (Bürgerliches Gesetzbuch): "If part of a legal transaction is null, the whole of the transaction is null, unless it be assumed that it would also have been transacted without the invalid part."] From this it followed, pursuant to Article 139 of the Civil Code, that the arbitration agreement was a nullity.

There were admittedly also so-called independent arbitration agreements, where the invalidity of the main contract did not involve the invalidity of the arbitration agreement. An independent arbitration agreement existed if the arbitral tribunal had to decide not only on claims arising from the existing main contract, but also on what were the main consequences of its invalidity. Arbitration agreements of this kind were the exception, however, because an independent arbitration agreement required "an unambiguous intention of the parties to this effect or other appropriate external circumstances." Since nothing could be established to that effect, the rule would apply that a non-independent arbitration agreement existed which pursuant to Article 139 of the Civil Code was ineffective, as was the lease.

The [Appeal Court] based its decision on the nullity of the value guarantee clause. There are objections to this approach.

The material levy clause certainly comes under Paragraph 3 phrase 2 of the Currency Law because the amount of the levy is determined "automatically" by the standard wage of a quarry worker.... The validity of the arbitration agreement should not be assessed under Article 139 of the Civil Code. If, like the Appeal Court, we were to regard the arbitration agreement as part of a unified legal transaction consisting of main contract and arbitration agreement, we would have to pose the question crucial for the application of Article 139 of the Civil Code, whether the arbitration agreement would have been concluded without the main contract. Posing this question makes no sense; it would always be answered in the negative.

---

17. This provision of the Currency law translates into English (emphasis supplied):

"Contracting parties may agree upon an obligation to pay money in a currency other than Deutschmark on the condition only that the agreement be approved by the authority competent to allow foreign exchange. *This rule applies also to pecuniary debts the amount of which, such as finally to be settled in Deutschmark, shall be calculated on the basis of such other currency or on the basis of a certain quantity of gold or of other goods or services.*"

It is rather a question of whether the parties agreed that the arbitration tribunal should decide not only on claims arising from the valid main contract, but also on the validity of the main contract (and claims arising from any invalidity); if the parties have also referred to the arbitral tribunal the decision on the effectiveness of the main contract, the ineffectiveness of the main contract of course cannot affect the existence of the arbitration agreement. It is not correct that in the present case the arbitration would be redundant because the parties were in agreement on the ineffectiveness of the main contract (as the Regional Court decided) because it is the claims arising directly from that ineffectiveness which are at issue.

It is therefore a question of how the arbitration agreement is to be interpreted. The Appeal Court also takes this into account, as already stated; however its argument on Article 139 of the Civil Code is incorrect, albeit immaterial. The decision therefore depends on what is meant by "differences of opinion or disputes arising from the contract" and by "matters of dispute" in Paragraph 1 of the arbitration agreement, i.e., whether this includes only claims arising from a valid main contract or also disputes on the validity of the latter or on the consequences of invalidity....

The wording of Paragraph 1 of the arbitration agreement would allow both interpretations. Arbitration clauses with identical wording or identical content, such as Paragraph 1 of the arbitration agreement contains, are frequently agreed. If we accept that the interpretation of an arbitration agreement is basically a matter for the trial judge we must face the fact that judicial practice will give different interpretations to identically worded clauses which continually recur and can be regarded as typical agreements. This is unsatisfactory. Haphazard interpretations should be avoided and a rule of construction should be established which prescribes to the judge "in cases of doubt" the parties' intention—either the restricted or the more comprehensive jurisdiction of the arbitral tribunal.

With continually recurring clauses ... the task of the court of third and last instance is to facilitate ... construction by such a rule. In the ... case law of the Federal Supreme Court many such rules have been developed (For example: the intention of the parties will be regularly to subject an arbitration agreement to the same law as the main contract ...). In reality the Appeal Court also resorted to such a rule of construction by designating as the norm the non independent arbitration agreement, which does not permit the arbitral tribunal to decide on the validity of the main contract, and by designating as the exception an arbitration agreement providing for a wider jurisdiction of the arbitral tribunal.

The Federal Supreme Court cannot agree with the position taken by the Appeal Court.... The Federal Supreme Court has not yet given a general ruling on the question whether in cases of doubt the narrower or wider construction of a clause as agreed here is to prevail. The Supreme Court has concerned itself with a similar clause, such as that on which Hamburg Friendly Arbitration is based. This clause states that the arbitration tribunal has to decide not only on quality questions, but also "on all matters of dispute arising from the transaction, in particular also on legal matters." This clause does not differ materially from the clause under discussion. It might appear that because of the expression "all matters of dispute," it is more comprehensive. This difference has no significance, however, for the question at issue here; neither the presence of the word "all" in the one clause nor its absence in the other clause can indicate whether the arbitral tribunal has to decide on the effectiveness of the main contract or not. The attaching of excessive importance to such wording is just as impractical as the distinction between the terms "from the contract" and "on the contract" considered by the Appeal Court.

The Hamburg Appeal Court has invariably interpreted the clause used in Hamburg Friendly Arbitration to mean that the arbitral tribunal is empowered to decide also on the validity of the main contract. The Supreme Court has approved this interpretation. This points to a rule of construction, according to which in cases of doubt the arbitral tribunal must be assumed to possess a more comprehensive jurisdiction. The Appeal Court discusses the established case law concerning Hamburg Friendly Arbitration, but just as with the established case law on other arbitration agreements contained in frequently used business terms, the Appeal Court attached no significance to it because "quasi-institutionalised arbitral tribunals or else established commercial usages" are there involved.

This means that also in these cases the jurisdiction of the arbitral tribunal is determined by the interpretation of the arbitration agreement contained in business terms. If in commercial dealings the agreement is interpreted as meaning a more comprehensive jurisdiction of the arbitral tribunal, this is nevertheless an indication that it is not in fact regarded the rule in commercial dealings to leave to the arbitral tribunal only the decision on claims from an effective contract. Since we are here concerned with the usual case, the question whether in cases of doubt such a limited jurisdiction is intended or not should be considered in the light of what reasonable parties in general regard as corresponding with their interests.... There is every reason to presume that reasonable parties will wish to have the relationships created by their contract and the claims arising therefrom, irrespective of whether their contract is effective or not, decided by the same tribunal and not by two different tribunals, i.e., the arbitral tribunal for the dispute on claims from a valid contract and the state tribunal for the dispute on the effectiveness of the contract and on the consequences of its ineffectiveness.

Experience shows that as soon as a dispute of any kind arises from a contract, objections are very often also raised against its validity. For example, if the interpretation of a contract is in dispute, one of the parties will soon come forward with the objection that the contract did not come into being because no valid meeting of the minds had been reached, or its declaration of intention was invalidated due to mistake; in such a case the same facts of the case usually have to be evaluated both for interpretation and for lack of intention. The fact that the assessment of these facts has to be entrusted to different tribunals according to one's approach will scarcely occur to the contracting parties.

Above all, however, the parties to an arbitration agreement will as a rule wish to avoid the unpleasant consequences of separate jurisdiction. For if the arbitral tribunal is not allowed to decide also on the effectiveness of the main contract, the situation is as follows: either it must, as soon as this point is disputed in the arbitration procedure, refrain from further activity and refer the parties for clarification of this dispute to the ordinary court; if the latter confirms the effectiveness of the main contract, the parties will have to return to the arbitration tribunal and continue the dispute there. Or the arbitral tribunal can, if it finds the main contract to be effective continue its proceedings ...); there is then the danger, however, that the state tribunal will find differently on the effectiveness of the main contract than the arbitral tribunal and the arbitral award will therefore be reversed. Both outcomes cannot be desirable to reasonable parties whose purpose in concluding an arbitration agreement is usually to accelerate a decision....

The Supreme Court arrives in the end to the conclusion that an arbitration clause such as the present one means in cases of doubt that the arbitral tribunal shall also decide on the question of the validity of the contract and on the claims arising in the event of nullity.... The plea that arbitration was agreed upon ... is therefore successful.

ALL-UNION EXPORT-IMPORT ASSOCIATION SOJUZNEFTEEXPORT (MOSCOW) v. JOC OIL, LTD

Award in Foreign Trade Arb. Comm'n at USSR Chamber of Commerce & Industry, Moscow Arb. Case No. 109/1980 of 9 July 1984, XVIII Y.B. Comm. Arb. 92 (1993)

[Sojuznefteexport (the "Association" or "SNE") was a foreign trade organization established under the laws of the former Union of Soviet Socialist Republics ("USSR"). In 1976, SNE entered into various agreements to sell quantities of oil to JOC Oil Limited ("JOC"), a Bermuda company. The purchase agreements incorporated SNE's standard conditions, which contained the following arbitration clause:

> "All disputes or differences which may arise out of this contract or in connection with it are to be settled, without recourse to the general Courts of law, in the Commission of the U.S.S.R. Chamber of Commerce and Industry in Moscow ["FTAC"], in conformity with the rules of procedure of the above Commission."

JOC took delivery of 33 oil shipments (worth approximately $100 million) without paying for them. Following JOC's non-payment, SNE initiated arbitration under the arbitration clause set forth above. JOC replied by claiming that the purchase agreement had not been executed by two authorized representatives of SNE and accordingly was void under Soviet law. JOC also alleged that, as a consequence, the arbitral tribunal lacked competence to adjudicate the dispute because the arbitration clause was void. SNE claimed that the sales agreement was not void and that, even if it were, the arbitration clause was separable, and the law applicable to that agreement did not require two signatures to be valid.]

1. The FTAC has confirmed the agreement of the parties as to the material law to be applied to the dispute between them. As this law, the parties have agreed upon Soviet law. The Commission has therefore decided the dispute being guided by the corresponding provisions of the Fundamentals of Civil Legislation of the USSR and of the Union Republics of 1961 and the Civil Code of the RSFSR of 1964....

2. According to Article 27 of the Civil Procedural Code of the RSFSR in cases contemplated by law of International Treaty, a dispute arising out of civil legal relationships, by agreement of the parties can be referred for resolution by an arbitration body, the Maritime Arbitration Commission or the FTAC at the Chamber of Commerce and Industry of the USSR. As stated in the statute on the FTAC, confirmed by the Decree of the Presidium of the Supreme Soviet of the USSR of the 16th April 1975, this Commission is a permanently functioning arbitration court and decides disputes arising from contractual and other civil legal relationships, arising between the subjects of law of different countries in relation to the implementation of foreign trade and of other international economic relationships. The FTAC considers disputes where there is a written agreement between the Parties to submit for its decision a dispute which has arisen or which may arise....

The Rules ... envisage different types of written agreements of the parties as to the submission of a dispute to the FTAC and do not require that this agreement be expressed in an independent document signed by the parties. The Rules also do not require fulfillment of those requirements which Soviet civil law, in accordance with articles 45 and 565 of the [Civil Code], require for the conclusion of a foreign trade transaction of which one party is a Soviet Organization. This provision of the Rules does not depart from Art. II(2) of the New York Convention in which it is stated that an agreement, establishing the arbitration procedure for hearing disputes, "shall include an arbitral clause in a contract or an arbitration agreement, signed by the parties or contained in an exchange of letters or telegrams."...

All this allows the Commission to recognize the arbitration clause contained in the contract signed in the name of the Association "Sojuznefteexport" by the Chairman of the Association V.E. Merkulow and in the name of the firm "JOC Oil" by John Deuss as a written agreement satisfying the requirements of the law—the Statute on the FTAC and its Rules as to the form of concluding such an agreement.

So far as the dispute is concerned which arose during the proceedings concerning the inter-relationship of the contract which established the rights and duties of the parties arising out of the sale of oil and oil products (the material-legal contract) and the arbitration agreement (the arbitration clause), that is to say as to whether the agreement is independent (autonomous) in relation to the contract independently of the decision as to the question of the validity or invalidity of the contract, the FTAC has come to the following conclusion. In the Rules of the FTAC there are no direct references to the fact that an arbitration agreement (arbitration clause) is autonomous in relation to the contract. But the above analysis of the Statute of the FTAC and of its Rules which have defined the competence of the Commission, and also the practice of the Commission, allows the conclusion to be drawn that the independence of an arbitration clause is not subject to doubt. Thus, in the ruling of the FTAC on the 29th January 1974, taken on hearing a dispute between a Soviet and an Indian organization, the arbitration agreement is treated as a procedural contract and not as an element (condition) of a material-legal contract (Arbitration Practice of the FTAC, Moscow 1979, part VII, page 68). The subject of an arbitration agreement (clause) is distinguished from the subject of a material-legal contract (of the contract of purchase and sale). The subject of the agreement is the obligation of the parties to submit the examination of a dispute between a plaintiff and defendant to arbitration (the FTAC) at the place where it sits, that is to say in Moscow, having excluded by that very fact the possibility of the resolution of the dispute in a state court.

Predominant in the literature is the recognition of the autonomy of an arbitration agreement, its independence in relation to the contract. Such is the point of view of the overwhelming majority of Soviet authors who have expressed themselves on this subject. The opinion of Soviet scholars are not unanimous but the Arbitration Commission considers as correct the opinion of those scholars, and this opinion is dominant, who recognize the autonomy of an arbitration clause, since this opinion relies upon the propositions of Soviet law cited above, from which there flows its autonomy as an independent procedural agreement....

The principle of the independence of an arbitration clause (in relation to the contract, to which the said clause relates), is now predominant both in doctrine as well as in practice. In a developed form, this principle has received its expression in the [1976] Arbitration Rules of UNCITRAL (Art. 21.2)....

Taking into account the cited facts and observations as to the nature of an arbitration agreement (clause), the Commission has come to the conclusion that, by virtue of its procedural content and independently of the form of its conclusion, it is autonomous in relation to the material-legal contract. An arbitration clause, included in a contract, means that there are regulated in it relationships different in legal nature, and that therefore the effect of the arbitration clause is separate from the effect of the remaining provisions of the foreign trade contract.

The requirements laid down for the recognition of the validity of the two contracts, which differ in their legal nature, need not coincide. Different also are the consequences of the recognition of these contracts as invalid. An arbitration agreement can be recognized as invalid only in the case where there are discovered in it defects in will (mistake, fraud and so on), the breach of the requirements of the law relating to the content and the form of an arbitration agreement which has been concluded. Such circumstances leading to the invalidity of an arbitration agreement do not exist and neither one of the parties stated its invalidity referring to such circumstances. [JOC Oil] considers the arbitration agreement as invalid for other reasons asserting that it is a component part of a contract which, in its opinion, as a whole (together with the arbitration clause) is invalid.

From this there follows the incorrectness in the objections relating to the fact that the New York Convention is applicable only to arbitration agreements on the basis of disputes arising out of specific contracts and therefore is inapplicable to contracts recognized as invalid. In Article II of the said Convention there is envisaged the enforcement of arbitral awards in relation to disputes which arise and can arise also in connection with other specific legal relationships, the object of which can be the subject of arbitration proceedings. This means, that since in connection with the invalidity of a contract, the applicable law envisages legal consequences, which are determined by a different non-contractual legal relationship but are connected with the invalid contract, the arbitrators have the right to examine the dispute and to rule upon it.

Proceeding from the above analysis of the Soviet material and procedural legislation applicable to the dispute in question, the Commission has recognized that an arbitration agreement (arbitration clause) is a procedural contract, independent from the material-legal contract and that therefore the question as to the validity or invalidity of this contract does not affect the agreement of the parties about the submission of the existing dispute to the jurisdiction of the FTAC. The Commission has come to the conclusion that the arbitration clause contained in the contract is valid and therefore in accordance with the right assigned to it has recognized itself as competent to hear the dispute as to its essence and to rule upon it.

3. The Commission has examined further the application of the representatives of the firm "JOC Oil" as to recognizing as invalid the contract of 17th November 1976 from which the dispute has arisen and has satisfied this application in view of the failure to observe the procedure for its signing (article 14 of the Fundamentals, article 45 of the [Civil Code]). [The tribunal concluded that the sales agreement was invalid because of failure to respect the two-signature rule for foreign trade organizations.]

4. On the question of the consequences of recognizing the contract of the 17th November 1976 as invalid, the representatives of the parties as pointed out in the deposition of the facts of the case, proceeded from a different approach to the question as to whether the recognition of the contract as invalid had any legal consequences and in the case of a positive answer to this question, as to what these consequences are.

In examining this question, the Commission established that according to article 14 of the Fundamentals (article 48 of the [Civil Code]) under an invalid transaction each of the parties is obligated to return to the other party everything received under the transaction and if it is impossible to return what has been received in kind, to reimburse its value in money if other consequences of the invalidity of the transaction are not set out in the law, that is to say bilateral (mutual) restitution must be effected.

The Arbitration Commission has confirmed further that, the recognition of the transaction as invalid does not mean that such a transaction does not give rise to any legal consequences, that it is nothing, legally amounting to a nullity, as asserted by the defendant on the main claim. As is evident from the content of article 48 of the [Civil Code], a court or arbitration tribunal in the event of a dispute must discuss the question of the consequences of the invalidity of a transaction and rule upon the same.

The assertion of the representatives of the Firm that the recognition of the contract as invalid must result in the refusal of the Arbitration Tribunal to hear the case on the basis that there has not arisen a legal relationship envisaged by the contract, is mistaken. It contradicts Soviet law applicable in this case, the practice of its application and the very concept of a transaction. In reality, a transaction, being a legal fact, is not always confined only to the expression of the will of the parties, directed to the achievement of a legal result, but gives rise, in the event of the breach of the requirements of the law, in relations to the content and form of the transaction, to other consequences envisaged by the law....

[The tribunal held that, although the underlying sales contract was void, Soviet principles of restitution applied. Under these principles, the tribunal concluded that "unilateral restitution" was required and awarded SNE the value of the oil shipped to JOC Oil, at prevailing oil prices at the time it was received by JOC Oil. It also awarded SNE all profits realized by JOC Oil from the sale of the oil (in an amount equal to market interest rates). This produced an award of approximately $200 million in SNE's favor. The tribunal did not award SNE another $120 million, which it claimed in lost profits.

The award was made in the then-USSR, and JOC Oil did not seek annulment in the USSR. Thereafter, SNE sought to enforce the award in Bermuda. The first instance court denied recognition on various grounds, including that the tribunal lacked jurisdiction. The court held that "based on the Tribunal's finding that the underlying contract was invalid *ab initio*, then under both Soviet and English law there never was any contract between the parties from the very onset; so that there never was an arbitration clause or agreement which could be submitted to arbitration." *Sojuznefteexport v. JOC Oil Co.*, 2 Mealey's Int'l Arb. Rep. 400, 486 (1987) (Bermuda Sup. Ct. 1987). This judgment was reversed on appeal in a 2-1 majority decision. *Sojuznefteexport v. JOC Oil Co.*, XV Y.B. Comm. Arb. 384 (Bermuda Ct. App. 1989). The dissenting judge said, in his opinion, that it was "quite ridiculous to suggest that this arbitration clause which formed part of that 'non-existent' contract would nevertheless, somehow, be deemed to have come into existence."]

BUCKEYE CHECK CASHING, INC. v. CARDEGNA
546 U.S. 440 (2006)

JUSTICE SCALIA. We decide whether a court or an arbitrator should consider the claim that a contract containing an arbitration provision is void for illegality.

Respondents John Cardegna and Donna Reuter entered into various deferred-payment transactions with petitioner Buckeye Check Cashing ("Buckeye"), in which they received cash in exchange for a personal check in the amount of the cash plus a finance charge. For each separate transaction they signed a "Deferred Deposit and Disclosure Agreement" ("Agreement"), which included the following arbitration provisions:

> "1. *Arbitration Disclosure* By signing this Agreement, you agree that if a dispute of any kind arises out of this Agreement or your application therefore or any instrument relating thereto, then either you or we or third-parties, involved can choose to have that dispute resolved by binding arbitration as set forth in Paragraph 2 below....

> 2. *Arbitration Provisions* Any claim, dispute, or controversy ... arising from or relating to this Agreement ... or the validity, enforceability, or scope of this Arbitration Provision or the entire Agreement (collectively "Claim"), shall be resolved, upon the election of you or us or said third-parties, by binding arbitration.... This arbitration agreement is made pursuant to a transaction involving interstate commerce, and shall be governed by the [FAA]. The arbitrator shall apply applicable substantive law constraint [sic] with the FAA and applicable statu[t]es of limitations and shall honor claims of privilege recognized by law...."

Respondents brought this putative class action in Florida state court, alleging that Buckeye charged usurious interest rates and that the Agreement violated various Florida lending and consumer-protection laws, rendering it criminal on its face. Buckeye moved to compel arbitration. The trial court denied the motion, holding that a court rather than an arbitrator should resolve a claim that a contract is illegal and void *ab initio*. [A Florida appellate court] reversed, holding that because respondents did not challenge the arbitration provision itself, but instead claimed that the entire contract was void, the agreement to arbitrate was enforceable, and the question of the contract's legality should go to the arbitrator. Respondents appealed, and the Florida Supreme Court reversed, reasoning that to enforce an agreement to arbitrate in a contract challenged as unlawful "'could breathe life into a contract that not only violates state law, but also is criminal in nature ...'" 894 So.2d 860 862 (2005). We granted certiorari [*i.e.*, discretionary review].

To overcome judicial resistance to arbitration, Congress enacted the [FAA]. Section 2 embodies the national policy favoring arbitration and places arbitration agreements on equal footing with all other contracts:

> "A written provision in ... a contract ... to settle by arbitration a controversy thereafter arising out of such contract ... or an agreement in writing to submit to arbitration an existing controversy arising out of such a contract ... shall be valid, irrevocable, and enforceable, save upon such grounds as exist at law or in equity for the revocation of any contract."

Challenges to the validity of arbitration agreements "upon such grounds as exist at law or in equity for the revocation of any contract" can be divided into two types. One type challenges specifically the validity of the agreement to arbitrate. *See, e.g., Southland Corp. v. Keating*, 465 U.S. 1, 4-5 (1984) (challenging the agreement to arbitrate as void under California law insofar as it purported to cover claims brought under the state Franchise Investment Law). The other challenges the contract as a whole, either on a ground that directly affects the entire agreement (*e.g.,* the agreement was fraudulently induced), or on the ground that the illegality of one of the contract's provisions renders the whole contract invalid.[18] ...

---

18. The issue of the contract's validity is different from the issue whether any agreement between the alleged obligor and obligee was ever concluded. Our opinion today addresses only the former, and does not

In *Prima Paint Corp. v. Flood & Conklin Mfg. Co.*, 388 U.S. 395 (1967), we addressed the question of who—court or arbitrator—decides these two types of challenges. The issue in the case was "whether a claim of fraud in the inducement of the entire contract is to be resolved by the federal court, or whether the matter is to be referred to the arbitrators." Guided by §4 of the FAA, we held that "if the claim is fraud in the inducement of the arbitration clause itself—an issue which goes to the making of the agreement to arbitrate—the federal court may proceed to adjudicate it. But the statutory language does not permit the federal court to consider claims of fraud in the inducement of the contract generally." We rejected the view that the question of "severability" was one of state law, so that if state law held the arbitration provision not to be severable a challenge to the contract as a whole would be decided by the court.

Subsequently, in *Southland Corp.*, we held that the FAA "create[d] a body of federal substantive law," which was "applicable in state and federal court." 465 U.S., at 12. We rejected the view that state law could bar enforcement of §2, even in the context of state-law claims brought in state court.

Prima Paint and *Southland* answer the question presented here by establishing three propositions. First, as a matter of substantive federal arbitration law, an arbitration provision is severable from the remainder of the contract. Second, unless the challenge is to the arbitration clause itself, the issue of the contract's validity is considered by the arbitrator in the first instance. Third, this arbitration law applies in state as well as federal courts. The parties have not requested, and we do not undertake, reconsideration of those holdings. Applying them …, we conclude that because respondents challenge the Agreement, but not specifically its arbitration provisions, those provisions are enforceable apart from the remainder of the contract. The challenge should therefore be considered by an arbitrator, not a court.

In declining to apply *Prima Paint's* rule of severability, the Florida Supreme Court relied on the distinction between void and voidable contracts. "Florida public policy and contract law," it concluded, permit "no severable, or salvageable, parts of a contract found illegal and void under Florida law." 894 So.2d, at 864. *Prima Paint* makes this conclusion irrelevant. That case rejected application of state severability rules to the arbitration agreement *without discussing* whether the challenge at issue would have rendered the contract void or voidable. *See* 388 U.S., at 400-404. Indeed, the opinion expressly disclaimed any need to decide what state-law remedy was available, (though Justice Black's dissent *asserted* that state law rendered the contract void). Likewise in *Southland*, which arose in state court, we did not ask whether the several challenges made there—fraud, misrepresentation, breach of contract, breach of fiduciary duty, and violation of the California Franchise Investment Law—would render the contract void or voidable. We simply rejected the proposition that the enforceability of the arbitration agreement turned on the state legislature's judgment concerning the forum for enforcement of the state-law cause of

---

speak to the issue decided in the cases cited by respondents (and by the Florida Supreme Court), which hold that it is for courts to decide whether the alleged obligor ever signed the contract, *Chastain v. Robinson-Humphrey Co.*, 957 F.2d 851 (CA11 1992), whether the signor lacked authority to commit the alleged principal, *Sandvik AB v. Advent Int'l Corp.*, 220 F.3d 99 (CA3 2000); *Sphere Drake Ins. Ltd. v. All American Ins. Co.*, 256 F.3d 587 (CA7 2001), and whether the signor lacked the mental capacity to assent, *Spahr v. Secco*, 330 F.3d 1266 (CA10 2003).

action. *See* 465 U.S. at 10. Here, we cannot accept the Florida Supreme Court's conclusion that enforceability of the arbitration agreement should turn on "Florida public policy and contract law," 894 So.2d at 864.

Respondents assert that *Prima Paint*'s rule of severability does not apply in state court. They argue that *Prima Paint* interpreted only §§3 and 4—two of the FAA's procedural provisions, which appear to apply by their terms only in federal court—but not §2, the only provision that we have applied in state court. This does not accurately describe *Prima Paint*. Although §4, in particular, had much to do with *Prima Paint*'s understanding of the rule of severability, *see* 388 U.S., at 403-404, this rule ultimately arises out of §2, the FAA's substantive command that arbitration agreements be treated like all other contracts. The rule of severability establishes how this equal-footing guarantee for "a written [arbitration] provision" is to be implemented. Respondents' reading of *Prima Paint* as establishing nothing more than a federal-court rule of procedure also runs contrary to *Southland*'s understanding of the case. One of the bases for *Southland*'s application of §2 in state court was precisely *Prima Paint*'s "reli[ance] for [its] holding on Congress' broad power to fashion substantive rules under the Commerce Clause." 465 U.S. at 11; *Prima Paint*, at 407 (Black, J., dissenting) ("the Court here holds that the [FAA], as a matter of *federal substantive law* ..." (emphasis added))....

Respondents point to the language of §2, which renders "valid, irrevocable, and enforceable" "a written provision in" or "an agreement in writing to submit to arbitration an existing controversy arising out of" a "contract." Since, respondents argue, the only arbitration agreements to which §2 applies are those involving a "contract," and since an agreement void *ab intitio* under state law is not a "contract," there is no "written provision" in or "controversy arising out of" a "contract," to which §2 can apply. This argument echoes Justice Black's dissent in *Prima Paint*: "Sections 2 and 3 of the Act assume the existence of a valid contract. They merely provide for enforcement where such a valid contract exists." We do not read "contract" so narrowly. The word appears four times in §2. Its last appearance is in the final clause, which allows a challenge to an arbitration provision "upon such grounds as exist at law or in equity for the revocation of any *contract*." (Emphasis added.) There can be no doubt that "contract" as used this last time must include contracts that later prove to be void. Otherwise, the grounds for revocation would be limited to those that rendered a contract voidable—which would mean (implausibly) that an arbitration agreement could be challenged as voidable but not as void. Because the sentence's final use of "contract" so obviously includes putative contracts, we will not read the same word earlier in the same sentence to have a more narrow meaning.[19]...

It is true, as respondents assert, that the *Prima Paint* rule permits a court to enforce an arbitration agreement in a contract that the arbitrator later finds to be void. But it is equally true that respondents' approach permits a court to deny effect to an arbitration provision in a contract that the court later finds to be perfectly enforceable. *Prima Paint* resolved this

---

19. Our more natural reading is confirmed by the use of the word "contract" elsewhere in the United States Code to refer to putative agreements, regardless of whether they are legal. For instance, the Sherman Act, 26 Stat. 209, as amended, states that "[e]very contract, combination..., or conspiracy, in restraint of trade [is] hereby declared to be illegal." 15 U.S.C. §1. Under respondents' reading of "contract," a bewildering circularity would result: A contract illegal because it was in restraint of trade would not be a "contract" at all, and thus the statutory prohibition would not apply.

conundrum—and resolved it in favor of the separate enforceability of arbitration provisions. We reaffirm today that, regardless of whether the challenge is brought in federal or state court, a challenge to the validity of the contract as a whole, and not specifically to the arbitration clause, must go to the arbitrator....

FIONA TRUST & HOLDING CO. v. PRIVALOV
[2007] UKHL 40 (House of Lords)

LORD HOFFMANN. This appeal concerns the scope and effect of arbitration clauses in eight charterparties in Shelltime 4 form made between eight companies forming part of the Sovcomflot group of companies (which is owned by the Russian state) and eight charterers. It is alleged by the owners that the charters were procured by the bribery of senior officers of the Sovcomflot group by a Mr Nikitin, who controlled ... the charterer companies.... [The owners] have purported to rescind the charters on this ground and the question is whether the issue of whether they were entitled to do so should be determined by arbitration or by a court. The owners have commenced court proceedings for a declaration that the charters have been validly rescinded and the charterers have applied for a stay under §9 of the Arbitration Act 1996. [The Court of Appeal granted the stay and this appeal followed.]

The case has been argued on the basis that there are two issues: first, whether, as a matter of construction, the arbitration clause is apt to cover the question of whether the contract was procured by bribery, secondly, whether it is possible for a party to be bound by submission to arbitration when he alleges that, but for the bribery, he would never have entered into the contract containing the arbitration clause....

I start by setting out the arbitration clause ...:

> "41(a) This charter shall be construed and the relations between the parties determined in accordance with the laws of England.
>
> (b) Any dispute arising under this charter shall be decided by the English courts to whose jurisdiction the parties hereby agree.
>
> (c) Notwithstanding the foregoing, but without prejudice to any party's right to arrest or maintain the arrest of any maritime property, either party may, by giving written notice of election to the other party, elect to have any such dispute referred ... to arbitration in London, one arbitrator to be nominated by Owners and the other by Charterers, and in case the arbitrators shall not agree to the decision of an umpire, whose decision shall be final and binding upon both parties. Arbitration shall take place in London in accordance with the London Maritime Association of Arbitrators, in accordance with the provisions of the Arbitration Act 1950, or any statutory modification or re-enactment thereof for the time being in force.
>
> (i) A party shall lose its right to make such an election only if: (a) it receives from the other party a written notice of dispute which (1) states expressly that a dispute has arisen out of this charter; (2) specifies the nature of the dispute; and (3) refers expressly to this clause 41(c) And (b) it fails to give notice of election to have the dispute referred to arbitration not later than 30 days from the date of receipt of such notice of dispute ..."

It will be observed that clause 41(b) is a jurisdiction clause in respect of "any dispute arising under this charter" which is then incorporated by reference (by the words "any such dispute") in the arbitration clause in 41(c). So the first question is whether clause 41(b) refers the question of whether the charters were procured by bribery to the jurisdiction of the English court. If it does, then a party may elect under clause 41(c) to have that question referred to arbitration. But I shall for the sake of convenience discuss the clause as if it was a simple arbitration clause. The owners say that for two reasons it does not apply. The first is that, as a matter of construction, the question is not a dispute arising under the charter. The second is that the jurisdiction and arbitration clause is liable to be rescinded and therefore not binding upon them....

Arbitration is consensual. It depends upon the intention of the parties as expressed in their agreement. Only the agreement can tell you what kind of disputes they intended to submit to arbitration. But the meaning which parties intended to express by the words which they used will be affected by the commercial background and the reader's understanding of the purpose for which the agreement was made. Businessmen in particular are assumed to have entered into agreements to achieve some rational commercial purpose and an understanding of this purpose will influence the way in which one interprets their language.

In approaching the question of construction, it is therefore necessary to inquire into the purpose of the arbitration clause. As to this, I think there can be no doubt. The parties have entered into a relationship, an agreement or what is alleged to be an agreement or what appears on its face to be an agreement, which may give rise to disputes. They want those disputes decided by a tribunal which they have chosen, commonly on the grounds of such matters as its neutrality, expertise and privacy, the availability of legal services at the seat of the arbitration and the unobtrusive efficiency of its supervisory law. Particularly in the case of international contracts, they want a quick and efficient adjudication and do not want to take the risks of delay, in too many cases, partiality, in proceedings before a national jurisdiction.

If one accepts that this is the purpose of an arbitration clause, its construction must be influenced by whether the parties, as rational businessmen, were likely to have intended that only some of the questions arising out of their relationship were to be submitted to arbitration and others were to be decided by national courts. Could they have intended that the question of whether the contract was repudiated should be decided by arbitration but the question of whether it was induced by misrepresentation should be decided by a court? If, as appears to be generally accepted, there is no rational basis upon which businessmen would be likely to wish to have questions of the validity or enforceability of the contract decided by one tribunal and questions about its performance decided by another, one would need to find very clear language before deciding that they must have had such an intention.

A proper approach to construction therefore requires the court to give effect, so far as the language used by the parties will permit, to the commercial purpose of the arbitration clause. But the same policy of giving effect to the commercial purpose also drives the approach of the courts (and the legislature) to the second question raised in this appeal, namely, whether there is any conceptual reason why parties who have agreed to submit the question of the validity of the contract to arbitration should not be allowed to do so.

There was for some time a view that arbitrators could never have jurisdiction to decide whether a contract was valid. If the contract was invalid, so was the arbitration clause. In *Overseas Union Ins. Ltd v. AA Mutual Int'l Ins. Co Ltd* [1988] 2 Lloyd's Rep 63, 66, Evans J said that this rule "owes as much to logic as it does to authority." But the logic of the proposition was denied by the Court of Appeal in *Harbour Assur. Co (UK) Ltd v. Kansa*

Gen. Int'l Ins. Co. [1993] QB 70, and the question was put beyond doubt by §7 of the Arbitration Act 1996[, which provides]:

> "Unless otherwise agreed by the parties, an arbitration agreement which forms or was intended to form part of another agreement (whether or not in writing) shall not be regarded as invalid, non-existent or ineffective because that other agreement is invalid, or did not come into existence or has become ineffective, and it shall for that purpose be treated as a distinct agreement."

This section shows a recognition by Parliament that, for the reasons I have given in discussing the approach to construction, businessmen frequently do want the question of whether their contract was valid, or came into existence, or has become ineffective, submitted to arbitration and that the law should not place conceptual obstacles in their way.

With that background, I turn to the question of construction. Your Lordships were referred to a number of cases in which various forms of words in arbitration clauses have been considered. Some of them draw a distinction between disputes "arising under" and "arising out of" the agreement. In *Heyman v. Darwins Ltd* [1942] AC 356, 399, Lord Porter said that the former had a narrower meaning than the latter but in *Union of India v. E B Aaby's Rederi A/S (The Evje)* [1975] AC 797, 814 Viscount Dilhorne and Lord Salmon said that they could not see the difference between them....

I do not propose to analyse these and other such cases any further because in my opinion the distinctions which they make reflect no credit upon English commercial law. It may be a great disappointment to the judges who explained so carefully the effects of the various linguistic nuances if they could learn that the draftsman of so widely used a standard form as Shelltime 4 obviously regarded the expressions "arising under this charter" in clause 41(b) and "arisen out of this charter" in clause 41(c)(1)(a)(i) as mutually interchangeable. So I applaud the opinion expressed ... in the Court of Appeal that the time has come to draw a line under the authorities to date and make a fresh start. I think that a fresh start is justified by the developments which have occurred in this branch of the law in recent years and in particular by the adoption of the principle of separability by Parliament in §7 of the 1996 Act. That section was obviously intended to enable the courts to give effect to the reasonable commercial expectations of the parties about the questions which they intended to be decided by arbitration. But §7 will not achieve its purpose if the courts adopt an approach to construction which is likely in many cases to defeat those expectations. The approach to construction therefore needs to be re-examined.

In my opinion the construction of an arbitration clause should start from the assumption that the parties, as rational businessmen, are likely to have intended any dispute arising out of the relationship into which they have entered or purported to enter to be decided by the same tribunal. The clause should be construed in accordance with this presumption unless the language makes it clear that certain questions were intended to be excluded from the arbitrator's jurisdiction. As Longmore LJ remarked: "if any businessman did want to exclude disputes about the validity of a contract, it would be comparatively easy to say so."

This appears to be the approach adopted in Germany: *see* the Bundesgerichtshof's Decision of 27 February 1970 (1990):

> "There is every reason to presume that reasonable parties will wish to have the relationships created by their contract and the claims arising therefrom, irrespective of whether their contract is effective or not, decided by the same tribunal and not by two different tribunals."

If one adopts this approach, the language of clause 41 of Shelltime 4 contains nothing to exclude disputes about the validity of the contract, whether on the grounds that it was procured by fraud, bribery, misrepresentation or anything else. In my opinion it therefore applies to the present dispute.

The next question is whether, in view of the allegation of bribery, the clause is binding upon the owners. They say that if they are right about the bribery, they were entitled to rescind the whole contract, including the arbitration clause. The arbitrator therefore has no jurisdiction and the dispute should be decided by the court.

The principle of separability enacted in §7 means that the invalidity or rescission of the main contract does not necessarily entail the invalidity or rescission of the arbitration agreement. The arbitration agreement must be treated as a "distinct agreement" and can be void or voidable only on grounds which relate directly to the arbitration agreement. Of course there may be cases in which the ground upon which the main agreement is invalid is identical with the ground upon which the arbitration agreement is invalid. For example, if the main agreement and the arbitration agreement are contained in the same document and one of the parties claims that he never agreed to anything in the document and that his signature was forged, that will be an attack on the validity of the arbitration agreement. But the ground of attack is not that the main agreement was invalid. It is that the signature to the arbitration agreement, as a "distinct agreement," was forged. Similarly, if a party alleges that someone who purported to sign as agent on his behalf had no authority whatever to conclude any agreement on his behalf, that is an attack on both the main agreement and the arbitration agreement.

On the other hand, if (as in this case) the allegation is that the agent exceeded his authority by entering into a main agreement in terms which were not authorised or for improper reasons, that is not necessarily an attack on the arbitration agreement. It would have to be shown that whatever the terms of the main agreement or the reasons for which the agent concluded it, he would have had no authority to enter into an arbitration agreement. Even if the allegation is that there was no concluded agreement (for example, that terms of the main agreement remained to be agreed) that is not necessarily an attack on the arbitration agreement. If the arbitration clause has been agreed, the parties will be presumed to have intended the question of whether there was a concluded main agreement to be decided by arbitration.

In the present case, it is alleged that the main agreement was in uncommercial terms which, together with other surrounding circumstances, give rise to the inference that an agent acting for the owners was bribed to consent to it. But that does not show that he was bribed to enter into the arbitration agreement. It would have been remarkable for him to enter into any charter without an arbitration agreement, whatever its other terms had been. [The owners argued] that but for the bribery, the owners would not have entered into any charter with the charterers and therefore would not have entered into an arbitration agreement. But that is in my opinion exactly the kind of argument which §7 was intended to prevent. It amounts to saying that because the main agreement and the arbitration agreement were bound up with each other, the invalidity of the main agreement should result in the invalidity of the arbitration agreement. The one should fall with the other because they would never have been separately concluded. But §7 in my opinion means that they must be treated as having been separately concluded and the arbitration agreement can be invalidated only on a ground which relates to the arbitration agreement and is not merely a consequence of the invalidity of the main agreement.

[The owners argued] that the approach to construction and separability adopted by the Court of Appeal infringed the owners' right of access to a court for the resolution of their civil disputes, contrary to Article 6 of the European Convention on Human Rights. I do not think there is anything in this point. The European Convention was not intended to destroy arbitration. Arbitration is based upon agreement and the parties can by agreement waive the right to a court. If it appears upon a fair construction of the charter that they have agreed to the arbitration of a particular dispute, there is no infringement of their Convention right.

For these reasons, … I would hold that the charterers are entitled to a stay of the proceedings to rescind the charters and dismiss the appeal.

LORD HOPE OF CRAIGHEAD…. No contract of this kind is complete without a clause which identifies the law to be applied and the methods to be used for the determination of disputes. Its purpose is to avoid the expense and delay of having to argue about these matters later. It is the kind of clause to which ordinary businessmen readily give their agreement so long as its general meaning is clear. They are unlikely to trouble themselves too much about its precise language or to wish to explore the way it has been interpreted in the numerous authorities, not all of which speak with one voice. Of course, the court must do what it can to provide charterers and shipowners with legal certainty at the negotiation stage as to what they are agreeing to. But there is no conflict between that proposition and [a liberal approach to] interpretation of jurisdiction and arbitration clauses in international commercial contracts. The proposition that any jurisdiction or arbitration clause in an international commercial contract should be liberally construed promotes legal certainty. It serves to underline the golden rule that if the parties wish to have issues as to the validity of their contract decided by one tribunal and issues as to its meaning or performance decided by another, they must say so expressly. Otherwise they will be taken to have agreed on a single tribunal for the resolution of all such disputes….

The arbitration clause … indicates to the reader that he need not trouble himself with fussy distinctions as to what the words "arising under" and "arising out of" may mean. Taken overall, the wording indicates that arbitration may be chosen as a one-stop method of adjudication for the determination of all disputes. Disputes about validity, after all, are no less appropriate for determination by an arbitrator than any other kind of dispute that may arise. So I do not think that there is anything in the appellants' point that it must be assumed that when the charters were entered into one party was entirely ignorant that they were induced by bribery. The purpose of the clause is to provide for the determination of disputes of all kinds, whether or not they were foreseen at the time when the contract was entered into.

Then there are consequences that would follow, if the appellants are right. It is not just that the parties would be deprived of the benefit of having all their disputes decided in one forum. The jurisdiction clause does not say where disputes about the validity of the contract are to be determined, if this is not to be in the forum which is expressly mentioned. The default position is that such claims would have to be brought in the jurisdiction where their opponents were incorporated, wherever and however unreliable that might be, while claims for breach of contract have to be brought in England…. If the parties have confidence in their chosen jurisdiction for one purpose, why should they not have confidence in it for the other? Why, having chosen their jurisdiction for one purpose, should they leave the question which court is to have jurisdiction for the other purpose unspoken, with all the risks that this may give rise to? For them, everything is to be gained by avoiding litigation in two different jurisdictions....

The Court of Appeal said that the time had come for a fresh start to be made, at any rate for cases arising in an international commercial context. It has indeed been clear for many years that the trend of recent authority has risked isolating the approach that English law takes to the wording of such clauses from that which is taken internationally. It makes sense in the context of international commerce for decisions about their effect to be informed by what has been decided elsewhere....

In *AT&T Technologies Inc. v. Communications Workers of America*, 475 U.S. 643 (1986), the U.S. Supreme Court said that, in the absence of any express provision excluding a particular grievance from arbitration, only the most forceful evidence of a purpose to exclude the claim from arbitration could prevail. In *Threlkeld & Co., Inc. v. Metallgesellschaft Ltd (London)*, 923 F.2d 245 (2d Cir. 1991), the court observed that federal arbitration policy required that any doubts concerning the scope of arbitral issues should be resolved in favour of arbitration and that arbitration clauses should be construed as broadly as possible. In *Comandate Marine Corp. v. Pan Australia Shipping Pty Ltd* [2006] FCAFC 192 (Australian Fed. Ct.), the Federal Court of Australia said that a liberal approach to the words chosen by the parties was underpinned by the sensible commercial presumption that the parties did not intend the inconvenience of having possible disputes from their transaction being heard in two places, particularly when they were operating in a truly international market. This approach to the issue of construction is now firmly embedded as part of the law of international commerce. I agree with the Court of Appeal that it must now be accepted as part of our law too.

It is in the light of these observations that the issue of severability should be viewed also. Section 7 of the Arbitration Act 1996 reproduces in English law the principle that was laid down by §4 of the U.S. [FAA]. That section provides that, on being satisfied that the making of the agreement for arbitration or the failure to comply therewith is not in issue, the court shall make an order directing the parties to proceed to arbitration. Section 7 uses slightly different language, but it is to the same effect. The validity, existence or effectiveness of the arbitration agreement is not dependent upon the effectiveness, existence or validity of the underlying substantive contract unless the parties have agreed to this. The purpose of these provisions, as the U.S. Supreme Court observed in *Prima Paint Corp. v. Flood & Conklin Mfg Co.*, 388 U.S. 395 (1967), is that the arbitration procedure, when selected by the parties to a contract, should be speedy and not subject to delay and obstruction in the courts. The statutory language, it said, did not permit the court to consider claims of fraud in the inducement of the contract generally. It could consider only issues relating to the making and performance of the agreement to arbitrate.

The appellants' case is that, as there was no real consent to the charterparties because they were induced by bribery, there was no real consent to the arbitration clauses. They submit that a line does not have to be drawn between matters which might impeach the arbitration clause and those which affect the main contract. What is needed is an analysis of whether the matters that affect the main contract are also matters which affect the validity of the arbitration clause. As the respondents point out, this is a causation argument. The appellants say that no substantive distinction can be drawn between various situations where the complaint is made that there was no real consent to the transaction. It would be contrary to the policy of the law, which is to deter bribery, that acts of the person who is alleged to have been bribed should deprive the innocent party of access to a court for determination of the issue whether the contract was induced by bribery.

But, ... this case is different from a dispute as to whether there was ever a contract at all. As everyone knows, an arbitral award possesses no binding force except that which is derived from the joint mandate of the contracting parties. Everything depends on their contract, and if there was no contract to go to arbitration at all an arbitrator's award can have no validity. So, where the arbitration agreement is set out in the same document as the main contract, the issue whether there was an agreement at all may indeed affect all parts of it. Issues as to whether the entire agreement was procured by impersonation or by forgery, for example, are unlikely to be severable from the arbitration clause.

That is not this case, however. The appellants' argument was not that there was no contract at all, but that they were entitled to rescind the contract including the arbitration agreement because the contract was induced by bribery. Allegations of that kind, if sound, may affect the validity of the main agreement. But they do not undermine the validity of the arbitration agreement as a distinct agreement. The doctrine of separability requires direct impeachment of the arbitration agreement before it can be set aside. This is an exacting test. The argument must be based on facts which are specific to the arbitration agreement. Allegations that are parasitical to a challenge to the validity to the main agreement will not do. That being the situation in this case, the agreement to go to arbitration must be given effect....

NOTES

1. *Historic authorities denying existence of separability presumption*—Kulukundis. Consider the U.S. court's decision in *Kulukundis*. What is its view of the separability presumption? Consider the court's statement that: "As the arbitration clause here is an integral part of the charter party, the court, in determining that the parties agreed to that clause, must necessarily first have found that the charter party exists." Although the court's opinion arose in the context of a claim that no underlying contract (or arbitration agreement) was ever formed, note the breadth of its rationale. What does the court mean that the "arbitration clause here is an integral part of the charter party"? Suppose that the charter party was formed, but is invalid (for example, because of fraud, unconscionability, formal defects, impossibility)? Under the *Kulukundis* rationale, what does the invalidity of the underlying contract do to the arbitration clause? Recall that it is treated as "an integral part" of the underlying contract. Can you support the *Kulukundis* result with a different rationale?

    Note that the *Kulukundis* decision considers both the scope of the parties' arbitration agreement (did it purport to encompass disputes about the existence and validity of the underlying charter) and the treatment of such an arbitration agreement under the FAA. What did the *Kulukundis* court conclude regarding the scope of the arbitration clause? Compare the analyses of the scope of the arbitration clause in the Bundesgerichtshof's *Judgment of 27 February 1970* and the House of Lords' decision in *Fiona Trust*.

2. *Tobler's approach to separability presumption.* The Swiss Federal Tribunal's opinion in *Tobler* is an early application of the separability presumption. In what sense does the Federal Tribunal treat the arbitration agreement as separable? What is the rationale

adopted by the court for this result? What is meant by the concept of a "procedural" agreement? In what sense is an arbitration agreement a "procedural" agreement? In what sense isn't it? How would the *Tobler* court have decided *Kulukundis*?

3. JOC Oil's *approach to separability presumption.* The award in *JOC Oil* is a leading example of application of the separability presumption. What was the practical importance of the tribunal's adoption of the separability presumption? Rephrase in your own words the tribunal's statement of the separability presumption. Does it differ from that in Article 16 of the UNCITRAL Model Law, §§6 and 7 of the English Arbitration Act or Article 178(3) of the SLPIL, excerpted at pp. 90, 113 & 158 of the Documentary Supplement? Note that, following the *JOC Oil* award, the Arbitration Rules of the Arbitration Court of the USSR Chamber of Commerce and Industry were amended to provide "An arbitration clause shall be considered to have legal force irrespective of the validity of the contract of which it is a component part." *See* Gardner, *The Doctrine of Separability in Soviet Arbitration Law: An Analysis of* Sojuznefteexport v. JOC Oil Co., 28 Colum. J. Transnat'l L. 301 (1990).

4. Buckeye's *approach to separability presumption. Buckeye*, and the U.S. Supreme Court's earlier decision in *Prima Paint*, are routinely cited for the proposition that, under the FAA, an arbitration clause is separable from the underlying contract that contains it. *See infra* pp. 278-80, 404-05, 416-20. Where precisely in *Buckeye* does the Court "adopt" the separability presumption? Consider carefully the language of §§2-4. Does anything in these provisions require application of the separability presumption? *See also infra* pp. 278-80; *Granite Rock Co. v. Int'l Bhd of Teamsters*, 130 S.Ct. 2847, 2857 (2010) ("courts must treat the arbitration clause as severable from the contract in which it appears").

    Compare the analysis of the separability doctrine in *Buckeye* with that in *JOC Oil*. Are there differences in the two analyses?

5. Fiona Trust's *approach to separability presumption.* Consider the approach to the separability presumption in *Fiona Trust*. Does the House of Lords rely on the language of the English Arbitration Act, 1996, to justify the separability presumption? Or on something else? Compare the language of §§6 and 7 of the English Arbitration Act, 1996, with §§2-4 of the FAA, excerpted at pp. 113 & 103-04 of the Documentary Supplement. How do they differ? Compare also Articles 7, 8 and 16 of the UNCITRAL Model Law. What were the practical consequences of adopting the separability presumption in *Fiona Trust*? How would the House of Lords have decided *Kulukundis*?

6. *German Bundesgerichtshof's* Judgment of 27 February 1970 *approach to separability presumption.* Consider the *Judgment of 27 February 1970*. What rationale does the Bundesgerichtshof adopt for the separability presumption? *See also Judgment of 12 March 1998*, XXIX Y.B. Comm. Arb. 663, 667 (2004) (Hanseatisches Oberlandesgericht Hamburg) ("nullity of the main contract, if there is such, does not affect the arbitration clause"). More recently, the Bundesgerichtshof has held that §1040(1) of the ZPO, adopting the Model Law, "codifies a basic principle of international arbitration.... The arbitration agreement is autonomous from the underlying contract." *Judgment of 27 November 2008*, 2009 HmbSchRZ 5 (German Bundesgerichtshof).

7. *Rationales for separability presumption.* What is the basis for the presumption that an agreement to arbitrate is "separable" from the parties' underlying contract—the par-

ties' intent, the nature of the agreement to arbitrate, the command of national law or the New York Convention, the needs of the international legal system, or something else?

(a) *Parties' express agreement as basis for separability presumption.* One possible source for the separability presumption is the parties' express agreement. This occurs most frequently where an arbitration clause incorporates institutional rules—like the UNCITRAL or ICC arbitration rules—which provide that an arbitration clause is separable from the parties' underlying contract. Consider Article 23 of the UNCITRAL Rules, Article 6 of the ICC Rules and Article 23 of the LCIA Rules, excerpted at pp. 170, 184-85 & 269-70 of the Documentary Supplement. Do these provisions clearly adopt the separability presumption? Are there differences between the various statements of the doctrine in each set of rules? Explain any such differences.

(b) *Parties' implied agreement as basis for separability presumption.* The separability presumption can also be justified on grounds of party intent even where institutional rules or the arbitration agreement itself do not expressly provide for such a result. Why would parties generally intend their arbitration clause to be "separable"? Consider the practical consequences of *not* accepting the separability presumption (including as described in *Judgment of 27 February 1970* and *Fiona Trust*). What might happen if every challenge to the continuing validity of a commercial contract also resulted in a challenge to the validity of the parties' associated arbitration agreement?

It is argued that: (a) parties to arbitration agreements generally "intend to require arbitration of any dispute not otherwise settled, including disputes over the validity of the contract or treaty"; (b) without the separability presumption, "it would always be open to a party to an agreement containing an arbitration clause to vitiate its arbitration obligation by the simple expedient of declaring the agreement void"; and (c) "the very concept and phrase 'arbitration agreement' itself imports the existence of a separate or at any rate separable agreement, which is or can be divorced from the body of the principal agreement if needs be." S. Schwebel, *International Arbitration: Three Salient Problems* 3-6 (1987). Is this a persuasive basis for concluding that parties ordinarily intend their arbitration clause to be separable?

Consider the following explanation of the separability presumption in *Harbour Assur. Co. (U.K.) v. Kansa Gen. Int'l Ins. Co. Ltd,* 1 Lloyds Rep. 81, 92-93 (QB) (English High Ct. 1992):

> First, there is the imperative of giving effect to the wishes of the parties unless there are compelling reasons of principle why it is not possible to do so…. Secondly, if the arbitration clause is not held to survive the invalidity of the contract, a party is afforded the opportunity to evade his obligation to arbitrate by the simple expedient of alleging that the contract is void. In such cases courts of law then inevitably become involved in deciding the substance of a dispute. Moreover, in international transactions where the neutrality of the arbitral process is highly prized, the collapse of this consensual method of dispute resolution compels a party to resort to national courts where in the real world the badge of neutrality is sometimes perceived to be absent. For parties the perceived effectiveness of the neutral arbitral process is often a vital condition in the process of negotiation of the contract. If that perception is absent, it will often present a formidable hurdle to the conclusion of

the transaction. A full recognition of the separability principle tends to facilitate international trade.

Is this persuasive? Consider also the explanations in *Judgment of 27 February 1970* and *Fiona Trust*.

(c) *"Procedural" or "ancillary" character of arbitration agreement.* Some authorities rely on the "procedural" character of the dispute resolution provisions of an arbitration agreement to justify its "separable" or "independent" nature. Consider the tribunal's analysis in *JOC Oil*. What were the stated reasons, under Soviet law, for treating an arbitration agreement as separable? What does the arbitral tribunal mean by a "material-legal" contract and a "procedural" arbitration agreement?

Compare the differences in the nature of the obligations imposed by a foreign trade contract (*e.g.*, to buy and sell oil) and an arbitration agreement (*i.e.*, to resolve disputes by arbitration). Is it likely that the parties would have regarded these two sets of obligations as separable? Why? Consider again the analysis in *Tobler*. How does it characterize the nature of the agreement to arbitrate?

Compare the following reasoning in *Westacre Inv. Inc. v. Jugoimp.-SDPR Holdings Co. Ltd*, [1998] 4 All ER 570, 582:

> These characteristics of an arbitration agreement which are in one sense independent of the underlying or substantive contract have often led to the characterisation of an arbitration agreement ... as a 'separate' contract.... For an agreement to arbitrate within an underlying contract is in origin and function parasitic. It is ancillary to the underlying contract for its only function is to provide machinery to resolve disputes as to the primary and secondary obligations arising under that contract. The primary obligations under the agreement to arbitrate exist only for the purpose of informing the parties by means of an award what are their rights and obligations under the underlying contract.

Why, in fact, should arbitration clauses be regarded as "separable" or "independent" from the agreements in which they appear? What does it mean to treat an arbitration clause as "ancillary" to the underlying contract, providing only "machinery to resolve disputes"? Consider again the distinction between "material-legal" and "procedural" agreements in *JOC Oil* and *Tobler*. Are not the "procedural" or "dispute resolution" provisions of arbitration clauses intimately interrelated to the "substantive" terms of underlying agreements? What aspects of an arbitration clause suggest that parties would likely regard it as independent or separable from their underlying agreement?

(d) *National law as basis for separability presumption.* Article 16(1) of the UNCITRAL Model Law, §§6 and 7 of the English Arbitration Act, 1996 and Article 178(3) of the SLPIL provide that an arbitration clause is separable from the underlying contract in which it appears. Compare the language of each provision, excerpted at pp. 90, 113 & 158 of the Documentary Supplement. How do they differ? How does each provision characterize the consequences of the separability presumption?

Consider §§2-4 of the FAA, excerpted at pp. 103-04 of the Documentary Supplement. Do these provisions address the question whether an arbitration clause is a separable agreement? Consider the interpretation of the FAA adopted in *Buck-*

eye. What role does the FAA's text have in the Court's analysis? What role did statutory language have in *JOC Oil*? In the *Judgment of 27 February 1970*?

(e) *Needs of international arbitral process as basis for separability presumption.* Aside from reliance on particular institutional rules, arbitration agreements, or statutory provisions of national law, rationales for the separability presumption also rest on practical considerations. Thus, it is said, the separability presumption is necessary in order to prevent challenges to the existence, validity, or continued effect of an underlying contract from derailing the arbitral process. See the quotes above from Judge Schwebel and *Harbour Assurance*. Compare the contrary view in *Kulukundis*.

Why exactly is the separability presumption necessary in order to prevent challenges to the underlying contract from derailing the arbitral process? Would it not be possible, even absent the separability presumption, for an arbitrator to rule on claims that the contract containing the arbitration clause was invalid? If national law (or the international requirements of the New York Convention) permitted arbitrators to decide challenges to the validity or existence of the arbitration agreement, would the separability presumption be necessary to prevent jurisdictional challenges from derailing the arbitral process? (The subject of an arbitral tribunal's competence to consider challenges to its own jurisdiction is discussed below. *See infra* pp. 218-87.)

8. *Consequences of separability presumption.* What are the practical consequences of concluding, like the arbitration statutes and other materials excerpted above, that an arbitration agreement is presumptively "separable" from the parties' underlying contract? Consider the following possibilities, to which we return in subsequent sections.

(a) *Nonexistence or invalidity of underlying contract does not necessarily invalidate arbitration agreement.* One vitally-important consequence of the separability presumption is that a party's challenge to the existence or validity of the underlying contract does not necessarily affect the existence or validity of the arbitration clause. Even if the underlying contract is nonexistent or invalid, the associated arbitration agreement may be valid: the two agreements (the underlying contract and the agreement to arbitrate) are different, "separable" (or "autonomous") agreements.

Consider the analysis, from two rather different perspectives, of the Soviet tribunal in *JOC Oil* and the U.S. Supreme Court in *Buckeye*. Both the arbitral tribunal and the Court held that a claim that the parties' underlying contract was invalid did not provide grounds for challenging the "separable" arbitration clause contained within the underlying contract. *See infra* pp. 355-75, 393-474. Compare the analyses in *Tobler* and the *Judgment of 27 February 1970*.

Consider how Articles 7, 8 and 16 of the UNCITRAL Model Law, excerpted at pp. 87-88 & 90 of the Documentary Supplement, address this issue. What effect, if any, does the invalidity of the parties' underlying contract have on the validity of their arbitration clause under the Model Law? Is the answer clear? Compare §§6 and 7 of the English Arbitration Act, 1996, excerpted at p. 113 of the Documentary Supplement. How does it differ from the Model Law?

(b) *Invalidity of arbitration agreement does not necessarily affect underlying contract.* Conversely, where the arbitration clause is invalid or illegal, the separability presumption provides that this does not necessarily infect the validity of the underlying contract. The underlying contract can be valid and enforceable, in national courts, without regard to the invalidity of the arbitration clause. How could the arbitration clause be invalid if the underlying contract is valid? Suppose parties crossed out the article of the contract containing the arbitration clause? Suppose the arbitration clause was invalid because it was indefinite, unconscionable, or procured by duress, even though the underlying contract suffered no such defects?

(c) *Law governing arbitration clause may be different from that governing underlying contract.* An arbitration agreement can be governed by a different national law, or a different body of substantive legal rules, from that applicable to the parties' underlying contract. *See infra* pp. 287-315. One explanation for this result is the separability presumption, which postulates two separate agreements, which can readily be governed by two different sets of laws.

Consider Article 178(2) of the SLPIL, excerpted at p. 158 of the Documentary Supplement. What does Article 178(2) provide with respect to the law governing an arbitration agreement? Consider also the award in *JOC Oil*. What substantive rules applied to the parties' underlying foreign trade contract? To their arbitration agreement?

(d) *Arbitration clause may survive termination or expiry of underlying contract.* Parties not infrequently commence arbitral proceedings after their underlying contract has expired or been terminated. In most jurisdictions, there is no general obstacle to this, provided that the claims arise from conduct during the term of the agreement. *See infra* pp. 532-33. Although not always directly attributed to the separability presumption, that rule is one explanation for an arbitration clause's survival after termination of the underlying agreement.

(e) *Separability presumption arguably implies arbitrator's power ("competence-competence") to consider his or her own jurisdiction.* Many arbitration statutes and institutional rules link the separability presumption with the principle that the arbitrator has jurisdiction to decide challenges to his or her own jurisdiction. This doctrine is often referred to as the "competence-competence" or "Kompetenz-Kompetenz" doctrine. *See infra* pp. 271-72.

Recall the discussions in *Judgment of 27 February 1970*, *Fiona Trust*, Schwebel and *Harbour Assurance*, about the importance of the separability presumption in preventing challenges to the underlying contract from derailing the arbitral process. *See supra* pp. 212-15. Is the separability presumption in fact necessary to prevent challenges to the existence or validity of the underlying contract from halting the arbitral process? Suppose national law provides that arbitrators may consider challenges to their own jurisdiction, including challenges to the validity of the arbitration agreement itself. Is the separability doctrine necessary, in these circumstances, to permit the arbitrators to consider challenges to the parties' underlying contract?

Consider how the arbitration statutes excerpted above deal with arbitrators' competence to consider challenges to their own jurisdiction. *See* UNCITRAL Model Law, Art. 16(1). *See also* 2012 ICC Rules, Art. 6; 2010 UNCITRAL Rules, Art. 23. Compare the approach of §§6 and 7 of the English Arbitration Act, 1996, excerpted at p. 113 of the Documentary Supplement. Does the English Arbitration

Act link the separability of the arbitration agreement to the arbitrators' competence-competence? Or only to the substantive validity of the arbitration agreement? Consider the House of Lords' analysis in *Fiona Trust*. Does it adopt the same approach?

9. *Criticism of rationales for separability presumption.* Although the separability presumption is widely accepted, it is also subject to criticism. As *Kulukundis* and *Buckeye* illustrate, parties not infrequently deny the very existence of the underlying contract containing an arbitration clause. For example, suppose that a party denies that it executed or otherwise assented to the underlying contract. How can the separability presumption aid in arguments that the arbitration clause, contained in that contract, is nonetheless valid and binding on that party? If a party claims that there simply never was an underlying contract—of any sort—doesn't this challenge necessarily also apply to the arbitration clause contained in the contract?

Consider the analysis in *JOC Oil*. The arbitrators concluded that the parties' underlying foreign trade contract was invalid because it failed to satisfy a "two-signature" requirement. Nonetheless, the tribunal also held that the parties' arbitration clause was valid. How did the tribunal justify this conclusion? Note also the analysis in *Tobler*.

Compare the reasoning in *Kulukundis*. Compare also:

> "[I]f an agreement contains an obligation to arbitrate disputes arising under it, but the agreement is invalid or no longer in force, the obligation to arbitrate disappears with the agreement of which it is a part. If the agreement was never entered into at all, its arbitration clause never came into force. If the agreement was not validly entered into, then, *prima facie*, it is invalid as a whole, as must be all of its parts, including its arbitration clause." S. Schwebel, *International Arbitration: Three Salient Problems* 1 (1987).

Why is this not irrefutable? Surely, if the parties' alleged contract was never agreed to, then none of it—arbitration clause included—is binding on the "parties." Before finally making up your mind, wait until you have examined the materials below, *see infra* pp. 355-75.

10. *Relevance of foreign and international decisions.* Consider the authorities relied upon in *Fiona Trust*. What is the relevance, in interpreting the English Arbitration Act, of German and U.S. decisions? What does the opinion say? Should other national courts also consider "foreign" judicial decisions in interpreting national arbitration legislation, and the New York Convention, as applied to international arbitration issues?

11. *Separability presumption in investment arbitration.* Does the separability presumption apply to arbitration clauses in investment contracts? Consider: *Plama Consortium Ltd v. Repub. of Bulgaria, Decision on Jurisdiction in ICSID Case No. ARB/03/24 of 8 February 2005*, ¶212 ("the nowadays generally accepted principle of the separability (autonomy) of the arbitration clause").

Recall the structure of BITs, *supra* pp. 43-44 & *infra* pp. 511-16, in which a host state makes a standing offer to arbitrate with specified classes of foreign investors. Aren't the resulting arbitration agreements necessarily separable? Note that in many such cases, the host state and foreign investor will have no contractual relationship.

12. *Separability presumption in inter-state arbitration.* Does the separability presumption apply to arbitration clauses in treaties and other inter-state instruments? Is there any reason that the same considerations that apply in the context of international com-

mercial arbitration agreements do not have equal force in the state-to-state context? Consider Article 73 of the 1907 Hague Convention. What does it suggest regarding the separability of arbitration agreements in the state-to-state context?

C. ALLOCATION OF COMPETENCE TO DECIDE DISPUTES OVER INTERPRETATION AND VALIDITY OF INTERNATIONAL ARBITRATION AGREEMENTS

A second issue concerning international arbitration agreements is the allocation of authority between arbitrators and national courts to decide disputes over the interpretation, validity and enforceability of arbitration agreements.[20] That is, "who decides" disputes over the formation, validity, or interpretation of arbitration clauses? In particular, do arbitrators have the authority to consider and/or decide disputes over their own jurisdiction? If so, how is the authority to resolve jurisdictional disputes allocated between arbitrators and national courts, and what avenues of judicial review of arbitrators' jurisdictional decisions are available? Excerpted below are materials addressing this subject.

SWEDISH ARBITRATION ACT
§§2, 34(1)

2. The arbitrators may rule on their own jurisdiction to decide the dispute. The aforesaid shall not prevent a court from determining such a question at the request of a party. The arbitrators may continue the arbitral proceedings pending the determination by the court.

Notwithstanding that the arbitrators have, in a decision during the proceedings, determined that they possess jurisdiction to resolve the dispute, such decision is not binding. The provisions of sections 34 and 36 shall apply in respect of an action to challenge an arbitration award which entails a decision in respect of jurisdiction.

34. An award which may not be challenged in accordance with §36 shall, following an application, be wholly or partially set aside upon motion of a party: (1) if it is not covered by a valid arbitration agreement between the parties.

KULUKUNDIS SHIPPING CO., SA v. AMTORG TRADING CORP.
126 F.2d 978 (2d Cir. 1942)

[excerpted above at pp. 191-93]

FINAL AWARD IN ICC CASE NO. 5294
XIV Y.B. Comm. Arb. 137 (1988)

KARRER, Arbitrator. [A Danish contractor entered into an agreement with an Egyptian sub-contractor ("Agreement") for the construction of an abattoir. Disputes arose, and the

---

20. *See* G. Born, *International Commercial Arbitration* 1077-237 (2d ed. 2014). *See also* Bermann, *The "Gateway" Problem in International Commercial Arbitration*, 37 Yale J. Int'l L. 1 (2012); Drahozal, Buckeye Check Cashing *and the Separability Doctrine*, 1 Y.B. Arb. & Med. 55 (2009); Rau, *Arbitral Power and the Limits of Contract: The New Trilogy*, 22 Am. Rev. Int'l Arb. 435 (2011).

Danish contractor commenced an ICC arbitration. The Egyptian subcontractor did not participate in the arbitral proceedings. Its Egyptian counsel sent various communications to the arbitrator, raising jurisdictional objections. The arbitrator made the following award.]

Since Zurich is the place of the arbitration, the procedure is governed by the ICC Rules and the Zurich Rules of Civil Procedure…. Since this arbitration was … commenced before 1 July 1985, it is still the former Zurich law (more particularly §§238-257 of the Zurich Rules of Civil Procedure as enacted on 13 June 1976) which governs. This is of practical importance mainly because of the necessity of a formally separate award on jurisdiction with a different type of appeal than against the award on the merits.

The decision on his own—disputed—jurisdiction is to be taken by the arbitrator himself. (§241 Zurich Rules of Civil Procedure and Article 8(3) ICC Rules.) [Section 241 of the Zurich Rules of Civil Procedure of 13 June 1976 reads: "The Court of Arbitration may rule on its own jurisdiction pursuant to Article III even when the validity of the arbitration agreement is contested."]

The arbitration clause invoked by claimant is contained in Article 14 of the Agreement … and reads as follows: "Any disputes and deviations which cannot be solved amicably between the parties shall be resolved and settled by arbitration under the rules of conciliation and arbitration of the International Chamber of Commerce, Zurich, Switzerland, in accordance with Swiss law of the Canton of Zurich." This clause could, in and of itself, give rise to a doubt inasmuch as it refers to the rules of conciliation and arbitration of the "International Chamber of Commerce, Zurich, Switzerland": the International Chamber of Commerce has its seat in Paris and there is no International Chamber of Commerce in Zurich.

For a correct construction of the clause, its background must be considered. The Agreement … was intimately connected with the main contract between claimant and the Egyptian [employer] of 26 March 1983 …; the latter formed an "integral part" of the former … and was, therefore known to both parties. The main contract contains, as Annex F, also an arbitration clause (which runs to one and a half pages). It provides for arbitration in Zurich with application of Swiss laws, but by an ad hoc arbitral tribunal of three members, the election of which is carefully described. Article 14 of the Agreement … which is relevant differs clearly in providing for "arbitration under the Rules of Conciliation and Arbitration of the International Chamber of Commerce, Zurich"; i.e., for institutional, rather than ad hoc arbitration, but it also refers to Swiss law "of the Canton of Zurich." The term "Rules of Conciliation and Arbitration" is generally used distinctively for the arbitration rules of the—only—International Chamber of Commerce (with seat in Paris), which is also widely known throughout the world for its arbitration organization. The rules of the local Zurich Chamber of Commerce are, on the other side, known as "rules of *mediation* and arbitration." Under these circumstances it must be concluded that the true meaning of the clause applicable here in an arbitration in Zurich under the ICC Rules with Swiss/Zurich law applicable to the substance of the case. This construction is concordant with at least one decision of a Zurich court and with other ICC cases, where similar clauses had been construed to refer to arbitrations taking place in Zurich under the Rules of the ICC (in Paris). The organization of the present arbitration … conforms exactly to the clause.

Defendant also appears to [argue] that the arbitration clause is deficient and violates Egyptian "*ordre public*" by not appointing the arbitrator itself. The exact argument …

[appears] obliquely in a copy of a request by defendant to [an] Egyptian Court…. There, defendant claims that the arbitration clause in case is invalid because it does not comply with Article 502(3) of the Egyptian Code of Civil Procedure, which provides that arbitrators should be appointed … in the agreement on arbitration….[21]

It is undoubtedly true that, in the present case, the arbitration clause did not nominate the arbitrator directly but only provided for ICC arbitration, and that the arbitrator was—pursuant to the ICC Rules—nominated by the ICC. This does not, however, make the arbitration clause invalid. It is not governed by Egyptian law, but by the *lex fori* of the arbitrator…. It may be noted that also under Article 22 of the Egyptian Civil Code … the law applicable to the arbitral procedure will be the law of the place where the arbitration is held. [Article 22 of the Egyptian Civil Code reads: "Principles of competence of courts and all questions of procedure are governed by the law of the country in which the action is brought, or in which the proceedings are taken."] Under the applicable procedural law (ICC Rules and Zurich Code of Civil Procedure in the 1976 version) it is self-evident that the agreement to arbitrate is binding even without nomination of the arbitrators by the parties in that agreement….

It should also be noted that on 26 April 1982 the Egyptian Cour de Cassation held that Article 502(3) of the Egyptian Code of Civil Procedure could not be used in the case of an agreement to arbitrate in England and that, furthermore, a foreign law which was different from Article 502(3) Egyptian Code of Civil Procedure would not violate public policy (and would therefore not be unenforceable in Egypt)….

Defendant's [claim] that the arbitration clause is invalid for not confirming to Article 502(3) of the Egyptian Code of Civil Procedure is, therefore, unfounded….

[B]y telex of 20 November 1985, Mr [A], on behalf of the defendant, informed the arbitrator that defendant had introduced an action to declare the arbitration clause void introduced at the [Egyptian court] and requested a suspension of the arbitration until a decision of that litigation in Egypt. By telex of 29 January 1987, Mr [B], on behalf of defendant, referred to a Court Order by the [Egyptian Court] ordering the holding of all arbitration procedures until a decision in a further procedure in the same court. No order of any Egyptian Court was actually ever notified or submitted to the arbitrator either directly or by either of the parties. This is, however, immaterial. As the arbitrator pointed out already in his telex of 21 November 1985 to Mr [A] (with copy to the claimant), court proceedings in Egypt did and do not have any direct influence on the present arbitration proceedings, since Egyptian Courts would not have jurisdiction of either these proceedings or the arbitrator. They certainly do not have any influence on the arbitrator's jurisdiction in the present case.

Based on the foregoing considerations, the result is that there is a valid arbitration agreement for ICC arbitration in Zurich and that, therefore, the arbitrator has jurisdiction….

21. Article 502(3) of the Egyptian Code of Civil Procedure reads:

"The arbitrator cannot be a minor (not possessing full legal capacity) or subject to curatorship or deprived from his civil rights as a result of criminal penalty or declared bankrupt unless he has his status restored. In case of plurality of arbitrators, their number should be in all cases uneven. Otherwise, the arbitration is null. Without prejudice to what is provided for in special laws, the appointment of the arbitrators has to be contained in the arbitration agreement or in a separate agreement." [Translation by Prof. Ahmed El-Kosheri.]

JUDGMENT OF 7 DECEMBER 1994, V 2000 v. PROJECT XJ 220 LTD
1996 Rev. arb. 245 (Paris Cour d'appel), aff'd, Judgment of 21 May 1997, Renault v. V 2000, 1997 Rev. arb. 537 (French Cour de cassation)

[During the course of 1989, Project XJ 220 ("Project"), an English company, planned to produce and market a new automobile (Jaguar XJ Type 220 limited edition), provided that at least 220 purchases were agreed. Jaguar France, a French company, agreed to use its French distribution network to market the new automobile in France. In January 1990, the fortuitously-named Philippe Renault signed an offer to purchase, titled "Application Form," in English for the benefit of Project, as well as a French translation made by Jaguar France of the terms and conditions applicable to the contract and appearing on the back of the application form. Renault committed himself to purchase a vehicle of the type XJ 220 at the price of roughly $500,000 on January 1, 1990, payable in three installments, with a price index adjustment. When Renault signed his application, he also paid roughly $100,000 by check, payable to the order of Jaguar France. On March 15, 1990, Renault was informed that his offer had been accepted and that the vehicle would be delivered within nine months. Renault later changed his mind and sought to cancel his order. He sued Project and Jaguar France before the Tribunal de Grande Instance of Paris to nullify the contract and obtain a refund of the amounts paid. Project and Jaguar France challenged the jurisdiction of that court by invoking the arbitration clause contained in Article 14 of the contract, which gave jurisdiction to an arbitrator appointed by the President of the Law Society in London in case of a dispute.

The first instance court dismissed the jurisdictional objection. It held that the Application Form was not binding because it was written in a foreign language, was almost illegible, and was neither signed nor initialed by Renault. It also held that the French translation of the Application Form was initialed by Renault and was a binding contract. Additionally, Renault had knowledge of Article 14, providing for arbitration in case of a dispute. However, the court also held that "the sale of the Jaguar XJ 220 vehicle does not involve the interests of international trade" and that "the arbitration clause of Article 14" was void. Project and Jaguar France appealed.]

Whereas under Article 1458 of the New Code of Civil Procedure ("NCCP"), applicable to both domestic arbitrations and international arbitration: "When a dispute referred to an arbitral tribunal in compliance with an arbitration agreement is brought before a state court, the latter must declare that it has no jurisdiction. If the arbitral tribunal is not yet seized, the court must also decline jurisdiction unless the arbitration agreement is manifestly null."

Whereas Renault argues precisely that the arbitration clause contained in Article 14 of the "Application Form" is void: [i] because it is a domestic arbitration and it is not a merchant, [ii] because he has not accepted it, [iii] due to the insufficient description of the arbitral procedure, [iv] because the dispute is not capable of arbitration under French domestic law and international public law as it involves the public policy regulation protecting consumers.

[Whereas,] the first instance judge considered that it could not be an international arbitration because "the purchase from a foreign company through a French company, exclusive importer of this foreign brands, of goods produced abroad, but in a limited edition, albeit expensive, but isolated by an individual who does not sell after having transformed or not, but intend it for personal use does not constitute an economic activity in an international meaning";

Considering that the resolution of the dispute indeed depends on the domestic or international nature of the arbitration;

Considering that the domestic or international nature of the arbitration derives exclusively from the nature of the economic transaction in question involving the interests of international trade, regardless of place of arbitration, the law applicable to the merits or the nationality of the parties to contract;

Considering in this case, that it is for the benefit of the English company Project that Renault signed an offer to purchase ...; that this offer has been accepted by it; that it is this company which would have built a vehicle in the United Kingdom which would have been then imported into France; that it is also with it that Renault has directly corresponded thereafter; [that] it is [Project] which received or should have received the final settlement price either paid directly by the client (2nd and 3rd installments) or advanced for commercial reasons by the company Jaguar France on behalf of latter (1st installment);

Whereas it may therefore be concluded that regardless of the legal role played by the company Jaguar France in the completion of the transaction, the contract signed, which provided a transfer of goods and money across borders, has involved the interests of international trade within the meaning of Article 1492 of the new Code of Civil Procedure;

[Whereas,] in the international order, the arbitration clause is lawful as such, pursuant to the general principal of autonomy of the arbitration agreement, substantive rule which gives it an own effectiveness regardless of the law applicable to the contract in which it is stipulated or the parties to this contract, subject to the only exception of international public policy;

Considering therefore that the mixed nature of the contract in which it appears is not likely to make it clearly void;

Considering further that in international relations, the arbitrators are the only one entitled to rule on their own jurisdiction, on the validity and the extent of their nomination; that they have in particular jurisdiction to decide on their own jurisdiction regarding to the arbitrability of the dispute with regard to international public policy, being observed that it is not excluded merely because a mandatory provision is applicable to the disputed legal relations, and that they also have the power to apply the principles and rules belonging to this public policy and to sanction under the control of the annulment judge its non-respect such as the one resulting from a breach of good faith which should govern the relations between international trading partners;

Considering that it follows that neither the possible applicability to the case of consumer protection rules, nor the allegation of fraud put forward by Renault against his contracting party(ies) are likely in themselves to exclude arbitral jurisdiction;

Considering finally that it is undisputed that Renault initialed the French translation of the terms and conditions of Project on the back of the application form and in particular page 4 where the arbitration clause at issue is reproduced clearly and legibly; that he therefore cannot seriously claim to have completely ignored it and the arbitrators are the only one to decide on the question whether the initials of a document which is not the agreement itself constitutes the necessary consent to their nomination;

Considering further that §1443 of the new Code of Civil Procedure, which provides the invalidity of an arbitration clause which does not provide a procedure for the nomination of arbitrators, does not apply to international arbitration;

Considering that the various grounds invoked by Mr. Philippe Renault to prevent the enforcement of the arbitration clause in its relations with Project are without force; that the said clause is not clearly void, but has on the contrary to be applied;...

Considering that Jaguar France, the rights of which were transferred to the company is V 2000, which Renault claims it is his contracting party, is directly interested in the dispute; that although it is not a signatory, it has been informed of the agreement at issue—which was translated on its initiative—and also of the existence of the arbitration clause which it claims itself to benefit;

But whereas in the law of international arbitration, the effects of the arbitration clause extends to the parties directly involved in the performance of the contract since their situation and their activities make assume the fact that they had knowledge of the existence and of the scope of the clause so that the arbitrator may decide on all economic and legal aspects of the dispute;

Considering that pursuant this rule, the appeal lodged by the company Jaguar France must be admitted; ...

Says that this court has no jurisdiction to hear the dispute between Renault and Project and Jaguar France and refers the parties to another authority....

SHIN-ETSU CHEMICAL CO. LTD v. AKSH OPTIFIBRE LTD
XXXI Y.B. Comm. Arb. 747 (2006) (Indian S.Ct. 2005)

[On November 16 and 18, 2000, Shin-Etsu Chemical Co. ("Shin-Etsu") and Aksh Optifibre Ltd ("Aksh") entered into a sale agreement ("the agreement") containing an arbitration clause providing for ICC arbitration in Tokyo, Japan. The clause also provided that the agreement was governed by the laws of Japan. Shin-Etsu terminated the agreement by letter dated December 31, 2002, and initiated arbitration proceedings in Japan. Aksh then initiated litigation in Indian courts seeking an injunction for cancellation of the agreement or a declaration that the agreement, including the arbitration clause, was void, inoperative and incapable of performance and could not be given effect. Shin-Etsu applied under §8 of the Indian Arbitration and Conciliation Act 1996 ("the Act") for an order that Aksh submit to the ongoing arbitration in Japan. The Indian trial court allowed Shin-Etsu's application and referred the parties to arbitration. Aksh challenged the order of the trial court, and the High Court set aside the decision of the trial court, holding that Art. 45 of the Act applied. Shin-Etsu appealed to the Supreme Court.]

Y.K. SABHARWAL, J., Dissenting. The interpretation of §45 of the Act falls for determination in this matter. Section 45 is as under:

> "45. *Power of judicial authority to refer parties to arbitration.* Notwithstanding anything contained in Part I or in the Code of Civil Procedure, 1908 (5 of 1908), a judicial authority, when seized of an action in a manner in respect of which the parties have made an agreement referred to in §44, shall, at the request of one of the parties or any person claiming through or under him, refer the parties to arbitration, unless it finds that the said agreement is null and void, inoperative or incapable of being performed."

The real question for consideration is as to the nature of adjudication that is contemplated by §45 when the objection about the agreement being "null and void, inoperative or incapable of being performed" is raised before a judicial authority. Should the judicial authority while exercising power under §45 decide the objection on a *prima facie* view of the matter and render a *prima facie* finding or a final finding on merits on affording parties such opportunity as the justice of the case may demand having regard to facts of the case?

The question is important and at the same time not free from difficulty. World over the opinion is divided. The courts in some of the countries have preferred the view that the adjudication should be *prima facie* so as to be raised again before the arbitral forum and others have preferred a final adjudication.

Under §45 of the Act, the judicial authority has to mandatorily refer the parties to arbitration, if conditions specified in the section are fulfilled and the agreement is not found to be null and void, inoperative or incapable of being performed…. The 1996 Act was enacted considering the international scenario as is evident from its preamble…:

> "WHEREAS the United Nations Commission on International Trade Law (UNCITRAL) has adopted the UNCITRAL Model Law on International Commercial Arbitration in 1985;
>
> AND WHEREAS the General Assembly of the United Nations has recommended that all countries give due consideration to the said Model Law, in view of the desirability of uniformity of the law of arbitral procedures and the specific needs of international commercial arbitration practice; …
>
> AND WHEREAS the said Model Law … make significant contribution to the establishment of a unified legal framework for the fair and efficient settlement of disputes arising in international commercial relations;
>
> AND WHEREAS it is expedient to make law respecting arbitration and conciliation, taking into account the aforesaid Model Law …"

[The dissenting Justice of the Indian Supreme Court referred to §8 of the Act, which provides for stays of litigation where an arbitration agreement provides for arbitration in India.] Under the Old Arbitration Act (§34 of the Arbitration Act, 1940), the court had discretion in the matter of grant of stay of legal proceedings where there was an arbitration agreement on being satisfied that the arbitration agreement exists factually and legally, and disputes between the parties are in regard to the matter agreed to be referred to arbitration. The court in exercise of its discretion could also decline an order of stay despite existence of the aforesaid conditions, depending upon the facts and circumstances of the case….

Section 8 of the Act is a departure from §34 of the old Act. Under [§8] the judicial authority has no discretion. It is mandatory for the judicial authority to refer the parties to arbitration on the existence of conditions stipulated in the section. Unlike §45, the judicial authority under §8 has not been conferred the power to refuse reference to arbitration on the ground of invalidity of the agreement. It is evident that the object is to avoid delay and accelerate reference to arbitration leaving the parties to raise objections, if any, to the validity of the arbitration agreement before the arbitral forum and/or post award under §34 of the Act….

Before this Court, learned counsel for the parties have rightly taken the stand that only §45 is applicable and §8 has no applicability. It is evident that there has been no adjudication of the application by the trial court in terms of §45 of the Act. The trial court has not gone into the question, *prima facie* or finally, as to the agreement being null and void, inoperative or incapable of being performed, which was the objection raised by the first respondent in reply to the application of the appellant. Thus, on the ingredients of §45, there was no adjudication. Therefore, the direction of the High Court for fresh adjudication of application of the appellant having regard to the provisions of §45 of the Act cannot be faulted. It is also necessary to issue directions for expeditious adjudication of the said application by the trial court but after first determining the scope of adjudication in exercise of power under §45.

[The] appellant ... contends that the consideration by the judicial authority under §45 has to be on a *prima facie* view of the matter based on examination of the plaint and any documents attached thereto, reply to the application for reference and any documents attached thereto and the affidavits filed by the parties. The court, on a *prima facie* examination of the pleadings and documents, should come to the conclusion as to whether the arbitration agreement is null or void, inoperative or incapable of being performed. Learned counsel submits that final determination on merits in some cases may even require recording of evidence and proceedings may turn out to be a full-fledged trial thereby defeating the very purpose for the enactment of the Act. It is urged that the final determination can be made if such objections are raised before the arbitral forum and/or post-award by the court.

On the other hand, ... the first respondent ... contends that §45 of the Act should be interpreted so as to give full effect to the opening non-obstante clause and the wordings of §45 which are entirely different from §8 in their effect and operation. It is urged that §45 cannot be construed in a way that it becomes indistinguishable from §8. It is further submitted that under §45, if an issue is raised before the court regarding the legality or validity of the agreement, then the court must give a finding on the issue. The contention is that the court would make an order of reference to arbitration only if the arbitration agreement is legal and valid....

Section 45 uses the expression "shall" in respect of referring the parties to arbitration, unless judicial authority finds that the said agreement is null and void, inoperative or incapable of being performed. The term "shall" in its ordinary significance is mandatory.... The words "shall" and "unless" appearing in §45 mandate that before referring the parties to arbitration, the judicial authority should be satisfied that the arbitration agreement is not null and void, inoperative or incapable of being performed.... Section 45 is clear; there is no doubt, ambiguity or vagueness in it.

[The dissenting Justice noted that the language of §45 of the Act is substantially the same as that of Article II(3) of the New York Convention.] Clearly §45 casts an obligation upon the judicial authority when seized of the matter to record a finding as to the validity of the arbitration agreement as stipulated in the section and there is nothing to suggest either from the language of the section or otherwise that the finding to be recorded is to be only *ex facie* or *prima facie*.

It is true that §5 limits judicial intervention in the manner provided therein. It accelerates the arbitral process by curtailing chances of delay that may be caused in court proceedings. But, at the same time, it is also clear that though §§8 and 45 both deal with the power of judicial authority to refer parties to arbitration, in the former which deals with domestic arbitration, no provision has been made for examining at that stage the validity of the arbitration agreement whereas under §45 which deals with arbitrations to which the New York Convention applies, a specific provision has been made to examine the validity of the arbitration agreement in the manner provided in §45.... Unlike §8 which provides that the application shall be moved not later than when submitting the first statement of the substance of the dispute, under §45 there is no such limitation. The apparent reason is that insofar as domestic arbitration is concerned, the legislature intended to achieve speedy reference of disputes to the arbitral tribunal and left most of the matters to be raised before the arbitrators or post-award. In case of foreign arbitration, however, in its wisdom the legislature left the question relating to the validity of the arbitration agreement being examined by the court. One of the main reasons for the departure being the heavy expense involved in such arbitrations which may be unnecessary if the arbitration agreement is to be invalidated in the manner prescribed in §45. In view of the aforesaid, adopting liberal approach and restricting the determination by judicial authority about validity of agreement only from *prima facie* angle, would amount to adding words to §45 without there being any ambiguity or vagueness therein.

The traditional approach has been to allow a court, where a dispute has been brought despite an arbitration agreement, to fully rule on the existence and validity of the arbitration agreement. This approach would ensure that the parties are not proceeding on an invalid agreement as this would be a fruitless exercise involving much time and expenditure. In some countries, however, the traditional approach has changed. The liberal approach which seems to be gaining increasing popularity in many legal systems both statutorily as well as through judicial interpretation is to restrict the review of validity of the arbitration agreement at a *prima facie* level. For final review the parties may raise issue before the arbitral forum or post-award....

The Geneva Protocol (Art. IV(1), the New York Convention (Art. II(3)) as well as the UNCITRAL Model Law (Art. 8), like §45 of the Act, have similarly ambiguous phraseology capable of either interpretation. It is true that the courts in ... Ontario and Hong Kong, both of which have based their law on the UNCITRAL Model Law (like India), have adopted a liberal approach to the issue.... It is clear from a plain reading of Hong Kong and English provisions that both confer discretion on the court, unlike §45 of the Act, which is mandatory. It is evident from the words "may" and "satisfied" used in the Hong Kong provision and also from the language used in §32 of the English Arbitration Act, 1996, that the intention in the said two jurisdictions was to confer on the court discretionary powers indicative of limited review from a *prima facie* point of view.... The American approach ... favors a traditional approach of final review of the court. [*See Comptek Telecomm v. IVD Corp.*, XXII Y.B. Comm. Arb. 905 and *SMG Swedish Machine Group v. Swedish Machine Group*, XVIII Y.B. Comm. Arb. 457 (N.D. Ill. 1970).]

It may be noted that both approaches have their own advantage and disadvantage. The approach whereby the court finally decides on merits on the issue of existence and validity of the arbitration agreement results in a certain degree of time and cost avoidance. It may prevent parties to wait for several months or in some cases years before knowing the final outcome of the dispute regarding jurisdiction. It will often take that long for the arbitrators and then the courts to reach their decisions. The same considerations of cost and time explain the position taken ... under §32(2) of the 1996 English Arbitration Act provides that the parties may agree (or, if the parties fail to agree, the arbitral tribunal may agree) that it would be more efficient to have the question resolved immediately by the courts.

I am of the view that Indian Legislature has consciously adopted a conventional approach so as to save the huge expense involved in international commercial arbitration as compared to domestic arbitration. In view of the aforesaid discussion, I am of the view that under §45 of the Act, the determination has to be on merits, final and binding and not *prima facie*....

Turning to the present case, I direct that the application filed by the appellant before the trial court would be treated as an application under §45 of the Act. Having regard to the nature of controversy in the present case, parties would be given opportunity to file documents and affidavits by way of evidence. No oral evidence would be examined.... [C]onsidering that the application has been pending for nearly two years, I direct its disposal within a period of two months....

Before concluding, this Court also deems it necessary to issue general directions for expeditious disposal of petitions/applications filed so as to challenge the validity of the arbitration agreement under §45. Ordinarily, such cases shall be decided on the basis of affidavits and other relevant documents and without oral evidence. There may, however, be few exceptional cases where it may become necessary to grant opportunity to the parties to lead oral evidence. In both eventualities, the judicial authority is required to decide the issue expeditiously within a fixed time-frame and not to treat such matters like regular civil suits. The object of arbitration including international commercial arbitration is expedition. The object of the Act would be defeated if international commercial disputes remain pending in court for months and years before even commencement of arbitration. Accordingly, I direct that any application that may be filed under §45 of the Act must be decided within three months of its filing. In rare and exceptional cases, the judicial authority may extend the time by another three months but by sending a report to the superior/Appellate Authority setting out the reasons for such extension....

B.N. SRIKRISHNA, J. I have had the benefit of carefully considering the erudite judgment delivered by my esteemed and learned Brother Sabharwal, J. Regretfully, I find myself in the unenviable position of having to disagree with the views expressed therein.... The core issue in this case is: Whether the finding of the court made under §45 of the Act that the arbitration agreement, falling within the definition of §44 of the Act, is or is not "null and void, inoperative or incapable of being performed" should be a final expression of the view of the court or should it be a *prima facie* view formed without a full-fledged trial?

The contrast in language between §§8 and 45 of the Act has been rightly noticed by my learned Brother. Section 8, which leaves no discretion in the court in the matter of referring parties to arbitration, does not apply to the present case, as we are concerned with Part II of the Act. On the other hand, §45 which is directly applicable to the present case, empowers the court to refuse a reference to arbitration if it "finds" that the arbitration agreement is "null and void, inoperative or incapable of being performed." ...

[N]o one can doubt that Part II of the 1996 Act is intended to opt for the international arbitration regime to meet the challenges of international trade and commerce, nor can it be doubted that §45 offers a greater discretion to the court for judicial intervention at the pre-reference stage. Despite all this, the question would still remain as to whether the discretion available for the court for interference, even under §45 of the Act, should be exercised on a *prima facie* view of the nature of the arbitral agreement or should it be on a final finding?

True, that there is nothing in §45 which suggests that the finding as to the nature of the arbitral agreement has to be *ex facie* or *prima facie*. In my view, however, this is an inescapable inference from an *ex visceribus* interpretation of the statute....

There are distinct advantages in veering to the view that §45 does not require a final determinative finding by the court. First, under the Rules of Arbitration of the [ICC], as in the present case, invariably the arbitral tribunal is vested with the power to rule upon its own jurisdiction. Even if the court takes the view that the arbitral agreement is not vitiated or that it is not invalid, inoperative or unenforceable, based upon purely *prima facie* view, nothing prevents the arbitrator from trying the issue fully and rendering a final decision thereupon. If the arbitrator finds the agreement valid, there is no problem as the arbitration will proceed and the award will be made. However, if the arbitrator finds the agreement invalid, inoperative or void, this means that the party who wanted to proceed for arbitration was given an opportunity of proceeding to arbitration, and the arbitrator after fully trying the issue has found that there is no scope for arbitration….

Treating the finding under §45 as final results in a paradoxical situation. A final decision rendered by the competent court on the nature of the arbitral agreement may have to be ignored by the arbitral tribunal, which would be entitled to decide the issue afresh on the material presented to it. It may also lead to another curious result, that the competent court in the jurisdiction where the arbitration proceeds (Japan, as in the present case) would have to reckon with the fully binding effect of a finding made under §45 by a competent court in India arrived at by following a summary procedure without admitting all relevant evidence….

[In cases where the arbitration agreement is governed by non-Indian law,] it would not only be unfeasible to prove foreign law exclusively through affidavits, but it would also entail enormous expenditure of time and money. [This is] exemplified in the U.S. case of *SMG Swedish Machine Group v. Swedish Machine Group*, [XVIII Y.B. Comm. Arb. 457 (1993) (N.D. Ill. 1991)]. In this case, it was held by the U.S. court that the validity or existence of the arbitration agreement would have to be conclusively determined by the court itself at the pre-award stage. The law applicable to the arbitration agreement was Swedish law and therefore the validity of the agreement had to be determined in accordance with this law. The court reviewed the Swedish law opinions submitted by both parties, but found them poorly documented. When parties submitted new opinions, these were found to be mutually contradictory. Finally, the court had to conduct a hearing where parties could provide proof of their true intentions as to the issues. Thus, similar difficulties, delays and costs may be encountered by the trial court in the present case if it has to give a final finding (after conducting a full-fledged trial) on the validity of the arbitration agreement at the pre-reference stage under §45.

On the other hand, if one were to take the view that the finding under §45 is only a *prima facie* view, then all these difficulties could be obviated. Neither the arbitral tribunal, nor the court enforcing the arbitral award may consider itself bound by the *prima facie* view expressed under §45 of the Act. The difficulty of having to *conclusively* prove the applicable foreign law at a trial would also be obviated….

The importance of carrying forward the objectives underlying the Model Law can hardly be gainsaid. There is evident dearth of guiding Indian precedent which might be useful in interpreting §45 of the Act. Hence, it becomes necessary to seek light from foreign judgments interpreting corresponding provisions that have been modelled on the Model Law. Now, for a survey of such foreign precedents.

It has rightly been noticed in the judgment of Brother Sabharwal, J. that different countries have approached the issue depending on their substantive and processual laws. It has been notice that the situation under the French Code of Civil Procedure favours a *prima facie* view, since under the Statute if the dispute is not before an arbitral tribunal, the French courts must decline jurisdiction unless the arbitration agreement is "patently void." Similarly, Art. 7 of the Swiss Private International Law Statute stipulates that the courts decline jurisdiction … "b. unless the court finds that the arbitral agreement is null and void, inoperative or incapable of being performed." This has been interpreted by the Swiss Federal Tribunal as restricting the court's review at the start of the proceedings to a *prima facie* verification of the existence and effectiveness of the arbitration clause. [*Fondation M. v. Banque X*, 1996 Bull. ASA 527 (Swiss Fed. Trib. 1996)]….

[I]n at least two common law jurisdictions, Ontario and Hong Kong, both of which have based their law on the Model Law (like India), the courts have adopted a "liberal approach" to the issue, namely that of *prima facie* view as to the existence and non-vitiation of the arbitral agreement before making a reference…. There is no doubt that in *Pacific Int'l Lines (Pte) Ltd v. Tsinlien Metals and Minerals Co. Ltd*, [XVIII Y.B. Comm. Arb. 180 (1993),] the High Court of Hong Kong was concerned precisely with the issue as to whether there was a valid arbitration agreement within the meaning of Art. 7 of the Model Law. The Court was of the view that there was a "plainly arguable" case to support the proposition that there was an arbitration agreement that complied with Art. 7 of the Model Law. The Court observed:

> "It follows, therefore, that if I am satisfied that there is a plainly arguable case to support the proposition and there was an arbitration agreement which complies with Art. 7 of the Model Law, I should proceed to appoint the arbitrator in the full knowledge that the defendants will not be precluded from raising the point before the arbitrator and having the matter reconsidered by the court consequent upon that preliminary ruling." …

[Citing *Rio Algom Ltd v. Sami Steel Ltd*, the Indian Supreme Court said that] the Ontario Court has clearly held that the court in the matter of interpretation of the existence and non-vitiation of the arbitral agreement has only a *prima facie* jurisdiction and is not required to render a final decision at that stage….

The suggestions made by learned Brother Sabharwal, J. to mollify some of the obvious drawbacks of the approach that he adopts, also need closer scrutiny. He has suggested a trial by affidavits as well as a fixed time-frame to reduce the possible delays ensuring from a protracted trial at the pre-reference stage. In my view, any attempt to mollify the significant adverse consequences of the determinative approach by enabling the court to render a final judgment only on the basis of affidavits, albeit within a fixed time-frame, may prove counter-productive.

There are several instances where affidavit evidence cannot aid in making a final determinative finding on the issue. For instance, where a defence taken is that the signature of a party was forged or that the agreement itself is entirely fabricated, I cannot conceive of the issue being satisfactorily determined fully and finally merely on the basis of affidavits without oral evidence. Correspondingly, if courts at the preliminary stage were to admit oral evidence, simply because forgery or the like is pleaded, the consequences are still troublesome. In fact, if the view postulated by learned Brother Sabharwal, J. were to prevail, then all international commercial arbitrations can be defeated by a totally bogus defence that the agreement is forged or fabricated. If such a defence were to be allowed, it would necessarily require a full-fledged trial (with oral evidence) at the pre-reference stage with all its consequential delay and expense. On the other hand, if only a *prima facie* view were to be taken, then the issue could still be examined in-depth after a full trial either before the arbitral tribunal or at any rate under §48(1)(a) when the enforceability of the ensuing award is questioned….

I fully agree with my learned Brother's view that the object of dispute resolution through arbitration, including international commercial arbitration, is expedition and that the object of the Act would be defeated if proceedings remain pending in court even after commencing of the arbitration. It is precisely for this reason that I am inclined to the view that at the pre-reference stage contemplated by §45, the court is required to take only a *prima facie* view for making the reference, leaving the parties to a full trial either before the arbitral tribunal or before the court at the post-award stage....

[A]s I have pointed out, adopting a final and determinative approach under §45 may not only prolong proceedings at the initial stage but also correspondingly increases costs and uncertainty for all the parties concerned. Finally, having regard to the structure of the Act, consequences arising from particular interpretations, judgments in other jurisdictions, as well as the opinion of learned authors on the subject, I am of the view that, the correct approach to be adopted under §45 at the pre-reference stage, is one of a *prima facie* finding by the trial court as to the validity or otherwise of the arbitration agreement....

BUCKEYE CHECK CASHING, INC. v. CARDEGNA
546 U.S. 440 (2006)

[excerpted above at pp. 201-05]

FIRST OPTIONS OF CHICAGO, INC. v. KAPLAN
514 U.S. 938 (1995)

JUSTICE BREYER. In this case we consider a question about how courts should review certain matters under the [FAA, including] how a district court should review an arbitrator's decision that the parties agreed to arbitrate a dispute....

The case concerns several related disputes between, on one side, First Options of Chicago, Inc., ..., on the other side, three parties: Manuel Kaplan; his wife Carol Kaplan; and his wholly owned investment company, MK Investments, Inc. (MKI), whose trading account First Options cleared. The disputes center around a "workout" agreement, embodied in four separate documents, which governs the "working out" of debts to First Options that MKI and the Kaplans incurred.... In 1989, after entering into the agreement, MKI lost an additional $1.5 million. First Options then took control of, and liquidated, certain MKI assets; demanded immediate payment of the entire MKI debt; and insisted that the Kaplans personally pay any deficiency. When its demands went unsatisfied, First Options sought arbitration....

MKI, having signed the only workout document (out of four) that contained an arbitration clause, accepted arbitration. The Kaplans, however, who had not personally signed that document, denied that their disagreement with First Options was arbitrable and filed written objections to that effect with the arbitration panel. The arbitrators decided that they had the power to rule on the merits of the parties' dispute, and did so in favor of First Options. The Kaplans then asked the Federal District Court to vacate the arbitration award, and First Options requested its confirmation. The court confirmed the award.... [O]n appeal the Court of Appeals for the Third Circuit agreed with the Kaplans that their dispute was not arbitrable; and it reversed the District Court's confirmation of the award against them. The Court of Appeals said that courts "should *independently* decide whether an arbitration panel has jurisdiction over the merits of any particular dispute." 19 F.3d at 1509 (emphasis added). First Options asked us to decide whether this is so (*i.e.*, whether courts, in "reviewing the arbitrators' decision on arbitrability," should "apply a *de novo* standard of review or the more deferential standard applied to arbitrators' decisions on the merits") when the objecting party submitted the issue to the arbitrators for decision.

The ... question—the standard of review applied to an arbitrator's decision about arbitrability—is a narrow one. To understand just how narrow, consider three types of disagreement present in this case. First, the Kaplans and First Options disagree about whether the Kaplans are personally liable for MKI's debt to First Options. That disagreement makes up the *merits* of the dispute. Second, they disagree about whether they agreed to arbitrate the merits. That disagreement is about the *arbitrability* of the dispute. Third, they disagree about *who should have the primary power to decide the second matter.* Does that power belong primarily to the arbitrators (because the court reviews their arbitrability decision deferentially) or to the court (because the court makes up its mind about arbitrability independently)? We consider here only this third question.

Although the question is a narrow one, it has a certain practical importance. That is because a party who has not agreed to arbitrate will normally have a right to a court's decision about the merits of its dispute (say, as here, its obligation under a contract). But, where the party has agreed to arbitrate, he or she, in effect, has relinquished much of that right's practical value. The party still can ask a court to review the arbitrator's decision, but the court will set that decision aside only in very unusual circumstances. *See, e.g.,* 9 U.S.C. §10 (award procured by corruption, fraud, or undue means; arbitrator exceeded his powers); *Wilko v. Swan,* 346 U.S. 427, 436-437 (1953) (parties bound by arbitrator's decision not in "manifest disregard" of the law), *overruled on other grounds, Rodriguez de Quijas v. Shearson/Am. Express, Inc.,* 490 U.S. 477 (1989). Hence, who—court or arbitrator—has the primary authority to decide whether a party has agreed to arbitrate can make a critical difference to a party resisting arbitration.

We believe the answer to the "who" question (*i.e.,* the standard-of-review question) is fairly simple. Just as the arbitrability of the merits of a dispute depends upon whether the parties agreed to arbitrate that dispute, *see, e.g., Mitsubishi Motors Corp. v. Soler Chrysler-Plymouth, Inc.,* 473 U.S. 614, 626 (1985), so the question "who has the primary power to decide arbitrability" turns upon what the parties agreed about *that* matter. Did the parties agree to submit the arbitrability question itself to arbitration? If so, then the court's standard in reviewing the arbitrator's decision about *that* matter should not differ from the standard courts apply when they review any other matter that parties have agreed to arbitrate. *AT&T Technologies, Inc. v. Communications Workers,* 475 U.S. 643, 649 (1986) (parties may agree to arbitrate arbitrability); *Steelworkers v. Warrior & Gulf Nav. Co.,* 363 U.S. 574, 583, n.7 (1960) (same). That is to say, the court should give considerable leeway to the arbitrator, setting aside his or her decision only in certain narrow circumstances. *See, e.g.,* 9 U.S.C. §10. If, on the other hand, the parties did *not* agree to submit the arbitrability question itself to arbitration, then the court should decide that question just as it would decide any other question that the parties did not submit to arbitration, namely independently. These two answers flow inexorably from the fact that arbitration is simply a matter of contract between the parties; it is a way to resolve those disputes—but only those disputes—that the parties have agreed to submit to arbitration.

We agree with First Options, therefore, that a court must defer to an arbitrator's arbitrability decision when the parties submitted that matter to arbitration. Nevertheless, that conclusion does not help First Options win this case. That is because a fair and complete answer to the standard-of-review question requires a word about how a court should decide whether the parties have agreed to submit the arbitrability issue to arbitration., that word makes clear that the Kaplans did not agree to arbitrate arbitrability here.

When deciding whether the parties agreed to arbitrate a certain matter (including arbitrability), courts generally (though with a qualification we discuss below) should apply ordinary state-law principles that govern the formation of contracts. The relevant state law here, for example, would require the court to see whether the parties objectively revealed an intent to submit the arbitrability issue to arbitration. *See, e.g., Estate of Jesmer v. Rohlev*, 609 N.E.2d 816, 820 (Ill. 1993) (law of state whose law governs the workout agreement); *Burkett v. Allstate Ins., Co.*, 534 A.2d 819, 823-824 (Pa. 1987) (law of the state where the Kaplans objected to arbitrability).

This Court, however, has (as we just said) added an important qualification, applicable when courts decide whether a party has agreed that arbitrators should decide arbitrability: Courts should not assume that the parties agreed to arbitrate arbitrability unless there is "clea[r] and unmistakabl[e]" evidence that they did so. *AT&T Technologies,* 475 U.S. at 649; *Warrior & Gulf,* 363 U.S. at 583, n.7. In this manner the law treats silence or ambiguity about the question "*who* (primarily) should decide arbitrability" differently from the way it treats silence or ambiguity about the question "*whether* a particular merits-related dispute is arbitrable because it is within the scope of a valid arbitration agreement"—for in respect to this latter question the law reverses the presumption. *See Mitsubishi,* 473 U.S. at 626 ("[A]ny doubts concerning the scope of arbitrable issues should be resolved in favor of arbitration").

But this difference in treatment is understandable. The latter question arises when the parties have a contract that provides for arbitration of some issues.... [G]iven the law's permissive policies in respect to arbitration, one can understand why the law would insist upon clarity before concluding that the parties did *not* want to arbitrate a related matter. On the other hand, the former question—the "who (primarily) should decide arbitrability" question—is rather arcane. A party often might not focus upon that question or upon the significance of having arbitrators decide the scope of their own powers. And, given the principle that a party can be forced to arbitrate only those issues it specifically has agreed to submit to arbitration, one can understand why courts might hesitate to interpret silence or ambiguity on the "who should decide arbitrability" point as giving the arbitrators that power, for doing so might too often force unwilling parties to arbitrate a matter they reasonably would have thought a judge, not an arbitrator, would decide.

On the record before us, First Options cannot show that the Kaplans clearly agreed to have the arbitrators decide *(i.e.,* to arbitrate) the question of arbitrability. First Options relies on the Kaplans' filing with the arbitrators a written memorandum objecting to the arbitrators' jurisdiction. But merely arguing the arbitrability issue to an arbitrator does not indicate a clear willingness to arbitrate that issue, *i.e.,* a willingness to be effectively bound by the arbitrator's decision on that point. To the contrary, insofar as the Kaplans were forcefully objecting to the arbitrators deciding their dispute with First Options, one naturally would think that they did *not* want the arbitrators to have binding authority over them. This conclusion draws added support from (1) an obvious explanation for the Kaplans' presence before the arbitrators (*i.e.,* that MKI, Mr. Kaplan's wholly owned firm, was arbitrating workout agreement matters); and (2) Third Circuit law that suggested [at the time] that the Kaplans might argue arbitrability to the arbitrators without losing their right to independent court review. *Teamsters v. Western Penn. Motor Carriers Ass'n*, 574 F.2d 783 (1978).

First Options makes several counterarguments: (1) that the Kaplans had other ways to get an independent court decision on the question of arbitrability without arguing the issue to the arbitrators (*e.g.*, by trying to enjoin the arbitration, or by refusing to participate in the arbitration, and then defending against a court petition First Options would have brought to compel arbitration, *see* 9 U.S.C. §4); (2) that permitting parties to argue arbitrability to an arbitrator without being bound by the result would cause delay and waste in the resolution of disputes; and (3) that the [FAA] therefore requires a presumption that the Kaplans agreed to be bound by the arbitrators' decision, not the contrary. The first of these points, however, while true, simply does not say anything about whether the Kaplans intended to be bound by the arbitrators' decision. The second point, too, is inconclusive, for factual circumstances vary too greatly to permit a confident conclusion about whether allowing the arbitrator to make an initial (but independently reviewable) arbitrability determination would, in general, slow down the dispute resolution process., the third point is legally erroneous, for there is no strong arbitration-related policy favoring First Options in respect to its particular argument here. After all, the basic objective in this area is not to resolve disputes in the quickest manner possible, no matter what the parties' wishes, but to ensure that commercial arbitration agreements, like other contracts, "'are enforced according to their terms,'" *Mastrobuono*, 514 U.S. at 1213, and according to the intentions of the parties, *Mitsubishi Motors*, 473 U.S. at 626. That policy favors the Kaplan, not First Options.

We conclude that, because the Kaplans did not clearly agree to submit the question of arbitrability to arbitration, the Court of Appeals was correct in finding that the arbitrability of the Kaplan/First Options dispute was subject to independent review by the courts....

BG GROUP PLC v. REPUBLIC OF ARGENTINA
134 S.Ct. 1198 (2014)

JUSTICE BREYER. Article 8 of an investment treaty between the United Kingdom and Argentina contains a dispute-resolution provision, applicable to disputes between one of those nations and an investor from the other. See Agreement for the Promotion and Protection of Investments, Art. 8(2), Dec. 11, 1990, 1765 U.N.T.S. 38 (hereinafter "Treaty"). The provision authorizes either party to submit a dispute "to the decision of the competent tribunal of the Contracting Party in whose territory the investment was made," *i.e.*, a local court. Art. 8(1). And it provides for arbitration

> "(i) where, after a period of eighteen months has elapsed from the moment when the dispute was submitted to the competent tribunal ..., the said tribunal has not given its final decision;
> [or] (ii) where the final decision of the aforementioned tribunal has been made but the Parties are still in dispute." Art. 8(2)(a).

The Treaty also entitles the parties to agree to proceed directly to arbitration. Art. 8(2)(b).

This case concerns the Treaty's arbitration clause, and specifically the local court litigation requirement set forth in Article 8(2)(a). The question before us is whether a court of the United States, in reviewing an arbitration award made under the Treaty, should interpret and apply the local litigation requirement *de novo*, or with the deference that courts ordinarily owe arbitration decisions. That is to say, who—court or arbitrator—bears primary responsibility for interpreting and applying the local litigation requirement to an underlying controversy? In our view, the matter is for the arbitrators, and courts must review their determinations with deference.

In the early 1990's, the petitioner, BG Group plc, a British firm, belonged to a consortium that bought a majority interest in an Argentine entity called MetroGAS. MetroGAS was a gas distribution company created by Argentine law in 1992, as a result of the government's privatization of its state-owned gas utility. Argentina distributed the utility's assets to new, private companies, one of which was MetroGAS. It awarded MetroGAS a 35year exclusive license to distribute natural gas in Buenos Aires, and it submitted a controlling interest in the company to international public tender. BG Group's consortium was the successful bidder. At about the same time, Argentina enacted statutes providing that its regulators would calculate gas "tariffs" in U.S. dollars, and that those tariffs would be set at levels sufficient to assure gas distribution firms, such as MetroGAS, a reasonable return.

In 2001 and 2002, Argentina, faced with an economic crisis, enacted new laws. Those laws changed the basis for calculating gas tariffs from dollars to pesos, at a rate of one peso per dollar. The exchange rate at the time was roughly three pesos to the dollar. The result was that MetroGAS' profits were quickly transformed into losses. BG Group believed that these changes (and several others) violated the Treaty; Argentina believed the contrary.

In 2003, BG Group, invoking Article 8 of the Treaty, sought arbitration. The parties appointed arbitrators; they agreed to site the arbitration in Washington, D.C.; and between 2004 and 2006, the arbitrators decided motions, received evidence, and conducted hearings. BG Group essentially claimed that Argentina's new laws and regulatory practices violated provisions in the Treaty forbidding the "expropriation" of investments and requiring that each nation give "fair and equitable treatment" to investors from the other. Argentina denied these claims, while also arguing that the arbitration tribunal lacked "jurisdiction" to hear the dispute. According to Argentina, the arbitrators lacked jurisdiction because: (1) BG Group was not a Treaty-protected "investor"; (2) BG Group's interest in MetroGAS was not a Treaty-protected "investment"; and (3) BG Group initiated arbitration without first litigating its claims in Argentina's courts, despite Article 8's requirement. In Argentina's view, "failure by BG to bring its grievance to Argentine courts for 18 months renders its claims in this arbitration inadmissible."

In late December 2007, [after deciding to consider and decide Argentina's jurisdictional objections together with the merits of the parties' dispute,] the arbitration panel reached a final decision. It began by determining that it had "jurisdiction" to consider the merits of the dispute. In support of that determination, the tribunal concluded that BG Group was an "investor," that its interest in MetroGAS amounted to a Treaty-protected "investment," and that Argentina's own conduct had waived, or excused, BG Group's failure to comply with Article 8's local litigation requirement. The panel pointed out that in 2002, the President of Argentina had issued a decree staying for 180 days the execution of its courts' final judgments (and injunctions) in suits claiming harm as a result of the new economic measures. In addition, Argentina had established a "renegotiation process" for public service contracts, such as its contract with MetroGAS, to alleviate the negative impact of the new economic measures. But Argentina had simultaneously barred from participation in that "process" firms that were litigating against Argentina in court or in arbitration. These measures, while not making litigation in Argentina's courts literally impossible, nonetheless "hindered" recourse "to the domestic judiciary" to the point where the Treaty implicitly excused compliance with the local litigation requirement. Requiring a private party in such circumstances to seek relief in Argentina's courts for 18 months, the panel concluded, would lead to "absurd and unreasonable result[s]."

On the merits, the arbitration panel agreed with Argentina that it had not "expropriate[d]" BG Group's investment, but also found that Argentina had denied BG Group "fair and equitable treatment." It awarded BG Group $185 million in damages.

In March 2008, both sides filed petitions for review in the District Court for the District of Columbia. BG Group sought to confirm the award under the New York Convention and the [FAA]. Argentina sought to vacate the award in part on the ground that the arbitrators lacked jurisdiction. See §10(a)(4) (a federal court may vacate an arbitral award "where the arbitrators exceeded their powers").

The District Court denied Argentina's claims and confirmed the award. But the Court of Appeals for the District of Columbia Circuit reversed. In the appeals court's view, the interpretation and application of Article 8's local litigation requirement was a matter for courts to decide *de novo, i.e.*, without deference to the views of the arbitrators. The Court of Appeals then went on to hold that the circumstances did not excuse BG Group's failure to comply with the requirement. Rather, BG Group must "commence a lawsuit in Argentina's courts and wait eighteen months before filing for arbitration." Because BG Group had not done so, the arbitrators lacked authority to decide the dispute. And the appeals court ordered the award vacated.

BG Group filed a petition for certiorari [*i.e.*, discretionary review]. Given the importance of the matter for international commercial arbitration, we granted the petition.

As we have said, the question before us is who—court or arbitrator—bears primary responsibility for interpreting and applying Article 8's local court litigation provision. Put in terms of standards of judicial review, should a United States court review the arbitrators' interpretation and application of the provision *de novo*, or with the deference that courts ordinarily show arbitral decisions on matters the parties have committed to arbitration? Compare, *e.g., First Options of Chicago, Inc. v. Kaplan*, 514 U.S. 938, 942 (1995) (example where a "court makes up its mind about [an issue] independently" because the parties did not agree it should be arbitrated), with *Oxford Health Plans LLC v. Sutter*, [133 S.Ct. 2064] (2013) (example where a court defers to arbitrators because the parties "'bargained for'" arbitral resolution of the question). See also *Hall Street Associates, LLC v. Mattel, Inc.*, 552 U.S. 576, 588 (2008) (on matters committed to arbitration, the [FAA] provides for "just the limited review needed to maintain arbitration's essential virtue of resolving disputes straightaway" and to prevent it from becoming "merely a prelude to a more cumbersome and time-consuming judicial review process").

In answering the question, we shall initially treat the document before us [*i.e.*, the U.K.-Argentina BIT] as if it were an ordinary contract between private parties. Were that so, we conclude, the matter would be for the arbitrators. We then ask whether the fact that the document in question is a treaty makes a critical difference. We conclude that it does not.

Where ordinary contracts are at issue, it is up to the parties to determine whether a particular matter is primarily for arbitrators or for courts to decide. See, *e.g., Steelworkers v. Warrior & Gulf Nav. Co.*, 363 U.S. 574, 582 (1960) ("[A]rbitration is a matter of contract and a party cannot be required to submit to arbitration any dispute which he has not agreed so to submit"). If the contract is silent on the matter of who primarily is to decide "threshold" questions about arbitration, courts determine the parties' intent with the help of presumptions.

On the one hand, courts presume that the parties intend courts, not arbitrators, to decide what we have called disputes about "arbitrability." These include questions such as "whether the parties are bound by a given arbitration clause," or "whether an arbitration clause in a concededly binding contract applies to a particular type of controversy." *Howsam v. Dean Witter Reynolds, Inc.*, 537 U.S. 79, 84 (2002). Accord, *Granite Rock Co. v. Teamsters*, 561 U.S. 287, 299-300 (2010) (disputes over "formation of the parties' arbitration agreement" and "its enforceability or applicability to the dispute" at issue are "matters … the court must resolve"); *First Options*, [514 U.S.] at 941, 943-947 (court should decide whether an arbitration clause applied to a party who "had not personally signed" the document containing it). See generally *AT&T Technologies, Inc. v. Communications Workers*, 475 U.S. 643, 649 (1986) ("Unless the parties clearly and unmistakably provide otherwise, the question of whether the parties agreed to arbitrate is to be decided by the court, not the arbitrator").

On the other hand, courts presume that the parties intend arbitrators, not courts, to decide disputes about the meaning and application of particular procedural preconditions for the use of arbitration. See *Howsam*, [537 U.S.] at 86 (courts assume parties "normally expect a forum-based decisionmaker to decide forum-specific *procedural* gateway matters" (emphasis added)). These procedural matters include claims of "waiver, delay, or a like defense to arbitrability." *Moses H. Cone Memorial Hospital v. Mercury Constr. Corp.*, 460 U.S. 1, 25 (1983). And they include the satisfaction of "'prerequisites such as time limits, notice, laches, estoppel, and other conditions precedent to an obligation to arbitrate.'" *Howsam*, [537 U.S.] at 85 (quoting the Revised Uniform Arbitration Act of 2000 §6, Comment 2, 7 U.L.A. 13 (Supp. 2002); emphasis deleted). See also §6(c) ("An arbitrator shall decide whether a condition precedent to arbitrability has been fulfilled"); §6, Comment 2 (explaining that this rule reflects "the holdings of the vast majority of state courts" and collecting cases).

The provision before us is of the latter, procedural, variety. The text and structure of the provision make clear that it operates as a procedural condition precedent to arbitration. It says that a dispute "shall be submitted to international arbitration" if "one of the Parties so requests," as long as "a period of eighteen months has elapsed" since the dispute was "submitted" to a local tribunal and the tribunal "has not given its final decision." It determines *when* the contractual duty to arbitrate arises, not *whether* there is a contractual duty to arbitrate at all. Neither does this language or other language in Article 8 give substantive weight to the local court's determinations on the matters at issue between the parties. To the contrary, Article 8 provides that *only* the "arbitration decision shall be final and binding on both Parties." The litigation provision is consequently a purely procedural requirement—a claims-processing rule that governs when the arbitration may begin, but not whether it may occur or what its substantive outcome will be on the issues in dispute. Moreover, the local litigation requirement is highly analogous to procedural provisions that both this Court and others have found are for arbitrators, not courts, primarily to interpret and to apply. See *Howsam*, [537 U.S.] at 85 (whether a party filed a notice of arbitration within the time limit provided by the rules of the chosen arbitral forum "is a matter presumptively for the arbitrator, not for the judge"); *John Wiley*, [376 U.S.] at 555-557 (same, in respect to a mandatory prearbitration grievance procedure that involved holding two conferences). See also *Dialysis Access Center, LLC v. RMS Lifeline, Inc.*, 638 F.3d 367, 383 (CA1 2011) (same, in respect to a prearbitration "good faith negotiations" requirement); *Lumbermens Mut. Cas. Co. v. Broadspire Management Servs., Inc.*, 623 F.3d 476, 481 (CA7 2010) (same, in respect to a prearbitration filing of a "Disagreement Notice").

Finally, as we later discuss in more detail, we can find nothing in Article 8 or elsewhere in the Treaty that might overcome the ordinary assumption. It nowhere demonstrates a contrary intent as to the delegation of decisional authority between judges and arbitrators. Thus, were the document an ordinary contract, it would call for arbitrators primarily to interpret and to apply the local litigation provision.

We now relax our ordinary contract assumption and ask whether the fact that the document before us is a treaty makes a critical difference to our analysis. The Solicitor General argues that it should. He says that the local litigation provision may be "a condition on the State's consent to enter into an arbitration agreement." He adds that courts should "review de novo the arbitral tribunal's resolution of objections based on an investor's non-compliance" with such a condition. And he recommends that we remand this case to the Court of Appeals to determine whether the court-exhaustion provision is such a condition.

We do not accept the Solicitor General's view as applied to the treaty before us. As a general matter, a treaty is a contract, though between nations. Its interpretation normally is, like a contract's interpretation, a matter of determining the parties' intent. *Air France v. Saks*, 470 U.S. 392, 399 (1985) (courts must give "the specific words of the treaty a meaning consistent with the shared expectations of the contracting parties"). And where, as here, a federal court is asked to interpret that intent pursuant to a motion to vacate or confirm an award made in the United States under the [FAA], it should normally apply the presumptions supplied by American law. See New York Convention, Art. V(1)(e) (award may be "set aside or suspended by a competent authority of the country in which, or under the law of which, that award was made"); Vandevelde, Bilateral Investment Treaties, at 446 (arbitral awards pursuant to treaties are "subject to review under the arbitration law of the state where the arbitration takes place");

The Solicitor General does not deny that the presumption discussed ... [above] (namely, the presumption that parties [to commercial contracts] intend procedural preconditions to arbitration to be resolved primarily by arbitrators), applies both to ordinary contracts and to similar provisions in treaties when those provisions are not also "conditions of consent." And, while we respect the Government's views about the proper interpretation of treaties, we have been unable to find any other authority or precedent suggesting that the use of the "consent" label in a treaty should make a critical difference in discerning the parties' intent about whether courts or arbitrators should interpret and apply the relevant provision.

We are willing to assume with the Solicitor General that the appearance of this label in a treaty can show that the parties, or one of them, thought the designated matter quite important. But that is unlikely to be conclusive. For parties often submit important matters to arbitration. And the word "consent" could be attached to a highly procedural precondition to arbitration, such as a waiting period of several months, which the parties are unlikely to have intended that courts apply without saying so. See, *e.g.*, Agreement on Encouragement and Reciprocal Protection of Investments, Art. 9, Netherlands-Slovenia, Sept. 24, 1996, Netherlands T.S. No. 296 ("Each Contracting Party hereby consents to submit any dispute ... which they can not [sic] solve amicably within three months ... to the International

Center for Settlement of Disputes for settlement by conciliation or arbitration"), online at www.rijksoverheid.nl/documenten-en-publicaties/besluiten/2006/10/17/slovenia.html (all Internet materials as visited on Feb. 28, 2014, and available in Clerk of Court's case file); Agreement for the Promotion and Protection of Investments, Art. 8(1), United King-dom-Egypt, June 11, 1975, 14 I.L.M. 1472 ("Each Contracting Party hereby consents to submit" a dispute to arbitration if "agreement cannot be reached within three months be-tween the parties"). While we leave the matter open for future argument, we do not now see why the presence of the term "consent" in a treaty warrants abandoning, or increasing the complexity of, our ordinary intent-determining framework. See *Howsam*, 537 U.S. at 83-85; *First Options*, 514 U.S. at 942-945; *John Wiley*, 376 U.S. at 546-549, 555-559.

In any event, the treaty before us does *not* state that the local litigation requirement is a "condition of consent" to arbitration. Thus, we need not, and do not, go beyond holding that, in the absence of explicit language in a treaty demonstrating that the parties intended a different delegation of authority, our ordinary interpretive framework applies. We leave for another day the question of interpreting treaties that refer to "conditions of consent" ex-plicitly. *See, e.g.,* U.S.-Korea Free Trade Agreement, Art. 11(18) (provision entitled "Conditions and Limitations on Consent of Each Party" and providing that "[n]o claim may be submitted to arbitration under this Section" unless the claimant waives in writing "any right" to press his claim before an "administrative tribunal or court"), available at www.ustr.gov/trade-agreements; North American Free Trade Agreement, Arts. 1121-1122, available at www.nafta-sec-alena.org (providing that each party's "[c]onsent to [a]rbitration" is conditioned on fulfillment of certain "procedures," one of which is a waiver by an investor of his right to litigate the claim being arbitrated). *See also* 2012 U.S. Model BIT, Art. 26 (entitled "Conditions and Limitations on Consent of Each Party"), available at www.state.gov/e/eb/ifd/bit. And we apply our ordinary presumption that the interpretation and application of procedural provisions such as the provision before us are primarily for the arbitrators.

A treaty may contain evidence that shows the parties had an intent contrary to our or-dinary presumptions about who should decide threshold issues related to arbitration. But the treaty before us does not show any such contrary intention. We concede that the local litigation requirement appears in ¶(1) of Article 8, while the Article does not mention ar-bitration until the subsequent paragraph, ¶(2). Moreover, a requirement that a party exhaust its remedies in a country's domestic courts before seeking to arbitrate may seem particu-larly important to a country offering protections to foreign investors. And the placing of an important matter prior to any mention of arbitration at least arguably suggests an intent by Argentina, the United Kingdom, or both, to have courts rather than arbitrators apply the litigation requirement.

These considerations, however, are outweighed by others. As discussed above, the text and structure of the litigation requirement set forth in Article 8 make clear that it is a pro-cedural condition precedent to arbitration—a sequential step that a party must follow be-fore giving notice of arbitration. The Treaty nowhere says that the provision is to operate as a substantive condition on the formation of the arbitration contract, or that it is a matter of such elevated importance that it is to be decided by courts. International arbitrators are likely more familiar than are judges with the expectations of foreign investors and recipient nations regarding the operation of the provision. See *Howsam*, [537 U.S.] at 85 (com-parative institutional expertise a factor in determining parties' likely intent). And the Treaty itself authorizes the use of international arbitration associations, the rules of which provide that arbitrators shall have the authority to interpret provisions of this kind. Art. 8(3) (providing that the parties may refer a dispute to the International Centre for the [sic] Settlement of Investment Disputes (ICSID) or to arbitrators appointed pursuant to the [UNCITRAL] arbitration rules); UNCITRAL Arbitration Rules, Art. 23(1) (rev. 2010 ed.) ("[A]rbitral tribunal shall have the power to rule on its own jurisdiction"); ICSID Convention, Regulations and Rules, Art. 41(1) (2006 ed.) ("Tribunal shall be the judge of its own competence"). Cf. *Howsam*, [537 U.S.] at 85 (giving weight to the parties' incorporation of the National Association of Securities Dealers' Code of Arbitration into their contract, which provided for similar arbitral authority, as evidence that they intended arbitrators to "interpret and apply the NASD time limit rule").

The upshot is that our ordinary presumption applies and it is not overcome. The interpretation and application of the local litigation provision is primarily for the arbitrators. Reviewing courts cannot review their decision *de novo*. Rather, they must do so with considerable deference.

The dissent interprets Article 8's local litigation provision differently. In its view, the provision sets forth not a condition precedent to arbitration in an already-binding arbitration contract (normally a matter for arbitrators to interpret), but a substantive condition on Argentina's consent to arbitration and thus on the contract's formation in the first place (normally something for courts to interpret). It reads the whole of Article 8 as a "unilateral standing offer" to arbitrate that Argentina and the United Kingdom each extends to investors of the other country. And it says that the local litigation requirement is one of the essential "'terms in which the offer was made.'"

While it is possible to read the provision in this way, doing so is not consistent with our case law interpreting similar provisions appearing in ordinary arbitration contracts. Consequently, interpreting the provision in such a manner would require us to treat treaties as warranting a different kind of analysis. And the dissent does so without supplying any different set of general principles that might guide that analysis. That is a matter of some concern in a world where foreign investment and related arbitration treaties increasingly matter.

Even were we to ignore our ordinary contract principles, however, we would not take the dissent's view. As we have explained, the local litigation provision on its face concerns arbitration's timing, not the Treaty's effective date; or whom its arbitration clause binds; or whether that arbitration clause covers a certain kind of dispute. Cf. *Granite Rock*, 561 U.S., at 296-303 (ratification date); *First Options*, 514 U.S., at 941, 943-947 (parties); *AT&T Technologies*, 475 U.S., at 651 (kind of dispute). The dissent points out that Article 8(2)(a) "does not simply require the parties to wait for 18 months before proceeding to arbitration," but instructs them to *do* something—to "submit their claims for adjudication." That is correct. But the something they must do has no direct impact on the resolution of their dispute, for as we previously pointed out, Article 8 provides that only the decision of the arbitrators (who need not give weight to the local court's decision) will be "final and binding." Art. 8(4). The provision, at base, is a claims-processing rule. And the dissent's efforts to imbue it with greater significance fall short.

The treatises to which the dissent refers also fail to support its position. Those authorities primarily describe how an offer to arbitrate in an investment treaty can be accepted, such as through an investor's filing of a notice of arbitration. *See* J. Salacuse, *The Law of*

Investment Treaties 381 (2010); Schreuer, *Consent to Arbitration*, in *The Oxford Handbook of International Investment Law* 830, 836-837 (P. Muchlinski, F. Ortino, & C. Schreuer eds. 2008). They do not endorse the dissent's reading of the local litigation provision or of provisions like it. To the contrary, the bulk of international authority supports our view that the provision functions as a purely procedural precondition to arbitrate. *See* 1 G. Born, *International Commercial Arbitration* 842 (2009) ("A substantial body of arbitral authority from investor-state disputes concludes that compliance with procedural mechanisms in an arbitration agreement (or bilateral investment treaty) is not ordinarily a jurisdictional pre-requisite")…. *See also* Schreuer, *Consent to Arbitration*, [in P. Muchlinski, F. Ortino, & C. Schreuer (eds.), *The Oxford Handbook of International Investment Law* 830, 846-848 (2008)] ("clauses of this kind … creat[e] a considerable burden to the party seeking arbitration with little chance of advancing the settlement of the dispute," and "the most likely effect of a clause of this kind is delay and additional cost").

In sum, we agree with the dissent that a sovereign's consent to arbitration is important. We also agree that sovereigns can condition their consent to arbitrate by writing various terms into their bilateral investment treaties. But that is not the issue. The question is whether the parties intended to give courts or arbitrators primary authority to interpret and apply a threshold provision in an arbitration contract—when the contract is silent as to the delegation of authority. We have already explained why we believe that where, as here, the provision resembles a claims-processing requirement and is not a requirement that affects the arbitration contract's validity or scope, we presume that the parties (even if they are sovereigns) intended to give that authority to the arbitrators.

Argentina correctly argues that it is nonetheless entitled to court review of the arbitrators' decision to excuse BG Group's noncompliance with the litigation requirement, and to take jurisdiction over the dispute. It asks us to provide that review, and it argues that even if the proper standard is "a [h]ighly [d]eferential" one, it should still prevail. Having the relevant materials before us, we shall provide that review. But we cannot agree with Argentina that the arbitrators "'exceeded their powers'" in concluding they had jurisdiction.

The arbitration panel made three relevant determinations: (1) "As a matter of treaty interpretation," the local litigation provision "cannot be construed as an absolute impediment to arbitration,"; (2) Argentina enacted laws that "hindered" "recourse to the domestic judiciary" by those "whose rights were allegedly affected by the emergency measures,"; that sought "to prevent any judicial interference with the emergency legislation,"; and that "excluded from the renegotiation process" for public service contracts "any licensee seeking judicial redress,"; (3) under these circumstances, it would be "absurd and unreasonable" to read Article 8 as requiring an investor to bring its grievance to a domestic court before arbitrating.

The first determination lies well within the arbitrators' interpretive authority. Construing the local litigation provision as an "absolute" requirement would mean Argentina could avoid arbitration by, say, passing a law that closed down its court system indefinitely or that prohibited investors from using its courts. Such an interpretation runs contrary to a basic objective of the investment treaty. Nor does Argentina argue for an absolute interpretation.

As to the second determination, Argentina does not argue that the facts set forth by the arbitrators are incorrect. Thus, we accept them as valid.

The third determination is more controversial. Argentina argues that neither the 180-day suspension of courts' issuances of final judgments nor its refusal to allow litigants (and those in arbitration) to use its contract renegotiation process, taken separately or together, warrants suspending or waiving the local litigation requirement. We would not necessarily characterize these actions as rendering a domestic court-exhaustion requirement "absurd and unreasonable," but at the same time we cannot say that the arbitrators' conclusions are barred by the Treaty. The arbitrators did not "'stra[y] from interpretation and application of the agreement'" or otherwise "'effectively "dispens[e]"'" their "'own brand of . . . justice.'" *Stolt-Nielsen SA v. AnimalFeeds Int'l Corp.*, 559 U.S. 662, 671 (2010) (providing that it is only when an arbitrator engages in such activity that "'his decision may be unenforceable'").

Consequently, we conclude that the arbitrators' jurisdictional determinations are lawful. The judgment of the Court of Appeals to the contrary is reversed. . . .

CHIEF JUSTICE ROBERTS, with whom JUSTICE KENNEDY joins, Dissenting. The Court begins by deciding a different case, "initially treat[ing] the document before us as if it were an ordinary contract between private parties." The "document before us," of course, is nothing of the sort. It is instead a treaty between two sovereign nations: the United Kingdom and Argentina. No investor is a party to the agreement. Having elided this rather important fact for much of its analysis, the majority finally "relax[es] [its] ordinary contract assumption and ask[s] whether the fact that the document before us is a treaty makes a critical difference to [its] analysis." It should come as no surprise that, after starting down the wrong road, the majority ends up at the wrong place.

I would start with the document that *is* before us and take it on its own terms. That document is a bilateral investment treaty between the United Kingdom and Argentina, in which Argentina agreed to take steps to encourage U.K. investors to invest within its borders (and the United Kingdom agreed to do the same with respect to Argentine investors). The Treaty does indeed contain a completed agreement for arbitration—between the signatory countries. The Treaty also includes, in Article 8, certain provisions for resolving any disputes that might arise between a signatory country and an investor, who is not a party to the agreement.

One such provision—completely ignored by the Court in its analysis—specifies that disputes may be resolved by arbitration when the host country and an investor "have so agreed." No one doubts that, as is the normal rule, whether there was such an agreement is for a court, not an arbitrator, to decide. See *First Options of Chicago, Inc. v. Kaplan*, 514 U.S. 938, 943-945 (1995).

When there is no express agreement between the host country and an investor, they must form an agreement in another way, before an obligation to arbitrate arises. The Treaty by itself cannot constitute an agreement to arbitrate with an investor. How could it? No investor is a party to that Treaty. Something else must happen to *create* an agreement where there was none before. Article 8(2)(a) makes clear what that something is: An investor must submit his dispute to the courts of the host country. After 18 months, or an unsatisfactory decision, the investor may then request arbitration.

Submitting the dispute to the courts is thus a condition to the formation of an agreement, not simply a matter of performing an existing agreement. Article 8(2)(a) constitutes in effect a unilateral *offer* to arbitrate, which an investor may accept by complying with its terms. To be sure, the local litigation requirement might not be absolute. In particular, an investor might argue that it was an implicit aspect of the unilateral offer that he be afforded a reasonable opportunity to submit his dispute to the local courts. Even then, however, the question would remain whether the investor has managed to form an arbitration agreement with the host country pursuant to Article 8(2)(a). That question under Article 8(2)(a) is—like the same question under Article 8(2)(b)—for a court, not an arbitrator, to decide. I respectfully dissent from the Court's contrary conclusion.

The majority acknowledges—but fails to heed—"the first principle that underscores all of our arbitration decisions: Arbitration is strictly 'a matter of consent.'" *Granite Rock Co. v. Teamsters*, 561 U.S. 287, 299 (2010) (quoting *Volt Information Sciences, Inc. v. Board of Trustees of Leland Stanford Junior Univ.*, 489 U.S. 468, 479 (1989)).... We have accordingly held that arbitration "is a way to resolve those disputes—but only those disputes—that the parties have agreed to submit to arbitration." *First Options of Chicago, Inc.*, [514 U.S.] at 943. The same "first principle" underlies arbitration pursuant to bilateral investment treaties. So only if Argentina agreed with BG Group to have an arbitrator resolve their dispute did the arbitrator in this case have any authority over the parties.

The majority opinion nowhere explains when and how Argentina agreed *with BG Group* to submit to arbitration. Instead, the majority seems to assume that, in agreeing with the United Kingdom to adopt Article 8 along with the rest of the Treaty, Argentina thereby formed an agreement with all potential U.K. investors (including BG Group) to submit all investment-related disputes to arbitration. That misunderstands Article 8 and trivializes the significance to a sovereign nation of subjecting itself to arbitration anywhere in the world, solely at the option of private parties.

The majority focuses throughout its opinion on what it calls the Treaty's "arbitration clause," but that provision does not stand alone. Rather, it is only part— and a subordinate part at that—of a broader dispute resolution provision. Article 8 is thus entitled "Settlement of Disputes Between an Investor and the Host State," and it opens without so much as mentioning arbitration. Instead it initially directs any disputing investor and signatory country (what the Treaty calls a "Contracting Party") to court. When "an investor of one Contracting Party and the other Contracting Party" have an investment-related dispute that has "not been amicably settled," the Treaty commands that the dispute "*shall be submitted*, at the request of one of the Parties to the dispute, to the decision of the competent tribunal of the Contracting Party in whose territory the investment was made." This provision could not be clearer: Before taking any other steps, an aggrieved investor must submit its dispute with a Contracting Party to that Contracting Party's own courts.

There are two routes to arbitration in Article 8(2)(a), and each passes through a Contracting Party's domestic courts. That is, the Treaty's arbitration provisions in Article 8(2)(a) presuppose that the parties have complied with the local litigation provision in Article 8(1). Specifically, a party may request arbitration only (1) "after a period of eighteen months has elapsed from the moment when the dispute was submitted to the competent tribunal of the Contracting Party in whose territory the investment was made" and "the said tribunal has not given its final decision," or (2) "where the final decision of the aforementioned tribunal has been made but the Parties are still in dispute." Either way, the obligation to arbitrate does not arise until the Contracting Party's courts have had a first crack at the dispute.

Article 8 provides a third route to arbitration in paragraph 8(2)(b)—namely, "where the Contracting Party and the investor of the other Contracting Party have so agreed." In contrast to the two routes in Article 8(2)(a), this one does not refer to the local litigation provision. That omission is significant. It makes clear that an investor can bypass local litigation only by obtaining the Contracting Party's explicit agreement to proceed directly to arbitration. Short of that, an investor has no choice but to litigate in the Contracting Party's courts for at least some period.

The structure of Article 8 confirms that the routes to arbitration in paragraph (2)(a) are just as much about eliciting a Contracting Party's consent to arbitrate as the route in paragraph 8(2)(b). Under Article 8(2)(b), the requisite consent is demonstrated by a specific agreement. Under Article 8(2)(a), the requisite consent is demonstrated by compliance with the requirement to resort to a country's local courts. Whereas Article 8(2)(a) is part of a completed *agreement* between Argentina and the United Kingdom, it constitutes only a unilateral standing *offer* by Argentina with respect to U.K. investors—an offer to submit to arbitration where certain conditions are met....

An offer must be accepted for a legally binding contract to be formed. And it is an "undeniable principle of the law of contracts, that an offer ... by one person to another, imposes no obligation upon the former, until it is accepted by the latter, *according to the terms in which the offer was made*. Any qualification of, or departure from, those terms, invalidates the offer." *Eliason v. Henshaw*, 4 Wheat. 225, 228 (1819) (emphasis added). This principle applies to international arbitration agreements just as it does to domestic commercial contracts.

By incorporating the local litigation provision in Article 8(1), paragraph 8(2)(a) establishes that provision as a term of Argentina's unilateral offer to arbitrate. To accept Argentina's offer, an investor must therefore first litigate its dispute in Argentina's courts—either to a "final decision" or for 18 months, whichever comes first. Unless the investor does so (or, perhaps, establishes a valid excuse for failing to do so, as discussed below), it has not accepted the terms of Argentina's offer to arbitrate, and thus has not formed an arbitration agreement with Argentina.[22]

Although the majority suggests that the local litigation requirement would not be a "condition of consent" even if the Treaty explicitly called it one, the Court's holding is limited to treaties that contain no such clear statement. But there is no reason to think that such a clear statement should be required, for we generally do not require "talismanic words" in treaties. *Medellín v. Texas*, 552 U.S. 491, 521 (2008). Indeed, another arbitral tribunal concluded that the local litigation requirement was a condition on Argentina's consent to arbitrate despite the absence of the sort of clear statement apparently contemplated by the majority. See *ICS Inspection & Control Servs. Ltd. v. Argentine Republic*, PCA Case No. 2010-9, Award on Jurisdiction, ¶262 (Feb. 10, 2012). Still other tribunals have reached the same conclusion with regard to similar litigation requirements in other Argentine bilateral investment treaties. See *Daimler Financial Servs. AG v. Argentine Republic*, ICSID Case No. ARB/05/1, Award, ¶¶193, 194 (Aug. 22, 2012); *Wintershall Aktiengesellschaft v. Argentine Republic*, ICSID Case No. ARB/04/14, Award, ¶116 (Dec. 8, 2008).

In the face of this authority, the majority quotes a treatise for the proposition that "'[a] substantial body of arbitral authority from investor-state disputes concludes that compliance with procedural mechanisms in an arbitration agreement (or bilateral investment

---

22. To be clear, the only question is whether BG Group formed an *arbitration* agreement with Argentina. To say that BG Group never formed such an agreement is not to call into question the validity of its various commercial agreements with Argentina.

treaty) is not ordinarily a jurisdictional prerequisite.'" *Ante,* at 16 (quoting 1 G. Born, *International Commercial Arbitration* 842 (2009)). But that simply restates the question. The whole issue is whether the local litigation requirement is a mere "procedural mechanism" or instead a condition on Argentina's consent to arbitrate.

BG Group concedes that other terms of Article 8(1) constitute conditions on Argentina's consent to arbitrate, even though they are not expressly labeled as such. The Court does not explain why the *only other term*—the litigation requirement—should be viewed differently.

Nor does the majority's reading accord with ordinary contract law, which treats language such as the word "after" in Article 8(2)(a)(i) as creating conditions, even though such language may not constitute a "clear statement." The majority seems to regard the local litigation requirement as a condition precedent to *performance* of the contract, rather than a condition precedent to *formation* of the contract. But that cannot be. Prior to the fulfillment of the local litigation requirement, there was no contract between Argentina *and BG Group* to be performed. The Treaty is not such an agreement, since BG Group is of course not a party to the Treaty. Neither the majority nor BG Group contends that the agreement is under Article 8(2)(b), the provision that applies "where the Contracting Party and the investor of the other Contracting Party have so agreed." An arbitration agreement must be *formed*, and Article 8(2)(a) spells out how an investor may do that: by submitting the dispute to local courts for 18 months or until a decision is rendered.

Moreover, the Treaty's local litigation requirement certainly does not resemble "time limits, notice, laches, estoppel," or the other kinds of provisions that are typically treated as conditions on the performance of an arbitration agreement, rather than prerequisites to formation. Revised Uniform Arbitration Act of 2000 §6(c), Comment 2, 7 U.L.A. 26 (2009). Unlike a time limit for submitting a claim to arbitration, see *Howsam v. Dean Witter Reynolds, Inc.*, 537 U.S. 79, 85 (2002), the litigation requirement does not simply regulate the timing of arbitration. As the majority recognizes, ... the provision does not simply require the parties to wait for 18 months before proceeding to arbitration, but instead requires them to submit their claims for adjudication during that period. And unlike a mandatory pre-arbitration grievance procedure, the litigation requirement sends the parties to court—and not just any court, but a court of the host country.

The law of international arbitration and domestic contract law lead to the same conclusion: Because paragraph (2)(a) of Article 8 constitutes only a unilateral standing offer by the Contracting Parties to each other's investors to submit to arbitration under certain conditions, an investor cannot form an arbitration agreement with a Contracting Party under the Treaty until the investor accepts the actual terms of the Contracting Party's offer. Absent a valid excuse, that means litigating its dispute in the Contracting Party's courts to a "final decision" or, barring that, for at least 18 months.

The nature of the obligations a sovereign incurs in agreeing to arbitrate with a private party confirms that the local litigation requirement is a condition on a signatory country's consent to arbitrate, and not merely a condition on performance of a pre-existing arbitration agreement. There are good reasons for any sovereign to condition its consent to arbitrate disputes on investors' first litigating their claims in the country's own courts for a specified period. It is no trifling matter for a sovereign nation to subject itself to suit by private parties; we do not presume that any country—including our own—takes that step lightly. Cf. *United States v. Bormes*, [133 S.Ct. 12] (2012) (Congress must "unequivocally express[]" its intent to waive the sovereign immunity of the United States (quoting *United States v. Nordic Village, Inc.*, 503 U.S. 30, 33 (1992)). But even where a sovereign nation has subjected itself to suit in its own courts, it is quite another thing for it to subject itself to international arbitration. Indeed, "[g]ranting a private party the right to bring an action against a sovereign state in an international tribunal regarding an investment dispute is a revolutionary innovation" whose "uniqueness and power should not be overlooked." That is so because of both the procedure and substance of investor-state arbitration.

Procedurally, paragraph (3) of Article 8 designates the [UNCITRAL] Arbitration Rules ... as the default rules governing the arbitration. Those rules authorize the Secretary-General of the Permanent Court of Arbitration at The Hague to designate an "appointing authority" who—absent agreement by the parties—can select the sole arbitrator (or, in the case of a three-member tribunal, the presiding arbitrator, where the arbitrators nominated by each of the parties cannot agree on a presiding arbitrator). The arbitrators, in turn, select the site of the arbitration (again, absent an agreement by the parties) and enjoy broad discretion in conducting the proceedings.

Substantively, by acquiescing to arbitration, a state permits private adjudicators to review its public policies and effectively annul the authoritative acts of its legislature, executive, and judiciary. Under Article 8, a Contracting Party grants to private adjudicators not necessarily of its own choosing, who can meet literally anywhere in the world, a power it typically reserves to its own courts, if it grants it at all: the power to sit in judgment on its sovereign acts. Given these stakes, one would expect the United Kingdom and Argentina to have taken particular care in specifying the limited circumstances in which foreign investors can trigger the Treaty's arbitration process. And that is precisely what they did in Article 8(2)(a), requiring investors to afford a country's own courts an initial opportunity to review the country's enactments and assess the country's compliance with its international obligations. Contrast this with Article 9, which provides for arbitration between the signatory countries of disputes under the Treaty without any preconditions. Argentina and the United Kingdom considered arbitration with particular foreign investors to be different in kind and to require special limitations on its use.

The majority regards the local litigation requirement as toothless simply because the Treaty does not require an arbitrator to "give substantive weight to the local court's determinations on the matters at issue between the parties." While it is true that an arbitrator need not defer to an Argentine court's judgment in an investor dispute, that does not deprive the litigation requirement of practical import. Most significant, the Treaty provides that an "arbitral tribunal shall decide the dispute in accordance with ... the laws of the Contracting Party involved in the dispute." I doubt that a tribunal would give no weight to an Argentine court's authoritative construction of Argentine law, rendered in the same dispute, just because it might not be formally bound to adopt that interpretation.

The local litigation requirement can also help to narrow the range of issues that remain in controversy by the time a dispute reaches arbitration. It might even induce the parties to settle along the way. And of course the investor might prevail, which could likewise obviate the need for arbitration....

Given that the Treaty's local litigation requirement is a condition on consent to arbitrate, it follows that whether an investor has complied with that requirement is a question a court must decide *de novo*, rather than an issue for the arbitrator to decide subject only to the most deferential judicial review. The logic is simple: Because an arbitrator's authority depends on the consent of the parties, the arbitrator should not as a rule be able to decide for himself whether the parties have in fact consented. Where the consent of the parties is in question, "reference of the gateway dispute to the court avoids the risk of forcing parties to arbitrate a matter that they may well not have agreed to arbitrate." *Howsam*, 537 U.S., at 83-84.

This principle is at the core of our arbitration precedents. See *Granite Rock Co.*, 561 U.S., at 299 (questions concerning "the formation of the parties' arbitration agreement" are for a court to decide *de novo*). The same principle is also embedded in the law of international commercial arbitration. [2 G. Born, *International Commercial Arbitration* 2792 (2009)] ("[W]here one party denies ever having made an arbitration agreement or challenges the validity of any such agreement, ... the possibility of de novo judicial review of any jurisdictional award in an annulment action is logically necessary"). See also *Restatement (Third) of U.S. Law of International Commercial Arbitration* §4-12(d)(1) (Tent. Draft No. 2, Apr. 16, 2012) ("a court determines de novo ... the existence of the arbitration agreement").

Indeed, the question in this case—whether BG Group accepted the terms of Argentina's offer to arbitrate—presents an issue of contract formation, which is the starkest form of the question whether the parties have agreed to arbitrate. In *Howsam v. Dean Witter Reynolds, Inc.*, we gave two examples of questions going to consent, which are for courts to decide: "whether the parties are bound by a given arbitration clause" and "whether an arbitration clause in a concededly binding contract applies to a particular type of controversy." ... In both examples, there is at least a putative arbitration agreement between *the parties to the dispute*. The only question is whether the agreement is truly binding or whether it covers the specific dispute. Here, by contrast, the question is whether the arbitration clause in the Treaty between the United Kingdom and Argentina gives rise to an arbitration agreement between Argentina *and BG Group* at all.

The majority never even starts down this path. Instead, it preempts the whole inquiry by concluding that the local litigation requirement is the kind of "procedural precondition" that parties typically expect an arbitrator to enforce. But as explained, the local litigation requirement does not resemble the requirements we have previously deemed presumptively procedural. It does not merely regulate the timing of arbitration. Nor does it send the parties to non-judicial forms of dispute resolution.

More importantly, all of the cases cited by the majority as examples of procedural provisions involve commercial contracts between two private parties. None of them—not a single one—involves an agreement between sovereigns or an agreement to which the person seeking to compel arbitration is not even a party. The Treaty, of course, is both of those things.

The majority suggests that I am applying "a different kind of analysis" from that governing private commercial contracts, just because what is at issue is a treaty. That is not so: The key point, which the majority never addresses, is that there is no completed agreement whatsoever between Argentina and BG Group. An agreement must be formed, and whether that has happened is—as it is in the private commercial contract context—an issue for a court to decide....

Nor has the majority pointed to evidence that would rebut this presumption by showing that Argentina "'clearly and unmistakably'" intended to have an arbitrator enforce the litigation requirement. *Howsam*, [537 U.S.] at 83 (quoting *AT&T Technologies, Inc. v.*

Communications Workers, 475 U.S. 643, 649 (1986)). As the majority notes, ... the Treaty incorporates certain arbitration rules that, in turn, authorize arbitrators to determine their own jurisdiction over a dispute. But those rules do not operate until a dispute is properly before an arbitral tribunal, and of course the whole question in this case is whether the dispute between BG Group and Argentina was before the arbitrators, given BG Group's failure to comply with the 18-month local litigation requirement. As a leading treatise has explained, "[i]f the parties have not validly agreed to any arbitration agreement at all, then they also have necessarily not agreed to institutional arbitration rules." [1 G. Born, *International Commercial Arbitration* 870 (2009).] "In these circumstances, provisions in institutional rules cannot confer any [such] authority upon an arbitral tribunal." *Ibid*....

Although the Court of Appeals got there by a slightly different route, it correctly concluded that a court must decide questions concerning the interpretation and application of the local litigation requirement *de novo*. At the same time, however, the court seems to have simply taken it for granted that, because BG Group did not submit its dispute to the local courts, the arbitral award in BG Group's favor was invalid. Indeed, the court addressed the issue in a perfunctory paragraph at the end of its opinion and saw "'only one possible outcome'": "that BG Group was required to commence a lawsuit in Argentina's courts and wait eighteen months before filing for arbitration."

That conclusion is not obvious. A leading treatise has indicated that "[i]t is a necessary implication from [a unilateral] offer that the offeror, in addition, makes a subsidiary offer by which he or she promises to accept a tender of performance." 1 Lord §5:14, at 1005. On this understanding, an offeree's failure to comply with an essential condition of the unilateral offer "will not bar an action, if failure to comply with the condition is due to the offeror's own fault." *Id.*, at 1005-1006.

It would be open to BG Group to argue before the Court of Appeals that this principle was incorporated into Article 8(2)(a) as an implicit aspect of Argentina's unilateral offer to arbitrate. Such an argument would find some support in the background principle of customary international law that a foreign individual injured by a host country must ordinarily exhaust local remedies—unless doing so would be "futile." In any event, the issue would be analyzed as one of contract formation, and therefore would be for the court to decide. I would accordingly vacate the decision of the Court of Appeals and remand the case for such an inquiry.

FIONA TRUST & HOLDING CO. v. PRIVALOV
[2007] UKHL 40 (House of Lords)

[excerpted above at pp. 205-11]

DALLAH REAL ESTATE & TOURISM HOLDING CO. v. MINISTRY OF RELIGIOUS AFFAIRS, GOVERNMENT OF PAKISTAN
[2010] UKSC 46 (U.K. S.Ct.)

LORD MANCE. This appeal arises from steps taken by the appellant, Dallah Real Estate and Tourism Holding Company ("Dallah"), to enforce in England a final award dated 23 June 2006 made in its favour in the sum of US$20,588,040 against the Government of Pakistan ("the Government") by an International Chamber of Commerce ("ICC") arbitral tribunal sitting in Paris. The Government has hitherto succeeded in resisting enforcement [in England] on the ground that "the arbitration agreement was not valid … under the law of the country where the award was made" (Arbitration Act 1996, §103(2)(b), [excerpted at p. 140 of the Documentary Supplement,] reflecting Article V(I)(a) of the New York Convention), that is under French law. Dallah now appeals.

The award was made against the Government on the basis that it was "a true party" to an Agreement dated 10 September 1996 expressed to be made between and signed on behalf of Dallah and Awami Hajj Trust ("the Trust"). The Agreement contains an arbitration clause referring disputes or differences between Dallah and the Trust to ICC arbitration. The tribunal in a first partial award dated 26 June 2001 concluded that the Government was a true party to the Agreement and as such bound by the arbitration clause, and so that the tribunal had jurisdiction to determine Dallah's claim against the Government. The central issue before the English courts is whether the Government can establish that, applying French law principles, there was no such "common intention" on the part of the Government and Dallah as would make the Government a party.

Dallah is a member of a group providing services for the Holy Places in Saudi Arabia. It had had long-standing commercial relations with the Government. By letter dated 15 February 1995, Mr Shezi Nackvi, a senior director in the Dallah group, made a proposal to the Government to provide housing for pilgrims on a 55-year lease with associated financing. The Government approved the proposal in principle, and a Memorandum of Understanding ("MOU") was concluded on 24 July 1995. Land was to be purchased and housing facilities were to be constructed at a total cost not exceeding US$242 million and the Government was to take a 99-year lease subject to Dallah arranging the necessary financing to be "secured by the Borrower designated by THE GOVERNMENT under the Sovereign Guarantee of THE GOVERNMENT." The lease and financing terms were to be communicated to the Government within 30 days for approval, and Dallah was to supply detailed specifications within 60 days of the date of such approval.

In the event, Dallah in November 1995 acquired a larger and more expensive plot of land than the MOU contemplated, and the timetable was also not maintained. Further, on 21 January 1996 the President of Pakistan promulgated Ordinance No VII establishing the Trust with effect from 14 February 1996. Under article 89(2) of the Constitution of Pakistan, an Ordinance so promulgated "shall stand repealed at the expiration of four months from its promulgation," although, under the same article, it should before then have been laid before Parliament, upon which it would have taken effect as a bill. In the event, Parliament appears never to have been involved, but further Ordinances were promulgated to recreate and continue the Trust, viz Ordinance No XLIX of 1996 on a date unknown (presumably prior to 21 May 1996) and No LXXXI of 1996 on 12 August 1996.

Under each Ordinance the Trust was to maintain a fund with a trustee bank, to be financed from contributions and savings by pilgrims (Hujjaj) and philanthropists, as well as by any income from investments or property. The Ordinances also assigned functions within the Trust to various public officers. They prescribed, in particular, that the secretary of the Ministry of Religious Affairs ("MORA") should act as secretary of the Board of Trustees and (unless some other person of integrity was appointed) as Managing Trustee of the Trust.

On 29 February 1996 Dallah wrote to the secretary of MORA with a revised proposal, increasing the cost to US$345 million to take account of the larger plot purchased, setting out options for a new legal and financial structure and stating:

"Legal issues

In order to comply with the legal requirements of the various entities involved, the structure will be as follows:

a) Government of Pakistan to set up AWAMI HAJJ TRUST

b) Trust will borrow the US$100 Million from Dallah Albaraka

c) Trust will make a down payment of US$100 million to Albaraka

d) Trust will enter into a lease to use these buildings during the Hajj period"

Annex A detailed the financial structure:

"Loan terms for down payment of US $100 Million—Approx 30% of project cost

Amount: US $100 Million

Borrower: Awami Hajj Trust

Guarantor: Government of Pakistan"

[Negotiations between Dallah and] the Government led to the signing of the Agreement between Dallah and the Trust on 10 September 1996 [(including a provision for the increased cost of land)].

Clause 27 [of the Agreement] provided that: "The Trust may assign or transfer its rights and obligations under this Agreement to the Government of Pakistan without the prior consent in writing of Dallah." The Agreement made no other references to the Government and was in terms introducing and setting out mutual obligations on the part of Dallah and the Trust. These included the arbitration clause:

"23. Any dispute or difference of any kind whatsoever between the Trust and Dallah arising out of or in connection with this Agreement shall be settled by arbitration held under the Rules of Conciliation and Arbitration of the International Chamber of Commerce, Paris, by three arbitrators appointed under such Rules."

[Two months later, on] 6 November 1996 Ms Benazir Bhutto's government fell from power [in Pakistan], and was replaced by that of Mr Nawaz Sharif. No further Ordinance was promulgated, and the Trust accordingly ceased to exist as a legal entity at midnight on 11 December 1996....

Dallah invoked ICC arbitration against the Government on 19 May 1998, nominating Lord Mustill as its arbitrator. It is common ground that the Government has throughout the arbitration denied being party to any arbitration agreement, maintained a jurisdictional reservation and not done anything to submit to the jurisdiction of the tribunal or waive its sovereign immunity. The ICC under its Rules appointed Justice Dr Nassim Hasan Shah to act as the Government's arbitrator and Dr Ghaleb Mahmassani to chair the tribunal. Terms of Reference, in which the Government refused to join, were signed by the arbitrators and Dallah in March 1999 and approved by the ICC in April 1999. The tribunal issued its first partial award on its own jurisdiction on 26 June 2001. A second partial award on liability was issued on 19 January 2004 and the final award on 23 June 2006. [Dallah sought to recognise and enforce the final award in England.]

The "validity" of the arbitration agreement depends in the present case upon whether there existed between Dallah and the Government any relevant arbitration agreement at all. Dallah's case is that the Government has at all times been an unnamed party to the Agreement containing the arbitration clause. Before the English courts, this case has been founded on a submission that it was the common intention of the parties that the Government should be such a party to the Agreement. Before the arbitral tribunal Dallah put the matter differently. It argued that either the Trust was the alter ego of the Government or the Government was the successor to the Trust or to the rights and obligations which the Trust had under the Agreement prior to its demise. Neither of these ways of putting the case is now pursued. Dallah did not argue before [the English trial court] that the Trust was the Government's alter ego, and it merely submitted that, if and so far as the Government behaved as if it were a successor to the Trust, this was relevant to the issue of common intention....

The issue regarding the existence of any relevant arbitration agreement falls to be determined by the [U.K.] Supreme Court as a United Kingdom court under provisions of national law which are contained in the Arbitration Act 1996 and reflect Article V(1)(a) of the New York Convention. The parties' submissions before the Supreme Court proceeded on the basis that, under §103(2)(b) of the 1996 Act and Article V(1)(a) of the Convention, the onus was and is on the Government to prove that it was not party to any such arbitration agreement. This was so, although the arbitration agreement upon which Dallah relies consists in an arbitration clause in the Agreement which on its face only applies as between Dallah and the Trust....

[The Court first considered Article V(1)(a)'s and §103(2)(b)'s text, providing for application of "the law of the country where the award was made."] It is common ground that the award was made in France and French law is relevant. But it is also common ground that this does not mean the French law that would be applied in relation to a purely domestic arbitration. In relation to an international arbitration, the experts on French law called ... by Dallah and the Government agreed ... that:

> "Under French law, the existence, validity and effectiveness of an arbitration agreement in an international arbitration ... need not be assessed on the basis of a national law, be it the law applicable to the main contract or any other law, and can be determined according to rules of transnational law."

The approach taken in French law appears in decisions of the Court of Appeal of Paris, in particular *Menicucci v. Mahieux* [1976] Rev. Crit. 507 (13 December 1975) and *Coumet et Ducler v. Polar-Rakennusos a Keythio* [1990] Rev. arb. 675 (8 March 1990), and later in the decision of the Cour de Cassation (1re Ch. Civ) (20 December 1993) in *Municipalité de Khoms El Mergeb v. Dalico* [1994] 1 Rev. arb. 116, where the court said that:

> "... by virtue of a substantive rule of international arbitration, the arbitration agreement is legally independent of the main contract containing or referring to it, and the existence and effectiveness of the arbitration agreement are to be assessed, subject to the mandatory rules of French law and international public policy, on the basis of the parties' common intention, there being no need to refer to any national law ..."

This language suggests that arbitration agreements derive their existence, validity and effect from supra-national law, without it being necessary to refer to any national law. If so, that would not avoid the need to have regard to French law as "the law of the country where the award was made" under Article V(1)(a) of the Convention and §103(2)(b) of the 1996 Act. The Cour de Cassation is, however, a national court, giving a French legal view of international arbitration; and Dallah and the Government agree that the true analysis is that French law recognises transnational principles as potentially applicable to determine the existence, validity and effectiveness of an international arbitration agreement, such principles being part of French law.

[The Court next considered the content of French law "as regards the existence and validity of an arbitration agreement."] The parties' experts on French law were agreed that a French court would apply a test of common intention to an issue of jurisdiction…. [In their] joint memorandum …, the experts agreed upon the following statement:

> "Under French law, in order to determine whether an arbitration clause upon which the jurisdiction of an arbitral tribunal is founded extends to a person who is neither a named party nor a signatory to the underlying agreement containing that clause, it is necessary to find out whether all the parties to the arbitration proceedings, including that person, had the common intention (whether express or implied) to be bound by the said agreement and, as a result, by the arbitration clause therein. The existence of a common intention of the parties is determined in the light of the facts of the case. To this effect, the courts will consider the involvement and behaviour of all the parties during the negotiation, performance and, if applicable, termination of the underlying agreement." …

The experts' agreement summarises a *jurisprudence constante* in the French courts. The Cour de Cassation endorsed a test of common intention in the case of *Dalico* [(excerpted above at pp. 182-83)]…. [In *Judgment of 11 January 1990, Orri v. Société des Lubrifiants Elf Aquitaine*, [1992] Jur Fr 95, the Paris Court of Appeal] put the position as follows:

> "According to the customary practices of international trade, the arbitration clause inserted into an international contract has its own validity and effectiveness which require that its application be extended to the parties directly involved in the performance of the contract and any disputes which may result therefrom, provided that it is established that their contractual situation, their activities and the normal commercial relations existing between the parties allow it to be presumed that they have accepted the arbitration clause of which they knew the existence and scope, even though they were not signatories of the contract containing it."

This then is the test which must be satisfied before the French court will conclude that a third person is an unnamed party to an international arbitration agreement. It is difficult to conceive that any more relaxed test would be consistent with justice and reasonable commercial expectations, however international the arbitration or transnational the principles applied.

[The Court then considered the nature and standard of judicial review of a recognition court under Article V(1)(a) and the relevance of a the arbitral tribunal's jurisdictional ruling. Dallah argued] that the only court with any standing to undertake a full examination of the tribunal's jurisdiction would be a French court on an application to set aside the award for lack of jurisdiction….

In [Dallah's] submission, any enforcing court (other than the court of the seat of the arbitration) should adopt a different approach. It should do no more than "review" the tribunal's jurisdiction and the precedent question whether there was ever any arbitration agreement binding on the Government. The nature of the suggested review should be "flexible and nuanced" according to the circumstances [and] militates in favour of a limited review. [Dallah] submits that the tribunal had power to consider and rule on its own jurisdiction (*Kompetenz-Kompetenz* or *compétence-compétence*), that it did so after full and close examination, and that its first partial award on jurisdiction should be given strong "evidential" effect. In these circumstances, [Dallah] submits, a court should refuse to become further involved, at least when the tribunal's conclusions could be regarded on their face as plausible or "reasonably supportable."

At times, Dallah has put its case regarding the first partial award even higher. In … oral submissions, [Dallah] went so far as to suggest that the first partial award was itself an award entitled to recognition and enforcement under the New York Convention. No application for its recognition or enforcement has in fact been made (the present proceedings concern only the final award), but, quite apart from that, the suggestion carries Dallah nowhere. First, (in the absence of any agreement to submit the question of arbitrability itself to arbitration) I do not regard the New York Convention as concerned with preliminary awards on jurisdiction…. Dallah could not satisfy even the conditions of Article IV(1) of the Convention and §102(1)(b) of the 1996 Act requiring the production of an agreement under which the parties agreed to submit the question of arbitrability to the tribunal—let alone resist an application under Article V(1)(a) and §103(2)(b) on the ground that the parties had never agreed to submit that question to the binding jurisdiction of the tribunal….

Dallah's stance … cannot therefore be accepted. Arbitration of the kind with which this appeal is concerned is consensual—the manifestation of parties' choice to submit present or future issues between them to arbitration. Arbitrators (like many other decision-making bodies) may from time to time find themselves faced with challenges to their role or powers, and have in that event to consider the existence and extent of their authority to decide particular issues involving particular persons. But, absent specific authority to do this, they cannot by their own decision on such matters create or extend the authority conferred upon them. Of course, it is *possible* for parties to agree to submit to arbitrators (as it is possible for them to agree to submit to a court) the very question of arbitrability—that is a question arising as to whether they had previously agreed to submit to arbitration (before a different or even the same arbitrators) a substantive issue arising between them. But such an agreement is not simply rare, it involves specific agreement (indeed "clear and unmistakable evidence" in the view of the United States Supreme Court in *First Options of Chicago, Inc. v. Kaplan* 514 U.S. 938, 944 (1995) per Breyer J), and, absent any agreement to submit the question of arbitrability itself to arbitration, "the court should decide that question just as it would decide any other question that the parties did not submit to arbitration, namely, independently."

Leaving aside the rare case of an agreement to submit the question of arbitrability itself to arbitration, the concept of competence-competence is "applied in slightly different ways around the world," but it "says nothing about judicial review" and "it appears that every country adhering to the competence-competence principle allows some form of judicial review of the arbitrator's jurisdictional decision …": *China Minmetals Materials Import and Export Co., Ltd. v. Chi Mei Corporation* 334 F 3d 274, 288 (2003), where some of the nuances (principally relating to the time at which courts review arbitrators' jurisdiction) were examined. In *China Minmetals* it was again held, following *First Options*, that under United States law the court "must make an independent determination of the agreement's validity and therefore of the arbitrability of the dispute, at least in the absence of a waiver precluding the defense." English law is well-established in the same sense, as Devlin J explained in *Christopher Brown Ltd v. Genossenschaft Österreichischer* [1954] 1 QB 8, 12-13 …:

> "It is not the law that arbitrators, if their jurisdiction is challenged or questioned, are bound immediately to refuse to act until their jurisdiction has been determined by some court which has power to determine it finally. Nor is it the law that they are bound to go on without in-

vestigating the merits of the challenge and to determine the matter in dispute, leaving the question of their jurisdiction to be held over until it is determined by some court which had power to determine it. They might then be merely wasting their time and everybody else's. They are not obliged to take either of those courses. They are entitled to inquire into the merits of the issue whether they have jurisdiction or not, not for the purpose of reaching any conclusion which will be binding upon the parties—because that they cannot do—but for the purpose of satisfying themselves as a preliminary matter whether they ought to go on with the arbitration or not. If it became abundantly clear to them, on looking into the matter, that they obviously had no jurisdiction as, for example, it would be if the submission which was produced was not signed, or not properly executed, or something of that sort, then they might well take the view that they were not going to go on with the hearing at all. They are entitled, in short, to make their own inquiries in order to determine their own course of action, and the result of that inquiry has no effect whatsoever upon the rights of the parties." ...

An arbitral tribunal's decision as to the existence of its own jurisdiction cannot therefore bind a party who has not submitted the question of arbitrability to the tribunal. This leaves for consideration the nature of the exercise which a court should undertake where there has been no such submission and the court is asked to enforce an award. Domestically, there is no doubt that, whether or not a party's challenge to the jurisdiction has been raised, argued and decided before the arbitrator, a party who has not submitted to the arbitrator's jurisdiction is entitled to a full judicial determination on evidence of an issue of jurisdiction before the English court, on an application made in time for that purpose under §67 of the Arbitration Act 1996, just as he would be entitled under §72 if he had taken no part before the arbitrator: *see, e.g., Azov Shipping Co. v. Baltic Shipping Co.* [1999] 1 Lloyd's Rep 68. The English and French legal positions thus coincide: see the *Pyramids* case [setting forth the French approach, referred to *infra* p. 267].

The question is whether the position differs when an English court is asked to enforce a foreign award.... It is true that Article V(1)(e) of the Convention and §103(2)(f) of the 1996 Act recognise the courts of "the country in which, or under the law of which" an award was made as the courts where an application to set aside or suspend an award may appropriately be made; and also that Article VI and §103(5) permit a court in any other country where recognition or enforcement of the award is sought to adjourn, if it considers it proper, pending resolution of any such application. But Article V(1)(a) and §103(2)(b) are framed as free-standing and categoric alternative grounds to Article V(1)(e) of the Convention and §103(2)(f) for resisting recognition or enforcement. Neither Article V(1)(a) nor §103(2)(b) hints at any restriction on the nature of the exercise open, either to the person resisting enforcement or to the court asked to enforce an award, when the validity (sc. existence) of the supposed arbitration agreement is in issue. The onus may be on the person resisting recognition or enforcement, but the language enables such person to do so by proving (or furnishing proof) of the non-existence of any arbitration agreement. This language points strongly to ordinary judicial determination of that issue. Nor do Article VI and §103(5) contain any suggestion that a person resisting recognition or enforcement in one country has any obligation to seek to set aside the award in the other country where it was made.

None of this is in any way surprising. The very issue is whether the person resisting enforcement had agreed to submit to arbitration in that country. Such a person has, as I have indicated, no obligation to recognise the tribunal's activity or the country where the tribunal conceives itself to be entitled to carry on its activity. Further, what matters, self-evidently, to *both* parties is the enforceability of the award in the country where enforcement is sought. Since Dallah has chosen to seek to enforce in England, it does not lie well in its mouth to complain that the Government ought to have taken steps in France. It is true that successful resistance by the Government to enforcement in England would not have the effect of setting aside the award in France. But that says nothing about whether there was actually any agreement by the Government to arbitrate in France or about whether the French award would actually prove binding in France if and when that question were to be examined there. Whether it is binding in France could only be decided in French court proceedings to recognise or enforce, such as those which Dallah has now begun. I note, however, that an English judgment holding that the award is not valid could prove significant in relation to such proceedings, if French courts recognise any principle similar to the English principle of issue estoppel. But that is a matter for the French courts to decide.

The nature of the present exercise is, in my opinion, also unaffected where an arbitral tribunal has either assumed or, after full deliberation, concluded that it had jurisdiction. There is in law no distinction between these situations. The tribunal's own view of its jurisdiction has no legal or evidential value, when the issue is whether the tribunal had any legitimate authority in relation to the Government at all. This is so however full was the evidence before it and however carefully deliberated was its conclusion. It is also so whatever the composition of the tribunal—a comment made in view of Dallah's repeated (but no more attractive for that) submission that weight should be given to the tribunal's "eminence," "high standing and great experience." The scheme of the New York Convention, reflected in §§101-103 of the 1996 Act may give limited *prima facie* credit to apparently valid arbitration awards based on apparently valid and applicable arbitration agreements, by throwing on the person resisting enforcement the onus of proving one of the matters set out in Article V(1) and §103. But that is as far as it goes in law. Dallah starts with advantage of service, it does not also start fifteen or thirty love up.

This is not to say that a court seised of an issue under Article V(1)(a) and §103(2)(b) will not examine, both carefully and with interest, the reasoning and conclusion of an arbitral tribunal which has undertaken a similar examination. Courts welcome useful assistance. The correct position is well-summarised by the following paragraph which I quote from the Government's written case:

> "Under §103(2)(b) of the 1996 Act / Art V.1(a) NYC, when the issue is initial consent to arbitration, the Court must determine for itself whether or not the objecting party actually consented. The objecting party has the burden of proof, which it may seek to discharge as it sees fit. In making its determination, the Court may have regard to the reasoning and findings of the alleged arbitral tribunal, if they are helpful, but it is neither bound nor restricted by them."

The above principles have already been applied to the facts of this case at two previous instances. Not surprisingly, therefore, most of the emphasis of Dallah's written case and oral submissions before the Supreme Court was on the submissions of principle which have already been considered. In the circumstances and in the light of the careful examination of the whole history in the courts below, it is unnecessary to go once again into every detail. Each of the courts below has paid close attention to the arbitral tribunal's reasoning and conclusions, before concluding that the tribunal lacked jurisdiction to make the final award now sought to be enforced. Their examination of the case took place by reference to the same principles that a French court would, on the expert evidence, apply if and when called upon to examine the existence of an arbitration agreement between Dallah and the Government. It took account of the whole history, including the Government's close involvement with and interest in the project from the original proposal onwards, the negotiation and signature of the MOU with the Government, the creation by the Government of the Trust and the re-structuring of the project to introduce the Trust, the negotiation and signature of the Agreement between Dallah and the Trust, the subsequent correspondence, the three sets of proceedings in Pakistan and the arbitration proceedings.

The arbitral tribunal set out its approach to the issue of jurisdiction in the opening paragraphs of its first partial award. Dallah and the Government had argued for a single law governing both arbitral jurisdiction and the substance of the issues: the law of Saudi Arabia in Dallah's submission and the law of Pakistan in the Government's. The tribunal distinguished between jurisdiction and substance, relying on the principle of autonomy of arbitral agreements, and rejected both the suggested national laws. It held that:

> "3. Judicial as well as Arbitral case law now clearly recognise that, as a result of the principle of autonomy, the rules of law, applicable to an arbitration agreement, may differ from those governing the main contract, and that, in the absence of specific indication by the parties, such rules need not be linked to a particular national law (French Cour de Cassation, 1er civ., Dec. 20, 1993, Dalico), but may consist of those transnational general principles which the Arbitrators would consider to meet the fundamental requirements of justice in international trade....
>
> By reason of the international character of the Arbitration Agreement coupled with the choice, under the main Agreement, of institutional arbitration under the ICC Rules without any reference in such Agreement to any national law, the Tribunal will decide on the matter of its jurisdiction and on all issues relating to the validity and scope of the Arbitration Agreement and therefore on whether the Defendant is a party to such Agreement and to this Arbitration, by reference to those transnational general principles and usages reflecting the fundamental requirements of justice in international trade and the concept of good faith in business."

As to what this meant in practice, the tribunal noted that:

> "a non-signatory may be bound by an arbitration agreement, by virtue of any one of a number of legal theories such as representation, assignment, succession, alter ego or the theory of group of companies."

It recorded that Dallah's primary case was that the Trust was an alter ego of the Government, but went on immediately to say that:

> "To arbitrate this disputed issue, the Arbitral Tribunal believes that it is very difficult to reason exclusively on the basis of juristic and abstract legal principles and provisions and to decide such issue by merely relying on general considerations of legal theory."

The tribunal then described the setting up and organisation of the Trust. It concluded that the rules and regulations provided in the Ordinance did "not contain sufficient evidence that would permit it to disregard the Trust's legal entity and to consider that the Trust and the Government are one such entity," and were "fully consistent with the general features of the regulations of public entities," and that "Such control of the Trust by the Government is not, in itself, sufficiently pertinent to impair the distinct legal personality enjoyed by the Trust or to lead to the disregard of such personality, and therefore to the extension of the Arbitration Agreement from the Trust to the Government." The tribunal, or Dr Shah and Lord Mustill, added that "particular caution must be observed where the party sought to be joined as defendant is a state or state body."

The tribunal continued:

> "5. In fact, any reply to the present issue relating to whether or not the Present Defendant is a Party to the Arbitration Agreement depends on the factual circumstances of the case and requires a close scrutiny of the conduct and of the actions of the parties before, during and after the implementation of the main Agreement in order to determine whether the Defendant may be, through its role in the negotiation, performance and termination of such Agreement, considered as a party thereto, and hence to the Arbitration Agreement. The control exercised by the State over the Trust becomes, within that framework, an element of evidence of the interest and the role that the party exercising such control has in the performance of the agreement concluded by the Trust, and provides the backdrop for understanding the true intentions of the parties.
>
> 6. Arbitral as well as judicial case-law has widely recognised that, in international arbitration, the effects of the arbitration clause may extend to parties that did not actually sign the main contract but that were directly involved in the negotiation and performance of such contract, such involvement raising the presumption that the common intention of all parties was that the non-signatory party would be a true party to such contract and would be bound by the arbitration agreement." ...

In this light, the tribunal examined in turn the position prior to, at signature of, and during performance of the Agreement, and during the period after the Trust lapsed. At each point, it focused on the Government's conduct. It considered that it was "clearly established" that the Trust was organically and operationally under the Government's strict control, that its financial and administrative independence was largely theoretical, and that everything concerning the Agreement was at all times "performed by the [Government] concurrently with the Trust" and that "the Trust functions ... reverted back logically to" the Government, after the Trust ceased to exist. The tribunal's examination led it to conclude that:

> "The Trust, in spite of its distinct legal personality in theory, appears thus in fact and in conduct to have been considered—and to have acted—as a part and a division of the Defendant to which it is fully assimilated, a temporary instrument that has been created by a political decision of the Defendant for specific activities which the Defendant wanted to perform, and which was cancelled also by a political decision of the Defendant. Therefore, the Trust appears as having been no more than the alter ego of the Defendant which appears, in substance, as the real party in interest, and therefore as the proper party to the Agreement and to the Arbitration with the Claimant."

The tribunal went on to say that the Government's behaviour, as "in actual fact the party that was involved in the negotiation, implementation and termination of the Agreement ... before, during and after the existence of the Trust," "shows and proves that the [Government] has always been—and considered itself to be—a true party to the Agreement...." The tribunal acknowledged that "Certainly, many of the above mentioned factual elements, if isolated and taken into a fragmented way, may not be construed as sufficiently conclusive for the purpose of this section," but it recorded that Dr Mahmassani believed that, when looked at "globally as a whole, such elements constitute a comprehensive set of evidence that may be relied upon to conclude that the Defendant is a true party to the Agreement," and that "While joining in this conclusion Dr Shah and Lord Mustill note that they do so with some hesitation, considering that the case lies very close to the line."

The tribunal's ultimate conclusion on jurisdiction was thus expressed as a finding (in which two of the arbitrators only narrowly concurred) that the Trust was the alter ego of the Government, making the Government a "true party" to the Agreement. That, as I have said, is not now Dallah's case. But Dallah points out that the tribunal's reasoning for its ultimate finding, and the lengthy analysis of conduct and events which the tribunal undertook, can be traced back to [earlier parts of its] award, where the tribunal identified a test of common intention to be derived from judicial and arbitral case-law. How these strands of thought relate is not to my mind clear. There is a considerable difference between a finding (and between the evidence relevant to a finding) that one of two contracting parties is the alter ego of a third person and a finding that it was the common intention of the other party to the contract that the third person should be a party to the contract made with the first party. The former depends on the characteristics and relationship of the first contracting party and the third person. The latter depends on a common intention on the part of the second contracting party and the third person (and possibly also on the part of the first contracting party, although no-one has suggested that the Trust in the present case did not concur in any common intention that Dallah and the Government may be found to have had). Since the tribunal focused throughout on the Trust and Government and their relationship and conduct, and ended with a conclusion that the former was the alter ego of the latter, it is not clear how far the tribunal was in fact examining or making any finding about any *common* intention of Dallah and the Government. If it was, the weight attaching to the finding is diminished by the tribunal's failure to focus on Dallah's intention. The hesitation of two of the arbitrators about the conclusion they reached also suggests the possibility that even a slight difference in the correct analysis of the relevant conduct and events could have led the tribunal overall to a different conclusion.

More fundamentally, if and so far as the tribunal was applying a test of common intention, the test which it expressed ... differs, potentially significantly, from the principle recognised by the relevant French case-law on international arbitration. Although the tribunal must have viewed its test as a transnational general principle and usage, it appears likely that it also had the French case-law in mind. This is suggested by its use of the words "directly involved in" and "presumption," [and] by its earlier mention of the *Dalico* case.... In any event, in Dallah's submission, the tribunal applied principles which accord "broadly" with French law. But, the French legal test, ... is that an international arbitration clause [may be] extended to non-signatories directly involved in the performance of a contract:

> "provided that it is established that their contractual situation, their activities and the normal commercial relations existing between the parties allow it to be presumed that they have accepted the arbitration clause of which they knew the existence and scope."

In contrast, under the test stated by the tribunal ..., direct involvement in the negotiation and performance of the contract is *by itself* said to raise the presumption of a common intention that the non-signatory should be bound. The tribunal's test represents, on its face, a low threshold, which, if correct, would raise a presumption that many third persons were party to contracts deliberately structured so that they were not party.... I consider that [the English trial court] was therefore correct to doubt ... whether the tribunal had applied a test which accords with that recognised under French law.

I turn to the conduct of the Government and the events on which the tribunal relied. As to the Ordinance, the tribunal said that it regarded the Government's "organic control" of the Trust as "an element of evidence as to the true intention of the Defendant to run and control directly and indirectly the activities of the Trust, and to view such Trust as one of its instruments." [Dallah] accepts that [it] cannot rely on the last ten words. Dallah is not advancing a case of agency, and the Ordinance does not support a case of agency. The tribunal's comment at this point is on its face also inconsistent with the tribunal's earlier references to the normality of the control established by the Ordinance.

As to the negotiations leading up the Agreement, the courts below were in my view correct to observe that the fact that the Government was itself involved in negotiations and in the MOU and remained interested throughout in the project does not itself mean that the Government (or Dallah) intended that the Government should be party to the Agreement deliberately structured so as to be made, after the Trust's creation, between Dallah and the Trust.... Here, the structure of the Agreement made clear that the Government was distancing itself from any direct contractual involvement.... The Government's only role under the Agreement (in the absence of any assignment or transfer under clause 27) was to guarantee the Trust's loan obligations and to receive a counter-guarantee from the Trust and its trustee bank. Dallah was throughout this period advised by lawyers, Orr, Dignam & Co. The tribunal confined itself in relation to the Agreement to statements that (a) it was the Government which decided to "delegate" to the Trust the finalisation, signature and implementation of the Agreement, (b) the Government was "contractually involved in the Agreement," as the Government was "bound," under Article 2, to give its guarantee and (c) clause 27 authorised the Trust to assign its rights and obligations to the Government without Dallah's prior approval, such a clause being "normally used only when the assignee is very closely linked to the assignor or is under its total control ..." (no doubt true, but on its face irrelevant to the issue). The [tribunal's use of the terms] "delegate" and "bound" tend to beg the issue, and nothing in these statements lends any support to Dallah's case that the Agreement evidences or is even consistent with an intention on the part of either Dallah or the Government that the Government should be party to the Agreement. Nowhere did the tribunal address the deliberate change in structure and in parties from the MOU to the Agreement, the potential significance of which must have been obvious to Dallah and its lawyers, but which they accepted without demur.

As to performance of the Agreement, between April 1996 and September 1996, exchanges between Dallah and the Ministry of Religious Affairs ("MORA") of the Government culminated in agreement that one of Dallah's associate companies, Al-Baraka Islamic Investment Bank Ltd., should be appointed trustee bank to manage the Trust's fund as set out in each Ordinance ..., and in notification by letters dated 30 July and 9 September 1996 of such appointment by the Board of Trustees of the Trust. In subsequent letters dated 26 September and 4 November 1996, the MORA urged Mr Nackvi of the Dallah/Al-Baraka group to give wide publicity to the appointment and to the savings schemes proposed to be floated for the benefit of intending Hujjaj. By letter dated 22 October 1996 Dallah submitted to the MORA a specimen financing agreement for the Trust (never in fact approved or agreed), under one term of which the Trust would have confirmed that it was "under the control of" the Government. The Government's position and involvement in all these respects is clear but understandable, and again adds little if any support to the case for saying that, despite the obvious inference to the contrary deriving from the Agreement itself, any party intended or believed that the Government should be or was party to the Agreement.

The fact that the Trust never itself acquired any assets is neutral, since its acquisition of any property always depended upon the arrangement of financing through Dallah, which never occurred, and its acquisition of other funds was to depend on the savings and philanthropic schemes to be arranged through its trustee bank under the Ordinances, the time for which never came. It is scarcely surprising that in these circumstances the Trust never itself acquired its own letter-paper, and letters recording its activity were, like those reporting decisions of its Board of Trustees, written on MORA letter-paper.

At the forefront of Dallah's factual case before the Supreme Court, as below, were exchanges and events subsequent to the Trust's demise. One letter in particular, dated 19 January 1997, was described in Dallah's written case as playing "a pivotal role" in, and … "key" to the differing analyses of the tribunal and the courts below. The letter was written by Mr Lutfullah Mufti, signing himself simply as "Secretary," on MORA letter-paper, and faxed to Dallah on 20 January 1997. It read:

> "Pursuant to the above mentioned Agreement for the leasing of housing facilities in the holy city of Makkah, Kingdom of Saudi Arabia, you were required within ninety (90) days of the execution of the said Agreement to get the detailed specifications and drawings approved by the Trust. However, since you have failed to submit the specifications and drawings for the approval of the Trust to date you are in breach of a fundamental term of the Agreement which tantamounts to a repudiation of the whole Agreement which repudiation is hereby accepted.
>
> Moreover, the effectiveness of the Agreement was conditional upon your arranging the requisite financing facility amounting to U.S. $100,000,000.00 within thirty (30) days of the execution of the Agreement and your failure to do so has prevented the Agreement from becoming effective and as such there is no Agreement in law.
>
> This is without prejudice to the rights and remedies which may be available to us under the law."

Mr Lutfullah Mufti was secretary of MORA from 26 August 1993 to 19 December 1995 and from 23 December 1996 to 3 June 1998, and it will be recalled that, under each Ordinance, the secretary of MORA was at the same time secretary of the Trust. Also on 20 January 1997 Mr Mufti verified on oath the contents of a plaint issued in the name of the Trust as plaintiff to bring the first set of Pakistani proceedings against Dallah. The plaint set out the establishment of the Trust by Ordinance LXXXI of 1996 dated 12 August 1996 as a body having perpetual succession and asserted that Dallah had repudiated the Agreement by failing to submit detailed specifications and drawings within 90 days of the execution of the Agreement "which repudiation was accordingly accepted by the plaintiff vide its letter dated 19.01.1997." The Trust sought a declaration that, in consequence of the accepted repudiation, the Agreement was "not binding and is of no consequence upon the rights of the plaintiff" and a permanent injunction restraining Dallah "from claiming any right against the plaintiff." By an undated application, also verified by Mr Mufti, the Trust further sought an interlocutory injunction restraining Dallah "from representing or holding out itself to have any contractual relation with the applicant on the basis of the aforesaid repudiated Agreement."

Dallah made an application against the Trust for a stay of the Trust's proceedings in favour of arbitration under clause 23 of the Agreement. The application is missing from the [record], but a written reply to it was put in on behalf of the Trust. This averred, in terms consistent with the stance taken in the plaint (though less obviously consistent with the principle of the separability of arbitration clauses), that since "the plaintiff has challenged the very validity and existence of the agreement dated [10 September 1996], the instant application is, therefore, not maintainable." Mr Mufti deposed on oath that allegations evidently made by Dallah against the Trust in its application for a stay were "false" and that "the facts stated in the plaint are true and correct to the best of my knowledge and belief and are reiterated." In early 1998, the first set of Pakistan proceedings were brought to an end by a judgment which commenced by recording that:

> "Counsel for the defendant had objected at the last date of hearing that Awami Haj Trust was established [under §]3 of the Awami Haj Trust Ordinance, 1996 but at the time of institution of this suit Ordinance had elapsed, there was no more ordinance in the field and suit has been filed on behalf of same which was formed under the Ordinance after the lapse of Ordinance. Awami Haj Trust is plaintiff in this suit. After the lapse of Ordinance, the present plaintiff was no more a legal person in the eye of law."

The judge went on to record and reject the submission of counsel appearing for the Trust that the Trust continued to be able to file suit in respect of things done during the life of the Trust, adding:

> "Moreover the things done during the Ordinance can be sued and can sue by the parent department for which this Ordinance was issued by the government and that was ministry for religious affairs. Suit should have been filed by the Ministry of religious affairs…. [B]efore parting with this Order, I observe that the liabilities and duties against the present defendant can be agitated by the Ministry of Religious affairs government of Pakistan if any. Since the suit has not been filed by the legal person. The present plaintiff is no more a plaintiff in the eye of the law. Suit is dismissed…."

Dallah invoked ICC arbitration against the Government on 19 May 1998, on the basis that the Government was party to the Agreement. Notice of Dallah's request for arbitration was received by the Government on 29 May 1998, and on 2 June 1998 a second Pakistani suit was filed in the Government's name against Dallah, verified once again by Mr Mufti. Its terms were clearly drawn from those of the first suit, but it started by reciting that the Trust established under Ordinance No. LXXXI of 1996 "no longer remained in field" after the lapse of the Ordinance after four months, and that "The present suit is, therefore, being filed by Pakistan who issued the said Ordinance." The plaint went on to recite the Agreement, variously referring to "the parties" to it, to the Trust as a party, to "the plaintiff Trust," to "the plaintiff" and to Dallah's alleged repudiation "which repudiation was accordingly accepted by the plaintiff vide its letter dated 19.01.1997." It further asserted that, on account of such repudiation, the Agreement "is no longer binding on the plaintiff" and then:

> "14. That in January 1997, Awami Hajj Trust instituted a civil suit for declaration and permanent injunction against the defendant which suit was, however, dismissed vide order dated 21.02.1998 on the ground that after the lapse of the Ordinance, Awami Hajj Trust was no more a legal person and it could neither sue or be sued. The learned civil court, however observed that 'liabilities and duties against the defendant can be agitated by the Government of Pakistan' [sic]."

The plaint concluded by praying for a declaratory decree in favour of the plaintiff that the Agreement "stands repudiated on account of default of the defendant … and the same, as such, is not binding and is of no consequence upon the rights of the plaintiff" and by seeking a permanent injunction restraining Dallah "from claiming any right against the plaintiff under the said Agreement or representing or holding out that it has any contractual relationship with the plaintiff." An interim injunction in the same terms was obtained on 2 June 1998. On 5 June 1998 the Government, through its advocates, wrote to the ICC informing it of the proceedings and the interim injunction as well as relying on §35 of the Pakistan Arbitration Act 1940 in support of a contention that any further proceedings in the ICC arbitration would be "invalid" in the light of the Pakistan proceedings.

Dallah responded to the second set of Pakistan proceedings on 12 June 1998 with an application for a stay for arbitration, asserting that "the contract, admitted by the Plaintiff, which is complete, valid and fully effective between the parties, contains the following clause 23 ...," which was then set out. It pointed out, no doubt correctly, that the Government's plaint must be seen as a riposte to the recently notified request for ICC arbitration. The Government replied on 27 June 1998 to the effect that "there is no valid and effective Agreement between the parties. The application, as such, is incompetent and is liable to be dismissed." On 15 August 1998 the Government's advocates informed the ICC that the Government "has already declined to submit to the jurisdiction of the International Court of Arbitration" and spelled out that:

> "There is no contract or any arbitration agreement between our client and Dallah.... The contract and the arbitration agreement referred to by the Claimant were entered into between the Claimant and Awami Hajj Trust. The Trust has already ceased to exist after expiry of the period of the Ordinance under which it was established."

By a judgment dated 18 September 1998, the judge in the second set of Pakistan proceedings dismissed Dallah's application for a stay for arbitration on the ground that Dallah had "neither alleged nor placed on record any instrument of transfer of rights and obligations of the Trust in the name of the [Government]," which was not therefore prima facie bound by the Agreement dated 10 September 1996. Dallah appealed on the ground that the Government was "successor" to the Trust, but on 14 January 1999 the Government withdrew its suit, as it was apparently entitled to, in view of its commencement of the third set of Pakistani proceedings....

In the third set of proceedings the Government claimed against Dallah declarations to the effect, inter alia, that it was not successor to the Trust, had not taken over the Trust's responsibilities and was not a party to the Agreement or any arbitration agreement with Dallah. The claim was made under §33 of [Pakistan's] Arbitration Act 1940, which entitles a party to an arbitration agreement or any person claiming under such party to claim relief. Dallah's response was that, since the Government was denying that it was party to an arbitration agreement, it had no *locus standi* to make the claim. This response was upheld by judgment dated 19 June 1999, against the Government's argument that the purpose of §33 was to enable a party alleged to be party to an arbitration agreement to seek the relief it claimed. An appeal by the Government to the Lahore High Court was dismissed, again on the basis that the Government was not a party to the Agreement or arbitration agreement. An appeal to the Pakistan Supreme Court has apparently remained unresolved.

[The Court noted that the English trial court] said, in relation to the letter dated 19 January 1997 that, "logically" Mr Mufti "must, in fact, have been writing the letter in his capacity of Secretary to MORA, whatever he may have thought at the time," but [the English trial court] found it "possible to get a clearer indication of the state of mind of the [Government] at this stage" by reference to the proceedings begun by Mr Mufti on 20 January 1997. These indicated, in [the trial court's] view, that Mr Mufti thought that the

Trust had rights it could enforce, and that there was no intention on the part of the Government to be bound by the Agreement or to step into the shoes of the Trust. The Court of Appeal took a slightly different view. It observed that the fact that, after the Trust ceased to exist, Mr Mufti could not have been writing (as opposed, I add, to purporting to write) as secretary to the Board of Trustees did not necessarily mean that he was writing on behalf of the Government or that the Government viewed itself as a party to the Agreement. [The Court of Appeal] continued: "If, as I think likely, the letter was written in ignorance that the Trust had ceased to exist, it is almost certain that Dallah was equally unaware of the fact and that it was read and understood as written on behalf of the Trust."

[Dallah] challenges this reasoning as regards the Government, and invites attention to the letter on its face and to the Government's stance in the second set of Pakistan proceedings. But one obvious explanation of the letter, read with the first set of proceedings of which it was clearly the precursor, is that neither Mr Mufti nor indeed Dallah was at that stage conscious of the drastic effect under Pakistan law of the failure to repromulgate the Ordinance. Even if Mr Mufti was aware of the Trust's demise, he may well have believed (and one may understand why) that this could not affect the Trust's right to litigate matters arising during and out of the Trust's existence—which was the stance taken by counsel for the Trust when Dallah eventually realised and pointed out that the Trust had lapsed. However that may be, it seems clear that Mr Mufti was in January 1997 acting on the basis that and as if the Trust existed. Further, Dallah clearly cannot have appreciated that the Trust had ceased to exist until a late stage in the course of the first set of Pakistan proceedings.

The arbitral tribunal regarded the letter dated 19 January 1997 as "very significant because it confirmed in the clearest way possible that the Defendant [the Government], after the elapse of the Trust, regarded the Agreement with the Claimant as its own and considered itself as a party to such Agreement." It went on to say that the Government's position in the arbitration:

> "did not deal with the substance and contents of such letter, but was rather limited to a formal and very general challenge of the validity of said letter, on the ground that such letter was absolutely unauthorised, illegal and of no legal effect because all office bearers of the Trust, including the Secretary, had ceased to have any authority to act for the defunct Trust. Such challenge is however completely unfounded as the signatory of the letter of 19.1.97, Mr Lutfullah Mufti, did not sign such letter in his capacity as official of the Trust, to which anyhow the letter makes no reference at all, but in his capacity as Secretary of the Defendant *i.e.* the Ministry of Religious Affairs which is an integral part of the Government of Pakistan. As such, the signatory of the letter engages and binds the Government, as he has continued to bind it during the whole previous period where the Trust was in existence."

Several features of the arbitral tribunal's reliance on the letter are notable. First, the tribunal did not put the letter in its context. It did not mention the first set of proceedings at all in addressing the letter's significance....

Secondly, the tribunal rejected any idea that Mr Mufti was, when writing the letter, acting in a manner which was "absolutely unauthorised, illegal and of no legal effect." But that, on any view, was precisely what Mr Mufti can be seen, with hindsight, to have been doing, on the same day as the letter was faxed, by commencing the first set of proceedings in the Trust's name.

Thirdly, the tribunal's comments on the letter assume that the Government or Mr Mufti on its behalf was aware of the "elapse of the Trust" and believed that this ended any possibility of the Trust taking any legal stance or proceedings. That, for reasons I have indicated, cannot have been the case. He must at least have believed that it was still possible for action to be taken in the Trust's name in respect of matters arising from the Agreement.

Fourth, the tribunal, in this context as in others, did not address Dallah's state of mind, or its objective manifestation—an important point when considering a test based on common intention. The letter dated 19 January 1997 and faxed on 20 January 1997 cannot be read in a vacuum, particularly when the issue is whether the parties shared a common intention, manifested objectively, to treat the Government as a or the real party to the Agreement and arbitration clause. Read in the objectively established context which I have indicated, it is clear that it was written and intended as a letter setting out the Trust's position by someone who believed that the Trust continued either to exist or at least to have a sufficient existence in law to enable it to take a position on matters arising when the Ordinance was in force. This is precisely how the plaint of 20 January 1997 put the matter when it said that the "repudiation was accordingly accepted by the plaintiff [*i.e.* the Trust] vide its letter dated 19.01.1997." It makes no sense to suppose that Mr Mufti on one and the same day sent a letter intended to set out the Government's position and caused proceedings to be issued by the Trust on the basis that the letter was intended to set out the Trust's position. That Dallah also believed that the Trust continued to exist, certainly in a manner sufficient to enable it to pursue the proceedings, is confirmed by Dallah's application to stay the Trust's proceedings pending arbitration and is also (as I understood her) admitted by [Dallah]....

Finally, the search for a subjective common intention under the principle recognised by the French courts must be undertaken by examining, and so through the prism of, the parties' conduct. Account will in that sense necessarily be taken of good faith. The tribunal also described the "transnational general principles and usages," which it decided to apply, as "reflecting the fundamental requirements of justice in international trade and the concept of good faith in business," and this must also be true of the principle recognised by the French courts. As both [the English trial court and the Court of Appeal] said, ... if conduct interpreted as it would be understood in good faith does not indicate any such common intention, then it is impossible to see how "... a duty of good faith can operate to make someone a party to an arbitration who on other grounds could not be regarded as such." This remains so, whatever comments might or might not be made about the Government's conduct in allowing the Trust to lapse without providing for the position following its lapse.

In my view, the third re-examination by this court, in the light of the whole history, of the issue whether the Government was party to the Agreement, and so to its arbitration clause, leads to no different answer to that reached in the courts below. The arbitral tribunal's contrary reasoning is neither conclusive nor on examination persuasive in a contrary sense. As to the law, it is far from clear that the tribunal was directing its mind to common intention and, if it was, it approached the issue of common intention in terms differing significantly from those which a French court would adopt. In any event, as to the facts, there are a number of important respects in which the tribunal's analysis of the Government's conduct and the course of events cannot be accepted, and this is most notably so in relation to the significance of the letter dated 19 January 1997 and the second set of proceedings in Pakistan. The upshot is that the course of events does not justify a conclusion that it was Dallah's and the Government's common intention or belief that the Government should be or was a party to the Agreement, when the Agreement was deliberately structured to be, and was agreed, between Dallah and the Trust.

Dallah has a fall-back argument, which has also failed in both courts below. It is that §103(2) of the 1996 Act and Article V(1) of the New York Convention state that "Recognition and enforcement of the award may be refused" if the person against whom such is sought proves (or furnishes proof of) one of the specified matters. So, [Dallah] submits, it is open to a court which finds that there was no agreement to arbitrate to hold that an award made in purported pursuance of the non-existent agreement should nonetheless be enforced. In *Dardana Ltd v. Yukos Oil Co.* [2002] 1 All ER (Comm) 819 I suggested that the word "may" could not have a purely discretionary force and must in this context have been designed to enable the court to consider other circumstances, which might on some recognisable legal principle affect the prima facie right to have enforcement or recognition refused. I also suggested as possible examples of such circumstances another agreement or estoppel.

Section 103(2) and Article V in fact cover a wide spectrum of potential objections to enforcement or recognition, in relation to some of which it might be easier to invoke such discretion as the word "may" contains than it could be in any case where the objection is that there was never any applicable arbitration agreement between the parties to the award. Article II of the Convention and §§100(2) and 102(1) of the 1996 Act serve to underline the (in any event obviously fundamental) requirement that there should be a valid and existing arbitration agreement behind an award sought to be enforced or recognised. Absent some fresh circumstance such as another agreement or an estoppel, it would be a remarkable state of affairs if the word "may" enabled a court to enforce or recognise an award which it found to have been made without jurisdiction, under whatever law it held ought to be recognised and applied to determine that issue.

The factors relied upon by Dallah in support of its suggestion that a discretion should be exercised to enforce the present award amount for the most part to repetition of Dallah's arguments for saying that there was an arbitration agreement binding on the Government, or that an English court should do no more than consider whether there was a plausible or reasonably supportable basis for its case or for the tribunal's conclusion that it had jurisdiction. But Dallah has lost on such points, and it is impossible to re-deploy them here. The application of §103(2) and Article V(1) must be approached on the basis that there was no arbitration agreement binding on the Government and that the tribunal acted without jurisdiction. General complaints that the Government did not behave well, unrelated to any known legal principle, are equally unavailing in a context where the Government has proved that it was not party to any arbitration agreement. There is here no scope for reliance upon any discretion to refuse enforcement which the word "may" may perhaps in some other contexts provide.

It follows that [the English trial court] and the Court of Appeal were right in the conclusions they reached and that Dallah's appeal to this Court must be dismissed.

LORD COLLINS…. The final award is a Convention award which prima facie is entitled to enforcement in England under the Arbitration Act 1996, §101(2). The principal issue is whether the courts below were right to find that the Government has proved that on the proper application of French law (as the law of the country where the award was made, since there is no indication in the Agreement as to the law governing the arbitration agreement), it is not bound by the arbitration agreement.

To avoid any misunderstanding, it is important to dispel at once the mistaken notion … that this is a case in which the courts below have recognised that the arbitral tribunal had correctly applied the correct legal test under French law. On the contrary, one of the principal questions before all courts in this jurisdiction has been whether the tribunal had applied French law principles correctly or at all.

The main issue involves consideration of these questions: (a) the role of the doctrine that the arbitral tribunal has power to determine its own jurisdiction, or Kompetenz-Kompetenz, or compétence-compétence; (b) the application of arbitration agreements to non-signatories (including States) in French law, and the role of transnational law or rules of law in French law; (c) whether renvoi is permitted under the New York Convention (and therefore the 1996 Act) and whether the application by an English court of a reference by French law to transnational law or rules of law is a case of renvoi….

Although Article V(1)(a) (and §103(2)(b)) deals expressly only with the case where the arbitration agreement is not valid, the consistent international practice shows that there is no doubt that it also covers the case where a party claims that the agreement is not binding on it because that party was never a party to the arbitration agreement. Thus in *Dardana Ltd v. Yukos Oil Co* [2002] 2 Lloyd's Rep 326 it was accepted by the Court of Appeal that §103(2)(b) applied in a case where the question was whether a Swedish award was enforceable in England against Yukos on the basis that, although it was not a signatory, it had by its conduct rendered itself an additional party to the contract containing the arbitration agreement. In *Sarhank Group v. Oracle Corp*, 404 F 3d 657 (2d Cir 2005) the issue, on the enforcement of an Egyptian award, was whether a non-signatory parent company was bound by an arbitration agreement on the basis that its subsidiary, which had signed the agreement, was a mere shell; and in *China Minmetals Materials Import and Export Co Ltd v. Chi Mei Corp.,* 334 F 3d 274 (3d Cir 2003) enforcement of a Chinese award was resisted on the ground that the agreement was a forgery. See also [G.] Born, *International Commercial Arbitration* [2778-79] (2009).

In this case, because there was no "indication" by the parties of the law to which the arbitration agreement was subject, French law as the law of the country where the award was made, is the applicable law, subject to the relevance of transnational law or transnational rules under French law.

A central part of this appeal concerns the authority to be given to the decision of the arbitral tribunal as to its own jurisdiction, and the relevance in this connection of the doctrine of Kompetenz-Kompetenz or compétence-compétence. These terms may be comparatively new but the essence of what they express is old.

The principle was well established in international arbitration under public international law by the 18th century. In the famous case of *The Betsy* (1797) the question was raised as to the power of the commissioners under the Mixed Commissions organised under the Jay Treaty between United States and Great Britain of 19 November 1794 to determine their own jurisdiction. On 26 December 1796 Lord Loughborough LC had a meeting at his house with the American Commissioners and the American Ambassador. The Lord Chancellor expressed the view "that the doubt respecting the authority of the commissioners to settle their own jurisdiction, was absurd; and that they must necessarily decide upon cases being within, or without, their competency." While the point was under discussion, the American Commissioners filed opinions. Mr. Christopher Gore, the eminent American Commissioner, said: "A power to decide whether a Claim preferred to this Board is within its Jurisdiction, appears to me inherent in its very Constitution, and indispensably necessary to the discharge of any of its duties."

The principle has been recognised by the Permanent Court of International Justice and the International Court of Justice.... In the Advisory Opinion on the *Interpretation of the Greco-Turkish Agreement* (1928) Series B No 16, 20, the Permanent Court of International Justice said: "as a general rule, any body possessing jurisdictional powers has the right in the first place itself to determine the extent of its jurisdiction...." In the *Nottebohm* case, the International Court of Justice, after referring to the *Alabama* case in 1872, and the views of the rapporteur of the Hague Convention of 1899 for the Pacific Settlement of International Disputes, said: "it has been generally recognised ... that ... an international tribunal has the right to decide as to its own jurisdiction."

The principle that a tribunal has jurisdiction to determine its own jurisdiction does not deal with, or still less answer, the question whether the tribunal's determination of its own jurisdiction is subject to review, or, if it is subject to review, what that level of review is or should be. Thus the International Court's decision on jurisdiction is not subject to recourse, although the State which denies its jurisdiction may decline to take any part at all in the proceedings, or to take any further part after it has failed in its objections to the jurisdiction. By contrast, a decision of an ICSID tribunal (which "shall be the judge of its own competence") is subject to annulment on the grounds (inter alia) that the tribunal manifestly exceeded its powers, which includes lack of jurisdiction.

So also the principle that a tribunal in an international commercial arbitration has the power to consider its own jurisdiction is no doubt a general principle of law. It is a principle which is connected with, but not dependant upon, the principle that the arbitration agreement is separate from the contract of which it normally forms a part. But it does not follow that the tribunal has the exclusive power to determine its own jurisdiction, nor does it follow that the court of the seat may not determine whether the tribunal has jurisdiction before the tribunal has ruled on it. Nor does it follow that the question of jurisdiction may not be re-examined by the supervisory court of the seat in a challenge to the tribunal's ruling on jurisdiction. Still less does it mean that when the award comes to be enforced in another country, the foreign court may not re-examine the jurisdiction of the tribunal.

Thus Article 16(1) of the UNCITRAL Model Law ... provides that the arbitral tribunal may rule on its own jurisdiction, including any objections with respect to the existence or validity of the arbitration agreement. But by article 34(2) an arbitral award may be set aside by the court of the seat if an applicant furnishes proof that the agreement is not valid under the law to which the parties have subjected it, or, failing any indication thereon, under the law of the seat. Articles V and VI of the European Convention on International Commercial Arbitration of 1961 also preserve the respective rights of the tribunal and of the court to consider the question of the jurisdiction of the arbitrator.

Consequently in most national systems, arbitral tribunals are entitled to consider their own jurisdiction, and to do so in the form of an award. But the last word as to whether or not an alleged arbitral tribunal actually has jurisdiction will lie with a court, either in a challenge brought before the courts of the arbitral seat, where the determination may be set aside or annulled, or in a challenge to recognition or enforcement abroad. The degree of scrutiny, particularly as regards the factual enquiry, will depend on national law, subject to applicable international conventions....

There was sometimes said to be a rule in German law that an arbitral tribunal had the power to make a final ruling on its jurisdiction without any court control, but if it ever existed, there is no longer any such rule: [J.-F.] Poudret & [S.] Besson, *Comparative Law of International Arbitration* [¶457] (2d ed. 2007); [G.] Born, *International Commercial Arbitration* [907-10] (2009).

In France the combined effect of articles 1458, 1466 and 1495 of the New Code of Civil Procedure ("NCPC") is that, in an international arbitration conducted in France, the tribunal has power to rule on its jurisdiction if it is challenged. If judicial proceedings are brought in alleged breach of an arbitration agreement the court must declare that it has no jurisdiction unless the jurisdiction agreement is manifestly a nullity.

But the position is different once the arbitral tribunal has ruled on its jurisdiction. Its decision is not final and can be reviewed by the court hearing an action to set it aside. The French Cour d'appel seised of an action for annulment of an award made in France for lack of jurisdiction, or seised with an issue relating to the jurisdiction of a foreign tribunal or an appeal against an exequatur granted in respect of a foreign award, has the widest power to investigate the facts. In the *Pyramids* case (*République Arabe d'Egypte v. Southern Pacific Properties Ltd*, Paris Cour d'appel, 12 July 1984 (1985) 10 Yb Comm Arb 113; Cour de cassation, 6 January 1987 (1987) 26 ILM 1004) the question was whether a distinguished tribunal had been entitled to find that Egypt (as opposed to a State-owned entity responsible for tourism) was a party to an arbitration agreement. The Cour d'appel said that the arbitral tribunal had no power finally to decide the issue of its jurisdiction; if it decided the issue of the existence or of the validity of the arbitration agreement, nevertheless it only decided this question subject to the decision of the court on an application for the annulment of the award pursuant to article 1504, NCPC. The Cour de cassation confirmed that the Cour d'appel had been entitled ... "to examine as a matter of law and as a matter of fact all circumstances relevant to the alleged defects ... in particular, it is for the court to construe the contract in order to determine itself whether the arbitrator ruled in the absence of an arbitration agreement."

[The U.S. Supreme Court adopted a similar approach in] *First Options* ...:

> "If, on the other hand, the parties did *not* agree to submit the arbitrability question itself to arbitration, then the court should decide that question just as it would decide any other question that the parties did not submit to arbitration, namely, independently."

That flowed inexorably from the fact that arbitration was simply a matter of contract between the parties and was a way to resolve those disputes, but only those disputes, that the parties had agreed to submit to arbitration....

The position in England under the Arbitration Act 1996 as regards arbitrations the seat of which is in England is as follows. By §30(1) of the 1996 Act, which is headed "Competence of tribunal to rule on its own jurisdiction" the arbitral tribunal may rule on its own substantive jurisdiction, including the question whether there is a valid arbitration agreement. By §30(2) any such ruling may be challenged (among other circumstances) in accordance with the provisions of the Act. Section 32 gives the court jurisdiction to determine any preliminary point on jurisdiction but only if made with the agreement of all parties or with the permission of the tribunal, and the court is satisfied (among other conditions) that there is good reason why the matter should be decided by the court. By §67 a party to arbitral proceedings may challenge any award of the tribunal as to its substantive jurisdiction but the arbitral tribunal may continue the arbitral proceedings and make a further award while an application to the court is pending in relation to an award as to jurisdiction.

The consistent practice of the courts in England has been that they will examine or re-examine for themselves the jurisdiction of arbitrators. This can arise in a variety of contexts, including a challenge to the tribunal's jurisdiction under §67 of the 1996 Act, or in an application to stay judicial proceedings on the ground that the parties have agreed to arbitrate. Thus in *Azov Shipping Co v. Baltic Shipping Co* [1999] 1 Lloyd's Rep 68 [the court] decided that where there was a substantial issue of fact as to whether a party had entered into an arbitration agreement, then even if there had already been a full hearing before the arbitrator the court, on a challenge under §67, should not be in a worse position than the arbitrator for the purpose of determining the challenge. This decision has been consistently applied at first instance (*see, e.g., Peterson Farms Inc v. C&M Farming Ltd* [2004] 1 Lloyd's Rep 603) and is plainly right.

Where there is an application to stay proceedings under §9 of the 1996 Act, both in international and domestic cases, the court will determine the issue of whether there ever was an agreement to arbitrate. So also where an injunction was refused restraining an arbitrator from ruling on his own jurisdiction in a Geneva arbitration, the Court of Appeal recognised that the arbitrator could consider the question of his own jurisdiction, but that would only be a first step in determining that question, whether the subsequent steps took place in Switzerland or in England.

Consequently, in an international commercial arbitration a party which objects to the jurisdiction of the tribunal has two options. It can challenge the tribunal's jurisdiction in the courts of the arbitral seat; and it can resist enforcement in the court before which the award is brought for recognition and enforcement. These two options are not mutually exclusive, although in some cases a determination by the court of the seat may give rise to an issue estoppel or other preclusive effect in the court in which enforcement is sought. The fact that jurisdiction can no longer be challenged in the courts of the seat does not preclude consideration of the tribunal's jurisdiction by the enforcing court: *see, e.g., Svenska Petroleum Exploration AB v. Government of the Republic of Lithuania (No 2)* [2006] EWCA Civ 1529, ¶104; *Paklito Investment Ltd v. Klockner East Asia Ltd* [1993] 2 HKLR 39, 48.

Dallah's argument is that the enforcing court, faced with a decision by the tribunal that it has jurisdiction, should only conduct a limited review.... In essence the issue in this case is whether the English court should refuse to enforce the award on the basis that its views and interpretation of the same facts, applying the same principles of law, should be preferred to the decision of a former Law Lord and a doyen of international arbitration, a former Chief Justice of Pakistan and an eminent Lebanese lawyer.

Dallah relies in particular on international authorities relating to applications to annul awards on the basis that the matters decided by the arbitral tribunal exceeded the scope of the submission to arbitration. In *Parsons & Whittemore Overseas Co Inc v. Soc Gén de l'Industrie du Papier*, 508 F.2d 969 (2d Cir 1974) the Court of Appeals for the Second Circuit, in dealing with an attack on a Convention award based on Article V(1)(c), said ... that the objecting party must "overcome a powerful presumption that the arbitral body acted within its powers." That statement was applied by the British Columbia Court of Appeal, in a case under article 34 of the Model Law as enacted by the International

Commercial Arbitration Act, SBC 1986: *Quintette Coal Ltd v. Nippon Steel Corpn* [1991] 1 WWR 219 (BCCA).

These cases are of no assistance in the context of a challenge based on the initial jurisdiction of the tribunal and in particular when it is said that a party did not agree to arbitration. Nor is any assistance to be derived from Dallah's concept of "deference" to the tribunal's decision. There is simply no basis for departing from the plain language of article V(1)(a) as incorporated by §103(2)(b). It is true that the trend, both national and international, is to limit reconsideration of the findings of arbitral tribunals, both in fact and in law. It is also true that the Convention introduced a "pro-enforcement" policy for the recognition and enforcement of arbitral awards. The New York Convention took a number of significant steps to promote the enforceability of awards. The Geneva Convention placed upon the party seeking enforcement the burden of proving the conditions necessary for enforcement, one of which was that the award had to have become "final" in the country in which it was made. In practice in some countries it was thought that that could be done only by producing an order for leave to enforce (such as an exequatur) and then seeking a similar order in the country in which enforcement was sought, hence the notion of "double exequatur" (but in England it was decided, as late as 1959, that a foreign order was not required for the enforcement of a Geneva Convention award under the Arbitration Act 1950, §37. The New York Convention does not require double exequatur and the burden of proving the grounds for non-enforcement is firmly on the party resisting enforcement. Those grounds are exhaustive.

But article V safeguards fundamental rights including the right of a party which has not agreed to arbitration to object to the jurisdiction of the tribunal…. In *Kanoria v. Guinness* [2006] 1 Lloyd's Rep 701, 706, [the court] said that §103(2) concerns matters that go to the "fundamental structural integrity of the arbitration proceedings."

Nor is there anything to support Dallah's theory that the New York Convention accords primacy to the courts of the arbitral seat, in the sense that the supervisory court should be the only court entitled to carry out a re-hearing of the issue of the existence of a valid arbitration agreement; and that the exclusivity of the supervisory court in this regard ensures uniformity of application of the Convention. There is nothing in the Convention which imposes an obligation on a party seeking to resist an award on the ground of the non-existence of an arbitration agreement to challenge the award before the courts of the seat. It follows that the English court is entitled (and indeed bound) to revisit the question of the tribunal's decision on jurisdiction if the party resisting enforcement seeks to prove that there was no arbitration agreement binding upon it under the law of the country where the award was made.

One of the most controversial issues in international commercial arbitration is the effect of arbitration agreements on non-signatories…. The issue has arisen frequently in two contexts: the first is the context of groups of companies where non-signatories in the group may seek to take advantage of the arbitration agreement, or where the other party may seek to bind them to it. The second context is where a State-owned entity with separate legal personality is the signatory and it is sought to bind the State to the arbitration agreement. Arbitration is a consensual process, and in each type of case the result will depend on a combination of (a) the applicable law; (b) the legal principle which that law uses to supply the answer (which may include agency, alter ego, estoppel, third-party beneficiary); and (c) the facts of the individual case…. [Lord Collins summarized the applicable principles of

French international arbitration law, citing the joint memorandum of the experts and French doctrine and jurisprudence, including *Dalico, see supra* pp. 182-83.]

The parties [agree] that article V(1)(a) of the New York Convention established two conflict of laws rules. The first was the primary rule of party autonomy: the parties could choose the law which governed the validity of the arbitration agreement. In default of that agreement, the law by which to test validity was that of the country where the award to be enforced was made. Because they were to be treated as "uniform" conflict of laws rules, the reference to "the law of the country where the award was made" in article V(1)(a) of the New York Convention and the same words in §103(2)(b) of the 1996 Act must be directed at that country's substantive law rules, rather than its conflicts of law rules. [The trial court] also drew support from §46(2) in Part I of the 1996 Act, which defines "the law chosen by the parties" as "the substantive laws of that country and not its conflict of laws rules," and which was specifically inserted to avoid the problems of *renvoi*.... [The trial court] considered that the same approach was intended for §103(2)(b) in Part III of the 1996 Act, and that he should have regard to French substantive law and not its conflict of laws rules and that the principle of French law that the existence of an arbitration agreement in an international context may be determined by transnational law was a French conflict of laws rule....

The crucial facts have been set out fully by Lord Mance. The essential question is whether the Government has proved that there was no common intention (applying the French law principles) that it should be bound by the arbitration agreement. The essential [facts] lead to the inevitable conclusion that there was no such common intention....

The crucial finding [cited by the arbitral tribunal] was that after the dissolution of the Trust, the termination letter of 19 January 1997 was written on Ministry of Religious Affairs letterhead and signed by the Secretary of the Ministry, and confirmed in the clearest way possible that the Government regarded the Agreement with Dallah as its own and considered itself as a party to the Agreement and was entitled to exercise all rights and assume all responsibilities provided for under the Agreement. The signature of the letter could only be explained as evidence that the Government considered itself a party to the Agreement. But the Trust had no separate letterhead and it is plain from the surrounding circumstances, and particularly the way in which the 1997 Pakistan proceedings were commenced on behalf of the Trust, and verified by Mr Lutfullah Mufti, that the letter was written on behalf of the Trust and in ignorance of its dissolution.

The tribunal ignored the 1997 Pakistan proceedings, and relied on the 1998 Pakistan proceedings to find that they showed that the Government considered itself as a party to the Agreement. But it is clear that those proceedings were commenced at the erroneous suggestion of the Pakistan judge and shed no light on whether the parties intended that the Government should be bound by the Agreement or the arbitration agreement....

EUROPEAN CONVENTION ON HUMAN RIGHTS
Article 6(1)

In the determination of his civil rights and obligations or of any criminal charge against him, everyone is entitled to a fair and public hearing within a reasonable time by an independent and impartial tribunal established by law. Judgment shall be pronounced publicly by the press and public may be excluded from all or part of the trial in the interest of morals, public order or national security in a democratic society, where the interests of juveniles or the protection of the private life of the parties so require, or the extent strictly necessary in the opinion of the court in special circumstances where publicity would prejudice the interests of justice.

NOTES

1. *Challenges to arbitrators' jurisdiction.* Consider the disputes presented in the various cases excerpted above. In each case, one party challenged the existence or validity of the alleged agreement to arbitrate. Why might a party raise such a challenge? What benefits could a party obtain from a jurisdictional challenge? What are the potential consequences of such jurisdictional challenges for the dispute resolution process contemplated by the agreement to arbitrate? In terms of delay and cost?

2. *Different types of challenges to arbitrators' jurisdiction.* Note that there are several different types of jurisdictional challenges. List these different categories. What were the grounds asserted in *JOC Oil* and *Kulukundis* against the existence of a valid arbitration agreement? In *ICC Case No. 5294*? In *First Options*? In *BG Group*? In *Dallah*?

   Note the discussion in the first footnote in *Buckeye, supra* p. 202 n. 18, regarding at least some challenges to existence or formation (as distinguished from the scope or validity) of any arbitration agreement. Does the distinction drawn by the Supreme Court in the footnote affect the arbitrators' competence-competence under the FAA? Should it? Is there a difference between the arbitrators' competence to consider jurisdictional challenges in cases where a party denies ever having concluded any contract and cases where a party disputes the scope of an admittedly valid arbitration agreement? Are there reasons to treat jurisdictional objections challenging the *existence* of an arbitration agreement differently from objections regarding the *scope* or the *validity* of an arbitration agreement?

   Consider the discussions of the jurisdictional challenge in *BG Group*. Did the majority consider that the case involved a challenge to the existence or validity of an agreement to arbitrate? Did Chief Justice Roberts' dissent? *See also infra* pp. 279-83.

3. *Arbitrators' competence-competence and allocation of power to decide jurisdictional disputes under institutional rules.* Almost all institutional rules grant arbitrators broad power to consider and decide challenges to their own jurisdiction, frequently referred to as "competence-competence" or "Kompetenz-Kompetenz." Consider Article 6 of the ICC Rules, Article 23 of the UNCITRAL Rules and Article 23 of the LCIA Rules, excerpted at pp. 184-85, 170 & 269-70 of the Documentary Supplement. *See also* 2014 ICDR Rules, Art. 19. Compare the language of each of these sets of institutional rules. How clear is it under each provision that an arbitral tribunal may consider and decide its own jurisdiction? Do any of these rules directly address the allocation of competence between arbitrators and courts?

   What are the effects of institutional rules granting arbitrators competence-competence? What effect can such rules have if one party denies ever having concluded, or even negotiated, any arbitration agreement or other contract? How can institutional rules, which a party denies having agreed to, provide a putative arbitrator with any authority at all?

   Consider the discussion in the majority opinion and dissenting opinion in *BG Group* of the effects of incorporation of the UNCITRAL Rules on the allocation of jurisdictional competence. Is Chief Justice Roberts' analysis persuasive?

4.   *Arbitrators' competence-competence and allocation of power to decide jurisdictional disputes under national arbitration legislation.* Many arbitration statutes grant arbitrators authority to consider and decide (at least preliminarily) jurisdictional disputes. Compare §2 of the Swedish Arbitration Act, Articles 8 and 16 of the UNCITRAL Model Law, Articles 1448 and 1465 of the French Code of Civil Procedure, and §§30 and 32 of the English Arbitration Act, 1996, excerpted at pp. 88-90, 144-47 & 119-20 of the Documentary Supplement. How does each statute deal with the arbitrators' power to consider jurisdictional objections? Consider how each statute allocates the power to decide jurisdictional disputes between the arbitrators and a national court.

Compare the language of §§3, 4 and 202 of the FAA to the other statutes excerpted above. What does the FAA's text provide with regard to the arbitrators' power to decide jurisdictional disputes? The allocation of power to decide such disputes?

5.   *"Negative" and "positive" effects of arbitrators' competence-competence.* Some authorities distinguish between the "positive" and the "negative" effects of competence-competence. *See also infra* pp. 315-34. The positive effect of an arbitrator's competence-competence is that the arbitrator may consider and render decisions on jurisdictional objections; the negative effect of competence-competence is that a national court may be precluded from considering jurisdictional objections (or some jurisdictional objections) until the arbitrator has already decided them. Note that the negative effect of competence-competence is to prevent a party from seeking resolution of its jurisdictional objections in a public court—a result that implicates constitutional guarantees of judicial access. *See* European Convention on Human Rights, Art. 6, excerpted above at pp. 270-71; U.S. Constitution, Amendments 5, 14; *infra* pp. 320-34.

Note that, as observed in *Shin-Etsu* and *Dallah*, and as also discussed below, different legal systems adopt different formulations of the competence-competence doctrine, and of the positive and negative effects of that doctrine. *See infra* pp. 273-84. Note also that the positive and negative effects of competence-competence are often, but not necessarily always, mirror-images; as also discussed below, the fact that an arbitral tribunal possesses (positive) competence-competence often, but not necessarily, means that a national court may not also consider the same jurisdictional issues. How might it be that, while an arbitrator had competence-competence, a national court was not simultaneously prohibited from considering the same jurisdictional issue? *See infra* p. 274.

6.   *Arbitrators' competence-competence in inter-state arbitration.* Consider Article 73 of the 1907 Hague Convention, excerpted at p. 48 of the Documentary Supplement. Is there any reason that arbitral tribunals in inter-state disputes should not be granted competence-competence? There is a substantial body of authority recognizing the competence-competence of arbitrators in the inter-state context. *See, e.g.,* ILC, *Model Rules on Arbitral Procedure With A General Commentary*, Art. 1(3) (1958) ("If the arbitral tribunal has already been constituted, any dispute concerning arbitrability shall be referred to it."), Art. 9 ("The arbitral tribunal, which is the judge of its own competence, has the power to interpret the compromis and the other instruments on which that competence is based."); *Award in Case of the Betsey of 13 April 1797*, cited in J. Moore, *History and Digest of the International Arbitrations to Which the United States Has Been A Party* 327 (1898) ("the doubt respecting the authority of the

commissioners to settle their own jurisdiction was absurd; and that they must necessarily decide upon cases being within or without, their competency").

7. *Competence-competence in investment arbitration.* Note Article 41(1) of the ICSID Convention, which provides: "The Tribunal shall be the judge of its own competence." As noted above, this follows general principles of international law in commercial and state-to-state arbitration. At the same time, the ICSID Secretariat performs an extensive review of Requests for Arbitration aimed at confirming the existence of a *prima facie* jurisdictional basis before an arbitration may proceed under the ICSID Rules. C. Schreuer *et al., The ICSID Convention: A Commentary* Art. 41, ¶1 (2d ed. 2009). Is there any reason to think that competence-competence should be *more limited* in investment arbitration than commercial arbitration? That arbitrators' competence-competence should be *more extensive* in ICSID arbitrations than other proceedings? Consider what alternatives exist to arbitration in investment disputes; compare that to alternatives in commercial disputes.

Note the discussion of the arbitrators' competence in *BG Group.* Is there any suggestion that the arbitrators' competence-competence is more limited under a BIT than under a commercial arbitration agreement? Or does the Court say the opposite? Are you persuaded?

8. *Arbitrators' exercise of competence-competence.* In practice, international arbitrators virtually always conclude (absent clear agreement to the contrary) that they have the power to consider and decide (subject to later review by national courts) the extent of their own jurisdiction. That was the case in *JOC Oil* and *ICC Case No. 5294.* This reflects the positive effects of competence-competence.

Would it make sense to preclude arbitrators from considering and (at least provisionally) deciding jurisdictional challenges? Note that this is arguably what the *Kulukundis* court contemplated. What would the consequences of such an approach be? Consider the following explanation:

> "It is not the law that arbitrators, if their jurisdiction is challenged or questioned, are bound immediately to refuse to act until their jurisdiction has been determined by some court which has power to determine it finally. Nor is it the law that they are bound to go on without investigating the merits of the challenge and to determine the matter in dispute, leaving the question of their jurisdiction to be held over until it is determined by some Court which had power to determine it. They might then be merely wasting their time and everybody else's. They are not obliged to take either of those courses. They are entitled to inquire into the merits of the issue as to whether they have jurisdiction or not, not for the purpose of reaching any conclusion which will be binding upon the parties—because that they cannot do—but for the purpose of satisfying themselves as a preliminary matter about whether they ought to go on with the arbitration or not." *Christopher Brown Ltd v. Genossenschaft Österreichischer* [1954] 1 QB 8, 12-13 (English High Ct.).

Is this persuasive? Recall the discussions above, in Schwebel and *Harbour Assurance*, about the importance of preventing jurisdictional challenges from obstructing the arbitral process.

9. *Allocations of competence to decide jurisdictional disputes between arbitrators and national courts.* Despite the almost universal acceptance of the competence-competence doctrine, different arbitration statutes take divergent approaches to the allocation of competence to decide jurisdictional disputes between arbitrators and

national courts. Compare the approaches adopted in the Swedish Arbitration Act, the French Code of Civil Procedure, the English Arbitration Act, the U.S. FAA and the UNCITRAL Model Law. In general, how are they similar? How do they differ?

10. *Allocation of power to decide jurisdictional disputes under Swedish Arbitration Act and FAA: resolution of jurisdictional challenge in national court at any time.* Despite the arbitrators' power to rule on jurisdictional challenges, either party to the arbitration might be left free under national law to seek judicial resolution of a jurisdictional challenge whenever it chose, with national courts being empowered immediately to consider the challenge. What does §2 of the Swedish Arbitration Act provide for? What about §§3 and 4 of the FAA as interpreted by *Kulukundis*? As interpreted by *Buckeye*?

Note that there can be different types of jurisdictional disputes (*e.g.*, disputes over the existence of an arbitration agreement, disputes over the validity of an arbitration agreement and disputes over the scope of an arbitration agreement). Does §2 of the Swedish Arbitration Act treat different types of disputes differently?

Do either §2 of the Swedish Act or §§3 and 4 of the FAA *require* that national courts entertain and decide, on an interlocutory basis, all challenges to an arbitrator's jurisdiction? What reasons might there be for a court not to immediately entertain such challenges? What are the benefits of an interlocutory judicial determination of jurisdictional disputes?

If an arbitrator considers a jurisdictional objection, and makes an award, what is the status of that award under the Swedish Act? Are the parties able to seek judicial review of the arbitrators' jurisdictional determination? What is the meaning of §34(1) of the Swedish Act?

11. *Allocation of power to decide disputes over arbitration agreements under French law: only prima facie consideration of jurisdictional challenge by national court prior to arbitrators' decision.* Consider Articles 1448 and 1465 of the French Code of Civil Procedure and the decision of the Paris Cour d'appel in *V 2000*. Compare this approach to the allocation of power to decide jurisdictional disputes to that under the Swedish Arbitration Act. Note that, like the Swedish Act, Article 1465 expressly authorizes the arbitral tribunal to rule on its own jurisdiction (*i.e.*, to exercise competence-competence). In addition, Article 1448 also addresses the circumstances in which French courts may consider and decide jurisdictional disputes.

Under the first sentence of Article 1448, may a French court consider a jurisdictional challenge where an arbitration has already been commenced? Why not? What does *V 2000* provide about the competence of French courts in these circumstances? After an arbitration has been commenced, are there *any* circumstances under Article 1448 in which a French court may consider challenges to the formation, validity, or scope of an arbitration agreement prior to an arbitral award on these issues? What is the rationale for granting arbitral tribunals, once they have been constituted, virtually complete priority to consider jurisdictional objections?

Even if a dispute has not yet been submitted to arbitration, may French courts consider jurisdictional objections? What is meant by the reference in the first sentence of Article 1448 to an arbitration agreement that is "manifestly void or manifestly not applicable"? Does the French Code of Civil Procedure treat some types of jurisdictional challenge (*e.g.*, challenges to the existence of an arbitration agreement) differently from other types of jurisdictional objection (*e.g.*, challenges to the scope of an admittedly valid arbitration agreement)?

Is the approach taken in Articles 1448 and 1465 to the allocation of competence to decide jurisdictional objections a sensible one? Should arbitrators be granted priority to consider objections to their jurisdiction, before any judicial consideration of the issue? Note the result: a party, who denies ever having negotiated with or agreed to anything with its counter-party, can be forced to arbitrate with that entity, without having access to judicial remedies. This approach cannot be justified by the parties' "agreement," can it? What provides for this result? Does anything other than French law, specifically Article 1448, do so?

If arbitrators are granted priority to consider objections to their jurisdiction, before any judicial consideration of the issue, should there be any requirements applicable to the timing of a tribunal's consideration of jurisdictional issues (*i.e.*, that jurisdictional objections be decided as a preliminary matter)? Do Articles 1448 and 1465 impose any limits on the timing of a tribunal's jurisdictional decisions? Compare Article 186(3) of the SLPIL.

If the arbitrators render a jurisdictional award, what is the status of that award under the French Code of Civil Procedure? Is it subject to judicial review? What is the meaning of Article 1520(1) of the French Code? Is it conceivable that there would be no judicial review of jurisdictional awards? Does it matter whether or not the jurisdictional award upholds or rejects the arbitrators' jurisdiction?

12. *Allocation of power to decide jurisdictional disputes under UNCITRAL Model Law: divergent national approaches.* Consider the allocation of competence to decide jurisdictional objections under Articles 8 and 16 of the UNCITRAL Model Law, excerpted at pp. 88 & 90 of the Documentary Supplement.

(a) *Arbitrators' competence-competence under Article 16.* Like most arbitration legislation (recall Article 1465 of the French Code of Civil Procedure and §2 of the Swedish Arbitration Act), Article 16 of the Model Law authorizes arbitrators to consider and make awards regarding their own jurisdiction. Does Article 16 depend on whether the parties have expressly agreed to confer such power on the arbitrators? What if the parties expressly agree that the arbitrators shall *not* have such power? Is there any reason this agreement should not be respected? Compare §30 of the English Arbitration Act with Article 16. Are there any material differences?

(b) *Interlocutory judicial review of jurisdictional awards under Article 16.* Article 16(2) of the Model Law requires that any objection to the arbitral tribunal's jurisdiction be raised promptly. What is the purpose of this requirement?

Article 16(3) provides for an immediate interlocutory appeal to local courts in the arbitral seat from a tribunal's jurisdictional ruling. Is it wise to permit interlocutory judicial appeals on jurisdictional issues? What would the alternative be? How does Article 16(3) deal with the problem of potential delays in the arbitral process, resulting from judicial consideration of jurisdictional issues?

Note that Article 16(3) does not require an arbitral tribunal to rule immediately on challenges to its jurisdiction. A tribunal can reserve decision on such questions until its final award on the merits. In that event, what avenue(s) exist for judicial review of jurisdictional issues? Consider Article 34(2)(a)(i) of the Model Law.

Why should an arbitral tribunal be given the discretion to reserve jurisdictional issues until its final award on the merits? Note that this will oblige the party challenging the arbitral tribunal's jurisdiction to go to the expense of presenting its case to the tribunal on the merits. Note also that, as a practical matter, the vast majority of all disputes will settle before a final decision on the merits by the tribunal. How does this affect analysis?

(c) *Allocation of jurisdictional competence under Articles 8 and 16.* What does Article 8 of the Model Law provide with regard to a court's consideration of challenges to the arbitrators' jurisdiction? Does Article 8 forbid a court from considering challenges to an arbitral tribunal's jurisdiction? Or does it require courts to consider such challenges? What is meant by Article 8's requirement that a court "refer the parties to arbitration *unless it finds that the agreement is null and void, inoperative or incapable of being performed*"? Does Article 8 require courts to consider and resolve jurisdictional disputes before referring the parties to arbitration?

Consider the decision in *Shin-Etsu.* The court was interpreting national arbitration legislation that adopted the UNCITRAL Model Law. What precisely was the interpretation of Article 8 in *Shin-Etsu*? Compare the approach in *Shin-Etsu* with that under the French Code of Civil Procedure. How do these approaches differ? How are they similar?

Is it possible to read Article 8 of the Model Law as permitting a national court only to conduct a *prima facie* jurisdictional review, akin to that available under the French Code of Civil Procedure? For one view, *see* Bachand, *Does Article 8 of the Model Law Call for Full or Prima Facie Review of the Arbitral Tribunal's Jurisdiction?*, 22 Arb. Int'l 463, 472-73 (2006). Is this interpretation the most natural reading of Article 8? Would this interpretation be wise?

Is there a basis in the Model Law's text for distinguishing jurisdictional challenges to the *existence or validity* of any arbitration agreement from challenges to *the scope* of a concededly valid agreement to arbitrate? Consider carefully the text of Articles 8 and 34(2), excerpted at pp. 88 & 94-95 of the Documentary Supplement. Compare the following interpretation from *Dalimpex Ltd v. Janicki,* (2003) 64 O.R.(3d) 737 (Ontario Ct. App.):

> It is my view that the proper approach to be taken by the court on a motion pursuant to Article 8 is that set out by ... the British Columbia Court of Appeal in *Gulf Canada Resources Ltd v. Arochem Int'l Ltd,* (1992) 43 C.P.R.(3d) 390 (B.C. C.A.)...:

> Considering [Art.] 8(1) in relation to the provisions of [Art.] 16 and the jurisdiction conferred on the arbitral tribunal, in my opinion, it is not for the court on an application for a stay of proceedings to reach any final determination as to the scope of the arbitration agreement or whether a particular party to the legal proceedings is a party to the arbitration agreement, because those are matters within the jurisdiction of the arbitral tribunal. Only where it is clear that the dispute is outside the terms of the arbitration agreement, or that a party is not a party to the arbitration agreement, or that the application is out of time should the court reach any final determination in respect of such matters on an application for a stay of proceedings. Where it is arguable that the dispute falls within the terms of the arbitration agreement or where it is arguable that a party to the legal proceedings is a party to the arbitration agreement then, in my view, the stay should be granted and those

matters left to be determined by the arbitral tribunal.

An issue may also arise on an Article 8 motion as to whether the agreement is (a) null and void; (b) inoperative; or (c) incapable of being performed. In the same way, where it is clear that one of these situations exist, the court will make a determinative finding to that effect and dismiss the motion for referral. However, in cases where it is not clear, it may be preferable to leave any issue related to the 'existence or validity of the arbitration agreement' for the arbitral tribunal to determine in the first instance under Article 16. In my view, this deferential approach is consistent with both the wording of the legislation and the intention of the parties to refer their disputes to arbitration....

Note the court's discussion of the allocation of competence with regard to: (a) disputes about scope of the arbitration clause; and (b) disputes about existence or validity of the arbitration clause. Are the same standards applicable in each context? Are the standards absolute requirements, or do courts have a degree of discretion or judgment in deciding whether or not to make a *prima facie* or a final determination?

(d) *Nature of judicial review of jurisdictional awards under Model Law*. Does Article 34(2)(a)(i) permit judicial review of both positive and negative jurisdictional awards? Consider the following analysis from a German decision, holding that no judicial review is available of negative jurisdictional determinations by arbitrators:

"According to its wording, §1059(2) does not give an (independent) ground for setting aside in the event that the arbitral tribunal erroneously declines its jurisdiction, only the positive jurisdictional determination is regulated (§§1040(3), 1059(2)(1)(a) and (c)). This is no mistake in editing. The legislator considered the possibility of a setting aside proceeding against the procedural arbitral award denying jurisdiction, but it did not extend the catalogue of grounds for setting aside in this respect. There was no objective need for it. As any other (domestic) arbitral award, the arbitral award cognizing the lack of jurisdiction is subject to the setting aside in the cases of §1059(2)(1)(b) and (d)(2)—that are not given here. The claimant may initiate judicial setting aside of the procedural arbitral award, among other things, if the composition of the arbitral tribunal was improper, if the arbitral tribunal did not respect the right to be heard, or acted otherwise contrary to public policy. If the arbitral tribunal decided to be incompetent contrary to a valid and comprehensive arbitration agreement that covered the dispute, the claimant does not lack judicial protection if none of the grounds for setting aside of §1059(2) is applicable. The claimant may go to state courts. The Court of Appeal correctly pointed out that the reverse case in which an arbitral tribunal erroneously declared itself to be competent or exceeded its jurisdiction (§§1040(3), 1059(2)(1)(a) and (c)), is not comparable to the case at hand; in case of an incorrect assumption of jurisdiction the parties are deprived from their lawful judges, whereas in the case at hand, the dispute may be brought before the competent state court and thus before the lawful judge. The fact that this may complicate in individual cases the asserting of legal rights, does not lead to a different conclusion." *Judgment of 6 June 2002,* 2003 SchiedsVZ 39 (German Bundesgerichtshof).

Is this a satisfactory result? Identify the various things that are wrong with the German court's analysis.

13. *Allocation of power to decide jurisdictional disputes under Swiss Law on Private International Law*. Consider the allocation of jurisdictional competence under Article

186 of the SLPIL, excerpted at p. 159 of the Documentary Supplement. Like Article 16 of the UNCITRAL Model Law, Article 186 of the SLPIL provides that the arbitral tribunal shall have the competence to consider and make awards on its own jurisdiction (*i.e.*, competence-competence). Does this authority depend on the parties' arbitration agreement conferring competence-competence on the arbitrators?

Also, as under Article 16(3) of the Model Law, an arbitral award on jurisdiction is immediately appealable to Swiss courts. *See* SLPIL, Art. 190(2)(b). Unlike the Model Law, Article 186(3) of the SLPIL requires arbitrators "as a rule" to make a preliminary award on issues of their jurisdiction. Why impose such a limitation on the arbitrators' otherwise broad discretion over procedural issues? What are the respective costs and benefits of this "rule"? When might exceptions to the rule be warranted? Note that Article 186(3) gives arbitrators discretion to hear a dispute on the merits, preventing (or at least impeding) a jurisdictional dispute from being judicially-reviewed until a final award is made.

What possibilities exist under the SLPIL for interlocutory judicial consideration of jurisdictional disputes (other than under Article 190)? Suppose one party sues in local courts on the merits of a dispute that is supposedly subject to arbitration; will the court not be required to consider whether a valid arbitration agreement provides for arbitration of the dispute? Suppose a party requests a Swiss court to appoint an arbitrator. *See* SLPIL, Art. 179(3).

If an arbitral tribunal makes a jurisdictional determination, what avenues of judicial relief are available under the SLPIL? Consider Article 190(2)(b). Does it apply to both positive and negative jurisdictional decisions? Compare the German Bundesgerichtshof's approach *supra* p. 277.

14. *Allocation of power to decide jurisdictional disputes under FAA: role of parties' agreement.* Consider §§2-4 and 203 of the FAA, excerpted at pp. 103-04 & 107 of the Documentary Supplement. What do these provisions indicate regarding the arbitrators' competence-competence and the allocation of power to consider disputes over arbitration agreements? To what extent do these provisions expressly address the issue?

Does the text of §§2-4 and 203 provide that arbitrators may rule on disputes over the formation, validity, and scope of arbitration agreements (*i.e.*, that the arbitrators have competence-competence)? Do these provisions state that courts must make such rulings? Does anything in the FAA directly address questions of the arbitrator's competence, timing of arbitral awards, and timing of judicial review?

Consider how issues of competence-competence and the allocation of jurisdictional competence are addressed in *Buckeye, First Options* and *BG Group*. Do these decisions permit arbitrators to consider challenges to the existence, validity and scope of arbitration agreements? Under these decisions, and the FAA, do arbitrators have the competence-competence to consider jurisdictional challenges even where the parties' arbitration agreement does not expressly grant them such authority? Compare the approach in *Kulukundis*.

(a) *Historic U.S. authority concerning allocation of jurisdictional competence between arbitrators and courts.* Historically, many U.S. courts held that disputes over the existence or validity of arbitration agreements were for independent judicial resolution. Consider again the analysis in *Kulukundis*:

"If the issue of the existence of the charter party were left to the arbitrators and they found that it was never made, they would, unavoidably (unless they were insane), be obliged to conclude that the arbitration agreement had never been made. Such a conclusion would (1) negate the court's prior contrary decision on a subject which, admittedly, the Act commits to the court, and (2) would destroy the arbitrators' authority to decide anything and thus make their decision a nullity."

Is it in fact "insane" for arbitrators (or courts) to conclude that an arbitration agreement had been formed, even if an underlying contract had not? *See supra* p. 217 & *infra* pp. 355-75. If the arbitrators concluded that no arbitration agreement had been formed, is it correct that this would "negate the court's prior contrary decision" referring the dispute to arbitration? Wouldn't that depend on exactly what the court previously decided? Suppose that the court only decided that there was a *prima facie* case that an arbitration agreement existed? Likewise, if the arbitrators concluded that no arbitration agreement had been formed, is it correct that this would "destroy the arbitrators' authority to decide anything and thus make their decision a nullity"? Why would this be so? Wouldn't the arbitrators' award declining jurisdiction be binding on the parties? *See infra* pp. 280-81, 1159, 1214-15. Wouldn't that resolve their dispute?

(b) *Current U.S. law concerning allocation of jurisdictional competence between arbitrators and courts:* First Options, Buckeye *and* BG Group. *First Options, Buckeye* and *BG Group* reflect the current allocation of competence under the FAA between arbitrators and courts to resolve jurisdictional disputes over arbitration agreements. Note that the allocation of jurisdictional competence under these decisions depends on both the nature of the jurisdictional challenge (*Buckeye* and *BG Group*) and the terms of the parties' arbitration agreement (*First Options*). The relationship between these various considerations, and their effect on the allocation of jurisdictional competence, can be complex.

(c) Buckeye: *separability presumption and allocation of jurisdictional competence.* Consider the Court's decision in *Buckeye*. In what circumstances does the FAA permit interlocutory judicial consideration of a jurisdictional objection? Suppose a party claims that the parties' underlying contract was fraudulently induced. Is that claim to be initially resolved by the arbitrators or by a U.S. court? Suppose a party claims that the parties' underlying contract was illegal or has been frustrated. Is that claim to be initially resolved by the arbitrators or a U.S. court?

Consider the Court's statements in *Buckeye* that "because respondents challenge the [underlying] Agreement, and not specifically its arbitration provisions, those provisions are enforceable apart from the remainder of the contract," and "should therefore be considered by an arbitrator, not a court" and that "a challenge to the validity of the contract as a whole and not specifically to the arbitration clause, must go to the arbitrator." In what circumstances will a U.S. court be permitted, under the FAA, to consider claims that an arbitration agreement is invalid or illegal? Why wasn't the objection in *Buckeye* "a challenge to the validity of the contract as a whole and not specifically to the arbitration clause"? When would a challenge be directed "specifically to the arbitration clause"?

Consider the first footnote in *Buckeye*, *supra* p. 202 n. 18. Note the Court's statement that its general approach to the allocation of jurisdictional competence did not necessarily apply to the question "whether any agreement between the alleged obligor and obligee was ever concluded." Why is the allocation of jurisdictional competence treated differently in cases where there is a dispute whether any agreement at all was concluded? Note that this was the case in *Kulukundis*.

Consider the Court's (and Chief Justice Roberts') treatment of the allocation of jurisdictional competence in *BG Group*. Is it any different from that in *First Options* and *Buckeye*?

Compare the analysis in *First Options*, *Buckeye* and *BG Group* with that in *Fiona Trust*. Are there material differences in the approach to the allocation of jurisdictional competence? Compare these approaches to that under the French Code of Civil Procedure. What are the differences between the U.S. and the French approaches? Compare the U.S. approach to that under the Swedish Arbitration Act.

(d) First Options: *Agreement to arbitrate jurisdictional disputes*. The Court's opinion in *First Options* squarely recognizes the parties' autonomy to agree to permit an arbitrator to finally decide jurisdictional disputes. According to *First Options*:

> "Just as the arbitrability of the merits of a dispute depends upon whether the parties agreed to arbitrate that dispute, … so the question 'who has the primary power to decide arbitrability' turns upon what the parties agreed about *that* matter. Did the parties agree to submit the arbitrability question itself to arbitration?"

First Options also addressed the standard of review that applies under the FAA to an arbitral award ruling on "arbitrability" issues pursuant to an agreement to arbitrate such issues. According to the Court, where the parties have agreed to arbitrate a particular issue (including arbitrability questions): "A court will set [an award] aside only in very unusual circumstances." And:

> "Did the parties agree to submit the arbitrability question itself to arbitration? If so, then the court's standard for reviewing the arbitrator's decision about *that* matter should not differ from the standard courts apply when they review any other matter that parties have agreed to arbitrate…. That is to say, the court should give considerable leeway to the arbitrator, setting aside his or her decision only in certain narrow circumstances."

In contrast, where "the parties did *not* agree to submit the arbitrability question itself to arbitration, then the court should decide that question just as it would decide any other question that the parties did not submit to arbitration, namely independently." The standard of judicial review of arbitrators' jurisdictional rulings is discussed in greater detail below. *See infra* pp. 1159, 1214-15.

Is *First Options*' approach to standards of judicial review of jurisdictional awards wise? Consider the level of judicial review that would apply to an arbitrator's (a) interpretation of the scope of an arbitral clause; (b) determination that an arbitration agreement existed; and (c) determination that an arbitration agreement was valid. Is it appropriate to permit parties to agree to resolve jurisdictional disputes by arbitration? What are the advantages of such an approach? What are the disadvantages?

Does *BG Group* suggest any different approach to the standard of judicial review of the arbitrators' jurisdictional rulings than *First Options*? In the Court's view, did *BG Group* invoke a jurisdictional ruling?

Consider how *Dallah* addresses the question of agreements to arbitrate jurisdictional disputes. How does it differ from *First Options*?

(e) First Options' *presumptions for determining when parties will be deemed under FAA to have agreed to submit an "arbitrability question" to arbitration. First Options* set forth two important rules for determining whether an agreement to arbitrate "arbitrability questions" exists: (i) the existence of an agreement to arbitrate arbitrability questions requires "clear and unmistakable" evidence; and (ii) the scope of an existent arbitration agreement should be interpreted broadly, in favor of arbitrability. *See supra* pp. 232-33. What is the basis for the heightened standard of proof required by *First Options* for an agreement to arbitrate jurisdictional disputes? Why must a party seeking to arbitrate arbitrability questions adduce "clear and unmistakable" evidence of an agreement to this effect?

Is the *First Options* Court's standard consistent with the parties' likely expectations when making an arbitration agreement? Suppose that parties to an international contract insert an *ad hoc* arbitration clause in their agreement. If disputes arise about the (i) formation, (ii) validity, (iii) legality, and (iv) interpretation of the arbitration clause, how would the parties likely have intended each such category of disputes to be resolved? Would they have the same view with respect to each category? Should other national courts apply the "clear and unmistakable" evidence standard adopted in *First Options*?

(f) *Application of* First Options *to arbitration agreements incorporating institutional rules.* Consider the excerpts from the UNCITRAL, ICC and LCIA Rules. How does *First Options* apply to each set of Rules' treatment of an arbitral tribunal's authority to rule on its jurisdiction? Consider the following hypotheticals:

(i) The Kaplans' company had signed a workout agreement containing a concededly-valid ICC, UNCITRAL, or LCIA arbitration clause, and the company denied that the clause covered the parties' dispute.

(ii) The Kaplans had personally signed an agreement containing an ICC, UNCITRAL, or LCIA arbitration clause, but they alleged that the underlying agreement was fraudulently induced or invalid.

(iii) The Kaplans had personally signed an agreement containing an ICC, UNCITRAL, or LCIA clause, but they alleged that the arbitration clause itself was procured by fraud or otherwise invalid.

(iv) The Kaplans' company had signed an agreement containing an ICC, UNCITRAL, or LCIA clause, but the Kaplans did not sign the agreement and denied that they were personally bound by the agreement.

In each case, would the relevant institutional rules provide "clear and unmistakable" evidence of an agreement to arbitrate the jurisdictional challenge?

How does the Court in *BG Group* address the effect of institutional rules on the allocation of jurisdictional competence? Does the Court rely on the U.K.-Argentina BIT's incorporation of the UNCITRAL Rules? How does Chief Justice Roberts' dissent address the issue?

(g) *Application of* First Options' *requirement for "clear and unmistakable" evidence.* Consider how *First Options*' requirement of "clear and unmistakable" evidence of an agreement to arbitrate "arbitrability questions" would be applied to different types of challenges to arbitration agreements.

First, suppose a party denies that it ever entered into an alleged arbitration agreement, as in examples (iii) and (iv) in the preceding Note, and as the Kaplans did in *First Options*. In this case, how could there be "clear and unmistakable evidence" that the party agreed to arbitrate its jurisdictional defense (that no arbitration agreement involving it exists)? If a party denies that it ever formed any arbitration agreement, mustn't that claim be judicially resolved under §4 of the FAA? On the other hand, consider the language of (for example) Article 23 of the LCIA Rules. Does it not give the arbitrators power to decide the "initial existence" of the arbitration agreement? Does Article 23 not grant this power in a "clear and unmistakable" fashion? How does one decide if Article 23 was "clearly and unmistakably" agreed to by the parties? Consider Chief Justice Roberts' treatment of this issue in *BG Group*.

Second, suppose a party acknowledges that it executed an agreement containing an arbitration clause, but denies that this clause is valid, as a matter of law. Assume further that the clause in question is broadly-drafted, and either directly or through incorporation of institutional rules would clearly encompass disputes about its own validity (*e.g.*, as under the LCIA or UNCITRAL arbitration rules). Is this "clear and unmistakable" evidence of an intention to arbitrate questions of validity? Or does the expression of intent to arbitrate arbitrability issues have to be legally effective to satisfy the *First Option* standard?

Third, suppose a party acknowledges that it entered into a valid arbitration clause, but argues that the clause was subsequently terminated or revoked. Assuming a broadly-drafted arbitration clause, are such challenges arbitrable?

Fourth, note the treatment of what the Court regards as non-jurisdictional issues in *BG Group. See also infra* pp. 543-48.

(h) *Presumptively broad scope of valid arbitration agreement.* In contrast to its approach to determining the existence of an agreement to arbitrate arbitrability questions, *First Options* held that the substantive scope of a concededly existent arbitration clause will be interpreted in favor of arbitration: the "law ... insist[s] upon clarity before concluding that the parties did *not* want to arbitrate a related matter." This "pro-arbitration" rule of interpretation under the FAA is discussed in detail below. *See infra* pp. 526-28.

(i) *Wisdom of* First Options' *and* BG Group's *approach to allocation of power between arbitrators and courts.* Is *First Options*' basic approach to the allocation of competence between courts and arbitrators persuasive? Consider the following reaction to the Court's analysis:

> "While [the Court's analysis] may make sense in some contexts, for most situations it says either too much or too little. If awards may still be reviewed for excess of authority under the [FAA], judicial deference to arbitrators' decisions on jurisdiction may be an illusion. On the other hand, lawyers straining to give meaning to the *dictum* might interpret the pronouncement so broadly as to permit an inappropriate degree of arbitral autonomy, opening the door to more problems than it resolves." Park, *Determining Arbitral Jurisdiction: Allocation of Tasks Between Courts and Arbitrators*, 8 Am. Rev. Int'l Arb. 133, 137 (1997).

Is this persuasive? What exactly is the criticism of *First Options*? Note that, at almost the same time *First Options* was decided, Germany was adopting legislation that forbid parties from agreeing to arbitrate jurisdictional disputes: "the parties will no longer be authorized to exclude the competence of the German courts" and "the arbitrator's decision on his competence is always provisional." Berger, *The New German Arbitration Law in International Perspective*, 26 Forum Int'l 1, 9 (2000).

Are agreements to arbitrate jurisdictional disputes any different from other arbitration agreements? Consider the terms of Article II of the New York Convention. Are agreements to arbitrate jurisdictional disputes subject to Article II's protections? Does a Contracting State (like Germany) violate its obligations under the Convention by denying effect to an agreement to arbitrate jurisdictional disputes?

(j) *No interlocutory judicial review of arbitrators' jurisdictional rulings under FAA.* Although there are few reported decisions, lower U.S. courts appear reluctant to review interim jurisdictional awards. *See Transportación Marítima Mexicana, SA v. Compañía de Navegação Lloyd Brasileiro*, 636 F.Supp. 474 (S.D.N.Y. 1983). Is the U.S. approach a sensible one? Compare the approach under Article 16 of the UNCITRAL Model Law and Article 190 of the SLPIL. Why shouldn't courts entertain interlocutory challenges to interim jurisdictional awards? Consider the wasted resources if the tribunal incorrectly upholds its own jurisdiction. On the other hand, consider the delays that can result from preliminary litigation of arbitrability disputes. Are such delays inevitable? Consider UNCITRAL Model Law, Art. 16(3).

15. *Allocation of power to decide jurisdictional disputes under English Arbitration Act, 1996.* Consider the approach to the allocation of power to decide jurisdictional disputes in *Fiona Trust* and *Dallah*. How does the approach in *Fiona Trust* to the English courts' consideration of jurisdictional challenges compare to that in *First Options* and *Buckeye*, on the one hand, and *Shin-Etsu* and the *Judgment of 7 December 1994*, on the other? How does the approach in *Dallah* to review of an arbitral tribunal's jurisdictional rulings compare to that in *BG Group*?

16. *Allocation of power to decide jurisdictional disputes under European Convention.* Consider how Article V(3) of the European Convention, excerpted at p. 31 of the Documentary Supplement, allocates competence to decide jurisdictional disputes. Compare Article V(3) to the approaches adopted by (a) the Swedish Arbitration Act, (b) the French Code of Civil Procedure, and (c) decisions under the FAA. Which approach makes most sense?

Suppose an arbitral tribunal, composed of three Swiss practitioners, has been constituted and presented with detailed submissions regarding a jurisdictional dispute concerning the validity of an arbitration agreement governed by Swiss law. What are the reasons that a U.S. court might be reluctant to consider the same dispute, in an action brought under the FAA, prior to the arbitrators' decision? Suppose that no arbitral tribunal has been constituted, and a U.S. court is presented with a jurisdictional dispute governed by U.S. law. What are the reasons that the court might be prepared to entertain the dispute? How would the European Convention address these hypotheticals? Would it be sensible to treat the allocation of jurisdictional authority between arbitral tribunals and national courts as a matter akin to questions of *lis pendens*, with both national courts and arbitral tribunals considering issues of efficiency, relative expertise and the parties' expectations? *See* G. Born, *International Commercial Arbitration* 1197-98 (2d ed. 2014).

17. *Appropriate allocation of power between arbitrators and courts in deciding disputes over validity or applicability of international commercial arbitration agreements.* Which of the arbitration statutes or decisions discussed above adopts the most appropriate allocation of power between courts and arbitrators with respect to jurisdictional issues? Why? What are the respective strengths and weaknesses of different approaches?

18. *Choice of law governing competence-competence and allocation of jurisdictional authority.* What law should apply to determine an arbitral tribunal's competence-competence? To determine the allocation of competence to decide jurisdictional disputes?

   Consider the award in *ICC Case No. 5294*. Note the arbitrators' care in ascertaining what the local arbitration statute (*i.e.*, then, the Zurich Rules of Civil Procedure) provided with respect to the handling of jurisdictional issues by an arbitrator. Why, in an international arbitration, do arbitrators care what the arbitration statute in the arbitral seat says about their power to make jurisdictional decisions? What other approach might be adopted?

   To what arbitrations is Article 8 of the UNCITRAL Model Law applicable? Consider Article 1 of the Model Law. What law was applied by the courts (from Model Law jurisdictions) in *Rio Algom Ltd* and *Shin-Etsu*? In *Buckeye*, *BG Group*, *Fiona Trust* and *V 2000*?

   Consider the Court's analysis in *BG Group*. What law did the Court apply to the allocation of competence? Why?

19. *Relationship between separability doctrine and arbitrators' powers to rule on their own jurisdiction.* Note that the UNCITRAL Model Law and the institutional rules excerpted above treat the questions of competence-competence and separability as closely-related. Note that *Buckeye* and *Fiona Trust* also treat questions of separability and the allocation of jurisdictional competence as related. Is there, on a proper analysis, any necessary connection between the separability of the arbitration agreement and the allocation of jurisdictional competence? Could one exist without the other? Put differently, if a party challenges an arbitrator's jurisdiction, could the arbitrator decide whether he has jurisdiction even if the parties' arbitration agreement is not separable?

   Consider how the French Code of Civil Procedure approaches these issues. Consider also how Article V(3) of the European Convention approaches this subject. *Compare* Park, *Determining Arbitral Jurisdiction: Allocation of Tasks Between Courts and Arbitrators*, 8 Am. Rev. Int'l Arb. 133, 142-43 (1997):

   > "Competence-Competence analysis should not be confused with the principle of 'separability' …, by which the validity of an arbitration clause is determined independently of the validity of the basic commercial contract in which it is encapsulated…. Separability … says nothing about the validity of the arbitration clause itself. The fact that an arbitration clause *might* be valid notwithstanding infirmities in other contract terms does not mean that the clause necessarily *will* be valid, or that an arbitrator's erroneous decision on the clause's validity will escape judicial scrutiny. Separability and competence-competence intersect only in the sense that arbitrators who rule on their own jurisdiction (like courts deciding whether to allow an arbitration to go forward) will look to the arbitration clause alone, not to the entirety of the contract."

Is this persuasive?

20. *Arbitrators' personal interest in outcome of disputes over validity or applicability of arbitration agreements.* Arbitrators are not national court judges; they are usually private practitioners, of some sort, engaged in the business of providing services for a fee. Often, they face financial and competitive pressures to earn more money and handle more cases. That is true for many arbitrators suitable for international commercial disputes. On the other hand, it is recognized in many nations that judges and other governmental authorities ought not have a personal financial interest in the outcome of their official decisions. *Cf. Tumey v. Ohio*, 273 U.S. 510 (1927) (Due Process Clause of U.S. Constitution requires vacating criminal conviction where judge's income was affected by outcome of case). Suppose that a judge's compensation depended on how he decided an issue. Would that be just?

How does the foregoing affect your analysis of the appropriate allocation of power between arbitrators and national courts to consider jurisdictional challenges? Consider the following:

> "Our deference to arbitrators has gone beyond the bounds of common sense. I cannot understand the process of reasoning by which any court can leave to the unfettered discretion of an arbitrator the determination of whether there is any duty to arbitrate. I am even more mystified that a court could permit such unrestrained power to be exercised by the very person who will profit by deciding that an obligation to arbitrate survives, thus ensuring his own business. It is too much to expect even the most fair-minded arbitrator to be impartial when it comes to determining the extent of his own profit. We do not let judges make decisions which fix the extent of their fees, *see Tumey v. Ohio*, 273 U.S. 510 (1927). How, then, can we shut our eyes to the obvious self-interest of an arbitrator?" *Ottley v. Sheepshead Nursing Home*, 688 F.2d 883, 898 (2d Cir. 1982) (Newman, J., dissenting).

See also Trafalgar Shipping Co. v. Int'l Milling Co., 401 F.2d 568, 573 (2d Cir. 1968) ("Moreover, it is not likely that arbitrators can be altogether objective in deciding whether or not they ought to hear the merits. Once they have bitten into the enticing fruit of controversy, they are not apt to stay the satisfying of their appetite after one bite"). What response is there to this? Is there evidence that arbitrators will really ignore the evidence and law in order to make more money? Will parties select arbitrators who are known to make their decisions based on their financial self-interest?

21. *Waiver of jurisdictional objections.* Consider Article 16(2) of the UNCITRAL Model Law. What is the consequence of failing to raise an objection to the jurisdiction of the arbitral tribunal? Is it appropriate to provide that a party's fundamental rights of access to judicial remedies be capable of waiver? Of inadvertent waiver through inaction? What alternatives might there be?

22. *Consequences of challenging arbitrator's jurisdiction before arbitrator.* In *First Options,* the Kaplans made written submissions to the arbitrator asserting that they were not bound by the arbitration agreement between First Options and MKI. The Kaplans' submissions did not challenge the arbitrator's power to decide whether the Kaplans were bound by the disputed arbitration clause. The *First Options* Court nonetheless held that this conduct did not clearly establish that the Kaplans had agreed to arbitrate the question whether they were bound by the arbitration clause.

Was the *First Options* decision correct on the facts? Isn't the presentation of arguments—without any reservation of rights—to a decision-maker evidence of submission to the decision-maker's jurisdiction to decide those arguments? Note that the Supreme Court observed that the Kaplans' presence before the arbitral tribunal was explicable because of their ownership of MKI, and hence the apparent suggestion that their written submissions were less clearly evidence that they personally accepted the tribunal's authority. What if these circumstances were not present?

Note that the Government of Pakistan made jurisdictional submissions to the arbitral tribunal in *Dallah*. Did that constitute an agreement to arbitrate jurisdictional disputes?

23. *Effect of national court litigation on arbitral proceedings.* In *ICC Case No. 5294*, the Egyptian respondent apparently commenced litigation in Egyptian courts and obtained an order purporting to stay the arbitral proceedings (which were seated in Zurich). Many other national courts will similarly entertain actions to stay or enjoin international arbitration proceedings. *See infra* pp. 319-20, 664-69 for a discussion of U.S. approaches to this issue.

Consider how the arbitral tribunal in *ICC Case No. 5294* dealt with the alleged existence of Egyptian judicial proceedings. What attitude *should* an arbitral tribunal take with respect to parallel judicial proceedings or injunctions against the arbitral proceedings? Note that the arbitrator in *ICC Case No. 5294* states that the Egyptian judicial proceedings "do not have any influence on the arbitrator's jurisdiction in the present case." Why is this true? Suppose that the arbitration had been seated in Egypt rather than Zurich. Suppose that a Danish, rather than an Egyptian, court had issued the order staying the arbitration. Would the order still be irrelevant?

24. *Effect of New York Convention on appropriate stage for judicial consideration of disputes over arbitration agreement's interpretation or validity.* The New York Convention has been interpreted as not addressing the allocation of authority between national courts and arbitrators over jurisdictional disputes. *See* A. van den Berg, *The New York Convention of 1958* 145-46 (1981). Under this view, national courts can in principle either decide for themselves whether an arbitration agreement exists, or can leave such issues to arbitration (followed by judicial review). Is this view consistent with the text of Article II?

Suppose the parties' arbitration agreement grants the arbitral tribunal competence to decide a particular jurisdictional issue or that it incorporates institutional rules which specifically require jurisdictional issues to be resolved initially by the arbitrators. *See* 2012 ICC Rules, Art. 6; 2010 UNCITRAL Rules, Art. 23. Alternatively, suppose that, after a jurisdictional objection is raised, the parties agree that the arbitrators may finally resolve the dispute. Does Article II's requirement that Contracting States "recognize" arbitration agreements, and "refer" parties to arbitration, obligate courts to adhere to the arbitration agreements' or institutional rules' allocation of authority to decide jurisdictional issues? There is little authority considering the issue. In principle, however, why doesn't Article II of the Convention require enforcement of agreements to arbitrate jurisdictional disputes?

25. *Relevance of foreign and international decisions (revisited).* Consider the Indian Supreme Court's analysis in *Shin-Etsu*. What role do foreign decisions on international arbitration issues play in the Court's analysis? Compare the approaches in *Fiona Trust, BG Group* and *Dallah*.

26. *Allocation of jurisdictional competence in investment arbitration.* Consider the Court's analysis of the allocation of jurisdictional competence under the U.K.-Argentina BIT in *BG Group*. Is there any difference in the basic analysis applied by the Court under the BIT and under a commercial arbitration agreement? Is that appropriate? How, if at all, would analysis differ under the ICSID Convention?

Is the *BG Group* Court correct to treat a BIT in the same manner as a commercial contract? How might arbitration clauses in BITs differ from those in a commercial contract?

D. LAW APPLICABLE TO INTERNATIONAL ARBITRATION AGREEMENTS

Identifying the law applicable to an international commercial arbitration agreement is a complex but critically important subject.[23] The topic has given rise to extensive commentary, and equally extensive confusion. This confusion does not comport with the ideals of international arbitration, which seek to simplify, expedite and rationalize dispute resolution. Nonetheless, as a practical matter, the intricacies of the contemporary conflict of law doctrine must be understood while, as a theoretical matter, avenues for reducing confusion regarding choice of the law governing international arbitration agreements can profitably be explored.

As discussed elsewhere, the law applicable to the parties' arbitration agreement may be different from both the law applicable to the substance of the parties' underlying contract and to the arbitral procedure or proceedings.[24] This section focuses on the law applicable to the arbitration agreement. As described below, four alternatives for the law governing an international commercial arbitration agreement are of particular importance: (a) the law expressly or impliedly chosen by the parties to govern the arbitration agreement itself; (b) the law of the arbitral seat; (c) the law governing the underlying contract; and (d) the law of the forum where judicial enforcement of the agreement is sought. There is little uniformity among arbitral tribunals, courts, or commentators in choosing between these alternatives.

The choice of law applicable to international commercial arbitration agreements is affected by both the New York Convention and national law. Both sources arguably provide choice-of-law rules and/or substantive rules applicable to the formation, validity and interpretation of international arbitration agreements. Determining the interplay between the Convention's choice of law and substantive rules, and those of national law, can be complex. The materials excerpted below explore these complexities.

---

23. *See* G. Born, *International Commercial Arbitration* 472 (2d ed. 2014). *See also* Arzandeh & Hill, *Ascertaining the Proper Law of An Arbitration Clause Under English Law*, 5 J. Private Int'l L. 425 (2009); Bantekas, *The Proper Law of the Arbitration Clause: A Challenge to the Prevailing Orthodoxy*, 27 J. Int'l Arb. 1 (2010); di Pietro, *Applicable Laws Under the New York Convention*, in F. Ferrari & S. Kröll (eds.), *Conflict of Laws in International Arbitration* 63 (2011); Pearson, Sulamérica v. Enesa: *The Hidden Pro-Validation Approach Adopted by the English Courts With Respect to the Proper Law of the Arbitration Agreement*, 29 Arb. Int'l 115 (2013).

24. *See supra* pp. 90-93 & *infra* pp. 300-01; G. Born, *International Commercial Arbitration* 473-75 (2d ed. 2014).

JUDGMENT OF 30 MAY 1994
XX Y.B. Comm. Arb. 745 (1995) (Tokyo High Ct.)

The Japan Educational Corporation ("JEC") and Ringling Bros., a U.S. company ("Ringling"), concluded an agreement under which Ringling was to organize circus performances in Japan. The agreement contained a clause referring all disputes to ICC arbitration, to be held either in New York at the request of JEC or in Tokyo at the request of Ringling.

A dispute arose between the parties and JEC sought damages before the District Court of Tokyo, alleging that Mr. Feld, Ringling's representative, had deceived JEC as to [financial matters under the parties' contract.]... On 21 November 1990, Mr. Feld and Ringling obtained an injunction order from the U.S. District Court in New York City; the order enjoined JEC and its representative, Kazuhiko Morioka, from proceeding with the lawsuit in the Tokyo District Court and directed them to submit their claim to ICC arbitrators as provided for in the contract. JEC and its representative did not appear in the U.S. proceedings. The District Court of Tokyo referred the parties to arbitration, whereupon JEC appealed to the High Court of Tokyo. The High Court affirmed....

[Mr. Feld] argues that this lawsuit should be dismissed, since the arbitration agreement concluded between [JEC] and Ringling applies to the dispute, and the existence of an arbitration agreement bars court proceedings under the Japanese Code of Civil Procedure.... Neither party disputes the fact that an arbitration clause was concluded between [JEC] and Ringling. [JEC] alleges that the arbitration clause in the contract is null and void as it fails to indicate the competent arbitral institution in Japan. However, the arbitration clause provides that "disputes ... shall be submitted to arbitration in accordance with the rules and procedures of the ICC relating to the arbitration of commercial disputes" ..., (which is not disputed), and the ICC Rules provide that a request for arbitration may be filed with the Secretariat of the Arbitration Court in Paris through the National Committees. The arbitrators are appointed by the parties; if the parties cannot agree on the appointment, the Rules provide that the arbitrators are to be appointed according to a certain procedure.... It appears to this Court that there is a Japanese ICC National Committee in Tokyo. Hence, as long as the parties have agreed to submit their dispute to arbitration in accordance with the ICC arbitration rules and procedures, it is possible to file for arbitration in Japan and an arbitral award may be rendered, even if the parties have not agreed on the arbitral institution. Hence, this Court cannot agree with [JEC]'s contention.

An arbitration agreement is an agreement to have certain disputes concerning rights and obligations or a legal relationship finally settled out of court by arbitrators. The arbitration agreement shall provide for various matters which are necessary in order to proceed to arbitration, including which disputes are to be decided by arbitration. The law applicable to the parties' agreement on these matters concerns an agreement on a dispute resolution means, but still we are here within the ambit of the parties' autonomy, therefore, this applicable law is to be determined by the parties themselves (*Hourei* Art. 7(1)).[25] If the parties' will is unclear we must presume, as it is the nature of arbitration agreements to provide

---

25. Art. 7 of the Law Concerning the Application of Laws in General (*Hourei*), 1898 reads: "1. As regards the formation and effect of a juristic act, the question as to the law of which country is to govern shall be determined by the intention of the parties. 2. If the intention of the parties is uncertain, the law of the place where the act is done shall govern."

for given procedures in a given place, that the parties intend that the law of the place where the arbitration proceedings are held will apply. We find no facts sufficient to overrule this presumption.

An arbitration agreement affects court litigation on the same disputes that are to be referred to arbitration (normally to the effect of excluding litigation); such effect on litigation is to be determined, in general, under the law of the forum. The fact that an arbitration agreement bars litigation is a reflection of the fact that it provides that certain disputes are to be resolved not by litigation but by arbitration. We infer from the above that the extent to which an arbitration agreement bars litigation shall be determined in principle by the law governing the arbitration agreement. Therefore, if the arbitration agreement provides for more than one country as the place of arbitration (as is the case here), the issue of which law determines the scope of the litigation bar must be examined. Since arbitration and litigation are mutually complementary, and the parties have agreed on arbitration as a dispute resolution means, their choice should be respected....

The arbitration agreement provides that the place of arbitration shall be the country of the party against which arbitration proceedings are initiated. Thus, the party applying for court proceedings may be exempted from the exclusion effect of the arbitration agreement only if its claim would be held not to be subject to arbitration under the law applicable to the arbitration agreement in the country of the other party. In other words, in the light of what we have said on the law governing the arbitration agreement, only if claimant is unable to refer the dispute to arbitration under the law of the country of defendant.

The arbitration clause provides that the parties agree to settle all disputes concerning the interpretation and/or application of the contract (Performance Contract) concluded between [JEC] and Ringling by arbitration before an arbitral institution in the country of the defendant (i.e., an arbitral institution in either Tokyo or New York City). Hence, the validity of this lawsuit shall be determined by whether the underlying dispute falls within the scope of the arbitration clause under the law applicable in New York City, USA.

We then consider the following issue. [Mr. Feld], who represents Ringling, is not a party to the arbitration agreement, as mentioned above, neither is it explicitly provided that the disputes between [JEC] and the representative of Ringling shall be referred to arbitration. However, we find, on the basis of [undisputed documents filed in the proceedings], that the laws applicable to arbitration agreements in New York City are the [FAA] and the case law of the Federal Courts of the United States; that the latter indicates that the validity and scope of arbitration agreements is, in general, to be interpreted broadly; and that when an arbitration agreement is concluded, which provides that all disputes arising from a certain transaction are to be referred to arbitration, disputes concerning the behaviour of an individual who acts in the capacity of employee of one party to the transaction, as well as disputes based on fraud on the part of one party to induce the other party to conclude the contract, are deemed to fall within the scope of the arbitration agreement and are to be settled by arbitration.

The New York Federal District Court issued an order, which is now final and binding, following a petition filed by Ringling and [Mr. Feld] against [JEC] and its representative, Kazuhiko Morioka, seeking an order to compel arbitration in New York City as well as an injunction order. The order, issued on 21 November 1990, reads as follows: "(1) [JEC] and Kazuhiko Morioka are directed to proceed to arbitration in accordance with the Rules of the ICC pursuant to the arbitration provision in the Contract; (2) the claims filed by [JEC] in the present lawsuit fall within the scope of the arbitration agreement; (3) [JEC] and Kazuhiko Morioka are enjoined and restrained from further prosecution of this lawsuit, pending arbitration as required by the arbitration agreement." (Note, however, that [JEC] did not appear in court although it had been duly summoned)....

The provisions of the [FAA], the interpretation given by the Federal Courts of the scope (*ad personam* or *in rem*) of arbitration agreements and the fact that the order to compel arbitration has become final and binding lead us to hold that [JEC] may file for arbitration in the United States against [Mr. Feld] to recover the alleged damages which it is claiming in the present case.... We hold that [JEC] and Ringling agreed to refer the disputes under-lying the present lawsuit to arbitration in New York City. This agreement also binds [Mr. Feld], in the presence of this arbitration agreement, although governed by foreign law, the present case may not be decided in court. The defense submitted by [Mr. Feld] is well founded. Hence, we hold as described in the reasons that the judgment of the District Court refusing to hear this case is valid and we hereby deny [JEC]'s appeal.

JORDANIAN AMENDMENT TO THE MERCHANDISE MARITIME LAW
Law No. 35 of 1983

Regardless of whatever is contained in any other law, any agreement, or stipulation which bars the Jordanian courts from maintaining disputes relating to bills of lading or carriage of goods is null and void.

INTERIM AWARD IN ICC CASE NO. 6149
XX Y.B. Comm. Arb. 41 (1995)

[A Korean manufacturer entered into three contracts to supply an Iraqi buyer with goods. The goods were to be delivered in Iraq. The contracts contained the following arbitration clause: "Any dispute with regards to this contract will be solved cordially; otherwise by two arbitrators appointed by each side. In an eventual non agreement it will be governed by the laws and regulations of the International Chamber of Commerce in Paris whose ruling should be final." Disputes arose under the contract. In due course, the Korean seller commenced an arbitration under ICC Rules. The Iraqi purchaser raised jurisdictional ob-jections to the tribunal's jurisdiction, citing Jordanian Law No. 35 of 1983, excerpted above at p. 290. The tribunal rendered the following interim award:]

Section 2 of the Jordanian Law No. 35 … is not applicable to the arbitration agreements contained in the three contracts of sale. The arbitration agreements therefore have not been voided by said §2. But they are still valid and binding upon the parties thus being suscep-tible of serving as a legitimate basis for the exercise of the arbitral tribunal's jurisdiction over the subject-matter of this arbitration....

Section 2 of the Jordanian Law No. 35 is based upon motivations of Jordanian public policy. Its obvious purpose is to prevent Jordanian courts from being ousted of their ju-risdiction as far as certain matters are concerned, considered to be of primordial im-portance for the Jordanian public interest. The effect of the said §2 therefore is to deny *arbitrability* to all matters defined by it. Non-arbitrability means that a matter is not ca-pable of settlement by arbitration. (Art. II(1) of the [New York Convention]) Section 2 of the said law thus removes arbitrability from "all disputes relating to bills of lading or car-riage of goods."

National provisions on non-arbitrability of disputes are constituent parts of the public policy provisions of the issuing state. The question of whether ..., if so, to what extent an international arbitral tribunal has to apply national provisions on the non-arbitrability of certain matters [must] ... be answered on the basis of the doctrines dealing with the *validity of international arbitration agreements under national public policy provisions ....*

Such validity of international arbitration agreements depends upon *the proper law by which they are governed.* It may be disputed whether an arbitration agreement, as a matter of principle, is subject to the same proper law by which also the main contract is governed so that both, arbitration agreement and main contract, share the same proper law, or whether the proper law of the arbitration agreement has to be determined upon its own, i.e., irrespectively of the proper law of the main contract. This ... does not need to be decided within the present context. For both doctrines lead to the same result ..., i.e., to the non-applicability of ... Jordanian Law No. 35.

If the arbitral tribunal would follow the first doctrine and assume the proper law of the arbitration agreement to be identical with the proper law of the main contract, the validity of the three arbitration agreements here under consideration would hinge upon the proper law of the three sales contracts. It will be seen in the following section of this interim award that the said three sales contracts are certainly *not* governed by Jordanian law. Thus, under the afore-mentioned first doctrine, an application of the Jordanian Law No. 35 would be excluded.

The same conclusion would have to be drawn if the arbitral tribunal would follow the afore-mentioned second, alternative doctrine by which the proper law of an arbitration agreement would have to be determined upon its own, i.e., without having regard to the proper law of the main contract. Pursuant to Article 13(3) of the ICC Rules ..., failing any indication by the parties as to the applicable law, the arbitrator shall apply the law designated as the proper law by the rule of conflict which he deems appropriate. If, according to the second doctrine, the proper law of the three arbitration agreements could not necessarily be derived from the proper law of the three sales contracts themselves, the only other rule of conflicts of laws whose application would seem appropriate in the sense of the above-mentioned Article 13(3), would be the application of the law where the arbitration takes place and where the award is rendered.

This conclusion would be supported also by Article V(1)(a) for the [Convention].... According to ... Article V, the validity of the arbitration agreement has to be determined "under the law of the country where the award was made." In the case here under consideration, the above-mentioned second doctrine therefore would lead to the application of French law, i.e., of Arts. 1493-1495, 1442-1446 of the [NCCP]. Under these French provisions, the three arbitration agreements would be valid and binding. In other words: the application of §2 of the Jordanian Law No. 35 would again be excluded.

[Further, t]here can be no doubt that, if Jordanian courts would have to decide on the present subject-matter, such courts would have to apply §2 of the Jordanian Law No. 35. But when the parties to the three sales contracts, in exercising their rights of autonomy to choose an appropriate forum or arbitral tribunal for their eventual disputes, agreed upon the jurisdiction of the [ICC Court] in Paris, they obviously had the *intention to withdraw any jurisdiction from Korean, Jordanian and Iraqi state courts* and to subject all disputes resulting from their three sales contracts exclusively to the jurisdiction of the [ICC Court]. Such court, being an international arbitration body sitting in a state other than Jordan, is not necessarily bound by considerations of Jordanian domestic public policy at least insofar as Jordanian law is not applicable to the subject-matter. It would therefore run counter to the common intention of the parties at the time when they entered into the three sales contracts, if the arbitral tribunal would apply a public policy provision of Jordanian law while there had been a clear intention of the parties to remove this subject-matter from Jordanian domestic jurisdiction....

The arbitration agreements contained in the three sales contracts, when properly construed, also cover the present dispute.... This conclusion follows from the interpretation of the three arbitration agreements and is based upon the tacit intention of the parties. When the parties entered into their three sales contracts and when, at that time, they agreed upon the jurisdiction of the [ICC Court], they certainly had in mind to subject to arbitration all matters relating to these three contracts, without regard as to whether the subject-matter of an eventual request for arbitration would later be a claim for the specific performance of those contracts, or a claim for the assessment of damages resulting from a breach of those contracts, or a claim for the restitution of performances rendered without cause and therefore constituting unjust enrichment, or finally any other claim directly or indirectly related to the three contracts. It must be assumed that it was the tacit intention of the parties to invest the arbitral tribunal with jurisdiction over all disputes possibly deriving from, or being related to, their three sales contracts.

This reasoning becomes even more persuasive if one considers, hypothetically, the consequences of a decision to the contrary: If it were permissible for the parties to be engaged in arbitration proceedings before the [ICC Court] on one issue of the contracts, e.g., on a breach of them, at the same time, to sue each other before state courts, e.g., before a Jordanian or a Korean state court, on another issue, e.g., upon an unjust enrichment allegedly resulting from the undue performance of the contracts, a conflict between the award of the arbitral tribunal and the judgment of the state court might ensue. Such conflicts would be detrimental to the interests of the parties. The arbitral tribunal must therefore assume that the parties wanted to avoid such conflicts. Consequently their arbitration agreements must be construed in such a way as to exclude a concurrent jurisdiction of the arbitral tribunal and a state court on matters resulting from one and the same contracts. The present dispute therefore is covered by the arbitration agreements....

FINAL AWARD IN ICC CASE NO. 5294
XIV Y.B. Comm. Arb. 137 (1989)

[excerpted above at pp. 218-20]

XL INSURANCE LTD v. OWENS CORNING CORP.
[2000] 2 Lloyd's Rep. 500 (QB) (English High Ct.)

[XL Insurance Ltd ("XL") issued an insurance policy to Owens Corning Co. ("Owens Corning"). Disputes arose concerning coverage under the policy. The terms of the policy were unclear, particularly concerning dispute resolution and choice of law. The policy contained either "long-form" or "short-form" arbitration and choice-of-law provisions, but it was not clear which provisions had been incorporated into the policy. The long-form provisions were as follows:

ARBITRATION. Any dispute, controversy or claim arising out of or relating to this Policy or the breach, termination or invalidity thereof shall be finally and fully determined in London, England under the provisions of the Arbitration Act 1996 ("Act") and/or any statutory modifications or amendments thereof for the time being in force, by a Board composed of three arbitrators to be selected for each controversy as follows.... Without limiting the foregoing, the parties waive any right to appeal to, and/or seek collateral review of the decision of the Board of Arbitration by, any court or other body to the fullest extent permitted by the applicable law, including, without limitation, any right to make application to the court under §45 or to appeal under §69 of the Act.

GOVERNING LAW AND INTERPRETATION. This policy shall be construed in accordance with the internal laws of the State of New York, United States except in so far as such laws:

> A. pertain to regulation under the New York Insurance Law, or regulations issued by the Insurance Department of the State of New York pursuant thereto, applying to insurers doing insurance business, or issuance, delivery or procurement of policies of insurance, within the State of New York or as respects risks or insureds situated in the State of New York; or
>
> B. are inconsistent with any provision of this Policy. Provided, however, that the provisions, stipulations, exclusions and conditions of this Policy are to be construed in an even handed fashion as between the Insured and XL. Without limitation, where the language of this Policy is deemed to be ambiguous or otherwise unclear, the issues shall be resolved in the manner most consistent with the relevant provisions, stipulations, exclusions and conditions (without regard to authorship of the language, without any presumption or arbitrary interpretation or construction in favour of either the Insured or XL and without reference to parol or other extrinsic evidence).

The "short-form" provisions were as follows:

A. THE APPRAISAL AND SUIT AGAINST THE COMPANY clauses are deleted and replaced with XL's London Arbitration clause.

B. THE JURISDICTION clause will be deleted. XL's Policy shall be construed in accordance with the internal regulation laws of the State of New York (USA).

Litigation was commenced in English courts concerning whether the policy contained a valid arbitration clause. Portions of the English court's decision follow. In its discussion, the court left unresolved whether the "long-form" or the "short-form" of the dispute resolution and choice-of-law clause were agreed between the parties and considered each possibility.]

JUSTICE TOULSON. An arbitration clause in a contract is an agreement within an agreement.... It is a general principle of English private international law that it is for the parties to choose the law which is to govern their agreement to arbitrate and the arbitration proceedings, and that English law will respect their choice.... Parties' freedom of choice includes freedom to choose different systems of law to govern different aspects of their relationship....

In *Channel Tunnel Group Ltd v. Balfour Beatty Constr. Ltd*, [1993] 1 Lloyd's Rep. 291, 303-304, Lord Mustill said:

> "It is by now firmly established that more than one national system of law may bear upon an international arbitration. Thus, there is the proper law which regulates the substantive rights and duties of the parties to the contract from which the disputes has arisen. Exceptionally,

this may differ from the national law governing the interpretation of the agreement to submit the dispute to arbitration. Less exceptionally it may also differ from the national law which the parties have expressly or by implication selected to govern the relationship between themselves and the arbitrator in the conduct of the arbitration: the 'curial law' of the arbitration, as it is often called.... Certainly there may sometimes be an express choice of a curial law which is not the law of the place where the arbitration is to be held: but in the absence of an explicit choice of this kind, or at least some very strong pointer in the agreement to show that such a choice was intended, the inference that the parties when contracting to arbitrate in a particular place consented to having the arbitral process governed by the law of that place is irresistible."

I take the sentence beginning with the words "Less exceptionally it may also differ" to mean that it is less exceptional to find the proper law of an arbitration clause differing from the proper law of the parent contract where the curial law differs from that of the parent contract.... The reasons are not hard to seek. Arbitration law is all about a particular method of resolving disputes. Its substances and processes are closely intertwined. The Arbitration Act contains various provisions which could not readily be separated into boxes labelled substantive arbitration law or procedural law, because that would be an artificial division....

The heart of [Owens Corning's] submissions was that by their choice of law clause the parties chose New York law, which necessarily included the FAA, to govern among other things the formal validity of the arbitration clause; and that, if [its] submissions on the FAA are correct, the arbitration clause is invalid.... On that approach, the effect of one of the two special conditions was to invalidate the other....

The choice of law clause has to be considered in conjunction with the arbitration clause, by which the parties chose that any dispute relating to the policy should be determined not only in London, but expressly under the provisions of the Arbitration Act, with the modification that they waived any right to apply to the Court under §45 for the determination of a question of law arising in the course of the proceedings and any right of appeal under §69 on a point of law.

The shorter form of choice of law clause provided that the policy was to be construed in accordance with the internal regulation laws of New York. I take the reference to internal regulation laws to exclude New York conflict of law rules. In the absence of any reason to conclude otherwise, a provision that a contract is to be construed in accordance with a particular system of law would be taken as a choice of that law to govern all aspects of that contract. But for reasons to which I have adverted ..., New York law cannot have been intended to govern all aspects of the arbitration clause.

The longer form of choice of law clause provided that the policy should be construed in accordance with the internal laws of the state of New York, except (among other things) insofar as such laws are inconsistent with any provision of the policy.... [T]here is ... nothing to preclude parties from agreeing that a system of law shall govern one part of their agreement, but not another part, so long as the parts are severable.... An arbitration clause in a contract is severable, and there is therefore nothing to prevent parties to it from agreeing that the proper law of the parent agreement shall not apply to it if it would be invalid according to that law....

The parties cannot have intended by either form of choice of law clause that all aspects of the arbitration agreement should be governed by New York law, for that would be inconsistent with the stipulation in the arbitration clause that any dispute should be determined in London "under the provisions of the Arbitration Act 1996" (other than §§45 and 69). When, for example, the arbitration clause provided that an award should be a complete defence to any attempted appeal or litigation of the decision in the absence of serious irregularity under §68, it cannot have meant that such irregularity should be judged otherwise than by English law....

A relevant feature of the Act is its definition in §5 of the formal requirements of a valid arbitration agreement, which are less stringent than those of the FAA and which the present arbitration clause undoubtedly satisfies. The agreement has to be in writing, but §5(2) provides that there is an agreement in writing if the agreement is made in writing (whether or not it is signed by the parties), or if the agreement is made by exchange of communications in writing, or if the agreement is evidenced in writing. A second relevant feature of the Act is that under §30 the arbitral tribunal may rule on its own substantive jurisdiction, which expressly includes whether there is a valid arbitration agreement....

I concluded that by stipulating for arbitration in London under the provisions of the Act (other than §§45 and 69) the parties chose English law to govern the matters which fall within those provisions, including the formal validity of the arbitration clause and the jurisdiction of the arbitral tribunal; and by implication chose English law as a proper law of the arbitration clause (although that final step is further than is necessary for the purpose of determining this application)....

HAMLYN & CO. v. TALISKER DISTILLERY
[1894] AC 202 (House of Lords)

LORD HERSCHELL. My Lords, on [January 27, 1892], an agreement was entered into between Roderick Kemp & Co. of the Talisker Distillery, Carbost, Isle of Skye, and Hamlyn & Co. of London, under which Hamlyn & Co. were to supply to the distiller a patent drying machine which was to be worked by the distillery company, who were to bag up and deliver to Hamlyn & Co. dried grain free on board at Carbost to their order or otherwise as required. The agreement concludes with a clause in the following terms: "Should any dispute arise out of this contract the same to be settled by arbitration by two members of the London Corn Exchange, or their umpire, in the usual way." This agreement was made between the parties in England.

Shortly after the contract was entered into ... the present action was instituted ... in Scotland in respect of an alleged breach of contract. The defenders pleaded that the Court of Session had "no jurisdiction," and that "the action is excluded by the clause of reference in the memorandum of agreement." These pleas were repelled by the Lord Ordinary, and his judgment was affirmed....

It is not in controversy that the arbitration clause is, according to the law of England, a valid and binding contract between the parties, nor that according to the law of Scotland it is wholly invalid inasmuch as the arbiters are not named. The view taken by the majority of the Court below is thus expressed by Lord Adam: "So far as I see, nothing required to be done in England in implement and effect of the agreement, and of all and each of its stipulations, is to be determined by the *lex loci solutionis*, that is, by the law of Scotland."

It is not denied that the conclusion thus arrived at renders the arbitration clause wholly inoperative, and thus defeats the expressed intention of the parties, but this is treated as inevitably following from the rule of law that the rights of the parties must be wholly determined by the *lex loci solutionis*. I am not able altogether to agree with the view taken by the learned Lord that everything required to be done in implement of the contract was to be done in Scotland, inasmuch as it appears to me that the arbitration clause which I have read to your Lordships does not indicate that that part of the contract between the parties was to be implemented by performance in Scotland. That clause is as much a part of the contract as any other clause as any other clause of the contract, and certainly there is nothing on the face of it to indicate, but quite the contrary, that it was in the contemplation of the parties that it should be implemented in Scotland.

The learned judges in the Court below treat the *lex loci solutionis* of the main portion of the contract as conclusively determining that all the rights of the parties under the contract must be governed by the law of that place. I am unable to agree with them in this conclusion. Where a contract is entered into between parties residing in different places, where different systems of law prevail, it is a question, as it appears to me, in each case, with reference to what law the parties contracted, and according to what law it was their intention that their rights either under the whole or any part of the contract should be determined. In considering what law is to govern, no doubt the *lex loci solutionis* is a matter of great importance. The *lex loci contractus* is also of importance. In the present case the place of the contract was different from the place of its performance. It is not necessary to enter upon the inquiry … to which of these considerations the greatest weight is to be attribute, namely, the place where the contract was made, or the place where it is to be attributed, namely, the place where the contract was made, or the place where it is to be performed. In my view they are both matters which must be taken into consideration, but neither of them is, of itself, conclusive, and still less is it conclusive, as it appears to me, as to the particular law which was intended to govern particular parts of the contract between the parties. In this case, as in all such cases, the whole of the contract must be looked at and the rights under it must be regulated by the intention of the parties as appearing from the contract. It is perfectly competent to those who, under such circumstances as I have indicated are entering into a contract, to indicate by the terms which they employ, which system of law they intend to be applied to the construction of the contract and to the determination of the rights arising out of it.

Now in the present case it appears to me that the language of the arbitration clause indicates very clearly that the parties intended that the rights under that clause should be determined according to the law of England. As I have said, the contract was made there; one of the parties was residing there. Where under such circumstances the parties agree that any dispute arising out of their contract shall be "settled by arbitration by two members of the London Corn Exchange, or their umpire, in the usual way," it seems to me that they have indicated as clearly as it is possible their intention that that particular stipulation, which is a part of the contract between them, shall be interpreted according to and governed by the law, not of Scotland, but of England…. As I have already pointed out, the contract with reference to arbitration would have been absolutely null and void if it were to be governed by the law of Scotland. That cannot have been the intention of the parties; it is not reasonable to attribute that intention to them if the contract may be otherwise construed…. I see no difficulty whatever in construing the language used as an indication that the contract, or that term of it, was to be governed and regulated by the law of England.

But then it is said that the Scotch Court is asked to enforce a law which is against the public policy of the law of Scotland, and that although the parties may have so contracted the Courts in Scotland cannot be bound to enforce a contract which is against the policy of their law. I should be prepared to admit that an agreement which was opposed to a fundamental principle of the law of Scotland founded on considerations of public policy could not be relied upon and insisted upon in the Courts of Scotland; and if according to the law of Scotland the Courts never allowed their jurisdiction to try the merits of a case to be interfered with by an arbitration clause, there would be considerable force in the contention which was urged by the respondents. But that is not the case. The Courts in Scotland recognise the right of the parties to a contract to determine that any disputes under it shall be settled, not in the ordinary course of litigation, but by an arbitration tribunal selected by the parties. If in the present case the arbitrators had been named, the Courts in Scotland would have recognised and given effect to and enforced the arbitration clause, and would by reason of it have declined to enter upon a trial of the merits of the case. That being so, I have been unable to understand upon what fundamental principle of public policy the rule can be said to rest that where an arbitrator is not named an agreement between the parties to refer a matter to arbitration ought not to be enforced....

But then it is argued that an agreement to refer disputes to arbitration deals with the remedy and not with the rights of the parties, and that consequently the forum being Scotch the parties cannot by reason of the agreement into which they have entered interfere with the ordinary course of proceedings in the Courts of Scotland. Stated generally, I should not dispute that proposition so far as it lays down that the parties cannot, in a case where the merits fall to be determined in the Scotch Courts, insist, by virtue of an agreement, that those courts shall depart from their ordinary course of procedure. But that is not really the question which has to be determined in the present case. The question which has to be determined is whether it is a case in which the Courts of Scotland ought to entertain the merits and adjudicate upon them. If it were such a case, then no doubt the ordinary course of procedure in the Scotch Courts would have to be followed; but the preliminary question has to be determined whether by virtue of a valid clause of arbitration the proper course is for the Courts of Scotland not to adjudicate upon the merits of the case, but to leave the matter to be determined by the tribunal to which the parties have agreed to refer it. Viewed in that light, I can see no difficulty; and the argument that to give effect to this arbitration clause would interfere with the course of procedure in the forum in which the action is pending seems to me entirely to fail. For these reasons I move that the judgment appealed from be reversed.

LORD ASHBOURNE. I concur. The substantial question to be determined is whether the law of Scotland or the law of England is to be applied to the interpretation of the arbitration clause in question. One of the parties was a Scotch distiller, and the parties on the other side were merchants in London. The contract was made in England, and was (apart from the arbitration clause) to be performed in Scotland.... There is no absolute rule of law as to the way in which the intention of the parties to a contract with reference to the law of a particular place is to be ascertained. Were it not for the arbitration clause, I should assent to the conclusion that the parties contracted solely with a view to the application of the law of Scotland. Having regard, however, to the terms of that clause, I am led to the conclusion that the parties intended that it should be interpreted by the rules of the law of England alone. A contract which provided that disputes "should be settled by arbitration by two members of the London Corn Exchange, or their umpire, in the usual way," distinctly introduces a reference to well-known laws regulating such arbitrations, and those must be the laws of England. This interpretation gives due and full effect to every portion of the contract; whereas the arbitration clause becomes mere waste paper if it is held that the parties were contracting on the basis of the application of the law of Scotland, which would at once refuse to acknowledge the full efficacy of a clause so framed. It is more reasonable to hold that the parties contracted with the common intention of giving entire effect to every clause, rather than of mutilating or destroying one of the most important provisions.

JUDGMENT OF 20 DECEMBER 1993, MUNICIPALITÉ DE KHOMS EL MERGEB v. SOCIÉTÉ DALICO

1994 Rev. arb. 116 (French Cour de cassation)

[excerpted above at pp. 182-83]

LEDEE v. CERAMICHE RAGNO

684 F.2d 184 (1st Cir. 1982)

[excerpted above at pp. 181-82]

RHONE MEDITERRANEE COMPAGNIA FRANCESE DI ASSICURAZIONI E RIASSICURAZONI v. ACHILLE LAURO

712 F.2d 50 (3d Cir. 1983)

GIBBONS, Circuit Judge. Rhone Mediterranee Compagnia Francese di Assicurazioni E Riassicurazioni ("Rhone"), a casualty insurer, appeals from an order of the District Court of the Virgin Islands staying Rhone's action pending arbitration. The action results from a fire loss which occurred when the vessel Angelina Lauro burned at the dock of the East Indian Co. Ltd in Charlotte Amalie, St. Thomas. At the time of the fire the vessel was under time charter to Costa Armatori SpA ("Costa"), an Italian Corporation. Rhone insured Costa, and reimbursed it for property and fuel losses totalling over one million dollars. Rhone, as subrogee of Costa, sued the owner of the vessel, Achille Lauro, ("Lauro"), and its master, Antonio Scotto di Carlo, alleging breach of the Lauro-Costa time charter, unseaworthiness, and negligence of the crew. The district court granted defendants' motion for a stay of the action pending arbitration, and Rhone appeals....

As subrogee, Rhone stands in place of its insured, the time charterer Costa. In the time charter contract there is a clause:

> "23. Arbitration. Any dispute arising under the Charter to be referred to arbitration in London (or such other place as may be agreed according to box 24) one arbitrator to be nominated by the Owners and the other by the Charterers, and in case the Arbitrators shall not agree then to the decision of an Umpire to be appointed by them, the award of the Arbitrators or the Umpire to be final and binding upon both parties.
> Box 24. Place of arbitration (only to be filled in if place other than London agreed (cl. 23) NAPOLI."

All the parties to the time charter agreement and the lawsuit are Italian. Italy and the United States are parties to the [New York] Convention. The [FAA] implements the United States' accession ... to the Convention by providing that it "shall be enforced in United States courts in accordance with this chapter." 9 U.S.C. §201. [Rhone does not dispute that the Convention is applicable.]

What Rhone does contend is that under the terms of the Convention the arbitration clause in issue is unenforceable. Rhone's argument proceeds from a somewhat ambiguous provision in Article II(3) of the Convention [which the court quoted in full.] ... Rhone contends that when the arbitration clause refers to a place of arbitration, here Naples, Italy, the law of that place is determinative. It then relies on the affidavit of an expert on Italian law which states that in Italy an arbitration clause calling for an even number of arbitrators is null and void, even if, as in this case there is a provision for their designation of a tie breaker.

The ambiguity in Article II(3) of the Convention with respect to governing law contrasts with Article V, dealing with enforcement of awards. Article V(1)(a) permits refusal of recognition and enforcement of an award if the "agreement is not valid under the law to which the parties have subjected it or, failing any indication thereon, under the law of the country where the award was made." ... Thus Article V unambiguously refers the forum in which enforcement of an award is sought to the law chosen by the parties, or the law of the place of the award.

Rhone and the defendants suggest different conclusions that should be drawn from the differences between Article II and Article V. Rhone suggests that the choice of law rule of Article V should be read into Article II. The defendants urge that in the absence of a specific reference Article II should be read so as to permit the forum, when asked to refer a dispute to arbitration, to apply its own law respecting validity of the arbitration clause....

None of the limited secondary literature sheds so clear a light as to suggest a certain answer. However, we conclude that the meaning of Article II(3) which is most consistent with the overall purposes of the Convention is that an agreement to arbitrate is "null and void" only (1) when it is subject to an internationally recognized defense such as duress, mistake, fraud, or waiver, *see Ledee v. Ceramiche Ragno*; *I.T.A.D. Associates, Inc. v. Podar Bros.*, 636 F.2d 75 (4th Cir. 1981), or (2) when it contravenes fundamental policies of the forum state. The "null and void" language must be read narrowly, for the signatory nations have jointly declared a general policy of enforceability of agreements to arbitrate....

[S]ignatory nations have effectively declared a joint policy that presumes the enforceability of agreements to arbitrate. Neither the parochial interests of the forum state, nor those of states having more significant relationships with the dispute, should be permitted to supersede that presumption. The policy of the Convention is best served by an approach which leads to upholding agreements to arbitrate. The rule of one state as to the required number of arbitrators does not implicate the fundamental concerns of either the international system or forum, and hence the agreement is not void.

Rhone urges that this rule may result in a Neapolitan arbitration award which, because of Italy's odd number of arbitrators rule, the Italian courts would not enforce. The defendants insist that even in Italy this procedural rule on arbitration is waivable and a resulting award will be enforced. Even if that is not the law of Italy, however, Rhone's objection does not compel the conclusion that we should read Article II(3) as it suggests. The parties did agree to a non-judicial dispute resolution mechanism, and the basic purpose of the Convention is to discourage signatory states from disregarding such agreements. Rhone is not faced with an Italian public policy disfavoring arbitration, but only with an Italian procedural rule of arbitration which may have been overlooked by the drafters of the time charter agreement. Certainly the parties are free to structure the arbitration so as to comply with the Italian procedural rule by having the designated arbitrators select a third member before rather than after impasse. Even if that is not accomplished an award may still result, which can be enforced outside Italy.

Rhone urges that Article V(1)(d) prohibits such enforcement outside Italy, because it refers a non-Italian forum to the law of Italy. We disagree. Section 1 says only that "enforcement of an award may be refused" on the basis of the law of the country where it was made. Where, as here, the law of such a country generally favors enforcement of arbitration awards, and the defect is at best one of a procedural nature, Article V(1) certainly permits another forum to disregard the defect and enforce. That is especially the case when defendants come before the court, relying on Article II, seek a stay of the action in favor of arbitration. They will hardly be in a position to rely on Italy's odd number of arbitrators rule if Rhone seeks to enforce an award in the District Court of the Virgin Islands.[26]

The forum law implicitly referenced by Article II(3) is the law of the United States, not the local law of the Virgin Islands or of a state. That law favors enforcement of arbitration clauses. *Scherk v. Alberto-Culver Co.*, 417 U.S. 506 (1974).... Since no federal law imposes an odd number of arbitrators rule—the only defect relied upon by Rhone—the district court did not err in staying the suit for breach of the time charter agreement pending arbitration....

BG GROUP PLC v. REPUBLIC OF ARGENTINA
134 S.Ct. 1198 (2014)

[excerpted above at pp. 233-47]

DALLAH REAL ESTATE & TOURISM HOLDING CO. v. MINISTRY OF RELIGIOUS AFFAIRS, GOVERNMENT OF PAKISTAN
[2010] UKSC 46 (U.K. S.Ct.)

[excerpted above at pp. 247-70]

NOTES

1. *Separability presumption and choice of law applicable to arbitration agreements.* As we have seen, an arbitration agreement is almost universally regarded as "separable" from the underlying contract to which it relates. *See supra* pp. 190-218. One consequence of this is that the arbitration clause of a contract may be governed by a different substantive law from that applicable to the underlying contract. Consider the award in *ICC Case No. 6149*. How does the tribunal approach the effect of the separability presumption on the choice of law applicable to the arbitration agreement? Compare the analyses in *Judgment of 30 May 1994*, *Owens Corning* and *Talisker*.

Consider Article V(1)(a) of the New York Convention. What does it provide regarding the law applicable to the arbitration agreement? Compare Article VI(2) of the European Convention, excerpted at p. 32 of the Documentary Supplement. Do both

---

26. Had Rhone so requested it would have been proper for the district court to condition its stay order on the defendants' agreement to reform the arbitration clause so as to satisfy Italy's procedural requirement. Since no such request was made we do not consider whether, had it been made, we would remand for such a modification.

Articles V(1)(a) and VI(2) provide for the application of a potentially different law to the arbitration agreement than to the underlying contract? Explain how.

Does the separability presumption mean that the law applicable to the arbitration clause is *necessarily* different from that applicable to the underlying contract? Or merely that differing laws *may* apply? If the latter, then what choice-of-law rules govern selection of the law governing the arbitration agreement? Consider:

> "[A]ll contracts which provide for arbitration and contain a foreign element may involve three potentially relevant systems of law: (1) the law governing the substantive contract; (2) the law governing the agreement to arbitrate and the performance of that agreement; (3) the law governing the conduct of the arbitration. In the majority of the cases all three will be the same, but (1) will often be different from (2) and (3) and occasionally, but rarely, (2) may also differ from (3). That is exactly the case here." *M.S. Dozco India P. Ltd v. M/S Doosan Infracore Co.*, [2010] INSC 839, ¶¶12-13 (Indian S.Ct.) (quoting *Naviera Amazonica Peruana SA v. Cia Internacional de Seguros del Peru* [1988] 1 Lloyd's Rep. 116, 119 (English Ct. App.)).

Why does it make sense for different laws to apply to the arbitration agreement and the underlying contract? What reasons might justify such a result? Consider in particular the analyses in *Talisker*, *Dalico* and *Ledee*. Are there reasons for applying special "pro-enforcement" or "validation" choice-of-law rules to international arbitration agreements?

2. *Issues governed by law applicable to arbitration agreement.* The law governing an arbitration agreement is usually regarded as applicable to the agreement's: (a) formation; (b) substantive validity; and (c) interpretation. *Cf. Restatement (Second) Conflict of Laws* §218 comment a (1971); L. Collins (ed.), *Dicey, Morris and Collins on The Conflict of Laws* ¶16-0228 (15th ed. 2012) ("The law governing the arbitration agreement will determine its validity, effect, and interpretation."). Issues of formal validity, nonarbitrability and the effects of the arbitration agreement may be subject to other national laws. *See infra* pp. 315-34, 375-92 & 475-510.

3. *Application of law of judicial enforcement forum to validity of arbitration agreements.* Historically, many authorities held that an arbitration agreement was governed by the law of the judicial forum where enforcement of the agreement was sought. That approach (referred to briefly in *Talisker*) regarded the validity and enforceability of an arbitration agreement as a "procedural" or "remedial" matter, governed by the law of the judicial forum in which the agreement was invoked. *See Ferrara SpA v. United Grain Growers Ltd*, 441 F.Supp. 778, 781 n.2 (S.D.N.Y. 1977) (dicta that judicial enforcement forum's laws should apply, on grounds that New York Convention's legislative history contemplates this and it "is consistent … with the view that enforceability of an agreement to arbitrate relates to the law of remedies and is therefore governed by the law of the forum."); *Sinva, Inc. v. Merrill Lynch, Pierce, Fenner & Smith, Inc.*, 253 F.Supp. 359, 364 (S.D.N.Y. 1966) ("New York for conflicts purposes treats issues concerning arbitrability as part of its 'law of remedies,' so that New York local law would apply in the case at bar, rather than the law of England or France which have greater contacts with the transactions involved here.").

Under this approach, what substantive law would apply to the arbitration agreements at issue in *Ledee* and *Rhone*? What law would have applied in *Judgment of 30 May 1994*? How does this compare with the law actually applied by the courts in each case? What are the arguments in favor of applying the law of the enforcement forum to the substantive validity of the arbitration agreement? What are the disadvantages?

4. *Parties' autonomy to select law applicable to substantive validity of arbitration agreement.* Consider Article V(1)(a) of the New York Convention. What does it provide with regard to the parties' autonomy to choose the law applicable to the arbitration agreement? Compare Article VI(2)(a) of the European Convention.

    Note the parties' broad autonomy, under most developed legal systems, to select the law governing their commercial contracts. *See infra* pp. 988-90. Is there any reason to treat the parties' autonomy to select the law governing their arbitration agreements less favorably? Note that Article V(1)(a) of the New York Convention and Article VI(2) of the European Convention both impose international obligations on Contracting States to recognize the parties' selection of the law governing an international arbitration agreement.

5. *Limits on parties' autonomy to select law applicable to arbitration agreement.* Are there limits to the parties' autonomy to select the law applicable to their arbitration agreement? Suppose that national law limits the enforceability or validity of arbitration agreements in particular circumstances (*e.g.,* consumer or labor disputes). *See supra* pp. 186-90 & *infra* pp. 436-60. Should parties be permitted to contract out of such limitations?

    Consider *Award in ICC Case No. 6149.* Suppose that the parties had expressly agreed that French (or some other non-Jordanian) law governed their arbitration agreement. The tribunal would fairly clearly have concluded—as it did even without a direct choice-of-law clause—that Jordanian Law No. 35 did not apply. But Jordanian Law No. 35 was enacted to advance substantial national policies of Jordan with regard to the enforceability of arbitration agreements. Why should parties be permitted to contract out of such vital national rules in cases with significant connections to Jordan? How would a Jordanian court have resolved the question whether the arbitration agreement in *ICC Case No. 6149* was valid? Does that have any relevance to an arbitral tribunal's resolution of the same question?

    Suppose that a nation's law invalidates arbitration agreements in consumer transactions or employment relations. *See infra* pp. 446-60. If parties to such transactions agree to arbitrate, but subject their arbitration agreement to foreign law (which does not contain similar limitations), is their agreement enforceable? Does it matter where the arbitral seat is located? Does it matter whether the decision is made by (a) a local arbitral tribunal; (b) a foreign arbitral tribunal; (c) a local court; or (d) a foreign court? Should it matter? If different decision-makers reach different conclusions, won't the objectives of international arbitration (including uniform, enforceable results and efficiency) be frustrated?

6. *Choice of law applicable to arbitration clause where underlying contract contains choice-of-law clause.* International contracts frequently contain choice-of-law clauses that apply to the contract generally. In principle, these choice-of-law clauses can be drafted broadly enough to encompass the arbitration clause contained in the parties' contract, even though it is "separable." For example: "All of the provisions of this contract (Articles 1-21, including the arbitration clause in Article 19) shall be governed by the law of State X." Often, however, choice-of-law clauses are drafted more

narrowly: "This agreement shall be governed by the law of State X." This type of formulation arguably does *not* encompass a "separable" arbitration agreement.

What approach should be taken to "general" choice-of-law clauses? Assume that, in contrast to the first choice-of-law provision in the foregoing paragraph, the language of the parties' agreement does not expressly state that the clause applies to the arbitration agreement. Is it likely that the parties to such a general choice-of-law clause intended their chosen law to apply to a "separable" arbitration agreement? Or is it more likely that the parties intended their chosen law *not* to apply to the arbitration clause?

Is it likely that most commercial parties have ever heard of the separability presumption? If there is no meaningful evidence of the parties' intent, and one merely has a general choice-of-law clause and an ordinary arbitration clause, should the law selected by the parties to govern their underlying contract also apply to their separable arbitration clause? Do you know enough to answer the question? Do you want to know what outcome would result from application of the law chosen by a general choice-of-law clause to the arbitration agreement? Why? Do you also want to know the nationalities of the parties, the applicable law they chose, and the location of their arbitral seat? Why?

Consider the following hypotheticals:

(i) French and German parties agree to arbitrate in Germany and to a general choice-of-law clause selecting German law.

(ii) French and German parties agree to arbitrate in Switzerland and to a general choice-of-law clause selecting Swiss law.

(iii) French and German parties agree to arbitrate in Switzerland and to a general choice-of-law clause selecting German law.

(iv) French and German parties agree to arbitrate in France and to a general choice-of-law clause selecting German law.

(v) French and German parties agree to arbitrate, without selecting an arbitral seat, and to a general choice-of-law clause selecting (i) Swiss; (ii) French; or (iii) German law.

(vi) French and German parties agree to arbitrate in England and to a general choice-of-law clause selecting Swiss law.

(vii) French and German parties agree to arbitrate in Switzerland and to a general choice-of-law clause selecting Russian law. Russian law invalidates the arbitration clause, while Swiss law upholds it.

(viii) French and German parties agree to arbitrate in Russia and to a general choice-of-law clause selecting Swiss law. Russian law invalidates the arbitration clause, while Swiss law upholds it.

Authorities regarding the effects of a general choice-of-law clause on the law governing the arbitration agreement are divided. What rule did the Bundesgerichtshof state with regard to this issue in *Judgment of 27 February 1970, supra* pp. 194-98? What rule did the Japanese court apply in *Judgment of 30 May 1994*? And what rule was applied in *Owens Corning*?

Some authorities have interpreted general choice-of-law clauses as extending to "separable" arbitration provisions contained within an underlying contract. *See Union of India v. McDonnell Douglas Corp.* [1993] 2 Lloyd's Rep. 48, 50 ("The parties may make an express choice of law to govern their commercial bargain and that choice may also be made of the law to govern the agreement to arbitrate. In the present case it is my view that by Art. 11 the parties have chosen the law of India not only to govern the rights and obligations arising out of their commercial bargain but also the rights and obligations arising out of their agreement to arbitrate."); *Final Award in ICC Case No. 6379*, XVII Y.B. Comm. Arb. 212, 215 (1992) (applying law governing underlying contract, not law of arbitral seat); *Final Award in ICC Case No. 3572*, XIV Y.B. Comm. Arb. 111 (1989) (applying law chosen by parties to govern underlying contract).

On the other hand, other authorities refuse to apply a general choice-of-law clause to the arbitration clause, particularly where the parties' chosen law would invalidate the clause, instead usually applying the law of the arbitral seat. *Final Award in ICC Case No. 5294*, XIV Y.B. Comm. Arb. 137, 140-41 (1989) (applying law of arbitral seat, not law governing underlying contract); *Final Award in ICC Case No. 6162*, XVII Y.B. Comm. Arb. 153 (1992) (applying Swiss law, as law of arbitral seat, to arbitration agreement; refusing to apply substantive law governing underlying agreement). Consider again the decision in *Judgment of 30 May 1994*.

Which of these two approaches is more sensible? In answering this question, does it matter whether the law governing the underlying contract gives effect to the parties' arbitration agreement (as opposed to rendering it invalid)? Consider the analysis in *Talisker*; what were the reasons expressed for applying English law (the law of the arbitral seat) to the arbitration agreement? Would it make sense to conclude that the parties' choice-of-law clause, selected to govern their underlying commercial relations, was intended to apply to their separable arbitration agreement, in circumstances where that law invalidated their agreement to arbitrate? Is that what parties likely would have intended in including a general choice-of-law clause in their underlying contract?

7. *Law applicable to arbitration agreement in absence of choice by parties.* In many cases, parties do not agree on the law applicable to their arbitration agreement. They either do not include a choice-of-law clause in their contract or that clause will be held not to apply to the separable arbitration agreement. In these circumstances, what law should apply to the parties' arbitration agreement? Authorities have arrived at a wide array of different conclusions, and choice-of-law rules, in answering this question.

(a) *Most significant relationship and closest connection standards.* Where the parties have not agreed upon an applicable law, a number of contemporary arbitral awards, judicial decisions and commentaries have applied generally-applicable choice-of-law standards to the arbitration agreement, including the most significant relationship and closest connection standards. Thus, §218 of the *Restatement (Second) Conflict of Laws* provides that the "validity of an arbitration agreement, and the rights created thereby," are to be determined by applying the generally applicable conflicts rules of §187 and §188. Section 218 explains, in comment a, that: "Whether a judicial action may be maintained in violation of the provisions of an arbitration agreement should be determined not by the local law of the forum but rather by the law selected by application of [§§187 and 188]." *Restatement (Second) Conflict of Laws* §218 comment a (1971). As discussed elsewhere, §§187 and 188 of the *Restatement* generally give effect to the parties' contractual choice of law or, failing such agreement, provide for application of the law of the state with the most significant relationship to the parties' agreement (*i.e.*, here, the parties' arbitration clause). *See infra* pp. 507, 990-91.

Review §§187 and 188 and consider how they would apply to an arbitration agreement. Recall the separability presumption and consider its effect upon choice of law analysis under the *Restatement*'s "most significant relationship" standard. What state will ordinarily have the most significant relationship to an agreement to arbitrate? Note the observation in *Talisker* about the place where the arbitration agreement will be performed. Where is that?

What exactly does it mean to refer to the "most significant relationship," or "closest connection," of the arbitration agreement? What jurisdictions are plausible contenders for this role? Is there any real alternative other than: (a) the law of the arbitral seat; or (b) the law governing the underlying contract? As between these two choices, how does one prefer one, rather than the other, as having a "closer" or "more significant" relationship to the arbitration agreement? Note the comments in *Talisker* about the difficulties in assigning priority to either the *lex loci solutionis* or the *lex loci contractus*; does the same observation apply here? Do either of these standards really engage with the underlying policies of the New York Convention and the parties' objectives in selecting international arbitration as a means to resolve their disputes? How would you describe these objectives? What sort of choice-of-law rule do these objectives suggest is appropriate?

(b) *Substantive law of arbitral seat.* A number of authorities have held that, absent contrary choice by the parties, the substantive validity of the arbitration agreement is governed by the law of the arbitral seat. What is the rationale for this result?

First, as discussed below, Article V(1)(a) of the New York Convention arguably provides for application of the law of the arbitral seat to arbitration agreements (absent contrary choice by the parties). *See infra* pp. 308-10. Note that Article V(1)(a)—which applies by its terms to the recognition of arbitral awards (not the enforcement of arbitration agreements)—provides that an arbitral award may be denied recognition if the parties' arbitration agreement was "not valid under the law to which the parties have subjected it or, failing any indication thereon, under the law of the country where the award was made." A number of authorities have relied upon Article V(1)(a)'s choice of law rule in considering whether to stay litigation pending an arbitration. *See* G. Born, *International Commercial Arbitration* 477-79, 493-502, 562-68 (2d ed. 2014). Is it appropriate to apply Article V(1)(a)'s choice-of-law rule outside the context of recognition of arbitral awards? What alternative is there?

Compare the choice-of-law analysis of the Tokyo High Court in the *Judgment of 30 May 1994*: "If the parties' will is unclear we must presume, as it is the nature of arbitration agreements to provide for given procedures in a given place, that the parties intend that the law of the place where the arbitration proceedings are held will apply." This result can again be explained as an implied choice of law by the parties (through their selection of the arbitral seat). If the parties' choice of the arbitral seat is treated as an implied choice of law, are other factors then also relevant to the parties' implied choice? For example, the law governing the underlying contract, the connections of the underlying commercial contract with different jurisdictions?

Alternatively, the arbitral seat can be said to have the most significant relationship with the parties' arbitration clause. Why is it that the arbitration agreement might be said to have its most significant relationship, or closest connection, with the arbitral seat? Why is the agreement to arbitrate not more closely connected to the underlying commercial contract, and the law governing that contract, which the parties' arbitration agreement relates to?

Is it sensible to apply the law of the arbitral seat to an arbitration agreement where the parties have not otherwise agreed on the governing law? Consider the hypotheticals set forth above. *See supra* p. 303.

What law did the Court in *BG Group* apply to the arbitration agreement? What was the Court's rationale for doing so? Was it that the United States was the arbitral seat? Apart from being the arbitral seat, what connection did the United States have with the parties' dispute? With the BIT? What law would Chief Justice Roberts have applied to the formation and validity of the arbitration agreement?

What law did the Court in *Dallah* apply to the arbitration agreement? Why?

(c) *Cumulative application of all potentially applicable laws.* How does the tribunal in *ICC Case No. 6149* approach the question of the law applicable to the arbitration agreement? *See Final Award in ICC Case No. 5485*, XIV Y.B. Comm. Arb. 156 (1989) (applying, cumulatively, ICC Rules, arbitral seat's law, law governing underlying contract and trade usages); *Award in ICC Case No. 4145*, XII Y.B. Comm. Arb. 97 (1987) (applying substantive laws chosen by parties and law of arbitral seat; finding all satisfied). The same approach is also sometimes taken to the substantive law governing the parties' dispute. *See infra* p. 975. The sequential or cumulative approach is comforting, but provides no guidance when a "true conflict" exists. If the potentially-applicable substantive laws yield differing results, then (it is said) some choice must be made among them. In that case, what rules of preference should be adopted?

At the end of the day, as noted above, selecting the law governing the parties' arbitration clause (absent express agreement) usually requires choosing between two principal alternatives—the substantive law of the underlying contract or the law of the arbitral seat. Does the cumulative choice-of-law method provide any assistance in resolving this choice? Is it unfair to say that the cumulative choice-of-law method provides no assistance except in those cases where no assistance is needed, because all conceivably applicable laws provide for the same result in any case?

(d) *"Validation" principle.* In practice, a prevailing theme of decisions dealing with the law governing arbitration agreements has been the so-called validation principle. Arbitrators and courts strive (both expressly and otherwise) to apply a law that will give effect to the parties' international arbitration agreement.

Consider Article 178(2) of the SLPIL, excerpted at p. 158 of the Documentary Supplement, which prescribes a special conflict of laws rule for the substantive validity of arbitration agreements. Under this rule, an agreement to arbitrate in Switzerland is valid if its validity would be recognized under either (i) the law chosen by the parties to govern the arbitration agreement, (ii) the law governing the merits of the parties' dispute, or (iii) Swiss substantive law. Article 178(2) adopts a variation of the validation principle. What is the rationale for this approach? *See also* Netherlands Code of Civil Procedure, Art. 166 ("an arbitration agreement is substantially valid if it is valid in accordance with the law that the parties have chosen or the law of the place of arbitration, or, if the parties made no choice of law, in accordance with the law applicable to the legal relationship to which the arbitration agreement relates"); Spanish Arbitration Act, 2011, Art. 9(6) ("When the arbitration is international, the arbitration agreement shall be valid and the dispute may be subject to arbitration if the requirements stipulated by the law chosen by the parties to govern the arbitration agreement, the law applicable to the substance of the dispute, or Spanish law, are fulfilled."); Algerian Code of Civil and Administrative Procedure, Art. 458 bis 1, ¶3 (same).

Compare the House of Lords' analysis in *Talisker* to the rationale underlying Article 178(2). Consider again the *Owens Corning* case; assume that the FAA and New York law contained a form requirement that would have invalidated the arbitration clause? Would that have been relevant to the English court's choice-of-law analysis? *See also Judgment of 26 August 2008*, XXXIV Y.B. Comm. Arb. 404, 405 (2009) (Austrian Oberster Gerichtshof) ("If the wording of the declaration of intent allows for two equally plausible interpretations, the interpretation which favors the validity of the arbitration agreement and its applicability to a certain dispute is to be preferred.").

Is the validation principle wise? Is the validation principle consistent with the parties' objectives in agreeing to an international arbitration agreement? Are there particular policy objectives that are furthered by generously enforcing arbitration agreements in international transactions?

Compare the approach of Article 178(2) and the validation principle to that of Article V(1)(a) of the Convention. Is Article 178(2) consistent with Article V(1)(a)? Why?

(e) *International principles.* Consider the analysis of the French Cour de cassation in *Dalico.* Note that the Cour de cassation does not apply a national law—French or otherwise—to the validity of the arbitration agreement. What law does the Cour de cassation apply to the arbitration agreement? *See also Award in ICC Case No. 8938,* XXIV Y.B. Comm. Arb. 174, 176 (1999) (the arbitration agreement's "existence and validity are to be ascertained, taking into account the mandatory rules of national law and international public policy, in the light of the common intention of the parties, without necessarily referring to a state law"); *Judgment of 24 February 1994,* XXII Y.B. Comm. Arb. 682, 686 (1997) (Paris Cour d'appel) ("For the arbitration clause … to be valid it is sufficient to establish that it is an international contract which has been concluded in conformity with the needs and conditions of international trade usages.").

What is the rationale for applying international law principles to the substantive validity of an international arbitration agreement? Consider Article V(1)(a) of the New York Convention and Article VI(2) of the European Convention. Does either instrument contemplate application of international—rather than national—law to the arbitration agreement? What exactly would the content of international law principles be? What would be the source of rules defining principles of contract formation, fraud, impossibility, unconscionability and the like?

What law did the parties appear to choose in *Dalico*? To what parts of the parties' agreement was this law applicable? Suppose that the parties' choice-of-law agreement extended to their arbitration agreement. Would it still have been appropriate for the *Dalico* court to apply international law?

What law did the Court in *Dallah* apply to the arbitration agreement? Did it apply French law? Or something else?

8. *Choice-of-law rules applicable to international arbitration agreements subject to New York Convention.* What effect does the New York Convention have on the choice of law applicable to arbitration agreements falling within its scope? Note that Article V(1)(a) addresses this issue, in the context of recognition of arbitral awards. Consider how the decisions in *Rhone* and *Ledee* address the choice of law governing the arbitration agreement under the Convention.

(a) *Uniform international substantive standards under Article II.* Can Article II be interpreted as setting forth a uniform international standard for when an arbitration agreement is valid under the Convention? Under this view, Article II would establish a substantive defense to arbitration agreements, applicable when those agreements are "null and void" within the meaning of Article II. If this uniform international standard were not satisfied, then enforcement of the agreement under Article II would be required (subject to the Convention's other exceptions). Is this a wise interpretation of Article II? Would it advance the goals of the Convention?

Does the text of Article II provide a sound basis for a uniform international definition of "null and void"? Does the half-sentence reference to agreements which are "null and void, inoperative, or incapable of being performed" provide an adequate basis for deciding cases? If the Convention's drafters had intended to create an international definition of "null and void," wouldn't they have included a more detailed formulation (referring, for example, to fraud, duress, unconscionability, etc.)? Or could such rules evolve over time, as courts gained experience in applying the Convention? What law would apply to the existence and validity of investment arbitration agreements under the ICSID Convention and of inter-state arbitration agreements? Could not similar international principles apply under the New York Convention?

If Article II does not establish a uniform international definition of "null and void," then what purpose does Article II serve? If individual nations can establish whatever defenses they wish, under local law, to arbitration agreements, then what is accomplished by Article II's obligation to "recognize" arbitration agreements? Suppose a Contracting State provides that arbitration agreements are "null and void" if: (a) not affirmed in writing after a dispute arises; (b) not approved by a designated government authority; (c) opposed by a local national; or (d) contrary to national interests. What effect does Article II have in these cases? How would the tribunal in *ICC Case No. 6149* respond to the foregoing queries? How would the *Ledee* court respond?

(b) *Article II overrides discriminatory national law.* An alternative interpretation of Article II would conclude that generally-applicable contract law defenses (under national law) would determine whether an arbitration clause is "null and void," but that Article II would override national law defenses which are not based on generally-applicable contract law rules. Consider the *Ledee* opinion. Does it adopt the approach outlined above? Is this persuasive? What textual objections can be made to the *Ledee* result?

Recall that Article V contains choice-of-law rules for international arbitration agreements which (by their terms) apply at the stage of enforcing arbitral awards. Would it make sense for Article II to impose a uniform set of international substantive rules governing the formation and validity of international arbitration agreements, while Article V left individual states freedom to apply potentially more restrictive national laws to deny enforcement to awards based on those agreements? What rationale might support such a result? Does it matter that non-recognition under Article V(1)(a) is permissive, not mandatory? *See infra* pp. 1184-85, 1196.

In addition to *Rhone*, a number of courts have refused to apply foreign laws, including the law of the arbitral seat, singling out arbitration agreements for special burdens. *See, e.g., Doe v. Royal Caribbean Cruises, Ltd*, 180 F.Appx. 893, 894 (11th Cir. 2006); *Becker Autoradio U.S.A., Inc. v. Becker Autoradiowerk GmbH*, 585 F.2d 39, 43 n.8 (3d Cir. 1978) (dicta that U.S. court would not apply "the law of state X [that] will not enforce, or gives very limited effect to arbitration clauses"); *Marchetto v. DeKalb Genetics Corp.*, 711 F.Supp. 936 (N.D. Ill. 1989) (rejecting claim that arbitration agreement was void under Italian law because it applied to tort claims and because non-parties were sued: "the possibility that Italian law might divest a panel of Italian arbitrators is not determinative"); *Ferrara SpA v. United Grain Growers*, Ltd, 441 F.Supp. 778, 781 (S.D.N.Y. 1977) (refusing to give effect to "purported Italian law rule [that] appears to be a special requirement governing agreements to arbitrate, but inapplicable to other contractual terms and conditions"). Why should U.S. courts give effect to arbitration agreements that are invalid under the law of the arbitral seat?

Is this refusal by U.S. courts to apply the law of a foreign arbitral seat justifiable? Is the position of U.S. courts consistent with Article V(1)(a) of the New York Convention? Explain why. What is the source of the rule in *Rhone* and *Ledee* that only "internationally neutral" defenses are available to challenge an international arbitration agreement?

Under *Rhone*'s analysis, what kinds of foreign laws would be applied to render an arbitration agreement invalid? Would *Rhone* permit defenses of fraudulent inducement, waiver, unconscionability, or illegality? What effect would the *Rhone* court have given to an Italian statute that mirrored the Puerto Rican statute in *Ledee*?

Assume that *Ledee* is correct that only defenses that are "neutral on an international scale" can be relied on to demonstrate the invalidity of an arbitration agreement. Why was the Puerto Rican law in *Ledee* not "internationally neutral"? If both Italy and Puerto Rico (or the United States) forbid agreements to arbitrate franchise disputes, would that be an "internationally neutral" defense? What if most countries do so? Or does *Ledee* forbid *any* national law that singles out arbitration agreements for special disfavor, no matter how widely accepted such a rule is?

What defines the content of "international neutral" defenses like fraud, mistake, duress, and waiver? Does the *Ledee* court contemplate some international standard of fraud or waiver that each nation must apply? Alternatively, does *Ledee* regard the requirement of international neutrality as essentially negative, preempting various parochial defenses, but leaving it to national law (such as the FAA) to define the details of internationally neutral defenses?

Compare the *Ledee* choice-of-law analysis with that in *Dalico*. What are the differences in the two approaches? What are the similarities? What purposes do each approach serve?

What if parties select foreign law to govern the validity and scope of their arbitration agreement? Shouldn't that choice be respected (*i.e.*, by applying the chosen national law instead of international principles)? How would *Rhone* have been decided if the parties had expressly selected Italian law to govern their arbitration agreement? Would it be fair to interpret the parties' choice-of-law clause as selecting a national law, but including and subject to limitations imposed by the New York Convention?

9. *U.S. court decisions applying federal common law or state law rules to arbitration agreements subject to New York Convention.* Some U.S. decisions appear to apply more traditional choice-of-law rules to international arbitration agreements (rather than the requirements of international neutrality adopted in *Ledee* and *Rhone*). Thus, some U.S. courts apply substantive rules of federal common law to the formation and validity of international arbitration agreements that are subject to the Convention. *See, e.g., Int'l Paper Co. v. Schwabedissen Maschinen & Anlagen GmbH*, 206 F.3d 411, 417 n.4 (4th Cir. 2000); *David L. Threlkeld & Co. v. Metallgesellschaft Ltd*, 923 F.2d 245, 249-50 (2d Cir. 1991); *Glencore Ltd v. Degussa Eng'd Carbons LP*, 848 F.Supp.2d 410, 435-36 (S.D.N.Y. 2012); *Copape Produtos de Pétroleo Ltda v. Glencore Ltd*, 2012 WL 398596 (S.D.N.Y.) (applying federal common law, comprised of generally-accepted principles of contract law and Uniform Commercial Code, to determine existence and validity of arbitration agreement); *Nanosolutions, LLC v. Prajza*, 793 F.Supp.2d 46, 54 n.5 (D.D.C. 2011) ("[i]n cases arising under the New York Convention, ... there are 'compelling reasons to apply federal law, which is already well developed, to the question of whether an agreement to arbitrate is enforceable'") (quoting *Smith/Enron Cogeneration LP, Inc. v. Smith Cogeneration Int'l, Inc.*, 198 F.3d 88, 96 (2d Cir. 1999)).

Other U.S. courts have applied the law of either the arbitral seat or the parties' underlying contract. *See, e.g., Motorola Credit Corp. v. Uzan*, 388 F.3d 39, 51 (2d Cir. 2004) ("respecting the parties' choice-of-law is fully consistent with the purposes of the FAA"); *Sphere Drake Ltd v. Clarendon Nat'l Ins. Co.*, 263 F.3d 26, 32, n.3 (2d Cir. 2001) (FAA "does not preempt choice-of-law clause"); *Karaha Bodas Co. v. Perusahaan Pertambangan Minyak Dan Gas Bumi Negara*, 364 F.3d 274, 292 n.43 (5th Cir. 2004) ("Certain sections and comments of the *Restatement* ... support a determination that Swiss law applied to the arbitration agreement."); *Todd v. S.S. Mut. Underwriting Ass'n, Ltd*, 2011 WL 1226464 (E.D. La.) (applying state choice-of-law rules to validity of international arbitration agreement, which court interpreted to require application of parties' chosen English law); *FR 8 Singapore Pty Ltd v. Albacore Maritime*

Inc., 754 F.Supp.2d 628, 636 (S.D.N.Y. 2010); *Nissho Iwai Corp. v. MV Joy Sea*, 2002 A.M.C. 1305, 1311 (E.D. La. 2002).

10. *Law applicable to arbitration agreement under institutional rules.* In general, institutional rules provide little guidance in selecting the law applicable to the parties' arbitration agreement. Indeed, provisions of institutional rules dealing with applicable law are usually directed at the law governing the merits of the parties' dispute. *See, e.g.*, 2010 UNCITRAL Rules, Art. 35; 2012 ICC Rules, Art. 21; 2014 ICDR Rules, Art. 31. Compare Article 16(4) of the LCIA Rules ("The law applicable to the Arbitration Agreement ... shall be the law applicable at the seat of arbitration, unless and to the extent that the parties have agreed in writing on the application of other laws or rules of law and such agreement is not prohibited by the law applicable at the arbitral seat."). Which approach is preferable? Which law is likely to be applied in the absence of such provision as in the LCIA Rules?

11. *Choice of law applicable to validity of arbitration agreement under Article II.* Consider again what law applies to the validity of an arbitration agreement under Article II of the New York Convention. There are four possibilities: (a) a uniform international substantive rule, derived from Article II, prescribing when a valid arbitration agreement exists; (b) an international substantive rule, derived from Article II, prohibiting (or "preempting") national laws that discriminated against arbitration agreements; (c) an international choice-of-law rule, based on the choice-of-law rule in Article V; and (d) national choice-of-law rules (choosing the law of the arbitral seat, the law of the underlying contract, or another law).

(a) *Uniform international definition of "agreement" in Article II(2).* One possibility is that Article II(2) might be read as establishing a single, uniform definition of "agreement," which would be mandatorily-applicable in all Contracting States. Under this analysis, the formation and validity of an arbitration agreement, otherwise subject to the Convention, would be governed directly by Article II itself. Article II's standards would occupy the entire field of legal rules governing the formation of arbitration agreements and override national (or state) law on the subject. Friedland & Hornick, *The Relevance of International Standards in the Enforcement of Arbitration Agreements Under the New York Convention,* 6 Am. Rev. Int'l Arb. 149 (1995) ("With regard to Article II, the Convention calls for the development by and among the courts of signatory nations of unified *international* standards to govern key issues such as what constitutes a binding arbitration agreement."). Would such an approach be wise? Would it advance the Convention's purposes? Is it justified by the Convention's text? What purpose does Article V(1)(a)'s choice-of-law rule have, if the Convention prescribes a uniform international substantive standard?

Suppose a Contracting State adopted stringent requirements for the formation or validity of international arbitration agreements (*e.g.*, an arbitration agreement is only properly formed if it is negotiated between the parties, if it is genuinely neutral, or if is established by clear and convincing evidence). Would it be desirable for the Convention to override such national law requirements?

Note that substantive rules of national law governing contract formation are usually detailed. *See, e.g., Restatement (Second) Contracts* §§17-109 (1981); UNIDROIT Principles of International Commercial Contracts. Is the brief text of

Article II(2) an adequate substitute for developed national regimes of contract law? How would issues such as offer and acceptance, capacity, formalities and consideration be dealt with? Consider the possibility of looking to international sources for rules on these issues, such as the Vienna Convention of International Sale of Goods or the UNIDROIT Principles of International Commercial Contracts. Why do there need to be complicated rules governing the formation and validity of arbitration agreements, especially given the pro-arbitration policies of the Convention?

Note that French courts have successfully applied international standards to arbitration agreements for some decades. *See Dalico, supra* pp. 182-83. Note also that, in the context of investment arbitration, many arbitral tribunals have successfully applied rules of international law to the formation and validity of arbitration agreements. *See* C. Schreuer *et al.*, *The ICSID Convention: A Commentary* Art. 25, ¶525 (2d ed. 2009). Compare the decision in *BG Group*. What law does the Court apply?

(b) *Article II overrides discriminatory national law*. As discussed below, in the United States, the FAA has been interpreted to preempt state law rules that single out arbitration agreements for specially demanding treatment. *See infra* pp. 365-67. For example, the FAA has been interpreted as preempting state law requirements that arbitration agreements be conspicuously placed, in capital letters, on the first page of any contract. *See Doctor's Assocs. Inc. v. Casarotto*, 517 U.S. 681 (1996). This result has been based upon §2's command that arbitration agreements "shall be valid, irrevocable, and enforceable, save upon such grounds as exist at law or in equity for the revocation of *any contract*." U.S. FAA, 9 U.S.C. §2. State law rules that subject arbitration agreements to more demanding treatment than "any contract" are preempted. *See infra* pp. 53-54, 56-59, 365-67.

Why isn't a similar approach appropriate under Article II of the Convention? Like §2 of the FAA, Article II requires Contracting States to "recognize" written arbitration agreements, and "refer the parties to arbitration," except where the agreement is "null and void, inoperative or incapable of being performed." As with §2 of the FAA, would not Article II's purposes be served by reading it to preempt national law rules which disfavor arbitration agreements? If national law may unilaterally block or disfavor the formation of arbitration agreements, what is the point of Article II(1)'s requirement that arbitration agreements be recognized?

Consider the award in *ICC Case No. 6149*. Does that award interpret the Convention as overriding rules of national law that discriminate against arbitration agreements? Consider the court's analysis in *Ledee* of Article II(3)'s exception for arbitration agreements that are "null and void." How does *Ledee* give meaning to this provision? As discussed above, the *Ledee* court appears to interpret the Convention as overriding national law rules of contract validity that discriminate against arbitration agreements. *See supra* pp. 308-10. Is this a wise approach? Compare it to an approach (discussed above at pp. 307-08) that would interpret Article II as establishing a uniform set of substantive contract law rules governing arbitration agreements. What are the relative advantages and disadvantages of each approach?

(c) *Choice-of-law rules under Article V.* As *ICC Case No. 6149* illustrates, Article V(1)(a) of the Convention sets forth choice-of-law rules that apply at the stage of enforcing arbitral awards. *See supra* p. 309. These rules require application of the law the parties selected to apply to their arbitration clause or, in the absence of such a choice, the law of the arbitral seat. Some authorities have concluded that Article V(1)(a)'s choice-of-law rules should apply to the enforcement of arbitration agreements (as well as awards). *See* A. van den Berg, *The New York Convention of 1958* 126-28 (1981); *Judgment of 21 March 1995*, XXII Y.B. Comm. Arb. 800 (1997) (Swiss Fed. Trib.) (applying Article V(1)(a) conflicts rules, on grounds that "where the New York Convention applies, reference should be made, for all issues which concern the validity of the arbitration and are not regulated by the Convention itself, to the law to be determined according to Article V(1)(a)"). Note the application of Article V(1)(a)'s choice-of-law rules in *ICC Case No. 6149*. Consider:

> "preliminary issues concerning the validity of an arbitration agreement may not be decided according to the lex fori. Hence, where the New York Convention applies, reference should be made, for all issues which concern the validity of an arbitration agreement and are not regulated by the Convention itself, to the law to be determined according to Art. V(1)(a) of the New York Convention." *Judgment of 21 March 1995*, XXII Y.B. Comm. Arb. 800, 804-05 (1997) (Swiss Fed. Trib.).

Consider again the wisdom of applying Article V(1)(a)'s choice-of-law rules to determine what national law applies to the formation and validity of an arbitration agreement. Would the application of such choice-of-law rules be consistent with the uniform interpretation of Article II(2) outlined above? Would it be consistent with a conclusion that Article II overrides national law that discriminates against arbitration agreements? How?

(d) *National choice-of-law rules.* Finally, Article II might be interpreted to leave questions about the formation and validity of arbitration clauses entirely to national law, with respect to both substantive and choice-of-law rules. That is, Article II would require Contracting States to recognize arbitration agreements, but only when national law provides that such an agreement has been formed and is valid. Would this interpretation of Article II advance the Convention's purposes? Is it consistent with the text of Article II?

As discussed above, national choice-of-law rules generally provide for application of one of the following alternatives to issues concerning formation and validity of arbitration agreements: (a) law of the judicial enforcement forum; (b) law chosen by the parties to govern the arbitration agreement; (c) law of the arbitral seat; (d) cumulative application of potentially applicable laws; or (e) validation principle. *See supra* pp. 304-08. What law did the *Owens Corning* court apply to the putative arbitration agreement? What law would have applied if the litigation had taken place in Italy? France? What law did the Japanese court apply in *Judgment of 30 May 1994*?

(e) *ALI Restatement (Third) approach.* The draft of the ALI's *Restatement (Third) U.S. Law of International Commercial Arbitration* would prescribe a default rule for the law governing the substantive validity of international arbitration agreements that requires application of the law selected by a general choice-of-law clause in the parties' underlying contract:

> "If the parties have not agreed upon a body of law to govern the arbitration agreement (either expressly or impliedly), a general choice-of-law clause in the contract that includes the arbitration agreement determines the applicable law. If the parties have not selected any law to govern the arbitration agreement or to govern the contract generally, the law of the seat of arbitration, without resort to its choice-of-law rules, governs the matters submitted to arbitration." *Restatement (Third) U.S. Law of International Commercial Arbitration* §4-14 comment b (Tent. Draft No. 2 2012)

Is this formulation well-considered? Consider the fact that, in cases where "the parties have not agreed upon a body of law to govern the arbitration agreement (either expressly or impliedly)," then Article V(1)(a)'s second prong prescribes a mandatory international default rule. That default rule, which was one of the Convention's major innovations, is the law of the arbitral seat, not the law governing the underlying contract. Is it consistent with the Convention the proposed *Restatement* to reject this default rule, in favor of either the law governing the underlying contract, the law of the enforcement forum, or otherwise?

12. *Law applicable to inter-state arbitration agreements.* What law applies to an agreement between states to arbitrate? Consider the arbitration provisions of the 1907 Hague Convention, excerpted at pp. 43-50 of the Documentary Supplement. Is there any suggestion what law applies to agreements to arbitrate falling under the Convention? Could the law of one (or both) of the states that are party to an international arbitration agreement govern that agreement? Is there any question but that international law governs inter-state arbitration agreements?

13. *Law applicable to international investment arbitration agreements.* What law applies to an arbitration agreement subject to the ICSID Convention? Consider Article 42 of the Convention. What bearing does it have on the law applicable to an agreement to arbitrate under ICSID's auspices? Suppose that the arbitration agreement is in a direct investment contract, between the host state and investor; alternatively, suppose that the only source of the arbitration agreement is the relevant BIT.

Does the choice of international law in Article 42 of the Convention apply to the separable arbitration agreement? *See* C. Schreuer *et al., The ICSID Convention: A Commentary* Art. 25, ¶¶579-585 (2009). Consider the following:

> Parties' arbitration agreement, contained in investor's investment application, governed by "the normal expectations of the parties, as they may be established in view of the agreement as a whole, and of the aim and the spirit of the Washington Convention as well as of the Indonesian legislation and behaviour." *Amco v. Indonesia, Decision on Jurisdiction in ICSID Case No. ARB/81/1 of 25 September 1983*, ¶¶18, 21-23.

> Parties' arbitration agreement, contained in investment contract, governed by international law: "The question of whether the parties have effectively expressed their consent to ICSID jurisdiction is not to be answered by reference to national law. It is governed by international law as set out in Article 25(1) of the ICSID Convention." *ČSOB v. Slovakia, Decision on Jurisdiction in ICSID Case No. ARB/97/4 of 24 May 1999*, ¶¶35, 49-55.

Are these views persuasive? What law, other than international law, might govern an investment agreement?

Consider the Court's analysis in *BG Group*. Is it persuasive? Do the Court and Chief Justice Roberts adopt the same position?

14. *Law applicable to international commercial arbitration agreements revisited.* If international law is capable of governing inter-state and international investment arbitration agreements, then why would it not be capable of governing international commercial arbitration agreements? Is there anything odd about the notion of a common body of international principles governing the formation, validity, effects and interpretation of international arbitration agreements—regardless of their particular characterization?

E. EFFECTS OF INTERNATIONAL ARBITRATION AGREEMENTS

A valid international arbitration agreement produces important legal effects for its parties, as well as for national courts and arbitrators. These effects are both positive and negative: the positive effects include the obligation to participate in good faith in the arbitration of disputes pursuant to the arbitration agreement, while the negative effects include the obligation not to pursue dispute resolution in national courts or similar forums.[27] These effects are the consequence of the parties' agreements, as enforced by international conventions and national arbitration legislation, which uniformly provide for such consequences.

1. *Positive Effects of International Arbitration Agreements: Obligation to Arbitrate in Good Faith*

The most fundamental objective and effect of an international arbitration agreement is to obligate the parties to participate in good faith and cooperatively in the arbitration of their disputes pursuant to that agreement. As one early authority put it:

> the principal effect of an arbitration clause is not the exclusion of jurisdiction of state courts, but the transfer of the right of adjudication to an arbitral tribunal: This positive effect of the agreement legally arises in the state where the arbitral tribunal is sitting according to the agreement. The negative effect, *i.e.*, the exclusion of jurisdiction of state courts, is nothing but a consequence of the positive effect.[28]

As discussed above, this positive obligation is a *sui generis* one—requiring parties whose underlying commercial or other relations have deteriorated to the point of litigation to cooperate together, in good faith, in an adjudicatory procedure that will finally resolve

---

27. *See* G. Born, *International Commercial Arbitration* 1253-306 (2d ed. 2014). The negative effects of an arbitration agreement include the waiver of rights of access to public courts. As discussed below, these rights are accorded constitutional or statutory protections in many jurisdictions. *See infra* pp. 327-29.

28. *Judgment of 2 October 1931*, DFT 57 I 295 (Swiss Fed. Trib.), quoted in van Houtte, *Parallel Proceedings Before State Courts and Arbitration Tribunals*, in Arbitral Tribunals or State Courts: Who Must Defer to Whom? 35, 42 (ASA Spec. Series No. 15 2001). *See also Judgment of 8 August 1990*, XVII Y.B. Comm. Arb. 545 (1992) (Italian Corte di Cassazione) (referring to effects of arbitration agreement: "its positive effects, *i.e.*, referral of the dispute to arbitrators, and its negative effects, *i.e.*, exclusion of court jurisdiction in the Contracting States").

their disputes, either for or against one of the parties.[29] The basis and content of this positive obligation, which is in many respects a unique and striking one, are examined below.

ALL-UNION EXPORT-IMPORT ASSOCIATION SOJUZNEFTEEXPORT (MOSCOW) v. JOC OIL, LTD

Award in Foreign Trade Arb. Comm'n at USSR Chamber of Commerce & Industry, Moscow Arb. Case No. 109/1980 of 9 July 1984, XVIII Y.B. Comm. Arb. 92 (1993)

[excerpted above at pp. 198-201]

JUDGMENT OF 30 MAY 1994

XX Y.B. Comm. Arb. 745 (1995) (Tokyo High Ct.)

[excerpted above at pp. 288-90]

NOTES

1. *Positive obligations imposed by agreement to arbitrate.* What obligations does an agreement to arbitrate impose on its parties? Recall that an agreement to arbitrate typically provides, essentially: "all disputes relating to this contract shall be finally resolved by arbitration." What does this agreement require the parties to do? Not to do? Consider the discussions in *JOC Oil* and *Judgment of 30 May 1994* of the effects of an arbitration agreement.

2. *Positive obligations imposed by agreement to arbitrate under New York Convention.* Is there anything in the New York Convention that imposes a positive obligation to arbitrate? Note that the positive obligations imposed by an arbitration agreement are only implicitly recognized in the Convention and other international commercial arbitration conventions. Both Article II(1) of the Convention and Article 1 of the Geneva Protocol require Contracting States to "recognize" written agreements by which parties undertake "to submit to arbitration" specified disputes. Geneva Protocol, Art. I; New York Convention, Art. II(1). In the words of Article II(1) of the Convention, Contracting States "shall recognize an agreement in writing under which the parties *undertake to submit to arbitration* all or any differences...."

   The premise of these provisions is that the parties' obligation to arbitrate includes, most importantly, the affirmative duty to accept the submission of their disputes to arbitration ("undertake to submit") and to participate cooperatively in arbitral proceedings to resolve such disputes. In agreeing to arbitrate, the parties do not merely negatively waive their legal rights or access to judicial remedies, *see infra* pp. 320-34, but instead affirmatively agree to participate in the resolution of their disputes through the arbitral process, which has *sui generis* characteristics. This positive obligation to participate in a mutually-established, adjudicative dispute resolution process is at the foundation of the arbitration agreement.

   The positive obligation to arbitrate is dealt with under the Geneva Protocol, New York Convention and other international commercial arbitration conventions by giv-

---

29. *See supra* pp. 131-34.

ing effect to the parties' agreement—that is, by requiring "recognition" of that agreement—rather than by stating a generally-applicable and abstract "obligation to arbitrate." This approach to the positive duty to arbitrate is consistent with the basic consensual and contractual character of the international arbitral process. *See supra* pp. 116-37, 177.

3. *Positive obligations of agreement to arbitrate under national arbitration legislation.* The parties' positive obligation to participate in arbitrating their differences is also impliedly recognized in national legal systems, which generally parallel and implement the approach taken to this issue by the New York Convention. Thus, Article 7(1) of the UNCITRAL Model Law defines an arbitration agreement as "an agreement by the parties to *submit to arbitration* all or certain disputes...." Similarly, Article 8(1) of the Model Law provides "A court before which an action is brought in a matter which is the subject of an arbitration agreement shall, if a party so requests ... *refer the parties to arbitration*...." As with the Convention, these provisions do not create free-standing duties to arbitrate, but instead give effect to the parties' contractual obligations to submit to the resolution of their disputes by arbitration (rather than litigation) and to participate affirmatively in the arbitration to which the parties are referred.

4. *Positive obligations of agreement to arbitrate under 1907 Hague Convention.* To what extent does the 1907 Hague Convention impose a positive obligation to arbitrate? Consider Articles 37, 52 and 53, excerpted at pp. 43 & 46 of the Documentary Supplement.

5. *Source of positive obligations to arbitrate.* If neither international arbitration conventions nor national arbitration legislation is the source of positive obligations to arbitrate, what is that source? Is there anything other than the parties' agreement to arbitrate?

    In the inter-state context, is there a potential external source, other than the parties' arbitration agreement itself, of a positive obligation to arbitrate? Consider Article 1 of the 1907 Hague Convention. Consider Article 33 of the United Nations Charter, excerpted above at p. 117.

6. *Content of positive obligations to arbitrate.* An arbitration agreement is not merely a negative undertaking not to litigate, but a positive obligation to take part in a *sui generis* dispute resolution process that requires a substantial degree of cooperation (*e.g.*, in constituting a tribunal, paying the arbitrators, agreeing upon an arbitral procedure, obeying the arbitral procedure (notwithstanding the absence of direct coercive powers of the arbitral tribunal) and complying with the award). When a party agrees to arbitrate, it impliedly, but necessarily, agrees to participate cooperatively in all of these aspects of the arbitral process. National courts have emphasized that an arbitration agreement imposes obligations to make use of, and participate cooperatively in, the arbitral process. For example, English courts hold that there is an implied term in an agreement to arbitrate that the parties must cooperate in accordance with applicable arbitral rules in the conduct of the arbitration. The House of Lords has reasoned:

> "the obligation is, in my view, mutual: it obliges each party to cooperate with the other in taking appropriate steps to keep the procedure in the arbitration moving, whether he happens to be the claimant or the respondent in the particular dispute.... [I]t is in my view a necessary implication from their having agreed that the arbitrator shall resolve their dispute that both parties, respondent as well as claimant, are under a mutual obligation to one another to join in applying to the arbitrator for appropriate directions to

put an end to the delay." *Bremer Vulkan Schiffbau und Maschinenfabrik v. S. India Shipping Corp.* [1981] AC 909, 982-83, 985 (House of Lords).

A Swiss Federal Tribunal decision adopted similar conclusions, emphasizing obligations of good faith: "One of the aims of arbitration is to come to a fast resolution of the disputes submitted to it. The parties who agree to arbitration are bound by the rules of good faith to avoid any conduct which might delay without absolute necessity the normal conduct of the arbitral proceedings." *Judgment of 10 May 1982*, DFT 108 Ia 197, 201 (Swiss Fed. Trib.).

Compare the provisions of the 1907 Hague Convention, particularly Articles 37, 52 and 53. Do these provisions imply similar obligations to participate in good faith in the arbitral process? Consider: ILC, *Draft on Arbitral Procedure Prepared by the International Law Commission at Its Fourth Session, 1952*, U.N. Doc. A/CN.4/59, Art. 1(3) (1952) ("The undertaking [to arbitrate] constitutes a legal obligation which must be carried out in good faith, whatever the nature of the agreement from which results"). *See also id.* at Art. 15(2) ("The parties shall cooperate with one another and with the tribunal in the production of evidence and comply with the measures ordered by the tribunal for this purpose.").

Arbitral tribunals have adopted similar conclusions regarding the parties' obligation to arbitrate in good faith. *Unpublished Award*, excerpted in Habegger, *Document Production: An Overview of Swiss Court and Arbitration Practice*, in ICC, *Document Production in International Arbitration* 21, 28-29 (2006) (parties' disclosure obligations "correspond[] to a generally acknowledged procedural rule in international arbitration deriving from the obligation of the parties to cooperate in good faith in the proceedings"). In the words of one award: "According to good faith, the parties to an international arbitration must in particular facilitate the proceedings and abstain from all delaying tactics." *Award in ICC Case No. 8486*, XXIV Y.B. Comm. Arb. 162, 172 (1999).

Consider the character of the positive obligation to arbitrate. Compare it to other contractual obligations (*e.g.*, to deliver goods, provide services, pay money). How does the positive obligation to "arbitrate" differ? Recall the definition of "arbitration," *supra* pp. 131-34. Is the positive obligation to arbitrate an unusual one? Note that arbitrations only arise when the parties have a "dispute," *supra* pp. 148-58, which they are unable to settle and which they submit to a third party. Isn't the obligation to cooperate together with an adverse party, in these circumstances, unusual?

7. *Particular aspects of positive obligations under arbitration agreement.* What exactly does the obligation to participate in good faith in the arbitral process mean? The precise contours of the obligation to participate cooperatively and in good faith in the arbitral process are unsettled. They have been held to include:

(i) participating in the constitution of the arbitral tribunal. *See, e.g., Safond Shipping Sdn Bhd v. E. Asia Sawmill Corp.*, [1993] HKCFI 151, ¶19 (H.K. Ct. First Inst.) ("All the time and expense have been caused by (a) the defendant's flagrant breach of its contractual obligations to arbitrate any dispute that may arise and in connection therewith to appoint an arbitrator when called upon to do so and (b) its complete defiance of these proceedings brought simply to give effect to the agreed dispute resolution mechanism."). *See also Uganda Post Ltd v. R.4 Int'l Ltd*, [2009] UGCADER 5

(Ugandan Ctr Arb. & Disp. Resol.) (parties have mutual obligation to participate in constitution of arbitral tribunal).

(ii) paying the arbitrators' fees and any required advances. *See, e.g.*, Wenger, in S. Berti *et al.* (eds.), *International Arbitration in Switzerland* Art. 178, ¶71 (2000) ("An arbitration agreement contains the implicit obligation that each party make an advance payment towards the prospective costs of the arbitral proceedings in the amount ordered by the arbitral tribunal....").

(iii) cooperating with the arbitrators in relation to procedural matters. S*ee, e.g.*, *Judgment of 21 November 2003*, DFT 130 III 66, 72 (Swiss Fed. Trib.) ("the parties are required—pursuant to the obligation to act in good faith and the prohibition of abuse of rights, which is also valid in procedural law—to raise any objection they have with respect to the jurisdiction or the composition of the arbitral tribunal at the earliest possible stage.").

(iv) not obstructing or delaying the arbitral process and instead cooperating to make it efficient and effective. *See, e.g.*, *Paul Wilson & Co. A/S v. Partenreederei Hannah Blumenthal* [1983] 1 AC 854, 887 (House of Lords) ("[a] mutual obligation of co-operation between both parties" to arbitration agreement).

(v) complying with disclosure requests and orders. *See, e.g.*, Unpublished Award, excerpted in Habegger, *Document Production: An Overview of Swiss Court and Arbitration Practice*, in ICC, *Document Production in International Arbitration* 21, 28-29 (2006) (parties' disclosure obligations "correspond[] to a generally acknowledged procedural rule in international arbitration deriving from the obligation of the parties to cooperate in good faith in the proceedings").

(vi) complying with arbitral award. 1907 Hague Convention, Arts. 37, 81.

Note that these obligations apply in circumstances where a commercial relationship has produced an intractable dispute and one party requires a neutral decision-maker, to force the other party to comply with its (alleged) obligations. Consider how "cooperation" between the parties works in this process. Can it?

8. *Enforcement of positive obligations to arbitrate.* How are the positive obligations under an agreement to arbitrate enforced? As noted above, Article II(3) of the New York Convention provides that, if a valid arbitration agreement exists, Contracting States shall "refer the parties to arbitration." The wording of that phrase fairly strongly suggests an obligation on national courts to affirmatively order or direct the parties to proceed with the arbitration of their dispute (rather than merely an obligation, like that arguably provided in Article II(1), *infra* pp. 320-34, not to permit litigation to proceed).

Does anything in the UNCITRAL Model Law provide for the enforcement of arbitration agreements by way of orders directing a party specifically to perform the positive aspects of such agreements? How are arbitration agreements enforced under the Model Law?

Consider §§4 and 206 of the FAA, excerpted at pp. 103-04 & 108 of the Documentary Supplement. What do they provide with regard to enforcement of an agreement to arbitrate? Note that these provisions empower a U.S. court to grant an order requiring a party to arbitrate pursuant to its arbitration agreement. In the words of one U.S. court, a request for affirmative relief under §4 (or §206) "is simply a request for an order compelling specific performance of part of a contract." *Joseph Muller Corp. v. Commonwealth Petrochem., Inc.*, 334 F.Supp. 1013 (S.D.N.Y. 1971).

Are there differences between a stay of litigation and an order affirmatively compelling arbitration? Consider the following excerpt from the *Kulukundis* decision: "The first merely arrests further action by the court itself in the suit until something outside the suit has occurred; but the court does not order that it shall be done. The second ... affirmatively orders that someone do (or refrain from doing) some act outside the suit." *Kulukundis Shipping Co. SA v. Amtorg Trading Corp.*, 126 F.2d 978, 987 (2d Cir. 1942).

U.S. courts have emphasized that the issuance of an order compelling arbitration under §§4 and 206 is not a matter of discretion, but a legal right (guaranteed by the FAA) on the part of the party invoking the arbitration clause:

> "So long as the parties are bound to arbitrate and the district court has personal jurisdiction over them, the court is under an unflagging, nondiscretionary duty to grant a timely motion to compel arbitration and thereby enforce the New York Convention as provided in chapter 2 of the FAA, even though the agreement in question requires arbitration in a distant forum." *InterGen NV v. Grina*, 344 F.3d 134, 142 (1st Cir. 2003).

See G. Born, *International Commercial Arbitration* 1265-69 (2d ed. 2014). Is it appropriate for national courts to issue affirmative orders compelling arbitration? Is doing so required by Article II of the Convention? If not, is it nonetheless a constructive remedy, which maximizes compliance with international arbitration agreements?

Some commentators have remarked that "specific performance is ... not an appropriate remedy" for breach of an arbitration agreement and that "it is not practical to force a party to take part in arbitration proceedings." J. Lew, L. Mistelis & S. Kröll, *Comparative International Commercial Arbitration* ¶7-84 (2003). Is that correct? Aren't injunctions requiring compliance with affirmative contractual obligations issued all the time? What risks arise from an order compelling arbitration? Does this not require compelling a particular kind of arbitration (*e.g.*, in a particular place, according to particular rules, before a particular tribunal)? If so, does this undesirably involve a national court in the arbitral process? Are there ways to avoid this risk?

9. *Enforcement of positive obligations to arbitrate under Inter-American Convention.* Compare Article 3 of the Inter-American Convention with Article II of the New York Convention. Note the absence of any obligation to "refer" parties to arbitration in Article 3. What is the consequence of that? Does the provision, in Article 1 of the Inter-American Convention, that arbitration agreements are "valid" accomplish the same result? Why or why not?

2. Negative Effects of International Arbitration Agreements: Obligation Not to Litigate

An international arbitration agreement also has negative effects, which are almost precisely the mirror-image of its positive effects. That is, with regard to virtually all of the disputes that a party is obligated positively to resolve by arbitration, a comparable negative obligation exists forbidding litigation of such matters. As discussed below, this obligation is set forth in and enforced by international arbitration conventions and national legislation.

JUDGMENT OF 30 MAY 1994
XX Y.B. Comm. Arb. 745 (1995) (Tokyo High Ct.)

[excerpted above at pp. 288-90]

JUDGMENT OF 7 SEPTEMBER 2005, HOTELS.COM v. ZUZ TOURISM LTD
XXXI Y.B. Comm. Arb. 791 (2006) (Israeli S.Ct.)

[excerpted above at pp. 183-86]

WSG NIMBUS PTE LTD v. BOARD OF CONTROL FOR CRICKET IN SRI LANKA
[2002] 3 SLR 603 (Singapore High Ct.)

LEE SEIU KIN JC. The plaintiffs are a company incorporated in Singapore. The defendants are the national association for cricket in Sri Lanka constituted pursuant to the Sri Lankan Sports Law No. 25…. [T]he parties entered into an agreement, called the "Master Rights Agreement" ("MRA"), under which the Plaintiffs obtained the commercial rights (including broadcasting … rights outside Sri Lanka) to cricket matches between the Sri Lankan national cricket team and visiting test playing sides for 14 tours in the period January 2001 to December 2003. Clause 19 of the MRA provides for English law to be the governing law and makes a reference to arbitration in Singapore in accord with the Arbitration Rules of the Singapore International Arbitration Centre ("SIAC")…. [Disputes arose between the parties, with the plaintiffs commencing arbitration under the MRA and the defendants initiating litigation in Sri Lankan courts. The plaintiffs sought an antisuit injunction from the Singaporean courts against the defendant proceeding with the Sri Lankan suit.]

[The Singapore court first considered] whether clause 19 of the MRA is an arbitration agreement falling within the definition of that term in the Act. That definition is found in §2 and it provides as follows: "'arbitration agreement' means an agreement in writing referred to in Article 7 of the Model Law…." [The court then quoted Article 7(1) of the UNCITRAL Model Law.]

Clause 19 of the MRA is entitled "LAW/ARBITRATION" and provides as follows:

> "This Agreement shall be governed by and construed in accordance with the laws of England and Wales. In the event that the parties have a dispute over any term or otherwise relating to this Agreement they shall use their best endeavors to resolve it through good faith negotiations. In the event that they fail to do so after 14 days then either party may elect to submit such matter to arbitration in Singapore in accordance with the Arbitration Rules of the Singapore International Arbitration Centre ('SIAC Rules') for the time being in force which rules are deemed to be incorporated by reference with this clause to the exclusive jurisdiction of which the parties shall be deemed to have consented. Any arbitration shall be referred to three arbitrators, one arbitrator being appointed by each party and the other being appointed by the Chairman of the SIAC and shall be conducted in the English language."

The Defendants had submitted to the Colombo High Court that the words "may elect" in Clause 19 confers on the parties a wide discretion in that either of them may elect for arbitration or to go to the courts and there was no reason to give the word "may" a mandatory meaning. Since §5 of the Sri Lankan Arbitration Act applies only when there is a compulsory arbitration clause, Clause 19 was not an arbitration agreement within the meaning of that Act. The Defendants had made an election to litigate when they commenced the action in the Colombo Court.

In my view, this submission hinges on taking the word "may" out of the context of Clause 19, after associating that word with the notions of discretion and a lack of any mandatory meaning, these notions are then linked with the word "arbitration" to arrive at the conclusion that there is no compulsory arbitration clause. But in order to arrive at the proper construction of Clause 19 it is necessary to consider the provision in its entirety and see how the words relate to one another to convey the intention of the parties. Taking this approach, the first sentence deals with the governing law which is to be English law. The remainder of the clause relates directly to arbitration and on a plain reading, this is what it provides. In the event of a dispute, the parties are required first of all to use their best endeavors to resolve it through good faith negotiations. It is only if this is unsuccessful after 14 days that the right is given to either party to elect to submit the dispute to arbitration. Upon such an election, both parties are bound to submit to arbitration in Singapore in accordance with the Arbitration Rules of the SIAC…. While it is true that under Clause 19, there is no compulsion to arbitrate until an election is made, once a party makes such election, arbitration is mandatory in respect of that dispute.

Another problem with the Defendants' submission is that there is no express mention in Clause 19 of any election to resolve the dispute by court action nor that once any party takes out an action in court, the other party is precluded from electing to submit the dispute to arbitration. It is the right of a party to a contractual dispute to commence an action in a court of competent jurisdiction for the determination of his claims. But this is subject to any agreement that the parties shall resolve such disputes by way of arbitration. If there is such an agreement then the court may, on the defendant's application, stay the action on that ground. This is certainly the position in Singapore and it is not disputed that it is so in Sri Lanka. When Clause 19 is construed within this legal matrix, it is clear that it is not a question of making an election for arbitration or litigation, but whether any party has opted for arbitration….

The question whether a clause which confers the parties an option to arbitrate is an arbitration agreement was considered in *Westfal-Larsen & Co A/S v. Ikerigi Compania Naviera SA*, [1983] 1 All ER 382. The contract there contained the following arbitration clause:

> "Any dispute arising under this charter shall be decided by the English courts to whose jurisdiction the parties agree whatever their domicile may be: Provided that either party may elect to have the dispute referred to the arbitration of a single arbitrator in London in accordance with the provisions of the Arbitration Act, 1950, or any statutory modification or re-enactment thereof for the time being in force. Such election shall be made by written notice by one party to the other not later than 21 days after receipt of a notice given by one party to the other of a dispute having arisen under this charter."

Bingham J held that by itself this did not constitute an agreement to arbitrate. It merely confers an option which may but need not be exercised. But once a party duly elects to refer the dispute to arbitration, a binding arbitration agreement comes into existence. He held that the arbitration clause was an "arbitration agreement" within the meaning of §32 of the UK Arbitration Act 1950….

In the light of these authorities, it is clear that an agreement in which the parties have the option to elect for arbitration which, if made, binds the other parties to submit to arbitration is an arbitration agreement within the meaning of the Act. This is plainly in accord with the policy behind the Act which is to promote the resolution of disputes by arbitration where the parties have agreed to achieve it by this method. I would therefore hold that Clause 19 is an arbitration agreement for the purpose of this application....

As I have determined that Clause 19 is an arbitration agreement, the Defendants become subject to the jurisdiction of this court. The Defendants submit that even so, the anti-suit injunction should not be granted on the ground that it does not fall within §12(6) of the Act read with §12(1)(g). These provisions state as follows:

> "12(1) Without prejudice to the powers set out in any other provision of this Act and in the Model Law, an arbitral tribunal shall have powers to make orders or give directions to any party for: (a) security for costs; (b) discovery of documents and interrogatories; (c) giving of evidence by affidavit; (d) the preservation, interim custody or sale of any property which is or forms part of the subject-matter of the dispute; (da) samples to be taken from, or any observation to be made of or experiment conducted upon, any property which is or forms part of this subject-matter of the dispute; (db) the preservation and interim custody of any evidence for the purposes of the proceedings; (e) securing the amount in dispute; (f) ensuring that any award which may be made in the arbitral proceedings is not rendered ineffectual by the dissipation of assets by a party; and (g) an interim injunction of any other interim measure....
>
> (6) The High Court or a Judge thereof shall have, for the purpose of and in relation to an arbitration to which this Part applies, the same power of making orders in respect of any of the matters set out in subsection (1) as it has for the purpose of and in relation to an action or matter in the court." ...

In the present case the Defendants submit that there is no reference to arbitration on the question of their entitlement to commence the [Sri Lankan litigation.] In the Plaintiffs' Notice of Arbitration, they refer to three matters in dispute, i.e., (i) the purported termination by the Defendants of the MRA and the Terms of Settlement on grounds that the Plaintiffs had breached ... the Terms of Settlement; (ii) the commencement of negotiations by the Defendants with third parties on the commercial rights the subject matter of the MRA; and (iii) interference with the rights of the Plaintiffs under its team sponsorship agreement with Ceylon Tea Services Ltd by instructing the latter to withhold payment of certain sums owed to the Plaintiffs. The Defendants contend the Plaintiffs did not refer to arbitration the question of their breach of the arbitration agreement by taking out the second action in the Colombo High Court. Therefore, [they argue] the anti-suit injunction cannot be an interim measure to maintain the status quo in relation to a dispute referred to the arbitral tribunal until it has had an opportunity to adjudicate upon it....

There is an arbitration clause in the MRA in which the parties agree to submit to arbitration in Singapore upon the election of any one of them. The Defendants purport to terminate the contract and the Plaintiffs dispute that they are entitled to do so. The Defendants then commence proceedings in the Colombo High Court, *inter alia*, for damages for breach of the MRA.... The Plaintiffs elect to refer these disputes to arbitration. There is therefore a reference to arbitration in respect of the disputes between the parties and the Plaintiffs have sought in this [action] an anti-suit injunction to prevent the Defendants from proceeding with the second action in the Colombo High Court....

The Defendants next submit that, even if there is jurisdiction under §12(6), the court ought not to have exercised its discretion to grant the anti-suit injunction. They rely on

Sokana Indus. Inc. v. Freyre & Co. [[1994] 2 Lloyd's Rep. 57 (Comm) (English High Ct.)] in which Colman J said that such discretion should be exercised sparingly:

> "There is no doubt that the English Courts can, in appropriate cases, restrain by injunction the conduct of proceedings in a foreign court. Where a contract contained an arbitration clause referring all relevant disputes to arbitration in England, and the claimant had started an arbitration in England and then commences proceedings in a foreign court making the same claim as had been advanced in the arbitration, the invocation of the foreign court's jurisdiction would be a breach of the arbitration agreement in English law. However, the fact that the pursuit of such proceedings would amount to a breach of contract would not automatically entitle the other party to an injunction in the English Courts. The court has a discretion whether to grant such an order.... Such a direction should be exercised in favor of an injunction only with caution.... The English Courts will not lightly interfere with the conduct of proceedings in a foreign court, even if that conduct is in breach of a contract to arbitrate.
>
> In the present case, there are already on foot in the Florida proceedings steps taken by the plaintiffs to challenge the jurisdiction of those courts. If those steps are successful, the action will not proceed and the defendants will have to pursue their claims in the arbitration. Having regard to the fact that this arbitration agreement falls within Art. 1 of the New York Convention, to which both the United States and Britain are parties, it would be extremely surprising if the United States had not given effect to that convention by enabling both the Federal Court and State Courts mandatorily to stay actions in breach of agreements for foreign arbitration. Accordingly, on the face of it, the plaintiffs should be able to obtain a mandatory stay of the Florida action. In view of there already being before those courts applications challenging their jurisdiction, I am firmly of the view that, at least at this stage, the English Courts should not interfere with those proceedings by granting an injunction. The U.S. courts must in such circumstances be left in control over their own proceedings.... Apart from the New York Convention, there are strong arguments for declining to exercise the jurisdiction to grant an injunction in this case. They are that it is appropriate that the Florida Courts should be seized of disputes under a contract governed by the law of Florida, further, that the joinder of Den Norske Bank as a co-defendant in the Florida proceedings means that, at least theoretically, the enjoining of the defendants from pursuing such proceedings against the plaintiffs will lead to multiplicity of litigation on the same issue with different parties involved.... Finally, the issues in the arbitration and the evidence in the case appear to be located in or near to Florida and not in England." ...

In the present case, with the greatest of respect, it would appear to me that if Clause 19 is an arbitration agreement, continuation of the proceedings in the Colombo High Court would constitute a breach by Sri Lanka of her obligations under [Article II of] the New York Convention....

The submission in Clause 19 is to arbitration under the SIAC Rules. Rule 26.1 provides as follows: "The Tribunal shall have the power to rule on its own jurisdiction, including any objections with respect to the existence, termination or validity of the arbitration agreement...." Therefore the parties would be deemed to have agreed that any dispute as to the jurisdiction of the arbitral tribunal be determined by the tribunal.

As the Plaintiffs' application was made under the Arbitration Act, it would be instructive to consider the parliamentary materials to divine the legislative intention.... The following are excerpts from the speech of the Parliamentary Secretary to the Minister for Law when he moved the Bill a second time (emphasis added):

> "...This Bill will facilitate the settlement of commercial disputes in Singapore. As Singapore

businessmen expand overseas, there will be greater contacts with foreign parties. Currently, foreign businessmen are uncomfortable with unfamiliar arbitration laws and excessive intervention from local courts if they select Singapore as a venue for arbitration. They will therefore *welcome the application of the Model Law in Singapore…."*

It can be seen that one major purpose of the Bill is to promote Singapore as an international centre for arbitration by facilitating arbitrations that are held here…. There are many formidable competitors in this area and the Act was enacted to enhance Singapore's position as a centre for international legal services and international arbitrations. The intention of the Bill is to promote the growth of Singapore as a venue for international arbitrations and the courts must do their part by taking a robust approach when faced with applications under §12(6)….

I should add that this is entirely consistent with the principle that parties be made to abide by their agreement to arbitrate. Furthermore, the New York Convention obliges state parties to uphold arbitration agreements and awards. Such an agreement is often contravened by a party commencing an action in its home courts. Once the court is satisfied that there is an arbitration agreement, it has a duty to uphold that agreement and prevent any breach of it. Accordingly, I am of the opinion that the anti-suit injunction should be continued until further order….

IBETO PETROCHEMICAL INDUSTRIES LTD v. M/T BEFFEN
475 F.3d 56 (2d Cir. 2007)

MINER, Circuit Judge…. Ibeto Petrochemical Industries Limited ("Ibeto") appeals from an Order entered in the U.S. District Court for the Southern District of New York (Scheindlin, J.) in an action arising out of the contamination by seawater of a shipment of oil being carried by motor tanker. The Order granted the motions of … M/T Beffen ("the Beffen") and … ("Bryggen") (collectively "defendants") to stay this action, to compel arbitration, and to enjoin an action pending in Nigeria…. For the reasons that follow, we … affirm the Order in part and modify it in part.

On February 6, 2004, the … Beffen departed Paulsboro, New Jersey, carrying a cargo of base oil for delivery to Lagos, Nigeria. A Bill of Lading for the shipment issued on that date indicated that the shipper was Chemlube International, Inc. ("Chemlube") and that the cargo was destined for delivery to Ibeto in Lagos. The Bill of Lading incorporated the Charter Agreement between Chemlube and Bryggen for carriage of the shipment aboard the Beffen as follows: "This shipment is carried under and pursuant to the terms of the Charter Party dated 31 December 2003 between Chemlube International, Inc. as Charterer and Bryggen Shipping and Trading A/S as Owner and all conditions and exceptions whatsoever thereto." The Charter Party Fixture incorporated the provisions of two other documents—the standard form "Asbatankvoy" Tanker Charter Party and the "Chemlube Terms" dated September 2002. The Asbatankvoy provisions included the following:

> "Any and all differences and disputes of whatsoever nature arising out of this Charter shall be put to arbitration in the City of New York or in the City of London whichever place is specified in Part I of this charter pursuant to the laws relating to arbitration there in force, before a board of three persons, consisting of one arbitrator to be appointed by the Owner, one by the Charterer and one by the two so chosen. The decision of any two of the three on any point or points shall be final. Either party hereto may call for such arbitration by service upon any officer of the other, wherever he may be found, of a written notice specifying the

name and address of the arbitrator chosen by the first moving party and a brief description of the disputes or differences which such party desires to put to arbitration."

The Chemlube Terms included a provision for "arbitration to be in London, English law to apply."

The base oil shipment allegedly was contaminated with seawater when the Beffen arrived in the Port of Lagos on March 5, 2004. Ibeto, as receiver of the shipment, instituted an action against Bryggen and the Beffen in the Federal District Court of Nigeria on March 19, 2004. [Ibeto also subsequently commenced an arbitration against the defendants in London and litigation against the defendants in U.S. courts. The defendants sought, among other things, a stay of the U.S. litigation based upon the arbitration clause (quoted above) and an injunction against the Nigerian litigation. The District Court held that Ibeto and the defendants were bound by a valid arbitration agreement and issued an antisuit against Ibeto's Nigerian litigation.]

[The Court of Appeals first held that, although] the Charter Party was entered into by Chemlube and Bryggen, its terms, including the provision for arbitration, were incorporated by reference in the Bill of Lading directing delivery from Chemlube to Ibeto in Lagos. According to the Bill of Lading, the shipment was "carried under and pursuant to the terms of the Charter Party dated 31 December 2003 between Chemlube International, Inc. as Charterer and Bryggen Shipping and Trading A/S as Owner and all conditions and exceptions whatsoever thereto." It was the Charter Party Fixture that incorporated the standard form Asbatankvoy Tanker Charter Party, which called for arbitration, and the Chemlube terms that provided for London as the place of arbitration and for the application of English law.... [The court held that these references validly incorporated the agreement to arbitrate and that Ibeto and the defendants were bound by the agreement's terms. The Court of Appeals then considered the District Court's antisuit injunction against Ibeto's pursuit of its Nigerian litigation.] ...

Ibeto's contention that the [antisuit] injunction was inappropriate ... properly was rejected by the District Court. In issuing the injunction, the District Court carefully applied the test, set forth in *China Trade & Dev. Corp. v. M.V. Choong Yong*, 837 F.2d 33, 35-36 (2d Cir. 1987), for injunctions against suits in foreign jurisdictions. Pursuant to the *China Trade* test,

> "[a]n anti-suit injunction against parallel litigation may be imposed only if: (A) the parties are the same in both matters, and (B) resolution of the case before the enjoining court is dispositive of the action to be enjoined. *China Trade*, 837 F.2d at 35. Once past this threshold, courts are directed to consider a number of additional factors, including whether the foreign action threatens the jurisdiction or the strong public policies of the enjoining forum." *In re Millenium Seacarriers, Inc.*, 458 F.3d 92, 97 n.4 (2d Cir. 2006) (quoting *Paramedics Electromedicina v. G.E. Med. Sys. Info. Techs., Inc.*, 369 F.3d 645, 652 (2d Cir. 2004)).

The "threshold" described is clearly met in this case, for the parties are the same in this matter and in the Nigerian proceeding and the resolution by arbitration of the case before the District Court is dispositive of the Nigerian proceeding. The factors then to be considered under the *China Trade* test are the following:

> "(1) frustration of a policy in the enjoining forum; (2) the foreign action would be vexatious; (3) a threat to the issuing court's in rem or quasi in rem jurisdiction; (4) the proceedings in the other forum prejudice other equitable considerations; or (5) adjudication of the same

issues in separate actions would result in delay, inconvenience, expense, inconsistency, or a race to judgment."

In the *China Trade* case, we found that the factors having "greater significance" there were threats to the enjoining forum's jurisdiction and to its strong public policies. Finding no such threats, we determined that the equitable factors of that case were "not sufficient to overcome the restraint and caution required by international comity." ...

Applying all the factors, the District Court found that the general federal policy favoring arbitration might be frustrated by the Nigerian litigation; widely disparate results might obtain because the Nigerian Courts would not apply the provisions of COGSA; a race to judgment could be provoked by the disparity; equitable considerations such as deterring forum shopping favor the injunction; and "it is likely that adjudication of the same issues in two separate actions would result in inconvenience, inconsistency, and a possible race to judgment." The District Court foresaw "considerable inconvenience" in the movement of witnesses between the two venues. The District Court determined, however, that the threat to jurisdiction factor did not apply since "both courts have in personam jurisdiction over the parties." We agree with the foregoing analysis of the District Court in applying the *China Trade* factors and add our observation that the policy favoring arbitration is a strong one in the federal courts. Accordingly, the injunction is fully justified in this case. We note, however, that the District Court's application of the principle that "'an anti-suit injunction may be proper where a party initiates foreign proceedings in an attempt to sidestep arbitration,'" *Ibeto*, 412 F.Supp. 2d at 289 (quoting *LAIF X SPRL v. Axtel, S.A. de C.V.,* 390 F.3d 194, 199 (2d Cir. 2004)), is not warranted here, where the proceeding in Nigeria was first in time.

The foregoing having been said, we reiterate our understanding that due regard for principles of international comity and reciprocity require a delicate touch in the issuance of anti-foreign suit injunctions, that such injunctions should be used sparingly, and that the pendency of a suit involving the same parties and same issues does not alone form the basis for such an injunction. Having these caveats in mind, we think that the injunction in this case cuts much too broadly.

The learned District Court wrote only that "defendants' motion to enjoin the Nigerian action is granted." The injunction should be directed specifically to the parties, for it is only the parties before a federal court who may be enjoined from prosecuting a suit in a foreign country.... Moreover, there is no need for the permanent injunction that the District Court seems to have issued. The parties need to be enjoined from proceeding in the courts of Nigeria only until the conclusion of the London arbitration and the consequent resolution of the still-pending case in the District Court. The District Court should modify its injunction with a specificity consonant with this determination.

NOTES

1. *Negative obligations imposed by arbitration agreement.* In addition to the positive obligations imposed by an agreement to arbitrate, what negative obligations does such an agreement impose? What does an arbitration agreement forbid the parties from doing? As noted above, an agreement to arbitrate typically provides, essentially: "the parties agree that all disputes relating to this contract shall be finally resolved by arbitration." Does this formulation, by its terms, forbid the parties from doing anything?

2. *Negative obligations of arbitration agreement under ICSID Convention.* Consider Articles 26 and 27 of the ICSID Convention, excerpted at p. 19 of the Documentary Supplement. What negative obligations do they impose? Note that Article 26 excludes other remedies "unless otherwise stated." Does Article 26 impose a mandatory rule, or is it a presumption about the parties' intent? Compare Article 27. What is the purpose of Articles 26 and 27?

3. *Negative obligations of arbitration agreement under 1907 Hague Convention.* Is there anything analogous to Articles 26 and 27 of the ICSID Convention in the 1907 Hague Convention? Why does the Hague Convention differ in its treatment of arbitration, in this respect, from the ICSID Convention? Are there, nonetheless, negative obligations imposed on states by their agreements to arbitrate? How would you phrase those obligations?

4. *Negative obligations of arbitration agreement under New York Convention.* As discussed above, Articles II(1) and II(3) of the New York Convention provide for Contracting States to "recognize" agreements to arbitrate and to "refer the parties to arbitration." These provisions enforce the negative effects of an arbitration agreement, by requiring either the stay (*i.e.*, suspension) of national court litigation or the dismissal of such litigation. Note the comment in the Israeli Supreme Court decision, in *Hotels.com*, that: "Article II(3) of the Convention states in mandatory language that the court 'shall ... refer' the parties to arbitration, unless one of the exceptions listed in the section is present. It appears that the manner in which both provisions were drafted leads to a single conclusion: that if one of the three exceptions mentioned in Article II(3) does not appear, the court is as a rule required to order a stay of the proceedings...."

   Compare how international arbitration agreements are dealt with, as compared to domestic arbitration agreements, under Israeli law. *See also Answers in Genesis of Kentucky, Inc. v. Creation Ministries*, 556 F.3d 459, 469 (6th Cir. 2009) ("The language of [Article II(3)] and its statutory incorporation provide for no exceptions. When any party seeks arbitration, if the agreement falls within the [New York Convention], we must compel the arbitration unless the agreement is 'null and void, inoperative, or incapable of being performed.'"); *I.T.A.D. Assocs., Inc. v. Podar Bros.*, 636 F.2d 75, 77 (4th Cir. 1981) (Article II(3) "clearly mandates the referral of the ... dispute to arbitration unless one of the enumerated exceptions is applicable"); G. Born, *International Commercial Arbitration* 1271 (2d ed. 2014).

5. *Negative obligations imposed by arbitration agreement under national arbitration legislation.* Article 8(1) of the UNCITRAL Model Law is representative of national arbitration legislation's treatment of the negative effects of an arbitration agreement. As discussed above, Article 8(1) imposes an obligation identical to that in Article II of the Convention, requiring courts to "refer the parties to arbitration." This precludes a national court from entertaining a dispute on the merits, if the parties have agreed to arbitrate it, and instead requires that the parties be referred to arbitration. Compare §3 of the FAA and §9 of the English Arbitration Act.

6. *Content of negative obligations under international arbitration agreement.* What precisely is the content of the negative obligations imposed by an agreement to arbitrate? What negative obligations are imposed upon the parties to an international commercial arbitration agreement?

Consider how the negative effects of an arbitration agreement are described in *Judgment of 30 May 1994* and *Judgment of 27 February 1970. Compare Judgment of 2 October 1931*, DFT 57 I 295 (Swiss Fed. Trib.) (holding that the "negative effect" of an arbitration agreement "is the exclusion of the State courts' jurisdiction"). Consider the following discussion, of the importance of these negative effects, by a U.S. court under the domestic FAA:

> "Contracts to arbitrate are not to be avoided by allowing one party to ignore the contract and resort to the courts. Such a course could lead to prolonged litigation, one of the very risks the parties, by contracting for arbitration, sought to eliminate." *Southland Corp. v. Keating*, 465 U.S. 1, 7 (1984).

Consider again Article 26 of the ICSID Convention. What negative effects does it impose?

7. *Waiver of right of access to judicial remedies*. Consider further the most fundamental negative obligation of an agreement to arbitrate—the obligation not to litigate a dispute. What rights does a party forego in agreeing to arbitrate? Consider Article 6 of the European Convention on Human Rights. Note that all developed legal systems have comparable guarantees of access to judicial remedies for citizens. *See also* U.S. Constitution, Amendments 5, 14.

What role should these guarantees of public access have in interpreting and giving effect to arbitration agreements? To *international* arbitration agreements?

8. *Exclusivity of arbitration as means for dispute resolution*. Consider again Article 26 of the ICSID Convention. Note that it provides that, where the parties have agreed to ICSID arbitration, that is the exclusive forum for resolving their investment dispute. Is the same obligation imposed by commercial arbitration agreements?

Most arbitration clauses do not provide expressly that "all disputes shall be resolved by arbitration, *to the exclusion of national courts*." Is this negative obligation nonetheless imposed impliedly by arbitration agreements? Recall that one of the fundamental purposes of international arbitration agreements is to centralize the parties' disputes in a single forum for final resolution, *supra* pp. 111-12. Would this objective be achieved if parallel national court proceedings were permitted? Should the waiver of fundamental right of access to judicial remedies be implied?

Consider the arbitration agreements excerpted in *JOC Oil, Buckeye* and *Nimbus, supra* pp. 198, 202 & 321. Do these provisions expressly address the negative obligations imposed by the agreement to arbitrate? Note also that some institutional rules contain provisions implying the exclusivity of the arbitral process. *See, e.g.*, 2012 ICC Rules, Art. 34(6); 2014 LCIA Rules, Arts. 23(5), 26(8).

9. *Non-exclusive agreement to arbitrate*. At least in theory, an arbitration agreement might be "non-exclusive." That is, like a forum selection clause, an arbitration agreement might permit either party to commence binding arbitration, but not forbid other forms of dispute resolution (such as litigation in national courts). Is it likely that this is what parties might intend in entering into an arbitration agreement? Why not? Consider how such an argument was received in *Judgment of 30 May 1994*.

10. *Contrast between exclusive character of forum selection and arbitration agreements*. In the United States, forum selection clauses are presumptively permissive. That is, an agreement to submit disputes to the courts of State X will allow litigation in State X, but will not exclude litigation in other states that possess jurisdiction under applicable

law. *See* G. Born & P. Rutledge, *International Civil Litigation in United States Courts* 462-63 (5th ed. 2011). Compare the U.S. approach to the interpretation of forum selection agreements with the interpretation of arbitration agreements. Are arbitration clauses presumptively exclusive or presumptively permissive? As we have seen, the answer is clearly the former; indeed, the contrary is virtually never even argued. *See supra* pp. 289-90. Why?

11. *Enforcement of negative obligations under agreement to arbitrate*. A party's commencement of litigation of claims, subject to an arbitration agreement, is in almost all cases a breach of that agreement, in particular, its negative obligations. That breach, like other violations of contractual obligations, entitles the non-breaching party to relief. What relief is the non-breaching party entitled to for the breach of an agreement to arbitrate?

(a) *Mandatory stay of litigation*. Consider Article II(3) of the New York Convention and Article 8 of the UNCITRAL Model Law, excerpted at pp. 2 & 88 of the Documentary Supplement. What do they provide as relief for a party's commencement of litigation in breach of an agreement to arbitrate? Why should the breach of an arbitration agreement be remedied through an order for specific performance? Isn't an award of monetary damages an adequate remedy?

Note that Article II(3) of the Convention does not leave national courts with any discretion to deny a dismissal or stay of local judicial proceedings where an arbitration agreement is enforceable under the Convention. Rather, it mandatorily requires that national courts "shall" refer parties to arbitration. Consider how the court in *Hotels.com* addresses this issue. *See also Answers in Genesis of Ky., Inc. v. Creation Ministries Int'l, Ltd*, 556 F.3d 459, 469 (6th Cir. 2009) ("there is nothing discretionary about Article II(3) of the Convention") (quoting *McCreary Tire & Rubber Co. v. CEAT SpA*, 501 F.2d 1032, 1037 (3d Cir. 1974)); *InterGen NV v. Grina*, 344 F.3d 134, 141 (1st Cir. 2003) ("Given this regime, it clearly appears that enforcing arbitration clauses under the New York Convention is an obligation, not a matter committed to district court discretion."). Note that *Hotels.com* suggests that a stay of litigation might be denied in exceptional cases. What types of cases might it be referring to?

Similarly, consider Article 8 of the UNCITRAL Model Law and §3 of the FAA. What relief do they provide for breaches of an agreement to arbitrate? *Compare Danisco A/S Denmark v. Novo Nordisk A/S*, 2003 U.S. Dist. LEXIS 1842, at *2 (S.D.N.Y.) ("The Act 'leaves no room for the exercise of discretion by a district court, but instead mandates that district courts shall direct the parties to proceed to an arbitration on issues as to which an arbitration agreement has been signed.'"); English Arbitration Act, 1996, §9(4) ("the court shall grant a stay unless satisfied that the arbitration agreement is null and void, inoperative, or incapable of being performed"); *A. Sanderson & Son v. Armour & Co. Ltd* 1922 SLT 285 (House of Lords) ("If the parties have contracted to arbitrate, to arbitration they must go."); *Kaverit Steel & Crane Ltd v. Kone Corp.*, XIX Y.B. Comm. Arb. 643, 645 (1994) (Alberta Ct. App. 1992) ("the statute commands that what may go to arbitration shall go. No convenience test limits reference."). Why is a stay of litigation not only available, but mandatory, for breach of an agreement to arbitrate? Note that Article II of the New York Convention is relatively unique among international law instruments, in obligating Contracting States not only to recognize a particular type of agreement, but also mandatorily to enforce those agreements in specified ways. What is the purpose of this enforcement regime?

(b) *Dismissal of litigation.* Is there any reason that Article II of the Convention and Article 8 of the Model Law cannot be complied with by dismissing a litigation (rather than suspending or staying it)? Is there an argument that Article II requires a dismissal?

(c) *Antisuit injunctions.* Suppose that a party is able to pursue litigation of a dispute, which is subject to arbitration, in a national court which does not honor, or fully honor, its undertakings in the New York Convention. In that event, a stay of the underlying litigation in one (or several) national courts, which honor the Convention, may be only a partial, and ultimately ineffective, remedy for enforcing the international arbitration agreement. What other forms of relief are possible?

Consider the decision in *WSG Nimbus. See also SulAmérica Cia Nacional De Seguros SA v. Enesa Engenharia SA* [2012] EWCA Civ 638 (English Ct. App.) (injunction restraining Brazilian litigation based on English arbitration agreement); *Aggeliki Charis Compania Maritima SA v. Pagnan SpA* [1995] 1 Lloyd's Rep. 87, 96 (English Ct. App.) ("in my judgment there is no good reason for diffidence in granting an injunction to restrain foreign proceedings [brought in violation of an arbitration agreement] on the clear and simple ground that the defendant has promised not to bring them.... I cannot accept the proposition that any Court would be offended by the grant of an injunction to restrain a party from invoking a jurisdiction which he had promised not to invoke and which it was its own duty to decline."); *Elektrim SA v. Vivendi Universal SA* [2007] EWHC 571, ¶52 (Comm) (English High Ct.) ("the court has jurisdiction ... to grant an injunction to restrain a party from engaging in court proceedings in another jurisdiction, in breach of an English arbitration clause").

What must be established in order to obtain an antisuit injunction in Singapore? What is the court's rationale in *WSG Nimbus* for permitting an antisuit injunction? Is it persuasive? Putting aside questions regarding the character of the parties' dispute resolution clause, and assuming that it was an agreement to arbitrate, is an antisuit order, forbidding litigation of arbitrable claims, appropriate? What effect does such an order have on the judicial functions of a foreign state? Is it appropriate for one state's courts to effectively forbid proceedings in another state's courts?

There are grave reservations about antisuit injunctions in some law systems. In one action, a German court declared that an English antisuit injunction, aimed at restraining proceedings brought in Germany in violation of an arbitration clause, was a violation of German public policy:

"such injunctions constitute an infringement of the jurisdiction of Germany because the German courts alone decide, in accordance with the procedural laws governing them and in accordance with existing international agreements, whether they are competent to adjudicate on a matter or whether they must respect the jurisdiction of another domestic or a foreign court (including arbitration courts).... These rights are safeguarded by the Germany procedural codes, in many respects, by the [German Constitution]. The courts must give effect to these rights. Instructions from foreign courts to the parties concerning the manner in which the proceedings are to be conducted and their subject-matter are likely to impede the German courts in fulfilling this task." *Judgment of 10 January 1996, 3 VA 11/95, Re the Enforcement of an English Anti-Suit Injunction* [1997] I.L.Pr. 320 (Oberlandesgericht Düsseldorf).

The Court upheld the refusal of the relevant German authorities to effect service of English process on the respondent in Germany (as had been requested under the Hague Service Convention).

Note that antisuit orders are directed against the parties to a foreign litigation (and not the foreign court itself), but are intended to have the effect of precluding the litigation from proceeding in the foreign court. G. Born & P. Rutledge, *International Civil Litigation in United States Courts* 567 (5th ed. 2011). Is this a sufficient justification for an antisuit injunction?

Is there a middle ground between the Singapore (and English) approach to antisuit orders and that of Germany (and many other civil law jurisdictions)? Consider the standard for an antisuit injunction articulated by the U.S. Court of Appeals in *Ibeto*. Based on the language used by the Court for this standard, is it easier or more difficult to obtain an antisuit injunction in the United States or in Singapore? Consider the U.S. court's stated concerns regarding comity and interference with foreign judicial proceedings. Are these valid concerns? In contrast to *Ibeto*, other U.S. courts have declined to issue antisuit injunctions against foreign proceedings brought in violation of agreements to arbitrate. *See, e.g., LAIF X SPRL v. Axtel, SA de CV*, 390 F.3d 194 (2d Cir. 2004); *Comverse, Inc. v. Am. Telecomms., Inc. Chile SA*, 2006 U.S. Dist. LEXIS 76791 (S.D.N.Y.) (declining to issue antisuit injunction against proceedings before Chilean antitrust authorities); *Empresa Generadora de Electricidad ITABO, SA v. Corporación Dominicana*, 2005 WL 1705080, at *8 (S.D.N.Y.); *Pepsico Inc. v. Oficina Central de Asesoria y Ayuda Tecnica, CA*, 945 F.Supp. 69, 71 (S.D.N.Y. 1996) ("in the absence of any challenge to the adequacy of the Venezuelan legal process ... the Venezuelan court that already has the issue of arbitrability before it ought to be afforded the initial opportunity to determine this threshold question of Venezuelan law before a non-Venezuelan court is called upon to do so"). *Compare Hunt v. Mobil Oil Corp.*, 583 F.Supp. 1092, 1094-95 (S.D.N.Y. 1984) (enjoining litigation brought in parallel to arbitration as "clearly designed to lay the ground work of an attack upon a final award by the arbitrators"; "to permit the continuance of the current state actions with the avowed purpose of extensive discovery of facts from [an arbitrator], other arbitrators, third parties and the AAA as to the fees and alleged bases for disqualification would unduly delay and interfere with the pending arbitration").

Compare what the U.S. court in *Ibeto* actually ordered to the language it used regarding international comity. Where was the arbitral seat in *Ibeto*? What court would have been the natural place to seek an antisuit injunction against the Nigerian litigation? Does it make sense for a court outside the arbitral seat to enjoin litigation allegedly brought in violation of the agreement to arbitrate?

If it is appropriate for a national court to issue an antisuit order, would it be appropriate for an arbitral tribunal to issue an antisuit order? For example, if litigation in breach of the parties' arbitration agreement, pursuant to which the tribunal was appointed, was initiated? *See* G. Born, *International Commercial Arbitration* 2501-03 (2d ed. 2014).

(d) *Damages for breach of agreement to arbitrate.* Most contractual breaches are remedied through awards of money damages to the non-breaching, injured party. Why is this not the appropriate means of relief for breach of an agreement to arbitrate? Consider *OT Africa Line Ltd v. MAGIC Sportswear Corp.* [2005] EWCA Civ. 710, ¶33 (English Ct. App.) ("damages will not be easily calculable and can indeed only be calculated by comparing the advantages and disadvantages of the respective fora. This is likely to involve an even graver breach of comity than the granting of an antisuit injunction").

Recall, as discussed above, that the only means for enforcing arbitration agreements in some common law jurisdictions prior to the 1920s was by actions for damages. *See supra* pp. 16-19, 21-26; *Red Cross Line v. Atl. Fruit Co.*, 264 U.S. 109, 118 (1924) ("an agreement to arbitrate was legal in New York and damages were recoverable for a breach thereof"); *Payton v. Hurst Eye, Ear, Nose & Throat Hosp.*, 318 S.W.2d 726, 731 (Tex. Ct. App. 1958) (under Texas common law, a party "could not compel an arbitration ... and is relegated to a suit for damages for any breach of the arbitration clause"). One of the fundamental reforms of the Geneva Protocol, adopted by the New York Convention, was to provide for specific performance of agreements to arbitrate. *See supra* pp. 30-39. If actions for damages are not the sole means for enforcing agreements to arbitrate, are they nonetheless an available means? For an ironic negative answer, see *Wells v. Entre Computer Ctrs, Inc.*, 915 F.2d 1566 (4th Cir. 1990) (court knows of no case "in which a court has awarded damages because a plaintiff brought suit in a forum other than the one to which it had contractually agreed").

(e) *Discretionary stay of litigation.* Note that the court in *Hotels.com* held that a mandatory, not discretionary, stay was required. Are there circumstances in which a discretionary stay might be appropriate, even if the standards for a mandatory stay (under Article II of the New York Convention and national law) were not satisfied? What circumstances might these be? Consider litigations involving some issues that are subject to arbitration and others that are not; consider litigations involving some parties that are involved in an arbitration and others that are not, *infra* pp. 592-94. *See also* G. Born, *International Commercial Arbitration* 1286-88 (2d ed. 2014); *Dale Metals Corp. v. Kiwa Chem. Indus. Co.*, 442 F.Supp. 78 (S.D.N.Y. 1977).

12. *Involvement in dispute of non-parties to arbitration agreement.* It is often the case that an international commercial dispute will involve multiple parties, only some of whom are bound by an arbitration agreement. In these circumstances, will the arbitration agreement be given effect, notwithstanding the absence of important parties in the arbitration? Consider how *Hotels.com* addresses this issue. Note also how the Japanese court in *Judgment of 30 May 1994* avoided needing to address this issue.

Like these decisions, other national courts have generally required the arbitration of disputes, notwithstanding the absence of important parties from the arbitration agreement and proceedings. *See, e.g., Moses H. Cone Memorial Hosp. v. Mercury Constr. Corp.*, 460 U.S. 1, 20 (1983) ("an arbitration agreement must be enforced notwithstanding the presence of other persons who are parties to the underlying dispute but not the arbitration agreement"); *Baggesen v. Am. Skandia Life Assur. Corp.*, 235 F.Supp.2d 30 (D. Mass. 2002) (refusing to allow litigation of arbitrable dispute when dispute involved non-party to arbitration agreement); *Air Freight Servs., Inc. v. Air Cargo Transp., Inc.*, 919 F.Supp. 321 (N.D. Ill. 1996) ("a plaintiff cannot avoid an arbitration agreement simply by adding as a defendant a person not a party to the arbitration agreement; that person still can obtain a stay of litigation pending arbitration").

Can a non-party to an arbitration agreement be forced to arbitrate? Consider the analysis in *Hotels.com* and *Judgment of 30 May 1994*. This topic is discussed in greater detail in Chapter 6 below. If non-parties cannot be required to arbitrate, to what extent does that affect the efficiency and efficacy of arbitration agreements?

CHAPTER 4

FORMATION AND VALIDITY OF INTERNATIONAL ARBITRATION AGREEMENTS

The formation and validity of international arbitration agreements are of vital importance to the arbitral process. Both issues arise in many international arbitration cases and can have a decisive impact on the course of arbitral proceedings. This chapter provides an overview of issues relating to the formation and validity of international arbitration agreements, focusing on international commercial arbitration agreements, but also considering inter-state and investor-state agreements to arbitrate.

First, the chapter examines the formation of international arbitration agreements, including the essential terms of agreements to arbitrate, the formation of arbitration agreements, standards of proof and tacit consent. Second, the chapter considers the formal validity of international arbitration agreements. Third, the chapter addresses the substantive validity of international arbitration agreements, including the presumptive validity of such agreements under the New York Convention, and the substantive bases for challenging the validity of international arbitration agreements. Fourth, the chapter explores the nonarbitrability doctrine, which provides that certain types of disputes may not be arbitrated. Finally, the chapter addresses agreements to arbitrate investment disputes, focusing on "arbitration without privity."

A. FORMATION OF INTERNATIONAL ARBITRATION AGREEMENTS

Although parties frequently agree to arbitrate, they also sometimes reconsider that commitment when disputes arise, and instead seek to litigate their claims in more familiar local courts. Ultimately, the efficacy of any arbitration agreement will depend on the parties' ability to enforce that agreement. As discussed above, the enforceability of international arbitration agreements has undergone important changes over the past century, evolving from a position of relative disfavor in some leading jurisdictions to one of essentially universal favor and encouragement.[1] This pro-arbitration enforcement regime for international arbitration agreements is of fundamental importance to the efficacy of the arbitral process, by ensuring that agreements to arbitrate can be enforced predictably and expeditiously in forums around the world.

1. Essential Terms of International Arbitration Agreements

In order for a valid international arbitration agreement to be formed, agreement must be reached on a core of essential issues. These rights and obligations are reflected in the definitions of "agreements to arbitrate" under international arbitration conventions[2] and

---

1. *See supra* pp. 19-67, 177-90; G. Born, *International Commercial Arbitration* 637 (2d ed. 2014).
2. These are discussed above. *See supra* pp. 116-17, 130-37.

national arbitration legislation,[3] and are elaborated by national courts and other authorities.[4] (As discussed above, arbitration is a process by which parties consensually submit a dispute to a non-governmental decision-maker, selected by or for the parties, to render a binding decision resolving a dispute in accordance with neutral, judicial procedures affording the parties an opportunity to be heard.[5]) The materials excerpted below consider what, in light of this definition, constitutes the essential elements of an arbitration agreement. What elements must the parties agree upon, in order to validly conclude an agreement to arbitrate; conversely, what elements are not essential, although they may be useful or advisable?

JUDGMENT OF 3 FEBRUARY 1990
XVII Y.B. Comm. Arb. 542 (1992) (Genoa Corte di Appello)

Samara and Coppola entered into a charter party containing a clause reading: "General average/arbitration, if any, in London in the usual manner." When a dispute arose, Coppola initiated court proceedings in Italy. The Court of First Instance held that it had jurisdiction to hear the case, and decided on the merits. The Court of Appeal reversed the lower court's decision, for the reasons set out below.

In order to establish the validity and efficacy of a clause for foreign arbitration in a contract to which an Italian national or company is a party, we must exclusively consider Art. II of the New York Convention, which establishes a uniform law. As far as the form of the clause is concerned, this Convention deems it sufficient that it be contained in an agreement signed by the parties or in an exchange of letters or telegrams. Stricter formal provisions of the place where the contract has been concluded (in this case Italy) do not apply (*in casu*, Art. 1341 CC, which provides for the specific approval in writing of the arbitration clause). Art. II does not provide for an autonomous discipline regulating the validity of the arbitration clause; it only provides, at [Art. II(3)], that the national court can ignore the effects of the arbitration clause [on court proceedings] when the clause is "null and void, inoperative or incapable of being performed."

The law applicable to the issue of the validity of the arbitration clause is either the law chosen by the parties in their contract or the law applicable to the arbitral proceedings. This principle can clearly be inferred from Art. V of the Convention, according to which recognition of the arbitral award shall be denied only when the arbitration clause is not valid under the law to which the parties have subjected it or, failing any indication thereon, under the law of the country where the award was made. Considering the *eadem ratio* and the close connection between the two provisions mentioned above, the criteria for the evaluation of the arbitration clause which are to be applied in enforcement proceedings must also be applied when the clause is invoked in order to derogate from the jurisdiction of the national courts. The uniform discipline laid down in the Convention is of the autonomous and exclusive nature; hence, it bars [the courts] from referring to national provisions referred to by the private international law norms of the forum (the so-called *lex*

---

3. These are also discussed above. *See supra* pp. 116-17, 131-37.
4. *See supra* pp. 116-37.
5. *See also supra* pp. 131-32.

fori), save in the case of the evaluation of the arbitrability of the subject matter, provided for in Art. V(2).

On the basis of the aforesaid, concerning the validity of the arbitral clause, we hold that [the arbitral clause at issue] is valid. Notwithstanding the contrary opinion of the Court of First Instance, this clause is not null and void on the strength of Art. 809 CCP,[6] which requires that the number of the arbitrators and the manner of their appointment be indicated in the arbitral clause, because there is no similar provision in the law regulating the arbitration—that is, English law. On the contrary, certain provisions in English law are to be applied when the number and powers of the arbitrators, or the manner of their appointment, are not indicated (see §6 of the Arbitration Act).

Nor can it be said that the clause is null and void because the referral to general average [in the arbitral clause] indicates that the parties only agreed to refer to arbitration the disputes concerning general average—which is not the case here. Neither the general nor the literal grounds on which the restrictive interpretation given by the Court of First Instance is based can be shared. If the parties had intended to provide for arbitration only in the case of general average, it would have been more effective and clear to amend clause 12 of the contract, concerning general average, instead of adding a clause to the contract....

E. GAILLARD & J. SAVAGE, *FOUCHARD GAILLARD GOLDMAN ON INTERNATIONAL COMMERCIAL ARBITRATION*
§486 (1999)

A "blank clause" (*clause blanche*) is one which contains no indication, whether directly or by reference to arbitration rules or to an arbitral institution, as to how the arbitrators are to be appointed. This is the case where, for example, the clause merely states "Resolution of disputes: arbitration, Paris."

In French domestic arbitration law, such clauses will be held ineffective. Article [1443(2)] of the New Code of Civil Procedure provides that the arbitration agreement must "either appoint the arbitrator or arbitrators or provide for a mechanism for their appointment," failing which the clause is void.[7] However, such clauses are valid in French international arbitration law. There is no French statutory provision requiring the parties to an international arbitration agreement to themselves specify a mechanism for appointing the arbitrators. Further, French case law has consistently confirmed that Article 1443 ... "does not apply to international arbitration."[8] In practice, the French courts will interpret such clauses as providing for *ad hoc* arbitration in which any difficulties with the composition of the arbitral tribunal will be resolved by the President of the Paris *Tribunal de grande in-*

---

6. Art. 809 of the [pre-2006] Italian Code of Civil Procedure [read]: "There may be either one or more arbitrators, provided that their number be always uneven. The submission or arbitration clause shall state who are to be the arbitrators or establish the number of arbitrators and the manner in which they are to be appointed. These provisions must be observed under penalty or nullity."

7. ... Cass. com., *Jan. 18, 1994, Nègre v. Aux délices de Bourgogne*, 1994 Rev. arb. 536, and observations by P. Fouchard.

8. *See* CA Paris, *Nov. 14, 1991, Consorts Legrand v. European Country Hotels Ltd*, 1994 Rev. arb. 545, 2d decision, and observations by P. Fouchard; CA Paris, *Dec. 7, 1994, V 2000 v. Renault*, 1996 Rev. arb. 245, and C. Jarrosson's note.

stance, under Article 1493 of the New Code of Civil Procedure.... That is not to say, however, that blank clauses are to be recommended.

The pathological element of a blank clause really only emerges where the arbitration agreement contains no detail linking the blank clause, by the choice of a seat or a procedural law, to a country whose courts are able to appoint the arbitrators. An example will be a clause stipulating that "any disputes arising from the interpretation of the present contract will be settled by an arbitral tribunal sitting in a country other than that of each of the parties." It is not clear whether the French courts, for instance, would agree to rule on a request to appoint arbitrators if confronted with an arbitration agreement of that kind between two non-French parties, one of which sought to commence arbitration in France. In order for the courts to agree to carry out such an appointment, the clause would have to be interpreted as containing an agreement between the parties whereby, in the event of a dispute, the plaintiff would be entitled to choose the seat of arbitration. If France were the chosen seat, the courts would then be able to apply Article 1493 ..., which empowers the President of the Paris Tribunal of First Instance to rule on any difficulty encountered in the constitution of the arbitral tribunal. In the above example, this result could be obtained by an *a contrario* interpretation of the arbitration agreement, the parties having excluded the jurisdiction of the courts of each of their home countries. However, the courts' response to this line of reasoning remains uncertain.

LUCKY-GOLDSTAR INTERNATIONAL (H.K.) LTD v. NG MOO KEE ENGINEERING LTD
[1994] Arb. & Disp. Resol. L.J. 49 (H.K. Ct. First Inst.)

I have before me an application for a stay of these proceedings pursuant to the provisions of Article 8 of the Model Law. Both plaintiff and defendant are Hong Kong companies having their place of business in Hong Kong. The plaintiff is a subsidiary of a well-known Korean company which trades under the name of "Lucky Goldstar." ... It will soon become apparent that [the parties] have agreed that the place of arbitration is to be outside that state.

By a written agreement dated 3 December 1990, the plaintiffs sold to the defendants five sets of elevators. The contract contained the following dispute resolution clause:

"Claims: Any claims by Buyer of whatever nature arising under this contract shall be made by cable within thirty (30) days after arrival of the merchandise at the destination specified in the bills of lading.... Any dispute or difference arising out of or relating to this contract, or the breach thereof which cannot be settled amicably without undue delay by the interested parties shall be arbitrated in the 3rd Country, under the rule of the 3rd Country and in accordance with the rules of procedure of the International Commercial Arbitration Association. The award shall be final and binding upon both parties."

The defendants seek to rely on the arbitration agreement and thus they seek a stay of these proceedings under Article 8 of the Model Law....

The parties appear to agree that the phrase "3rd Country" which appears in the arbitration clause means any country other than Hong Kong and probably Korea. No evidence was put in as to what was intended by the use of this phrase. For all I know it might have been intended to convey to the parties using this clause that a specific 3rd country had to be inserted where those words appeared. Be that as it may, the conditions of this contract were the standard terms and conditions used by the plaintiff's Korean head office with the deletion of the word "Korea" which was replaced by the words "3rd Country." It is also common ground between the parties that the International Commercial Arbitration Association referred to in the arbitration clause is a non-existent organization. No useful purpose can be served by speculating as to what was actually intended by the use of these words.

[The plaintiffs] attempted to argue that there was no binding arbitration agreement on the grounds that a common mistake had been made. [They] submitted that when the parties have agreed to undertake arbitration only in certain circumstances, and according to certain rules and those rules turn out to be non-existent, the consent to arbitration is therefore nullified…. I cannot accept this argument. It is perfectly clear that the parties, by this clause, intended to arbitrate any disputes that might arise under this contract. This agreement is not nullified because they chose the rules of the non-existent organization. It must be noted that the clause refers to arbitration in the 3rd country "under the rule of the 3rd Country *and* in accordance with the rules of procedure of…." The word "rule" must mean "law." As there are no rules and this non-existent organization the arbitration has to be conducted under the law of the 3rd country chosen by the plaintiff. In this regard, they are in the fortunate position of being able to choose a country whose law and practice of arbitration is acceptable to them and no doubt they will also take into account whether that country has ratified the New York Convention.

I do not, and cannot, accept that this agreement to arbitrate is nullified in the manner suggested. [The plaintiffs] turn[] to the words used in Article 8 of the Model Law and attempts to argue that this arbitration agreement is "inoperative or incapable of being performed" was taken from the New York Convention…. Professor Albert Jan van den Berg, in his book on The New York Arbitration Convention 1958, in dealing with the word "inoperative" stated at page 158:

> "The word 'inoperative' can be deemed to cover those cases where the arbitration agreement has ceased to have effect. The ceasing of effect to the arbitration agreement may occur for a variety of reasons. One reason may be that the parties have implicitly or explicitly revoked the agreement to arbitrate. Another may be that the same dispute between the same parties had already been decided in arbitration or court proceedings (… *res judicata*)."

He goes on to give other examples … where the award has been set aside or there is stalemate in voting of the arbitrators or the award has not been rendered within the prescribed time limit. Further he suggests that a settlement reached before the commencement of arbitration may have the effect of rendering the arbitration agreement inoperative…. As to the phrase "incapable of being performed," Professor van den Berg is of the view that this would seem to apply to a case where the arbitration cannot be effectively set in motion. The clause may be too vague or perhaps other terms in the contract contradict the parties' intention to arbitrate. He suggests that if an arbitrator specifically named in the arbitration agreement refuses to act or if an appointing authority refuses to appoint, it might be concluded that the arbitration agreement is "incapable of being performed." However, that would only apply if the curial law of the state where the arbitration was taking place had no provision equivalent to … Article 11 of the Model Law [permitting judicial selection of an arbitrator, *see infra* pp. 705-06]….

Having considered all of [the plaintiffs'] arguments, I cannot see how it can be said that this arbitration clause is "inoperative or incapable of being performed." True, it is, that there will be no arbitration under the rules of the International Commercial Arbitration Association, but there will be an arbitration under the law of the place of arbitration chosen by the plaintiffs and they have a very wide choice indeed. The parties have made their intentions to arbitrate perfectly plain in this clause. If the use only of the word "arbitration" is sufficient to create a binding arbitration agreement then, *a fortiori*, this clause is valid (*see Hobbs Padgett & Co. (Reins.) Ltd v. J.C. Kirkland Ltd* [1969] 2 Lloyds Rep. 547, 549).

I believe that the correct approach in this case is to satisfy myself that the parties have clearly expressed the intention to arbitrate any dispute which may arise under this contract. I am so satisfied: I am also satisfied that they have chosen the law of the place of arbitration to govern the arbitration even though that place has not yet been chosen by the plaintiffs. As to the reference to the non-existent arbitration institution and rules, I believe that the correct approach is simply to ignore it. I can give no effect to it and I reject all reference to it so as to be able to give effect to the clear intention of the parties.

I further reject [the plaintiffs'] submission that both parties only agreed to arbitrate if it was to be under these non-existent set of rules. The defendants would seem to have had no choice but to accept the plaintiffs' standard terms and conditions and they can be forgiven for thinking that an organization as large as Lucky-Goldstar knew what they were talking about. [The plaintiffs] submit[] that I cannot salvage this arbitration agreement by ignoring reference to the non-existent organization, because the seat of this arbitration is going to be outside Hong Kong and thus only Articles 8 and 9 of the Model Law apply. However, [they] did concede that I could and, indeed, had to construe this agreement, and that is all I believe I am doing using canons of construction applied by the law of the state exercising jurisdiction under article 8.

Having decided that this arbitration agreement is not "null and void inoperative or incapable of being performed," I have no choice under article 8 but to stay these proceedings, which I do accordingly. Before parting with this case, I would like to add the following. This is not the first case with which I have had to deal where the arbitration clause has left something to be desired. Many contract drafters seem to have difficulty in the fairly simple task of drafting an arbitration clause or even replicating a standard form clause. Arbitral institutions and associations go to the trouble of drafting standard form arbitration clauses and disseminating them for the benefit of users, yet in far too high a percentage of cases something goes wrong. The former Secretary General of the ICC told an audience in Hong Kong a few years ago that only in a very small number of cases which came to the ICC, did the parties manage to replicate accurately in their contract the standard ICC clause. A badly-drafted clause leads to disputes and wasted costs, both of which are anathema to the arbitral process. In many cases in this region, I imagine the problem is caused by contract drafters not drafting in their native tongue and this problem is appreciated. However, anything that can be done to ensure that arbitration clauses are clear, meaningful and effective would enhance the arbitration process quite considerably....

Since drafting this judgment my attention has been drawn to a decision from New York which is of interest to the matters raised in this application. *In Laboratories Grossman v. Forest Laboratories*, 295 NYS2d 756, the parties agreed to arbitrate under the rules of a non-existent organization.... [T]he Supreme Court of New York ordered a hearing to determine the parties' true intent. If their true intent was not to arbitrate under the rules of the organization put forward by the respondent then the Court had to determine,

> "whether the dominant purpose of the agreement was to settle disputes by arbitration, rather than the instrumentally through which arbitration should be effected.... In such event, there being no viable organization named in the agreement through which arbitration may be had,

the court may direct arbitration before such tribunal as it may determine would be the most appropriate in the circumstances."

I think that this is a useful test and when applied to the facts before me, I have no doubt that the parties' dominant intention was to settle disputes by arbitration rather than the instrumentality through which arbitration was to be conducted. This is clear from the fact that the organization referred to was a non-existent and further, unlike in the case cited, neither party deposed to intending any specific alternative arbitral institution.... I therefore grant the stay sought by the defendants....

LEA TAI TEXTILE CO. v. MANNING FABRICS, INC.
411 F.Supp. 1404 (S.D.N.Y. 1975)

DUFFY, District Judge.... Petitioner, Lea Tai Textiles, Ltd ("Lea Tai"), is a corporation organized under the laws of Hong Kong where it has its principal place of business. Respondent, Manning Fabrics, Inc. ("Manning"), is a New York corporation with its principal place of business in St. Paul, North Carolina.... From November 1973 to April 1974, the parties entered into a series of contracts for the sale of cotton cloth. Manning would send a purchase order from its New York office to Lea Tai in Hong Kong. Lea Tai, in turn, mailed confirmations to Manning. In September of 1974, Lea Tai shipped 400,000 yards of cotton duck and 120,000 yards of cotton sateen to Manning. Lea Tai alleges that due to changing market conditions Manning wrongfully refused to accept the goods. Manning argues that after an August, 1974 shipment of defective goods it instructed Lea Tai to cease further shipments. Manning filed suit in the Court of Common Pleas, State of South Carolina.... Lea Tai seeks to stay this suit and compel arbitration in New York. Manning contends that no agreement to arbitrate was ever made.

The Act provides that a party aggrieved by another's failure to arbitrate may petition a U.S. District Court to compel arbitration, 9 U.S.C. §4[:] "If the making of the arbitration agreement ... be in issue, the court shall proceed summarily to trial thereof." Although the existence of the arbitration agreement is in dispute, the essential facts are not and thus the matter can be disposed of without plenary hearing.

In determining the validity of a contract to arbitrate, the Court of Appeals for this Circuit has consistently held that federal rather than state law controls. *Robert Lawrence Co. v. Devonshire Fabrics, Inc.*, 271 F.2d 402 (2d Cir.); *Coenen v. R. W. Pressprich & Co.*, 453 F.2d 1209 (2d Cir. 1972). In the context of this case the conflict of law inquiry is more of an academic pursuit. Although Congress did not substitute the Uniform Commercial Code ("U.C.C.") for the federal common law of contracts, the Code is nevertheless "a most appropriate source of federal law." *In re Yale Express System, Inc.*, 370 F.2d 433, 435 (2d Cir. 1966)....

Turning to the existence of a contract to arbitrate, I am faced with the not uncommon exchange of inconsistent forms between a buyer and a seller. Both parties apparently concede the existence of a series of valid contracts for the sale of goods, they argue whether an arbitration clause was made a part thereof. Manning's order form under which Lea Tai seeks to compel arbitration provides as follows:

"11. ARBITRATION: Any controversy arising out of or relating to this contract shall be settled by arbitration in the City of New York in accordance with the Rules then obtaining of the American Arbitration Association or the General Arbitration Counsel [sic] of the Textile

Industry, whichever shall be first selected by the party instituting the arbitration…. The parties consent to the jurisdiction of the Supreme Court of the State of New York and the United States District Court for the Southern District of New York for all purposes in connection with said arbitration…."

Lea Tai's confirmation form, labelled a "contract," contains an arbitration clause different from Manning's:

"12. ARBITRATION…. Should any dispute arise between the Buyers and the Sellers in relation to this Contract which they are unable themselves to settle the same shall be referred to the arbitration of two arbitrators; one to be appointed by the Sellers and the other by the Buyers, and the provisions of the Hong Kong Code of Civil Procedure as to a reference to two arbitrators shall apply."

Thus, the parties now seek me to decide whether they agreed to arbitrate and if so which clause controls. U.C.C. 2-207(1) provides that a confirmation may operate as an acceptance even though its terms differ from that of the offer: "A definite and seasonable expression of acceptance or a written confirmation which is sent within a reasonable time operates as an acceptance even though it states terms additional to or different from those offered or agreed upon, unless acceptance is expressly made conditional on assent to the additional or different terms." [U.C.C. 2-207(2)] outlines the effect of the conflicting term:

"The additional terms are to be construed as proposals for addition to the contract. Between merchants such terms become part of the contract unless: (a) the offer expressly limits acceptance to the terms of the offer; (b) they materially alter it;[9] or (c) notification of objection to them has already been given or is given within a reasonable time after notice of them is received."

The Official Comment to the section clearly indicates that a conflicting clause is to be considered as a notification of objection for the purposes of U.C.C. §2-207(2)(c)…. Since the arbitration clauses are in hopeless conflict, I find that no contract to arbitrate was made.

This result suggested by the U.C.C. has a solid basis in logic and reason. While there is a strong federal policy favoring arbitration, … it remains a creature of contract. This Court will not impose its will on parties whose intentions are in clear conflict on this important issue. Arbitration under the Code of Hong Kong rather than the laws of New York may well affect important substantive rights. It is irrelevant to the issues of contract formation that the Hong Kong seller now concludes that it would be willing to arbitrate in New York….

JUDGMENT OF 21 NOVEMBER 2003
DFT 130 III 66 (Swiss Fed. Trib.)

The parties concluded … an exclusive distributor agreement which contains the following arbitration clause in Article 22.2:

---

9. There is a difference of opinion on the question of whether the inclusion of an arbitration clause in an acceptance is a per se material alteration of the offer. *Compare Matter of Doughboy Industries, Inc.*, 233 N.Y.S.2d 488, 495-96 (1st Dep't 1962) (Brietel, J.) *with Dorton v. Collins & Aikman Corp.*, 453 F.2d 1161, 1169 (6th Cir. 1972); *In re Wolfkill Feed & Fertilizer Corp.* (N.Y. County Sup. Ct.), New York Law Journal 16 (May 16, 1975).

"The parties agree that any dispute or difference which may arise out of this Agreement or the execution or interpretation of any of the clauses hereof shall be settled amicably. If such dispute or difference cannot be settled in the aforementioned manner they shall be finally settled under the Rules of Conciliation and Arbitration of the Zurich Chamber of Commerce, Zurich/ Switzerland, in accordance with the UNCITRAL Arbitration Rules. The number of arbitrators shall be three (3). ICC shall be the Appointing Authority acting in accordance with the rules adopted by ICC for that purpose."

In August 2002, the respondent initiated at the Zurich Chamber of Commerce ("ZCC") an arbitration against the appellant.... [T]he president of the Chamber of Commerce appointed the lawyer Dr. Rudolf Tschäni as president of the tribunal on 16 September 2002. On 19 September 2002, he selected [four Swiss lawyers] as potential members of the arbitral tribunal. On 23 October 2002, the president of the arbitral tribunal submitted to the parties a draft Order of Constitution, were he listed in addition to himself and [two of the four Swiss lawyers] as members of the arbitral tribunal. He ordered inter alia the following: "Both parties are invited to submit their comments or objections with regard to the aforementioned draft or the appointment of the arbitrators on or before November 1, 2002. Otherwise, the order of constitution will be issued in this form." On 31 October 2002, the respondent informed the president of the tribunal that it had no comments or objections. The appellant did not [reply] within the period allotted.

On 12 November 2002, the arbitral tribunal sent the parties the "Order of Constitution" dated 5 November 2002 in its original form. By this order, the parties were called for advance payment of court fees each for CHF 100,000. The respondent paid, the appellant did not. On 20 February 2003, the president of the arbitral tribunal asked the respondent to pay the share of the appellant or to dismiss the arbitration (Article 55 of the ZCC Arbitration Rules). The respondent paid the outstanding half of the advance.

In the Order of Constitution the arbitral tribunal had set a deadline for the appellant to reply until 26 November 2002. The appellant asked for an extension of that deadline and stressed at the same time that its request for an extension did not imply the recognition of the jurisdiction of the arbitral tribunal. On 13 January 2003, the appellant filed a motion to limit the procedure on the question of jurisdiction for the time being. The appellant objected to the arbitral tribunal's jurisdiction on the grounds that the tribunal was not constituted validly.... [T]he arbitral tribunal issued an interim decision and order in which it recognized to be constituted properly ("The Arbitral Tribunal is properly constituted"). The appellant [appealed to the Swiss Federal Tribunal, which rejected the appeal].

The appellant asserts that the arbitral tribunal had no jurisdiction due to lack of a valid arbitration agreement [citing Article 190(2)(b) of the Swiss Law on Private International Law ("SLPIL")]. [The appellant argued that the arbitration was invalid because it referred to] three different rules of arbitration (ZCC Arbitration Rules, UNCITRAL Arbitration Rules and ICC Arbitration Rules), [and therefore] contained contradictory orders, which could not be interpreted in a compatible way. Consensus between the parties on the contents of the arbitration agreement was therefore not identifiable and the agreement therefore was invalid.

Article 178 of the SLPIL deals with the formal requirements of the arbitration clause and determines the law applicable to its substantive validity, especially as regards its conclusion, its scope and its expiry. The provision does not refer to the main characteristics and to the necessary content of an arbitration clause. In line with the traditional concept of private arbitration, this is to be understood as an agreement by which two or more identified or identifiable parties agree to subject one or more existing or certain future disputes in a binding way and under the exclusion of state court litigation to an arbitral tribunal in accordance with a directly or indirectly identified legal order. A general requirement of an arbitration agreement is also its clarity and certainty regarding the private jurisdiction, i.e., the arbitral tribunal that is appointed to make the decision, must be determined either clearly or at least be determinable. Provisions in arbitration agreements that are incomplete, unclear or contradictory are considered to be pathological clauses. If they do not contain mandatory elements of the arbitration agreement, namely the binding reference of the decision on the dispute to private arbitration, they do not necessarily lead to its invalidity. Instead, in these circumstances, a solution has to be found by interpretation or at most by amending the contract in accordance with general contract law; a solution that respects the basic intent of the parties, to be bound by an arbitration clause. If the parties intended the seat of the arbitration in Switzerland, they may regulate the constitution of the arbitral tribunal themselves [citing Article 179(1) of the SLPIL]. This order can be made individually ad hoc or through reference to institutional arbitration rules. If there is no such agreement, the judge at the arbitral seat can be requested to decide on this issue. He can determine in analogy of Swiss law the appointment, dismissal or replacement of arbitrators [citing Article 179(2) of the SLPIL].

The arbitration agreement is interpreted in the same manner and according to the same general principles as other declarations of intent. The determining factor is primarily the agreed actual subjective understanding of the parties regarding their declarations to one another. If such an actual intention of the parties can not be identified, the arbitration agreement has to be interpreted objectively, i.e. the presumed intention of the parties has to be determined based upon how the respective addressee of the statements would and could have understood the statements in good faith. If it is established as a result of this interpretation that the parties wanted their dispute to be excluded from state jurisdiction and that they wanted to bring their case to arbitration, but differences remain regarding the settlement of the process of the arbitration, the validation principle ("*Utilitätsgedanke*") applies. This principle states that a contractual interpretation which justifies and gives effect to an arbitration clause must be found. Accordingly, an imprecise or faulty description of the arbitral tribunal does not mean that the arbitration agreement is invalid if it can be determined by interpretation, which arbitration tribunal the parties have designated. Similarly and based on Article 179(2) of the SLPIL the state judge in the place where the parties have chosen the arbitral seat has jurisdiction to appoint the arbitral tribunal if the parties have not selected the arbitrators or a means for doing so. This judicial appointment of the arbitral tribunal requires that the parties have determined the arbitral seat.

The arbitration agreement [in this case] is unambiguous and clear insofar as the parties have excluded any possible disputes arising out of their exclusive distributor agreement form the jurisdiction of any court and agreed upon a private arbitration instead. With the primary reference to the conciliation and arbitration rules of the Zurich Chamber of Commerce the parties have agreed upon an institutional arbitral tribunal based in Zurich. The fact that the arbitration agreement refers to arbitration under the ZCC Arbitration Rules "in accordance with the UNCITRAL Arbitration Rules" shall be interpreted based on the principles of good faith and validation ("*Utilitätsprinzip*"), [which indicates that the parties intended] that the primary procedural law was to be complemented. This does not appear to be an incurable pathological clause. However the arbitration clause creates a possible conflict of competence regarding the appointment of the arbitral tribunal, insofar as it provides for a three person arbitral tribunal, appointed by the [ICC] in Paris and according to the ICC Rules, and insofar as these rules do not tolerate the primary applicable ZCC-Arbitration Rules.

According to Article 11(2) of the ZCC Arbitration Rules the President of the ZCC appoints the chairman of the tribunal, in principle from a list of the Board of the ZCC. The other two arbitrators shall be appointed by the parties, provided that they have agreed to this in writing; failing such agreement, the President of the arbitral tribunal shall appoint the two remaining arbitrators based on a list provided by the President of the ZCC (Article 12(1) and (3) of the ZCC Arbitration Rules). According to Article 8(4) of the ICC Rules, each party shall appoint one arbitrator who must be confirmed by the ICC Court. The third and presiding arbitrator shall be appointed by the ICC Court, unless the parties agreed upon a different designation process. In this case, the appointment by the parties requires a confirmation of Court (Article 9 of the ICC Rules).

The two sets of arbitral rules [ICC and ZCC] are in conflict because they both refer to an institutional arbitral tribunal, which is administered, selected and controlled by the applicable arbitral institution (ZCC, ICC). The two regimes are thus incompatible insofar as the arbitration can only belong to one of the two institutions. It therefore raises the question of whether this incompatibility leads to the invalidity of the arbitration clause. This is also a question of the interpretation of the contract. According to the theory of good faith reliance, the arbitration agreement has to be understood to mean that the parties wanted any dispute arising from their agreement to be decided by the ZCC arbitral tribunal. This follows from the selection in the first place of the ZCC Arbitration Rules and from Zurich being explicitly designated as the arbitral seat, and also from the fact that the ICC Rules are not generally selected, but only for the appointment of the arbitrator. The agreed procedures for the appointment of the arbitrators are, however, excluded by the choice of a non-ICC arbitration, because there is a lack of administration by the ICC in such circumstances. In that regard, a part of the arbitration agreement is impossible to perform. But, by virtue of the clear intention of the parties to settle their disputes by private arbitration, this partial impossibility does not lead to the complete ineffectiveness of the arbitration agreement or the lack of jurisdiction of the ZCC arbitral tribunal…. [H]aving regard to the purpose of the arbitration agreement, simply deleting the appointment provision in favor of the ZCC Arbitration Rules, which enjoy contractual priority, is entirely reasonable; this conclusion is supported by the statutory appointment provisions set forth in Article 179(2) of the SLPIL. Consequently, the claim of lack of jurisdiction of the arbitral tribunal for lack of a valid arbitration agreement as unfounded.

HOOGOVENS IJMUIDEN VERKOOPKANTOOR BV v. MV SEA CATTLEYA

852 F.Supp. 6 (S.D.N.Y. 1994)

WHITMAN KNAPP, Senior District Judge. This is an admiralty action relating to damage caused to steel coils during their carriage from the Netherlands to the United States. Defendant Van Ommeren Bulk Shipping BV ("Van Ommeren"), one of the parties which shipped the coil, moves pursuant to the [New York] Convention to stay proceedings against it pending arbitration in the Netherlands…. Van Ommeren asserts that according to the terms of the charter party which and plaintiff entered into on January 12, 1989, in Ijmuiden,

Netherlands, for the purpose of shipping plaintiff's steel coils to Bridgeport, Connecticut, plaintiff must arbitrate its cargo damage claim in the Netherlands. Clause 2 of that charter states: "General Average and arbitration to be settled in the Netherlands." Van Ommeren interprets this clause to require the parties to submit all disputes arising in connection with the charter to arbitration in the Netherlands[, citing] *Oriental Commercial & Shipping Co. v. Rosseel NV*, 609 F.Supp. 75, 77 (S.D.N.Y. 1985).

In *Rosseel*, defendant moved to compel arbitration under the [New York] Convention, based on the clause in a sales contract, "Arbitration: If required in New York City." Applying federal law to determine whether or not the parties to a foreign contract have agreed to arbitrate, the court ruled that the clause bound the parties to arbitration of all claims arising with respect to the contract. It reasoned that "[a]rbitration clauses must be interpreted broadly, and all doubts as to whether a dispute is encompassed by a particular clause must be resolved in favor of arbitration, even where the problem is the construction of the contract language itself."

Plaintiff, on the other hand, asserts that the clause merely states the parties' choice of situs for any arbitration relating to the charter, if the parties were to voluntarily decide to arbitrate claims, or if such arbitration were otherwise required. Alternatively, plaintiff suggests that the clause only requires the parties to arbitrate general average claims in the Netherlands, no such claims being asserted in this suit.

Regretfully, we must disagree with [the court's] interpretation of a very similar clause in *Rosseel*.... The first inquiry in a case governed by the [New York] Convention is whether or not the parties have made "any agreement in writing arbitrate the subject in dispute." *Filanto, SpA v. Chilewich Intern. Corp.*, 789 F.Supp. 1229, 1236 (S.D.N.Y. 1992), quoting *Ledee v. Ceramiche Ragno*, 684 F.2d 184, 186-87 (1st Cir. 1982). Where no such agreement exists, the court has no jurisdiction under the Convention and its implementing legislation to stay a federal action or to compel arbitration. We find that clause 24 of the January 1989 charter party is no more than an agreement that, if arbitration were to be conducted whether voluntarily agreed upon or required by some other contractual clause, it would proceed in the Netherlands. Therefore, we have no authority under the [New York] Convention to stay proceedings against Van Ommeren pending arbitration.

JUDGMENT OF 1 FEBRUARY 1979
1980 Rev. arb. 97 (Paris Tribunal de grande instance)

On 28 January 1947, Techniques de l'Ingénieur (T.I.) and Sofel concluded a contract drafted on headed paper of T.I. for the distribution of a book edited by T.I. that Sofel was to publish. Article 7 of the contract reads: "Jurisdiction selections: in case of disagreement [sic] the parties must refer the matter to the Fédération française de la Publicité. In case of dispute, the Court of Seine will have exclusive jurisdiction." A dispute arose between the parties and Sofel referred it, pursuant the arbitration clause of Article 7, to a Federal Commission of Mediation and Arbitration of the Fédération Nationale de la Publicité. T.I. defaulted in the arbitration and the Arbitral Commission nominated an arbitrator on behalf of the defaulting party, pursuant to the Commission's rules. T.I. was held liable for damages in an award of 8 March 1978....

T.I. argues that article 7 is ambiguous and contradictory because it seems either to give jurisdiction to the Seine Court while at the same time obliges the parties to refer the matter to an Arbitral Commission or to make an untenable distinction between disagreement and dispute. T.I. asserts that this clause is void.... Sofel, on the other side, considers the arbitration clause valid, although acknowledging its ambiguity. Relying on Article 1196 of the Civil Code, Sofel argues that one must go beyond the literal meaning of the words and seek the common intention of the contracting parties to establish the arbitrators' jurisdiction. [The court held:]

Whereas arbitration is a possibility offered to contracting parties that expressly agree thereto, which excludes the otherwise applicable jurisdiction of state courts;

Whereas in this case the ambiguous arbitration clause should be interpreted in light of the fact that if the parties did not wish to resort to arbitration they would not have referred to the possibility of resorting to arbitrators; but, whereas by including an arbitration clause in their agreement, the parties manifested their intention to refer difficulties arising from the contract to the Fédération de la Publicité;

Whereas article 7 is captioned "Jurisdiction selections (plural)," which reveals the parties' intent to refer their disputes to arbitration, and which also explains the conditional form of the last sentence of the clause, which means that if there were no resort to arbitrators, the Court of Seine would be the second instance that would hear an eventual dispute;

Whereas the company T.I. which drafted the contract on its headed paper cannot claim an ambiguity stemming from its own doing and cannot assert a different interpretation of the common intent of the parties; that consequently the arbitration clause being valid, the judgment of 8 March 1978 is lawful and the appeal of T.I is ill-founded....

WSG NIMBUS PTE LTD v. BOARD OF CONTROL FOR CRICKET IN SRI LANKA

[2002] 3 SLR 603, 637 (Singapore High Ct.)

[excerpted above at pp. 321-25]

INT'L LAW COMMISSION MODEL RULES ON ARBITRAL PROCEDURE
Article 2

2(1). Unless there are earlier agreements which suffice for the purpose, for example in the understanding to arbitrate itself, the parties having recourse to arbitration shall conclude a *compromis* which shall specify, as a minimum: (a) The undertaking to arbitrate according to which the dispute is to be submitted to the arbitrators; (b) The subject-matter of the dispute and, if possible, the points on which the parties are or are not agreed; (c) The method of constituting the tribunal and the number of arbitrators.

2(2). In addition, the *compromis* shall include any other provisions deemed desirable by the parties, in particular: (i) The rules of law and the principles to be applied by the tribunal, and the right, if any, conferred on it to decide *ex aequo et bono* as though it had legislative functions in the matter; (ii) The power, if any, of the tribunal to make recommendations to the parties; (iii) Such power as may be conferred on the tribunal to make its own rules of procedure; (iv) The procedure to be followed by the tribunal; provided that, once constituted, the tribunal shall be free to override any provisions of the *compromis* which may prevent it from rendering its award; (v) The number of members required for the constitution of a *quorum* for the conduct of the hearings; (vi) The majority required for the award; (vii) The time limit within which the award shall be rendered; (viii) The right of the members of the tribunal to attach dissenting or individual opinions to the award, or any prohibition of such opinions; (ix) The languages to be employed in the course of the proceedings; (x) The manner in which the costs and disbursements shall be apportioned; (xi) The services which the International Court of Justice may be asked to render. This enumeration is not intended to be exhaustive.

NOTES

1. *Diversity of arbitration agreements and "pathological" arbitration clauses.* Consider the model arbitration clauses of the UNCITRAL, ICC, LCIA and other institutions, excerpted at pp. 297-99 of the Documentary Supplement. Compare these provisions with the arbitration agreements in the cases excerpted above. Agreements to arbitrate are, like other contracts, products of the parties' negotiations and drafting, and thus differ widely, depending on the parties' interests, needs, skill and foresight. Consider the court's comments at the end of the *Lucky-Goldstar* opinion, expressing concern at the inability of parties to make use of model institutional rules and the frequency with which potentially "pathological" (*i.e.*, invalid) arbitration provisions are encountered. Why does this occur? Note from the cases excerpted above that non-specialist drafters often attempt to create specially-tailored solutions for particular transactions.

   Note also that arbitration clauses are, to a considerable extent, relatively formulaic; even if drafted by different parties, for different transactions, arbitration clauses almost always involve similar provisions and language. What are the provisions that recur in model (and other) international arbitration agreements? Recall the German Bundesgerichtshof's observations in its *27 February 1970* decision, *supra* pp. 194-98 about the formulaic character of agreements to arbitrate. What conclusions did the Court draw from this observation about the proper approach to interpreting arbitration agreements? Are those conclusions valid?

2. *Minimum essential terms of agreement to arbitrate.* What terms are required in order for a valid agreement to arbitrate to exist? Suppose that the parties to a contract agree "Disputes to be arbitrated." Is that sufficient to constitute a binding arbitration agreement? What about the scope of the disputes to be arbitrated; the place of arbitration; the means of selecting the arbitrators; the applicable law? Are none of these terms necessary to form a binding arbitration agreement? Why not?

   Consider the results in *Judgment of 3 February 1990* and *Hoogovens*. Can you draft a more skeletal arbitration clause? Should these provisions be sufficient to form a binding arbitration agreement? For other examples of decisions upholding skeletal clauses, see *CNA Reins. Co., Ltd v. Trustmark Ins. Co.*, 2001 WL 648948, at *6 (N.D. Ill.) (upholding phrase "Arbitration clause" in contract); *Bauer Int'l Corp. v. Etablissements Soules & Cie.*, 303 N.Y.S.2d 884 (N.Y. 1969) (upholding: "Arbitration in New York"); *Schulze & Burch Biscuit Co. v. Tree Top, Inc.*, 831 F.2d 709, 715-16 (7th Cir. 1987) (upholding: "All disputes under this transaction shall be arbitrated in the usual manner"); *Hobbs, Padgett & Co. (Reins.) Ltd v. JC Kirkland Ltd* [1969] 2 Lloyd's Rep. 547 (English Ct. App.) (upholding: "Suitable arbitration clause"); *Judgment of 21 November 1983*, X Y.B. Comm. Arb. 478 (1985) (Italian Corte di Cassazione) (upholding: "Arbitration. In London if necessary").

Compare the results in *Judgment of 3 February 1990* and *Hoogovens*. Which decision is wiser? What exactly is it that is required to form an arbitration agreement? Is it simply an exchange of promises to resolve disputes by "arbitration"?

Note that both the *Judgment of 3 February 1990* and *Hoogovens* involved a specialized industry with substantial trade custom. How relevant is that to deciding whether or not the parties concluded a valid arbitration agreement?

3. *"Blank clauses."* Consider the excerpt from *Fouchard Gaillard Goldman on International Commercial Arbitration* dealing with "blank clauses"—that is, agreements that do not specify either an arbitral seat or a means of selecting the arbitrators (either directly or through incorporation of institutional rules). Give an example of a "blank clause." Why is it that a "blank clause" should arguably not be a valid agreement to arbitrate?

Suppose that a Swiss and a Russian party agree to a contract containing a "blank arbitration clause." Is that clause incapable of being implemented? Where would the arbitration be seated? If the parties did not agree upon the identity (or identities) of the arbitrator(s), how would they be selected? Would not the courts of either Russia or Switzerland be capable of specifying the arbitral seat and appointing the arbitrators? What if both Swiss and Russian courts purported to fulfill these functions? Is the risk of inconsistent national court implementations of the arbitration clause sufficient to conclude that it is invalid? Why is it that "blank clauses" are invalid under French domestic arbitration law, but not under French international arbitration law? Does that make sense?

Is it appropriate to conclude that a clause providing only "Arbitration in New York," is a valid agreement to arbitrate? What else is arguably required in order for the clause to be valid? How will arbitrators be selected? What procedures will govern the arbitration? Which law will be applied? Is the failure of the parties' clause to address these issues sufficient grounds for concluding that it is not a binding agreement to arbitrate?

4. *International Law Commission's requirements for validity of inter-state arbitration agreements*. Consider Article 2 of the ILC Model Rules on Arbitral Procedure. What are identified as the essential elements of an agreement to arbitrate between states by the ILC? Why are these elements so important? Should the same elements be required for an international commercial arbitration agreement?

5. *Choice of law governing essential elements of international arbitration agreements*. What law governs requirements for the essential elements of an international commercial arbitration agreement? Is it Article II of the New York Convention? Does Article II specify, expressly or impliedly, the essential elements of an arbitration agreement? Suppose State A required that an international arbitration agreement specify all of the arbitrators, the details of the arbitral procedure and the precise nature of the parties' claims. Would that requirement comply with Article II of the Convention?

Consider the choice-of-law rules governing the validity of international arbitration agreements under the New York Convention. *See supra* pp. 308-10 & *infra* pp. 367, 407, 420. Do those rules apply to determination of the essential elements of an agreement to arbitrate?

6. *Indefinite or internally-contradictory arbitration agreements.* Suppose that an arbitration clause does address various aspects of the arbitral process, but does so in an ambiguous or indefinite manner. Does this affect the validity of the arbitration clause? Consider the following "pathological" arbitration clauses. What is wrong with each one? Is each such defect sufficient to invalidate the entire arbitration agreement, or only parts of it?

    "All disputes arising in connection with the present agreement shall be submitted in the first instance to arbitration. The arbitrator shall be a well-known chamber of commerce (like the International Chamber of Commerce) designated by mutual agreement between buyer and seller." W. Craig, W. Park & J. Paulsson, *International Chamber of Commerce Arbitration* ¶9.06 (3d ed. 2000).

    "For all claims of disputes arising out of this agreement which could not be amicably settled between the parties, is competent the arbitrage for export trade at the Federal Chamber of Commerce in Beograd. In the case that the buyer is accused, the Chamber of Commerce in New York [which does not exist] is competent." *Astra Footwear Indus. v. Harwyn Int'l, Inc.*, 442 F.Supp. 907 (S.D.N.Y. 1978).

    "All disputes arising in connection with the present agreement should be resolved by negotiation and friendly settlement. If this method of resolution should be impracticable, the disputed questions shall be decided in accordance with the Rules of Arbitration of the ICC in Paris. In the event the proceedings were not able to decide the question for any reason whatsoever, the judicial courts of the injured party shall decide the dispute on a legal basis." W. Craig, W, Park & J. Paulsson, *International Chamber of Commerce Arbitration* ¶9.02 (3d ed. 2000).

    "In case of dispute (contestation) the parties undertake to submit to arbitration but in case of litigation the Tribunal de la Seine shall have exclusive jurisdiction." W. Craig, W, Park & J. Paulsson, *International Chamber of Commerce Arbitration* ¶9.02 (3d ed. 2000).

    "All disputes arising in connection with the present contract (contract) shall be finally settled by arbitration. Arbitration to be held outside the United States of America shall be conducted in accordance with the Rules of Arbitration of the International Chamber of Commerce, unless by written agreement of the parties, they adopt the Rules of the American Arbitration Association. Arbitration to be held in the United States of America shall be conducted in accordance with the Rules of the American Arbitration Association, unless by written agreement of the parties, they adopt the rules of Arbitration of the International Chamber of Commerce." *Batson Yarn & Fabric Mach. Group, Inc. v. Saurer-Allma GmbH-Allgauer Maschinenbau*, 311 F.Supp. 68 (D.S.C. 1970).

    "If there will arise disputes or differences by fulfilling the present contract, the Parties will take measure to solve them in a friendly way. In case the parties do not come to an agreement to solve the existing differences, they are to be settled by the Court of Arbitration of Budapest, Hungary in accordance with the Rules of the International Chamber of Commerce." *Award in Court of Arbitration at the Hungarian Chamber of Commerce and Industry Case No. V-99130*, excerpted in T. Várady, J. Barceló & A. von Mehren, *International Commercial Arbitration* 92 (4th ed. 2009).

7. *Agreement referring to nonexistent arbitral institution.* Consider the issue in *Lucky-Goldstar*—where the parties' agreement provided for arbitration pursuant to the rules of a nonexistent institution. Is the Hong Kong court's analysis persuasive? Is it

satisfactory to conclude that the parties were prepared to be bound by an *ad hoc* arbitration clause, when they provided for a (defective) form of institutional arbitration? *Compare Nat'l Material Trading v. Tang Indus., Inc.*, 1997 WL 915000, at *6 (D.S.C.) (clause invalid where it provided "[a]ny disputes or differences that may arise out of or in connection with this contract shall be referred to the Court of Arbitration at the Chamber of Commerce and Industry of Switzerland and settled in conformity with the rules and procedures of said Commission"; there is no such institution as the "Court of Arbitration at the Chamber of Commerce and Industry of Switzerland"); *Judgment of 24 January 1996, Harper Robinson v. Société Int'le de Maintenance et de Réalisation*, 1997 Rev. arb. 82 (Grenoble Cour d'appel) (refusing to uphold clause providing for arbitration with nonexistent appointing authority).

8. *Agreement referring to two arbitral seats or arbitral institutions*. Following the adage that one can have too much of a good thing, some arbitration clauses specify not just one, but two (or more), arbitral seats or institutions. Consider the clauses in *Judgment of 21 November 2003* and *Lucky-Goldstar.* Are such provisions invalid? Are the courts' analyses persuasive? Recall the authority suggesting that "blank clauses" are invalid. If a blank clause, not specifying an arbitral seat, were invalid, would the same result apply to a clause that fails to specify a definite arbitral seat or institution, by instead specifying multiple seats and institutions?

Conversely, if a blank clause is valid in a particular legal system, then why should a clause specifying contradictory arbitral seats or institutions not also be valid? Consider *Star Shipping AS v. China Nat'l Foreign Trade Transp. Corp.* [1993] 2 Lloyd's Rep. 445 (English Ct. App.) (upholding clause providing "any dispute arising under the charter is to be referred to arbitration in Beijing or London in the defendant's option"); *Warnes SA v. Harvic Int'l Ltd*, 1993 WL 228028 (S.D.N.Y.) ("an agreement on a nonexistent arbitration forum is the equivalent of an agreement to arbitrate which does not specify a forum; since the parties had the intent to arbitrate even in the absence of a properly designated forum"); *Peters Fabrics, Inc. v. Jantzen, Inc.*, 582 F.Supp. 1287, 1291 (S.D.N.Y. 1984) (competing forms providing for AAA and GAC arbitrations, held to constitute agreement to arbitrate); *Award of Arbitration Court Attached to Chamber for Foreign Trade, Berlin of 17 March 1982*, VIII Y.B. Comm. Arb. 128, 131 (1983) ("The arbitrators interpret the clause as an optional one which allows the Plaintiff the choice of applying to any arbitration court of the three mentioned countries....").

In *Lea Tai*, the parties had exchanged writings that purported to designate two different arbitral seats (and two different appointing institutions). How does that differ from a case where the parties agree to a single text, which contains multiple or inconsistent arbitral seats or mechanisms? Is there a way that the apparently conflicting provisions in *Lea Tai* could have been reconciled? Could the claimant have been left with its option of where to initiate an arbitration? Assuming the two provisions were in conflict, does that mean that the parties did not agree to arbitrate? On what basis could the parties have been held to have concluded a binding arbitration agreement in *Lea Tai*? *Compare I.T.A.D. Assocs., Inc. v. Podar Bros.*, 636 F.2d 75 (4th Cir. 1981) (competing forms providing for arbitration in, respectively, New York and India, held to constitute agreement to arbitrate and trial court left to determine seat).

9. *Agreements containing both arbitration clauses and forum selection clauses*. Suppose that the parties' contract contains both an arbitration clause and a choice of forum clause. Does this invalidate both provisions? Does it invalidate the arbitration clause?

    Consider the decision in *Judgment of 1 February 1979*. Is it well-reasoned? Consider also *Paul Smith Ltd v. H & S Int'l Holding Inc.*, [1991] 2 Lloyd's Rep. 127 (QB) (English High Ct.) (upholding agreement where one clause provided that disputes "shall be adjudicated upon" under the ICC Rules, while another clause provided that the "Courts of England shall have exclusive jurisdiction"; reference to English courts held to be a designation of the courts with supervisory jurisdiction (to appoint and remove arbitrators and entertain actions to set aside awards)). Are these conclusions appropriate? Is there not an argument that the parties were simply confused in both these cases? If so, is confusion enough to form a valid arbitration agreement? What motivates the courts' conclusions in such cases? Recall the observations in Note 1 above.

10. *Arbitration agreements with defective specifications of arbitral institution or seat.* Consider again the decisions in *Lucky-Goldstar* and *Judgment of 21 November 2003*, and *Award in ICC Case No. 5294*, excerpted above. Are these well-reasoned? If the parties agreed to a particular, specifically-negotiated arbitral process, should they be assumed to have also agreed to other arbitral processes when their chosen mechanism cannot be implemented? Consider the court's analysis at the conclusion of the *Lucky-Goldstar* opinion. How does that compare with the Swiss Federal Tribunal's analysis in *Judgment of 21 November 2003*? Is that analysis persuasive? *See also infra* pp. 652-53, 655-56, 663-69.

    The tribunal's willingness in *ICC Case No. 5294* to minimize imperfections in the parties' arbitration agreement is consistent with most awards on the issue. *See Preliminary Award in Zurich Chamber of Commerce Case of 25 November 1994*, XXII Y.B. Comm. Arb. 211 (1997) ("international trade arbitration organization in Zurich" held to mean arbitration under Zurich Chamber of Commerce International Arbitration Rules); *Final Award in ICC Case No. 5294 of 22 February 1988*, XIV Y.B. Comm. Arb. 137 (1989) ("rules of conciliation and arbitration of the International Chamber of Commerce, Zurich, Switzerland" held to mean ICC arbitration seated in Zurich); *Award in ICC Case No. 5103*, reprinted in S. Jarvin, Y. Derains & J. Arnaldez, *Collection of ICC Arbitral Awards*, *1986-1990*, at 361 (1994) (reference to Paris Chamber of Commerce interpreted as reference to ICC).

11. *Arbitration agreements referring to unavailable, deceased, or incompetent arbitrators*. Arbitration clauses sometimes specify the identity of the arbitrator(s) in advance. This is often unwise, because the nature of future disputes may not be foreseen by the parties (rendering their choice of arbitrator(s) inappropriate) or the specified arbitrators may die or become unavailable or incompetent. In the latter case, what is the status of the parties' arbitration agreement? Does the unavailability of the contemplated arbitrator render the arbitration agreement invalid, or does it call for selecting a new arbitrator? *See Stinson v. Am.'s Home Place, Inc.*, 108 F.Supp.2d 1278, 1285 (M.D. Ala. 2000) ("Although the arbitrator specified in [the contract] is not now available to resolve their dispute, there is no indication that the choice of that particular arbitrator was central to the arbitration clause. In such cases §5 [of the FAA] dictates that the court choose another arbitrator and enforce the arbitration clause.");

Judgment of 16 April 1984, 1986 Rev. arb. 596 (Swiss Fed. Trib.) (Swiss courts uphold ICC's appointment of arbitrator after Director General of World Health refuses to accept parties' designation).

12. *Arbitration agreements containing other defects.* The creativity of parties in drafting arbitration agreements is almost unlimited, with all variety of errors finding their way into arbitration clauses. How forgiving should courts and arbitral tribunals be in deciding whether these errors invalidate the agreement to arbitrate? Consider the courts' patience in *Lucky-Goldstar* and *Judgment of 1 February 1979. See also Mangistaumunaigaz Oil v. United World Trade Inc.* [1995] 1 Lloyd's Rep. 617 (Comm) (English High Ct.) (phrase "if any" disregarded as surplusage in clause providing "arbitration, if any, by ICC Rules in London"). A New Zealand decision recently expressed this general approach in cogent terms, invoking the

> "general principle that Courts should uphold arbitration, by striving to give effect to the intention of parties to submit disputes to arbitration, and not allow any inconsistencies or uncertainties in the wording or operation of the arbitration clause to thwart that intention." *Marnell Corrao Assocs. Inc. v. Sensation Yachts Ltd*, [2000] 15 PRNZ 608, ¶61-62 (Auckland High Ct.).

Is this appropriate? *Compare Branham v. CIGNA Healthcare of Ohio*, 692 N.E.2d 137, 139-40 (Ohio 1998) (holding that arbitration agreement was ambiguous and invalid where the agreement provided that "any controversy between GROUP, a Subscriber or Dependent (whether a minor or adult) or the heirs-at-law or personal representatives (including any of their agents, employees, or providers), arising out of or in connection with this Agreement shall, upon written notice by one party to another, be submitted to arbitration"; clause was ambiguous because the preposition "between" lacked a second object and thus, it was unclear which disputes were covered); *Jiampietro v. Utica Alloys, Inc.*, 576 N.Y.S.2d 733, 733 (N.Y. App. Div. 1991) ("The agreement to arbitrate is ambiguous and unenforceable because the 'schedule' containing the list of sanctions available upon a breach of the underlying agreement is inconsistent with an agreement to arbitrate.").

13. *Consequences of defective term in arbitration agreement.* Suppose that one term of an arbitration clause is invalid, for example, because it selects a deceased arbitrator or a nonexistent appointing authority. Is the remainder of the arbitration agreement still valid? Consider:

> "Where one term of an arbitration agreement has failed, the decision between substituting a new term for the failed provision and refusing to enforce the agreement altogether turns on the intent of the parties at the time the agreement was executed, as determined from the language of the contract and the surrounding circumstances.... to the extent the court can infer that the essential term of the provision is the agreement to arbitrate, that agreement will be enforced despite the failure of one of the terms of the bargain. If, on the other hand, it is clear that the failed term is not an ancillary logistical concern but rather is as important a consideration as the agreement to arbitrate itself, a court will not sever the failed term from the rest of the agreement and the entire arbitration provision will fail." *Zechman v. Merrill Lynch, Pierce, Fenner & Smith, Inc.*, 742 F.Supp. 1359, 1364 (N.D. Ill. 1990).

Consider the similar approach at the conclusion of the *Lucky-Goldstar* opinion. Is that a sensible approach?

14. *Reliance on foreign authorities*. Note the court's reliance in *Lucky-Goldstar* on U.S. authorities. Compare that approach discussed above in the *Shin-Etsu* decision. Does it make particular sense to consider foreign decisions in addressing the validity and interpretation of international arbitration agreements? Why?

15. *Arbitration clauses with undefined scope*. Suppose an arbitration clause provides "Disputes shall be arbitrated in Paris in accordance with the AAA Commercial Arbitration Rules." Is the absence of any express delimitation of the scope of the arbitration agreement fatal to the validity of the arbitration clause? Recall the discussion above of the requirement, under the New York Convention, that the arbitration agreement involve a "defined legal relationship." *See also supra* pp. 148-58.

Is it not possible, and commercially-sensible, to interpret the provision as encompassing disputes related to the parties' contract? Recall the court's analysis in *Roose Indus., supra* pp. 149-50. How did the court interpret a potentially unlimited agreement to arbitrate? *See also Tritonia Shipping Inc. v. S. Nelson Forest Prods. Corp.* [1966] 1 Lloyd's Rep. 114 (English Ct. App.) (court rejects challenge to clause providing "Arbitration to be settled in London," reasoning that it meant "any dispute under this charter party to be settled by arbitration in London"). On the other hand, is it not equally possible to interpret the provision as encompassing only contractual disputes arising directly under the terms of the parties' contract (not non-contractual disputes)? *Compare Lovisa Constr. Co. v. County of Suffolk*, 485 N.Y.S.2d 309, 310 (N.Y. Sup. Ct. 1985) (scope of issues to be submitted to arbitration were ambiguous and rendered agreement to arbitrate unenforceable).

Consider Article 2(1)(b) of the ILC Model Rules. What is the rationale for this requirement?

16. *"Optional" and "non-binding" agreements to arbitrate*. Parties sometimes agree only to consider arbitration as an alternative or optional means of dispute resolution, but not to require mandatory submission of future disputes to arbitration. For example, parties could agree: "If both parties mutually agree, after a dispute under this contract arises, to resolve such dispute by arbitration, then the following procedures shall apply." Would such a provision require either party to submit to arbitration of a dispute? Compare the foregoing hypothetical with the putative arbitration clauses in *WSG Nimbus* and *Hoogovens*. How are the provisions in those cases different from the hypothetical?

Consider the Singaporean court's analysis in *WSG Nimbus*. Does it adopt a persuasive interpretation of the parties' likely intentions? Note the court's explanation that "While it is true that under clause 19, there is no compulsion to arbitrate until an election is made, once a party makes such election, arbitration is mandatory in respect of that dispute." Does this make sense? What point would be served by a purely non-binding arbitration clause? *See also Bonnot v. Congress of Indep. Unions Local #14*, 331 F.2d 355, 359 (8th Cir. 1964) ("may" gives either party the option of requiring arbitration); *Canadian Nat'l Railway Co. v. Lovat Tunnel Equip.*, (1999) 174 D.L.R.(4th) 385 (Ontario Ct. App.) (clause providing that "the parties may refer any dispute under this agreement to arbitration" is mandatory arbitration agreement).

Consider the court's opinion in *Hoogovens*. Is the court's analysis persuasive? Why should arbitration agreements be regarded as presumptively mandatory? Was the parties' agreement in *Hoogovens* clearly non-mandatory? Compare the clause in *Judgment of 3 February 1990*.

2. Formation of International Arbitration Agreements

International arbitration agreements, like other categories of contracts, give rise to issues of contract formation (particularly issues of consent).[10] In turn, these issues require consideration of rules of substantive contractual validity, as well as choice-of-law, separability and competence-competence principles. The materials excerpted below explore the issues raised in disputes over the formation of international arbitration agreements.

KULUKUNDIS SHIPPING CO., SA v. AMTORG TRADING CORP.
126 F.2d 978 (2d Cir. 1942)

[excerpted above at pp. 191-93]

REPUBLIC OF NICARAGUA v. STANDARD FRUIT CO.
937 F.2d 469 (9th Cir. 1991)

FERGUSON, Judge. The Republic of Nicaragua appeals from two orders of the district court which denied its motion to compel international arbitration of a contract dispute and granted summary judgment to Standard Fruit Company ("SFC") and its two parent companies, Standard Fruit and Steamship Company ("Steamship") and Castle & Cooke, Inc. ("C&C"), [referred to collectively as "Standard,"] on Nicaragua's breach of contract claim. Nicaragua ... argues [on appeal] that the questions of whether a document entitled "Memorandum of Intent" was a valid contract and whether SFC was bound by that contract should have been referred to arbitration in the first instance, not decided by the district court. Secondly, it contends that disputed issues of material fact exist on the question of whether the Memorandum of Intent was a binding contract for the purchase and sale of bananas, or merely an "agreement to agree" at some later date....

We hold that although it was the court's responsibility to determine the threshold question of arbitrability, the district court improperly looked to the validity of the contract as a whole and erroneously determined that the parties had not agreed to arbitrate this dispute. Instead, it should have considered only the validity and scope of the arbitration clause itself. In addition, the district court ignored strong evidence in the record that both parties intended to be bound by the arbitration clause. As all doubts over the scope of an arbitration clause must be resolved in favor of arbitration, and in light of the strong federal policy favoring arbitration in international commercial disputes, Nicaragua's motion to compel arbitration should have been granted. Whether the Memorandum was binding, whether it covered banana purchases, and whether SFC was bound by it are all questions properly left to the arbitrators....

Since 1970, defendant SFC has been involved in the production and purchase of bananas in western Nicaragua.... In 1979, the Sandinistas overthrew the Somoza government in Nicaragua, forming a new "Government of National Reconstruction," led by a three-person junta. The Sandinistas wished to assume closer control over the banana in-

---

10. *See* G. Born, *International Commercial Arbitration* 738-818 (2d ed. 2014).

dustry, and eventually to transfer SFC's shares in [certain banana plantation] partnerships to the Nicaraguan government.... [In due course,] Nicaragua promulgated "Decree No. 608," which declared that the banana industry was to become a state monopoly, that all plantation leases would be transferred to a new government agency, and that all preexisting lease, partnership, and fruit purchase contracts were nullified. SFC interpreted this decree as an expropriation of its business, and immediately ceased all operations in Nicaragua.... Both sides were surprised and upset by the issuance of the decree and the almost immediate withdrawal of SFC, with the bananas still ripe on the trees and ready to pick. As a result, Nicaragua requested a "summit meeting" at which SFC and its two parent companies, Steamship and C&C, could sort out their differences ... and come back to the country....

The meeting commenced in San Francisco on Friday, January 9, 1981, and continued for three days of intense negotiations, led by C&C Vice President and General Counsel Robert Moore (principal draftsman of the Memorandum) and Norton Tennille, Nicaragua's legal counsel. On Sunday, January 11, a document entitled "Memorandum of Intent" was executed by two officers of C&C, two officers of Steamship, and two Ministers of Trade and a member of the ruling junta of Nicaragua. Sousane and other SFC representatives participated in the negotiations but did not sign the document.

The Memorandum, termed an "agreement in principle," contained an arbitration provision, and envisioned the renegotiation and replacement of four operating contracts between SFC and "the competent Nicaraguan national entity." These were to include a detailed fruit purchase contract, a technical assistance contract, the transfer of SFC's shares in the production societies, and Nicaragua's purchase of SFC's assets in the country. The Memorandum also established the essential elements of the fruit purchase contract: a price term ($4.30 per box...), the length of the contract (five years ...), and stated that it would cover all the first-quality bananas produced by the Nicaraguan growers....

Within a week after the Memorandum was signed, SFC returned to Nicaragua and resumed its operations there. In addition, it began negotiating with Nicaraguan officials regarding the technical assistance and fruit purchase contracts referred to in the Memorandum, as well as the share transfers and asset buy-outs. Many subsequent drafts of these four documents were exchanged, some similar to the Memorandum and some not, although none were ever finalized and executed. Throughout the negotiations and for the next 22 months, SFC complied with the terms of the Memorandum as though it were bound by it. For example, it began paying $4.30 per box of bananas.... During this period, C&C and SFC produced and disseminated a number of documents which referred to the Memorandum as "a contract," a "commitment," or "a final agreement," several of which were signed and/or approved by Robert Moore. These included a C&C press release sent out the day after the Memorandum was signed, SEC reports, Annual Reports, letters, [etc.]. Although SFC, Steamship, C&C, and Nicaragua all acted as though the Memorandum was binding for almost two years, the implementing contracts were never finalized, and SFC left Nicaragua for good on October 25, 1982.

The arbitration clause [contained in the Memorandum] states that: "Any and all disputes arising under the arrangements contemplated hereunder ... will be referred to mutually agreed mechanisms or procedures of international arbitration, such as the rules of the London Arbitration Association." Nicaragua admits that this clause is less than crystal clear and in fact refers to an association which does not exist. However, it introduced a letter written by Robert Moore, principal draftsman of the Memorandum, to explain the inconsistency. The letter, written to Nicaragua's representative only three weeks after the negotiations, described the "deep sense of urgency on both sides," the "exceedingly tight time schedule," and the "highly political nature of the agreement (from the Nicaraguan standpoint)." It explained that, during the negotiations themselves, neither side could remember the name of the arbitration body in London, and stated: "What resulted was *an agreement for providing for arbitration* but without finally fixing the forum or an automatic method of transmitting disputes." Moore suggested "we would be better off agreeing in advance that Paragraph IV was to be read and interpreted to provide for arbitration by [a certain] agency," and concluded "I am sure you will agree that it is best done *in the infancy of the agreement and at a time that negotiations of the implementing agreements are being worked out*." (Emphasis added.)[11] Although this letter seems to suggest both that C&C intended the clause to be binding and that the parties intentionally left it vague because they could not remember the name of the London arbitration agency, the district court disregarded this evidence.

The district court applied a three-part test for arbitrability: "first, whether the parties entered into a contract; second, that the contract included an agreement to arbitrate disputes, and third, that the disputes covered by the arbitration agreement included those which are before the Court." It then proceeded to find that the Memorandum as a whole was not a binding contract, that the arbitration provision was not a present agreement to submit to arbitration, but merely "a provision declaring the expectations of the parties that contracts to be negotiated later would include agreements to arbitrate." ... The court [also] determined that the phrase "all arrangements contemplated hereunder" in Paragraph IV referred only to the "implementing agreements" subsequently to be negotiated, executed, and performed in Nicaragua, and not to the Memorandum itself....

Section 2 [of the FAA] ... embodies a clear federal policy of requiring arbitration unless the agreement to arbitrate is not part of a contract evidencing interstate commerce or is revocable "upon such grounds as exist at law or in equity for the revocation of any contract." ... [T]his "'liberal federal policy favoring arbitration agreements' ... is at bottom a policy guaranteeing the enforcement of private contractual arrangements." *Mitsubishi Motors Corp. v. Soler Chrysler-Plymouth, Inc.*, 473 U.S. 614, 625 (1985) (quoting *Moses H. Cone*, 460 U.S. at 24). "Thus, as with any other contract, the parties' intentions are generously construed as to issues of arbitrability." *Id.* at 626. Therefore, the only issue properly before the district court was whether the parties had entered into a contract ... committing both sides to arbitrate the issue of the contract's validity....

Nicaragua's primary claim [on appeal] is that the three-part test applied to determine whether the parties had in fact agreed to arbitrate violates *Prima Paint*, which expressly held that courts may not consider challenges to a contract's validity or enforceability as defenses against arbitration.... In the instant case, the district court made a preliminary "Factual Conclusion" that the Memorandum "was not intended as a binding contract," in direct opposition to the *Prima Paint* rule.[12] ... [This holding relied] chiefly on the trial

---

11. Attached to the letter was a very explicit page-long "substitute arbitration clause," providing for arbitration in London pursuant to the Arbitration Act of Great Britain [sic].

12. The district court reasoned that an arbitrator can derive his or her power only from a contract, so that when there is a challenge to the existence of the contract itself, the court must first decide whether there is a

testimony of Robert Moore, who drafted most of the Memorandum, and on what the court termed the "unambiguous" language of the document itself. However, as Nicaragua correctly points out, Moore's testimony directly conflicts with contemporary documents in the record, which should have precluded any summary judgment. As a matter of law, the key language in Paragraph IV seems highly ambiguous, since it refers to "the arrangements contemplated hereunder," and thus requires extensive inquiry into just what arrangements are being referred to....

[We repeat] *Prima Paint*'s clear directive that courts disregard surrounding contract language and "consider only issues relating to the making and performance of the agreement to arbitrate." 388 U.S. at 404. The correct analysis is set forth in *Sauer-Getriebe KG v. White Hydraulics, Inc.*, 715 F.2d 348, 350 (7th Cir. 1983):

> "White argues that if there is no contract to buy and sell motors there is no agreement to arbitrate. The conclusion does not follow its premise. The agreement to arbitrate and the agreement to buy and sell motors are separate. Sauer's promise to arbitrate was given in exchange for White's promise to arbitrate and each promise was sufficient consideration for the other." *Ibid.*

There, the Seventh Circuit ordered arbitration despite the facts that the district court had found the contract "vague and ambiguous," and construed it against its drafter. *See also Teledyne, Inc. v. Kone Corp.*, 892 F.2d 1404, 1410 (9th Cir. 1990). Thus, in the absence of any evidence that Paragraph IV of the Memorandum was intended as non-severable, we must strictly enforce any agreement to arbitrate, regardless of where it is found. Under *Prima Paint* and *Teledyne*, we hold that the district court erred in considering the contract as a whole to determine the threshold question of whether Nicaragua may enforce the arbitration agreement contained in Paragraph IV....

The next question is whether Paragraph IV in fact constitutes an agreement to arbitrate, and whether it encompasses the dispute at hand. The district court stated that the parties had not made any present agreement to submit all disputes under the Memorandum to arbitration, but merely agreed to include such clauses in future contracts.... It is unclear whether [this] statement[] [was] based on the language of the Memorandum itself, or on the evidence of the parties' intent developed during the evidentiary hearing. In any case, since "the issue of arbitrability 'is to be determined by the contract entered into by the parties,' the task before this court remains one of contractual interpretation." However, because of the presumption of arbitrability established by the Supreme Court, courts must be careful not to overreach and decide the merits of an arbitrable claim. Our role is strictly limited to determining arbitrability and enforcing agreements to arbitrate, leaving the merits of the claim and any defenses to the arbitrator. Here, the district court disregarded "the emphatic federal policy in favor of arbitral dispute resolution [which] applies with special force in the field of international commerce." *Mitsubishi Motors Corp.*, 473 U.S. at 631....

The district court also found that the clause's "lack of specificity" mitigated against its enforcement. However, the clear weight of authority holds that the most minimal indication of the parties' intent to arbitrate must be given full effect, especially in international disputes. *See, e.g., Bauhinia Corp. v. China Nat'l Mach. and Equip. Co.*, 819 F.2d 247 (9th

---

valid contract between the parties. Although this appears logical, it goes beyond the requirements of the statute and violates the clear directive of *Prima Paint*, 388 U.S. at 404....

Cir. 1987) (arbitration ordered where contract contained two incomplete and contradictory arbitration clauses); *Mediterranean Enter., Inc. v. Ssangyong Corp.*, 708 F.2d 1458, 1462-63 (9th Cir. 1983) (broadly construing scope of Korean arbitration clause under the Act). Under this analysis, Paragraph IV here was not too vague to be given effect, especially when considered in light of Robert Moore's letter explaining the ambiguity.... Nicaragua's motion to compel arbitration is granted, and the case remanded to determine the appropriate arbitral agency.

JUDGMENT OF 30 MARCH 1993, NOKIA-MAILLEFER SA v. MAZZER
XXI Y.B. Comm. Arb. 681 (1996) (Vaud Tribunal Cantonal)

[On March 30, 1988, Nokia-Maillefer SA ("Nokia"), a Swiss company, sent one Mr. Mazzer, an Italian businessman, a confirmation of an order which he had placed. The confirmation referred to Nokia's enclosed general conditions of sale, which contained a forum-selection clause choosing Swiss courts. On March 31, 1988, Leasindustria, an Italian financing company, replied to Nokia by sending a purchase order to which its general conditions of purchase were annexed. Article 10 of the general conditions included a forum selection clause providing for "jurisdiction of Milan courts." Two months later, Nokia returned the purchase order, replacing the word "Milan" in Article 10 with "International Chamber of Commerce, Paris." By a telex to Leasindustria, Mr. Mazzer accepted the modification. When a dispute arose, the Italian buyer commenced court proceedings before a Swiss court in the Canton of Vaud, where Nokia was headquartered. Nokia requested the Court to refer the dispute to arbitration.]

The dispute is whether Article 10 of the purchase order, as modified, is a valid arbitration clause. The autonomy of the arbitration clause as to the contract in which it is contained or to which it refers is unanimously recognized. Hence, to the exception of cases where a ground for nullity of the contract also affects the clause, the validity of the arbitration clause must be examined separately.

An arbitration clause can only be validly concluded where there is a common intention of the parties to refer a possible dispute to arbitration. The existence of such an agreement must be ascertained according to the general principles of the Code of Obligations, in particular Art. 2 CO.[13] Considering the important consequences of an arbitration agreement, the court shall beware of finding too easily that such an agreement has been concluded.

In the present case, the ... question of the authority having jurisdiction to decide on a possible dispute has been dealt with in different stages in two different documents, one of which has been modified by one party. In the annex to the confirmation of order ... which it sent on 30 March 1988 to [Mr.] Mazzer, Nokia enclosed the general conditions of sale which, at no. 17.1, provided that the forum be at the seat of the supplier. Subsequently, the general conditions of purchase annexed to the purchase order sent on 31 March 1988 by

---

13. Article 2 of the Swiss Code of Obligations reads: "When the parties have agreed with regard to all essential points, it is presumed that a reservation of ancillary points is not meant to affect the binding nature of the contract. Where agreement with regard to such ancillary points so reserved is not reached, the judge shall determine them in accordance with the nature of the transaction. The foregoing shall not affect the provisions regarding the form of contracts (Arts. 9-16)."

Leasindustria initially provided that the parties agreed to accept the jurisdiction of the Milan courts over all possible disputes. Lastly, Milan was replaced by "International Chamber of Commerce, Paris." Thus, the question of the authority having jurisdiction to decide on a possible dispute has not been provided for straightaway in a clear and indisputable manner.

In this evolutionary and uncertain context, there is no common intent on arbitration unless the "final" arbitration clause, that is, Article 10 as modified, has a manifest and certain meaning. It is at least necessary that a common intent of the parties can be deduced from their expressions. Considering the clause, it is not possible to ascertain the common intent of the parties, in particular as to the arbitration agreement. Initially, the clause at issue provides under "forum" for the jurisdiction of the (State) courts of Milan. Only the term "Milan" has been replaced by "International Chamber of Commerce, Paris," with no mention of the fact that the jurisdiction of the courts is excluded and replaced by private arbitration.

The jurisdiction of the [ICC] in Paris cannot be deemed to be tantamount to the appointment of an arbitrator, as the word arbitrator or arbitration does not appear and the [ICC] itself does not act as arbitrator. Only physical persons may be arbitrators, to the exclusion of legal entities or collectivités; in particular, a Chamber of Commerce cannot be appointed as arbitrator. Appellant must bear the consequences of the ambiguity and obscurity of the alleged clause, which it modified with the intention of transforming a *prorogatio fori* into an arbitration clause functioning also as arbitration agreement. Appellee's agreement as to the modifications does not clear away the uncertainty as to the meaning of the clause and, consequently, of the agreement. In a context in which it should not be held too easily that an agreement has been concluded, we cannot accept an unclear clause as proof of an agreement having an uncertain subject matter. Hence, we must hold that the parties did not conclude a valid arbitration agreement....

BUCKEYE CHECK CASHING, INC. v. CARDEGNA
546 U.S. 440 (2006)

[excerpted above at pp. 201-05]

INTERIM AWARD IN ICC CASE NO. 6149
XX Y.B. Comm. Arb. 41 (1995)

[excerpted above at pp. 290-92]

FIRST OPTIONS OF CHICAGO v. KAPLAN
514 U.S. 938 (1995)

[excerpted above at pp. 230-33]

BG GROUP PLC v. REPUBLIC OF ARGENTINA
134 S.Ct. 1198 (2014)

[excerpted above at pp. 233-47]

NOTES

1. *Applicability of separability presumption in disputes over formation of underlying contract.* As discussed above, most arbitration regimes recognize the separability presumption. *See supra* pp. 190-218. Under the separability presumption, an arbitration clause is viewed as presumptively separable from the parties' underlying contract. As a consequence, defects in the formation of the underlying contract do not necessarily affect the formation of the arbitration clause. *See supra* pp. 215-17. Suppose one party denies ever having negotiated, agreed, or signed any contract (containing a putative arbitration clause) with another party. If those claims were true, how could the parties have concluded a valid arbitration clause? Is there some manner in which the "separable" agreement to arbitrate could be formed, even if the underlying contract was not?

   (a) *Authorities holding that arbitration clause may not validly be formed if underlying contract is not.* Some authorities (particularly early ones) hold that non-formation of the underlying contract necessarily entails non-formation of the arbitration clause. Consider the analysis in *Kulukundis.* Note the remark that it would be "insane" to think that an arbitration agreement was concluded if the underlying charter was not. *See also Pollux Marine Agencies v. Louis Dreyfus Corp.,* 455 F.Supp. 211, 219 (S.D.N.Y. 1978) ("something can be severed only from something else that exists. How can the Court 'sever' an arbitration clause from a non-existent charter party?"); Svernlöv, *What Isn't, Ain't,* 25 J. World Trade 37, 38 (1991) ("Where it is alleged that no agreement has been entered into, the application of the separability doctrine is more doubtful. If the principal agreement was never entered into, the arbitration agreement contained therein must be affected by the invalidity as well."). Are these views persuasive? What response would the authors of *JOC Oil* and *Standard Fruit* give to the foregoing analyses?

   (b) *Authorities holding that arbitration clause has been validly formed although underlying contract has not.* Despite the authorities cited in the preceding note, valid arbitration agreements have been found in a number of cases where no underlying contract had been concluded. *See, e.g., Sphere Drake Ins. Ltd v. All Am. Ins. Co.,* 256 F.3d 587, 591-92 (7th Cir. 2001) ("if they have agreed on nothing else, they have agreed to arbitrate"); *Colfax Envelope Corp. v. Local No. 458-3M, etc.,* 20 F.3d 750, 754-55 (7th Cir. 1994) (despite no meeting of minds on underlying contract "there was a meeting of the minds on the mode of arbitrating disputes between the parties" and "the parties had agreed to arbitrate their claims"); *Judgment of 27 September 1985, O.P.A.T.I. v. Larsen, Inc.,* Case No. L 8169 (Paris Cour d'appel), described in M. de Boisséson, *Le droit français de l'arbitrage interne et internationale* 825 (2d ed. 1990) and E. Gaillard & J. Savage (eds.), *Fouchard Gaillard Goldman on International Commercial Arbitration* 933 (1999) (valid arbitration agreement where some provisions were noted "draft," but not arbitration provision).

2. *Rationales for concluding that parties formed valid arbitration agreement even if they did not validly conclude underlying contract.* As already noted, the separability presumption provides that the parties may form a valid, separable agreement to arbitrate, even if they do not conclude a valid underlying contract. *See supra* pp. 215-17. The

separability presumption has a number of consequences for formation of arbitration agreements.

(a) *Intentions relevant to formation of arbitration agreement.* One consequence of the separability presumption concerns the intentions that are relevant to formation of the arbitration agreement. Specifically, the relevant issue for contract formation purposes is whether the parties intended to form an agreement to arbitrate; these intentions are not necessarily identical to the parties' intentions to form their underlying contract. Are there circumstances in which one might conclude that the parties intended to form an arbitration agreement, but did not intend to form the underlying contract? Or vice versa? Consider the facts in *Standard Fruit* and *JOC Oil*. Compare the facts in *Kulukundis*. How likely is it that parties would want to conclude an arbitration agreement, without concluding any underlying commercial contract?

Suppose Party A sends Party B a draft contract, containing an arbitration clause. Party B responds, without signing the draft, saying "No deal—your terms are not acceptable." Is there any reason to think that the parties formed an agreement to arbitrate? Are Party B's intentions, as to both the underlying contract and the arbitration clause, not clear? How does one determine what Party B's intentions with regard to the arbitration agreement were?

Suppose that a party's claim that no underlying contract exists rests on an alleged failure to agree on certain essential terms (such as price) or on an alleged intention of the parties that any agreement be consummated in a later formal contract. In these cases, might one conclude that an agreement to arbitrate was reached, even though other related agreements were not? Can it be that, in some cases, an agreement to arbitrate crystallizes out of precontractual negotiations before the overall agreement is consummated? Consider, in this regard, the facts of the *Standard Fruit* and *Nokia* cases. How would the Swiss court have decided *Standard Fruit*? How would the U.S. court have decided *Nokia*?

How do the issues regarding formation of arbitration agreements presented in *Standard Fruit* and *Nokia* differ? Did *Nokia* concern the validity of the underlying contract? Was there any question about the underlying contract's validity in *Nokia*?

(b) *Different national laws applicable to formation of arbitration agreement and underlying contract.* As discussed above, it is not uncommon for different laws to be applied to the arbitration agreement and the underlying contract. *See supra* pp. 90-93, 287, 300-01. Would it not, therefore, be possible for the underlying contract to have not been properly formed (under one national law), but the arbitration agreement to have been properly formed (under identical facts, but a different national law)?

Recall Article 178 of the SLPIL and the validation principle, *supra* pp. 306-07. Also recall the possible application of uniform international substantive rules to the formation of arbitration agreements under Article II of the New York Convention, which might differ from the national law rules governing formation of an underlying contract. *See supra* pp. 307-12.

(c) *Different substantive rules of contract formation applicable to arbitration agreement and underlying contract.* It is also possible that different rules of contract formation would apply to the underlying contract and the arbitration agreement. This can be true even if the same national law applies to both issues. Consider *JOC Oil*, which concluded that different rules of contract law applied to the formation and validity of the arbitration agreement and underlying contract.

(d) *Different standards of proof for formation of arbitration agreement and underlying contract.* Suppose different standards of proof applied to the formation of arbitration agreements as compared to other agreements. Would there be any basis for requiring different standards of proof? For example, might the pro-enforcement policies of the New York Convention and modern arbitration legislation permit a conclusion that an arbitration agreement had been validly formed even if an underlying contract had not? Is it possible that in signifying their assent to international arbitration provisions, parties evince a particular desire that their "agreement" be recognized, without legal technicalities of national laws? Why? Is this (partially) an explanation for the result in *Standard Fruit*?

3. *Standards of proof for establishing existence of arbitration agreement.* What standard of proof should apply to the formation of international arbitration agreements? Suppose, for example, that one party adduces some evidence that an arbitration agreement was formed, which its counterparty partially rebuts. Should the same degree of clarity and certainty be required for arbitration agreements as for underlying substantive contracts? *See supra* pp. 361-63.

(a) *Heightened standard of proof.* Consider the analysis in *Nokia*. Does the Swiss court in effect adopt a heightened standard of proof for arbitration agreements, as compared to other types of contracts? *See Final Award in ICC Case No. 7453*, XXII Y.B. Comm. Arb. 107 (1997) ("consent of each party must be unambiguously demonstrable"); *Schubtex, Inc. v. Allen Snyder, Inc.*, 424 N.Y.S.2d 133 (N.Y. 1979) ("a litigant ought not to be forced into arbitration and, thus, denied the procedural and substantive rights otherwise available in a judicial forum, absent evidence of an express intention to be so bound"); *Judgment of 10 March 2000*, XXVI Y.B. Comm. Arb. 816 (2001) (Italian Corte di Cassazione) (requiring "*unambiguous intention of both parties* to refer disputes ... to foreign arbitrators" and "parties must sign the arbitral clause and ... their unequivocal intention to refer the dispute to arbitrators must appear unambiguously") (emphasis added).

What is the rationale for requiring a heightened standard of proof or certainty for arbitration agreements? Recall Article 6 of the European Convention on Human Rights, excerpted above at pp. 270-71. Note the importance attached to access to judicial remedies. Consider how this is relied upon in *Nokia*. Is it persuasive to argue that parties should be held to have given up their (important) rights of access to judicial protections only where they have clearly agreed to do so?

For a Swiss decision, more explicitly relying on the concept of constitutional access to public courts than *Nokia*, consider:

"Constitutional law (in Switzerland, Article 30(1) of the Federal Constitution applies) as well as treaty law (see Article 6(1) of the European Convention on Human Rights) afford each natural person and legal entity the right to be heard before a court established on the basis of statutory law. By submitting to arbitration a party waives such right. Since this constitutes a deviation of a constitutional right one must not conclude readily that the parties concluded an arbitration agreement if that issue is disputed. Rather, one has to make sure whether an arbitration agreement exists that binds the parties. Only where these prerequisites are satisfied, the parties can be required to bear the consequences of their choice (in particular the constraints on their rights to appeal)." *Judgment of 16 October 2001*, 2002 Rev. arb. 753, 756 (Swiss Fed. Trib.).

See also Judgment of 20 January 2006, Case No. LJN:AU4523 (Dutch Hoge Raad) (relying on Article 6 of ECHR to conclude that an arbitration agreement must be clear and unequivocal); *Kloss v. Jones*, 54 P.3d 1 (Mont. 2002), *partial rehearing*, 57 P.3d 41 (Mont. 2002) (relying on Montana state constitution to invalidate a domestic arbitration agreement, reasoning that arbitration "is at one and the same time an 'open attack' on the right of jury trial and a 'secret machination' causing forfeiture" of "sacred" and "inviolable" rights to judicial access protected by Montana Constitution).

Is this rationale of safeguarding access to courts persuasive in commercial matters? Are companies not sophisticated parties who require no protection in matters of forum selection? Is the rationale of safeguarding access to courts persuasive in international cases? In international cases, are there not by definition two sets of courts—whose access to which is to be safeguarded? In terms of ensuring a neutral dispute resolution forum, with equal access to justice, is arbitration less or more desirable than one party's home courts?

(b) *Reduced standard of proof.* Alternatively, one might reason that the pro-arbitration policies of the Convention and national law warrant a lower standard of proof of formation of arbitration agreements, as compared to other contracts. The result in *Standard Fruit* is arguably representative of this view. Compare the *Standard Fruit* analysis (and result) to that in *Nokia*. Which is wiser?

(c) *Neutral standard of proof.* A third approach is to reject either an "anti-arbitration" or a "pro-arbitration" standard of proof for establishing the existence of an international arbitration agreement. Many authorities effectively adopt this approach by not considering issues concerning the standard of proof or by simply applying generally-applicable rules regarding contract formation. As one U.S. court declared: "[T]he purpose of the FAA was to make arbitration agreements as enforceable as other contracts, *not more so*." *In re Kellogg Brown & Root Inc.*, 166 S.W.3d 732 (Tex. 2005) (quoting *Bridas SAPIC v. Gov't of Turkmenistan*, 345 F.3d 347, 354 n.4 (5th Cir. 2003)) (emphasis added). Some commentators endorse this approach, saying it is "inappropriate to resort to a general principle of interpretation *in favorem validitatis* or *in favorem jurisdictionis*," because "there is no place here for the logic of principle and exception" and "it remains perfectly legitimate to choose to have one's international disputes settled by the courts." E. Gaillard & J. Savage (eds.), *Fouchard Gaillard Goldman on International Commercial Arbitration* ¶481 (1999). Is this analysis persuasive? Why not?

(d) *Doubtful relevance of pro-arbitration approach to interpretation of arbitration agreements to disputes over formation of arbitration agreement.* In *Standard Fruit*, there was a separate challenge to the existence of any agreement to arbitrate. The court appears to have decided the claim itself, but by applying the FAA's presumption that all doubts as to interpretation of the scope of an arbitration agreement are to be resolved in favor of arbitration. *See infra* pp. 527-29. Is this analysis persuasive? Compare the analysis in *First Options*, which distinguished between the presumptions applicable to interpretation of an existent arbitration agreement and those applicable to the formation of an arbitration agreement. *See supra* pp. 230-33. *See also Heinhuis v. Venture Assocs. Inc.*, 1991 U.S. Dist. LEXIS 8190, at *8-9 (E.D. La.) (refusing to apply presumption of arbitrability to question "whether the arbitration clause is part of the parties' contractual agreement at all"); *DeMarco Cal. Fabrics, Inc. v. Nygard Int'l, Ltd*, 1990 U.S. Dist. LEXIS 3842, at *9 (S.D.N.Y.) ("federal policy favoring arbitration is most applicable in determining the scope of arbitration agreements, rather than whether an arbitration agreement actually exists"); *Astor Chocolate Corp. v. Mikroverk Ltd*, 704 F.Supp. 30, 33 n.4 (E.D.N.Y. 1989) (pro-arbitration "policy argument would seem inapplicable" to dispute concerning "existence of the arbitration clause").

Is it appropriate to apply a presumption that arbitration agreements will be interpreted broadly to the question whether an arbitration agreement actually exists? Would doing so mean that if there is any doubt concerning, for example, a claim that one party forged the other party's signature on a submission agreement, arbitration must be compelled? If so, is that appropriate?

4. *Standard of proof for establishing existence of arbitration agreement under FAA*. What must be demonstrated under the FAA to establish the existence of an arbitration agreement? If there is a dispute over the formation or existence of an arbitration agreement, what presumptions (or default rules) should apply? That is, if it is unclear whether the parties have agreed to arbitrate, should doubts be resolved in favor of, or against, arbitration? Should the same standards of proof apply as those used for underlying commercial contracts?

   (a) *Generally-applicable state contract law. First Options* indicates that the formation of arbitration agreements under the domestic FAA is governed by generally applicable contract law rules. *See supra* pp. 56-57, 232 & *infra* p. 366. These rules, almost by definition, would apply the same standards of proof to the formation of arbitration agreements as to the formation of other contracts. *See, e.g., Kresock v. Bankers Trust Co.*, 21 F.3d 176, 178 (7th Cir. 1994) ("An agreement to arbitrate is treated like any other contract"); *Singer v. Smith Barney Shearson*, 926 F.Supp. 183, 187 (S.D. Fla. 1996) ("arbitration agreements are no more than contracts to which the usual rules of contract interpretation apply").

   (b) *State law presumptions requiring clear evidence of existence of arbitration agreement*. In some U.S. states, local law purportedly imposes unusually rigorous standards of proof with respect to arbitration agreements. That is, no agreement to arbitrate will be found in the absence of clear evidence of such an agreement. *See, e.g., Computer Assocs. Int'l Inc. v. Com-Tech Assocs.*, 658 N.Y.S.2d 322, 381 (N.Y. App. Div. 1997) (A party who agrees to arbitration "waives in large part many of his normal rights under the procedural and substantive law of the State, and it would be unfair to infer such a significant waiver on the basis of anything less than a clear indication of intent"); *Massey v. Galvan*, 822 S.W.2d 309, 316 (Tex. App. 1992) ("No party is under a duty to arbitrate unless by clear language he has previously agreed to do so; and it must clearly appear that the intention of the parties was to submit their dispute to an arbitration panel and to be bound by the panel's decision"); *Matter of Doughboy Indus.*, 233 N.Y.S.2d 488, 492 (N.Y. App.

Div. 1962) ("threshold for clarity of agreement to arbitrate is greater than with respect to other contractual terms").

(c) *Preemptive effect of domestic FAA on state law requirements of heightened evidence of arbitration agreement.* Does the domestic FAA permit state (or foreign) law rules which require clear evidence of arbitration agreements? Recall the domestic FAA's requirement that arbitration agreements be subjected to the same generally-applicable rules that apply to other agreements. *See supra* pp. 56-57, 232, 365. Does this preempt the application of state law presumptions which require heightened proof of an agreement to arbitrate as compared to other contracts? Lower courts have (correctly) held that the domestic FAA preempts such state law rules. *See, e.g., PaineWebber Inc. v. Bybyk*, 81 F.3d 1193, 1198 (2d Cir. 1996) ("[FAA] creates a body of federal substantive law of arbitrability, applicable to any arbitration agreement within the coverage of the Act"); *Progressive Cas. Ins. Co. v. C.A. Reaseguradora Nacional de Venezuela*, 991 F.2d 42, 46, 48 (2d Cir. 1993).

(d) *"Pro-arbitration" standard of proof of formation of arbitration agreement arguably applicable under domestic FAA.* It could also be that the domestic FAA requires, as a matter of federal law, a *lower* standard of proof for the existence of an arbitration agreement than for other types of contracts. *First Options* makes no reference to any such rule (and likely suggests the contrary, by its reliance on state law rules of contract formation). Nonetheless, would the domestic FAA's "pro-arbitration" policies not be advanced by a rule allowing arbitration agreements to be established more easily than other contracts? Is this consistent with the text of §2 of the FAA?

Lower U.S. federal courts have not clearly analyzed the question of what presumptions (if any) should apply to the existence of an agreement to arbitrate. Authority (usually unreasoned) can be found for both the view that arbitration agreements must be established by clear evidence and for the view that doubts will be resolved in favor of the existence of an arbitration agreement. *Compare Kresock,* 21 F.3d at 178 ("An agreement to arbitrate is treated like any other contract") *with Ins. Co. of North Am. v. ABB Power Generation, Inc.*, 925 F.Supp. 1053, 1058 (S.D.N.Y. 1996) ("courts resolve ambiguities against finding the existence of an agreement to arbitrate") *and with Standard Fruit,* 937 F.2d 469, 478 (9th Cir. 1991) ("the most minimal indication of the parties' intent to arbitrate must be given full effect").

(e) *"Pro-arbitration" standard of proof arguably applicable to international arbitration agreements under second chapter of FAA.* As we have seen, the formation of international arbitration agreements under the New York Convention and the second chapter of the FAA is ordinarily held to be governed by federal common law rules, formulated specifically for arbitration agreements. *See supra* pp. 56-57, 310-11. Do these federal common law rules impose less demanding rules of contract formation or a lower standard of proof for arbitration agreements than for other contracts? What rationale would support such a result?

Consider the U.S. authorities declaring that particularly weighty "pro-arbitration" policies are applicable under the New York Convention and the second chapter of the FAA. *See supra* pp. 189, 312. Don't these policies argue for federal common law rules of contract formation that facilitate the entry into international arbitration agreements? Is *Standard Fruit* an example of such a rule? Does such a rule of "easy" formation of international arbitration agreements make the result (if not the stated rationale) of *Standard Fruit* more understandable?

(f) *"Clear and unmistakable evidence" of agreement to arbitrate not required under domestic FAA. First Options* arguably imposes a requirement that the existence of domestic arbitration agreements be established through "clear and unmistakable" evidence. Put differently, is *First Options'* "clear and unmistakable" evidence test applicable only to agreements to arbitrate "questions of arbitrability" or does it extend to the existence of *any* arbitration agreement (including agreements to arbitrate substantive issues)?

Do you agree that the opinion will probably be interpreted as meaning: (a) the existence of any arbitration agreement is to be determined without resort to any presumptions, simply applying state-law (or otherwise applicable) contract rules; (b) the existence of an agreement to arbitrate disputes about the formation or validity of arbitration agreements ("arbitrability questions") is determined in light of a requirement for "clear and unmistakable" evidence of such an agreement; (c) the scope of an existent arbitration agreement, as applied to substantive disputes, is determined in light of a "pro-arbitration" presumption; and (d) the scope of an existent arbitration agreement, as applied to disputes about jurisdiction or arbitrability, may or may not be determined in light of a requirement for "clear and unmistakable" evidence? Why or why not?

If the foregoing analysis of *First Options* were applicable to international arbitration agreements, then how should *Standard Fruit* have been resolved? Was there sufficient evidence that a binding arbitration agreement applicable to the merits of the parties' dispute existed to satisfy generally-applicable rules of contract law? Was there "clear and unmistakable" evidence of an agreement to arbitrate disputes over formation of the arbitration agreement?

5. *Law applicable to formation of arbitration agreement.* What substantive law applies to the formation of an international arbitration agreement? Consider what substantive law was applied to this issue in *JOC Oil, Standard Fruit, Nokia,* and *ICC Case No. 6149.*

Is there any reason that the law applicable to formation of the arbitration agreement would not be the same law that governs its validity? Suppose the putative arbitration agreement contains a choice-of-law provision providing that the agreement to arbitrate is governed by the law of State A. Under Article V(1)(a) of the Convention, is the parties' choice of law entitled to effect? What about the fact that one party denies having concluded the agreement to arbitrate—given that, how can there be a valid choice of law?

6. *Formation of arbitration agreements by conduct.* Most legal systems recognize that a party's assent to contractual terms may be established by its conduct or oral statements. For example, a party's performance of its putative contractual obligations is often regarded as a basis for finding assent to a disputed contract. Similarly, a party's conduct is sometimes argued to establish the existence of a valid arbitration agreement. (As discussed below, arbitration agreements are often subject to separate form

requirements, *infra* pp. 375-92, which may render an agreement formed by conduct invalid.)

In particular, numerous authorities have relied on a party's commencement of arbitral proceedings, or its participation without protest in such proceedings, as evidence of a valid arbitration agreement. Consider Article 16(2) of the UNCITRAL Model Law. *See Thomson-CSF, SA v. Am. Arbitration Ass'n*, 64 F.3d 773, 777 (2d Cir. 1995) ("party may be bound by an arbitration clause if its subsequent conduct indicates that it is assuming the obligation to arbitrate"); *Manes Org., Inc. v. Standard Dyeing & Finishing Co.*, 472 F.Supp. 687, 691 (S.D.N.Y. 1979) ("Manes contends that there is no enforceable agreement between the parties for arbitration. However, Manes is estopped to deny the parties for arbitration, when it is served its own Demand for Arbitration upon Standard in May, 1978, it relied on the very arbitration provision it now argues is invalid."); *Furness Withy Pty Ltd v. Metal Distrib. Ltd*, [1990] 1 Lloyd's Rep. 236, 243 (English Ct. App.) ("There are enough hazards in the process of obtaining and enforcing an arbitral award without the additional prospect that the respondent, having taken part all along, without a murmur of protest, may at the end argue that there never was an arbitration agreement in the first place. Nor would I wish him to be allowed to do so half way through when time has elapsed and money has been spent on pleadings, discovery and such like. The rule ought to be that if a person wishes to preserve his rights by taking part in an arbitration under protest, he must make his objection clear at the start, or at least at a very early stage. Otherwise, he ought to be bound.").

7.   *The* Standard Fruit *decision.* Is it sensible to conclude, as the *Standard Fruit* court does, that the parties' arbitration agreement is binding even if the underlying Memorandum of Intent is not? Suppose that *Standard Fruit* argued that the Memorandum of Intent was a forgery—that it had never discussed, much less signed, any such document. Would this really be irrelevant to Nicaragua's motion to compel arbitration? *See supra* pp. 361-63. If the Memorandum is not a binding contract, then how can the arbitration provision contained in it be binding?

The standard answer, of course, is that the arbitration agreement is separable, and therefore that it is supported by separate consideration (the exchange of promises to arbitrate), proved by separate evidence as to its existence, and subject to different rules of formation. *See supra* pp. 215-17, 361-63. Is that answer persuasive in cases involving claims that no underlying contract was formed? If the very existence of any contract is challenged, is that not necessarily relevant to the existence of an agreement to arbitrate? In concrete terms, if Standard Fruit and Nicaragua had no intention to be bound by the Memorandum of Intent, would they have intended to be bound by the Memorandum's arbitration clause? Does the *Standard Fruit* court address this difficulty?

Are the answers to the foregoing questions affected by the basis for the claim that no underlying contract exists? Compare a case where the parties have detailed negotiations and the issue is whether consent has been given to a binding contract with a case where one party denies any dealings at all with the other or claims that its signature was forged.

Even assuming that the binding character of the Memorandum is irrelevant to the existence of an arbitration agreement, Standard Fruit also specifically challenged the existence of the arbitration "agreement" itself. In particular, it argued that the arbitration clause was only a statement of intention to attempt to agree on an arbitration mechanism in the future. Did the *Standard Fruit* court offer any response to this argument? Consider the text of the clause. Note the parties' subsequent statements regarding the clause.

What are the limits of the *Standard Fruit* rationale? Suppose the Memorandum of Intent had not been signed, but Nicaragua argued it had been orally agreed to. Suppose the arbitration clause was contained in a draft prepared by Nicaragua, but not included in the unsigned Memorandum of Intent. Suppose Standard Fruit said it never attended the "summit" meeting.

8. *The* Nokia *decision.* Was the *Nokia* case correctly decided? What was the alleged defect in the provision to which the parties agreed (providing "jurisdiction of the International Chamber of Commerce, Paris")? What, other than an agreement to arbitrate, could this provision have been? Did the court attempt to give the provision any meaning? How does the issue presented in *Nokia* differ from cases, discussed above, where the parties' forms contained different arbitration clauses (*e.g.*, different seats, institutional rules, etc.)? *See supra* pp. 350-53.

Was there some other problem with the putative arbitration clause? Who agreed to it? Is there any suggestion that this vitiated the underlying contract?

9. *Exchanges of contractual documentation containing differing terms relating to arbitration.* As *Lea Tai* and *Nokia* illustrate, national courts have considered challenges to the existence of an arbitration agreement in a number of cases arising from the exchange of contractual documentation with differing dispute resolution terms. Such difficulties have been most common when merchants have exchanged differing sales and purchase forms, leading to what is sometimes referred to as the "battle of the forms."

(a) *Formation of arbitration agreement under U.C.C. §2-207.* Under §2-207(1) of the U.C.C., lower U.S. courts have held that the mere presence of an arbitration clause in one of the party's forms, but not the other's, does not necessarily prevent formation of a contract. *See, e.g., C. Itoh & Co. (Am.) Inc. v. Jordan Int'l Co.*, 552 F.2d 1228, 1235 (7th Cir. 1977); *Dorton v. Collins & Aikman Corp.*, 453 F.2d 1161 (6th Cir. 1972). If a contract is formed, §2-207 of the U.C.C. deals with additional terms contained in one party's form, providing generally that additional terms included in an expression of acceptance become part of the contract unless they either "materially alter" the offer or are objected to. Section 2-207(2) and (3) also provide that where the parties' conduct recognizes the existence of a contract, but their writings differ over material terms, the contract is limited to the provisions common to both writings.

In cases involving one writing that provides for arbitration, and another writing that does not, lower U.S. courts have generally relied on §2-207 to deny arbitration. They have done so on the theory that the arbitration clause was a material term that, under U.C.C. §2-207(2), is not included in the parties' contract. *See, e.g., S.E. Enameling Corp. v. Gen. Bronze Corp.*, 434 F.2d 330 (5th Cir. 1970); *Fairfield-Noble Corp. v. Pressman-Gutman Co.*, 475 F.Supp. 899 (S.D.N.Y. 1979).

Some courts have apparently taken a *per se* approach, reasoning that inclusion of an arbitration clause is always material, and that an arbitration clause is therefore never properly includible in the parties' contract under §2-207(2). *See, e.g., Marlene Indus. Corp. v. Carnac Textiles, Inc.*, 408 N.Y.S.2d 410, 413 (N.Y. 1978) (arbitration clause is always a material alteration; "unequivocal agreement" required before arbitration will be ordered); *Supak & Sons Mfg Co. v. Pervel Indus., Inc.*, 593 F.2d 135, 136-37 (4th Cir. 1979). Other lower courts have taken a case-by-case approach. *N&D Fashions, Inc. v. DHJ Indus., Inc.*, 548 F.2d 722, 766 (8th Cir. 1977) (whether addition of arbitration clause is material alteration is "question of fact to be resolved by the circumstances of each particular case"); *Dorton v. Collins & Aikman Corp.*, 453 F.2d 1161, 1169 & n.8 (6th Cir. 1972) (same).

Which approach is more consistent with the parties' likely intentions? In international cases? Should the proposal of an arbitration clause be regarded, either *per se* or presumptively, as a material alteration to the proposed contract? Does the answer to the question depend on either (i) the terms of the arbitration clause that is proposed (*i.e.*, is a "neutral" clause different from one that favors the proposing party); or (ii) what is standard or expected in the market at issue?

Does it make sense to apply §2-207 to the formation of arbitration agreements? Is it significant that §2-207 is contained in the U.C.C., applicable to sales agreements, not arbitration agreements? Does §2-207 nonetheless provide relevant rules governing the treatment of arbitration clauses contained in sales contracts?

How should one party's alterations to the text of an arbitration clause proposed by the adverse party be treated under §2-207? Should competing proposals for different arbitral seats, institutions, or applicable law be regarded as material alterations? What about different numbers of arbitrators or arbitral procedures (like language)?

(b) *Formation of arbitration agreement under other legal systems.* Section 1031(2) of the German version of the UNCITRAL Model Law provides that an agreement in writing exists "if the arbitration agreement is contained in a document transmitted from one party to the other party ... and—if no objection was raised in good time—the contents of such document are considered to be part of the contract in accordance with common usage." Contrast this approach to that under §2-207. Which approach is more consistent with the status of arbitration as a normal or preferred mode of international dispute resolution?

10. *Allocation of competence to decide disputes over formation of underlying contract.* Although the concepts are closely related, it is important to keep the allocation of jurisdictional competence analytically distinct from the substantive validity of the arbitration agreement. The former question involves who decides disputes whether the underlying contract, containing an arbitration agreement, was validly formed—an arbitrator or a national court? The latter issue concerns the answer to this question—whether or not the underlying contract and the arbitration agreement were validly formed. As discussed above, different legal systems have adopted different approaches to the allocation of jurisdictional competence between arbitral tribunals and national courts. *See supra* pp. 273-84. These allocations of jurisdictional competence apply, among other things, to disputes over the formation of the underlying contract containing an arbitration clause.

Is there any reason to treat disputes concerning the formation of the underlying contract any differently, for purposes of allocating jurisdictional competence, from disputes concerning the validity or legality of the underlying contract? Consider the following observation of the House of Lords in *Heyman v. Darwins Ltd* [1942] AC 356, 366 (Viscount Simon LC):

> "If the dispute is whether the contract which contains the clause has ever been entered into at all, that issue cannot go to arbitration under the clause, for the party who denies that he has ever entered into the contract is thereby denying that he has ever joined in the submission [to arbitration]."

For similar observations, *see Ashville Invs. Ltd v. Elmore Contractors Ltd* [1988] 3 WLR 867, 873 (English Ct. App.) ("it ... is a principle of law that an arbitrator does not have jurisdiction to rule upon the initial existence of the contract"); Svernlöv, *What Isn't, Ain't,* 25 J. World Trade 37, 49 (1991) ("carried to its extreme, ... the separability doctrine ... could give rise to a valid arbitral award even if two parties had never met, as long as one person alleged there was a contract between them containing an arbitration clause").

What is the response to the foregoing arguments? If the parties never entered into a contract, how can they be said to have agreed to an arbitration clause in that contract? And, if one party denies that it ever entered into either the underlying contract or the arbitration clause, how can the arbitrators have competence to decide the party's jurisdictional objection? As the following three Notes discuss, different legal systems have adopted different approaches to these questions.

11. *Allocation of competence to decide disputes over formation of underlying contract under prima facie jurisdiction standard.* As discussed above, some jurisdictions legislatively provide arbitrators with competence initially to consider all non-frivolous jurisdictional challenges, regardless of the character of these challenges. That is the approach adopted in France, as well as by some courts in India, Hong Kong and Canada. *See supra* pp. 274-75. Under this approach, the fact that a party denies concluding either the underlying contract or the arbitration agreement should be irrelevant to the tribunal's competence; national courts will only consider jurisdictional objections, whatever their character, on a *prima facie* basis, leaving all other jurisdictional objections for the arbitrators initially to consider and decide. *See supra* pp. 221-23.

Is this a sensible way of dealing with claims that no underlying contract, and no arbitration agreement, was ever formed? Is there anything wrong with requiring a party, who denies ever having concluded any contract of any sort, to arbitrate this denial? Note that the *prima facie* jurisdiction approach also applies when a party specifically denies that it concluded any agreement to arbitrate. *See supra* pp. 274-77.

12. *Allocation of competence to decide disputes over formation of underlying contract under FAA.* Other states (including the United States and England) allocate competence to decide jurisdictional disputes based, in part, on the nature of the jurisdictional objection. As discussed below, these states have encountered difficulty allocating jurisdictional competence over claims that no underlying contract, or no arbitration agreement, was ever formed. *See supra* pp. 278-81. The approach adopted in these states is reflected in decisions such as *Buckeye* and *Fiona Trust*, which hold that national courts will generally only consider claims that are directed specifically at the

putative agreement to arbitrate (and not at both the arbitration agreement and the underlying contract). *See supra* pp. 201-05, 205-11.

(a) Buckeye *revisited.* In the United States, the allocation of power between courts and arbitrators to decide disputes over the formation of the underlying contract under the FAA remains unclear, with divided lower court authority. *See also supra* pp. 278-81. As discussed above, the U.S. Supreme Court held in *Buckeye* that challenges to the validity of the underlying contract are generally for initial resolution by the arbitrators: "because respondents challenge the [underlying] Agreement, and not specifically its arbitration provisions, those provisions are enforceable apart from the remainder of the contract," and "should therefore be considered by an arbitrator, not a court." 546 U.S. at 446; *supra* p. 203. The Court also held that "a challenge to the validity of the contract as a whole, and not specifically to the arbitration clause, must go to the arbitrator." 546 U.S. at 449; *supra* p. 205. In addition, however, the Supreme Court reserved decision in *Buckeye* on the applicability of the separability presumption in cases where the presumption is "whether any agreement between the alleged obligor and obligee was ever concluded." 546 U.S. at 444 n. 1; *supra* p. 202, n. 18. The Court went out of its way to note that its decision did not address the correctness of cases "which hold that it is for courts to decide whether the alleged obligor ever signed the contract, whether the signer lacked authority to commit the alleged principal and whether the signor lacked the mental capacity to assent." *Ibid.*

How should jurisdictional competence be allocated under the FAA in cases where a party claims that no underlying contract was ever formed? Should parties be required to arbitrate claims that they never signed, or otherwise concluded, any agreement at all? What about claims that their signature on the putative underlying contract was forged? In fact, as discussed below, U.S. lower courts have arrived at widely varying answers to these questions.

(b) *Lower U.S. court decisions holding that arbitrators must resolve claim that no underlying contract exists.* The court in *Standard Fruit* holds that the arbitrators must decide whether the Memorandum (containing the alleged arbitration clause) is a binding contract. For other decisions requiring arbitration of challenges to the formation of the underlying contract, see *Alexander v. U.S. Credit Mgt, Inc.*, 384 F.Supp.2d 1003, 1007 (N.D. Tex. 2005) ("challenges claiming that—*as a whole*—a contract is illegal, is void as a matter of law, contains forged signatures, or was induced by fraud will generally not serve to defeat an arbitration clause"); *AmSouth Bank v. Bowens*, 351 F.Supp.2d 571, 575 (S.D. Miss. 2005) ("since the Bowenses' forgery allegation regards the customer agreement as a whole and not just the arbitration clause of the customer agreement, it is an issue that must be submitted to the arbitrator as part of the underlying dispute").

(c) *Lower U.S. court decisions holding that courts must resolve claim that no underlying contract exists.* In contrast, other lower U.S. court decisions have required judicial resolution of claims that there was never any underlying contract. According to one court: "There are, of course, certain issues, such as the existence of any agreement at all between the parties, which by their very nature cannot fall within the scope of arbitration." *Merritt-Chapman & Scott Corp. v. Penn. Turnpike Comm'n*, 387 F.2d 768, 771 n.5 (3d Cir. 1967). *See Opals on Ice Lingerie v.*

Bodylines, Inc., 2002 WL 718850, at *3 (E.D.N.Y.) ("if a party's signature were forged on a contract, it would be absurd to require arbitration if the party attacking the contract as void failed to allege that the arbitration clause itself was fraudulently obtained"); *Interocean Shipping Co. v. Nat'l Shipping & Trading Corp.*, 462 F.2d 673, 676 (2d Cir. 1972) ("There can be no doubt that the question of the very existence of the charter party which embodies the arbitration agreement requires judicial resolution under §4....").

(d) *Effect of* First Options *on resolution by U.S. courts of claims that no underlying contract exists*. What effect, if any, does *First Options* have on the allocation of power under the FAA to resolve claims that no underlying contract exists? As discussed elsewhere, the Court held that the parties could agree that disputes about the "arbitrability question" would be submitted to arbitration and that, if they did, this agreement would be entitled to effect. *See supra* pp. 280-81. In addition, however, *First Options* requires "clear and unmistakable" evidence of an agreement to submit "questions of arbitrability" to arbitration. *See supra* pp. 230-33. How does the *First Options* standard apply (if at all) to questions regarding the formation of the parties' underlying contract? How is it that a party could demonstrate clear and unmistakable evidence of an agreement to arbitrate jurisdictional disputes—when its counterparty denied ever concluding any agreement at all?

Most lower U.S. courts have concluded that *First Options'* "clear and unmistakable" evidence exception to the general rule that jurisdictional disputes are for judicial resolution is not available in disputes involving challenges to the formation of the underlying contract. *See Sanford v. MemberWorks, Inc.*, 483 F.3d 956 (9th Cir. 2007) (question of "existence" of arbitration agreement, as distinguished from "validity," is for court, rather than arbitrator); *Bank of Am., NA v. Diamond State Ins. Co.*, 38 F.Appx. 687, 689 (2d Cir. 2002) ("While the arbitration provisions state that issues concerning the 'formation and validity' of the contracts 'shall be submitted to arbitration,' it is not clear that this includes the question of the very existence of the contract"); *A.T. Cross Co. v. Royal Selangor(s) Pte, Ltd*, 217 F.Supp.2d 229, 234 (D.R.I. 2002) ("when plaintiff contends that no arbitration agreement was reached, the court, not an arbitrator, must determine the validity of the arbitration agreement").

Consider again Article 23 of the UNCITRAL Rules, Article 6 of the ICC Rules and Article 23 of the LCIA Rules, excerpted at pp. 170, 184-85 & 269-70 of the Documentary Supplement. How does each provision purport to deal with the allocation of jurisdictional competence to decide disputes over the formation of the underlying contract and the arbitration agreement? Note that most of these provisions grant the arbitrators power to resolve disputes over the "existence" and "validity" of arbitration agreements. What effect do these provisions have, under *First Options*, when a party denies that it ever entered into the arbitration agreement that incorporates them? *See also supra* pp. 281-82. How can parties have "agreed"—much less "clearly and unmistakably" agreed—to give an arbitrator power to determine whether the agreement vesting him with authority was properly formed?

Some have suggested that this is akin to the fable of Baron Munchhausen, who lifted himself from a swamp by his own pigtail. Less picturesquely, in order to decide that there is "clear and unmistakable" evidence of an agreement to arbitrate disputes over the formation of arbitration agreements, mustn't the court first decide that the parties in fact entered into an arbitration agreement? Doesn't this decision result in (and require) judicial resolution of the dispute over the formation of the arbitration agreement?

(e) *Wisdom of current approach to allocation of jurisdictional competence under FAA.* Consider the complexities and uncertainties that arise under *Buckeye* and *First Options* in cases involving disputes about formation of the underlying contract and arbitration agreement. Do these uncertainties contribute to the arbitral process? Compare the approach adopted under the FAA to that under French law. Which is preferable? Is there another approach that would be better?

13. Fiona Trust *revisited.* Consider again the House of Lords' decision in *Fiona Trust.* How does it deal with the allocation of jurisdictional competence in cases involving claims that no underlying contract was ever formed? For example, how does the House of Lords indicate that claims of forgery, or lack of authority of an agent, should be handled? Compare this to the approach in *Buckeye.* To the approach under a *prima facie* jurisdiction standard, such as in France.

14. *Formation of arbitration agreements by incorporation from other instruments.* International contracts frequently incorporate arbitration agreements or rules from other sources (*i.e.*, other contracts, trade association rules). This process of incorporation raises legal issues under applicable law.

(a) *Enforceability of incorporated arbitration agreements under UNCITRAL Model Law.* Consider Article 7(2) of the UNCITRAL Model Law, excerpted at p. 88 of the Documentary Supplement. What does it provide with regard to the formation of an arbitration agreement through incorporation by reference where "the reference is such as to make that clause part of the contract." Does Article 7(2) make any effort to address the question of what conditions must be satisfied to "make [the arbitration] clause part of the contract"?

Applying Article 7(2), most national courts have sought, in commercial settings, to give effect to both specific and general references to either arbitration provisions or to other contracts containing arbitration clauses. *See, e.g., Nanisivik Mines Ltd v. F.C.R.S. Shipping Ltd*, [1994] 2 FC 662, 667-68 (Ottawa Ct. App.) (arbitration clause in charter incorporated into bill of lading); *Guangdong New Tech. Imp. & Exp. Corp. v. Chiu Shing t/a B.C. Pty & Trading Co.*, XVIII Y.B. Comm. Arb. 385 (1993) (H.K. Ct. First Inst.) (upholding arbitration agreement where "there was a reference in a written contract to a document containing an arbitration clause," in compliance with Article 7(2) of Model Law); *Owners of the Annefield v. Owners of Cargo etc.*, [1971] 1 All ER 394, 406 (English Ct. App.) (where specific reference to arbitration clause exists, court will entertain "manipulation" of language to accommodate it to parties' transaction).

(b) *Enforceability of incorporated arbitration agreements under FAA.* It is also well-settled under the FAA in the United States that an agreement may validly incorporate an arbitration clause from another document. *R.J. O'Brien & Assoc. v. Pipkin*, 64 F.3d 257, 260 (7th Cir. 1995) ("A contract ... need not contain an explicit arbitration clause if it validly incorporates by reference an arbitration clause in another document"); *Gingiss Int'l, Inc. v. Bormet*, 58 F.3d 328, 331 (7th Cir. 1995) ("a sub-contract with a guarantor or surety may incorporate a duty to arbitrate by reference to an arbitration clause in a general contract"); *Cont'l U.K. Ltd v. Anagel Confidence Compania Naviera, SA*, 658 F.Supp. 809, 813 (S.D.N.Y. 1987) (if "party's arbitration clause is expressly incorporated into a bill of lading, non-signatories … who are linked to that bill through general principles of contract law or agency law may be bound"); *State Trading Corp. of India v. Grunstad Shipping Corp.*, 582 F.Supp. 1523 (S.D.N.Y. 1984) (arbitration clause in charter was incorporated into bill of lading).

(c) *Requirement of clarity or specificity regarding incorporated arbitration agreement.* Some national courts have required relative clarity from language incorporating an arbitration clause in another document. *See, e.g., PaineWebber, Inc. v. Bybyk*, 81 F.3d 1193 (2d Cir. 1996) (no incorporation of arbitration clause "unless it is clearly identified in the [principal] agreement"); *Weiner v. Mercury Artists Corp.*, 130 N.Y.S.2d 570, 571 (N.Y. App. Div. 1954) (one-page contract did not validly incorporate arbitration clause in 200-page pamphlet); *Fed. Bulk Carriers Inc. v. C. Itoh & Co.* [1989] 1 Lloyd's Rep. 103, 108 (English Ct. App.) ("it is clear that an arbitration clause is not directly germane to the shipment carriage and delivery of goods…. It is, therefore, not incorporated by general words in the bill of lading. If it is incorporated, it must either be by express words in the bill of lading itself … or by express words in the charterparty itself…. If it is desired to bring in an arbitration clause, it must be done explicitly in one document or the other"); *Judgment of 11 October 1989*, XV Y.B. Comm. Arb. 447, 448 (1990) (French Cour de Cassation) (requiring that "the existence of the [arbitration] clause be mentioned in the main contract, unless there exists between the parties a longstanding business relationship which ensures that they are properly aware of the written conditions normally governing their commercial relationships"). *Compare Century Indem. Co. v. Certain Underwriters at Lloyd's*, 584 F.3d 513 (3d Cir. 2009); *Sea Trade Maritime v. Hellenic Mut. War Rules Ass'n (Bermuda) Ltd* [2007] 1 Lloyd's Rep. 280, ¶65 (QB) (English High Ct.) ("English law accepts incorporation of standard terms by the use of general words …, particularly so when the terms are readily available and the question arises in the context of established dealers in a well-known market"); *Judgment of 4 May 2000*, XXVI Y.B. Comm. Arb. 277 (2001) (Italian Corte di Cassazione) (acceptance of arbitration clause, contained in annex referred to in main contract, was valid; no need for "specific approval" of clause).

3. *Formal Validity of International Arbitration Agreements*

The pro-arbitration legislative regimes of all leading international commercial arbitration conventions (including the New York, European and Inter-American Conventions) are limited to "written" agreements to arbitrate.[14] Article II of the New York Convention limits the Convention's coverage to arbitration agreements that are in "writing," while Article II(2) of the Convention defines an "agreement in writing" to include "an arbitral clause in a

---

14. *See* G. Born, *International Commercial Arbitration* 658-59 (2d ed. 2014).

contract or an arbitration agreement, signed by the parties or contained in an exchange of letters or telegrams."[15] The ICSID Convention is similar, in the investment context, requiring that agreements to arbitrate under ICSID auspices be in "writing."[16]

Although there are exceptions, many national arbitration statutes also contain "writing" requirements, sometimes expressed as rules regarding the formal validity of arbitration agreements.[17] Article 7(2) of the 1985 UNCITRAL Model Law provides that the "arbitration agreement shall be in writing,"[18] while §2 of the FAA applies the domestic U.S. arbitration statute to "written provision[s]" for arbitration.[19] These "writing" requirements have deep historical roots in most national legal systems,[20] as well as in many international instruments (although there are exceptions[21]). The materials excerpted below explore the "writing" requirements of the New York, Inter-American and ICSID Conventions and leading contemporary arbitration statutes.

SPHERE DRAKE INSURANCE PLC v. MARINE TOWING, INC.
16 F.3d 666 (5th Cir. 1994)

DUHE, Circuit Judge. Sphere Drake Insurance Plc sued Marine Towing, Inc. to stay litigation and compel arbitration of certain claims under a protection and indemnity policy. Defendant-Appellant Marine Towing, Inc. moved to dismiss for lack of jurisdiction. The district court denied Marine Towing's motion and ordered arbitration. Marine Towing appeals....

Marine Towing contracted Schade & Co. to acquire protection and indemnity insurance for its vessels. Schade eventually secured a policy from Sphere Drake, a London marine insurer. Before Schade delivered the policy to Marine Towing, but during the policy period, an insured vessel sank. Upon receiving the policy, Marine Towing discovered a provision requiring arbitration of coverage disputes in London. Marine Towing nevertheless sued Sphere Drake and Schade in state court for a declaration of rights under the policy and coverage. Sphere Drake removed the case to federal court and moved to compel arbitration and stay the litigation pending arbitration.... The court ... ordered arbitration, and stayed all litigation between the parties....

Marine Towing ... argues that the district court lacked jurisdiction under the Convention[22] because Marine Towing and Sphere Drake had no "agreement in writing" to arbitrate.[23] The Convention provides that the phrase "agreement in writing" shall include an arbitral clause in a contract or an arbitration agreement, signed by the parties or contained

---

15. Article 1 of the Inter-American Convention is similar.

16. ICSID Convention, Art. 25(1).

17. *See* G. Born, *International Commercial Arbitration* 658 (2d ed. 2014).

18. As discussed below, the 2006 Revision of the UNCITRAL Model Law included significant proposed changes to Article 7, which either eliminated or significantly relaxed the original writing requirement. *See infra* p. 391.

19. UNCITRAL Model Law Article 7(2); FAA 9 U.S.C. §2.

20. *See infra* pp. 383-84.

21. The Geneva Protocol and Geneva Convention did not contain any written form requirement.

22. A proceeding "falling under the Convention shall be deemed to arise under the laws and treaties of the United States," and original jurisdiction is in the district courts. 9 U.S.C. §203.

23. The Convention applies if there is "an agreement in writing" in which the parties undertake to submit their differences to arbitration. [New York] Convention, Art. II[(1)].

in an exchange of letters or telegrams." Marine Towing contends that, because it did not sign the insurance contract, the policy cannot provide the agreement in writing. Marine Towing would define an "agreement in writing" only as 1) a contract or other written agreement signed by the parties or 2) an exchange of correspondence between the parties demonstrating consent to arbitrate. We disagree with this interpretation of the Convention. We would outline the Convention definition of "agreement in writing" to include either (1) an arbitral clause in a contract or (2) an arbitration agreement, (a) signed by the parties or (b) contained in an exchange of letters or telegrams.

The insurance contract indisputably contains an arbitral clause. Because what is at issue here is an arbitral clause in a contract, the qualifications applicable to arbitration agreements do not apply. A signature is therefore not required. *But see Sen Mar, Inc. v. Tiger Petroleum Corp.*, 774 F.Supp. 879, 882 (S.D.N.Y. 1991) (requiring that arbitration clause be found in a signed writing or an exchange of letters to be enforceable). The district court properly did not require that the contract containing an arbitral provision be signed to constitute an agreement in writing under the Convention....

KAHN LUCAS LANCASTER, INC. v. LARK INTERNATIONAL LTD
186 F.3d 210 (2d Cir. 1999)

PARKER, Circuit Judge. Defendant-Appellant Lark International, Ltd ("Lark") appeals from a judgment of the U.S. District Court for the Southern District of New York (Denise L. Cote, Judge) … granting Plaintiff-Appellee Kahn Lucas Lancaster, Inc.'s ("Kahn Lucas") motion under 9 U.S.C. §206 and the [New York] Convention, as implemented, 9 U.S.C. §§201-08, to compel arbitration. The judgment was entered in accordance with an Opinion and Order of the district court, which held that arbitration clauses in certain purchase orders sent by Kahn Lucas to Lark were enforceable under the Convention and bound Lark, despite the fact that Lark had not signed the purchase orders. We reverse.

Lark is a Hong Kong corporation which acts as a purchasing agent for businesses seeking to buy and import clothing manufactured in Asia. Kahn Lucas is a New York corporation, with its principal place of business in New York, NY, engaged in the children's clothing business…. Kahn Lucas and Lark enjoyed a business relationship which began in 1988 and pursuant to which Lark would assist Kahn Lucas in arranging for overseas manufacturers to make garments ordered by Kahn Lucas. As part of this relationship, Lark processed Kahn Lucas's purchase orders and invoices. Pursuant to the terms of the purchase orders, as well as the parties' standing practice, the manufacturers would issue Kahn Lucas a seller's invoice for payment once the ordered garments were completed. Lark would then issue a separate invoice to Kahn Lucas for its commission, usually a set percentage of the amount charged by the manufacturer, on the order. Kahn Lucas paid both of these invoices through draw-downs on an existing letter of credit on which Lark was the named beneficiary. Lark would then remit payment to the manufacturer.

The dispute in this case arises from two purchase orders Kahn Lucas issued in early 1995 for children's fleece garments, manufactured in the Philippines, that it was to resell to Sears Roebuck, Inc. (the "Purchase Orders"). The Purchase Orders stated that the garments were "ordered from" Lark, listed "Lark International (Agent)" as seller, and were signed by Kahn Lucas. They were not signed by Lark. The Purchase Orders also clearly indicated that they contained a number of additional terms printed on the reverse side, and were made conditional upon the seller's acceptance of those terms. Included in these terms were clauses relating to arbitration [(the "Arbitration Clauses")], which stated:

> "Any controversy arising out of or relating to this Order ... shall be resolved by arbitration in the City of New York.... The parties consent to application of the New York or Federal Arbitration Statutes and to the jurisdiction of the Supreme Court of the State of New York, and of the United States District Court for the Southern District of New York, for all purposes in connection with said arbitration...."

Lark accepted the Purchase Orders without objection. In July 1995, the manufacturers issued final invoices relating to the ordered garments, and Lark issued its commission invoice. But citing defective garments and failed deliveries, Kahn Lucas refused to release funds to Lark to pay either the seller's invoices or Lark's commission invoice. Unable to achieve a satisfactory settlement with Lark and the manufacturers, Kahn Lucas sued Lark in the ... Southern District of New York, ... alleging breach of contract, breach of warranty, negligence, and breach of fiduciary duty.... [The U.S. District Court held that it lacked] personal jurisdiction over Lark to adjudicate the then-pending claims, but also held that, given the Arbitration Clauses, it would have personal jurisdiction over Lark if Kahn Lucas were to seek to compel arbitration. See *Kahn Lucas Lancaster, Inc. v. Lark Int'l Ltd.*, 956 F.Supp. 1131, 1139 (S.D.N.Y. 1997) ("*Kahn Lucas I*")....

By motion brought pursuant to 9 U.S.C. §206 and the Convention, Kahn Lucas converted its complaint into a motion to compel Lark to arbitrate the dispute in accordance with the Arbitration Clauses. Kahn Lucas also filed a demand for arbitration with the [AAA]. Lark opposed the motion to compel arbitration. Lark argued that it was not bound by the provisions of the Purchase Orders because the Purchase Orders were directed towards the sellers of the garments to which they related, namely the manufacturers, and not towards Lark. Lark also argued that the Arbitration Clauses were not enforceable under the Convention because Lark had not signed the Purchase Orders....

[T]he district court granted Kahn Lucas's motion to compel arbitration. *Kahn Lucas Lancaster, Inc. v. Lark Int'l Ltd.*, 1997 WL 458785 (S.D.N.Y.) ("*Kahn Lucas II*").... The court ... focused on whether the Arbitration Clauses were enforceable under the Convention so as to vest the court with jurisdiction under §203.... Although Lark had not signed the Purchase Orders, the district court held that the Purchase Orders represented an "arbitral clause in a contract," and therefore an "agreement in writing" to arbitrate sufficient to bring the dispute within [Articles II(1) and II(2) of] the Convention. In holding that an arbitral clause in a contract need not be signed by the parties to be enforceable under the Convention, the district court relied on the only appellate case interpreting this section of the Convention, *Sphere Drake Ins. plc* [*supra* pp. 376-77] (outlining, without much analysis, Article II(1) of the Convention as including "(1) an arbitral clause in a contract or (2) an arbitration agreement, (a) signed by the parties or (b) contained in an exchange of letters or telegrams"), and declined to follow *Sen Mar, Inc. v. Tiger Petroleum Corp.*, 774 F.Supp. 879, 882 (S.D.N.Y. 1991) ("An arbitration clause is enforceable only if it is found in a signed writing or an exchange of letters.").

The district court then turned to Lark's argument that it should not be bound by the Arbitration Clauses because it was not the seller of the garments. The district court held that the Purchase Orders embodied "an agreement between Kahn Lucas and Lark for the sale of goods, as opposed to an agreement between Kahn Lucas and the manufacturers." *Kahn Lucas II*, 1997 WL 458785 at *5. The district court relied on the fact that Kahn Lucas and Lark were the only parties mentioned on the Purchase Orders, and on the fact that Kahn Lucas was to pay Lark directly for the garments ultimately delivered under the Purchase Orders. Finally, the district court found that Lark was bound to the terms of the Purchase Orders despite the fact it did not sign them because it manifested assent to the Purchase Orders by performing under them, and that the subject of the dispute was therefore within the scope of the Arbitration Clauses.... Lark timely appealed.

On appeal, Lark ... [first] argues that in order to be enforceable under the terms of the Convention, any agreement to arbitrate, be it an "arbitral clause in a contract" or an "arbitration agreement," must be signed by the parties or contained in an exchange of letters or telegrams. Because the Purchase Orders were not signed by both parties, the argument continues, they are not "agreements in writing" enforceable under the Convention. Second, Lark argues that the district court erred in finding that it was bound by the terms of the Purchase Orders, including the Arbitration Clauses, because it was not the seller of the garments.

For the reasons that follow, we hold that the definition of "agreement in writing" in the Convention requires that such an agreement, whether it be an arbitration agreement or an arbitral clause in a contract, be signed by the parties or contained in a series of letters or telegrams. Therefore, the Arbitration Clauses are not enforceable under the Convention, and both the district court and this Court lack subject matter jurisdiction over the dispute. Because of this holding, we need not consider Lark's second argument, and we accordingly reverse the judgment of the district court and dismiss Kahn Lucas's motion to compel arbitration....

Treaties are construed in much the same manner as statutes.... [T]he obvious starting point in construing a treaty is its text. And the plain meaning of a text "will typically heed the commands of its punctuation." *United States Nat'l Bank*, 508 U.S. at 454; *see United States v. Ron Pair Enters., Inc.*, 489 U.S. 235, 241-42 (1989) (holding that the "grammatical structure of the statute," specifically the placement of commas, mandated a specific construction). Among the rules of punctuation applied in construing statutes is this: When a modifier is set off from a series of antecedents by a comma, the modifier should be read to apply to each of those antecedents. *See Bingham, Ltd. v. United States*, 724 F.2d 921, 925-26 n. 3 (11th Cir. 1984). As stated by the Eleventh Circuit, this rule is a "supplementary 'rule of punctuation,'" to the "doctrine of the last antecedent," which states that a modifier generally applies only to the nearest, or last, antecedent.[24] *See Bingham*, 724 F.2d at 925-26 n. 3. Of course, "these doctrines are not absolute rules," *id.* at 926 n. 3, and in applying them we are mindful of the Supreme Court's admonition that "a purported plain-meaning analysis based only on punctuation is necessarily incomplete and runs the risk of distorting a statute's true meaning." *United States Nat'l Bank*, 508 U.S. at 454.

In addition to utilizing rules of punctuation, we are aided in our plain-meaning analysis by the fact that the Convention exists in five official languages—French, Spanish, English, Chinese and Russian—of equal authenticity. Because one purpose of the Convention is to

---

24. These rules are illustrated by the following examples. Consider a sentence containing two antecedents—"A" and "B"—and one modifying phrase—"with C." The doctrine of the last antecedent suggests that if the sentence were structured "A or B with C," the phrase "with C" should be read to modify only "B." However, the "supplementary rule" of Bingham suggests that if the sentence were structured "A or B, with C," the phrase "with C" should be read to modify both "A" and "B."

unify the standards under which international agreements to arbitrate are observed, *Scherk v. Alberto-Culver Co.*, 417 U.S. 506, 520 n.15 (1974), we should, if possible, adhere to an interpretation consistent with all of the official languages. That said, some of the official languages provide more insight into the drafters' intent than others: Of the five official languages, English, French, and Spanish were the working languages of the United Nations Conference on International Commercial Arbitration, which drafted the Convention. All records of Conference meetings were kept in these working languages.

Finally, to the extent the drafters' intent is unclear from the text of the multiple versions of the Convention, we may turn to the Convention's legislative history for guidance. As noted above, Article II(1) of the Convention provides that each contracting state ... "shall recognize" an "agreement in writing" to arbitrate a given dispute. Article II(2), in turn, defines the term "agreement in writing" to include "an arbitral clause in a contract or an arbitration agreement, signed by the parties or contained in an exchange of letters or telegrams." Lark contends that the modifying clause "signed by the parties or contained in an exchange of letters or telegrams," modifies both: (1) "an arbitral clause in a contract" and (2) "an arbitration agreement" and, as a result, the dispute between the parties is not arbitrable due to the absence of Lark's signature on the Purchase Orders. Kahn Lucas contends, and the district court held, that "signed by the parties" modifies only the clause immediately preceding it, "an arbitration agreement," and not the previous clause. Thus, in Kahn Lucas's view, the unsigned Purchase Orders constitute an "agreement in writing" to arbitrate enforceable under the Convention.

As an initial matter, we must determine the meaning of the two elements in the series, namely "an arbitral clause in a contract" and "an arbitration agreement." We find the meaning of "an arbitral clause in a contract" to be self-evident. We also find that the phrase "an arbitration agreement," because it is used in conjunction with the phrase "an arbitral clause in a contract," refers to any agreement to arbitrate which is not a clause in a larger agreement, whether that agreement is part of a larger contractual relationship or is an entirely distinct agreement which relates to a non-contractual dispute. The parties agree that the Arbitration Clauses each constitute "an arbitral clause in a contract" and not "an arbitration agreement" under the Convention.

We turn, then, to the plain meaning of the English-language version of the Convention. Taking its lead from the Fifth Circuit's analysis in *Sphere Drake*, Kahn Lucas argues that the grammatical structure of §2 compels the conclusion that its dispute with Lark falls within the Convention. We disagree. Section 2 takes the structure "A or B, with C." This structure is exactly that to which the "supplementary rule of punctuation" expressed in *Bingham* applies. Grammatically, the comma immediately following "an arbitration agreement" serves to separate the series ("an arbitral clause in a contract or an arbitration agreement") from the modifying phrase ("signed by the parties or contained in an exchange of letters or telegrams"), and suggests that the modifying phrase is meant to apply to both elements in the series. Indeed, this comma can serve no other grammatical purpose. As a result, Kahn Lucas's reading of the statute would render the comma mere surplusage, a construction frowned upon.... [O]ther available interpretive tools strongly support the conclusion the punctuation suggests.

First, the plain language of the other working-language versions of the Convention compels the conclusion that, in order to be enforceable under the Convention, both an arbitral clause in a contract and an arbitration agreement must be signed by the parties or contained in an exchange of letters or telegrams. In the French and Spanish-language versions, the word for "signed" appears in the plural form, "*signés*" and "*firmados*" respectively. Because each of the two antecedents is couched in the singular, the modifier unambiguously applies to both of them. If ... only an arbitration agreement need be signed by the parties, the French-language version would utilize the verb "*signé*" and the Spanish "*firmado*."

[The court concluded that Chinese language text was similar to the French and Spanish; the Russian language text pointed to an opposite conclusion, but was dismissed by the court as anomalous.] ... Finally, to the extent the plain meanings of the non-English language versions of the Convention do not resolve any ambiguity that exists in the English-language version, the legislative history of Article II puts the matter to rest....

Accordingly, although we are cognizant that the Convention "should be interpreted broadly to effectuate its recognition and enforcement purposes," *Bergesen v. Joseph Muller Corp., 710 F.2d 928*, 933 (2d Cir. 1983), the rules governing our construction do not allow us to follow the Fifth Circuit's interpretation of Article II(2) as expressed in *Sphere Drake*.... [W]e hold that the modifying phrase "signed by the parties or contained in an exchange of letters or telegrams" applies to both "an arbitral clause in a contract" and "an arbitration agreement."

Having determined that the Convention requires that "an arbitral clause in a contract" be "signed by the parties or contained in an exchange of letters or telegrams," we turn to the application of the Convention to the facts of this case. As noted above, the Arbitration Clauses were contained in the Purchase Orders which were signed only by Kahn Lucas, and not by Lark. There is therefore no "arbitral clause in a contract ... signed by the parties." Further, Kahn Lucas does not contend that the Purchase Orders, even together with Lark's Confirmation of Order forms, represent "an arbitral clause in a contract ... contained in an exchange of letters or telegrams." As a result, there is no "agreement in writing" sufficient to bring this dispute within the scope of the Convention.... The judgment of the district court is reversed, and Kahn Lucas's motion to compel arbitration is dismissed with prejudice.

JUDGMENT OF 5 NOVEMBER 1985
XII Y.B. Comm. Arb. 511 (1987) (Swiss Fed. Trib.)

[On December 6, 1980, Tracomin and Sudan Oil Seeds ("SOS") entered into a commodity sale contract. After disputes arose, SOS asked Tracomin—by a telex dated May 18, 1981, by a subsequent letter dated July 4, and by a telex dated July 16—to submit the dispute to arbitration before the Arbitration Board of the Federation of Oils, Seeds and Fats Associations ("FOSFA") in London. By a letter dated July 21, Tracomin appointed its arbitrator, with express reference to SOS's most recent telex. The tribunal made an award against Tracomin.

Tracomin refused to comply with the award, and SOS sought to enforce it in Switzerland. Tracomin contended that the arbitration agreement, pursuant to which the award was made, was invalid under Articles II(1) and (2) of the New York Convention. The Swiss Federal Tribunal rejected Tracomin's objections.]

It results from [Article II(1) and II(2)] that a written agreement by which arbitration is agreed to between the parties can be either an arbitration clause or a submission agreement. The arbitration clause submits to arbitration a dispute which has not yet arisen but which could arise out of a legal relationship between the parties. On the contrary, the submission agreement is a contract which the parties conclude at the time when a dispute has arisen between them and whose object it is to have arbitrators decide on the dispute already arisen.

Both the arbitration clause and the submission agreement must be in a written form as described by Art. II(2) of the Convention. This provision prevails over national laws and constitutes a uniform law governing the form of the arbitration clause and the submission agreement. The recognition of the arbitration agreement cannot involve requirements which are less or more demanding than the form described by Art. II(2). It is true that, according to Art. VII of the Convention, parties can also avail themselves of more liberal conditions of recognition to the extent that they may invoke the law or treaties of the country where the award is relied upon. However, Art. VII is not applicable in the present case because the parties do not invoke any legal rule other than the Convention and the Court cannot substitute the grounds asserted by the parties.

In the absence of a signature of both parties, the arbitration clause or submission agreement can result from an exchange of letters or telegrams. The exchange of telexes must be assimilated to the exchange of telegrams. However, an exchange of messages is necessary. If a submission agreement is proposed in writing or telegram and is accepted orally or tacitly, the forms required by Art. II(2) are not satisfied.... [N]ot only must there be a written proposal to arbitrate but also a written acceptance from the other party which acceptance must be communicated to the party who made the proposal to arbitrate

In the present case, SOS made to Tracomin a proposal to submit to arbitration the dispute arising out of the failure to open a letter of credit in time for the last deliveries due under contract no. 10-80/81 of 6 December 1980, by telex of 18 May 1981, by letter of 4 July 1981 and by telex of 16 July 1981. Tracomin stated in its telex of 21 July 1981 that it designated its arbitrator in this dispute since it referred explicitly to the telex of 16 July of the counter party which telex recalled the telex of 18 May and the letter of 4 July. Accordingly, as from the moment that it had designated its arbitrator for the said dispute, it has expressed in the forms laid down in Art. II(2) that it accepted arbitration. One must therefore consider that the parties expressed in writing their will to submit to FOSFA arbitration the dispute arisen between them.... That dispute has effectively been submitted to the arbitrators and decided upon by award no. 2542 the enforcement of which is sought.

The arguments of Tracomin boil down to the argument that the arbitration clause in the contract nr. 10-80/81 of 6 December 1980 is not valid under Art. II of the New York Convention because this contract did not expressly refer to the possibility to submit to arbitration disputes which might arise out of its execution. This question can be left open because, even if an arbitration clause was not validly made at the time of conclusion of the contract, a submission agreement was in any case entered into by an exchange in writing once the dispute had arisen and was concretely defined in the messages of SOS of 18 May, 4 July and 16 July 1981 to which Tracomin referred in its message in response dated 21 July....

AWARD IN VIAC CASE NO. SCH-4366 OF 15 JUNE 1994
2 UNILEX, E. 199414, p. 331 (1994)

By the request of arbitration of 30 March 1993, the claimant [a company with place of business in Austria] applied for an award against the respondent [a company with place of business in Germany] for payment of a total of US$ [...]. It submitted that the respondent had not fulfilled its obligations on the basis of two contracts for the delivery of cold-rolled sheet concluded with the claimant, since it had either not taken delivery of or had not paid for part of the goods purchased.... The competence of the [VIAC] is founded on the last paragraphs of the two contracts concluded between the parties. According thereto, all disputes that cannot be settled amicably should be finally decided according to the [VIAC] Arbitral Rules by one or more arbitrators appointed in accordance with those rules.

It is true that the contracts—and thus the aforesaid arbitration clause—exist only in the acknowledgement of order sent by the claimant to the respondent, which the latter never countersigned. However, there can be no doubt of the validity of the arbitration clause. The fact that Article I(1) the [New York Convention], which applies in this case, provides that the agreement must be writing, does not mean that the arbitration clause must be contained in a contractual document signed by both parties. According to Article II(2), an "arbitral clause in a contract or an arbitration agreement, signed by the parties or contained in an exchange of letters or telegrams" is sufficient. The predominant view in international legal writings is that the requirement is therefore also met if the addressee replies in writing to the acknowledgement of an order in such a way that need only conclusively show that he accepts the acknowledgement of the order together with the arbitration clause mentioned therein, for example, if he expressly refers in subsequent letters or invoices to the contractual document in question. That is exactly what happened in the present case. Though initially the respondent only tacitly accepted the two acknowledgements of the order by the claimant, it subsequently—to be precise in a letter to the claimant of 19 January 1993—expressly referred to the relevant contracts ... and thus satisfied the requirement as to the written form of the arbitration clause contained therein.

Furthermore, in the present case, on the basis of the general legal principle of good faith, the respondent would be precluded from relying on the absence of an arbitration clause in writing for the purpose of negating the competence of the arbitral centre. Within a little less than three months, the respondent concluded three contracts with the claimant with essentially identical wording but never countersigned the acknowledgement of the orders together with the arbitration clause contained therein that were sent to it by the claimant. That did not prevent the respondent from relying on that specific arbitration clause and from entrusting [VIAC, which was] specified therein with the settlement of a dispute concerning the second of the three contracts. To rely on one occasion on the arbitration clause signed only by the opposing party in order to assert one's own claims and, on a second occasion, when the opposing party goes to law, to dispute the validity of an arbitration clause agreed upon in exactly the same form, would not be compatible with the requirement of the observance of good faith and fair business dealings, which is also fully valid within the scope of the New York Convention....

NOTES

1. *Distinction between formal requirements and substantive rules of contract formation.* The conclusion that an arbitration agreement was formed under applicable substantive law does not necessarily mean that the agreement is valid. Article II of the New York Convention, Article 7 of the UNCITRAL Model Law and a number of other instruments impose formal requirements on arbitration agreements, which can either render such agreements invalid or exclude otherwise validly-formed arbitration clauses from

the scope of the relevant legislation (*e.g.*, the New York Convention). Conversely, even if a putative arbitration agreement satisfies applicable formal requirements, it may not be substantively valid—either because the parties have not consented or because the contract is invalid (*e.g.*, by reason of mistake, unconscionability, or impossibility). This distinction is illustrated by *Lark*, where both the first instance and appellate courts distinguished between the questions of (a) the Convention's writing requirement; and (b) the parties' consent to the agreement to arbitrate.

2.   *Character of "writing" requirement in New York Convention.* Consider Article II of the Convention, excerpted at p. 1 of the Documentary Supplement. Does Article II impose a written form requirement, violation of which will render an agreement invalid? Or does Article II define the scope of the Convention (*i.e.*, specify those arbitration agreements that are subject to the Convention's pro-arbitration regime), while not affecting the validity of other arbitration agreements? Whatever its effects, what does Article II provide for with regard to the form of an arbitration agreement?

     Consider the approach to writing requirements of Article I(2)(a) of the European Convention, excerpted at p. 29 of the Documentary Supplement. Is this desirable? More desirable than that of the New York Convention?

3.   *Writing requirement in ICSID Convention.* Consider Article 25(1) of the ICSID Convention, excerpted at p. 18 of the Documentary Supplement. Note that it imposes a "writing" requirement on agreements to arbitrate under ICSID auspices. Compare the text of that requirement to that under Article II of the New York Convention. How do they differ? Compare Articles 52 and 53 of the 1907 Hague Convention, excerpted at p. 46 of the Documentary Supplement.

4.   *Rationale for requirements that arbitration agreements be in "writing."* The materials excerpted above include a number of different "writing" requirements for international arbitration agreements. In general terms, what do these differing requirements call for? Why?

     Suppose A and B agree orally to arbitrate an existing dispute between them before C, as arbitrator. Suppose C and D witness the oral agreement. Why should the agreement not be enforced? Recall the pro-arbitration policies of the New York Convention (and most national arbitration regimes). *See supra* pp. 30-39, 45-67, 177-90. Wouldn't those purposes be served by enforcing oral promises to arbitrate? Aren't other oral agreements generally enforceable under most developed legal systems?

     What aspects of arbitration agreements argue for a "writing" requirement? What policies are advanced by the requirement? One explanation is ensuring that parties are aware both of their waiver of otherwise-available judicial remedies when agreeing to arbitrate and of their commitment to arbitrate. *See supra* pp. 363-65; ILC, *Draft on Arbitral Procedure Prepared by the International Law Commission at Its Fourth Session*, 1952, U.N. Doc. A/CN.4/59, Arts. 1(3), 15(2) (1952) ("In view of the fundamental importance of the undertaking to arbitrate, paragraph 2 of this article implies that the undertaking may not be based on a mere verbal agreement."). This is sometimes referred to as a "warning" function of the written form requirement.

     Doesn't any contract involve a compromise or waiver of otherwise existing rights? If parties may agree orally to a $20 million sales transaction, why can't they agree orally to a $50,000 arbitration? What is special about arbitration agreements? If parties in an international transaction do not waive their rights of judicial access, then what are they left with? Isn't the risk of litigation in a counter-party's home forum, or multiplicitous litigation in different courts, also something the parties should be warned about?

Alternatively, the writing requirement is sometimes justified on evidentiary grounds—it ensures that adequate proof will be provided of an agreement to arbitrate. Is this persuasive? Are courts not capable of evaluating different forms of evidence (including oral evidence) and determining when agreements have been concluded, without the arbitrariness that accompanies a written form requirement?

Another potential explanation for a "writing" requirement is the impetus that it gives to the parties' consideration of, and agreement on, critical issues such as arbitral seat, language, institutional rules, and the like. Does the value of encouraging discussion of, and agreement on, these issues warrant refusal to enforce arbitration agreements that are not in the written form?

5. *Possible interpretations of "writing" requirement under Article II(2) of New York Convention.* What does Article II(2)'s "writing" requirement call for? Consider the interpretation adopted by *Sphere Drake*, reading Article II(2) as requiring *either* (i) an arbitral clause contained in a contract, *or* (ii) an arbitration agreement that is (A) signed by the parties, or (B) contained in an exchange of letters or telegrams. Is this interpretation of Article II(2) persuasive? What does the first category identified by *Sphere Drake* include? More to the point, what does it exclude? Anything? Doesn't "an arbitral clause in a contract" include oral contracts? Consider the text of Article II(2). Does it support, as a textual matter, the *Sphere Drake* interpretation?

For an alternative interpretation of Article II's "writing" requirement, consider: "Article II(2) may be divided into two alternatives for an arbitration agreement in writing: ... [1] an arbitral clause in a contract or a submission agreement, the contract or agreement being signed by the parties; ... [2] an arbitral clause in a contract or a submission agreement, contained in an exchange of letters or telegrams." A. van den Berg, *The New York Convention of 1958* 191 (1981). How does this differ from the formulation in *Sphere Drake*? Which is correct? Compare the alternative reasoning of the Second Circuit in *Lark*. Is the Second Circuit's analysis persuasive?

6. *Is Article II(2)'s "writing" requirement exclusive?* Consider again the text of Article II(2): "The term 'agreement in writing' shall include an arbitral clause in a contract or an arbitration agreement, signed by the parties or contained in an exchange of letters or telegrams." Does Article II(2) require arbitration agreements to satisfy the specific definition of an "agreement in writing" set out therein in order to benefit from the Convention's protections? Or, alternatively, does Article II(2) merely provide a non-exclusive (or non-exhaustive) list which illustrates some of the types of "agreements in writing" that satisfy Article II, without purporting to exclude all other types of agreements from the "agreement in writing" definition or the Convention's protections? Authorities are divided.

(a) *Authorities concluding that Article II(2)'s definition is not exclusive.* A number of authorities have concluded that Article II(2) merely lists some examples of the sorts of arbitration agreements that would satisfy the Convention's "agreement in writing" requirement, but does not exclude the conclusion that other types of agreements also satisfy the requirement. That is, Article II(2) contains a non-exclusive list of agreements that clearly satisfy the Convention's "writing" requirement, without prejudice to arguments that other types of agreements are also "agreements in writing," which are subject to the Convention. Consider:

> "While agreements of the type mentioned in Article II(2) are definitely within the ambit of the Convention, its application is not limited to such agreements. Others which constitute valid agreements in writing under the private international law of the forum are equally included." A. Samuel, *Jurisdictional Problems in International Commercial Arbitration* 83 (1989).

Is the non-exclusive interpretation of Article II(2)'s writing requirement wise? What are the benefits of extending the Convention to a broader range of arbitration agreements? The costs?

In connection with the 2006 revisions to the Model Law, UNCITRAL also adopted a Recommendation, which urged Contracting States to interpret Article II(2) as non-exclusive. UNCITRAL's July 2006 Recommendation recommends that "article II, paragraph 2, of the [New York Convention] be applied recognizing that the circumstances described therein are not exclusive." *Report of the UNCITRAL on the Work of Its Thirty-Ninth Session, Recommendation Regarding the Interpretation of Article II, Paragraph 2, and Article VII, Paragraph 1, of the Convention on the Recognition and Enforcement of Foreign Arbitral Awards*, U.N. Doc. A/61/17, Annex 2 (2006). Is this recommendation wise? What legal weight does it have?

(b) *Non-exclusive interpretations of Article II(2)*. Assume that Article II(2)'s definition of an "agreement in writing" is illustrative and not exclusive. What then does Article II mean, and, in particular, to what arbitration agreements does it apply? Two principal possibilities exist:

First, Article II(1)'s reference to an "agreement in writing" might establish a uniform, international standard for written arbitration agreements. This category would include, but not be limited to, the agreements listed in Article II(2). Agreements that satisfied Article II(2)'s standard (either by inclusion on Article II(2)'s list *or otherwise*) would be subject to Article II's basic rule of enforceability; other agreements would not be enforceable under Article II (although they might nonetheless be enforceable under national law).

Second, Article II(1)'s reference to an "agreement in writing" might permit national courts to extend the Convention's coverage under local law to agreements not listed in Article II(2). Other states that are party to the Convention could, but would not be obliged to, accept such extensions.

Which of the foregoing interpretations is more persuasive? Why?

(c) *Authorities concluding that Article II(2)'s definition is exclusive*. Some authorities have concluded that Article II(2)'s definition of what constitutes an "agreement in writing" is exclusive, exhaustively defining the entire category of agreements that satisfy Article II's "agreement in writing" requirement. *See Judgment of 21 March 1995*, XXII Y.B. Comm. Arb. 800, 804 (1997) (Swiss Fed. Trib.) ("the issue of (formal) validity is determined solely according to the Convention; the requirement of the written form according to Article II ... is to be interpreted independently, without the assistance of a national law"); A. van den Berg, *The New York Convention of 1958* 179 (1981). These authorities typically rely on the French (and Spanish) texts of the Convention. The French text of Article II(2) of the Convention is more clearly exclusive than the English text. It provides: "On entend par 'convention écrite' ...," most nearly translating into "The term 'agreement in writing' *means*...." The Spanish is to the same effect ("La expresión 'acuerdo por escrito' *denotará* ...). Compare the English text of Article II(2): "The term 'agreement in writing' shall include...." Is this formula not fairly clearly "non-exclusive"?

7. *Does Article II impose a maximum form requirement?* Does Article II of the Convention require national courts to recognize any agreement that meets or exceeds Article II's definition of an "agreement in writing"? That is, does Article II impose a "maximum" form requirement, precluding Contracting States from requiring more demanding formal requirements for international arbitration agreements? For example, would Article II prevent Contracting States from requiring that all (or some) international arbitration agreements be in all capital letters and separately initialed by the parties?

Virtually all national courts have concluded that Article II imposes a maximum form requirement, which Contracting States may not exceed. *See Judgment of 20 March 1997, ANC Maritime Co. v. W. of England etc.*, XXIII Y.B. Comm. Arb. 654, 655 (1998) (Greece S.Ct.) (Article II(2) "introduced a directly applicable substantive rule, which binds the States-Parties and does not allow the court, in the field of application of the Convention, the possibility to resort to another rule of substantive or private law in order to confirm the validity of the form of the conclusion of the agreement to arbitrate"); *Judgment of 5 July 1994*, XXI Y.B. Comm. Arb. 685 (1994) (Basel-Land Obergericht) ("[o]bviously, a Contracting State may not set stricter requirements as to form."). Is there any reason to doubt this conclusion? Could one argue that Article II has nothing to do with formal validity and merely defines what arbitration agreements the Convention applies to, without suggesting that those agreements are formally valid or that Contracting States are free to impose whatever form requirements they wish?

8. *Does Article II impose a minimum form requirement?* Suppose that a Contracting State imposes *less* demanding form requirements on international arbitration agreements than those under Article II. In practice, as discussed below, this is the case in an increasing number of jurisdictions, which often permit either oral or tacit arbitration agreements, or impose less stringent writing requirements than under Article II. In these cases, does Article II supersede national law, requiring that Article II's stricter form requirement be applied to invalidate the arbitration agreement (even if it would be formally valid under national law)?

There is authority to the effect that Article II(2) establishes a "minimum," as well as a maximum, form requirement and that this requirement supersedes national laws purporting to give effect to international arbitration agreements based on lesser form requirements. Consider the court's analysis in *Lark*—does it interpret Article II as imposing a minimum form requirement? *See also Judgment of 30 March 2000*, XXXI Y.B. Comm. Arb. 652, 656 (2006) (Oberlandesgericht Schleswig) ("no reliance can be placed on national law, be it more or less strict as to formal requirements"); *Judgment of 21 March 1995*, XXII Y.B. Comm. Arb. 800, 804 (1997) (Swiss Fed. Trib.) ("the issue of [formal] validity is determined solely according to the Convention; the requirement of the written form according to Article II of the New York Convention is to be interpreted independently, without the assistance of a national law").

Is this conclusion warranted? Is it consistent with the Convention's objectives? How can Article II be interpreted so that it does not impose a minimum form requirement?

First, consider Article VII(1), which provides that the Convention shall not "deprive any interested party of any right he may have to avail himself of an arbitral award in the manner and to the extent allowed by the law or the treaties of the country where such an award is sought to be relied upon." This provision ensures that the Convention does not, through the establishment of one set of guarantees as to the enforceability of arbitration awards (and, by analogy, agreements), override or undermine other protections granted by national law. Is this objective not implicated by Article II's form requirement? *See Judgment of 16 December 1992*, XXI Y.B. Comm. Arb. 535, 537 (1996) (Oberlandesgericht Cologne) (Article II(2) "does not provide for a uniform rule," because Article VII permits reliance on more lenient national law standards).

Note that, in addition to its Recommendation concerning the non-exclusive character of Article II(2), UNCITRAL also adopted a recommendation that embraced the foregoing interpretation of Article VII(1). The Recommendation urges states to apply Article VII(1) to allow "any interested party to avail itself of rights it may have, under the law or treaties of the country where an arbitration agreement is sought to be relied upon, to seek recognition of the validity of such an arbitration agreement." *UNCITRAL Recommendation Regarding Interpretation of Article II, Paragraph 2, and Article VII, Paragraph 1, of the Convention on the Recognition and Enforcement of Foreign Arbitral Awards*, U.N. Doc. A/61/17, Annex 2. Is this recommendation wise?

Second, consider again the question whether Article II(2) is exclusive. If Article II(2) is *not* exclusive, then is it possible that Article II would impose a minimum form requirement? Suppose that Article II imposes an autonomous, uniform international definition of "agreement in writing," as referred to in Article II(1). Although that definition would be more expansive than the non-exclusive list of arbitration agreements in Article II(2), it could still be a minimum standard (apart from Article VII(1)), couldn't it?

9. *What types of arbitration agreements satisfy Article II(2)?* Putting aside the question whether Article II(2) is exclusive, what categories of arbitration agreements fall within the description of an "agreement in writing" set out in Article II(2)? National courts and other authorities have reached differing conclusions. Note that it is a misnomer to say that Article II(2) contains a "writing" requirement; in fact, Article II(2) requires either a "signature" (on a signed contract) or an "exchange" of letters—requirements that go well beyond a mere writing requirement.

   (a) *Contract, signed by all parties, containing arbitration clause.* It is clear that Article II(2) is satisfied by a contract, which both parties sign, that contains a written arbitration clause as one of its terms. A. Samuel, *Jurisdictional Problems in International Commercial Arbitration* 82 (1989) ("If an arbitral clause appears in a contract which has been signed by the parties, or an arbitration agreement has been signed by them, the definition of an 'agreement in writing' ... is fulfilled."). Notwithstanding the separability presumption, there is no requirement that the arbitration clause itself be signed. (Should there be?) It is also clear that a submission agreement (by which the parties agree to refer an existing dispute to arbitration), which is signed by both parties, satisfies Article II(2)'s "writing" requirement.

(b) *Contract, not signed by parties, containing arbitration clause.* It is less clear whether an arbitration clause contained in an unsigned, but nonetheless agreed, written contract satisfies Article II(2)'s form requirement. The literal text of Article II(2) arguably requires that both a written contract containing an arbitration clause and a separate arbitration agreement be signed, with the result that an unsigned (but agreed) written contract or arbitration agreement is not subject to the Convention. Despite this, some authorities have reached different results, interpreting Article II(2) as not requiring that a contract containing an arbitration clause be signed (in contrast to a separate arbitration agreement, where a signature would be required). *Sphere Drake* is a leading example of this analysis; the court held that, in the case of an "arbitral clause in a contract, the qualifications applicable to arbitration agreements do not apply. A signature is therefore not required." Contrast the analysis in *Lark*. Which interpretation is more persuasive?

(c) *Exchanges of telexes, telegrams, emails, or similar communications, containing arbitration clause.* An arbitration agreement contained in an exchange of letters or telegrams may also satisfy Article II(2). Although different textual readings are possible, Article II(2) has not generally been interpreted to require that letters or telegrams (as distinguished from "contracts") be "signed." *See* A. Samuel, *Jurisdictional Problems in International Commercial Arbitration* 82 (1989) ("Where the arbitral clause or agreement is contained in an exchange of letters or telegrams, no signature is required for the conditions contained in Article II(2) to be satisfied."). What constitutes an "exchange" of letters? What types of communications fall within the category "letters or telegrams"?

Suppose that Lark had, in response to the purchase orders, sent Kahn Lucas a fax saying: "As discussed, we consent to the arbitration clause, but we still need to discuss price and delivery schedules, which we cannot accept." Would Article II require recognition of the arbitration agreement?

(d) *Oral or other non-written acceptance of written contract containing arbitration clause.* The most significant area of disagreement over Article II(2) concerns its application to oral or other non-written acceptances of a written offer, containing within it a written arbitration clause. Many authorities conclude that Article II(2) does not extend to oral, tacit, or other non-written acceptance of written contracts. *See Judgment of 18 September 2003*, XXX Y.B. Comm. Arb. 536, 538 (2005) (Oberlandesgericht Celle) ("oral or tacit agreement on the application of these general conditions of contract [containing an arbitration clause], does not satisfy the requirements as to form of Article II(2)"); *Moscow Dynamo v. Ovechkin*, 2006 U.S. Dist. LEXIS 1320 (D.D.C.) (Article II(2) not satisfied: "no ... written exchange of correspondence exists").

On the other hand, a few authorities have held that a written offer containing an arbitration agreement may be accepted tacitly, including by performance pursuant to the offer. *See Overseas Cosmos, Inc. v. NR Vessel Corp.*, 1997 U.S. Dist. LEXIS 19390, at *10 (S.D.N.Y.) ("While Article II ... requires that an agreement to arbitrate be in writing to be enforceable, 'it does not require that the writing be signed by the parties,' and 'ordinary contract principles dictate when the parties are bound by a written arbitration provision absent their signatures.'"); *Judgment of 26 June 1970, Israel Chem. & Phosphates Ltd v. NV Algemene Oliehandel*, I Y.B. Comm. Arb. 195 (1976) (Rotterdam Rechtbank).

(e) Sphere Drake *revisited*. Does Article II(2) exclude from its scope an arbitration clause in a written document that the parties have assented to in an exchange of letters (*i.e.*, in which both parties consent to be bound by the written, but unsigned, document)? The answer should be that this satisfies Article II(2). If so, must the assent in the parties' exchange of letters to the written (but unsigned) contract be express? The answer should be in the negative; nothing in Article II(2) imposes a requirement that assent be express, and the Convention's purposes would best be served if consent could be implied (as under ordinary contract law rules). Finally, if implied assent can be obtained from telexes and letters (and presumably other forms of writing), was *Sphere Drake* decided correctly (albeit for confused reasons)? That is, did the parties' written correspondence provide implied acceptance of a written document containing an arbitration clause?

(f) *Post-dispute "writing" agreeing to arbitrate.* Even if no valid written arbitration agreement exists, the parties' post-dispute conduct can constitute or acknowledge a written agreement to arbitrate. The least controversial example of this should be a party's signature on the Terms of Reference under the ICC Rules. *See supra* pp. 75-77. *But see Judgment of 16 December 1992*, XXI Y.B. Comm. Arb. 535 (1996) (Oberlandesgericht Cologne) (ICC Terms of Reference held not to satisfy Article II(2)'s "writing" requirement). Other examples also frequently occur, typically involving correspondence preceding or during an arbitration. *See Nghiem v. NEC Elec., Inc.*, 25 F.3d 1437, 1440 (9th Cir. 1994) (party's letter commencing arbitration constituted writing confirming arbitration agreement in unsigned employee handbook). (Note that, in addition to satisfying formal requirements, the parties' post-dispute "writings" must also satisfy applicable substantive requirements for formation of an agreement to arbitrate. *See infra* pp. 393-474.)

10. *"Writing" requirements under national arbitration legislation.* Arbitration statutes in most jurisdictions also impose formal requirements on international arbitration agreements. Historically, these requirements paralleled the provisions of Article II of the New York Convention, while more recent enactments have substantially reduced or eliminated such formal requirements.

(a) *"Writing" requirement under 1985 UNCITRAL Model Law.* Consider Article 7(2) of the UNCITRAL Model Law, as it was adopted in 1985, excerpted at p. 88 of the Documentary Supplement. How does Article 7(2)'s *"writing"* requirement compare to that of Article II(2) of the New York Convention? How would *Sphere Drake* and *Lark* be decided under Article 7(2)? Is Article 7(2) of the 1985 UNCITRAL Model Law broader or narrower than Article II(2) of the Convention?

(b) *"Writing" requirement under FAA.* As noted above, §2 of the FAA also contains a "writing" requirement. Consider the language of §2 (referring to a "written provision in any maritime transaction or a contract evidencing a transaction involving commerce"). Note also the separate reference in §2 to "an agreement in writing to submit to arbitration an existing controversy." What meaning do these phrases suggest? Are they broader or narrower than Article II(2)'s writing requirement? Section 2 has been interpreted as less stringent than that under Article II(2). Lower U.S. courts have held that the parties' acceptance—either orally or by conduct—of an unsigned, written contract containing an arbitration clause satisfies §2 of the FAA. *McAllister Bros., Inc. v. A & S Transp. Co.*, 621 F.2d 519, 524 (2d Cir. 1980); *Imptex Int'l Corp. v. Lorprint Inc.*, 625 F.Supp. 1572 (S.D.N.Y. 1986).

(c) *"Writing" requirement under French Code of Civil Procedure and Swedish Arbitration Act.* Consider Article 1507 of the French Code of Civil Procedure. Compare §1 of the Swedish Arbitration Act. Do they impose any form requirements for arbitration agreements?

(d) *"Writing" requirement under Swiss Law on Private International Law.* Consider Article 178(1) of the SLPIL, excerpted at p. 158 of the Documentary Supplement. How does its *"writing"* requirement compare to that of Article II(2)? With Article 7(2) of the UNCITRAL Model Law? How would *Sphere Drake* and *Lark* have been decided under Article 178(1)?

(e) *"Writing" requirement under 2006 Revisions of UNCITRAL Model Law.* Consider the 2006 revisions of the Model Law, excerpted at pp. 97-101 of the Documentary Supplement. What exactly does Option 2 for Article 7 of the revised Model Law provide? Does it impose any written form requirement at all?

Consider Option 1 of Article 7 of the 2006 Model Law. Although Option 1 retains a "writing" requirement, what is the substance of this requirement? What is the effect of the following text: "an arbitration agreement is in writing if its content is recorded in any form, whether or not the arbitration agreement or contract has been concluded orally, by conduct, or by other means"? Consider what types of written records might be made of agreements concluded orally, by conduct or otherwise.

What is the rationale for the 2006 revisions to Article 7 of the Model Law? Is it wise? Compare the New Zealand Arbitration Act, which provides in Article 7(1) of the First Schedule that "an arbitration agreement may be made orally or in writing," and Article 1681 of the Belgian Judicial Code (which has been amended in 2013 to eliminate the writing requirement), to §2A of the Singapore International Arbitration Act and §19(1) of the Hong Kong Arbitration Ordinance, incorporating Option 1 of Article 7 of the 2006 Model Law. Which option is preferable?

(f) *"Writing" requirement under institutional rules.* Consider Article 4(1)(e) of the 2012 ICC Rules, Article 1(1)(ii) of the 2014 LCIA Rules, Article 9(3) of the 2014 WIPO Rules and Article 2(3) of the 2014 ICDR Rules. How does Article 2(3) of the 2014 ICDR Rules correlate with Article 1 of the same rules, from which the "writing" requirement has been deleted by the 2014 amendments?

11. *Good faith and estoppel as grounds for satisfying writing requirement.* Suppose that Party A places a written order on its standard terms and conditions (containing an arbitration clause), and that Party B fulfils the order, but without sending a written confirmation; suppose further that Party A accepts Party B's performance, but that disputes later arise over payment. Can Party A invoke formal defects in the arbitration agreement if Party B seeks to initiate an arbitration? Or, is Party A estopped or pre-

vented by principles of good faith from challenging the formal validity of the arbitration agreement?

Consider the analysis in *Award in VIAC Case No. SCH-4366*. Is that persuasive? Suppose that there had been no letter acknowledging receipt of the two relevant contracts. Would applicable form requirements have been satisfied? *See also China Nanhai Oil Joint Serv. Corp. Shenzhen Branch v. Gee Tai Holdings Co.*, XX Y.B. Comm. Arb. 671 *et seq.* (1995) (H.K. Ct. First Inst. 1994) (doctrine of good faith and estoppel apply as international principles under Articles II(2) and V(1) of Convention: "on a true construction of the Convention there is indeed a duty of good faith" requiring award debtor to raise jurisdictional objection); *Jiangxi Provincial Metal & Minerals Imp. & Exp. Corp. v. Sulanser Co.*, [1995] 2 HKC 373 (H.K. Ct. First Inst.) (award debtor whose letters affirmed existence of arbitration agreement estopped from challenging validity of agreement); G. Born, *International Commercial Arbitration* 691-92 (2d ed. 2014).

12. *Non-statutory enforcement of unwritten arbitration agreement.* Suppose an arbitration agreement does not satisfy the writing requirement of either the New York Convention or national arbitration legislation. Does this mean that the unwritten arbitration agreement is therefore invalid and unenforceable? Do either Article II(2) of the Convention or §2 of the FAA provide that "arbitration agreements which do not satisfy the foregoing writing requirement are void"? In some states, it may be possible to enforce unwritten arbitration agreements under generally-applicable rules of contract law. Develop arguments for and against such enforcement.

13. *Applicability of New York Convention in arbitral proceedings.* The New York Convention is, by its terms, directed towards the actions of "Contracting States" and the decisions of national courts. See, for example, the provisions of Articles II(1), II(3), and V. Does the Convention apply in arbitral proceedings? If a party argues to an arbitrator that the Convention requires recognition of an arbitration agreement, is the arbitrator bound to apply the Convention? As *ICC Case No. 6149, supra* pp. 290-92, and *Award in VIAC Case No. SCH-4366* illustrate, arbitrators are often receptive to arguments based on the Convention.

On the other hand, some tribunals have refused to apply limitations imposed by the Convention (*e.g.*, Article II(2)'s writing requirement), reasoning that the Convention does not apply to arbitrators. Consider:

> "The Convention ... deals only with the recognition and enforcement in a Contracting State of arbitral awards made in another Contracting State. The Convention does not contain substantive provisions which are directly applicable to the determination as to the competence of arbitrators according to the law of the country in which the arbitral award is rendered. The arbitrators are therefore not bound by the Convention in determining their competence. The question whether in the present case there exists 'a written agreement' within the meaning of Article II(2) of the Convention therefore does not have to be answered by the arbitrators." *Award in Netherlands Oils, Fats, & Oilseeds Trade Ass'n Case of 20 March 1977*, III Y.B. Comm. Arb. 225 (1978).

Compare *Final Award in ICC Case No. 7626*, XXII Y.B. Comm. Arb. 132, 137 (1997) (applying "writing" requirement of Article II (2)). Is this persuasive? On what theory would the Convention apply to arbitral proceedings?

4. Substantive Validity of International Arbitration Agreements

It is elementary that an international arbitration agreement, like other contracts, gives rise to issues of substantive validity. In the vocabulary of the New York Convention and the UNCITRAL Model Law, the arbitration agreement may be "null and void," "inoperative," or "incapable of being performed."[25] Early commentators remarked that "[t]he invalidity of the arbitration agreement under the law applicable to it pursuant to Article V(1)(a) has scarcely ever been invoked, and never successfully."[26] This observation is no longer correct: there is now a substantial body of authority involving challenges to the substantive validity of international arbitration agreements, with a number of decisions upholding such challenges.[27]

The categories of substantive invalidity of arbitration agreements contained in the Convention and most developed national arbitration legislation are limited to cases where such agreements are invalid on generally-applicable contract law grounds (*e.g.*, mistake, fraud, unconscionability, impossibility, waiver). Importantly, these lists of grounds for challenging the substantive validity of arbitration agreements are exclusive: they provide exceptions to the presumptive validity of agreements to arbitrate.[28]

There are two basic categories of objections to the validity of international arbitration agreements. First, there can be challenges that parallel those which are available under generally-applicable contract law to contest the validity of any contract. In particular, these grounds include unconscionability or duress, fraudulent inducement or fraud, illegality, impossibility or changed circumstances, and waiver. Second, in some jurisdictions, special rules of invalidity apply to some categories of disputes (treating agreements to arbitrate differently from other types of contracts); these rules are frequently referred to under the doctrine of "nonarbitrability."

The first set of grounds for challenging the validity of arbitration agreements are examined immediately below. The second set is examined in the following section.[29] In both instances, the focus is on commercial arbitration agreements, rather than investment or inter-state arbitration agreements.

a. Unconscionability and Duress

Basic principles of contract law in most jurisdictions provide that unconscionable agreements, or agreements obtained through duress, are unenforceable. When international disputes arise, parties sometimes argue either that contracts containing arbitration provisions, or the arbitration agreements themselves, are unconscionable and that this precludes enforcement of the arbitration clause.[30] The following materials illustrate the application of rules regarding unconscionability, duress, and related doctrines to international commercial arbitration agreements.

---

25. *See* New York Convention, Arts. II(1), II(3); UNCITRAL Model Law, Arts. 7, 8(1); *infra* pp. 393-474. *See* G. Born, *International Commercial Arbitration* 833 (2d ed. 2014).

26. A. van den Berg, *The New York Arbitration Convention of 1958* 282 (1981).

27. *See* G. Born, *International Commercial Arbitration* 834 (2d ed. 2014).

28. *See supra* pp. 177-90 & *infra* pp. 393-474.

29. *See infra* pp. 475-510.

30. *See* G. Born, *International Commercial Arbitration* 856 (2d ed. 2014).

NETHERLANDS CODE OF CIVIL PROCEDURE
Article 1028(1)

If by agreement or otherwise one of the parties is given a privileged position with regard to the appointment of the arbitrator or arbitrators, the other party may, in derogation of the agreed appointment procedure, request the District Court judge hearing applications for interim relief to appoint the arbitrator or arbitrators.

BROWER v. GATEWAY 2000, INC.
676 N.Y.S.2d 569 (N.Y. App. Div. 1998)

MILONAS, Justice Presiding. Appellants are among the many consumers who purchased computers and software products from defendant Gateway 2000 through a direct-sales system, by mail or telephone order. As of July 3, 1995, it was Gateway's practice to include with the materials shipped to the purchaser along with the merchandise a copy of its "Standard Terms and Conditions Agreement" ... The Agreement begins with a "NOTE TO CUSTOMER," which provides, in slightly larger print than the remainder of the document, in a box that spans the width of the page: "This document contains Gateway 2000's Standard Terms and Conditions. By keeping your Gateway 2000 computer system beyond thirty (30) days after the date of delivery, you accept these Terms and Conditions." The document consists of 16 paragraphs, and, as is relevant to this appeal, paragraph 10 of the agreement, entitled "DISPUTE RESOLUTION," reads as follows:

> "Any dispute or controversy arising out of or relating to this Agreement or its interpretation shall be settled exclusively and finally by arbitration. The arbitration shall be conducted in accordance with the Rules of Conciliation and Arbitration of the International Chamber of Commerce. The arbitration shall be conducted in Chicago, Illinois, U.S.A. before a sole arbitrator. Any award rendered in any such arbitration proceeding shall be final and binding on each of the parties, and judgment may be entered thereon in a court of competent jurisdiction."

Plaintiffs commenced this action on behalf of themselves and others similarly situated for compensatory and punitive damages, alleging deceptive sales practices in seven causes of action, including breach of warranty, breach of contract, fraud and unfair trade practices. In particular, the allegations focused on Gateway's representations and advertising that promised "service when you need it," including around-the-clock free technical support.... According to plaintiffs, ... they unable to avail themselves of this offer because it was virtually impossible to get through to a technician....

Insofar as is relevant to appellants, who purchased their computers after July 3, 1995, Gateway moved to dismiss the complaint based on the arbitration clause in the Agreement. Appellants argued that the arbitration clause is invalid under U.C.C. 2-207, unconscionable under U.C.C. 2-302 and an unenforceable contract of adhesion. Specifically, they claimed that the provision was obscure; that a customer could not reasonably be expected to appreciate or investigate its meaning and effect; that the [ICC] was not a forum commonly used for consumer matters; and that because ICC headquarters were in France, it was particularly difficult to locate the organization and its rules. To illustrate just how inaccessible the forum was, appellants advised the court that the ICC was not registered with the Secretary of State, that efforts to locate and contact the ICC had been unsuccessful and that apparently the only way to attempt to contact the ICC was through the United States

Council for International Business, with which the ICC maintained some sort of relationship.

In support of their arguments, appellants submitted a copy of the ICC's Rules ... and contended that the cost of ICC arbitration was prohibitive, particularly given the amount of the typical consumer claim involved. For example, a claim of less than $50,000 required advance fees of $4,000 (more than the cost of most Gateway products), of which the $2000 registration fee was nonrefundable even if the consumer prevailed at the arbitration. Consumers would also incur travel expenses disproportionate to the damages sought, which appellants' counsel estimated would not exceed $1,000 per customer in this action, as well as bear the cost of Gateway's legal fees if the consumer did not prevail at the arbitration; in this respect, the ICC Rules follow the "loser pays" rule used in England. Also, although Chicago was designated as the site of the actual arbitration, all correspondence must be sent to ICC headquarters in France.

The [lower] court dismissed the complaint as to appellants based on the arbitration clause in the Agreements delivered with their computers. We agree with the court's decision ... in all respects but for the issue of the unconscionability of the designation of the ICC as the arbitration body.

First, the court properly rejected appellants' argument that the arbitration clause was invalid under U.C.C. 2-207. Appellants claim that when they placed their order they did not bargain for, much less accept, arbitration of any dispute, and therefore the arbitration clause in the agreement that accompanied the merchandise shipment was a "material alteration" of a preexisting oral agreement. Under U.C.C. 2-207(2), such a material alteration constitutes "proposals for addition to the contract" that become part of the contract only upon appellants' express acceptance. However, as the court correctly concluded, the clause was not a "material alteration" of an oral agreement, but, rather, simply one provision of the sole contract that existed between the parties. That contract, the court explained, was formed and acceptance was manifested not when the order was placed but only with the retention of the merchandise beyond the 30 days specified in the Agreement enclosed in the shipment of merchandise. Accordingly, the contract was outside the scope of U.C.C. 2-207.

In reaching its conclusion, the [trial] court took note of the litigation in Federal courts on this very issue, and, indeed, on this very arbitration clause. In *Hill v. Gateway 2000, Inc.*, 105 F.3d 1147 [(7th Cir. 1997)], plaintiffs in a class action contested the identical Gateway contract in dispute before us, including the enforceability of the arbitration clause. As that court framed the issue, the "[t]erms inside Gateway's box stand or fall together. If they constitute the parties' contract because the Hills had an opportunity to return the computer after reading them, then all must be enforced." The court then concluded that the contract was not formed with the placement of a telephone order or with the delivery of the goods. Instead, an enforceable contract was formed only with the consumer's decision to retain the merchandise beyond the 30-day period specified in the agreement. Thus, the agreement as a whole, including the arbitration clause, was enforceable....

Second, with respect to appellants' claim that the arbitration clause is unenforceable as a contract of adhesion, in that it involved no choice or negotiation on the part of the consumer but was a "take it or leave it" proposition, we find that this argument, too, was properly rejected by the [trial] court. Although the parties clearly do not possess equal bargaining power, this factor alone does not invalidate the contract as one of adhesion. As the [trial] court observed, with the ability to make the purchase elsewhere and the express option to return the goods, the consumer is not in a "take it or leave it" position at all; if any term of the agreement is unacceptable to the consumer, he or she can easily buy a competitor's product instead ... and reject Gateway's agreement by returning the merchandise. The consumer has 30 days to make that decision. Within that time, the consumer can inspect the goods and examine and seek clarification of the terms of the agreement; until those 30 days have elapsed, the consumer has the unqualified right to return the merchandise, because the goods or terms are unsatisfactory or for no reason at all.

While returning the goods to avoid the formation of the contract entails affirmative action on the part of the consumer, and even some expense, this may be seen as a trade-off for the convenience and savings for which the consumer presumably opted when he or she chose to make a purchase of such consequence by phone or mail as an alternative to on-site retail shopping. That a consumer does not read the agreement or thereafter claims he or she failed to understand or appreciate some term therein does not invalidate the contract any more than such claim would undo a contract formed under other circumstances....

Finally, we turn to appellants' argument that the [trial] court should have declared the contract unenforceable, pursuant to U.C.C. 2-302, on the ground that the arbitration clause is unconscionable due to the unduly burdensome procedure and cost for the individual consumer. The [trial] court found that while a class-action lawsuit ... may be a less costly alternative to the arbitration (which is generally less costly than litigation), that does not alter the binding effect of the valid arbitration clause contained in the agreement....

[U]nder New York law, unconscionability requires a showing that a contract is "both procedurally and substantively unconscionable when made." ... [T]here must be "some showing of 'an absence of meaningful choice on the part of one of the parties together with contract terms which are unreasonably favorable to the other party.'" The ... purpose of this doctrine is not to redress the inequality between the parties but simply to ensure that the more powerful party cannot "surprise" the other party with some overly oppressive term.

As to the procedural element, a court will look to the contract formation process to determine if in fact one party lacked any meaningful choice in entering into the contract, taking into consideration such factors as the setting of the transaction, the experience and education of the party claiming unconscionability, whether the contract contained "fine print," whether the seller used "high-pressured tactics" and any disparity in the parties' bargaining power. None of these factors supports appellants' claim here. Any purchaser has 30 days within which to thoroughly examine the contents of their shipment, including the terms of the Agreement, and seek clarification of any term therein. The Agreement itself, which is entitled in large print "STANDARD TERMS AND CONDITIONS AGREEMENT," consists of only three pages and 16 paragraphs, all of which appear in the same size print. Moreover, despite appellants' claims to the contrary, the arbitration clause is in no way "hidden" or "tucked away" within a complex document of inordinate length, nor is the option of returning the merchandise, to avoid the contract, somehow a "precarious" one. We also reject appellants' insinuation that, by using the word "standard," Gateway deliberately meant to convey to the consumer that the terms were standard within the industry, when the document clearly purports to be no more than Gateway's "standard terms and conditions."

With respect to the substantive element, which entails an examination of the substance of the agreement in order to determine whether the terms unreasonably favor one party, we do not find that the possible inconvenience of the chosen site (Chicago) alone rises to the level of unconscionability. We do find, however, that the excessive cost factor that is necessarily entailed in arbitrating before the ICC is unreasonable and surely serves to deter the individual consumer from invoking the process. Barred from resorting to the courts by the arbitration clause in the first instance, the designation of a financially prohibitive forum effectively bars consumers from this forum as well; consumers are thus left with no forum at all in which to resolve a dispute....

While it is true that, under New York law, unconscionability is generally predicated on the presence of both the procedural and substantive elements, the substantive element alone may be sufficient to render the terms of the provision at issue unenforceable. Excessive fees, such as those incurred under the ICC procedure, have been grounds for finding an arbitration provision unenforceable or commercially unreasonable (*see, e.g., Matter of Teleserve Systems*, 659 N.Y.S.2d 659).

In [another case involving a Gateway arbitration clause], the Federal District Court stated that it was "inclined to agree" with the argument that selection of the ICC rendered the clause unconscionable, but concluded that the issue was moot because Gateway had agreed to arbitrate before the [AAA]. The court accordingly granted Gateway's motion to compel arbitration.... Plaintiffs in that action ... contend that costs associated with the AAA process are also excessive, given the amount of the individual consumer's damages, and their motion for reconsideration of the court's decision has not yet been decided. While the AAA Rules and costs are not part of the record before us, the parties agree that there is a minimum, nonrefundable filing fee of $500, and appellants claim each consumer could spend in excess of $1,000 to arbitrate in this forum. Gateway's agreement to the substitution of the AAA is not limited to the [other case involving Gateway]. Gateway's brief includes the text of a new arbitration agreement that it claims has been extended to all customers, past, present and future (apparently through publication in a quarterly magazine sent to anyone who has ever purchased a Gateway product). The new arbitration agreement provides for the consumer's choice of the AAA or the ICC as the arbitral body and the designation of any location for the arbitration by agreement of the parties, which "shall not be unreasonably withheld." ...

As noted, however, appellants complain that the AAA fees are also excessive and thus in no way have they accepted defendant's offer (*see* U.C.C. 2-209); because they make the same claim as to the AAA as they did with respect to the ICC, the issue of unconscionability is not rendered moot, as defendant suggests. We cannot determine on this record whether the AAA process and costs would be so "egregiously oppressive" that they, too, would be unconscionable. Thus, we modify the order on appeal to the extent of finding that portion of the arbitration provision requiring arbitration before the ICC to be unconscionable and remand to Supreme Court so that the parties have the opportunity to seek appropriate substitution of an arbitrator pursuant to the FAA (9 U.S.C. §5)....

BAUTISTA v. STAR CRUISES, NORWEGIAN CRUISE LINE, LTD
396 F.3d 1289 (11th Cir. 2005) (also excerpted above at pp. 138-42)

RESTANI, Chief Judge. [The facts are excerpted above at pp. 138-42.] ... [W]e turn to the other relevant jurisdiction prerequisite, *i.e.*, that the party seeking arbitration provide "an agreement in writing" in which the parties undertake to submit the dispute to arbitration. Convention, Art. II(1). Agreements in writing include "an arbitral clause in a contract or an arbitration agreement, signed by the parties or contained in an exchange of letters or telegrams." Convention, Art. II(2).

NCL supplied the district court with copies of the employment agreement and the Standard Terms signed by each crewmember. Although Plaintiffs claim the crewmembers did not have an opportunity to review the entirety of the Standard Terms before signing, Plaintiffs do not dispute the veracity of the signatures. Accordingly, this documentation fulfills the jurisdictional prerequisite that the court be provided with an agreement to arbitrate signed by the parties. Plaintiffs try in vain to identify three reasons why the signed documents fail to constitute agreements in writing.

First, Plaintiffs impugn the incorporation of the Standard Terms into the employment agreement, citing decisions of other Circuits that interpret Article II(2) to require inclusion of an arbitration provision in a signed agreement or an exchange of letters or telegrams. *Std. Bent Glass*, 333 F.3d at 449; *Kahn Lucas Lancaster, Inc. v. Lark Int'l Ltd.*, 186 F.3d 210, 218 (2d Cir. 1999). This argument fails to address the fact that the crewmembers signed the Standard Terms, the document containing the arbitration provision.

Second, Plaintiffs assert that, in order to satisfy the agreement-in-writing requirement, NCL bears an "evidentiary burden" of establishing that the crewmembers knowingly agreed to arbitrate disputes arising from the employment relationship. The parties disagree as to whether the crewmembers were specifically notified of the arbitration provision, and each side supports its position with affidavits. Plaintiffs also emphasize the general solicitude of seamen reflected in the Jones Act.... Plaintiffs, however, offer no authority indicating that the Convention or the Convention Act impose upon the party seeking arbitration the burden of demonstrating notice of knowledgeable consent. To require such an evidentiary showing in every case would be to make an unfounded inference from the terms of the Convention and would be squarely at odds with a court's limited jurisdictional inquiry, an inquiry colored by a strong preference for arbitration. It is no better to style Plaintiffs' defective notice claim as an affirmative defense, as virtually every case would be susceptible to a dispute over whether the party resisting arbitration was aware of the arbitration provision when the party signed the agreement. In the limited jurisdictional inquiry prescribed by the Convention Act, we find it especially appropriate to abide by the general principle that "[o]ne who has executed a written contract and is ignorant of its contents cannot set up that ignorance to avoid the obligation absent fraud and misrepresentation." *Vulcan Painters v. MCI Constructors*, 41 F.3d 1457, 1461 (11th Cir. 1995)....

The Convention requires that courts enforce an agreement to arbitrate unless the agreement is "null and void, inoperative or incapable of being performed." Plaintiffs do not articulate their defenses in these terms, claiming instead that the arbitration provision is unconscionable and the underlying dispute is not arbitrable. For purposes of analysis, we style the former as a "null and void" claim and the latter as an "incapable of being performed" claim. "[T]he Convention's 'null and void' clause ... limits the bases upon which an international arbitration agreement may be challenged to standard breach-of-contract defenses." *DiMercurio v. Sphere Drake Ins. Plc*, 202 F.3d 71, 79 (1st Cir. 2000). The limited scope of the Convention's null and void clause "must be interpreted to encompass only those situations—such as fraud, mistake, duress, and waiver—that can be applied neutrally on an international scale." *Id.* at 80.

Plaintiffs do not claim fraud, mistake, duress or waiver. Instead, Plaintiffs allege that the crewmembers were put in a difficult "take it or leave it" situation when presented with the terms of the employment. Plaintiffs argue that state-law principles of unconscionability render the resulting agreements unconscionable. They support this position by citing ... *First Options,* 514 U.S. at 944 ("courts generally ... should apply ordinary state-law principles that govern the formation of contracts"). In [*First Options*], however, the Court applied the FAA, not the Convention. Domestic defenses to arbitration are transferable to a Convention Act case only if they fit within the limited scope of defenses described above. Such an approach is required by the unique circumstances of foreign arbitration: "concerns of international comity, respect for the capacities of foreign and transnational tribunals, and sensitivity to the need of the international commercial system for predictability in the resolution of disputes require that we enforce the parties' agreement even assuming that a contrary result would be forthcoming in a domestic context." *Mitsubishi*, 473 U.S. at 629. While it is plausible that economic hardship might make a prospective Filipino seaman susceptible to a hard bargain during the hiring process, Plaintiffs have not explained how this makes for a defense under the Convention. It is doubtful that there exists a precise, universal definition of the unequal bargaining power defense that may be applied effectively across the range of countries that are parties to the Convention, and absent any indication to the contrary, we decline to formulate one....[31]

JUDGMENT OF 17 FEBRUARY 1989
XV Y.B. Comm. Arb. 455 (1990) (Hanseatisches Oberlandesgericht)

[A German shipping company ordered from the respondent, a Japanese shipyard, the design and construction of a ship for a price of DM 46.5 million. The claimant, an assignee of the German shipping company, initiated litigation against the respondent in German courts on the ground that the price charged by the respondent was inflated since it included, among other things, a large commission which had been paid to a company in Monrovia, Liberia. The claimant also asserted that the interest which respondent received on the whole amount paid was excessive. The claimant alleged tortious misconduct by the respondent and based its claims for damages on German tort law.

The respondent objected to the German litigation on the ground that the claimant was bound by an arbitration clause in the shipbuilding contract, providing: "All disputes arising out of or in connection with this Contract shall be referred to and finally settled by arbitration held by The Japan Shipping Exchange, Inc. in accordance with the provisions of the Rules of Maritime Arbitration of the Exchange. Arbitration shall take place in Tokyo, in English language...." A German appellate court upheld the arbitration clause, in the judgment excerpted below.] ...

[T]he Japanese Civil Code of Procedure does not contain a provision similar to §1025(2) of the amended German Civil Code of Procedure. Pursuant to this section, an arbitration agreement is invalid if one of the parties has used any superiority it has by virtue of its economic or social position in order to constrain the other party to enter into the

---

31. This is not to say that the crewmembers were at the complete mercy of NCL. As noted above, the government of the Philippines, through the POEA, regulated the hiring process with the stated purpose of protecting the interests of seamen....

agreement or to accept conditions therein, resulting in one party having an advantage over the other in the procedure, in particular, with respect to the appointment of the arbitrators.... Beyond that, however, a German court has also to consider whether the arbitration agreement which is valid under foreign law corresponds to German public policy, because this correspondence determines whether a German citizen who calls upon a German court is to be given legal protection or whether protection is to be refused because of the jurisdiction of the arbitral tribunal which has been agreed upon. This Court considers the provision of §1025(2) as part of German public policy of the law on arbitration agreements. That provision prohibits "unconscionable" contracts which go against the judgment of all reasonable and fair men....

It is true that for the German party considerable difficulty is caused by the seat of the arbitral tribunal having been agreed upon in Tokyo given the great distance, the language problems and the foreign culture, whereas the Japanese defendant has the typical advantage of being on his homeground. But that would apply *mutatis mutandis* if a German city had been agreed upon as the seat of the arbitral tribunal. From that alone it cannot be concluded that an economic or social superiority was used. After all, the arbitral procedure must take place somewhere. However, it may be considered as a defect of the arbitration clause that the arbitral tribunal shall have its seat in the country of one of the contracting parties at all. An international arbitral procedure should in principle take place in a "neutral" third country under the chairmanship of someone from a third country. This is in fact required by the principle of "arm's length" or of "fair trial," which should also and especially apply in an arbitral procedure....

The reasons for this are obvious: If the arbitral procedure takes place in the country of one party, the chairman is, as a rule, a citizen of that country and, together with the arbitrator appointed by the party concerned gives rise to a national preponderance in the arbitral tribunal. Furthermore, the judicial control of the arbitral procedure—perhaps in a challenge procedure or if the arbitral award is attacked—will also be exercised by judge of one party's nationality, if one disregards the rare exceptions where the parties have waived the possibility of control by the courts from the beginning, as has recently been made possible in Belgium ... and in Switzerland (Article 192 of the new [SLPIL]).... There should, indeed, be no suspicion against an independent judge of a civilized country that he would not decide impartially and objectively and—if required by the legal situation—also in the disfavor of the party of his nationality, or even of his State itself. Nevertheless, such a judge is said to be impartial, but not "neutral." This means that despite all his personal integrity the judge is, so to speak, "biased" in respect of the legal culture of his country, its position of interest and its whole way of thinking, and that therefore in borderline cases his award *could* turn out different ... from the case in which a citizen of a third country were called upon to make the decision.

This view which—in any event with respect to the person of the chairman—has always been taken into due account worldwide in all football matches, has developed in the field of international arbitration, into a general principle of law. Currently, countless international arbitration proceedings take place in the country of one of the contracting parties with a non "neutral" chairman without—as far as can be seen—a court ever having taken offence at that and having declared a corresponding arbitration clause to be invalid. This is—still—acceptable to the international legal community. It is true that the practice of choosing a third country for international arbitration proceedings is predominant nowadays.... But a general belief in the necessity *(opinio necessitatis)* of proceeding in that way has not yet been formed. For example, Art. 2(6) [of the ICC Rules provides] that the sole arbitrator or the chairman of an arbitral tribunal should have the nationality of a different country. However, the second sentence allows exceptions to this principle. A "neutral" country as the seat of the arbitral tribunal is also not prescribed in these rules of arbitration which have been agreed upon worldwide. Consequently in this regard also, this Court cannot deny the validity of the arbitration clause under consideration....

The contracting parties have accepted arbitration of the "Japan Shipping Exchange, Inc." under the "Tokyo Maritime Arbitration Rules." The claimant has put forward nothing against this arbitration, and furthermore an analysis of the "Rules" by this Court has not given rise to any objections. In particular, the ability to be an arbitrator does not depend on the membership of a specific association which, if one party is a member and the other is not, would mean the invalidity of the arbitration clause.... The list of arbitrators is also open—at least pursuant to the "Ordinary Rules," which apply to a higher sum in dispute as is presently at stake.

JUDGMENT OF 26 JANUARY 1989

1989 NJW 1477 (German Bundesgerichtshof)

The claimant is liquidator of the assets of the former claimant (debtor). As part of a long business relationship, the debtor produced injection-molded parts for the defendant.... The parties' relationship was originally based on a contract of January 1, 1977. The contract provides that, at the defendant's option, a fast-track arbitral procedure could be used to resolve disputes. Sections 2 to 4 of the arbitration agreement annexed to the contract read...: "2 For the purposes of any dispute, Company G will choose a neutral person out of the economic sector or the legal sector as an arbitrator. The arbitrator will then decide the dispute definitely for both sides. The decision is immediately enforceable without any opposition. 3 (1) There must always be conducted only one procedure against each other. (2) If the proceedings are held before a court, lawyers must be appointed as counsel. (3) If an arbitration is carried out, the parties are represented by themselves exclusively. 4 The amount of dispute of each procedure is limited to a maximum of DM 7000." ...

If §4 of the arbitration agreement is interpreted as barring any claims in excess of DM 7000, then the arbitration agreement ... is ineffective because it constitutes an excessive restriction of the claimant's rights to legal remedy and is thus immoral *(contra bonos mores)*. According to the jurisprudence of the German Federal Supreme Court, §138(1) of the German Civil Code has the function of giving effect to the fundamental principles and basic standards of the legal system against abuses of the freedom of contract.... The present case relates to the ... serious matter of a restriction of rights of legal remedy before courts which has not yet been treated by the Federal Supreme Court. It derives from the rule-of-law principle of the [German Constitution] that an effective legal remedy must be ensured in civil disputes. This legal remedy must allow a comprehensive factual and legal analysis of the subject matter and a binding decision by a judge. An effective legal remedy also means that it can be obtained within reasonable time. Without an effective legal remedy the recognized legal rights of individuals would have but little practical importance. Because of its essential importance for the existence of the legal order, the legal remedy may be waived in advance even by party agreement in specific embodiments at the most, but not in the abstract.

In the present case, the parties have already restricted their legal remedies by having agreed to an arbitration clause. Although this is generally permitted by §1025(1) of the German Code of Civil Procedure—subject to §§1025(2) and 1027 of the Code of Civil Procedure—, it must not lead to a one-sided disadvantage of a party, and it must not deprive a party of essential legal remedies. That is, however, the case here. According to §13 III of the contract, the arbitration clause is drafted unilaterally in favor of the defendant; the defendant—and it alone—will be able to determine in each case at its own option whether court litigation or an arbitration procedure will be conducted. The defendant could therefore decide in each of the proceedings initiated by the claimant, that the other path must be taken. When conducting an arbitration proceeding in practice, the defendant shall be granted an inappropriate influence to the extent that it alone may select the single arbitrator.... Furthermore, §3 II and III of the arbitration agreement provide that the parties shall appoint lawyers as counsel in ordinary proceedings, whereas they must represent themselves in an arbitration; that violates §1034(1)(2) of the Code of Civil Procedure which provides that lawyers may not be excluded as representatives in arbitration proceedings and that agreements to the contrary are invalid ...; the defendant [also] thereby seeks to determine to some extent the choice of the parties' weapons.

An additional serious limitation arises from the fact that the parties may conduct "only one procedure against each other" according to §3 I of the arbitration agreement, whereas the amount in dispute of each proceeding is limited to DM 7,000 pursuant to §4.... [T]his means that a subject matter that exceeds the value of DM 7,000—provided for its divisibility—would have to be split among multiple processes, and that only after final judicial conclusion of the first procedure—possibly after several years of proceedings—a second procedure could be initiated, whereby the final clarification of a larger complex dispute could be postponed indefinitely; in case of doubt, this scheme would have again an one-sided impact in favor of the defendant, as the claimant [under German law] is obliged to perform in advance....

Taking all these factors together, it is clear that the legal remedy of the claimant is ... excessively restricted by the arbitration agreement, which is not compatible with the fundamental principles of existing law. This applies particularly to the commands and prohibitions to limit the subject of any proceedings to a maximum value of DM 7,000 or to set up several procedures simultaneously.... Legitimate interests of the defendant that could justify such a rule, are not apparent. Cost considerations may, in individual cases, make a partial claim seem advisable, they do however not justify a full commitment aiming thereto at the cost of a possibly endlessly deferred settlement of the entire complex....

The provisions of the arbitration agreement constitute a related indivisible unit and must be regarded in total as void....

GUTIERREZ v. ACADEMY CORP.
967 F.Supp. 945 (S.D. Tex. 1997)

KENT, District Judge. On March 24, 1997, Plaintiff filed her ... Complaint alleging that Defendant discriminated against her in violation of Title VII, and constructively discharged her. Now before the Court is Defendant's Motion to Stay Litigation and to Compel Arbitration.... [T]he Motion is GRANTED.

Plaintiff began working for Defendant in October, 1991. On May 2, 1992, Plaintiff signed a document entitled "Waiver, Release of Claims, Indemnification and Arbitration."

In exchange for receiving medical and other benefits under Defendant's Work Related Accident Program ..., Plaintiff agreed to submit to final and binding arbitration for "any and all disputes, claims and/or disagreements," specifically including "any claim of discrimination or other claim relating to any violation of the Texas Commission on Human Rights Act, Title VII of the Civil Rights Act, the Equal Pay Act, Age Discrimination in Employment Act, Rehabilitation Act or any other law." In the agreement, the parties specified that it would be governed by the FAA.

Despite her signing of this arbitration agreement, after Plaintiff was terminated, she filed suit against Defendant in this Court.... Defendant now seeks to compel Plaintiff to arbitrate her claims pursuant to her agreement and stay this action until the completion of the arbitration. Plaintiff opposes arbitration and alleges that ... the arbitration clause is unconscionable. Specifically, Plaintiff claims that on the day she signed the agreement, she asked to take the agreement home to her paralegal husband and to an attorney for legal advice but was told that she had to sign it that day or ... lose the opportunity for the benefits offered under the agreement. Moreover, Plaintiff claims that there was an inequality in bargaining positions when she signed the agreement....

This case presents a different set of facts than many compulsion of arbitration cases. In this case, the arbitration clause under which Plaintiff's claims fall is not simply a clause in an employment contract or other contract, as is true in many cases. Rather, it is part of an agreement the whole subject of which is arbitration, release of claims, and indemnification. The relevance of this distinction comes into play in deciding whether Plaintiff's complaints regarding the unconscionability of the agreement and the unequal bargaining positions are to be decided by the court or by an arbitrator. Most cases involving this issue concern arbitration clauses in employment or other contracts and hold that if a plaintiff's complaints regarding the enforceability of the clause relate to the entire contract, they must be decided by an arbitrator, but if they relate to the arbitration clause itself, the court must decide them. *See Rojas v. TK Comm., Inc.*, 87 F.3d 745 (5th Cir. 1996) (... because plaintiff's claim that her employment agreement was an unconscionable contract of adhesion related to the entire agreement, rather than just the arbitration clause, the FAA required that her claims be heard by an arbitrator); *R.M. Perez & Assoc., Inc. v. Welch*, 960 F.2d 534 (5th Cir. 1992) (... if a plaintiff's claim of fraud relates to the arbitration clause itself, the court should adjudicate the fraud claim, but if it relates to the entire agreement, the FAA requires that the fraud claim be decided by an arbitrator).

The Court follows these cases and holds that in a case such as this, involving an arbitration, release, and indemnification agreement, if a plaintiff's claims regarding the enforceability of the agreement relate to the entire agreement, they must be decided by an arbitrator. But where a plaintiff's claims are directed at particular clauses, this Court is obligated to interpret those clauses according to the law and decide the plaintiff's claims. In this case, Plaintiff's complaints regarding the enforceability of the agreement is an attack on the agreement and the formation of the agreement, not on any clause in particular. As stated above, Plaintiff contends that she was not given time to seek legal advice before signing the agreement and that there was an inequality in bargaining positions when the agreement was formed. The Court finds that it is for the arbitrator to decide whether Plaintiff's allegations are true and meritorious and whether they are sufficient to invalidate the entire agreement.

The Court would offer the arbitrator some guidance in evaluating the enforceability of an agreement such as the one in this case. It is important to ascertain whether this agreement was extended to all employees of like class and circumstance or whether it was offered to one or a few individual employees to forestall or impede those individuals' access to the courts. The Court would look harshly upon an attempt by an employer to forestall specific litigation by an individual by presenting him or her with such an agreement. The arbitrator also may want to consider whether the consideration for such an agreement was reasonable in the circumstances. Furthermore, it is important that the choice of responses were clearly presented to the employees and that the employer made them aware of the benefits and disadvantages of the choice made....

NOTES

1. *Unconscionability and duress under New York Convention.* Are unconscionability and duress available as defenses to the validity of an arbitration agreement under the New York Convention? Nothing in Article II or Article V refers specifically to either unconscionability or duress, right?

   Consider the analysis in *Bautista* of the possibility of unconscionability objections under the Convention. *See also Khan v. Parsons Global Servs. Ltd*, 480 F.Supp.2d 327, 340 (D.D.C. 2007) ("unconscionability is *not*—and indeed *cannot* be—a recognized defense to the enforceability of arbitration agreements falling under the Convention"; "by its very nature, the defense of unconscionability seeks to promote those very tenets that are contrary to a finding of certainty, namely: policy, fairness, and appeals to a court's discretion outside of the letter of the law"); *Judgment of 1 March 2011*, DFT 4A_514/2010, ¶4.1.2 to 4.2.1. (Swiss Fed. Trib.) ("[l]ike any other contract, an arbitration agreement may be affected by a vitiation of consent," including duress: "A duress in vitiation of consent exists where a person—a party or a third person—intentionally and unlawfully incites another person to enter into a legal act. Duress is based on the threat of future harm if the person refuses to comply; it vitiates the party's will at the stage of will formation."). Is this persuasive? Note that unconscionability is a well-settled ground for contractual invalidity in all jurisdictions, applied equally to both commercial contracts and arbitration agreements. Is unconscionability not one of the classic grounds for holding an arbitration agreement "null and void" under the Convention?

2. *Unconscionability and duress under UNCITRAL Model Law.* Note that unconscionability and duress are not referred to in Article 8 (or Articles 34 and 36) of the UNCITRAL Model Law. It is nonetheless clear that both defenses are recognized under the Model Law. *See* G. Born, *International Commercial Arbitration* 812-15, 856-66 (2d ed. 2014). *See also* Ware, *Arbitration and Unconscionability After* Doctor's Associates, Inc. v. Casarotto, 31 Wake Forest L. Rev. 1001 (1996). What is the source of the unconscionability and duress standards that are to be applied in Model Law jurisdictions? Is it local contract law? Or is it uniform standards of unconscionability and duress, derived from the character and purposes of the Model Law and the arbitral process? How relevant are unconscionability decisions, in one Model Law jurisdiction, in other Model Law jurisdictions?

3. *Application of separability presumption to claims that underlying contract is unconscionable.* Suppose a party complains that the price paid for goods, and the other

commercial terms of the underlying contract, were unconscionably one-sided. Does that claim have any consequences for the arbitration clause in the contract?

How does the separability presumption apply to the challenges to the agreement in *Gutierrez*? Was the underlying waiver agreement different from other types of commercial contracts? Does that affect application of the separability presumption? Why is it that the court decided in *Gutierrez* that the claimant's challenge did not concern the arbitration agreement, but only the parties underlying contract? What did that challenge allege? Compare the challenge in *Gateway*. What did the unconscionability claim focus on there?

How does the separability presumption apply to the challenges to the agreement in *Judgment of 26 January 1989* and *Judgment of 17 February 1989*? Was part of the challenge in each case directed at the parties' underlying contract? At the parties' arbitration agreement?

4. *Allocation of competence to decide claims that underlying contract is unconscionable*. Like other defenses to the validity of arbitration agreements, claims of unconscionability raise issues as to the respective roles and competence of courts and arbitrators.

(a) *Allocation of competence under FAA to decide claims that underlying contract is unconscionable*. Is there any reason that the analysis in *Buckeye* should not apply to claims of unconscionability? As *Gutierrez* illustrates, most U.S. courts have cited *Buckeye* and *Prima Paint* as authority for referring claims that the parties' underlying contract is unconscionable to arbitration. *See Jenkins v. First Am. Cash Advance of Ga., LLC*, 400 F.3d 868, 877 (11th Cir. 2005) ("FAA does not permit a federal court to consider claims alleging the contract as a whole was adhesive"); *Madol v. Dan Nelson Auto. Group*, 372 F.3d 997, 1000 (8th Cir. 2004) ("plaintiffs' arguments that their … transactions were generally unconscionable were subject to resolution by an arbitrator, absent a showing by the plaintiffs that the [arbitration clause], standing alone, was invalid"). Is this persuasive? Consider the court's decision in *Gutierrez*. Is it consistent with these decisions?

A few U.S. courts have treated claims that the parties' underlying contract is unconscionable as an issue for judicial resolution, and usually then rejected the claim. *Nagrampa v. MailCoups, Inc.*, 469 F.3d 1257, 1264 (9th Cir. 2006) (court, rather than arbitrator, addresses procedural unconscionability of underlying contract because California law "requires the court to consider, in the course of analyzing the validity of the arbitration provision, the circumstances surrounding the making of the entire agreement"); *Murphy v. Check 'N Go of Cal., Inc.*, 2007 WL 3016414 (Cal. App.) (refusing to require arbitration of claim that arbitration clause was unconscionable, notwithstanding provision for arbitration of "any assertion by you or us that this Agreement is substantively or procedurally unconscionable": "in this contract of adhesion, the provision for arbitrator determinations of unconscionability is unenforceable").

(b) *Allocation of competence to decide claims that underlying contract is unconscionable under prima facie jurisdiction standard*. How would unconscionability claims directed at the underlying contract be dealt with under French or Indian law? *See supra* pp. 274-75. Is an unconscionability claim directed at the underlying contract even a jurisdictional challenge to the validity of the arbitration agreement? If so, what standard would be applied in actions to enforce the arbitration agreement under French and Indian law?

(c) *Allocation of competence to decide claims that underlying contract is unconscionable under UNCITRAL Model Law.* Should an unconscionability claim directed at the underlying contract be regarded as a jurisdictional challenge under the Model Law? What was the approach of the German courts in *Judgment of 26 January 1989* and *Judgment of 17 February 1989*?

5. *Allocation of competence to decide claims that underlying contract was procured by duress.* Establishing duress generally requires a showing of a wrongful act or threat compelling a party's involuntary submission to an agreement—classically, a party who is forced to sign a contract at gunpoint. If the contract contains an arbitration clause, should a court or an arbitrator decide the claim of duress? *Compare Merrill Lynch, Pierce, Fenner & Smith, Inc. v. Haydu*, 637 F.2d 391, 398 (5th Cir. 1981) ("claims regarding duress and unconscionability are ones that ... would be decided by an arbitrator, not the district court, since they go to the formation of the entire contract rather than to the issue of misrepresentation in the signing of the arbitration agreement"); *Serv. Corp. Int'l v. Lopez*, 162 S.W.3d 801, 810 (Tex. App. 2005) ("duress ... issue relates to the contract as a whole and not solely the arbitration provision. It is therefore an issue to be decided in arbitration") *with Flannery v. Tri-State Div.*, 402 F.Supp.2d 819, 825 (E.D. Mich. 2005) ("duress argument ... questions whether the arbitrator could derive power from the clause contained in it").

How could a claim that a contract was procured by duress (*e.g.*, at gunpoint), if proven, not also impeach the validity of the arbitration agreement? Does this necessarily affect the allocation of jurisdictional competence to consider claims that the arbitration agreement is invalid?

6. *Allocation of competence to decide claims that arbitration agreement is unconscionable.* Consider the unconscionability claims in *Gateway, Judgment of 26 January 1989* and *Judgment of 17 February 1989*. Were these claims directed at the underlying contract, or the arbitration agreement? Compare the unconscionability claims in *Gutierrez*, which were directed at the underlying contract. How would the *Gutierrez* court have decided *Gateway*? And vice versa? To which agreement were the claims in *Bautista* directed?

How should the competence to decide claims that the arbitration agreement itself is unconscionable be allocated between the arbitral tribunal and national courts? Are there peculiarities about claims of unconscionability that make them inappropriate for arbitration? Note that claims of unconscionability, directed at arbitration clauses, will often concern the means of selecting the arbitrators or the arbitral procedures. The facts in *Judgment of 26 January 1989*, *Judgment of 17 February 1989* and *Gateway* illustrate this. If an arbitration clause is unconscionable, how can an arbitrator, selected and acting pursuant to the agreement, reasonably decide the unconscionability claim? Is this true of all unconscionability claims, or only some?

(a) *Allocation of competence under FAA over claims that arbitration agreement is unconscionable.* As *Gateway* illustrates, claims that the agreement to arbitrate itself was unconscionable are generally held to be the subject of judicial resolution under the FAA. Nonetheless, a few U.S. courts have required arbitration of claims that an arbitration clause is unconscionable. *See, e.g., WMX Tech., Inc. v. Jackson,*

932 F.Supp. 1372 (M.D. Ala. 1996) (alleged lack of mutuality claim could, as a matter of law, only apply to entire contract, and was, therefore, for judicial resolution). What justifies this?

What effect does *First Options* have on the allocation of competence under the FAA to decide claims that an arbitration agreement is unconscionable? Suppose that an arbitration clause provides specifically that unconscionability claims will be subject to arbitration. Does this constitute "clear and unmistakable" evidence of an agreement to arbitrate such claims? Or is that provision itself tainted by the unconscionability claim? Note that the arbitration clause in *Gateway* incorporated the ICC Rules. Consider Article 6 of the 1998 ICC Rules. What effect did the *Gateway* court give to Article 6? Is this consistent with *First Options?*

(b) *Allocation of competence to decide claims that arbitration agreement is unconscionable under prima facie jurisdiction standard.* How would unconscionability claims, directed at the arbitration agreement itself, be addressed under French or Indian law? In light of the issues raised concerning the ability of arbitrators to consider challenges to their own selection and procedures, is this approach wise?

(c) *Allocation of competence to decide claims that arbitration agreement is unconscionable under prima facie jurisdiction standard.* How would unconscionability claims, directed at the arbitration agreement itself, be addressed under the UNCITRAL Model Law? How should they?

7. *Choice of law applicable to unconscionability claims.* Claims of unconscionability present choice-of-law issues: what law defines the degree of unfairness which will invalidate an agreement? Consider what law the courts in *Gateway, Judgment of 26 January 1989* and *Judgment of 17 February 1989* applied to claims that the parties' arbitration agreement was unconscionable. Did any of these courts apply (a) the law governing the arbitration agreement, or (b) absent that, the law governing the underlying contract or the law of the arbitral seat? Why not?

Note the German courts' conclusions in *Judgment of 26 January 1989* and *Judgment of 17 February 1989* that issues of unconscionability, at least as directed to the parties' arbitration clause, implicated German public policies which were mandatorily applicable to protect German litigants. Is this analysis persuasive? Compare the approach in *Gateway.*

8. *Reluctance of national courts to find international arbitration agreements unconscionable.* As the court's decision in the *Judgment of 17 February 1989* illustrates, national courts have been reluctant to invalidate arbitration agreements on unconscionability grounds. For authority, *see Judgment of 14 July 1995*, XXI Y.B. Comm. Arb. 643, 645 (1996) (Hertogenbosch Gerechtshof) (rejecting claim that enforcement of arbitration clause would be "unjustly onerous": "an arbitration such as this is certainly not unusual and is frequently chosen for efficiency's sake"); *Grow Biz Int'l Inc. v. D.L.T. Holdings, Inc.*, XXX Y.B. Comm. Arb. 450 (2005) (Prince Edward Island S.Ct. 2001) (rejecting claim that party was "weaker party" and lacked mental capacity: "There is clear evidence that Tanton had legal advice, or had the opportunity to receive legal advice, when she signed the franchise agreement"); *Doctor's Assocs., Inc. v. Distajo*, 107 F.3d 126 (2d Cir. 1997) (rejecting claims that arbitration clause was unconscionable); *Doctor's Assocs., Inc. v. Stuart*, 85 F.3d 975 (2d Cir. 1996) (rejecting

claim that arbitration clause was unconscionable because of AAA's filing fees, cost of travelling to arbitral seat, arbitrator's fees and alleged bias of AAA).

Consider the result in *Gateway*. Is it correct to conclude that the arbitration agreement was unconscionable? Consider the notice to the purchaser, the purchaser's freedom to reject the clause and the use of internationally-recognized arbitral institutions. After Gateway accepted the AAA (in addition to the ICC) as the administering authority, was there a persuasive argument that the arbitration clause was unconscionable?

Compare the decision in *Judgment of 26 January 1989*. Was the German court correct in holding that the arbitration clause was unconscionable? What features of the clause were most objectionable?

9. *Grounds for holding arbitration agreements unconscionable*. Courts and arbitral tribunals have considered claims that arbitration agreements (or provisions thereof) are unconscionable in a variety of cases. Note that many unconscionability claims in U.S. courts arise in the context of consumer disputes which, in some European jurisdictions, may be nonarbitrable. *See infra* p. 458.

(a) *Form contracts and contracts of adhesion*. The fact that an arbitration clause was included in a form contract does not necessarily render the clause unenforceable. *Compare Coleman v. Prudential-Bache Sec., Inc.*, 802 F.2d 1350 (11th Cir. 1986) (arbitration clause in form contract not unconscionable) *with Aamco Transmissions Inc. v. Kunz*, (1991) 97 Sask. R. 5 (Saskatchewan Ct. App.) (refusing to recognize award made in United States on grounds that form contract signed by unsophisticated party was not binding). Note that the court in the *Judgment of 26 January 1989* was influenced by the fact that the arbitration agreement conferred substantial benefits on the party that drafted it. Compare the analysis in *Gateway*, rejecting claims that the arbitration clause was invalid because it was in a standard form contract. Aren't virtually all terms of many transactions prescribed by standard form contracts? If these terms are valid (*e.g.*, warranties, delivery terms), why shouldn't arbitration clauses also be valid?

(b) *Disparity in bargaining power*. U.S. and other courts have generally refused to hold arbitration agreements unconscionable merely because there was a disparity in the parties' bargaining power. *See Great W. Mortgage Corp. v. Peacock*, 110 F.3d 222 (3d Cir. 1997); *Gilmer v. Interstate/Johnson Lane Corp.*, 500 U.S. 20, 33 (1991) ("mere inequality in bargaining power" is not basis to hold arbitration agreements invalid in employment disputes). Consider the analysis in *Bautista* and *Gateway*.

(c) *Procedural advantages or defects*. Unconscionability claims are most likely to be accepted where a party with materially greater bargaining power obtains terms of an arbitration agreement that give it a disproportionate advantage (for example, with respect to selection of the arbitrators, fees, arbitral procedures, or waivers of substantive rights). That was the basic argument made in the *Judgment of 26 January 1989*. Was the challenge properly rejected? The alleged unfairness of the arbitral procedure was also the basic complaint in *Judgment of 26 January 1989*. What aspects of the arbitral procedure were most objectionable?

Suppose the arbitration clause in *Judgment of 26 January 1989* had only permitted the drafting party to select the arbitrator; would that be sufficient to invalidate the agreement? What if the arbitration agreement had only contained the DM 7,000 (approximately $2,500) limitation; would that have been unconscionable? What if the agreement had only conferred on the drafter the unilateral, asymmetrical right to choose between arbitration and litigation? *Compare Judgment of 22 March 2007*, DFT 4P.172/2006 (Swiss Fed. Trib.) (invalidating clause in arbitration clause in professional athletic association's rules waiving right to seek annulment of arbitral award); *Gonzalez v. Hughes Aircraft Employees Fed. Credit Union*, 82 Cal.Rptr.2d 526 (Cal. Ct. App. 1999) (arbitration clause unconscionable because of time limits for filing claims, limits on discovery and asymmetrical right to arbitrate); *Judgment of 24 September 1998*, 1999 NJW 282 (German Bundesgerichtshof) (undue procedural advantage where party was given right to choose between litigation in court and arbitration); *Judgment of 10 October 1991*, XIX Y.B. Comm. Arb. 200 (1994) (German Bundesgerichtshof) (invalidating arbitration clause providing only three days to notify seller of defects and requiring non-legally qualified arbitrators).

Other courts have rejected unconscionability claims based on alleged one-sidedness of various aspects of the arbitral procedures. *Webb v. Investacorp, Inc.*, 89 F.3d 252 (5th Cir. 1996) (rejecting claim that arbitral forum was more favorable and convenient to one party); *Doctor's Assocs., Inc. v. Stuart*, 85 F.3d 975 (2d Cir. 1996) (rejecting claim that clause was unconscionable because of AAA's fees, cost of travelling to arbitral seat, cost of arbitrator's fees and alleged bias of AAA); *Judgment of 31 January 2002*, II Gaz. Pal., Cahiers de l'arbitrage 303 (French Cour de cassation) (requirement that one party may select arbitrator, from a pre-agreed list, not unconscionable).

Some arbitration statutes address the fairness of the contractually-agreed appointment mechanism for arbitrators. In addition to the Netherlands Code of Civil Procedure, Art. 1028(1), *see* German ZPO, §1034(2) ("If the arbitration agreement grants preponderant rights to one party with regard to the composition of the arbitral tribunal which place the other party at a disadvantage, that other party may request the court to appoint the arbitrator or arbitrators in deviation from the nomination made, or from the agreed nomination procedure."). How would these provisions apply in *Gateway* and *Judgment of 26 January 1989*?

(d) *Costs of arbitral procedure.* As *Gateway* suggests, some courts have relied on the financial aspects of arbitral procedures in holding arbitration agreements unenforceable. *See, e.g., Cole v. Burns Int'l Sec. Serv.*, 105 F.3d 1465 (D.C. Cir. 1997) (arbitration clause, required as condition of employment, cannot validly require former employee to pay portion of arbitrators' fees). *Compare J.B. Harris Inc. v. Razei Bar Indus. Ltd*, 181 F.3d 82 (2d Cir. 1999) (rejecting argument that arbitration in Israel would be prohibitively expensive).

Is *Gateway*'s refusal to enforce the arbitration clause in question justified? Why is it that the ICC procedures were unconscionably expensive? Suppose that some of Gateway's customers were businesses. Would the ICC arbitration clause still be unenforceable? Suppose that a small, financially-strapped business had ordered 250 Gateway computers, at a total cost of $500,000. Would the applicable ICC arbitration clauses be unconscionable? Isn't the real problem in *Gateway* that it is hard to efficiently resolve a small consumer claim for several hundred dollars—either in arbitration or litigation?

Suppose that a party to an arbitration clause is based in a country affected by economic difficulties and that the hard currency needed to pay the ICC's fees cannot be obtained. Under the *Gateway* rationale, does this make the parties' arbitration agreement unenforceable?

(e) *Ignorance of arbitration clause.* Courts have generally rejected claims that an arbitration clause is invalid because a party was unaware of its presence in a contract it signed. Consider the analysis in *Bautista. See also Judgment 11 July 1992*, XXII Y.B. Comm. Arb. 715, 720 (1997) (Italian Corte di Cassazione) ("it is the party signing a contract in a foreign language who has the burden to ascertain the meaning of the clauses prepared by the other party"); *Judgment of 27 February 1989*, XVII Y.B. Comm. Arb. 581, 583 (1992) (Basel Appellationsgericht) ("appellant has signed a standard contract in English containing an unequivocal arbitral clause. This arbitral clause is valid even though the appellant allegedly did not read it"); *Cohen v. Wedbush, Noble, Cooke, Inc.*, 841 F.2d 282, 287-88 (9th Cir. 1988) ("We see no unfairness in expecting parties to read contracts before they sign them.... We are unable to understand how any person possessing a basic education and fluent in the English language could fail to grasp the meaning of that provision.").

10. *Asymmetrical arbitration agreements.* Claims of unconscionability are not infrequently made against so-called "asymmetrical" arbitration clauses, which permit one party to commence arbitration, or, at its option, litigation, but which do not allow the other party to do so. Confronted with a clause granting one party (but not the other) a unilateral right to commence arbitration, an early English case reasoned:

> "It seems to me that this is about as unlike an arbitration clause as anything that one could imagine. It is necessary in an arbitration clause that either party shall agree to refer disputes to arbitration, and it is an essential ingredient in that either party may in the event of a dispute arising refer it in the provided manner to arbitration. In other words, the clause must give bilateral rights of reference." *Baron v. Sunderland Corp.* [1966] 1 All ER 349, 351 (English Ct. App.).

Is this persuasive? In contrast, contemporary decisions generally reject arguments that asymmetrical arbitration agreements are invalid. *Barker v. Golf U.S.A.*, 154 F.3d 788, 792 (8th Cir. 1998) ("[U]nder Oklahoma law, mutuality of obligation is not required for arbitration clauses so long as the contract as a whole is supported by consideration"); *Doctor's Assocs., Inc. v. Distajo*, 66 F.3d 438, 453 (2d Cir. 1995) ("where the agreement to arbitrate is integrated into a larger unitary contract, the consideration for the contract as a whole covers the arbitration clause as well"); *Wilson Elec. Contractors, Inc. v. Minnotte Contracting Corp.*, 878 F.2d 167, 169 (6th Cir. 1989) ("Because the contract as a whole did not lack consideration, we see no grounds justifying the district court's decision, which appears to be pervaded by 'the old judicial hostility to arbitration.'"). Note the reliance in these decisions on provisions in the "contract as a whole" or the "larger unitary contract." Is this analysis of asymmetrical arbitration agreements consistent with the separability presumption? Are there other reasons for concluding that asymmetrical arbitration clauses are valid?

Some recent lower U.S. courts have relied on theories of unconscionability in holding asymmetrical arbitration clauses invalid, particularly in domestic matters involving consumers or employees. *Armendariz v. Found. Health PsychCare Serv., Inc.*, 6 P.3d 669, 770 (Cal. 2000) ("it is unfairly one-sided for an employer with superior bargaining power to impose arbitration on the employee as plaintiff but not to accept such limitations when it seeks to prosecute a claim against the employee, without at least some reasonable justification ... based on 'business realities'"); *Iwen v. U.S. West Direct*, 977 P.2d 989, 996 (Mont. 1999) (arbitration clause in form contract of telephone company, with consumer, held "completely one-sided" and unconscionable); *Arnold v. United Companies Lending Corp.*, 511 S.E.2d 854, 861 (W. Va. 1998) (in "contract between rabbits and foxes," an asymmetrical arbitration clause was "unreasonably favorable" to corporate lender than to unsophisticated consumer). Compare the German court's decision in *Judgment of 26 January 1989*. Should the asymmetrical character of an arbitration agreement be sufficient to invalidate it on unconscionability grounds? If not, what more should be required?

11. *Validity of arbitration agreement selecting inconvenient or otherwise objectionable arbitral seat.* Suppose that the parties' agreement selects an arbitral seat that is (or becomes) unreasonably inconvenient to one party. Is this inconvenience a ground for challenging the validity of the arbitration agreement, including on the basis of unconscionability or mistake? Recall the criticism, in *Prunier*, of an arbitration clause (in the mid-19th century) requiring small property disputes from all over France to be arbitrated in Paris. *See supra* pp. 178-79. In contrast, contemporary national court decisions have virtually always rejected claims based on the alleged expense and inconvenience of the arbitral seat (at least outside the consumer context). Consider the conclusion in the *Judgment of 17 February 1989*. Note the court's flirtation with suggestions that an arbitration seated in one party's home jurisdiction cannot be impartial. Is that a serious argument? *See infra* pp. 656-57, 1218-41.

Suppose that political, security, or other conditions in the contractually-selected arbitral seat change, making one party reluctant or unwilling to go there. Does that render the arbitration agreement invalid? Again, courts have virtually always answered in the negative. *See infra* pp. 421-35.

In one decision, a claim of unconscionability was rejected where a small U.S. company was forced to arbitrate before a Chinese state-related arbitral institution against a Chinese state entity. *China Res. Prods. (U.S.A.) Ltd v. Fayda Int'l, Inc.*, 747 F.Supp. 1101 (D. Del. 1990). The court noted that the party challenging the arbitration agreement had been aware of the connections between the proposed arbitral institution and its counterparty at the time it entered into the transaction. Compare *Judgment of 17 February 1989*.

12. *Consequences of unconscionability of one term in arbitration agreement.* What are the consequences of a conclusion, as in *Gateway*, that one term of an arbitration agreement is invalid on unconscionability grounds? Is the entire agreement to arbitrate invalid? Or is the offending term deleted or reformed? What does *Gateway* suggest? What does *Judgment of 26 January 1989* suggest?

13. *Court's intervention in merits of arbitrators' decision.* Consider the court's comments in the final paragraph of *Gutierrez* about the substance of the parties' dispute. What relevance, if any, does this have to the arbitrators' decision? Recall that the arbitrators'

mandate is to decide the parties' dispute in an adjudicative process, applying the law; don't the court's comments in *Gutierrez* reflect what the law is? Compare the principle of judicial non-intervention in the arbitral process, discussed below at pp. 797-810.

b. Fraudulent Inducement or Fraud

Two commonly invoked bases for objecting to the validity of international arbitration agreements are fraudulent inducement and fraud.[32] The materials excerpted below illustrate the resolution of claims that either the arbitration agreement or the underlying contract containing it was the product of fraud or fraudulent inducement.

FIONA TRUST & HOLDING CO. v. PRIVALOV
[2007] UKHL 40 (House of Lords)

[excerpted above at pp. 205-11]

JUDGMENT OF 30 MAY 1994
XX Y.B. Comm. Arb. 745 (1995) (Tokyo High Ct.)

[excerpted above at pp. 288-90]

REPUBLIC OF THE PHILIPPINES v. WESTINGHOUSE ELECTRIC CORP.
714 F.Supp. 1362 (D.N.J. 1989)

DEBEVOISE, District Judge. This is an action brought by the Republic of the Philippines and the National Power Corporation ("NPC"), the Philippine government agency responsible for electric power generation, against Westinghouse Electric Corporation ("WECOR"), a Pennsylvania corporation, [Burns & Roe, a New Jersey engineering firm, and other U.S. companies]. This case arises out of the construction of the 600-megawatt Philippines Nuclear Power Plant Unit 1 ("PNPP")…. The fifteen-count complaint alleges breach of contract, fraud, tortious interference with fiduciary duties, negligence, civil conspiracy, RICO violations, antitrust violations and various pendent state claims. Defendants moved to stay this action pending arbitration pursuant to contractual arbitration clauses and §3 of the [FAA] …

[Accepting plaintiffs' allegations,] in the summer of 1973, Ferdinand E. Marcos, then President of the Republic of the Philippines, announced his government's decision to build the nation's first nuclear powerplant…. Westinghouse sought the contract for the construction of the plant's nuclear steam supply system and Burns & Roe was interested in obtaining the architect/engineering ("A/E") contract for the project. Plaintiffs allege that … both Westinghouse and Burns & Roe concluded that the way in which business was done in the Philippines required the retention of a special sales representative ("SSR") who had both access to and influence in Malacanang, the presidential palace…. Since 1972, when Marcos declared a state of martial law, Marcos had ruled the nation largely by decree and his direct assent to such a high-profile project was considered essential. The complaint

---

32. G. Born, *International Commercial Arbitration* 846-53 (2d ed. 2014).

alleges that it was understood that the SSR would offer Marcos a "piece of the action" in order to obtain his endorsement of the bidders.

Westinghouse and Burns & Roe ultimately came to retain Herminio T. Disini as their SSR under separate agreements. Disini was a well-known Philippine businessman and close personal friend of President Marcos whose wife was also Mrs. Marcos cousin and personal physician.... Disini allegedly boasted to Burns & Roe that he could obtain a turnkey contract for PNPP project for Westinghouse including an A/E subcontract for Burns & Roe.

[Allegedly at Marcos' directive, the NPC entered into contract negotiations with Westinghouse. A government negotiating committee comprised of three technical, commercial and legal officials met with Westinghouse in lengthy negotiations. One government representative purportedly recalled, however, that Westinghouse refused to negotiate any critical contract terms: "... Westinghouse knew that it had the President's support and that NPC could not go to any other supplier for the nuclear plant. Therefore Westinghouse could get whatever terms it wanted, and NPC was powerless to bargain effectively...."

Among the terms in the Westinghouse draft contract considered by the legal panel, was the arbitration clause, Article 24. One member of the NPC negotiating committee recalled that Westinghouse was intransigent and indicated that the draft contract was nonnegotiable. Because of prior bad experience with arbitration, NPC wanted the procedural protection available in a judicial forum. Apparently Westinghouse continued to insist on the inclusion of the arbitration clause and the parties were soon at an impasse. According to plaintiffs, however, Marcos repeatedly intervened and, with minor changes to the arbitration clause and other provisions, the contract was eventually executed.] ...

The initial question raised by this motion is whether the plaintiffs' allegations of bribery may be considered in determining whether the action should be stayed pending arbitration. Defendants argue that under the doctrine announced by the Supreme Court in *Prima Paint Corp.*, the allegations are properly directed to the arbitration panel and not the court.... [U]nder either §3 or 4, the arbitration clause is to be treated as conceptually "separable" from the remainder of the contract. "[I]n passing upon a §3 application for a stay while the parties arbitrate, a federal court may consider only issues relating to the making and performance of the agreement to arbitrate." *Prima Paint*, 388 U.S. at 404....

The result in *Prima Paint* is not wholly logical. It leaves federal courts with the rather rare and narrow issue of whether fraud was directed specifically to the arbitration clause while passing the more frequent and usually more complex question of whether fraud was directed to the entire contract to the arbitration panel, a group chosen more for their technical knowledge than their legal skills. This approach also seems to run counter to §2's broad declaration that a written arbitration agreement be considered valid and enforceable "save upon such grounds as exist at law or equity for the revocation of any contract." Nonetheless, subsequent Supreme Court cases have confirmed that *Prima Paint* is alive and healthy and, if nothing else, the case has come to stand as an expression of the Court's militant determination to enforce arbitration agreements freely chosen by the parties. The challenge for the party who believes himself to be the victim of a fraud and wishes to fight it out in court is to demonstrate that the fraud was specifically directed to the arbitration clause or to convince the court to craft some exception to the *Prima Paint* doctrine.

Plaintiffs first argue that bribery should not be treated as fraud in the inducement but as a species of fraud in factum (or fraud in the execution) that vitiates NPC's assent to the agreement and makes the contract void *ab initio*. Plaintiffs, relying primarily upon *Cancanon v. Smith Barney, Harris Upham & Co.*, 805 F.2d 998 (11th Cir. 1986), argue that the defense of fraud in factum creates an exception to *Prima Paint*'s separability rule. *Cancanon* was a securities fraud action brought by purchasers of a money market account who alleged that the defendant brokerage firm wasted their principal in unauthorized trading. The account agreement, a form contract, contained an arbitration clause and the defendant moved for an order compelling arbitration.... Plaintiffs, who did not speak English, argued that since defendant represented that the contract was for a money market account, plaintiffs had never assented to a contract for a securities account. Plaintiffs argued that this fraud in factum, as opposed to fraud in the inducement, voided the entire contract including the arbitration clause and therefore overcame the *Prima Paint* separability doctrine. The *Cancanon* Court adopted the plaintiffs' position. Citing the *Restatement of Contracts*, the court observed that "[w]here misrepresentation of the character or essential terms of a proposed contract occurs, assent to the contract is impossible. In such a case there is no contract at all." Thus, "where the allegation is one of fraud in factum, *i.e.*, ineffective assent to the contract, the issue is not subject to resolution pursuant to an arbitration clause contained in the contract document."

Several other cases have taken positions consistent with this approach. In *Par-Knit Mills, Inc. v. Stockbridge Fabrics Co.*, 636 F.2d 51 (3d Cir. 1980), for instance, the defendant argued that certain documents, which the plaintiff contended were contracts, were signed only as confirmations of delivery dates. The court observed that the "mere execution of a document ... even assuming that it is executed by a corporate agent, does not negate the factual assertion that such signature was not intended to represent a contractual undertaking." If such a defense were mounted against a motion to compel arbitration under §4 of the Act, and if the allegations were set forth in an affidavit, a proceeding held before the case was committed to arbitration and limited to the issue of whether or not an agreement had been reached would be appropriate.

Even if allegations of fraud in factum created an exception to *Prima Paint* doctrine, however, the allegations in the complaint do not set forth such a claim. As the *Cancanon* court made clear, fraud in factum exists where there is a "misrepresentation of the character or essential terms" of a contract. As the authors of the *Restatement* expressed it: "If a misrepresentation as to the character or essential terms of a proposed contract induces conduct that appears to be a manifestation of assent by one who neither knows nor has reasonable opportunity to know of the character or essential terms of the proposed contract, his conduct is not effective as a manifestation of assent." *Restatement of Contracts (Second)* §163. As noted in explanatory comments accompanying this section, "[t]he party may believe that he is not assenting to any contract or that he is assenting to a contract entirely different from the proposed contract." *Id.*, comment a. *See also Langley v. Fed. Deposit Ins. Corp.*, 484 U.S. 86 (1987) (fraud in factum is "the sort of fraud that procures a party's signature to an instrument without knowledge of its true nature or contents"); *Southwest Admin., Inc. v. Rozay's Transfer*, 791 F.2d 769, 774 (9th Cir. 1986) ("[fraud in inducement] induces a party to assent to something he otherwise would not have; [fraud in factum] induces a party to believe the nature of his act is something entirely different than it actually is.").

These explanations demonstrate that the fraud in factum doctrine is inapposite in the present situation. There is no question but that the NPC officials negotiating the contract were fully aware of the nature of its terms; that is why they resisted the Westinghouse draft and why Marcos, in turn, was repeatedly forced to bring pressure to bear in order to override their opposition. Plaintiffs do not claim, nor can they, that they were duped or deceived as to the nature or terms of the agreement as they must in order to make out a claim for fraud in factum. They understood the contract all too well.

What plaintiffs' actually allege is a defense of duress or coercion: Marcos allegedly received payments in return for which he used his power and influence to force the NPC to assent to an oppressive, one-sided agreement. *Cancanon* itself, however, takes pains to distinguish these defenses from those of fraud in factum. In *Merrill Lynch, Pierce, Fenner & Smith v. Haydu*, 637 F.2d 391 (5th Cir. 1981), a stock brokerage customer who signed options trading agreements with arbitration clauses claimed that she had been distracted and coerced by high pressure sales talk amounting under the circumstances to confusion, undue influence and duress. The *Cancanon* court observed that "[t]hese were not allegations of ineffective assent, but rather of fraud in the inducement of a contract.... Thus the [*Haydu*] court properly held that these allegations were subject to resolution by arbitration."

Plaintiffs argue that coercion through bribery is a form of coercion so different in degree and kind that it rises to the level of fraud in factum. Perhaps there is some form of coercion so extreme that is equivalent to a lack of assent. That is not this case, however, and plaintiffs' attempts to force the doctrine to fit their allegations would contort the doctrine beyond recognition.

Alternatively, if plaintiffs could demonstrate that the coercion or duress were directed specifically to the arbitration clause, this would satisfy *Prima Paint* and it would be appropriate to have a hearing on this issue. It is clear that plaintiffs have raised a material issue of fact with respect to whether or not the "commission" payments specifically induced assent to the arbitration clause. As plaintiffs' own papers demonstrate, however, any payments ultimately received by Marcos could not be the basis for voiding the contract or any of its clauses since Marcos was not acting as a third party who coerced the NPC to contract but as the ultimate authority of the nation who had full power to commit the NPC to the contract. [The court considered in detail the political and legal structure of the Philippines in supporting this conclusion.] ...

[Finally, plaintiffs alleged that the powerplant contract was awarded in violation of Philippine competitive bidding rules.] Even if the award of the contract in derogation of ... competitive bidding requirements were illegal under Philippines law, this defense goes to the entire contract as a whole and not to the arbitration clause exclusively. Therefore, under the *Prima Paint* doctrine, this would be a matter for the arbitration panel to consider. In conclusion, plaintiffs' allegations of bribery, even if true, do not make the contract void or voidable since the recipient of the payments, Marcos, had the authority to compel NPC to contract with Westinghouse....

NOTES

1. *Fraudulent inducement/fraud under New York Convention*. Fraudulent inducement as a ground for non-enforcement of an arbitration agreement is not specifically mentioned in the New York Convention; for that matter, neither is fraud in the factum, duress, waiver, or illegality. Are these bases for non-enforcement encompassed within Articles II(3) and V(l)(a) of the Convention, which set forth exception to enforcement

for "null and void" or "invalid" arbitration agreements? Why didn't the *Westinghouse* court refer to the New York Convention?

2. *Fraudulent inducement/fraud under UNCITRAL Model Law.* As with the New York Convention, there is no specific reference in Article 8 (or Articles 34 and 36) of the Model Law to fraud as a basis for non-recognition of an arbitration agreement. Can there be any doubt but that a fraud defense is available? What are the sources for the standards of a fraud defense under the Model Law? Are they derived from the Model Law or from local law standards for fraud in other contexts?

3. *Application of separability presumption in disputes over alleged fraudulent inducement of underlying contract.* As *Fiona Trust, Judgment of 30 May 1994* and decisions such as *Prima Paint* illustrate, the separability presumption has frequently been applied to claims that the parties' underlying contract was fraudulently induced. *See Walter Rau Neusser Oel und Fett AG v. Cross Pac. Trading Ltd*, XXXI Y.B. Comm. Arb. 559 (2006) (Australian Fed. Ct. 2005) ("what is required for §7(5) to be engaged and to justify the matter of avoidance for fraud or otherwise not being referred to the arbitrator for decision, is that the fraud or vitiating conduct be directed to the arbitration clause itself" (citing *Prima Paint*); *Judgment of 3 October 1936, AB Norrköpings Trikåfabrik v. AB Per Persson*, 1936 NJA 521 (Swedish S.Ct.) (fraud in making of main contract has no effect on validity of arbitration clause); *Judgment of 13 February 1978*, VI Y.B. Comm. Arb. 228 (1981) (Naples Corte di Appello).

Why is it that fraudulent inducement to enter into the underlying contract does not also affect the arbitration clause? Suppose, as in *Judgment of 30 May 1994*, one party fraudulently misrepresented the quality of its services (or balance sheet). Does that impeach the parties' agreed dispute resolution mechanism? Does that sort of fraud make it less likely that the defrauded party would agree to arbitrate disputes with the fraudster? Why or why not? Suppose, as in *Fiona Trust*, one party fraudulently bribed employees of the other party in order to procure favorable commercial terms. Does that sort of fraud make it less likely that the defrauded party would agree to arbitrate disputes with the fraudster? How does the House of Lords address this issue?

4. *Allocation of competence to decide disputes over fraud in connection with underlying contract.* Disputes over the alleged fraudulent inducement of the parties' underlying contract raise issues of the allocation of competence.

(a) *Allocation of competence to resolve disputes over fraudulent inducement of underlying contract under FAA.* Note the various descriptions of *Prima Paint* in *Westinghouse, Buckeye* and other decisions. How did *Prima Paint* allocate competence to resolve disputes over the alleged fraudulent inducement of the parties' underlying contract? What role did the separability presumption play in the Court's analysis?

Following *Prima Paint*, U.S. courts have consistently held that a claim that the parties' underlying contract was fraudulently induced is to be resolved by the arbitrators. *See, e.g., Ferro Corp. v. Garrison Indus., Inc.*, 142 F.3d 926, 933 (6th Cir. 1998) ("[T]he arbitration agreement is effectively considered as a separate agreement which can be valid despite being contained in a fraudulently induced contract."); *In re Oil Spill by Amoco Cadiz*, 659 F.2d 789, 794 (7th Cir. 1981) ("a claim of fraud in the inducement of a contract is a matter for arbitration"); *Elliott v. Icon in the Gulch, LLC*, 2010 WL 2025456, at *2-3 (Tenn. Ct. App.) ("When an arbitration agreement in a contract is controlled by the FAA and contains a broad arbitration clause, claims of fraudulent inducement are subject to arbitration."). As *Buckeye* illustrates, U.S. decisions have distinguished between (i) fraud (or other) challenges directed to the parties' underlying contract or to both the underlying contract and the arbitration agreement, on the one hand, and (ii) fraud (or other) challenges directed specifically to the arbitration agreement. *See Moses H. Cone Mem. Hosp. v. Mercury Constr. Corp.*, 460 U.S. 1, 24 (1983); *Southland Corp. v. Keating*, 465 U.S. 1, 11 (1984); *Perry v. Thomas*, 482 U.S. 483, 491 n.8 (1987). In the context of fraud, does this distinction make sense? Consider again the facts in *Fiona Trust*. When one party allegedly bribed the employees of its counterparty, can this really be irrelevant to the formation of the arbitration agreement? Does it nonetheless make sense for such fraud claims to be heard, in the first instance, by the arbitrators?

(b) *Allocation of competence to decide disputes over fraudulent inducement of underlying contract under English Arbitration Act.* Consider the House of Lords decision in *Fiona Trust*. How does its analysis and rule compare to those in *Prima Paint* and *Buckeye*?

(c) *Allocation of competence to decide disputes over fraudulent inducement of underlying contract under prima facie jurisdiction standard.* Recall the *prima facie* jurisdiction approach to the allocation of jurisdictional competence in France, as well as in some Indian, Canadian and other courts. How would the facts in *Judgment of 30 May 1994*, *Prima Paint* and *Fiona Trust* be dealt with under this approach?

(d) *Allocation of competence to decide disputes over fraudulent inducement of underlying contract under Model Law.* How should competence be allocated under the Model Law over claims that the underlying contract was fraudulently induced?

5. *Does arbitration clause extend to claims that underlying contract was fraudulently induced? Prima Paint* and *Fiona Trust* both considered whether the parties' arbitration clause was broad enough to encompass claims that the underlying contract was procured by fraud. What did they conclude? Compare the interpretation of the arbitration clause in *Kulukundis, supra* pp. 191-93.

It will not always be the case that the parties' arbitration clause provides for arbitration of claims of fraudulent inducement. *Prima Paint* referred to a case in which the parties "intended to withhold such issues [*i.e.*, fraudulent inducement] from the arbitrators and to reserve them for judicial resolution." 388 U.S. at 403 n.9 (citing *El Hoss Eng'g & Transp. Co. v. Am. Indep. Oil Co.*, 289 F.2d 346 (2d Cir. 1961)). Consider the interpretative approach of *Fiona Trust*. Is that persuasive? Is that effectively the approach adopted under the FAA? *See infra* pp. 528-29.

6. *"Fraud in the factum" affecting underlying contract.* As *Westinghouse* illustrates, one party may claim that, because of "fraud in the factum," there was never any underlying contract at all—as opposed to a fraudulently induced contract. These sorts of claims involve allegations that one party's signature on the contract was forged or that a document was fraudulently substituted for another. Is there any reason to treat such claims differently from fraudulent inducement claims?

(a) *Allocation of competence to decide "fraud in the factum" claims under FAA.* U.S. courts have reached inconsistent results in dealing with claims that the parties' underlying contract was the product of fraud in the factum, such as forged signatures or falsified pages. In the words of one court, "where the allegation is one of fraud in the factum, *i.e.*, ineffective assent to the contract, the issue is not subject to resolution pursuant to an arbitration clause contained in the contract documents." *Cancanon v. Smith Barney, Harris, Upham & Co.*, 805 F.2d 998, 1000 (11th Cir. 1986). *See Solymar Invs., Ltd v. Banco Santander SA*, 672 F.3d 981, 994 (11th Cir. 2012) ("*Prima Paint* requires reference to an arbitrator for a general challenge to a contract on the grounds of fraud in the inducement."); *Opals on Ice Lingerie etc. v. Bodylines, Inc.*, 320 F.3d 362 (2d Cir. 2003); *Sphere Drake Ins. Ltd v. All Am. Ins. Co.*, 256 F.3d 587, 590 (7th Cir. 2001) ("a person whose signature was forged has never agreed to anything."); *Kyung In Lee v. Pac. Bullion (N.Y.) Inc.*, 788 F.Supp. 155, 157 (E.D.N.Y. 1992) ("if a party's signature were forged on a contract, it would be absurd to require arbitration if the party attacking the contract as void failed to allege that the arbitration clause itself was fraudulently obtained.").

In contrast, other U.S. courts have rejected the distinction between fraud in the factum and fraudulent inducement. These decisions have held that claims of fraud in the factum as to the underlying contract are generally for the arbitrators. *See Alexander v. U.S. Credit Mgt, Inc.*, 384 F.Supp.2d 1003, 1007 (N.D. Tex. 2005) ("challenges claiming that—*as a whole*—a contract is illegal, is void as a matter of law, contains forged signatures … will generally not serve to defeat an arbitration clause"); *AmSouth Bank v. Bowens*, 351 F.Supp.2d 571, 575 (S.D. Miss. 2005) ("since the Bowenses' forgery allegation regards the customer agreement as a whole and not just the arbitration clause of the customer agreement, it is an issue that must be submitted to the arbitrator").

Recall that the U.S. Supreme Court reserved decision in *Buckeye Check Cashing* on the applicability of the separability presumption in cases where the presumption is "whether any agreement between the alleged obligor and obligee was ever concluded." 546 U.S. at 444 n. l; *supra* p. 202 n. 18. The Court also went out of its way to note that its decision did not address the correctness of cases "which hold that it is for courts to decide whether the alleged obligor ever signed the contract, whether the signer lacked authority to commit the alleged principal and whether the signor lacked the mental capacity to assent." *Ibid*. How should the forgery of a signature, or other fraud in the factum, be dealt with under the FAA? Do such allegations necessarily affect the existence of the arbitration clause? Should such allegations be resolved in the first instance by arbitrators or by a court? Even if fraud in the factum allegations affect the existence and validity of the agreement to arbitrate, does this necessarily mean that a court should decide such claims in the first instance?

Why did the alleged bribery in *Westinghouse* not fall within the "fraud in the factum" doctrine? Assume that one contracting party bribes an officer of another contracting party to sign a contract. Would that not constitute deceit as to the essential terms of the agreement? Is it a satisfactory answer to say that the aggrieved contracting party knew that the contract had objectionable features, without knowing of the bribery?

(b) *Allocation of competence to decide "fraud in the factum" claims under English Arbitration Act*. Consider what the House of Lords suggested about fraud in the factum claims in *Fiona Trust*. Note that, as in *Buckeye*, the House of Lords commented that "Issues as to whether the entire agreement was procured by impersonation or by forgery ... are unlikely to be severable from the arbitration clause." *See supra* p. 210. Why is that? Is fraud by impersonation or forgery of contractual documentation so different from fraud by forgery and deceit regarding the parties' commercial transaction?

(c) *Allocation of competence to decide "fraud in the factum" claims under prima facie jurisdiction standard.* Recall again the *prima facie* jurisdiction approach to competence-competence in France, as well as in Indian, Canadian and other courts. How would claims of fraud in the factum be dealt with under this approach?

(d) *Allocation of competence to decide "fraud in the factum claims" under Model Law.* How should claims of fraud in the factum be dealt with under the Model Law? Note that India, Canada and Hong Kong are essentially Model Law jurisdictions—as is England. Which approach is appropriate?

7. *Allocation of competence to decide claims of fraudulent inducement of arbitration agreement.* Suppose that a party claims that it was fraudulently induced to enter into an arbitration agreement. For example, as in *Westinghouse*, a party may claim specifically that the inclusion of an arbitration clause in a contract was fraudulently induced. Who has the competence to resolve such claims? Preliminarily, how likely is such a claim?

(a) *Allocation of competence to decide claims of fraudulent inducement of arbitration agreement under FAA.* Under the FAA, where a party alleges that there was fraud in procuring the arbitration clause itself—as distinguished from the parties' underlying contract—that is generally an issue for judicial resolution. This was expressly recognized in *Prima Paint* and was reaffirmed in *Buckeye*, where the Court held that "a challenge to the validity of the contract as a whole and not specifically to the arbitration clause, must go to the arbitrator." 546 U.S. at 449.

Consistent with this analysis, U.S. courts have generally held that claims of fraud (and other types of invalidity or illegality) will be for judicial determination only when they are "specifically" directed at the arbitration clause itself, and not when they are directed generally at both the underlying contract and the arbitration clause. *Cancanon,* which is discussed in *Westinghouse,* is a good example of this. For other U.S. precedents, *see Sanford v. MemberWorks, Inc.*, 483 F.3d 956 (9th Cir. 2007) ("existence" of arbitration agreement, as distinguished from "validity," is for court); *A.T. Cross Co. v. Royal Selangor(s) PTE, Ltd*, 217 F.Supp.2d 229, 234 (D.R.I. 2002) ("when plaintiff contends that no arbitration agreement was reached, the court, not an arbitrator, must determine the validity of the arbitration agreement"). What does this mean in practice? Suppose one party is alleged to have fraudulently substituted the entire body of the contract (including the arbitration clause), or to have fraudulently misrepresented the contents of the entire contract (including the arbitration clause). Does this satisfy *Buckeye*?

(b) *Allocation of competence to decide claims of fraudulent inducement of arbitration agreement under English Arbitration Act.* Consider the holding in *Fiona Trust*: the "doctrine of separability requires direct impeachment of the arbitration agreement before it can be set aside," and this "is an exacting test." *See supra* p. 211. Further, the jurisdictional challenge "must be based on facts which are specific to the arbitration agreement," and that "[a]llegations that are parasitical to a challenge to the validity to the main agreement will not do." What does this mean in practice? How does one decide whether allegations "directly impeach" the arbitration clause, on the one hand, or are merely "parasitical to the challenge to the validity of the main agreement"?

(c) *Allocation of competence to decide claims of fraudulent inducement of the arbitration agreement under Model Law.* How should competence to decide claims of fraudulent inducement of the arbitration agreement be allocated under the Model Law?

(d) *The* Westinghouse *case.* Consider the *Westinghouse* case; how should the claim of fraudulent inducement of an arbitration clause be resolved? In *Westinghouse*, the plaintiffs alleged that the entire powerplant contract, but including specific demands regarding the arbitration clause, was fraudulently induced through secret bribes. Given that the bribes and intervention of President Marcos were allegedly directed to the arbitration clause specifically, as well as to other portions of the contract, was the *Buckeye* standard satisfied? Are there likely to be many cases in which a party targets fraudulent inducement *solely* at procuring an arbitration clause? Would someone really pay bribes for an agreement to arbitrate? Consider scenarios where this might not be far-fetched.

(e) *Effect of* First Options *on fraudulent inducement claims directed at arbitration agreement.* What effect does *First Options* have on the allocation of competence under the FAA to decide claims that an arbitration agreement was fraudulently induced? Suppose the arbitration clause provides expressly or by incorporation of institutional rules that disputes regarding its validity (including by reason of fraudulent inducement) are to be decided by the arbitrators. Suppose that this provision of the arbitration clause is said to have been fraudulently induced. In answering this hypothetical, recall *First Options'* requirement for "clear and unmistakable" evidence of an agreement to arbitrate questions of arbitrability. *See supra* pp. 230-33, 280-83. Would this standard be satisfied by incorporation of institutional rules granting arbitrators power to decide claims that the arbitration agreement itself was fraudulently induced?

8. *What law governs claims of fraud?* What law governs issues of fraud in connection with the (a) underlying contract, and (b) arbitration agreement? Consider again the discussions of the law governing the underlying contract and the arbitration agreement. *See supra* pp. 90-93, 287-315. Does the same substantive law necessarily govern claims of fraud of the underlying contract and the arbitration clause? Consider what the agreements in *Westinghouse* provided. What substantive laws should have applied to claims that the underlying contract and the arbitration clause were fraudulently induced?

What if an arbitration agreement contains a choice-of-law clause? Does the parties' chosen law apply to claims that the arbitration provision was fraudulently induced? *See Restatement (Second) Conflict of Laws* §201 comment c (1971) ("The fact that a contract was entered into by reason of misrepresentation—does not necessarily mean[] that a choice-of-law provision contained therein will be denied effect. This will only be done if the misrepresentation ... was responsible for the complainant's adherence to the provision.").

c. Impossibility, Frustration and Repudiation

All legal systems appear to recognize impossibility or frustration as an excuse for non-performance of a contractual obligation.[33] The impossibility and frustration doctrines are in principle applicable to international arbitration agreements, although in practice they are rarely applied. As with other generally-applicable contract law defenses, a recurrent issue is whether the separable agreement to arbitrate has been frustrated (as distinguished from whether the underlying contract has been frustrated or become impossible to perform).

The materials excerpted below explore issues relating to application of the impossibility and frustration doctrines to international arbitration agreements. They also examine the related doctrine of repudiation,[34] which is typically invoked where one party claims that an arbitration agreement has been repudiated by virtue of a counterparty's failure to honor its obligations under the agreement.

AWARDS IN ICC CASES NOS. 10373 & 10439

in Lalive, *The Transfer of Seat in International Arbitration*, in *Law and Justice in A Multistate World, Essays in Honor of Arthur T. von Mehren* 515 (2002)

[Professor Lalive discusses two (unpublished) ICC cases (*ICC Case Nos. 10373* and *10439*)] in a dispute involving an American corporation on the one hand and, on the other, the Republic of Serbia and a State enterprise of that country…. [T]he parties had chosen Belgrade as a place of arbitration in a contract entered into in 1990. Some nine years later, disputes arose between the parties, leading to claims and counterclaims, and the American corporation requested first the Arbitral Tribunal, and then the ICC "Court" of International Arbitration to consider its application to change the place of arbitration and designate Geneva instead of Belgrade….

A controversial procedural question arose, which should be mentioned in passing: who had *authority to decide* on the requested change of place? The Arbitration Tribunal or the arbitration institution, here the so-called ICC "Court" (in the absence of any specific provision in the ICC rules)? It was argued, on the Serbian side, surprisingly and hardly convincingly, that in cases where the place of arbitration has been agreed by the parties, *no one* has any authority to modify such a choice, even in the most extreme circumstances, since the ICC "Court" has merely "administrative," and not "judicial" functions! That theory was obviously contrary to the needs of practice and to common sense, as well as, it is submitted, any reasonable interpretation of the ICC Arbitration Rules. It was not adopted in the case under scrutiny, the ICC Court choosing to ask first the Arbitral Tribunal to render an interim award on the binding character, or not, of the original agreement selecting Belgrade….

[T]he request for transfer of seat was based on two grounds, one legal (an interpretation of the contractual clause choosing Belgrade), and the other factual, *i.e.*, the situation allegedly prevailing in Belgrade 2000 under the Milosevic regime. On the first point, it could safely be asserted that the initial choice of place had been, or must have been based on the common understanding or assumption that "Belgrade was, *and would remain*, a legal en-

---

33. G. Born, *International Commercial Arbitration* 890 (2d ed. 2014).
34. G. Born, *International Commercial Arbitration* 886-90 (2d ed. 2014).

vironment conductive to fair and effective international arbitration, in accordance with the ICC Rules." In other words, the arbitration agreement as a whole, and in particular its provision on the place or "seat," was based upon and implied the continuing *trust* of the parties in Belgrade legal environment in accord with the fundamental principles of international arbitration, *i.e.*, regarding the equal treatment of the parties, and the fairness, independence and impartiality of the proceedings and of the arbitrators. Trust in and respect of such fundamental principles (which would seem to be part and parcel of "transnational public policy," as well as a traditional component of the "national" and international public policy of most States), are obviously a precondition of any arbitration agreement, so much so that their mention appears superfluous and indeed futile in all "normal" cases.

But it was contended that arbitration in "Belgrade 2000" (allegedly the very antithesis of the place chosen in 1990 by the parties) was not, and could not be "normal," given the fact that "the Milosevic Government had degraded, intimidated, manipulated and purged the Yugoslav judiciary and [had] placed the Courts in the service of the Government's iron-fisted crackdown on political expression by citizens and its xenophobic hatred of the United States," with the result, among others, that any future award in favor of the claimant [which was an American pharmaceutical company owned or controlled by a well-known political opponent of S. Milosevic, of Yugoslav origin,] would inevitably be annulled in Belgrade. It was recognized by the applicant that the fact that a State is a party to an arbitration is not sufficient, as such and in itself, to justify or compel the transfer of the (agreed) place away from its own territory. But it was stressed that the dispute involved a *de facto* expropriation or confiscation of property by the direct action of the local judiciary (and not only with its apparent complicity). How then could the local courts act in an independent and objective "judicial" manner? And how could arbitrators meeting in "Belgrade 2000" and called upon to decide a "Serbian-American dispute" of some importance be, or feel, really free in an oppressive environment from (direct or indirect) psychological pressures if not from actual personal intimidation?

It should be remembered in this context that the standard of *independence* is an objective one. It suffices that, from an objective point of view, there could arise in the view of a reasonable man "justifiable doubts" as to the independence of the arbitrators. The latter, when exposed to (the risk of) interference by a totalitarian State (known to have eliminated its political opponents by murder and other violent means), runs clearly the risk of losing, *nolens volens*, at least the appearance of independence, and thus the trust of the parties, as well as the respect of international opinion....

First, it should be repeated that a mere transfer of the *place of hearings*, or the choice of another location for the tribunal's deliberations, (*e.g.*, ICC Rules, Art. 14(2), (3)) would obviously fail to answer the preoccupations of the party requesting a change of the "seat," having regard to the possible role of that notion with respect for the applicable procedural law, or for the role of its courts concerning the enforceability and finality of awards. Belgrade, again, is an appropriate illustration. In recent times it was public knowledge that a totalitarian regime led by a Stalinist clique controlled, in particular, the judiciary, the army and the police, and would have no compunction in causing the courts to set aside any unfavorable award which might be rendered against the State itself or a State enterprise. In such an environment, the position of a foreign party involved in a (contractual) dispute with the State, or one of its agencies, is indisputably *not equal* to that of the "State party." The equilibrium between the parties is clearly jeopardized, already during the proceedings themselves (even if the State is cautious enough not to appear to interfere directly …). This equilibrium is imperiled because of the likelihood that local courts will be able to set aside any award considered unsatisfactory by the State party to the arbitration.

The totalitarianism prevailing in recent times in Serbia (including the takeover of the judiciary by the government) endangered, and indeed destroyed, the *equality of the parties* in arbitration. It also affected the very independence of an arbitral tribunal sitting in Serbia and called upon to decide, as said above, a "Serbian-American dispute" of some importance (also involving a personal political opponent of S. Milosevic). Quite apart from the likelihood of threat of an annulment of a future award favorable to the foreign party, the mere knowledge of the violent methods used locally to silence opponents of the regime, [*i.e.*, high-profile assassinations in public places (*e.g.*, Arcan, Balatovic) or attempts (*e.g.*, V. Draskovic)], and the prevailing oppressive environment, could not fail to exercise a psychological pressure upon the minds of many, if not all, arbitrators. This fact should suffice, it is submitted, short of actual personal intimidation, to cast a doubt in the minds of a foreign party and in the general public's mind upon the "remaining" or lasting independence of the arbitrators. How, in such circumstances, could the arbitrators continue to enjoy the full confidence of all parties and be seen to exercise their functions completely, impartially and independently? …

A second fundamental change alleged by the foreign claimant was the unilateral assignment by the State of its contractual obligations to another (state-controlled) contractual partner, against the will of the foreign party. And a third, even more, fundamental change of circumstances, in the claimant's view, was the fact that the Serbian State, acting directly or through its own judiciary (and with its active assistance) had caused a *de facto* expropriation or confiscation of the foreign-owned enterprise. In other words, the State, or rather its State-controlled assignee (and allegedly new contracting party) had *caused* the disturbances and difficulties at the core of the dispute submitted to arbitration, thereby effectively frustrating or destroying the legitimate expectations of the parties (and in particular those of the non-Serbian, *i.e.*, foreign contracting party) regarding the neutrality of the place of arbitration….

[M]ention should be made of some of the (few) known arbitral precedents where a transfer of seat would appear to be, at least to the detached observer, quite justified on the basis of the *rebus sic stantibus* principle. But such "precedents" as known seem contradictory and not decisive. In general, arbitrators may be said to be and to have been very cautious, and understandably reluctant, to weaken the rule *pacta sunt servanda* and to excuse non-performance or adaptation by resorting to *rebus sic stantibus*. But it is doubtful whether the same solutions can be "transposed," so to speak, mechanically from the general field of non-performance or "adaptation" of (substantive) contractual obligations to the particular, procedural domain of the "choice of seat" clause (which … is in general little more than an ancillary modality, based on practical considerations of convenience).

In one of the cases where Teheran had been agreed upon (before 1979) as the place of arbitration, an international arbitral tribunal had no alternative, with regard to the troubled circumstances of the time in that city, but to transfer the seat to another country. In another case, the ICC Court unilaterally changed the place it (and not the parties) had previously fixed in Bangkok. What is remarkable is that the *ratio decidendi* was not any existing local threats to the security and independence of the arbitrators or the parties, but the fact that (in the absence of legislation) the award would not have been enforceable. In still another case, where the defending party was obstructing the arbitration in the Courts of Abu Dhabi, the contractual seat, the arbitrators proposed in their draft terms of reference a transfer to another country, but the ICC Court, with excessive but perhaps characteristic timidity, refused.... [1987 ASA Bull. 293]

In a recent ICC Award, an American company had requested that the (originally agreed) seat of arbitration in Belgrade be transferred to a neutral place, such as Geneva—in the circumstances described above, *i.e.*, because of the totalitarian Serbian regime. The Arbitral Tribunal did not have the courage ... to accept the request—which would, of course, have implied expressing a view on the nature of the Milosevic regime and its consequences on the "Rule of Law."...

One reason retained by the Tribunal was that the risk of annulment by the courts of the seat (in case of an award unfavorable to the Serbian party) did exist even at the time of execution of the arbitration agreement (although the award concedes that such a risk may have become a certainty in 1996 when Milosevic and his party took control). Furthermore, the Tribunal relies on *Hilmarton* and *Chromalloy* (notwithstanding cases like *Baker Marine* and *Martin I. Spier*) to reject the argument that an award hypothetically rendered in favor of the American claimant and annulled in Belgrade would not be enforced outside Serbia. More clearly controversial is ...:

> "Unlike the judge of a selected forum whose decision may not be impartial due to the political environment of that forum, the members of this Tribunal are totally independent from any Serbian authority, be it a governmental one or a judicial one. Indeed, the three arbitrators have been confirmed in their function by the ICC Court after having signed a declaration of independence and their removal or replacement remains within the sole competence of that Court. Furthermore, the three arbitrators are nationals of third countries and do not reside in Serbia; therefore, any possible threat from whatever Serbian or Yugoslav authority would have no impact on their decision, whatever it may be and whichever party it may favor. Under these circumstances, the award to be rendered shall be *free* from any governmental influence, intimidation etc. and that consideration is sufficient to find that the parties legitimate expectancies when signing the arbitration clause shall be totally implemented."

That the Arbitral Tribunal should find it convenient or necessary to reaffirm its own independence from Serbian influence is hardly surprising, but is it sufficient? A negative answer could be based, it is submitted, on several reasons [referring to the arguments outlined above].... The following conclusions may thus be drawn ...:

(a) There is no reason why a choice of place of arbitration contained in an arbitration clause should not, as a general rule, be interpreted *rebus sic stantibus* like any other contractual clause, and according to the common intention of the parties at the time when the contract was executed.

(b) When requested to decide a transfer of the (agreed) place of arbitration, the competent authority (arbitral tribunal, institution or judge) should pay due regard to all relevant circumstances and in particular to the fact that the choice of place is normally a modality of the arbitration agreement, secondary to the common intention of the parties to submit a future dispute to an effective arbitral process.

(c) The integrity of that process, and respect for fundamental principles of arbitration (*e.g.*, due process, equality of the parties, independence of the arbitrators), clearly require priority in a case where substantial and unforeseen change of circumstance would make it "unduly difficult" to carry on the arbitration at the agreed place....

GATOIL INTERNATIONAL v. NATIONAL IRANIAN OIL CO.
XVII Y.B. Comm. Arb. 587 (1992) (QB) (English High Ct. 1988)

On 17 April 1982, the parties entered into a written contract [("Contract")] for the purchase by Gatoil International Inc. ("Gatoil") from National Iranian Oil Company ("NIOC") of a quantity of oil during the period between 1 April and 31 December 1982. Section 8 of the Contract provided for arbitration as follows:

> "Any dispute between the parties arising out of this Contract shall be settled by arbitration in accordance with the laws of Iran. The party who wants to submit such a dispute to arbitration shall advise the other party in writing, stating therein its claim and nominating its arbitror [sic—corrected throughout as "arbitrator"]. The other party shall nominate a second arbitrator within 30 days after receiving the said advice. The two arbitrators thus appointed shall appoint a third arbitrator who shall be the president of the board of arbitration. Should the other party fail to appoint and nominate the second arbitrator or should the two arbitrators fail to agree on the appointment of the third arbitrator within 30 days, the interested party may request the President of the Appeal Court of Tehran, Iran, to appoint the second arbitrator or the third arbitrator as the case may be. The arbitrators appointed as per above provisions shall have broad experience with respect to the petroleum industry practices and oil marketing and be reasonably fluent in written and spoken English. The arbitration award may be issued by majority and shall be binding on both parties. The seat of arbitration shall be in Tehran, unless otherwise agreed by the parties."

Section 10 of the Contract provided that it would be governed and construed according to the laws of Iran.

A dispute arose between the parties regarding the delivery of oil and on 17 March 1987, Gatoil served a writ on NIOC. Gatoil did not wish to arbitrate in Tehran. NIOC was not willing to have the dispute litigated and was only prepared to arbitrate in Tehran. NIOC applied for a mandatory stay under §1(1) of the Arbitration Act 1975, which implements the New York Convention in the United Kingdom,[35] ... [§8 is] a non-domestic arbitration clause and the defendant is entitled, as of right, to a stay of the action under §1(1), unless the Court is satisfied that the arbitration agreement is null and void, inoperative or incapable of being performed....

The first argument relied upon by the plaintiff was directed to the description of the default appointer in the arbitration clause, namely the President of the Appeal Court of Tehran. No such person has existed since the revolution. By the post-revolutionary law, which abolished the Appeal Court, that Court's functions were transferred to the Municipal Court of Tehran, and the function of appointing an arbitrator where the parties are unable to agree is now exercisable by a Judge of that Municipal Court. The experts are also now agreed that if such an appointment had to be made, Art. 644(2) of the Civil Code of Procedure provides that it would have to be from amongst those residing or domiciled within

---

35. Sect. 1(1) of the Arbitration Act 1975 reads: "If any party to an arbitration agreement to which this section applies, or any person claiming through or under him, commences any legal proceedings in any court against any other party to the agreement, or any person claiming through or under him, in respect of any matter agreed to be referred, any party to the proceedings may at any time after appearance, and before delivering any pleadings or taking any other steps in the proceedings, apply to the court to stay the proceedings; and the court, unless satisfied that the arbitration agreement is null and void, inoperative or incapable of being performed or that there is not in fact any dispute between the parties with regard to the matter agreed to be referred, shall make an order staying the proceedings."

the jurisdiction of that Court, a restriction which would not have applied if the President of the Court of Appeal had been the default appointer. [Article 644(2) of the Iranian Civil Code of Procedure reads: "The following persons cannot be appointed as arbiter by drawing lots: ... 2. Persons not residing or domiciled within the territorial jurisdiction of the court which is appointing arbiters."]

Mr. Sabi, the Iranian lawyer engaged by the plaintiff, in his first affidavit pointed to Art. 232 of the Iranian Civil Code, which provides that in regard to contracts: "the following conditions are of no effect, though they do not nullify the contract itself: — Conditions which are impossible to fulfil." Mr. Sabi also relies upon Art. 190 of the Iranian Civil Code, which provides: "For validity of a contract, the following conditions are essential: The intention and mutual consent of both parties." Mr. Sabi says that §8, the arbitration clause, is a condition of the contract and that it lacks two vital elements necessary if it is to be capable of being performed, namely: (a) it is impossible to enforce the provisions relating to the appointment of the second and third arbitrators; and (b) the parties did not intend to constitute the Municipal Court, or a Judge thereof, as the default appointer.

I prefer the opinions expressed by Dr. Movahed and Professor Safai to the effect that §8 is not a condition of the contract but a collateral contract consisting of a number of different conditions or terms. If, as contended by the plaintiff, the condition relating to the default appointer is void, that does not nullify the rest of §8. The parties entered into this contract some two and a half years after the enactment of the Iranian law abolishing the pre-revolutionary Appeal Court and replacing it and its functions with the Municipal Court of Tehran. But as §8 itself is not nullified, and as the parties' mutual intention is to arbitrate further disputes, should they arise, in Tehran, according to the substantive and curial laws of Tehran, it seems to me that they must both be bound by the provisions of law as to the substitute default appointer....

The plaintiff has not appointed its own arbitrator as required by the opening paragraphs of §8.... The defendant is therefore not yet in a position when it is called upon to appoint its own arbitrator. If and when that arises, it seems obvious that it will do so.... It would then fall to the two appointed arbitrators to agree upon the appointment of the third. Only if they failed to agree upon the third appointment would a Judge of the Municipal Court be called upon to exercise his default function. I do not think that I should assume at this stage that the two appointees will not be able to agree upon the third arbitrator. The plaintiff suggests that the defendant's appointee will be likely to be obstructive in the knowledge that this must result in the Municipal Court being called upon to exercise its default function, and thus appoint a third arbitrator from within the restricted class, because this would be the defendant's wish, and the defendant is likely to be consulted by, and would be able to dictate the actions of, its own arbitrator. I am not prepared to assume in advance that the defendant's arbitrator will so abnegate his duty to act independently in agreeing an acceptable third arbitrator.

Even if, in the event, agreement as to the third arbitrator proves impossible and a Municipal Court Judge is called upon to exercise the default function, it is not inevitable that such appointee will have some connection with the defendant, as suggested in ... of Mr. Sabi's first affidavit, though the field of potential candidates will no doubt be more limited than the field which would theoretically have been available to the President of the Court of Appeal. I am not, therefore, prepared to hold that the arbitration clause is inoperative or incapable of being performed on this ground....

[An] alternative ground relied upon by the plaintiff is that, practically speaking, it is impossible for them to find a qualified arbitrator who is willing to go to Tehran. There are exhibited ... four replies from potential arbitrators who were approached in late 1986 and the early months of 1987. Each refused, and there is an unparticularised allegation that a number of other candidates have been approached and have refused. I am asked to infer that the result will be the same, whomsoever is approached and that the arbitration clause is incapable of being performed for that reason.

Of the four replies in evidence it would seem that two were not in any case properly qualified candidates. What can be said by the plaintiff is that despite the ceasefire in the Iran/Iraq war, the evidence of Mr. Sabi shows that Tehran remains an uncomfortable venue and that there are many reasons, good or supposed, which will deter many potential arbitrators from accepting appointment as the plaintiff's nominee. [NIOC accepted] that the plaintiff is in some difficulty in persuading an arbitrator of its choice to accept the appointment, but he contended that difficulty is not enough; the plaintiff has to show that no one suitable from the available field is prepared to accept the appointment. I do not accept that the plaintiff is required to go that far. It would be totally unrealistic to expect any plaintiff to show that it had exhausted the possible field. There must come a point far short of this where the Court can be satisfied on balance of probabilities that a corporation such as the plaintiff is unable, as a practical reality, to find an appointee of its choice who is willing to sit as an arbitrator in Tehran. But I am not satisfied that that point has been reached on the evidence before me.

The required qualifications of the arbitrators are that they should have broad experience of petroleum industry practice and be reasonably fluent in spoken and written English. There is no requirement that they should be legally qualified, though no doubt that would be desirable. Since English is, broadly speaking, the lingua franca of the oil industry worldwide, the potential field is enormous. I think that I am entitled to take judicial notice of the fact that there are likely to be English-speaking people, lawyers and/or oil company executives, all over the world, including of course the important areas of the Third World, who would be acceptable to the plaintiff as arbitrator, and who would not necessarily be deterred from sitting in Tehran…. The defendant was granted the stay it sought.

NATIONAL IRANIAN OIL CO. v. ASHLAND OIL, INC.
817 F.2d 326 (5th Cir. 1987) (also excerpted above at pp. 170-71)

GOLDBERG, Circuit Judge…. [The facts of the case are excerpted above at pp. 170-71. In summary, an Iranian state entity, NIOC, sought to enforce agreements to arbitrate which it had concluded with a U.S. company, Ashland. The arbitration clauses provided for arbitration in Tehran, Iran. In another portion of its opinion, *supra* pp. 170-71, the U.S. court held that the FAA did not permit arbitration to be compelled in Iran. NIOC, therefore, argued (ironically) that the parties' agreement on Tehran as the arbitral seat should be disregarded.]

NIOC also argues that, because it may be "inconvenient" for Ashland to participate in an arbitral proceeding in Iran, this impossibility (or commercial impracticability) renders the forum selection clause without force. NIOC … therefore asserts that the forum selection clause should be severed and Ashland compelled to perform the essential term of the bargain, viz., to participate in an arbitral proceeding (in Mississippi). This syllogism … is fatally flawed.

In *The Bremen v. Zapata Off-Shore Oil Co.*, [407 U.S. 1, 10-12 (1972)], the Supreme Court held ... that forum selection clauses must be strictly enforced, unless the enforcement would be "unreasonable," or unless the resisting party could show "countervailing" or "compelling" reasons why it should not be enforced. But the forum selection clause at issue in *The Bremen* did not relate to the choice of situs in an arbitral proceeding, rather it related to the parties' contractual choice of arbitration as opposed to litigation to resolve its disputes. Thus, in *Sam Reisfeld & Son Import Co. v. SA Eteco*, 530 F.2d 679 (5th Cir. 1976), we held that the test in *The Bremen* was inapposite respecting the enforcement of the choice of situs expressed in an arbitration agreement. In *Reisfeld*, a U.S. company argued that a forum selection clause designating Belgium as the situs of arbitration should not be enforced because "it is so unreasonable that it either vitiates the arbitration clause altogether or requires a transfer to a more neutral situs." We held that the forum selection clause contained in an arbitration provision must be enforced, even if unreasonable. A forum selection clause establishing the situs of arbitration must be enforced unless it conflicts with an "explicit provision of the [FAA]." ... NIOC['s] assertion of inconvenience or impossibility fails [this test].

Under traditional principles of contract law, NIOC's argument that the political atmosphere in Iran renders arbitration there impossible or impracticable certainly supplies an adequate predicate for finding the forum selection clause unenforceable and without effect. "Where only part of the obligor's performance is impracticable his duty to render the remaining part is unaffected if ... it is still practicable for him to render performance that is substantial." *Restatement (Second) of Contracts* §270. But impracticability is an argument upon which NIOC may not rely. In order to assert the doctrine of impossibility or commercial impracticability, the party wishing to assert such a defense must meet two conditions. First, "[t]he affected party must have no reason to know at the time the contract was made of the facts on which he [or she] relies." *Restatement (Second) of Contracts* §266, comment a.... [I]t simply is unimaginable that NIOC, part of the revolutionary government, could not reasonably have foreseen that Tehran would become a forum in which it is indisputably impossible for Americans to participate in any proceedings.

Second, a party may not rely on the doctrine of impossibility or impracticability "[i]f the event is due to the fault of the ... [party] himself [or herself]." *Restatement (Second) of Contracts* §261, comment d. Yet, as part of the revolutionary Government, NIOC certainly bears responsibility for creating the chain of events making it impossible for an American entity reasonably to travel to and to engage in quasi-judicial proceedings in Iran. Thus, NIOC cannot assert the doctrine of impossibility.

Even were NIOC able to rely on the fact that it is now impossible for Ashland to arbitrate in Iran, thus vitiating the forum selection clause, NIOC must show that the venue provision is severable from the rest of the arbitration agreement. Whether the agreement to arbitrate is entire or severable turns on the parties' intent at the time the agreement was executed, as determined from the language of the contract and the surrounding circumstances. NIOC must therefore show that the essence, the essential term, of the bargain was to arbitrate, while the situs of the arbitration was merely a minor consideration.

But the language of the standard form document—drafted by NIOC—belies any such argument. Not only did NIOC choose Tehran as the site of any arbitration, but the contract also provides that Iranian law governs the interpretation and rendition of any arbitral awards. The arbitration agreement also provides that, should one of the parties fail to appoint an arbitrator or should the two arbitrators fail to agree on a third arbitrator, "the interested party may request the *President of the Appeal Court of Tehran* to appoint the second arbitrator or the third arbitrator as the case may be." Indeed, the contract expressly provides that the entire agreement is to be interpreted by reference to Iranian law. The language of the contract thus makes self-evident the importance of Iranian law and Iranian institutions to NIOC. The language of the contract demonstrates that the parties intended the forum selection clause and the arbitral agreement to be entire, not divisible....

NIOC points to the weighty congressional policy favoring the use of arbitration if the parties have contractually agreed to resolve their disputes in this manner. This policy acquires special significance in the international context.... Therefore, we have repeatedly held that "arbitration should not be denied 'unless it can be said with positive assurance that an arbitration clause is not susceptible of an interpretation which would cover the dispute at issue.'" *Phillips Petroleum*, 794 F.2d at 1081 (quoting *Wick v. Atlantic Marine, Inc.*, 605 F.2d 166, 168 (5th Cir. 1979)). At the same time, a corollary "to th[is] principle[] is that the duty to submit a dispute to arbitration arises from contract, therefore a party cannot be compelled to arbitrate a dispute if he has not agreed to do so." *Lodge No. 2504*, 812 F.2d at 221. Thus, NIOC's appeal to congressional policy will not suffice to transform the plain words of the parties' agreement to arbitrate in Tehran, Iran to arbitrate in Jackson, Mississippi....

PARTIAL DECISION OF 2 APRIL 1992
1993 RIW 239 (Kassel Landgericht)

The claimant sought compensation for contractual breaches. The respondent refused to pay voluntarily, and the claimant sought judicial assistance. In this regard, with respect to the dissolution of the Socialist Federal Republic of Yugoslavia ("SFRJ") and the resulting war, due to which all postal and telecommunication connections where interrupted between Ljubljana—capital of the now independent state of Slovenia—and Belgrade/Serbia and due to which direct travel was made impossible, the claimant did not take action before the Court of Arbitration for Foreign Trade of the Economic Chamber of the SFRJ in Belgrade, which was provided for by Art. XII of a contract dated 27 February 1985. Simultaneously, as a measure of precaution, the claimant terminated the agreement on the basis of an important ground. The claimant argues that, as an institution of the Yugoslavian central government, the Economic Chamber of the SFRJ—and thereby its court of arbitration—will not be competent for a company seated in Slovenia. The claimant also argues, in any case, that it cannot be reasonably expected that it seek relief in a court now located in (undisputed) foreign hostile territory. The respondent argues that the claim is inadmissible by reason of the arbitration agreement contained in Art. XII of the agreement. The respondent also refers to ongoing negotiations between the European Community and the government in Belgrade, which are likely to produce near-peace conditions in the foreseeable future, which would enable the court of arbitration to resume action. The court upheld the claimant's action.

Section 1072a of the German Code of Civil Procedure does not preclude jurisdiction, because an arbitration agreement bars the competence of the state courts only insofar as one party thereby is not deprived of every legal remedy that in can be reasonably expected to pursue. According to its content, meaning and purpose an arbitration agreement shall only shift the legal settlement of certain disputes from public to private courts (of arbitration), but not impede it permanently nor exclude it entirely. Thus, if it appears that such an agreement is practically unfeasible—for whatever reason—each party is entitled to release itself from the contract on the ground of a concrete reason. According to principles of good faith, which apply with regard to the effective choice of German law between the parties, a termination due to an important reason is therefore in principle equally admissible for arbitration agreements as for other contracts involving continuing obligations. Due to the importance of the right to a legal remedy, the entitlement to a right of termination does not as a rule depend on the question whether arbitration has already been commenced or whether the terminating party is responsible for the unfeasibility of the arbitration. With the conclusion of an arbitration agreement a party waives, to a large extent, its right to fair trial and thereby its important fundamental right under … the German Constitution; this intention however, will generally not encompass a waiver of all legal remedies before state courts in cases where the arbitration agreement is impossible to perform. Rather, in such a situation, a right to extraordinary termination is justified …, as well as on the basis of a general principle of the rule of law, that a social state under the rule of law cannot accept to expel its citizens to a lawless space not at all controlled by the state.

From the principle of the rule of law in the German Constitution, the guarantee of an effective legal remedy applies to civil litigation, which in principle must enable a comprehensive factual and legal assessment of the dispute as well as a binding judicial decision. For an effective legal remedy it is necessary that such a remedy will be obtained within a reasonable period of time, since otherwise the individual rights recognized by jurisprudence would have little value. Due to its material significance for the existence of the legal order the right to a legal remedy can, therefore, be waived by a party agreement at most in individual specific arrangements, but may not be waived in its substance from the outset. Since each arbitration aims to settle the dispute between the parties in the near future by rendering an award, the termination of this agreement must be permissible if circumstances appear to prevent arbitration from being an effective legal remedy.

Such a situation is to be assumed in the present case, because such radical changes have occurred since the conclusion of the contract that the claimant may not be relegated to the form of dispute resolution provided in the contract. It may be left undecided whether the Foreign Trade Arbitration Court at the Economic Chamber of the SFRJ in Belgrade is able to function at all; that is because that court would, even if still functioning, not be accessible for the claimant in an appropriate manner. It is not seriously disputed that at present all postal and telecommunications links between Ljubljana and the seat of the tribunal are interrupted or that travel from Slovenia to Serbia is only possible by a detour through Hungary. Furthermore, it is common ground between the parties that the separated states of the former Socialist Federative Republic of Yugoslavia are essentially in a state of war, whereas credible indications for the expected return to "near-peace circumstance" "within a foreseeable" have neither been demonstrated by the respondent nor are otherwise apparent. Considering the fact that the agreed court of arbitration, contrary to the circumstances present at conclusion of the contract, is now, from the perspective of the claimant, an organ of a hostile, foreign power and cannot be reached to the extent necessary for the proper conduct of the arbitration, it would exceed the limits of the principle of sanctity of contract if, subject to entirely different circumstances, one nevertheless permanently bound the claimant to the arbitration agreement.

ASTRA FOOTWEAR INDUSTRY v. HARWYN INTERNATIONAL
442 F.Supp. 907 (S.D.N.Y. 1978)

Pierce, District Judge. Petitioner Astra Footwear brings this action to compel arbitration to resolve a contract dispute which has arisen between the parties. Petitioner is a footwear manufacturer ... in Zagreb, Yugoslavia; respondent is a footwear distributor ... in New York. In May, 1975 the parties entered into an agreement under which petitioner agreed to sell ... and respondent agreed to purchase 13,400 pairs of shoes. Petitioner alleges that it has shipped footwear pursuant to the agreement, but that respondent has refused to pay.... Petitioner seeks to compel arbitration before the [ICC].... In so requesting, petitioner relies on paragraph 12 of the contract, which provides:

> "12. Disputes: For all claims of disputes arising out of this agreement which could not be amicably settled between the parties, is competent the arbitrage for export trade at the Federal Chamber of Commerce in Beograd. [sic] In the case that the buyer is accused, the Chamber of Commerce in New York is competent."

It is petitioner's position that in designating the "Chamber of Commerce in New York," the parties were referring to the [ICC], which is based in Paris and has offices in New York.[36] Petitioner further indicates that should the Court determine that the ICC was not agreed to, it stands ready to arbitrate before any arbitrator appointed by the Court, including the [AAA].

In reply, respondent maintains that the agreement refers to and the parties intended the New York Chamber of Commerce ("NYCC") to arbitrate disputes arising thereunder. In support of its position, respondent asserts that prior to entering into this agreement it had never before done business with a Communist concern, and therefore was careful to choose an arbitration body—NYCC—that would best protect its interests. It appears that the NYCC ceased to arbitrate disputes in April, 1973 when it merged to become the New York Chamber of Commerce & Industry ("NYCCI"). It is respondent's position that the naming of NYCC was "an integral part of the substantive rights bargained for by Harwyn," and that in light of NYCCI's inability to hear the dispute, the agreement to arbitrate has been vitiated and the petition must be dismissed.

Respondent argues that the question of whether the agreement was to arbitrate in general or was to arbitrate before a particular organization is an issue mandating a jury trial under 9 U.S.C. §4. To support this position, respondent cites a New York case,[37] *Laboratorios Gross, SA v. Forest Lab., Inc.*, 295 N.Y.S.2d 756 (1st Dep't 1986) which dealt with a closely analogous fact situation. There the parties agreed to arbitrate "in accordance with the rules and procedures of the Pan American Arbitration Association," an organization which had never in fact existed.... The Court, in ordering a hearing to determine the parties' intent stated: "the issue to be decided is whether the dominant purpose of the agreement was to settle disputes by arbitration, rather than the instrumentality through which

---

36. Petitioner in fact approached the [ICC] in January 1977 and requested arbitration before that body. The ICC denied petitioner's request since it was not the organization specified in the agreement and respondent refused to consent to ICC jurisdiction.

37. The New York statutes relevant to this inquiry are N.Y. C.P.L.R. §§7503 & 7504 (McKinney 1963). They are similar to the [FAA], in providing for a trial where there is a question regarding the making of an agreement to arbitrate and in providing for Court appointment of a substitute arbitrator. However, the federal statute, 9 U.S.C. §4, provides for trial by jury if one is demanded.

arbitration should be effected." However, the intent of the parties was necessary only to determine the appropriate arbitrator to appoint.

Petitioner, on the other hand, has cited ... *Delma Eng'g Corp. v. K & L Constr. Co.*, 174 N.Y.S.2d 620 (2d Dep't 1958), *aff'd*, 181 N.Y.S.2d 794 (1958), which has a factual situation bearing greater resemblance to the present case than does *Laboratorios*. The contract in *Delma* provided for arbitration before the New York Building Congress which refused to take the case because it had discontinued arbitration procedures.... The Appellate Division rejected the argument that since the provisions for arbitration had failed, the parties were relegated to their remedies in court. Instead, the court held that there was a dominant intent to arbitrate and not merely to arbitrate before particular arbitrators. Without requiring a trial on the question of intent, the appellate court directed the lower court to appoint three arbitrators of its own selection, pursuant to the New York statute.

The Court of Appeals ... has stated that what a party must show in order to place the making of an arbitration agreement in issue or to make a genuine issue entitling a party to trial by jury is "an unequivocal denial that the agreement had been made ... and some evidence should have been produced to substantiate the denial." *Interocean Shipping Co. v. Nat'l Shipping & Trading Corp.*, 462 F.2d 673, 676 (2d Cir. 1972). In *Interocean*, the party opposing arbitration denied the very existence of the contract that contained the arbitration clause. In the present case, respondent's main objection to arbitration appears to be fear that the arbitrator would not support American business interests.[38] Respondent has not unequivocally denied that an arbitration agreement was made in the present case. From the language of the contract and the position of the parties, the Court finds that an arbitration agreement was made and that the making of such agreement is not in issue here.

The Court further finds that by the term "Chamber of Commerce in New York" the parties intended the NYCC, and not the [ICC] which has an office in New York. Respondent has pointed out that even the petitioner, when seeking arbitration applied first to the NYCCI. In addition, the [ICC] when approached as an arbitrator [sic] also suggested that the parties try the NYCC.

Since the NYCC no longer arbitrates and the [ICC] was not specified in the agreement, petitioner next requested that the Court appoint an arbitrator pursuant to 9 U.S.C. §5.... However, respondent contends that "[w]hile there is a strong policy favoring arbitration ... it remains a creature of contract. [The Court should] not impose its will on parties whose intentions are in clear conflict on this important issue." *Lea Tai Textile Co. v. Manning Fabrics, Inc.*, 411 F.Supp. 1404, 1407 (S.D.N.Y. 1975). But respondent's reliance on *Lea Tai* is misplaced. In that case, Judge Duffy held that there was no agreement to arbitrate since buyer and seller had exchanged forms with "hopelessly" inconsistent arbitration terms. In the present case, as had been noted, it is undisputed that the parties did agree to arbitrate albeit before the "Chamber of Commerce in New York." The Court finds that 9 U.S.C. §5 was drafted to provide a solution to the problem caused when the arbitrator selected by the parties cannot or will not perform. In view of the federal policy to construe liberally arbitration clauses and to resolve doubts in favor of arbitration, the Court con-

---

38. Respondent apparently feels that the [ICC] would not be as protective of the interests of American businesses as would the NYCC. However, although preferring the [ICC], petitioner is willing to appear before any arbitrator including the [AAA], which apparently should alleviate respondent's fears of the arbitrator being prejudiced against American businesses.

cludes that it cannot ignore the plain language of 9 U.S.C. §5, nor do the equities of the case[39] warrant doing so. The Court thus agrees to appoint an arbitrator pursuant to 9 U.S.C. §5. Accordingly, petitioner's motion to arbitrate is hereby granted. The only matter remaining is the appointment of a substitute arbitrator. The parties are invited to submit in writing to the Court by January 26, 1978 the names of possible alternate arbitrators. Should the parties fail together in agreeing upon one arbitrator, the Court will designate one....

NOTES

1. *Impossibility and frustration under New York Convention.* The New York Convention expressly recognizes the possibility that agreements to arbitrate may be rendered impossible to perform. Article II(3) of the Convention contemplates the non-recognition of agreements which are "incapable of being performed." What standard does Article II(3) require to be met in order to deny recognition of an arbitration agreement? Consider the three conclusions reached by Professor Lalive. What standard would Professor Lalive prescribe for a showing of changed circumstances or *rebus sic stantibus*? Does he require a showing that the arbitration agreement is "incapable of being performed"? Or something less demanding?

2. *Impossibility and frustration under UNCITRAL Model Law.* Article 8(1) of the Model Law, excerpted at p. 88 of the Documentary Supplement, contains the same formulation as the New York Convention, providing for non-recognition of agreements to arbitrate that are "incapable of being performed." Does Article 8(1) prescribe a uniform and autonomous definition of the phrase "incapable of being performed," or does it refer to local standards of impossibility and frustration? Consider again Professor Lalive's standard for changed circumstances.

3. *Impossibility or frustration of underlying contract.* Suppose that German and Venezuelan companies are party to a long-term contract (concluded in the mid-1990s) to develop natural resources in Venezuela; assume political events in the years thereafter have rendered performance of the contract impossible; finally, assume the contract provides for arbitration of disputes relating to the contract in New York. Is there any reason to think that the arbitration clause in the long-term contract has also been frustrated?

   Most national courts have relied on the separability presumption in concluding that claims of impossibility and frustration do not affect the associated arbitration clause. *Judgment of 22 September 1977*, BGHZ 69, 260, 263-64 (German Bundesgerichtshof); *Unionmut. Stock Life Ins. Co. of Am. v. Beneficial Life Ins. Co.*, 774 F.2d 524, 529 (1st Cir. 1985) (fact that a party's "attempt to rescind the entire agreement is based on the grounds of frustration of purpose rather than on fraud in the inducement does not change applicability of the severability doctrine"); *Island Territory*

---

39. *But cf. Cia de Navegacion Omsil, SA v. Hugo Neu Corp.*, 359 F.Supp. 898 (S.D.N.Y. 1973). Court did not appoint arbitrator when one arbitrator on three person panel died, but instead ordered parties to select a new panel. The Court noted that it would not be fair for the appointed arbitrator—"respondent's arbitrator"—to join in the deliberations after a series of hearings and meetings had transpired without him. "The two remaining arbitrators, 'petitioner's' and neutral, have worked together and been exposed to each other's influence. The results of that may have been good, bad, or nil for respondent.... It is not fair or fitting to impose the risk, which respondent never agreed to accept, by judicial command." *Id.* at 899.

of Curacao v. Solitron Devices, Inc., 356 F.Supp. 1, 11 (S.D.N.Y. 1973), *aff'd,* 489 F.2d 1313 (2d Cir. 1973) (claim of frustration of underlying contract does not impeach arbitration clause). What is the most plausible argument you could make that the arbitration agreement is affected by frustration of the underlying contract?

4. *Standards for impossibility or frustration of arbitration agreement.* What standards of impossibility and/or changed circumstances should be adopted with regard to agreements to arbitrate? Consider Professor Lalive's proposed standard: a substantial and unforeseen change in circumstances that makes it "unduly difficult" to perform the agreement to arbitrate. What about a substantial and unforeseen change in circumstance that makes the arbitration materially less favorable to one party? Materially more expensive? Under Professor Lalive's standard, what sorts of circumstances might constitute frustration of the agreement to arbitrate?

Compare Professor Lalive's analysis to that of the court in *Gatoil.* How would Professor Lalive have decided *Gatoil*? How would the English court have decided the ICC cases, involving an agreement selecting Belgrade as the arbitral seat, which Professor Lalive discusses? Which standard, that of Professor Lalive or that of *Gatoil,* is more appropriate? Contrast the English court's analysis in *Gatoil* to NIOC's position in the U.S. proceedings described in *NIOC.*

Consider also the *Partial Decision of 2 April 1992.* What is the court's standard for frustration? What is the rationale for this standard? Is it persuasive? How does it compare to the standards of Professor Lalive and *Gatoil*? The standard in *NIOC*?

Consider Professor Lalive's comment that the choice of the arbitral seat "is in general little more than an ancillary modality, based on practical considerations of convenience." Is that correct? What are the consequences of selecting the arbitral seat? *See infra* pp. 599-625. Do they concern "little more" than matters of "convenience"? If the selection of the arbitral seat is more than a matter of "convenience," should it be more difficult to conclude that it can be disregarded on the basis of changed circumstances?

5. *Impossibility or frustration because agreed arbitral institution is unavailable.* Suppose parties agree to arbitrate under institutional rules and, thereafter, the institution is unable or unwilling to administer the arbitration. Is the agreement to arbitrate frustrated? Consider the analysis in *Astra Footwear. See also Sumitomo Heavy Indus. Ltd v. Oil & Natural Gas Comm'n* [1994] 1 Lloyd's Rep. 45 (QB) (English High Ct.) (arbitration agreement not frustrated where, although parties agreed to ICC arbitration, they provided for two arbitrators and an "umpire," which the ICC refused to permit; court held that the arbitration could proceed in accordance with the ICC Rules, without the ICC as administering authority); *Judgment of 16 April 1984,* 1986 Rev. arb. 596 (Swiss Fed. Trib.) (Swiss courts uphold ICC's nomination of arbitrator after Director General of World Health Organization declined to act as appointing authority). See also the decisions referred to above, where agreements to arbitrate were upheld where they selected a nonexistent arbitral institution as appointing authority, *supra* pp. 350-52. Is the result in *Astra Footwear* persuasive? Why wasn't the respondent correct that the arbitration agreement had been frustrated?

6. *Impossibility or frustration because agreed arbitrator is unavailable.* Suppose the parties' agreement selects a named individual as sole arbitrator, but the individual dies or is unavailable. Has the agreement to arbitrate been frustrated? *Ballas v. Mann,* 82

N.Y.S.2d 426, 446 (N.Y. Sup.. Ct. 1948) ("a proper construction of the contract is that the intention to arbitrate is the dominant intention, the personality of the arbitrator being an auxiliary incident rather than the essence, and that frustration of that dominant intention is not to be permitted merely because the precise method of accomplishing that intent has become impossible; and under those circumstances the court may give effect to the dominant intention through the agency of an arbitrator chosen by itself"). Is that persuasive? If the parties thought it was important enough to, unusually, specify the arbitrator in the arbitration clause, should they be required to arbitrate before someone else?

7. *Impossibility or frustration because of changed circumstances in arbitral seat*. Note that both the ICC Court of Arbitration and the English court in *Gatoil* rejected arguments that changed circumstances in the arbitral seat frustrated the parties' agreement on the seat. Most other authorities have also rejected arguments that the agreed arbitral seat should be changed based on changed circumstances.

    Contrast the court's analysis in *Partial Decision of 2 April 1992*. Was it appropriate to hold that the agreement to arbitrate was frustrated? Note that arbitrators have the power, under most national laws and institutional rules, to hold hearings outside the arbitral seat. *See infra* pp. 624, 638. Could hearings have been held outside the arbitral seat in *Partial Decision of 2 April 1992*? Would this meet the claimant's concerns? Who would select the arbitrators under the clause? Would holding hearings outside the arbitral seat address (or fully address) the concerns raised by Professor Lalive regarding the choice of Belgrade as the arbitral seat?

    Is it appropriate to impose a demanding changed circumstances standard in the context of events affecting the neutrality of the arbitral seat? Where changed circumstances give rise to legitimate concerns regarding the neutrality of the courts of the arbitral seat, should this be sufficient to conclude that the parties' choice of the seat has been frustrated?

8. *Remedy if term of arbitration agreement is frustrated*. Suppose one term of an arbitration clause is frustrated (*e.g.*, choice of arbitral seat or arbitrator). What is the consequence of that conclusion? Is the agreement to arbitrate itself invalid or frustrated? Or does it mean that the term which cannot be implemented as agreed can be replaced? For example, if a tribunal or court concluded that it was impossible or fundamentally unfair to proceed with arbitration in Teheran or Belgrade, could (or must) it then select an alternative seat? Or, if the parties' agreed arbitrator becomes unavailable, could a court select a replacement? Consider the court's analysis of this issue in *NIOC*.

9. *Termination of arbitration agreement*. May a party terminate an arbitration agreement? If so, on what grounds? Consider the court's decision in *Partial Decision of 2 April 1992*. Was it appropriate to permit termination?

    Suppose a party refuses to comply with a concededly valid agreement to arbitrate (for example, by not paying its share of the arbitrators' fees or by refusing to comply with disclosure orders). Should this sort of conduct permit the other party to declare that the arbitration agreement has been repudiated and, therefore, proceed with its claims in its own home courts? If not, what sort of conduct should justify a conclusion that an arbitration agreement has been repudiated?

d. Illegality

It is hornbook law in developed legal systems that an illegal agreement is generally not enforceable.[40] The grounds for illegality claims include trade sanctions, prohibitions against trading with the enemy, competition law rules, anti-money laundering regulations, and securities or banking laws.[41] Illegality claims are frequently based on alleged illegality arising from the parties' underlying contract. These types of claims, directed at the parties' underlying contract, give rise to questions concerning the separability doctrine, the allocation of power between national courts and arbitrators, and the choice of applicable law.

In addition, national law in many countries imposes various restrictions on the validity of arbitration agreements, which are not applicable to other types of contracts.[42] That is, national law will permit parties to enter into underlying contracts dealing with particular subjects (*e.g.*, oil concessions or consumer contracts), but will not permit (or give effect to) agreements to arbitrate those subjects. For example, national law may deny effect to agreements to arbitrate certain types of employment or consumer disputes, securities claims, bankruptcy issues, and the like.[43] These types of legislative provisions are often dealt with under the "nonarbitrability" doctrine (discussed below).

JUDGMENT OF 27 FEBRUARY 1970
6 Arb. Int'l 79 (German Bundesgerichtshof)

[excerpted above at pp. 194-98]

BUCKEYE CHECK CASHING, INC. v. CARDEGNA
546 U.S. 440 (2006)

[excerpted above at pp. 201-05]

JUDGMENT OF 7 MAY 1994, FINCANTIERI-CANTIERI NAVALI ITALIANI SPA v. MIN. OF DEF., ARMAMENT & SUPPLY DIRECTORATE OF IRAQ
XXI Y.B. Comm. Arb. 594 (1996) (Genoa Corte di Appello)

[The Republic of Iraq, through the Armament and Supply Directorate of its Ministry of Defense (the "Iraqi parties"), entered into contracts with shipbuilders Fincantieri-Cantieri Navali Italiani SpA and Oto Melara SpA (the "Italian parties") for the supply of corvettes. All contracts contained a clause for ICC arbitration in Paris. An embargo against Iraq was declared by the UN Security Council in August 1990, following the invasion of Kuwait; embargo legislation was issued thereafter by the EU and Italy restricting weapons trade with Iraq. At that time, most of the corvettes had not yet been built or delivered.

The Italian parties commenced proceedings against Iraq in the Court of First Instance of Genoa, seeking termination and damages. The Iraqi parties objected to the Court's jurisdiction and claimed that the dispute should be referred to arbitration. The Italian parties

---

40. G. Born, *International Commercial Arbitration* 896 (2d ed. 2014).
41. G. Born, *International Commercial Arbitration* 973-95 (2d ed. 2014).
42. *See supra* pp. 186-88 & *infra* pp. 446-60, 475-510.
43. *See infra* pp. 446-60, 475-510.

replied that the parties' dispute concerned matters which were not arbitrable. They claimed that arbitrability must be ascertained under Italian law, relying on Art. 806 of the Italian Code of Civil Procedure (CCP),[44] according to which only disputes concerning rights which the parties may freely dispose of ("be the subject of a compromise") may be referred to arbitration. They alleged that, due to the [EU and Italian] embargo legislation, the parties could [no longer] freely dispose of the contractual rights at issue. On December 9, 1992, the Court of First Instance of Genoa held that it had no jurisdiction. It held that arbitration is excluded under Art. 806 CCP only when it directly affects *diritti indisponibili* (rights of which the parties may not freely dispose) by bringing about a result which is forbidden by the law (here, delivery of the corvettes). It found that the parties' dispute did not directly affect such rights, because the claimants were only seeking termination of the contracts and damages. The Italian parties appealed to the Court of Appeal of Genoa, which reversed, in an opinion excerpted below.]

Each of the contracts at issue contains a clause, according to which "any dispute which may arise under the present contract ... shall be finally settled according to the Conciliation and Arbitration Rules of the Paris Chamber of Commerce by three arbitrators appointed according to the said Rules." The validity of this clause must be ascertained according to the [New York Convention], which derogates from the fundamental principle in the Code [of Civil Procedure] that the jurisdiction of Italian courts cannot be excluded by agreement (to the exception of limitatively listed cases ...). Art. II provides that the Contracting States shall recognize the agreement in writing under which the parties undertake to submit to arbitration all or any differences related to a defined legal relationship and concerning "a subject matter capable of settlement by arbitration." Correspondingly, the court of a Contracting State, when seized of an action in a matter in respect of which the parties have made any such agreement, "shall refer the parties to arbitration" at the request of one of the parties, unless it finds that the agreement is null and void, inoperative or incapable of being performed....

[The Italian parties maintain] that the dispute falls outside the scope of the arbitration clause because of its subject matter, that is, because the parties may not freely dispose of it.... [In] Italian law: (1) according to Art. 806 CCP, the parties may by a "submission to arbitration" have arbitrators settle "the disputes arising between them," with the exception of those disputes ... "that cannot be the subject of a compromise;" (2) according to Art. 808, the parties may, by an arbitral clause "in the contract or by subsequent agreement, establish that the disputes arising from that contract be settled by arbitrators, provided that these disputes may be the subject of a submission to arbitration;" (3) according to Art. 1966 CC, a compromise is null and void when the parties may not freely dispose of the rights which are the subject matter of the dispute, either by these rights' nature or by express provision of the law.

It is beyond doubt that the rights deriving from the contracts between [the parties] could be freely disposed of at the time when the arbitral clause was stipulated. It is equally beyond doubt that they could not when this action was commenced, as a consequence of the international measures sanctioning Iraq's aggression of Kuwait and of the legislative

---

44. Art. 806 of the [pre-2006] Italian Code of Civil Procedure read: "Submission to arbitration. The parties may have arbitrators settle the disputes arising between them, excepting those ... regarding issues of personal status and marital separation and those others that cannot be the subject of a compromise." ...

measures implementing them in our country…. The Court of First Instance of Genoa did not deny that according to the law applicable to the merits [these rights] could not be freely disposed of, in the sense of and for the reasons mentioned above: it denied that this could be an obstacle for referring the dispute to arbitration…. The Court held that … "claimants … essentially seek a declaration that the supply contracts are frustrated as a result of the lack of performance by the MOD and the Republic of Iraq, as well as damages; both requests do not affect the prohibition to dispose of the rights as provided for in the said legislation."

We do not agree with the lower court … that "any dispute on the validity or termination of the contract, which does not lead to a decision on *diritti indisponibili*, cannot be deemed to fall outside the jurisdiction of the arbitrators." The Court of First Instance bases this principle [on an Italian Supreme Court decision] … which reads:

> "For an arbitral clause concerning disputes on *diritti indisponibili* to be null and void … it is necessary that the contract containing the clause (which clause remains autonomous) affects such rights by transferring, renouncing them etc. in violation of the law. It is also necessary that the disputes arising from that contract, if negotiated by the parties or settled by arbitrators, affect *diritti indisponibili*, i.e., that the agreement of the parties or the arbitral decision disposes of them in violation of the law. Any other dispute—including a dispute on the validity of the contract concerning allegedly *indisponibili* rights—which does not lead to this result, as well as any other ground for the contract's invalidity, falls within the arbitrators' jurisdiction, as the related decision would have a merely declaratory nature…. Since any dispute on the validity of the contract which does not involve a decision on *diritti indisponibili* falls within the arbitrators' jurisdiction, it may be that the award denying such ground for invalidity as raised by the parties in the arbitration is null and void; it is no question here of the arbitral clause being null and void and the arbitrators lacking jurisdiction."

The decision of the Supreme Court—which is made less clear by the confusion between [*ab initio*] nullity and invalidity of the contract—concerns the autonomy of the arbitral clause from the underlying contract and its independence from the latter's defects. Consequently, it concerns the role played in national arbitration by *indisponibili* contractual rights, both as a ground for the objection that the arbitral clause is null and void and as a ground for setting aside the award under Art. 829(1)(1) CCP. [Article 829 of the pre-2006 Italian Code of Civil Procedure read in relevant part: "One may institute proceedings on the ground of nullity, notwithstanding any waiver, in the following cases: (1) if the submission is void…."] This does not affect the role which the *diritti indisponibili* may otherwise play with respect to the arbitrators' failure to observe the rules of law, which may be censured according to Art. 829(2) CCP. [Article 829(2) of the pre-2006 Italian Code of Civil Procedure read: "One may also make recourse on the ground of nullity where the arbitrators, when making their decision, have not observed the rules of law, unless the parties have authorized them to decide according to equity or unless they have declared that there may be no recourse against the award."] However, in the present case there is no question of nullity, since the original validity of the arbitral clause is neither challenged nor seriously challengeable: at the time of the clauses' conclusion all formal and substantial conditions were met and the parties could freely dispose of their contractual rights. As we have seen, this situation came to an end later on….

We do not see a substantial difference between national and international arbitration as to the nature of the arbitral clause, which pertains … to the intrinsic nature of [arbitration], that is, in our best doctrine, a contract with essentially procedural effects. In the objection to and subsequent declaration of lack of jurisdiction we recognize the submission to arbitration and the referral to arbitrators mentioned in the Convention, respectively. The New York Convention does indeed recognize both effects of arbitral agreements and clauses: the positive effect (referral to arbitration when requirements are met) and the negative effect (consequent exclusion of the jurisdiction of the courts of the Contracting States).

There is no doubt that, although the Convention's language is subjectively and objectively very broad, the derogation from court jurisdiction must be interpreted in the light of the other provisions of the Convention and in particular of the fundamental provision of Art. I. According to Art. I, derogation is possible only when the arbitration proceedings aim at a decision which is enforceable under the Convention, particularly as to the requirement that the dispute be arbitrable. If the dispute cannot by settled by arbitration, a derogation is not possible and State courts … again have jurisdiction. Art. V(2)(a) of the Convention, which denies recognition and enforcement to those arbitral awards which, according to the law of the State where recognition or enforcement is sought, concern a non-arbitrable dispute, leads to the same conclusion.

For the present purpose it is sufficient to answer the question whether, at the time of commencing this action …, the arbitral clause in the contracts was "null and void, inoperative or incapable of being performed." The answer must be sought in Italian law, according to the jurisprudential principle that, when an objection for foreign arbitration is raised in court proceedings concerning a contractual dispute, the arbitrability of the dispute must be ascertained according to Italian law as this question directly affects jurisdiction, and the court seized of the action can only deny jurisdiction on the basis of its own legal system. This also corresponds to the principles expressed in Arts. II and V of the [Convention]. Hence, the answer to the question [of arbitrability] can only be that the dispute was not arbitrable due to [the Italian embargo].

The dispute is further non-arbitrable under EC Rule no. 3541/1992 of 7 December 1992…. Art. 21 of this Rule forbids [parties] to meet or take any measure to meet Iraqi requests to perform in any way under contracts or transactions falling under Resolution No. 686/1990 and following of the UN Security Council [the UN embargo legislation]. Art. 1.2 explains that "request" means a request made in or out of court, before or after the date of entry into force of the Rule; that "transaction" … generically means negotiation, and that this provision, in the light of its ratio, must be interpreted in the sense that it forbids not only meeting a request but also any (voluntary) act aiming at meeting it. This *jus superveniens* is worth mentioning: even where the answer given above to the question of jurisdiction were uncertain under the [Italian] legislation …, [this EC Rule] would make the arbitral clause null and void….

This solution finds no obstacle in the fact that claimants' main claim aimed at terminating the contracts, not at obtaining performance under them. Also in this case, referral of the dispute to the arbitrators could have affected … rights which international and national embargo legislation had made *indisponibili*. Indeed, if the claim had been accepted and the contracts terminated, a restitution … would have been effected which was prohibited under the above legislation. Further, as a set-off had been claimed, in case termination were granted, between the Iraqi parties' credits for advance payments made and their allegedly higher debts, the arbitration could have led to meeting [Iraqi requests] in violation of the said supranational legislation. Also, an hypothetical arbitral award against the claimants, denying termination of the contract, would have recognized the continuing validity of the contracts, thereby affecting, in a contrary but similar manner, *diritti indisponibili*.

The Court of First Instance of Genoa apparently missed this point and held the arbitral clause (which we hold to be null and void) to be valid. It reasoned that the Italian claimants' claim that the contract was frustrated due to the Iraqi parties' behaviour, and their connected request for damages, if and when granted by award, would not affect *diritti indisponibili* as there would be no actual transfer of property nor delivery of the contractual goods to the Iraqi parties. The Court further ignored the possibility that the arbitrators would reach the opposite solution, which would be as capable of (otherwise) affecting *diritti indisponibili*.

In its reasoning on the issue of jurisdiction the Court of First Instance apparently anticipated its own evaluation, incidentally but unequivocally made when dealing with the merits, that "performance under the main contract (has) become impossible not due to the suppliers but solely to the embargo legislation caused by Iraq's aggression of Kuwait" and that "there exists sure proof that nonperformance under the contracts was due to force majeure independent of [the Iraqi parties]." … [This explanation] cannot justify the fact that [the Court] did not consider the effect of the request for termination on the *diritti indisponibili* at issue; otherwise, the logical and juridical order of preliminary questions of jurisdiction and questions on the merits would be unacceptably subverted: when dealing with the issue of jurisdiction, the court must consider it *in abstracto* and in the light of all potential outcomes of the examination of the merits, and this latter must be logically subsequent and totally independent.

Also, the Court of First Instance should not have distinguished … the delivery of warfare goods from the mere regulation of monetary aspects of the same relationship through a money transfer from the Italian to the Iraqi party as activities capable of causing a situation not allowed under the embargo legislation. Such distinction is at odds with the supranational legislation issued in the historical situation at hand, which legislation is very far-reaching as it not only prohibits the supply of weapons and accessories to Iraq: it also juridically and commercially isolates that State….

FINAL AWARD IN ICC CASE NO. 5294
XIV Y.B. Comm. Arb. 137 (1980)

[excerpted above at pp. 218-20]

INTERIM AWARD IN ICC CASE NO. 6149
XX Y.B. Comm. Arb. 41 (1995)

[excerpted above at pp. 290-92]

NOTES

1. *Application of separability presumption to claims that underlying contract is illegal.* How does the separability presumption apply to challenges to the legality of the underlying contract? Does the alleged illegality of the underlying contract mean that the arbitration clause is void?

(a) *Authorities holding that illegality of underlying contract invalidates arbitration clause*. Some authorities have held that the illegality of the underlying contract invalidates the arbitration clause contained in the contract. *Judgment of 15 June 1987*, 1987 NJW 3193 (German Bundesgerichtshof) (arbitration clause invalid because underlying contract violated German Stock Exchange Law); *Alabama Catalog Sales v. Harris*, 794 So.2d 312 (Ala. 2000) (because claim of illegal "pay-day loans" challenges "the very existence of the contracts," illegality claim impeaches arbitration clause); *Nature's 10 Jewelers v. Gunderson*, 648 N.W.2d 804 (S.D. 2002) (franchise agreement was void, because not registered with state regulatory authority and franchisor cannot invoke "benefit from the arbitration clause in the illegal contract").

(b) *Illegality in* Fincantieri. Consider the decision in *Fincantieri*. What was the basis for the appellate court's reversal of the first instance court? Was there any claim that either the underlying contract or the arbitration agreement itself was illegal when concluded? Was there any claim that the arbitration agreement itself subsequently became illegal, either under Italian or EU regulations? Compare the reasoning of the Genoa court with that of the first instance court and the Italian Supreme Court (in the quoted passage, *supra* p. 438). Is it oversimplifying analysis to say that the Genoa appellate court holds that, since the award might produce a result that violated Italian or EU mandatory legislation (forbidding commercial transactions with Iraq), the arbitration clause was void? Wouldn't an award that produced a result that violated Italian or EU mandatory law be subject to annulment or non-recognition on public policy grounds? *See infra* pp. 1161-63, 1250-60.

(c) *Authorities holding that illegality of underlying contract does not invalidate arbitration clause.* In contrast to the decision in *Fincantieri*, a number of authorities have held that the illegality of a contract does not invalidate an arbitration clause contained in the contract. Consider the result in the German Bundesgerichtshof's *Judgment of 27 February 1970*. Was there a claim that the underlying lease contract was void for illegality? Did that claim invalidate the arbitration clause? Might the arbitrators make an award that would raise issues under the German currency regulations? Consider also the result in *Buckeye*. For similar decisions, *see Hodge Bros., Inc. v. DeLong Co.*, 942 F.Supp. 412 (W.D. Wis. 1996) ("A party may not invalidate an arbitration clause by attacking the legality of the underlying contract containing that clause."); *Judgment of 7 May 1963, Ets Raymond Gosset v. Frère Carapelli SpA*, JCP G 1963, II, 13 ("the arbitration agreement, whether concluded separately or included in the contract to which it relates, shall, save in exceptional circumstances ..., have full legal autonomy and shall not be affected by the fact that the aforementioned contract may be invalid"); *Interim Award in ICC Case No. 4145*, XII Y.B. Comm. Arb. 97, 100 (1987) ("question of validity or nullity of the main contract, for reasons of public policy, illegality or otherwise, is one of merits and not of jurisdiction, the validity of the arbitration clause having to be considered separately from the validity of the main contract").

(d) *Illegality in* Buckeye. Suppose the underlying contract in *Buckeye* is illegal; would that result in the invalidity of the agreement to arbitrate contained within that contract? What does the U.S. Supreme Court hold? How does the reasoning of the

Supreme Court compare to that of the Genoa appellate court in *Fincantieri*? To the German Bundesgerichtshof in *Judgment of 27 February 1970*?

Does the *Buckeye* holding apply to all claims of illegality? If a band of robbers agree to divide their loot, and to arbitrate any resulting disagreements, does the separability presumption insulate the arbitration clause from the illegality of the underlying contract? Does it make sense to say that no claims of illegality, directed at the underlying contract, ever affect the validity of the associated arbitration agreement? Is it not possible that some such claims do necessarily affect the agreement to arbitrate (*e.g.*, the bank robbers or terrorists' agreements)?

(e) Fincantieri *revisited*. What if the embargo in *Fincantieri* prohibited any arbitration between EU and Iraqi entities? Would there be any doubt then that the arbitration agreement was void for illegality? Consider the Genoa court's reference to UN Resolution No. 686/1990. Does the court interpret the resolution as forbidding arbitration with Iraqi entities? If so, would that provide a more satisfactory basis for the court's conclusion? What effect would Article II of the Convention have on the UN resolution?

2. *Allocation of competence to decide disputes over legality of underlying contract.* Like other disputes over the validity of international arbitration agreements, challenges to the legality of both arbitration clauses and underlying contracts give rise to questions regarding the allocation of competence to resolve such disputes.

(a) *Allocation of competence to decide disputes over legality of underlying contract under FAA.* The allocation of competence to decide claims that the underlying contract is illegal under the FAA is closely related to the separability presumption. Consider the *Buckeye* decision: under the Supreme Court's analysis, who has competence to decide claims that the underlying contract is illegal—the arbitrators or the court? Compare the *Westinghouse* decision. Note that the court rejected, in the final paragraph of the opinion excerpted above, the argument that it should decide challenges to the legality of the parties' underlying agreement. *See supra* p. 415. What is the basis for the *Westinghouse* decision?

A number of lower U.S. courts have reached the same result as that in *Westinghouse*, typically relying on the separability presumption. *See, e.g., Snowden v. CheckPoint Check Cashing*, 290 F.3d 631 (4th Cir. 2002) (claims that loan agreement was usurious "do not relate specifically to the Arbitration Agreement" and are therefore for arbitral, not judicial, determination); *Bess v. Check Express*, 294 F.3d 1298 (11th Cir. 2002) (claims that usurious loans were illegal did not concern "the arbitration agreement specifically," and "an arbitrator should decide those questions"); *Nat'l Rail Passenger Corp. v. Consolidated Rail Corp.*, 892 F.2d 1066 (D.C. Cir. 1990) ("if the parties have validly agreed to submit a dispute to arbitration, we see no reason not to enforce that agreement. If the arbitrator construes the contract so as to require someone to commit an illegal act, a court can then refuse to enforce the arbitrator's decision. A court cannot, however, bypass the arbitration process simply because a public policy issue might arise."). Contrary to *Westinghouse* and *Buckeye*, a few lower U.S. courts (usually applying state law) have held that challenges to the legality of the underlying contract require judicial resolution. *See, e.g., Durst v. Abrash*, 253 N.Y.S.2d 351 (N.Y. App. Div. 1964), *aff'd*, 266 N.Y.S.2d 806 (N.Y. 1966) ("If usurious agreements could be made enforceable by the simple device of employing arbitration clauses the courts would be surrendering their control over public policy."); *Kramer & Uchitelle, Inc. v. Eddington Fabrics Corp.*, 43 N.E.2d 493 (N.Y. 1942) (no arbitration under contract void under price control regulations).

Does it make sense to conclude, as *Buckeye* apparently does, that all claims of illegality directed at the underlying contract must be for initial determination by the arbitrators? Are there not instances in which arbitral consideration of an issue concerning the illegality of the underlying contract would be forbidden by either national law or public policy?

(b) *Allocation of competence to decide disputes over legality of underlying contract under English Arbitration Act.* Consider the following excerpt from a leading English decision on the allocation of authority to consider claims of illegality in connection with an arbitration agreement:

> "[In] *Harbour Assur. Co (UK) Ltd v. Kansa Gen. Int'l Ins. Co* ... the Court of Appeal held that the arbitration clause in an insurance contract was separate from the main contract with the effect that (a) invalidity of the main contract did not deprive the arbitrator of jurisdiction, and (b) the arbitrator had jurisdiction to decide the question of illegality of the main contract. But the fact that in a contract alleged to be illegal the arbitration clause may not itself be infected by the illegality, does not mean that it is always so, and does not mean that an arbitration agreement that is separate may not be void for illegality. There may be illegal or immoral dealings which are, from an English law perspective, incapable of being arbitrated because an agreement to arbitrate them would itself be illegal or contrary to public policy under English law. The English court would not recognize an agreement between the highwaymen to arbitrate their differences any more than it would recognize the original agreement to split the proceeds.... [The court cited] a case concerned with betting and an arbitration provision collateral to that contract, *Joe Lee Ltd v. Lord Dalmeny* [1927] 1 Ch 300, [which] recognized the possibility of an agreement containing any arbitration clause of such a nature that the arbitration clause itself was invalid. It must also follow that an arbitration agreement made separately in relation to an illegal or immoral dispute would not be recognized." *Soleimany v. Soleimany* [1999] QB 785 (English Ct. App.).

Compare the following English decision, rendered in the same year as *Soleimany*:

> "There can be no doubt that as a matter of language the arbitration clause in the consultancy agreement was expressed in terms wide enough to cover the issue whether the agreement was illegal and void by reason of a common or unilateral intention to bribe Kuwaiti officials. The approach to the question whether as a matter of English public policy an agreement to arbitrate that issue should be treated as enforceable must be determined by considerations similar to those deployed by the United States Supreme Court in the context of statutory illegality in relation to the antitrust legislation in *Mitsubishi Motors Corp.* It is necessary to consider both on the one hand the desirability of giving effect to the public policy against enforcement of corrupt transactions and on the other hand the public policy of sustaining international arbitration agreements. One consequence of the arbitrators being accorded jurisdiction might be that they gave effect to a contract which on the face of the award was held to involve the payment of bribes. It would then be a matter for consideration at the enforcement stage whether, although the

arbitrators had jurisdiction to determine the issue, the award should be enforced because they had exceeded their jurisdiction in giving effect to an illegal contract or had misconducted themselves or because enforcement would be contrary to public policy. If, however, the arbitrators found facts on the basis of which they rightly concluded that the underlying contract did not involve the payment of bribes, their award would ordinarily be enforced notwithstanding that it might be objected that their findings of fact were in truth mistaken. Thus, in determining whether English public policy would deny jurisdiction to arbitrators to determine the illegality issue consideration has to be given to the weight that ought to be attached to the risk that arbitrators might reach the wrong decision in a way which could not be challenged and thereby give effect to an underlying contract which the courts would have declined to enforce.

In the present case, the parties selected arbitration by an impressively competent international body, the ICC. The English court would be entitled to assume that arbitrators appointed were of undoubted competence and ability, well able to understand and determine the particular issue of illegality arising in this case. That issue involves no consideration of complex principle of law capable only of being safely determined by an English court. Insofar as it involves determination of questions of fact, that is an everyday feature of international arbitration. The opportunity for erroneous and uncorrectable findings of fact arises in all international arbitration. If much weight were to be attached to that consideration it is difficult to see that arbitrators would ever be accorded jurisdiction to determine issues of illegality." *Westacre Inv. Inc. v. Jugoimp.-SPDR Holdings Co.* [1998] 4 All ER 570, 593 (QB) (English High Ct.).

Consider the analysis in *Soleimany* and *Westacre*. How does it compare with that in *Buckeye*? To that of the Genoa appellate court in *Fincantieri*? Do the English courts hold that *all* claims of illegality directed at the underlying contract are subject initially to arbitration? What factors appear to be relevant to deciding this issue?

(c) *Allocation of competence to decide disputes over legality of underlying contract under prima facie jurisdiction standard.* How would claims of illegality directed at the underlying contract be dealt with under the *prima facie* jurisdiction rule applied in France, India and elsewhere? *See supra* pp. 274-75. Does it make sense to say that all claims of illegality, no matter what their character, will be subject only to a *prima facie* jurisdiction test?

(d) *Allocation of competence to decide disputes over legality of underlying contract under UNCITRAL Model Law.* How should claims of illegality directed at the underlying contract be dealt with under the Model Law? Does anything in Articles 8 or 16 resolve the issue? To what sources should a court in a Model Law jurisdiction look in resolving this issue? Decisions such as those in *Fincantieri, Buckeye* and *Westacre*?

3. *Provisions of national law rendering certain categories of arbitration agreements illegal.* Many legal systems contain restrictions directed specifically towards arbitration agreements (as distinct from underlying contracts). These include, for example, prohibitions against arbitration of certain consumer, employment, distributorship and domestic relations disputes. *See infra* pp. 446-60, 475-510. These provisions virtually never carry criminal sanctions, but instead provide that agreements to arbitrate are unenforceable as applied to certain types of disputes or if contained in specified types

of agreements. (Note the U.N. resolution referred to by the Genoa appellate court in *Fincantieri*; if it extended to arbitrations, it would be an example of a regulation rendering certain categories of arbitration agreements illegal.) Rules of illegality directed specifically towards arbitration agreements are generally categorized under the heading of nonarbitrability, which is discussed below. *See infra* pp. 475-510. How do these provisions compare to an illegality claim directed at the parties' underlying contract?

4. *Allocation of competence to resolve disputes over legality of arbitration agreement.* Suppose one party to an arbitration agreement challenges the legality of that agreement itself. Can or must an arbitrator resolve this challenge? Compare this question to the allocation of competence over other issues (such as formation and fraud). *See supra* pp. 370-74, 416-20. Recall the standard set forth in *Buckeye* for allocating competence between arbitrators and U.S. courts. Suppose a claim of illegality is directed specifically at the agreement to arbitrate (*e.g.*, the arbitration clause was an integral part of a price-fixing conspiracy or a money-laundering scheme). Would this claim be subject initially to arbitration? Suppose that neither party initiates litigation in national courts, claiming or denying the illegality of the arbitration agreement; mustn't the arbitral tribunal consider the issue of illegality?

5. *Applying* First Options' *allocation of power between courts and arbitrators to resolve disputes over legality of arbitration agreement.* As discussed above, *First Options* requires judicial resolution of questions of arbitrability unless there is "clear and unmistakable" evidence that the parties have agreed to arbitrate these issues. *See supra* pp. 230-33, 280-83. It is unclear how *First Options* applies to disputes about the legality of an arbitration agreement.

Suppose the arbitration clause in *Westinghouse* included a sentence providing that: "All disputes relating to the formation and validity of this arbitration agreement (including the legality thereof) shall be resolved by the arbitrators." Is this "clear and unmistakable" evidence of an agreement to arbitrate issues of legality? What if a party challenges the legality, and thus validity, of the arbitration agreement containing this clause? Mustn't a court decide the challenge? Suppose the arbitration clause provided for arbitration under the 2012 ICC Rules, and specifically Article 6 thereof. Does Article 6 provide "clear and unmistakable" evidence of an agreement to arbitrate claims that the parties' arbitration agreement was illegal?

6. *Choice of law applicable to claims that arbitration agreement is illegal.* What substantive law was applied to illegality claims in each of the decisions excerpted above? What choice-of-law rules were applied to select this substantive law?

What law did the court apply in *Westinghouse* to the issue of illegality? The court in *Fincantieri*? What law did the arbitrators in *ICC Case No. 5294* and *ICC Case No. 6149* apply to the issue of illegality? Note the tribunal's effort, in each case, to reject the illegality claim under all conceivably applicable laws. Which law, in each case, does the tribunal appear to have regarded as primarily applicable?

Consider the choice-of-law issues that arise in connection with international arbitration agreements. *See supra* pp. 90-93, 287-315. Do questions of legality give rise to special choice-of-law issues? *See Restatement (Second) Conflict of Laws* §202(2) (1971) ("When performance is illegal in the place of performance, the contract will usually be denied enforcement."). Is the place of performance the arbitral seat? Or where the underlying contract is performed?

7. *Treatment of illegality claims in* Westinghouse. The *Westinghouse* court summarily dismisses the argument that illegality of the underlying powerplant contract—for failure to follow Philippine competitive bidding rules—precluded arbitration. Treating illegality like fraudulent inducement in *Prima Paint*, the *Westinghouse* court held that challenges to the legality of the underlying contract did not affect the arbitration clause and that those claims were, therefore, subject to arbitration. Is this sensible? Is the analysis affected at all by the fact that the Philippines was invoking its own law to invalidate a contract it made?

8. *Arbitrators' refusal to accept jurisdiction in corruption cases*. Arbitral tribunals have sometimes invoked "international" public policy as a basis for refusing to exercise jurisdiction—essentially declaring particular disputes nonarbitrable. Several well-publicized awards arose out of disputes over what were alleged to be contracts for the payment of illegal bribes. In one such case, when a party to such a contract pursued an arbitration to recover amounts owing, the tribunal declined to hear the dispute, holding:

> "It cannot be contested that there exists a general principle of law recognized by civilized nations that contracts which seriously violate bonos mores or international public policy are invalid or at least unenforceable and that they cannot be sanctioned by courts or arbitrators.... Thus, jurisdiction must be declined in this case.... In concluding that I have no jurisdiction, guidance has been sought from general principles denying arbitrators to entertain disputes of this nature rather than from any national rules on arbitrability." J. Lew, *Applicable Law in International Commercial Arbitration* 553-55 (1978) (summarizing and excerpting award by Lagergren in *ICC Case 1110 of 1963*).

In recent years, however, the practice of tribunals has more often been to take jurisdiction in cases involving illegal contracts, but to hold the agreement void:

> "[A]rbitral jurisprudence has evolved profoundly in respect of contracts contrary to public policy.... Old awards considered that such disputes were not susceptible of being submitted to arbitration (*ICC Case No. 1110 of 1963*.) However, in recent awards, arbitrators have systematically refused to reject their jurisdiction and have decided, when necessary, upon the nullity of the underlying contract (*ICC Case Nos. 2730, ... 2930, ... [and] 3916*)." Schwartz, *The Domain of Arbitration and Issues of Arbitrability: The View From the ICC*, in Tenth Joint ICC/AAA/ICSID Colloquium on International Arbitration (1993), at 4 n.6 (quoting unpublished ICC award).

Is there anything wrong with arbitrators deciding claims of corruption or bribery? Recall the House of Lords' discussion of this issue in *Fiona Trust. See supra* pp. 205-11.

e. Consumer Disputes, Employment Contracts and Bankruptcy

There is substantial diversity in the treatment, under national legal systems, of agreements to arbitrate consumer claims, employment disputes and matters involving bankrupt parties.[45] As the materials excerpted below illustrate, different states adopt substantially different approaches to each of these categories of disputes.

Historically, many national legal systems refused to enforce agreements to arbitrate labor disputes. Despite the rejection of historic prohibitions against arbitration in other contexts, some European jurisdictions continue to treat labor disputes as nonarbitrable (with some exceptions), including Belgium,[46] Italy[47] and France.[48] Similar legislation exists in other jurisdictions.[49]

In contrast, a very different approach is taken in the United States. In general, U.S. federal law and policy have long affirmatively encouraged arbitration of many labor disputes,[50] as a specialized mode of dispute resolution regarded by both U.S. legislative and judicial opinion as superior to that of litigation, while imposing only narrow nonarbitrability limits on some forms of employer-employee disputes. Thus, as discussed above, §1 of the U.S. FAA excludes from the Act's coverage agreements arising from a limited range of employment relations—involving "contracts of employment of seamen, railroad employees, or any other class of workers engaged in foreign or interstate commerce."[51]

As the materials excerpted below illustrate, different legal systems also take different approaches towards the arbitration of "consumer" disputes. ("Consumer" disputes are defined generally as disputes between a consumer (or a non-merchant) and a merchant or commercial party, sometimes with a limited amount in controversy.) In broad outline, U.S. law currently recognizes the validity of agreements to arbitrate between consumers and businesses and permits the arbitration of both existing and future consumer disputes, subject to restrictions based on principles of unconscionability and due notice, while some other jurisdictions forbid or regulate (through statutory provisions) agreements to arbitrate future consumer disputes. Even in jurisdictions that do not give general effect to consumer arbitration agreements, there is a considerable diversity in the treatment of restrictions and prohibitions in different states.

Finally, parties to international arbitration agreements sometimes end up in some form of bankruptcy or insolvency, often in their home jurisdiction.[52] Is a party who has been declared bankrupt bound by preexisting arbitration agreements? If not, in what circumstances is the bankrupt's agreement to arbitrate invalid? As detailed in the following materials, different legislative regimes and judicial decisions have reached different conclusions in addressing these questions.

---

45. G. Born, *International Commercial Arbitration* 1009 *et seq.* (2d ed. 2014).

46. Belgian Judicial Code, Art. 1676(5).

47. Italian Code of Civil Procedure, Art. 806; *Judgment of 30 April 1980*, VII Y.B. Comm. Arb. 341 (1980) (Genoa Pretore).

48. *See Judgment of 13 September 1993*, XX Y.B. Comm. Arb. 656 (1995) (Grenoble Cour d'appel), Note, Moreau, ("arbitration agreement included in an international individual employment agreement is valid").

49. *See* Japanese Arbitration Law, Supplementary Provisions, Art. 4 ("for the time being," agreements to arbitrate certain "individual labor-related disputes" shall be "null and void").

50. *See* T. Bornstein, A. Gosline & M. Greenbaum, *Labor and Employment Arbitration* §1.04 (2007).

51. U.S. FAA, 9 U.S.C. §1. The exclusion has been held to apply only to employees engaged in transportation industries. *Circuit City Stores, Inc. v. Adams*, 532 U.S. 105, 107 (2001). As discussed above, the provision has also been held inapplicable in the context of international arbitration agreements subject to the New York Convention. *See supra* pp. 138-42.

52. *See* G. Born, *International Commercial Arbitration* 995 (2d ed. 2014).

BELGIAN JUDICIAL CODE
Article 1676(5)

Without prejudice to the exceptions provided for in the law, an arbitration agreement concluded before a dispute has arisen, which dispute falls within the competence of the Labor Tribunal as determined in Articles 578 to 583 is *ipso jure* null.

ITALIAN CODE OF CIVIL PROCEDURE
Article 806

The parties may have arbitrators resolve the disputes arising between them provided the subject matter does not concern rights which may not be disposed of, except in case of express prohibition by law.

Disputes provided for in Article 409 [labor disputes] may be decided by arbitrators only if so provided by law or by collective labor contracts or agreements.

JAPANESE ARBITRATION LAW
Supplementary Provisions, Article 4

For the time being until otherwise enacted, any arbitration agreements concluded following the enforcement of this Law, the subject of which constitutes individual labor-related disputes (which means individual labor-related disputes as described in article 1 of the Law on Promoting the Resolution of Individual Labor Disputes) that may arise in the future, shall be null and void.

ARKANSAS CODE, 2010
§16-108-201

[excerpted above at p. 180]

BAUTISTA v. STAR CRUISES, NORWEGIAN CRUISE LINE, LTD
396 F.3d 1289 (11th Cir. 2005)

[excerpted above at pp. 138-42 & 397-99]

JUDGMENT OF 28 NOVEMBER 2011, HATEM TAMIMI v. MÉDECINS SANS FRONTIÈRES
Case No. 409/2011 (Ramallah Ct. App.)

[The Palestinian court decided not to revert to arbitration law according to the company's policy manual, which stated that arbitration be the mechanism for settling disputes, and decided that it should only look to the substantial law governing the dispute—labor law.]

The lawsuit is a claim of labor rights which means that what governs this case is the Labor Law and not the arbitration law or any other law…. [T]he policy manual of the appellant company is not binding on the employee except to the extent it complies with the provisions of the Labor Law…. [E]ven if we assume that the employee agreed to refer the dispute to arbitration under the terms and conditions of the policy manual, which are contrary to the law which stated the employee's rights, how can we apply such agreement and discard the law? ...

The arbitration term in the policy manual is contrary to the Labor Law Article 127, which grants the employee the right to litigate in Article 63 even if it was mentioned pertaining injuries ... which means ultimately the employee can resort to courts.... The policy manual the employee signed will not prohibit him to go to courts, this agreement (policy manual) is contrary to the legal provision, the term in the agreement shall be void and what is in compliance with the law shall remain.... Therefore the first instance judge's decision not to accept the case was incorrect.

[On appeal, the cassation court ruled that it could not hear the case because this decision is a preliminary one that is not final in order to be reviewed by the cassation court. However, it did mention that a wrong decision made by the appellate court cannot be corrected by a decision without competence by the cassation court. When the case was sent back to the first instance court, the court ruled to stop the court proceedings and refer the case to arbitration.]

EU UNFAIR TERMS IN CONSUMER CONTRACTS DIRECTIVE
93/13/EEC, Official Journal L095, 21/04/1993 P.0029-0034, Articles 1-3, Annex

1(1). The purpose of this Directive is to approximate the laws, regulation and administrative provisions of the Member States relating to unfair terms in contracts concluded between a seller or supplier and a consumer.

1(2). The contractual terms which reflect mandatory statutory or regulatory provisions and the provisions or principles of international conventions to which the Member States or the Community are party, particularly in the transport area, shall not be subject to the provisions of this Directive.

2. For the purposes of this Directive: (a) "unfair terms" means the contractual terms defined in Article 3; (b) "consumer" means any natural person who, in contracts covered by this Directive, is acting for purposes which are outside his trade, business or profession; (c) "seller or supplier" means any natural or legal person who, in contracts covered by this Directive, is acting for purposes relating to his trade, business or profession, whether publicly owned or privately owned.

3(1). A contractual term which has not been individually negotiated shall be regarded as unfair if, contrary to the requirement of good faith, it causes a significant imbalance in the parties' rights and obligations arising under the contract, to the detriment of the consumer.

3(2). A term shall always be regarded as not individually negotiated where it has been drafted in advance and the consumer has therefore not been able to influence the substance of the term, particularly in the context of a pre-formulated standard contract. The fact that certain aspects of a term or one specific term have been individually negotiated shall not exclude the application of this Article to the rest of a contract if an overall assessment of the contract indicates that it is nevertheless a pre-formulated standard contract. Where any seller or supplier claims that a standard term has been individually negotiated, the burden of proof in this respect shall be incumbent on him.

3(3). The Annex shall contain an indicative and non-exhaustive list of the terms which may be regarded as unfair....

Annex (Terms Referred to in Article 3(3)(1)). Terms which have the object or effect of: (a) excluding or limiting the legal liability of a seller or supplier in the event of the death or a consumer or personal injury to the latter resulting from an act or omission of that seller or supplier; (b) excluding or hindering the consumer's right to take legal action or exercise any other legal remedy, particularly by requiring the consumer to take disputes exclusively to arbitration not covered by legal provisions, unduly restricting the evidence available to him or imposing on him a burden of proof which, according to the applicable law, should lie with another party to the contract....

QUÉBEC CONSUMER PROTECTION ACT
§§1(e), 11

1(e). "consumer" means a natural person, except a merchant who obtains goods or services for the purposes of his business....

11(1). Any stipulation that obliges the consumer to refer a dispute to arbitration, that restricts the consumer's right to go before a court, in particular by prohibiting the consumer from bringing a class action, or that deprives the consumer of the right to be a member of a group bringing a class action is prohibited. If a dispute arises after a contract has been entered into, the consumer may then agree to refer the dispute to arbitration.

ONTARIO CONSUMER PROTECTION ACT
S.O. 2002, c. 30, §§1, 6-8

1. In this Act, "consumer" means an individual acting for personal, family or household purposes and does not include a person who is acting for business purposes; "consumer agreement" means an agreement between a supplier and a consumer in which the supplier agrees to supply goods or services for payment; ...

6. Nothing in this Act shall be interpreted to limit any right or remedy that a consumer may have in law.

7(1). The substantive and procedural rights given under this Act apply despite any agreement or waiver to the contrary.

7(2). Without limiting the generality of subsection (1), any term or acknowledgment in a consumer agreement or a related agreement that requires or has the effect of requiring that disputes arising out of a consumer agreement be submitted to arbitration is invalid insofar as it prevents a consumer from exercising a right to commence an action in the Superior Court of Justice given under this Act.

7(3). Despite subsections (1) and (2), after a dispute over which a consumer may commence an action in the Superior Court of Justice arises, the consumer, the supplier and any other person involved in the dispute may agree to resolve the dispute using any procedure that is available in law.

7(4). A settlement or decision that results from the procedure agreed to under subsection (3) is as binding on the parties as such a settlement or decision would be if it were reached in respect of a dispute concerning an agreement to which this Act does not apply.

7(5). Subsection 7(1) of the *Arbitration Act, 1991* does not apply in respect of any proceeding to which subsection (2) applies unless, after the dispute arises, the consumer agrees to submit the dispute to arbitration.

8(1). A consumer may commence a proceeding on behalf of members of a class under the *Class Proceedings Act, 1992* or may become a member of a class in such a proceeding in respect of a dispute arising out of a consumer agreement despite any term or acknowledgment in the consumer agreement or a related agreement that purports to prevent or has the effect of preventing the consumer from commencing or becoming a member of a class proceeding....

POLISH BANKRUPTCY LAW
Articles 142, 147

An arbitration agreement concluded by the bankrupt shall lose its force from the date of the declaration of bankruptcy and pending proceedings shall be subject to discontinuance.

IN RE MARCIA L. PATE
198 B.R. 841 (Bankr. S.D. Ga. 1996)

DALIS, U.S. Bankruptcy Judge. Marcia L. Pate (hereinafter "Debtor") brings this adversary proceeding against Melvin Williams Manufactured Homes, Inc. and Greentree Financial Corporation (hereinafter "Greentree") asserting state law claims for violation of the Uniform Commercial Code—Sales as adopted in Georgia, Georgia Motor Vehicle Sales Finance Act and fraud and for violation of the Federal Truth in Lending Act arising out of the Debtor's purchase and financing of a mobile home from the Defendants. The Defendants answered the complaint and Defendant Greentree filed a motion to stay the adversary proceedings and to compel the Debtor to submit the claims to arbitration.... The motion is granted.

The claims asserted by the Debtor are core proceedings [within the jurisdiction of the bankruptcy court.] ... Defendant Greentree filed a secured claim in the amount of $38,996.19 in the Debtor's Chapter 13 case. Additionally, the claims asserted by the Debtor against both Defendants arose before the bankruptcy filing, constitute assets of the estate, and this adversary proceeding therefore affects the liquidation of estate assets. The arbitration clause included in the sales contract reads as follows:

> "18. ARBITRATION: All disputes, claims or controversies arising from or relating to this Contract or the relationships which result from this Contract, or the validity of its arbitration clause or the entire Contract, shall be resolved by binding arbitration by one arbitrator selected by Assignee with consent of the Buyer(s). This arbitration contract is made pursuant to a transaction in interstate commerce, and shall be governed by the Federal Arbitration Act at 9 U.S.C. §1. Judgment upon the award may be entered in any court having jurisdiction. The parties agree and understand that they chose arbitration instead of litigation to resolve disputes. The parties understand that they have a right or opportunity to litigate disputes through a court, but they prefer to resolve their disputes through arbitration, except as pro-

vided herein. **THE PARTIES VOLUNTARILY AND KNOWINGLY WAIVE ANY RIGHT THEY HAVE TO A JURY TRIAL EITHER PURSUANT TO ARBITRATION UNDER THIS CLAUSE OR PURSUANT TO A COURT ACTION BY ASSIGNEE (AS PROVIDED HEREIN)**. The parties agree and understand that all disputes arising under case law, statutory law and all other laws including, but not limited to, all contract, tort and property disputes will be subject to binding arbitration in accord with this Contract. The parties agree and understand that the arbitrator shall have all powers provided by the law and the Contract. These powers include all legal and equitable remedies including, but not limited to, money damages, declaratory relief and injunctive relief. Notwithstanding anything hereunto the contrary, Assignee retains an option to use judicial or non-judicial relief to enforce a security agreement relating to the Manufactured Home secured in a transaction underlying this arbitration agreement, to enforce the monetary obligation secured by the Manufactured Home or to foreclose on the Manufactured Home. Such judicial relief would take the form of a lawsuit. The institution and maintenance of an action for judicial relief in a court to foreclose upon any collateral, to obtain monetary judgment or to enforce the security agreement shall not constitute a waiver of the right of any party to compel arbitration regarding any other dispute or remedy subject to arbitration in this Contract, including the filing of counterclaim in a suit brought by Assignee pursuant to this provision." ...

The parties concede that Georgia law applies to this contract. The Debtor asserts that under Georgia law the arbitration clause lacks mutuality of obligation because it forces the Debtor to arbitrate any claims she may have against the Defendants but preserves the Defendants' right to bring an action in court to enforce the security agreement or to collect any amounts payable under the contract. Georgia law does not require a contract to provide for mutual obligations if the contract provides additional consideration to support one party's obligation. *Brack v. Brownlee*, 273 S.E.2d 390 (Ga. 1981). "Where there is no other consideration for a contract, the mutual promises must be binding on both parties, for the reason that only a binding promise is sufficient consideration for a promise of the other party." However, "where there is any other consideration for a contract so that each promise does not depend upon the other for consideration, mutuality of obligation is not essential." The Debtor does not dispute that the parties have provided each other with consideration beyond the promise to arbitrate some of the claims arising between them. Therefore, the commitment to arbitrate does not have to be mutually binding upon all parties....

The final issue for consideration is whether enforcing the arbitration clause under the FAA conflicts with the policies and goals of the Bankruptcy Code.... The [FAA] established a "federal policy favoring arbitration." *Moses H. Cone Mem. Hosp. v. Mercury Const. Corp.*, 460 U.S. 1, 24. Congress established the Bankruptcy Code as a means of providing debtors an efficient, costs effective means of obtaining a fresh start and for dispute adjudication. Congress' intent in the Bankruptcy Reform Act of 1978 was to reduce "... unnecessary delays, expenses, and duplications of effort ... in bankruptcy cases." *Zimmerman v. Continental Airlines, Inc.*, 712 F.2d 55, 58 (3d Cir. 1983) (bankruptcy court has discretion to compel parties to arbitrate issues). *But see Hays and Co. v. Merrill Lynch, Pierce, Fenner & Smith, Inc.*, 885 F.2d 1149 (3d Cir. 1989) (bankruptcy courts lack discretion to deny arbitration in non-core proceedings). Although the rationale of *Zimmerman* was repudiated in *Hays*, *Hays* dealt with a non-core proceeding and recognized that the court "must carefully determine whether any underlying purpose of the Bankruptcy Code would be adversely affected by enforcing an arbitration clause and that ... such a clause [must be enforced] unless that effect would seriously jeopardize the objectives of that [Bankruptcy] Code." However, general assertions that the Bankruptcy Code was "designed to consolidate jurisdiction over property of the debtor and reflects a policy favoring a unified and consistent exercise of jurisdiction and supervision over the debtor and the debtor's estate," or that allowing arbitration would affect the overall administration of the estate by causing inefficient delay, duplicative proceedings, or a collateral effect of such arbitration on estate administration are insufficient to override the general federal policy favoring arbitration.

In this case no specific adverse effect can be shown. The Debtor's underlying Chapter 13 [plan recognized Greentree's claim]: "Debtor shall make regular post-petition payments as they come due to creditors (named below) holding security interest in Debtor's residence. Any claim filed for pre-petition arrearage on such obligations shall be paid by distributions from the Chapter 13 trustee. Greentree Financial." Defendant Greentree has an allowed, unobjected to, secure claim in the Chapter 13 case reflecting a principal balance due as of the Chapter 13 filing of $38,996.19.... By order filed December 6, 1995 I granted Defendant Greentree's motion for relief from the stay of 11 U.S.C. §362 in order to foreclose its security interest in the mobile home that is the subject matter of the contract between the parties at issue in this adversary proceeding.... With the grant of relief from the stay of 11 U.S.C. §362, the Chapter 13 trustee will make no further distributions to Greentree under the Debtor's plan. Relief from the stay of §362 having taking the administration of the debt to Greentree outside the distribution scheme of the Chapter 13 case, no other creditor interests are affected. The Plaintiff has failed to meet her burden of proof by a preponderance of the evidence that this court should exercise its discretion by refusing to permit arbitration of this core proceeding, the Plaintiff has failed to establish any adverse effect on the administration of this case by permitting the contractually agreed to arbitration to go forward....

IN RE UNITED STATES LINES, INC.
197 F.3d 631 (2d Cir. 1999)

WALKER, Circuit Judge. The United States Lines, Inc. and the United States Lines (S.A.) Inc., Reorganization Trust (the "Trust") sued in the Bankruptcy Court for the Southern District of New York ... seeking a declaratory judgment to establish the Trust's rights under various insurance contracts [containing arbitration agreements, which the insurers (referred to as "Clubs") sought to enforce]. The bankruptcy court held that the action was within its core jurisdiction and denied the defendants' motion to compel arbitration of the proceedings. The District Court ... reversed and held that the insurance contract disputes were not core proceedings [and ordered] arbitration to go forward.... We now reverse and remand....

The parties have entered into valid agreements to arbitrate their contract disputes, some of which call for international arbitration. Arbitration is favored in our judicial system, and the [FAA] mandates enforcement of valid arbitration agreements. The arbitration preference is particularly strong for international arbitration agreements. *See Mitsubishi Motors*, 473 U.S. at 629 ("Concerns of international comity, respect for the capacities of foreign and transnational tribunals, and sensitivity to the need of the international commercial system for predictability in the resolution of disputes require enforce[ment of] the parties' [arbitration] agreement, even assuming that a contrary result would be forthcoming in a domestic context."). The Clubs [*i.e.*, the insurers] therefore argue that the bankruptcy court cannot enjoin arbitration of the proceedings. We disagree.

"Like any statutory directive, the [FAA's] mandate may be overridden by a contrary congressional command." *Shearson/Am. Express,* 482 U.S. at 226. That is true even where arbitration is sought subject to an international arbitration agreement. The [New York] Convention "which requires the recognition of agreements to arbitration that involve 'subject matter capable of settlement by arbitration,' contemplates exceptions to arbitrability grounded in domestic law." *Mitsubishi*, 473 U.S. at 639 n. 21. "If Congress did intend to limit or prohibit waiver of a judicial forum for a particular claim such an intent will be deductible from [the statute's] text or legislative history, or from an inherent conflict between arbitration and the statute's underlying purposes." *Shearson/Am. Express*, 482 U.S. at 227. In the bankruptcy setting, congressional intent to permit a bankruptcy court to enjoin arbitration is sufficiently clear to override even international arbitration agreements.

The Bankruptcy Court has broad, well-established powers ... to preserve the integrity of the reorganization process. Section 105 of the Bankruptcy Code states that where it has jurisdiction, the bankruptcy "court may issue *any* order, process, or judgment that is necessary or appropriate to carry out the provisions of the title." 11 U.S.C. §105(a) (emphasis added). The language of §362, the automatic stay provision, is equally encompassing: "Except as provided in subsection (b) of this section, a petition [for bankruptcy protection].... operates as a stay, applicable to all entities, of—the commencement or continuation ... of a judicial, administrative or other action or proceeding against the debtor...." 11 U.S.C. §362(a)(1). "As the legislative history of the automatic stay provision reveals, the scope of §362(a)(1) is broad, staying all proceedings, including arbitration...." *FAA v. Gull Air, Inc.*, 890 F.2d 1255, 1262 (1st Cir. 1989). Finally, one of the core purposes of bankruptcy "effectuated by §§362 and 105 of the Code" is to "allow the bankruptcy court to centralize all disputes concerning property of the debtor's estate so that reorganization can proceed efficiently, unimpeded by uncoordinated proceedings in other arenas." *Shugrue v. Air Line Pilots Ass'n Int'l*, 992 F.2d 984, 989 (2d Cir. 1990). However, by not granting the bankruptcy court exclusive jurisdiction over non-core matters, "it is clear that the 1984 Congress did not envision all bankruptcy related matters being adjudicated in a single bankruptcy court." *Hays & Co. v. Merrill Lynch, Pierce, Fenner & Smith, Inc.*, 885 F.2d 1149, 1157 (3d Cir. 1989).

Thus, there will be occasions where a dispute involving both the Bankruptcy Code and the [FAA], "presents a conflict of near polar extremes: bankruptcy policy experts an inexorable pull towards centralization while arbitration policy advocates a decentralized approach towards dispute resolution." *Societe Nationale Algerienne Pour La Recherche v. Distrigas Corp.*, 80 B.R. 606, 610 (D. Mass. 1987). Such a conflict is lessened in non-core proceedings which are unlikely to present a conflict sufficient to override by implications the presumption in favor of arbitration. Core proceedings implicate more pressing bankruptcy concerns, but even a determination that a proceeding is core will not automatically give the bankruptcy court discretion to stay arbitration. "Certainly not all core bankruptcy proceedings are premised on provisions of the Code that 'inherently conflict' with the [FAA]; nor would arbitration of such proceedings necessarily jeopardize the objectives of the Bankruptcy Code." *Ins. Co. of N. Am. v. NGC Settlement Trust etc.*, 118 F.3d 1056, 1067 (5th Cir. 1997). However, there are circumstances in which a bankruptcy court may stay arbitration, and in this case the bankruptcy court was correct that it had discretion to do so.

In exercising its discretion over whether, in core proceedings, arbitration provisions ought to be denied effect, the bankruptcy court must still "carefully determine whether any underlying purpose of the Bankruptcy Code would be adversely affected by enforcing an arbitration clause." *Hays & Co.*, 885 F.2d at 1161. The [FAA] as interpreted by the Supreme Court dictates that an arbitration clause should be enforced "unless [doing so] would seriously jeopardize the objectives of the Code." ... Where the bankruptcy court has properly considered the conflicting policies in accordance with law, we acknowledge its exercise of discretion and show due deference to its determination that arbitration will seriously jeopardize a particular core bankruptcy proceeding. We see no basis for disturbing the bankruptcy court's determination ... here.

[T]he declaratory judgment proceedings [in bankruptcy court] are integral to the bankruptcy court's ability to preserve and equitably distribute the Trust's assets. Furthermore, ... the bankruptcy court is the preferable venue in which to handle mass tort actions involving claims against an insolvent debtor. The need for a centralized proceedings is further augmented by the complex factual scenario, involving multiple claims, policies and insurers. The bankruptcy court was not clearly erroneous in finding that "arbitration of the disputes raised in the Complaint would prejudice the Trust's efforts to preserve the Trust as a means to compensate claimants." It was within the bankruptcy court's discretion to refuse to refer the declaratory judgment proceedings, which it properly found to be core, to arbitration....

NOTES

1. *Historic prohibitions against arbitration of labor and employment disputes.* Consider Article 1676(5) of the Belgian Judicial Code and Article 806 of the Italian Code of Civil Procedure. What is the policy rationale underlying these provisions? What is it about disputes between employers and employees that made the Belgian and Italian legislatures conclude that arbitration was unsuitable to resolve them? Is it the factual character of these disputes (*e.g.*, the facts are difficult to gather)? Is it the legal character (*e.g.*, the law is very complex)? Is it the effects on third-party rights? Or is it ensuring protection for a particular societal group? Is the object of this protection a generous recovery for members of the protected group? Or is that too cynical?

    What is the effect of Article 1676(5) and Article 806? Do they render all arbitration agreements between employers and employees nonarbitrable? What about agreements to arbitrate disputes that have already arisen? What about disputes not falling into the jurisdiction of specialized tribunals? Compare Article 4 of the Supplementary Provisions of the Japanese Arbitration Law. What is its scope? Why might the Japanese law only be applicable "for the time being"?

    Consider recent developments in Italian labor legislation: Law No. 183 of November 4, 2010 and Decree No. 276 of September 10, 2003 provide that arbitration clauses in employment agreements are valid if they are regulated by a collective labor agreement and have been approved by a Certification Commission and that the arbitration clause cannot relate to disputes arising out of termination of employment. Is such a system desirable?

2. *Nonarbitrability versus contractual invalidity*. By their terms, do the Belgian, Italian and Japanese statutory provisions state rules of contractual invalidity or nonarbitrability? Note that rules of contractual invalidity generally invalidate an arbitration agreement, providing that it has no binding effects in any circumstances; in contrast, the nonarbitrability doctrine provides that certain disputes may not be arbitrated, notwithstanding an otherwise valid agreement to arbitrate, which may be enforced with respect to other claims. *See infra* pp. 475, 479-83.

    The Belgian and Japanese statutes both provide that certain arbitration agreements are "null and void" or "null." Is it in fact specified categories of agreements that are rendered null? Suppose an arbitration agreement includes both the category of disputes covered by the legislation and other, arbitrable categories of disputes. Would the agreement to arbitrate be valid as to the latter categories of disputes? Compare the texts of Article 806 of the Italian Code of Civil Procedure and Article 31(10) of Law No. 183 of November 4, 2010 ("the arbitration clause, under penalty of nullity, must be certified in accordance with the provisions of Title VIII of the Legislative decree of 10 September 2003 No. 276, by certification authorities").

    Why is it relevant to consider whether a legislative enactment provides a rule of contractual invalidity or rule of nonarbitrability? Are the same choice-of-law rules necessarily applicable in both cases? *See supra* pp. 287-315 & *infra* pp. 499-510.

3. *U.S. approach to arbitration of labor and employment disputes*. Consider the approach to labor disputes in the U.S. FAA and, in particular, *Bautista*. What explains the differences between the Belgian/Italian/Japanese approach and that of the United States? Note that U.S. law and policy has long encouraged arbitration of many labor disputes, as a specialized mode of dispute resolution regarded by both U.S. legislative and judicial opinion as superior to that of litigation, while imposing only narrow nonarbitrability limits on some forms of employer-employee disputes. *See* T. Bornstein, A. Gosline & M. Greenbaum, *Labor and Employment Arbitration* §1.04 (2007); *United Steelworkers of Am. v. Enter. Wheel & Car Corp.*, 363 U.S. 593 (1960). Is there anything surprising about the fact that different jurisdictions adopt different means of dealing with labor issues?

4. *Potential risks of employee-employer arbitration*. Are there inherent risks in arbitration between employers and employees? What are those risks? Is the risk that a party with disproportionate bargaining power, who is a repeat player in a particular type of dispute, will unfairly bias the arbitral process in its own favor? Who is likely the more frequent repeat player in the employment context? What about union representatives for employees? Law firms specializing in employment claims?

    For one example of a one-sided arbitration agreement in the employment context, involving a form arbitration agreement between Hooters (a fast-food chain) and its employees, see:

    > "The Hooters rules when taken as a whole, however, are so one-sided that their only possible purpose is to undermine the neutrality of the proceeding. The rules require the employee to provide the company notice of her claim at the outset, including 'the nature of the Claim' and 'the specific act(s) or omissions(s) which are the basis of the Claim.' Hooters, on the other hand, is not required to file any responsive pleadings or to notice its defenses. Additionally, at the time of filing this notice, the employee must provide the company with a list of all fact witnesses with a brief summary of the facts known to each. The company, however, is not required to reciprocate.

The Hooters rules also provide a mechanism for selecting a panel of three arbitrators that is crafted to ensure a biased decisionmaker. The employee and Hooters each select an arbitrator, and the two arbitrators in turn select a third. Good enough, except that the employee's arbitrator and the third arbitrator must be selected from a list of arbitrators created exclusively by Hooters. This gives Hooters control over the entire panel and places no limits whatsoever on whom Hooters can put on the list. Under the rules, Hooters is free to devise lists of partial arbitrators who have existing relationships, financial or familial, with Hooters and its management. In fact, the rules do not even prohibit Hooters from placing its managers themselves on the list. Further, nothing in the rules restricts Hooters from punishing arbitrators who rule against the company by removing them from the list. Given the unrestricted control that one party (Hooters) has over the panel, the selection of an impartial decision maker would be a surprising result.

Nor is fairness to be found once the proceedings are begun. Although Hooters may expand the scope of arbitration to any matter, 'whether related or not to the Employee's Claim,' the employee cannot raise 'any matter not included in the Notice of Claim.' Similarly, Hooters is permitted to move for summary dismissal of employee claims before a hearing is held whereas the employee is not permitted to seek summary judgment. Hooters, but not the employee, may record the arbitration hearing 'by audio or videotaping or by verbatim transcription.' The rules also grant Hooters the right to bring suit in court to vacate or modify an arbitral award when it can show, by a preponderance of the evidence, that the panel exceeded its authority. No such right is granted to the employee.

In addition, the rules provide that upon 30 days notice Hooters, but not the employee, may cancel the agreement to arbitrate. Moreover, Hooters reserves the right to modify the rules, 'in whole or in part,' whenever it wishes and 'without notice' to the employee. Nothing in the rules even prohibits Hooters from changing the rules in the middle of an arbitration proceeding." *Hooters of Am., Inc. v. Phillips*, 173 F.3d 933, 938-39 (4th Cir. 1999).

How are the risks of one-side arbitration procedures best dealt with? Note that the court in *Hooters* invalidated the provisions referred to above: "By promulgating this system of warped rules, Hooters so skewed the process in its favor that Phillips has been denied arbitration in any meaningful sense of the word. To uphold the promulgation of this aberrational scheme under the heading of arbitration would undermine, not advance, the federal policy favoring alternative dispute resolution. This we refuse to do." Can't one-sided arbitration agreements in the employment arbitration context be invalidated, just as one-sided agreements in other contexts can be invalidated? What are the costs of a blanket prohibition against arbitration between employers and employees?

5. *Prohibitions against arbitration of disputes under consumer contracts.* Consider the excerpts from the EU's Unfair Terms in Consumer Contracts Directive, which subjects the provisions of standard form consumer contracts to statutory fairness requirements. Among other things, the Directive provides that a provision is *prima facie* unfair, and therefore invalid, if it "requir[es] the consumer to take disputes exclusively to arbitration not covered by legal provision." EU Council Directive 93/13/EEC, O.J. L 095, 23/04/1993, at 29, Annex 1(q). Although the critical phrase, "by legal provision," is not defined, some EU Member States have implemented this provision by adopting legislation that deems arbitration clauses in form contracts unfair (and therefore invalid) if they require binding arbitration of future disputes involving claims for less

than specified sums (*e.g.*, approximately $10,000). *E.g.*, Office of Fair Trading, *Unfair Contract Terms Guidance*, ¶¶17.2 to 17.3 (2008) (United Kingdom). What is the rationale for this provision? Is it based on sound policy or simple politics?

6. *Current U.S. approach to arbitration of consumer disputes.* Consider the approach to consumer disputes adopted in *Buckeye* and *Marcia Pate*. Again, what explains this difference between the EU/Canadian approach? Consider the following, by a U.S. court, rejecting challenges to the validity of an arbitration clause included in form agreements used with consumers:

    "Ours is not a bazaar economy, in which the terms of every transaction, or even of most transactions are individually dickered; ... [F]orm contracts enable enormous savings in transaction costs, and the abuses to which they occasionally give rise can be controlled without altering traditional doctrines, provided those doctrines are interpreted flexibly, realistically." *N.W. Nat'l Ins. Co. v. Donovan*, 916 F.2d 372, 377 (7th Cir. 1990) (Posner, J.).

    What are the abuses that Judge Posner refers to? How would these abuses manifest themselves in the context of arbitration agreements? For some examples, in addition to those in the *Hooters* case, see *McMullen v. Meijer, Inc.*, 355 F.3d 485, 490 (6th Cir. 2004) (procedure allowing employer exclusive control over the pool of potential arbitrators); *Broemmer v. Abortion Serv. of Phoenix, Ltd*, 840 P.2d 1013 (Ariz. 1992) (requirement that arbitrator be licensed medical doctor, in medical malpractice dispute, unconscionable).

    What is required in order that traditional principles of contract law can control those abuses? Would this be sufficient? Recall the statutory protections against one-sided arbitration agreements in some European jurisdictions. *See supra* pp. 393-412. Recall also the decisions in *Judgment of 26 January 1989*, *Gateway* and *Hooters*. Is there any reason to think that doctrines of unconscionability and duress do not provide adequate protections for consumers?

7. *Alternative approaches to arbitration of consumer disputes.* Consider the approaches adopted for the arbitration of consumer disputes in Ontario, Québec and Japan. How do these approaches differ from that in the European Union? What explains the different approaches? Which is preferable? If consumer arbitration is to be limited, which approach is preferable?

    What are the costs of a blanket legal prohibition against all pre-dispute labor and consumer arbitration agreements? If one accepts that arbitration is potentially cheaper, quicker and more expert than litigation, won't a blanket prohibition deny parties that want these benefits of the opportunity to obtain them? Is there a better way to protect against the potential abuses of employment or consumer relations than a blanket prohibition against pre-dispute arbitration agreements? Can an approach similar to that in *Brower v. Gateway* be adopted in legislation? How?

8. *Treatment of consumer and labor disputes under UNCITRAL Model Law.* How does the Model Law deal with consumer and labor disputes? Consider Article 1(5), which provides that "this Law shall not affect any other law of this State by virtue of which certain disputes may not be submitted to arbitration ..." Note that the Ontario and Québec legislation has been adopted in jurisdictions that have adopted the Model Law.

9. *Proposed legislation affecting arbitration of consumer disputes in United States.* For the past several years, legislation has been proposed in the U.S. Congress that would

limit the extent to which consumer, employment and some other disputes may be arbitrated. The so-called "Arbitration Fairness Act" has been proposed in various forms, one example of which would provide:

> (a) IN GENERAL. Notwithstanding any other provision of this title, no predispute arbitration agreement shall be valid or enforceable if it requires arbitration of an employment dispute, consumer dispute, antitrust dispute, or civil rights dispute.

"Consumer disputes" are defined to include "a dispute an individual who seeks or acquires real or personal property, services (including services relating to securities and other investments), money, or credit for personal, family, or household purposes and the seller or provider of such property, services, money, or credit." Is this proposal wise? Is it consistent with U.S. obligations under the New York Convention?

10. *Validity of legislation invalidating pre-dispute agreements to arbitrate consumer or employment disputes under New York Convention.* Recall that Articles II(1) and II(3) of the New York Convention require Contracting States to recognize agreements to arbitrate and refer the parties to such agreement to arbitration. *See supra* pp. 177-90, 315-34. Should the New York Convention be interpreted as imposing international limits on a Contracting State's ability to restrict agreements to arbitrate labor and consumer disputes? What about limits in international settings?

Note that the Convention only requires recognition of agreements to arbitrate disputes that are not "null and void." If legislation provides that agreements to arbitrate labor and consumer disputes are null and void, how can such legislation be inconsistent with Article II? Suppose a Contracting State enacted legislation providing that all arbitration agreements are null and void; would that be consistent with Article II? Why not? What is the distinction between that legislation and the labor and consumer statutes in Europe and elsewhere? Does that distinction make a difference? In general, what is the nationality of consumers and workers supposedly protected by nonarbitrability provisions? Of multinational vendors and employers? Is that relevant?

11. *Arbitration of bankruptcy-related disputes.* Parties to international transactions are not infrequently placed into bankruptcy or insolvency under national law. These proceedings often entail some form of judicial or administrative protection against the claims of creditors; in many jurisdictions, only national courts (often specialized courts) have the authority to commence, administer and wind-up bankruptcy proceedings, including proceedings that liquidate a bankrupt company, reschedule its liabilities, operate it under receivership or administration, or distribute payments to creditors. Disputes concerning these "core" bankruptcy functions are almost universally considered nonarbitrable, whether in domestic or international arbitrations. *See* Kaufmann-Kohler & Lévy, *Insolvency and International Arbitration*, in H. Peter, N. Jeandin & J. Kilborn (eds.), *The Challenges of Insolvency Law Reform in the 21st Century* 257, 262-63 (2006); Mantilla-Serrano, *International Arbitration and Insolvency Proceedings*, 11 Arb. Int'l 51, 65 (1995). Thus, parties could not agree to arbitrate whether or not an entity is to be declared bankrupt or whether a judicially-sanctioned liquidation plan, paying creditors a pro rata share of their claims, is to be adopted.

Suppose, however, that a bankrupt entity is a party to a contract containing an arbitration clause, and disputes have arisen under that contract. Does the fact that the party has become bankrupt invalidate the arbitration agreement or render the parties' dispute nonarbitrable?

12. *Legislation invalidating arbitration agreements of bankrupt parties.* Consider the Polish bankruptcy legislation. What does it provide? *Compare* Latvian Civil Procedure Law, Art. 487(8) (disputes "regarding the rights and obligations of persons with respect to whom insolvency or bankruptcy proceedings have been initiated before the making of the award by the arbitral tribunal" are not arbitrable). What is the rationale of these statutes? Is it appropriate for a company, which promises to arbitrate with a counterparty, to be permitted to resile from that commitment because it encounters serious financial difficulties? What is the rationale for transferring all pending disputes, including arbitrations, to a single forum (the bankruptcy proceeding)? Is it, in part, because that forum will be predisposed towards the debtor? Assuming this is appropriate in domestic settings, is it appropriate in international settings, where the parties have bargained for a nationally neutral proceeding?

13. *Approach to bankruptcy issues under FAA.* Consider the court's analysis in *Pate* and *United States Lines*. Contrast the U.S. approach to that in Poland and Latvia. Which is preferable? What are the advantages and disadvantages of each?

14. *Choice of law governing validity of agreement to arbitrate by bankrupt entity.* Suppose that a Polish company agrees to arbitrate in Switzerland (against a non-Polish company) and then subsequently becomes bankrupt. What effect does Article 147 have on the agreement to arbitrate? Does the bankruptcy of the Polish company affect its capacity to conclude a valid arbitration agreement? Does it matter whether the arbitral seat is in Poland or abroad? What law governs issues of capacity? In an arbitration seated outside Poland? *See infra* p. 470. Alternatively, does the Polish legislation concern the substantive validity of the arbitration agreement, as a question of frustration or illegality? If so, what law governs these issues?

  Compare Syska (Elektrim SA) v. Vivendi Universal SA [2009] EWCA Civ 677 (English Ct. App.) *with Judgment of 31 May 2009,* 28 ASA Bull. 104 (2010) (Swiss Fed. Trib.).

  Suppose that Polish legislation invalidates agreements to arbitrate, but not other contracts of Polish companies. Suppose that Polish legislation does not invalidate forum selection clauses or does not invalidate forum selection clauses selecting Polish courts. Do any of these circumstances raise questions about the consistency of the hypothesized legislation with the New York Convention? On what basis?

15. *Asymmetrical arbitration agreements.* Recall the discussion regarding the unconscionability of arbitration clauses. *See supra* pp. 393-412. Consider the arbitration clause in *Marcia Pate.* Note that it preserved Greentree's rights to litigate against Pate, while obligating Pate to arbitrate her claims. Is this asymmetric arrangement valid? Consider the court's response in *Pate.* Do you agree? Is there anything fundamentally unfair about an agreement that allows one party, but not the other, to litigate? What about an asymmetric agreement where there are other indicia of unfairness?

f. Lack of Capacity

A party's lack of capacity to have entered into an arbitration agreement is universally recognized as a basis for resisting enforcement of the agreement.[53] The requirement, in Article II of the New York Convention, for an "arbitration agreement" and its exception for "null and void" agreements readily encompass lack of capacity claims. Likewise, Article V(1)(a) of the Convention permits national courts to deny recognition to an award if the parties to the arbitration agreement "were, under the law applicable to them, under some incapacity."

The requirement that a party have had capacity to enter into a binding arbitration agreement is little different from the role of capacity in other areas of the law. Generally-applicable contract defenses going to capacity—such as incompetence, minority, and lack of corporate authorization—are frequently applied in the context of arbitration agreements, just as they are elsewhere.[54] In addition, however, some national laws impose special requirements with respect to the capacity of parties to enter into arbitration agreements (*i.e.*, restrictions on the power of government entities to arbitrate certain disputes). The materials excerpted below illustrate the ways in which issues of capacity arise in international arbitration.

CENTROAMERICANOS, SA v. REFINADORA COSTARRICENSE DE PETROLEOS, SA
1989 U.S. Dist. LEXIS 5429 (S.D.N.Y.)

EDELSTEIN, District Judge. Petitioner, Buques Centroamericanos, SA ("Bucesa"), has filed the instant petition to confirm an arbitration award against respondent Refinadora Costarricense de Petroleos, SA ("Recope"), pursuant to the [FAA] and the [New York] Convention.

Both Recope and Bucesa are Costa Rican corporations. They entered an affreightment agreement for the transport of crude oil from the Caribbean to Costa Rica. The agreement contained a broad arbitration clause that provided for the submission to arbitration in New York or London of "[a]ny and all differences and disputes of whatsoever nature arising out of this Charter." A dispute arose over the contract and Bucesa initiated an arbitration proceeding.... [A] panel of three arbitrators ... awarded Bucesa $243,779.44 plus interest against Recope.

Recope contends that the award should not be confirmed on the ground that the arbitration agreement was invalid. According to respondent, Recope is and, at the time it entered the agreement, was a corporation wholly owned by the Government of Costa Rica. Recope contends that under the laws of Costa Rica an agreement to arbitrate by a government-owned corporation must be approved by the Costa Rican legislature. Recope contends that this agreement is null and void because it was not approved by the legislature.

Recope acknowledges that it raised the same arguments before the arbitrator and that they were rejected. Its legal basis for opposing the confirmation by this court is Article V(1)(a) of the Convention.... Recope thus concludes that the arbitration agreement was

---

53. *See* G. Born, *International Commercial Arbitration* 725 (2d ed. 2014).
54. *See* G. Born, *International Commercial Arbitration* 727 (2d ed. 2014).

invalid and that Recope was "under some incapacity," namely the purported bar under the laws of Costa Rica....

As noted, the issues raised by Recope were also raised before the arbitrators. Arbitrators have the power to decide all questions necessary to dispose of the issue submitted. The arbitrators in this case found that the arbitration agreement, by its terms was governed by the laws of New York and further, that under the laws of New York the agreement is enforceable. Finally, the arbitrators found that by entering into the agreement to arbitrate and by attending three arbitration hearings Recope had waived any sovereign immunity it might have had.

The findings of an arbitrator are not to be disturbed unless they are in "manifest disregard" of the law. *Wilko v. Swan*, 346 U.S. 427, 436 (1953). To review arbitration awards *de novo* would frustrate the very purpose of arbitration. The findings of the arbitrators were not only not in manifest disregard, but are well founded on the law and correct. The parties voluntarily entered an arbitration agreement specifying that New York law would govern the agreement. Recope participated in three hearings before the arbitrators and submitted to them the same issues it raises now before this court. Now it comes before this court and contends that the arbitrators had no authority to make the findings that they made. This position is simply not tenable. The court finds that the arbitrators' award was well founded and that none of the grounds articulated in Article V of the Convention have been proved by Recope....

CONSTITUTION OF ISLAMIC REPUBLIC OF IRAN
Article 139

[T]he resolution of disputes concerning state property, or the submission of such disputes to arbitration, shall in each case be subject to approval by the Council of Ministers and must be notified to Parliament. Cases in which one party to the dispute is foreign, as well as important domestic disputes, must also be approved by Parliament.

B.V. BUREAU WIJSMULLER v. UNITED STATES OF AMERICA AS OWNER OF THE WARSHIP JULIUS A. FURER
1976 A.M.C. 2514 (S.D.N.Y. 1976)

HAIGHT, District Judge. Plaintiff B.V. Bureau Wijsmuller ("Wijsmuller"), a professional marine salvage company, moves this court for an order, pursuant to [§206 of the FAA] directing defendant United States of America to proceed to arbitration of plaintiff's salvage claim in London, in accordance with the terms of a Lloyd's open form salvage agreement ("LOF") signed by the Captain of defendant's warship Julius A. Furer prior to rendition by Wijsmuller of the salvage services which form the subject matter of this action. The Government contends that it is not bound by the LOF or the provisions for arbitration which it contains. Accordingly, the Government contends, the motion to compel arbitration must be denied, and the case go forward in this court pursuant to the provisions of the Public Vessels Act, 46 U.S.C. §78.... The court concludes that the United States is not bound by the LOF, and accordingly is not required to participate in arbitration of Wijsmuller's claim for salvage....

The Julius A. Furer is a warship of the United States Navy. On June 30, 1974 the vessel stranded off the coast of The Netherlands. Plaintiff Wijsmuller, one of the leading maritime salvage companies in the world, directed four salvage tugs to the assistance of the Furer. Before commencing assistance to the warship, Wijsmuller's representative ... obtained the signature of the Captain of the Furer, Commander S.H. Edwards, to the LOF, also known as the Lloyd's "no cure-no pay" salvage agreement, or the Lloyd's Standard Form of Salvage Agreement. It does not appear from the papers before me that Commander Edwards consulted higher authority before signing the LOF....

The LOF, known throughout the maritime industry and in use by salvors for many years, provides for submission of the salvor's claim for salvage compensation to binding arbitration in London, before an arbitrator appointed by the Committee of Lloyd's. The arbitration agreement ... provides that the arbitration will be held in accordance with English law. The LOF also provides for the giving of security by the owner of the salved property (ship or cargo)....

The Furer was freed from the strand on July 1, 1974. Wijsmuller filed its complaint in this court, pursuant to the Public Vessels Act, which provides: "A libel in personam in admiralty may be brought against the United States, or a petition impleading the United States, for damages caused by a public vessel of the United States, and for compensation for towage and salvage services, including contract salvage, rendered to public vessel of the United States...." In its complaint, Wijsmuller reserved the right to demand arbitration in accordance with the LOF. By its present motion, Wijsmuller seeks an order directing the United States to proceed to arbitration before Mr. G.R.A. Darling, Q.C., the arbitrator appointed by Lloyd's. The Government, while conceding that "during the period of the strand, the plaintiff provided some assistance during attempts to float the Furer," has consistently taken the position that it is not bound by the terms of the LOF, and is not required to submit to arbitration before Mr. Darling or anyone else in London. The Government contends that Wijsmuller's salvage compensation must be fixed by this court in accordance with principles of maritime law declared by the federal courts sitting in admiralty....

Absent an express waiver of sovereign immunity, no suit lies against the sovereign. Prior to execution of the Public Vessels Act and its related statutes, the only means of pressing an affirmative claim against the United States for the acts of one of its vessels was by a special act of Congress. The armor of sovereign immunity has now been put aside by the statutes in question; but it is equally well settled that suits against the United States must conform strictly to the provisions of the enabling statutes. The initial question, therefore, is whether by enacting the Public Vessels Act Congress intended to waive the sovereign immunity of the United States in such a manner as to require the Government to submit to arbitration in London, in accordance with contractual terms such as those contained in the LOF. That question must clearly be answered in the negative. While the Public Vessels Act permits suits against the United States for salvage services rendered to one of its public vessels, the venue of such a suit is the U.S. District Court.... Arbitration in London, before an arbitrator appointed by the Committee of Lloyd's or any other body, is entirely inconsistent with the statutory scheme....

The fact that Commander Edwards, the commanding officer of the Furer, signed the LOF is of no legal consequence. Indeed, it would have made no difference if the Chief of Naval Operations had chanced to be upon the Furer, and had executed the contract himself. That is because only the Congress can remove or tailor the armor of the sovereign's immunity from suit; no officer or representative, regardless of rank, good intentions, or innocent misapprehension of his powers, has the requisite authority. In *United States v. Shaw*,

309 U.S. 495, 500 ([1940]), the Supreme Court stated generally that: "Without specific statutory consent, no suit may be brought against the United States. No officer by his action can confer jurisdiction. Even when suits are authorized they must be brought only in designated courts." ...

Wijsmuller also contends that the United States is bound to arbitrate ... as the result of ... 46 U.S.C. §786:

> "The Attorney General of the United States is authorized to arbitrate, compromise, or settle any claim on which a libel or cross libel would lie under the provisions of this chapter, and for which a libel or cross libel has actually been filed."

This argument is specious. The statute does no more than to confer authority upon the Attorney General to arbitrate claims which would otherwise be justiciable in the district courts. By no stretch of the imagination can such limited authority be expanded so as to include the distinguished arbitrator appointed by the Committee of Lloyd's. Accepting arguendo the doubtful proposition that the Attorney General has the authority to delegate his arbitrator's function to the Lloyd's arbitrator, the record in this case makes it clear that he declines to do so.

But Wijsmuller contends that all the foregoing principles and lines of authority are changed by the adherence of the United States, in 1970, to the [New York] Convention.... [A]dherence by the United States to the Convention reflects an expression of public policy in favor of resolving international commercial disputes through arbitration. However, it does not follow that by adhering to the Convention the United States agreed to do away with limitations upon the waiver of sovereign immunity contained in other statutes. Certainly, neither the Convention nor the implementing statute contain express provisions to that effect, the argument must therefore be one of necessary implication. But there are formidable obstacles in the path of such an implication.

Thus, Article XIV of the Convention provides: "A Contracting State shall not be entitled to avail itself of the present Convention against other Contracting States except to the extent that it is itself bound to apply the Convention." This provision recognizes that a "Contracting State" may or may not be bound by the provisions of the Convention, depending upon its expressions of will or intent on the point. Furthermore, adherence of the United States to the Convention was accompanied by the following [commercial] reservation [quoted *supra* p. 138].

Whatever uncertainties may arise when agencies of government engage in commercial transactions, relations arising out of the activities of warships have never been regarded as "commercial" within the context of sovereign immunity. In addition, the Convention itself recognizes [in Article II(3)] that in certain circumstances the forum court may decline to enforce an agreement providing for arbitration elsewhere.... While the cases cited in this section hold that the "null and void" concept is to be given a narrow construction within the context of arbitration agreements in commercial contracts between private parties, I have no hesitation in holding that the present arbitration agreement, contained in the LOF contract, is "null and void" in respect of the United States because of the sovereign immunity principles discussed previously....

RESTATEMENT (SECOND) CONFLICT OF LAWS
§198 (1971)

(1) The capacity of the parties to contract is determined by the law selected by application of the [generally applicable choice-of-law principles set forth in] §§187-188.

(2) The capacity of a party to contract will usually be upheld if he has such capacity under the local law of the state of his domicile.

BENTELER v. STATE OF BELGIUM
Ad Hoc Award of 18 November 1983, 1989 Rev. arb. 339

[This preliminary award was rendered by a panel of three arbitrators in a dispute relating to a Protocol of Agreement entered into by the Belgian State of the first part, Dipl. Ing. E. Benteler KG and H. Benteler KG from the Federal Republic of Germany ("Benteler") of the second part, and A.B.C. SA ("ABC") of the third part. The Protocol, signed in Brussels on February 4, 1980, related to the industrial and financial restructuring of ABC. Art. 14 of the Protocol contains an arbitration clause which reads as follows:]

> "*Arbitration.* All disputes between the State and Benteler that could arise out of this agreement, shall be decided by a final and binding award issued by an arbitral tribunal. It can rule *ex aequo et bono*…. The arbitral tribunal shall consist of three members…. The arbitral tribunal shall have its situs at the president's domicile…."

After a major dispute occurred between Benteler and the Belgian State, the former started arbitration proceedings. The latter raised the invalidity of the arbitration clause from the outset, arguing that it was prevented from submitting to arbitration by Art. 1676 of the Belgian [Judicial] Code….

In its first brief, the Belgian State evoked Art. 1676(2) of the new Belgian [Judicial] Code, which reads as follows: "With the exception of public law legal entities, whoever has legal capacity or power to compromise can enter into an arbitration agreement. The State may enter such agreement when a treaty allows it to resort to arbitration."

The Belgian State [argued] that such prohibition of submitting to arbitration in matters prone to be communicated to the Ministère Public already appeared in well-known texts, Arts. 84 and 1003 of the 1806 French Code of Civil Procedure, which remained force in Belgium until the adoption of the present [Judicial] Code. This text … has always been interpreted in the sense of a rigorous prohibition…. It is true that in a famous line of cases, in particular in *Trésor Public v. Galakis* (1966 Rev. arb. 99), the French Cour de Cassation considered that the prohibition of submitting to arbitration only applied to domestic legal relations and that it was not a matter of international public order. However, this precedent is not applicable under Belgian law since the prohibition of submitting to arbitration has been maintained in the [Judicial] Code, adopted after the *Galakis* case…. Several authors have indeed deplored this decision, which leaves Belgian law behind in the liberalisation of international arbitration, but the prohibition so confirmed is absolute. However, even in matters of international arbitration, the State's ability to compromise is a question of capacity, which can only be solved in the eyes of national law. In view of the text of Art. 1676, which reserves exceptions deriving from a treaty, there is no room, under Belgian law, for the distinction adopted by French case law between domestic arbitration and international arbitration….

Benteler ... invoked Art. II(1) of the [European Convention], to which both Belgium and Germany have adhered. Under Art. I(1)(a), the European Convention applies to "arbitration agreements concluded for the purpose of settling disputes arising from international trade between physical or legal persons having, when concluding the agreement, their habitual place of residence or their seat in different Contracting States." Under Art. II(1), in such cases, "qualified legal entities, under the law applicable to them, as 'public law legal entities', have the right to enter legitimately into arbitration agreements." In ratifying the European Convention, Belgium used the reservation allowed by Art. II(2) of the Convention to limit this right to arbitration agreements entered into by the State. The European Convention, Benteler concluded, applies ... to the arbitration clause contained in the Protocol.

As a subsidiary argument, Benteler claimed that Art. 1676 of the [Judicial] Code does not apply to international arbitration, particularly when it does not take place in Belgium. Belgium case law decisions invoked by the State all relate to domestic arbitration. Belgian commentators, on the other hand, generally agree with the jurisprudence of the French Cour de Cassation, which states a material rule of international law widely applied by the arbitrators of international commerce. Finally, added Benteler, in the event Art. 1676 is applicable in the case at stake, the attitude of the Belgian State, which invokes a provision of its domestic law against a foreign party, is in all hypotheses contrary to international public order. The sanction of such an attitude must consist in a declaration of competence by the arbitral tribunal.

In its answering brief, the Belgian State did not deny that the European Convention is in principle applicable between the parties, but only on the condition that it is a matter of an international commercial operation. In fact, claimed the Belgian State, the Protocol does not relate to a commercial operation, in the meaning of Belgian law; [rather, the Protocol] determines the restructuring of a Belgian company by several operations having to take place in Belgium. There is thus no international element in the services arising from the contract, at least between the Belgian State and Benteler. The presence of a foreign partner is not enough to give them the international character required by the Convention.

In its reply brief, Benteler contested that the definition of commercial act distinctive to domestic Belgian law, applies to the interpretation of the European Convention. On the contrary, this Convention, given its international character, calls for the notion of international commercial operations in a broad sense, as is in particular accepted in international commercial arbitration. From this point of view, it is beyond doubt that the Protocol constitutes an act of international commerce....

The problem submitted to the arbitral tribunal thus concentrated ... on the question of knowing whether the dispute referred to it as a substantive issue springs from international commercial operations, within the meaning of Art. I(1)(a) of the European Convention. Both parties agree that under this reservation the European Convention applies by right to the arbitration agreement which constitutes Art. 14 of the Protocol.... This clause indeed appears in a contract concluded between the Belgian State and two German companies having their seat in Germany. Both Belgium and the Federal Republic ratified the European Convention. Belgium used the option left open under Art. II(2) by reserving to the Belgian State the power of compromising only in international matters....

To answer the only contested issue, which is the character of the dispute, it is important to first remember that ... the European Convention springs from the objective in the

Preamble: "Desirous of promoting the development of European trade, by, as far as possible, removing certain difficulties that may impede the organization and operation of international commercial arbitration in relations between physical or legal persons of different European countries." ... It would indeed be contrary to the very object of the Convention to admit that its terms have to be interpreted according to notions of domestic law, because such an interpretation would lead to the very type of difficulties the Convention's drafters wanted to avoid. The notion of act of commerce is the best example of that, since it would not be difficult to imagine that a deal be considered as commercial in one of the signatory countries whose domestic law would have a broad congestion of acts of commerce, and not in another which, like Belgium, draws its inspiration from the tradition of French commercial law. In this respect, it is significant that the European Convention did not allow any reservation as to the notion of commercial operations, unlike the New York Convention, which allows the States to limit its application to the disputes considered as commercial by their domestic law, a reservation that Belgium has not used in any case. One cannot better define it than to refer to the formula envisaged during the preparatory work of the European Convention, that is to say operations characterized by movements of goods, services or currencies across the borders.... [The Convention] ... applies only in matters of arbitration relating to operations of international commerce. It seemed more prudent not to define this notion, which will generally be characterized by a movement of goods, services or currencies across borders.

In the case at stake, the Protocol provides for the admission of Benteler of the shareholding of an industrial company, the conditions of the increase of its shares, its participation in the reorganization and the management of ABC as well as in the commercialisation of its products. In a broad sense, it is a question of a joint venture agreement, including a shareholders' agreement, management and collaboration agreements. Whatever is the qualification of such type of contract under Belgian Law, it is undisputedly a question of a commercial agreement within the meaning of Art. I of the European Convention. Joint venture agreements are indeed one of the means typical of international commercial law.

Is the issue at stake an agreement relating to international commerce? ... Analyzing the Protocol in as much as it concerns the relationships of the State and of Benteler, the [Belgian] State underlines that they exclusively affect the stockholding, the reorganization and the functioning of a Belgian company, and that in this respect, all the parties' undertakings had to be executed in Belgium.... The arbitral tribunal cannot follow the Belgian State in this analysis. The Protocol is a tripartite contract and not the reunion of two contracts, one between the State and Benteler, the other between Benteler and ABC. It must be regarded as a whole. Apart from Benteler's extraneity, which, by itself, would perhaps already justify the application of the European Convention, the contract presents numerous aspects characterized by movements of goods, services or currencies across borders: transfers of funds between Benteler and ABC, Benteler's participation in ABC's capital, transfer of shares by the State of Benteler, the availability to the Belgian company ABC of the technical and commercial know-how of the German companies, etc. Considered as a whole, the Protocol unquestionably concerns interests of international commerce, within the meaning of Art. I(1)(a) of the European Convention.

The Belgian State also invoked the fact that its intervention in the restructuring of the steel industry and, in particular, in that of the ABC company was not a commercial operation, but an operation with a political character, demanded by public interest and, moreover, based on the legislation. Without going that far, the argument of the Belgian State on this point repeats the classical distinction in public international law between acts performed *jure imperii* or *jure gestionis*. As does Benteler, the arbitral tribunal does not underestimate the political justification of the Belgian State's intervention. The arbitral tribunal could not ignore the very serious problems the steel industry is posing the Belgian government, nor the gravity of the situation it has to face. It is obvious that the State's intervention in ABC's restructuring has nothing in itself of the character of a commercial investment. But that is not the question. These considerations relate to the motives of such intervention. By contrast, both parties agreed that the Protocol fully had the character of a private law agreement, resorting to private law techniques....

The arbitral tribunal consequently accepts that, notwithstanding its political justification, the conclusion by the Belgian State of the Protocol constitutes a private law act, giving rise to private law rights, obligations and means....

It is useful to note, although this motive is not necessary to the solution, that this conclusion is in no way contrary to the domestic law arbitration system in Belgium since Art. 1676(2), in fine reserves as well international treaties. It is [also] useful to point out that other considerations confirm the conclusion this arbitral tribunal draws solely from the European Convention. From a more general point of view, it is important to stress that Art. II of the European Convention, which forms the basis of public law legal entities' capacity to resort to arbitration, is in no way exceptional. It is indeed, to the contrary, a principle more and more generally accepted in international arbitration law.... In this arbitration, both parties repeated the well known development of the jurisprudence of the French Cour de Cassation, as it culminated in the *Galakis* case.... Another technique, used in France and in other countries, is the submission of the State's capacity to enter into an arbitration agreement to the law of the contract and not to its national law.

A third formula, very widely used by international commercial arbitrators, consists in considering the prohibition on arbitration as being contrary to international public order. In consequence, the State which has subscribed to an arbitration clause or an arbitration agreement would act contrary to international public order in later invoking the incompatibility of such an obligation with its domestic legal order. Without going that far, one can also conceive that the international arbitrator dismiss the argument based on this prohibition when the circumstances of the case are such that the State would go *contra factum proprium* in raising it.... However that may be, the arbitral tribunal does not have to rule on this issue, Art. II of the European Convention being enough to justify its decision. On the other hand, this brief reminder of the present state of international arbitration law can only reinforce, if needed, the interpretation given to this Convention in the dispute referred to [the arbitral tribunal].

NOTES

1. *Lack of capacity under New York Convention.* Consider Article II of the New York Convention, excerpted at p. 1 of the Documentary Supplement, which deals with recognition of arbitration agreements, and does not make express reference to lack of capacity as a ground for challenging an agreement to arbitrate. Most authorities have concluded, however, that lack of capacity is a ground for challenging the validity of an arbitration agreement under Article II. Many authorities (like *Wijsmuller*) have also

cited Article V(1)(a) of the Convention in connection with challenges to arbitration agreements based upon a lack of capacity. As noted above, Article V(1)(a) permits non-recognition of awards if the parties to an arbitration agreement "were, under the law applicable to them, under some incapacity."

Is there any reason not to apply Article V(1)(a) by analogy to the recognition of arbitration agreements? Would it make sense to say that the Convention's drafters intended to exclude lack of capacity as a defense to enforcement of an arbitration agreement, while permitting it for awards?

2. *Lack of capacity under UNCITRAL Model Law.* Consider Articles 8, 34(2)(a) and 36(1)(a) of the UNCITRAL Model Law. How does the Model Law deal with issues of capacity? Is there any reference to the issue of capacity in Article 8? Note that the Model Law also permits non-recognition of an award if it resulted from an arbitration agreement where a party was "under some incapacity." UNCITRAL Model Law, Arts. 34(2)(a)(i), 36(1)(a)(i). As under the New York Convention, is there any reason not to apply the same defense at the stage of enforcing the agreement to arbitrate?

3. *Application of separability presumption to claims that party lacked capacity to conclude underlying contract.* Suppose a party lacks the capacity to conclude the underlying contract (for example, because the party is a minor, is mentally incompetent, or otherwise). Does this lack of capacity also affect the associated arbitration clause? What about the separability presumption, providing that the agreement to arbitrate is presumptively separate from the underlying contract? If someone is mentally incompetent, how can they conclude a binding arbitration agreement? Even as part of a larger contract?

4. *Allocation of competence to decide issues of capacity.* Who decides challenges to the capacity of a party to enter into an underlying contract? As in other contexts, the answer varies depending on the legal system in which the question arises.

   (a) *Allocation of competence to decide issues of capacity under FAA.* As discussed above, U.S. courts have interpreted the FAA as generally providing for judicial resolution of claims of contractual defects only where those claims are directed "specifically" at the arbitration agreement (and not at the underlying contract or at both the underlying contract and the arbitration clause). *See supra* pp. 370-74, 419-20. How would this general rule be applied to the hypotheticals in Note 3 above?

   Recall that the U.S. Supreme Court went out of its way in *Buckeye* to note that its decision did not address the correctness of cases "which hold that it is for courts to decide whether the alleged obligor ever signed the contract, whether the signor lacked authority to commit the alleged principal and whether the signor lacked the mental capacity to assent." 546 U.S. at 444 n. l; *supra* p. 202 n. 18. How should these issues be resolved? U.S. lower courts have reached divergent conclusions. *Compare Hosp. Dist. No. 1 v. Cerner Corp.*, 2012 WL 996932, at *1 (D. Kan.) ("issue of a party's mental capacity to enter into a contract generally, which contract contains an arbitration provision, is one for the Court in the first instance") *and Amirmotazedi v. Viacom, Inc.*, 2011 U.S. Dist. LEXIS 23667, at *16-17 (D.D.C.) ("Plaintiff challenges the making of the Arbitration Agreement on the grounds of intoxication.... Because this mental capacity defense goes to the formation, or the 'making' of the Arbitration Agreement, under §4 of the FAA it must be decided by this Court.") *and CitiFin., Inc. v. Brown*, 2001 WL 1530352, at *5 (N.D. Miss.) ("issue of John Brown's mental incompetence goes directly to the making of the arbitration agreement. If he could not read or understand the arbitration agreement, he certainly could not consent to it. Under *Prima Paint*, if an issue 'goes to the "making" of the agreement to arbitrate the federal court may proceed to adjudicate it.'") *with Sommers v. Cuddy*, 2009 WL 873983, at *3 (D. Nev.) (plaintiffs' argument concerning lack of mental capacity to enter into any agreements challenged contract as whole, and not just arbitration provision, thus making it an issue for arbitrator to decide) *and Primerica Life Ins. Co. v. Brown*, 304 F.3d 469 (5th Cir. 2002) (claim of mental incapacity is "not a specific challenge to the arbitration clause") *and In re Steger Energy Corp.*, 2002 WL 663645 (Tex. App.) (court required arbitration of claim that party was "incompetent at the time he signed the contracts—in the early stages of Alzheimer's," on grounds that "the defense asserted relates to the contract as a whole" and does not "specifically relate to the arbitration agreement itself").

How did the *Wijsmuller* court proceed with respect to the allocation of competence to resolve the United States' capacity objection? What differences are there between disputes concerning capacity and disputes concerning fraud, formation, illegality, or unconscionability? Would it have made sense to permit Mr. Darling to resolve this claim in the first instance?

(b) *Allocation of competence to decide claims of incapacity under prima facie jurisdiction standards.* How would competence be allocated under French, Indian, or Hong Kong law to decide the claim that a party to an arbitration agreement lacked capacity?

(c) *Allocation of competence to resolve disputes over capacity under UNCITRAL Model Law.* How should competence to resolve disputes over capacity be resolved under the Model Law?

5. *Choice of law governing capacity.* Disputes about a party's capacity raise choice-of-law questions: is capacity determined by the law of the party's domicile or place of incorporation, by the law governing the party's arbitration agreement, or by some other law? Note that Article V(1)(a) of the Convention and Articles 34(2)(a)(i) and 36(1)(a)(i) of the Model Law appear to contemplate a different choice-of-law rule from that applicable generally to the substantive validity of the arbitration agreement. *See supra* pp. 90-93, 287-315.

Note the provision in Article V(1)(a) of the Convention that the capacity of the parties is determined "under the law applicable to them" (and the comparable references in Articles 34(2)(a)(i) and 36(1)(a)(i)). Do these provisions prescribe a choice-of-law rule? Or is the choice of law left to local conflicts rules? When the Convention and the Model Law refer to the "law applicable to them" is it referring to the personal law of the parties—as distinguished from the law governing the arbitration agreement generally?

6. *Validation principle.* As discussed above, some authorities apply a "validation" principle to selecting the law applicable to international arbitration agreements. *See supra* pp. 306-07. Should the same principle apply to issues of capacity?

Compare §198 of the *Restatement (Second) Conflict of Laws* (1971) with Article 177(2) of the SLPIL, excerpted at p. 158 of the Documentary Supplement. Also compare Article V(1)(a) of the Convention and Article 34(2)(a)(i) of the Model Law. Is Article 34(2)(a)(i) inconsistent with application of the validation principle to issues of capacity?

7. *Law applied in* Centroamericanos *and* Wijsmuller. Did the court in *Centroamericanos* apply the law of Costa Rica? Should it have? Suppose the parties' agreement contained a choice-of-law clause selecting some law other than that of Costa Rica. Consider what law the court in *Wijsmuller* applied to issues of capacity. Was there a choice-of-law clause in *Wijsmuller*? Why did it not require application of English law to determine the capacity of the United States to enter into an arbitration agreement?

8. *Law applied in* Benteler. What law applied to determine the question of capacity in *Benteler*? Was it Belgian law? In the first instance? What result did the tribunal indicate would apply in *Benteler* under Belgian law?

9. *Purported limitations on state's capacity to enter into arbitration agreements.* Most developed legal systems recognize the capacity of states to conclude binding arbitration agreements. G. Born, *International Commercial Arbitration* 727-33 (2d ed. 2014). Article II(1) of the European Convention is representative, providing that "legal persons considered by the law which is applicable to them as 'legal persons of public law' have the right to conclude valid arbitration agreements." What are the policies underlying this provision?

Contrast with this general approach Article 139 of the Constitution of the Islamic Republic of Iran. Compare Article 139 with the statement of U.S. sovereign immunity articulated in *Wijsmuller* and Article 1676(2) of the Belgian Judicial Code (as quoted in *Benteler*). How do the U.S., Belgian and Iranian approaches to arbitration agreements binding the state differ? See also Articles 1676(2)-(3) of the Belgian Judicial Code as currently in force.

States can ordinarily waive their sovereign immunity, including, for example, by entering into an agreement to arbitrate particular matters. Why did the arbitration agreement in *Wijsmuller* not constitute such a waiver? Does the legislation cited by *Wijsmuller* suggest that entering into an agreement to arbitrate does not waive U.S. immunity?

10. *State's inability to rely on its own law to invalidate agreement to arbitrate.* Consider Article 177(2) of the SLPIL, excerpted at p. 158 of the Documentary Supplement. Does Article 177(2) state a choice-of-law rule? Suppose the arbitration clause in *Wijsmuller* had selected Switzerland as the arbitral seat; would Article 177(2) have permitted the United States to claim sovereign immunity or lack of capacity?

Consider the decision in *Benteler*. What is the basis for its conclusion that states are generally not entitled to rely on domestic legislation to invalidate their own agreement to arbitrate? Is this a rule based on the European Convention? On Belgian law? *See also Interim Award in ICC Case No. 7263*, XXII Y.B. Comm. Arb. 92, 100 (1997) (states and public bodies "cannot avail themselves of the incapacity and lack of authorization deriving from their national laws"); *Judgment of 21 June 1983*, XXI Y.B. Comm. Arb. 627 (1996) (Casablanca Cour d'appel) ("Doctrine and jurisprudence constantly recognize the validity of an arbitration agreement concluded by a State or State agency where the contract for which the arbitration agreement is concluded is an international contract and is governed by private law"). What explains the rule in

Benteler? Are private parties permitted to rely on their own incapacity to invalidate their arbitration agreements? Why are states so different?

Suppose that Iran, or an Iranian state entity, enters into a contract containing an arbitration clause, and subsequently argues that the clause is invalid because of Article 139 of the Iranian Constitution. How would that claim be dealt with under *Benteler*? Does the same analysis apply in *Wijsmuller*?

g. Waiver of Right to Arbitrate

Like other contractual rights, the right to arbitrate is subject to waiver. Waiver has been recognized by national courts as a defense to enforcement of arbitration agreements under Article II(3) of the New York Convention and national arbitration legislation.[55] The following materials explore the waiver of rights to arbitrate.

STONE v. E.F. HUTTON & CO.
898 F.2d 1542 (11th Cir. 1990)

HODGES, District Judge.... The case involved alleged Federal and Florida securities law violations, as well as allegations of common law fraud, negligence, and breach of fiduciary obligations. The Defendants, E.F. Hutton & Company ("Hutton"), contend that the action should be referred to arbitration ... since the parties have previously consented to arbitration in a E.F. Hutton "customer's agreement" executed by the Plaintiff on April 8, 1976. Paragraph seven of the agreement provides as follows: "Any controversy arising out of or relating to my account, to transactions between us or to this agreement or the breach thereof, shall be settled by arbitration in accordance with the rules, then in effect, of the New York Stock Exchange, Inc. or the National Association of Securities Dealers, Inc. as I may elect." ...

A party may be deemed to have waived its right to arbitrate a dispute "when a party seeking arbitration substantially invokes the judicial process to the detriment or prejudice of the other party." *Miller Brewing Co. v. Fort Worth Dist. Co.*, 781 F.2d 494, 497 (5th Cir. 1986). The use of pre-trial discovery procedures by a party seeking arbitration may sufficiently prejudice the legal position of an opposing party so as to constitute a waiver of the party's right to arbitration. However, "because federal law favors arbitration, any party arguing waiver of arbitration bears a heavy burden of proof." *Belke v. Merrill Lynch, Pierce, Fenner & Smith*, 693 F.2d 1023, 1025 (11th Cir. 1982). Furthermore, "any doubts concerning the scope of arbitrable issues should be resolved in favor of arbitration." *Moses H. Cone Mem. Hosp. v. Mercury Constr. Corp.*, 460 U.S. 1, 24-25 (1983).

Plaintiff contends that the Defendant, Hutton, waived its right to arbitration by conducting discovery in preparation for trial and waiting more than two years after the Supreme Court's decision in *McMahon* before requesting that the case be referred to arbitration.... Hutton deposed the Plaintiff on November 17, 1987, and on January 28, 1988, and also responded to a request for production of documents by Plaintiff in January, 1989.... [A]s of the date of his response, Plaintiff had recently submitted to all Defendants a third and fourth set of interrogatories and a third request for production of documents, and that both Hutton and the Plaintiff had scheduled depositions of the parties to this action

---

55. *See* G. Born, *International Commercial Arbitration* 870-81 (2d ed. 2014).

for the month of July, 1989. The Court further notes that the discovery completion date of August 1, pre-trial conference date of August 24, and trial date of September 4, 11, or 18, 1989, were set in its Order dated November 20, 1988. Yet Defendant's motion to refer this action to arbitration was not filed until June 14, 1989.

In *Benoay v. Prudential-Bache Sec., Inc.*, 805 F.2d 1437 (11th Cir. 1986), the court stated that mere participation in discovery does not cause prejudice sufficient to constitute a waiver where the request for arbitration was timely. In *Benoay*, the court held that since the request for arbitration was made only ten weeks after the right to seek arbitration had accrued, the request was timely and that no waiver had occurred.... [S]ince the case was reactivated on September 29, 1987, and Hutton filed its motion to refer this action to arbitration on June 14, 1989, Hutton delayed over one year and eight months before seeking to enforce its arbitration agreement. The Court concludes that a one year and eight month delay renders Hutton's motion untimely. During this period of time, Hutton engaged in discovery typical of a party preparing for trial. Significant prejudice to Plaintiff's legal position may be inferred from the extent of discovery conducted in this case. Since the Defendant's request for arbitration was untimely, the Defendant will be deemed to have waived its right to compel arbitration....

NOTES

1. *Waiver under New York Convention.* Does anything in Article II permit non-recognition of arbitration agreements based on claims that the agreement has been waived? Should rights to arbitrate be waivable? Are rights to arbitrate any different, in this respect, from other contractual rights?

2. *Waiver under UNCITRAL Model Law.* Consider Article 8(1) of the UNCITRAL Model Law, excerpted at p. 88 of the Documentary Supplement. Article 8(1) provides for the enforcement of arbitration agreements by national courts, provided that the party invoking the agreement requests its enforcement "not later than when submitting his first statement on the substance of the dispute." Is this an appropriate standard for waiver?

    Note that Article 8(1) provides a relatively clear-cut standard for determining when waiver may occur. What does this standard mean (*i.e.*, what is the "first statement on the substance of the dispute")? Is it a pleading? A letter? A statement? *Compare Restore Int'l Corp. v. K.I.P. Kuester Int'l Prods. Corp.*, [1999] B.C.J. No. 257 (B.C. Sup. Ct.) (filing defense to counterclaim waives right to arbitration) *and 429545 B.C. Ltd v. Herlihy*, [1998] B.C.J. No. 1801 (B.C. Sup. Ct.) (filing defense without reference to arbitration clause constitutes waiver) *with Bilta v. Nazir* [2010] EWHC 1086 (Ch) (English High Ct.) (defendant may correspond with claimant and/or make application for extending time for defense without waiving right to arbitrate) *and Navionics Inc. v. Flota Maritima Mexicana SA*, (1989) 26 FTR 148 (Canadian Fed. Ct.) (filing statement of defense, which does not refer to arbitration, in order to avoid default judgment held not to constitute waiver) *and No. 363 Dynamic Endeavours Inc. v. 34718 B.C. Ltd*, (1993) 81 B.C.L.R. 359 (B.C. Ct. App.) (seeking discovery on merits in litigation is not waiver) *and Globe Union Indus. Corp. v. G.A.P. Mktg Corp.*, [1995] 2 W.W.R. 696 (B.C. Sup. Ct.) (contesting application for interim relief in court does not constitute waiver) *and Chok Yick Interior Design & Eng'g Co. Ltd v. Fortune World Enters. Ltd*, [2010] HKCFI 84 (H.K. Ct. First Inst.) (plaintiff who commenced court proceedings has not waived right to stay proceedings pending arbitration). Does Article 8 mean that waiver *necessarily* will occur if a party does not raise the agreement to arbitrate in its "first statement on the substance of the dispute"? What if there is no prejudice to the adverse party?

Does Article 8 make clear what the legal consequences of waiver are? A number of authorities appear to have held that waiver necessarily entails a loss of the right to arbitrate under Article 8(1). *See, e.g., Ruhrkohle Handel Inter GmbH v. Fed. Calumet*, [1992] 3 FC 98, 105 (Canadian Fed. Ct. App.) ("very objective standard that must be met"); *Stancroft Trust Ltd v. Can-Asia Capital Co. Ltd*, [1990] 3 W.W.R. 665, 671 (B.C. Ct. App.).

3. *Waiver under FAA*. Consider the decision in *Stone v. E.F. Hutton*. What standard does the court articulate for waiver under the FAA? For other formulations, *see Repub. Ins. Co. v. PAICO Receivables, LLC*, 383 F.3d 341, 343-45 (5th Cir. 2004) ("Waiver will be found when the party seeking arbitration substantially invokes the judicial process to the detriment or prejudice of the other party. There is a strong presumption against finding a waiver of arbitration, and the party claiming that the right to arbitrate has been waived bears a heavy burden."); *Great W. Mortg. Corp. v. Peacock*, 110 F.3d 222, 233 (3d Cir. 1997) ("A party waives the right to compel arbitration only in the following circumstances: when the parties have engaged in a lengthy course of litigation, when extensive discovery has occurred, and when prejudice to the party resisting arbitration can be shown"); *Pirito v. Penn Eng'g World Holdings*, 833 F.Supp.2d 455, 468 (E.D. Pa. 2011) ("prejudice and the purposes of arbitration should guide the waiver inquiry").

Note that U.S. law disfavors, reasonably strongly, the finding of a waiver of rights to arbitrate. *See, e.g., Moses H. Cone Mem. Hosp. v. Mercury Constr. Corp.*, 460 U.S. 1, 24-25 (1983) ("[a]s a matter of federal law, any doubts concerning the scope of arbitrable issues should be resolved in favor of arbitration, whether the problem at hand is the construction of the contract language itself or an allegation of waiver, delay, or a like defense to arbitrability"); *Rush v. Oppenheimer & Co.*, 779 F.2d 885, 887 (2d Cir. 1985) ("Given this dominant federal policy favoring arbitration, waiver of the right to compel arbitration due to participation in litigation may be found only when prejudice to the other party is demonstrated."); *Nokia Corp. v. AU Optronics Corp.*, 2011 WL 2650689, at *8 (N.D. Cal.) (policy disfavoring waiver); *Khan v. Parsons Global Servs., Ltd*, 480 F.Supp.2d 327, 332 (D.D.C. 2009) ("If the Court is faced with any ambiguity with regard to the scope of the waiver, the Court must resolve the ambiguity in favor of arbitration.").

Is the FAA standard stricter than that under the UNCITRAL Model Law (*i.e.*, is it easier to waive rights under the FAA or the Model Law)? Does the FAA require a showing of prejudice? Under the FAA, does a party necessarily waive rights to arbitrate by failing to raise them in its first substantive submission? What must a party do to waive its rights?

4. *Appropriate standard of waiver*. What approach to the topic of waiver of rights to arbitrate is appropriate—that of the Model Law or of U.S. courts? Is it preferable to have a clear, bright-line test, or should decisions be made on a case-by-case basis? Who makes most decisions about litigating versus arbitrating a dispute—the client or the lawyers? Does this affect the standard relevant to waiver?

B. NONARBITRABILITY DOCTRINE

1. *Introduction to Nonarbitrability Doctrine*

As described above, the New York Convention contains various exceptions to the general obligation, set forth in Article II, to enforce written arbitration agreements.[56] In particular, Article II(1) does not require arbitration of disputes that are not "capable of settlement by arbitration." Similarly, Article V(2)(a) provides that an arbitral award need not be recognized if "[t]he subject matter of the difference is not capable of settlement by arbitration under the law" of the country where recognition is sought. Together, these provisions permit the assertion of nonarbitrability defenses to the enforcement of arbitration agreements and awards under the Convention. Other international commercial arbitration conventions and treaties contain similar exceptions.[57]

Like the New York Convention, legislation in virtually all nations treats some categories of claims as incapable of resolution by arbitration. The UNCITRAL Model Law is representative, resting on the premise that specified categories of disputes may be treated as not capable of settlement by arbitration (or "nonarbitrable").[58]

The types of claims that are nonarbitrable differ from nation to nation. Claims are ordinarily deemed "nonarbitrable" because of their perceived public importance or a felt need for formal judicial procedures and protections. Among other things, various nations refuse to permit arbitration of disputes concerning labor or employment grievances, intellectual property, competition (antitrust) claims, real estate, domestic relations and franchise relations. More broadly, legislation in some states at least nominally forbids arbitration of "all matters in the realm of public policy."[59]

For many of the early decades of the 20th century, the nonarbitrability doctrine flourished. National courts concluded that a wider variety of claims or types of disputes were nonarbitrable, invoking a host of expansive, sometimes ill-defined conceptions of public policy. This is illustrated by the materials excerpted below.

ARKANSAS CODE, 2010
§16-108-201

[excerpted above at p. 180]

JORDANIAN AMENDMENT TO THE MERCHANDISE MARITIME LAW
Law No. 35 of 1983

[excerpted above at p. 290]

---

56. *See supra* pp. 393-474.

57. *See* Inter-American Convention, Art. 5(2)(a); 1961 European Convention, Art. VI(2); G. Born, *International Commercial Arbitration* 946 (2d ed. 2014).

58. UNCITRAL Model Law, Arts. 1(5), 34(2)(b)(i), 36(1)(b)(i); G. Born, *International Commercial Arbitration* 959-60 (2d ed. 2014).

59. *See, e.g.*, French Civil Code, Art. 2060; Québec Civil Code, Art. 2639.

AWARD IN ICC CASE NO. 6149
XX Y.B. Comm. Arb. 41 (1995)

[excerpted above at pp. 290-92]

WILKO v. SWAN
346 U.S. 427 (1953)

JUSTICE REED. This action by petitioner, a customer, against respondents, partners in a securities brokerage firm, was brought in the ... Southern District of New York, to recover damages under §12(2) of the Securities Act of 1933. The complaint alleged that ... petitioner was induced by Hayden, Stone and Company to purchase 1,600 shares of the common stock of Air Associates ... by false representations.... [T]he respondent moved to stay the trial of the action pursuant to §3 of the [FAA] until an arbitration in accordance with the terms of identical margin agreements was had.... [The applicable arbitration clause provided: "Any controversy arising between us under this contract shall be determined by arbitration pursuant to the Arbitration Law of the State of New York, and under the rules of either the Arbitration Committee of the Chamber of Commerce of the State of New York, or of the American Arbitration Association, or of the Arbitration Committee of the New York Stock Exchange or such other Exchange as may have jurisdiction over the matter in dispute, as I may elect...."] Finding that the margin agreements provide that arbitration should be the method of settling all future controversies, the District Court held that the agreement to arbitrate deprived petitioner of the advantageous court remedy afforded by the Securities Act, and denied the stay. A divided Court of Appeals concluded that the Act did not prohibit the agreement to refer future controversies to arbitration, and reversed.

The question is whether an agreement to arbitrate a future controversy is a "condition, stipulation, or provision binding any person acquiring any security to waive compliance with any provision" of the Securities Act which §14 declares "void." ... In response to a Presidential message urging that there be added to the ancient rule of *caveat emptor* the further doctrine of "let the seller also beware," Congress passed the Securities Act of 1933.... To effectuate this policy, §12(2) created a special right to recover for misrepresentation which differs substantially from the common-law action in that the seller is made to assume the burden of proving lack of scienter. The Act's special right is enforceable in any court of competent jurisdiction—federal or state—and removal from a state court is prohibited. If suit be brought in a federal court, the purchaser has a wide choice of venue [and] the privilege of nation-wide service of process.... Petitioner argues that §14 shows that the purpose of Congress was to assure that sellers could not maneuver buyers into a position that might weaken their ability to recover under the Securities Act.... He reasons that the arbitration paragraph of the margin agreement is a stipulation that waives "compliance with" the provision of the Securities Act, ... conferring jurisdiction of suits and special powers. [15 U.S.C. §77v(a). §22(a) provides: "The district courts of the United States ... shall have jurisdiction ... concurrent with State and Territorial courts, of all suits in equity and actions at law brought to enforce any liability or duty created by this subchapter. Any such suit or action may be brought in the district wherein the defendant is found or is an inhabitant or transacts business, or in the district where the sale took place, if the defendant participated therein, and process in such cases may be served in any other district of which the defendant is an inhabitant or wherever the defendant may be found...."]

Respondent asserts that arbitration is merely a form of trial to be used in lieu of a trial at law, and therefore no conflict exists between the Securities Act and the [FAA] either in their language or in the congressional purposes in their enactment. Each may function within its own scope, the former to protect investors and the latter to simplify recovery for actionable violations of law by issuers or dealers in securities. Respondent is in agreement with the Court of Appeals that the margin agreement arbitration paragraph does not relieve the seller from either liability or burden of proof imposed by the Securities Act. We agree that in so far as the award in arbitration may be affected by legal requirements, statutes or common law, rather than by considerations of fairness, the provisions of the Securities Act control. This is true even though this proposed agreement has no requirement that the arbitrators follow the law....

The words of §14 void any "stipulation" waiving compliance with any "provision" of the Securities Act. This arrangement to arbitrate is a "stipulation," and we think the right to select the judicial forum is the kind of "provision" that cannot be waived under §14 of the Securities Act.... While a buyer and seller of securities, under some circumstances, may deal at arm's length on equal terms, it is clear that the Securities Act was drafted with an eye to the disadvantages under which buyers labor.... When the security buyer, prior to any violation of the Securities Act, waives his right to sue in courts, he gives up more than would a participant in other business transactions. The security buyer has a wider choice of courts and venue. He thus surrenders one of the advantages the Act gives him and surrenders it at a time when he is less able to judge the weight of the handicap the Securities Act places upon his adversary.

Even though the provisions of the Securities Act, advantageous to the buyer, apply, their effectiveness in application is lessened in arbitration as compared to judicial proceedings. Determination of the quality of a commodity or the amount of money due under a contract is not the type of issue here involved. This case requires subjective findings on the purpose and knowledge of an alleged violator of the Act. They must be not only determined but applied by the arbitrators without judicial instruction on the law. As their award may be made without explanation of their reasons and without a complete record of their proceedings, the arbitrators' conception of the legal meaning of such statutory requirements as "burden of proof," "reasonable care" or "material fact" cannot be examined. Power to vacate an award is limited. While it may be true, as the Court of Appeals thought, that a failure of the arbitrators to decide in accordance with the provisions of the Securities Act would "constitute grounds for vacating the award pursuant to §10 of the FAA," that failure would need to be made clearly to appear. In unrestricted submissions, such as the present margin agreements envisage, the interpretations of the law by the arbitrators in contrast to manifest disregard are not subject, in the federal courts, to judicial review for error in interpretation. The [FAA] contains no provision for judicial determination of legal issues such as is found in the English law. As the protective provisions of the Securities Act require the exercise of judicial direction to fairly assure their effectiveness, it seems to us that Congress must have intended §14 to apply to waiver of judicial trial and review....

JUSTICE JACKSON, Concurring. I agree with the Court's opinion insofar as it construes the Securities Act to prohibit waiver of a judicial remedy in favor of arbitration by agreement made before any controversy arose. I think thereafter the parties could agree upon arbitration....

JUDGMENT OF 18 JULY 1987
XVII Y.B. Comm. Arb. 534 (1992) (Bologna Tribunale)

[The case arose from an Italian company's (Coveme) termination of its distribution agreement ("Agreement") with a French manufacturer (CFI); following termination, CFI informed Coveme that it was bound by a non-competition clause in the terminated Agreement, and Coveme filed suit in Italy seeking a declaration that the non-competition clause violated EC competition laws. CFI sought a stay pending arbitration.]

We must firstly ascertain whether the Italian courts have jurisdiction to hear the dispute between Coveme and CFI, because the latter relies on the last clause in the [Agreement], according to which all disputes arising under the contract are referred to arbitration before the [ICC]. CFI ... also maintains that Italian law does not apply to the issue of the arbitrability of the matter, and that French law applies (the contract was concluded in Paris). According to Article 27 of the Preliminary Dispositions to the Civil Code[60] and [the New York Convention], there is no doubt that, contrary to defendant's theory, Italian law applies to review arbitrability. Italian law regulates the jurisdiction issue and the form of the proceedings (Article 27) and also applies to the court's review of the jurisdiction issue under Articles II and V of the said Convention.

Authoritative doctrine and case law[61] make clear that Article II(3) of the said Convention provides that jurisdiction must be denied if the arbitration clause is null and void, inoperative or incapable of being performed, and that this review can only take place in light of the national law. This principle becomes even clearer if Article II(3) is read in conjunction with Article V(2)(a), which subordinates the efficacy of the arbitral award to the requirement that its subject matter be capable of settlement by arbitration, according to the law of the State where recognition and enforcement are sought. This provision not only applies to the field which it directly regulates (the efficacy of an arbitral award already rendered); it also applies when the court obtains its own jurisdiction in the presence of an arbitration clause or agreement for international arbitration. It would be totally useless to recognize the jurisdiction of the arbitrator if the award, when rendered, could in no way be enforced in the legal system of the court which has jurisdiction.

This said, we must ascertain whether, according to Articles 806[62] and 808 CCP, it is possible to arbitrate the issue of the nullity of the clause in the [Agreement], according to which Coveme could not sell similar products for a period of two years following the termination of the contract. This nullity would ensue from the clause's being at odds with imperative provisions of EC competition law, particularly ... Article 85 of the EEC Treaty, which provides for the nullity of all agreements which can hinder trade among Member States.... According to this thesis, the nullity of the clause concerns the clause's conflict

---

60. Article 27 of the Preliminary Provisions to the Italian Civil Code read: "Jurisdiction and form of the proceedings are regulated by the law of the place where the proceedings are held."

61. The Court of First Instance referred to the decision rendered by the Supreme Court on 27 April 1979, *Compagnia Generale Costruzioni COGECO SpA v. Piersanti*, VI Y.B. Comm. Arb. 229-30 (1981).

62. Article 806 of the Italian Code of Civil Procedure then in force is excerpted above at p. 437.

with imperative provisions and cannot, therefore, … be capable of settlement by arbitration.

The Court holds that this thesis must be accepted, leaving aside any examination on the merits…. Indeed, it has been noted by authoritative doctrine that according to Article 806 CCP, which refers to Article 1966 CC, only the courts can decide matters in which the freedom of the parties to settle their disputes is limited by provisions of public law and public interest. It is beyond doubt that this is the case here, because it is the conflict with imperative provisions that are relied upon [by Coveme]. Hence, the parties are not free to settle the issue of this nullity, which could be objected to by any interested party and also *ex officio*. All agreements on this issue would also be null and void…. We hold that the arbitration clause is null and void as far as this nullity is concerned…. [T]he courts have jurisdiction to hear the case….

NOTES

1. *UNCITRAL Model Law's treatment of nonarbitrability*. Consider how the Model Law, excerpted at pp. 86-96 of the Documentary Supplement, treats the subject of nonarbitrability. Note that Articles 1(5), 34(2)(b)(i) and 36(1)(b)(i) recognize the possibility of a nonarbitrability exception to the general obligation to recognize and enforce arbitration agreements and awards. Does the Model Law define what categories of disputes are nonarbitrable? If a Model Law jurisdiction chooses to treat particular categories of disputes as nonarbitrable, how should it do so?

2. *Differences in national law treatments of nonarbitrability*. Compare the different national authorities, both legislative and judicial, providing that various categories of claims are nonarbitrable. Recall that Article 806 of the Italian Code of Civil Procedure provides that labor and similar disputes are, with some exceptions, nonarbitrable. Compare those categories to the Arkansas statute, which excluded "personal injury or tort matters, employer-employee disputes, [and claims by] any insured or beneficiary under any insurance policy or annuity contract." *See supra* p. 180. Note also the Jordanian legislation.

   What explains the significant differences taken in different jurisdictions to the categories of claims that are treated as nonarbitrable? Is there any underlying theme or unifying principles for the nonarbitrability exceptions adopted in different nations? Do these exceptions have a principled basis, or are they simply the product of domestic politics, where particular interest groups secure advantageous legislative treatment with regard to dispute resolution mechanisms and forum selection? If the latter, how should such legislative advantages be regarded under the New York Convention and other international instruments?

3. *Potential nonarbitrability of sovereignty and natural resource disputes in developing countries*. As we have seen, historically, many developing countries, or at least portions of their governmental and legal communities, viewed international arbitration with reserve and occasional hostility. Recall Decision 24 of the Andean Commission. *See supra* pp. 179, 186-88. Among other things, international arbitration was (and, to some extent, still is) seen as dominated by Western interests and arbitrators, insensitive to the policies of developing nations, and unacceptably expensive for non-Western entities. *See, e.g.*, Sornarajah, *The UNCITRAL Model Law: A Third World Viewpoint*, 6 J. Int'l Arb. 7 (1989); Kassis, *The Questionable Validity of Arbitration and Awards*

Under the Rules of the International Chamber of Commerce, 6(2) J. Int'l Arb. 79 (1989).

Among other things, it was urged that disputes involving significant sovereign interests (like natural resource projects) be deemed nonarbitrable. What are the pros and cons of this proposal? From whose perspective? Recall that one of the objectives of the international arbitral process is to provide a neutral method for dispute resolution. What is the objective of nonarbitrability rules providing that natural resource disputes can only be heard in local courts?

4. *Rationale for nonarbitrability doctrine*. Why is there a nonarbitrability doctrine? Consider the reasons advanced by *Wilko* for concluding that federal securities claims are nonarbitrable, and by the Bologna court for holding EU competition law defenses nonarbitrable. Are these reasons persuasive? Why can't Contracting States rely on existing, generally-applicable principles of contract law to invalidate arbitration agreements they don't like?

(a) *Public values*. In both *Wilko* and the Bologna decision, the courts reasoned that the claims at issue embodied "public" values that had importance transcending the particular plaintiff's case. Aren't all statutory claims important? Don't common law and civil law systems of contract and tort law embody vital "public" values? Why is Mr. Wilko's securities fraud claim more important than the claim of a victim of an environmental disaster, fraudulent real estate practices, or breach of a billion-dollar contract? If nonarbitrability is concerned about ensuring "good" results in cases of major public importance, what about forbidding agreements to arbitrate disputes with a value of more than $500 million? Would that make sense?

(b) *Arbitral procedures*. *Wilko* also emphasizes the differences between judicial and arbitral procedures—limited discovery, no jury, no appellate review, and informal evidentiary and pleading rules. It was, of course, these characteristics of arbitration that have prompted Congress and other national legislatures to enact national arbitration statutes (like the FAA), encouraging arbitration. *See supra* pp. 44-67. Do these features of the arbitral process argue against the arbitrability of some categories of claims? Consider the following description of the arbitral process, drawn from a U.S. Supreme Court opinion holding that employment discrimination claims are nonarbitrable:

> "Arbitral procedures, while well suited to the resolution of contractual disputes, make arbitration a comparatively inappropriate forum for the final resolution of rights created by Title VII. This conclusion rests first on the special role of the arbitrator, whose task is to effectuate the intent of the parties rather than the requirements of enacted legislation. Where the collective-bargaining agreement conflicts with Title VII, the arbitrator must follow the agreement.... [T]he specialized competence of arbitrators pertains primarily to the law of the shop, not the law of the land. Parties usually choose an arbitrator because they trust his knowledge and judgment concerning the demands and norms of industrial relations. On the other hand, the resolution of statutory or constitutional issues is a primary responsibility of courts, and judicial construction has proved especially necessary with respect to Title VII, whose broad language frequently can be given meaning only by reference to public law concepts. Moreover, the factfinding process in arbitration usually is not equivalent to judicial factfinding. The record of the arbitration proceedings is not as complete; the usual rules of evidence do not apply;

and rights and procedures common to civil trials, such as discovery, compulsory process, cross-examination, and testimony under oath, are often severely limited or unavailable. And as this Court has recognized, 'arbitrators have no obligation to the court to give their reasons for an award.' *United Steelworkers of Am. v. Enterprise Wheel & Car Corp.*, 363 U.S. at 598. Indeed, it is the informality of arbitral procedure that enables it to function as an efficient, inexpensive, and expeditious means for dispute resolution. This same characteristic, however, makes arbitration a less appropriate forum for final resolution of Title VII issues than the federal courts...." *Alexander v. Gardner-Denver Co.*, 415 U.S. 36, 58 (1974).

Recall also the *Prunier* decision and Joseph Story's description of the arbitration process in 1845, as "*rusticum judicium.*" *See supra* pp. 16-26, 178-79, 186-88. Are these observations correct? Are they reasons for providing that certain categories of claims may not be arbitrated?

(c) *Unequal bargaining power*. There are suggestions in various nonarbitrability discussions that the doctrine is related to unconscionability—certain classes of litigants will not be permitted to waive particular statutory protections against economically powerful entities. Note, for example, the prevalence of the nonarbitrability doctrine in investor, consumer, and employment contexts. *See supra* pp. 446-60; *Am. Safety Equip. Corp. v. J.P. Maguire & Co.*, 391 F.2d 821 (2d Cir. 1968). Are these reasons for forbidding arbitration of particular categories of disputes—or for applying traditional rules of unconscionability and requirements of procedural fairness? These rules are discussed above. *See supra* pp. 393-412.

(d) *Legislative intent*. At least in the United States, the touchstone of the nonarbitrability doctrine is what Congress intended: did it want a particular statutory claim to be excluded from the FAA's general regime? That partially explains *Wilko*, which relied on language of §14 of the Securities Act, forbidding waiver of rights under the Act.

5. *Nonarbitrability of agreements to arbitrate future, not existing, disputes*. Historically, agreements to arbitrate *future* disputes were often the focus of anti-arbitration sentiment. *See supra* pp. 16-26, 186-88. Note that most nonarbitrability rules apply only to agreements to arbitrate *future* disputes. *See* Justice Jackson's concurrence in *Wilko*. Recall also the legislation, discussed above, in Belgium, Arkansas and elsewhere, limiting pre-dispute agreements to arbitrate consumer and other claims—but permitting post-dispute agreements to arbitrate these claims. Does this distinction between the arbitrability of existing and future disputes make sense? Private parties are, of course, generally free to settle law suits they have commenced concerning almost any kind of claim (including employment, consumer, securities, and domestic relations claims). They are also free to settle such claims before commencing litigation. If parties are free to settle a pending litigation, why wouldn't they be permitted to agree to arbitrate it?

If a dispute can satisfactorily be resolved by arbitration *after* it has arisen, why could the same dispute not have been the subject of a pre-dispute agreement to arbitrate? If post-dispute agreements to arbitrate are permitted, aren't concerns about supposed defects in the arbitral process just window-dressing? Aren't disparities in bargaining power and lack of informed consent the only basis for prohibiting pre-dispute arbitration agreements?

Note that one of the central principles of the New York Convention and the UNCITRAL Model Law was to require recognition of agreements to arbitrate *future* disputes. *See* New York Convention, Art. II; UNCITRAL Model Law, Art. 7; *supra* pp. 30-39, 189-90. Does the application of the nonarbitrability doctrine to categories of future disputes violate the Convention?

6. *Authority of arbitrators to consider public law claims.* Why couldn't the arbitrator in *Wilko* have resolved federal securities law claims exactly like a U.S. district judge would have? Couldn't the arbitrator in *Judgment of 18 July 1987* have considered and resolved the EC competition law claims? Note that the *Wilko* Court accepted that the arbitrator could have considered securities claims, but for §14 of the Securities Act, just as he could consider contract claims. Note also the decision in *ICC Case No. 6149*.

Compare the apparently different attitude towards this topic in *Alexander v. Gardner-Denver Co.*, quoted above, suggesting that an arbitrator cannot consider "public laws":

> "The arbitrator, however, has no general authority to invoke public laws that conflict with the bargain between the parties:[63] 'An arbitrator is confined to interpretation and application of the collective bargaining agreement; he does not sit to dispense his own brand of industrial justice. He may of course look for guidance from many sources, yet his award is legitimate only so long as it draws its essence from the collective bargaining agreement.... *United Steelworkers of Am. v. Enterprise Wheel & Car Corp.*, 363 U.S. 593, 597 (1960).' If an arbitral decision is based 'solely upon the arbitrator's view of the requirements of enacted legislation,' rather than on an interpretation of the collective-bargaining agreement, the arbitrator has 'exceeded the scope of the submission,' and the award will not be enforced." 415 U.S. at 56-57.

Is it correct that an arbitrator cannot consider statutory (or other non-contractual) claims? Suppose these claims fall within the scope of the parties' arbitration agreement? As discussed below, contemporary decisions have decisively rejected the *Alexander* view of arbitral authority.

7. *Wisdom of nonarbitrability exceptions.* Consider the policies articulated for different nonarbitrability exceptions. Are these persuasive? Why is it that arbitrators could not be trusted to resolve consumer, labor, competition/antitrust, securities and similar disputes? Note that, in fact, arbitrators are generally permitted to resolve such disputes, provided that they are already in existence when the parties agree to arbitrate them. What are the costs of not permitting parties to agree in advance that arbitrators may resolve such disputes?

8. *Consistency of nonarbitrability legislation with New York Convention.* Article II(1) of the Convention does not require recognition of arbitration agreements as applied to disputes that are not "capable of settlement by arbitration," while Article V(2)(a) provides that an award need not be recognized if "[t]he subject matter of the difference

---

63. "A proper conception of the arbitrator's function is basic. He is not a public tribunal imposed upon the parties by superior authority which the parties are obliged to accept. He has no general charter to administer justice for a community which transcends the parties. He is rather part of a system of self-government created by and confined to the parties. He serves their pleasure only, to administer the rule of law established by their collective agreement." Shulman, *Reason, Contract, and Law in Labor Relations*, 68 Harv. L. Rev. 999, 1016 (1955). [Footnote in original.]

is not capable of settlement by arbitration under the law" of the country where recognition is sought. What do Articles II(1) and V(2)(a) permit Contracting States to do? Do these provisions affect the validity of agreements to arbitrate? Or do they affect the enforceability of arbitration agreements as applied to particular categories of disputes? If the latter, do Articles II(1) and V(2)(a) provide an escape valve that permits individual Contracting States to deny recognition of arbitration agreements and arbitral awards in particular circumstances, without affecting the validity of the agreement or award in other Contracting States? Consider how this would work. For example, what if the arbitral seat in *Wilko* were in Spain; the arbitral seat in *Judgment of 18 July 1987* in Miami? Would Spanish and U.S. courts be obligated to enforce the agreements?

2. *Contemporary Status of Nonarbitrability Doctrine*

During the 1980s, many national courts in developed jurisdictions brought the expansion of the nonarbitrability doctrine to a fairly decisive end.[64] In Europe, a series of judicial decisions held that EU competition claims were arbitrable (subject to subsequent judicial review).[65] Similar conclusions were reached by U.S. and other national courts with respect to competition laws and other "public law" claims.[66] The materials excerpted below illustrate the decline of the nonarbitrability doctrine in recent decades.

SCHERK v. ALBERTO-CULVER CO.
417 U.S. 506 (1974)

JUSTICE STEWART. Alberto-Culver Co., the respondent, is an American company incorporated in Delaware with its principal office in Illinois. It manufactures and distributes toiletries.... During the 1960's Alberto Culver ... approached the petitioner Fritz Scherk, a German citizen residing at the time of [this litigation] in Switzerland. Scherk was the owner of three interrelated business entities, organized under the laws of Germany and Liechtenstein.... [After negotiations in Europe and the United States,] a contract was signed in Vienna, Austria, which provided for the transfer of the ownership of Scherk's enterprises to Alberto-Culver, along with all rights held by these enterprises to trademarks in cosmetic goods.... In addition, the contract contained an arbitration clause providing that "any controversy or claim [that] shall arise out of this agreement or the breach thereof" would be referred to arbitration before the [ICC] in Paris, France, and that "[t]he laws of the State of Illinois, USA shall apply to and govern this agreement, its interpretation and performance." ...

Nearly one year [after closing] Alberto-Culver allegedly discovered that the trademark rights purchased under the contract were subject to substantial encumbrances.... [Thereafter,] Alberto-Culver commenced this action for damages and other relief in a Federal

---

64. *See* G. Born, *International Commercial Arbitration* 964 *et seq.* (2d ed. 2014).

65. *Nordsee Deutsche Hochseefischerei GmbH v. Reederei Mond Hochseefischerei AG*, [1982] ECR 1095; *Eco Swiss China Time Ltd v. Benetton Int'l NV*, Case No. C-126/97, [1999] E.C.R. I-3055 (E.C.J.).

66. *Hi-Fert Pty Ltd v. Kiukiang Maritime Carriers*, [1998] FCA 1485 (Australian Fed. Ct.) (rejecting argument that claims under Australian Trade Practices Act are nonarbitrable); *Attorney Gen. of N.Z. v. Mobil Oil N.Z. Ltd*, [1989] 2 NZLR 649 (N.Z. High Ct.) (New Zealand competition law claims held arbitrable).

District Court in Illinois, contending that Scherk's fraudulent representations concerning the status of the trademark rights constituted violations of §10(b) of the Securities Exchange Act of 1934.... In response, Scherk filed a motion to ... to stay the action pending arbitration ... Alberto-Culver, in turn, opposed this motion.... [T]he District Court denied Scherk's motion to dismiss, and ... granted a preliminary order enjoining Scherk from proceeding with arbitration, [citing] *Wilko*....

In *Wilko*, this Court ... found that "[t]wo policies, not easily reconcilable, are involved in this case." On the one hand, the [FAA] stressed "the need for avoiding the delay and expense of litigation," and directed that [arbitration] agreements be "valid, irrevocable, and enforceable" in federal courts. On the other hand, the Securities Act of 1933 was "[d]esigned to protect investors" ... by creating "a special right to recover for misrepresentation...." In particular, ... [the] Court ruled that an agreement to arbitrate "is a 'stipulation,' and the right to select the judicial forum is the kind of 'provision' that cannot be waived under §14 of the Securities Act." ...

Alberto-Culver, relying on this precedent, contends that ... its agreement to arbitrate disputes arising under the contract with Scherk is similarly unenforceable.... [T]he respondent's reliance on *Wilko* in this case ignores the significant and, we find, crucial differences between the agreement involved in *Wilko* and the one signed by the parties here. Alberto-Culver's contract ... was a truly international agreement. Alberto-Culver is an American corporation with its principal place of business and the vast bulk of its activity in this country, while Scherk is a citizen of Germany whose companies were organized under the laws of Germany and Liechtenstein. The negotiations leading to the signing of the contract in Austria and to the closing in Switzerland took place in the United States, England and Germany.... Finally, and most significantly, the subject matter of the contract concerned the sale of business enterprises organized under the laws of and primarily situated in European countries, whose activities were largely, if not entirely, directed to European markets.

Such a contract involves considerations and policies significantly different from those found controlling in *Wilko*. In *Wilko*, quite apart from the arbitration provision, there was no question but that the laws of the United States generally, and the federal securities laws in particular, would govern disputes arising out of the stock-purchase agreement. The parties, the negotiations, and the subject matter of the contract were all situated in this country, and no credible claim could have been entertained that any international conflict-of-laws problems would arise. In this case, by contrast, in the absence of the arbitration provision considerable uncertainty existed at the time of the agreement, and still exists, concerning the law applicable to the resolution of disputes arising out of the contract.

Such uncertainty will almost inevitably exist with respect to any contract touching two or more countries, each with its own substantive laws and conflict-of-laws rules. A contractual provision specifying in advance the forum in which disputes shall be litigated and the law to be applied is, therefore, an almost indispensable precondition to achievement of the orderliness and predictability essential to any international business transaction. Furthermore, such a provision obviates the danger that a dispute under the agreement might be submitted to a forum hostile to the interests of one of the parties or unfamiliar with the problem area involved.[67]

A parochial refusal by the courts of one country to enforce an international arbitration agreement would not only frustrate these purposes, but would invite unseemly and mutually destructive jockeying by the parties to secure tactical litigation advantages. In the present case, for example, it is not inconceivable that if Scherk had anticipated that Alberto-Culver would be able in this country to enjoin resort to arbitration he might have sought an order in France or some other country enjoining Alberto-Culver from proceeding with its litigation in the United States. Whatever recognition the courts of this country might ultimately have granted to the order of the foreign court, the dicey atmosphere of such a legal no-man's-land would surely damage the fabric of international commerce and trade, and imperil the willingness and ability of businessmen to enter into international commercial agreements.... In *Wilko* the Court reasoned that "[w]hen the security buyer, prior to any violation of the Securities Act waives his right to sue in courts, he gives up more than would a participant in other business transactions. The security buyer has a wider choice of courts and venue. He thus surrenders one of the advantages the Act gives him...." In the context of an international contract, however, these advantages become chimerical since, as indicated above, an opposing party may by speedy resort to a foreign court block or hinder access to the American court of the purchaser's choice.

[Recalling *Bremen v. Zapata Off-Shore Co.*, 407 U.S. 1 (1972), upholding a forum selection clause, the Court reasoned that an] agreement to arbitrate before a specified tribunal is, in effect, a specialized kind of forum-selection clause that posits not only the situs of suit but also the procedure to be used in resolving the dispute. The invalidation of such an agreement in the case before us would not only allow the respondent to repudiate its solemn promise but would, as well, reflect a "parochial concept that all disputes must be resolved under our laws and in our courts.... We cannot have trade and commerce in world markets and international waters exclusively on our terms governed by our laws, and resolved in our courts."[68] For all these reasons we hold that the agreement of the parties in this case to arbitrate any dispute arising out of their international commercial transaction is to be respected and enforced by the federal courts in accord with the explicit provisions of the [FAA].[69]

---

67. *See* Quigley, *Accession by the United States to the United Nations Convention on the Recognition and Enforcement of Foreign Arbitral Awards*, 70 Yale L.J. 1049, 1051 (1961). For example, while the arbitration agreement involved here provided that the controversies arising out of the agreement be resolved under "[t]he laws of the State of Illinois," a determination of the existence and extent of fraud concerning the trademarks would necessarily involve an understanding of foreign law on that subject.

68. In The Bremen we noted that forum-selection clauses "should be given full effect" when "a freely negotiated private international agreement [is] unaffected by fraud ... ." This qualification does not mean that any time a dispute arising out of a transaction is based upon an allegation of fraud, as in this case, the clause is unenforceable. Rather, it means that an arbitration or forum-selection clause in a contract is not enforceable if the inclusion of that clause in the contract was the product of fraud or coercion. Cf. *Prima Paint Corp. v. Flood & Conklin Mfg. Co.*, 388 U.S. 395. Although we do not decide the question, presumably the type of fraud alleged here could be raised, under Article V of the [New York] Convention, in challenging the enforcement of whatever arbitral award is produced through arbitration [citing Article V(2)(b) of the Convention].

69. Our conclusion today is confirmed by international developments and domestic legislation in the area of commercial arbitration subsequent to the Wilko decision.... In 1970 the United States acceded to the [New

JUSTICE DOUGLAS, Dissenting.... There has been much support for arbitration of disputes; and it may be the superior way of settling some disagreements. If A and B were quarrelling over a trademark and there was an arbitration clause in the contract, the policy of Congress in implementing the [New York] Convention would prevail. But the [FAA] does not substitute an arbiter for the settlement of disputes under the 1933 and 1934 Acts. Article II(3) of the Convention [permits U.S. courts to decline to enforce agreements that are "null and void, inoperative or incapable of being performed.]⁷⁰ But §29(a) of the 1934 Act makes agreements to arbitrate liabilities under §10 of the Act "void" and "inoperative." Congress has specified a precise way whereby big and small investors will be protected and the rules under which the Alberto-Culvers of this Nation shall operate. They or their lawyers cannot waive those statutory conditions, for our corporate giants are not principalities of power but guardians of a host of wards unable to care for themselves. It is these wards that the 1934 Act tries to protect.... It is important that American standards of fairness in security dealings govern the destinies of American investors until Congress changes these standards....

When a defendant, as alleged here, has, through proscribed acts within our territory, brought itself within the ken of federal securities regulation, a fact not disputed here, those laws—including the controlling principles of *Wilko*—apply whether the defendant is foreign or American, and whether or not there are transnational elements in the dealings. Those laws are rendered a chimera when foreign corporations or funds—unlike domestic defendants—can nullify them by virtue of arbitration clauses which send defrauded American investors to the uncertainty of arbitration on foreign soil, or, if those investors cannot afford to arbitrate their claims in a far-off forum, to no remedy at all....

MITSUBISHI MOTORS CORP. v. SOLER CHRYSLER-PLYMOUTH, INC.
473 U.S. 614 (1985) (also excerpted below at pp. 522-25)

JUSTICE BLACKMUN. The principal question presented by these cases is the arbitrability, pursuant to the [FAA] and the [New York] Convention of claims arising under the Sherman

---

York Convention], and Congress passed Chapter 2 of the [FAA] in order to implement the Convention.... The goal of the Convention, and the principal purpose underlying American adoption and implementation of it, was to encourage the recognition and enforcement of commercial arbitration agreements in international contracts and to unify the standards by which agreements to arbitrate are observed and arbitral awards are enforced in the signatory countries.... In their discussion of Article [II of the Convention], the delegates to the Convention voiced frequent concern that courts of signatory countries in which an agreement to arbitrate is sought to be enforced should not be permitted to decline enforcement of such agreements on the basis of parochial views of their desirability or in a manner that would diminish the mutually binding nature of the agreements. Without reaching the issue of whether the Convention, apart from the considerations expressed in this opinion, would require of its own force that the agreement to arbitrate be enforced in the present case, we think that this country's adoption and ratification of the Convention and the passage of Chapter 2 of the [FAA] provide strongly persuasive evidence of congressional policy consistent with the decision we reach today.

70. The Convention also permits that arbitral awards not be recognized and enforced when a court in the country where enforcement is sought finds that "[t]he recognition or enforcement of the award would be contrary to the public policy of that country." Article V(2)(b). It also provides that recognition of an award may be refused when the arbitration agreement "is not valid under the law to which the parties have subjected it," in this case the laws of Illinois. Article V(1)(a).

Act, 15 U.S.C. §1 *et seq.*, and encompassed within a valid arbitration clause in an agreement embodying an international commercial transaction.

[Mitsubishi Motors Corporation ("Mitsubishi") is a Japanese corporation that manufactures automobiles in Japan. Mitsubishi is a joint venture between Chrysler International ("CISA"), a Swiss corporation owned by Chrysler Corporation, and Mitsubishi Heavy Industries, a Japanese corporation. Soler Chrysler-Plymouth, Inc. ("Soler"), is a Puerto Rico corporation. Soler entered into a distributor agreement with CISA that provided for the sale by Soler of Mitsubishi-manufactured vehicles within a designated area. At the same time, CISA, Soler, and Mitsubishi entered into a sales procedure agreement ("sales agreement") that provided for the direct sale of Mitsubishi products to Soler and governed the terms and conditions of such sales. Paragraph VI of the Sales Agreement, labeled Arbitration of Certain Matters, provides:

> "All disputes, controversies or differences which may arise between [Mitsubishi] and [Soler] out of or in relation to Articles I-B through V of this Agreement or for the breach thereof, shall be finally settled by arbitration in Japan in accordance with the rules and regulations of the Japan Commercial Arbitration Association."

Soler failed to maintain the sales volume specified in its agreements and requested that Mitsubishi delay or cancel shipment of several orders. Mitsubishi and CISA refused, and Mitsubishi later brought an action against Soler in the District of Puerto Rico under the [FAA] and the Convention. Mitsubishi sought an order, pursuant to 9 U.S.C. §§4 and 201, to compel arbitration. Shortly after filing the complaint, Mitsubishi filed a request for arbitration before the Japan Commercial Arbitration Association, seeking damages from Soler for breach of the parties' sales agreement. Soler denied the allegations and counterclaimed against both Mitsubishi and CISA under the Sherman Act; the Puerto Rico competition statute; and the Puerto Rico Dealers' Contract Act. In the counterclaim premised on the Sherman Act, Soler alleged that Mitsubishi and CISA had conspired to divide markets in restraint of trade. The Court of Appeals held that antitrust claims were "non-arbitrable" and permitted Soler's suit to proceed. The Supreme Court first concluded that the parties' arbitration agreement encompassed Soler's antitrust claims. *See* pp. 486-92.]

We now turn to consider whether Soler's antitrust claims are non-arbitrable even though it has agreed to arbitrate them. In holding that they are not, the Court of Appeals followed the decision of the Second Circuit in *Am. Safety Equip. Corp. v. J.P. Maguire & Co.*, 391 F.2d 821 (1968). Notwithstanding the absence of any explicit support for such an exception in either the Sherman Act or the [FAA], the Second Circuit there reasoned that "the pervasive public interest in enforcement of the antitrust laws, and the nature of the claims that arise in such cases, combine to make ... antitrust claims ... inappropriate for arbitration." We find it unnecessary to assess the legitimacy of the *American Safety* doctrine as applied to agreements to arbitrate arising from domestic transactions. As in *Scherk v. Alberto-Culver Co.*, we conclude that concerns of international comity, respect for the capacities of foreign and transnational tribunals, and sensitivity to the need of the international commercial system for predictability in the resolution of disputes require that we enforce the parties' agreement, even assuming that a contrary result would be forthcoming in a domestic context.

Even before *Scherk*, this Court had recognized the utility of forum selection clauses in international transactions. [One example is the Court's decision in *Bremen*, which] clearly eschewed a provincial solicitude for the jurisdiction of domestic forums.... *Bremen* and *Scherk* establish a strong presumption in favor of enforcement of freely negotiated contractual choice-of-forum provisions. Here, as in *Scherk*, that presumption is reinforced by the emphatic federal policy in favor of arbitral dispute resolution. And at least since this Nation's accession in 1970 to the Convention ... that federal policy applies with special force in the field of international commerce. Thus, we must weigh the concerns of *American Safety* against a strong belief in the efficacy of arbitral procedures for the resolution of international commercial disputes and an equal commitment to the enforcement of freely negotiated choice-of-forum clauses.

At the outset, we confess to some skepticism of certain aspects of the *American Safety* doctrine. As distilled by the First Circuit, the doctrine comprises four ingredients[, all of which we find insufficient.].... [First, the] mere appearance of an antitrust dispute does not alone warrant invalidation of the selected forum on the undemonstrated assumption that the arbitration clause is tainted. A party resisting arbitration of course may attack directly the validity of the agreement to arbitrate. Moreover, the party may attempt to make a showing that would warrant setting aside the forum-selection clause—that the agreement was "[a]ffected by fraud, undue influence, or overweening bargaining power"; that "enforcement would be unreasonable and unjust"; or that proceedings "in the contractual forum will be so gravely difficult and inconvenient that [the resisting party] will for all practical purposes be deprived of his day in court." *Bremen*, 407 U.S. at 12, 15, 18. But absent such a showing—and none was attempted here—there is no basis for assuming the forum inadequate or its selection unfair.

[Second,] potential complexity should not suffice to ward off arbitration. We might well have some doubt that even the courts following *American Safety* subscribe fully to the view that antitrust matters are inherently insusceptible to resolution by arbitration, as these same courts have agreed that an undertaking to arbitrate antitrust claims entered into after the dispute arises is acceptable.... [A]daptability and access to expertise are hallmarks of arbitration. The anticipated subject matter of the dispute may be taken into account when the arbitrators are appointed, and arbitral rules typically provide for the participation of experts either employed by the parties or appointed by the tribunal....

[Third,] we also reject the proposition that an arbitration panel will pose too great a danger of innate hostility to the constraints on business conduct that antitrust law imposes. International arbitrators frequently are drawn from the legal as well as the business community; where the dispute has an important legal component, the parties and the arbitral body with whose assistance they have agreed to settle their dispute can be expected to select arbitrators accordingly.

We are left, then, with the core of the *American Safety* doctrine—the fundamental importance to American democratic capitalism of the regime of the antitrust laws. Without doubt, the private cause of action plays a central role in enforcing this regime.... The treble-damages provision wielded by the private litigant is a chief tool in the antitrust enforcement scheme, posing a crucial deterrent to potential violators. The importance of the private damages remedy, however, does not compel the conclusion that it may not be sought outside an American court. Notwithstanding its important incidental policing function, the treble-damages cause of action conferred on private parties by §4 of the Clayton Act, and pursued by Soler here by way of its third counterclaim, seeks primarily to enable an injured competitor to gain compensation for that injury. "§4 ... is in essence a remedial provision." ...

There is no reason to assume at the outset of the dispute that international arbitration will not provide an adequate mechanism. To be sure, the international arbitral tribunal owes no prior allegiance to the legal norms of particular states; hence, it has no direct obligation to vindicate their statutory dictates. The tribunal, however, is bound to effectuate the intentions of the parties. Where the parties have agreed that the arbitral body is to decide a defined set of claims which includes, as in these cases, those arising from the application of American antitrust law, the tribunal therefore should be bound to decide that dispute in accord with the national law giving rise to the claim.[71] And so long as the prospective litigant effectively may vindicate its statutory cause of action in the arbitral forum, the statute will continue to serve both its remedial and deterrent function.

Having permitted the arbitration to go forward, the national courts of the United States will have the opportunity at the award enforcement stage to ensure that the legitimate interest in the enforcement of the antitrust laws has been addressed. The Convention reserves to each signatory country the right to refuse enforcement of an award where the "recognition or enforcement of the award would be contrary to the public policy of that country." Article V(2)(b). While the efficacy of the arbitral process requires that substantive review at the award-enforcement stage remain minimal, it would not require intrusive inquiry to ascertain that the tribunal took cognizance of the antitrust claims and actually decided them.[72]

As international trade has expanded in recent decades, so too has the use of international arbitration to resolve disputes arising in the course of that trade.... If [international arbitral institutions] are to take a central place in the international legal order, national courts will need to "shake off the old judicial hostility to arbitration," and also their customary and understandable unwillingness to cede jurisdiction of a claim arising under domestic law to

71. In addition to the clause providing for arbitration before the Japan Commercial Arbitration Association, the Sales Agreement includes a choice-of-law clause which reads: "This Agreement is made in, and will be governed by and construed in all respects according to the laws of the Swiss Confederation as if entirely performed therein." The United States raises the possibility that the arbitral panel will read this provision not simply to govern interpretation of the contract terms, but wholly to displace American law even where it otherwise would apply. The International Chamber of Commerce opines that it is "[c]onceivabl[e], although we believe it unlikely, [that] the arbitrators could consider Soler's affirmative claim of anticompetitive conduct by CISA and Mitsubishi to fall within the purview of this choice-of-law provision, with the result that it would be decided under Swiss law rather than the U.S. Sherman Act." At oral argument, however, counsel for Mitsubishi conceded that American law applied to the antitrust claims and represented that the claims had been submitted to the arbitration panel in Japan on that basis. The record confirms that before the decision of the Court of Appeals the arbitral panel had taken these claims under submission.

We therefore have no occasion to speculate on this matter at this stage in proceedings, when Mitsubishi seeks to enforce the agreement to arbitrate, not to enforce an award. Nor need we consider now the effect of an arbitral tribunal's failure to take cognizance of the statutory cause of action on the claimant's capacity to reinitiate suit in federal court. We merely note that in the event the choice-of-forum and choice-of-law clauses operated in tandem as a prospective waiver of a party's right to pursue statutory remedies for antitrust violations, we would have little hesitation in condemning the agreement as against public policy.

72. We note, for example that the rules of the Japan Commercial Arbitration Association provide for the taking of a "summary" of each hearing, Rule 28.1; for the stenographic recording of the proceedings where the tribunal so orders or a party requests one, Rule 28.2; and for a statement of reasons for the award unless the parties agree otherwise, Rule 36.1(4).

a foreign or transnational tribunal. To this extent, at least, it will be necessary for national courts to subordinate domestic notions of arbitrability to the international policy favoring commercial arbitration.[73] Accordingly, we "require this representative of the American business community to honor its bargain," by holding this agreement to arbitrate "enforce[able] ... in accord with the explicit provisions of the [FAA]."

JUSTICE STEVENS, Dissenting.... [The] Court has repeatedly held that a decision by Congress to create a special statutory remedy renders a private agreement to arbitrate a federal statutory claim unenforceable. Thus, ... the express statutory remedy provided in the Ku Klux Act of 1871, the express statutory remedy in the Securities Act of 1933, the express statutory remedy in the Fair Labor Standards Act, and the express statutory remedy in Title VII of the Civil Rights Act of 1964, each provided the Court with convincing evidence that Congress did not intend the protections afforded by the statute to be administered by a private arbitrator. The reasons that motivated those decisions apply with special force to the federal policy that is protected by the antitrust laws.... It was Chief Justice Hughes who characterized the Sherman Antitrust Act as "a charter of freedom" that may fairly be compared to a constitutional provision. *See Appalachian Coals, Inc. v. United States*, 228 U.S. 344, 359-360 (1933)....

[I]t is not surprising that all of the federal courts that have considered the question have uniformly and unhesitatingly concluded that agreements to arbitrate federal antitrust issues are not enforceable. In a landmark opinion ..., Judge Feinberg wrote:

"A claim under the antitrust laws is not merely a private matter. The Sherman Act is designed to promote the national interest in a competitive economy; thus, the plaintiff asserting his rights under the Act has been likened to a private attorney-general who protects the public's interest.... Antitrust violations can affect hundreds of thousands—perhaps millions—of people and inflict staggering economic damage.... We do not believe that Congress intended such claims to be resolved elsewhere than in the courts.... [I]t is also proper to ask whether contracts of adhesion between alleged monopolists and their customers should determine the forum for trying antitrust violations." *Am. Safety Equip.*, 391 F.2d at

---

73. We do not quarrel with the Court of Appeals' conclusion that Article II(1) of the Convention, which requires the recognition of agreements to arbitrate that involve "subject matter capable of settlement by arbitration," contemplates exceptions to arbitrability grounded in domestic law. And it appears that before acceding to the Convention the Senate was advised by a State Department memorandum that the Convention provided for such exceptions.

In acceding to the Convention the Senate restricted its applicability to commercial matters, in accord with Article I(3). Yet in implementing the Convention by amendments to the [FAA], Congress did not specify any matters it intended to exclude from its scope. In Scherk, this Court recited Article II(1), including the language relied upon by the Court of Appeals, but paid heed to the Convention delegates' "frequent[ly voiced] concern that courts of signatory countries in which an agreement to arbitrate is sought to be enforced should not be permitted to decline enforcement of such agreements on the basis of parochial views of their desirability or in a manner that would diminish the mutually binding nature of the agreements." There, moreover, the Court dealt arguendo with an exception to arbitrability grounded in express congressional language; here, in contrast, we face a judicially implied exception. The utility of the Convention in promoting the process of international commercial arbitration depends upon the willingness of national courts to let go of matters they normally would think of as their own. Doubtless, Congress may specify categories of claims it wishes to reserve for decision by our own courts without contravening this Nation's obligations under the Convention. But we decline to subvert the spirit of the United States' accession to the Convention by recognizing subject-matter exceptions where Congress has not expressly directed the courts to do so.

826-27....

[Awards] are only reviewable for manifest disregard of the law, 9 U.S.C. §10, 207, and the rudimentary procedures which make arbitration so desirable in the context of a private dispute often mean that the record is so inadequate that the arbitrator's decision is virtually unreviewable.[74] Despotic decision-making of this kind is fine for parties who are willing to agree in advance to settle for a best approximation of the correct result in order to resolve quickly and inexpensively any contractual dispute that may arise in an ongoing commercial relationship. Such informality, however, is simply unacceptable when every error may have devastating consequences for important businesses in our national economy and may undermine their ability to compete in world markets.[75] Instead of "muffling a grievance in the cloakroom of arbitration," the public interest in free competitive markets would be better served by having the issues resolved "in the light of impartial public court adjudication."

The Court assumes for the purposes of its decision that the antitrust issues would not be arbitrable if this were a purely domestic dispute, but holds that the international character of the controversy makes it arbitrable. The holding rests on vague concerns for the international implications of its decision and a misguided application of *Scherk v. Alberto-Culver Co.*... As the Court acknowledges, the only treaty relevant here is the [New York Convention].... However, the United States, as *amicus curiae*, advises the Court that the Convention "clearly contemplates" that signatory nations will enforce domestic laws prohibiting the arbitration of certain subject matters. This interpretation is ... beyond doubt.... [R]eading Articles II and V together, the Convention provides that agreements to arbitrate disputes which are non-arbitrable under domestic law need not be honored, nor awards rendered under them enforced.

It is clear then that the international obligations of the United States permit us to honor Congress' commitment to the exclusive resolution of antitrust disputes in the federal courts. The Court today refuses to do so, offering only vague concerns for comity among nations. The courts of other nations, on the other hand, have applied the exception provided in the Convention, and refused to enforce agreements to arbitrate specific subject matters of concern to them.[76] It may be that the subject-matter exception to the Convention ought to be reserved—as a matter of domestic law—for matters of the greatest public interest which involve concerns that are shared by other nations. The Sherman Act's commitment

---

74. The arbitration procedure in this case does not provide any right to evidentiary discovery or a written decision, and requires that all proceedings be closed to the public. Moreover, Japanese arbitrators do not have the power of compulsory process to secure witnesses and documents, nor do witnesses who are available testify under oath. Cf. 9 U.S.C. §7 (arbitrators may summon witnesses to attend proceedings and seek enforcement in a district court).

75. The great risk, of course, is that the arbitrator will condemn business practices under the antitrust laws that are efficient in a free competitive market. In the absence of a reviewable record, a reviewing district court would not be able to undo the damage wrought. Even a Government suit or an action by a private party might not be available to set aside the award.

76. For example, the Cour de Cassation in Belgium has held that disputes arising under a Belgian statute limiting the unilateral termination of exclusive distributorships are not arbitrable under the Convention in that country, *Audi-NSU Auto Union A.G. v. SA Adelin Petit & Cie.* (1979), in 5 Yearbook Commercial Arbitration 257, 259 (1980), and the Corte di Cassazione in Italy has held that labor disputes are not arbitrable under the Convention in that country, *Compagnia Generale Costruzioni v. Persanti*, 6 Y.B. Comm. Arb. 229, 230 (1981).

to free competitive markets is among our most important civil policies. This commitment, shared by other nations which are signatory to the Convention, is hardly the sort of parochial concern that we should decline to enforce in the interest of international comity....

ECO SWISS CHINA TIME LTD v. BENETTON INTERNATIONAL NV
Case No. C-126/97, [1999] E.C.R. I-3055 (E.C.J.)

[The European Court of Justice first considered] whether a national court to which application is made for annulment of an arbitration award must grant such an application where, in its view, that award is in fact contrary to Article 85 of the Treaty although, under domestic procedural rules, it may grant such an application only on a limited number of grounds, one of them being inconsistency with public policy, which, according to the applicable national law, is not generally to be invoked on the sole ground that, because of the terms or the enforcement of an arbitration award, effect will not be given to a prohibition laid down by domestic competition law. It is to be noted, first of all, that, where questions of Community law are raised in an arbitration resorted to by agreement, the ordinary courts may have to examine those questions, in particular during review of the arbitration award, which may be more or less extensive depending on the circumstances and which they are obliged to carry out in the event of an appeal, for setting aside, for leave to enforce an award or upon any other form of action or review available under the relevant national legislation.... [I]t is for those national courts and tribunals to ascertain whether it is necessary for them to make a reference to the Court under Article 177 of the Treaty in order to obtain an interpretation or assessment of the validity of provisions of Community law which they may need to apply when reviewing an arbitration award....

Next, it is in the interest of efficient arbitration proceedings that review of arbitration awards should be limited in scope and that annulment of or refusal to recognize an award should be possible only in exceptional circumstances. However, according to Article 3(g) of the EC Treaty ..., Article 85 of the Treaty constitutes a fundamental provision which is essential for the accomplishment of the tasks entrusted to the Community and, in particular, for the functioning of the internal market. The importance of such a provision led the framers of the Treaty to provide expressly, in Article 85(2) of the Treaty, that any agreements or decisions prohibited pursuant to that article are to be automatically void. It follows that where its domestic rules of procedure require a national court to grant an application for annulment of an arbitration award where such an application is founded on failure to observe national rules of public policy, it must also grant such an application where it is founded on failure to comply with the prohibition laid down in Article 85(1) of the Treaty.

That conclusion is not affected by the fact that the New York Convention ... which has been ratified by all the Member States, provides that recognition and enforcement of an arbitration award may be refused only on certain specific grounds, namely where the award does not fall within the terms of the submission to arbitration or goes beyond its scope, where the award is not binding on the parties or where recognition or enforcement of the award would be contrary to the public policy of the country where such recognition and enforcement are sought (Article V(1)(c) and (e) and II(b) of the Convention). For the reasons stated ... above, the provisions of Article 85 of the Treaty may be regarded as a matter of public policy within the meaning of the Convention.

Lastly, it should be recalled that … arbitrators, unlike national courts and tribunals, are not in a position to request this Court to give a preliminary ruling on questions of interpretation of Community law. However, it is manifestly in the interest of the Community legal order that, in order to forestall differences of interpretation, every Community provision should be given a uniform interpretation, irrespective of the circumstances in which it is to be applied. It follows that, in the circumstances of the present case … Community law requires that questions concerning the interpretation of the prohibition laid down in Article 85(1) of the Treaty should be open to examination by national courts when asked to determine the validity of an arbitration award and that it should be possible for those questions to be referred, if necessary, to the Court of Justice for a preliminary ruling. The answer … must therefore be that a national court to which application is made for annulment of an arbitration award must grant that application if it considers that the award in question is in fact contrary to Article 85 of the Treaty, where its domestic rules of procedure require it to grant an application for annulment founded on failure to observe national rules of public policy….

[Next, the ECJ considered] whether Community law requires a national court to refrain from applying domestic rules of procedure according to which an interim arbitration award which is in the nature of a final award and in respect of which no application for annulment has been made within the prescribed time-limit acquires the force of *res judicata* and may no longer be called in question by a subsequent arbitration award, even if this is necessary in order to examine, in proceedings for annulment of the subsequent award, whether an agreement which the interim award held to be valid in law is nevertheless void under Article 85 of the Treaty. According to the relevant domestic rules of procedure, application for annulment of an interim arbitration award which is in the nature of a final award may be made within a period of three months following the lodging of that award at the registry of the court having jurisdiction in the matter. Such a period, which does not seem excessively short compared with those prescribed in the legal systems of the other Member States, does not render excessively difficult or virtually impossible the exercise of rights conferred by Community law…. In those circumstances, Community law does not require a national court to refrain from applying such rules, even if this is necessary in order to examine, in proceedings for annulment of a subsequent arbitration award, whether an agreement which the interim award held to be valid in law is nevertheless void under Article 85 of the Treaty.

The answer … must therefore be that Community law does not require a national court to refrain from applying domestic rules of procedure according to which an interim arbitration award which is in the nature of a final award and in respect of which no application for annulment has been made within the prescribed time-limit acquires the force of *res judicata* and may no longer be called in question by a subsequent arbitration award, even if this is necessary in order to examine, in proceedings for annulment of a subsequent arbitration award, whether an agreement which the interim award held to be valid in law is nevertheless void under Article 85 of the Treaty….

JUDGMENT OF 7 MAY 1994, FINCANTIERI-CANTIERI NAVALI ITALIANI SPA v. MIN. OF DEF., ARMAMENT & SUPPLY DIRECTORATE OF IRAQ

XXI Y.B. Comm. Arb. 594 (1996) (Genoa Corte di Appello)

[excerpted above at pp. 436-40]

NOTES

1. *New York Convention's exception for matters "not capable of settlement by arbitration."* Could the U.S. Supreme Court, consistently with the New York Convention, have held that U.S. federal securities and antitrust claims are not arbitrable? In footnotes, the Court in *Scherk* and *Mitsubishi* concluded that the Convention does not require enforcement of agreements to arbitrate a "subject matter [not] capable of settlement by arbitration." *See supra* pp. 486 n. 70, 490 n. 73. Moreover, the Court in both cases concluded that the Convention would not have prohibited a holding that securities and antitrust claims were nonarbitrable. Is that correct?

2. *Nonarbitrability exception to enforcement of arbitration agreements under New York Convention.* Article II of the Convention is not well-drafted. Article II(1) provides that an arbitration agreement need not be enforced if it concerns a "subject matter [not] capable of settlement by arbitration," and Article V(2) repeats that exception in the context of recognition of awards. In contrast, Article II(3) requires courts to refer parties to agreements without mentioning any "nonarbitrability" exception. Does that mean that arbitration agreements must be enforced even if they pertain to nonarbitrable claims? As Justice Douglas observed in his dissent in *Scherk*:

   > "When Article II(3) was being discussed, the Israeli delegate pointed out that while a court could, under the draft Convention as it then stood, refuse enforcement of an award which was incompatible with public policy, 'the court had to refer parties to arbitration whether or not such reference was lawful or incompatible with public policy.' … [T]he Article was … adopted without any words linking agreements to the awards enforceable under the Convention." 417 U.S. 506, 530-31 n.10 (1973) (Douglas, J., dissenting) (citing Haight, *Convention on the Recognition and Enforcement of Foreign Arbitral Awards: Summary Analysis of Record of United Nations Conference*, May/June 1958 (1958)).

   Notwithstanding the Convention's language and drafting history, all the opinions in *Scherk* and *Mitsubishi*, like the opinions in *Eco Swiss* and *Fincantieri*, concluded that Contracting States may refuse to refer parties to arbitration on "nonarbitrability" grounds, even though Article II(3) does not itself contain such an exception. Is that a fair reading of Article II—including Article II(1)? What would be the logic of a different reading? Would it make sense to require courts to refer parties to arbitration on a claim that could produce an award that some Contracting States might refuse to recognize on nonarbitrability grounds? In what states would the award be treated as dealing with a nonarbitrable subject matter?

3. *Eco Swiss's nonarbitrability decision.* The European Court of Justice ("ECJ") has made clear that EU competition claims and defenses may be arbitrated (subject to subsequent judicial review). In a 1982 decision, the ECJ said, "if questions of Community law are raised in an arbitration resorted to by agreement the ordinary courts may be called upon to examine them either in the context of their collaboration with arbitration tribunals, in particular in order to assist them in certain procedural matters or to interpret the law applicable, or in the course of a review of an arbitration award—which may be more or less extensive depending on the circumstances—and which they may be required to effect in case of an appeal for objection, in proceedings for leave to issue the execution or by any other method of recourse available under the relevant national legislation." *Nordsee Deutsche Hochseefischerei GmbH v. Reederei*

Mond Hochseefischerei AG & Co. KG, [1982] ECR 1095, ¶14 (E.C.J.). That left little doubt that arbitrators were competent to, and would, consider and decide competition law claims (subject to subsequent judicial review). Similarly, in *Eco Swiss*, the ECJ again acknowledged that arbitrators could consider EU competition claims (subject again to judicial review of any resulting award).

Consider the ECJ's analysis in *Eco Swiss*. Does the ECJ consider expressly whether agreements to arbitrate EU competition law disputes are arbitrable? Whether pre-dispute agreements to arbitrate EU competition law disputes are valid? What exactly does the ECJ hold? Compare the ECJ's analysis to that of the U.S. Supreme Court. In what manner does the ECJ indicate that EU competition law claims are different from other kinds of claims?

4. *Scherk's nonarbitrability decision.* What did the Court hold in *Scherk* regarding the arbitrability of a U.S. securities law claim in a domestic setting? Consider *Scherk's* reliance on possible conflicts between U.S. and foreign laws and decisions. Is this persuasive? Consider the language of §§14 and 29 in the Securities Act and the Securities Exchange Act, relied upon in *Wilko. See supra* pp. 476-78, 483-86. Does this provision not clearly forbid agreements to waive access to federal courts? Does this provision exclude claims involving international transactions? Note that *Scherk* concluded that the New York Convention left U.S. courts free not to require arbitration of securities law claims. Should *Scherk* have been decided differently?

5. *Mitsubishi's nonarbitrability decision.* What exactly did the Court hold in *Mitsubishi*? Consider the first and last paragraphs of the opinion. Why are "international" cases different from domestic ones? Is it because of the New York Convention? Consider the following explanation from *Mitsubishi*: "The utility of the Convention in promoting the process of international commercial arbitration depends upon the willingness of national courts to let go of matters they normally would think of as their own.... [W]e decline to subvert the spirit of the United States' accession to the Convention by recognizing subject matter exceptions where Congress has not expressly directed the courts to do so." Similar reasoning underlies the decision in *Scherk*. Is that persuasive? What exactly does it mean? Is it an interpretation of the Convention? An interpretation of domestic legislation?

Exactly what are the special needs for predictability in the "international commercial system" that the Court relies on in *Mitsubishi* and *Scherk*? Consider the dissents (by Justice Douglas in *Scherk* and Justice Stevens in *Mitsubishi*). Note that other nations also distinguish between domestic and international arbitration and the scope of public policy defenses in each. *See, e.g.*, Carbonneau, *The Elaboration of A French Court Doctrine on International Commercial Arbitration: A Study in Liberal Civilian Judicial Creativity*, 55 Tulane L. Rev. 1 (1980).

More recent U.S. Supreme Court decisions have rejected nonarbitrability defenses even in the purely domestic context. *See Shearson/American Express v. McMahon*, 482 U.S. 220 (1987) (Securities Exchange Act and RICO claims arbitrable, even in purely domestic context); *Rodriguez de Quijas v. Shearson/American Express, Inc.*, 490 U.S. 477 (1989) (Securities Act claims arbitrable); G. Born, *International Commercial Arbitration* 964-69 (2d ed. 2014).

6. *Criticism of* Mitsubishi *and* Scherk. Although the decision was applauded in many circles, *Mitsubishi* has also provoked criticism. Consider the following:

"if such fundamental issues as antitrust matters (and RICO claims) can be submitted to arbitration, what possible limits could there be to the reach of arbitrability in the international … context? The confusing and potentially dangerous shift of domestic public law concerns to the enforcement stage is likely to be ineffectual, destined to act as the shadow of a safeguard rather than a genuine means of protection…. The Court's rush to eradicate all national legal constraints not only compromises legitimate national concerns, but also threatens the integrity of international arbitral adjudication itself, frustrating its normal tendency to seek guidance and appropriate limits from external factors." Carbonneau, *The Exuberant Pathway to Quixotic Internationalism: Assessing the Folly of Mitsubishi*, 19 Vand. J. Trans. L. 263, 297-98 (1986).

Compare Park, *Private Adjudicators and the Public Interest: The Expanding Scope of International Arbitration*, 12 Brook. J. Int'l L. 629, (1986); Lowenfeld, *The* Mitsubishi *Case: Another View*, 2 Arb. Int'l 178 (1986). Do you agree? Do *Mitsubishi* and *Scherk* advance or obstruct the international arbitral process?

7. *Procedural efficacy of arbitration of "public law" claims.* Does the arbitral process allow for adequate presentation and consideration of securities, antitrust, and similar "public law" claims? Consider the arguments made by the various justices in *Wilko*, *Scherk* and *Mitsubishi*. Consider also whether the Court's view that arbitral procedures are effective, in *Scherk* and *Mitsubishi*, extends beyond the international context. If arbitration can resolve international antitrust and securities claims, why can't it also resolve domestic ones?

   (a) *Arbitral procedures.* Consider again the comments in *Alexander*, and the dissents in *Scherk* and *Mitsubishi*, regarding the alleged defects in arbitral procedures. Note the aspects of arbitration which trouble these critics—no U.S.-style discovery, no appeal, confidentiality, non-judicial decision-maker, no formal rules of evidence, and (sometimes, in the United States) no reasoned award. Do these features of arbitration amount to what Justice Stevens terms "despotic decision-making" in his *Mitsubishi* dissent? How is it that these procedural features of arbitration allegedly make it ill-suited for resolving public law claims (as distinguished from contract claims)? What disadvantages do arbitrators and arbitral procedures have when compared to lay juries? How does the Court treat these procedural complaints in *Scherk* and *Mitsubishi*? *See Shearson/American Express, Inc. v. McMahon*, 482 U.S. 220 (1987) ("the mistrust of arbitration that formed the basis for the *Wilko* opinion in 1953 is difficult to square with the assessment of arbitration that has prevailed since that time").

   (b) *Arbitrators need not be lawyers qualified to practice the law applicable to dispute.* Arbitrators are often lawyers (or retired judges), but they are not always lawyers qualified to practice in the jurisdiction whose law governs the parties' dispute. For example, in *Mitsubishi*, there was no requirement that the arbitrators be qualified to practice U.S. law (much less experts in U.S. antitrust law). Does that affect the arbitrability of U.S. antitrust claims? Suppose that a tribunal of French, English, and Egyptian arbitrators is required to decide issues under the Sherman or Clayton Acts. Will they fairly and competently be able to decide such claims? *See* Lowenfeld, *The* Mitsubishi *Case: Another View*, 2 Arb. Int'l 178, 181-82 (1986) (an arbitrator can "learn enough U.S. antitrust law (or European competition law) in the course of an arbitration to be able to resolve the questions put to him"); *Mitsubishi Motors*, 473 U.S. at 633-34 n.18 ("The obstacles confronted by the arbitration panel in this case, however, should be no greater than those confronted by any judicial or arbitral tribunal required to determine foreign law."). How does an international tribunal compare to a U.S. federal judge? A jury?

(c) *Limited discovery in arbitration.* Although discovery is available in arbitration, it is often more limited in scope than in U.S. litigation, typically does not permit pre-trial depositions, hardly ever extends to third parties, and is often not enforced through compulsory process. *See infra* pp. 831-51. Note the widely-held view that "the heart of any United States antitrust case is the discovery of business documents. Without them there is virtually no case." *In re Uranium Antitrust Lit.*, 480 F.Supp. 1138, 1155 (N.D. Ill. 1979). Does this cast doubt on the *Mitsubishi* holding?

(d) *Minimal substantive review.* As discussed below, in most jurisdictions judicial review of the arbitrators' substantive decisions is either nonexistent or highly deferential. *See infra* pp. 1164-69. For example, only if the arbitrator "manifestly disregards" the law will a U.S. court disturb the award; in UNCITRAL Model Law jurisdictions, even minimal judicial review will ordinarily not be available. *See infra* pp. 1164-68, 1194-99. Does the almost unreviewable authority of arbitrators on substantive issues argue against permitting them to hear public law claims?

(e) *Confidentiality.* Note Justice Stevens' statement that: "Instead of 'muffling a grievance in the cloakroom of arbitration,' the public interest in free competitive markets would be better served by having the issues resolved 'in the light of impartial public court adjudication.'" Why is this? Is it grounds for holding antitrust claims nonarbitrable? Could arbitral hearings be public? *See infra* pp. 851-70.

8. *Future versus existing disputes (revisited).* *Mitsubishi* reasons that, if arbitration can satisfactorily resolve an existing dispute, then there is no reason that arbitral procedures cannot suffice for future disputes. Isn't that a compelling point? How does Justice Stevens' dissent reply to this? *See supra* pp. 490-92. What does this suggest generally about the nonarbitrability doctrine?

9. *Fincantieri's "nonarbitrability" decision.* What exactly did the Genoa appellate court hold in *Fincantieri*? Did it hold that claims regarding UN and EU sanctions were nonarbitrable under Articles II(1) and V(2)(a)? Or that an arbitration of such claims was illegal? How does *Fincantieri*'s analysis compare with that in *Eco Swiss* and *Mitsubishi*? Why shouldn't an arbitrator be able correctly to apply public law and to determine on which of the parties' claims he may rule? *See also Belship Navigation, Inc. v. Sealift, Inc.*, 95 Civ. 2748, 1995 WL 447656 (S.D.N.Y.) (contract made in 1994 *void ab initio* due to Cuban Assets Control Regulations of 1963, but arbitration agreement valid; issue of nonarbitrability not raised); *Soeximex SAS v. Agrocorp Int'l Pte Ltd* [2011] EWHC 2743 (Comm) (English High Ct.) (arbitrators have to address issues related to effect of trade sanctions on parties' relationship); *Compagnie Nationale Air France v. Libyan Arab Airlines*, 2003 CanLII 35834 (Québec Ct. App.) (contract affected by economic sanctions against Libya terminated; Air France invoked nonarbitrability of dispute; tribunal accepted jurisdiction: "no nonarbitrability of the dispute whatever resulting either from transnational public order, from French law (law of the merits), or from Canadian law (law of seat)"; courts upheld—see, in particular, the position of the court of first instance: "the question really raised by Air France concerns the non-admissibility of LAA's requests and not the nonarbitrability

of the dispute"); Audit, *L'effet des sanctions économiques internationales sur l'arbitrage international*, in E. Loquin & S. Manciaux (eds.), *L'ordre public et l'arbitrage* 143, 147-50 (2014); Geisinger *et al.*, *The Impact of International Trade Sanctions on Contractual Obligations and on International Commercial Arbitration*, Int'l. Bus. L. J. 4, 405-37 (2012).

10. *"Second look" doctrine in* Mitsubishi *and* Eco Swiss. The Court in *Mitsubishi* contemplated a so-called "second look" by U.S. courts at the arbitral tribunal's application of U.S. antitrust law: "Having permitted the arbitration to go forward, the national courts of the United States will have the opportunity at the award-enforcement stage to ensure that the legitimate interest in the enforcement of the antitrust laws has been addressed." *See supra* p. 489. *Eco Swiss* also stresses that national courts may review awards dealing with EC competition law issues. Is this so-called "second look" doctrine wise? What kind of review is contemplated?

From a procedural perspective, is it correct that particular courts will in fact have an opportunity to take a "second look" at an arbitrator's antitrust decision? For example, awards made outside the United States, but dealing with the U.S. antitrust laws, ordinarily will be subject to annulment only where they were made, and not in U.S. courts. *See infra* pp. 1099-112. Moreover, the prevailing party may seek enforcement of the award outside the United States, and not in U.S. courts. Ultimately, the sole opportunity for a "second look" might well be in a renewed antitrust action in U.S. courts, where the prevailing party in the arbitration would be obliged to raise the award as preclusive. If U.S. antitrust law was raised as a defense, which the arbitral tribunal rejected, instead making a monetary award in the claimant's favor, the award might well be enforced outside the United States and no U.S. court would ever have reason to review the merits of the tribunal's decision. Is that problematic? Why or why not?

11. *Scope of "second look" at award*. What does it mean to have a "second look" at the arbitrators' decision? Does it mean that the reviewing court—wherever that may be—will consider the substance of U.S. antitrust and EU competition law issues *de novo*? If so, what would this do to the arbitral process? What would be the point of arbitrating a public law dispute if the losing party were free to relitigate it *de novo* in court?

Mitsubishi indicated that non-recognition of an award would be appropriate if the tribunal did not take "cognizance of the antitrust claims and actually decide[] them." *Mitsubishi* also held that a U.S. court reviewing the award could engage in only "minimal" "substantive review." 473 U.S. at 638. This is consistent with U.S. law regarding the enforcement of domestic arbitral awards, which only permits non-enforcement for a panel's "manifest disregard of law" (and perhaps not even that). *See infra* pp. 1165-68. Would this "minimal" substantive review be permitted? In an annulment (vacatur) action? In a recognition action?

What if U.S. (or any national) courts defer almost entirely to awards dealing with public law claims? *See* Park, *Private Adjudicators and the Public Interest: The Expanding Scope of International Arbitration*, 12 Brook. J. Int'l L. 629, 642 (1986) ("The 'second look' doctrine is a problematic safety valve for ensuring that public law issues receive proper consideration. If it calls for review on the merits, it disrupts the arbitral process. But if it calls only for a mechanical examination of the face of the award, it may not provide an effective check on an arbitrator who mentions the Sherman Act before he proceeds to ignore it."). Is it problematic if there is only limited judicial scrutiny in a "second look" at awards in public law disputes? What other mechanisms are available for enforcing public laws? Are there antitrust (competition law), securities and other regulators with the capability to bring their own enforcement actions? Is this relevant?

If the judicial review occurs in a recognition action, does the New York Convention permit even a minimal level of substantive review of the arbitrators' decision? Note, as discussed in detail below, that the Convention requires the enforcement of foreign arbitral awards, subject to specified exceptions—which do not include the arbitrators' mistake as to law or fact. *See infra* pp. 1195-99. Would the "public policy" exception to the Convention permit non-recognition of an award that misapplied national public laws?

Consider the following critique of *Mitsubishi*:

"Buried at the end of footnote 19 is probably the main message delivered by the Supreme Court in this decision: it is perfectly permissible to arbitrate foreign antitrust claims so long as the arbitrators will, no matter what the law chosen by the parties for governing their dispute says, apply U.S. laws to such claims. Otherwise enforcement of the award might well be denied. I do not want to discuss here the rather strange views of the Supreme Court of the grounds on which enforcement of an award could be refused in the United States, a country which is a party to and bound by the 1958 New York Convention. I would like merely to notice that we have here a magnificent example of an attempt to export U.S. substantive laws where they had no place up to now; in international arbitration proceedings held outside the United States under an arbitration agreement providing for a non-U.S. law as law governing the dispute. If the price for *Mitsubishi* is this dilution of parties' freedom and extension of U.S. substantive laws operated in tandem, I doubt that users of international arbitration can afford to pay it." Werner, *A Swiss Comment on Mitsubishi*, 3 J. Int'l Arb. 81 (1986).

Is that persuasive?

12. *Showing required for nonarbitrability under* Mitsubishi. What standard did *Mitsubishi* formulate for holding a statutory claim nonarbitrable? Note the Court's comment that "We must assume that if Congress intended the substantive protection afforded by a given statute to include protection against waiver of the right to a judicial forum, that intention will be deducible from text or legislative history." The Court also said that claims will be deemed arbitrable unless Congress "expressly directed" a contrary result. Is this standard appropriate?

13. *Law governing nonarbitrability defense to enforcement of arbitration agreement.* What law governs the question of nonarbitrability when a court considers a claim that an international arbitration agreement, subject to the Convention, should not be enforced on nonarbitrability grounds? What law applied to this issue in *Mitsubishi, Scherk, Eco Swiss* and *Fincantieri*? Is the issue of nonarbitrability governed by the Convention? Or by national law?

(a) *National laws potentially applicable to issue of nonarbitrability.* Assuming that national law is applicable to this issue, what state's law should be applied to the question of nonarbitrability? Should nonarbitrability be governed by the law of: (a) the state whose substantive law governs the parties' relations; (b) the state where the arbitration agreement is sought to be enforced; (c) the state where the arbitral award will be enforced; or (d) the arbitral seat? For example, if a U.S. court is asked to enforce an agreement to arbitrate, providing for arbitration of EU competition claims in an arbitration seated in Paris, what law should apply? Suppose that the litigation is brought in Paris. In Germany. Suppose that the issue of nonarbitrability arises before the tribunal in the arbitration. In each case, what law applies?

(b) *Possible application of judicial enforcement forum's law to determine nonarbitrability.* As discussed below, Article V(2)(a) of the Convention provides that enforcement may be denied an award if the "subject matter of the difference is not capable of settlement by arbitration *under the law of that country*." If Article V(2)(a) permits an award to be denied enforcement based upon the law of the judicial enforcement forum, should Article II(1) incorporate a similar reference to national law? What state's national law? Note that Article V(2)(a) refers to the nonarbitrability rules for *an award*. How would this rule apply in the context of *arbitration agreements*? Would it provide for application of the law of the judicial enforcement forum for the arbitration agreement, or the law of the place where the award is expected to be enforced?

If one applied the law of the judicial enforcement forum, would it not mean that every national court would apply a different (*i.e.*, its own) nonarbitrability law to the enforcement of an arbitration agreement? Is there something wrong with that? Note that the nonarbitrability exception is in the nature of an "escape valve," like the public policy doctrine, to the general obligation to recognize and enforce arbitral awards under the Convention. Is it unusual that this exception would be defined by the law of the judicial enforcement forum, as it is under Article V(2)(a)?

Does it make sense to apply the law of the judicial enforcement forum in all cases? Suppose that Russian and German parties agree to arbitrate in France and their dispute involves Russian competition law claims; assume also that Russian law provides that Russian competition law claims are nonarbitrable. If the arbitration agreement is sought to be enforced in the United States, does it make sense for U.S. courts to apply *Mitsubishi* and standards developed with regard to U.S. antitrust laws to Russian competition law claims? On the other hand, should U.S. courts give effect to Russia's rule of nonarbitrability? If nonarbitrability is treated as an exceptional escape valve, relieving Contracting States of their obligation to recognize arbitration agreements and arbitral awards in limited circumstances, should U.S. courts give effect to the Russian nonarbitrability rule? Or should that rule apply only in Russian courts?

(c) *Possible application of law of arbitral seat.* Does it make sense to apply the law of the arbitral seat to issues of nonarbitrability? Consider again the hypothetical in which Russian and German parties agree to arbitrate Russian competition law claims in Paris. Is there any reason to apply French nonarbitrability rules to the issue of nonarbitrability? In U.S. courts? In German courts? What about French courts? Does the way that France treats the arbitration of French or EU competition law claims have anything to do with how Russia treats the arbitrability of Russian competition law claims?

(d) *Possible application of uniform international standard to determine nonarbitrability under New York Convention.* Can Article II(1) of the New York Convention be interpreted as establishing a uniform international definition of those disputes whose subject matter is "capable of settlement by arbitration"? Under this view, Contracting States would be obliged to enforce arbitration agreements except where they concerned a subject matter falling within Article II(1)'s uniform, international definition of nonarbitrability. Even if national law provided that a dispute was nonarbitrable, the arbitration agreement would be enforceable (under Article II) if Article II(1)'s international definition of nonarbitrability was not satisfied.

Can Articles II(1) and V(2)(a) be interpreted as imposing a uniform international definition of what disputes are "not capable of settlement by arbitration"? Would such a reading be consistent with the text of Article V(2)(a), referring to the law of the recognition forum? Does the same rule necessarily apply under Article II(1)? Would an interpretation of Article II(1) as imposing a uniform international definition of disputes not capable of settlement by arbitration be consistent with the historic practices of Contracting States to adopt nonarbitrability rules without reference to international limits?

(e) *Possible limits on nonarbitrability doctrine under New York Convention.* If the Convention does not prescribe a uniform international standard of nonarbitrability, are there any limits under the Convention on the categories of disputes a Contracting State may treat as nonarbitrable? Suppose a Contracting State declares *all* disputes nonarbitrable. Would that violate the state's commitment under Article II(1) to recognize agreements to arbitrate? Suppose a Contracting State declares all disputes covered by agreements to arbitrate future disputes nonarbitrable. Or, suppose a state declares that all disputes involving amounts in dispute of more than $15 million are nonarbitrable, or all disputes of less than $15 million.

Even if Articles II(1) and V(2)(a) do not impose a uniform international definition of nonarbitrable disputes, could the Convention nonetheless impose limits on nonarbitrability exceptions adopted by Contracting States? If you were going to interpret the Convention as imposing implied limits on a Contracting State's right to declare disputes nonarbitrable, how would you go about formulating such limits? Recall *Ledee*'s analysis of Article II(3). *Ledee* concludes that Article II imposes an international standard of neutrality that "preempts" or supersedes national laws that single out arbitration agreements for special disfavor. *See also Meadows Indem. Co. v. Baccala & Shoop Ins. Serv., Inc.*, 1991 U.S. Dist. LEXIS 4144 (E.D.N.Y.) ("determination of whether a type of claim is 'not capable of settlement by arbitration' under Article II(1) must be made on an international scale, with reference to the laws of the countries party to the Convention"); *supra* pp. 190, 306-10. How would the *Ledee* analysis take account of Article V(2)(a)'s reference to the law of the enforcement forum?

How would the *Ledee* analysis apply? Consider the hypotheticals discussed above, with Russian and German parties agreeing to arbitrate Russian competition claims in France. If Russian courts treat these claims as nonarbitrable, what effect should French, German, or U.S. courts give to that position? Suppose that Russian courts permit competition claims to be arbitrated if the arbitral seat is in Russia, but not if it is abroad. How would *Ledee* treat such a rule? Suppose, alternatively,

Russian and German parties have agreed to arbitrate bankruptcy issues that are treated as nonarbitrable in Russia, as well as in France, Germany and elsewhere.

3. Contemporary Nonarbitrability, Choice-of-Law and Enforcement Issues

As a consequence of legislative actions and judicial decisions in developed jurisdictions during the past three decades, most public law claims are capable of being arbitrated.[77] For example, after *Mitsubishi*, antitrust claims cannot be litigated in a U.S. court when they are subject to a valid arbitration agreement, but instead must be arbitrated. The same conclusion applies to EU competition claims, and to national competition law claims in most European and other developed jurisdictions.[78]

National court decisions expanding the arbitrability of public law claims raise a cluster of complex issues. First, international commercial arbitration often presents difficult choice-of-law questions, including questions relating to the law applicable to the substance of the parties' dispute. These choice-of-law questions must be resolved, among other things, to select the applicable law for public law claims (whether antitrust, securities, or otherwise) asserted by a party in arbitration. They must also be resolved to determine what effect should be given, both in terms of interpretation and enforceability, to choice-of-law clauses selecting particular nations' laws in cases where public law claims are asserted.

Second, beyond choice-of-law questions, the role of national courts that are requested to recognize or annul awards where antitrust (or other public law) claims were raised remains unsettled. Are traditional national law standards relating to the recognition and annulment of arbitral awards applicable? Or are these rules rendered inapplicable, or modified, when awards in the public law context are reviewed?

ROBY v. CORP. OF LLOYD'S
996 F.2d 1353 (2d Cir. 1993)

MESKILL, Circuit Judge. [This case arose from the financial misfortunes of Lloyds of London ("Lloyd's"). Lloyd's is an insurance market, located in London, that is similar to the New York Stock Exchange; it has various governing bodies that promulgate regulations and enforce compliance therewith by "syndicates." Syndicates are investment vehicles that attract investors and use capital obtained from investors to finance insurance activities. In the late 1980s, many Lloyd's syndicates sustained very substantial losses, in part because of the need to pay amounts owed to insureds.

The present case arose when a large number of U.S. residents filed suit in the United States against Lloyd's. The plaintiffs were all "Names" in Lloyd's—that is, investors in Lloyd's syndicates that provided funds to underwrite insurance risk. The plaintiffs had all been solicited, in the United States, by Lloyd's representatives, and had agreed to invest in particular Lloyd's syndicates. All Names, and all the plaintiffs, signed several agreements that contained broad choice-of-law and choice-of-forum clauses. The "General Undertaking" between each Name and the governing bodies of Lloyd's provided: "Each party hereto irrevocably agrees that the courts of England shall have exclusive jurisdiction to settle any dispute and/or controversy of whatsoever nature arising out of or relating to the

---

77. G. Born, *International Commercial Arbitration* 1039-43 (2d ed. 2014).
78. G. Born, *International Commercial Arbitration* 977-80 (2d ed. 2014).

[Name's] membership of and/or underwriting of insurance business at, Lloyd's." Another section of the General Undertaking provided in equally broad terms that English law governed disputes between the parties.

A "Members' Agent's Agreement" between the Names and other Lloyd's entities provided: "Any dispute, difference, question or claim relating to this Agreement which may arise between the Agent and the Name shall be referred at the request of either party to arbitration in London...." It also contained an English choice-of-law clause.

Notwithstanding these provisions, disappointed U.S. Names filed suit against Lloyd's and many entities connected to it in U.S. federal courts. They asserted claims under the U.S. securities laws and RICO claims; they did not assert common law fraud claims or claims under English law. On appeal from a district court decision holding that the plaintiffs' claims had to be arbitrated or submitted to the English courts, the Second Circuit considered the Names' argument that the arbitration clauses/choice-of-law clauses in their agreements either did not reach their U.S. statutory claims, or, if they did, those clauses were unenforceable. The Court of Appeals assumed for purposes of its decision that the plaintiffs had stated cognizable claims under the U.S. securities laws.]

The Roby Names first contended that, because the choice of law clauses require the application of English law, the Roby Names' U.S. statutory claims cannot possibly be covered under the agreements. It defies reason to suggest that a plaintiff may circumvent forum selection and arbitration clauses merely by stating claims under laws not recognized by the forum selected in the agreement. A plaintiff simply would have to allege violations of his country's tort law or his country's statutory law or his country's property law in order to render nugatory any forum selection clause that implicitly or explicitly required the application of the law of another jurisdiction. We refuse to allow a party's solemn promise to be defeated by artful pleading. In the absence of other considerations, the agreement to submit to arbitration or the jurisdiction of the English courts must be enforced even if that agreement tacitly includes the forfeiture of some claims that could have been brought in a different forum....

The Roby Names argue that the public policy codified in the antiwaiver provisions of the securities laws renders unenforceable any agreement that effectively eliminates compliance with those laws. The Securities Act provides that "any ... stipulation ... binding any person acquiring any security to waive compliance with any provision of this subchapter ... shall be void." 15 U.S.C. §77n. Similarly, the Securities Exchange Act states, "any ... stipulation ... binding any person to waive compliance with any provision of this chapter or of any rule or regulation thereunder ... shall be void." 15 U.S.C. §78cc(a).

According to the undisputed testimony of a British [sic] attorney, neither an English court nor an English arbitrator would apply the U.S. securities laws, because English conflict of law rules do not permit recognition of foreign tort or statutory law. From this, the Roby Names conclude that the contract clauses work to waive compliance with the securities laws and therefore are void. We note at the outset that *Wilko v. Swan*, 346 U.S. 427 (1953), has been squarely overruled. *See Rodriguez de Quijas v. Shearson/American Express*, 490 U.S. 477, 484 (1989). *Wilko* held that an agreement to arbitrate future controversies was void under the antiwaiver provision of the Securities Act. We do not doubt that judicial hostility to arbitration has receded dramatically since 1953 and that the arbitral forum is perfectly competent to protect litigants' substantive rights. In the words of the *Mitsubishi* Court, quoted by both the *Rodriguez* and *McMahon* Courts, "by agreeing to arbitrate a statutory claim, a party does not forgo the substantive rights afforded by the statute; it only submits to their resolution in an arbitral, rather than a judicial, forum." 473 U.S. at 628. If the Roby Names objected merely to the choice of an arbitral rather than a judicial forum, we would reject their claim immediately, citing *Rodriguez* and *McMahon*. However, the Roby Names argue that they have been forced to forgo the substantive protections afforded by the securities laws, not simply the judicial forum. We therefore do not believe that *Rodriguez* and *McMahon* are controlling....

The Tenth Circuit recently addressed this exact issue in a similar context in *Riley v. Kingsley Underwriting Agencies, Ltd.*, 969 F.2d 953 (10th Cir.). Relying primarily on ... *Carnival Cruise Lines v. Shute*, 113 L.Ed.2d 622 (1991); *Mitsubishi*, 473 U.S. at 614; *Scherk*, 417 U.S. at 506; [and] *Bremen*, 407 U.S. at 1, the *Riley* Court concluded that "when an agreement is truly international, as here, and reflects numerous contacts with the foreign forum, the Supreme Court has quite clearly held that the parties' choice of law and forum selection provisions will be given effect." 969 F.2d at 957. While we agree with the ultimate result in *Riley*, we are reluctant to interpret the Supreme Court's precedent quite so broadly.

The Supreme Court certainly has indicated that forum selection and choice of law clauses are presumptively valid where the underlying transaction is fundamentally international in character. *See, e.g., Bremen*, 407 U.S. at 15.[79] ... This presumption of validity may be overcome, however, by a clear showing that the clauses are "unreasonable" under the circumstances." *Bremen*, 407 U.S. at 10. The Supreme Court has construed this exception narrowly: forum selection and choice of law clauses are "unreasonable" (1) if their incorporation into the agreement was the result of fraud or overreaching; (2) if the complaining party "will for all practical purposes be deprived of his day in court," due to the grave inconvenience or unfairness of the selected forum; (3) if the fundamental unfairness of the chosen law may deprive the plaintiff of a remedy; or (4) if the clauses contravene a strong public policy of the forum state.

[The court readily found that the first three criteria did not argue for non-recognition of the parties' agreements.] We depart somewhat from the *Riley* Court with respect to the fourth factor. We believe that there is a serious question whether U.S. public policy has been subverted by the Lloyd's clauses.... The Supreme Court in *Bremen* wrote, "[a] contractual choice-of-forum clause should be held unenforceable if enforcement would contravene a strong public policy of the forum in which suit is brought." 407 U.S. at 15. By including antiwaiver provisions in the securities laws, Congress made clear its intention that the public policies incorporated into those laws should not be thwarted. The framers of the securities laws were concerned principally with reversing the common law rule favoring "caveat emptor." To this end, the securities laws are aimed at prospectively protecting American investors from injury by demanding "full and fair disclosure" from issuers. Private actions exist under the securities laws not because Congress had an

---

79. The analysis is no different for the arbitration clauses. Indeed, an arbitration clause is merely a specialized type of forum selection clause. *See Scherk*, 417 U.S. at 519. We might have referred to the [New York] Convention, for further support with respect to the arbitration clauses; however, because we are not entirely persuaded that the [Convention] applies in the securities context, we prefer to rest our decision on different grounds. Because we understand the Roby Names to complain primarily that the United States securities laws will not be applied and not that the arbitration forum is particularly inappropriate in their case, we do not believe a detailed analysis of the [Convention] is necessary.

overwhelming desire to shift losses after the fact, but rather because private actions provide a potent means of deterring the exploitation of American investors. We believe therefore that the public policies of the securities laws would be contravened if the applicable foreign law failed adequately to deter issuers from exploiting American investors.

In this sense, the securities laws somewhat resemble the antitrust laws at issue in *Mitsubishi*. The *Mitsubishi* Court enforced a clause providing that all disputes arising under a contract between a Puerto Rican corporation and a Japanese corporation be submitted for arbitration.... The Court recognized that private actions under the Sherman Act, play a "central role" in promoting the national interest in a competitive economy. Like private actions in the securities context, private actions under the Sherman Act serve primarily a deterrent purpose. Nevertheless, the *Mitsubishi* Court held that a Japanese arbitration panel, applying U.S. antitrust law, adequately would further the deterrent purpose of the Sherman Act.... The Court indicated quite clearly in dicta, however, that "in the event the choice-of-forum and choice-of-law clauses operated in tandem as a prospective waiver of a party's right to pursue statutory remedies for antitrust violations, we would have little hesitation in condemning the agreement as against public policy."

We are concerned in the present case that the Roby Names' contract clauses may operate "in tandem" as a prospective waiver of the statutory remedies for securities violations, thereby circumventing the strong and expansive public policy in deterring such violations. We are cognizant of the important reasons for enforcing such clauses in Lloyd's' agreements. Lloyd's is a British concern which raises capital in over 80 nations. Its operations are clearly international in scope. There can be no doubt that the contract clauses mitigate the uncertainty regarding choice of law and forum inherent in the multinational affairs of Lloyd's. Comity also weighs in favor of enforcing the clauses. Yet we do not believe that a U.S. court can in good conscience enforce clauses that subvert a strong national policy, particularly one that for over fifty years has served as the foundation for the U.S. financial markets and business community. In this case, the victims of Lloyd's' alleged securities violations are hundreds of individual American investors, most of whom were actively solicited in the United States by Lloyd's representatives. We believe that if the Roby Names were able to show that available remedies in England are insufficient to deter British issuers from exploiting American investors through fraud, misrepresentation or inadequate disclosure, we would not hesitate to condemn the choice of law, forum selection and arbitration clauses as against public policy. For the reasons set forth ... below, however, we conclude that the Roby Names have failed to make such a showing. We are satisfied not only that the Roby Names have several adequate remedies in England to vindicate their substantive rights, but also that in this case the policies of ensuring full and fair disclosure and deterring the exploitation of U.S. investors have not been subverted....

English common law provides remedies for knowing or reckless deceit, negligent misrepresentation, and even innocent misrepresentation.... While the Roby Names might have been able to sue "controlling persons" under the U.S. securities laws and establish liability without proving reliance, it certainly is not unfair for English law to require proof of actual misconduct and reliance. Furthermore, we are skeptical that "controlling person" liability could be established against many of the defendants here....

Finally, although ... §14 of the Lloyd's Act of 1982 exempts the Corporation of Lloyd's (and its officers and employees) from liability, no other entity within Lloyd's is exempt. Moreover, even the Corporation of Lloyd's is not exempt for acts "done in bad faith." ...

We conclude that the Roby Names have adequate remedies in England to vindicate their statutory fraud and misrepresentation claims.... That RICO provides treble damages and seeks to deter persistent misconduct does not dissuade us from our view that the Roby Names' contract clauses must be enforced. As we have explained, the Roby Names have adequate potential remedies in England and there are significant disincentives to deter English issuers from unfairly exploiting American investors. Although the remedies and disincentives might be magnified by the application of RICO, we cannot say that application of English law would subvert the policies underlying that statute....

CONVENTION ON THE LAW APPLICABLE TO CONTRACTUAL OBLIGATIONS ("ROME CONVENTION")
Articles 3(3), 7(1) (1980)

3(3). The fact that the parties have chosen a foreign law, whether or not accompanied by the choice of a foreign tribunal, shall not, where all the other elements connected with the situation at the time of the choice are relevant to one country only, prejudice the application of rules of the law of that country which cannot be derogated from by the contract, hereinafter called "mandatory rules."

7(1). When applying under this Convention the law of a country, effect may be given to the mandatory rules of the law of another country with which the situation has a close connection if, and in so far as, under the law of the latter country, those rules must be applied whatever the law applicable to the contract. In considering whether to give effect to those mandatory rules, regard shall be had to their nature and purpose and to the consequences of their application or non-application.

REGULATION ON THE LAW APPLICABLE TO CONTRACTUAL OBLIGATIONS ("ROME I REGULATION")
Article 9 (2008)

9(1). Overriding mandatory provisions are provisions the respect for which is regarded as crucial by a country for safeguarding its public interests, such as its political, social or economic organisation, to such an extent that they are applicable to any situation falling within their scope, irrespective of the law otherwise applicable to the contract under this Regulation.

9(2). Nothing in this Regulation shall restrict the application of the overriding mandatory provisions of the law of the forum.

9(3). Effect may be given to the overriding mandatory provisions of the law of the country where the obligations arising out of the contract have to be or have been performed, in so far as those overriding mandatory provisions render the performance of the contract unlawful. In considering whether to give effect to those provisions, regard shall be had to their nature and purpose and to the consequences of their application or non-application.

RESTATEMENT (SECOND) CONFLICT OF LAWS
§187 (1971)

187(1). The law of the state chosen by the parties to govern their contractual rights and duties will be applied if the particular issue is one which the parties could have resolved by an explicit provision in their agreement directed to that issue.

187(2). The law of the state chosen by the parties to govern their contractual rights and duties will be applied, even if the particular issue is one which the parties could not have resolved by an explicit provision in their agreement directed to that issue, unless either

(a) the chosen state has no substantial relationship to the parties or the transaction and there is no other reasonable basis for the parties' choice, or

(b) the application of the law of the chosen state would be contrary to a fundamental policy of a state which has a materially greater interest than the chosen state in the determination of the particular issue and which under the rule of §188, would be the state of the applicable law in the absence of an effective choice of law by the parties.

187(3). In the absence of a contrary indication of intention, the reference is to the local law of the state of the chosen law.

NOTES

1. *Authority of arbitrators to consider public law claims (revisited)*. Recall the discussion above regarding the authority of arbitrators to consider and decide claims involving public law or public policy. *See supra* pp. 482, 494-99. What is the basis for the arbitrators' authority to consider such claims? Is it any different from the arbitrators' authority to consider other matters falling within the scope of the parties' agreement to arbitrate?

2. *Effect of choice-of-law agreement on arbitrators' authority to consider public law claims*. As noted elsewhere, international agreements often contain choice-of-law clauses, as well as arbitration agreements. *See supra* p. 89 & *infra* p. 983. That was true, for example, in *Scherk*, *Mitsubishi* and *Roby*. Suppose an agreement with an arbitration clause also contains a choice-of-law clause that selects a particular national law (that of State A) and that excludes the national laws of other jurisdictions (those of States B, C and D), as the law applicable to disputes between the parties. How should an arbitrator resolve antitrust or other public law claims arising under the laws of States B, C and D when such a choice-of-law clause exists?

   For example, how should the arbitral tribunal in *Mitsubishi* handle the antitrust claims asserted by Soler? Given the parties' choice-of-law clause (selecting Swiss law), could the tribunal have applied U.S. antitrust laws? On what legal theory? Consider Justice Blackmun's suggestion that:

   > [T]he international arbitral tribunal owes no prior allegiance to the legal norms of particular states; hence, it has no direct obligation to vindicate their statutory dictates. The tribunal, however, is bound to effectuate the intentions of the parties. Where the parties have agreed that the arbitral body is to decide a defined set of claims which includes, as in these cases, those arising from the application of American antitrust law, the tribunal therefore should be bound to decide that dispute in accord with the national law giving rise to the claim.

Is that persuasive? Where did the parties in *Mitsubishi* agree that the arbitrators were to "decide a defined set of claims" that include U.S. antitrust claims? Why is it that U.S. antitrust laws should have been intended to apply to the parties' dispute—when the parties agreed to a choice-of-law clause selecting Swiss substantive law? Is the Court distinguishing between (a) the scope of the agreement to arbitrate (encompassing all claims relating to the parties' contract), and (b) the applicable substantive law? Just considering the scope of the parties' arbitration agreement, did the parties agree to arbitrate a category of claims that would include U.S. antitrust claims, as well as any other claims that apply under applicable conflict of laws rules?

3. *Conflict of laws rules and claims under mandatory law or public policy.* What conflict of laws rules might provide for application of mandatory national laws or public policies other than those selected by the parties? (This issue is addressed in detail below at pp. 979-81, 1000-04.) Consider *Restatement (Second) Conflict of Laws* §187 (1971) and Articles 3 and 9 of the Rome I Regulation. Under these rules, the parties' designation of a national law to govern their relations will not operate to override mandatory national laws of other countries that have sufficiently close connections to the parties' dispute. Is it appropriate for an arbitral tribunal to ignore the parties' chosen law in favor of "foreign" mandatory laws and policies, which the parties did not select? *See also infra* pp. 979-81.

4. *Validity of choice-of-law clause excluding mandatory law or public policy.* How will a national court, asked to enforce an arbitration agreement or arbitral award dealing with mandatory law (*e.g.*, antitrust) claims, react if the arbitral tribunal refused to apply the relevant mandatory law? For example, what if the parties' agreement provided expressly that the relevant mandatory law claims were waived and that no relief could be granted on them? In a footnote, the *Mitsubishi* Court suggests that, where U.S. antitrust claims are concerned, such an arbitration agreement or award would not be enforced:

> "in the event the choice-of-forum and choice-of-law clauses operated in tandem as a prospective waiver of a party's right to pursue statutory remedies for antitrust violations, we would have little hesitation in condemning the agreement as against public policy." 473 U.S. at 637 n.21.

What authority supports the *Mitsubishi* Court's refusal to enforce a contractual waiver of antitrust claims? Is it merely an interpretation of the antitrust laws? Would such a refusal be permitted by the New York Convention? *See* Article V(2).

5. *Interpretation of choice-of-law clauses affecting mandatory law or public policy claims.* Consider the Swiss choice-of-law clause in *Mitsubishi* and the English choice-of-law clause in *Roby*. Were there any differences in the two clauses? Were the two clauses interpreted as producing different results? Was the *Mitsubishi* clause interpreted to exclude U.S. antitrust claims? Was the *Roby* clause interpreted to exclude U.S. securities claims? Should a court ordinarily err on the side of extending ambiguous choice-of-law clauses to exclude, or to leave standing, claims under the mandatory law of foreign legal systems? *See infra* pp. 508-10, 979-81.

6. *The* Roby *decision.* The decision in *Roby* has been followed, almost uniformly, in a series of U.S. appellate decisions involving federal securities, antitrust and other statutory claims. *See Richards v. Lloyd's of London*, 135 F.3d 1289, 1295 (9th Cir.

1998); *Haynsworth v. Corp.*, 121 F.3d 956, 969 (5th Cir. 1997); *Allen v. Lloyd's of London*, 94 F.3d 923, 929 (4th Cir. 1996). *See also S.K.I. Beer Corp. v. Baltika Brewery*, 612 F.3d 705, 712(2d Cir. 2010) (speculation as to application of U.S. law by foreign court did not justify non-enforcement of forum selection clause). What exactly does the *Roby* court hold? Is its holding persuasive?

(a) *Prospective waivers of statutory rights.* Does *Roby* comport with the Court's comment in *Mitsubishi* about the impermissibility of "prospective waivers" of antitrust claims? Does *Roby* permit the prospective waiver of securities law claims, at least when some roughly comparable remedy is provided by the applicable foreign law? Reread Justice Douglas' dissent in *Scherk*: "When a foreign corporation undertakes fraudulent action which subjects it to the jurisdiction of our federal securities laws, nothing justifies the conclusion that only a diluted version of those laws protects American investors." Does *Roby* permit such dilution?

Is the rule adopted in *Roby* for securities law claims applicable also to other types of statutory claims? Are securities law claims entitled to less protection under U.S. law than antitrust claims? Note that although the securities laws contain provisions specifically forbidding waivers of their protections, *see Wilko, supra* pp. 476-78, no analogous provision exists under the antitrust laws.

(b) *Importance of foreign remedies.* Under *Roby*, when is a waiver of U.S. mandatory law claims permitted? Does the *Roby* analysis extend outside the context of U.S. securities law claims (for example, also providing a model for analyzing waivers or exclusions of U.S. and EU antitrust claims)? Under the *Roby* standards, how is a U.S. court to conclude that foreign law and remedies are sufficiently comparable to U.S. ones to permit an exclusion of the U.S. claims?

7. *Treble or other statutory damages in international arbitration.* The *Mitsubishi* Court left it to the arbitrators to decide whether to award treble damages. Suppose an arbitral tribunal that hears U.S. antitrust claims applies substantive U.S. antitrust laws, but refuses to award treble damages. Would *Mitsubishi* permit Soler to renew its U.S. judicial action or would U.S. courts recognize the arbitral award as a bar to Soler's action? Compare *Mitsubishi*'s emphasis on the preservation through arbitration of "statutory remedies," which presumably include treble damages, with its emphasis on the "remedial" purpose of the antitrust laws. Consider the following comment from one proponent of international commercial arbitration:

> "As to the trebling of damages, my instinct, without any real authority, is that the rest of the world views treble damages in antitrust cases as in some sense penal, and that arbitrators do not award—possibly even lack authority to award—penal damages. Where an allegation of violation of antitrust laws is raised, it seems reasonable to establish at the outset—*i.e.*, in the submission agreement or terms of reference—that the counterclaimant is entitled in the arbitration only to actual damages…. Whether at a later stage the successful counterclaimant could assert in a civil action his entitlement to treble damages, and how much, if any, of the determination in the arbitration would be regarded as *res judicata*, may be left for the time being as an unresolved issue." Lowenfeld, *The* Mitsubishi *Case: Another View*, 2 Arb. Int'l 178, 189 (1986).

Lower U.S. courts have thus far reached divergent results as to the obligation of arbitrators to award treble damages where a federal statute provides for such relief. *Compare Simula, Inc. v. Autoliv, Inc.*, 1999 U.S. App. LEXIS 8273 (9th Cir.) ("remedies in a foreign forum need not be identical") *and Life of Am. Ins. Co. v. Aetna Life Ins. Co.*, 744 F.2d 409 (5th Cir. 1984) (declining to decide in §4 proceeding whether treble damages were awardable under state law: "Until arbitration establishes that Life of America is entitled to damages but must be denied treble damages, its asserted rights under Texas law have not been impaired") *with PPG Indus., Inc. v. Pilkington plc*, 825 F.Supp. 1465 (D. Ariz. 1993) ("the Court directs that any damages determination, or arbitral award, made by the arbitrators shall be determined according to U.S. antitrust law irrespective of any conflict that may exist between those laws and the laws of England.").

8.   *Arbitration agreement enforced notwithstanding doubts about arbitral tribunal's application of foreign mandatory law.* Suppose that it is uncertain whether the arbitral tribunal will apply an allegedly applicable foreign mandatory law. Is that uncertainty sufficient to deny enforcement of the arbitration agreement under *Mitsubishi* (or parallel rules in other jurisdictions)? Or should courts refer parties to arbitration, permitting the arbitral tribunal an opportunity to apply (or not apply) allegedly applicable mandatory law?

     U.S. courts have generally rejected requests that they decline to order arbitration if it is unclear that the arbitrators will hear mandatory law claims. *See, e.g., Simula, Inc. v. Autoliv, Inc.*, 175 F.3d 716, 723 n.4 (9th Cir. 1999) ("[I]t is possible that the Swiss Tribunal might apply U.S. antitrust law to the dispute…. Moreover, even if Swiss law is applied to the dispute, there has been no showing that it will not provide Simula with sufficient protection"); *George Fischer Foundry Sys., Inc. v. Adolph H. Hottinger Maschinenbau GmbH*, 55 F.3d 1206, 1210 (6th Cir. 1995) ("*Mitsubishi* stands for the proposition that arbitration should go forward even if there is a chance that U.S. antitrust statutory rights will not be fully recognized … because the Zurich [arbitral] tribunal has yet to decide what law it will apply, this case is not ripe for review."); *Dziennik v. Sealift, Inc.*, 2010 WL 1191993, at *7 (E.D.N.Y.) (possibility that "'the foreign arbitrators might apply [foreign] law which, depending on the proper construction of [the federal statute in issue], might reduce respondents' legal obligations,' does not provide an adequate basis upon which to declare the relevant arbitration agreement unenforceable") (quoting *Vimar Seguros y Reaseguros, SA v. M/V Sky Reefer*, 515 U.S. 528, 541 (1995)). Is this approach appropriate? Does it unacceptably delay vindication of statutory rights? Make them uncertain?

9.   *Judicial "supervision" of arbitration of mandatory law claims.* Under most contemporary arbitration regimes, national courts are generally forbidden from intervening in or considering interlocutory challenges to ongoing arbitrations, save in exceptional circumstances. *See infra* pp. 797-810. Nevertheless, some U.S. courts have proceeded differently where U.S. mandatory law claims are involved. In particular, some courts have ordered the parties to submit such claims, under U.S. law, to arbitration and to furnish periodic reports on the progress of the arbitration. *Cole v. Burns Int'l Sec. Servs.*, 105 F.3d 1465 (D.C. Cir. 1997) (ordering arbitration of Title VII dispute, but imposing "procedural safeguards," including "more than minimal discovery," punitive damages, and employee's exemption from paying arbitrators' fees); *MEL v. Gotaas-Larsen Shipping Corp.*, No. 89-0602-CIV (S.D. Fla. July 17, 1990) (requiring reports every three months on progress of London arbitration of federal securities claims).

C. ARBITRATION AGREEMENTS IN INVESTOR-STATE DISPUTES

As noted above, it is frequently said that international arbitration is "consensual" or that every international arbitration "requires an international arbitration agreement." These observations are largely accurate. The overwhelming majority of international arbitrations arise from arbitration clauses and, without an arbitration agreement, there is no legal basis for an international arbitration.[80] That has also historically been true in the investment context, where the ICSID Convention provided (in Article 25) for the recognition of agreements to arbitrate investment disputes under ICSID auspices.[81]

Despite this general principle, it is not correct that international arbitration invariably requires an arbitration agreement—at least in the traditional sense of the term. There are instances in which disputes can be arbitrated, and in which there exists a legal obligation to arbitrate, even without an international arbitration agreement. In particular, contemporary "bilateral investment treaties" ("BITs") or "investment protection treaties" frequently create treaty-based rights (and obligations) to arbitrate various categories of international disputes.[82] In the words of one commentator, BITs provide the basis for "arbitration without privity."[83]

The past decade has seen a dramatic increase in the number and scope of BITs, particularly between developed, capital-exporting states and developing or emerging market states. Germany, the United Kingdom, Switzerland, the Netherlands, and the United States all have entered into substantial numbers of bilateral investment treaties with various states around the world.[84] In 1999, there were more than 1,300 BITs in force[85]; by 2014, the figure exceeded 2,100.[86]

Typically, BITs contain requirements that each state afford nationals of the other state either "national" or "most favored nation" status and that each state refrain from expropriatory or otherwise arbitrary conduct with respect to the investments of the other state's nationals.[87] A key feature of the past decade's wave of BITs has been provisions granting foreign investors (from one contracting state) the right to initiate international arbitration against either the host state (the other contracting state) or its instrumentalities. For example, a BIT between the United States and Haiti might provide that U.S. investors in Haiti could pursue claims against the Haitian state for violations of the BIT's protections in international arbitration—even without any arbitration agreement (or any contract at all)

---

80. *See supra* pp. 177, 335-474.

81. *See* G. Born, *International Commercial Arbitration* 124-25 (2d ed. 2014); C. Schreuer *et al.*, *The ICSID Convention: A Commentary* Art. 25, ¶247 (2d ed. 2009).

82. For commentary on BITs, *see* Comeaux & Kinsella, *Reducing Political Right in Developing Countries: Bilateral Investment Treaties, Stabilization Clauses, and MIGA & OPIC Investment Insurance*, 15 N.Y.L. Sch. J. Int'l & Comp. L. 1 (1994); Kishoiyian, The *Utility of Bilateral Investment Treaties in the Formulation of Customary International Law*, 14 Nw. J. Int'l L. & Bus. 327 (1994); C. Schreuer *et al.*, *The ICSID Convention: A Commentary* (2d ed. 2009); Unegbu, *BITs and ICC Arbitration*, 16(2) J. Int'l Arb. 93 (1999).

83. Paulsson, *Arbitration Without Privity*, 10 ICSID L. Rev. 232 (1995).

84. ICSID, *Bilateral Investment Treaties* 1959-1996 51 (1997).

85. Parra, *The Role of ICSID in the Settlement of International Investment Disputes*, 16 ICSID News 1 (1999).

86. *See* investmentpolicyhub.unctad.org/IIA.

87. C. Dugan *et al.*, *Investor-State Arbitration* 413-15 (2008); C. Schreuer *et al.*, *The ICSID Convention: A Commentary* Art. 25 ¶¶567-577 (2d ed. 2009).

with Haiti or any Haitian state entity. The following materials illustrate the dispute resolution provisions of contemporary BITs.

DECISION 24 OF THE ANDEAN COMMISSION CONCERNING TREATMENT OF FOREIGN CAPITAL
Article 51, 10 I.L.M. 152 (1971)

[excerpted above at p. 179]

UNITED STATES OF AMERICA-HAITI TREATY CONCERNING THE ENCOURAGEMENT & RECIPROCAL PROTECTION OF INVESTMENTS
Article 7(3)

7(3)(a). The national or company concerned may choose to consent in writing to the submission of the dispute to the International Chamber of Commerce ("ICC"), for settlement by conciliation or binding arbitration, at any time after six months from the date upon which the dispute arose, provided:

(i) the dispute has not, for any reason, been submitted for resolution in accordance with any applicable dispute resolution procedures previously agreed to by the parties to the dispute; and

(ii) the national or company concerned has not brought the dispute before the courts of Justice or administrative tribunals or agencies of competent jurisdiction of the Party that is a party to the dispute.

Once the national or company concerned has so consented, either party to the dispute may institute proceedings before the ICC. If the parties disagree over whether conciliation or binding arbitration is the more appropriate procedure to be employed, the opinion of the national or company concerned shall prevail.

7(3)(b). Each party hereby consents to the submission of an investment dispute to the ICC for settlement by conciliation or binding arbitration.

7(3)(c). Conciliation or binding arbitration of such disputes shall be done in accordance with the provisions of the Regulations and Rules of the ICC.

7(3)(d). In case of arbitration between the party and a national or company of the other party, the ICC, consistent with its rules, shall determine the venue for arbitration. The venue for arbitration shall be in a State which is a party to the New York Convention on the Recognition and Enforcement of Foreign Arbitral Awards. Moreover, each Party shall provide for enforcement within its territory of ICC arbitral awards.

SPAIN-ALGERIA AGREEMENT ON THE PROMOTION & RECIPROCAL PROTECTION OF INVESTMENTS
Article 11(2)

If the controversy cannot be resolved in this way [amicable means] within six months from the date of written advice mentioned in paragraph 1, the controversy may be submitted at the choice of the investor:

—to an arbitral tribunal, according to the Rules of Arbitration of the Arbitration Institute of the Chamber of Commerce of Stockholm;

—to the Court of Arbitration of the International Chamber of Commerce in Paris;

—to an "ad hoc" arbitral tribunal established by the Rules of Arbitration of the United Nations Commission on International Trade Law (UNCITRAL);

—to the International Centre for the Settlement of Disputes Concerning Investments Between States and Citizens of Other States," open to signature in Washington on 18 March 1965, when each Member State to the present agreement has become signatory to such agreement.

BG GROUP PLC v. REPUBLIC OF ARGENTINA
134 S.Ct. 1198 (2014)

[excerpted above at pp. 233-47]

NOTES

1. *Historic hostility of some developing states to international arbitration.* As discussed above, some developing states historically regarded international arbitration with a high degree of mistrust. Decision 24 of the Andean Commission is one example of this. What are the costs and risks to developing countries of agreeing to international arbitration with foreign investors? Does the United States or France agree to international arbitration when foreign investors acquire U.S. or French firms or undertake major projects in those countries? If not, why should Nigeria, Saudi Arabia, India, or Brazil do so when U.S. or French firms invest there? What are the costs and risks to developing countries of not agreeing to international arbitration with foreign investors?

2. *Abandonment of hostility of developing countries to international arbitration.* As detailed above, during the past two decades, much of the hostility of developing states to international arbitration has dissipated. *See supra* pp. 44-45, 188-89. In addition to adopting "pro-arbitration" arbitration legislation, many developing states have entered into BITs. Consider the basic structure and consequences of a BIT. Is it wise for a developing state to enter into such a treaty? Why or why not? What are the costs and benefits of a BIT?

3. *"Arbitration without privity."* Consider Article VII(3) of the U.S.-Haiti BIT. What does Article VII(3) grant to foreign investors (from a signatory state) with respect to international arbitration? Compare Article 11(2) of the Spain-Algeria BIT to Article VII(3) of the U.S.-Haiti BIT. Also compare Article 8 of the U.K./Bosnia-Herzegovina BIT, excerpted at p. 76 of the Documentary Supplement, and the Model U.S. BIT. For a more detailed analysis, *see* Unegbu, *BITs and ICC Arbitration*, 16 J. Int'l Arb. 93 (1999); C. McLachlan, L. Shore & M. Weiniger, *International Investment Arbitration* (2007); R. Dolzer & M. Stevens, *Bilateral Investment Treaties* (1995).

   Suppose Company A invests $100 million in a plant in Haiti and the Haitian government subsequently imposes very high tax rates on foreign investors. What does Article VII(3) of the U.S.-Haiti BIT permit the U.S. investor to do? What would Article 11(2) of the Spain-Algeria BIT and Article 8 of the U.K./Bosnia-Herzegovina BIT permit in analogous circumstances? Would it matter, in either case, that the foreign investor's investment agreement did not contain any dispute resolution or arbitration clause? Which BIT (U.S.-Haiti; Spain-Algeria; U.K./Bosnia-Herzegovina) offers broader and more certain rights with respect to international arbitration?

4. *Nature of "arbitration agreement" under a BIT.* Is it correct to say that there is no arbitration agreement when an investor proceeds with a claim under a BIT? Or is there an agreement to arbitrate that is formed through the host state's offer to arbitrate (contained in the BIT (or, sometimes, national investment protection legislation)) and the foreign investor's acceptance of that offer by commencing an arbitration? Consider:

> "Finally, BGT's consent to the submission of the dispute to ICSID arbitration under Article 8(1) of the BIT, or §23.2 of the TIA, is constituted by the Request for Arbitration, therefore perfecting the parties' arbitration agreement." *Biwater Gauff (Tanzania) Ltd v. Tanzania, Award in ICSID Case No. ARB/05/22 of 24 July 2008*, ¶258.

> "It is well established that arbitration pursuant to an investment treaty such as the ECT requires an arbitration agreement. However, this arbitration agreement is not created by a contemporaneous exchange of promises between the parties in the manner of a commercial arbitration agreement. Rather, often offer and acceptance are separated in time and form. The State parties make an open offer of arbitration to investors of the other party or parties in the Treaty itself, which can be accepted by an investor when a dispute arises. Only at this time is there mutual consent to arbitration and therefore the Arbitral Tribunal has jurisdiction over the dispute (see, for example, *Banco Int'l, Inc. v. Argentine Republic*, ICSID ARB/97/96 'Preliminary Decision on Jurisdiction' December 18, 1998, paragraph 44; 40 ILM 457 (Mar. 2001)." *AMTO LLC v. Ukraine, Final Award in SCC Case No. 080/2005 of 26 March 2008*, ¶46.

Consider also the analysis of the U.S. Supreme Court of formation of an agreement to arbitrate in *BG Group*. Note in particular the Court's discussion of Argentina's "standing offer" to arbitrate.

Are these analyses persuasive? Is it accurate to describe the dispute resolution mechanism under a BIT as giving rise to an "arbitration agreement"? Should one instead regard the relationship as in the nature of a regulatory mechanism for resolving investment disputes—given that one party is a state, whose conduct as a state is challenged? Does that take into account the fact that the parties are of different nationalities and are both subject to international law?

When is a host state's "offer" to arbitrate under a BIT accepted by a foreign investor? Is it when the foreign investor commences an arbitration? Files a notice of dispute? Makes a protected investment? What does *BG Group* suggest? Would it be more accurate to say that an offer to arbitrate is accepted when an investment is made? Does the answer depend on the language of the BIT?

5. *Choice of arbitration to resolve investment disputes.* Why do many (most) BITs provide for the resolution of investment disputes by international arbitration? Why do contracting states not provide for resolution of such disputes in their own courts? How neutral would that be? How attractive to investors? What other forums could be used for the resolution of investment disputes (other than international arbitration)? What about the International Court of Justice? What about a special "International Investment Tribunal"? What advantages and disadvantages would this have?

Comparison between investment arbitrations under BITs and commercial arbitrations under contractual dispute resolution mechanisms. Contrast the dispute resolution mechanism that exists for investment arbitration under many BITs (*i.e.*, "arbitration without privity") and the dispute resolution mechanisms that exist in the international commercial context. How do BITs differ from the New York (and Inter-American) Convention(s)? What explains these differences?

Could you imagine "arbitration without privity" for commercial disputes? Suppose the G-20 States agreed that, absent contrary agreement between the parties, all international commercial disputes between their nationals involving more than €5 million would be submitted to arbitration pursuant to the UNCITRAL Rules. Would that be sensible? What information would you need to answer this question? *See also* Born, *BITs, BATs and Buts*, available at www.globalarbitrationreview.com.

6. *Interaction between BITs and contractual dispute resolution provisions.* Suppose that a foreign investment agreement does contain a dispute resolution provision. How does this interact with the dispute resolution rights granted in a BIT? Consider what Article VII(3) of the U.S.-Haiti BIT provides in this regard. For example, in the foregoing hypothetical, suppose that a U.S. investor agreed that all disputes arising from its investment agreement would be resolved in Haitian courts. How would Article 11(2) of the Spain-Algeria BIT and Article 8 of the U.K./Bosnia-Herzegovina BIT deal with such a provision?

7. *Choice of multiple arbitral forums.* Consider again Article 11(2) of the Spain-Algeria BIT and Article 8 of the U.K./Bosnia-Herzegovina BIT. Note that each permits multiple arbitral forums which the foreign investor can choose between. What is the purpose of granting the foreign investor a choice, unilaterally, between the Stockholm Chamber of Commerce, the ICC, an *ad hoc* UNCITRAL tribunal, and ICSID? If an agreement between two private parties granted one party and not the other such options, would it be enforceable? Would it be accepted in negotiations? Systemically, is there any risk that the relevant arbitral institutions will take undesirable steps to compete for foreign investors' business? How might they do so? Recall also the concerns about one-sided commercial arbitration agreements. *See supra* pp. 408-10.

8. *Unilateral character of arbitration under BITs.* What sorts of claims can be brought under most BITs? Who can bring such claims? Is there any basis for a host state to bring claims against an investor under a BIT? Is the unilateral character of dispute resolution under BITs problematic? Why or why not? Again, note the concerns about asymmetrical arbitration agreements. *See supra* pp. 410-11.

9. *Standing to invoke arbitration under BITs.* Who can invoke the arbitration remedies provided for under a BIT? The answer, of course, depends on what the particular BIT provides. Virtually all BITs provide, however, that arbitration remedies (and substantive rights) are extended to "nationals" of one signatory state vis-à-vis the other signatory state. That is, a U.S. "national" may invoke the U.S.-Haiti BIT against Haiti, but a French or a Haitian national may not.

Who is a "national" for purposes of a BIT? Again, the answer depends on the particular BIT and its definitional provisions (if any). In general, however, BITs look to citizenship (for natural persons) and incorporation and/or ownership (for juridical persons). Typically, companies incorporated under the laws of third states are not able to invoke rights (including arbitration remedies) granted by a BIT between two countries.

10. *"Cooling off periods" and "local litigation" requirements.* Note the "cooling off periods" of six months in Article VII(a) of the U.S.-Haiti BIT and Article 11(2) of the Spain-Algeria BIT. Compare the "local litigation" requirement in Article 8(2)(a) of the U.K.-Argentina BIT, at issue in the *BG Group* decision. What is the purpose of the requirements?

Who should have the competence to determine whether an investor has complied (and must comply) with either a "cooling off" period or a "local litigation" requirement? The arbitral tribunal or an annulment court? What did the *BG Group* decision hold? Is that persuasive? Consider Chief Justice Roberts's dissent. Is that persuasive?

Recall the treatment of similar issues in the context of international *commercial* arbitrations. How relevant is that?

Putting aside the allocation of competence, what standard of review should apply in an annulment action to a tribunal's determination that a cooling off period had been complied with? Waived? Rendered futile? Should any different standards apply to a local litigation requirement?

Note how Chief Justice Roberts' dissent in *BG Group* suggests the question of compliance with the local litigation requirement should be resolved. Is that persuasive? How hard a case was *BG Group*?

11. *Legislation implementing ICSID Convention.* "Arbitration without privity" is also possible under ICSID, at least as implemented by foreign investment protection legislation in some states. Although national implementing legislation varies widely, in some states, foreign investors are granted a right (even absent any contractual arbitration provision) to arbitrate pursuant to the ICSID Rules against the host state with respect to ICSID investment disputes. The host state's legislation is regarded as an "offer" to arbitrate, which is accepted by the investor's commencement of arbitral proceedings. *See* C. Dugan *et al., Investor-State Arbitration* 230-36 (2008); Parra, *Principles Government Foreign Investment, as Reflected in National Investment Codes*, 7 ICSID Rev. 428 (1992).

CHAPTER 5
INTERPRETATION OF INTERNATIONAL ARBITRATION AGREEMENTS

Under the New York Convention, other international arbitration instruments, and most national arbitration regimes, parties enjoy broad autonomy to draft international arbitration agreements in the fashion they desire. The parties' autonomy inevitably produces a wide range of different arbitration agreements. Arbitration clauses can be very short (a few words) or quite long (many pages); they may be drafted in various languages and with varying degrees of skill and linguistic proficiency; they may incorporate model clauses, either in whole or part, or start from scratch; they may provide for arbitration of no disputes, some contractual disputes, all contractual disputes, or virtually all disputes (contractual, tort, or otherwise) connected to their relationship; they may provide for either *ad hoc* or institutional arbitration; they may designate an arbitral seat; they may select the arbitrators, impose limitations on the identities of the arbitrators, or designate an appointing authority; and they may otherwise structure the arbitration process.[1]

The interpretation of the arbitration agreements that parties negotiate and draft is, in practice, frequently required and is of critical importance to the international arbitral process. Questions of interpretation often concern the scope of arbitration clauses, but can also include other topics (such as the incorporation of institutional rules). This chapter examines the interpretation of international arbitration agreements, focusing particularly on international commercial arbitration agreements.

A. SCOPE OF INTERNATIONAL ARBITRATION AGREEMENTS

The most frequent, and important, issue that arises in the interpretation of international arbitration agreements relates to the "scope" of the parties' agreement; that is, what category of disputes or claims have the parties agreed to submit to arbitration? Disputes frequently arise concerning the application of arbitration agreements to particular contract claims or, even more commonly, non-contractual claims based upon tort or statutory protections.

1. Rules of Construction for International Arbitration Agreements

The following materials examine the issues that arise in connection with the interpretation of international arbitration agreements, particularly with regard to their scope. They also examine both the choice-of-law rules and the substantive principles of contract construction that arise in disputes over the interpretation of arbitration agreements.

---

1. *See supra* pp. 84-90; Böckstiegel, *The Role of Party Autonomy in International Arbitration*, 54(2) Disp. Resol. J. 24 (1997); G. Born, *International Commercial Arbitration* 204-10 (2d ed. 2014); Zhang, *Party Autonomy and Beyond: An International Perspective of Contractual Choice of Law*, 20 Emory Int'l L. Rev. 511 (2006).

MEDITERRANEAN ENTERPRISES, INC. v. SSANGYONG CORP.
708 F.2d 1458 (9th Cir. 1983)

NELSON, Circuit Judge. Defendant-appellant Ssangyong Construction Co. ("Ssangyong") appeals the district court's interlocutory order staying the action and sending to arbitration certain issues raised in a complaint filed by plaintiff-appellee Mediterranean Enterprises, Inc. ("MEI"). Ssangyong contends that the district court improperly interpreted the scope of the arbitration clause in a contract between the parties....

MEI, a California corporation, provides engineering services for modular housing projects in developing countries. In May, 1978, MEI was invited by the Saudi Arabian Royal Commission to bid on certain construction projects in Saudi Arabia. In connection with this invitation, MEI contacted Ssangyong, a Korean contractor. On September 9, 1978, in Los Angeles, MEI and Ssangyong signed a "Preliminary Agreement for Formation of a Joint Venture" ("the Agreement"). The arbitration clause in the Agreement provides as follows: "Any disputes arising hereunder or following the formation of joint venture [sic] shall be settled through binding arbitration pursuant to the Korean U.S. Arbitration Agreement, with arbitration to take place in Seoul, Korea."

Subsequently, MEI and Ssangyong entered into an Agency Agreement ... with Trac Enterprises, providing that Trac would serve as the agent of the joint venture in Saudi Arabia. The contemplated MEI-Ssangyong joint venture was never actually formed.... MEI alleges that Ssangyong used the Agreement merely to gain access to the Saudi projects, and wrongfully commenced the projects in association with Trac (named as a defendant [by MEI in its complaint]) rather than with MEI. Ssangyong claims that no breach occurred....

MEI commenced this action in district court. The complaint contains six counts against Ssangyong: breach of contract and breach of fiduciary duty (counts 1, 2 and 4), inducing and conspiracy to induce breach of contract [the Trac Agency Agreement] (count 7), quantum meruit (count 8), and conversion (count 9).... [T]he district court rejected MEI's contention that Ssangyong had fraudulently inserted the words "arising hereunder or" in the arbitration clause ... [Thereafter, following a hearing, the district court issued the following order concerning the scope of the arbitration clause:] "The issues raised by Counts 1, 2 and 4 of [MEI's] Complaint against [Ssangyong] are found to be arbitrable and are ordered to arbitration between the said parties pursuant to paragraph 16 of the [Agreement]...."

Ssangyong argues that federal policy favors the enforcement of arbitration agreements, especially in international business transactions. MEI does not dispute the existence of such a federal policy, but counters by arguing that "arbitration is a matter of contract and a party cannot be required to submit to arbitration any dispute which he has not agreed to submit," quoting *United Steel Workers v. Warrior & Gulf Nav. Co.*, 363 U.S. 574, 582 (1960). Both statements are sound and not at all irreconcilable. Ultimately, the issue of arbitrability "is to be determined by the contract entered into by the parties." The task before this court remains one of contractual interpretation. Ssangyong argues that the arbitration clause "was designed to cover 'any' disputes between the parties." MEI argues that the phrase "arising hereunder" means "arising under the contract itself" and was not intended to cover "matters or claims independent of the contract or collateral thereto." Neither side points to, and additional research has not uncovered, cases in this circuit which define "arising hereunder" in the context of an arbitration agreement. However, we are persuaded by a line of cases from the Second Circuit that MEI's interpretation is the more reasonable one.[2]

We interpret "arising hereunder" as synonymous with "arising under the Agreement." The phrase "arising under" has been called "relatively narrow as arbitration clauses go." *Sinva, Inc. v. Merrill, Lynch, Pierce, Fenner & Smith, Inc.*, 253 F.Supp. 359, 364 (S.D.N.Y. 1966). In *In re Kinoshita & Co.*, 287 F.2d 951, 953 (2d Cir. 1961), Judge Medina concluded that when an arbitration clause "refers to disputes or controversies 'under' or 'arising out of' the contract," arbitration is restricted to "disputes and controversies relating to the interpretation of the contract and matters of performance." Judge Medina reasoned that the phrase "arising under" is narrower in scope than the phrase "arising out of or relating to," the standard language recommended by the [AAA]....

In *Michele Amoruso e Figli v. Fisheries Dev. Corp.*, 499 F.Supp. 1074, 1080 (S.D.N.Y. 1980), the court discussed the Supreme Court's interpretation of an arbitration clause, noting that "arising out of or relating to this agreement" had been labelled a "broad arbitration clause." The court went on to say that in the case before it, "the clause is limited to differences or disputes 'arising out of this Agreement'; notably, it omits reference to disputes 'relating to' the agreements. The omission is significant in the Second Circuit." The omission should be significant in this circuit as well. The standard clause suggested in the U.S.-Korean Commercial Arbitration Agreement contains the phrase, "out of or in relation to or in connection with this contract, or for the breach thereof." We have no difficulty finding that "arising under" is intended to cover a much narrower scope of disputes, *i.e.*, only those relating to the interpretation and performance of the contract itself.

In light of our interpretation of the arbitration clause in the Agreement, we must next decide whether the district court properly sent "the issued raised by" counts 1, 2 and 4 to arbitration. This entails examining MEI's complaint to determine the extent to which the counts against Ssangyong refer to disputes or controversies relating to the interpretation and performance of the contract itself. Counts 1, 2 and 4 alleging breach of the Agreement and breach of the fiduciary duty created by the Agreement, clearly fall within the scope of the arbitration clause, and are thus proper subjects for arbitration. However, counts 7, 8 and 9 appear to raise issues that are either primarily or wholly outside the scope of the arbitration clause. Count 7 alleges that Ssangyong induced and conspired to induce breach of the Trac Agency Agreement, a separate and distinct contract. Ssangyong's alleged conduct appears to relate only peripherally to the MEI-Ssangyong Agreement, and could have been accomplished even if the Agreement did not exist. Count 7 therefore alleges activity and raises issues which are predominantly unrelated to the central conflict over the interpretation and performance of the Agreement.

Count 8 sets forth a claim in quantum meruit, which by its own terms rests on the theory that services were performed and accepted pursuant to an implied contract or "quasi-contract." An action does not lie on an implied contract where there exists between the

---

2. The cases cited by Ssangyong in support of its broad interpretation are unpersuasive. Most cited cases involved arbitration clauses which were drafted in broader terms and intended to cover a broader spectrum of disputes than the clause involved here. *See*, *e.g.*, *Griffin v. Semperit of Am., Inc.*, 414 F.Supp. 1384, 1387 (S.D. Tex. 1978) (clause read "[a]ny controversy or claim arising out of or relating to this agreement"); *Acevedo Maldonado v. PPG Indus., Inc.*, 514 F.2d 614, 616 (1st Cir. 1975) (same); *Altshul Stern & Co., v. Mitsui Bussan Kaisha, Ltd*, 385 F.2d 158, 159 (2d Cir. 1967) (clause read "any dispute ... arising out of or relating to this contract or the breach thereof").

parties a valid express contract which covers the identical subject matter.... Thus, by definition, count 8 does not directly relate to the interpretation and performance of the Agreement itself.

Count 9 alleges that Ssangyong converted to its own use and benefit certain prequalification documents delivered by MEI. The Agreement provides only that each of the parties would bear his own costs at the prequalification stage. MEI's claim that Ssangyong misappropriated these documents appears to raise issues largely distinct from the central conflict over the interpretation and performance of the Agreement itself.

By sending the "issues raised by" counts 1, 2 and 4 to arbitration, the district court authorized the arbitrator, in accordance with the expressed intention of the parties, to decide those issues relating to the interpretation and performance of the Agreement. Counts 1, 2 and 4 appear to be completely arbitrable. By deciding those issues necessary to resolve counts 1, 2 and 4, the arbitrator might well decide issues which bear in some way on the court's ultimate disposition of counts 7, 8 and 9. Nothing in the district court's order, or in this opinion would bar such a result. The arbitrator's award, if it clearly exceeds the scope of his authority by deciding a matter not within the ambit of the arbitration clause, will not be given effect by the court. After the district court receives the results of the arbitration, it should proceed to adjudicate those issues which fall outside the scope of the arbitration clause....

HI-FERT PTY LTD v. KIUKIANG MARITIME CARRIERS INC.
(1998) 90 FCR 1 (Australian Fed. Ct.)

BEAUMONT J. [Disputes arose under a charter party, in which both contractual claims (for breach of the charter party's terms) and non-contractual claims (for alleged breaches of statutory duties and misrepresentations in connection with concluding the charter party) were asserted. The Federal Court of Australia considered whether the non-contractual claims were within the scope of the arbitration agreement.

The arbitration clause of the charter (clause 34) provides]:

> "Any dispute arising from this charter or any Bill of Lading issued hereunder shall be settled in accordance with the provisions of the Arbitration Act, 1950, and any subsequent Acts, in London, each party appointing an Arbitrator, and the two Arbitrators in the event of disagreement appointing an Umpire whose decision shall be final and binding upon both parties hereto. This Charter Party shall be governed by and construed in accordance with English Law. The Arbitrators and Umpire shall be commercial men normally engaged in the Shipping Industry...."

[T]he appellants have made a number of claims in the alternative, including the "Non-Contractual Claims" which are based on representations said to have been made in Australia by one Australian company to another in September 1995 as to the inspection system which had been adopted. These representations are said (a) to constitute misleading and deceptive conduct contrary to §52 of the Trade Practices Act 1974; (b) to have been made negligently; and (c) to involve the breach of a collateral warranty.

The words in the provision which are presently material are: "[a]ny dispute arising from this charter or any Bill of Lading issued hereunder...." Since the contract's chosen proper law is English law, that law will govern its interpretation. It appears that there is no English authority on the words "arising from" in the present kind of context and that these are not terms of art or words that have a special or technical significance. In my opinion, for our purposes the key expression in the provision is the preposition "from." In the present context this preposition is used to show the origin of something (see *The Cambridge International Dictionary of English*).

What was the origin of the "non-contractual claims"? In my opinion, their origin was the making of the specific representations alleged to have been made in September 1995 rather than the charter party or bill of lading.... [W]hilst the charter party and the bill of lading are background matters, their terms and their operation are not ingredients in the "Non-Contractual Claims." In that sense, those claims are independent and free-standing.

This conclusion is reinforced by a consideration of the practicalities which the parties clearly had in mind. In choosing arbitrators with commercial backgrounds, the parties indicated a choice for the practical solution of disputes of the kind referred to the arbitrators. But to read clause 34 as contemplating a reference to such persons of a problem of considerable private international legal complexity, let alone the application of a foreign (Australian) law in the form of the Trade Practices legislation, would seem to contradict a desire for a practical outcome. We should not attribute such a bizarre intention to these parties. It is not likely that they intended to refer to these arbitrators in London any dispute however remotely connected with the charter party or the bill of lading and however special its legal characteristics in terms of English law. It appears that there is no counterpart of the *Trade Practices Act* in England. The consumer protection provisions in Part V of the *Trade Practices Act* were derived from American legislation and constitute an exhaustive code in the field covered.... In these circumstances, I need not consider the questions that would have arisen had I been of the view that clause 34 was, on its true construction, capable of applying to "Non-Contractual Claims." ...

EMMETT, J.... [W]here there is a dispute as to a claim in respect of conduct which is antecedent to the making of a contract, I do not consider that such a dispute can be said to arise *from* the contract in question. In relation to the Addendum Contract, for example, the conduct complained of by Hi-Fert was antecedent to and did not depend upon the contractual relationship that existed by reason of the Addendum Contract. That latter contractual relationship was induced by the conduct complained of. In the present case, the Non-Contractual Claims are not generated by the Charter Contract. They will not be resolved by examining the Charter Contract but by considering and assessing evidence external to it. They do not *arise out of* the Charter Contract nor do they *arise from* the Charter Contract....

In the present case, the parties have chosen restricted language to describe those disputes which are to be settled by arbitration. The question is whether the Non-Contractual Claims can fairly be said to arise "*from*" the Charter Contract. The Alleged Representations, which are the basis of the Non-Contractual Claims, had nothing to do with the performance of the Charter Contract by WBC. WBC did not own or operate the Kiukiang Career. The Alleged Representations were concerned only with the question of extending the Charter Contract for the purposes of fixing the Kiukiang Career. The Charter Contract was no more than background to the making of the Alleged Representations which, having been acted upon, led to its terms being attracted to the arrangement relating to the Kiukiang Career. Accordingly, I consider that none of the Non-Contractual Claims arise *from* the Charter Contract. Therefore, they are not subject to clause 34.

MITSUBISHI MOTORS CORP. v. SOLER CHRYSLER-PLYMOUTH, INC.
473 U.S. 614 (1985) (also excerpted above at pp. 486-92)

JUSTICE BLACKMUN. [Mitsubishi Motors Corporation ("Mitsubishi") is a Japanese corporation that manufactures automobiles in Japan. Mitsubishi is a joint venture between Chrysler International ("CISA"), a Swiss corporation owned by Chrysler Corporation, and Mitsubishi Heavy Industries, a Japanese corporation. Soler Chrysler-Plymouth, Inc. ("Soler"), is a Puerto Rico corporation. Soler entered into a distributor agreement with CISA that provided for the sale by Soler of Mitsubishi-manufactured vehicles within a designated area. At the same time, CISA, Soler, and Mitsubishi entered into a sales procedure agreement ("sales agreement") that provided for the direct sale of Mitsubishi products to Soler and governed the terms and conditions of such sales.

Paragraph VI of the Sales Agreement, labelled Arbitration of Certain Matters, provides:

> "All disputes, controversies or differences which may arise between [Mitsubishi] and [Soler] out of or in relation to Articles I-B through V of this Agreement or for the breach thereof, shall be finally settled by arbitration in Japan in accordance with the rules and regulations of the Japan Commercial Arbitration Association."

Soler failed to maintain the sales volume specified in its agreements and requested that Mitsubishi delay or cancel shipment of several orders. Mitsubishi and CISA refused, and Mitsubishi later brought an action against Soler in the District of Puerto Rico under the FAA and the Convention. Mitsubishi sought an order to compel arbitration. Shortly after filing the complaint, Mitsubishi filed a request for arbitration before the Japan Commercial Arbitration Association seeking damages from Soler for breach of the parties' sales agreement. Soler denied the allegations and counterclaimed against both Mitsubishi and CISA under the Sherman Act; the Puerto Rico competition statute; common law defamation rules; and the Puerto Rico Dealers' Contract Act. In the counterclaim premised on the Sherman Act, Soler alleged that Mitsubishi and CISA had conspired to divide markets in restraint of trade.][3]

At the outset, we address the contention raised in Soler's cross-petition that the arbitration clause at issue may not be read to encompass the statutory counterclaims stated in its answer to the complaint. In making this argument, Soler does not question the Court of Appeals' application of Paragraph VI of the Sales Agreement to the disputes involved here as a matter of standard contract interpretation.[4] Instead, it argues that as a matter of law a

---

3. The District Court found that the arbitration clause did not cover the fourth and six counterclaims, which sought damages for defamation, or the allegations in the seventh counterclaim concerning discriminatory treatment and the establishment of minimum-sales volumes. Accordingly, it retained jurisdiction over those portions of the litigation. In addition, because no arbitration agreement between Soler and CISA existed, the court retained jurisdiction, insofar as they sought relief from CISA, over the first, second, third, and ninth counterclaims, which raised claims under the Puerto Rico Dealers' Contracts Act, the federal Automobile Dealers' Day in Court Act, the Sherman Act, and the Puerto Rico competition statute, respectively. These aspects of the District Court's ruling were not appealed and are not before this Court.

4. ... Soler does suggest that, because the title of the clause referred only to "certain matters," and the clause itself specifically referred only to "Articles I-B through V," it should be read narrowly to exclude the statutory claims. Soler ignores the inclusion within those "certain matters" of "[a]ll disputes, controversies or differences which may arise between [Mitsubishi] and [Soler] out of or in relation to [the specified provisions] or for the breach thereof." Contrary to Soler's suggestion, the exclusion of some areas of possible dispute from the scope of an arbitration clause does not serve to restrict the reach of an otherwise broad clause

court may not construe an arbitration agreement to encompass claims arising out of statutes designed to protect a class to which the party resisting arbitration belongs "unless [that party] has expressly agreed" to arbitrate those claims, by which Soler presumably means that the arbitration clause must specifically mention the statute giving rise to the claims that a party to the clause seeks to arbitrate....

We do not agree, for we find no warrant in the [FAA] for implying in every contract within its ken a presumption against arbitration of statutory claims. The [FAA]'s center-piece provision makes a written agreement to arbitrate "in any maritime transaction or a contract evidencing a transaction involving commerce ... valid, irrevocable, and enforceable, save upon such grounds as exist at law or in equity for the revocation of any contract." 9 U.S.C. §2. The "liberal federal policy favoring arbitration agreements," *Moses H. Cone Mem. Hosp. v. Mercury Constr. Corp.*, 460 U.S. 1, 24 (1983), manifested by this provision and the Act as a whole, is at bottom a policy guaranteeing the enforcement of private contractual arrangements: the Act simply "creates a body of federal substantive law establishing and regulating the duty to honor an agreement to arbitrate." ...

Accordingly, the first task of a court asked to compel arbitration of a dispute is to determine whether the parties agreed to arbitrate that dispute. The court is to make this determination by applying the "federal substantive law of arbitrability, applicable to any arbitration agreement within the coverage of the Act." And that body of law counsels

> "that questions of arbitrability must be addressed with a healthy regard for the federal policy favoring arbitration.... The [FAA] establishes that, as a matter of federal law, any doubts concerning the scope of arbitrable issues should be resolved in favor of arbitration, whether the problem at hand is the construction of the contract language itself or an allegation of waiver, delay, or a like defense to arbitrability."

Thus, as with any other contract, the parties' intentions control, but those intentions are generously construed as to issues of arbitrability. There is no reason to depart from these guidelines where a party bound by an arbitration agreement raises claims founded on statutory rights.... The [FAA] provides no basis for disfavoring agreements to arbitrate statutory claims by skewing the otherwise hospitable inquiry into arbitrability.

That is not to say that all controversies implicating statutory rights are suitable for arbitration. There is no reason to distort the process of contract interpretation, however, in order to ferret out the inappropriate. Just as it is the congressional policy manifested in the [FAA] that requires courts liberally to construe the scope of arbitration agreements covered by that Act, it is the congressional intention expressed in some other statute on which the courts must rely to identify any category of claims as to which agreements to arbitrate will be held unenforceable. For that reason, Soler's concern for statutorily protected classes provides no reason to color the lens through which the arbitration clause is read. By agreeing to arbitrate a statutory claim, a party does not forgo the substantive rights afforded by the statute; it only submits to their resolution in an arbitral, rather than a judicial, forum. It trades the procedures and opportunity for review of the courtroom for the simplicity, informality, and expedition of arbitration. We must assume that if Congress intended the substantive protection afforded by a given statute to include protection against waiver of

---

in the areas in which it was intended to operate. Thus, insofar as the allegations underlying the statutory claims touch matters covered by the enumerated articles, the Court of Appeals properly resolved any doubts in favor of arbitrability."

the right to a judicial forum, that intention will be deducible from text or legislative history....

JUSTICE STEVENS, Dissenting.... [First,] as a matter of ordinary contract interpretation, there are at least two reasons why that clause does not apply to Soler's antitrust claim against Chrysler and Mitsubishi. First, the clause only applies to two-party disputes between Soler and Mitsubishi. The antitrust violation alleged in Soler's counterclaim is a three-party dispute. Soler has joined both Chrysler and its associated company, Mitsubishi, as counterdefendants.... Only by stretching the language of the arbitration clause far beyond its ordinary meaning could one possibly conclude that it encompasses this three-party dispute.

Second, the clause only applies to disputes "which may arise between MMC and BUYER out of or in relation to Articles I-B through V of this Agreement or the breach thereof...." Thus, disputes relating to only 5 out of a total of 15 Articles in the Sales Procedure Agreement are arbitrable. Those five Articles cover: (1) the terms and conditions of direct sales (matter such as the scheduling of orders, deliveries, and payment); (2) technical and engineering changes; (3) compliance by Mitsubishi with customs laws and regulations, and Soler's obligation to inform Mitsubishi of relevant local laws; (4) trademarks and patent rights; and (5) Mitsubishi's right to cease production of any products. It is immediately obvious that Soler's antitrust claim did not arise out of Articles I-B through V and it is not a claim "for the breach thereof." The question is whether it is a dispute "in relation to" those Articles....

The federal policy favoring arbitration cannot sustain the weight that the Court assigns to it. A clause requiring arbitration of all claims "relating to" a contract surely could not encompass a claim that the arbitration clause was itself part of a contract in restraint of trade. Nor in my judgment should it be read to encompass a claim that relies, not on a failure to perform the contract, but on an independent violation of federal law. The matters asserted by way of defense do not control the character, or the source, of the claim that Soler has asserted.[5] Accordingly, simply as a matter of ordinary contract interpretation, I would hold that Soler's antitrust claim is not arbitrable....

[Second,] until today all of our cases enforcing agreements to arbitrate under the [FAA] have involved contract claims. In one, the party claiming a breach of contractual warranties also claimed that the breach amounted to fraud actionable under §10(b) of the Securities Exchange Act of 1934. *Scherk v. Alberto-Culver Co.* But this is the first time the Court has considered the question whether a standard arbitration clause referring to claims arising out of or relating to a contract should be construed to cover statutory claims that have only an indirect relationship to the contract. In my opinion, neither the Congress that enacted the [FAA] in 1925, nor the many parties who have agreed to such standard clauses, could have anticipated the Court's answer to that question.

On several occasions we have drawn a distinction between statutory rights and contractual rights and refused to hold that an arbitration barred the assertion of a statutory right. Thus, in Alexander v. Gardner Denver Co., 415 U.S. 36 (1974), we held that the arbitration of a claim of employment discrimination would not bar an employee's statutory

---

5. Even if Mitsubishi can prove that it did not violate any provision of the contract, such proof would not necessarily constitute a defense to the antitrust claim....

right to damages under Title VII of the Civil Rights Act of 1964 ... notwithstanding the strong federal policy favoring the arbitration of labor disputes.... In view of the Court's repeated recognition of the distinction between federal statutory rights and contractual rights, together with the undisputed historical fact that arbitration has functioned almost entirely in either the area of labor disputes or in "ordinary disputes between merchants as to questions of fact," it is reasonable to assume that most lawyers and executives would not expect the language in the standard arbitration clause to cover federal statutory claims. Thus, in my opinion, both a fair respect for the importance of the interests that Congress has identified as worthy of federal statutory protection, and a fair appraisal of the most likely understanding of the parties who sign agreements containing standard arbitration clauses, support a presumption that such clauses do not apply to federal statutory claims....

ROOSE INDUSTRIES LTD v. READY MIXED CONCRETE LTD
[1974] 2 NZLR 246 (Wellington Ct. App.)

[excerpted above at pp. 149-50]

JUDGMENT OF 3 FEBRUARY 1990
XVII Y.B. Comm. Arb. 542 (1992) (Genoa Corte di Appello)

[excerpted above at pp. 336-37]

FIONA TRUST & HOLDING CO. v. PRIVALOV
[2007] UKHL 40 (House of Lords)

[excerpted above at pp. 205-11]

JUDGMENT OF 27 FEBRUARY 1970
6 Arb. Int'l 79 (German Bundesgerichtshof)

[excerpted above at pp. 194-98]

INTERIM AWARD IN ICC CASE NO. 6149
XX Y.B. Comm. Arb. 41 (1995)

[excerpted above at pp. 290-92]

ITALIAN CODE OF CIVIL PROCEDURE
Article 808-quater

In case of doubt, the arbitration agreement shall be interpreted in the sense that the arbitral jurisdiction extends to all disputes arising from the contract or from the relationships to which the agreement refers.

BG GROUP PLC v. REPUBLIC OF ARGENTINA
134 S.Ct. 1198 (2014)

[excerpted above at pp. 233-47]

JUDGMENT OF 30 MARCH 1993, NOKIA-MAILLEFER SA v. MAZZER
XXI Y.B. Comm. Arb. 681 (1996) (Vaud Tribunal Cantonal)

[excerpted above at pp. 359-60]

NOTES

1. *Scope of agreement to arbitrate.* Even if the parties have concluded a valid agreement to arbitrate, that agreement may not encompass a particular dispute. One court put the issue as follows:

> "Imagine a contract for construction of a one room log cabin. The parties agreed that disputes over the glass used in the windows would be subject to arbitration. If the owner were to sue the builder on broad breach of contract and tort causes of action, alleging drafty walls, a leaky roof, and a complete lack of wooden flooring, it would defy logic to force the owner to submit the entire dispute to arbitration, when all he had agreed to arbitrate was disputes over window glass." *Mesquite Lake Assocs. v. Lurgi Corp.*, 754 F.Supp. 161 (N.D. Cal. 1991).

Is there any doubt about the correctness of this reasoning? Might it not be more efficient to require parties to arbitrate disputes that are related to matters falling within their agreement to arbitrate, even if those disputes are not themselves covered by the arbitration agreement? What is wrong with that analysis?

2. *Rules of construction of scope of arbitration agreements.* Rules of construction play an important role in the arbitral process; to a greater extent than many other contractual provisions, arbitration clauses are relatively formulaic and deal with unforeseen and fluid events. Most arbitration agreements provide "All disputes arising out of this contract shall be finally resolved by arbitration" or "All disputes and controversies relating to this contract shall be finally resolved by arbitration." Applying these formulae to often unpredictable and complex facts seldom produces clear-cut results. Equally, it is trite to observe that most arbitration clauses are included in the parties' contract relatively late in the negotiating process, without detailed consideration of their likely future impact.

As a consequence, the parties' contractual language will seldom expressly resolve issues relating to the coverage of an arbitration clause. Instead, general rules of interpretation and presumptions regarding the parties' intent play an important role in ascertaining the meaning of such agreements. Recall the discussion of this issue in the *Judgment of 27 February 1970.* To what extent is it appropriate to attempt to formulate general rules of construction for international arbitration agreements? How would these rules apply in an international context? Do U.S. businessmen and lawyers have the same expectations and understandings as Peruvian, Singaporean or Czech businessmen and lawyers?

3. *Language of international arbitration agreements.* To what extent does interpretation of the scope of an international arbitration agreement turn on the language of the

agreement? Is the text of an agreement not the starting point for any interpretative analysis? Many courts have questioned efforts to distinguish between different linguistic formulations used in arbitration provisions. Note in particular the analysis in *Fiona Trust*, rejecting efforts at fine interpretation of arbitration agreements. Note also the approach in *Mitsubishi Motors* and the *Judgment of 27 February 1970*. Compare the approach in *Ssangyong* and *Hi-Fert*.

Is it sensible to distinguish between formulations such as "arising under" and "in connection with" or "relating to"? Do you think that, in general, parties really intend different meanings to attach to these different terms? As a general rule, what presumption about the intended scope of an arbitration clause makes sense? That the parties wanted all disputes having some connection to their contractual relations and dealings to be arbitrated? Isn't this consistent with arbitration's promise of a single, efficient dispute resolution mechanism? Note the reasoning in *Fiona Trust*, *Judgment of 27 February 1970*, and *ICC Case No. 6149*. Note also the reasoning in *Roose*. On the other hand, if one does not pay attention to the specific wording of arbitration agreements, and draw distinctions between various phrases, how is one to ascertain the parties' intentions?

4. *Authorities adopting restrictive interpretation of scope of arbitration agreement.* Some authorities hold that arbitration clauses must be interpreted restrictively, resolving doubts about the coverage of particular disputes against coverage. *See, e.g., Award in ICC Case No. 7920*, XXIII Y.B. Comm. Arb. 80 (1998) (scope of arbitration clause is to be interpreted "strictly," but validity of clause is governed by "principle of effectiveness"); *Flood v. Country Mut. Ins. Co.*, 41 Ill. 2d 91, 94 (1968) ("clear language" required; "arbitration agreements will not be extended by construction or implication"); *Shuffman v. Rudd Plastic Fabrics Corp.*, 407 N.Y.S.2d 565, 566 (N.Y. App. Div. 1978) ("If equivocal, the scope of a commercial arbitration clause must be read conservatively"). These state law rules are almost unanimously held to be preempted under the FAA. *See supra* pp. 56-57, 365-67; *Progressive Cas. Ins. Co. v. CA Reaseguradora Nacional de Venezuela*, 991 F.2d 42 (2d Cir. 1993).

Consider the analyses in *Ssangyong* and *Hi-Fert*. What is the rationale for a restrictive interpretative approach to arbitration agreements? What do you make of the argument that, since arbitration involves a waiver of fundamental civil rights of access to judicial remedies, agreements to arbitrate should be interpreted narrowly?

5. *Neutral interpretation of scope of arbitration agreement.* Other authorities have held that arbitration agreements should be interpreted without resort to either a "pro-arbitration" or "restrictive" presumption. *See, e.g., Amco Asia Corp. v. Indonesia, Decision on Jurisdiction in ICSID Case No. ARB/81/1 of 25 September 1983*, 23 I.L.M. 359 (1984) ("a convention to arbitrate is not to be construed *restrictively*, nor, as a matter of act, *broadly* or *liberally*. It is to be construed in a way which leads to find out and to respect the common will of the parties."). Is the decision in *Ssangyong* an example of a neutral approach to interpretation of arbitration agreements? What is the rationale for interpreting arbitration agreements neither restrictively nor liberally, but simply in accordance with their language? How often is the language of arbitration agreements particularly instructive about their intended scope?

6. *"Pro-arbitration" bias of interpretation of international arbitration agreements.* In a number of jurisdictions, national law provides that international arbitration agree-

ments should be interpreted in light of a strong "pro-arbitration" presumption. Consider *Mitsubishi*, *Fiona Trust*, and *Judgment of 27 February 1970*. What approach does each of these decisions adopt to interpretation of arbitration agreements?

Mitsubishi held that "any doubts concerning the scope of arbitrable issues should be resolved in favor of arbitration." Or, as the Court put it even more expansively in *United Steelworkers of Am. v. Warrior & Gulf Nav. Co.*, 363 U.S. 574, 582-83 (1960), arbitration must be compelled unless the court can say with "positive assurance that the arbitration clause is not susceptible to an interpretation that covers the asserted dispute." How does this standard compare to that in *Fiona Trust*? In the *Judgment of 27 February 1970*?

Consider the approach of Article 808-quater of the Italian Code of Civil Procedure. How does this provision approach the interpretation of arbitration agreements?

7.   *Rationale for "pro-arbitration" rules of interpretation.* Do either national arbitration statutes or the New York Convention contain legislative provisions governing the interpretation of arbitration agreements? If not, then what authorizes national courts to develop presumptions governing the construction of international arbitration agreements? Does a presumption interpreting arbitration clauses expansively, in favor of arbitration, accord with the likely intent of private parties?

Consider the rationale for a pro-arbitration rule of construction outlined in *Fiona Trust*. What exactly are the reasons for interpreting an arbitration clause expansively? Compare the analysis in *Mitsubishi* and *First Options*. How does this differ from that in *Fiona Trust*?

What are the reasons in favor of "one-stop shopping"? Consider what happens to the parties' disputes in *Ssangyong* (in particular, the final paragraphs of the opinion). Does this make commercial sense? Does it comport with the parties' objectives in agreeing to arbitrate?

8.   *"Pro-arbitration" bias in interpreting international arbitration agreements under New York Convention.* Are there particular reasons for interpreting international arbitration agreements, as distinguished from domestic agreements to arbitrate, expansively? What would these reasons be? Note that U.S. judicial decisions under the New York Convention have adopted an especially broad federal pro-arbitration approach to interpretation, *see, e.g., Sourcing Unlimited, Inc. v. Asimco Int'l, Inc.*, 526 F.3d 38, 45 (1st Cir. 2008) ("the policy in favor of arbitration is even stronger in the context of international business transactions"); *Simula, Inc. v. Autoliv, Inc.*, 1999 U.S. App. LEXIS 8273 (9th Cir.) ("strong federal policy favoring arbitral dispute resolution ... applie[s] with special force in the field of international contracts"); *Pennzoil Exploration & Prod. Co. v. Ramco Energy Ltd*, 139 F.3d 1061, 1065 (5th Cir. 1998) ("[presumption of arbitrability] applies with special force in the field of international commerce"). Is this approach justified?

9.   *Interpretation of arbitration agreement with exceptions.* What does it mean to interpret an arbitration agreement "expansively" or in a "pro-arbitration" manner? Suppose an arbitration agreement contains exclusions. For example, what if an arbitration clause provides that "all disputes relating to this contract, except for disputes under Article V hereof, shall be finally resolved by arbitration." Should a "pro-arbitration" presumption still apply? Why?

Note that the arbitration clause in *Mitsubishi* was drafted narrowly ("All disputes, controversies or differences which *may arise between [Mitsubishi] and [Soler] out of or in relation to Articles I-B through V* of this Agreement or for the breach thereof, shall be finally settled by arbitration…."). If the parties have drafted their arbitration clause narrowly, or with specified exception, why should they be presumed to have wanted an expansive arbitration agreement? Are the policies underlying a pro-arbitration rule of construction nonetheless applicable? *Compare Louis Dreyfus Negoce SA v. Blystad Shipping & Trading Inc.*, 252 F.3d 218, 224 (2d Cir. 2001) ("Where the arbitration clause is narrow, a collateral matter will generally be ruled beyond its purview"); *Chevron U.S.A., Inc. v. Consolidated Edison Co.*, 872 F.2d 534, 537-38 (2d Cir. 1989) ("even a narrow arbitration clause must be construed in light of the presumption in favor of arbitration"); *Advanstar Commc'ns Inc. v. Beckley-Cardy, Inc.*, 1994 WL 176981, at *3 (S.D.N.Y.) ("A narrow arbitration clause must be construed in favor of arbitration").

10. *Interpretation distinguished from validity or formation.* When do "pro-arbitration" rules of interpretation apply? Consider *BG Group* and *Nokia*. What rules of construction and standards of proof are applied in each case? Recall the discussion regarding the standard of proof of a valid agreement to arbitrate. *See supra* pp. 363-67, 375-92.

    Recall the *BG Group* decision, excerpted above at pp. 233-47. Did it present a question of interpretation of the "arbitration agreement"? Do the same considerations that apply to the scope of an arbitration agreement also apply to issues of formation?

11. *Relevance of generally applicable rules of contract interpretation.* Aside from the "pro-arbitration" presumption of many developed national arbitration regimes, what rules of construction apply to arbitration agreements? What rules of construction were applied in *First Options*? Is there any reason that generally applicable rules of contract construction should not apply?

12. *Standard formulae in arbitration clauses.* There are a limited number of fairly standard formulae used in arbitration clauses to describe the scope of such provisions. The most common formulae are examined below.

    (a) *"Relating to."* A number of lower courts have concluded that the phrase "relating to" extends an arbitration clause to a broad range of disputes. *Pennzoil Exploration. & Prod. Co.*, 139 F.3d 1061 ("relating to" language in arbitration agreement is "broad"; clause not limited to claims under contract, and also reaches claims that "'touch' matters covered by" the contract); *Am. Recovery Corp. v. Computerized Thermal Imaging, Inc.*, 96 F.3d 88, 93 (4th Cir. 1996) ("arising out of or relating to" parties' agreement is "broad" language, covering "all disputes having a significant relationship to the consulting agreement regardless of whether those claims implicated the terms of the consulting agreement").

    (b) *"In connection with."* Various authorities have commented on the "in connection with" formula, usually in ways that suggest it is broad. *See Simula, Inc. v. Autoliv, Inc.*, 1999 U.S. App. LEXIS 8273 (9th Cir.) ("in connection" formula "must be interpreted liberally"); *J.J. Ryan & Sons v. Rhone Poulenc Textile, SA*, 863 F.2d 315, 321-22 (4th Cir. 1988) (clause covering "'all disputes arising in connection with the present contract' must be construed to encompass a broad scope of arbitrable issues…. It embraces every dispute between the parties having a significant relationship to the contract regardless of the label attached to the dispute.").

(c) *"Arising under."* The *Ssangyong* court holds that arbitration clauses using the formulation "arising under" are "narrow" and do not encompass various tort claims that do not directly involve application of the parties' contractual commitments. Other courts have adopted similar positions. *See Belke v. Merrill Lynch, Pierce, Fenner & Smith*, 693 F.2d 1023, 1028 (11th Cir. 1982) ("An arbitration clause covering disputes arising out of the contract or business between the parties evinces a clear intent to cover more than just those matters set forth in the contract."); *Ashville Invs. Ltd v. Elmer Contractors Ltd* [1988] 3 WLR 867 (English Ct. App.) (misrepresentation claims not caught by "arising under" language, but were covered by "in connection therewith").

(d) *"Arising out of."* National courts and arbitral tribunals are divided in their interpretations of "arising out of" clauses. Some courts have concluded that this formula is narrow, equating it with "arising under" provisions. *Tracer Research Corp. v. Nat'l Environmental Servs. Co.*, 42 F.3d 1292 (9th Cir. 1994) ("The 'arising out of' language is of the same limited scope as the 'arising under' language" and does not reach misappropriation of trade secrets claim); *Ethiopian Oilseeds & Pulses Corp. v. Rio Del Mar Foods Inc.*, [1990] 1 QB 86 (English High Ct.). Other authorities suggest that "arising out of" is broader than "arising under." *Am. Recovery Corp. v. Computerized Thermal Imaging, Inc.*, 96 F.3d 88, 93 (4th Cir. 1996).

13. *Distinction between scope of arbitration clause and scope of related choice-of-law clause.* As discussed above, it is common (and advisable) for international contracts to contain both an arbitration clause and a choice-of-law clause. *See infra* p. 983. The two provisions are closely related and must frequently be applied to the same issues. Nonetheless, as a practical matter, arbitration clauses and choice-of-law clauses are often drafted in differing terms. For example, choice-of-law clauses sometimes provide that the parties' "agreement shall be governed by the law of State X," while arbitration clauses often apply to "all disputes relating to" the parties' agreement.

It is generally well-settled that choice-of-law clauses and arbitration clauses may, if the parties so agree, have different scopes. *S+L+H SpA v. Miller-St. Nazianz, Inc.*, 988 F.2d 1518 (7th Cir. 1993) (disputes excluded from contracts' choice-of-law clause nonetheless subject to contract's arbitration clause). Why would parties agree to such an arrangement? Should an agreement's choice-of-law clause and its arbitration clause be presumed to have identical scopes, absent clear contrary evidence? Why?

14. *Application of arbitration agreements to statutory claims.* Parties to international arbitration agreements frequently assert claims based on statutory protections under national law. As *Mitsubishi* illustrates, these claims often raise questions concerning the scope of the parties' arbitration agreement.

(a) *Arbitrability of statutory claims.* As *Mitsubishi* illustrates, there is no absolute prohibition in most developed jurisdictions against the arbitration of non-contractual statutory claims. Note that Article II(1) of the New York Convention defines the Convention's scope as extending to agreements to arbitrate "any differences which have arisen or which may arise between [the parties] in respect of a defined legal relationship, whether contractual or not." That formulation clearly extends to non-contractual—and therefore statutory—claims. Does the decision in *Hi-Fert* question this conclusion?

As discussed below, national courts have also long held that some types of statutory claims are "nonarbitrable"—that is, that particular statutory rights cannot be the subject of a binding arbitration agreement. For a discussion of the nonarbitrability doctrine, *see supra* pp. 475-510.

(b) *"Pro-arbitration" rule of interpretation applicable to statutory claims. Mitsubishi* held that the parties had clearly intended to arbitrate the antitrust claims asserted by Soler. *Mitsubishi* also rejected any presumption that an arbitration clause would not extend to statutory claims. On the contrary, *Mitsubishi* held that the FAA's "pro-arbitration" rule of interpretation is fully applicable to statutory and other non-contractual claims. *Mitsubishi,* 473 U.S. at 626 ("There is no reason to depart from these [pro-arbitration] guidelines where a party bound by an arbitration agreement raises claims founded on statutory rights"). *See also Good(e) Bus. Sys., Inc. v. Raytheon Co.,* 614 F.Supp. 428 (W.D. Wisc. 1985) ("there is no presumption against arbitration of statutory claims"); *Singer v. Jefferies & Co.,* 571 N.Y.S.2d 680, 683 (N.Y. 1991) ("A court's obligation under the [FAA] to liberally interpret and enforce arbitration agreements is not diminished when the underlying controversy involves a violation of a Federal statute").

Are the foregoing decisions persuasive? Do you believe that parties ordinarily consider the existence and arbitrability of statutory claims—not based on the contract itself—when they include an arbitration provision in their agreement? Should "pro-arbitration" biases also apply to statutory claims? With any modifications? Compare Justice Stevens' dissent in *Mitsubishi* and the court's analysis in *Hi-Fert.*

15. *Arbitrability of tort claims.* It is common for disputes to arise in international arbitration over the arbitrability of common law tort claims. In a footnote, *Mitsubishi* observed that the district court held that the parties' arbitration clause did not cover common law defamation claims asserted against Mitsubishi and CISA by Soler. As a result, the parties' arbitration clause failed to achieve the objective of consolidating all litigation in a single forum. How could the language of the parties' arbitration agreement in *Mitsubishi* have been improved, so as to cover defamation claims?

(a) *Arbitrability of tort claims.* There is no general bar under the laws of most jurisdictions to inclusion of tort claims within the scope of an arbitration clause. *See supra* pp. 483-502 and *infra* pp. 531-32. In addition, it is frequently said that a party may not defeat an arbitration clause by casting its claims in tort, rather than contract. *Ford v. NYLcare Health Plans of the Gulf Coast, Inc.,* 141 F.3d 243, 250-51 (5th Cir. 1998) ("Basing the arbitrability of an action merely on the legal label attached to it would allow artful pleading to dodge arbitration of a dispute otherwise 'arising out of or relating to' (or legally dependent on) the underlying contract. To avoid this contrivance, courts look at the facts giving rise to the action and to whether the action 'could be maintained without reference to the contract'...."); *Collins & Aikman Prods. Co. v. Building Sys., Inc.,* 58 F.3d 16, 22 (2d Cir. 1995) (plaintiff cannot "'avoid the broad language of [an] arbitration clause by the casting of its complaint in tort'").

(b) *"Pro-arbitration" presumptions applicable to tort claims.* As *Mitsubishi* indicates, the FAA's "pro-arbitration" presumption is fully applicable to common law tort claims. *Nylcare Health Plans,* 141 F.3d at 250-51; *Collins & Aikman Prods. Co.,*

58 F.3d at 22. The same conclusion applies under the analysis in *Fiona Trust*. How would the court in *Hi-Fert Pty Ltd* deal with this issue?

(c) *Tort claims under particular arbitration agreements*. Numerous decisions have held that particular tort claims were within the scope of particular arbitration agreements. *See, e.g., Hicks v. Cadle Co.*, 355 F.Appx 186 (10th Cir. 2009) (claims for defamation and intentional infliction of emotional distress); *Judgment of 16 November 1987*, XVI Y.B. Comm. Arb. 585 (1991) (Italian Corte di Cassazione) (tort, unjust enrichment and restitution claims); *Judgment of 3 May 1980*, VIII Y.B. Comm. Arb. 394 (1983) (Yokohama Dist. Ct.) (tort claims); *Partial Award in ICC Case No. 7319*, XXIV Y.B. Comm. Arb. 141 (1999) (unfair competition claim).

On the other hand, tort claims have also frequently been held to fall outside the scope of the parties' arbitration agreement. *See, e.g., Cape Flattery Ltd v. Titan Maritime LLC*, 647 F.3d 914, 924 (9th Cir. 2011) ("arising under" arbitration clause must be interpreted narrowly and does not encompass "tort claim based on Hawaii and maritime tort law"); *N. Cal. Newspaper Guild Local 52 v. Sacramento Union*, 856 F.2d 1381, 1383 (9th Cir. 1998) (clause "limit[ing] arbitrable disputes to those involving 'application of' the agreement" only covered disputes "involving construction of the substantive provisions of the contract"); *Award in Italian Arbitration Association Case No. 41/92 of 1993*, XXII Y.B. Comm. Arb. 178 (1997) (only claims under parties' contract held arbitrable).

(d) *What approach should be taken to arbitrability of tort claims*? What is the right approach to determining whether tort claims are arbitrable? If parties' arbitration clauses are generally silent, or if one questions the wisdom of fine distinctions between formulae such as "arising under" and "relating to," what criteria can be used to decide whether the parties agreed to arbitrate a particular tort claim? For some efforts to articulate general presumptions, *see Kroll v. Doctor's Assocs., Inc.*, 3 F.3d 1167, 1170 (7th Cir. 1993) ("touchstone of arbitrability in such situations is the relationship of the tort alleged to the subject matter of the arbitration clause"); *Aspero v. Shearson Am. Express, Inc.*, 768 F.2d 106, 109 (6th Cir. 1985) (claim "goes to the core" of parties' contractual relations); *Becker Autoradio (U.S.A.), Inc. v. Becker Autoradiowerk GmbH*, 585 F.2d 39, 47 (3d Cir. 1978) (claim "derive[s] from the [contractual] relationship"). Consider also the general formulae in *Roose* and Article 808-quater of the Italian Code of Civil Procedure.

16. *Disputes arising after contract terminated*. The fact that a dispute does not arise, and a party does not assert claims, until after the parties' contract has terminated does not necessarily prevent the dispute from being arbitrated pursuant to an arbitration clause in the underlying (and expired) contract. A leading U.S. decision on the issue is *Nolde Bros., Inc. v. Bakery & Confectionery Workers Union*, 430 U.S. 243, 250 (1977), where the Court held that "the parties' obligations under their arbitration clause survived contract termination when the dispute was over an obligation arguably created by the expired agreement." This is arguably a consequence of the separability presumption, permitting the arbitration agreement to survive the underlying contract. Is there any reason to conclude, as a matter of interpretation, that the parties would not have intended their arbitration clause to survive and continue to provide a means of

resolving disputes that arose during the course of their contractual dealings, even after those dealings conclude?

17. *Disputes arising before arbitration agreement is made.* It is, of course, possible to conclude an arbitration agreement that applies to an existing dispute. Indeed, in earlier eras, so-called "submission agreements" were the only form of arbitration agreement that were enforceable. *See supra* pp. 16-28, 186-88.

Parties sometimes enter into commercial contracts, containing ordinary arbitration clauses, which are later invoked with respect to disputes arising before the contract was made. This gives rise to interpretative questions as to whether the arbitration clause was intended to have retroactive application. *See Zink v. Merrill Lynch, Pierce, Fenner & Smith, Inc.*, 13 F.3d 330 (10th Cir. 1993) (rejecting "contention that an agreement to arbitrate a dispute must pre-date the actions giving rise to the dispute"); *Whisler v. H.J. Meyers & Co.*, 948 F.Supp. 798 (N.D. Ill. 1996) (arbitration clause covers disputes arising "out of transactions that occurred prior to signing of agreement"). Is there any reason that an arbitration agreement should not be interpreted to apply to disputes pre-dating conclusion of the agreement to arbitrate?

18. *Disputes involving multiple agreements.* As *Ssangyong* illustrates, disputes arise in which the parties have entered in a number of different agreements, each with (or without) a separate dispute resolution mechanism. This can create interpretative questions, as well as procedural quagmires, with parallel or overlapping arbitrations under different rules. Many national courts have in principle been willing to conclude that disputes under one agreement are arbitrable, if the parties have so agreed, under an arbitration provision of a different agreement. *See, e.g., ARW Exploration Corp. v. Aguirre,* 45 F.3d 1455 (10th Cir. 1995) (where 5 of 6 related agreements included arbitration clauses, disputes under 6th agreement could be arbitrated); *Becker Autoradio U.S.A., Inc. v. Becker Autoradiowerk GmbH*, 585 F.2d 39 (3d Cir. 1978) (dispute over subsequent oral agreement subject to arbitration provision in prior written agreement); *Hart Enter. Int'l, Inc. v. Anhui Provincial Imp. & Exp. Corp.*, 888 F.Supp. 587 (S.D.N.Y. 1995) (arbitration clause in sales agreement applied to claims arising from subsequent settlement agreement (which did not contain an arbitration clause)); *Judgment of 20 September 2011*, 30(2) ASA Bull. 449, 454-55 (2012) (Swiss Fed. Trib.) (arbitration clause in contract extends to disputes under related contracts).

On the other hand, the existence of a separate arbitration provision in a related agreement is presumably strong evidence that disputes under that agreement were meant to be arbitrated under its dispute resolution provisions—not those of some other contract. *Nordin v. Nutri/Sys., Inc.*, 897 F.2d 339, 345 (8th Cir. 1990); *Netherlands Curacao Co., NV v. Kenton Corp.*, 366 F.Supp. 744 (S.D.N.Y. 1973). Suppose that Contract A has an ICC arbitration clause and Contract B, which is closely related, has an AAA arbitration clause. Should disputes under the two contracts be regarded as subject to arbitration under either one of the individual contract's arbitration clauses? Why or why not?

19. *Interpretation of "unlimited" arbitration agreements.* Consider the arbitration clause at issue in *Roose*. Note that its literal terms provided for arbitration of all disputes between two named parties. Why didn't the court give effect to those literal words? Suppose a dispute arose that had to do with a completely different, unrelated contract between the same parties; would the clause quoted above apply? Is the *Roose* court's

gloss on what the parties intended persuasive? Can you think of another gloss? Does there need to be a gloss? Compare the approach of Article 808-quater of the Italian Code of Civil Procedure.

20. *Interpretation of investment arbitration agreements.* The rules of construction discussed above were developed in the context of international commercial arbitration agreements. Should the same rules apply in an investment arbitration? Suppose the question is whether a dispute is covered by Article 8 of the U.K./Bosnia-Herzegovina BIT or Article 25 of the ICSID Convention. Should those provisions be interpreted in a pro-arbitration fashion? What about an arbitration clause in an investment contract? A provision in national foreign investment legislation?

21. *Interpretation of inter-state arbitration agreements.* To what extent do the rules of interpretation developed in commercial arbitration contexts apply to the interpretation of inter-state arbitration agreements? Note that there may not be the same presumption of one-stop shopping. What other structural differences are there in the inter-state and commercial contexts that arguably affect rules of construction?

2. Allocation of Competence to Interpret International Arbitration Agreements

The interpretation of international arbitration agreements also raises questions regarding the allocation of jurisdictional competence to decide disputes over the scope of such agreements. That is, who (a court or arbitral tribunal) decides disputes over the scope of an international arbitration agreement? The materials excerpted below explore this question.

FIRST OPTIONS OF CHICAGO v. KAPLAN
514 U.S. 938 (1995)

[excerpted above at pp. 230-33]

APOLLO COMPUTER, INC. v. BERG
886 F.2d 469 (1st Cir. 1989)

TORRUELLA, Circuit Judge. The plaintiff appeals from a district court order refusing its request for a permanent stay of arbitration proceedings.... Apollo Computer, Inc. ("Apollo") and Dicoscan Distributed Computing Scandinavia AB ("Dico") entered into an agreement granting Dico, a Swedish company ..., the right to distribute Apollo's computers in four Scandinavian countries. Helge Berg and Lars Arvid Skoog, the defendants in this action, signed the agreement on Dico's behalf in their respective capacities as its chairman and president. The agreement contained a clause stating that all disputes arising out of or in connection with the agreement would be settled in accordance with the [1988 ICC] Rules, and another clause that stated that the agreement was to be governed by Massachusetts law. The agreement also provided that it could not be assigned by Dico without the written consent of Apollo.

In September 1984, ... Apollo notified Dico that it intended to terminate the agreement, effective immediately. Dico then filed for protection from its creditors under Swedish bankruptcy law and subsequently entered into liquidation, with its affairs being handled by its trustee in bankruptcy. The trustee assigned Dico's right to bring claims for damages against Apollo to the defendants. In May 1988, the defendants filed a complaint and a request for arbitration with the ICC.... Apollo rejected arbitration, claiming that there was no agreement to arbitrate between it and the defendants, and that assignment of Dico's contractual right to arbitrate was precluded by the agreement's nonassignment clause. The ICC requested both parties to submit briefs on the issue. On December 15, 1988, the ICC's Court of Arbitration decided that pursuant to its rules, the arbitrator should resolve the issue of arbitrability, and directed the parties to commence arbitration proceedings to resolve that issue and, if necessary, the merits.

[Apollo] sought a permanent stay of the arbitration ... on the grounds that there is not an arbitration agreement between the parties.... [T]he district court denied the request to stay arbitration.... The district court first decided that the parties had explicitly agreed to have the issue of arbitrability decided by the arbitrator. Notwithstanding this conclusion, the court then proceeded to analyze the issue of arbitrability itself. It determined that Dico would have the right to seek arbitration of the underlying claims if it had pursued them on its own behalf. The only remaining issue, the court reasoned, was whether the agreement's nonassignment clause prevented the defendants from asserting Dico's right to arbitrate. The court ruled that it did not because, under Massachusetts law, a general nonassignment clause will be construed as barring only the delegation of duties, not the assignment of rights....

We ... find that the parties contracted to submit issues of arbitrability to the arbitrator.... Both parties agree that under the [FAA], the general rule is that the arbitrability of a dispute is to be determined by the court. *See Necchi v. Necchi Sewing Machine Sales Corp.*, 348 F.2d 693, 696 (2d Cir. 1965) (Marshall, J.); *AT&T Technologies, Inc. v. Communications Workers*, 475 U.S. 643, 649 (1986). Parties may, however, agree to allow the arbitrator to decide both whether a particular dispute is arbitrable as well as the merits of the dispute. *See Necchi*, 348 F.2d at 696.

In this case, the parties agreed that all disputes arising out of or in connection with their contract would be settled by binding arbitration "in accordance with the rules of arbitration of the International Chamber of Commerce." Article 8.3 of the ICC's [1988] Rules of Arbitration states:

> "Should one of the parties raise one or more pleas concerning the existence or validity of the agreement to arbitrate, and should the [International Court of Arbitration of the ICC] be satisfied of the prima facie existence of such an agreement, the [Court of Arbitration of the ICC] may, without prejudice to the admissibility or merits of the plea or pleas, decide that the arbitration shall proceed. In such a case, any decision as to the arbitrator's jurisdiction shall be taken by the arbitrator himself."

Article 8.4 of the ICC's [1988] Rules of Arbitration states:

> "Unless otherwise provided, the arbitrator shall not cease to have jurisdiction by reason of any claim that the contract is null and void or allegation that it is inexistent provided that he upholds the validity of the agreement to arbitrate. He shall continue to have jurisdiction, even though the contract itself may be inexistent or null and void, to determine the respective rights of the parties and to adjudicate upon their claims and pleas."

The contract therefore delegates to the arbitrator decisions about the arbitrability of disputes involving the existence and validity of a prima facie agreement to arbitrate. Both the ICC's Court of Arbitration and the district court determined that a prima facie agreement to arbitrate existed. Therefore, they reasoned, Article 8.3 requires the arbitrator to determine the validity of the arbitration agreement in this specific instance—in other words, decide whether the arbitration agreement applies to disputes between Apollo and the assignees of Dico.

Apollo did not discuss this issue in its brief. At oral argument, it averred that Article 8.3 is inapplicable because no prima facie agreement to arbitrate exists between it and the defendants. We are unpersuaded by this argument. The relevant agreement here is the one between Apollo and Dico. The defendants claim that Dico's right to compel arbitration under that agreement has been assigned to them. We find that they have made the prima facie showing required by Article 8.3. Whether the right to compel arbitration survives the termination of the agreement, and if so, whether that right was validly assigned to the defendants and whether it can be enforced by them against Apollo are issues relating to the continued existence and validity of the agreement.

Ordinarily, Apollo would be entitled to have these issues resolved by a court. By contracting to have all disputes resolved according to the Rules of the ICC, however, Apollo agreed to be bound by Articles 8.3 and 8.4. These provisions clearly and unmistakably allow the arbitrator to determine her own jurisdiction when, as here, there exists a *prima facie* agreement to arbitrate whose continued existence and validity is being questioned. The arbitrator should decide whether a valid arbitration agreement exists between Apollo and the defendants under the terms of the contract between Apollo and Dico. Consequently, without expressing any opinion on the merits of the issues raised by Apollo, we affirm the district court's order denying a permanent stay of the arbitration proceedings.

NOTES

1. *Respective roles of courts and arbitrators in interpreting international arbitration agreements.* Compare the respective roles of the court and the arbitral tribunal in interpreting the scope of the arbitration agreements in *Mitsubishi, Hi-Fert,* and *Ssangyong,* on the one hand, and *Apollo Computer,* on the other. Is it the court or the arbitrator that decides the scope of the parties' arbitration clause in each case? Are the first three decisions consistent with the fourth one? Note that *Ssangyong* holds that certain claims are outside the scope of the arbitration agreement and shall not be arbitrated. Would that result have been possible under the analysis in *Apollo*? Are there material differences between the arbitration agreements in the three cases that might explain the different approaches? Between the types of claims or disputes that are at issue?

2. *Rationale for allocations of competence to interpret scope of arbitration agreements.* What is the rationale for a national court to interpret the scope of an international arbitration agreement? What is the rationale for the arbitral tribunal doing so? Suppose that the parties' arbitration agreement specifically provides that the arbitrators are to resolve disputes about its scope. Then what result? Suppose that the validity of the arbitration agreement is conceded by both parties. In this case, haven't the parties clearly agreed to arbitrate questions about the scope of the arbitrators' competence? Is such an agreement not binding under Article II of the New York Convention and Article 8 of the UNCITRAL Model Law?

   Suppose, however, that the parties have not expressly agreed that the arbitrators will resolve disputes about the scope of their arbitration agreement. Is such an agreement nonetheless implied? Is not judicial interpretation of the scope of the parties' arbitration agreement—in a national court, likely of one party—inconsistent with the basic purpose of international arbitration? If the parties have entered into a valid arbitration agreement, where the arbitrators will decide some significant category of disputes, is it not likely that they intended the arbitrators to decide where their competence ends? Would this be a sensible presumption?

3. *Allocation of competence under FAA to interpret scope of arbitration clause.* Reread *First Options* and *Apollo*. How do they allocate competence to interpret the scope of an arbitration agreement?

   (a) First Options'*presumption that questions of "arbitrability" are for judicial resolution.* As discussed above, the Supreme Court held in *First Options* that disputes concerning "arbitrability questions" can in principle be dispatched to the arbitrator for decision, but that whether or not this will be ordered depends upon what the parties' arbitration agreement was intended to mean and upon presumptions which apply to ascertaining the parties' intent. *See supra* pp. 230-33, 280-83. The Court adopted a presumption in *First Options* that arbitration agreements do not ordinarily submit questions of arbitrability to the arbitrators. According to the *First Options* Court, only "clear and unmistakable" evidence will support a conclusion that "arbitrability" questions must be arbitrated. *See supra* pp. 281-82. Note that *Apollo* (a pre-*First Options* decision) expressly adopted a similar presumption that disputes over the scope of an arbitration agreement are to be resolved by courts, not arbitrators, but then held that the presumption had been rebutted by virtue of the ICC Rules.

   (b) *Applicability of* First Options'*presumption for judicial resolution of arbitrability questions to interpretation of scope of arbitration agreement.* Should the *First Options'* presumption in favor of judicial resolution of arbitrability questions apply to the interpretation of the scope of a concededly existent and valid arbitration agreement? Consider the rationale in *First Options* for the presumption. If the parties have agreed to arbitrate their disputes rather than litigate them, isn't it more likely that they assumed that arbitrators would resolve questions about how far their arbitration clause reached? Recall that, in international transactions, parties often agree to arbitrate in order to avoid national court proceedings in either party's home forum. *See supra* p. 111. Does this support a presumption that the scope of international arbitration agreements should be resolved by the arbitrators?

   In *Granite Rock Co. v. Int'l Bhd of Teamsters*, 130 S.Ct. 2847 (2010), the U.S. Supreme Court made clear that the *First Options* presumptive allocation of competence applied to issues of interpretation of an arbitration agreement. The Court held: "Under that framework, a court may order arbitration of a particular dispute only where the court is satisfied that the parties agreed to arbitrate *that dispute*. To satisfy itself that such agreement exists, the court must resolve any issue that calls into question the formation or applicability of the specific arbitration clause that a party seeks to have the court enforce. Where there is no provision validly committing them to an arbitrator, these issues typically concern the scope of the arbitration clause and its enforceability. In addition, these issues always include whether the clause was agreed to, and may include when that agreement was formed." *Id.* at 2856 (emphasis in original). Similarly, most U.S. lower courts have held that *First Options* does apply to disputes about the scope of an arbitration clause, but have also frequently found that *First Options'* presumption in favor of judicial resolution has been overcome, citing a variety of rationales (discussed below). *See also Toledo Tech., Inc. v. INA Walzlager Schaeffer KG*, 1999 WL 681557 (N.D. Ohio) (interpretation of arbitration clause subject to arbitration under *First Options*); *Port Auth. of N.Y. & N.J. v. Office of the Contract Arbitrator*, 660 N.Y.S.2d 408 (N.Y. App. Div. 1997) (same); *In re Ras Sec. Corp.*, 674 N.Y.S.2d 303 (N.Y. App. Div. 1998) (same).

(c) *Consequences of conclusion that parties agreed to arbitrate disputes regarding interpretation of scope of arbitration agreement.* Recall the consequences, under the FAA, of a conclusion that the parties agreed to arbitrate a question of "arbitrability." Under *First Options*, such an agreement authorizes the arbitrators to finally resolve the issue in question, subject to only very limited judicial review. *See supra* pp. 230-33, 280-81. Given these consequences, *First Options* required that agreements to arbitrate "arbitrability" questions require "clear and unmistakable" evidence. Does this rationale apply (or apply fully) to agreements to arbitrate disputes over interpretation?

4. *Application of* First Options' *allocation of competence where institutional rules grant arbitrators power to interpret scope of parties' arbitration agreement.* As discussed above, leading institutional rules grant arbitral tribunals authority to determine challenges to their own jurisdiction, including disputes over the scope of an arbitration clause. *See supra* p. 271; 2012 ICC Rules, Art. 6; 2014 LCIA Rules, Art. 23.

(a) *ICC Rules.* As *Apollo* indicates, Article 8(3) of the 1988 ICC Rules provided that the ICC International Court of Arbitration would decide challenges to the "prima facie" jurisdiction of an ICC arbitral tribunal and that "any decision as to the arbitrator's jurisdiction shall be taken by the arbitrator himself"; Article 8(4) provided that the arbitrator shall have jurisdiction notwithstanding claims that the parties' contract is void or nonexistent. (Article 6 of the 2012 ICC Rules contains substantially identical provisions. *See* pp. 184-85 of the Documentary Supplement.) *Apollo* interprets Articles 8(3) and 8(4) of the 1988 ICC Rules as delegating to the arbitrator the power to decide disputes over the scope of the arbitration agreement. Note that the 1998 and 2012 ICC Rules expressly provide that decisions on the scope of the arbitration agreement are for the arbitral tribunal to make. *See also Qualcomm, Inc. v. Nokia Corp.*, 466 F.3d 1366, 1374 (Fed. Cir. 2006) ("the parties clearly and unmistakably intended to delegate arbitrability questions to an arbitrator as evidenced by their incorporation of the AAA Rules"); *Contec Corp.*, 398 F.3d at 208; *Shaw Group Inc. v. Triplefine Int'l Corp.*, 322 F.3d 115, 118, 125 (2d Cir. 2003) (ICC arbitration clause "clearly and unmistakably evidences the parties' intent to arbitrate questions of arbitrability"); *Société Generale v. Raytheon European Mgt & Sys. Co.*, 643 F.2d 863, 869 (1st Cir. 1981); *Daiei Inc. v. U.S. Shoe Corp.*, 755 F.Supp. 299, 303 (D. Haw. 1991). *Compare J.J. Ryan & Sons v. Rhone Poulenc Textile SA*, 863 F.2d 315, 318-19 (4th Cir. 1988) (directly considering scope of ICC arbitration clause without reference to Article 8); *Butler Prods. Co. v. Unistrut Corp.*, 367 F.2d 733 (7th Cir. 1966); *Andrew Martin Marine Corp. v. Stork-Werkspoor Diesel BV*, 480 F.Supp. 1270 (D. La. 1979) (interpreting ICC clause broadly, but without reference to Article 8).

Is *Apollo*'s interpretation of the Articles 8(3) and 8(4) of the 1988 ICC Rules (equivalent to Articles 6(3)-(5) and 6(9) of 2012 ICC Rules) a fair reading of those provisions? Is any other interpretation plausible? Note again the consequence of concluding, under *First Options*, that the parties agreed to arbitrate disputes about the scope of their arbitration clause; such an agreement permits the arbitral tribunal to finally resolve the (jurisdictional) issue in question, subject to only minimal judicial review. Is this what the ICC Rules should be permitted as allowing?

(b) *Other institutional arbitration rules.* Compare Articles 6(3)-(5) and 6(9) of the 2012 ICC Rules and Article 23(1) of the LCIA Rules with Article 23(1) of the UNCITRAL Rules, excerpted at pp. 184-85, 269 & 170 of the Documentary Supplement. Does the latter provision accomplish the same thing? Is this treatment of the issue of jurisdiction a reason for or against selecting such rules?

(c) *Criticism of reliance on institutional arbitration rules under* First Options. U.S. decisions relying on *First Options* and the ICC (and other) institutional rules to grant arbitral tribunals competence finally to resolve jurisdictional disputes have been criticized on the grounds that the rules are not intended to authorize arbitrators to make final and binding jurisdictional decisions. *See* Rau, *Everything You Really Need to Know About "Separability" in Seventeen Simple Propositions*, 14 Am. Rev. Int'l Arb. 1, 107-09 & n.323 (2003) ("It seems obvious that such a provision [like Art. 6 of the ICC Rules granting arbitrators competence to rule on their own jurisdiction] is meant to restate the notion of *compétence/compétence* and as such is deeply rooted in the premises and presuppositions of European procedural law—that is, it is apparently not intended in any way to amount to a final allocation of decision-making authority.... In an alien legal environment, seeing arbitration primarily as an extension of contract law and having only *First Options* to look to, American courts and commentators seem regularly to miss the point. So they have tended to view Art. 6 broadly as a grant to arbitrators—similar in effect to the ... AAA Rules—of the power to make a binding determination of their own jurisdiction."). Is that persuasive?

Consider the following:

> "[T]he more appropriate analysis is that the *First Options* standard can be satisfied by the incorporation of institutional rules, like the ICC and UNCITRAL Rules, but only if those rules include both (a) an express grant of authority to decide jurisdictional issues; and (b) an express waiver of rights of recourse from the tribunal's awards, and that this would only permit the arbitrators to finally resolve a jurisdictional dispute in cases involving challenges to the scope of the arbitrators' jurisdiction." G. Born, *International Commercial Arbitration* 1169 (2d ed. 2014).

Is this persuasive?

5. *Application of* First Options *where parties agree to "broad" arbitration clause.* Some lower U.S. court decisions have distinguished between "broad" and "narrow" arbitration clauses. These courts have held that, under a "broad" clause, the arbitrator is granted authority to decide whether particular claims are subject to arbitration, while the latter requires a judicial determination: "Simply stated, a court should compel arbitration, and permit the arbitrator to decide whether the dispute falls within the clause, if the clause is 'broad.' In contrast, if the clause is 'narrow,' arbitration should not be compelled unless the court determines that the dispute falls within the clause. Specific words and phrases alone may not be determinative although words of limitations would indicate a narrower clause. The tone of the clause as a whole must be

considered." *Prudential Lines, Inc. v. Exxon Corp.*, 704 F.2d 59, 64 (2d Cir. 1983). *See Lebanon Chem. Corp. v. United Farmers Plant Food, Inc.*, 179 F.3d 1095 (8th Cir. 1999) ("court deciding arbitrability under a broad agreement [to arbitrate] leaves for the arbitrator the issue of whether the controversy in question relates to the agreement containing the arbitration clause, i.e., the scope of the clause."); *Paine Webber, Inc. v. Bybyk*, 81 F.3d 1193 (2d Cir. 1996) ("broad" arbitration clause indicates that "parties intended to arbitrate issues of arbitrability"); *Nationwide Gen. Ins. Co. v. Investors Ins. Co.*, 371 N.Y.S.2d 463, 467 (N.Y. 1975) ("[p]enetrating definitive analysis of the scope of the agreement must be left to the arbitrators").

If *First Options* were applicable, does the parties' agreement on a "broad" arbitration clause constitute "clear and unmistakable" evidence of an intention to arbitrate disputes about the scope of their arbitration clause? Note that *First Options'* requirement of "clear and unmistakable" evidence may not apply to disputes about the scope of an arbitration clause (as distinct from dispute about the existence of validity of an arbitration agreement). *See supra* pp. 537-38.

6. *Application of* First Options *where parties' underlying contract must be interpreted.* Disputes about the scope of an arbitration clause can require interpretation of the parties' underlying contract. For example, in determining whether a particular claim or dispute "arises from" or "relates to" a contract, it may be necessary to determine what substantive obligations the underlying contract imposes. It is almost universally acknowledged, however, that it is for the arbitrators to determine what substantive obligations an underlying contract imposes. Judicial resolution of such issues, for purposes of deciding disputes about the scope of an arbitration clause, threatens to encroach on the undisputed domain of the arbitrators.

Some courts have relied on the foregoing analysis in remitting disputes over the scope of arbitration agreements to the arbitrators. *See, e.g., Sharon Steel Corp. v. Jewell Coal & Coke Co.*, 735 F.2d 775 (3d Cir. 1984) ("[T]he Federal Arbitration Act gives the arbitrator the power to determine the scope of the arbitration clause as well as the substantive merits of the claim.... [A] case in which the scope of arbitrability affects the merits of the claim is a strong[] candidate for an arbitration."); *Nat'l R.R. Passenger Corp. v. Chesapeake & Ohio Ry. Co.*, 551 F.2d 136, 140 (7th Cir. 1977) ("'When the judiciary undertakes to determine the merits of a grievance under the guise of interpreting the ... (arbitration clause), it usurps a function which ... is entrusted to the arbitration tribunal.'"), quoting *United Steelworkers of Am. v. Am. Mfg Co.*, 363 U.S. 564, 569 (1960). Is this persuasive? Even if one does not grant the arbitrators competence to finally decide a scope dispute, doesn't this analysis suggest that courts should allow arbitrators to initially consider such issues?

7. *Allocation of competence to decide scope of arbitration agreement under UNCITRAL Model Law.* Consider the court's analysis in *Dalimpex, supra* pp. 276-77. What does the court hold with regard to its competence to decide disputes regarding the scope of an arbitration agreement prior to any arbitral decision? Is this interpretation supported by the language of the Model Law? Consider carefully the text of Articles 8 and 34(2) of the Model Law, excerpted at pp. 88 & 94 of the Documentary Supplement. How does the approach in *Dalimpex* differ from that in *Apollo* and *First Options*? Is the arbitrators' interpretation of the scope of the arbitration agreement, following *Apollo*,

subject to *de novo* judicial review? What about the arbitrators' interpretation under *Dalimpex*?

8. *Allocation of competence to decide scope of arbitration agreement under prima facie jurisdiction standard.* Recall the *prima facie* jurisdiction approach of French, Indian, and other courts to the allocation of competence to resolve challenges to the arbitrators' jurisdiction. *See supra* pp. 274-75, 275-77. Is there any reason that this general approach should not apply to disputes over the scope of an arbitration clause? If there is a concededly valid arbitration clause (*i.e.,* there is no claim that the clause is "manifestly null"), is there any basis for interlocutory judicial consideration of the scope of the arbitration agreement under French law? What are the consequences of an arbitral decision regarding the scope of the parties' arbitration agreement under French law?

9. *Appropriate allocation of competence to decide disputes regarding scope of arbitration agreement.* Which of the various approaches to the allocation of competence to decide disputes regarding the interpretation of international arbitration agreements is preferable? Should arbitrators ever be permitted to finally decide disputes regarding the scope of arbitration agreements? What if that is what the parties agree? How clear should the parties' agreement on this issue need to be? Does Article II of the New York Convention permit a Contracting State to deny effect to an agreement to arbitrate disputes over the agreement's scope?

B. INTERPRETATION OF PROCEDURAL AND RELATED ISSUES IN INTERNATIONAL ARBITRATION AGREEMENTS

As discussed above, several issues—other than those relating to the scope of such agreements—frequently recur in interpreting international arbitration agreements. In particular, disputes not infrequently arise as to whether an arbitration agreement is mandatory or optional and as to whether a party must exhaust pre-arbitration steps (such as negotiations) prior to commencing an arbitration.[6] Excerpted below are materials that illustrate these issues.

FINAL AWARD IN ICC CASE NO. 8445
XXVI Y.B. Comm. Arb. 167 (2001)

Claimant and defendant entered into a know-how/technology licensing contract in which the defendant granted Claimant a non-exclusive license to produce and sell six "contract products" in return for a series of payments. As licensor, defendant was obliged to provide claimant with specific documentation within three months of entering into the agreement. Claimant paid the initial sum. A disagreement arose concerning whether the documentation specified in the agreement was provided for…. The agreement provided for ICC arbitration and the application of Indian law. Arbitration was initiated in Zurich, Switzerland. [A] legal action initiated by claimant in a local court in India was dismissed pending the outcome of this arbitration….

---

6. Berger, *Law and Practice of Escalation Clauses*, 22 Arb. Int'l 1 (2006); G. Born, *International Commercial Arbitration* 278-81, 916-18 (2d ed. 2014); Figuera, *Multi-Tiered Dispute Resolution Clauses in ICC Arbitration*, 14(1) ICC ICArb. Bull. 82 (2003).

As a preliminary matter, the arbitrators must address the contention made by defendant that claimant has not made any effort to settle the dispute amicably, as called for in ... the Agreement, and that this arbitration has therefore been brought prematurely. In this connection, the arbitrators have considered the history of the relations between the parties, since the signature of the Agreement and the exchanges of correspondence, including claimant's letter ... expressing its dissatisfaction, and suggesting termination with compensation to be paid by defendant. This letter was presumably sent before receipt of defendant's letter ... restricting the use of the brand name, but after successive delays in getting a reply to earlier letters. After receiving defendant's letter ... claimant immediately replied to defendant, rejecting defendant's proposal, and reiterating its desire to terminate with compensation. There were several further letters, with each party maintaining its position. Those positions were far apart, with little prospect of a compromise, and the defendant did not respond to claimant's last proposal for a meeting in India. Again this background, claimant brought an action before the Indian Court, ostensibly to preclude defendant from entering into arrangements for the same products with the third parties. Thereafter, litigation having been commenced, the possibility of any amicable settlement was even more remote. This is particularly true in view of the length of time which had elapsed since the signature of the Agreement, the increasingly acrimonious exchanges of letters between the parties, and the large sums eventually demanded by claimant.

The arbitrators are of the opinion that a clause calling for attempts to settle a dispute amicably are primarily expression of intention, and must be viewed in the light of the circumstances. They should not be applied to oblige the parties to engage in fruitless negotiations or to delay an orderly resolution of the dispute. Accordingly, the arbitrators have determined that there was not obligation on the claimant to carry out further efforts to find an amicable solution, and that the commencement of these arbitration proceedings was neither premature nor improper....

GONE TO THE BEACH LLC v. CHOICEPOINT SERVICES, INC.
2007 WL 2768256 (W.D. Tenn.)

JON P. MCCALLA, District Judge.... This case arises out of an asset purchase agreement ("the Agreement") between Plaintiff, Gone to the Beach, LLC ("GTTB"), and Defendants Choicepoint Services, Inc. and its wholly owned subsidiary, Rapsheets Acquisition Corp. (collectively "Defendants"). The parties entered into the Agreement on March 31, 2004, whereby Plaintiff sold substantially all of the assets of its business to Defendants. According to the Agreement, Plaintiff was to receive $20,400,000 as a base price and an earnout payment not to exceed $15,000,000 based on the business' financial performance in 2004. Defendants agreed to operate the business for the remainder of 2004 "in the ordinary course consistent with [Plaintiff's] past practice." On June 10, 2005, Defendants notified Plaintiff that the earnout payment would be only $27,858. Plaintiff contends that Defendants did not operate the business in accordance with the Agreement, and thereby diminished the value of the earnout payment....

The Agreement specifies that "[a]ny controversy, claim, or question of interpretation in dispute ... arising out of or relating to this Agreement" must be settled by arbitration in Atlanta, Georgia. The Agreement further provides that if any calculations related to the earnout payment are disputed, they must be resolved by an audit firm in Birmingham, Alabama.

Plaintiff views Defendants' alleged failure to abide by the terms of the Agreement as a matter of contract interpretation. Accordingly, on August 30, 2005, Plaintiff made a demand for arbitration in Atlanta, Georgia, and identified an arbitrator. According to Plaintiff, Defendants objected to arbitration, stating that they were only amenable to having an arbitrator determine whether the issues raised by Plaintiff were in fact arbitrable. Defendants contend that the only dispute between the parties concerns the amount of the earnout payment, and therefore, this is an accounting matter that should be resolved by the audit firm in Birmingham, rather than by arbitration. [Plaintiff filed the instant complaint [seeking a] declaratory judgment as to the arbitrability of the issues in this case. Both parties agree that this matter should either go to arbitration in Atlanta or to the audit firm in Birmingham....

"[T]he question of arbitrability ... is undeniably an issue for judicial determination." *AT&T Technologies, Inc. v. Communications Workers of America*, 475 U.S. 643, 649.... [The Court cited *Buckeye, supra* pp. 201-05, and reasoned that the decision] involved a general arbitration agreement, similar to the general arbitration clause in this case.... In *Certain Underwriters at Lloyd's London v. Westchester Fire Ins. Co.*, 489 F.3d 580 (3d Cir. 2007), the issue ... was "whether an arbitrator or a court should decide whether coverage disputes under essentially identical insurance contracts should be arbitrated separately ... or collectively...." As is the case here, the question was "'not whether the parties wanted a judge or an arbitrator to decide *whether they agreed to arbitrate a matter*,' but rather 'what *kind of arbitration proceeding* the parties agreed to.'" *Id.* at 587 (*quoting Green Tree Fin. Corp. v. Bazzle*, 539 U.S. 444 [(2003)]). The Third Circuit held that this question should be resolved by the arbitrator. Similarly the ... Fourth Circuit has held that "only when there is a question regarding whether the parties should be arbitrating at all" is there a question of arbitrability for the court to address. *Dockser v. Schwartzberg*, 433 F.3d 421, 426 (4th Cir. 2006).

In this case the parties agree that the only issue for the court to resolve is not whether arbitration is appropriate, but what kind of arbitration is required under the contract. This issue of contract interpretation is not properly before the court. Accordingly, the Court DENIES both Motions for Summary Judgment and DISMISSES Plaintiff's claims without prejudice for determination by the arbitrator....

ASTRA FOOTWEAR INDUSTRY v. HARWYN INTERNATIONAL
442 F.Supp. 907 (S.D.N.Y. 1978)

[excerpted above at pp. 431-33]

BG GROUP PLC v. REPUBLIC OF ARGENTINA
134 S.Ct. 1198 (2014)

[excerpted above at pp. 233-47]

NOTES

1. *Procedural requirements of arbitration agreement.* Arbitration agreements not infrequently contain various procedural steps that are to be followed prior to or contemporaneous with commencement of the arbitration. For example, arbitration

agreements often require that, prior to commencing arbitration, the parties attempt to resolve their disputes in good faith negotiations or to mediate their differences. *See* Figuera, *Multi-Tiered Dispute Resolution Clauses in ICC Arbitration*, 14(1) ICC ICArb. Bull. 82 (2003); Berger, *Law and Practice of Escalation Clauses*, 22 Arb. Int'l 1 (2006); G. Born, *International Commercial Arbitration* 278-81, 916-18 (2d ed. 2014). Other arbitration clauses impose contractual time-limits on the commencement of arbitral proceedings (*e.g.*, arbitration must be commenced within three months of a dispute arising).

2.   *Multi-tiered arbitration agreements or escalation clauses*. Parties sometimes include a "multi-tier" dispute resolution procedure in their contracts. "Escalation clauses provide that, in the event of a dispute between the parties, dispute resolution is to proceed through a sequence of 'multi-step levels' of dispute resolution processes. Arbitral proceedings will not be initiated until the end of such sequences. As a preliminary phase to arbitral proceedings, informal discussions or formal negotiations between technicians or decision-makers at management level, mediation proceedings, expert adjudication by a 'Dispute Review Expert' (DRE), a 'Dispute Adjudication Board' (DAB) or a 'Dispute Review Board' (DRB) will usually be agreed upon. The clauses thereby combine adversarial procedures with proceedings derived from the artillery of Alternative Dispute Resolution ..., resulting in a system of multi-tiered dispute resolution tailor-made for each contract." Berger, *Law and Practice of Escalation Clauses*, 22 Arb. Int'l 1 (2006). Consider, for example, the following:

> The Parties agree to make all reasonable efforts to settle any dispute arising out of or relating to this Agreement by referring such dispute to their respective senior managers for a period of not less than 30 days following receipt of written notice describing such dispute from any other Party. In the event that the dispute is not resolved during such 30 day period, the Parties agree to submit such dispute to arbitration under [the ICC Rules].

> The parties shall use their best efforts to resolve all disputes relating to this Agreement by amicable negotiations. If either party gives notice to the other party that a dispute has arisen, and the parties are unable within thirty (30) days of such notice to resolve the dispute, then it shall be referred to [the Vice-President for Sales] of Seller and [the Vice-President for Quality Control] of Buyer. If these officers are unable within thirty (30) days to resolve the dispute, then it shall be referred to the [Chief Executive Officers] of Seller and Buyer. If the Chief Executive Officers of Seller and Buyer are unable within thirty (30) days to resolve the dispute, then either party may submit the dispute to arbitration in accordance with the provisions of Article X hereof.

> In the event any disputes arise between the Parties relating to this Agreement, X's and Y's Project Managers shall use their best good faith efforts to reach a reasonable, equitable and mutually agreed upon resolution of the item or items in dispute. In the event that the Project Managers cannot so resolve the disputed item(s) within fifteen days, the Parties shall use their best good faith efforts to agree, within a further ten day period, upon an appropriate method of non-judicial dispute resolution, including mediation or arbitration. In the event that the Parties shall decide that any disputed item(s) shall be resolved by arbitration, such arbitral proceedings shall be governed by the [ICC Rules].

As *ICC Case No. 8445* illustrates, these types of procedural requirements can give rise to questions of interpreting the arbitration agreement and ascertaining the consequences of non-compliance with its procedural provisions.

3. *Is an agreement to negotiate enforceable?* Is an agreement to negotiate possible future disputes enforceable? Is it anything more than an "agreement to agree," which is unenforceable in many legal systems? *See* G. Born, *International Commercial Arbitration* 918-23 (2d ed. 2014). Consider:

> "There is then no bargain except to negotiate, and negotiations may be fruitless and end without any contract ensuing; yet even then in strict theory, there is a contract (if there is good consideration) to negotiate, though in the event of repudiation by one party the damages may be nominal, unless a jury think that the opportunity to negotiate was of some appreciable value to the injured party" *Hillas & Co. Ltd v. Arcos Ltd* [1932] All ER 494, 505-07 (House of Lords).

Is this persuasive? For a more recent, and representative, view, consider:

> "An obligation to undertake discussions about a subject in an honest and genuine attempt to reach an identified result is not incomplete. It may be referable to a standard concerned with conduct assessed by subjective standards, but that does not make the standard or compliance with the standard impossible of assessment. Honesty is such a standard…. The assertion that each party has an unfettered right to have regard to any of its own interests on any basis begs the question as to what constraint the party may have imposed on itself by freely entering into a given contract. If what is required by the voluntarily assumed constraint is that a party negotiate honestly and genuinely with a view to resolution of a dispute with fidelity to the bargain, there is no inherent inconsistency with negotiation, so constrained. To say, as Lord Ackner did [in describing the historic common law rule], that a party is entitled not to continue with, or withdraw from, negotiations at any time and for any reason assumes that there is no relevant constraint on the negotiation or the manner of its conduct by the bargain that has been freely entered into. Here, the restraint is a requirement to meet and engage in genuine and good faith negotiations." *United Group Rail Servs. Ltd v. Rail Corp. N.S.W.*, [2009] NSWCA 177, ¶65 (N.S.W. Ct. App.).

Which approach to agreements to negotiate is more appropriate? Assuming that an agreement to negotiate is enforceable, should it be regarded as mandatory or merely precatory? If an agreement to negotiate is enforceable, what obligation does it impose—an obligation to discuss or an obligation to agree upon a particular result? *See* G. Born, *International Commercial Arbitration,* 922-28 (2d ed. 2014). If the former, is such an "obligation" really likely to have been intended to be mandatory?

Consider the following:

> "The better view would be to acknowledge more explicitly and consistently the imperfect and aspirational character of agreements to negotiate and the importance of ensuring parties access to justice. Adopting this analysis would limit the treatment of pre-arbitration procedural requirements as "conditions precedent" or "jurisdictional bars" to very rare cases, where the parties' agreement permits no other characterization. This would allow pre-arbitration procedural requirements to serve their intended objectives—of facilitating amicable settlement—without frustrating the adjudicative process of resolving parties' disputes." Born & Šćekić, *Pre-Arbitration Procedural Requirements: "A Dismal Swamp"*, in *Liber Amicorum in Honour of Charles Brower* (forthcoming 2015).

Is that persuasive?

4. *Is compliance with procedural requirements in arbitration agreement a jurisdictional requirement?* It is sometimes argued that the claimant's failure to comply with the

procedural requirements of the arbitration agreement constitutes a jurisdictional defect which denies an arbitral tribunal authority to proceed with the arbitral proceedings (or that constitutes a repudiation of the arbitration agreement). *See, e.g.*, Várady, *The Courtesy Trap Arbitration "If No Amicable Settlement Can Be Reached,"* 14(4) J. Int'l Arb. 5 (1997). Suppose, for example, the claimant in an arbitration pursuant to the clauses quoted in the preceding Note fails to conduct the contemplated negotiations, mediation, or other pre-arbitration dispute resolution steps. What is the consequence of this non-compliance? If the claimant nonetheless commences an arbitration without having complied with provisions to negotiate or mediate, must the arbitration be dismissed?

Consider the tribunal's conclusion in *ICC Case No. 8445*. Although the award does not reproduce the parties' dispute resolution agreement, that agreement provided that the parties would negotiate in good faith before commencing an arbitration—something that did not occur. What are the consequences of such non-compliance with dispute resolution procedures set forth in an agreement to arbitrate? Should the answer depend on the language of the arbitration agreement? Should a provision for negotiations or conciliation be regarded as mandatory? Note the statement in *ICC Case No. 8445* that the provisions for pre-arbitration negotiation "are primarily expression of intention." What does that mean? What if the provision is drafted in mandatory terms ("the parties *shall* meet and negotiate")? Assuming that a mandatory obligation of this character is breached, is dismissal of an arbitration the appropriate remedy? What other remedies might exist?

What if the right to arbitrate is conditioned on compliance with an obligation to negotiate ("*only if* the parties are unable to resolve their dispute through good faith negotiations after 30 days, *then* either party may refer the dispute to arbitration ...")? If the parties have agreed that no arbitration may be commenced prior to completion of specified dispute resolution mechanisms, does an arbitral tribunal have the authority to proceed with the arbitration?

What if the parties' agreement is silent or ambiguous about the consequences of non-compliance with obligations to negotiate or conciliate? What should the parties be assumed to have intended? That the arbitral tribunal should have competence to fashion an appropriate remedy? *See also Judgment of 15 March 1999*, 20 ASA Bull. 373, 374 (Kassationsgericht Zurich) (2002) (obligation to mediate was substantive obligation, but did not prevent procedural commencement of arbitration); *Int'l Ass'n of Bridge, Structural v. EFCO Corp.*, 359 F.3d 954, 956-57 (8th Cir. 2004) (compliance with procedural prerequisites in arbitration agreement is not condition for arbitration, but substantive issue for the arbitrators). For different approaches, compare *Judgment of 6 July 2000*, 2001 Rev. arb. 749 (French Cour de cassation) (claim inadmissible because contractual conciliation not pursued); *HIM Portland, LLC v. DeVito Builders, Inc.*, 317 F.3d 41 (1st Cir. 2003) ("Because the parties intentionally conditioned arbitration upon either party's request for mediation, we conclude that [claimant's] failure to request mediation precludes it from compelling arbitration"); *White v. Kampner*, 641 A.2d 1381, 1385 (Conn. 1994) ("trial court correctly interpreted the contractual language to require satisfaction of the provisions of the mandatory negotiation clause as a condition precedent to arbitration, and correctly determined that this arbitrability issue was one for the courts to determine").

5. *Futility of negotiations or mediation.* Suppose the claimant does not comply with a mandatory obligation to negotiate (or conciliate/mediate), but claims that doing so would have been futile. Does that affect the consequences resulting from non-compliance? Consider the tribunal's reasoning in *ICC Case No. 8445.* Note its observation that the clause "should not be applied to oblige the parties to engage in fruitless negotiations or to delay an orderly resolution of the dispute." *See Cumberland & York Distrib. v. Coors Brewing Co.*, 2002 WL 193323, at *4 (D. Me.) (even where the contract included "a term requiring mediation ... as a condition precedent to arbitration," court held that "surely a party may not be allowed to prolong resolution of a dispute by insisting on a term of the agreement that, reasonably construed, can only lead to further delay").

6. *Pre-arbitration procedural requirements in investment arbitration.* Many BITs contain arbitration procedural requirements that arguably must be satisfied before an arbitration may be commenced under the BIT.

    (a) *Cooling off periods.* Many BITs contain provisions regarding pre-arbitration "cooling off" periods, during which negotiations or conciliation of the parties' dispute must be sought. For example:

    > "Disputes between the Contracting Parties concerning the interpretation or application of this Agreement shall, as far as possible, be settled amicably or through consultations, mediation or conciliation. Should the Contracting Parties agree on a controversial issue, a written understanding shall be drafted and approved by the Contracting Parties." Agreement between the United Mexican States and the Republic of Austria on the Promotion and Protection of Investments (2001), Art. 20.

    > "(1) Any investment dispute shall form the subject of a written notification, accompanied by a sufficiently detailed memorandum which will be submitted by one of the Parties to such investment dispute, to the other Party. Such dispute shall preferably be settled amicably by direct consultation between the Parties to the dispute or through pursuit of local, non-judicial or administrative remedies. In the absence of such settlement the dispute shall be submitted to conciliation between the Contracting Parties to this Agreement through diplomatic channels. (2) If any such dispute cannot be settled within six months of a written notification being submitted by one party to the dispute to the other party as provided for in paragraph I of this Article, such dispute shall at the request of either party to the dispute be submitted to conciliation or arbitration by [ICSID] under the [ICSID Convention]. (3) In the event of disagreement as to whether conciliation or arbitration is the more appropriate procedure, the national or company affected shall have the right to choose. (4) Each Contracting Party hereby irrevocably consents to submit to the Centre any legal dispute arising between that Contracting Party and a national or company of the other Contracting Party concerning an investment of the latter in the territory of the former...." Agreement Between the Belgo-Luxembourg Economic Union and the Democratic Socialist Republic of Sri Lanka for the Promotion and Protection of Investments (1984), Art. 10.

    > "(1) Before a disputing investor may submit a claim to arbitration, the disputing parties shall first hold consultations in an attempt to settle a claim amicably. (2) Consultations shall be held within 30 days of the submission of the notice of intent to submit a claim to arbitration, unless the disputing parties otherwise agree." Agreement between the Government of Canada and the Government of the Republic of Peru for the Promotion and Protection of Investments (2007), Art. 25.

What are the consequences of non-compliance with a negotiation requirement or a cooling-off period (*e.g.*, a request for arbitration is filed less than six months before notice of a dispute is given)? Should non-compliance result in dismissal of the arbitration or is it merely a procedural infraction that can be dealt with through other procedural directions (*e.g.*, delay in procedural time-table; order to negotiate)?

Further, is an agreement to negotiate enforceable? Intended to be mandatory? Consider also Article 7(3)(a) of the U.S.-Haiti BIT, excerpted above at p. 512; Articles 11(1) and (2) of the Spain-Algeria BIT, excerpted above at pp. 512-13; and Article 23 of the 2012 U.S. Model BIT, available at www.state.gov/e/eb/ifd/bit. Contrast with Investment Chapter of Agreement Between Japan and the Republic of Singapore for a New-Age Economic Partnership, Art. 82(2) ("In the event of an investment dispute, such investment dispute shall, as far as possible, be settled amicably through consultations between the parties to the investment dispute"). Should the consequences for non-compliance with procedural requirements differ between these various provisions? Why?

Most BIT awards have rejected claims that non-compliance with these sorts of procedural requirements for negotiations during a "cooling off" period constitutes jurisdictional defects requiring dismissal of arbitral proceedings. *See, e.g., Spyridon Roussalis v. Romania, Award in ICSID Case No. ARB/06/1 of 7 December 2011*, ¶335-337; *Abaclat v. Argentine Repub., Decision on Jurisdiction and Admissibility in ICSID Case No. ARB/07/5 of 4 August 2011*, ¶564-565; *Salini Costruttori v. Morocco, Decision on Jurisdiction in ICSID Case No. ARB/00/4 of 23 July 2001*, 42 I.L.M. 609, 612 (2003); *Am. Mfg & Trading v. Repub. of Zaire, ICSID Award No. ARB/93/1 of 21 February 1997*, 36 I.L.M. 1531, 1545 (1997); Schreuer, *Travelling the BIT Route, of Waiting Periods, Umbrella Clauses and Forks in the Road*, 5 J. World Inv. & Trade 231, 235 (2004). Is there any reason to treat pre-arbitration obligations to negotiate or conciliate in the investment context differently from in the commercial context?

(b) *Local litigation requirements.* Other BITs contain provisions requiring claims to be litigated in local courts for specified periods before they are submitted to arbitration under the BIT. Consider, for example, Article 8 of the U.K.-Argentina BIT, at issue in *BG Group.*

What should the consequences of non-compliance with a local litigation requirement be? Should non-compliance be a "jurisdictional" defect, requiring dismissal of the arbitration, or a "procedural" infraction or issue of "admissibility," that does not require (or permit) dismissal of the arbitration?

Consider the discussion of this issue by the Court and Chief Justice Roberts's dissent in *BG Group*. Which analysis is more persuasive? Why?

7. *Allocation of competence to interpret procedural requirements of arbitration clause.* Suppose one party claims that an arbitration agreement bars commencement of arbitral proceedings, because the agreement's procedural requirements have not been satisfied. Are such objections for a national court, or an arbitral tribunal, to resolve? Do such objections involve questions of interpretation of the arbitration agreement or substantive defenses? Or both?

8. *Allocation of competence to interpret procedural requirements of arbitration clause under UNCITRAL Model Law*. Does anything in the Model Law address the question of non-compliance with pre-arbitration procedural requirements? Consider Articles 7, 8, and 16, excerpted at pp. 87-90 of the Documentary Supplement. To what sources should courts in Model Law jurisdictions look in interpreting procedural requirements in arbitration agreements and deciding the consequences of non-compliance with such requirements?

9. *Allocation of competence to interpret procedural requirements of arbitration clause under FAA*. U.S. courts have generally refused to consider claims that procedural requirements imposed by an arbitration clause were satisfied, reasoning that this issue is one for the arbitrators. *See Paine Webber v. Elahi*, 87 F.3d 589 (1st Cir. 1996) (timeliness of arbitration under institutional rules is issue for arbitral tribunal); *Int'l Ass'n of Machinists v. Gen. Elec. Co.*, 865 F.2d 902, 904 (7th Cir. 1989) ("arbitrator is not the judge of his own authority—though ... there is an exception: the arbitrator, like any other adjudicator, is empowered to decide whether the parties have taken whatever procedural steps are required to preserve their right to arbitrate a particular dispute"); *Del E. Webb Constr. v. Richardson Hosp. Auth.*, 823 F.2d 145, 149 (5th Cir. 1987) ("question of compliance with procedural prerequisites to arbitration under a bargaining agreement is for the arbitrator"); *Town Cove Jersey City Urban Renewal, Inc. v. Procida Constr. Corp.*, 1996 WL 337293, at *2 (S.D.N.Y.) ("Whether or not a condition precedent to arbitration has been satisfied is a procedural matter for the arbitrator to decide."). Consider the application of this principle in *BG Group*. Is it persuasive?

10. *Disputes over appropriate institutional rules or appointing authority*. Consider the issue presented in *Astra Footwear* and *Gone to the Beach*. The parties had agreed to arbitrate, but they disagreed over the content of their agreed arbitral procedure. Who should decide such disputes—a national court or an arbitral tribunal? *Compare OEMSDF Inc. v. Europe Israel Ltd*, [1999] O.J. No. 3594 (Ontario Super. Ct.) (court considers and decides question whether arbitration agreement provides for LCIA or ICC arbitration). If the arbitral tribunal is to resolve disputes over the arbitral procedures, which one? Suppose that, in *Gone to the Beach*, the two alternative dispute resolution mechanisms were (a) an AAA arbitration; and (b) an ICC arbitration. If interpretation of the parties' arbitration agreement is for the arbitral tribunal, which arbitral tribunal? Must such disputes be resolved by a court? What did *Gone to the Beach* decide? What did *Astra Footwear* decide? Which is preferable? How is the dispute resolution agreement in *Gone to the Beach* different from an agreement allegedly providing for two different forms of institutional arbitration?

11. *Non-compliance with time-limits for asserting claims or commencing arbitration*. Some arbitration provisions contain time-limits for the assertion of claims or the initiation of arbitrations. Consider the following:

> "All disputes arising out of or relating to this Agreement may be submitted to arbitration under [the ICC Rules] within 12 months of the date on which such dispute arises."

What is the consequence of non-compliance with such a provision? Consider *Judgment of 17 August 1995*, 14 ASA Bull. 673 (1996) (Swiss Fed. Trib.) (annulling award where arbitrators had held that claim had been brought within contractually specified 30-day period after dispute arose; court concluded that dispute had arisen earlier than tribunal held, and therefore held that the arbitrators exceeded their jurisdiction). If claim is asserted outside a contractually specified period for bringing claims, is that a jurisdictional or a substantive issue? If, for example, the arbitrators wrongly conclude that a claim is not time-barred by an applicable statute of limitations, is that an excess of jurisdiction? Or is it a mistake in applying the substantive law applicable to the parties' dispute? *See infra* pp. 1160, 1217-18.

12. *Allocation of competence to decide disputes over time-limits for asserting claims or commencing arbitration.* Who should decide claims that an arbitration has not been commenced within contractually agreed time-limits—the arbitral tribunal or a national court? Is such a claim a jurisdictional challenge (affecting the arbitrators' jurisdictional authority) or a substantive defense (not affecting the arbitrators' jurisdictional authority, but instead how they exercise that authority)? If an arbitral tribunal decides a claim that an arbitration was commenced outside of contractually permitted time periods, what level of scrutiny should apply to its decision in a subsequent annulment or non-recognition action? *See infra* pp. 1159-69, 1198-99, 1211-18.

CHAPTER 6

NON-SIGNATORIES AND INTERNATIONAL ARBITRATION AGREEMENTS

As we have seen, virtually all international and national legal regimes regard arbitration as consensual and provide that only the parties to an arbitration agreement are obliged to comply with that agreement.[1] In most cases, the parties to an arbitration agreement are—and are only—the entities that executed the underlying contract containing the arbitration clause.[2] Nevertheless, some cases involve claims that entities which have not formally executed a contract (so-called "non-signatories") are bound by its arbitration clause. This chapter examines the issues that arise in determining whether a non-signatory is bound, or benefitted, by an agreement to arbitrate.[3]

A. NON-SIGNATORIES TO ARBITRATION AGREEMENTS

A variety of legal theories have been invoked to bind non-signatories to arbitration agreements. These include alter ego and agency principles, assignment and other transfer doctrines, third-party beneficiary status, estoppel, assumption and ratification, implied consent and guarantor relations.[4] The materials excerpted below illustrate the application of these legal theories to determining the identity of the parties to international arbitration agreements and the scope of the arbitrators' jurisdiction.

BRIDAS SAPIC v. GOVERNMENT OF TURKMENISTAN
345 F.3d 347 (5th Cir. 2003)

BENAVIDES, Circuit Judge. Plaintiffs-appellees, Bridas SAPIC, Bridas Energy International, Ltd, Intercontinental Oil & Gas Ventures, Ltd, and Bridas Corporation (collectively, "Bridas") originally brought this action to confirm an international arbitration award rendered in Bridas's favor against Defendants-appellants, Government of Turkmenistan ("the Government" or "Turkmenistan"), Concern Balkannebitgaz-Senegat, and State Concern Turkmenneft (collectively "Turkmenneft").

Bridas, an Argentinian corporation, entered into a joint venture agreement ("JVA" or "the agreement") on February 10, 1993, with a production association, Turkmenneft, formed and owned by the Government at the time that the JVA was signed. The Govern-

---

1. See supra pp. 116-37 & infra pp. 573-74. The principal exception to this rule is the possibility of so-called "arbitration without privity" under BITs. See supra pp. 511-16.

2. G. Born, *International Commercial Arbitration* 1406-10 (2d ed. 2014).

3. A separate issue is whether an entity that is a party to a multiparty arbitration agreement may properly be made a party to a particular arbitration that is commenced under the agreement. For example, if A, B and C are parties to an arbitration agreement, and an arbitration is brought only between A and C, can B either voluntarily intervene or be non-voluntarily joined by A or C? We discuss this issue below. See *infra* pp. 933-60.

4. See *infra* pp. 575-86.

ment itself was not a signatory to the agreement. The JVA designated Bridas as the "Foreign Party," and Turkmenneft as the "Turkmenian Party." Over time, the Government substituted various other entities to serve as the Turkmenian Party, ultimately resting with State Concern Turkmenneft and Concern Balkannebitgaz-Senegat (collectively, "Turkmenneft").

The JVA created a joint venture entity called Joint Venture Keimir ("JVK"). JVK was established "for the purpose of conducting hydrocarbon operations in an area in southwestern Turkmenistan, known generally as Keimir." The relevant part of Article XXIV of the agreement stipulates that "any dispute, controversy or claim arising out of or in relation to or in connection with the agreement ... shall be exclusively and finally settled by arbitration, and any Party may submit such a dispute, controversy or claim to arbitration." The parties further agreed that any arbitration would be "conducted in accordance with the Rules of Conciliation and Arbitration of the International Chamber of Commerce as amended from time to time." The law governing the interpretation of the agreement was to be the law of England.

Bridas claims that in November 1995, the Government "ordered Bridas to suspend further work in Keimir, and prohibited Bridas from making imports and exports in or from Turkmenistan." Consequently, on April 16, 1996, Bridas initiated an arbitration proceeding against Appellants with the [ICC].... Turkmenistan argued to the ICC Court of Arbitration that it was not a proper party to the arbitration because, among other reasons, it did not sign the JVA and was thus not a party to the arbitration clause contained within it. The ICC Court subsequently confirmed by letter that the arbitrators themselves would determine whether the Government was subject to their jurisdiction. The dispute was subsequently referred to a three-person tribunal. Although the arbitration agreement contemplated that the arbitration proceeding would be held in Stockholm, Sweden, the parties instead agreed to arbitration proceedings in Houston, Texas.

The arbitral proceedings ... involved 19 days of hearings, various expert reports, testimony concerning damages, and extensive legal briefing. On June 25, 1999, a two-person majority of the Tribunal issued its First Partial Award ("FPA"). The FPA held that (1) the arbitrators had jurisdiction to determine whether they had jurisdiction over the Government, and (2) that "the Government [was] a proper party to the arbitration." The Tribunal also ruled that Appellants had repudiated the JVA. The FPA stated: "If [Bridas] were to accept repudiatory conduct by the [Defendants] and [Turkmenistan] and thus to bring the [joint venture] agreement to an end, their damages would be calculated on a loss-of-bargain basis, involving 218,560,935 barrels of oil equivalent at a net-back price of $10.50 per barrel, using a discount rate of 10.446% based on a contract term of 25 years." In a letter dated July 5, 1999, Bridas formally accepted the Defendant's repudiation of the JVA.

On October 21, 1999, the arbitrators issued their Second Partial Award ("SPA"). In its SPA, the same two-person majority held that the Tribunal had "the jurisdiction to consider and make an award concerning [Bridas's] claim for damages arising out of their acceptance of the repudiatory conduct of the [appellants]." The Third Partial Award ("TPA") was rendered on September 2, 2000. In the TPA, the same two-person majority clarified its previous rulings in the FPA and calculated damages for Bridas. The Tribunal ... awarded a grand total of $495,000,000 in damages to Bridas. The Final Award was issued on January 26, 2001.

Bridas initiated this lawsuit on July 7, 1999, when it filed its application for confirmation of the FPA. The Government and Turkmenneft, in response, filed motions to dismiss the application for confirmation and to vacate and refuse confirmation of the FPA. On December 22, 2000, Turkmenneft, conditionally joined by the Government, moved to vacate or modify both the TPA and the Final Award. The district court denied Appellants' motions to vacate or modify the FPA, TPA, and the Final Award. The Government and Turkmenneft appealed the district court's judgment....

The first issue we address is whether the Tribunal properly exercised jurisdiction over the Government.... The parties agree that federal common law governs the determination of this issue. In order to be subject to arbitral jurisdiction, a party must generally be a signatory to a contract containing an arbitration clause. [*Westmoreland v. Sadoux*, 299 F.3d 462, 465 (5th Cir. 2002) (holding that arbitration agreements "must be in writing and signed by the parties" and may apply to nonsignatories only "in rare circumstances"). Accord *Grigson v. Creative Artists Agency, LLC*, 210 F.3d 524, 528 (5th Cir. 2000) (noting that "arbitration is a matter of contract and cannot, in general, be required for a matter involving an arbitration agreement nonsignatory").] Even though the Government did not sign the JVA, the Tribunal held that the Government was bound to arbitrate the dispute with Bridas because (1) the Government had not taken any steps to extricate itself from the proceedings and (2) its evaluation of the evidence revealed at least 22 commitments in the JVA "that only the Government could give or fulfill."

The district court, because it did not find "clear and unmistakable" evidence that the parties agreed that the Tribunal would determine its own jurisdiction, undertook an independent review of whether the Government was bound to arbitrate with Bridas. *First Options,* 514 U.S. at 944-47. Whether a party is bound by an arbitration agreement is generally considered an issue for the courts, not the arbitrator, "unless the parties clearly and unmistakably provide otherwise." *AT&T Technologies,* 475 U.S. at 649. The district court concluded that despite the Government's nonsignatory status, principles of agency and equitable estoppel bound the Government to the JVA.

As a preliminary matter, we will address Bridas's assertion that the Government waived its right to contest the Tribunal's jurisdiction because it voluntarily took part in the arbitration through Turkmenneft.... [W]hile it is rare that we are asked to decide a jurisdictional issue such as this one after the proceedings have concluded, neither the fact that the Government "allowed the proceeding to continue" over its objection, nor its "virtual representation" at the arbitration by Turkmenneft, waive its right to dispute the Tribunal's jurisdiction in court. *See, e.g., First Options,* 514 U.S. at 946-47....

We begin our review by considering the terms of the JVA. Who is actually bound by an arbitration agreement is a function of the intent of the parties, as expressed in the terms of the agreement. It is apparent that the four corners of the agreement do not bind the Government to arbitrate this dispute. The Government did not sign the JVA, nor was it defined as a party in the agreement. The agreement describes the framework for the relationship between two parties: the "Foreign Party," defined as Bridas, and the "Turkmenian Party," defined as Turkmenneft. Considering that the purpose of the joint venture was to develop the hydro-carbon resources of a nation whose economy and land is dominated by the Government, the Government itself is not mentioned frequently in the agreement. Corporations commonly elect to establish "liability insulating entities" to enter into particular types of transactions, and the structure of the JVA indicates that this was exactly what the

Government intended to do with respect to the JVA. The agreement itself does not signal an intention to bind the Government to its terms, and thus to arbitrate this dispute.

Nevertheless, federal courts have held that so long as there is some written agreement to arbitrate, a third party may be bound to submit to arbitration. Ordinary principles of contract and agency law may be called upon to bind a non-signatory to an agreement whose terms have not clearly done so. *See E.I. DuPont de Nemours & Co. v. Rhone Poulenc*, 269 F.3d 187 (3d Cir. 2001); *Thomson-C.S.F., S.A. v. Am. Arbitration Ass'n*, 64 F.3d 773, 776 (2d Cir. 1995). Six theories for binding a nonsignatory to an arbitration agreement have been recognized: (a) incorporation by reference; (b) assumption; (c) agency; (d) veil-piercing/alter ego; (e) estoppel; and (f) third-party beneficiary. *Thomson-C.S.F.*, 64 F.3d at 776; *DuPont*, 269 F.3d at 195-97....

The district court held that the Government was bound to arbitrate the dispute with Bridas because Turkmenneft signed the JVA as an agent of the Government.... [T]he district court's holding that Turkmenneft is an agent of the Government does not withstand our review, regardless of the standard applied. Turkmenneft is entitled to a "presumption of independent status." *Hester Int'l Corp. v. Federal Republic of Nigeria*, 879 F.2d 170, 176 (5th Cir. 1989). Bridas, therefore, carried the burden of proving that Turkmenneft signed the JVA as an agent of the Government. Agency is "the fiduciary relation which results from the manifestation of consent by one person to another that the other shall act on his behalf and subject to his control, and consent by the other so to act." *Restatement (Second) of Agency* §1(1) (1958). An agency relationship may be demonstrated by "written or spoken words or conduct, by the principal, communicated either to the agent (actual authority) or to the third party (apparent authority)." *Hester*, 879 F.2d at 181. If Turkmenneft indeed signed the JVA in its capacity as the Government's agent, the Government would be bound by the JVA's arbitration requirement.

The district court primarily relied upon three pieces of evidence to support its determination that Turkmenneft signed the JVA as the Government's agent. First, it pointed to a letter from Mr. Suyunov, Deputy Chairman of the Council of Ministers of Turkmenistan, and Mr. Ishanov, Chairman of the Turkmenian Party, that confirmed, during negotiation of the JVA, that "all Joint Venture Keimir rights ... established in the organization documents are fully and completely guaranteed by the Government, and there is no additional need for any further decisions, decrees, or approvals." Second, the district court referred to Article 22.3 of the JVA which states that the "interests, rights and obligation of Turkmenistan" are represented by the Turkmenian Party. Third, the district court relied upon a statement made in a 1996 letter by the Government's Ministry of Oil and Gas to the director general of JVK and JVY (another joint venture with Bridas), that "the Ministry is the Turkmenian Party."

Given the language and structure of the JVA, these evidentiary findings are insufficient to support an agency determination. First, typically a guarantor cannot be compelled to arbitrate on the basis of an arbitration clause in a contract to which it is not a party. *Interocean Shipping Co. v. Nat'l Shipping & Trading Co.*, 523 F.2d 527, 539 (2d Cir. 1975). Second, a statement of representation, such as that in Article 22.3, in the midst of a provision regarding oral modifications of the agreement, is not remarkable. "All corporations to some degree represent their owners," and Turkmenneft is an oil company wholly owned by Turkmenistan. *Hester*, 879 F.2d at 180. As we have held in the past, such a statement does not establish an agency relationship. And third, the 1996 letter from the Ministry, while probative of how the Government conceived of its role in JVK in 1996, does not overcome the fact that the preamble to the JVA defines the Turkmenian Party as Turkmenneft—a "legal entity within the meaning of the laws of Turkmenistan"—not the Government or the Ministry. The JVA was signed in 1993, before the Ministry penned the letter that Bridas claims demonstrates that Turkmenneft signed the JVA as an agent.

Arbitration agreements apply to nonsignatories only in rare circumstances. We are simply unable to conclude that the parties, one a multi-national corporation who has negotiated joint venture agreements in the past, and the other, a sovereign nation, both represented by able counsel, intended Turkmenneft to sign the JVA as an agent of the Government in the absence of clearer language.... "The mere fact that one is dealing with an agent, whether the agency be general or special, should be a danger signal, and, like a railroad crossing, suggests the duty to stop, look, and listen, and he who would bind the principal is bound to ascertain, not only the fact of agency, but the nature and extent of the authority[.]" *Standard Accident Ins. Co. v. Simpson*, 64 F.2d 583, 589 (4th Cir. 1933). Had Bridas truly felt that Turkmenneft was signing the agreement not for itself but on behalf of the Government, it had the obligation to make that fact clear on the face of the agreement. This could have been accomplished in a myriad of ways. Bridas could have requested that the Government sign the agreement, or inserted a prominent and direct statement as to Turkmenneft's status.... Bridas was doubtlessly well aware of the risks inherent in investing in countries of the former Soviet Union in 1993, and the possibility that its investment would be swept away in political turmoil. We will not bind the Government to the agreement, simply because Bridas lost a gamble that it was willing to take. To do otherwise would vitiate the predictability of the legal backdrop against which the parties voluntarily agreed to do business.

Bridas has set forth ample evidence regarding the extent to which Turkmenneft was controlled by the Government subsequent to the signing of the JVA. Such evidence, however, does not establish that Turkmenneft had the apparent authority to bind the Government in 1993. Bridas did not satisfy its burden in this regard, and the district court's holding that Turkmenneft signed the JVA as an agent of the Government was clearly erroneous.

Courts occasionally apply the alter ego doctrine and agency principles as if they were interchangeable. The two theories are, however, distinct. Under the alter ego doctrine, a corporation may be bound by an agreement entered into by its subsidiary regardless of the agreement's structure or the subsidiary's attempts to bind itself alone to its terms, "when their conduct demonstrates a virtual abandonment of separateness." *Thomson-C.S.F.*, 64 F.3d at 777. This is due to the doctrine's strong link to equity. The laws of agency, in contrast, are not equitable in nature, but contractual, and do not necessarily bend in favor of justice. Courts are thus comparatively free from the moorings of the parties' agreements when considering whether an alter ego finding is warranted. This is not to say that the decision to apply the alter ego doctrine to bind a parent is made routinely. "Courts do not lightly pierce the corporate veil even in deference to the strong policy favoring arbitration." *ARW Exploration Corp. v. Aguirre*, 45 F.3d 1455, 1461 (10th Cir. 1995). The corporate veil may be pierced to hold an alter ego liable for the commitments of its instrumentality only if (1) the owner exercised complete control over the corporation with respect to the transaction at issue and (2) such control was used to commit a fraud or wrong that injured the party seeking to pierce the veil.

The district court held, in a brief paragraph, that the Government was not the alter ego of Turkmenneft. After finding that the evidence reveals that Turkmenneft was controlled by the Government, the court stated, "despite this control ... Bridas has not offered evidence proving 'an absence of corporate formalities.' Moreover, there is no indication of 'an intermingling of corporate finances and directorship' between Turkmenneft and the government. Thus, Turkmenistan cannot be bound under an alter ego theory."

The district court erred in premising its conclusion solely upon the existence of corporate formalities and an absence of comingling of funds and directors. Alter ego determinations are highly fact-based, and require considering the totality of the circumstances in which the instrumentality functions. No single factor is determinative.... Because the district court failed to take into account all of the aspects of the relationship between the Government and Turkmenneft, it committed an error of law and must reconsider the issue on remand.[5]

The district court, relying on *Grigson v. Creative Artists Agency, LLC*, 210 F.3d 524, 527 (5th Cir. 2000), held that a nonsignatory may be equitably estopped from asserting that it is not bound by an arbitration agreement when the signatory raises allegations of substantially interdependent and concerted misconduct against both a nonsignatory and one or more of the signatories to the contract. As the Government correctly points out, the district court misapplied the "intertwined claims" theory of equitable estoppel.... In *Grigson*, we estopped a *signatory* plaintiff from relying upon the defendants' status as a nonsignatory to prevent the *defendants* from compelling arbitration under the agreement. We justified applying equitable estoppel in *Grigson* in part because to do otherwise would permit the signatory plaintiff to have it both ways. "[The plaintiff] cannot, on the one hand, seek to hold the nonsignatory liable pursuant to duties imposed by the agreement, which contains an arbitration provision, but, on the other hand, deny arbitration's applicability because the defendant is a nonsignatory." *Grigson*, 210 F.3d at 528.

The rationale of *Grigson* does not apply to the circumstances of this case. Here, the Government, unlike the estopped party in *Grigson*, did not sign a contract containing an arbitration provision and never sued Bridas on the agreement.... The Second Circuit has

---

5. Once it has been determined that the corporate form was used to effect fraud or another wrong upon a third-party, alter ego determinations revolve around issues of control and use. On remand, the court should explore the totality of the environment in which Turkmenneft operated, including those factors normally explored in the context of parent-subsidiary alter ego claims, such as whether: (1) the parent and subsidiary have common stock ownership; (2) the parent and subsidiary have common directors or officers; (3) the parent and subsidiary have common business departments; (4) the parent and subsidiary file consolidated financial statements; (5) the parent finances the subsidiary; (6) the parent caused the incorporation of the subsidiary; (7) the subsidiary operated with grossly inadequate capital; (8) the parent pays salaries and other expenses of subsidiary; (9) the subsidiary receives no business except that given by the parent; (10) the parent uses the subsidiary's property as its own; (11) the daily operations of the two corporations are not kept separate; (12) the subsidiary does not observe corporate formalities. Additional factors include: (1) whether the directors of the "subsidiary" act in the primary and independent interest of the "parent"; (2) whether others pay or guarantee debts of the dominated corporation; and (3) whether the alleged dominator deals with the dominated corporation at arms length.

While the preceding considerations are adaptable to a certain degree to the context of a sovereign government and its instrumentality, the district court should also consider the factors that we take into account when determining if a state agency is the "alter ego" of a state for 11th amendment sovereign immunity purposes: (1) whether state statutes and case law view the entity as an arm of the state; (2) the source of the entity's funding; (3) the entity's degree of local autonomy; (4) whether the entity is concerned primarily with local, as opposed to statewide, problems; (5) whether the entity has the authority to sue and be sued in its own name; and (6) whether the entity has the right to hold and use property.

expressly stated that the *Grigson* version of estoppel applies only to prevent "a *signatory* from avoiding arbitration with a nonsignatory when the issues the *nonsignatory is seeking to resolve in arbitration are intertwined with the agreement that the estopped party has signed.*" *Thomson-CSF,* 64 F.3d at 779 (emphasis added). "Because arbitration is guided by contract principles, the reverse is not also true: a signatory may not estop a non-signatory from avoiding arbitration regardless of how closely affiliated that nonsignatory is with another signing party." *MAG Portfolio Consult,* 268 F.3d at 62....

As the Government correctly notes, the result in *Grigson* and similar cases makes sense because the parties resisting arbitration had expressly agreed to arbitrate claims of the very type that they asserted against the nonsignatory. "It is more foreseeable, and thus more reasonable, that a party who has actually agreed in writing to arbitrate claims with someone might be compelled to broaden the scope of his agreement to include others." The simple fact that *Bridas's* claims against Turkmenneft and the Government are inextricably intertwined ... is insufficient, standing alone, to justify the application of equitable estoppel to the *Government's* assertion that it is not subject to the Tribunal's jurisdiction. Were this to become the case, this expanded version of equitable estoppel would "threaten to overwhelm the fundamental premise that a party cannot be compelled to arbitrate a matter without its agreement." The district court thus abused its discretion in applying the intertwined claims theory of equitable estoppel....

Bridas, however, contends that the district court's decision may nonetheless be affirmed on the basis of the "direct benefits" version of estoppel. Direct benefits estoppel applies when a nonsignatory "knowingly exploits the agreement containing the arbitration clause." *DuPont,* 269 F.3d at 199. *See Deloitte Noraudit A/S v. Deloitte Haskins & Sells*, U.S., 9 F.3d 1060, 1064 (2d Cir. 1993) (holding that nonsignatory local affiliate, who used a trade name pursuant to an agreement that it ratified which contained an arbitration clause, was estopped from relying on its nonsignatory status to avoid arbitrating under the agreement); *Am. Bureau of Shipping v. Tencara Shipyard SPA*, 170 F.3d 349, 353 (2d Cir. 1999) (binding nonsignatory to a contract under which it received direct benefits of lower insurance and the ability to sail under the French flag).

There is an important distinction, however, between cases where the courts seriously consider applying direct benefits estoppel, and the case at bar. In the former, the nonsignatory had brought suit against a signatory premised in part upon the agreement. Here, it is undisputed that the Government has not sued Bridas under the agreement. The Government has thus not "exploited" the JVA to the degree that the cases that consider applying this version of estoppel require....

While very similar to estoppel, the third-party beneficiary doctrine is distinct:

> "Under third party beneficiary theory, a court must look to the intentions of the parties at the time the contract was executed. Under the equitable estoppel theory, a court looks to the parties' conduct after the contract was executed. Thus, the snapshot this Court examines under equitable estoppel is much later in time than the snapshot for third party beneficiary analysis." *DuPont,* 269 F.3d at 200 n.7.

It is not enough, therefore, that the Government benefitted from the existence of the JVA. "The fact that a person is directly affected by the parties' conduct, or that he may have a substantial interest in a contract's enforcement, does not make him a third-party beneficiary." *Id.*

Parties are presumed to be contracting for themselves only. *Fleetwood Enter. Inc. v. Gaskamp*, 280 F.3d 1069, 1075-76 (5th Cir. 2002). This presumption may be overcome only if the intent to make someone a third-party beneficiary is "clearly written or evidenced in the contract." *Id*. For the same reasons given *supra*, the JVA simply does not evince the requisite clear intent to benefit the Government, other than to the degree ordinarily expected when an instrumentality of a sovereign enters into a contract to develop the country's natural resources. The JVA's integration clause, moreover, specifies that the terms of the agreement apply only to the parties, defined as the Turkmenian Party (i.e. Turkmenneft) and Bridas.

Furthermore, we are again reluctant to bind the Government to the terms of the JVA on a third-party beneficiary theory because the Government has never filed a claim against Bridas premised upon the agreement, or otherwise sought to enforce its terms. Bridas has not brought to our attention a case where a third-party beneficiary has been bound to arbitrate a dispute, arising under an agreement to which it is not a party, that the third-party itself did not initiate in court. We decline to do so for the first time today....

BRIDAS SAPIC v. GOVERNMENT OF TURKMENISTAN
447 F.3d 411 (5th Cir. 2006)

[On remand, the District Court found that the Government was not an alter ego of Turkmenneft, and vacated the award. Bridas appealed. The Court of Appeals reconsidered the facts and found that "the totality of the record demonstrates that the Government should be bound as an alter ego of State Concern Turkmenneft," because the Government both committed fraud or injustice and used the financial dependence of Turkmenneft to perpetrate such wrong. Accordingly, the Court of Appeals reversed the District Court's judgment and recognized the award.]

INTERIM AWARD IN ICC CASE NO. 4131
IX Y.B. Comm. Arb. 131 (1984)

SANDERS, GOLDMAN & VASSEUR, Arbitrators. [Dow Chemical Company is incorporated in the United States. It owns 100 percent, either directly or indirectly, of Dow Chemical (Venezuela), Dow Chemical AG, Dow Chemical Europe, and Dow Chemical France. In 1965, Dow Chemical (Venezuela) entered into a contract with a French company for the distribution of equipment in France. Dow Chemical (Venezuela) later assigned the contract to Dow Chemical AG. In 1968, Dow Chemical Europe entered into a similar contract with different French companies. The 1965 and 1968 agreements each contained an ICC arbitration clause.

Both the 1965 and the 1968 agreement was eventually assigned by Dow's original French counter-party to Isover Saint Gobain, a French company. Both agreements permitted any subsidiary of the Dow Chemical Company to make deliveries contemplated by the agreements. In practice, Dow Chemical France made the deliveries. Disputes arose between the parties, and Isover brought several lawsuits against various Dow Chemical entities in French courts. As a consequence, various Dow entities filed a Request for Arbitration against Isover; the claimants were Dow Chemical Company, Dow Chemical AG, Dow Chemical Europe, and Dow Chemical France. Isover challenged the tribunal's jurisdiction to hear claims asserted by Dow Chemical Company and Dow Chemical

France, as well as the standing of Dow Chemical AG and Dow Chemical Europe. The tribunal issued an interim award, which is excerpted below.] ...

Considering that it is not disputed that the arbitration clauses relied upon by the claimants are contained in contracts that have been signed by neither Dow Chemical (France) nor Dow Chemical Company; that these two companies, nonetheless, maintain that they may invoke them, by reason both of the factual context of the conclusion and performance of the contracts, and of the fact that these companies, along with the signatories of the contracts, are part of a group of which Dow Chemical Company is the parent company, the three others being its daughter and granddaughters, entirely controlled by the former;

Considering, thus, that the jurisdictional objection and, in consequence, the related objection as to the admissibility of the action give rise to the issue of the scope and effects of the relevant arbitration clause. Therefore, the sources of law appropriate to the determination of said scope and said effects should be defined;

Considering that the Defendant, in fact, has argued that the arbitration clause contained in the 1968 contract, according to which "any difference arising under this agreement will be settled ... , according to French law ..." should be interpreted to mean not only that the merits of the dispute should be determined by reference to French law but also the scope and the effects of the arbitration agreement;

Considering, however, that in referring to the ICC Rules, the parties incorporated its provisions concerning the arbitral tribunal's authority to decide as to its own jurisdiction, which provisions do not refer to the application of any national law. The reference to French law could therefore concern only the merits of the dispute;

Considering that the sources of law applicable to determine the scope and the effects of an arbitration clause providing for international arbitration do not necessarily coincide with the law applicable to the merits of a dispute submitted to such arbitration. Although this law or these rules of law may in certain cases concern the merits of the dispute as well as the arbitration agreement, it is perfectly possible that in other cases, the latter, because of its autonomy, is governed—not only as to its scope, but also as to its effects—by its own specific sources of law, distinct from those that govern the merits of the dispute;

Considering that this is particularly the case—unless the parties have expressly agreed otherwise—with respect to an arbitration clause referring to the ICC Rules;

Considering in effect that these Rules, in their 1975 version (whose applicability to this case, given the dates of the litigious contracts, will be decided in due course), contain provisions relating to the proper law to be applied to the merits of the dispute (Article 13(3)), but are silent on this subject in their prior version. However, both versions of the [ICC] Rules contain practically identical provisions (1955 [ICC] Rules, Article 13; 1975 [ICC] Rules, "Arbitration" section, Article 8) concerning the arbitrator's competence to decide on his own jurisdiction. These provisions establish in particular, the principle of the complete autonomy of the arbitration clause (paragraph 4 of both texts) and confer on the arbitrator the power to take any decision as to his own jurisdiction upon the Court's determination that the arbitration will take place (paragraph 3) without obliging him to apply any national law whatever in order to do so.

Considering that the tribunal shall, accordingly, determine the scope and effects of the arbitration clauses in question, and thereby reach its decision in regarding jurisdiction, by reference to the common intent of the parties to these proceedings, such as it appears from the circumstances that surround the conclusion and characterize the performance, and later the termination of the contracts in which they appear. In doing so, the tribunal, following, in particular, French case law relating to international arbitration should also take into account, usages conforming to the needs of international commerce, in particular, in the presence of a group of companies;

Considering that in conformity with the "General rule" set forth in Article 31 (1955 version) and Article 26 of the "Arbitration" Section of the ICC Rules, the tribunal will however make every effort to make sure that the award is enforceable at law. To this end, it will assure itself that the solution it adopts is compatible with international public policy, in particular, in France....

Considering that in conformity with the preceding it is appropriate, in order to determine the scope and the effects of the arbitration clauses relied upon, to examine in succession the circumstances under which the negotiation, the performance and the termination of the contracts in which these claims appear, took place and to explore thereafter the possible bearing, in this context, of the fact that the claimants are part of a group of companies....

Considering that in point of fact Dow Chemical France at the time of signature of the 1965 contracts as well as the negotiations which led to the 1968 contract, appeared to be at the center of the organization of the contractual relationship with the companies succeeded by the present Defendant. Moreover, this relationship could not have been formed without the approval of the American parent company, which owned the trademarks under which the relevant products were to be marketed in France.

That this analysis reveals that neither the "Sellers" nor the "Distributors" attached the slightest importance to the choice of the company within the Dow Group that would sign the contracts. It is significant to note that none of the documents produced contains any trace of a discussion on this subject. In reality all the entities of the Dow Group involved in distribution in France understood themselves to be contracting with the distributor or distributors in France and likewise, it was with the aggregate of these entities that the present defendant's predecessors understood themselves to be contracting....

Considering that—as it has been mentioned above—the distribution agreement of 1965 as well as the one of 1968 designated first of all Dow France for delivery of the products to distributors. Although it has been provided for that deliveries could also be effectuated, at the choice of the "seller," by other subsidiaries of Dow Chemical Company, it is to be noted that, in fact, it has not been sustained that this option has ever been used. It has always been Dow France which has assured the execution of the contracts; ... Dow France, therefore, played in the execution of the contracts an equally preponderant role as it did in the establishment of the contractual relations....

[It also] appears, as was the case with respect to the conclusion and performance of the distribution agreements, that Dow Chemical France played an essential role in the termination of the 1968 contract, which had been substituted for the 1965 contract; that all of these factors permit the conclusion that Dow Chemical France was a party to each of these contracts and, consequently, to the arbitration clauses they contained; that the same conclusion should be reached with respect to Dow Chemical Company by reason of its ownership of the trademarks under which the products were marketed, and its absolute control over those of its subsidiaries that were directly involved, or could under the contracts have become involved in the conclusion, performance, or termination of the litigious distribution agreements.

Considering that the Defendant adopted the same position in its brief of 1 July 1980 before the Court of Appeal of Paris, in support of its motion for the compulsory joinder of inter alia Dow Chemical Company. That the Defendant there in fact wrote as follows: "Whereas Dow Chemical Company, owner to the patents and organizer of the manufacturing and distribution of Roofmate, decided and conceived the modalities of the manufacturing and distribution of said product, thus engaging its direct liability."

Considering that in the circumstances of this case, the application of the arbitration clauses to Dow Chemical Company may also be justified, as we shall now show, by the fact that the contracts containing these clauses concern, in the context of a group of companies, a parent company and certain of its subsidiaries. The same fact could justify, if necessary, the application of the arbitration clause to Dow Chemical France.

Considering that it is indisputable—and in fact not disputed—that Dow Chemical Company has and exercises absolute control over its subsidiaries having either signed the relevant contracts or, like Dow Chemical France, effectively and individually participated in their conclusion, their performance, and their termination;

Considering that irrespective of the distinct juridical identity of each of its members, a group of companies constitutes one and the same economic reality (une réalité économique unique) of which the arbitral tribunal should take account when it rules on its own jurisdiction subject to Article 13 (1955 version) or Article 8 (1975 version) of the ICC Rules.

Considering, in particular, that the arbitration clause expressly accepted by certain of the companies of the group should bind the other companies which, by virtue of their role in the conclusion, performance, or termination of the contracts containing said clauses, and in accordance with the mutual intention of all parties to the proceedings, appear to have been veritable parties to these contracts or to have been principally concerned by them and the disputes to which they may give rise.

Considering that ICC arbitral tribunals have already pronounced themselves to this effect (see *Award in ICC Case No. 2375 of 1975*, 1976 J.D.I. 978). The decisions of these tribunals progressively create case law which should be taken into account, because it draws conclusions from economic reality and conforms to the needs of international commerce, to which rules specific to international arbitration, themselves successively elaborated should respond.

Considering that it is true that in another award (*Award in ICC Case No. 2138 of 1974*, 1975 J.D.I. 934) the arbitral tribunal refused to extend an arbitration clause signed by one company to another company of the same group. However, in so doing it based itself on the factor "that it was not established that Company X" (which the tribunal had determined was neither a signatory nor a party to the contract) "would have accepted the arbitration clause if it had signed the contract directly." Considering that in the absence of such a showing, the tribunal did not allow application of the arbitration clause; but that in the present case, the circumstances and the documents analyzed above show that such application conforms to the mutual intent of the parties.

That it is not without interest to recall that an American arbitral tribunal recently reached a similar result, referring to U.S. national court decisions and observing that "it is neither sensible nor practical to exclude (from the arbitral jurisdiction) the claims of companies who have an interest in the venture and who are members of the same corporate family." (*Partial Final Award No. 1510*, VII Y.B. Comm. Arb. 151 (Society of Maritime Arbitrators 28 November 1980).)

Considering finally that in a matter directly connected with the issues litigated in the present arbitration, the Court of Appeal in Paris on 5 February 1982 held that it lacked jurisdiction to hear Isover Saint Gobain's motion for the compulsory joinder of not only Dow Chemical Europe (which signed the 1968 distribution contract), but also Dow Chemical Company (U.S.A.) and "(referred) Isover Saint Gobain to the proper jurisdiction of the arbitral tribunal of the ICC in Paris." In order to justify this decision, the Court of Appeal stated "that Isover Saint Gobain cannot dispute the fact that the litigation is pending and that its claims against Dow Company and Dow Europe in their relations inter se flow directly from the two contracts" (of 1965 and 1968);

It is true that by the same decision the Court reached a decision on the merits as regards Dow Chemical France. However, in that case, the said company had been sued on the grounds of quasi-tortious liability, and did not invoke the arbitration clauses and did not contest jurisdiction.

In conclusion, it is appropriate for the tribunal to assume jurisdiction over the claim brought not only by Dow Chemical AG (Zürich) and Dow Chemical Europe, but also by Dow Chemical Company (U.S.A.) and Dow Chemical France.

In so doing, the tribunal contradicts no principle nor any rule of international "public policy," in particular, that of the French legal system. The latter is not based on any principle, nor does it contain any rule of such a stature, that would prohibit giving to an arbitration clause implicating companies that are legally distinct but form part of a group of companies, the scope attributed to it by the present award. To the contrary, by taking into account, in reaching this result, the needs of international commerce to which the rules of international arbitration should be responsive, the tribunal follows the example of French case law to which express reference was made in the report to the Prime Minister explaining the purposes of the Decree of May 12, 1981.

Considering that, as has been recalled, the alleged non-admissibility of the claims of Dow Chemical AG and Dow Chemical Europe invoked by the Defendant is connected by the arbitrators' Terms of Reference, to the decision sought from the tribunal on its jurisdiction with respect to the two other Claimants;

Considering that the tribunal will reject the challenge to its jurisdiction, it will as a result, not at present uphold the challenge to the admissibility of the action. This decision will not, however, preclude a future ruling by the tribunal on the existence or the absence of interest to institute an action as far as one or both of the Claimants in question, are concerned or a possible finding that the claims of one or both of them may not be heard due to an absence of direct interest in the cause of action.

FOR THESE REASONS, the Tribunal: 1. Assumes jurisdiction to decide the claims of the four Claimants. 2. Rejects, for the present, the Defendant's challenge to the admissibility of the action of Dow Chemical AG (Zürich) and Dow Chemical Europe....

AWARD IN ICC CASE NO. 8385

in J.-J. Arnaldez, Y. Derains & D. Hascher (eds.), *Collection of ICC Arbitral Awards 1996-2000* **474 (2003)**

[X, a company incorporated in Maine, and Y, a Belgian corporation, entered into a contract providing for X to provide its know-how and services to Y for the purpose of building a factory in Bulgaria. The agreement contained an ICC arbitration clause. Disputes subsequently arose over Y's alleged non-payment of royalties. X initiated an ICC arbitration against Y and, because Y was insolvent, Y's parent corporation, Z, another Belgian corporation. The sole arbitrator decided that Z's corporate veil should be lifted under principles of *lex mercatoria*.]

Z has filed what it called a motion for special appearance "for the sole purpose of demonstrating that it was unduly designated as Defendant." It also asked the Tribunal to make a decision on the issues raised by this special appearance in limine litis. The Tribunal has rejected this request based on the fact that a proper assessment required an analysis of the facts and that Z would be free to defend itself on the merits without giving up in anyway on its objections regarding the jurisdiction of the tribunal. Of course, Z's defense as to the merits of the dispute was to be the same as Y's, especially given the fact Y and Z are represented by the same counsel. In any case, Z had the same opportunities as Y in order to defend itself and cannot argue to the contrary. The tribunal's refusal to decide in limine litis on Z's objection regarding the tribunal's jurisdiction is justified since the tribunal was informed and able to make a decision on this request only after it had heard the parties' pleadings on the merits.

It must be underlined that the claims against Z raise two questions: first, can Z be a party to this arbitration and, second, can Z be held liable for Y's debt? The answer to those two questions depends on determining whether Z could be bound by Y's contracts and the obligations resulting from said contracts....

The first point to solve concerns the applicable law. The conflict rule provided by article 15 of the contract [which provided: "New York state law, United States, shall apply"] cannot be considered applicable to solving this issue. Indeed, one must first determine whether Z is bound by the contract, including article 15, and said determination must be carried out pursuant a law other than the one specified in the contract. Referring to article 15 in order to determine the applicable law would amount to putting the cart before the horse. The applicable law should be determined by referring to the appropriate conflict rule other than the one provided by the contract.

In fact, the situation the tribunal is facing is the same faced by an ad hoc tribunal which does not possess any contractual indication as to the applicable law. A tribunal in such a situation could wish to share the analysis that would be followed by a tribunal having its sit at the place of arbitration and apply the law of the seat. It is generally accepted that a tribunal shall apply the law of the place where it sits.... Applying the lex fori is thus not unreasonable. However, the place of arbitration is often chosen with neutrality concerns in mind and does not have any particular connection to the parties. In this case, Y and Z are Belgian corporations and X a Maine corporation headquartered in Connecticut. Applying the New York conflict rule simply because the tribunal sits in New York is thus not necessarily reasonable.

It is true that the tribunal's situation is the same as a state tribunal in a neutral forum and which has jurisdiction pursuant to a choice of forum clause. But this does not mean that the tribunal should apply the conflict rule of the lex fori that would be applied by a state tribunal which jurisdiction would solely depend on a choice of forum clause. On the contrary, the state tribunal should ask itself, as an arbitral tribunal would, whether, even in this case, the conflict rule of the lex fori should be applied. The tribunal considers that, in the case of a neutral forum such as this one, the automatic application of the conflict rule of the place of arbitration must be rejected and the tribunal shall apply the law, and if necessary the private international law, which is the most appropriate in those circumstances. That is, the law that best fits the need of the international business community, which does not conflict with the legitimate expectations of the parties, which generates uniform results and offer a reasonable solution to the dispute.

In this case, the tribunal, when trying to determine the applicable law, will examine New York law where the tribunal sits, the law of Belgium, where the place of conclusion of the contract as well as the main establishments of Y and Z are located, and also the principles of law developed by the international community. The application of New York state law is justified since it has been chosen by X and Y in article 15 of the contract. It must be determined whether Z should be bound by this choice as it was made by a third party under its complete control, as demonstrated below. Furthermore, the application of New York law would not contradict the parties' legitimate expectations most directly involved, and would give rise to uniform results. Finally, New York state law is sufficiently developed in order to decide the case at issue.

Belgian law is also a real contender as the applicable law since it is the law of the place of conclusion and of the main establishment of Z and Y. The fact that the law of the place of conclusion applies to incidents taking place during the lifetime of the corporation is a sound argument. In fact, it is the law of the incorporation that determines the extent to which a corporation can be deemed to have a separate legal existence and the application of the law of the place of incorporation guarantees the foreseeability and uniformity of the result.... Yet, a distinction must be drawn between questions involving the relationship between the corporations and its shareholders or its managers and directors, or the relationship between the corporation and third parties,...Whilst it can be fair and reasonable to bring a corporation, its shareholders, directors and managers under the law of incorporation when dealing with their internal relationship, the third parties dealing with those corporations cannot be considered as getting bound by taking the risk of being governed by the law of the state of incorporation. This is particularly true for third parties coming from other countries who will not necessarily be fully informed about the law of the State of incorporation.

Indeed, in [the context of] international relations, the tribunal considers that it is preferable to apply rules that fit the conditions of the international market and which achieve a reasonable balance between the trust a corporation bestows upon its distinct legal personality and the protection of persons who can be the victims of manipulations by a parent corporation using its subsidiary as a shield from a creditor. Applying international principles offers many advantages. They can be applied in uniform fashion and are independent from the particularities of each national law. They take into account the needs of international relations and allow a fruitful exchange between systems that are sometimes overly linked to conceptual distinctions and those that are seeking a pragmatic and fair solution to specific cases. It thus constitutes a unique and ideal opportunity to apply what is increasingly referred to as *lex mercatoria*. Even though the tribunal considers that it is preferable to apply the principles of international commerce dictated by the needs of the international market, it comes to the conclusion that the result is the same regardless of the application of New York law, Belgian law or of international principles. Those three systems recognize, at least in certain situations, that the corporate veil can be lifted and the tribunal concludes that, considering the particular circumstances of this dispute, those three systems allow for the veil to be lifted.

Whether or not one lifts the corporate veil depends on many factors in each case. Certain elements are almost always necessary. They include a significant amount of control of the subsidiary's actions by the parent company or the shareholder and the insolvency of the subsidiary. But this is not generally sufficient. The end of significant activity of the subsidiary and its directors is equally a factor which facilitates the lifting of the corporate veil. And if the control and effective management of the subsidiary by the parent company has contributed towards making a remedy against the above mentioned subsidiary elusive, the lifting of the corporate veil becomes even more important. Unlawful conduct towards the person seeking to lift the corporate veil by the subsidiary upon the instigation of the parent company is another factor that can facilitate the lifting of the corporate veil. The question that one must ultimately answer is when the legal fiction of corporate legal personality must bow to the reality of human behavior and cease protecting those who hide behind the corporate veil as a way of promoting their own interests at the expense of those who have traded with the company....

In light of the above mentioned facts, Z, in the present case, is bound by the arbitration clause and liable for Y's debts towards the claimant according to the law of the State of New York, Belgian law and the law of the international commercial community.

The law of New York is very well summarized in the cases of *Carte Blanche (Singapore) Pte vs. Diners Club Int'l, Inc.*, 2 F.3d 24 (2d Cir. 1993) and *Passalacque Builders Inc. vs. Resnick Dev. South Inc.*, 933 F.2d 131 (2d Cir 1991). It should be noted that this line of case law states several factors that are mostly superficial ..., such as knowing whether separate corporate documents are kept, though in the present case, there are very substantial factors that argue in favor of lifting the corporate veil.

Lifting the corporate veil is a relatively new concept in civil law countries. Belgium is not an exception. The traditional approach has been to apply the conceptual methodology more or less to the facts which as a result, has prevented a swift consensus to a global doctrine in relation to the lifting of the corporate veil. However, Belgian law recognizes that an abuse of power when in control of a company can justify the person who exercised it as being considered liable for the obligations of the said company. Furthermore a parent company can, in particular circumstances, be considered as having employed its subsidiary as an agent. The use of these different constructions arrives at the same result as the one produced by lifting the corporate veil (Verougstrate, I, *Het Waterdicht Beschot*, in *Liber Amicorum Jan Ronse, E. Story-Scientia*, 19; *De Smedt v. P V B A Duerinckx*, RAC, 1990-10, 884 (Court of Cassation, 1990)). The well-known *Badger* case demonstrates Belgium's approval of the principle of lifting the corporate veil. In this case, the American parent company denied all responsibility of its insolvent subsidiary in relation to its pensions obligations. Belgium rigorously pursued the parent company which, in the end, was forced to face up to its obligations. Lowenfeld, *International Litigation and the Quest for Reasonableness* 245 Academy of International Law 138-144 (1994-I). In the present case, the tribunal considers that a Belgian tribunal, according to Belgian law, would consider Z bound by the contract's arbitration clause and that Z would be obligated to honor the obligations of Y vis-à-vis the claimant.

However, while the tribunal considers that, according to the law of the State of New York and Belgian law, Z is to be held responsible in relation to the contract and the agreement ..., the decision to this effect must in the first place be based on the law applicable to the international commercial community. It believes that, for the reasons already mentioned above ..., it is this law that must guide the decision of the tribunal. There is no doubt that the international community has developed a law in relation to this question. In many international disputes, arbitral tribunals, while applying international principles, have lifted the corporate veil. It is important to remember the remarkable precedent and to emphasize the authority of the decision taken by a group of distinguished arbitrators (Professors Sanders, Goldman and Vasseur) in the case of *Dow Chemical v. Isover Saint Gobain, ICC Case No. 4131* (1982). In this case, the tribunal, in lifting the corporate veil, according to international principles, stated that:

> "The decisions of these tribunals ... have progressively formed an established jurisprudence which should be taken into account since the jurisprudence has taken to heart the consequences of the economic reality and is in conformity with the needs of international commerce, which must respond to specific rules, themselves progressively elaborated, by international arbitration."

Significantly, in the case determined by that tribunal, the principal circumstances on which the tribunal was founded were that the subsidiary of which the corporate veil were to be lifted was part of a company group that constituted "one and the same economic reality" and that the parent company exercised such total control over the subsidiary that it executed and terminated contracts of its subsidiary. By way of comparison, in the present case, as we see above ..., there are numerous significant circumstances which provide even more reasons to lift the corporate veil. For other international precedents of application of international principles to this question. *See also Westland Helicopters Limited vs. AOI, etc., ICC Case No. 3879/AS*, in which the tribunal, confronted with an international entity deprived of financial resources, declared liable the states which created that entity and considered that: "Equity, in common with the principles of international law, allows the corporate veil to be lifted, in order to protect third parties against an abuse which would be to their detriment." ...

JUDGMENT OF 30 MAY 1994
XX Y.B. Comm. Arb. 745 (1995) (Tokyo High Ct.)

[excerpted above at pp. 288-90]

PETERSON FARMS INC. v. C&M FARMING LTD
[2004] 1 Lloyd's Rep. 603 (Comm) (English High Ct.)

MR. JUSTICE LANGLEY. The claimant ("Peterson") seeks a declaration that certain findings in an ICC Arbitration Award were made without jurisdiction. The application is made under §67 of the Arbitration Act 1996 [excerpted in Documentary Supplement at p. 131].

The arbitration involved a claim for damages by the respondent ("C&M") as claimant against Peterson as respondent arising out of the sale by Peterson of live poultry. C&M is an Indian company. It changed its name from "Nasik" in the course of the material events. Peterson is a company organized under the laws of the State of Arkansas, U.S.A. The sales of poultry were made under a written contract entitled "Sales Right Agreement" made on September 7, 1996 ("the Agreement"). Clause 17 of the Agreement provided that: "All disputes ... which may arise between the parties out of or in relation to or in connection with this agreement or for the breach thereof, shall be finally settled by International

Chamber of Commerce, U.K." Clause 19 of the Agreement provided: "This agreement shall be interpreted and construed in accordance with the laws of Arkansas, U.S.A."

The poultry was infected with an avian virus. C&M claimed some U.S. $16 million in damages. C&M initiated the arbitration by a Request dated April 27, 2000. The appointed tribunal was Joel Hirschhorn, Judge Abraham Gafni and Julian D.M. Lew as Chairman.... The Final Award ... was dated March 10, 2003. The tribunal awarded C&M damages in the sum of U.S. $6,747,217.

Under the Agreement Peterson sold to C&M male "grandparent" birds. C&M mated the birds to produce "parent" males which it would sell on as hatching eggs or day-old chicks. Those sales were made both to other "C&M group entities" (60 per cent) and (40 per cent) to other purchasers. The other C&M group entities used the parent males to breed with parent females to produce broiler chicks which they would sell on as chicks or hatching eggs. The award of damages was made up of two parts: i. Losses suffered by C&M itself, consisting of lost sales because of the reduced numbers of parent male chicks and hatching eggs it was able to produce and lost market share and loss of future profits. The total of this award ("the grandparent loss") was U.S. $1,222,448. There is no challenge to this part of the award. ii. Losses suffered by the other C&M group entities consisting also of lost sales, lost market share and loss of future profits ("the parent losses") in the total sum of U.S. $5,524,768. It is this part of the award which is the subject of Peterson's challenge. Essentially it is Peterson's submission that the tribunal had no jurisdiction to entertain claims by entities which were not named as parties to the Agreement.

The jurisdiction issue was before the tribunal itself. Entirely sensibly, it was agreed that the issue should be dealt with in the course of the hearing and in the award.... The tribunal had jurisdiction to rule on its own substantial jurisdiction as there was no contrary agreement: §30. It ... dealt with jurisdiction in its award on the merits: pars. 78 to 102 and Section Fa of the Final Award. It ruled that it did have jurisdiction to consider and determine the damages claims of the other entities not named as parties to the Agreement....

The tribunal decided that it had jurisdiction on two bases: i. First, and primarily, by application of what has come to be known as "the group of companies doctrine." The "doctrine" finds its origin in the [*Interim ICC Award in Case No. 4131*] in which the claimants were a number of companies in the Dow Chemical "group;" and ii. Second, on the basis that C&M entered into the Agreement as agent for the other entities in the group who were thus parties to the Agreement and the arbitration clause contained in it....

The tribunal recorded Peterson's submissions that C&M had not mentioned a principal and agent relationship and that reliance on the group of companies doctrine was misplaced because identification of the parties to the Agreement was a matter of substantive law governed by Arkansas law. The Award continues:

"86. The tribunal does not accept Peterson's arguments. Under the doctrine of separability, an arbitration agreement is separable and autonomous from the underlying contract in which it appears. The autonomy of arbitration agreements has become a universal principle in the realm of international commercial arbitration. A corollary to the separability doctrine is that the law applicable to the arbitration agreement may differ from the law applicable both to the substance of the contract underlying the dispute and to the arbitral proceedings themselves. The right of C&M to make claims for the C&M Group is a question of interpretation of the arbitration agreement contained in the Agreement, including the intention of the parties. In the absence of any choice of law made by the parties with regard to the arbitration agreement itself, this tribunal will determine this question in accordance with the common intent of the parties.

87. The Tribunal considers that Peterson was aware throughout the negotiating period and at the time of contracting that it was dealing with the C&M Group. Furthermore, Peterson intended to deal with C&M Group. This is apparent from the correspondence and internal reports [and a draft Sales Right Agreement]....

92. The Tribunal considers that it was logical to have the name of one member of that group as the contracting partner with Peterson. One company had to take formal legal responsibility for the contract with Peterson. C&M Group, as such, was not a legal entity and therefore could not contract in its own name. There would have been greater uncertainty had it sought to do so. Nasik contracted on behalf of and as agent for the whole C&M Group. This was clearly understood by Peterson.

93. The Tribunal does not consider that it is legally precluded from considering C&M's damages claims to cover and embrace the damages of all C&M Group companies. The group of companies doctrine provides that an arbitration agreement signed by one company in a group of companies entitles (or obligates) affiliate non-signatory companies, if the circumstances surrounding negotiation, execution and termination of the agreement show that the mutual intention of all the parties was to bind the non-signatories. Following the *Dow Chemical* decision ... the Tribunal recognised that because a group of companies constitute the same "economic reality" one company in the group can bind the other members to an agreement if such a result conforms to the mutual intentions of all the parties and reflects the good usage of international commerce. The Tribunal considers that such circumstances are present in this case....

96.... Thus, Peterson was aware not only of the integrated nature of the poultry business but also that an agreement with Nasik would impact the operations of all of the C&M Group.... Peterson, therefore, was aware of the integrated nature of the poultry business. It also fully recognised and expected that on the international level, providing grandparent level stock to a company like Nasik was but the first step in the process under which Nasik would, through the integrated complex of businesses of which it was a part, complete the further production and distribution of the Peterson Breed. In short, it understood that the Agreement with Nasik was, in effect, an agreement with and would impact the operations of all the entities comprising the C&M Group.

100. In summary, the record of correspondence between the parties and internal documents of Peterson, the preliminary documents exchanged between the parties, and the general nature of the poultry business demonstrate that Peterson intended to enter into and perform under a contract with all the entities forming the C&M Group of companies. Peterson knew that it was contracting with the group as a whole and that its product would be used in an integrated operation that involved all members of the C&M Group. The Tribunal considers that C&M is fully entitled to claim all damages suffered by the C&M Group and arising out of the contractual relationship with Peterson...."

In my judgment, the tribunal's approach to the issue is open to a number of substantial criticisms and is seriously flawed in law. The predicate (par. 86) of the tribunal's approach was that the Agreement contained no choice of law with regard to the arbitration agreement in cl. 17. Yet, as the tribunal also and rightly recognized, the issue raised a question of interpretation of the Agreement and such questions were expressly subject to Arkansas law by cl. 19. The identification of the parties to an agreement is a question of substantive not procedural law.

"The autonomy" of the arbitration agreement is not in point. The question is whether it is governed by Arkansas law. In my judgment it plainly is. There was, therefore, no basis for the tribunal to apply any other law whether supposedly derived from "the common intent of the parties" or not. The common intent was indeed expressed in the Agreement: that is both English and Arkansas law. The "law" the tribunal derived from its approach was not the proper law of the Agreement nor even the law of the chosen place of the arbitration but, in effect, the group of companies doctrine itself.

[The C&M group] submitted that the tribunal's approach was in accord with §46 of the 1996 Act. It is not. Section 46(1)(a) sets out the basic rule that the tribunal "shall" decide the dispute in accordance with the law chosen by the parties as applicable to the substance of the dispute. That was Arkansas law. Section 46(1)(b) provides only that "if the parties agree" the tribunal shall decide in accordance with that agreement. There was no relevant agreement within this provision. It was (a) not (b) which should have been applied.

The reference to an early draft of the Agreement ... is in fact mistaken. Not only was the draft just that, but it in fact named as party another supposed corporate entity "C&M Group" which it transpired did not exist. C&M was the named party in the final agreement in recognition of that.

The reasoning of the tribunal in par. 92 is in my judgment [also inconsistent]. Far from there being "greater uncertainty" had the Agreement named "C&M Group" as a party, on the tribunal's reasoning that would have been both accurate and well understood. In contrast the nomination of Nasik on that reasoning created or at least increased any uncertainty. The last two sentences of par. 92 represent all that the tribunal said about "agency." Not only do those sentences ignore the fact that no case in agency was ever advanced by C&M before the tribunal but had there been an agency relationship between C&M and "the whole C&M Group" there would have been no need for C&M to advance the Group of Companies doctrine as it did nor for "one company to take formal legal responsibility for the contract." That company could indeed have signed as agent as well as for itself. In my judgment, therefore, the tribunal's award on this issue cannot stand....

It was not suggested to the tribunal that the Group of Companies doctrine was recognized by Arkansas law. The witness statements prepared for this appeal by Ms. Stewart and Mr. Hollingsworth addressing Arkansas law are plainly at odds on a number of matters. Those matters include the question whether or not Arkansas law would by one legal route or another permit resort by the tribunal to the doctrine.... In the context of the Group of Companies doctrine the agreement was that Arkansas law was the same as English law. As I have already said, English law treats the issue as one subject to the chosen proper law of the Agreement and that excludes the doctrine which forms no part of English law.

The principles of the law of agency in Arkansas law are also in substance the same as those of English law. The questions whether there is a relationship of principal and agent and whether an agent acted as such are questions of fact. Unsurprisingly, as agency was not alleged or addressed in the evidence before the tribunal, there was no evidence to establish either fact. Indeed the evidence and commercial reality was to the contrary and there is no further evidence on the matter before me.

The Agreement itself is drafted and signed in terms of an agreement between the two named companies. Clause 10 forbad assignment of the rights acquired by C&M to any other entity. It contains no reference to any other companies or entities. It is true ... that the restriction on C&M selling any other "meat-type Male Parent" in Clause 6 was arguably ineffective unless it applied to other group entities but I think that is of no real significance. Clause 12, in contrast, restricted sales by C&M of "Peterson Male Parents" to third parties outside the agreed territory "directly or indirectly." The evidence was that C&M itself sold parent chicks to other group entities which bought them from C&M. That was the basis on which, albeit not pursued or proved before the tribunal, it was said that C&M was liable to indemnify those entities. It was also the basis on which C&M itself recovered damages (included in the award which is not challenged) for the loss of sales to those entities. That is consistent with the relationship of buyer and seller, not principal and agent, along the chain starting with C&M purchasing the grandparent chicks from Peterson.

In commercial terms the creation of a corporate structure is by definition designed to create separate legal entities for entirely legitimate purposes which would often if not usually be defeated by any general agency relationship between them. Moreover the corollary of C&M acting as agent for the other group entities named would be that those entities would themselves be bound by C&M's obligations under the Agreement, including the obligation to pay for the chicks. That would extend, for example, to Mr. D'Souza personally insofar as he was a partner in any of those entities.... [T]he only identification of those entities for which it is said C&M acted as agent in entering into the Agreement are those who happened subsequently to suffer losses when the infected poultry was delivered. In my judgment the Award cannot be sustained on the basis of agency. There is no evidence to support it and the evidence there is contradicts it....

Peterson is entitled to have that part of the Award which awarded payment of losses by other C&M group entities set aside for want of jurisdiction....

JUDGMENT OF 17 FEBRUARY 2011, GOV'T OF PAKISTAN, MIN. OF RELIGIOUS AFFAIRS v. DALLAH REAL ESTATE & TOURISM HLDG CO.
XXXVI Y.B. Comm. Arb. 590 (Paris Cour d'appel)

I. Sole Ground for Annulment: Lack of Arbitration Agreement (Art. 1502(1) [N]CCP) [6]
The Government of Pakistan, Ministry of Religious Affairs (the "MORA") claims that the arbitration clause in the Agreement of 10 September 1996 cannot be invoked against it; in its opinion, the arbitral tribunal held that it had jurisdiction by mistakenly finding that in accordance with transnational principles the MORA is but a ministerial department of the Government of Pakistan without an autonomous juridical personality, and further that it was the Pakistani party to the Memorandum of Understanding ("MOU") that preceded the Agreement. The MORA contends that the [MOU] of 24 July 1995 and the Agreement of 10 September 1996 are completely independent, that the MOU expired before the creation of the Trust and was replaced by the Agreement; that it was neither the intention nor the common will of the parties that the MORA be a party thereto; that arbitration clauses must be interpreted strictly, and that the Agreement was signed only by the Trust created by the Government of Pakistan for the financial and material organization of pilgrimages of its nationals to Mecca.

---

6. Article 1502(1) of the French [New] Code of Civil Procedure provide[d]:

"Appeal of a court decision granting recognition or enforcement is only available on the following grounds: (1) if the arbitrator has rendered his decision in the absence of an arbitration agreement or on the basis of an arbitration agreement that is invalid or that has expired;...."

The MORA argues that the First Award shows that there were differences among the arbitrators and that [arbitrators] Shah and Mustill only agreed after hesitations with the conclusion that [the MORA] was a party to the Agreement and thus to the dispute. Claimant adds that the English court seized by Dallah with proceedings to enforce the final award [denied leave to recognize and enforce the award] in the United Kingdom at the request of the Government of Pakistan, that the Court of Appeal confirmed this decision on 20 July 2009 and that the Supreme Court rejected Dallah's appeal on 3 November 2010.

By a letter of 16 February 1995 …, Dallah informed the MORA that the King of Saudi Arabia and the Keeper of the Holy Sites entrusted [Dallah] with the maintenance of those sites and that [Dallah] was authorized to offer a long-term lease of a complex for hosting pilgrims to Islamic governments. It proposed to the Government of Pakistan to lease several plots of land at Mecca on which Dallah would build a housing complex; Dallah would also provide financing. On 15 July 1995, Dallah submitted the financial conditions for the project to the [Pakistani] Ministry of Finances. The project was concretely realized by the conclusion of a MOU on 24 July 1995 between the President of the Republic of Pakistan, through Mr. Lutfullah Mufti, Secretary of the MORA, on the one hand, and Dallah, through Mr. Nackvi, on the other.

Dallah undertook under the MOU to purchase plots of land at Mecca and build lodgings thereon for Pakistani pilgrims; [the lodgings] were to be leased to the Government of Pakistan for 99 years. Dallah would also provide the financing for the operation as provided for in its offer of 16 February 1995. Pursuant to Art. 4 of the MOU, Dallah was to supply within 90 days to the Government of Pakistan, for its approval, the terms and conditions of the lease and the financing plan; pursuant to Art. 5, the financing was to be given to an entity ("the Borrower") designated by the Government of Pakistan. Pursuant to Art. 28, the Government of Pakistan reserved the faculty to grant the managing and the maintenance of the housing complex to one or more persons or legal entities or to a Trust, which would be the Borrower.

Since the signature of the MOU on 24 July 1995 until the signature of the Agreement, Dallah had dealings only with the Government of Pakistan, to which it sent the draft lease between the Government of Pakistan and Dallah on 17 August 1995. The financial proposal was not approved by the Government, and the MOU expired on 17 November 1995.

The President of the Islamic Republic of Pakistan issued an ordnance [sic] on 31 January 1996, notified on 14 February 1996, which created a Trust called Awami Hajj Trust, a "statutory corporation" under Pakistani law having essentially the aim of "mobilizing the savings of pilgrims," "financing the costs of the pilgrimage," investing the savings of the pilgrims in order to "obtain maximum returns and compound interest" and taking and "adopting measures facilitating the realization of the pilgrimage by the members." Art. 10 of the Ordnance [sic] provided that the Trust would have at its disposal a fund, the Awami Hajj Fund, financed by savings of pilgrims, donations and investment income managed by a bank (the Trustee Bank) which would be responsible for collecting the savings and investing the assets of the fund. The Trust was incorporated; the Minister of Religious Affairs, the secretary of the MORA, Mr. Lutfullah Mufti, and the Minister of Finances were members of its Board of Trustees.

During the pre-contractual phase, which lasted over six months, Dallah detailed in several correspondences the roles assigned to the future contracting parties—collecting savings of pilgrims and donations by the Trust, advance by Dallah given to the Trust, guarantee by the Government of Pakistan for the reimbursement of Dallah's US$ 100 million financing. In Mr. Nackvi's letter of 29 February 1996 and its annexe A, Dallah described its financing plan and expressly proposed to the Government of Pakistan a second option, for five years from the signature of the Agreement, in view of the construction of additional lodgings for 45,000 pilgrims. The financial division of the MORA asked questions in respect of this proposal in a letter of 4 April 1996.

The MORA also relies on a letter of 15 March 1996 to the Al Rajhi Banking and Investment Group, in which Dallah presented the fund indicating the Trust as the Pakistani contracting party, in support of its argument that Dallah accepted that [the MORA] was the only co-contracting party. However, on 4 April [1996] the MORA wrote to the presidents of [certain] banks, inviting them to express their interest to become the Trustee Bank, indicating that "the Government wishes to appoint as Trustee Bank...." On 14 April, the Albaraka Islamic Investment Bank of the Dallah group [the Albaraka Bank] presented its candidacy to the MORA, which accepted delivery [of the offer] on 23 April and invited Mr. Nackvi to present his proposal at the Ministry's offices. After exchanging several communications—particularly a letter of Dallah to the MORA dated 23 May 1996, recording the discussions which took place with the Ministry of Finances—on 30 July 1996 the MORA, on stationery of the Government of Pakistan, informed Dallah that the Albaraka Bank had been appointed and confirmed that it agreed with the "B plan" proposed by Dallah, concerning the free lodging of 12,000 pilgrims for the "Government of Pakistan," with "the Government of Pakistan" having to pay US$ 395 per pilgrim for the remaining pilgrims."

It is true that when presenting the contractual provisions to its lawyers, who were charged with drafting the Agreement, Dallah mentioned the Trust as the Pakistani party, but the negotiations took place solely between Dallah and the MORA, not the Trust, until the day before the Agreement was signed (letter of 8 September 1996 of Dallah to the Ministry). Moreover, on 30 July 1996 Mr. Nackvi clearly indicated to the president of the Dallah group that approving the envisaged financial operation was the Ministry's decision and informed him that the Prime Minister would hold a meeting on this issue on 15 June. In fact, a press article of 17 July 1996 tells of the meeting of the Board of Trustees, presided by the Prime Minister of Pakistan, who was not, however, one of its members.

The MORA argues that since the Trust, which was juridically and financially independent, concluded the Agreement, including the arbitration clause, with Dallah, "the acts of the Trust cannot be attributed to the Government of Pakistan," which excludes that it was "the true party to the Agreement," and that this was the common intention of the parties.

However, in the period of contractual performance, two functionaries of the MORA who held no position within the Trust addressed to Dallah within six weeks of each other, on 26 September and 4 November 1996, letters concerning the savings plans which were to be offered to the pilgrims, the announcement of the advertising information campaign to be launched by the Albaraka Bank to make itself known as the Trustee Bank with the public, and a request for a copy of the agreement between the [Albaraka Bank] and the Muslim Commercial Bank concerning the use of [the latter's] network of agencies for collecting the savings. No reason can justify the intervention of these two state functionaries.

Further, the Trust ceased to legally exist on 12 December 1996 because the presidential decree was not re-issued.

On 19 January 1997, Mr. Lutfullah Mufti informed Dallah, on stationery of the MORA, that: "according to the above-mentioned Agreement for the lease of a lodgings complex in the holy city of Mecca, you were obliged, within 90 days from the Agreement, to have the detailed specifications approved by the Trust" and "you failed in your obligation to supply the specifications and plans for the approval of the Trust, you are in breach of a fundamental clause of the Agreement which equals a repudiation of the totality of the Agreement, a repudiation that is accepted hereby." No confusion is possible because Mr. Lutfullah Mufti was also secretary of the Board of Trustees or because the Trust did not have its own stationery. Everything in this letter indicates in what quality the Ministry in whose name he accepts the repudiation of the Agreement acted.

It is irrelevant in this respect that Mr. Lutfullah commenced proceedings in an Islamabad court in the name of the Trust. By having its high official denounce Dallah's breach of contract on 19 January 1997, the MORA behaved as if it were a party to the Agreement.

This involvement of the MORA, without there being record of acts performed by the Trust, as well as [the MORA's] behavior at the time of the pre-contractual negotiations, confirm that the creation of the Trust was purely formal and that the MORA, as argued by Dallah, behaved as the true Pakistani party to the financial operation.

As a consequence, the [Government of Pakistan's claim] that the arbitral tribunal incorrectly extended the arbitration clause to the MORA and held that it had jurisdiction is unfounded. Hence, the applications for setting aside the award on jurisdiction of 26 June 2001 rendered in Paris and consequently the two following awards of 19 January 2004 and 23 June 2006 are dismissed....

DALLAH REAL ESTATE & TOURISM HOLDING CO. v. MINISTRY OF RELIGIOUS AFFAIRS, GOVERNMENT OF PAKISTAN

[2010] UKSC 46 (U.K. S.Ct.)

[excerpted above at pp. 247-70]

NOTES

1. *Only parties to arbitration agreement are bound or entitled to arbitrate.* Consider the language of Article II(1) of the New York Convention and Article 7(1) of the UNCITRAL Model Law. Article II(1) of the Convention provides that Contracting States "shall recognize an agreement in writing under which *the parties* undertake to submit [their disputes] to arbitration," while Article 7(1) of the Model Law defines an arbitration agreement as "an agreement by *the parties* to submit to arbitration all or certain disputes which have arisen or which may arise *between them*." Note the courts' analyses in *Bridas* and *Peterson Farms*. As with Article II(1) and Article 7(1), both courts refuse to require (or permit) entities that are not parties to the arbitration agreement to arbitrate. Is there any question but that an arbitration agreement only binds (and benefits) the parties to that agreement? Is any other approach conceivable?

   Note that in national court litigation, all entities that are involved in a dispute will ordinarily be subject to joinder in litigation concerning the dispute. Consider the following:

   "Contrary to litigation in front of state courts where any interested party can join or be adjoined to protect its interests, in arbitration only those who are parties to the arbitration agreement expressed in writing could appear in the arbitral proceedings either as claimants or as defendants. This basic rule, inherent in the essentially voluntary nature of arbitration, is recognized internationally by virtue of Article II of the New York Convention." *Banque Arabe et Internationale d'Investissement v. Inter-Arab Inv. Guar. Corp.*, *Ad Hoc Award of 17 November 1994,* XXI Y.B. Comm. Arb. 13, 18 (1996).

Can you imagine a different approach to the question of who is bound or benefitted by an arbitration agreement? What if any entity whose presence would materially contribute to expeditious, final resolution of the dispute could be joined to, or could join, an arbitration, regardless whether that entity had consented to arbitrate? Are there suggestions of such an approach in *ICC Case No. 4131* and *ICC Case No. 8385*?

2. *Signatories to "arbitration agreement."* What is the most obvious, and reliable, way to determine who the parties to an arbitration agreement are? Is it not by ascertaining what parties have expressed their consent to be bound by the agreement, by executing the agreement to arbitrate? Consider the courts' remarks on this issue in *Bridas* and *Dallah*. (Recall also the formal requirements of the New York Convention and many arbitration statutes, *supra* pp. 375-92 & *infra* pp. 586-58, often requiring that arbitration agreements be signed.)

How frequently are arbitration agreements—as distinguished from the underlying contract with which they are associated—actually signed? In fact, it is very rare for parties to separately sign their agreements to arbitrate, instead executing the contract in which an arbitration clause appears. How then does one determine the "signatories" to an agreement to arbitrate? Does this question present any real practical difficulty? Consider the following analysis from one arbitral award:

> "It is generally accepted that if a third party is bound by the same obligations stipulated by a party to a contract and this contract contains an arbitration clause or, in relation to it, an arbitration agreement exists, such a third party is also bound by the arbitration clause, or arbitration agreement, even if it did not sign it." *Award in ICC Case No. 9762,* XXIX Y.B. Comm. Arb. 26 (2004).

Is there any reason to think that someone who signs a contract containing an arbitration clause does not mean for its signature to constitute consent to the clause?

3. *Non-signatories may be bound by arbitration agreement.* Although the most common manner in which a party may be bound by an arbitration agreement is by signing it, this is not the only way to become a party to an agreement to arbitrate. Consider the court's comment in *Bridas* that "federal courts have held that so long as there is some written agreement to arbitrate, a third party may be bound to submit to arbitration. Ordinary principles of contract and agency law may be called upon to bind a non-signatory to an agreement whose terms have not clearly done so."

How is it that general "principles of contract and agency law" apply to bind a non-signatory to an agreement to arbitrate? In particular, is a non-signatory bound by the arbitration clause because the non-signatory becomes a party to the underlying contract (for example, if the underlying contract is assigned to a non-signatory or because a non-signatory merges with a signatory)? Or is a non-signatory bound by the arbitration clause because it becomes a party only to the arbitration agreement itself? Or are both avenues possible ways for a non-signatory to be bound by an arbitration agreement?

4. *Distinction between jurisdiction and substantive liability.* Note that it is possible for a non-signatory to be bound by an underlying commercial contract, but not the associated arbitration clause. Note, conversely, that a non-signatory might be bound by an arbitration clause, but not the associated commercial contract. Construct hypotheticals in which each result is plausible. Consider the discussion of this issue in *ICC Case No. 8385.*

5. *Alter ego status or veil-piercing as basis for subjecting a non-signatory to arbitration agreement.* A number of authorities have concluded that a party that has not executed or otherwise directly assented to a contract containing an arbitration provision may nonetheless be bound by the provision, albeit only in exceptional cases, if that party is an "alter ego" of an entity that did execute the agreement. Phrased differently, an entity may be bound by an agreement (including an arbitration agreement) executed by a corporate affiliate if its "corporate veil" is "pierced," subjecting one party to the contractual and other liabilities of the first. The ICJ has explained the doctrine as follows:

> "the process of 'lifting the corporate veil' or 'disregarding the legal entity' has been found justified and equitable in certain circumstances or for certain purposes. The wealth of practice already accumulated on the subject in municipal law indicates that the veil is lifted, for instance, to prevent misuse of the privileges of legal personality, as in certain cases of fraud or malfeasance, to protect third persons such as creditor or purchaser, or to prevent the evasion of legal requirements or of obligations." *Case Concerning the Barcelona Traction, Light & Power Co.*, 1970 I.C.J. 3, 38-39 (I.C.J.).

Consider the comparable discussions of the veil-piercing doctrine in *Bridas* and *ICC Case No. 8385.*

(a) *Standard for establishing alter ego status.* Standards for veil-piercing or alter ego status vary, in and among different legal systems, but generally require evidence that one entity dominated the day-to-day actions of another entity and/or that it exercised this power to work fraud or other serious injustice upon a third party. Consider the standards that are set forth in *Bridas* and *ICC Case No. 8385.* How do they differ? How are they similar?

(b) *Presumption of separate corporate identity.* The standard for establishing alter ego status or piercing the corporate veil in most legal systems is difficult to satisfy. The starting point is a strong presumption that a parent corporation and its affiliates are legally separate and distinct entities and that a company is legally independent from its shareholders. *See, e.g., Bridas*, 345 F.3d at 356 ("presumption of independent status"); *Am. Renaissance Lines, Inc. v. Saxis SS Co.*, 502 F.2d 674, 677 (2d Cir. 1974) ("absent findings of fraud or bad faith, a corporation … is entitled to a presumption of separateness from a sister corporation … even if both are owned and controlled by the same individuals"); *Salomon v. A Salomon & Co Ltd* [1897] AC 22, HL 31 (House of Lords) ("once a company is legally incorporated it must be treated like any other independent person with its rights and liabilities appropriate to itself … whatever may have been the ideas or schemes of those who brought it into existence"). What is the reason for this presumption? Note that: "Normally, the corporation is an insulator from liability on claims of creditors…. Limited liability is the rule not the exception; and on that assumption large undertakings are rested, vast enterprises are launched, and huge sums of capital attracted." *Anderson v. Abbott*, 321 U.S. 349, 362 (1944). Compare the similar reasoning in *Bridas* and *Peterson Farms*. Does this rationale really apply to veil-piercing for jurisdictional purposes (as distinguished from veil-piercing to impose substantive liability)?

(c) *Standards for overcoming presumption of separate corporate identity*. Although standards in various jurisdictions differ, most authorities have held that two basic inquiries are relevant to overcoming the presumption of separate corporate identity: (i) the extent of domination and control of a corporate affiliate, including disregard of corporate formalities; and (ii) fraudulent or otherwise abusive misuse of that control to the injury of adverse parties. *See, e.g., Faiza Ben Hashem v. Abdulhadi Ali Shayif* [2008] EWHC 2380, ¶¶166-184 (English High Ct.) ("in the various cases to which I have referred, the attempt to pierce the veil succeeded only in … cases [involving] the twin features of *control* and *impropriety*"; "[t]hese cases can be contrasted with the cases where the claim failed … each of these cases lacked at least one of the necessary ingredients"). See also cases referred to in G. Born, *International Commercial Arbitration* 1431-44 (2d ed. 2014). Why is not one company's "domination" of another sufficient to pierce the corporate veil—why is some form of abusive conduct also typically required? Should it be? Should the standard for piercing the corporate veil be different for jurisdictional purposes (*i.e.*, for binding a party to an arbitration agreement) than for purposes of substantive liability (*i.e.*, for holding a party liable for breaches of the underlying contract)?

Consider the following rationale, from a maritime award made in a U.S.-seated arbitration:

> "It has been argued by some that the charter party arbitration simply provides for the adjudication of disputes between Owner and Charterer and that no other party may enter the proceedings unless it does so with the express consent of the two so named…. [I]t is neither sensible nor practical to exclude the claims of companies who have an interest in the venture and who are members of the same corporate family. The practicality of such an approach is apparent. The major shipping organizations often charter through a subsidiary company, ship their cargoes through another and sometimes consign them to other related companies. To consider the arbitration clause as one which limits the right to arbitrate to the chartering subsidiary and to no other company within the same corporate family involved in the venture is to narrowly restrict the parties' apparent intention to arbitrate their differences. We consider our conclusion in this respect to be consistent with the more recent court decisions in on this matter. [The tribunal held that all members of the Mobil Oil Group were bound by the arbitration clause.]" *MAP Tankers, Inc. v. Mobil Tankers, Ltd, Partial Final Award in SMA Case No. 1510 of 28 November 1980*, VII Y.B. Comm. Arb. 151 (1982).

Is that rationale persuasive? Is it alter ego analysis? Or something else?

Should the standards for veil-piercing be lower in tort cases? Consider *Adams v. Cape Indus. plc* [1990] Ch. 433, 545 (English Ct. App.), where the technical application of the veil-piercing doctrine had the effect that hundreds of employees suffering from an incurable professional disease were denied enforcement of the judgment awarding them compensation ("we do not accept as a matter of law that the court is entitled to lift the corporate veil as against a defendant company which is the member of a corporate group merely because the corporate structure has been used so as to ensure that the legal liability (if any) in respect of particular future activities of the group (and correspondingly the risk of enforcement of that liability) will fall on another member of the group rather than the defendant company. Whether or not this is desirable, the right to use a corporate structure in this manner is inherent in our corporate law. Mr. Morison urged on us that the purpose of the operation was in substance that Cape would have the practical benefit of the group's asbestos trade in the United States of America without the risks of tortious liability. This may be so. However, in our judgment, Cape was in law entitled to organise the group's affairs in that manner and ... to expect that the court would apply the principle of *Salomon v. A. Salomon & Co. Ltd* [1897] A.C. 22 in the ordinary way"). The court applied the rule that, in order for the veil to be pierced, the requirement that the company structure has been used in order to evade an existing liability should be satisfied. Consider the facts and the procedural history of *Adams v. Cape*—can it be said that the liability in question was purely a future one? Where is the borderline?

(d) *Factors relevant to control or domination.* Different authorities have identified a variety of factors that are relevant to establishing control or domination for purposes of piercing the corporate veil. Note the various factors identified in *Bridas* and *ICC Case No. 8385.* For additional lists, see *Carte Blanche (Singapore) Pte Ltd v. Diners Club Int'l, Inc.*, 2 F.3d 24 (2d Cir. 1993) (absence of corporate formalities; inadequate capitalization; financial dealings between parent and subsidiary; overlap in ownership, officers, directors, and personnel; common office space, address, and phone numbers; business discretion of allegedly dominated company; whether companies deal with each other at arms' length; whether companies are separate profit centers; parent's payment or guarantee of subsidiary's debts; subsidiary's use of parent's property); G. Born, *International Commercial Arbitration* 1431-44 (2d ed. 2014). How do these factors compare to those relevant to the "group of companies" doctrine?

(e) *Showing of fraud or its equivalent.* Even if a company is controlled or dominated by another company or individual, many authorities (including *Bridas*) hold that there must be a showing of fraud or similarly abusive conduct in order to bind a non-signatory to an arbitration agreement. *Freeman v. Complex Computing Co.*, 119 F.3d 1044, 1053 (2d Cir. 1997) ("While complete domination of the corporation is the key to piercing the corporate veil, ... such domination, standing alone, is not enough; some showing of a wrongful or unjust act toward plaintiff is required."); *Interocean Shipping Co. v. Nat'l Shipping & Trading Corp.*, 523 F.2d 527, 539 (2d Cir. 1975) (even if company has "no mind of its own," showing of fraud or something akin to fraud is needed); *Judgment of 11 June 1991, Orri v. Société des Lubrifiants Elf Aquitaine*, 1992 Rev. arb. 73 (French Cour de cassation civ. 1e); *Ord v. Belhaven Pubs Ltd* [1998] 2 BCLC 447 (English Ct. App.) ("The approach of the judge in the present case was simply to look to the economic unit, to disregard the distinction between the legal entities that were involved and then to say: since the company cannot pay, the shareholders ... should be made to pay instead. That of course is radically at odds with the whole concept of corporate personality and limited liability and the decision of the House of Lords in *Salomon v. Salomon* [1897] AC 22. On the question of lifting the corporate veil ... they were of the view that there must be some impropriety before the corporate veil can be pierced.... in the present case no impropriety is alleged"). Other authorities (in some countries) hold, however, that a sufficient showing of control and domination or other factors may independently justify piercing the corporate veil. *See, e.g., Middendorf v. Fuqua Indus., Inc.*, 623 F.2d 13, 17 (6th Cir. 1980); *Del Santo v. Bristol County Stadium, Inc.*, 273 F.2d 605, 608 (1st Cir. 1960); P. I. Blumberg *et al., Blumberg on Corporate Groups* Chapter 12 (2005 & Update 2014); Strasser, *Piercing the Veil in Corporate Groups*, 37 Conn. L. Rev. 637 (2005) (citing cases). Which approach is wiser?

(f) *Law applicable to veil-piercing.* What law applies to determine whether the corporate veil may be pierced? What law is applied in *Bridas*? In *ICC Case No. 8385*? Why? Consider also *ICC Case No. 8163*, 16(2) ICC ICArb. Bull. 77 (2005) (seat in France, applicable substantive law German; German law applied to veil-piercing); *Final Award in ICC Case No. 7626*, in J.-J. Arnaldez, Y. Derains & D. Hascher (eds.), *Collection of ICC Arbitral Awards 1996-2000* 122, 124 (2003) (law applicable to the arbitration clause as chosen by the parties); *Judgment of 16 October 2003*, 22 ASA Bull. 364 (2004) (Swiss Fed. Trib.) (arbitral tribunal applied Lebanese law governing the main contract, interpreting this law in light of *lex mercatoria* being part of French law, which is cognate to Lebanese law); *Aloe Vera of Am., Inc. v. Asianic Food (S) Pte Ltd*, [2006] SGHC 78 (Singapore High Ct.) (law of Arizona, to which the parties subjected the underlying contract).

Is the law applicable to determine whether the corporate veil may be lifted the law of the state of incorporation of the subsidiary company, whose separate corporate identity would be set aside? Is it the law of the place of incorporation (or domicile) of the shareholder, who is to be subjected to the arbitration agreement? Is it the law of the place where the acts of control and/or abusive conduct occurred? Is it the law chosen by the parties' underlying contract? Is the choice of any jurisdiction's law satisfactory in most settings, where conduct occurs in multiple different jurisdictions, without any clear center of gravity? Would it be preferable to apply an international standard of veil-piercing? Is that what was done in *ICC Case No. 8385*? What about in *Bridas*? What does the principle of party autonomy suggest?

Contrast the choice-of-law analysis in *ICC Case No. 8385* and *Aloe Vera v. Asianic Food*. Is the law chosen by the parties to govern their underlying contract a sensible choice for the law governing veil-piercing of one party to the contract?

What considerations are relevant to selecting the law applicable to veil-piercing? Is the fact that the non-signatory in veil-piercing cases usually has a close connection with the controlled signatory persuasive enough to apply the law, in the explicit or implied choice of which the non-signatory formally did not participate? Why or why not?

6. *Agency as basis for subjecting a non-signatory to arbitration agreement.* The simplest, least controversial circumstance in which a non-signatory will be bound by an arbitration agreement is when an agent executes a contract on behalf of its principal. It is well settled, under all developed legal systems, that one party (an "agent") may in certain circumstances legally bind another party (a "principal") by its acts. Among other things, an agent may enter into contracts, which will be legally binding on its

principal, although not necessarily on the agent. *See* G. Born, *International Commercial Arbitration* 1419-20 (2d ed. 2014); Hanotiau, *Problems Raised by Complex Arbitrations Involving Multiple Contracts-Parties-Issues—An Analysis*, 18 J. Int'l Arb. 251, 258-60 (2001).

(a) *Principal bound by arbitration clause in contract executed by agent.* As *Bridas* illustrates, most jurisdictions hold that a principal may be bound by an arbitration clause contained in a contract executed on its behalf by an agent. The least controversial example of this is where a disclosed agent, with all parties' consent, executes an agreement on behalf of its principal, with the purpose of binding (only) its principal. More difficult issues arise, as in *Bridas* and *Peterson Farms*, when one party is alleged, after-the-fact, to have been the undisclosed agent of a non-signatory.

As *Bridas* illustrates, most authorities have applied generally applicable agency law in determining whether a non-signatory is bound by an arbitration agreement. *See InterGen NV v. Grina*, 344 F.3d at 142-43, 147-48 ("[i]t is hornbook law that an agent can commit its (nonsignatory) principal to an arbitration agreement"; applying "traditional principles of agency law"); *Judgment of 22 December 1992*, 14 ASA Bull. 646, 649 (Swiss Fed. Trib.) (1996) (citing generally applicable principle of reliance to conclude that under Spanish law, no special mandate was required for agent to bind principal to arbitration agreement).

(b) *Agent's right to invoke arbitration clause in principal's contract.* In most cases, an agency relationship will be alleged as binding a non-signatory principal to an arbitration clause. That was the result unsuccessfully sought in *Bridas* and *Peterson Farms*. Nonetheless, some authorities have held that an agent may invoke an arbitration clause contained in a contract which it executes on behalf of a principal. *Arnold v. Arnold Corp.*, 920 F.2d 1269, 1282 (6th Cir. 1990) (applying "the well-settled principle affording agents the benefits of arbitration agreements made by their principal"). What is the rationale for such conclusions? Note that, in most cases, there will be no direct evidence of the parties' actual intentions for an agent to be benefitted by its principal's arbitration clause. Why should such an intention be presumed? If an agent is benefitted by an arbitration agreement, is it also bound by that agreement?

(c) *Law applicable to agency relation.* What law applies to determine whether an agency relation, binding a principal to its agent's arbitration agreement, existed? Is it the law governing the validity of the arbitration agreement? The law governing the underlying contract? The law of the agency relation? What does *Bridas* hold? What is the most appropriate choice-of-law rule? Consider the facts in *Peterson Farms*, where the arbitration agreement was held to be governed by Arkansas law. What law would have applied to determine the existence of an agency relationship between C&M and its corporate affiliates?

(d) *Apparent or ostensible authority.* Closely related to agency as a basis for concluding that an entity is party to an arbitration clause is the doctrine of ostensible or apparent authority (sometimes referred to as the "principle of appearance" or "*mandat apparent*"). Under this doctrine, a party may be bound by another entity's acts purportedly on its behalf, even where those acts were unauthorized, if the putative principal created the appearance of authority, leading a counter-party reasonably to believe that authorization actually existed. *See* G. Born, *International Commercial Arbitration* 1424-27 (2d ed. 2014); E. Gaillard & J. Savage (eds.), *Fouchard Gaillard Goldman on International Commercial Arbitration* ¶470 (1999); *Kett v. Shannon*, [1987] ILRM 364, ¶8 (Irish S.Ct.) ("Ostensible authority, on the other hand, derives not from any consensual arrangement between the principal and the agent, but is founded on a representation made by the principal to the third party which is intended to convey, and does convey, to the third party that the arrangement entered into under the apparent authority of the agent will be binding on the principal."). In particular, this theory can bind the "apparent" principal to a contract (including an arbitration clause) entered into putatively on its behalf by the "apparent" agent. Note that the apparent authority doctrine does not rest on principles of consent, but is more akin to estoppel or veil-piercing, by mandating that in certain circumstances a party will be bound by an arbitration agreement even if it did not intend to be. Do the same choice-of-law considerations apply to questions of apparent authority as to questions of actual authority? Are the choice-of-law considerations closer to those in veil-piercing settings?

(e) *Agency and alter ego distinguished.* What is the difference between alter ego and agency theories? Consider application of each theory to the facts in (i) *Bridas*; (ii) *Peterson Farms*; (iii) *ICC Case No. 4131*; and (iv) *ICC Case No. 8385*.

7. *Implied consent.* Under most developed legal systems, an entity may become a party to a contract, including an arbitration agreement, impliedly—typically, either by conduct or non-explicit declarations, as well as by express agreement or formal execution of an agreement. Where a party conducts itself as if it were a party to a commercial contract, by playing a substantial role in negotiations and/or performance of the contract, it may be held to have impliedly consented to be bound by the contract. *See* G. Born, *International Commercial Arbitration* 1427-31 (2d ed. 2014). Which theory does the Paris Cour d'appel apply in *Dallah*, upholding the arbitral award? Is it the alter ego theory? The theory of implied consent? Is it different from the theory relied upon by the arbitral tribunal in the same case?

What law did the arbitral tribunal apply in *Dallah*? What law did the French annulment court apply? The English recognition court?

8. *Guarantor relationship as basis for subjecting non-signatory to arbitration agreement.* Commercial arrangements sometimes involve one party (Party A) guaranteeing the performance or liability of another party (Party B), thereby permitting Party B's contractual counter-party (Party C) to assert claims directly against Party A, in the event of non-performance by Party B. If such a guarantee relationship exists, with respect to a contract containing an arbitration clause, is the guarantor party to that arbitration agreement? Note that the guarantor often will not be a signatory to the guaranteed contract between Party B and Party C.

Most authorities hold that a guarantor relationship may potentially have the effect of making the guarantor a party to an arbitration clause in the underlying contract, but that this is a question of the parties' intentions, which will vary from case to case. *Compare Kvaerner v. Bank of Tokyo Mitsubishi*, 210 F.3d 262, 265 (4th Cir. 2000) (compelling guarantor to arbitrate dispute on underlying contract because guaranty agreement mandated that "the same 'rights and remedies'" be available to parties as under contract) *with Compania Espanola de Petroleos SA v. Nereus Shipping, SA*, 527

F.2d 966, 973 (2d Cir. 1975) ("[t]he determination of whether a guarantor is bound by an arbitration clause contained in the original contract necessarily turns on the language chosen by the parties in the guaranty"; distinguishing broader language in guaranty and arbitration clauses at issue from narrower language of such clauses in other cases). *See* G. Born, *International Commercial Arbitration* 1459-63 (2d ed. 2014).

Note the comment in *Bridas* that the guarantor of a contract "typically" will not be bound by the agreement to arbitrate in that contract. *See supra* p. 554. What justifies this assumption? Isn't the arbitration clause one of the provisions that the guarantor has guaranteed? Suppose the guarantee is reflected in a separate contract between the guarantor and the party benefitting from the guarantee. Suppose the guarantor signs the guaranteed contract, with the statement: "Party A guarantees the full performance of all provisions of the contract." Do the two cases present different considerations?

9. *Transfers of arbitration agreements.* There are a number of circumstances in which an arbitration agreement may be transferred from its original signatories to a non-signatory, resulting in the non-signatory being bound and benefitted by the agreement to arbitrate.

(a) *Assignment of arbitration agreement.* Contracts are frequently transferred from one party to another by way of assignment or novation. In these circumstances, disputes sometimes arise as to whether the transferee or assignee of a contract is bound by an arbitration clause contained in the transferred/assigned agreement. *See* G. Born, *International Commercial Arbitration* 1465-71 (2d ed. 2014); Girsberger & Hausmaninger, *Assignment of Rights and Agreement to Arbitrate*, 8 Arb. Int'l 121 (1992); Yang, *Who Is A Party? The Case of the Non-Signatory (Assignment)*, 2005 Asian Disp. Resol. 43. Should an agreement to arbitrate be assignable? Could one argue that the obligation to arbitrate is "personal" or "unique," and that it should either not be assignable or should be capable of assignment only by very clear language? *See Cotton Club Estates Ltd v. Woodside Estates Co.* [1928] 2 KB 463 (English K.B.) ("The arbitration clause is a personal covenant, and cannot be transferred; nor indeed was it transferred in any sense in this case. The arbitration clause remained in full force and effect as between the original parties").

Most authorities agree that an assignment of a contract should in principle have the effect of transferring the arbitration clause contained in the contract, as one part of the parties' agreement, to the assignee, at least absent some sort of contractual term indicating a contrary intention or some sort of legal prohibition that renders the assignment ineffective. Should there be a presumption that assignment of the underlying contract transfers the arbitration clause? Or the contrary assumption? Or should it simply be a question of the parties' intentions? How likely is it that the parties will express their intentions regarding transfer of the arbitration clause? Suppose that a U.S. company enters into a contract with a German company containing an agreement to arbitrate under CIETAC Rules in China; if one of the parties later assigns the contract to a Chinese state-owned entity, should the arbitration agreement be deemed to have been assigned? Consider: *Award in ICC Case No. 9801*, discussed in Grigera Naón, *Choice-of-Law Problems in International Commercial Arbitration*, 289 Recueil des Cours 9, 147 (2001) ("an arbitration clause must be considered an ancillary right (Nebenrecht) to the assigned principal rights which … follows the assigned rights.").

(b) *Ratification*. A non-signatory party may be bound by an arbitration clause if it has ratified or assumed that provision. *See, e.g., Thomson-CSF, SA v. Am. Arbitration Ass'n*, 64 F.3d 773 (2d Cir. 1995) ("party may be bound by an arbitration clause if its subsequent conduct indicates that it is assuming the obligation to arbitrate"); *Gvozdenovic v. United Air Lines, Inc.*, 933 F.2d 1100, 1105 (2d Cir. 1991); *Day v. Fortune Hi-Tech Mktg*, 2012 WL 588768, at *3 (E.D. Ky.) (non-signatories assented to arbitration clause in contract by ratifying contract through their conduct and accepting benefits thereunder); *Judgment of 19 May 2003*, 22 ASA Bull. 344, 348 (Swiss Fed. Trib.) (2004) ("retroactive approval"). Consider how the separability presumption applies in the context of ratification/assumption. Does every assumption of underlying contractual obligations also constitute an assumption of the arbitration clause? Is some specific assumption of obligations to arbitrate required? Compare the issues raised by guarantees of contractual obligations.

(c) *Merger or universal succession*. It is well settled that an entity that does not execute an arbitration agreement may become a party thereto by way of legal succession. *E.g., Judgment of 19 May 2003*, 22 ASA Bull. 344, 348 (Swiss Fed. Trib.) (2004) ("in principle, an arbitration clause is binding only on those parties which have entered into a contractual agreement to submit to arbitration, whether directly or indirectly through their representatives. Exceptions to this rule arise in cases of legal succession, subsequent ratification of the arbitration clause or piercing the corporate veil of the legal entity in case of abusive denial of the clause."). *See* G. Born, *International Commercial Arbitration* 1463-65 (2d ed. 2014). The most common means of such succession is by a company's merger or combination with the original party to an agreement. If Company Z is merged into Company A, with the latter acquiring all the assets and liabilities of the former, is there any reason to conclude that Company A does not assume the arbitration agreements associated with Company Z's contracts? What law applies to this issue? Is it necessarily the law governing the original agreement to arbitrate?

10. *Corporate officers and directors*. Some national courts have adopted specialized rules with regard to the application of arbitration clauses to officers and directors of companies that have executed the arbitration agreement. In virtually all such cases, the officers and directors of the corporate party will not be parties to the relevant contract. Even in cases where a company's officers or directors execute a contract on behalf of the company, they do not ordinarily thereby become parties to the contract. *See* G. Born, *International Commercial Arbitration* 1478-80 (2d ed. 2014); *Judgment of 23 October 2003, Société Kocak Ilac Fabrikasi AS v. SA Labs. Besins Int'l*, 2006 Rev. arb. 149, 152 (Paris Cour d'appel) (setting aside award against officer of corporate party; officer's "will to be bound by the arbitration agreement could not be inferred only from his signature of the contract."). Suppose litigation relating to the underlying dispute includes the officers and directors (or other agents) of one or both parties, with claims being asserted personally against individual officers and directors. In these cases, officers and directors frequently seek to invoke the arbitration clause (or, conversely, may have the clause invoked against them).

Some courts have permitted the employees of a corporate party to invoke the arbitration clause in that party's underlying commercial contracts, notwithstanding the fact that the individual employees are not parties to the underlying contract under ordinary contractual principles. These decisions have held that corporate employees, sued for actions taken in the course of their employment, may invoke arbitration clauses contained in their employer's contracts with the adverse third party. *Pritzker v. Merrill Lynch, Pierce, Fenner & Smith*, 7 F.3d 1110 (3d Cir. 1993) (company can only act through employees and officers, and "an arbitration agreement would be of little value if it did not extend to them"); *Nesslage v. York Sec., Inc.*, 823 F.2d 231, 233 (8th Cir. 1987) (employees of company that concluded arbitration clause were third-party beneficiaries of agreement).

Consider the treatment of Mr. Feld in *Judgment of 30 May 1994*. Was Mr. Feld a party to the relevant contract? Why was he permitted to invoke the contract's arbitration clause? What is the rationale for extending an agreement to arbitrate to corporate officers and directors? Is it what the parties intended? Intended about their underlying contract or the arbitration agreement? *Compare Westmoreland v. Sadoux*, 299 F.3d 462, 467 (5th Cir. 2002) ("courts must not offer contracts to arbitrate to parties who failed to negotiate them before trouble arrives. To do so frustrates the ability of persons to settle their affairs against a predictable backdrop of legal rules—the cardinal principle to all dispute resolution.").

11. *The "group of companies" doctrine*. The *Dow* award is widely cited as establishing the "group of companies" doctrine. That doctrine holds that companies which form part of an integrated economic "group" ("one and the same economic reality") may, in some circumstances, be bound by one another's arbitration agreements. *See* G. Born, *International Commercial Arbitration* 1444-55 (2d ed. 2014); Savage & Leen, *Family Ties: When Arbitration Agreements Bind Non-Signatory Affiliate Companies*, 2003 Asian Disp. Resol. 16; Wilske, Shore & Ahrens, *The "Group of Companies Doctrine"—Where Is It Headed?*, 17 Am. Rev. Int'l Arb. 73 (2006).

   (a) *Rationale for group of companies doctrine*. What exactly is the rationale for the group of companies doctrine? A more recent award summarizes the theory as follows:

   "When concluding, performing, nonperforming and renegotiating their contractual relations with [defendants], the three claimant companies appear, pursuant to the common intention of all parties engaged in the procedure, to have been real parties to all the contracts. In its formulation and in its spirit, this analysis is based on a remarkable and approved tendency of arbitral rulings favoring acknowledgement, under those circumstances, of the unity of the group.... The security of international commercial relations requires that account should be taken of its economic reality and that all the companies of the group should be held liable one for all and all for one for the debts of which they either directly or indirectly have profited at this occasion." *Award in ICC Case No. 5103*, 1988 J.D.I. 1206 (quoted and translated in Sandrock, *Arbitration Agreements and Groups of Companies*, 27 Int'l Law. 941, 944 (1993)).

   Is this persuasive? Does the group of companies doctrine provide that a non-signatory is bound by the parties' underlying contract? Or does it provide that the non-signatory is bound only by the agreement to arbitrate? Note that the group of companies doctrine was developed in arbitral awards (and has only been applied in that context); in that regard, the doctrine is unlike veil-piercing, agency, assignment, and similar doctrines, which are generally applicable rules, not developed or applicable specifically in arbitral contexts.

Does the group of companies doctrine depend on the parties' intentions? Only the parties' intentions?

(b) *Group of companies doctrine and alter ego theory compared*. Compare the "group of companies" doctrine to the alter ego theory. Which rule is more expansive (i.e., which rule more likely will subject non-signatories to an arbitration agreement)? What precisely was the basis of the award in *Dow*? What if Isover had not asserted in French courts that all the Dow companies were liable under the underlying agreements? How does the group of companies doctrine compare to principles of agency?

(c) *Law applicable to group of companies doctrine*. What law provides the basis for the group of companies doctrine, as formulated in *Dow*? Is it national law or international law? If it is the latter, what are the sources of this law? What law did the *Dow* award apply? Note that the *Dow* arbitration was seated in France. Recall that, under French arbitration law, the law applicable to an international arbitration agreement is "international law," *supra* pp. 307-08, 311-12. Would the tribunal have applied the same law to the group of companies doctrine if it were seated elsewhere—for example, Germany? England?

What law did the court in *Peterson Farms* apply to determine whether the group of companies doctrine could be applied? Note that *Peterson Farms* involved an action to annul an award made in England; suppose that the award in *Peterson Farms* had been made in France. Would the English court have nonetheless refused to apply the group of companies doctrine? Suppose that the parties' agreement to arbitrate was governed by French law.

(d) *Criticism of group of companies doctrine*. Consider the criticism of the group of companies doctrine in *Peterson Farms*. Is that criticism warranted?

12. *Estoppel as basis for subjecting non-signatory to arbitration agreement*. Particularly in common law jurisdictions, "estoppel" is a well-recognized legal doctrine, which can be invoked to preclude parties from denying that they are party to arbitration (or other) agreements. In these jurisdictions, estoppel is defined in various ways, but generally means that a party is precluded by considerations of good faith from acting inconsistently with its own statements or conduct. *See* G. Born, *International Commercial Arbitration* 1472-77 (2d ed. 2014); J. Lew, L. Mistelis & S. Kröll, *Comparative International Commercial Arbitration* ¶7-30 (2003).

A number of authorities have applied estoppel to permit a non-signatory to invoke an arbitration agreement against its signatories: where a signatory claims rights under a contract, which contains an arbitration clause, against a non-signatory, it may be estopped from denying that the non-signatory is a party to the arbitration provision. *See, e.g., Thomson-CSF, SA v. Am. Arbitration Ass'n*, 64 F.3d 773 (2d Cir. 1995) (courts "willing to estop a signatory from avoiding arbitration with a nonsignatory when the issues the nonsignatory is seeking to resolve in arbitration are intertwined with the agreement that the estopped party has signed"); *Sunkist Soft Drinks, Inc. v. Sunkist Growers, Inc.*, 10 F.3d 753 (11th Cir. 1993) (party that asserts claim under contract equitably estopped from denying it is party to contract's arbitration clause).

Conversely, a signatory to a contract, which contains an arbitration clause, may be permitted to invoke that clause against a non-signatory that has claimed rights under the contract. *See, e.g., Int'l Paper Co. v. Schwabedissen Maschinen & Anlagen GmbH*, 206 F.3d 411, 418 (4th Cir. 2000) (non-signatory bound by arbitration clause because "a party may be estopped from asserting that the lack of his signature on a written contract precludes enforcement of the contract's arbitration clause when he has consistently maintained that other provisions of the same contract should be enforced to benefit him"); *Tepper Realty Co. v. Mosaic Tile Co.*, 259 F.Supp. 688, 692 (S.D.N.Y. 1966) ("In short, [plaintiff] cannot have it both ways. It cannot rely on the contract when it works to its advantage and ignore it when it works to its disadvantage."). Consider the discussion of estoppel in *Bridas*. Do you agree with the court's conclusion that non-signatories may more readily rely on estoppel against signatories than vice-versa? What sense does this make?

13. *Third-party beneficiary status as basis for subjecting non-signatory to arbitration agreement.* In many legal systems, non-parties to a contract may, in certain circumstances, invoke the benefits of that contract as third-party beneficiaries. In such circumstances, the third party may either be able to invoke or be bound by an arbitration clause contained in the contract. *See, e.g., Tractor-Trailer Supply Co. v. NCR Corp.*, 873 S.W.2d 627 (Mo. Ct. App. 1994) (third-party beneficiary that invokes contract is bound by its arbitration clause); *Nisshin Shipping Co. v. Cleaves & Co.* [2004] 1 All ER (Comm) 481 (QB) (English High Ct.) (brokers, who had status as third-party beneficiaries of charters, entitled to arbitrate against party thereto).

As in many other non-signatory contexts, the decisive factor in third-party beneficiary analysis is generally the parties' intentions; in some contexts, it may be apparent that the parties did not intend for the third-party beneficiary to be bound or benefitted by the arbitration agreement. *See, e.g., McCarthy v. Azure*, 22 F.3d 351, 362 n.16 (1st Cir. 1994) ("Because third-party beneficiary status constitutes an exception to the general rule that a contract does not grant enforceable rights to non-signatories, a person aspiring to such status must show with special clarity that the contracting parties intended to confer a benefit on him": declining to extend arbitration agreement to non-signatory claiming to be third-party beneficiary because agreement did not evidence such intent, and requirements for binding third-party beneficiary "are not satisfied merely because a third party will benefit from performance of the contract"); *Judgment of 19 April 2011*, DFT 4A_44/2011 (Swiss Fed. Trib.) (third-party beneficiary was subject to arbitration clause where this was common intention of parties and beneficiary, together with signatories, initiated arbitration, thereby agreeing to be bound by clause). In general, what should one assume about a third-party beneficiary's status under an arbitration clause, contained in the contract that benefits him? What would considerations of efficiency and centralized dispute resolution suggest?

In addition, some courts have required that the third party be entitled to, and assert, contractual rights under a contract in order to be subject to its arbitration clause. See *Fortress Value v. Blue Skye* [2012] EWHC 1486 (Comm) (English High Ct.) (non-signatory defendants could not claim benefit of arbitration agreement because they did not assert *claims* arising out of substantive provisions of contract but only sought to rely on limitations as contractual *defense*); *Judgment of 8 March 2012*, DFT

4A_627/2011 (Swiss Fed. Trib.) (no third party beneficiary status where alleged third party beneficiary was not granted direct rights).

14. *Choice-of-law issues in determining parties to arbitration agreement.* What law governs the question whether a non-signatory is bound by an arbitration agreement? As *Dow, ICC Case No. 8385,* and *Peterson Farms* illustrate, choice-of-law issues frequently arise in disputes over the identities of the parties to international arbitration agreements.

(a) *Effect of separability doctrine on choice-of-law analysis.* As discussed above, the separability doctrine permits the application of one law to the parties' underlying contract and another law to the arbitration clause contained in that contract. *See supra* pp. 90-93, 287, 300-01. *Dow* illustrates this point well. What law applied to the underlying contract in *Dow*? To the arbitration clause? Consider the choice of law analysis in *ICC Case No. 8385.* What law did the tribunal, the English courts and the French courts consider applicable to the arbitration agreement in *Dallah*?

Recall the discussion above regarding the laws that are ordinarily applicable to the arbitration agreement (assuming no express choice of this law by the parties): (i) the law applicable to the parties' underlying contract; or (ii) the law of the arbitral seat. *See supra* pp. 304-08. Consider again the arguments in favor of each. Is there any reason to prefer one or the other alternative more strongly in the context of determining the law governing the identity of the parties to an arbitration agreement? Is the law applicable to the validity of the arbitration agreement necessarily the same law that should govern the question whether a non-signatory is bound by the arbitration clause? Why or why not?

(b) *Relevance of legal theory invoked against non-signatory to choice-of-law analysis.* As detailed in the preceding Notes, different legal theories can be invoked to subject non-signatories to an arbitration agreement. For example, would the same law necessarily govern (i) veil-piercing and alter ego status; (ii) agency; (iii) third-party beneficiary status; (iv) guarantee claims; (v) group of companies; and (vi) implied consent claims?

Suppose that A and B enter into an arbitration agreement that is expressly governed by the laws of State X. Does the law of State X necessarily govern the question whether C is an alter ego of B or whether C guaranteed B's obligations under the arbitration agreement? Suppose that C and B are both companies incorporated in State Y; what law applies to the companies' alter ego status? Suppose that, in the same hypothetical, the underlying contract is governed by the laws of State Z, and C is a third party beneficiary to the underlying contract under the laws of State Z; should the laws of State X or State Z govern whether C is bound by the arbitration clause?

(c) *Choice of law in* Peterson Farms. What law did the English court hold applicable to the arbitration agreement in *Peterson Farms*? Where was the arbitral seat? Why does the court conclude that the choice-of-law clause in the parties' underlying contract applied to the arbitration agreement? Compare *ICC Case No. 8385.*

15. *Application of form requirements to non-signatory issues.* Application of the theories discussed above to bind a non-signatory to an agreement to arbitrate raises questions of compliance with applicable formal requirements for a "written" arbitration agreement. *See supra* pp. 375-92, 574. Note that the decisions in *Bridas, Dow, Peterson*

Farms, *Dallah* and *ICC Case No. 8385*, do not address issues of form. Suppose that the *Bridas* and *Peterson Farms* courts had applied alter ego or other theories to hold that non-signatories were bound by the relevant arbitration agreements. Would the formal requirements of Article II of the New York Convention have been satisfied? Of Article 7 of the UNCITRAL Model Law? How were these formal requirements satisfied in *Dow* and *ICC Case No. 8385*?

If they are applicable, how are the written form and signature requirements of Article II of the New York Convention (and Article 7 of the 1985 UNCITRAL Model Law) satisfied with respect to the "non-signatories" that are held bound by agreements to arbitrate? Does not, by definition, a non-signatory not sign the arbitration agreement (*e.g.*, in alter ego, group of companies, estoppel, merger, and third-party beneficiary contexts)? What theory can you articulate for why Article II's form requirement would be satisfied in each of these contexts?

Is it correct to assume that Article II's form requirement must be satisfied with respect to the question of what parties are bound by the arbitration agreement, as distinguished from the question whether there was a valid arbitration agreement between its original signatories? Consider the following rationale:

> "this formal [writing] requirement only applies to the arbitration agreement itself, that is to the agreement ... by which the initial parties have reciprocally expressed their common will to submit the dispute to arbitration. As to the question of the subjective scope of an arbitration agreement formally valid [under this writing requirement] the issue is to determine which are the parties which are bound by the agreement and eventually determine if one or several third parties which are not mentioned therein nevertheless enter into its scope *ratione personae*...." *Judgment of 16 October 2003*, DFT 129 III 736 (Swiss Fed. Trib.).

Is this persuasive? What is the purpose of the form requirement? *See also Arthur Andersen LLP v. Carlisle*, 556 U.S. 624, 630 (2009) ("'traditional principles' of state law allow a contract to be enforced by or against nonparties to the contract through 'assumption, piercing the corporate veil, alter ego, incorporation by reference, third party beneficiary theories, waiver and estoppel'.... If a written arbitration provision is made enforceable against ... a third party under state contract law, the [FAA's writing requirement is] fulfilled").

16. *Characterization of non-signatory issues.* Should the identity of the parties to the arbitration agreement be characterized as a question of formation or existence of a valid agreement to arbitrate or a question of the agreement's scope? What are the legal consequences of each characterization? Consider: *First Options of Chicago, Inc. v. Kaplan*, 514 U.S. 938, 944 (1995) (holding, in case involving non-signatory issue: "When deciding whether the parties agreed to arbitrate a certain matter (including arbitrability), courts generally ... should apply ordinary state-law principles that govern the formation of contracts."); *Dallah Real Estate & Tourism Holding Co. v. Ministry of Religious Affairs, Gov't of Pakistan* [2010] UKSC 46, ¶11 (U.K. S.Ct.) ("The 'validity' of the arbitration agreement depends in the present case upon whether there existed between Dallah and the Government any relevant arbitration agreement at all"); *Judgment of 19 August 2008*, DFT 4A_128/2008, ¶4.1.1 (Swiss Fed. Trib.) ("The question as to the subjective bearing of an arbitration agreement—at issue is which parties are bound by the agreement and to determine to what extent one

or several third parties not mentioned there nonetheless fall within its scope *ratione personae*—relates to the substance and accordingly must be resolved in light of [Article 178(2) of the SLPIL]"); *Aloe Vera of Am., Inc. v. Asianic Food (S) Pte Ltd*, [2006] SGHC 78 (Singapore High Ct.) (refusing to consider argument that non-signatory was not bound by arbitration agreement under Article V(1)(c), on grounds that Article V(1)(c) of the New York Convention, concerned the "scope of the arbitration agreement, rather than ... whether a particular person was party to that agreement" and considering (but rejecting on the facts) the question whether the arbitration agreement bound the non-signatory).

B. ALLOCATION OF COMPETENCE TO DECIDE NON-SIGNATORY ISSUES

Non-signatory issues also raise questions concerning the allocation of jurisdictional competence between arbitral tribunals and national courts. In particular, who should be permitted initially to consider and decide whether a non-signatory is bound by an arbitration agreement—the arbitrators or a national court? The materials excerpted below consider this issue.

ORIENTAL COMMERCIAL & SHIPPING CO. (U.K.) LTD v. ROSSEEL, NV
609 F.Supp. 75 (S.D.N.Y. 1985)

LEISURE, District Judge. Defendant moves pursuant to Article II(3) of the New York Convention and 9 U.S.C. §206 to compel arbitration.... Rosseel NV ("Rosseel"), a Belgian corporation, entered into a contract to purchase specified oil from Oriental Commercial and Shipping Co. (U.K.) Ltd ("Oriental U.K."). The oil was apparently never delivered and Rosseel alleges damages as a result. Oriental Commercial and Shipping Co. Ltd ("Oriental SA") is a Saudi Arabian company with ... representative offices located throughout the world. The Bokhari family owns both Oriental SA and Oriental U.K. but neither corporation owns shares of the other. Oriental SA was not a signatory to the contract of sale between Oriental U.K. and Rosseel.

Rosseel served its Notice of Intention to Arbitrate upon Oriental U.K. and Oriental SA demanding arbitration under the contract. Oriental SA responded with a petition to stay arbitration....

The arbitration provision in the contract is the only contract term here in dispute. Oriental U.K.'s telex to Rosseel stated the terms of the agreement which included the following provision: "Arbitration: If required in New York City." Oriental U.K. and Oriental SA claim that the wording of the phrase is insufficient to create an enforceable arbitration provision.... Additionally, Oriental SA claims the arbitration clause is enforceable, if at all, between Oriental U.K. and Rosseel only....

[The court first held that the arbitration clause was valid and encompassed the dispute.] It is within the province of this Court to determine whether Oriental SA, although not formally a party to the arbitration agreement, should be made a party to the arbitration proceeding in addition to *Rosseel* and *Oriental U.K. Orion Shipping & Trading Co. v. Eastern States Petroleum Corp.*, 312 F.2d 299 (2d Cir. 1983). Ordinary contract and agency principles determine which parties are bound by an arbitration agreement, and parties can become contractually bound absent their signatures. Rosseel suggests two theories to support its contention that Oriental SA should be made a party to the arbitration proceeding. The first is that Oriental U.K. is merely the alter ego of Oriental SA. The second alleges that Oriental U.K. acted as Oriental SA's agent in contracting with Rosseel. Rosseel claims that either theory allows this Court to pierce the corporative veil and bind Oriental SA to the arbitration agreement.

To apply the alter ego doctrine to justify the disregard of a corporate entity, the court must determine that there is such unity of interest and ownership that separate personalities of the corporations no longer exist, and that failure to disregard the corporate form would result in fraud or injustice. However, a stringent showing is required before a court will pierce the corporate veil. The courts do not lightly disregard the separate existence of related corporations, even in deference to a strong policy favoring arbitration of private commercial disputes. *Coastal States Trading, Inc. v. Zenith Navigation SA*, 446 F.Supp. 330, 387 (S.D.N.Y. 1977).

There are insufficient facts before the Court to determine whether Oriental SA should be made a party to the arbitration proceeding. Consequently, by June 1, 1985 the parties shall complete discovery on the issue of whether Oriental SA is a party to the arbitration agreement with regard to this transaction. At that time the Court shall conduct an evidentiary hearing on this issue.

The Court notes that an alternative procedure ... may be useful to expedite resolution of this matter. With the assistance of this Court, if required, the parties may stipulate that a final determination of whether Oriental SA is bound by the arbitration agreement would be stayed pending arbitration of Rosseel's claims against both companies. Oriental SA would fully participate in the arbitration proceedings. If Rosseel prevails in its claim, and Oriental U.K. alone is unable or unwilling to satisfy the arbitration award, this Court, upon Rosseel's motion, will order discovery to proceed in the manner set forth above. An evidentiary hearing would then be held to determine whether Oriental SA was a party to the arbitration agreement and thus bound by the arbitration award. If the parties agree to this latter procedure, the matter will be referred to the [AAA]. Otherwise, Rosseel's motion for appointing of an arbitrator is stayed pending this Court's determination of the identity of the parties....

BUILDERS FEDERAL (H.K.) LTD v. TURNER CONSTRUCTION
655 F.Supp. 1400 (S.D.N.Y. 1987)

HAIGHT, District Judge. [Builders Federal (Hong Kong) Ltd ("Builders Federal") is a Hong Kong corporation. Turner Construction ("Turner") and Turner International Industries, Inc. ("Turner International") are incorporated in the United States; Turner owned 100 percent of a Singapore company, Turner (East Asia) Pte Ltd ("TEA"); TEA was the main contractor for a major construction project in Singapore. Builders Federal was a subcontractor to TEA, pursuant to an agreement between TEA, Builder Federal and other subcontractors; Turner and Turner International were not parties to the subcontract. The subcontract contained an arbitration clause, providing for arbitration in Singapore. In addition the clause provided that:

> "... if the dispute or difference between the Contractor and the Subcontractor is substantially the same as a matter which is a dispute or difference between the Contractor and the Employer under the Main Contract the Contractor and the Sub-Contractor hereby agree that such dispute or difference shall be referred to arbitration pursuant to the terms of the Main Contract."

Disputes arose during the construction project and TEA ceased work. An action was commenced in Singapore courts by Builders Federal against TEA seeking to compel arbitration of disputes between them. TEA refused to arbitrate with Builders Federal on the grounds that the disputes had to be heard pursuant to an arbitration clause in its main contract. Builders Federal and other subcontractors filed a petition in U.S. district court seeking an order compelling Turner, TEA, and various of their affiliates to proceed with arbitration in Singapore and a declaration that each of these entities was bound to arbitrate. The court refused to grant the relief requested, reasoning as follows]....

The briefs of counsel debate at some length just what claims plaintiffs are asserting. Plaintiffs' basic premise ... is that defendants are liable for TEA's contractual obligations (including the obligation to arbitrate) because TEA is their alter ego. Defendants, for their part, appear to characterize the plaintiffs' theory as one of implied guaranty of TEA's performance. Both theories of liability may, in appropriate circumstances, support an order to compel arbitration....

It is clear that plaintiffs state a viable claim under the alter ego theory. The petition is replete with allegations that defendants exercised dominance and control over TEA, and that TEA was under-capitalized. Those allegations are not sufficient of themselves to "pierce a corporate veil" so as to visit upon parent corporations the obligations of a subsidiary. *Walkovszky v. Carlton*, 276 N.Y.S.2d 585 (1966). But the petition alleges more than that. It alleges that the subcontract between plaintiff's and TEA obligated TEA to make certain payments to plaintiffs upon termination of the main contract; and that defendants decided that TEA would breach those obligations, sending implementing instructions to TEA. These allegations, even in the absence of allegations of fraud requiring Rule 9(b) particularity, are sufficient to state a claim for alter ego liability. The petition states a viable claim falling within this Court's subject matter jurisdiction.

In the alternative, defendants ask that proceedings in this Court be stayed pending completion of the arbitration proceedings in Singapore. I will grant that application, subject to the conditions set forth below.... When the existence of any agreement obligating anyone to arbitrate anywhere is at issue, then by definition the [trial under §4 of the FAA] must precede the arbitration. But that is not necessarily so when an arbitration agreement concededly exists, undisputedly binding named parties to arbitrate, and the §4 petitioner claims that non-signatories to the contract are also bound to arbitrate. In those circumstances an arbitration will in any event take place between the named parties to the contract. If the prevailing party's award is not satisfied by the other party, the prevailing party may subsequently proceed against the non-signatory, either as guarantor of the named party's obligations or on an alter ego theory.... [T]he Second Circuit's ... holdings ... prompted Judge Carter of this Court in *Cochin Refineries Ltd v. Triton Shipping Inc.*, S.D.N.Y. 74 Civ. 216 (March 19, 1974), to stay a corporate veil piercing effort until resolution of the arbitration between the named parties. Judge Carter wrote: "If plaintiff prevails against Triton at arbitration, and the latter is unable to satisfy the judgment award, plaintiff's action against the other defendants will still be pending. It will be time enough at that time for a trial to determine whether these defendants are bound."

I declined to follow Judge Carter's lead in *Hidrocarburos y Derivados, CA v. Lemos*, 453 F.Supp. 160, 173-74 (S.D.N.Y. 1977). But in that case, the non-signatory party flatly declared that it would not be bound by any award in the arbitration involving the company for whose performance the non-signatory party was said to be liable. Furthermore, the signatory party was pressing affirmative claims against the §4 petitioner. 453 F.Supp. 174 at n.31. In those circumstances, it seemed to me right to direct that New York arbitrators determine in advance of the arbitration whether the non-signatory parties would be fully bound by the arbitration, both in respect of an obligation to arbitrate and the quantum of the arbitrators' award....

In the case at bar, were I to "proceed summarily" at this time to the trial of plaintiff's petition, it would have a disruptive effect upon the pending judicial and arbitral proceedings in Singapore, the agreed-upon situs of the arbitration. Plaintiffs' brief seeks to minimize that disruption, but it appears to me both real and significant. Plaintiffs' discovery demands in aid of its alter ego theory are far-reaching, in respect of both document production and answers to interrogatories. The taking of depositions of TEA and defendants' officers and employees cannot be far behind. I say this not in criticism of the litigation tactics of plaintiffs' counsel here, but in recognition that such litigation would in all likelihood disrupt and delay the rather stringent procedural deadlines imposed by Mr. Gardam, the Singapore arbitrator.... This Court's order, adding three additional corporate parties to the Singapore proceedings, would constitute an intrusive action against which comity counsels.

Quite apart from these considerations, resolution of the issues in the Singapore arbitration may well limit or narrow the issues here. That is a sufficient basis for this Court to exercise its inherent power "to control the disposition of the cases on its docket with economy of time and effort for itself, for counsel and for litigants." There is ample authority in this circuit for staying suits here on alleged guarantees given by corporate parents pending arbitration abroad between plaintiff and subsidiary.

The concerns this Court addressed in *Hidrocarburos,* are alleviated by the present defendants' willingness, expressed through counsel, to waive any "due process" arguments arising out of their desired non-participation in the Singapore arbitration. I will exact that undertaking as a condition for a stay of these proceedings.... In addition, this court directs in an exercise of its equitable powers that the defendants take no steps which would hamper the progress of the Singapore arbitration, or serve to impede its completion within a reasonable time. In making that direction, I do not mean to preclude such litigation steps as TEA may be advised by their Singapore counsel to pursue. My focus will be upon possible bad-faith obstructionism generated by the corporate parents.... On these terms and conditions and in the exercise of my discretion, I grant a stay of proceedings under the petition and complaint, including discovery....

BRIDAS SAPIC v. GOVERNMENT OF TURKMENISTAN
345 F.3d 347 (5th Cir. 2003)

[excerpted above at pp. 551-58]

PETERSON FARMS INC. v. C&M FARMING LTD
[2004] 1 Lloyd's Rep. 603 (Comm) (English High Ct. 2004)

[excerpted above at pp. 566-70]

DALLAH REAL ESTATE & TOURISM HOLDING CO. v. MINISTRY OF RELIGIOUS AFFAIRS, GOVERNMENT OF PAKISTAN
[2010] UKSC 46 (U.K. S.Ct.)
[excerpted above at pp. 247-70]

JUDGMENT OF 17 FEBRUARY 2011, GOV'T OF PAKISTAN, MIN. OF RELIGIOUS AFFAIRS v. DALLAH REAL ESTATE & TOURISM HLDG CO.
XXXVI Y.B. Comm. Arb. 590 (Paris Cour d'appel)
[excerpted above at pp. 570-73]

NOTES

1. *Allocation of competence to consider identity of parties to arbitration agreement.* As with other disputes over the enforceability and interpretation of arbitration clauses, disputes over the identities of the parties to an arbitration agreement give rise to debates concerning the allocation of competence between national courts and arbitrators.

   (a) *Arbitral awards considering arbitrators' competence to determine parties to arbitration agreement.* The tribunals in *Dow* and *ICC Case No. 8385*, excerpted above at pp. 558-62 & 562-66, readily concluded that it had the authority to decide whether the parties' arbitration agreements were binding on particular parties. Other international tribunals have agreed. *See Partial Award in ICC Case No. 4402*, IX Y.B. Comm. Arb. 138, 139 (1984). *See also supra* pp. 218-87.

   What was the rationale for the tribunal's conclusion in *Dow* that it possessed competence to determine the parties to the relevant arbitration agreement? What role did the ICC Rules (and particularly Article 8 of the 1975 ICC Rules) play in the tribunal's conclusion? Is there any reason to think that arbitrators would not have competence to determine the parties to an arbitration clause? How (if at all) do disputes regarding the identity of the parties to an arbitration clause differ from other disputes over the validity and interpretation of arbitration agreements?

   (b) *Arbitrators' competence to consider identity of parties to arbitration agreement under national arbitration statutes.* As discussed above, most arbitration statutes address the allocation of competence between courts and arbitrators to decide disputes over the validity and interpretation of arbitration agreements. *See supra* pp. 272-84. Consider Articles 7, 8 and 16 of the UNCITRAL Model Law, Articles 1448 and 1465 of the French Code of Civil Procedure and Articles 178 and 186 of the SLPIL, excerpted at pp. 87-90, 144-47 & 158-59 of the Documentary Supplement. How does each provision deal with the allocation of competence to determine the parties to an arbitration agreement?

   (c) *Court decisions holding that arbitrators can consider identity of parties to arbitration agreement.* In *Builders Federal*, the court upheld an arbitrator's power to decide, subject to subsequent judicial review, what parties are bound by an arbitration clause. Consider the court's reasoning. Does the court discuss how the parties' arbitration clause submitted disputes to arbitration over the parties to the arbitration agreement? Consider also the English and French court decisions, reviewing the arbitrators' award in *Dallah*.

(d) *Court decisions holding that arbitrators cannot consider identity of parties to arbitration agreement.* In apparent contrast to *Builders Federal*, *Oriental Commercial* and other courts have suggested that arbitrators should not consider the identity of the parties to an arbitration agreement. *See also ARW Exploration Corp. v. Aguirre*, 45 F.3d 1455, 1461 (10th Cir. 1995) ("It is the province of the court, not the arbitrator, to determine whether a party has a duty to arbitrate"); *Microchip Tech. Inc. v. U.S. Philips Corp.*, 367 F.3d 1350 (Fed. Cir. 2004) (court must determine whether non-signatory is successor corporation before compelling arbitration); *Orion Shipping & Trading Co. v. E. States Petroleum Corp.*, 312 F.2d 299, 301 (2d Cir. 1983); *Fiat SpA v. Ministry of Fin. & Planning*, 1989 U.S. Dist. LEXIS 11995 (S.D.N.Y.) ("the determination as to whether to afford relief against FIAT, a non-party to the arbitration clause, was not the arbitrator's to make"). What is the rationale for this result?

(e) *Allocation of competence to consider identity of parties to arbitration agreement under FAA.* Review the analysis in *First Options*, excerpted above at pp. 230-33. Does anything in *First Options* suggest that an arbitral tribunal cannot consider the identity of the parties to an arbitration agreement? Does *First Options* instead address the finality of the arbitrator's award after such consideration occurs?

(f) *Judicial abstention from considering identity of parties to arbitration agreement under FAA.* The *Builders Federal* court declined to consider whether to compel the various Turner entities, which had not executed the arbitration agreement, to participate in the Singapore arbitration. In doing so, the court cited considerations of comity and deference to the Singapore arbitral proceedings. Was this a sensible decision? Is this the same conclusion as a decision that the parties had agreed to arbitrate arbitrability issues? Does the FAA permit the abstention practiced in *Builders Federal*? Other U.S. lower courts have concluded that it does not and have compelled the joinder of non-signatories. *O & Y Landmark Assocs. of Va. v. Nordheimer*, 725 F.Supp. 578 (D.D.C. 1989). Note that, in *Builders Federal*, the court only agreed to abstain from deciding the proper parties to the arbitration after extracting commitments from the non-signatories to be bound by the award. Is this appropriate? Is it less of an interference in the Singapore arbitration than compelling the non-signatories to arbitrate? Why would the Turner companies have agreed to such an arrangement? Consider the issue of discovery in the Singapore arbitration.

(g) *Allocation of competence to consider identity of parties to arbitration agreement under prima facie jurisdiction standard.* Consider again the approach to the allocation of jurisdictional competence to consider the existence and validity of an arbitration agreement under French law. *See supra* pp. 274-75. Is there any reason not to apply the general French approach to consideration of the identity of the parties to an arbitration agreement?

(h) *Allocation of competence to consider identity of parties to arbitration agreement under UNCITRAL Model Law.* Consider again the approach to the allocation of jurisdictional competence to consider the existence and validity of an arbitration agreement under the Model Law. *See supra* pp. 275-77. Again, is there any reason that this approach should not apply to consideration of the identity of the parties to an arbitration agreement?

2. *Finality of arbitral award determining identity of parties to arbitration agreement*. If an arbitral tribunal considers the identity of the parties to an arbitration clause, what are the effects of its jurisdictional award? Is the award a final resolution of the identity of the parties to the arbitration agreement, or is it subject to subsequent judicial review? If the latter, what standard of judicial review is appropriate?

    (a) *Finality of arbitral award determining identity of parties to arbitration agreement under FAA*. Consider the court's decision in *Bridas*. Does the court treat the arbitrators' award regarding the identity of the parties to the arbitration agreement as final? Or is the award subject to judicial review? Under what standard?

        Does the *Bridas* court recognize circumstances in which the arbitrators' decision regarding the identity of the parties to the arbitration agreement would be final? When? Recall the *First Options* holding that, where there is "clear and unmistakable" evidence of an agreement to arbitrate disputes over the identity of the parties to an arbitration agreement, the arbitrators' resolution of this issue is final, subject to only minimal judicial review in a vacatur action. *See supra* pp. 230-33, 280-83. When will there be "clear and unmistakable" evidence of an agreement to arbitrate disputes over the identity of parties to the arbitration agreement? What might constitute "clear and unmistakable" evidence that a party had agreed to arbitrate arbitrability issues? Wouldn't such evidence necessarily require showing (in court) that the company was a party to the arbitration agreement itself? *See supra* pp. 281-83, 373-74.

    (b) *Finality of arbitral award determining identity of parties to arbitration agreement under UNCITRAL Model Law*. Consider the court's decision in *Peterson Farms* under the English Arbitration Act. Does the court treat the arbitrators' determination of the identity of the parties to the arbitration agreement as binding? What standard of review does the court appear to apply? Compare the standard of review of the English court in *Dallah*. Note that *Dallah* involved recognition of a foreign award, not annulment of an award made in England.

    (c) *Finality of arbitral award determining identity of parties to arbitration agreement under French law*. What standard of review did the Paris Cour d'appel apply in *Dallah*?

    (d) *Appropriate standard of judicial review of arbitral award determining identity of parties to arbitration agreement*. What is the appropriate standard of judicial review of an arbitral award's determination of the identity of the parties to an arbitration agreement? Is *de novo* judicial review appropriate? Is complete judicial deference to the arbitrators' decision appropriate? Is there a sensible middle ground?

3. *Determining parties to arbitration agreement in action to enforce arbitral award*. Suppose that an arbitral award is made against one party and then is sought to be enforced against another entity. May a party seek to enforce an award made against one entity against another entity? For a negative answer, *see IMC Aviation Solutions Pty Ltd v. Altain Khuder LLC*, [2011] VSCA 248 (Victoria Ct. App). A few courts have suggested, however, that where factual issues are simple, an award made against one party can be enforced against another entity. *See Productos Mercantiles etc. v. Faberge USA, Inc.*, No. 92 Civ. 7916 (S.D.N.Y. Sept. 14, 1993) (alter ego liability can be considered in §9 action to confirm award, where "factual determination at issue is not

complex"); *Int'l Ass'n of Machinists, Inc. v. Numberale Stamp & Tool Co.*, 1987 U.S. Dist. LEXIS 12736 (S.D.N.Y.); *In re Arbitration Between Bowen & 39 Broadway Assocs.*, 1992 WL 73480 (S.D.N.Y.); *Orlogin, Inc. v. U.S. Watch Co.*, 1990 U.S. Dist. LEXIS 7794, at *17 (S.D.N.Y.).

Some courts have also suggested that an arbitral award can be enforced, after it has been confirmed against one party, against another party. *See Carte Blanche (Singapore) Pte, Ltd v. Diners Club Int'l Inc.*, 2 F.3d 24 (2d Cir. 1993); *Cecil's, Inc. v. Morris Mechanical Enters., Inc.*, 735 F.2d 437 (11th Cir. 1984) (award enforced against non-signatory subcontractor); *Orion Shipping & Trading Co. v. E. States Petroleum Corp.*, 312 F.2d 299 (2d Cir. 1963); *Gilberg Switzer & Assocs. v. Nat'l Housing P'ship, Ltd*, 641 F.Supp. 150 (D. Conn. 1986) (award enforced against general partner and third-party defendant). Other courts regard a party's failure to join a non-party to an arbitration as a waiver of any right to enforce the award against the non-party. *Brownko Int'l, Inc. v. Ogden Steel Co.*, 585 F.Supp. 1432 (S.D.N.Y. 1983) (where party to arbitration tried to join third party, but abandoned effort, it cannot later attempt to enforce award against that third party).

PART II
INTERNATIONAL ARBITRATION PROCEEDINGS

CHAPTER 7
SELECTION OF ARBITRAL SEAT IN INTERNATIONAL ARBITRATION

A critical issue in any international arbitration is the location of the arbitral seat (or place of arbitration). This chapter examines practical and legal issues arising in connection with the selection of the arbitral seat. First, the chapter examines the meaning and importance of the choice of the arbitral seat. Second, the chapter addresses the selection of the arbitral seat by agreement of the parties, including the enforceability of such agreements. Third, the chapter discusses the selection of the arbitral seat by the arbitral tribunal or by an arbitral institution. Finally, the chapter examines the role of national courts in selecting an arbitral seat.

A. MEANING AND IMPORTANCE OF ARBITRAL SEAT IN INTERNATIONAL ARBITRATION

The location of the arbitral seat is a critical issue in any international arbitration.[1] The location of the arbitral seat can have profound legal and practical consequences, and can materially alter the course of dispute resolution. In the words of one English judicial decision, "[i]n international commercial arbitration the place or seat of arbitration is always of paramount importance."[2]

The significance of the arbitral seat includes relatively mundane issues of convenience and cost. Although such factors are often given undue weight, they can be important to the conduct and outcome of an arbitration. Moreover, factors such as visa requirements, availability of air or other transportation, hearing facilities, hotel accommodations, support staff (such as interpreters, stenographers, secretaries), and the like can bear heavily on the smooth progress of an arbitration.

Much more significant than convenience and cost is the effect of the law of the arbitral seat, and particularly the arbitration legislation of the arbitral seat, on the arbitration. In most legal systems, the arbitration legislation of a state is territorial in scope, regulating arbitrations that have their seat within the territory of that state and not other arbitrations (that have their seats outside national territory).[3] As discussed below, the territorial scope of national arbitration legislation is fundamental to the international arbitral process.[4]

The arbitration legislation of the arbitral seat governs a number of "internal" and "external" matters relating to arbitral proceedings. The "internal" matters potentially governed

---

1. G. Born, *International Commercial Arbitration* 345-46, 1536-43, 2051-66 (2d ed. 2014); G. Petrochilos, *Procedural Law in International Arbitration* 20 (2004).

2. *Star Shipping AS v. China Nat'l Foreign Trade Transp. Corp.* [1993] 2 Lloyd's Rep. 445, 452 (English Ct. App.).

3. *See infra* pp. 619-20; G. Born, *International Commercial Arbitration* 345-48 (2d ed. 2014); M. Storme & F. De Ly, *The Place of Arbitration* (1992).

4. *See infra* pp. 619-25.

by the arbitral seat's law include: (a) the parties' autonomy to agree on substantive and procedural issues; (b) standards of procedural fairness in arbitral proceedings; (c) timetable of arbitral proceedings; (d) consolidation, joinder and intervention; (e) conduct of hearings, including the parties' opportunities to be heard and the examination of witnesses; (f) rights of lawyers to appear, and their ethical obligations, in the arbitral proceedings; (g) pleading and evidentiary rules; (h) permissibility and administration of oaths; (i) disclosure, "discovery," and related issues; (j) confidentiality, (k) rights and duties of arbitrators, (l) arbitrators' remedial powers, including to grant provisional measures; (m) arbitrators' relations with the parties, including liability, ethical standards, appointment and removal; and (n) form, making and publication of the award.[5] In addition, and less clearly, the law of the arbitral seat sometimes governs: (o) "interpretation and enforceability of the parties' arbitration agreement (including issues of nonarbitrability)" (p) conflict of laws rules applicable to the substance of the dispute; and (q) quasi-substantive issues, such as rules concerning interest and costs of legal representation.

The "external" matters potentially governed by the law of the arbitral seat concern judicial supervision of the arbitral proceedings by the courts of the arbitral seat. Among other things, these include: (a) arbitrators' competence-competence and the allocation of competence to consider and decide jurisdictional challenges between arbitral tribunals and national courts; (b) annulment of arbitral awards; (c) selection of arbitrators; (d) removal and replacement of arbitrators; (e) evidence-taking in aid of the arbitration; and (f) provisional measures in support of the arbitration.[6] In most instances, "external" matters entail affirmative actions of the local courts of the arbitral seat, which consider and decide applications seeking judicial intervention in, or support for, the arbitral process (*e.g.*, annulling an award; selecting an arbitrator).

The materials excerpted below examine the concept of the arbitral seat in international commercial arbitration. They consider the territorial scope of national arbitration legislation, the consequences of selecting an arbitral seat and an overview of the selection of the arbitral seat.

PT GARUDA INDONESIA v. BIRGEN AIR
[2002] 1 SLR 393 (Singapore Ct. App.)

CHAO HICK TIN JA. This was an appeal against the decision of the High Court setting aside an order of the assistant registrar granting leave to the appellant to serve an originating motion out of jurisdiction on the respondent....

The facts giving rise to the institution of this originating motion were largely undisputed. The appellant ("Garuda"), an Indonesian company, and the respondent ("Birgen"), a Belgium company entered into an agreement dated 20 January 1996 whereby Birgen agreed to lease one DC 10-30 aircraft to Garuda for use by pilgrims to Saudi Arabia for the Hajj ("the lease agreement"). The lease agreement expressly provided that the governing law would be the law of Indonesia and that disputes arising therefrom were to be referred for arbitration in Jakarta. Subsequently a dispute arose because Birgen proposed to sub-

---

5. *See* G. Born, *International Commercial Arbitration* 1531 (2d ed. 2014).
6. *See* G. Born, *International Commercial Arbitration* 1532-33 (2d ed. 2014); *infra* pp. 620-21.

stitute the aircraft under the lease agreement and the dispute was referred to arbitration in accordance with the terms thereof, with Garuda as the claimant and Birgen, the respondent.

The arbitral tribunal consisted of Dr. Clyde Croft, as Chairman, and Professor Priyatna Abdurrasyid and Professor Nurkut Inan as co-arbitrators. From February 1999, the tribunal, through its Chairman, Dr. Croft, sought to set dates for the hearing of the arbitration. As regards the place of hearing, the Chairman informed the parties on 24 February that the tribunal thought that Jakarta was not an appropriate place given the then situation prevailing in Indonesia and proposed that the tribunal should sit in Zurich. On 11 and 12 March 1999, Birgen and Garuda respectively responded but neither made any comment on the tribunal's proposal to have the hearing in Zurich. On 30 March 1999, Dr. Croft proposed that the hearing of the arbitration be carried out in Singapore rather than in Zurich.

On 7 April 1999, M/s Donald H Bunker and Associates ("Donald Bunker"), the lawyers for Birgen, replied requesting that the tribunal proceed to decide the case on the basis of the documents without any hearing but if that request were not granted then they were agreeable, *inter alia*, that "Jakarta is not an appropriate place for the hearing and accepts the tribunal's proposal to sit in Singapore."

On 21 May 1999, Dr. Croft wrote to the lawyers for the parties asking for their comments on certain matters, including Birgen's application for "documents only arbitration." Nevertheless, he also notified the parties that "the tribunal had decided that this matter will be heard on 4, 5 and 6 August 1999 in Singapore." On 10 June 1999 Gani Djemat & Partners ("Gani Djemat"), lawyers for Garuda, wrote indicating, *inter alia*, that they agreed that "the hearing to take place on 4, 5 and 6 August 1999 in Singapore." On 23 July 1999 by another letter to both Donald Bunker and Gani Djemat, the lawyers for the parties, Dr. Croft reiterated that "a hearing will take place in Singapore" on the appointed dates.

The hearing was duly held in Singapore and a final award, dated 15 February 2000, was handed down which was signed by two members, Dr. Croft and Prof. Inan. The third member, Prof. Abdurrasyid, declined to sign it and rendered a dissenting opinion. The final award stated that it was delivered at Jakarta and the tribunal in ¶39 also made the following comments: "It had not been suggested by either of the parties, nor is it the view of the arbitral tribunal, that the use of Singapore as a convenient place for the hearing had any substantive or procedural impact on the proceedings." ...

On 3 February 2001, Garuda filed a notice of originating motion ("OM") in the High Court in Singapore to set aside the final award and the addendum, and for various other reliefs. The application was based on §24 of the International Arbitration Act ("the IA Act") and Art. 34 of the Model Law. Article 34 sets out the grounds upon which an award governed by the Model Law may be set aside by the court. Section 24 sets out grounds, additional to those in Art. 34, upon which the High Court may set aside an award. In the view of the judge below, §24 and Art. 34 are closely linked—if Art. 34 is not applicable to an arbitration, then §24 will also not be applicable. We agree with this construction.... [The lower court also held that there were no grounds for serving Birgen out of the jurisdiction. In coming to his decision, the judge below found: ... "This was not a proper case to grant leave to Garuda to serve the papers out of jurisdiction as the place of arbitration remained at Jakarta."] ...

[Under Singapore law, Garuda could only serve its motion outside of the jurisdiction if it could show, "first, that there were merits in the case and, second, that Singapore was a forum conveniens."] Birgen's case was that Garuda failed to satisfy both requirements by reason of the fact that the place of arbitration was not Singapore but Jakarta and thus Singapore courts did not have jurisdiction in the matter. However, the position taken by Garuda was that the parties had subsequently agreed to change "the place of arbitration" to Singapore....

Garuda relied upon the IA Act, an Act to make provision for the conduct of international commercial arbitrations based on the [UNCITRAL] Model Law. By §3(1) of the IA Act, the Model Law (except Ch. VIII thereof) shall have the force of law in Singapore. Section 24 empowers the Singapore High Court to set aside the award of an arbitral tribunal in certain specified circumstances, other than those described in Art. 34 of the Model Law.

Some of the relevant provisions of the Model Law are the following [quoting Article 1(2), 20 and 31(3)] ... From Arts. 1(2) and 20 it will be seen that unless Singapore is the "place of arbitration" the Singapore courts can only intervene in relation to an arbitration governed by the Model Law in the limited instances set out in Arts. 8, 9, 35 and 36. Thus, Art. 34 only applies if an arbitration has its "place of arbitration" in Singapore.

Garuda did not dispute that the Model Law is only applicable where the place of arbitration is Singapore. Their main plank of argument was that Singapore was the place of arbitration and not Jakarta and thus, the Model Law applied.

It should be apparent from Art. 20 that there is a distinction between "place of arbitration" and the place where the arbitral tribunal carries on hearing witnesses, experts or the parties, namely, the "venue of hearing." The place of arbitration is a matter to be agreed by the parties. Where they have so agreed, the place of arbitration does not change even though the tribunal may meet to hear witnesses or do any other things in relation to the arbitration at a location other than the place of arbitration.

Thus the place of arbitration does not change merely because the tribunal holds its hearing at a different place or places. It only changes where the parties so agree. The significance of the place of arbitration lies in the fact that for legal reasons the arbitration is to be regarded as situated in that state or territory. It identifies a state or territory whose laws will govern the arbitral process. The following passage of Kerr LJ in *Naviera Amazonica Peruana SA v. Compania Internacional de Seguros del Peru* [1988] 1 Lloyd's Rep. 116 ("the *Amazonica* case"), while it did not relate to the Model Law, is nevertheless germane: "... it seems clear that the submissions advanced below confused the legal 'seat' etc. of an arbitration with the geographically convenient place or places for holding hearings. This distinction is nowadays a common feature of international arbitrations...." ... It will be seen that the English concept of "seat of arbitration" is the same as "place of arbitration" under the Model Law.

While the agreement to change the place of arbitration may be implied, it must be clear. This is in the interest of certainty. By choosing the "place of arbitration" the parties would have also thereby decided on the law which is to govern the arbitration proceedings.

We shall now refer to the relevant provisions of the lease agreement which have a bearing on the question of the place of arbitration.

"Clause 16.8: Governing Law
   This Agreement shall in all respects be governed by, and construed in accordance with, the laws of the Republic of Indonesia, including all matters of construction, validity and performance.

Clause 16.9: Arbitration
   In the event that a commercial controversy or claim ... such controversy or claim shall be

settled by arbitration held before a board of three qualified arbiters. *The parties agree that such arbitration shall be held in Jakarta, Indonesia* and conducted in the English language in accordance with the Rules of Conciliation and Arbitration of the [ICC]."

Next we turn to the terms of reference of the arbitration which the parties had agreed. The following are pertinent:

"6 Place of Arbitration
    6.1 The place of arbitration is Jakarta, Indonesia.
    6.2 The arbitral Tribunal and the Parties may convene at any other location if necessary, for example, for a view."

From these two documents, it is clear that the parties had agreed that the governing law of the lease agreement was Indonesian law and that the place of arbitration was Jakarta. So was there a subsequent agreement to alter the place of arbitration? We have ... set out the relevant correspondence. It would be recalled that in February 1999 the tribunal first suggested, in view of the turmoil in Indonesia, that it should sit in Zurich. It was on 30 March 1999 that the tribunal proposed Singapore in place of Zurich. On 7 April 1999 the lawyers for Birgen replied accepting the tribunal's proposal to sit in Singapore. There was no reply from Garuda on the proposal. On 21 May 1999, the tribunal informed the parties of the hearing in Singapore on 4-6 August 1999. It was only on 10 June 1999 that the lawyers for Garuda, Gani Djemat, replied stating that they agreed to the hearing in Singapore on the specified dates. The hearing was accordingly held here.

From these, Garuda contended that there was an implied agreement to change the place of arbitration, and thus the *lex fori*, or curial law, from Jakarta to Singapore and they relied upon the *Amazonica* case. But this authority is hardly relevant. In *Amazonica*, the plaintiffs insured their vessels with the defendants. The policy provided that the city of Lima was to have jurisdiction over all disputes. However, it also provided that arbitration was to be governed by the conditions and laws of England. A dispute arose between the parties and the issue for determination by the court was whether the arbitration was to be held in London or Lima. Quite clearly there was ambiguity in the clauses of the policy.

At first instance, the High Court ruled that the arbitration was to be held in Lima but governed by English law as the *lex fori*. The Court of Appeal reversed that decision and held that the seat of arbitration should be London where it would be governed by English law, thereby avoiding the situation of an arbitration in country X being governed by the law of country Y. The Court of Appeal made the following proposition:

"*Prima facie*, i.e., in the absence of some express and clear provision to the contrary, it must follow that an agreement that the curial or procedural law of an arbitration is to be the law of X has the consequence that X is also to be the 'seat' of the arbitration. The *lex fori* is then the law of X, and accordingly X is the agreed forum of the arbitration. A further consequence is then that the Courts which are competent to control or assist the arbitration are the Courts exercising jurisdiction at X."

Also relying on the *Amazonica* case, and in view of the fact that the parties agreed to the tribunal's suggestion of having the hearing in Singapore, Garuda made the alternative contention that it followed that the parties had chosen Singapore law as the law governing the arbitration, the curial law, and had thereby also impliedly chosen Singapore as the "place of arbitration." This argument is circular and is also flawed because it is based on the false premise that the parties had chosen Singapore law as the curial law. In fact, the parties made no such choice. By stating in the lease agreement and the terms of reference, that the place of arbitration was Jakarta, it must follow that the curial law would be Indonesian law. The curial law would be Singapore law only if it was established that the parties had agreed to alter the "place of arbitration" from Jakarta to Singapore.

The second case relied upon by Garuda was *Union of India v. McDonnell Douglas Corp* [1993] 2 Lloyd's Rep. 48 where the contract provided that the arbitration should be conducted in accordance with the procedures provided in the Indian Arbitration Act 1940 and that the seat of arbitration proceedings should be in London. The issue was whether the law governing the arbitration proceedings was English or Indian law. The court was of the view that by specifying London as the seat of arbitration, it was reasonable to assume from that choice that they attached some importance to the relevant laws of England, Saville J stated:

> "It is clear from the authorities cited above that English law does admit of at least the theoretical possibility that the parties are free to choose to hold their arbitration in one country but subject to the procedural laws of another, but against this is the undoubted fact that such an agreement is calculated to give rise to great difficulties and complexities, as Lord Justice Kerr observed in the *Amazonica* decision....
>
> [I]t seems to me that by their agreement, the parties have chosen English law as the law to govern their arbitration proceedings, while contractually importing from the Indian Act those provisions of that Act which are concerned with the internal conduct of their arbitration and which are not inconsistent with the choice of English arbitral procedural law."

The court also felt that the jurisdiction of the English court under the Arbitration Acts over an arbitration in England could not be excluded by agreement between the parties to apply the laws of another country. We would emphasise that the court was there referring to an arbitration where the seat was in England. This was not the situation here. Clearly, if it was established that the parties had agreed to change the "place of arbitration" to Singapore, then it must follow that the curial law would be Singapore law.

It is incontrovertible that parties are at liberty to change the place of arbitration. In *ABB Lummus Global v. Keppel Fels* [1999] 2 Lloyd's Rep. 24, there was such an express agreement to alter the place of arbitration from Singapore to London. *ABB Lummus* [therefore] cannot help us determine whether the parties here had, in fact, agreed to change the place of arbitration. We were unable to accept Garuda's contention that just because the parties eventually agreed with the arbitrators' suggestion that the hearing be held in Singapore, there was in consequence such an agreement to alter the place of arbitration from Jakarta to Singapore. What was changed was the "venue of hearing." This comes out clearly from the language of the correspondence.

In our opinion, Garuda's argument failed to give effect to the provisions of Art. 20(2) of the Model Law which expressly authorise the tribunal to meet at any place, other than the agreed place of arbitration, to hear witnesses and the parties. The opening words of Art. 20(2), "notwithstanding the provisions of paragraph (1) of this Article," clearly mean that such a hearing by the tribunal at a different location from that of the place of arbitration does not alter what was the agreed place of arbitration....

Garuda seemed to have placed great emphasis on the fact that the hearing of the arbitration was held entirely in Singapore and nowhere else. But an arbitration proceeding does not comprise only of the oral hearing and the submission. It encompasses an entire process, commencing from the appointment of the arbitrator or arbitrators to the rendering of the final award.

While both *Amazonica* and *Union Bank of India* did not involve the Model Law, and could be distinguished on that basis, the real differentiating feature there lies in the fact that in both those cases the relevant clauses were far from clear. We have alluded to that before. But in the instant case, the lease agreement was abundantly clear: the lease agreement was to be governed by Indonesian law and the place of arbitration was Jakarta, which must also mean that the arbitration proceedings were subject to Indonesian law.

In the result, Art. 34 of the Model Law and §24 of the IA Act did not apply to the final award. [Therefore,] there was no basis for Garuda to file [its application to annul the award] in the Singapore High Court....

KARAHA BODAS CO., LLC v. PERUSAHAAN PERTAMBANGAN MINYAK DAN GAS BUMI NEGARA
364 F.3d 274 (5th Cir. 2004)

ROSENTHAL, District Judge. Thirty years ago, the U.S. Supreme Court recognized that "[a] contractual provision specifying in advance the forum in which disputes shall be litigated and the law to be applied is ... an almost indispensable precondition to achievement of the orderliness and predictability essential to any international business transaction.... Such a provision obviates the danger that a dispute under the agreement might be submitted to a forum hostile to the interests of one of the parties or unfamiliar with the problem area involved." [*Scherk v. Alberto-Culver Co.*, 417 U.S. 506, 516 (1974).] When, as here, parties to international commercial contracts agree to arbitrate future disputes in a neutral forum, orderliness and predictability also depend on the procedures for reviewing and enforcing arbitral awards that may result. This appeal arises from an arbitral award (the "Award") made in Geneva, Switzerland, involving contracts negotiated and allegedly breached in Indonesia. The Award imposed liability and damages against Perusahaan Pertambangan Minyak Dan Gas Bumi Negara ("Pertamina") ... in favor of Karaha Bodas Company, LLC ("KBC"), a Cayman Islands company. KBC filed this suit in the federal district court in Texas to enforce the Award under the [New York] Convention, and filed enforcement actions in Hong Kong and Canada as well. While those enforcement proceedings were pending, Pertamina appealed the Award in the Swiss courts, seeking annulment. When that effort failed, and after the Texas district court granted summary judgment enforcing the Award, Pertamina obtained an order from an Indonesian court annulling the Award. Pertamina appealed to this court....

Pertamina urges this court to reverse the district court's decision enforcing the Award on several grounds under the New York Convention. We conclude that the record forecloses Pertamina's arguments that procedural violations ... during the arbitration preclude enforcement. We reject Pertamina's argument that the Indonesian court's order annulling the Award bars its enforcement under the Convention; this argument is inconsistent with the arbitration agreements Pertamina signed and with its earlier position that Switzerland, the neutral forum the parties selected, had exclusive jurisdiction over an annulment proceeding. We reject Pertamina's efforts to delay or avoid enforcement of the Award as evidencing a disregard for the international commercial arbitration procedures it agreed to follow....

KBC explores and develops geothermal energy sources and builds electric generating stations using geothermal sources. Pertamina is an oil, gas, and geothermal energy company owned by the Republic of Indonesia. In November 1994, KBC signed two contracts to produce electricity from geothermal sources in Indonesia. Under the Joint Operation Contract ("JOC"), KBC had the right to develop geothermal energy sources in the Karaha area of Indonesia; Pertamina was to manage the project and receive the electricity generated. Under the Energy Sales Contract ("ESC"), PLN agreed to purchase from Pertamina the energy generated by KBC's facilities. Both contracts contained almost identical broad arbitration clauses, requiring the parties to arbitrate any disputes in Geneva, Switzerland under the [UNCITRAL] Rules.[7]

On September 20, 1997, the government of Indonesia temporarily suspended the project because of the country's financial crisis. The government of Indonesia indefinitely suspended the project on January 10, 1998. On February 10, 1998, KBC notified Pertamina and PLN that the government's indefinite suspension constituted an event of force majeure under the contracts. KBC initiated arbitration proceedings on April 30, 1998. In its notice of arbitration, KBC appointed Professor Piero Bernardini, vice-chair of the [ICC's] International Court of Arbitration and member of the [LCIA], to serve as an arbitrator. Pertamina, however, did not designate an arbitrator in the contractually allotted thirty days. The JOC and ESC both provided that if a party failed to appoint an arbitrator within thirty days, the Secretary-General of [ICSID] was to make the appointment. After notifying Pertamina, PLN, and the government of Indonesia, the ICSID appointed Dr. Ahmed El-Kosheri, another vice-chair of the ICC, as the second arbitrator. As specified in the JOC

7. Article 13.2(2) of the arbitration provision of the JOC provided:

"If the Dispute cannot be settled within thirty (30) working days by mutual discussions as contemplated by Article 13.1 hereof, the Dispute shall finally be settled by an arbitral tribunal (the "Tribunal") under the UNCITRAL arbitration rules ... Each Party will appoint an arbitrator within thirty (30) days after the date of a request to initiate arbitration, who will then jointly appoint a third arbitrator within thirty (30) days of the date of the appointment of the second arbitrator to act as Chairman of the Tribunal. Arbitrators not appointed within the time limits set forth in the preceding sentence shall be appointed by the Secretary General of the International Center for Settlement of Investment Disputes. Both Parties undertake to implement the arbitration award. The site of the arbitration shall be Geneva, Switzerland. The language of the arbitration shall be English. The Parties expressly agree to waive [certain Indonesian procedural laws]...."

Section 8.2(a) of the ESC's arbitration provision similarly read:

"If the Dispute cannot be settled within forty-five calendar (45) days by mutual discussions as contemplated by §8.1 hereof, the Dispute shall finally be settled by an arbitral tribunal (the "Tribunal") under the UNCITRAL arbitration rules ... PLN on one hand, and [KBC] and PERTAMINA on the other hand, will each appoint one arbitrator, in each case within thirty (30) days after the date of a request to initiate arbitration, who will then jointly appoint a third arbitrator within thirty (30) days of the date of the appointment of the second arbitrator, to act as Chairman of the Tribunal. Arbitrators not appointed within the time limits set forth in the preceding sentence shall be appointed by the Secretary General of the International Center for Settlement of Investment Disputes, upon the request of any Party. All Parties undertake to implement the arbitration award. The site of the arbitration shall be Geneva, Switzerland. The language of the arbitration shall be English. The Parties expressly agree to waive the applicability of [certain Indonesian procedural laws]...."

Both contracts contained the following additional arbitration language:

"The award rendered in any arbitration commenced hereunder shall be final and binding upon the Parties and judgment thereon may be entered in any court having jurisdiction for its enforcement. The Parties hereby renounce their right to appeal from the decision of the arbitral panel and agree that in accordance with §641 of the Indonesian Code of Civil Procedure [neither] Party shall appeal to any court from the decision of the arbitral panel and accordingly the Parties hereby waive the applicability of [certain Indonesian laws]. In addition, the Parties agree that [neither] Party shall have any right to commence or maintain any suit or legal proceeding concerning a [dispute hereunder until the] dispute has been determined in accordance with the arbitration procedure provided for herein and then only to enforce or facilitate the execution of the award rendered in such arbitration."

and ESC, the two appointed arbitrators then selected the chairman of the arbitration panel, Yves Derains, the former Secretary-General of the ICC.

Pertamina raised threshold challenges to the Tribunal's consolidation of the claims KBC raised under the JOC and the ESC into one arbitration proceeding and to the selection of the panel.... [T]he Tribunal issued a Preliminary Award, rejecting Pertamina's threshold challenges and ruling that the government of Indonesia was not a party to the contracts or to the arbitration proceeding. KBC filed its Revised Statement of Claim in November 1999. Pertamina received a number of extensions before it filed its reply to the Revised Statement of Claim in April 2000. KBC filed a rebuttal to that reply in May 2000. In response to KBC's rebuttal, Pertamina sought additional discovery and a continuance of the proceedings, claiming that KBC had raised assertions and added elements to its case-in-chief not contained in the Revised Statement of Claim.

From the outset, the parties vigorously disputed whether KBC could have obtained financing to build the project if the government of Indonesia had not issued the suspension decree. Pertamina contended that KBC could not have built the project—and therefore suffered no damages from the government decree suspending the work—because the precarious situation in Indonesia effectively made the necessary financing unavailable. Pertamina asserted that KBC's rebuttal introduced a new theory as to how project financing could have been obtained. KBC changed from focusing on the availability of third-party financing and argued in the rebuttal that one of its direct investors, FPL Energy ("FPL"), would have provided project financing if no other source was available. Shortly before the scheduled hearing, Pertamina sought discovery of documents relating to FPL's asserted willingness to finance the project.... [T]he Tribunal denied Pertamina's request to obtain this discovery before the hearing and denied the request for a continuance. The Tribunal stated that it would decide at the conclusion of the hearing "whether any adjustment to the proceeding" would be required because of the discovery requested. The hearing on the merits proceeded as scheduled in June 2000....

During the hearing, Pertamina and PLN cross-examined KBC's witnesses, including two witnesses who testified about KBC's ability to finance the project, Robert McGrath, Treasurer of FPL Group, Inc., and Leslie Gelber, former Vice-President of Development at FPL Energy. Both witnesses submitted declarations stating that "FPL Energy was prepared in 1998 to provide bridge financing or direct capital to continue the Project through the phases of the Project that were scheduled to be completed during Indonesia's period of instability." At the hearing, counsel for Pertamina specifically questioned McGrath about the availability of project financing from FPL. During that questioning, a Tribunal member asked McGrath whether the investment in the project was protected by a form of political risk insurance. McGrath responded, "I am not sure of that. I know there were some discussions at the time, but I don't recollect as to whether it was or wasn't." Counsel for Pertamina asked no follow-up questions. At the end of the hearing, counsel for Pertamina declined to pursue the previously requested discovery and stated that the record had been "fully" made.

In the Final Award, the Tribunal ... interpreted the contracts as "putting the consequences of a Governmental decision which prevents the performance of the contract at Pertamina's ... sole risk." The Tribunal awarded KBC $111.1 million, the amount KBC had expended on the project, and $150 million in lost profits. The Tribunal explained in detail why it rejected the lost profits amount KBC sought—$512.5 million—and how it arrived at the amount awarded.

In February 2001, Pertamina appealed the Award to the Supreme Court of Switzerland. While that appeal was pending, KBC initiated this suit in the federal district court to enforce the Award. Pertamina challenged enforcement of the Award in the federal district court on four grounds under Article V of the New York Convention: (1) the procedure for selecting the arbitrators was not in accordance with the agreement of the parties; (2) the Tribunal improperly consolidated the claims into one arbitration; (3) Pertamina was "unable to present its case" to the Tribunal; and (4) enforcement of the ... Award would violate the public policy of the United States....

Pertamina continued its appeal seeking annulment of the Award to the [Swiss Federal Tribunal] while the enforcement action was pending in the district court in Texas. The Texas district court slowed the proceedings in deference to Pertamina's request that the Swiss court first be allowed to decide whether to annul the Award. In April 2001, the Swiss [Federal Tribunal] dismissed Pertamina's claim because of untimely payment of costs.... In December 2001, the district court enforced the Award, rejecting each of Pertamina's grounds for refusal.... The district court [also] denied Pertamina's Rule 56(f) request for additional discovery....

Having failed in its effort to annul the Award in the Swiss courts, Pertamina filed suit in Indonesia seeking annulment. In August 2002, an Indonesian court annulled the Award. KBC continued with enforcement suits in Hong Kong and Canada. In October 2002, ... Pertamina discovered in the Canadian proceeding that FPL and one other KBC investor, Caithness, had held a political risk insurance policy covering the KBC project through Lloyd's of London. Pertamina also learned that Lloyd's had paid $75 million under that insurance policy to FPL and Caithness for the losses resulting from the Indonesian government's suspension of the project.

In December 2002, Pertamina filed a motion in the district court to vacate the judgment on three grounds: (1) newly-discovered evidence of the political risk insurance policy ...; (2) the Indonesian court's annulment of the underlying arbitral Award ...; and (3) satisfaction of judgment to the extent of the $75 million insurance payment.... Pertamina argued that the existence of political risk insurance coverage in favor of FPL undermined KBC's claims that the contracts allocated political risks to Pertamina and that FPL would have financed the project in order to avoid losing its earlier investment. Additionally, Pertamina argued that the payment of the insurance proceeds undermined the Tribunal's determination of damages.... [T]he district court denied the motion, finding that Pertamina failed to show that KBC had misled the tribunal or that KBC's failure to produce the political risk insurance policy violated the rules governing the arbitration. The district court also rejected Pertamina's claim that Indonesia had primary jurisdiction to decide to annul the Award and declined to give effect to the Indonesian court's annulment order as a defense to enforcement.... Finally, the district court rejected Pertamina's argument that the amount of the Award should be offset by the $75 million insurance payment.

This appeal followed. Pertamina argues that the Tribunal improperly consolidated the claims into one arbitration proceeding; the selection of the arbitrators violated the JOC and ESC; the Tribunal denied Pertamina a fair opportunity to present its case because the Tribunal reversed part of its Preliminary Award without notice, denied Pertamina's request to postpone the arbitration, and denied Pertamina's discovery requests; the Award is contrary to public policy because it violated the international law abuse of rights doctrine and because the district court's decision holds Pertamina liable for complying with Indonesian law; and the Indonesian court's annulment of the arbitral Award is a defense to enforcement under the New York Convention. Each ground is addressed below.

The New York Convention provides a carefully structured framework for the review and enforcement of international arbitral awards. Only a court in a country with primary jurisdiction over an arbitral award may annul that award. Courts in other countries have secondary jurisdiction; a court in a country with secondary jurisdiction is limited to deciding whether the award may be enforced in that country. The Convention "mandates very different regimes for the review of arbitral awards (1) in the [countries] in which, or under the law of which, the award was made, and (2) in other [countries] where recognition and enforcement are sought." [*Yusuf Ahmed Alghanim & Sons, WLL v. Toys "R" Us, Inc.*, 126 F.3d 15, 23 (2d Cir. 1997) (quoted in *Karaha Bodas Co.*, 335 F.3d at 364).] Under the Convention, "the country in which, or under the [arbitration] law of which, [an] award was made" is said to have primary jurisdiction over the arbitration award. All other signatory states are secondary jurisdictions, in which parties can only contest whether that state should enforce the arbitral award. It is clear that the district court had secondary jurisdiction....

Article V enumerates specific grounds on which a court with secondary jurisdiction may refuse enforcement. In contrast to the limited authority of secondary-jurisdiction courts to review an arbitral award, courts of primary jurisdiction, usually the courts of the country of the arbitral situs, have much broader discretion to set aside an award. While courts of a primary jurisdiction country may apply their own domestic law in evaluating a request to annul or set aside an arbitral award, courts in countries of secondary jurisdiction may refuse enforcement only on the grounds specified in Article V.

The New York Convention and the implementing legislation, Chapter 2 of the [FAA] provide that a secondary jurisdiction court must enforce an arbitration award unless it finds one of the grounds for refusal or deferral of recognition or enforcement specified in the Convention. [9 U.S.C. §207]. The court may not refuse to enforce an arbitral award solely on the ground that the arbitrator may have made a mistake of law or fact. "Absent extraordinary circumstances, a confirming court is not to reconsider an arbitrator's findings." [*Europcar Italia, SpA v. Maiellano Tours, Inc.*, 156 F.3d 310, 315 (2d Cir. 1998); *Nat'l Wrecking Co. v. Int'l Bhd of Teamsters*, 990 F.2d 957, 960 (7th Cir. 1993).] The party defending against enforcement of the arbitral award bears the burden of proof. Defenses to enforcement under the ... Convention are construed narrowly, "to encourage the recognition and enforcement of commercial arbitration agreements in international contracts...." [*Imperial Ethiopian Gov't v. Baruch-Foster Corp.*, 535 F.2d 334, 335 (5th Cir. 1976); *Parsons & Whittemore Overseas Co., Inc. v. Societe Generale de l'Industrie du Papier*, 508 F.2d 969, 974, 976 (2d Cir. 1974).]

In the JOC and ESC, the parties stipulated that "the site of the arbitration shall be Geneva." The Tribunal concluded that under the arbitration agreements, Swiss procedural law applied as the law of the arbitral forum.[8] From 1998 to April 2002, Pertamina consistently

---

8. The Tribunal specifically cited Swiss procedural law in its Preliminary Award. The Tribunal first cited Swiss law regarding the intentions of parties to a contract to help guide its determination whether the government of Indonesia was a party to the JOC and ESC. The Tribunal cited the Swiss concept of "connexity" in

and repeatedly took the position before the Tribunal, the Swiss courts, and the U.S. district court, that Swiss procedural law applied to the arbitration. In April 2002, after the Swiss court had rejected Pertamina's annulment proceeding and the district court had held the Award enforceable in the United States, Pertamina moved in the district court for a stay of the Award pending the outcome of the annulment proceeding Pertamina had filed in Indonesia. For the first time, Pertamina raised in the district court the argument that Indonesian, not Swiss, procedural law had applied to the arbitration. Pertamina took this position in the district court as part of its argument that Indonesia had primary jurisdiction over the Award and therefore had the authority to set it aside rather than merely decline to enforce it.

Article V(1)(e) of the Convention provides that a court of secondary jurisdiction may refuse to enforce an arbitral award if it "has been set aside or suspended by a competent authority of the country in which, or under the law of which, that award was made." Courts have held that the language, "'the competent authority of the country … under the law of which, that award was made' refers exclusively to procedural and not substantive law, and more precisely, to the regimen or scheme of arbitral procedural law under which the arbitration was conducted, and not the substantive law … applied in the case." [*Int'l Standard Elec. Corp. v. Bridas Sociedad Anonima Petrolera*, 745 F.Supp. 172, 178 (S.D.N.Y. 1990); *Toys "R" Us*, 126 F.3d at 21; *M & C Corp. v. Erwin Behr GmbH & Co.*, 87 F.3d 844, 848 (6th Cir. 1996).] In this appeal, Pertamina and the Republic of Indonesia (the "Republic"), as amicus, argue that the Tribunal and the district court erred in finding that Swiss procedural law, rather than Indonesian procedural law, applied. Pertamina and the Republic argue that in the arbitration agreements, the parties chose Indonesian procedural, as well as substantive, law to govern the arbitration. [They] assert that, as a result: (1) the arbitration must be examined for compliance with Indonesian procedural law; and (2) the Indonesian court had primary jurisdiction to annul the Award, providing a defense to enforcement in the United States. KBC responds that the Tribunal properly interpreted the parties' contracts in deciding that Swiss procedural law applied and the district court properly applied the Convention in affirming that decision. This court agrees with KBC.

Under the Convention, the rulings of the Tribunal interpreting the parties' contract are entitled to deference. Unless the Tribunal manifestly disregarded the parties' agreement or the law, there is no basis to set aside the determination that Swiss procedural law applied. The parties' arbitration agreements specified that the site of the arbitration was Geneva, Switzerland and that the arbitration would proceed under the UNCITRAL Rules. Those Rules specify that the "arbitral tribunal shall apply the law designated by the parties as applicable to the substance of the dispute." [1976 UNCITRAL Rules, Art. 33(1)]. It is undisputed that the parties specified that Indonesian substantive law would apply.[9] It is also undisputed that the contracts specified the site of the arbitration as Switzerland. The contracts did not otherwise expressly identify the procedural law that would apply to the arbitration. The parties did refer to certain Indonesian Civil Procedure Rules in the

concluding that KBC could consolidate its claims under the contracts into a single arbitration proceeding. Finally, the Tribunal referred to Swiss common law suggesting that arbitrators are not agents in determining that the selection of Tribunal arbitrators was appropriate under the agreements. The Final Award stated that it was "made in Geneva."

9. Article 20 of the JOC and §12.1 of the ESC each provided: "This Contract shall be governed by the laws and regulations of [the] Republic of Indonesia."

contracts.[10] Pertamina and the Republic argue that these references evidence an intent that while Switzerland would be the place of the arbitration, Indonesian procedural law would apply as the *lex arbitri*.

Under the Convention, an agreement specifying the place of the arbitration creates a presumption that the procedural law of that place applies to the arbitration. Authorities on international arbitration describe an agreement providing that one country will be the site of the arbitration but the proceedings will be held under the arbitration law of another country by terms such as "exceptional"; "almost unknown"; a "purely academic invention"; "almost never used in practice"; a possibility "more theoretical than real"; and a "once-in-a-blue-moon set of circumstances." Commentators note that such an agreement would be complex, inconvenient, and inconsistent with the selection of a neutral forum as the arbitral forum.[11]

In the JOC and ESC, the parties expressly agreed that Switzerland would be the site for the arbitration. This agreement presumptively selected Swiss procedural law to apply to the arbitration. There is no express agreement in the JOC or ESC that Indonesia would be the country "under the law of which" the arbitration was to be conducted and the Award was to be made. The Tribunal recognized the parties' selection of Switzerland by issuing the Award as "made in Geneva." In selecting Switzerland as the site of the arbitration, the parties were not choosing a physical place for the arbitration to occur, but rather the place where the award would be "made." Under Article 16(1) of the [1976] UNCITRAL Rules, the "place" designated for an arbitration is the legal rather than physical location of the forum. The arbitration proceeding in this case physically occurred in Paris, but the Award was "made in" Geneva, the place of the arbitration in the legal sense and the presumptive source of the applicable procedural law. The references in the contracts to certain Indonesian civil procedure rules [*supra* p. 611 n. 10] do not rebut the strong presumption that Swiss procedural law applied to the arbitration. These references fall far short of an express designation of Indonesian procedural law necessary to rebut the strong presumption that designating the place of the arbitration also designates the law under which the award is made.

---

10. Pertamina and the Republic rely on the following contractual provisions for their position:

"The parties expressly agree to waive the applicability of (a) Article 650.2 of the Indonesian Code of Civil Procedure so that the appointment of the arbitrator shall not terminate as of the sixth (6th) Month after the date(s) of their appointments and (b) the second sentence of Article 620.1 of the Indonesian Code of Civil Procedure so that the arbitration need not be completed within the specific time." JOC at Art. 13.2(a); ESC at §8.2(a).

"In accordance with §631 of the Indonesian Code of Civil Procedure, the Parties agree that the Tribunal need not be bound by strict rules of law where they consider the application thereof to particular matters to be inconsistent with the spirit of this Contract and the underlying intent of the Parties, and as to such matters their conclusion shall reflect their judgment of the correct interpretation of all relevant terms hereof and the correct and just enforcement of this Contract in accordance with such terms." JOC at Art. 13.2(b); ESC at §8.2(b).

"The parties hereby renounce their right to appeal from the decision of the arbitral panel and agree that in accordance with §641 of the Indonesian Code of Civil Procedure neither Party shall appeal to any court ... and accordingly the Parties hereby waive the applicability of Articles 15 and 108 of the Law No. 1 of 1950 and any other provision of Indonesian law and regulations that would otherwise give the right to appeal the decisions of the arbitral panel." JOC at Art. 13.2(d); ESC at §8.2(d).

11. *See, e.g.*, Gary B. Born, *International Commercial Arbitration: Commentary and Materials* 761 (2d ed. 2001). Few reported cases involve arbitration clauses that separate the law of the forum state and the *lex arbitri*....

Pertamina and the Republic have belatedly asserted that the district court should have conducted a choice-of-law analysis to determine the law that would apply to the interpretation of the parties' contracts, rather than analyze the contracts under the Convention. Pertamina and the Republic assert that the result of such an analysis would have been to identify Indonesian law as the decisional law under which to interpret the contracts. This argument is inconsistent with the position Pertamina—and its experts on interpreting international commercial arbitration agreements—took earlier in this case, that the district court should review the Tribunal's interpretation of the contracts under the Convention. A court conducts the multifactor choice-of-law analysis Pertamina now advocates in the absence of an effective choice of law by the parties to an arbitration agreement. In the JOC and ESC, the parties presumptively chose Swiss procedural law as the *lex arbitri* when they designated Switzerland as the site of the arbitration, and that presumption is unrebutted.[12]

As the district court, another panel of this court, and the Hong Kong Court of First Instance have all recognized, Pertamina's previous arguments that Swiss arbitral law applied strongly evidence the parties' contractual intent. Pertamina represented to the Tribunal that Swiss procedural law applied. As but one example, Pertamina cited Swiss procedural law in arguing that the Tribunal could not consolidate the claims under the JOC and ESC into one proceeding. Pertamina at no point argued to the Tribunal that Indonesian procedural law applied. Pertamina initially sought to set aside the Award in a Swiss court. Pertamina asked the Texas district court to stay its enforcement proceeding until Pertamina's appeal in Switzerland was resolved. In making this argument, Pertamina stated that "the arbitration … was conducted according to the laws of Switzerland, and the Swiss court is empowered to vacate an award rendered in Switzerland … KBC is asking this Court to act prematurely to confirm an award that might be overturned in the country whose law governed the arbitration."…

The combination of the parties' selection of Switzerland as the site of the arbitration; the failure clearly or expressly to choose Indonesian arbitral law in their agreements, as required to select arbitral law other than that of the place of the arbitration; and the clear evidence provided by the parties' own conduct that they intended Swiss law to apply to the arbitration, amply supports the district court's determination that the Tribunal properly applied Swiss procedural law….

Under Article V(1)(d) of the Convention, a court may refuse to enforce an arbitration award if "the composition of the arbitral authority or the arbitral procedure was not in accordance with the agreement of the parties, or, failing such agreement, was not in accordance with the law of the country where the arbitration took place." Pertamina argues that because the JOC and ESC were separate contracts with separate arbitration clauses, and because neither contract expressly allowed the consolidation of claims, the Tribunal improperly consolidated the claims into one arbitration proceeding. Pertamina also contends on appeal that because Indonesian rather than Swiss procedural law governed the

---

12. Certain sections and comments of the Restatement also support a determination that Swiss law applied to the arbitration agreement. *See, e.g., id.* at §188 (incorporating REST, (2D) CONFL. §6, which requires consideration of the relevant policies of the forum); *id.* at §218 cmt. b (suggesting that the arbitration forum may have the most significant relationship to the arbitration and that a contractual provision requiring arbitration to occur in a certain forum may evidence an intention by the parties that the local law of their forum should govern).

arbitration, the Tribunal's reliance on Swiss procedural law to consolidate the claims was erroneous.

The Tribunal carefully analyzed the parties' contracts in concluding that a consolidated arbitration of KBC's claims against Pertamina and PLN under the JOC and ESC was appropriate. In factual findings set out in the Preliminary Award, the Tribunal set out the basis for concluding that the two contracts were integrated such that "the parties did not contemplate the performance of two independent contracts but the performance of a single project consisting of two closely related parties."[13] The Tribunal continued:

> "In such circumstances, the conclusion of this Arbitral Tribunal is that KBC's single action should be admitted, provided it is appropriate. The Arbitral Tribunal has not the slightest doubt in this respect. Due to the integration of the two contracts and the fact that the Presidential Decrees, the consequences of which are at the origin of the dispute, affected both of them, the initiation of two separate arbitrations would be artificial and would generate the risk of contradictory decisions. Moreover, it would increase the costs of all the parties involved, an element of special weight in the light of difficulties faced by the Indonesian economy...."

The record provides ample support for the Tribunal's ... conclusion that the two contracts were integrated such that the parties contemplated a single arbitration.

The Tribunal cited the Swiss law of concept of "connexity" in analyzing the legal relations among KBC and Pertamina under the JOC and KBC, Pertamina, and PLN under the ESC as one of the factors justifying the consolidation of claims under the two contracts into one arbitration proceeding. The Tribunal concluded that the relationship of the JOC and ESC exceeded the standard of "connexity" under Swiss law. "The use of the word 'connexity' to describe the relationship between the JOC and ESC would be an understatement. In reality, the two contracts are integrated." Courts and arbitration tribunals have recognized that claims arising under integrated contracts may be consolidated into single arbitrations. [*See, e.g., Conn. Gen. Life Ins. Co. v. SunLife Assur. Co. of Canada*, 210 F.3d 771, 774 (7th Cir. 2000); *Maxum Founds. v. Salus Corp.*, 817 F.2d 1086, 1087-88 (4th Cir. 1987).] The Tribunal cited one other factor that supported consolidation: "appropriateness." The parties agreed to the application of the UNCITRAL Rules, which permit a tribunal to conduct an arbitration "in such manner as it considers appropriate." [1976 UNCITRAL Rules, Art. 15(1); 2010 UNCITRAL Rules, Art. 17(1).] ...

Courts are reluctant to set aside arbitral awards under the Convention based on procedural violations, reflected in cases holding that the Convention embodies a pro-enforcement bias. The Tribunal emphasized in its Preliminary Award that although the claims would be consolidated, "the position of each party has to be considered independently when discussing the substance of the case, on the basis of their respective legal and contractual situations." The record reflects that the Tribunal kept this promise. There is

---

13. Article 15.3 of the ESC provided that "the terms of [the ESC] and the Joint Operation Contract constitute the entire agreement between the parties hereto." Article 1.2 of the JOC stated that "each such Energy Sales Contract shall be an integral part of this contract, and to the extent the provisions of the Energy Sales Contract obligate the parties hereto, shall be deemed incorporated into this contract for all purposes." Pertamina and KBC entered into the JOC and ESC on the same day. The JOC and the ESC contained virtually identical arbitration provisions.

no prejudice arising from the consolidation that would justify a refusal to enforce the Award.

Under Article V(1)(d), a court may refuse enforcement of an arbitral award if the composition of the tribunal is not in accordance with the parties' agreement. The JOC provided for the appointment of arbitrators, as follows:

> "Each Party [KBC and Pertamina] will appoint an arbitrator within thirty (30) days after the date of a request to initiate arbitration, who will then jointly appoint a third arbitrator within thirty (30) days of the date of the appointment of the second arbitrator, to act as Chairman of the Tribunal. Arbitrators not appointed within the time limits set forth in the preceding sentence shall be appointed by the Secretary General of the [ICSID]."

The ESC procedure ... was slightly different:

> "PLN on one hand, and [KBC] and PERTAMINA, on the other hand, will each appoint one arbitrator, in each case within thirty (30) days after the date of a request to initiate arbitration, who will then jointly appoint a third arbitrator within thirty (30) days of the date of the appointment of the second arbitrator, to act as Chairman of the Tribunal. Arbitrators not appointed within the time limits set forth in the preceding sentence shall be appointed by the Secretary General of the [ICSID, upon the request of any Party."

Each contract required the appointment of arbitrators within thirty days of the notice of arbitration and provided for appointment by the ICSID in the event that a party did not do so. In its notice of arbitration sent to Pertamina, KBC appointed Professor Piero Bernardini to serve as an arbitrator. Pertamina did not designate an arbitrator within thirty days, nor did it object to KBC's selection at that time. By letter dated June 2, 1998, KBC notified the ICSID of Pertamina's inaction and requested the appointment of a second arbitrator under the default appointment provisions of the contracts. Pertamina did not respond to this letter. The ICSID questioned KBC about the consolidation of claims under the JOC and the ESC and KBC's unilateral appointment of an arbitrator. KBC responded by letter dated June 22, 1998. The ICSID confirmed receipt of KBC's letters and in a June 29, 1998 letter to all parties, recapped the prior correspondence, noted Pertamina's failure to respond, and expressed its intent to grant KBC's request to appoint the second arbitrator. The ICSID Secretary-General identified Dr. Ahmed El-Kosheri as its candidate and asked for any objections by July 13, 1998. The ICSID sent all the preceding correspondence to PLN by courier and to Pertamina by fax and courier. Despite the Secretary-General's invitation to do so, neither Pertamina nor PLN lodged objections or responses to the proposed appointment. On July 13, 1998, having received no communications from Pertamina, the ICSID notified Pertamina and PLN of its intent to appoint Dr. El-Kosheri and made the appointment on July 15, 1998. Under the JOC and ESC, Professor Bernardini and Dr. El-Kosheri then selected the chairman of the arbitration panel, Yves Derains.

In its Preliminary Award, the Tribunal rejected Pertamina's argument that KBC's selection of an arbitrator violated the ESC's requirement that KBC and Pertamina jointly make the nomination. The Tribunal found that the parties intended to limit that requirement to disputes in which PLN was opposed to KBC and Pertamina. Because the ESC did not expressly address the method for appointing arbitrators when KBC and Pertamina opposed each other, the Tribunal found that UNCITRAL Rules for appointment applied. The Tribunal ruled that the appointment procedures used did not violate these rules or create an inequality of treatment. The Tribunal emphasized Pertamina's failure to nominate an arbitrator or object to those nominated. The district court agreed with the Tribunal ... and added that Pertamina had failed to demonstrate any prejudice from the appointment proceedings.

On appeal, Pertamina reasserts its argument that KBC's unilateral selection of an arbitrator violated the ESC's requirement that "PLN on the one hand and [KBC] and Pertamina, on the other hand, will each appoint one arbitrator." Pertamina contends that its interests would always be aligned with KBC under the ESC, which required PLN to purchase from Pertamina the electricity that KBC provided, and that this explains the contractual requirement that KBC and Pertamina agree on an arbitrator in a dispute arising under that contract. In response, KBC argues that the Tribunal correctly found that a dispute between KBC and Pertamina was possible under the ESC, but in the event of such a dispute, the ESC did not provide a procedure for choosing an arbitrator. KBC asserts that the Tribunal correctly found that the general UNCITRAL Rules for selecting an arbitrator would apply, under which KBC, Pertamina, and PLN would each appoint an arbitrator....

The ESC arbitration clause refers to "any dispute or difference of any kind whatsoever" arising among "the Parties." Section 2 of the ESC defines "parties" to include PLN, Pertamina, and KBC. By its terms, the arbitration clause covers a dispute between KBC and Pertamina arising under the ESC, as well as a dispute in which the interests of KBC and Pertamina are aligned. If the ESC required KBC and Pertamina jointly to select an arbitrator for disputes in which KBC and Pertamina were opposed, as Pertamina contends, Pertamina could effectively block arbitration under the ESC simply by refusing to agree with KBC to the selection of an arbitrator. Such an interpretation would make the ESC arbitration clause illusory.

In addition, Pertamina had numerous opportunities early in the proceedings to object to KBC's selection of Professor Bernardini as an arbitrator and to nominate its own arbitrator. Pertamina did not challenge the composition of the arbitral panel until after the entire panel had been selected and seated. Pertamina's failure timely to object to Professor Bernardini's selection and to nominate its own arbitrator was, as the district court noted, a strategic decision that Pertamina should not now be able to assert as a defense to enforcing the Award.[14]

Pertamina has failed to meet its burden of showing that the Tribunal was improperly constituted. The Tribunal reasonably interpreted the ESC's arbitration provisions and reasonably applied the UNCITRAL arbitration rules. Despite numerous opportunities, Pertamina failed to challenge the Tribunal's composition until after the arbitrators were selected. The procedural infirmities Pertamina alleges do not provide grounds for denying enforcement of the Award.

Under Article V(1)(b), enforcement of a foreign arbitral award may be denied if the party challenging the award was "not given proper notice of the appointment of the arbitrator or of the arbitration proceedings or was otherwise unable to present [its] case." Article V(1)(b) "essentially sanctions the application of the forum state's standards of due process," in this case, U.S. standards of due process. [*Iran Aircraft Indus. v. Avco Corp.*, 980 F.2d 141, 145 (2d Cir. 1992) (quoting *Parsons & Whittemore Overseas*, 508 F.2d at

---

14. Pertamina apparently argued to the Tribunal that it did not name an arbitrator because it was contesting the legitimacy of the arbitration and further contended that it did not receive certain correspondence from ICSID regarding KBC's request that the ICSID appoint a second arbitrator. Pertamina, however, did not make these arguments before the district court.

975).] A fundamentally fair hearing requires that a party to a foreign arbitration be able to present its case. A fundamentally fair hearing is one that "meets 'the minimal requirements of fairness'—adequate notice, a hearing on the evidence, and an impartial decision by the arbitrator." The parties must have an opportunity to be heard "at a meaningful time and in a meaningful manner." "The right to due process does not include the complete set of procedural rights guaranteed by the Federal Rules of Civil Procedure."

Pertamina first contends that the Tribunal reversed the Preliminary Award in the Final Award without notice, denying Pertamina the opportunity to be "meaningfully heard." ... The Final Award shows that the Tribunal considered and rejected Pertamina's argument in making its liability decision.... In this enforcement proceeding, Pertamina is essentially repeating the arguments it made to the Tribunal. The fact that those arguments were presented to and considered by the Tribunal is inconsistent with Pertamina's claim that it had no notice of the need to make the argument to that Tribunal or the opportunity to do so. Pertamina did not suffer the fundamental unfairness it claims, so as to support a refusal to enforce the Award.

To challenge KBC's contention that FPL was willing to finance the project, Pertamina sought in the arbitration ... a continuance and discovery of [various categories of] documents from KBC, FPL, and Caithness regarding the financing of the KBC project.... The Tribunal denied Pertamina's request. After Pertamina discovered that FPL and certain other investors in KBC owned a political risk insurance policy underwritten by Lloyd's of London, which had paid $75 million after the project suspension, Pertamina sought reconsideration of the district court's [decision enforcing the Award]. The district court found that Pertamina's inability to introduce evidence of the insurance policy at the arbitration did not prevent the presentation of its case to the Tribunal. The district court also held that KBC's failure to bring the insurance policy to the Tribunal's attention did not make enforcing the Award a violation of public policy. We agree.

"An 'arbitrator is not bound to hear all of the evidence tendered by the parties ... [He] must give each of the parties to the dispute an adequate opportunity to present its evidence and arguments.'" [*Generica Ltd v. Pharm. Basics, Inc.*, 125 F.3d 1123 (7th Cir. 1997) (quoting *Hoteles Condado Beach, La Concha & Convention Ctr v. Union de Tronquistas Local 901*, 763 F.2d 34, 39 (1st Cir. 1985)); *see Slaney v. Int'l Amateur Athletic Fed'n*, 244 F.3d 580, 592 (7th Cir. 2001) (cautioning that "parties that have chosen to remedy their disputes through arbitration rather than litigation should not expect the same procedures they would find in the judicial arena").] It is appropriate to vacate an ... award if the exclusion of relevant evidence deprives a party of a fair hearing. "Every failure of an arbitrator to receive relevant evidence does not constitute misconduct requiring vacatur of an arbitrator's award. A federal court may vacate an arbitrator's award only if the arbitrator's refusal to hear pertinent and material evidence prejudices the rights of the parties to the arbitration proceedings." [*Hoteles Condado Beach*, 763 F.2d at 40.]

Although the Tribunal denied Pertamina the specific discovery it sought on the issue of FPL financing, Pertamina was able to cross-examine the KBC witnesses who testified that FPL was willing to provide financing for the project, Leslie Gelber and Robert McGrath. Before those witnesses testified, Pertamina had already presented substantial evidence ... as to why KBC would not have been able to secure financing for the project, emphasizing the depressed state of the Indonesian economy and its unattractiveness to investors. Pertamina argued to the Tribunal that KBC had presented no documentary evidence of FPL's willingness to finance the project and asserted that FPL would have required such a high rate of interest because of the risk involved as to make the KBC venture unprofitable. The Tribunal found that "the issue remained open in 1998 of the terms and conditions upon which financing could have been obtained for the Project development." The Tribunal noted that "the worsening of the economic and political situation in Indonesia at the time has to be taken into account as regards both the conditions at which financing could have been obtained and possible delays in arranging the same." ... The Tribunal found the testimony of KBC's witnesses on financing credible, stating that it had "no reason ... to cast doubts about KBC's readiness, directly and/or through its shareholders, to make provision thereof." In determining the lost profits, the Tribunal considered all the risks of the project, including the potential difficulties in arranging financing that Pertamina cited, and "significantly reduced" the amount of lost profits claimed by KBC.

In *Generica, Ltd v. Pharm. Basics, Inc.*, the party opposing enforcement of an international arbitration award argued that the tribunal curtailed cross-examination of a witness, in violation of the party's due process right to present its case. The tribunal, recognizing that it had curtailed the cross-examination, placed diminished reliance on the witness's testimony. The court found that by limiting the reliance on the witness's testimony, the arbitrators eliminated the possibility of prejudice to the party claiming a due process violation. The court confirmed the award. As in *Generica*, the Tribunal appears to have given all the evidence as to damages, including the availability of financing, appropriate weight in determining liability and damages.

In *Tempo Shain Corp. v. Bertek, Inc.*, [120 F.3d 16 (2d Cir. 1997)], the arbitral panel did not allow a potential witness to testify on the basis that the witness's testimony was cumulative. The court vacated the arbitral award. The record showed that the witness would have testified to facts that only he could have known, making his testimony essential. Similarly, in *Hoteles Condado Beach v. Union de Tronquistas Local* 901, [763 F.2d 34 (1st Cir. 1985)], the court vacated an award because the arbitral panel refused to give any weight to the only evidence available to the losing party. In the present case, by contrast, the Tribunal's language in the Final Award and the record show that the testimony about FPL's willingness to provide financing was only one factor relevant to damages. KBC raised the possibility of FPL's direct financing only in response to Pertamina's affirmative defense that KBC could not have financed the project. Pertamina did not seek discovery on KBC's efforts to finance the project in the arbitration proceeding until after KBC filed its rebuttal to the response to the Statement of Claim, despite the fact that Pertamina raised the issue as an affirmative defense.

The record shows that the Tribunal's refusal to grant a continuance and additional pre-hearing discovery did not "so affect the rights of [Pertamina] that it may be said that [it] was deprived of a fair hearing." [*Newark Stereotypers' Union No. 18 v. Newark Morning Ledger Co.*, 397 F.2d 594, 599 (3d Cir. 1968).] Pertamina was able to present comprehensive evidence of investment conditions in Indonesia and expert opinions on the availability of financing, as well as cross-examine Gelber and McGrath on FPL's asserted willingness and ability to provide financing....

The Tribunal asked McGrath whether FPL had purchased "OPIC insurance," a form of political risk insurance. McGrath responded that he did not know the answer to the question. Pertamina's counsel did not follow up on the Tribunal's questioning. At the conclusion of the hearing, the Tribunal chair asked the parties whether the discovery requests were "maintained, all of them, part of them, because we would like to know on what we have to decide." The response from counsel for Pertamina was as follows:

> "The purpose of discovery is to prepare for the hearing, it is not to supplement the record after the hearing. So I think the discovery requests are moot, and if discovery is now permitted, then you have to re-open the proceedings and so on. So I treated, notwithstanding the fact that it was theoretically open, I treated this request as effectively being denied, and we went forward. Our request went to the purported financial ability, the purported financing that would have been made available and other things, and I think the record on that has been fully made. I am prepared to rest on that record, and so I think the discovery requests should no longer be in the picture."

The parties submitted extensive post trial briefs. In the Final Award, issued in December 2000, the Tribunal stated that all parties had "waived their respective requests for discovery" at the conclusion of the hearing…. The record supports the Tribunal's conclusion that the discovery requests made before the hearing had been waived. Pertamina did not ask for discovery into political risk insurance until … its Rule 60(b) motion in the district court.

The Tribunal's denial of a continuance and additional discovery did not prevent Pertamina from presenting its case, so as to deprive it of a fair hearing. Pertamina presented ample evidence in support of its position that KBC would be unable to find financing. The Tribunal considered Pertamina's evidence and gave it considerable weight, awarding KBC damages substantially lower than the amount it sought. Pertamina has failed to show the prejudice required to decline enforcement of the Award on this ground….

Pertamina filed an annulment action in the Central District Court of Jakarta, Indonesia in March 2002. That court annulled the Award on August 27, 2002. Pertamina now contends that the Indonesian court's annulment is a defense to enforcement under the New York Convention. KBC responds that Indonesia cannot be a proper forum for annulment because Switzerland is the country of primary jurisdiction.

Pertamina argues that the Convention permits more than one country to have primary jurisdiction over an arbitration award. Pertamina contends that the Convention's language permitting annulment by a court in "the country in which, or under the law of which, that award was made" allows for two potential primary jurisdiction countries—the country who hosted the arbitration proceeding, and the country whose arbitral procedural law governed that proceeding.[15] … Pertamina suggests that both Switzerland (the host country) and Indonesia (the country of governing law) have primary jurisdiction over the arbitration in this case.

Pertamina correctly observes that the Convention provides two tests for determining which country has primary jurisdiction over an arbitration award: a country in which an award is made, and a country under the law of which an award is made. The Convention suggests the potential for more than one country of primary jurisdiction. Courts and scholars have noted as much. Pertamina cites one such scholar as support for its position:

> "Ambiguity is derived from the fact that the formula does not indicate whether the party

---

15. The language, "'the competent authority of the country … under the law of which, that award was made' refers exclusively to procedural and not substantive law, and more precisely, to the regimen or scheme of arbitral procedural law under which the arbitration was conducted, and not the substantive law … applied in the case." *Int'l Standard Elec. Corp.*, 745 F.Supp. at 178; *[Toys "R" Us,]* 126 F.3d at 21; *M & C Corp.*, 87 F.3d at 848.

seeking the annulment of the award must choose between the court at the seat of the arbitration and the one located in the country under the law of which the award is made—if the two are distinct—or whether it may seek annulment jointly or alternatively before both courts ... Article V(1)(e) of the New York Convention could [] be construed as referring to the courts of only one country while giving the party seeking the annulment the possibility to choose between the two countries should the two be distinct." [H. Gharavi, *The International Effectiveness of the Annulment of An Arbitral Award* (2002).]

Although an arbitration agreement may make more than one country eligible for primary jurisdiction under the New York Convention, the predominant view is that the Convention permits only one in any given case. "Many commentators and foreign courts have concluded that an action to set aside an award can be brought only under the domestic law of the arbitral forum." [*Toys "R" Us*, 126 F.3d at 22 (citing commentary that the country of origin of the award is the only country with primary jurisdiction).] Pertamina's expert on international arbitration filed a report in the district court, stating that "there can be only one country in which the courts have jurisdiction over an annulment." [*Supplemental Expert Report of Albert Jan van den Berg*, p. 20.] In its motion ... to set aside judgment under Rule 60(b), Pertamina conceded that "[a] primary jurisdiction has exclusive authority to nullify an award on the basis of its own arbitration law." Such "exclusive" primary jurisdiction in the courts of a single country is consistent with the [Convention]'s purpose; facilitates the "orderliness and predictability" necessary to international commercial agreements; and implements the parties' choice of a neutral forum.

In this case, both of the New York Convention criteria for the country with primary jurisdiction point to Switzerland—and only to Switzerland. The Award was made in Switzerland and was made under Swiss procedural law. The parties' arbitration agreement designated Switzerland as the site for the arbitration. This designation presumptively designated Swiss procedural law as the *lex arbitri*, in the absence of any express statement making another country's procedural law applicable.... Under the ... Convention, the parties' arbitration agreement, and this record, Switzerland had primary jurisdiction over the Award. Because Indonesia did not have primary jurisdiction to set aside the Award, this court affirms the district court's conclusion that the Indonesian court's annulment ruling is not a defense to enforcement under the ... Convention....

Pertamina's challenges to the district court's decision affirming the Award are without merit. The summary judgment enforcing the Award is affirmed.

NOTES

1. *Territorial scope of national arbitration legislation.* Consider the scope of the UNCITRAL Model Law, the English Arbitration Act and the SLPIL. What arbitrations does the Model Law (other than Articles 35 and 36) apply to? Consider Articles 1(2) and 18-20, excerpted at pp. 86 & 90-91 of the Documentary Supplement. What arbitrations does the SLPIL (other than Article 194) apply to? Consider Articles 176(1), 176(3) and 182 of the SLPIL, excerpted at pp. 157-59 of the Documentary Supplement. Suppose the Model Law is enacted in State A. Does the Model Law apply generally to arbitrations where the place of arbitration is outside State A? What about the SLPIL—does it apply to arbitrations seated outside Switzerland?

   Note that, under Article 1(2), most of the Model Law's provisions apply only to arbitrations that are seated in the jurisdiction that adopted the Model Law (State A, in the above example). What exceptions are there to this general rule? Consider the same question under Article 176(1) of the SLPIL.

What is the rationale for the territorial scope of the UNCITRAL Model Law? Is it based on notions of territorial sovereignty—*i.e.*, that a state enjoys sovereign regulatory authority over actions occurring within its territory and not elsewhere? Consider:

> "it is still always necessary to connect the conduct of the arbitral proceedings to a national legal system, which will regulate, for example, the extent of autonomy which the parties are permitted to exercise in selecting the arbitral procedure (and any mandatory rules from which the parties cannot derogate); the assistance which the national courts will provide to the arbitration in the grant of provisional measure, collection of evidence etc.; and procedures for the review of awards." L. Collins (ed.), *Dicey, Morris & Collins on The Conflict of Laws* ¶16-009 (15th ed. 2012).

See also Mann, *Lex Facit Arbitrum,* reprinted in 2 Arb. Int'l 241, 244 (1986) ("every arbitration is a national arbitration, that is to say, subject to a specific system of national law"); Rubins, *The Arbitral Seat Is No Fiction: A Brief Reply to Tatsuya Nakamura's Commentary,* 16(1) Mealey's Int'l Arb. Rep. 23, 24-26 (2001) ("at its present stage of development, arbitration would not be served by a divorce from geography and State-based jurisprudence"). Compare:

> "The strict territorial criterion, governing the bulk of the provisions of the Model Law, was adopted for the sake of certainty and in view of the following facts. The place of arbitration is used as the exclusive criterion by the great majority of national laws...."
> *Explanatory Note by the UNCITRAL Secretariat on the Model Law on International Commercial Arbitration, as amended in 2006* ¶14 (2008).

What alternatives are there to the territorial scope of national arbitration legislation? Suppose that the SLPIL purported to govern arbitrations seated in Singapore.

2. *Concept of "arbitral seat."* What does it mean to refer to the "arbitral seat"? (The arbitral seat is also variously termed the "place of arbitration," "*siège*," "*Ort*," arbitral "*situs*," "*locus arbitri*," or arbitral "forum.") Is the arbitral seat just the place where the arbitration (and its hearings) take place physically? Or is it something different? Note the definition of the arbitral seat in §3 of the English Arbitration Act, 1996, excerpted at p. 112 of the Documentary Supplement. Compare Article 1(2) of the Model Law. Consider the Singaporean court's analysis in *Garuda.* As you read the following Notes, continue to consider what it means to refer to the arbitral seat.

3. *"Internal" and "external" procedural issues governed by law of arbitral seat.* Consider what issues are governed by the law of the arbitral seat. For example, what issues affecting an arbitration with its seat in a Model Law jurisdiction are governed by the Model Law?

   (a) *"External" issues.* Some issues that are addressed by the Model Law and other national arbitration legislation can be described as "external." They concern the relationship between the arbitral process and the courts and law of the arbitral seat and, in particular, the limited number of circumstances in which courts in the arbitral seat may exercise a judicial supervision role over the arbitral process. Among other things, "external" issues include the power of local courts to appoint arbitrators (Model Law, Art. 11), to remove arbitrators (Model Law, Art. 13), to consider jurisdictional issues (Model Law, Art. 16), to assist in evidence-taking

(Model Law, Art. 27), and to annul arbitral awards (Model Law, Art. 34). Are there other "external" issues that are governed by the law of the arbitral seat?

(b) *"Internal" issues.* Other issues that are addressed by national arbitration legislation can be described as "internal." These issues concern the conduct of the arbitration proceedings, rather than (the limited) instances where national courts intervene in the arbitral process. In general, the law of the arbitral seat addresses "internal" issues by imposing basic guarantees regarding party autonomy and due process. For example, Articles 18 and 19 of the Model Law provide mandatory requirements regarding the equal treatment of the parties and the recognition of the parties' procedural autonomy. Are there any other instances in which the Model Law addresses "internal" issues in the arbitral process?

4. *Mandatory character of law of arbitral seat.* Suppose the arbitral seat is in State A. Are the parties able to agree to exclude the arbitration legislation of State A? Consider two types of exclusion: (a) the parties agree that the law of State A will not apply to the arbitration and, instead, the procedural law of the arbitration will be that of State B; or (b) the parties agree to exclude particular provisions of the arbitration legislation of State A, such as the appointment or removal of arbitrators by State A courts. Are either or both types of agreement valid? What law is relevant to determining this question?

Consider the English Arbitration Act. Does it permit parties to an English-seated arbitration to contract out of the provisions of the Act? Note §4(1) of the Act, which provides that various provisions of the Act are "mandatory" and have "effect notwithstanding any agreement to the contrary." That provision expressly precludes the parties from contracting out of the Act's basic framework; among other things, this does not permit parties to an English-seated arbitration to exclude application of the Act's basic provisions regarding the court's supervisory powers (including power to extend time limits, remove arbitrators, consider jurisdictional objections, assist in evidence-taking, secure attendance of witnesses and annul awards) or the tribunal's duties of fairness. English Arbitration Act, 1996, §§12, 24, 31, 32, 43, 67-68, excerpted at pp. 113-32 of the Documentary Supplement.

Does the UNCITRAL Model Law permit the parties to an arbitration agreement, seating the arbitration in a Model Law jurisdiction, to contract out of the statute's terms? Is there any equivalent to §4(1) of the English Arbitration Act? Should such a prohibition nonetheless be implied? Or would such an implication contradict the basic premise of party autonomy in international arbitration?

5. *Effect of Articles II and V(1)(d) of New York Convention.* Does the New York Convention permit Contracting States to impose mandatory limitations on the parties' autonomy, forbidding parties from contracting out of the arbitration legislation of the arbitral seat? What provisions of the Convention might restrict the ability of a Contracting State to impose such limitations?

Consider Article V(1)(d) of the Convention, providing that awards may be denied recognition if the arbitral procedures were not in accordance with the parties' agreement; consider also Article II(1), obligating Contracting States to recognize agreements to arbitrate. Do these provisions have the effect of requiring Contracting States to give effect to the parties' agreed arbitral procedures—including provisions contracting out of the arbitration legislation of the arbitral seat? Suppose the parties agreed to arbitrate in State A, but provided that the courts of State A would not be competent to appoint or remove arbitrators and that, instead, the courts of State B would exercise such authority. If State A's arbitration legislation denied effect to such an agreement—as with §4(1) of the English Arbitration Act—would that be consistent with Articles II(1) and V(1)(d) of the Convention?

6. *Selection of foreign procedural law*. The decisions in *Garuda* and *Karaha Bodas* refer to the possibility of the parties choosing a foreign procedural law to govern their arbitration. That is, although the arbitral seat is in State A, the parties agree that the procedural law of the arbitration (variously also called the curial law or the *lex arbitri*) shall be that of State B. As the *Karaha Bodas* decision makes clear, it is unusual for parties to agree to arbitrate in one place, subject to the procedural law of another state. The choice of a foreign procedural law is discussed below, *see infra* pp. 625-40.

7. *Ascertaining location of arbitral seat—place the parties have agreed*. Where is the arbitral seat located? This is often a straight-forward question: the arbitral seat is the place that the parties have agreed upon as the arbitral seat or place of arbitration. Consider Article 20(1) of the Model Law, which provides that the "place of arbitration" is located where the parties have agreed. Compare Article 176(1) of the SLPIL, excerpted at p. 157 of the Documentary Supplement. Consider how the *Garuda* court analyzes the question where the arbitral seat is located. The selection of the arbitral seat by the parties is discussed in greater detail below, *see infra* pp 640-58. Where was the arbitral seat in *Garuda*? In *Karaha Bodas*? How difficult is this question in each case?

8. *Ascertaining location of arbitral seat—the place chosen pursuant to procedures the parties have agreed*. Arbitration agreements sometimes do not specify the seat (or place) of the arbitration, and instead incorporate institutional rules which provide a mechanism for selecting the arbitral seat—usually that the arbitral institution or the arbitral tribunal shall select the seat. This mode of selecting the seat is discussed in greater detail below, *see infra* pp. 653-55.

9. *Ascertaining location of arbitral seat—absent agreement, place the arbitrators have chosen*. Arbitration agreements sometimes do not specify either the seat (or place) of the arbitration or any means for selecting the seat (for example, pursuant to the provisions of institutional rules). In these circumstances, how is the arbitral seat selected? Consider Article 20(1) of the UNCITRAL Model Law and Article 176(3) of SLPIL, providing that the arbitral tribunal shall, in the absence of agreement by the parties, select the arbitral seat. Is there any other means for selecting the arbitral seat in these circumstances?

10. *Issues affected by choice of arbitral seat and procedural law of arbitration*. What issues are affected by designation of the arbitral seat? Consider the following:

    (a) *Where award is "made" under New York Convention*. The arbitral seat is usually (but not always) the place where the arbitral award will be "made" for purposes of the New York Convention. *See infra* pp. 1086-87. This has significant legal consequences for the enforceability of arbitral awards outside the country where they are rendered. If a state is party to the Convention, awards made within its territory will generally be subject to the Convention's pro-enforcement rules in other Contracting States; conversely, if a state is *not* party to the Convention, its awards often will not enjoy the benefits of the Convention, and may instead be subject to parochial or archaic domestic legislation when sought to be enforced abroad. *See infra* pp. 1093-99.

(b) *Supervisory jurisdiction*. As *Karaha Bodas* illustrates, the courts of the arbitral seat will almost always possess supervisory (or primary) jurisdiction over the arbitral process. This includes the "external" issues detailed above, *supra* pp. 620-21, such as selection and removal of arbitrators, assistance in evidence-taking, and annulment of arbitral awards.

(c) *Forum and standards for annulment of awards*. The national courts in the arbitral seat are usually competent (and exclusively competent) to entertain actions to annul or set aside the arbitral award. Note the analysis to this effect in *Garuda* and *Karaha Bodas*, and *infra* pp. 1099-12. The scope and extent of judicial review of an award is primarily a matter of national law that varies from country to country. Under many national arbitration regimes, an arbitral award is subject to little or no review of the merits of the tribunal's decision and little review of the arbitral procedures. *See infra* pp. 1156-63. In contrast, other states permit relatively extensive review of the merits of arbitral awards and of the procedures used in the arbitration, either explicitly or in the form of extensive public policy inquiries. *See infra* pp. 1163-68.

(d) *Effects on selection of arbitrators*. The selection of an arbitral seat will often have a material influence on the selection of the arbitrators. Some states impose idiosyncratic nationality or religion requirements on the identities of arbitrators, *infra* pp. 696, 712-14, 732-40, the number of arbitrators, *infra* pp. 687-88, or procedures for selecting and removing arbitrators, *infra* pp. 715-16, 758-76. Even absent such laws, choosing the arbitral seat often has an important indirect effect on the identity, nationality and legal training of the arbitrators, who are more likely to be drawn from the arbitral seat than otherwise. *See infra* pp. 698-99. In turn, this will often influence the parties' selections of co-arbitrators or their agreement on a sole or presiding arbitrator. Consider why this might occur.

(e) *Effects on choice of procedural and substantive laws*. The local law of the arbitral seat may have a material influence on the substantive or procedural issues that arise in the arbitration. For example, local law may purport to mandatorily impose particular choice-of-law, *infra* pp. 969-73, or particular rules regarding the arbitral procedures, *infra* pp. 793-95. Further, although local procedural rules (applicable in national court litigation) should not be understood to apply to international arbitral proceedings with a local seat, *infra* pp. 634, 639, local law can nonetheless have an important indirect impact on the arbitral procedures. As a practical matter, it is sometimes the case that local procedural rules and practices will influence the arbitrators' procedural decisions (*e.g.*, an international arbitration seated in England, with English substantive law applying, will more likely entail common law document disclosure and cross-examination than an arbitration seated in Switzerland with Swiss substantive law applying), *infra* pp. 818-19.

(f) *Convenience and cost*. The selection of the arbitral seat is also relevant to issues of logistics, cost and convenience. If the hearings are conducted in an expensive place (*e.g.*, where hotels, meetings rooms, or support services are costly), this might preclude some individuals or other parties from pursuing their claims or presenting their defenses. Conversely, an inconvenient forum without developed support facilities can make the arbitral process cumbersome and inefficient.

11. *Arbitral tribunal may hold hearings at places other than arbitral seat.* Consider what occurred in *Garuda*: the arbitral tribunal held hearings in Singapore, notwithstanding the fact that the arbitral seat was Indonesia. Compare what occurred with regard to the location of the arbitral hearings in *Karaha Bodas*. In each case, was there any question that the holding of hearings outside the arbitral seat was permitted? Did holding hearings outside the arbitral seat affect the location of the seat or have other significant legal consequences? Consider also Article 18(2) of the 2010 UNCITRAL Rules, Article 18(2) of the 2012 ICC Rules and Article 16(3) of the 2014 LCIA Rules, excerpted at pp. 168, 189 & 265 of the Documentary Supplement. What power does each provision give to the arbitral tribunal and in what circumstances could this power be used?

    Why would it not merely be simpler to provide that the tribunal can change the place or seat of the arbitration? What are the differences in the legal consequences of changing the arbitral seat and of changing the place where hearings and meetings are held? *See supra* pp. 620-24.

12. *Territorial scope of national arbitration legislation revisited.* Recall the discussion above of the foundational principle that national arbitration legislation is territorial in scope. What exactly does that mean? Note that most arbitration legislation applies to arbitrations that have their "arbitral seat" in national territory. *See supra* pp. 619-20; UNCITRAL Model Law, Art. 1(2); English Arbitration Act, 1996, §§2, 3; SLPIL, Art. 176(1).

    Note also, however, that the concept of the arbitral seat has almost nothing to do with physical actions within territorial boundaries; the arbitral seat is where the parties agree that it is, even if nothing in the arbitral process takes place physically on the territory of the arbitral seat. What then is the rationale for the territorial scope of arbitration legislation? Does it have to do with national sovereignty? Or with providing a stable and predictable international legal regime for international arbitration?

13. *"A-national" arbitration.* It is often said that an arbitration proceeding *must* be governed by the law of some nation. As noted above, the late Dr. F.A. Mann is routinely cited for his declaration that "every arbitration is subject to the law of a given State." Mann, *Lex Facit Arbitrum*, reprinted in 2 Arb. Int'l 241 (1986). List the various ways in which this statement is ambiguous. List the ways in which it is misleading. Try and formulate an interpretation of the statement that is both accurate and useful.

    Some commentators have suggested that an arbitration does not need to be governed by a national law. *See* Paulsson, *Delocalisation of International Commercial Arbitration: When and Why It Matters*, 32 Int'l & Comp. L. Q. 53 (1983). What would it mean to conclude that an international arbitration need not be governed by any national law? Would it mean, using the terminology of *Karaha Bodas*, that the law and courts of the arbitral seat have no "primary jurisdiction" over the arbitration? Is that imaginable? That no national court could annul the award? Remove or appoint arbitrators? Consider: *Kloeckner Industrien-Anlagen GmbH v. Kien Tat Sdn Bhd*, 3 Malayan L.J. 183 (Malaysian High Ct. 1990) (holding, under Malaysian arbitration legislation, that Malaysian courts had no "jurisdiction to exercise supervisory function over arbitration proceedings held" under the Rules of the Regional Centre for Arbitration at Kuala Lumpur).

14. *Arbitral seat in inter-state arbitrations*. The concept of the arbitral seat in inter-state arbitrations is generally less significant than in international commercial arbitrations. Consider:

> "The Tribunal's place of session is selected by the parties. Failing this selection the Tribunal sits at The Hague. The place thus fixed cannot, except in case of necessity, be changed by the Tribunal without the assent of the parties." 1899 Hague Convention, Art. 36.

> Note the general recognition of the parties' autonomy to select the "place of session," coupled with a default choice (of the Hague, Netherlands); note also, however, the tribunal's authority "in case of necessity," to move the place of the arbitral sessions.

> What is the legal significance of the "place of session"? Does the "place of session" have the same significance as the "arbitral seat" in a commercial arbitration? In an inter-state arbitration (for example, between the United States and India), would national courts in the place where the arbitration was conducted have the authority to review and annul an award? Would national arbitration legislation apply to awards in an inter-state arbitration? Why not?

15. *Arbitral seat in investment arbitrations*. Consider Articles 62 and 63 of the ICSID Convention. What do they provide with regard to the arbitral seat? What is the legal significance of the fact that ICSID "arbitration proceedings shall be held" in a particular place? Are the legal consequences of conducting an ICSID arbitration in a particular place the same as locating the arbitral seat in a commercial arbitration in that place? In particular, can an ICSID award be annulled by a national court in the place where the arbitration is conducted? *See* ICSID Convention, Arts. 50-54, excerpted at pp. 23-25 of the Documentary Supplement. Can ICSID arbitrators be removed by a national court in the place where the arbitration is conducted? *See* ICSID Convention, Art. 56-58, excerpted at p. 25 of the Documentary Supplement. If not, what would be so unimaginable about an a-national international commercial arbitration?

B. APPLICABLE PROCEDURAL LAW IN INTERNATIONAL ARBITRATION

Particularly in international commercial arbitration, national arbitration legislation, judicial decisions and academic commentary frequently refer to the "procedural law of the arbitration." As noted above, the procedural law of the arbitration is sometimes referred to as the "curial law," the "*lex arbitri*," or the "*loi de l'arbitrage*."[16]

The term "procedural law" is not uniformly defined, but typically encompasses a range of "internal" and "external" issues (outlined above) that are central to the arbitral process.[17] Importantly, the procedural law of the arbitration is almost always the arbitration legislation of the arbitral seat; in the words of one authority, a foreign procedural law (other than that of the arbitral seat) applies to an arbitration only "once in a blue moon."[18] Nonetheless, parties theoretically have the freedom to select a foreign procedural law,[19] and there are

---

16. *See supra* pp. 621-22; G. Born, *International Commercial Arbitration* 1533, 1598-604 (2d ed. 2014).

17. As discussed above, these issues are ordinarily addressed by national arbitration legislation applicable to arbitrations seated on local territory. *See supra* pp. 619-20, 624-25.

18. Hunter, *Case and Comment: International Arbitration*, [1988] Lloyd's Mar. & Com. L.Q. 23, 26.

19. *See* G. Born, *International Commercial Arbitration* 1533-34 (2d ed. 2014).

rare cases where the parties attempt to agree upon a foreign procedural law. Where it is permitted, the application of a foreign procedural law to an arbitration can have significant consequences, altering the legal standards which are otherwise applicable to the "internal" and "external" aspects of the arbitral process.

Determining whether the parties have agreed to a foreign procedural law raises difficult issues, which are explored in the materials below. Equally, the parties' choice of a foreign procedural law raises issues of validity—with many states imposing significant restrictions on parties' ability to contract out of the arbitration law of the arbitral seat, whether by selecting a foreign procedural law or otherwise. The materials excerpted below explore the concepts of the procedural law of the arbitration and the choice of a foreign procedural law.

KARAHA BODAS CO., LLC v. PERUSAHAAN PERTAMBANGAN MINYAK DAN GAS BUMI NEGARA

364 F.3d 274 (5th Cir. 2004)

[excerpted above at pp. 605-19]

UNION OF INDIA v. MCDONNELL DOUGLAS CORP.
[1993] 2 Lloyd's Rep. 48 (Comm) (English High Ct.)

MR. JUSTICE SAVILLE. By a written agreement dated July 30, 1987 the plaintiffs contracted with the defendants for the latter to undertake services for the former in and about the launch of a space satellite. Article 11 of the agreement provided that the agreement was to be governed by, interpreted and construed in accordance with the laws of India. The agreement also contained an arbitration clause (Art. 8) in the following terms:

> "In the event of a dispute or difference arising out of or in connection with this Agreement, which cannot be resolved by amicable settlement, the same shall be referred to an Arbitration Tribunal consisting of three members. Either Party shall give notice to the other regarding its decision to refer the matter to arbitration. Within 30 days of such notice, one Arbitrator shall be nominated by each Party and the third Arbitrator shall be nominated by agreement between the Parties to this Agreement. If no such agreement is reached within 60 days of the mentioned notice, the President of the [ICC] shall be requested to nominate the third Arbitrator. The third Arbitrator shall not be a citizen of the country of either Party to this Agreement. The arbitration shall be conducted in accordance with the procedure provided in the Indian Arbitration Act of 1940 or any reenactment or modification thereof.... The seat of the arbitration proceedings shall be London, United Kingdom...."

[The parties'] dispute or difference has been referred to arbitration under the provisions of Art. 8. The hearing before the arbitrators is presently fixed to begin in London on Jan. 11, 1993. The question before me is as to the law governing the arbitration proceedings....

In essence the plaintiffs contend that the words: "The arbitration shall be conducted in accordance with the procedure provided in the Indian Arbitration Act 1940" make clear that the parties have chosen Indian law, or at least those parts of Indian law found in the 1940 Act, to govern any arbitration proceedings arising under Art. 8. The defendants, on the other hand, contend that by stipulating London as the "seat" of any arbitration proceedings under Art. 8, the parties have made clear not merely that any arbitration will take place in London, but that English law will govern the arbitration proceedings.

An arbitration clause in a commercial contract like the present one is an agreement inside an agreement. The parties make their commercial bargain, *i.e.*, exchange promises in relation to the subject matter of the transaction, but in addition agree on a private tribunal to resolve any issues that may arise between them. The parties may make an express choice of the law to govern their commercial bargain and that choice may also be made of the law to govern their agreement to arbitrate. In the present case it is my view that by Art. 11 the parties have chosen the law of India not only to govern the rights and obligations arising out of their commercial bargain but also the rights and obligations arising out of their agreement to arbitrate. In legal terms, therefore, the proper law of both the commercial bargain and the arbitration agreement is the law of India.

The fact that the law of India is the proper law of the arbitration agreement does not, however, necessarily entail that the law governing the arbitration proceedings themselves is also the law of India, unless there is in that agreement some effective express or implied term to that effect. In other words, it is, subject to one proviso, open to the parties to agree that their agreement to arbitrate disputes will be governed by one law, but that the procedures to be adopted in any arbitration under that agreement will be governed by another law: *see James Miller & Partners v. Whitworth Street Estates (Manchester) Ltd* [1970] 1 Lloyd's Rep. 269 [(House of Lords)]. Thus, in an international bargain of the present kind, the parties, subject to the proviso mentioned (to which I shall return below) may make a choice of a law to govern their commercial bargain, of a law to govern their arbitration agreement, and of a law to govern the procedures in any arbitration held under that agreement. In theory at least … the parties could chose a different law for each of these purposes.

If the parties do not make an express choice of procedural law to govern their arbitration, then the Court will consider whether they have made an implicit choice. In this circumstance the fact that the parties have agreed to a place for the arbitration is a very strong pointer that implicitly they must have chosen the law of that place to govern the procedures of the arbitration. The reason for this is essentially one of common sense. By choosing a country in which to arbitrate the parties have, *ex hypothesi*, created a close connection between the arbitration and that country and it is reasonable to assume from their choice that they attached some importance to the relevant laws of that country, i.e. those laws which would be relevant to an arbitration conducted in that country….

In the present case, … the defendants place[] great stress on the fact that the parties have expressly selected London as the "seat" and not just the place of the arbitration. The word "seat," [they] suggest[], is a legal term of art, meaning the legal place of the arbitration proceedings. By choosing the legal place of the arbitration proceedings the parties ipso facto choose the laws of that place to govern their arbitration proceedings. Indeed, although the choice of a "seat" also indicates the geographical place for the arbitration, this does not mean that the parties have limited themselves to that place…. [I]t may often be convenient to hold meetings or even hearings in other countries. This does not mean that the "seat" of the arbitration changes with each change of country. The legal place of the arbitration remains the same even if the physical place changes from time to time, unless of course the parties agree to change it. In short, [the defendants] suggested that the word "seat" carried with it much more clearly the meaning conveyed by the French word "*siège*" than the English word "place" though [its] submission was that this word too in an arbitration agreement would be primarily concerned with the legal rather than the physical place of the arbitration.

[The plaintiff] accepted that in the absence of agreement to the contrary, the choice of a "seat" would carry with it the choice of the law of that place as the law governing the arbitration proceedings, though [it] categorized that result as arising from implication rather than from the meaning of the word "seat" itself. In the present case, however, [the plaintiff's] submission was that the parties, by stipulating that the arbitration should be conducted in accordance with the procedure provided in the Indian Arbitration Act, had made an express choice of Indian law to govern the arbitration proceedings and that this choice must, on ordinary principles, prevail over anything inconsistent that might otherwise be implied.

These arguments are nicely balanced. It is clear from the authorities cited above that English law does admit of at least the theoretical possibility that the parties are free to choose to hold their arbitration in one country but subject to the procedural laws of another, but against this is the undoubted fact that such an agreement is calculated to give rise to great difficulties and complexities.... For example (and this is the proviso to which I referred earlier in this judgment) it seems to me that the jurisdiction of the English Court under the Arbitration Acts over an arbitration in this country cannot be excluded by an agreement between the parties to apply the laws of another country, or indeed by any other means unless such is sanctioned by those Acts themselves. Thus, to my mind, there can be no question in this case that the English Courts would be deprived of all jurisdiction over the arbitration. However, much of that jurisdiction is discretionary in character so that if the Court were convinced that the parties had chosen the procedural law of another country, then it might well be slow to interfere with the arbitral process. Again, for the sake of avoiding parallel Court proceedings, the Court might be minded to regard the choice of a foreign legal procedure as amounting to an exclusion agreement within the meaning of §3 of the Arbitration Act, 1979 [permitting parties to exclude certain grounds for annulment of awards made in England]. Be that as it may, the choice of a procedural law different from the law of the place of the arbitration will, at least where that place is this country, necessarily mean that the parties have actually chosen to have their arbitral proceedings at least potentially governed both by their express choice and by the laws of this country.

Such a state of affairs is clearly highly unsatisfactory: indeed in *Black Clawson Int'l Ltd v. Papierwerke Waldhof-Aschaffenburg AG* [1981] 2 Lloyd's Rep. 446, 453, Mr. Justice Mustill (as he then was) described the converse situation (i.e. a foreign arbitration suggested to be governed by English procedural law) as producing an absurd result. In the end, therefore, the question is whether the parties have agreed to such a potentially unsatisfactory method of regulating their arbitration procedures. In my judgment, they have not because, as [the defendants] submitted, there is a way of reconciling the phrase relied upon by [the plaintiff] with the choice of London as the seat of the arbitration, namely by reading that phrase as referring to the internal conduct of the arbitration as opposed to the external supervision of the arbitration by the Courts. The word used in the phrase relied upon by [the plaintiff] is "conducted" which I agree with [the defendants] is more apt to describe the way in which the parties and the tribunal are to carry on their proceedings than the supervision of those proceedings by the Indian courts, for example through the Special Case provisions of the Indian Act. It is true, as [the plaintiff] pointed out, that this would mean that only §3 and Schedule 1 of the Indian Act would be applicable (though many of the other provisions are still to be found in the English statutes and so would be applicable in the English Courts) but the construction for which [the plaintiff] contends would, to my mind, not only have the unsatisfactory and possibly absurd results to which I have referred, but would also necessarily give the word "seat" a meaning which excluded any choice of London as the legal place for the arbitration. In my view, such a change from the ordinary meaning to be given to that word in an international arbitration agreement (the ordinary meaning being that submitted by [the defendants]) cannot be accepted, unless the other provisions of the agreement show clearly that this is what the parties intended. I am not persuaded that this is the case here. On the contrary, for the reasons given, it seems to me that by their agreement the parties have chosen English law as the law to govern their arbitration proceedings, while contractually importing from the Indian Act those provisions of that Act which are concerned with the internal conduct of their arbitration and which are not inconsistent with the choice of English arbitral procedural law.

The question ... before me is whether upon the proper construction of Art. 8 ... the pending arbitration between the parties an any award made by the arbitral tribunal is subject to the supervisory jurisdiction of the Indian Courts or the English Courts. For the reasons given my answer to this question is that it is the latter.

PRELIMINARY AWARD IN ICC CASE NO. 5505
XIII Y.B. Comm. Arb. 110 (1988)

G. MULLER, Arbitrator. [The claimant was a Mozambique purchaser; the respondent was a Netherlands seller. The parties entered into a contract for the sale of seed potatoes, which contained the following provision: "[the parties] must finally undertake to submit the matter according to the regulation for agreement and arbitration of the [ICC] to one or more arbitrators as per the said laws. The arbitration will take place in Switzerland, the law applicable is that known in England." Disputes arose under the contract and arbitration ensued. The parties disagreed about the meaning of the words "the law applicable is that known in England."]

The parties to an agreement are free, under the [1988] ICC Rules [Article 13(3)], to adopt the substantive law which should govern their agreement and an arbitral tribunal has to apply the law so adopted. It is only if there is no designation by the parties of the applicable law that the arbitral tribunal shall resort to a rule of conflict of laws. An arbitral tribunal should probably also deviate from the law chosen by the parties if it would appear that such a choice, if applied by the arbitral tribunal, could prevent that the award be implemented (Article 26 of the ICC Rules.)

In making [the] decision [as to applicable law], one has first to select which system or principles of law one has to apply. One could construe the disputed sentence by applying English law as being the law presumably chosen by the parties, or by applying Swiss law as the "*lex fori*," or by resorting to principles of law generally admitted. It does not seem adequate to apply English law to determine the issue as it could lead to preempting the solution. Therefore, the arbitrator will be guided by Swiss law and general principles of law. It has to be noted that in the present instance there is no absolute need to resort to a specific system of law to construe the said sentence. Under Swiss law, the wording of contracts forms the basis of their construction, but Swiss judges also look at all the circumstances which seem appropriate to establish the common intention of the parties [and various other rules of construction]....

The arbitrator is of the opinion that the parties to the contract did not include inadvertently the said sentence.... In the said context, one may elaborate four possible meanings, that is [a] a choice of substantive law; [b] a choice of procedural law; [c] a choice of a rule of conflict of laws; and [d] a choice of a law to determine the validity and effect of the arbitration clause.... In reviewing the possible meanings of the disputed sentence, the arbitrator will apply the following test: How could that sentence be understood in good faith by a reasonable man active in the international trade? [Initially], the arbitrator notes that the word "law" appears twice in the arbitration clause.... The first reference is to "as per said laws." The "said laws" obviously refer to the [ICC] Rules.... The second reference to the word "law" appears in the disputed sentence, in connection with the word "applicable." The defendants allege that "the law applicable" could refer to "as per said laws." This does not seem, however, to be a valid construction of these words....

It is quite uncommon to find in an arbitration clause an indication of the law which shall govern the procedure under which the arbitration shall take place. Parties adopting an arbitration clause expect mostly to escape procedural particularities of local courts; the designation of a municipal law is most often contrary to the advantages sought in an arbitration clause.

In this case, the choice of the ICC Rules was well sufficient to settle the problems of procedure (Article 11 of the [ICC] Rules). The choice of Switzerland as the place of arbitration implied in any case the application of the Swiss mandatory provisions. Nothing indicates that the parties could have reason to avoid the application of Swiss procedural law and to choose specifically English procedural law. Moreover, such a choice could bring with it numerous difficulties. Therefore, quite clearly, if the parties intended a reference to procedural law, they would have made it plain and would not have used the words "the law applicable" which designate ordinarily the substantive law. Further, one cannot understand why the parties would have chosen such an extraordinary law of procedure under the circumstances, but not a substantive law....

It seems unlikely that parties to an international contract choose a rule of conflict of laws, but not the substantive law: it is hard to understand how the parties cannot agree to a proper law, but can agree to the rules of conflict that determine the proper law. This may sometimes happen, but for certain reasons. In this case, there is no evidence of any reason of that kind. Further, one may assume that, if the parties had in mind to refer to a rule of conflict of laws, as opposed to a substantive law, they would have made it clear. Finally, it would have been contradictory and therefore unreasonable to choose at the same time a rule of conflict of laws and a substantive law, as this is assumed by the defendants....

Parties may submit an arbitration agreement to a law which is not the substantive law of the main contract. But in that case, they almost always designate the law governing the arbitration agreement and the law applying to the contract. If not, they indicate that the selected law applies specifically to the arbitration agreement. Obviously, the parties to an international contract are likely to have in mind the problems of jurisdiction or arbitration, possibly of substantive law, but not of the law governing the arbitration clause itself, which is mostly thought to be governed either by the selected law or by the *"lex fori"* (the law of the place of arbitration). In this case, there is no evidence that the parties might have intended or at least had reasons to submit the arbitration clause to a specific law....

Universally, the words "the law applicable" or "the law which applies" are used in the context of the determination of the substantive law governing private international relationships (example: Article 13(3) of [1988 ICC] Rules.) In contracts containing no arbitration clause, the choice of the "applicable law" unambiguously refers to the substantive law, the procedure being in any case governed by the "*lex fori.*" The word "substantive" therefore never or very rarely appears in connection with the expression "the law applicable," although always implied….

The parties had valid reasons to refer to the substantive law known in England. English law is neutral; its provisions are adapted to the needs of international commerce; it is fairly well accessible and known to lawyers of other countries, such as Switzerland, Mozambique, and the Netherlands; English is far more common than Dutch, Portuguese, or even French. The arbitrator is therefore of the opinion that a reasonable man active in the international trade should have understood the disputed sentence as a reference to a substantive law. Although somewhat unusual, the expression "the law known in England" is not ambiguous. It is wide enough to include, as appropriate, international rules and usages recognized in England….

The argument has been made by the defendants that a clause of choice of substantive law should be clear and unambiguous. Under Swiss law, the choice of the applicable law is considered as the result of a contract between the parties, which is separate from the main contract. This "choice of law" is not subject to any formality and can be express or implied…. In this case, the arbitrator [also] finds that the express election in favor of English law is sufficiently clear to be regarded….

The defendants allege that the parties were not free to choose English law as the law applicable to their contract, for there being no connection between the matter and English law. Whether English law is a valid choice of law has to be scrutinized both under Swiss law and English law. Under Swiss law, the freedom of the parties as to their choice of the applicable law has not been finally settled. Swiss courts do not require the existence of a "natural connection between the matter and the chosen law" and recognize the validity of a choice of law in each case where the parties have a reasonable interest in the application of the chosen law. Such an interest exists for example when the chosen law contains a regulation of the matter which seems appropriate, when the parties are willing to submit their relationship to certain usages assuming the application of the chosen law or when the contract is in connection with another business submitted on the chosen law. It does not seem that any decision of a Swiss court has ever denied the existence of a reasonable interest of the parties in the application of a chosen law….

Under English law, the question of the connection between the matter and the chosen law seems to be somewhat controversial. There seems to be no reported case in which an English court refused to give effect to an express choice of law because of the deficient connection between the contract and the chosen law. In *Vita Food Products Inc. v. Unus Shipping Co.* (1939, AC 277 (PC)), it was stated that "a connection with English law is not, as a matter of principle, essential." In this decision, the judge mentioned in particular the importance of English law in international commercial relationships, even unconnected with England. He considered it reasonable for the parties to commercial contracts to submit their transaction to English law, although that law might have nothing to do with the facts of the particular case.

Swiss and English laws largely reflect the international practice.

"In most countries, the parties to transnational contracts enjoy a large degree of autonomy in selecting the proper law of their contract. Except in those situations in which compliance with mandatory rules is required, the parties are generally free to choose by way of express stipulation the law applicable to their relationship. In the overwhelming majority of cases, the law stipulated applicable is the domestic law of a specific country to which the contracts bears some connection or the law of a 'third' country selected for reason of expertise (such as English law in regard to maritime matters) or of neutrality (such as Swedish, Swiss, or French law)...." G. Delaume, *Transnational Contracts* Chapter VII, p. 2.

In this case, the arbitrator finds that the parties have a reasonable interest in the application of English law. The choice of English substantive law cannot be held invalid for there being no connection between the matter and English law.

There is further no indication that the choice of English substantive law was made to escape some mandatory provisions of the laws of the Netherlands or Mozambique. Nor is there any indication that an award which would be based on English substantive law would not be enforceable in the Netherlands or in the Mozambique. Therefore, the arbitrator considers that the parties have made a valid choice in favor of English substantive law. In accordance with Article 13(3) of the [1988 ICC] Rules, the arbitrator shall apply English substantive law.

SAPPHIRE INT'L PETROLEUM LTD v. NATIONAL IRANIAN OIL CO.
Award in Ad Hoc Case of 15 March 1963, 35 I.L.R. 136 (1963)

CAVIN, Sole Arbitrator. Article 39 of the [parties'] agreement provides that ... the only way of settling any difference concerning the interpretation or performance of the agreement is arbitration of the kind set out in Article 41 of the agreement. The parties have thus unequivocally shown their mutual desire to use arbitration in order to obtain a decision which will settle once and for all their possible differences concerning the interpretation and performance of the agreement, including claims for damages. [Among other things, the parties' arbitration] clause provides for the determination of a seat for the arbitration, which is a necessary element in the activity of any judicial authority. The judicial authority thus conferred upon the arbitrator necessarily implies that the arbitration should be governed by a law of procedure, and that it should be subject to the supervision of a State authority, such as the judicial sovereignty of a State.

Authority is to be found, in doctrine and case law, which gives the parties the right to make a free choice of the law of procedure to be applied to the arbitration, as for example, the State to whose judicial sovereignty the arbitration is submitted, or in other words "the location" of the arbitration. In the present case the parties agreed to leave the arbitrator free to determine the seat of the arbitration, if they failed to agree it themselves. Thus by agreeing beforehand to whatever seat was fixed by the arbitrator, who would make his choice under express delegation from the parties, they committed themselves to accept the law of procedure which results from his choice. In this case it is the law of [the Swiss canton of] Vaud, since the seat of the arbitration has been fixed at Lausanne [located in Vaud].

Even if this interpretation of the parties' intention is wrong, the rule is that, in default of agreement by the parties, the arbitration is submitted to the judicial sovereignty of the seat of the arbitration at the place where the case is heard. Resolution of the Institute of International Law, Articles 8, 9, 10, 12; Geneva Protocol, Article 2. Thus, in the present case, Lausanne is at the same time the headquarters of the judicial authority which has jurisdiction to appoint the arbitrator, the seat of the arbitration, the domicile of the sole arbitrator, and the place where all the arbitration procedure up to and including judgment has taken place.

The present arbitration, then, is governed by the law of procedure of Vaud and is subject to the judicial sovereignty of Vaud. Therefore, as far as procedure is concerned, it is subject to the binding rules of the Code of Civil Procedure of Vaud, and in particular to the 8th Title of this Code. The case has been heard in accordance with the rules prescribed by the Order of June 13, 1961, in which the arbitrator laid down the arbitral procedure, as he was entitled to do under Article 41(7) of the agreement if the parties failed to agree upon the procedure to follow, and in accordance with Article 511 of the Code of Civil Procedure of Vaud. Article I of the above Order laid down that the Federal Law of Civil Procedure of December 4, 1947, was applicable where there was no contrary provision in the Order.

The defendant NIOC has refused to co-operate in the procedure and has deliberately made default. Article 41(8), of the agreement lays down that the absence or default of one party should not be an obstacle to the arbitral proceedings in any of their stages. Accordingly, despite the default of the defendant, the arbitrator has proceeded to hear the case and to give judgment on the merits.

According to Article 15 of the arbitrator's Order, which is in accordance with Article 12 of the Federal Law of Civil Procedure, the default of one party and the omission of a procedural step simply means that the case proceeds without the step which had been omitted. By virtue of Article 3 of the Federal Law of Civil Procedure, the judge cannot base his judgment on facts other than those which have been alleged during the case. As a result, the present award is based upon the facts pleaded by the plaintiff, who alone has taken part in the procedure. But in applying these rules, the arbitrator has accepted only those facts which have been satisfactorily proved to him during the procedure....

NOTES

1. *Procedural law of arbitration distinguished from law governing arbitration agreement and law governing underlying contract.* It is important to distinguish the procedural law governing the arbitration from other laws relevant to the arbitral process, including the law governing the arbitration agreement and the law governing the underlying contract and/or substance of the parties' dispute. Consider how the courts in *Karaha Bodas* and *Union of India* and the tribunal in *ICC Case No. 5505* distinguish between these categories.

2. *Procedural law of arbitration distinguished from arbitral procedures.* It is also critical to distinguish between the *procedural law* governing the arbitration and the *procedures* applied in the arbitral proceedings. As detailed below, most contemporary arbitration statutes impose virtually no specific procedural requirements on the arbitration proceedings and prescribe only very general due process requirements. *See infra* pp. 786-95. In most cases, the parties and the arbitrators are left almost entirely free by national arbitration legislation to formulate whatever procedures and procedural rules they deem best-suited for their arbitration. *See infra* pp. 788-90, 793-95. The procedures which are adopted in particular cases by the parties and arbitrators constitute the arbitral procedures; in contrast, the procedural law of the arbitration generally refers to the arbitration legislation of a jurisdiction, which in most developed jurisdictions prescribes only minimal procedures for an arbitration, and instead leaves the parties

and the arbitrators to tailor such procedures to their particular arbitration. *See supra* pp. 620-21 & *infra* pp. 636-37, 638-39.

3. *Procedural law of arbitration distinguished from local rules of civil procedure in arbitral seat.* It is also important to distinguish between the arbitration legislation in the arbitral seat and the local rules of civil procedure applicable in judicial proceedings in the arbitral seat. The "procedural law" of the arbitration refers to the former, and not to the latter, which are only applicable to litigations in national courts, not to international arbitrations seated on local territory. *See* G. Born, *International Commercial Arbitration* 1530-34 (2d ed. 2014); Kaufmann-Kohler, *Identifying and Applying the Law Governing the Arbitration Procedure—The Role of the Law of the Place of Arbitration,* in A. van den Berg (ed.), *Improving the Efficiency of Arbitration Agreements and Awards: 40 Years of Application of the New York Convention* 336 (ICCA Congress Series No. 9 1999); G. Petrochilos, *Procedural Law in International Arbitration* (2004).

4. *Parties' autonomy to agree on foreign procedural law.* Are parties permitted to agree to select a foreign procedural law, so that the law of State B provides the procedural law for an arbitration seated in State A? If so, will the arbitration law of the arbitral seat impose limitations on the parties' autonomy to contract out of its provisions? Are there different answers for different issues governed by the procedural law of the arbitration (*e.g.*, the various "internal" and "external" issues discussed above)?

    (a) *Parties' general autonomy to agree on foreign procedural law.* How did *Karaha Bodas* and *Union of India* deal with the parties' autonomy to select a foreign procedural law for the arbitration? Note that *Union of India* held: "[t]here is ... no reason in theory which precludes parties to agree that an arbitration shall be held at a place or in country X but subject to the procedural laws of Y," quoting *Naviera Amazonica Peruana SA v. Compania Internacional De Seguros del Peru* [1988] 1 Lloyd's Rep. 116, 119. Consider Article 182(1) of the SLPIL, which provides: "[t]he parties may, directly or by reference to arbitration rules, determine the arbitral procedure; they may also submit it to a procedural law of their choice." Consider also the tribunal's conclusion in *Sapphire. See also Nat'l Thermal Power Corp. v. Singer Co.*, XVIII Y.B. Comm. Arb. 403, 407 (1993) (Indian S.Ct. 1992) ("if the parties have specifically chosen the law governing the conduct and procedure of arbitration, the arbitration proceedings will be conducted in accordance with that law so long as it is not contrary to the public policy or the mandatory requirements of the law of the country in which the arbitration is held."). Why are parties permitted to select a foreign procedural law for their arbitration? What purposes do such agreements serve? What risks do they entail?

    (b) *Limitations on parties' autonomy to agree upon foreign procedural law.* Is the parties' autonomy to agree upon a foreign procedural law unlimited? What does the *Union of India* court mean when it says: "it seems to me that the jurisdiction of the English Court under the Arbitration Acts over an arbitration in this country cannot be excluded by an agreement between the parties to apply the laws of another country, or indeed by any other means unless such is sanctioned by those Acts themselves. Thus, to my mind, there can be no question in this case that the English Courts would be deprived of all jurisdiction over the arbitration." Why would there be "no question" that the parties could not deprive the English courts of all jurisdiction over the arbitration? What jurisdiction would the English courts mandatorily retain? Consider the provisions of the English Arbitration Act, 1996. Do they permit parties to an arbitration seated in England to contract out of English arbitration law, whether by choice of a foreign procedural law or otherwise? Consider in particular §4(1) and Schedule 1 of the Arbitration Act, 1996, excerpted at pp. 112 & 141-42 of the Documentary Supplement; what provisions of the Act are mandatory for arbitrations seated in England?

Consider the provisions of the UNCITRAL Model Law, excerpted at pp. 88-96 of the Documentary Supplement. Does it permit the parties to an arbitration seated in a Model Law jurisdiction to select a foreign procedural law? What is the meaning of Article 1(2) of the Model Law? Can the parties to an arbitration seated in State A (a UNCITRAL Model Law state) agree that the following functions will be governed by the law of State B (as applied by the courts of State B): (a) selection and removal of arbitrators; (b) annulment of arbitral awards; (c) provision of judicial assistance in aid of the arbitration? Does the text of the Model Law address these issues?

Note that the tribunal in *ICC Case No. 5505* goes out of its way to say that the mandatory provisions of the law of the arbitral seat (Switzerland) apply even where the parties agree on a foreign procedural law. Consider Article 182 of the SLPIL. Are there limitations on the parties' freedom to select a foreign procedural law?

(c) *Parties' autonomy under FAA to agree on foreign procedural law.* In the United States, the text of the FAA does not expressly address the question whether parties to an international arbitration may agree to a foreign procedural law. As *Karaha Bodas* indicates, the few U.S. authorities to consider directly whether the FAA permits parties to agree upon the procedural law governing their arbitration answer in the affirmative. *Remy Amerique, Inc. v. Touzet Distr.*, SARL, 816 F.Supp. 213, 216-17 (S.D.N.Y. 1993) ("parties are free to include in their agreement a choice-of-law provision which impacts upon procedural rules"); *Intercarbon Bermuda, Ltd v. Caltex Trading & Transp. Corp.*, 146 F.R.D. 64, 72 (S.D.N.Y. 1993) ("agreement between the parties here did not establish any particular arbitral procedure, so the question is whether the procedure was in accordance with the law of the United States"); *Restatement (Second) Conflict of Laws* §220 comment c (1971). There is no direct U.S. precedent on the extent to which agreement on a foreign procedural law would affect the authority of U.S. courts to exercise powers of judicial supervision—including annulment of awards and selection of arbitrators—in connection with arbitrations conducted in the United States. There is also no direct U.S. precedent on the extent to which agreement on a foreign procedural law would override otherwise applicable U.S. standards of procedural fairness in U.S.-seated arbitrations. How should these issues be dealt with?

(d) *Rationale for mandatory restrictions on choice of foreign procedural law.* Why do countries, such as England and Switzerland, require application of local arbitration legislation to arbitrations conducted locally? What values or objectives are served by such an approach? Suppose two large, highly-sophisticated international companies (*e.g.*, U.S. and Argentine) agree to arbitrate in England, but want U.S. (or Argentine) procedural rules to apply. Why should England's legislature refuse to permit this? What provisions of local arbitration law should be regarded as mandatory? Consider first "external" procedural issues and then "internal" ones. Note the provisions that the English Arbitration Act treats as mandatory.

(e) *Parties' autonomy to select foreign procedural law revisited.* How much autonomy should parties have to select a foreign procedural law? Recall that the concept of an "arbitral seat" is a legal construct: an arbitration can be conducted completely outside the arbitral seat, without anything ever occurring in the territory of the arbitral seat. *See supra* p. 624. If the parties are free to select an arbitral seat that has nothing to do with actual territorial boundaries and physical conduct, why are they not free to select a different procedural law from that of their notional arbitral seat? If an inter-state or investment arbitration can be conducted with no supervision at all by the courts of the arbitral seat, why can't an international commercial arbitration?

5. *Potential consequences of parties' choice of foreign procedural law.* Assume the parties to an arbitration seated in State A choose a foreign procedural law (that of State B) for their arbitration and that this choice is given full effect. What are the consequences of this choice? What courts may annul the arbitral award, and pursuant to what legal standards? Consider the decision in *Karaha Bohas.* What courts may appoint arbitrators (assuming that the parties have not done so)? What courts may remove arbitrators? What legal standards apply to issues such as the fairness of the arbitral proceedings, the confidentiality of the arbitral proceedings and the rights of counsel to appear in the arbitral proceedings?

6. *Reasons for selecting foreign procedural law.* Why might parties choose a procedural law to govern an arbitration that is different from the law of the arbitral seat? What benefits might this provide? Suppose a U.S. and a German company wish to arbitrate any disputes that arise between them at the location of a construction project on which they are collaborating in Saudi Arabia, but that they wish to apply German (or U.S.) procedural rules in such an arbitration. Is this preference understandable? Suppose the U.S. and German company wish to arbitrate in Saudi Arabia, but do not want Saudi courts to have the power to annul the award. Are there reasons that they might have this preference? Suppose a Russian company enters into a joint venture with a Brazilian company; the Russian company is willing to arbitrate in Miami, but insists that Russian courts have the power to decide applications to annul any award. Is this a plausible negotiating position?

If parties do not want their arbitration to be governed by the arbitration law of the arbitral seat, why don't they select a different arbitral seat? Note that, as discussed above, arbitral proceedings can be conducted outside of the arbitral seat. *See supra* p. 624. If parties want their arbitration to be governed by the procedural law of State B, why don't they just agree upon State B as the arbitral seat and conduct hearings elsewhere (in State A or wherever)?

7. *Interpretation of choice-of-law clauses.* Consider the choice-of-law clause at issue in *ICC Case No. 5505.* How did the arbitral tribunal interpret this provision? Is that a sensible interpretation of the parties' agreement? *Compare Judgment of 1 February 1996, Osuuskunta METEX Andelslag VS v. Türkiye Elektrik Kurumu Genel Müdürlügü Gen. Directorate, Ankara,* XXII Y.B. Comm. Arb. 807 (1997) (Turkish Yargitay) (interpreting Turkish choice-of-law clause in underlying contract as select-

ing Turkish law as procedural law of arbitration seated in Switzerland). Compare the similar issues that arise with respect to the effect of a choice-of-law clause in the underlying contract on the law governing the arbitration agreement. As discussed above, parties sometimes intend a general choice-of-law clause to encompass the arbitration clause in their contract (even though it is separable). *See supra* pp. 90-93, 287-315. Does the same view apply to the procedural law governing the arbitral proceedings?

When will a choice-of-law clause be interpreted as selecting a foreign procedural law to govern the arbitral proceedings? Suppose the parties agree that the arbitral seat shall be in State A, and also include one of the following provisions in their agreement:

"The arbitration and the arbitral proceedings shall be governed by the law of State B."

"The procedural law of the arbitration shall be the law of State B."

As noted above, these types of provisions are rare. If the parties included such a provision in their agreement, would they be interpreted as selecting a foreign procedural law? Consider the text of the parties' agreements in *Karaha Bodas* and *Union of India*. Did the parties' agreements choose a foreign procedural law?

8. *Presumption against choice of foreign procedural law.* As discussed in *Karaha Bodas, Union of India* and *ICC Case No. 5505*, the procedural law of the arbitration will virtually always be the arbitration law of the arbitral seat. Parties almost never include a choice-of-law provision in their arbitration agreement specifying a foreign procedural law. And, as the same decisions also illustrate, general choice-of-law provisions are virtually never interpreted as selecting a foreign procedural law for the arbitration.

Consider the choice-of-law provision in *Union of India*. Is there not a serious argument that this provision was intended to select the procedural law of the arbitration? What is meant by the following sentence, included in the arbitration agreement in *Union of India*: "The arbitration shall be conducted in accordance with the procedure provided in the Indian Arbitration Act of 1940 or any reenactment or modification thereof"? If that language does not constitute the choice of Indian law as the procedural law of the arbitration, then what would? How does the (English) court interpret this sentence? Consider §§3, 33, 34 and 53 of the English Arbitration Act, 1996 (enacted after the *Union of India* decision, and excerpted at pp. 112, 121 & 127 of the Documentary Supplement); how would *Union of India* be decided under the 1996 Act?

Consider again the choice-of-law and other provisions of the agreement in *Karaha Bodas*. Is there not a serious argument that these provisions were intended to select Indonesian law as the procedural law of the arbitration? What else would explain the language used by the parties?

Where the parties have chosen an arbitral seat, and not chosen any procedural law governing the arbitration, what law will provide the procedural law of the arbitration? Consider the answers provided in *Union of India* and in *Sapphire*. Is there any doubt as to the correctness of this analysis?

Note the court's holding in *Karaha Bodas* that there is a presumption in favor of application of the law of the arbitral seat as the procedural law of the arbitration: "Under the New York Convention, an agreement specifying the place of the arbitration creates a presumption that the procedural law of that place applies to the arbitration." *Karaha Bodas Co.*, 364 F.3d at 291. *See also Compagnie d'Armement Maritime SA v.*

Compagnie Tunisienne de Navigation SA [1971] A.C. 572, 604 (House of Lords) ("An express choice of forum by the parties to a contract necessarily implies an intention that their disputes shall be settled in accordance with the procedural law of the selected forum and operates as if it were also an express choice of the curial law of the contract."). Is the presumption that the law of the arbitral seat provides the procedural law of the arbitration appropriate? What do you think parties usually expect, as to applicable procedural law, when they site an arbitration in a particular country?

9. *Effect of New York Convention on parties' autonomy to select foreign procedural law.* Consider Articles II(1) and V(1)(d) of the New York Convention, excerpted at pp. 1-2 of the Documentary Supplement. Article II(1) obliges Contracting States to give effect to agreements to arbitrate, while Article V(1)(d) provides that an award may be denied recognition if "[t]he composition of the arbitral authority or the arbitral procedure was not in accordance with the agreement of the parties, or, failing such agreement, was not in accordance with the law of the country where the arbitration took place." What effect do these provisions have on an agreement by the parties selecting the procedural law of an arbitration? Do they require Contracting States to give effect to the parties' selection of a foreign procedural law to govern an arbitration? That is, if a national law forbids or does not enforce the parties' selection of the procedural law governing an arbitration, does this violate the Convention?

Note that Article V(1)(d) merely allows Contracting States to refuse to recognize arbitral awards that disregard the parties' agreed arbitral procedures and does not expressly require Contracting States affirmatively to give effect to the parties' agreed arbitral procedures. What about Article II(1)? Does Article II(1)'s reference to the parties' arbitration agreement include their agreement on a foreign procedural law? Is there any reason it should not?

10. *Applicable procedural law not ordinarily affected by holding hearings elsewhere for convenience.* As discussed above, most institutional rules and national laws permit arbitral tribunals to conduct hearings at locations other than the arbitral seat. *See supra* p. 624. As a consequence, parties often agree to arbitration in State X, but thereafter, arbitral proceedings are physically conducted in other places, for reasons of convenience, without any intention to change either the arbitral seat or the procedural law applicable to the arbitration. *See supra* p. 636 and *infra* pp. 638, 652-55. When this occurs, is the procedural law affected by the location of the hearings?

Virtually all authority answers the foregoing question in the negative. Consider the analysis in *Garuda* (and the conduct of the arbitration in *Karaha Bodas*). Even the late Francis Mann, *Lex Facit Arbitrum, reprinted in*, 2 Arb. Int'l 241, 248 (1986), who attached overriding weight to the arbitral seat's law, wrote: "For the convenience of arbitrators or parties or for other reasons hearings may be held in different places. Such a practice will not ordinarily involve a change of the seat and, therefore, of the lex fori." *See also* Hirsch, *The Place of Arbitration and the Lex Arbitri*, 34 Arb. J. 43, 45 (1979); Park, *The Lex Loci Arbitri and International Commercial Arbitration*, 32 Int'l & Comp. L.Q. 21 (1983).

On the other hand, if an arbitral proceeding is physically conducted in a particular jurisdiction, are that jurisdiction's laws really irrelevant to the arbitral proceedings? What about basic standards of procedural fairness? What about prohibitions against swearing an oath or penalties for perjury?

11. *Meaning of parties' choice of procedural law governing the arbitration.* Although it rarely occurs, suppose the parties agree that the law of State A should govern the arbitral proceedings. What does this agreement mean? Does it mean that rules of civil procedure applicable in local judicial proceedings in State A should be binding on the arbitral tribunal? Or does it mean that the arbitration legislation and arbitration law of State A should apply? For analysis, see *ICC Case No. 5505*. Compare the reasoning in *Sapphire*. Which decision is more persuasive?

    (a) *Applicability of local rules of civil procedure.* Note the procedural law applied by the tribunal in *Sapphire*. In general, *Sapphire's* resort to the domestic rules of civil procedure applicable in local courts for the procedural law of an international arbitration is unusual, particularly in contemporary international commercial arbitration. Why is that so? Why wouldn't it make sense to apply relatively detailed (and predictable) local rules of civil procedure in international arbitrations? Is this application of judicial procedures what parties intend in agreeing to arbitrate?

    (b) *Applicability of national arbitration statute.* In contrast to *Sapphire*, most contemporary authorities interpret an agreement selecting a national law as the procedural law in an international arbitration as agreement on the arbitration statute of the seat, rather than the local rules of judicial procedure. In many jurisdictions, the local arbitration statute (i) will *not* specify detailed procedural rules that apply in particular arbitral proceedings, (ii) will allow the parties substantial autonomy to agree upon procedural rules, and (iii) may set out a few general procedural principles (*e.g.*, equality of treatment, adversarial procedure, and an opportunity for all parties to be heard). *See infra* pp. 793-95. Consider in this regard the UNCITRAL Model Law and SLPIL, excerpted at pp. 85-96 & 157-60 of the Documentary Supplement.

12. *Refusal of foreign procedural law selected by parties to allow itself to be chosen.* The national legal regime that the parties select for the procedural law may not permit itself to be selected, at least in some respects, for application to a foreign arbitration. That is particularly true with respect to the so-called "external" procedural law of the arbitration, focusing on judicial supervision of and assistance to the arbitral process. Thus, English courts have held that, even where parties have agreed to conduct an arbitration in a foreign state, with English law providing the applicable procedural law, English courts will not appoint an arbitrator (although they would do so in an "English" arbitration in England). *Naviera Amazonica Peruana SA v. Compania Internacional De Seguros del Peru* [1988] 1 Lloyd's Rep. 116, 119.

    Would a court in an UNCITRAL Model Law jurisdiction be permitted, by the Model Law, to exercise supervisory functions with respect to an arbitration seated in another state? Consider again the text of Article 1(2), excerpted at p. 86 of the Documentary Supplement. Note that the provisions of the Model Law generally apply "*only* if the place of arbitration is in the territory of this State." Why might national courts refuse to exercise supervisory power in support of an international arbitration located abroad, if the parties desired their aid?

13. *Potential conflicts in jurisdiction arising from selection of foreign procedural law.* Consider what might have occurred in *Union of India* if the English court had held that Indian law was the procedural law of an arbitration conducted in London; among other things, this would have meant that Indian courts (applying Indian law) could annul

awards made by the tribunal in London. *See supra* pp. 622-23 & *infra* pp. 1091-92, 1157-58. Is this a desirable result? Suppose Indian law (the procedural law) requires acts that English law (the arbitral seat's law) forbids—or vice versa. Suppose English courts confirm the award while Indian courts annul it. *See infra* p. 1110. Note the remarks in *Union of India* about the confusion resulting from application of multiple procedural laws to the same arbitration. Or, as one court reasoned, permitting an action to annul an award in two jurisdictions: "would be a recipe for litigation and (what is worse) confusion which cannot have been intended by the parties.... It could scarcely be supposed that a party aggrieved by one part of an award could proceed in one jurisdiction and a party aggrieved by another part of an award could proceed in another jurisdiction." *C v. D* [2007] EWCA Civ. 1282 (English Ct. App.). Is this so bizarre? What if it is what the parties agreed? Note the court's observations in *Karaha Bodas* about the possibility of awards being annulled in two different jurisdictions.

C. SELECTION OF ARBITRAL SEAT BY PARTIES' AGREEMENT OR ARBITRAL TRIBUNAL IN INTERNATIONAL ARBITRATION

For the reasons discussed above, it is both common (and very advisable) for international arbitration agreements to designate the arbitral seat.[20] Alternatively, the parties may agree upon institutional rules that permit either an appointing authority or the arbitral tribunal to choose the arbitral seat. As detailed below, most national arbitration statutes and institutional rules permit parties to specify their arbitral seat by agreement.

DUBAI ISLAMIC BANK PJSC v. PAYMENTECH MERCHANT SERVS. INC.
[2001] 1 All ER (Comm) 514 (English High Ct.)

AIKENS J. This case raises [a] new and interesting point[] concerning the application of the [English] Arbitration Act 1996.... [H]ow should the court apply §3 when determining what is the "juridical seat of the arbitration," if neither the parties to the arbitration agreement nor any arbitral or other institutions have designated the "seat" of the arbitration? ... [This question arises] upon the application of the respondent [seeking] the following relief: ... an order setting aside the award under §67, [§68 or §69] of the 1996 Act....

The applicant ("the bank") is a public joint stock company whose business is and was that of the Islamic banking. Its business is conducted from premises in Dubai and in the United Arab Emirates ("the UAE").... The bank operated a payment card scheme pursuant to a written agreement between Visa International Service Association ("VISA") and the bank which was concluded in England on 13 December 1990. That agreement incorporated

---

20. *See supra* p. 87. More than 80% of all ICC arbitrations involve agreements specifying the arbitral seat. *See, e.g., 2011-2013 ICC Statistical Reports* (2012-2014) (in 2013, arbitral seat was chosen by parties in 88.5% of cases; in remaining 11.5% of cases, place of arbitration was fixed by Court; in 2012, 90% and 10%; in 2011, 87% and 13); J. Fry, S. Greenberg & F. Mazza, *Secretariat's Guide to ICC Arbitration* ¶3-678, Table 28 (2012) (in 88% of ICC arbitrations commenced between 2007 and 2011, there has been agreement with respect to arbitral seat, either in contract's arbitration clause or by subsequent agreement of parties); Jarvin, *The Place of Arbitration—A Review of the ICC Court's Guiding Principles and Practice When Fixing the Place of Arbitration*, 7(2) ICC ICArb. Bull. 54 (1996); Verbist, *The Practice of the ICC International Court of Arbitration With Regard to the Fixing of the Place of Arbitration*, 12 Arb. Int'l 347 (1996).

by reference the by-laws and operating regulations of VISA which were then in force or might come into force from time to time.

The respondent ("Paymentech") is also a member of VISA. Paymentech's business is that of credit card payment processing, which includes payments made pursuant to the VISA credit card system.... It is an "acquirer," which means that it can "sign" a merchant and process a merchant's VISA card transaction through the VISA system. [The court described a complex process in which authorization for a credit card transaction is obtained in the VISA system.]

If there is a dispute about a particular transaction then a process called "chargeback and representment" is instigated.... If the acquirer is ... not satisfied [with the results of this process,] then it may initiate an arbitration procedure to resolve the dispute. The VISA International Operating Regulations set out the system for resolving disputes between card issuers and acquirers at ch 7.7 of vol. 1.... There are two tiers of arbitration. At the first tier arbitrations are conducted by the VISA International Arbitration Committee. At the second tier, which is an appellate level that only operates in limited circumstances, the arbitrations are conducted by VISA's international board of directors.... There are no provisions indicating (expressly or impliedly) what law governs the arbitration provisions in the regulations or the arbitral procedure itself. Indeed there is no proper law provision in the regulations at all. There is no specific reference to either the "seat" or the place of any arbitration under the regulations....

The regulation ... details "Filing Procedures." In a case such as this which involves two VISA members that are of different regions, the "Requesting Member" must file its arbitration request with the filing authority. In this case that authority will be VISA in California. Arbitration documentation has to be sent to the VISA International Arbitration/Compliance Committee in California. If the request is held to be valid, then VISA will notify both the requesting member and the opposing member and will forward a copy of the case to the opposing member. The opposing member is entitled to forward any additional information or substantiating documentation to VISA and the requesting member. The arbitration committee will use all available information in making its decision. It will notify the members of its decision.

[Following this decision, there] is the appeal process. This is available in respect of disputed amounts of over US$100,000, but only if the member wishing to appeal can provide new evidence. Then the matter will be dealt with by the VISA international board, acting as the appeal authority. [I]nternational board appeals will be submitted to the arbitration/compliance committee for consideration prior to board review.

In 1997/8 a large-scale fraud was perpetrated on the bank by its chief executive officer with the assistance of other personnel in the bank. One of the people allegedly involved in the fraud (but not a bank employee) was Mr Foutanga Babadi Sissoko. He held a VISA card that had been issued by the bank. Between November 1997 and January 1998 Mr Sissoko's VISA card was used for 18 purchases of jewellery at Mayor's Fine Jewellers in Miami, Florida, USA. The total involved in the 18 transactions was US$1,064,000. The bank says that the misuse of the VISA credit card was such that Mayor's accounts department and/or its vice president at the time (Mr Leon Benzrihem) must have colluded with Mr Sissoko to misuse the VISA card....

The bank challenged its liability to pay the sum of US$1,064,000, using the chargeback and representment procedure [and then the arbitration procedure] laid down in the VISA regulations.... The arbitration procedure before the VISA International Arbitration Committee (the VIAC) was conducted entirely on paper. The bank answered various questions put to it by the VIAC. On 16 and 17 March 1999 the VIAC issued two awards that were in Paymentech's favour. The VIAC held that there was no evidence of any collusion between Mayor's employees and Mr Sissoko to defraud the bank. It also held that ... the bank had failed to support the chargeback with the required documentation. Accordingly, Paymentech's account was credited with the sum in dispute.

In May 1999 the bank appealed to the VISA international board of directors. The bank submitted a series of lengthy written submissions through its lawyers.... There was no oral hearing before the international board of directors.... [T]he matter was heard at an international board meeting that took place in London on 8 November 1999.... No formal awards were produced by the board. Instead, after the board meeting, the assistant secretary to the board advised Miss Kris Misfeldt, the director of VISA International Arbitration and Compliance, of the board's unanimous decision. The board decided to dismiss the appeals and upheld the VIAC's awards.

On 15 November 1999 Miss Misfeldt wrote to the bank (from an office in San Francisco, California, USA), informing it of the international board's decision. The letter first sets out the reasons why the VIAC had reached its decision against the bank. The letter then states that (in accordance with the appeal procedure), the arbitration committee had considered further information that had been submitted by the bank at the appeal stage, before the matter was reviewed by the board. The arbitration committee had concluded that this further information did not conclusively demonstrate: "a purposeful attempt by the merchant to defraud the Issuer and did not meet Visa's traditional view of merchant collusion, such as counterfeit card schemes intended to defraud the broader Visa payment system." The letter then stated that the international board of directors had agreed with this view. The letter continued: "As all permissible actions with the Visa Arbitration process have been exhausted, Visa International now considers the matter closed. The Issuer will retain responsibility for all transactions and case processing fees associated with the above reference cases."

This letter was received by Jonathan Rosenn of Fine & Associates, the Florida lawyers acting for the bank, on 29 November 1999.... [Mr. Rosenn inquired] of VISA where the international board of VISA sat when it made its decision [and] was told by Miss Misfeldt that it was in London....

[The bank applied to the English courts to annul the award] under §§67, 68 and 69 of the 1996 Act.... Whether the bank can pursue these applications depends on ... [whether] for the purposes of §§2 and 3 of the 1996 Act, is the "seat of the arbitration" in England and Wales? ... Both parties agree that the court has no jurisdiction to hear or determine the bank's applications under §§67 to 69 unless the court is satisfied that the seat of the arbitrations is in England and Wales....

By §53 of the 1996 Act: "Unless otherwise agreed by the parties, where the seat of the arbitration is in England and Wales ... any award in the proceedings shall be treated as made there, regardless of where it was signed, despatched or delivered to any of the parties." In this case it is agreed that there was no particular agreement by the parties as to the place where the relevant awards were made.... Therefore the English court can only consider the bank's applications if the bank establishes that the seat of the arbitrations was in England, so that (under §53) the awards will be treated as having been made in England.

Section 3 of the 1996 Act provides:

"In this Part 'the seat of the arbitration' means the juridical seat of the arbitration designated—(a) by the parties to the arbitration agreement, or (b) by any arbitral or other institution or person vested by the parties with powers in that regard, or (c) by the arbitral tribunal if so authorised by the parties, or determined in the absence of any such designation, having regard to the parties' agreement and all the relevant circumstances."

It is accepted that none of the circumstances set out in (a), (b) or (c) of §3 apply in this case. In particular it is agreed that there is nothing in the arbitration provisions of the VISA regulations that identifies the seat of any arbitration conducted under the regulations.... Therefore it is for the court to determine the seat of the arbitration "having regard to the parties' agreement and all the relevant circumstances." ...

Paymentech submitted as follows.... The "seat" of the arbitration is its "juridical seat," as opposed to the physical place where the proceedings generally or particular hearings occur. The "seat" is the central point of the arbitration or its centre of gravity, viewed overall.... The court is entitled to look at the arbitration agreement of the parties and the conduct of the reference from the beginning to the end as part of "all the relevant circumstances" within §3.... [T]he court must reach an objective view of where the "seat" of the particular arbitration is located....

[Paymentech argued that,] although the VISA regulations make no specific reference to a "seat," place or governing law of arbitrations ..., the centre of gravity of any arbitrations under those provisions is clearly at the VISA headquarters in California. That is where the request for arbitration must be filed and the arbitration documentation must be sent in accordance with the VISA regulations. VISA headquarters will notify the members of the process and the arbitration committee's decision.... In particular, in relation to the appeal procedure: (a) the notification of appeal was sent by the bank to VISA in California; (b) the lengthy submissions of the bank were sent by its lawyers, Fine & Associates, to VISA in California; (c) Paymentech's responses were sent to VISA in California; (d) the procedure on appeal is dealt with by VISA's director of arbitration and compliance, Miss Misfeldt, who is based in California; (e) the appeal had to be dealt with by the international board as part of the agenda for one of its four monthly meetings. The location of the board meeting at which the appeal is heard will be adventitious. In fact it was London; (f) the decision of the international board on the appeal was notified to the parties from VISA in California....

[The] bank submitted the following.... The task of the court under §3 is to make an objective determination of the "seat." The parties' intention (in the absence of an express choice of "seat") is irrelevant.... The court can take all factors into account in deciding the location of the seat.... In a case involving transnational trade and services such as this one, the location of the seat of the arbitration can (and frequently will) be different from the country whose law governs either the substantive contract or the law governing the parties' arbitration agreement.... The relevant arbitration is the appeal process.... The key factor here that makes England the seat of the appeal arbitration is that the appeal was held, heard and determined by the appellate tribunal (the international board of VISA) in London. There are no countervailing factors that make California the seat.... The fact that all correspondence concerning the arbitration was routed through the administrative centre of VISA in California is not a strong factor. All ICC arbitrations are organised through Paris; it does not make France the seat of all ICC arbitrations....

It is clear from §2(1) of the 1996 Act that the concept is used in order to define which arbitrations will be subject to the statutory regime in Pt 1 of the 1996 Act. Part 1 of the 1996 Act gives the English court important powers in relation to arbitration proceedings which will be exercisable at different states of an arbitration. Therefore, in general, only those arbitrations that have their "seat" in England and Wales should be subject to the exercise of the court's powers in Pt 1 of the 1996 Act. The 1996 Act uses the concept of the "seat" as the test for the exercise of Pt 1 powers rather than the choice of procedural law made by the parties in their arbitration agreement.... Section 4(1) and (2) stipulate that there will be "mandatory" and "non-mandatory" provisions in Pt 1. The Pt 1 regime applies "whether or not the law applicable to the parties' agreement is the law of England and Wales.... But if the parties have chosen another procedural law for the arbitration or particular aspects of it, then, in relation to non-mandatory provisions in Pt 1, the effect will be as if the parties had made a specific agreement dealing with those matters." English Arbitration Act, §4(5).

Section 3 states that "the seat of the arbitration means the juridical seat of the arbitration." It is clear that "seat" is intended to refer to some state of territory; hence the reference to "the seat of the arbitration [being] in England and Wales" in §2(1) of the 1996 Act.... [T]he location contemplated is a particular state or territory which is associated with a recognisable and distinct system of law. So the "juridical seat of the arbitration" means the state or territory where, for legal purposes, "the arbitration" is to be regarded as situated....

[T]he powers conferred on the court by Pt 1 ... are exercisable at different stages in the arbitral process. The power to appoint an arbitrator (§18) will arise usually at the start of the process. The power to remove an arbitrator (§24) could be exercised at any stage up to and even after an award. Self-evidently the powers of the court in relation to awards (§§66-70) will only be exercisable at the end of the arbitration process. I draw attention to these factors only to emphasise the point that the issue of whether an English court can exercise these various powers depends (with exceptions) on the answer to the threshold question of whether, in accordance with §§2 and 3, the "seat" of "the arbitration" is England and Wales? ...

The key circumstance that the bank relies on is that the actual appeal hearing by the international board took place at the board meeting in London on 8 November 1999. The only other "English connections" that the bank can rely on really have nothing to do with the individual appeal arbitration at all. First, there is the English connection concerning the original agreement between the bank and VISA. Secondly there is the fact that the point of contract generally between the bank and VISA was the VISA centre at Basingstoke. Thirdly there is the point that, at the start of the payment procedure, the bank as issuer would have received a request for authorisation from Basingstoke and (if it had been given) it would have gone to Basingstoke....

[The question of where the "seat" is located concerns the seat of] the individual arbitration with which the case is particularly concerned.... In this case the relevant arbitration is clearly the appeal arbitration.... So I am concerned with discovering the "seat" of that individual appeal "arbitration."

The next question is at what stage of the relevant arbitration does the court have to examine "the parties' agreement and all the relevant circumstances" in order to determine the "seat of the arbitration." As I have already pointed out, the issue of the jurisdiction of the court to exercise one of its Pt 1 powers might arise at either an early or a late stage of the arbitral process. Thus if the issue arose when the court was being invited to appoint an arbitrator under §18, then there might be very much fewer "relevant circumstances" … to consider compared with a case when the issue arose after an award had been made.

[Paymentech] accepted that once the "seat" has been determined for §3 purposes, then it cannot move, unless the parties agree that it should or one of the mechanisms set out in §3 is operated…. In *Union of India* [*supra* pp. 626-29], which was a case before the 1996 Act, Saville J took the view that once the "seat" of the arbitration was fixed it could not move unless the parties agreed to change it. In a case under the 1996 Act, *ABB Lummus Global Ltd v. Keppel Fels Ltd* [1999] 2 Lloyd's Rep 24 at 33, Clarke J said that he agreed with Saville J's view…. I respectfully agree with both judges…. My conclusion … is that if the court has to determine the "juridical seat of the arbitration" in the circumstances set out in §3, then it must do so at the point at which the relevant arbitration begins. In this case that point would be when the bank invoked the appeal process in May 1999 and Paymentech submitted to it.

My reasons for this conclusion … are the following…. Under English law an arbitration must always have a "seat." As the Departmental Advisory Committee on Arbitration Law Report on the Arbitration Bill commented: "English law does not at present recognise the concept of an arbitration which has no seat and we do not recommend that it should do so." This means that an arbitration must have a seat when the arbitration starts. In this case that must mean that a "seat" must exist when the appeal process started in May 1999…. Once an arbitration starts and it has a "seat" then I cannot see how it can be changed, unless it is by one of the mechanisms envisaged in §3…. It would be contrary to the whole idea of a "juridical seat" that its location should somehow be peripatetic. The purpose of locating a "seat" of an arbitration under the 1996 Act is to identify a state or territory whose laws will (subject to exceptions) govern the arbitral process. If the "seat" could change from one point in the arbitral process to the next then the parties would never know whether the English court could exercise its Pt 1 powers…. The procedural law regime of an arbitration surely cannot change capriciously from one point in the arbitral process to the next…. Therefore … if the particular mechanisms identified in §3 are not used, then once a "seat" has been identified, it cannot move.

If this conclusion is correct, then I have to examine the "agreement of the parties and all the relevant circumstances" as at May 1999. The reference to the "the parties' agreement" means, I think, the agreement that contains the original contract to submit disputes to arbitration…. If this is correct, then "the parties' agreement" here must mean the VISA regulations. They contain the agreement to submit disputes to the VISA arbitration process and the arbitration appeal process. I take the phrase "all the relevant circumstances" to mean … that a court has to have regard to any connections with one or more particular countries that can be identified in relation to: (i) the parties; (ii) the dispute which will be the subject of the arbitration; (iii) the proposed procedures in the arbitration, including (if known) the place of interlocutory and final hearings; and (iv) the issue of the award or awards.

If I consider those matters then it is clear that the "seat" of the appeal arbitration process is not in England, but is probably located in California. Thus—(1) Paymentech is based in Texas. The bank is based in Dubai. VISA is based in California. (2) The VISA regulations have no express proper law provisions either as to the substantive regulations or as to the appeal arbitration process between members. (3) The VISA worldwide payment card scheme has its headquarters in California. (4) The dispute arose out of transactions in

Florida. Although the bank had to grant authorisation for those transactions (as issuer) through Basingstoke, Paymentech had to deal with its authorisation (as acquirer) through California. (5) The regulations appear to contemplate that the appeal arbitral process will be handled through the VISA offices in California. Thus it is contemplated that notifications will be sent there; the process will be handled by the arbitration and compliance department in California. The merits will be considered by the arbitration committee which is based at VISA headquarters in California before being considered by the board. It is contemplated that the board will consider the merits of the appeal at a board meeting which could be anywhere in the world. (6) The regulations appear to contemplate that notification of the result of the appeal process will be handled by VISA headquarters in California.

Is this conclusion on the "seat of the arbitration" altered if … [a] court should consider circumstances relating to all the subsequent stages in the arbitral process in order to determine the "seat" of the arbitration? In my view this cannot alter my conclusion that the "seat" of the appeal arbitration is not in England and is probably in California. The reasons for this conclusion are the following. (1) The only additional factor pointing to England as the "seat" is that the international board meeting at which the appeal of the bank was heard took place in London. But the location of the board meeting was adventitious. It was not contemplated by anyone, in the bank, VISA or Paymentech, that the appeal would necessarily be heard in London. (2) Nor was the fact that the hearing was in London of any particular significance. The preparatory administrative work for the appeal and the consideration by the arbitration committee were not done in London. It was done in California. After the decision of the international board the parties were informed by Miss Misfeldt of the result by letter from the VISA office in California.…

Therefore, on either approach, I have concluded that "the seat" of the appeal arbitration is this case was not in England and Wales. Accordingly the court has no jurisdiction in this case to exercise the powers set out in §§67 to 69 of Pt 1 of the 1996 Act.…

PT GARUDA INDONESIA v. BIRGEN AIR
[2002] 1 SLR 393 (Singapore Ct. App.)

[excerpted above at pp. 600-05]

IN THE MATTER OF CHARLES R. STEVENS v. COUDERT BROTHERS
662 N.Y.S.2d 42 (N.Y. App. Div. 1997)

The arbitration agreement in issue provides for arbitration pursuant to the Rules of the [AAA], except that "whenever any of the foreign branches of [respondent law] firm shall be involved in [a] dispute or controversy [arising under respondent's partnership agreement], such arbitration shall take place in the city where the foreign branch has its principal office, if the New York principal office shall have requested the arbitration." Because several of respondent's foreign branch offices are "involved" in its claim that petitioner, among other things, wrongfully recruited its attorneys to another firm, there is no city where "the" foreign branch office is located and it therefore cannot be said that respondent failed to comply with the agreement by demanding arbitration in New York. Where parties have agreed to arbitration, courts should proceed with "great caution" in interfering with the processes of the selected tribunal, particularly with respect to procedural threshold questions such as venue (*Matter of D.M.C. Constr. Corp. v. Nash Steel Corp.*, 51 A.D.2d

1040, 1041 [dissenting mem], *rev'd on dissenting mem* 41 N.Y.2d 855). The parties having agreed to arbitrate their dispute pursuant to the Rules of the American Arbitration Association, and there being no clear violation of the exception to that agreement for foreign branch offices, the issue of venue was properly referred to the AAA for resolution....

ADF GROUP INC. v. UNITED STATES OF AMERICA
Procedural Order No. 2 Concerning the Place of Arbitration in ICSID Case No. ARB(AF)/00/1 of 1 July 2001

FELICIANO, LAMM & DE MESTRAL. At our first session held by video-conference with the parties and their respective counsel, it was noted that the parties had not been able to agree on the location of the place of arbitration of the instant case, having agreed only that the place of arbitration, for reasons of cost and convenience, should be located either in Canada or in the United States. Nevertheless, the parties agreed that the question of the proper place of arbitration should be determined by the Tribunal, after the parties have each had an opportunity to submit a written memorial to the Tribunal....

The Claimant requests us to designate Montreal, in the Province of Québec, Canada, as the place of arbitration in the instant case. The Respondent submits that we should instead select Washington D.C. as the place of arbitration.

Article 1130 of the North American Free Trade Agreement ("NAFTA") provides that

"[u]nless the disputing parties agree otherwise, a Tribunal shall hold an arbitration *in the territory of a Party that is a party to the New York Convention*, selected in accordance with: (a) the ICSID Additional Facility Rules if the arbitration is under those Rules or the ICSID Convention; or (b) the UNCITRAL Arbitration Rules if the arbitration is under those Rules." (Emphasis supplied.)

Both the United States of America and Canada are parties to the [New York Convention].... Article 21 of the ICSID Arbitration (Additional Facility) Rules reads in full as follows:

"Determination of Place of Arbitration
(1) Subject to Article 20 of these Rules the place of arbitration shall be determined by the Arbitral Tribunal after consultation with the parties and the Secretariat.
(2) The Arbitral Tribunal may meet at any place it deems appropriate for the inspection of goods, other property or documents. It may also visit any place connected with the dispute or conduct inquiries there. The parties shall be given sufficient notice to enable them to be present at such inspection or visit.
(3) The award shall be made at the place of arbitration."

Article 20 of the ICSID Arbitration (Additional Facility) Rules, entitled "Limitation on Choice of Forum," requires no more than that arbitration proceedings be held "only in States that are parties to the [New York Convention]." Clearly, Article 20 does not bring us very far in approaching the issue of an appropriate place of arbitration.

The [1976] UNCITRAL Rules, the other set of arbitration rules referred to in Article 1130 of the NAFTA, provide only the most general guidance on this matter:

"Place of Arbitration Article 16.
(1) Unless the parties have agreed upon the place where the arbitration is to be held, such place shall be determined by the arbitral tribunal, *having regard to the circumstances of the arbitration*...." (Emphasis added.)

Fortunately, the UNCITRAL Notes on Organizing Arbitral Proceedings ("UNCITRAL Notes") are substantially more helpful, even though they do not bind either the disputing parties or the Arbitral Tribunal:

> "3. Place of Arbitration (a) Determination of the place of arbitration, if not already agreed upon by the parties ... 22. Various factual and legal factors influence the choice of the place of arbitration, and their relative importance varies from case to case. Among the more prominent factors are: (a) suitability of the law on arbitral procedure of the place of arbitration; (b) whether there is a multilateral or bilateral treaty on enforcement of arbitral awards between the State where the arbitration takes place and the State or States where the award may have to be enforced; (c) convenience of the parties and the arbitrators, including the travel distances; (d) availability and cost of support services needed; and (e) location of the subject-matter in dispute and proximity of evidence...."

Both the Claimant and the Respondent agree that we may and should take into consideration the kinds of factors identified as pertinent in ¶22 of the UNCITRAL Notes. We will do so seriatim.

The first factor that bears consideration is the "suitability of the law on arbitral procedure of (a proposed) place of arbitration." The Claimant begins its case for Montreal as an appropriate place of arbitration with the general proposition that a "suitable" domestic legal system is one which is "supportive" of arbitration and that a jurisdiction which creates "uncertainty in arbitration by permitting a myriad of legal challenges to an award" is not supportive. In the view of the Claimant, a "supportive" jurisdiction provides a legal environment that sets out "clear, predictable and limited procedures for challenging an award along with an effective mechanism for recognition and enforcement of an award."

For its part, the United States stresses its broad commitment to "facilitating international arbitration" and the recognition by the United States Supreme Court of an "emphatic federal policy in favor of arbitral dispute resolution" (*Mitsubishi Motors*, 473 US at 631. That Court held that "concerns of *international comity, respect for the capacities of foreign and transnational tribunals and sensitivity to the need of the international commercial system for predictability* in the resolution of disputes *require that we enforce the parties' agreement*, even assuming that a contrary result would be forth coming in a domestic context." (473 US at 629; emphasis added.) ...

[T]he "suitability" in international arbitration of the law on arbitral procedure of a suggested place of arbitration, has multiple dimensions. These dimensions include the extent to which that law, *e.g.*, protects the integrity of and gives effect to the parties' arbitration agreement; accords broad discretion to the parties and to the arbitrators they choose to determine and control the conduct of arbitration proceedings; provides for the availability of interim measures of protection and of means of compelling the production of documents and other evidence and the attendance of reluctant witnesses; consistently recognizes and enforces, in accordance with the terms of widely accepted international conventions, international arbitral awards when rendered; insists on principled restraint in establishing grounds for reviewing and setting aside international arbitral awards; and so on. The Claimant has tended to focus and distinguish between two aspects of the *lex arbitri*: (a) recognition and enforcement of arbitral awards; and (b) review by the courts of the *locus arbitri* of such awards in actions to modify or set aside and vacate those awards....

In respect of the recognition and enforcement of international awards, including awards issued under the NAFTA and ICSID (Additional Facility) Rules, the parties agree that the laws of the United States and the laws of Canada and the Province of Québec render applicable the pertinent provisions of the New York Convention. Both Canada and the United States, in their respective reservations to the Convention, had determined that they would apply the Convention only to arbitral proceedings arising out of disputes which are considered as "commercial" under their respective national laws. Article 1136(7) of the NAFTA, however, provides that "[a] claim that is submitted to arbitration under this §[B] shall be considered to arise out of a commercial relationship or transaction for purposes of Article 1 of the New York Convention and Article 1 of the Inter-American Convention." Accordingly, the parties are agreed that the laws of both the United States and of Canada (and of Québec Province) concerning international arbitrations are equally "suitable" so far as concerns the recognition and enforcement of the ensuing awards.

In respect of review by a national court in the place of arbitration of an international arbitral award, it is suggested by the Claimant that the "deeming provision" of Article 1136(7) of the NAFTA "might not reach actions to review and set aside Chapter Eleven awards in situations where domestic review remedies were limited to awards in commercial arbitration." The Claimant points out that Canada amended its Federal Commercial Arbitration Act to "deem" Chapter Eleven awards "to be commercial for the purposes of actions to review (such) award(s)," while the United States made no similar amendment to its own FAA.... The Claimant goes on to elaborate that actions in a U.S. Federal Court to review and set aside arbitral awards are governed by Chapter 1 ("General Provisions") of the FAA, the grounds for vacating such awards being set out in [§10], while actions for recognition and enforcement are governed by Chapter 2 (referring to the New York Convention) and Chapter 3 (referring to the Inter-American Convention).... Neither Chapter 2 ... nor the New York Convention, the Claimant contends, provides for actions to review and set aside arbitral awards. Although §208 does provide for application of Chapter 1 to actions brought under Chapter 2 "to the extent that Chapter [1] is not in conflict with this Chapter [2] or the [New York] Convention," Claimant argues that whether an action initiated in the United States to set aside a Chapter Eleven award can be considered "an application or proceeding brought under [Chapter 2]" is a "serious question." Accordingly, the Claimant characterizes U.S. law on this matter as "unclear" and affected with "uncertainty," a condition tending to "undermine the authority of the Tribunal and its eventual award" by possible "post award litigation" which "will severely test judicial deference to international arbitration awards" and which renders U.S. arbitration law as "unsuitable."

Upon the other hand, the Claimant submits that Québec law clearly provides for, and identifies the grounds of, judicial review of Chapter Eleven awards. Québec's arbitration law is said to be based on the UNCITRAL Model Law and does not distinguish between "commercial" and "non-commercial" arbitration and hence is "unclouded by the uncertainty resulting from the debate whether Chapter Eleven arbitrations are international commercial arbitrations."

The United States, for its part, rejects the Claimant's contentions summed up above. The United States stresses, firstly, that it is "impossible" at this stage of "Chapter Eleven's evolution" for any party to have "absolute certainty as to the legal regime governing review of a Chapter Eleven award," whether such review takes place in Canada or in the United States. At the time of its Final Observations, no decision in a proceeding to review a Chapter Eleven award had, according to the United States, been rendered, even in a first instance court, in any of the NAFTA Parties. The United States goes on to note that the

Attorney-General of Canada has gone on record in *United Mexican States v. Metalclad Corp.*, recently before the British Columbia Supreme Court, as contending that "in interpreting NAFTA, Chapter Eleven tribunals should not attract extensive judicial deference and should not be protected by a higher standard of judicial review." The Claimant has not, in the view of the United States, adduced any basis for believing that an action in Québec to review a Chapter Eleven award would not be subject to similar questions as to the applicable standard of judicial review....

The United States also, perhaps more importantly, directly controverts the correctness of the Claimant's description of the condition of U.S. law in this respect and states outright that "suitable procedures for review of a Chapter Eleven award are available in the United States under both federal and D.C. law, regardless of whether the award is deemed commercial for purposes of review." The clear statement is made, albeit in a footnote, that "under §208 of the U.S. FAA, Chapter 1 of the FAA, and specifically §10 governing vacatur of awards, would apply to Chapter Eleven awards made in the United States." ...

After extensive consideration of the submissions of both parties, we are unpersuaded that we must characterize the U.S. [FAA] as an "unsuitable" *lex arbitri* or as a less "suitable" *lex arbitri* than the Canadian or Québec law on international arbitration. In the absence of U.S. case law directly addressing the specific issue raised here by the Claimant, we do not consider that the Claimant has adequately documented its description of the relevant U.S. law as infected, as it were, by a "lack of clarity" which "undermines the authority of the Tribunal and its eventual award and promises to multiply post award litigation." We would also note that the distinction heavily stressed by the Claimant between an action to review and set aside a Chapter Eleven award and an action for recognition and enforcement of such an award may not, in certain situations, be as important as might be supposed. The grounds for vacating an arbitral award under 9 U.S.C. Chapter 1, §10 and those for setting aside an award under Article 34 of the UNCITRAL Model Law on the one hand, and the grounds specified in the New York Convention for resisting an action for recognition and enforcement of an award on the other hand, exhibit overlapping in significant degree.... We do not believe that the Claimant has provided us with sufficient basis for refusing to join the tribunals in the *Methanex* and *Ethyl* cases in holding that Canadian law and United States law relating to international arbitration, are equally "suitable" for purposes of determining an appropriate place of arbitration. (*Ethyl Corp. v. Canada*, 38 ILM 700 (1999, May No. 3); *Methanex Corp. v. United States of America, Written Reasons for the Tribunal's Decision of 7th September 2000 on the Place of Arbitration, December 21, 2000*).

We turn now to the second factor listed in ¶22 of the UNCITRAL Notes: the existence of a multilateral or bilateral treaty on enforcement of arbitral awards between the State where the arbitration takes place and the State or States where the award may have to be enforced. Since both the United States and Canada are parties to the New York Convention, this factor is moot in the present case.

The third UNCITRAL Notes factor is the convenience of the parties and the arbitrators. The convenience, or relative inconvenience, of the arbitrators offers no real guidance in this case. Two of the three arbitrators reside or hold office outside the United States. Similarly, two of the three arbitrators reside or hold office outside Canada. Thus, whether the place of arbitration be in Canada or in the United States, two of the arbitrators would have to travel to one or the other State.... In respect of the parties, however, the relative inconvenience of travelling to Montreal or to Washington D.C. may not be as finely balanced. At this stage, we are not informed as to how many officials, counsel, representatives and witnesses of one or the other party would have to travel to Montreal or Washington D.C., as the case may be. The United States submits that the convenience of the parties favors Washington D.C. over Montreal because the United States, qua party, is comprised of numerous agencies of which at least seven are concerned with or involved in the instant dispute. Presumably, all seven agencies are based in Washington D.C. So far as Claimant is concerned, it may well be that some of its officials or representatives involved in this dispute are based in Virginia, though others would presumably be located in Québec or elsewhere in Canada. We should, at the same time, note that the Tribunal may, when necessary or appropriate, meet in Montreal or any other place to hear particular witnesses and facilitate the presentation of evidence, upon request of either party and with prior notice to and agreement of both parties. On balance, in the circumstances of this case, we believe that the submission of the United States on this point, is not unreasonable, even though the relative inconvenience of a State, as a party, is not necessarily compelling.

The next UNCITRAL factor relates to the availability and cost of support services needed. In principle, there may well be no significant difference between Montreal and Washington D.C. in respect of the availability of arbitration support services in one or the other city. It appears to us, however, that because the ICSID is administering this case and providing the services of the Secretary of the Tribunal, the over-all costs of the arbitration support involved are likely to be substantially less in Washington D.C. than in Montreal. The opinion of the ICSID, solicited by us and conveyed to us by our Secretary, is to that effect.

The UNCITRAL Notes refer, lastly, to the location of the subject-matter of the dispute and proximity of evidence. The question of "proximity" of testimonial and documentary "evidence" has been substantially dealt with above under the rubric of the convenience of the parties.... [T]he "subject-matter" of the present dispute may be seen to refer to, essentially, the claims made by the Claimant about the consistency or lack of consistency of certain measures (or applications thereof) taken by the Respondent United States with certain provisions of Chapter Eleven of the NAFTA. To the extent that such claims can be regarded as having a "location" or situs anywhere, we consider that those claims may, for purposes of determining an appropriate place of arbitration, be deemed to be located in the place where the United States authorities, to whom they are addressed, are based....

We come finally to the element of "neutrality" of the place of arbitration. It is our belief that Washington D.C. is properly regarded as a "neutral" place of arbitration, notwithstanding that it is the capital of the Respondent Party. Our perspective on this last point is rooted in the belief that the ICSID is, and is widely perceived to be, a "neutral" forum and institution. The policy imperatives which drive parties proceeding to international arbitration to seek a "neutral" forum are, in our opinion, satisfied by choosing the city in which the ICSID is located which also happens to be the capital of the United States.

For all the foregoing considerations, the Tribunal determines to designate Washington D.C. as the place of arbitration in the instant case. The Tribunal may also meet in Montreal or any other place, when necessary or appropriate, to hear particular witnesses and facilitate the presentation of evidence, upon request of either party and with notice to and the agreement of both parties.

NOTES

1. *Selection of arbitral seat in international arbitration agreement.* As noted above, international arbitration agreements frequently specify the arbitral seat. Why is this so? What considerations argue in favor of attempting to reach agreement on an arbitral seat? Why might it be difficult to reach agreement on the arbitral seat?

2. *Effect of parties' agreement on arbitral seat under national arbitration statutes.* What effect is given to the parties' selection of an arbitral seat in their international commercial arbitration agreement by national arbitration legislation? Consider Article 20(1) of the UNCITRAL Model Law, excerpted at p. 91 of the Documentary Supplement, providing: "The parties are free to agree on the place of arbitration." Compare Article 176(3) of the SLPIL, excerpted at p. 157 of the Documentary Supplement. What is the rationale for permitting parties to select their arbitral seat by agreement? Suppose the arbitrators believe the parties have not wisely chosen the arbitral seat; do they have the power to change the seat?

   Should there be any limits on this freedom? Can you posit a case where the parties' agreement on the arbitral seat should not be given effect? Suppose the arbitral seat is geographically remote and costly, imposing disproportionate expense and inconvenience on a financially weak party. Suppose the arbitral seat is in one party's home jurisdiction, whose courts often display a bias towards local parties. On what grounds might a party challenge an agreement selecting an arbitral seat in these circumstances?

   Suppose national law purports to invalidate any agreement selecting a foreign arbitral seat (and to instead require the arbitration to be conducted locally). Is such a provision consistent with the New York Convention? Recall the discussion above of Articles II(1) and V(1)(d) of the Convention, excerpted at pp. 1-2 of the Documentary Supplement. *See supra* pp. 638-39. Do these provisions have the effect of forbidding Contracting States from denying effect to the parties' choice of the arbitral seat? Should they?

3. *Effect of parties' agreement on arbitral seat under institutional rules.* Consider Article 18 of the 2010 UNCITRAL Rules, Article 18 of the 2012 ICC Rules, Article 16 of the 2014 LCIA Rules and, excerpted at pp. 168, 189 & 265 of the Documentary Supplement. What effect do the UNCITRAL, LCIA and ICC Rules give to the parties' choice of an arbitral seat? Suppose a tribunal is appointed and, after considering the dispute, decides that the parties picked the "wrong" arbitral seat. What power does the tribunal have under the ICC and UNCITRAL Rules to change the arbitral seat?

4. *Implied selection of arbitral seat.* The parties' selection of the arbitral seat may be implied, as well as express. Consider the analysis in *Dubai Islamic Bank*. What factors are relevant to determining the existence of an implied choice of the arbitral seat by the parties? Did the *Dubai Islamic Bank* court reach the correct conclusion as to the parties' choice of an arbitral seat?

   Consider the Singaporean court's analysis in *Garuda*. What factors did the court consider in deciding whether the parties had agreed to move the arbitral seat? Did the Singaporean court reach the correct conclusion?

   Note that the possibility of an implied choice or change of the arbitral seat allows national courts to play a potentially significant role in selecting the arbitral seat. What would constitute an implied choice of the arbitral seat? Would a choice-of-law clause, selecting the substantive law governing the parties' underlying contract, constitute an implied choice of the arbitral seat? Would the selection of a language of the arbitration constitute an implied choice of the arbitral seat (*e.g.*, Russian, Chinese)?

Would the selection of an arbitral institution based in a particular country amount to an implied choice of that country as the arbitral seat? For example, would agreement to arbitrate under the ICC Rules amount to an implied choice of Paris as the arbitral seat? Consider how the *Dubai Islamic Bank* court deals with this suggestion. Does the *ADF Group* decision in fact rely upon an implied choice of the arbitral seat, through selection of ICSID as the administering authority?

5. *What place(s) should a party select as arbitral seat?* Assume you represent a Swiss company considering whether to enter into four separate international contracts with, respectively, a Russian, a U.S., a Pakistani and an English company. What place would you wish to specify as an arbitral seat in each of the four agreements? Would the same arbitral seat be appropriate in all four contracts? If you could not obtain your first choice, what would your second choice be? Suppose that each of the above counter-parties is state-related. Does that affect your analysis?

Which of the following factors should be considered by a party in selecting an arbitral seat, and in what order of priority? (a) the seat is located within a New York Convention Contracting State; (b) the seat has a supportive international arbitration statute; (c) the seat has a well-developed legal system on issues relating to the substance of the parties' dispute; (d) the courts in the seat will review arbitral awards with a high degree of deference; (e) the seat will permit foreign lawyers to appear in arbitrations conducted there; (f) the seat has good hotels, food and weather; and (g) the seat is located in your counter-party's principal place of business.

The past decade has witnessed the promotion of "new" arbitral seats, notably in Dubai, Miami, Kuala Lumpur, Seoul and elsewhere. These locations all offer a combination of modern arbitration legislation, a new or reinvigorated national arbitral institution and governmental support for facilities and the like. These seats are attracting increasing interest from users, particularly in local and regional transactions and disputes.

6. *Selection of arbitral seat by arbitral institution or arbitrators (absent agreement by parties).* Suppose parties are unable to agree on an arbitral seat in their arbitration agreement (or otherwise) and instead agree only that their arbitration will be conducted in accordance with a set of institutional arbitration rules. How is the seat selected?

   (a) *Institutional rules providing for selection of arbitral seat by arbitral institution.* Some institutional rules provide for the selection of the arbitral seat by the arbitral institution (absent contrary agreement by the parties). See Article 18(1) of the ICC Rules, excerpted at p. 189 of the Documentary Supplement. What are the advantages of such an approach? What advantages might an arbitral institution have over an arbitral tribunal in selecting an arbitral seat? Over a national court?

   (b) *Institutional rules providing for selection of arbitral seat by arbitrators.* Consider Article 18(1) of the UNCITRAL Rules, excerpted at p. 168 of the Documentary Supplement, providing that the arbitral tribunal is to select the arbitral seat (absent contrary agreement). See also Article 16 of the LCIA Rules, providing that in absence of contrary agreement, the seat is London, unless the tribunal decides otherwise after consulting with the parties. Is this preferable to the approach of the ICC Rules? Why or why not?

Note the approach taken under NAFTA to selection of the arbitral seat. Would it be preferable for ICSID to select the arbitral seat in NAFTA arbitrations? Note that the *ADF Group* tribunal consulted with ICSID. Consider the tribunal's decision in *ADF Group*; is selection of the arbitral seat an adjudicative function?

(c) *Institutional rules providing for selection of arbitral seat by institution, subject to confirmation by arbitrators*. Consider Article 17 of the ICDR Rules, excerpted at p. 220 of the Documentary Supplement. What advantages does Article 17 have when compared to the ICC, LCIA and UNCITRAL rules?

7. *Effect of national arbitration law on selection of arbitral seat by arbitral institution or tribunal*. What effect do Article 20(1) of the Model Law and Article 176(3) of the SLPIL give to institutional rules that provide for selection of an arbitral seat by the arbitral institution? Is there any reason that the parties' agreement on institutional rules, providing a mechanism for selecting the arbitral seat, should not be entitled to the same effect as an agreement directly specifying the arbitral seat?

8. *Effect of FAA on selection of arbitral seat by arbitral institution or tribunal*. What effect do §§4, 206 and 303 of the FAA, excerpted at pp. 103-04, 108 & 109 of the Documentary Supplement, give to agreements incorporating institutional rules that provide a mechanism for selecting the arbitral seat? *See infra* pp. 658-69. Consider the result in *Coudert*. Recall that Article 17 of the ICDR Rules provides for the AAA/ICDR to make an initial choice of forum, subject to subsequent confirmation or alteration by the tribunal. What effect does the *Coudert* court give to the parties' agreement to these provisions? How else might *Coudert* have been decided? Could the court have interpreted the parties' agreement to constitute selection of a particular arbitral seat—considering the factors identified in *Dubai Islamic Bank*—rather than leaving this issue to the AAA and arbitral tribunal? What would argue for, and against, such an approach?

Consider §§4 and 206 of the U.S. FAA, excerpted at pp. 103-04 & 108 of the Documentary Supplement. Do §§4 and 206 impose an obligation on U.S. courts to interpret the arbitration agreement as it relates to selection of the arbitral seat, and then to order the parties to arbitrate in that seat? A number of other lower courts have held that §§4 and 206 impose such an obligation. *See, e.g., Euro-Mec Imp., Inc. v. Pantrem & Co., SpA*, 1992 WL 350211, at *5 (E.D. Pa.) ("upon the request of defendant, this Court must refer the parties to arbitration in Geneva"); *Tenn. Imps., Inc. v. Filippi*, 745 F.Supp. 1314, 1320 (M.D. Tenn. 1990) (court "must refer the parties to arbitration"); *PaineWebber Inc. v. Pitchford*, 721 F.Supp. 542, 551 (S.D.N.Y. 1989) (holding that agreement to arbitrate "'before the [AAA] in the City of New York' … specifically states the venue of such arbitration proceedings"). The *Tolaram Fibers* decision, excerpted below, is an example of such a decision. *See supra* pp. 662-63. Is this approach consistent with that in *Coudert*?

9. *Factors relevant to selection of arbitral seat where parties have failed to agree on seat*. If the parties have not agreed on the arbitral seat, what factors should an arbitral institution or tribunal consider in determining the location of the seat? Note the approach of the UNCITRAL Notes on Organizing Arbitral Proceedings, quoted in *ADF*

Group. See supra p. 648. In contrast, consider the approach of the AAA/ICDR, listing factors that determine the choice of an arbitral "locale" in international cases:

> "(1) Location of parties and attorneys. (2) Location of witness and documents. (3) Location of records. (4) Location of the site, place or materials and the possible necessity of an on-site inspection. (5) Consideration of relative difficulty in traveling and cost to the parties. (6) Place of performance of contract. (7) Place of previous court actions. (8) Location of most appropriate panel. (9) Any other reasonable arguments that might affect the locale determination." AAA/ICDR, *Locale Determinations in International Cases*, available at www.adr.org.

Which of these AAA/ICDR and UNCITRAL factors are most important? What other reasonable arguments might affect the selection of a seat? Should the governing law be taken into account? Should a neutral seat for the parties be considered? Why? Should an arbitral institution apply a presumption that the claimant's choice of forum should be rarely disturbed? Do these answers change if one party is a sovereign entity?

10. *Institutional rules specifying presumptive (or definitive) arbitral seat.* Some institutional rules provide that, absent contrary agreement, the arbitral seat shall be in a specified location. Consider Article 16(2) of the LCIA Rules, excerpted at p. 265 of the Documentary Supplement. *See also* 2013 VIAC Rules, Art. 25(1) ("Unless the parties agree or have agreed otherwise (1) the place of arbitration shall be Vienna"). Is that wise or attractive to users? Is it reasonably within their contemplation when choosing an arbitral institution? Does consideration of a long list of factors really produce a better choice of arbitral seat? Consider the *ADF Group* decision.

11. *Drafting agreement specifying arbitral seat.* If the parties are agreed on where they want their arbitration(s) to be seated, the terms of that agreement can (and should) be simple. The model clauses recommended by leading arbitral institutions generally provide: "The place of arbitration shall be [New York, U.S.A.]," or "the seat of the arbitration shall be [Paris, France]." *See, e.g.*, *UNCITRAL Model Arbitration Clause for Contracts*, 2010 UNCITRAL Rules, Annex ("The place of arbitration shall be …[town or country]"); *LCIA Recommended Clauses, Future Disputes*, available at www.lcia.org ("The seat, or legal place, of the arbitration shall be [City and/or Country]").

Consider the following provisions. What is problematic about each of them?

"The arbitration hearings shall be held in New York, U.S.A."

"The venue of the arbitration shall be Singapore."

"The place of the arbitration is Switzerland."

"The seat of the arbitration shall be in the location specified by the Respondent."

Consider the parties' correspondence in *Garuda* for further examples of ambiguities in language addressing the location of the arbitration.

12. *Form requirements for agreement selecting arbitral seat.* Suppose the parties' arbitration agreement does not specify an arbitral seat, but the parties' lawyers agree in a telephone call that the arbitration will be seated in Hong Kong. Suppose alternatively that, in *Garuda*, the parties' lawyers had agreed orally that the arbitral seat would be moved to Singapore. Are either of these agreements valid? Or must an agreement on the seat satisfy the same written form requirements that apply to the arbitration

agreement itself? What arguments are there for applying a form requirement to agreements on the arbitral seat? Against?

13. *Changing the arbitral seat by parties' agreement.* As *Garuda* illustrates, parties sometimes jointly reconsider an earlier selection of the arbitral seat and seek to substitute a new seat by agreement. If no arbitrators have been selected, changing the seat by mutual agreement is usually non-controversial. Do either *Garuda* or *Dubai Islamic Bank* suggest any reason that the parties' agreement, moving the arbitral seat, should not be given effect?

How should the question whether the parties agreed to change the arbitral seat be approached? Should there be a presumption against such changes? Why or why not? Note the emphasis on legal certainty as the principle reason for the concept of an arbitral seat. What does that suggest about changes to the arbitral seat?

Suppose an arbitral tribunal has been selected, on the expectation that the arbitral seat is State A, and the parties then agree to change the seat to State B. Suppose further that State B is inconvenient to one or more arbitrators, or inhospitable (for example, requiring an Indian arbitrator to sit in Pakistan). What if all three arbitrators refuse to accept the parties' new seat? What if only one of the arbitrators refuses?

14. *Defense to arbitration based on claim that arbitral seat is inconvenient.* In some national court litigation (particularly common law systems), the doctrine of *forum non conveniens* permits a party to obtain dismissal of claims in a forum (where it is subject to personal jurisdiction) on the grounds that the forum is grossly inconvenient. *See, e.g.,* G. Born & P. Rutledge, *International Civil Litigation in United States Courts* 365-94 (5th ed. 2011). Similarly, a party may resist enforcement of a forum selection clause on the grounds that it designates an unreasonably inconvenient forum. *Id.* at 499-511. In general, analogous defenses are not available in national courts to the enforcement of international arbitration agreements selecting particular forums.

(a) *National court decisions involving claims that agreed arbitral seat is forum non conveniens.* There is little reported precedent upholding challenges in national courts to contractually-agreed arbitral seats. For one decision refusing to recognize the parties' choice of the arbitral seat, *see M/S V/O Tractoroexport Moscow v. M/S Tarapore & Co.,* [1971] All India Rep. 1 (Indian S.Ct.) (upholding injunction against arbitration in Moscow: "The current restrictions imposed by the Government of India on the availability of foreign exchange ... will make it virtually impossible for the Indian Firm to take its witnesses to Moscow for examination before the Arbitral tribunal and to otherwise properly conduct the proceedings there").

Most decisions reject claims that the parties' choice of the arbitral seat should not be recognized on grounds of convenience. *See, e.g., Bliss Corp. Ltd v. Kobe Steel Ltd,* unreported decision (N.S.W. Sup. Ct. 1987) ("Having regard to the substantial practical considerations in favor of holding the arbitration in Tokyo and the contractual provision that it be held there, I would not ... impose a condition that the whole of the arbitration be held in New South Wales. This would be an unwarranted interference with the discretion of the arbitrators. The conduct of the arbitration is their province."), quoted in Rogers, *Forum Non Conveniens in Arbitration,* 4 Arb. Int'l 240, 252 (1988); *USM Corp. v. GKN Fasteners,* Ltd, 574 F.2d 17, 20 (1st Cir. 1978) ("if every party who signed an arbitration clause could later come into court and attempt to defeat the clause on the basis of its unfairness or unreasonableness, the advantages attendant on arbitration rather than litigation would be largely lost."); *Redshaw Credit Corp. v. Ins. Prof'ls, Inc.*, 709 F.Supp. 1032, 1035 (D. Kan. 1989) (no *forum non conveniens* defense under FAA; arbitration "clause must be enforced even if the result is unreasonable"). *See also supra* pp. 411, 435, discussing inconvenient arbitral seat as grounds for an unconscionability defense.

(b) *Wisdom of no forum non conveniens defense to agreement on arbitral seat.* Is the refusal to permit a *forum non conveniens* defense to agreements selecting the arbitral seat wise? Why should courts lend their assistance to the enforcement of agreements selecting "unreasonable" foreign arbitral seats? Consider: "It is submitted that, strictly confined, as it should be, to instances where proper opportunity for vindicating the rights of the parties demands it, the reserve power of the courts to negate forum selection or transfer the place of hearing should be maintained and exercised." Rogers, *Forum Non Conveniens in Arbitration*, 4 Arb. Int'l 240, 254 (1988). Is that correct? Is there any reason that gross inconvenience and unreasonableness should matter less in the arbitration context than in the forum selection context? Who will decide claims of *forum non conveniens*? If the answer is national courts, isn't expensive, multiplicitous litigation likely to ensue? As a matter of policy, why should different defenses be available for forum selection clauses than for arbitration clauses?

(c) *Forum non conveniens under UNCITRAL Model Law and New York Convention.* Does either the Model Law or the New York Convention permit a *forum non conveniens* defense? Is an agreement selecting a grossly inconvenient or unreasonable arbitral seat "null and void"? Or "revocable"? If not, do Article 8 of the Model Law and Article II of the Convention foreclose any *forum non conveniens* defense?

(d) *Consequences of concluding that arbitral seat is grossly inconvenient.* Assume both that a *forum non conveniens* defense is recognized and that the parties' selection of a particular arbitral seat is so grossly inconvenient as to be invalid. What is the appropriate remedy? Should arbitration be ordered elsewhere (and if so, where)? Or, should the entire arbitration agreement be invalidated? Note that a tribunal would ordinarily have the power to order hearings at places other than the seat. *See supra* p. 624. Is this an appropriate (or the appropriate) remedy for an inconvenient arbitral seat?

15. *Changed circumstances in arbitral seat.* Suppose a previously-designated arbitral seat becomes extremely onerous because of political developments (as in *Gatoil, NIOC* and *Partial Decision of 2 April 1992*). Would a different seat be justified or merely a change in the place of the hearings? Under what circumstances? Recall the discussion above regarding frustration and impossibility affecting the agreement to arbitrate. *See supra* p. 435.

16. *Selection of arbitral seat in investment and inter-state arbitration.* Consider the decision in *ADF Group*. Why is it that NAFTA does not specify the arbitral seat for all NAFTA proceedings? The United States, Canada and Mexico could, for example, have agreed that all NAFTA arbitrations will be seated in the territory of the respondent state. Why isn't that done?

Consider the Abyei Arbitration Agreement between the Government of Sudan and the SPLM/A, excerpted at pp. 79-84 of the Documentary Supplement. What does it provide with regard to the arbitral seat? Why were Sudan and the SPLM/A able to agree upon the arbitral seat and the United States, Canada and Mexico unable to do so in NAFTA?

D. SELECTION OF ARBITRAL SEAT BY NATIONAL COURTS IN INTERNATIONAL ARBITRATION

Despite the wisdom of selecting an arbitral seat, parties not infrequently fail to designate either the arbitral seat or a means of selecting a seat in their arbitration agreement. Worse, they may enter into agreements that are ambiguous or internally contradictory as to the seat of the arbitration. In some such cases, parties may be able to agree upon an arbitral seat after a dispute arises.

Nonetheless, if the parties are unable to agree upon the location of the arbitral seat, or a means of selecting one, then national law and national courts may play a role in selection of the arbitral seat.[21] As the materials excerpted below illustrate, most developed national arbitration regimes, including the UNCITRAL Model Law, allow national courts only a very limited role in selecting the arbitral seat. The principal exception to this approach is the United States, where the FAA grants U.S. courts a broad, if unsettled, authority to select the arbitral seat.

SWEDISH ARBITRATION ACT
§47

Arbitral proceedings in accordance with this Act may be commenced in Sweden, where the arbitration agreement provides that the proceedings shall take place in Sweden, or where the arbitrators or an arbitration institution pursuant to the agreement have determined that the proceedings shall take place in Sweden, or the opposing party otherwise consents thereto. Arbitral proceedings in accordance with this Act may also be commenced in Sweden against a party which is domiciled in Sweden or is otherwise subject to jurisdiction of the Swedish courts with regard to the matter in dispute, unless the arbitration agreement provides that the proceedings shall take place abroad. In other cases, arbitral proceedings in accordance with this Act may not take place in Sweden.

JAPANESE ARBITRATION LAW
Article 8(1)

Even if the place of arbitration has not been designated, [applications for specified judicial assistance] may be made when there is a possibility that the place of arbitration will be in the territory of Japan and the applicant or counterparty's general forum … is in the territory of Japan.

---

21. *See* G. Born, *International Commercial Arbitration* 2094-119 (2d ed. 2014).

ECONO-CAR INTERNATIONAL, INC. v. ANTILLES CAR RENTALS, INC.
499 F.2d 1391 (3d Cir. 1974)

ADAMS, Circuit Judge.... The controversy prompting this appeal centers upon a franchise agreement between Econo-Car International, Inc., the franchisor, and Antilles Car Rentals, Inc., the franchisee.... [Disputes arose under the agreement.] Econo-Car advised Antilles that it desired to submit the [parties'] various disagreements to the process of arbitral resolution pursuant to paragraph 15 of the franchise agreement.[22] Antilles refused to submit the disputes to arbitration, and Econo-Car thereupon filed petition in the district court for the Virgin Islands to compel arbitration.... [The] court ordered Antilles to "enter into arbitration proceedings in the City of New York in accordance with the terms of the [franchise] agreement." ...

On this appeal, Antilles challenges the district court's order on several grounds.... Under the order's terms the contemplated arbitration is to take place in New York City, as specifically provided in the agreement between the parties. Section 4 of the [FAA] permits a party to request an order requiring arbitration "in the manner provided for in such agreement." But §4 also provides that the arbitration "shall be within the district in which the petition for an order directing such arbitration is filed." In a case like the present, where the agreement provides for arbitration outside the district in which the petition is filed, §4 can create a perplexing dilemma: a district court might not be able to order arbitration strictly in accordance with the terms of the agreement, as one portion of §4 seems to require, without contravening a second portion of §4.

While any directive in §4 that arbitration be conducted according to the terms of the agreement is implicit at best, the requirement that arbitration take place in the district court where the petition is filed is clear and unequivocal. Certainly the saving of resources occasioned by the geographic concentration of all proceedings provides an appropriate legislative basis for this limitation on the district court's power. We recognize that if the statutory language referring to the terms of the arbitration agreement is also given a restrictive reading, a party who seeks arbitration in a district court properly having venue may well be unable to secure an arbitration order in such district court in circumstances like those presented by this case. Despite the somewhat paradoxical situation thus possibly created, we are inclined to heed the unambiguous statutory language limiting the district court's power to order arbitration outside of the district. We hold, therefore, that the district court erred in ordering arbitration to take place in New York City.[23] ...

---

22. Paragraph 15 of the contract provides as follows: "It is mutually agreed that the parties hereto will submit any controversy or claim arising out of or relating to this agreement, or the breach thereof, to arbitration in the City of New York and shall abide by the provisions and rules of the 'Rules of American Arbitration Association' and that any judgment upon any award rendered by the arbitrator may be entered in any court having jurisdiction thereof and all cost and expenses will be paid by the parties hereto according to said rules."

23. We note that had Econo-Car brought this suit initially in a district court in New York, such court, it appears, would view the agreement to arbitrate in New York as a waiver of any possible objections Antilles might make to the court's venue. See *Joseph Muller Corp. Zurich v. Commonwealth Petrochemicals, Inc.*, 334 F.Supp. 1013, 1021 (S.D.N.Y. 1971); *Lawn v. Franklin*, 328 F.Supp. 791, 793-94 (S.D.N.Y. 1971).

LEA TAI TEXTILE CO. v. MANNING FABRICS, INC.
411 F.Supp. 1404 (S.D.N.Y. 1975)

[excerpted above at pp. 341-42]

BAUHINIA CORP. v. CHINA NATIONAL MACHINERY & EQUIPMENT IMPORT & EXPORT CORP.
819 F.2d 247 (9th Cir. 1987)

TANG, Circuit Judge. China National Machinery & Equipment Import and Export Corporation ("CMEC") appeals an order of the district court compelling arbitration of a contract dispute between CMEC and Bauhinia Corp. Bauhinia sued CMEC for breach of contract and CMEC moved to compel arbitration before the China Council for the Promotion of International Trade ("CCPIT") in Peking. The district court granted the motion to compel arbitration, but ordered arbitration before the [AAA].

Bauhinia is a California corporation founded by Mr. Abbies Tsang who fled the People's Republic of China in 1974. CMEC is a Chinese state trading organization. In 1981 and 1982 Bauhinia contracted to purchase nails from CMEC. The parties executed the contracts in California for delivery to [the United States.] CMEC failed to deliver the nails claiming that an edict from the People's Republic of China prevented performance. After Bauhinia filed suit in district court, CMEC moved to compel arbitration invoking arbitration clauses in the contracts. The first contract, written in Chinese, provides "[i]n case quality problems occurs, the both sides shall have consultation as soon as possible to resolve it." The other two contracts, written in English, contain the following clause:

> "All disputes in connection with the execution of this Contract shall be settled through friendly negotiations. In case an arbitration is necessary and is to be held in Peking, the case in dispute shall then be submitted for arbitration to the Foreign Trade Arbitration Commission of the China Council for the Promotion of International Trade, Peking, in accordance with the 'Provisional Rules of Procedure of the Foreign Trade Arbitration Commission of the China Council for the Promotion of International Trade.' ...
>
> In case the Arbitration is to take place at [BLANK] either party shall appoint one arbitrator, and the arbitrators thus appointed shall nominate a third person as umpire, to form an arbitration committee. The award of the Arbitration Committee shall be accepted as final by both Parties. The Arbitrators and the umpire shall be confined to persons of Chinese or [BLANK] Nationality."

On November 18, 1985, the district court granted CMEC's motion to compel arbitration and further ordered the parties to submit the matter to the [AAA] pursuant to the [AAA]'s rules and regulations.... The order does not state the court's reason for designating the AAA instead of CCPIT. At the hearing the judge indicated that the contract clearly called for arbitration but was ambiguous as to whether arbitration was mandated in Peking or some other location. He expressed concerns that Mr. Tsang might be subjected to personal danger if forced to return to China and that the CCPIT would not provide a "speedy, thorough, informal, neutral decision making process," consistent with the parties' intent in seeking arbitration. CMEC appeals that part of the order designating AAA instead of CCPIT as the arbitration agency. It argues that the district court erred in overriding the parties' choice of arbitrator, CCPIT....

Federal law governs arbitration issues in agreements affecting interstate and foreign commerce.... The contract here expressly calls for arbitration. In light of the strong federal policy favoring arbitration, we conclude that the trial judge did not err in ordering the parties to submit the matter to arbitration. The more difficult question, however, is whether the court properly ordered arbitration before the AAA. The clauses do not expressly choose a forum. The clauses consist of two paragraphs. The first paragraph reads *"in case* arbitration is necessary and is to be held in Peking...."* (Emphasis added.) Likewise, the second paragraph begins: *"In case* arbitration is to take place at [BLANK]...."* (Emphasis added.) CMEC argues that by failing to complete the blanks in the second paragraph, the parties implicitly chose the Peking forum.... Furthermore, argues CMEC, most of the witnesses, evidence and law are in the People's Republic of China; Mr. Tsang negotiated the contracts in the People's Republic of China; and the CCPIT is an impartial agency....

In construing arbitration clauses, standard contract principles apply.... We agree with the district court that this contract is ambiguous. The two paragraphs are mutually exclusive. The document lacks any indication what forum the parties intended to select. Furthermore, the record offers no evidence of an implied agreement to select a particular forum. The record permits only one conclusion, that the parties intended to leave the issue open.

At the hearing, the judge indicated that he found the contract ambiguous on the forum issue. He then asked the parties to "resolve the problem of when, where and how without court intervention.... If you don't think you can do so, tell me and I'll issue an order that orders arbitration be taken at the forum and under the requirements set forth by the Court." The parties failed to resolve the issue so the court ordered arbitration before the AAA.

In the absence of a term specifying location, a district court can only order arbitration within its district. Chapter 2 of Title 9 codifies the [New York] Convention.... §206 empowers a district court to "direct that arbitration be held in accordance with the agreement at any place therein provided for, whether that place is within or without the United States." However, by its terms, §206 does not permit a court to designate a foreign forum when the agreement fails to designate a place. Chapter 1 of the [FAA] applies to international agreements to the extent that Chapter 1 does not conflict with Chapter 2. 9 U.S.C. §208. Under Chapter 1, the arbitration proceedings "shall be within the district in which the petition for an order directing such arbitration is filed."[24] Therefore, under the statutory regime, the only place that the district court could order arbitration is the Eastern District of California. We conclude that the court acted reasonably. The contracts left the location open. The judge gave the parties an opportunity to resolve the matter themselves. When they failed to do so, he took the only action within his power....

NATIONAL IRANIAN OIL CO. v. ASHLAND OIL, INC.
817 F.2d 326 (5th Cir. 1987)

[excerpted above at pp. 170-71 & 427-29]

---

24. 9 U.S.C. §4. Section 206 only applies to international agreements. We express no opinion on whether a district court may order arbitration outside the district in cases of interstate agreements that expressly specify location. *See Snyder v. Smith*, 736 F.2d 409, 420 (7th Cir. 1984); *Mgt Recruiters of Albany, Inc. v. Mgt Recruiters. Int'l, Inc.*, 643 F.Supp. 750, 753 (N.D.N.Y. 1986).

TOLARAM FIBERS, INC. v. DEUTSCHE ENGINEERING DER VOEST-ALPINE INDUSTRIEANLAGENBAU GMBH
1991 U.S. Dist. LEXIS 3565 (M.D.N.C.)

ELIASON, U.S. Magistrate. Defendant Barmag AG ("Barmag") moves, pursuant to the [FAA,] to compel arbitration and to stay this action pending the completion of arbitration. Plaintiff filed this action in state court and it was removed to this Court by defendant Deutsche Engineering der Voest-Alpine Industrieanlagenbau GmbH ("Deutsche Engineering") ...

Defendant Barmag shows through an affidavit that the parties entered into a contract which provided in paragraph 12 that any contract disputes were to be decided in accordance with the [ICC] Rules.... Consequently, ... Barmag argues the Court should grant the motion to compel arbitration and stay proceedings. Plaintiff does not dispute defendant Barmag's claim that this action is subject to the parties' arbitration clause and that defendant's motion to compel arbitration and to stay the proceedings in this Court should be granted. Rather, plaintiff states that the claims against Barmag are based upon allegations made by defendant Deutsche Engineering. Therefore, it adds that judicial economy will only be served if Deutsche Engineering also requests that the proceedings be referred to arbitration and that the proceedings against both Deutsche Engineering and Barmag be coordinated. Finally, because the equipment is located in Ashboro, North Carolina, plaintiff requests that the arbitration forum be set for Randolph County, North Carolina.

Defendant Barmag opposes any such limitation on the arbitration forum. It claims that to require arbitration to be held in Randolph County, North Carolina, would be tantamount to rewriting the arbitration clause which is forbidden. It argues that plaintiff must direct its request to the ICC because Article 12 of the ICC Rules grants the arbitral court, absent agreement by the parties, the power to fix the place of arbitration. Defendant Barmag further points out that the ICC Rules do not present any obstacle to coordinated proceedings....

Upon motion of a party, §3 of the Act permits a court to stay court proceedings pending arbitration should it find an issue referable to arbitration under the parties' contract. A §3 order does not concern itself with the place of arbitration. Rather, the court merely enters an order staying proceedings until such arbitration proceedings are completed. Section 4 grants the Court the power to compel arbitration. However, it requires that the arbitration be held in the district issuing the order. *Econo-Car Int'l, Inc. v. Antilles Car Rentals, Inc.*, 499 F.2d 1391 (3d Cir. 1974); *Continental Grain Co. v. Dant & Russell, Inc.*, 118 F.2d 967 (9th Cir. 1941). A party may not misuse §4 by filing a lawsuit in a district and then seek to compel arbitration in that district in contravention to a forum selection clause in the arbitration agreement which directs arbitration to be conducted elsewhere. *Snyder v. Smith*, 736 F.2d 409, 419-20 (7th Cir. 1984). In such an instance, the Court may dismiss the petition, or upon a motion under §3, stay the proceedings pending completion of the arbitration elsewhere....

[T]he Fifth Circuit, in a series of cases, has concluded that when the party seeking to enforce arbitration did not initiate the action, a district court has authority under §4 to compel arbitration outside of the district in accordance with a specific arbitration forum selection clause. Therefore, the Court may perhaps still entertain defendant Barmag's motion to compel arbitration in the place listed in the forum selection clause of the arbitration agreement and, if necessary, compel arbitration in another judicial district....

The Fifth Circuit cases involve interstate agreements for arbitration at specific places in the United States as opposed to an international agreement not setting out a specific place, as in the present case. The forum selection clause of the instant contract does not identify a specific place for the arbitration. In fact, the contract does not even contain a forum selection clause. It merely says arbitration will be conducted pursuant to ICC Rules. And, Article 12 of the ICC Rules merely states that: "The place of arbitration shall be fixed by the [arbitration?] Court, unless agreed upon by the parties." Furthermore, the contract is an international one, involving foreign parties. The defendants are German corporations and plaintiff is a North Carolina corporation. Thus, it is possible that the arbitration could be directed to take place not just outside of this judicial district but outside of the country. The Ninth Circuit confronted such a scenario in *Bauhinia Corp.*, [*supra* pp. 660-61]....

Having found the forum selection clause of the arbitration agreement to be ambiguous, the *Bauhinia Corp.* court noted that pursuant to §4 of the Act, a district court can only order arbitration within its district. However, since the case involved a possible foreign arbitration, it also looked to the provisions of the [New York] Convention. It noted that §206 of that Convention empowers a district court to order arbitration in accordance with the agreement whether that place be within or without the United States. However, that section does not permit the court to designate a forum if the agreement fails to do so. The court then reasoned that Chapter 1 of the [FAA] applies to international agreements to the extent that it does not conflict with Chapter 2.... Under Chapter 1, when a court enters an order compelling arbitration, the proceedings must be conducted within the district in which the petition to enforce it is filed. 9 U.S.C. §4. The court, therefore, concluded that when an international contract left the location of the arbitration forum open, and a petition is brought to enforce an arbitration contract, the district court must resort to Chapter 1 and order arbitration within its own district.

The *Bauhinia Corp.* reasoning applies to the international contract before this Court. Here, defendant Barmag fails to show that the place of arbitration has been fixed. It never identifies a specific place. It merely points to a forum selection clause of the ICC Rules which are mentioned in paragraph 12 of the contract. The ICC Rules merely say that the [ICC] court will fix the place of arbitration unless agreed to by the parties. This clause does not select a definite forum. The Court finds that this forum selection clause is not sufficiently specific so as to come with §206 of the Act. The provisions of Chapters 1 and 2 of the [FAA] require the Court to compel arbitration to be held in this district unless there is a specific place designated in the forum selection clause of the arbitration contract.

Defendant Barmag has not shown that the contract specifies a specific place. At most, it demonstrates that there is a specific method for forum selection under ICC Rules. That is not sufficient. Arbitration will be compelled, but in this district....

NOTES

1. *No general authority under most arbitration statutes for national court to select arbitral seat in absence of agreement by parties.* Few national arbitration statutes grant local courts the power to select an arbitral seat. Consider Article 20 of the UNCITRAL Model Law, excerpted at p. 91 of the Documentary Supplement. What power does it grant local courts to select an arbitral seat? Compare Article 176 of the SLPIL, excerpted at p. 157 of the Documentary Supplement. Do Swiss courts play any role in

selecting the arbitral seat when the parties have not agreed upon the location of the seat?

How does the Model Law deal with the choice of the arbitral seat if the parties have not agreed upon either the location of the seat or a means of selecting it? Recall that, where the parties have not otherwise agreed, Article 20(1) provides for the arbitral tribunal to select the arbitral seat; Article 176(3) of the SLPIL is to the same effect.

2. *Potential circularity of national arbitration statutes.* Suppose the parties have agreed to arbitrate, but have not (a) agreed to incorporate a set of institutional rules, or (b) agreed upon an arbitral seat, or (c) agreed upon the identities or a means of selecting the arbitrators. In this circumstance, how do Article 20(1) of the Model Law and Article 176(3) of the SLPIL function?

    If the parties have not agreed upon a means to select the arbitrators, then who will appoint the arbitrators? Note that, under both the Model Law and the SLPIL, local courts can only appoint an arbitrator if the arbitral seat is within national territory. *See infra* pp. 708-09. If there is no arbitral tribunal, then who, under provisions such as Article 20(1) of the Model Law and Article 176(3) of the SLPIL, will select the arbitral seat? Are the parties not stuck in a Catch-22 situation—without an arbitral tribunal, there can be no selection of the arbitral seat, and without an arbitral seat, there is no means of selecting the arbitral tribunal. In part, as a consequence, some national arbitration regimes hold that "blank" arbitration clauses, which do not specify an arbitral seat or a means of selecting the arbitral seat, are invalid. *See supra* pp. 337-38, 349; E. Gaillard & J. Savage (eds.), *Fouchard Gaillard Goldman on International Commercial Arbitration* ¶486 (1999).

3. *National arbitration legislation addressing problem of arbitration agreements that do not specify arbitral seat or means of selecting arbitrators.* In a few states, arbitration legislation provides for local courts to select the arbitral seat if the parties have not agreed upon either a seat or a means for selecting a seat. Consider the Swedish and Japanese arbitration legislation, excerpted above. What do these statutes provide? How do they differ? Is either one of these statutes sensible from a policy perspective?

4. *Role of U.S. courts in selecting arbitral seat under FAA.* In contrast to most jurisdictions, U.S. courts can play a significant role in selection of the arbitral seat in international arbitrations. Litigation in U.S. courts over the location of the arbitral seat typically arises in actions to compel arbitration under §4, §206, or §303 of the FAA. These sections provide U.S. courts the authority to compel arbitration, by affirmatively ordering a recalcitrant party to arbitrate. As discussed above, these provisions of the FAA are unusual; most jurisdictions do not enforce arbitration agreements by affirmatively ordering that the parties arbitrate. *See supra* pp. 319-20.

    Is it sensible, as a matter of policy, for U.S. courts to compel arbitration in a particular seat? Contrast this approach to that under the Model Law, where national courts instead stay litigation, allowing the arbitral process to proceed, with the arbitrators or arbitral institution selecting the arbitral seat. Which approach is preferable?

5. *U.S. district court's power under §4 to order arbitration outside its district.* U.S. judicial authority interpreting §4 of the FAA is divided, with different courts reaching significantly different conclusions. How did the court in *Econo-Car* interpret §4? Did the court conclude that a district court had the power under §4 of the FAA to order arbitration outside of its own judicial district?

Like *Econo-Car*, a number of other U.S. courts have concluded that §4 does not permit a U.S. district court to compel parties to arbitrate outside the judicial district where the court is located—even when that is what the parties' arbitration agreement unambiguously provides. *See, e.g., Mgt Recruiters Int'l, Inc. v. Bloor*, 129 F.3d 851, 854 (6th Cir. 1997) ("We agree with the majority of courts that have recognized that, where the parties have agreed to arbitrate in a particular forum, only a district court in that forum has jurisdiction to compel arbitration pursuant to §4."); *Merrill Lynch, Pierce Fenner & Smith, Inc. v. Lauer*, 49 F.3d 323, 327 (7th Cir. 1995)("Section 4 clearly requires a geographic link between the site of the arbitration and the district which, by compelling arbitration or directing its scope, exercises preliminary control …"). In contrast to *Econo-Car*, some lower U.S. courts have concluded that §4 does permit an order compelling arbitration in another U.S. judicial district (or abroad)—but only if the parties' arbitration agreement specifically provides for arbitration there. *See, e.g., Jones v. Sea Tow Servs. Freeport N.Y., Inc.*, 828 F.Supp. 1002 (E.D.N.Y. 1993), *rev'd on other grounds*, 30 F.3d 360 (2d Cir. 1994); *G.B. Michael v. SS Thanasis*, 311 F.Supp. 170 (N.D. Cal. 1970).

Other lower U.S. courts have concluded that arbitration can be ordered in another judicial district—but only if the party seeking the §4 order did not commence the litigation in which the extraterritorial order is sought, and instead is defending against a suit brought against it in federal court on the merits by invoking the arbitration agreement. *See, e.g., Nat'l Iranian Oil Co. v. Ashland Oil, Inc.*, 817 F.2d 326, 330-32 (5th Cir. 1987); *M & I Elec. Indus. Inc. v. Rapistem Demag Corp.*, 814 F.Supp. 545 (E.D. Tex. 1993) (party cannot resist arbitration in order to provoke §4 motion to compel in a judicial district other than the arbitral seat).

6. *Rationale for territorial limits on §4 power to order arbitration.* Why did *Econo-Car* hold that a district court could only order arbitration within the district where it is located? According to *Econo-Car*, §4 is internally inconsistent. The section's literal terms "can create a perplexing dilemma: a district court might not be able to order arbitration strictly in accordance with the terms of the agreement, as one portion of §4 seems to require, without contravening a second portion of §4."Is §4 actually so confused? Consider the court's explanation in *Jones*, 828 F.Supp. at 1013: "The two clauses of §4 are easily reconciled by a close reading of the statutory language: the court in the district in which the petition was filed must 'hear' the parties concerning whether the 'making of the agreement for arbitration' is at issue; once that 'hearing' or 'proceeding' takes place, the court must order arbitration in accordance with the agreement." Is that persuasive?

Is the conclusion in *Econo-Car*, that §4 only permits a court to compel arbitration in its own district, compelled by the language of §4? Is it desirable? Consider the following excerpt from *Econo-Car*:

> "While any directive in [§]4 that arbitration be conducted according to the terms of the agreement is implicit at best, the requirement that arbitration take place in the district court where the petition is filed is clear and unequivocal. Certainly the saving of resources occasioned by the geographic concentration of all proceedings provides an appropriate legislative basis for this limitation on the district court's power."

If the parties have designated an arbitral seat that is *within the United States*, is there any real difficulty with the position taken in the foregoing excerpt? What can a party that wants to compel arbitration do? It can file suit in the judicial district where the arbitral seat is located, right? Suppose, however, the arbitral seat is *outside the United States*?

7. *U.S. district court's power under §206 to order arbitration outside its district.* Consistent with the plain language of §206, *Tolaram* and other lower courts have held that they have the power under §206, at least in some circumstances (discussed below), to order arbitration outside their judicial districts. Indeed, the legislative history of §206 makes it clear that the provision was intended specifically to correct §4's territorial limitation. *Foreign Arbitral Awards*, S. Rep. No. 91-702, 91st Cong., 2d Sess. 7 (1970) (Statement of Richard D. Kearney).

(a) *Power of U.S. district court under §206 to order arbitration abroad in accordance with parties' arbitration agreement.* As *Tolaram* suggests, lower courts have unanimously concluded that §206 authorizes U.S. district courts to compel arbitration outside both their district and the United States, provided that the parties' agreement designates a foreign arbitral forum. *See, e.g., Jain v. de Mere,* 51 F.3d 686 (7th Cir. 1995) ("If the [international arbitration] agreement calls for arbitration outside of the district in which the action is brought, the limits of §4 directly conflict with the district court's powers under §206, and §208 would render §4 inapplicable"). As discussed in the following Notes, however, determining whether the parties have provided for a foreign arbitral seat, within the meaning of §206, has proven difficult.

(b) *No power of U.S. district court under §206 to order arbitration abroad if parties have not agreed on foreign arbitral seat. Tolaram* also holds that, if the parties have not agreed upon a foreign arbitral seat, then §206 does not grant a district court power to compel arbitration abroad. Other courts have also held that §206 grants no authority to order arbitration abroad if the parties have not agreed upon—"provided for," in §206's phrase—the arbitral seat. *See, e.g., Jain v. de Mere,* 51 F.3d 686 (7th Cir. 1995); *Bauhinia Corp. v. China Nat'l Mach. & Equip. Imp. & Exp. Corp.,* 819 F.2d 247 (9th Cir. 1987); *Prograph Int'l Inc. v. Barhydt,* 928 F.Supp. 983 (N.D. Cal. 1996) (where arbitration agreement subject to Convention does not specify arbitral seat, U.S. court may compel arbitration in United States).

(c) *Incorporation of §4 in actions under Chapter 2 of FAA when §206 is not applicable.* As we have seen, cases arise when §206 is not applicable to enforce an arbitration agreement that is subject to the New York Convention—typically, because the parties have not agreed upon an arbitral seat. *See supra* pp. 664-66. When this occurs, §208 provides for the residual applicability of §4 "to the extent that [it] is not in conflict with this chapter [2 of the FAA] or the Convention as ratified by the United States." U.S. FAA, 9 U.S.C. §208. *See, e.g., Jain v. de Mere,* 51 F.3d 686 (7th Cir. 1995); *Bauhinia Corp. v. China Nat'l Mach. & Equip. Imp. & Exp. Corp.,* 819 F.2d 247 (9th Cir. 1987), excerpted above at pp. 660-61. One court explained the application of §4 to an international arbitration agreement, which does not specify the arbitral seat, as follows:

> "Section 4 … , which requires that the court direct that arbitration take place in its district, conflicts with §206 … , which requires the court to direct that arbitration be held in accordance with the agreement of the parties whenever the parties to an international agreement have chosen a location for arbitration. However, …

[where] the parties have failed to choose a place for arbitration, §4 … does not conflict with [§206], and accordingly has been applied." *Capitol Converting Co. v. Curioni*, 1989 WL 152832, at *1 (N.D. Ill.).

When §4 is incorporated into chapter 2, is it appropriate to incorporate it wholesale? In particular, is there not a reasonable argument that §4's purported prohibition against orders compelling arbitration outside the judicial district is inconsistent with the purposes of the New York Convention? What about the limits in §206?

8. *Lower U.S. court decisions refusing to order arbitration abroad under §206 pursuant to parties' agreement to institutional rules providing for selection of arbitral seat by appointing authority.* As *Tolaram* illustrates, some U.S. courts have held that an agreement to arbitrate pursuant to institutional rules which grant the arbitral institution (or arbitrator) authority to select an arbitral seat does not provide a basis for a §206 order compelling arbitration in a foreign seat chosen by the institution or the arbitrator(s). Wasn't *Tolaram* plainly wrong in holding that the parties' agreement to the ICC Rules "is not sufficiently specific so as to come within §206"?

The *Tolaram* court also refused to compel arbitration in the seat selected by the ICC because it could not be certain that the seat would be a signatory to the New York Convention. Does the *Tolaram* conclusion follow from that premise? Can't the ICC seat-selection process go forward, and if the ICC selects a forum to which §206 does not permit an order compelling arbitration, then no such order will issue; if the ICC picks a forum within §206's ambit, an order may issue. Could the *Tolaram* court have waited until the ICC had selected a specific arbitral seat and then ordered arbitration in that place?

9. *Lower U.S. court decisions ordering arbitration in U.S. judicial district notwithstanding parties' agreement to institutional rules providing for selection of arbitral seat by appointing authority.* In addition to refusing to compel arbitration in a seat selected by the ICC, the *Tolaram* court also compelled arbitration in its own judicial district. If a company agrees to ICC arbitration, without agreeing on an arbitral seat, and wishes for the arbitration to take place in the United States, what might it do after *Tolaram*?

Compare the approach in *Tolaram* with that under Article 20(1) of the UNCITRAL Model Law and Article 176(3) of the SLPIL. Which legislative approach is wiser?

Is *Tolaram* consistent with U.S. obligations under Article II(1) of the New York Convention, requiring that courts in Contracting States recognize agreements to arbitrate? Is not the agreement to arbitrate in accordance with the ICC or AAA Rules, including rules for the selection of the arbitral seat, entitled to recognition under Article II(1)? By ordering arbitration in the United States rather than in the place selected by the ICC, doesn't *Tolaram* violate both the parties' agreement to arbitrate and Article II(1) and II(3) of the Convention? In *Tolaram*, will an award made in North Carolina against the German company likely be enforceable in Germany? Should it be? Consider Article V(1)(d) of the Convention.

Note that there were alternatives to the course taken by the *Tolaram* court—even if one accepted the view that §206 would not permit an order compelling arbitration abroad. An alternative course would have been merely to grant a §3 stay and leave the ICC proceedings free to go forward. If one party declined to participate in arbitral proceedings in the forum selected by the ICC, it would face a potential default award. This is effectively the course taken by Article 20(1) of the Model Law and Article 176(3) of the SLPIL. This was also essentially the course adopted by the court in *Coudert, supra* pp. 646-47. Is it preferable to the course taken in *Tolaram*?

10. *U.S. lower court decisions abstaining from selecting arbitral seat where parties' agreement incorporates institutional rules providing for selection of arbitral seat by appointing authority.* In contrast to *Tolaram*, some lower U.S. courts have refused to select an arbitral seat and order arbitration there if the parties' arbitration agreement incorporates institutional rules permitting the arbitration institution to designate the seat. In *Shearson Lehman Bros., Inc. v. Brady*, 783 F.Supp. 1490 (D. Mass. 1991), for example, the court considered whether to select an arbitral seat, and compel arbitration there, when the parties had agreed to AAA Rules without specifying an arbitral seat. The court refused to do so, holding that "abstention" in deference to the AAA was appropriate:

> "The inherent risks of cost and delay before arbitration could commence, should a trial court undertake to decide, subject to appeal to higher courts, disputes concerning where an application must be filed and where the arbitration must be held, are fundamentally inconsistent with the parties' agreement to resolve their disputes by arbitration…. [The] AAA is prepared to decide the appropriate situs of the arbitration pursuant to a number of neutral, commonsense factors, including the location of the parties, the location of the witnesses and documents, a consideration of the relative cost to the parties, the place of performance of the contract, and the laws applicable to the parties. This process seems likely to be fair and far less expensive than threshold determination of the issue of situs in courts."

Isn't that exactly right? For similar conclusions, *see, e.g., UBS Fin. Servs. Inc., v. W. Va. Univ. Hosps., Inc.*, 660 F.3d 643, 654 (2d Cir. 2011) ("venue is a procedural issue arbitrators should address"); *Imaging Tech. Solutions, LLC v. Tech Data Corp.*, 1999 WL 493075, at *1 (E.D. La.) (compelling arbitration but refusing to fix arbitral seat, instead holding that seat would be determined by the AAA, which had the power under its rules to do so); *Modern Drop Forge Co. v. Eumuco Hasenclever GmbH*, 1997 WL 323660 (N.D. Ill.) (refusing to fix seat of arbitration within or without judicial district under §4 of the FAA and holding that the determination of seat would be left to the ICC); *Prudential Sec. Inc. v. Thomas*, 793 F.Supp. 764, 767-68 (W.D. Tenn. 1992) ("the agreement of the parties provides that the [AAA] is the proper entity to determine whether the parties have agreed on a location for the arbitration proceedings, and, if not, to determine that location under its Rule 11 [providing that arbitral tribunal will fix locale in absence of agreement by parties].").

Recall also the reasoning in *Coudert, supra* pp. 646-47.

11. *Lower U.S. court decisions ordering arbitration under §§4 and 206 in local judicial district where parties have not agreed on a foreign arbitral seat.* Some U.S. lower courts have ordered arbitration in the local judicial district in cases where the parties have agreed to arbitrate, but have not clearly or validly agreed to an arbitral seat. For example, *Bauhinia* holds that a district court lacks power under §206 to compel arbitration outside its judicial district if the parties have not agreed upon an arbitral seat. *Bauhinia* also held that the district judge had power—without any such agreement on the arbitral seat between the parties—to compel arbitration in its own judicial district.

"In the absence of a term specifying location, a district court can only order arbitration *within its district*." 819 F.2d at 250 (emphasis added).

Other courts have done the same. *See, e.g., Jain v. de Mere*, 51 F.3d 686 (7th Cir. 1995) (§206 does not apply where arbitration agreement designates no arbitral seat, and §4 "not only permits but requires a court to compel arbitration in its own district when no other forum is specified"); *Schulze & Burch Biscuit Co. v. Tree Top, Inc.*, 831 F.2d 709, 716 (7th Cir. 1987) (where parties agreed only that "All disputes under this transaction shall be arbitrated in the usual manner," arbitration would be compelled in district where §4 motion was filed); *Beauperthuy v. 24 Hour Fitness USA, Inc.*, 2011 WL 6014438 (N.D. Cal.) (court can compel arbitration in own district where arbitration clause provides for no arbitral seat); *Prograph Int'l Inc. v. Barhydt*, 928 F.Supp. 983 (N.D. Cal. 1996) (where arbitration agreement subject to Convention does not specify arbitral seat, U.S. court may compel arbitration in United States); *Rosgoscirc v. Circus Show Corp.*, 1993 U.S. Dist. LEXIS 9797 (S.D.N.Y.) (ordering arbitration under §206 and §4 in district court's district, where parties had agreed to arbitrate before nonexistent institution in Netherlands); *Oil Basins Ltd v. Broken Hill Proprietary Co.*, 613 F.Supp. 483 (S.D.N.Y. 1985) ("the place of arbitration is not designated in the contract and it is readily apparent that the parties are not in agreement as to the place to proceed.... Accordingly, the Court grants plaintiff's motion to compel arbitration in New York").

Assuming that the parties have in fact not selected an arbitral seat, or a means of choosing such a seat (by either an arbitral institution or the arbitrators), is there anything wrong with the approach in *Bauhinia*? Compare the approaches in the Japanese and Swedish legislation excerpted above. Which is preferable?

Was the court in *Bauhinia* correct when it concluded that the parties had not agreed upon a foreign arbitral seat? Was there another interpretation of the parties' agreement? To what extent should a court attempt to interpret the parties' arbitration agreement to identify an implied choice of arbitral seat? Recall the analyses in *Garuda* and *Dubai Islamic Bank*.

12. *Wisdom of national court compelling arbitration in specified place when parties have not agreed on arbitral seat*. If the parties have not agreed—either expressly or impliedly—upon an arbitral seat, *should* a national court pick the seat for them? In the international context, is it appropriate for a court in one country to designate the place where the parties will arbitrate if they have not agreed upon an arbitral seat? Recall how the UNCITRAL Model Law and the SLPIL approach this question. *See supra* pp. 663-64. What are the costs and risks of national courts selecting the arbitral seat in international arbitrations?

What is the consequence if national courts do *not* designate the arbitral seat? If the consequence is no arbitration, should national courts not seek to effectuate the parties' basic agreement to arbitrate rather than to litigate? Recall the Swedish and Japanese legislation excerpted above. How do these legislative provisions differ from the approach of U.S. courts? Note that, absent agreement on an arbitral seat, the Swedish legislation permits arbitration in Sweden where the respondent is Swedish, while the Japanese legislation permits arbitration in Japan where either the claimant or the respondent is Japanese. How do these provisions compare to the U.S. approach?

CHAPTER 8
SELECTION, CHALLENGE AND REPLACEMENT OF ARBITRATORS IN INTERNATIONAL ARBITRATION

The selection and removal of arbitrators is one of the most important aspects of international arbitral proceedings.[1] This chapter first examines the selection of arbitrators, including by the parties' agreement and by non-judicial appointing authorities. Second, the chapter considers the role of national courts in selecting arbitrators. Third, the chapter discusses requirements regarding the identities of arbitrators, including requirements regarding impartiality and independence, contractually-imposed requirements and other requirements. Fourth, the chapter addresses the procedures for challenging and removing arbitrators, focusing first on non-judicial appointing authorities and then considering appointment by national courts. Finally, the chapter discusses the problems presented by "truncated" tribunals, where one or more members of the tribunal refuse to participate in rendering an award.

A. SELECTION OF ARBITRATORS BY PARTIES OR APPOINTING AUTHORITY IN INTERNATIONAL ARBITRATION

One of the characteristic features of international arbitration is that there is no standing or pre-established "court" or tribunal to which disputes generally may be submitted. That is particularly true in international commercial arbitration, but it is also true in investment and inter-state arbitrations. The absence of any standing tribunal contrasts with national courts and many international tribunals (such as the International Court of Justice), which have a preexisting complement of judges who are assigned randomly to cases and generally-applicable, comprehensive procedural rules. In contrast, for most arbitral proceedings, an arbitral tribunal must be separately constituted by the parties (or otherwise), in accordance with the terms of the arbitration agreement and applicable law.

1. Parties' Autonomy in Selection of Arbitrators

As with other aspects of the international arbitral process, a dominant characteristic of the selection of the tribunal is the principle of party autonomy. As illustrated below, international arbitration conventions, national law and institutional rules all accord parties broad autonomy both to agree directly upon the arbitrators in "their" arbitration and to agree on indirect mechanisms for selecting such arbitrators. This autonomy is subject to only limited restrictions, directed at ensuring an impartial arbitral tribunal and safeguarding other similarly-important national and international public policies.

---

1. *See* G. Born, *International Commercial Arbitration* 1638 *et seq.* (2d ed. 2014); Carter, *The Selection of Arbitrators*, 5 Am. Rev. Int'l Arb. 84 (1994); C. Rogers, *Ethics in International Arbitration* 60-74 (2014); Rogers, *The Vocation of the International Arbitrator*, 20 Am. U. Int'l L. Rev. 957 (2005).

Many international commercial arbitration agreements provide a procedural mechanism for the selection of the arbitrator(s)—either expressly or by incorporating institutional arbitration rules. The almost universal contractual mechanism for selecting an arbitrator is designation of a neutral "appointing authority" to choose the arbitrator(s), if the parties cannot agree directly upon the identity of the arbitrators.[2] All leading institutional rules provide for such a role by the sponsoring institution when parties agree to arbitrate under the institution's rules.[3] As discussed below, international arbitration conventions and most national arbitration statutes give effect to agreements by which parties provide for the selection of arbitrators either by an appointing authority or by other means.

GENEVA PROTOCOL
Article 2 (1923)

The arbitral procedure, including the constitution of the arbitral tribunal, shall be governed by the will of the parties and by the law of the country in whose territory the arbitration takes place. The Contracting States agree to facilitate all steps in the procedure which require to be taken in their own territories, in accordance with the provisions of their law governing arbitral procedure applicable to existing differences.

SUMUKAN LTD v. COMMONWEALTH SECRETARIAT
[2007] EWCA Civ. 1148 (English Ct. App.)

LORD JUSTICE WALLER. By an award dated 25 April 2005, arbitrators ruled in favour of The Commonwealth Secretariat ("CMS") that on a proper construction of a contract between them, and Sumukan Ltd ("Sumukan"), the title in certain software had become that of CMS. Sumukan made various attacks on the validity of that award, attacking the substantive jurisdiction of the arbitrators under §67 of the Arbitration Act 1996 ("the Act"), attacking the award on the basis of irregularity under §68 of that Act.... Sumukan ... say that the effect of the contract they signed was ... to compel them to arbitrate before a tribunal effectively appointed by the other contracting party CMS giving rise to a perception of partiality, and that even in the process of that tribunal being appointed the procedures which might have protected them to some extent against any lack of independence or impartiality were not complied with.

CMS's answer ... [supported by the Tribunal] is that Sumukan are bound by the contract they signed; that the suggestion of any perceived lack of independence or impartiality is misplaced since the Tribunal appointed was of the highest calibre and clearly totally impartial; any failure to comply with procedures was not of a character that could undermine

---

2. This mechanism is also adopted in inter-state arbitrations, with treaties or arbitration agreements typically specifying a particular institution (*e.g.*, the Permanent Court of Arbitration) or individual (*e.g.*, the President of the International Court of Justice) to select arbitrators where the parties are unable to agree. *See infra* pp. 701-02.

3. *See supra* pp. 87-88 & *infra* pp. 689-99; 2010 UNCITRAL Rules, Arts. 6-10; 2012 ICC Rules, Arts. 11-13; 2014 LCIA Rules, Arts. 5-9. In investment arbitrations, the ICSID Rules provide a similar mechanism, for selection of the arbitrator(s) if the parties cannot agree upon their identity. ICSID Rules, Art. 4; ICSID Convention, Art. 38. Alternatively, some neutral individual or office-holder—like the Secretary-General of the ICC or the Permanent Court of Arbitration—can be designated as an appointing authority.

the jurisdiction of the Tribunal which sat and heard the arbitration; and in any event they say Sumukan went ahead with the arbitration in circumstances where with reasonable diligence they could have discovered any of the points now taken, and are precluded from complaining now by §73 of the 1996 Act....

[The parties'] contract contained an arbitration clause in the following terms: "The Secretariat and the consultant shall endeavour to settle by negotiation and agreement any dispute which arises in connection with this contract. Failing such agreement the dispute shall be referred to the Commonwealth Secretariat Arbitral Tribunal [CSAT] for settlement by arbitration in accordance with its statute which forms part of this contract and is available on request." That clause referred to "its statute," [which was,] available on request as forming part of the contract.... [T]he material terms of that statute [as it existed in 1999] were:

"Article II

1. The Tribunal shall hear and pass judgment upon any application brought by: (a) a member of the staff of the Commonwealth Secretariat, (b) the Commonwealth Secretariat, (c) any person who enters into a contract in writing with the Commonwealth Secretariat, which alleges the non-observance of the contract....

Article IV

1. The Tribunal shall normally be composed of one member who shall be the President or if the President is for any reason unable to sit, some other member of the Tribunal designated by the President.

2. In exceptional cases where, in the opinion of the President the complexity of the matter requires it, the Tribunal shall sit as a three-member Tribunal empanelled by and including the President but no two members may be nationals of the same country....

4. The members of the Tribunal, all of whom shall be Commonwealth nationals, shall be of high moral character and must: a. Hold or be qualified to hold high judicial office in a Commonwealth country; b. Be jurisconsults of recognised competence with experience as such....

5. The president of the Tribunal and four other persons shall be appointed by the Commonwealth Secretary General on a regionally representative basis after consultation with governments and the Commonwealth Secretariat Staff Association to be available to serve as members of the Tribunal. Each appointment shall be for a period of three years and may be extended for further periods of three years....

7. The President of the Tribunal shall hold office until a successor is appointed.

Article XIII

The present statute may be amended by the Secretary-General. Before making any amendment, the Secretary-General shall seek the views of the President and shall consult with Commonwealth governments and the Commonwealth Secretariat Staff Association...."

[Sumukan] suggested that "it would be an unusual and onerous term in a contract that an arbitration be conducted by a panel wholly appointed by one side and under statutes capable of being changed at any time by that one side." [Sumukan] suggested that such terms would not be of contractual affect if they were not drawn to Sumukan's attention.... This was a commercial contract. True, Sumukan had no choice as to the terms of the contract so far as arbitration was concerned but that is a common feature of and the reality of many commercial contracts. Sumukan are not a consumer with the protection of consumer legislation and are bound by the terms of the contract they made. It follows they were bound to accept a Tribunal appointed in accordance with the relevant statute to which the term refers.

As we will see there may be room for argument as to which that statute was, and what it requires. I will come to that. But what seems to me to flow from that first point is important. If ... Sumukan would seek to attack the award on the basis that a procedure in accordance with the statute could not produce an impartial tribunal, and that on that basis there was a serious irregularity (relying on §68(2)(a) taken together with §33 of the Act), that attack is doomed to failure. Having agreed to it, they must be taken to have waived any objection....

The most difficult part of the case arises out of the fact that it is accepted that there was a degree of non-compliance with the relevant statute in the appointment both as a member and then as President of the CMS arbitral panel, Professor Chappel. It was he that presided over the Tribunal of three which sat and made the award. The key issues on the appeal are (1) whether any non-compliance with the relevant statute was such as to affect the substantive jurisdiction of the panel that sat and made its award; and (2) if so, whether CMS can succeed in their arguments that any failures to comply with the statute was cured in some way, or that the failures could with reasonable diligence have been discovered by Sumukan, so as preclude reliance on them by virtue of §73....

[The court provided a chronology of Professor Chappell's appointment both as a member of the Panel and as President thereof. In sum, Professor Chappell was inadvertently appointed to these positions without consultations among the members of the Commonwealth governments as required by Article 4(5) of the 1999 statute. Sumukan commenced its arbitration against CMS in 2003. In July 2004, Professor Chappell determined that the constitution of the tribunal to hear Sumukan's claim should be himself, Ms. Weekes, and Dame Joan Sawyer, and Sumukan was notified accordingly. A hearing was held in February 2005, following which the tribunal made an award in favor of CMS, rejecting Sumukan's claims.]

Any arbitration tribunal was to be presided over by the President of the Panel, and indeed the persons to sit on the Tribunal were selected by that President. If therefore there was a defect in the appointment of the President so as to make his appointment to the Panel invalid, that would as it seems to me have an effect on the substantive jurisdiction of the arbitrators. Furthermore if the arbitrators were to be selected from a Panel, and if there was a procedure for the appointment of the Panel aimed at guarding against any apparent lack of independence, it seems to me right that a substantial failure to comply with that procedure should have an effect on the jurisdiction of the tribunal itself.

It is accepted by CMS that prior to Professor Chappell being appointed as a member of the Panel there was no consultation with member states under Article IV(4) of the 1999 statute; it is accepted that prior to his appointment as President in 2001 there was no consultation with member states under Article IV(4).... It follows there has been non-compliance with the appointment procedure. [The CMS statutes] were incorporated into the contract between Sumukan and the CMS, and Sumukan are prima facie entitled to have the agreed procedure for appointment of any arbitrator complied with. Thus once non-compliance is established it is for CMS to show that a failure to comply with the relevant statute was either inconsequential in some way or cured by the fact that the States clearly knew he was acting as a member and as a President and made no protest; or to show that the procedural failure was of a kind which did not lead to an invalid appointment. This latter they seek to do in reliance on the nature of the provision as surplusage or because they submit that a de facto principle applies in arbitration so as to cloak the tribunal that sat with jurisdiction....

We were referred to a number of cases [which] demonstrat[e] that the court will wrestle to avoid setting aside an otherwise perfectly good decision by virtue of non-compliance with a provision which really does not matter. In the instant case it seems to me that the correct question is whether, as a matter of contract, compliance with the obligation to consult member states was a provision simply for the benefit of the Commonwealth Governments so that they could check whether a fair balance between different parts of the world was being kept, or whether the provision was also for the benefit of those who might become involved in arbitration with CMS in the sense that the requirement to consult might assist in promoting the independence of panelists from whom arbitrators were to be drawn. I accept ... that the main point of the requirement to consult was probably to enable member states to see that the balance of representation on the panel between different parts of the world was maintained. However CMS have difficulty in arguing that the provision had nothing to do with promoting the independence of the arbitrators or the President. Their own skeleton argument paragraph 63 says that one aim was to promote "independence"....

In my view, Sumukan are entitled to say that even if they must be taken to have agreed to a tribunal appointed without any input from them, and with a major influence of the party with whom they were contracting, they were at least entitled to rely on compliance with any measure that might protect even to a small degree the independence of the panel or the President. I should add, although the statute contemplated appointees of very high calibre that fact does not preclude Sumukan being entitled to so insist. I would thus hold unless the lack of consultation was cured or was something which Sumukan are precluded by §73 from relying on, Sumukan should succeed in their appeal.

Was any lack of consultation cured? ... In truth ... curing the lack of consultation is not pressed with any vigour [by CMS] and rightly. Informing the member states of a fait accompli cannot equate with consultation intended to take place before an appointment has been made. I would not hold that any failure to consult had been cured.

Does the de facto concept apply? I do not think it does in the arbitration context. The question is whether the agreement under which the arbitrators have been appointed has been complied with. Where one party has failed to abide by the procedure required for appointing the President it lies ill in his mouth to seek to rely on any de facto arguments. I understand an argument that it is unsatisfactory to allow an arbitration to go ahead with the costs incurred, and indeed the more unsatisfactory for the person who loses only to take a point on jurisdiction once they have lost, but it is §73 which will assist in that regard if it applies and not an appeal to a de facto principle.

I turn therefore to §73 [dealing with waiver of objections]. [Is it possible] to find that Sumukan could not with reasonable diligence have discovered the lack of validity? This again is not straightforward. As one sees from the language of the 1996 Act, e.g. §31, the Act is concerned that substantive jurisdiction points should be taken before expense and time is incurred. It could be said to be an obvious point to check whether the appointment procedures have been complied with....

However the [lower court] found that it would be wrong to construe §73 so as to hold that Sumukan could with reasonable diligence have discovered facts which it neither knew nor believed nor had grounds to suspect. Indeed since CMS were under the statute to be instrumental in carrying out the requisite procedures, and since it seems CMS did appreciate that the procedures had not been gone through, it can be said with some force it was for CMS to draw the matters to Sumukan's attention and seek a waiver. Sumukan were (it might legitimately be said) entitled to rely on the fact that CMS would not be suggesting a particular Tribunal unless the procedures had been complied with.... I would uphold the [lower court's] decision on this aspect. It thus follows that this award must be set aside and the matter remitted to a differently and properly constituted tribunal....

LORD JUSTICE SEDLEY.... In my judgment the requirement for consultation with the Commonwealth governments about the appointment of the president and members of the arbitral tribunal is a real and important safeguard for anyone with a claim against the Commonwealth Secretariat. The unusual set-up is dictated by the need to provide a forum which will impartially and bindingly adjudicate on disputes involving the London-based Secretariat without requiring the sovereign states which make up the Commonwealth to submit to the jurisdiction of the ordinary courts. The solution, underpinned by legislation, is an arbitral tribunal appointed entirely by the Secretariat, to which anyone who contracts with the Secretariat must agree to submit disputes. This makes the suitability and impartiality of the tribunal a critical safeguard for a party who of necessity has no say in its constitution.

How then could consultation with the governments make any difference to an appointment? [CMS] submits that it is tokenism and of no material consequence.... I strongly disagree.... [W]hile some officials ... may nod it through without further debate, others may very well want to consider, first, the suitability of the particular candidate and, secondly and in any event, whether there is someone preferable. Take Professor Chappell. His integrity and ability are undoubted, but his CV shows him to be a criminologist with no background in contract law or arbitration, albeit strong recent experience as deputy president of the Australian Federal Administrative Appeals Tribunal. While it would have been noted that the CMS tribunal's workload to date had concerned only staff issues, it might also have been noted that it potentially included anyone who had a contractual dispute with the Secretariat. It is therefore perfectly possible that, had the governments been consulted, someone with more experience of arbitration and contract law might have been proposed and ... appointed as president. While this in no way undermines the standing of Professor Chappell ..., it illustrates how important it is from the point of view of those who have no choice about the arbitration procedure or its personnel that the prescribed filters on appointment are used, so that the best candidate whom the collective knowledge of the member states can suggest is approached.... I would therefore hold that the appointment procedure exists at least in part for the protection of parties to arbitrations against the Secretariat. The departure from it rendered Professor Chappell's participation as president in Sumukan's arbitration unlawful and the award a nullity....

CERTAIN UNDERWRITERS AT LLOYD'S LONDON v. ARGONAUT INSURANCE CO.
500 F.3d 571 (7th Cir. 2007)

RIPPLE, Circuit Judge. Certain Underwriters at Lloyd's London ("Underwriters") entered into a reinsurance contract with Argonaut Insurance Company ("Argonaut"). A dispute over coverage arose, and Argonaut demanded arbitration in accordance with the contract. Further disputes arose related to the arbitration, and Underwriters ... sought an order confirming a panel of arbitrators. The district court ... confirmed the panel of arbitrators. Argonaut timely appeals.... [W]e affirm....

Underwriters, a reinsurance syndicate ..., entered into certain reinsurance contracts, or "treaties," with Argonaut, a California-based insurer. The treaties contain an arbitration provision as well as a further clause that details the responsibilities of the parties in selecting the arbitration panel...:

> "If any dispute shall arise between the Company and the Underwriters with reference to the interpretation of this Agreement ..., this dispute shall be referred to three arbitrators, one to be chosen by each party and the third by the two so chosen. If either party refuses or neglects to appoint an arbitrator within thirty days after receipt of written notice from the other party requesting it to do so, the requesting party may nominate two arbitrators, who shall choose the third."

[After coverage disputes arose,] Argonaut sent an arbitration demand. That demand, made on August 4, 2004, included a request that Underwriters name its arbitrator within 30 days. Underwriters complied with the deadline and named its arbitrator on September 3. On August 6, 2004, before Underwriters nominated its arbitrator, it sent a demand that Argonaut nominate its arbitrator. Consistent with the treaty, Underwriters' demand also invoked the thirty-day time limit; although the demand did not specifically so note, the expiration of Argonaut's thirty-day period would come on Sunday, September 5, 2004. That day, however, came and went without any word from Argonaut regarding its nomination of an arbitrator. The following day, Monday, September 6, was Labor Day, a legal holiday in the United States, where Argonaut is located and where the arbitration proceedings were to take place, but a normal business day in the United Kingdom, where the Underwriters syndicate is based. On that day, one day after the expiration of thirty calendar days from the date of Underwriters' request for Argonaut's naming of an arbitrator, Underwriters faxed a letter to Argonaut invoking the default provision of the treaty's arbitration clause and naming a second arbitrator.

In response, on Tuesday, September 7, thirty-two days after the demand had been made, counsel for Argonaut first sent an e-mail to Underwriters, representing that Argonaut's named arbitrator *had been* selected properly on the previous Friday, and notice thereof sent to Underwriters the previous week. Later in the day on the 7th, when it became clear that, in fact, no notice had been sent during the previous week, Argonaut faxed a new letter to Underwriters naming its arbitrator. In that letter, Argonaut claimed it was not bound by the strict thirty-day deadline because its terminus was a Sunday followed by a legal holiday; instead, it claimed that it was not obligated to name the arbitrator on Sunday or on Monday and that the Tuesday, September 7, notice was a timely nomination of the second arbitrator within the meaning of the treaty.

Because of the competing demands for arbitrators, Underwriters filed a petition in the district court under 9 U.S.C. §5 for an order confirming the appointment of its two nominees as arbitrators in its dispute with Argonaut.... The court granted summary judgment for Underwriters.... [Argonaut appealed.]

[The Court first addressed] the most significant issue presented by this case: Whether, in interpreting an arbitration agreement that falls within the New York Convention, but that contains no choice-of-law provision, we should apply a federal common law rule of decision or, through the use of choice-of-law principles, determine what appropriate state law should govern.... Underwriters chiefly argues for the application of federal substantive law while Argonaut primarily seeks to have the law of California govern the present dispute....

A United States delegation participated in the 1958 negotiations [of the New York Convention;] ... that delegation recommended against the United States becoming an original signatory to the Convention. In part, the delegation was concerned that the Convention would "override the arbitration laws of a substantial number of States and entail changes in State and possibly Federal court procedures." ... [T]welve years after it initially was opened for signature, the United States acceded to the treaty.... The concern for an unintended effect on domestic laws, which had counselled against the participation of the United States in 1958, was addressed in the implementation. Specifically, §202 of the FAA expressly limits the application of the Convention to disputes involving a foreign party, or, if only disputes involving exclusively United States citizens are involved, to circumstances in which the dispute has a "reasonable relation with one or more foreign states." Further the implementing legislation makes clear that the standards contained in the FAA apply to disputes under the Convention "to the extent [the FAA] is not in conflict with [the Convention as implemented] or the Convention as ratified by the United States" although the Convention is codified as part of the FAA. 9 U.S.C. §208. Therefore, although the Convention would displace certain domestic laws, it would do so only in the narrow context of truly international disputes; within that narrow context, where appropriate, federal arbitration law under the FAA would fill the gaps left by the Convention.... With this history in mind, we turn now to the primary issue in the present case: What substantive law should be applied to interpret the terms of an arbitration agreement under the Convention when the parties have not included an explicit choice-of-law provision in their contract? ...

[W]hen our sister circuits have been confronted with issues relating to agreements under the Convention—whether the question be arbitrability or enforcement or some other question—they appear to have resolved those issues by employing federal rules of decision, particularly when the parties have not provided otherwise by their contract.... Argonaut urges that these cases, primarily addressed to arbitrability of disputes, have no application to the present dispute, which is concededly arbitrable. We cannot agree. The interpretation of the portion of the arbitration clause related to the appointment of arbitrators seems to us very closely aligned with the other issues of interpretation of arbitration agreements under the Convention; such questions present an equally compelling case for a uniform federal rule in the absence of direction to use another law selected by the parties themselves.... "The goal of the Convention, and the principal purpose underlying American adoption and implementation of it, was to encourage the recognition and enforcement of commercial arbitration agreements in international contracts *and to unify the standards by which agreements to arbitrate are observed* and arbitral awards are enforced in the signatory countries." *Scherk*, 417 U.S. at 520 n.15 (emphasis added).... [T]his overarching federal concern with the uniformity of treatment of international arbitration agreements requires that the issue before us be resolved by a federal common law rule, rather than by a state rule of decision....

In light of the recognition by the Supreme Court and by our sister circuits that uniformity in determining the manner by which agreements to arbitrate will be enforced is a critical objective of the Convention, we hold that, in this circumstance, the injection of a parochial rule that interprets a contractual deadline other than by its plain wording is contrary to the interests of the United States as embodied the Convention. Underwriters has identified a specific objective of federal law, namely, to ensure uniform enforcement of agreements to arbitrate. Were we to conclude that state law provided the applicable rule of decision in this case, we would sanction an interpretation of the contract that permitted, necessarily, *non*-uniform results.[4] ...

In the absence of a choice-of-law provision, we conclude that parties are to be bound to the explicit language of arbitration clauses, with no state-specific exceptions that would extend otherwise clear contractual deadlines. Of course, sophisticated commercial parties such as these may provide by contract that thirty days does not include Sundays and holidays, or that a contract with a terminus for performance on a Sunday or holiday (as recognized by some identifiable body—state, federal or otherwise) may be timely performed on the next business day. However, in the absence of such an agreement, or an agreement to apply particular parochial rules of interpretation, we believe a uniform federal rule that enforces strongly arbitration deadlines under the Convention is necessary and appropriate.

[The Court of Appeals affirmed the District Court's judgment confirming the identities of the arbitrators.] ...

KARAHA BODAS CO., LLC v. PERUSAHAAN PERTAMBANGAN MINYAK DAN GAS BUMI NEGARA
364 F.3d 274 (5th Cir. 2004)

[excerpted above at pp. 605-19]

JIVRAJ v. HASHWANI
[2011] UKSC 40 (U.K. S.Ct.)

[excerpted above at pp. 117-24]

AMERICO LIFE, INC. v. MYER
2014 WL 2789429 (Tex.)

JUSTICE BROWN. In 1998, Robert Myer and Strider Marketing Group, Inc. (collectively "Myer") sold a collection of insurance companies to the petitioners (collectively "Americo"). The parties agreed on an up-front payment to Myer for the businesses and executed a "trailer agreement" to provide for additional payments based on the businesses' future

---

4. We note that Argonaut's suggestion, that California law should apply and that it would extend the contract deadline, would permit such an extension of the deadline not only for Sundays and for national holidays, such as Labor Day, but also for Cesar Chavez Day (March 31) and Admission Day (September 9). *See* Cal. Gov. Code §6700(f), (j). Under this interpretation, in Illinois, Casimir Pulaski Day (March 1) would be exempted. *See* 205 ILCS 630/17(a) (defining holidays); 5 ILCS 70/1.11 (providing that when the time within which an act required by law to be performed ends on a day designated as a holiday by the state, it may be performed on the next business day). In Hawaii, Argonaut may have had the benefit of Prince Jonah Kuhio Kalanianaole Day (March 26) and King Kamehameha I Day (June 11), *see* Hi. Rev. Stat. §8-1 (listing holidays), *id.* §1-32 (providing that acts required by contract to be performed on a particular day, which fall on a holiday, may be performed on the next business day). The application of local rules such as these necessarily would defeat the uniformity goals of the Convention.

performance. The trailer agreement included an arbitration clause with six paragraphs of terms agreed upon by the parties, including:

> "3.3 Arbitration. In the event of any dispute arising after the date of this Agreement among the parties hereto with reference to any transaction contemplated by this Agreement the same shall be referred to three arbitrators. Americo shall appoint one arbitrator and Myer shall appoint one arbitrator and such two arbitrators to select the third…. Each arbitrator shall be a knowledgeable, independent businessperson or professional….
>
> The arbitration proceedings shall be conducted in accordance with the commercial arbitration rules of the American Arbitration Association, except that Americo and Myer each shall be entitled to take discovery as provided under Federal Rules of Civil Procedure Nos. 28 through 36 during a period of 90 days after the final arbitrator is appointed and the arbitrators shall have the power to issue subpoenas, compel discovery, award sanctions and grant injunctive relief. The arbitrators shall be entitled to retain a lawyer to advise them as to legal matters, but such lawyer shall have none of the relationships to Americo or Myer (or any of their Affiliates) that are proscribed above for arbitrators."

The agreement combines terms expressly chosen by the parties with the incorporation by reference of American Arbitration Association rules to govern the arbitration proceeding. When the parties executed their agreement, AAA rules did not require arbitrator-impartiality, but by the time Americo invoked arbitration in 2005 after disputes arose concerning the additional payments to Myer, the AAA rules by default required that "[a]ny arbitrator shall be impartial and independent … and shall be subject to disqualification for … partiality or lack of independence…." AAA Commercial Arbitration Rules R-17(a)(I) (2003).

Myer alleged that Americo's first-choice arbitrator, Ernest Figari, Jr., was partial toward Americo, and successfully moved the AAA to disqualify him. Americo objected to Figari's disqualification but named another arbitrator, about whom Myer likewise complained, and whom the AAA likewise struck. Myer did not object to Americo's third appointee, who ultimately served on the panel. The arbitration proceeding resulted in a unanimous award in Myer's favor amounting to just over $26 million in payments due, breach-of-contract damages, and attorneys' fees.

When Myer moved to confirm the award in the trial court, Americo renewed its objection to Figari's disqualification. Americo argued that in disqualifying Figari for partiality, the AAA failed to follow the arbitrator-selection process specified in the parties' agreement, which provided only that "each arbitrator shall be a knowledgeable, independent businessperson or professional." The trial court determined the arbitration agreement was ambiguous but ultimately agreed with Americo's reading and vacated the award. [After various appellate proceedings, the Texas Court of Appeals reversed, confirming the award.] …

Arbitrators derive their power from the parties' agreement to submit to arbitration. They have no independent source of jurisdiction apart from the parties' consent. Accordingly, arbitrators must be selected pursuant to the method specified in the parties' agreement. *Brook v. Peak Int'l, Ltd*, 294 F.3d 668, 672-73 (5th Cir. 2002). An arbitration panel selected contrary to the contract-specified method lacks jurisdiction over the dispute. Accordingly, courts "do not hesitate to vacate an award when an arbitrator is not selected according to the contract-specified method." *Bulko v. Morgan Stanley DW Inc.*, 450 F.3d 622, 625 (5th Cir. 2006). So we look to the arbitration agreement to determine what the parties specified concerning the arbitrator-selection process….

In their agreement, the parties directly addressed the issue of arbitrator qualifications and agreed on a short list of requirements, namely that each arbitrator must be a "knowledgeable, independent businessperson or professional." Americo argues the court of appeals improperly added "impartial" to the parties' list of qualifications. Myer counters that because "independent" and "impartial" are essentially synonymous, Americo was always obligated to name an impartial arbitrator.

We disagree that "independent" may be read interchangeably with "impartial." Various dictionary definitions might support some overlap between the two words, but when applied in the arbitration context, they carry distinct meanings. The parties in this case agreed to "tripartite arbitration," through which each party would directly appoint an arbitrator, and the two party-appointed arbitrators would agree on a third panelist. This method was commonplace when the parties executed their agreement in 1998. *See Burlington N. R.R. Co. v. TUCO Inc.*, 960 S.W.2d 629, 630 & n.2 (Tex. 1997) (describing the method as "often-used"). In a tripartite arbitration, each party-appointed arbitrator ordinarily advocates for the appointing party, and only the third arbitrator is considered neutral.... *Lozano v. Md. Cas. Co.*, 850 F.2d 1470, 1472 (11th Cir. 1988) (per curiam) ("An arbitrator appointed by a party is a partisan only one step removed from the controversy and need not be impartial.")....

The AAA rules in place when the agreement was executed likewise reflect the prevalence of this practice. At that time, the rules provided that "[u]nless the parties agree otherwise, an arbitrator selected unilaterally by one party is a party-appointed arbitrator and not subject to disqualification pursuant to §19." AAA Commercial Arbitration Rules §12 (1996). Section 19 contained procedures to challenge arbitrators for partiality. *See id.*, §19. Accordingly, the AAA rules presumed party-appointed arbitrators were non-neutral, and the parties would have to "agree otherwise" to rebut this presumption.

The only indication the parties sought to "agree otherwise" is their requirement that party-appointed arbitrators be "independent." Americo argues that the parties chose the word "independent" not to require impartiality, but to proscribe arbitrators employed by or otherwise under the control of one of the parties. Americo's argument is certainly plausible; the practice of appointing arbitrators who are somehow formally associated with the party appointing them is not unheard of. *See, e.g.,* [*Matter of Astoria Med. Group*, 182 N.E.2d 85, 86 (N.Y. 1962)] (party appointed "one of the incorporators of [the company] and its president from 1950 to 1957" who was at the time "a member of its board of directors and one of its paid consultants")....

The industry norm for tripartite arbitrators when the parties executed their agreement was that party-appointed arbitrators were advocates, and the AAA rules in place at that time presumed such arbitrators would not be impartial unless the parties specifically agreed otherwise. Given the pervasiveness of the practice, and the clear AAA presumption the parties had to rebut, we believe the parties would have done more than require its arbitrators to be "independent" if they wished them to be impartial. "Independent" and "impartial" are not interchangeable in this context, and therefore we conclude the parties did not intend to require impartiality of party-appointed arbitrators.

Having concluded the terms of the agreement do not require impartial party-appointed arbitrators, we turn to the effect of the incorporated-by-reference AAA rules on arbitrator qualifications. There is no dispute the AAA rules would govern matters on which the agreement is silent. The question is whether AAA rules on arbitrator qualifications can, as the court of appeals concluded, supplement terms agreed on by the parties that specifically speak to the same point.

The court of appeals reasoned that the rules and the agreement "can be read together and harmonized to avoid any irreconcilable conflict." In other words, because "impartial" could be added without negating any expressly chosen qualifications, it was proper to do so to effectuate all the agreement's provisions. But this cannot be the end of our inquiry, or the specifically chosen terms of any agreement would be hopelessly open-ended whenever outside rules are incorporated by reference.

When an arbitration agreement incorporates by reference outside rules, "the specific provisions in the arbitration agreement take precedence and the arbitration rules are incorporated only to the extent that they do not conflict with the express provisions of the arbitration agreement." The [FAA], which the parties agree governs their agreement, requires that if an agreement provides "a method of naming or appointing an arbitrator or arbitrators or an umpire, such method shall be followed." 9 U.S.C. §5. Similarly, the AAA rules in effect when the parties executed their agreement, as well as when arbitration was invoked, both provide that "[i]f the agreement of the parties names an arbitrator or specifies a method of appointing an arbitrator, that designation or method shall be followed." AAA Commercial Arbitration Rules §14 (1996), R-12 (2003).

Any attempt to harmonize the AAA impartiality rule with the parties' expressly chosen arbitrator qualifications misses the point. We do not construe "conflict" between an agreement and incorporated rules so narrowly as to find it exists only if the rule contradicts the agreement. A conflict can exist when an agreement and incorporated rules speak to the same point. Even if both can be followed without contradiction, they conflict because the parties have already addressed the matter and are not in need of gap-filling from the AAA rules. When the agreement and incorporated rules speak to the same point, the agreement's voice is the only to be heard.

Here, the parties chose a short list of arbitrator qualifications, and in doing so we must assume they spoke comprehensively. The parties chose "knowledgeable" and "independent" but not "impartial," and we think they meant not only what they said but also what they did not say. And though we can concede the parties embraced some uncertainty by adopting AAA rules that were subject to change, we cannot conceive that they agreed to be bound by rules that would alter the express terms of their agreement. Nor can we imagine they took the trouble to expressly agree on some terms if their decision to incorporate AAA rules would leave those terms open to alteration. The AAA impartiality rule conflicts with the parties' agreement because the parties spoke on the matter and did not choose impartiality. When such a conflict arises, the agreement controls....

Because the AAA disqualified Americo's first-choice arbitrator for partiality, the arbitration panel was formed contrary to the express terms of the arbitration agreement. The panel, therefore, exceeded its authority when it resolved the parties' dispute. Because the arbitrators exceeded their authority, the arbitration award must be vacated. *See* 9 U.S.C. §10(a); *Bulko*, 450 F.3d at 625....

JUDGMENT OF 24 FEBRUARY 1994
XXII Y.B. Comm. Arb. 682 (1997) (Paris Cour d'appel)

The French company, Bec Frères SA, and the Tunisian company, Grands Travaux d'Afrique, formed a group of companies ("Group") and successfully bid on the tender offered by the Tunisian Ministry of Public Works ("Ministry") for the construction of two road segments. The two contracts which they were awarded each contained an arbitration clause providing, *inter alia*, that disputes would be examined in the framework of Tunisian jurisprudence and, subsidiarily, French jurisprudence relating to public works. The arbitration clauses also provided that the arbitral tribunal was to consist of two arbitrators, one to be appointed by each party.

Difficulties arose between the parties which eventually resulted in the contract being terminated by the Ministry. [An arbitration was commenced and, after procedural disputes, the Group appointed one arbitrator and the Tunisian courts appointed a second arbitrator (following the Ministry's failure to do so). Thereafter,] the arbitrators informed the parties that in order to conform with Art. 263 of the Tunisian Code of Civil and Commercial Procedure ("CCCP") which requires an uneven number of arbitrators, they had appointed Mr. Revaclier as third arbitrator. [After further procedural disputes, the three arbitrators made an award in favor of the Group. The Ministry resisted recognition of the award in France, on the grounds that the tribunal had not been constituted in accordance with the parties' agreement.]

The Ministry points out that the arbitration clause provides that all disputes will be submitted to an arbitral tribunal of two arbitrators, each of the parties appointing its arbitrator. Art. 263 CCCP prescribes that there be an uneven number when there is more than one arbitrator. They contend that the arbitrators exceeded their powers when they appointed a third arbitrator as neither the arbitration agreement nor the Tunisian procedural law confer such a power. The Group responded that the arbitrators proceeded in this way in order to comply with the Tunisian procedural law which prescribes that there be an uneven number and that they used their powers to make the arbitration clause effective. The will of the parties expressed in the arbitration clause to submit their future disputes to two arbitrators designated by them cannot frustrate the provisions of Art. 263 of the CCCP which prescribes an uneven number of arbitrators. The two arbitrators did nothing more than make themselves subject to the ... mandatory law....

NOTES

1. *Parties' autonomy under New York Convention to select arbitrators.* Consider Article 2 of the Geneva Protocol and Articles II and V(1)(d) of the New York Convention, excerpted at pp. 1-2 of the Documentary Supplement. How does Article 2 of the Geneva Protocol deal with the parties' autonomy to constitute the arbitral tribunal? What are the respective roles of the parties' procedural agreements and the law of the arbitral seat under Article 2? Compare Article V(1)(d) of the New York Convention. What are the respective roles of the parties' procedural agreements and the law of the arbitral seat under Article V(1)(d)?

   Compare Article 45 of the 1907 Hague Convention, excerpted at p. 44 of the Documentary Supplement. Note that it also rests on the principle that the parties are generally free to select the arbitrators to resolve their dispute. Is there any reason that party autonomy should be entitled to greater respect in inter-state than commercial arbitrations? To lesser respect?

2. *Parties' autonomy under national arbitration legislation to select arbitrators.* Consider Article 11 of the UNCITRAL Model Law and Article 179 of the SLPIL, excerpted at pp. 88-89 & 158 of the Documentary Supplement. Compare §5 of the FAA,

which begins by providing that "[i]f in the agreement provision be made for a method of naming or appointing an arbitrator or arbitrators or an umpire such method shall be followed." What effect do these provisions give to the parties' agreement on the identity of the arbitrators? To the parties' agreement on an appointing authority or other mechanism for selecting arbitrators?

Consider how the decisions in *Sumukan, Americo, Certain Underwriters* and *Jivraj* recognized the parties' autonomy to select arbitrators. Note that in *Sumukan*, one party (the Commonwealth Secretariat) was permitted to select all the members of tribunals that decided claims against it; note the court's flat rejection of objections that this was unfair. Note also the court's decision in *Certain Underwriters*, that the parties' agreement on 30 days would be strictly enforced—even if the consequence was one party appointing two members of the tribunal. Likewise, note the deference accorded the parties' religious requirement in *Jivraj* and "partiality" requirement in *Americo*. Why is party autonomy accorded such deference?

3. *Rationale for parties' autonomy to select arbitrators.* Why do most national laws grant parties the autonomy to agree upon the identity, or means of selecting, individual arbitrators? What benefits are derived from permitting litigants to mutually agree upon the identity of the person who will decide their dispute? Does this necessarily ensure a more expert or legally-sound outcome? A more efficient proceeding? A greater chance of settlement? A result that will be voluntarily accepted by the losing party?

Suppose the parties have a construction or reinsurance dispute, governed by New York law, with relevant documents and witness testimony in French and English. Or a complex joint venture dispute involving Mexican corporate law issues. What sorts of individuals are best placed to resolve these disputes in an expert manner? In a manner that the parties both respect? Suppose the parties to a dispute are from France and the United States. Would it be desirable for the decision-maker to be either French or U.S. in nationality? Why or why not?

Are parties able to designate individual judges on a national court to resolve their dispute? Why not? Suppose a particular judge had very relevant legal or other experience and the confidence of the parties. Why would it not make sense for the parties to be able to select that judge (if they mutually agreed)?

4. *Parties' autonomy to select arbitrators through agreement on appointing authority.* The parties' autonomy to select their arbitrators extends to—and is very frequently exercised by—agreeing upon an "appointing authority" that will select the arbitrators. Consider, for example, Article 2 of the Inter-American Convention: "Arbitrators shall be appointed in the manner agreed upon by the parties. Their appointment may be delegated to a third party, whether a natural or juridical person." *See also* European Convention, Art. IV(1)(b). National arbitration legislation is similar. *See, e.g.*, FAA, 9 U.S.C. §5 ("If in the [arbitration] agreement provision be made for a method of naming or appointing an arbitrator or arbitrators ... such method shall be followed...."); UNCITRAL Model Law, Art. 11(2). *See also Judgment of 23 June 1988*, 1988 Rev. arb. 657 (Paris Tribunal de grande instance) ("by choosing the Paris Arbitral Chamber as the institution responsible for organizing their arbitration, [the parties] agreed to adhere to its procedural rules and thereby empowered the institution to organize the arbitral proceedings in accordance with those rules, and to resolve any difficulties which might arise").

If a national court were authorized to appoint arbitrators without regard to the parties' agreed means of appointment, would this be consistent with the principles of party autonomy underlying Articles II and V(1)(d) of the New York Convention? *See supra* pp. 637-38, 652, 667. If one national court were to make such appointments, in international cases, would not other national courts also be free to do so? What consequences would this have for the arbitral process?

5. *Exceptions to parties' autonomy to select arbitrators.* Should the parties' autonomy to select the arbitrator(s) be unlimited? If not, what types of exceptions to that autonomy should be recognized?

    (a) *Unacceptably one-sided procedures for constituting tribunal.* Suppose that the parties agree that one party may unilaterally select the arbitrator(s). Suppose that the parties agree that the CEO or General Counsel of one party will serve as arbitrator. Consider how complaints about the impartiality of the tribunal were addressed in *Sumukan.* These issues are considered in greater detail below. *See infra* pp. 698-99, 713-14, 739-40. *See also supra* pp. 408-09. Suppose that the parties agree to a name to be randomly selected from a telephone book. *See supra* pp. 352-53, 393-412, 434-35, 671-72.

    (b) *Capacity limitations.* Suppose the parties select an arbitrator who is not legally-competent (*e.g.,* 15 years old) or a convicted criminal (*e.g.,* serving a prison sentence for fraud). *See infra* pp. 712-13.

    (c) *Experience requirements.* Suppose national law requires that arbitrators be legally-qualified. *See infra* p. 713. Note again that Articles 44 and 45 of the 1907 Hague Convention provided for the selection of arbitrators from a previously compiled list of arbitrators. This limits the parties' autonomy to choose precisely the arbitrators that they consider appropriate for a particular dispute. What is the rationale for this limitation? Would comparable limits be appropriate in international commercial arbitration?

    (d) *Impartiality requirements.* Consider the Texas Supreme Court's conclusion that the parties' agreement for partial co-arbitrators was binding and enforceable under the FAA. As discussed below, other jurisdictions may reach different conclusions.

6. *Consequences of violations of parties' agreement regarding selection of arbitrators.* Suppose the parties agree to a particular procedure for selecting the arbitrator(s) and that procedure is not followed. What are the consequences for the award?

    (a) *Contractual consequences.* Note the consequences in *Certain Underwriters* of Argonaut's failure to appoint an arbitrator within the contractual 30-day period. Some arbitration clauses provide that a party's failure to appoint a co-arbitrator entitles its counter-party to designate its co-arbitrator as presiding arbitrator. G. Born, *International Commercial Arbitration* 1647-48 (2d ed. 2014).

    (b) *Removal of arbitrator(s).* If the parties' agreed procedures for selecting the arbitrators are not complied with, one course of action is to remove the arbitrator(s) from the tribunal, either through judicial or institutional challenge. This was essentially the course taken in *Certain Underwriters* (albeit, in reverse, with one party seeking judicial confirmation of the composition of the tribunal, rather than judicial removal of one of the arbitrators) and *Jivraj.* The challenge and removal of arbitrators under national law and institutional rules are discussed below. *See infra* pp. 758-76.

(c) *Annulment of arbitral award.* Consider Article 34(2)(a)(iv) of the UNCITRAL Model Law, excerpted at p. 94 of the Documentary Supplement. Note how a provision paralleling Article 34(2)(a)(iv) was invoked in *Sumukan* and *Americo.* What were the consequences of non-compliance with the parties' agreement regarding selection of the arbitrator(s)? Is this the appropriate result? After an entire arbitration has been conducted, without any apparent procedural unfairness, should complaints about the means of constitution of the tribunal be permitted? Consider the analysis in *Sumukan* and the "*de facto* concept."

Are there circumstances in which violations of the parties' agreement regarding selection of the arbitrators should not result in annulment or non-recognition of the eventual award? What circumstances might these be? Suppose that there is a minor deviation from the parties' agreed arbitral procedures. Suppose that the co-arbitrators are given 15 days to agree upon a presiding arbitrator, after which a specified appointing authority will make the selection; if the co-arbitrators select a presiding arbitrator after 18 days, should a subsequent award by the tribunal be annulled?

(d) *Non-recognition of arbitral award.* Consider Article V(1)(d) of the New York Convention and Article 36(1)(a)(iv) of the UNCITRAL Model Law, excerpted at pp. 2 & 95 of the Documentary Supplement. Note how Article V(1)(d) was invoked in *Karaha Bodas.* Should the standard for denying recognition of an award because of non-compliance with agreed procedures for constituting the tribunal be the same as that for annulling an award on the same grounds? Why might standards for annulment and non-recognition differ?

7. *Conflicts between parties' agreed procedures for constituting arbitral tribunal and mandatory law of arbitral seat.* Suppose the parties' arbitration clause provides for constitution of a tribunal that would violate mandatory law in the arbitral seat. For example, what if the parties agree to a presiding arbitrator who is a non-Muslim, when legislation in the arbitral seat requires that arbitrators all be of the Muslim faith? What if, as in *Judgment of 24 February 1994*, the parties agree to arbitrate before an even number of arbitrators, when legislation in the arbitral seat requires an odd number of arbitrators? *See infra* pp. 687-88 & 712-13. Consider the lower court's analysis in *Jivraj.*

Consider Article 34(2)(a)(iv) of the Model Law. What does Article 34(2)(a)(iv) provide for when the parties' agreement regarding constitution of the tribunal conflicts with the law of the arbitral seat? If the parties have agreed to a particular procedure, does Article 34(2)(a)(iv) permit annulment of the award because local law regarding constitution of the tribunal requires a different procedure? Consider again the hypotheticals in the preceding Note.

Consider again Article V(1)(d) of the Convention and Article 36(1)(a)(iv) of the Model Law. Note that they contain the same language, with regard to non-recognition of awards, as contained in Article 34(2)(a)(iv), with regard to annulment of awards. How did the French Cour d'appel apply Article V(1)(d) in the *Judgment of 24 February 1994*? Didn't the parties' agreement provide for an arbitral tribunal constituted in a different manner than that which was adopted? Doesn't Article V(1)(d) provide for non-recognition in these circumstances?

8. *Parties' autonomy to select number of arbitrator(s).* One aspect of the parties' autonomy to select the arbitrator(s) is choosing the number of arbitrators. Consider Article 10(1) of the Model Law, excerpted at p. 88 of the Documentary Supplement. It reflects the general principle, under most arbitration statutes, that parties are free to select the number of arbitrators. Parties could theoretically choose almost any number of arbitrators (and historically have, as illustrated by agreements to arbitrate in Antiquity before tribunals composed of dozens or hundreds of arbitrators). *See* G. Born, *International Commercial Arbitration* 9 (2d ed. 2014) (describing arbitral tribunals of 600 Milesians, 334 Larissaeans, and 204 Cnidians). Could a proceeding before hundreds (or even dozens) of arbitrators really be an arbitration? Why or why not? Recall the definition of arbitration, *supra* pp. 116-37.

9. *Limitations on parties' autonomy to select number of arbitrators.* What if parties wish to arbitrate before two (or four) arbitrators? In a few jurisdictions, agreements to arbitrate before tribunals with an even number of arbitrators are invalid (and, typically, will be subject to revision, by the addition of another arbitrator). *See, e.g.,* Italian Code of Civil Procedure, Art. 809; French Code of Civil Procedure, Art. 1451 (in domestic cases); Netherlands Code of Civil Procedure, Art. 1026(3) ("If the parties have agreed on an even number of arbitrators, the arbitrators shall appoint an additional arbitrator who shall act as the chairman of the arbitral tribunal"); 1966 European Uniform Law on Arbitration, Art. 5 ("(1) The arbitral tribunal shall be composed of an uneven number of arbitrators. There may be a sole arbitrator. (2) If the arbitration agreement provides for an even number of arbitrators an additional arbitrator shall be appointed."); *Judgment of 13 September 1995*, 1995 Rev. arb. 630 (Paris Cour d'appel) (agreement providing for arbitration before two arbitrators and, if two arbitrators do not agree, an umpire, is null and void).

   Are these legislative restrictions on the parties' autonomy wise? What if a tribunal of two (or some other even number of) arbitrators reached a "tie," with each arbitrator insisting on a different result? How would deadlocks among the arbitrators be broken? Is it accurate to state that deadlocks would not, or would hardly ever, be broken? Considering the deliberations of a two-person tribunal pragmatically, how might such a tribunal reach unanimous decisions? If parties want such a procedure, why can't they agree to it? Note the comment, quoted *infra* p. 1233, that parties can (probably) agree to trial by a panel of three monkeys. If so, why not two?

   There are examples of highly successful arbitrations conducted by two arbitrators. After very substantial disputes arose between IBM and Fujitsu regarding their respective intellectual property rights, the two parties arbitrated their disputes before two arbitrators. The parties did so notwithstanding existing arbitration agreements providing for a tribunal of three arbitrators. Ultimately, the two-member tribunal issued awards requiring Fujitsu to pay billions of dollars in compensation to IBM, while granting it access (under strictly controlled conditions) to, and use of, IBM's intellectual property. The awards were implemented between the parties. *See* Mnookin & Greenberg, *Lessons of the IBM-Fujitsu Arbitration: How Disputants Can Work Together to Solve Deeper Conflicts*, 4(3) Disp. Resol. Mag. 16, 18 (1998); Bühring-Uhle, *The IBM-Fujitsu Arbitration: A Landmark in Innovative Dispute Resolution*, 2 Am. Rev. Int'l Arb. 113 (1991). If parties believe that a two (or four) person tribunal is likely to solve their dispute in satisfactory ways, why should they be forbidden from agreeing to such a mechanism? What should happen if the mechanism fails to produce a resolution?

Are prohibitions on agreements for an even number of arbitrators consistent with the parties' procedural autonomy under Articles II and V(1)(d) of the New York Convention? Consider the *Judgment of 24 February 1994*. Note that the parties' agreement provided for arbitration before two arbitrators. How many arbitrators did the tribunal ultimately comprise? Was this in accordance with the parties' agreement? Is there any way to interpret the parties' agreement consistently with a three-person tribunal? Was the action of the two initial arbitrators wise? What else could they have done? Was the decision of the Paris Cour d'appel wise?

10. *Number of arbitrators in international commercial arbitrations.* Recall that most arbitration legislation recognizes the parties' autonomy to select the number of arbitrators that will hear their dispute. In practice, virtually all international commercial arbitrations involve tribunals consisting of one or three arbitrators. Why might that be? What alternatives exist?

    What are the advantages and disadvantages, respectively, of tribunals consisting of one and three arbitrators? In a case involving multiple legal systems, what does a three-person tribunal permit? In a case involving a complex technical background, what would a three-person tribunal permit? What are the possible procedural safeguards and benefits of a three (or five) person tribunal? What are the possible procedural and logistical disadvantages of a three (or five) person tribunal? Is it possible categorically to prefer one number of arbitrators over another number?

11. *Number of arbitrators in inter-state arbitrations.* Consider the number of arbitrators agreed to in the *Alabama Arbitration* and *Abyei Arbitration. See* Treaty of Washington, Art. I and Abyei Arbitration Agreement, Art. 5, excerpted at pp. 65 & 80-82 of the Documentary Supplement. How many arbitrators are provided for in each agreement? What reasons might explain the different preferences regarding the number of arbitrators in commercial and inter-state arbitrations?

12. *Approaches to number of arbitrators where parties have not so agreed.* Parties sometimes do not agree on the number of arbitrators for disputes under their agreements. In the absence of agreement, both national law and institutional rules provide fallback rules or presumptions regarding the number of arbitrators.

    (a) *Number of arbitrators under national arbitration statutes.* Section 5 of the FAA provides that, where the parties have not agreed upon the number of arbitrators, "the arbitration shall be by a single arbitrator." Compare the different approach, adopting a presumption in favor of three arbitrators, in the UNCITRAL Model Law, Article 10(2). *Compare* Netherlands Code of Civil Procedure, Art. 1026(2), providing that the number of arbitrators shall be designated on a case-by-case basis by the court. Which default rule is more appropriate? Why?

    (b) *Number of arbitrators under institutional arbitration rules.* Compare the approaches of Article 7 of the 2010 UNCITRAL Rules and Article 12 of the 2012 ICC Rules to the number of arbitrators. *See also* 2012 Swiss Rules, Art. 6(2) ("As a rule, the Court shall refer the case to a sole arbitrator, unless the complexity of the subject matter and/or the amount in dispute justify that the case be referred to a three-member arbitral tribunal."). Again, which of the various approaches is wisest?

2. *Exercise of Parties' Autonomy to Select Arbitrators*

As important as the parties' autonomy to select the arbitrators, either directly or by agreement upon an appointing authority or other selection mechanism, is how this autonomy is exercised. The parties' selection of the arbitrator(s) occurs against a complex background of legal rules and tactical considerations.

Among other things, in selecting an arbitrator, parties must consider the procedural mechanisms set forth in their arbitration clause (including any institutional rules). They must also consider any applicable legal standards regarding the qualification and independence of arbitrators (discussed in detail below[5]), including national law, the arbitration clause and any institutional rules. In addition, parties must consider what personal characteristics, qualifications, and experience they would like an arbitrator to have, as well as how the appointing authority would likely exercise its authority to select an arbitrator in the absence of an agreement between the parties. The materials excerpted below explore the various issues that arise in the parties' exercise of their autonomy to select the arbitrator(s) in an international arbitration.

O. GLOSSNER, *SOCIOLOGICAL ASPECTS OF INTERNATIONAL COMMERCIAL ARBITRATION*
in P. Sanders (ed.), *The Art of Arbitration* 143, 144-46 (1982)

"L'arbitrage vaut ce que vaut l'arbitre!" This phrase has a proverbial quality. To be an arbitrator is to exercise an honourable function. It is not a profession, although there are institutions which train arbitrators aiming more at the non-lawyer as it is not necessary that the arbitrator be a lawyer. He can be just as well a technical expert or an engineer. But he must be a person of knowledge and high moral standard. He must be able to appease parties who may quarrel over a contract. He may possibly have to see that the parties agree to a settlement. It is only natural that the parties listen more attentively to someone who speaks to them from a position of experience, knowledge, or reputation. To be an arbitrator is a noble task, which challenges the whole personality, all of its intellectual and physical capacities. He is entrusted by virtue of a contract with the parties to an arbitration to deal with their property, to decide on their investment, to present conclusions with far-reaching consequences, which can only be challenged, if there is proof that the parties' basic rights of due process have been violated. The responsibility of an arbitrator is immense. If he fails there is practically no remedy available, because most laws do not allow one to sue an arbitrator for a wrong decision and, what is decisive, arbitrators cannot grant compensation for a possible damage caused to a party, even if they could be sued, for lack of means. This is what makes it difficult to believe that amiable composition, a foster child of French legal intellect, where the arbitrator is his own master in the decision making process, but for the mandatory provisions of the law, is in practice a recommendable form of arbitration. No one can finally appraise the arbitrator's sense of justice and feeling for practical needs until decision has been rendered by him. It seems better to have the arbitrator observe controllable legal standards.

---

5. *See infra* pp. 716-58.

JIVRAJ v. HASHWANI
[2011] UKSC 40 (U.K. S.Ct.)

[excerpted above at pp. 117-24]

2010 NAI RULES
Article 14

14(1) As soon as possible … the Administrator shall communicate to each of the parties an identical list of names. If one arbitrator is to be appointed, the list shall contain not less than three names; if three arbitrators are to be appointed, the list shall contain not less than nine names.

14(2) Each party may delete from this list the names of persons against whom he has overriding objections, and number the remaining names in the order of his preference.

14(3) If a list is not returned to the Administrator within two weeks after its dispatch to a party, it will be assumed that all persons appearing on it are equally acceptable to that party for appointment as arbitrator.

14(4) As soon as possible after receipt of the lists, or failing this, after expiration of the period of time referred to in the previous paragraph, the Administrator shall, taking into account the preferences and/or objections expressed by the parties, invite one or three persons from the list, as the case may be, to act as arbitrators.

14(5) If and to the extent that lists which have been returned show an insufficient number of persons who are acceptable as arbitrator to each of the parties, the Administrator shall be authorized to invite directly one or more other persons to act as arbitrator. The same shall apply if a person is not able or does not wish to accept the Administrator's invitation to act as arbitrator, or if there appear to be other reasons precluding him from acting as arbitrator, and there remain on the lists an insufficient number of persons who are acceptable as arbitrator to each of the parties.

14(6) If the arbitral tribunal is composed of three arbitrators, the arbitrators shall choose a chairman from amongst themselves, if necessary….

14(7) If the parties agreed only to the appointment of arbitrator(s) by the [NAI], without referring to arbitration by the [NAI] or arbitration in accordance with the [NAI] Rules, such appointment shall take place in accordance with the provisions of this article unless the parties agreed to another method of appointment by the [NAI].

14(8) For the application of the provisions of this article, the Administrator preferably shall draw the names of persons from the General Panel of Arbitrators which is established, expanded and amended by the NAI….

IBA RULES OF ETHICS FOR INTERNATIONAL ARBITRATORS
Article 5(1)

When approached with a view to appointment, a prospective arbitrator should make sufficient enquiries in order to inform himself whether there may be any justifiable doubts regarding his impartiality or independence; whether he is competent to determine the issues in dispute; and whether he is able to give the arbitration the time and attention required. He may also respond to enquiries from those approaching him, provided that such enquiries are designed to determine his suitability and availability for the appointment and provided that the merits of the case are not discussed. In the event that a prospective sole arbitrator or presiding arbitrator is approached by one party alone, or by one arbitrator chosen unilaterally by a party (a "party-nominated" arbitrator), he should ascertain that the other party or parties, or the other arbitrator, has consented to the manner in which he has been approached. In such circumstances he should, in writing or orally, inform the other party or parties, or the other arbitrator, of the substance of the initial conversation.

2014 IBA GUIDELINES ON CONFLICTS OF INTEREST IN INTERNATIONAL ARBITRATION
Green List

[excerpted in Documentary Supplement at pp. 377-78]

[The IBA Guidelines include a "Green List" of circumstances "where no appearance and no actual conflict of interest exists…."]

XL INSURANCE LTD v. TOYOTA MOTOR SALES U.S.A. INC.
Unreported judgment of 14 July 1999 (QB) (English High Ct.)

MR. JUSTICE AIKENS. This is an application by XL Insurance Ltd … for the appointment of a third arbitrator because the two arbitrators appointed by the parties in a dispute which has arisen between them are unable to agree the identity of the third arbitrator….

The applicant is a major insurer of excess liability risks. It is incorporated in Bermuda. Its business is based there. The two Respondents are in the Toyota group of companies…. XL was set up by a number of large United States corporations in 1986 to provide excess liability coverage for those corporations…. I am told that XL provides excess coverage in the present case for Toyota (Vermont) for the level of $25m to $100m. Toyota have made claims on XL in respect of Toyota's alleged liability to third parties arising out of personal injuries…. The issues in the arbitration are likely to cover at least four areas. First, there are coverage issues turning upon the proper interpretation of the policy…. The second issue is XL's asserted right to rescind the policy for misrepresentation. The third issue is whether XL by its conduct has waived or is otherwise barred from asserting a right to rescind. The fourth issue concerns delay in responding to notices given by Toyota concerning claims….

[D]isputes under the policy are to be determined in London under the provision of the Arbitration Act 1950 or its successors. The board is to be composed of three arbitrators to be selected in respect of each dispute that arises…. Each party is entitled to nominate its own arbitrator. Then, within a specified period, those two arbitrators that have been nominated by the parties are themselves to nominate a third arbitrator. The clause then goes on to provide that if the two arbitrators fail to agree on a third arbitrator then the parties may apply to a judge of the High Court of England…. Condition V(q) … provides that the substantive law that governs the policy is "the internal laws of the State of New York." However, there are certain restrictions that are imposed under the terms of the clause, which if they are operative means that all the laws of New York which otherwise might apply would not do so with regard to this policy....

On 4 September 1998 Toyota made its demand for arbitration to XL. Toyota stated that it had selected Robert Saylor as its party nominated arbitrator. He is a well-known United States lawyer. His background is one of acting for claimants in respect of insurance claims. On 5 October XL wrote to Toyota to nominate Mr. Stewart Boyd QC as their party nominated arbitrator. Mr. Boyd is ... a very well-known English Queen's Counsel who has a particular experience in insurance generally and also in arbitration. It was then for the two arbitrators to agree on a third. Most unfortunately, as things have turned out, the U.S. attorneys acting for XL suggested in a letter of 8 October 1998 that any arbitrator appointed by the two arbitrators should be subject to the parties' approval. In effect, although the suggestion was never formally adopted by both sides, that is precisely what has happened. The only problem is that none of the suggested names has met with both parties' approval.

What has happened is that each side has, whether consciously or not, seen some disadvantage in names put forward by the other side. Furthermore, each side has sought to ensure that the third arbitrator has qualities which it thinks are particularly important in the context of this arbitration. Not surprisingly, each side has different views on what it regards as the most important characteristics. Because it has proved impossible (inevitably) for the parties to find one Colossus who bestrides all the qualities that each wants, this application to the court became inevitable.

The qualities that the party have identified and, indeed, identified before me in argument are as follows. Toyota said that it was important, if not paramount, for the third arbitrator to have some knowledge of United States tort law and practice. Furthermore, in Toyota's view, the third arbitrator should have experience and knowledge of New York and other of U.S. insurance law. On XL's side it was said that the third arbitrator should be preferably someone who comes from or has particular experience of English arbitration in practice, and also English arbitration law. In XL's view the third arbitrator should also have particular experience in relation to international arbitration practice as conducted in London.

In the course of the correspondence between Mr. Saylor and Mr. Boyd and the parties various names were canvassed. I should identify them for present purposes. First, Judge Renfrew was suggested by Mr. Boyd. He is a former U.S. District Judge. He has also, in the course of his distinguished career, acted as a United States attorney in practice, and has been a Vice President for Legal Affairs for the Standard Oil Company of California, subsequently renamed Chevron.... He was accepted by Mr. Saylor but was rejected when his name was put to Hanson & Peters, attorneys acting for XL. In particular, they thought it objectionable that he had for ten years served as a director general, counsel and vice president of Chevron Corporation.

Next Judge Estey was suggested by XL. He was rejected by Toyota. He is a former justice of the Supreme Court of Canada.... [I]t was thought unlikely he would have sufficient knowledge of the U.S. tort claims. The third name that has come to the fore is that of Lord Mustill. His name was suggested by XL. It was rejected by Toyota on the grounds that he too would be unlikely to have sufficient knowledge of U.S. tort law and practice or New York, or other U.S. insurance law and practice....

Two other U.S. candidates were suggested by Toyota. First, Mr. Fisk who is a partner in the distinguished law firm of Davis, Polk & Wardell. Secondly, Professor Young who is a distinguished U.S. academic lawyer. The last name that has been put forward is that of Mr.

Yves Fortier QC.... He is a distinguished Canadian lawyer and diplomat. He is the current chairman of the [LCIA]. XL have objected to him on the personal ground that he is currently the chair of another arbitral tribunal which is dealing with a claim by Ford Motors against XL. That case deals with many issues which are said to be very similar to those in the present dispute. XL are concerned that it might be difficult in practice for him to keep these matters entirely distinct if he had to deal with the two cases....

Under §18 of the 1996 Act the court has a discretion in who it should appoint when exercising the power that it has under that section. This discretion is not fettered by §18 of the Act. It is also not fettered by the terms of the clause in the policy with which I am concerned.... In my view, the relevant factors in the present case are these. First, the parties have chosen London for the seat of the arbitration. They have done so, so it appears to me, because it is a neutral and independent venue.

Secondly, because the parties have chosen London as the arbitration venue, English law will be the curial law of that arbitration. Again, it seems to me that they have chosen that law because it will be neutral and independent. They have I think deliberately chosen the curial law to be different and independent from the substantive law of the contract, i.e., New York law.

The third factor is that the parties have chosen New York law as the substantive law of the contract, but have done so with modifications.... Those are specific terms and I am satisfied that the parties chose those in conjunction with a London arbitration venue in order to ensure that they could be considered dispassionately and independently by the tribunal that is appointed.

The fourth factor which appears to me to be relevant is that the parties in the policy deliberately left it to the two arbitrators to agree on the identity of the third. The wording of the clause makes it clear to my mind that the parties themselves were to have no part in the choice of the third arbitrator. In my view it is important, unless there is some overriding question of conflict of interest, that the parties do not have any say in the appointment of the third arbitrator. Moreover, I think it is important that the views of the parties should not in fact or have the appearance of interfering with the two arbitrators' choice. Otherwise, in my view, it subverts the whole purpose of the clause.

Even more importantly, I think if the parties do appear to have some influence on the choice of the third party it detracts from the position of the two arbitrators. Once they are appointed as arbitrators they are entirely independent of the parties. To my mind they must be seen to be independent and must remain independent. Therefore, in my view, one or other or both parties' view as to who is thought to be a proper third arbitrator are irrelevant and must be seen to be irrelevant.

Having considered these factors it seems to me that the overriding consideration for the court in exercising its discretion is to choose the best person for the job bearing in mind these factors. The qualities needed in the present case, as perhaps in every case, are threefold. First, the third arbitrator, who will inevitably be chairman, must be able to deal properly with the substantive issues that arise in the arbitration. Secondly, he must be able as chainman to deal with any procedural issues that arise in the course of the reference as best he can. In this context one has to bear in mind that the arbitration is in London and will be governed by English law as the curial law. Thirdly, the third arbitrator as chairman must command the full respect and confidence of both sides. I think that none of these three qualities is more important than the other two. They all bear equal weight....

How then should I apply those factors and the overriding consideration I have referred to in this case? To my mind the leading candidates as things now stand must be Lord Mustill and Judge Renfrew. I understand both are willing to be appointed as third arbitrator. To my mind both have all the qualities that I have identified. I think it is, in the circumstances, most unfortunate that this matter has had to come to court at all for the present application to be determined. Having considered the matter very carefully I think that I should order that Lord Mustill should be appointed as the third arbitrator.... First, XL have objected to Judge Renfrew. I have already referred to the grounds upon which they have objected to him. They are not, in my view, good grounds, but I do not think that it is proper that in a large and serious arbitration such as this the matter should go forward with one party feeling from the outset unhappy about the identity of the chairman of the tribunal. There is no similar personal objection to Lord Mustill on Toyota's part.

The second reason why I have decided that Lord Mustill should be appointed is that when one examines the reasons why Toyota initially wanted a US lawyer as the third arbitrator they do not stand close examination. Once it was conceded by them that they were prepared to countenance a non-US lawyer, such as Mr. Fortier, being appointed, he does not meet their supposed requirements. He has no close experience of U.S. tort law. As [XL's counsel] said in argument, "It is one thing to have first hand experience. It is another thing to have it, as English lawyers frequently do in commercial matters, at second hands." Mr. Fortier does not have first hand experience as a US trial lawyer, and if Toyota were prepared to countenance him, then it suggests that they did not after all regard this as a paramount consideration. Secondly, Mr. Fortier does not have an intimate first hand knowledge of U.S. or New York insurance law. This also suggests that ultimately Toyota did not regard this as of paramount importance.

This means, to my mind, that ultimately Toyota have to accept that although having experience of US tort law and United States insurance law and New York insurance law may be valuable qualities, they are not paramount. Ultimately it is the ability to deal with all the issues of substance and to act as an effective chairman with the respect of the parties that matters. In my view Lord Mustill is very well qualified to do the job that he will have to do. I should add as a postscript that the U.S. lawyers of XL should not regard my decision as a victory for their view. Lord Mustill is absolutely independent and he will, I am sure, have no a priori views in favour of either the merits of the case or any particular aspect of procedure. He is, in my judgment, simply the right man for the job in this case.

NOTES

1. *Importance of selection of arbitrator.* Consider the excerpt from Glossner. It is frequently said that the most important decision that a party makes in an arbitration is the selection of an arbitrator. Why is that so? Consider the different individuals from your law school, your personal background and from your professional acquaintances who might serve as an arbitrator. What strengths and weaknesses does each have? How big a difference would the choice of one or the other make? *See* Bishop & Reed, *Practical Guidelines for Interviewing, Selecting and Challenging Party-Appointed Arbitrators in International Commercial Arbitration*, 14 Arb. Int'l 395 (1998); D. Caron & L. Caplan, *The UNCITRAL Arbitration Rules: A Commentary* 144-45 (2d ed. 2013); Seppälä, *Obtaining the Right International Arbitral Tribunal: A Practitioner's View*,

22(10) Mealey's Int'l Arb. Rep. 1 (2007); Webster, *Selection of Arbitrators in A Nutshell*, 19 J. Int'l Arb. 261 (2002).

Consider the arbitration agreement in *Jivraj*. How important was the identity of the arbitrators to the parties? Why? Why do you think Sir Anthony Evans was appointed?

2. *Selection of arbitrators under leading institutional arbitration rules.* Recall that most national arbitration regimes recognize the parties' autonomy to agree to procedures regarding constitution of the arbitral tribunal. *See supra* pp. 683-85. That autonomy extends to agreeing upon institutional rules providing mechanisms for selecting the arbitrators. Not surprisingly, different institutional rules provide for different mechanisms for selection of the arbitrators.

Consider the excerpt from the NAI Rules. Consider also Articles 7-10 of the UNCITRAL Rules and Articles 11-13 of the ICC Rules, excerpted at pp. 165-66 & 186-88 of the Documentary Supplement. How do these mechanisms for selecting arbitrators differ and how are they similar? Consider the list procedure in the NAI, ICDR and UNCITRAL Rules. What are the advantages and disadvantages of such an approach? Role-play the selection of arbitrators using a list procedure. Consider again the Swiss Federal Tribunal's *Judgment of 21 November 2003, supra* p. 342-45. Note the method that was provided for under the Zurich Chamber of Commerce Arbitration Rules for selecting the arbitrators. What are the advantages and disadvantages of such an approach?

3. *Selection of arbitrator in parties' arbitration agreement.* It is possible to name a specific individual as an arbitrator in an arbitration agreement made before any dispute has arisen between the parties (*e.g.,* "The arbitrator shall be Ms. Natascha Born."). Note the approving reference to such an approach in §5 of the FAA.

National courts have generally enforced agreements making pre-dispute selections of arbitrators (subject, of course, to otherwise applicable challenges to the validity of the agreement and the independence of the arbitrator). *See, e.g., Aviall, Inc. v. Ryder Sys., Inc.,* 913 F.Supp. 826, 833 (S.D.N.Y. 1996) ("when parties have validly contracted to have a particular arbitrator resolve their disputes, federal courts are loath to alter that selection"); *Judgment of 26 May 1994,* XXIII Y.B. Comm. Arb. 754, 761 (1998) (Affoltern am Albis Bezirksgericht) ("it is not forbidden to appoint the arbitrator(s) already in the arbitration clause. This is, however, a risky practice"). What risks do parties run when naming a specific individual as arbitrator in their pre-dispute arbitration agreement? What advantages and disadvantages does such an approach have?

4. *Selection of arbitrators in post-dispute negotiations between parties.* After a dispute has arisen, parties may find it difficult to agree on much, if anything. Nonetheless, parties to international disputes are not infrequently able to reach post-dispute agreement on a sole or presiding arbitrator. This can be done either in direct discussions between the parties (or their counsel) or through the party-nominated arbitrators in three-person arbitral tribunals. *See infra* pp. 700-01. Why might hostile adversaries be able to agree upon a sole or presiding arbitrator? What is the alternative? Might it be worse? Why?

In practice, parties fairly frequently agree upon the identities of "their" arbitrator(s). In roughly 21% of ICC cases in 2013 involving sole arbitrators, the arbitrator was chosen by agreement of the parties themselves. ICC, *2013 Statistical Report,*

25(1) ICC ICArb. Bull. 5, 6 (2014). In contrast, in cases involving three arbitrators, the parties or the co-arbitrators were able to agree upon the presiding arbitrator in 60% of ICC cases in 2013. *Ibid.* What explains the significant difference in the ability of parties to agree upon a presiding arbitrator (in a three-person tribunal) and upon a sole arbitrator? Consider the *XL Insurance* decision and its allocation of authority for selecting the presiding arbitrator. Is it likely that the arbitrators, rather than the parties themselves, would be able to agree more readily upon a presiding arbitrator? Why? *See also infra* pp. 696-98.

5. *Importance of national law to selection of arbitrators.* Parties to international arbitrations must take potentially-applicable national law requirements (discussed below at pp. 709-58) into account in making their selections of arbitrators. Consider the following hypothetical:

> Company A is headquartered in State 1. Company B is headquartered in State 2. Companies A and B enter into a contract with an arbitration clause providing for arbitration in State 3, with the parties' underlying contract being subject to the substantive laws of State 4. State 1 has an arbitration statute identical to §5 of the FAA, but also providing (like the Saudi and Ecuadorean legislation (now repealed), or the Uzbek legislation, *infra* pp. 711): "All arbitrators shall be nationals of State 1." State 2 has an arbitration law providing that recognition shall be denied an arbitral award if the arbitrator was not "independent." States 3 and 4 have arbitration statutes identical to the UNCITRAL Model Law. The language of the arbitration is not specified.

You represent Company B, which is preparing to commence an arbitration (not under any institutional rules) against Company A. Consider the following: (a) how many arbitrators will there be, assuming nothing in the parties' agreement resolves the issues; (b) what requirements apply to the arbitrators in terms of nationality and independence/impartiality; and (c) what relevance, if any, does the likely place of enforcement of an award have? What if State 3 had the same arbitration law as State 1 or State 2?

6. *Party's selection of party-nominated arbitrator.* Consider Article 11(3) of the UNCITRAL Model Law. How does it provide for selection of co-arbitrators in a three-person tribunal? Even apart from Article 11(3), it is common for international arbitration agreements, and most institutional rules, to expressly permit each party (in two-party disputes) to nominate a co-arbitrator, where three arbitrators are called for. All developed arbitration legislation gives effect to such agreements, consistent with general principles of party autonomy in the field. *See, e.g.*, UNCITRAL Model Law, Arts. 11(2), 11(3)(a); SLPIL, Art. 179(1).

   (a) *Rationale for party-nominated co-arbitrators.* What is the rationale for permitting one party unilaterally to designate an arbitrator in arbitrations involving three (or five) person tribunals? Is this not a fairly extraordinary power—to select one of the persons who will be empowered to make a binding decision regarding the parties' dispute? Consider:

   > "It is critical to appreciate why party-nominated co-arbitrators have been a distinguishing feature of international arbitration for centuries, and why party-nominated co-arbitrators continue to be provided for in institutional rules from every legal system and culture. Considered in their proper international context, par-

ty-nominated co-arbitrators are an essential means of ensuring the expert, efficient and internationally-neutral arbitral procedure which is a central object of the parties' agreement to arbitrate.

Party nomination of co-arbitrators seeks to guarantee that the tribunal in an international dispute will include individuals who speak each party's native tongue, understand the cultural, economic and political environment in which that party acted, appreciate the procedural expectations (and misconceptions) that the party may have, and otherwise are likely to seek to understand and fully appreciate the nuances of that party's case. Put concretely, when a Northern European company arbitrates against a Middle Eastern counterpart, it is entirely appropriate—and indeed essential to a truly neutral international dispute resolution procedure—that each party be able to select a member of the tribunal reflecting its national, legal, cultural and linguistic background and capable of fully appreciating its perspective on the dispute....

Experience teaches that the most efficient and effective way of selecting an appropriate tribunal is for the parties—who have the greatest incentive and information to do their jobs well—to play a leading role in the process. Although not perfect, the most efficient and equitable way of accomplishing this, in a three-person tribunal, is the simple, time-tested and balanced approach of each of the parties unilaterally selecting one arbitrator and then agreement being sought on a presiding arbitrator. In effect, party nomination of co-arbitrators is a means of quality control, aimed in part at ensuring that the members of the tribunal have the requisite experience and ability." G. Born, *International Commercial Arbitration* 1809-10 (2d ed. 2014).

Is that persuasive? What are the costs of party-nominated co-arbitrators? What alternatives might exist?

Consider the approaches to nominating the members of the arbitral tribunal in the Treaty of Washington and Abyei Arbitration Agreement, excerpted at pp. 65 & 80-82 of the Documentary Supplement. Why is it that each of the parties in these disputes wanted the ability to nominate one (or two) of the members of the arbitral tribunal?

(b) *Considerations affecting choice of co-arbitrator.* Consider again the hypothetical in Note 5 above. As counsel to Company B, what considerations would influence your selection of a party-arbitrator? Important considerations can include a party's confidence in the personal competence, time availability, and integrity of an individual, as well as the individual's arbitration experience and knowledge of a particular industry or type of contract. Putting these points aside, what type of individual should Company B consider? Should the individual be qualified to practice law in State 3? Should the individual be qualified to practice law in State 4? What nationality will the presiding arbitrator have? How does that affect Company B's choice of a co-arbitrator? *See* 2010 UNCITRAL Rules, Art. 6(7); 2012 ICC Rules, Arts. 13(1), (3), (5); 2014 LCIA Rules, Arts. 6, 7, excerpted at pp. 165, 187-88 and 258 of the Documentary Supplement.

More generally, what is it that a party wants from a co-arbitrator? Is it a neutral, objective and dispassionate judge? Is it a partisan advocate? Something else? Consider: "When I am representing a client in an arbitration, what I am really looking for in a party-nominated arbitrator is someone with the maximum predisposition towards my client, but with the minimum appearance of bias." Hunter,

Ethics of the International Arbitrator, 53 Arb. 219, 223 (1987). Why is it important to have a "minimum appearance of bias"? Imagine yourself as a presiding arbitrator: how would you be influenced by the views, respectively, of an objective and neutral co-arbitrator and a partisan and predisposed co-arbitrator? *Compare* Lowenfeld, *The Party-Appointed Arbitrator in International Controversies: Some Reflections*, 30 Tex. Int'l L. J. 59 (1995); *infra* pp. 749-55.

(c) *Role of arbitrator's nationalities.* The role of nationality is important in the selection of international arbitrators. Note that most leading arbitral institutions will not select as presiding arbitrator a person with the nationality of one of the parties. Compare in this regard Article 6(7) of the 2010 UNCITRAL Rules and Article 13(5) of the 2012 ICC Rules. *See also infra* p. 712. (Note also that, in practice, some arbitral institutions are reluctant to select as presiding arbitrator a person with the nationality of one of the co-arbitrators.) Why is it generally inappropriate to select a presiding arbitrator with the same nationality as one of the parties? Is it not frequently the case in international litigations that the presiding judge (and appellate judges) will be of the nationality of one, but not the other, of the parties? Why is arbitration different? How does the likely nationality of the presiding arbitrator affect your choice of a co-arbitrator selected by one of the parties?

What does "nationality" mean? Are Germans and French nationals of the European Union? Are Austrians the same nationality as Bavarians? Is a U.S. citizen of Mexican descent and cultural background the same nationality as a Mexican? As a Maine resident of Irish or African descent?

(d) *Arbitrator's competence in applicable substantive law.* Note that the applicable substantive law in the above hypothetical is that of State 4. How would that affect Company B's choice of an arbitrator?

(e) *Personal characteristics.* As much as anything else, the personal characteristics of arbitrators play a vital role in selection. Recall the examples, set out above, of various types of disputes that may be arbitrated. *See supra* p. 684. Consider again selecting co-arbitrators (and a presiding arbitrator) from your law school colleagues and instructors. Who would you most want? Why? Who would you least want? Why? Does it depend on your case—how strong, or complex, it is?

(f) *Likely identity of presiding arbitrator.* The suitability of a co-arbitrator in a particular matter will often depend in part on the identity of the presiding arbitrator. However, the presiding arbitrator will virtually never be chosen until *after* selection of the co-arbitrators. Nonetheless, speculation about the likely identity, nationality and other characteristics of a future presiding arbitrator will inevitably influence choice of a co-arbitrator. For example, in the exercise referred to in the previous subparagraph, how would your thinking be influenced if you thought that the presiding arbitrator would be (i) your professor; (ii) your law school dean; (iii) me; or (iv) another.

(g) *Timing considerations.* Note the timetables pursuant to which co-arbitrators must be selected under various institutional rules. What advantages does a respondent have? Are there any ways that a claimant might avoid this?

7. *Institutional confirmation of party-nominated arbitrators.* Under some institutional rules, parties may only "nominate" a co-arbitrator, who must then be confirmed and "appointed" by the relevant institution. What is the reason for this? Consider how

different institutional rules deal with this topic. In particular, compare Article 9(1) of the UNCITRAL Rules with Articles 12 and 13 of the ICC Rules. Which is preferable? Why? What might be grounds for an arbitral institution refusing to confirm a party's nomination of an arbitrator?

8. *Consequences of party failing to nominate arbitrator under institutional rules.* Suppose a party intends to nominate a co-arbitrator, either directly by the arbitration agreement or indirectly by institutional rules which it incorporates. Suppose further that the party fails to make the nomination. What are the consequences of this failure?

   Consider the treatment of defaults in nominating an arbitrator in the ICC and UNCITRAL Rules. Suppose one party nominates an arbitrator and the other does not. Is it procedurally fair to proceed with an arbitral process where one party selects one of the arbitrators, but the other party selects none of the arbitrators? What alternatives exist? Suppose the arbitral process were stayed pending both parties' nominations; wouldn't most respondents be delighted? Suppose all three arbitrators were chosen by the appointing authority.

   Some arbitration agreements provide that, if one party fails to nominate an arbitrator, the other party may make the nomination itself—thus, choosing the two co-arbitrators, who would then in turn ordinarily select the presiding arbitrator. Is this approach fair? What if all three arbitrators are required to be "independent"? What if a party misses the time deadline for making an appointment by a few days? Recall the results of late nomination in *Certain Underwriters*.

9. *Consequences of party's failure to nominate arbitrator under national law.* If a party fails to nominate an arbitrator, and if the agreement provides no default rule in these circumstances (in contrast to the agreement in *Certain Underwriters*), applicable national law can impose severe consequences. These can include forfeiture of the right to make a nomination.

   (a) *Consequences of party's failure to nominate arbitrator under FAA.* U.S. courts have generally been lenient in excusing delays in the appointment of an arbitrator, at least where no bad faith delay or other improper motive existed. Rather than compelling a party to proceed to arbitration before arbitrators selected by its adversary, U.S. courts have granted the tardy party additional time to appoint an arbitrator and ordered arbitration before the resulting panel. *See Ancon Ins. Co. v. GE Reins. Corp.*, 480 F.Supp.2d 1278 (D. Kan. 2007) (court refused to enforce clause in arbitration agreement, permitting party to select counter-party's co-arbitrator, because it considered that time was not of the essence, and that five day delay of one party in appointment did not result from bad faith); *New England Reins. Corp. v. Tenn. Ins. Co.*, 780 F.Supp. 73 (D. Mass. 1991) (party's eight-day delay in appointing arbitrator held not to waive right to appoint); *Compania Portorafti Commerciale v. Kaiser Int'l*, 616 F.Supp. 236, 238 (S.D.N.Y. 1985) ("so minor a delay, uncomplicated by indications of bad faith, does not in equity deprive a party to an arbitration clause of its contracted for right to appoint an arbitrator of its choosing ... unless the contract makes time of the essence").

   Nonetheless, as *Certain Underwriters* suggests, some U.S. courts have interpreted arbitration agreements strictly, holding that the failure to comply with time limits for nominating an arbitrator results in loss of the right to make a nomination. *Universal Reins. Corp. v. Allstate Ins. Co.*, 16 F.3d 125, 129 (7th Cir. 1994) (party's failure to nominate arbitrator within 30-day period waived its right to do so and, under arbitration agreement, entitled other party to make nomination; "the agreement is crystal clear, specifying a particular course for the appointment of a second arbitrator when one of the parties fails to make its selection within thirty days").

   (b) *Consequences of party's failure to nominate arbitrator under English Arbitration Act.* Consider §17 of the English Arbitration Act, 1996, excerpted at pp. 115-16 of the Documentary Supplement, which provides that if a party fails to nominate a co-arbitrator within the agreed time limits, then (absent contrary agreement) its counter-party may elect to treat its nominated co-arbitrator as a sole arbitrator. Is this result appropriate? What are the advantages and disadvantages of the English rule?

   Should an award, made by a sole arbitrator appointed unilaterally by one party, be recognizable in other jurisdictions? Consider Article V(1)(d) of the New York Convention. *See infra* pp. 1218-41.

10. *Selection of presiding arbitrator.* After selection of the co-arbitrators, in a three-person tribunal, the presiding arbitrator must be chosen. Suppose an arbitration clause provides simply for a three-person tribunal, without any further details. Assuming no further agreements between the parties, how would appointment of the arbitrators proceed under the ICC Rules? How would appointment proceed under the UNCITRAL Rules? If you were drafting an arbitration agreement, which approach would you prefer?

11. *Procedure for selecting presiding arbitrator.* There are numerous procedures for attempting to reach agreement on a presiding arbitrator. Additionally, the appointing authority (if one exists) can play various different roles in the discussions. For example, any of the following alternatives can be used:

   (a) the two co-arbitrators agree in direct discussions, without the parties being present, on a presiding arbitrator and inform the parties;

   (b) the two co-arbitrators discuss the choice of a presiding arbitrator directly, without the parties being present, but each of the co-arbitrators can "consult" with his or her nominating party, with agreement only being reached after the parties approve the selection;

   (c) the same as (b), except the parties may express a preference, but not veto candidates;

   (d) the parties' representatives discuss the choice of a presiding arbitrator directly, without involvement of the co-arbitrators;

   (e) the co-arbitrators agree, in discussions not involving either party, on a list of five potential presiding arbitrators, with each party being entitled to strike two names from the list, leaving the remaining name as the presiding arbitrator;

   (f) the parties themselves directly exchange lists of persons whom they would accept, with any common name being deemed accepted.

   What are the advantages and disadvantages of these various mechanisms? Suppose you were a co-arbitrator nominated by a party (*e.g.*, Company B in the hypothetical in Note 5 above). How would you go about fulfilling your task of choosing a presiding arbitrator? What information would you want and with whom would you like to communicate? Why?

Compare the 2010 UNCITRAL Rules, which provide for a "list-procedure" in Article 8 in which the appointing authority sends both parties an identical list of at least three names; each party deletes names it finds unacceptable and numbers the remaining names in order of preference. Based on this, the appointing authority selects the prospective arbitrator with the greatest support. Use this procedure in connection with the hypothetical in Note 5.

12. *Limitations on parties' involvement in selecting presiding arbitrator.* Assuming that the co-arbitrators and/or parties are granted some role in selecting the presiding arbitrator, what limits are there to how the co-arbitrators and parties conduct themselves during the selection process? Consider *XL Insurance.* What does the English court hold with regard to the co-arbitrator's right to discuss selection of the presiding arbitrator with his or her nominating party? Are such discussions absolutely forbidden? Are there limits on the nature of such discussions?

   Is the court's conclusion in *XL Insurance*, that parties may play only a limited role in selection of the presiding arbitrator, persuasive? What was the basis for the court's conclusion—the parties' arbitration agreement or the English Arbitration Act? What if the parties' arbitration agreement provides expressly that the parties themselves may agree upon the identity of the presiding arbitrator? What if the parties agree that the co-arbitrators may (or must) consult with their respective nominating parties? Under *XL Insurance*'s analysis, is this permitted by the English Arbitration Act? Is there any indication that this is what the parties' arbitration agreement in *XL Insurance* required? Did the parties' conduct in *XL Insurance*, on both sides, indicate that the parties considered that they were to be involved in the selection of a presiding arbitrator? How should silence by the parties regarding their involvement in the co-arbitrators' selection of a presiding arbitrator be interpreted? Should silence be interpreted as permitting or excluding (as in *XL Insurance*) party involvement in selecting the presiding arbitrator?

   Is it a wise policy to exclude the parties from the co-arbitrators' decision-making regarding selection of a presiding arbitrator? What benefits and costs does participation by the parties (or their counsel) provide? At the outset of the arbitration, do the co-arbitrators know the case and issues as well as the parties (and their counsel)? Do the co-arbitrators have the same incentives as the parties (and their counsel) in selecting the presiding arbitrator?

   Suppose that two co-arbitrators agree upon a prospective presiding arbitrator. Should each of them inform the party that nominated him? Must they? Can they? What purposes would be served by such disclosure? Should such information be given before or after the two co-arbitrators have agreed upon the identity of the presiding arbitrator? What if a party objects to a prospective presiding arbitrator? What if a party objects repeatedly and uniformly to every proposal by the co-arbitrators? Why might a party do so?

   Consider the approach to selection of a presiding arbitrator in Canon III(B)(2) of the AAA/ABA Code of Ethics. See also the IBA Guidelines on Conflicts of Interest. How does this compare to the approach in *XL Insurance*? Which approach is preferable?

13. *Role of appointing authority in selecting presiding or sole arbitrator.* Suppose parties (or co-arbitrators) are unable to agree on selection of a sole arbitrator (or presiding

arbitrator). Who then makes the selection? Consider who selects the sole or presiding arbitrator, in the absence of agreement by the parties, under Article 11 of the Model Law. The role of national courts in selecting arbitrators is discussed above at pp. 702-09.

Consider who selects the sole or presiding arbitrator under the UNCITRAL Rules. Compare the selection of the sole or presiding arbitrator under the ICC Rules. What advantages or disadvantages are there to each approach?

14. *Appointing authority in inter-state arbitrations.* Consider the selection of the presiding arbitrator in Article I of the Treaty of Washington, excerpted at p. 65 of the Documentary Supplement. Why do you think that the parties adopted this approach?

Consider Articles 44 and 45 of the 1907 Hague Convention. If the parties (and co-arbitrators) are unable to agree upon a presiding arbitrator, how will he or she be chosen? Why isn't the International Bureau selected as the appointing authority? What advantages does Article 45's mechanism provide? What disadvantages? If you represented a respondent, which mechanism would you prefer?

Compare Articles 8-10 of the PCA Rules, excerpted at pp. 282-83 of the Documentary Supplement. What is the mechanism for selecting arbitrators if the parties are unable to agree upon the composition of a tribunal? How does this compare with the Hague Convention?

Compare the provision for inter-state arbitration in Article 9 of the U.K./Bosnia-Herzegovina BIT, excerpted at pp. 76-77 of the Documentary Supplement. How are the arbitrators selected there? How does that provision compare to the way in which arbitrators are selected in a BIT arbitration between a state (*e.g.*, the United Kingdom) and an investor (*e.g.*, a Bosnian national)? Why is there a difference?

B. SELECTION OF ARBITRATORS BY NATIONAL COURTS IN INTERNATIONAL ARBITRATION

Most developed arbitration statutes permit appointment of arbitrators by a national court in international arbitrations, but only in narrow circumstances.[6] In general, judicial appointment of arbitrators is limited to cases where the parties have not agreed upon means for selecting the tribunal or where their agreed means have failed to function. The availability of judicial appointment of arbitrators as a default mechanism ensures that arbitral proceedings can be pursued, even in the face of what would otherwise be grave difficulties in constituting the tribunal. At the same time, unless carefully exercised, the availability of judicial appointment authority creates risks of disregarding the parties' procedural agreement(s) and of premature and/or conflicting actions by one or more national courts.

JUDGMENT OF 18 JANUARY 1991
1996 Rev. arb. 503 (Paris Tribunal de grande instance)

In order to settle a dispute between Mannesmann Demag AG ("MII"), Mannesmann Anlagenbau Dusseldorf ("MAB") and Chérifienne des Pétroles ("SCP"), the latter [filed a

---

6. *See* G. Born, *International Commercial Arbitration* 1712 (2d ed. 2014).

Request for Arbitration with] the ICC and appointed Professor F as arbitrator; ... the defendants [MII and MAB] appointed C. as arbitrator; ... on recommendation of the Greek National Committee ..., the [ICC] International Court of Arbitration appointed M.B., a Greek national, as third arbitrator and chairman of the arbitral tribunal; this decision was announced to the parties on 19 October [1990] and was confirmed by letter on 31 October 1990;

Considering the conditions of M.B's appointment by the ICC to be wrong and invalid, ... SCP [initiate suit against] the respondents and the ICC before the President of the Paris Tribunal de Grande Instance [under] Articles 1493(2), 1495 and 1455 of the [1981] NCCP; [SCP] argues that, from the moment the arbitral proceedings were carried out, it informed the Court orally that it was opposed to the appointment of a European national as the third arbitrator because both defendants have their head office in Europe; [SCP] considers that, by appointing a Greek national residing in the EU as [presiding arbitrator], the [ICC] Court breached its own rules and violated one of the parties' express intent; consequently [SCP] requests us "to enjoin the ICC to appoint a non-European national as President in order to complete the arbitral tribunal, and to do so within a month"; ... SCP claims that the President of the Paris Tribunal de Grande Instance has jurisdiction over, on the one hand, an international arbitration sitting in Paris and for which the provisions of Articles 1493 and 1506 of the NCCP must apply auxiliary to the ICC Rules, and on the other hand, over a difficulty affecting the constitution of the arbitral tribunal once the irregularity of this constitution is alleged; [SCP] firstly argues that the [ICC] Court breached its own rules, particularly Article 2(6)(3) which stipulates that "the sole arbitrator or the President of the arbitral tribunal shall be chosen from a different state than the ones from which the parties originate ...," unless the circumstances "justify it and the parties are not opposed to it"; [SCP] declares that a Greek President belongs to the same political, judicial and economic group as both defendants to the arbitration, which "usefully makes both European defendants benefit from a tribunal composed of two European arbitrators out three"; ... [SCP argues:] "the reality of European citizenship" which is unquestionable within the European community and is established in particular by belonging to the same legal order, is assimilated to a nationality in the sense of Article 2(6)(3) of the ICC Rules; considering M.B.'s personality, who has exercised very important functions at the time of Greece's accession to the European Union, SCP considers that "[the third arbitrator's] appointment" constitutes an alteration of the rules and the spirit of international commercial arbitration;

Secondly, [SCP argues] that in deciding like it did, the [ICC] Court deliberately breached the instruction that it received from [SCP], and argues that all factual circumstances demonstrate that the Court was fully aware of it; it also refers to Article 1455 of the NCCP which stipulates that the arbitrator appointed by a settled center of arbitration must be accepted by all the parties; finally, SCP considers that, in order to ensure full transparency of the decision, the [ICC] Court should have exercised the current practice of national jurisdictions and centers of arbitration, which consists in referring to the parties for advice on the personalities likely to be chosen, so as to reach full consensus and mutual trust;

[T]he defendants and the ICC objected to the competence of the national jurisdiction referred to by arguing that since the arbitral tribunal was definitely constituted, the President of the Paris Tribunal de Grande Instance does not, in the present case, have the power to interfere in the dispute as it falls under the exclusive interpretation of the arbitrators; they observe that Article 1493 of the NCCP applies "except conflicting clause" agreed by the parties; since [the parties] agreed to the ICC Rules, which expressly stipulate: "the Court decides 'with no recourse on appointment, confirmation, removal or 'substitution of an arbitrator,'" the Paris Tribunal de Grande Instance has no jurisdiction to decide; finally, the defendants argue that the present interim hearing constitutes in reality a claim to remove the arbitrator, the assessment of which falls only within the [ICC] Court's jurisdiction; on a subsidiary basis, the defendants consider the claimant's allegations to be ill-founded;

[The Tribunal de Grande Instance held:] Whereas the seat of the present international arbitration is Paris, if constitution of the arbitral tribunal becomes difficult, the President of the Paris Tribunal de Grande Instance has jurisdiction to take the appropriate measures;

That this provision does not limit the national judge's intervention to the constitution of the arbitral tribunal *ab initio* but also empowers him, with respect to the parties' common intent, to resolve a difficulty relating to a subsequent event affecting the constitution of the arbitral tribunal which would prevent [the judge] from exercising his decision power; That however, once the arbitral tribunal is constituted, the President of the Tribunal de Grande Instance's mission to assist and technically cooperate to arbitration [does not include the power] to interfere with the arbitrators' jurisdictional prerogatives which fall within their own and autonomous legitimacy, nor to substitute for the settled center of arbitration, except recognized or established deficiency of the latter, to organize and carry out the arbitral proceedings in compliance with the parties' agreement;

Whereas in the present case, the arbitral tribunal was constituted following the [ICC] Court's decision dated 10 October 1990, which was notified to the parties on 19 and 31 October 1990; and that throughout its objection relating to the appointment of M.B., SCP criticizes the validity of this appointment which necessarily affects the validity of the arbitral tribunal's nomination and consequently its decision-making power;

That finally, the provisions of Article 1455 of the NCCP, auxiliary to the parties' intent, are not applicable in the present matter since the ICC Rules, agreed to as a primary source to resolve the procedure, stipulate that there is no possible recourse against the Court's decision on appointment of arbitrators; Consequently, the present dispute only falls within the arbitrators' competence, who may possibly decide on the validity of their nomination, provided [subsequent] recourse against their award; ... In view of Article 1493(2) of the NCCP; [The Paris Tribunal de Grande Instance] declares itself incompetent to decide SCP's claims....

ASTRA FOOTWEAR INDUSTRY v. HARWYN INTERNATIONAL
442 F.Supp. 907 (S.D.N.Y. 1978)

[excerpted above at pp. 431-33]

PARTIAL DECISION OF 2 APRIL 1992
1993 RIW 239 (Kassel Landgericht)

[excerpted above at pp. 429-30]

GATOIL INTERNATIONAL INC. v. NATIONAL IRANIAN OIL CO.
XVII Y.B. Comm. Arb. 587 (1992) (English High Ct. 1988)

[excerpted above at pp. 425-27]

XL INSURANCE LTD V. TOYOTA MOTOR SALES U.S.A. INC.
Unreported judgment of 14 July 1999 (QB) (English High Ct.)

[excerpted above at pp. 691-94]

NOTES

1. *National courts' authority to appoint arbitrators in absence of parties' agreement.* Consider Article 11 of the UNCITRAL Model Law, excerpted at pp. 88-89 of the Documentary Supplement. In what circumstances does Article 11 permit a court to appoint an arbitrator? Compare Article 179 of the SLPIL, excerpted at p. 158 of the Documentary Supplement.

   Like other arbitration statutes, §5 and §206 of the FAA authorize a district court to "designate and appoint an arbitrator or arbitrators" or to "appoint arbitrators." Section 206, by its terms, only authorizes the appointment of arbitrators "in accordance with the provisions of the [arbitration] agreement." This arguably would not allow judicial appointment where an agreement failed to specify an appointment mechanism (which, of course, is the one time when judicial appointment is really useful). Notwithstanding this drafting, it is clear that §§5 and 206, taken together, authorize the appointment of arbitrator(s) in international arbitrations when the parties have neither selected an arbitrator nor a contractual appointment mechanism. *Jain v. de Mere*, 51 F.3d 686 (7th Cir. 1995) (§5 of FAA incorporated into FAA's second chapter and permits appointment of arbitrator when parties have not agreed on means of appointment). Consider the court's action in *Astra*.

   What is the appropriate role of national courts in appointing arbitrators in international matters? Should national courts be free to appoint arbitrators in any case where justice demands, provided the arbitration has a jurisdictional nexus to the country in question? Why not? What if the parties have agreed upon an arbitrator or upon a means of selecting an arbitrator (*e.g.*, through incorporation of institutional rules)? Should national courts still be permitted to appoint the arbitrator? *See supra* pp. 683-87.

2. *Appointment of arbitrator by national court when parties have not agreed upon appointing authority.* As described above, parties do not always agree upon an arbitrator or an appointing authority. *See supra* pp. 695-96. Alternatively, a party may refuse to comply with a contractual mechanism for selecting arbitrators, or the appointing authority agreed to by the parties may refuse or be unable to act. In those circumstances, most arbitration statutes provide for appointment of an arbitrator(s) by a national court, acting in a default role. Consider again Article 11 of the Model Law, Article 179 of the SLPIL and §§5 and 206 of the FAA.

3. *Appointment of arbitrator by national court when party refuses to appoint co-arbitrator.* In cases involving three-member tribunals, one party will occasionally fail to appoint a co-arbitrator, either through neglect or a desire to frustrate the arbitral process. As we have seen, institutional rules provide mechanisms for selecting an arbitrator notwithstanding a party's inaction. *See supra* p. 699. Similarly, national arbitration laws also provide appointment alternatives (for *ad hoc* arbitrations or when an appointing authority also refuses to act). Article 11(4)(a) of the Model Law is an example of such legislation. Similarly, §5 of the FAA specifically permits court ap-

pointment of an arbitrator where "any party [to the arbitration agreement] shall fail to avail himself of" his right to appoint. For cases where the court exercised this power, *see, e.g., Pac. Reins. Mgt Corp. v. Ohio Reins. Corp.*, 814 F.2d 1324 (9th Cir. 1987); *Neptune Maritime, Ltd v. H & J Isbrandtsen, Ltd*, 559 F.Supp. 531, 533 (S.D.N.Y. 1983); *Judgment of 7 June 2007*, 2008 SchiedsVZ 200, 201 (Kammergericht Berlin). *See also supra* pp. 699-700.

4. *Judicial appointment of arbitrator when contractual appointment mechanism breaks down*. Suppose the parties' agreed mechanism for appointing a tribunal breaks down or appears to reach impasse. Consider Article 11(4)(c) of the UNCITRAL Model Law. Compare §5 of the FAA.

    How clear must it be that the parties' agreed contractual appointment mechanism will not function, before a judicial appointment will be made? One U.S. decision reversed a lower court order under §5 of the FAA, directing that the appointing authority, specified in the institutional rules incorporated into the parties' arbitration agreement, select the entire tribunal; instead, the appellate court ordered the parties to comply with their arbitration agreement by appointing co-arbitrators who, in turn, were to attempt to select a presiding arbitrator, before court appointment would be made. *Cargill Rice, Inc. v. Empresa Nicaraguense Dealimentos Basicos*, 25 F.3d 223 (4th Cir. 1994). *Compare Pac. Reins. Mgt Corp. v. Ohio Reins. Corp.*, 814 F.2d 1324, 1327, 1329 (9th Cir. 1987) (affirming district court's appointment of "umpire," notwithstanding parties' failure to conclude contractual selection process: "the contractual selection method seemed doomed from the start" and parties had received "ample time and opportunity to comply with their own agreement") *with Judgment of 29 January 2009*, 2010 SchiedsVZ 168, 169 (Oberlandesgericht München) (no judicial appointment of arbitrator until parties' agreed appointment procedure fails) *and Philips H.K. Ltd v. Hyundai Elec. Indus. Co.*, [1993] Arb. & Disp. Resol. L.J. 174 (H.K. High Ct.) (refusing to appoint arbitrator, pursuant to ambiguous ICC arbitration clause, where ICC had not been approached to appoint arbitrator). *See also ATSA of Cal., Inc. v. Cont'l Ins. Co.*, 702 F.2d 172 (9th Cir. 1983), 754 F.2d 1394 (9th Cir. 1985). Consider the facts in *Astra* and *XL Insurance*. Would there have been any point to waiting for the parties to make further efforts to select an arbitrator? Consider the facts in *Gatoil*: note that England was not the arbitral seat.

5. *Judicial appointment of arbitrator when agreed appointing authority refuses to act*. Suppose the parties select an appointing authority, but it refuses to act (like the ICC in *Astra*). If the parties' agreed contractual appointing authority will no longer act, is the entire agreement to arbitrate invalid? Will a court appoint an arbitrator or will it conclude that the arbitration agreement is no longer valid (on grounds of frustration or otherwise)? *See supra* pp. 434-35. Consider the *Astra* court's analysis.

    Suppose that, where the parties' agreed appointing authority refuses to act, an arbitral institution makes an appointment. Is this permitted? What gives the institution authority to make an appointment? *See Judgment of 16 April 1984*, 1986 Rev. arb. 596 (Swiss Fed. Trib.) (in arbitration under ICC Rules, upholding ICC's nomination of arbitrator after contractually-agreed Director General of World Health Organization declined to act as appointing authority); *Preliminary Award in ICC Case No. 2321*, I Y.B. Comm. Arb. 133, 139 (1976) (clause providing for arbitration under ICC Rules also selects "Chairman" of ICC to appoint sole arbitrator; when ICC Chairman refused to make appointment, ICC International Court of Arbitration did so, and one party challenged appointment: "when inserting an arbitration clause in their contract the intention of the parties must be presumed to have been willing to establish an effective machinery for the settlement of disputes … [when the parties' agreed method of selecting an arbitrator] proved to be ineffective because of the refusal of the chairman to appoint an arbitrator, [the parties] must be said to have failed to nominate an arbitrator by common agreement. Then, according to Art. 7(2) of the [ICC] Rules, the arbitrator shall be appointed by the Court.").

6. *Judicial appointment of arbitrator when agreement on appointing authority is indefinite or internally inconsistent.* Parties sometimes attempt to designate an appointing authority (or procedure) in their arbitration agreement, but do so in either an incoherent or internally inconsistent fashion. This was one of the issues in *Astra*. If an arbitration clause contains an indefinite, inconsistent, or otherwise defective appointment mechanism, what are the consequences of this defect on the arbitration agreement generally? In particular, is the defective provision severed from the remainder of the clause (which is then enforced, with a national court appointing an arbitrator), or is the entire arbitration agreement invalid? This issue is discussed above. *See supra* pp. 353, 411, 435; G. Born, *International Commercial Arbitration* 1723-25 (2d ed. 2014).

Are decisions such as *Astra*, which salvage a partially-defective arbitration agreement, wise? In international arbitrations, selection of the appointing authority is a crucial decision. After unsuccessful negotiations on the seat and/or appointing authority, parties sometimes are unable to agree upon an arbitration clause and either omit any reference to dispute resolution mechanisms in their contract or agree to a forum selection clause. If purported agreement on issues such as the appointing authority turns out to be absent, should one assume that both parties still wanted to arbitrate?

7. *Judicial appointment of arbitrator when parties' agreement on appointing authority is frustrated.* Recall the facts in *Partial Decision of 2 April 1992* and *Gatoil*, where fundamental changes occurred affecting the parties' agreed appointing authority. When do such changes result in frustration of the parties' agreement on the appointing authority? *See supra* pp. 434-35. If the parties' agreement on the appointing authority is frustrated, is the remainder of the parties' arbitration agreement also invalidated? If not, does national law authorize judicial appointment of an arbitrator? Consider the results in *Gatoil*.

8. *Judicial appointment of arbitrator when arbitrator specified in parties' agreement cannot or will not serve.* Although it is usually inadvisable, parties sometimes provide in their arbitration agreement that a particular individual will act as arbitrator. *See supra* p. 695. That individual occasionally cannot (because of a conflict or otherwise) or will not serve. In those circumstances, assuming the parties cannot reach an agreement on a new choice and have not agreed upon an appointing authority, most national arbitration legislation (including §5 of the FAA) permits judicial appointment. (Note that these circumstances again raise the question whether the parties' agreement to arbitrate remains binding. *See supra* pp. 353, 411, 434-35.)

9. *National courts' ability to appoint appropriate international arbitrators.* Consider the advantages and disadvantages of the appointment of international arbitrators by a national court. What experience and expertise does a national court judge have in se-

lecting suitable international arbitrators? Compare that expertise and experience to the abilities of leading arbitral institutions. Consider also the possibilities of parochial or other predispositions, both of national courts and arbitral institutions.

Note the conclusion in *XL Insurance*. Is the English court's result—appointment of an English arbitrator—surprising? Consider its discussion of the parties' objections to previous proposals. *See also Quintette Coal Ltd v. Nippon Steel Corp.*, [1988] B.C.J. No. 492 (B.C. Sup. Ct.) (appointing Canadian presiding arbitrator in dispute between Canadian and Japanese parties, over objections of Japanese party), *aff'd*, [1988] CanLII 2923 (B.C. Ct. App.), modified by the British Columbia International Commercial Arbitration Act, §11(9). What types of individuals are national courts most familiar with? Most confident with to discharge their duties?

Consider the reasoning in *XL Insurance*. Is the selection of an arbitrator a judicial function? What resources does a court have to make a selection of an arbitrator? Note that the *XL Insurance* court relied on the names already exchanged between the parties. Is that wise? Note that the court approved one name (Lord Mustill) that had been exchanged, but not accepted, by the parties. Is that wise? How would the court have gone about trying to identify additional candidates with the appropriate experience?

Who would you prefer to appoint arbitrators in a case involving your client? Does it depend on the identity of the client and the national court making the selection? Does it depend only on these factors? Consider Articles 6(1), 11(3) and 11(5) of the Russian Law on International Commercial Arbitration, which provide that appointments of arbitrators, where the parties have not agreed upon an arbitrator or means of selecting an arbitrator, shall be performed by "the President of the Chamber of Commerce and Industry of the Russian Federation." Is this a wise approach?

10. *What national court has competence to appoint an arbitrator(s)?* Suppose parties do not agree on an arbitrator or appointing authority. What national court has jurisdiction to appoint an arbitrator? Assume Party A, domiciled in State 1, agrees to arbitrate with Party B, domiciled in State 2, and the arbitral seat is State 3. Can the courts of State 1, State 2, or State 3 appoint the missing arbitrator(s)? Can more than one state's courts do so? What problems would arise if the courts of more than one state could appoint an arbitrator?

   (a) *Jurisdictional limits on judicial appointment of arbitrators under UNCITRAL Model Law.* Consider Article 11 of the UNCITRAL Model Law. When does Article 11 permit a local court to appoint an arbitrator in an international arbitration? Does Article 11 authorize a court to appoint an arbitrator in a foreign-seated arbitration? Compare Article 179 of the SLPIL.

   (b) *Jurisdictional limits on judicial appointment of arbitrators under §5 of FAA.* Consider §5 of the FAA. If the parties have agreed to arbitrate in a particular place in the United States, will §5 permit the district court at that place to appoint an arbitrator(s)? *See Ore & Chem. Corp. v. Stinnes Interoil, Inc.*, 611 F.Supp. 237 (S.D.N.Y. 1985); *Masthead Mac Drilling Corp. v. Fleck*, 549 F.Supp. 854 (S.D.N.Y. 1982). Does §5 authorize a U.S. court to appoint an arbitrator in an arbitration seated outside the United States?

   (c) *Jurisdictional limits on judicial appointment of arbitrators under §206 of FAA.* Under §206 of the FAA, the power to appoint arbitrators is granted in the same section as, and appears coextensive with, the power to compel arbitration. As discussed above, §206 permits orders compelling arbitration in U.S. judicial districts other than the arbitral seat. *See supra* pp. 658-69. Does §206 therefore permit U.S. courts to appoint arbitrators for foreign arbitrations? What happened in *Astra*? *See also United States Lines, Inc. v. Liverpool & London SS etc.*, 833 F.Supp. 350 (S.D.N.Y. 1993). As to a U.S. court's related power in such circumstances to specify the arbitral seat, *see supra* pp. 664-69. Suppose the parties have not agreed upon either arbitrators or an arbitral seat, or upon means of choosing either. In a dispute between two U.S. companies, what objection would there be to a U.S. court appointing an arbitrator? Suppose that a dispute involves a U.S. and a French (or Somali) company, and no arbitral seat is specified. What objection would there be to a U.S. court appointing an arbitrator?

(d) *Applicability of §206 where parties have agreed on foreign arbitral seat.* If the parties have agreed on a foreign arbitral seat, may a U.S. court appoint an arbitrator? If a §206 action is brought because one party refuses to arbitrate, the court can generally compel arbitration in the foreign seat under §206. *See supra* pp. 619-24. Given the inclusion of an appointment power in §206, does the U.S. court also have the power to select an arbitrator for the foreign arbitration? If it exists, should such a power be exercised? Compare the approach under the UNCITRAL Model Law and SLPIL.

11. *Exercise of authority to appoint arbitrator in foreign arbitration.* Assuming a national court has the power to appoint arbitrators in both local and "foreign" arbitrations, as under §206 of the FAA, when should it use that power? Suppose one party to an international arbitration seated in London is a U.S. entity and the other is not (*e.g.*, French or Somali). Assuming both parties are subject to U.S. personal jurisdiction, *should* a U.S. court exercise the power to appoint an arbitrator in the London arbitration? What about French (or Somali) courts? What about English courts? What national court, in this hypothetical, is the sensible one to make an appointment? Should a U.S. court's exercise of its power depend on the power (and jurisdiction) of English courts to appoint an arbitrator?

12. *Judicial consideration of jurisdictional objections prior to appointment of arbitrator.* Suppose that, when a national court is asked to appoint an arbitrator, one party challenges the existence, validity, or scope of the arbitration agreement. Should the court entertain such challenges or leave them for the arbitrators? Does Article 11 of the UNCITRAL Model Law provide any guidance? Consider Article 179(3) of the SLPIL, excerpted at p. 158 of the Documentary Supplement. What does it prescribe? Is that wise? *See also supra* pp. 285-86; Portuguese Law No. 31/86 of 1986, Art. 12(4) ("If the arbitration agreement is manifestly void, the president of the court of appeal shall declare that the appointment of the arbitrators ... shall not take place....") (repealed). Should disputes about the scope of the arbitration agreement be considered at all by a national court in the appointment process? Why or why not?

C. IDENTITY REQUIREMENTS FOR ARBITRATORS IN INTERNATIONAL ARBITRATION

As discussed above, the principle of party autonomy is central to the process of selecting arbitrators in international arbitration. Nonetheless, there are limits to the parties' freedom to choose the arbitrators or the procedures for selecting the arbitrators.

These limits can arise variously from international arbitration conventions, national law and institutional rules. These restrictions include a range of different limits concerning nationality, experience, qualifications (*i.e.*, legally-trained) and independence or impartiality. Additionally, there are instances in which the parties' arbitration agreement (together with any institutional rules that are incorporated) may limit a party's freedom to select an arbitrator in a particular case.

1. Restrictions on Arbitrators' Nationality, Qualifications and Experience

The materials excerpted in this section illustrate restrictions that national arbitration legislation imposes concerning arbitrators' nationality, qualifications and experience. These materials do not address requirements regarding the arbitrators' independence and impartiality, which are discussed separately in the following section.[7]

NETHERLANDS CODE OF CIVIL PROCEDURE
Articles 1023, 1028

1023. Any natural person of legal capacity may be appointed as arbitrator. Unless the parties have agreed otherwise in view of the impartiality (objectivity) and independence of the arbitral tribunal, no person shall be precluded from appointment by reason of his nationality.

1028(1). If by agreement one of the parties is given a privileged position with regard to the appointment of the arbitrator or arbitrators, the other party may, in derogation of the agreed appointment procedure, request the District Court judge hearing applications for interim relief to appoint the arbitrator or arbitrators.

1028(2). A party shall be required to file the request as mentioned in paragraph (1) within three months after the commencement of the arbitration, failing to do so it will lose the right to rely upon the privileged position with regard to the appointment of the arbitrator or arbitrators at a later stage in the arbitral proceedings or before the court. The parties can extend this period by agreement.

1028(3). The other party shall be given an opportunity to be heard....

CHINESE ARBITRATION LAW
Article 13

An arbitration commission shall appoint its arbitrators from among righteous and upright persons. An arbitrator shall meet one of the conditions set forth below: (1) To have been engaged in arbitration work for at least eight years; (2) To have worked as a lawyer for at least eight years; (3) To have served as a judge for at least eight years; (4) To have been engaged in legal research or legal education, possessing a senior professional title; or (5) To have acquired the knowledge of law, engaged in the professional work in the field of economy and trade, etc., possessing a senior professional title or having an equivalent

---

7. *See infra* pp. 716-58.

professional level. An arbitration commission shall have a register of arbitrators in different specializations.

RULES FOR THE IMPLEMENTATION OF THE SAUDI ARABIAN ARBITRATION REGULATION, 1985
§3 (repealed)

The arbitrator shall be a Saudi national or Muslim expatriate from the free professional section or others. The arbitrator may also be an employee of the state, provided approval of the department to which he belongs is obtained. In the case of more than one arbitrator, the umpire shall have a knowledge of Sharia rules, commercial regulations, customs and traditions applicable to Saudi Arabia.

SAUDI ARABIAN ARBITRATION LAW, 2012
Article 14

The arbitrator shall: (1) be of full legal capacity; (2) be of good conduct and reputation; (3) hold at least a college degree in Shari'a or law. If the arbitral tribunal consists of more than one arbitrator, it is sufficient that the chairman of the tribunal satisfies this condition.

ECUADORIAN ORGANIC LAW OF THE JUDICIARY, 1974
Articles 89, 90 (repealed)

89. To be appointed as an arbitrator, a person must be Ecuadorian from birth, doctor of jurisprudence or lawyer in the exercise of the profession and in full exercise of its citizenship rights. To act as *amiable compositeur*, such requirements are not needed, but one must be Ecuadorian in the exercise of one's citizenship rights.

90. The following people cannot act as arbitrators: (1) The President of the Republic, the Ministers of State, the Magistrates of the Courts and the Ordinary and Special Judges; (2) Whoever has a direct interest in the controversy; (3) The spouse and family members within the fourth degree of consanguinity or the second by affinity, of any of the parties; (4) Intimate friends or manifest enemies of any of the parties; and, (5) Those designated in article 4 of this Law [the absolutely deaf, mute, blind, valetudinarian, mentally ill, drug addict, friar and minister of any religion, legally incapable].

UZBEK LAW ON ARBITRATION TRIBUNALS
Article 14

To be elected (appointed) as arbitrator, a person must be a citizen of the Republic of Uzbekistan.... A sole arbitrator must have higher legal education. If the tribunal consists of more than one arbitrator, the presiding arbitrator must have higher legal education....

JIVRAJ v. HASHWANI
[2011] UKSC 40 (U.K. S.Ct.)

[excerpted above at pp. 117-24]

JUDGMENT OF 26 JANUARY 1989
1989 NJW 1477 (German Bundesgerichtshof)
[excerpted above at pp. 401-02]

NOTES

1. *Requirements imposed by national law with regard to arbitrator's identity.* National law may impose limits on the identities of arbitrators in international commercial arbitrations. For example, in some countries, arbitrators must be either local nationals, qualified to practice local law, or of a particular religious faith. In other states, arbitrators must not have been convicted of prescribed crimes, have been adjudged bankrupt, be a minor, or hold various public offices.

   Consider the restrictions imposed by §3 of the Saudi Arbitration Regulation, 1985 (now repealed), Articles 89 and 90 of the Ecuadorian Organic Law (now repealed) and Article 14 of the Uzbek Law on Arbitral Tribunals. What are the policies underlying these restrictions? Are they appropriate in international commercial arbitration? Compare Article 11(1) of the UNCITRAL Model Law with the Saudi, Ecuadorian and Uzbek legislation. Also compare Article 1023 of the Netherlands Code of Civil Procedure. What are the differences, if any, between these legislative restrictions?

2. *Legislative requirements regarding arbitrators' nationality.* Consider Article 11(1) of the Model Law, excerpted at p. 88 of the Documentary Supplement. Is this a wise legislative guarantee? Why or why not?

   Consider again the provisions of §3 of the Saudi Arbitration Regulation, 1985, Articles 89 and 90 of the Ecuadorian Organic Law and Article 14 of the Uzbek Law on Arbitral Tribunals. These enactments require(d) that arbitrators be local nationals, including (apparently) in international arbitrations seated on local territory. Note that this requirement applied to both co-arbitrators and presiding (and sole) arbitrators. (Is there any way to read the Saudi regulation so as *not* to require Muslim arbitrators? How?)

   If Saudi and Ecuadorian law required local nationals as arbitrators (which Uzbek law still does) or imposed a requirement for Muslim faith, is this an appropriate limitation on the parties' autonomy to select the arbitrators? Is it consistent with the objectives of parties in agreeing to international arbitration (of securing an expert, neutral dispute resolution mechanism)? Consider again the provisions of Articles II and V(1)(d) of the New York Convention. Does the Convention permit a Contracting State to deny effect to the parties' agreement to arbitrate before arbitrators who they have selected? Or before a sole arbitrator of a neutral nationality?

   Compare the provisions of institutional rules (and some arbitration legislation (*e.g.*, UNCITRAL Model Law, Art. 11(5)) providing that the presiding or sole arbitrator be of a neutral nationality, different from that of either of the parties. What does Article III of the European Convention provide? How do such provisions differ from the Saudi, Ecuadorian and Uzbek legislation excerpted above?

3. *Legislative prohibitions against national court judges serving as arbitrators.* In some jurisdictions, persons holding office as judges in local courts are prohibited from serving as arbitrators, including in international arbitrations. French Decree 93-21 of 7 January 1993, modified by Decree 94-314 of 20 April 1994, Art. 37 ("The participa-

tion of a judge in arbitration is subject to an preliminary exemption in accordance with [French administrative regulations]. An exemption is necessary for each arbitration."). In the United States, the FAA imposes no capacity restrictions, but active judges are prohibited by canons of judicial conduct from acting as arbitrators. ABA Code of Judicial Conduct, Canon 5(E).

What is the purpose of legislative prohibitions on judges serving as arbitrators? Is it appropriate to forbid parties from selecting sitting judges as arbitrators? What if the arbitration is seated abroad? Suppose a national court judge sits as an arbitrator in a foreign-seated arbitration, in violation of the law of the country where she serves as a judge. Should this affect the validity of the resulting arbitral award? Suppose a U.S. judge—who is forbidden by statute or public policy in the United States from acting as an arbitrator—sits as arbitrator in Finland—where Finnish judges can sit as arbitrators. Is the U.S. judge's resulting award enforceable? In Finland? In the United States?

4. *Legislative requirements that arbitrators be natural persons*. Legislation in some jurisdictions prohibits juridical persons from serving as arbitrators. Consider Article 1450 of the French Code of Civil Procedure and Article 1023 of the Netherlands Code of Civil Procedure. Are these provisions well-considered? Suppose parties wanted, for example, an accountancy firm or investment bank to arbitrate their dispute. Should that agreement be denied effect? What are the reasons for and against such a prohibition? Would an award made in France or the Netherlands by an accountancy firm, pursuant to the parties' agreement to arbitrate before such a firm, be recognizable in other jurisdictions under Article V of the New York Convention? What if Dutch or French courts replaced the accountancy firm with a natural person as the arbitrator? Would the award be subject to non-recognition under Article V(1)(d)?

5. *Legislative requirements that arbitrators have legal capacity*. Many arbitration statutes require that arbitrators have legal capacity. Consider, for example, Article 1023 of the Netherlands Code of Civil Procedure and Article 1450 of the French Code of Civil Procedure. Are these requirements wise? How does it compare to the Uzbek nationality requirements?

6. *Legislative requirements that arbitrators be legally-qualified*. Some national arbitration regimes require that the arbitrators (or, at least, the presiding arbitrator) be legally-qualified. Consider Article 13 of the Chinese Arbitration Law. *See* Spanish Arbitration Act, 2011, Art. 15(1) ("Unless otherwise agreed by the parties, in arbitrations that are not to be decided *ex aequo et bono*, when the arbitration is conducted by a sole arbitrator, such person will be required to be a lawyer.... When the arbitration is to be conducted by three or more arbitrators, at least one must be a lawyer."); Colombian Arbitration Act, 2013, Art. 7 ("the arbitrators shall fulfill, as a minimum, the same requirements applicable to the justices of Superior Tribunals"). Again, how does this requirement differ from requirements that the arbitrators have local nationality or a particular religious faith? What if the requirement for legal qualification is interpreted, as to arbitrations seated locally, as a requirement that the arbitrator(s) be qualified to practice law locally?

7. *Legislative requirements that arbitrators be chosen in procedurally fair manner*. Consider Article 1028 of the Netherlands Code of Civil Procedure. Compare the similar legislation discussed above at p. 409. What impact does this provision have on the structuring of agreements for the selection of arbitrators? Is Article 1028 a desirable

legislative provision? How should arbitration legislation, which lacks explicit requirements such as Article 1028, be interpreted?

For comparable requirements of procedural fairness in other jurisdictions, *see, e.g., Hooters of Am., Inc. v. Phillips*, 173 F.3d 933 (4th Cir. 1999) (arbitrators selected from list prepared by employer: "given the unrestricted control that [the employer] has over the panel, the selection of an impartial decision maker would be a surprising result"); *Harold Allen's Mobile Home Factory Outlet, Inc. v. Butler*, 825 So.2d 779, 783-85 (Ala. 2002) ("the portion of the arbitration agreement in this case excluding one of the parties from selection of the arbitrator is unconscionable. Such provision offends fundamental notions of fairness"); *Judgment of 11 November 1981*, DFT 107 Ia 155, 158 (Swiss Fed. Trib.) ("The Federal Tribunal … has developed principles, under which conditions an arbitral tribunal sufficiently safeguards impartial and independent adjudication. The most important of these principles … is that no party may have a preponderant influence on the appointment of the tribunal."); *Judgment of 17 April 1978*, IV Y.B. Comm. Arb. 282, 282 (1979) (Italian Corte di Cassazione) ("an arbitral clause which provides that a sole arbitrator shall be appointed by one of the parties only is invalid").

Review the provisions regarding selection of arbitrators, discussed above at p. 408-09, which have been held unconscionable by different national courts. What if: (a) one party is permitted to select the sole or presiding arbitrator; (b) one party is permitted to select all the (three) arbitrators; (c) one party draws up a list of possible arbitrators, from which an appointing authority must select the sole or presiding arbitrator; (d) one party imposes a requirement regarding the identity of the arbitrator(s), such as professional requirements. Which of these provisions raise the most issues from an unconscionability perspective?

8. *Choice of law governing legislative requirements for arbitrators' qualifications.* When is a national arbitration statute requiring that the arbitrators have a particular nationality, religion, or legal capacity applicable? Did the (now repealed) Saudi or Ecuadorian statutes excerpted above purport to apply to arbitrations seated outside Saudi Arabia or Ecuador? Suppose a Saudi company arbitrated against a Canadian company in Switzerland. Did Saudi law purport to require that the arbitrators be Saudis? Suppose a Belgian company arbitrates against a Saudi company in Switzerland. Does Belgian law require that the arbitrators have legal capacity?

9. *Contractual requirements regarding arbitrators' qualifications.* Apart from legislative requirements regarding arbitrators' capacity, nationality, or the like, parties also sometimes agree to contractual requirements regarding the arbitrators. These can include nationality requirements (or prohibitions), language requirements, expertise requirements and independence and impartiality requirements. Consider the following examples:

> "Arbitrators shall be commercial persons and not practising lawyers, except where two arbitrators by these rules are to appoint a third, that third arbitrator may be a practising lawyer…." 2013 Vancouver Maritime Arbitrators Association Rules, Art. 6.

> "To qualify as an arbitrator, an individual must be (1) an employee, or active partner, principal, officer or director of a member firm eligible to arbitrate disputes under these rules …; and (2) [should be] commercially disinterested with respect to the particular dispute…. (d) Arbitrators also shall be selected with a view to forming arbitration

committees experienced in the type of trade or transaction involved in the case." 2014 National Grain and Feed Association Arbitration Rules, Rules 5(c), (d).

"[P]ersons designated to serve on the Panels shall be persons of high moral character and recognized competence in the fields of law, commerce, industry or finance, who may be relied upon to exercise independent judgment. Competence in the field of law should be of particular importance in the case of persons on the Panel of arbitrators." ICSID Convention, Art. 14(1)

"The arbitrators shall be fluent in Spanish and English and shall have experience in telecommunications joint ventures."

"Where the parties are of different nationalities, a sole arbitrator or the presiding arbitrator shall not have the same nationality as any party unless the parties who are not of the same nationality as the arbitral candidate all agree in writing otherwise." 2014 LCIA Rules, Art. 6(1).

What effect should be given to these contractual requirements? Consider the general validity of parties' agreements regarding the selection of the arbitrators, *supra* pp. 683-84. Is there any reason to treat contractual requirements regarding expertise, qualifications, or nationality differently? *See* G. Born, *International Commercial Arbitration* 1737 *et seq.* (2d ed. 2014).

10. *Effect of parties' agreement on legislative requirements regarding arbitrators' qualifications.* What effect does the parties' agreement have on legislative requirements regarding the arbitrator's qualifications (*e.g.*, nationality, legal capacity, legal qualification)? Suppose parties to an arbitration in Saudi Arabia had agreed to non-Muslim arbitrators or parties to an arbitration seated in China agreed to arbitrators who were not legally-qualified. Would the parties' agreement override the contrary legislative requirement in the arbitral seat? Does the answer to this question depend on the nature of the legislative requirement?

    What is the effect of Article II of the New York Convention on legislative requirements that contradict the parties' agreement regarding the arbitrators' qualifications? Suppose the parties to an international arbitration seated in China agree upon non-legally-qualified arbitrators. Does Article II of the Convention require giving effect to that agreement, notwithstanding contrary Chinese law? What are the arguments for and against this conclusion? Consider also whether Article II required giving effect to the parties' agreement on non-Saudi arbitrators, notwithstanding contrary Saudi law, in an international arbitration seated in Saudi Arabia.

11. *Procedural mechanisms for implementing legislative and contractual requirements regarding arbitrators' qualifications.* Suppose an arbitrator in an arbitration seated in the Netherlands lacks legal capacity or has been chosen in a procedurally unfair manner. How and where is the relevant Dutch legislative requirement (regarding capacity or a procedurally-fair means of selection) implemented? Conversely, suppose that an arbitrator seated in Saudi Arabia lacked the legislatively-mandated nationality and religion. Again, how and where would the relevant Saudi legislative requirement be implemented?

    One avenue for implementing national legislative requirements for arbitrators is by means of an interlocutory challenge to the arbitrator, which (if successful) would result in the arbitrator's removal. The procedural mechanisms for challenging arbitrators on an interlocutory basis are discussed below. *See infra* pp. 758-76. An alternative avenue for implementing national legislative requirements for arbitrators is by means of an action to annul the arbitrators' award or to deny recognition of the award. These possibilities are also discussed below. *See infra* pp. 1160-61, 1242-50.

12. *Requirements for arbitrators' qualifications in investment arbitrations.* Consider Articles 12-14 and 38-40 of the ICSID Convention, excerpted at pp. 16 & 21-22 of the Documentary Supplement. What limits do these provisions place on the selection of arbitrators? Why? Compare these limits to those in international commercial arbitrations. What explains the differences?

13. *Requirements for arbitrators' qualifications in inter-state arbitrations.* Consider Articles 44 and 45 of the 1907 Hague Convention, excerpted at p. 44 of the Documentary Supplement. What limitations do these provisions place on the identities of arbitrators? What is the rationale for these limits? Compare the limitations contained in Articles 8-10 of the PCA Rules, excerpted at pp. 282-83 of the Documentary Supplement. Note in particular Article 8(3). What explains the differences between the 1907 Hague Convention and the PCA Rules? Contrast the PCA Rules with the ICSID Convention. What explains the differences?

2. Requirements for Arbitrators' Independence and Impartiality

Virtually all national arbitration statutes and institutional rules require arbitrators in international arbitrations to satisfy requirements of independence and impartiality. An arbitrator's failure to satisfy these requirements can result in his or her interlocutory removal during the arbitration[8] or in annulment or non-recognition of his or her award.[9] Although most arbitration statutes and institutional rules impose requirements of impartiality and independence, the content of these requirements varies significantly between legal systems and institutional rules.

VERITAS SHIPPING LTD v. ANGLO-CANADIAN CEMENT, LTD
[1966] 1 Lloyds Rep. 76 (QB) (English High Ct.)

MR. JUSTICE MCNAIR. In this matter … Veritas Shipping Corporation [("Veritas") moves] for an order that Dr. W. K. Wallersteiner, the arbitrator appointed by Anglo-Canadian Cement, Ltd., [("Anglo)"] in the reference to arbitration between Veritas and Anglo … be removed and that an arbitrator be appointed on behalf of Anglo….

Veritas were the owners and Anglo the charterers in a charter-party in the Gencon form dated May 11, 1964, which charter-party contained by Clause 30 an arbitration clause to the following effect: "Any dispute arising under this Charter Party shall be referred to arbitration in London. One arbitrator to be nominated by the Owners and the other by the Charterers. In case such arbitrators cannot agree, then the dispute to be referred to the decision of an Umpire who shall be appointed by said arbitrators…." Disputes arose between the parties, the shipowners advancing a claim amount to a sum of just under £10,000 in respect of freight and demurrage. The shipowners, Veritas, are a Panamanian company and Anglo are a company incorporated in Nigeria.

---

8. *See infra* pp. 758-76.
9. *See infra* pp. 1160-61 & 1242-50.

These disputes having arisen, correspondence took place, and the correspondence on behalf of Anglo ... was conducted by Dr. W.K. Wallersteiner as their managing director. Correspondence proceeded for a long time. Finally the shipowners appointed Mr. R.A. Clyde as their arbitrator and called upon Anglo to appoint their arbitrator. In response to that request, they received a letter from Anglo signed by Dr. W.K. Wallersteiner as their managing director appointing the same Dr. W.K. Wallersteiner as the arbitrator to act on their behalf in this arbitration. The shipowners, through their representatives, objected to this appointment on the grounds of the close connection that Dr. Wallersteiner had with Anglo and, indeed, with this particular dispute or series of disputes, which, they said, disqualified him from acting as an arbitrator under this clause. In the course of further correspondence between the representatives of Anglo and Dr. Wallersteiner personally, Dr. Wallersteiner refused to withdraw and Anglo refused to appoint anybody in his stead....

[B]y this motion the shipowners seek the assistance of the Court to get the arbitration properly constituted. The order they ask for is that the Court should remove Dr. W.K. Wallersteiner under §23 of the Arbitration Act on the ground that Dr. Wallersteiner has misconducted himself in the arbitration in not only allowing himself to be appointed as arbitrator but, having appointed himself, having as managing director of Anglo signed the letter appointing him to act. Without making any reflections upon the propriety and skill of Dr. Wallersteiner, I am quite satisfied that it would be quite wrong for him to be allowed to continue to act as arbitrator in a dispute of this nature. It is quite true that under the clause, if the two arbitrators disagree and the matter is referred to the umpire for his decision, the arbitrators, according to the customary way in which these matters are dealt with in the City of London, may if they so wish act as advocates. They need not do so but there is nothing wrong in them doing so. Until that moment arrives, the arbitrators must not only act judicially and show no bias at all but must also appear to be in a position to act judicially and without any bias. Accordingly, in the exercise of my discretion, I remove Dr. W.K. Wallersteiner from his position as arbitrator in this matter.

The motion also asks that, if he is removed, an arbitrator should be appointed in his place on behalf of Anglo in this arbitration. That power so to do is contained in §25(1) of the Arbitration Act of 1950 [and the court exercised it.]

COMMONWEALTH COATINGS CORP. v. CONTINENTAL CASUALTY CO.
393 U.S. 145 (1968)

JUSTICE BLACK.... The petitioner, Commonwealth Coatings Corporation, a subcontractor, sued the sureties on the prime contractor's bond to recover money alleged to be due for a painting job. The contract for painting contained an agreement to arbitrate such controversies. Pursuant to this agreement petitioner appointed one arbitrator, the prime contractor appointed a second, and these two together selected the third arbitrator. This third arbitrator, the supposedly neutral member of the panel, conducted a large business in Puerto Rico, in which he served as an engineering consultant for various people in connection with building construction projects. One of his regular customers in this business was the prime contractor that petitioner sued in this case. This relationship with the prime contractor was in a sense sporadic in that the arbitrator's services were used only from time to time at irregular intervals, and there had been no dealings between them for about a year immediately preceding the arbitration. Nevertheless, the prime contractor's patronage was repeated and significant, involving fees of about $12,000 over a period of four or five years, and the relationship even went so far as to include the rendering of services on the very projects involved in this lawsuit. An arbitration was held, but the facts concerning the close business connections between the third arbitrator and the prime contractor were unknown to petitioner and were never revealed to it by this arbitrator, by the prime contractor, or by anyone else until after an award had been made. Petitioner challenged the award on this ground, among others, but the District Court refused to set aside the award. The Court of Appeals affirmed....

Section 10 [of the FAA] sets out the conditions upon which awards can be vacated. The two courts below held, however, that §10 could not be construed in such a way as to justify vacating the award in this case. We disagree and reverse.

Section 10 does authorize vacation of an award where it was "procured by corruption, fraud, or undue means" or "[w]here there was evident partiality ... in the arbitrators." These provisions show a desire of Congress to provide not merely for any arbitration but for an impartial one. It is true that petitioner does not charge before us that the third arbitrator was actually guilty of fraud or bias in deciding this case, and we have no reason, apart from the undisclosed business relationship, to suspect him of any improper motives. But neither this arbitrator nor the prime contractor gave to petitioner even an intimation of the close financial relations that had existed between them for a period of years. We have no doubt that if a litigant could show that a foreman of a jury or a judge in a court of justice had, unknown to the litigant, any such relationship, the judgment would be subject to challenge. This is shown beyond doubt by *Tumey v. Ohio*, 273 U.S. 510 (1927), where this Court held that a conviction could not stand because a small part of the judge's income consisted of court fees collected from convicted defendants. Although in *Tumey* it appeared the amount of the judge's compensation actually depended on whether he decided for one side or the other, that is too small a distinction to allow this manifest violation of the strict morality and fairness Congress would have expected on the part of the arbitrator and the other party in this case. Nor should it be at all relevant, as the Court of Appeals apparently thought it was here, that "[t]he payments received were a very small part of [the arbitrator's] income...." For in *Tumey* the Court held that a decision should be set aside where there is "the slightest pecuniary interest" on the part of the judge, and specifically rejected the State's contention that the compensation involved there was "so small that it is not to be regarded as likely to influence improperly a judicial officer in the discharge of his duty...." Since in the case of courts this is a constitutional principle, we can see no basis for refusing to find the same concept in the broad statutory language that governs arbitration proceedings.... It is true that arbitrators cannot sever all their ties with the business world, since they are not expected to get all their income from their work deciding cases, but we should, if anything, be even more scrupulous to safeguard the impartiality of arbitrators than judges, since the former have completely free rein to decide the law as well as the facts and are not subject to appellate review. We can perceive no way in which the effectiveness of the arbitration process will be hampered by the simple requirement that arbitrators disclose to the parties any dealings that might create an impression of possible bias.

While not controlling in this case, §18 of the Rules of the [AAA], in effect at the time of this arbitration, is highly significant. It provided as follows:

"Section 18. Disclosure by Arbitrator of Disqualification – At the time of receiving his notice of appointment, the prospective Arbitrator is requested to disclose any circumstances likely to create a presumption of bias or which he believes might disqualify him as an impartial Arbitrator. Upon receipt of such information, the Tribunal Clerk shall immediately disclose it to the parties, who if willing to proceed under the circumstances disclosed, shall, in writing, so advise the Tribunal Clerk. If either party declines to waive the presumptive disqualification, the vacancy thus created shall be filled in accordance with the applicable provisions of this Rule."

And based on the same principle as this [AAA] rule is that part of the 33d Canon Judicial Ethics which provides:

"33. Social Relations.... [A judge] should, however, in pending or prospective litigation before him be particularly careful to avoid such action as may reasonably tend to awaken the suspicion that his social or business relations or friendships, constitute an element in influencing his judicial conduct."

This rule of arbitration and this canon of judicial ethics rest on the premise that any tribunal permitted by law to try cases and controversies not only must be unbiased but also must avoid even the appearance of bias. We cannot believe that it was the purpose of Congress to authorize litigants to submit their cases and controversies to arbitration boards that might reasonably be thought biased against one litigant and favorable to another....

MR. JUSTICE WHITE, Concurring. While I am glad to join my Brother Black's opinion in this case, I desire to make these additional remarks. The Court does not decide today that arbitrators are to be held to the standards of judicial decorum of Article III judges, or indeed of any judges. It is often because they are men of affairs, not apart from but of the marketplace, that they are effective in their adjudicatory functions. This does not mean the judiciary must overlook outright chicanery in giving effect to their awards; that would be an abdication of our responsibility. But it does mean that arbitrators are not automatically disqualified by a business relationship with the parties before them if both parties are informed of the relationship in advance, or if they are unaware of the facts but the relationship is trivial. I see no reason automatically to disqualify the best informed and most capable potential arbitrators.

The arbitration process functions best when an amicable and trusting atmosphere is preserved and there is voluntary compliance with the decree, without need for judicial enforcement. This end is best served by establishing an atmosphere of frankness at the outset, through disclosure by the arbitrator of any financial transactions which he has had or is negotiating with either of the parties. In many cases the arbitrator might believe the business relationship to be so insubstantial that to make a point of revealing it would suggest he is indeed easily swayed, and perhaps a partisan of that party.[10] But if the law requires the disclosure, no such imputation can arise. And it is far better that the relationship be disclosed at the outset, when the parties are free to reject the arbitrator or accept him with knowledge of the relationship and continuing faith in his objectivity, than to have the relationship come to light after the arbitration, when a suspicious or disgruntled party can seize on it as a pretext for invalidating the award. The judiciary should minimize its role in arbitration as judge of the arbitrator's impartiality. That role is best consigned to the parties,

---

10. In fact, the District Court found on the basis of the record and petitioner's admissions that the arbitrator in this case was entirely fair and impartial. I do not read the majority opinion as questioning this finding in any way.

who are the architects of their own arbitration process, and are far better informed of the prevailing ethical standards and reputations within their business.

Of course, an arbitrator's business relationships may be diverse indeed, involving more or less remote commercial connections with great numbers of people. He cannot be expected to provide the parties with his complete and unexpurgated business biography. But it is enough for present purposes to hold, as the Court does, that where the arbitrator has a substantial interest in a firm which has done more than trivial business with a party, that fact must be disclosed. If arbitrators err on the side of disclosure as they should, it will not be difficult for courts to identify those undisclosed relationships which are too insubstantial to warrant vacating an award.

MR. JUSTICE FORTAS, Dissenting. I dissent, and would affirm the judgment. The facts in this case do not lend themselves to the Court's ruling. The Court sets aside the arbitration award despite the fact that the award is unanimous and no claim is made of actual partiality, unfairness, bias, or fraud.

Each party appointed an arbitrator and the third arbitrator was chosen by those two. The controversy relates to the third arbitrator. The third arbitrator was not asked about business connections with either party. Petitioner's complaint is that he failed to volunteer information about professional services rendered by him to the other party to the contract, the most recent of which were performed over a year before the arbitration. Both courts below held, and petitioner concedes, that the third arbitrator was innocent of any actual partiality, or bias, or improper motive. There is no suggestion of concealment as distinguished from the innocent failure to volunteer information.

The third arbitrator is a leading and respected consulting engineer who has performed services for "most of the contractors in Puerto Rico." He was well known to petitioner's counsel and they were personal friends. Petitioner's counsel candidly admitted that if he had been told about the arbitrator's prior relationship "I don't think I would have objected because I know Mr. Capacete [the arbitrator]."

Clearly, the District Judge's conclusion, affirmed by the Court of Appeals for the First Circuit, was correct, that "the arbitrators conducted fair, impartial hearings; that they reached a proper determination of the issues before them and that plaintiff's objections represent a 'situation where the losing party to an arbitration is now clutching at straws in an attempt to avoid the results of the arbitration to which it became a party.'" The Court nevertheless orders that the arbitration award be set aside. It uses this singularly inappropriate case to announce a per se rule that in my judgment has no basis in the applicable statute or jurisprudential principles: that, regardless of the agreement between the parties, if an arbitrator has any prior business relationship with one of the parties of which he fails to inform the other party, however innocently, the arbitration award is always subject to being set aside. This is so even where the award is unanimous; where there is no suggestion that the nondisclosure indicates partiality or bias; and where it is conceded that there was in fact no irregularity, unfairness, bias or partiality....

I agree that failure of an arbitrator to volunteer information about business dealings with one party will, prima facie, support a claim of partiality or bias. But where there is no suggestion that the nondisclosure was calculated, and where the complaining party disclaims any imputation of partiality, bias, or misconduct, the presumption clearly is overcome.[11] I do not believe that it is either necessary, appropriate, or permissible to rule, as the Court does, that regardless of the facts, innocent failure to volunteer information constitutes the "evident partiality" necessary under §10(b) of the [FAA] to set aside an award. "Evident partiality" means what it says: conduct—or at least an attitude or disposition—by the arbitrator favoring one party rather than the other.... [Here,] all agree that the arbitrator was innocent of either "evident partiality" or anything approaching it....

SPHERE DRAKE INSURANCE LTD v. ALL AM. LIFE INSURANCE CO.
307 F.3d 617 (7th Cir. 2002)

EASTERBROOK, Circuit Judge. [Disputes arose over the validity of six reinsurance contracts between All American Life Insurance Co. ("All American") and Sphere Drake Insurance Ltd ("Sphere Drake").] Sphere Drake submitted [these disputes] to arbitration at All American's insistence. The arbitration was conducted under the auspices of the Association Internationale de Droits des Assurances ("AIDA") and its U.S. affiliate, the AIDA Reinsurance and Insurance Arbitration Society ("ARIAS I U.S."), which uses tripartite panels. Each insurer names one member of the panel, and these two choose a neutral (called the "umpire") to break ties. All American designated Robert M. Mangino, and Sphere Drake named Ronald A. Jacks. They chose Robert M. Huggins as the umpire. All three have considerable experience in international reinsurance arbitration, having served on at least 35 panels. Mangino and Jacks are founding directors of ARIAS I U.S.; Jacks is a former president of the U.S. chapter of AIDA. All three have served as umpires; Jacks has been chosen for that duty more than 25 times by party-named arbitrators who relied on his reputation for legal acumen and impartiality. Huggins decided that Sphere Drake was entitled to victory on the ground that All American had disavowed Stirling Cooke Brown Reinsurance Brokers as its agent.... But Huggins concluded that if All American was not bound (because Stirling Cooke lacked authority to act on its behalf) then Sphere Drake could not be bound either. Jacks joined him to make a majority; Mangino dissented. Having demanded arbitration, All American decided that it did not like the result and asked a court to set aside the award—which it did, on the ground that Jacks displayed "evident partiality," one of the few grounds for refusing to enforce an award. 9 U.S.C. §10(a)(2).

As far as we can see, this is the first time since the [FAA] was enacted in 1925 that a federal court has set aside an award because a party-appointed arbitrator on a tripartite panel, as opposed to a neutral, displayed "evident partiality." The lack of precedent is unsurprising, because in the main party-appointed arbitrators are *supposed* to be advocates. In labor arbitration a union may name as its arbitrator the business manager of the local union, and the employer its vice-president for labor relations. Yet no one believes that the predictable loyalty of these designees spoils the award. *See Astoria Med. Group v. Health Ins. Plan of Greater New York*, 227 N.Y.S.2d 401 (1962). Cf. *United Transp. Union v. Gateway W. Ry.*, 284 F.3d 710 (7th Cir. 2002). This is so because the parties are entitled to waive the

---

11. At the time of the contract and the arbitration herein, §18 of the [AAA] Rules, which the Court quotes, was phrased merely in terms of a "request" that the arbitrator "disclose any circumstances likely to create a presumption of bias or which he believes might disqualify him as an impartial Arbitrator." In 1964, the rule was changed to provide that "the prospective neutral Arbitrator shall disclose any circumstances likely to create a presumption of bias or which he believes might disqualify him as an impartial Arbitrator."

protection of §10(a)(2), as they can waive almost any other statutory entitlement. The [FAA] makes arbitration agreements enforceable to the same extent as other contracts, so courts must "enforce privately negotiated agreements to arbitrate, like other contracts, in accordance with their terms." *Volt Info. Sciences, Inc. v. Stanford Univ.*, 489 U.S. 468, 478 (1989).

Parties are free to choose for themselves to what lengths they will go in quest of impartiality. Section 10(a)(2) just states the presumptive rule, subject to variation by mutual consent. Industry arbitration, the modern law merchant, often uses panels composed of industry insiders, the better to understand the trade's norms of doing business and the consequences of proposed lines of decision. The more experience the panel has, and the smaller the number of repeat players, the more likely it is that the panel will contain some actual or potential friends, counselors, or business rivals of the parties. Yet all participants may think the expertise-impartiality tradeoff worthwhile; the [FAA] does not fasten on every industry the model of the disinterested generalist judge. To the extent that an agreement entitles parties to select interested (even beholden) arbitrators, §10(a)(2) has no role to play.

There remains the question whether this was such an agreement, to which the answer is yes and no. Party-appointed arbitrators are entitled under the ARIAS I U.S. rules to engage in *ex parte* discussions with their principals until the case is taken under advisement, but they are supposed thereafter to be impartial adjudicators. The parties assume that as a result Sphere Drake could not have appointed one of its current employees as its arbitrator. (Whether that assumption is correct depends on ARIAS I U.S. rules and practices; we need not pursue the issue.) Still, Jacks was not, and never has been, one of Sphere Drake's employees. He is a retired lawyer, until recently a partner of Mayer, Brown & Platt.... The district court deemed Jacks "evidently partial" because four years before the arbitration, while still at Mayer Brown, Jacks had been engaged by the Bermuda subsidiary of Sphere Drake (a U.K. company) as counsel on an unrelated matter that landed in arbitration but was settled before decision. It emerged in discovery compelled by the district court that Jacks had billed about 380 hours for that matter. The judge deemed Sphere Drake (U.K.) his real client because its financial interests were at stake, even though the Bermuda subsidiary signed the engagement letter and paid the fees, and even though Jacks himself thought that most of his billable time related to corporate counseling rather than to the arbitration.

Let us suppose that the district judge's inferences are sound—that Jacks spent two months of equivalent full-time service as counsel for Sphere Drake in an international insurance arbitration, four years before the unrelated arbitration with All American. Even if Jacks had been the umpire, this would not have implied "evident partiality." Indeed, Jacks could have served as a federal judge in this case without challenge on grounds of partiality, and the scope of disqualification under §10(a)(2) is considerably more confined than the rule applicable to judges. *See Health Serv. Mgt Corp. v. Hughes*, 975 F.2d 1253 (7th Cir. 1992); *Int'l Produce, Inc. v. A/S Rosshavet*, 638 F.2d 548 (2d Cir. 1981). "Evident partiality" under §10(a)(2) is a subset of the conditions that disqualify a federal judge under 28 U.S.C. §455(b). A judge can't hold even a single share of a party's stock, but this would not imply "evident partiality" for purposes of §10(a)(2). The parties themselves evinced this understanding. Before the arbitration began, umpire Huggins revealed that he was an investor in American International Group, which recently had made a bid to acquire All

American—yet neither side thought that this imperiled Huggins' ability to serve as the neutral.

A federal judge would be disqualified on account of prior legal work "[w]here in private practice he served as lawyer in the matter in controversy, or a lawyer with whom he previously practiced law served during such association as a lawyer concerning the matter, or the judge or such lawyer has been a material witness...." 28 U.S.C. §455(b)(2). Jacks fits none of these categories. The work he did for Sphere Drake was unrelated to the controversy with All American; no partner of Mayer Brown served "during such association" (that is, while Jacks also was a partner) as a lawyer in this dispute between Sphere Drake and All American (indeed, Sphere Drake has been represented throughout by a firm other than Mayer Brown); and neither Jacks nor any lawyer at Mayer Brown is a "material witness" in this case. Arbitration differs from adjudication, among many other ways, because the "appearance of partiality" ground of disqualification for judges does not apply to arbitrators; only *evident* partiality, not appearances or risks, spoils an award. Still, a judge's former representation of a litigant does not imply any need to disqualify under §455(a) because "his impartiality might reasonably be questioned." *See Nat'l Auto Brokers Corp. v. General Motors Corp.*, 572 F.2d 953 (2d Cir. 1978). Nothing in the Code of Conduct for federal judges makes prior representation of a litigant a disqualifying event. The norm among new appointees to the bench is that once two years pass, perhaps even earlier, a judge is free to sit in controversies involving former clients. *See* Committee on Codes of Conduct, *Judicial Ethics Compendium* §3.6-5.

If Jacks could have served as a federal judge in this case, it is impossible to see how his background could demonstrate "evident partiality" within the meaning of §10(a)(2). "Evident partiality" for a party-appointed arbitrator must be limited to conduct in transgression of contractual limitations. No claim is made, however, that Jacks' past violated the contractual restrictions for ARIAS I U.S. arbitration. Nonetheless, All American insists that all of this is irrelevant. The problem as All American sees it is not that Jacks was partial, but that he did not disclose before the arbitration the extent of his involvement in the unrelated proceedings four years earlier. All American attributes this rule to *Commonwealth Coatings Corp. v. Continental Casualty Co.*, 393 U.S. 145 (1968).

At the arbitrators' initial meeting, where Huggins disclosed that he had a potential financial interest in All American, Jacks said only that he had "known of Sphere Drake over the years." Before the arbitration got under way, Jacks sent a letter stating that he had neglected a more concrete connection. He wrote:

> "several years ago I provided limited corporate advice to Jonathan Crawley, then President of Sphere Drake's Bermuda subsidiary. In that capacity I recommended that my former law firm, Mayer, Brown, & Platt, be retained to represent Sphere Drake (Bermuda) Ltd in an arbitration ... involving a set of wholly unrelated issues which were settled shortly after the initial meeting of the Panel and Counsel."

The district judge faulted this on several counts. First, the word "former" could be read to mean that Mayer Brown was Jacks' "former" firm at the time he made the recommendation, rather than (as was correct) at the time he wrote the letter. Second, Jacks did not reveal that when the firm took him up on the recommendation, he personally rendered legal services in the arbitration. Third, the letter did not reveal that Sphere Drake (U.K.), the parent corporation, was the real party in interest in the arbitration. Finally, the letter did not reveal the number of hours Jacks devoted to the case and left the impression that his involvement had been negligible.

Once again, let us suppose that the letter was deficient in all of these respects. How do these shortcomings demonstrate "evident partiality" when, as we have observed already, the full truth would not have disclosed even a risk of partiality? The district court treated candid and complete disclosure as a requirement in addition to disinterest. Yet that position has no purchase in the language of §10(a)(2)—or for that matter in judicial practice. A federal judge is not required to disclose his role as counsel to one litigant in an unrelated matter many years ago. Since disclosure, though often prudent, is not thought *essential* to impartial judicial service, it is hard to see how a disclosure requirement could be deemed implicit in §10(a)(2), which, to repeat, addresses only a subset of the circumstances that would disqualify a judge.

Commonwealth Coatings observes that disclosure at the outset often avoids later controversies—as Huggins's disclosure did. One can only imagine what Sphere Drake would be saying now had Huggins kept his mouth shut and then supported All American's position. Disclosure in *Commonwealth Coatings* itself would have averted a problem that spoiled an award. The neutral in a tripartite arbitration was engaged in *ongoing* business relations with one of the parties, "and the relationship even went so far as to include the rendering of services on the very projects involved in this lawsuit." 393 U.S. at 146. The Court held that being on one side's payroll is a form of partiality condemned by §10(a)(2). The Justices urged arbitrators to disclose their business dealings so that similar problems would not recur.

Commonwealth Coatings did not hold, as All American would have it, that disclosure is compulsory for its own sake, and its absence fatal even if the arbitrator meets judicial standards of impartiality. *See United States Wrestling Federation v. Wrestling Divisional of AAU, Inc.*, 605 F.2d 313 (7th Cir. 1979) (holding an award valid even though the neutral failed to disclose that his law firm had represented one of the parties on a regular basis). Nor did *Commonwealth Coatings* so much as hint that party-appointed arbitrators are governed by the norms under which neutrals operate. The point of *Commonwealth Coatings* is that the sort of financial entanglements that would disqualify a judge will cause problems for a neutral under §10(a)(2) unless disclosure is made and the parties' consent obtained.

Disclosure by a neutral may serve purposes other than flagging potential conflicts. One gets to *be* a neutral only by agreement of the party-appointed arbitrators. A potential neutral may have contractual obligations to reveal information to those who select him. Failure to comply with a contractual requirement designed to facilitate the search for an acceptable neutral might imply that the neutral exceeded his authority, spoiling the award under 9 U.S.C. §10(a)(4). But Mangino had no power to remove Jacks, and we have not been given any reason to think that umpire Huggins wanted more information from Jacks in order to know what to make of Jacks' arguments during the panel's deliberations. For someone in Jacks' position—a party-appointed arbitrator, and one who could have presided in court under the standards of §455—failure to make a full disclosure may sully his reputation for candor but does not demonstrate "evident partiality" and thus does not spoil the award.

AMERICO LIFE, INC. v. MYER
2014 WL 2789429 (Tex.)

[excerpted above at pp. 679-82]

ASM SHIPPING LTD OF INDIA v. TTMI LTD OF ENGLAND
[2005] EWHC 2238 (Comm) (English High Ct.)

MORISON J. This is an application made under §68 of the [English] Arbitration Act 1996. The arbitration arose out of disputes between owners ASM Shipping Ltd of India ("the owners") and charterers, TTMI Ltd of England ("the charterers"). The essential ground upon which this application is based is that one of the three arbitrators, namely X QC (nominated by the other two arbitrators) should have recused himself....

[The application to remove X arose during a preliminary hearing in the arbitration, with X sitting as presiding arbitrator. At the outset of the hearing, Mr. Moustakas, a key witness for the owners, thought he recognized X. Later on the first day of the hearing, Mr. Moustakas recalled that X had acted as counsel for another charterer seven months earlier in an action in English courts ("the B case") to compel disclosure of documents from another shipowner, for whom Mr. Moustakas had acted as a broker. In the B case, serious allegations had allegedly been made against Mr. Moustakas, including claims that he had deliberately failed to disclosure material documents and had fraudulently falsified other documents. The law firm that represented the charterer in the B case, and instructed X as counsel in that litigation, was representing the charterer in the pending arbitration, where X was the presiding arbitrator.

After recognizing X, Mr. Moustakas raised concerns about X's impartiality with the law firm representing the owners (on the grounds that X had been involved in making serious allegations against Mr. Moustakas in the B case). The owners' lawyers did not raise Mr. Moustakas' concerns with the arbitrators, apparently because Mr. Moustakas began to testify immediately after raising his concerns (thus making it difficult for the owners' lawyers to pursue their concerns because the witnesses were sequestered during their testimony). At the conclusion of Mr. Moustakas' testimony, on the second day of the arbitration, X informed the parties that he had been involved in previous proceedings adverse to Mr. Moustakas. Later that day, the owners' lawyers objected to X serving as presiding arbitrator on the grounds that X could not impartially consider Mr. Moustakas' testimony given his recent involvement in the B case in challenging Mr. Moustakas' credibility.

X responded to the owners' objection the next day, reading a prepared statement that acknowledged his role in the B case. X denied, as far as he was aware, that any allegations of impropriety had been made against Mr. Moustakas: "I do not recall making or Waterson Hicks [the law firm instructing X] or their clients making any allegation of producing fraudulent and fabricated document...." X also denied ever having met or seen Mr. Moustakas. X's statement explained that X was involved only in an initial application for disclosure, which resulted in a consent order, and that he had no further involvement in the case. X refused to withdraw: "nothing relating to that case [the B case] gives rise to any doubt in my mind as to the propriety of Mr. Moustakas' conduct."

In subsequent correspondence, the owners and X maintained their previous views. X maintained that he was "unaware" of the allegations made against Mr. Moustakas in the B case. He said: "had I recused myself a substantial way into the hearing and an umpire had to be re-appointed, costs would indeed have been wasted.... On the basis of the information provided by the Claimant and for the reasons already given I did not think I was entitled to recuse myself."] ...

Both parties agreed that the test for apparent bias is that stated in *Porter v. Magill* [2002] 1 All ER 465: namely, the test of what a fair-minded and informed observer would conclude having considered the facts. It is this notional person who must be asked whether (s)he would conclude that there was a real possibility that the tribunal was biased. In *R v. Gough* [1993] 2 All ER 724, 737, Lord Goff of Chieveley said that he thought:

> "it unnecessary, in formulating the appropriate test, to require that the court should look at the matter through the eyes of a reasonable man, because the court in cases such as these personifies the reasonable man; and in any event the court has first to ascertain the relevant circumstances from the available evidence, knowledge of which would not necessarily be available to an observer in court at the relevant time. Finally, for the avoidance of doubt, I prefer to state the test in terms of real danger rather than real likelihood, to ensure that the court is thinking in terms of possibility rather than probability of bias."

The new test, using the words "real possibility" as opposed to "real danger," was not significantly different in that respect; although the imposition of a fair minded observer (to bring the test into line with Strasbourg jurisprudence) was different. The threshold is "a real possibility of unconscious bias."

As Lord Steyn's judgment in *Lawal v. Northern Spirit Ltd* [2004] 1 All ER 187, illuminates, the position of barristers who take up part-time judicial appointments can cause difficulties.... It is no longer necessary, in my judgment, to draw a distinction between cases where there is a foreign party and those where there is not. The objective observer is there to ensure an even handed approach to apparent bias, whatever the nationality of the parties. The only possible justification for treating foreign parties differently could be on the basis that they may not understand as well as an indigenous party the way the legal professions in England are organised or their conventions and rules of conduct.... The interpolation of the observer does, I think, make it unnecessary in future to have to give special regard to foreigners. "In determination of their rights and liabilities, civil or criminal, everyone is entitled to a fair hearing by an impartial tribunal. That right ... is properly described as fundamental." *Locabail (UK) Ltd v. Bayfield Prop. Ltd* [2000] 1 All ER 65, 69. The entitlement to that right is universal (see for example art. 12(2) of the UNCITRAL Model Law) and not parochial and it is not to be determined by awareness or otherwise of local rules and customs.

In my judgment, if the properly informed independent observer concluded that there was a real possibility of bias, then I would regard that as a species of "serious irregularity" which has caused substantial injustice to the applicant. I do not accept [the] submission that even if that conclusion was reached the court must then inquire as to whether substantial injustice has been caused. In my judgment there can be no more serious or substantial injustice than having a tribunal which was not, *ex hypothesi*, impartial, determine parties' rights. The right to a fair hearing by an impartial tribunal is fundamental; the Act is founded upon that principle and the Act must be construed accordingly. In these circumstances, upon a proper construction of §§1, 33 and 68(1) and (2), if the tribunal were not impartial, then the requirements of §68(1) and (2) are satisfied. I profoundly disagree with ... *Groundshire v. VHE Constr.* [2001] 1 BLR 395 [which said that "the court is only to interfere on the grounds of serious irregularity in the form of unfairness if the court considers, not speculates, that the irregularity or unfairness has caused or will cause substantial injustice to the applicant."] It is contrary to fundamental principles to hold that an arbitral award made by a tribunal which was not impartial is to be enforced unless it can be shown that the bias has caused prejudice. The problem with unconscious bias is that it is inherently difficult to prove and the statements made about it by the judges themselves cannot be tested. Nor can the court know whether the bias actually made any difference or not.

The [2004] International Bar Association guidelines [cited by the charterer] do not purport to be comprehensive and as the working party added "nor could they be" ((¶7)). The guidelines are to be "applied with robust commonsense and without pedantic and unduly formalistic interpretation" (see ¶6). I am not impressed by the points [the charterer] made on these lists [(i.e., that the prior representation by X is not on the Red List)]. They come close to the point in issue. The question at issue is not whether what happened fell within the Red List or not. Barristers in practice who take up part-time judicial appointments are not … mentioned in the lists at all. But that says nothing about the true answer to the questions in this case.

I start with the question whether as a result of X's involvement in the B case he should have recused himself when objection was taken on the second day of the arbitration. The facts which the independent observer would have known are…: (1) In the B arbitration he was instructed by the same solicitors who were instructed on the charterers' behalf in the present arbitration; (2) in the B arbitration there were serious allegations made against Mr. Moustakas in relation to disclosure of documents and to his failure to make proper disclosure and to the authenticity of documents in his possession; (3) The extent of X's knowledge of these allegations in the B case is not entirely clear and would ultimately depend upon seeing the instructions (which have not been made available) which were given to him in connection with the application for disclosure which he made to the court. The observer would know that X said in his prepared statement to the tribunal that he did not "recall" (and that the note for his oral submissions did not refer to) making, or Waterson Hicks or their clients making, any allegation of producing fraudulent and fabricated documents and threatening forensic investigation "but again I have no basis for thinking that any such allegation, even if made, was ever substantiated." (4) Immediately Mr. Moustakas knew X's name, he was concerned about his involvement with the same solicitors in the B case. It is not clear whether Mr. Moustakas recognized X before he was told his name nor whether Mr. Moustakas had seen X at the B hearing. The evidence on this is equivocal; but the immediacy of his concern when he knew who X was (whether as the umpire or not) is a fact. (5) In the present arbitration, there was a "heavy" challenge to the way disclosure had been handled [with the owners accused of "suppressing" documents and engaging in "disgraceful" tactics.]. (6) These sorts of points had been made by the same solicitors in the B arbitration, and the uncomfortable feeling which Mr. Moustakas had that X would or might have detected a "pattern" of misbehaviour in relation to disclosure based upon his knowledge acquired as a barrister in the B action was genuine. (7) The objection to X was not an attempt to disrupt the arbitration, as the owners had indicated their wish to continue with the two appointed arbitrators and without an umpire and, unless they disagreed, a replacement umpire was not needed.

In my judgment, the independent observer would share the feeling of discomfort expressed by Mr. Moustakas and concluded that there was a real possibility that the tribunal was biased. I pay no attention to the evidence of the other two arbitrators that had they sat on their own the result would have been the same simply because such evidence is not relevant to the issue which the objective observer must decide. The question is whether X should have recused himself at the beginning of the third day, by which time the arbitration had not been completed and the other two arbitrators would have retained an open mind as to the result.

It is true that in specialist arbitrations prior contact between parties and their lawyers and arbitrators is to be expected. The mere fact, for example, that a person selected as arbitrator had previously had a trade dispute with one of the parties would not thereby have caused an objectionable situation. But even in such a case, much would depend on the facts: if the dispute had involved allegations of dishonesty of a similar nature to the allegations in the second arbitration, the position could well be different. Again, there would be no problem with a barrister sitting as an arbitrator in a case in which an expert witness whom he had previously cross-examined was to give evidence. But, again, if the contact had been a short time before, and allegations of dishonesty had been made, the position could be different.

The Armageddon theory espoused by [the charterers], were this application to succeed, is unreal. In this case there was a pattern of complaint amounting to dishonesty in relation to disclosure being made by the same solicitors in each case; and X had played a part in the B disclosure exercise seven months before the arbitration.... [This] persuades me, for the reasons I have given that X should have recused himself after objection was taken.

In reaching my conclusion I have not taken into account any of the interlocutory decisions which the tribunal had made which at some stage had led to an allegation of actual bias. The position is clear, I think. If the decisions were to be challenged on grounds of prejudice or bias, then that is one thing. But they were not. In those circumstances I cannot take into account any feeling which Mr. Moustakas and his team may have felt that "odd" or unusual interlocutory decisions were being made (for example in relation to security for costs)....

I turn to the final question which relates to waiver. The point may have some significance since the interim award dealt only with certain preliminary issues. The arbitral process is not yet at an end.... If the right to object to X was waived through conduct, does that waiver apply only to the award which has already been made or does it apply to the whole arbitration so that X can continue to sit as an umpire in relation to the future conduct of the case? ...

I reject [the charterers'] submission that the owners had somehow waived their rights at 2.00 p.m. on the first day. The reality is that the arbitration was about to resume at that time; Mr. Moustakas had had only a brief word with the partner in the [law firm], although he had spoken more fully to [a junior lawyer]; [the lead trial counsel] had not been consulted. In those circumstances the owners cannot, in my view, be criticised for letting Mr. Moustakas start his evidence. It is common ground that after that moment it was not really feasible for further instructions to be taken from him until after his evidence had been completed. The completion of his evidence coincided with X making his disclosure. In my judgment, when the case resumed on the third day, after X had declined to recuse himself, [the lead trial counsel] should have indicated that that decision was not acceptable and that an application would be made to the court to have him removed but that the hearing should be concluded, without prejudice to owners' rights. Following the hearing, an application should have been made to this court under §24.... Instead what happened was a continuing objection to X conducted in correspondence. An interim award was made and owners took it up. In my judgment, by taking up the award, at the very least, the owners had lost any right they may have had to object to X's continued involvement in that part of the arbitral process. It is unacceptable to write making further objections after the hearing was concluded. X had made his decision not to recuse himself, rightly or wrongly, at the beginning of the third day. The owners were faced with a straight choice: come to the court and complain and seek his removal as a decision maker or let the matter drop. They could not get themselves into a position whereby if the award was in their favour they would drop their objection but make it in the event that the award went against them. A "heads we win and tails you lose" position is not permissible in law as §73 makes clear....

In my view, given the facts and conclusions I have stated, X should not continue to act in this matter. I have not heard argument about the continuation of the other two arbitrators but would express the hope that they could continue....

JUDGMENT OF 9 FEBRUARY 1998
16 ASA Bull. 634 (1998) (Swiss Fed. Trib.)

[A contract for technical management of ships was concluded between I SA, a Swiss company, and V, the Chief Executive Officer of a company specialized in the technical management of ships. In order to perform this contract, the two companies created a joint venture in Singapore: G. Pte Ltd, which had its capital divided between I SA (51%) and a Panamanian Company controlled by V (49%). Disputes arose under the contract and, in December 1993, V initiated the arbitral proceedings. A three-person tribunal was constituted, seated in Geneva. I SA appointed Arbitrator G, V appointed Arbitrator X, and Arbitrator Y was designated as the president of the arbitral tribunal.

In December 1995, the tribunal issued a partial award upholding] its competence over the claims of I SA. The tribunal also rejected those claims and ordered the liquidation of the joint venture through the buyback by V of the shares owned ... by G. In September 1996, I SA requested that Arbitrator G resign as an arbitrator relying on the fact that Arbitrator G and Mr. M were both partners in the same law firm, and that Mr. M was representing N Bank in its lawsuit against EPC Ltd, a company in the group of companies to which I SA belonged. The chief executive officer of I SA said he was scandalized by the aggressive litigating style of Mr. M in the *EPC Ltd* case. The first instance court rejected I SA's claim, explaining that although the claim was admissible, the "uneasiness" generated was not sufficient to justify any lack of independency of G. On June 24, 1997, the arbitral tribunal rendered an award ordering I SA to pay V $1,468,376, plus costs. I SA sought to annul the award under Article 190 of the SLPIL.]

Precedents limit the scope of the Federal Tribunal's control when asked to rule on the incompatibility of the award with public policy, as defined by Art. 190(2)(e) [of the SLPIL]. When it comes to international arbitration, an award will not be set aside on the ground that it was based on findings of arbitrary facts or because it is amounting to an untenable judicial decision. On the other hand, it would be possible when the result achieved collides with public policy. That is to say, that it is not sufficient that the grounds it is based on collide with public policy; the same consequences have to be drawn from its solution. Public policy, when referred to through Art. 190(2)(e), has to be understood as an universal notion—and not as a domestic one—that aims to preclude any incompatibility with legal or moral fundamental principles as recognized by every civilized state....

Art. 180(1)(c) addresses the case of a challenge of arbitrators when reasonable doubts can be drawn up from the circumstances regarding its lack of independence. Doubts about the independence have to be demonstrated by objective factual observations that would lead any reasonable observer to have suspicions about the arbitrator independence. That excludes subjective reactions from one party about a potential lack of independence. However the line of precedents of the Federal Tribunal suggested that since an award is considered as equivalent to a Court judgment, the same safeguards must apply to both of them. Hence, the principles of Federal Tribunal decisions regarding challenge of judges apply similarly to arbitrators. But the Court must also take into account the contextual differences between arbitration and court litigation, namely as arbitration usually involves individuals with closer relationships.

The Court rejects any complaints alleged by the parties grounded on a lack of safe-guards as provided by Art. 6 of the [European Convention on Human Rights]. Such a ruling is justified by the fact that when deciding to submit their dispute to arbitration the parties must be considered as having accepted the consequences of such a choice.... [The court referred to domestic Swiss legislation providing for challenges to Swiss judges in Swiss judicial proceedings.] When alleging that a judge is biased, the determining element in deciding whether or not such challenge has to be upheld is to be found in the objectiveness of the observations of the parties.

In order to comply with the principle of good faith, as stated in Art. 180(2), the reason justifying the challenge has to be raised before the arbitral tribunal and communicated to the other party as soon as it is discovered.... [A]lthough there is no express deadline in Art. 180(2), a party that does not react immediately loses its right to raise this reason for challenge later.

In the present case, the appellant challenges G's service on the arbitral tribunal because he is a partner of Mr. M. It is suggested this could shatter "the feeling of trust a party has to have toward the arbitrator," especially in the circumstance where the two companies in the R group of companies have to be considered as one due to the prominent position of their director and main shareholder. From the precedents it can be derived that when applying to arbitration [domestic Swiss legislation regarding removal of judges] and Art. 6.1 [of the European Convention on Human Rights], the Federal Court has to take into account the economic and professional relationships between a party, or its counsel, and an arbitrator in order to admit only in exceptional circumstances a reason justifying the removal of the arbitrator. In the present case, the Court reaches the conclusion that insofar as the factual circumstances do not justify an objective reason likely to create any suspicion as regards to a lack of independence of Me G., the latter may remain in place. The Federal Court adds that even if it would not have been able to reject the claims on the basis stated above, it would definitely have reached the same conclusion by pointing out that the claim was too belated in respect of Art. 180(2) and in respect of the principle of good faith....

ICS INSPECTION & CONTROL SERVICES LTD (U.K.) v. REPUBLIC OF ARGENTINA

Decision on Challenge to Arbitrator in Ad Hoc Case of 17 December 2009

[ICS Inspection Control Services Ltd ("ICS") commenced an investment arbitration against the Republic of Argentina under the Agreement between the Government of the United Kingdom of Great Britain and Northern Ireland and the Government of The Republic of Argentina for the Promotion and Protection of Investments, signed December 11, 1990 (the "Treaty"). The arbitration was conducted, pursuant to Article 8(3) of the Treaty, under the 1976 UNCITRAL Rules, before a three-person tribunal. ICS appointed Mr. A as an arbitrator. In accordance with Article 9 of the UNCITRAL Rules, Mr. A made the following disclosure to the Parties:

1. My law firm, Sidley Austin LLP, has in the past represented PWC Logistics, which I understand may be, or may have been, an affiliate or a parent of ICS, the Claimant in this case. My firm no longer represents PWC Logistics. The last invoices issued to PWC Logistics date back to 2005. The total billings amounted to less than $60,000. The representation had no relation to the present case (to the extent of my knowledge of the facts of the present case, which is based in the Notice of Arbitration). I was not involved in any way in that representation.

2. My law firm and I personally are involved in the ICSID case of *Compañía de Aguas del Aconquija SA and Vivendi SA v. Argentine Republic*, ICSID Case No. ARB/97/3, where my law firm and I represent Claimants and are adverse to the Argentine Republic. The subject matter of the Vivendi dispute is not related to the subject matter of this case.

3. I do not believe that these circumstances affect my impartiality and independence as an arbitrator in this case.

Argentina challenged the appointment of Mr. A pursuant to Article 10(1) of the 1976 UNCITRAL Rules and requested that the Secretary-General of the Permanent Court of Arbitration designate an appointing authority to decide the Respondent's challenge. The Secretary-General appointed Mr. Jernej Sekolec, appointing authority, and after receiving written submissions, Mr. Sekolec issued the following decision.]

[I] sustain the challenge against Mr. A as arbitrator in the above-referenced matter for the following reasons:

In his disclosure, Mr. A indicates that he and his law firm currently represent the claimants in the long-running investment treaty proceedings, *Compañía de Aguas del Aconquija SA and Vivendi SA v. Argentine Republic* (the "*Vivendi* case"). This puts Mr. A in a situation of adversity towards Argentina, a situation that is often a source of justified concerns and that I believe should in principle be avoided, except where circumstances exist that eliminate any justifiable doubts as to the arbitrator's impartiality or independence.

It is noted that, in their submissions on the challenge, both Parties have referred to the [2004] IBA Guidelines. Although the [2004] IBA Guidelines have no binding status in the present proceedings, they reflect international best practices and offer examples of situations that may give rise to objectively justifiable doubts as to an arbitrator's impartiality or independence. Specifically, in support of its challenge, the Respondent relied on the scenario set forth at §3.4.1 of the "Orange List" of the [2004] IBA Guidelines which provides that circumstances in which "[t]he arbitrator's law firm is currently acting adverse to one of the parties or an affiliate of one of the parties" may give rise to justifiable doubts as to the arbitrator's impartiality or independence. I also note that the scenario posited at §3.1.2 of the "Orange List" provides that circumstances in which "[t]he arbitrator has within the past three years served as counsel against one of the parties or an affiliate of one of the parties in an unrelated matter" may give rise to justifiable doubts as to the arbitrator's impartiality or independence. Given that the facts underlying Mr. A's disclosure are reflected in both of these scenarios, I am of the opinion that the conflict in question is sufficiently serious to give rise to objectively justifiable doubts as to Mr. A's impartiality and independence.

It has been argued in opposition to the challenge, *inter alia*, that the *Vivendi* case may soon come to a close and is unrelated to the present case. However, I do not consider that these circumstances resolve all justifiable doubts. While no more action appears to be required from Mr. A in the current annulment proceedings in the above case, I do not consider that this possibility entirely negates Mr. A's conflict as envisaged in §3.4.1 of the [2004] IBA Guidelines inasmuch as the possibility exists that the case may continue in some form and engage Mr. A's firm's continued representation.

As to the relation between the cases, I note again that this is not merely a case in which the arbitrator's law firm is acting adversely to one of the parties in the dispute, but rather a case where the arbitrator has personally and recently acted adversely to one of the parties to the dispute. The scenario set forth in §3.1.2 of the [2004] IBA Guidelines provides that past, personal representation against one of the parties "in an unrelated matter" can be sufficient to give rise to justifiable doubts. Moreover, while the Claimant has argued that the cases are unrelated and there are technical differences between the issues raised in the two cases, they are not entirely dissimilar. Both matters are investment protection actions of considerable magnitude which raise broadly similar concerns against the same State party in a manner that reinforces any justifiable doubts as to the Arbitrator's impartiality or independence.

I wish to add that I find no reason to doubt Mr. A's personal intention to act impartially and independently but that, for the reasons stated above, it is prudent that another arbitrator be appointed by the Claimant....

NOTES

1. *Requirements for impartiality of arbitrators under New York Convention.* Does anything in the New York Convention require that arbitrators be impartial or independent? Do any of the exceptions in Articles V(1) and V(2) of the Convention provide an express basis for denying recognition to an award based on an arbitrator's lack of independence or impartiality?

    As discussed below, most national courts have found no difficulty in treating an arbitrator's lack of independence and impartiality as a potential basis for non-recognition of an award under the New York Convention (and parallel provisions of the Inter-American Convention). *See infra* pp. 1242-50. What provisions of Article V of the New York Convention might permit non-recognition of an award based upon an arbitrator's lack of impartiality? Is there anything in the Convention that could affirmatively require that arbitrators be independent and impartial? What relevance do Articles II(1) and II(3) have for the arbitrators' independence and impartiality? What if the parties' arbitration agreement requires that the arbitrators be independent and/or impartial? Do Articles II(1) and II(3) require Contracting States to give effect to this agreement? What if the parties' agreement expressly permits some (or all) arbitrators not to be impartial? Do Articles II(1) and II(3) require Contracting States to give effect to this agreement?

2. *Requirements for impartiality of arbitrators under ICSID Convention.* Consider Articles 14 and 56-58 of the ICSID Convention, excerpted at pp. 16 & 25 of the Documentary Supplement. What requirements do they impose with regard to the

impartiality of arbitrators in ICSID arbitrations? Contrast the approach under the New York Convention. What explains the differences?

3. *Requirements for impartiality of arbitrators in inter-state arbitrations.* Consider the 1907 Hague Convention, excerpted at pp. 37-52 of the Documentary Supplement. Is there any mechanism for challenging arbitrators? Is there any express requirement for impartiality and independence? Why not? Note the distinction between the "Tribunal" and the "Umpire" in Articles 45 and 57. What does that imply? Compare Articles 11 and 12 of the 2012 PCA Rules with the 1907 Hague Convention. What explains the differences?

4. *Requirements for impartiality of arbitrators under national arbitration legislation.* Most arbitration statutes impose requirements of independence and impartiality on arbitrators. Consider Article 11 of the UNCITRAL Model Law, excerpted at pp. 88-89 of the Documentary Supplement. What substantive obligations of independence does Article 11 impose on arbitrators? Note that violation of these obligations provides the basis for an interlocutory challenge to the arbitrator under Articles 12 and 13 of the Model Law. Compare the grounds for annulment of an arbitral award under Article 34 of the Model Law and the grounds for non-recognition of an award under Article 36 of the Model Law. What are the differences among these provisions?

Compare Article 11 of the Model Law with Article 180 of the SLPIL and §10(b) of the FAA, excerpted at p. 105 of the Documentary Supplement. What are the differences between these various standards for the independence and impartiality of arbitrators? Compare the approach under the Model Law to §8 of the Swedish Arbitration Act:

> "An arbitrator shall be impartial. If a party so requests, an arbitrator shall be discharged if there exists any circumstance which may diminish confidence in the arbitrator's impartiality. Such a circumstance shall always be deemed to exist: (1) where the arbitrator or a person closely associated to him is a party, or otherwise may expect benefit or detriment worth attention, as a result of the outcome of the dispute; (2) where the arbitrator or a person closely associated to him is the director of a company or any other association which is a party, or otherwise represents a party or any other person who may expect benefit or detriment worth attention as a result of the outcome of the dispute; (3) where the arbitrator has taken a position in the dispute, as an expert or otherwise, or has assisted a party in the preparation or conduct of his case in the dispute; or (4) where the arbitrator has received or demanded compensation in violation of §39, second paragraph."

Is this approach more desirable than that of the UNCITRAL Model Law? How does it differ? Which of the foregoing legislative provisions is most desirable?

Consider the following excerpts addressing the arbitrators' obligations of impartiality and independence:

> "an independent mind is indispensable in the exercise of adjudicative power, whatever the source of that power may be and it is one of the essential qualities of an arbitrator." *Judgment of 13 April 1972*, 1975 Rev. arb. 235 (French Cour de cassation civ. 2e).

> "All legal arbiters are bound to apply the law as they understand it to the facts of individual cases as they find them. They must do so without fear or favor, affection or ill-will, that is, without partiality or prejudice. Justice is portrayed as blind not because she ignores the facts and circumstances of individual cases, but because she shuts her

eyes to all considerations extraneous to the particular case." *Locabail (U.K.) Ltd v. Bayfield Prop. Ltd* [2000] Q.B. 451 (English Ct. App.).

"the independence of the arbitrator is essential to his judicial role, in that from the time of his appointment he assumes the status of a judge, which excludes, in its very nature, any relation of dependence, particularly with the parties. Further, the circumstances relied on to challenge that independence must constitute, through the existence of material or intellectual links, a situation which is liable to affect the judgment of the arbitrator by creating a definite risk of bias in favor of a party to the arbitration." *Judgment of 2 June 1989*, 1991 Rev. arb. 87 (Paris Cour d'appel).

Are these appropriate standards? How, if at all, do they differ from one another? How do they differ from Article 11?

Can an arbitrator ever be a completely blank slate, without any relevant prior experiences or views about the issues and subject matter of the parties' dispute? *See, e.g.*, Bedjaoui, *The Arbitrator: One Man—Three Roles*, 5(1) J. Int'l Arb. 7, 8 (1998) (an arbitrator "is neither a robot nor an inanimate object. Before considering him as a judge, the arbitrator as a man [sic] should be borne in mind.... Like all men, an arbitrator has a conscience which gives him a certain outlook on the world. He cannot detach himself from all the emotional ties which, consciously or unconsciously, may influence his thoughts."). What does this suggest about the content of the standards of impartiality and independence that apply to arbitrators? Is it inevitable that an arbitrator will have intellectual and emotional predispositions towards one party's position?

Compare the grounds for removal of an arbitrator under Article 11 of the Model Law with those under Articles 56 and 58 of the ICSID Convention, excerpted at pp. 88-89 & 25 of the Documentary Supplement. Which regime provides the stricter requirements for impartiality and independence? Which regime provides for more clearly objective and effective enforcement? What explains these differences? Which regime is preferable?

5. *Requirements for independence and impartiality of arbitrators under UNCITRAL Model Law.* What is meant by the standard contained in Article 11 of the Model Law—permitting an arbitrator to be challenged if "circumstances exist that give rise to justifiable doubts as to his impartiality or independence"? What are "justifiable *doubts*"—a 51% chance of bias? 49%? 25%? What makes a doubt "justifiable"? Whose doubts are relevant to determining whether "justifiable doubts" exist—the subjective doubts of the parties? The objective doubts of a reasonable party? The objective doubts of a reasonable onlooker? Consider how Article 11's standard (or its equivalent) is phrased and applied in *ASM Shipping* and *ICS v. Argentina*.

What do the terms "impartiality or independence" in Article 11 mean? Does Article 11's standard require that an arbitrator be entirely free of any predisposition with regard to the parties or the issues in dispute in the arbitration? Would that be true of anyone? Suppose a Russian party appoints a Russian co-arbitrator. Is the Russian co-arbitrator independent and impartial with regard to the Russian party? Suppose an insurance company, in a dispute between the insurance company and an insured, appoints as co-arbitrator a lawyer who ordinarily represents insurance companies. Is the co-arbitrator independent and impartial?

6. Commonwealth Coatings *and impartiality of arbitrators under FAA §10(b)*. The leading U.S. domestic decision on the lack of independence (or "bias") of arbitrators is *Commonwealth Coatings*. There, the U.S. Supreme Court vacated an award because the "requirements of impartiality" of arbitrators under FAA §10(b) had not been satisfied. In particular, the Court relied on the fact that the "neutral" chairman had failed to disclose his four-to-five year consulting relationship with one party to the arbitration—which had earned him $12,000, including compensation on "the very projects involved in" the arbitration. Note that there was no suggestion that the arbitrator was in fact "guilty of fraud or bias in deciding this case." Rather, the sole basis for annulling the award was the undisclosed business relationship with one of the parties. Is *Commonwealth Coatings* correctly decided on its facts? Consider Justice Fortas' dissent. Why is it not correct? How would *Commonwealth Coatings* be decided under Article 11 of the Model Law? (What about under Article 34?)

   What exactly is the Supreme Court's holding in *Commonwealth Coatings?* Is it set forth in Justice Black's opinion, or in Justice White's? U.S. lower courts have encountered understandable difficulty in deriving some generally applicable standard of impartiality from *Commonwealth Coatings. See Positive Software Solutions, Inc. v. New Century Mortg. Corp.*, 476 F.3d 278, 281 (5th Cir. 2007) ("Reasonable minds can agree that *Commonwealth Coatings*, like many plurality-plus Supreme Court decisions, is not pellucid."); *Morelite Constr. Corp. v. N.Y.C. Dist. Council*, 748 F.2d 79 (2d Cir. 1984).

   Compare the analyses in *Commonwealth Coatings* and *Americo*. Are the two decisions reconcilable? How?

   What should be the general rule regarding arbitrator independence under the FAA? In *Morelite Constr. Corp.*, the court adopted a requirement that "a reasonable person would have to conclude that an arbitrator was partial to one party to the arbitration." In *Sheet Metal Workers etc. v. Kinney Air Conditioning Co.*, 756 F.2d 742, 745-46 (9th Cir. 1988), the court concluded an award would be annulled where there was "a reasonable impression of partiality." How, if at all, do these standards differ from one another? Compare the analysis in *Sphere Drake*. What standard of impartiality does the Seventh Circuit formulate? Does the court articulate a single uniform standard of impartiality, or the possibility of multiple standards?

   How, if at all, do these (various) standards under the FAA differ from Article 11 of the UNCITRAL Model Law? From the standard applied in *ASM Shipping Ltd of India* excerpted above?

   Note that *Commonwealth Coating* involved an action to annul an arbitral award after the arbitration had been concluded, rather than an application to remove an arbitrator before the arbitration had been conducted. Should this affect the standard of impartiality and independence that is applied to the arbitrators?

7. *"Independence" and "impartiality."* Article 11 of the UNCITRAL Model Law requires arbitrators to be both independent and impartial. Compare Article 180 of the SLPIL (requiring only that an arbitrator be "independent") and §24(1)(a) of the English Arbitration Act (requiring only that an arbitrator be "impartial"). What is the difference between "independence" and "impartiality"? Is there a difference?

   Note that some authorities regard "independence" as concerned only with objective, external matters, involving the question whether an arbitrator has connections or relationships with a party (or its counsel) which render him or her "dependent" on the party; in contrast, "impartiality" is said to be concerned with subjective biases and predispositions, involving the question whether an arbitrator is able to neutrally and fairly decide a dispute. *See* U.K. Departmental Advisory Committee on Arbitration Law, *Report on the Arbitration Bill* ¶¶102-104 (1996) ("It seems to us that lack of independence, unless it gives rise to justifiable doubts about the impartiality of the arbitrator, is of no significance. The latter is, of course, the first of our grounds for removal. If lack of independence were to be included, then this could only be justified if it covered cases where the lack of independence did not give rise to justifiable doubts about impartiality, for otherwise there would be no point including lack of independence as a separate ground."); D. Caron & L. Caplan, *The UNCITRAL Arbitration Rules: A Commentary* 213 (2d ed. 2013) ("In general, impartiality means that an arbitrator will not favor one party more than another, while independence requires that the arbitrator remain free from the control of either party."). Do these distinctions make sense?

Consider the discussion of "impartiality" and "independence" in *Americo*. Is it persuasive? Why or why not?

What is the purpose of requirements for "independence"? How is it that an arbitrator's "impartiality" can be ascertained? Is there any way, as a practical matter, to ascertain an arbitrator's true subjective impartiality except by considering his or her external independence from the parties? *See Morelite Constr. Corp. v. N.Y.C. Dist. Council*, 748 F.2d 79, 84 (2d Cir. 1984) ("Bias is always difficult, and indeed often impossible, to 'prove.' Unless an arbitrator publicly announces his partiality, or is overheard in a moment of private admission, it is difficult to imagine how 'proof' would be obtained."). Doesn't this mean that lack of impartiality can usually only be inferred from external relations, statements, or actions—that is, from the arbitrator's lack of "independence"?

8. *"Appearance" of partiality*. Suppose there is an "appearance" of partiality or bias, but that the arbitrator is nonetheless impartial and independent. Should the existence of a partial appearance be sufficient to warrant removal of the arbitrator? What would be the reasons supporting such a conclusion? How does the court in *Sphere Drake* dispose of this issue? For other suggestions that an appearance of partiality is not sufficient to warrant removal of an arbitrator or annulment of an award, *see Apperson v. Fleet Carrier Corp.*, 879 F.2d 1344, 1358 (6th Cir. 1989) (rejecting "appearance of bias" as basis for challenging award under §10(b)); *Freedom Investors Corp. v. Hadath*, 2012 U.S. Dist. LEXIS 15129, at *11 (S.D.N.Y.) ("[A]n arbitrator is disqualified only when a reasonable person, considering all of the circumstances, would have to conclude that an arbitrator was partial to one side.... To vacate an arbitration award where nothing more than an appearance of bias is alleged would be automatically to disqualify the best informed and most capable potential arbitrators."); *Hunt v. Mobil Oil Corp.*, 654 F.Supp. 1487, 1497-98 (S.D.N.Y. 1987) ("'Evident partiality' means more than a mere appearance of bias"); *AT&T Corp. v. Saudi Cable Co.* [2000] 2 Lloyd's Rep. 127 (English Ct. App.) ("The court considers on all the material which is placed before it whether there is any real danger of unconscious bias on the part of the decision maker."); *Judgment of 1 February 2001*, XXIX Y.B. Comm. Arb. 700, 701 (2004) (German Bundesgerichtshof).

Recall, as discussed above, that "bias" or lack of impartiality can virtually never be proven, at least if it connotes a subjective state-of-mind of the arbitrator. Is it useful to state broadly that a mere "appearance" of bias is not grounds for challenging an arbitrator's impartiality? Isn't such an "appearance" just what the concept of "independence" concerns?

9. *Relevance of stage of arbitral proceedings at which arbitrator's independence and impartiality is challenged.* Suppose that a party objects to an arbitrator's impartiality and independence immediately after the arbitrator is nominated. That is what occurred, for example, in *ICS* and *Veritas Shipping*. Should the standard of independence and impartiality applicable at this stage of the arbitral proceedings be the same as that applicable to a challenge made after three years of arbitral proceedings and several interim or partial awards? That is what occurred in *Commonwealth Coatings, Sphere Drake*, and *Judgment of 9 February 1998.*

    Even apart from considerations of waiver, *infra* pp. 770-71, 773, should the same standard of independence and impartiality be applicable to removal of an arbitrator as to annulment or non-recognition of an arbitral award? What argument(s) support application of different standards at different stages in the arbitral proceedings? Is there anything in the language of Article 11 of the UNCITRAL Model Law that might support different standards of independence and impartiality?

10. *Relevance of impartiality standards for national court judges to international arbitrators.* What is the relevance of ethical standards for national court judges to the requirements of impartiality and independence applicable to international arbitrators?

    (a) *Authorities requiring same standards of impartiality for arbitrators as for judges.* In some countries, arbitrators have been subject to the same standards of impartiality as national court judges. *See, e.g.,* Québec Code of Civil Procedure, Arts. 234, 235, 942; Luxembourg Code of Civil Procedure, Art. 378; *Judgment of 14 November 1990*, 1991 Rev. arb. 75 (French Cour de cassation civ. 2e) (standards of impartiality prescribed for judges under Article 341 of French New Code of Civil Procedure applicable to arbitrators). What is the rationale for these requirements? If an arbitrator performs an adjudicatory function, should he or she not be subject to the same standards of impartiality and independence as other judicial officers? Are there differences between the role of an arbitrator and that of a judge, which might require a different result?

    Consider the analysis in *Judgment of 9 February 1998.* What does the court conclude about the applicability of standards for judicial impartiality under Swiss law and the European Convention on Human Rights? What is the rationale for this analysis? Note that the Federal Tribunal remarks that these standards must be applied with regard to the "contextual differences between arbitration and Court litigation." What does that mean?

    (b) *Authorities requiring lower standards of independence and impartiality for arbitrators than judges.* Justices White and Fortas conclude in *Commonwealth Coatings* that arbitrators should presumptively be held to a lower standard of impartiality than judges. Compare the court's analysis in *Sphere Drake*. For similar conclusions, *see Reeves Bros., Inc. v. Capital-Mercury Shirt Corp.*, 962 F.Supp. 408 (S.D.N.Y. 1997) ("Arbitrators are ... held to a lower standard of impartiality than Article III judges"); *Areca, Inc. v. Oppenheimer & Co.*, 960 F.Supp. 52, 56

(S.D.N.Y. 1997) ("less stringent standards for disqualification of arbitrators than for federal judges").

Recall that, unlike judges, arbitrators are not subject to appellate review, to governmental disclosure obligations, to democratic appointment or confirmation, or other related requirements. Recall also that arbitrators can (and do) decide important public law claims and that they often need not render reasoned awards. Does this suggest that arbitrators ought to be held to higher—or at least equivalent—ethical standards than judges?

What are the disadvantages of imposing rigorous ethical standards on arbitrators? Consider the following: "The unique role of arbitrators, whose special expertise arises from wide experience in their fields, sometimes leads to a gain of their professional knowledge and skill at the cost of the appearance of less than complete impartiality." *Pitta v. Hotel Ass'n of N.Y. City, Inc.*, 806 F.2d 419, 423 (2d Cir. 1986). *See also Morelite Constr. Corp.*, 748 F.2d at 83 ("Familiarity with a discipline often comes at the expense of complete impartiality. Some commercial fields are quite narrow, and a given expert may be expected to have formed strong views on certain topics, published articles in the field and so forth. Moreover, specific areas tend to breed tightly knit professional communities. Key members are known to one another, and in fact may work with, or for, one another, from time to time."). Compare the similar observations in *Commonwealth Coatings* and *Judgment of 9 February 1998. See also AT&T Corp. v. Saudi Cable Co.* [2000] 2 Lloyd's Rep. 127, 135 (English Ct. App.) ("The courts are responsible for the provision of public justice. If there are two standards I would expect a lower threshold [for bias or lack of independence] to apply to courts of law than applies to a private tribunal whose 'judges' are selected by the parties. After all, there is an overriding public interest in the integrity of the administration of justice in the courts").

Are there really so few lawyers, academics, and judges that obtaining qualified arbitrators requires lowering ethical standards? Why is there fairly robust competition for appointments among would-be arbitrators if there are insufficient potential arbitrators?

(c) *Authorities requiring higher standards of impartiality for arbitrators than judges*. Some authorities have concluded that arbitrators should be subject to higher standards of independence and impartiality than judges. Note that Justice Black's opinion in *Commonwealth Coatings* required that arbitrators be "even more scrupulous" than national court judges. Similarly, *see* Nariman, *Standards of Behaviour of Arbitrators*, 4 Arb. Int'l 311, 311-12 (1988): "standards of behaviour expected of arbitrators … are no less stringent than those demanded of judges; in fact, arbitrators are expected to behave a shade better since judges are institutionally insulated by the established court-system, their judgments being also subjected to the corrective scrutiny of an appeal" Is this conclusion persuasive? What justifies the general conclusion that "arbitrators are expected to behave" better than judges? Expected by whom? The parties to the arbitration agreement? In all cases?

(d) *Relevance of standards of impartiality of judges to international arbitrators*. Is it in fact useful to look to standards of independence and impartiality applicable to domestic court judges in determining standards of impartiality and independence for international arbitrators? Note that, in international disputes, parties will almost always come from different legal systems, with differing standards of judicial independence and impartiality; note also that parties to arbitration agreements will often share common expectations regarding the independence and impartiality of "their" arbitrators (*e.g.*, when they agree to institutional rules specifying such standards). Given these characteristics of the arbitral process, how useful are domestic standards for judicial impartiality?

Consider again the analysis in *Judgment of 9 February 1998*. Would it be permissible for a national court to ignore fundamental legal (European Convention on Human Rights) protections in adopting standards for international arbitrators? Are those standards in fact applicable to international arbitration? If not, do they nonetheless provide guidance? What about the standards of impartiality and independence developed in inter-state arbitration; do they also provide guidance?

11. *Relevance of parties' agreement to standards of independence and impartiality of arbitrators.* Suppose that the parties expressly or impliedly agree that their arbitrator(s) will be bound by standards of impartiality and independence that are more (or, alternatively, that are less) rigorous than those applicable to national court judges. Should this agreement be respected? Why or why not?

Note the analysis in *Sphere Drake*. How important are the parties' expectations regarding the arbitrators' impartiality in Judge Easterbrook's analysis? Consider the following discussion, by Judge Posner in *Merit Ins. Co. v. Leatherby Ins. Co.*, 714 F.2d 673, 679-81 (7th Cir. 1983):

> If Leatherby had wanted its dispute with Merit resolved by an Article III judge … it would not have inserted an arbitration clause in the contract, or having done so move for arbitration against Merit's wishes. Leatherby wanted something different from judicial dispute resolution. It wanted dispute resolution by experts in the insurance industry, who were bound to have greater knowledge of the parties, based on previous professional experience, than an Article III judge, or a jury…. It is no surprise, therefore, that the standards for disqualification in the [AAA's] Commercial Arbitration Rules and the Code of Ethics for Arbitrators are not so stringent as those in the federal statutes on judges…. (In fact the arbitration rules and code do not contain any standards for disqualification as such, though such standards are implicit in the disclosure requirements of the AAA's Rules and the AAA-ABA Code.)
>
> The [AAA] is in competition not only with other private arbitration services but with the courts in providing—in the case of the private services, selling—an attractive form of dispute settlement. It may set its standards as high or as low as it thinks its customers want. The statute has a different purpose—to make arbitration effective by putting the coercive force of the federal courts behind arbitration decrees that effect interstate commerce or are otherwise of federal concern…. The statute does not provide a dispute settlement mechanism; it facilitates private dispute settlement. The standards for judicial intervention are therefore narrowly drawn to assure the basic integrity of the arbitration process without meddling in it. Section 10 is full of words like corruption and misbehavior and fraud. The standards it sets are minimum ones…. The fact that the AAA went beyond the statutory standards in drafting its own code of ethics does not lower the threshold for judicial intervention.

Is Judge Posner's analysis persuasive? Are there not two propositions at work in Judge Posner's analysis: (a) by agreeing to arbitrate, parties impliedly agree to lower requirements of impartiality than those applicable to U.S. judges; and (b) the parties' agreement to these lower standards of impartiality should be given effect? Do you agree with both of these propositions? Compare the Texas Supreme Court's analysis in *Americo*.

What is the source for the conclusion that parties impliedly expect arbitrators to meet lower standards of independence and impartiality than judges? Are the general statutory grounds for annulment of a domestic award reliable grounds for determining the content of parties' expectations in all cases? In particular, in international cases? Do all parties in all cases agree to lower standards of impartiality for the arbitrators? Suppose the parties' arbitration agreement expressly imposes rigorous standards of impartiality? For example, suppose the parties' arbitration agreement provides "No arbitrator shall be of the same nationality as any party and no arbitrator shall have had any prior professional or commercial relations with any of the parties or their counsel." Consider Articles 7 to 12 of the UNCITRAL Rules, Articles 11 to 13 of the ICC Rules and the IBA Guidelines, excerpted at pp. 165-67, 186-88 & 363-78 of the Documentary Supplement. Do these provisions support Judge Posner's view that parties impliedly agree to reduced standards of impartiality for arbitrators? Doesn't it depend on the individual parties and the terms of their agreement?

Suppose the parties do expressly (or impliedly) agree to reduced standards of impartiality and independence for arbitrators. How far does Judge Posner's rationale in *Merit Insurance* extend? What if parties agree that a sole arbitrator (or presiding arbitrator) may be an employee of one party, for example, one party's General Counsel? Would Judge Posner permit that employee to serve as an arbitrator? Would Judge Posner have permitted Dr. Wallersteiner to have served as a party-nominated arbitrator in *Veritas Shipping*?

12. *Validity of advance waiver of impartiality obligations.* Suppose the parties agree expressly to an arbitral tribunal that is not impartial; is that agreement valid? Consider the analysis in *Americo*. What would the result have been in *Americo* if the presiding arbitrator had been, pursuant to the parties' agreement, partial to one party?

The UNCITRAL Model Law omits any grounds for parties to contract out of Article 12's impartiality standards. Does that mean that the parties are not free to agree to alternative standards of independence and impartiality than those specified in Article 12? Note that the English Arbitration Act includes standards of impartiality and the judicial power to remove arbitrators for a lack of impartiality among the Act's mandatory provisions. English Arbitration Act, 1996, §§4(1), 24, 33(1), Schedule 1; R. Merkin, *Arbitration Law* ¶¶10.27 to 10.28 (1991 & Update August 2014).

Consider the relevance of Articles II and V(1)(d) of the New York Convention to determining whether the parties may agree to the standards of impartiality and independence of the arbitrators. If the parties' arbitration agreement provides for arbitration before an individual having commercial relationships with both parties, should that agreement not be given effect pursuant to Articles II(1) and II(3)? Suppose that the parties' agreement in *Veritas Shipping* provided for arbitration before Dr. Wallersteiner, as sole arbitrator.

Also consider the IBA Guidelines on Conflicts of Interest, General Standards 3(b) and 4(b). Are these provisions wise?

13. *What standards of impartiality should be required for arbitrators under national law?* Given the foregoing discussion, what standards of impartiality and independence *should* be imposed by national law on international arbitrators? To what extent should these standards be defined by the parties' agreement? To what extent should these standards be imposed by external statutory requirements?

14. *Choice-of-law issues relating to impartiality requirements imposed by national law.* As with other requirements relating to the identity of arbitrators, independence and impartiality requirements imposed by national law raise choice-of-law issues. That is, to what international arbitrations (and which arbitrators) are a particular country's requirements concerning independence applicable? Put concretely, suppose Parties 1 and 2, from States A and B, agree to arbitrate in State C. What state's requirements for independence and impartiality apply to the arbitrators—State A, B, or C's? Does the answer differ depending upon whether (a) a party seeks to challenge an arbitrator, or (b) a party seeks to deny recognition of an arbitral award?

    To what arbitrations are the independence and impartiality requirements of Article 11 of the UNCITRAL Model Law applicable? *See* UNCITRAL Model Law, Art. 1. Virtually all authorities conclude that the law governing the requirements applicable to arbitrators' capacity, nationality and independence/impartiality is that of the arbitral seat. *See* G. Born, *International Commercial Arbitration* 1824-26 (2d ed. 2014). What about the law governing the arbitration agreement?

15. *Impartiality requirements under institutional rules.* In addition to legislative requirements imposed by national law, most institutional arbitration rules also impose requirements of independence and impartiality on the arbitrators. Consider Articles 11 and 12 of the UNCITRAL Rules and Article 11 of the ICC Rules, excerpted at p. 186 of the Documentary Supplement. How does each set of rules define the arbitrator's independence obligations? What differences exist between the rules? Compare the foregoing approaches to Rules 13-20 of the AAA Rules, excerpted at pp. 235-38 of the Documentary Supplement. Consider carefully the differences under the UNCITRAL and ICC Rules, on the one hand, and the AAA Commercial Rules, on the other.

    Suppose that institutional rules (or the parties' arbitration agreement) contain provisions regarding impartiality that are *more* demanding than those imposed by applicable national law? Is there any reason that the parties' agreement to heightened requirements of impartiality should not be given effect? Does Article 12 of the UNCITRAL Model Law provide any basis for the parties to impose heightened requirements of independence and impartiality? Suppose that the institutional rules (or the parties' agreement) impose *less* demanding standards of impartiality than applicable national law. Are the parties able to contract for lower standards of independence than those required by generally-applicable arbitration legislation? What does Article 12 of the Model Law suggest?

    Why is it that different sets of institutional rules specify different standards of impartiality and independence? Is it because this is what different categories of users desire? If so, why should parties be forbidden from making these choices?

16. *Declarations of independence.* In ancient Greece, arbitrators were required to swear an oath of impartiality, often in a religious sanctuary, before hearing evidence or, in other accounts, before deliberating. *See* M. Tod, *International Arbitration Amongst the Greeks* 115-16 (1913). Various formulations of oaths were used, including:

"By Zeus and Lycian Apollo and Earth, I will judge the case to which the contesting parties have sworn in accordance with the justest judgment, and I will not judge according to a witness if he does not seem to be bearing true witness; nor have I received gifts from any one on account of this trial, neither I myself nor any one else, man or woman, on my behalf, in any way or under any pretext whatsoever. If I swear truly, may to be well with me, if falsely, the reverse." *Ibid.*

What was the purpose of this oath? Compare the modern version of the arbitrators' oath, illustrated by the ICC Arbitrator's Statement of Acceptance, Availability, Impartiality and Independence, excerpted at pp. 325-26 of the Documentary Supplement. As discussed below, witnesses in international arbitrations are required, under potential criminal penalties, to testify honestly and, in many cases, are required to swear oaths or affirmations to that effect. *See infra* pp. 837-38, 839-51, 1035. Why shouldn't arbitrators be required to do the same? Note the ancient Greek practice.

17. *IBA Guidelines on Conflicts of Interest.* Read the IBA Guidelines, which were amended in 2014 and are excerpted at pp. 363-78 of the Documentary Supplement, focusing on their basic structure and procedural requirements, rather than the particular terms of the Red, Orange and Green Lists. Outline what the basic terms of the Guidelines require. Compare the IBA Guidelines to the provisions of Article 12 of the UNCITRAL Model Law and Articles 11-15 of the ICC Rules. What are the differences in each? What are their respective advantages and disadvantages?

What is the legal status of the IBA Guidelines? Note that the appointing authority in *ICS* relied upon the Guidelines as useful guidance. Is that appropriate? Recall Judge Easterbrook's analysis, and reliance on the parties' expectations, in *Sphere Drake.* Aren't the IBA Guidelines relevant to determining the parties' expectations in contemporary international arbitrations?

What is the difference between items that are on the Orange and Red Lists? Note that there are waivable and non-waivable sections of the Red List. What are the differences between the waivable Red List and non-waivable Red List? Between the waivable Red List and the Orange List?

Note that many items on the Orange List have time periods associated with them. What if circumstances fall outside the time period specified (*e.g.*, three years); is that event or relationship then on the Green List? Is it irrelevant to consideration of the arbitrator's independence and impartiality?

Are the IBA Guidelines appropriate for investment arbitration? For inter-state arbitration? Why or why not? The 2004 IBA Guidelines have (recently) been applied in challenge decisions in investment arbitrations. In addition to *ICS,* see *Alpha Projektholding GmbH v. Ukraine, Decision on Respondent's Proposal to Disqualify Arbitrator Dr. Yoram Turbowicz in ICSID Case No. ARB/07/16 of 10 March 2010* and *Perenco Ecuador Ltd v. Repub. of Ecuador, Decision on Challenge to Arbitrator in PCA Case No. IR-2009/1 of 8 December 2009.* Note that the Guidelines state that they "apply to international … investment arbitration." 2014 Guidelines, Introduction, ¶5.

18. *Commonly-invoked bases for lack of arbitrator independence or impartiality.* A number of bases for challenging an arbitrator's independence and impartiality recur frequently in practice.

(a) *General statements of requirement that arbitrators be independent and impartial.* Different national courts and other authorities have adopted different general standards of impartiality. Recall the requirement, imposed by Article 11 of the

UNCITRAL Model Law, that an arbitrator may be challenged where "circumstances exist that give rise to justifiable doubts as to his impartiality or independence." Consider also the formulations quoted above at pp. 733-34. How much guidance do these formulations provide in particular cases? What are "justifiable doubts"? Are they nonetheless useful in defining the purpose of decisions regarding an arbitrator's independence and impartiality?

(b) *Judge in own cause.* It is elementary that a party may not be an arbitrator in its own case ("*nemo debet esse iudex in propria causa*"). *See Judgment of 31 January 1907*, DFT 33 I 143, 146 (Swiss Fed. Trib.) ("It is a fundamental principle of every well-regulated judicature that nobody can be a judge in his own cause.") According to the IBA Guidelines, "no one is allowed to be his or her own judge, there cannot be identity between an arbitrator and a party." 2014 IBA Guidelines, Explanation to General Standard 2(d). Can there be any doubt that a party should not be permitted to act as an arbitrator in its own case? What if the other party agrees?

(c) *Financial interest in arbitration.* Another clear basis for finding a lack of impartiality, effectively involving an arbitrator acting as a judge in his or her own cause, is the arbitrator's material financial interest in the arbitration. This includes cases where the arbitrator would profit from his or her own decision or had an ownership interest in a party to the arbitration. *See* 2014 IBA Guidelines, Non-Waivable Red List 1.3 (non-waivable conflict where "the arbitrator has a significant financial or personal interest in one of the parties, or the outcome of the case."); Swedish Arbitration Act, §8(1) (arbitrator "may expect benefit or detriment worth attention, as a result of the outcome of the dispute"); *Rand v. Readington*, 13 N.H. 72 (N.H. Super. 1842) (award annulled because prevailing party was indebted to arbitrators and amounts received were pledged to repay arbitrators' claims); *Judgment of 9 April 1992, Société Annahold BV & D. Frydman v. Société l'Oréal*, 1996 Rev. arb. 483 (Paris Cour d'appel) (award annulled because arbitrator had not disclosed having served for several years as financial consultant of company belonging to same group as party). In cases involving an arbitrator's ownership of de minimis number of shares of a party, courts have generally rejected partiality claims. *Standard Tankers (Bahamas) Co. v. Motor Tank Vessel, AKTI*, 438 F.Supp. 153, 160 (E.D.N.Y. 1977).

(d) *Present or past employment by party.* As *Veritas Shipping* illustrates, an arbitrator's present employment by a party should presumptively be a *per se* basis for finding bias. *See, e.g.*, 2014 IBA Guidelines, Explanation to General Standard 2(d), Non-Waivable Red List 1.1, 1.2 (including position in third-party funder of party); Swedish Arbitration Act, §8(2) ("director of a company"); *Judgment of 20 October 1994*, 1996 Rev. arb. 442 (Paris Cour d'appel) (arbitrator was supervisor of one of the parties to the arbitral proceedings); *Judgment of 15 January 1988*, 1988 Rev. arb. 316 (Paris Tribunal de grande instance) (arbitrator was paid technical consultant for one party at time of arbitration). *Compare Logy Enters. Ltd v. Haikou City Bonded Area Wansen Prods. Trading Co.*, XXIII Y.B. Comm. Arb. 660 (1998) (H.K. Ct. App. 1997) (arbitrator's status as official of state entity related to one party does not constitute bias); *Transocean Shipping Agency Ltd v. Black Sea Shipping*, XXIII Y.B. Comm. Arb. 713 (1998) (Indian Ct. App. 1998) (Indian public policy does not require non-recognition of Ukrainian arbitral award made by sole arbitrator who was an officer of one of the parties); *Judgment of 11 July 1992*, XXII Y.B. Comm. Arb. 715 (1982) (Italian Corte di Cassazione) (fact that co-arbitrator for defaulting party was appointed by adverse party (Romanian state entity) and was Romanian state official does not constitute bias).

It is less clear whether an arbitrator's past employment or retention as counsel on unrelated matters will presumptively sustain a finding of a lack of independence or impartiality. *See, e.g.*, 2014 IBA Guidelines, Orange List 3.1, 3.4.2; *Employers Ins. of Wausau v. Nat'l Union Fire Ins.*, 933 F.2d 1481 (9th Cir. 1991); *Imperial Ethiopian Gov't v. Baruch-Foster Corp.*, 535 F.2d 334, 337 (5th Cir. 1976) ("neutral" arbitrator advised party on unrelated matter in past); *Austin S. I, Ltd v. Barton-Malow Co.*, 799 F.Supp. 1135 (M.D. Fla. 1992) (fact that arbitrator had briefly collaborated with party, five years earlier in a different job, to make business development presentation not grounds for finding partiality); *Fertilizer Corp. of India v. IDI Mgt Inc.*, 517 F.Supp. 948 (S.D. Ohio 1981) (party-appointed arbitrator had acted as counsel for party on several past occasions); *Judgment of 27 January 2005*, 2005 SchiedsVZ 159 (Oberlandesgericht Dresden) (lack of independence where sole arbitrator acted as counsel for party in pending court proceedings); *Decision in SCC Case 177/2012*, described in F. Mutis Tellez, *Arbitrator's Independence and Impartiality: A Review of SCC Board Decisions on Challenges to Arbitrators (2010-2012)* 12 (2013) (sustaining challenge based on arbitrator's representation of claimant in dispute before national courts until few months prior to filing of arbitration).

(e) *Direct, substantial business relationship*. If an arbitrator has substantial, undisclosed business dealings with a party, a lack of independence and impartiality can presumptively be found. 2014 IBA Guidelines, Non-Waivable Red List 1.3, Waivable Red List 2.3.4, 2.3.6, 2.3.9, Orange List 3.5.4; *Olson v. Merrill Lynch, Pierce, Fenner & Smith, Inc.*, 51 F.3d 157 (8th Cir. 1995) (annulling award where arbitrators failed to disclose that their employers had ongoing business relations with one party); *Petroleum Cargo Carriers Ltd v. Unitas, Inc.*, 220 N.Y.S.2d 724 (N.Y. Sup. Ct. 1961), *aff'd*, 224 N.Y.S.2d 654 (N.Y. App. Div. 1962) (award annulled because arbitrator's firm received $350,000 in commissions from party); *Judgment of 23 March 1995*, 1996 Rev. arb. 446 (Paris Cour d'appel) (filing of patent and incorporation of company by arbitrator and party); *Judgment of 9 April 1992*, 1996 Rev. arb. 483 (Paris Cour d'appel) (arbitrator was consultant to affiliate of party). *Compare Woods v. Saturn Distrib. Corp.*, 78 F.3d 424 (9th Cir. 1996) (rejecting claim of partiality based on financial relationship of arbitrator with party which was disclosed); *Cook Indus., Inc. v. C. Itoh & Co. (Am.) Inc.*, 449 F.2d 106 (2d Cir. 1971) (award upheld where arbitrator was employee of company with significant business dealings with party).

(f) *Family or personal relationship*. A familial or other close personal relationship (or enmity) between an arbitrator and a party or a party's principal, counsel, third-party funder or key witness can also sustain a finding of bias. *See* 2014 IBA Guidelines, Non-Waivable Red List 1.3, Waivable Red List 2.2.2, 2.2.3, 2.3.8, Orange List 3.3.6, 3.3.7, 4.4.3, 3.4.4; *Judgment of 12 January 1999*, 1999 Rev. arb. 381 (Paris Cour d'appel) (arbitrator was stepfather of the party's counsel); *Judgment of 26 October 1966*, DFT 92 I 271 (Swiss Fed. Trib.) (arbitrator removed because his wife was associate at one party's law firm). A personal relationship between an arbitrator and a party, principal, or lawyer can also result in disqualification of an arbitrator or annulment of an award. For one salacious example, *see Suite Sharing: Arbitrator's Friendship With Winning Lawyer Imperils Huge Victory*, Wall Street J. (Feb. 14, 1990), at A1 (presiding male arbitrator spent two nights in hotel room of prevailing party's female counsel). *See also Pac. & Arctic Ry. & Nav. Co. v. United Transp. Union*, 952 F.2d 1144, 1148 (9th Cir. 1991) (award annulled where presiding arbitrator was friend of president of party to arbitration and dined together (at party's expense) with president before hearing); *Judgment of 9 September 2010*, Case No. I CSK 535/09 (Polish S.Ct.) (annulling award where co-arbitrator was social friend of party that nominated him and had previously acted as counsel for party's wife and related company).

(g) *Law firm "conflicts."* Arbitrators are often members of law firms. Although the arbitrator himself or herself may not represent, or have previously represented, one of the parties to the arbitration, partners or other colleagues in his or her law firm may do so, or have done so. It appears settled, under most developed legal systems, that the arbitrator's law firm's conflicts will be relevant to assessing his or her independence and impartiality. 2014 IBA Guidelines, General Standard 6(a), Non-Waivable Red List 1.4, Waivable Red List 2.3.3, 2.3.5, 2.3.6, Orange List 3.1.4, 3.2.1, 3.2.2, 3.2.3, 3.3.4, 3.4.1. In general, however, courts have been reluctant to uphold challenges or annul awards where an arbitrator was not personally involved in representations that were unrelated to the arbitration. *See, e.g., Reed & Martin, Inc. v. Westinghouse Elec. Corp.*, 439 F.2d 1268 (2d Cir. 1971) (award confirmed despite arbitrator's affiliation with law firm that represented client with interest on legal issue identical to that of one party to arbitration); *Standard Tankers (Bahamas) Co. v. Motor Tank Vessel AKTI*, 438 F.Supp. 153, 160 (E.D.N.Y. 1977) ("the fact that Smith's firm includes greater than twenty attorneys and that he was not directly involved in the legal decisions regarding the majority of the actions described above (in which [Smith's law firm represented one party]) substantiate the conclusion that these 'relationships' do not satisfy the statutory prerequisite"). Nonetheless, there are exceptions, particularly in more recent U.S. decisions. *Schmitz v. Zilveti*, 20 F.3d 1043, 1049 (9th Cir. 1994) (vacating award because arbitrator's law firm represented parent company of party to arbitration). *Cf. Beebe Med. Ctr, Inc. v. Insight Health Serv. Corp.*, 751 A.2d 426 (Del. Ch. 1999) (where law firm representing services provider simultaneously represented arbitrator as local counsel in another matter, award would be vacated even if arbitrator was unaware of the simultaneous representation).

Suppose, midway into an arbitration, one party hires the law firm with which the chairman (or the other party's arbitrator) is associated. Can it challenge the arbitrator's impartiality? Can the other party do so? *See also infra* pp. 1034-35.

(h) *Prior involvement in parties' dispute.* Another presumptive basis for finding a lack of impartiality is an arbitrator's prior involvement in the parties' dispute, either as a corporate officer or other decision-maker, lawyer, or witness. Note that this was the case in *Veritas Shipping*. Thus, the IBA Guidelines on Conflicts of Interest provide that an "arbitrator [who] had a prior involvement in the dispute" is subject to a Waivable Red List conflict. 2014 IBA Guidelines, Waivable Red List 2.1.2.

But see Employers Ins. of Wausau v. Nat'l Union Fire Ins. Co., 933 F.2d 1481, 1488-89 (9th Cir. 1991) (no bias where party-appointed arbitrator had previously provided legal advice to party on an issue in the arbitration); *Modern Brokerage Corp. v. Mass. Bonding & Ins. Co.*, 56 F.Supp. 696 (S.D.N.Y. 1944).

(i) *Arbitrator's conduct during arbitral proceedings as evidence of bias.* An arbitrator's acts and comments during the arbitral proceedings can either constitute misconduct or evidence of bias. Commentators sometimes cite the example of an arbitrator, in a proceeding between Italian and Norwegian parties who remarked, in quite direct terms, that Italians were not reliable witnesses. Paulsson, *Securing the Integrity, Impartiality and Independence of Arbitrators: Judicial Intervention*, 1993 Y.B. Arb. Inst. Stock. Cham. Comm. 91, 93 ("Italians are all liars in these cases.").

In practice, however, national courts have generally rejected claims that an arbitrator's conduct was evidence of improper bias. *Judgment of 24 November 1994*, XXI Y.B. Comm. Arb. 635 (1996) (Rotterdam Rechtbank) (rejecting challenge to award based on alleged improper *ex parte* contacts by tribunal); *Judgment of 24 February 1994*, XXII Y.B. Comm. Arb. 682 (1997) (Paris Cour d'appel) (arbitrators' refusal to suspend arbitral proceedings pending resolution of judicial challenge not evidence of bias); *Fort Hill Builders, Inc. v. Nat'l Grange Mut. Ins. Co.*, 866 F.2d 11 (1st Cir. 1989) (award upheld despite repeated hostile interruptions by arbitrator of one party's counsel); *Areca, Inc. v. Oppenheimer & Co.*, 960 F.Supp. 52 (S.D.N.Y. 1997) ("evident partiality may not be shown by alleged procedural or evidentiary errors, by legitimate efforts to move the case along, or by failure to follow the rules of evidence"). Consider also the tribunal's actions in *Certain Underwriters*.

(j) *Interviews of arbitrators.* It is well-settled that a party (or its counsel) may interview a prospective arbitrator in order to determine his or her availability, experience, and lack of conflicts. *See* IBA Ethics, Art. 5(1); AAA/ABA Code of Ethics, Canon III(B). Such discussions may not properly involve any material discussion of the merits of the case (beyond an overview sufficient to enable the prospective arbitrator to indicate whether he or she has relevant experience). *See ibid*; 2014 IBA Guidelines, Green List 4.4.1; *supra* pp. 696-702 & *infra* pp. 746-47. Lack of impartiality has sometimes been presumptively found where an arbitrator has discussed the merits of the case with a party prior to appointment and indicated his views. *Metropolitan Prop. & Cas. Ins. Co. v. J.C. Penney Cas. Ins. Co.*, 780 F.Supp. 885 (D. Conn. 1991). Parties and a co-arbitrator are also generally permitted (and even encouraged) to discuss the selection of a possible presiding arbitrator where the arbitration agreement provides for the co-arbitrators to make this selection.

(k) *Ex parte contacts.* Most institutional rules, as well as the IBA and AAA/ABA codes of ethics, forbid *ex parte* contacts between the tribunal and the parties concerning the substance of the arbitration. Even in the absence of institutional rules, undisclosed *ex parte* contacts concerning the merits of the parties' dispute are presumptively regarded as improper. For lower court decisions annulling awards for *ex parte* contacts, *see Totem Marine Tug & Barge, Inc. v. North Am. Towing, Inc.*, 607 F.2d 649 (5th Cir. 1979) (arbitrator engaged in *ex parte* communications with one party's lawyers, without notifying adverse party); *United Food & Commercial Workers Int'l Union v. SIPCO, Inc.*, 1992 U.S. Dist. LEXIS 21332 (D. Iowa) (annulling award where arbitrator engaged in *ex parte* communications after hearing and made use of *ex parte* evidence); *Judgment of 3 April 1975*, II Y.B. Comm. Arb. 241 (1977) (Hanseatisches Oberlandesgericht Hamburg) (refusing to enforce award on public policy grounds, based on material violation of German procedural standards as consequence of arbitrator's consideration of ex parte communications); *Carolina-Va. Fashion Exhibitors, Inc. v. Gunter*, 230 S.E.2d 380 (N.C. 1976) (annulling award based on arbitrators' *ex parte* inspection of property).

What if the *ex parte* contacts concerned the substance of the arbitration, but involved an issue that was ultimately not material? *See Glass, Molders, Pottery, etc. v. Excelsior Foundry Co.*, 56 F.3d 844, 846 (7th Cir. 1995) ("An *ex parte* contact is not an automatic ground for vacating [an arbitral] award"); *Schwartz v. Merrill Lynch*, 2010 U.S. Dist. LEXIS 12264, at *7 (S.D.N.Y.) ("To vacate an award on the basis of ex parte communications between a panel member and a witness or interested party, the petitioner must make a two-part showing. First, the ex parte conversation must have deprived the petitioner of a fair hearing and in-fluenced the outcome of the arbitration. Second, petitioner must show that the subject matter of the conversation [went] to the heart of the dispute's merits."); *Spector v. Torenberg*, 852 F.Supp. 201, 209 (S.D.N.Y. 1994) (to annul award based upon *ex parte* contacts "a party must show that this conversation deprived him of a hearing and influenced the outcome of the arbitration"). Are these conclusions sensible? Doesn't the existence of *ex parte* contacts indicate partiality? And therefore warrant removal? Should the same requirement exist in the context of an action to remove an arbitrator (as distinguished from an action to annul an award)?

If the parties agree to permit *ex parte* contacts between party-appointed arbitrators and parties, should this be permitted? *See Employers Ins. of Wausau v. Nat'l Union Fire Ins. Co.*, 933 F.2d 1481, 1490-91 (9th Cir. 1991) (no misconduct where panel permitted (and both parties engaged in) *ex parte* contacts between party-appointed arbitrators and parties); *Sunkist Soft Drinks, Inc. v. Sunkist Growers*, 10 F.3d 753, 759 (11th Cir. 1993) (party-nominated arbitrator attended meetings with nominating party and counsel, including witness preparation and strategy; court held that this was "not only unobjectionable, but commonplace").

(l) *Recurrent arbitral appointments by same party.* If an arbitrator is repeatedly ap-pointed by the same party or lawyer, this may give rise to justifiable doubts con-cerning his or her impartiality. On the other hand, repeated appointments may be the result of an arbitrator's (independent) quality. *Compare Andros Compania Maritima, SA v. Marc Rich & Co.*, 579 F.2d 691 (2d Cir. 1978) (upholding award where presiding arbitrator had frequently appointed, and been appointed by, one party-appointed arbitrator) *with Neaman v. Kaiser Found. Hosp.*, 11 Cal.Rptr.2d 879, 883-84 (Cal. App. 1992) (award annulled where "neutral" arbitrator failed to disclose that on five prior occasions he served as party-appointed arbitrator to one of the parties). The IBA Guidelines require disclosure of repeat appointments of an arbitrator by the same party or the same legal counsel if they are sufficiently fre-quent (*e.g.*, more than three appointments in the past three years), and provide for the possibility of challenges in these circumstances. 2014 IBA Guidelines, Orange List 3.1.3 ("The arbitrator has, within the past three years, been appointed as arbitrator on two or more occasions by one of the parties, or an affiliate of one of the parties."), 3.3.8 ("The arbitrator has, within the past three years, been appointed on more than three occasions by the same counsel, or the same law firm."). Moreover, the IBA Guidelines provide for disclosure of the fact of having served within three years as arbitrator in an unrelated dispute involving one of the parties, regardless of the appointment procedure. 2014 IBA Guidelines, Orange List 3.1.5. Is this approach wise?

(m) *Public expressions of opinion.* It is sometimes argued that an arbitrator's public statements of his or her opinion concerning matters raised in the arbitration will be grounds for removal. *See* Levine, *Dealing With Arbitrator "Issue Conflicts" in International Arbitration*, 61 Disp. Resol. J. 60 (2006). In almost every instance, statements of legal philosophy, interpretation, or approaches to particular issues are not considered even relevant to the arbitrator's independence or impartiality. *See* 2014 IBA Guidelines, Green List 4.1.1; Bishop & Reed, *Practical Guidelines for Interviewing, Selecting and Challenging Party-Appointed Arbitrators in International Commercial Arbitration*, 14 Arb. Int'l 395, 412-13 (1998). Every lawyer has—whether expressed or unexpressed—views about legal issues which may be relevant in arbitral proceedings; indeed, it is desirable that the tribunal include individuals who are experienced in the matters in dispute, which necessarily involves the formulation of thoughts and positions. On the other hand, a public expression of views about the particular dispute (as opposed to general legal issues) involved in the arbitration is often held as grounds to remove an arbitrator, and the same result may follow from an expression of views about a particular party. For a recent decision, in the context of investment arbitration, where an arbitrator's public remarks were used as the basis for a challenge, *see Perenco Ecuador Ltd v. Repub. of Ecuador, Decision on Challenge to Arbitrator in PCA Case No. IR-2009/1 of 8 December 2009.*

19. *Disclosure requirements on arbitrators and prospective arbitrators under national law.* Most developed arbitration regimes require prospective arbitrators to disclose potential grounds for challenging their impartiality and independence. Consider Article 12(1) of the UNCITRAL Model Law. Consider also Justice Black's plurality opinion in *Commonwealth Coatings*, which held that arbitrators must "disclose to the parties any dealings that might create an impression of possible bias." What is the rationale for requiring disclosure of potential conflicts by arbitrators and prospective arbitrators? Why can't arbitrators be trusted unilaterally to decide whether they are impartial—after all, they are trusted to make decisions on the merits and on jurisdiction?

What disclosure requirements do *Commonwealth Coatings* impose on arbitrators? How do those requirements compare with those under the Model Law?

Suppose an arbitrator is aware of a business relationship with a party, but does not investigate or disclose it. Does that compromise the arbitrator's impartiality? Under *Commonwealth Coatings*? Under the Model Law? Consider: *Applied Indus. Materials Corp. v. Ovalar Makine Ticaret ve Sanayi, AS*, 492 F.3d 132, 138 (2d Cir. 2007) ("where an arbitrator has reason to believe that a nontrivial conflict of interest might exist, he must (1) investigate the conflict (which may reveal information that must be disclosed ...) or (2) disclose his reasons for believing that there might be a conflict and his intention not to investigate"; "when an arbitrator knows of a potential conflict, a failure to either investigate or disclose an intention not to investigate is indicative of evident partiality."). Is this an appropriate standard? What alternative might there be?

Note that virtually all developed jurisdictions, other than England, impose a disclosure duty by statute or judicial authority. The drafters of the English Arbitration Act, 1996, concluded that a disclosure and challenge process would unduly delay constitution of the arbitral tribunal. R. Merkin, *Arbitration Law* ¶10.23 (1991 & Update August 2014). Is that wise? Is there any question but that arbitrators and potential arbitrators should be required to disclose potential conflicts to the parties? What would be the source of such a requirement? Is it what the parties impliedly expect?

20. *Disclosure requirements on arbitrators and prospective arbitrators under institutional rules.* Note that many institutional rules expressly require that prospective arbitrators disclose any potential conflicts or grounds for disqualification. Compare Article 11 of the UNCITRAL Rules and Article 11(2) of the ICC Rules, excerpted at pp. 166 & 186 of the Documentary Supplement. Consider also General Standard 3(c) of the IBA Guidelines on Conflicts of Interest. What is the scope of disclosure imposed by each of these various provisions?

What is the scope of an arbitrator's disclosure obligations? Is the arbitrator required to disclose only matters that would result in his or her removal, or a broader category of matters? What would make sense? What do Articles 11 and 12 of the Model Law provide?

21. *Disclosure under IBA Guidelines.* Consider an arbitrator's disclosure obligations under the IBA Guidelines. Must items on the Green List be disclosed? What if a number of items appear, for a prospective arbitrator, on the Green List; do they still not need to be disclosed? Must items on the Orange List be disclosed? Is that an absolute requirement, or may an arbitrator exercise judgment? What about items on the waivable Red List?

Suppose an arbitrator makes "friends" on Facebook or LinkedIn. Under what circumstances would their relationship be subject to disclosure? Consider IBA Guidelines, Green List 4.3.1 and 4.4.4. How do these provisions correlate with Orange List 3.3.6 and 3.4.3, from which the criteria of "close personal friendship" have been removed in the 2014 Guidelines? *See also* 2014 IBA Guidelines, Explanation to General Standard 3(a), Introduction, ¶¶1-3; *Judgment of 10 March 2011*, *Tecso v. Neoelectra*, 2011 Rev. arb. 569 (Paris Cour d'appel) (Facebook connection between arbitrator and counsel after rendering award does not raise reasonable doubts as to impartiality); *Judgment of 31 January 2012*, DFT 4A_672/2011 (Swiss Fed. Trib.) (proof of strong and intense friendship casting doubt on judge's ability to make own decision required to justify recusal of judge).

22. *Differing approaches under national arbitration legislation and institutional rules to impartiality obligations of party-nominated arbitrators and presiding arbitrator.* Different national arbitration regimes take different approaches to the respective impartiality obligations of party-nominated co-arbitrators, on the one hand, and presiding or sole arbitrators, on the other. These differences are paralleled by differences on the same topic among institutional rules.

(a) *Historic U.S. approach of providing different standards of independence for "party-nominated" and "neutral" arbitrators.* Section 10(a)(2) of the FAA does not make any express distinction between the standards of impartiality applicable to party-nominated arbitrators and other, "neutral" arbitrators. On the contrary, §10(a)(2) permits an award to be annulled for "evident partiality ... in the arbitrators, *or either of them.*" U.S. FAA, 9 U.S.C. §10(a)(2) (emphasis added). A few federal courts have suggested that this implies that a uniform standard of impartiality applies to all the arbitrators. *See, e.g., Standard Tankers (Bahamas) Co. v. Motor Tank Vessel AKTI*, 438 F.Supp. 153, 159 (E.D.N.Y. 1977).

Despite the foregoing, party-nominated arbitrators in the United States were historically presumed (absent contrary agreement) to have a degree of partiality towards the party that appointed them. In this regard, note that the disqualified arbitrator in *Commonwealth Coatings* was the "neutral" chairman of a three-person tribunal. Consider the decision in *Sphere Drake*. How does the court regard the co-arbitrator's role? What is the basis for the Court's view of the role of co-arbitrators? Is it the FAA? The parties' agreement? Their implied expectations? Compare the decision in *Americo*.

Other U.S. courts have reached similar conclusions. *See Sunkist Soft Drinks, Inc. v. Sunkist Growers, Inc.*, 10 F.3d 753 (11th Cir. 1993) ("Mr. Meyers, as a party-appointed arbitrator, may be predisposed or sympathetic toward [the] position" of the party that nominated him); *Cia de Navegacion Omsil, SA v. Hugo Neu Corp.*, 359 F.Supp. 898, 899 (S.D.N.Y. 1973) ("As everyone knows, the party's named arbitrator is an amalgam of judge and advocate"); *Stef Shipping Corp. v. Norris Grain Co.*, 209 F.Supp. 249 (S.D.N.Y. 1962) (party-appointed arbitrators "are partisans once removed from the actual controversy"); *Petrol Corp. v. Groupement D'Achat des Carburants*, 84 F.Supp. 446, 448 (S.D.N.Y. 1949) ("no reason appears why the parties could not mutually agree to let one arbitrator decide the issue, thus treating him as an umpire and the other arbitrators as advocates and agents of the parties designating them").

(b) *Party-nominated and "neutral" arbitrators under 1999 AAA Commercial Rules.* As the decision in *Americo* illustrates, until 2003, the AAA Rules provided for presumptively different standards of independence and impartiality for co-arbitrators and presiding arbitrators (termed, tellingly, "neutrals"). *See* 1999 AAA Rules, Rule 12(b) ("Unless the parties agree otherwise, an arbitrator selected unilaterally by one party is a party-appointed arbitrator and is not subject to disqualification pursuant to Section R-19."). *See also* 1977 AAA/ABA Code of Ethics, Canon VII ("In some types of arbitration in which there are three arbitrators, it is customary for each party, acting alone, to appoint one arbitrator. The third arbitrator is then appointed by agreement either of the parties or of the two arbitrators, or, failing such agreement, by an independent institution or individual. In some of these types of arbitration, all three arbitrators are customarily considered to be neutral and are expected to observe the same standards of ethical conduct. However, there are also many types of tripartite arbitration in which it has been the practice that the two arbitrators appointed by the parties are not considered to be neutral and are expected to observe many but not all of the same ethical standards as the neutral third arbitrator. For the purposes of this code, an arbitrator appointed by one party who is not expected to observe all of the same standards as the third arbitrator is referred to as a "non-neutral arbitrator." This Canon VII describes the ethical obligations that non-neutral party-appointed arbitrators should observe and those that are not applicable to them.").

Note also the discussion of the AAA Rules in *Americo*.

(c) *Wisdom of historic U.S. distinction between "party-appointed" and "neutral" arbitrators.* Was it wise to permit party-nominated arbitrators to be presumptively less independent than the presiding (or sole) arbitrator? If the parties desire non-neutral party-nominated arbitrators, why interfere with their choice? Is it in fact clear that parties desire non-neutral party-nominated co-arbitrators? Including in international cases? Why might parties desire partial co-arbitrators?

(d) *No distinction between independence obligations of party-nominated and "neutral" arbitrators under most national arbitration statutes.* In contrast to the customary approach to arbitration in the United States, most national arbitration regimes formally impose the same standards of independence on both party-nominated and presiding (or sole) arbitrators. Consider Article 12 of the UNCITRAL Model Law and Article 180 of the SLPIL. Do they distinguish between party-nominated and presiding (or sole) arbitrators? As indicated above, there is authority under the Model Law and in some other jurisdictions that statutory standards of impartiality and independence are mandatory—not subject to alteration or exclusion by agreement. *See supra* p. 740. J.-F. Poudret & S. Besson, *Comparative Law of International Arbitration* ¶425 (2d ed. 2007) ("The statutory grounds guaranteeing the independence and/or the impartiality of the arbitrators are minimum requirements which the parties cannot waive in advance and which an arbitral institution must respect in contractual challenge proceedings.").

(e) *Treatment of "party-nominated" and "neutral" arbitrators under institutional rules.* As with arbitration legislation outside the United States, most institutional rules outside the United States require that all arbitrators be independent and impartial. Compare the AAA Rules to Article 11(1) of the ICC Rules and Articles 11-13 of the UNCITRAL Rules. Compare also the approach of the IBA Guidelines. Are there different standards of impartiality for party-nominated and other arbitrators under any of these rules?

On the other hand, consider the following excerpts from an ICC Report:

> "The theme of our discussion is focused upon the independence of the arbitrators, which is deemed a pillar of the arbitral system, and on the standards of behavior by which the arbitrators are most likely to preserve it…. [The Report is] based on the assumption that impartiality is to be expected from both the party-appointed arbitrator as well as the third arbitrator. I am aware that in many a circumstance the parties do not expect their appointee to act neutrally and impartially. If this is their wish, they should hasten to make the proper disclosure beforehand; otherwise, it is dutiful to assume that also the party-appointed arbitrator(s) should be neutral and act impartially…. I readily concede, also in light of existing practices, a margin of discretion in allowing departure from the basic canon of neutrality. As regards impartiality, however, the acceptance of possible deviations must be reduced to a bare minimum.
>
> It has been said that the arbitrator may be partial but not dishonest. I understand

this statement as an ethical justification only if partiality is the result of some bona fide (*i.e.*, justifiably negligent) conduct. However, if one relinquishes the ethical outlook, an arbitrator who is innocently partial cannot be accepted in the framework of fair and orderly proceedings. This would allow tolerance of a lack of independence which, though morally admissible, would betray the arbitral function at its very roots.

A slightly different conclusion may be reached with reference to neutrality. It is acceptable that one party seek, in terms of legal and cultural extraction, greater intellectual propinquity with its appointed arbitrator. This, however, does not adversely affect "per se" the independence of the arbitrator. Non-neutral arbitrators, therefore, do not necessarily antagonize the nature of arbitration, as traditionally envisaged, provided however, that the same rules apply, by mutual agreement of the parties, to all appointees, in full transparency and without hidden or overt discriminations. In conclusion, any lack of independence due to cultural hurdles in principle, should be proven in each individual instance." G. Bernini (ed.), *Report on Neutrality, Impartiality and Independence* 31-37 (1991).

What does this suggest about the meaning of the requirement that the party-nominated co-arbitrators be independent and impartial? Does independence and impartiality have the same meaning for co-arbitrators as for sole and presiding arbitrators under this analysis?

(f) *Contemporary treatment of "party-nominated" and "neutral" arbitrators in United States*. Reacting to international approaches to the subject, there have been significant changes to the U.S. treatment of party-nominated co-arbitrators during the past decade. In 2004, the AAA/ABA Code of Ethics for Arbitrators in Commercial Disputes was amended to specifically alter historic domestic U.S. approaches and impose duties of independence and impartiality on co-arbitrators. A new "Note on Neutrality" to the Code of Ethics explained:

"it is preferable for all arbitrators including any party-appointed arbitrators to be neutral, that is independent and impartial, and to comply with the same ethical standards. This expectation generally is essential in arbitrations where the parties, the nature of the dispute, or the enforcement of any resulting award may have international aspects.... This Code establishes a presumption of neutrality for all arbitrators, including party-appointed arbitrators, which applies unless the parties' agreement, the arbitration rules agreed to by the parties or applicable laws provide otherwise."

Consistent with this, the AAA/ABA Code of Ethics was revised to impose the same ethical obligations on all arbitrators, including co-arbitrators, unless the parties agreed to the contrary. *See* AAA/ABA Code of Ethics for Arbitrators in Commercial Disputes, Canons IX and X, excerpted at pp. 334-37 of the Documentary Supplement. At the same time, the AAA amended its domestic Commercial Rules to provide that (absent contrary agreement) all arbitrators were required to be independent and impartial. 2013 AAA Rules, R-13(b), R-18.

Consider Canon X and Rules 12 and 17, excerpted above. What exactly do they provide with regard to partial co-arbitrators? Canon X permits Canon X arbitrators to be "predisposed toward the party who appointed them." What is meant by "predisposed"? What restrictions are placed on the conduct of Canon X arbitrators?

Taken together, the foregoing developments have laid the basis for a significant shift in U.S. approaches to arbitrators' ethics in both domestic and international arbitrations. At the same time, the tradition of presumptively partial party-nominated arbitrators has thus far been retained in some other domestic U.S. institutional arbitration rules (*See, e.g.*, ARIAS U.S. Code of Conduct, Canon II, comment ("Although party-appointed arbitrators may be initially predisposed toward the position of the party who appointed them (unless prohibited by the contract), they should avoid reaching a final judgment … until after both parties have had a full and fair opportunity to present their respective positions and the panel has fully deliberated the issues. Arbitrators should advise the appointing party, when accepting an appointment, that they will ultimately decide issues presented in the arbitration objectively."), and, less clearly, the Revised Uniform Arbitration Act. Revised Uniform Arbitration Act, §12 (2000)). Do either the AAA/ABA Code of Ethics or the 2013 AAA Rules prohibit parties from agreeing upon the use of "non-neutral" co-arbitrators? What requirements are imposed on the use of non-neutral co-arbitrators?

Note the AAA's actions, as appointing authority, in *Americo*. Note in particular the effect of the revised AAA Rules on the AAA's actions. Was the Texas Supreme Court's interpretation of the parties' arbitration agreement in *Americo* persuasive? What version of the AAA Rules applied? What did those Rules provide?

(g) *Continuing differences between national approaches to impartiality of party-nominated arbitrators.* Despite recent changes, the contemporary U.S. approach to the impartiality of party-nominated arbitrators continues to differ from that in some other jurisdictions. In particular, a number of jurisdictions do not permit parties to agree upon "non-neutral" co-arbitrators, as permitted under the 2013 AAA Rules and AAA/ABA Code of Ethics. That appears to be true in England, France and elsewhere. *See supra* pp. 740, 751. G. Born, *International Commercial Arbitration* 1796 *et seq.* (2d ed. 2014).

Consider how *Americo* would have been decided by an English court if the arbitral seat had been London. Would the AAA's refusal to confirm a partial co-arbitrator have been upheld? Is that wise?

Which approach is wiser—the historic U.S. approach (permitting presumptively partial co-arbitrators), the contemporary U.S. approach (permitting partial co-arbitrators, but only where expressly agreed), or the Model Law approach (forbidding partial co-arbitrators, even where agreed)? Why? In cases where one party is permitted unilaterally to select a co-arbitrator, do you really think that the co-arbitrator will be entirely neutral? If not, would it not be better to openly acknowledge the co-arbitrators' "real" attitude and role?

For a contrary view, *see* Tupman, *Challenge and Disqualification of Arbitrators in International Commercial Arbitration,* 38 Int'l & Comp. L.Q. 26, 49 (1989): "Unquestionably all members of the tribunal in international arbitration should be held to the same standard of independence, whether appointed by a party or not. The concept of a non-neutral arbitrator as it exists in some common law systems simply has no place where the parties are of different nationalities and might lose faith in the arbitral process if a foreign, apparently lesser, standard were applied."

Is that correct? Recall the discussion above of the historic (and contemporary) practice of permitting parties to nominate the co-arbitrators when the arbitral tribunal consists of three (or more) arbitrators. *See supra* pp. 7-10, 13, 696-98. Recall also the excerpt above from the ICC's *Report on Neutrality, Impartiality and Independence. See supra* pp. 751-52. What are the reasons for permitting the parties to select "their" arbitrators? Consider the following excerpts from the drafting history of the Statute of the International Court of Justice, addressing the role of party-nominated *ad hoc* judges on the Court:

> "[W]e consider that it is essential to retain [party-nominated ad hoc judges]. Countries will not in fact feel full confidence in the decision of the Court in a case in which they are concerned if the Court includes no Judge of their own nationality, particularly if it includes a Judge of the nationality of the other party. Moreover, while national Judges are not, or should not be, representatives on the Court of the case of their own country, they fulfil a useful function in supplying local knowledge and a national point of view." United Nations, *Report of the Informal Inter-Allied Committee on the Future of the Permanent Court of International Justice*, at ¶39, 39 Am. J. Int'l L. 1, 11 (Supp. 1945).

What are the consequences of permitting the parties unilaterally to nominate the co-arbitrators? Is it entirely frank to insist that parties expect co-arbitrators to have the same degree of impartiality as presiding or sole arbitrators? Note that one of the least-publicized statistics concerning international arbitration is the almost complete absence of any cases in which a co-arbitrator has dissented from an award in favor of "his" or "her" nominating party (coupled with the relatively unremarkable nature of dissenting opinions by co-arbitrators against awards against "their" nominating parties). Consider Rau, *The Culture of American Arbitration and the Lessons of ADR*, 40 Tex. Int'l L.J. 449, 460 (2005) ("A mythology that promotes the belief that conscience and professional judgment—regardless whether this is taken as empirical description or (more likely) as mere aspiration—seems calculated only to increase the dangers of self-deception and sandbagging. All of this, to paraphrase La Rochefoucauld, is nothing but the homage that vice pays to virtue."); Sheppard, *A New Era of Arbitrator Ethics for the United States: The 2004 Revision to the AAA/ABA Code of Ethics for Arbitrators in Commercial Disputes*, 21 Arb. Int'l 91 (2005).

Which of the above approaches to the co-arbitrators' impartiality—the historic U.S. approach, the current U.S. approach, or the Model Law approach—is wiser? Suppose parties expressly agree to partisan co-arbitrators. Is there something so fundamentally unfair in such a means of dispute resolution that the parties' agreement is invalid? Recall that (a) for decades, that system was used in U.S. and other legal systems, and (b) many experienced practitioners conclude that co-arbitrators in international arbitrations often demonstrate a measure of predisposition towards their nominating parties. If parties desire, and agree, that their disputes should be resolved by a tribunal including partial co-arbitrators, should this be forbidden?

Is it consistent with Articles II and V(1)(d) of the New York Convention to deny effect to parties' agreements to arbitrate with partisan co-arbitrators? Would an award made in an arbitration with mandatorily-required impartial co-arbitrators, despite the parties' agreement on partial co-arbitrators, be subject to non-recognition under Article V(1)(d)? Would that award be made "in accordance with the agreement of the parties" if partial co-arbitrators are forbidden?

(h) *Ethical standards for non-neutral arbitrators.* Even where non-neutral party-nominated arbitrators are permitted, U.S. law imposes minimum standards of conduct:

> "Partisan he may be, but not dishonest. Like all arbitrators, the arbitrator selected by a party must (unless the requirement is waived) take the prescribed oath that he will 'faithfully and fairly … hear and examine the matters in controversy and … make a just award according to the best of [his] understanding.' And, if either one of the party-appointed arbitrators fails to act in accordance with such oath, the award may be attacked on the ground that it is the product of "evident partiality or corruption." *Astoria Medical Group v. Health Ins. Plan*, 11 N.Y.2d 128, 136 (N.Y. 1962).

> *See also Aetna Cas. & Surety Co. v. Grabbert*, 590 A.2d 88, 93-94 (R.I. 1991) (requiring "ethical obligation to act in good faith and with integrity and fairness").

23. *Party-nominated co-arbitrators in inter-state arbitrations.* Recall the *Alabama Arbitration*, conducted pursuant to the Treaty of Washington, *supra* pp. 6, 104. As discussed above, Article I of the Treaty of Washington permitted the United States and United Kingdom to nominate one arbitrator to the five-person tribunal. *See supra* p. 9. The United States nominated Mr. Charles Francis Adams, a U.S. diplomat who had served as U.S. ambassador to the United Kingdom during the Civil War and who, in that position, had extensive personal involvement in the United States' ultimately unsuccessful efforts to persuade the United Kingdom not to permit the Alabama to be constructed or to leave U.K. waters. *See* Bingham, *The Alabama Claims Arbitration*, 54 Int'l & Comp. L.Q. 1, 3-7, 16-18 (2005). Consider Adams's prior involvement under the IBA Guidelines; could he be successfully challenged? Is it relevant that there was no U.K. objection to Adams's appointment and participation as an arbitrator in the *Alabama Arbitration*? *Id.* at 16.

Note that the United Kingdom appointed Sir Alexander Cockburn, then the Lord Chief Justice of England, as an arbitrator. After the *Alabama Arbitration* concluded, Cockburn wrote: "I have always considered the Treaty of Washington—with the arbitration and the three rules—as a *grievous* mistake; and when applied to by the Government to undertake the office of British arbitrator did not hesitate to express my dislike of the Treaty." *Id.* at 17 (quoting Cockburn to Russell, Oct. 6, 1872, PRO 30/22/17A at the National Archives) (emphasis in original). During the arbitration, Lord Cockburn wrote to senior U.K. government officials from the Geneva arbitral proceedings as follows:

> "Things have gone badly with us here. I saw from our first sitting in July that they would. We could not have had a worse man than Staempfli [the Swiss-appointed arbitrator]—or next to him than the President [the Italian-nominated arbitrator]. The first a furious Republican, hating monarchical government, and ministries in which men of rank take part, ignorant as a horse and obstinate as a mule. The second vapid, and all anxiety to give a decision which shall produce an effect in the world…. Baron Itajuba is of a far better stamp, but was not sufficiently informed and very indolent…." F. Hackett, *Reminiscences of the Geneva Tribunal of Arbitration* 281 (1911) (quoting Cockburn to Granville).

Cockburn dissented from the tribunal's decision in the *Alabama Arbitration* (and refused to sign the award); among other things, his dissent said: "Sitting on this Tribunal as in some sense the representative of Great Britain, I cannot allow these statements to go forth to the world without giving them the most positive and unqualified contradiction."

Consider Cockburn's statements, prior to accepting the U.K. nomination, during the arbitration, and in his dissent, under the IBA Guidelines and UNCITRAL Model Law; could he successfully have been challenged? Did the apparent lack of impartiality on the part of either Mr. Adams or Lord Cockburn frustrate the *Alabama Arbitration*? Is there any reason that an arbitral tribunal cannot function with party-nominated arbitrators who are not impartial? What limits should there be on the co-arbitrators' actions and predispositions?

Consider the excerpt above from the drafting history of the ICJ Statute. *See supra* p. 754. Are co-arbitrators in inter-state arbitrations subject to different standards of independence and impartiality than in commercial arbitrations? What would justify such an approach?

Consider the following excerpt from an award rendered in 1876, shortly after Mr. Adams and Lord Cockburn served in the *Alabama Arbitration*:

> "It is argued by counsel that the act of the U.S. Government in recognizing Zuloaga is conclusive upon Mr. Commissioner Wadsworth, because he is the 'judicial representative of the United States in this Commission....' It is scarcely necessary to remark that this view is founded upon a total misconception of the nature and character of the office of a commissioner under the convention between the United States and Mexico. Mr. Commissioner Wadsworth is not a 'judicial representative of the United States in this Commission,' nor 'a judicial officer' of that government. The authority which he possesses he derives from both the United States and Mexico, and is obliged to exercise it impartially for the benefit of both. He would possess neither office nor authority without the consent and concurrence of both nations, and is not more bound by the official acts or municipal regulations of the United States than by those of Mexico. He derives his appointment to a place on the board—a place created by the action of both governments—from the Government of the United States, indeed, but is no more bound by this appointment to represent the interests of the United States than those of Mexico, and no more bound by the acts of that government than his colleague on the board, or their umpire. He is an impartial arbiter selected by the United States and Mexico, nor more the officer of the former than of the latter." *J.G.A. McKenny (U.S.A.) v. Mexico, Award of 1876*, in J. Moore, *History and Digest of the International Arbitrations to Which United States Has Been A Party* (1898).

Is this position consistent with the behavior of the United States in appointing Mr. Adams to the *Alabama Arbitration* tribunal? Of the United Kingdom in appointing Lord Cockburn?

24. *Party-nominated co-arbitrators in investment arbitrations.* What standards of independence and impartiality apply to co-arbitrators in investment arbitrations? Recall Article 57 of the ICSID Convention. What is meant by the requirement for "a manifest lack of the qualities" required by Article 14(1) of the ICSID Convention? Consider the *ICS* removal decision.

25. *Practical applications of independence and impartiality standards.* Review the decisions in each of the cases excerpted above. Which decisions do you believe were correct? Which do you disagree with?

Consider the following hypotheticals under the independence and impartiality standards set out in the various materials excerpted above. In each case, consider whether the circumstances outlined (i) must be disclosed by an arbitrator or prospective arbitrator; (ii) are grounds for removal of an arbitrator; and (iii) are grounds for annulment of an award.

(a) Suppose an arbitrator is in-house counsel to a party.

(b) Suppose an arbitrator is outside counsel to a party. Consider separately cases where the lawyer has advised on the dispute subject to arbitration and where he has advised on an entirely unrelated matter.

(c) Suppose an arbitrator was formerly employed as an officer of a party. Alternatively, suppose an arbitrator was formerly retained as outside counsel by a party. In each case, does it matter: (a) when the employment or retention occurred and how long it lasted; (b) how senior the employment position was or how large and/or remunerative the retention was; (c) whether the employment or retention related to the dispute subject to arbitration?

(d) Suppose an arbitrator is related by blood or marriage to principals of a party (for example, is the cousin of the CFO of one party).

(e) Suppose an arbitrator would derive economic benefit from the outcome of the arbitration. For example, suppose (a) the arbitrator has a "contingent" fee arrangement whereby he will be paid extra amounts if a party prevails; or (b) the arbitrator owns shares in a party.

(f) Suppose the parties each pay "their" co-arbitrator his fees as an arbitrator and one party pays its arbitrator a higher hourly rate than the other.

(g) Suppose an arbitrator is a partner in a law firm that represents a party, although the arbitrator himself is not involved in the representation. Does it matter: (a) whether the representation is ongoing; (b) how substantial the representation is; (c) whether the representation is related to the dispute subject to arbitration?

(h) Suppose an arbitrator is employed by a state party (for example, is a judge or senior member of the Ministry of Justice of a state respondent).

(i) Suppose an arbitrator is of the same religious faith as one party and not the other (for example, in a dispute between Egyptian or Pakistani parties and Israeli parties, the arbitrator is a U.S. national of Arab descent and Muslim belief or a French national of Jewish descent and belief).

(j) Suppose an arbitrator knows the principals of a party socially. Suppose there is a close personal friendship. Suppose the friendship has been or is intimate. Suppose there is intense personal dislike. Suppose a male arbitrator and the male counsel that appoints him are gay. Suppose a female arbitrator and the male counsel that appoints her are heterosexual.

(k) Suppose a sole arbitrator (or all three arbitrators) have dinner with one party and its counsel and "much wine was drunk," during which the arbitration was discussed. Consider *Re Hopper* [1867] 2 Lloyd's Rep. 367 (QB) (English High Ct.) (upholding award without enthusiasm).

(l) Suppose an arbitrator is presently serving as co-arbitrator for a party in another matter. Suppose he did so in the past. Suppose an arbitrator is a chairman in one arbitration, where lawyer X represents a party, and lawyer X then appoints the arbitrator as co-arbitrator in a second arbitration.

(m) Suppose an arbitrator knows the lawyers representing a party. Suppose he is advising those lawyers on an unrelated matter. Suppose he is serving as a co-arbitrator in another matter, monitored by those lawyers. What if he did so in the past?

Which hypotheticals would involve an arbitrator breaching his obligations of independence under leading national laws or institutional rules? Would your answers be any different with respect to presiding arbitrators, rather than co-arbitrators?

26. *Relevance of arbitrator's independence obligations during appointment process.* Consider the procedures set forth in the UNCITRAL, ICC and ICDR Rules for the nomination of arbitrators. Role-play the process of nominating co-arbitrators, including interviews between the party's counsel and two prospective nominees for co-arbitrators. In doing so, assume that each of the prospective co-arbitrators affirmatively want to be appointed because of the money they will earn. Note the statements of independence that must be submitted by an arbitrator under most institutional rules.

Consider the role of (a) counsel who is considering nominating a particular co-arbitrator; and (b) counsel whose opposite number (*i.e.*, opposing counsel) has nominated a particular co-arbitrator. How do the independence obligations (and other qualification requirements) applicable to the co-arbitrators affect your conduct? What should, or must, you do to ascertain compliance with such obligations or requirements?

D. PROCEDURES FOR CHALLENGING ARBITRATORS IN INTERNATIONAL ARBITRATION

Most national arbitration statutes and institutional rules provide mechanisms that permit parties to challenge arbitrators during the arbitral process.[12] These procedural mechanisms are designed principally to permit interlocutory challenges to arbitrators based on a lack of independence or impartiality, but can sometimes also be used to raise other challenges. As detailed in the following materials, the interplay between the challenge mechanisms available under national law and institutional rules raises difficult questions.

JIVRAJ v. HASHWANI
[2011] UKSC 40 (U.K. S.Ct.)

[excerpted above at pp. 117-24]

---

12. *See* G. Born, *International Commercial Arbitration* 1913-36 (2d ed. 2014); C. Rogers, *Ethics in International Arbitration* 77-78 (2014); Rogers, *Regulating International Arbitrators: A Functional Approach to Developing Standards of Conduct*, 41 Stan. J. Int'l L. 53 (2005); Smith, *Impartiality of the Party-Appointed Arbitrator*, 6 Arb. Int'l 320 (1990).

CERTAIN UNDERWRITERS AT LLOYD'S v. ARGONAUT INSURANCE CO.
264 F.Supp.2d 926 (N.D. Cal. 2003)

CHEN, Magistrate.... Petitioners Certain Underwriters at Lloyd's, London, Highlands Insurance Company, and London & Edinburgh General Insurance Company ("Certain Underwriters") seek to disqualify George Gottheimer, Jr., the neutral umpire ("Umpire") of a pending arbitration proceeding between Certain Underwriters and Argonaut Insurance Company ("Argonaut") and to vacate certain interim orders issued by the Umpire. Respondent Argonaut moves to dismiss, pursuant to Rule 12(b)(6), or to stay, until after the arbitration hearing, both ... motions.

The parties entered into certain reinsurance agreements ("the Treaty"). The pending arbitration arose from a dispute regarding coverage under the Treaty. Argonaut had submitted claims to Certain Underwriters in the approximate amount of $2.5 million for legal expenses from an underlying coverage action between Argonaut and an alleged insured. Certain Underwriters denied coverage and initiated arbitration proceedings against Argonaut.... Each party appointed a party arbitrator, and these party arbitrators nominated two candidates for the umpire position. George M. Gottheimer was selected as the Umpire. The Treaty contains an arbitration clause requiring that disputes be resolved in San Francisco.

The parties and the arbitration panel held an organizational meeting on November 25, 2002. Prior to this meeting the parties exchanged their respective preliminary position statements, and Argonaut claimed that Certain Underwriters was obligated to pay it $2,535,491.32 for legal expenses incurred in connection with the underlying insurance coverage litigation.... Moreover, Argonaut contended it was entitled to immediate payment under the Treaty....

At the meeting the Umpire asked [about] a California insurer's annual filing requirements with the California Insurance Commissioner pursuant to Cal. Insurance Code §§922.22 *et seq.* [An insurer's] failure to receive payment [of reinsurance recoveries] before the end of the year has adverse implications for reporting purposes. At the organizational meeting, the [tribunal] orally issued Interim Order No. 1:

> "[W]e order the Petitioner to establish an escrow in the amount of $2,535,491.32 to be held by counsel for the Respondent under the control of the Panel and that the escrow be established by December 31, 2002. The form of the escrow to be mutually agreed upon by the parties and if they cannot agree on the form of the escrow, that the Panel be contacted immediately and then we will order what form will be necessary." ...

The December 31, 2002 deadline was apparently set with the reporting requirements in mind. On December 18, 2002, more than three weeks after the organizational meeting, Certain Underwriters informed Argonaut's counsel that it would be complying with Interim Order No. 1 by filing a $2.5 million dollar bond.... On December 24, 2002, Argonaut's counsel e-mailed Certain Underwriters counsel expressing its view that the bond was inadequate vis-à-vis California year-end relief from penalties for uncollected reinsurance. Argonaut also filed a motion with the panel to require interim payment or posting of letter of credit by Certain Underwriters by December 31, 2002. That motion was served on Certain Underwriters the afternoon of Christmas eve, but Certain Underwriters' attorneys' office was closed early for the holiday. The Umpire e-mailed the parties that same afternoon and informed them that it would respond to the motion soon.

On December 26, 2002, the Umpire e-mailed the parties, stating that the panel was is-suing Interim Order No. 2 because the parties had not been able to agree to the form of the escrow. Interim Order No. 2 required Certain Underwriters to "either make an interim cash payment or post a Letter of Credit in the amount of $2,535,491.32" with five conditions.... On December 27, 2002 counsel for Certain Underwriters e-mailed the Umpire and oppos-ing counsel, stating that because of the Christmas holiday it had not reviewed Argonaut's motion prior to the issuance of Interim Order No. 2, to which it was now objecting. The Umpire responded indicating that he had not heard from Certain Underwriters between December 24 and 26, that Interim Order No. 2 was designed to allow Argonaut to avoid a penalty to surplus, and that the order would stand unless the parties could mutually agree to a suitable funding arrangement.

On December 30, 2002, counsel for Certain Underwriters responded to the previous e-mail by reiterating its belief that Interim Order No. 1 was designed to provide potential payment rather than actual payment to Argonaut. Certain Underwriters also objected to Interim Order No. 2, arguing that Interim Order No. 2 was in irreconcilable conflict with Interim Order No. 1, and that the arbitration panel had effectively resolved a disputed coverage issue in Argonaut's favor without a hearing on the merits and before Certain Underwriters could obtain and review the necessary files from Argonaut.

On December 31, 2002, the Umpire took Certain Underwriters' correspondence under advisement, acknowledging that the penalty to surplus matter "raises other issues." That same day, counsel for Argonaut [replied].... The arbitration panel considered counsels' correspondence of December 30 and 31. Interim Order No. 2 was then modified on January 2, 2003, requiring Certain Underwriters to comply within 10 days, but also requiring that if Argonaut draws on the letter of credit, the arbitration panel would require Argonaut to establish an escrow in the same amount, to be held by counsel for Certain Underwriters, but under control of the panel....

On January 3, 2003, Certain Underwriters again challenged the propriety of Interim Order No. 2, and requested that it be stayed. This request by the panel was denied the same day.... On January 13, 2003 the Umpire again directed Certain Underwriters to comply with Interim Order No. 2. Certain Underwriters requested the opportunity for additional briefing regarding applicability of the California Insurance Code as well as the punitive nature of the Panel's order. The next day the Umpire declared, "... further briefing is un-necessary as Petitioners had ample time to brief the issues, and would be duplicative. Ac-cordingly, the Panel's ruling of January 13, 2003 and Interim Order No. 2 must be complied with without further delay."

With Certain Underwriters still not having complied with Interim Order No. 2, on Jan-uary 22, 2003, Argonaut moved for $10,000 per day in sanctions to commence as of Jan-uary 17. On January 27, 2003, Certain Underwriters moved for the panel to remove the Umpire, alleging that there were justifiable doubts about Mr. Gottheimer's impartiality. On January 29, Certain Underwriters also opposed the motion for sanctions, arguing that ... the sanctions would not draw their essence from the Treaty. Argonaut replied regarding sanctions on January 30, 2003, arguing that the panel must be granted broad latitude in interpreting the contract, and that sanctions were permissible because the parties had not agreed to limit the remedies that would be available to the panel.

On January 31, 2003, the panel stayed the motion for sanctions pending the parties' agreement to submit to an independent consultant chosen by the panel (Paul Dassenko) to examine the penalty to surplus question. Certain Underwriters objected to the designation of Dassenko as the independent consultant because he was an Argonaut-appointed arbitrator in other reinsurance arbitrations pending with Certain Underwriters. While not opposing Dassenko, Argonaut pointed out that Dassenko had recently [been] retained as the opposing arbitrator and had ruled contrary to Argonaut's interests in [an unrelated] litigation. The panel found that Dassenko also served as Certain Underwriters' appointed arbitrator in two matters. The panel overruled the objection to the consultant and denied the petition to remove the Umpire.

On February 7, 2003, the panel issued Interim Order No. 3, which imposed sanctions on Certain Underwriters of $10,000 a day, dating back to January 17, 2003, for each day in which Certain Underwriters are not in compliance with Interim Order No. 2. The panel also ruled that "If the Petitioners comply with Interim Order No. 2 on a timely basis, the Panel will revisit the sanctions ... and give consideration to the premium Petitioners paid for the bond." The panel ordered the bond obtained by Certain Underwriters returned upon compliance with Interim Order No. 2.... Certain Underwriters filed an action ... to disqualify the arbitration Umpire and to vacate Interim Orders No. 2 and No. 3....

At the hearing, counsel for Certain Underwriters acknowledged there are, to his knowledge, no federal cases in which a court has issued an order disqualifying a neutral arbitrator once arbitration had commenced but prior to a final arbitration award.... [O]ther courts have consistently held that courts do not have the power under the FAA to disqualify an arbitrator while proceedings are pending. *See Gulf Guaranty Life Ins. Co. v. Connecticut Gen. Life Ins. Co.*, 304 F.3d 476, 490 (5th Cir. 2002) ("[E]ven where arbitrator bias is at issue, the FAA does not provide for removal of an arbitrator from service prior to an award, but only for potential vacatur of any award ... the FAA appears not to endorse court power to remove an arbitrator for any reason prior to issuance of an arbitral award."). There is a strong basis in FAA policy for such a rule. As ... noted in *Gulf Guaranty*:

> "A 'prime objective of arbitration law is to permit a just and expeditious result with a minimum of judicial interference' and any other such rule could 'spawn endless applications to the courts and indefinite delay' and that otherwise 'there would be no assurance that the party seeking removal would be satisfied with the removed arbitrator's successor and would not bring yet another proceeding to disqualify him or her.'" 304 F.3d at 492 (quoting *Marc Rich & Co. v. Transmarine Seaways Corp.*, 443 F.Supp. 386, 387-388 (S.D.N.Y. 1995)).

Disqualifying an arbitrator can be highly disruptive to the expeditious arbitration process fostered by the FAA.

Certain Underwriters argue that the Ninth Circuit's decision in *Pacific Reins. Mgt Corp. v. Ohio Reins. Corp.*, 935 F.2d 1019 (9th Cir. 1991), though not directly on point, suggests that disqualification is proper, because interim orders such as those issued herein are "final" for purposes of judicial review, and that disqualification after issuance of a "final" award is appropriate. In *Pacific Reins.*, the arbitration panel issued an interim order requiring members of a reinsurance pool to contribute to an escrow account during the pendency of the arbitration as security for any final award. The Ninth Circuit held that the district court had the power to review such an interim award. The Ninth Circuit recognized that temporary equitable relief may be essential to preserving assets or enforcing performance, and that such relief needs to be judicially enforceable at the time it is granted in order to be meaningful. It was in this context that the *Pacific Reins.* panel ruled that court enforcement of interim equitable awards "is not an 'undue intrusion upon the arbitral process,' but is essential to preserve the integrity of that process." *Id.* at 1023. Moreover, the issues regarding the interim award were self-contained and distinct from the merits of the arbitration. *Pacific Reins.* thus concluded such an award, though interim, was sufficiently "final" to permit judicial review under the FAA.

Certain Underwriters argue that since an interim order (as was issued here) can be treated as a final award pursuant to *Pacific Reins.*, the door should be open for a court to remove an arbitrator for bias after such an award. The Court disagrees. Even though an interim award may itself be deemed final for purposes of judicial review, the fact remains that the arbitration proceedings are still pending. Thus, *Pacific Reins.* [is] inapposite. Rather than facilitating the arbitral process, judicial intervention in the form of disqualifying an arbitrator during the pendency of the arbitration would thwart the "prime objective of arbitration law [which] is to permit a just and expeditious result with a minimum of judicial interference." *Gulf Guaranty*, 304 F.3d at 492.... While judicial review and enforcement of an interim award is not an "undue intrusion upon the arbitral process" (935 F.2d at 1023), judicial disqualification of an arbitrator during the pendency of arbitration is. Simply put, the policy rationale in *Pacific Reins.* does not diminish the reasoning and conclusion of the Fifth Circuit's analysis in *Gulf Guaranty*.

Finally, the Court notes that under *Pacific Reins.* and the FAA, Certain Underwriters has a remedy for bias—it can obtain judicial review of the merits of the award. That, rather than disqualification, is the appropriate remedy for any alleged error due to bias. Indeed, as noted below, evident partiality of the arbitrator is one ground for vacating an award under the FAA. Accordingly, Certain Underwriters' motion to disqualify the neutral Umpire is denied.

Unlike an arbitrator disqualification motion, this Court has authority under the FAA to review and vacate an arbitration panel's interim order that *e.g.* sets up an escrow account or requires a party to post a letter of credit as interim security pending arbitration. *Pacific Reins*, 935 F.2d at 1022-23; [*Yasuda Fire & Marine Ins. Co. of Europe v. Continental Cas. Co.*, 37 F.3d 345, 348-351 (7th Cir. 1994)]. As noted above, such an order is sufficiently "final" to permit judicial review.

This scope of this Court's review, pursuant to the FAA, is limited; it may vacate an award on only the following [grounds specified in §10 of the FAA].... [The Court considered whether the arbitral tribunal's Interim Award No. 2 was subject to vacatur for "evident partiality" under 9 U.S.C. §10(a)(2).] There are two standards for what constitutes "evident partiality." First, where an arbitrator fails to disclose relevant facts, such as the arbitrator's relationship with a party or counsel, vacatur is appropriate when the non-disclosure gives the impression of bias in favour of one party. *Woods v. Saturn Distrib. Corp.*, 78 F.3d 424, 427 (9th Cir. 1996); *Schmitz v. Zilveti*, 20 F.3d 1043, 1047 (9th Cir. 1994).... However, in this case, Certain Underwriters do not allege that Interim Order No. 2 should be vacated because the Umpire failed to disclose facts that give the impression of a conflict of interest.

Thus, the Court applies the second, more stringent, standard which governs cases involving allegations of actual bias. In actual bias cases, the mere appearance of impropriety is not enough; rather, "the party alleging evident partiality must establish specific facts which indicate improper motives." *Woods*, 78 F.3d at 427.... The bias of an arbitrator must be "direct and definite." *Sofia Shipping Co. Ltd v. Amoco Transp. Co.*, 628 F.Supp. 116, 119 (S.D.N.Y. 1986).... In this case, Certain Underwriters do not point out any extrinsic evidence that the Umpire has a secret relationship with Argonaut or possessed some pre-existing bias against Certain Underwriters. Rather, Certain Underwriters argues that the Umpire's rulings evidence a bias against it. In particular, Certain Underwriters contend that the Umpire was particularly solicitous of Argonaut's need for the interim payment because of the penalty to surplus problem, and that this concern drove the timing and the substance of Interim Order No. 2. Yet, the Court cannot presume that Mr. Gottheimer was motivated by an extrajudicial bias. It may have reflected his preliminary view that there was a substantial likelihood that Argonaut would prevail on the merits and that the interim payment to which Argonaut may have been entitled was necessary in order to prevent prejudice resulting from reporting requirements....

The Court finds that a significant factor weighing against a finding of evident partiality is that Interim Order No. 2 was modified by the arbitration panel soon after receiving objections for Certain Underwriters. As modified, the order requires that if Argonaut drew on the letter of credit, it would have to establish an escrow in the same amount, under control of the panel, in order to protect Certain Underwriters' ultimate position in the arbitration. In any event, the fact that an arbitrator "consistently relied on evidence and reached conclusions favorable" to one party, is not enough establish "evident partiality." *Bell Aerospace Co. v. Local 516*, 500 F.2d 921, 923 (2d Cir. 1974). There is no evidence here that the Umpire "was predisposed to favor either party, or that he acted out of any improper motives." *Id.* Petitioners have not set forth "specific facts which indicate improper motives." *Woods*, 78 F.3d at 427.

Certain Underwriters also contend that the Umpire engaged in numerous procedural irregularities which evidence bias. It argues that Interim Order No. 2 was issued without proper notice and without the opportunity for Certain Underwriters to respond. However, the panel indicated at the November 25, 2002 organizational meeting that the form of the escrow was to be mutually agreed upon by the parties and that if the parties were unable to agree to a mutually acceptable form of escrow the panel was to be informed immediately so that it could direct what form would be necessary. The impending December 31, 2002 deadline for reporting purposes was looming, and the panel and parties were aware of that fact. Immediate notification after the organizational meeting as to an acceptable form of escrow did not occur; Certain Underwriters did not inform opposing counsel until December 18, 2002 that it would be filing a bond. Argonaut objected six days later. Given the limited time frame and the fast approaching December 31 deadline, the Court cannot presume that the panel acted with improper purpose in issuing Interim Order No. 2 on such an expedited basis....

Moreover, as previously noted, the Umpire and the panel did entertain the subsequent filings of Certain Underwriters immediately thereafter, and the panel modified the order in an important respect to protect Certain Underwriters' interests, requiring Argonaut to establish an escrow if it were to draw on the letter of credit. The panel's revised order of January 2, 2003 also gave Certain Underwriters ten additional business days to comply. Interim Order No. 3, imposing a daily penalty for non-compliance with Interim Order No. 2 as modified, was not issued until after Certain Underwriters were afforded several weeks within which to comply with Interim Order No. 2. In summary, the rigorous standard for evident partiality is not met here....

Certain Underwriters argue that the arbitration panel did not have the authority to issue Interim Order No. 3 which imposed sanctions of $10,000 per day for non-compliance with

Interim Order No. 2, and that Order No. 3 derives from misconduct. As noted above, the Court finds the proceedings were not infected by any misconduct by the Umpire or the panel. Certain Underwriters were afforded ample opportunity to object to and comply with these interim orders. Thus, the question before the Court is whether the Umpire and the panel exceeded its powers in issuing Interim Order No. 3.

Interim Order No. 3 was issued by the panel on February 7, 2003, after objections to Interim Order No. 2 were filed and considered by the panel, and after Argonaut moved for sanctions on January 22. Interim Order No. 3 required the following:

> "Petitioners, jointly and severally, are ordered to pay Respondent, in addition to the amount set forth in Interim Order No. 2, the additional sum of $10,000.00 for every day that they [Certain Underwriters] are not in compliance with that Order, commencing on January 17, 2003, the first day following the date on which payment was to have been made or letter or credit established."

The threshold question is whether arbitrators have the authority to sanction non-compliance with their orders. In *Pacific Reins.*, the Ninth Circuit stated "Arbitrators have no power to enforce their decisions. Only courts have that power." 935 F.2d at 1023. Arguably, this language could be interpreted broadly to mean that the imposition of sanctions, one method of "enforcing" an order, is not authorized under the FAA. However, the language could also simply mean that arbitrators do not have the ability to effectuate execution of an award as courts have the power to issue *e.g.* writs of execution and attachment.

The Court is persuaded that the language of *Pacific Reins.* should be narrowly construed. A number of courts have held that arbitrators have authority to sanction outrageous conduct or non-compliance with its interim orders. In *Polin v. Kellwood Co.*, 103 F.Supp.2d 238 (S.D.N.Y. 2000), the arbitration panel rendered a final award entitling the defendant to half of its expenses, including attorney fees, as a sanction for outrageous conduct and refusal to respond to the panel's questions by plaintiff's counsel. In *Konkar Maritime Enter., SA v. Compagnie Belge D'Affretement*, 668 F.Supp. 267, 274 (S.D.N.Y. 1987), the court ruled that "it was not improper for the Panel to consider respondent's failure to comply with its interim order" in assessing 85% of the costs against the party that had ignored an escrow account order. In both *Polin* and *Konkar*, the courts found that the final allocation of fees and costs which reflected the panel's effective imposition of sanctions was within the grant of authority conferred by the arbitration agreement upon the arbitrators. Accordingly, there is no categorical ban to an arbitrator's imposition of sanctions for non-compliance with his or her orders. The more specific question in the case at bar is whether the daily sanctions imposed by Interim Order No. 3 exceeded the panel's authority. There are two possible sources for such power: authority that inheres in the FAA itself and the arbitration contract as construed in light of FAA policy.

The Court concludes the FAA does not affirmatively grant inherent authority to impose the sanction contained in Interim Order No. 3 for several reasons. First, the imposition of a fine of $10,000 per day for each day of non-compliance with Interim Order No. 2 is akin to civil contempt issued by a court. In an analogous context, the courts have found that non-Article III magistrate judges do not have the inherent power to punish for contempt. Their contempt power derives solely from a statutory grant of authority. Nothing in the explicit language of the FAA authorizes such inherent power upon arbitrators.

Second, the imposition of the equivalent of civil contempt, imposing a daily penalty for a non-compliance of an interim order, could burden a party's right to pursue judicial review of a "final" interim order such as Interim Order No. 2—a right established in *Pacific Reins.* Such a sanction imposes a substantial risk on the appealing party—given the time it takes to seek judicial review and obtain a ruling, it risks incurring a substantial fine in the event it does not obtain vacation of the order. As of the date of this Order for instance, the fine under Interim Order No. 3 is approximately $900,000. Such a risk could pose a substantial impediment to judicial review and undermine the FAA policies the court in *Pacific Reins.* sought to vindicate.

This is not to say that the parties cannot agree by arbitration contract to confer on the arbitrator power to impose monetary sanctions for non-compliance. Even if judicial review and enforcement of an interim order were available under *Pacific Reins.*, in light of the strong public policy favoring expeditious arbitration the parties should not be barred from consensually conferring such power on the arbitrator; enforcement via sanctions by the arbitrator is likely to be more efficient than mandating judicial review and enforcement in every instance. However, where the nature of the sanction involved seeks to coerce compliance at the expense of a party's right under the FAA to seek judicial review, as in the instant case, the potential for conflict with FAA policy counsels in favor of requiring that any intent of the parties to afford contempt-like power on the arbitrator must be clearly evident.

There is no clear grant of authority to impose mounting punitive sanctions equivalent to civil contempt in the Treaty herein even though the panel's grant of authority is generally broad.[13] Indeed, unlike *Polin* and *Konkar*, the sanction was not imposed under the auspices of the arbitrators' power under the governing agreement to allocating fees and costs. Indeed, the Treaty in the instant case mandates that the expense of the arbitration be equally divided. Moreover, unlike the allocation of costs in *Konkar*, Interim Order No. 3 was far more punitive in nature.

In addition, the amount of the daily sanctions imposed—$10,000 per day—does not relate to any provision in the Treaty. Pressed at oral argument, Argonaut's counsel could not point to any specific basis for the level of fine imposed. Thus, it cannot fairly be said that Interim Order No. 3 "draw[s] its essence" from the Treaty as interpreted in view of FAA policy. Moreover, the Court finds that the figure of $10,000 per day was arbitrary and appears to have been based on "some body of thought, or feeling, or policy, or law that is outside the contract." *Yasuda*, 37 F.3d at 349.

Accordingly, because there is no basis in either the FAA or the arbitration agreement for the sanctions imposed under Interim Order No. 3, the arbitration panel exceeded its powers in issuing said order. For the reasons stated above, the Court denies the petition to disqualify the Umpire, confirms Interim Order No. 2 and vacates Interim Order No. 3 . . . .

JUDGMENT OF 9 FEBRUARY 1998
16 ASA Bull. 634 (1998) (Swiss Fed. Trib.)

[excerpted above at pp. 729-30]

---

13. [Reinsurance Treaty,] Art. 15 ("The arbitrators shall consider this Agreement an honorable engagement rather than merely a legal obligation; they are relieved of all judicial formalities and may abstain from following the strict rules of law.").

ASM SHIPPING LTD OF INDIA v. TTMI LTD OF ENGLAND
[2005] EWHC 2238 (Comm) (English High Ct.)

[excerpted above at pp. 725-29]

AAOT FOREIGN ECONOMIC ASS'N (VO) TECHNOSTROYEXPORT v. INT'L DEVELOPMENT & TRADE SERVICES, INC.
139 F.3d 980 (2d Cir. 1999)

SCHWARZER, Senior District Judge. We must decide whether the District Court for the Southern District of New York erred in confirming two international arbitration awards rendered by an allegedly corrupt tribunal where the losing party, knowing the relevant facts, chose to participate fully in the proceedings without disclosing those facts until after the adverse awards had been rendered.

In 1991 and 1992 appellant International Development and Trade Services, Inc. ("IDTS") entered into contracts for the purchase of non-ferrous metals from appellee AAOT Foreign Economic Association (VO) Technostroyexport ("Techno"). Disputes arose over IDTS's performance under the contracts. The disputes were submitted to arbitration pursuant to the contracts' arbitration clauses which provided for arbitration before the International Court of Commercial Arbitration of the Chamber of Commerce and Industry of the Russian Federation in Moscow. Hearings were held before a tribunal appointed by the Arbitration Court which rendered awards in favor of Techno of approximately $200 million. Techno filed a petition in the district court to confirm the awards under the [New York] Convention. IDTS opposed enforcement of the awards under Article V(2)(b) of the Convention as "contrary to the public policy" of the United States.[14] The district court rejected IDTS's contention and entered judgment confirming the awards. This appeal followed....

The factual showing on which IDTS founded its opposition may be briefly summarized. Following the initiation of the arbitration proceedings, IDTS sent an interpreter—Tamara Sicular—to Moscow to file papers, clarify the status of the cases and gain an understanding of the procedures that would be followed. On July 14, 1993, Sicular met with Sergey Orlov, the Secretary of the Arbitration Court, and his superior at the Chamber of Commerce. According to IDTS, Sicular, on her own initiative and to test the integrity of the court, asked Orlov whether the court could be "bought." Orlov responded affirmatively and offered to "fix" the cases for IDTS in exchange for a substantial payment. His superior later that day told Sicular he would personally assist IDTS "sort out" the arbitration. On the next day, Orlov presented Sicular with his plan which called for a payment of $1 million for which he would rig the tribunal. There followed a series of communications with Orlov over the next two months in which Sicular ostensibly sought to gather further evidence and establish that the Arbitration Court and its officials were corrupt. They ended inconclusively in

---

14. On appeal, IDTS also argues that it was denied due process, relying on Article V.1(b) which provides that recognition and enforcement may be denied when a party "was otherwise unable to present its case." Although IDTS did raise a due process concern to the district court in sur-reply memorandum, it did so only as part of a response to Techno's waiver argument and did not squarely present to the district court the argument it now presents to this Court. Therefore, IDTS did not properly raise this point in the district court; in any event, we do not reach it.

September 1993, without any payment being made. Sicular passed all of this information on to IDTS president Edith Reich prior to the commencement of any arbitration hearings. The Arbitration Court held hearings beginning in December 1994 and ending in September 1995. IDTS, represented by several attorneys, participated actively. The final awards in favor of Techno were rendered in March 1996.

In November 1996, Techno filed its petition to confirm the awards in the district court. In its opposition to the petition, IDTS for the first time disclosed the offer to bribe the Arbitration Court—the sting, as IDTS describes it—in support of its contention that enforcement of an award rendered by a corrupt tribunal would be contrary to the public policy of the United States. The district court determined that IDTS's allegations failed to establish that the Arbitration Court was not impartial in these cases; that the use of the public policy exception is not appropriate ...; and that IDTS waived its right to assert the public policy exception where it had knowledge of the facts but remained silent until an adverse award was rendered. Because we agree with the court's third ground, it is unnecessary for us to consider ... [the other grounds].

The settled law of this circuit precludes attacks on the qualifications of arbitrators on grounds previously known but not raised until after an award has been rendered. "Where a party has knowledge of facts possibly indicating bias or partiality on the part of an arbitrator he cannot remain silent and later object to the award of the arbitrators on that ground. His silence constitutes a waiver of the objection." *Ilios Shipping & Trading Corp. v. Am. Anthracite & Bituminous Coal Corp.*, 148 F.Supp. 698, 700 (S.D.N.Y.), *aff'd*, 245 F.2d 873 (2d Cir. 1957). This law of waiver controls the outcome of this appeal. It is undisputed that IDTS had knowledge of concrete facts possibly indicating the corruption of the Arbitration Court—namely, the apparent willingness of some members of the Arbitration Court to take bribes. Despite this knowledge, IDTS remained silent. Accordingly, it cannot now object to the award based on these facts. IDTS contends that it cannot be charged with waiver because it did not voluntarily and intentionally waive its right to a corruption-free tribunal. It argues that any attempt to seek relief would have been futile: from the tribunal because it was corrupt, from the Arbitration Court because its officials were corrupt and because its rules precluded it, and from the Russian courts because the applicable law did not permit it. We express no view on the validity of these contentions. But even if they are valid, it was incumbent on IDTS to notify opposing counsel. It is no answer, as IDTS claims, that it was unlikely that Techno would agree to the charge of corruption of the tribunal or to surrender any perceived resulting advantage. Had Techno insisted in the face of IDTS's charges on proceeding with the arbitration as arranged, IDTS would have preserved its objections and been free to raise them in any later confirmation proceeding. Instead IDTS tried to put the case in a posture in which, as the district judge aptly characterized it, "Heads I win, tails you lose." We therefore conclude that IDTS waived whatever objections it had to the tribunal and affirm....

NOTES

1. *Frequency of challenges to arbitrators.* Institutional statistics suggest that challenges to arbitrators have been increasing in recent years. ICC statistics indicate that 82 challenges to arbitrators were made in the five years between 1995 and 1999 (roughly 16 challenges per year), 140 challenges were made in the five years between 2000 and 2004 (28 per year), 148 challenges were made in the four years between 2005 and

2008 (37 per year), and 269 challenges were made in the four years between 2009 and 2013 (54 per year). The rate of challenges per 100 pending ICC cases increased similarly, from 1.8 between 1994 and 1998, to 2.5 between 1999 and 2003, to 3.1 between 2004 and 2008, and 3.6 between 2009 and 2013. *2002-2013 ICC Statistical Reports* (2003-2014); G. Born, *International Commercial Arbitration* 1855 (2d ed. 2014).

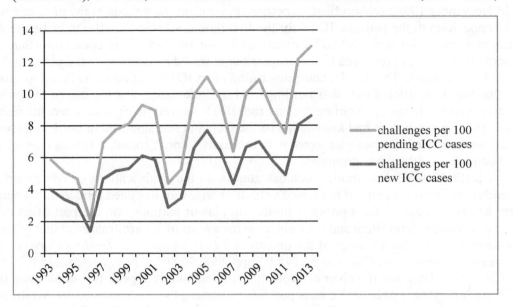

Other institutions anecdotally report similar experiences. Despite these developments, challenges to arbitrators still occur only in a minority of all cases and are upheld in significantly fewer.

2. *Interlocutory judicial removal of arbitrators under national arbitration statutes.* Consider Articles 12 and 13 of the UNCITRAL Model Law, Article 1456 of the French Code of Civil Procedure and Article 180 of the SLPIL, excerpted at pp. 89, 145 & 158 of the Documentary Supplement. Note that all three statutes permit interlocutory challenges of arbitrators in national courts. Note also that, in *Jivraj, ASM Shipping* and *Veritas*, judicial challenges to one of the arbitrators were permitted by English law and that, in *Judgment of 9 February 1998*, a challenge under Article 180 of the SLPIL is described. Note also that each of these statutory regimes imposes strict constraints on the timing of judicial challenges and appellate review of decisions regarding such challenges; these constraints are designed to produce an immediate decision on any challenge and to minimize delays and interference in the arbitral process.

Consider the procedure provided for in Articles 13(2) and 13(3) of the Model Law. Under Article 13(2), who decides challenges to an arbitrator in the first instance? Is it appropriate for an arbitral tribunal to consider challenges to one of its own members? What if all of the members of the tribunal are challenged? Or, what if there is a sole arbitrator who decides on that challenge in the first instance? Does the possibility of subsequent judicial review of the arbitrator's(s') decision address any concerns?

3. *Interlocutory judicial challenge to arbitrator only available in arbitral seat.* What international arbitrations are subject to the possibility of interlocutory judicial removal under Article 12 of the UNCITRAL Model Law? Under Article 180 of the SLPIL? *See*

UNCITRAL Model Law, Art. 1(2); SLPIL, Art. 176(1), excerpted at pp. 86 & 157 of the Documentary Supplement.

Suppose parties from Chile and Malaysia agree to arbitrate in Singapore. May either party seek interlocutory judicial removal of the arbitrators in the courts of either Chile or Malaysia? If both Chile and Malaysia had enacted the UNCITRAL Model Law, what provisions would require this result? Suppose that Chile and Malaysia had not adopted the Model Law, and that local law in each state *would* permit removal of an arbitrator in an arbitration seated abroad. Does anything in the New York Convention prohibit such actions? *See infra* pp. 1099-112.

4. *No interlocutory judicial challenges to arbitrators under FAA.* Consider the decision in *Certain Underwriters* regarding the possibility of pursuing an interlocutory action in U.S. courts to remove an arbitrator. As the decision illustrates, U.S. courts generally interpret the FAA as forbidding interlocutory judicial challenges to arbitrators. *See Larry's United Super, Inc. v. Werries*, 253 F.3d 1083, 1085 (8th Cir. 2001) (no judicial removal of arbitrator under FAA); *Aviall, Inc. v. Ryder Sys., Inc.*, 113 F.3d 892 (2d Cir. 1997) ("it is well established that a district court cannot entertain an attack upon the qualifications or partiality of arbitrators until after the conclusion of the arbitration and the rendition of the award"); *Florasynth, Inc. v. Pickholz*, 750 F.2d 171 (2d Cir. 1984) ("[FAA] does not provide for judicial scrutiny of an arbitrator's qualifications to serve, other than in a proceeding to confirm or vacate an award, which necessarily occurs after the arbitrator has rendered his service."). *See also Trustmark, Inc. v. John Hancock Life Ins. Co.*, 2011 U.S. App. LEXIS 1931 (7th Cir.) (refusing to enjoin arbitration on grounds that co-arbitrator had participated in prior, closely-related arbitration; relying in part on fact that arbitrators were not required (in domestic U.S. reinsurance arbitration) to be impartial)

Suppose a party or an appointing authority selects, or refuses to remove, an arbitrator who is manifestly biased and partial. Should a court not have the power to remove the arbitrator and direct a new appointment? Suppose the facts alleged in *Technostroyexport* occurred with respect to an arbitration seated in the United States and IDTS sought judicial relief in a U.S. court. Suppose Dr. Wallersteiner from the *Veritas* case was appointed as a sole arbitrator. Does it make any sense for U.S. courts to be required to stand by as a blatantly biased arbitrator conducts proceedings?

Consider the results in *Certain Underwriters*, where the U.S. court (a) refuses to consider a challenge to the impartiality of the arbitral tribunal, on the grounds that it is interlocutory; and (b) entertains a challenge to the arbitral tribunal's interim measures, on the grounds that they are final. *See also infra* pp. 900-03, 1118 for more detailed discussion of the latter holding. Can it really be that an arbitral tribunal's decisions can be considered in an annulment (vacatur) action, but the composition of the arbitral tribunal cannot be? Compare the broadly comparable facts in *ASM Shipping*.

5. *Lower U.S. court decisions asserting equitable power to review selection of arbitrator on interlocutory basis.* Notwithstanding the majority view, some U.S. courts have held open (without deciding) the possibility of a general "equitable power" to issue interlocutory orders removing or replacing arbitrators. *See, e.g., Michaels v. Mariforum Shipping SA*, 624 F.2d 411, 415 n.5 (2d Cir. 1980); *Aviall, Inc. v. Ryder Sys., Inc.*, 913 F.Supp. 826, 828 (S.D.N.Y. 1996) (judicial power to disqualify arbitrator prior to award when "one party has deceived the other, ... unforeseen intervening events have

frustrated parties' intent, ... or the unmistakable partiality of the arbitrator will render arbitration a mere prelude to subsequent litigation"). Thus, in a few cases, usually citing extreme circumstances, U.S. courts have removed arbitrators in interlocutory actions. *Metropolitan Cas. Ins. Co. v. J.C. Penny Cas. Ins. Co.*, 780 F.Supp. 885 (D. Conn. 1991) (interlocutory order removing arbitrator who had "fiduciary relationship" with party); *Third Nat'l Bank v. Wedge Groups, Inc.*, 749 F.Supp. 851 (M.D. Tenn. 1990) (interlocutory order removing arbitrator who had discussed issues with party before nomination); *Christina Blouse Corp. v. Int'l Ladies Garment Workers' Union*, 492 F.Supp. 508 (S.D.N.Y. 1980) (arbitrator named in contract possessed relationship with one party, which was concealed from other party when contract was signed).

6. *Wisdom of national arbitration statutes permitting interlocutory judicial removal of arbitrators.* Is it wise to permit interlocutory judicial review of an arbitrator's bias or qualifications, as the UNCITRAL Model Law, SLPIL, French Code of Civil Procedure and most other developed arbitration statutes contemplate? Is this a more sensible approach than that taken under the FAA by *Certain Underwriters*? What are the respective advantages and disadvantages of each approach?

   Note the concerns stated by the *Certain Underwriters* court, that interlocutory judicial challenges of arbitrators "might spawn endless applications and indefinite delay" and that "there could be no assurance that [a party] would not bring yet another proceeding to disqualify" any arbitrator that might be selected. Are these concerns realistic? Sufficient to justify a prohibition against *any* interlocutory judicial relief? Is it not intolerable to permit an adjudicatory proceeding to go forward with a manifestly biased decision-maker? Is it sufficient to respond that the biased decision-maker's award can be annulled? What are the costs of permitting such an arbitration to go forward? After an arbitration has been fully conducted, are there pressures on the reviewing court not to overturn an otherwise acceptable award, based on doubts about an arbitrator's impartiality? Is it possible for a biased arbitrator to make procedural rulings in the course of an arbitration (regarding, for example, disclosure or provisional measures) which could have very substantial consequences for a party, even if the arbitrator's final award is annulled?

   What are the potential costs arising from permitting interlocutory judicial challenge of an arbitrator? Note that the UNCITRAL Model Law and SLPIL contain specific procedural safeguards on judicial removal proceedings, to ensure that the arbitral proceedings are not delayed.

7. *Waiver of objections under national law to arbitrator's lack of independence or improper constitution of tribunal.* Consider the challenge provisions in Article 13 of the UNCITRAL Model Law and Article 180 of the SLPIL, excerpted at pp. 89 & 158 of the Documentary Supplement. Note the requirements for timely challenges. What is the reason for these requirements? What are the consequences of failing to comply with these timing requirements?

   Consider the concluding comment by the Swiss Federal Tribunal in its *Judgment of 9 February 1998*. Why was it that the complaining party would have waived its objection to the arbitrator in question? Consider also the court's analysis in *ASM Shipping*. What exactly did the charterer waive? Why didn't it waive its objections to the presiding arbitrator? Why was there no waiver in *Certain Underwriters*?

Although not generally permitting interlocutory judicial challenges to arbitrators, U.S. courts have held that a party must object to an arbitrator's partiality in a timely fashion, or risk waiving the right to object in subsequent actions to annul the arbitrator's award. *See, e.g., Dealer Computer Servs., Inc. v. Michael Motor Co.*, 485 F.Appx. 724, 727 (5th Cir. 2012) ("A party seeking to vacate an arbitration award based on an arbitrator's evident partiality generally must object during the arbitration proceeding. Its failure to do so results in waiver of its right to object."); *Health Servs. Mgt Corp. v. Hughes*, 975 F.2d 1253 (7th Cir. 1992) (objection to arbitrator's impartiality in arbitral proceedings will preserve party's objection, even where party proceeds with arbitration after its objection is overruled); *Hayne, Miller & Farmi, Inc. v. Flume*, 888 F.Supp. 949, 953 (E.D. Wis. 1995) ("Where a party was fully aware of facts which could possibly indicate arbitrator partiality at the time of the arbitration hearing and that party fails to make an objection during the course of the hearing, it waives its right to object"). Consider the *Technostroyexport* case. Was it correctly decided? Why?

Note that the allegations of corruption were assumed correct for purposes of the appeal (and are also consistent with many reports from comparable international settings, *supra* pp. 100-01). Is the right to object to a corrupt arbitrator waivable? Should it be? Consider the Non-Waivable Red List under the IBA Guidelines. Should a party be permitted to challenge the award on such grounds, as in *Technostroyexport*? If not, are such grounds really non-waivable?

Note that the allegations in *Technostroyexport* were directed towards the Russian appointing authority and arbitral institution, not the arbitrators themselves. How does this affect waiver analysis? If the U.S. party had come into possession of information that the presiding arbitrator was corrupt, is it appropriate to require it to act upon that information in a timely fashion upon pain of waiving the objection? Why? To whom would the U.S. party direct its challenge? *Technostroyexport* involved alleged corruption of the appointing authority itself. To whom would the U.S. party direct its "challenge"?

8. *Duty on party to investigate for arbitrator's bias.* Is a party to an arbitration required to investigate at the outset of an arbitration to determine whether a prospective or newly-appointed arbitrator is partial? National courts have sometimes said that parties are not generally obliged to seek out possible bases of bias of an arbitrator in order to preserve a later challenge. *See Merit Ins. Co. v. Leatherby Ins. Co.*, 714 F.2d 673, 683 (7th Cir.); *U.S. Wrestling Fed'n v. Wrestling Div. of AAU, Inc.*, 605 F.2d 313, 321 (7th Cir. 1979).

Is that view appropriate? Suppose review of an arbitrator's online biography, on his or her law firm's website, would reveal a conflict. Should a party that fails to consider this information be permitted, if it later is informed of the information, to rely on that information to challenge the arbitrator? Suppose the challenge comes after 18 months of arbitration, in which the tribunal has rendered unfavorable partial decisions against the challenging party.

Some U.S. courts have held that a waiver of objections to an arbitrator's independence and impartiality will occur where a party had only constructive knowledge. *See Dealer Computer Serv., Inc. v. Michael Motor Co.*, 485 F.Appx. 724, 728 (5th Cir. 2012). Others have required that a party have actual knowledge of the alleged basis for an arbitrator's alleged conflict of interest for waiver to occur. *See Middlesex Mut. Ins. Co. v. Levine*, 675 F.2d 1197, 1204 (11th Cir. 1982).

9. *Procedures under institutional rules for interlocutory challenge and removal of arbitrators*. Most institutional rules contain procedures for interlocutory challenges to, and removals of, arbitrators. Consider Articles 12-14 of the UNCITRAL Rules, Article 14 of the ICC Rules and Article 10 of the LCIA Rules. Note how the challenge procedures operate under each set of rules, including the time limits.

What is the procedure for such decision-making, and what are the parties' opportunities to be heard? What opportunity is there for written submissions? Oral submissions? Live witnesses or an evidentiary hearing? Discovery? The short answer, under all these institutional rules, is that a party can submit a written presentation regarding its challenge, and that is it (*i.e.*, there is no discovery and no evidentiary or other hearing). An arbitrator who is challenged may respond, as may the other party, but no further procedures exist. Is the foregoing appropriate? Would this sort of procedure satisfy due process or adversarial procedure standards in many other contexts? What are the advantages and disadvantages of the procedure?

Is a decision by the ICC on a challenge to an arbitrator under the ICC Rules reasoned? Is it public? Compare the approach under the LCIA Rules. *See* Nicholas & Partasides, *LCIA Court Decisions on Challenges to Arbitrators: A Proposal to Publish*, 23 Arb. Int'l 1 (2007). Which is wiser? Why? What benefits does a reasoned explanation provide? At what costs? Note that the challenge decision in *ICS* was published.

Who do you think parties would prefer to have decide upon the challenge to an arbitrator—a national court in the arbitral seat or an institutional appointing authority? Why? Recall the discussion of the costs and benefits of different means of appointing arbitrators (*e.g.*, national court appointment versus appointment by an institutional appointing authority). *See supra* pp. 707-08. Do the same costs and benefits exist in the context of challenges to arbitrators?

10. *Standards for challenging arbitrators under institutional rules*. Consider again the grounds for challenging arbitrators under each of the leading sets of institutional rules. Which set of rules provides the broadest grounds for challenging an arbitrator? Note the reference in the ICC Rules to challenges based on an "alleged lack of impartiality or independence, *or otherwise*." What might fall within the latter category?

11. *Who decides challenges to arbitrators under institutional rules?* Consider the identity of the person(s) who decide(s) challenges to arbitrators under most institutional rules. Why doesn't the arbitral tribunal itself (either with or without the participation of the challenged arbitrator) decide challenges? At least preliminarily? Is it appropriate for challenges to be decided essentially by administrative committees whose membership is often secret?

In practice, challenges to arbitrators are much more likely to succeed if made prior to confirmation, rather than during the course of the arbitral proceedings. Note the timing of the challenge in *ICS*. Various surveys of ICC practice suggest that approximately 70% of pre-appointment objections are accepted, while less than 10% of post-appointment challenges succeed. W. Craig, W. Park & J. Paulsson, *International Chamber of Commerce Arbitration* 204 (2000). Consider what explains this disparity.

12. *Representative bases for challenges under institutional rules.* Consider again the hypotheticals set forth above at pp. 757-58, positing various possible grounds for questioning an arbitrator's independence. In reviewing these hypotheticals, consider whether or not you would bring a challenge based on the stated facts.

13. *Challenging arbitrators in investment arbitrations.* What is the procedural mechanism for challenging an arbitrator in an ICSID arbitration? Consider Article 58 of the ICSID Convention. Note that the "other members of the ... Tribunal" first consider any challenge and, if they cannot agree, "the Chairman [the President of the World Bank] shall take that decision." Is this a sensible procedure? Why or why not?

    A number of BITs and FTAs (or individual investment agreements) have altered this procedure to provide, for example, that the Secretary-General of the PCA or the Secretary-General of ICSID either makes or appoints an appointing authority to make any challenge decision. See, for example, the procedure followed in *Perenco* (where the Secretary-General of the PCA decided the challenge in accordance with a letter agreement between the parties); the procedure followed in *Gallo v. Canada, Decision on Challenge to Arbitrator in NAFTA Case of 14 October 2009* (acting Secretary-General of ICSID decided challenge in accordance with NAFTA and Article 12(1)(b) of 1976 UNCITRAL Rules); and the procedure followed in *ICS* (the Secretary-General of the PCA designated an appointing authority to decide the challenge in accordance with the UK-Argentina BIT and Article 12(1)(c) of the 1976 UNCITRAL Rules, which provides that, where the parties have not previously designated an appointing authority for the arbitration and cannot agree upon one, the Secretary-General of the PCA will do so).

14. *Practical implications of challenging arbitrators.* Consider a party's reactions if, during the process of selecting a tribunal, it discovers grounds for challenging either (a) another party's co-arbitrator, or (b) the presiding arbitrator. What happens if a challenge is made, but fails? What happens if a challenge succeeds? What are the benefits of a successful challenge? The costs? What are the costs of an unsuccessful challenge? Does your view of the costs of failure depend upon whether it is the presiding arbitrator who is challenged? Consider the reactions of the presiding arbitrator to both a successful and an unsuccessful challenge to a co-arbitrator. How do you think Mr. Gottheimer was disposed after the challenge against him was made? And failed?

15. *Waiver of objections under institutional rules based on arbitrator's lack of impartiality.* Consider the procedural requirements of institutional rules, including particularly the timing requirements for making challenges based upon lack of independence. Note in particular Article 13(1) of the 2010 UNCITRAL Rules and Article 14(2) of the 2012 ICC Rules. Are the requirements wise? Why or why not?

16. *Party's ability to remove arbitrator it nominated under institutional rules.* Most institutional rules vest the appointing authority with power to both confirm and remove party-nominated arbitrators. *See, e.g.,* 2010 UNCITRAL Rules, Arts. 8, 13; 2012 ICC Rules, Arts. 11-14. After a party's nominee has been confirmed, he or she cannot ordinarily be removed by that party, and must instead be challenged (like any other arbitrator). Indeed, under most institutional rules, a party cannot challenge the arbitrator it appointed except for reasons it became aware of following the appointment. 2010 UNCITRAL Rules, Art. 12(2).

Can both parties acting together remove an arbitrator? Consider Canon II(G) of the AAA/ABA Code of Ethics, requiring an arbitrator to resign if requested by both parties. Compare the UNCITRAL, LCIA and ICC Rules. Consider Article 13(2) of the UNCITRAL Model Law.

17. *Institutional finality clauses and judicial review of appointing authority's resolution of challenge.* Consider Article 11(4) of the 2012 ICC Rules. There are similar finality clauses in many other institutional rules. What is the purpose of such provisions?

Are provisions providing for the finality of institutional challenge and appointment decisions valid? Does this amount to permitting parties contractually to adopt whatever standards of impartiality they wish? As discussed above, in many jurisdictions, the parties' autonomy to contract out of requirements regarding the arbitrators' independence and impartiality is limited by local mandatory law. *See supra* pp. 739-40. Should the same be true with regard to the parties' autonomy to agree to institutional challenge mechanisms? How are institutional challenge mechanisms different from agreement on partisan or corrupt arbitrators?

18. *Relationship between interlocutory judicial challenges and institutional challenge procedures.* As we have seen, most arbitration statutes provide mechanisms for interlocutory judicial challenges to arbitrators; similarly, most institutional rules provide procedures for interlocutory challenges to arbitrators before an appointing authority. *See supra* p. 772. Assuming that there is in principle a possibility for interlocutory judicial challenge of an arbitrator, should such *judicial* challenges be available where the parties have agreed to an *institutional* challenge mechanism?

Consider the approach of the UNCITRAL Model Law (in Article 13(3)). If the parties agree to arbitrate pursuant to institutional rules, providing an institutional challenge mechanism, may a party nonetheless pursue an interlocutory judicial challenge under Article 13(3)? In what cases? Is that wise? What alternative might be adopted?

Consider the approach under Articles 179 and 180 of the SLPIL. If a party agrees to an institutional challenge procedure, may it also pursue a judicial challenge under Article 180? *See Judgment of 18 August 1992*, DFT 118 II 359 (Swiss Fed. Trib.) ("It is correct that an appeal directly against a decision of refusal of a private body such as the [ICC] is not possible," but objections to the arbitrator's independence may be considered in annulment action). *See also* French Code of Civil Procedure, Art. 1456; Swedish Arbitration Law, § 11 ("The parties may agree that a motion as referred to in Art. 10(1) [permitting challenge of arbitrator before appointing authority] shall be conclusively determined by an arbitration institution.").

Where parties have agreed for an arbitral institution to resolve challenges to the arbitrators, and where the applicable institutional rules contain a finality provision (*e.g.*, 2012 ICC Rules, Art. 11(4)), should an interlocutory judicial challenge (*e.g.*, UNCITRAL Model Law, Art. 13(3)) be available? Why or why not?

Even if interlocutory judicial review is available, should courts defer to the results of an institutional challenge? *Compare* Paulsson, *Securing the Integrity, Impartiality and Independence of Arbitrators: Judicial Intervention*, 1993 Y.B. Arb. Inst. Stock. Cham. Comm. 91, 95 ("Nor should courts, in the context of institutional arbitration, be encouraged to intervene in the process ... before the award is rendered, [although] ... earlier court intervention in the case of *ad hoc* arbitration is another matter.") *with*

AT&T Corp. v. Saudi Cable Co. [2000] 2 Lloyd's Rep. 127, 137 (English Ct. App.) ("I do not accept the view ... the finality provision means that the English courts have no power to review the decision of the ICC Court in a challenge to an arbitrator").

19. *Vacancies on arbitral tribunal.* During the course of an arbitration, one of the members of the tribunal may die, resign, or otherwise leave a vacancy on the tribunal. How is the vacancy to be filled? Consider the UNCITRAL Model Law. What does it provide regarding the filling of vacancies on a tribunal? Consider the UNCITRAL Rules and the ICC Rules. What do they provide? Is this a sensible approach? Suppose a party nominates a partial co-arbitrator who is subsequently removed. Should that party be permitted to nominate another co-arbitrator? Why or why not?

20. *Truncated arbitral tribunals.* Suppose one arbitrator on a three-person tribunal refuses to continue to participate in deliberations with his or her colleagues on the tribunal. Alternatively, suppose an arbitrator resigns from his or her position on the tribunal. In each case, suppose the arbitrator's non-participation or resignation occurs after it appears that his or her colleagues on the tribunal have decided to rule against the party that nominated the arbitrator in question. In these circumstances, may the tribunal continue as a "truncated tribunal" (*i.e.*, with only two participating members) or must the non-participating arbitrator be removed and replaced? How long will this take?

If a co-arbitrator has resigned during the course of deliberations, why shouldn't the resulting vacancy be filled in the usual manner under applicable law and institutional rules? *See supra* pp. 694-702. Suppose the co-arbitrator in question resigned, in bad faith, as a means of obstructing an award against the party that nominated him or her. Should that resignation be permitted to delay the making of an award? Suppose the co-arbitrator in question is removed, a replacement co-arbitrator is nominated (by the party that nominated the original co-arbitrator) and that replacement arbitrator then resigns. How long should this be required to continue?

Consider Article 15(5) of the ICC Rules, excerpted at p. 189 of the Documentary Supplement. What does it permit? Compare Article 12(1) of the LCIA Rules:

> In exceptional circumstances, where an arbitrator without good cause refuses or persistently fails to participate in the deliberations of an Arbitral Tribunal, the remaining arbitrators jointly may decide (after their written notice of such refusal or failure to the LCIA Court, the parties and the absent arbitrator) to continue the arbitration (including the making of any award) notwithstanding the absence of that other arbitrator, subject to the written approval of the LCIA Court.

Contrast the UNCITRAL Rules. Do they contain any comparable provision, permitting two arbitrators to continue as a truncated tribunal or providing for institutional nomination of a replacement co-arbitrator? Is this wise? Do the ICC Rules and LCIA Rules adopt sensible solutions to cases of arbitrator misconduct?

Suppose an ICC or LCIA arbitration is seated in a jurisdiction that has adopted the UNCITRAL Model Law. Is there an argument that Article 15(5) of the ICC Rules or Article 12(1) of the LCIA Rules would violate mandatory provisions of the Model Law? What provisions?

Suppose parties have agreed to an *ad hoc* arbitration (or to an arbitration under UNCITRAL Rules) in an UNCITRAL Model Law jurisdiction. If an arbitrator refused to participate in further hearings or deliberations, would the two remaining arbitrators be permitted to proceed in the arbitrator's absence? Would the appointing authority be permitted to remove the misbehaving arbitrator and appoint a replacement (rather than allowing the party that originally nominated the misbehaving arbitrator to do so)? Why or why not?

Two members of a panel of the Iran-U.S. Claims Tribunal held that they were permitted to proceed without the participation of the third arbitrator (a co-arbitrator nominated by Iran) under arbitration rules based on the UNCITRAL Rules. They reasoned:

> "this is in accordance with the established practice of the Tribunal to continue its work and make awards despite the failure of one arbitrator to participate. The practice of the Tribunal in this respect is necessary to prevent disruption and frustration by one Member of the Tribunal's performance of its functions and is fully in accordance with recognized principles of international law." *Uiterwyk Corp. v. Islamic Repub. of Iran, Award in IUSCT Case No. 375-381-1 of 6 July 1988*, 19 Iran-US C.T.R. 107, ¶30 (1988).

Is this persuasive? If the parties' arbitration agreement provides for arbitration before three (not two) arbitrators, and for replacement of arbitrators in the same manner they were selected, is it appropriate to permit two arbitrators to resolve the parties' dispute? Does this not contradict the parties' agreement? Query what the parties intended in cases where a co-arbitrator deliberately seeks to frustrate an award. *See also* G. Born, *International Commercial Arbitration* 1955 *et seq.* (2d ed. 2014); Schwebel, *The Authority of A Truncated Tribunal*, in A. van den Berg (ed.), *Improving the Efficiency of Arbitration Agreements and Awards: 40 Years of Application of the New York Convention* 314 (1999).

21. *Improper conditions on resignation.* Suppose an arbitrator attempts to resign and, in doing so, attaches a condition to his resignation. For example, suppose an arbitrator resigns on the condition that his successor is appointed by the party that nominated him. Is such a condition effective? In an early ICSID arbitration, Sir John Foster resigned from an ICSID tribunal on the condition that his successor be appointed by the party that appointed him. Eisemann, *The Double Sanction of the ICSID Convention for Agreements or Understandings Between An Arbitrator and the Party Appointing Him*, 23 Annuaire Français de Droit Int'l 436 (1977). The remaining two arbitrators on the tribunal refused to accept the condition and therefore withheld their consent to Foster's resignation pursuant to Article 56 of the ICSID Convention. As a consequence, Foster's successor was selected by the Secretary-General of ICSID, rather than by the party that nominated him. Is this a harsh sanction? What if Foster had simply been removed for lack of impartiality? *See* ICSID Convention, Art. 58, second sentence. Is a harsher result appropriate in the circumstances of an attempted conditional resignation? Why or why not?

CHAPTER 9

PROCEDURAL ISSUES IN INTERNATIONAL ARBITRATION

This chapter explores the procedural aspects of international arbitral proceedings in commercial, investment and inter-state settings. First, the chapter considers the choice of procedures in international arbitration, including the autonomy of parties to select procedures, the limits on that autonomy and the discretion of arbitral tribunals to establish arbitral procedures. Second, the chapter considers the principle of judicial non-intervention in arbitral proceedings. Third, the chapter explores how parties and arbitral tribunals customarily approach various significant "procedural" issues in practice, such as scheduling, the taking and admissibility of evidence, disclosure or discovery, and the like. Fourth, the chapter considers in greater detail the subject of disclosure in international arbitration. Finally, the chapter considers the related topics of confidentiality and transparency in international arbitration.

A. APPLICABLE PROCEDURAL RULES IN INTERNATIONAL ARBITRATION

Historically, it was frequently said or assumed that arbitrators were required to apply the domestic procedural rules applicable in national courts in the arbitral seat.[1] For the most part, it is now widely accepted that the domestic procedural rules of local courts are not applicable—mandatorily or otherwise—in international arbitrations seated on local territory.[2] Rather, one of the most fundamental characteristics of contemporary international arbitration is the parties' broad freedom to agree upon the procedures to be followed in their arbitration. As explained below, this principle is acknowledged in the New York Convention (and other international instruments concerning arbitration);[3] it is guaranteed by arbitration statutes in many developed jurisdictions;[4] it is confirmed in the decisions of national courts and arbitral tribunals;[5] and it is contained in and facilitated by the rules of most leading arbitration institutions.[6]

As discussed below, the autonomy of parties to choose their own arbitral procedures (like their autonomy to choose the applicable procedural law of the arbitration) in international commercial arbitrations is often qualified by the mandatory requirements of applicable national law. In leading arbitral forums, these requirements are ordinarily minimal.

---

1. *See Sapphire Int'l Petroleum Ltd v. Nat'l Iranian Oil Co.*, 35 I.L.R. 136 (1963).

2. *See* G. Born, *International Commercial Arbitration* 2130-38, 2150-53, 2161-62 (2d ed. 2014).

3. *See infra* pp. 789-90; New York Convention, Arts. II, V(1)(d); G. Born, *International Commercial Arbitration* 2156-59 (2d ed. 2014).

4. *See infra* pp. 788-89; UNCITRAL Model Law, Art. 19; English Arbitration Act, 1996, §§34-38; SLPIL, Art. 182(1) & (2); G. Born, *International Commercial Arbitration* 2132-36 (2d ed. 2014).

5. *See infra* pp. 782-85, 788-89; *Final Award in ICC Case No. 7626*, XXII Y.B. Comm. Arb. 132 (1997); G. Born, *International Commercial Arbitration* 2132-38 (2d ed. 2014).

6. *See infra* p. 791; 2012 ICC Rules, Art. 19; G. Born, *International Commercial Arbitration* 2138-40, 2149-53 (2d ed. 2014).

"As a speedy and informal alternative to litigation, arbitration resolves disputes without confinement to many of the procedural and evidentiary structures that protect the integrity of formal trials."[7] Nevertheless, most jurisdictions require that arbitral proceedings satisfy at least some minimal standards of procedural fairness and equality.

Jurisdictions typically impose their own standard of procedural fairness in the international commercial arbitration context, variously termed "due process," the "right to be heard," "natural justice," or "procedural public policy." Both in verbal formulation and in specific application, these standards differ from country to country. For the most part, however, differences among national standards of procedural fairness in developed arbitral centers are not significant, in part because of a desire by national courts to accommodate the needs of international arbitration and to avoid parochial procedural requirements.

Although national law in most developed states will permit the parties to agree upon the arbitral procedures, subject only to minimal due process or procedural regularity requirements, parties often do not agree in advance on detailed procedural rules. At most, international commercial arbitration agreements will provide for arbitration pursuant to a set of institutional rules, which will ordinarily supply only a broad procedural framework.[8] Filling in the considerable gaps in this framework will be left to the subsequent agreement of the parties or, when they cannot agree, the arbitral tribunal.

Where the parties have not agreed upon particular (or any) procedural matters, most national arbitration laws, and institutional rules, grant the tribunal in an international arbitration substantial discretion to establish arbitral procedures. This authority has enormous practical importance because it is a rare case where the parties to an arbitration will find common ground on all of the procedural issues that confront them.

The following materials examine both the parties' autonomy to select arbitral procedures and the tribunal's discretion, absent agreement by the parties, to prescribe procedures in an international arbitration. The materials also explore the mandatory limits, imposed by national and international law, on the parties' procedural autonomy and the arbitrators' procedural discretion.

BELGIAN JUDICIAL CODE
Articles 1699, 1700, 1708

1699. Notwithstanding any agreement to the contrary, the parties shall be treated with equality and each party shall be given a full opportunity of presenting his case, pleas in law and arguments in conformity with the principle of adversarial proceedings. The arbitral tribunal shall ensure that this requirement as well as the principle of fairness of the debates are respected.

1700(1). The parties are free to agree on the procedure to be followed by the arbitral tribunal in conducting the proceedings.

1700(2). Failing such agreement, the arbitral tribunal may, subject to the provisions of Part 6 of this Code, determine the rules of procedure applicable to the arbitration in such manner as it considers appropriate.

---

7. *Forsythe Int'l, SA v. Gibbs Oil Co.*, 915 F.2d 1017, 1022 (5th Cir. 1990).
8. *See* G. Born, *International Commercial Arbitration* 2145 (2d ed. 2014).

1700(3). Unless otherwise agreed by the parties, the arbitral tribunal shall freely assess the admissibility and weight of the evidence.

1700(4). The arbitral tribunal shall set the necessary investigative measures unless the parties authorise it to entrust this task to one of its members. It may hear any person and such hearing shall be taken without oath. If a party holds a piece of evidence, the arbitral tribunal may enjoin it to disclose the evidence according to such terms as the arbitral tribunal shall decide and, if necessary, on pain of a penalty payment.

1700(5). With the exception of applications relating to authentic instruments, the arbitral tribunal shall have the power to rule on applications to verify the authenticity of documents and to rule on allegedly forged documents. For applications relating to authentic instruments, the arbitral tribunal shall leave it to the parties to refer the matter to the Court of First Instance within a given time limit. In the circumstances referred to in §2, the time limits of the arbitral proceedings are automatically suspended until such time as the arbitral tribunal has been informed by the most diligent party of the final court decision on the incident.

1708. With the approval of the arbitral tribunal, a party may apply to the Court of First Instance ruling as in summary proceedings to order all necessary measures for the taking of evidence in accordance with article 1680, paragraph 4.

GUATEMALAN CODE OF CIVIL AND COMMERCIAL PROCEDURE, 1963
Articles 287, 288 (repealed)

287. *Mandatory Nature of the Proceedings.* The arbitral proceedings shall be conducted in accordance with the provisions of the following articles and may not be modified under any circumstances by agreement of the parties.

288. *De Jure Arbitration.* Arbitral proceedings shall be conducted in accordance with the following rules:

(1) Arbitrators shall grant the parties a period of time, which may not exceed one-fourth of the period fixed in the deed embodying the submission, in order to state in writing their claims, submit the documents on which such claims are based, and produce, also in writing, any other means of evidence, attaching as many copies as there are parties;

(2) Copies of the documents submitted by each party shall be handed over to the other parties, granting them another period of time, which may not exceed one-fourth of the period fixed in the deed embodying the submission, in order to file answers, submit the documents, and produce the evidence necessary to rebut the arguments of the opponent;

(3) Arbitrators shall take the evidence they deem necessary to prove those facts having a direct and known bearing on settlement of the dispute submitted to arbitration. The time limit for the taking of evidence may not exceed one-fourth of the total period designated in the deed embodying the submission;

(4) Any type of evidence may be taken during arbitration even on the initiative of the arbitrators, in accordance with the general rules of evidence of this Code. For evidence that may not be taken by the arbitrators themselves, the arbitrators shall request assistance from the court of first instance of the place of arbitration, which shall take any measures deemed suitable for the purpose;

(5) Once the evidence has been taken, the arbitrators shall personally hear the parties or the lawyers representing them; and

(6) Finally, in accordance with the law, the arbitrators shall render the award on each of the points submitted to their decision within the remaining part of the period of time designated in the submission.

SAPPHIRE INT'L PETROLEUM LTD v. NATIONAL IRANIAN OIL CO.
Ad Hoc Award of 15 March 1963, 35 I.L.R. 136 (1967)

[excerpted above at pp. 632-33]

INTERIM AWARD IN ICC CASE NO. 5029
XII Y.B. Comm. Arb. 113 (1987)

MALMBERG, FLETCHER-COOKE, ZAAZOUE, Arbitrators. [Two French companies entered into a joint venture with two Egyptian companies. The joint venture thereafter entered into a contract to construct certain civil works in Egypt. Article 5(1)(b) of the Contract provided: "The Contract shall be deemed to be an Egyptian Contract and shall be governed by and construed according to the laws in force in Egypt." Article 67 of the agreement contained an arbitration clause, providing for arbitration under ICC Rules. The agreement did not specify an arbitral seat. Disputes arose, and the French companies filed a request for arbitration under the ICC Arbitration Rules against the Egyptian employer. Pursuant to Article 12 of the 1975 ICC Rules, the ICC selected the Netherlands as the arbitral seat.

The defendant argued that Egyptian law of civil procedure governed the arbitration proceedings. It reasoned that the choice of law clause in Article 5 covered both substantive and procedural subjects, including issues relating to the arbitration. According to defendant, the text of Article 67 of the agreement "clearly expressed the intention of the parties that the arbitration is a local arbitration and not international" and "that it is internal and not external." The claimant agreed with the defendant that Egyptian law rules of interpretation should be applied to the parties' contract, but distinguished between substantive and procedural law. According to the claimant substantive law is governed by the law chosen by the parties (*i.e.*, Egyptian law), but procedural law is governed by the mandatory provisions of the place of arbitration (*i.e.*, Dutch arbitration law).]

The choice of law clause contained in Article 5(1)(b) of the Contract must be interpreted in accordance with the rules of contract interpretation of Egyptian law, in particular Articles 150 *et seq.* of the Egyptian Civil Code.[9] The Arbitral Tribunal will follow these rules of interpretation in respect of all the jurisdictional issues.

The Arbitral Tribunal holds that the law governing the arbitration is the arbitration law of the Netherlands. The Arbitral Tribunal notes at the outset that the Contract is a truly international contract involving parties of different nationalities (*i.e.*, French and Egyp-

---

9. Article 150 of the Egyptian Civil Code provides:

"When the wording of a contract is clear, it cannot be deviated from in order to ascertain by means of interpretation the intention of the parties. When a contract has to be construed, it is necessary to ascertain the common intention of the parties and to go beyond the literal meaning of words, taking into account the nature of the transaction as well as that loyalty and confidence which should exist between the parties in accordance with commercial usage."

tian), the movement of equipment and services across national frontiers, and the payment in different currencies.... The international character of the Contract is inconsistent with the defendant's allegation that the parties intended to provide for domestic, internal (*i.e.*, Egyptian) arbitration. Such intent cannot be derived from the choice of law clause contained in Article 5(1)(b) of the Contract, providing for the applicability of Egyptian law, whilst Article 67, providing for arbitration under the [ICC Rules], clearly expresses the contrary. As it is recognized in virtually all legal systems around the world, a basic distinction must be made between the law governing the substance and the law governing the procedure. That distinction is also recognized in Egyptian conflict of laws: whereas Article 19 of the Egyptian Civil Code provides for the law governing the substance of the dispute, Article 22 is concerned with the law governing the procedure. Accordingly, if the parties had wished that the arbitration be governed by Egyptian procedural law, they should have made a specific agreement thereon. Article 5(1)(b) of the Contract is not such a provision as it does not mention specifically that arbitration is governed by Egyptian law. Failing such agreement, the arbitration law of the place governs the arbitration. This principle is in accordance with Article V(1)(a), (d) and (e) of the New York Convention to which Egypt and the Netherlands have adhered.

The agreement of the parties in arbitration under the [ICC Rules] in Clause 67 meant that, failing their agreement on the place of arbitration, they gave, under Article 12 of the Rules, a mandate to the Court of Arbitration to fix the place of arbitration on their behalf. It is to be noted that defendant itself proposed in the alternative The Hague as the place of arbitration. The prevailing interpretation of the [ICC Rules] nowadays, is also that the mandatory provisions of the arbitration law of the place of arbitration govern the arbitration, irrespective of the law governing the substance. Whereas Article 13(3) of the Rules contains the contractual conflict of laws rules for determining the law governing the substance of the dispute, Article 11 is concerned with the rules governing the proceedings [and specifically requires observance of the mandatory procedural requirements of the seat.] ...

The Arbitral Tribunal emphasizes that the applicability of Dutch arbitration law in the present case by no means implies that the Dutch rules concerning proceeding before Dutch State Courts are applicable. According to Dutch arbitration law, parties are free to agree on the rules of procedure and, failing such agreement, the arbitrator determines the conduct of the proceedings, subject to a few necessary mandatory provisions. By referring to the [ICC Rules], the parties have "internationalized" the arbitration within this legal framework....

FINAL AWARD IN ICC CASE NO. 7626
XXII Y.B. Comm. Arb. 132 (1997)

[An Austrian company ("Company A") entered into a technical cooperation agreement with another Austrian company ("Company B"). The agreement required Company A to provide technical assistance to Company B. Disputes about this assistance arose, and Company B commenced arbitral proceedings against Company A under the ICC Rules. The arbitral seat was England.] There is one procedural issue which we deal with at the outset: the admissibility of the diaries of Dr. Y and Dr. V [an employee of Company A]. Company B has objected to its admission in this arbitration on the basis of §21 of the Indian Evidence Act.

Dr. Y and Dr. V kept a daily notebook into which they contemporaneously summarized items of business significance. They entered into that notebook comments and issues discussed with Mr. X at various meetings. Company A presented a copy of the relevant pages of the notebook recording notes of the meetings with Mr. X.... At the hearing the Tribunal requested and were provided with a copy of the German text from the notebooks, with a transcription and English translation. Dr. Y had his notebook with him and referred to it during the hearing. He gave evidence and ... explained to the Tribunal what various notes meant and the context in which they were recorded.... Mr. X also had notebooks with him to which he referred and to which no objection was expressed. Mr. X's notebooks were not offered as supporting evidence by Company B.

Company B argues that Dr. Y's diary entries are inadmissible in evidence in this arbitration. It submits that except for statements recorded in books in the course of business by a person who is dead, admissions made in a written record such as a diary cannot be presented and relied upon by the party who keeps or made the diary. Company B referred us to §21 of the Indian Evidence Act which provides: "Admissions are relevant and may be proved as against the person who makes them, or his representative in interest; but they cannot be proved by or on behalf of the person who makes them or by his representative in interest...." Section 32 of the Indian Evidence Act provides that written evidence may be relied on in certain circumstances where the maker of the statement is dead or not easily available.

This is an international arbitration procedure. The strict rules of evidence, as they apply in England where the Tribunal is sitting, or in India, do not apply. In accordance with the power given to the arbitrators in the Terms of Reference, and under the ICC Rules, the Tribunal has the right to determine whether and what evidence shall be admitted. The Tribunal considers that the diary notes of Dr. Y and Dr. V are admissible. They were used as an aide memoire by Dr. Y as to what occurred and were explained to the Tribunal. Company B had the opportunity to cross-examine him on that evidence. It is up to the Tribunal to give to those diary notes whatever credence and weight it considers appropriate. The notes are not in themselves proof of what was discussed, but do indicate and support the evidence given by Dr. Y. Furthermore, and in any event, the Tribunal does not consider that the Indian Evidence Act has any relevance to the conduct of and the admission of evidence in this arbitration....

CARD v. STRATTON OAKMONT, INC.
933 F.Supp. 806 (D. Minn. 1996)

DAVIS, District Judge. In his Statement of Claim [in the arbitration], Petitioner made references to a civil complaint for Preliminary and Permanent Injunction filed by the [U.S. Securities and Exchange Commission ("SEC")] against Stratton Oakmont [and certain related matters]. Respondents assert that consideration of these SEC proceeding in the ... arbitration, by the panel, evidences partiality and a manifest disregard of the law. In support of this argument, Respondents cite [domestic U.S. judicial decisions which] granted motions to strike from complaints ... references to SEC consent judgments or SEC complaints pursuant to the applicable Federal Rules of Evidence. Petitioner argues, and this Court agrees, that reliance on [these decisions] is misplaced as the Federal Rules of Evidence do not apply to arbitration proceedings.

We commence by discussing what arbitration is and what it is not. Arbitration is a creature born of a contract between the parties who are desirous of avoiding litigation in a court of law. Arbitration requires the parties agree to rules of arbitration. Frequently, rules of arbitration specifically exclude the application of judicial rules of evidence. Instead, the arbitrators determine the materiality and relevance of all evidence offered. Arbitrators are not judges of a court nor are they subject to the general superintending power of a court. Arbitration provides neither the procedural protections nor the assurance of the proper application of substantive law offered by the judicial system. Those who choose to resolve dispute by arbitration can expect no more than they have agreed. One choosing arbitration should not expect the full panoply of procedural and substantive protection offered by a court of law. In short, "by agreeing to arbitrate, a party 'trades the procedures and opportunity for review of the courtroom for the [perceived] simplicity, informality, and expedition of arbitration.'" [In deciding whether communicating settlement offers to the arbitrators was grounds for vacating an award, the court held that such conduct fell within the broad procedural rule of arbitration and that the court did not have the power to draft a contract between the parties or the power to impose judicial rules of evidence on an arbitration proceeding.]

In the present case, the Submission Agreements entered into by the parties provided that arbitration would proceed in accordance with the Constitution, By-Laws, Rules, Regulations and/or Code of Arbitration Procedure of the sponsoring organization, NASD. Section 34 of the Code of Arbitration Procedure, which governs NASD arbitration proceedings, provides the following: "Evidence. The arbitrators shall determine the materiality and relevance of any evidence proffered and shall not be bound by the rules governing the admissibility of evidence." Section 35 provides: "Interpretations of Provisions of Code and Enforcement of Arbitrator Rulings. The arbitrators shall be empowered to interpret and determine the application of all provisions under this Code and to take appropriate action to obtain compliance with any ruling by the arbitrators. Such interpretations and actions to obtain compliance shall be final and binding upon the parties." These sections make clear that the panel had the authority and discretion to determine materiality and relevance without reference to the judicial rules of evidence and that the decision to accept such evidence by the panel is final and binding upon Respondents. Accordingly, this Court has no power to judicially impose its rules of evidence on this arbitration proceeding.

Respondents also argue that the panel improperly failed to make a tape recording of Petitioner's cross examination. Section 37 of the Code of Arbitration Procedure provides:

"A verbatim record by stenographic reporter or a tape recording of all arbitration hearings shall be kept. If a party or parties to a dispute elected to have the record transcribed, the costs of such transcription shall be borne by the party or parties making the request unless the arbitrators direct otherwise. The arbitrators may also direct that the record be transcribed. If the record is transcribed at the request of any party, a copy shall be provided to the arbitrators."

Respondents assert that a verbatim record of the arbitration hearings was kept by tape recording, except for a significant portion of the hearing—Petitioner's cross-examination. Respondents argue that failure to record Petitioner's cross-examination constitutes misbehavior by the panel and further evidences the prejudice to Respondents as a result of the panel's numerous misdeeds.

Respondents do not point to any authority supporting their argument that an arbitration award may be vacated because a verbatim record of a portion of an arbitration proceeding was not made. There is no evidence before the Court that the panel purposefully orchestrated the failure of the tape record while Petitioner was cross-examined. Respondents argue, however, that the particular portion not recorded is so critical to its ability to have the award vacated that it clearly establishes partiality. Assuming Respondent could point to portions of Petitioner's cross-examination that completely contradict his claims of excessive trading, such evidence could be used to vacate the award as it is not proper for this Court to revisit the arguments and evidence presented to the arbitrators. In reviewing an arbitration award, this Court must focus on whether the arbitral process itself was flawed, not the result.

Furthermore, even though §37 of the Code of Arbitration Procedure may have been by its literal terms violated by the panel it does not follow that the award must be nullified as the Code does not have the force of law. Respondents must point to a statutory violation to warrant vacation of an arbitral award, not a violation of the Code of Arbitration Procedure....

CORPORACION TRANSNACIONAL DE INVERSIONES, SA DE CV v. STET INTERNATIONAL, SPA
(2000) 49 O.R.(3d) 414 (Ontario Ct. App.)

By the Court: ... The appellants ... argued that Lax J. erred in failing to find that the appellants had been unable to present their case within the meaning of Article 34(a)(ii) of the Model Law.... The appellants accepted the statement of principle ... in *Schreter v. Gasmac Inc.* (1992), 7 O.R.(3d) 608, 623 (Gen. Div.):

> "The concept of imposing our public policy on foreign awards is to guard against enforcement of an award *which offends our local principles of justice and fairness in a fundamental way*, and in a way which the parties could attribute to the fact that the award was made in another jurisdiction where the procedural or substantive rules diverge markedly from our own, or where there was ignorance or corruption on the part of the tribunal which could not be seem to be tolerated or condoned by our courts."

We are satisfied that the procedure followed by the tribunal did not offend our principles of justice and fairness in a fundamental way. We are also satisfied that the appellants were not deprived of an adequate opportunity to present their case....

We are satisfied that the manner in which the UTISA/STET agreements were to be disclosed did not infringe the principles of fundamental justice nor deprive the appellants of the opportunity to present their case. Prior to the final hearing, the tribunal ordered that the respondents disclose information concerning the agreements whether or not the appellants had signed a confidentiality agreement. The respondents provided this information to the appellants [by supplying redacted versions of the agreements] and the tribunal found that the respondents had complied with its order. The appellants made no complaint about the disclosure at the final hearing. They now argue that only full and timely disclosure of the actual agreements could meet the principles of fundamental justice. There are at least three problems with these submissions.

First, the agreements could have been obtained by the execution of a confidentiality agreement. The appellants made no good faith attempt to pursue this avenue for obtaining the agreements. They raised spurious objections to the respondents' form of confidentiality agreement and did not provide an alternative form of agreement to the respondents. Second, as Lax J. said, "how can it be said that the [appellants] were denied equality of treatment or that the Tribunal acted in a manner inconsistent with Ontario public policy when the Tribunal was never asked to determine the relevancy of the redacted portions or to order their production?"

Finally, had the appellants not withdrawn from the arbitration, they would have had the same access to the information, including the agreements, as did the tribunal during the testimony of the respondents' witness. This is not speculation, as argued by the appellants. It follows from the terms of Article 25(c) of the Model Law and Article 15(2) of the [1988 ICC Rules]. The latter provides that if one of the parties is absent without valid excuse the arbitrator shall proceed with the arbitration and "such proceedings shall be deemed to have been conducted in the presence of all parties." It hardly offends our notions of fundamental justice if a party that had the opportunity to present its case and meet the opposing case forfeits that opportunity by withdrawing from the arbitration. This argument is entirely without merit.

We are also satisfied that in the circumstances, and given the tribunal's right to control its own procedure and ensure the orderly conduct of the arbitration (albeit in a manner consistent with Article 18), there was no breach of the principles of fundamental justice because of the absence of the Cuban witnesses. We reject the submission that the appellants' counsel was misled by the May 8 letter from the chairman. As Lax J. held, the tribunal had no power to compel evidence from Cuban witnesses nor to issue letters rogatory. The appellants' right to apply to the Ontario courts for letters rogatory to obtain the Cuban evidence did not depend upon interpretation of Ontario law but flowed from Article 27 of the Model Law....

Moreover, it was open to the tribunal to find that the appellants had been given an adequate opportunity to obtain this evidence in one form or another. Well before the final hearing, the tribunal had proposed a variety of alternatives so that the evidence could be produced. The appellants made no attempt to obtain a further adjournment of the hearing to pursue attempts to obtain the Cuban evidence. Rather, they withdrew from the arbitration on the basis that there had been a settlement. The tribunal's response to the appellants' attempts to obtain the Cuban evidence did not breach the principles of fundamental justice nor offend public policy.

NOTES

1. *Objectives of arbitral procedures.* What are the parties' procedural objectives in agreeing to international arbitration? Do the parties desire that the local rules of civil procedure in their respective home jurisdictions be replicated? That the rules of civil procedure of the arbitral seat be applied? What sort of procedure do parties want in an international arbitration? Consider the following options: (a) internationally-neutral procedural rules or rules from the home jurisdiction of one party or the other; (b) flexible procedures, tailored to the parties' particular dispute, or civil litigation procedures used in domestic litigations. What are the advantages and disadvantages of each? Consider §§33 and 34 of the English Arbitration Act, 1996, excerpted at p. 121 of the Documentary Supplement. What do they suggest about the objectives of the arbitral process? Can the provisions be improved?

2. *Domestic civil procedure rules of arbitral seat not generally applicable in international arbitrations.* Historically, it was often said that international arbitrators were obliged to apply the civil procedure rules applicable in local courts. This view is reflected in the arguments unsuccessfully made in *ICC Case No. 5029* and *ICC Case No.*

7626. It is also reflected in the commentary, as late as 1989, by two distinguished English commentators:

> "It is widely believed that an arbitrator, merely because he is an arbitrator, is empowered to act on evidence which would not be strictly admissible in a Court of Law. This is not so. Arbitrators are bound by the law of England, and the rules regarding admissibility of evidence are part of that law. Thus, if an arbitrator admits evidence which is inadmissible, he commits an error of law which may be appealed against. Furthermore, if the arbitrator deliberately accepts evidence which is obviously inadmissible, he commits misconduct and the award will be set aside, at any rate if the evidence is important." M. Mustill & S. Boyd, *Commercial Arbitration* 352 (2d ed. 1989).

Compare the similar rationale of the tribunal in *Sapphire*: "The present arbitration, then, is governed by the law of procedure of Vaud and is subject to the judicial sovereignty of Vaud. Therefore, as far as procedure is concerned, it is subject to the binding rules of the Code of Civil Procedure of Vaud of November 20, 1911, and in particular to the 8th Title of this Code."

As the decisions in *ICC Case No. 5029* and *ICC Case No. 7626* illustrate, however, most contemporary authorities reject the view that the local procedural rules of the arbitral seat's domestic courts must be applied in international arbitrations. In the words of one authority:

> "The law of the place of arbitration had at one time a very material relationship with the procedure to be adopted in an arbitration, including international arbitration. However, that influence has been diluted. The law of the major centers of arbitration eschews prescribing procedure." Webster, *Evolving Principles in Enforcing Awards Subject to Annulment Proceedings*, 23 J. Int'l Arb. 201, 222 (2006).

Would the arbitration in *Card* have been more just if the Federal Rules of Evidence had applied? Would the arbitration in *ICC Case No. 7626* have been more fair if English (or Indian) rules of evidence had applied?

Note that, under most legal systems, arbitrators are *not* free to ignore applicable national substantive law unless the parties have expressly permitted them to decide *ex aequo et bono*. *See infra* pp. 1020-21. If international arbitrators are not permitted to ignore national substantive law, why should they be permitted to ignore national procedural rules? Is there a principled distinction between procedural and substantive issues in this regard?

Some institutional rules expressly state that some procedures applicable to national court proceedings are not appropriate in arbitration. *See* 2014 ICDR Rules, Art. 21(10). Is this justified? *Compare* 2012 ICC Rules, Art. 19(1).

3. *No generally-applicable code of procedure for international commercial arbitrations*. In most international commercial arbitrations, there is no preexisting or generally-applicable code of procedural rules that govern conduct of the arbitral proceedings. As discussed above, it is well-settled in virtually all developed jurisdictions that arbitrators are not required to apply local civil procedure rules applicable in national court litigation, in an international arbitration. *See supra* p. 786. Further, in *ad hoc* arbitrations, there will often be no procedural rules of any sort incorporated into the parties' arbitration agreement.

Consider the statutory provisions regarding arbitral procedures excerpted above. Do Articles 18 and 19 of the UNCITRAL Model Law, Article 182 of the SLPIL, Article 1509 of the French CCP or §§33 and 34 of the English Arbitration Act prescribe any general code of procedure for international arbitrations? Does the FAA do so?

In almost all jurisdictions, the tribunal and the parties will ordinarily have full discretion to establish the course of the proceedings (subject only to the requirements of mandatory national law, which, as discussed below, are very limited in most developed jurisdictions). *See infra* pp. 793-95. In institutional settings, most arbitral institutions—notably the ICC, AAA/ICDR, LCIA and ICSID—have promulgated rules that apply to arbitrations where the parties have adopted those rules in their arbitration agreement or otherwise. In addition, the UNCITRAL Rules are available for selection by parties who desire an essentially *ad hoc* arbitration, but supplemented by a skeletal procedural framework and an appointing authority. *See supra* pp. 72-74. Each of these sets of institutional rules gives some structure to the arbitral process by providing a general procedural framework for the conduct of the arbitration, but they leave the overwhelming bulk of issues relating to the arbitral process unaddressed, for resolution by the parties and arbitral tribunal.

Is this absence of any general procedural code, applicable in all international arbitrations, desirable? Consider the suggestion by one commentator that "a formal system of procedure designed specifically for arbitration would be a good idea." Silberman, *International Arbitration: Comments From A Critic*, 13 Am. Rev. Int'l Arb. 9, 13 (2002). *See* Park, *Arbitration's Protean Nature: The Value of Rules and the Risks of Discretion*, 19 Arb. Int'l 279 (2003). Is that a desirable suggestion? Or does it contradict some of the basic objectives of the arbitral process? Consider the following:

> "Procedure is no unalterable course of conduct to which all tribunals must adhere. It should always be adapted to facilitate the course of the particular arbitration and to enable the economical accomplishment of its task within the time fixed. In each arbitration the rules of procedure should be designed to reconcile the divergence of national viewpoints concerning procedure, to require of litigants no more procedural steps than are necessary to enable a satisfactory disposal of the particular case, to conserve litigants' interests from injury by departures from the contemplated course of proceedings, and to bring the arbitration to the speediest possible end compatible with justice. Only through a conscious and careful adaptation of procedural rules to the requirements of each arbitration as it arises will the procedural ills of international arbitration be minimized and its utility as a means for the settlement of disputes between states be fostered." Carlston, *Procedural Problems in International Arbitration*, 39 Am. J. Int'l L. 426, 448 (1945).

See also ICC, *Controlling Time and Costs in International Arbitration* 6 (2d ed. 2012) ("experience shows that in practice it is difficult at the time of drafting the [arbitration] clause to predict with a reasonable degree of certainty the nature of disputes and the procedures that will be suitable for those disputes").

Would arbitrations be fairer and more efficient if—as in national courts—a single, predictable, tested, and refined set of procedural rules applied in all cases? Is justice or efficiency really served by having part-time arbitrators re-invent the procedural wheel anew in every case? What benefits does such procedural flexibility provide? Note that there is a huge diversity of disputes (*e.g.*, construction, insurance, joint venture, banking, shipping) and a huge diversity of parties (*e.g.*, European, North American, Asian, African; major companies, small businesses, individuals) that participate in international arbitrations. How does this bear on the suitability of a uniform international code of arbitral procedures?

4. *Differences between arbitral procedures and litigation procedures.* As a general matter, it is elementary that arbitral proceedings are different from judicial proceedings. That is illustrated by *Card* and *Corporacion Transnacional.* One of the reasons that some parties choose to arbitrate is their desire to obtain the comparative informality, flexibility and occasional speed of arbitration. In theory, a party "trades the procedures and opportunity for review of the courtroom for the simplicity, informality, and expedition of arbitration." *Mitsubishi,* 473 U.S. at 628. *See infra* pp. 815-30. Consider also:

> "Arbitration may or may not be a desirable substitute for trials in courts; as to that the parties must decide in each instance. But when they have adopted it, they must be content with its informalities; they may not hedge it about with those procedural limitations which it is precisely its purpose to avoid. They must content themselves with looser approximations to the enforcement of their rights than those that the law accords them, when they resort to its machinery." *Am. Almond Prods. Co. v. Consolidated Pecan Sales, Co.,* 144 F.2d 448, 450 (2d Cir. 1944).

Particularly in major matters, the contrast between litigation and arbitration can be exaggerated and the procedures of an arbitration can assume a fairly "judicial" cast. "Though litigation is compulsory and arbitration is consensual, both are judicial processes of an adversarial character." Nariman, *Standards of Behaviour of Arbitrators,* 4 Arb. Int'l 311, 311 (1988). Tribunals and parties often conclude that complex cases require considerable issue definition, scheduling, and the like, and it is very common in international arbitration to encounter written pleadings, briefs, testimony under oath, cross-examination, verbatim transcripts, and a measure of disclosure or discovery. Indeed, some contemporary critics of arbitration argue that it has lost the informality and expedition that once characterized it and urge reforms returning to less judicial procedures. Hobeck, Mahnken & Koebke, *Time for Woolf Reforms in International Construction Arbitration,* 2008 Int'l Arb. L. Rev. 84; Wetter, *The Present Status of the International Court of Arbitration of the ICC: An Appraisal,* 1 Am. Rev. Int'l Arb. 91, 101 (1990).

5. *Parties' autonomy to choose arbitral procedures under UNCITRAL Model Law.* Articles 18 and 19 of the UNCITRAL Model Law, excerpted at pp. 90-91 of the Documentary Supplement, illustrate the prevailing approach in most developed legal systems to the parties' autonomy to choose the procedures applicable in an international arbitration. Consider the extent to which the parties' procedural autonomy will be honored under the Model Law. Compare the parties' procedural autonomy under the SLPIL and the Belgian Judicial Code. Are there any differences between the parties' autonomy under either of these provisions and the Model Law? What about §§33 and 34 of the English Arbitration Act?

The Canadian Supreme Court recently remarked, with regard to the parties' autonomy to select the arbitral procedures under the Model Law:

> "the parties to an arbitration agreement are free, subject to any mandatory provision by which they are bound, to choose any place, form and procedures they consider appropriate. They can choose cyberspace and establish their own rules." *Dell Computer Corp. v. Union des consommateurs,* 2007 SCC 34, ¶52 (Canadian S.Ct.).

Why do contemporary legal systems allow parties this procedural freedom? What advantages are gained? What are the costs? Are parties permitted to design their own litigation procedures when litigating in national courts? Why not? Should arbitration be different? Is it appropriate that questions of procedural regularity and due process be resolved through private bargaining and agreement? Does this not compromise the quality of civil justice? Why should courts enforce agreements to use arbitrary or inefficient procedures?

Should there be limits on the parties' autonomy over arbitral procedures? Would the optimal solution be for national legislatures or regulatory authorities to develop neutral, objective and predictable procedural rules that can be applied uniformly in every case? Why or why not?

6. *Parties' autonomy to choose arbitral procedures under FAA.* As *Card* illustrates, the FAA has long been interpreted to grant parties to arbitrations seated in the United States broad freedom to choose the arbitral procedures applicable in their proceedings. The text of the FAA does not contain any express affirmative recognition of the parties' freedom to select the arbitral procedure. Nonetheless, U.S. courts have afforded parties relatively broad freedom to designate procedural rules governing the arbitral process in both domestic and international arbitrations. This is reflected in numerous U.S. judicial decisions, like that in *Card*, rejecting challenges to arbitral awards based on procedural objections and declining to interfere on an interlocutory basis with the parties' agreed procedural regime. *See infra* pp. 808-10, 831-32.

7. *Parties' autonomy to choose arbitral procedures under New York Convention.* What effect does the New York Convention have on the parties' autonomy to choose arbitral procedures? Consider Article V(1)(d) , excerpted at p. 2 of the Documentary Supplement. Does it require Contracting States to respect the parties' procedural autonomy? Or merely provide a basis for non-recognition of awards if the parties' procedural autonomy is not respected?

Consider Article II of the Convention. What effect does it have on the obligations of Contracting States to respect the parties' procedural autonomy? As discussed above, Articles II(1) and (3) require Contracting States to recognize valid arbitration agreements and refer the parties to arbitration pursuant to such agreements. *See supra* pp. 189, 316-17. As discussed above, this obligation extends to all material terms of an agreement to arbitrate—including the parties' agreement regarding arbitral seat, number of arbitrators, institutional rules and arbitral procedures. *See supra* pp. 637-38, 652, 666, 683-85. Does the Convention place any limits on Contracting States' obligation to give effect to the parties' procedural autonomy? Note the exceptions to the obligation to recognize foreign arbitral awards in Articles V(1)(b) and V(2)(b). What effect do these provisions have on the parties' procedural autonomy?

8. *Parties' autonomy to choose arbitral procedures under European Convention.* The European Convention provides in Article IV(1)(b)(iii) that parties shall be free "to lay down the procedure to be followed by the arbitrators." Like Article V(1)(d) of the New York Convention, Article IX(1)(d) provides for the non-recognition of awards if the procedure followed by the tribunal departed from that agreed by the parties. Note also the exception for non-recognition in Article XI(1)(b).

9. *Parties' autonomy to choose arbitral procedures under ICSID Convention.* Consider Article 44 of the ICSID Convention and the ICSID Arbitration Rules. What is the role

of party autonomy in ICSID arbitrations? Are parties permitted to agree to omit or alter procedures provided for by the Convention? Consider the terms of Articles 41 through 47 of the Convention. What scope do they permit for the parties' procedural autonomy?

10. *Parties' autonomy to choose arbitral procedures in inter-state arbitrations.* Consider Article 51 of the 1907 Hague Convention, excerpted at p. 45 of the Documentary Supplement. What is the role of party autonomy in the selection of arbitral procedures in inter-state arbitrations? What is the nature of the procedural provisions in Articles 51 and following of the Hague Convention—do these prescribe mandatory procedural rules or default provisions? Should there be limits to the parties' procedural autonomy in inter-state arbitrations? What would be the source of such limits? Note also the "fast-track" arbitral process in Articles 86 to 90 of the 1907 Hague Convention.

11. *Parties' lack of autonomy to choose arbitral procedures in some national arbitration regimes.* Consider the former Guatemalan Code of Civil and Commercial Procedure, excerpted above, and the approach that it took to arbitral procedures. Was this desirable? Did it not provide predictability? And avoid the risk of arbitrary or unfair arbitral procedures?

Suppose the parties agree to arbitrate in a jurisdiction that imposes a mandatory procedural code on the parties without regard to their agreement on the arbitral procedures, as was the case in Guatemala. Was Guatemala's application of its procedural code consistent with Articles II and V(1)(d) of the New York Convention? Suppose the arbitrators had complied with the Guatemalan procedural code, and made an award adverse to the respondent; if the claimant attempted to enforce the award abroad, what could the respondent do? Suppose the arbitrators did not comply with the Guatemalan procedural code, and made an award adverse to the respondent; suppose further that the Guatemalan courts annulled the award (on the grounds that the arbitral procedures were not in accordance with Guatemalan law). What could the claimant do?

12. *Application of court procedures in arbitration as default option.* Some national laws still provide for the application of the rules of national procedural laws in arbitration, if the parties have not agreed on different rules. Consider Article 751 of the Argentine Code of Civil and Commercial Procedure ("If neither in the arbitral agreement nor in the *compromiso* nor in a later agreement of the parties procedural rules have been established, the arbitrators shall abide by the rules of ordinary ... proceedings") and Article 490 of the Uruguayan General Code of Procedure ("The parties may agree upon procedures that they consider most appropriate. Absent such agreement by the parties or if a particular matter is not covered by the indicated procedures, the arbitrators shall apply the provisions of this Code for ordinary proceedings."). Are these provisions wise? Do these provisions apply in institutional arbitrations? Consider Article 3 of the Inter-American Convention. *See supra* pp. 39-40 & *infra* p. 797.

13. *Parties' autonomy to choose arbitral procedures under institutional rules.* Consider the procedural provisions of leading institutional rules. *See* 2010 UNCITRAL Rules, Arts. 17-32; 2012 ICC Rules, Arts. 16-29; 2014 LCIA Rules, Arts. 14-25; ICSID Rules, Arts. 36-52 (all excerpted in the Documentary Supplement). What approach do these provisions take to the parties' autonomy to choose arbitral procedures? Do these rules all adopt precisely the same approach? Which rules would you prefer to apply as an arbitrator? Which rules provide most flexibility? Least flexibility?

14. *Impact of selection of arbitral seat on procedural rules in international arbitration*. As discussed above, the parties' selection of the arbitral seat will, among other things, affect the parties' autonomy to choose their own arbitral procedures. *See supra* pp. 620-24. Compare the differences between Swiss and U.S. law, on the one hand, and the excerpted Guatemalan statute (now repealed), on the other, with respect to the parties' freedom to agree upon arbitral procedures. Would you rather arbitrate in Switzerland or Guatemala? Does the answer depend on the dispute and who you represent?

15. *Procedural frameworks under institutional arbitration rules*. Compare briefly the procedural frameworks provided for in leading institutional rules—UNCITRAL, ICC, LCIA, AAA, ICDR and ICSID. Note the similarities and differences in arbitral procedures under them. Note also the many procedural issues and details that are *not* addressed by most institutional rules.

16. *Procedural frameworks under international arbitration agreements*. Although they are free to do so, parties seldom include detailed procedural provisions in their international commercial arbitration agreements. At most, agreements to arbitrate future disputes will address matters such as a "fast-track" proceeding, *infra* p. 796, the scope of disclosure, *infra* pp. 823-25, 835-36, the language of the arbitration, *infra* p. 816, and the allocation of the costs of the arbitration. *See* Bond, *How to Draft An Arbitration Clause Revisited*, 1 ICC ICArb. Bull. 14 (1990); G. Born, *International Commercial Arbitration* 2128-29, 2283-85, 2296, 3086-88 (2d ed. 2014); Townsend, *Drafting Arbitration Clauses*, 58 Disp. Resol. J. 1 (2003). Why is that? Is it wise?

    Consider the terms of the Treaty of Washington and the Abyei Arbitration Agreement, excerpted at pp. 65-66 & 80-83 of the Documentary Supplement. Note that Articles II, III, and IV prescribe a relatively detailed procedural schedule for the *Alabama Arbitration*. Compare Articles 4-8 of the Abyei Arbitration Agreement. Why is it that the parties chose, and were able, to agree to relatively detailed procedural regimes in the two arbitrations? Note that both agreements involved existing disputes. Compare the situation of parties that agree to arbitrate future disputes.

17. *Arbitrators' authority under national law to prescribe arbitral procedures in absence of parties' agreement*. Suppose the parties are unable to agree upon procedures for their arbitration. Who then is responsible under national law for establishing the arbitral procedures?

    Consider the excerpts from the UNCITRAL Model Law (particularly Articles 19(2) and 24(1)) and the SLPIL (Article 182(2)), giving the arbitral tribunal broad powers to adopt arbitral procedures. Consider the court's analysis, under the Model Law, in *Corporacion Transnacional*. Consider also: "Parties who choose arbitral tribunals desire more flexible and informal proceedings than those offered by the courts, especially in Germanic legal systems." *Judgment of 26 May 1994*, XXIII Y.B. Comm. Arb. 754 (1998) (Bezirksgericht Affoltern am Albis). *See also Judgment of 25 June 1992*, XXII Y.B. Comm. Arb. 619 (1997) (Austrian Oberster Gerichtshof) ("parties may determine the arbitral procedure in the arbitration agreement or in a separate written agreement. Lacking such agreement, the arbitrators decide on the procedure.").

    Compare the approach to the arbitral tribunal's procedural authority in the (now repealed) Guatemalan Code of Civil and Commercial Procedure. How did the Guatemalan statute differ from its UNCITRAL and Swiss counterparts? Which basic approach is preferable?

Compare the approach under the Belgian Judicial Code. Is it preferable to that under the Model Law? In what ways does the Code constrain the arbitrators' procedural authority? Are these desirable constraints?

18. *Arbitrators' authority under FAA to prescribe arbitral procedures in absence of parties' agreement.* As *Card* demonstrates, the FAA allows arbitrators broad discretion to adopt procedures and regulate the arbitral proceedings. *See infra* pp. 793-94, 808-10, 831-35, 1233-34; *Transp. Workers Union v. Philadelphia Trans. Co.*, 283 F.Supp. 597, 600 (E.D. Pa. 1968) ("Although arbitration hearings are of quasi-judicial nature, the prime virtue of arbitration is its informality, and it would be inappropriate for courts to mandate rigid compliance with procedural rules."). Is it appropriate to grant arbitrators such broad procedural discretion? Recall the adage, "Power tends to corrupt, and absolute power corrupts absolutely." Does that apply to arbitrators' procedural power?

19. *Arbitrators' authority under institutional arbitration rules to adopt arbitral procedure.* Consider Article 19 of the ICC Rules, Articles 14(2) and (5) of the LCIA Rules, and Article 17(1) of the UNCITRAL Rules. What procedural powers do these provisions grant to arbitrators? Is this wise? What alternatives are there?

What limitations do these provisions place on the arbitral tribunal's power to adopt arbitral procedures? How do these limitations vary among the leading institutional rules?

20. *Arbitral tribunal's interpretation of procedural authority under institutional arbitration rules.* The award in *ICC Case No. 7626* illustrates how international arbitral tribunals typically interpret their procedural authority under institutional rules. Compare the court's analysis in *Card* of the arbitral tribunal's powers on procedural issues under the NASD Code of Arbitration Procedure. *See also infra* pp. 808-10, 1231-41.

21. *Effect on arbitral procedures of choice-of-law clause selecting procedural law applicable to arbitral proceedings.* Suppose the parties expressly agree that the procedural law of the arbitral seat will apply to the arbitral proceedings. For example: "The arbitral proceedings shall be governed by the law of State X." Alternatively, suppose the parties agree to arbitration rules containing a provision to the same effect (*e.g.*, the LCIA Rules). What does such a clause mean for the arbitral procedures?

As discussed above, most authorities interpret choice-of-law clauses selecting the procedural law of the arbitration as *not* incorporating local rules of civil procedure. *See supra* p. 639. Instead, such clauses are interpreted as making applicable the arbitration legislation of the arbitral seat (which, in turn, in most developed states, typically affords the parties and arbitral tribunal broad discretion to adopt procedural rules). *See supra* pp. 619-20, 634, 786, 788-90. Is this persuasive? If the parties take the relatively rare step of specifying the procedural law of the arbitral seat, shouldn't this imply the procedural rules of the arbitral seat's courts?

Consider again the analysis in *Sapphire* and compare it with the results in *ICC Case Nos. 7626* and *5029*. The tribunal's application of the local procedural rules of the arbitral seat's courts in *Sapphire* is unusual by contemporary standards; the tribunals' refusals in *ICC Case Nos. 7626* and *5029* are much more representative of contemporary practice.

22. *Wisdom of applying domestic procedural rules of arbitral seat's courts in international arbitration.* What approach *should* an arbitrator take to the local procedural rules of the arbitral seat's courts? Just because the arbitrator *must* not apply these rules does not mean he *should* not. Consider *ICC Case No. 7626* and *Card.* Why is it that English rules of evidence should not have been applied by the tribunal in *ICC Case No. 7626*? Wouldn't these rules provide a predictable, neutral set of procedures for both parties?

    In international disputes between parties from different nations, the litigants may have dramatically different procedural expectations and wishes (reflecting their respective backgrounds). Consider whether either the Austrian or Indian party in *ICC Case No. 7626* was likely familiar with English procedural or evidentiary rules.

    Recall the aspirations of arbitration to provide an expeditious, uncomplicated means of dispute resolution tailored to the needs of particular disputes. *See supra* pp. 108-09. Note that the Federal Rules of Evidence (at issue in *Card*) were designed with a particular context (*e.g.*, public jury trials) in mind; the same is true of other national procedural rules. As suggested above, are rules designed for this sort of specialized context likely to be appropriate for an international arbitration, which is intended to be culturally neutral?

23. *Mandatory procedural requirements of arbitral seat.* Notwithstanding the parties' procedural autonomy, and the arbitral tribunal's general procedural discretion, almost every nation has basic procedural norms that cannot be ignored. These procedural norms will apply to arbitrations seated within that state, and will be given effect principally in actions to annul the arbitral award or remove an arbitrator.

    (a) *Mandatory procedural requirements of UNCITRAL Model Law.* Note the references to mandatory law in Article 18 of the UNCITRAL Model Law. What procedural requirements does Article 18 impose? On what category of arbitrations? Compare Article 182(3) of the SLPIL.

    (b) *Mandatory procedural requirements under FAA.* What mandatory procedural requirements apply to arbitrations conducted in the United States? Should the same procedural rules apply in an international arbitration, seated in the United States, as in a domestic U.S. litigation? A domestic U.S. arbitration? An international arbitration seated abroad? Why or why not?

        U.S. courts have not clearly articulated what minimum procedural requirements apply to arbitrations seated in the United States. A number of U.S. authorities suggest that arbitral procedures must comport with the Due Process Clause (which requires only fairly broad compliance with principles of fairness, due notice, and equality of treatment). *See infra* pp. 1159-61, 1231-34. Other U.S. courts have suggested that even the Due Process Clause's general limits do not apply in arbitrations, on the grounds that arbitrations do not constitute state action. *See FDIC v. Air Fla. Sys., Inc.,* 822 F.2d 833, 842 n.9 (9th Cir. 1987) (arbitration is "private, not state, action" and not subject to the due process clause)*; Elmore v. Chicago & Ill.Midland Ry. Co.,* 782 F.2d 94, 96 (7th Cir. 1986) (same).

    (c) *Enforcement of arbitral seat's mandatory procedural requirements.* How will the mandatory procedural norms of the arbitral seat be enforced? *See* UNCITRAL Model Law, Art. 34(2)(a)(ii); SLPIL, Art. 190(2)(d); U.S. FAA, 9 U.S.C. §10. Note, however, that *Card* and *Corporacion Transnacional* illustrate the strict standards that need to be satisfied to justify annulment of an award. *See infra* pp. 1159-61, 1169-70.

24. *Mandatory procedural requirements of judicial recognition forum.* Consider Articles V(1)(b) and V(2)(b) of the New York Convention. Note that a denial of an opportunity to be heard, or a procedural unfairness amounting to a violation of the enforcement forum's public policy, will provide grounds for non-recognition of an award. *See infra* pp. 1218-41, 1260. To what extent can an arbitral tribunal anticipate procedural objections to recognition when conducting an arbitration?

25. *Content of mandatory procedural requirements under national arbitration legislation.* Consider the mandatory procedural requirements imposed by Article 18 of the UNCITRAL Model Law, Article 1699 of the Belgian Judicial Code, Article 182(3) of the SLPIL and the FAA. What procedural obligations do these provisions impose? What is the value of imposing these requirements? What exactly do these requirements demand? Consider ways in which these procedural requirements might be violated.

What does Article 18 of the Model Law mean when it requires that the parties "*shall be treated with equality and each party shall be given a full opportunity of presenting his case*"? Is this provision a mandatory requirement, or may it be overridden or varied by contrary agreement by the parties? Consider Articles 19(1), 34(2)(a)(ii) and 36(1)(a)(ii) of the Model Law. Similarly, Article 182(3) of the SLPIL provides: "Regardless of the procedure chosen, the arbitral tribunal shall ensure equal treatment of the parties and the right of both parties to be heard in adversarial proceedings."

What do these various procedural protections mean in practice? Note the courts' interpretation in *Card* and *Corporacion Transnacional*. Consider: "Short of authorizing trial by battle or ordeal or, more doubtfully, by a panel of three monkeys, parties can stipulate to whatever procedures they want to govern the arbitration of their disputes; parties are as free to specify idiosyncratic terms of arbitration as they are to specify any other terms in their contract." *Baravati v. Josephthal, Lyon & Ross, Inc.*, 28 F.3d 704, 709 (7th Cir. 1994). Compare the following comments of the Swiss Federal Tribunal:

> "It should be underlined that procedural public policy will constitute only a simple exclusion provision namely that it will merely have a protective function and will not generate any positive rules. This is because the legislature did not desire that procedural public policy should be extensively interpreted and that there should arise a code of arbitral procedure to which the procedure, as freely selected by the parties, should be subjected." *Judgment of 30 December 1994*, 13 ASA Bull. 217, 221 (Swiss Fed. Trib.) (1995).

Consider how these procedural guarantees apply to the following hypotheticals:

(a) In a case involving a $50 million fraud claim, the arbitrators refuse to permit either party to call witnesses from the other party (leaving each party free to nominate those of its employees that will give evidence); the arbitrators also refuse to permit either party to cross-examine the other party's witnesses; the presiding arbitrator briefly questions both parties' witnesses, but refuses to consider questions suggested by either party.

(b) In a case where the claimant has ten witnesses and the respondents three witnesses, the arbitrators give the claimant 75% of the hearing time and the respondent 25%.

(c) In a case involving complex contractual claims and factual issues, as well as choice-of-law disputes, the tribunal imposes a 15-page limit on all written submissions, permitting one pre-hearing submission and one post-hearing submission (both simultaneous).

(d) In a case involving $2.5 million in dispute, the tribunal refuses to conduct an oral hearing.

(e) The parties' arbitration agreement provides that one party may be represented by lawyers, but the other side may not.

(f) The parties' arbitration agreement provides that one party's witnesses may be cross-examined but the other party's witnesses may not. Alternatively, the parties' arbitration agreement permits one party to obtain discovery, but not the other party.

26. *Arbitrator's failure to comply with applicable institutional (or other) arbitration rules.* Suppose an arbitral tribunal fails to comply with the (fairly minimal) procedural requirements set out in the applicable institutional arbitration rules. Note that this is, apparently, what occurred under the NASD Code of Arbitration Procedure in *Card.* Should the resulting arbitral award be annulled? In all cases? This is discussed in detail below, *see infra* pp. 832, 838, 1160-61.

As discussed above, Article V(1)(d) of the New York Convention allows for non-recognition of an arbitral award where the "arbitral procedure was not in accordance with the agreement of the parties." National law is generally the same. *See* UNCITRAL Model Law, Arts. 19, 36(1)(a)(iv); FAA §10(c); SLPIL, Arts. 182(2), 189, 190(2)(d). What does it mean for a procedure to not be "in accordance with the agreement of the parties"? Does that mean *any* non-compliance? We discuss this below as well, *see infra* pp. 1238-40.

27. *Allocation of power to adopt arbitral procedures between arbitrators and parties.* Suppose the parties are agreed on one procedural approach or issue, and the arbitral tribunal disagrees. For example, suppose both parties desire a two-week hearing and broad document discovery, while the tribunal wants only a three-day hearing and minimal document discovery. Who decides what procedure is adopted?

In practice, some sort of negotiated compromise is almost always reached on most procedural "disputes" between the parties and the arbitrators. But who has the authority to decide the issue if no compromise is struck? Compare the ICC, LCIA and UNCITRAL Rules. What are the differences in their approaches? Which approach is most desirable? Compare the UNCITRAL Model Law and the SLPIL with Article 1700 of the Belgian Judicial Code.

Consider the following comments by an experienced international arbitrator:

"I would advocate the existence of ... a right for the arbitrator to lead—even lead firmly, when necessary—in establishing the arbitral procedures over the heads of counsel on both sides. The arbitrator does not have a judge's power to regulate procedures unilaterally, nor should he or she forget that party autonomy may be the most important arbitral principle of all. The scope for persuasion by the arbitrator before making a ruling is large, and the need to impose procedures should thus be rare. But it is possible—at least for one with a common law background—to imagine situations in which counsel for both sides may slide toward extended and acrimonious evidentiary procedures that could be shortened or avoided by an arbitrator who was prepared to 'just say no.'" Carter, *The Rights and Duties of the Arbitrator: Six Aspects of the Rule of Reasonableness*, in ICC, *The Status of the Arbitrator* 24, 31 (ICC ICArb. Bull. Spec. Supp. 1995).

Is this appropriate? Or is it a usurpation of the parties' procedural autonomy? *See also* Pryles, *Limits to Party Autonomy in Arbitral Procedure*, 24 J. Int'l Arb. 327 (2007); Veeder, *Whose Arbitration Is It Anyway: The Parties or the Arbitration Tribunal—An Interesting Question?*, in L. Newman & R. Hill (eds.), *The Leading Arbitrators' Guide to International Arbitration* 347 (2d ed. 2008).

28. *Mandatory time limits for award under national arbitration legislation.* An exception to the arbitrators' procedural discretion is the existence, in some arbitration statutes, of time limits for rendering a final award (which must be complied with in order to avoid annulment of the award). *See, e.g.,* Belgian Judicial Code, Art. 1713(2) (six months from constitution of tribunal, unless otherwise agreed by the parties); Luxembourg Code of Civil Procedure, Arts. 1228, 1233 (three months from date of submission to arbitration, unless otherwise agreed); Spanish Arbitration Act, 2011, Art. 37(2) ("Unless otherwise agreed by the parties, the arbitrators must decide the dispute within six months from the date of filing of the [statement of defense].... Unless otherwise agreed by the parties, the arbitrators may extend this term by a period not exceeding two months, by way of a reasoned decision.... [T]he expiration of this period without delivery of a final award shall not affect the arbitration agreement or the validity of the award, without prejudice to any liability that may be incurred by the arbitrators."); Romanian Code of Civil Procedure, Art. 567 ("If the parties have not provided otherwise, the arbitral tribunal must render the award not later than 6 months from its constitution, under the sanction of lapse of the arbitration.... [T]he parties may agree in writing to extend the time limit for the arbitration. The arbitral tribunal can decide, for a justifiable reason, to extend the time limit for the arbitration once, for no more than 3 months. The time limit for the arbitration shall be automatically extended by 3 months upon the death of one of the parties."). Compare also the (atypical) Guatemalan arbitration legislation (now repealed), *supra* pp. 779-80.

As a practical matter, tribunals will virtually always comply with such legislative requirements. Suppose, however, that a tribunal in an international arbitration does not do so—instead exercising its procedural authority under the parties' arbitration agreement to conclude that more time is necessary to afford the parties an opportunity to present their cases. Is the mandatory time limit under national law consistent with the New York Convention (Articles V(1)(d) and II)? What if the parties' arbitration agreement or applicable institutional rules grant the tribunal authority to extend time limits for the arbitration?

29. *Arbitrator's authority under ICSID Convention to prescribe arbitral procedures in absence of parties' agreement.* In an investment arbitration under ICSID, what is the scope of the arbitrators' procedural authority where the parties have not agreed upon a procedural matter? Consider the second sentence of Article 44 of the ICSID Convention. Are there any mandatory limits on the arbitrators' authority over procedural matters in an ICSID arbitration? Consider Article 52(1)(b) and (d) of the ICSID Convention. What is the source of the "fundamental rule[s] of procedure" referred to in Article 52?

30. *Arbitrator's authority in inter-state arbitrations to prescribe arbitral procedures in absence of parties' agreement.* Consider the arbitral tribunal's authority under the 1907 Hague Convention. What limits are there on the tribunal's procedural authority under Article 74 of the Convention? Consider the other procedural provisions of the Convention. To what extent was it envisaged that the arbitral tribunal could deviate from these provisions?

31. *Non-participation in arbitral proceedings.* Parties will sometimes fail to participate in an arbitration, either accidentally or deliberately. *See* Donahey, *Defending the Arbitration Against Sabotage,* 13 J. Int'l Arb. 93 (1996). Consider how various institutional rules deal with the possibility of default by one party to an arbitration. *See* 2012 ICC Rules, Art. 6(8); 2014 LCIA Rules, Art. 15(8); 2010 UNCITRAL Rules, Art. 30. What powers do these provisions grant to the arbitrators in cases of default? How should such powers be exercised? As *Corporacion Transnacional* illustrates, if a party defaults, the tribunal will ordinarily proceed on an *ex parte* basis, ensuring that the defaulting party receives notice of the ongoing proceedings. Is an arbitral tribunal a court, empowered to issue a default judgment predicated solely on one party's non-participation? Or, is it responsible for deciding the issues presented to it and rendering a decision, regardless whether both parties participate? If the tribunal makes an award, what is the relevance of the defaulting party's non-participation in both annulment and recognition proceedings? What does *Corporacion Transnacional* suggest? *See infra* pp. 1240-41.

32. *Procedural rules under Inter-American Convention.* Note Article 3 of the Inter-American Convention. Under Article 3, absent express contrary agreement by the parties, the Inter-American Commercial Arbitration Commission's Rules will apply to any arbitration governed by the Convention. (The IACAC Rules closely parallel the UNCITRAL Rules. *See supra* pp. 39-40.) Is this a wise default solution? Why shouldn't the New York Convention do the same?

B. LIMITED GROUNDS FOR INTERLOCUTORY JUDICIAL REVIEW OF ARBITRATORS' PROCEDURAL DECISIONS

During the course of an arbitration, countless significant procedural and substantive decisions are made by the arbitrators (or appointing authority). Depending on the case, an arbitral seat may be selected; arbitrators may be appointed, challenged, or removed; the language of the arbitration will be chosen; procedural rules will be fixed (or amended); provisional measures may be granted; disclosure may be requested and ordered; jurisdictional and choice-of-law decisions may be made; and preliminary substantive decisions may be reached.

One party or the other is usually unhappy with each preliminary decision. If there is an opportunity, the disappointed party may seek interlocutory judicial review of the arbitrators' ruling. The extent to which interlocutory judicial review of an interim decision of an arbitral tribunal is available is ordinarily governed by the national law in the place where relief is sought. As discussed elsewhere, judicial review of arbitrators' awards or orders will almost always be available only in the arbitral seat.[10]

This section examines the general principle that national courts may not interfere with the procedural conduct of an international commercial arbitration proceeding. Under this principle of judicial non-intervention, national courts will generally not review procedural orders or decisions of arbitrators on an interlocutory basis, and will instead reserve any judicial review until the final award. The policy underlying this approach is to permit arbitral proceedings to be conducted expeditiously (without the delay that interlocutory judicial review entails) and without the second-guessing of arbitral decisions by national courts. The same principle of judicial non-interference applies even more emphatically in investment and interstate arbitrations.

STANTON v. PAINE WEBBER JACKSON & CURTIS INC.
685 F.Supp. 1241 (S.D. Fla. 1988)

GONZALEZ, District Judge.... Plaintiffs seek an order enjoining the defendants, Paine Webber Jackson & Curtis, Inc. ("Paine Webber) and Robert Diamond ("Diamond") from requesting the issuance of and serving subpoenas for the attendance of witnesses or production of documents, other than for attendance or production before the arbitration panel.

Plaintiffs brought the underlying action against Paine Webber and Diamond for violations of the Commodity Exchange Act, Florida securities laws, and common law. Defendants moved for, and this court ordered arbitration of plaintiff's claims pursuant to the FAA.... A hearing before the [AAA] panel is scheduled to begin shortly. Defendants Paine Webber and Diamond have requested that the arbitration panel issue subpoenas duces tecum to various third parties. The documents sought are records of commodities accounts maintained by plaintiffs with firms other than Paine Webber and plaintiffs' tax returns. Defendants claim that production of these documents is necessary because they tend to disprove plaintiffs' claims of unsophistication and financial unsuitability.

It appears from plaintiffs' Motion that the arbitrators have issued several of the subpoenas requested. The subpoenas require pre-hearing production of documents to the defendants. Plaintiffs contend that the issuance of these subpoenas to third parties violates the law and the production of documents constitutes impermissible pre-hearing discovery.

Plaintiffs are correct that all discovery between parties must be stayed by the court pending arbitration. *See Suarez-Valdez v. Shearson/American Express, Inc.*, 845 F.2d 950, 951 (11th Cir. 1988). "An agreement to arbitrate is an agreement to proceed under arbitration and not under court rules." *Id.* However, the court can find no support for plaintiffs' contention that the court may interfere with the procedures of the arbitration panel. The [FAA] sets forth the district courts' powers to enforce arbitration agreements. These include the power to (1) stay court proceedings when an issue therein is arbitrable (9 U.S.C. §3); (2) compel such issues to arbitration (9 U.S.C. §4); (3) enforce summons issued by arbitrators (9 U.S.C. §7); and (4) confirm, vacate, modify, or correct an arbitration award (9 U.S.C. §§9-13). Nothing in the Act contemplates interference by the court in an ongoing arbitration proceeding. *See Foremost Yarn Mills, Inc. v. Rose Mills, Inc.*, 25 F.R.D. 9, 11

---

10. *See supra* pp. 620-21, 622-23, 634-35 & *infra* pp. 1099-112; G. Born, *International Commercial Arbitration* 1550-52, 2905 (2d ed. 2014).

(E.D. Pa. 1960) ("it is clearly evident that the [FAA] does not in any wise attempt to regulate the procedures before the arbitrators or prescribe rules or regulations with respect to hearings before arbitrators").

The FAA does provide the parties with some protection from the arbitrators' acts. When the arbitrators have by their misbehavior prejudiced the rights of any party or have exceeded their powers, the court may vacate an award made by the arbitrators. 9 U.S.C. §10. The procedures and standards for vacating an award must be followed. However, the plaintiffs are not seeking to vacate an award by the arbitrators. They are asking the court to impose judicial control over the arbitration proceedings. Such action by the court would vitiate the purposes of the FAA: "to facilitate and expedite the resolution of disputes, ease court congestion, and provide disputants with a less costly alternative to litigation." *Recognition Equip., Inc. v. NCR Corp.*, 532 F.Supp. 271, 275 (N.D. Tex. 1981).

Furthermore, the court finds that under the FAA, the arbitrators may order and conduct such discovery as they find necessary. *See Corcoran v. Shearson/American Express, Inc.*, 596 F.Supp. 1113, 1117 (N.D. Ga. 1984*); Mississippi Power Co. v. Peabody Coal Co.*, 69 F.R.D. 558 (S.D. Miss. 1976) (arbitrator, in his discretion, may permit and supervise discovery he deems necessary); *see also* 9 U.S.C. §7 (arbitrators may issue summons to bring witnesses and documents before them). Plaintiffs' contention that §7 of the [FAA] only permits the arbitrators to compel witnesses at the hearing, and prohibits pre-hearing appearances, is unfounded....

MOBIL OIL INDONESIA INC. v. ASAMERA (INDONESIA) LTD
392 N.Y.S.2d 614 (N.Y. App. 1977), *rev'd on other grounds*, 401 N.Y.S.2d 186 (1977)

In this action involving contract rights to explore and produce vast petroleum reserves, the parties seek a determination of which procedural rules shall govern arbitration of their disputes. The contract, dated July 16, 1968, contained a broad arbitration clause providing that "[a]ny dispute arising out of or relating to this Agreement shall be settled by arbitration in accordance with the Rules of the [ICC]" and designated New York City as the place of arbitration. At the time the agreement was executed, and indeed at the time of institution on November 6, 1974 of the arbitration, the 1955 Rules were in force. On June 1, 1975, after arbitration had commenced, new Rules were put into effect (1975 Rules). Following several meetings to prepare the "Terms of Reference" which would govern the arbitral proceeding, at which counsel, the parties, and the three arbitrators were present, a majority of the arbitrators ruled that all proceedings thereafter would be conducted under the 1975 Rules.

On October 31, 1975 petitioner-respondent applied to the ICC Court of Arbitration for a direction that the arbitrators apply the 1955 Rules. The Court refused to interfere, held that it was for the arbitrators to decide the procedural issue presented, and directed the arbitrators to formalize their decision. On March 30, 1976 the arbitrators, again by a majority vote, ruled in an interlocutory award that the 1975 Rules were applicable. They concluded the parties intended to refer to the Rules as they were from time to time and that the general principle, as well as New York law, is to apply procedural rules as they exist at the time the procedural issues arise. The dissenting arbitrator, the esteemed former Judge John Van Voorhis, likewise seeking the intent of the parties, found the parties intended the 1955 Rules to apply. It is submitted, as the Court below found, that prehearing discovery is permitted under the 1975 Rules but not under the 1955 Rules....

That the parties agreed to arbitrate is undisputed as is the fact that the issues raised on arbitration bear a reasonable relationship to the contract. Furthermore, that the arbitrators' result is rational, although it may not have been the result others would have reached is beyond peradventure. The parties agreed to be bound by the [ICC Rules] and it was for the arbitrators to determine which [ICC Rules] intended. Despite petitioner's position to the contrary, no evidence is presented that greater restriction exists on the authority of an ICC arbitrator than on the authority of any other commercial arbitrator under the Rules of the [AAA]. Nor is any limitation of the arbitrators' broad powers found in the agreement itself.

Under the broad arbitration clause in the case at bar, questions of interpretation are for the arbitrators to decide and this is so even if the contract determination affects the very ground rules of the arbitration. If, for example, the agreement provided for arbitration pursuant to New York law, a determination by the arbitrators would not be overturned because the arbitrators applied the substantive law as of the time of arbitration rather than as of the time of agreement, or vice versa. Such determination as to substantive law goes no more nor less to the parties' agreement to arbitrate than a provision as to which procedural rules to apply. It follows logically and naturally that the determination of the parties' intention as to procedural rules is gauged by the same standard applied to substantive rules: Did the parties agree to arbitrate and did the arbitrators make a rational determination of which procedural rules to apply? As the answer to both portions of the question is in the affirmative, it was improper for the Court below to impose its judgment in the place and stead of the arbitrators.

ELEKTRIM SA v. VIVENDI UNIVERSAL SA
[2007] EWHC 571 (QB) (English High Ct.)

MR. JUSTICE AIKENS. In this action Elektrim [SA ("Elektrim")] claims an order for a final injunction … to restrain each of the defendants from pursuing an arbitration … that is currently being conducted before the [LCIA] ("LCIA Arbitration"). Elektrim claims that the injunction should continue until the final determination of an ICC Arbitration which is under way in Geneva. The LCIA Arbitration was started in August 2003 by two of the defendants in the current action, the two Vivendi companies ("Vivendi") as Claimants. It is against Elektrim and two other companies. The ICC Arbitration was also started by Vivendi and two other companies by a Request dated 13 April 2006. In that arbitration, Elektrim and eight other companies are the defendants. The injunction is sought on the ground that the relief claimed by the defendants in this action (or at least the two Vivendi companies) in the LCIA Arbitration is inconsistent with the position adopted and the relief sought in the ICC Arbitration. Elektrim claims that the simultaneous pursuit of both arbitrations by the Vivendi companies is vexatious and oppressive to Elektrim….

Elektrim and Vivendi are two protagonists in a complicated and very hard fought corporate campaign in several theatres of war for the control of Polska Telefonia Cyfrowa Sp. z.o.o. ("PTC"). [PTC is a joint venture, established by Elektrim, Deutsche Telekom ("DT") and others in 1995, that runs the largest mobile telecoms network in Poland. In 1999, Elektrim purported, in violation of the PTC joint venture agreements, to transfer its PTC shares to a new company, Elektrim Telecommunikacja Sp. z.o.o. ("Telco"—the third defendant in the present action). Telco was a new joint venture company established by Elektrim and Vivendi.

The purported transfer of Elektrim's PTC shares to Telco gave rise to complex disputes among DT, Elektrim and Telco, including various arbitrations and litigations in Polish and other courts. Among other things, Vivendi commenced the LCIA Arbitration against Elektrim pursuant to a "Third Investment Agreement" between Vivendi and Elektrim ("TIA"); the LCIA Arbitration was seated in London and English substantive law was applicable. In the LCIA Arbitration, Vivendi sought monetary damages and other relief against Elektrim based upon alleged breaches of the terms of the TIA. Subsequently, after abortive settlement discussions between Vivendi, Elektrim and DT, Vivendi commenced an ICC arbitration against Elektrim, DT and others, alleging that the parties had concluded a binding settlement agreement ("Settlement Agreement") that settled all of their disputes concerning PTC, including the disputes between Vivendi and Elektrim under the TIA. The ICC Arbitration was seated in Geneva, Switzerland and the applicable substantive law was Swiss law. Following Vivendi's commencement of the ICC Arbitration, Elektrim sought to stay the LCIA Arbitration, based upon the pending ICC arbitration.]

On 21 April 2006, the Polish lawyers acting for Elektrim (Soltysinski Kawecki and Szlezak—"SKS") wrote to the LCIA arbitrators and informed them of Vivendi's request to the ICC and the nature of the relief sought by Vivendi in the proposed ICC arbitration. The letter continued: "… the ICC arbitration directly impacts the present proceedings. In … the event that Vivendi and the other ICC claimants are correct … the present arbitration should be settled and terminated on the terms set forth in the pertinent agreements. Therefore Elektrim respectfully requests the Arbitral Tribunal to stay the present arbitration proceedings … until the ICC arbitration is finally resolved…." On 28 April 2006, Salans, the lawyers acting for Vivendi, wrote to the LCIA arbitrators opposing the application for a stay…. The letter urges the LCIA Arbitrators to proceed….

On 9 May 2006 the LCIA Arbitrators issued their ruling on Elektrim's application. The tribunal … stated: "Given that there is no agreement between the parties on the stay of the proceedings, the arbitral tribunal shall issue its Partial Award and set a date for a conference call with parties to discuss the next steps of the proceedings." …

[Elektrim's lawyers subsequently wrote again to the LCIA Arbitrators,] summarized Vivendi's case in the ICC Arbitration and asserted that Vivendi's pursuit of the LCIA Arbitration "… is wholly inconsistent with its case and the relief that it is seeking in the ICC Arbitration." The letter continues:

"1. The very basis for the LCIA arbitration, namely a dispute in relation to the TIA, depends upon the outcome of the ICC arbitration. If, as Vivendi allege, there was a settlement agreement concluded on or about 26 March 2006, all disputes, concerning the TIA have been settled and the LCIA arbitration must cease.

2. Vivendi's continued pursuit of its claims in the LCIA arbitration simultaneously with the pursuit of its claim in the ICC arbitration (a) expose Elektrim to the risk of wholly inconsistent awards and, indeed, double jeopardy and (b) forces Elektrim to devote huge amounts of management time and resources to fighting what could turn out (on Vivendi's own case) to be an entirely baseless and futile proceeding.

3. It follows, as a matter of logic, fairness and common-sense, that the ICC arbitration must reach a conclusion on the existence of the alleged settlement agreement before any further steps in the LCIA arbitration is taken by any party. It is and cannot be right that Elektrim is required, pending the ICC Tribunal's determination to continue to fight an arbitration which Vivendi claims has been and must be terminated. It is abusive and unconscionable. For the above reasons, Elektrim calls upon Vivendi either (a) finally to

withdraw its claims in the ICC arbitration (and finally to terminate that arbitration) or (b) to stay the LCIA arbitration pending the outcome of the ICC arbitration...."

The letter also stated that if the Tribunal was not prepared to make [such an] order, then Elektrim would: "... be forced to make an application for an injunction ... enjoining Vivendi and the Tribunal from proceeding with the LCIA arbitration pending the outcome of the ICC Arbitration." ...

[T]he LCIA Tribunal rejected this application for a stay in a letter sent to the parties on 17 January 2007. This decision was confirmed in the Tribunal's Procedural Order Number 8, dated 22 January 2007.... The Tribunal noted that similar requests for a stay had been made by Elektrim in April and May 2006, which the Tribunal had refused. [After the LCIA arbitrators refused to stay the LCIA arbitration, Elektrim sought an injunction from the English courts against the LCIA arbitration. The court's opinion denying the request is excerpted below.]

I think that it is helpful to begin by asking: what Elektrim is trying to achieve by this action? Although the action is for a final injunction to restrain the LCIA arbitration pending the outcome of the ICC arbitration, its real aim is "case management" of the two arbitrations. Elektrim does not claim that the LCIA arbitration must stop for all time. Elektrim simply does not wish to fight in these two theatres of war at once. Presumably it judges the ICC arbitration to be the better battle ground at present and its chances of success there are greater....

I do not intend to explore generally the question of whether the court has any jurisdiction at all ... to grant either interim or final injunctions to restrain arbitrations that are subject to the 1996 Act. I must assume that there is such a jurisdiction, given the comments of the Court of Appeal in the cases of *Cetelem SA v. Roust Holdings Ltd* [2005] 2 Lloyd's Rep 494; and *Weissfisch v. Julius* [2006] 1 Lloyd's Rep 716....

There is no dispute, of course, that the court has jurisdiction ... to grant an injunction to restrain a party from engaging in court proceedings in another jurisdiction, in breach of an English arbitration clause in a contract by which the parties are bound. [*See, e.g., Aggeliki Charis Compania Maritima SA v. Pagnan SpA ("The Angelic Grace")* [1995] 1 Lloyd's Rep 87 at 96 per Millett LJ....] But in this case [Elektrim] urges the court to [grant an injunction] for a very different purpose. It is to grant a final injunction to restrain the prosecution of an arbitration whose seat is in England, so is governed by Part 1 of the 1996 Act. The LCIA arbitration results from an admittedly valid arbitration clause which is itself a term in a contract (the TIA) which the arbitrators have held is valid and binding on Elektrim and Vivendi. As far as the English courts are concerned, Elektrim cannot challenge either the validity of the TIA, nor the validity of the current LCIA arbitration, nor the authority of the arbitrators. Elektrim does not try to do any of those things in the present proceedings.

It seems to me that there are two initial difficulties that Elektrim has to overcome before the court could consider granting an injunction to restrain an arbitration that is governed by the 1996 Act. First, it must demonstrate that the prosecution of the LCIA arbitration is an act which would entitle the court to invoke the jurisdiction to grant injunctions [under English statutory authority, being §37 of the Supreme Court Act 1981 ("SCA"). Section 37(1) of the SCA provides: "(1) The High Court may by order (whether interlocutory or final) grant an injunction or appoint a receiver in all cases where it appears to the court to be just and convenient to do so...."] Secondly, it must show that the grant of an injunction to restrain the LCIA proceedings is consistent with the statutory scheme of the 1996 Act. In my view, Elektrim faces great difficulties in respect of each of these issues....

Although the present case involves a claim for a final injunction to restrain an arbitration, I think it is useful at this stage to consider, by analogy, the basis on which the court grants an injunction (often interim) to restrain *proceedings* in a foreign court. An injunction can be granted on one of two bases. First, if the proceedings are an infringement of a legal or equitable right of a party; secondly, where those proceedings are vexatious, oppressive or unconscionable. The first analysis is usually applied to cases where the parties have contractually agreed to submit disputes to a particular court or to arbitration and one party has started proceedings in breach of that agreement. The second analysis applies where there is no such agreement but the court concludes that the ends of justice require an injunction to restrain foreign proceedings that are vexatious or oppressive. In each case the court has a discretion to grant or refuse the injunction sought, depending on the particular facts of the case.

[Elektrim] did not argue that there was any different juridical basis ... to grant an injunction to restrain an arbitration. Indeed, [its] argument is that the continuation of the LCIA Arbitration is vexatious and oppressive to Elektrim. So, the first difficulty for Elektrim is this: what legal or equitable right of Elektrim has been infringed by Vivendi that entitles the court to consider restraining the LCIA Arbitration from continuing? Alternatively, on what basis is it vexatious or oppressive or unconscionable towards Elektrim for Vivendi to continue the LCIA Arbitration, so as to entitle the court to consider restraining the LCIA Arbitration from continuing? ... [T]he court has to be satisfied (on a balance of probabilities) that Elektrim has demonstrated that one or other of these bases exists....

Elektrim [claims] a legal or equitable right to have a fully and unquestionably enforceable award, which right is reflected in the duty placed on the tribunal by Article 32 of the LCIA Rules. Elektrim has a right not to be oppressed or vexed by having to face the LCIA and the ICC arbitrations and Polish proceedings at once in the present circumstances. Whilst I can follow the first stage, I cannot accept the second stage of that submission as a satisfactory analysis.

Elektrim and Vivendi agreed to the arbitration clause in the TIA. The current LCIA Arbitration was set up by agreement between the parties once disputes had arisen concerning the TIA. The LCIA Arbitration has continued by the agreement of the parties until Elektrim issued the present proceedings. Neither the existence of the LCIA Arbitration nor its prosecution can be characterized as being in breach of any legal or equitable right of Elektrim. It is, in fact, the opposite. The resolution of disputes concerning the TIA through an LCIA Arbitration is what the parties agreed to do by their contract in the TIA.

I fail to see how the fact that Vivendi has started the ICC Arbitration after the start of the LCIA Arbitration can create a new legal or equitable right for Elektrim in respect of the LCIA Arbitration that might allow the court to invoke its jurisdiction under §37. So far as I can see, only two possible arguments might be raised. The first is that there is an implied term of the LCIA Arbitration agreement that if another arbitration is started between the same parties, but not relating to the same subject-matter as the existing arbitration, then the parties have a right to call a halt to the LCIA Arbitration. Such an implied term is neither reasonable nor necessary to the working of the LCIA arbitration agreement....

The second possible argument is Elektrim has a legal right to the conduct of the LCIA Arbitration by the arbitrators in a manner consistent with their duties as set out in

§§33(1)(a) and (b) and (2) of the 1996 Act [Documentary Supplement at p. 121]. I will assume that parties to an arbitration have a legal right that the arbitrators who have been appointed will carry out their duties in accordance with §33. Elektrim's argument in this case would have to be that the LCIA arbitrators have failed in the exercise of their statutory duty by refusing (three times) to stay the LCIA Arbitration pending resolution of the ICC arbitration. But in my view there are two reasons why, even assuming such a breach of duty, it could not permit the invocation of the court's jurisdiction to grant an injunction using §37.

First, it was well established under the old [English legislation for international arbitration (the Arbitration Act, 1975)] that the court did not have a general supervisory role over arbitrations at their interlocutory stage beyond that granted by the Arbitration Acts.... [*See the Bremer Vulcan case* [1981] AC 909 at 979 per Lord Diplock.] Therefore there was no scope to invoke the court's jurisdiction to grant injunctions to compel arbitrators to take a particular course in the reference. That rule must remain the case under the 1996 Act. The position is emphasized by the provisions of §1(c) of the Act, which stipulates that *"in matters governed by this Part the court should not intervene except as provided by this Part."*

Secondly, the 1996 Act itself provides the remedy for a breach of the §33 duty. Either before the award is made or after it is made, the party that alleges it is aggrieved can apply to remove the arbitrator or challenge the award, under (respectively) §§24 (1)(d)(i) or 68(2)(b). The first section permits an application to the court to remove the arbitrator for a refusal or failure properly to conduct the proceedings. The second section permits a challenge to the award on the basis that there has been a serious irregularity because of the tribunal's failure to comply with §33. In either case there is no need for the court to interfere with the arbitral process by granting an injunction pursuant to the powers in §37.

The next question is can Elektrim demonstrate that continuation of the LCIA Arbitration now that the ICC Arbitration has started is oppressive or vexatious? The only basis on which it can seriously do so is by asserting that it should not have to face two arbitrations at once. However, it is clear that the two arbitrations concern different subject matters. The LCIA Arbitration is dealing with disputes concerning the TIA. The ICC Arbitration is dealing with disputes concerning the Settlement Agreement. Neither arbitration could deal with the subject matter of the disputes that is being dealt with by the other. Both arbitrations were started pursuant to contracts by which the parties agreed to resolve disputes concerning them by arbitration.

Therefore, ... Elektrim has failed to demonstrate any legal basis on which the court could invoke the jurisdiction to grant an injunction. But Elektrim's position is made even weaker, in my view, when the question of the court's power to grant an "anti-arbitration" injunction is put in the context of the 1996 Act.

Arbitrations that fall within the 1996 Act are the result of agreements between two (or possibly more) parties to resolve legal disputes through a private impartial tribunal. Such arbitrations are, by definition, consensual.... I have already noted that under the pre-1996 Act regime, it was well established that the courts did not have a general supervisory power to intervene in arbitrations before an award was made, either by injunction or some other method. That remains the position. Section 1(c) of the Act is an express statutory warning[11] to the courts not to intervene except as provided in Part 1 of the 1996 Act. That reflects the underlying principles of the 1996 Act of party autonomy and the minimum of interference in the arbitral process by the courts, at least before an award is made.

In my view the whole structure of Part 1 also suggests that the scope for the court to intervene by injunction before an award is made by arbitrators is very limited. First, §44(2)(e), is the only express provision in Part 1 giving the courts the power to grant interim injunctions in aid of an arbitration, but the scope for obtaining one is limited. [Elektrim] accepted that the power given to the court to grant interim injunctions in §44(2)(e) was of no use to [it] in the current action.

Secondly, the only other express reference to the court granting an injunction is in §72. That section permits a person who is alleged to be a party to arbitral proceedings but who has taken no part in them to question in court proceedings the validity of the arbitration agreement, the constitution of the tribunal and the terms of the reference to arbitration. The court proceedings can be for either a declaration or an injunction or other appropriate relief. Again, [Elektrim] accepted that this section was no use to [it] in this action.

Thirdly, Part 1 of the Act contemplates that once matters are referred to arbitration, it is the arbitral tribunal that will generally deal with issues of their jurisdiction and the procedure in the arbitration up to an award…. [Section] 33 lays a statutory duty upon the tribunal to adopt procedures suitable to the circumstances of a particular case, avoiding unnecessary delay or expense, so as to provide a fair means for the resolution of the matters that are to be determined. Section 34(1) stipulates that it is for the tribunal to decide "*all procedural and evidential matters, subject to the rights of the parties to agree any matter.*" Section 34(2)(a) provides that procedural matters will include "*when and where any part of the proceedings is to be held.*" It is clear, therefore, that the Act contemplates that the tribunal will consider and decide such matters as whether there should be an adjournment or a stay of the arbitral proceedings. That is consistent with the general approach of the 1996 Act, which is to give as much power as possible to the parties and the arbitrators and to reduce the role of the courts to that of a supporter of the arbitration process up to an award being made….

In the present case, the LCIA arbitrators have not only to comply with the statutory duty under §33, but also a duty to the parties by virtue of Article 14(1)(i) and (ii) of the LCIA Rules. This only serves to reinforce my conclusion that in the present case the LCIA tribunal itself should decide whether or not those proceedings should continue or should await the outcome of the ICC arbitration. The tribunal has the power to do so and it is the body chosen by the parties to decide the dispute that has arisen between Vivendi and Elektrim concerning the TIA.

Against this background, I have concluded that even if Elektrim could establish that one of its legal or equitable rights had been infringed or was threatened by the continuation of the LCIA Arbitration pending the outcome of the ICC arbitration, or even if it could establish that the continuation of the LCIA Arbitration was otherwise vexatious, oppressive or unconscionable, … the court should not invoke the power to grant an injunction….

---

11. I use the word "warning" rather than "prohibition," because §1(c) says "…the court should not intervene…." The conditional mood implies that there might be circumstances where it should intervene other than as provided for in Part 1 of the Act.

I should note that [Vivendi] submitted that the grant of an injunction to restrain the LCIA arbitration would mean that the court was acting contrary to the U.K.'s obligations, as a Contracting State, under the New York Convention on the recognition and enforcement of foreign arbitral awards, 1958. In view of the decision I have reached apart from the New York Convention arguments [of Vivendi], I do not need to comment on them.

Having decided, on the basis of the first two issues, that no injunction should be granted, strictly speaking there is no need for me to decide the third question I have posed. As I have already said, I am not satisfied that the continuation of the LCIA Arbitration is vexatious or oppressive or unconscionable. The reason for the two arbitrations carrying on at the same time is that Vivendi wishes to claim that the Settlement Agreement is valid and to do so it must start the ICC Arbitration, whereas Elektrim claims it is not and the TIA subsists. So Vivendi has little choice but to continue with the LCIA Arbitration which is dealing with the parties disputes under the TIA.... It is simply inevitable that there will be multi-party, multi-tribunal litigation or arbitration in the circumstances of the war for the PTC shares that is going on.... [The Court also concluded that Elektrim had delayed for ten months in seeking an anti-arbitration injunction.] In these circumstances it would be unjust, in my view, to grant Elektrim an injunction to restrain the continuation of the LCIA arbitration....

NOTES

1. *Arbitrators' authority to issue interim orders or awards.* Most national arbitration legislation expressly or impliedly permits arbitrators to make various types of interim procedural rulings, orders, or awards. These can concern such matters as the applicable law, jurisdictional objections, the time and manner for making submissions, the time and manner of hearings, discovery, the admissibility of evidence, and requests for extensions of time. The arbitral tribunal's interim award in *Mobil Oil*, deciding what version of the ICC Rules was applicable, is a good example. *See* UNCITRAL Model Law, Arts. 16, 17, 19, 24, 29; SLPIL, Arts. 182, 183, 186, 188.

   Many interim rulings are denominated as "orders" or "instructions" or simply take the form of letters from the tribunal to the parties. *See infra* pp. 816-17. These rulings differ from "awards" in that they do not adopt the form of awards (*e.g.*, signed by all arbitrators, state reasons, etc.) and are (as discussed below) not generally subject to judicial review. In addition, such rulings are not subject to provisions of institutional rules (*e.g.*, the ICC Rules) requiring institutional review of awards or imposing formal requirements. Importantly, as discussed below, many such orders are—in contrast to final awards—not subject to independent judicial review or annulment in national courts. *See infra* pp. 806-10.

2. *Limits on judicial intervention in international arbitral proceedings under UNCITRAL Model Law.* Article 5 of the Model Law is a leading example of legislation imposing limits on interlocutory judicial intervention in international arbitral proceedings, whether by review of a tribunal's interim orders or otherwise. Article 5 provides that "[i]n matters governed by this Law, *no court shall intervene except where so provided in this Law.*" (Emphasis added.) The Model Law then sets forth limited circumstances involving judicial support for the arbitral process (*e.g.*, resolving jurisdictional objections, assisting in constitution of the tribunal, granting provisional relief, considering applications to annul arbitral awards), but not permitting judicial supervision of pro-

cedural decisions through interlocutory appeals or otherwise. UNCITRAL Model Law, Arts. 8, 9, 11(3), 13, 14(1), 16(3), 17, 27, 34 and 36.

In the words of one court in a Model Law jurisdiction: "Article 5 of the Model Law expressly limits the scope for judicial intervention except by application to set aside the award or to resist enforcement of an award under one or more of the limited grounds specified in Articles 34 or 36." *Corporacion Transnacional de Inversiones, SA de CV v. STET Int'l, SpA*, (1999) 45 O.R.(3d) 183 (Ontario Super. Ct.), excerpted above at pp. 784-85. Or, as a court in another Model Law jurisdiction held, rejecting a request that it review a tribunal's interim decisions: "It is premature, in effect, at this stage of proceedings, to ask the Superior Court of Québec to intervene on questions that can eventually, and only, be remitted to it after a final arbitral award has been made…. [The] Court is not clothed with the power to examine [these questions] at this moment, but only once the final arbitral decision has been rendered." *Compagnie Nationale Air France v. Libyan Arab Airlines*, [2000] R.J.Q. 717 (Québec Super. Ct.). *See also Judgment of 4 December 1994*, XXII Y.B. Comm. Arb. 263 (1997) (Austrian Oberster Gerichtshof) (vacating injunction requiring arbitrators to conduct arbitration in German and English, rather than only in English (as the tribunal had ordered): "Court review of orders for directions by the arbitral tribunal is not provided for; this would also be in contradiction with the sense and purpose of arbitral proceedings"); *Bancol etc. v. Bancolombia etc.*, 123 F.Supp.2d 771 (S.D.N.Y. 2000) ("the court's authority to direct or oversee [an] arbitration is narrowly confined. In particular, it has little or no power to afford interlocutory review of procedural matters, let alone to determine at the outset what procedural rules are to be applied…. '[P]rocedural' questions which grow out of the dispute and bear on its final disposition should be left to the arbitrator."); *K/S A/S Bill Biakh v. Hyundai Corp.* [1988] 1 Lloyd's Rep. 187 (Comm) (English High Ct.) ("In the interests of expedition and finality of arbitral proceedings, it is of first importance that judicial intrusion in the arbitral process should be kept to a minimum. A judicial power to correct during the course of the reference procedural rulings of an arbitrator which are within his jurisdiction is unknown in advanced arbitration systems….").

3. *National arbitration legislation limiting judicial confirmation or review to "final" awards.* Consider the FAA and the SLPIL. Do they contain any limitation equivalent to Article 5 of the UNCITRAL Model Law? Note the limitations on the types of arbitral rulings that may be reviewed under Article 190(1) and 190(3) of the SLPIL and §§9 and 10 of the FAA. *See infra* pp. 1116-18. The limitation of judicial review (or confirmation) to "final" awards serves the same basic purpose as Article 5 of the UNCITRAL Model Law.

Consider the court's reasoning in *Elektrim*. What was the basis for the principle of judicial non-intervention under English law? Compare Article 5 of the Model Law and §1(c) of the English Arbitration Act. Consider Articles 34-36 of the UNCITRAL Model Law. Compare §§67-69 of the English Arbitration Act. What sorts of rulings by an arbitral tribunal may be the subject of actions to set aside? Could the tribunal's orders denying a stay in *Elektrim* have been subject to an annulment action?

Would the analysis in *Elektrim* have been any different if the LCIA arbitration had been seated outside of England? Suppose that the English court had been asked to stay the ICC arbitration. Would it have been harder, or easier, to obtain an injunction? Why?

4. *Rationale for limits on interlocutory judicial review.* The rationale for limits on interlocutory judicial review is that a "court should not 'hold itself open as an appellate tribunal' since applications for interlocutory relief 'result only in a waste of time, the interruption of the arbitration proceeding, and ... delaying tactics in a proceeding that is supposed to produce a speedy decision.'" *Michaels v. Mariforum Shipping, SA,* 624 F.2d 411, 414 (2d Cir. 1980) (quoting *Compania Panemena Maritima v. J.E. Hurley Lumber Co.,* 244 F.2d 286, 288-89 (2d Cir. 1957)). Or, in the words of *Mobil Oil,* "for the court to entertain review of intermediary arbitration decisions involving procedure or any other interlocutory matter, would disjoint and unduly delay the proceedings, thereby thwarting the very purpose" of arbitration. *See supra* pp. 799-800.

Is the foregoing rationale persuasive? If the arbitrators have committed some gross procedural or other interlocutory error, is it not better to know sooner rather than later? What is the cost of such knowledge? Particularly in international arbitration?

Are there any circumstances in which interlocutory judicial intervention in an international arbitration should be permitted? Suppose an arbitrator refuses to permit one party to proffer critical evidence, in undeniable breach of clear provisions in the parties' arbitration agreement. Suppose a sole arbitrator persists in having indefensible *ex parte* contacts about the merits of the dispute with one party. Should such procedural errors go uncorrected? How might they be redressed?

What if, in *Elektrim,* Vivendi had agreed in the Settlement Agreement to stay the LCIA Arbitration, and Elektrim sought to enforce that agreement. If Vivendi refused to comply with its agreement to stay the arbitration, should a court in the arbitral seat have the authority to enjoin the arbitral proceedings? Or should the decision whether or not to do so be for the arbitral tribunal? Be subject to subsequent judicial review of their award?

What if, in *Mobil Oil,* the parties' arbitration agreement had provided unambiguously for the application of the 1975 ICC Rules? What if the tribunal's refusal to apply the 1975 ICC Rules inflicted enormous cost and irreparable damage on one party? Is it appropriate for the arbitral proceedings to proceed on a fundamentally flawed and highly damaging basis, without the possibility of judicial intervention? Note that an arbitrator may be challenged and removed in an interlocutory judicial action. *See supra* pp. 758-75. Why can't a defective procedural decision also be corrected?

What if an arbitral tribunal appointed pursuant to the ICC (or AAA) Rules refused to apply those rules? Would it be appropriate for interlocutory judicial review to be available? Why or why not?

5. *Interim arbitral decisions generally not subject to interlocutory actions to vacate under §10 of FAA.* As *Stanton* and *Mobil Oil* illustrate, if the arbitrators render an interim decision (for example, limited to issues of choice of law or liability) that is not intended to be a final disposition of part of the parties' dispute, then no provision of the FAA confers any power of interlocutory judicial review. Lower U.S. courts have refused to review interim decisions on subjects such as an arbitrator's partiality, selection of arbitral seat, discovery or evidentiary orders, provisional measures, choice of law, and jurisdiction. *See, e.g., In re Y & A Group Sec. Litg.,* 38 F.3d 380 (8th Cir. 1994) ("the usual rule is that under the FAA no appeal [sic] can be taken to the district

court [from an award] until a final decision is rendered"); *Compania Panemena Maritima v. J.E. Hurley Lumber Co.*, 244 F.2d 286, 288-89 (2d Cir. 1957) (refusing to permit interim judicial review of arbitrators' evidentiary ruling); *Yasuda Fire & Marine Ins. Co. v. Cont'l Cas. Co.*, 840 F.Supp. 578 (N.D. Ill. 1993) (arbitrators' order that discovery not be shared with non-parties is not final award subject to FAA §10 vacatur); *Ligon Nationwide, Inc. v. Alton Bean*, 761 F.Supp. 633 (S.D. Ind. 1991) (refusing to permit action to annul award that request for arbitration was timely filed and could be amended: "Without question, the two 'awards' appealed herein are not final. They do not decide either liability or damages; their nature is purely procedural and precursory to a final arbitration.").

6. *Possibility of interlocutory judicial intervention in exceptional circumstances.* Notwithstanding the general rule against interlocutory judicial intervention in the arbitral process, there are a limited number of exceptional circumstances where such intervention is available.

   (a) *Selection or removal of arbitrators.* Consider Articles 11, 12 and 13 of the UNCITRAL Model Law and Article 180 of the SLPIL. What do these provisions permit by way of interlocutory judicial intervention in the arbitral process? Why? What safeguards are placed on such judicial intervention? *See also supra* pp. 768-71.

   (b) *Interlocutory jurisdictional decisions.* Consider Article 16 of the UNCITRAL Model Law (particularly Article 16(3)) and Articles 186 and 190(2)(b) of the SLPIL. What do they provide with respect to interlocutory judicial decisions on the arbitrators' jurisdiction? Why? What safeguards are placed on such judicial intervention? *See also supra* pp. 275-78. Note also the possibilities for interlocutory judicial consideration of jurisdictional objections under the FAA. *See supra* pp. 278-83.

   (c) *Provisional measures.* The UNCITRAL Model Law and other developed arbitration statutes permit national courts to issue provisional measures in aid of an international arbitration. UNCITRAL Model Law, Art. 9; SLPIL, Art. 183(2); *infra* pp. 904-32. Alternatively, the arbitral tribunal may itself grant provisional measures; if enforcement of tribunal-ordered provisional measures is sought, national courts will review the tribunal's decision (under applicable standards for judicial review). *See infra* pp. 896-904.

   (d) *Evidence-taking.* The UNCITRAL Model Law provides for national courts to provide interlocutory judicial assistance to international arbitral tribunals. *See* UNCITRAL Model Law, Art. 27; SLPIL, Art. 184(2); *infra* pp. 839-51. Note that judicial assistance is generally available only when requested or authorized by the arbitral tribunal. *Compare* U.S. FAA, §7.

   (e) *Other circumstances.* Note the court's observation in *Elektrim* that §1(c) of the English Arbitration Act is only a "warning," and that circumstances permitting interlocutory judicial intervention might arise. (Compare Article 5 of the Model Law.) Should such an open-ended authority exist?

7. *New York Convention limits on interlocutory judicial intervention in international arbitration proceedings.* Consider the argument, referred to in *Elektrim*, that the New York Convention prohibited the English courts from enjoining the LCIA Arbitration. What provisions of the Convention would that argument be based upon? Article II? In

what respect would English courts be failing to recognize the parties' arbitration agreement (for example, in the TIA)?

Would the Convention argument be any stronger if the seat of the LCIA Arbitration had been outside of England?

8. *Orders by national courts supervising arbitration.* After compelling arbitration or staying litigation, a few U.S. lower courts have taken steps to supervise arbitral proceedings. *Nederlandse Erts-Tankersmaatschappij NV v. Isbrandtsen Co.*, 339 F.2d 440 (2d Cir. 1964); *PPG Indus., Inc. v. Pilkington plc*, 825 F.Supp. 1465 (D. Ariz. 1993) ("the Court directs that any damages determination, or arbitral award, made by the arbitrators shall be determined according to U.S. antitrust law irrespective of any conflict that may exist between those laws and the laws of England."); *Euro-Mec Imp., Inc. v. Pantrem & C., SpA*, 1992 WL 350211 (E.D. Pa.) ("The parties must reach agreement within forty-five (45) days on how the arbitration will proceed in Geneva and inform the court of their agreement; the court will order the location and terms of arbitration"). Nevertheless, the concept of judicial supervision of the arbitral process is alien to the promise of swift, non-national dispute resolution by international arbitration. Are these decisions consistent with prohibitions against interlocutory judicial review of interim arbitral rulings?

9. *Judicial non-interference in ICSID arbitrations.* The principle of judicial non-interference is made express in investment arbitrations by the ICSID Convention. Consider Articles 26, 27 and 53 of the Convention. Is there any room for national court involvement in an ICSID arbitration? Do national courts play any role in: (a) determining jurisdictional disputes; (b) selecting or removing arbitrators; (c) granting provisional measures; (d) assisting in evidence-taking; or (e) reviewing and confirming awards? Contrast this to the international arbitral process under the New York Convention.

C. ARBITRATORS' EXERCISE OF PROCEDURAL AUTHORITY IN INTERNATIONAL ARBITRATION

As we have seen, national law and institutional rules grant arbitral tribunals substantial discretion over the arbitral procedures (absent contrary agreement by the parties).[12] As discussed below, the manner in which an arbitral tribunal actually exercises its discretion in practice turns on the identity and background of the arbitrators, the desires of the parties, the nature of the dispute, the need for and utility of different procedural mechanisms or orders (*e.g.*, disclosure, a site inspection), and the costs and delays that will result from ordering a particular course of action. The tribunal's exercise of its discretion plays a highly significant role in the procedural conduct of the arbitration, influencing most aspects of the procedural timetable and scheduling of the arbitration. The materials excerpted below explore international arbitral tribunals' exercise of their procedural authority.

UNCITRAL NOTES ON ORGANIZING ARBITRAL PROCEEDINGS

[excerpted in Documentary Supplement at pp. 301-19]

12. *See supra* pp. 791-95.

REPRESENTATIVE PROCEDURAL ORDER IN ICC ARBITRATION

[excerpted in Documentary Supplement at pp. 321-23]

2010 IBA RULES ON THE TAKING OF EVIDENCE IN INTERNATIONAL ARBITRATION

[excerpted in Documentary Supplement at pp. 351-62]

MEDITERRANEAN AND MIDDLE EAST INSTITUTE OF ARBITRATION STANDARD RULES OF EVIDENCE

Article 5

5(1) Each party shall deliver to the arbitrator, and exchange with the other parties, a list of all the classes of its documents related to the dispute.

5(2) The other party shall be entitled to request, within 30 days after receipt of such list, a full list of the documents of one or more of such classes (List of Documents) and to inspect one or more of such documents, inspection to take place in such a way as to minimize the inconveniences to the other parties; the applicant shall advance the costs related to discovery, as fixed by the arbitrator.

5(3) In case of refusal to provide the List of Documents or to allow inspection within 30 days after receipt of the notice to this effect, the other party shall be entitled to apply to the arbitrator for an Order of Discovery. The parties are entitled to be heard on such application.

5(4) Before issuing such an order, the Arbitrator shall satisfy himself that such documents are not irrelevant to the dispute, and that the application does not aim totally or partially to confuse the matter through the production of quantity of unnecessary documents. An application for discovery will have to be examined by the Arbitrator by proceeding to test the relevance of a portion of such documents. On a party's application, before or after his order, the Arbitrator shall conduct a hearing at which the application or his order will be discussed.

5(5) Whenever the arbitrator, after such an examination, has the impression that a large number of the documents, production of which is sought, is irrelevant, he shall be entitled to appoint a lawyer as his expert to divide the documents in three classes; those which he considers relevant, the irrelevant ones and those which might be relevant. The party which seeks production of documents, the relevance of which has been challenged, will have to advance the costs of the expert and to deposit an amount that covers the costs caused to the other party by its inspection (such as the time spent by the other side's staff to attend inspection of the documents which are found irrelevant). All the costs caused by the inspection of the irrelevant documents are to be borne by the party which has applied for their production, even if its claim is eventually successful. Likewise the Arbitrator may, on application, appoint an expert to divide already produced documents into said three categories and to report on them and place the expert and the Arbitrator's costs and the other parties' costs to the charge of the party which has produced irrelevant documents even if the claim of that party succeeds.

5(6) Apart from general discovery, the production of specific documents may be ordered by the Arbitrator on a party's application at any stage of the proceedings until the hearing for the final addresses of the parties to the Arbitrator.

5(7) Before deciding on the application, the arbitrator shall invite the parties to file their written arguments or to be heard if they so wish.

5(8) The unjustified refusal by a party to discover documents as well as the refusal of a party to testify may be used by the Arbitrator as one of the elements of his decision.

PROCEDURAL ORDER IN ICC CASE NO. 7170

in D. Hascher, *Collection of Procedural Decisions in ICC Arbitration 1993-1996* 56 (1997)

Regarding the testimony of Mr. [X]
  1. If plaintiff so requests the testimony of Mr. [X] shall be taken.
  2. Mr. [X] can testify close to his home, before a public notary, in Italian, if necessary.
  3. The Tribunal will not be present.
  4. Counsel for defendant may be present and may put questions. In that case simultaneous translation is to be provided into English, provisionally at the expense of the plaintiff.
  5. An English-language transcript of all declarations shall be provided, authenticated by the notary public and by a qualified translator and shall be sent to the parties, the Tribunal and the Secretariat by [date] at the latest.
  6. Counsel for the plaintiff should send per telefax a proposal with all specifications at their earliest convenience and addressed to counsel for defendant, the Tribunal and the Secretariat.

PROCEDURAL ORDER IN ICC CASE NO. 5542

in D. Hascher, *Collection of Procedural Decisions in ICC Arbitration 1993-1996* 63 (1997)

[The arbitration occurred under ICC Rules, with its seat in Ethiopia. The chairman of the tribunal was a civil lawyer.] In their Submission on the merits of [date], Claimant required the Defendant: "to disclose all documents passing between itself and the [Bank]," and "to disclose all documents in their possess or control relating to this contract." The second request was directed to the Engineer as well. The grounds for the Claimant's request was that "(it) understands the continued non-payment of the foreign currency element of Certificates Nos. [A] and [B] and [C] subsequently Certificates Nos. [D] and [E] has arisen as a result of an instruction issued to the [Bank] by the Defendant." As to the second request, Claimants stated that

> "(it) understands the Defendant instructed the Engineer to issue a certificate under Clause 63.1 immediately it (the Defendant) received the notice of termination by the Claimant."

The certificate thus referred to is the document issued by the Engineer which allows the Employer, according to clause 63.1 of the General Conditions of the contract in dispute, "after giving 14 days' notice in writing to the Contractor (to) enter upon the Site and the

Works and expel the Contractor therefrom," which the Employer actually did in the instant case.

By telex of [date], solicitors to Defendant, objected that Claimant's application for "discovery" was premature, and that the "discovery" required would "involve the generation of massive number of copy documents many of which are probably not relevant to the matter in issue in the arbitration." In its "Submission for hearing on [date]," Claimant stated again that it "required to see" the documents indicated in its Submission in the merits, however limiting the request as to the documents passed between the Defendant and the Engineer to those which were passed from [a particular date] to the present date.

In its own Submission of [date], Defendant relied on article 249 of the Ethiopian Code of Civil Procedure, stating that this provision gives "power to the Courts to require the presentation of any document in the absence of which the Court considers the issues of the case cannot be correctly framed." However, Defendant stated that Ethiopian Courts, "exercise this power not at the request of the Claimant but on their own initiative" and that they do so "very rarely," and only when "they are convinced of the relevance and importance of the documents." Defendant concluded that under the Ethiopian law of procedure, which he considers to be applicable "to the present dispute," Claimant's request was not to be granted, "since" (the latter) "did not request for the disclosure of specific documents (title, date, reference number, etc.) and did not show the relevance of disclosure of all documents without exception" (relevance which, says the Defendant, "cannot be reasonably presumed").

Finally, at the hearing of [date], Claimant amended its request for disclosure in the following terms:

> "All documents passing between the Defendant and the Engineer relating to or in any way referring to: (a) Any request by the Claimant, for an extension of time the contract period, (b) the issue by the Engineer of a certificate under clause 63.1 of the Conditions of Contract of Civil Works.
>
> All documents passing between the Defendant and the [Bank] relating to or in any way referring to any instruction or similar request by the Defendant to the [Bank] not to make payment to the Claimant of any of certificates Nos. [A-E] inclusive...."

The parties have agreed in the Terms of Reference, that:

> "(t) rules governing the proceedings before the arbitrators shall be those resulting from the [ICC Rules], as published by the latter in 1975, and, where these Rules are silent, any rules which the arbitral tribunal may settle, whether or not reference is thereby made to a municipal procedural law to be applied in the arbitration."

Following to the execution of the Terms of Reference, amended [ICC Rules] were published by the ICC, which entered in force on 1st January 1988. However, it is not necessary to enter here into the discussion of the applicability of the Rules *ratione temporis*, since their provisions which are relevant in the instant case (namely Articles 24 and 26, already referred to, and article 14-1, 1st sentence, to which reference will be made hereunder) are identical in the 1975 and in the 1988 versions.

Now, while the ICC Rules do not contain any provision dealing with "discovery" properly speaking, it is enough to recall here that according to Article 4(1) "(t)he arbitrator shall proceed within as short a time as possible to establish the facts of the case by all appropriate measures." This provision allows the arbitrators to ask the parties to produce the documents in their possession or control, which in their view are relevant to the case.

Moreover, one might notice, *ex abundente cautela*, that as the Defendant recalls itself, article 249 of the Ethiopian Code of Civil Procedure does confer such power on the Ethiopian Courts, which shows that such a measure—being, indeed discovery by inspection of one party's files—is not alien to Ethiopian law. In addition, the Tribunal stresses that no request or injunction for production of documents might be addressed by an arbitral tribunal to third parties, on which such a tribunal has no jurisdiction of whatever kind.

In the circumstances of the case, the Tribunal considers that the amended request for disclosure of documents, such as presented by the Claimant during the hearing of [date], may furnish a basis to an order to [be] issued in this respect. However, the same is to be restricted by deciding that the documents passing between the Defendant and the Engineer relating to the implementation of clause 63.1 of the Conditions of Contract are those relating or referring to the certificate referred to by the Defendant in its letter of [date], this certificate being the only one which may be relevant to the issue of the expulsion of the Contractor by the Employer. As to the documents passing by the Defendant and the [Bank], they would be relevant only insofar as they concern the foreign currency element of Certificates Nos. [A-E] inclusive.

Consequently, disclosure of documents is hereby ordered by the Tribunal within the limits thus indicated. Further, it is hereby ordered that the Claimant is not entitled to any inspection of the Defendant's files.

FINAL AWARD IN ICC CASE NO. 7626
XXII Y.B. Comm. Arb. 132 (1997)

[excerpted above at pp. 781-82]

CERTAIN UNDERWRITERS AT LLOYD'S v. ARGONAUT INSURANCE CO.
264 F.Supp.2d 926 (N.D. Cal. 2003)

[excerpted above at pp. 759-65]

PARKER v. UNITED MEXICAN STATES (U.S.A. v. MEXICO)
4 R.I.A.A. 35, 39 (General Claims Commission 1926)

For the future guidance of the respective Agents, the Commission announces that, however appropriate may be the technical rules of evidence obtaining in the jurisdiction of either the United States or Mexico as applied to the conduct of trials in their municipal courts, they have no place in regulating the admissibility of and in the weighing of evidence before this international tribunal. There are many reasons why such technical rules have no application here, among them being that this Commission is without power to summon witnesses or issue processes for the taking of depositions with which municipal tribunals are usually clothed. The Commission expressly decides that municipal restrictive rules of adjective law or of evidence cannot be here introduced and given effect by clothing them in such phrases as "universal principles of law," or "the general theory of law," and the like. On the contrary, the greatest liberality will obtain in the admission of evidence before this Commission with the view of discovering the whole truth with respect to each claim submitted.

As an international tribunal, the Commission denies the existence in international procedure of rules governing the burden of proof borrowed from municipal procedure. On the contrary, it holds that it is the duty of the respective Agencies to cooperate in searching out and presenting to this tribunal all facts throwing any light on the merits of the claim presented. The Commission denies the "right" of the respondent merely to wait in silence in cases where it is reasonable that it should speak. To illustrate, in this case the Mexican Agency could much more readily than the American Agency ascertain who among the men ordering typewriting materials from Parker and signing the receipts of delivery held official positions at the time they so ordered and signed, and who did not. On the other hand, the Commission rejects the contention that evidence put forward by the claimant and not rebutted by the respondent must necessarily be considered as conclusive. But, when the claimant has established a *prima facie* case and the respondent has offered no evidence in rebuttal the latter may not insist that the former pile up evidence to establish its allegations beyond a reasonable doubt without pointing out some reason for doubting. While ordinarily it is incumbent upon the party who alleges a fact to introduce evidence to establish it, yet before this Commission this rule does not relieve the respondent from its obligation to lay before the Commission all evidence within its possession to establish the truth, whatever it may be.

For the future guidance of the Agents of both Governments, it is proper to here point out that the parties before this Commission are sovereign Nations who are in honor bound to make full disclosures of the facts in each case so far as such facts are within their knowledge, or can reasonably be ascertained by them. The Commission, therefore, will confidently rely upon each Agent to lay before it all of the facts that can reasonably be ascertained by him concerning each case no matter what their effect may be. In any case where evidence which would probably influence its decision is peculiarly within the knowledge of the claimant or of the respondent Government, the failure to produce it, unexplained, may be taken into account by the Commission in reaching a decision. The absence of international rules relative to a division of the burden of proof between the parties is especially obvious in international arbitrations between Governments in their own right, as in those cases the distinction between a plaintiff and a respondent often is unknown, and both parties often have to file their pleadings at the same time. Neither the Hague Convention of 1907 for the Pacific Settlement of International Disputes, to which the United States and Mexico are both parties, nor the statute rules of the Permanent Court of International Justice at the Hague contain any provision as to a burden of proof. On the contrary, article 75 of the said Hague Convention of 1907 affirms the tenet adopted by providing that "The parties undertake to supply the tribunal as fully as they consider possible, with all the information required for deciding the case."

NOTES

1. *UNCITRAL Notes on Organizing Arbitral Proceedings*. An example of institutional guidance for management of international arbitrations is provided by the 1996 UNCITRAL "Notes on Organizing Arbitral Proceedings" (the "UNCITRAL Notes"). The Notes are a reference tool to be used during the initial stages of an arbitration, aimed at producing a well-organized, efficient arbitral proceeding by identifying issues for the tribunal and the parties to address. The UNCITRAL Notes confirm the tribunal's discretion as to the management of proceedings (subject to the applicable arbitration agreement or rules). With regard to the tribunal's decision-making process on procedural matters, the Notes envisage that a tribunal could theoretically issue

procedural orders without consultation with the parties in appropriate circumstances. In most international arbitrations, however, the parties will expect to be, and must be, consulted on many (if not all) procedural matters and given an opportunity to present their views.

Among other things, the UNCITRAL Notes suggest early consideration of:

(a) adoption of procedural rules (¶¶14-16);

(b) language of the arbitration, translations and costs (¶¶17-20);

(c) seat of the arbitration and location of hearings (¶¶21-23);

(d) administrative matters and appointment of a secretary (¶¶24-27);

(e) deposits for costs and arbitrators' fees (¶¶28-30);

(f) communications and confidentiality (¶¶31-37);

(g) timetable for written submissions, evidence (documentary and physical), witness testimony (fact and expert) and hearing (¶¶38-42, 48-49, 55-58, 60-68, 74-77);

(h) hearing procedures (¶¶74-85);

(i) possible settlement issues (¶47); and

(j) issue definition (¶¶43-46).

What are the benefits of considering and discussing these matters between the parties and arbitral tribunal at the outset of the arbitration? What other issues should an arbitral tribunal consider? Is there any reason to criticize the UNCITRAL Notes? Consider Fouchard, *Une initiative contestable de la CNUDCI*, 1994 Rev. arb. 461 (distinguished French arbitration academic criticizes Notes as limiting flexibility of arbitral process, forcing tribunal and parties to "foresee the unforeseeable" and provoking unnecessary disputes at early stage of proceedings).

2. *Language of the arbitration.* An essential preliminary issue is the language of the arbitration—which can have an enormous practical impact on the conduct of the arbitral proceedings, the composition of the arbitral tribunal and counsel's efficacy. Many arbitration agreements specify the language of the arbitral proceedings (and, less frequently, the award). Absent such agreement, most institutional rules expressly authorize the arbitral tribunal to select a language or languages for the arbitration. *See, e.g.*, 2010 UNCITRAL Rules, Art. 19; 2012 ICC Rules, Art. 20; 2014 LCIA Rules, Art. 17. Arbitrators will often select the language of the underlying contract to govern the arbitral proceedings (*see* ICC Rules, Art. 20). There are important exceptions, however, where institutional arbitration rules dictate a particular language (absent contrary agreement by the parties). *See* Polish Chamber of Commerce Arbitration Rules, Art. 21(1) (presumption of Polish); 2011 Hungarian Chamber of Commerce Court of Arbitration Rules of Proceedings, Art. 9(3) (Hungarian).

If the parties have not agreed upon the language of the arbitration, the arbitral tribunal will ordinarily have the authority to prescribe it. *See, e.g.*, UNCITRAL Model Law, Art. 22(1). What if national law in the arbitral seat purported to override the parties' agreement on the language of the arbitration; would that be consistent with Article II of the New York Convention? What issues would that raise under Article V(1)(d) of the Convention?

3. *Initial procedural conference.* After the arbitral tribunal is constituted, one of its first steps will often be to hold an initial procedural conference with the parties. Some arbitrators consider this essential, and insist on an early meeting, in person, between the

tribunal and the parties (or their counsel). At the initial meeting, the tribunal will make introductions and discuss the organization of further arbitral proceedings.

In practice, tribunals frequently dispense with physical meetings in contemporary international arbitration. If the arbitrators and/or counsel reside in different countries, as is often the case, scheduling a prompt initial meeting can be difficult. The meeting itself can often entail substantial expense (for transportation, accommodation and the like). At the same time, experienced practitioners question the benefits of a physical meeting to discuss procedural matters. Modern technology permits video conferencing or telephonic meetings where interactions may be at least as focused and constructive, if properly managed, as in a physical meeting.

In either case, it is important for the tribunal to conduct a preliminary conference of some sort with the parties and counsel. Oral discussion of procedural and organizational issues is often essential to identifying mutually-acceptable approaches and time-saving schedules. The issues discussed are those identified above, in the UNCITRAL Notes, together with any additional matters specific to the parties' dispute. Although discussion of these various issues need not occur in the same room, real-time discussion with the tribunal is usually necessary.

During the parties' discussions at the initial procedural conference, agreement will often be reached on some or many aspects of the arbitral proceedings (*e.g.*, nature and timing of written submissions, date and duration of evidentiary hearing, need for experts). Where agreement is not possible, the parties will typically argue to the tribunal why their preferred procedural approach should be adopted. At or following the procedural conference, the tribunal will typically make a procedural order, setting out the timetable for the arbitral proceedings.

Some institutional arbitration rules provide for an initial procedural meeting either as a compulsory or an optional stage of arbitral proceedings. Compare Article 24 of the ICC Rules and Article 40 of the WIPO Rules with Article 14(1) of the LCIA Rules. Is it wise to make the initial meeting compulsory?

4. *Initial procedural order.* It is essential for the tribunal to establish a procedural timetable at the outset of the arbitration. For the most part, arbitration legislation does not address the contents or timing of a procedural timetable for the arbitration. These matters are instead left to the parties' agreement or, absent such agreement, the tribunal's directions. (Recall, however, the mandatory time limits under some national arbitration legislation, *supra* p. 796, and the (former) Guatemalan mandatory procedural regime, *supra* pp. 779-80.)

Consider the Representative Procedural Order in ICC Arbitration, excerpted at pp. 321-23 of the Documentary Supplement, which is representative of contemporary practice. What are the key elements in the Order? Consider the positions of the Claimant and the Respondent. Where do you think that disagreement likely arose in discussing the procedural timetable? Consider what different approaches to particular issues (*e.g.*, number and nature of filings, timing of disclosure, timing of witness evidence) might benefit one party or the other.

Compare the procedures set forth in the Treaty of Washington and the Abyei Arbitration Agreement, excerpted at pp. 65-66 & 80-83 of the Documentary Supplement, to those contained in the Procedural Order. How do these procedures differ? How are they similar? What might explain the differences?

5. *ICC Terms of Reference.* Consider Article 23 of the ICC Rules. Note the Terms of Reference that the arbitrators must draw up. What are the document's contents? What purpose might the Terms of Reference serve? Is it wise? Worth the effort? Consider: Wetter, *The Present Status of the International Court of Arbitration of the ICC: An Appraisal*, 1 Am. Rev. Int'l Arb. 91, 101-02 (1990) ("One of the most controversial and antiquated relics in the ICC Rules ... The terms of reference should indicate with precision the issues in dispute, but this is not always possible.... A troubling aspect of the practice is the time and thus the expense that the exercise entails, mostly without producing tangible results towards advancing a resolution of the case.... [T]he fact that no other arbitral institution, no other arbitration rules, and, to the writer's knowledge, no ad hoc tribunals require terms of reference is sufficient proof that the notion is ill-conceived and that the requirement should be abolished in the interest of both economy and justice."). Do you agree with this critique?

6. *Arbitrator's exercise of power to prescribe arbitral procedures.* In some cases, the parties' procedural freedom and the arbitrators' authority can produce a happy marriage of civil law, common law, and other procedures that is relatively efficient and effective. It can also allow the parties to agree upon, or the tribunal to order, innovative or other procedures specially adapted to their particular dispute. In other cases, particularly where irresponsible party behavior coincides with a reticent or incompetent tribunal, it can yield a morass of procedural confusion and inconsistency.

    As a practical matter, a tribunal's use of its discretion to adopt arbitral procedures will often be influenced significantly by the arbitrators' legal training, experience, personality, and other personal characteristics. These factors are summarized below.

    (a) *Arbitrators' legal background and training.* The legal training and experience of an arbitrator can significantly affect his approach to arbitral procedures. As discussed below, arbitrators with common law backgrounds will likely approach procedural issues differently from those with civil law backgrounds; arbitrators with Islamic, socialist, or non-Western backgrounds will take yet other approaches. *See* Wetter, *The Conduct of Arbitration*, 2(1) J. Int'l Arb. 7 (1985); E. Gaillard *et al.*, *Transnational Rules in International Arbitration* (1993); ICC, *Taking of Evidence in International Arbitral Proceedings* (1990); *Overview of Methods of Presenting Evidence in Different Legal Systems*, ICCA Congress Series No. 7 (1996).

    In general, arbitrators with civil law backgrounds can be expected to adopt more "inquisitorial" procedures, with somewhat less scope for adversarial procedures than is familiar to U.S. lawyers. Borris, *Common Law and Civil Law: Fundamental Differences and Their Impact on Arbitration*, 2 Arb. & Disp. Resol. L.J. 92 (1995); Patocchi & Meakin, *Procedure and Taking of Evidence in International Commercial Arbitration: The Interaction of Civil Law and Common Law Procedures*, 7 Int'l Bus. L.J. 884 (1996). Arbitrators from common law jurisdictions will be inclined to adopt "adversarial" procedures more broadly similar to those prevailing in U.S. litigation—such as broad, party-initiated discovery, depositions, lengthy oral hearings, counsel-controlled cross-examination, and the like.

    In some cases, arbitrators may not be legally-qualified. *See supra* p. 713. This is very common in some nations and in some industries, where arbitrators are often businessmen experienced in a trade or non-legal experts. The use of lay arbitrators is much less common in international arbitration, where legal training is often (and rightly) perceived as critical to the handling of conflict of laws, jurisdictional, and related issues. Obviously, a lay arbitrator will have a fundamentally different procedural approach than most lawyers.

(b) *Personal characteristics of arbitrators.* The importance of the differences between civil law, common law, and other backgrounds can be exaggerated. Intangible, individual characteristics of the arbitrators—age, temperament, ego, intelligence, time commitments, and interest—significantly influence procedural preferences. For example, an elderly academic who is unenthusiastic about factual details will approach procedural issues very differently from a compulsively-busy, underemployed practitioner who likes to impress with his grasp of minutiae. Arbitrators with long attention spans and keen memories approach procedures differently from those with different thought processes. Individuals who value control of events will prescribe a different procedure from those who don't. And arbitrators with substantial experience will take different approaches than novices.

Consider, from among your classmates (and various faculty instructor(s)) who you would want as an arbitrator in the following cases:

(1) You represent Company A in a case where it needs to obtain discovery of complex facts and then present a detailed (and boring) factual argument.

(2) You represent Company A in a case where it plans to make personal attacks on the integrity and honesty of a contracting partner and its management.

(3) You represent Company A where it has a powerful, but complex, legal claim, and is concerned that its counter-party intends to respond with obfuscation and a blizzard of incidental, prejudicial facts.

(4) You represent State A in an arbitration against another state over territorial boundaries. The arbitration is a matter of fundamental national importance to State A.

Change sides in each example and suppose you represent the counter-party.

(c) *Nature of dispute.* A number of other factors also influence a tribunal's decisions about arbitral procedures. Most importantly, the specifics of the parties' dispute often significantly affect arbitral procedures. Indeed, one of the advantages of arbitration is the possibility of tailoring procedures to a specific set of factual and legal issues to provide an efficient and accurate fact-finding mechanism. *See supra* pp. 108-11.

(d) *International procedures.* While influenced by their legal training, experienced arbitrators in cases with parties of diverse nationalities will often seek to arrive at procedural decisions that are "international," rather than replicating parochial procedural rules in local courts. Several sets of self-avowedly "international" procedural rules, suitable for use in international arbitrations, exist. *See, e.g.,* 2010 IBA Rules on the Taking of Evidence in International Commercial Arbitration; ALI/UNIDROIT Transnational Principles of Civil Procedure. These procedures are considered below. *See infra* pp. 819-28.

7. *Differing approaches to evidence-taking and disclosure in civil law and common law jurisdictions.* There are important differences between civil law and common law approaches to evidence-taking and disclosure. Although other factors are also significant, these differences have a material effect on the arbitral procedures adopted by

tribunals; common law practitioners will sometimes gravitate to common law procedures, with civil law practitioners likewise favoring what is familiar to them.

(a) *Evidence-taking and disclosure in civil law jurisdictions*. In most civil law jurisdictions, inquisitorial traditions do not provide for party-initiated (or other) disclosure. Consider the observation of Claude Reymond, a leading Swiss arbitrator: "[w]e react to the notion of discovery, be it English or, worse, American style, as an invasion of privacy by the court which is only acceptable in criminal cases." Reymond, *Civil Law and Common Law: Which Is the Most Inquisitorial? A Civil Lawyer's Response*, 5 Arb. Int'l 357 (1989). A tribunal composed entirely of civil lawyers, particularly civil lawyers with limited international experience, will not infrequently be reluctant to order disclosure and skeptical about the benefits of such a procedure. Indeed, only a decade ago, a well-known civil law practitioner said "[i]t is perhaps an exaggeration, but not a big one, to state categorically that discovery does not exist in international commercial arbitration, with the possible exception of instances where both parties are represented by common lawyers." Briner, *Domestic Arbitration: Practice in Continental Europe and Its Lessons for Arbitration in England*, 13 Arb. Int'l 155, 160-61 (1997). That view was difficult to sustain when made, and certainly does not reflect contemporary practice. It does, however, suggest the approach historically adopted towards international arbitration by more traditionally-minded civil law practitioners.

Civil law jurisdictions also did not generally permit either direct examination or cross-examination of witnesses. Indeed, witness testimony was (and remains) comparatively unusual in many civil law proceedings: "the idea of a witness being presented by the lawyer for a party in the question-and-answer format of common law direct examination is vaguely distasteful to civil lawyers." Elsing & Townsend, *Bridging the Common Law-Civil Law Divide in Arbitration*, 18 Arb. Int'l 59, 62 (2002). More generally, evidence-taking in civil law jurisdictions is largely controlled by the court, and the parties have virtually no right to demand relevant materials from one another or from witnesses; equally, civil law courts seldom ordered (or order) parties to produce materials that they had not voluntarily proffered as evidence.

(b) *Evidence-taking and disclosure in common law jurisdictions*. On the other hand, evidence-taking in common law jurisdictions permits much broader, party-initiated disclosure and attaches much greater importance to witness testimony, permitting each party to present and examine factual and expert witnesses. Many common law practitioners view discovery as a necessary and desirable feature of dispute resolution; common law arbitrators will often be reluctant to deny either party the opportunity to seek disclosure. O'Malley & Conway, *Document Discovery in International Arbitration—Getting the Documents You Need*, 18 Transnat'l Law. 371 (2004); Jones, *The Accretion of Federal Power in Labor Arbitration—The Example of Arbitral Discovery*, 116 U. Pa. L. Rev. 830 (1968) (characterizing limited discovery in arbitration as return to "sporting theory of justice"). Thus, a tribunal of three English or U.S.-trained arbitrators will, in all likelihood, assume that the parties should be permitted to exchange disclosure requests and that some substantial measure of document disclosure is essential to a fair and reliable proceeding.

Similarly, common law practitioners often regard cross-examination as "the greatest legal engine ever invented for the discovery of truth." *See, e.g.,* J. Wigmore, *Evidence* §1367, at 32 (J. Chadbourn Rev. 1974); *United States v. Salerno*, 505 U.S. 317 (1992) (Stevens, J. dissenting) ("Even if one does not completely agree with Wigmore's assertion ... one must admit that in the Anglo-American legal system cross examination is the principal means of undermining the credibility of a witness whose testimony is false or inaccurate"). In domestic litigation in common law states, counsel are subject to few limits on their cross-examination of witnesses, and they are most comfortable when the same approach is used in international arbitration.

(c) *"International" approaches to disclosure.* While influenced by their legal training, experienced arbitrators in cases with parties of diverse nationalities will usually seek to arrive at procedural decisions that are "international," rather than replicating parochial procedural rules in local courts. G. Born, *International Commercial Arbitration* 2208 (2d ed. 2014). The IBA Rules on the Taking of Evidence in International Arbitration, excerpted at pp. 351-62 of the Documentary Supplement, is one common source for such international approaches to disclosure and other aspects of evidence-taking. As one experienced authority has remarked, a touch over-optimistically:

> "in international cases, tribunals strive to look for cross-cultural solutions.... The salutary impetus to meet legitimate expectations leads to harmonization and to the avoidance of the peculiarities of national law." Paulsson, *Differing Approaches in International Arbitration Procedures: A Harmonization of Basic Notions*, 1 ADR Currents 17, 18-19 (1996).

This is particularly true in cases involving "multinational" tribunals, with members of different nationalities and backgrounds, and parties and counsel from different jurisdictions. In these circumstances, tribunals will seek to fashion arbitral procedures that do not mimic those of either party's or counsel's home jurisdiction, but that instead provide an internationally-neutral procedural framework (consistent with the parties' objectives in agreeing to arbitrate their disputes). Bernardini, *The Role of the International Arbitrator*, 20 Arb. Int'l 113, 119 (2004) ("the tendency is to organize a model of arbitration which, by establishing a strict co-operation between the arbitrator and the parties, produces an economic and efficient proceeding respectful at the same time of the equality of the parties and their right to be heard.").

At the same time, experienced arbitrators (properly) avoid merely "splitting the difference" between competing procedural desires and proposals (except, perhaps, in fixing time deadlines). Doing so will ultimately satisfy no one and can produce the worst of both worlds:

> "The arbitrators should not confuse flexibility with compromise. Having chosen one system, the arbitrators may modify it in the interest of efficiency, but should not try to marry it to the other system. Tribunals sometimes try to operate both systems at once, either out of mutual courtesy between the members of the tribunal, or because of the misplaced feeling that this will be more fair in cases where the parties come from countries with widely differing concepts of procedure. Experience shows that this attempt to amalgamate the two systems invariably produces a so-

lution which embodies the weakest features of each systems; and it almost always guarantees misunderstandings and confusion." Mustill, *Arbitral Proceedings*, Paper delivered at the ICC Arbitration Seminar in Malbun, 6 (24 November 1976), quoted in W. Craig, W. Park & J. Paulsson, *International Chamber of Commerce Arbitration* ¶23.04 (3d ed. 2000).

8. *Written witness statements.* Note that the Representative Procedural Order provides for written witness statements. Consider the provisions of the IBA Rules on the Taking of Evidence dealing with witness statements. What is the process for preparing a witness statement? What are the risks and benefits of the use of written witness statements? Consider: Veeder, *Introduction*, in L. Lévy & V.V. Veeder (eds.), *Arbitration and Oral Evidence* 7-9 (2004) ("Written witness statements can bear little relation to the independent recollection of the factual witness, with draft after draft being crafted by the party's lawyer or the party itself, with the witness's written evidence becoming nothing more than special pleading, usually expressed at considerable length. It rarely contains the actual unassisted recollection of the witness expressed in his or her own actual words."); P. Sanders, *Quo Vadis Arbitration?* 262 (1999) ("Drawn up with the party or its legal advisers the witness may be influenced in formulating his or her Statement which has to be signed and affirmed by him or her as being the truth. In my opinion, the Witness Statements preceding the hearings of the witnesses in person are not in accordance with the expectations of many parties in an international arbitration."). Why are written witness statements used? Are these criticism well-founded?

Suppose that an arbitration is seated in State A, with the parties' underlying contract governed by the law of State B. If one party argues that the civil procedure rules of State B forbid submission of evidence by witness statements, what weight should the tribunal give to the argument? Consider: *W. Co. of N. Am. v. Oil & Natural Gas Comm'n, Interim Award in Ad Hoc Case of 17 October 1985*, XIII Y.B. Comm. Arb. 5, 13-14 (1988) ("While I entirely accept that arbitrators (and umpires) are bound to have regard to certain fundamental evidential precepts they are clearly not in my view bound either by the letter of the [Indian] Code of Civil Procedure or by the strictly procedural rules of evidence which may apply elsewhere. It is the observance of the rules of natural justice that is paramount in the proper conduct of [an] arbitration...."). What if it had been English law that forbade witness statements?

9. *Witness examination: direct and cross-examination.* Consider the provisions of the IBA Rules on the Taking of Evidence dealing with witness examination. Who conducts the examination? Subject to what limits? What are the advantages and disadvantages of this process? Is it more like a common law system or a civil law system?

10. *Allocation of hearing time.* Should there be an oral evidentiary hearing in ordinary international arbitrations? What factors are relevant to deciding this question? If there is a hearing, how much time should be scheduled for it? Again, what factors are relevant to deciding this question? How is time allocated between the parties?

In many common law traditions, trial lawyers face few constraints on the amount of time they are allotted to question witnesses and present their cases. As one seasoned U.S. authority describes:

> "Litigators from the United States are accustomed to having appellate courts establish strict time-limits for oral argument, but expect trial courts and arbitral tribunals to allow

whatever amount of time is reasonably needed by the parties to present their evidence and arguments, without regard to pre-set timetable. Appellate courts are seen as being able to limit the length of oral argument because they have the relatively narrow task of deciding only issues of law based on the written record of the trial in the court below. This contrasts with trial courts which are perceived as being unable to establish schedules in advance because of the difficulty in predicting the number of witnesses that may be presented, the time required for examination and cross-examination or the strategies counsel may choose to adopt as the case proceeds." Holtzmann, *Streamlining Arbitral Proceedings: Some Techniques of the Iran-U.S. Claims Tribunal*, 11 Arb. Int'l 39, 46-47 (1995).

In contrast, trials in civil law systems are often focused almost entirely on the presentation of documents and formal statements of position. Time limits are short and the opportunity (and expectation) for witness examination minimal or nonexistent.

Marrying these differing traditions is a difficult task. It is clear, though, that most contemporary international arbitral tribunals accept neither approach and instead adopt a procedural model that permits meaningful witness examination and oral advocacy, while also imposing time limits and forcing the parties to manage their time wisely. An illustration of a "normal time" allocation from the Iran-U.S. Claims Tribunal, which is similar to that in many other international contexts, is again instructive:

> One Day Hearing: Normal Time
>   Introduction by the Chairman 9:30
>   Claimant's First Round Presentation 1 1/2 hour maximum
>   Respondent's First Round Presentation 1 1/2 hour maximum
>   Lunch
>   Questions by Arbitrators 15:00
>   Rebuttal Presentation by Claimant 45 minutes maximum
>   Rebuttal Presentation by Respondent 45 minutes maximum
>   Further Questions by Arbitrators, if any

Memorandum from Prof. K.-H. Böckstiegel, May 26, 1987, quoted in Holtzmann, *Streamlining Arbitral Proceedings: Some Techniques of the Iran-U.S. Claims Tribunal*, 11 Arb. Int'l 39, 47 (1995). What do you think of Professor Böckstiegel's proposed allocation of time? What is his guiding principle? How would you alter the proposed allocations?

11. *Characteristics of disclosure in international arbitration.* A vitally-important aspect of many arbitrations is the disclosure (or discovery) process. Although generalizations are risky, as a practical matter, disclosure in international arbitration often has several recurrent features.

    (a) *No automatic right to disclosure: control of tribunal over disclosure.* Consider the extent to which disclosure in international arbitration is—or is not—party-initiated under the institutional rules, national laws, and various model rules excerpted above. Do parties have an automatic right to obtain disclosure? Note how the diary pages which were at the heart of the procedural dispute in *ICC Case No. 7626* were produced.

        Compare Article 3 of the IBA Rules and the disclosure provisions of the Standard Rules of Evidence with the pretrial discovery provisions of the U.S. Federal Rules of Civil Procedure; if you were counsel for a party in an arbitration that was anxious to obtain broad discovery, would you prefer the above arbitration rules or the Federal Rules? Note that most institutional arbitration rules do not grant the parties the general right to make discovery demands on other parties (or non-parties) as a matter of course. Discovery instead generally occurs only if ordered by the tribunal, usually as part of its initial procedural timetable for the arbitral proceedings.

(b) *Limited scope of "discovery" in international arbitration as compared to disclosure in common law jurisdictions.* In practice, discovery or disclosure in international arbitration is ordinarily more limited than that in common law litigation. Even in common law jurisdictions discovery tends to be more limited in arbitration than litigation. *See United Nuclear Corp. v. Gen. Atomic Co.*, 597 P.2d 290, 302 (N.M. 1979) ("As a general rule, discovery is very limited in arbitration proceedings."); *O.R. Sec., Inc. v. Prof'l Planning Assoc.*, 857 F.2d 742, 747-48 (11th Cir. 1988) ("Arbitration proceedings are summary in nature to effectuate the national policy of favoring arbitration, and they require 'expeditious and summary hearing, with only restricted inquiry into factual issues'"). Indeed, the very term "discovery" is often a misnomer when used in connection with international arbitration.

Consider the scope of the "discovery" that was ordered in *ICC Case No. 5542*. Compare the scope of the tribunal's ultimate order to that originally sought, and to what would be available under U.S., English, or other common law procedures. What were the differences between what was sought and what was ordered? Note also the procedural background of the "discovery" order, which included an explanation at an oral hearing for why the requested materials were important. Consider the showing that is required under the IBA Rules on the Taking of Evidence to obtain disclosure of a document. Is it enough that the document is relevant to the parties' claims? What more is required?

(c) *Commonly-used approaches to disclosure in international arbitration.* Where no agreement between the parties is reached, the arbitrators will usually issue a procedural order at the outset of the arbitration defining the scope and mechanisms of disclosure. They will do so after hearing from the parties what legal and factual issues the case presents, and how each would prefer evidence-taking to be structured. At least in significant cases, it is common for the tribunal to order each party to produce, at a fairly early stage in proceedings, documents and other materials on which it wishes to rely; these are often attached to the parties' written submission (titled "Brief," "Memorial," "Statement of Claims"). Each party will then review its counter-party's submissions and, where "disclosure" is permitted, request that additional documents or categories of documents be disclosed. The tribunal will often suggest that the parties comply with such requests, subject to its own views concerning relevance, materiality, privilege, and the like. As a practical matter, many requests will be for specific documents and, where U.S.-style requests for categories of documents are made, stricter standards of relevance are very likely to be applied. If the tribunal's initial suggestion does not resolve matters, it may then hear a party's application for a more formal disclosure order. Note that this is what ultimately transpired in *ICC Case No. 5542*. Compare also Article 3 of the IBA Rules.

(d) *Impact of procedural law applicable to arbitration on disclosure.* As discussed below, the procedural law applicable to the arbitration has a potentially significant impact on disclosure. *See infra* pp. 831-35. As a practical matter, the applicable procedural law will often be that of the arbitral seat. Arbitrators will almost always take care to ensure that they act in accordance with the arbitration statute of the arbitral seat. Note the provisions of Article 1(1) of the IBA Rules.

Consider what weight the arbitral tribunal in *ICC Case No. 5542* gave to the Ethiopian Code of Civil Procedure (note that the arbitral seat was Ethiopia). What exactly was the importance of the Ethiopian Code of Civil Procedure in the tribunal's analysis in *ICC Case No. 5542*? Consider also the weight that the arbitral tribunal in *ICC Case No. 7626* gave to the procedural law of the arbitration in determining issues of evidence-taking. Note the tribunal's discussion of what nation's law (England or India) provided the procedural law of the arbitration in *ICC Case No. 7626*.

(e) *Importance of institutional rules to exercise of arbitral tribunal's disclosure authority.* Also critical to an international arbitral tribunal's exercise of disclosure authority are the terms of any applicable institutional rules. As the order in *ICC Case No. 5542* illustrates, the ICC Rules have generally been understood by arbitral tribunals as authorizing discovery orders. *See also infra* pp. 835-37. Arbitral tribunals typically rely upon the general grant of evidence-taking authority in institutional rules as the primary basis for any discovery orders they make.

(f) *Disclosure orders generally limited to parties to the arbitration.* Disclosure orders in international arbitration are ordinarily limited to the parties to the arbitration. Disclosure is seldom sought or ordered from non-parties. The order in *ICC Case No. 5542* is a good example of this approach.

The limitation of disclosure orders in international arbitration to the parties is in substantial part a result of limits on the arbitral tribunal's power. The powers conferred by the arbitration agreement and any institutional rules it incorporates extend only to the parties to that agreement. *See infra* p. 833. As discussed below, there are instances in which national law may grant arbitrators power to take evidence from non-parties, either with or without judicial assistance from national courts, but this authority is infrequently exercised. *See infra* pp. 833, 846-48. Note how Article 3(9) of the IBA Rules deals with possible disclosure by or discovery from non-parties. What does Article 3(9) mean?

(g) *Document disclosure in international arbitration.* The most common and significant mode of disclosure in international arbitration is document disclosure. Consider the procedural order in *ICC Case No. 5542*. It illustrates the reluctance that many tribunals display when requested to order document disclosure. Note the tribunal's refusal to order one party to permit the other to inspect its files. Note also the tribunal's concern regarding the materiality of the documents requested.

12. *Compelling attendance of party's witness at evidentiary hearings.* Suppose one party submits a written witness statement from a senior employee, which is directly relevant to the parties' dispute, but the party indicates that the witness will not be available for an oral hearing before the tribunal. What power does a tribunal have to compel attendance of the party's witness at a hearing? Consider the tribunal's authority under

the ICC, LCIA, AAA, UNCITRAL and IBA Rules. Consider also the arbitration legislation discussed below at pp. 839-51.

One course of action is for a tribunal to order a party to produce employees whose written testimony it has procured. What if the witness is not an employee or otherwise subject to the control of either party? What if a party indicates that it does not intend to rely on the testimony of an employee who clearly possesses material information about the disputed matters? What can the other party do? What can the tribunal do?

Consider Article 4(10) of the IBA Rules. What if the arbitrators wish to question someone who the parties have agreed need not appear at the hearing?

What limitations are there upon the tribunal accepting into evidence (and relying upon) a written witness statement from an individual who did not appear at a hearing or submit to cross-examination? What obligations are there on a tribunal to accept the written witness statement of a material witness, even if he or she is not available for cross-examination? Consider Article 4(7) of the IBA Rules.

13. *Transcript and protocol.* Consider the provisions of the institutional rules excerpted above. Do any of these rules require the taking of a transcript of oral proceedings? Should they? Who decides, in a particular arbitration, whether a verbatim transcript will be required? The parties? The tribunal? What if the parties don't want to pay for a transcript, but the tribunal believes that one is necessary?

Note that, in common law jurisdictions, verbatim transcripts are the rule in national court (and many arbitral) proceedings. In contrast, in many civil law jurisdictions, the presiding judge will prepare a "protocol" or "minute" of the oral proceedings (summarizing the evidence and/or arguments). *See* G. Born, *International Commercial Arbitration* 2292 (2d ed. 2014); P. Sanders, *ICC Comparative Arbitration Practice and Public Policy* 137-40 (1987). How should a tribunal exercise its discretion to order the taking of a verbatim transcript? Does it depend on the size of the case? The importance of the oral evidence? The customary approach of courts in the arbitral seat? Should oral testimony of witnesses be treated differently from oral argument by counsel?

14. *Sanctions for failure to comply with arbitrators' procedural order.* Consider what sanctions, if any, a tribunal may impose under various national arbitration statutes against a party that refuses to comply with its procedural orders (including disclosure orders). In particular, consider Article 1700 of the Belgian Judicial Code, Article 1467(3) of the French Code of Civil Procedure and Article 184 of the SLPIL.

Consider the court's opinion in *Certain Underwriters.* What did Interim Order No. 3, issued by the arbitral tribunal, provide? Why did the U.S. court vacate (annul) the order? In what circumstances could an arbitral tribunal properly make such an order? Are there other types of sanctions that an arbitral tribunal could make, without express authorization from the parties? Is the analysis in *Certain Underwriters* wise? Why or why not?

If an arbitral tribunal cannot impose coercive sanctions, how effective are the other enforcement powers available to the tribunal? Consider the various provisions of the IBA Rules relating to sanctions for failure to comply with disclosure obligations, including Articles 4(7), 5(5), 9(5) and 9(6). Again, how effective are the arbitrators' powers?

Although it is at least theoretically possible in many jurisdictions, arbitrators seldom seek judicial enforcement of discovery orders. Consider Article 1708 of the Belgian Judicial Code and Article 184 of the SLPIL. We discuss the topic of judicial assistance to arbitral tribunals in detail below. *See infra* pp. 832-33, 839-51.

Rather than impose sanctions or seek judicial enforcement of discovery orders, arbitrators are much more likely to draw adverse inferences from a party's refusal to produce requested documents or witnesses. *See* IBA Rules, Arts. 4(7), 5(5), 9(5) and 9(6); *Forsythe Int'l, SA v. Gibbs Oil Co.*, 915 F.2d 1017, 1023 n.8 (5th Cir. 1990) ("Arbitrators may ... devise appropriate sanctions for abuse of the arbitration process"); *Bigge Crane & Rigging Co. v. Docutel Corp.*, 371 F.Supp. 240, 246 (E.D.N.Y. 1973). Is this a significant sanction?

Consider also Article 37(5) of the 2012 ICC Rules, Article 28(4) of the LCIA Rules and Article 34 of the 2014 ICDR Rules, discussing the tribunal's powers to allocate costs. Do they provide a sufficient incentive for the parties to comply with the tribunal's disclosure orders?

15. *Site inspections.* In some cases, visits by the arbitrators to a particular site may be necessary or appropriate. Such inspections will virtually always occur with the agreement of the parties, whose representatives will attend. Video recordings, photographs and other records of the visit can be made. Consider Article 7 of the IBA Rules. What practices does Article 7 forbid? (For an example of problems that may occur during a site inspection, *see infra* pp. 842-44.)

16. *Witness conferences.* Various procedural innovations have been suggested to improve the quality of witness examination in international arbitration. One approach is "witness-conferencing," where two or more witnesses are simultaneously and collectively examined concerning the same set of issues or events. The purpose of witness-conferencing is to confront two or more witnesses on the same topic with potentially-contradictory testimony, in order to identify areas of agreement, force concessions and evaluate the credibility of differing contentions. *See* Peter, *Witness Conferencing Revisited,* in S. Bond (ed.), *Arbitral Procedure at the Dawn of the New Millennium, Reports of the International Colloquium of CEPANI* 156 *et seq.* (2004); Hunter, *Expert Conferencing and New Methods*, in A. van den Berg (ed.), *International Arbitration 2006: Back to Basics?* (ICCA Congress Series 2007).

Consider the possibility of witness conferencing from the perspective of counsel for one party. What do you like about the mechanism? What do you fear? Consider the possibility from the perspective of the tribunal. If you were counsel, how would you prepare your witnesses for witness-conferencing?

17. *Party representatives as witnesses.* In some jurisdictions, national law limits the ability of party representatives (*e.g.*, the parties themselves, if natural persons, or officers, directors, or employees of juridical entities) to provide witness evidence. Other jurisdictions adopt different rules, including allowing such testimony subject to the fact-finder's weighing of a witness's credibility. How should these sorts of evidentiary restrictions be applied in international arbitrations? Consider the following dissent by an Iranian judge, protesting against the admission of testimony from a party in an arbitration before the Iran-U.S. Claims Tribunal:

"Although the Tribunal acknowledges that the Claimant has presented no evidence or documentation in order to establish its nationality, the majority has exempted the

Claimant from the obligation to do so. Without the slightest legal basis, it has accepted the assertions solely on the basis of the statements of Mr. Jennings himself, who is an interested party in his claim and thus it has made it clear that its Award is invalid. Is it not unfair and oppressive that the unsubstantiated statements by the Claimant in an international forum be accepted as establishing its allegations, and that such a considerable sum be awarded against a sovereign government merely on the basis of an allegation brought against it? Indubitably, those persons with an interest in the Tribunal's arbitration will not relax their vigilance and will not readily overlook such high-handed decisions, nor will the international legal system, closely following the Tribunal's decision." *Economy Forms Corp. v. Islamic Repub. of Iran, Award in IUSCT Case No. 55-165-1 of 14 June 1983, Dissenting Opinion of Mahmoud M. Kashani of 1 December 1983*, 3 Iran-US C.T.R. 42 (1983).

Compare Article 4(2) of the IBA Rules, excerpted at p. 356 of the Documentary Supplement.

18. *Privileges in tribunal-ordered disclosure.* An important feature of evidence-taking in many national litigation systems is the treatment of various sorts of privileges—most significantly, the attorney-client privilege and various privileges attaching to settlement discussions and communications between counsel. There is limited authority concerning the appropriate treatment of privileges when disclosure is ordered by the tribunal in an international arbitration.

   (a) *Availability of privileges in international arbitration.* As a practical matter, most international arbitral tribunals give effect to otherwise-available privileges under applicable law. *ICC Case No. 7626* is a representative example.

   (b) *Availability of privileges in arbitration under FAA.* In general, lower U.S. courts have assumed that otherwise-applicable privileges are unaffected either by the parties' agreement to arbitrate or the fact that it is the arbitral tribunal (rather than a court) that has ordered discovery. *See Robbins v. Day*, 954 F.2d 679 (11th Cir. 1992); *W. Employers Ins. Co. v. Merit Ins. Co.*, 492 F.Supp. 53 (N.D. Ill. 1979) (assuming that accountants' privilege was applicable to subpoenas issued by arbitral tribunal, at least where judicial enforcement of subpoena was sought).

   Is it appropriate to apply generally-applicable privilege rules in an arbitral proceeding? Does an agreement to arbitrate constitute a waiver of privileges, on the theory that accepting the informality of arbitral procedures also abandons legal privileges? Or are privileges like other substantive legal rights, which are given full effect in the arbitral process?

   (c) *Choice of law governing privileges.* Assuming that privileges can, in principle, be asserted in arbitration, what law governs the existence and scope of a privilege? Alternatives include the procedural law of the arbitration, the law most closely connected to the allegedly privileged communications (*e.g.*, where they were made or received), the law governing the parties' arbitration agreement, and the law of the judicial forum where enforcement of the arbitrators' disclosure orders is sought. *ICC Case No. 7626* involved a choice-of-law question affecting an issue related to privileges; specifically, what law governed admissibility of a party's representative's diary? Consider the possible laws applicable to this issue. How should the issue have been analyzed?

   Another possibility is an international privilege standard, not based upon a particular national law. Such an international rule could provide a substantive standard (analogous to a national law definition of privilege for communications with legal advisers). Alternatively, some authorities have proposed a different form of international standard, providing that both parties will be subject to the same privilege rules—regardless of the location of their communications or the legal qualifications of their legal advisers; rather, the "most favorable privilege," granting the greatest protection from compulsory disclosure, applicable to either party would be applied uniformly to both (or all) parties. *See* 2014 ICDR Rules, Art. 22. What is the logic of this approach?

19. *Oral submissions.* Most international arbitrations will involve oral submissions by the parties' counsel to the arbitral tribunal. These submissions often take the form of "Openings" (or Opening Submissions, Presentations, or Speeches) or "Closings." Counsel will present the parties' respective positions on evidentiary and legal matters, and respond to questions from the arbitrators. For an example of oral submissions, in the Abyei Arbitration, *see* www.wx4all.net/pca.

20. *Admission and evaluation of evidence in inter-state arbitration.* Consider the excerpts from *Parker v. United Mexican States.* As the award illustrates, arbitrators in inter-state arbitrations enjoy broad discretion to make evidentiary decisions on subjects such as admissibility, weight and credibility of evidence, usually without reference to local national evidentiary rules. *See also Shufelt v. Guatemala (Guatemala v. U.S.A.),* 2 R.I.A.A. 1083 (1930) ("On the question of evidence over which there was some argument, I may point out that in considering the cases quoted on both sides it is clear that international courts are by no means as strict as municipal courts and cannot be bound by municipal rules in the receipt and admission of evidence. The evidential value of any evidence produced is for the international tribunal to decide under all the circumstances of the case."); ICSID Rules, Rule 34(1) ("The Tribunal shall be the judge of the admissibility of any evidence adduced and of its probative value.").

What law governed the tribunal's admission and evaluation of evidence in *Parker*? Would a different approach arguably be required in a more ordinary commercial arbitration, as contrasted to a claims commission established by international treaty (as in *Parker*)?

As a practical matter, the tribunal's approach in *Parker* is illustrative of the reluctance of arbitrators in international commercial arbitrations, as well as inter-state arbitrations, to rely on strict rules of evidence drawn from national law. For a more detailed discussion, *see infra* pp. 831-32. International arbitral tribunals are nonetheless frequently requested to apply national evidentiary rules. Is doing so wise? Is the analysis in *Parker* persuasive? What other reasons are there against (and for) applying strict rules of evidence drawn from national law? Recall the historically "informal" character of international arbitration. *See supra* pp. 785-88.

If a national evidentiary rule is to be applied, what state's law is applicable? Possibilities include the law governing the underlying contract, the arbitration agreement, and the arbitral procedure. In practice, the procedural law of the arbitration would ordinarily govern issues relating to the admissibility and weighing of evidence. *See supra* pp. 620-21, 623.

If a tribunal does not apply national law evidentiary rules, does it then apply no rules at all? If so, would this be acting *ex aequo et bono*? If not, what determines the content of the tribunal's international evidentiary rules?

21. *Procedures in inter-state arbitration.* Consider again the procedural arrangements, set forth in the Treaty of Washington and Abyei Arbitration Agreement, excerpted at pp. 65-66 & 80-83 of the Documentary Supplement. How do these procedures compare with those in international commercial arbitrations?

D. EVIDENCE-TAKING AND DISCLOSURE IN INTERNATIONAL ARBITRATION

The taking and presentation of evidence (including disclosure or discovery) are as important in international arbitration as they are in litigation.[13] The manner in which evidence is taken and presented in international arbitration depends on a variety of factors. Particularly important are the terms of the parties' arbitration agreement, any applicable institutional rules, and the procedural law governing the arbitration. Equally important are the identity and attitude of the arbitral tribunal, which will typically possess broad discretion in adopting procedures for taking and presenting evidence. Finally, the taking of evidence in international arbitration can also be significantly affected by the actions of national courts, which may have the power to either assist arbitral tribunals in taking evidence or offer alternative means for obtaining evidentiary materials.

This section first examines the evidence-taking and disclosure provisions of leading institutional rules and national arbitration statutes, and the authority that these provisions grant to international arbitral tribunals. Second, the section considers the impact of national arbitration legislation on the evidence-taking and disclosure powers of international arbitral tribunals.

1. Authority of International Arbitral Tribunals Over Evidence-Taking and Disclosure

There is great diversity in the modes of taking evidence in international arbitration. In a considerable number of cases, the parties will agree to a relatively consensual process for both the taking and presentation of evidence in the arbitration. These agreements can produce many different forms of evidence-taking. For example, there can be agreement that each party will rely on its own documents and witnesses, with no right to seek disclosure or discovery from the other party. Alternatively, parties can voluntarily agree to the disclosure to one another of certain categories of information or documents.[14]

If voluntary evidence-taking does not occur, the manner of evidence-taking and evidence-presentation in international arbitration is subject to the parties' arbitration agreement, any applicable institutional rules, applicable national law and the discretion of the arbitrators. The interplay between these various sources of authority can be complex.[15] As a practical matter, however, it will often mean that the arbitral tribunal will have fairly substantial discretion to define the manner of evidence-taking. The way in which that discretion is actually exercised varies substantially among arbitral proceedings. The materials excerpted below explore these aspects of the taking of evidence, including disclosure, in contemporary international arbitrations, focusing in particular on international commercial arbitrations.

---

13. *See* G. Born, *International Commercial Arbitration* 2307 (2d ed. 2014).

14. *See* G. Born, *International Commercial Arbitration* 2321, 2325, (2d ed. 2014); Böckstiegel, *Presenting Evidence in International Arbitration*, 16 ICSID Rev. 1 (2001); Pietrowski, *Evidence in International Arbitration*, 22 Arb. Int'l 373 (2006).

15. *See* G. Born, *International Commercial Arbitration* 2321 (2d ed. 2014).

BELGIAN JUDICIAL CODE
Article 1700

[excerpted above at pp. 778-79]

GUATEMALAN CODE OF CIVIL AND COMMERCIAL PROCEDURE, 1963
Articles 287, 288 (repealed)

[excerpted above at pp. 779-80]

2010 IBA RULES ON THE TAKING OF EVIDENCE IN INTERNATIONAL ARBITRATION

[excerpted in Documentary Supplement at pp. 351-62]

FINAL AWARD IN ICC CASE NO. 7626
XXII Y.B. Comm. Arb. 132 (1997)

[excerpted above at pp. 781-82]

CORPORACION TRANSNACIONAL DE INVERSIONES, SA DE CV v. STET INTERNATIONAL, SPA
(2000) 49 O.R(3d) 414 (Ontario Ct. App.)

[excerpted above at pp. 784-85]

NOTES

1. *Inapplicability of local rules of civil procedure to disclosure and evidence-taking in international arbitrations.* What national law applies to subjects of evidence-taking and disclosure in an international arbitration? Is it the local civil procedure rules of the arbitral seat, applicable in domestic court proceedings? Why shouldn't such rules apply in international arbitration?

   It is well-settled in most jurisdictions that local civil procedure rules do not apply to locally-seated international arbitrations. In the United States, for example, the Federal Rules of Civil Procedure are not applicable in international or other arbitrations seated in the United States (unless otherwise agreed by the parties). *Great Scott Supermkts, Inc. v. Local Union No. 337*, 363 F.Supp. 1351, 1354 (E.D. Mich. 1973); *Commercial Solvents Corp. v. Louisiana Liquid Fertilizer Co.*, 20 F.R.D. 359 (S.D.N.Y. 1957); *Foremost Yarn Mills, Inc. v. Rose Mills, Inc.*, 25 F.R.D. 9 (E.D. Pa. 1960). *See also McDonald v. City of W. Branch*, 466 U.S. 284, 292 (1984) (quoting *Alexander v. Gardner-Denver Co.*, 415 U.S. 36, 58 n.19 (1974)) ("Arbitral factfinding is generally not equivalent to judicial factfinding.... [T]he record of the arbitration proceedings is not as complete; the usual rules of evidence do not apply; and rights and procedures common to civil trials, such as discovery, compulsory process, cross-examination, and testimony under oath, are often severely limited or unavailable."). Rather, the subjects of evidence-taking and disclosure are governed by the arbitration legislation of the arbitral seat, together with the parties' arbitration agreement and any incorporated institutional rules.

2. *Parties' autonomy under national arbitration legislation with respect to evidence-taking procedures.* Consider Articles 18, 19(1), and 24(1) of the UNCITRAL Model Law and Article 182 of the SLPIL, excerpted at pp. 90-91 & 158-59 of the Documentary Supplement; consider also Article 1700 of the Belgian Judicial Code. As discussed above, these provisions grant the parties broad freedom to agree upon the arbitral procedures. *See supra* pp. 786-89. Is there any specific reference to the parties' autonomy with regard to evidence-taking or disclosure? Is there any reason to think that the parties' autonomy does not extend to these subjects? Compare the different approach of the (now repealed) Guatemalan legislation to evidence-taking. Is there anything to recommend the latter approach in the context of evidence-taking?

3. *Arbitral tribunal's authority under national arbitration legislation with respect to evidence-taking procedures absent agreement of parties.* Consider Articles 19(2), 24(1) and 27 of the UNCITRAL Model Law, excerpted at pp. 90-92 of the Documentary Supplement. Note that these provisions grant arbitrators broad power—where the parties have not otherwise agreed—over "taking evidence" (Article 27) and evaluating evidence (Article 19(2)). Does the Model Law authorize arbitral tribunals to order the parties to make disclosure of documents or other materials? Is there any reference to "disclosure" or "discovery" in the Model Law? Consider Article 26(1)(b). Is there any reason to think that arbitrators would have the power to order parties to disclose materials to experts, but not to the tribunal or the adverse party?

   Compare the Model Law with Article 182 of the SLPIL and §7 of the FAA. Which of these statutes expressly authorize the arbitrators to order the parties to provide disclosure or discovery of documents or other materials? Should such an authority be implied? What *should* a national arbitration statute ideally provide regarding evidence-taking and disclosure in an international arbitration? Who should be in control of such evidence-taking—an arbitral tribunal or a national court?

   Consider the following: "Any order for discovery, which may not be based on a respective agreement by the parties, would probably be seen as a violation of due process, at least if one party belongs to a civil law system." Weigand, in F.-B. Weigand (ed.), *Practitioner's Handbook on International Arbitration* 80 *et seq.* (2002). How exactly would a tribunal's order requiring disclosure of relevant evidence violate a party's due process rights?

4. *National arbitration statutes forbidding arbitrators from ordering disclosure or discovery.* In some civil law jurisdictions, arbitrators are forbidden by statute from ordering unwilling parties to disclose information. Consider Article 1700(4) of the Belgian Judicial Code. Is this a desirable procedural regime for obtaining disclosure of information in arbitration? Note that Article 1708 requires application by (or on behalf of) the arbitral tribunal to national courts and that it transfers decisions about the need for and appropriate scope of disclosure away from the arbitral tribunal. Is this efficient? Consistent with the parties' objectives in agreeing to arbitrate?

5. *National arbitration statutes authorizing judicial assistance in taking evidence in aid of arbitration.* What happens if an arbitral tribunal orders disclosure or other forms of evidence-taking, and a party refuses to comply? What powers does the tribunal have in these circumstances? Note the arbitrators' power under the arbitration legislation ex-

cerpted above to apply to national courts for judicial assistance in compelling a party to give discovery. Note also that the arbitrators can, in turn, authorize the parties to seek judicial assistance in ordering discovery. Consider, for example, Article 1708 of the Belgian Judicial Code. Is this approach appropriate? Compare §7 of the FAA.

Do arbitral tribunals have any other power, beyond seeking judicial assistance, to require compliance with their disclosure orders? Recall the decision in *Certain Underwriters, supra* pp. 759-65, ordering sanctions against a party for non-compliance with provisional measures ordered by a tribunal. Should a tribunal have the authority to sanction a party that refuses to comply with disclosure orders? Consider Article 1700(4) of the Belgian Judicial Code and Article 1467(3) of the French Code of Civil Procedure. *See also supra* pp. 826-27 for discussions of a tribunal's power to draw adverse inferences and allocate costs.

6. *Arbitrators' power to order disclosure or discovery generally limited to parties.* Suppose A and B are parties to an arbitration, but critical evidence is in the hands of C. Under the UNCITRAL Model Law, the SLPIL and the Belgian Judicial Code, is the arbitral tribunal empowered to order C to provide the evidence? Do the institutional rules excerpted above purport to provide the tribunal with this authority? If A and B are the only parties to the arbitration agreement, would C be bound by these rules, even if they granted the tribunal power to seek discovery from non-parties? What might be the source of the arbitrators' power to order disclosure from non-parties? As discussed below, national law may in some cases give arbitrators power to order discovery from non-parties. *See infra* pp. 846-47.

7. *Scope of permitted discovery or disclosure in arbitration under national arbitration statutes.* What is the scope of "discovery" affirmatively authorized under the UNCITRAL Model Law and FAA? Note that each law refers to "taking evidence," not to "discovery." Is this choice of language significant? How broad a discovery order may a tribunal make? Can a tribunal only compel the production of documents that are admissible and material as evidence, or can it order production of materials that appear generally relevant to the parties' dispute or that might lead to the discovery of evidence? Can a tribunal compel pre-hearing oral depositions and pre-hearing production of documents? Or, is the tribunal limited to requiring that evidence be adduced at a hearing? *See also infra* pp. 833-35, 837-38.

8. *Discovery authority of arbitrators under FAA.* Consider §7 of the FAA.

   (a) *Scope of arbitrators' power under FAA §7 to order "discovery."* Section 7 of the FAA provides that the arbitrators "may summon in writing any person to attend before them or any of them as a witness and in a proper case to bring with him or them any book, record, document, or paper which may be deemed material as evidence in the case." What is the scope of "discovery" that a tribunal is authorized to order under §7? What is the meaning of the phrase "deemed material as evidence in the case"?

   In considering the scope of judicial assistance in ordering "discovery" under §7, lower U.S. courts have reached divergent conclusions. Some courts have held that §7 does not permit a tribunal to order "discovery," but only to require the production of "evidence" at a hearing. Consider the comment in *Oceanic Transport* that:

   "However great a respect we owe the arbitrators, it is a fact that when the statute [§7 of the FAA] imposed upon the District Court the duty to determine whether or not to compel the attendance of a witness and his production of papers, it imposed upon the Court the duty to determine whether or not the proposed evidence is material."

For similar decisions, *see Integrity Ins. Co. v. Am. Centennial Ins. Co.*, 885 F.Supp. 69 (S.D.N.Y. 1995) ("an arbitrator does not have the authority to compel nonparty witnesses to appear for pre-arbitration depositions"); *Wilkes-Barre Publishing Co. v. Newspaper Guild of Wilkes-Barre*, 559 F.Supp. 875 (M.D. Pa. 1982) (refusing to enforce subpoena under §7 for "anything [one party] wants," and remanding to arbitrator for relevance determination); *Local Lodge 1746 etc. v. Pratt & Whitney Div.*, 329 F.Supp. 283 (D. Conn. 1971) (enforcing arbitrator's subpoena, but requiring in camera review by arbitrator and only permitting arbitrator to provide parties with "relevant evidence in the dispute"; "Arbitration has never afforded to litigants complete freedom to delve into and explore at will, the adversary party's files under the pretense of pre-trial discovery.").

Other U.S. courts have been reluctant to second-guess arbitrators' determinations concerning materiality and have enforced what appear to be fairly broad pre-hearing discovery orders issued by arbitrators. Consider the decision in *Stanton, supra* pp. 798-99, 808-09, refusing to interfere with an arbitral tribunal's pre-hearing discovery orders. *See also Meadows Indem. Co. v. Nutmeg Ins. Co.*, 157 F.R.D. 42 (M.D. Tenn. 1994) (upholding arbitrators' pre-hearing subpoena requiring document production by non-party witness under §7 of FAA: "power of the panel to compel production of documents from third-parties for the purposes of a hearing implicitly authorizes the lesser power to compel such documents for arbitration purposes prior to a hearing"); *Commercial Metals Co. v. Int'l Union Marine Corp.*, 318 F.Supp. 1334 (S.D.N.Y. 1970) (enforcing subpoena for materials because they might be relevant to arbitration).

(b) *Relationship between FAA §7 and parties' agreement.* What is the relationship between §7 and the parties' agreement or the institutional rules agreed to by the parties? First, if the parties' arbitration agreement (or institutional rules it incorporates) permits *broader* discovery than that contemplated by §7, does §7 limit the effect of the parties' agreement on the arbitrators' power? Second, if the parties' arbitration agreement permits only limited discovery (narrower than that provided for by §7), does this limit the otherwise-available scope of discovery?

Consider the scope of "discovery" contemplated under the various institutional rules set forth above. (Note that none of the rules actually refers to "discovery.") Do the rules contain limits on the scope of allowable discovery that may be ordered by the arbitrators? How does §7 of the FAA, which permits arbitrators to subpoena "material" evidence, compare with the standards set forth in the institutional rules excerpted above?

(c) *What arbitrations does FAA §7 apply to?* As noted above, in the absence of agreement between the parties forbidding discovery, §7 would appear to provide affirmative authority to an arbitral tribunal to order at least some discovery. *See supra* pp. 833-34. What arbitrations and arbitrators enjoy the benefit of this grant of authority to order discovery? For example, is §7 applicable to an arbitration in London between two U.S. companies, in a dispute governed by English law? Note that §7 permits petitions for enforcement of arbitrators' subpoenas to "the United

States district court for the district in which such arbitrators, or a majority of them, are sitting." *See Thompson v. Zavin*, 607 F.Supp. 780 (C.D. Cal. 1984) (§7 "restricted to the district in which the arbitrators sit").

Does a tribunal have the authority, over the objection of one party, to move the place where it "sits" to somewhere other than the arbitral seat? Recall the discussion above at pp. 624, 638, concerning the tribunal's authority to hold hearings outside the arbitral seat for convenience. *See* Gorske, *An Arbitrator Looks at Expediting the Large, Complex Case*, 5 Ohio St. J. Disp. Resol. 381, 385 (1990) (describing how parties and arbitrators moved arbitration hearing temporarily to locale of unwilling third party, so that §7 discovery could be ordered).

9. *Power of arbitral tribunal to order discovery or disclosure under institutional arbitration rules.* An arbitral tribunal's power to order evidence-taking and/or discovery is defined in part by the parties' arbitration agreement and any applicable institutional rules. Consider whether the various institutional rules set forth above grant the arbitral tribunal the right to order discovery. Which rules do so and which do not? Do the rules impose any limits on the scope of discovery? On the manner and procedures of discovery? *See infra* pp. 836-37 for a more detailed discussion.

Compare the ICC Rules, the UNCITRAL Rules and the AAA Commercial Rules. Consider the following criticism (by a common law practitioner): "the [UNCITRAL] Rules do not constitute anything like an evenly balanced compromise between different jurisdictions, being heavily slanted towards continental practice, and do not empower the tribunal to order general discovery of relevant documents. Indeed, the only power that exists in this context is a very limited one of ordering discovery in relation to matters on which expert evidence may be called." Morgan, *Discovery in Arbitration*, 3(3) J. Int'l Arb. 9, 21-22 (1986). Is that criticism accurate?

Also read the IBA Rules. How do they compare with the institutional rules set forth above? Which rules permit a tribunal to order the broadest scope of discovery? Which rules, if any, would permit a tribunal to order U.S.-style discovery like that permitted by the Federal Rules of Civil Procedure? Which, if any, would forbid such action?

10. *Express provision in arbitration agreement concerning discovery ordered by arbitral tribunal.* In relatively rare cases, the parties will include a provision in their arbitration agreement dealing expressly with discovery. This most frequently will occur by the incorporation of the IBA Rules or some other preexisting set of rules. Alternatively, the parties can also draft their own provisions dealing with discovery for inclusion in the arbitration agreement. The following excerpts illustrate efforts by parties to deal with discovery contractually:

"The Arbitration hearing will be held in The Hague, Holland, except that, to the extent that the dispute pertains to the local market, business practices, or requires evidence primarily obtainable in the Licensed Territory [the USA], the parties authorize the arbitrators to conduct all or part of the proceedings in the Licensed Territory...." *Remy Amerique, Inc. v. Touzet Distrib., SARL*, 816 F.Supp. 213, 215 (S.D.N.Y. 1993).

"In order to resolve the disputes hereunder expeditiously and economically, the parties will confer and cooperate with each other on necessary and reasonable discovery, based on the types of discovery set forth in Rules 26-37 of the Federal Rules of Civil Procedure, but which shall be conducted in such a way as to limit the burdensomeness, delay, and expense of the conventional discovery processes." Baker & Stabile, *Arbitration of Antitrust Claims: Opportunities and Hazards for Corporate Counsel*, 48 Bus. Law. 395

(1993).

"In conducting the arbitration, each party agrees it will produce at the request of counsel for the other party, without objections other than those based on physical or legal impossibility or the attorney-client or a similar privilege recognized in the jurisdiction in which the arbitration is conducted: (a) all documents or classes of documents and physical objects in the responding party's control or to which it has access that the requesting party believes relevant to the just determination of the dispute, and (b) a statement of the expected testimony from any person on whose statements the responding party will rely, covering all points to which such person is expected to testify. The parties shall, in good faith, with the assistance and subject to the order of the arbitrator(s) if necessary, agree on procedures to permit such production to be conducted in a manner that enables access to the requested statements, documents and things that are relevant to the proceedings, and nevertheless avoids unnecessary expense or disruption to the business of the parties, for the primary purpose of assuring the orderly and prompt resolution of the dispute referred to arbitration. The arbitrators may draw adverse inferences from the failure of a party to produce tangible evidence or a statement from an expected witness." Ehrenhaft, *Discovery in International Arbitration Proceedings*, 9 Private Invs. Abroad 1 (2000).

What are the advantages and disadvantages of each provision?

11. *Authority of arbitrators under institutional arbitration rules to order disclosure or discovery.* Consider the various institutional rules excerpted at pp. 161-295 of the Documentary Supplement. What powers do they grant arbitrators to order the parties to provide disclosure or discovery to one another and/or the tribunal?

   (a) *Authority of arbitral tribunal under LCIA Rules.* Consider Articles 22(1)(iv) and (v) of the 2014 LCIA Rules. What powers do they provide to an LCIA arbitral tribunal to order the parties to disclose documents and other materials to one another? Is there any doubt about this?

   (b) *Authority of arbitral tribunal under ICC Rules.* Although Article 25 of the 2012 ICC Rules does not expressly permit arbitrators to order discovery, does an ICC tribunal have the implied authority to do so? The answer is generally in the affirmative. Consider paragraphs 25(1) and 25(5). For interpretations of earlier versions of the ICC Rules, *see* W. Craig, W. Park & J. Paulsson, *International Chamber of Commerce Arbitration* §26.01 (2d ed. 1990) (discussing 1988 ICC Rules: "This authority [to order production of documents] is implicit in the arbitrator's mandate under Article 14(1) ... to establish the facts 'by all appropriate means.'"); Hanotiau, *Document Production in International Arbitration: A Tentative Definition of "Best Practices,"* in ICC, *Document Production in International Arbitration* 113, 114 (2006) ("The [1998] ICC Rules ... permit the parties to request documents and provide the arbitral tribunal with the power to order production"). See also interpretations of the ICC Rules in *Mobil Oil*.

   (c) *Authority of arbitral tribunal under UNCITRAL Rules.* Consider Article 27(3) of the UNCITRAL Rules. What powers to order disclosure or discovery does it grant to arbitrators? What are the limits on this power? Compare it to the LCIA and ICDR Rules.

   (d) *Authority of arbitral tribunal under AAA and ICDR Rules.* Consider Rule 22 of the domestic 2013 AAA Rules and Articles 20(4) and 21 of the 2014 ICDR Rules. Are there any advantages in these rules as compared to the UNCITRAL, ICC, or LCIA

Rules? Do any grant the power to order pre-hearing discovery? For a decision under a prior version of the AAA Rules, which did not authorize pre-hearing discovery, *see Chiarella v. Viscount Indus. Co.*, 1993 WL 497967 (S.D.N.Y.) (interpreting AAA Commercial Rules to permit pre-hearing discovery: "Although this language does not specifically authorize an arbitrator to order pre-hearing discovery, it confers on arbitrators broad powers to ensure that evidence is presented at arbitration hearings in such a manner as to ensure that legal and factual issues are sufficiently developed. Plaintiff has cited no authority explicitly limiting the power of an arbitrator to order discovery under the AAA rules or to order the in camera inspection of documents.").

12. *Depositions in international arbitration.* A common feature of U.S. litigation is the deposition on oral examination. In U.S. practice, a deposition involves the oral questioning of a party or witness, under oath and with a verbatim transcript, by an attorney for a party. The party or witness is accompanied by his or her attorney, who has limited rights to object to particular questions. Depositions ordinarily take place well in advance of hearings and are not attended by the judge (or tribunal). The transcript of the deposition can, in certain circumstances, be used as evidence at subsequent hearings.

Depositions are not infrequently used in domestic U.S. arbitrations, but are much less common in international arbitration. In cases where U.S. counsel are involved, parties sometimes voluntarily agree to reciprocal depositions of the parties' officers and relevant employees. In international cases involving non-U.S. counsel, and particularly counsel from civil law jurisdictions, oral depositions are virtually unheard of. Is a tribunal's authority to order depositions, over a party's objections, any different from its authority to order document production? Why, as a practical matter, are arbitrators less willing to do so?

Consider *ICC Case No. 7170*. The practical impact of the order is almost identical to that of a U.S.-style deposition. Consider the various issues that needed to be resolved for this "civil law deposition" to proceed. Who would be permitted to examine—and cross-examine—the witness? What language would be used? On what topics could questions be asked? What if the witness refused to answer certain questions? What record would be kept of the deposition? Note that the deposition will occur outside the tribunal's presence. Is this appropriate?

What provisions do the IBA Rules make for depositions? What is an "Evidentiary Hearing"? Consider the various provisions of the Belgian Judicial Code, the SLPIL, the UNCITRAL Model Law, and the FAA. To what extent does each permit or forbid depositions? *See also* 2014 ICDR Rules, Art. 21(10).

13. *Depositions under §7 of FAA.* Section 7 of the FAA expressly permits witnesses to be summoned to testify before the tribunal (i.e., at an evidentiary hearing). There is no express provision in §7 for pre-hearing depositions, either before the tribunal or in its absence. Some U.S. courts have therefore concluded that §7 does not authorize arbitrators to order pre-hearing discovery. *COMSAT Corp. v. Nat'l Science Found.*, 190 F.3d 269, 275-76 (4th Cir. 1999); *Atmel Corp. v. LM Ericsson Telefon, AB*, 371 F.Supp.2d 402, 403 (S.D.N.Y. 2005). Other U.S. courts have upheld tribunal-ordered pre-hearing depositions. *Amgen, Inc. v. Kidney Ctr of Del. County*, 879 F.Supp. 878 (N.D. Ill. 1995) (FAA permits arbitrator to order third party discovery), *dismissed on appeal*, 101 F.3d 110 (7th Cir. 1996); *Stanton v. Paine Webber Jackson & Curtis, Inc.*,

685 F.Supp. 1241, 1242-43 (S.D. Fla. 1988) (a court may rely on §7 to uphold tribunal-ordered depositions).

14. *Possible obligation of arbitrators to order disclosure or discovery.* Suppose the parties' arbitration agreement requires that discovery be permitted, but the tribunal refused to order discovery (on the grounds it was too expensive and time-consuming). Is the tribunal's action a violation of its obligations? *See* UNCITRAL Model Law, Art. 19(1). What remedy does a party have for the tribunal's refusal? *See* UNCITRAL Model Law, Arts. 34(2)(a)(iv), 36(1)(a)(iv); New York Convention, Art. V(1)(d).

Suppose the parties' arbitration agreement did not address the question of disclosure, but that discovery was essential in a particular case to a party's opportunity to present its case. Would this violate the tribunal's obligations to conduct the arbitration fairly? *See supra* pp. 793-95 & *infra* pp. 1159-61, 1218-41; UNCITRAL Model Law, Art. 18. *See also Chevron Transp. Corp. v. Astro Vencedor Compania Naviera*, 300 F.Supp. 179 (S.D.N.Y. 1969) ("affirmative duty of arbitrators to insure that relevant documentary evidence in the hands of one party is fully and timely made available to the other side before the hearing is closed"). *Compare Judgment of 21 January 1997, Nu Swift plc v. White Knight I SA*, Mealey's Int'l Arb. Rep., at E-1 (Paris Cour d'appel) (rejecting proceedings to annul award on grounds that tribunal refused to order document discovery); *Hyman v. Pottberg's Executors*, 101 F.2d 262, 265 (2d Cir. 1939) ("It is at best very doubtful whether the failure to require the production of this evidence could be regarded as a refusal 'to hear evidence pertinent and material within §10(c)'"); *Asiatic Petroleum Corp. v. New England Petroleum*, 410 N.Y.S.2d 91 (N.Y. App. Div. 1978) ("It is the law that an award may not be vacated for [the tribunal's] refusal to enforce the subpoenas."). Are these responses too sweeping?

15. *Disclosure in ICSID investment arbitrations.* What authority does an arbitral tribunal have to order disclosure in an arbitration under the ICSID Convention? Consider Article 43, excerpted at p. 22 of the Documentary Supplement. Compare Article 43 to the ICC and UNCITRAL Rules. Does it provide more expressly for disclosure than such rules?

16. *Disclosure in inter-state arbitrations.* What authority does an arbitral tribunal have to order disclosure in an inter-state arbitration under the 1907 Hague Convention? Consider Articles 68 and 69, excerpted at p. 48 of the Documentary Supplement. *See also* ILC, *Memorandum on Arbitral Procedure, Prepared by the Secretariat*, U.N. Doc. A/CN.4/35, II Y.B. I.L.C. 157, 165, 173-74 (1950) (describing powers of arbitral tribunals to require additional documents and information from parties); ILC, *Draft on Arbitral Procedure Prepared by the International Law Commission at Its Fourth Session*, U.N. Doc. A/CN.4/59, Arts. 15(2), 15(3) (1952) ("(2) The parties shall co-operate with one another and with the tribunal in the production of evidence and shall comply with the measures ordered by the tribunal for this purpose ... (3) The tribunal shall have the power at any stage of the proceedings to call for such evidence as it may deem necessary").

Is there any reason an arbitral tribunal should not have the power to order disclosure in inter-state arbitrations? Isn't access to the relevant factual circumstances of the parties' dispute essential to a just decision? What reasons might argue against disclosure in inter-state arbitration? Consider Crawford, *Advocacy Before the International Court of Justice and Other International Tribunals in State-to-State Cases*, in R.

Bishop (ed.), *The Art of Advocacy in International Arbitration* 11, 35 (2004) ("In pure inter-state litigation, discovery is very unusual and the relatively few attempts that have been made by one state to get access to documents of the other have generally been ineffective.").

2. *Discovery Ordered by National Courts in Aid of Arbitration at Request of Tribunal or Party*

This section examines the circumstances in which an arbitral tribunal or a party itself may obtain discovery from a national court. As discussed in the materials excerpted below, §7 of the FAA, Article 27 of the UNCITRAL Model Law, and Article 184 of the SLPIL all permit arbitrators or parties to an international arbitration to obtain judicial assistance in taking evidence for use in the arbitration. The materials excerpted below also discuss the availability of U.S. judicial assistance under 28 U.S.C. §1782 in international arbitrations.

28 UNITED STATES CODE §1782

Assistance to foreign and international tribunals and to litigants before such tribunals

(a) The district court of the district in which a person resides or is found may order him to give his testimony or statement or to produce a document or other thing for use in a proceeding in a foreign or international tribunal. The order may be made pursuant to a letter rogatory issued, or request made, by a foreign or international tribunal or upon the application of any interested person and may direct that the testimony or statement be given, or the document or other thing be produced, before a person appointed by the court. By virtue of his appointment, the person appointed has power to administer any necessary oath and take the testimony or statement. The order may prescribe the practice and procedure, which may be in whole or part the practice and procedure of the foreign country or the international tribunal, for taking the testimony or statement or producing the document or other thing.... A person may not be compelled to give his testimony or statement or to produce a document or other thing in violation of any legally applicable privilege.

OCEANIC TRANSP. CORP. OF MONROVIA v. ALCOA STEAMSHIP CO.
129 F.Supp. 160 (S.D.N.Y. 1954)

CLANCY, District Judge. This motion to punish for contempt a subpoenaed witness that failed to respond is denied. The witness conveyed to the parties in writing its informed opinion that unless directed by the Court it would not answer the subpoena. [Section 7 of the FAA] provides that in such case the District Court may compel the attendance of the witness if it be "a proper case" to justify the issuance of the subpoena. The Court must then rule, among other things, whether or not the subpoenaed material would be material as evidence. The Court is unable to recognize why the matter subpoenaed from the protesting witness is or can be material or even relevant evidence in this case. It was the plaintiff's task to establish its materiality. I say this even though it appears in the papers that the request for a subpoena to issue was argued before the arbitrators and it is apparently their judgment that some evidence, material to the case before them, would be supplied. However great a respect we owe the arbitrators, it is a fact that when the statute imposed upon the District Court the duty to determine whether or not to compel the attendance of a witness and his production of papers, it imposed upon the Court the duty to determine whether or not the proposed evidence is material. [The Court rejected the tribunal's conclusion that the requested items were material.] ...

It follows from all this that the motion to punish for contempt is denied. And, it also follows from what has been said that this is not a proper case for the subpoena's issuance. The motion to vacate is therefore granted....

COMMERCIAL SOLVENTS CORP. v. LA. LIQUID FERTILIZER CO.
20 F.R.D. 359 (S.D.N.Y. 1957)

BICKS, District Judge. This motion was brought on by Commercial Solvents Corporation ("petitioner") to vacate ... an ex parte order issued,[16] and a notice of taking certain depositions.... Pursuant to a provision in a written contract between the parties evidencing a transaction involving commerce to settle by arbitration controversies thereafter arising out of such contract or transaction,[17] petitioner mailed to Louisiana Liquid Fertilizer Co., Inc. ("respondent"), a demand for arbitration.... Respondent submitted an answering statement in accordance with the rules of the [AAA].... Then followed the respondent's notice of taking the depositions of five employees of petitioner in the State of Louisiana, pursuant to the Federal Rules of Civil Procedure.

Respondent's position is that it is essential that it have this means of obtaining information allegedly peculiarly within the knowledge of employees of petitioner residing in Louisiana in order adequately to prepare for the hearing to be held before the arbitrators. It is argued that since the [FAA] does not provide a procedure for depositions and discovery, Rule 81(a)(3) of the Federal Rules of Civil Procedure,[18] fills the void and authorizes application of the federal discovery rules for the purposes for which they are here sought to be invoked.... At this stage, in the instant matter, the parties have submitted to arbitration, there is no proceeding pending in another court relating to the matter submitted to arbitration, and there has been no occasion to initiate any of the proceedings expressly authorized in the Act. Rule 81(a)(3), it is to be noted, authorizes the application of the Federal Rules "in proceedings under Title 9, U.S.C." By its attempted invocation of that Rule under the present circumstances, respondent has failed to note the distinction between "matters of procedure" and "proceedings" as those terms are employed in the Rule. Application of the federal rules in proceedings under the [FAA] to supply "matters of procedure" not provided for therein, is authorized. Rule 81(a)(3) comes into play, however, only in proceedings under the Act. The instant matter involves none.

16. The order recites: "Ordered that the Clerk of this Court be and he hereby is directed to accept for filing notices for the taking of depositions herein on behalf of Louisiana Liquid Fertilizer Company, Inc."

17. The arbitration provision in the contract reads:

"19. Any controversy of claim arising out of or relating to this agreement, or a breach thereof, shall be settled by arbitration in New York, New York, in accordance with the Commercial Arbitration Rules, then obtaining, of the [AAA], and judgment upon the award rendered may be entered in any court having jurisdiction thereof."

18. Insofar as here material Rule 81(a)(3) provides as follows: "In proceedings under Title 9, U.S.C., relating to arbitration ... these rules apply ... to the extent that matters of procedure are not provided for in [that statute]...."

Respondent urges that it is entitled to avail itself of the discovery rules because, save for the agreement to arbitrate, the federal courts would have jurisdiction of the subject matter of a suit arising out of the controversy between the parties and in such a suit the federal discovery rules would obtain. The argument contains its own answer. By voluntarily becoming a party to a contract in which arbitration was the agreed mode for settling disputes thereunder respondent chose to avail itself of procedures peculiar to the arbitral process rather than those used in judicial determinations.... Arbitration may well have advantages[19] but where the converse results a party having chosen to arbitrate cannot then vacillate and successfully urge a preference for a unique combination of litigation and arbitration. The proposition that "[a]rbitration is merely a form of trial, to be adopted in the action itself, in place of the trial at common law ...," *Murray Oil Prod. Co. v. Mitsui & Co.*, 146 F.2d 381, 383 (2d Cir. 1944), which stated thus broadly might indicate the propriety of pre-hearing discovery in arbitration, was rejected by the Supreme Court in *Bernhardt v. Polygraphic Co.*, 350 U.S. 198 (1956) ...: "the remedy by arbitration, whatever its merits or shortcomings, substantially affects the cause of action.... The nature of the tribunal where suits are tried is an important part of the parcel of rights behind a cause of action. The change from a court of law to an arbitration panel may make a radical difference in ultimate result."

The fundamental differences between the fact-finding process of a judicial tribunal and those of a panel of arbitrators demonstrate the need of pretrial discovery in the one and its superfluity and utter incompatibility in the other.... As Judge Learned Hand said in *Am. Almond Products Co. v. Consolidated Pecan Sales*, 144 F.2d 448, 451 (2d Cir. 1944): "Arbitration may or may not be a desirable substitute for trials in courts; as to that the parties must decide in each instance. But when they have adopted it, they must be content with its informalities; they may not hedge it about with those procedural limitations which it is precisely its purpose to avoid. They must content themselves with looser approximations to the enforcement of their rights than those that the law accords them, when they resort to its machinery."

For matters of procedure relating to the hearings before the arbitrators we refer not to the [Federal] Rules of Civil Procedure but to the Commercial Arbitration Rules of the [AAA] which the parties agreed should control. Section 30 of those rules provides: "The parties may offer such evidence as they desire and shall produce such additional evidence as the Arbitrator may deem necessary to an understanding and determination of the dispute." While the arbitrators could not perhaps compel the attendance of the witnesses whose depositions are sought to be taken because service of subpoenas could not be made upon them within the Southern District of New York or within 100 miles of the place the hearing is to be held, 9 U.S.C. §7; Rule 45(e)(1), Fed. R. Civ. P., they may be relied on to draw such inferences from the failure of the petitioner to produce them as they in their unreviewable judgment think the circumstances justify. Mere suggestion as to the testi-

---

19. Overenthusiastic sponsors of the method, however, have had ample warning that it should be resorted to with care: "The more enthusiastic of those sponsors have thought of arbitration as a universal panacea. We doubt whether it will cure corns or bring general beatitude. Few panaceas work as well as advertised." *Kulukundis Shipping Co. v. Amtorg Trading Corp.*, 126 F.2d 978, 987 n.32 (2d Cir. 1942). "Arbitration sometimes involves perils that even surpass the 'perils of the seas.'" *In re Canadian Gulf Line, Ltd*, 2 Cir., 1938, 98 F.2d 711, 714.

mony these witnesses would give if available at the hearing would in an arbitration hearing probably cast the onus upon the petitioner to negative the unsupported assertion that if called their testimony would be unfavorable to its position. Fortunately or otherwise, depending on one's views as to the soundness of the broad claims made by arbitration enthusiasts, almost "anything goes" before arbitrators.

Respondent's reliance upon cases decided by the New York Supreme Court under the state arbitration statute is misplaced. Firstly, they depend on express statutory authority. *See Interocean Mercantile Corp. v. Buell*, 201 N.Y.S. 753 (App. Div. 1923); New York Civil Practice Act, §§1459 and 308. Further, notwithstanding such authority, the state court will not grant examinations before trial in arbitration proceedings except under extraordinary circumstances. *See In re Schwartz*, 217 N.Y.S. 233 (N.Y. Sup. Ct. 1925); *In re Katz*, 160 N.Y.S.2d 159 (App. Div. 1957).... Reason and authority compel that in federal courts pre-hearing examinations under court aegis in matters pending before arbitration tribunals are unwarranted.

KOCH FUEL INTERNATIONAL INC. v. M/V SOUTH STAR
118 F.R.D. 318 (E.D.N.Y. 1987)

DEARIE, District Judge. This admiralty claim ... requires the Court to revisit an issue that has attracted some controversy: whether discovery can be had on the subject matter of a dispute that is to be arbitrated. For the reasons stated below, the Court finds that this case presents the exceptional circumstances warranting the limited discovery now authorized.

On December 28, 1987, the plaintiff applied to this Court for an order of arrest and an order allowing expedited discovery of the defendant ship. This Court signed an order ... granting the relief requested based on plaintiff's representations that the defendant ship, a foreign vessel, was preparing to leave the local port and that the arrest and discovery were necessary to secure its claim and also to substantiate the allegations in its complaint that the defendants had converted a portion of the plaintiff's cargo of fuel oil....

On December 29, 1987, attorneys for both parties appeared before this Court pursuant to an application by defendant M/V SOUTH STAR to vacate the order signed the previous day. At that conference the defendant alleged that the contract between the parties provided for the resolution of any dispute through arbitration in London under English law. The defendant did agree, however, to certain limited discovery notwithstanding the existence of the arbitration agreement. Specifically, defendant agreed to produce the vessel's records and to permit an inspection of the vessel by plaintiff's authorized surveyors. Defendant strenuously objected, however, to plaintiff's application to take brief depositions of a limited number of crew members. Defendant argues that depositions should not be allowed because they are not utilized under English law in the arbitration. Indeed, defendant argues that depositions are "anathema" to this method of dispute resolution in England....

Plaintiff, on the other hand, insists that in this setting the records and inspection are insufficient and that the depositions of a small group of those with knowledge concerning the shipment is necessary to prove its claims. More specifically, plaintiff argues that the testimony of the various crew members might well provide some of the most important evidence in this dispute, and that if the depositions are not taken now, testimony of these individuals will never be had—in arbitration or otherwise. Plaintiff alleges that the deposition request is not a mere fishing expedition in search of any relevant facts. Rather, plaintiff points out, it has already obtained certain information from certain crew members supporting its position. In addition, plaintiff represents that it has evidence of attempts to frustrate a surveyor's efforts to calculate the extent of the losses by tampering with certain internal systems of the vessel. These matters, plaintiff urges, are the matters to be pursued at deposition. Finally, plaintiff claims the depositions would be completed in one day, thus allowing for the release of the merchant vessel pursuant to an agreement of the parties.

The issue before the Court, then, is whether limited discovery in the form of the depositions should be allowed where the parties have agreed to arbitrate their dispute and where the testimony sought is that of crew members preparing to depart the country who will thus most likely be unavailable to provide testimony in this dispute in the future.... [I]t is not without some significance to note that defendant's counsel have provided no assurances that any of the crew members will be made available to plaintiff in the future.

Although discovery on the subject matter of a dispute to be arbitrated generally has been denied, *Commercial Solvents Corp. v. Louisiana Liquid Fertilizer Co.*, 20 F.R.D. 359 (S.D.N.Y. 1957), courts have recognized that discovery may be appropriate in exceptional circumstances. *See, e.g., E.C. Ernst, Inc. v. Potlatch Corp.*, 462 F.Supp. 694, 695 n.1 (S.D.N.Y. 1978); *Bergen Shipping Co. v. Japan Marine Services, Ltd*, 386 F.Supp. 430, 435 n.8 (S.D.N.Y. 1974); *Ferro Union Corp. v. SS Ionic Coast*, 43 F.R.D. 11 (S.D. Tex. 1967). One of the "exceptional circumstances" in which discovery has been deemed proper is where a vessel with crew members possessing particular knowledge of the dispute is about to leave port. *See e.g., Bergen Shipping Co.*, 386 F.Supp. at 435 n.8; *Ferro Union Corp.*, [43 F.R.D. at] at 14. This Court believes that the facts here meet the "exceptional circumstances" test.

Although this case may be routine in the sense that it represents a relatively garden variety commercial dispute as defendant argues, for discovery purposes the circumstances are hardly routine. The only persons possessing first-hand knowledge of the facts recited and alleged in plaintiff's verified complaint are the crewmen and executive officers of the M/V SOUTH STAR, none of whom is an American citizen and all of whom will presumably be unavailable once the ship leaves the United States. Here, plaintiff seeks only minimal deposition discovery. In the words of the *Ferro Union* court, "this court cannot conceive how defendants can be harmed by allowing the depositions to proceed...." 43 F.R.D. at 14.

Defendant's argument that the relevant facts are discoverable through alternative methods, such as inspection by authorized surveyors, is not convincing. Although the physical and documentary evidence may show a diversion of the cargo, it may not show with certainty the theft through usage that is alleged in the complaint. Defendant's contention that deposition testimony is improper here because it is not used under English arbitration is similarly unconvincing.

The Court is well aware of the strong federal policy favoring arbitration. The Court is also aware that arbitration should not generally be encumbered by protracted discovery or other procedural mechanisms. *See Commercial Solvents Corp.*, 20 F.R.D. at 361. However, in deferring to the arbitration forum in accordance with the parties' agreement, the Court should not blindfold the arbitrators and frustrate, perhaps irreparably, the fact-finding process by failing to afford the parties a brief opportunity to preserve evanescent evidence. This Court finds applicable the cogent reasoning of the *Ferro Union* court in a case strikingly similar to the one at bar:

"[T]o allow [the deposition discovery] to proceed would, it seems to this court, be an aid to the ultimate arbitration proceedings. This decision does not mean that the arbitrators who might be ultimately appointed to determine this matter should or should not consider the results of the discovery here allowed. This decision does mean, however, that potentially valuable information will be available for the arbitrators to consider if they so desire. To deny discovery here could well mean that the information sought would never be available to the arbitrators or, if available, only at great expense." 43 F.R.D. at 14.

In sum, defendant's request to vacate the order allowing discovery is denied. Plaintiff shall be permitted a physical inspection of the ship and appropriate access to its records pursuant to the agreement between the parties. In addition, plaintiff shall be permitted the brief depositions of the five individuals requested.

IN RE ARBITRATION IN LONDON, ENGLAND BETWEEN NORFOLK SOUTHERN CORP. ET AL. & ACE BERMUDA LTD
2009 U.S. Dist. LEXIS 49827 (N.D. Ill.)

BUCKLO, District Judge. Before me is a motion by Norfolk Southern Corporation, Norfolk Southern Railway Company, and General Security Insurance Company (collectively, "movants") seeking an order to require Scott Carey, former counsel to ACE Bermuda Ltd ("ACE"), to appear for a deposition in Chicago so that his testimony may be used in connection with an ongoing arbitration in London, England. Movants request this relief under 28 U.S.C. §1782.... I deny their motion.

The parties' underlying dispute relates to insurance coverage for losses incurred in connection with a train derailment in Graniteville, South Carolina. Mr. Carey represented certain insurance and reinsurance companies, including ACE, and movants assert that he has personal knowledge of facts relevant to the parties' dispute. The London arbitration is being conducted pursuant to arbitration provisions in a reinsurance policy issued by ACE, in which General Security Insurance Company is the "Named Entity" and Norfolk Southern Corporation is the "Named Insured." Movants assert that §1782 authorizes me to order Mr. Carey to provide deposition testimony for use in the London arbitration, and that I should exercise my statutory discretion to do so. Mr. Carey opposes the motion, arguing that the statute does not authorize me to grant the relief movants seek, and that even if it does, I should decline to exercise my discretion to compel his deposition.... Mr. Carey's opposition to the motion focuses on the statutory meaning of the phrase "a foreign or international tribunal."

As discussed in the leading [U.S.] Supreme Court case interpreting §1782, *Intel Corp. v. Advanced Micro Devices, Inc.*, 542 U.S. 241 (2004), the statute "is the product of congressional efforts, over the span of nearly 150 years, to provide federal-court assistance in gathering evidence for use in foreign tribunals." ... The scope of authorized assistance was broadened in 1948 with the passage of legislation that became §1782. The new statute authorized courts to assist in evidence-gathering in connection with "any civil action" pending in a "court in a foreign country...." The statute was further broadened the following year, when Congress replaced the phrase "civil action" with the phrase "judicial proceeding." "[P]rompted by the growth of international commerce," §1782 was completely revised in 1964. The 1964 revisions deleted the phrase "in any judicial proceeding pending in any court in a foreign country," replacing it with the text that appears in the statute's current form: "in a proceeding in a foreign or international tribunal." In *Intel*, the Court clarified that this phrase encompassed "administrative and quasi-judicial proceedings" such as those at issue in that case, where the party asserting §1782 sought to obtain evidence to support a complaint filed in the Directorate-General for Competition ("DG Competition") of the Commission of the [then-EC].

The parties agree that *Intel* does not expressly resolve whether private arbitrations fall within the scope of §1782. Relying on precedent from the Second and Fifth Circuits ..., however, Mr. Carey argues that "only governmental entities, such as administrative or investigative courts, acting as state instrumentalities or with the authority of the state" fall within the purview of §1782.... This is, indeed, what the Second and Fifth Circuits concluded in *Nat'l Broadcasting Co. v. Bear Stearns & Co.*, 165 F.3d 184, 189 (2d Cir. 1999) and *Republic of Kazakhstan v. Biedermann Int'l*, 168 F.3d 880 (5th Cir. 1999) ("[t]here is no contemporaneous evidence that Congress contemplated extending §1782 to the then-novel arena of international commercial arbitration."). Of course, both of these cases predate *Intel*, and movants point out that the majority of courts to have considered, post-*Intel*, whether private arbitral tribunals fall within the ambit of §1782 have concluded that they do.... A minority of courts, however, have held that private arbitrations remain outside the scope of the statute....

Having reviewed the cited cases and closely considered the Court's analysis in *Intel*, I conclude that the arbitration at issue in this case is outside the scope of §1782. It is true, as some courts have noted, that the *Intel* Court both "emphasized Congress's intent to expand the applicable scope of §1782(a)," [*In re Babcock Borsig AG*, 583 F.Supp.2d 233, 240 (D. Mass. 2008)], and favorably quoted, albeit in dictum, a definition of the statutory term "tribunal" that expressly includes "arbitral tribunals." *Id.*, citing *Intel*, 542 U.S. at 258 ("'[t]he term "tribunal" ... includes investigating magistrates, administrative and arbitral tribunals, and quasi-judicial agencies, as well as conventional civil, commercial, criminal, and administrative courts,'" (quoting Smit, *International Litigation under the United States Code*, 65 Colum. L. Rev. 1015, 1026 n.71 (1965))). Nevertheless, although the *Intel* Court acknowledged the ways in which Congress has progressively broadened the scope §1782, it stopped short of declaring that any foreign body exercising adjudicatory power falls within the purview of the statute. Indeed, the ellipses in the Court's citation to Smit (without which Smit's definition reads, "[t]he term 'tribunal' *embraces all bodies exercising adjudicatory powers*, and includes investigating magistrates, administrative and arbitral tribunals, and quasi-judicial agencies, as well as conventional civil, commercial, criminal, and administrative courts" (emphasis added)), suggest that the Court was not willing to embrace the full breadth of Smit's definition. Moreover, as the analysis in *In re Matter of the Application of Oxus Gold PLC*[, 2006 WL 2927615 (D.N.J.),] illustrates, a reasoned distinction can be made between arbitrations such as those conducted by UNCITRAL, "a body operating under the United Nations and established by its member states," and purely private arbitrations established by private contract. *Id.* at *6. While the private arbitral tribunal at issue here likely falls within the scope of "all bodies exercising adjudicatory powers," the *Intel* Court's language did not endorse such a broad definition of "tribunal." Accordingly, I interpret the *Intel* Court's reference to "arbitral tribunals" as including state-sponsored arbitral bodies but excluding purely private arbitrations. *See also Kazakhstan*, 168 F.3d at 882 ("References in the United States Code to 'arbitral tribunals' almost uniformly concern an adjunct of a foreign government or international agency.") Further support for this interpretation is the *Intel* Court's discussion of the role that DG Competition plays in enforcing European law, and the relationship of DG Competition to the major European judicial authorities, the Court of First Instance and the European Court of Justice. The Court explained that DG Competition's "overriding" responsibility is to conduct investigations, either sua sponte or pursuant to a complaint, into alleged violations of [EU] competition laws. *Intel*, 542 U.S. at 254....

At several points in its analysis, the *Intel* Court emphasized the relevance of the ultimate reviewability of DG Competition's decisions by European courts to its conclusion that DG Competition itself fell within the purview of §1782. *Id.* at 255 ("the statute authorizes, but does not require, a federal district court to provide assistance to a complainant in a [EC] proceeding that leads to a dispositive ruling, *i.e.*, a final administrative action both re-sponsive to the complaint *and reviewable in court*." (emphasis added)), 259 ("we hold that §1782(a) requires only that a dispositive ruling by the Commission, *reviewable by the European courts*, be within reasonable contemplation.") (Emphasis added.) By contrast, private arbitrations are generally considered alternatives to, rather than precursors to, formal litigation. Indeed, it is common for arbitration provisions in private contracts to include a waiver of review by courts. Indeed, that is the case here. The section of ACE's reinsurance policy captioned "ARBITRATION" states that the decision of the "Board" (as previously defined) is final and binding on the parties, and that "Such decision shall be a complete defense to any attempted appeal or litigation of such decision in the absence of fraud or collusion. Without limiting the foregoing, the parties waive any right to appeal to, and/or seek collateral review of the decision of the Board of Arbitration by any court or other body to the fullest extent permitted by applicable law." It is clear from this text that the very narrow circumstances in which the Board's decisions may be subject to review does not allow for judicial review of the merits of the parties' dispute. Accordingly, the "arbitral tribunal" at issue here does not fall within the definition the Supreme Court em-braced in its *Intel* dictum. For the foregoing reasons, ... I am without authority to order the relief movants seek....

NOTES

1. *Arbitrator's ability under national law to obtain judicial assistance from courts.* Consider Article 27 of the UNCITRAL Model Law and Article 184 of the SLPIL, excerpted at pp. 92 & 159 of the Documentary Supplement. Also consider Article 1708 of the Belgian Judicial Code and former Article 288(4) of the Guatemalan Code, excerpted above at pp. 779-80. How does each statute define an arbitrator's power to obtain judicial assistance in aid of its discovery orders? What is the scope of the ju-dicial assistance that is available to the tribunal under each statute? Under each statute, is an arbitrator entitled to apply to courts located outside the place where the arbitra-tion is seated for assistance in taking evidence? To the courts of the arbitral seat? What are the applicable procedures? Can the parties agree to exclude the tribunal's evi-dence-taking power?

2. *Inapplicability of local rules of judicial procedure to permit court-ordered discovery in aid of international arbitration proceedings.* In most instances, local rules of judi-cial procedure are not applicable either in arbitral proceedings, *see supra* pp. 786, 831-32, or to permit court-ordered discovery in aid of arbitral proceedings. Thus, lower U.S. courts have uniformly held that Rule 81(a)(3) does not make the Federal Rules of Civil Procedure available for court-ordered discovery in aid of arbitration proceedings, but instead deals only with the Rules' applicability in judicial proceed-ings to compel, or in aid of, arbitration, or to enforce or vacate an arbitral award. In

addition to *Commercial Solvents*, *see Penn Tanker Co. v. C.H.Z. Rolimpex Warszawa*, 199 F.Supp. 716 (S.D.N.Y. 1961); *Foremost Yarn Mills, Inc. v. Rose Mills, Inc.*, 25 F.R.D. 9 (E.D. Pa. 1960). *Compare Complaint of Koala Shipping & Trading Inc.*, 587 F.Supp. 140, 143 (S.D.N.Y. 1984).

3. *Section 7 of FAA grants arbitral tribunal power to seek court-ordered discovery*. As we have seen, §7 of the FAA grants an arbitral tribunal authority to order testimony and document production in certain circumstances. *See supra* pp. 833-35. If those orders are not complied with, §7 authorizes the tribunal to seek judicial assistance in compelling compliance. Compare the rights of arbitrators to seek judicial assistance under other national laws, excerpted above, such as the UNCITRAL Model Law, the SLPIL, the Belgian Judicial Code and the (now repealed) Guatemalan Code of Civil and Commercial Procedure. Which approach is most desirable? *Should* arbitrators have the power, absent express agreement by the parties, to seek judicially-ordered discovery?

4. *No interlocutory judicial review of arbitral tribunal's discovery rulings in national courts*. As discussed above, if an arbitral tribunal refuses to order disclosure requested by a party, the tribunal's ruling cannot be the subject of interlocutory judicial review. *See supra* pp. 797-810. Suppose an arbitral tribunal concludes that it is appropriate to seek judicial assistance in obtaining disclosure, and an application is made to courts in the arbitral seat under Article 27 of the Model Law or Article 184 of the SLPIL. Will judicial consideration of the tribunal's authority to order the requested disclosure occur in the course of considering the tribunal's request?

If a tribunal does not seek judicial assistance under §7 of the FAA, U.S. courts have usually refused to intervene in an ongoing arbitration because of alleged improprieties or deficiencies in the discovery orders of the tribunal. Consider how this issue is addressed in both *Stanton* and *Mobil Oil*. In contrast, as described below, some lower courts have refused to enforce discovery orders by tribunals under §7 of the FAA on the grounds that they exceeded the scope of that provision. *See supra* pp. 833-34.

5. *General inability of parties to arbitration to seek court-ordered evidence-taking or disclosure from adverse parties*. To what extent may parties to an arbitration, as distinguished from the arbitral tribunal, seek judicial assistance in evidence-taking or disclosure?

(a) *Parties' inability under UNCITRAL Model Law to seek court-ordered discovery*. Consider again Article 27 of the Model Law and Article 184 of the SLPIL. Do these provisions permit parties to an arbitration to seek judicial assistance in evidence-taking or disclosure?

(b) *Parties' general inability to seek court-ordered discovery under FAA §7*. Why didn't the courts in *Commercial Solvents* and *M/V South Star* rely on §7 of the FAA? Note that §7 permits the arbitral tribunal to order discovery, not the parties themselves. Lower courts have almost uniformly held, as a matter of federal law, that court-ordered discovery at a party's request, for use in an arbitration, is ordinarily improper. *E.g., Burton v. Bush*, 614 F.2d 389 (4th Cir. 1980) ("While an arbitration panel may subpoena documents or witnesses, the litigating parties have no comparable privilege."); *Hires Parts Serv., Inc. v. NCR Corp.*, 859 F.Supp. 319 (N.D. Ind. 1994) (staying district court discovery pending arbitration: "permitting discovery on two levels, district court level and arbitration level, is a great waste of resources and frustrates the basic purpose of [the FAA]"). Why is this distinction drawn in §7? What policies does it serve?

Consider the rationale of *Commercial Solvents* in refusing to order discovery requested by a party to a pending arbitration. Why shouldn't a national court order such discovery? *Commercial Solvents* cites two factors in denying a party's request for court-ordered discovery: (a) the risk of judicial interference in the arbitral process; and (b) the fact that, in agreeing to arbitrate, parties impliedly agree to forego the benefits and avoid the costs of judicial discovery. Are these sufficient reasons for preventing access to the full truth?

6. *Court-ordered discovery under FAA §7 in aid of arbitration at request of party in "exceptional circumstances."* Consider the opinion in *South Star*. Is the result wise? Is the objective of avoiding judicial interference in the arbitral process threatened by the "exceptional circumstances" rule recognized in *South Star*? How exceptional were the circumstances in *South Star*? Note that the underlying dispute involved fraud claims.

Most U.S. courts have, as a matter of federal law, permitted discovery in aid of arbitration only in limited cases involving something akin to "exceptional circumstances." *See, e.g., Ferro Union Corp. v. S.S. Ionic Coast*, 43 F.R.D. 11 (S.D. Tex. 1967) (depositions of sailors about to leave jurisdiction; "To deny discovery here could well mean that the information sought would never be available to the arbitrators or, if available, only at great expense."); *Bergen Shipping Co. v. Japan Marine Serv., Ltd*, 386 F.Supp. 430 (S.D.N.Y. 1974) (vessel about to leave jurisdiction); *Vespe Contracting Co. v. Anvan Corp.*, 399 F.Supp. 516, 522 (E.D. Pa. 1975) (construction work would destroy evidence).

In order to satisfy the "exceptional circumstances" exception to §7, U.S. courts have generally required a fairly compelling demonstration of need for particular evidence, that otherwise will likely be unavailable, in circumstances in which the arbitral tribunal itself is not constituted or is otherwise unable to take or safeguard the evidence. *See, e.g., Levin v. Ripple Twist Mills, Inc.*, 416 F.Supp. 876, 881-82 (E.D. Pa. 1976); *Miss. Power Co. v. Peabody Coal Co.*, 69 F.R.D. 558, 566-68 (S.D. Miss. 1976); *Vespe Contracting Co. v. Anvan Corp.*, 399 F.Supp. 516, 522 (E.D. Pa. 1975) (arbitral tribunal not constituted and evidence was "disappearing" as construction work progressed). Can court-ordered discovery in exceptional circumstances be viewed as a form of court-ordered provisional relief in aid of arbitration? *See infra* pp. 904-32. If so, does that warrant judicial involvement, at the request of a party, in ordering disclosure?

A few U.S. courts have found what appear to be fairly routine requests for pre-arbitration discovery to be sufficiently "exceptional" to grant relief. These decisions have typically emphasized the absence of any delay to the arbitral process resulting from court-ordered discovery. *See, e.g., Local 66 v. Leona Lee Corp.*, 434 F.2d 192 (5th Cir. 1970) (apparently not requiring any showing of exceptional circumstance); *Bigge Crane & Rigging Co. v. Docutel Corp.*, 371 F.Supp. 240 (E.D.N.Y. 1973) (relying on size of claim, minimal cost of court-ordered discovery, and absence of any showing that arbitration would be delayed). Is this application of §7 of the FAA appropriate?

7. *Court-ordered discovery under FAA §7 in aid of foreign arbitration.* In *South Star*, the court ordered discovery in aid of a foreign arbitration (seated in England). Is it ap-

propriate for a U.S. court to order discovery in aid of foreign arbitrations conducted outside the United States? Recall that under §7, an arbitrator can only obtain judicial assistance in the district where he or she "sits." Is it relevant to the availability of U.S. court-ordered discovery in aid of a foreign arbitration that comparable discovery would not be available under the foreign procedural law of the arbitration? If the foreign procedural law does not permit court-ordered discovery at a party's request, doesn't the *South Star* result threaten to interfere both with the parties' expectations and the conduct of the arbitration under the (foreign) curial law? Suppose that the vessel owner in *South Star* was guilty of fraud?

8. *Availability of 28 U.S.C. §1782 for obtaining discovery in aid of arbitration.* Consider §1782. How might it be used in an international arbitration?

   (a) *Is an international commercial arbitral tribunal a "tribunal" under §1782?* What is a "foreign or international tribunal" under §1782? Why wouldn't an ICC-appointed or AAA-appointed tribunal qualify as an "international tribunal"? An UNCITRAL-appointed tribunal?

   Early U.S. decisions addressing this issue were divided. *Compare In re Application of Medway Power Ltd*, 985 F.Supp. 402 (S.D.N.Y. 1997) (international commercial arbitration tribunal not "tribunal" under §1782); *In re Application of the Repub. of Kazakhstan*, 168 F.3d 880 (5th Cir. 1999) (same) *with In re Application of Technostroyexport*, 853 F.Supp. 695, 697 (S.D.N.Y. 1994) ("arbitrator or arbitration panel is a 'tribunal' under §1782"). *See also In re Trygg-Hansa Ins. Co.*, 1995 WL 505339 (E.D. La.) (apparently treating party to foreign arbitration as "interested party" for purposes of §1782).

   Consider the analysis of §1782 in *Norfolk Southern* and in particular its interpretation of the phrase "tribunal." It is, of course, clear that the phrase "tribunal" is widely considered as encompassing commercial arbitration tribunals. See, for example, the ICC, LCIA and 2010 UNCITRAL Rules. Why is it that the *Norfolk Southern* court concludes that the term "tribunal" in §1782 does not include these tribunals? What do you make of the argument that an arbitral tribunal is not a "tribunal" because its awards are not subject to appreciable judicial review?

   Note the court's explanation that "the analysis in … *Oxus Gold plc* illustrates [that] a reasoned distinction can be made between arbitrations such as those conducted by UNCITRAL, 'a body operating under the United Nations and established by its member states,' and purely private arbitrations established by private contract." Does this make any sense? How is it that an arbitral tribunal constituted under the UNCITRAL Rules—which have force solely by being incorporated into the parties' "private" agreement to arbitrate, *supra* pp. 72-74—is different from a "private arbitration[] established by private contract"? More importantly, don't both tribunals function within the international treaty framework of the New York Convention—which, unlike the UNCITRAL Rules, does have the force of public law?

   (b) *Is an investment tribunal a "tribunal" under §1782?* Is an investment tribunal constituted under the ICSID Convention or a BIT a "tribunal" for purposes of §1782? Note that *In re Oxus Gold plc*, 2007 WL 1037387 (D.N.J.) involved a BIT arbitration and that the court suggested in dicta that a commercial arbitral tribunal would be treated differently. Can one treat arbitral tribunals constituted under BITs as different types of "tribunals" than arbitral tribunals constituted purely by private agreement? Would this make much sense, given the purposes of §1782?

(c) *Intel Corp. v. Advanced Micro Devices.* The U.S. Supreme Court's 2004 decision in *Intel Corp.* adopted an expansive view of §1782, holding that the provision extended to "administrative and quasi-judicial proceedings abroad," including specifically competition law investigations of the European Commission. *Intel Corp.*, 542 U.S. at 258. As the decision in *Norfolk Southern* illustrates, the same rationale has been extended by some lower courts to apply §1782 to foreign arbitral tribunals in commercial arbitrations. *In re Application of Babcock Borsig AG*, 583 F.Supp.2d 233 (D. Mass. 2008); *Comisión Ejecutiva v. Nejapa Power Co.*, LLC, 2008 WL 4809035 (D. Del.); *In re Roz Trading Ltd*, 469 F.Supp.2d 1221 (N.D. Ga. 2006) (arbitral tribunal under VIAC Rules is "tribunal" for purposes of §1782).

As *Norfolk Southern* also indicates, other U.S. courts have reached contrary conclusions, holding or suggesting that a commercial arbitral tribunal would not be a "tribunal" for purposes of §1782. *El Paso Corp. v. La Comisión Ejecutiva*, No. 08-20771 (5th Cir. Aug. 6, 2009) (UNCITRAL commercial arbitral tribunal not "tribunal" under §1782).

(d) *How should §1782 be interpreted?* Does the *Norfolk Southern* conclusion serve the purposes of Congress? Of international commercial arbitration? What policy grounds does the court cite in support of its holding? What risk is there that arbitral proceedings would become less efficient if §1782 applied to international arbitrations? Note that *Norfolk Southern* involved an application for discovery by a party to arbitral proceedings, rather than by an arbitral tribunal itself. Would party-initiated discovery in U.S. courts under §1782 threaten to delay and complicate arbitral proceedings? Would discovery requested by the arbitral tribunal have the same risk?

(e) *What arbitral tribunals might utilize §1782?* Suppose that §1782 is available in connection with arbitral proceedings; is it only available to a tribunal sitting outside the United States? When §1782 refers to a "foreign or international" tribunal, could that encompass a tribunal sitting in the United States? Recall the discussion of awards not considered to be "domestic" under the New York Convention. *See supra* pp. 158-69, *infra* pp. 1072-93. Why wouldn't a tribunal, sitting in the United States, but whose award would be nondomestic, be regarded as "international" under §1782?

9. *Availability of 28 U.S.C. §1782 to "interested parties."* Note that §1782 permits assistance to both the "foreign or international tribunal" and "any interested person." In light of the rationale of *Commercial Solvents*, is it reasonable to interpret §1782 as permitting parties to an arbitration to unilaterally obtain judicial assistance? Is there some reason that parties to foreign arbitrations should have greater access to discovery orders from U.S. courts under §1782 than parties to domestic arbitrations under FAA §7? Note that §1782 was enacted to provide U.S. judicial assistance to foreign tribunals and litigants, in the hopes that foreign courts would reciprocate. Arguably, the expectation was that foreign tribunals and/or courts could control the discovery efforts of parties to foreign arbitrations if that was thought necessary.

Even if authority to order party-requested discovery under §1782 exists, should it be exercised? And if so, in what circumstances? Recall the considerations discussed in

Commercial Solvents underlying limits on judicially-ordered discovery for parties to arbitrations. Those considerations are entirely applicable to applications for discovery under §1782 by parties to an arbitration. If §1782 is interpreted to permit judicial assistance in aid of arbitrations, it should be limited to restrict discovery efforts by parties (as opposed to the arbitral tribunal).

10. *Restrictions in arbitration agreement on applications by parties for court-ordered discovery.* Consider Article 22(2) of the 2014 LCIA Rules. What is the effect of this provision? Are there similar provisions in the other institutional rules? Is it an implied requirement of agreeing to arbitration that the parties forego access to court-ordered discovery? Assuming that it is not, is the LCIA's prohibition a desirable one? Compare Article 27 of the UNCITRAL Model Law.

    Is there any need for an express authorization in the parties' arbitration agreement or any applicable institutional rules to permit an arbitrator (as opposed to a party) to seek court enforcement of his discovery orders (for example, under §7 of the FAA)? Is there any such authorization in the institutional rules excerpted above?

E. CONFIDENTIALITY AND TRANSPARENCY IN INTERNATIONAL ARBITRATION

The confidentiality of international arbitration proceedings is a contentious and unsettled subject.[20] A number of authorities regard confidentiality as an essential aspect of the arbitral process, which assists in the effective, efficient resolution of international disputes, and which must be given legal effect.[21] At the same time, a substantial body of critics deny that confidentiality is a necessary or particularly beneficial feature of international arbitral proceedings, or that parties have any general legally-enforceable right to confidential arbitral proceedings.[22] This section explores the nature and scope of confidentiality obligations in international arbitration, including the divergent approaches that are taken in different legal systems, in different commercial settings, and in different types of arbitrations (i.e., commercial, investment, inter-state).

HASSNEH INSURANCE CO. OF ISRAEL v. MEW
[1993] 2 Lloyd's Rep. 243 (QB) (English High Ct.)

MR. JUSTICE COLMAN. This is a claim for an injunction to restrain disclosure by the defendant of certain documents engendered in the course of an arbitration between the

---

20. G. Born, *International Commercial Arbitration* 2783 *et seq.* (2d ed. 2014).

21. *See, e.g.*, Neill, *Confidentiality in Arbitration*, 12 Arb. Int'l 287, 315-16 (1995) (if English law "no longer regarded the privacy and confidentiality of arbitration proceedings ... as a fundamental characteristic of the agreement to arbitrate ... there would be a flight of arbitrations from this country to more hospitable climes"); Knahr & Reinisch, *Transparency Versus Confidentiality in International Investment Arbitration—The* Biwater Gauff *Compromise*, 6 L. & Prac. Int'l Cts. & Tribs. 97, 109 (2007) ("Confidentiality is generally regarded as one of the hallmarks of (commercial) arbitration and usually ranks high among the perceived main advantages of arbitration over other forms of dispute settlement").

22. *See, e.g.*, Naimark & Keer, *International Private Commercial Arbitration—Expectations and Perceptions of Attorneys and Business People*, in C. Drahozal & R. Naimark (eds.), *Towards A Science of International Arbitration: Collected Empirical Research* 43 (2005); *Expert Report of Dr. Julian D.M. Lew (in* Esso/BHP v. Plowman*)*, 11 Arb. Int'l 283, 285 (1995).

plaintiffs and the defendant. The issues to which it gives rise are of considerable importance to those concerned with the conduct of commercial litigation and arbitration in London, particularly in the insurance and reinsurance markets and in relation to shipping and commodity trading transactions....

[The plaintiff, Hassneh Insurance Co. of Israel ("Hassneh") entered into reinsurance contracts with the defendant, Steuart Mew ("Mew"). The reinsurance contract was placed for Mew with Hassneh by C.E. Heath and Co. ("Heath"), an insurance broker. After Mew incurred losses, it sought payments from Hassneh under its reinsurance contracts; Hassneh refused payment, leading to disputes and an arbitration, commenced by Mew against Hassneh, which was conducted in England under the English Arbitration Act. The arbitral tribunal substantially rejected Mew's claims in an award made against it and in favor of Hassneh.

Mew subsequently brought claims in English court against Heath, for alleged negligence in placing its reinsurance with Hassneh. In its litigation, Mew indicated its intention to disclose the arbitral award made in the Mew-Hassneh arbitration; Mew did not indicate any intention to disclose other documents in the arbitration (e.g., written submissions, witness statements, transcripts), but did not exclude the possibility. Hassneh objected and sought an injunction from the English courts to forbid Mew from disclosure of either the arbitral award (other than selected portions) or any of the other documents from the Mew-Hassneh arbitration.] ...

The starting point for any consideration of this subject must be to investigate the nature and scope of the duty of confidence which applies in relation to arbitrations and the documents in them. Surprisingly, there is little authority on the point, at least in English law. In the *Eastern Saga*, [1984] 2 Lloyd's Rep. 373, 379, Mr. Justice Leggatt said:

> "The concept of private arbitration derives simply from the fact that the parties have agreed to submit to arbitration particular disputes arising between them and only between them. It is implicit in this that strangers shall be excluded from the hearing and conduct of the arbitration and that neither the tribunal nor any of the parties can insist that the dispute shall be heard or determined concurrently with or even in consonance with another dispute, however convenient that course may be to the parties seeking it and however closely associated with each other the disputes in question may be."

The most extensive and indeed most recent consideration of the point is that of the Court of Appeal in *Dolling-Baker v. Merrett*, [1990] 1 W.L.R. 1205, 1213, when Lord Justice Parker ... stated:

> "We were invited, therefore, to consider whether this was a case where there ought to be production. It is not contended on behalf of the first defendant that the fact that the documents were prepared for or used in an arbitration, or consist of transcripts or notes of evidence given, or the award, confers immunity. It could not, in my judgment, successfully be so contended. Nor is it contended that the documents constitute confidential documents in the sense that 'confidentiality' and 'confidential' documents have been used in the court. What is relied upon is, in effect, the essentially private nature of an arbitration, coupled with the implied obligation of a party who obtains documents on discovery not to use them for any purpose other than the dispute in which they were obtained. As between parties to an arbitration, although the proceedings are consensual and may thus be regarded as wholly voluntary, their very nature is such that there must, in my judgment, be some implied obligation on both parties not to disclose or use for any other purpose any documents prepared for and used in the arbitration, or disclosed or produced in the course of the arbitration, or

transcripts or notes of the evidence in the arbitration or the award, and indeed not to disclose in any other way what evidence had been given by any witness in the arbitration, save with the consent of the other party, or pursuant to an order or leave of the court. That qualification is necessary, just as it is in the case of the implied obligation of secrecy between banker and customer.

It will be appreciated that I do not intend in the foregoing to give a precise definition of the extent of the obligation. It is unnecessary to do so in the present case. It must be perfectly apparent that, for example, the fact that a document is used in an arbitration does not *confer* on it any confidentiality or privilege which can be availed of in subsequent proceedings. If it is a relevant document, its relevance remains. For that the obligation exists in some form appears to me to be abundantly apparent.... It is a question of an implied obligation arising out of the nature of arbitration itself. Where a question arises as to production of documents or indeed discovery by list or affidavit, the court must, it appears to me, have regard to the existence of the implied obligation, whatever its precise limits may be. If it is satisfied that despite the implied obligation, disclosure and inspection is necessary for the fair disposal of the action, that consideration must prevail. But in reaching a conclusion, the court should consider amongst other things whether there are other and possibly less costly ways of obtaining the information which is sought which do not involve any breach of the implied undertaking."

It is to be observed that Lord Justice Parker identifies an "implied obligation" as the basis for the confidentiality attaching to documents used in or engendered in the course of an arbitration. Such an obligation can exist only because it is implied in the agreement to arbitrate and like any other implied term must be capable of reasonably precise definition. The implication of the term must be based on custom or business efficacy.

If the parties to an English law contract refer their disputes to arbitration they are entitled to assume at the least that the hearing will be conducted in private. That assumption arises from a practice which has been universal in London for hundreds of years and, I believe, undisputed. It is a practice which represents an important advantage of arbitration over the Courts as a means of dispute resolution. The informality attaching to a hearing held in private and the candour to which it may give rise is an essential ingredient of arbitration, so essential that if privacy were denied by an officious bystander, I have no doubt that, in the case of practically every arbitration agreement, both the parties would object.

If it be correct that there is at least an implied term in every agreement to arbitrate that the hearing shall be held in private, the requirement of privacy must in principle extend to documents which are created for the purpose of that hearing. The most obvious example is a note or transcript of the evidence. The disclosure to a third party of such documents would be almost equivalent to opening the door of the arbitration room to that third party. Similarly witness statements, being so closely related to the hearing, must be within the obligation of confidentiality. So also must outline submissions tendered to the arbitrator. If outline submissions, then so must pleadings be included.

Then one comes to a somewhat wider group of documents: those documents which are disclosed as produced by one party to another by reason of the application to the arbitrator of the English rules of discovery of documents. In the context of litigation there is an implied "undertaking" by each party not to use any document disclosed in that litigation for any purpose, save in relation to the litigation in which the document was disclosed.... Such undertaking arises regardless of whether there is a pre-existing contract between the parties to the litigation. In as much as the parties to an English law arbitration impliedly agree to use English discovery procedure, or at least to submit to the possibility that such procedure will apply, it must by implication be their mutual obligation to accord to documents disclosed for the purposes of the arbitration the same confidentiality which would attach to those documents if they were litigating their disputes as distinct from arbitrating them. The fact that the proceedings are in private lends weight to the necessity for that implication.

Then one comes to the award itself, which in this case incorporated reasons, a practice which in English commercial arbitration is usual, if not invariable, in accordance with the provisions of the Arbitration Act, 1979. There are important distinctions between the reasoned award and the other documents which I have already considered.

First, the reasoned award, containing the arbitrator's determination of the issues between the parties which have been referred, identifies the rights and duties of the parties inter se in relation to which they have been in dispute. In so far as it awards that one party shall pay, or do something for the benefit of the other, it gives rise to an independent contractual obligation to perform the award. In as much as it contains the arbitrator's reasons it explains how that obligation arises.

Second, the award by reason of the Arbitration Acts, 1950 and 1979 is subject to the supervisory jurisdiction of the English Courts. It can be set aside or remitted to the arbitrator, for example, for misconduct. It can be the subject of an appeal on a point of law. For these purposes the award may have to be brought into open Court and the consequence of that will usually be that its contents are reproduced in the judgment which will be public and may well be published in the law reports. If one obliterated from the law reports all those cases where a substantial part of an arbitration award had been published for all to read one would be deprived of a massive part of the development of English commercial law, particularly in the fields of carriage of goods by sea and commodity sales contracts.

Thirdly, awards can be enforced in the English Courts by the summary procedure provided for by §26 of the Arbitration Act 1950 or by an action on the award. If the latter course is adopted the award will be opened to the Court in open Court and may therefore, be the subject of a law report which anybody can read.

Accordingly these three factors invest an award with two characteristics not associated with the other documents. First, an award is an identification of the parties' respective rights and obligations and secondly it is at least potentially a public document for the purposes of supervision by the Courts or enforcement in them. It follows, in my judgment, that any definition of the scope of the duty of confidence which attaches to an arbitration award—and I include the reasons—which omitted to take account of such significant characteristics would be defective. Since the duty of confidence must be based on an implied term of the agreement to arbitrate, that term must have regard to the purposes for which awards may be expected to be used in the ordinary course of commerce and in the ordinary application of English arbitration law.

I consider first the ordinary course of commerce. There are many circumstances where one party to an arbitration may require to establish against a third party that the arbitrating party is or has been under an obligation to satisfy an award. One example is where an insurer must establish his liability to the primary assured for the purpose of claiming on his reinsurers. Another in the context of the insurance market is where an assured under a professional indemnity policy has to establish that he has become liable for breach of his professional duty and needs to place before the insurer an award which has been made against him to this effect. In the quite different field of ship-chartering a head charterer may be able to make good his claim against the ship-owner only by reference to an arbitration award made against the head charterer in favour of a sub-charterer.... In all these cases the arbitrating party may require for the purposes of establishing his legal rights against the third party to produce that award against him to that third party. The suggestion by an officious bystander of a duty of confidentiality which precluded the use of arbitration awards for the establishment by arbitrating parties of their rights against third parties, unless the leave of a Court were first obtained, would be unlikely to be enthusiastically received by the commercial community....

[The Court analogized the confidentiality of arbitral proceedings to the confidentiality owed by a bank to its customer.] Implicit in ... formulations of the scope of the duty of confidence is that the bank should be able to disclose the information if to withhold it would or might prejudice the bank in the establishment or protection of its own legal rights vis-à-vis the customer or third parties. The essence of the matter is that it might need to disclose the information either as the foundation of a defence to a claim by a third party, or as the basis for a cause of action against a third party. In my judgment a similar qualification must be implied as a matter of business efficacy in the duty of confidence arising under an agreement to arbitrate. If it is reasonably necessary for the establishment or protection of an arbitrating party's legal rights vis-à-vis a third party, in the sense which I have described, that the award should be disclosed to that third party in order to found a defence or as the basis for a cause of action, so to disclose it would not be a breach of the duty of confidence.

Is there any justification for treating the reasons differently from the formal parts of the award? After all, the reasons may contain references to the pleadings, the submissions and the evidence, all of which material would in the ordinary way be subject to the duty of confidence. On the other hand, the bald conclusion reached by the formal award will in many cases be insufficiently explicit for the purpose of the protection of the arbitrating party's rights against the third party. It is not merely that the award may not be fully comprehensible without reference to the reasons, but that the process of reasoning leading to the arbitrator's conclusion may be the particular feature of the award which gives rise to the right against the third party.... Accordingly, I conclude that the exception to the duty of confidentiality which I have held to apply by implication to arbitration awards applies equally to the reasons, if it is reasonably necessary for the protection of an arbitrating party's rights vis-à-vis a third party that the award should be disclosed to that third party, so to disclose it, including its reasons, would not be a breach of the duty of confidence....

[The Court also reasoned that the decision in *Dolling-Baker* did not involve or consider disclosures to a third party, and its analysis had to be considered against that background.] Therefore, I conclude in the present case that if, as asserted, it is reasonably necessary for the establishment by the defendant of his causes of action against Heath that he should disclose or in his pleadings quote from the arbitration award, including the reasons, ... he should be entitled to do so, without editing either the award or the reasons and without having to apply to the Court for leave to do so....

[Although no request was made for disclosure of other documents from the arbitration, the Court nonetheless briefly addressed the principles regarding such documents (i.e., "pleadings, witness statements, disclosed documents in the arbitration and transcripts").] It is reasonably clear that, as I have held, such documents are subject to a duty of confidence. They are merely the materials which were used to give rise to the award which defined the rights and obligations of the parties to the arbitration. Accordingly, that qualification to the duty of confidentiality based on the reasonable necessity for the protection of an arbitrating party's rights against a third party cannot be expected to apply to them. It is the final determination of rights expressed in the award which is pertinent as against third parties, no the raw materials for that determination. The relevant exception in the case of such documents is an order or leave of the Court. This is the conclusion arrived at by the Court of Appeal in *Dolling-Baker*....

[T]he documents engendered by or in the course of an arbitration to which an obligation of confidence attaches, cannot in principle have any different status from any other documents which are the subject of a duty of confidence.... [The] course envisaged ... in *Dolling-Baker* is for the Court to resolve the conflicting interests on the one hand of protecting the confidential status of the documents, and on the other of facilitating production of documents in compliance with the discovery obligation and for the purpose of protecting the rights of the party in possession. The [appropriate] course ... is that the party in possession should first invite the consent of the other arbitrating party to disclosure of the documents and in the absence of such consent he should decline to permit those documents to be inspected by the third party unless the third party has first obtained an order from the Court to that effect. The documents having been listed and therefore conceded to be relevant, it will then be for the party seeking inspection to apply to the Court for [a disclosure] order. The Court must then consider the evidential significance of the documents in the context of the pending proceedings and investigate whether it is appropriate to preserve the confidentiality of the documents by leaving it to the parties to the action to prove their case on the basis of alternative evidence, or to override the duty of confidentiality in the interests of "disposing fairly of the cause or matter or saving costs in the action."

There is ... in my judgment nothing to justify the voluntary disclosure to a third party of such arbitration documents, other than the award, in anticipation of the commencement of proceedings by or against that third party. To disclose such documents without the consent of the other arbitrating party would be a breach of the obligation of confidence. In the absence of such consent the arbitrating party should proceed to discovery in proceedings by or against the third party, list the document, if relevant, and then decline to permit inspection except upon an order by the Court.... Accordingly, if it were in issue whether the defendant might now disclose such documents to Heath it would be appropriate for them to be enjoined from so doing in the absence of an undertaking not to do so prior to obtaining the plaintiffs' consent or an order for inspection ... being made upon Heath's application in future proceedings....

ESSO AUSTRALIA RESOURCES LTD v. PLOWMAN
XXI Y.B. Comm. Arb. 137 (1996) (Australian High Ct. 1995)

CHIEF JUSTICE MASON. This appeal raises the important question whether an arbitrating party is under an obligation of confidence in relation to documents and information disclosed in, and for the purposes of, a private arbitration.... [Esso/BHP contracted to sell natural gas to two public utilities—the Gas and Fuel Corporation of Victoria ("GFC") and the State Electricity Commission of Victoria ("SEC")—pursuant to the GFC Sales Agreement and the SEC Sales Agreement. Both agreements contained a price adjustment clause. Esso/BHP sought a price adjustment, which the utilities refused, and the dispute was referred to arbitration pursuant to arbitration clauses in the sales agreements, which provided for arbitration in Australia.

While the arbitrations were pending, the Australian Minister for Energy and Minerals brought an action before the Supreme Court of Victoria against Esso/BHP and the utilities seeking a declaration "that any and all information disclosed to [GFC] in the course of its arbitration with [the appellants] is not subject to any obligation of confidence." The Minister also sought a declaration that neither sales agreement contained any obligation on the parties not to disclose to third parties not party to the arbitration any of the following: (a) pleadings, other documents, evidence, and transcript; (b) the award and the reasons for the award. It appeared that the Minister sought a substantial body of commercial, technical, and marketing information.

The appellants counterclaimed for a declaration that the arbitration be conducted in private and the documents and information supplied by any of the parties to the other party be treated in confidence. Esso/BHP argued that "an arbitration agreement includes a term implied by law that the arbitration be conducted in private in that strangers are to be excluded from the hearing," and that "it is an incident of a private arbitration that a party is not entitled to disclose, otherwise than for the purposes of the arbitration, information and documents disclosed to that party by the opposing party for the purposes of the arbitration with which that party would not otherwise have been supplied, unless disclosure is authorized by statute." In response, the Minister argued that "an implied term restricting disclosure of information is not an incident of all private arbitrations and cannot be supported on grounds of necessity, reasonableness or common sense."] ...

It is well settled that when parties submit their dispute to a private arbitral tribunal of their own choice, in the absence of some manifestation of a contrary intention, they confer upon that tribunal a discretion as to the procedure to be adopted in reaching its decision. No doubt the conferral of that power upon the tribunal is incidental to the power which it is given to determine the dispute submitted to the tribunal. Section 14 of the Commercial Arbitration Act 1984 (Vict.) specifically empowers the arbitrator or umpire to: "conduct proceedings under [the] agreement in such manner as the arbitrator or umpire thinks fit." ... There is no reason to doubt that an arbitrator, in the exercise of power with respect to procedural matters, can decide who shall be present at the hearing of the arbitration. But that power is not a free-standing power; it is a power to decide who is entitled to attend, having regard to the provisions of the relevant contract.

Subject to any manifestation of a contrary intention arising from the provisions or the nature of an agreement to submit a dispute to arbitration, the arbitration held pursuant to the agreement is private in the sense that it is not open to the public.... The arbitrator will exclude strangers from the hearing unless the parties consent to attendance by a stranger.[*Oxford Shipping Co. v. Nippon Yusen Kaisha* [1984] 3 All ER 835, 842 (English High Ct.); *Bibby Bulk Carriers v. Cansulex Ltd* [1989] QB 155, 166-167 (English High Ct.).] Persons whose presence is necessary for the proper conduct of the arbitration are not strangers in the relevant sense. Thus, persons claiming through or attending on behalf of the parties, those assisting a party in the presentation of the case, and a shorthand writer to take notes may appear. It does not matter much whether this characteristic of privacy is an ordinary incident of the arbitration, that is, an incident of the subject matter upon which the parties have agreed, or whether it is an implied term of the agreement. For the most part, the authorities refer to it as an implied term. But, for my part, I prefer to describe the private character of the hearing as something that inheres in the subject matter of the agreement to submit disputes to arbitration rather than attribute that character to an implied term. That view better accords with the history of arbitrations....

[T]he efficacy of a private arbitration as an expeditious and commercially attractive form of dispute resolution depends, at least in part, upon its private nature. Hence the efficacy of a private arbitration will be damaged, even defeated, if proceedings in the arbitration are made public by the disclosure of documents relating to the arbitration. As one text writer has observed:

> "There would be little point in excluding the public from an arbitration hearing if it were open to a party to make public, for example in the press, or on television, an account of what was said or done at the hearing. It is suggested that a party would be entitled to an injunction to restrain the other party from such publication. And the same principle must apply to the arbitration as a whole, including the pleadings or statements of case, expert reports or witness proofs that have been exchanged, as well as to evidence given orally at a hearing." [Bernstein, *Handbook of Arbitration Practice* (1987) at ¶13.6.3.]

It was on this basis that the English Court of Appeal, in *Dolling-Baker* [*v. Merrett*, [1990] 1 W.L.R. 1205], restrained a party to an arbitration from disclosing on discovery in a subsequent action documents relating to the arbitration. The documents consisted of documents prepared for or used in the arbitration, transcripts and notes of evidence given and the award. [The Court], after referring to "the essentially private nature of an arbitration," said:

> "As between parties to an arbitration, ... their very nature is such that there must ... be some implied obligation on both parties not to disclose or use for any other purpose any documents prepared for and used in the arbitration, or disclosed or produced in the course of the arbitration, or transcripts or notes of the evidence in the arbitration or the award, and indeed not to disclose in any other way what evidence had been given by any witness in the arbitration, save with the consent of the other party, or pursuant to an order or leave of the court."

[The Court] went on to emphasize that the obligation arose out of the "nature of arbitration itself."

On the other hand, the Minister argues that, while it is one thing to say that the hearing is private in the sense that strangers are excluded, it is another thing to say that it is confidential. The Minister points to the fact that, before *Dolling-Baker*, there was no decision suggesting that an arbitration hearing was confidential as distinct from private. Further, in Australia and the United States, there is no support in the decided cases for the existence of such an obligation of confidence. Indeed, in the United States, the decided cases are inconsistent with the proposition that confidentiality is a characteristic of arbitration proceedings [*Industrotech Constructors Inc. v. Duke Univ.*, 314 S.E.2d 272, 274 (N.C. Ct. App. 1984); *Giacobazzi Grandi Vini SpA v. Renfield Corp.*, 1987 U.S. Dist. LEXIS 1783 (S.D.N.Y.); *U.S.A. v. Panhandle E. Corp.*, 118 FRD 346 (D. Del. 1988)] and, in Australia, there is a decision implicitly denying the existence of an obligation of confidentiality. [*Alliance v. Australian Gas Light Co.*, (1983) 34 SASR 215 at 229-32 (Australian High Ct.).] And members of the profession with experience in the field of arbitration have expressed in this very case conflicting views on the question whether the parties come under an obligation not to disclose the proceedings. To that may be added the comment that, if such an obligation had formed part of the law, one would have expected it to have been recognized and enforced by judicial decision long before *Dolling-Baker*.

Moreover, it has to be acknowledged that, for various reasons, complete confidentiality of the proceedings in an arbitration cannot be achieved. First, it is common ground between the parties that no obligation of confidence attaches to witnesses who are therefore at liberty to disclose to third parties what they know of the proceedings. Secondly, there are various circumstances in which an award made in an arbitration, or the proceedings in an arbitration, may come before a court involving disclosure to the court by a party to the arbitration and publication of the court proceedings. Thus, ... an award made under an arbitration agreement may be enforced in the same manner as a judgment or order of that Court to the same effect. An award may become subject to judicial review. The Supreme Court may determine a preliminary point of law arising in the arbitration, and may remove an arbitrator or umpire. And the Court has the same power to make interlocutory orders for the purposes of and in relation to arbitration proceedings as it has for the purposes of and in relation to proceedings in the Court. Thirdly, there are other circumstances in which an arbitrating party must be entitled to disclose to a third party the existence and details of the proceedings and the award. An arbitrating party may be bound under a policy of insurance to disclose to the insurer matters involved in the arbitration proceedings which are material to the risk insured against. Likewise, an arbitrating party may be obliged to disclose the existence and nature of arbitration proceedings as well as the award made in the proceedings because the disclosure is necessary in order to state accurately what are the assets and liabilities of the party or to give an indication of its future prospects. Such a disclosure may be necessary in order to comply with the statutory requirements regulating the provision of financial information by corporations or with stock exchange requirements....

The illustrations just given are but some of the instances in which a party to an arbitration could legitimately and justifiably disclose the proceedings, or some aspect of the proceedings, of an arbitration. Granted the various circumstances in which disclosure can legitimately take place, two questions necessarily arise. First, is there a legal basis for holding that there is an obligation not to disclose? Secondly, if so, how is the obligation to be defined and what are the exceptions to it?

An obligation not to disclose may arise from an express contractual provision. If the parties wished to secure the confidentiality of the materials prepared for or used in the arbitration and of the transcripts and notes of evidence given, they could insert a provision to that effect in their arbitration agreement. Importantly, such a provision would bind the parties and the arbitrator, but not others. Witnesses, for example, would be under no obligation of confidentiality.

Absent such a provision, it is difficult to resist the conclusion that, historically, an agreement to arbitrate gave rise to an arbitration which was private in the sense that strangers were not entitled to attend the hearing. Privacy in that sense went some distance in bringing about confidentiality because strangers were not in a position to publish the proceedings or any part of them. That confidentiality, though it was not grounded initially in any legal right or obligation, was a consequential benefit or advantage attaching to arbitration which made it an attractive mode of dispute resolution. There is, accordingly, a case for saying that, in the course of evolution, the private arbitration has advanced to the stage where confidentiality has become one of its essential attributes so that confidentiality is a characteristic or quality that inheres in arbitration.

Despite the view taken in *Dolling-Baker* and subsequently ... in *Hassneh*, I do not consider that, in Australia, having regard to the various matters to which I have referred, we are justified in concluding that confidentiality is an essential attribute of a private arbitration imposing an obligation on each party not to disclose the proceedings or documents and information provided in and for the purposes of the arbitration. The appellants' argument was designed to establish that an agreement to arbitrate contains an implied term that each party will not disclose information provided in and for the purposes of the arbitration. The argument was that the implication was to be made as a matter of law in all private agreements for arbitration unless presumably the agreement provided otherwise.... [T]he case for an implied term must be rejected for the very reasons I have given for rejecting the view that confidentiality is an essential characteristic of a private arbitration. In the context of such an arbitration, once it is accepted that confidentiality is not such a characteristic, there can be no basis for implication as a matter of necessity....

[Given these conclusions], I do not need to consider whether the difficulties in defining the exceptions to any implied term forbidding disclosure are such as to preclude the implication of such a term. That the difficulties are considerable was acknowledged both by the Court of Appeal in *Dolling-Baker* and ... in *Hassneh*.... [The latter decision] expressed the qualification applicable to arbitration agreements in these terms:

> "If it is reasonably necessary for the establishment or protection of an arbitrating party's legal rights *vis-à-vis* a third party, in the sense which I have described, that the award should be disclosed to that third party in order to found a defence or as the basis for a cause of action, so to disclose it would not be a breach of the duty of confidence."

For my part, if an obligation of confidence existed by virtue of the fact that the information was provided in and for the purposes of arbitration, this statement of the qualification seems unduly narrow. It does not recognize that there may be circumstances, in which third parties and the public have a legitimate interest in knowing what has transpired in an arbitration, which would give rise to a "public interest" exception....

In relation to documents produced by one party to another in the course of discovery in proceedings in a court, there is an implied undertaking, springing from the nature of discovery, by each party not to use any document disclosed for any purpose otherwise than in relation to the litigation in which it is disclosed.... Because an undertaking is implied, it has not been the practice to condition the making of orders in that way. The implied undertaking is subject to the qualification that once material is adduced in evidence in court proceedings it becomes part of the public domain, unless the court restrains publication of it.

It would be inequitable if a party were compelled by court process to produce private documents for the purposes of the litigation yet be exposed to publication of them for other purposes. No doubt the implied obligation must yield to inconsistent statutory provisions and to the requirements of curial process in other litigation, e.g. discovery and inspection, but that circumstance is not a reason for denying the existence of the implied obligation.

The next step is to say that a similar obligation arises in an arbitration. In England it has been held that, because the parties to an English law arbitration submit to the possibility that the English discovery procedure will apply to their arbitration, by implication they must be mutually obliged: "to accord to documents disclosed for the purposes of the arbitration the same confidentiality which would attach to those documents if they were litigating their disputes as distinct from arbitrating them." [*Hassneh Ins.* [1993] 2 Lloyd's Rep. at 247 per Colman J.]

I see no reason to disagree with this statement. But, consistently with the principle as it applies in court proceedings, the obligation of confidentiality attaches only in relation to documents which are produced by a party compulsorily pursuant to a direction by the arbitrator. And the obligation is necessarily subject to the public's legitimate interest in obtaining information about the affairs of public authorities. The existence of this obligation does not provide a basis for the wide-ranging obligation of confidentiality which the appellants seek to apply to all documents and information provided in and for the purposes of an arbitration. If the judgments in *Dolling-Baker* and *Hassneh* are to be taken as expressing a contrary view, I do not accept them....

BRENNAN J.... If a party to an arbitration agreement be under any obligation of confidentiality, the obligation must be contractual in origin. A term imposing an obligation of confidentiality could be expressed in an arbitration agreement but such a term would be unusual. Nor is such an obligation imposed by the Commercial Arbitration Act 1984 (Vict.). A term is implied only where, inter alia, it is necessary to give to the contract "such business efficacy as the parties must have intended." [*Luxor (Eastbourne) Ltd. v. Cooper* [1941] AC 108 at 137 (House of Lords).] The intended business efficacy must be inferred "from the very nature of the transaction." ...

In the present case, the Minister has a statutory right under the State Electricity Commission Act 1958 (Vict.) ("SEC Act") to obtain information from the State Electricity Commission of Victoria ("SECV"). It is the duty of SECV to furnish the Minister with the information required under that subclause and that duty cannot be defeated by any contractual duty to keep documents or information confidential. Any implied obligation of confidentiality must be qualified accordingly. Further, the Gas and Fuel Corporation of Victoria ("GFC") and SECV are public authorities. They are engaged in the supply of energy in the State of Victoria. The award to be made in the respective arbitrations will affect the price of the energy supplied by the appellants to GFC and SECV and by them to the public. The public generally has a real interest in the outcome, and perhaps in the progress, of each arbitration which the relevant public authority has a duty to satisfy. GFC and SECV have a duty—possibly a legal duty in the case of SECV but at least a moral duty in the case of both public authorities—to account to the public for the manner in which they perform their functions. Public authorities are not to be taken, prima facie, to have bound themselves to refrain from giving an account of their functions in an appropriate way: sometimes by giving information to the public directly, sometimes by giving information to a Minister, to a government department or to some other public authority....

In the ordinary course of administration of the relevant Acts and in the performance by GFC and SECV of their respective functions, information on energy matters would have to be passed from GFC and SECV respectively to the Minister, and vice versa. Neither GFC nor SECV could be taken to have impliedly undertaken to keep confidential from the Government or the Minister documents or information relevant to the administration of the energy portfolio. The implied obligation of confidentiality is qualified accordingly....

BIWATER GAUFF (TANZANIA) LTD v. UNITED REPUBLIC OF TANZANIA
Procedural Order No. 3 in ICSID Case No. ARB/05/22 of 29 September 2006

On 2 August 2005, the Claimant, Biwater Gauff (Tanzania) Ltd. ("BGT") filed a request for arbitration [pursuant to the ICSID Convention and the United Kingdom-Tanzanian BIT] with respect to a dispute with the Respondent, the United Republic of Tanzania ("the UROT") arising out of a series of alleged breaches by the UROT of its obligations under both international and domestic law concerning foreign investment which, according to BGT, are said to have caused loss to BGT in the region of US$ 20 to 25 million. [In the arbitral proceedings, BGT sought provisional measures from the arbitral tribunal, prohibiting the UROT from publicly disclosing material produced in or for the arbitration (*e.g.*, materials produced in disclosure, documentary evidence, memorials and other written submissions, and correspondence).] The determination of this application for provisional measures entails a careful balancing between two competing interests: (i) the need for transparency in treaty proceedings such as these, and (ii) the need to protect the procedural integrity of the arbitration. In order properly to strike this balance, it is important at the outset to clearly identify the nature of each interest.

Considerations of confidentiality and privacy have not played the same role in the field of investment arbitration, as they have in international commercial arbitration. Without doubt, there is now a marked tendency towards transparency in treaty arbitration.

Agreement of the Parties: Parties are free, of course, to conclude any agreements they choose concerning confidentiality. Any such agreements would give rise to rights that are susceptible of protection by way of provision measures or other appropriate relief. There has been no general agreement in this regard in this case, and there is no provision on confidentiality in the [UK-Tanzania BIT] pursuant to which these proceedings have been brought....

No General Per Se Rule: In the absence of any agreement between the parties on this issue, there is no provision imposing a general duty of confidentiality in ICSID arbitration, whether in the ICSID Convention, any of the applicable Rules or otherwise. Equally, however, there is no provision imposing a general rule of transparency or non-confidentiality in any of these sources.

The position of ICSID with respect to transparency has evolved from the old Rules to the new Rules, in force since 10 April 2006, and which govern these proceedings as of that date. The changes mainly concern briefs *amicus curiae* and the attendance of third parties at the hearing (e.g., the new Rule 37(2)). However, ... they clearly reflect an overall trend in this field towards transparency. As matters now stand, the ICSID Convention and the Administrative and Financial Regulations and Rules only contain limitations on specific aspects of confidentiality and privacy, as follows:

> (a) Article 48(5) of the ICSID Convention provides that: "The Centre shall not publish the award without the consent of the parties." ... [T]his provision deals by its terms only with publication by the Centre itself....
>
> (b) Regulation 22(2) of the Administrative and Financial Regulations provides that the Secretary-General of ICSID shall only arrange for the publication of (i) arbitral awards or (ii) the minutes and other records of proceedings, if both parties to a proceeding so consent. Again, this provision by its terms is addressed only to the Secretary-General.
>
> (c) Rule 32(2) of the new ICSID Arbitration Rules provides that the hearing may be opened by the Tribunal to other persons besides the disputing parties, their agents, counsel and advocates, witnesses and experts and officers of the Tribunal—provided that no party objects....

These provisions require (subject to contrary agreement) the privacy of the arbitral hearing—a central element of the arbitral process. At the same time, the foregoing provisions focus on the actions of ICSID and arbitral tribunals, and do not expressly address the actions of the parties themselves. There is no provision in the ICSID Arbitration Rules which expressly provides for the confidentiality of pleadings, documents or other information submitted by the parties during the arbitration. On the contrary, the official annotations accompanying the original version of the ICSID Arbitration Rules (which are not binding, and do not form part of the Rules) state that the parties are not prohibited from publishing their pleadings, but that they may agree not to do so *"if they feel that publication may exacerbate the dispute"* (Rule 30, Note F, 1 ICSID Reports 93)....

UNCITRAL Rules: Under Article 25(4) of the [1976] UNCITRAL Rules, hearings are to be held *in camera* unless the parties agree otherwise. Under Article 32(5), awards are to be made public only with the consent of both parties. Aside from these two provision, there are no other provisions expressly imposing a general duty of confidentiality, or prohibiting disclosure of documents prepared for or disclosed in the arbitration. In *S.D. Myers Inc. v. Canada*, (Procedural Order No. 16 of 13 May 2000), the Tribunal operating under the [1976] UNCITRAL Rules distinguished treaty arbitrations from private commercial arbitrations, as follows (¶8):

> "The Tribunal considers that, whatever may be the position in private consensual arbitrations between commercial parties, it has not been established that *any general principle* of confidentiality exists in an arbitration such as that currently before this tribunal. The main argument in favour of confidentiality is founded on a supposed implied term in the arbitration agreement. The present arbitration is taking place pursuant to a provision in an international treaty, not pursuant to an arbitration agreement between disputing parties."

At the same time, the Tribunal did impose restrictions on hearings and materials that formed part of the hearings. Insofar as NAFTA arbitration are concerned, the Tribunal's holdings may have to be reconsidered in light of the subsequent FTC Interpretation of 2001. These considerations, and the accepted need for greater transparency in this field, generally militate against the type of provisional measures for which the Claimant now contends. However, there exist other specific, and analytically distinct, interests that may militate in favour of restrictions. These are addressed below....

It is now settled in both treaty and international commercial arbitration that an arbitral tribunal is entitled to direct the parties not to take any step that might (1) harm or prejudice the integrity of the proceedings, or (2) aggravate or exacerbate the dispute. Both may be seen as a particular type of provisional measure (as, for example, in Article 17 of the newly revised UNCITRAL Model Law, which refers to the prevention of *"current or imminent harm or prejudice to the arbitral process itself"*), or simply as a facet of the tribunal's overall procedural powers and its responsibility for its own process. Both concerns have a number of aspects, which can be articulated in various ways, such as the need to: [a] preserve the Tribunal's mission and mandate to determine finally the issues between the parties; [b] preserve the proper functioning of the dispute settlement procedure; [c] preserve and promote a relationship of trust and confidence between the parties; [d] ensure the orderly unfolding of the arbitration process; [e] ensure a level playing field; [f] minimize the scope for any external pressure on any party, witness, expert or other participant in the process; [g] avoid "trial by media."

It is self-evident that the prosecution of a dispute in the media or in other public fora, or the uneven reporting and disclosure of documents or other parts of the record in parallel with a pending arbitration, may aggravate or exacerbate the dispute and may impact upon the integrity of the procedure. This is all the more so in very public cases, such as this one, where issues of wider interest are raised, and where there is already substantial media coverage, some of which already being the subject of complaint by the parties.

Whilst it is in the wider public interest to ensure that accurate information about the parties' dispute and its resolution is broadcast, this is not always easy to achieve. That is particularly true while an arbitration is ongoing, and an arbitral record has yet to be completed.... Importantly, these are not concerns that are inconsistent for all time with transparency—since they are limited in duration, and do not impact beyond the end of the proceedings themselves. Once the arbitration has finally concluded, most restrictions would not normally continue to apply. While the proceedings remain pending, however, there is an obvious tension between the interests in transparency and in procedural integrity....

The UROT asserts that none of the rights or interests identified by BGT are actually the subject of any existing threat, such as to warrant the imposition of provisional measures at this stage. It is true that the risks to the integrity of these proceedings, and the danger of an aggravation or exacerbation of this dispute, have yet to manifest themselves in concrete terms. Neither party has demonstrated that it has yet been inhibited, in fact, from participating fully in these proceedings or that any of the existing arbitration procedures have been hindered or impaired by the publicity that has occurred to date. In truth, BGT's complaint amounts to a concern about the risk of future prejudice, or the potential risks to the arbitral process as it unfolds hereafter.

The Tribunal disagrees, however, with the suggestion that actual harm must be manifested before any measures may be taken. Its mandate and responsibility includes ensuring that the proceedings will be conducted in the future in a regular, fair and orderly manner (including by issuing and enforcing procedural directions to that effect). Among other things, its mandate extends to ensuring that potential inhibitions and unfairness do not arise; equally, its mandate extends to attempting to reduce the risk of future aggravation and exacerbation of the dispute, which necessarily involves probabilities, not certainties. Given the media campaign that has already been fought on both sides of this case (by many entities beyond the parties to this arbitration), and the general media interest that already exists, the Tribunal is satisfied that there exists a sufficient risk of harm or prejudice, as well as aggravation, in this case to warrant some form of control.

Equally, however, given the public nature of this dispute and the range of interests that are potentially affected, including interests in transparency and public information, the Tribunal is also of the view that, as far as possible, any restrictions must be carefully and narrowly delimited.... Having carefully considered each category of documents and information involved in Claimant's request for provisional measures, the Tribunal concludes that an appropriate balance between the competing interests, at least for the time being, is as follows:

i. General Discussion about the Case[:] Subject to the restrictions on disclosure of specific documents set out below, neither party should be prevented from engaging in general discussion about the case in public, provided that any such public discussion is restricted to what is necessary (for example, pursuant to the Republic's duty to provide the public with information concerning governmental and public affairs), and is not used as an instrument to further antagonize the parties, exacerbate their differences, unduly pressure one of them, or render the resolution of the dispute potentially more difficult. Part of the UROT's opposition to the measures sought by BGT is based upon a concern that there ought not to be any: "*curtailment of a sovereign State's right (and obligation) to inform the public about a matter of great public importance and comment*" The Tribunal agrees with this, and considers that the direction ... above adequately caters for UROT's concern.

ii. Awards[:] In light of the parties' agreement ... that the Centre may publish awards at such time and in such manner as it deems fit, there is no need for any direction in this regard.

iii. Decisions, Orders and Directions of the Tribunal (other than Awards)[:] Given the treatment of awards, and the treatment of such materials in investment arbitration generally, the presumption should be in favour of allowing the publication of the Tribunal's Decisions, Orders and Directions. Publication of the Tribunal's decisions also, as a general matter, will be less likely to aggravate or exacerbate a dispute, or to exert undue pressure on one party, than publication of parties' pleading or release of other documentary materials. However, the nature and subject matter of Decisions, Orders and Directions varies enormously, and for some it may still be inappropriate to allow wider distribution. It follows that this category ought to be considered by the Tribunal on a case-by-case basis as such determinations are made. In the exercise of this mandate, the Tribunal considers it important that no confidentiality restriction be imposed upon this Procedural Order No. 3, given the need to explain to parties with interests in transparency the precise basis upon which the Tribunal is proceeding.

iv. Minutes or Records of Hearings[:] The Tribunal considers itself responsible to ensure that the hearing is conducted in an efficient manner, to resolve the parties' dispute fairly and impartially. The publication of minutes or records of hearings has at least the potential to affect the procedural integrity and efficiency of the hearing itself. Indeed: (a) Regulation 22(2) of the Administrative and Financial Regulations provides that the Secretary-General of ICSID shall only arrange for the publication of the minutes and other records of proceedings if both parties to a proceeding so consent, and; (b) Rule 32(2) of the new ICSID Arbitration Rules provides that the hearing may not be opened by the Tribunal to third parties of a party objects. Accordingly, it is appropriate that minutes or records of hearings should not be disclosed unless the parties so agree, or the Tribunal so directs.

v. Documents Disclosed in the Proceedings[:] No restriction is appropriate upon the publication by one party of its own documents, even if those documents have been produced in the arbitral proceedings pursuant to a disclosure exercise, or otherwise. (Of course, if there are separate contractual or other confidentiality restrictions on such publication, then the nature, applicability and enforceability of those restrictions would need to be raised and considered. No such restrictions have been suggested in this case.) However, in the interests of procedural integrity, the Tribunal does consider it appropriate to restrict publication or distribution of documents that have been produced in the arbitration by the opposing party. The interests of transparency are here outweighed, since the threat of wide publication may well undermine the document production process itself, as well as the overall arbitration procedure. The production of documents by a party, whether in response to a disclosure request or otherwise, is made for the purpose of resolving the parties' dispute and the presumption is that materials disclosed in this manner should be used only for such purpose.

vi. Pleadings/Written Memorials[:] Given that (a) the pleadings and written memorials are likely to detail documents that have been produced pursuant to a disclosure exercise, and (b) any uneven publication or distribution of pleadings or memorials is likely to give a misleading impression about these proceedings, this category of documents should be restricted, pending conclusion of the proceedings (or agreement between the parties, or further order by the Tribunal). The same restriction ought to apply to witness statements and expert reports attached to pleadings and written memorials....

vii. Correspondence Between the Parties and/or the Arbitral Tribunal Exchanged in Respect of the Arbitral Proceedings[:] This is a category in which the needs of transparency (if any) are outweighed by the requirements of procedural integrity. Correspondence between the parties and/or the Arbitral Tribunal will usually concern the very conduct of the process itself, rather than issues of substance, and as such do not warrant wider distribution. It follows that this is an appropriate category for restriction.

Continued Review: In order to ensure that the balance between the competing interests is maintained, the Tribunal considers it appropriate to keep each category under continued review. To this end, pending the conclusion of these proceedings, the Tribunal will act as a "gate-keeper" on disclosures. Thus, if new circumstances arise, and the parties are unable to reach agreement, the parties remain at liberty to apply to vary these directions on a case-by-case basis. In the interests of efficiency, the Tribunal expects that such applications would be made only in well-justified circumstances, supported by concrete explanations.

Restrictions on Both Parties: As will be clear, the analysis above leads to a form of order different to that requested by BGT. In particular, it is an order that must as a matter of fairness, equality of treatment and non-aggravation of the parties' dispute apply equally to both parties....

ARBITRATION AGREEMENT BETWEEN THE GOVERNMENT OF SUDAN AND THE SUDAN PEOPLE'S LIBERATION MOVEMENT/ARMY ON DELIMITING THE ABYEI AREA
Articles 1.1, 8.4, 8.6, 9.3 (2008)

[excerpted in Documentary Supplement at pp. 79-84]

NOTES

1. *Privacy versus confidentiality*. What is the difference between the "privacy" and the "confidentiality" of arbitrations? Consider the court's discussion of these issues in *Esso Australia*. Can an arbitration be private without being confidential? What does this entail?

2. *General absence of provisions regarding confidentiality in international arbitration instruments*. Does anything in the New York Convention address the confidentiality of international commercial arbitrations? Consider also the European and Inter-American Conventions. Does anything in the ICSID Convention address confidentiality in investment arbitrations? What relevance, if any, does this have to the question whether or not international commercial or investment arbitrations are confidential?

3. *General absence of provisions regarding confidentiality in national arbitration legislation*. Consider the texts of leading arbitration statutes. Does anything in the UNCITRAL Model Law, the SLPIL, the English Arbitration Act, French Code of Civil Procedure, or the FAA address the question of confidentiality in international arbitrations? For example, does anything in any of these legislative instruments ad-

dress the right of third parties to attend arbitral hearings? The publication of the arbitral award? The obligation (or not) of the parties to treat the arbitration as confidential? What relevance, if any, does this have to the question whether or not international commercial arbitrations are confidential?

Unusually, some arbitration statutes do address the subject of confidentiality. *See, e.g.*, Hong Kong Arbitration Ordinance, 2013, §18(1) (Unless otherwise agreed by the parties, no party may publish, disclose or communicate any information relating to (a) the arbitral proceedings under the arbitration agreement; or (b) an award made in those arbitral proceedings"); Spanish Arbitration Act, 2011, Art. 24(2) ("The arbitrators, the parties and the arbitral institutions, if applicable, are obliged to maintain the confidentiality of information coming to their knowledge in the course of the arbitral proceedings."); New Zealand Arbitration Act, Art. 14B(1) ("Every arbitration agreement to which this section applies is deemed to provide that the parties and the arbitral tribunal must not disclose confidential information").

4. *Importance (or non-importance) of confidentiality to parties agreeing upon international commercial arbitration.* In the absence of legislative provisions, to what extent do parties have an expectation that their international commercial arbitrations will be confidential? To what extent is the expectation that their arbitrations will be confidential a reason that parties agree to arbitrate? Consider: *UNCITRAL Notes on Organizing Arbitral Proceedings*, ¶31 ("It is widely viewed that confidentiality is one of the advantageous and helpful features of arbitration"); C. Bühring-Uhle, *A Survey on Arbitration and Settlement in International Business Disputes* in C. Drahozal & R. Naimark (eds.), *Towards A Science of International Arbitration: Collected Empirical Research* 25, 35 (2005) (confidentiality identified by survey respondents as third most important feature of international arbitration). *See also supra* pp. 99-114.

5. *Parties' autonomy to agree upon confidentiality of arbitration.* Suppose the parties' agreement to arbitrate includes an express confidentiality provision. Is there any reason to doubt that this agreement is valid? Consider: *Report of the Secretary-General on Possible Features of A Model Law on International Commercial Arbitration,* U.N. Doc. A/CN.9/207, ¶17 (1981) (confidentiality "may be left to the agreement of the parties or the arbitration rules chosen by the parties"). Consider how the Australian court in *Esso Australia* and the ICSID tribunal in *Biwater-Gauff* address the issue. Are there any doubts as to the parties' autonomy to agree upon the confidentiality of "their" arbitration? Who exactly is bound by such an agreement—the parties to the arbitration? The arbitrators? The witnesses? Third parties?

If the parties' arbitration agreement does provide for confidentiality, does Article II of the New York Convention require Contracting States to give effect to this agreement?

6. *Provisions regarding confidentiality in institutional rules.* Consider the UNCITRAL, ICC and LCIA Rules. How does each deal with confidentiality? What are the differences between each set of rules? Note the provisions of the UNCITRAL and ICC Rules concerning attendance at hearings, publication of awards and deliberations of arbitrators. How do these provisions contrast with Article 30(1) of the LCIA Rules? *Compare* 2012 Swiss Rules, Art. 44(1) ("Unless the parties expressly agree in writing to the contrary, the parties undertake to keep confidential all awards and orders as well as all materials submitted by another party in the framework of the arbitral proceed-

ings not already in the public domain, except and to the extent that a disclosure may be required of a party by a legal duty, to protect or pursue a legal right or to enforce or challenge an award in legal proceedings before a judicial authority."). *See also* 2013 HKIAC Rules, Art. 42; 2014 JCAA Rules, Art. 38; 2010 SCC Rules, Art. 46; 2014 WIPO Rules, Arts. 75-78.

If confidentiality is so important to parties, why don't the UNCITRAL and ICC Rules provide expressly for broad confidentiality obligations on the parties? Wouldn't this be ensuring that the parties' expectations are realized? Is the omission sufficiently compensated by the tribunal's power to make orders on confidentiality?

7. *Implied obligations of confidentiality in international commercial arbitration.* Consider the analysis in *Hassneh*. Is it persuasive to conclude that, where the parties have not otherwise agreed, there is an implied obligation of confidentiality on the parties to an international commercial arbitration? What is there in the nature of an arbitration that supports implying such an obligation? (Note that parties are free to agree expressly on the confidentiality of arbitral proceedings, either directly in their agreement to arbitrate or by incorporating institutional arbitration rules that provide for confidentiality.)

   Compare the analysis of implied confidentiality obligations in *Esso Australia*. Is it preferable to that in *Hassneh*? Is it possible to reconcile, at least partially, the decisions in *Hassneh* and *Esso Australia*? Where was the arbitration in *Hassneh* seated? Where was the arbitration in *Esso Australia* seated? Did the Australian court address the implied obligations of confidentiality in an English-seated arbitration? Did *Hassneh* involve a third-party request for disclosure? Or a party's effort to use, on its own initiative, materials from an arbitration? What did *Esso Australia* involve? How would *Esso Australia* have been decided under the standards in *Hassneh* and *Dolling-Baker*?

   When commercial parties engage in business litigation in national courts, do they have an implied expectation of confidentiality? Why not? What if they conclude a forum selection agreement? What is it about arbitration that arguably supports an implied expectation, and obligation, of confidentiality? To what extent is history a reliable basis for concluding that parties have implied expectations of confidentiality? Note the observation in *Esso Australia* that, until recently, there were no judicial decisions recognizing the confidentiality of arbitrations. What does that suggest?

8. *Differing confidentiality obligations for differing categories of documents.* Consider how the *Hassneh* court deals with different types of documents and the confidentiality obligations applicable to each. Is an award entitled to the same confidentiality as other documents connected to the arbitration? What about the parties' written submissions and arguments? The witness statements and testimony? The documents produced in disclosure? Why is it that different obligations of confidentiality attach to each? Compare the approach in *Biwater*.

9. *Confidentiality and third-party rights (to disclosure or otherwise).* Assuming that the parties' arbitration agreement imposes either express or implied obligations of confidentiality, does that prevent third parties from obtaining documents from the arbitration in disclosure (or through other mechanisms)? If the arbitral award, or submissions in the arbitration, are relevant and material to the issues in another litigation or arbitration, can a party withhold them merely because it is subject to confidentiality obligations? Note that many commercial agreements contain broad confidentiality

provisions, which do not insulate a party from providing disclosure of relevant documents falling within the confidentiality provision. To what extent does this explain the result in *Esso Australia*? How did the procedural posture of the parties differ in *Hassneh* from that in *Esso Australia*?

10. *Choice of law governing confidentiality in international commercial arbitration.* What law governs the parties' confidentiality obligations in an international commercial arbitration? Is it the law of the arbitral seat (where the arbitral hearings are presumptively held) or the law governing the arbitration agreement? If the rationale for implied confidentiality obligations is that they arise from the parties' agreement to arbitrate, shouldn't the law governing the arbitration agreement be applicable?

    What law did the Court in *Hassneh* apply to issues of confidentiality? Why? What law did the Court in *Esso Australia* apply? Why?

11. *Obligations of confidentiality in investment arbitration.* Note that many investment arbitrations are relatively public, with the parties' written submissions and the tribunal's orders and awards typically being available on the websites of ICSID and others. *See* icsid.worldbank.org; ita.law.uvic.ca (Investment Treaty Arbitration).

    Compare the approaches in *Hassneh* and *Esso Australia* to that in *Biwater*. What was the basis for the tribunal's confidentiality order in *Biwater*? Did it conclude that there was a general obligation of confidentiality in investment arbitration? What justified its confidentiality order? Is this persuasive?

    Why should there be different implied confidentiality obligations in investment arbitration than in commercial arbitration? Consider:

    > "The Tribunal considers that, whatever may be the position in private consensual arbitration between commercial parties, it has not been established that any general principle of confidentiality exists in an arbitration such as that currently before this tribunal. The main argument in favor of confidentiality is founded on a supposed implied term in the arbitration agreement. The present arbitration is taking place pursuant to a provision in an international treaty, not pursuant to an arbitration agreement between disputing parties." *S.D. Myers Inc. v. Canada,* NAFTA Procedural Order No. 16 of 13 May 2000, ¶8.

    Is that persuasive? What differences exist in the two types of arbitrations that would justify differences in the treatment of confidentiality?

12. *Obligations of confidentiality in inter-state arbitration.* Consider Article 66 of the 1907 Hague Convention, excerpted at p. 48 of the Documentary Supplement. Note that it provides that the arbitration hearings "are only public if it be so decided by the Tribunal, with the assent of the parties." Why is that? Is there a particular need for arbitral hearings in inter-state disputes to be private? Compare Article 80 of the 1907 Convention. What does it provide with regard to the arbitral award? Why would the Convention make this provision?

    Consider Articles 8.6 and 8.7 of the Abyei Arbitration Agreement, excerpted at p. 83 of the Documentary Supplement. What do these provisions provide with regard to the confidentiality—or non-confidentiality—of the parties' arbitral proceedings? Are the parties' written submissions public? The award? Note that the oral hearings in the Abyei Arbitration were webcast. *See* www.wx4all.net/pca.

    Contrast the confidentiality provisions of the 1907 Hague Convention and the 2008 Abyei Arbitration Agreement. Why did the parties to the Abyei Arbitration Agreement provide for public submissions and public hearings? Why is it that parties to a state-to-state arbitration might wish for the arbitral proceedings to be public? How are these considerations different from those in an international commercial arbitration? Why not webcast international commercial arbitrations to whoever wanted to watch them? Would this improve the arbitral process?

Recall the *Rainbow Warrior* arbitration between Greenpeace and the Republic of France. *See supra* pp. 105-06. Those arbitral proceedings were confidential, pursuant to the parties' agreement; among other things, the parties' written submissions and the arbitral award were not made public. Why not?

In the *Alabama Arbitration*, the United States published copies of its memorial in the arbitration and circulated them widely in European diplomatic circles, while the United Kingdom also took steps to appeal to public opinion:

> "With commendable foresight, Mr. Davis had caused the Case and a large part of the accompanying documents to be printed both in English and in French, a precaution which was not adopted by the other side. Our Agent was aware, too, how vital was it that Continental Europe should possess exact and trustworthy information as to the issue in controversy. He had the Case printed in Spanish. He also printed it in English (as well as in French) at the Brockhaus Press of [Leipzig], in octavo form, with a full index. Copies of the Case thus reproduced were distributed judiciously in several countries.... [After submissions of the parties' initial memorials,] England had now adopted the policy of trying her case in the newspapers. Public opinion adverse to the United States might have gained considerable headway upon the Continent, had not our Agent kept a vigilant eye upon the press of Great Britain, as well as noted day by day what the newspapers of the principal cities of the rest of Europe were saying upon the topic of the '*Alabama* Claims.' Mr. Davis took care that there should frequently appear in Continental journals of the largest influence articles setting forth substantially the American Case, with the contentions of the United States, as they really existed. This undertaking, upon which our Agent bestowed time and thought, had the effect of bringing about results that were to an eminent degree satisfactory."

Why would the United State have taken these various steps to publicize its memorial? Was this improper? What about the United Kingdom's effort to "try its case in the newspapers"? What risks, if any, did these efforts pose to the arbitral process? If the United States had sought permission in advance from the arbitral tribunal, how should the tribunal have ruled? Does anything in the Treaty of Washington address the issue? Would the United Kingdom have been well-advised to distribute its memorial as well?

CHAPTER 10

PROVISIONAL MEASURES IN INTERNATIONAL ARBITRATION

This chapter addresses the subject of provisional or interim measures of protection ("provisional measures"),[1] designed to protect parties or property during the pendency of international arbitral proceedings. Properly defined, "provisional measures" are awards or orders issued for the purpose of protecting one or both parties to a dispute from damage during the arbitral process. Most often, provisional measures are "intended to preserve a factual or legal situation so as to safeguard rights the recognition of which is sought from the [tribunal] having jurisdiction as to the substance of the case."[2] Additionally, provisional measures of protection can extend beyond merely preserving the factual or legal status quo, to require restoring a previous state of affairs or taking new actions.[3]

This chapter first explores the extent to which international arbitral tribunals, in both commercial and investment arbitrations, are authorized to grant provisional relief and the circumstances in which they will be willing to do so. Second, the chapter considers when national courts may grant interim relief in aid of international arbitrations. Among other things, the chapter examines whether the New York Convention forbids judicial orders granting provisional measures in aid of international commercial arbitrations, the effect of institutional rules on court-ordered provisional measures, and the circumstances in which national courts will exercise their powers to grant provisional relief in aid of arbitration (whether seated locally or abroad). Finally, the chapter considers the enforceability in national courts of provisional measures ordered by international arbitral tribunals.

A. ARBITRATORS' AUTHORITY TO ORDER PROVISIONAL MEASURES IN INTERNATIONAL ARBITRATION

The threshold question for a party seeking pre-award relief in an international arbitration is whether the tribunal possesses the authority to order interim relief. In general, that requires consulting three sources: (a) any applicable international arbitration convention, particu-

---

1. Provisional measures are also variously referred to as provisional relief or remedies, interim relief or remedies, conservatory measures, or prejudgment or pre-award relief. *See* G. Born, *International Commercial Arbitration* 2428 (2d ed. 2014); Brower & Tupman, *Court-Ordered Provisional Measures Under the New York Convention*, 80 Am. J. Int'l L. 24 (1986); Caron, *Interim Measures of Protection: Theory and Practice in Light of the Iran-United States Claims Tribunal*, 46 Zeitschrift für ausländisches öffentliches Recht und Völkerrecht 465 (1986); Collins, *Provisional and Protective Measures in International Litigation*, 234 Recueil des Cours 9 (1992).

2. *Van Uden Maritime BV v. Kommanditgesellschaft in Firma Deco-Line*, Case No. C-391/95, [1998] E.C.R. I-7091, 7133 (E.C.J.).

3. *See infra* pp. 892-95; G. Born, *International Commercial Arbitration* 2491-503 (2d ed. 2014); ICC, *Conservatory and Provisional Measures in International Arbitration* (1993).

larly the New York Convention; (b) applicable national law; and (c) the parties' arbitration agreement, including any relevant institutional arbitration rules.[4]

1. *Effect of National Arbitration Legislation on Arbitrators' Authority to Order Provisional Measures*

For the most part, international arbitration conventions have little to say about the authority of arbitrators to order provisional measures. The New York Convention contains no provision expressly referring to awards of provisional measures by arbitrators.[5] The Inter-American Convention is the same. The European Convention does address the general subject of provisional relief, but only provides: "[a] request for interim measures or measures of conservation addressed to a judicial authority shall not be deemed incompatible with the arbitration agreement, or regarded as a submission of the substance of the case to the court."[6] Like the New York Convention, the European Convention does not address whether or when an arbitral tribunal may grant provisional measures.

There are significant differences among national arbitration laws on the subject of tribunal-ordered provisional relief. In some nations, like Argentina, Italy and China, national arbitration law contains a mandatory prohibition against arbitrators from ordering provisional relief; following early 20th century statutory models, the granting of provisional measures in these jurisdictions is reserved exclusively to local courts, which are specifically authorized to issue provisional relief in aid of arbitration.[7] Other arbitration regimes, like those in UNCITRAL Model Law jurisdictions, France, Switzerland and the United States, authorize arbitrators to grant provisional measures (absent contrary agreement) and provide for judicial enforcement of such orders.[8]

The following materials illustrate the varying approaches that national laws take to tribunal-ordered provisional measures in international arbitration, focusing particularly on international commercial arbitration. In reviewing these materials, consider the extent to which the availability of tribunal-ordered provisional relief under national law is left to the parties' arbitration agreement, as well as the existence of any presumptions where the parties' agreement is not clear in this issue.

---

4. *See* G. Born, *International Commercial Arbitration* 2429 (2d ed. 2014); Brower & Tupman, *Court-Ordered Provisional Measures Under the New York Convention*, 80 Am. J. Int'l L. 24 (1986).

5. As discussed in detail below, however, some U.S. courts have interpreted Article II of the New York Convention as forbidding the courts of Contracting States from ordering prejudgment attachment. *See infra* pp. 910-12.

6. European Convention, Art. VI(4).

7. Argentine Code of Civil and Commercial Procedure, Art. 753; Italian Code of Civil Procedure, Art. 818; Chinese Arbitration Law, Art. 68. *See* G. Born, *International Commercial Arbitration* 2427, 2432-33, 2459, 2538 (2d ed. 2014).

8. UNCITRAL Model Law, Art. 17; French Code of Civil Procedure, Art. 1468; SLPIL, Arts. 183, 184. *See* G. Born, *International Commercial Arbitration* 2431-40, 2516-22 (2d ed. 2014); Donovan, *Powers of the Arbitrators to Issue Procedural Orders, Including Interim Measures of Protection, and the Obligations of Parties to Abide by Such Orders*, 10(1) ICC ICArb. Bull. 57 (1999).

ARGENTINE CODE OF CIVIL AND COMMERCIAL PROCEDURE
Article 753

Arbitrators cannot order compulsory measures or measures leading to enforcement. They must request them from the judge who will have to lend the support of his jurisdictional powers for the most swift and effective carrying out of the arbitral proceedings.

ITALIAN CODE OF CIVIL PROCEDURE
Article 818

The arbitrators may not grant attachment or other interim measures of protection, unless otherwise provided by law.

SWISS INTERCANTONAL CONCORDAT, 1969
Article 26 (generally superseded by SLPIL, Article 183)

26(1). The public judicial authorities alone have jurisdiction to make provisional orders.

26(2). However, the parties may voluntarily submit to provisional orders proposed by the arbitral tribunal.

NOTES

1. *Rationale for historic prohibitions under national laws against awards of provisional measures by arbitrators.* Consider Article 26 of the Swiss Intercantonal Concordat, Article 753 of the Argentine Code of Civil and Commercial Procedure and Article 818 of the Italian Code of Civil Procedure. All three sections forbid arbitrators from granting provisional relief and reserve that power to the courts. What is the rationale for that prohibition? If an arbitral tribunal can be trusted to resolve the merits of the parties' dispute, why can't it be permitted to order provisional measures that merely preserve the status quo? Are there particular reasons to doubt the efficacy and fairness of arbitral procedures in such matters (as compared to judicial procedures)?

    What consequences does an approach forbidding arbitrators from granting provisional measures have for the efficacy of the arbitral process? For example, what sort of issues will a court need to decide in granting provisional measures? What effect will judicial disposition of these issues have on the arbitrators' consideration of the parties' dispute?

    Suppose the parties' agreement to arbitrate provides expressly that the arbitrators shall have the authority to issue provisional measures. (As discussed below, that is the case with arbitration clauses that incorporate most institutional rules, which expressly authorize arbitral tribunals to grant provisional relief. *See infra* pp. 877-83.) In these instances, if a national arbitration statute forbids the arbitral tribunal from ordering provisional measures, as in Italy or Argentina, is this consistent with Articles V(1)(d) and II of the New York Convention?

2. *Trend of national arbitration legislation towards permitting arbitrators to grant provisional relief (unless otherwise agreed).* Consider Articles 183 and 184 of the SLPIL, excerpted at p. 159 of the Documentary Supplement, and compare them to Article 26 of the Swiss Intercantonal Concordat; also consider Article 17 of the UNCITRAL

Model Law, including the 2006 revisions to Article 17, excerpted at pp. 90 & 98-101 of the Documentary Supplement. In general, most developed arbitration statutes have moved towards permitting arbitrators to grant provisional relief, provided that the parties have not otherwise agreed. *See* G. Born, *International Commercial Arbitration* 2433-40 (2d ed. 2014); Fry, *Interim Measures of Protection: Recent Developments and the Way Ahead*, 2003 Int'l Arb. L. Rev. 153; Rau, *Provisional Relief in Arbitration: How Things Stand in the United States*, 22 J. Int'l Arb. 1 (2005). What explains this trend?

3. *Authority of arbitral tribunal under UNCITRAL Model Law and most other modern arbitration legislation to order provisional relief (unless parties have otherwise agreed).* Consider Article 17 of the UNCITRAL Model Law, including the 2006 revisions to Article 17. Compare Article 183 of the SLPIL. How does each provision deal with the arbitral tribunal's power to grant provisional measures? Is this an issue that the parties may regulate by agreement? If the parties' arbitration agreement does not expressly deal with the tribunal's power to award provisional measures, then what is the presumptive rule—that provisional measures may be issued by the arbitrators or that they may not be? What is the rationale of this approach?

4. *Authority of arbitral tribunal under most U.S. judicial decisions to order provisional relief (unless parties have agreed otherwise).* The FAA is silent on the arbitrators' powers to order provisional measures. Nonetheless, most U.S. courts have recognized the power of an arbitrator under the FAA to order provisional measures in aid of a domestic arbitration, provided that this is contemplated by the parties' agreement. *See Next Step Med. Co. v. Johnson & Johnson Int'l*, 619 F.3d 67, 70 (1st Cir. 2010) ("[a]rbitrators normally have the power to grant interim relief unless the parties specify otherwise in the contract"); *Pac. Reins. Mgt Corp. v. Ohio Reins. Corp.*, 935 F.2d 1019, 1022-23 (9th Cir. 1991) ("Temporary equitable relief in arbitration may be essential to preserve assets or enforce performance which, if not preserved or enforced, may render a final award meaningless"); *Island Creek Coal Sales Co. v. Gainesville*, 729 F.2d 1046, 1049 (6th Cir. 1984) (absent contrary provision in state law or parties' agreement, tribunal may award interim injunctive relief); *Certain Underwriters at Lloyd's, London v. Argonaut Ins. Co., supra* pp. 759-65.

    Despite this general approach, a few lower U.S. courts have held that arbitrators generally lack the power to issue provisional relief in aid of a domestic arbitration unless the parties have expressly authorized them to do so. *See Swift Indus., Inc. v. Botany Indus., Inc.*, 466 F.2d 1125, 1134 (3d Cir. 1972) (parties' agreement did not authorize tribunal to award provisional relief); *Carolina Power & Light Co. v. Uranex*, 451 F.Supp. 1044 (N.D. Cal. 1977) (dicta). *See also Charles Constr. Co. v. Derderian*, 586 N.E.2d 992 (Mass. 1992) (AAA Rules held not to permit tribunal-ordered provisional measures). No U.S. court appears to have held that parties are forbidden by the FAA from agreeing to vest arbitrators with power to award interim relief in aid of a domestic arbitration. Most U.S. decisions impliedly reject any such conclusion. *See* cases cited *supra* p. 874 and *infra* pp. 880-81. Indeed, a refusal to recognize an agreement giving arbitrators power to grant interim relief would be contrary to the FAA's rule that arbitration agreements are enforceable. *See supra* pp. 189, 320-21.

5. *Limits under national law on arbitrators' authority to grant provisional relief.* National law may authorize arbitrators to grant provisional measures only within speci-

fied limits. For example, as discussed below, Article 17 of the 1985 UNCITRAL Model Law limits provisional measures to those that are "necessary" and that concern the "subject-matter of the dispute." *See infra* p. 875. Contrast the language of Article 183(1) of the SLPIL. Which approach is preferable?

6. *Limits under Article 17 of UNCITRAL Model Law on arbitrators' authority to grant provisional relief.* Consider the original text of Article 17 of the Model Law, as adopted in 1985. Note that the original text of Article 17 arguably placed restrictions on a tribunal's powers to order interim relief (*i.e.*, such relief must be "necessary" and "in respect of the subject-matter of the dispute").

   (a) *Relief must be "necessary."* What does Article 17 mean when it provides that interim measures must be those that the tribunal considers "necessary"? Does this impose a substantive limitation on the interim relief that a tribunal may order? Or is it merely a grant of discretion?

   (b) *"In respect of the subject-matter of the dispute."* The original text of the Model Law grants arbitral tribunals the power to issue provisional measures that they "consider necessary *in respect of the subject-matter of the dispute*." Does this language limit the arbitrators' authority to grant provisional measures? Consider: Huntley, *The Scope of Article 17: Interim Measures under the UNCITRAL Model Law*, 740 PLI/Lit. 1181, 78 (2005) (urging "narrow interpretation" of subject-matter of the dispute: "a broad interpretation of the subject matter could lead to a slippery slope whereby [the] tribunal will define the all-encompassing term to include anything and everything"); A. Redfern & M. Hunter (eds.), *Law and Practice of International Commercial Arbitration* ¶7-26 (4th ed. 2004) ("measures contemplated relate to preserving or selling of goods rather than, for instance, preventing the flight of assets"). Is this the only interpretation of Article 17? Is it consistent with the Model Law's objectives?

   (c) *2006 Revisions to Article 17.* The 2006 Revisions of the Model Law amended Article 17(1) to omit the requirement that relief be "in respect of the subject-matter of the dispute." What explains this amendment?

7. *Arbitrators' authority to grant provisional relief is ordinarily concurrent with national court authority.* Note that Articles 9 and 17 of the UNCITRAL Model Law contemplate concurrent authority of the arbitral tribunal and national courts to order provisional relief. Articles 183 and 184 of the SLPIL are similar. Is it wise to permit two separate sources for provisional measures? Or does it encourage forum-shopping and jurisdictional disputes? Does the answer depend on whether it is the parties or the arbitrators that may seek judicial relief? Does it depend on when judicial relief is sought?

8. *Arbitrators lack authority to issue provisional measures against non-parties.* An arbitrator's powers are virtually always limited to the parties to the arbitration. As a consequence, the arbitrator generally will not have the power to order, for example, attachment of property held by a third party. G. Born, *International Commercial Arbitration* 1406-10, 2445-46 (2d ed. 2014); D. Caron, L. Caplan & M. Pellonpää, *The UNCITRAL Arbitration Rules: A Commentary* 517 (2d ed. 2013) ("an arbitral tribunal's jurisdiction encompasses only the parties before it [and] interim measures may not be directed to non-parties").

9. *Arbitrators lack authority directly to enforce their provisional measures.* If a party refuses to comply with tribunal-ordered provisional measures, can the arbitrators directly enforce those measures? How would that be done? As with final relief, an arbitral tribunal lacks direct coercive power to compel compliance with its awards or orders of provisional measures, and application for enforcement must be made to national courts. See, for example, the language of Article 183(2) of the SLPIL.

10. *Arbitral tribunal lacks authority to order provisional measures until it is constituted.* An arbitral tribunal obviously cannot issue provisional measures until it has been constituted. This is implied by arbitration legislation limiting the power to grant provisional measures to "arbitral tribunals" (not appointing authorities or individual arbitrators). *See, e.g.*, UNCITRAL Model Law, Art. 17; SLPIL, Arts. 183, 184. Until an arbitral tribunal has been legally-constituted, it has no powers and cannot issue provisional measures. This has important practical implications because, *supra* pp. 694-702, the process of constituting the arbitral tribunal can take weeks or months—during which time there is no tribunal that is able to order provisional relief. *See also infra* pp. 882-83, 904.

    Consider the discussion of "emergency arbitrators," under some recently-amended arbitration rules. *See infra* pp. 882-83.

11. *Judicial enforcement and review of tribunal-ordered provisional relief.* A corollary of recognition of an arbitrator's power to grant provisional relief is the availability of judicial enforcement of such orders. Consider how Articles 35 and 36 of the UNCITRAL Model Law, Articles 188-192 of the SLPIL and §§9 and 10 of the FAA provide for enforcement of awards of provisional relief. As discussed below, national courts in most developed jurisdictions will enforce provisional measures awarded by arbitral tribunals. *See infra* pp. 896-904. Arbitral awards of provisional measures are also subject to judicial review, just as other arbitral awards are. *See infra* pp. 902, 1117-20, 1134-73.

12. *Choice of law applicable to arbitral tribunal's power to grant provisional measures.* What law applies to determine an arbitrator's power to grant interim relief in an international arbitration? There is little authority on the law applicable to an arbitrator's power to grant provisional measures. Most precedent looks to the law of the arbitral seat. *See Interim Award in NAI Case No. 1694 of 12 December 1996*, XXIII Y.B. Comm. Arb. 97 (1998) (applying law of arbitral seat to arbitral tribunal's power to grant provisional measures).

    What law would govern the arbitrators' power to grant provisional measures in an arbitration seated in Argentina? Does Article 753 of the Argentine Code of Civil and Commercial Procedure apply? Suppose parties agree to arbitrate in Switzerland and their dispute arises under a contract governed by Italian law. Does Article 818 of the Italian Code of Civil Procedure apply? Or does Article 183 of the SLPIL apply? Isn't the latter choice clearly correct? *See supra* pp. 619-21, 634-38 & *infra* pp. 888-89.

13. *Arbitral tribunal's authority to grant provisional relief in ICSID investment arbitration.* Consider Article 47 of the ICSID Convention, excerpted at p. 23 of the Documentary Supplement. Is there any doubt about the authority of ICSID tribunals to grant at least some form of provisional relief? What is meant by the term "recommend any provisional measures"? Does Article 47 appear to contemplate mandatory orders of provisional relief—or just precatory recommendations? Despite Article 47's phrasing,

ICSID arbitral awards have interpreted the provision as permitting the ordering of binding provisional measures. *See, e.g., Occidental Petroleum Corp. v. Repub. of Ecuador, Decision on Provisional Measures in ICSID Case No. ARB/06/11 of 17 August 2007,* ¶58 ("The Tribunal wishes to make clear for the avoidance of doubt that, although Article 47 of the ICSID Convention uses the word 'recommend,' the Tribunal is, in fact, empowered to order provisional measures. This has been recognized by numerous international tribunals...."); *Tokios Tokelés v. Ukraine, Procedural Order No. 1 in ICSID Case No. ARB/02/18 of 1 July 2003,* ¶4; *Maritime Int'l Nominees Est. v. Guinea, Award in ICSID Case No. ARB/84/4 of 6 January 1988* ("In view of Article 47 and the applicable ICSID Rules, the Tribunal will take into account in its award the consequences of any failure by MINE to abide by these recommendations"); *Judgment of 27 September 1985, Guinea v. Maritime Int'l Nominees Est.*, 24 I.L.M. 1639 (1985) (Antwerp Rechtbank) ("according to Article 26 of the [ICSID Convention,] any possibility to introduce an action before the national courts of one of the contracting States ... is excluded for the contracting parties including the possibility to institute proceedings to obtain an attachment").

14. *Arbitral tribunal's authority to grant provisional relief in inter-state arbitration.* Consider the 1907 Hague Convention, especially Articles 37-48, excerpted at pp. 43-45 of the Documentary Supplement. What powers, if any, did arbitral tribunals have to grant provisional relief in inter-state arbitrations? Did the notion that parties would honor any award imply a submission to the arbitral tribunal's authority to issue provisional measures ensuring that the award could have practical meaning? Compare Article 26 of the PCA Rules, excerpted at pp. 287-88 of the Documentary Supplement. Note that Article 26 expressly provides that the tribunal shall have the authority to grant provisional measures. What explains the differences from the 1907 Hague Convention?

2. Effect of Institutional Arbitration Rules on Arbitrators' Authority to Order Provisional Measures

As described above, national arbitration statutes generally neither forbid arbitrators from granting provisional measures nor require that they have the power to do so. Rather, under most arbitration statutes, arbitrators have the authority to order provisional relief (and courts may enforce tribunal-ordered provisional measures), provided this authority is not excluded in the parties' arbitration agreement.[9] As a consequence, an arbitrator's power to order interim relief often turns largely on the terms of the parties' arbitration agreement, any applicable institutional rules and presumptions about the parties' likely intentions.

In practice, it is unusual (although by no means unheard of) for the parties' arbitration agreement expressly to address the subject of provisional relief. Thus, the power of an arbitrator under most national laws to order provisional relief usually turns upon the institutional rules (if any) selected by the parties. As the following materials illustrate, many institutional rules expressly address the power of a tribunal to grant interim relief. Nonetheless, in *ad hoc* arbitrations, or where institutional rules do not deal with the subject of provisional relief, interpretation of the parties' arbitration agreement and application of presumptions under national law will be required.

---

9. *See supra* pp. 873-77; G. Born, *International Commercial Arbitration* 2511-19 (2d ed. 2014).

CHARLES CONSTRUCTION CO. v. DERDERIAN
586 N.E.2d 992 (Mass. 1992)

WILKINS, Judge. Because the applicable arbitration rules did not authorize them to do so, the arbitrators had no authority to enter an interim order directing a party to provide security toward the payment of any award the arbitrators might eventually enter. We, therefore, affirm Superior Court judgments vacating the arbitrators' interim order for security. That award had directed James Derderian, as trustee of Parkman Realty Trust, to furnish a $1,000,000 irrevocable letter of credit, payable on demand, to the [AAA], as security for the payment of any arbitration award that might be entered against Derderian, as trustee, in the arbitration proceeding.... Charles Construction Co., Inc., seeks enforcement of the interim arbitration award in one of the actions before us, and Derderian seeks an order vacating that award in the other.

In October, 1984, Derderian, as owner of property in Brookline ("owner"), and Charles, as construction manager ("contractor"), entered into an associated general contractors' standard form of agreement pursuant to which a condominium and parking garage were to be constructed. That agreement provided for the arbitration of certain claims, disputes, and other matters arising out of the agreement "in accordance with the Construction Industry Arbitration Rules of the [AAA] then obtaining." Disputes did arise, and they were submitted to arbitration. The owner asserted claims for more than $2,800,000, and the contractor for more than $1,170,000. Hearings commenced in September, 1987, and continued intermittently until January, 1990, when the contractor requested the panel to issue an order for interim security. On February 16, 1990, in an interim order, the arbitrators, purporting to act under §34 of the construction industry arbitration rules, ordered the owner to provide the security that we have previously described. There is no contractual provision apart from the arbitration rules on which the contractor relies. He points to no statutory authorization for the arbitrators' award of interim relief. The owner contends first that, if Charles is to obtain relief before the arbitration proceeding is concluded, it must come from a court.

We reject the owner's claim that the contractor's only avenue for obtaining interim relief is through a court order independent of the arbitration proceeding. We have indeed upheld the entry of protective court orders even though a dispute between the parties is subject to arbitration. *See Hull Mun. Lighting Plant v. Massachusetts Mun. Wholesale Elec. Co.*, 399 Mass. 640, 648-649 (1987) (preliminary injunction upheld requiring contractual payments to continue while dispute is arbitrated pursuant to court order); *Salvucci v. Sheehan*, 349 Mass. 659, 663 (1965) (bill to reach and apply fraudulently conveyed property may be maintained before arbitration proceeding is concluded). If, however, there is an express agreement that authorizes an arbitrator to grant interim relief, including any authorization set forth in arbitration rules incorporated by agreement of the parties, there is no reason why an arbitrator may not act under that authority. Indeed, in such an instance, the court might be obliged both to defer to the parties' agreement to submit the matter of interim relief to arbitration and to give any subsequent interim order the same deferential treatment that must be accorded to an arbitrator's final order. Of course, a statute could authorize an arbitrator to grant interim relief. Therefore, if the arbitrators had contractual or statutory authority to issue an interim order, the contractor properly could have sought such an order from them and was not limited to asking for interim relief from a court.

There is little authority on the question whether, absent any controlling statute or agreement of the parties, an arbitrator has implicit authority to order a party to provide security, during the pendency of the arbitration, against the possibility of a decision adverse to that party....[10] We agree in general that, in the absence of an agreement or statute to the contrary, an arbitrator has inherent authority to order a party to provide security while the arbitration is continuing. It is reasonable to assume that parties, in agreeing to arbitration, implicitly intended that the arbitration not be fruitless and that interim orders to preserve the status quo or to make meaningful relief possible would be proper. In such a circumstance, the arbitrator's authority to act would reasonably be implied from the agreement to arbitrate itself.

This general principle has no application in this case because we construe the construction industry arbitration rules of the [AAA], which the contract incorporates by reference, to restrict the authority of an arbitrator to provide interim relief. To justify the issuance of the interim order, the contractor relies on §34 of the arbitration rules, the same authority that the arbitrators relied on when issuing their order. Section 34, as it was in effect when the interim order for security was entered in February, 1990, is entitled "Interim Measures," and states: "The arbitrator may issue such orders for interim relief as may be deemed necessary to safeguard the property that is the subject matter of the arbitration without prejudice to the rights of the parties or to the final determination of the dispute."[11] No property was the subject matter of the arbitration. The arbitration was not a dispute over specific property but rather concerned claims of breach of contract. The fact that the owner would be obliged to satisfy any arbitration award against him from assets of the Parkman Realty Trust does not make those assets "the subject matter of the arbitration." We do not give §34 such an expansive reading. If the drafters of §34 for the [AAA] had intended that an arbitrator have authority to issue a preliminary order that a party provide security, the rule would not have been written as it was, referring only to property that is the subject matter of the arbitration.[12]

There is another arbitration rule to which the contractor points but on which it relies only by a casual assertion. Section 43 of the construction industry arbitration rules, entitled "Scope of Award," permits an arbitrator to "grant any remedy or relief that the arbitrator deems just and equitable and within the scope of the agreement of the parties...." That rule cannot authorize interim relief of the sort that the arbitrators awarded in this case. Section 43 does not explicitly refer to interim relief, and, if were to be read to do so, it would render unnecessary §34, a rule that appears to deal explicitly and comprehensively with the subject of interim measures. Moreover, whatever just and equitable relief is granted must be "within the scope of the agreement of the parties." That language seems to be focused on

10. *Compare* Rodman, *Commercial Arbitration* §26.1 (West 1984 & Supp. 1989) ("Generally, with the exception of maritime cases, provisional remedies such as attachments or compulsory bonds are not available in arbitration") *with* 4 Business Law Monographs 5-6 (M. Bender 1989) ("Once the parties agree to submit their dispute to arbitration, the power of the arbitrator to govern the proceedings before him includes the power to grant provisional remedies").

11. Previously §34, in effect on January 1, 1986 (and perhaps earlier), was headed "Conservation of Property" instead of "Interim Measures," but it was substantially the same as the rule quoted above. The prior rule did not have the words "for interim relief" after the word "orders." The parties do not argue which rules are applicable, and we need not decide.

12. The conclusion of the court in *Pacific Reins. Mgt Corp. v. Ohio Reins. Corp.*, 935 F.2d. 1019, 1022-23 & n.1 (9th Cir. 1991), that the rule identical to §34 in the AAA commercial arbitration rules "contemplates interim equitable relief in appropriate circumstances" is correct, but that rule does not justify an interim order that a party provide security pending the arbitrator's decision.

the arbitrator's final disposition (unless perhaps the parties explicitly agreed to grant the arbitrators the right to grant interim relief).[13]

CERTAIN UNDERWRITERS AT LLOYD'S v. ARGONAUT INSURANCE CO.
264 F.Supp.2d 926 (N.D. Cal. 2003)
[excerpted above at pp. 759-65]

NOTES

1. *Institutional rules relating to provisional relief.* Consider Article 26 of the UNCITRAL Rules, Article 28 of the ICC Rules, Rule 37 of the AAA Rules and Article 25 of the LCIA Rules, excerpted at pp. 170-71, 192, 241-42 & 271-72 of the Documentary Supplement. What are the differences between these various approaches? What are the respective advantages and disadvantages of each approach?

2. *Presumptions concerning parties' intentions as to provisional measures in absence of express agreement.* As described above, the UNCITRAL Model Law, the SLPIL and the FAA (as well as most other leading national arbitration statutes) permit arbitrators to order provisional relief—provided that the parties have not otherwise agreed. *See supra* pp. 873-77. In a significant number of cases, however, neither the parties' agreement nor the institutional arbitration rules that they designate expressly address the power of arbitrators to order provisional measures. *See, e.g., Charles Constr.*, 586 N.E.2d 992, excerpted above at pp. 878-80; 1988 ICC Rules, Art. 8(5), excerpted below at p. 913. In the absence of evidence regarding an express or implied agreement, what legal rule should govern the availability of tribunal-ordered provisional measures? That is, when the parties' agreement is silent, should or should not arbitrators be presumed to have been intended to have the power to order provisional relief?

  (a) *Presumption that arbitrators lack authority to grant provisional relief (unless otherwise agreed).* Some authorities hold that an arbitral tribunal lacks the power to grant provisional measures, unless otherwise agreed. In *Swift Indus., Inc. v. Botany Indus., Inc.*, 466 F.2d 1125 (3d Cir. 1972), the court held that the arbitrator lacked the power to order provisional relief:

  > We have sought to distill from the Agreement the essence of the arbitrator's authority. Whatever that authority may be, it is clear to us that it does not include the authority to award a six million dollar cash bond to cover a liability which contrary to the requirements of the applicable breach of warranty clause, has not yet been (and may not be) "*incurred or suffered*," in a situation where the parties did not provide for such security in their agreement, although they might have done so. In our view, to award, as an adjunct to declaratory relief, a form of prejudgment execution which the Agreement by its lack of reference to security seems to exclude

---

13. The statement in *Island Creek Coal Sales Co. v. Gainesville*, 729 F.2d 1046, 1049 (6th Cir. 1984), that §43 authorizes an arbitrator to order specific performance to preserve the status quo during arbitration may be correct (unless the contract expressly prevents such relief), especially as to the party who commenced the proceeding in order to discover whether he could depart from the status quo. That opinion does not, however, say that §43 supports an order of the sort entered in the case before us.

rather than to intend, is to eclipse the framework of the agreement and to venture onto unprotected ground. We subscribe to the observations ... that the draftsmen may be unable to perceive in advance what specific remedy should be awarded to meet a particular contingency and that in arbitration flexibility is important. But the principle of flexibility of relief cannot be permitted to obscure or to effect a metamorphosis of the claim itself. That untoward event would occur if we were to permit the arbitrator's award to stand in this case.

Is this persuasive? As a general presumption about an arbitrator's lack of authority to grant interim relief?

(b) *Presumption that arbitrators possess authority to grant provisional relief (unless otherwise agreed).* In contrast, consider again Article 17 of the UNCITRAL Model Law (both the 1985 and 2006 versions) and Article 183 of the SLPIL, excerpted at pp. 90, 98-100 & 159 of the Documentary Supplement. *See supra* pp. 873-75. What presumption does each provision adopt? Also consider *Charles Construction.* What approach does the court take to the burden of establishing the existence or nonexistence of an agreement to permit the tribunal to award provisional relief? How does the presumption adopted in *Charles Construction* differ (if at all) from that in the UNCITRAL Model Law and the SLPIL?

What is the presumption in *Charles Construction* concerning the arbitrator's power to order provisional measures when the parties have not agreed to institutional arbitration rules? Should a similar approach be taken to institutional rules under the UNCITRAL Model Law and SLPIL? If the parties have agreed to institutional arbitration rules, what does *Charles Construction* presume concerning the arbitrator's power to award provisional relief?

What approach does the court take in *Certain Underwriters* to the arbitrators' presumptive authority (or "inherent" authority) to grant provisional measures? Note the court's refusal to annul Interim Order No. 2. Why did the court annul Interim Order No. 3? Was it because the arbitral tribunal lacked authority to issue provisional measures? Or because of the particular character of the sanctions imposed by Interim Order No. 3?

3. *What presumption should be adopted regarding arbitrator's authority to grant provisional relief?* Which approach to the arbitrator's implied authority—the UNCITRAL Model Law's, *Charles Construction*'s, *Certain Underwriters*', or *Swift*'s—is preferable? Would it be better to take an approach not accepted in either the Model Law or *Charles Construction*—i.e., that the tribunal presumptively does not enjoy power to award provisional relief, absent an affirmative showing of an express or implied agreement to that effect? What are the likely expectations of the parties in the absence of an express agreement? What approach is most likely to produce a fair and efficient dispute-resolution process?

4. *U.S. judicial decisions concluding that arbitrators presumptively possess implied authority to grant provisional relief (unless otherwise agreed).* As noted above, most U.S. courts have adopted a position similar to that of the UNCITRAL Model Law—i.e., that parties will generally be presumed, absent contrary agreement, to have conferred the power to award provisional relief on their arbitrator, even where institutional arbitration rules are involved. *See supra* pp. 874, 881. The opinions in *Charles Construction* and *Certain Underwriters* illustrate this approach. Is this approach wise? Is there a better presumptive rule?

Most commentators on international arbitration also conclude that arbitrators presumptively have the power to order provisional relief (unless otherwise agreed): "The authority of arbitrators to grant conservatory and provisional measures stems from their inherent powers to conduct the arbitral proceedings and, more specifically, any additional authority granted to them in the contract between the parties." Hoellering, *The Practices and Experience of the American Arbitration Association*, in ICC, *Conservatory and Provisional Measures in International Arbitration* 31 (1993). *See also* Higgins, *Interim Measures in Transnational Maritime Arbitration*, 65 Tulane L. Rev. 1519, 1535-36 (1991) ("By expressly consenting to the arbitration of their dispute, the parties implicitly accord to the arbitrators a general grant of power to exercise any authority necessary to reach a determination on the merits of the dispute.").

5. *Arbitrators' power to grant provisional measures under ICC Rules.* The ICC Rules were revised in 1998 to more directly address the arbitral tribunal's power to grant provisional measures. Consider Article 8(5) of the 1988 version of the ICC Rules. Does this provision affirmatively grant an arbitrator power to award interim relief? *See* Schwartz, *The Practices and Experiences of the ICC Court*, in ICC, *Conservatory and Provisional Measures in International Arbitration* 46 (1993) ("the arbitrators themselves are not expressly authorized to issue [provisional] measures"). How would Article 8(5) of the 1988 ICC Rules be interpreted under the analysis in *Charles Construction*? In *Certain Underwriters*? Compare Article 28 of the 2012 ICC Rules and Article 23 of the 1998 ICC Rules to their predecessor in the 1988 ICC Rules. Note that Article 28 of the 2012 Rules and Article 23 of the 1998 Rules expressly grant the arbitral tribunal authority to order "interim or conservatory measures." Was this a desirable change to the ICC Rules? Compare Article 28 of the 2012 ICC Rules with Article 25 of the 2014 LCIA Rules. Which approach is wiser?

6. *Interpretation of other leading institutional rules.* Consider again Article 26 of the 2010 UNCITRAL Rules, Article 25 of the 2014 LCIA Rules and Article 28 of the 2012 ICC Rules. How would each be interpreted under the analysis in *Charles Construction*? Under *Certain Underwriters*? Consider Article R-37 of the 2013 AAA Commercial Rules, which replaces the version of the AAA Rules at issue in *Charles Construction*. Would the case be decided differently under the new rule?

7. *ICC Rules for A Pre-Arbitral Referee Procedure.* Some arbitral institutions have adopted specialized rules that seek to provide a non-judicial mechanism for obtaining urgently-needed provisional relief. The ICC Rules for a Pre-Arbitral Referee Procedure were an early example of such efforts. *See* Hausmaninger, *The ICC Rules for A Pre-Arbitral Referee Procedure: A Step Towards Solving the Problem of Provisional Relief in International Commercial Arbitration*, 7 ICSID Rev. 82 (1992). These rules were used rarely (less than a dozen instances). That was because parties must specifically agree to the use of this specialized procedure; the procedures are not included within the ICC Rules. Given the realities of litigation, this agreement cannot often be expected to occur after a dispute has arisen; on the other hand, at earlier stages, parties are not generally sufficiently focused on the procedural intricacies of future disputes to make provision for specialized issues.

8. *Institutional rules providing for urgent provisional relief by "emergency arbitrators."* An alternative and improved approach to that of the ICC's Pre-Arbitral Referee Procedure involves so-called "emergency arbitrators" appointed on a fast-track basis

solely to decide claims for urgent interim relief before the arbitral tribunal is constituted. A number of sets of institutional rules have been recently revised to provide for "emergency arbitrators," including the ICC Rules (Art. 29 and Appx. V), ICDR Rules (Art. 6), LCIA Rules (Art. 9B), HKIAC Rules (Schedule 4), NAI Rules (Art. 42a), SCC Rules (Appx. II), SCC Rules for Expedited Arbitrations (Appx. II), SIAC Rules (Rule 26(2) & Schedule 1), Swiss Rules (Art. 43), CIETAC Rules (Art. 23 & Appx. III) and WIPO Rules (Art. 49). Each of these sets of rules provides for the appointment, in cases of urgency, of a sole arbitrator to resolve requests for provisional measures prior to constitution of the full arbitral tribunal. *See, e.g.,* 2014 ICDR Rules, Art. 6 ("Emergency Measures of Protection," involving appointment of special "emergency arbitrator"); 2010 NAI Rules, Art. 42. As soon as the full tribunal is constituted, the arbitrator responsible for considering initial requests for provisional measures ceases to play any further role in the arbitral proceedings. *See, e.g.,* 2014 ICDR Rules, Art. 6(5); 2013 HKIAC Rules, Schedule 4, ¶20. Because the provisions do not require a separate agreement by the parties to this mechanism, they offer a reasonable prospect of being used in actual dispute resolution. Is this an appropriate approach towards providing for provisional relief? What are its advantages and disadvantages?

9. *Characterizing "emergency arbitrators."* Is an "emergency arbitrator" really an arbitrator? Recall the definition of "arbitration." *See supra* pp. 131-37 & *infra* pp. 1059-61. How does dispute "resolution" by an emergency "arbitrator" resemble "arbitration"? How does it differ?

   Is a decision of an emergency arbitrator an award? Subject to annulment under national law? To recognition under the New York Convention? Why or why not?

10. *Arbitrators' authority to order security and counter-security.* A key feature of provisional relief is security—either for ultimate liability or for attorneys' fees and other legal costs—and counter-security—for the damages caused by provisional measures granted for a party that ultimately is unsuccessful. Note that this was the type of interim relief addressed in *Charles Construction* and *Certain Underwriters.* Consider the institutional rules set forth above; what provisions do these rules make for security orders by tribunals?

3. Arbitrators' Exercise of Authority to Order Provisional Relief

Assuming an arbitrator possesses the power to order provisional relief, how do arbitrators choose to exercise that authority? The short answer is that arbitrators were historically hesitant to grant provisional relief, even when authorized by national law to do so, but that in recent years tribunals have shown greater decisiveness.[14] Nonetheless, the circumstances in which arbitrators will grant interim relief vary widely, depending on the applicable law(s), relevant contractual terms and the tribunal's assessment of discretionary considerations. The following materials illustrate how arbitral tribunals assess these circumstances.

---

14. *See* G. Born, *International Commercial Arbitration* 2461-62 (2d ed. 2014).

DECISION OF GENEVA CHAMBER OF COMMERCE OF 25 SEPTEMBER 1997

19 ASA Bull. 745 (2001)

This arbitration was initiated on 21 October 1996, by A SpA (hereinafter "Claimant" or "A"), a company registered in Italy, against B. A.G. (hereinafter "Defendant" or "B"), a company registered in Germany, under the Arbitration Rules of the Geneva Chamber of Commerce and Industry. A claims from B [a specified sum in] damages. B moves for the dismissal of A's claim and counterclaims for restitution of amounts paid to A, i.e., [a sum] plus [another specified sum] plus an award for lost profits....

In a letter dated 26 March 1997, Defendant informed the Arbitral Tribunal that A had gone into voluntary liquidation on 20 December 1996, and that Mr. R. of Bologna had been appointed as liquidator. This prompted Defendant to request the Tribunal (a) to order a stay of proceedings, and (b) to order A "to provide security for costs by way of a cash deposit or a bank guarantee issued by a first class bank in an appropriate amount to be determined to the Arbitral Tribunal for the compensation of attorney's fees it may be ordered to pay to B. Such security for costs to be provided either in cash or by an irrevocable bank guarantee issued by a first class bank." The motion for suspension was later withdrawn. In an answer ... Claimant ... moved for dismissal of Defendant's request for a *cautio*. On the Tribunal's directions, each party then filed short briefs on the Defendant's motion for security for costs.... The Arbitral Tribunal, having met for deliberation, now issues the following ruling.

The parties are of opposite views as to the authority of an Arbitral Tribunal to issue an order requiring a party to furnish security for costs. Defendant appears to consider it as a matter of course; it does not quote any authority in support of its motion. By contrast, Claimant contends that, in international as well as in municipal arbitration, arbitrators sitting in Switzerland have no authority to order security for costs. In its view, such is the conclusion to be derived from a review of Swiss legal writing. This view was further adopted in four reported decisions of arbitrators sitting in Switzerland.

It is a fact that, in Swiss legal writing, there is a widespread opinion that there is no room for security for costs in arbitration. This seems to be the prevailing view in municipal arbitration under the Concordat. [Some authorities] are less categorical, but their reluctance seems to proceed from the fact that security for costs is unusual in ordinary court proceedings and should not be expected in arbitration. At this junction, it should be remembered that security for costs has practically disappeared from the State Courts of continental Europe, due to the widespread acceptance of relevant Hague Conventions (1905, then 1954). This explains, to some extent at least, the reluctance of Swiss legal writers as to its use in arbitration. It should be further noted that most of the writers aptly quoted by Claimant have addressed the problem from a municipal rather than from an international point of view. By contrast, three of the four decisions relied upon by Claimant have been issued in international arbitration....

The third decision quoted by Claimant is the most detailed and the most recent. [1995 ASA Bull. 529]. [T]he learned arbitrator formed the view that ["in general, commentary and case law are hostile to security for costs (*cautio judicatum solvi*) with regard to arbitration"]. There is furthermore no mention of it in most arbitration rules, Art. 15.2 [of the 1985 LCIA Rules] being an exception. As for the [SLPIL], it does not mention it either way. Turning then to general considerations, the learned arbitrator holds the view that if the parties had contemplated the possibility of security for costs, they would have mentioned it in the arbitration clause, all the more so that, by definition, international arbitration arises between parties established in different countries. He further holds that the possibility of enforcing an award for costs under the New York Convention is an additional reason for dismissing the motion.

The Tribunal cannot but share the view expressed in that decision as to the legal situation under the [SLPIL]. The wide terms of Art. 182(2) are such that it could not be contended that they deprive the arbitrators from the authority to order security for costs. The same is true for Art. 19 of the Arbitration Rules of the Geneva Chamber of Commerce. The further fact that the Act grants the arbitrator the power to order provisional measures allows the conclusion that an order for security for costs would not be alien to the spirit of the Act. The question whether the arbitrator has such authority and, if so, at what conditions he may make such an order depends therefore on more general considerations.

In this respect, the Tribunal does not consider as binding the opinions expressed by the majority of Swiss legal writers, since they deal mainly with municipal, e.g., Concordat arbitration, and are clearly impressed by the disappearance of security for costs from the State Courts. But international arbitration is not restricted to the shores of Swiss lakes. There are precedents in international arbitration which actually ordered security for costs. Thus, in 1990, in an ICC arbitration (No. 6697), the Arbitral Tribunal issues a detailed decision in which its authority to issue such an order was affirmed. [1992 Rev. arb. 143.] Similarly, another decision in another ICC arbitration required security for costs from both Claimant and Counter-Claimant (ICC arbitration No. 6682, 1993).

It should further be remembered that in England, one of the major centres of international, mainly professional, arbitration, security for costs is in daily use. Under the previous Arbitration Act, the power to order it [lay] with the Courts, and the exercise of this power in ICC arbitration gave rise to the well-known dispute that followed the decision of the House of Lords in *Ken Ren* [1994] 2 WLR 631. Under the Arbitration Act, 1996, §38(3), this power was transferred to the arbitrator.

Contrary therefore to the view expressed in Switzerland, security for costs is resorted to in international arbitration, and arbitrators have issued orders, therefore. As already said, the authority to issue such an order in international arbitration located in Switzerland may be derived from Art. 182(2) and 183 of the Act.

The question is not therefore whether but when an arbitrator may require from a party to give security for costs. It is obvious that registration or domicile of the party outside the place of arbitration cannot justify such an order, since such situation is in the essence of international arbitration. It should be furthermore taken into consideration, that international arbitration arises in connection with contracts or other operations of international trade, in the wide sense of the world, which imply greater risks than domestic trade. Such risks are to be borne by the parties including, in the view of this Tribunal, the risk of the other party failing into financial difficulties up to and including bankruptcy. By contrast, it may happen that a party takes certain steps in order to divest itself from its assets so as to be just an empty shell in case it loses the arbitration. Such manoeuvres, contrary to good faith, could justify an order for security for costs. Another instance is provided by the facts in *Ken Ren*: an important arbitration is launched by a company that is just an empty shell; if it wins, it cashes the award; if it loses, it will not pay anything.

In the particular circumstances of this case, the shareholders of A have decided to go into liquidation. In the view of the Tribunal, it is a commercial risk that has to be borne by Defendant. It has neither been alleged nor proved that this decision was made in circumstances amounting to bad faith. The liquidator of the Claimant company has the powers and the responsibilities prescribed by Italian law. It is the responsibility of the Defendant to take whatever steps that are open to creditors under Italian law in order to safeguard its rights as possible creditor. In summary, the decision of A to go into voluntary liquidation does not go beyond the commercial risks to be borne by the parties in an international contract. In the light of the foregoing, the Tribunal comes to the conclusion that there is no ground for the issuance of an order for security for costs.... The Arbitral Tribunal dismisses Defendant's motion for security for costs....

INTERIM AWARD IN ICC CASE NO. 8786
11(1) ICC ICArb. Bull. 81 (2000)

The dispute arose in connection with Defendant's cancellation of order for ready-made clothes from Claimant. Claimant argued that the orders were cancelled shortly prior to delivery of the goods, despite its having submitted samples found to be acceptable. It claimed damages for unusable materials, loss of profit and costs. Defendant invoked late performance by Claimant, arguing that it had been forced to terminate the contract on account of Claimant's failure to respect delivery dates and its refusal to grant a price reduction for such failure. Defendant in its turn claimed damages for loss of profit and various costs, and contested those requested by Claimant. In the arbitration proceedings before a sole arbitrator, Defendant asked for an interim award on security. The Arbitral Tribunal rejected this request [reasoning as follows].

Both parties have agreed to the applicability of the following procedural rules.... [a] the rules set forth in article 8 of the Terms of Reference; [b] the ICC [Rules]; [c] the provisions of chapter 12 of the [SLPIL]). [T]he Defendant and Counter-claimant has filed a brief, seeking the following relief: ... "1. The Claimant must provide adequate security for the counterclaim by establishing a[n] irrevocable bank guarantee that will be unconditionally released to the Defendant upon presentation of the final award in the present arbitration in the amount awarded to the Defendant." Defendant argues in essence that security measures [are] necessary because of "Claimant's failure to cooperate" in the ... arbitration proceedings.... The Defendant believes "that should the award in the instant case be in its favor the Claimant will not voluntarily comply such an award." In its brief ... the Defendant quotes *Decision 96/627* of February 1, 1996, rendered by the 15th Legal Department of the Turkish Court of Appeals.... Also a case study of Dr. Felix R. Ehrat of February 2, 1996, about "Practical Enforcement Experience in Turkey" ... is quoted. Quoting [these sources], the Defendant [claims] that "the chances of a foreign party to obtain recognition of an arbitral award in Turkey are less than slim." ...

In its brief ... the Claimant and Counter-defendant does not agree with the Defendant's request for security measures. The Claimant asks for more respect for the Turkish Courts and maintains that the Defendant's request is unacceptable because "[t]he Defendant's Attorney is acting like he has won the trial already and by doing this the Arbitration is becoming more complex." ...

Decision 96/627 quoted by the Defendant and Counter-claimant ... must be distinguished from the situation in the present arbitration.... The Turkish Court of Appeals ...

found that the Arbitral Tribunal had violated the arbitration agreements between the parties, because the Arbitral Tribunal [came] to the conclusion that the wording "Turkish laws in force" was to be understood as a choice of Turkish *substantive* law only. The Turkish Court concluded that the parties had also agreed on the choice of *procedural* law. Therefore, it held that the reservation of Art. V(i)(d) of the New York Convention was applicable.... Because the Commercial Court of Ankara found that Turkish substance and procedural law was applicable, it held that the arbitral award did not qualify as a "foreign" award within the meaning of Art. 1 of the Convention [and therefore could be annulled by Turkish courts, notwithstanding the fact that the arbitration was seated in Switzerland]....

In the present arbitration, however, there exists a clear agreement concerning the applicable substantive and procedural law ... between Defendant and Claimant. Thus, *Decision 96/627* must be distinguished from the present arbitration with respect to the procedural and substantive law applicable to the dispute. In the present matter, none of the parties has ever maintained so far that Turkish substantive and/or procedural law should be applicable to the dispute. [Likewise,] none of the parties has maintained so far that an award should not qualify as a "foreign" award in the sense of Art. 1 [of the] Convention.... Based on the above considerations the Arbitral Tribunal concludes that Defendant has failed to show that, as a direct consequence of *Decision 96/627*, an award rendered in its favor would not be enforceable.... Defendant, therefore, has further failed to show on a prima facie basis that its chances to obtain recognition of an award in the present matter in Turkey "are less than slim." ...

The Terms of Reference as well as the ICC Rules do not contain any specific rule concerning security measures (cf, however, ... below regarding Art. 8(5) ICC Rules). Art. 183 [of the SLPIL] contains rules regarding ... provisional and protective measures. One possible measure is to order the deposit of security [citing Swiss academic commentary regarding Article 183 of the SLPIL]. As a consequence, a security measure as requested by the Defendant is basically possible. Thus, it has to be examined, whether such a measure would be justified in the present matter.

It is undisputed that to "preserve the legitimate rights of the requesting party, the measures must be 'necessary.' This requirement is satisfied only if the delay in the adjudication of the main claim caused by the arbitral proceedings would lead to a 'substantial' (but not necessarily 'irreparable' as known in common law doctrine) prejudice for the requesting party...." "The Arbitral Tribunal may only order provisional measures, if the requesting party has substantial *threat of a not easily reparable prejudice*" [citing K. Berger, *International Economic Arbitration* 336 (1993).] Furthermore, it is required that "the facts supporting the request for interim measures have to be substantiated by *prima facie* evidence." The Defendant has failed to produce *prima facie* evidence for its allegation that an arbitral Award rendered in its favor would not be enforceable in Turkey.... Thus, the Defendant has failed to sufficiently substantiate the existence of a not easily reparable prejudice.

A further precondition for an interim award on security is that provisional and protective measures have to be *urgently needed*. The Defendant did not allege nor show that provisional and protective measures in the present arbitration are urgently needed.

The Arbitral Tribunal therefore concludes that Defendant has failed to show that the prerequisites under Art. 183 for the relief sought are fulfilled in the present matter. Finally, the Arbitral Tribunal wishes to emphasize that the Defendant is "at liberty to apply to any competent judicial authority for interim or conservatory measures, and [he] shall not by so doing be held to infringe the agreement to arbitrate or to affect the relevant powers reserved to the arbitrator." (Art. 8(5), ICC Rules). Once the file is transmitted to the arbitrator, Art. 8(5) [of the] ICC Rules provides for "exceptional circumstances" as precondition to order such measures. Whether exceptional circumstances are given in the present matter would have to be decided by the competent authorities in accordance with their local law. Thus the Defendant is free to try to seek "interim or conservatory measures" directly from the competent authorities in Turkey or in any other competent jurisdiction....

The Arbitral Tribunal directs and awards as follows: ... Defendant and Counter-claimant's request for an interim award on security ... is hereby dismissed....

CERTAIN UNDERWRITERS AT LLOYD'S v. ARGONAUT INSURANCE CO.
264 F.Supp.2d 926 (N.D. Cal. 2003)

[excerpted above at pp. 759-65]

NOTES

1. *General absence of legislative standards governing exercise of arbitrators' authority to grant provisional measures.* Consider Article 17 of the 1985 UNCITRAL Model Law and Article 183 of the SLPIL, excerpted at pp. 90 & 159 of the Documentary Supplement. Does either provision address the question of what standards are applicable to an arbitrator's grant of provisional measures? Compare the U.S. FAA. How are arbitrators, whose authority derives from these statutory provisions, to determine whether or not to exercise that authority by granting interim relief? What is the legal source of standards governing an arbitrator's decision whether or not to grant provisional relief?

2. *Choice of law governing arbitrators' exercise of authority to grant provisional measures.* As discussed above, the law governing the arbitral tribunal's authority to grant provisional measures is ordinarily that of the arbitral seat. *See supra* p. 876. Note that the *Geneva Award* looks to Swiss law to determine whether the arbitrators had the power to issue a particular type of provisional measures (security for costs).

    Is the law of the arbitral seat necessarily the law that governs the *exercise*—as distinguished from the *existence*—of the arbitrators' authority? Is there any reason that a different law should apply to the arbitral tribunal's *authority* to order provisional measures and the *exercise* of that authority? What law did the *Geneva Award* look to in deciding whether to exercise its authority to grant security for costs?

    In particular, three principal choices are possible for the law governing the exercise of authority to order provisional measures: (1) the law of the arbitral seat; (2) the law governing the parties' underlying contract or relationship; or (3) international standards. There are authorities adopting each of these choices of law (or, alternatively, looking to the laws of multiple jurisdictions). *Compare Interim Award in ICC Case No. 7544*, 11(1) ICC ICArb. Bull. 56 (2000) (considering French domestic standards as "helpful as a pointer") with *Interim Award in ICC Case No. 8879*, 11(1) ICC ICArb. Bull. 84, 89 (2000) ("... both the laws of Ontario (*lex fori*) and Mexico (*lex contractus*) expressly grant arbitrators that authority in substantially the same terms as Article 17 of the UNCITRAL Model Law ...") and *Decision of 25 September 1997*, 19 ASA

Bull. 745 (2001) (considering international practice as to whether request for interim relief should be granted).

Consider the *Geneva Award*. Is its application of standards drawn from international practice appropriate? What are the benefits of applying such standards? How would a tribunal determine the contents of these international standards? Consider the *Interim Award in ICC Case No. 8786*. What law does it apply to the question of the standards for granting interim relief?

Does it make sense for the standards for granting provisional measures to be ascertained according to the law of the arbitral seat? That would mean that the availability and extent of provisional measures would depend on the location of the arbitral seat—is that appropriate? Recall that most arbitration legislation does not contain standards governing the grant of interim relief by an arbitral tribunal. *See supra* p. 888. To what body of law, within the arbitral seat, should an arbitral tribunal then look in determining whether or not to grant provisional relief? Does it make sense to look to the standards applicable in local courts for provisional measures?

Alternatively, does it make sense for the availability and extent of interim relief to be determined by the law governing the underlying contract? If the parties' disputes involved claims under different contracts, or both tort and contract claims, governed by different substantive laws, wouldn't this mean that different standards for provisional relief applied to different disputes? Is this sensible?

3. *Choice of law governing standards for provisional measures under Article 17A of 2006 UNCITRAL Model Law*. Revised Article 17A of the 2006 Model Law, excerpted at pp. 98-99 of the Documentary Supplement, provides that a party seeking interim measures must satisfy the tribunal that specified conditions exist (irreparable harm outweighing possible injury to other party and reasonable possibility of success on the merits). Does this suggest what law would govern the tribunal's exercise of power to order provisional measures? Is it a sensible approach to the choice-of-law issue?

4. *Standards for provisional measures*. Stated generally, most international arbitral tribunals require showings of (a) serious or irreparable harm to the claimant; (b) urgency; and (c) no prejudgment of the merits, while some tribunals also require the claimant to establish a *prima facie* case on the merits. Considered more closely, many arbitral tribunals also look to the nature of the provisional measures that are requested, and the relative injury to be suffered by each party, in deciding whether to grant such measures. In particular, some provisional measures (*e.g.*, preserving the status quo or ordering performance of a contract or other legal obligation) will typically require strong showings of serious injury, urgency and a *prima facie* case, while other provisional measures (*e.g.*, preservation of evidence, enforcement of confidentiality obligations, security for costs) are unlikely to demand the same showings.

(a) *Serious or irreparable harm*. Consider *ICC Case No. 8786*. What standard does the tribunal require in order to grant provisional measures? What is meant by the requirement that "the delay in the adjudication of the main claim caused by the arbitral proceedings would lead to a 'substantial' (but not necessarily 'irreparable' as known in common law doctrine) prejudice for the requesting party?" What is the source of this standard? Is it based on any legal rules, set forth in any legal system? If not, what is it based on?

Consider the following excerpt from a leading ICSID award: "a provisional measure is necessary where the actions of a party 'are capable of causing or of threatening irreparable prejudice to the rights invoked.'" *Tokios Tokelés v. Ukraine, Procedural Order No. 3, ICSID Case No. ARB/02/18*, ¶8. When will a delay in paying a monetary claim ever constitute "irreparable" prejudice? If only "substantial" harm, rather than "irreparable" damage, is required, how substantial must the harm be?

(b) *Urgency*. Consider again *ICC Case No. 8786*. Note the requirement that the party seeking interim relief demonstrate that the need for such measures is "urgent." What does this requirement mean and how does it differ from the requirement that serious harm will be suffered if interim relief is not granted? Again, what legal system defines how urgent harm must be before provisional measures will be warranted?

(c) *No prejudgment of merits*. It is often said that provisional measures will only be granted if doing so does not "prejudge the merits" of the dispute. That is, "an arbitral tribunal must refrain from prejudging the merits of the case." Lew, *Commentary on Interim and Conservatory Measures in ICC Arbitration Cases*, 11(1) ICC ICArb. Bull. 23, 27 (2000). What does this formulation mean? Does it argue against the tribunal making a decision that might prejudice or bias its final decision on the merits, or does it argue against the tribunal granting the same relief that is requested on the merits? If the former, should it not be clear that a tribunal's interim decision on provisional measures is just that—a temporary decision that does not bind, or even predispose, the arbitrators with regard to their final decision? If the latter, is not interim relief necessarily different from final relief, in that it is by definition only temporary and subject to revision? What purpose does the "no prejudgment" rule serve?

(d) *Prima facie basis for claim*. Some authorities have held that the party requesting interim relief must demonstrate a *prima facie* case on the merits of its claim (or, in other formulations, a probability of prevailing on its claim). According to one award: "The present Arbitral Tribunal is not a referee jurisdiction, but a jurisdiction of the merits seized of provisional measures.... a serious dispute does not prevent a broader appreciation, although on a provisional basis, of the respective arguments of the parties." *Partial Award in Unidentified ICC Case*, quoted in Schwartz, *The Practices and Experience of the ICC Court,* in ICC, *Conservatory and Provisional Measures in International Arbitration* 45, 60 (1993). Did the tribunal examine the existence of a *prima facie* case in *ICC Case No. 8786* or the *Geneva Award*? Is it appropriate for a tribunal to consider the merits of the parties' claims at a preliminary stage? Consider: J. Lew, L. Mistelis & S. Kröll, *Comparative International Commercial Arbitration* ¶23-62 (2003) ("To avoid any appearance of prejudgment arbitrators are invariably reluctant to express their views on the merits before they have considered at least a significant amount of the evidence presented by the parties. For this reason the merits of the case rarely play any direct role in determining whether or not interim relief is granted.").

(e) *Balancing of interests*. Many awards concerning provisional measures do not appear fully to discuss the real considerations underlying the tribunal's conclusions. Consider the following:

"In fact, even this formulation ['substantial' harm] obscures more complex considerations. On close examination, tribunals appear to consider the extent to which (a) the claimant will suffer serious injury during the arbitral proceedings; (b) the extent to which such injury appears compensable in a final award; and (c) the extent to which it is just or fair that the burden or risk of loss during the arbitral proceedings fall on one party or another (including considerations such as whether one party is seeking to alter the existing status quo to its advantage during the arbitral proceeding, the likelihood of success of each party on the merits of its case, and the relative hardship to each of the parties if provisional measures are or are not granted). Some authorities refer to this, accurately, as a 'balancing of interests' or a 'balancing of hardships.'" G. Born, *International Commercial Arbitration* 2471 (2d ed. 2014).

Is it appropriate for arbitrators to engage (generally without discussion) in this "balancing of interests"? Does this amount to a form of arbitration *ex aequo et bono*? Is it what commercial parties expect and want?

Suppose a claimant, asserting a *prima facie* credible claim, appears likely to suffer serious (but not irreparable) injury as a consequence of steps threatened by the respondent to alter the existing status quo. Should provisional measures be likely? Suppose the respondent's actions appear designed to make ultimate enforcement of an award more difficult (*e.g.*, transferring disputed property outside the ordinary course of business) and/or the respondent does not appear likely to suffer material harm from a grant of provisional measures. Conversely, suppose a respondent is merely pursuing business in the ordinary course, its contemplated actions appear unaffected by litigation considerations and it will suffer demonstrable damage from the requested provisional measures? Should provisional measures presumptively be available?

Suppose a claimant licensee has failed to present a *prima facie* case of wrongful termination of a license agreement, while the respondent licensor has presented a comprehensive defense as to why it was contractually entitled to terminate. Should this affect a tribunal's willingness to order the respondent licensor to continue to permit use of licensed property and to supply updates on a provisional basis during the pendency of the arbitration? Conversely, if the claimant licensee has advanced a very thorough case as to wrongful termination, countered by no serious argument or evidence from the respondent licensor, should provisional measures be more readily granted?

(f) *Different standards for different types of interim relief.* Does it make sense to apply the same requirements to all types of interim relief? Suppose a party seeks an interim order permitting third-party inspection of disputed goods or damaged property, or preservation of documentary evidence. Are the same standards appropriate in considering such requests as are appropriate when a party requests monetary security for payment of its claim?

5. *Arbitrators' "discretion" to order provisional measures.* It is sometimes said that arbitrators have "discretion" whether or not to order provisional measures. According to one commentator, "arbitral tribunals have very wide discretion in determining the appropriate measure." Yesilirmak, *Interim and Conservatory Measures in ICC Arbitral Practice*, 11(1) ICC ICArb. Bull. 31, 33 (2000). Or, "[i]n international arbitration, there are no clear guidelines to the types of relief available or when they should be

granted." Lew, *Commentary on Interim and Conservatory Measures in ICC Arbitration Cases,* 11(1) ICC ICArb. Bull. 23, 26 (2000). Is it appropriate that significant legal matters—the availability of security over substantial claims, the right to market a product or use intellectual property—be left to the arbitrators' discretion? Again, does this amount to arbitrators exercising the power to decide *ex aequo et bono* (which requires the parties' express consent, *see infra* pp. 1020-21)?

6. *Security for underlying claims or costs of arbitration.* Consider *ICC Case No. 8786* and the *Geneva Award.* What interim relief is sought in each case? How does the relief differ? Which relief is more onerous for the party against whom it is sought? Consider also the relief ordered by the tribunal in *Charles Construction, supra* pp. 878-80. What interim measures were obtained in each case? Compare Interim Order No. 2 in *Certain Underwriters.* What interim measures were obtained there? What explains the different approaches of the various arbitral tribunals?

    Consider the tribunal's observation in the *Geneva Award* about obstacles to obtaining security for the amount of a party's legal costs: the risks that a counterparty will be unable to pay an award of costs "are to be borne by the parties, including, in the view of this Tribunal, the risk of the other party failing into financial difficulties, up to and including bankruptcy." Is that a persuasive reason for withholding interim relief? Or, on the contrary, should the risks of international commerce argue for more expansive possibilities for provisional relief? Does the same rationale, as that cited by the *Geneva Award,* also apply to requests for security for an underlying claim?

    When might it be appropriate to order security for legal costs? How does the *Geneva Award* answer this question? When might it be appropriate to order security for an underlying claim? Suppose that, in *ICC Case No. 8786,* it was clear that Turkish courts would not recognize the tribunal's award. Would it have then been appropriate to order security for the underlying claim? What would the tribunal likely have concluded? Consider:

    > "the creditor's normal impatience to see his claim satisfied or at least secured, or the normal risk that the debtor's ability to pay his debts might deteriorate in the course of the proceedings, are not sufficient to justify provisional payment or security measures. In the absence of factual circumstances which call for an urgent remedy against the foreseeable risk of an aggravation of the situation, provisional payments and providing security in view of the final award fall outside the scope of provisional and protective measures...." *Partial Award in Unidentified ICC Case,* quoted in Schwartz, *The Practices and Experience of the ICC Court,* in ICC, *Conservatory and Provisional Measures in International Arbitration* 45, 61 (1993).

    See also On Time Staffing, LLC v. Nat'l Union Fire Ins. Co., 2011 U.S. Dist. LEXIS 50689 (S.D.N.Y.) ("The [arbitral tribunal], in the absence of language in the arbitration agreement expressly to the contrary, possesses the inherent authority to preserve the integrity of the arbitration process to which the parties have agreed by, if warranted, requiring the posting of pre-hearing security.... Otherwise, an [arbitral tribunal] with a well-founded concern that a party was financially unable to satisfy an eventual award would have no recourse to protect itself against the risk that its significant expenditures of time and effort would be for naught."). Is it appropriate to grant interim relief against parties from Contracting States that do not honor their obligations under the

New York Convention? Recall the discussion of the reciprocity requirement. *See supra* pp. 169-75 & *infra* pp. 1093-99.

7. *Orders requiring performance of contractual or other obligations.* Arbitrators sometimes order what common law practitioners refer to as "specific performance," requiring a party to perform specified acts pursuant to a preexisting contractual or other legal obligation. In some institutional rules, such orders qualify as ordering "on a provisional basis … any relief which the Arbitral Tribunal would have power to grant in an award." 2014 LCIA Rules, Art. 25(1)(iii). For example, a party may be ordered to continue to perform contractual obligations (*e.g.*, shipping products, providing intellectual property) or to ensure the claimant's enjoyment of its rights (*e.g.*, voting shares in compliance with a shareholders agreement). *See, e.g., Interim Award in ICC Case No. 8894*, 11(1) ICC ICArb. Bull. 94, 97-98 (2000) (party ordered to petition administrative authority to cancel import permission); *Award in ICC Case No. 6503*, 122 J.D.I. (Clunet) 1022 (1995) (order to continue executing a long term contract pending award).

How does an order requiring continued performance of a contract compare with an order to post security for a claim? Should different showings be required to obtain each? Why or why not?

8. *Orders preserving status quo.* One common form of interim relief is an order preserving the status quo between the parties (or, alternatively, preserving specified contractual or legal relations or factual circumstances). (This form of interim relief is referred to in Article 17(2)(a) of the 2006 UNCITRAL Model Law.) For example, a party may be ordered not to take certain steps—terminating an agreement, disclosing trade secrets, calling a letter of credit, or using disputed intellectual property—pending a decision on the merits. *See, e.g., Award in ICC Case No. 3896*, X Y.B. Comm. Arb. 47 (1985) ("the best solution, in the Arbitral Tribunal's opinion, would involve the maintenance, in so far as possible, of the 'status quo ante,' that is, the situation which existed at the moment when Terms of Reference Nos. 1 and 2 were signed."); *Final Award in ICC Case No. 7895* 11(1) ICC ICArb. Bull. 64, 65 (2000) (party ordered to refrain from selling other party's products); *Final Award in ICC Case No. 9324* (party ordered to reimburse amount of letter of credit if it were called), in Lew, *Commentary on Interim and Conservatory Measures in ICC Arbitration Cases*, 11(1) ICC ICArb. Bull. 23, 29 (2000). Alternatively, a tribunal may order the parties generally not to take steps that alter the contractual status quo. *See, e.g.*, UNCITRAL Model Law, 2006 Revision, Art. 17(2)(a) ("maintain or restore the status quo pending determination of the dispute").

Examples of such relief are described as follows:

> "an example of an existing right [justifying provisional measures] would be an interest in a piece of property, the ownership of which is in dispute. A provisional measure could be ordered to require that the property not be sold or alienated before the final award of the arbitral tribunal. Such an order would preserve the *status quo* of the property, thus preserving the rights of the party in the property." *Emilio Augustin Maffezini v. Kingdom of Spain, Procedural Order No. 2 in ICSID Case No. ARB/97/7 of 28 October 1999*, ¶14.

Orders preserving the status quo are often cited as the prime examples of appropriate interim measures in international arbitration: "[p]rovisional measures, as a rule, aim at avoiding or preventing a modification of the state of facts or law of the subject matter of the dispute which could render more difficult or impossible later performance." *Extract From A Procedural Order in ICC Arbitration No. 12 of 1989*, 12 ASA Bull. 142 (1994).

Interim relief preserving the status quo has been particularly common in investment arbitration. *See, e.g., Plama Consortium Ltd v. Repub. of Bulgaria, Order in ICSID Case No. ARB/03/24 of 6 September 2005*, ¶38 (provisional measures appropriate "to preserve the status quo"); C. Schreuer *et al., The ICSID Convention: A Commentary* Art. 47, ¶157 (2d ed. 2009) ("The references in the *travaux préparatoires* [of the ICSID Convention] to the preservation of the *status quo* ... are an expression of the principle that in the course of litigation the parties must refrain from taking steps that might affect the rights of the side which are the object of the proceedings on the merits. This is particularly so where ... a business is at stake which may be damaged through unilateral action...."). Is there any reason to conclude that orders preserving the status quo are more appropriate in investment arbitrations than in commercial arbitrations?

Should the same showing be required to obtain an order preserving the status quo as an order requiring posting of security for a party's underlying claim? How are the two types of relief different?

9. *Orders prohibiting aggravation of parties' dispute.* One type of provisional measure preserving the status quo is an order prohibiting actions that would aggravate or exacerbate the parties' dispute. (Note that this sort of relief is referred to in Article 17(2)(b) of the 2006 Revision to the UNCITRAL Model Law.) Such orders may be directed towards forbidding public statements (potentially in breach of confidentiality obligations), obstructing or interfering with contractual performance, continuing to breach contractual obligations, and the like.

The principle that arbitrators may take steps to prohibit aggravation of a dispute is well-described in the order of one tribunal: "As held by several ICC awards, provisional measures may be ordered not only in order to prevent irreparable damage but also to avoid aggravation of the dispute submitted to arbitration." *Order in ICC Case No. 7388*, in Reiner, *Les mesures provisoires et conservatoires et l'Arbitrage international, notamment l'Arbitrage CCI*, 125 J.D.I. (Clunet) 853, 889 n.82 (1998). *See also Award in ICC Case No. 3896*, X Y.B. Comm. Arb. 47 (1985) ("[T]he Arbitral Tribunal considers that there exists, undeniably, the risk of the dispute before it becoming aggravated or magnified, and that the parties should, in the same spirit of goodwill that they have already demonstrated in signing the Terms of Reference refrain from any action likely to widen or aggravate the dispute, or to complicate the task of the Tribunal or even to make more difficult, one way or another, the observance of the final arbitral award."). The principle has been stated by an ICSID tribunal as follows: "The parties to a dispute over which ICSID has jurisdiction must ... refrain from any action of any kind which might aggravate or extend the dispute." *Tokios Tokelés v. Ukraine, Order No. 1 in ICSID Case No. ARB/02/18 1 July 2003*, ¶2. *See Quiborax SA v. Plurinat'l State of Bolivia, Decision on Provisional Measures in ICSID Case No. ARB/06/2 of 26 February 2010*, ¶117 ("rights to be preserved by provisional measures are not limited to those which form the subject matter of the dispute, but may extend to procedural rights, including the general right to the preservation of the status quo and to the non-aggravation of the dispute…. [T]hese latter rights are self-standing rights.").

What is the rationale for this type of interim relief? Should the same showing be required to obtain an order forbidding aggravation of the parties' dispute as is required for an order to provide security for the underlying claim in the arbitration?

10. *Orders for preservation or inspection of property or evidence.* Another form of provisional relief involves orders for the preservation or inspection of property (typically for evidentiary purposes). (This form of interim relief is contemplated by Article 17(2)(d) of the 2006 Revisions to the UNCITRAL Model Law.) Such orders can include the appointment of a neutral third person charged with taking specified actions. For example, an independent expert can be appointed to inspect goods or other property and provide a factual report about its condition. *See, e.g.,* 2010 UNCITRAL Rules, Arts. 26(1), (2); 2012 ICC Rules, Arts. 28(1); 2014 LCIA Rules, Arts. 22(1)(iv), 25(1)(ii). Recall the interim relief ordered (by a court) in *South Star, supra* pp. 842-44.

Again, should this form of interim relief require the same showing as an order to perform a contract or post security for a party's underlying claim? What showing should be required to order preservation or inspection of property? Should a showing of serious injury, *prima facie* claims, or urgency be required?

11. *Standards for provisional measures under Article 17A of 2006 UNCITRAL Model Law.* Consider again Article 17A of the 2006 Revisions of the UNCITRAL Model Law. What standards does Article 17A provide for an arbitrator's grant of interim relief? Note the requirement for a showing that "harm not adequately reparable by an award of damages is likely" and that "such harm substantially outweighs the harm that is likely to result to the party against who the measure is directed if the measure is granted." Note also the requirement of "a reasonable possibility that the requesting party will succeed on the merits of the claim." Does the standard set forth in Article 17A make sense? How does it compare to the standards developed by arbitral tribunals? Does Article 17A provide for the possibility of different standards for different types of interim relief? Should it?

12. *Ex parte provisional measures.* It is not uncommon in national court proceedings for interim relief to be issued on an *ex parte* basis. This type of relief is appropriate where a party could suffer serious damage through a single, rapidly-completed action by its counter-party—for example, calling a letter of credit, transferring needed security to third parties, or destroying critical evidence. Despite its arguable practical utility, there is substantial controversy surrounding an arbitral tribunal's *ex parte* consideration of requests for interim relief. As discussed above, most national laws and institutional rules guarantee all parties an opportunity to be heard and equality of treatment. *See supra* pp. 793-95 & *infra* pp. 1159-63, 1218-41. *Ex parte* relief runs strongly counter to these requirements.

Despite this, the 2006 revisions to the UNCITRAL Model Law expressly permit *ex parte* provisional measures in limited circumstances. The amendments (to Article 17B(1) of the Model Law) provide for "preliminary orders" that may be applied for "without notice to any other party." Article 17B and 17C provide that *ex parte* preliminary orders may be issued where the arbitrators conclude that "prior disclosure of the request for the interim measure to the party against whom it is directed risks frustrating the purpose of the measure." UNCITRAL Model Law, 2006 Revision, Art. 17B(2).

The 2006 revisions to the Model Law were controversial, and as of 2014 about a dozen jurisdictions have incorporated them. *Compare* van Houtte, *Ten Reasons Against A Proposal for Ex Parte Interim Measures of Protection in Arbitration*, 20 Arb. Int'l 85 (2004) *with* Castello, *Arbitral Ex Parte Interim Relief: The View In Favor*, 58 Disp. Resol. J. 60 (2003). What are the arguments for and against inclusion of *ex parte* provisional measures in the 2006 revisions to the Model Law? Can an *ex parte* order, issued by the arbitral tribunal, have coercive effects? *See supra* p. 876. What does this mean for the practical utility of *ex parte* orders by the arbitrators? Consider Article 17C(1). Given this provision, what good are *ex parte* provisional orders from a tribunal? *See also* 2012 Swiss Rules, Art. 26(3). Is this a desirable development?

13. *Security as condition for grant of provisional measures*. Consider Article 17 of the UNCITRAL Model Law and Article 183(3) of the SLPIL. The grant of interim relief is generally conditioned on the posting of security by the party requesting such measures, to preserve the adverse party's ability to recover damages resulting from provisional measures that prove to have been wrongfully requested. For example, if a party successfully obtains interim relief forbidding its counterparty's sale of a product or use of intellectual property, it may be required to post security sufficient to cover monetary damage claims for lost sales or profits.

14. *Form of decision granting provisional measures*. If a tribunal concludes that interim measures are appropriate, questions arise as to what form such measures should take. In principle, interim relief can be granted as either an order or an award. (The differences between these forms are discussed below. *See supra* pp. 806-10, *infra* pp. 1062-66.) Article 28(1) of the ICC Rules permits arbitrators to grant provisional measures either by order or by award. 2012 ICC Rules, Art. 28(1) ("Any such measure shall take the form of an order, giving reasons, or of an award, as the Arbitral Tribunal considers appropriate."). Should the form of the decision affect the availability of judicial review? Judicial enforcement?

15. *Availability of court-ordered provisional measures*. Consider the tribunal's reliance on Article 8(5) of the 1988 ICC Rules in *ICC Case No. 8786*. The availability of court-ordered provisional measures, in parallel to tribunal-ordered provisional measures, is discussed below. *See infra* pp. 904-32. Does the availability of court-ordered provisional measures provide a persuasive reason for a tribunal not to order provisional relief? Would the same argument not work in reverse?

B. JUDICIAL ENFORCEMENT OF PROVISIONAL MEASURES ORDERED BY ARBITRATORS IN INTERNATIONAL ARBITRATION

As discussed above, arbitrators lack the authority, under virtually all national legal regimes, coercively to enforce their orders.[15] "The most important and obvious such difference [between court-ordered and tribunal-ordered provisional measures] is that orders given by arbitrators are not self-executing, like those of courts, and must generally take the

---

15. *See supra* p. 876; G. Born, *International Commercial Arbitration* 2446-48, 2511-12 (2d ed. 2014).

form of directions to the parties to perform or refrain from performing certain acts."[16] Accordingly, if a party refuses to comply with tribunal-ordered provisional measures, judicial enforcement may be essential to effectuating those measures.

Many national arbitration statutes do not expressly address the judicial enforceability of tribunal-ordered provisional measures issue, leaving enforcement of tribunal-ordered provisional measures to general statutory provisions regarding arbitral awards. That was the case with the original text of the 1985 UNCITRAL Model Law, as well as a number of other arbitration statutes. Under such legislation, the enforcement of tribunal-ordered provisional relief has given rise to significant uncertainties. In part because of these issues, some jurisdictions have enacted specialized legislation providing for judicial enforcement of tribunal-ordered provisional measures, including many Model Law jurisdictions.[17] Similarly, the Model Law was revised in 2006 along similar lines to permit specialized enforcement of "orders" of provisional relief.

CHARLES CONSTRUCTION CO. v. DERDERIAN
586 N.E.2d 992 (Mass. 1992)

[excerpted above at pp. 878-80]

CERTAIN UNDERWRITERS AT LLOYD'S v. ARGONAUT INSURANCE CO.
264 F.Supp.2d 926 (N.D. Cal. 2003)

[excerpted above at pp. 759-65]

SPERRY INTERNATIONAL TRADE, INC. v. GOVERNMENT OF ISRAEL
689 F.2d 301 (2d Cir. 1982)

KEARSE, Circuit Judge. [The] Government of Israel ("Israel") appeals from an order of the U.S. District Court for the Southern District of New York … confirming an arbitration award in a proceeding between Israel and petitioner-appellee Sperry International Trade, Inc. ("Sperry"). Because we conclude that the award was within the arbitrators' powers and did not disregard the law, we affirm….

In July 1978, [Sperry] … and Israel executed a contract (the "Contract") requiring Sperry to design and construct a communication system for the Israeli Air Force. As contemplated by paragraph 59 of the Contract, Sperry caused Citibank, NA ("Citibank") to open a clean irrevocable letter of credit in Israel's favor for a sum eventually set at approximately $15 million. Paragraph 59 gave Israel the right to draw on this letter of credit, to the extent of its payments to Sperry, upon presentation of a sight draft and Israel's own "certification that it is entitled to the amount covered by such draft by reason of a clear and substantial breach" of the Contract….

---

16. Schwartz, *The Practices and Experience of the ICC Court*, in ICC, *Conservatory and Provisional Measures in International Arbitration* 59 (1993).

17. *See, e.g.*, California Code of Civil Procedure, §1297.92; English Arbitration Act, 1996, §44(2); Belgian Judicial Code, Art. 1696; German ZPO, §1041(2); Hong Kong Arbitration Ordinance, 2013, §61; Ontario International Commercial Arbitration Act, §9; Indian Arbitration and Conciliation Act, Art. 9; Mexican Commercial Code, Art. 1479.

Paragraph 45 of the Contract provided that all Contract disputes that could not be resolved by negotiation were to be submitted to arbitration in accordance with the rules of the [AAA]. On August 3, 1981, Sperry initiated arbitration proceedings, seeking a declaration that Israel had breached its contractual obligations and demanding damages of approximately $10 million. Sperry alleged that its attempts to perform its obligations under the Contract had been seriously and substantially frustrated by wrongful actions and inactions of Israel. Israel denied Sperry's allegations and asserted eleven counterclaims, claiming, inter alia, nonperformance of the Contract by Sperry.

On September 11, 1981, Sperry instituted suit in the district court to compel arbitration and to enjoin Israel from drawing on the letter of credit pending a decision by the arbitrators. The district court enjoined Israel from making the certification that would enable it to draw on the letter of credit, "pending an early ruling by the arbitrators" as to "whether it is equitable and proper in the circumstances that Israel shall or shall not draw on the letter of credit." On January 21, 1982, we reversed the district court's order granting the preliminary injunction because Sperry had made no showing that it would be irreparably injured in the absence of such an injunction.... *Sperry I*, 670 F.2d at 11 & n.4.

On January 27, 1981, Israel [demanded payment of the letter of credit. Sperry sought an attachment of the proceeds of the letter of credit in U.S. courts and provisional relief before the arbitral tribunal.] ... On February 8, the arbitration panel held its first hearing and considered Sperry's motion to require Israel to withdraw its certification and demand for payment, and to enjoin it permanently from drawing down the letter of credit. Early on the morning of February 9, the arbitrators made their award on these issues (the "Award"), ordering that the proceeds of the letter of credit be held in an escrow account in the joint names of Israel and Sperry.[18] ...

Sperry stated that it would move for an order confirming the arbitrators' Award, and that if the Award were confirmed, the attachment [it had sought] would become "essentially moot and unnecessary." On February 10 Judge Cannella vacated the attachment on the ground "that the attachment [was] unnecessary to the security of [Sperry]." ... Judge Cannella also stayed Israel "from taking any further action to collect the proceeds of [the] letter of credit ..." pending a hearing on Sperry's motion to confirm the arbitrators' award.

---

18. The Award provided, in relevant part, as follows:

"Upon the motion of [Sperry], in an arbitration before this Tribunal commenced by a Demand for Arbitration dated August 3, 1981 (as amended), for injunctive relief with respect to a Letter of Credit (no. WCG-150297) purchased by [Sperry] from Citibank, NA, or the proceeds thereof, and for other relief, and upon hearing and considering the arguments presented and the large number of documents submitted (directly or, during the month prior to the hearing, through the American Arbitration Association) on behalf of [Sperry] and [Israel] in favor of and in opposition to such injunctive and other relief;

Now, upon due consideration, the arbitrators order as follows:

1. The proceeds of said Letter of Credit shall be paid into an escrow account ("Escrow Account") in the joint names of [Sperry] and [Israel] with such bank or other entity in the United States of America as shall be agreed upon in writing by [Sperry] and [Israel] prior to the release of such proceeds by Citibank, NA or, in default of such agreement, with Citibank, NA...." [The order also prescribed the terms of the Escrow Account. It also provided:] "8. This order shall constitute an Award of the arbitrators and either party is at liberty to apply forthwith to the United States District Court for the Southern District of New York for confirmation and/or enforcement thereof."

Sperry's motion to confirm the Award was heard ... on February 18, and was opposed by Israel.... [The District Court] rejected all of Israel's arguments[19] in a reasoned opinion and confirmed the Award. On this appeal, Israel renews its [effort to vacate the] Award. We disagree and affirm....

It is beyond cavil that the scope of the district court's review of an arbitration award is limited. Under 9 U.S.C. §9, "the court must grant ... an order [confirming an arbitration award] unless the award is vacated, modified, or corrected as prescribed in [9 U.S.C. §§10 and 11]." Section 10 permits the court to vacate an award only in specific situations [which the court quoted], ...[20] Israel argues that the arbitrators exceeded their powers, in violation of §10(d), and that the Award was made in manifest disregard of the law. Israel bases these contentions on our decision in *Sperry I*, vacating the preliminary injunction issued by the district court and issuing our mandate promptly, which it construes as having established (a) that, as a matter of law, Sperry was not entitled to any restraint for any period of time on Israel's right to the $15 million represented by the letter of credit, and (b) that Israel should have the immediate right to those funds without having to relitigate the issue before the Arbitrators. On this view of *Sperry I*, Israel argues that the arbitrators were barred from prohibiting Israel from drawing down the letter of credit, and that in making the Award the arbitrators exceeded their powers and manifestly disregarded such principles as res judicata, collateral estoppel, and law of the case....

Israel has rather badly misstated our decision. In *Sperry I* we reiterated the standard criteria that govern the district courts' granting of preliminary injunctions, *see Jackson Dairy, Inc. v. H.P. Hood & Sons, Inc.*, 596 F.2d 70, 72 (2d Cir. 1979), and ruled that Sperry had failed to prove the likelihood of irreparable injury required to obtain such relief, because the only potential harm it had shown was strictly monetary. This was the only ground of our decision. Nowhere did we state that Israel had a right to the funds or suggest that Sperry had breached the Contract in such a way as to give Israel the right to draw down the letter of credit. Indeed, we expressly declined to state a view as to such issues as Sperry's likelihood of prevailing on the merits and the seriousness of the dispute as to the merits of Sperry's claim. And the question of what powers the arbitrators might have to interpret the Contract or to rule in any way on the propriety of any certification Israel might make was not before us. To the extent, therefore, that Israel's contention that the arbitrators exceeded their powers or manifestly disregarded the law depends on the proposition that the Award was somehow foreclosed by *Sperry I*, it fails because of Israel's false premise.

19. Israel also contended that the Award was an interim decision not ripe for confirmation, *Michaels v. Mariforum Shipping, SA*, 624 F.2d 411, 413-15 (2d Cir. 1980).... On this appeal Israel has abandoned its prematurity argument, which had been rejected by Judge Pollack because (a) the Award itself stated that either party could seek confirmation, indicating that it was a final decision as to the severable issues regarding the letter of credit, *see Moyer v. Van-Dye-Way Corp.*, 126 F.2d 339, 341 (3d Cir. 1942); *Puerto Rico Maritime Shipping Authority v. Star Lines Ltd*, 454 F.Supp. 368, 372-73 (S.D.N.Y. 1978), and (b) the Contract provides that any arbitration award "shall be deemed final and may be enforced." ...

20. Paragraph 45 of the Contract requires the arbitrators to "interpret the contract in accordance with the substantive laws of the State of New York," and paragraph 62 provides that the Contract "shall be interpreted, and the legal rights of the parties ... shall be determined, in accordance with the laws [of the State of New York]." Under New York law the power of a court to vacate an arbitrator's award is no greater than the power of a federal court under 9 U.S.C. §§9 and 10....

Nor do we find merit in Israel's contention that under New York law the arbitrators had no power to prevent Israel's sole possession of proceeds of the letter of credit pending a decision on the merits of the contractual claims and counterclaims. Preliminarily, we note that, [consistent with AAA practice] ... the arbitrators gave no explanation for the Award. We are thus left to theorize as to the basis of the Award, and New York law requires that all reasonable efforts be made to find a ground on which to sustain it. *See Fudickar v. Guardian Mutual Life Ins. Co.*, 62 N.Y. 392, 401 (1875) ("It is a settled principle governing this subject, and which ought never to be lost sight of, that all reasonable intendments and presumptions are indulged in support of awards."). One quite reasonable explanation of the Award comes quickly to mind: that is, that the arbitrators' view was that any breach of the Contract by Sperry had not been so "clear and substantial" (Contract paragraph 59) as to allow Israel in good faith to draw down the letter of credit, and that any breach of the Contract by Israel was not so egregious as to relieve Sperry of its contractual obligation to provide security for its own performance of the Contract. We have been cited to no principle of law, from New York or elsewhere, preventing the arbitrators in such circumstances from ruling that the $15 million be held in the names of both parties until the contract disputes are determined.

Rather, New York law gives arbitrators substantial power to fashion remedies that they believe will do justice between the parties. Thus, in *Sprinzen v. Nomberg*, 415 N.Y.S.2d 974 [(1979)], the New York Court of Appeals stated as follows: "An arbitrator's paramount responsibility is to reach an equitable result, and the courts will not assume the role of overseers to mold the award to conform to their sense of justice. Thus, an arbitrator's award will not be vacated for errors of law and fact committed by the arbitrator." ...

Under New York law arbitrators have power to fashion relief that a court might not properly grant. In *Rochester City School Dist. v. Rochester Teachers Ass'n*, 394 N.Y.S.2d 179 (1977), the court reversed the vacation of an arbitration award that ordered the petitioner school district to grant sabbaticals to certain teachers, stating as follows:

> "In the final analysis 'Arbitrators may do justice' and the award may well reflect the spirit rather than the letter of the agreement.... Thus courts may not set aside an award because they feel that the arbitrator's interpretation disregards the apparent, or even the plain, meaning of the words or resulted from a misapplication of settled legal principles. In other words a court may not vacate an award because the arbitrator has exceeded the power the court would have, or would have had if the parties had chosen to litigate, rather than to arbitrate the dispute. Those who have chosen arbitration as their forum should recognize that arbitration procedures and awards often differ from what may be expected in courts of law."

In sum, *Sperry I* did not foreclose the arbitrators' Award, and we are aware of no provision of law contravened by the Award. Accordingly, we concur in the district court's ruling that Israel has failed to advance any valid basis for denying Sperry's motion to confirm the Award....

NOTES

1. *Do provisional measures constitute "binding" or "final" awards?* As discussed in detail below, the provisions of national arbitration legislation providing for confirmation and annulment of arbitral awards generally apply only to awards that are "binding" or "final." *See supra* pp. 806-10 & *infra* pp. 1113-23. Similarly, the New York Convention applies only to awards that are "binding." *See infra* pp. 1118-21,

1250. If an arbitrator's decision granting interim relief constitutes a "final" or "binding" award, then generally-applicable legislative regimes for confirming and challenging awards apply to the decision—enabling relatively effective judicial enforcement of it; conversely, if these regimes do not apply, then enforcement will ordinarily be difficult.

Is a decision granting provisional relief "final" or "binding" for purposes of national arbitration legislation and the New York Convention? In one sense, "provisional" measures are by definition not the tribunal's ultimate disposition of the parties' dispute; provisional measures are instead intended to preserve the parties' rights until their dispute can be resolved. Does this mean that provisional measures should not be considered to be "final" or "binding"? And therefore not subject to judicial enforcement? Consider:

> "whilst it is true that a valid interlocutory order is in one sense 'binding' on the parties to the arbitration agreement ... an interlocutory order which may be rescinded, suspended, varied or reopened by the tribunal which pronounced it is not 'final' and binding on the parties.... [T]he New York Convention ... applies to final and binding awards. Provisional or interim measures are not final." *Resort Condominiums Int'l Inc. v. Bolwell*, XX Y.B. Comm. Arb. 628 (1995) (Queensland Sup. Ct. 1993).

Is this persuasive? Does it make sense, from the perspective of an effective arbitral process, for provisional measures to be subject to judicial enforcement?

In *Sperry*, Israel argued in the district court that the tribunal's order of provisional relief was not enforceable because it was only an interim, and not a final, award. What did *Sperry* hold? Is the court's analysis persuasive? What about the fact that the tribunal may withdraw or alter the interim relief—doesn't that prevent such measures from being final or binding? Consider the following:

> "such an award is not 'interim' in the sense of being an 'intermediate' step toward a further end. Rather, it is an end in itself, for its very purpose is to clarify the parties' rights in the 'interim' period pending a final decision on the merits ... [I]f an arbitral award of equitable relief based upon a finding of irreparable harm is to have any meaning at all, the parties must be capable of enforcing or vacating it at the time it is made." *Southern Seas Nav. Ltd v. Petroleos Mexicanos of Mexico City*, 606 F.Supp. 692 (S.D.N.Y. 1985).

See also Yasuda Fire & Marine Ins. v. Cont'l Cas. Co., 37 F.3d 345 (7th Cir. 1994) ("The arbitration panel's order compelling Yasuda to post a letter of credit as interim security pending arbitration is an award subject to both confirmation and vacation under the FAA.")

Is that persuasive? Putting aside questions of statutory interpretation, what are the risks of treating provisional measures as "final" and "binding"? If provisional measures are "final" and "binding," then would procedural timetables and similar types of rulings also be?

Recall the provision for "emergency arbitrators" under some institutional arbitration rules. *See supra* pp. 882-83. Are rulings by an emergency arbitrator "awards"? Why or why not? How do such rulings differ from decisions by an arbitral tribunal regarding interim relief?

2. *Enforceability of tribunal-ordered provisional measures under FAA.* Although there are few decided cases, lower U.S. courts generally have been willing to confirm and

enforce arbitral awards of provisional measures. In addition to *Certain Underwriters* and *Sperry, see Arrowhead Global Solutions, Inc. v. Datapath, Inc.*, 166 F.Appx. 39, 41 (4th Cir. 2006) (preliminary injunctive order confirmed); *Publicis Commc'ns v. True N. Commc'ns, Inc.*, 206 F.3d 725 (7th Cir. 2000) (confirming and enforcing interim relief); *Yasuda Fire & Marine Ins. Co.*, 37 F.3d 345 (confirming interim order that reinsurer post letter of credit as security); *CE Int'l Res. Holdings LLC v. SA Minerals Ltd*, 2012 U.S. Dist. LEXIS 176158 (S.D.N.Y.) (order freezing respondent's assets as security for claims in arbitration is final award for purposes of confirmation); *Century Indem. Co. v. Certain Underwriters at Lloyd's London*, 2012 WL 104773 (S.D.N.Y.) (interim award is final, and can be recognized, if it definitely disposes of independent claim even though it does not dispose of all claims; interim order of security or preservation of assets are final).

3. *Enforceability of tribunal-ordered provisional measures under 1985 UNCITRAL Model Law*. Consider Articles 17, 34-36 of the original 1985 Model Law. How do these provisions deal with the enforcement of tribunal-ordered provisional measures? Does anything in Article 35 provide that interim or provisional awards cannot be enforced? Does Article 35 require that awards be "binding" or "final"? What about Article 36(1)(a)(v)?

4. *Enforceability of tribunal-ordered provisional measures under New York Convention*. Consider Articles III, IV and V of the New York Convention. *See also infra* pp. 1189-99, 1199-1266. Does the Convention apply to an arbitral tribunal's decisions granting (or withholding) provisional measures? For one view, consider the following excerpt from preparatory materials for the 2006 revisions of the Model Law: *Note of the Secretariat on the Possible Future Work in the Area of International Commercial Arbitration*, U.N. Doc. A/CN.9/460, ¶121 (1999) ("The prevailing view, confirmed ... by case law in some States, appears to be that the Convention does not apply to interim awards.").

5. *Standard of judicial review of arbitrators' substantive decision to award provisional measures*. If an award of interim relief may be enforced, like other arbitral awards, then it may also be challenged—either in an action to annul the award or in a defense to an action to enforce the award. When an award of provisional measures is challenged, what are the grounds for resisting enforcement? Are these the same grounds that apply generally to all arbitral awards? *See infra* pp. 1134-73, 1199-1266 for a discussion of these grounds.

    What standard of judicial review was applied in *Sperry*? In *Certain Underwriters*? Is this appropriate? Are there aspects of an award of provisional relief that argue for different standards? More demanding? Less demanding?

6. *Excess of authority in ordering provisional measures*. One basis for denying enforcement of an arbitral award is the arbitrators' excess of authority. *See infra* pp. 1200-18. As *Charles Construction* and *Certain Underwriters* illustrate, the "excess of authority" defense raises special issues in the context of provisional measures. These issues are discussed in detail above, *see supra* pp. 873-75, 881.

7. *Specialized national arbitration legislation permitting enforcement of tribunal-ordered provisional measures*. The uncertainties surrounding the enforceability of provisional measures as "awards" has prompted legislative efforts to provide specialized means for enforcing such measures, outside the context of regimes for en-

forcing final awards. These sorts of legislative solutions typically provide for enforcement of tribunal-ordered interim relief by courts in the arbitral seat. They do not typically address enforcement of a foreign tribunal's interim orders.

Consider Article 183(2) of the SLPIL. It provides that if a party does not comply with tribunal-ordered provisional measures, "the arbitral tribunal may request the assistance of the competent court." Compare this to the approach under FAA, which contemplates that a party to the arbitration, as opposed to the tribunal, will seek to enforce interim arbitral awards. Which approach is wiser? What are the costs and the benefits of the arbitrators (rather than a party) seeking enforcement of an interim order?

Other arbitration statutes adopt broadly similar approaches. Section 1041(2) of German legislation implementing the Model Law provides: "the court may, at the request of a party, permit enforcement of a measure … unless application for a corresponding interim measure has already been made to a court. [The enforcing court] may recast such an order if necessary for the purpose of enforcing the measure." German ZPO, §1041(2). *See also* English Arbitration Act, 1996, §42(1); Netherlands Code of Civil Procedure, Art. 1043b; Belgian Judicial Code, Art. 1696(1); Singapore International Arbitration Act, 2012, §12(6); Hong Kong Arbitration Ordinance, 2013, §61; Mexican Commercial Code, Art. 1479. Compare these different approaches to ensuring that tribunal-ordered provisional measures are enforceable. Why do states so consistently take steps to ensure that tribunal-ordered provisional measures are judicially-enforceable?

Some recent legislation is aimed at ensuring the enforcement of interim measures ordered by emergency arbitrators. *See* Netherlands Code of Civil Procedure, Arts. 1043b(2), (4); Singapore International Arbitration Act, 2012, §§2(1), 12(6); Hong Kong Arbitration Ordinance, 2013, §22B. Which is preferable? Is there any difference in territorial enforceability of interim measures ordered by emergency arbitrators in these jurisdictions?

8. *Specialized regime for enforcement of tribunal-ordered provisional measures under 2006 revisions to UNCITRAL Model Law.* Consider how the Model Law's 2006 revisions deal with the enforcement of tribunal-ordered provisional measures. Article 17H(1) provides that "[a]n interim measure issued by an arbitral tribunal shall be recognized as binding and, unless otherwise provided by the arbitral tribunal, enforced upon application to the competent court." The provision goes on to provide that enforcement may be sought "irrespective of the country in which it was issued," permitting provisional measures to be enforced outside the arbitral seat. The enforceability of provisional measures under Article 17H is subject to exceptions, detailed in Article 17I. Consider these exceptions. How do they differ from those generally-applicable to arbitral awards? Is the approach to enforcement of tribunal-ordered provisional measures in revised Article 17 sensible? How does it compare to the approach under the FAA?

9. *Relation between request for court-ordered provisional relief and request for tribunal-ordered provisional relief.* In *Sperry*, Sperry initially sought injunctive relief from the federal courts in New York; that request was ultimately denied. What effect did the denial of court-ordered provisional measures have on Sperry's request for tribunal-ordered provisional measures? What effect *should* the denial of court-ordered

provisional relief have had? Are the issues in the two fora the same? If Sperry elected to seek provisional relief first from a court, should it be bound by that refusal? *See infra* pp. 924-25 for further discussion.

10. *Tribunal's authority to enforce its provisional measures.* What authority, if any, does an arbitral tribunal have to enforce its own provisional measures? Consider the decision in *Certain Underwriters*. Does it exclude all forms of sanctions by an arbitral tribunal, aimed at enforcing compliance with its provisional measures? Should it? *See supra* pp. 826-27, 832-33. Note the statement of an ICSID tribunal in *Maritime Int'l Nominees Est. v. Guinea, Award in ICSID Case No. ARB/84/4 of 6 January 1988*, 4 ICSID Rep. 61, 69 (1997), that "In view of Article 47 and the applicable ICSID Rules, the Tribunal will take into account in its award the consequences of any failure by MINE to abide by these recommendations." To what extent may a tribunal take a party's non-compliance with provisional orders into account in its final award?

C. NATIONAL COURTS' AUTHORITY TO ORDER PROVISIONAL MEASURES IN AID OF INTERNATIONAL ARBITRATION

As outlined above, the arbitral tribunal is not the only source of provisional relief in an international arbitration: in addition, national courts generally possess concurrent authority to grant provisional measures in connection with arbitral proceedings.[21] This section considers when such relief is available.

As noted above, until the arbitral tribunal is in place, there is no prospect of obtaining provisional relief from it. Efforts by a number of arbitral institutions to provide pre-arbitral mechanisms for non-judicial emergency relief have begun to address this, but numerous *ad hoc* and other arbitrations continue not to offer such avenues for interim relief in the arbitral process. And, where attachments and other provisional measures binding third parties are concerned, arbitrators can virtually never provide effective relief.[22]

As a consequence, parties to international arbitration agreements who require urgent relief at the outset of a dispute must often seek the assistance of national courts. Like other issues relating to judicial assistance for an international arbitration, three sources of authority bear on a court's decision whether to grant provisional measures in aid of an international arbitration: (a) the New York Convention and other applicable international conventions; (b) applicable national arbitration legislation; and (c) any applicable institutional rules, together with other relevant provisions of the arbitration agreement.[23]

1. Effect of New York Convention on Authority of National Courts to Grant Provisional Measures in Aid of International Arbitration

The New York Convention does not contain any provision dealing expressly with interim relief (whether granted by an arbitral tribunal or a court). As described above, however, the Convention does require in Article II(3) that courts of Contracting States enforce arbitra-

---

21. *See supra* p. 875; G. Born, *International Commercial Arbitration* 2456-57, 2522-28, 2538-49 (2d ed. 2014).

22. *See supra* pp. 875-76; G. Born, *International Commercial Arbitration* 2445-46, 2492 (2d ed. 2014).

23. *See* G. Born, *International Commercial Arbitration* 2454-55, 2561-63 (2d ed. 2014).

tion agreements.[24] The impact of Article II(3) on court-ordered provisional measures in aid of arbitration is unsettled, particularly in the United States.

A few U.S. courts have interpreted Article II(3) of the Convention as forbidding national courts from ordering attachments prior to the commencement of arbitration pursuant to a preexisting arbitration agreement.[25] Other U.S. judicial decisions have expressly refused to adopt that reading of Article II(3), as have almost all non-U.S. decisions and academic commentary.[26]

The seminal decision holding that Article II(3) forbids court-ordered provisional relief in aid of arbitration was *McCreary Tire & Rubber Co. v. CEAT, SpA.*[27] The case arose from a distribution agreement that went awry, triggering disputes falling within a provision calling for ICC arbitration in Belgium. The U.S. party (McCreary) then commenced litigation, on the merits, in federal district court in Massachusetts; the district court stayed the action and ordered arbitration. Undeterred, McCreary next commenced a new action in federal district court in Pennsylvania, reasserting its underlying breach of contract claims against CEAT and, in addition, seeking to attach sums owed to CEAT by a Pittsburgh bank. On appeal, the Third Circuit held that no attachment should be granted and that arbitration should be compelled.

The *McCreary* court rested its decision on Article II(3) of the New York Convention and on its understanding of the parties' arbitration agreement:

> "What is plainly there to see is that [McCreary's federal court action] is a violation of McCreary's agreement to submit the underlying disputes to arbitration…. This complaint does not seek to enforce an arbitration award by foreign attachment. It seeks to bypass the agreed upon method of settling disputes. Such a bypass is prohibited by the Convention…. The Convention forbids the courts of a contracting state from entertaining a suit which violates an agreement to arbitrate. Thus, the contention that arbitration is merely another method of trial, to which state provisional remedies should equally apply, is unavailable…. Permitting a continued resort to foreign attachment in breach of the agreement is inconsistent with that purpose."[28]

In short, the *McCreary* court concluded that McCreary's U.S. judicial action for provisional relief was designed to frustrate the arbitral process that it had agreed to and, therefore, that the Convention precluded the suit and the request for attachment.

McCreary was followed, and extended, in other U.S. decisions. For example, the New York Court of Appeals held in *Cooper v. Ateliers de la Motobecane, SA*,[29] excerpted below, that the Convention foreclosed an attachment action that was apparently part of an effort to circumvent arbitration. In addition, however, subsequent decisions also applied the

---

24. *See supra* pp. 189, 316-17. In particular, Article II(3) provides: "The court of a Contracting State, when seized of an action in a matter in respect of which the parties have made an agreement within the meaning of this article, shall, at the request of one of the parties, refer the parties to arbitration, unless it finds that the said agreement is null and void, inoperative or incapable of being performed."

25. *See infra* pp. 906-08, 910-12; *I.T.A.D. Assoc. Inc. v. Podar Bros.*, 636 F.2d 75 (4th Cir. 1981); *McCreary Tire & Rubber Co. v. CEAT SpA*, 501 F.2d 1032 (3d Cir. 1974); *Cooper v. Ateliers de la Motobecane, SA*, 442 N.E.2d 1239 (N.Y. 1982).

26. *See* authorities cited at *infra* p. 912.

27. 501 F.2d 1032 (3d Cir. 1974).

28. 501 F.2d at 1038.

29. 456 N.Y.S.2d 728 (N.Y. 1982).

McCreary/Cooper rationale where court-ordered provisional measures were fairly clearly in aid of a pending arbitration (rather than in circumvention of it).[30] In contrast, other lower U.S. courts have refused to follow *McCreary* and *Cooper*. They have concluded that Article II(3) of the Convention does not speak to the question of provisional relief in aid of arbitration. *Uranex*, excerpted below at pp. 909-10, is a seminal example of this authority.[31]

COOPER v. ATELIERS DE LA MOTOBECANE, SA
442 N.E.2d 1239 (N.Y. 1982)

COOKE, Chief Judge. The [New York] Convention was drafted to minimize the uncertainty of enforcing arbitration agreements and to avoid the vagaries of foreign law for international traders. This policy would be defeated by allowing a party, contrary to contract, to bring multiple suits and to obtain an order of attachment before arbitration....

Plaintiff and others not here involved entered into a contract with defendant, a French corporation, to establish a New York corporation to distribute defendant's products. The agreement provided that plaintiff and others could each tender his or her shares for repurchase to defendant or the New York corporation, the two being jointly and severally obligated to buy such shares according to a price-setting formula. Disputes over valuation were to be resolved by arbitration in Switzerland.

In April, 1978, plaintiff tendered his shares for repurchase. Negotiations ensued until defendant finally demanded arbitration. In September, 1978, plaintiff sought a permanent stay of arbitration [and eventually] ... the Appellate Division ... issued a stay [in "Action I."] ... During the pendency of Action I, in January, 1979, plaintiff commenced this action for a money judgment ("Action II") and obtained an *ex parte* attachment of a debt owed by the New York corporation to defendant.... [The New York] Supreme Court confirmed the attachment [as did the Appellate Division]....

It has long been the policy in New York to encourage the use of arbitration "as an easy, expeditious and inexpensive method of settling disputes, and as tending to prevent litigation." *Fudickar v. Guardian Mut. Life Ins. Co.*, 62 N.Y. 392, 399. This support has not diminished over the last century. The desirability of arbitration is enhanced in the context of international trade, where the complexity of litigation is often compounded by lack of familiarity with foreign procedures and law. Thus, resolving disputes through arbitration allows all parties to avoid unknown risks inherent in resorting to a foreign justice system.

The prevalent problem in international contracts containing arbitration clauses has been in enforcing the agreement to arbitrate. The old antagonism to arbitration is shared by many countries, so that there is often uncertainty whether a contracting party may be compelled to arbitrate or whether an arbitrator's award may be enforced.... It was against this background that the [New York] Convention was drafted.... When an action is brought in court and a party asserts the arbitration agreement, the court "shall ... refer the parties to arbitration, unless it finds that the said agreement is null and void, inoperative or incapable of being performed." Article II(3). Moreover, foreign arbitration awards are to be enforced

---

30. *See infra* pp. 910-12; *Drexel Burnham Lambert Inc. v. Ruebsamen*, 139 A.D.2d 323 (N.Y. App. Div. 1988).

31. *Carolina Power & Light Co. v. Uranex*, 451 F.Supp. 1044 (N.D. Cal. 1977). *See infra* pp. 912-13.

on the same terms as domestic awards. Article III…. Moreover, if enforcement is opposed, the proponent of the award may request that the other party be ordered to give suitable security. This gives the courts a tool to discourage attempts to avoid arbitration awards which attempts are made merely as obstructionist tactics.

The provisional remedy of attachment is, in part, a device to secure the payment of a money judgment. It is available only in an action for damages (*see* CPLR 6201). Under the appropriate circumstances, it can be obtained in a matter that is subject to arbitration: an order of attachment will remain valid if it was obtained with notice or has been confirmed in a contract action before a defendant obtains a stay of proceedings because the underlying controversy is subject to arbitration. *See Am. Reserve Ins. Co. v. China Ins. Co.*, 297 N.Y. 322, 326-327 [(N.Y. 1948)]. It should be noted, however, that attachment would not be available in a proceeding to compel arbitration (*see* CPLR 7503(a)) as that is not an action seeking a money judgment.

It is open to dispute whether attachment is even necessary in the arbitration context. Arbitration, as part of the contracting process, is subject to the same implicit assumptions of good faith and honesty that permeate the entire relationship. Voluntary compliance with arbitral awards may be as high as 85%. Moreover, parties are free to include security clauses (*e.g.*, performance bonds or creating escrow accounts) in their agreements to arbitrate. The Convention apparently considered the problem and saw no need to provide for prearbitration security. Moreover, the list of signatory countries provides assurance to a contracting party that it will be able to enforce an arbitral award almost anywhere in the world. More important here, however, is the injection of uncertainty—the antithesis of the Convention's purpose—that would occur by permitting attachments and judicial proceedings. Once again, the foreign business entity would be subject to foreign laws with which it is unfamiliar.

The Convention was implemented in the United States in 1970. This act amended the [FAA] by re-enacting the earlier sections and denominating them "Chapter 1," and adding "Chapter 2" to provide a vehicle for enforcing the [New York] Convention. In *McCreary Tire*, the Third Circuit ruled that the language "refer the parties to arbitration" precludes the courts from acting in any capacity except to order arbitration, and therefore an order of attachment could not be issued. To hold otherwise would defeat the purpose of the Convention (*accord I.T.A.D. Assoc. v. Podar Bros.*, 636 F.2d 75 (4th Cir.); *Metropolitan World Tanker Corp. v. P.N. Pertambangan Minjakdangas Bumi Nasional*, 427 F.Supp. 2 (S.D.N.Y.)).

Plaintiff relies on a number of cases to the contrary (see *Paramount Carriers Corp. v. Cook Indus.*, 465 F.Supp. 599 (S.D.N.Y.); *Compania de Navegacion y Financiera Bosnia, SA v. National Unity Mar. Salvage Corp.*, 457 F.Supp. 1013 (S.D.N.Y. [(1978)]); *Carolina Power & Light Co. v. Uranex*, 451 F.Supp. 1044 (N.D. Cal.)). Most of these cases are distinguishable, however. The implementing statute provides that normal Federal arbitration law applies to the extent it is not inconsistent with the Convention [9 U.S.C. §208]. That law specifically permits attachment to be used in admiralty cases [9 U.S.C. §8]. In all of the cases relied on by plaintiff, except for *National Unity Mar.* and *Carolina Power*, the courts relied on §8 in approving attachment in a case arising out of a maritime contract…. Only in Carolina Power did the court allow attachment in a case not involving a maritime contract falling under the Convention. That court rejected McCreary's reasoning that it must divest itself of jurisdiction. Instead, concerned that the plaintiff would be unable to enforce an eventual arbitral award, the District Court approved the security attachment, a rationale that, as discussed above, is not compelling.

The controversy now before this court demonstrates the soundness of the decisions reached by the Third and Fourth Circuits. Defendant agreed to arbitrate disputes, but instead has become embroiled in two lawsuits. Action II, the instant case, is nothing more than plaintiff's attempt to circumvent Special Term's ruling in Action I denying the stay of arbitration. Indeed, the chronology of events indicates that the order of attachment should never have [been] issued at all, as the underlying dispute is subject to arbitration.

Whenever a matter of foreign relations is involved, one must consider the mirror image of a particular situation. Is it desirable to subject American property overseas to whatever rules of attachment and other judicial process may apply in some foreign country when our citizen has agreed to arbitrate a dispute? ... Permitting this type of attachment to stand would expose American business to that risk in other countries. The essence of arbitration is resolving disputes without the interference of the judicial process and its strictures. When international trade is involved, this essence is enhanced by the desire to avoid unfamiliar foreign law. The Convention has considered the problems and created a solution, one that does not contemplate significant judicial intervention until after an arbitral award is made. The purpose and policy of the Convention will be best carried out by restricting prearbitration judicial action to determining whether arbitration should be compelled.

MEYER, Dissenting. Respectfully, I dissent.... In response to the majority I add that: (1) nothing in the Convention or in the history of its negotiation or its implementation by Congress suggests that the word "refer" as used in §3 of article II of the Convention was intended to foreclose the use of attachment where permitted by the law of the jurisdiction in which the attachment is obtained; (2) in light of the majority's concessions that foreign arbitration awards are enforced on the same terms as domestic awards, that there are circumstances under which a domestic award may be enforced under our law through use of a preaward attachment, and that the Convention speaks only in terms of postaward security, and of the fact that the Convention does not specifically address the subject of preaward attachment, the Convention cannot properly be said to have proscribed such an attachment by implication; and (3) the use of attachment in maritime contract cases arbitrated under the Federal statute cannot properly be distinguished from arbitration-related attachment permitted under State statutory and decisional law, for the Convention makes no distinction; it either permits or proscribes both. In my view, absent more specific language of proscription in the Convention, it permits both.

NEW YORK CIVIL PRACTICE LAW AND RULES
§7502(c)

Provisional remedies. The supreme court in the county in which an arbitration is pending or in a county specified in subdivision (a) of this section, may entertain an application for an order of attachment or for a preliminary injunction in connection with an arbitration that is pending or that is to be commenced inside or outside this state, whether or not it is subject to the United Nations convention on the recognition and enforcement of foreign arbitral awards, but only upon the ground that the award to which the applicant may be entitled may be rendered ineffectual without such provisional relief.... The provisions of article 62 and 63 of this chapter [relating to attachments and injunctions] shall apply to the application, including those relating to undertakings and to the time for commencement of an action (arbitration shall be deemed an action for this purpose) if the application is made before commencement, except that the sole ground for the granting of the remedy shall be stated above....

CAROLINA POWER & LIGHT CO. v. URANEX
451 F.Supp. 1044 (N.D. Cal. 1977)

PECKHAM, Chief Judge. In 1973 Carolina Power & Light Company ("CP&L"), a North Carolina public utility company, contracted with defendant Uranex for the delivery of uranium concentrates to CP&L during the period 1977 to 1986. Uranex is a French *groupement d'interet economique* that markets uranium internationally. Following the recent and dramatic rise in the price of uranium fuel in the world market, Uranex either would not or could not deliver at the contract price, and requested renegotiation....

Earlier this year CP&L filed the present action against Uranex, and proceeded *ex parte* to attach an 85 million dollar debt owed to Uranex by Homestake Mining Company ("Homestake"), a San Francisco based corporation that markets uranium throughout the United States. The 85 million dollars is due to Uranex pursuant to a uranium supply contract between Homestake and Uranex, and has no relationship to the present litigation except as a potential source for CP&L to satisfy any judgment that might issue. But for the attachment the funds would have been transferred out of the country in the ordinary course of business.

The contract between CP&L and Uranex provides that disputes are to be submitted to arbitration in New York. At the time this lawsuit was filed CP&L sought to compel Uranex to enter arbitration. Since that time, however, Uranex voluntarily has entered arbitration and those proceedings are now going on in New York. Both parties agree that because of the arbitration agreement this court cannot adjudicate the merits of the dispute, but CP&L contends that the court should stay this action and maintain the attachment in order to protect any award that CP&L might receive in the New York arbitration. CP&L claims that Uranex has no other assets in this country with which to satisfy a judgment, and Uranex apparently does not dispute this proposition....

In 1970 the United States became a party to the [New York] Convention which provides generally that member nations will enforce provisions for arbitration in international commercial agreements and recognize arbitral awards made in other member nations. France is also a contracting nation to the Convention. There is little question that the Convention would apply to the contract at issue in this litigation. As described above, both Uranex and CP&L agree that they must pursue arbitration in New York as provided in the arbitration clause of their contract. Uranex, however, argues that it would be inconsistent with the Convention for this court to maintain the attachment pending the arbitration.[32]

___

32. Uranex also argues that a prejudgment attachment is inconsistent with the agreement of the parties. Article 11 of the contract between Uranex and CP&L, however, provides only that:

> "Arbitration. Any controversy or claim arising out of this Agreement, or the breach thereof, which the parties are unable to settle by mutual consultation, shall be settled by arbitration by three impartial Arbitrators, all of whom shall be attorneys, in accordance with the Rules of the American Arbitration Association, and judgment upon the award rendered by the Arbitrators may be entered in any court having jurisdiction thereof. The arbitration shall take place in New York, New York."

The Convention and its implementing statutes contain no reference to prejudgment attachment, and provide little guidance in this controversy.... Uranex, however, relies upon the decisions of the Third Circuit in *McCreary Tire & Rubber Co*.... At least one district court has chosen to follow the rationale of the *McCreary* opinion in applying the Convention to prejudgment attachments. See *Metropolitan World Tanker, Corp. v. P.N. Pertambangan Minjakdangas Bumi Nasional (P.M. Pertamina)*, 427 F.Supp. 2 (S.D.N.Y. 1975). This court, however, does not find the reasoning of *McCreary* convincing.... [N]othing in the text of the Convention itself suggests that it precludes prejudgment attachment. The [FAA], 9 U.S.C. §§1 et. seq. (1970), which operates much like the Convention for domestic agreements involving maritime or interstate commerce, does not prohibit maintenance of a prejudgment attachment during a stay pending arbitration:

> "After declaring (§2 [of the FAA]) such agreements [to arbitrate] to be enforceable, Congress, in succeeding sections, implemented the declared policy.... [I]t would seem there is nothing to prevent the plaintiff from commencing the action by attachment if such procedure is available under the applicable law." *Barge "Anaconda" v. American Sugar Refining Co.*, 322 U.S. 42, 44-45 (1944).

The *McCreary* court [did not persuasively] distinguish the [FAA] from the Convention.... [T]he court notes that the [FAA] only directs courts to "stay the trial of the action," while the Convention requires a court to "refer the parties to arbitration." 501 F.2d at 1038. From this difference the *McCreary* court apparently concludes that while the [FAA] might permit ... maintenance of a prejudgment attachment pending arbitration, application of the Convention completely ousts the court of jurisdiction. The use of the general term "refer," however, might reflect little more than the fact that the Convention must be applied in many very different legal systems, and possibly in circumstances where the use of the technical term "stay" would not be a meaningful directive....

In sum, this court will not follow the reasoning of *McCreary, supra*. There is no indication in either the text or the apparent policies of the Convention that resort to prejudgment attachment was to be precluded....

HALKI SHIPPING CORP. v. SOPEX OILS LTD
[1998] 1 Lloyd's Rep. 49 (QB) (English High Ct.)

[excerpted above at pp. 150-54]

NOTES

1.   Cooper *and* McCreary*: Article II(3) forbids court-ordered provisional relief in aid of arbitration.* The holding of *McCreary* and *Cooper* is that Article II(3) divests national courts of jurisdiction to order attachment in aid of arbitration, or to do anything else other than refer the parties to arbitration. As *McCreary* said, "the purpose and policy of

---

Hence, prejudgment attachment can be considered inconsistent with the agreement only if one decides that such attachment is inherently inconsistent with any agreement to arbitrate. In that sense defendant's argument premised on the contract is actually identical with defendant's argument premised on the Convention. Insofar as defendant's contractual argument might be considered separately, the court finds it to be without basis.

the [New York] Convention will be best carried out by restricting prearbitration judicial actions to determining whether arbitration should be compelled." A number of lower courts have followed the language of *Cooper* in holding that Article II(3) of the Convention prohibits national courts from ever ordering pre-award attachments in aid of an international arbitration that is subject to the Convention. *See I.T.A.D. Assocs. Inc. v. Podar Bros.*, 636 F.2d 75 (4th Cir. 1981); *Metropolitan World Tanker Corp. v. P.N. Pertambangan Minjakdangas Bumi Nasional*, 427 F.Supp. 2 (S.D.N.Y. 1975) (attachment); *Drexel Burnham Lambert Inc. v. Ruebsamen*, 139 A.D.2d 323 (N.Y. App. Div. 1988); *Shah v. Eastern Silk Indus. Ltd*, 493 N.Y.S.2d 150 (N.Y. App. Div. 1985).

2. *Stated rationale of* Cooper *and* McCreary*: Article II(3) of New York Convention forbids national court from ordering pre-award provisional measures in aid of arbitration.* It is important, in analyzing *McCreary* and *Cooper*, to recall their facts. In both decisions, two circumstances were present: (a) the party seeking attachment was resisting arbitration and was held by the court to be seeking attachment as a means of litigating, rather than arbitrating, the parties' underlying dispute; and (b) the arbitral seat was outside of the United States, within another New York Convention State (Belgium in *McCreary*; Switzerland in *Cooper*).

Put aside these two factors, however, and consider for the moment *only* the stated rationale for the *Cooper* opinion: Article II(3) of the Convention forbids court-ordered attachment in aid of arbitration. Is that a sensible rule? As we have seen, provisional relief is often necessary in order to ensure that the arbitral process functions and that the parties' rights are respected. As we have seen, however, arbitrators often cannot provide provisional relief—especially where they are not yet in place—and they generally cannot order attachments (as to third parties). *See supra* pp. 874-76. Given this, does the *Cooper* rationale further the arbitral process, as the Court contends, or does it impede the process, by denying what may be the only realistic means of preserving the status quo?

Consider the argument, advanced in *Cooper*, that parties to an arbitration agreement bargained to exclude the involvement of national courts, and that permitting court-ordered provisional measures would be inconsistent with this basic bargain. Is this correct? Recall the historic rule (still followed in a few jurisdictions) that arbitrators could not order provisional measures, which could only be obtained from national courts. *See supra* p. 873. Also, consider Article 9 of the UNCITRAL Model Law, which reflects the generally prevailing view that authority to order provisional measures is concurrent (shared by national courts and arbitral tribunals). *See supra* p. 875. *See also* European Convention, Art. VI(4). The *Cooper* court also reasons that provisional measures are not really very important in arbitration. That is simply wrong. Provisional relief is often of critical importance in international disputes. *See supra* pp. 888-96.

More plausible is *Cooper*'s suggestion that parties should be left to agree specifically to allow national courts to order pre-award security measures. That argument at least focuses properly on the primacy of the parties' agreement and the needs of the arbitral process. But does anything in *Cooper* justify the court's allocation of the burden of proof and its requirement for an express agreement to permit court-ordered provisional measures? Is it not more likely that, absent contrary agreement, the parties intended, and justice would be served by, the availability of court-ordered interim relief that is genuinely in aid of arbitration?

3. *Authorities rejecting conclusion that Article II(3) forbids court-ordered provisional relief.* The weight of lower U.S. authority has followed *Uranex* and rejected the argument that Article II(3) forbids all court-ordered interim relief in aid of arbitration. For other decisions adopting the *Uranex* position, *see China Nat'l Metal Prods. etc. v. Apex Digital, Inc.,* 155 F.Supp.2d 1174, 1179 (C.D. Cal. 2001) ("The court disagrees with ... *McCreary* and concludes that Article II(3) ... does not deprive the court of subject matter jurisdiction over this action and particularly to order provisional relief, e.g., a pre-arbitral award writ of attachment pending reference to arbitration and pending the conclusion of the arbitration proceedings."); *Filanto SpA v. Chilewich Int'l Corp.,* 789 F.Supp. 1229 (S.D.N.Y. 1992) (*McCreary* is "facially absurd"), *app. dismissed,* 984 F.2d 58 (2d Cir. 1993); G. Born, *International Commercial Arbitration* 2524-37 (2d ed. 2014); Rau, *Provisional Relief in Arbitration: How Things Stand in the United States,* 22 J. Int'l Arb. 1 (2005).

Similarly, virtually all non-U.S. authorities reject the conclusion that Article II(3) of the New York Convention precludes court-ordered provisional measures in aid of arbitration. For a representative example, consider:

> "I am unable to agree with those decisions in the United States (there has been no citation of authority on this point from any other foreign source) which form one side of a division of authority as yet unresolved by the [U.S.] Supreme Court. These decisions are to the effect that interim measures must necessarily be in conflict with the obligations assumed by the subscribing nations to the New York Convention, because they 'bypass the agreed upon method of settling disputes': *see McCreary Tire & Rubber Co. v. CEAT SpA....* I prefer the view that when properly used such measures serve to reinforce the agreed method, not to bypass it." *Channel Tunnel Group Ltd v. Balfour Beatty Constr. Ltd* [1993] AC 334, 354 (House of Lords) (rejecting *Cooper* reading of Article II(3)).

See also A. van den Berg, *The New York Arbitration Convention of 1958* 139-40 (1981) ("no doubt as to the possibility of a pre-award attachment, that is to say an attachment before or during the arbitration, in order to secure the subject matter in dispute or the payment under the award if rendered in favor of the party who has applied for the attachment"). Consider these criticisms of the rationale in *McCreary* and *Cooper.* Are they correct? Completely correct?

4. *New York legislative response to* Cooper. The interpretation of the Convention in *Cooper* was widely criticized in New York (and elsewhere). As a consequence, §7502 of the New York Civil Practice Law and Rules was amended (and then re-amended in 2005), adding a new sub-paragraph (c), excerpted above. Subparagraph (c) permits New York state courts to grant attachments and preliminary injunctive relief "in connection with an arbitration that is pending or that is to be commenced inside or outside this state, whether or not it is subject to the United Nations convention on the recognition and enforcement of foreign arbitral awards," provided that an arbitral award may be rendered ineffectual without interim relief.

Section 7502(c) is, of course, a state statute. Does *state* legislation affect the interpretation of the New York Convention (*i.e., federal* law) in *Cooper* and *McCreary*? What does enactment of §7502(c) suggest about the assessment of the need for provisional measures in *Cooper* and *McCreary*? *See Sojitz Corp. v. Prithvi Info. Solutions Ltd*, 891 N.Y.S.2d 622 (N.Y. Sup. Ct. 2011) (relying on §7502(c) as basis for attachment of assets in New York in aid of arbitration subject to New York Convention).

5. *Rationale of* Uranex*: Article II(3) permits court-ordered attachments in aid of arbitration.* Consider the rationale of *Uranex*. What does the court conclude Article II(3) means? Suppose a foreign court entertains an attachment action in circumstances like those in *McCreary* and *Cooper*, and grants an attachment that is plainly intended to frustrate the arbitral process. Would Article II(3) of the Convention forbid such actions? In *Uranex*, however, note that there was no evidence that the pre-award attachment was designed to do anything other than secure an eventual arbitral award (and hence, aid the arbitral process). Although the rationale articulated in *Cooper* and *McCreary* would not permit such an attachment, *Uranex* does. Which interpretation of the Convention—*Uranex* or *Cooper/McCreary*—is sounder?

6. McCreary *and* Cooper *revisited: effect of Article II(3) where parties' arbitration agreement is violated.* Consider again the specific results—as opposed to the stated rationale—in *McCreary* and *Cooper*. Was it not clear in each case that the judicial attachment action was an effort to circumvent the arbitration process that the parties had agreed upon? Note that the *McCreary* court specifically grounded its holding—that Article II(3) of the Convention would be violated by the attachment—on its conclusion that the attachment action "breached" the parties' arbitration agreement. Assuming that an attachment (or other) action in a national court does violate the parties' arbitration agreement, then the results in both *Cooper* and *McCreary* are unexceptional—and indeed both desirable and mandated by Article II(3). It is no more inappropriate to refuse to entertain such an action than it would be to entertain an action on the merits in violation of the parties' arbitration agreement. Indeed, the basic reading of Article II(3) adopted by *McCreary*—that Article II(3) forbids actions in national courts in violation of the parties' arbitration agreement—also appears sound.

Note that, while parts of the rationale and the specific results in *Cooper* and *McCreary* can be explained as involving litigation that was designed to frustrate the arbitral process, subsequent decisions cannot. In these cases, Article II(3) was invoked where it was clear that court-ordered provisional measures were not intended to circumvent the arbitral process. *See Drexel Burnham Lambert Inc. v. Ruebsamen*, 139 A.D.2d 323 (N.Y. App. Div. 1988) (attachment solely in aid of arbitration); *Shah v. Eastern Silk Indus. Ltd*, 493 N.Y.S.2d 150 (N.Y. App. Div. 1985); *Faberge Int'l Inc. v. Di Pino*, 491 N.Y.S.2d 345 (N.Y. App. Div. 1985); *I.T.A.D. Assoc., Inc. v. Podar Bros.*, 636 F.2d 75 (4th Cir. 1981).

7. Cooper *and* McCreary *revisited again: was the parties' arbitration agreement violated?* Note that both *Cooper* and *McCreary* involved ICC arbitrations and, therefore, that Article 8(5) of the then-prevailing 1988 ICC Rules was applicable. Article 8(5) of the 1988 ICC Rules provided:

> Before the file is transmitted to the arbitrators, and in exceptional circumstances even thereafter, the parties shall be at liberty to apply to any competent judicial authority for interim or conservatory measures, and they shall not by so doing be held to infringe the agreement to arbitrate or to affect the relevant powers reserved to the arbitrator.

What light does Article 8(5) shed upon the correctness of the conclusion in *McCreary* that the attachment action was a violation of the parties' arbitration agreement? Even though the ICC Rules provided that seeking attachment does not, *in principle,* violate the parties' arbitration agreement, does that mean that it *never* does? Even where the attachment is part of a scheme to substitute litigation in national courts for arbitration?

8. *Arbitration agreements permitting court-ordered provisional relief.* The *Cooper* court suggests that the parties could have specifically agreed to permit court-ordered provisional measures. (The court's suggestion ignores the fact that, by agreeing to ICC arbitration (and Article 8(5) of the 1988 ICC Rules), the parties in *Cooper* did just that.) Thus, *Cooper* rests on a court's obligation under Article II(3) of the Convention to refer the parties to arbitration, pursuant to their agreement to arbitrate; even under the *Cooper* rationale, Article II(3) would appear to permit court-ordered provisional measures when that is what the parties specifically agreed.

    If the parties' agreement does expressly permit court-ordered provisional measures, it must still be interpreted. Suppose the parties in *Cooper* had agreed: "either party shall have the right at any time to seek provisional measures from any national court in aid of arbitration hereunder." Would that clause, or any similar language, have allowed the attachment actions in either *Cooper* or *McCreary*? Do general clauses permitting parties to seek court-ordered provisional measures apply where judicial actions for provisional measures are designed to frustrate the arbitral process? *See also infra* pp. 914, 925-32.

9. *Proper application of Article II(3) to provisional relief.* Consider the following approach to Article II(3). First, a correct resolution of any dispute over a national court's authority to order provisional relief in aid of an arbitration requires interpreting the parties' arbitration agreement and any applicable institutional rules: do the parties' agreement and any applicable rules permit pre-award court-ordered provisional measures, and if so, which ones?

    Second, if the parties' agreement and applicable institutional rules provide no express answer, what should the parties be presumed to have intended? Absent express contrary language, the presumption should be that court-ordered provisional relief in aid of arbitration is permitted, but efforts to circumvent arbitration are not.

    Third, is the request for pre-award court-ordered interim relief in a particular case consistent with, or inconsistent with, the parties' arbitration agreement? This requires analysis of both the relevant arbitration agreement and the relevant request for court-ordered provisional measures.

    Only with these three conclusions in hand can Article II(3) sensibly be considered: that consideration should generally conclude that Article II(3) does not forbid court-ordered pre-award provisional measures in aid of arbitration, except when they are contrary to the terms of the parties' arbitration agreement or applicable institutional rules. Conversely, Article II(3) should forbid court-ordered provisional relief that is intended to frustrate or circumvent the arbitral process or that is contrary to the parties' agreement. This analysis places a premium on deciding when a request for provisional relief is "in aid" of arbitration, rather than an effort to circumvent it. Resolution of this question will depend on the timing of a request, the availability of provisional relief from the arbitrators, the extent to which provisional measures will effectively resolve the underlying dispute and the hardship suffered by the parties. Is this approach persuasive?

10. *What national court is competent to order an attachment in aid of an international arbitration?* As noted above, in *McCreary* and *Cooper* the parties had agreed to arbitrate their disputes outside the United States—in Belgium and Switzerland, respectively. What relevance, if any, does that have for the power of a *U.S. court* to order pre-award provisional measures under the New York Convention?

    Is there anything in the Convention that suggests that only the court where the arbitration proceeding will be conducted should have the authority to order pre-award attachment? Would that be a sensible rule? Is it likely that jurisdictional disputes, forum-shopping, multiplicitous litigation, or other ills will result from a different rule? Is there any basis, however, for finding such a rule in the text of the Convention? The question of what nation's courts can or should entertain requests for provisional relief in aid of arbitration is considered in detail below. *See infra* pp. 925-32.

11. *Effect of New York Convention on court-ordered attachment or other measures in aid of execution of arbitral award.* Suppose that an arbitration goes forward, without provisional measures, and produces an award. The prevailing party then has the award confirmed, for example, in the United States; if the losing party refuses to pay, does the Convention interpose any obstacle to court-ordered measures in aid of execution? Even under the interpretation of Article II(3) of the Convention adopted in *Cooper*? *See* Sanders, *Consolidated Commentary*, XIV Y.B. Comm. Arb. 528, 570 (1989) ("no court has doubted that an attachment in connection with the enforcement of an arbitral award, in order to secure payment under the award, is compatible with the Convention."); *Cooper v. Ateliers de la Motobecane SA*, 442 N.E.2d 1239 (N.Y. 1982). In fact, not only does the Convention not *preclude* court-ordered attachment in aid of execution of an arbitral award, it arguably *requires* such action—at least if it is available in purely domestic arbitration matters.

12. *Effect of New York Convention on judicial enforcement of tribunal-ordered provisional measures.* Suppose a party obtains provisional measures from the arbitrators (as *Cooper* would appear to require). If those measures are not complied with, does the New York Convention forbid or restrict judicial enforcement of the interim relief? Under the interpretation of Article II(3) adopted in *Cooper*? Would this not be an ironic result? *See Ministry of Fin. & Planning v. Onyx Dev. Corp.*, 1989 U.S. Dist. LEXIS 11995 (S.D.N.Y.) (permitting judicial enforcement). *See also supra* pp. 896-904, 910-15.

13. *Summary dispositions by national courts.* Recall the decision in *Halki, supra* pp. 150-54. There, the English court considered whether to follow authority permitting a national court to grant summary judgment for a claimant, notwithstanding the parties' agreement to arbitrate, where there was no credible defense by the respondent to the claimant's claims. Compare the judicial power exercised pursuant to this line of precedent to the grant of provisional measures in aid of an arbitration. What is the difference between a grant of summary judgment in favor of the claimant (or respondent) and a grant of provisional relief in aid of the arbitration?

14. *Prohibition against court-ordered provisional measures under ICSID Convention.* One arbitral regime that excludes court-ordered provisional measures in aid of arbitration is ICSID. Consider Article 26 of the ICSID Convention, excerpted at p. 19 of the Documentary Supplement. Article 26 has been interpreted by several ICSID arbitral tribunals and other authorities as precluding actions seeking provisional measures

from a national court. *Holiday Inns SA, Occidental Petroleum Corp. v. Gov't of Morocco, Award in ICSID Case No. ARB/72/1 of 1 July 1973; Judgment of 27 September 1985, Guinea v. Maritime Int'l Nominees Est.*, 24 I.L.M. 1639 (1985) (Antwerp Rechtbank); *Maritime Int'l Nominees Est. v. Guinea, Award in ICSID Case No. ARB/84/4 of 6 January 1988*, 4 ICSID Rep. 61, 69 (1997) ("The Tribunal recommends that MINE withdraw and terminate any and all judicial proceedings commenced before national jurisdictions and refrain from commencing any further proceedings in connection with this dispute.... The Tribunal recommends in addition that MINE withdraw all other provisional measures before national jurisdictions (including any seizures or attachments of the property of the Republic of Guinea whatever their judicial designation and whatever the method) and that MINE refrain from seeking additional provisional measures before any national jurisdiction.").

What is the rationale for extending Article 26 of the ICSID Convention to provisional measures? Is this wise? What aspects of the ICSID regime argue for this application of Article 26?

When might parties have "otherwise" agreed to court-ordered interim relief in aid of an ICSID arbitration? Note that Rule 39(6) of the ICSID Arbitration Rules provides: "Nothing in this Rule shall prevent the parties, provided that they have so stipulated in the agreement recording their consent, from requesting any judicial or other authority to order provisional measures, prior to or after the institution of the proceedings, for the preservation of their respective rights and interests."

2. *Effect of National Arbitration Legislation on Authority of National Courts to Grant Provisional Measures in Aid of International Arbitration*

The concurrent jurisdiction of national courts and arbitral tribunals to issue provisional measures is provided for by many arbitration statutes.[33] Although a few national laws are to the contrary (reserving interim relief to courts alone[34]), the overwhelming weight of arbitration legislation and judicial authority is that both arbitral tribunals and national courts may (absent contrary agreement) issue provisional measures in connection with an international arbitration.[35] The materials excerpted below explore the issues raised under national law by requests for court-ordered interim relief in aid of international arbitrations.

ROGERS, BURGUN, SHAHINE & DESCHLER, INC. v. DONGSAN CONSTRUCTION CO.
598 F.Supp. 754 (S.D.N.Y. 1984)

KRAM, District Judge. Rogers, Burgun, Shahine & Deschler, Inc. ("RBSD") is a New York corporation engaged in business as architectural designers of hospitals. Dongsan Construction Company, Ltd. ("Dongsan") is a Korean corporation, with offices in New Jersey, engaged in business as general contractors in construction projects.

In 1982, Saudi Arabia undertook to build a hospital in Jubail. Dongsan secured the main contract on this project. Dongsan subcontracted a portion of the architectural and engi-

---

33. *See* G. Born, *International Commercial Arbitration* 2451, 2538-51 (2d ed. 2014).
34. *See supra* pp. 872-73 (Italy, Argentina, China).
35. *See supra* pp. 873-75.

neering design work on the project to RBSD (the "Subcontract"). Under the Subcontract, RBSD agreed to perform certain services, some of which RBSD, in turn, subcontracted to other entities. In return for those services, Dongsan agreed to pay RBSD some $2,596,086. Dongsan further agreed to pay RBSD twenty per cent of that amount ($519,217) in advance of RBSD's performance. In order to secure this advance payment, RBSD provided Dongsan a Letter to Guarantee from Bank Al-Jazira in the full amount of the advance payment. The amount guaranteed by this letter was to decrease periodically commensurate with the percentage of work performed by RBSD and paid for by Dongsan. The Subcontract also provided in broad terms for resolution of disputes by arbitration in Paris, France, under the [ICC Rules].[36]

RBSD has performed some of the services required by the Subcontract and Dongsan has paid RBSD for that work. Pursuant to the terms of the Letter of Guarantee, the amount currently secured is $155,766.... [A] dispute arose with respect to RBSD's performance.... RBSD claims that the dispute concerns a very small portion of the work performed or owing.... Dongsan notified RBSD that it intended to complete certain of RBSD's obligations itself, effecting a partial termination of the Subcontract as modified. Additionally, Dongsan indicated that it would withhold the remaining balance due RBSD under the Subcontract to set-off the anticipated expenses in completing those parts of RBSD's services it had terminated. RBSD claims that it has substantially performed all of its obligations due to date, that it is owed some $752,865 for actual and tendered performance, and that it is entitled to the release of the remaining $155,766 held by way of the Letter of Guarantee....

RBSD filed the complaint herein on November 5, 1984, alleging breach of contract by Dongsan and seeking inter alia the $908,631 allegedly owed to RBSD by Dongsan and a preliminary injunction enjoining Dongsan from calling the Letter of Guarantee.... On November 21, 1984, Dongsan filed its motion to dismiss or stay this action pending arbitration of the disputes herein. [The Court first held that RBSD's claims were subject to arbitration.]...

The fact that this dispute is to be arbitrated does not deprive the Court of its authority to provide provisional remedies. *See Erving v. Virginia Squires Basketball Club*, 349 F.Supp. 716, 719-29 (E.D.N.Y.), *aff'd*, 468 F.2d 1064, 1067 (2d Cir. 1972). The Court must, therefore, decide if this is "a proper case" for an injunction. *Erving*, 468 F.2d at 1067. The standards governing the issuance of a preliminary injunction are well established in this Circuit. A preliminary injunction will issue only upon

> "a showing of (a) irreparable harm and (b) either (1) likelihood of success on the merits or (2) sufficiently serious questions going to the merits to make them a fair ground for litigation and a balance of hardships tipping decidedly toward the party requesting the preliminary relief." *Jackson Dairy, Inc. v. H.P. Hood & Sons Inc.*, 596 F.2d 70, 72 (2d Cir. 1979).

---

36. Article XVI of the subcontract provides...:

> "If at any time either party considers that any question, dispute or difference whatsoever has arisen between the parties herein in relation to or in conjunction with this Agreement then that party may give to the other party notice in writing of the existence of such question, dispute or difference and, unless it shall have been amicably resolved within one month from the date of such notice, the same shall be referred to arbitration to be finally settled under the Rules of Conciliation and Arbitration of the [ICC], unless otherwise agreed, in Paris, France."

I find that the second prong test has been met in the present case. The relief sought in this case is minimal. RBSD seeks only to preserve the status quo with respect to the Letter of Guarantee. "The status quo has been frequently defined as the last uncontested status which preceded the pending controversy." *Flood v. Kuhn*, 309 F.Supp. 793, 798 (S.D.N.Y. 1970), *aff'd*, 443 F.2d 264 (2d Cir. 1971), *aff'd*, 407 U.S. 258 (1972). The last uncontested status in this case found Dongsan holding a Letter of Guarantee for $155,766 with RBSD holding that sum to indemnify Bank Al-Jazira for the letter should it be called. Dongsan's argument that the status quo would be preserved by allowing it to call the letter and take the $155,766 secured thereby is unavailing.[37] RBSD seeks only to prevent Dongsan from calling this letter.[38]

The contract dispute involves nearly one million dollars. Dongsan is a Korean corporation with apparently no fixed assets in the United States. Dongsan does maintain an office in New Jersey and a large amount of liquid assets in bank accounts in New York and New Jersey. Those assets, however, because they are all liquid, could easily be depleted or removed from the United States. If that were to occur, RBSD's ability to recover in this Court or any arbitration award obtained in Paris would be frustrated.

With respect to the Letter of Guarantee, the potential for frustration of RBSD's recovery is doubled. The monies securing the letter are currently in RBSD's possession. If Dongsan is permitted to call the letter, those assets would be transferred, essentially, from RBSD to Dongsan. Any arbitral determination that RBSD is entitled to recover from Dongsan, or that Dongsan was not entitled to call the letter, would be meaningless if Dongsan were to transfer its liquid assets, increased by the monies securing the letter, out of the reach of this Court. Since there would then be no adequate remedy at law for RBSD in this Court, the Court finds that there could be irreparable harm to RBSD if Dongsan is not enjoined from calling the letter.

Dongsan's argument that RBSD would be able to enforce any arbitration award in Korea does not change this finding. RBSD would still have no adequate remedy at law here, in this Court…. [T]he federal courts [have] held that legal remedies in state courts did not suffice to make injunctive relief in federal courts unavailable. The absence of legal remedy is to be determined in this Court. If the availability of legal remedies in state court is not sufficient to preclude injunctive relief here, a fortiori the availability of a legal remedy in a foreign country is not sufficient.[39]

37. Dongsan also argues that the status quo will be upset if it "is unable to *maintain* its security in the form of the Letter of Guarantee" (emphasis added), presumably because the Letter might expire by its own terms and Dongsan would be left with nothing. RBSD has, however, agreed to secure an extension of the Letter for the duration of the arbitration. RBSD is directed to do so and to file proof of such extension with the Court by December 15, 1984. Thus, the status quo will be maintained.

38. The underlying dispute involves nearly one million dollars, RBSD has not attempted to restrain Dongsan from doing anything with assets valued near that amount to secure any potential judgment. Rather it has merely sought to avoid increasing the amounts potentially unrecoverable from Dongsan.

39. The Court notes that there is some question about the availability of prejudgment attachment under the Convention. *Compare Carolina Power & Light v. Uranex*, 451 F.Supp. 1044 (N.D. Cal. 1977) (yes) *with Metropolitan World Tanker Corp. v. P.N. Pertambangan Minjakdangas Bumi Nasional*, 427 F.Supp. 2 (S.D.N.Y. 1975) (no). However, the relief sought here is not an attachment. Dongsan is in no way restricted in its use or possession of its assets, but only in its power to gather more assets from RBSD leaving RBSD with only the recourse of recovery in Korea.

The parties are in hot dispute about the underlying contractual claims. Plaintiff claims it is due nearly $1,000,000. Defendant asserts that plaintiff's obligation to indemnify could total $10,000,000. Certainly this is sufficient to establish serious questions going to the merits for the arbitrator's decision.

Finally, the Court finds that the balance of hardships tips decidedly toward RBSD. If the status quo is maintained, defendant feels no hardship whatsoever. Dongsan maintains security in the sum of $155,766 should the arbitrators determine that it is entitled to any or all of that sum (or more), and loses nothing that it currently has. If the status quo is not maintained, and Dongsan is permitted to call the letter RBSD stands to lose its own money (the $155,766) without recourse here.

Accordingly, RBSD's motion is granted. RBSD is to file proof of extension of the Letter of Guarantee for one year (to be extended further if necessary) by December 15, 1984. Dongsan ... is hereby enjoined from directing the Bank Al-Jazira to honor or pay the Letter of Guarantee....

BORDEN, INC. v. MEIJI MILK PRODUCTS CO.
919 F.2d 822 (2d Cir. 1990)

TIMBERS, Circuit Judge. [Borden, Inc. ("Borden"),] a New Jersey corporation with offices in New York City, is a multi-national corporation engaged in the manufacture and distribution of food, dairy and consumer products ... throughout the world. [Appellee Meiji Milk Products Co. ("Meiji")], a Japanese corporation with offices in New York City, is engaged in the manufacture of ... milk products in Japan and other parts of the world. In 1983, Borden and Meiji entered into a Trademark License and Technical Assistance Agreement (the "agreement"), pursuant to which Borden licensed the use of its name and logo to Meiji to be used on a variety of margarine products manufactured and sold by Meiji in Japan for a period of seven years. The agreement, which was performed entirely in Japan, expired by its terms on October 3, 1990.

For the past seven years, Meiji has sold a number of margarine products bearing the Borden trademark. The formulas and techniques used to manufacture the margarine products are owned by Meiji. Meiji has obtained protection under Japanese Design Patent law for the margarine packaging it has used. Although the agreement has now expired, Meiji continues to market margarine, in Japan, in the packaging it had been using while the agreement was in force, but now without any use of the Borden trademark or logo. Borden contends that the use of the packaging is an "appropriation" in violation of the agreement.

Section 16 of the agreement specifically provides that all disputes arising in connection with the agreement shall be finally settled by arbitration pursuant to the Japanese-American Trade Arbitration Agreement.... [O]n August 24, 1990, Borden filed a demand for arbitration, alleging that Meiji had breached the agreement and unfairly competed with Borden. Meiji contends that Japanese patent law authorizes its continued use of the packaging and asserts that the agreement between the parties is silent as to any use by Meiji of packaging after termination of that agreement. The site of arbitration—which will be either New York or Japan—has not yet been determined.

On August 30, 1990, Borden commenced this action in the Southern District of New York, alleging claims for breach of contract and wrongful destruction of goodwill. Borden sought to compel arbitration pursuant to 9 U.S.C. §206. It also sought a preliminary injunction against Meiji's use of the disputed packaging.... [The district court had granted a temporary restraining order but refused to grant a preliminary injunction, instead dismissing Borden's action on *forum non conveniens* grounds. Borden appealed.] ...

As a threshold matter, we address the question of the court's subject matter jurisdiction to entertain the application for preliminary injunctive relief in aid of arbitration.... Meiji's argument is that, since the agreement between the parties contains an arbitration clause, the Convention is applicable [and, therefore, that the court lacks jurisdiction to grant provisional relief].... Borden concedes that the Convention is applicable, but argues that the Convention does not oust the court of jurisdiction to issue an injunction in aid of arbitration. We agree.

Federal courts are charged with enforcing the Convention. 9 U.S.C. §201. Specifically, a court may direct that "arbitration be held in accordance with the agreement at any place therein provided for.... Such court may also appoint arbitrators...." §206.... Meiji argues that a court's jurisdiction is limited to compelling arbitration or confirming an arbitration award. In the instant case, however, Borden specifically invoked §206, seeking to have the district court compel arbitration and appoint arbitrators. We hold that entertaining an application for a preliminary injunction in aid of arbitration is consistent with the court's powers pursuant to §206. *Cf. McCreary Tire & Rubber Co. v. CEAT SpA* (district court order refusing to vacate an attachment reversed, because underlying complaint sought to bypass arbitration altogether and "the Convention forbids the courts of a contracting state from entertaining a suit which violates an agreement to arbitrate"); *Int'l Shipping Co. v. Hydra Offshore, Inc.*, 875 F.2d 388, 391 n.5 (2d Cir. 1989) (district court properly held that jurisdiction could not be premised on the Convention because "the party invoking its provisions did not seek either to compel arbitration or to enforce an arbitral award").

In the instant case, far from trying to bypass arbitration, Borden sought to have the court compel arbitration. New York law specifically provides for provisional remedies in connection with an arbitrable controversy, N.Y. Civil Practice Law & Rules ("CPLR") §7502(c) (McKinney Supp. 1990), and the equitable powers of federal courts include the authority to grant it. *Murray Oil Products Co. v. Mitsui & Co.*, 146 F.2d 381 (2d Cir. 1944). Entertaining an application for such a remedy, moreover, is not precluded by the Convention but rather is consistent with its provisions and its spirit. In *Murray*, we held that an arbitration clause "does not deprive the promisee of the usual provisional remedies...." *Id.* at 384. We held that the desire for speedy decisions in arbitration "is entirely consistent with a desire to make as effective as possible recovery upon awards, after they have been made, which is what provisional remedies do." *Id.* We hold that the district court [possessed] subject matter jurisdiction....

Our review of the district court's dismissal [on the ground of *forum non conveniens*] is extremely limited. [*Piper Aircraft Co. v. Reyno*, 454 U.S. 235, 257 (1981)].... The district court in the instant case carefully considered the ... factors [set forth in *Gulf Oil Corp. v. Gilbert*, 330 U.S. 501, 508-09 (1947).] It found that only the Japanese market and consumers are affected by the parties' dispute and that all necessary fact witnesses are in Japan. The court found further that an injunction issued in Japan clearly would be enforceable there, whereas one obtained in this country might not be. Examining the public interests at stake, the court found that Japan has a much greater interest in the litigation than does the United States.... Under the circumstances of the instant case, we hold that the court's decision to dismiss in light of the *Gilbert* factors was sufficiently justified.

Borden asserts that the court's application of the *Gilbert* factors was "misplaced" in the first instance because Meiji allegedly failed to meet, "at the outset," its burden of showing the availability of an adequate remedy in Japan. We reject this contention....

Borden claims that the district court failed to recognize the limited, emergency nature of the relief it was seeking, *i.e.*, a preliminary injunction in aid of arbitration. Borden claims that there is no provision for such a remedy in Japan when the arbitration is pending outside Japan. Borden's implication that arbitration currently is pending in New York is itself disingenuous. In fact, a determination has not yet been made whether the underlying arbitration will be in New York or in Japan. Moreover, even if the arbitration were to proceed in the United States, the record relied upon by the court indicates a good possibility that a Japanese court would grant preliminary relief even if the underlying arbitration were going forward in New York. The court explicitly found that "there has been an adequate showing on Meiji's part that there is an alternative remedy available to Borden in the Japanese courts." This finding is adequately supported by the record.

Third, although Borden suggests that, in order for Japan to be considered an adequate forum, Japan must provide precisely the same remedies and in the same time-frame, this simply is not so. Rather, "some inconvenience or the unavailability of beneficial litigation procedures similar to those available in the federal district courts does not render an alternative forum inadequate." *Shields v. Mi Ryung Constr. Co.*, 508 F.Supp. 891, 895 (S.D.N.Y. 1981).

We do agree with Borden, however, that its rights would be unduly prejudiced if it were forced to wait years or even months to have a Japanese court review its application for some measure of temporary relief. The district court ordered that Borden may move to restore this action if preliminary injunctions prove to be unavailable in Japan. In dismissing the action only conditionally, the court sought to protect Borden's rights. In order to provide a further measure of protection to Borden, we modify the district court's order so that Borden may reapply for a preliminary injunction in the Southern District of New York if the Japanese court does not decide Borden's application within 60 days after it is submitted. Meiji agreed to this modification ... at oral argument....

NOTES

1. Dongsan *and* Borden—*injunctive relief versus attachment under New York Convention.* In contrast to *Cooper* and *McCreary*, the courts in *Dongsan* and *Borden* were both willing, in principle, to grant provisional relief in aid of international arbitrations subject to the New York Convention. *Borden* specifically considered the *McCreary* rationale and rejected it as applied to injunctive relief (as distinguished from attachments). Is there any principled basis for distinguishing between the effect of Article II(3) of the Convention on an attachment and a preliminary injunction? Consider the final footnote to the *Dongsan* opinion, *supra* p. 918 n. 39. Is there a principled basis for holding that Article II(3) forbids attachments (because they restrict a party's use of its property), but permits injunctions (because they may only restrict a party's ability to acquire additional assets)? Does anything in Article II(3) or the rationale of *Cooper* and *McCreary* support this distinction?

2. *Choice of law governing court-ordered provisional relief in aid of arbitration.* What law applies to the availability of interim relief in aid of arbitration from a national court? Is there any question but that the applicable law is that of the judicial forum?

Consider Article 183(2) of the SLPIL, excerpted at p. 159 of the Documentary Supplement. Consider also Article 17J of the 2006 revisions to the Model Law, excerpted at p. 101 of the Documentary Supplement.

3. *Availability of court-ordered provisional relief under original 1985 UNCITRAL Model Law.* Consider Article 17 of the original Model Law. What effect does it have on the power of a national court to grant provisional measures in aid of an international arbitration? What other sources of law would be relevant to determining whether a local court would be willing to grant provisional measures?

4. *Availability of court-ordered provisional relief under 2006 revisions to UNCITRAL Model Law.* Consider Article 17J of the 2006 revisions to the Model Law. It provides that a national court "shall have the same power of issuing an interim measure in relation to arbitration proceedings" as exist with regard to judicial proceedings. What was the reason for this revision to the Model Law? Is it appropriate? What does it mean?

5. *Availability of court-ordered provisional measures in aid of arbitration under FAA.* Assume: (a) the New York Convention does not forbid court-ordered provisional measures in aid of arbitration; and (b) under applicable U.S. standards for injunctive relief, provisional measures could otherwise be granted. Even then, does the FAA permit such relief, and, if so, does the FAA alter the availability or scope of provisional measures?

   (a) *Lower court decisions holding court-ordered provisional measures available under FAA.* A number of lower U.S. courts have held, under the domestic FAA, that they possess the authority to order injunctive relief in aid of arbitration, at least in certain circumstances. *See, e.g., Teradyne, Inc. v. Mostek Corp.*, 797 F.2d 43, 51 (1st Cir. 1986) ("district court can grant injunctive relief in an arbitrable dispute pending arbitration"); *Rose-Lino Bev. Distrib. v. Coca-Cola Bottling Co.*, 749 F.2d 124, 125 (2d Cir. 1984) ("fact that a dispute is to be arbitrated ... does not absolve the court of its obligation to consider the merits of a requested preliminary injunction"). For one explanation of the rationale of these decisions, consider:

   > "The Courts are not limited in their equity powers to the specific function of enforcing arbitration agreements but may exercise those powers required to preserve the status quo of the subject matter in controversy pending the enforcement of the arbitration provision. To rule otherwise would in effect permit a party to take the law into its own hands while the proceeding is carried on as a result of the specific direction of the Court [compelling arbitration].... It would be an oddity in the law if the Court, after compelling a party to live up to his undertaking to arbitrate, had to stand idly by during the pendency of the arbitration which it has just directed and permit him to assert his 'right to breach a contract and to substitute payment of damages for non-performance.'" *Albatross S.S. Co. v. Manning Bros.*, 95 F.Supp. 459, 463 (S.D.N.Y. 1951).

   Is this persuasive?

   (b) *Lower court decisions holding court-ordered provisional measures not available under FAA.* A few lower courts have concluded that §§3 and 4 of the FAA—like the *McCreary/Cooper* interpretation of Article II(3) of the Convention—impliedly preclude court-ordered provisional relief in aid of arbitration absent contrary agreement. *See, e.g., Merrill Lynch, Pierce, Fenner & Smith, Inc. v. Hovey*, 726 F.2d 1286 (8th Cir. 1984) (absent agreement permitting court-ordered provisional measures, "unmistakably clear congressional purpose" was to bar them); *Merrill Lynch, Pierce, Fenner & Smith v. DeCaro*, 577 F.Supp. 616, 625 (W.D. Mo. 1983).

(c) *Standards under FAA for availability of preliminary injunction in aid of arbitration.* There is no language in the FAA that addresses the subject of court-ordered interim relief in aid of arbitration. In *Dongsan* and *Borden*, the courts applied generally-applicable federal standards for injunctive relief. Compare Article 17J of the 2006 revisions to the Model Law. Is it appropriate to apply generally-applicable standards for obtaining preliminary injunctions where the relief is in aid of arbitration? Is there no need to take into account the possibility of obtaining relief from the arbitral tribunal or the risk of interfering with the arbitral process?

6. *Limitations imposed by institutional rules on national courts' grant of provisional measures in aid of arbitration.* The parties' arbitration agreement or institutional rules incorporated by it may impose, or purport to impose, limits on the authority of national courts to grant provisional measures. These limits may be expressly included in the parties' arbitration agreement. More likely, they will be included in institutional rules incorporated into the parties' agreement. In this regard, consider the rules excerpted above.

(a) *ICC Rules.* A leading example of institutional rules limiting court-ordered provisional measures is Article 28(2) of the 2012 ICC Rules, excerpted at p. 192 of the Documentary Supplement. (Article 8(5) of the 1988 and Article 23(2) of the 1998 ICC Rules were broadly similar.) Article 28(2) of the 2012 ICC Rules imposes limits on the right of the parties to seek provisional relief from national courts. The provision attempts to make it clear that, prior to constitution of the arbitral tribunal, requests for court-ordered provisional measures are permitted; after the tribunal is constituted, however, judicial relief is permitted only in "appropriate circumstances." And, under Article 28(2), only "interim or conservatory measures" are provided for.

What should qualify as "appropriate circumstances"? Note that Article 8(5) of the 1988 ICC Rules permitted court-ordered provisional measures, after the arbitral tribunal had received the file, only in "exceptional circumstances." Who decides whether "appropriate" or "exceptional" circumstances permitting court-ordered provisional measures are satisfied? The arbitrator? A court? Suppose, after a tribunal is constituted and the Terms of Reference are finalized, a party seeks court-ordered provisional measures. What is the party's obligation to inform the arbitral tribunal?

(b) *UNCITRAL Rules.* Consider Article 26(9) of the UNCITRAL Rules, excerpted at p. 171 of the Documentary Supplement. What effect does it have on requests for court-ordered provisional measures? Is there any difference, express or implied, between requests made before and those made after a tribunal is constituted?

(c) *LCIA Rules.* Consider Article 25(3) of the 2014 LCIA Rules, excerpted at pp. 271-72 of the Documentary Supplement. What effect does it have on requests for court-ordered provisional measures? Compare Article 25(3) to the 2012 ICC Rules. Which is preferable?

7. *Parties' right to seek provisional measures from both national courts and arbitral tribunals.* Note that the corollary of concurrent jurisdiction of arbitral tribunals and

national courts to issue provisional measures is the ability of parties to decide where to seek provisional relief; that includes the ability of parties to decide whether to seek provisional relief from both a national court and an arbitral tribunal. Is this appropriate? Does it permit unfair or inefficient forum-shopping?

8. *Agreements limiting or excluding court-ordered provisional measures.* Suppose the parties' arbitration agreement excludes all recourse to national courts for interim relief. Is such an exclusion subject to challenge as contrary to public policy? *See* Hausmaninger, *The ICC Rules for A Pre-Arbitral Referee Procedure: A Step Towards Solving the Problem of Provisional Relief in International Commercial Arbitration*, 7 ICSID Rev. 82 (1992) (suggesting parties cannot exclude court-ordered provisional relief because arbitral relief is inadequate); *Anaconda v. Am. Sugar Refining Co.*, 322 U.S. 42 (1944). Note, however, that under *McCreary*, the exclusion of court-ordered interim relief is not merely permitted but required, supposedly by the New York Convention. How likely is it that parties would really intend to exclude court-ordered provisional measures in aid of arbitration? How should this influence interpretation of agreements purportedly excluding any right to seek court-ordered interim relief in aid of arbitration?

9. *Preclusive effect of court-ordered provisional measures.* Suppose a national court orders provisional relief in aid of an arbitration, and the arbitral tribunal is thereafter constituted; suppose further that one or both parties request that the tribunal reexamine the subject of provisional relief and withdraw (or extend) the court-ordered interim relief. Conversely, suppose interim relief is sought from a court, but it refuses to grant that relief; suppose the party who sought relief subsequently asks for the same relief from the arbitral tribunal.

Some arbitral tribunals have concluded that an earlier court decision granting (or denying) provisional measures is either binding on a tribunal considering the same request or, alternatively, entitled to a high degree of deference. One tribunal concluded that it was "not competent to lift such sequestration [of property ordered by a national court] or to order the defendants to renounce it." *Award in Unidentified ICC Case*, in Schwartz, *The Practices and Experience of the ICC Court,* in ICC, *Conservatory and Provisional Measures in International Arbitration* 45, 57 (1993). Another tribunal reasoned:

> "If the state court orders or declines to order a measure, the parties cannot subsequently resort to the arbitral tribunal to obtain a more favorable ruling, and vice versa. Even if the state court was first approached solely for the reason that the arbitral tribunal was not yet properly constituted, the tribunal cannot later on, after its constitution, reverse or modify the measure ordered by the state judge. What if a subsequent request for reversal or modification of an order is based on changed circumstances? Arguably, such a request should be dealt with by the arbitral tribunal once it is constituted." *Order No. 5 Regarding Claimant's Request for Interim Relief in ICC Case of 2 April 2002*, 21 ASA Bull. 810, 816 (2003).

Is this persuasive? Should a prior court decision be preclusive in a subsequent arbitration? Is it relevant that the court applies its own law, *supra* pp. 921-23, often taking into account the exceptional nature of court-ordered provisional measures in connection with an arbitration, rather than applying international standards? Would you agree with the following:

"Properly understood, a national court's decision on provisional measures should be regarded as supportive of the arbitral process, available in circumstances where an arbitral tribunal is unable to act, but subject to subsequent decisions of the arbitral tribunal; this accords with the arbitral tribunal's authority to conduct the dispute resolution process and finally resolve the parties' dispute." G. Born, *International Commercial Arbitration* 2505 (2d ed. 2014).

Some national courts have qualified grants of provisional measures in aid of arbitration, to make clear that the arbitral tribunal, when constituted, may revisit the issue. *See, e.g., Merrill Lynch v. Salvano*, 999 F.2d 211 (7th Cir. 1993) (issuing provisional measures "only until the arbitration panel is able to address whether the [relief] should remain in effect. Once assembled, an arbitration panel can enter whatever temporary injunctive relief it deems necessary to maintain the status quo"); *PLD Telekom Inc. v. Commerzbank AG*, unreported decision (2000) (QB) (English High Ct.) (arbitrators may reconsider grant of court-ordered provisional measures).

10. *When is a request for court-ordered provisional measures a waiver of a party's right to arbitrate?* As we have seen, the right to arbitrate can be waived. *See supra* pp. 472-74. When does a request for provisional measures from a court waive a party's right to enforce the parties' arbitration agreement (or, alternatively, a party's right to seek provisional measures from the arbitrators)?

What does Article 9 of the UNCITRAL Model Law provide regarding a party's waiver or violation of its agreement to arbitrate by seeking court-ordered provisional measures? Consider Article VI(4) of the European Convention, excerpted at p. 32 of the Documentary Supplement. How does it compare to Article 9 of the Model Law? Compare the similar approach of U.S. courts under the FAA. *See, e.g., Sauer-Getriebe KG v. White Hydraulics, Inc.*, 715 F.2d 348, 349-50 (7th Cir. 1984); *Rogers, Burgun, Shahine & Deschler, Inc. v. Dongsan Constr. Co., Lt*d, 598 F.Supp. 754, 757-58 (S.D.N.Y. 1984); *United Nuclear Corp. v. Gen. Atomic Co.*, 597 P.2d 290 (N.M. 1979). Most institutional rules also provide that a request for court-ordered provisional measures does not independently constitute a waiver of rights under an arbitration agreement. 2010 UNCITRAL Rules, Art. 26(9); 2012 ICC Rules, Art. 28(2); 2013 AAA Rules, Rule 37(c); 2012 Swiss Rules, Art. 26(5).

Do these provisions mean that *no* request for court-ordered provisional measures can constitute a waiver of a right to arbitrate? Or do they mean that, where the parties have simply agreed to arbitrate (without excluding court-ordered provisional measures), an application for court-ordered provisional measures is *not necessarily* a waiver of the right to arbitrate? Suppose, however, that the parties have agreed to exclude court-ordered provisional measures or that a party seeks court-ordered provisional measures in an effort to circumvent an arbitration clause. In these circumstances, can a party's application for court-ordered provisional measures be contrary to its agreement to arbitrate and, under applicable law, a waiver of its arbitration rights?

D. APPROPRIATE NATIONAL COURT TO GRANT PRE-AWARD PROVISIONAL MEASURES IN AID OF INTERNATIONAL ARBITRATION

Assuming the parties' agreement does not exclude court-ordered interim relief in aid of an international arbitration, the question arises as to what national court(s) should have the jurisdiction to grant such relief. In particular, should such jurisdiction be limited to the courts of the arbitral seat, or should provisional relief in aid of arbitration also be available in other courts? And, if jurisdiction to order interim relief in aid of a foreign arbitration exists, should it be exercised? The following materials explore how national courts have approached these questions.

CHANNEL TUNNEL GROUP LTD v. BALFOUR BEATTY CONSTR. LTD
[1993] AC 334 (House of Lords)

LORD MUSTILL. [Channel Tunnel Group Limited ("appellants") won a concession from the U.K. and French governments to construct a tunnel under the English Channel. Balfour Beatty Construction Limited and others ("respondents") entered into a construction contract with appellants to commission the Tunnel. The contract contained the following arbitration and choice-of-law clauses:

"67(1).... If any dispute or difference shall arise between the employer and the contractor during the progress of the works ... then ... such dispute or difference shall at the instance of either the employer or the contractor in the first place be referred in writing to and be settled by a panel of three persons (acting as independent experts but not as arbitrators) who shall unless otherwise agreed by both the employer and the contractor within a period of 90 days after being requested in writing by either party to do so, and after such investigation as the panel think fit, state their decision in writing and give notice of the same to the employer and the contractor....

67(2).... The contractor shall in every case continue to proceed with the works with all due diligence and the contractor and the employer shall both give effect forthwith to every such decision of the panel (provided that such decision shall have been made unanimously) unless and until the same shall be revised by arbitration as hereinafter provided. Such unanimous decision shall be final and binding upon the contractor and the employer unless the dispute or difference has been referred to arbitration as hereinafter provided.

67(3).... [If either party is dissatisfied with the experts' decision, or if the experts render no decision, or if the experts' decision is not obeyed,] then either the employer or the contractor may ... notify the other party in writing that the dispute or difference is to be referred to arbitration....

67(4).... All disputes or differences in respect of which a notice has been given under Clause 67(3) by either party that such dispute or difference is to be referred to arbitration and any other dispute or difference of any kind whatsoever which shall arise between the employer or the Maître oeuvre and the contractor in connection with or arising out of the contract, or the execution of the works or after their completion and whether before or after the termination, abandonment, or breach of the contract shall be finally settled under the Rules of Conciliation and Arbitration of the [ICC] by three arbitrators appointed under such Rules. The employer and the contractor shall each nominate and appoint one arbitrator and the third arbitrator shall be appointed by the [ICC]. The seat of such arbitration shall be Brussels....

68. The construction, validity and performance of the contract shall in all respects be governed by and interpreted in accordance with the principles common to both English law and French law, and in the absence of such common principles by such general principles of international trade law as have been applied by national and international

tribunals. Subject in all cases, with respect to the works to be respectively performed in the French and in the English part of the site, to the respective French or English public policy (ordre public) provisions."

Disputes arose over the price payable for work relating to the cooling system. The respondents demanded more money than the appellants were willing to pay, and when that demand failed, threatened to cease work. In response, the appellants commenced an action in the English courts, seeking an injunction forbidding the respondents from ceasing work. The respondents moved to stay the English judicial proceedings under the English Arbitration Act, 1975.... The Court of Appeal stayed the injunction proceeding and indicated that it would not uphold the granting of injunction.

The House of Lords first held that the English courts had the power to stay the injunction proceedings in favor of the expert/arbitration mechanism in the construction contract. First, English courts possess inherent power to stay their proceedings in deference to foreign judicial or arbitral proceedings; that discretion should be exercised where "large commercial enterprises, negotiating at arms' length in the light of long experience of construction contracts," agree to arbitration. Second, §1 of the 1975 Arbitration Act would appear to require a stay pending the expert and arbitral process. The House of Lords went on to consider whether an interim injunction, pending the experts' decision or the arbitral award, could be issued by an English court.]

Thus far, the question has been whether the appellant's claim for a final injunction should be allowed to proceed to trial in the High Court. [If not,] a difficult and important question will arise concerning the power of the court to order the respondents back to work pending the decision of the panel or, as the case may be, the arbitrators.... [First, appellants argue that an injunction could be issued under §12(6)(h) of the Arbitration Act 1950, which provides that "The High Court shall have, for the purpose of and in relation to a reference, the same power of making orders in respect of ... (h) interim injunction ... as it has for the purpose of and in relation to an action in the High Court."]

It is by now firmly established that more than one national system of law may bear upon an international arbitration. Thus, there is the proper law which regulates the substantive rights and duties of the parties to the contract from which the dispute has arisen. Exceptionally, this may differ from the national law governing the interpretation of the agreement to submit the dispute to arbitration. Less exceptionally it may also differ from the national law which the parties have expressly or by implication selected to govern the relationship between themselves and the arbitrator in the conduct of the arbitration: the "curial law" of the arbitration as it is often called. The construction contract [in this case] provides an example. The proper substantive law of this contract is the law, if such it can be called, chosen in clause 68. But the curial law must I believe be the law of Belgium. Certainly there may sometimes be an express choice of a curial law which is not the law of the place where the arbitration is to be held: but in the absence of an explicit choice of this kind, or at least some very strong pointer in the agreement to show that such a choice was intended, the inference that the parties when contracting to arbitrate in a particular place consented to having the arbitral process governed by the law of that place is irresistible....

[A] national court may ... be invited, as in the present case, to play a secondary role, not in the direct enforcement of the contract to arbitrate, but in the taking of measures to make the work of the chosen tribunal more effective. Here, the matter is before the court solely because the court happens to have under its own procedural rules the power to assert a personal jurisdiction over the parties, and to enforce protective measures against them. Any court satisfying this requirement will serve the purpose, whether or not it has any prior connection with the arbitral agreement or the arbitral process. In the present case, the English court has been drawn into this dispute only because it happens to have territorial jurisdiction over the respondents, and the means to enforce its order against them. The French court would have served just as well, and if the present application had been made in Paris we should have found the French court considering the same questions as have been canvassed on this appeal....

The distinction between the internal and external application of national arbitration laws is important. In my opinion, when deciding whether a statutory or other power is capable of being exercised by the English court in relation to clause 67, and if it is so capable whether it should in fact be so exercised, the court should bear constantly in mind that English law, like French law, is a stranger to this Belgian arbitration, and that the respondents are not before the English court by choice. In such a situation the court should be very cautious in its approach both to the existence and to the exercise of supervisory and supportive measures, lest it cut across the grain of the chosen curial law. Thus, in the present instance I believe that we should approach §12 of the Act of 1950 by asking—Can Parliament have intended that the power to grant an interim injunction should be exercised in respect of an arbitration conducted abroad under a law which is not the law of England? ... It seems to me absolutely plain ... that Parliament cannot have intended these provisions to apply to a foreign arbitration. I can see no reason why Parliament should have had the least concern to regulate the conduct of an arbitration carried on abroad pursuant to a foreign arbitral law....

[Second, appellants relied on §37(l) of the Supreme Court Act 1981 as providing authority to issue an interim injunction. Section 37(l) provides that "the High Court may by order (whether interlocutory or final) grant an injunction in all cases in which it appears to the court to be just and convenient to do so." The House of Lords concluded that the High Court possessed the power under this provision to issue an injunction in aid of a foreign arbitration. In addition, the House of Lords reasoned:] I am unable to agree with those decisions in the United States (there has been no citation of authority on this point from any other foreign source) which form one side of a division of authority as yet unresolved by the [U.S.] Supreme Court. These decisions are to the effect that interim measures must necessarily be in conflict with the obligations assumed by the subscribing nations to the New York Convention, because they "bypass the agreed upon method of settling disputes": *see McCreary Tire*.... I prefer the view that when properly used such measures serve to reinforce the agreed method, not to bypass it....

On the assumption that the court does have power to grant the appellants an injunction, a decision on whether the power should be exercised requires the making of certain assumptions.... Only one item of substantive relief was claimed by the writ, and although this was cast in negative form it was in substance a claim for a final mandatory injunction: or, what seems to me the same thing, an order for specific performance of the respondents' obligation to work continuously on the contract. Absent any evidence of Belgian law, we must also assume that this is an order which the panel and arbitrators would have power to make, if minded to do so. How long the proceedings will take is impossible to predict, apart from saying that if the appellants had gone straight to the panel in October 1991 rather than starting an action, the clause 67 proceedings would no doubt have been comfortably finished by now. At all events, we should in my opinion assume that if the panel rules in favor of the appellants the respondents will appeal to the arbitrators, and that a final ruling on the claim is not likely to emerge for some considerable time....

Amidst all these assumptions, there is one hard fact which I believe to be conclusive, namely that the injunction claimed from the English court is the same as the injunction to be claimed from the panel and the arbitrators, except that the former is described as interlocutory or interim. In reality its interim character is largely illusory, for as it seems to me an injunction granted in November 1991, and a fortiori an injunction granted today, would largely pre-empt the very decision of the panel and arbitrators whose support forms the raison d'être of the injunction. By the time that the award of the panel or arbitrators is ultimately made, with the respondents having continued to work meanwhile it will be of very modest practical value, except as the basis for a claim in damages by the respondents....

In these circumstances, I do not consider that the English court would be justified in granting the very far-reaching relief which the appellants claim. It is true that mandatory interlocutory relief may be granted even where it substantially overlaps the final relief claimed in the action; and I also accept that it is possible for the court at the pre-trial stage of a dispute arising under a construction contract to order the defendant to continue with a performance of the works. But the court should approach the making of such an order with the utmost caution, and should be prepared to act only when the balance of advantage plainly favors the grant of relief.... There is always a tension when the court is asked to order, by way of interim relief in support of an arbitration, a remedy of the same kind as will ultimately be sought from the arbitrators: between, on the one hand, the need for the court to make a tentative assessment of the merits in order to decide whether the plaintiff's claim is strong enough to merit protection, and on the other the duty of the court to respect the choice of tribunal which both parties have made, and not to take out of the hands of the arbitrators (or other decision-makers) a power of decision which the parties have entrusted to them alone. In the present instance I consider that the latter consideration must prevail. The court has stayed the action so that the panel and the arbitrators can decide whether to order a final mandatory injunction. If the court now itself orders an interlocutory mandatory injunction, there will be very little left for the arbitrators to decide.

Any doubts on this score are to my mind resolved by the choice of the English rather than the Belgian courts as the source of interim relief. Whatever exactly is meant by the words "competent judicial authority" in article 8.5 of the ICC Rules, the Belgian court must surely be the natural court for the source of interim relief.... Apparently no application for interim relief has been made to the court in Brussels.... If the appellants had wished to say that the Belgian court would have been unable or unwilling to grant relief, and that the English court is the only avenue of recourse, it was for them to prove it, and they have not done so. Moreover, even if evidence to this effect had been adduced I doubt whether it would have altered my opinion. This is not a case where a party to a standard form of contract finds himself burdened with an inappropriate arbitration clause to which he had not previously given his attention. I have no doubt that the dispute-resolution mechanisms of clause 67 were the subject of careful thought and negotiation. The parties chose an indeterminate "law" to govern their substantive rights; an elaborate process for ascertaining those rights; and a location for that process outside the territories of the participants. This conspicuously neutral, "a-national" and extra-judicial structure may well have been the right choice for the special needs of the Channel Tunnel venture. But whether it was right or wrong, it is the choice which the parties have made. The appellants now regret that choice. To push their claim for mandatory relief through the mechanisms of clause 67 is too slow and cumbersome to suit their purpose, and they now wish to obtain far reaching relief through the judicial means which they have been so scrupulous to exclude. Notwithstanding that the court can and should in the right case provide reinforcement for the arbitral process by granting interim relief I am quite satisfied that this is not such a case, and that to order an injunction here would be to act contrary both to the general tenor of the construction contract and to the spirit of international arbitration....

BORDEN, INC. v. MEIJI MILK PRODUCTS CO.
919 F.2d 822 (2d Cir. 1990)

[excerpted above at pp. 919-21]

NOTES

1. *Authority of national court under UNCITRAL Model Law to order provisional measures in aid of international arbitration seated in another country.* Does a court in State A have the authority to order provisional measures in aid of an arbitration seated in State B (with the law of State B providing the procedural law of the arbitration)? Consider Articles 1(2) and 9 of the original Model Law, excerpted at pp. 86-88 of the Documentary Supplement. What do these provisions suggest about the power of a national court to order provisional measures in aid of a foreign-seated arbitration? *See TLC Multimedia Inc. v. Core Curriculum Tech., Inc.,* [1998] B.C.J. No. 1656 (B.C. Sup. Ct.) (court has power under Article 9 of Model Law to grant provisional measures in aid of foreign arbitration). Is the statutory language clear? If not, should the text be interpreted as authorizing provisional measures in aid of foreign-seated arbitrations?

2. *Authority of national court under 2006 revisions to UNCITRAL Model Law to order provisional measures in aid of international arbitration seated in another country.* Consider Article 17J of the 2006 revisions to the Model Law. Does its language leave any doubt as to the power of a national court, in a Model Law jurisdiction, to order provisional measures in aid of an arbitration seated abroad?

3. *Authority of U.S. courts under FAA to order provisional measures in aid of international arbitration seated outside United States.* Consider the court's assumption in *Borden,* that it had authority to issue provisional measures in aid of a foreign arbitration. *See also Deiulemar Compagnia di Navigazione SpA v. M/V Allegra,* 198 F.3d 473 (4th Cir. 1999) (inspection of vessel, located in United States, ordered in aid of arbitration seated in London); *Tampimex Oil Ltd v. Latina Trading Corp.,* 558 F.Supp. 1201 (S.D.N.Y. 1983) (granting attachment of New York bank account in aid of arbitration in London); *Atlas Chartering Servs. Inc. v. World Trade Group, Inc.,* 453 F.Supp. 861, 863 (S.D.N.Y. 1978) (granting attachment of funds in two accounts in New York banks in aid of arbitration in London). Is there anything in the FAA that supports (or contradicts) this conclusion? Consider §201 of the FAA, excerpted at p. 107 of the Documentary Supplement.

4. *Should a national court ever order provisional measures in aid of an international arbitration seated in another country?* Consider the various arguments set out in the *Channel Tunnel* case against an English court's interference, by ordering provisional

measures in aid of arbitration, in a Belgian arbitration. Should a court in State A *ever* grant provisional measures in aid of an arbitration to be conducted in State B with the law of State B as the procedural law of the arbitration? If a court does so, will it not risk intruding unacceptably upon the supervisory functions of the courts of State B? Does the possibility of seeking provisional measures in foreign courts open the door to unjust and inefficient forum-shopping? Why can't the courts of the arbitral seat (State B) be given exclusive competence over the decision whether to issue provisional relief in aid of arbitration seated in that state? Consider the facts in *South Star, supra* pp. 842-44. Did they warrant an order of interim relief in aid of a foreign arbitration? *See also BALCO* (Indian S.Ct. 2012) ("In a foreign seated international commercial arbitration, no application for interim relief would be maintainable under §9 or any other provision, as applicability of Part I of the [Indian] Arbitration Act, 1996 is limited to all arbitrations which take place in India"), *supra* pp. 1073-81. Is this a reasonable approach?

5. *"Foreign" court-ordered provisional measures when "domestic" court cannot grant effective relief.* Note that the courts of the state where the arbitration is seated may not be in a position to grant effective provisional relief. Particularly where attachment or similar remedies are sought, only the jurisdiction where the defendant's assets are located may be able to grant meaningful provisional relief. That is because security measures often have only territorial effect and, even when they purport to apply extraterritorially, enforcement may be impossible. *See* G. Born, *International Commercial Arbitration* 2481-83, 2524-37, 2555-57 (2d ed. 2014). In those circumstances, according exclusive jurisdiction to the state where the arbitration is seated may not be warranted. Even assuming this is correct, and proven, is it relevant whether courts in the arbitral seat would grant provisional measures if the assets in question were within their jurisdiction?

In cases involving *in personam* relief—as in *Borden* and *Channel Tunnel*—is there any reason that courts of nations other than those of the arbitral seat should entertain actions for provisional relief? Both *Borden* and *Channel Tunnel* resolve this question by concluding (under U.S. and English law, respectively) that a court has the power to grant provisional relief in aid of a foreign (or potentially foreign) arbitration. Is that resolution persuasive? What are the reasons for and against it?

6. *Exercise of authority to order provisional relief in aid of foreign-seated arbitration.* While affirming the power to order provisional measures in aid of a foreign-seated arbitration, both *Borden* and *Channel Tunnel* refused to exercise that power on the facts before them. Both courts cited various factors counseling for this result.

Consider the factors cited by the English and U.S. courts. Are the factors the same? Which set of factors is more relevant to the question whether a particular national court should grant relief? Are all of the factors relevant? In addition, is it relevant whether (a) the arbitral tribunal is constituted and functioning; (b) if not, the reasons for that; (c) the attitude of the tribunal towards the request for relief; and (d) the availability of effective provisional measures from other courts? If you could consider only one of the above factors, which would it be?

What factors *should* be relevant to a decision by a court in one country to grant provisional measures in aid of an arbitration conducted in another country? Is it not relevant, as suggested above, that the court is asked to take action with respect to an asset located within its jurisdiction, which the courts of the arbitral forum could not reach?

7. Borden *revisited—provisional relief when arbitral forum has not been selected*. Note that in *Borden* the arbitral seat had not yet been designated, and New York might well have been the seat of the arbitration. If the arbitral seat were New York, what effect should this have on the availability of provisional measures in a U.S. court? Suppose the arbitration were seated in New York. In that case, should the New York court have granted the requested relief? Was *Borden* correctly decided?

8. *Law governing request for provisional measures in aid of foreign-seated arbitration*. If a court has the authority to grant provisional relief in aid of a foreign arbitration, should it apply its own law or a foreign law in determining whether such relief is appropriate? Recall that the law applicable to a court's decision whether to grant provisional measures in aid of arbitration is generally the law of the judicial forum. *See supra* pp. 921-23. Is there any reason a different rule should apply in the context of provisional measures in aid of a foreign arbitration? What law did *Borden* and *Channel Tunnel* apply? What law does Article 17J of the 2006 revisions to the Model Law provide for?

   Consider *Castelan v. M/V Mercantil Parati*, 1991 U.S. Dist. LEXIS 6472 (D.N.J.), where the parties' agreement provided for arbitration in London, under English law. The district court concluded that, under English law, the plaintiff in the U.S. action could not have obtained provisional relief from an English court; nevertheless, because U.S. standards for maritime arrest were satisfied, the court arrested the defendant's vessel in aid of the arbitration. Is that appropriate? If the primary reason to permit courts to aid foreign arbitrations is necessity and convenience, shouldn't the courts apply the same substantive rules as those under the law of the arbitral seat?

CHAPTER 11

MULTIPARTY ISSUES IN INTERNATIONAL ARBITRATION

International business transactions are frequently multiparty in nature; in turn, this makes it likely that international commercial disputes will also be multiparty. Although empirical evidence is limited, it appears that a significant and increasing number of international arbitrations involve multiparty disputes,[1] with roughly a third of all ICC arbitrations involving multiple parties.[2] This chapter examines the questions that arise from multiparty issues in international arbitration, focusing particularly on the questions of joinder, consolidation and intervention in international commercial arbitrations.

A. CONSOLIDATION, JOINDER AND INTERVENTION UNDER NATIONAL ARBITRATION LEGISLATION

In national court litigation, a variety of mechanisms exist for consolidating the claims between different parties to a dispute into a single judicial proceeding, or for permitting intervention or joinder of additional parties into an ongoing proceeding. For example, if A, B and C enter into related contracts (A with B and B with C), separate actions between A versus B and B versus C can often be consolidated into a single action; alternatively, C can intervene in, or be joined in, an action between A and B. In each of these instances, there is generally no requirement that all parties consent to such consolidation, joinder, or intervention. Rather, typically based on considerations of fairness and efficiency, national courts have broad discretion to order consolidation or joinder or permit intervention.

Rules regarding consolidation, joinder and intervention in national court litigation are intended to permit proceedings to occur more efficiently and to avoid the possibility of inconsistent results. These considerations are at least partially applicable in the context of arbitration. In general, however, consolidation, joinder and intervention in international arbitration raise additional or different issues than in national court litigation.

Permitting consolidation of separate international arbitrations, and joinder or intervention of additional parties into an international arbitration, can provide some obvious advantages.[3] First, as with litigations, a single arbitration can in some circumstances be more

---

1. Between 1984 and 1988, approximately 21% of the Requests for Arbitration filed with the ICC involved more than two parties. Bond, *The Experience of the ICC International Court of Arbitration*, in ICC, *Multiparty Arbitration* 37, 40 (1991).

2. In 2002, nearly 33% of all new ICC Requests for Arbitration involved multiple parties. Whitesell & Silva-Romero, *Multiparty and Multicontract Arbitration: Recent ICC Experience*, in ICC, *Complex Arbitrations* 7 (ICC ICArb. Bull. Spec. Supp. 2003). The proportion of multiparty cases has remained generally constant. Between 2003 and 2013 the number of new multiparty ICC cases was between 29% and 33%. *2003-2013 ICC Statistical Reports* (2004-2014).

3. B. Hanotiau, *Complex Arbitrations* (2006); ICC, *Multi-Party Arbitration: Views from International Arbitration Specialists* (1991); Thomson, *Arbitration Theory & Practice: A Survey of AAA Construction Arbitrators*, 23 Hofstra L. Rev. 137, 165-67 (1994) (83% of domestic U.S. construction arbitrators favor

efficient than two or more separate arbitrations. A single proceeding permits savings of overall legal fees, witness's time, preparation efforts and other expenses. Moreover, a single arbitral proceeding avoids the unique expenses associated with multiple arbitral tribunals—each of whose members must be compensated by the parties. According to one authority: "[O]n the whole it seems reasonable to conclude that the consolidation of closely-related disputes, where essentially the same evidence will be presented, will result in significant savings of both time and money."[4]

Second, a consolidated arbitral proceeding reduces the risk of inconsistent results in two or more separate arbitrations. One party to a tripartite dispute may be found liable to another party in one arbitration, while in a second arbitration the same party may be denied recovery from a different party on a theory inconsistent with the rationale of the first proceeding.[5] Worse, one tribunal may issue injunctive relief inconsistent with that of another tribunal—for example, requiring a party to do something that another tribunal forbids. Neither result is likely in a consolidated arbitration.

On the other hand, consolidation, joinder and intervention in arbitration also have disadvantages, which may outweigh their perceived benefits and which may, in particular cases, favor one party at the expense of a counter-party. Although "[l]ack of chronological coordination, potentially conflicting findings and the possibility of diverging judgments may cast disfavor upon arbitration," care must be taken to ensure that "the remedy [is not] worse than the evil."[6]

First, consolidating arbitrations involving multiple parties, or permitting joinder, can raise significant problems with respect to the composition of the arbitral tribunal.[7] Many arbitrations involve three-person tribunals, with each party nominating one member of the tribunal, and the two party-nominated arbitrators agreeing upon a third (or the appointing authority selecting a third) arbitrator.[8] If there are three (or more) parties to the arbitration

---

power to consolidate all interested parties); Thomson, *The Forum's Survey on the Current and Proposed AIA A201, Dispute Resolution Provisions*, 16(3) Constr. L. 3 (1996) (construction practitioners favor multiparty proceedings and consolidation). *See also* G. Born, *International Commercial Arbitration* 2567 (2d ed. 2014).

4. Chiu, *Consolidation of Arbitral Proceedings and International Commercial Arbitration*, 7(2) J. Int'l Arb. 53, 55 (1990). *But see* Hascher, *Consolidation of Arbitration by American Courts: Fostering or Hampering International Commercial Arbitration?*, 1(2) J. Int'l Arb. 127, 136 (1984) ("Consolidated proceedings are more time-consuming and more costly than unconsolidated proceedings, since additional parties and arbitrators are involved. Matters are enormously complicated by the incorporation of separate disputes in a single arbitration proceeding.").

5. *See* G. Born, *International Commercial Arbitration* 2567 (2d ed. 2014). For example, a construction project may involve an owner, a contractor and a sub-contractor, or a sale of goods may involve a purchaser, a seller and the seller's supplier. In these examples, the contractor and the seller will likely wish to ensure that complaints made by the owner or purchaser can be passed along directly to the sub-contractor or supplier, so that the contractor or seller is not held to one standard of performance, while being unable to claim corresponding performance from its sub-contractor or supplier. Although differences in the parties' contracts may require such a result, permitting consolidated proceedings would minimize the risk of injustice or inadvertently inconsistent results, while also potentially permitting savings of time and costs. *See also* ICC, *Multi-Party Arbitration: Views from International Arbitration Specialists* (1991).

6. Bernini, *Overview of the Issues*, in ICC, *Multiparty Arbitration* 161, 163 (1991).

7. If the parties have all agreed to a sole arbitrator, then the constitution of the tribunal in multiparty cases is not particularly difficult: all the parties can attempt to agree on an acceptable individual, or, if no agreement can be reached, the appointing authority can appoint an acceptable person. *See supra* pp. 696-702.

8. *See supra* pp. 687-88, 696-702.

who all have distinct interests, which prevents two (or more) parties on what is nominally the "same" side from agreeing upon a joint nomination, then the foregoing model does not work.[9]

Of course, *all* the members of the tribunal could be appointed by the appointing authority.[10] But this solution denies each party the opportunity it would otherwise enjoy to participate in selecting the tribunal.[11] That is a significant change in customary arbitral procedure, which not all parties may desire.[12]

Second, as discussed above, parties frequently have expectations that their arbitral proceedings will be confidential, and some national laws and institutional rules presumptively require such treatment.[13] The joinder of additional parties into a dispute between two (or more) parties entails a real, albeit limited, loss of confidentiality. Although this may be warranted, or outweighed by other considerations, it can also be inconsistent with the parties' agreement to arbitrate, raising concerns not present in litigation.

Third, although multiparty arbitral proceedings may be more efficient as a general matter, the savings will not always be distributed evenly among the parties. In particular instances, some parties' costs may actually increase because of consolidation or joinder, even though other parties' legal costs (or total legal costs) are decreased.[14] Moreover, a multiparty arbitration may well take longer than a simple two-party proceeding, thus potentially delaying enforcement of a party's rights.

These conflicting considerations have created significant challenges in the treatment of issues of consolidation, intervention and joinder in international arbitration. Both national courts and arbitral tribunals (as well as arbitral institutions) have struggled to reconcile these considerations. This section of the chapter considers how national legislatures and courts have addressed these issues.

In many jurisdictions, arbitration legislation does not deal expressly with consolidation, joinder, or intervention. That is true under the UNCITRAL Model Law, as well as under most other modern arbitration statutes. As discussed below, judicial authority in these (and other) jurisdictions does deal with these topics, often in ways not dissimilar from statutory solutions in the few states that legislatively address the subject.[15]

Where national legislation does address the subjects of consolidation and joinder, it can take one of several forms.[16] In most cases, as in judicial decisions under the Model Law

---

9. If no joint appointment is possible, either one or more parties must forego the right to appoint an arbitrator, or all three parties must be permitted to nominate an arbitrator. The former solution is unacceptably one-sided, *see supra* p. 685 & *infra* pp. 958-59, while the latter is impracticable and, additionally, likely one-sided (even where three parties have distinct interests, there will likely be majority views on particular issues).

10. *See supra* pp. 684-85, 701-02 and *infra* pp. 958-59.

11. *See supra* pp. 696-97 and *infra* pp. 958-59.

12. Expanding the size of the tribunal is usually also problematic, because it increases expense, creates logistical difficulties and poses risks of deadlocked results.

13. *See supra* pp. 851-70.

14. That can be the case, for example, if the party is required to be present throughout a consolidated arbitration rather than only in a single, unconsolidated arbitration or if it is required to deal with the procedural complexities that arise from multiparty proceedings.

15. *See infra* pp. 944-47; G. Born, *International Commercial Arbitration* 2573-96 (2d ed. 2014); B. Hanotiau, *Complex Arbitrations* 163 & n.397, 179 (2006).

16. *See infra* pp. 936-39, 944; G. Born, *International Commercial Arbitration* 2573-96 (2d ed. 2014).

and U.S. FAA, the approach taken by national legislation is that consolidation and join-der/intervention may be ordered by an arbitral tribunal or a national court, but only pur-suant to the parties' (unanimous) agreement thereto; if the parties have not so agreed, both the tribunal and local courts will lack the authority under national law to order either con-solidation or joinder/intervention. In a few instances, however, national courts can be granted the power to consolidate arbitrations even without the parties' agreement—as the Netherlands and Massachusetts legislation excerpted below illustrate.

BRITISH COLUMBIA INTERNATIONAL COMMERCIAL ARBITRATION ACT
§§27(2), (3)

27(2). If the parties to 2 or more arbitration agreements have agreed, in their respective arbitration agreements or otherwise, to consolidate the arbitrations arising out of those arbitration agreements, the Supreme Court may, on application by one party with the con-sent of all the other parties to those arbitration agreements, do one or more of the follow-ing:

(a) order the arbitrations to be consolidated on terms the court considers just and nec-essary;

(b) if all the parties cannot agree on an arbitral tribunal for the consolidated arbitration, appoint an arbitral tribunal in accordance with §11(8);

(c) if all the parties cannot agree on any other matter necessary to conduct the consoli-dated arbitration, make any other order it considers necessary.

27(3). Nothing in this section is to be construed as preventing the parties to 2 or more ar-bitrations from agreeing to consolidate those arbitrations and taking any steps that are necessary to effect that consolidation.

NETHERLANDS CODE OF CIVIL PROCEDURE
Article 1046

1046(1). If arbitral proceedings are pending in the Netherlands, any of the parties may request a third party designated for this purpose by the parties to order consolidation with other pending arbitral proceedings in or outside the Netherlands, unless the parties have agreed otherwise. In the absence of the third party having been designated for this purpose by the parties, either party may request the District Court judge hearing applications for interim relief in Amsterdam to order a consolidation of arbitral proceedings pending in the Netherlands with other arbitral proceedings pending in the Netherlands, unless the parties have agreed otherwise.

1046(2). Consolidation may be ordered to the extent that it shall not cause unreasonable delay of the pending arbitral proceedings, also taking into consideration the stage of the pending proceedings and whether there is such a close connection between the arbitral proceedings that a proper process of justice requires them to be dealt with and adjudicated simultaneously, in order to avoid rendering incompatible decisions in separate proceed-ings.

1046(3). The designated third party or the judge hearing applications for interim relief may wholly or partially grant or refuse the request, after giving all parties and, if appointed, the arbitrators an opportunity to be heard. His decision shall be communicated in writing to all parties and the arbitral tribunals involved.

1046(4). If the third party or the judge hearing applications for interim relief orders consolidation, the parties shall, in consultation with each other, appoint one arbitrator or an uneven number of arbitrators and determine the procedural rules which shall apply to the consolidated proceedings. If, within the period of time prescribed by the third party or the judge hearing applications for interim relief, the parties have not reached agreement on the above, the third party or the judge hearing applications for interim relief shall, at the request of any of the parties, appoint the arbitrator or arbitrators and, if necessary, determine the procedural rules which shall apply to the consolidated proceedings. The third party or the judge hearing applications for interim relief shall determine the remuneration for the work already carried out by the arbitrator or arbitrators whose mandate is terminated by reason of the consolidation. Article 1027(4) shall apply accordingly.

MASSACHUSETTS GENERAL LAWS ANNOTATED
Chapter 251, §2A

A party aggrieved by the failure or refusal of another to agree to consolidate one arbitration proceeding with another or others, for which the method of appointment of the arbitrator or arbitrators is the same, or to sever one arbitration proceeding from another or others, may apply to the superior court for an order for such consolidation or such severance. The court shall proceed summarily to the determination of the issue so raised. If a claimant under §29 of chapter 149 applies for an order for consolidation or severance of such proceedings, the issue shall be decided under the applicable provisions of said §29 of said chapter 149 governing consolidation or severance of such actions; otherwise the issue shall be decided under the Massachusetts Rules of Civil Procedure governing consolidation and severance of trials and the court shall issue an order accordingly. No provision in any arbitration agreement shall bar or prevent action by the court under this section.

CALIFORNIA CODE OF CIVIL PROCEDURE
§1281.3

A party to an arbitration agreement may petition the court to consolidate separate arbitration proceedings, and the court may order consolidation of separate arbitration proceedings when: (1) separate arbitration agreements or proceedings exist between the parties; or one party is a party to a separate arbitration agreement or proceeding with a third party; (2) the disputes arise from the same transaction or series of related transactions; and (3) there is a common issue or issues of law or fact creating the possibility of conflicting rulings by more than one arbitrator or panel of arbitrators.

If all of the applicable arbitration agreements name the same arbitrator, arbitration panel, or arbitration tribunal, the court, if it orders consolidation, shall order all matters to be heard before the arbitrator, panel, or tribunal agreed to by the parties. If the applicable arbitration agreements name separate arbitrators, panels, or tribunals, the court, if it orders consolidation, shall, in the absence of an agreed method of selection by all parties to the consolidated arbitration, appoint an arbitrator in accord with the procedures set forth in §1281.6.

In the event that the arbitration agreements in consolidated proceedings contain inconsistent provisions, the court shall resolve such conflicts and determine the rights and duties of the various parties to achieve substantial justice under all the circumstances.

The court may exercise its discretion under this section to deny consolidation of separate arbitration proceedings or to consolidate separate arbitration proceedings only as to certain issues, leaving other issues to be resolved in separate proceedings....

HONG KONG ARBITRATION ORDINANCE, 2013
§99; Schedule 2, §2

99. An arbitration agreement may provide expressly that any or all of the following provisions are to apply ... (b) §2 of Schedule 2; ...

Schedule 2, §2(1). If, in relation to 2 or more arbitral proceedings, it appears to the Court—(a) that a common question of law or fact arises in both or all of them; (b) that the rights to relief claimed in those arbitral proceedings are in respect of or arise out of the same transaction or series of transactions; or (c) that for any other reason it is desirable to make an order under this section, the Court may, on the application of any party to those arbitral proceedings—(d) order those arbitral proceedings—(i) to be consolidated on such terms as it thinks just; or (ii) to be heard at the same time or one immediately after another; or (e) order any of those arbitral proceedings to be stayed until after the determination of any other of them.

2(2). If the Court orders arbitral proceedings to be consolidated under subsection (1)(d)(i) or to be heard at the same time or one immediately after another under subsection (1)(d)(ii), the Court has the power—(a) to make consequential directions as to the payment of costs in those arbitral proceedings; and (b) if—(i) all parties to those arbitral proceedings are in agreement as to the choice of arbitrator for those arbitral proceedings, to appoint that arbitrator; or (ii) the parties cannot agree as to the choice of arbitrator for those arbitral proceedings, to appoint an arbitrator for those arbitral proceedings (and, in the case of arbitral proceedings to be heard at the same time or one immediately after another, to appoint the same arbitrator for those arbitral proceedings).

2(3). If the Court makes an appointment of an arbitrator under subsection (2) for the arbitral proceedings to be consolidated or to be heard at the same time or one immediately after another, any appointment of any other arbitrator that has been made for any of those arbitral proceedings ceases to have effect for all purposes on and from the appointment under subsection (2).

2(4). The arbitral tribunal hearing the arbitral proceedings that are consolidated under subsection (1)(d)(i) has the power under sections 74 and 75 in relation to the costs of those arbitral proceedings....

BELGIAN JUDICIAL CODE
Article 1709

1709(1). Any interested third party may apply to the arbitral tribunal to join the proceedings. The request must be put to the arbitral tribunal in writing, and the tribunal shall communicate it to the parties.

1709(2). A party may call upon a third party to join the proceedings.

1709(3). In any event, the admissibility of such joinder requires an arbitration agreement between the third party and the parties involved in the arbitration. Moreover, such joinder is subject to the unanimous consent of the arbitral tribunal.

U.K. OF GREAT BRITAIN & NORTHERN IRELAND v. BOEING CO.
998 F.2d 68 (2d Cir. 1993)

MESKILL, Chief Judge. This is an appeal from a judgment ... granting the motion of ... Government of the United Kingdom ... ("United Kingdom"), to consolidate an [AAA] arbitration proceeding between the United Kingdom and ... The Boeing Company ("Boeing") with a separate AAA arbitration proceeding between the United Kingdom and respondent Textron, Inc. ("Textron"). The district court held that it has the authority ... to compel consolidation of separate arbitration proceedings when the proceedings involve the same questions of fact and law, even in the absence of the parties' consent to consolidation. We hold that a district court cannot order consolidation of arbitration proceedings arising from separate agreements to arbitrate absent the parties' agreement to allow such consolidation....

This case ... arises from a January 1989 ground testing incident in which a military helicopter owned by the United Kingdom was damaged. The incident occurred during Boeing's testing of a new electronic fuel control system ("FADEC") that had been designed by Textron and installed in the helicopter by Boeing. The helicopter had been manufactured by Boeing and its engine had been manufactured by Textron.

Boeing and Textron have separate contracts with the United Kingdom governing long-standing relationships that each company has with the United Kingdom.... The relevant arbitration agreement between the United Kingdom and Boeing is contained in a 1981 base contract.... The relevant arbitration agreement between the United Kingdom and Textron is contained in a 1985 contract relating specifically to the design and development of FADEC. The contracts contain identical arbitration clauses ...:

> "Any controversy or claim arising out of or relating to this contract, or the breach thereof, shall be settled by arbitration in New York City by three arbitrators in accordance with the Rules of the [AAA], and judgment upon the award rendered by the Arbitrators may be entered in any court having jurisdiction thereof." ...

[T]he United Kingdom filed Demands for Arbitration with the AAA against Boeing and Textron for its losses resulting from the January 1989 ground testing incident. Both before and after filing the Demands for Arbitration, the United Kingdom requested that Boeing and Textron consent to consolidation of the arbitration proceedings. Boeing refused, alleging that consolidation would lead to undue expense and effort on its behalf because of the alleged simplicity of the issues involved in its arbitration with the United Kingdom compared to those in the United Kingdom/Textron arbitration. The AAA informed the

United Kingdom that it will not order consolidation of arbitration proceedings without the consent of all parties.... [T]he United Kingdom filed a Petition to Compel Consolidated Arbitration in the U.S. District Court for the Southern District of New York [which] ... granted the United Kingdom's Petition....

The United Kingdom urges, and the district court held, that our decision in *Compania Espanola de Petroleos, SA v. Nereus Shipping, SA*, 527 F.2d 966 (2d Cir. 1975) ("*Nereus*"), definitively established in this Circuit the district court's authority pursuant to the FAA and the Federal Rules of Civil Procedure to consolidate arbitration proceedings that turn on the same questions of fact and law.... [T]he facts in *Nereus* were much different than the facts in this case, and the district court erred in applying the *Nereus* holding.

In *Nereus*, a ... Charter Party, was signed by Nereus, as owner, and Hideca, as charterer. The Charter Party contained a detailed arbitration clause somewhat similar to the one contained in the United Kingdom contracts. Five months later, Addendum No. 2 to the Charter Party was signed by Nereus, Hideca and Cepsa, as guarantor. The addendum provided that "should HIDECA default in payment or performance of its obligations under the Charter Party, [Cepsa] will perform the balance of the contract and assume the rights and obligations of HIDECA on the same terms and conditions as contained in the Charter Party." Later, ... complications developed causing Nereus to give notice to Cepsa that it felt Hideca was in default and asking Cepsa to perform the balance of the Charter Party. A month later Nereus demanded arbitration with Hideca and Hideca consented. Several weeks after that, Nereus demanded arbitration with Cepsa. Cepsa, however, rejected the demand, claiming that it had not agreed to arbitrate. Cepsa filed suit in the district court seeking a declaratory judgment that it had not agreed to arbitrate disputes. The district court disagreed with Cepsa and held that Cepsa had consented to arbitrate disputes in signing Addendum No. 2, which the court held incorporated the arbitration clause of the Charter Party. Several months later Hideca filed suit seeking to restrain the Cepsa/Nereus arbitration until after the conclusion of the Hideca/Nereus arbitration. In this second action, one of the parties requested consolidation of the two arbitrations and the district court granted the request to compel consolidation.

On appeal, we affirmed the district court's order compelling consolidation and reformed the arbitration provision from which both arbitrations arose to provide for five arbitrators instead of three, one to be selected by each of the three parties and the remaining two arbitrators to be selected by the three arbitrators already selected. We held that a guarantor can be bound by an arbitration clause contained in the original contract when broad and inclusive guarantee language is employed, such as the language of Addendum No. 2.

Nereus is distinguishable from the case before us. In *Nereus*, all three parties signed Addendum No. 2, which incorporated the provisions of the Charter Party, including the arbitration provision. We held that in signing the addendum, Cepsa had agreed to "assume the rights and obligations" of Hideca, including the obligation to participate in arbitration over any disputes. Thus, all three parties were in arbitration pursuant to a single arbitration agreement. We determined that the intention of the signatories to Addendum No. 2 would be most closely adhered to with a single arbitration proceeding. In contrast, in the case before us, Boeing and Textron are in arbitration with the United Kingdom pursuant to two distinct agreements to arbitrate contained in two distinct contracts. Neither agreement contains any provision for consolidation. Boeing never agreed to participate in arbitration with Textron, and vice-versa. We simply have no grounds to conclude that the parties consented to consolidated arbitration. The district court is without authority to consolidate the two actions based upon the mere fact that the disputes contain similar or identical issues of fact and law. *Volt Info. Sciences v. Bd of Trustees*, 489 U.S. 468, 478 (1989) ("[FAA] simply requires courts to enforce privately negotiated agreements to arbitrate, like other contracts, in accordance with their terms.").

As the district court and the United Kingdom point out, in our holding in *Nereus* we also relied on the Federal Rules of Civil Procedure and the "liberal purposes" of the FAA.... However, as we explain below, recent Supreme Court case law has undermined our previous conclusion that the FAA's "liberal purposes" and the Federal Rules of Civil Procedure allow us to consolidate arbitration proceedings absent consent. To the extent that *Nereus* relied on that conclusion it is no longer good law.

The United Kingdom brought this federal action under the FAA, asserting that the district court has authority to compel consolidation pursuant to the FAA and the Federal Rules of Civil Procedure, Rules 42(a) and 81(a)(3). The relevant section of the FAA provides, in pertinent part:

"A party aggrieved by the alleged failure, neglect, or refusal of another to arbitrate under a written agreement for arbitration may petition any U.S. district court ... for an order directing that such arbitration proceed in the manner provided for in such agreement.... [U]pon being satisfied that the making of the agreement for arbitration or the failure to comply therewith is not in issue, the court shall make an order directing the parties to proceed to arbitration in accordance with the terms of the agreement." 9 U.S.C. §4.

Boeing takes the position that the district court did not have the authority under the FAA to compel consolidation because ..., given the court's narrowly circumscribed role in private arbitrations to merely "direct[] the parties to proceed to arbitration in accordance with the terms of the agreement," the district court is without authority to direct consolidation when consolidation is not provided for in the agreements. We ... now hold that the FAA does not authorize consolidation of arbitration proceedings unless doing so would be "in accordance with the terms of the agreement." 9 U.S.C. §4.

In *Nereus*, we found authority to consolidate arbitration proceedings in "the liberal purposes of the [FAA]," 527 F.2d at 975, and we based our finding on our prior decision in *Robert Lawrence Co. v. Devonshire Fabrics*, 271 F.2d 402 (2d Cir. 1959). We stated in *Robert Lawrence* that: "any doubts as to the construction of the [FAA] ought to be resolved in line with its liberal policy of promoting arbitration both to accord with the original intention of the parties and to help ease the current congestion of court calendars. Such policy has been consistently reiterated by the federal courts and we think it deserves to be heartily endorsed." 271 F.2d at 410. Cases decided in the Supreme Court since our decisions in *Robert Lawrence* and *Nereus* have undermined our interpretation of the purposes of the FAA. *See Volt Info. Sciences*; *Dean Witter Reynolds Inc. v. Byrd*, 470 U.S. 213 (1985); *Moses H. Cone Mem. Hosp. v. Mercury Constr. Corp.*, 460 U.S. 1 (1983). These cases concluded that the FAA was intended merely to assure the enforcement of privately negotiated arbitration agreements, despite possible inefficiencies created by such enforcement.

The Supreme Court affirmed an order requiring enforcement of an arbitration agreement in *Moses H. Cone*, even though arbitration would result in bifurcated proceedings because not all of the parties to the dispute were parties to the arbitration agreement. In words quite relevant to the case at hand, the Supreme Court stated that "under the [FAA], an arbitration agreement must be enforced notwithstanding the presence of other persons who are parties to the underlying dispute but not to the arbitration agreement." Subsequently in *Byrd*, the Supreme Court explained in detail the limited purposes behind the FAA:

"... We therefore reject the suggestion that the overriding goal of the [FAA] was to promote the expeditious resolution of claims. The [FAA], after all, does not mandate the arbitration of all claims, but merely the enforcement—upon the motion of one of the parties—of privately negotiated arbitration agreements. The House Report accompanying the [FAA] makes clear that its purpose was to place an arbitration agreement "upon the same footing as other contracts, where it belongs," H.R. Rep. No. 96, 68th Cong., 1st Sess. 1 (1924).... The preeminent concern of Congress in passing the [FAA] was to enforce private agreements into which parties had entered, and that concern requires that we rigorously enforce agreements to arbitrate, even if the result is 'piecemeal' litigation, at least absent a countervailing policy manifested in another federal statute." 470 U.S. at 219-21.

Four years later the Supreme Court reemphasized its position by stating that the FAA "simply requires courts to enforce privately negotiated agreements to arbitrate, like other contracts, in accordance with their terms." *Volt*, 489 U.S. at 478.

Each of our sister circuit courts to have considered the question since these Supreme Court decisions has held that district courts do not have the authority under the FAA to consolidate arbitrations absent the parties' consent. In *Weyerhaeuser Co. v. Western Seas Shipping Co.*, 743 F.2d 635 (9th Cir. 1984), the Ninth Circuit declined to compel consolidation, stating:

"The district court correctly held that our authority under the [FAA] is narrowly circumscribed.... We can only determine whether a written arbitration agreement exists, and if it does, enforce it 'in accordance with its terms.' As the district court noted, this provision 'comports with the statute's underlying premise that arbitration is a creature of contract,' and that 'an agreement to arbitrate before a special tribunal is, in effect, a specialized kind of forum-selection clause that posits not only the situs of suit but also the procedure to be used in resolving the dispute.' *Scherk*, 417 U.S. at 519."

Similarly, the Sixth Circuit has made clear that "a court is not permitted to interfere with private arbitration arrangements in order to impose its own view of speed and economy. This is the ease even where the result would be the possibly inefficient maintenance of separate proceedings." *Am. Centennial Ins. Co. v. Nat'l Cas. Co.*, 951 F.2d 107, 108 (6th Cir. 1991).

The United Kingdom also claims that the district court has the authority to compel consolidation ... pursuant to the Federal Rules of Civil Procedure, Rules 42(a) and 81(a)(3).... We hold that these rules are not applicable to the case before us. Rule 42(a) provides, in pertinent part, that "when actions involving a common question of law or fact are pending before the court ... it may order all the actions consolidated." Rule 81(a)(3) provides, in pertinent part, that "in proceedings under Title 9, U.S.C., relating to arbitration, ... [the Federal Rules] apply only to the extent that matters of procedure are not provided for in those statutes." ... Rule 81(a)(3) merely allows the application of the Federal Rules of Civil Procedure to judicial proceedings that are before a court pursuant to U.S.C. Title 9, to the extent that Title 9 does not provide appropriate procedural rules. Rule 81(a)(3) clearly does not import the Federal Rules of Civil Procedure to the private arbitration proceedings that underlie the Title 9 proceedings....

The United Kingdom also makes much of the inefficiencies and possible inconsistent determinations that may result if the U.K./Boeing and U.K./Textron arbitrations are allowed to proceed separately. Although these may be valid concerns to the United Kingdom, they do not provide us with the authority to reform the private contracts which underlie this dispute. If contracting parties wish to have all disputes that arise from the same factual situation arbitrated in a single proceeding, they can simply provide for consolidated arbitration in the arbitration clauses to which they are a party. *Volt*, 489 U.S. at 479 ("Arbitration under the [FAA] is a matter of consent, not coercion, and parties are generally free to structure their arbitration agreements as they see fit. Just as they may limit by contract the issues which they will arbitrate, ... so too may they specify by contract the rules under which that arbitration will be conducted.").

We reverse ... and ... hold that the district court cannot consolidate arbitration proceedings arising from separate agreements to arbitrate, absent the parties' agreement to allow such consolidation....

KARAHA BODAS CO., LLC v. PERUSAHAAN PERTAMBANGAN MINYAK DAN GAS BUMI NEGARA
364 F.3d 274 (5th Cir. 2004)

[excerpted above at pp. 605-19]

NOTES

1. *Advantages and disadvantages of consolidation, joinder and intervention.* What are the advantages of consolidation of separate arbitrations? What are the disadvantages? Are these benefits distributed equally among the parties? Consider how they might not be.

    Consolidation (and joinder/intervention) is permitted liberally in many national court systems. That is presumably because of judgments that these mechanisms are just and efficient. Given that, what reason is there not to adopt a similar approach to consolidation (and joinder or intervention) in the context of arbitration? What should be the role of the parties' consent in determining whether or not separate arbitrations may be consolidated? How reliably can "consent" to consolidation (and related mechanisms) be ascertained? Do parties really consider these issues? Have genuine intentions regarding them?

2. *Consolidation and Article II of New York Convention.* How does Article II of the New York Convention, excerpted at p. 1 of the Documentary Supplement, affect issues of consolidation? Suppose an arbitration agreement expressly permits (or requires) the consolidation of related proceedings. Does Article II require courts in Contracting States to give effect to this agreement? Is the parties' agreement regarding consolidation part of the "agreement in writing under which the parties undertake to submit to arbitration" of specified disputes? If so, isn't the language of Articles II(1) and II(3) clear?

    What if the parties' arbitration agreement forbids consolidation? Does the Convention require Contracting States' courts to refuse consolidation? What if the arbitration agreement purports to allow national courts to consolidate related arbitrations? Does the Convention require enforcement?

3. *No provisions dealing with consolidation, joinder and intervention in UNCITRAL Model Law or FAA.* Most arbitration statutes do not deal expressly with issues of consolidation, joinder, or intervention. Consider, for example, the UNCITRAL Model Law and the FAA. Neither statute expressly addresses the subject of court-ordered consolidation. If a statute does not deal with consolidation or related issues, what approach *should* a court adopt to these subjects? To what extent should this be a question of giving effect to the provisions concerning consolidation in the parties' arbitration agreement(s)—which would be given effect through Articles 7 and 8 of the Model Law and §4 of the FAA?

4. *National arbitration legislation permitting consolidation only where parties' agreement provides for consolidation.* Consider §27(2) of the British Columbia International Commercial Arbitration Act, §35 of the English Arbitration Act and §99 and Schedule 2, §2 of the Hong Kong Arbitration Ordinance. What do they provide with regard to consolidation of related arbitrations? Do these provisions permit consolidation of arbitrations in the absence of the parties' agreement to do so? Why do the Hong Kong and the British Columbia laws provide for affirmative judicial involvement in the consolidation process? What advantages does this provide? What might happen without judicial involvement?

5. *National arbitration legislation permitting consolidation even where parties' agreement does not provide for consolidation.* Consider Article 1046 of the Netherlands Code of Civil Procedure. How does it deal with issues of court-ordered consolidation? Is the parties' consent to consolidated arbitrations required? Is this a wise approach? What limits are there on the Dutch courts' authority to consolidate arbitrations? Compare §2A of the Massachusetts statute. How does it differ from the Netherlands Code? Which approach is wiser?

6. *National arbitration legislation permitting joinder even where parties' agreement does not provide for joinder.* Consider Article 1709 of the Belgian Judicial Code. Would joinder be permitted in absence of such statutory provisions, where all parties concerned are bound by the same arbitration agreement?

7. *Court-ordered consolidation of arbitrations where parties' agreement does not provide for consolidation.* Prior to *Boeing,* a number of lower U.S. courts had held that the FAA contains an implied grant of authority to courts to order the consolidation of separate arbitrations—even if the parties have not agreed to permit court-ordered consolidation. The seminal decision was *Compania Espanola de Petroleos, SA v. Nereus Shipping, SA,* 527 F.2d 966 (2d Cir. 1975), discussed in *Boeing,* where the Second Circuit ordered three parties to participate in a consolidated arbitration. Without relying on the fact that all three parties were bound by the same agreement, the court reasoned broadly that "we think the liberal purposes of the [FAA] clearly require that this Act be interpreted so as to permit and even to encourage the consolidation of arbitration proceedings in proper cases."

As *Boeing* observes, *Nereus* involved unusual facts—a two-party arbitration agreement, which was held to bind a "non-party" guarantor. All three parties were therefore bound by the same arbitration agreement—on a guarantor theory—and had therefore arguably agreed to a single arbitration involving all such parties. Nevertheless, after *Nereus,* a number of decisions ordered consolidation in the absence of a common arbitration agreement binding all of the parties. *See, e.g., P/R Clipper Gas v.*

PPG Indus., 804 F.Supp. 570, 575 (S.D.N.Y. 1992); *N. River Ins. Co. v. Philadelphia Reins. Corp.*, 1991 WL 90735 (S.D.N.Y.). This was essentially the factual background for the lower court's consolidation order in *Boeing* (there was no "single arbitration agreement" binding the United Kingdom, Boeing and Textron).

8. *No court-ordered consolidation under FAA if parties' agreement affirmatively forbids consolidation.* If the parties' arbitration agreement affirmatively forbids consolidation, then the rationale of *Nereus* and its progeny would not allow consolidation; rather, *Nereus* and its progeny held that consolidation was authorized by the FAA, provided that the parties had not otherwise agreed. *Sociedad Anonima de Navegacion Petrolera v. Cia. de Petroleos de Chile SA*, 634 F.Supp. 805 (S.D.N.Y. 1986). What is the rationale for this result? Is it required by §4 of the FAA and Article II(1) and II(3) of the New York Convention?

9. *Lower U.S. court decisions holding that FAA does not authorize consolidation of arbitrations absent parties' agreement.* Consistent with *Boeing*, the weight of lower court precedent rejects the rationale of *Nereus*, concluding that the FAA does not authorize the court-ordered consolidation of arbitrations in the absence of the parties' affirmative agreement to permit consolidation. *See, e.g., Champ v. Siegel Trading Co.*, 55 F.3d 269 (7th Cir. 1995) (no consolidation of arbitration without consolidation provision in arbitration agreement); *Am. Centennial Ins. Co. v. Nat'l Cas. Co.*, 951 F.2d 107 (6th Cir. 1991) ("district court is without power to consolidate arbitration proceedings, over the objection of a party to the arbitration agreement, when the agreement is silent regarding consolidation").

   As *Boeing* illustrates, even the Second Circuit eventually abandoned decisions reading *Nereus* broadly. Assuming the parties are silent regarding consolidation, what should they be assumed to have impliedly intended? That mechanisms available in all national courts for ensuring just, efficient dispute resolution are also available in arbitrations? That arbitral proceedings would be separate no matter how inefficient?

10. *Lower U.S. court decisions holding that FAA authorizes consolidation of arbitrations if parties have agreed to consolidation.* A corollary of holding, as *Boeing* does, that the FAA *forbids* court-ordered consolidation if the arbitration agreement does not so provide is that §4 requires court-ordered consolidation if all the parties have so agreed. Several lower courts have concluded in particular cases that, if the parties had agreed to consolidated arbitrations, orders for consolidation would be issued. *See, e.g., Protective Life Ins. Corp. v. Lincoln Nat'l Life Ins. Co.*, 873 F.2d 281 (11th Cir. 1989) ("sole question for the district court is whether there is a written agreement among the parties providing for consolidated arbitration"; concluding two separate contracts (A with B; B with C) did not provide for consolidated arbitration); *Del E. Webb Constr. v. Richardson Hosp. Auth.*, 823 F.2d 145, 150 (5th Cir. 1987) ("the court must determine only whether the contract provides for consolidated arbitration, a question free of the underlying facts"). Is there any doubt about the correctness of this conclusion? If the parties' agreement provides that arbitrations will or may be consolidated, isn't that agreement entitled to the same respect as other aspects of the arbitration agreement?

11. *Determining when parties have agreed to consolidated arbitration.* If the parties' intentions are the decisive consideration, what should be required in order to find that the parties agreed to consolidated arbitrations?

(a) *Need to identify parties' implied agreement.* Note that in virtually all cases the parties' arbitration agreement will not expressly address the subject of consolidation. In unusual cases, an agreement will contemplate multiparty arbitration and include specially-drafted provisions for commencing arbitration, appointing arbitrators, consolidation and/or joinder, and the like. For examples of multiparty agreements, which usually permit some forms of consolidation or intervention, *see* Bartels, *Multiparty Arbitration Clauses*, 2 J. Int'l Arb. 61 (1985); Wetter, *A Multiparty Arbitration Scheme for International Joint Ventures*, 3 Arb. Int'l 2 (1987); Wetter, *Six Multiparty Arbitration Clauses*, in ICC, *Multi-Party Arbitration* 117 (1991). More likely, institutional rules may expressly address the subjects of consolidation, joinder and intervention. *See infra* pp. 950-60. In most cases, however, the parties' agreements will simply be silent on issues of consolidation and joinder/intervention.

What are the relevant factors in ascertaining the parties' implied intentions regarding consolidation? Is there any basis in the parties' separate agreements to arbitrate for a conclusion that the parties all impliedly agreed to consolidation in circumstances where this would be just and efficient? Wouldn't businessmen in fact want such a (just and efficient) solution?

As described above, many two-party arbitrations contemplate that the parties will each appoint a party-appointed arbitrator, who will then select a chairman. To varying degrees, arbitration agreements and institutional rules provide for this procedure. *See supra* pp. 687-88, 696-702. Would parties desire consolidation if this would entail loss of the right to appoint an arbitrator—for example, if an arbitral institution or court selects a neutral sole arbitrator or all three members of a three-person tribunal?

Recall the discussion above about confidentiality in international arbitration. *See supra* pp. 851-70. If two arbitrations, involving differing parties, are consolidated, then it is likely that aspects of the arbitral proceedings that likely would have remained confidential will not, correct? Is that a significant enough cost to warrant refusing consolidation that would otherwise be just and efficient?

(b) *Possible requirement for an express consolidation agreement.* One U.S. court has suggested that consolidation can only be ordered if the parties expressly agreed to that. *Ore & Chem. Corp. v. Stinnes Interoil, Inc.*, 606 F.Supp. 1510 (S.D.N.Y. 1985). Should express agreement to consolidation be required? Why?

(c) *Possible requirement for implied agreement to consolidation.* As already noted, in most cases the parties' arbitration agreement will not address the question of consolidation. In these circumstances, will an implied agreement to permit consolidation be sufficient? Most authorities have answered in the affirmative. In one court's words, a court has "no power to order ... consolidation if the parties' contract does not authorize it ... [b]ut in deciding whether the contract does authorize it the court may resort to the usual methods of contract interpretation." *Conn. Gen. Life Ins. Co. v. Sun Life Assur. Co.*, 210 F.3d 771 (7th Cir. 2000). *See also Maxum Found., Inc. v. Salus Corp.*, 817 F.2d 1086, 1087 (4th Cir. 1987) (finding agreement to consolidated arbitration, even though no "unambiguous[]" provision to that effect); *Matter of Coastal Shipping Ltd & S. Petroleum Tankers Ltd*, 812 F.Supp. 396, 402-03 (S.D.N.Y. 1993) (inquiring whether the parties' agreement provides for consolidation "either directly or by implication" and stating that "[a]n agreement to consolidate may be implied by: (1) the language of the arbitration clause ... (2) the amendments or addenda to the agreement ... (3) the course of dealing between the parties ... or (4) incorporation of rules that permit consolidation"). Is it appropriate to permit consolidation based upon an implied agreement? Aren't many contractual terms implied? Why not a consolidation provision?

(d) *Consolidation where all parties are bound by single arbitration agreement.* Consider the rationales of *Nereus* and *Boeing*. In both cases, the parties' agreements were silent concerning consolidation. Why, in *Nereus*, should the parties be assumed to have agreed to consolidation? Is it enough that all three parties agreed to the same arbitration agreement? *Compare P/R Clipper Gas v. PPG Indus., Inc.*, 804 F.Supp. 570 (S.D.N.Y. 1992) (district court has power to consolidate arbitrations, based on identical arbitration clauses covering "all" disputes). Doesn't the parties' joint acceptance of a single dispute resolution mechanism, to deal with disputes under a single contractual relationship, strongly suggest that they expected a unified, rather than fragmented, proceeding?

(e) *Consolidation where all parties are bound by interrelated agreements.* Consider the premise underlying *Boeing*: if three or more parties sign a single arbitration agreement, they consent to court-ordered consolidation of all disputes encompassed by the agreement, but if they do not sign the same agreement, they do not consent to *any* consolidation. Why does this presumption make sense? Why, in *Boeing*, should the parties be assumed *not* to have agreed to arbitration? Should the parties in two inter-related contracts be presumed to have agreed to consolidated arbitration?

Consider the facts in *Karaha Bodas* and the tribunal's decision to consolidate the two arbitrations. Would the *Boeing* court have agreed that the parties' two agreements provided for consolidation? Note that there were separate agreements involving separate parties in *Karaha Bodas*. Was the tribunal correct in *Karaha Bodas* that consolidation was permitted? What was its rationale?

In other cases, the existence of a tripartite contractual relationship, with an Owner, Contractor, and Sub-contractor, was held to permit consolidation. *See Maxum Found., Inc. v. Salus Corp.*, 817 F.2d 1086 (4th Cir. 1987); *Gavlik Constr. Co. v. H.F. Campbell Co.*, 526 F.2d 777 (3d Cir. 1975). Although each agreement contained an arbitration clause, neither the principal contract nor the subcontract provided for consolidated arbitration. Nevertheless, the courts held that the broad provisions of the arbitration clauses in both contracts contemplated arbitration of disputes between all three parties to both agreements (notwithstanding the fact that the two contracts each had only two parties (A with B; B with C)). Consider the dispute in *Boeing*. Would this rationale have applied in *Boeing*? Would it not make eminent practical sense to consolidate the two arbitrations in *Boeing*? Would not the parties' expectations have been that consolidation would occur?

12. *Consolidation and Article V(1)(d) of New York Convention.* Suppose the parties' arbitration agreement forbids consolidation of related arbitrations, but the tribunal(s) nonetheless consolidate two or more arbitrations, and then make an award stated to be binding on all parties to the consolidated arbitration. Is the award subject to recogni-

tion under the New York Convention? Consider Article V(1)(d), excerpted at p. 2 of the Documentary Supplement.

Consider again the decision in *Karaha Bodas*. What conclusion would have been reached if the court had found that consolidation was *not* permitted by the parties' agreement? *See Nicor Int'l Corp. v. El Paso Corp.*, 292 F.Supp.2d 1357, 1374 (S.D. Fla. 2003); *Judgment of 7 March 1990*, 1991 Rev. arb. 326 (Versailles Cour d'appel) (annulling award concluding that different arbitration clauses in different contracts could be amalgamated and a single arbitration conducted; rather, each arbitration agreement, and its parties, needed to be considered separately).

What deference (if any) did the *Karaha Bodas* court accord to the arbitral tribunal's decision to consolidate? Is any deference appropriate? Note that in *Boeing*, no arbitral tribunal had considered the question whether or not consolidation was permitted (and appropriate); in fact, the AAA had declined to consolidate. What would the result in *Boeing* have been if a tribunal had determined that consolidation or join-der/intervention was permitted and appropriate? Would that determination have been entitled to any deference?

What if, in *Karaha Bodas*, the tribunal had refused to consolidate the arbitrations and, subsequently, the award debtor had sought annulment or non-recognition of the award because the parties' agreement to consolidate had not been respected? Isn't an Article V(1)(d) defense available in these circumstances as well?

13. *Non-recognition of arbitral award where consolidation is based on law of arbitral seat.* Suppose an award is made by a tribunal in an arbitration that is consolidated, contrary to the parties' agreement, pursuant to legislation like that in Massachusetts. Is that award subject to non-recognition pursuant to Article V(1)(d)? Is the award made in accordance with the parties' agreed arbitral procedures? Can the parties' agreement to arbitrate in a state that provides for mandatory consolidation, absent or contrary to the parties' agreement, be interpreted as consent to such judicial authority? If not, can the exercise of such authority be regarded as a reason, discretionarily, not to deny recognition under Article V(1)(d)?

14. *Consolidating arbitrations with different arbitral seats.* Suppose two or more arbitra-tions are initiated, or could be initiated, between three or more parties to different contracts and the designated arbitral seats are in different countries. Can arbitrations with different seats properly be consolidated? Is it likely that parties would agree to the consolidation of arbitrations in these circumstances? For a lower U.S. court decision, ordering a consolidated arbitration where arbitrations with different arbitral seats were involved, *see Elmarina, Inc. v. Comexas, NV*, 679 F.Supp. 388 (S.D.N.Y. 1988). Compare the approach to court-ordered consolidation under Article 1046 of the Netherlands Code of Civil Procedure. How does Article 1046 deal with "foreign" ar-bitrations? Why? Which approach is wiser?

15. *Consolidating arbitrations under different institutional rules.* Where parties have en-tered into contracts containing differing dispute resolution provisions (including arbi-tration provisions specifying different sets of institutional rules), then there will generally be little basis for concluding that they impliedly consented to consolidation, joinder, or intervention. On the contrary, by selecting divergent arbitration procedures (*e.g.*, ICC Rules in one arbitration; CIETAC Rules in another), arbitral seats and/or appointing authorities, the parties expressed their preference for incompatible dispute

resolution mechanisms, which ordinarily do not admit of the possibility of mandatory consolidation. *See, e.g., Rolls-Royce Indus. Power, Inc. v. Zurn EPC Servs., Inc.,* 2001 WL 1397881 (N.D. Ill.) (no consent to consolidation where parties agreed to different arbitral regimes); *Cont'l Energy Assocs. v. Asea Brown Boveri, Inc.,* 192 A.D.2d 467 (N.Y. App. Div. 1993) (no abuse of discretion to deny consolidation of arbitrations under different rules); *Stewart Tenants Corp. v. Diesel Constr. Co.,* 229 N.Y.S.2d 204 (N.Y. App. Div. 1962) (declining to consolidate arbitration between two parties before one arbitral institution with second arbitration between same parties, before different institution).

16. *Allocation of authority to order consolidation between national courts and arbitrators.* Who should decide issues of consolidation or joinder in the first instance—the arbitral tribunal(s) or a court? Given the effect of consolidation on the procedural conduct of an arbitration, and the relevance of procedural issues to deciding whether to order consolidation, is not an arbitral tribunal much better placed to deal with issues of consolidation than a court?

What basis, if any, is there under the UNCITRAL Model Law for a court to order consolidation of arbitrations? Or to order the joinder or intervention of a party in an arbitration? Doesn't the general rule of judicial non-intervention, reflected in Article 5 of the Model Law, preclude judicial involvement in issues such as consolidation? *See supra* pp. 806-07. The only opportunity for judicial consideration of arbitral decisions regarding consolidation and joinder/intervention comes at the stage of enforcing an award.

Compare the respective roles of arbitrators and courts in *Boeing* and *Karaha Bodas.* The grant of authority to U.S. courts under the FAA, to affirmatively compel arbitration, permits U.S. judicial involvement in consolidation, joinder and intervention prior to the award-enforcement stage—as in *Boeing.* Nonetheless, some U.S. courts have held that the question whether to consolidate arbitrations, pursuant to the parties' agreement, is for the arbitrators (and not a court) to decide. *See, e.g., Certain Underwriters at Lloyd's London v. Westchester Fire Ins. Co.,* 489 F.3d 580 (3d Cir. 2007); *Shaw's Supermarkets, Inc. v. United Food & Commercial Workers Union,* 321 F.3d 251 (1st Cir. 2003) ("The issue before us is who should make the determination as to whether to consolidate the three grievances into a single arbitration: the arbitrator or a federal court.... this is a procedural matter for the arbitrator."). Other U.S. courts have taken the opposite view, concluding in particular cases that, if the parties agree upon consolidation, judicial orders for consolidation are both permissible and required under the FAA. *See, e.g., Conn. Gen. Life Ins. Co. v. Sun Life Assur. Co.,* 210 F.3d 771 (7th Cir. 2000) (interpreting arbitration agreement to permit court-ordered consolidation); *Protective Life Ins. Corp. v. Lincoln Nat'l Life Ins. Corp.,* 873 F.2d 281 (11th Cir. 1989); *Del E. Webb Constr. v. Richardson Hosp. Auth.,* 823 F.2d 145, 150 (5th Cir. 1987) ("question of consolidation ... is for the district court because the court must determine only whether the contract provides for consolidated arbitration, a question free of the underlying facts").

Which of these approaches is preferable? Are national courts or international arbitral tribunals better-situated to decide issues of consolidation? Why? Note that, even if the power to order consolidation (or joinder/intervention) exists, this is a discretionary authority. *See infra* pp. 959-60. There may well be powerful reasons of efficiency and fairness not to consolidate two (or more) arbitrations, even if they theoretically could be consolidated. Who should exercise this discretionary authority—the courts or the arbitrators?

B. CONSOLIDATION, JOINDER AND INTERVENTION UNDER INSTITUTIONAL ARBITRATION RULES

As noted above, arbitration agreements rarely address the subjects of consolidation, joinder and intervention expressly. Some institutional rules do address these issues, particularly in recent versions, as the materials excerpted below illustrate; this includes the ICC, ICDR, LCIA, JCAA, HKIAC, Swiss, VIAC, CIETAC and WIPO Rules. However, many institutional rules are still silent on the questions of consolidation, intervention and joinder. For example, the UNCITRAL and SIAC Rules only contain provisions on joinder, while SCC Rules only deal with consolidation.

PARTIAL AWARD IN ICC CASE NO. 5625
excerpted in ICC, *Multi-Party Arbitration* 41-42

[This award arose from a Request for Arbitration filed by A against B. The dispute arose from a contract, containing an arbitration clause, between A, B, and C. B replied to A's Request by seeking to join both C and D (which was the controlling company of A) as additional claimants. B also sought to add E as an additional respondent, on the theory that E was its controlling company. Among other things, B relied upon various decisions permitting arbitrations to be commenced against the alter egos of formal parties to an arbitration agreement. The tribunal rejected B's efforts to join additional parties, reasoning as follows.]

The question whether a person is or not bound by an agreement to arbitrate, and the debate whether and under what circumstances companies belonging to one group are bound by an agreement to arbitrate which has been signed by other companies belonging to that same group, can only arise in a situation where they identify themselves as claimants, or are being identified by a claimant as defendants, in a Request for Arbitration. The [1975 ICC Rules] leave no doubt as to who is, or are, to be identified as a claimant/claimants: it is that person that submits, on the basis of Article 3 a Request for Arbitration. In this particular case the Request for Arbitration has been submitted by (A) and by it only.

Neither do the rules leave any doubt as to who is, or are, the defendant/defendants: it is that person which is being identified as such in the Request. In this particular case the Request for Arbitration identifies as the defendant (B) and it only.... From (Article 5 of the ICC Rules) it follows that a counter-claim is a claim by the Defendant,—that is: the person identified as such by the Claimant in its Request for Arbitration —, against the Claimant,—that is: the person that has submitted the Request and identified himself as being the Claimant.

That follows not only from the text of Article 5, but is moreover in conformity with the meaning of the word counter-claim and the way that mechanism is understood in many national legislations.... It is up to the interested person involved to determine whether it wishes to be a claimant in a procedure and one can only be drawn as a defendant in a procedure through the mechanisms thereto prescribed, *i.e.*, in this case through the mechanism of Article 3 of the Rules.... There is one way only in which one can become a party in an arbitral procedure under the ICC Rules: that is by way of Article 3, by a Request in which one constitutes oneself a claimant or is being identified by such a claimant as a defendant.... Under the ICC Rules, the Arbitrators once they have been nominated, have no discretion to add as parties to the arbitration Claimant(s) or Defendant(s) who were not identified as such in the Request for Arbitration.

2010 NAI ARBITRATION RULES
Article 41

41(1). A third party who has an interest in outcome of arbitral proceedings to which these rules apply may request the arbitral tribunal for permission to join the proceedings or to intervene therein.

41(2). Such request shall be filed with the Administrator in six copies. The Administrator shall communicate a copy of the request to the parties and to the arbitral tribunal.

41(3). A party who claims to be indemnified by a third party may serve a notice of joinder on such a party. A copy of the notice shall be sent without delay to the arbitral tribunal, the other party and the Administrator.

41(4). The joinder, intervention or joinder for the claim of indemnity may only be permitted by the arbitral tribunal, having heard the parties and the third party, if the third party accedes to the arbitration agreement by an agreement in writing between him and the parties to the arbitration agreement. On the grant of request for joinder, intervention or joinder for the claim of indemnity, the third party becomes a party to the arbitral proceedings.

41(5). In case of a request or notice as referred to in paragraphs (1) and (3), respectively, the arbitral tribunal may suspend the proceedings. After the suspension, the proceedings shall be resumed in the manner as determined by the arbitral tribunal, unless the parties have agreed otherwise....

2012 SWISS INTERNATIONAL ARBITRATION RULES
Article 4

4(1). Where a Notice of Arbitration is submitted between parties already involved in other arbitral proceedings pending under these Rules, the Court may decide, after consulting with the parties and any confirmed arbitrator in all proceedings, that the new case shall be consolidated with pending arbitral proceedings. The Court may proceed in the same way where a Notice of Arbitration is submitted between parties that are not identical to the parties in the pending arbitral proceedings. When rendering its decision, the Court shall take into account all relevant circumstances, including the links between the cases and the progress already made in the pending arbitral proceedings. Where the Court decides to consolidate the new case with the pending arbitral proceedings, the parties to all proceedings shall be deemed to have waived their right to designate an arbitrator, and the Court may revoke the appointment and confirmation of arbitrators and apply the provisions of Section II (Composition of the Arbitral Tribunal).

4(2). Where one or more third persons request to participate in arbitral proceedings already pending under these Rules or where a party to pending arbitral proceedings under these rules requests that one or more third persons participate in the arbitration, the arbitral tribunal shall decide on such request, after consulting with all of the parties, including the person or persons to be joined, taking into account all relevant circumstances.

2013 HKIAC RULES
Articles 27, 28

27(1). The arbitral tribunal shall have the power to allow an additional party to be joined to the arbitration provided that, prima facie, the additional party is bound by an arbitration agreement under these Rules giving rise to the arbitration, including any arbitration under Article 28 or 29.

27(2). The arbitral tribunal's decision pursuant to Article 27.1 is without prejudice to its power to subsequently decide any question as to its jurisdiction arising from such decision.

27(3). A party wishing to join an additional party to the arbitration shall submit a Request for Joinder to HKIAC. HKIAC may fix a time limit for the submission of a Request for Joinder.

27(4). The Request for Joinder shall include the following: [a] the case reference of the existing arbitration; [b] the names and addresses, telephone numbers, and email addresses of each of the parties, including the additional party; [c] a request that the additional party be joined to the arbitration; [d] a reference to the contract(s) or other legal instrument(s) out of or in relation to which the request arises; [e] a statement of the facts supporting the request; [f] the points at issue; [g] the legal arguments supporting the request; [h] the relief or remedy sought; and [i] confirmation that copies of the Request for Joinder and any exhibits included therewith have been or are being served simultaneously on all other parties and the arbitral tribunal, where applicable, by one or more means of service to be identified in such confirmation. A copy of the contract(s), and of the arbitration agreement(s) if not contained in the contract(s), shall be annexed to the Request for Joinder.

27(5). Within 15 days of receiving the Request for Joinder, the additional party shall submit to HKIAC an Answer to the Request for Joinder. The Answer to the Request for Joinder shall include the following: [a] the name, address, telephone and fax numbers, and email address of the additional party and its counsel (if different from the description contained in the Request for Joinder); [b] any plea that the arbitral tribunal has been improperly constituted and/or lacks jurisdiction over the additional party; [c] the additional party's comments on the particulars set forth in the Request for Joinder, pursuant to Article 27.4(a) to (g); [d] the additional party's answer to the relief or remedy sought in the Request for Joinder, pursuant to Article 27.4(h); [e] details of any claims by the additional party against any other party to the arbitration; and [f] confirmation that copies of the Answer to the Request for Joinder and any exhibits included therewith have been or are being served simultaneously on all other parties and the arbitral tribunal, where applicable, by one or more means of service to be identified in such confirmation.

27(6). A third party wishing to be joined as an additional party to the arbitration shall submit a Request for Joinder to HKIAC. The provisions of Article 27.4 shall apply to such Request for Joinder.

27(7). Within 15 days of receiving a Request for Joinder pursuant to Article 27.3 or 27.6, the parties shall submit their comments on the Request for Joinder to HKIAC. Such comments may include (without limitation) the following particulars: (a) any plea that the arbitral tribunal lacks jurisdiction over the additional party; (b) comments on the particulars set forth in the Request for Joinder, pursuant to Article 27.4(a) to (g); (c) answer to the relief or remedy sought in the Request for Joinder, pursuant to Article 27.4(h); (d) details of any claims against the additional party; and (e) confirmation that copies of the comments have been or are being served simultaneously on all other parties and the arbitral tribunal, where applicable, by one or more means of service to be identified in such confirmation.

27(8). Where HKIAC receives a Request for Joinder before the date on which the arbitral tribunal is confirmed, HKIAC may decide whether, prima facie, the additional party is bound by an arbitration agreement under these Rules giving rise to the arbitration, including any arbitration under Article 28 or 29. If so, HKIAC may join the additional party to the arbitration. Any question as to the jurisdiction of the arbitral tribunal arising from HKIAC's decision under this Article 27.8 shall be decided by the arbitral tribunal once confirmed, pursuant to Article 19.1.

27(9). HKIAC's decision pursuant to Article 27.8 is without prejudice to the admissibility or merits of any party's pleas.

27(10). Where an additional party is joined to the arbitration, the date on which the Request for Joinder is received by HKIAC shall be deemed to be the date on which the arbitration in respect of the additional party commences.

27(11). Where an additional party is joined to the arbitration before the date on which the arbitral tribunal is confirmed, all parties to the arbitration shall be deemed to have waived their right to designate an arbitrator, and HKIAC may revoke the appointment of any arbitrators already designated or confirmed. In these circumstances, HKIAC shall appoint the arbitral tribunal.

27(12). The revocation of the appointment of an arbitrator under Article 27.11 is without prejudice to: [a] the validity of any act done or order made by that arbitrator before his or her appointment was revoked; and [b] his or her entitlement to be paid his or her fees and expenses subject to Schedule 2 or 3 as applicable.

27(13). The parties waive any objection, on the basis of any decision to join an additional party to the arbitration, to the validity and/or enforcement of any award made by the arbitral tribunal in the arbitration, in so far as such waiver can validly be made.

27(14). HKIAC may adjust its Administrative Fees and the arbitral tribunal's fees (where appropriate) after a Request for Joinder has been submitted.

28(1). HKIAC shall have the power, at the request of a party (the "Request for Consolidation") and after consulting with the parties and any confirmed arbitrators, to consolidate two or more arbitrations pending under these Rules where: [a] the parties agree to consolidate; or [b] all of the claims in the arbitrations are made under the same arbitration agreement; or [c] the claims are made under more than one arbitration agreement, a common question of law or fact arises in both or all of the arbitrations, the rights to relief claimed are in respect of, or arise out of, the same transaction or series of transactions, and HKIAC finds the arbitration agreements to be compatible.

28(2). The party making the request shall provide copies of the Request for Consolidation to all other parties and to any confirmed arbitrators.

28(3). In deciding whether to consolidate, HKIAC shall take into account the circumstances of the case. Relevant factors may include, but are not limited to, whether one or more arbitrators have been designated or confirmed in more than one of the arbitrations, and if so, whether the same or different arbitrators have been confirmed.

28(4). Where HKIAC decides to consolidate two or more arbitrations, the arbitrations shall be consolidated into the arbitration that commenced first, unless all parties agree or HKIAC decides otherwise taking into account the circumstances of the case. HKIAC shall provide copies of such decision to all parties and to any confirmed arbitrators in all arbitrations.

28(5). The consolidation of two or more arbitrations is without prejudice to the validity of any act done or order made by a court in support of the relevant arbitration before it was consolidated.

28(6). Where HKIAC decides to consolidate two or more arbitrations, the parties to all such arbitrations shall be deemed to have waived their right to designate an arbitrator, and HKIAC may revoke the appointment of any arbitrators already designated or confirmed. In these circumstances, HKIAC shall appoint the arbitral tribunal in respect of the consolidated proceedings.

28(7). The revocation of the appointment of an arbitrator under Article 28.6 is without prejudice to: [a] the validity of any act done or order made by that arbitrator before his or her appointment was revoked; [b] his or her entitlement to be paid his or her fees and expenses subject to Schedule 2 or 3 as applicable; and [c] the date when any claim or defence was raised for the purpose of applying any limitation bar or any similar rule or provision.

28(8). The parties waive any objection, on the basis of HKIAC's decision to consolidate, to the validity and/or enforcement of any award made by the arbitral tribunal in the consolidated proceedings, in so far as such waiver can validly be made.

28(9). HKIAC may adjust its Administrative Fees and the arbitral tribunal's fees (where appropriate) after a Request for Consolidation has been submitted.

JUDGMENT OF 7 JANUARY 1992, SOCIÉTÉS BKMI ET SIEMENS v. SOCIÉTÉ DUTCO

119 J.D.I. (Clunet) 707 (1992) (French Cour de cassation)

[Siemens AG (Siemens), BKMI Industrienlagen GmbH (BKMI), and Dutco Construction Company (Dutco) entered into a consortium agreement on March 21, 1981, for the construction of a cement plant in Oman. In 1986, Dutco commenced an ICC arbitration against Siemens and BKMI, and the latter two parties appointed a single arbitrator, but under protest and with all due reservations. In a partial award, the arbitral tribunal affirmed that it had been validly constituted and that it could continue as a multiparty arbitration and that it had been properly constituted. The Paris Cour d'appel upheld the award in a decision of May 5, 1989. The Cour de Cassation overturned the decision of the Cour d'appel and referred the case to the Versailles Cour d'appel, holding that the principle of equality of the parties in appointing arbitrators is a matter of public policy and can be waived only after the dispute has arisen.]

In view of Arts. 1502(2) and 1504 of the [French] New Code of Civil Procedure[17] and Art. 6 of the Civil Code [Art. 6 of the French Civil Code read: "One may not waive by private agreement laws which involve public policy and morality."];

Considering that the principle of the equality of the parties in the appointment of arbitrators is a matter of public policy (*ordre public*) which can be waived only after a dispute has arisen;

Considering that ... a consortium agreement was concluded between Dutco (Dubai) and two German companies, BKMI and Siemens, for the construction of a cement plant in Oman; that is was stipulated in that agreement that all differences would be settled according to the [ICC Rules] by three arbitrators to be appointed according to the ICC Rules; that upon the single request for arbitration submitted by Dutco against its two contractual partners separately in respect of separate credits concerning the two firms, an arbitral tribunal was constituted consisting of three arbitrators, one of whom was appointed—under protest and with all due reservations—jointly by the two defendants; that the arbitral tribunal decided that it had been regularly constituted and that the arbitral procedure should be continued in the form of a multi-party arbitration against the two defendants;

Considering that in rejecting the request for annulment of the award in question submitted by BKMI and Siemens, the contested judgment held that the arbitral clause contained in the agreement binding the three companies unambiguously expressed the common will of the parties to such a contract to submit differences arising from their agreement to three arbitrators, and that it follows necessarily from the multi-party nature of the contract itself, entailing the foreseeable possibility of differences which might oppose the three partners, that the parties had accepted the possibility of a single tribunal composed of three arbitrators deciding on a dispute among the three partners, including the arrangements that such a situation would entail;

Considering that the judgment was in violation of the above-mentioned provisions of law; For these reasons, ... the decision of 5 May 1989 is annulled....

NOTES

1. *Importance of institutional rules' provisions regarding consolidation, joinder and intervention.* As discussed above, few arbitration agreements expressly address issues of consolidation, joinder, or intervention. *See supra* pp. 945-47. Consequently, the provisions of leading institutional rules play a significant role in determining how issues of consolidation, joinder and intervention are resolved. Putting aside what the

---

17. Arts. 1502(2) and 1504 of the [pre-2011] French New Code of Civil Procedure [read]:

"*Article 1502.* An appeal against a decision granting recognition or enforcement may be brought only in the following cases: ... If the arbitral tribunal was irregularly composed or the sole arbitrator irregularly appointed...."

"*Article 1504.* An arbitral award rendered in France in international arbitral proceedings is subject to an action to set aside on the grounds set forth in Article 1502. An order to enforce such an award may not be appealed in any manner. However, the action to set aside encompasses *ipso jure*, within the limits of the terms of the action of which the Court of Appeal has been seized, appeal against the decision of the enforcement judge having issued such an order, or having declined jurisdiction."

various institutional rules excerpted above provide, what *should* such rules provide? What would be the ideal solution for issues of consolidation, joinder and intervention?

2. *Consolidation under ICC Rules.* Consider Article 10 of the ICC Rules, excerpted at p. 186 of the Documentary Supplement. Under what circumstances may a tribunal "consolidate" (or join) two proceedings? What conditions must exist for consolidation to occur? Who makes decisions regarding consolidation?

    Suppose A and B sue C in one ICC arbitration and that C sues A, B and D in a second ICC arbitration. Do the two arbitrations involve the "same parties"? If not, may the two arbitrations be consolidated under Article 10? Suppose A and B sue C and B sues C. Then what? Suppose A and B sue C and that A sues C and B. What if A and B sue C and D under Contract 1, in one ICC arbitration, and C and D sue A and B under Contract 2, in a second ICC arbitration. Do the two arbitrations involve the same "legal relationship"? May the two arbitrations be consolidated under Article 10? Can Article 9 be used in this situation? Are there any limitations on this? What if one arbitration is under the ICC Rules and the second is *ad hoc*; may the two arbitrations be consolidated in the absence of the parties' agreement?

3. *Joinder and intervention under ICC Rules.* Does Article 7 of the ICC Rules permit C to intervene in an arbitration commenced by A against B? Does it permit A (or B) to join C in an ongoing arbitration? Who decides whether there is an arbitration agreement binding on the parties and what standard is applied?

    As *ICC Case No. 5625* illustrates, institutional practice at the ICC in principle permitted the claimant to structure "its" arbitration as it chose, naming (or not naming) the other parties to the arbitration that it thought fit (provided that they were parties to the arbitration agreement). The parties named as respondents could not join additional parties as co-respondents, nor implead additional parties as claimants or counter-claim respondents. That was true even if the additional parties sought to be joined were parties to the same contracts and arbitration agreements. *See* M. Bühler & T. Webster, *Handbook of ICC Arbitration: Commentary, Precedents, Materials* 74 (2d ed. 2008) (ICC Rules "basically leave the Claimant with the right to designate the parties to the arbitration"). As *ICC Case No. 5625* illustrates, this practice rested in part on a technical reading of the ICC Rules, but also on concerns that are generally applicable outside the ICC context:

    > "The [ICC] Court's position has been based ... [on] the insuperable problems that could arise from permitting a defendant to add parties to an arbitration over the objections of the claimant. Thus, should the arbitral tribunal already have been constituted, the subsequent addition of a party which had had no opportunity to participate in the selection of the arbitral tribunal would present obvious difficulties for the eventual enforcement of an award against such party." Bond, *The Experience of the ICC International Court of Arbitration*, reprinted in ICC, *Multi-Party Arbitration* 37, 41-42 (1991).

    Was the ICC approach wise? Are the interests of justice and efficiency served by the approach? Are the problems with joinder and intervention so great?

    In recent years, the ICC Court relaxed its historic position and permitted joinder of new parties to an arbitration by a respondent in limited circumstances. Whitesell & Silva-Romero, *Multiparty and Multicontract Arbitration: Recent ICC Experience*, in ICC, *Complex Arbitrations* 7, 10-11 (ICC ICArb. Bull. Spec. Supp. 2003). In practice, the ICC Court would permit joinder if: (a) the third party had signed the arbitration agreement; (b) claims were asserted against the new party; and (c) no steps had been taken towards constitution of the arbitral tribunal. In addition, there were unique circumstances in which joinder was permitted despite a failure to establish one of the three requirements.

More recently, Article 7 of the ICC Rules was amended to provide expressly for joinder of additional parties to an ICC arbitration, in general under the conditions previously used in the ICC Court's practice. Article 7 of the 2012 ICC Rules allows a party to join an additional party before the appointment of any arbitrator, provided that the additional party is party to the arbitration agreement. Article 7 does not permit additional parties to be joined after confirmation of the arbitrators "unless all parties, including the additional party, otherwise agree." Article 7(1) also confers power on the ICC Secretariat to fix a time limit for submission of a "Request for Joinder." Are these conditions appropriate? For an alternative approach, see Rule 52 of the 2014 JCAA Rules.

4. *NAI Rules*. Compare Article 41 of the NAI Rules to the ICC Rules and practice. Does Article 41 permit intervention without the consent of all parties? Suppose A sues B in an NAI arbitration, and C serves notice claiming an interest in the outcome and requesting that it be joined. If C was not a signatory to the arbitration agreement (between A and B), can it be joined? In order for C to join, what must occur? Who makes the decision regarding joinder? What if A and/or B object to C's joinder?

5. *LCIA Rules*. Compare Article 22 of the LCIA Rules, excerpted at pp. 268-69 of the Documentary Supplement, with Article 7 of the ICC Rules and Article 41 of the NAI Rules. Who makes decisions regarding joinder? When is joinder permitted under the LCIA Rules? Consider the example given in Note 4 above. Would joinder be permitted under the LCIA Rules? What if only A and C wish C to be joined—does B's objection prevent C's joinder?

Consider the provisions on consolidation in Article 22 of the LCIA Rules and compare them with the relevant provisions in the ICC, ICDR and Swiss Rules. Is there any reason for the additional limitation on consolidation contained in Article 22(1)(x) of the 2014 LCIA Rules?

6. *Swiss International Arbitration Rules*. Consider Article 4 of the Swiss Rules. Who makes decisions regarding consolidation under Article 4(1)? Who makes decisions under Article 4(2)? Consider the hypotheticals in Note 4 above. How would each be resolved under the Swiss Rules? Which approach—that of the Swiss Rules or the ICC—is preferable?

Suppose that A sues B in a Swiss Rules arbitration and that B sues C in a second Swiss Rules arbitration, under a separate contract; suppose further that the first (*A v. B*) arbitration is underway and that the (three-person) tribunal has already been constituted. If the second arbitration (*B v. C*) is consolidated with the first arbitration, does C have any influence on the selection of the arbitrators? If not, is that acceptable? Is it appropriate to regard C's agreement to arbitrate under the Swiss Rules (in the B-C contract) as a waiver of the right to participate in selection of the arbitrators?

Consider the tribunal's authority to join third parties under Article 4(2). Suppose A sues B in a Swiss Rules arbitration, and that B is party with C to a contract with an *ad hoc* arbitration clause; if B requests the arbitrators in the *A v. B* arbitration to join C, may the arbitrators do so? Has C agreed to the *A v. B* contract and arbitration clause?

Has C agreed to the Swiss Rules in any form? What permits the arbitrators to assert jurisdiction over C? Suppose that C seeks to join the *A v. B* arbitration, but that A and B oppose; may the arbitrators nonetheless join C?

7. *ICDR Rules.* Compare Article 7 of the ICDR Rules with Article 7 of the ICC Rules; also compare Article 8 of the ICDR Rules with Article 10 of the ICC Rules. Is there any material difference between the provisions on joinder and consolidation in these rules? Does the appointment of a consolidation arbitrator provide any advantages, in comparison with the same functions being exercised by a permanent institutional body? What is the purpose of vesting a consolidation arbitrator with these functions and to what extent does the provision fulfil it? Is the additional flexibility in the constitution of the arbitral tribunal for the consolidated proceedings in Article 8(6) of the ICDR Rules a desirable development or is the approach of the ICC Rules preferable? Why? *See also* 2013 HKIAC Rules, Arts. 28(4), (6).

8. *Other institutional rules.* Compare Article 15 of the VIAC Rules and Article 18 of HKIAC Rules with Article 4(1) of the Swiss Rules and Article 10 of the ICC Rules. Can two arbitrations be consolidated under VIAC or HKIAC Rules if the parties to those arbitrations are not identical?

   See Articles 11-13 of the CEPANI Rules. Is it possible to join C to an arbitration between A and B if there is no single arbitration agreement binding all the three parties, but there exist arbitration agreements between A and B and between A and C? How?

   Consider the UNCITRAL, AAA, SCC and SIAC Rules. What provisions does each set of rules make for consolidation, joinder and intervention? If a set of institutional rules (and arbitration agreement) is silent regarding consolidation or joinder, what powers does this provide the arbitral tribunal? *See supra* pp. 945-49.

9. *Allocation of authority to order consolidation between courts and arbitrators revisited.* As discussed above, there is limited authority, considering the allocation of power between courts and arbitral tribunals, to order consolidation. *See supra* pp. 949-50. Where institutional rules provide for the arbitral institution or tribunal to resolve issues of consolidation or joinder/intervention, is there any question but that it is for the institution and tribunal, not national courts, to resolve? In all cases?

10. *Appointment of arbitrators in multiparty disputes.* Many arbitration clauses give each "party" the right to appoint one member of a three-person arbitral tribunal. When a party commences arbitration against two other parties under such a clause, there is no completely satisfactory way of dealing with appointment issues.

    Permitting the claimant to appoint one arbitrator and two (or more) respondents jointly to appoint a second arbitrator denies each respondent the opportunity to select "its" arbitrator. Worse, if one respondent's interests are in fact aligned with the claimant's, requiring joint selection by the two "respondents" may be perceived to be seriously tainted. On the other hand, permitting each respondent to select an arbitrator could permit two respondents with aligned interests to choose arbitrators with a controlling vote. Where more than two respondents (or claimants) are involved, it would be impossible to accommodate individually appointed arbitrators with a three-person tribunal.

    Finally, denying *any* of the three (or more) parties the right to select an arbitrator denies all parties the right to a significant voice in constituting the tribunal; as discussed elsewhere, that right is an important feature of contemporary international commercial arbitration. *See* de Boisséson, *Constituting An Arbitral Tribunal*, in ICC, *Multi-Party Arbitration* 147, 150 (1991) ("the right of each party to appoint an arbitrator appears to be mandatory and substantially linked to arbitration"); *supra* pp. 696-98. Nevertheless, neutral selection of all three tribunal members, by the appointing authority, appears to do least violence to the parties' expectations regarding the arbitral process in multiparty cases.

Consider how the appointment of arbitrators in multiparty cases is dealt with under Article 12 of the 2012 ICC Rules and Article 8 of the 2014 LCIA Rules. Read each rule carefully. How, if at all, do they differ? Suppose A sues B, C and D, and B and C agree on a jointly nominated arbitrator, but D does not. Can B and C appoint "their" arbitrator? Can D appoint "its" arbitrator? If not, can A appoint "its" arbitrator? What if D's interests are really aligned with those of A?

11. *The* Dutco *decision.* Consider the result and reasoning in *Dutco.* Why did the French Cour de cassation annul the award? Consider the Court's statement that "the principle of the equality of the parties in the designation of arbitrators is a matter of public policy; it can be waived only after the dispute has arisen." How was it that the principle of equality in selecting the arbitrators was supposedly violated in *Dutco*?

Note that the parties' agreement to the ICC Rules (in the arbitration clause of their underlying contract) provided for exactly the method of constituting the tribunal that was used: a sole claimant nominated one co-arbitrator, while the two respondents were required to agree on a co-arbitrator. (Note that the same approach would have been taken if two claimants had initiated the arbitration against a single respondent.) The French Cour de cassation holds that agreement in advance to the ICC Rules was not sufficient to waive a party's right to equality of treatment in the constitution of the arbitral tribunal. Is that holding persuasive? Is there any reason to think that the parties—all major, sophisticated commercial entities—did not understand what rights they were waiving? Is there any reason to think that one of the three parties lost more, in agreeing to the ICC Rules, than the others?

Is the *Dutco* decision consistent with Articles II(3) and V(1)(d) of the New York Convention? At a minimum, where sophisticated commercial parties have expressly agreed to arbitral procedures that may deny them the opportunity to participate in selecting an arbitral tribunal, then an automatic invalidation of all such advance waivers arguably invites non-recognition of an award under Article V(1)(d). Does France violate the Convention, though, by refusing to give effect to the parties' agreement (without claims of one-sidedness or unconscionability) to institutional rules regarding constitution of the tribunal?

Consider the application of the *Dutco* rationale in the context of joinder and consolidation. With regard to consolidation, does the solution in Article 8 of the ICDR Rules resolve the issues presented in *Dutco*? Compare with Article 10 of the ICC Rules.

12. *Exercise of power to order consolidation or joinder/intervention.* Assuming an arbitral tribunal (or court) possesses the power to order consolidation or joinder/intervention, questions arise as to when this power should be exercised. There will be many instances in which, although consolidation or joinder/intervention is possible, it would be unjust and inefficient. Suppose, for example, an arbitration has proceeded for three

years, with extensive disclosure and pre-hearing submissions, and is on the eve of the main evidentiary hearing; if an affiliate of one party seeks to join the arbitration at this stage, or to consolidate the arbitration with a newly commenced arbitration at this stage, there would be strong reasons to deny the request.

Some arbitration statutes and rules provide a measure of guidance, although much is left to the tribunal or court's discretion. *See, e.g.,* Netherlands Code of Civil Procedure, Article 1046(2); Florida Statutes §682.033 (2013) ("(1) ... upon motion of a party to an agreement to arbitrate or to an arbitration proceeding, the court may order consolidation of separate arbitration proceedings as to all or some of the claims if: ... (b) The claims subject to the agreements to arbitrate arise in substantial part from the same transaction or series of related transactions; (c) The existence of a common issue of law or fact creates the possibility of conflicting decisions in the separate arbitration proceedings; and (d) Prejudice resulting from a failure to consolidate is not outweighed by the risk of undue delay or prejudice to the rights of or hardship to parties opposing consolidation. (2) The court may order consolidation of separate arbitration proceedings as to some claims and allow other claims to be resolved in separate arbitration proceedings...."); Revised Uniform Arbitration Act, §10(a) (2000) (the court "may" order consolidation if certain criteria are met); Hong Kong Arbitration Ordinance, 2013, Schedule 2 Art. 2(1); Victoria Commercial Arbitration Act, 2011, Art. 27C(8) ("Before making an order under this section, the arbitral tribunal or tribunals concerned must take into account whether any party would or might suffer substantial hardship if the order were made"); 2010 UNCITRAL Rules, Art. 17(5) ("The arbitral tribunal may, at the request of any party, allow one or more third persons to be joined in the arbitration ... unless the arbitral tribunal finds ... that joinder should not be permitted because of prejudice to any of those parties"); 2012 ICC Rules, Art. 10 ("In deciding whether to consolidate, the Court may take into account any circumstances it considers to be relevant...."); 2014 ICDR Rules, Art. 8(3) ("In deciding whether to consolidate, the consolidation arbitrator ... may take into account all relevant circumstances, including: (a) applicable law; (b) whether one or more arbitrators have been appointed in more than one of the arbitrations and, if so, whether the same or different persons have been appointed; (c) the progress already made in the arbitrations; (d) whether the arbitrations raise common issues of law and/or facts; and (e) whether the consolidation of the arbitrations would serve the interests of justice and efficiency."); 2013 HKIAC Rules, Art. 28(3) ("In deciding whether to consolidate, HKIAC shall take into account the circumstances of the case"); 2014 JCAA Rules, Rule 53 ("The arbitral tribunal may, at the written request of a Party and when it finds it necessary, consolidate and hear the pending claim(s) with the other claim(s) (as to which no arbitral tribunal has been constituted), if: ... (3) ... (a) the same or a similar question of fact or law arises from the claims; ... (c) the arbitral proceedings are capable of being conducted in a single proceeding with regard to the place of arbitration, the number of arbitrators, language(s), and other issues governed by the Arbitration Agreements under which the claims arise.").

How should this discretion be exercised? Where it is based on statutory provisions, should it be exercised by national courts or by arbitral tribunals/institutions?

CHAPTER 12
CHOICE OF SUBSTANTIVE LAW IN INTERNATIONAL ARBITRATION

This chapter examines the choice of substantive law applied to the merits of the parties' dispute in an international arbitration. The chapter first considers the choice of substantive law by international arbitrators in the absence of any agreement by the parties as to the law governing their dispute, including the examination of principal choice-of-law rules applied in international commercial and investment arbitration. Second, the chapter considers the choice of substantive law where parties have agreed to a choice-of-law clause selecting the applicable law, including the conflict of laws principles applicable to the validity and enforceability of such agreements. Third, the chapter considers the interpretation of choice-of-law agreements.

Parties often choose international arbitration to resolve their disputes because they desire enhanced certainty and predictability about their legal rights. Among other things, private parties want a stable, predictable substantive legal regime and a single, neutral procedural framework.[1] These objectives are particularly important in international commercial matters, where the needs for predictability and stability are particularly acute.

International arbitration seeks to provide comparative predictability with respect to both substantive and procedural matters,[2] often by combining a choice-of-law clause with an arbitration agreement. As explained by the U.S. Supreme Court in *Scherk v. Alberto-Culver Co.*:

> uncertainty will almost inevitably exist with respect to any contract touching two or more countries, each with its own substantive laws and conflict-of-laws rules. A contractual provision specifying in advance the forum in which disputes shall be litigated and the law to be applied is, therefore, an almost indispensable precondition to achievement of the orderliness and predictability essential to any international business transaction.[3]

There is considerable force to this analysis. Nevertheless, while arbitrating international disputes offers advantages over litigation in national courts, it sometimes can also generate choice-of-law questions that are potentially as complex as those in litigation. The choice-of-law complexities that arise in international arbitration do not comport with the ideals of predictability and efficiency of the arbitral process. In the words of one commentator:

> The freedom [that arbitrators have in choosing the applicable law] has been useful in some cases. However, it has also led to some unpredictability. With the growing use of international arbitration this uncertainty has become a matter of concern to parties. They see no

---

1. *See supra* pp. 108-12; Grigera Naón, *Choice-of-Law Problems in International Commercial Arbitration*, 289 Recueil des Cours 9 (2001); G. Born, *International Commercial Arbitration* 2616 (2d ed. 2014).
2. *See supra* pp. 109-11.
3. *Scherk v. Alberto-Culver Co.*, 417 U.S. 506, 516-17 (1974).

attraction in unpredictable conflict-of-laws rules. They need some degree of certainty as to the law applicable, when drafting their contracts ... and when resorting to arbitration.[4]

As discussed above, it is necessary to distinguish between several different conflict of laws issues that arise in the international arbitral process.[5] In international arbitration, questions can arise about any of the following applicable laws: (1) the substantive law applicable to the merits of the parties' dispute, including the validity, enforceability and interpretation of the underlying contract and the law governing any non-contractual claims; (2) the substantive law applicable to the parties' arbitration agreement (as distinguished from the parties' underlying contract), including its validity, enforceability and interpretation; (3) the law applicable to the arbitral proceeding, including its procedural conduct (*i.e.*, the "procedural law" or "curial law"); and (4) the conflict of laws rules that are to be applied in selecting each of the foregoing laws.[6]

As also discussed above, it is possible for each of the foregoing laws to be that of a different state.[7] The possibility of applying different national laws to different substantive and procedural issues raised in an arbitration can be seen as a peculiarly complex example of *dépeçage*.[8] This chapter concerns only the substantive law applicable in international arbitration to the merits of the parties' dispute (and not the substantive law applicable to the parties' arbitration agreement or the procedural law applicable in the arbitration).

A. CHOICE OF LAW GOVERNING MERITS OF PARTIES' DISPUTE IN ABSENCE OF AGREEMENT ON APPLICABLE LAW

In a substantial number of cases, the parties to an international dispute will not have agreed, either in their underlying contract or otherwise, upon the substantive law governing their relations. In these circumstances, an arbitral tribunal will be required to select the applicable substantive law, either applying some set of conflict of laws rules or "directly" applying a substantive law.[9]

International arbitration regimes take differing approaches to selection of the applicable substantive law. In principle, six basic choice-of-law approaches can be identified in contemporary arbitration regimes: (a) although long regarded as archaic, the law of the arbitral seat may mandatorily require arbitrators to apply either local conflict of laws rules (appli-

---

4. Lando, *Conflict-of-Law Rules for Arbitrators*, in *Festschrift für Konrad Zweigert* 157, 159 (1981).

5. *See supra* pp. 90-93.

6. *See supra* pp. 90-93, 287-315, 625-40; G. Born, *International Commercial Arbitration* 2618 (2d ed. 2014); E. Gaillard & J. Savage (eds.), *Fouchard Gaillard Goldman on International Commercial Arbitration* ¶¶1171-1177 (1999). *See also Naviera Amazonica Peruana SA v. Compania Internacional de Seguros del Peru* [1988] 1 Lloyd's Rep. 116, 118 (English Ct. App.) ("All contracts which provide for arbitration and contain a foreign element may involve three potentially relevant systems of law. (1) The law governing the substantive contract. (2) The law governing the agreement to arbitrate and the performance of that agreement. (3) The law governing the conduct of the arbitration. In the majority of cases all three will be the same. But (1) will often be different from (2) and (3). And occasionally, but rarely, (2) may also differ from (3).").

7. *See supra* pp. 90-93.

8. *Dépeçage* refers to the application of different national laws to different aspects of a contractual or other legal relationship. *See Restatement (Second) Conflict of Laws* §218 comment b (1971); L. Collins (ed.), *Dicey, Morris & Collins on the Conflict of Laws* ¶32-047 (15th ed. 2012); G. Born, *International Commercial Arbitration* 2618-25, 2749-54 (2d ed. 2014).

9. *See* G. Born, *International Commercial Arbitration* 2625-48 (2d ed. 2014); Yu, *Choice of Laws for Arbitrators—Two Steps or Three?*, 2001 Int'l Arb. L. Rev. 152.

cable in national courts) or (b) local substantive law;[10] (c) some arbitration legislation imposes specialized choice-of-law rules on arbitral tribunals seated within national territory (albeit ordinarily via very general formulae that leave tribunals with broad freedom to select an applicable law);[11] (d) a number of contemporary statutes authorize arbitrators to apply the choice-of-law rules they consider "applicable" or "appropriate";[12] (e) some legislation grants arbitrators the power "directly" to apply whatever substantive rules of law they consider appropriate, without applying conflict of laws principles;[13] and (f) a nation's law may dictate that particular claims or defenses must be heard by the arbitrator under mandatory national law.

Institutional rules also vary, but generally grant arbitrators broad flexibility in selecting an applicable substantive law (in the absence of agreement by the parties). Some rules provide for the arbitrators to apply the law selected by those conflict of laws rules that they consider "applicable."[14] Other rules permit the tribunal to apply directly the substantive law it considers "appropriate" or "applicable," without reference to any conflict of laws rules.[15]

In some cases, national law and/or institutional rules provide relatively clear guidance or directions to the arbitral tribunal in selecting the applicable substantive law—as, for example, with an arbitration where the parties have agreed to institutional rules prescribing a choice-of-law rule[16] or seated the arbitration in a jurisdiction that prescribes a specific, mandatory conflicts rule for international arbitrations.[17] In most cases, however, arbitrators are either expressly or impliedly granted broad powers (absent a choice-of-law agreement) with regard to choosing the applicable substantive law—including the authority to apply

10. *See* J. Lew, *Applicable Law in International Commercial Arbitration* 245-84 (1978); Mann, *Lex Facit Arbitrum*, reprinted in, 2 Arb. Int'l 241, 248 (1986).

11. SLPIL, Art. 187(1); *infra* p. 969.

12. *See* Danish Arbitration Act, §28(2) ("apply to law determined by the conflict of law rules which is considers applicable"); New Zealand Arbitration Act, 28(2) ("apply the law determined by the conflict of laws rules which it considers applicable"); Greek International Commercial Arbitration Law, Art. 28(2) (same). *See also* L. Collins (ed.), *Dicey, Morris and Collins on The Conflict of Laws* ¶¶16-055 *et seq.* (15th ed. 2012); de Boisséson, *The Arbitration Act 1996 and the New ICC Arbitration Rules 1998: A Comparative Approach*, 1998 Int'l Arb. L. Rev. 68; R. Merkin, *Arbitration Law* ¶¶7.39 to 7.46 (1991 & Update April 2014); Shackleton, *The Applicable Law in International Arbitration Under the New English Arbitration Act 1996*, 13 Arb. Int'l 375 (1997); Yu, *Choice of Laws for Arbitrators—Two Steps or Three?*, 2001 Int'l Arb. L. Rev. 152.

13. French Code of Civil Procedure, Art. 1511. *See Judgment of 13 July 1989, Compania Valenciana de Cementos Portland v. Primary Coal*, 1990 Rev. arb. 663 (Paris Cour d'appel), Note, Lagarde ("To determine the law applicable to the merits, the arbitrator is not required to apply a conflicts rule of a specific national legislation.").

14. 1976 UNCITRAL Rules, Art. 33(1) ("apply the law determined by the conflict of laws rules which it considers applicable"); IACAC Rules, Art. 30(1); CIDRA Rules, Art. 32(1).

15. 2010 UNCITRAL Rules, Art. 35(1) ("apply the rules of law which it determines to be appropriate"); 2012 ICC Rules, Art. 21(1); 2014 ICDR Rules, Art. 31(1); 2014 LCIA Rules, Art. 22(3); 2011 ACICA Arbitration Rules, Art. 34(1); 2015 CIETAC Rules, Art. 49(2); 2010 NAI Rules, Art. 46; 2012 PCA Rules, Art. 35(1); 2010 SCC Rules, Art. 22(1); 2013 SIAC Rules, Art. 27(1); 2013 VIAC Rules, Art. 27(2); 2014 WIPO Rules, Art. 61(a).

16. *See, e.g.*, DIS Rules, §23(2); 2012 Swiss Rules, Art. 33(1); 2011 Cairo Regional Centre for International Commercial Arbitration Rules, Art. 35(1); *infra* pp. 964, 970-71.

17. *See infra* p. 969; SLPIL, Art. 187; German ZPO, §1051(2); Japanese Arbitration Law, Art. 36.

the conflict of laws rules that they deem "applicable"[18] or the substantive rules that they deem "appropriate."[19] The resulting latitude has produced a considerable range of choice-of-law decisions by arbitral tribunals, outlined in the materials excerpted below.

JAPANESE ARBITRATION LAW
Article 36

36(1). The arbitral tribunal shall decide the dispute in accordance with such rules of law as are agreed by the parties as applicable to the substance of the dispute. In such case, any designation of the law or legal system of a given State shall be construed, unless otherwise expressed, as directly referring to the substantive law of that State and not to its conflict of laws rules.

36(2). Failing agreement as provided in the preceding paragraph, the arbitral tribunal shall apply the substantive law of the State with which the civil dispute subject to the arbitral proceedings is most closely connected.

36(3). Notwithstanding the provisions prescribed in the preceding two paragraphs, the arbitral tribunal shall decide *ex aequo et bono* only if the parties have expressly authorized it to do so.

36(4). Where there is a contract relating to the civil dispute subject to the arbitral proceedings, the arbitral tribunal shall decide in accordance with the terms of such contract and shall take into account the usages, if any, that may apply to the civil dispute.

2012 SWISS INTERNATIONAL ARBITRATION RULES
Article 33(1)

The arbitral tribunal shall decide the case in accordance with the rules of law agreed upon by the parties or, in the absence of a choice of law, by applying the rules of law with which the dispute has the closest connection.

FINAL AWARD IN ICC CASE NO. 5460
XIII Y.B. Comm. Arb. 104 (1988)

[The arbitration was between an Austrian equipment franchisor and a South African franchisee. The dispute arose out of a franchise agreement, which included a clause submitting the parties "to the jurisdiction of the [ICC], as the arbitration court," but did not select an arbitral seat. The ICC Court of Arbitration selected London as the arbitral seat and appointed the arbitrator. Excerpts of his default award follow.]

The place of this arbitration is London, and on any question of choice of law I must therefore apply the relevant rules of the private international law of England. Under those rules, questions of performance or breach of a contract fall to be determined in accordance with what we call the "proper law" of the contract. Unlike the laws of some other countries,

---

18. *See infra* pp. 975-76. As discussed above, this is what the UNCITRAL Model Law and most institutional rules provide. *See infra* pp. 969-70.

19. French Code of Civil Procedure, Art. 1511; *infra* pp. 969-70.

the principal consideration here is not the *lex loci contractus*, but rather the law of the place with which the contract has its closest connection—which, in practice, means the place in which the principal obligations under the contract are to be performed.

In the present case, virtually all the obligations of both parties fell to be performed in South Africa. It was there that the claimant's drawings and other documents were to be delivered; it was there that the defendants had to obtain the appropriate exchange control consent before dispatching the royalties to claimant; above all, it was there that the equipment was to be made and sold. On any commercial view, the principal place of performance of this Contract, and the place with which it had its closest connection, was South Africa. Insofar as it may be necessary for the purposes of this award, I therefore hold that the proper law of the Contract was South African law.

Under the rules of English private international law, foreign law is a question of fact, to be established by expert evidence; failing evidence to the contrary, English private international law compels me to assume that any foreign law is the same as English domestic law. Neither party has furnished me with any evidence about the South African substantive law of contract. Accordingly, I am bound to assume that it does not differ from the law of England....

AWARD IN ICC CASE NO. 4237
X Y.B. Comm. Arb. 52 (1985)

[The claimant was a Syrian state entity; the respondent was a Ghanaian state entity. The claimant contracted to purchase various wood products from the respondent. The products were not shipped according to schedule, and the claimant sought damages, first in a Syrian court and then in an ICC arbitration. The parties signed Terms of Reference selecting Paris as the arbitral seat and "French International Arbitration Law" as the procedural law. They disagreed as to the applicable substantive law.]

The question of the law applicable to the substance of the dispute poses the preliminary question which conflict of laws rules are to be applied in order to determine this law. Claimants relied on Syrian conflict of laws rules ... (*i.e.*, application of Syrian law because contract was signed in Syria). However, Claimants overlook the fact that this arbitration is expressly subjected to French International Arbitration Law, which Law, as rightly pointed out by Defendants, contains conflict rules for determining the law applicable to the substance of the dispute. The Arbitrator notes that it is controverted in literature whether an international arbitrator should apply the conflict rules of the law applicable to the arbitration, but since the new French law itself contains conflicts rules the Arbitrator feels himself obliged to follow these rules. Article 1496 of the [French NCCP] provides: "The arbitrator shall decide the dispute according to the rules of law chosen by the parties; in the absence of such a choice, he shall decide according to such rules as he deems appropriate."

As no documents submitted by the parties ... point to "rules of law chosen by the parties," the Arbitrator shall, in virtue of Article 1496, have to determine which are the appropriate rules governing the substance of the dispute. This poses the question which rules of law are appropriate. It is argued in literature that international arbitrators should, to the extent possible, apply the *lex mercatoria*. Leaving aside that its contents are not easy to determine, neither party has argued that a *lex mercatoria* should be applied. Rather, each party strenuously argued on the basis of a national law, *i.e.*, Syrian and Ghanaian/English law respectively. Accordingly, the Arbitrator shall follow the implied desire of the parties to apply a national law.

Within the framework of the conflict rules contained in Article 1496 ..., Article 13(3) of the ICC Rules constitutes a contractual elaboration of the conflicts rules contained in Article 1496.... In other words, Article 13(3) of the ICC Rules specifies how the Arbitrator has to determine the appropriate rules. Consequently, and admittedly this is rather complicated, the Arbitrator is, [by] virtue of Article 13(3) ..., again obliged to determine conflict rules in order to arrive at the law governing the substance of the dispute. But this time the Arbitrator is not bound to follow conflict rules of a national system of law as Article 13(3) constitutes contractual conflict rules contained in international arbitration rules.

In view of the international character of the present arbitration, the Arbitrator deems it appropriate to apply those conflict rules which are generally followed in international arbitrations of the kind under consideration. The decided international awards published so far show a preference for the conflict rule according to which the contract is governed by the law of the country with which it has the closest connection. The country with which it has the closest connection is the country where the party who has to carry out the most characteristic performance has its head office. In the case of a contract for the sale of goods on C & F conditions, the most characteristic performance has to be carried out by the seller. Accordingly, Ghanaian law would in principle be applicable. However, Defendants argued that English law should be applied. As Defendants' arguments are convincing and English law is not different from Ghanaian law, especially since Ghana has enacted the English Sale of Goods Act, the Arbitrator accepts that the dispute is to be resolved on the basis of English law....

AWARD IN ICC CASE NO. 2930
IX Y.B. Comm. Arb. 105 (1982)

[After citing Article 13(3) of the 1975 ICC Rules, for the proposition that it was free to select the appropriate conflicts rules, the tribunal reasoned as follows.] [T]he most authoritative present-day doctrine and international arbitration jurisprudence admit that in determining the substantive law, the arbitrator may leave aside the application of the conflict rules of the forum. The arbitral tribunal thus enjoys wide, and even discretionary, powers in the choice of the applicable law.... [I]t is authorized to refer to the different systems of conflict of laws at its disposal, it is by no means obliged to give preference to one of them above another. In the choice of the applicable law, the arbitral tribunal will also take into consideration the results of the work of the Commission on International Commercial Practice of the ICC which were presented at the Congress in Stockholm on October 9, 1981, in the form of draft rules on the law applicable to international contracts. The arbitral tribunal will also take into account the Convention on the Law Applicable to the International Sale of Goods, ... and ratified ... by France and Switzerland.... Article 3 of the Convention [provides] that the sale shall be governed by the domestic law of the country in which the seller has his habitual residence at the time when he receives the order, but, nevertheless, the sale shall be governed by the domestic law of the country in which the buyer has his habitual residence, if it is in that country that the order was received by the seller.

The private international law provisions of Switzerland, France, and Yugoslavia at the present time all refer to similar criteria in looking for the law applicable to contractual obligations. The first task should be the determination of the most characteristic performance of the contract(s) under examination. The second task is to determine with which territory is the performance most closely connected, or to use a very meaningful phrase of the Swiss Federal Tribunal, to locate the "centre of gravity" of the contract. This solution was also relied upon by the [Rome] Convention on the Law Applicable to Contractual Obligations....

[T]he arbitral tribunal observes that the aggregate of contracts which it has to examine is indisputably closely connected, and even very closely connected, with Yugoslavia and as one single law should be applicable to the entirety of the contractual obligations of the parties, the connection with Yugoslav law prevails without any doubt. [In addition,] any contract concerning import into Yugoslavia or export from Yugoslavia is subject to the mandatory provisions of [Yugoslav Law of 1972 Controlling Imports and Exports.]...

AWARD IN ICC CASE NO. 4491
2(1) J. Int'l Arb. 75 (1985)

The Plaintiff submits that the Defendant cannot [raise statute of limitations defenses] because Finnish law is the relevant law, and ... there is no Limitation Act under Finnish law.... However, the arbitration is taking place in London, and English law is the *lex fori*. In questions of limitation the provisions of the *lex fori* must be taken into account—see for example *British Linen Co. v. Drummond*, 10 B. & C. 903, 912 [(English K.B. 1830)]. The Limitation Act 1980 applies the Act and any other limitation enactment to English arbitrations. I must apply the Limitation Act 1980 even though Finnish law has no enactment—assuming for this purpose, that Finnish law is the proper law of the licensing agreement. The relevant period for a contractual claim or for an account is six years from the date on which the cause of action accrued: sections 5 and 23 of the Limitation Act 1980. The arbitration must therefore have been commenced within six years of the date when the cause of action accrued.

PRELIMINARY AWARD IN ICC CASE NO. 4132
X Y.B. Comm. Arb. 49 (1985)

[The dispute arose out of a Supply Agreement between the Claimant, an Italian supplier, and the Defendant, a South Korean buyer. The agreement provided for ICC arbitration and did not contain a governing law clause. The Claimant alleged various breaches of contract by the Defendant, who invoked statutory protections of Korean law, including Korean antitrust, unfair competition and price control statutes. The Defendant also relied on EU competition law.]

The Agreement has been executed and performed partly in Italy and partly in Korea. At the time the Agreement was made the parties did not express themselves as to the law that would govern their contractual relationship. Lacking such choice-of-law by the parties and all further direct points of contact which could be decisive for the determination of the governing law, the Centre of Gravity test, as proposed by the defendant, could indeed be relevant in order to decide this question....

Claimant has granted to defendant the right to use their technical know-how relating to the manufacture of [the product], on an exclusive basis in the Republic of Korea. Defendant purchased from Claimant the raw materials required for the production of [the product] in Korea. Taking these special elements of the Agreement into account this Tribunal is satisfied that the Agreement is for a larger part to be performed in Korea and that for that reason Korean private law should prevail as the law governing the Agreement....

[W]hatever national private law may govern the Agreement, the latter is likely to affect the domain of Korean (public) law, so that this Tribunal must determine whether Korean law as invoked by the Defendant is applicable to the Agreement, even if it does not govern it. However, the national public law as invoked by the Defendant in this case (antitrust law, price law, fair trade law) is by nature of public order. Usually, the very application of these public laws is based upon considerations of national public policy. It is for this reason that this Arbitral Tribunal is not free directly to apply the Korean public law as invoked by the Defendant when such considerations of public policy would be involved to an appreciable extent.

On the other hand, the tribunal is empowered to apply national public law insofar as the Tribunal is satisfied that in the circumstances of the case pursuant to published jurisprudence of the competent national courts and/or the published and stated policy of the competent national authorities the acts under consideration of the Arbitral Tribunal are deemed null and void and unenforceable as prohibited by any relevant national public law. As a consequence of this, the party which in arbitral proceedings appeals to any national public law must prove that this law, indeed, is applicable in the case, and to what extent.... Since the Defendant did not provide sufficient evidence as to the [elements of a Korean statutory claim,] the Tribunal is of the opinion that the Defendant did not sufficiently prove his case....

[W]ith respect to national public laws also the rules on competition (Article 85 *et seq.*) of the Treaty [of Rome] are of public order and part of the public policy of the Community. As far as the possible application of those rules on competition of the Treaty in this arbitral case is concerned, the Tribunal refers, *mutatis mutandis*, to its considerations here above.... Pursuant to Article 85(2) of the Treaty ... all agreements between undertakings, decisions by associations of undertakings, and concerted practices in violation of Article 85 ... are prohibited and shall be automatically void. If this Tribunal will find that the Agreement in whole or in part contravenes Article 85 ..., the consequence thereof is likely to be that the relevant clauses, if not the Agreement *in toto*, are deemed void, and unenforceable. With reference to its considerations hereabove, the Tribunal must, therefore, on its own initiative investigate whether the Agreement comes under the prohibition of Article 85(1)....

According to pertinent decisions of the [European Court of Justice] pertaining of Article 85 ... the prohibition, as contained in the first paragraph of this Article, is applicable only in so far as the relevant agreements, decisions by associations of undertakings, and concerted practices have as their object or effect the prevention, restriction, or distortion of competition within the common market of the Community and may affect trade between Member States, to an appreciable extent. Since the Agreement is a contract between an Italian and a Korean undertaking and was for larger part performed in Korea, this Tribunal is not satisfied that the Agreement may affect trade between Member States and that the Agreement, particularly its clause 2, has as its object or effect a prevention, restriction or distortion of competition within the common market of the Community, to any appreciable extent. Therefore, the Tribunal ... does not accept the applicability of Article 85 of the Treaty to the Agreement....

NOTES

1. *Arbitrators' selection of substantive law applicable to merits of parties' dispute.* All of the decisions excerpted above provide, absent agreement by the parties, for the arbitrators to select the substantive law applicable in an arbitration (subject to very limited judicial review in annulment or recognition proceedings). Consider also Article 28 of the UNCITRAL Model Law and Article 187 of the Swiss Law on Private International Law, as well as Article 35 of the UNCITRAL Rules and Article 21(1) of the ICC Rules, excerpted at pp. 92 & 159 and pp. 174 & 190 of the Documentary Supplement. What alternatives exist for this means of selecting the applicable law and how would they work? Are they desirable? Could national courts play a positive role in this process?

2. *Choice of substantive law in international arbitration under New York and European Conventions.* What do the New York Convention and Inter-American Convention provide with regard to the choice of the substantive law governing the parties' dispute? Recall that both Conventions address the law governing the arbitration agreement. *See supra* pp. 302, 308-14. Why is the law governing the substance of the parties' dispute treated differently?

    Compare the European Convention, excerpted at pp. 29-36 of the Documentary Supplement. What is the point of Article VII(2)? What does it prevent? Would Article VII(2) permit a Contracting State to require arbitrators to apply local substantive law in any locally-seated arbitration? To apply local conflict of laws rules? Compare the approach of the ICSID Convention. Would it be desirable for the New York and Inter-American Conventions to have a choice-of-law provision like that in the ICSID Convention? What would it provide?

3. *Arbitrators' choice of substantive law under UNCITRAL Model Law.* What does Article 28(2) of the Model Law, excerpted at p. 92 of the Documentary Supplement, permit arbitrators to do? Does it permit arbitrators to "directly" apply a substantive law, without first considering choice-of-laws rules? *See infra* pp. 971-72, 977.

4. *Arbitrators' choice of substantive law under SLPIL.* Consider Article 187(1) of the SLPIL, excerpted at p. 159 of the Documentary Supplement. How does Article 187(1) differ from Article 28(2) of the Model Law? Do arbitrators in a Swiss-seated arbitration, where the parties have not chosen the applicable law, have freedom to apply the conflict of laws rules they consider appropriate? Or must they apply the conflicts rule contained in Article 187(1)?

    Other states have adopted statutory provisions comparable to Article 187(1), including Germany, Japan and Egypt. *See* German ZPO, §1051(2) ("Where the parties to the dispute failed to determine which statutory provisions are to be applied, the arbitral tribunal is to apply the laws of that state to which the subject matter of the proceedings has the closest ties"); Japanese Arbitration Law, Art. 36; Egyptian Arbitration Law, Art. 39(2). What are the benefits of the approach adopted by the SLPIL? What are the disadvantages?

5. *Arbitrators' choice of substantive law under national arbitration legislation providing for "direct" choice of law.* Some arbitration legislation grants arbitrators power "directly" to apply whatever substantive rules of law they consider appropriate, without applying conflict of laws principles. Consider Article 1511 of the French Code of Civil Procedure. Other legislation, in Europe and elsewhere, is similar. *See* Hungarian Ar-

bitration Act, §49(2) ("the applicable law shall be determined by the arbitral tribunal"); Indian Arbitration and Conciliation Act, Art. 28(1)(b)(iii) ("apply the rules of law it considers to be appropriate given all the circumstances surrounding the dispute"); Netherlands Code of Civil Procedure, Art. 1054(2) ("in accordance with the rules of law it considers appropriate").

How does Article 1511 differ from the UNCITRAL Model Law and the SLPIL? How is it similar to each instrument? What are the benefits of Article 1511's "direct" application approach? What are the drawbacks?

6. *Arbitrators' choice of substantive law under institutional arbitration rules.* Institutional rules are as diverse, in their treatment of the choice of the applicable substantive law, as national arbitration statutes. Consider Article 35 of the UNCITRAL Rules, excerpted at p. 174 of the Documentary Supplement. How does it compare with the UNCITRAL Model Law's approach? Compare Article 21 of the ICC Rules, excerpted at p. 190 of the Documentary Supplement. How does it differ from the UNCITRAL Rules?

Compare Article 33(1) of the Swiss Rules. *See also* DIS Rules, §23(2) ("the law of the State with which the subject-matter of the proceedings is most closely connected"). How does Article 33(1) of the Swiss Rules limit the arbitrators' freedom to choose the applicable substantive law? Also compare Article 33(1) of the Swiss Rules with Article 187 of the SLPIL. Does Article 187 require a rule such as Article 33(1)?

7. *Interaction between arbitral seat's conflict of laws rules and institutional rules granting arbitrators authority to select conflicts rules.* As noted above, many institutional rules (including the UNCITRAL, ICC, AAA and LCIA Rules) grant arbitrators authority to select the applicable law that they deem appropriate, either "directly" or through the application of the choice-of-laws rules that the arbitrators consider appropriate. *See supra* pp. 962-64. What effect do these institutional rules have where the arbitration legislation of the arbitral seat prescribes a particular choice-of-law rule (*e.g.*, Switzerland)?

As discussed below, most legal systems permit parties to agree on the substantive law governing their dispute. *See infra* pp. 988-90. Does this recognition of party autonomy to select the applicable substantive law apply to the selection of choice-of-law rules, rather than of the substantive law itself? For example, can an ICC arbitrator in an arbitration in Switzerland (without an express choice-of-law clause) apply a conflict of laws rule other than the "closest connection" formula in Article 187(1) of the SLPIL? What does the arbitrator in *ICC Case No. 4237* conclude about Article 13(3) of the 1975 ICC Rules? *See also* D. Caron & L. Caplan, *The UNCITRAL Arbitration Rules: A Commentary* 118-19 (2d ed. 2012); Karrer, in S. Berti *et al.* (eds.), *International Arbitration in Switzerland* Art. 187, ¶¶118, 144 (2000) (agreement to ICC Rules supersedes Article 187's "closest connection" formula).

8. *Mandatory application of conflict of laws rules of arbitral seat.* The historic view in many states was that international arbitral tribunals were mandatorily required to apply the arbitral seat's choice-of-law rules. This conclusion was reached even in the absence of arbitration legislation, like that in Switzerland or Germany, expressly requiring the arbitrators to apply a specified conflicts rule; rather, these authorities concluded that the arbitrators were bound to apply the generally-applicable conflicts rules applicable in the courts of the arbitral seat. (A variation of this rule (discussed

below) was that the arbitral seat's substantive laws were mandatorily applicable to the merits of the parties' dispute.) *See* G. Born, *International Commercial Arbitration* 2629-31, 2637 (2d ed. 2014).

For an example of a broader rule that the arbitral seat's conflicts rules must always be applied, consider the 1957 Resolution of the Institute of International Law: "The rules of choice of law in the state of the seat of the arbitral tribunal must be followed to settle the law applicable to the substance of the dispute." Institute of International Law, *Resolution on Arbitration in Private International Law 1957 (Amsterdam), Tableau des Résolutions Adoptées (1957-1991)* 237, at Art. 11(1) (1992).

Consider *ICC Case No. 5460.* What did it conclude regarding the obligation of an arbitral tribunal seated in England to apply English private international law rules to select the substantive law? What is the legal basis for this conclusion? Compare the conclusion in *ICC Case No. 2930.* How does the arbitral tribunal deal with the suggestion that they are bound to apply the conflicts rules of the arbitral seat? Compare also *ICC Case No. 4491.*

9.   *Rationale for arbitrator's application of seat's conflict of laws rules.* What was the rationale for the historic rule requiring arbitrators to apply the conflicts rules of the arbitral seat? Was this a requirement imposed by some international standard? Was it a requirement imposed by the law of the arbitral seat? Was it required by the parties' agreement to arbitrate?

Some traditional authorities reasoned that the conflicts rules of the arbitral seat were binding because they provided the procedural law (or "*lex fori*") for the arbitral proceedings. This was the theory of the 1957 Resolution of the Institute of International Law, quoted above. Consider:

> "In the legal sense, no international commercial arbitration exists. Just as, notwithstanding its notoriously misleading name, every system of private international law is a system of national law, every arbitration is a national arbitration, that is to say, subject to a specific system of national law.... No one has ever or anywhere been able to point to any provision or legal principle which would permit individuals to act outside the confines of a system of municipal law.... [E]very arbitration is necessarily subject to the law of a given state.... The law of the arbitration tribunal's seat initially governs the whole of the tribunal's life and work. *In particular, it governs* the validity of the submission, the creation and composition of the tribunal, *the rules of the conflict of laws to be followed by it*, its procedure, the making and publication of its award." Mann, *Lex Facit Arbitrum*, reprinted in 2 Arb. Int'l 241, 244-45, 248 (1986) (emphasis added).

Is this persuasive? What is the source of the requirement that arbitrators must apply the conflicts rules of the seat? Does not Professor Mann assume that it is the law of the arbitral seat that imposes this requirement (that arbitrators apply the conflicts rules of the arbitral seat)? Is this in fact what contemporary arbitration legislation provides?

Recall that many contemporary arbitration statutes do not require arbitrators in arbitrations seated locally to apply local conflict of laws rules; on the contrary, as discussed above, these statutes grant arbitrators broad authority to select the conflicts rules that they consider appropriate. *See supra* pp. 962-64, 970-71. Consider in this regard Article 28(2) of the UNCITRAL Model Law. Consider also arbitration legislation, like the French Code of Civil Procedure, permitting arbitrators to "directly" apply the substantive law that they consider appropriate, without any choice-of-law analysis.

Consider again Article VII(1) of the European Convention. Does it require that arbitrators apply the conflicts rules of the arbitral seat? Does Article VII(1) permit a Contracting State to require international arbitral tribunals, seated locally, to apply the conflicts rules of the seat?

10. *Erosion of support for requirement that arbitrators apply conflict of laws rules of arbitral seat.* The historic rule that arbitrators were required to apply the conflicts rules of the arbitral seat was eroded during the second half of the 20th century. As *ICC Case No. 2930* and (arguably) *ICC Case No. 4237* illustrate, arbitrators frequently concluded that they were not bound by the conflicts rules of the seat. Similarly, many commentators concluded that the arbitral tribunal is not equivalent to a national court and is not bound by the "*lex fori.*" In the words of one award, "the arbitration tribunal does not have a *lex fori.*" *Saudi Arabia v. Arabian Am. Oil Co., Ad Hoc Award of 23 August 1958*. Or, as another award reasoned:

> "it is highly debatable whether a preferred choice of the *situs* of the arbitration is sufficient to indicate a choice of governing law. There has for several years been a distinct tendency in international arbitration to disregard this element, chiefly on the ground that the choice of the place of arbitration may be influenced by a number of practical considerations that have no bearing on the issue of applicable law." *Award in SCC Case No. 117/1999 of 2001*, 2002:1 Stockholm Arb. Rep. 59, 64.

Consider:

> "The arbitrator exercises a private mission, conferred contractually, and it is only by a rather artificial interpretation that one can say that his powers arise from—and even then very indirectly—a tolerance of the State of the place of arbitration, or rather of the various States involved (States of the parties, of the *siège*, of the probable places of execution of the award), which accept the institution of arbitration, or of the community of nations, notably those which have ratified international treaties in the matter. Would it not be to force the international arbitrator into a kind of Procrustean bed if he were assimilated to a State judge, who is imperatively bound to the system of private international law of the country where he sits and from which he derives his power of decision?" Lalive, *Les règles de conflits de lois appliquées au fond du litige par l'arbitre international siégant en Suisse,* 1976 Rev. arb. 155.

Is this persuasive? If the arbitral seat's conflicts rules do not apply, what rules do? Are there no legal standards that guide the arbitrators' choice of law? As a matter of policy, *should* the conflict of laws rules of the arbitral seat be mandatorily applicable by the arbitrators? Is that likely to be what the parties intended?

Consider the discussion below concerning the parties' implied choice of the arbitral seat's substantive law. *See infra* pp. 973-74. Is there any reason to think that the parties might have intended the conflicts rules of the arbitral seat to apply to their dispute? What conflict of laws rules other than those of the arbitral seat might the parties think applicable?

11. *Enduring significance of arbitral seat's conflict of laws rules.* While there has been an erosion of the traditional "arbitral seat" rule, the announcements that the rule has been wholly abandoned are wrong. Arbitrators continue in many cases to apply the choice-of-law rules of the arbitral seat, based either on local legislation prescribing this method or on theories of implied choice. *See, e.g., Final Award in ICC Case No. 9771*, XXIX Y.B. Comm. Arb. 46, ¶18 (2004) ("The indication of Stockholm as the

place of arbitration could be interpreted as an indication of the will of the parties to let the law of the place of arbitration govern their contract. In this case nothing seems to warrant such a conclusion. It does, however, support the conclusion that Swedish conflict of law rules should apply to determine the applicable law."); *Award in ICC Case No. 8619*, in Grigera Naón, *Choice-of-Law Problems in International Commercial Arbitration*, 289 Recueil des Cours 9, 230 n.230 (2001) ("It can be reasonably argued that the parties who fail to explicitly agree on an applicable substantive law, but agree on arbitration at a specified place pursuant to specified arbitration rules and procedures … impliedly also agree—or at least impliedly accept a determination to that effect—on the conflict of laws rules of the law of the jurisdiction in which the place of arbitration is located"); *Award in ICC Case No. 1598*, in S. Jarvin & Y. Derains (eds.), *Collection of ICC Arbitral Awards 1974-1985* 19 (1990) (tribunal sitting in Switzerland applies Swiss law (Article 178(2)) to uphold Swiss choice-of-law clause).

Is the continuing reliance on the conflicts rules of the arbitral seat, by some national arbitration legislation and arbitral awards, appropriate? What alternatives are there to applying the conflicts rules of the arbitral seat?

12. *Application of substantive laws of arbitral seat.* Historically, a number of authorities concluded that arbitrators were required to apply the substantive law of the arbitral seat. In the words of a mid-20th century U.S. commentator, "[i]t is widely held that the parties who have chosen a place of arbitration have thus *impliedly agreed on the applicability of both the procedural and substantive law of that place.*" A. Ehrenzweig, *Conflict of Laws* 540 (1962) (emphasis added). Likewise, English courts historically held that designation of England as arbitral seat constituted agreement on English substantive law. *Tzortzis & Sykias v. Monark Line A/B* [1968] 1 Lloyd's Rep. 337, 413 (English Ct. App.) (selection of England as arbitral seat "raises an irresistible inference which overrides all other factors"); *Norske Atlas Ins. Co. v. London Gen. Ins. Co.* [1927] 2 Lloyd's Rep. 104 (English Ct. App.). Is *ICC Case No. 4491* an example of a tribunal's application of the substantive law of the arbitral seat?

13. *Rationale for application of arbitral seat's substantive law.* Consider the following quotation from the *Restatement (Second) Conflict of Laws* §218 comment b (1971), explaining application of the arbitral seat's substantive laws:

> "Provision by the parties in a contract that arbitration shall take place in a certain state may provide some evidence of an intention on their part that the local law of this state should govern the contract as a whole. This is true not only because the provision shows that the parties had this particular state in mind; it is also true because the parties must presumably have recognized that arbitrators sitting in that state would have a natural tendency to apply its local law."

In some European jurisdictions, these results were explained on the grounds of *qui elegit arbitrum elegit ius*—as in the United States, the parties were presumed to have intended application of the seat's conflicts or substantive rules. G. Born, *International Commercial Arbitration* 2637-39 (2d ed. 2014).

Is the foregoing rationale persuasive? Perhaps it was (and still is) where the parties to a straightforward, two-party contract agree to arbitrate in one party's home state. As described above, however, in contemporary international arbitration it is common for arbitrations to be conducted in a neutral state and for the law of a different state from either the arbitral seat or the parties' domiciles to provide the substantive law. A nation is usually selected as the arbitral seat because of its *arbitration law*, its convenience, and its neutrality—and not its substantive law. *See supra* pp. 620, 622-24, 652-55.

Do these considerations significantly undermine explanations of the traditional seat rule based on the parties' implied choice? If the parties selected a "neutral" state as their arbitral seat, and have not selected the applicable law, is it reasonable to conclude that they also expected the "neutral" substantive law of the arbitral seat to apply? Wouldn't this conclusion make particular sense in light of the complexities and uncertainties of contemporary conflict of laws analysis and the desire of most businesses for an efficient, predictable and neutral resolution of their international disputes? How would this analysis apply where the parties have agreed to arbitrate in one party's domicile, without selecting an applicable substantive law?

14. *Erosion of support for automatic application of seat's substantive law.* Just as the rule requiring application of the arbitral seat's conflicts rules eroded, so did the rule requiring automatic application of the arbitral seat's substantive law. As one decision said: "It is appropriate to eliminate forthwith the law of the forum, whose connection with the case is purely fortuitous." *Award in ICC Case No. 1422*, 101 J.D.I. (Clunet*)* 884 (1974). *See also supra* pp. 786, 972.

Note that in *ICC Case No. 5460*, the ICC International Court of Arbitration—not the parties—selected the arbitral seat. What force does the theory of an implied choice of law have in such cases? Particularly where the arbitral seat is selected by the arbitral institution, the parties may have had no conceivable reason to contemplate the application of its substantive (or choice-of-law) rules. This can produce anomalous results. An example involves a German and an English company arbitrating in Switzerland, in a dispute where both German and English conflicts rules would have selected English law, but Swiss conflicts rules selected German law. Cohn, *The Rules of Arbitration of the International Chamber of Commerce*, 14 Int'l & Comp. L.Q. 132, 162 (1965).

15. *Other conflict of laws rules applied by contemporary arbitral tribunals.* Against this historical background, choice-of-law rules other than those of the arbitral seat are frequently applied in contemporary awards selecting the applicable substantive law. Unfortunately, while several alternatives to the traditional "arbitral seat" rule can be identified, there is not yet a consensus regarding any of these alternatives (or even a clear trend towards any solution). As a result, substantial uncertainty often surrounds the selection of the applicable substantive law by international arbitral tribunals.

   (a) *"International" conflict of laws rules.* The arbitrators in *ICC Case No. 2930* applied what they characterized as "international" conflict of laws rules. Other authorities have also adopted this approach. *See* G. Born, *International Commercial Arbitration* 2651 (2d ed. 2014). What is likely contemplated by the parties to an international contract who select international arbitration as a means of resolving their disputes (principally for reasons of neutrality, efficiency, and effective international enforcement)? Is it likely that they bargained for the conflict of laws rules of the arbitral seat or that they intended to engage in lengthy future debate about the intricacies of conflicts rules in different jurisdictions? Do "international" conflicts rules provide a uniform, neutral formula that satisfies the parties' expectations?

What content does an "international" conflict of laws rule have? What sources should one consult in answering this question? Do developed nations share certain basic principles relating to choice of law? How does the tribunal in *ICC Case No. 2930* suggest that such principles are to be ascertained? Are the difficulties in ascertaining the content of "international" conflicts principles any greater than those of ascertaining the content of domestic conflicts principles?

In practice, arbitrators have looked to international conventions on choice-of-law issues even when those conventions are not, by their terms, directly applicable. In particular, tribunals have relied on the International Sale of Goods Convention (cited in *ICC Case No. 2930*) and the Rome Convention on the Law Applicable to Contractual Obligations (cited in *ICC Case No. 6379*, *infra* pp. 993-94). Compare the development of so-called *lex mercatoria* and "general principles of law," *infra* pp. 977-78, 1019-20.

(b) *Cumulative application of national conflict of laws rules*. As *ICC Case No. 2930* suggests, arbitrators sometimes purport to apply the conflicts rules of each of the states with a connection to the dispute. G. Born, *International Commercial Arbitration* 2649-50 (2d ed. 2014). As a practical matter, this "cumulative" approach often concludes that all the relevant conflicts rules select the same national law. When this occurs, it demonstrates a particular type of "false conflict." Grigera Naón, *Choice-of-Law Problems in International Commercial Arbitration*, 289 Recueil des Cours 9, 191 (2001) ("Tribunals normally make special efforts to show that the substantive solution found for the dispute is either one pointed out by the private international law systems of the national jurisdictions reasonably connected with the dispute (false '*conflit de systèmes*') or by a generally accepted conflict-of-laws rule").

It is also said that, on a practical level, the cumulative approach provides some insulation against a challenge to the award for failure to apply the proper conflict of laws rules. *Compare* W. Craig, W. Park & J. Paulsson, *International Chamber of Commerce Arbitration* 326-27 (3d ed. 2000) ("The cumulative method is particularly apt for use in the arbitral process…. [T]he arbitrators are able to infuse an international element into the proceedings and assure both parties that the issue has not been determined by the narrow application of the system of a single state, whose relationship to the dispute is not necessarily predominant.").

If all potentially-applicable conflicts rules point towards application of the same substantive law, then the choice-of-law issue is easy; indeed, in these circumstances, there is no need for the "cumulative" method, since any choice-of-law rule produces the same result. Suppose, however, that the potentially-relevant conflict of laws rules point towards two or more different national laws. In that case, does the "cumulative" method provide any basis for choosing between the competing alternatives? If not, then how is the appropriate conflict of laws rule to be selected?

(c) *Application of conflicts rule that arbitrators consider "appropriate."* Contemporary arbitral tribunals frequently apply the conflict of laws rule that the tribunal considers "appropriate." *See, e.g., Award in ICC Case No. 8385*, in J.-J. Arnaldez, Y. Derains & D. Hascher (eds.), *Collection of ICC Arbitral Awards 1996-2000* 474, 478 (2003) (tribunal "should apply the law, and if necessary the private international law, that is most appropriate in the circumstances"); *BP Co. Ltd v. Libyan Arab Repub., Award on Merits in Ad Hoc Case of 10 October 1973*, V Y.B. Comm. Arb. 143, 148 (1980) (tribunal "is at liberty to choose the conflicts of laws rules that it deems applicable, having regard to all the circumstances of the case"). Recall that this is the standard prescribed by Article 28(2) of the Model Law and by a number of institutional rules. *See supra* pp. 962-64, 970.

What does it mean to apply the "appropriate" conflicts rule? Is that a legal standard? How does one go about determining whether a particular conflicts rule is "appropriate" or not? Does one look at connecting factors with specific jurisdictions? At the content of the substantive laws chosen? At international principles? What is there, if anything, that ensures consistency and predictability in choice-of-law decisions under this standard?

(d) *Application of conflicts rules of state with closest connection to dispute*. Another approach to the choice of the substantive law by arbitral tribunals involves selecting the conflict of laws system of the state that is most closely connected to the merits of the parties' dispute. *See, e.g., Final Award in ICC Case No. 5885*, 1(2) ICC ICArb. Bull. 23 (1990); *Interim Award in ICC Case No. 6149*, XX Y.B. Comm. Arb. 41 (1995). Note that a leading choice-of-law standard is the "closest connection" test, which provides for application of the substantive law of the state with the closest connection to the dispute. Does it make sense to apply the *conflicts rules*—as distinct from the *substantive laws*—of the state with the closest connection to a dispute? Does this introduce unnecessary and confusing complexity?

(e) *Application of substantive law of state with closest connection to dispute*. As discussed above, some arbitration legislation prescribes a "closest connection" standard for arbitrators seated on national territory (*e.g.*, Germany, Switzerland, Japan, Egypt). *See supra* p. 969. Even where no such statutory rule applies, some awards have applied a "closest connection" choice-of-law rule. *See Award in ICC Case No. 4237*, X Y.B. Comm. Arb. 52 (1985) ("awards published so far show a preference for the conflict rule according to which the contract is governed by the law of the country with which it has the closest connection"). This approach draws support, as to the choice-of-law analysis applicable to contracts, from the related approaches of the Rome Convention and Rome I Regulation (most "closely connected") and *Restatement (Second) Conflict of Laws* ("most significant relationship"). *See* G. Born, *International Commercial Arbitration* 2653-54 (2d ed. 2014).

(f) *"Direct" application of substantive law*. As already discussed, some arbitration legislation (Article 1511 of the French Code of Civil Procedure) and institutional rules (Article 21(1) of the 2012 ICC Rules) permit "direct" application by the arbitrators of the substantive law that they determine to be "appropriate." *See supra* pp. 962-64, 969-70. A number of awards have adopted this approach. *See* G. Born, *International Commercial Arbitration* 2646-47 (2d ed. 2014). How is a tribunal to determine what substantive rules are "appropriate"? Can a tribunal do so without applying conflict of laws rules? If so, what defines what law is "appropriate"? Does Article 21(1) contribute to the predictable, efficient resolution of international business disputes?

16. *Uncertainty about choice of applicable substantive law.* As the foregoing materials suggest, the choice of applicable substantive law in international arbitration is often surrounded by uncertainty. That is not consistent with the ideal of predictability, particularly as concerns applicable law, that international arbitration promises. *Scherk v. Alberto-Culver Co.*, 417 U.S. 506, 516-17 (1974); *supra* pp. 961-62. Consider the comment at *supra* pp. 961-62 regarding the unpredictability of some contemporary conflicts analyses. What alternatives are available?

17. *What conflict of laws rules should international arbitrators apply?* In light of the possibilities, outlined above, what conflict of laws rules *should* be applied by international arbitrators? In some cases, as described above, the arbitration legislation of the arbitral seat will impose a conflicts rule (*e.g.*, Switzerland, Germany). In those instances, and assuming that the parties have not agreed to institutional rules specifying a different standard, the arbitral tribunal has no choice but to apply the statutory standard. Right?

    If the arbitration is seated in a jurisdiction that does not impose a conflict of laws rule on the tribunal, then what conflicts rule should the arbitrators apply? What rule is likely to provide the greatest degree of predictability, neutrality and efficiency?

    Are national conflict of laws rules appropriate for application in international arbitrations? Are they instead designed for, and properly limited to, litigation in national courts? Consider:

    > "the choice of law process constitutes an attempt to localize a legal issue, i.e., to link a contractual arrangement with a national legal system to govern the legal relationship between the parties. Consequently, the traditional conflict of laws rules in general provide for the application of a certain national law. By contrast, modern conflict of laws rules for international arbitration recognize that it is often inappropriate to localize legal issues arising out of an international contract…. It has also been suggested that law is merely a non-mandatory model for the arbitrator and that there may be no obligation for an arbitrator to apply it." M. Blessing, *Introduction to Arbitration: Swiss and International Perspectives* ¶630 (1999).

    Is this correct? Do parties who agree to international arbitration generally regard law as a "non-mandatory model"? If parties intend national substantive laws to apply in arbitral proceedings, why wouldn't they intend national choice-of-law rules to do so? Which national choice-of-law rule is best-suited for application in international arbitration?

18. *Application of non-national systems of law.* Application of either a choice-of-law system or "direct" application of a substantive law results in the application of some set of legal rules; in most cases, this will be the national law of a particular state. Nonetheless, a few arbitral tribunals have applied so-called non-national legal systems or rules of law—including *lex mercatoria*, general principles of law, the UNIDROIT Principles of International Commercial Contracts, or the Principles of European Contract Law ("PECL"). *See, e.g., Award in ICC Case No. 3131*, in S. Jarvin & Y. Derains (eds.), *Collection of ICC Arbitral Awards 1974-1985* 122 (1990) ("Faced with the difficulty of choosing a national law the application of which is sufficiently compelling, the Tribunal considered it was appropriate, given the international nature of the agreement to leave aside any compelling nature to a specific legislation, be it Turkish or French, and apply the lex mercatoria"); *Award in SCC in Case No. 117/1999 of*

2001, 2002:1 Stockholm Arb. Rep. 59 (tribunal held that the "parties in this case deliberately refrained from agreeing on the applicable law" governing their contract and found that the dispute at hand should be decided on the basis of "such rules of law that have found their way into international codifications...."); *Final Award in ICC Case No. 10422*, 130 J.D.I. (Clunet) 1142 (2003) ("The arbitral tribunal, in view of the fact that the parties apparently wanted a neutral solution, decided to apply 'general principles and rules of international contracts, *i.e.*, the so-called *lex mercatoria*'").

Do the arbitration statutes excerpted above permit application of a non-national system of law (absent the parties' agreement thereto)? Consider the UNCITRAL Model Law. Note that Article 28(2) provides for the arbitrators to apply the "law" chosen by the conflicts rules they consider appropriate. Compare Article 28(1), which provides for the arbitrators to apply the "rules of law" selected by the parties' agreement. *See infra* p. 1018. The reference to "*rules of law*," rather than merely "*law*," has been interpreted as permitting parties to select non-national legal systems (such as *lex mercatoria* or the UNIDROIT Principles) in their choice-of-law agreements. *Report of the Secretary-General on the Analytical Commentary on Draft Text of A Model Law on International Commercial Arbitration*, U.N. Doc. A/CN.9/264, XVI Y.B. UNCITRAL 104, 132-33 (1985).

In contrast, Article 28(2) of the Model Law provides for the arbitrators to apply the "*law*" determined by applicable conflicts rules. That difference in the text of Articles 28(1) and 28(2) suggests, and has been interpreted as requiring, that arbitrators may not—in the absence of a choice-of-law agreement selecting such a legal system—apply non-national rules of law. H. Holtzmann & J. Neuhaus, *A Guide to the UNCITRAL Model Law on International Commercial Arbitration* 764-807 (1989); P. Sanders, *The Work of UNCITRAL on Arbitration and Conciliation* 117 (2d ed. 2004). *Compare* Derains, *The Application of Transnational Rules in ICC Arbitral Awards*, 5 World Arb. & Med. Rev. 173, 174-75 (2011) ("For many years, international arbitrators, in particular those acting under the auspices of the [ICC] have been applying transnational rules in their awards in order to resolve disputes submitted to them.... It is no longer disputed that, in most countries, international arbitrators may apply transnational rules to the merits of a dispute without putting the validity of their award in danger, even in the absence of a choice-of-law agreement expressly selecting such norms.").

Just considering the language of Articles 28(1) and 28(2), is there a real difference between "law" and "rules of law"? Does it make sense to permit the parties to agree upon a non-national system of law, but not to permit arbitrators to apply such a system, absent the parties' agreement? Compare the treatment of *ex aequo et bono* decisions. *See infra* pp. 1020-21.

In a few jurisdictions, including Switzerland, India, Algeria, Ontario and Lebanon, legislation has been adopted that modifies Article 28(2) of the Model Law to refer to "*rules of law*." SLPIL, Art. 187(1); Indian Arbitration and Conciliation Act, Art. 28(1)(b)(iii); Lebanese New Code of Civil Procedure, Art. 813; Ontario Arbitration Act, §32(1). This change has generally been intended to authorize arbitrators to select a non-national legal system or set of non-national rules to govern a dispute, even in the absence of an agreement to this effect. Is this a wise legislative choice?

19. *Application of mandatory law and public policy in arbitration.* Consider the analysis in *ICC Case No. 4132.* How does the choice-of-law issue considered by the tribunal differ from that in the other awards excerpted above? What law governed the parties' agreement? What laws did the tribunal nonetheless consider potentially applicable to the parties' dispute? Would it have been possible for *both* Korean and EU competition laws to apply? Why didn't the tribunal actually apply EU public law? Would the tribunal have done so if the jurisdictional requirements of EU competition law were satisfied?

What would have authorized the arbitrators to apply Korean or EU public laws? EU law was not the law applicable to the parties' contract (which was governed by Korean law). What would have empowered the tribunal to nonetheless apply EU law? Note that the arbitral seat was in the EU. Does that affect the applicability of EU competition law? Suppose the issue was whether U.S. antitrust law was applicable. What was the choice-of-law analysis by which the tribunal considered whether EU competition law was applicable? Did the tribunal consider Korean conflicts rules? Other national conflicts rules? Or did the tribunal simply consider the applicability, under EU law, of EU competition legislation? How would this differ from other types of choice-of-law analysis in international arbitration?

20. *Arbitrators' authority to apply public policy.* May an arbitrator resolve a claim or defense based on a "mandatory" public policy or statutory duty imposed by a legal system other than that selected by the parties?

(a) *Traditional view that arbitrators could not consider claims or defenses based on public policy or statutory protections.* As discussed below, *see infra* pp. 979-80, during the early part of the 20th century, many national courts held that arbitrators were forbidden from considering non-contractual claims based on public policy. The following passage from a U.S. decision is illustrative:

"As the proctor of the bargain, the arbitrator's task is to effectuate the intent of the parties.... The arbitrator ... has no general authority to invoke public laws that conflict with the bargain between the parties:

'An arbitrator is confined to interpretation and application of the ... agreement; he does not sit to dispense his own brand of ... justice. He may of course look for guidance from many sources, yet his award is legitimate only so long as it draws its essence from the ... agreement. When the arbitrator's words manifest an infidelity to this obligation, courts have no choice but to refuse enforcement of the award.' *United Steelworkers of Am. v. Enter. Wheel & Car Corp.*, 363 U.S. 593, 597 (1960).

If an arbitral decision is based 'solely upon the arbitrator's view of the requirements of enacted legislation,' rather than on an interpretation of the collective-bargaining agreement, the arbitrator has 'exceeded the scope of the submission,' and the award will not be enforced. Thus, the arbitrator has authority to resolve only questions of contractual rights, and this authority remains regardless of whether certain contractual rights are similar to, or duplicative of, the substantive rights secured by [a federal statute]." *Alexander v. Gardner-Denver Co.*, 415 U.S. 36, 56-57 (1974).

At the same time, as discussed above, national courts also held that many claims (and defenses) based on mandatory public laws were nonarbitrable, instead being reserved to national court litigation. *See supra* pp. 475-83. Is this traditional approach to mandatory law claims (and defenses) persuasive? Why should an arbitration agreement be interpreted as encompassing only the parties' contractual rights, and not their other legal rights (including their statutory rights)?

(b) *Contemporary view that arbitrators can consider claims and defenses based on public policy or statutory protections.* As also discussed above, during the last three decades, courts in most developed jurisdictions have abandoned traditional restrictions on the power of arbitrators to consider public policy and statutory claims and related concepts of nonarbitrability. *See supra* pp. 483-510. As *ICC Case No. 6379* illustrates, arbitrators now routinely consider claims (and defenses) based on mandatory public laws and policies. *See also Trade & Transp., Inc. v. Valero Refining Co., Final Award in SMA Case No. 2699 of 23 August 1990*, XVIII Y.B. Comm. Arb. 124 (1993) (arbitral award in excess of $500,000 for violations of RICO).

Why should these conclusions be accepted? Why should "private" arbitrators be empowered to decide important issues of public policy? In confidential proceedings and awards? Without normal judicial review?

21. *Rationales for arbitrators' consideration of public policy and mandatory law claims.* What is the basis for the trend in most jurisdictions towards permitting consideration of mandatory law and public policy claims by arbitrators? What is the source of an arbitral tribunal's authority to consider and decide such claims?

(a) *Parties' arbitration agreement as source of authority to consider public policy and mandatory law claims.* An arbitration agreement typically grants arbitrators power to resolve "all disputes" relating to the parties' contract; as a matter of interpretation, that formulation usually encompasses disputes based on statutory and other non-contractual claims, provided they have a sufficient factual nexus to the parties' contract. *See supra* pp. 529-32, for authorities holding that such non-contractual claims fall within the scope of an arbitration clause. Only if one implies an exclusion—"all disputes except disputes based on tort or non-contractual claims"—would most arbitration agreements fail as a matter of interpretation to grant the arbitrators the power to resolve such claims.

Many authorities have concluded that, if the parties' arbitration agreement encompasses public law claims, that agreement will ordinarily be a sufficient justification for the arbitrators' power to resolve such claims. Under this view, the parties will have granted the arbitrator the authority to resolve all disputes, including public law disputes, and, unless some legislative instrument forbids that grant, it should be enforced. As the U.S. Supreme Court reasoned in *Mitsubishi Motors,* excerpted above at pp. 486-92:

> "[T]he international arbitral tribunal owes no prior allegiance to the legal norms of particular states [and] has no direct obligation to vindicate their statutory dictates. The tribunal, however, is bound to effectuate the intentions of the parties. Where the parties have agreed that the arbitral body is to decide a defined set of claims which includes, as in these cases, those arising from the application of American antitrust law, the tribunal therefore should be bound to decide that dispute in accord with the national law giving rise to the claim." 473 U.S. at 636-37.

Is this analysis persuasive? *See also* De Ly, Friedman & Radicati di Brozolo, *International Law Association International Commercial Arbitration Committee*

Report and Recommendations on Ascertaining the Contents of the Applicable Law in International Arbitration, 26 Arb. Int'l 193, 216 (2010) ("public policy constrains contractual and arbitral freedom, and may impose limitations or restrictions that the parties cannot agree to disregard"); Rivkin, *The U.S. Situation*, in ICC, *Competition and Arbitration Law* 140 (1993) ("The tribunal must consider all issues falling within the scope of the arbitration clause in the agreement including an antitrust counterclaim if it falls within the scope of the arbitration clause.").

Conversely, if the parties' arbitration clause does *not* encompass particular statutory or public policy claims, then the arbitrators cannot consider these claims. International commercial arbitration is consensual: the parties can only be required to arbitrate that which they have agreed to arbitrate. *See supra* pp. 177, 517, 526.

(b) *Arbitrators' obligation to render enforceable award.* Consider the argument referred to in *ICC Award No. 4132*, that an arbitrator's overriding duty is to render an enforceable award, and impliedly that this requires consideration of public policy defenses and claims. For a similar formulation:

> "Although arbitrators are neither guardians of the public order nor invested by the State with the mission of applying its mandatory rules, they ought nevertheless have an incentive to do so out of a sense of duty to the survival of international arbitration as an institution.... [A]rbitrators should pay heed to the future of their award. They should consider that if they do not apply a mandatory rule of law, the award will in all likelihood be refused enforcement in the country which promulgated that rule. It often turns out that that country is the one, or at least one of several, exercising a de facto control over the situation; it is not reasonable to disregard its attitude." Mayer, *Mandatory Rules of Law in International Arbitration*, 2 Arb. Int'l 274, 284-86 (1986).

Is this persuasive? First, should the parties' rights turn on an arbitrator's "sense of duty to the survival of international arbitration as an institution"? Second, how persuasive is the argument that public policies and mandatory laws must be considered in order to ensure an enforceable award? Article 41 of the 2012 ICC Rules requires the arbitrator to "make every effort" to render an enforceable award. If the parties have not agreed to institutional rules containing such a provision, is there nonetheless an implied expectation or duty to do so? Should this general duty override a specific choice-of-law clause? Should the arbitrator's primary duty be to render an award in accordance with the parties' arbitration agreement, even if it proves unenforceable in some places, rather than a universally enforceable award that disregards the parties' agreement?

22. *Distinction between matters of "substance" and "procedure."* What issues are subject to (a) the "substantive" law selected by the arbitrators' choice-of-law analysis, and (b) the "procedural" law governing the arbitral proceedings? For example, what law applies to issues such as burden of proof, admissibility and weight of evidence, conduct of hearings, evidentiary privileges, availability and amount of interest, and limitations periods? Are these matters of "substance" or "procedure"? *See infra* pp. 982, 1013-14.

Why does the distinction between "substance" and "procedure" matter? Recall the discussion above regarding the law applicable to the arbitral proceedings (the "procedural law of the arbitration" or "*lex arbitri*"). *See supra* pp. 625-40.

Consider the award in *ICC Case No. 4491*. How is the statute of limitations issue categorized? What law would have applied to the issue if it were "substantive"?

The distinction between substantive and procedural issues is elusive even within national legal systems. In the international context, where multiple characterizations exist, the distinction is even more complex. Suppose, in *ICC Case No. 4491*, that Finnish law characterized the statute of limitations issue as substantive. Suppose the parties' underlying contract in *ICC Case No. 4491* contained a choice-of-law clause selecting Finnish law. Would that clause have covered the statute of limitations issue? What law would apply to answering this question?

23. *National court decisions refusing to review arbitrators' choice-of-law decisions*. Neither the New York Convention nor most arbitration statutes expressly permit non-recognition of an award because the arbitrators erred in their choice-of-law analysis. Rather, in the absence of a choice-of-law agreement, the arbitrators' choice-of-law decisions are subsumed within their rulings on the merits of the parties' dispute, and thus subject to the general presumption in favor of recognition under the Convention and most developed arbitration legislation. *See infra* pp. 1113-25, 1164-66, 1189-99.

The same deference to arbitrators' choice-of-law decisions also applies under most national arbitration regimes in annulment actions. Thus, except where statutory protections or public policy issues are involved, judicial review of arbitrators' choice-of-law decisions concerning the substantive law applicable to the merits of the parties' dispute is usually minimal. *See, e.g., ATSA of Cal., Inc. v. Cont'l Ins. Co.*, 754 F.2d 1394, 1396 (9th Cir. 1985) (reversing trial court's holding that Egyptian law should apply, on grounds that arbitrator had authority to determine applicable law); *B v. A* [2010] EWHC 1626, ¶25 (Comm) (English High Ct.) (rejecting challenge to award on basis that arbitrators applied wrong substantive law); *Judgment of 22 October 1991, Compania Valenciana de Cementos Portland v. Primary Coal Inc.*, 1992 Rev. arb. 457 (French Cour de cassation), *Note*, Lagarde ("The Court of Appeal was not required … to examine how the arbitrator determined and implemented the rule of law that was applied."); *Judgment of 18 September 1997*, XXV Y.B. Comm. Arb. 641 (2000) (Landesgericht Hamburg) (defense to recognition based on excess of authority, based on application of wrong substantive law, rejected: "dealing with an objection relating to an [alleged] excess of authority would lead, in the present case, to reviewing the interpretation of the choice of law clause and indirectly to reviewing the correctness of the arbitral award as to the merits"). Recall the *Karaha Bodas* decision and the U.S. court's deference to the arbitrators' determination of the applicable procedural law, *supra* p. 610.

Is this appropriate? Is there any argument that choice-of-law decisions should be subject to more intensive judicial review in annulment (or recognition) actions than other decisions?

24. *Choice of substantive law in investment arbitration*. Consider Article 42 of the ICSID Convention, excerpted at p. 22 of the Documentary Supplement. Compare the ICSID Convention's approach, of including a choice-of-law rule, to that under the New York Convention. What explains the different approaches? Which is preferable?

What does Article 42 provide with regard to the law applicable in investment arbitrations under the ICSID Convention? What is meant by Article 42(1)'s statement that "the Tribunal shall apply the law of the Contracting State party to the dispute (including its rules on the conflict of laws) and such rules of international law as may be applicable"? Note the reference to the law of the Contracting State, including its conflict of laws rules. Compare this to the anti-*renvoi* approach to choice-of-law agreements in the commercial context. *See infra* p. 1014. What is meant by the reference to "such rules of international law as may be applicable"?

25. *Choice of substantive law in inter-state arbitration.* Inter-state arbitrations, between states and/or state-like entities, raise special choice-of-law considerations, because of the (arguable) existence of a single, specialized body of law applicable to disputes between such parties (being public international law). Nonetheless, note the choice-of-law provisions in the Treaty of Washington (in Article VI) and in the Abyei Arbitration Agreement (in Article 3). Consider each of these choice-of-law provisions. Why did the parties agree to them? Can you identify other inter-state circumstances in which similar choice-of-law agreements might be constructive? What law would apply in the absence of such provisions?

B. CHOICE OF LAW GOVERNING MERITS OF PARTIES' DISPUTE PURSUANT TO CHOICE-OF-LAW AGREEMENT

International arbitration agreements often include, or accompany, an express choice-of-law provision addressing the substantive law applicable to the parties' contract and relationship.[20] Prior agreement on the governing substantive law increases the predictability of the parties' relationship and, in some cases, selection of a particular nation's law may provide important advantages to one or the other party. Where a choice-of-law clause exists, three significant issues arise: (a) is the choice-of-law agreement enforceable; (b) if so, subject to what exceptions; and (c) how is the choice-of-law clause to be interpreted? The materials excerpted below explore each of these issues.

1. *Presumptive Validity of Parties' Choice of Law in International Arbitration*

The basic principle, recognized in most national and international instruments, is that choice-of-law agreements are presumptively valid and enforceable.[21] This principle is reflected in a wide variety of legislative and other sources, excerpted below, and is generally subject only to limited exceptions.

---

20. In ICC arbitrations, the parties' contract reportedly contained choice-of-law clauses in 90% of all cases in 2013 (88% in 2012). ICC, *2013 ICC Statistical Report* 5 (2014). *See Award in ICC Case No. 5466*, in Grigera Naón, *Choice-of-Law Problems in International Commercial Arbitration*, 289 Recueil des Cours 9, 234 n.247 (2001) ("It is rather exceptional that a construction contract with a total value of nearly $40 million does not contain an express choice-of-law clause"); G. Born, *International Commercial Arbitration* 2671(2d ed. 2014).

21. *See* G. Born, *International Commercial Arbitration* 2671-83 (2d ed. 2014).

REGULATION ON THE LAW APPLICABLE TO CONTRACTUAL OBLIGATIONS ("ROME I REGULATION")
Articles 3, 9 (2008)

3(1). A contract shall be governed by the law chosen by the parties. The choice shall be made expressly or clearly demonstrated by the terms of the contract or the circumstances of the case. By their choice the parties can select the law applicable to the whole or to part only of the contract.

3(2). The parties may at any time agree to subject the contract to a law other than that which previously governed it, whether as a result of an earlier choice made under this Article or of other provisions of this Regulation. Any change in the law to be applied that is made after the conclusion of the contract shall not prejudice its formal validity under Article 11 or adversely affect the rights of third parties.

3(3). Where all other elements relevant to the situation at the time of the choice are located in a country other than the country whose law has been chosen, the choice of the parties shall not prejudice the application of provisions of the law of that other country which cannot be derogated from by agreement.

3(4). Where all other elements relevant to the situation at the time of the choice are located in one or more Member States, the parties' choice of applicable law other than that of a Member State shall not prejudice the application of provisions of Community law, where appropriate as implemented in the Member State of the forum, which cannot be derogated from by agreement.

3(5). The existence and validity of the consent of the parties as to the choice of the applicable law shall be determined in accordance with the provisions of Articles 10, 11 and 13.

9(1). Overriding mandatory provisions are provisions the respect for which is regarded as crucial by a country for safeguarding its public interests, such as its political, social or economic organisation, to such an extent that they are applicable to any situation falling within their scope, irrespective of the law otherwise applicable to the contract under this Regulation.

9(2). Nothing in this Regulation shall restrict the application of the overriding mandatory provisions of the law of the forum.

9(3). Effect may be given to the overriding mandatory provisions of the law of the country where the obligations arising out of the contract have to be or have been performed, in so far as those overriding mandatory provisions render the performance of the contract unlawful. In considering whether to give effect to those provisions, regard shall be had to their nature and purpose and to the consequences of their application or non-application.

RESTATEMENT (SECOND) CONFLICT OF LAWS
§187 (1971)

[excerpted above at p. 507]

SECOND INTERIM AWARD IN ICC CASE NO. 4145
XII Y.B. Comm. Arb. 97 (1987)

[The claimant was a Middle Eastern public entity. The respondent was a South Asian construction company. The respondent contracted to construct buildings for the claimant. The parties' agreement contained an ICC arbitration clause and a choice-of-law clause: "The validity and construction of this Agreement shall be governed by the laws of the Canton of Geneva or country X, or both." In arbitral proceedings, the claimant contended that Swiss law governed the parties' dispute, while the respondent argued for the law of country X.]

The principle of autonomy—widely recognized—allows the parties to choose any law to rule their contract, even if not obviously related with [it]. This is what the parties have done in mentioning Swiss law, although at first sight less related with the Agreement than the law of country X. Such mention of Swiss law in the first place (before the law of country X) is in this respect an important indication. Moreover, Swiss law constitutes a highly sophisticated system of law, which answers all the questions that may arise from the interpretation or fulfillment of an agreement of the kind of the one entered into. On the other hand, the law of country X, might partially or totally affect the validity of the Agreement. It is then reasonable to assume that from two possible laws, the parties would choose the law which would uphold the validity of the Agreement. It is also a general and widely recognized principle that from two legal solutions, the judge will choose the one which favors the validity of an agreement (*favor negotii*).

In these circumstances, the arbitrators definitely decided to choose Swiss law as the applicable law, assuming that this choice corresponds to what the parties had in mind by inserting the above mentioned provision in Article 11 of the Agreement. (There is no reason to envisage the cumulative application of both Swiss law and the law of country X to the Agreement, such solution being rejected by most of the authors)....

PRELIMINARY AWARD IN ICC CASE NO. 5505
XIII Y.B. Comm. Arb. 110 (1988)

[excerpted above at pp. 629-32]

RULER OF QATAR v. INTERNATIONAL MARINE OIL CO. LTD
Award of June 1953, 20 I.L.R. 534 (1953)

SIR ALFRED BUCKNILL, Referee. On the 5 August 1949, an Agreement in writing hereafter called the Principal Agreement was made between His Excellency the Shaikh of Qatar of the first part, hereafter called the Ruler, and Sir Hugh Weightman on behalf of the Central Mining and Investment Corporation, a company registered in accordance with English law, and Robert Morton Allan Jr. on behalf of the Superior Oil Company, a California corporation, parties of the second part. They were acting as agents for a company to be formed, namely, the International Marine Oil Company, to whom in October, 1950, the parties of the second part assigned all their rights and obligations under the Principal Agreement. This Company is the Respondent to this Arbitration. Meanwhile the Ruler had assigned all his rights and obligations under the Principal Agreement to his son, His Excellency Shaikh

Ali Bin Abdulla Al-Thani, who then succeeded as Ruler of Qatar, and is the Claimant in this Arbitration.

By the terms of the Principal Agreement any doubt or dispute arising between the parties concerning the interpretation of the Agreement or concerning the rights or liabilities of either party under it, were to be referred to two arbitrators, and to a Referee chosen by them. In 1952 disputes and doubts arose; the parties nominated their arbitrators, and they then nominated me, the Right Honourable Sir Alfred Bucknill, a member of Her Majesty's Privy Council, to be the Referee.

Article 2 of the Agreement refers to the Proclamation issued by the Ruler of Qatar on [June 8, 1949], claiming jurisdiction and control over an area of the sea-bed and subsoil lying beneath the high seas of the Persian Gulf contiguous to the territorial waters of Qatar, states that he is satisfied that in respect of such area no prior obligation exists towards an individual or Company, and grants to the Company in conformity with this Agreement for a period of sixty five years from the date of signature hereof, the sole and exclusive right to explore for, drill for, develop, produce, transport and dispose of oil and/or gas or other kindred substances within the area described in Article 3. The Article ends by saying: "It is understood and agreed that this Agreement is subject to any rights which may be established under an existing concession in accordance with the machinery provided for in said concession." ...

Article 4 states: "On the date of signature of this Agreement, the Company shall pay to the Ruler the sum of Rupees 500,000. No part of this amount shall be returnable under any circumstances whatever." Article 5 states:

> "The Company shall pay to the Ruler annually the sum of Rupees 1,000,000, the first payment to be made one year after the date of signature of this Agreement. Upon discovery of oil in commercial quantities this annual rental shall cease, but the amount payable thereafter to the Ruler as royalty under the terms of Article 8 hereof shall in no circumstances be less than the sum of Rupees 1,000,000 annually. For this purpose calculations shall be made on the expiry of each period of twelve months from the date of signature of this agreement. When oil is discovered in commercial quantities in the concession area the Company shall, if the Ruler so desires, make a loan to him of Rupees 1,000,000. The Company shall have the right to recover such loan by deduction from up to one half of the royalties accruing thereafter to the Ruler, provided that the amount paid to the Ruler in any one year shall not in consequence be reduced below the sum of Rupees 1,000,000 as provided above."

The Principal Agreement defined "discovery of oil in commercial quantities" as "the time when a well or wells are drilled, tested and found capable of producing no less than 15,000 barrels of oil of satisfactory quality per day, for thirty consecutive days, according to good oil field practice." The Principal Agreement was drawn up in Arabic and in English. Article 30 stated that: "This Agreement has been written in the Arabic and English languages, each of which has equal validity, but is understood that the Ruler will refer to the Arabic text...."

The crucial issue on this Arbitration was whether the parties intended that the first payment of Rupees 1,000,000 to be made one year after 5th August, 1949, was to be a payment in respect of the year 5th August, 1949, to 5th August, 1950, or a payment in respect of the year 5th August, 1950, to 5th August, 1951. The Claimant argued that this sum of rupees 1,000,000 which was payable on each 5th August was in the nature of rent for the past twelve months, whereas the Respondent Company argued that the sum was a payment for the future twelve months.... At the conclusion of the arguments, the Arbitrators submitted to me certain questions on which they asked for my decision. I need not set out the exact words of the questions, but merely give the gist of them.

The first question was whether the proper law to be applied in the construction of the Principal Agreement is Islamic law or the principles of natural justice and equity. On this point the remarks of Mr. Justice Hardy, a Member of the Supreme Court of Oklahoma, in the case of *Bearman v. Dux Oil Co.*, decided in 1917, and quoted to me, are apt. The case concerned an oil concession, and Mr. Justice Hardy ... said:

> "On the construction of contracts, it is the duty of the Court to place itself as far as possible in the situation of the parties at the time their minds met upon the terms of the agreement, and from a consideration of the writing itself ascertain their intention, and if this cannot be done by the instrument itself, the circumstances under which it was made and the subject matter to which it relates may be considered, and with these aids, it is the duty of the Court so to interpret the contract as to give effect to the mental intention of the parties as it existed at the time of contracting, so far as that intention is ascertainable and lawful."

There is nothing in the Principal or Supplemental Agreements which throws a clear light upon the intention of the parties on this point. If one considers the subject matter of the contract, it is oil to be taken out of ground within the jurisdiction of the Ruler. That fact, together with the fact that the Ruler is a party to the contract and had, in effect, the right to nominate Qatar as the place where any arbitration arising out of the contract should sit, and the fact that the agreement was written in Arabic as well as English, points to Islamic law, that being the law administered at Qatar, as the appropriate law.

On the other hand, there are at least two weighty considerations against that view. One is that in my opinion, after hearing the evidence of the two experts in Islamic law, Mr. Anderson and Professor Milliot, "there is no settled body of legal principles in Qatar applicable to the construction of modern commercial instruments" to quote and adapt the words of Lord Asquith of Bishopstone, in his award as Referee in an Arbitration in 1951 in which the Shaikh of Abu Dhabi, a territory immediately adjacent to Qatar and in fact much larger than Qatar, was a party, and the Arbitration concerned the interpretation of words in an oil concession contract. [*See I.L.R., 1951*, Case No. 37.] I need not set out the evidence before me about the origin, history and development of Islamic law as applied in Qatar or as to the legal procedure in that country. I have no reason to suppose that Islamic law is not administered there strictly, but I am satisfied that the law does not contain any principles which would be sufficient to interpret this particular contract.

Arising out of that reason is the second reason, which is that both experts agreed that certain parts of the contract, if Islamic law was applicable, would be open to the grave criticism of being invalid. According to Professor Milliot, the Principal Agreement was full of irregularities from end to end according to Islamic law, as applied in Qatar. This is a cogent reason for saying that such law does not contain a body of legal principles applicable to a modern commercial contract of this kind. I cannot think that the Ruler intended Islamic law to apply to a contract upon which he intended to enter, under which he was to receive considerable sums of money, although Islamic law would declare that the transaction was wholly or partially void. Still less would the Ruler so intend, and at the same time stipulate that these sums when paid were not to be repaid under any circumstances whatever. I am sure that Sir Hugh Weightman and Mr. Allan did not intend Islamic law to apply. In my opinion neither party intended Islamic law to apply, and intended that the agreement was to be governed by "the principles of justice, equity and good conscience" as indeed each party pleads in Claim and Answer, alternatively to Islamic law, in the case of the Claimant.

[The Referee then held that "Islamic law does not govern the Principal Agreement" and that the Agreement was valid.]

NOTES

1. *Need to select and apply conflict of laws rules even where choice-of-law provision exists.* Like other contractual terms, choice-of-law provisions must be interpreted and enforced. Determining what law to apply to interpret and give effect to a choice-of-law clause requires resort to some set of rules of construction and validity, just as with other types of agreement. In turn, that requires application of some set of conflict of laws rules, to select the applicable rules of construction and validity. What conflict of laws rules are applied to the choice-of-law clauses in the above awards? Is the method of selecting conflict of laws rules any different where a choice-of-law clause exists than where it does not?

2. *Applicability of conflicts rules of arbitral seat to validity and interpretation of choice-of-law agreement.* Consider the various arbitration statutes excerpted above. Under these statutes, what law applies to the validity of a choice-of-law clause? Is there any reason to doubt the appropriateness of this choice? If the parties' underlying contract provides that it is governed by State X's law, with the arbitration seated in State Y, can it be argued that State X's law should also supply the conflicts rules to determine the validity and meaning of the choice-of-law clause? What if State Y's law will not give effect to the choice-of-law clause, but State X's law will?

3. *Presumptive validity of choice-of-law agreement selecting substantive law.* To what extent is the parties' autonomy to select the substantive law governing their relations recognized in international commercial arbitration?

    (a) *Presumptive validity of choice-of-law agreement selecting substantive law under New York and European Conventions.* Does the New York Convention address the validity of choice-of-law agreements selecting the substantive law governing the merits of the parties' dispute? What about Article V(1)(a), discussed above at pp. 302, 308-14? Does it not recognize the parties' autonomy to choose the law governing their agreement? What agreement?

    Consider Article VII(1) of the European Convention, excerpted at pp. 32 of the Documentary Supplement. How does Article VII(1) differ from Article V(1)(a) of the New York Convention? *See also* ICSID Convention, Art. 42 ("The Tribunal shall decide a dispute in accordance with such rules of law as may be agreed by the parties."). *See also Tjong Very Sumito v. Antig Invs. Pte Ltd*, [2009] SGCA 41, ¶28 (Singapore Ct. App.) ("the need to respect party autonomy … in deciding … the substantive law to govern the contract, has been accepted as the cornerstone underlying judicial non-intervention in arbitration."); *Bhatia Int'l v. Bulk Trading SA*, [2002] 4 SCC 105, ¶25 (Indian S.Ct.) ("in international commercial arbitrations parties are at liberty to choose, expressly or by necessary implication, the law and the procedure to be made applicable.").

    (b) *Presumptive validity of choice-of-law agreement selecting substantive law under national arbitration legislation.* National arbitration legislation also generally recognizes the presumptive validity of agreements selecting the law governing the substance of the parties' dispute. Consider Article 28(1) of the Model Law, Article 1511 of the French Code of Civil Procedure, Article 187(1) of the SLPIL, excerpted at pp. 92, 153 & 159 of the Documentary Supplement, and Article 36 of the Japanese Arbitration Law. Do these provisions limit the parties' autonomy to select the substantive law governing their dispute? Consider the scope of the parties' autonomy under these provisions—is it limited to choice of the law governing the parties' contract?

    Legislation in some states does not (expressly) provide a conflicts rule regarding choice-of-law agreements in international arbitrations, but courts in these states have found no difficulty applying the same rules that govern choice-of-law agreements. In the United States, the FAA is silent with regard to the validity of choice-of-law agreements, but under the laws of most U.S. states, and under federal common law rules applicable in matters subject to the New York Convention, such agreements are presumptively valid. *See* G. Born, *International Commercial Arbitration* 2678-80 (2d ed. 2014).

(c) *Presumptive validity of choice-of-law agreement selecting substantive law under institutional rules.* Recognition of party autonomy in the choice of substantive law is also the approach of leading institutional rules. Consider Article 35(1) of the UNCITRAL Rules and Article 21(1) of the ICC Rules, excerpted at pp. 174 & 190 of the Documentary Supplement. *See also* 2014 ICDR Rules, Art. 31(1); 2014 LCIA Rules, Art. 22(3); 2012 Swiss Rules, Art. 33(1). What is the effect of these rules? Do they enhance the presumptive validity or enforceability of particular choice-of-law agreements? How would that be?

(d) *Presumptive validity of choice-of-law agreement selecting substantive law.* Consider *ICC Case No. 4145* and *ICC Case No. 5505*. The awards are consistent with a considerable body of authority, reaching similar conclusions about the parties' autonomy to select the substantive law governing their relations.

(e) *Rationale for parties' autonomy to select substantive law.* Is it appropriate for private parties to be afforded substantial autonomy to specify the substantive law applicable to their relations? Are there societal interests implicated, beyond those of the autonomous "parties"? What about the employees, shareholders, lenders, suppliers, taxing authorities, and communities surrounding the "party"? Are not the interests of such entities directly affected by purported choices of law made by corporate managers? Does the lack of any meaningful judicial (or other) review of arbitral awards heighten these concerns about party autonomy?

    Is it in fact correct that contracting parties obtain vital certainty from a choice-of-law clause? Consider how poorly-drafted the choice-of-law clauses in some of the foregoing awards are. Is it likely that the parties had any idea what the scope of these clauses was, whether the clauses were enforceable, or what the content of the law they might have thought they picked was? If in fact choice-of-law agreements do not provide much certainty, why enforce them?

(f) *Exceptions to presumptive validity of parties' choice-of-law agreement selecting substantive law.* Consider the following: "[p]arty autonomy in arbitration is quite unlimited. Whatever restrictions different legal systems may place on the right of the parties to choose the law to govern their relations, those limitations can only bind the courts of that legal system." J. Lew, *Applicable Law in International*

Commercial Arbitration 126 (1978). Is it correct that limitations on the parties' autonomy (discussed below) are irrelevant in international arbitration, and instead are applicable only in national courts? Is it likely that national legislatures, in enacting mandatory laws or legislation giving effect to public policies, intend that arbitrators are not bound by these rules?

4. *National laws invalidating or disfavoring choice-of-law agreements.* Despite wide-spread recognition of party autonomy, there have been dissenting currents. The Calvo and Drago doctrines provided that states could not compromise their sovereignty by either submitting to "foreign" dispute resolution mechanisms or laws. Hershey, *The Calvo and Drago Doctrines*, 1 Am. J. Int'l L. 26 (1907). In most parts of the world, these ideas lost currency by at least the 1980s; nonetheless, political climates are cyclical, and there have been efforts in recent years in some states to invalidate or withdraw from agreements providing for either international arbitration or application of a foreign law. Cremades, *Resurgence of the Calvo Doctrine in Latin America*, 7 Bus. L. Int'l 53 (2006); Grigera Naón, *Arbitration and Latin America: Progress and Setbacks*, 21 Arb. Int'l 127 (2005). Why might a state refuse to give effect to choice-of-law clauses? Compare the reasons a state might refuse to give effect to international arbitration agreements. *See supra* pp. 335-474.

Suppose an arbitration is seated in a state whose law does not give effect to choice-of-law agreements. Must the arbitral tribunal give effect to the local law invalidating choice-of-law clauses? On what basis could it decline? Does the New York Convention obligate the tribunal to give effect to the choice-of-law agreement? What provision?

Suppose an arbitration is seated in a state that gives effect to choice-of-law clauses, but the parties' transaction occurred principally in a state that does not permit such agreements. Would this restriction apply to the validity of the choice-of-law clause in the arbitration?

5. *Validation principle.* The tribunals in *ICC Case No. 4145* and *Ruler of Qatar* refer to the validation principle, which selects the law of the state that will enforce the parties' agreement. Similar approaches exist under many developed national legal systems. *See* G. Born, *International Commercial Arbitration* 2687-89 (2d ed. 2014). Recall the discussion above, concerning application of the validation principle to international arbitration agreements. *See supra* pp. 306-07. Is the validation principle appropriate in either context? Why?

6. *"Reasonable relation" requirements in international arbitration.* Historically, a few jurisdictions have conditioned the validity of choice-of-law agreements on the existence of a "reasonable relationship" between the parties' transaction and their chosen law. *See* G. Born, *International Commercial Arbitration* 2724-29 (2d ed. 2014).

(a) *The "reasonable relationship" requirement.* Consider §187 of the *Restatement (Second) Conflict of Laws*: it provides that the parties' chosen law must be applied unless, among other things, "the chosen state has no substantial relationship to the parties or the transaction and there is no other reasonable basis for the parties' choice." Comment f provides that §187's requirement for a "reasonable basis" can be satisfied by the choice of a neutral, developed law: "The parties to a multistate contract may have a reasonable basis for choosing a state with which the contract has no substantial relationship. For example, when contracting in countries whose legal systems are strange to them as well as relatively immature, the parties should be able to choose a law on the ground that they know it well and that it is sufficiently developed." Does §187 impose a reasonableness requirement on the parties' choice of substantive law? What is meant by a "substantial relationship" to the parties or transaction or some other "reasonable basis" for the parties' chosen law?

Section 1-105(1) of the U.S. Uniform Commercial Code ("U.C.C.") historically imposed a similar "reasonable relation" test. The original U.C.C. required a "reasonable relationship" between a contract and the state whose law was selected by a choice-of-law clause. *See* U.S. U.C.C. §1-105(1). This requirement was significantly restricted in the revised version of the Code, adopted in 2001. The revised version of the U.C.C. contains a "reasonable relationship" requirement, but only with respect to "consumer" transactions (where many jurisdictions refuse to enforce choice-of-law clauses); it also requires that a choice-of-law clause not deprive consumers of the protection of any mandatory rule of law designed to safeguard their interests. Finally, with respect to wholly "domestic transactions" between businesses, the revised U.C.C. does not permit foreign law to be the chosen law. U.C.C. §§1-301 (c), (e), (f).

Even as revised, does the U.C.C. impose a sensible limitation on choice-of-law agreements? If two businesses wish to select a foreign law to govern their transaction, even if it is purely domestic, why should that not be permitted? What if the two parties do business in a market where a foreign legal system is highly-developed and provides predictable rules?

(b) *Arbitrators generally do not apply reasonable relation requirements.* As *ICC Case No. 5505* illustrates, it is sometimes argued that the parties' choice-of-law agreement should not be enforced because the chosen law is not "related" to the parties' dispute. Such arguments almost inevitably meet the fate of that in *ICC Case No. 5505.*

(c) *Reasonable relationship requirement of arbitral seat.* Suppose an ICC arbitration is seated in a U.S. jurisdiction, where the original U.C.C. is in force; if the parties' choice-of-law clause provides for application of English or Swiss law, should that clause be given effect by the arbitral tribunal? If so, what grounds can be advanced for that conclusion? What conflicts rules must the tribunal apply? Should the tribunal apply?

(d) *Reasonable relationship requirement of state whose conflict of laws rules apply.* If an arbitrator decides to apply the conflict of laws rules of some state that requires a reasonable relationship, can he or she ignore that requirement? Is there any basis for an arbitrator to apply national conflicts rules differently from a national court? Recall the basic aims of arbitration—neutrality, efficiency, and international enforceability, detached as much as possible from the parochial features of any particular legal system. Are they relevant to the foregoing question?

7. *Requirements that choice-of-law clause be express or conspicuous.* As *ICC Case No. 5505* suggests, parties sometimes contest the validity of choice-of-law agreements in arbitration on the grounds that they fail to comply with local law requirements that such agreements be express, specific, or conspicuous. In *ICC Case No. 5505*, the tribunal concluded that Swiss law did not contain a requirement that choice-of-law clauses be explicit. Suppose that Swiss conflicts law *did* contain such a requirement

for choice-of-law agreements. Would arbitrators in a Swiss arbitration have been obliged to apply it? What does Article 187(1) of the SLPIL provide? Article 28(1) of the Model Law?

8. *Internally-inconsistent or contradictory choice-of-law clauses.* Suppose the parties' choice-of-law agreement is internally inconsistent, providing, for example, "this contract shall be governed by the law of the parties' principal place of business," in a case where the parties have two or more principal places of business in different states. Or suppose the choice-of-law clause provides: "the contract shall be governed by the law referred to in Annex A," and Annex A lists three different states. In these instances, is there any choice-of-law agreement? If not, does this have any consequences for the parties' arbitration agreement? The underlying contract? *See Compagnie d'Armement Maritime SA v. Compagnie Tunisienne de Navigation SA* [1971] AC 572 (choice of law of vessel's flag, where vessels had multiple flags) (House of Lords); *Morgan Home Fashions, Inc. v. UTI, U.S., Inc.*, 2004 WL 1950370, at *3 (D.N.J.) (choice of law "of the State shown on the reverse side thereof" read against drafter when two states were referred to).

9. *Choice-of-law agreements selecting law of an "incomplete" legal system.* Parties occasionally argue that a choice-of-law clause cannot be given effect because it selects a law that is "incomplete" or "ill-developed." Although little commentary adopts this position, a few arbitral awards arguably do so. Consider *Ruler of Qatar.* The award is similar to that in another proceeding, cited in *Ruler of Qatar*, where the tribunal rejected a choice-of-law agreement selecting the (then uncodified) law of Abu Dhabi in favor of "English municipal law," because the latter is "so firmly grounded in reason as to form part of this broad body of jurisprudence—this modern law of nature." *Petroleum Dev. Ltd v. Sheikh of Abu Dhabi, Ad Hoc Award of August 1951*, 1 Int'l & Comp. L.Q. 247, 251 (1952).

   Is the "incomplete" character of a legal system a legitimate basis for denying effect to a choice-of-law clause? By what standard does one conclude that a law is "incomplete"? Does the concept invite parochial favoritism of local law (and local parties)? Note that parties are free to agree to arbitration *ex aequo et bono*, where no legal rules are applied. *See infra* pp. 1020-21. If parties can agree to no legal rules, can't they agree to an incomplete set of legal rules?

10. *Choice-of-law agreement selecting law that would result in annulment of award.* Suppose one party argues that the parties' contractually-agreed law would, if applied, result in annulment of the award. Is this grounds for refusing to apply the parties' agreed law? Consider how the tribunal in *ICC Case No. 5505* refers to this possibility. Suppose a Swiss company enters into a contract, governed by Swiss law, with a Venezuelan state entity, with disputes to be resolved by ICC arbitration in Venezuela. Does the possibility that Venezuelan courts would refuse to honor the parties' choice-of-law clause mean the arbitrators should refuse to do so? Why or why not?

2. Public Policy Limitations on Parties' Choice of Law in International Arbitration

Issues of "public policy" or "mandatory law" play significant roles in international commercial arbitration. As discussed elsewhere, the New York Convention and other international arbitration instruments permit non-recognition of awards that conflict with the "public policy" of the enforcing state.[22] In addition, however, "public policy" is not infrequently invoked in arbitral proceedings themselves, in support of arguments either that a choice-of-law clause should not be given effect or that a particular mandatory national (or other) law should be applied. The materials excerpted below examine this latter application of principles of public policy.

FINAL AWARD IN ICC CASE NO. 6379
XVII Y.B. Comm. Arb. 212 (1992)

[The arbitration involved an Italian manufacturer and a Belgian distributor who had entered into a distribution agreement that provided for ICC arbitration and that selected Italian law as the governing law. The arbitral seat was Köln, Germany. The dispute arose from the manufacturer's termination of the distributor, who then commenced arbitration asserting, among other things, that it had not received the notice required by Belgian law.] ...

In general, arbitrators are more cautious than national courts in relying on public policy notions to override a bargained-for choice-of-law agreement. That is in part because arbitrators derive their authority from private contractual relations and in part because tribunals are aware that parties select arbitration to ensure an internationally neutral, consensual means to resolve their disputes. Over-anxious application of national public policies would be inconsistent with this.

The common intention of the parties, expressed in Clause 27 of the Contract, was to choose Italian law as the law applicable to the substance of any dispute; it cannot be disregarded in the present case. Defendant [the Belgian distributor] maintains that claimant, which was in a stronger bargaining position, forced it to accept these contractual provisions. However, defendant does not show in which way these provisions bring about an imbalance.... At the moment of entering into the Contract, the parties were free to decide as they did. We hold that the Contract is governed by Italian law. Hence, the validity of the arbitral clause must be ascertained according to Italian law. According to the Italian Supreme Court, the provisions on jurisdiction of the New York Convention prevail over national law in the Italian legal system. Hence, the validity of a clause for foreign arbitration must be ascertained according to Article II of the New York Convention [and under Article II the clause is enforceable]....

Defendant recognizes in principle that the parties have chosen Italian law to apply to their contract. However, it invokes [Articles 4 and 6 of Belgian Law of 27 July 1961, as modified by Belgian Law of 13 April 1971], contending that these provisions are "provisions of mandatory application" and relying on the mandatory nature of provisions concerning the modalities and consequences of the termination of a distributorship contract for reasons other than gross negligence. [Article 4 provides that an agent "who has suffered damages as a result of the termination of a distributorship contract having effect in the whole or part of the Belgian territory, may always initiate court proceedings in Belgium [under Belgian substantive law,"] while Article 6 provides that these protections "apply notwithstanding any agreement to the contrary...."]

---

22. New York Convention, Art. V(2)(b); Inter-American Convention, Art. 5(2)(b). These provisions are discussed below, *see infra* pp. 1250-60.

Defendant mentions in this context Article 7 of the Rome Convention on the Law Applicable to Contractual Obligations [compare Article 9 of the Rome I Regulation, *supra* p. 984]. Defendant alleges that, under Article 7 above-mentioned, Clause 29 of the Contract is null and void, inoperative or incapable of being performed, in the sense of Article II(3) of the New York Convention.... The Rome Convention has not entered into force. Arbitral clauses are expressly excluded from its scope of application (Article I(2)(d)). Hence, the Rome Convention cannot be applied....

The [European Convention], which has become part of the Italian legal system and which prevails over internal provisions, allows the parties to agree on the law applicable to their contract (Article VII). It provides that the validity of the arbitral clause must be ascertained according to the law chosen by the parties (Article 6(2)), *i.e.*, in the present case, according to Italian law. The [European] Convention makes no exception for foreign provisions of mandatory application.

According to Italian law, the Belgian law of 1961/1971 [concerning distribution agreements] does not prevail over Italian law and, therefore, does not prevail either on the contractual provisions freely agreed upon by the parties.... Further considerations confirm this outcome. In international arbitration, an Arbitral Tribunal is not an institution under the legal system of a State.... [The arbitrator also questioned whether the Belgian law was meant to apply in cases of arbitrations involving agreements to apply foreign law.]

[After concluding that the arbitration agreement was enforceable, the Tribunal proceeded to apply Italian law, again rejecting the argument that mandatory provisions of Belgian law should apply.] As the Rome Convention is not yet in force and the theory according to which a foreign mandatory law is to be respected is not recognized in Italian law as applicable to the present case which concerns an exclusive distributorship, there is no mandatory provision or public policy provision in Italian law that imposes a longer notification period between the producer and the distributor. On the contrary, the contractually agreed upon period should be respected.... Consequently, the provisions of Belgian law providing for a longer notification period for the distributor shall not be applied by the arbitrator....

FINAL AWARD IN ICC CASE NO. 5622
XIX Y.B. Comm. Arb. 105 (1994)

[The respondent submitted a bid to Algerian authorities for certain public works. It also concluded a Protocol of Agreement with the claimant, under which claimant was to give legal and fiscal advice to respondent and to coordinate its subcontractors, assisting respondent to obtain the contract with the Algerian authorities. Respondent was to pay claimant a percentage of the price of its contract with the Algerian authorities. The Protocol of Agreement contained an ICC arbitration clause and a Swiss choice-of-law clause. Respondent obtained the contract with the Algerian authorities. It paid claimant 50% of the agreed fee but refused to pay the remaining 50%, alleging that claimant's performance had been deficient. Claimant initiated an ICC arbitration. Respondent sought dismissal on the grounds that the Protocol of Agreement violated mandatory law (*loi de police*) of Algeria on intermediary activities and sought an award of its legal costs in the arbitration.]

There is no written evidence allowing us to determine exactly what claimant did, so that we must rely only on the testimony by claimant's witnesses, to which unfortunately the testimony given by defendant's managers who participated in the conclusion of the Protocol of Agreement cannot be opposed. In fact, one of the characteristics of this case is the absence of tangible evidence: claimant's file, which could have provided us with many interesting elements, has been stolen ..., and the people who played a key role within the defendant company have been dismissed. The parties have not called them as witnesses, which is, to say the least, strange. Apparently, one of the key witnesses was traumatized by his imprisonment in Algeria! However, it is possible to define more or less clearly claimant's activities on the basis of the testimonies given. It appears from the witnesses' testimonies that claimant developed both activities resembling the provision of more or less confidential commercial information, and activities consisting of using its influence on some Algerian authorities, against payment, in order to have defendant's bid preferred to bids from other companies. According to witness C, 85% of claimant's work consisted of the latter activities....

[T]here exists in Switzerland no special law concerning the issues connected to the traffic in influence.... In the present case, defendant alleges that claimant developed activities consisting of using its contacts with people in Algeria who could grant defendant the contract ..., possibly paid bribes and in any case violated Algerian Law No. 78-02 of 11 February 1978 on the State Monopoly on Foreign Trade, thereby violating either Swiss or international public policy. The Arbitral Tribunal holds that the activities developed by claimant essentially resembled the supply of more or less confidential and discreet commercial information, together with the use of claimant's influence on the Algerian authorities. Hence, we can ask ourselves whether claimant's activities were contrary to fair trading and, therefore, to *bonos mores*.

According to Art. 20(1) [of the Swiss Code of Obligations], "a contract providing for an impossibility, having illegal contents or violating *bonos mores* is null and void." ... We must note, however, that the [Swiss Federal Tribunal] has not yet examined, to our knowledge, a case of trading in influence. The existing jurisprudence highlights two aspects: 1. In all cases a group of people had a common interest (awarding a contract, inheritance, exchange of goods between members); 2. Some of these persons had, on the strength of hidden agreements, interfered with the rights of other members of the group. In the present case, claimant did not conclude a secret agreement with another company interested in the contract with the Algerian authorities, with the aim of altering the allocation rules. Claimant did try to use its influence on the Algerian authorities, but this attempt is not per se a violation of fair trading, at least as interpreted by the [Swiss Federal Tribunal]....

Now it happens that nowadays, especially in certain fields (armaments, sale of know-how, aviation, etc.), ... [that] the manager of an enterprise or the board of a company is tempted to use various means, and particularly bribes, that is, "any offer (or request) concerning the granting of a hidden and not-owed material advantage to the employee of a third party with the aim of influencing this third party in favour of the donor." Many enterprises, in fact, establish reserves for bribes, either by creating a "bribery fund" or by including this practice in the budget. For instance, bribes may be deducted from taxes in the Federal Republic of Germany.

Now, we may ask ourselves whether the conclusion of the contract between defendant and the Algerian authorities depended on bribes paid by claimant. It is important to give an answer to this question, because if this were the case the contract would be null and void. The [Swiss Federal Tribunal] has affirmed this principle on several occasions.

The issue of bribery has been discussed at the hearings; ... one of claimant's witnesses, B, maintained that the Algerian authorities were not bribed. On the other hand, at the same hearing, B also said that when [the representatives of Algeria] were in France, "they were taken care of." Also, the correspondence between the former General Manager of defendant and claimant ambiguously mentions payments "which would have been made by defendant directly to local representatives," payments which were to be deducted from claimant's fee. Further, the high commission fee could indicate that there has been bribery (*see* the U.S. jurisprudence cited below). In the present case, bribery has not been proved beyond doubt. It is true that it is possible to prove something through indirect evidence.... However, it is necessary that a sufficient ensemble of indirect evidence be collected to allow the judge to base his decision on something more than likely facts, *i.e.*, facts which have not been proven. Thus, evidence of bribery has not been given and the indirect evidence is not sufficiently relevant.

I shall not list the activities prohibited by Algerian Law No. 78-02 of 11 February 1978 on the State Monopoly on Foreign Trade, but it is important to emphasize that the Law aims at prohibiting all trading in influence and especially all interventions which can affect real or supposed relationships within Algeria and its bodies. Of course, assistance is still possible on the conditions indicated by Art. 21 of the same Law. The Law aims at "moralizing" somewhat the trading in influence. The issue is whether claimant's activities in Algeria violated Algerian Law No. 78-02 ... and the effect of this violation under Swiss law....

If we consider claimant's activities, we can reasonably hold that the Law of Algeria has been violated. In fact, claimant's Administrator, when describing the coordination work which was provided for in the Protocol of Agreement, said that claimant's collaborator checked how defendant's offer was proceeding through the various departments of [the Ministry], in order to make sure that defendant's offer would be preferred to the offers made by its competitors. Furthermore, claimant affirms that its task was, through its contacts in Algeria, to obtain the granting of the contract. It also says that claimant's representatives sustained important relations with persons from Algeria whom they had met at receptions and various meetings....

First of all, illegality in the sense of Art. 20(1) [of the Swiss Code of Obligations] requires that provisions of Swiss law be violated. Hence, violation of foreign law provisions must be examined from the point of view of a possible affront to morality.

The [Swiss Federal Tribunal has] ... held that: the violation of foreign ... provisions on foreign currency was not an affront to morality in the sense of Art. 20(1). The [Federal Tribunal] held that the foreign provision concerned must protect individual and community interests generally acknowledged to be fundamental, or else juridical interests which are, from an ethical point of view, more important than contractual freedom.... Such is the case, for instance, regarding the battle against drugs or the trade in women. The [Federal Tribunal] held that currency regulations which, due to their contents, are of a pure commercial nature, are not provisions of the kind indicated above.... The fight against the trading in influence is not an exclusive concern of Algeria. In fact, on the national level, most European States have adopted special corruption legislation..... This intention to stop or at least restrict practices which are considered contrary to fair trading is echoed by Swiss criminal law, which sanctions active (Art. 288 Swiss Penal Code) and passive (Art. 315 Swiss Penal Code) corruption, and also the unfair management of public interests (Art. 314 Swiss Penal

Code). It is unanimously recognized that trading in influence is a practice which must be sanctioned and does not deserve any juridical protection....

It ensues from these considerations that the Law of Algeria does not have the sole aim of serving the interest of Algeria—as is the case in the ... above-mentioned [Swiss Federal Tribunal] cases—but that it aims at guaranteeing healthy and fair commercial practices and at fighting against corruption in general. In fact, the Law of Algeria lays down a general principle which must be respected by all legal systems wishing to fight corruption. This is why the violation of this Law, which concerns international public policy, is contrary to the notion of morality based on Art. 20(1), which is part of Swiss public policy. Hence, the brokerage contract is null and void in its entirety since, according to claimant's collaborator, 85% of claimant's activities aimed at obtaining the contract with the Algerian authorities for defendant, collecting information and legal and fiscal advice being only a marginal activity.

This solution recalls the solution developed in US jurisprudence, which is very abundant in this field.... [Summarizing U.S. authority, the award noted that corruption often involves intervention of a local agent, often incorporated in a foreign jurisdiction (particularly one with strict commercial secrecy legislation), acting to obtain a government contract, in return for commissions, generally disproportionate to the amount of work rendered.] Apart from the striking parallels with the case at issue, the various judgments cited above show, if it were needed, that there exists a real political will to moralize commercial transactions and to ban traffic in influence from commercial life. Thus, declaring the contract concluded between claimant and defendant null and void is in keeping with the wish expressed by the US courts to stop activities which are contrary to public policy. In fact, this solution also lines up with the effort of the [ICC], aiming at "promoting high ethics in commercial transactions, both at a national and an international level, and to favour the growth of international trade in a context of fair competition," [citing an ICC policy statement].

Now that we have found that the brokerage contract and consequently the Protocol of Agreement concluded between defendant and claimant are null and void, it is important that we examine the consequences of this nullity on the validity of the arbitral clause contained in the contract.... [In an early case,] the sole arbitrator, Mr. Lagergren, held that, since the contract concluded between the parties was null and void, he should decline jurisdiction and should not hear the merits of the case.... [The tribunal quoted Lagergren's award: "... it cannot be contested that there exists a general principle of law recognised by civilised nations that contracts which seriously violate *bonos mores* or international public policy are invalid or at least unenforceable and that they cannot be sanctioned by court or arbitrators. This principle is especially apt for use before international arbitration tribunals that lack a 'law of the forum' in the ordinary sense of the term.... Whether one is taking the point of view of good government or that of commercial ethics it is impossible to close one's eyes to the probable destination of amounts of this magnitude, and to the destructive effect thereof on the business pattern with consequent impairment of industrial progress. Such corruption is an international evil; it is contrary to good morals and to an international public policy common to the community of nations.... Parties who ally themselves in an enterprise of the present nature must realise that they have forfeited any right to ask for the assistance of the machinery of justice (national courts or arbitral tribunals) in settling their disputes."] ...

[A second case] concerned a dispute between an intermediary and a company which had obtained a public contract in a developing country, the intermediary requested payment of the balance of his fee. The appointed arbitrator reasoned ... "Clearly, performance by claimant could only mean the use of its influence on those who had the possibility and the right to decide with whom State A would conclude a contract. It is of little importance, as far as the validity of the agreement between the parties is concerned, whether the influence was used in order to exclude a competitor who had offered more favourable conditions or to remind an official of his duty to accept the best offer or else to induce the choice of claimant's offer among equivalent offers." [In contrast to] Judge Lagergren, the arbitrator entered into the merits of the case, found that he had jurisdiction and then dismissed the claim for the payment of the commission....

This second solution, which is admitted and recognized today by doctrine and jurisprudence, is to be preferred, since it makes it possible to declare null and void all contracts which are illicit or contrary to morality. In the present case, this second solution has consequently been followed by the arbitral tribunal. Also, its jurisdiction is not invalidated by the Protocol of Agreement being declared null and void.

No party to a contract can file a claim based on a contract which is null and void. In fact, Art. 20(1) implies the application of the adage *in pari turpitudine melior est pars possidentis*.... Recovery is thus excluded if the party has performed under a contract which is illicit or contrary to morality.... Further, when a contract is null and void because it is illicit or contrary to morality, the arbitrator cannot grant the parties' claims without becoming somewhat of an "accomplice," a role which he must refuse to play! ... Consequently, if defendant filed a claim for recovery of the sums paid [to defendant], that claim would be denied.

Is this result shocking? In our opinion, the answer is that it is not, since claimant did not prove that it performed as provided for in the Protocol of Agreement, that is, as a legal and fiscal advisor. The file, which could have proved it, has been stolen, a fact that claimant did not mention when filing its request for arbitration! Claimant further alleges that defendant obtained the contract thanks to claimant's intervention with the competent authorities.... It also recognizes that it has been paid for these activities. Now, as we have seen, these activities violate the Law of Algeria which prohibits the trading in influence and thereby violate the notion of morality laid down in Art. 20(1), and Swiss public policy. Hence, the contract between claimant and defendant is null and void and the fate of claimant's claim must be that of all claims arising from contracts which are null and void on the ground of violation of morality, according to the adage: *nemo auditur suam turpitudinem allegans*. Claimant's claim must, therefore, be denied.

As to the costs and fees of the arbitration, according to Art. 20(1) of the ICC Rules ... leaves the arbitrator totally free to apportion the costs in equity.... Since claimant's claim has been denied in its entirety, claimant shall bear all costs. On the other hand, defendant's behaviour has not been flawless either, and the Arbitrator denies its claim for damages for the following reasons: Due to the immoral contents of claimant's activities—which, it is true, did not correspond with the activities provided for in the Protocol of Agreement, but were tacitly approved of by defendant in so far as defendant paid 50% of the agreed fee—it would be shocking if defendant did not bear its own expenses. In fact, the above-mentioned adage *nemo auditur suam turpitudinem allegans* can also by analogy be opposed to defendant. [The defendant also did not fully disclose facts regarding the parties' relationship and actions.] The behaviour of defendant in these proceedings is, in the Arbitrator's opinion, as reprehensible as that of claimant. Defendant's claim for compensation for the costs of the procedure does not deserve to be granted: if the Arbitrator granted it, he would again become an "accomplice" by refunding expenses to a party to which the above-mentioned adage applies....

PRELIMINARY AWARD IN ICC CASE NO. 4132
X Y.B. Comm. Arb. 49 (1985)

[excerpted above at pp. 967-68]

FINAL AWARD IN ICC CASE NO. 5946
XVI Y.B. Comm. Arb. 97 (1991)

[The dispute involved a French company, which bottled and supplied wine, and a U.S. company, which distributed wine. The two parties entered into an exclusive agency agreement appointing the U.S. company as distributor in the United States for certain brands of wine supplied by the French company. The Agreement contained a choice-of-law clause that provided: "This Agreement is made in New York, New York, and shall be construed in accordance with the laws of New York."]

[The U.S. company] claims exemplary damages of U.S.$ 100,000 for claimant's alleged unilateral and unprovoked termination of the Agreement, its commencement of litigation instead of arbitration, and its refusal to resolve this dispute. To the extent that respondent has sustained and proven legal expenses in connection with claimant's unjustified bringing suit before the Federal Court in New York, respondent is already compensated [by a separate award of compensatory damages]. Damages that go beyond compensatory damages to constitute a punishment of the wrongdoer (punitive or exemplary damages) are considered contrary to Swiss public policy, which must be respected by an arbitral tribunal sitting in Switzerland even if the arbitral tribunal must decide a dispute according to a law that may allow punitive or exemplary damages as such (see Article 135(2) [of the Swiss Law on Private International Law], which refuses to allow enforcement of a judgment awarding damages that cannot be awarded in Switzerland....) In addition, it must also be emphasized that even if an award of punitive damages were not found inconsistent with Swiss public policy, respondent has not proven that under New York law a claim for such punitive or exemplary damages would lie ...

NOTES

1. *Distinction between validity of arbitration agreement and validity of choice-of-law clause.* Note that the tribunal in *ICC Case No. 6379* considers two issues: (a) at the outset of its award, whether the parties' arbitration clause was valid and enforceable, notwithstanding Belgian mandatory law; and (b) in more detail, whether to give effect to the choice-of-law clause, selecting Italian law, or to apply mandatory Belgian law. What law does the tribunal apply to the first issue? Does that law include the New York Convention? What law does the tribunal apply to the second issue?

2. *Arbitrators' authority to apply mandatory law and public policy revisited.* Recall the nonarbitrability doctrine and the arbitrators' authority to consider mandatory law and

public policy claims. *See supra* pp. 483-510, 979-81. Consider again the sources of the arbitrators' authority to apply mandatory laws and public policies to override the parties' contract.

3.   *Application of mandatory law and public policy of legal system selected by parties' choice-of-law agreement.* Suppose the parties' choice-of-law agreement selects the law of State X. Is it controversial for a tribunal then to apply the public policy or mandatory law of State X to override or supplement the parties' underlying contract? By choosing the law of State X, don't the parties choose the mandatory laws and public policies of State X? *See* G. Born, *International Commercial Arbitration* 2707-08 (2d ed. 2014).

4.   *Application of mandatory law and public policy of legal system that is not selected by parties' choice-of-law agreement.* Consider *ICC Case No. 5946*, where the arbitrator held that the mandatory law and public policy of the arbitral seat (Switzerland) forbid an award of punitive damages under the substantive law agreed to by the parties (New York). What authorized the tribunal to apply the public policy of the arbitral seat to override the parties' choice of substantive law? Recall the discussion of the traditional approach, under which the conflict of laws rule of the seat is applicable in the arbitration. *See supra* pp. 970-73. Can application of the seat's public policies be justified as a form of contract interpretation? By agreeing upon State A as the arbitral seat, have parties impliedly agreed on the application of its conflicts rules and public policies, even where inconsistent with the parties' choice-of-law clause?

Suppose a tribunal is asked to apply a mandatory law or public policy other than that chosen by the parties' choice-of-law agreement or of the arbitral seat. For example, suppose a tribunal, seated in State A, with a choice-of-law agreement selecting the law of State B, is asked to apply the mandatory law or public policy of State C. What would justify application of the law of a state that is neither the arbitral seat nor the parties' choice? Consider the facts in *ICC Case No. 6379*. Note that the parties' underlying contract was governed by Italian law, but that the claimant relied on Belgian mandatory law. What would have permitted the arbitral tribunal to apply Belgian mandatory law, notwithstanding the parties' contrary agreement? Is the source of the arbitrators' authority to apply a mandatory law different from that agreed by the parties any different from the source of its authority to apply a mandatory law to invalidate the substantive terms of the parties' agreement?

Would an arbitrator have authority to consider a claim under the competition law of State X if the parties' arbitration clause provided: "Under no circumstances, shall the arbitral tribunal consider or make any award based upon the competition law of State X." Does it matter where the tribunal is seated?

5.   *Arbitrators' refusals to apply mandatory law and public policy of legal system that is not selected by parties' choice-of-law agreement.* Consider the tribunal's decision in *ICC Case No. 6379*. Why did the tribunal refuse to apply the Belgian distributorship statute? Was the Belgian statute applicable by its own terms (*i.e.*, would a Belgian court, presented with the same facts, have applied the Belgian statute)? Compare the tribunal's approach to application of the EU competition laws in *ICC Case No. 4132*, *supra* pp. 967-68.

Note the tribunal's statement in *ICC Case No. 6379* that "arbitrators are more cautious than national courts in relying on public policy notions to override a bargained-for choice-of-law agreement." Compare the tribunal's observation to that of the traditional view, *supra* pp. 979-80, that arbitrators lacked the authority to apply any mandatory law or public policy.

Consider the reliance on Article VII of the European Convention in *ICC Case No. 6379*. Does the absence of any reference to public policy in Article VII mean that there are no circumstances in which a tribunal may, in an arbitration subject to the Convention, apply a mandatory law or public policy not selected by the parties' choice-of-law agreement?

Consider also the discussion of the Rome Convention in *ICC Case No. 6379*. Note that the Rome Convention had not, at the time of the arbitration, yet come into force; the Convention subsequently came into force in EU Member States, and was then superseded (for almost all EU Member States) by the substantially similar Rome I Regulation. What if the Rome Convention or the Rome I Regulation had been in force when *ICC Case No. 6379* was decided? Would the tribunal have then applied the Belgian legislation? Why is it that the Rome Convention was itself applicable, as a conflict of laws rule, in *ICC Case No. 6379*?

6. *Arbitrators' application of mandatory law and public policy of legal system that is not selected by parties' choice-of-law agreement.* In contrast to *ICC Case No. 6379*, most tribunals and other authorities agree that, at least in some circumstances, arbitrators are permitted (and perhaps required) to apply mandatory national laws and public policies notwithstanding choice-of-law clauses selecting a different nation's laws. *See* G. Born, *International Commercial Arbitration* 2712-16 (2d ed. 2014); *Mitsubishi Motors Corp. v. Soler Chrysler-Plymouth Inc.*, 473 U.S. 614, 637 n.19 (1985) (tribunal seated in Japan will apply U.S. antitrust laws, notwithstanding Swiss choice-of-law clause); Maniruzzaman, *International Arbitrator and Mandatory Public Law Rules in the Context of State Contracts: An Overview*, 7 J. Int'l Arb. 53, 55-58 (1990); Lando, *The Law Applicable to the Merits of the Dispute*, in *Essays on International Commercial Arbitration* 128 (1989).

Consider the awards in *ICC Case No. 4132* and *ICC Case No. 5622*. Was the tribunal in each case prepared, in principle, to apply a mandatory law or public policy other than that of the legal system selected by the parties' choice-of-law agreement? How did the approaches of the two tribunals differ? What was the relationship between Algerian and Swiss law in *ICC Case No. 5622*?

7. *Choice of law governing public policy and statutory claims and defenses.* If an arbitral tribunal has the authority to apply mandatory laws and public policies other than those of the legal system selected by the parties' choice-of-law agreement, how does a tribunal determine which nation's policies and law it should apply?

(a) *Need for choice-of-law analysis with respect to public policy issues.* Some authorities appear to have suggested that mandatory laws or public policies *must* be applied, without any choice-of-law analysis to determine whether they are applicable. *See, e.g.,* Mayer, *Mandatory Rules of Law in International Arbitration*, 2 Arb. Int'l 274, 275-77 (1986) ("a mandatory rule (*loi de police* in French) is an imperative provision of law which must be applied in an international relationship irrespective of the law that governs that relationship. To put it another way: mandatory rules of law are a matter of public policy (*ordre public*) and moreover reflect a public policy so commanding that they must be applied even if the general body of law to which they belong is not competent by application of the relevant rule of conflict of laws."). Would such a view be correct? Or is it necessary to determine whether, in fact, a public policy or mandatory law was intended by the legislature that enacted it to apply to particular circumstances? For example, would EU or U.S. "mandatory" competition law purport to apply to a domestic Zambian transaction? Even if a national mandatory law purports, by its own terms, to apply in a particular case, may there not be circumstances in which the arbitral tribunal may not apply it? For example, even if EU or U.S. antitrust laws purported to apply to a wholly foreign transaction, will applicable national or international conflicts rules give effect to that? Compare the analysis in *ICC Case No. 5946*, where the tribunal concluded that applicable Swiss conflicts rules forbid application of New York law.

(b) *Scope of mandatory law or public policy.* A particular state's public policy or mandatory law may not, by its own terms, be applicable to an international dispute. For example, suppose that an arbitration is seated in State X between State A and State B companies, involving conduct occurring entirely in State Y. Suppose one party relies on the competition laws of State Z. Would State Z's mandatory law or public policy be applicable to the underlying dispute? Consider *ICC Case No. 4132*, where the tribunal concluded that, by its own terms, EU competition law did not apply to the parties' conduct and transactions. Also consider *ICC Case No. 6379*, where the arbitrator suggested that Belgian statutory rules did not, by their own terms, apply to international transactions. If a state's mandatory law does not, by its own terms, extend to a particular set of facts or transaction, is there any reason to apply it? Does it matter if the arbitral seat is located within that state?

(c) *Public policy and mandatory law limitations imposed by substantive law of arbitral seat on parties' choice-of-law agreement.* Consider again *ICC Case No. 5946*. Note the tribunal's application of the mandatory law and public policy of the arbitral seat to deny effect to the parties' choice-of-law agreement. Is the tribunal's conclusion persuasive? Why should the mandatory law and public policy of the arbitral seat, on matters of substantive public policy, override the parties' agreement on the substantive law governing their relations? *Compare* Karrer, in S. Berti et al. (eds.), *International Arbitration in Switzerland* Art. 187, ¶¶163, 175 (2000) (Swiss public policy against punitive damages would not apply in arbitration, seated in Switzerland, of dispute having no other connection to Switzerland).

Under most conflict of laws systems, private choice-of-law agreements are unenforceable when they result in application of a rule that violates the forum's mandatory laws or public policies. *See supra* pp. 989-90, 979-81; *Restatement (Second) Conflict of Laws* §187 (1971); *See* G. Born & P. Rutledge, *International Civil Litigation in United States Courts* 760-61 (5th ed. 2011). Note, however, that the arbitral seat may have nothing to do with the parties' underlying dispute. *See supra* pp. 652-58. For example, an arbitration seated in State X may involve contractual dealings in States A, B and C. In such cases, the substantive public policies of the arbitral seat (State X) are irrelevant to the parties' dispute—while those of States A, B and C (where the dispute occurred) may be highly relevant. Moreover, by their own terms, the public policies and mandatory laws of the arbitral seat may not be applicable to the parties' dispute. In *ICC Case No. 5946*, for example, what connection did Switzerland's policy against punitive damages have to a dispute governed by New York law that involved no conduct in or affecting Switzerland?

Consider also the case where an arbitral institution or tribunal (rather than the parties) designates the arbitral seat. In such cases, should the mandatory law or public policy of the seat apply to override the parties' chosen law?

(d) *Public policy and mandatory law limitations imposed by applicable conflict of laws rules on parties' choice-of-law.* Many conflicts systems provide, in certain circumstances, for a forum court's application of "foreign" public policies to supplement or override the parties' agreement. Article 7 of the Rome Convention, cited in *ICC Case No. 6379*, (and now superseded by Article 9 of the Rome I Regulation) is one example of such a conflicts rule. Section 187 of the *Restatement (Second) Conflict of Laws* (1971) is another. Section 187(2)(b) provides that the parties' chosen law will ordinarily be applied, unless:

> (b) application of the law of the chosen state would be contrary to a fundamental policy of a state which has a materially greater interest than the chosen state in the determination of the particular issue and which, under the [general choice-of-law] rule of §188, would be the state of the applicable law in the absence of an effective choice of law by the parties.

Also consider the two following alternatives to the application of foreign public policies, which were proposed as Draft Recommendations on the Law Applicable to International Contracts of the Working Group of the ICC's Commission on Law and Commercial Practices in 1980:

> Alternative 1: Even when the arbitrator does not apply the law of a certain country as the law governing the contract he may nevertheless give effect to mandatory rules of the law of that country if the contract or the parties have a close contact to that country and if and in so far as under its law those rules must be applied whatever may be the law applicable to the contract. On considering whether to give effect to these mandatory rules, regard shall be had to their nature and purpose and to the consequences of their application or non-application.

> Alternative 2: Even when the arbitrator does not apply the law of a certain country as the law applicable to the contract he may nevertheless give effect to the mandatory rules of the law of that country if the contract or parties have a close contact to the country in question especially when the arbitral award is likely to be enforced there, and if and in so far as under the law of that country those rules must be applied whatever be the law applicable to the contract.

Suppose an arbitral tribunal, seated in State X, applies the conflicts rules of State X to determine the validity of the parties' choice-of-law clause. Suppose further that, like Article 9 of the Rome I Regulation or §187(2)(b) of the *Restatement*, State X's conflicts rules permit (or require) application of the mandatory law or public policy of another state (*i.e.*, State Y). Should the tribunal apply the mandatory law or public policy of State Y?

Note that, pursuant to the conflicts rules in Article 9 of the Rome I Regulation and §187 of the *Restatement*, a mandatory law or public policy would only be applicable if the state in question had a significant connection to the parties' dispute. Under these rules, how would *ICC Case No. 5946* have been resolved? Compare the draft ICC proposals.

In *ICC Case No. 4132*, the arbitrator considered whether public policy/statutory rights of a country other than the arbitral seat or the parties' chosen substantive law could be applied. Based on the facts presented in the award, how would Article 9 of the Rome I Regulation and §187(2)(b) of the *Restatement* have been applied? Compare the draft ICC proposals.

(e) *Conflict between public policy and mandatory law limitations and applicable conflict of laws rules*. Suppose the mandatory law or public policy of one state purports, by its own terms, to apply to a transaction. Assume further, though, that the conflicts rules of the arbitral seat do not provide for application of that mandatory law. Suppose, for example, that parties from States A and B agree to arbitrate in State X, with their contract subject to the law of State Y, but one party then relies on EU competition law; what conclusion should the tribunal reach if, while EU competition laws purport to apply, the conflicts rules of both State X and State Y refuse to apply EU competition law?

What rules *should* an arbitrator use in determining when to apply a "foreign" public policy? Should the arbitrator look to the conflict of laws rules he initially concluded were applicable to select a substantive law governing the parties' contract? Should he look to the relevant foreign state's definition of its public policies? Or is there some "international" set of conflict of laws rules that he should consult? What might these rules be?

(f) *Enforcement issues*. Suppose a party relies on a mandatory law or public policy, but the tribunal refuses to apply that law. May the unsuccessful party then pursue claims based on that law or public policy in national courts? For example, in *ICC Case No. 6379*, could the Belgian distributor pursue its claims in Belgian courts? Or, could the claimant in *ICC Case No. 5946* pursue claims for punitive damages in New York courts? *See supra* pp. 509-10, discussing the availability of treble damages in arbitration of U.S. antitrust claims.

8. *Corruption and bribery*. Consider the tribunal's analysis in *ICC Case No. 5622*. Does the tribunal rely on Swiss law to conclude that the Protocol is invalid? Does the Protocol violate any provision of Swiss domestic law? Does the tribunal rely on Algerian law? Why does the tribunal rely on international developments, including ICC policy statements and U.S. judicial decisions? What relevance do these have to the issues before the tribunal?

Suppose you represent the claimant in *ICC Case No. 5622*. Construct the best argument to annul the award. Consider the grounds for annulment under Article 34 of the UNCITRAL Model Law and Article 190 of the SLPIL, excerpted at pp. 94-95 & 160 of the Documentary Supplement. *See infra* pp. 1155-69.

9. *Arbitrators' sua sponte consideration of mandatory law and public policy issues*. Note that the tribunal in *ICC Case No. 5622* appears to have raised on its own accord at least some of the mandatory law and public policy arguments discussed in its award. Is this appropriate? If neither party relies on mandatory law or public policy claims, what is the source of the tribunal's authority to do so? What procedural safeguards should a tribunal afford the parties if it *sua sponte* raises issues of mandatory law or public policy?

10. *Consequences of decision that mandatory law invalidates parties' contract*. Consider the results of the decision in *ICC Case No. 5622*. The tribunal considered (a) declining

jurisdiction, citing an early award by Gunnar Lagergren adopting this approach to a claim based upon a contract to pay corrupt bribes; and (b) accepting jurisdiction, but dismissing the claim. What are the arguments for and against each course of action? Which course was adopted in *ICC Case No. 5622*? Was this appropriate?

11. *Purported "supervisory" role of national courts in arbitration of public policy disputes.* As described elsewhere, U.S. courts not infrequently entertain actions to compel arbitration and issue orders requiring compliance with an arbitration agreement. *See supra* pp. 319-20, 664-69. These orders can include orders to arbitrate statutory claims—such as claims based on U.S. securities or antitrust laws. *See Mitsubishi Motors Corp. v. Soler Chrysler-Plymouth Inc.*, 473 U.S. 614 (1985); *supra* pp. 494-98, 510. In doing so, U.S. courts have sometimes imposed conditions on the arbitration of these claims. Consider, for example, the excerpt below from the court's opinion compelling arbitration in *PPG Indus. v. Pilkington plc*, 825 F.Supp. 1465 (D. Ariz. 1993):

> the Court may, and certainly will, withdraw the reference to arbitration if U.S. antitrust law does not govern the substantive resolution of [the plaintiff's claims.] In addition, the Court directs that any damages determination, or arbitral award, made by the arbitrators shall be determined according to U.S. antitrust law irrespective of any conflict that may exist between those laws and the laws of England. Finally, the Court will retain jurisdiction over this matter in order to ensure that the arbitration directed by this Order is conducted in accordance with the Order.

> Is such an order wise? Permitted by the New York Convention? How should a foreign arbitral tribunal respond to such orders?

3. *Interpretation and Content of Choice-of-Law Agreements*

Assuming that a choice-of-law clause is valid and enforceable, it also must be interpreted. A number of interpretative issues recurrently arise with regard to choice-of-law agreements in international arbitration. The materials excerpted below explore these issues.

REGULATION ON THE LAW APPLICABLE TO CONTRACTUAL OBLIGATIONS ("ROME I REGULATION")

Articles 3, 9 (2008)

[excerpted above at p. 984]

RESTATEMENT (SECOND) CONFLICT OF LAWS

§187 (1971)

[excerpted above at p. 507]

PRELIMINARY AWARD IN ICC CASE NO. 5505

XIII Y.B. Comm. Arb. 110 (1988)

[excerpted above at pp. 629-32]

AWARD IN ICC CASE NO. 6618

discussed in Grigera Naón, *Choice-of-Law Problems in International Commercial Arbitration*, 289 Recueil des Cours 9, 263 (2001)

The dispute arose out of a distribution contract showing a choice-of-law clause referring to the law of Washington State as proper law. Claimant's claim was based on tortious interference of contract, which both under the *lex arbitri* and the proper law has to be characterized, as pointed out by the Arbitral Tribunal, as a tort. However, after finding that the tort claim arose out "of behavior which ... constituted" a contractual breach and was related to the performance of the contract, the Arbitral Tribunal concluded that the tort issues raised by Claimant were to be governed by the proper law of the contract. [The Tribunal also emphasized that the case involved a "false conflict"]:

> The issue of which law governs, however, is probably academic. The parties have not pointed out, and I have failed to find, any indication that the law of any other jurisdiction which arguably might control the dispute ... is significantly different from the law of Washington.... Even if one were to conclude that the law where the alleged wrong occurred governed, there is something to be said for returning to Washington State law, in any event, since it was from Seattle that the termination fax was dispatched.

COMPAGNIE D'ARMEMENT MARITIME SA v. COMPAGNIE TUNISIENNE DE NAVIGATION SA

[1971] AC 572 (House of Lords)

LORD DIPLOCK. My Lords, this appeal is about a "tonnage contract" for the carriage by sea of 300,000/350,000 tons of light crude oil between two ports in Tunisia in shipments of 16,000/25,000 tons between March and December 1967.... The parties were a French company as carriers and a Tunisian company as shippers. The French company owned four tankers and through a subsidiary company controlled a fifth in 16,000/25,000 ton range. All these vessels flew the French flag. The contract was negotiated in Paris at a meeting of the presidents of the two companies arranged by French shipbrokers employed by the Tunisian company. The negotiations were conducted in the French language. The written contract was prepared by the shipbrokers. They used for this purpose a printed form of tanker voyage charterparty in the English language which is widely used for tanker fixtures on the Baltic Exchange in London and in other chartering centres abroad. They adapted it to a "tonnage contract" by adding typed clauses on an attached slip. The only attached clause which matters for the purposes of this appeal reads as follows: "28—This Charter-Party covers the transport of minimum 300,000/ Maximum 350,000 long tons of light crude oil—exact quantity at Charterers' option. Shipments to be effected in tonnage owned, controlled or chartered by the Compagnie d'Armement Maritime S.A. of 16,000/25,000 tons 10% more less at Owners' option." It was found as a fact by the arbitrators that it was contemplated at the time the contract was entered into that vessels owned by the French company would be used at least primarily to perform the contract.

The printed form of tanker voyage charter-party to which the slip was attached is intended for use for a single voyage charter in a named vessel flying a named flag and contains no provision for a substitute vessel. In it the French company were described as "Owners" and the Tunisian company as "Charterers" but the space for the name of the vessel and the nationality of the flag was not filled in. Instead there was a reference to clause 28. The other blanks in the printed form were filled in with appropriate typed words and some minor deletions and additions were made to some of the printed words themselves. Freight was payable in French francs in Paris. Clause 13 (the "proper law clause") and clause 18 (the "London arbitration clause") were left as printed [and] read:

> 13. This contract shall be governed by the laws of the Flag of the Vessel carrying the goods, except in cases of average or general average, when same to be settled according to the York-Antwerp Rules, 1950.

> 18. Any dispute arising during execution of this Charter-Party shall be settled in London, Owners and Charterers each appointing an Arbitrator—Merchant or Broker—and the two thus chosen, if they cannot agree, shall nominate an Umpire—Merchant or Broker—whose decision shall be final. Should one of the parties neglect or refuse to appoint an Arbitrator within 21 days after receipt of request from the other party, the single Arbitrator appointed shall have the right to decide alone....

The French company did not in fact use for the carriage on the first six voyages under the contract their own vessels or that of their subsidiary company, as had been contemplated at the time the contract was made. They chartered other vessels which flew a number of different flags. Only one was French. After the sixth voyage the Arab-Israeli war broke out and the French company ceased to perform the contract. This gave rise to disputes between the parties which were referred to two arbitrators in London under clause 18.

The rights of the parties in the event of repudiation of a contract are not the same under English law as they are under French [and Tunisian] law.... So a preliminary question was raised in the arbitration as to whether the substantive law applicable to the contract was English law or French law....

The very experienced commercial arbitrators appointed by each party were in agreement that the substantive law to be applied was French law.... Their award was upheld by Megaw J..... His judgment, however, was reversed by the Court of Appeal. They held unanimously that the proper law of the contract was English law....

The Court of Appeal treated the case as governed by the principle, which they had recently laid down in *Tzortzis v. Monark Line A/B* [1968] 1 WLR 406, that when a contract contains a London arbitration clause the resulting implication that the parties intended that the substantive law applicable should be English law can only be rebutted by an express provision to the contrary. They considered that clause 13 of the printed form was inapplicable to a "tonnage contract" that permitted performance by chartered vessels which might fly flags of a number of different countries. They accordingly treated clause 13 as non-existent and the contract was left with no express provision to contradict the implication resulting from the inclusion of the London arbitration clause....

I think that the Court of Appeal erred both in holding that clause 13 was to be ignored, and in the conclusive effect upon the proper law of the contract which they ascribed to the presence of clause 18, the London arbitration clause. When parties enter into an agreement which they intend to give rise to legally enforceable rights and liabilities, they must *ex necessitate* contemplate that there will be some system of law by reference to which their mutual rights and liabilities will be determined, *i.e.*, the substantive or "proper" law of their agreement; and also that the procedure by which disputes about their rights and liabilities will be resolved will also be regulated by some system of law, *i.e.*, the curial law of their agreement. By "proper law" in this context is meant the system of law which governs the interpretation and the validity of the contract and the mode of performance and the consequences of breaches of the contract. If English law is the "proper law," the contract will be interpreted, if the language so permits, as requiring the mode of performance of any part of the contract to conform with the law of the country in which that part of the performance is to take place. This does not, however, mean that the English court is applying foreign law. It is applying an English rule of construction to the interpretation of the contract.

English law accords to the parties to a contract a wide liberty to choose both the proper law and the curial law which is to be applicable to it. If the parties exercise that choice as respects either the proper law or the curial law or both, the English courts will give effect to their choice unless it would be contrary to public policy to do so. But it is a liberty to choose—not a compulsion—and if the parties do not exercise it as respects the proper law applicable to their contract the Court itself will determine what is the proper law.

The first stage, therefore, when any question arises between parties to a contract as to the proper law applicable to it, is to determine whether the parties intended by their contract to exercise any choice at all and, if they did, to determine what was the system of law which they selected. In determining this the English Court applies the ordinary rules of English law relating to the construction of contracts.

If, applying these rules, the Court reaches the conclusion that the parties did not intend to exercise any choice of proper law, or is unable to identify what their choice was, it becomes necessary for the Court to proceed to the second stage, of determining itself what is the proper law applicable. In doing so, the Court applies the English rule of the conflict of laws relating to the proper law of the contract. This is that the proper law is that system of law with which the transaction has its closest and most real connection....

Similarly with choice of curial law. This generally takes the form of a provision in the contract for submission to arbitration of disputes arising out of it.... An express choice of forum by the parties to a contract necessarily implies an intention that their disputes shall be settled in accordance with the procedural law of the selected forum and operates as if it were also an express choice of the curial law of the contract. If the parties have made no choice of forum, an English Court can only apply English procedural law in any disputes under the contract in which it is invited to adjudicate....

It is not now open to question that if parties to a commercial contract have agreed expressly upon the system of law of one country as the proper law of their contract and have selected a different curial law by providing expressly that disputes under the contract shall be submitted to arbitration in another country, the arbitrators must apply as the proper law of the contract that system of law upon which the parties have expressly agreed. But the cases which have given rise to difficulty are those where the parties have made a choice of curial law by a clause of their contract expressly agreeing to arbitration in a particular country but have made no express provision as to the proper law applicable to the contract....

Where the only express choice of law in a contract is that of curial law, resulting from the inclusion in the contract of a provision for arbitration in a particular country, an intention of the parties to exercise their right also to choose the proper law of the contract and, if so, the proper law which they have chosen, can only be deduced by implication from what they have expressly agreed and the circumstances in and in relation to which their agreement was made. The fact that they have expressly chosen to submit their disputes under the contract to a particular arbitral forum of itself gives rise to a strong inference that they intended that their mutual rights and obligations under the contract should be determined by reference to the domestic law of the country in which the arbitration takes place, since this is the law, with which arbitrators sitting there may be supposed to be most familiar. But this is an inference only. It may be destroyed by inferences to the contrary to be drawn from other express provisions of the contract or relevant surrounding circumstances, and those inferences may be so compelling as to lead to the identification of another system of law which the parties must have intended to be the proper law of the contract.

That the presence of an arbitration clause, though powerfully persuasive, was not conclusive of an intention to choose the curial law as the proper law of the contract was clearly recognised ... in *Hamlyn & Co. v. Talisker Distillery* [1894] AC 202 and was never doubted until after *Kwik Hoo Tong* [1927] AC 604.... [Nonetheless, subsequent English authority held that]: "An express choice of a tribunal is an implied choice of the proper law." [*e.g., Vita Food Products Inc. v. Unus Shipping Co. Ltd.* [1939] AC 277, 290].... Nevertheless, strong though the implication [that the choice of England as the arbitral seat is a choice of English substantive law] may be, it can be negatived by the other terms of the contract when the contract, as it must be, is construed as a whole in the light of the surrounding circumstances. It is clearly negatived by an express term prescribing some other law than the curial law as the proper law, and it may also be negatived by an overwhelming implication from the other terms all pointing to one single other system of law as the proper law of the contract as distinct from the curial law....

I turn, then, ... to determine, by applying ordinary rules of construction of contracts, whether the parties intended to exercise any choice as to the proper law as distinct from the curial law of their contract and, if so, what their choice was. Although not in all respects apt for the purposes of a "tonnage contract," they selected as appropriate to embody the terms on which they had agreed a printed form which included clauses 13 and 18 providing for one system of law to be the proper law of the contract and another system of law to be the curial law, and neither of these clauses did they strike out. Two things it seems to me are clear. First, that clause 18 was not intended to operate as a choice of the proper law of the contract but only as a choice of the curial law. Secondly, that clause 13, when the form was used for the purpose for which it was primarily designed, viz., a single voyage charter, was intended to operate as a choice for the proper law of the contract of a system of law with which the transaction would have a close and real connection, viz., the law of the flag of the carrying vessel. From this I conclude that the parties did not intend to choose as the proper law of the contract English law with which their transaction had no real connection whatever, apart from the arbitration clause itself; and also that the system of law which they did intend to choose as the proper law was one which would have a close and real connection with their transaction.

Whether they succeeded in expressing that choice in words which, when read in the light of the surrounding circumstances, are sufficiently clear to enable the Court to identify it must be decided by applying the ordinary rules of construction of commercial contracts. If they have failed, then the Court must proceed to the second stage of applying the positive rule of English law that, in the absence of choice by the parties themselves, the proper law of a contract is that system of law with which the transaction has its closest and most real connection. In determining this, the arbitration clause should be taken into consideration merely as indicating some actual connection which the transaction has with English law, and not as an exercise of a choice of English law as the proper law of the contract; for to treat it as that would be contrary to the intention of the parties....

By clause 13 when used for a single voyage charter the parties clearly intended to choose the system of law with which the contract had its connection through the nationality of the carrying vessel. Had the parties contemplated that the contract would be performed exclusively by vessels owned or controlled by the French company there could be no question but that the parties intended to choose French law as the proper law of their contract. Is the Court to treat the clause as meaningless simply because, notwithstanding that they did contemplate that vessels owned by the French company would be used primarily to perform the contract, they also contemplated that there might be exceptional occasions on which chartered vessels might be used? It does not seem to me that from the business point of view this could make any significant difference so far as choice of proper law was concerned; and I accordingly agree with Megaw J. that in its application to this tonnage contract clause 13 should be construed by analogy as if it read: "This Contract shall be governed by the laws of the Flag of the Vessels of the Owners, except." etc.

I recognise that this is a matter upon which different conclusions may be reached.... But if I am wrong, and the parties by using an inappropriate printed form have failed to make their actual choice of proper law clear, the same result is, in my view, reached by proceeding to the second stage of the inquiry and applying the positive rule of English law that, where the parties have not themselves exercised their choice, the proper law of a contract is the system of law with which it has its closest and most real connection.

As I have already said [in a portion of the opinion that is not excerpted], for the purposes of this transaction France and Tunisia may be regarded as sharing a common system of law. That was the system of law of the place where each party resided, of the place where the contract was negotiated and made, of the ports of shipment and of discharge, of the place of payment and was the law of the flag of the vessels which the parties contemplated would be used at least primarily for the carriage. The only connection of the transaction with English law was provided by an arbitration clause which was intended to operate only as a choice of curial law. Clearly French law was the system of law with which the contract had its closest and most real connection.

My Lords, in the instant case any implication that the arbitration clause was intended to operate as a choice of proper law as distinct from curial law was negatived by the retention in the contract of clause 13. I do not wish to throw any doubt upon the proposition that an arbitration clause is generally intended by the parties to operate as a choice of the proper law of the contract as well as the curial law and should be so construed unless there are compelling indications to the contrary in the other terms of the contract or the surrounding circumstances of the transaction. The mere fact that there are other systems of law with which the transaction has a closer connection is not sufficient to rebut the implication. In international transactions, particularly on commodity markets where the same shipment of goods may be bought and sold many times before delivery of the actual goods to the last buyer, it is of great commercial convenience that all the contracts relating to such sales should be subject to the same proper law irrespective of the place of shipment or discharge, the residence or nationality of the parties, or the place where the contract was made. This is the basis on which commodity markets operate and the choice of arbitral forum is understood as being intended as a choice of proper law. But strong as the implication may be, it can be rebutted as other implications of intention can be rebutted. It is not a positive rule of law which is independent of the intentions of the parties. In the instant case I am satisfied that it has been rebutted, and I would allow the appeal.

STATE OF KUWAIT v. AMERICAN INDEPENDENT OIL CO.
Ad Hoc Award of 24 March 1982, 21 I.L.M. 976 (1982)

[The Government of the State of Kuwait ("Government") and the American Independent Oil Company ("Aminoil") entered into a long-term concession agreement for the production of oil in parts of Kuwait. In 1977, the Government nationalized Aminoil's assets. The Government and Aminoil subsequently agreed to arbitrate disputes arising from the nationalization. The arbitral tribunal considered the law applicable to the parties' dispute as a preliminary issue.] ...

The Parties have approached the question of "the applicable law" by distinguishing the procedural law of the arbitration—or law governing the arbitration as a whole—and the law governing the substantive issues in the case. On these topics they have furnished rival analyses and concepts which, on the scientific and academic levels, possess very great interest; but the Tribunal, in carrying out the function entrusted to it, has not experienced any difficulty as to the determination of the applicable law. The essential reason for this is twofold: the Parties themselves by their mutual arbitral commitments, have defined with adequate clarity what the applicable law is; and the legal systems that either do, or may, call for consideration in this connection have characteristics such that, for this case, the solution of the problem becomes easy.

With regard to the law governing the arbitral procedure in the broadest sense, it is not open to doubt that the Parties have chosen the French legal system for everything that is implied in the statement in Article IV.1 of the Arbitration Agreement to the effect that the proceedings are subject to "any mandatory provisions of the procedural law of the place where the arbitration is held" (namely Paris); and both Parties "expressly waive all rights to recourse to any Court, except such rights as cannot be waived by the law of the place of arbitration" (Article V).

But this does not in the least entail of itself a general submission to the law of the tribunal's seat which was designated as Paris. In actual fact the Parties themselves, in the Arbitration Agreement, provided the means of settling the essential procedural rules, when they conferred on the Tribunal the power to "prescribe the procedure applicable to the arbitration on the basis of natural justice and of such principles of transnational arbitration procedure as it may find applicable" (Article IV.1), which was done by the Rules adopted on 16 July, 1980. Having regard to the way in which the Tribunal has been constituted, its international or rather, transnational character is apparent. It must also be stressed that French law has always been very liberal concerning the procedural law of arbitral tribunals, and has left this to the free choice of the Parties who, often, have not had recourse to any one given national systems. French law has thus befriended arbitrations the transnational character of which has been well in evidence....

Respecting the law applicable to the substantive issues in the dispute ... the question is equally simple in the present case. It can hardly be contested but that the law of Kuwait applies to many matters over which it is the law most directly involved. But this conclusion, based on good sense as well as law, does not carry any all-embracing consequences with it,—and this for two reasons. The first is that Kuwait law is a highly evolved system as to which the Government has been at pains to stress that "established public international law is necessarily a part of the law of Kuwait." In their turn the general principles of law are part of public international law—(Article 38.1(c) of the Statute of the [ICJ]),—and that this specifically applies to Kuwait oil concessions, duly results from the clauses included in these. For instance, in the 1973 Agreement between the Parties, First Annex, Second Part, XII the following provision is to be found:

> "The parties base their relations with regard to the agreements between them on the principle of goodwill and good faith. Taking account of the different nationalities of the parties, the agreements between them shall be given effect, and must be interpreted and applied, in conformity with principles common to the laws of Kuwait and of the State of New York, United States of America, and in the absence of such common principles, then in conformity with the principles of law normally recognized by civilized states in general, including those which have been applied by international tribunals."

Although the Parties did not, in the course of the present arbitral proceedings, make any reference to this particular text, it is of all the more interest to note that the ideas it embodies are so isolated features of Kuwait practice.

Equally, the Offshore Concession Agreement of the Arabian Oil Company, contains the same provision, except that reference is made to the principles common to Kuwait and to Japanese law (Article 39). The Oil Concession Agreement with the Kuwait National Petroleum Company and Hispanica de Petroleos, concluded in 1967, refers to the principles common to Kuwait and to Spanish law. Yet it would be quite unrealistic to suppose that these three Concessions were governed by three different régimes. Clearly, it must have been the general principles of law that were chiefly present to the minds of the Government of Kuwait and its associates.

But there is a second consideration which has greatly eased the task of the Tribunal, namely that the Parties have themselves, in effect, indicated in the Arbitration Agreement what the applicable law is. Article III.2 of the Agreement provides that: "The law governing the substantive issues between the Parties shall be determined by the Tribunal, having regard to the quality of the Parties, the transnational character of their relations and the principles of law and practice prevailing in the modern world."

Although it may in theory be possible for a litigation to be governed by an assemblage of rules different from that which, before the Arbitration, governed the situations and matters that are the object of the litigation, there must be a presumption that this is not the case. Thus, to the extent that Article III.2 of the Arbitration Agreement calls for interpretation, such an interpretation ought to be based on that provision which not only was freely chosen by the Parties in 1973, but also reflects the spirit which has underlain the carrying on of the oil concessions in Kuwait. Article III.2, with good reason, makes it clear that Kuwait is a sovereign State entrusted with the interests of a national community, the law of which constitutes an essential part of intra-community relations within the State. At the same time, by referring to the transnational character of relations with the concessionaire, and to the general principles of law, this Article brings out the wealth and fertility of the set of legal rules that the Tribunal is called upon to apply.

The different sources of the law thus to be applied are not—at least in the present case—in contradiction with one another. Indeed, if, as recalled above, international law constitutes an integral part of the law of Kuwait, the general principles of law correspondingly recognize the rights of the State in its capacity of supreme protector of the general interest. If the different legal elements involved do not always and everywhere blend as successfully as in the present case, it is nevertheless on taking advantage of their resources, and encouraging their trend towards unification, that the future of a truly international economic order in the investment field will depend....

NOTES

1. *Law governing interpretation of choice-of-law clause in international arbitration.* What law governs the interpretation of a choice-of-law agreement in an international arbitration? In national court litigation, what law governs the interpretation of a choice-of-law agreement? Consider the analysis in *Compagnie d'Armement*. What law did the English court apply to interpret the parties' (alleged) choice-of-law agreement? Should an arbitral tribunal simply apply the conflicts rules of the arbitral seat in the same way that a national court applies its own conflicts rules, to interpret a putative choice-of-law clause? Why not?

   What conflicts rules should a tribunal apply to interpret a choice-of-law clause? The law of the arbitral seat? The law putatively chosen by the choice-of-law clause? Is there any reason that a different law should apply to interpretation of a choice-of-law clause than to the validity of such a clause?

2. *What conflict of laws question does a choice-of-law agreement answer?* As discussed elsewhere, and illustrated by the decision in *Compagnie d'Armement*, parties are free to choose the law governing their underlying contract, *supra* pp. 983-90, their arbitration agreement, *supra* pp. 301-02, and the arbitral proceedings, *supra* pp. 633-38. Assuming the parties have validly concluded a choice-of-law clause, what conflict of laws question(s) does that clause address?

   Is determining the issues addressed by a choice-of-law clause not essentially a question of interpreting the choice-of-law clause to determine what the parties intended? Does this not principally require considering the language that the parties used? As *ICC Case No. 5505* demonstrates, it can, at least theoretically, be unclear from the text of a choice-of-law provision whether it was meant to select (a) the substantive law governing the underlying contract, (b) the substantive law governing the arbitration agreement, (c) the procedural law of the arbitration, or (d) the conflict of laws rules to be applied by the tribunal. (These legal regimes are discussed above. *See supra* pp. 90-93, 287-315, 625-40.)

3. *Choice-of-law clause does not ordinarily refer to procedural law.* Should a choice-of-law clause be interpreted as selecting the procedural law of the arbitration? Would it be unusual for the parties to select the law governing the arbitral proceedings? To do so in addition to selecting the arbitral seat? What purposes would be served by selecting the procedural law of the arbitration?

   The arbitrator in *ICC Case No. 5505* concludes that, when parties choose a law, they usually mean to choose the substantive law governing their dispute. Is that conclusion sound? Why or why not? Note the observation in *ICC Case No. 5505* that "such a choice [of a foreign procedural law] could bring with it numerous difficulties." What difficulties does the tribunal have in mind? Would it be appropriate to conclude that there is a presumption that a choice-of-law clause is intended to address the substantive law governing the parties' contract? *See also supra* pp. 636-37, 1107-08.

   Recall the discussion in the context of interpreting the scope of arbitration clauses of the problems with fine linguistic analysis of different formulations (*e.g.*, "arising under" versus "relating to"). *See supra* pp. 526-30. Does the same rationale argue for not attempting to draw fine lines between different formulations of choice-of-law clauses and instead presuming that such provisions address the substantive law applicable to the parties' underlying contract?

4. *Choice-of-law clause does not ordinarily refer to law governing arbitration agreement.* Would it be unusual for parties to select the law governing their arbitration agreement? To do so without selecting the law governing their underlying contract? Arbitral awards (and national court decisions) virtually never conclude that the parties' choice-of-law clause was intended only to select the law governing the arbitration agreement. *See supra* pp. 303-05; G. Born, *International Commercial Arbitration* 580-83 (2d ed. 2014). Is that result appropriate?

5. *Choice-of-law clause does not ordinarily refer to conflict of laws rules.* As *ICC Case No. 5505* indicates, it is theoretically possible that the parties would agree to choose a conflict of laws system, rather than a body of substantive law. Why might commercial parties wish to do so? Why might they not wish to do so? What answers would such a choice of law provide? Arbitral awards (and national court decisions) virtually never conclude that the parties' choice-of-law clause was intended to select a conflict of laws system. *See* G. Born, *International Commercial Arbitration* 2736 (2d ed. 2014). Is that result appropriate?

6. *Choice-of-law clause does not ordinarily include conflict of laws rules of designated legal system.* Does a choice-of-law clause selecting the law of State A refer merely to the substantive law of State A, or also to the choice-of-law rules of State A? If the latter, then choice-of-law clauses would lead parties to a renewed conflict of laws debate. How does the tribunal in the *ICC Case No. 5505* resolve this issue?

    In general, most authorities interpret choice-of-law clauses as not referring to the conflicts rules of the designated legal system. For example, Article 28(1) of the UNCITRAL Model Law provides that "[a]ny designation of the law or legal system of a given State shall be construed, unless otherwise expressed, as directly referring to the substantive law of that State *and not to its conflict of laws rules*." *See also* Rome I Regulation, Art. 20 ("The application of the law of any country specified by this Regulation means the application of the rules of law in force in that country other than its rules of private international law, unless provided otherwise in this Regulation."); *Restatement (Second) Conflict of Laws* §186 comment b (1971) ("... the reference, in the absence of a contrary indication of intention (*see* §187 comment b), is to the 'local law' of the state of the applicable law and not to that state's 'law' which means the totality of its law including its choice-of-law rules ..."). Is this the only plausible approach to the issue? Make the best counter-argument that you can.

7. *Scope of choice-of-law clauses.* Parties not infrequently dispute the scope of particular choice-of-law provisions. Specifically, it is often argued that a contractually-chosen law applies only to issues or claims based directly on the parties' contract, and not to "extra-contractual" issues (like tort claims, unfair competition claims, and related statutory claims) or to "procedural" issues. Compare the discussion above concerning the scope of arbitration clauses and their application to extra-contractual claims, *supra* pp. 530-32.

8. *Hypotheticals relating to scope of choice-of-law clauses.* Suppose A and B enter into a distribution agreement providing that B will distribute A's products in State Y. In due course, A claims that B failed to fulfill its obligations to act as a loyal and competent distributor. A asserts claims against B based on: (a) breach of contract; (b) breach of common law fiduciary and agency principles under the law of State Y, based on the parties' contractual relation, but imposed by common law tort and agency law; (c)

violation of a statutory protection provided by the law of State Y against unfair competition. B defends on the grounds that the law of State X governs the dispute. The case also raises questions regarding: (d) the applicable statute of limitations; and (e) the burden of proof. What results under the following choice-of-law clauses?

"This agreement shall be construed according to the laws of State X."

"This agreement shall be governed by the laws of State X."

"This agreement shall be deemed to have been made and performed in State X and all disputes arising under this agreement shall be governed by the laws of State X (excluding the conflict of laws rules of State X)."

"All disputes arising out of or relating to this agreement (including its formation, performance, breach and termination) shall be governed exclusively by the laws of State X."

To what extent should resolution of these hypotheticals depend on the precise language of the parties' choice-of-law clause? Recall the interpretation of the scope of arbitration agreements. *See supra* pp. 526-30. Should the same presumption, that the parties intend their dispute resolution provision to extend broadly to all their disputes, also apply to choice-of-law agreements? Why or why not? How are arbitration (or forum selection) clauses different from choice-of-law clauses? Does this affect analysis?

Consider the excerpt from the *ICC Case No. 6618*. The tribunal does not supply the parties' choice-of-law clause. Assuming it read "this contract shall be governed by Washington law," does this clause reach a claim for tortious interference with contractual relations? What is the parties' likely intent?

9. *Scope of choice-of-law clause versus scope of arbitration clause.* In practice, choice-of-law clauses are often drafted in narrower terms than forum selection or arbitration agreements. As discussed above, arbitration clauses often extend to all disputes "relating to" or "arising in connection with" the parties' contract. *See supra* pp. 529-30. By their terms, these formulations usually reach extra-contractual claims, such as those sounding in tort, as well as contractual ones. In contrast, as the hypotheticals provided above illustrate, choice-of-law clauses are often drafted less expansively, providing only that the underlying contract shall be "governed by," or, more narrowly, "construed under," a specified law.

To what extent, if any, should the language of the parties' arbitration clause be relevant to interpreting their choice-of-law clause? If the former is broader, does that argue for interpreting the choice-of-law clause more broadly (to match the scope of the arbitration agreement), or more narrowly (since the parties chose different formulations for the two provisions)?

Some choice-of-law clauses are drafted broadly, attempting to include non-contractual claims (as well as contractual ones): "all disputes arising out of or relating to this agreement shall be governed exclusively by the laws of State D." Does this really mean that all tort and statutory breach claims are to be governed by the law governing the parties' contract?

10. *Choice-of-law clause generally limited to matters of "substance," not "procedure."* Assuming a choice-of-law clause is interpreted to apply to the substantive law governing the parties' contract (and, perhaps, related extra-contractual matters), what

matters does this concretely include? Some national courts have held that a "contractual" choice-of-law provision is ordinarily "deemed to import only substantive law, ... not procedural law." *Woodling v. Garrett Corp.*, 813 F.2d 543, 551 (2d Cir. 1987). *See also S.C. Ins. Co. v. Assurantie NV* [1987] AC 24 (House of Lords).

For example, most choice-of-law clauses have not been regarded as extending to burdens of proof, pleading requirements, discovery mechanisms, or joinder of parties. *See, e.g., Woodling v. Garrett Corp.*, 813 F.2d 543, 552 (2d Cir. 1987) (burden of proof not within scope of choice-of-law clause); *Gambar Enter., Inc. v. Kelly Ser., Inc.*, 418 N.Y.S.2d 818, 822 (N.Y. App. Div. 1979) (pleading requirements not within choice-of-law clause). *Compare Judgment of 8 November 1951*, 1952 NJW 142, 143 (German Bundesgerichtshof) (law applicable to the merits determines burden of proof). Other questions, such as statutes of limitations, rights to legal expenses and entitlement to interest raise more difficult issues; they are sometimes regarded as substantive (and thus subject to commonly-used choice-of-law provisions) and sometimes treated as procedural (and thus arguably subject to the forum's rules). *See* G. Born, *International Commercial Arbitration* 2737-38 (2d ed. 2014).

11. *Exclusivity of choice-of-law clause.* Suppose the choice-of-law clause provides, as commonly occurs, that disputes "shall be governed by the law of State X." Does this choice-of-law provision exclude claims based on some other state's laws? That is, if the parties agree that Swiss law governs their relations, do they thereby intend to *forbid* a U.S. tort, German securities, or EU competition law claim from being asserted? Would the result be any different if the parties' choice-of-law clause provided that all disputes "arising out of or in connection with the Agreement shall be governed *exclusively* by the law of State X"? Is analysis affected if some other state recognizes claims that are not recognized by the law of State X?

For example, suppose a U.S. and an English company enter into an agreement, to be performed largely in the United States, providing that all disputes shall be resolved under English law. Suppose various U.S. state and federal laws provide for claims that either do not exist under English law or are different under English law (*e.g.*, federal and state statutory securities claims and state common law fraud claims). What is the effect of the parties' choice-of-law clause selecting a non-U.S. law if one party attempts to bring claims in an arbitration based on the application of mandatory U.S. law to conduct occurring in the United States? For one judicial treatment of this issue, see *Roby v. Corp. of Lloyd's*, 996 F.2d 1353 (2d Cir. 1993), *supra* pp. 502-06.

The foregoing hypothetical raises, in the first instance, issues of interpretation: does the choice-of-law clause extend to the claims/disputes in question? If so, was the parties' choice of law meant to be exclusive (*i.e.*, that only claims under the parties' chosen law could be asserted)? These questions require interpretation of the particular language of the parties' choice-of-law provision. But, assuming that no clear answer is apparent from the provision's specific wording, are there any more general expectations or interests that might give rise to presumptions regarding the parties' intent? Would parties generally want to exclude claims recognized under the law of the place where the conduct occurred? Would they generally want a single law to apply to all their disputes?

12. *Implied choice-of-law agreements.* As with other types of agreements, a choice-of-law agreement may be implied, as well as express. Consider Article 3(1) of the Rome I

Regulation. What does it provide regarding the possibility of implied choice-of-law agreements?

Other authorities are similar. *See Restatement (Second) Conflict of Laws* §187 comment a (1971) ("[E]ven when the contract does not refer to any state, the forum may nevertheless be able to conclude from its provisions that the parties did wish to have the law of a particular state applied. So the fact that the contract contains legal expressions, or makes reference to legal doctrines, that are peculiar to the local law of a particular state may provide persuasive evidence that the parties wished to have this law applied."). Compare Hague Convention of 15 June 1955 on the Law Applicable to International Sales of Goods, Art. 2(2) ("unambiguously result from the provision of the contract").

Is there any reason to think that implied choice-of-law agreements should either not be permitted or should be found only in rare cases? What is meant by the concept that the parties "impliedly" choose the legal system governing their contract? What are examples of where this might occur?

13. *Standard of proof for implied choice-of-law agreement.* What standard of proof should be required to establish the existence of an implied choice-of-law agreement? Consider Article 3(1) of the Rome I Regulation and Article 2(2) of the Hague Convention on the Law Applicable to International Sales of Goods. Do they require a particular degree of clarity for an implied choice-of-law agreement? Is this appropriate? Why or why not?

14. *Choice of arbitral seat as implied choice-of-law agreement.* Suppose the parties' arbitration clause specifies State A as the arbitral seat and there is no choice-of-law clause. Does selection of the arbitral seat constitute an implied choice of the substantive law governing the parties' contract?

Consider *Compagnie d'Armement.* Is its analysis persuasive? Does the court hold that the choice of an arbitral seat always includes an implied choice of substantive law? Or only sometimes? If only sometimes, what is necessary for the choice of the seat to also constitute an implied choice of substantive law? What if the seat is the center for a particular type of commercial activity (*e.g.*, New York or London for insurance matters; Hamburg for maritime matters)? Does that make it likely that the substantive law of that place was impliedly chosen by the parties?

In what circumstances, under *Compagnie d'Armement*, will the choice of England as the arbitral seat not constitute an implied choice of English substantive law? Note that the parties' contract in *Compagnie d'Armement* included a specific choice-of-law provision selecting the substantive law governing the parties' contract (which was not English law). Was this not fairly substantial evidence of the parties' implied (or, very arguably, express) intentions regarding the choice of substantive law? Note the court's observation, in the final paragraph of its opinion, that the choice of England as the arbitral seat continues presumptively to constitute an implied choice of the substantive law governing the parties' contract. What does it take to overcome this presumption?

Compare *Compagnie d'Armement* with standards for implied choice-of-law agreements in Article 3(1) of the Rome I Regulation and Article 2(2) of the Hague Convention on the Law Applicable to International Sales of Goods. Would the same results be reached, with regard to the implied choice of the substantive law of the arbitral seat, under these instruments as under English law?

15. *Choice of non-national legal system.* Suppose a choice-of-law clause selects the law of a non-national legal system—that is, rather than choosing the law of State A (*e.g.*, Singapore or New York), the clause selects "general principles of law," the UNIDROIT Principles of Contract Law, "principles common to the laws of states A and B," or "*lex mercatoria.*" Is such a choice of substantive law valid?

Some authorities take the view that a choice-of-law agreement can only validly select a *national* legal system to provide the "law" governing a contract. In the words of one critic: "It is difficult to imagine a more dangerous, more undesirable and more ill-founded view which denies any measure of predictability and certainty and confers upon parties to an international commercial contract or their arbitrators powers that no system of law permits and no court could exercise." Mann, *England Rejects "Delocalised" Contracts and Arbitration*, 33 Int'l & Comp. L.Q. 193, 197 (1984).

In contrast, consider Article 28(1) of the UNCITRAL Model Law, excerpted at p. 92 of the Documentary Supplement. Compare its terms with Article 28(2), which provides that, in the absence of agreement by the parties, the tribunal shall "apply the law determined by the conflict of laws rules which it considers applicable." The latter formulation refers to "the law," selected by "conflict of laws rules," in contrast to the "rules of law" permitted by Article 28(1). As discussed above, the reference to "*rules of law,*" rather than merely "*law,*" has been interpreted as permitting parties validly to select non-national legal systems (such as *lex mercatoria* or the UNIDROIT Principles) in their choice-of-law agreements. *See supra* pp. 977-78. Should parties' agreements on a non-national legal system to govern their contract be upheld? What exactly is a non-national legal system? Can it constitute law?

16. *Choice of "international" or "general" principles of law in investment arbitration.* Private parties frequently enter into investment contracts with sovereign states. The most significant categories include concession agreements (where a private firm develops and exploits natural resources) and construction contracts for an infrastructure project. Private parties are often reluctant to submit to the laws of a host state where major investments within that state are concerned. In those circumstances, the host state's laws can become potential sources of unilateral advantage, rather than a neutral legal framework. As a consequence, private parties often negotiate choice-of-law agreements selecting the law of a neutral state, which the host state cannot unilaterally alter to suit its commercial purposes. *See* G. Born, *International Commercial Arbitration* 2767 (2d ed. 2014). Conversely, many nations (both developed and developing) prefer not to submit themselves to foreign law. That is true both for commercial reasons and for reasons of ideology or nationalism. As a result, contracts between private investors and foreign sovereigns sometimes contain choice-of-law provisions that select either "international law," "general principles of law," or some combination of local national law and international law.

Consider how the arbitral tribunal in *Kuwait v. Aminoil* interprets the parties' choice-of-law clause. *See also Libyan Am. Oil Co. v. Libyan Arab Repub., Ad Hoc Award of 12 April 1977*, VI Y.B. Comm. Arb. 89 (1981); *BP Co. Ltd v. Libyan Arab Repub., Award on Merits in Ad Hoc Case of 10 October 1973*, V Y.B. Comm. Arb. 143 (1980); *Texas Overseas Petroleum Co. v. Libyan Arab Repub., Ad Hoc Award of 19 January 1977*, 17 I.L.M. 1 (1978). What are the legal consequences of the tribunal's interpretation? Suppose the parties had simply agreed that the law of Kuwait governed their contractual relations. Would that have had different consequences from a choice of "international" law? What if Kuwait enacted expropriatory legislation or took arbitrary state actions?

Suppose two private commercial parties conclude a contract. Would it be advisable for them to agree that the contract shall be governed by "general principles of law"? Why or why not? What security and certainty would such a formulation provide? How might the relationship between a foreign investor and a host state differ from that between two private commercial parties?

Consider again Article 42 of the ICSID Convention, excerpted at p. 22 of the Documentary Supplement. Note the choice-of-law provision formulated there. How does that formulation compare with those in the choice-of-law agreements in *Kuwait v. Aminoil*?

17. *Lex mercatoria.* The tribunal in *ICC Case No. 4237* considers (but rejects) the possibility of applying *lex mercatoria*, or "merchants' law," to resolve the parties' dispute.

(a) *Definitions of lex mercatoria. Lex mercatoria* is defined in a variety of ways. Most ambitiously, it is a category of international law, separate from any national legal order, derived from and applicable to international commercial dealings. Less sweeping definitions characterize *lex mercatoria* as a body of substantive rules concerning international trade, derived principally from arbitral awards and international conventions. *See* G. Born, *International Commercial Arbitration* 2759-65 (2d ed. 2014); B. Goldman, *The Applicable Law: General Principles of Law—The Lex Mercatoria*, in *Contemporary Problems in International Arbitration* 113 (J. Lew ed. 1986); Mustill, *The New Lex Mercatoria*, 4 Arb. Int'l 86 (1988).

There is substantial debate about the content of any body of "law" termed *lex mercatoria*. Consider:

> "The proponents of the *lex mercatoria* claim it to be the law of the international business community: which must mean the law unanimously adopted by all countries engaged upon international commerce. Such a claim would have been sustainable two centuries ago. But the international business community is now immeasurably enlarged. What principles of trade law, apart from those which are so general as to be useless, are common to the legal systems of the members of such a community? How could the arbitrators … amass the necessary materials on the laws of, say, Brazil, China, the Soviet Union, Australia, Nigeria, and Iraq?" Mustill, *The New Lex Mercatoria*, 4 Int'l Arb. 86, 89, 92-93 (1988).

Can *lex mercatoria* not develop in particular regions or industries, even if a universal *lex mercatoria* has not developed? In a dispute between U.S. and European companies, who cares what Nigerian or Iraqi law says?

The development of *lex mercatoria* is often said to have been fueled by the desire of international businesses to avoid unpredictable quirks of local law, as well as the uncertainties of choice-of-law analysis. "Application of ideosyncratic [sic] provisions of foreign law, or of foreign law provisions addressed to purely domestic conditions, does not serve the purposes of international business." Smit, *Substance and Procedure in International Arbitration: The Development of A New Legal Order*, 65 Tulane L. Rev. 1309, 1312 (1991). Despite (or, perhaps, because of) this, businesses in practice virtually never agree to choice-of-law provisions selecting *lex mercatoria*. Why is that? In a commercial transaction between two private parties, would it be sensible to provide for the parties' agreement to be governed by *lex mercatoria*? Why or why not? What about an investment agreement between a foreign investor and a host state or host state entity?

(b) *Enforceability of arbitral awards based on lex mercatoria*. There is controversy as to the enforceability of such awards based on *lex mercatoria* in some jurisdictions. In England, for example, the traditional view was apparently that awards based on *lex mercatoria* were unenforceable. Mustill, *Contemporary Problems in International Commercial Arbitration: A Response*, 17 Int'l Bus. Law. 161, 161-62 (1989). More recently, however, judicial decisions have strongly suggested that most courts would enforce foreign arbitral awards based on *lex mercatoria*. *Deutsche Schachtbau- und Tiefbohrgesellschaft mbH v. Ras Al Khaimah Nat'l Oil Co.* [1987] 2 Lloyd's Rep. 246 (giving effect to award based on "internationally accepted principles of law governing contractual relations"); *Ministry of Defense v. Gould, Inc.*, 887 F.2d 1357 (9th Cir. 1989).

What would be the argument under the New York Convention for denying recognition to an award based on *lex mercatoria*? For annulling the award under Article 34 of the UNCITRAL Model Law? Suppose the parties' choice-of-law agreement selected *lex mercatoria*? Would analysis be different if it did not?

18. *Split choice-of-law clauses*. Some choice-of-law agreements attempt to specify different substantive national laws for different aspects of the parties' contract or contractual relationship. (This process is sometimes referred to as "*dépeçage*.") One national law may be applied to payment obligations, or to intellectual property rights, while another national law applies to other matters. Consider, for example, the choice-of-law clause in the *Channel Tunnel* decision, *supra* pp. 926-27. *See also* G. Born, *International Commercial Arbitration* 2751 (2d ed. 2014). Is there any reason to doubt the validity of split choice-of-law clauses? The wisdom of such provisions? What difficulties could they produce?

19. *Floating choice-of-law clause*. Parties sometimes draft choice-of-law agreements to provide a "floating" choice of law, which may vary in accordance with future developments. In particular, choice-of-law clauses sometimes provide that, in a claim brought by Party A, the arbitration will be seated in the home state of Party B, and the parties' dispute will be governed by the laws of Party B's home jurisdiction. The notion underlying these provisions is one of "rough justice," that also seeks to discourage the bringing of claims. Is this a sensible approach? Recall the arbitration clauses that provided that the arbitral seat was in the jurisdiction of the respondent (whichever party that might be). *See supra* pp. 288-90. Is that more or less sensible than use of the same approach in the choice-of-law context?

20. *Amiable compositeur/ex aequo et bono*. Some arbitration agreements provide for arbitration "*ex aequo et bono*" or for an arbitrator to act as "*amiable compositeur*." The essential principle of each term is that arbitrators are not obliged ultimately to decide the parties' dispute in accordance with a strict application of legal rules; rather, the arbitrators are expected to decide in light of general notions of fairness, equity, and justice. Rubino-Sammartano, *Amicable Compositeur (Joint Mandate to Settle) and Ex Bono et Aequo (Discretional Authority to Mitigate Strict Law)*, 9 J. Int. Arb. 5 (1992); Kerr, *Equity Arbitration in England*, 2 Am. Rev. Int'l Arb. 377 (1993).

Are agreements providing for arbitration *ex aequo et bono* valid? Consider Article VII(2) of the European Convention, excerpted at p. 32 of the Documentary Supplement. Note that the Convention leaves to national law the validity of agreements empowering the arbitrator to act as *amiable compositeur*. Consider also UNCITRAL Model Law, Art. 28(3). *Compare* SLPIL, Art. 187(2) ("The parties may authorize the arbitral tribunal to decide *ex aequo et bono*."); French Code of Civil Procedure, Art. 1512 ("The arbitral tribunal shall rule as *amiable compositeur* if the parties have conferred this mission upon it").

Similarly, most institutional rules authorize arbitrators to decide *ex aequo et bono*, but only if the parties specifically agree to such provisions. See Article 35(2) of the UNCITRAL Rules and Article 21(3) of the ICC Rules, excerpted at pp. 174 & 190 of the Documentary Supplement. Is it appropriate to require heightened clarity in order to permit arbitration *ex aequo et bono*? Why or why not? Is it advisable for private commercial parties to agree to arbitration *ex aequo et bono*? Why or why not? Suppose the parties' agreement contains no choice-of-law provision. Does that indicate they are willing to have their dispute decided *ex aequo et bono*?

Historically, arbitration in the United States and some other jurisdictions bore many resemblances to arbitration *ex aequo et bono* or *amiable composition*. Arbitrators were neither required to give reasoned awards nor to apply statutory protections, and their decisions were not reviewable for errors of law (or fact). See the excerpt of Joseph Story's description of arbitration, *supra* p. 24. Why might parties desire such a form of dispute resolution? If the arbitrators are free to make a decision based on general equitable notions, is there as much need for detailed legal and evidentiary submissions? Is it also possible for the dispute resolution mechanism to proceed rapidly and, therefore, cheaply?

The ICSID Convention is more flexible, providing in Article 42(3) that the tribunal's obligation to apply the law selected by that parties "shall not prejudice the power of the Tribunal to decide a dispute *ex aequo et bono* if the parties so agree." Is there any reason to conclude that arbitration *ex aequo et bono* should be regarded differently in commercial and investment arbitrations? What about inter-state arbitrations?

21. *Judicial review of arbitrators' choice of substantive law revisited.* Recall the discussion above of the deference accorded to choice-of-law decisions by arbitral tribunals, *supra* p. 982. Consider the approach in *Compagnie d'Armement*; does the English court accord any deference to the arbitrators' interpretation of the parties' choice-of-law agreement? The reason for this lay in the approach, under then-applicable English arbitration legislation, to review of arbitral awards made in England. Under English law and practice at the time, *de novo* judicial review of questions of English law was available through a "case stated" procedure; unless parties contractually excluded it, English courts would (as in *Compagnie d'Armement*) review the arbitrators' substantive decisions *de novo*. As discussed below, this approach has been altered under the English Arbitration Act, 1996, which provides only for much more limited judicial review. *See infra* p. 1168.

CHAPTER 13

LEGAL REPRESENTATION AND PROFESSIONAL RESPONSIBILITY IN INTERNATIONAL ARBITRATION

The topic of representation in international arbitral proceedings gives rise to important practical and theoretical issues.[1] First, to what extent may—and do—individual states impose restrictions on the identities of the representatives who appear in international arbitral proceedings conducted within national territory? Second, what ethical limitations, or other constraints imposed by rules of professional responsibility, apply to representatives in international arbitrations? This chapter examines both topics.

A. RIGHT TO SELECT COUNSEL IN INTERNATIONAL ARBITRATION

An important practical and theoretical question is the parties' right to counsel, of their choosing, in international arbitral proceedings. As discussed below, many institutional arbitration rules provide that parties may be represented in arbitral proceedings, either expressly or impliedly guaranteeing the parties' freedom to be represented by persons of their choice.[2] Similarly, in many developed jurisdictions, national law imposes no (or virtually no) limitations on the identities of persons that may serve as a party's representative in international arbitrations. That is generally true in the United States, as well as most European, Asian and many Middle Eastern jurisdictions.[3] In some international instruments (*e.g.*, the Inter-American Convention and IACAC Rules, the 1907 Hague Convention), the parties' right to counsel of their choice is also guaranteed.[4]

Nonetheless, a few countries impose (or have imposed) limitations on the identities of legal representatives permitted to appear in arbitrations (including international arbitrations) conducted within national territory. Most frequently, these limitations take the form of rules against the "unauthorized practice of law," which are interpreted to require that legal representatives in an international arbitration be admitted to the local bar in the arbitral seat.

---

1. *See* G. Born, *International Commercial Arbitration* 2832-893 (2d ed. 2014); Menkel-Meadow, *Ethics Issues in Arbitration and Related Dispute Resolution Processes: What's Happening and What's Not*, 56 U. Miami L. Rev. 949 (2002); C. Rogers, *Ethics in International Arbitration* 99-138 (2014); Rogers, *Context and Institutional Structure in Attorney Regulation: Constructing An Enforcement Regime for International Arbitration*, 39 Stan. J. Int'l L. 1 (2003).

2. 2010 UNCITRAL Rules, Art. 5; 2012 ICC Rules, Art. 26(4); 2014 LCIA Rules, Art. 18.

3. In a few countries, the freedom of parties to select their legal representatives in international arbitration is expressly confirmed by statute. English Arbitration Act, 1996, §36; German ZPO, §1042; Hong Kong Arbitration Ordinance, 2013, §63; Australian International Arbitration Act, §29(2).

4. Inter-American Convention, Art. 3; IACAC Rules, Art. 4; 1907 Hague Convention, Arts. 62, 70, 71.

MICHIGAN COMPILED LAWS
§600.916(1)

A person shall not practice law or engage in the law business, shall not in any manner whatsoever lead others to believe that he or she is authorized to practice law or to engage in the law business, and shall not in any manner whatsoever represent or designate himself or herself as an attorney and counselor, attorney at law, or lawyer, unless the person is regularly licensed and authorized to practice law in this state. A person who violates this section is guilty of contempt of the [court] in which the violation occurred, and upon conviction is punishable as provided by law. This section does not apply to a person who is duly licensed and authorized to practice law in another state while temporarily in this state and engaged in a particular matter.

WILLIAMSON v. JOHN D. QUINN CONSTRUCTION CO.
537 F.Supp. 613 (S.D.N.Y. 1982)

EDWARD WEINFELD, District Judge. [The John D. Quinn Construction Company (Quinn) was involved in a construction-related arbitration with another company. Initially, a New York law firm represented Quinn. During the arbitration, Quinn allegedly authorized the New York law firm to retain Williamson PA, a two-member New Jersey law firm with expertise in construction litigation, to assist in the representation. According to the terms of the retention agreement, David Williamson, a partner admitted in both New York and New Jersey, would supervise all activities and strategy; Michael Rehill, an associate admitted only in New Jersey, would be responsible for day-to-day services. Following completion of the arbitration, Quinn refused to pay Williamson PA and argued, among other things, that neither Williamson PA nor Mr. Rehill was authorized to practice in New York.]

There remains Quinn's claim that Williamson PA is foreclosed from recovery of any fees because Michael Rehill, who performed the bulk of the services, was not admitted to practice in this State and Williamson PA likewise is not authorized to practice in this State. Plaintiff's services were rendered solely in the arbitration proceeding. An arbitration tribunal is not a court of record; its rules of evidence and procedures differ from those of courts of record; its fact finding process is not equivalent to judicial fact finding; it has no provision for the admission pro hac vice of local or out-of-state attorneys. In *Spanos v. Skouras Theatres Corp.*, Judge Friendly held that an attorney not admitted to practice law in New York could recover fees for legal services even though he had not been admitted pro hac vice because "there is not the slightest reason to suppose that if (a motion had been made it) would have been denied." [364 F.2d 161, 168 (2d Cir. 1966).] This observation applies with even greater force with respect to an arbitration proceeding which is of such an informal nature....

[T]he issue has been addressed by the Association of the Bar of The City of New York [which] considered generally the issue of legal representation before arbitration tribunals. The report states "(i)t should be noted that no support has to date been found in judicial decision, statute or ethical code for the proposition that representation of a party in any kind of arbitration amounts to the practice of law." The report concludes "the Committee is of the opinion that representation of a party in an arbitration proceeding by a non-lawyer or a lawyer from another jurisdiction is not the unauthorized practice of law." Quinn has cited no case nor has the Court's independent research disclosed any to the contrary....

LAWLER, MATUSKY & SKELLER v. ATTORNEY GENERAL OF BARBADOS

Civil Case No. 320 of 1981 (Barbados High Ct. 1983)

[An arbitration was seated in Barbados. One party wished to be represented by Mr. Kannry, who was admitted to practice law in jurisdictions other than Barbados, but not in Barbados. The other party prompted the Attorney General of Barbados to file an action precluding Mr. Kannry from acting in the arbitration.] It is submitted on behalf of the Attorney General that if Mr. Kannry were to represent the claimants at the arbitration hearings in Barbados, he would be practising law in breach of §12(1)(a); and that the arbitrator cannot authorize or permit Mr. Kannry to do any act which would be in contravention of the law of Barbados. My task therefore is to determine whether representation of a party at a hearing in Barbados in a private arbitration constitutes the practice of law within the meaning of the Act....

Far from the Legal Profession Act disclosing in clear and unambiguous terms the intention to reserve exclusively to attorneys-at-law advocacy and like functions, the indications are that it was not Parliament's intention to make such a significant change in the law. In my judgement the Act did not affect the powers of an arbitrator in a private arbitration to regulate its procedure or the common law right of a party, if permitted by the arbitrator, to be represented by someone chosen by him. The findings of the arbitrator disclose, that, in giving his ruling, he took into account Mr. Kannry's qualifications and references, general as well as in the particular case, his own experience and the possibility of prejudice being caused to the claimants if they were deprived of Mr. Kannry's continued assistance. In my opinion these were all matters which he could properly take into consideration and it cannot be said that he exercised his discretion in any improper manner.... [Therefore, t]he Arbitrator had and still has, the power in law to determine and has correctly and validly determined that the applicants are entitled to be represented at hearings in Barbados by Mr. Jack Kannry, a person not registered under the provisions of the Legal Profession Act.

The Arbitration Act ... governs the proceedings and the High Court of Barbados has jurisdiction under the Act and common law to control them. The Court may set aside an award where the arbitrator misconducts himself or the proceedings or where an arbitration or award has been improperly procured (§26). The court may on application give relief where an arbitrator is not impartial or there is a dispute whether a party has been guilty of fraud (§27). And at common law the court may intervene if there is a breach of the rules of natural justice. There are good reasons therefore for requiring an attorney-at-law registered in Barbados to be associated with Mr. Kannry. Any applications to the court would be dealt with by someone acquainted with the case. The reasons given by the arbitrator for directing that Mr. Kannry be assisted by a Barbados attorney-at-law at all hearings were to enable Mr. Kannry to be advised on Barbadian law. It seems to me that the considerations I mentioned earlier are more to the point. However that may be, the arbitrator's direction is in my opinion sensible. I would therefore answer the second question by saying that the arbitrator could permit the applicants to be represented by Mr. Kannry and could also permit such representation subject to the proviso that Mr. Kannry be associated with an attorney-at-law registered under the Legal Profession Act.

JUDGMENT OF 23 MAY 1995
Case No. 704/1995 (Jordanian Cour de cassation)

After revision and deliberation, we found that the [appellant at cassation] attended all arbitration procedures, and the award was rendered in his presence as apparent in the minutes of the arbitration sessions and in the arbitral award. He was accompanied with his [attorney]. As for the arbitration agreement it is a provision in the Contracting Agreement that the appellant had signed by himself. Therefore the arbitration agreement and arbitration procedures were all conducted properly and are not affected by any reason for annulment. The Bar Association Law does not require the parties to be represented before arbitral tribunals by lawyers, and they are not requested to submit pleas to arbitrators signed by lawyers, in accordance with Article 41 of the Jordanian Bar Association Law.

SINGAPORE LEGAL PROFESSION ACT
§§32(1), 33(1)

32(1). Subject to this Part and Part IXA, no person shall practise as an advocate and solicitor or do any act as an advocate or a solicitor unless (a) his name is on the roll; and (b) he has in force a practising certificate.

33(1). Any unauthorised person who (a) acts as an advocate or a solicitor or agent for any party to proceedings or as such advocate, solicitor or agent (i) sues out any writ, summons or process; (ii) commences, carries on, solicits or defends any action, suit or other proceeding in the name of any other person or in his own name in any of the courts in Singapore; or (iii) draws or prepares any document or instrument relating to any proceeding in the courts in Singapore … shall be guilty of an offence and shall be liable on conviction to a fine not exceeding $25,000 or to imprisonment for a term not exceeding 6 months or to both….

BUILDERS FEDERAL (H.K.) LTD v. TURNER (EAST ASIA) PTE LTD
5(3) J. Int'l Arb. 139 (1988) (Singapore High Ct. 1988)

This is an application … for the continuation of an interim injunction … restraining Messrs Debevoise and Plimpton, a firm of New York attorneys (herein called "D&P") … from acting or appearing on behalf of the Respondents in an arbitration in Singapore between the Applicants and the Respondents….

The Applicants, a company incorporated in Singapore, were the main contractors for the building project known as "The Gateway Project…." The Respondents were the sub-contractors for the construction of the curtain walls for the Gateway Project…. [Disputes arose between Applicants and Respondents, which] were referred to arbitration and one Douglas Smith [an accountant living in London] … was on 9 April 1987 appointed by the court as the sole arbitrator.

On 25 June 1987, the solicitors for the Applicants received from D&P by facsimile transmission a letter also dated 25 June 1987 from D&P in New York to the arbitrator in London stating, inter alia, that they represented the Respondents in the arbitration…. On 1 July 1987, D&P informed the arbitrator that they were ready to attend a preliminary meeting at an early date and suggested London as the most satisfactory venue. In this letter, D&P stated that they were "acting as counsel for [both Respondents]." On 7 July 1987,

D&P submitted under a covering letter the Respondents' Statement of Claim…. The cover page and the final page of the Statement of Claim each bear the description of D&P as "Attorneys for Claimants." The arbitrator subsequently fixed the preliminary meeting to be held in Singapore, as the proper venue, on 20 August 1987. On 6 August 1987, D&P wrote to the arbitrator stating its intention to attend the preliminary meeting in Singapore as fixed by the arbitrator. On 18 August 1987, the solicitors for the Applicants commenced these proceedings and on the same day obtained ex parte an interim injunction restraining D&P from acting or appearing in the said arbitration on the ground that such representation or appearance at the arbitration in Singapore would contravene the Legal Profession Act….

[It is undisputed that]: (1) D&P are American attorneys having an office in New York and have not been admitted as advocates and solicitors of the Supreme Court of Singapore. (2) D&P are employed by the Respondents as attorneys and counsel for the said arbitration. (3) The arbitration clause (Clause 22) in the sub-contract provides specifically that the arbitration be in accordance with the Arbitration Act of Singapore; the procedure of the arbitration is also governed by the law of Singapore and the arbitration is subject to the supervision of the courts of Singapore as provided by the Arbitration Act. (4) The sub-contract is also governed by the law of Singapore….

The case for the Applicants is that D&P, by so acting for the Respondents, have contravened and, by intending to so act in the arbitration proceedings will contravene either §29(1) or §30(1) of the Legal Profession Act ("the Act"). Counsel for the Law Society, who appeared by the leave of the court, supports the case for the Applicants.

The case for the Respondents is that the Act has no application to arbitration proceedings and that foreign lawyers and non-lawyers are not prohibited by the Act from representing parties to arbitration proceedings in Singapore. In so far as D&P are concerned, it is not disputed that they would be providing one or more of the following services to the Respondents in the arbitration proceedings i.e. (i) advising the Respondents on their rights and liabilities under the sub-contract; (ii) the drafting of such documents as may be required for the arbitration; (iii) leading evidence on behalf of Respondents and cross-examining the Applicants' witnesses; and (iv) making submissions on the law and on the facts before the arbitrator. It is also common ground that the purpose of this application is to obtain from this court a ruling to determine D&P's status and also because the issue is one of public interest in the light of the Government's intention to promote Singapore as an international arbitration centre….

I now turn to §§29 and 30 of the Act…. Section 29(1) provides the foundation for the case for the Applicants…. The submission is that D&P's role at the arbitration proceedings would amount to either (a) practising as advocates and solicitors or (b) doing an act or acts as advocates and solicitors. Alternatively, it was submitted that D&P's role would amount to acting as advocates or as solicitors to proceedings under §30(1)(a) of the Act. None of the relevant expressions in §§29(1) and 30(1) … i.e. "practising as an advocate and solicitor," "do any act as an advocate and solicitor" and "act as an advocate or solicitor," has been defined…. The categories of legal services are not closed nor do they remain static for all time. They change from time to time to meet the needs of society…. [In my view,] (a) an act is an act of an advocate and solicitor when it is customarily (whether by history or tradition) within his exclusive function to provide e.g. giving advice on legal rights and obligations, drafting contracts and pleadings and pleading in a court of law; [or] (b) a person acts as an advocate and/or solicitor if, by reason of his being an advocate and solicitor, he is employed to act as such in any matter connected with his profession. In this case, ... [t]he answer is beyond any doubt. Firstly, the services D&P intend to provide to the Respondents are services customarily provided by advocates and solicitors ... and, indeed, may be said to constitute the core services of the legal profession. Secondly, D&P's employment in the arbitration ... is in connection with their profession as attorneys and because they are attorneys. They are not being employed to act as experts in the science of building construction ... or in some other non-legal capacity.

Counsel for the Respondents ... sought to avoid the consequences of such a conclusion by contending that arbitration proceedings are fundamentally different from proceedings in a court of law (in that the former is consensual whereas the latter is not and that the arbitrator is the master of the procedure in such proceedings) and that the Act has no application to arbitration proceedings. He contended ... that the expression "practise" in §29(1) implies regularity ... and that D&P by acting in the arbitration on this single occasion cannot be said to practise as advocates and solicitors.... I ... do not accept the argument that D&P would not be practising as advocates and solicitors because they are acting in only one arbitration. It is true that D&P are acting in only one dispute but it is a dispute of a substantial character which may take a long time to be resolved by arbitration and/or in further proceedings by way of appeal. The degree and duration of D&P's participation are relevant factors to be taken into account.... That type of service distinguishes from a case where D&P give legal advice and no more on an isolated occasion and, in my view, amounts to practising as advocates and solicitors in Singapore....

Counsel's final submission is that the Act is intended to protect the public but not persons who voluntarily agree to have their disputes resolved through arbitration rather than by a court of law and that if the law allows them to settle their differences in this manner, they must be free to choose who will represent them without any restriction being placed on their choice. I do not agree with these submissions. In my view, §30(1) is not restricted to proceedings in a court of law.... The primary object of the Act is to protect the public from claims to legal services by unauthorised persons. Parties who prefer to have their disputes resolved through arbitration rather than by court proceedings are no less members of the public. Their common law right to retain whomsoever (from the category of unauthorised persons) they desire or prefer for their legal services in arbitration proceedings in Singapore has, in my view, been taken away by the Act.... For the above reasons, I am of the view that D&P's representation of the Respondents at the arbitration proceedings in Singapore will contravene §29(1) and/or §30(1) of the Act. Accordingly, the Applicants succeed in this application....

SINGAPORE LEGAL PROFESSION (AMENDMENT) BILL (2004)
§35

Sections 32 and 33 shall not extend to (a) any arbitrator or umpire lawfully acting in any arbitration proceedings; (b) any person representing any party in arbitration proceedings; or (c) the giving of advice, preparation of documents and any other assistance in relation to or arising out of arbitration proceedings except for the right of audience in court proceedings. (2) In this section, "arbitration proceedings" means proceedings in an arbitration which—(a) is governed by the Arbitration Act or the International Arbitration Act; or (b) would have been governed by either the Arbitration Act or the International Arbitration Act had the place of arbitration been in Singapore.

SECOND READING SPEECH ON SINGAPORE LEGAL PROFESSION (AMENDMENT) BILL 2004

S. Jayakumar, Minister of Law (2004)

Mr. Speaker, Sir, I beg to move, that the Bill be now read a second time.... This Bill amends the Legal Profession Act to promote Singapore as an arbitration venue and to allow lawyers to practice on a free-lance basis similar to a locum. Sir, in 1992, we amended the Legal Profession Act to allow foreign counsel to argue arbitration cases involving Singapore law. When we did that, we also provided they should appear jointly with a Singapore lawyer. Arbitration has since grown into a major form of dispute settlement, and is increasingly becoming an attractive alternative mechanism to resolve large commercial disputes.

We have made good progress in promoting Singapore as an arbitration centre. We are already a major arbitration centre but our aim is to make Singapore the location of choice for arbitration in the Asia-Pacific region. To further promote this objective, we have reviewed the requirement for foreign counsel to appear jointly with a Singapore lawyer. There is no similar restriction in the laws of the UK, Hong Kong, Malaysia and Australia. It is a requirement which puts us at a disadvantage with jurisdictions that do not have it, as may be a factor against the use of Singapore as an arbitration venue. Foreign parties are more likely to recommend or choose a place with less restrictions. To be competitive in this field, we need to remove this requirement, and allow foreign counsel the choice of appearing without local counsel. This amendment does not mean that local lawyers will be excluded altogether. Foreign counsel may still choose to appear with a Singapore lawyer, for example, where there are complex issues of Singapore law. If they choose to appear on their own, it would be prudent for them to engage a Singapore lawyer for advice on Singapore law.

2014 GAFTA ARBITRATION RULES

Article 16(2)

Where there is no [express agreement between the parties that they may engage legal representatives] they are nevertheless free to engage legal representatives to represent them in the written proceedings but not to appear on their behalf at oral hearings. The costs of engaging legal representatives in such circumstances shall not be recoverable even if claimed.

ICS INSPECTION & CONTROL SERVICES LTD (U.K.) v. REPUBLIC OF ARGENTINA

Decision on Challenge to Arbitrator in PCA Case No. 2010-9 of 17 December 2009

[excerpted above at pp. 730-32]

NOTES

1. *Prohibitions on unauthorized practice of law*. Consider Michigan Compiled Laws §600.916, which is similar to statutes in many U.S. and non-U.S. jurisdictions. What impact does §600.916 have on a non-U.S. practitioner appearing in a Michigan pro-

ceeding? What is the logic of such prohibitions? Consider the following: "the goals of ethical regulation are to guide, punish, and deter attorney conduct in an effort to protect client and third parties, and to ensure the proper functioning of the state adjudicatory apparatus." Rogers, *Context and Institutional Structure in Attorney Regulation: Constructing An Enforcement Regime for International Arbitration*, 39 Stan. J. Int'l L. 1, 20 (2003). If foreigners can provide music, software, cars, or aircraft in the United States, why not legal services? If Volkswagen or Sony wanted to be represented by their European or Japanese counsel in a U.S. or African litigation, what would be wrong with that?

U.S. courts generally require attorneys appearing before them to be members of the relevant bar. Often, U.S. counsel will secure "admission *pro hac vice*," that is, admission limited for a particular matter following a formal application to the court. In these situations, counsel must certify that he will observe the rules of the court and, in most cases, appear alongside local counsel admitted to the local bar. *See* DiSabatino, *Attorney's Right to Appear Pro Hac Vice in State Court*, 20 A.L.R.4th 855 (2005); Rydstrom, *Attorney's Right to Appear Pro Hac Vice in Federal Court*, 33 A.L.R. Fed. 799 (2004). What purposes does this requirement serve? Is it legitimate?

2. *Representation in international arbitration and unauthorized practice of law*—Williamson. Putting aside litigations in national courts, how do unauthorized practice regulations apply to lawyers acting as counsel in international arbitrations? Despite the seemingly broad sweep of such provisions, U.S. and foreign courts are divided over whether they restrict representation before international arbitral tribunals. (Note, preliminarily, that in some jurisdictions and industry settings, it is common for non-lawyers to act as party representatives in arbitral proceedings. *See infra* pp. 1030-34.)

Williamson holds that representation by an attorney in an arbitration does not constitute the unauthorized practice of law. Other decisions have reached similar conclusions. *See, e.g., Prudential Equity Group, LLC v. Ajamie*, 538 F.Supp.2d 605, 607-08 (S.D.N.Y. 2008) (rejecting argument that counsel not authorized to practice law in New York could not recover attorney's fees in New York-seated arbitration); *Superadio LP v. Winstar Radio Prods., LLC*, 844 N.E.2d 246 (Mass. 2006) (rejecting annulment of award on grounds that prevailing party was represented by counsel not authorized to practice law in Massachusetts); *Mscisz v. Kashner Davidson Sec. Corp.*, 844 N.E.2d 614 (Mass. 2006) (rejecting request for declaration that counsel not authorized to practice law in Massachusetts could not appear in arbitration); Eastman, *International Decision:* Birbrower, Montalbano, Condon & Frank v. Superior Court, 94 Am. J. Int'l L. 400, 403 n.21 (2000) (this view of an arbitration exception "though sparsely represented in case law, had seemed to prevail in the United States").

Why exactly is this so? What is the practice of law? Doesn't it consist—as the court in *Builders Federal* reasons—of matters like preparing witnesses, drafting pleadings and examining witnesses? Doesn't it also consist of matters like offering one's opinion on the legal consequences of certain actions, as in *Williamson*? If so, why does it make a difference that these acts occur in the context of an arbitration (as opposed to litigation)?

In one oft-cited U.S. decision, *Birbrower, Montalbano, Condon & Frank v. Superior Court*, 949 P.2d 1 (Cal. 1998), the California Supreme Court refused to hold that the state's unauthorized practice of law statute contained a domestic arbitration exception (the statute did contain a narrow international arbitration exception but did not contain a similar exception for domestic arbitration):

> "We decline ... to craft an arbitration exception to [California's] prohibition of the unlicensed practice of law in this state. Any exception for arbitration is best left to the Legislature, which has the authority to determine qualifications for admission to the State Bar and to decide what constitutes the practice of law. Even though the Legislature has spoken with respect to international arbitration and conciliation, it has not enacted a similar rule for private arbitration proceedings. Of course, private arbitration and other alternative dispute resolution practices are important aspects of our justice system. [California's law], however, articulates a strong public policy favoring the practice of law in California by licensed State Bar members. In the face of the Legislature's silence, we will not create an arbitration exception under the facts presented." 949 P.2d at 9.

This provoked a spirited dissent:

> "Representing another in an arbitration proceeding does not invariably present difficult or doubtful legal questions that require a trained legal mind for their resolution. Under California law, arbitrators are 'not ordinarily constrained to decide according to the rule of law....' Thus, arbitrators, 'unless specifically required to act in conformity with rules of law, may base their decision upon broad principles of justice and equity, and in doing so may expressly or impliedly reject a claim that a party might successfully have asserted in a judicial action.' They "'are not bound to award on principles of dry law, but may decide on principles of equity and good conscience, and make their award *ex aequo et bono.*'" ... Moreover, an arbitrator in California can award any remedy 'arguably based' on 'the contract's general subject matter, framework or intent.' This means that 'an arbitrator in a commercial contract dispute may award an essentially unlimited range of remedies, whether or not a court could award them if it decided the same dispute, so long as it can be said that the relief draws its 'essence' from the contract and not some other source.' To summarize ... arbitration proceedings are not governed or constrained by the rule of law; therefore, representation of another in an arbitration proceeding, including the activities necessary to prepare for the arbitration hearing, does not necessarily require a trained legal mind." *Id.* at 17 (Kennard, J., dissenting).

As noted above, *Birbrower* did not apply to international arbitrations, where a separate statutory provision exempted such proceedings from California's unauthorized practice of law regulations. Cal. C.C.P. §1297.351. *See also* Conn. Gen. Stat. §51-88(d)(3); R. Regulating Fla. Bar 1-3.11 comment ("This rule applies to arbitration proceedings held in Florida where [one] or both parties are being represented by a lawyer admitted in another U.S. jurisdiction or a non-U.S. jurisdiction.... However, entire portions of subdivision (d) and subdivision (e) do not apply to international arbitrations."). Is it not peculiar that an attorney from Canada, India, Russia, or Korea can appear in an international arbitration in California, but that an attorney from Arizona or Oregon cannot appear in a domestic arbitration in the same state? What explains this disparate treatment?

Following *Birbrower*, the California Legislature largely abrogated its holding by statute. A new provision, Cal. C.C.P. §1282.4(c)(11), permitted out-of-state lawyers to represent parties in domestic arbitrations conducted in California, subject to registration requirements and, most notably, identification of a California lawyer to serve as "the attorney of record." Why was the Legislature so concerned about ensuring that out-of-state lawyers could practice in the state? Wouldn't one expect a state to be more concerned about protecting its citizens from lawyers, not admitted to the state bar, practicing within its borders (or, more cynically, protecting local lawyers from outside competition through robust enforcement of its local rules of professional responsibility)?

3. *Representation in international arbitration and unauthorized practice of law*—Builders Federal. In contrast to *Williamson*, courts in a few jurisdictions have refused to graft an "arbitration exception" onto unauthorized practice of law statutes. Consider the court's analysis in *Builders Federal*. As a matter of statutory construction, is there anything surprising or objectionable about the court's decision? Would it really make any sense to say that since a foreign lawyer only engages in a single arbitration, he is not engaged in the practice of law as an advocate? How else might one conclude that representation in an international arbitration does not constitute the practice of law?

Note the residence (London) and occupation (chartered accountant) of the arbitrator in *Builders Federal*—who was not legally qualified. Is it anomalous that an arbitrator could sit in a Singapore arbitration, without being admitted to practice law in Singapore, but the lawyers could not? Why or why not?

The *Builders Federal* decision attracted substantial adverse commentary after it was issued. Lowenfeld, *Singapore and the Local Bar: Aberration or Ill Omen*, 5 J. Int'l Arb. 71 (1988); Rivkin, *Restrictions on Foreign Counsel in International Arbitrations*, XVI Y.B. Comm. Arb. 402, 404 (1991) ("As long as … foreign counsel cannot represent their clients in arbitration proceedings there, … Singapore is less likely to be chosen as the situs of arbitration by parties contemplating arbitration."). Despite this, some other jurisdictions have adopted similar rules. *See* Chilean Organic Code of Tribunals, Art. 526 (incrementally lifting Chile's restriction to permit foreign national residents who completed all of their legal studies in Chile to practice as a lawyer, but not other foreign nationals).

What is the rationale for requirements that parties be represented in arbitrations by locally qualified lawyers? Is it naked protectionism or parochialism? Note, again, that the arbitrator in *Builders Federal* was an accountant, not qualified to practice law in Singapore. Consider one observer's comment that it is important "not only for the international arbitration community, but for the much larger international business community, for international arbitration not to become clogged by the vested interests of a local bar. Only if it fends off or limits the spread of localism will arbitration live up to its promise of assistance and support to the continuing growth of international trade, finance, and investment." Lowenfeld, *Singapore and the Local Bar: Aberration or Ill Omen*, 5(3) J. Int'l Arb. 71 (1988).

An arbitral award made in a particular nation becomes an expression of that state's sovereignty. The award is treated under the New York Convention as having been made in that state, is subject to judicial supervision and actions to annul in that state (and not elsewhere), and is entitled to recognition in other nations because it was made in that state (under the New York Convention and other international treaties). Does not a state, therefore, have a material interest in ensuring that the proceeding that produces an award is entirely regular, transparent and fair? Is not the imposition of strict, policeable professional requirements, such as the requirement of admission to the local bar, a good way to accomplish this? Are there less restrictive alternatives? Why should nations be expected to adopt such alternatives?

Who would enforce ethical standards on foreign lawyers appearing in local arbitration? The arbitral tribunal? The local bar association or courts? The foreign lawyers' bar association or home courts? Does not a requirement of local admission solve all these problems? At what cost?

4. *Legislative reactions to* Builders Federal. In time, *Builders Federal* provoked legislative reactions. At first, the amended legislation continued to require that local Singapore counsel be retained in matters involving Singapore law. *See* Singapore Legal Profession (Amendment No. 2) Act of 1991. Consider the Singaporean legislative materials excerpted above. What does the revised legislation provide? What is the principal concern underlying the Singaporean legislative reaction?

5. *Requirements for joint representation.* Consider the opinion in *Lawler*. What did the court conclude was required under the Barbados Legal Profession Act?

In some jurisdictions, there are requirements that, if foreign lawyers appear in an arbitration seated locally, they be assisted by local counsel (at least in some circumstances). Note the concluding sentence of the *Lawler* decision; note also that, following *Builders Federal*, Singapore revised its law to permit joint representation. Is joint representation what was contemplated there? Is it wise? What are the advantages and disadvantages of requirements of joint representation?

Suppose you were in-house counsel for a Swiss company with a dispute, likely subject to Singapore substantive law, being arbitrated in Singapore. Putting aside what Singapore law compels, would you be content with your usual outside Swiss counsel to run the case alone? Why or why not? Consider the last sentences of the Singaporean legislative materials excerpted above.

6. *Freedom under most national laws for parties to international arbitrations to select legal representatives from foreign jurisdictions.* Many jurisdictions allow parties to international arbitrations to select legal representatives from either the local bar or from foreign jurisdictions. That is, in these jurisdictions, a representative in an international arbitration does not need to be locally-qualified. *See, e.g.,* Swiss ZPO, Art. 373(5) ("Every party has the right to be represented."); Austrian ZPO, §594(3) ("The parties may be represented or advised by persons of their choosing. This right cannot be excluded or limited."); Polkinghorne, *The Right of Representation in A Foreign Venue,* 4 Arb. Int'l 333 (1988). Consider the decision of the Jordanian Cour de cassation.

Even in states that historically limited the right to counsel in international arbitrations, recent legislative and regulatory amendments have frequently removed such limitations. For example, institutional arbitration rules in Japan were amended to confirm that non-Japanese counsel may serve as counsel in international arbitrations seated in Japan. 2014 JCAA Rules, Art. 10 ("A Party may be represented or assisted by any person of its choice in arbitral proceedings under the Rules."). *See also* Nakamura, *Continuing Misconceptions of International Commercial Arbitration in Japan,* 18 J. Int'l Arb. 641, 642-43 (2001). Similar developments occurred in China. Houzhi & Shengchang, *China,* in J. Paulsson (ed.), *International Handbook on Commercial Arbitration* 26 (1984 & Update 1998).

7. *Freedom under institutional rules of parties to select legal representatives.* Consider the various arbitration agreements encountered in previous readings. Do any of these clauses address the question of legal representation? Why or why not? As noted above, most institutional rules provide that the parties may be represented by legal or other agents or advisers, and either expressly or impliedly grant the parties freedom to select these advisers. Article 4 of the IACAC Rules is a good example. *Compare* 2010 UNCITRAL Rules, Art. 5; 2012 ICC Rules, Art. 26(4); 2014 LCIA Rules, Art. 18; ICSID Rules, Rule 18(1).

    What legal effect do these provisions—which are ultimately contractual agreements between the parties—have? Would an arbitration agreement that purported to grant both parties freedom to be represented by foreign counsel override local law prohibitions? If not, would there be a right in damages against the party that invoked local law to invalidate the parties' agreement? If a party was denied its choice of (foreign) counsel, in violation of the parties' agreement, would the eventual award be enforceable outside the arbitral seat? Consider Article V(1)(d) of the New York Convention. *See infra* pp. 1218-41.

8. *International limitations on power of states to forbid representation by foreign counsel in international arbitration.* Consider whether states are entirely free to restrict the freedom of foreign counsel to appear in international arbitrations. Note the combined effect of Article 4 of the IACAC Rules and Article 3 of the Inter-American Convention, excerpted at p. 9 of the Documentary Supplement. Does this require Contracting States to give effect to Article 4 of the IACAC Rules, permitting parties freely to select their legal representatives?

    Consider the combined effect of Article II of the New York Convention and provisions of institutional rules allowing parties to select their legal representatives. Does Article II's requirement, that Contracting States recognize agreements to arbitrate, mean that Contracting State are required to give effect to provisions of arbitration agreements or institutional rules guaranteeing parties the right to counsel of their choice?

9. *Limitations on right to counsel.* Suppose an arbitral tribunal schedules hearings, or dates for written filings, that preclude a party's preferred legal counsel from attending the hearing or completing the submissions. Although tribunals often exhibit flexibility in such circumstances, there are cases where arbitrators will order a hearing to proceed, or a submission to be filed, even if a party's counsel claims unavailability. Do these sorts of orders deny a party its right to select counsel of its choice?

    Consider: "if a party's first choice is not available, his second choice will still be a lawyer or other person chosen by him. The right to be represented exists but must not be abused." U.K. Department Advisory Committee on Arbitration Law, *Report on the Arbitration Bill* ¶184 (1997). Suppose a party is arbitrarily subject to procedural rulings that effectively deny it the counsel of its preference, or that exclude counsel on the basis of discrimination with regard to nationality, religion, or place of qualification. Does this implicate the parties' right to legal representation in the arbitration? What would be the consequences of such a denial?

    Suppose a party wishes to use counsel to represent it in an international arbitration that previously represented the adverse party, in the same, or closely related, matter. Would it violate the party's right to counsel if a national court, or the arbitral tribunal, forbid the party's preferred counsel from representing it? What would such a refusal be based upon? *See infra* pp. 1049-50.

10. *Allocation of competence between national courts and arbitrators with respect to local restrictions on foreign lawyers*. Who possesses the competence to interpret and enforce local restrictions on representation by foreign lawyers in an international arbitration—the local court, the local bar association, or the arbitral tribunal? What did the court in *Lawler* decide? What would the arbitral tribunal in the underlying dispute in *Lawler* have the freedom to do? What could it not do?

     How should competence to enforce local bar restrictions be allocated? What is wrong with the arbitrators doing so?

11. *Institutional rules prohibiting or limiting right to counsel*. Consider Article 16(2) of the 2014 GAFTA Rules. *See also* Brand, *Professional Responsibility in A Transnational Transactions Practice*, 17 J. L. & Com. 301, 334-35 (1998). Is the parties' agreement that neither party may be represented by legal counsel during the arbitration valid and enforceable? Would this be against public policy?

12. *Institutional rules limiting right to change legal representatives*. Consider Article 18 of the LCIA Rules. What are the reasons for the provisions requiring the tribunal's approval of a change to a party's legal representatives? See also the IBA Guidelines on Conflicts of Interest, General Standard 7(b), requiring a party to disclose any change in its legal team and any relevant relationships of the new counsel. If such disclosure is made, what result might ensue, if the applicable arbitration rules do not contain provisions like Article 18 of the LCIA Rules?

13. *Freedom to select counsel in inter-state arbitrations*. Consider Article 62 of the 1907 Hague Convention and Article 5 of the 2012 PCA Rules, excerpted at pp. 47 & 281 of the Documentary Supplement. Contrast the guarantee of a right to counsel in these instruments with the silence on the subject in the New York Convention. What explains the difference? Note also Articles 70 and 71 of the Hague Convention, guaranteeing counsel's right to participate actively in the arbitral proceedings.

B. STANDARDS AND SUPERVISION OF PROFESSIONAL CONDUCT IN INTERNATIONAL ARBITRATION

A subject of increasing importance is the standards for professional conduct of lawyers (and other participants) in international arbitrations and the identities of the authorities responsible for administering those standards. These standards have a variety of different sources.[5]

For example, local legislation may forbid arbitrators from administering oaths[6] or may criminalize false statements to an arbitral tribunal.[7] Violation of these statutory provisions may result in criminal fines or other penalties.

---

5. *See* G. Born, *International Commercial Arbitration* 2850-93 (2d ed. 2014); C. Rogers, *Ethics in International Arbitration* 74-90, 132-37, 162-65 (2014); Rogers, *Context and Institutional Structure in Attorney Regulation: Constructing An Enforcement Regime for International Arbitration*, 39 Stan. J. Int'l L. 1 (2003); Vagts, *International Legal Ethics and Professional Responsibility*, 92 Am. Soc'y Int'l L. Proc. 378 (1998).

6. *See, e.g.*, Swedish Arbitration Act, §25 ("arbitrators may not administer oaths ... or otherwise use compulsory measures in order to obtain requested evidence").

Alternatively, codes of professional responsibility or ethics regulate the activities of members of a jurisdiction's legal profession, often including when they provide legal services outside of that jurisdiction. For example, a lawyer admitted to practice in State A may be (and usually is) governed by the professional responsibility rules of State A when involved in international arbitral proceedings in State B. At the same time, the laws or regulations of State B may also purport to regulate the conduct of foreign-qualified lawyers participating in an arbitration in State B. In both cases, professional, civil and other sanctions may be imposed for violations of applicable law.

DISTRICT OF COLUMBIA BAR OPINION (1979)
p. 79, in *Code of Professional Responsibility and Opinions of the D.C. Bar Legal Ethics Committee* 138 (1991)

We have been asked to delineate the ethical limitations upon a lawyer's participation in preparing the testimony of witnesses. The specific inquiry before us arises out of the adjudicatory hearings before a federal regulatory agency. The agency's rules of practice provide that direct testimony of witnesses is to be submitted in written form prior to the hearing session at which the testimony is offered; at that session, the witness adopts the testimony and attests that it is true and correct ... and then is offered for cross-examination.... The ... questions ... are whether it is ethically proper for a lawyer actually to write the testimony the witness will adopt under oath; whether, if so, the lawyer may include in such testimony information that the lawyer has initially secured from sources other than the witness; and whether ... the lawyer may engage in "practice cross-examination exercises" intended to prepare the witness for questions that may be asked at the hearing....

Submission of direct testimony in written form in advance of a hearing at which the witness is subject to questioning about the testimony is a frequent and familiar pattern, but it is by no means the only kind of setting in which lawyers are called upon to assist in the preparation of a witness's testimony. Written testimony is offered in a variety of forms and circumstances; in answers to written interrogatories, for instance; and in all sorts of affidavits. Lawyers are almost invariably involved in the preparation of the former, and frequently in the latter as well....

In addition, lawyers commonly, and quite properly, prepare witnesses for testimony that is to be given orally in its entirety. In consequence, questions of whether a lawyer may properly suggest the language in which a witness's testimony will be case, or suggest subjects for inclusion in testimony, do not arise solely in connection with written testimony. For this reason also, the inquirer's questions about "practice cross-examination exercises" is narrower than it needs to be: there may equally well be practice direct examination. In sum, the ethical issues raised by the inquiry before us apply more broadly than is implied by the particular questions put by the inquirer.... [T]he questions may usefully be rephrased as follows:

---

7. *See, e.g.,* Swiss Criminal Code, Art. 307(1) ("Whoever testifies in [court] proceedings as a witness of fact, expert witness or translator and gives false testimony as to the facts, provides false expertise or false translation shall be sentenced to the penitentiary for up to five years or imprisoned."). Article 309 of the Criminal Code extends these provisions to arbitration proceedings.

(1) What are the ethical limitations on a lawyer's suggesting the actual language in which a witness's testimony is to be presented, whether in written form or otherwise?

(2) What are the ethical limitations on a lawyer's suggesting that a witness's testimony include information that was not initially furnished to the lawyer by the witness?

(3) What are the ethical limitations on a lawyer's preparing a witness for the presentation of testimony under live examination, whether direct or cross, and whether by practice questioning or otherwise?

A single prohibitory principle governs the answer to all three of these questions: it is, simply, that a lawyer may not prepare, or assist in preparing, testimony that he or she knows, or ought to know, is false or misleading. So long as this prohibition is not transgressed, a lawyer may properly suggest language as well as the substance of testimony, and may indeed, should do whatever is feasible to prepare his or her witnesses for examination.

The governing ethical provisions, which are cast in quite general terms, appear to be EC 7-26 and DR 7-102(A)(4), (6) and (7). The Ethical Consideration reads as follows:

> The law and Disciplinary Rules prohibit the use of fraudulent, false or perjured testimony or evidence. A lawyer who knowingly participates in introduction of such testimony or evidence is subject to discipline. A lawyer should, however, present any admissible evidence his client desires to have presented unless he knows, or from facts within his knowledge should know, that such testimony or evidence is false, fraudulent, or perjured.

The disciplinary provisions are these: ...

> DR 7-102(A) In his representation of a client, a lawyer shall not: ... (4) Knowingly use perjured testimony or false evidence.... (6) Participate in the creating or preservation of evidence when he knows or it is obvious that the evidence is false. (7) Counsel or assist his client in conduct that the lawyer knows to be illegal or fraudulent.

Curiously, there appear to be no decisions by bar ethics committees directly addressing the line of demarcation between permissible and impermissible lawyer participation in the preparation of testimony from the perspective involved in this inquiry, focusing on the lawyer's conduct rather than on the nature of the testimony; and while there is some authority from other sources, it is scant, and not brightly illuminating. In any event, it seems to us clear that the proper focus is indeed on the substance of the witness's testimony which the lawyer has, in one way or another, assisted in shaping; and not on the manner of the lawyer's involvement. In this regard, the pertinent provisions of the Code, quoted above, do not call for an excessively close analysis. They employ the terms "false," "fraudulent" and "perjured," the terms "testimony" and "evidence," and the terms "illegal" and "fraudulent," in a manner that suggests, not that fine differences are intended, but that the terms are used casually and interchangeably. We think therefore, that all of these provisions, so far as here pertinent, are to the same effect: that a lawyer may not ethically participate in the preparation of testimony that he or she knows, or ought to know, as false or misleading.

It follows, therefore—to address the first question here raised—that the fact that the particular words in which testimony, whether written or oral, is cast originated with a lawyer rather than the witness whose testimony it is has no significance so long as the substance of that testimony is not, so far as the lawyer knows or ought to know, false or misleading. If the particular words suggested by the lawyer, even though not literally false, are calculated to convey a misleading impression, this would be equally impermissible from the ethical point of view. Herein, indeed, lies the principal hazard (leaving aside outright subornation of perjury) in a lawyer's suggesting particular forms of language to a witness to instead of leaving the witness to articulate his or her thought wholly without prompting: there may be differences in nuance among variant phrasings of the same substantive point, which are so significant as to make one version misleading while another is not. Yet it is obvious that by the same token, choice of words may also improve the clarity and precision of a statement: even subtle changes of shading may as readily improve testimony as impair it. The fact that a lawyer suggests particular language to a witness means only that the lawyer may be affecting the testimony in these respects. It is not, we think, a matter of undue difficulty for a reasonably competent and conscientious lawyer to discern the line of impermissibility, where truth shades into untruth, and to refrain from crossing it.

We note that in the particular circumstances giving rise to this inquiry, there is some built-in assurance against hazards of this kind, to be found in the fact that the testimony will be subject to cross-examination—which, of course, may properly probe the extent of the lawyer's participation in the actual drafting of the direct testimony, including whether language used by the witness originated with the lawyer rather than the witness, what other language was considered but rejected, the nuances involved, and so forth....

The second question raised by the inquiry—as to the propriety of a lawyer's suggesting the inclusion in a witness's testimony of information not initially secured from the witness—may, again, arise not only with respect to written testimony but with oral testimony as well. In either case, it appears to us that the governing consideration for ethical purposes is whether the substance of the testimony is something the witness can truthfully and properly testify to. If he or she is willing and (as respects his or her state of knowledge) able honestly so to testify, the fact that the inclusion of a particular point of substance will initially suggested by the lawyer rather than the witness seems to us wholly without significance. There are two principal hazards here. One hazard is the possibility of undue suggestion: that is, the risk that the witness may thoughtlessly adopt testimony offered by the lawyer simply because it is so offered, without considering whether it is testimony that he or she may appropriately give under oath. The other hazard is the possibility of a suggestion or implication in the witness's resulting testimony that the witness is testifying on a particular matter of his own knowledge when this is not in fact the case. For reasons explained above, these hazards are likely to be somewhat less serious in a case like the one giving rise to the present inquiry, where cross-examination can inquire into the source of the testimony, and test its truth and genuineness, than in the numerous situations where written testimony will probably not be followed by any examination of the witness at all....

We turn, finally, to the extent of the lawyer's proper participation in preparing a witness for giving live testimony—whether the testimony is only to be under cross-examination, as in the particular circumstances giving rise to the present inquiry, or, as is more usually the case, direct examination as well. Here again it appears to us that the only touchstones are the truth and genuineness of the testimony to be given. The mere fact of a lawyer's having prepared the witness for the presentation of testimony is simply irrelevant: indeed, a lawyer who did not prepare his or her witness for testimony, having had an opportunity to do so, would not be doing his or her professional job properly. This is so if the witness is also a client; but it is no less so if the witness is merely one who is offered by the lawyer on the client's behalf. *See Hamdi & Ibrahim Mango Co. v. Fire Ass'n of Philadelphia*, 20 F.R.D. 181, 182-83 (S.D.N.Y. 1957):

[It] could scarcely be suggested that it would be improper for counsel who called the witness to review with him prior to the deposition the testimony to be elicited. It is usual and legitimate practice for ethical and diligent counsel to confer with a witness whom he is about to call prior to his giving testimony, whether the testimony is to be given on deposition or at trial. Wigmore recognizes 'the absolute necessity of such a conference for legitimate purposes' as part of intelligent and thorough preparation for trial. *3 Wigmore on Evidence*, (3d Edition) §788. In such a preliminary conference counsel will usually, in more or less general terms, ask the witness the same questions as he expects to put to him on the stand. He will also, particularly in a case involving complicated transactions and numerous documents, review with the witness the pertinent documents, but for the purpose of refreshing the witness' recollection and to familiarize him with those which are expected to be offered in evidence. This sort of preparation is essential to the proper presentation of a case and to avoid surprise.

It matters not at all that the preparation of such testimony takes the form of "practice" examination or cross-examination. What does matter is that whatever the mode of witness preparation chosen, the lawyer does not engage in suppressing, distorting or falsifying the testimony that the witness will give....

VAN HOUTTE, *COUNSEL-WITNESS RELATIONS AND PROFESSIONAL MISCONDUCT IN CIVIL LAW SYSTEMS*
19 Arb. Int'l 457 (2003)

In order to understand the counsel-witness relations in civil law arbitrations one first needs to understand how civil law courts handle witnesses in a manner in which the parties' counsel is in a supporting role. Indeed, the arbitration situation in civil law countries envisage that arbitrators will deal with witnesses in the same way as judges do, with counsel as mere "walk-ons." However, in practice—and under Anglo-American influence—counsel in civil law arbitrations play an active role in the presentation of witness evidence, an approach that stands at right angles to the civil law legal tradition....

It is an essential feature of civil law proceedings that the courts assume the obligation to investigate the case themselves and to find the "truth." In the past, civil law courts investigated a case without any contribution from counsel, not only in criminal matters, but also in civil and commercial matters. A 19-century French *avocat*, for instance, was not allowed to interfere with the court's "*instruction de l'affaire*" in a commercial dispute. When the court heard a witness, the *avocat* could thus not attend the hearing. *A fortiori* he must not visit prospective witnesses to learn what they had to say, and less still, influence their statements. The rules, undoubtedly, have become less strict. Nevertheless some of the underlying philosophy has somehow survived. Indeed, nowadays civil law courts still see it as their task to lead the investigation in the case. However in most continental European countries (Austria, Germany, the Netherlands, Sweden) counsel may approach and meet a prospective witness. In Belgium, France, Italy and Switzerland on the other hand, the Rules of Conduct of the Bar still forbid consent to interview prospective witnesses.

In fact, however, in civil and commercial court proceedings witnesses are not much used. They are of secondary importance. For civil matters, the Code Napoleon Article 1341, for example, has significantly curbed the possibility of using witness testimony to contradict written documents. Although the same strict rule does not exist for commercial matters, where witness evidence is more generally admitted, in commercial matters witness testimony is also rarely submitted. In 30 years of commercial litigation, I have known only two instances where a Belgian court has heard witnesses. Moreover, if a witness nonetheless has to be heard, in most civil law countries the courts have kept a preponderant—if not exclusive—role: it is the judge who carries out the witness examination. Generally, neither the parties nor their counsel have the opportunity to question the witness directly. A party usually forwards its questions to the judge, who then has full discretion in deciding whether to put the question to the witness. In many jurisdictions, the parties and their counsel cannot even interrupt a witness.

Traditionally witnesses had a similar minor role in civil law arbitration. Arbitrators restricted witness evidence in the same way as courts. A Belgian arbitration treatise thus admonished arbitrators to admit witness evidence in civil and commercial matters only when the law allowed for such evidence. In fact, witnesses were only used in arbitration when there was no written evidence available. It is also quite striking ... that a leading French treatise on arbitration, Jean Robert's *L'arbitrage*, in its 1983 edition, did not discuss witness evidence at all.

Whenever arbitrators hear witnesses, they follow as much as possible the same modalities as a court would. Depending on the applicable arbitration law, they administer an oath; they exclude as witnesses persons who are too closely linked to the parties; they and not the parties question the witness and draft minutes of the hearing. Arbitrators—or even only one of them—sometimes examine the witnesses in the absence of the parties and their counsel. In the event, the arbitrators will submit a "*procès-verbal*" of the examination to the parties so that they are aware of its outcome. Whenever a witness refuses to appear before the arbitrators, depending on the applicable law, the state court can either order the witness to appear before the arbitral tribunal, or can question the witness itself.

In their sociological exploration of the arbitration world, Dezalay and Garth described how Anglo-American lawyers, who play a preponderant role in present-day arbitration, have modelled their international arbitration proceedings on American court practice and have turned transnational arbitration into offshore American-style litigation. [Y. Dezalay & G. Garth, *Dealing with Virtue* 53 (1996).] The intensive reliance on witnesses and their cross-examination by counsel is part of this change. At first some European arbitrators considered cross-examination of witnesses "barbaric" and "primitive." Others, however, soon "began to realize that parties seemed to like the cross-examination" and were open to this new approach. Consequently, in Europe witnesses are now becoming a substantial element in arbitration proceedings, not only for transatlantic or cross-Channel cases, but also for continental European disputes and even for purely domestic disputes. Occasionally, a continental European arbitrator may still insist that it will be he, and not counsel, who will put the questions to the witness. This implies that counsel cannot question the witness in direct and cross-examination but can only prompt the Chairman of the Tribunal to ask questions that counsel would put to the witness—a somewhat boring, demanding and time-consuming exercise. After a few questions, however, reasonableness generally prevails over formality, and counsel address the witness direction.

For modern continental European arbitrators witness evidence, production of witness lists, submission of witness statements, examination in chief, cross-examination, re-examination and further cross-examination have become an inherent part of the arbitration proceedings. The IBA Rules on Evidence ..., meant in the first instance to bring procedural gaps between civil and common law on the presentation of evidence, are often also used for intra-continental European disputes, and even in purely domestic arbitrations. In brief, continental European arbitrators, rooted in the inquisitorial tradition, have discovered the benefits of adversarial questioning. That allows many of them to combine the best of the continental European tradition with Anglo-American approaches. In a first stage they will often thus allow counsel to examine the witnesses; at the end they may themselves question the witness directly....

PARTIAL AWARD IN ICC CASE NO. 8879

discussed in Grigera Naón, *Choice-of-Law Problems in International Commercial Arbitration*, 289 Recueil des Cours 9, 157-58 (2001)

Claimant A—a U.S. company—retained a law firm in the Latin American country of all Respondents (Country R) in order to obtain legal advice related to the subject matter of the arbitration concerning an investment in … Respondent B. In part on the basis of such advice—which indicated that such investment did not require prior governmental authorization under the laws of Country B and was based on the review of certain documents pertaining to Respondent B, including its by-laws—Claimant A decided to invest in the share capital of Respondent B. That advice was rendered before the initiation of the arbitration. After arbitral proceedings were initiated by Claimants, it turned out that (i) the very law firm that rendered advice to Claimant A had been retained as counsel for the Respondents in the arbitral proceedings; and (ii) counsel for Respondents raised as one of the defenses against Claimants' claims the invalidity under the laws of Country R of the very by-laws of Respondent B on which it based its legal opinion rendered to Claimant A (which did not contain reservations as to the validity of such by-laws).

Consequently, Claimant A—based on provisions in the Civil and Criminal Codes as well as the Code of Ethics of Country R where both Respondent B and its counsel are based and the laws of which were the subject-matter of the legal advice given to Claimant A—requested the exclusion of Respondents' counsel from the arbitral proceedings. Those provisions indicated: (a) an attorney retained by one party may not simultaneously or thereafter represent another party in the same controversy even if he or she terminates the previous representation; and (b) a law firm must refrain from participating in a case where it would be in the position to disclose or take advantage of privileged information it has previously received from a client....

[T]he Arbitral Tribunal sitting in Canada was of the view that (a) the claims of Claimant A against counsel for Respondents did not fall within the scope of the arbitration clause only concerning Claimants and Respondents and should rather be the subject of "domestic proceedings" (presumably in Country R) under the provisions of Country R invoked by Claimant A; (b) a decision of the Arbitral Tribunal to exclude Respondents' counsel from the arbitral proceedings would deprive Respondents from freely choosing their counsel and damage the interests of such counsel although he is not bound by an arbitration agreement; and (c) even if *arguendo* the Arbitral Tribunal had concluded that the dispute between Claimant A and counsel for Respondents falls within the scope of the arbitration agreement, it would have found the dispute to be non-arbitrable, since it requires adjudicating on "the criminal consequences of alleged advocate misconduct." The Arbitral Tribunal also expressed doubts as to the application of the code of ethics of a domestic private bar association "in the context of an international arbitration proceeding."

BIDERMANN INDUSTRIES LICENSING, INC. v. AVMAR NV
N.Y. L.J. 23 (N.Y. Sup. Ct.) (Oct. 26, 1990)

Petitioner Bidermann Industries, Inc. ("BILI"), makes this application for an order pursuant to CPLR §7503 staying the arbitration demanded by respondents, Avmar NV ("Avmar"), Leit Moti, Inc. ("LMI") and Karl Lagerfeld ("Lagerfeld"), as to the issue of whether BILI's counsel, Coudert Brothers, should be disqualified from representing them in the arbitration proceedings pending between BILI and the respondents. The issue presented is one of apparent first impression: May the issue of attorney disqualification be determined in an arbitration, or is it a matter exclusively within the province and jurisdiction of the courts? ...

BILI ... argues that the issue of disqualification is not arbitrable because it is not within the scope of the arbitration agreement executed between BILI and the respondents. Further, BILI contends it is against public policy to arbitrate the ethical obligations of attorneys, since that is within the exclusive jurisdiction of the courts. Respondents argue that the arbitration provision encompasses any dispute arising out of the agreements or their alleged breach. They also contend that the issue of disqualification is a procedural issue in the arbitration and as such is clearly within the province of the arbitrators to decide.

Pursuant to the license agreement executed by the parties, BILI and respondents agreed that:

> "Any controversy, dispute or claim arising out of or relating to this Agreement, or the breach thereof, shall be settled by arbitration which shall be held in the City of New York in accordance with the rules of the [AAA] and judgment upon the award rendered by the arbitrator(s) may be entered in any court having jurisdiction thereof."

The license agreement ... deals with the contractual obligations and aspects of trademark use and design services....

Generally, New York favors arbitration. "Those who agree to arbitrate should be made to keep their solemn written promises." *Matter of Grayson-Robinson Stores, Inc.*, 8 N.Y.2d 133, 138 (1960). It is the strong policy of this state to encourage use of arbitration as an easy expeditious method of settling dispute which, ideally, dispenses with the need for protracted litigation.... It is a threshold question for the courts, however, ... "to determine whether the parties agreed to submit their disputes to arbitration, [and] if so, whether the particular disputes come within the scope of their agreement." *County of Rockland v. Primiano Constr. Co.*, 51 N.Y.2d 1 (1980). An arbitration agreement will be enforced by the courts provided it does not transgress a provision or statute or violate public policy.... "Public policy, whether derived from, and whether explicit or implicit in statute or decisional law, or in neither, may also restrict the freedom to arbitrate." *Susquehanna Valley etc. v. Susquehanna Valley Teacher's Ass'n*, 37 N.Y.2d 614, 616-617 (1975). It is for courts to decide whether the enforcement of an agreement to arbitrate would contravene an important public policy.

Where an important interest of public at large is likely to be affected by the resolution of a dispute, decision by arbitration is inappropriate, notwithstanding agreement by parties to the dispute. For example, even if child custody and visitation agreements provide for arbitration as the forum for dispute resolution, the courts have jurisdiction to consider the issues de novo.... Violations of state antitrust laws are not arbitrable, ... nor are violations of criminal law ... and matters involving civil penalties.... Similarly, the regulation of attorneys, and determinations as to whether clients should be deprived of counsel of their choice as a result of professional responsibilities and ethical obligations, implicate fundamental public interests and policies which should be reserved for the courts and should not be subject to arbitration.... Among the competing public interests which must be balanced against a client's right to counsel of her choice is "the courts' duty to protect the integrity of the judicial system and preserve the ethical standards of the legal profession." *Matter of Abrams*, 62 N.Y.2d 183, 196 (1984).

The general policy favoring arbitration ... must be balanced against the important policy favoring judicial determination of attorney disqualification. While jurisdiction to discipline an attorney for misconduct is vested exclusively in the Appellate Division, disqualification in a particular matter should be sought in the court in which the motion is pending.... The court has the inherent power to disqualify an attorney for a party upon a finding that it is improper for him to represent the litigant or to participate in a proceedings....

Although no New York case specifically precludes arbitration of attorney disqualification issues, a number of cases imply that attorney conduct is the exclusive province of the courts. A New York City Council regulation involving the sale of taxicabs, which limited the usual and normal privileges of attorneys, was held invalid because regulation of conduct of attorneys was found to be vested in the courts.... In *Erdheim v. Selkowe*, 51 A.D.2d 705 (1st Dept. 1976), the Appellate Division ... held that arbitrators have no jurisdiction to discipline attorneys, as this is within the exclusive jurisdiction of the Appellate Division.... Based on these cases which indicate that attorney regulation questions should be addressed in the courts, I hold that the issue of attorney disqualification is not appropriate for arbitration.

ABA MODEL RULES OF PROFESSIONAL CONDUCT
Rules 5.5(c), 8.5(b)

5.5(c). A lawyer admitted in another United States jurisdiction, and not disbarred or suspended from practice in any jurisdiction, may provide legal services on a temporary basis in this jurisdiction that ... (3) are in or reasonably related to a pending or potential arbitration, mediation or other alternative dispute resolution proceeding in this or another jurisdiction, if the services arise out of or are reasonably related to the lawyer's practice in a jurisdiction in which the lawyer is admitted to practice and are not services for which the forum requires pro hac vice admission....

8.5(b). In any exercise of the disciplinary authority of this jurisdiction, the rules of professional conduct to be applied shall be as follows: (1) for conduct in connection with a matter pending before a tribunal, the rules of the jurisdiction in which the tribunal sits, unless the rules of the tribunal provide otherwise; and (2) for any other conduct, the rules of the jurisdiction in which the lawyer's conduct occurred, or, if the predominant effect of the conduct is in a different jurisdiction, the rules of that jurisdiction shall be applied to the conduct. A lawyer shall not be subject to discipline if the lawyer's conduct conforms to the rules of a jurisdiction in which the lawyer reasonably believes the predominant effect of the lawyer's conduct will occur.

2013 IBA GUIDELINES ON PARTY REPRESENTATION IN
INTERNATIONAL ARBITRATION

[excerpted in Documentary Supplementat pp. 339-49]

HRVATSKA ELEKTROPRIVREDA, DD v. REPUBLIC OF SLOVENIA
Tribunal's Ruling Regarding Participation of David Mildon QC in Further Stages of Proceeding in ICSID Case ARB/05/24 of 6 May 2008

[In the course of an investment arbitration under the ICSID Convention, the respondent (represented by an English law firm) added an English barrister (Mr. Mildon QC) to its legal team about ten weeks before the evidentiary hearing. Mr. Mildon was a member of the same barrister's chambers as the presiding arbitrator. Mr. Mildon's addition to the respondent's legal team was notified to the tribunal (and the claimant) shortly before the main evidentiary hearing was scheduled to begin. The claimant immediately objected, arguing that Mr. Mildon's membership in the same chambers as the presiding arbitrator compromised the independence of the tribunal and that Mr. Mildon should, therefore, be disqualified from further participation as counsel in the arbitral proceedings. The respondent replied that there was no basis to the application, on the grounds that the tribunal lacked authority to disqualify counsel and, in any event, that barristers are independent practitioners and that Mr. Mildon's participation in the arbitration did not affect the tribunal's independence or the integrity of the proceedings. The respondent relied on the following description of Mr. Mildon (and the presiding arbitrator's) chambers, from its Web site and promotional materials:

> "Essex Court Chambers is a leading set of Barristers Chambers specialising in commercial, international and European law. Its members advise and act in a broad range of litigation, arbitration, and dispute resolution worldwide. Chambers is not a firm, nor are its members partners or employees. Rather, Chambers contains the separate, self-contained offices of individual barristers, each self-employed and working separately. Indeed, (as in all specialist sets) individual Barristers within Chambers are commonly retained by opposing sides in the same dispute, both in litigation and arbitration. As well as acting on opposing sides, individuals regularly appear in front of other members acting as Deputy Judges or Arbitrators. Members of Chambers may be instructed individually or in a team to provide a wide range and level of expertise in both contentious and non-contentious work."

Neither the claimant nor the respondent sought to challenge the presiding arbitrator (and, on the contrary, affirmatively requested that he remain in his position). The arbitral tribunal granted the claimant's application to disqualify Mr. Mildon, reasoning *inter alia* as follows:]

The ICSID Convention in Article 14 demands that arbitrators "be relied upon to exercise independent judgment." ICSID Arbitration Rule 6 requires them to "judge fairly." The objection in this case is not predicated on any actual lack of independence or impartiality, but on apprehensions of the appearance of impropriety. In the interest of the legitimacy of these proceedings, the arbitrators consider that the Claimant is entitled to make [its] objection [that Mr. Mildon's participation in the proceedings created an appearance of impropriety] and that it is well founded.

The consequences of this conclusion are not straight-forward. For an international system like that of ICSID, it seems unacceptable for the solution to reside in the individual national bodies which regulate the work of professional service providers, because that might lead to inconsistent or indeed arbitrary outcomes depending on the attitudes of such bodies, or the content (or lack of relevant content) of their rules. It would moreover be disruptive to interrupt international cases to ascertain the position taken by such bodies.

The ICSID Convention and Rules do not, however, explicitly give the power to tribunals to exclude counsel. To the contrary, we readily accept that as a general rule parties may seek such representation as they see fit—and that this is a fundamental principle. Even fundamental principles must, however, give way to overriding exceptions. In this case, the overriding principle is that of the immutability of properly constituted tribunals (Article 56(1) of the ICSID Convention). To be concrete: although the Respondent in this case was free to select its legal team as it saw fit prior to the constitution of the Tribunal, it was not entitled subsequently amend the composition of its legal team in such a fashion as to imperil the Tribunal's status or legitimacy....

[The Tribunal identified a principle of the "immutability of arbitral tribunals," which limited to the maximum extent possible alterations in the composition of ICSID tribunals during the course of the arbitration.] The present case involves ... an initiative undertaken by one of the litigants, which only at an extremely late stage has disclosed the involvement of counsel whose presence is for all practical purposes incompatible with the maintenance of the Tribunal in its present proper composition. The Tribunal is concerned—indeed, compelled—to preserve the integrity of the proceedings and, ultimately, its Award. Undoubtedly, one of the "fundamental rules of procedure" referred to in Article 52(l)(d) of the ICSID Convention is that the proceedings should not be tainted by any justifiable doubt as to the impartiality or independence of any Tribunal member. [Applying this standard,] Mr. Mildon's QC's continued participation in the proceedings could indeed lead a reasonable observer to form such a justifiable doubt in the present circumstances. [The tribunal cited the fact that barrister "chambers themselves have evolved in the modern market place for professional services with the consequence that they often present themselves with a collective connotation." As a consequence, the participation of one member of the chambers in an investment arbitration chaired by another member of chambers gave rise to an unacceptable appearance of impropriety.]

The Tribunal does not believe there is a hard-and-fast rule to the effect that barristers from the same Chambers are always precluded from being involved as, respectively, counsel and arbitrator in the same case. Equally, however, there is no absolute rule to opposite effect. The justifiability of an apprehension of partiality depends on all relevant circumstances. Here, those circumstances include, first, the fact that the London Chambers system is wholly foreign to the Claimant; second, the Respondent's conscious decision not to inform the Claimant or the Tribunal of Mr. Mildon's involvement in the case, following his engagement in February of this year, third, the tardiness of the Respondent's announcement of Mr. Mildon's involvement and, finally, the Respondent's subsequent insistent refusal to disclose the scope of Mr. Mildon's involvement, a matter of days before the commencement of the hearing on the merits. The last three matters were errors of judgment on the Respondent's part and have created an atmosphere of apprehension and mistrust which it is important to dispel.

The Tribunal's conclusion about the substantial risk of a justifiable apprehension of partiality leads to a stark choice: either the President's resignation (which, as noted, neither Party desires), or directions that Mr. Mildon QC cease to participate in the proceedings. In the light of the cardinal rule of immutability of Tribunals, (Article 56(1) of the Convention), resignation of its President is a course of action that the Tribunal simply cannot endorse in the present circumstances.

The Tribunal disagrees with the contention of Respondent that it has no inherent powers in this regard. It considers that as a judicial formation governed by public international law, the Tribunal has an inherent power to take measures to preserve the integrity of its proceedings. In part, that inherent power finds a textual foothold in Article 44 of the Convention, which authorizes the Tribunal to decide "any question of procedure" not expressly dealt with in the Convention, the ICSID Arbitration Rules or "any rule agreed by the parties." More broadly, there is an "inherent power of an international court to deal with any issues necessary for the conduct of matters falling within its jurisdiction"; that power "exists independently of any statutory reference." In the specific circumstances of the present case, it is in the Tribunal's view both necessary and appropriate to take action under its inherent power.

In light of the fundamental rule enshrined in Article 56(1) ... and given its inherent procedural powers confirmed by Article 44, the Arbitral Tribunal hereby decides that the participation of Mr. Mildon QC in this case would be inappropriate and improper. We appreciate that the Respondent was under a misapprehension in this regard and will, by making appropriate procedural adjustments, ensure that the Respondent's ability to present its case will not be adversely affected by this ruling....

NOTES

1. *Professional responsibility codes and international practice.* The bar associations or other regulatory authorities of almost every developed country have adopted codes of conduct or professional responsibility governing the professional activities of lawyers admitted to provide legal services in that jurisdiction. *See, e.g.,* ABA Model Rules of Professional Conduct; Council of Bars and Law Societies of Europe Code of Conduct for European Lawyers; C. Rogers, *Ethics in International Arbitration* 87-88 (2014); Terry, *An Introduction to the European Community's Legal Ethics Code,* 7 Geo. J. Legal Ethics 1 (1993-1994); Toulmin, *A Worldwide Common Code for Professional Ethics?,* 15 Fordham Int'l L. Rev. 673 (1992). These rules generally regulate, among other things: (a) quality of representation ("zealous" representation of client interests; definition of malpractice); (b) conflicts of interest; (c) compensation (disclosure, contingent fee arrangements, rates); (d) confidentiality and privilege; (e) relations with other counsel and courts; (f) publicity and advertising. As explained in the Preamble to the ABA Model Rules of Professional Conduct:

   "The [legal] profession has a responsibility to assure that its regulations are conceived in the public interest and not in furtherance of parochial or self-interested concerns of the bar.... The[] principles [reflected in the professional standards] include the lawyer's obligation zealously to protect and pursue a client's legitimate interests, within the bounds of the law, while maintaining a professional, courteous and civil attitude toward all persons involved in the legal system." ABA Model Rules of Professional Conduct, Preamble ¶¶9, 11.

   For similar principles, *see* Council of Bars and Law Societies of Europe Code of Conduct for European Lawyers, Art. 1.1. Inevitably, different jurisdictions take very different approaches to particular issues, including matters such as conflicts of interest, permissibility of particular fee arrangements, contact with and "preparation of" witnesses, and privilege. *See* Rogers, *Lawyers Without Borders*, 30 U. Pa. J. Int'l L. 1035 (2009); Vagts, *Professional Responsibility in Transborder Practice: Conflict and Resolution*, 13 Geo. J. Legal Ethics 677, 683, 688 (2000).

2. *Professional responsibility codes and international arbitration.* Many professional conduct rules either expressly or impliedly regulate attorney activity during arbitration, including international arbitration. *See, e.g.,* Council of Bars and Law Societies of Europe Code of Conduct for European Lawyers, Art. 4.5 ("The rules governing a lawyer's relations with the courts apply also to the lawyer's relations with arbitrators"); N.Y. Judiciary Law (Appx.: Code of Prof. Resp. §1200.1(f)). Where this is the case, counsel remains accountable to his local bar association for his conduct during the arbitration and can be subject to disciplinary sanctions for violating the applicable rules of professional conduct. For example, a Minnesota attorney was suspended from the practice of law for six months after presenting misleading documentation in support of a client's arbitration proceeding in violation of Minnesota Rules of Professional Conduct 3.3(a)(4). *See In re Disciplinary Action Against Zotaley*, 546 N.W.2d 16, 20 (Minn. 1996). *See also Brunswick v. Statewide Grievance Comm.*, 2006 WL 895007 (Conn. Super. Ct.).

State rules of professional conduct may also regulate the activities of lawyers serving as arbitrators. In addition to the generally applicable rules of professional conduct, some states have enacted specific ethics rules for domestic and international arbitrators. *See, e.g.,* North Carolina Bar Association Dispute Resolution Section & Its Committee on Ethics and Professionalism Canons of Ethics for Arbitrators; California Rules of Court Ethics Standards for Neutral Arbitrators in Contractual Arbitration. *See* Gabriel, *Ethics for Commercial Arbitrators: Basic Principles and Emerging Standards*, 5 Wyo. L. Rev. 453 (2005); Glick, *California Arbitration Reform*, 38 U.S.F. L. Rev. 119 (2003).

How likely is it that a bar association in one state will closely supervise activities of members of that bar abroad, in a presumptively confidential arbitration? What standards would a bar association apply in these circumstances? How much expertise would the bar association have in regulating legal counsel's conduct in these proceedings?

To what extent are the substantive standards of professional conduct applicable in domestic settings (principally litigation) appropriate for international arbitral proceedings? Does it matter if the arbitral proceedings are conducted in another state from that in which the lawyer in question is qualified? Does it matter if the other lawyer(s) in the arbitration is qualified in different states, subject to different standards of professional responsibility? Why or why not? Before making up your mind on these issues, consider the specific issues discussed below.

3. *Choice-of-law issues affecting professional responsibility.* The multiplicity of statutes and professional rules that might govern the duties of counsel in an international arbitration gives rise to complex choice-of-law issues. What law governs issues of professional responsibility in an international arbitration? What conflict of laws rules determine the applicable substantive rules of professional responsibility in international arbitration?

Suppose a U.S. lawyer, practicing from the Washington, D.C. office of a multinational law firm, represents a U.S. company in an arbitration seated in England against a Chinese company represented by English lawyers practicing in Moscow and London. What law should govern issues of: (a) conflicts of interest; (b) witness preparation; (c) attorney-client privilege or other forms of legal privilege; (d) the permissibility of contingent fees; and (e) candor towards the tribunal? English law and professional responsibility rules (as that of the arbitral seat)? U.S. law and professional responsibility rules (for the U.S. lawyers) and English law and professional responsibility rules (for the English lawyers)? Russian law (as the law governing the underlying contract)?

There is very little developed commentary or authority on the foregoing questions, which can have considerable importance in actual practice. Different national rules of professional responsibility adopt different approaches to choice-of-law issues. *Compare* ABA Model Rules of Professional Conduct, Rule 8.5(b) (in a matter before a tribunal, the tribunal's rules presumptively apply; in other matters, the rules of the jurisdiction where the alleged misconduct occurred presumptively apply) *with* EC Directive 98-5, Art. 6 (Feb. 16, 1998) (where lawyers from one member state are practicing in another member state, they are subject to the host state's rules of professional conduct for activities occurring there, irrespective of the obligations of their home state). For a thoughtful discussion of Rule 8.5 and the issues it raises, *see* Rogers, *Lawyers Without Borders*, 30 U. Pa. J. Int'l L. 1035 (2009).

Is it possible for lawyers from different jurisdictions to be subject to different ethical restraints in the same arbitration? *See* ABA Model Rules of Professional Conduct, Rule 8.5 comment 7 ("The choice of law provision applies to lawyers engaged in transnational practice, unless international law, treaties or other agreements between competent regulatory authorities in the affected jurisdictions provide otherwise."). If so, wouldn't that favor the attorney from the jurisdiction with more liberal rules regarding attorney activity? What if it were a multinational law firm with partners from different jurisdictions, which had conflicting disclosure obligations?

4. *IBA Guidelines on Party Representation.* Consider the 2013 IBA Guidelines on Party Representation in International Arbitration, excerpted at pp. 339-49 of the Documentary Supplement. What are the principal obligations that the Guidelines would impose on counsel?

Are the Guidelines mandatorily applicable? How might the Guidelines be applied in an arbitration? How might they be relevant?

What is the relationship between the Guidelines and the rules of professional responsibility of the jurisdiction where counsel is admitted? The rules of the professional responsibility of the arbitral seat?

Are the Guidelines useful? Why or why not?

5. *Witness interviews and preparation.* Consider the discussion of witness preparation and cross-examination exercises in D.C. Bar Opinion 79. How does it treat the question of drafting affidavits or written witness statements? The subject of preparation and practice for cross-examination? As D.C. Bar Opinion 79 indicates, it is elementary in U.S. litigation that lawyers will carefully interview potential witnesses and will subsequently prepare them for testimony. Indeed, the Opinion notes that failure to do so could well constitute a violation of an attorney's obligation to zealously represent his or her client. As an experienced U.S. litigator puts it: "in the world in which I have practiced law the failure of counsel adequately to prepare the witness both for direct

and cross-examination would be regarded as a serious dereliction of professional duty." Rifkind, *Practices of the Horseshed*, in L. Lévy & V.V. Veeder, *Arbitration and Oral Evidence* 55 (2004).

Consider the discussion of civil law approaches to witness preparation and cross-examination in Professor van Houtte's article. Compare these approaches to those in the United States (and most other common law jurisdictions). In contrast to U.S. practice, in some civil law jurisdictions it is unethical or even potentially criminal to assist a witness in preparing his or her testimony. Damaska, *Presentation of Evidence and Fact-finding Precision*, 123 U. Pa. L. Rev. 1083, 1088-89 (1975); Vagts, *The International Legal Profession: A Need for More Governance?*, 90 Am. J. Int'l L. 250, 260 (1996). Suppose you are a U.S.-qualified lawyer advising a German client in an arbitration, seated in Belgium, with three civil law arbitrators. How should you approach the question of preparing written witness statements? Preparing the witness for cross-examination?

The 2010 IBA Rules on the Taking of Evidence and some institutional arbitration rules attempt to address the problems arising from different approaches to witness interviews and preparation. For example, Article 4(3) of the IBA Rules provides: "It shall not be improper for a Party, its officers, employees, legal advisors or other representatives to interview its witnesses or potential witnesses and to discuss their prospective testimony with them." *See also* 2014 LCIA Rules, Art. 20(5); 2012 Swiss Rules, Art. 25(2) ("It is not improper for a party, its officers, employees, legal advisors or counsel to interview witnesses, potential witnesses or expert witnesses"). What is the difference? Consider Guidelines 20 and 21 of the IBA Guidelines on Party Representation. By its terms, Article 4(3) of the IBA Rules permits witness interviews but does not address the subjects of witness "preparation" or "familiarization."

Do the IBA Rules or institutional rules override otherwise-applicable national rules of professional responsibility? Even if they do not, how do they affect the likelihood that state bar associations or regulatory authorities would take steps to punish witness preparation or interviews?

6. *Conflicts of interest.* Most national rules of professional responsibility contain provisions regarding conflicts of interest, which preclude lawyers from representing clients in certain matters because of their responsibilities to other parties. ABA Model Rules of Professional Conduct, Rules 1.07 to 1.11; Council of Bars and Law Societies of Europe Code of Conduct for European Lawyers, Art. 3.2. As with other matters of professional responsibility, different jurisdictions have developed different conflict of interest standards. For example, some states may permit a lawyer to represent Party A against Party B, even if the lawyer (or his or her law firm) represents Party B in an unrelated matter; other states may forbid or impose conditions on such representations. *See, e.g.,* ABA Model Rules of Professional Conduct, Rules 1.07 to 1.11; 2011 English Solicitors' Regulation Authority Code of Conduct, Chapter 3; German Bundesrechtsanwaltsordnung (Federal Lawyers' Act), §43a(4).

Different legal systems also adopt different mechanisms for enforcing conflict of interest rules. In some legal regimes, national courts bear the primary responsibility for "disqualification" motions, to prevent a lawyer from proceeding with a representation in breach of his or her ethical duties. Note that the *Bidermann* court acknowledged the authority of New York courts to disqualify lawyers appearing before them.

See also Talecris Biotherapeutics, Inc. v. Baxter Int'l Inc., 491 F.Supp. 2d 510 (D. Del. 2007) (court has power to supervise professional conduct of attorneys appearing before it, which includes power to disqualify attorney). In many jurisdictions, the local bar association or a judicial committee has primary responsibility for conducting disciplinary proceedings, which can indirectly force counsel not to proceed with a representation.

Consider the arbitral tribunal's decision in *ICC Case No. 8879*. What law did the claimant rely upon in order to attempt to disqualify the respondents' counsel? What did the arbitral tribunal hold in response to the claimant's request? Why is it that the claimant's request to disqualify the respondent's counsel supposedly did not fall within the scope of the agreement to arbitrate? Was this not a dispute between the claimant and respondent? Did it not relate to the parties' agreement (*e.g.*, what legal representatives could represent a party in disputes under the contract's arbitration clause)?

Is a tribunal not responsible for ensuring the fairness of the arbitral proceedings before it? Would it be fair for Respondent R, in *ICC Case No. 8879*, to be represented by Claimant's former counsel on the underlying contract?

Consider *Hrvatska*. Note that the tribunal disqualifies counsel for one party, ordering that he not appear in future proceedings. Is this approach—of permitting the arbitrators to decide applications to disqualify counsel—more persuasive than that in *ICC Case No. 8879*? What was the source of the tribunal's authority to disqualify Mr. Mildon in *Hrvatska*? Would any tribunal have this authority? Or only an investment arbitration tribunal in an ICSID arbitration? Would a tribunal in an inter-state arbitration have authority to disqualify counsel?

Was the decision to disqualify Mr. Mildon correct? Note that the tribunal acknowledges the "fundamental" importance of a party's right to choose counsel. *See supra* p. 1045. Note also the three factors that the tribunal relies upon at the end of its order; do these establish genuine questions of the tribunal's impartiality or are they expressions of frustration with the respondent's procedural actions? Consider the tribunal's analysis of the "conflict" arising from Mr. Mildon's membership in the same barrister's chambers as the presiding arbitrator. Is this persuasive? Is there a difference between disqualifying counsel based on their violation of local rules of professional responsibility (as in *ICC Case No. 8879*) and based on their effect on the tribunal's independence (as in *Hrvatska*)? Does this distinction make a difference?

What do the IBA Guidelines on Party Representation provide with respect to conflicts of interest? Why is that? Note Guidelines 4 and 5.

Consider the position taken in the IBA Guidelines on Conflicts of Interest with respect to disclosure of counsel's and arbitrators' membership in barristers' chambers. Compare General Standard 7(b) with the Explanation to General Standard 6(a).

7. *Privilege and communications with opposing counsel.* The privileged character of lawyer-client communications is an important feature of most legal systems. Many jurisdictions take very different approaches to the types of communications (and actors) entitled to privilege, the scope of privilege and the possibility of waivers of privilege. Rogers, *Fit and Function in Legal Ethics: Developing A Code of Conduct for International Arbitration*, 23 Mich. J. Int'l L. 341, 371 (2002). In some jurisdictions, privileges will be relatively narrow (*e.g.*, communications with an in-house

lawyer may not be privileged, or the types of communications that are privileged may be limited); in other cases, privileges may be broad (*e.g.*, communications between opposing counsel may be inadmissible and confidential as between counsel). *Ibid.* These issues can be particularly important in the context of discovery or disclosure during the arbitral proceedings, and are discussed above. *See supra* pp. 828-29.

Suppose an English company communicates, in London, with its English lawyers about English law advice. If the company is later involved in arbitral proceedings seated in Switzerland (or New York), against a German counter-party, what law should apply to the question of whether the communications were privileged? English, Swiss (or New York), something else? What if the underlying contract is governed by German law? What if the advice rendered by the English law firm concerned German, not English, law?

Should the decisions be based on the privilege rules of the relevant legal advisers' jurisdictions? If there are doubts about arbitrators' authority to disqualify counsel, are there doubts about arbitrators' authority to decide privilege issues? Is there any reason to treat the arbitrators' authority with regard to the two issues differently?

8. *Settlement communications.* In many jurisdictions, settlement communications between parties or their representatives are generally not admissible in legal proceedings, at least to prove liability or damages. *See* U.S. Federal Rules of Evidence, Rule 408; California Evidence Code §1152; New York Civil Practice Law & Rules §4547; *Barnetson v. Framlington Group Ltd* [2007] EWCA Civ. 502 (English Ct. App.); Vaver, *"Without Prejudice" Communications—Their Admissibility and Effect,* 9 U. B.C. L. Rev. 85, 97-101 (1974). Nonetheless, rules governing the definition and disclosure of settlement communications differ materially among jurisdictions.

There may be instances in which one jurisdiction's law or ethical rules forbids certain uses of a communication, while another jurisdiction's law or ethical rules requires counsel to attempt to introduce the communication (as part of his or her obligation to represent the client zealously). For example, in some jurisdictions (*e.g.*, Italy and France), labeling a communication as "confidential" is presumed to mean that the receiving attorney cannot disclose the document to the adjudicating tribunal and can require that confidentiality be maintained even against the receiving attorney's client. *See* Rogers, *Fit and Function in Legal Ethics: Developing A Code of Conduct for International Arbitration,* 23 Mich. J. Int'l L. 341, 373 (2002); C. Rogers, *Ethics in International Arbitration* 111-32 (2014). At the same time, such correspondence could very readily contain information that a U.S. lawyer would be ethically obliged to convey to a tribunal (*e.g.*, if it contains concessions) or to a client (*e.g.*, if it touches on issues of settlement). *See ibid.*; ABA Model Rules of Professional Conduct, Rule 1.3 ("A lawyer shall act with reasonable diligence and promptness in representing a client."), Rule 1.4 (requiring attorney to "keep a client reasonably informed about the status of a matter" and to "explain a matter to the extent reasonably necessary to permit the client to make informed decisions about the representation").

Suppose a U.S. (or English) lawyer represents a U.S. (or English) party in an arbitration seated in Italy and that the Italian lawyers (for the Italian counter-party) send a document entitled "confidential" to the U.S. (or English) lawyer, making significant concessions about the merits of the parties' dispute and offering a settlement. Are the U.S. (or English) lawyers permitted (or required) to disclose the letter to their client?

To the arbitrators? What law governs this issue? Italian? U.S. (or English)? Who would have the authority to resolve these issues?

What do the IBA Guidelines on Party Representation provide with respect to settlement communications? To privilege issues more generally? Why?

9. *Contingent fees.* In many jurisdictions outside the United States, "contingent fee" arrangements are either flatly prohibited or stringently regulated (*e.g.*, to limit the size of any premium or the circumstances in which such arrangements may be used). *See, e.g.*, Council of Bars and Law Societies of Europe Code of Conduct for European Lawyers, Art. 3.3.1 ("A lawyer shall not be entitled to make a *pactum de quota litis*."), Art. 3.3.2 ("By '*pactum de quota litis*' is meant an agreement between a lawyer and the client entered into prior to final conclusion of a matter to which the client is a party, by virtue of which the client undertakes to pay the lawyer a share of the result regardless of whether this is represented by a sum of money or by any other benefit achieved by the client upon the conclusion of the matter."), Art. 3.3.3 ("'*Pactum de quota litis*' does not include an agreement that fees be charged in proportion to the value of a matter handled by the lawyer if this is in accordance with an officially approved fee scale or under the control of the Competent Authority having jurisdiction over the lawyer.").

In contrast, contingent fee arrangements are not only permitted in most U.S. litigation but are considered an almost essential aspect of a fair procedure (designed to ensure adequate representation for parties with limited resources). *See* Maurer *et al.*, *Attorney Fee Arrangements: The U.S. and Western European Perspectives*, 19 Nw. J. Int'l L. & Bus. 272 (1999); Vagts, *Professional Responsibility in Transborder Practice: Conflict and Resolution*, 13 Geo. J. Legal Ethics, 677, 683.

There are circumstances in which a contingent fee agreement could violate local law prohibitions in the arbitral seat against champerty, or exceed the permitted terms of such agreements, exposing either a party or counsel to civil or criminal liability. For example, English law imposes relatively stringent prohibitions against contingency fee arrangements. *See Bevan Ashford v. Geoff Yeandle* [1998] 3 All ER 238 (QB) (English High Ct.) (prohibition on contingency fees on the basis of champerty extends to arbitration); Miller, *Conditional Fees and Section 65 of the Arbitration Act 1996*, 149 New L.J. 140 (2000). Similar prohibitions on contingent fee arrangements have recently been upheld in other common law jurisdictions, including Hong Kong and Singapore. *See Otech Pakistan Pvt Ltd v. Clough Eng'g Ltd*, [2006] SGCA 46 (Singapore Ct. App.) (champerty applies to arbitration); *Unruh v. Seeberger*, [2007] 2 HKLRD 414 (H.K. Ct. Fin. App.) (rule against champerty applicable in international arbitration, but the particular contract under consideration was not champertous).

Suppose a U.S. plaintiffs' lawyer represents a U.S. company in a London-seated international arbitration. May the U.S. lawyer enter into a contingent fee agreement with the U.S. party? Why or why not? What are the risks in doing so? Note that most contingent fee agreements would need to be disclosed in submissions on costs at the conclusion of the arbitration and could result in disallowance of a party's claim for its legal costs and/or for claims against the lawyer for the opposing party's costs. *See* G. Born, *International Commercial Arbitration* 3086-3101 (2d ed. 2014).

10. *Candor and honesty to tribunal.* Most rules of professional conduct require lawyers to comply with basic obligations of candor and fairness towards tribunals and counter-parties. *See, e.g.*, ABA Model Rules of Professional Conduct, Rules 3.3, 3.4; Swiss

Bar Association Rules of Professional Conduct, Art. 1; 2011 English Solicitors' Regulation Authority Code of Conduct, Chapter 5.

How is this rule enforced in international arbitration? There are instances in which violations of these standards of candor in an arbitration can result in discipline of attorneys by the local bar associations to which they are admitted. *See In re Disciplinary Action Against Zotaley*, 546 N.W.2d 16, 21 (Minn. 1996) (Minnesota attorney suspended from the practice of law for six months after presenting misleading documentation in domestic arbitration). As already observed, however, the efficacy of such enforcement mechanisms is questionable in the context of international arbitration, where distance, confidentiality and complexity will often result in local bar authorities being unaware of misconduct, ill-suited to assessing complex, atypical issues and reluctant to sanction counsel for conduct in unfamiliar circumstances.

In some instances, national law in the arbitral seat imposes obligations of honesty on counsel (as well as witnesses) in international arbitrations. For example, it is a criminal offense in Switzerland to provide false testimony as to factual matters or false expert evidence to an arbitral tribunal sitting in Switzerland. Swiss Criminal Code, Arts. 307, 309. Legislation in other countries is similar. *See, e.g.*, English Arbitration Act, 1996, §68; French Law No. 71-1130 of 31 December 1971, Art. 3 (lawyer's duty to practice his profession with dignity and integrity); French Criminal Code, Art. 313-1 (fraud); Austrian Criminal Code, Art. 146. In general, however, criminal law enforcement is an unsatisfactory means for regulating misconduct by witnesses or counsel; it is an extreme remedy, which, therefore, is (often properly) very rarely utilized, even in egregious cases.

What should an arbitral tribunal that detects fraud or perjury do in response? May it draw adverse inferences or exclude evidence? May it impose cost-shifting sanctions? May it discipline or impose sanctions on legal counsel (as opposed to parties) who engage in misconduct? Recall the sanctions imposed by the tribunal in *Certain Underwriters*, *supra* pp. 759-65. Consider: *Pope & Talbot, Inc. v. Gov't of Canada, Decision in NAFTA Case of 27 September 2000* (tribunal imposes costs on party because of its counsel's disclosure of confidential materials from arbitration).

Note the provisions of Guidelines 7 and 8 of the IBA Guidelines on Party Representation on communications with arbitrators and Guidelines 9 to 11 on submissions to the arbitral tribunal.

11. *Use of confidential information.* Suppose that counsel in an international arbitration comes into possession of confidential materials belonging to a counter-party. *See, e.g.*, F. Hackett, *Reminiscences of the Geneva Tribunal of Arbitration* 105 n.1 (1911) ("[A member of the U.S. legal team was given] a copy of the Case of the United States [before it was filed,] a secret document to be most carefully guarded. As luck had it, however, when the carriage was driven up to the hotel, this copy was missing; it had dropped into the street. Search was in vain. Somebody found it who, knowing its value, took the precious document to the British Legation, and there disposed of it, it is understood, at a bargain. Then it is supposed to have promptly found its way to London."). What ethical rules prescribe whether or not the material can be used by counsel? Or, alternatively, must be used by counsel? What role, if any, does the arbitral tribunal have in specifying such rules?

12. *Forum selection and arbitrability questions relating to ethical and professional issues in international arbitration.* Putting aside what substantive standards apply to professional responsibility obligations in international arbitration, what forum should apply these standards (and decide what standards apply)? Should the arbitrators do so? Does an international arbitral tribunal have the authority to decide issues of professional responsibility? Note that different nations have differing sources (*i.e.*, statutory, self-regulatory) of ethical and professional responsibility rules.

    Suppose a French partner in a New York law firm, who is based in the firm's London office, represents a French company in an arbitration seated in Stockholm under ICC Rules against a Danish company. Suppose further that the Danish company was a former client of the French lawyer and that it objects to his representation of an adverse party in the Stockholm arbitration. If the lawyer does not withdraw, who should decide whether the objection is merited? The French bar? The New York bar (responsible for regulating the French lawyer's New York partners)? The English Law Society (responsible for regulating foreign lawyers practising in England and Wales)? The Stockholm bar or courts (since Stockholm is the arbitral seat)? New York or Danish courts (in an action brought by the Danish company on contractual or fiduciary duty theories)?

    Should a local court or bar association in the place where a lawyer is qualified have competence to decide issues relating to his or her conduct in an international arbitration seated elsewhere? What problems would arise from such a conclusion? Could different legal representatives, on opposing sides of the same international arbitration, be subject to differing ethical rules? Is that a problem? Could one legal representative be subject to multiple ethical regimes?

    Consider the result and analysis in *Bidermann*. Is the court's analysis of the arbitrability of ethical issues wise? Why should conflicts issues be nonarbitrable? Couldn't arbitral tribunals interpret and apply national ethical rules (just as they interpret and apply national substantive law)? What is there about ethical issues that arguably makes them nonarbitrable? Compare the analysis in *Bidermann* with that in *ICC Case No. 8879*. Contrast these analyses with that in *Hrvatska*. Considering the latter decision, is there anything to suggest that arbitrators cannot in fact make disqualification decisions based on violations of ethical rules?

    What about integrating rules of professional responsibility into institutional arbitration rules? *See* Rogers, *Context and Institutional Structure in Attorney Regulation: Constructing An Enforcement Regime for International Arbitration*, 39 Stan. J. Int'l L. 1 (2003). Suppose the ICC Rules provided that the ICC would decide ethical issues raised during an arbitration with respect to the parties' legal representatives. Would this be a good idea? Would it be enforceable? As against whom?

13. *Attorney malpractice and international arbitration.* In addition to unauthorized practice of law statutes and ethical rules, malpractice lawsuits provide another, albeit indirect, method of regulating attorney conduct during an arbitration. In *Williamson*, *supra* p. 1024, the construction company also sued Williamson PA for malpractice based on the firm's advice during the arbitration. Do malpractice suits serve as a beneficial means of regulating attorney misconduct during arbitration? Aren't they the ultimate measure of whether the attorney is adequately safeguarding the client's interests?

14. *Immunity of arbitrators and counsel in ICSID arbitral proceedings*. Consider Articles 21 and 22 of the ICSID Convention. Give examples of the types of claims that would be barred in national courts by these provisions. Why does the Convention preclude such claims? What mechanisms are there for dealing with attorney misconduct? Should a similar regime be adopted for commercial arbitrations? What would be the benefits? The costs?

15. *A "Code of Arbitrator Conduct"?* Assuming the foregoing statutes, rules and causes of action do not adequately regulate arbitrators' activities, should international *arbitrators* be subject to a transnational code of conduct? Consider the ABA/AAA Code of Ethics for Arbitrators in Commercial Disputes, excerpted at pp. 327-37 of the Documentary Supplement. To what extent does the Code of Ethics provide meaningful guidance for arbitrators? What alternatives would be preferable? Compare the IBA Guidelines on Conflicts of Interest.

    Would an international code of conduct provide a degree of uniformity and predictability to questions of professional responsibility? If so, how exactly would it work? Who would administer and enforce it? How would it relate to domestic statutes and rules governing arbitrator conduct? To rules of the arbitral institution?

PART III
INTERNATIONAL ARBITRAL AWARDS

CHAPTER 14

LEGAL FRAMEWORK FOR INTERNATIONAL ARBITRAL AWARDS

This chapter addresses the legal framework applicable to international arbitral awards. First, the chapter examines the definition of arbitral "awards" and the formal requirements applicable to international awards. Second, the chapter considers the jurisdictional requirements under leading international and national legal regimes for international arbitral awards—including requirements regarding a commercial relationship, for "foreign," "nondomestic," or "international" awards and for reciprocity. Third, the chapter discusses the limits placed by leading international and national legal regimes on actions to challenge awards—including, in particular, actions to annul, correct, or interpret awards in international commercial arbitrations.

A. DEFINITION OF "ARBITRAL AWARD"

The final step in the arbitration proceedings involves the making of the award. Once a final award is made, the tribunal's mandate is substantially concluded. The tribunal becomes *functus officio*, and its responsibilities (and authority) cease to exist, except in very circumscribed ways.[1] Thereafter, the award generally has *res judicata* and other binding preclusive effects of its own force,[2] while compliance with, and enforcement of, the award become matters for the parties and national courts.[3]

Arbitral awards are not "advisory" instruments, but binding, enforceable instruments similar to national court judgments.[4] In most cases, parties voluntarily comply with awards: empirical studies and anecdotal evidence indicate that the percentage of voluntary compliance with arbitral awards exceeds 90% of international cases.[5] This reflects the parties' contractual undertakings to arbitrate and to comply with the resulting arbitral

---

1. *See* G. Born, *International Commercial Arbitration* 3115-24 (2d ed. 2014); Chiu, *Final, Interim, Interlocutory or Partial Award: Misnomers Apt to Mislead*, 13 Sing. Acad. L.J. 461 (2001).

2. *See* G. Born, *International Commercial Arbitration* 2898-901 (2d ed. 2014); ILA International Commercial Arbitration Committee, *Final Report on Lis Pendens and Arbitration* (72d Conference, Toronto 2006); *infra* pp. 1113-25.

3. *See* G. Born, *International Commercial Arbitration* 2898-901 (2d ed. 2014); *infra* pp. 1060-61, 1125-87, 1189-99.

4. *See* G. Born, *International Commercial Arbitration* 2898-901 (2d ed. 2014); Brower & Sharpe, *Multiple and Conflicting Arbitral Awards*, 4 J. World Inv. 211 (2003). Parties occasionally agree to dispute resolution processes whereby a neutral person (or panel) will render a purely advisory, non-binding opinion. In even more unusual cases, parties may refer to this process as "arbitration." As discussed above, this reference is ineffective to convert what is a form of mediation or conciliation (producing a non-binding recommendation) into something regarded by international conventions and national law as arbitration. *See supra* pp. 131-35.

5. *See* Lalive, *Enforcing Awards*, in ICC, *60 Years of ICC Arbitration* 317, 319 (1984) (voluntary compliance with ICC awards exceeds 90%); Kerr, *Concord and Conflict in International Arbitration*, 13 Arb. Int'l 121, 127 (1997) (voluntary compliance plus successful court enforcement exceeds 98%).

award, the efficacy of the arbitral process (which leaves parties believing that their dispute has been fairly resolved), and the likelihood that the award can be coercively enforced. Moreover, in particular contexts, there are specific commercial pressures for parties to comply with awards, such as with awards under some trade association arbitration rules that encourage "voluntary" compliance by members.[6]

Nevertheless, not all international arbitral awards are voluntarily complied with. The ultimate test of any arbitration is, therefore, its ability to render an award that, if necessary, will be recognized and enforced in relevant national courts—including, if necessary, through coercive mechanisms of execution, attachment and garnishment. If an award cannot be successfully enforced, then the parties' arbitration agreement and investment in the arbitral proceedings will have been for naught. Fortunately, in most cases, the recognition and enforcement of awards is straightforward and speedy; the recognition and enforcement of international arbitral awards is discussed below.[7]

At the same time, like other legal proceedings, arbitrations may be imperfect and can leave one party aggrieved. A party in this position may wish to take steps to have the award corrected or, alternatively, judicially reviewed and set aside—just as a party that has lost in litigation may seek appellate review. In contrast to the relative ease and efficiency of recognizing and enforcing foreign awards, efforts to set aside or annul an international arbitral award frequently face substantial obstacles and succeed only in rare cases.[8] The annulment of international arbitral awards, as well as the correction, interpretation and supplementation of such awards, is also discussed below.[9]

The enforcement regimes of the New York Convention and other international instruments apply only to "arbitral awards" and not to other categories of decisions or determinations (such as expert determinations, judgments, or conciliation reports or recommendations). Article I(1) of the New York Convention provides that the Convention applies to "the recognition and enforcement of *arbitral awards*," while Article III of the Convention also deals only with "*arbitral awards*."[10] The Inter-American and European Conventions are to the same effect,[11] as is the ICSID Convention.[12]

---

6. For example, compliance with awards made in arbitrations mandated by the rules of various commodities associations such as GAFTA (Grain and Feed Trade Association) and RSA (Refined Sugar Association) have particular commercial weight. The GAFTA Rules provide that, in the event of a member's non-compliance with an award, the GAFTA Council may circulate a notice informing the Association's membership of the refusal to comply. 2014 GAFTA Rules, Art. 22(1) ("In the event of any party to an arbitration or an appeal held under these Rules neglecting or refusing to carry out or abide by a final award of the tribunal or board of appeal made under these Rules, the Council of GAFTA may post on the GAFTA Notice Board, Web-site, and/or circulate amongst Members in any way thought fit notification to that effect. The parties to any such arbitration or appeal shall be deemed to have consented to the Council taking such action as aforesaid."); RSA Rules, Art. 16.

7. *See infra* pp. 1189-266.

8. *See* G. Born, *International Commercial Arbitration* 2893 (2d ed. 2014); Reinisch, *The Use and Limits of Res Judicata and Lis Pendens as Procedural Tools to Avoid Conflicting Dispute Settlement Outcomes*, 3 L. & Prac. Int'l Cts. & Tribs. 37 (2004).

9. *See infra* pp. 1125-87.

10. New York Convention, Arts. I(1), III (emphasis added).

11. Inter-American Convention, Art. 4 ("arbitral decision or award"), Art. 5 ("decision"); 1961 European Convention, Art. I(1)(b) ("awards"), Art. VIII ("award"), Art. IX ("arbitral award").

12. ICSID Convention, Arts. 48-55.

Legislation in developed jurisdictions, including the UNCITRAL Model Law, is also generally applicable only to awards (and not other instruments).[13] Only "arbitral awards," and not other instruments, are subject to annulment, correction, or interpretation, or recognition and enforcement under most national arbitration statutes.

Despite the importance of the concept of an "arbitral award," neither international arbitration conventions nor national arbitration legislation contain express definitions of what constitutes an arbitral "award," nor what distinguishes an "award" from other arbitral decisions.[14] The materials excerpted below explore these issues, as well as the formal requirements applicable to arbitral awards.

BELGIAN JUDICIAL CODE
Article 1713

1713(1). The arbitral tribunal shall make a final decision or render interlocutory decisions by way of one or several awards.

1713(2). The parties may determine the time limit within which the Arbitral Tribunal must render its award, or the terms for setting such a time limit. Failing this, if the arbitral tribunal is late in rendering its award, and a period of six months has elapsed between the date on which the last arbitrator has been appointed, the President of the Court of First Instance, at the request of one of the parties, may impose a time limit on the arbitral tribunal in accordance with article 1680, paragraph 3. The mission of the arbitrators ends if the arbitral tribunal has not rendered its award at the expiry of this time limit.

1713(3). The award shall be made in writing and shall be signed by the arbitrator. In arbitral proceedings with more than one arbitrator, the signatures of the majority of all members of the arbitral tribunal shall suffice, provided that the reason for any omitted signature is stated.

1713(4). The award shall state the reasons upon which it is based.

1713(5). In addition to the decision itself, the award shall contain, inter alia:
     a) the names and domiciles of the arbitrators;
     b) the names and domiciles of the parties;
     c) the object of the dispute;
     d) the date on which the award is rendered;
     e) the place of arbitration determined in accordance with article 1701, paragraph 1, and the place where the award is rendered.

1713(6). The final award shall fix the costs of the arbitration and decide which of the parties shall bear them or in what proportion they shall be borne by the parties. Unless otherwise agreed by the parties, these costs shall include the fees and expenses of the arbitrators, the fees and expenses of the parties' counsel and representatives, the costs of services rendered by the instances in charge of the administration of the arbitration and all other expenses arising from the arbitral proceedings.

---

13. G. Born, *International Commercial Arbitration* 2918-19, 2923 (2d ed. 2014).
14. This treatment of the definition of "arbitral awards" parallels that of "arbitration agreements," where little statutory guidance exists. *See supra* pp. 116-17, 130-31.

1713(7). The arbitral tribunal may order a party to pay a penalty. Articles 1385 *bis* through *octies* shall apply mutatis mutandis.

1713(8). Once the arbitral award has been rendered, a copy shall be sent, in accordance with article 1678, paragraph 1, to each party by the sole arbitrator or by the chairman of the arbitral tribunal, who shall moreover ensure that each party receives an original copy if the method of communication retained in accordance with article 1678, paragraph 1 did not entail the delivery of such an original. He shall file the original copy with the court clerk of the Court of First Instance, and shall notify the parties of this filing.

1713(9). The award shall have the same effect as a court decision in the relationship between the parties.

NOTES

1. *Form requirements for award under New York Convention.* Recall that the New York Convention applies only to arbitration agreements that satisfy Article II's "writing" requirement. *See supra* pp. 375-92. Does the Convention impose any comparable form requirements for awards? Consider Article IV(1)(a), excerpted at p. 2 of the Documentary Supplement. Does Article IV(1)(a) impliedly require that awards be in written form? Does the Convention apply to awards that are not in written form (*e.g.*, oral awards)?

    Does anything in the Convention preclude a Contracting State from imposing form requirements on awards, including requirements that go beyond the written form? For example, suppose a Contracting State required that all awards be in triplicate, with signatures and seals on each page, in the official language of the relevant state, and that awards not meeting this standard would not be recognized. Does the Convention permit such requirements?

2. *Form requirements for award under ICSID Convention.* What formal requirements are imposed by the ICSID Convention on arbitral awards in investment arbitrations? Consider Article 48, excerpted at p. 23 of the Documentary Supplement. What else must be done, formally, with an ICSID award after it is made? Compare the treatment of the award under the New York Convention.

    Consider also Articles 79 and 80 of the 1907 Hague Convention, excerpted at p. 49 of the Documentary Supplement. How do the form requirements of the Convention compare to those in international commercial and investment arbitration? Consider what is done with an award when and after it is made. What explains these differences?

3. *Form requirements for award under national arbitration legislation.* Most arbitration statutes impose form requirements for arbitral awards (the FAA being a notable exception). Consider Article 31 of the UNCITRAL Model Law, excerpted at p. 93 of the Documentary Supplement. What form requirements does Article 31 impose on international arbitral awards? What is the purpose of these requirements? Compare the Model Law with Article 1481 of the French Code of Civil Procedure, excerpted at p. 149 of the Documentary Supplement, and Article 1713 of the Belgian Judicial Code. What are the differences?

    To what extent may the form requirements of Article 31 be altered by the parties' agreement? Suppose parties agree that no signatures are required on the award. Suppose parties agree that no reasons must be included in the award. Why are signatures treated differently from reasons?

4. *Signature requirements.* Some arbitration statutes require that all the arbitrators sign the award. What if one arbitrator refuses? Does this prevent the award from being valid? In most jurisdictions, the award may, if necessary, be signed by a majority of the arbitrators. *See, e.g.,* UNCITRAL Model Law, Art. 31(1); French Code of Civil Procedure, Art. 1513; Belgian Judicial Code, Art. 1713(3); Netherlands Code of Civil Procedure, Arts. 1057(2), (3).

   Compare ICSID Convention, Art. 48(2). Alternatively, an award may be signed by the chairman alone in some jurisdictions. French Code of Civil Procedure, Art. 1513; SLPIL, Art. 189. Where one arbitrator refuses to sign the award, an explanation of the refusal is sometimes required (by the majority or chairman of the tribunal).

5. *Scope of application of form requirements for awards under national arbitration legislation.* To what awards are the form requirements discussed in the preceding Note applicable? Suppose Parties 1 and 2, from States X and Y, agree to arbitrate in State Z. Are the form requirements of States X and Y applicable to an award made in State Z—or are only the form requirements of State Z applicable to that award? Consider Article 1(2) of the UNCITRAL Model Law, excerpted at p. 86 of the Documentary Supplement. Does the question of what state's form requirements apply to an award arise under the ICSID Convention?

6. *Consequences of failure to comply with form requirement in award.* Suppose a commercial arbitral award does not comply with the form requirements of the arbitration statute of the arbitral seat. What are the consequences of that non-compliance? In particular, is an otherwise valid and binding award subject to annulment because it lacks a date or an indication of the place of arbitration?

   Consider Article 34 of the UNCITRAL Model Law, excerpted at pp. 94-95 of the Documentary Supplement. What does it provide with regard to annulment of an award—and, in particular, does Article 34 provide for annulment of an award for formal defects? Consider also Article 1717(3) of the Belgian Judicial Code. What do they provide with regard to annulment of an award for formal defects? Which formal defects will result in annulment and which will not?

   What mechanisms other than annulment are available to deal with formal defects in an award? Consider Article 33(1) of the Model Law, which permits corrections to an award in limited circumstances. Is there any reason Article 33(1) could not be used to correct formal defects in an award?

   How does the ICSID Convention deal with formal defects in an ICSID award? Consider Articles 51 and 52 of the Convention.

7. *Requirements for reasoned awards under national arbitration statutes.* Consider Article 31(2) of the UNCITRAL Model Law. Does it require an award to be "reasoned"? Are parties permitted to dispense, by agreement, with the requirement for a reasoned award? Why might parties wish to do so?

   If the parties' arbitration agreement does not expressly require that the arbitrators provide reasons, should such a requirement be assumed? Consider Article VIII of the European Convention, which provides that the parties "shall be presumed to have agreed that reasons shall be given for the award," except where: (a) they "expressly declare" to the contrary or (b) they "have assented to an arbitration procedure under which it is not customary to give reasons for awards," and neither party requests reasons.

8. *No requirement under FAA that arbitrators render reasoned awards.* In the United States, domestic practice was historically not to issue reasoned awards. Under U.S. domestic arbitration law, including the FAA, unreasoned awards are enforceable (at least where institutional rules or the parties' agreement do not require a reasoned award). *See United Steelworkers of Am. v. Enter. Wheel & Car Corp.*, 363 U.S. 593, 598 (1960) ("Arbitrators have no obligation to the court to give their reasons for an award"); *Eljer Mfg Inc. v. Kowin Dev. Corp.*, 14 F.3d 1250 (7th Cir. 1994) ("an arbitrator is simply not required to state the reasons for his decision"); *Virgin Islands Nursing Ass'n v. Schneider*, 668 F.2d 221 (3d Cir. 1981) (rejecting argument that court should "exercise [its] supervisory power to enunciate a new requirement that arbitrators file written opinions, or, at least, findings of fact").

9. *Requirement in parties' agreement or institutional arbitration rules for reasoned award.* Most institutional arbitration rules require reasoned awards. *See* 2010 UNCITRAL Rules, Art. 34(3); 2012 ICC Rules, Art. 31(2); 2014 LCIA Rules, Art. 26(2). Where the parties' arbitration agreement (including any incorporated institutional rules) requires a reasoned award, what should the remedy be for non-compliance with this requirement? Should this warrant annulment of the award? Consider Article 34(2)(a)(iv) of the UNCITRAL Model Law. If the tribunal fails to provide reasons required by the parties' agreement, can one say that the "arbitral procedure was not in accordance with the agreement of the parties"?

10. *Reasons for requiring reasoned awards.* Why do many arbitration statutes and international conventions require a reasoned award? Is this consistent with efforts to encourage and facilitate arbitration as a means of dispute-resolution? How? Consider the following:

> "By the end of the judgment the whole of the judge's thinking on the facts and the law should have been laid bare, that all who run may read. It should be fair to assume that he has not been led to his decision by matters he has not mentioned. No cards regarded by him as significant should remain face downwards or in the pack. His decision may later be held to have been right or wrong, but at least there should be no real doubt what he decided or why." Bingham, *Reasons and Reasons for Reasons,* 4 Arb. Int'l 141, 145 (1988).

> *See also* Carbonneau, *Rendering of Awards With Reasons*: *The Elaboration of A Common Law of International Transactions,* 23 Colum. J. Transnat'l L. 579 (1984-1985). Is this rationale persuasive? Does it justify treating the requirement for reasons as (a) a mandatory requirement, from which the parties may not deviate; or (b) a presumptive requirement, from which the parties may deviate but only by express contrary agreement?

11. *Meaning of requirement for reasoned award.* What does the requirement for a reasoned award entail? How lengthy, detailed, comprehensive, or erudite must an award be to satisfy a requirement for reasons? Consider the following explanation of the requirement for a reasoned award:

> "All that is necessary is that the arbitrators should set out what, on their view of the evidence, did or did not happen and should explain succinctly why, in the light of what happened, they have reached their decision and what that decision is. This is all that is

meant by a 'reasoned award.'" *Bremer Handelsgesellschaft v. Westzucker* [1981] 2 Lloyd's Rep. 130, 123 (English Ct. App.).

Is that persuasive? What else might be required of a reasoned award? Does the requirement for a reasoned award mean that the award must be correctly reasoned? Well-reasoned? If awards were required to be correctly reasoned, would this not impose a basis for substantive review of the merits of the arbitrators' decision?

12. *Annulment of unreasoned award.* Suppose an arbitral tribunal fails to provide a reasoned award or its reasoning is held insufficient. What is the consequence of this failure? Is a failure of a tribunal to provide reasons for its award grounds for annulment under Article 34 of the UNCITRAL Model Law? For non-recognition under Article 36? Compare Articles 1713(4), 1717(3)(a)(iv) and 1721(1)(a)(iv) of the Belgian Judicial Code. Are parties permitted to contract out of the requirement for a reasoned award? Is the tribunal's failure to provide reasons a basis for annulment of the award?

Consider the following Swiss decision:

"In addition, Art. 190(2) [of the SLPIL, providing grounds for setting aside an award] does not know the grounds of a lack of reasons. One can also not deduce a mandatory requirement for reasons from the right to be heard within the meaning of Article 190(2)(d). The lack of reasons also does not violate public policy. If the lack of reasons does not even constitute a ground for annulment under Art. 190(2), it can equally not hinder enforcement." *Judgment of 9 December 2003*, DFT 130 III 125, 130 (Swiss Fed. Trib.).

Should an award be subject to annulment if it is unreasoned? Why or why not? Should an unreasoned award automatically be subject to annulment or only in some circumstances?

13. *Recognition of unreasoned foreign awards.* Suppose an award is made in a jurisdiction that does not require reasoned awards (*e.g.,* the United States). May that unreasoned award be recognized in a jurisdiction that requires reasoned awards in locally-seated arbitrations? Should the unreasoned award be recognized? *Compare* Belgian Judicial Code, Art. 1721(1)(a)(iv); *Judgment of 29 January 1958*, 47 Rev. crit. Dr. intl. priv. 148 (Nancy Cour d'appel) (1958) ("failure to give reasons, although contrary in principle to French procedure is not contrary to French international public policy, if it is permitted by the foreign law"); *Judgment of 30 September 1999*, XXXI Y.B. Comm. Arb. 640, 648 (2006) (Hanseatisches Oberlandesgericht Bremen) (foreign award was scantily-reasoned and "would hardly meet the requirements of German domestic procedural public policy," but this was not grounds for non-recognition under Article V(2)(b): "In the case of foreign arbitral awards, it must be borne in mind that the deciding arbitrators come from different legal cultures and follow the customs of their procedural systems when writing reasons."); *Bay Hotel & Resort Ltd v. Cavalier Constr. Co.,* [2001] UKPC 34 (Turks & Caicos Privy Council) (award made in United States was not reasoned, by either English standards or by standard that "the loser should be told not only that he has lost but also why he has lost"; nonetheless, award was recognized on grounds that "however lean and unembellished, the award with its supplement must be found to have been reasoned within the meaning of the [AAA] institutional rules" pursuant to which it was made); *Judgment of 8 October 1977*, IV Y.B. Comm. Arb. 289, 292 (1979) (Florence Corte di Appello) ("fact that the reason-

ing constitutes a principle of the Italian Constitution is not important because what is fundamental in Italian law of procedure may not be considered as such by foreign legislative and judicial authorities").

14. *Requirement for reasoning under ICSID Convention.* Consider the requirement for reasoned awards in Articles 48(3) and 52(1)(e) of the ICSID Convention. What is the content of the requirement for reasoning under the Convention? Consider:

> "Provided that the reasons given by a tribunal can be followed and relate to the issues that were before the tribunal, their correctness is beside the point.... Moreover, reasons may be stated succinctly or at length, and different legal traditions differ in their modes of expressing reasons.... In the Committee's view, annulment under Article 52(1)(e) should only occur in a clear case. This entails two conditions: first, the failure to state reasons must leave the decision on a particular point essentially lacking in any expressed rationale; and second, that point must itself be necessary to the tribunal's decision." *Compañía de Aguas del Aconquija SA & Vivendi Universal SA v. Argentine Repub., Ad Hoc Committee Judgment on Application for Annulment Submitted by CAA Against Arbitral Award in ICSID Case No. ARB/97/3 Rendered on 21 November 2000 of 3 July 2002*, 6 ICSID Rep. 340, 358 (2002).

Consider also:

> "an insistence on a very detailed standard and a culturally unique ratiocinative style for the reasoning requirement would open up many awards to challenges of nullification and undermine the entire process of international arbitration. Hence, there would appear to be very compelling reasons for the substantially reduced requirement found in international arbitral practice and adopted in the text of Article 52 of the ICSID Convention." Reisman, *The Breakdown of the Control Mechanism in ICSID Arbitration*, Duke L.J. 739, 792 (1989).

Is this appropriate? Should there be differences in the standard for reasoning in ICSID investment arbitrations and commercial arbitrations? What about inter-state arbitrations? Compare Article 79 of the 1907 Hague Convention, excerpted at p. 49 of the Documentary Supplement.

15. *Requirement for reasoning under international law.* Consider the award in the *Abyei Arbitration. Abyei Arbitration (Gov't of Sudan v. Sudan Peoples' Liberation Movement/Army), Final Award in PCA Case of 22 July 2009.* Note how it articulates the requirement for reasoned awards. What is the source of this requirement? Compare the requirement to that under the ICSID Convention and national arbitration legislation applicable to international commercial arbitrations.

16. *Majority awards.* Suppose the members of a three-person tribunal are unable to agree upon a common result. If only two of the three arbitrators agree to the substance (and text) of an award, may they issue a majority award? In a commercial arbitration, what law would govern this issue (for example, in an arbitration seated in State A)?

Consider Article 29 of the UNCITRAL Model Law, excerpted at pp. 92-93 of the Documentary Supplement. What does it permit a majority of the tribunal to do? Is this sensible? What if the parties agree to a contrary result, requiring that all three arbitrators agree to the award? Would you recommend such a requirement?

What if the tribunal is unable to produce a majority award? For example, in a case involving claims by A against B and C, suppose one arbitrator concludes that A is entitled to no recovery, one arbitrator concludes that A may recover from B (but not C), and one arbitrator concludes that A may recover from C (but not B). Can an award be made in these circumstances? For example, can an award be made under Article 29 of the Model Law? *Compare* English Arbitration Act, 1996, §20(4) (permitting awards by presiding arbitrator); 2012 ICC Rules, Art. 31(1) (same); 2014 LCIA Rules, Art. 26(5) (same); SLPIL, Art. 189(2) (same). Is it appropriate to permit awards by the presiding arbitrator alone, when no majority award is possible? *Compare* ICSID Convention, Art. 48(1); 1907 Hague Convention, Arts. 78, 79.

17. *Permissibility of dissenting opinions.* Suppose one arbitrator feels strongly that the tribunal has reached an incorrect and indefensible result. Note that the arbitrator might, in principle, refuse to sign the award; is that an appropriate course of action? Note that the arbitrator might also, in principle, issue a dissenting opinion; is that an appropriate course of action?

Some institutional rules expressly permit dissenting (and concurring) opinions. *See, e.g.,* ICSID Rules, Rule 47(3); 2015 CIETAC Rules, Art. 49(5). Suppose no such express provision exists. May an arbitrator issue a dissenting opinion in these circumstances? What might argue against an arbitrator issuing a dissent? Does this violate the confidentiality of the arbitral tribunal's deliberations? Does it contradict the arbitrators' obligation to deliberate collegially? To act impartially and independently? Consider: Geimer, in R. Zöller (ed.), *Zivilprozessordnung* §1052, ¶5 (30th ed. 2014) ("Absent different agreement by the parties, the arbitrators have to keep the secrecy of deliberations (including the voting result).... A dissenting opinion is only admitted given express permission in the parties' arbitration agreement."); J. Robert, *L'arbitrage: Droit interne, Droit international privé* 360 (5th ed. 1983) ("Although it is customary under a certain number of foreign laws, notably Anglo-Saxon, the dissenting opinion is prohibited in French domestic law since it violates the secrecy of the tribunal's deliberations"). Are these points persuasive?

Consider the provisions for dissenting opinions in investment arbitration. ICSID Convention, Art. 48(4). Compare the approach in inter-state arbitrations. *See* 1899 Hague Convention, Art. 52 ("The Award, given by a majority of votes, is accompanied by a statement of reasons. It is drawn up in writing and signed by each member of the Tribunal. Those members who are in the minority may record their dissent when signing."). *Compare* Articles 78 and 79 of the 1907 Hague Convention, excerpted at p. 49 of the Documentary Supplement. Is there any reason that dissents should be permitted in investment or inter-state arbitrations but not in commercial arbitrations? In advance? Or vice versa?

Note that, in the *Alabama Arbitration*, Lord Cockburn announced that he was submitting a dissenting opinion at the tribunal's formal presentation of its award to the parties: "At this point, Sir Alexander Cockburn arose, and in a clear, musical voice, said that he held in his hand a paper setting forth his reasons for not joining his colleagues in assenting to the award. With that he produced a bulky collection of sheets ... and, handing it to the Secretary, expressed a wish that the 'Opinion' be annexed to the Protocol. It did not appear that any one of his colleagues had seen Sir Alexander's dissenting opinion. But it was no time for technicalities; and Count Sclopis politely replied that the desire of the Arbitrator from Great Britain should be gratified." F. Hackett, *Reminiscences of the Geneva Arbitration Tribunal* 342-43 (1911). Should a dissenting arbitrator provide a copy of the dissent to his or her colleagues? Why or why not? Must he or she do so?

18. *Character and purpose of dissenting opinions.* Suppose an arbitrator does decide to dissent. What is the purpose of such a dissent? Are there any limits, either legal or prudential, on a dissenting opinion? Consider:

> "I regret that I am unable to concur with the conclusions of the Tribunal contained in the *Dispositif* of the Award or to agree, in general, with the reasoning deployed by the majority to arrive at those conclusions. Indeed, and I say this with great respect to my learned colleagues, I find the underlying logic of the Award singularly unpersuasive (let alone convincing), self-contradicting, result-oriented, in many respects cavalier, insufficiently critical and unsupported by evidence, and indeed flying in the face of overwhelming contrary evidence. In other words.... [the Award is] as far in excess of mandate as it is removed from historical (and contemporary) reality. I must therefore dissent." *Abyei Arbitration (Gov't of Sudan v. Sudan Peoples' Liberation Movement/Army), Dissenting Opinion of His Excellency Judge Awn Shawkat Al-Khasawneh in PCA Case of 22 July 2009,* 1.

Compare the dissent by Lord Cockburn in the *Alabama Arbitration* (accompanied by a refusal to sign the tribunal's award). *See supra* pp. 755-56, 1068; Bingham, *The Alabama Claims Arbitration,* 54 Int'l & Comp. L.Q. 1, 23 (2005).

Is it appropriate for a dissenting arbitrator to challenge the validity of the tribunal's award? What objections might be made to this? Should there be either legal or prudential limits to the nature of the dissenting opinion's criticisms of the tribunal's award?

19. *Awards drafted by third parties.* Suppose that the arbitrators do not draft their award themselves, but instead delegate this to a third party (*e.g.*, a secretary to the tribunal, an expert). Consider *Judgment of 7 June 1989, Sacheri v. Robotto,* XVI Y.B. Comm. Arb. 156 (1991) (Italian Corte di Cassazione) ("The issue is whether Italian procedural law allows arbitrators in *arbitrato rituale* [*i.e.*, formal arbitration] to delegate an expert to decide legal issues which are essential to the decision-making process. This question must be answered in the negative.... [T]here is a difference within the framework of the *arbitrato rituale* between arbitrators who decided according to rules of law and arbitrators called upon to decide *ex aequo et bono.* Under Italian procedural law it does not seem possible to allow the former to delegate a third person to assess the legal issues which are relevant for the decision-making process.").

Don't judges in national courts often rely upon law clerks to draft their opinions? (They do.) What is different about arbitrators? What if an arbitral tribunal relies upon a draft section of their award, prepared by an acknowledged expert, more experienced and capable, on particular issues raised by the parties' dispute? What is wrong with that? What if the tribunal informs the parties?

Note the suggestion in *Judgment of 7 June 1989* that it might be permissible to delegate an arbitrator's duties to a third party if the arbitrator was to decide *ex aequo et bono.* What sense does that make? If the arbitrator is unconstrained by law (*i.e.*, can decide *ex aequo et bono, supra* pp. 1020-21), isn't it more, not less, important that the arbitrator decide personally? Why or why not?

20. *Consent awards.* If parties succeed in reaching a negotiated resolution of their dispute(s), one option is to simply dismiss the arbitration, recording the terms of the settlement in an agreement to this effect. Alternatively, however, parties may wish to

obtain a "consent award" (or "award on agreed terms"), which records some or all of the terms of their settlement. A consent award is often perceived as providing a greater degree of certainty and enforceability than a simple settlement agreement; in particular, a consent award may be capable of being enforced as an award (*e.g.*, if it contains a payment obligation), rather than requiring suit for breach of contract.

Many arbitration statutes provide expressly for the possibility of consent awards. Article 30(1) of the UNCITRAL Model Law provides that, if the parties reach a settlement during the arbitration, the tribunal "shall ... if requested by the parties and not objected to by the arbitral tribunal, record the settlement in the form of an arbitral award on agreed terms." Similar provisions exist in other arbitration legislation or are accepted by national court decisions. *See, e.g.*, English Arbitration Act, 1996, §51; Japanese Arbitration Law, Art. 38(1); G. Born, *International Commercial Arbitration* 3021-27 (2d ed. 2014); Kreindler, *Settlement Agreements and Arbitration in the Context of the ICC Rules*, 9(2) ICC ICArb. Bull. 22 (1998); Tchakoua, *The Status of the Arbitral Award by Consent: The Limits of the Useful*, 2002 RDAI/IBLJ 775. Most institutional rules also provide expressly that arbitral tribunals may make consent awards if requested to do so by the parties. *See* 2010 UNCITRAL Rules, Art. 36(1) ("The arbitral tribunal is not obliged to give reasons for such an award."); 2014 LCIA Rules, Art. 26(9). *See also* 2012 ICC Rules, Art. 32. Why might an arbitral tribunal refuse to make a consent award? Must an arbitral tribunal do anything to explain or justify its decision not to make a consent award? Does the tribunal have to determine whether the settlement between the parties was actually reached during the proceedings and not before? Why?

Both national laws and institutional rules provide that the general requirement that arbitral awards be "reasoned" does not apply to consent awards. UNCITRAL Model Law, Art. 31(2); English Arbitration Act, 1996, §52(4); 2010 UNCITRAL Rules, Art. 36(1); 2014 LCIA Rules, Art. 26(9). Why is that? Is that rule appropriate? Should a consent award be subject to recognition and enforcement, like other arbitral awards? Is a consent award an adjudicated decision? Should that be required for recognition?

21. *Requirements under national law for deposit of awards.* Does anything in the New York Convention require that arbitral awards be deposited with a local court or notary in the arbitral seat? Does anything in Articles 30 through 36 of the UNCITRAL Model Law impose such a requirement? Consider Article 193 of the SLPIL, excerpted at p. 160 of the Documentary Supplement. Is the deposit of an award required by Article 193? Imposed as a condition of validity or enforcement of the award? Compare Article 1713(8) of the Belgian Judicial Code. What is the purpose of these provisions? What effect do they have on the validity of the award (*i.e.*, what if the chairman of the tribunal neglects to deposit the award)? Note that the non-deposit of the award is generally not included among the grounds for annulment of an award. *See infra* pp. 1134-73. What effect do provisions requiring deposit of an award have on the finality of the award? *See infra* pp. 1163-64.

B. JURISDICTIONAL REQUIREMENTS OF INTERNATIONAL ARBITRAL AWARDS UNDER INTERNATIONAL AND NATIONAL ARBITRATION REGIMES

After an international arbitral award is made, international conventions and national arbitration statutes provide five basic legal avenues that may be taken with respect to the award. These five avenues can be taken independently or, on occasion, pursued in parallel, sometimes with different parties initiating different proceedings.

First, a party to the arbitration may seek a "correction" or "interpretation" of the award by the tribunal.[15] The circumstances in which such relief is available are very limited (and constitute one of the narrow exceptions to the general principle that an arbitral tribunal becomes *functus officio* after making its final award). If an award is corrected or interpreted, the correction or interpretation becomes a part of the tribunal's final award, then subject to further actions in national courts.

Second, the prevailing party in the arbitration may commence proceedings in the national courts of the arbitral seat to "confirm" or "recognize" the award (*e.g.*, to obtain *exequatur*). The successful confirmation of the award will usually provide the basis for the entry of a judgment of the local court based on the underlying award.[16] The confirmation of an award in the arbitral seat may occasionally be a defensive act (*e.g.*, to comply with local requirements providing that awards can only be confirmed within a certain period after they are made);[17] much more frequently, confirmation is a step towards further actions, and specifically, towards "enforcement" of the relief granted in the award (*e.g.*, execution against the award-debtor's assets).

After confirmation of an award in the arbitral seat, the resulting judgment can either be "enforced" in local courts (typically in the same manner as a domestic court judgment) or it can be taken to another state for "recognition" and enforcement in accordance with its legislation for recognizing and enforcing foreign judgments.[18]

---

15. *See, e.g.*, UNCITRAL Model Law, Art. 33; *infra* pp. 1125-34. *See also* G. Born, *International Commercial Arbitration* 3124-48 (2d ed. 2014); Gaitis, *International and Domestic Arbitration Procedure: The Need for A Rule Providing A Limited Opportunity for Arbitral Reconsideration of Reasoned Awards*, 15 Am. Rev. Int'l Arb. 1, 80 (2004).

16. *See, e.g.*, UNCITRAL Model Law, Art. 35; U.S. FAA, 9 U.S.C. §9; SLPIL, Art. 193; *infra* pp. 1073, 1099, 1190. *See also* G. Born, *International Commercial Arbitration* 2903-04 (2d ed. 2014).

17. *See, e.g.*, U.S. FAA, 9 U.S.C. §9 (award may be confirmed for one year following date it was made). In some jurisdictions, an award's effects may depend on its first being recognized or confirmed, so that applying for confirmation will often be undertaken even if no further steps are contemplated (*e.g.*, by a successful respondent, to ensure that the claimant does not attempt to relitigate the issue subsequently).

18. *See* G. Born, *International Commercial Arbitration* 2905-08 (2d ed. 2014); H. Gharavi, *The International Effectiveness of the Annulment of An Arbitral Award* (2002); *infra* p. 1199. As this description indicates, "recognition" refers to judicial acceptance or confirmation of an award (or foreign court judgment) and the entry of a local court judgment accepting or confirming the operative terms of the foreign award, while "enforcement" refers to the subsequent reliance of local national courts on this judgment for execution, attachment, garnishment and similar remedies. G. Born, *International Commercial Arbitration* 2905-08 (2d ed. 2014); *Astro Nusantara Int'l BV v. PT Ayunda Prima Mitra*, [2012] SGHC 212, 70 (Singapore High Ct.) ("Recognition and enforcement of arbitral awards are concerned with giving effect to such awards. There is a difference between 'recognition' per se and 'recognition and enforcement.' An award may be recognised without being enforced, but a court cannot enforce an award which it does not recognise.").

Third, an award can be taken to a state outside the arbitral seat, to be "recognized" (and then "enforced") in that state's courts, without first being confirmed in the seat. Recognition of a foreign award occurs in the form of a local national court judgment, which gives the award full legal force within the local legal system (in the same manner that a foreign judgment is recognized).[19]

As discussed below, one of the fundamental reforms of the New York Convention was to remove the requirement of "double *exequatur*," which had required an award to be confirmed in the arbitral seat before it could be recognized or enforced abroad.[20] Under the Convention, an award is capable of recognition outside the arbitral seat even if it has not been recognized or confirmed in the seat. Indeed, there will be circumstances in which an arbitral award may (and will) be recognized abroad even if it has been set aside in the arbitral seat.[21]

Once the award is recognized in a foreign state, the resulting judgment can then ordinarily be given effect in the courts of that state in the same manner as a judgment of that state's courts. This includes coercively "enforcing" the award or judgment against the assets of the award- or judgment-debtor, in accordance with local legislation governing execution and enforcement of judgments.[22] It also includes giving the award or judgment preclusive effect in the courts of the foreign state (in accordance with local legislation regarding the preclusive effects of foreign awards and/or judgments).[23]

Fourth, the unsuccessful party in the arbitration may commence proceedings, in the national courts of the arbitral seat, to "set aside," "annul," or "vacate" the award.[24] If successful, such an action generally has the legal effect of nullifying the award within the domestic legal regime of the arbitral seat, much the way that an appellate decision vacates a trial court judgment. After an award is annulled or set aside, it cannot be enforced locally in the courts of the arbitral seat.

Nonetheless, despite the annulment of an award, the better view is that the award still exists—both as a matter of fact and (potentially) as a matter of law in other legal systems outside the arbitral seat.[25] It remains open in principle to the successful party in the arbitration to attempt to have the award recognized, notwithstanding its annulment, in courts outside the arbitral seat. Equally, it remains open in principle to the successful party in the arbitration to rely on the award for preclusive effects in foreign court proceedings, irrespective of the award's annulment in the arbitral seat. In both instances, the annulment of the award in the arbitral seat, and the reasons for that annulment, may be relied upon to

---

19. *See* G. Born, *International Commercial Arbitration* 2905-07 (2d ed. 2014); *infra* pp. 1189-99.

20. *See* G. Born, *International Commercial Arbitration* 3411-17, 3424-25 (2d ed. 2014); Quigley, *Accession by the United States to the United Nations Convention on the Recognition and Enforcement of Foreign Arbitral Awards*, 70 Yale L.J. 1049, 1054 (1961); A. van den Berg, *The New York Arbitration Convention of 1958* 266-67 (1981); *infra* pp. 1196-97.

21. *See infra* pp. 1174-87.

22. See *infra* pp. 1113-25; G. Born, *International Commercial Arbitration* 2907-08 (2d ed. 2014); Harnik, *Recognition and Enforcement of Foreign Arbitral Awards*, 31 Am. J. Comp. L. 703 (1983).

23. *See* G. Born, *International Commercial Arbitration* 2908-09; 3739-73 (2d ed. 2014).

24. *See, e.g.,* U.S. FAA, 9 U.S.C. §10; UNCITRAL Model Law, Art. 34; SLPIL, Art. 190; *infra* pp. 1099-112, 1134-73. *See also* G. Born, *International Commercial Arbitration* 2905 (2d ed. 2014).

25. *See* G. Born, *International Commercial Arbitration* 3390-92 (2d ed. 2014); H. Gharavi, *The International Effectiveness of the Annulment of An Arbitral Award* (2002); *infra* pp. 1182-84.

resist recognition and enforcement of the award, but the annulment is not necessarily independently sufficient to preclude recognition of the award in other states.

Finally, in some instances it is not possible for an arbitral award to be recognized or enforced as an award. This can result from a failure to timely confirm it in the arbitral seat or to recognize it elsewhere, from formal defects, or from valid substantive grounds for resisting confirmation or recognition of the award.[26] Even in such cases, the award may nonetheless continue to have limited legal effect under national law. For example, the award may be the basis for a contract action under national law or may be admissible as evidence in an action on the merits of the parties' underlying dispute.[27]

Critical to the recognition, enforcement and annulment of an arbitral award under the foregoing regime (or otherwise) is the question of what (if any) international arbitration convention and national arbitration statute applies to the award. In the context of commercial arbitration, resolving these questions requires determining whether an award: (a) arises from a "commercial" and "defined legal" relationship; (b) qualifies as a "foreign," "nondomestic," or "international" award; (c) satisfies any applicable reciprocity requirements; and (d) is "binding" or "final." Each of these requirements is examined below.

1. "Commercial" and "Defined Legal" Relationships

The New York and Inter-American Conventions, as well as many national arbitration statutes, apply only to arbitration agreements and awards arising from "commercial" and "defined legal" relationships. These requirements are discussed above, in the context of arbitration agreements.[28] In general, neither requirement has presented significant issues concerning the applicability of the Conventions to arbitral awards differing from those applicable to arbitration agreements.[29]

2. "Foreign," "Nondomestic" and "International" Awards

Many international arbitration conventions and national arbitration statutes are applicable only to international arbitral awards (as distinguished from purely domestic awards). As a consequence, the applicability of the generally favorable enforcement regimes of these instruments will depend on characterization of an award's status as "foreign," "nondomestic," or "international."

The New York Convention applies only to so-called "foreign" and "nondomestic" awards.[30] Article I(1) provides:

> "This Convention shall apply to the recognition and enforcement of arbitral awards made in the territory of a State other than the State where the recognition and enforcement of such awards are sought, and arising out of differences between persons, whether physical or legal. It shall also apply to arbitral awards not considered as domestic awards in the State where their recognition and enforcement are sought."

26. *See* G. Born, *International Commercial Arbitration* 3380-81 (2d ed. 2014).

27. *See* G. Born, *International Commercial Arbitration* 3447 (2d ed. 2014).

28. *See supra* pp. 137-48, 148-58; G. Born, *International Commercial Arbitration* 2938-41 (2d ed. 2014).

29. G. Born, *International Commercial Arbitration* 2940-41 (2d ed. 2014).

30. G. Born, *International Commercial Arbitration* 2941-42 (2d ed. 2014); Pryles, *Foreign Awards and the New York Convention*, 9 Arb. Int'l 259 (1993); van den Berg, *When Is An Arbitral Award Non-Domestic Under the New York Convention of 1958?*, 6 Pace L. Rev. 25 (1985).

The Convention only applies to awards falling within Article I(1)'s jurisdictional requirements—that is, (a) awards "made in the territory of a State other than the State where the recognition and enforcement of such awards are sought" (*i.e.*, "foreign" awards), and (b) "awards not considered as domestic awards in the State where their recognition and enforcement are sought" (*i.e.*, "nondomestic" awards).

National arbitration legislation also applies differently depending on the status of an award as "international," "foreign," or "domestic." First, as discussed above, the UNCITRAL Model Law applies only to "international commercial arbitration," and not to purely domestic arbitration; other national arbitration regimes are similar.[31] In this respect, the characterization of an award as "international" or "domestic" determines whether or not international arbitration statutes (like the Model Law) are applicable, rather than domestic legislation.

Second, and additionally, the UNCITRAL Model Law sets forth separate enforcement regimes for "foreign" arbitral awards that, in international commercial arbitrations, are made outside the enforcement state (the recognition provisions of Articles 35 and 36), and for awards, again in international commercial arbitrations, which are made within the enforcement state (the annulment provisions of Article 34).[32] Similarly, other arbitration statutes distinguish between the treatment of "foreign" arbitral awards, which are subject only to recognition, and awards made locally, which are subject to annulment (as well as correction and interpretation) and confirmation.[33] The materials excerpted below examine the application of these various requirements.

BHARAT ALUMINIUM CO. ("BALCO") v. KAISER ALUMINIUM TECHNICAL SERVICE, INC.
[2012] C.A. No. 7019 of 2005 (Indian S.Ct.)

SURINDER SINGH NIJJAR, J. An agreement dated 22nd April, 1993 was executed between the appellant and the respondent [Kaiser Aluminium Technical Service, Inc. ("Kaiser")], under which the respondent was to supply and install a computer based system for Shelter Modernization at Balco's Korba Shelter. The agreement contained an arbitration clause for resolution of disputes arising out of the contract. The arbitration clause contained in Articles 17 and 22 was as under:

"Article 17.1—Any dispute or claim arising out of or relating to this Agreement shall be in the first instance, endeavour to be settled amicably by negotiation between the parties hereto and failing which the same will be settled by arbitration pursuant to the English Arbitration Law and subsequent amendments thereto.

Article 17.2—The arbitration proceedings shall be carried out by two Arbitrators one appointed by BALCO and one by KATSI chosen freely and without any bias. The court of Arbitration shall be held wholly in London, England and shall use English language in the proceeding. The findings and award of the Court of Arbitration shall be final and binding upon the parties.

Article 22—Governing Law—This agreement will be governed by the prevailing law of

---

31. *See supra* pp. 158-59, 166-67; UNCITRAL Model Law, Art. 1.
32. *See supra* pp. 619-20, 623; UNCITRAL Model Law, Arts. 34, 35.
33. *See, e.g.*, SLPIL, Arts. 190, 194; Japanese Arbitration Law, Art. 3.

India and in case of Arbitration, the English law shall apply."

The aforesaid clause itself indicates that by reason of the agreement between the parties, the governing law of the agreement was the prevailing law of India. However, the settlement procedure for adjudication of rights or obligations under the agreement was by way of arbitration in London and the English Arbitration Law was made applicable to such proceedings. Therefore, the *lex fori* for the arbitration is English Law but the substantive law will be Indian Law.

Disputes arose between the parties with regard to the performance of the agreement. Claim was made by the appellant for return of its investment in the modernization programme, loss, profits and other sums. The respondent made a claim for unclaimed instalments plus interest and damages for breach of intellectual property rights. Negotiations to reach a settlement of the disputes between the parties were unsuccessful and a written notice of request for arbitration was issued by the respondent to the appellant by a notice dated 13th November, 1997. The disputes were duly referred to arbitration which was held in England. The arbitral tribunal made two awards dated 10th November, 2002 and 12th November, 2002 in England. The appellant thereafter filed applications [in Indian courts] under §34 of the [Indian] Arbitration Act, 1996 for setting aside the aforesaid two awards in the Court of the learned District Judge, Bilaspur.... [The Indian Supreme Court considered whether Indian courts had the authority to annul the awards.]

Resolution of disputes through arbitration was not unknown in India even in ancient times. Simply stated, settlement of disputes through arbitration is the alternate system of resolution of disputes whereby the parties to a dispute get the same settled through the intervention of a third party. The role of the court is limited to the extent of regulating the process. During the ancient era of Hindu Law in India, there were several machineries for settlement of disputes between the parties. These were known as *Kulani* (village council), *Sreni* (corporation) and *Puga* (assembly). [*See* P.V. Kane, III *History of Dharmasastra* 242.] Likewise, commercial matters were decided by Mahajans and Chambers. The resolution of disputes through the panchayat was a different system of arbitration subordinate to the courts of law.... The law of arbitration in India remained static [from 1899 through 1996].

The disastrous results which ensued from the abuse of the [Indian Arbitration Act, 1940] are noticed by this Court in the case of *Guru Nanak Foundation v. M/s. Rattan Singh & Sons.* [1981 (4) SCC 634] Justice D.A. Desai speaking for the court expressed the concern and anguish of the court about the way in which the proceedings under the 1940 Act, are conducted and without an exception challenged in courts. His Lordship observed:

"Interminable, time consuming, complex and expensive court procedures impelled jurists to search for an alternative forum, less formal, more effective and speedy for resolution of disputes avoiding procedural claptrap and this led them to Arbitration Act, 1940 ("Act" for short). However, the way in which the proceedings under the Act are conducted and without an exception challenged in Courts, *has made lawyers laugh and legal philosophers weep.* (Emphasis supplied.) Experience shows and law reports bear ample testimony that the proceedings under the Act have become highly technical accompanied by unending prolixity, at every stage providing a legal trap to the unwary. Informal forum chosen by the parties for expeditious disposal of their disputes has by the decisions of the Courts been clothed with 'legalese' of unforeseeable complexity. This case amply demonstrates the same."

Difficulties were also being faced in the International sphere of Trade and Commerce. With the growth of International Trade and Commerce, there was an increase in disputes arising out of such transactions being adjudicated through Arbitration. One of the problems faced in such Arbitration, related to recognition and enforcement of an Arbitral Award made in one country by the Courts of other countries. This difficulty was sought to be removed through various International Conventions, [including the Geneva Protocol and the Geneva Convention, both of which India signed. Thereafter, India ratified the New York Convention but] failed to keep pace with the developments at the international level.

The Arbitration Act, 1996, based closely on the UNCITRAL Model Law, was intended to remedy those legislative shortcomings. The Act is one *"to consolidate and amend the law relating to domestic arbitration, international commercial arbitration and enforcement of foreign arbitral awards as also to define the law relating to conciliation and for matters connected therewith or incidental thereto."*

Internationally, the Arbitration Law developed in different countries to cater for the felt needs of a particular country. This necessarily led to considerable disparity in the National Laws on arbitration. Therefore, a need was felt for improvement and harmonization as National Laws which were, often, particularly inappropriate for resolving international commercial arbitration disputes. The explanatory note by the UNCITRAL Secretariat refers to the recurring inadequacies to be found in outdated National Laws, which included provisions that equate the arbitral process with Court litigation and fragmentary provisions that failed to address all relevant substantive law issues…. There was [sic] also unexpected and undesired restrictions found in National Laws, which would prevent the parties, for example, from submitting future disputes to arbitration. The Model Law was intended to reduce the risk of such possible frustration, difficulties or surprise…. With these objects in view, the UNCITRAL Model Law … was adopted [in 1985]. The General Assembly in its Resolution 40 of 1972 on 11th December, 1985 recommended that "all States give due consideration to the Model Law on international commercial arbitration, in view of the desirability of uniformity of the law of arbitral procedures and the specific needs of international commercial arbitration practice." The aim and the objective of the [Indian] Arbitration Act, 1996 is to give effect to the UNCITRAL Model Laws.

[The principal issue addressed by the Indian Supreme Court was whether Part I of the Indian Arbitration Act, including its grant of authority to annul arbitral awards and to otherwise exercise supervisory jurisdiction over arbitral proceedings, applied to arbitrations seated in London. The Court held that Part I of the Act applied only to arbitrations seated in India and that only Part II of the Act, dealing with recognition and enforcement of foreign arbitral awards, applied to arbitrations seated outside India.

The appellants relied on the decisions in *NTPC, supra* pp. 1102-06 and *Bhatia Int'l v. Bulk Trading SA*, (2004) 2 SCC 105, which held that Indian courts had authority to annul awards made outside India, at least where that authority had not been excluded by express agreement. The Indian Supreme Court rejected the argument reasoning:] With utmost respect, upon consideration of the entire matter, we are unable to support the conclusions recorded by this Court in both the judgments i.e. *Bhatia International* and *Venture Global Engineering*….

A plain reading of §1 shows that the Arbitration Act, 1996 extends to [the] whole of India, but the provisions relating to domestic arbitrations, contained in Part I, are not extended to the State of Jammu and Kashmir. [The same logic applies to awards made in foreign states.] ...

We are unable to accept the submission of the learned counsel for the appellants that the omission of the word "only" from §2(2) [,which parallels Article 1(2) of the UNCITRAL Model Law], indicates that applicability of Part I of the Arbitration Act, 1996 is not limited to the arbitrations that take place in India....

> [The] UNCITRAL Model Law has unequivocally accepted the territorial principle. Similarly, the Arbitration Act, 1996 has also adopted the territorial principle, thereby limiting the applicability of Part I to arbitrations, which take place in India...."Article 1(2): The provisions of this law, except Articles 8, 9, 17(H), 17(I), 17(J), 35 and 36 apply "*only*" if the place of arbitration is in the territories of this State."

The aforesaid article is a model and a guide to all the States, which have accepted the UNCITRAL Model Laws....

It must be pointed out that the law of the seat or place where the arbitration is held, is normally the law to govern that arbitration. The territorial link between the place of arbitration and the law governing that arbitration is well established in the international instruments, namely, the New York Convention of 1958 and the UNCITRAL Model Law of 1985.... [T]he 1923 Geneva Protocol states: "The arbitral procedure, including the constitution of the arbitral tribunal, shall be governed by the will of the parties and by the law of the country in whose territory the arbitration takes place." [Art. 2]. The New York Convention maintains the reference to "the law of the country where the arbitration took place '(Article V(1)(d))' and, synonymously to "the law of the country where the award is made" [Article V(1)(a) and (e)]. The aforesaid observations clearly show that New York Convention continues the clear territorial link between the place of arbitration and the law governing that arbitration.... [T]his territorial link is again maintained in the Model Law which provides in Article 1(2) that "the provision of this law, except Articles 8, 9, 35 and 36 apply only if the place of arbitration is in the territory of the State." Just as the Arbitration Act, 1996 maintains the territorial link between the place of arbitration and its law of arbitration, the law in Switzerland and England also maintain a clear link between the seat of arbitration and the *lex arbitri*. [citing SLPIL, Art. 176(1).] [W]e are of the opinion that the views expressed by the learned counsel for the appellants are not supported by the provisions of the Arbitration Act, 1996. Section 2(7) of the Arbitration Act, 1996 reads thus:

> "An arbitral award made under this Part shall be considered as a domestic award."

In our opinion, the aforesaid provision does not, in any manner, relax the territorial principal [sic] adopted by [the] Arbitration Act, 1996. It certainly does not introduce the concept of a delocalized arbitration into the Arbitration Act, 1996. It must be remembered that Part I of the Arbitration Act, 1996 applies not only to purely domestic arbitrations, i.e., where none of the parties are in any way "foreign" but also to "international commercial arbitrations" covered within §2(1)(f) held in India. The term "domestic award" can be used in two senses: one to distinguish it from "international award," and the other to distinguish it from a "foreign award." It must also be remembered that "foreign award" may well be a domestic award in the country in which it is rendered. As the whole of the Arbitration Act, 1996 is designed to give different treatments to the awards made in India and those made outside India, the distinction is necessarily to be made between the terms "domestic awards" and "foreign awards." ... Therefore, it seems clear that the object of §2(7) is to distinguish the domestic award covered under Part I of the Arbitration Act, 1996 from the *"foreign award"* covered under Part II of the aforesaid Act; and not to distinguish the *"domestic award"* from an *"international award"* rendered in India. In other words, the provision highlights, if anything, a clear distinction between Part I and Part II as being applicable in completely different fields and with no overlapping provisions....

The territoriality principle of the Arbitration Act, 1996, precludes Part I from being applicable to a foreign seated arbitration, even if the agreement purports to provide that the Arbitration proceedings will be governed by the Arbitration Act, 1996....

We now come to §20, [derived from the UNCITRAL Model Law,] which is as under:-

"20. Place of arbitration

(1) The parties are free to agree on the place of arbitration.

(2) Failing any agreement referred to in sub-section (1), the place of arbitration shall be determined by the arbitral tribunal having regard to the circumstances of the case, including the convenience of the parties.

(3) Notwithstanding sub-section (1) or sub-section (2), the arbitral tribunal may, unless otherwise agreed by the parties, meet at any place it considers appropriate for consultation among its members, for hearing witnesses, experts or the parties, or for inspection of documents, good or other property."

A plain reading of §20 leaves no room for doubt that where the place of arbitration is in India, the parties are free to agree to any "place" or "seat" within India, be it Delhi, Mumbai etc. In the absence of the parties' agreement thereto, §20(2) authorizes the tribunal to determine the place/seat of such arbitration. Section 20(3) enables the tribunal to meet at any place for conducting hearings at a place of convenience in matters such as consultations among its members for hearing witnesses, experts or the parties.

The fixation of the most convenient "venue" is taken care of by §20(3).... True, that in an international commercial arbitration, having a seat in India, hearings may be necessitated outside India. In such circumstances, the hearing of the arbitration will be conducted at the venue fixed by the parties, but it would not have the effect of changing the seat of arbitration which would remain in India....

We may point out here that the distinction between "seat" and "venue" would be quite crucial in the event, the arbitration agreement designates a foreign country as the "seat"/"place" of the arbitration and also select the Arbitration Act, 1996 as the curial law/law governing the arbitration proceedings. It would be a matter of construction of the individual agreement to decide whether:

(i) The designated foreign "seat" would be read as in fact only providing for a "venue"/"place" where the hearings would be held, in view of the choice of Arbitration Act, 1996 as being the *curial law*—OR (ii) Whether the specific designation of a foreign seat, necessarily carrying with it the choice of that country's Arbitration / *curial law*, would prevail over and subsume the conflicting selection choice by the parties of the Arbitration Act, 1996.

ONLY if the agreement of the parties is construed to provide for the "seat"/"place" of Arbitration being in India—would Part I of the Arbitration Act, 1996 be applicable. If the agreement is held to provide for a "seat"/"place" outside India, Part I would be inapplicable to the extent inconsistent with the arbitration law of the seat, even if the agreement purports to provide that the Arbitration Act, 1996 shall govern the arbitration proceedings....

[The Court considered a number of cases where English and other courts held that the law of the arbitral seat governed the arbitral proceedings, including *C v. D* [2007] EWCA Civ. 1282 (English Ct. App.), *Sulamerica CIA Nacional de Seguros SA v. Enesa Engenharia SA* [2012] WL 14764 (QB) (English High Ct.) and *Braes of Doune Wind Farm (Scotland) Ltd v. Alfred McAlpine Bus. Servs. Ltd* [2008] EWHC 426 (TCC) (English High Ct.).] The legal position that emerges from a conspectus of all the decisions, seems to be, that the choice of another country as the seat of arbitration inevitably imports an acceptance that the law of that country relating to the conduct and supervision of arbitrations will apply to the proceedings.

It would, therefore, follow that if the arbitration agreement is found or held to provide for a seat / place of arbitration outside India, then the provision that the Arbitration Act, 1996 would govern the arbitration proceedings, would not make Part I of the Arbitration Act, 1996 applicable or enable Indian Courts to exercise supervisory jurisdiction over the arbitration or the award. It would only mean that the parties have contractually imported from the Arbitration Act, 1996, those provisions which are concerned with the internal conduct of their arbitration and which are not inconsistent with the mandatory provisions of the English Procedural Law/Curial Law. This necessarily follows from the fact that Part I applies only to arbitrations having their seat / place in India....

Much emphasis has been laid by the learned counsel for the appellants on the expression that enforcement of a foreign award may be refused when the award "has been set aside or suspended ..." "under the law of which" that award was made. The aforesaid words and expressions appear in §[48(1)(e), paralleling Article V(1)(e) of the New York Convention], which is contained in Part II of the Arbitration Act, 1996 under the title "enforcement of certain foreign awards." The Courts in India under Chapter I of Part II of the aforesaid Act have limited powers to refuse the enforcement of foreign awards given under the New York Convention. A reading of Article V(1)(e) [§48(1)(e)] makes it clear that only the courts in the country "in which the award was made" and the courts "under the law of which the award was made" (hereinafter referred to as the "first alternative" and the "second alternative" respectively) would be competent to suspend/annul the New York Convention awards.... [The appellants] submitted that the two countries identified in "alternative one" and "alternative two," would have concurrent jurisdiction to annul the award. In our opinion, interpreting the provision in the manner suggested ... would lead to very serious practical problems....

Accepting the submission ... would lead to unnecessary confusion. There can be only one Court with jurisdiction to set aside the award. There is a public policy consideration apparent, favouring the interpretation that, only one Court would have jurisdiction to set aside the arbitral award. This public policy aspect was considered by the Court of Appeal in England in the case of *C v. D* [which held: "[Permitting actions for annulment in two different forums] would be a recipe for litigation and (what is worse) confusion which cannot have been intended by the parties."] The observation of the Court of Appeal in Paragraph 16 of the judgment has already been reproduced earlier in this judgment.

It was pointed out by the Court of Appeal [in *C v. D*] that accepting more than one jurisdiction for judicial remedies in respect of an award would be a recipe for litigation and confusion. "Similarly, in the case of a single complaint about an award, it could not be supposed that the aggrieved party could complain in one jurisdiction and the satisfied party be entitled to ask the other jurisdiction to declare its satisfaction with the award." ...

The expression "under the law" has also generated a great deal of controversy as to whether it applies to "the law governing the substantive contract" or "the law governing the arbitration agreement" or limited only to the procedural laws of the country in which the award is made. The consistent view of the international commentators seems to be that the "second alternative" refers to the procedural law of the arbitration rather than "law governing the arbitration agreement" or "underlying contract." This is even otherwise evident from the phrase "under the law, that award was made," which refers to the process of making the award (i.e., the arbitration proceeding), rather than to the formation or validity of the arbitration agreement.

Gary B. Born in his treatise titled International Commercial Arbitration [(2009)] takes the view in Chapter 21 that the correct interpretation of Article V(1)(e)'s "second alternative" is that it relates exclusively to procedural law of the arbitration which produced an award and not to other possible laws (such as the substantive law governing the parties underlying dispute or governing the parties' arbitration agreement). He further notices that courts have generally been extremely reluctant to conclude that the parties have agreed upon a procedural law other than that of the arbitral seat. Consequently, according to Born, although it is theoretically possible for an award to be subject to annulment outside the arbitral seat, by virtue of Article V(1)(e)'s "second alternative," in reality this is a highly unusual "once-in-a-blue-moon" occurrence.... In our opinion, the views expressed by the learned author are in consonance with the scheme and the spirit in which the New York Convention was formulated. The underlying motivation of the New York Convention was to reduce the hurdles and produce a uniform, simple and speedy system for enforcement of foreign arbitral award. Therefore, it seems to be accepted by the commentators and the courts in different jurisdictions that the language of Article V(1)(e) referring to the "second alternative" is to the country applying the procedural law of arbitration if different from the arbitral forum and not the substantive law governing the underlying contract between the parties. [The Court reviewed decisions from a variety of foreign jurisdictions which, it held. Reached the same result.]

The correct position under the New York Convention is described very clearly and concisely by Gary B. Born in his book International Commercial Arbitration 1260 [(2009)] as follows:

> "This provision is vitally important for the international arbitral process, because it significantly restricts the extent of national court review of international arbitral awards in annulment actions, limiting such review only to the courts of the arbitral seat (that is, the state where the award is made or the state whose procedural law is selected by the parties to govern the arbitration). In so doing, the Convention ensures that courts outside the arbitral seat may not purport to annul an international award, thereby materially limiting the role of such courts in supervising or overseeing the procedures utilized in international arbitrations.
>
> At the same time, the New York Convention also allows the courts of the arbitral seat wide powers with regard to the annulment of arbitral awards made locally. The Convention generally permits the courts of the arbitral seat to annul an arbitral award on any grounds available under local law, while limiting the grounds for non-recognition of Convention awards in courts outside the arbitral seat to those specified in Article V of the Convention. This has the effect of permitting the courts of the arbitral seat substantially greater scope than courts of other states to affect the conduct or outcome of an international arbitration through the vehicle of annulment actions. *Together with the other provisions of Articles II and V, this allocation of annulment authority confirms the (continued) special importance of the arbi-*

tral seat in the international arbitral process under the New York Convention." (Emphasis supplied.)

In our opinion, the aforesaid is the correct way to interpret the expressions "country where the award was made" and the "country under the law of which the award was made." We are unable to accept the submission of [the appellants] that the provision confers concurrent jurisdiction in both the fora. "Second alternative" is available only on the failure of the "first alternative." The expression *under the law* is the reference only to the *procedural law/curial law* of the country in which the award was made and under the law of which the award was made. It has no reference to the substantive law of the contract between the parties. In such view of the matter, we have no hesitation in rejecting the submission of the learned counsel for the appellants.

At this stage, we may notice that in spite of the aforesaid international understanding of the second limb of Article V(1) (e), this Court has proceeded on a number of occasions to annul an award on the basis that parties had chosen Indian Law to govern the substance of their dispute. The aforesaid view has been expressed in *Bhatia International* and *Venture Global Engineering*. In our opinion, accepting such an interpretation would be to ignore the spirit underlying the New York Convention which embodies a consensus evolved to encourage consensual resolution of complicated, intricate and in many cases very sensitive International Commercial Disputes. Therefore, the interpretation which hinders such a process ought not to be accepted. This also seems to be the view of the national courts in different jurisdictions across the world. For the reasons stated above, we are also unable to agree with the conclusions recorded by this Court in *Venture Global Engineering* that the foreign award could be annulled on the exclusive grounds that the Indian law governed the substance of the dispute. Such an opinion is not borne out by the huge body of judicial precedents in different jurisdictions of the world....

[I]t is patent that there is no existing provision under the [Code of Civil Procedure] or under the Arbitration Act, 1996 for a Court to grant interim measures in terms of §9, in arbitrations which take place outside India.... In view of the above discussion, we are of the considered opinion that the Arbitration Act, 1996 has accepted the territoriality principle which has been adopted in the UNCITRAL Model Law. Section 2(2) makes a declaration that Part I of the Arbitration Act, 1996 shall apply to all arbitrations which take place within India. We are of the considered opinion that Part I of the Arbitration Act, 1996 would have no application to International Commercial Arbitration held outside India. Therefore, such awards would only be subject to the jurisdiction of the Indian courts when the same are sought to be enforced in India in accordance with the provisions contained in Part II of the Arbitration Act, 1996.... With utmost respect, we are unable to agree with the conclusions recorded in the judgments of this Court in *Bhatia International* and *Venture Global Engineering*....

In a foreign seated international commercial arbitration, no application for interim relief would be maintainable under §9 or any other provision, as applicability of Part I of the Arbitration Act, 1996 is limited to all arbitrations which take place in India.... We conclude that Part I of the Arbitration Act, 1996 is applicable only to *all the arbitrations* which take place within the territory of India.

The judgment in *Bhatia International* was rendered by this Court on 13th March, 2002. Since then, the aforesaid judgment has been followed by all the High Courts as well as by this Court on numerous occasions. In fact, the judgment in *Venture Global Engineering* has been rendered on 10th January, 2008 in terms of the ratio of the decision in *Bhatia International*. Thus, in order to do complete justice, we hereby order, that the law now declared by this Court shall apply prospectively, to all the arbitration agreements executed hereafter....

BRIER v. NORTHSTAR MARINE INC.
1992 WL 350292 (D.N.J.)

[excerpted above at pp. 162-64]

BERGESEN v. JOSEPH MULLER CORP.
710 F.2d 929 (2d Cir. 1983)

[excerpted above at pp. 159-62]

YUSUF AHMED ALGHANIM & SONS, WLL v. TOYS "R" US, INC.
126 F.3d 15 (2d Cir. 1997)

MINER, Circuit Judge. Appeal from a judgment entered in the U.S. District Court for the Southern District of New York denying respondents' cross-motion to vacate or modify an arbitration award and granting the petition to confirm the award. The [district] court found that while the petition for confirmation was brought under the [New York] Convention, respondents' cross-motion to vacate or modify the award was properly brought under the [FAA], and thus those claims were governed by the [FAA's] implied grounds for vacatur. Nonetheless, the court granted the petition to confirm the award, finding that respondents' allegations of error in the arbitral award were without merit.... [W]e affirm.

In November of 1982, respondent-appellant Toys "R" Us, Inc. (... "Toys 'R' Us") and petitioner-appellee Yusuf Ahmed Alghanim & Sons, WLL ("Alghanim"), a privately owned Kuwaiti business, entered into a License and Technical Assistance Agreement (the "agreement") and a Supply Agreement. Through the agreement, Toys "R" Us granted Alghanim a limited right to open Toys "R" Us stores and use its trademarks in Kuwait and 13 other countries located in and around the Middle East (the "territory"). Toys "R" Us further agreed to supply Alghanim with its technology, expertise and assistance in the toy business. [Disputes arose between Toys "R" Us and Alghanim, leading the former to terminate the agreement and contract with a new Kuwaiti distributor.]... Toys "R" Us invoked the dispute-resolution mechanism in the agreement, initiating an arbitration before the [AAA]. Toys "R" Us sought a declaration that the agreement was terminated on December 31, 1993. Alghanim responded by counterclaiming for breach of contract.... On July 11, 1996, the arbitrator awarded Alghanim $46.44 million for lost profits under the agreement....

Alghanim petitioned the district court to confirm the award under the [New York] Convention. Toys "R" Us cross-moved to vacate or modify the award under the FAA, arguing that the award was clearly irrational, in manifest disregard of the law, and in manifest disregard of the terms of the agreement. The district court concluded that "[t]he Convention and the FAA afford overlapping coverage, and the fact that a petition to confirm is brought under the Convention does not foreclose a cross-motion to vacate under the FAA, and the Court will consider [Toys "R" Us's] cross-motion under the standards of the FAA." ... [T]he district court confirmed the award.... This appeal followed....

Toys "R" Us argues that the district court correctly determined that the provisions of the FAA apply to its cross-motion to vacate or modify the arbitral award. In particular, Toys "R" Us contends that the FAA and the Convention have overlapping coverage. Thus, Toys "R" Us argues, even though the petition to confirm the arbitral award was brought under the Convention, the FAA's implied grounds for vacatur should apply to Toys "R" Us's cross-motion to vacate or modify because the cross-motion was brought under the FAA. We agree that the FAA governs Toys "R" Us's cross-motion.

Neither party seriously disputes the applicability of the Convention to this case and it is clear to us that the Convention does apply. The Convention provides that it will apply "to the recognition and enforcement of arbitral awards made in the territory of a State other than the State where the recognition and enforcement of such awards are sought, and arising out of differences between persons, whether physical or legal. *It shall also apply to arbitral awards not considered as domestic awards in the State where their recognition and enforcement are sought.*" Convention Art. I(1) (emphasis added). The Convention does not define nondomestic awards. *See Bergesen* [*supra* pp. 159-62].... In *Bergesen*, we held "that awards 'not considered as domestic' denotes awards which are subject to the Convention not because made abroad, but because made within the legal framework of another country, *e.g.*, pronounced in accordance with foreign law or involving parties domiciled or having their principal place of business outside the enforcing jurisdiction." The Seventh Circuit similarly has interpreted §202 to mean that "any commercial arbitral agreement, unless it is between two United States citizens, involves property located in the United States, and has no reasonable relationship with one or more foreign states, falls under the Convention." *Jain v. de Mere*, 51 F.3d 686, 689 (7th Cir.).

The Convention's applicability in this case is clear. The dispute giving rise to this appeal involved two nondomestic parties and one [U.S.] corporation, and principally involved conduct and contract performance in the Middle East. Thus, we consider the arbitral award leading to this action a non-domestic award and thus within the scope of the Convention.

Toys "R" Us argues that the district court properly found that it had the authority under the Convention to apply the FAA's implied grounds for setting aside the award. We agree. Under the Convention [sic], the district court's role in reviewing a foreign arbitral award is strictly limited: "The court shall confirm the award unless it finds one of the grounds for refusal or deferral of recognition or enforcement of the award specified in the said Convention." 9 U.S.C. §207. Enforcement may also be refused if "[t]he subject matter of the difference is not capable of settlement by arbitration," or if "recognition or enforcement of the award would be contrary to the public policy" of the country in which enforcement or recognition is sought. [Article V's] seven grounds are the only grounds explicitly provided under the Convention.

In determining the availability of the FAA's implied grounds for setting aside, the text of the Convention leaves us with two questions: (1) whether, in addition to the Convention's express grounds for refusal, other grounds can be read into the Convention by implication, much as American courts have read implied grounds for relief into the FAA, and (2) whether, under Article V(1)(e), the courts of the United States are authorized to apply United States procedural arbitral law, *i.e.*, the FAA, to nondomestic awards rendered in the United States. We answer the first question in the negative and the second in the affirmative.

We have held that the FAA and the Convention have "overlapping coverage" to the extent that they do not conflict. *Bergesen*; *see* 9 U.S.C. §208 (FAA may apply to actions brought under the Convention "to the extent that [the FAA] is not in conflict with [9 U.S.C. §§201-208] or the Convention as ratified by the United States"); *Lander Co. v. MMP Invs., Inc.*, 107 F.3d 476, 481 (7th Cir. 1997). However, by that same token, to the extent that the Convention prescribes the exclusive grounds for relief from an award under the Convention, that application of the FAA's implied grounds would be in conflict, and is thus precluded. *See, e.g., M & C Corp. v. Erwin Behr GmbH & Co., KG*, 87 F.3d 844, 851 (6th Cir. 1996)....

There is now considerable case law holding that, in an action to confirm an award rendered in, or under the law of, a foreign jurisdiction, the grounds for relief enumerated in Article V of the Convention are the only grounds available for setting aside an arbitral award.... This conclusion is consistent with the Convention's pro-enforcement bias. *See, e.g., Scherk* [*supra* p. 485].... We join these courts in declining to read into the Convention the FAA's implied defenses to confirmation of an arbitral award.

Although Article V provides the exclusive grounds for refusing confirmation under the Convention, one of those exclusive grounds is where "[t]he award ... has been set aside or suspended by a competent authority of the country in which, or under the law of which, that award was made." New York Convention Art. V(1)(e). Those courts holding that implied defenses were inapplicable under the Convention did so in the context of petitions to confirm awards rendered abroad. These courts were not presented with the question whether Article V(1)(e) authorizes an action to set aside an arbitral award under the domestic law of the state in which, or under which, the award was rendered. We, however, are faced head-on with that question in the case before us, because the arbitral award in this case was rendered in the United States, and both confirmation and vacatur were then sought in the United States. We read Article V(1)(e) ... to allow a court in the country under whose law the arbitration was conducted to apply domestic arbitral law, in this case the FAA, to a motion to set aside or vacate that arbitral award. The district court in *Spector v. Torenberg*, 852 F.Supp. 201 (S.D.N.Y. 1994), reached the same conclusion ..., reasoning that, because the Convention allows the district court to refuse to enforce an award that has been vacated by a competent authority in the country where the award was rendered, the court may apply FAA standards to a motion to vacate a nondomestic award rendered in the United States.

Our conclusion also is consistent with the reasoning of courts that have refused to apply non-Convention grounds for relief where awards were rendered outside the United States. For example, the Sixth Circuit in *M & C* concluded that it should not apply the FAA's implied grounds for vacatur, because the United States did not provide the law of the arbitration for the purposes of Article V(1)(e) of the Convention. 87 F.3d at 849. Similarly, in *Int'l Standard Electric Corp. v. Bridas etc.*, 754 F.Supp. 172 (S.D.N.Y. 1990), the district court decided that only the state under whose procedural law the arbitration was conducted has jurisdiction under Article V(1)(e) to vacate the award, whereas on a petition for confirmation made in any other state, only the defenses to confirmation listed in Article V of the Convention are available. This interpretation of Article V(1)(e) also finds support in the scholarly work of commentators on the Convention and in the judicial decisions of our sister signatories to the Convention. There appears to be no dispute among these authorities that an action to set aside an international arbitral award, as contemplated by Article V(1)(e), is controlled by the domestic law of the rendering state....

There is no indication in the Convention of any intention to deprive the rendering state of its supervisory authority over an arbitral award, including its authority to set aside that award under domestic law. The Convention succeeded and replaced the Geneva Convention. The primary defect of the Geneva Convention was that it required an award first to be recognized in the rendering state before it could be enforced abroad, the so-called requirement of "double *exequatur*." The Convention eliminated this problem by eradicating the requirement that a court in the rendering state recognize an award before it could be taken and enforced abroad. In so doing, the Convention intentionally "liberalized procedures for enforcing foreign arbitral awards."

Nonetheless, under the Convention, the power and authority of the local courts of the rendering state remain of paramount importance. "What the Convention did not do ... was provide any international mechanism to insure the validity of the award where rendered. This was left to the provisions of local law. The Convention provides no restraint whatsoever on the control functions of local courts at the seat of arbitration." [Craig, *Some Trends and Developments in the Laws and Practice of International Commercial Arbitration*, 30 Tex. Int'l L.J. 1, 11 (1995).] Another commentator explained: "Significantly, [Article V(1)(e)] fails to specify the grounds upon which the rendering State may set aside or suspend the award. While it would have provided greater reliability to the enforcement of awards under the Convention had the available grounds been defined in some way, such action would have constituted meddling with national procedure for handling domestic awards, a subject beyond the competence of the Conference." Quigley, *Accession by the United States to the United Nations Convention on the Recognition and Enforcement of Foreign Arbitral Awards*, 70 Yale L.J. 1049, 1070 (1961). From the plain language and history of the Convention, it is thus apparent that a party may seek to vacate or set aside an award in the state in which, or under the law of which, the award is rendered. Moreover, the language and history of the Convention make it clear that such a motion is to be governed by domestic law of the rendering state, despite the fact that the award is nondomestic within the meaning of the Convention as we have interpreted it in *Bergesen*.

In sum, we conclude that the Convention mandates very different regimes for the review of arbitral awards (1) in the state in which, or under the law of which, the award was made, and (2) in other states where recognition and enforcement are sought. The Convention specifically contemplates that the state in which, or under the law of which, the award is made, will be free to set aside or modify an award in accordance with its domestic arbitral law and its full panoply of express and implied grounds for relief. *See* Convention Art. V(1)(e). However, the Convention is equally clear that when an action for enforcement is brought in a foreign state, the state may refuse to enforce the award only on the grounds explicitly set forth in Article V of the Convention....

NOTES

1. *Jurisdictional requirements for awards under Article I of New York Convention.* Consider Articles I and V of the New York Convention, excerpted at pp. 1-2 of the Documentary Supplement. Broadly speaking, what categories of awards does the Convention apply to? Any awards? Any awards made in another nation? In another Contracting State? Any other awards? In general terms, what is the difference between a "foreign" and a "nondomestic" award?

Compare Article I of the New York Convention with Article I of the European Convention, excerpted at pp. 1 & 29 of the Documentary Supplement. How are the two instruments different in their jurisdictional requirements for arbitral awards? What is the purpose of limiting the scope of the New York and the European Conventions to certain categories of awards? Compare the treatment of "arbitration agreements" under the New York Convention. *See supra* pp. 158-59, 164-66.

2. *No express jurisdictional requirements for awards under Inter-American Convention.* The Inter-American Convention does not contain any express jurisdictional requirements for those awards that are subject to its provisions. (In particular, and in contrast to the New York Convention, nothing limits the Inter-American Convention to "foreign" and "nondomestic" awards.) Does that mean that the Inter-American Convention applies to *all* awards in the courts of signatory states? Would this be sensible? Consider the title and preamble to the Inter-American Convention. Do they limit the Convention to "international" arbitral awards? *See supra* p. 166. How should "international" awards be defined?

3. *Article I of New York Convention: "foreign" awards.* Consider the first jurisdictional basis, under Article I, for concluding that an award is subject to the New York Convention. Under Article I, the Convention will apply to awards "made in the territory of a State other than the State where the recognition and enforcement of such awards are sought"—that is, the Convention will be applicable to recognition proceedings in a Contracting State's courts if the proceedings involve an award which is "foreign" in that State.

When will an award be "foreign" under Article I of the Convention? Note that an award is "foreign" in a particular Contracting State when the award is "made" in a different state. Note also that an award which is "foreign" in one state need not be "foreign" in other states; that is, an award "made" in State A will be "foreign" in State B (and State C) but *not* in State A. Why does the Convention apply primarily to "foreign" awards, made outside the territory of a Contracting State, and not to awards made within that Contracting State? What are the consequences of applying the Convention to a particular award? *See infra* pp. 1099-112, 1189-99.

4. *When is an award "foreign" under New York Convention?* When will an award be "foreign" for purposes of Article I of the New York Convention? What is the source of the legal rules that apply to determine if an award is "foreign"?

(a) *Authorities holding that all awards "made" outside the judicial enforcement forum are "foreign."* Many authorities have interpreted Article I as categorically applying the Convention to *all* awards made outside the Contracting State where recognition is sought. In the words of one commentator, the "Convention always applies to the recognition and enforcement of an arbitral award made in another state …, whilst it may, in addition, apply to the recognition and enforcement of an arbitral award made in the State where the recognition and enforcement are sought if such an award is considered non-domestic." van den Berg, *When Is An Arbitral Award Non-Domestic Under the New York Convention of 1958?*, 6 Pace L. Rev. 25, 39 (1985). *See also Hiscox v. Outhwaite* [1992] 1 AC 562 (House of Lords) ("in the negotiations leading to the Convention there emerged divergent views between the delegates about the appropriate criterion for determining to what awards the Convention should apply and that the school of thought which favoured the simple, if arbitrary, geographical test of where the award was made ultimately won the day, but subject to a compromise addition which included also awards not considered as 'domestic' in the enforcing state"); G. Petrochilos, *Procedural Law in International Arbitration* 347 (2004) ("all awards made outside the territory of the enforcement forum are Convention awards"). Is this conclusion not what the plain language of Article I(1) requires?

(b) *Determining where award is "made."* Where is an award "made" for purposes of Article I? Does Article I provide that an award is "made" where the arbitral hearings are held? Where the award is signed?

Recall the discussion in Chapter 7 above of the arbitral seat, *supra* pp. 599-625, 640-58. As discussed above, virtually all contemporary authorities hold that an award is "made" at the seat of the arbitration, either as specified in the arbitration agreement or subsequently by the arbitral tribunal or institution. *See supra* pp. 622-23. Thus, the English Arbitration Act, 1996, provides that "where the seat of the arbitration is in England and Wales or Northern Ireland, any award in the proceedings shall be treated as made there, regardless of where it was signed, dispatched, or delivered to any of the parties." English Arbitration Act, 1996, §53. Articles 1(2) and 31(3) of the UNCITRAL Model Law achieve the same result, providing that an award shall be deemed to have been made at the "place of arbitration" agreed by parties (or selected by the arbitrators or appointing authority). Other developed jurisdictions adopt the same approach. G. Born, *International Commercial Arbitration* 2945-48 (2d ed. 2014).

Recall that it is very common for hearings to be held, for the convenience of the arbitrators and parties, at a place other than the seat of the arbitration selected in the arbitration agreement. *See supra* p. 624. As also discussed above, virtually all authorities hold that an award continues to be "made" in the arbitral seat, despite the fact that hearings or deliberations are held outside the arbitral seat. *See supra* pp. 622-24.

Nonetheless, there have been a few idiosyncratic decisions holding that an award is "made" where it was signed or where hearings were conducted for convenience. *Hiscox v. Outhwaite* [1992] 1 AC 562 (House of Lords) (award "made" where it was signed, rather than in arbitral seat; decision since overruled by English Arbitration Act, 1996); *Judgment of 28 February 2005, Titan Corp. v. Alcatel CIT SA*, XXX Y.B. Comm. Arb. 139 (2005) (Svea Ct. App.) (award "made" where hearings were conducted for convenience, rather than in arbitral seat), *overruled*, *Judgment of 12 November 2010, RosInvestCo UK Ltd v. Russian Fed'n*, XXXVI Y.B. Comm. Arb. 334, 336 (2011) (Swedish S.Ct.). *See also* Mann, *Where Is An Award "Made"?*, 1 Arb. Int'l 107 (1985) ("an award is 'made' at the place at which the arbitration is held, *i.e.*, the arbitral seat. It is by no means necessarily identical with the place or places where hearings are being held or where the parties or the arbitrators reside. It is rather the place fixed in the contract or the submission or the minutes of the hearing or is found to be the central point of the arbitral proceedings.").

What is the consequence, under the Convention, of concluding that an award is "made" in a particular jurisdiction? What effect does this have on the places where the award will be "foreign"? On the place where an action to annul the award may be brought?

(c) *Does Article I prescribe a uniform international standard defining where an award is "made"?* Does the New York Convention prescribe a uniform international standard for determining where an arbitral award is "made"? For example, would the Convention permit a Contracting State to treat any award made by a tribunal that included one of its nationals as made within that Contracting State? Any award that applies the state's substantive law as made within that state? Does the Convention prescribe a uniform rule, providing that awards are "made" in the parties' agreed arbitral seat? What purposes would be served by such a rule?

(d) *Authorities concluding that some awards made outside the judicial enforcement forum are not "foreign."* Are there circumstances in which an award made outside the territory of a Contracting State will not be "foreign" within that State? For example, are there circumstances in which an award made in State A will not be "foreign" in State B (or State C)?

Consider the analysis in *Northstar. Northstar* involved enforcement of an arbitration agreement (rather than an award). Under the *Northstar* rationale, however, would an award made in England between two U.S. parties necessarily be subject to the Convention in U.S. courts? Relying on §202 of the FAA, *Northstar* suggested that some awards made outside the United States will not be "foreign" awards; in particular, §202 provides that, in cases involving U.S. citizens, a "reasonable relation" with a foreign state is required for an award to be subject to the Convention. Other U.S. courts have reached similar conclusions, holding or suggesting that awards in domestic U.S. disputes, between U.S. nationals and under U.S. law, will not be "foreign," even if they are made abroad. *See, e.g., Jones v. Sea Tow Servs. Freeport NY, Inc.*, 30 F.3d 360 (2d Cir. 1994); *Ensco Offshore Co. v. Titan Marine LLC*, 370 F.Supp. 2d 594, 598-601 (S.D. Tex. 2005); *Reinholtz v. Retriever Marine Towing & Salvage*, 1993 WL 414719 (S.D. Fla.), *aff'd*, 46 F.3d 71 (11th Cir. 1995).

Similarly, in *Nat'l Thermal Power Corp. v. Singer Co.*, XVIII Y.B. Comm. Arb. 403, 409 (1993) (Indian S.Ct. 1992), the Indian Supreme Court held that an award made in England was a domestic Indian award, not a "foreign" award subject to the Convention, because it was rendered pursuant to an arbitration agreement governed by Indian law: "An award is 'foreign' not merely because it is made in the territory of a foreign State, but because it is made in such a territory on an arbitration agreement not governed by the law of India." *See infra* pp. 1102-06, 1108-09.

Significantly, however, in *BALCO*, the Indian Supreme Court recently disavowed this position, overruling several decades of Indian authority and holding that an award was "made" in the contractual arbitral seat and that, where the arbitral seat was outside India, the award would be treated as a "foreign" award in Indian courts.

Are the *Northstar* and *National Thermal* holdings consistent with the Convention? Does Article I(1) permit nations to say that some awards made abroad are not "foreign"? If so, what potential threats does this pose to the Convention? What, for example, would prevent a Contracting State from treating awards in all disputes governed by its substantive law as "domestic" and not "foreign"? What consequences would this have for the Convention?

Consider *Northstar* again. What exactly is the court's rationale? What types of agreements and awards does the court's holding encompass? Suppose the parties had both been sophisticated companies. Would the result have been any different? Is the *Northstar* reasoning persuasive? Suppose a U.S. company's Indian subsidiary enters into a contract with an Indian company, with an arbitration clause providing for arbitration in Switzerland. Should the resulting award be deemed "foreign" in India? Does *Northstar* jeopardize this?

Why was the U.S. court reluctant in *Northstar* to treat an award in a dispute between two U.S. residents (with no foreign connections), which involved purely U.S. conduct, as "foreign"? Was the court in fact concerned that the Convention might be used to circumvent important U.S. public policies (and, in particular, that a party with overweening economic leverage might force a weaker counter-party to accept this)? If this is the concern, what does the Convention permit the court to do in a recognition action? Consider Articles V(2)(a) and (b) of the Convention. How might these provisions address the U.S. court's apparent concerns?

5. *Article I of New York Convention: award made in a Contracting State can be subject to the Convention in that State if it is "nondomestic."* As noted above, the Convention does not necessarily apply only to awards that are "foreign" in a Contracting State. In addition, Article I provides that the Convention will apply to "nondomestic" awards in certain circumstances.

Some commentators have said that "the question what constitutes a non-domestic award within the meaning of the New York Convention is one of the most complicated issues posed by this Treaty." van den Berg, *When Is An Arbitral Award Non-Domestic Under the New York Convention of 1958?*, 6 Pace L. Rev. 25, 26 (1985). As *Bergesen* suggests, the language of Article I(1) was a compromise. During drafting of the Convention, various civil law states initially opposed a territorial criteria that defined awards based on where they were made. In contrast, common law and Eastern European states at first favored variations of the territorial requirement of Article I(1)'s first clause. The final version of the Convention sought to bridge these two views.

Preliminary drafts of the Convention adopted the "territorial" perspective and provided that it would apply to "the recognition and enforcement of arbitral awards *made in the territory of a State other than the State in which such awards are relied upon.*" *Report of the Committee on the Enforcement of International Arbitral Awards*, U.N. Doc. E/2704, Annex, Art. 1 (1955) (emphasis added). French, German and other civil law delegates criticized this proposal, on the grounds that:

"If it was agreed that the place where the award was made should not be considered a determining factor ... whether an award was to be regarded as national [*i.e.*, domestic] or foreign could be made dependent on the nationality of parties, the subject of the dispute, or the rules of procedure applied. The last seemed to constitute the most appropriate defining factor. The nature, and hence the nationality, of an arbitral award would then be derived from the rules of procedure under which it had been made. Moreover, it should be noted that those rules depended to a large extent, at least in German law, on the will of the parties and, failing that, on the arbitral body itself...." *Summary Record of the United Nations Conference on International Commercial Arbitration, Fourth Meeting*, U.N. Doc. E/CONF.26/SR.4 (1958) (Mr. Bulow, Federal

Republic of Germany).

The German delegate subsequently commented that if two German parties conduct an arbitration in London, subject to German law as the curial law, then, under German law, the award would not be foreign, but domestic. *Id.* at III.C.28. Other delegates agreed, and a number of civil law states proposed the following amendment: "This Convention shall apply to the recognition and enforcement of arbitral awards other than those considered as domestic in the country in which they are relied upon." *Id.* at III.B.1.2. In response to these criticisms, a Working Group was established to draft a compromise acceptable to all parties. The "compromise" was essentially the same as Article I(1) as finally adopted:

> "This Convention shall apply to the recognition and enforcement of arbitral awards made in the territory of a State other than the State where the recognition and enforcement of such awards are sought, and arising out of disputes or differences between physical and legal persons. It shall also apply to arbitral awards not considered as domestic awards in the State where the recognition and enforcement are sought." *Id.* at III.B.4.2.

This was scarcely a compromise: "In fact, the compromise reached at the New York Conference was in favour of the territorialists." van den Berg, *When Is An Arbitral Award Non-Domestic Under the New York Convention of 1958?*, 6 Pace L. Rev. 25, 39 (1985). That is because the non-territorial criteria for defining the Convention's application, contained in the second sentence of Article I(1), was an *extension* of the Convention; in addition to the non-territorial criteria added in the second sentence of Article I(1), the Convention was applicable, through the first sentence of Article I(1), which was retained, to all awards made in foreign countries. "[T]he New York Convention always applies to the recognition and enforcement of an arbitral award made in another State ..., whilst it may, in addition, apply to the recognition and enforcement or an arbitral award made in the State where the recognition and enforcement are sought if such an award is considered nondomestic." *Ibid.*

6. *Rationale of* Bergesen. Relying on Article I(1)'s second sentence, *Bergesen* and *Toys-R-Us* hold that awards made in the United States were "nondomestic" under Article I(1) and, therefore, subject to the Convention and its implementing legislation. Other U.S. courts have also held that awards made in the United States may be "nondomestic." *See, e.g., S&T Oil Equip. & Mach., Ltd v. Juridica Invs. Ltd*, 456 F.Appx 481 (5th Cir. 2012); *Karaha Bodas Co., v. Perusahaan Pertambangan*, 364 F.3d 274, 287-88 (5th Cir. 2004); *Jacada (Europe), Ltd v. Int'l Mktg Strategies, Inc.*, 401 F.3d 701, 705-10 (6th Cir. 2005). Are *Bergesen* and its progeny correctly decided? Note that virtually no other Contracting State has defined any category of awards as "nondomestic." G. Born, *International Commercial Arbitration* 2944-45 (2d ed. 2014).

(a) *No definition of "nondomestic" award in Convention.* The *Bergesen* court first reasoned that the Convention simply "did not define non-domestic awards," thereby leaving it to Contracting States to adopt their own definitions. Is that correct? Is there anything in the Convention or its purposes that would forbid the United States from regarding awards made in New York under U.S. arbitration law as nondomestic, and thus subjecting those awards to the Convention in U.S. courts? What if the United States were to regard *every* award as nondomestic?

Would this undermine the Convention or adversely affect other Contracting States?

Is not the real threat to the Convention the opposite: narrow national court definitions of "foreign" and "nondomestic" awards that place inappropriately restrictive limits on the Convention's scope? *See* the *Northstar* decision and the Indian Supreme Court's decision in *National Thermal Power*, holding awards made outside India "domestic" in certain circumstances, *infra* pp. 1102-06, 1108-09.

(b) *How should "nondomestic" awards be defined?* Assuming that the Convention permits the definition of nondomestic awards adopted in *Bergesen*, is that a wise decision? Should not U.S. and other courts be mindful of the legislative history and purpose of the Convention in defining "nondomestic" awards? The Convention's legislative history strongly suggests, as outlined above, that "nondomestic" awards were intended to be those that, while made within a state's territory, were made pursuant to the arbitration law of another country; an example, discussed above, would be two Germans arbitrating in Germany with English law as the procedural law of the arbitration. *See supra* p. 1088-89. Should U.S. law define "nondomestic" awards as awards made outside the United States, but with the FAA being chosen as the procedural law of the arbitration?

(c) *Definition of "nondomestic" in §202 of the FAA*. After concluding that the Convention left each Contracting State free to define "nondomestic," *Bergesen* turned to §202 of the FAA for the U.S. definition of the term. Section 202 provides that, if a U.S. arbitration involves only U.S. citizens, the Convention may be applicable, but only if the parties' "relationship involves property located abroad, envisages performance or enforcement abroad, or has some other reasonable relation with one or more foreign states." U.S. FAA, 9 U.S.C. §202. Note that the second sentence of §202 provides that the Convention will *not* apply to certain agreements and awards. *See supra* pp. 167-68 for an explanation of Congress's purposes in enacting §202, indicating that the section was intended to exclude certain primarily domestic disputes from the Convention's scope.

Section 202's "reasonable relationship" standard was derived from §1-105 of the U.S. Uniform Commercial Code. *See* Foreign Arbitral Awards, S. Rep. No. 91-702, 91st Cong., 2d Sess. 6 (1970) (Appx.; Statement of Richard D. Kearney) ("The reasonable relationship criterion is taken from the general provisions of the Uniform Commercial Code [1-105(1).]"). As noted above, §1-105 (in its original version) provided that the law chosen by a contractual choice-of-law clause must be reasonably related to the parties' transaction. *See supra* pp. 167-68, 990-91. This "reasonable relationship" standard appears to be that which was adopted by the court in *Bergesen*.

Consider the *Bergesen* court's reliance on §202 to define a "nondomestic" award under Article I(1). Did Congress in fact "spell out its definition" of a nondomestic award in §202, as *Bergesen* concluded? Is §202 nonetheless relevant to fashioning a definition of "nondomestic" awards under U.S. law? Are the Convention's goals furthered by adopting *Bergesen*'s reading of §202?

(d) *Standards for determining when awards "made" in United States will be "nondomestic" after Bergesen*. Under *Bergesen*'s analysis, how would §202's "reasonable relationship" standard be applied to define what awards are "nondomestic"? What if an arbitration involved one or more foreign nationals (rather than only U.S. nationals); would an award made in the United States always be "nondomestic"? What if an arbitration involved a dispute where some of the contractual performance occurred abroad? Where foreign substantive law governed the dispute? Won't a "reasonable relationship" requirement result in treating a substantial number of awards made in the United States as "nondomestic"?

7. *Consequences under New York Convention of classifying award as "foreign" or "nondomestic."* What are the consequences of treating an award as "foreign" or "nondomestic" under the Convention?

(a) *"Foreign" and "nondomestic" awards presumptively entitled to recognition under Article III and can be denied recognition only on grounds specified in Article V.* As *Toys-R-Us* explains, if an award is "foreign" or "nondomestic" in a particular Contracting State, it will be subject to Article III, requiring that the State presumptively recognize and enforce the award. In addition, a "foreign" or "nondomestic" award will ordinarily be subject to non-recognition and non-enforcement only if one of the exceptions set forth in Article V of the Convention is applicable. *See supra* pp. 33-39 and *infra* pp. 1189-99, 1199-266. In contrast, as *Toys-R-Us* holds, an award that is not "foreign" can generally be annulled on any grounds available under local law. *See supra* pp. 622-23, 639-40 and *infra* pp. 1157-58.

(b) *"Foreign" award cannot be annulled outside of arbitral seat.* If an award is "foreign" in a Contracting State, then that State may not entertain an application to annul the award under local law. Rather, the award may only be annulled where the award was made, in the arbitral seat. *See infra* pp. 1099-112. Recall the discussion of this structural aspect of the Convention in *Karaha Bodas*. *See supra* pp. 609-12.

(c) *Possibility of annulling "nondomestic" award in arbitral seat under local law.* Does the Convention permit a "nondomestic" award to be annulled in the arbitral seat (which treats the award as "nondomestic")? Or, if an award is characterized as "nondomestic" in a particular Contracting State, is it then subject only to recognition or non-recognition under Article V of the Convention, and not to annulment? If annulment of a "nondomestic" award in the arbitral seat is permitted, what grounds may be relied upon to annul the award—any grounds permitted under local law or only grounds permitted for non-recognition under Article V of the Convention?

Toys-R-Us addressed these issues and concluded that the Convention (and §207 of the FAA) permits actions under the first chapter of the FAA to annul a "nondomestic" award, made in the United States, applying the FAA's vacatur standards. What is the rationale supporting this conclusion? Note that characterizing an award as "nondomestic" does not affect the place where the award was "made"; in *Bergesen*, the award was still "made" in New York, even though the award is "nondomestic." If an award is made in a particular Contracting State, does Article V(1)(e) of the Convention permit actions to annul the award in that state—including actions to annul on grounds not specified in Article V of the Convention? *See infra* pp. 1106-10, 1157-58; *Hebei Imp. & Exp. Corp. v. Polytek Eng'g Co.*, [1999] 2 HCK 205 (H.K. Ct. Fin. App.) (New York Convention "distinguishes between proceedings to set aside an award in the court of supervisory jurisdiction … and proceedings in the court of enforcement. Proceedings to set aside are governed by the law under which the award was made up or the law of the place where it was made, while proceedings in the court of enforcement are governed by the law of that forum"). What in the Convention would prohibit an annulment action in a Contracting State if an award is "made" in that state? What effect does designating an award of "nondomestic" have? If a state were free to annul "nondomestic" awards under local law, would the designation of such awards as "nondomestic" have any meaning at all?

In *Toys-R-Us*, the court held that a "nondomestic" award, made in the United States, could be annulled on all of the grounds permitted under the FAA for domestic awards, including manifest disregard. Other U.S. courts have apparently adopted this analysis, holding that §10 grounds are available for annulling a nondomestic award made in the United States. *See, e.g., Zeiler v. Deitsch*, 500 F.3d 157, 164 (2d Cir. 2007); *Jacada (Europe), Ltd, v. Int'l Mktg Strategies, Inc.*, 401 F.3d 701, 709-10 (6th Cir. 2005); *Lucent Techs., Inc. v. Tatung Co.*, 379 F.3d 24 (2d Cir. 2004); *Banco de Seguros del Estado v. Mut. Marine Office, Inc.*, 344 F.3d 255 (2d Cir. 2003). In contrast, other authorities have concluded, usually without significant discussion, that only Article V grounds are available in actions in the arbitral seat to annul "nondomestic" awards. *See Indus. Risk Insurers v. M.A.N. Gutehoffnungshütte GmbH*, 141 F.3d 1434 (11th Cir. 1998) (only grounds enumerated in Article V may be basis for vacating award subject to Convention, including "nondomestic" awards made in United States); *Costa v. Celebrity Cruises, Inc.*, 768 F.Supp.2d 1237, 1240 (S.D. Fla. 2011) (where Convention award is made in United States, "any additional grounds for vacating an arbitration award as may be contained in Chapter 1 of the FAA or the FIAA are strictly inapplicable…. Although this may not be the rule in other circuits, it is the rule in the Eleventh Circuit").

Which approach *should* national courts take to the debate described above (and addressed in *Toys-R-Us)*? If an award is treated by a Contracting State as "nondomestic," should the award then be subject to annulment under local law in that state? If the award can be annulled, what is the meaning of its categorization as "nondomestic"? Should the characterization of an award as "nondomestic" mean that the award should be treated under the Convention as if it were a "foreign" award? Wouldn't that mean not subjecting the award to annulment in local courts, and only permitting actions to recognize and enforce the award? If a U.S. court does not have authority to annul a "nondomestic" award made in the United States, what Contracting State would have such authority? Any state? Would it be acceptable for there to be awards not subject to annulment anywhere? *See infra* pp. 1158-59.

(d) *Possible limits on grounds for annulment of "nondomestic" award in arbitral seat under local law*. Even if an award that is "nondomestic" in a Contracting State can be subject to an annulment action in that state, should domestic grounds for annulling awards be available in such an annulment action (without regard to Article V of the Convention)? If an award can be annulled pursuant to local law, what is the point of characterizing the award as "nondomestic"? Would it make sense for the characterization of an award as "nondomestic" to have no meaning? Was

Toys-R-Us correctly decided? What application does §208 of the FAA have to an annulment action in cases involving "nondomestic" awards made in the United States? Can §208 be interpreted to limit the grounds for annulment available under the domestic FAA?

8. *Distinctions between "international" and "non-international" arbitrations in national arbitration legislation.* Consider Article 1 of the UNCITRAL Model Law and Article 176 of the SLPIL, excerpted at pp. 86 & 157 of the Documentary Supplement. Note that each statute is limited to arbitrations with an "international" character. What types of arbitrations does this exclude? Why? *See supra* pp. 166-67.

9. *Different enforcement regimes for "foreign" and "non-foreign" arbitral awards under national arbitration legislation.* Even outside the context of the New York Convention (and other international instruments), the place where an arbitral award is made is important for enforcement purposes. In most developed states, an arbitral award will only be subject to an action to annul or set aside in local courts if it was "made" within that state. Consider Articles 34-36 of the UNCITRAL Model Law, excerpted at pp. 94-96 of the Documentary Supplement. Compare Articles 190 and 194 of the SLPIL, excerpted at p. 160 of the Documentary Supplement. *See supra* pp. 619-20, 622-24. If an award was "made" elsewhere (*i.e.*, if it is "foreign"), then it will be subject only to legislative provisions dealing with the recognition of "foreign" arbitral awards, such as Article 35 of the UNCITRAL Model Law and Article 194 of the SLPIL.

Compare the regime for review of ICSID awards under Articles 52 and 54 of the ICSID Convention. For purposes of review of an award, does it matter where an ICSID award is "made" or whether it is "foreign" or not?

3. *Reciprocity Requirements Under International Conventions and National Arbitration Legislation*

Reciprocity plays a role in many aspects of private international law.[34] That is less true with respect to the enforcement of arbitral awards than in other contexts, but the principle of reciprocity still has important applications in some contexts affecting international awards. As described above, the New York Convention permits Contracting States to make reciprocity reservations.[35] Article I(3) provides that Contracting States may declare that they "will apply the Convention, on the basis of reciprocity, to the recognition and enforcement of only those awards made in the territory of another Contracting State." In addition, Article XIV of the Convention contains a separate, more general reciprocity provision: "A Contracting State shall not be entitled to avail itself of the present Convention against other Contracting States except to the extent that it is itself bound to apply the Convention."

As we have also seen, the United States and many other Contracting States have made reciprocity reservations under the Convention.[36] The U.S. reservation provides that the United States will apply the Convention, on the basis of reciprocity, to the recognition and

---

34. *See supra* p. 169; G. Born, *International Commercial Arbitration* 2970 (2d ed. 2014).

35. *See supra* pp. 169-71; G. Born, *International Commercial Arbitration* 343-44, 2970-78 (2d ed. 2014). Similarly, the Geneva Convention of 1927 was applicable only to awards made in other Contracting States. *See supra* pp. 30-32.

36. *See supra* p. 171.

enforcement of "only those awards made in the territory of another Contracting State."[37] The materials excerpted below explore the application of this, and other, reciprocity reservation(s).

<hr>

FERTILIZER CORP. OF INDIA v. IDI MANAGEMENT, INC.
517 F.Supp. 948 (S.D. Ohio 1981)

<hr>

SPIEGEL, District Judge. [Fertilizer Corporation of India (FCI) was a wholly owned entity of the Republic of India; IDI Management, Inc. (IDI) was an Ohio corporation engaged in designing fertilizer plants. IDI designed a plant near Bombay for FCI, pursuant to an agreement containing an ICC arbitration clause. Disputes arose and FCI sought arbitration; arbitral proceedings were conducted in India, and the tribunal issued a unanimous award in favor of FCI in an amount of approximately $1.3 million. IDI refused to satisfy the award, and FCI commenced enforcement proceedings in U.S. district court in Ohio.]

IDI argues that India would not enforce the Nitrophosphate Award had it been rendered in the United States in IDI's favor and that therefore the reciprocity between India and the United States required by the Convention is absent. India has adopted various evasive devices, IDI submits, to avoid enforcement of awards adverse to Indian parties.... Article I(3) of the Convention states that contracting states may choose to apply the Convention only to legal relationships considered "commercial" under the law of the acceding state, and may also choose to apply the Convention only to awards made in another contracting state's territory. Both India and the United States chose to adopt these restrictions. Citing *Indian Organic Chem., Ltd v. Chemtex Fibers, Inc.*, A.I.R. 1978 Bombay 106, IDI alleges that India has narrowly defined the term "commercial" so as to exclude many or most legal relationships which would be considered "commercial" in the normal sense of the word. IDI argues further that Article XIV of the Convention sweeps broadly and, in effect, requires this Court to determine the extent to which India is applying the Convention and to react in like manner.

FCI contends that the concept of reciprocity does not apply to the commercial reservation, citing the fact that the phrase "on the basis of reciprocity" appears in the first sentence of Article I(3), but does not appear in the second sentence, the "commercial" reservation. Furthermore, it cites legislative history for the proposition that Article XIV does not apply at all to Article I, which has its own reciprocity clause. In the alternative, if Article XIV does apply to the entire Convention, it must be read literally. Article XIV says that a contracting state may avail itself of the Convention only "*to the extent that it is itself* bound to apply the Convention" (emphasis added). Whereas IDI reads "bound to apply" as "applies," FCI urges a reading which would allow a contracting state which had not, for example, adopted the "commercial" reservation to do so when faced with an award rendered in a country which had adopted that reservation. Under FCI's interpretation of reciprocity, all that is required, since the United States has adopted the first reservation of Article I(3),

<hr>

37. 9 U.S.C.A. §201. The complete text of the U.S. reservation is reproduced at *supra* p. 171. *See also Restatement (Third) U.S. Law of International Commercial Arbitration* §4-5 (Tent. Draft No. 2 2012) ("Recognition or enforcement of a Convention award is subject to a requirement of reciprocity. The requirement is satisfied if the seat of the arbitration that produced the award is a Contracting State to the applicable Convention. Recognition or enforcement of a Convention award is not subject to any other reciprocity requirement.").

is to determine that India is a signatory to the Convention, and since the United States had adopted the second reservation, to determine that the contract in question is commercial under the laws of the United States. If more is required, FCI asserts that the contract would also be considered commercial by most courts in India and that *Chemtex* is an aberration.

The Court is persuaded that the reciprocity required by the Convention is satisfied in this case. With regard to the wording of Article I(3), it is an elementary rule of statutory construction that where express language is used in one part of a statute, its commission from another part is presumed to be deliberate. It is undisputed that India is a signatory to the Convention; therefore, the reciprocity of the first sentence in question is satisfied. It is equally undisputed that the contract between the parties is considered commercial under the laws of the United States; thus, the requirement of the second sentence is met.

As to Article XIV, Leonard Quigley has said, "The adoption of this Article [XIV] gives states a defensive right to take advantage of another state's reservations with regard to territorial, federal or other provisions." Quigley, *Accession by the United States to the United Nations Convention on the Recognition and Enforcement of Foreign Arbitral Awards*, 70 Yale L.J. 1049, 1074 (1961). Quigley also mentions that this clause "presumably will also cover the case where the courts of a State have placed a restrictive interpretation upon its obligations under the Convention," but we do not find this comment determinative. In any case, we are satisfied that the Indian courts are not engaged in a devious policy to subvert the Convention by denying non-Indians their just awards. [An arbitral award in favor of the U.S. company in a related case] helps persuade us that the Indian judiciary is functioning in a responsible manner. Moreover, FCI has cited other cases and arbitrations showing that Indian courts will enforce awards against Indian parties and that Indian parties do arbitrate outside of India. As IDI itself has counseled, United States courts should "construe exceptions narrowly lest foreign courts use holdings against application of the Convention as a reason for refusing enforcement of awards made in the United States." ...

NATIONAL IRANIAN OIL CO. v. ASHLAND OIL, INC.
817 F.2d 326 (5th Cir. 1987)

[excerpted above at pp. 170-71 & 427-29]

NOTES

1. *Reciprocity reservations under New York Convention.* Article I(3) of the New York Convention does not forbid the enforcement of foreign awards based upon a lack of reciprocity. It merely permits Contracting States, which have made a reciprocity reservation, to deny recognition and enforcement to otherwise valid awards based upon a lack of reciprocity. The United States and many other Convention signatories have adopted reciprocity reservations under Article I(3). *See supra* p. 171. Is this wise? Is it supportive of the international arbitral process?

2. *Reciprocity under Article I(3) based on where award "made."* As we have seen, reciprocity with respect to awards under Article I(3) of the Convention has been held to be determined by reference to the place where an arbitration is conducted and the award is made, not to the parties' nationalities. *See supra* pp. 171-73; *E.A.S.T., Inc. of Stamford, Conn. v. M/V Alaia*, 876 F.2d 1168, 1172 (5th Cir. 1989) ("The principle of

reciprocity is thus concerned with the forum in which the arbitration will occur and whether that forum state is a signatory to the Convention—not whether both parties to the dispute are nationals of signatory states."). *See also Restatement (Third) U.S. Law of International Commercial Arbitration* §4-5 comment a (Tent. Draft No. 2 2012) ("Satisfaction of this reciprocity requirement depends on the seat of the arbitration and not the nationality of the parties, the law governing the substance of the dispute, or the place where the arbitration hearing is held or other procedural steps are taken.").

For example, suppose a Taiwanese company arbitrates with a U.S. company and the arbitration is seated in Switzerland (which, like the United States, but unlike Taiwan, has ratified the Convention). In this case, an award made in Switzerland in favor of the Taiwanese company would be enforceable in accordance with the Convention in the United States (and in other Convention signatories). *See Iran Aircraft Indus. v. Avco Corp.*, 980 F.2d 141 (2d Cir. 1992) (Convention applicable to award made in Netherlands against U.S. company in favor of Iranian company, when Iran was not Contracting State to Convention). Similarly, an award in favor of the U.S. company would be enforceable in other Convention States against the Taiwanese company. Importantly, however, neither award would be enforceable under the Convention in Taiwan.

If the above hypothetical arbitration were conducted in Taiwan (or another state that had not acceded to the Convention) then the award would not be enforceable as a matter of right under the Convention in the United States—because of the U.S. reciprocity reservation. *See Nat'l Iranian Oil Co. v. Ashland Oil, Inc.*, 817 F.2d 326 (5th Cir. 1987). Nor would the Taiwanese award be enforceable under the Convention in other Contracting States with a reciprocity reservation (even if the award were in favor of the U.S. party). Note, however, that enforcement might still be possible under local, non-Convention law. *See infra* p. 1196.

3. *Rationale for reciprocity reservations under Article I(3).* A reciprocity reservation presumably rests on a judgment that it is both unjust and impolitic for a nation's courts to apply the Convention's pro-enforcement provisions to an award made in a foreign country that would not apply the Convention to enforce a local award: simply put, if "they" won't enforce "our" awards, "we" won't enforce "theirs." Why exactly is that so? *See also supra* p. 174.

Consider the foregoing question from a U.S. perspective. What sorts of parties are most likely to be the subject of enforcement actions in U.S. courts? The answer is generally U.S. companies, which will be more likely than foreign companies to have attachable assets in the United States. What sorts of companies are most likely to be the subject of enforcement actions in the foreign country where the award was made? The answer is probably that there is not any particular correlation between the nation where a foreign award is made and the nationality of the losing party to the arbitration; England, Switzerland, France, Singapore and other nations are routinely selected as arbitral seats by companies with no local connection. Thus, the result of the U.S. reciprocity reservation is that awards made in Switzerland and other Convention States will be entitled to reciprocity in the United States, even: (a) if such Swiss awards are made in favor of entities from countries that are not parties to the Convention, (b) if such awards can, therefore, generally not be enforced in the home jurisdictions of such companies, where they are most likely to have assets, and (c) though enforcement of such awards in Switzerland will likely not be of practical value to the U.S. company, because there is no particular reason to think that there will be assets of nationals from non-member states there that can be enforced against.

Given all this, what purpose does the reciprocity reservation serve? Would it not be better to adopt a reciprocity reservation defined by reference to the parties' nationalities? For example, if Taiwan will not enforce a U.S. award (or the award of any other nation) under the Convention, then the United States will not enforce an award in favor of a Taiwanese entity. Note that the sometimes-maligned reciprocity exception to the enforcement of foreign judgments is structured in this fashion. That is, foreign court judgments against a U.S. national are only enforced in favor of a national of the foreign forum if the foreign forum's courts would recognize U.S. judgments against citizens of the foreign forum. *See Hilton v. Guyot*, 159 U.S. 113 (1895); G. Born & P. Rutledge, *International Civil Litigation in United States Courts* 1098-99 (5th ed. 2011).

Would Article I(3) permit a reciprocity reservation defined on the basis of the parties' nationalities? Should it? If so, could the United States and other countries change their reciprocity reservations to focus on the parties' nationalities?

4. *Reciprocity under Article XIV of New York Convention.* What effect does Article XIV of the Convention have?

    (a) *Who can invoke Article XIV?* Putting aside what Article XIV means, who can enforce it and where is it applicable? In particular, can a private litigant invoke the provision in recognition or enforcement proceedings? *Fertilizer Corp.* assumed that Article XIV could be invoked by a private party in a national court. Note, however, that the Article's language appears directed at the rights of Contracting States against one another, not at the rights of private parties. *See Restatement (Third) U.S. Law of International Commercial Arbitration* §4-5 comment b & Reporters' Note b (Tent. Draft No. 2 2012) ("By its terms ... Article XIV addresses only the rights of one Contracting State vis-à-vis another under the Convention, and does not purport to apply to private-party actions to enforce awards brought in national courts."). Some commentators have nonetheless concluded that Article XIV applies in private litigation. Quigley, *Accession by the United States to the United Nations Convention on the Recognition and Enforcement of Foreign Arbitral Awards*, 70 Yale L.J. 1049, 1074 (1961); A. van den Berg, *The New York Convention of 1958* 13-15 (1981). Is this wise? Wouldn't Article XIV then duplicate Article I(3)?

    (b) *Possible interpretations of Article XIV.* Article XIV is broadly drafted, and there is uncertainty as to its meaning. Assuming the provision is available to private parties in national court proceedings, consider the following possible applications:

        (1) State X regards antitrust and competition law claims as arbitrable, but State Y does not; nevertheless, suppose an arbitral tribunal sitting in State Z (a Contracting State) renders an award against a State X company, in favor of a State Y company, based on State X and State Z antitrust law. Does the reciprocity reservation allow State X courts to deny recognition because the award would be unenforceable in State Y?

        (2) State B treats natural resource agreements as "commercial," but suppose State A does not. State A is a Contracting State, but its courts have refused to enforce

awards, arising out of natural resource agreements, made in other Contracting States against State A government entities, on the grounds that they are not commercial. An arbitral tribunal in State A issues an award in favor of a State A government corporation and against a State B company, holding that it breached a natural resource agreement; must a State B court enforce the award?

(3) State C is a Contracting State, but its courts will not enforce awards for interest at punitive rates. Suppose a tribunal makes an award in State C for punitive interest in favor of a State C company, and enforcement is sought in State D. State D courts ordinarily would enforce such awards; must a State D court enforce the award?

(c) *Possible application of Article XIV on basis of nationality.* Reread Article XIV. Note that the text of Article XIV differs from that of Article I(3)'s provision for reciprocity reservations; specifically, Article XIV is not confined expressly to non-recognition of awards made in the territory of non-Contracting States. Note also that, under traditional principles of public international law, a nation may espouse the rights of its nationals, and not others, when a foreign state acts in violation of its international obligations towards them. *See Restatement (Third) Foreign Relations Law* §§711-712, 901-902 (1987). Does that mean, in examples (i), (ii) and (iii) above, that Article XIV's reciprocity exception could be invoked even if States Z, A and C are Contracting States? More broadly, does Article XIV permit U.S. courts to refuse to recognize awards rendered in favor of nationals of states that are not party to the Convention? Note the policy considerations supporting such an interpretation. *See supra* pp. 1096-97.

(d) *Article XIV held not to permit inquiry into foreign state's actual application of Convention.* What interpretation of Article XIV does *Fertilizer Corp.* adopt? Suppose it was clear that the courts of State A simply did not, as a practical matter, honor State A's commitments under the Convention. Note that in the context of the recognition of foreign judgments, U.S. courts inquire into the actual treatment, in practice, of U.S. judgments by foreign courts. G. Born & P. Rutledge, *International Civil Litigation in United States Courts* 1099 (5th ed. 2011). Note also that enforcing arbitral awards—in a fashion consistent with the Convention's requirements—in some parts of the world is generally difficult. Given the purposes of the reciprocity reservation, why shouldn't the courts of Contracting States engage in at least some scrutiny of how foreign courts actually apply the Convention? For one view, *see* R. von Mehren, *The Enforcement of Arbitral Awards Under Conventions and United States Law*, 9 Yale J. World Pub. Order 343, 352 (1983) (terming *Fertilizer Corp.* "correct" because it discourages "needless litigation").

5. *Absence of provision for reciprocity reservation from Inter-American Convention.* As discussed above, there is no provision in the Inter-American Convention for reciprocity reservations. *See supra* p. 174. Is that wise?

Note, however, that §304 of the FAA imposes a reciprocity limitation on the Inter-American Convention in U.S. courts. Is this statutory limitation consistent with the Convention? Suppose a national of Colombia (which is a party to the Inter-American Convention) obtains an award against a U.S. company in a state that is not a party to the Inter-American Convention. Is the Convention applicable to enforcement of the award in U.S. courts? Under §304 of the FAA?

6. *Does the absence of reciprocity affect recognition and enforcement of non-Convention awards?* A party can seek to enforce an award made in a non-Convention State in Contracting States under the domestic law of those States (for example, in the United States, under either U.S. state law or §9 of the FAA). In deciding whether to enforce the award under domestic law, is it relevant that the award was made in a state that has not ratified the Convention? Why or why not?

As discussed above, the common law rule in the United States in the context of enforcing foreign court judgments was historically (and generally still is) that U.S. courts would only enforce such judgments on the basis of reciprocity. G. Born & P. Rutledge, *International Civil Litigation in United States Courts* 1094-102 (5th ed. 2011); *supra* pp. 1096-97. Note also the determination of the President and Congress that national interests would be served by a U.S. reciprocity reservation under Article I(3) of the Convention, as well as Congress's judgment in enacting §304. Should these determinations about U.S. interests influence decisions under state law or the domestic FAA?

7. *Absence of reciprocity requirement in national arbitration legislation.* Consider Articles 35 and 36 of the UNCITRAL Model Law. Do they impose any reciprocity requirement? Compare Article 194 of the SLPIL.

C. LIMITS ON FORUMS FOR ANNULMENT OF INTERNATIONAL ARBITRAL AWARDS

As noted above, the New York Convention limits the judicial enforcement forums in which an action to annul or set aside an award may be pursued. In particular, an annulment action may only be pursued in: (a) the country "in which ... that award was made," and (b) the country "under the law of which ... that award was made."[38] The Inter-American Convention contains similar provisions.[39]

Pursuant to these provisions, the "model" procedure for judicial actions to annul (or, alternatively, confirm) an award subject to the New York (or Inter-American) Convention is straightforward. If the award is made in State A, under the laws of State A, it will be subject to an action to annul in State A (but not elsewhere).[40] An action to confirm the award can be brought in State A, but need not be; actions to recognize and enforce the award can also be brought in other nations. The action to annul in State A can be based on any ground available under State A's laws, without regard to the Convention's exceptions, but defenses to actions to recognize and enforce the award in courts outside State A are limited to the bases for non-recognition set forth in the Convention.[41] The following materials consider how this "model" is constructed.

---

38. *See* New York Convention, Arts. V(1)(e) and VI; *supra* pp. 620-21, 634-36 & *infra* pp. 1106-09.

39. Inter-American Convention, Art. 5(1)(e).

40. *See supra* pp. 620-21, 1071 and *infra* pp. 1106-09, 1134-73; G. Born, *International Commercial Arbitration* 2988-3002, 3008-09 (2d ed. 2014). If the award is made in State A, but under the laws of State B, it will be subject to an action to annul in State B (and, perhaps, also in State A). *See infra* pp. 1106-09.

41. *See supra* pp. 1070-72 and *infra* pp. 1157-58, 1195-97; G. Born, *International Commercial Arbitration* 3008-09 (2d ed. 2014).

PT GARUDA INDONESIA v. BIRGEN AIR
[2002] SGCA 12 (Singapore Ct. App.)

[excerpted above at pp. 600-05]

KARAHA BODAS CO., LLC v. PERUSAHAAN PERTAMBANGAN MINYAK DAN GAS BUMI NEGARA
364 F.3d 274 (5th Cir. 2004)

[excerpted above at pp. 605-19]

UNION OF INDIA v. MCDONNELL DOUGLAS CORP.
[1993] 2 Lloyd's Rep. 48 (QB) (English High Ct.)

[excerpted above at pp. 626-29]

INTERNATIONAL STANDARD ELECTRIC CORP. v. BRIDAS SAPIC
745 F.Supp. 172 (S.D.N.Y. 1990)

CONBOY, District Judge. In this action, the parties seek, on the one side, to vacate a foreign arbitration award, and, on the other, to enforce that award pursuant to [the New York Convention]. Petitioner, International Standard Electric Corporation ("ISEC"), is a wholly owned subsidiary of the International Telephone and Telegraph Company ("ITT"). Respondent Bridas Sociedad Anonima Petrolera, Industrial Y Comercial ("Bridas") is a corporation organized and doing business in Argentina.... [ITT] conducted its international business through ISEC, [which] in turn controlled more than 50% of the Argentine telecommunications market through its wholly owned subsidiary, Compania Standard Electric Argentina S.A. ("CSEA"). In 1978, ISEC offered, and Bridas accepted 25% participation in CSEA for $7.5 million. The parties entered into a Shareholders Agreement (the "Agreement") ... to control the terms of their arrangement. Chapter 11 of the Agreement provides that "[a]ll disputes connected to this Agreement ... shall be settled or finally decided by one or more arbitrators appointed by the [ICC] in accordance with the Rules of Conciliation and Arbitration." Chapter 8 of the Agreement provides that the Agreement would be "governed by and construed under and in accordance with the laws of the State of New York." ...

Bridas filed with the [ICC] in Paris a Request for Arbitration.... Mexico City was designated [by the ICC] as the place of the arbitration.... ISEC filed "Objections to Jurisdiction" with the Arbitral Panel, asserting lack of jurisdiction over three of the four claims set forth in Bridas' complaint. [T]he Arbitral Panel conducted a hearing in Mexico City, heard argument on the jurisdictional question, and in conjunction with the parties drafted the Terms of Reference, which were then signed by the parties.... [After hearings and briefing,] the Panel, in accordance with the rules which require the advance review and approval by the ICC International Court of Arbitration, signed the final Award, which was released and issued to the parties on January 16, 1990. The Arbitral Award ("Award") ... awarded Bridas damages of $6,793,000 with interest at 12%....

ISEC filed a petition in this Court to vacate and refuse recognition and enforcement of the Award.... Bridas has cross-petitioned to dismiss ISEC's petition to vacate on the grounds that this Court lacks subject matter jurisdiction to grant such relief under the Convention.... Bridas further cross-petitions to enforce the Award pursuant to Article III of the Convention.

We will first address the question of whether, under the binding terms of the New York Convention, we lack subject matter jurisdiction to vacate a foreign arbitral award. The situs of the Award in this case was Mexico City, a location chosen by the [ICC] pursuant to rules of procedure explicitly agreed to by the parties. Since the parties here are an American Company and an Argentine Company, it is not difficult to understand why the Mexican capital was selected as the place to conduct the arbitration.

Bridas argues that, under the New York Convention, only the courts of the place of arbitration, in this case the Courts of Mexico, have jurisdiction to vacate or set aside an arbitral award. ISEC argues that under the Convention both the courts of the place of arbitration and the courts of the place whose substantive law has been applied, in this case the courts of the United States, have jurisdiction to vacate or set aside an arbitral award.

Under Article V(1)(e) of the Convention, "an application for the setting aside or suspension of the award" can be made only to the courts or the "competent authority of the country in which, *or under the law of which,* that award was made." (Emphasis added.) ISEC argues that "the competent authority of the country ... under the law of which [the] award was made," refers to the country the substantive law of which, as opposed to the procedural law of which, was applied by the arbitrators. Hence, ISEC insists that since the arbitrators applied substantive New York law, we have jurisdiction to vacate the award. ISEC cites only one case to support this expansive reading of the Convention, *Laminoirs-Trefileries-Cableries de Lens v. Southwire Co.,* 484 F.Supp. 1063 (N.D. Ga. 1980). That case, however, did not involve a foreign award under the Convention, and did not implicate the jurisdictional question here raised, since there the parties' substantive and procedural choice of law, and the situs of the arbitration were both New York. It seems plain that the Convention does not address, contemplate or encompass a challenge to an award in the courts of the state where the award was rendered, since the relation of the courts to the arbitral proceeding is not an international, but a wholly domestic one, at least insofar as the Convention is concerned. Whether such an arbitration would be considered international because of the parties' nationalities under the [FAA], is irrelevant.

Bridas has cited ... *Am. Constr. Mach. & Equip. Corp. v. Mechanised Constr. of Pakistan Ltd,* 659 F.Supp. 426 (S.D.N.Y.), *aff'd,* 828 F.2d 117 (2d Cir. 1987), as authority against the ISEC position. This case involved a dispute between a Cayman Islands company and a Pakistani company, arguably controlled by Pakistani substantive law and arbitrated in Geneva. Judge Keenan was asked to decline enforcement of the award on the ground that a challenge to it was pending in the courts of Pakistan. He ruled that "[t]he law under which this award was made was Swiss law because the award was rendered in Geneva *pursuant to Geneva procedural law.*" 659 F.Supp. at 429 (emphasis added). This analysis was expressly affirmed in the Court of Appeals....

We conclude that the phrase in the Convention "[the country] under the laws of which that award was made" undoubtedly referenced the complex thicket of the procedural law of arbitration obtaining in the numerous and diverse jurisdictions of the dozens of nations in attendance at the time the Convention was being debated. Even today, over three decades after these debates were conducted, there are broad variations in the international community on how arbitrations are to be conducted and under what customs, rules, statutes or court decisions, that is, under what "competent authority." Indeed, some signatory nations have highly specialized arbitration procedures, as is the case with the United States, while many others have nothing beyond generalized civil practice to govern arbitration.... [T]he language in dispute reflects the delegates' practical insight that parties to an international arbitration might prefer to equalize travel distance and costs to witnesses by selecting as a situs forum A, midpoint between two cities or two continents, and submit themselves to a different procedural law by selecting the arbitration procedure of forum B.

> "The 'competent authority' as mentioned in Article V(1)(e) for entertaining the action of setting aside the award is virtually always the court of the country in which the award was made. The phrase 'or under the law of which' the award was made refers to the theoretical case that on the basis of an agreement of the parties *the award is governed by an arbitration law which is different from the arbitration law of the country in which the award was made*." A. van den Berg, *The New York Arbitration Convention of 1958* 350 (Kluwer 1981) (emphasis added)....

It is clear, we believe, that any suggestion that a Court has jurisdiction to set aside a foreign award based upon the use of its domestic, substantive law in the foreign arbitration defies the logic both of the Convention debates and of the final text, and ignores the nature of the international arbitral system.... Decisions of foreign courts deciding cases under the Convention uniformly support the view that the clause in question means procedural and not substantive (*i.e.*, in most cases contract) law [citing decisions from six countries.]

Finally, we should observe that the core of petitioner's argument, that a generalized supervisory interest of a state in the application of its domestic substantive law (in most arbitrations the law of contract) in a foreign proceeding, is wholly out of step with the universal concept of arbitration in all nations. The whole point of arbitration is that the merits of the dispute will not be reviewed in the courts, wherever they be located. Indeed, this principle is so deeply imbedded in American, and specifically, federal jurisprudence, that no further elaboration of the case law is necessary. That this was the animating principle of the Convention, that the Courts should review arbitrations for procedural regularity but resist inquiry into the substantive merits of awards, is clear from the notes on this subject by the Secretary-General of the United Nations. Accordingly, we hold that the contested language in Article V(1)(e) of the Convention, "... the competent authority of the country under the law of which, [the] award was made" refers exclusively to procedural and not substantive law, and more precisely, to the regimen or scheme of arbitral procedural law under which the arbitration was conducted, and not the substantive law of contract which was applied in the case. In this case, the parties subjected themselves to the procedural law of Mexico. Hence, since the situs, or forum of the arbitration is Mexico, and the governing procedural law is that of Mexico, only the courts of Mexico have jurisdiction under the Convention to vacate the award. ISEC's petition to vacate the award is therefore dismissed....

NATIONAL THERMAL POWER CORP. v. SINGER CO.
7 Mealey's Int'l Arb. Rep. C1 (Indian S.Ct. 1992)

THOMMEN, Justice. The National Thermal Power Corporation ("NTPC") appeals from the judgment of the Delhi High Court ... dismissing the NTPC's application to set aside an interim award made at London by a tribunal constituted by the [ICC] in terms of the contract made in New Delhi between the NTPC and the respondent—the Singer Company ("Singer")—for the supply of equipment, erection and commissioning of certain works in India. The High Court held that the award was not governed by the [Indian] Arbitration Act, 1940; the arbitration agreement on which the award was made was not governed by the law of India; the award fell within the ambit of the Foreign Awards (Recognition and Enforcement) Act, 1961 (Act 45 of 1961) (the "Foreign Awards Act"); [and] London being the seat of arbitration, English Courts alone had jurisdiction to set aside the award....

The NTPC and the Singer entered into two formal agreements.... The General Terms and Conditions of Contract ... (the "General Terms") are expressly incorporated in the agreements and they state: "the laws applicable to this Contract shall be the laws in force in India. The Courts of Delhi shall have exclusive jurisdiction in all matters arising under this Contract." (7.2). The General Terms deal with the special responsibilities of foreign contractors ... [Clause 27(7) provides:]

In the event of foreign Contractor, the arbitration shall be conducted by three arbitrators, one each to be nominated by the Owner and the Contractor and the third to be named by the President of the [ICC], Paris. Save as above all Rules of Conciliation and Arbitration of the [ICC] shall apply to such arbitrations. The arbitration shall be conducted at such places as the arbitrators may determine.

In respect of an Indian Contractor, sub-clauses 6.2 of clause 27 says that the arbitration shall be conducted at New Delhi in accordance with the provisions of the Arbitration Act, 1940. It reads: "The arbitration shall be conducted in accordance with the provisions of the Indian Arbitration Act, 1940 or any statutory modification thereof. The venue of arbitration shall be New Delhi, India." The General Terms further provide: "the Contract shall in all respects be construed and governed according to Indian laws." (32.3). The formal agreements which the parties executed ... contain a specific provision for settlement of disputes. Article 4.1 provides:

Settlement of Disputes: It is specifically agreed by and between the parties that all the differences or disputes arising out of the contract or touching the subject matter of the contract, shall be decided by process of settlement and arbitration as specified in clause 26.0 and 27.0 excluding 27.6.1 and 17.6.2, of the General Conditions of the Contract....

[T]he dispute which arose between the parties was referred to an Arbitral Tribunal constituted in terms of the [ICC Rules]. In accordance with Article 12 of those Rules, the ICC Court chose London to be the place of arbitration.... The award was made in London as an interim award in an arbitration between the NTPC and a foreign contractor on a contract governed by the law of India and made in India for its performance solely in India.

The fundamental question is whether the arbitration agreement contained in the contract is governed by the law of India so as to save it from the ambit of the Foreign Awards Act and attract the provisions of the Arbitration Act, 1940. [India has ratified the New York Convention, which is implemented by the Indian "Foreign Awards Act."] Which is the law which governs the agreement on which the award has been made? ...

[The court identified two different legal systems potentially applicable in arbitral proceedings:] (a) the law governing the arbitration agreement, namely, its proper law; and (b) the law governing the conduct of the arbitration, namely, is procedural law. The proper law of the arbitration agreement is normally the same as the proper law of the contract. It is only in exceptional cases that it is not so even where the proper law of the contract is expressly chosen by the parties. Where, however, there is no express choice of the law governing the contract as a whole, or the arbitration agreement as such, a presumption may arise that the law of the country where the arbitration is agreed to be held is the proper law of the arbitration agreement. But that is only a rebuttable presumption.... The validity, effect, and interpretation of the arbitration agreement are governed by its proper law.... The parties have the freedom to choose the law governing an international commercial arbitration agreement ... as well as the procedural law governing the conduct of the arbitration.... Where there is no express choice of the law governing the contract as a whole, or the arbitration agreement in particular, there is, in the absence of any contrary indication, a presumption that the parties have intended that the proper law of the contract as well as the law governing the arbitration agreement are the same as the law of the country in which the arbitration is agreed to be held. On the other hand, where the proper law of the contract is expressly chosen by the parties, as in the present case, such law must, in the absence of an unmistakable intention to the contrary, govern the arbitration agreement which, though collateral or ancillary to the main contract, is nevertheless a part of such contract....

[T]he arbitration proceedings are conducted, in the absence of any agreement to the contrary, in accordance with the law of the country in which the arbitration is held. On the other hand, if the parties have specifically chosen the law governing the conduct and procedure of arbitration, the arbitration proceedings will be conducted in accordance with that law so long as it is not contrary to the public policy or the mandatory requirements of the law of the country in which the arbitration is held. If no such choice has been made by the parties, expressly or by necessary implication, the procedural aspect of the conduct of arbitration (as distinguished from the substantive agreement to arbitrate) will be determined by the law of the place or seat of arbitration. Where, however, the parties have, as in the instant case, stipulated that the arbitration between them will be conducted in accordance with the ICC Rules, those rules, being in many respects self-contained or self-regulating and constituting a contractual code of procedure, will govern the conduct of the arbitration, except insofar as they conflict with the mandatory requirements of the proper law of arbitration, or of the procedural law of the seat of arbitration. To such an extent the appropriate courts of the seat of arbitration, which in the present case are the competent English courts, will have jurisdiction in respect of procedural matters concerning the conduct of arbitration. But the overriding principle is that the courts of the country whose substantive laws govern the arbitration agreement are the competent courts in respect of all matters arising under the arbitration agreement, and the jurisdiction exercised by the courts of the seat of arbitration is merely concurrent and not exclusive and strictly limited to matters of procedure. All other matters in respect of the arbitration agreements fall within the exclusive competence of the courts of the country whose laws govern the arbitration agreement.

The proper law of the contract in the present case being expressly stipulated to be the laws in force in India and the exclusive jurisdiction of the courts in Delhi in all matters arising under the contract having been specifically accepted, and the parties not having chosen expressly or by implication a law different from the Indian law in regard to the agreement contained in the arbitration clause, the proper law governing the arbitration agreement is indeed the law in force in India, and the competent courts of this country must necessarily have jurisdiction over all matters concerning arbitration. Neither the rules of procedure for the conduct of arbitration contractually chosen by the parties (the ICC Rules) nor the mandatory requirements of the procedure followed in the courts of the country in which the arbitration is held can in any manner supersede the overriding jurisdiction and control of the Indian law and the Indian courts.

This means, questions such as the jurisdiction of the arbitrator to decide a particular issue or the continuance of an arbitration or the frustration of the arbitration agreement, its validity, effect, and interpretation are determined exclusively by the proper law of the arbitration agreement, which, in the present case, is Indian law. The procedural powers and duties of the arbitrators, as for example, whether they must hear oral evidence, whether the evidence of one party should be recorded necessarily in the presence of the other party, whether there is a right of cross-examination of witnesses, the special requirements of notice, the remedies available to a party in respect of security for costs or for discovery etc. are matters regulated in accordance with the rules chosen by the parties to the extent that those rules are applicable and sufficient and are not repugnant to the requirements of the procedural law and practice of the seat of arbitration....

An award rendered in the territory of a foreign State may be regarded as a domestic award in India where it is sought to be enforced by reason of Indian law being the proper law governing the arbitration agreement in terms of which the award was made. The Foreign Awards Act, incorporating the New York Convention, leaves no room for doubt on the point.... A "foreign award," as defined under the Foreign Awards Act, 1961 means an award ... on differences arising between persons out of legal relationships, whether contractual or not, which are considered to be commercial under the law in force in India. To qualify as a foreign award under the Act, the award should have been made in pursuance of an agreement in writing for arbitration to be governed by the [New York Convention] and not to be governed by the law of India. Furthermore, such an award should have been made outside India in the territory of a foreign State notified by the Government of India as having made reciprocal provisions for enforcement of the Convention. These are the conditions which must be satisfied to qualify an award as a "foreign award" (§2 read with §9).

An award is "foreign" not merely because it is made in the territory of a foreign State, but because it is made in such a territory on an arbitration agreement not governed by the law of India. An award made on an arbitration agreement governed by the law of India, though rendered outside India, is attracted by the saving clause in §9 of the Foreign Awards Act and is, therefore, not treated in India as a "foreign award." [Section 9 of the Foreign Awards Act contains a "savings clause," which excepts certain awards from the Act's coverage. Section 9 provides that "[n]othing in this Act shall ... apply to any award made on an arbitration agreement governed by the law of India."] A "foreign award" is (subject to §7) recognized and enforceable in India "as if it were an award made on a matter referred to arbitration in India" (§4).... The Foreign Awards Act contains a specific provision to exclude its operation to what may be regarded as a "domestic award" in the sense of the award having been made on an arbitration agreement governed by the law of India, although the dispute was with a foreigner and the arbitration was held and the award was made in a foreign State. Such an award necessarily falls under the Arbitration Act, 1940, and is amenable to the jurisdiction of the Indian Courts and controlled by the Indian system of law just as in the case of any other domestic award, except that the proceedings held abroad and leading to the award were in certain respects amenable to be controlled by the public policy and the mandatory requirements of the law of the place of arbitration and the competent courts of that place....

Significantly, London was chosen as the place of arbitration by reason of Article 12 of the ICC Rules which reads: "The place of arbitration shall be fixed by the International Court of Arbitration, unless agreed upon by the parties." The parties had never expressed their intention to choose London as the arbitral forum.... London has no significant connection with the contract or the parties except that it is a neutral place and the Chairman of the Arbitral Tribunal is a resident there.... The arbitration clause must be considered together with the rest of the contract and the relevant surrounding circumstances. In the present case, as seen above, the choice of the place of arbitration was, as far as the parties are concerned, merely accidental in so far as they had not expressed any intention in regard to it and the choice was made by the ICC Court for reasons totally unconnected with either party to the contract....

All substantive rights arising under the agreement including that which is contained in the arbitration clause are, in our view, governed by the laws of India. In respect of the actual conduct of arbitration, the procedural law of England may be applicable to the extent that the ICC Rules are insufficient or repugnant to the public policy or other mandatory provisions of the laws in force in England. Nevertheless, the jurisdiction exercisable by the English courts and the applicability of the laws of that country in procedural matters must be viewed as concurrent and consistent with the jurisdiction of the competent Indian courts and the operation of Indian laws in all matters concerning arbitration in so far as the main contract as well as that which is contained in the arbitration clause are governed by the laws of India.

The Delhi High Court was wrong in treating the award in question as a foreign award. The Foreign Awards Act has no application to the award by reason of the specific exclusion contained in §9 of that Act. The award is governed by the laws in force in India, including the Arbitration Act, 1940. Accordingly, we set aside the impugned judgment of the Delhi High Court....

BHARAT ALUMINIUM CO. ("BALCO") v. KAISER ALUMINIUM TECHNICAL SERVICE, INC.

C.A. No. 7019 OF 2005 (Indian S.Ct. 2012)

[excerpted above at pp. 1073-81]

NOTES

1. *Articles V(1)(e) and VI of New York Convention limit available fora for annulling award.* Article V(1)(e) of the Convention permits a court in a Contracting State to deny recognition of an award that has been annulled in either: (a) the state in which the award was "made," or (b) the state "under the laws of which" the award was "made." Similarly, Article VI of the Convention permits a court to stay proceedings to enforce an award if an application to annul the award is pending before the "competent authority referred to in Article V(1)(e)."

   Nothing in Articles V and VI, or the remainder of the Convention, expressly requires that actions to annul an award be brought only in these two fora. Nonetheless, *Karaha Bodas*, *Garuda* and *Union of India* all held that the effect of these two articles and the overall enforcement scheme of the Convention was to limit the fora for annulment actions. Similarly, commentators and other national courts have virtually unanimously concluded that the Convention forbids actions to annul an award except in the country where it was "made" or "under the laws of which" it was made. *See* G. Born, *International Commercial Arbitration* 2988-93 (2d ed. 2014); *Judgment of 24 November 1993*, XXI Y.B. Comm. Arb. 617 (1996) (Luxembourg Cour Supérieure de Justice) (setting aside application can be made only in "the country of rendition" of award); *Judgment of 24 November 1994*, XXI Y.B. Comm. Arb. 635 (1996) (Rotterdam Rechtbank) ("as the arbitral awards have been rendered in Israel, the Israeli courts have exclusive jurisdiction over an application for setting aside").

Consider again the court's discussion of primary and secondary jurisdiction in *Karaha Bodas*. What is meant by "primary jurisdiction"? What may a court with primary jurisdiction over an arbitration do? What may a court with "secondary jurisdiction" do? What may it not do?

Does the language of Articles V(1)(e) and VI of the Convention support the *Garuda* and *Karaha Bodas* interpretations? Are the policies of the Convention served by limiting the forums in which an annulment action can be brought? What would be the consequences if no such limit existed?

2. *Article V(1)(e) of New York Convention—identifying the state "under the laws of which" award was "made."* As we have seen, Article V(1)(e) permits non-recognition of an award that has been set aside or suspended by the competent authority in the state "under the laws of which" the award was "made." Article VI permits deferral of enforcement proceedings if a similar action to annul has been commenced. *See Fertilizer Corp., supra* pp. 1094-95. It is important, therefore, to determine "under [whose] laws" an award was made. As discussed above, international arbitrations can involve application of various different national laws, including: (a) the substantive law governing the parties' underlying dispute (in *Bridas*, New York; in *NTPC*, Indian; in *Karaha Bodas*, Indonesian); (b) the law governing the parties' arbitration agreement (in *Bridas*, not identified; in *NTPC*, purportedly Indian, but, under most conflicts rules, English; in *Karaha Bodas*, Swiss); (c) the procedural law of the arbitration (in *Bridas*, apparently Mexican; in *NTPC*, purportedly both English and Indian; in *Karaha Bodas*, Swiss); and (d) the choice-of-law rules for selecting the foregoing laws. *See supra* pp. 90-93. To which of these various laws does Article V(1)(e) refer?

(a) *Authorities holding that award is made "under" procedural law of the arbitration.* Interpreting the second limb of Article V(1)(e), *Bridas* holds that this clause refers to the arbitration law of the arbitral seat—that is, to the procedural law of the arbitration. What result does *Karaha Bodas* reach with regard to this question? Is this result wise?

(b) *Presumption that procedural law of arbitration is that of arbitral seat.* In the overwhelming majority of cases, the procedural law of the arbitration will be the law of arbitral seat (and the state where the award is made). *See supra* pp. 636-38. The *Union of India* and *Karaha Bodas* decisions reflect this strong presumption that the procedural law of the arbitration will be the law of the arbitral seat—except, perhaps, for "once in a blue moon." It is theoretically possible that the parties seek to agree that the law of some country other than the arbitral seat should govern the proceedings. *See supra* pp. 625-40. That is what the courts rejected in *Union of India* and *Karaha Bodas*. Among other things, it also is arguably what the Indian court held had occurred in *NTPC*. Suppose the parties in *Bridas* had agreed, for example, that the arbitration was to be conducted in Mexico subject to New York arbitration law. Where then, according to the *Bridas* opinion, could actions to annul have been brought?

How strong is the presumption that the procedural law of the arbitration is that of the arbitral seat? How do the courts in *Karaha Bodas* and *Union of India* state the presumption? What are the reasons underlying the presumption? Are these reasons persuasive?

(c) *Authorities holding that award is made "under" law governing arbitration agreement.* Why did the *NTPC* court conclude that the arbitral award could be annulled in India? Note the court's conclusion that "the overriding principle is that the courts of the country whose substantive laws govern the arbitration agreement are the competent courts in respect of all matters arising under the arbitration agreement." Also note the court's reliance on §9(b) of the Indian Foreign Awards Act 1961, providing that "any award made on an arbitration agreement governed by the law of India" shall be subject to annulment under domestic Indian law. The *NTPC* court's rationale, and the so-called "savings provision" of §9(b), have been vigorously criticized:

> "[This is an example] of parochial overreaching by a national legal system. It is hoped that the trend will be reversed in India, and not copied elsewhere. For now, India stands alone in this respect; no other legal system has adopted such an aggressively nationalistic posture." Paulsson, *The New York Convention's Misadventures in India*, 7 Mealey's Int'l Arb. Rep. (June 1992).

Is that criticism warranted? Why shouldn't the law governing the arbitration agreement be the law "under which" an award is made for purposes of Article V(1)(e)?

Consider the Indian Supreme Court's analysis in *BALCO*. How does it compare with that in *NTPC*?

(d) *No authority holding that award is made "under" substantive law governing parties' dispute.* *Bridas* rejected the argument that an award is made "under" the law of the country whose substantive law governs the parties' contract. Other authorities also reject that interpretation. *See supra* pp. 636-37, 1013. Why shouldn't courts of the country whose law governed the parties' substantive rights be competent to annul awards disposing of those rights?

(e) *New York Convention constraints on national law definitions of when award is made "under" national law.* *Bridas* holds that Article V(1)(e)—not merely U.S. law—provides that an award is made "under" the procedural law of the arbitration. *Karaha Bodas* adopts a similar view of the Convention. According to this rationale, other Contracting States to the Convention must reach the same conclusion. Does the language of Article V(1)(e), or other provisions of the Convention, require such a result? Do the purposes do so?

(f) *Is* NTPC *consistent with the Convention?* Is the *NTPC* rationale—that an award can be annulled in the country whose law governs the arbitration agreement—consistent with that in *Karaha Bodas* and *Bridas*? Is the rationale of *NTPC* permitted by the Convention?

Is the result in *NTPC*—as opposed to the rationale—consistent with *Bridas*? Consider the parties' agreement in *NTPC*—expressly accepting the "exclusive" jurisdiction of Indian courts. These factors do not dictate a conclusion that Indian law was the procedural law governing the arbitration, "under" which the award was made; the presumption relied on in *Karaha Bodas* and *Union of India*, that the parties would not select a foreign procedural law from outside the arbitral seat, is a formidable one. But would the parties' agreement in *NTPC* permit concluding that Indian law was the procedural law governing the arbitration? If the court's analysis in *NTPC* had relied simply upon the parties' "agreement" on Indian law as the procedural law, would it be objectionable? Alternatively, why isn't the parties' acceptance of the exclusive jurisdiction of the Indian courts—presumably over annulment—a sufficient basis for the decision in *NTPC*?

Consider again the Indian Supreme Court's analysis in *BALCO*. What weight does it attach to the New York Convention? Decisions of other Contracting States?

(g) *What nation's courts should be competent to entertain actions to annul an award?* Is it sensible to interpret Article V(1)(e) as assigning authority to annul awards to the courts of the state: (i) whose law provided the procedural law governing the arbitration; (ii) whose substantive law governs the parties' underlying dispute; or (iii) whose law governs the parties' arbitration agreement? What makes the procedural law governing the arbitration a reasonable interpretation of Article V(1)(e)? In *Bridas*, for example, the award was based on an application of New York substantive law to the merits of the parties' dispute. Would it not make the most sense for a New York judge to provide such judicial review of an award as the Convention permits? Consider the bases set forth in developed arbitration legislation (such as Article 34 of the UNCITRAL Model Law), for annulling awards. Do these bases concern matters of procedure or of substance? Do they concern the existence of an arbitration agreement? Given the types of review contemplated by the Convention, and most arbitration statutes, what nation's courts *should* have the authority to annul an award?

(h) *Identifying the state "under the laws of which" award is made in* Karaha Bodas *and* Bridas. Consider the analysis of the arbitration agreement in *Karaha Bodas*. Put aside the parties' previous positions before the arbitrators and Swiss courts. Just considering the parties' agreement, is it correct to conclude that the procedural law of the arbitration was not Indonesian law? How should one interpret the references to Indonesian civil procedure rules in the arbitration agreement?

Why was the award in *Bridas* made "under" Mexican law? Did the parties have anything to do with Mexico? Did their contract select Mexican law? In fact, Mexico became the arbitral seat because the ICC picked it, as contemplated by the ICC Rules when parties have not selected an arbitral seat. Is that a sufficient basis for according Mexican courts the substantial, and unique, review powers that *Bridas* produces?

Compare the result in *NTPC*. Should the award there have been deemed to be made "under" English or Indian law? Note that England was the arbitral seat as a result of the ICC's decision. Is that relevant?

3. *Can an award be "made" in several places for purposes of Article V(1)(e)?* Under Article V(1)(e), an action to annul an award may be entertained in the country where the award is "made." *See supra* pp. 622-23, 1106-07. When arbitration hearings are held for convenience in several countries or when the arbitrators (being of different nationalities) sign the award in different countries, where is the award made? *See su-*

pra pp. 624, 1063. Could one argue that the award is "made" in each of those countries—and thus subject to an action to annul in each of them? Would the Convention's purposes be well served by such a conclusion, or should an arbitral award be deemed to be "made" in only one place? *See* Mann, *Where Is An Award "Made"?*, 1 Arb. Int'l 107, 108 (1985) ("If there are three arbitrators who hold an arbitration in London, but meet in Paris to consider their award, and sign it at their respective residences, viz, New York, Geneva and Tokyo, the award should be treated as 'made' in London, even if the each arbitrator has indicated the place where he has signed it.").

4. *Awards subject to action to annul in two places.* Under Article V(1)(e) of the New York Convention, an award can arguably be annulled either in the country where it was made or in the country under whose procedural law the arbitration was conducted. As we have seen, these can be different countries. *See Naviera Amazonica Peruana SA v. Compania Internacional de Seguros del Peru* [1988] Lloyd's Rep. 116 (English Ct. App.) ("There is … no reason in theory which precludes parties to agree that an arbitration shall be held at a place or in country X but subject to the procedural laws of Y."); *supra* pp. 625-40. If an award is made in State A, under the laws of State B, then are challenges permitted under Article V(1)(e) in *both* states? What if the two states' courts reach different results? What should a third state, asked to enforce the award, do?

   The court in *Union of India* labored hard to avoid interpreting the parties' agreement as selecting a procedural law different from that of the arbitral seat. Underlying the court's analysis was the view that "absurd" results would follow from applying a "foreign" procedural law to govern the arbitration. What are these "absurd" results? What does *NTPC* suggest about an English court's power to annul the award in that case?

5. *Responses to actions to annul commenced in forums other than those permitted in Article V(1)(e).* Suppose that the *NTPC* rationale was applied in a case where the sole basis for an action to annul in India was the applicability of Indian law (under Indian conflicts rules) to the arbitration agreement. Under *Bridas* and most other authorities, the Convention would not permit Indian courts to entertain an annulment action in these circumstances. What could the party resisting involvement of the Indian courts do in the foregoing hypothetical? Which course would be most effective?

   (a) *Forum court's refusal to entertain action to annul.* An award creditor can request a court outside the arbitral seat not to entertain the annulment action, arguing that the New York Convention denies it jurisdiction. Such a denial then occurred in *Bridas*, *Garuda* and the Delhi High Court's decision (reversed on appeal) in *NTPC*. This is the most effective way to enforce the Convention's fora restrictions, but it relies on the willingness of national courts to abstain from exercising jurisdiction. As the Indian appellate court's decision in *NTPC* illustrates, that does not always happen.

   (b) *Action to confirm in arbitral seat.* One course of action would be to seek to confirm the arbitral award in the arbitral seat (in *NTPC*, England). If successful, the judgment could be used both to demonstrate the finality of the award and as an independent basis for recovery (or defense). *See supra* pp. 1070-72.

   (c) *Antisuit injunction.* Another course of action would be to seek an antisuit injunction in the arbitral seat against actions to annul the award elsewhere. See *supra* pp. 331-33 for discussion of antisuit injunctions against foreign litigation of claims that are subject to arbitration. Should it be easier or more difficult to get an injunction against efforts, in violation of the Convention, to annul an award outside the arbitral seat than to obtain an injunction against litigation in violation of an agreement to arbitrate? For a U.S. decision, in the *Karaha Bodas* case, refusing to enjoin (wrongful) litigation in Indonesia to annul the Swiss award, *see Karaha Bodas Co. v. Perusahaan Pertambangan Minyak Dan Gas Bumi Negara*, 335 F.3d 357 (5th Cir. 2003).

(d) *Litigation on the merits.* Another course would be to commence litigation of the underlying dispute in a national court, relying on the improper action to annul the award in a forum prohibited by the Convention as a waiver of arbitration. For discussions of waiver or repudiation of arbitration agreements, see *supra* pp. 435, 472-74.

(e) *Rulings by arbitral tribunal.* It may be possible to obtain rulings from the arbitral tribunal that discourage resort to improper judicial fora. Note that in *NTPC* the tribunal had found that English law was the curial law; query what would have occurred if the tribunal had also concluded that the parties' arbitration agreement was governed by English law. Alternatively, could the party whose award was annulled, in an improper forum, assert a claim before the arbitral tribunal for damages occasioned by the wrongful annulment action? Note that any new award would doubtless itself be annulled in the improper judicial forum, but might be enforceable elsewhere.

(f) *Refusal to recognize judgment annulling award.* If an improper judicial forum annuls an award and/or issues a judgment on the parties' dispute, the recognition of those judgments in other forums can be resisted. For example, in *NTPC*, if the Indian trial court annulled the award, English or other courts might disregard the Indian judgment. For an example, *see Am. Constr. Mach. & Equip. Corp. v. Mechanised Constr. of Pakistan Ltd*, 659 F.Supp. 426 (S.D.N.Y. 1987) (refusing to recognize Pakistani judgment purporting to annul award made in Geneva), *aff'd*, 828 F.2d 117 (2d Cir. 1987); *Karaha Bodas Co. v. Perusahaan Pertambangan Minyak Dan Gas Bumi Negara*, XXVIII Y.B. Comm. Arb. 752 (2003) (H.K. Ct. First Inst. 2003) (refusing to recognize Indonesian judgment purporting to annul award made in Switzerland). The only exception to this is where the parties have agreed to a procedural law for the arbitration of a country other than the arbitral seat. If this occurs, then Articles V(1)(e) and VI permit the state whose procedural law was chosen to consider actions to annul the award.

6. *Possible limits under Inter-American Convention on fora for annulling award.* Consider Articles 5(1)(e) and 6 of the Inter-American Convention, excerpted at pp. 9-10 of the Documentary Supplement. Do they permit an argument that the Inter-American Convention imposes the same limits on an action to annul awards as the New York Convention?

7. *Where can an action to vacate under §10 of the FAA be brought?* Section 10 of the FAA provides that the "United States district court in and for the district wherein the award was made may make an order vacating the award."

(a) *Lower U.S. court decisions holding that actions to vacate awards under FAA §10 can only be brought in district court where award was made.* Lower courts originally struggled with §10's reference to the district court where the award was made. Some U.S. lower courts concluded that the reference was a mandatory restriction on venue and that an action to vacate an award under the FAA could be commenced exclusively in the district where the award was made. *See Central Valley Typographical Union No. 46 v. McClatchy Newspapers*, 762 F.2d 741, 743-44 (9th Cir. 1985); *Enserch International Exploration, Inc. v. Attock Oil Co.*, 656 F. Supp. 1162, 1165. (N.D. Tex. 1987). Other lower courts interpreted the language as permissive or non-exclusive, not providing a restraint on venue for actions to annul an award. *See Sutter Corp. v. P & P Industries, Inc.*, 125 F.3d 914, 917-18 (5th Cir. 1997); *Smiga v. Dean Witter Reynolds, Inc.*, 766 F.2d 698, 706 (2nd Cir. 1985); *In re VMS Securities Litigation*, 21 F.3d 139, 142,145 (7th Cir. 1994).

(b) Cortez Byrd Chips, Inc. v. Bill Harbert Construction*: no limitation on venue in actions to vacate, modify or confirm awards.* The Supreme Court interpreted §10 of the FAA in *Cortez Byrd Chips, Inc. v. Bill Harbert Constr. Co.,* 529 U.S. 193 (U.S. S. Ct. 2000), holding that the FAA's venue provisions should be interpreted as "permissive" and not imposing a restriction on venue. Consider the text of §10. Is the Court's interpretation persuasive? Does it make sense that actions to vacate awards can be brought anywhere that satisfies (liberal) general venue provisions? What about actions to confirm awards?

(c) *No basis under FAA for vacating awards made outside United States but "under" U.S. law.* As discussed above, Article V(1)(e) of the Convention permits actions to vacate an award to be brought in the country "under" whose law the award was made. Does *Cortez*'s interpretation of §10 alter this rule? Suppose an award is made in Bulgaria or Belgium. Can an action to vacate be pursued in a U.S. court under §10? Suppose an arbitration is conducted outside the United States, with the parties expressly selecting the FAA (or the law of a U.S. state) as the procedural law of the arbitration. Does the FAA provide a basis to annul the award? Nothing in the FAA's express language suggests an affirmative response to this question. Is this a sensible result?

8. *Limitations on fora to annul ICSID awards.* Consider Articles 52 and 54 of the ICSID Convention, excerpted at pp. 24-25 of the Documentary Supplement. Where may actions to annul ICSID awards be pursued? Compare this regime to that under the New York Convention. Which is preferable? Note that a distinctive structural feature of both regimes is that of limiting significantly the potential fora for annulling arbitral awards. Why? Which instrument accomplishes this objective better?

CHAPTER 15

ANNULMENT AND REVISION OF INTERNATIONAL ARBITRAL AWARDS

This chapter examines issues relating to the finality of international arbitral awards and the mechanisms for challenging that finality, particularly annulment of awards. First, the chapter examines the presumptive finality and *res judicata* effects of awards under both the New York Convention and most national arbitration statutes. Second, the chapter considers the *functus officio* doctrine and the correction, interpretation and supplementation of awards. Third, the chapter examines the substantive grounds that are available for annulling (or setting aside) awards in the arbitral seat, in particular under national arbitration legislation, together with the international limitations on these grounds for annulment. Fourth, the chapter considers the consequences of a judicial decision in the arbitral seat annulling an international award.

A. PRESUMPTIVE FINALITY AND PRECLUSIVE EFFECTS OF INTERNATIONAL ARBITRAL AWARDS

One of the fundamental objectives of international arbitration is to provide a final, binding resolution of the parties' dispute.[1] Essential to achieving this objective is the preclusive effect of arbitral awards: if parties are not bound by the results of the awards made against them—either dismissing or upholding their claims or declaring their conduct wrongful or lawful—then those awards do not achieve their intended purpose and are of limited practical value.

Consequently, *res judicata* and related principles of preclusion are widely accepted as applying to the awards of international arbitral tribunals.[2] As formulated by one award, "[t]he sanctity of *res judicata* attached to a final decision of an international tribunal is an essential and settled rule of international law."[3] The same principle has been acknowledged, in the inter-state context, by the International Court of Justice.[4]

---

1. *See supra* pp. 109, 111-12, 527-28.

2. *See Trail Smelter Arbitration (U.S. v. Canada), Award of 16 April 1938 & 11 March 1941*, III R.I.A.A. 1905, 1950 (1941); *Effect of Awards of Compensation Made by the United Nations Administrative Tribunal*, [1954] I.C.J. Rep. 47, 53 (I.C.J.) (*res judicata* is "well-established and generally recognized principle of law"); G. Born, *International Commercial Arbitration* 3739 (2d ed. 2014).

3. *Trail Smelter Arbitration (U.S. v. Canada), Award of 16 April 1938 & 11 March 1941*, III R.I.A.A. 1905, 1950 (1941). See *infra* pp. 1116-20.

4. *Case Concerning the Arbitral Award Made by the King of Spain on 23 December 1906 (Honduras v. Nicaragua)*, [1960] I.C.J. Rep. 192 (I.C.J.). *See also Qatar v. Bahrain, Dissenting Opinion of Torres Bernardez in Maritime Delimitation and Territorial Questions*, [2001] I.C.J. Rep. 40, 364 (I.C.J.) ("*Res judicata* is precisely a notion of procedural law intrinsically linked to the form adopted by the procedure and decision concerned and the jurisdictional character of the organ adopting it ... [i]ndependently of the name given to it (arbitration, adjudication, enquiry, etc.)").

Although it is widely recognized that arbitral awards have binding, *res judicata* effects, the precise nature of those effects (and of their legal sources) is debated. Internationally, Article III of the New York Convention provides that "[e]ach Contracting State shall recognize arbitral awards as binding and enforce them in accordance with the rules of procedure of the territory where the award is relied upon, under the conditions laid down in the following articles [particularly Article V]."[5] Comparable provisions apply in other international commercial arbitration conventions.[6] Despite this, it is unclear what preclusive effects are mandated by Article III, or cognate provisions, with relatively few authorities having addressed the preclusive effects of either the New York Convention or other international instruments.

Instead, rules of preclusion in international commercial arbitration have been developed almost entirely as a matter of national law, typically by reference to rules of preclusion developed for judicial judgments in national court proceedings. As the materials excerpted below illustrate, in most legal systems, awards made in international commercial arbitrations are accorded the same preclusive effects that national court judgments receive under national law. This is implied under Article 35(1) of the UNCITRAL Model Law and express under parallel provisions of the German and Japanese arbitration statutes, excerpted below. Compare the provisions of the ICSID and 1907 Hague Conventions, which adopt broadly similar, but not identical, approaches in the investment and inter-state contexts.

GERMAN ZPO
§1055

The arbitral award has the same effect between the parties as a final and binding court judgment.

JAPANESE ARBITRATION LAW
Article 45(1)

An arbitral award (irrespective of whether or not the place of arbitration is in the territory of Japan …) shall have the same effect as a final and conclusive judgment.

CERTAIN UNDERWRITERS AT LLOYD'S v. ARGONAUT INSURANCE CO.
264 F.Supp. 2d 926 (N.D. Cal. 2003)

[excerpted above at pp. 759-65]

FERTILIZER CORP. OF INDIA v. IDI MANAGEMENT, INC.
517 F.Supp. 948 (S.D. Ohio 1981)

Spiegel, District Judge. [The facts of the case are excerpted above at pp. 1094-95.] … IDI's fourth defense is that the [Award] is not enforceable because it is not binding within the Convention's meaning. The Convention covers this point in Article V(1)(e) which provides

---

5. New York Convention, Art. III.
6. Inter-American Convention, Art. 4. *See also* ICSID Convention, Art. 53(1).

for a refusal to enforce if: "(e) the award has not yet become binding on the parties, or has been set aside or suspended by a competent authority of the country in which, or under the law of which, that award was made." IDI argues that the award is not binding until it has been reviewed by an Indian court for errors of law. The award is presently before the Indian courts for a ruling, among other things, on whether the arbitrators could award consequential damages despite an express contract clause to the contrary. While [IDI contends that] American courts review arbitration awards only for errors which are totally irrational or in manifest disregard of law, Indian courts review "speaking awards" for any error of law. IDI contends that this kind of review is one on the merits and that it prevents any meaningful binding effect or finality.

FCI counters that under Indian law, both statutory and decisional, as well as under the ICC Rules and under the parties' contract, an arbitral award is final and binding. They argue that merely because an award has been challenged in an Indian court, its binding effect is not destroyed, just as a district court decision is binding on the parties, even though it is appealable, and a judgment may be executed unless the loser posts an appeal or supersedeas bond. FCI maintains that the Convention itself distinguishes, in Article V and Article VI, between a successful challenge and one that is merely pending....

[The district court reviewed the parties' agreement (which provided that all disputes will be "finally" settled by arbitration), the 1955 and 1975 ICC Rules (which provided that arbitral awards "shall be final"), and Indian law (which it understood to provide, albeit not unequivocally, that "an award is binding on the parties when made").] We find that the [Award] is final and binding, for purposes of the Convention. Therefore, Article V(1)(e) does not apply to prevent enforcement. We note the comment of Professor Gerald Aksen, General Counsel of the [AAA]: "The award will be considered 'binding' for the purposes of the Convention if no further recourse may be had to another arbitral tribunal (that is, an appeals tribunal). The fact that recourse may be had to a court of law does not prevent the award from being 'binding.'" ... Aksen, *American Arbitration Accession Arrives in the Age of Aquarius*, 3 Sw. U. L. Rev. 1, 11 (1971)....

[The court continued, quoting] Article VI [of the Convention and then holding that] this appears to be an unfettered grant of discretion; the Court has been unable to discover any standard on which a decision to adjourn should be based, other than to ascertain that an application to set aside or suspend the award has been made. Here, it is undisputed that IDI has made such an application in India....

We believe it is important ... to consider the purpose of the Convention. The primary thrust of the Convention is to make enforcement of arbitral awards more simple by liberalizing enforcement procedures, limiting defenses, and placing the burden of proof on the party opposing enforcement.... [The court noted that IDI had obtained an award in a related arbitration against FCI, but that the award was also on appeal in India and that IDI had not been able to recover.] [I]n order to avoid the possibility of an inconsistent result, this Court has determined to adjourn its decision on enforcement of the [Award] until the Indian courts decide with finality whether the award is correct under Indian law. FCI, of course, may apply to this Court for suitable security, as provided by Article VI. When we are informed that the Indian courts have reviewed the [Award] and rendered a decision, we will proceed to either grant or deny enforcement based on that decision....

NOTES

1. *Divergent approaches to preclusion under national legal systems.* Civil and common law legal systems adopt different rules of preclusion, both in the context of national court judgments and otherwise. These differences are complex, and vary from jurisdiction to jurisdiction.

    Most common law jurisdictions recognize two basic types of preclusion: *res judicata* (or "claim preclusion") and issue estoppel (or "collateral estoppel" or "issue preclusion"). The doctrine of *res judicata* provides that a judicial judgment accepting or rejecting a particular "claim" is binding upon the parties to the proceeding that produced the judgment. That is, a party that has asserted a claim unsuccessfully will be precluded from attempting to assert that claim again against the same defendant, while a party which has had a claim adjudicated against it will be precluded from asserting the non-existence of the claim against the successful plaintiff. In general, the notion of a "claim" or "cause of action," which is subject to preclusion, is defined to include all rights of legal action that arise out of a single set of facts or a single transaction: this has the effect of extending the preclusive effects of a *res judicata* [bar] beyond those claims that were actually litigated concerning a particular transaction in a prior litigation, to also reach claims that might have been litigated (even if they were not). *See* P. Barnett, *Res Judicata, Estoppel and Foreign Judgments* 120-121 (2001); G. Born, *International Commercial Arbitration* 3735 (2d ed. 2014).

    Distinct from the doctrine of *res judicata* in common law jurisdictions is that of issue preclusion. Issue preclusion prevents a party from relitigating, against a counter-party, an issue of fact or law that was previously contested and decided in a litigation between the same parties. The issue in question must have actually been litigated between the parties and must have been significant to the court's decision in the earlier judgment; issues that were not litigated or that were merely *obiter dictum* (not decisive) in the earlier judgment will ordinarily not be subject to issue preclusion. *See* P. Barnett, *Res Judicata, Estoppel and Foreign Judgments* 137 (2001); G. Born, *International Commercial Arbitration* 3736 (2d ed. 2014).

    The basic principle of preclusion in civil law states is that of *res judicata* (or claim preclusion). This principle is statutorily expressed in the French Code of Civil Procedure (which parallels that in a number of other civil law jurisdictions) in the following terms:

    > "The judgment which decides in its holdings all or part of the main issue, or one which rules upon the procedural plea seeking a peremptory declaration of inadmissibility or any other incidental application, shall from the time of its pronouncement, become *res judicata* with regard to the dispute which it determines." French Code of Civil Procedure, Art. 480.

    Additionally, "[i]t is necessary that the thing claimed be the same; that the claim be based on the same grounds; that the claim be between the same parties and brought by them and against them in the same capacity." French Civil Code, Art. 1351. Consistent with these provisions, most civil law states apply a relatively restricted doctrine of *res judicata* (in comparison to common law jurisdictions). A "triple identity" requirement—of the same claim, same legal grounds and same parties—must generally be satisfied before an action will be precluded by a prior judgment. *See* G. Born, *Inter-*

national Commercial Arbitration 3738 (2d ed. 2014); De Ly & Sheppard, *ILA Interim Report on Res Judicata and Arbitration*, 25 Arb. Int'l 35, 48-51 (2009).

It is frequently said that there is no doctrine of issue preclusion in civil law jurisdictions. ILA International Commercial Arbitration Committee, *Interim Report: Res Judicata and Arbitration* 14 (Berlin 2004) ("There is no notion of issue estoppel or preclusion (as in the Common Law)"). That conclusion has surface appeal, but appears to ignore the way in which principles of *res judicata* give preclusive effect in civil law jurisdictions to aspects of a judgment's (or an award's) reasoning: as one authority puts it, "the reasons for a decision may partake of the *res judicata* effect that applies to the operative part, whenever such reasons are a necessary adjunct to such operative part." B. Hanotiau, *Complex Arbitrations* ¶534 (2006). This rule is similar, in most respects, to principles of issue estoppel or collateral estoppel as applied in common law jurisdictions.

2. *Practical importance of preclusive effects of awards.* As a practical matter, how important are the preclusive effects of awards? Recall the reasons that commercial parties agree to arbitrate their international disputes—including the desire to finally and efficiently resolve their disputes in a single, centralized forum, without the jurisdictional disputes and multiplicitous proceedings that characterize international litigation. *See supra* pp. 109, 111-12. To what extent would these objectives be achievable if arbitral awards did not have preclusive effects? What if an award had no *res judicata* effect between the parties—what would be the practical consequence? What if an award had no collateral estoppel or issue estoppel effects—again, what would be the practical consequences?

3. *Finality and preclusive effects of awards under UNCITRAL Model Law.* Article 35(1) of the UNCITRAL Model Law, excerpted at p. 95 of the Documentary Supplement, provides that "[a]n arbitral award, irrespective of the country in which it was made, shall be recognized as binding...." The drafting history of the Model Law explains that, under Article 35(1), "an award shall be recognized as binding, which means, although this is not expressly stated, binding between the parties and from the date of the award." *Report of the Secretary-General on the Analytical Commentary on Draft Text of A Model Law on International Commercial Arbitration,* U.N. Doc. A/CN.9/264, Art. 35, ¶4 (1985). What does it mean to "recognize" an award as "binding"? Does this mean that the parties are legally prohibited from challenging the award? Consider the provisions of Articles 33 and 34. Does Article 35 preclude a party's exercise of its rights under Articles 33 and 34?

Is an award "binding" under Article 35(1) before the time period required for seeking a correction or annulment (under Articles 33 and 34) has expired? What if an award is annulled under Article 34—is it still "binding"? Why not?

If an award is "binding" under Article 35(1), what precisely does that mean? Does it mean that the award has preclusive effects—often referred to as having "*res judicata*" and "collateral estoppel" (or issue estoppel) effects? Compare the text of Article 35(1) with the German and Japanese arbitration statutes. What meaning—other than the preclusive effects of an award—could be ascribed to the term "binding" in Article 35?

4. *Finality and res judicata effects of awards under other national arbitration legislation.* Consider the provisions of the German and Japanese arbitration laws. What do

the excerpted sections provide with regard to the legal consequences of an award? *See* Belgian Judicial Code, Art. 1713(9) ("The award shall have the same effect as a court decision in the relationship between the parties."); Netherlands Code of Civil Procedure, Art. 1059(1) ("Decisions relating to the legal relationship which is in dispute and are comprised in a final arbitration award, have the force of *res judicata* in other legal proceedings between the same parties from the day on which they are rendered.").

Why should awards have the same *res judicata* and other preclusive effects as a national court judgment? Are there not vital differences between the arbitral and litigation processes (*e.g.*, public court proceedings, institutional judiciary, appellate review)? Do these differences argue for less extensive preclusive effects for awards? Why or why not?

Conversely, consider the objectives that lead parties to agree to arbitrate their disputes—including the desire to obtain a single, centralized dispute resolution mechanism and to avoid multiplicitous litigation in multiple forums. *See supra* pp. 109, 111-12, 527-28. Do these objectives argue in favor of narrower—or broader—rules of preclusion in arbitration than in national court litigation?

From when exactly do arbitral awards have *res judicata* effect? From when the tribunal decides the dispute? From when the tribunal completes its award? Signs its award? Delivers the award to the parties? Deposits the award with a local court? *See supra* p. 1069. From when any challenge to annulment is rejected? *See infra* pp. 1125-34, 1134-73.

5. *Finality and preclusive effects of awards under Inter-American Convention.* Consider Article 4 of the Inter-American Convention, excerpted at p. 9 of the Documentary Supplement. How does Article 4 compare with Article III of the New York Convention? Which approach is preferable?

6. *Finality and preclusive effects of awards under Article III of New York Convention.* Do the provisions of the New York Convention expressly address the finality or other legal consequences of an award? Consider Article V(1)(e) of the Convention. Note that one of the grounds for non-recognition of an award is that it "has not yet become binding on the parties" (discussed below at pp. 1120-22). Note that, as with other exceptions to recognition under Article V, the burden of proving that an award has not yet become binding is on the party resisting recognition.

Consider Article III of the Convention. Does Article III require Contracting States to grant awards *res judicata* or other preclusive effects? How clear is Article III's text? Would Article III leave Contracting States free to afford arbitral awards no (or *de minimis*) preclusive effect—for example, by treating awards as having no *res judicata* effect and instead as allowing relitigation of disputes without regard to the results of prior arbitral proceedings? Would this not frustrate the purpose of the Convention? Note that Article V of the Convention enumerates a limited number of exceptions to the obligation, under Article III, to recognize awards. *See infra* pp. 1189-90, 1195-97. Would it not frustrate the purpose of Articles III and V if Contracting States were free to define their recognition of awards as essentially meaningless—permitting relitigation of disputes which had already been decided in the award?

Assuming that the Convention requires Contracting States to accord awards some measure of *res judicata* or other preclusive effect, what defines the character and scope of that effect? Does Article III prescribe any particular *res judicata* or preclusion standards? What does it mean for an award to be recognized as "binding" under Article III? To what sources might one look in defining the preclusion standards of Article III? Consider the following:

"If the New York Convention is understood as requiring Contracting States to afford some measure of preclusive effect to arbitral awards, the decisive issue is determining the content of this preclusion principle. Article III of the Convention should not be interpreted to prescribe particular rules of preclusion, but instead to provide a constitutional statement of principle—mandating recognition of the "binding" effects of arbitral awards—that must be elaborated over time by national courts and arbitral tribunals.

Most clearly, Article III would forbid the courts of a Contracting State from denying any preclusive effect to arbitral awards, permitting litigants to relitigate claims or issues that were rejected in arbitral proceedings and awards between the same parties. This result … would make a mockery of the Convention's requirement that Contracting States "recognize" the "binding" effect of arbitral awards, permitting states to say that awards have binding effect, but that the effects which are binding are non-existent. That is contrary to both the language and fundamental purposes of the Convention.

It is inherent in the nature of an agreement to arbitrate, and the concept of an arbitral award, that such an award will have binding, and thus preclusive, effects. Equally, it would be inherently contrary to the obligations to recognize an arbitration agreement and an arbitral award for a state to deny preclusive effects to a valid award and instead to entertain litigation of disputes that the parties had both agreed to arbitrate and arbitrated. That would contradict the obligation to recognize agreements to finally resolve disputes by arbitration, as well as the obligation to recognize awards setting forth such resolutions.

Beyond this, the Convention's objectives of ensuring the final, binding resolution of international disputes, and the effective recognition of arbitral awards, argue in favor of presumptively affording at least the same preclusive effects to arbitral awards as accorded national court judgments: where the parties have agreed to resolution of their disputes in a single, centralized forum, specifically to avoid the costs and delays of multiplicitous litigations in national courts, the Convention's requirement that Contracting States recognize such agreements, and the resulting awards, imply at least equally broad principles of preclusion as those applicable to national court judgments, which rest on a structural premise of multiple possible forums and proceedings. Indeed, a substantial argument can be made that presumptively broader preclusion rules are required, as between the parties, for international arbitral awards than for national court judgments.

The precise contours of the international preclusion rules, mandated by the New York Convention, which are applicable in particular cases is to be developed by national courts in light of general principles of international law and the parties' expectations in particular cases. Fundamental to this analysis, however, is the obligation presumptively to treat arbitral awards no less favorably, insofar as preclusive effects are concerned, than national court judgments and to give effect to the terms and objectives of the parties' agreement to arbitrate. As discussed below, most developed jurisdictions have applied rules of preclusion to international arbitral awards which are consistent with this analysis, generally treating such awards as identical for preclusion purposes to national court judgments.

More controversially, principles of preclusion mandated by the New York Convention should generally prevent parties from relitigating a dispute that has been resolved by an arbitral award—regardless whether particular claims arising out of that dispute were or were not asserted in earlier arbitral proceedings. So long as claims were within the scope of the parties' arbitration agreement, and were related to affirmative claims that the party asserted, a party should not be permitted to hold back claims for relitigation in subsequent proceedings: permitting this to occur contradicts the parties' objective of a speedy, final resolution of their disputes in a single forum, and instead rewards, and thereby encourages, technical pleadings and multiplicitous dispute resolution proceedings.

The better view of the Convention is that it should permit parties only "one bite at the cherry" (or apple), as required in developed common law preclusion systems. This analysis would entail a broader view of *res judicata* principles than ordinarily taken in some civil law jurisdictions, but that is appropriate in light of the New York Convention's requirements and the objectives of the arbitral process." G. Born, *International Commercial Arbitration* 3746 (2d ed. 2014).

Is that persuasive? Are some of these conclusions more persuasive than others? Which ones?

7. *Consequences of parties' arbitration agreement for preclusive effects of award.* To what extent are the preclusive effects of awards affected by the terms of the parties' arbitration agreement? For example, suppose the arbitration agreement provides that the award will be binding only if neither party objects to it, and commences proceedings in a state court, within 30 days after it is made. Will the award be binding before the 30 day period has expired? After the 30 day period has expired, without either party objecting?

8. *Finality of awards under ICSID Convention.* Consider Article 53(1) of the ICSID Convention. How does that provision compare with the New York Convention? Which instrument provides more clearly for finality? Which instrument more clearly provides a uniform international rule of finality? Which approach is preferable?

9. *Finality of awards in inter-state arbitration.* Consider Article 81 of the 1907 Hague Convention, excerpted at p. 49 of the Documentary Supplement. Again, how does this provision compare with the New York Convention (and the ICSID Convention)? Is there any reason that inter-state awards should enjoy greater finality and preclusive effects than commercial awards?

10. *Non-recognition of awards that are not "binding" under Article V(1)(e) of New York Convention.* Consider Article V(1)(e) of the New York Convention, excerpted at p. 2 of the Documentary Supplement, which permits Contracting States to deny recognition of awards that "have not yet become binding on the parties." What exactly does it mean for an award to be "binding" under Article V(1)(e)? Consider the analysis of the "binding" award requirement in *Fertilizer Corp.* Why is it that the award in *Fertilizer Corp.* was "binding" under Article V? Was it because that is what the parties agreed, either expressly or by reference to ICC Rules? Is it because Indian law, as the law of the arbitral seat, provided that the award was binding? Is it because U.S. law deemed the award binding? Or is it for some other reason?

Consider the following possibilities—an award is "binding" for purposes of Article V(1)(e) when: (a) it is made by the arbitral tribunal, without regard to possible judicial or other review; (b) it is made by the tribunal, provided that no internal appellate review within the arbitral institution has been invoked; (c) it is made by the tribunal, and the time for seeking *de novo* judicial review of the merits of the award under local law (in an action to annul) in the arbitral seat has expired, or any application for such review has been denied; (d) it is made by the tribunal, and the time for seeking limited judicial review under local law in the arbitral seat has expired, or any application for such review has been denied; (e) it is made by the tribunal, and the award has been confirmed by a local court in the arbitral seat; or (f) it is made by the tribunal, and appellate review of any of the avenues of judicial review in paragraphs (a)-(e) has been exhausted, or the time for doing so has expired. Which of these interpretations is most consistent with the Convention's purposes? Which interpretation reflects the approach of the Geneva Convention (which, as noted above, the New York Convention rejected, *supra* pp. 32-39 & *infra* pp. 1195-97)?

11. *Authorities holding awards "binding" under Article V(1)(e) even if they are subject to annulment action in arbitral seat.* Suppose an award is potentially subject to an action to annul in the jurisdiction where it was made; alternatively, suppose an action to annul the award has been filed and is pending. Can the award still be "binding"? What did *Fertilizer Corp.* hold? *See Judgment of 8 January 1995*, XXII Y.B. Comm. Arb. 789 (1997) (Swiss Fed. Trib.) ("Nor is it decisive that a request to have the award set aside or suspended, even if it has suspensive effect, is pending," citing Article VI); Aksen, *American Arbitration Accession Arrives in the Age of Aquarius*, 3 Sw. U. L. Rev. 1, 11 (1971) ("The fact that recourse may be had to a court of law does not prevent the award from being binding.").

Consider Article VI of the Convention. What does it suggest about the effects of an annulment action on an award's status as "binding" under Article V(1)(e)? Does it make sense for an award to be subject to recognition when a court in the arbitral seat may still annul it?

12. *Authorities holding awards "binding" under Article V(1)(e) if they are not subject to judicial review of merits of arbitrators' decision.* Some authorities conclude that only the availability of judicial review on the merits of the arbitrator's decision in its country of origin prevents an award from being binding:

> In most cases, an award can be deemed binding and enforceable under the Convention as soon as it is rendered. Those cases where it would not be binding would include specific cases where the law of the home jurisdiction permits judicial appeal on the merits or the rules of the arbitral institution permit review within the institution.

Craig, *Uses and Abuses of Appeal From Awards*, 4 Arb. Int'l 174, 187 (1988). *See also Judgment of 12 July 1984*, X Y.B. Comm. Arb. 487 (1985) (Amsterdam Rechtbank) ("An arbitral award is not binding if it is open to appeal on the merits before a judge or an appeal arbitral tribunal").

Note that these authorities apparently distinguish between *de novo* judicial review of the merits of an award under local law—which will prevent the award from being "binding"—and more limited judicial review (for example, along the lines permitted in an action to annul under Article 34 of the UNCITRAL Model Law), which will not. Is this a sensible distinction? Is there any basis for it in the text of Article VI? Given the pro-enforcement bias of the Convention, is it unusual for judicial review of the merits of the arbitral decision to block enforcement abroad, while more limited review does not?

13. *Authorities suggesting that awards are "binding" under Article V(1)(e) if they are not subject to review by another arbitral tribunal.* Some institutional rules provide for the possibility of appeal from an award to an appellate arbitral tribunal (for example, as under the ICSID Convention). As the quotation excepted above from Mr. Aksen in

Fertilizer Corp. suggests, some authorities have concluded that an award is "binding" unless it is subject to appellate review by another arbitral tribunal. Is this a sensible rule? Note that in the vast majority of cases, no "appellate" review by another arbitral body is provided for.

14. *Effect under Article V(1)(e) of agreement that award shall be "final."* Should Article V(1)(e) be interpreted to provide that awards are "binding" when that is what the parties agreed? That is, even if an award was subject to various forms of judicial or appellate review, if the parties agreed that the award was binding (or final) and could be enforced, then the award would be treated as "binding" for purposes of Article V(1)(e). Note that many institutional rules provide that awards are final and binding upon the parties as soon as they are made. *See, e.g.,* 2010 UNCITRAL Rules, Art. 34(2) ("shall be final and binding on the parties"); 2012 ICC Rules, Art. 34(6) ("Every award shall be binding on the parties.... the parties undertake to carry out any award without delay and shall be deemed to have waived their right to any form of recourse insofar as such waiver can validly be made."). As *Fertilizer Corp.* illustrates, contractual provisions sometimes say the same thing. What effect should such contractual provisions have? Do they mean that the award is binding, regardless of what the law of the arbitral seat provides? Why or why not?

15. *Drafting history of Article V(1)(e).* The drafting history of the New York Convention sheds some light on the meaning of a "binding" award. First, as discussed above, the Convention's drafters plainly wished to dispense with the double *exequatur* requirement. *See supra* pp. 35-36. Second, a working party responsible for the language that became Article V(1)(e) thought that an award would not be binding if "ordinary means of recourse" were available against it. 22 U.N. ESCOR 13, U.N. Doc. E/CONF.26/SR.17 (1958). That formulation is unclear, but arguably suggests that some sort of *de novo* judicial review on the merits (and not merely the review in an annulment action) must be available to preclude an award from being binding, while not clearly specifying the character of the judicial review that would have this effect. On the other hand, the formulation could suggest merely that any "ordinary" process of seeking to annul an award—through whatever means are available—would render it non-binding, while extraordinary actions to reopen or set aside awards (such as actions based on after-discovered evidence) would not. Which view is more consistent with the Convention and its purposes?

16. *Article VI's provision for suspending enforcement proceedings pending conclusion of action to annul in arbitral seat.* Suppose an award is made in Switzerland, under Swiss law, and is subject to an annulment action brought by the losing party in Swiss courts; suppose further that, while the action to annul is pending, the prevailing party seeks to enforce the award in Singapore. Can the award properly be recognized in Singapore, and, if so, should it be? Under the Convention, must it be?

Article VI of the Convention grants courts the power to adjourn enforcement proceedings pending the resolution of actions to set an award aside in its country of origin. As *Fertilizer Corp.* suggests, many courts have found this an attractive alternative and have granted Article VI stays. *Rive, SA v. Briggs of Cancun, Inc.*, 2000 WL 98127 (E.D. La.) (staying enforcement, but requiring security); *Caribbean Trading & Fidelity Corp. v. Nigerian Nat'l Petroleum Corp.*, 1990 U.S. Dist. LEXIS 17198 (S.D.N.Y.)

(same); *Spier v. Calzaturificio Tecnica SpA*, 663 F.Supp. 871, 874 (S.D.N.Y. 1987) (same).

Does the desirability of an Article VI adjournment depend on the likelihood that the foreign court will annul the award? Consider: A. van den Berg, *The New York Convention of 1958* 380-81 (1981) (Article VI "implies that the respondent has the burden of giving some summary proof that the award is tainted by a defect which is likely to cause its setting aside in the country of origin"). Does the wisdom of adjournment depend on the balance of hardship suffered by each of the parties as a result of a stay?

Does the wisdom of granting an Article VI stay depend on what bases are available in the arbitral seat for annulling the award? Suppose a State A and a State B party arbitrate, with the seat in State B; after the State A party prevails, State B courts begin *de novo* review of the merits of the arbitrators' decision. Should foreign courts postpone enforcement against the State B entity while the State B court retries the substance of the parties' dispute?

17. *Role of judicial precedent in international arbitration.* The role of judicial precedent varies in different legal systems, with courts in some states according substantial weight to the statements of law in prior judicial decisions and other legal systems according less weight to prior decisions. Thus, common law states are frequently said to recognize prior judicial decisions as "binding precedent," adopting a firm rule of *stare decisis*, derived from the notion of *stare decisis et non quieta movere*—"to stand by and adhere to decisions and not disturb what is settled." In contrast, civil law states are said to afford less weight to judicial precedent (and greater importance to codified statutory authority): "The conventional view in continental Europe is that the courts are bound by statutory laws only, not however by precedents." P. Forstmoser, *Einführung in das Recht* 411-14 (2003). Despite this, many commentators conclude that the differences between the treatments of precedent in civil and common law systems are overstated, and that both systems afford substantial weight to prior decisions. G. Born, *International Commercial Arbitration* 3810-17 (2d ed. 2014) (citing authorities).

What role should precedent have in international arbitration? Suppose that an arbitral tribunal, seated in a common law state and applying the substantive law of that state, is presented with judicial decisions from that common law system. What weight should the arbitrators accord to the judicial decisions? Does it depend on what weight the courts of the arbitral seat would accord to the decisions? Suppose the same tribunal, applying the same (common law) substantive law, is seated in a civil law state. Should that affect the weight to be accorded to the common law authorities?

Suppose an arbitral tribunal, seated in a civil law state and applying the substantive law of that state, is presented with judicial decisions of that civil law system. What weight should the arbitrators accord to those judicial authorities? Should they accord the same weight to those authorities as would a court in the arbitral seat? More or less weight?

Consider the following remarks:

"By its whole nature and constitution, an arbitral tribunal is far more ready, and far freer than a conventional judicial tribunal to deal with the actual case in front of it. An arbitral tribunal is usually established to deal with a particular case. Once it has pronounced its decision, its function is over. In such cases, there is less need to be concerned with consistency of decisions. There is more scope for tailoring the award to the particular merits of the dispute…." Redfern, *International Commercial Arbitration: Winning the*

Battle, Private Investors Abroad 11-1, 11-12 (1989).

"the arbitrators should be entitled to go a step further than the foreign judge and disregard even long-standing case-law of the highest court if the result does not conform with the needs of international trade and commerce, provided there is sufficient support in foreign doctrine for the result he endeavors to achieve in the case before him." Berger, *The International Arbitrators' Application of Precedents,* 9(4) J. Int'l Arb. 5, 15 (1992).

Are these views consistent with the objectives of the arbitral process? Recall that, save where parties have agreed to arbitration *ex aequo et bono*, the arbitrators' mandate is to resolve the parties' dispute in an adjudicative manner, in accordance with applicable law. If a national legal system accords judicial decisions binding precedential weight, then shouldn't arbitrators give those decisions the same effect as would a court in that system? Is it acceptable to permit arbitrators to disregard applicable substantive law, based on their assessment of "the needs of international trade and commerce"?

18. *Role of arbitral precedent in international arbitration.* What role should the decisions of previous arbitral tribunals have in defining the applicable substantive law in later arbitrations? It is sometimes said that arbitral awards have no role as precedent: "[I]n both [Common and Civil law] systems, the prior decision of an arbitral tribunal on a question of law has no precedential value." Sheppard, *Res Judicata and Estoppel*, in B. Cremades & J. Lew (eds.), *Parallel State and Arbitral Procedures in International Arbitration* 219, 222 (2005).

Recall that many arbitral awards are confidential and, therefore, are never published or otherwise made available to non-parties. In these instances, it is obvious that an award can have no precedential effects. But assume an award is made public—why should it not have similar precedential effects to those of a national court? For example, if a three-person tribunal, composed of respected English (or Singaporean) arbitrators, carefully considers an issue of English (or Singaporean) commercial law and unanimously makes a reasoned award, should that award have the same precedential weight as a decision by an English (or Singaporean) court? Recall that one of the reasons parties agree to arbitrate is to obtain an expert, commercially-sophisticated decision; why should those decisions not have broader precedential authority?

Reliance on prior arbitral decisions, as a form of decisive precedent, can be observed in the context of maritime and international construction arbitrations, where awards are not only followed, but often published in industry circles for precisely this purpose. O'Brien, *Maritime Arbitration*, 14 Forum 222, 227 (1978-1979); Berger, *The International Arbitrators' Application of Precedents,* 9 J. Int'l Arb. 5, 20 (1992). Why shouldn't the same approach apply more broadly?

19. *Role of arbitral precedent in investment arbitration.* Note that many awards in investment arbitrations are public. *See supra* p. 869. Does this argue for according them greater precedential effect than might be the case in commercial arbitrations? Consider the following refusal, by a tribunal in an investment arbitration, to accord precedential authority to prior awards:

"there is no doctrine of precedent in international law, if by precedent is meant a rule of the binding effect of a single decision. There is no hierarchy of international tribunals, and even if there were, there is no good reason for allowing the first tribunal in time to resolve issues for all later tribunals." *SGS Société Gén. de Surveillance SA v. Repub. of Philippines, Decision on Jurisdiction in ICSID Case No. ARB/02/6 of 29 January 2004*, 8 ICSID Rep. 515, 545 (2004).

Is this appropriate? Compare the following:

"The decisions of these tribunals [addressing jurisdiction over non-signatories] progressively create case-law which should be taken into account, because it draws conclusions from economic reality and conforms to the needs of international commerce, to which rules specific to international arbitration, themselves successively formulated should respond." *Interim Award in ICC Case No. 4131*, IX Y.B. Comm. Arb. 131, 136 (1984).

What are the various arguments for and against according precedential authority to arbitral awards? Which view prevails? In commercial arbitration? In investment arbitration? If arbitrators should afford precedential authority to prior awards, what about national courts?

B. CORRECTION, INTERPRETATION AND SUPPLEMENTATION OF INTERNATIONAL ARBITRAL AWARDS

Human fallibility guarantees that virtually all arbitral awards will have mistakes, omissions, or ambiguities. These will range from typographical errors, to inaccurate references to evidence or legal authorities, to *non sequiturs* or unpersuasive analysis, to outright confusions of parties or mathematical miscalculations of amounts; they also may involve failures by the arbitrators to address particular arguments, claims, or evidence. These errors usually concern minor or incidental issues and have little or no relevance to the tribunal's ultimate awards of damages or other relief. In some cases, however, errors can concern very fundamental points that lie at the heart of the tribunal's reasoning or award.

Most obviously, an award's damage calculations may contain arithmetic mistakes or an undisputed fact relevant to a damages award may be erroneously recorded (*e.g.*, the number of lost sales in a particular year, the cost of purchasing replacement goods);[7] alternatively, it may be clear that the tribunal failed to address one of the claims presented by the parties. In these instances, a party may wish to seek correction or supplementation of the award in order to change the quantum of monetary damages that were awarded or to address the neglected issue(s).

Historically, there were significant reservations about permitting arbitrators to correct, supplement, or interpret their awards. Immediately upon making their award (which was, as discussed above, final and binding), arbitrators became "*functus officio*," and lost the capacity to take further steps, including to correct or interpret their award.[8] Accordingly, many modern arbitration statutes provide mechanisms that allow parties to request (and arbitrators to make) "corrections" to, "interpretations" of, or "supplementations" to an award. In most states, the circumstances in which these types of changes can be made are

---

7. For examples, *see Hyle v. Doctor's Assocs., Inc.*, 198 F.3d 368 (2d Cir. 1999) (tribunal assessed damages against wrong party); *Judgment of 12 January 2005*, DFT 131 III 164 (Swiss Fed. Trib.) (rejecting an application to set aside an award rectifying the amount to be paid from $71,100,000 (as provided in the initial award) to $107,500,000).

8. *See* G. Born, *International Commercial Arbitration* 3115 (2d ed. 2014).

very narrowly circumscribed. Nonetheless, as the materials excerpted below illustrate, the existence of these powers provide grounds for addressing obvious slips or miscalculations, omissions, or uncertainties that could otherwise cause injustice or lead to annulment of the award.

LA VALE PLAZA, INC. v. R.S. NOONAN, INC.
378 F.2d 569 (3d Cir. 1967)

FREEDMAN, Circuit Judge.... Appellant, La Vale Plaza, Inc., contracted for the construction of a shopping center by R.S. Noonan, Inc. Because a dispute arose regarding the amount due it, Noonan filed with the [AAA] a demand for arbitration under the provisions of the contract.[9] ... [T]he arbitrators rendered an award in favor of Noonan in the amount of $30,861.64. Their award expressly declared that it was "in full settlement of all claims submitted to this arbitration one against the other." Two months later, La Vale brought the present action to recover the amount of $25,568.02 which it alleged was due it as the difference between the award and a deposit of $56,429.66 which it had delivered to Noonan during the pendency of the arbitration proceedings in order to obtain a continuance of one of the hearings. Noonan in its answer alleged on the contrary that the $56,429.66 was a partial payment on account and left a balance in dispute which was decided by the award. Curiously enough, Noonan filed no counterclaim for the recovery of the amount of the award.

The district judge held that the dispute whether the sum of $56,429.66 was a deposit or a payment of account raised a material question of fact and ... denied Noonan's motion for summary judgment. In doing so, however, he ordered *sua sponte* that the award be resubmitted to the arbitrators for clarification of its meaning. For his power to do this the district judge relied on §11 of the [Pennsylvania] Arbitration Act of April 25, 1927, which authorizes a court on the application of any party to an arbitration to modify and correct an award or resubmit it, "where the award is imperfect in matter of form not affecting the merits of the controversy."[10] The court held that the Act of 1927 was applicable because the arbitration clause of the contract provided that it was to be enforceable under the "prevailing arbitration law." Appellant contends that this was error because this was a common law arbitration and that under it the court has no power to resubmit an award to arbitrators for clarification....

In 1927 Pennsylvania adopted with some modifications the Uniform Arbitration Act.... The Act provides in general for the enforcement of a provision in any written contract,

---

9. Article 40 of the contract provides: "All disputes, claims or questions subject to arbitration under this contract shall be submitted to arbitration in accordance with the provisions, then obtaining, of the [AAA], and this agreement shall be specifically enforceable under the prevailing arbitration law, and judgment upon the award rendered may be entered in the court of the forum, state or federal, having jurisdiction. It is mutually agreed that the decision of the arbitrators shall be a condition precedent to any right of legal action that either party may have against the other."

10. 5 Purdon's Pa. Stat. Annot. §171. Section 10(d) of the Act of 1927 is also relevant. It authorizes the court to vacate an award upon the application of any party to the arbitration and if the time within which the agreement required the award to be made has not expired, to direct a rehearing by the arbitrators, *inter alia,* "where the arbitrators exceeded their powers or so imperfectly executed them that a final and definite award upon the subject matter submitted was not made." 5 Purdon's Pa. Stat. Annot. §170.

except a contract for personal services, to settle by arbitration a controversy which may thereafter arise out of the contract and for the enforcement of an agreement in writing to submit an existing controversy to arbitration. Because the Act of 1927 makes a number of changes in the earlier practice in arbitration and prescribes grounds for the vacation and modification and correction of awards by the court it has become increasingly important to determine whether a particular arbitration proceeding is subject to the provisions of the Act of 1927 or is to be deemed a common law arbitration.... The present contract contains no reference to the Act of 1927, and the language of Article 40 that disputes under the contract should be arbitrated in accordance with the existing practice of the [AAA] does not indicate the intention of the parties that the provisions of the Act should apply. Nor does the further language that the contract "shall be specifically enforceable under the prevailing arbitration law" bring the arbitration under the Act of 1927.... Since it is clear that the Act of 1927 does not apply and that this was a common law arbitration, the question is whether in such a case the district judge had power to order the award resubmitted for clarification by the arbitrators.

The general principle in a common law arbitration is that the arbitrators are the final judges for both the facts and the law and their decision will not be disturbed for a mistake of fact or of law. This is one of the fundamental distinctions between common law and statutory arbitration under the Act of 1927. It is presumed that in not providing affirmatively for the application of the Act of 1927 the parties to an arbitration intend the common law principle to prevail. It is equally fundamental common law principle that once an arbitrator has made and published a final award his authority is exhausted and he is *functus officio* and can do nothing more in regard to the subject matter of the arbitration. The policy which lies behind this is an unwillingness to permit one who is not a judicial officer and who acts informally and sporadically, to re-examine a final decision which he has already rendered, because of the potential evil of outside communication and unilateral influence which might affect a new conclusion. The continuity of judicial office and the tradition which surrounds judicial conduct is lacking in the isolated activity of an arbitrator, although even here the vast increase in the arbitration of labor disputes has created the office of the specialized professional arbitrator. This policy of finality, founded on practical considerations, is nourished by the primitive view of the solemnity of all judgments. From it, reinforced by the enormous fines which King Edward I levied to replenish his treasury on his judges for erasing or altering their records, came the ancient common law rule that a judgment, once enrolled on parchment, was unalterable even for the correction of a manifest mistake. [3 Blackstone Commentaries, *409-410.]

The principle that an award once rendered is final contains its own limitation, however, and it therefore has been recognized in common law arbitration that the arbitrator can correct a mistake which is apparent on the face of his award. Similarly, where the award does not adjudicate an issue which has been submitted, then as to such an issue the arbitrator has not exhausted his function and it remains open to him for subsequent determination. In such a case the arbitrator is not exposed to any greater risk of impropriety than would normally exist during the pendency of the arbitration proceedings, a risk which is inherent in the submission of disputes to non judicial determination. The Pennsylvania courts therefore have recognized that an arbitrator may complete a common law arbitration if the award is not complete, even over the objection of one of the parties. Thus, in *Frederick v. Margwarth*, 221 Pa. 418 (1908), plaintiff sued on an award in his favor made by an arbitrator.... The court sustained the defense that the award was invalid because it was not coextensive with the submission, since the arbitrator had failed to pass on a number of disputed matters that had been submitted to him. Thereupon the arbitrator, on notice to the parties, went forward with the completion of his award, on which the plaintiff brought a new action. The Supreme Court of Pennsylvania rejected the defense that the arbitrator's authority ended with the making of the first award ...:

> "The rule undoubtedly is that, when an arbitrator has made and delivered his award, the special power conferred upon him ends. But an award must be final, complete, and coextensive with the terms of the submission. The arbitrator, through mistake, failed to consider and decide a part of the dispute submitted to him, and the award was invalid because incomplete. But the agreement as still in force, and it was competent for the arbitrator to finish his work by making a full and complete award...."

Where the award, although seemingly compete, leaves doubt whether the submission has been fully executed, an ambiguity arises which the arbitrator is entitled to clarify. The resolution of such an ambiguity is not within the policy which forbids an arbitrator to redetermine an issue which he has already decided, for there is no opportunity for redetermination on the merits of what has already been decided. Instead, the clarification of an ambiguity closely resembles the correction of a mistake apparent on the face of the award and the determination of an issue which the arbitrators had failed to decide. Thus, in the present case the arbitrators will act only to remove the cloud of doubt as to whether they considered the payment of $56,429.66 in making their award and will in no way reopen the merits of the controversy.

The remaining question is whether the court in which the arbitrator's award is offered to sustain a claim or defense may take cognizance of the dispute over its finality, and finding that its clarification would not in any way violate any policy relating to arbitration and would be within the arbitrators' power to pursue on their own motion, may resubmit it to the arbitrators for such purpose. When awards are made under a rule of court, the decisions in Pennsylvania sustain the power of the court to order resubmission to the same referee for the correction of an informality or even an ambiguity. In *Refowich v. Rice*, 4 Pennypacker 449 (Pa. 1883), the Supreme Court of Pennsylvania held that the court below could not alter the award of arbitrators based on their subsequent testimony of their intention to award full costs in a slander action, rather than the nominal costs prescribed by a colonial statute. Justice Paxton said, however, that "had the award been recommitted to the arbitrators, and amended so as to give full costs, there would have been no difficulty. But there was no action by the arbitrators as such. Their award could only be amended by themselves, acting in their official character as arbitrators, upon a recommittal of it to them by the court." What was involved in that case apparently as not a common law arbitration, but the procedural vehicle should be as equally applicable in a common law arbitration as in a statutory one.... [There] is no indication that Pennsylvania intends that the common law of arbitration should be frozen as it was prior to 1836 and that the common law is to be deprived of its traditional capacity for development and growth. Indeed, there is no reason why we may not look to Pennsylvania's statutes, which explicitly permit resubmission of an award, for their reflection of a public policy on which courts may properly draw in administering the gradualist development of the common law. If the common law of arbitration should be fixed as it was a century or more ago and incapable of growth, the increasing body of arbitrations on commercial contracts and on construction contracts like the one before us, establishing arbitration under the auspices of the [AAA], would be condemned to stagnation, beyond the reach of progressive judicial development…. Moreover, it would be strange if a court which finds an ambiguity in an award should be powerless to order its resubmission to the arbitrators although the arbitrators themselves admittedly have the authority to clarify the ambiguity and if necessary to complete their action under the submission. [The court affirmed the trial court's decision re-submitting the award to the tribunal.] …

JAPANESE ARBITRATION LAW
Article 40(3)

The mandate of the arbitral tribunal terminates with the termination of the arbitral proceedings. Provided, the acts prescribed in the provisions of articles 41 through 43 may be made [concerning corrections, interpretations and supplementations].

JUDGMENT OF 12 JANUARY 2005
DFT 131 III 164 (Swiss Fed. Trib.)

[This case concerns] a pending arbitration … subject to the [ICC Rules] between company B as claimant and company A as defendant…. On 24 March 2004, the arbitral tribunal, composed of three arbitrators acting unanimously, rendered a partial award which fixed the price of the 49 shares of company C to an amount of 73,100,000 US\$ …, which A was ordered to pay to B, provided a deduction of 27,000,000 US\$ as payment on account on 28 February 2002 and provided a transit account of 855,556.17 US\$ which corresponds to the defendant's claim for compensation…. [A applied to annul the award, citing Arts. 190(2)(a), (d) and (e) of the SLPIL. The Swiss Federal Tribunal dismissed the application.]…

On 7 April 2004, B lodged a request for amendment to the ICC regarding the partial award…. On 18 August 2004, the arbitral tribunal, acting unanimously, notified to the parties an addendum dated 27 July 2004, whereby [the arbitrators] partially admitted the above request, fixed the price of C's 49 shares to 107,500,000 US\$ and consequently amended … the partial award's operative part. In order to justify this amendment, the arbitrators conceded that, as the result of a twofold inadvertence, they, on the one hand, took into consideration C and D's consolidated expenses twice, and on the other hand, used the plus sign instead of the minus sign at the time of the valuation of D's minor shareholders' participations. [A applied to annul the addendum to the award dated July 27, 2004, under Articles 190(2)(a), (d) and (e).]….

Contrary to [an] additional award [which supplements the original award], [a] corrective award does not add anything to the initial award. Because it is accessory to [the initial award], it has the same fate and will be null and void ipso facto if the initial award is annulled. Thus it is not a new award, but a decision which forms an "integral part of the award," according to the [ICC Rules] … Thus it goes without saying that the successful party in the arbitration proceedings will not proceed to total enforcement of the pecuniary sanctions imposed by the initial and the corrective awards, which would amount to claim twice the amount of the allotment….

In accordance with its accessory nature, the corrective award complies with the legal status of the initial award. Like in the present case, when the [corrective] award is not the final one, the admissibility of an immediate appeal to the Federal Tribunal against this award is subject to the same conditions as the ... complaint brought against the partial award.... Awards rectifying a final or a partial award *stricto sensu* will be [subject] to immediate appeal in all the cases provided for in [Article 190(2) ... in the same manner as other awards].

When determining which grounds for complaint may be invoked against a corrective award [under Article 190(2)], one must not ignore the limited scope of the amendment procedure, as well as the fact that an award has already been rendered. Indeed, for this purpose a preexisting award is a matter of particular importance. Because it acquires the authority of *res judicata* from the moment it is issued to the parties, this initial award may only be challenged through a specific legal ground, for reasons exhaustively listed [in Article 190] and within a [reasonable] deadline which cannot be extended. The purpose of the amendment procedure is not to modify this system and provide the parties with an alternative to challenge the initial award. It must not be interpreted as an additional means of appeal. It is only designed to correct a substantive error (error in calculation, clerical mistake, misprint, etc.) which affects the initial award, in contrast to an error in reasoning or a mistake in law, without infringing on the *res judicata* authority of this award. Restricting in the same manner the possibility to challenge the corrective award, complies with the purpose of this procedure. Thus, the ... complaint against this award may only be aimed at the rectification in itself....

When a ... complaint is lodged against a corrective award ... the claimant can claim that the corrective award was rendered in irregular terms [Art. 190(2)(a)]); that the tribunal unjustly accepted or declined jurisdiction to correct the initial award, or that it exceeded jurisdiction in the matter and amended the actual content of the award [Art. 190(2)(b)]; that by issuing a corrective award, [the tribunal] adjudicated *ultra petita* or omitted to decide on a count of the request for amendment [Art. 190(2)(c)]; that the amendment procedure infringed on the equality of the parties [principle] or their right to be heard [Art. 190(2)(d)]; finally, that the corrective award is incompatible with substantive (theoretical assumption) or procedural (more probable) public policy [Art. 190(2)(e)]. However, if one party neglected to challenge the initial award in due time or if his claim was unsuccessful, it is impossible for him to challenge this initial award, for the first time or on another ground, by means of a ... complaint ... against the corrective award....

As a general rule, [the] procedures [for correcting an award and seeking annulment of an award] must not interfere with one another. Thus, an application for [correction] of the initial award will not adjourn the deadline for challenging such award.... In the absence of appeal or if the ... complaint lodged against the initial award is set aside or declared inadmissible, the corrective award will substitute to the initial award. If the request for amendment is not accepted, the first award will continue to have effect. In any event, the corrective award *lato sensu* will be subject to a ... complaint pursuant to the conditions mentioned above. Assuming that this recourse is admitted and the corrective award is annulled, the initial award will revive. If the ... complaint against the initial award is admitted and the said award is annulled, the corrective award—where the request for annulment is admitted—will be null and void ipso facto because it formed an integral part of an award which was annulled....

Because the addendum of 27 July 2004 is of the same nature as the award rendered on 24 March 2004, it also constitutes a partial award subject to immediate appeal to the Federal Tribunal pursuant to [Article 190(2)].... The claimant mainly resumes the grounds previously raised in [an] appeal against the initial award, [an appeal that was rejected] by the Federal Tribunal in its decision of 6 October 2004.... To that extent, i.e. for most of the criticisms which were expressed in the present appeal, such appeal is inadmissible. Regarding the award of 24 March 2004, it goes without saying [that the present appeal is inadmissible] because the time limit for appeal was passed when it was lodged; for that matter, the claimant attempted—with no success—to have the said award annulled by challenging it separately before expiry of the time limit. But the present appeal is also inadmissible because it attacks the addendum of 27 July 2004 with identical grounds to those raised in the first appeal. Indeed, for the reasons mentioned above, it is impossible to call into question the *res judicata* effect of the initial award through an appeal against the corrective award. The purpose of such appeal can only be the corrective award and the admissible objections can only relate to the procedure for amendment and/or to the content of the said award.

[Here, it] seems that a good many of the alleged new objections expressed in the second appeal consist in reality only of a slightly different presentation from those previously submitted to the Federal Tribunal. In these conditions, the ... court will not get involved in all the objections which, even remotely, relate to the way to determine the value of the company of which 49 shares were sold by the respondent to the claimant and as a result of this evaluation.... The only genuinely new ground of the claimant is to reproach the arbitral tribunal for admitting an error in the addendum, the rectification of which led to a 34,400,000 US$ (i.e. 47%) increase of the sold shares' price compared to the one which was fixed in the first award. However, the extent of the rectification made by the arbitrators to the prejudice of the claimant does not involve violation of the safeguards which result from [Article 190(2)]. The omission of one figure in the allocated amount could therefore lead to a major rectification of the amount at issue. [The court cited a case where the omission of a "0" from the sums awards resulted in a 900% error, requiring correction.]

Therefore, it was for the claimant to specify why the rectification made in the present case fell under the scope of one of the reasons for appeal listed in [Article 190(2)]. He did not do so.... [T]he present appeal is entirely inadmissible.

NOTES

1.   *"Functus officio" doctrine*. It was historically the case, in many states, that an arbitral tribunal lost its capacity to act—including its power to correct, interpret, or supplement an award it had made—after the arbitrators had rendered their final award. In the phrase used in some jurisdictions, the tribunal became *"functus officio." See, e.g., U.S. Life Ins. Co. v. Superior Nat'l Ins. Co.*, 591 F.3d 1167, 1178 n.11 (9th Cir. 2010); *Judgment of 2 May 2012*, DFT 4A_14 2012 (Swiss Fed. Trib.) ("once the final award is issued, the arbitral tribunal sees its jurisdiction disappear and becomes functus officio, with some exceptions"); Webster, *Functus Officio and Remand in International Arbitration*, 27 ASA Bull. 441, 441 (2009) ("The principle that an arbitral tribunal is functus officio when it renders its final award is sacrosanct, subject to limited exceptions for correction and interpretation of awards and in some cases to remedial action with respect to awards.").

In one court's words: "The term [*functus officio*] is Latin for 'office performed' and in the law of arbitration means that once an arbitrator has issued his final award he may not revise it." *Glass Molders, Pottery, etc. v. Excelsior Foundry Co.*, 56 F.3d 844 (7th Cir. 1995). The *functus officio* doctrine is distinguished from an arbitrator's premature resignation or removal prior to conclusion of the arbitration, thereby terminating his or her mandate before it has been completed. *See supra* pp. 775-76. The term *functus officio* refers instead to a tribunal's completion of its mandate at the end of an arbitration, by making an award with *res judicata* effect. *See supra* pp. 1113-25.

2. *Rationale for functus officio doctrine*. Why does it make sense for the arbitrators to become *functus officio* after they have made their final award? A national court judge does not cease to hold office after he or she renders a judgment; why should an arbitrator? Are there policies that argue for limiting the arbitrators' competence in this manner? Consider the rationale in *La Vale Plaza*. Is this persuasive? Some U.S. courts have questioned whether the *functus officio* doctrine serves any continued purpose. *Glass, Molders, etc.*, 56 F.3d 844 (questioning *functus officio* doctrine; "perhaps the time has come to discard the rule").

   Compare how modern arbitration statutes deal with the arbitrators' completion of their mandate and subsequent authorities (for example, UNCITRAL Model Law, Art. 32; Japanese Arbitration Law, Art. 40(3)). Do these statutes provide for effectively the same results as the *functus officio* doctrine? Compare also Article 81 of the 1907 Hague Convention.

3. *Arbitrators' inherent authority to correct or interpret award*. Suppose neither the arbitration legislation of the arbitral seat nor the parties' arbitration agreement (including any institutional rules) addresses the question of the arbitrators' authority to correct or interpret awards. Do the arbitrators have the authority to make such corrections or interpretations? Or does the *functus officio* doctrine forbid a tribunal from taking such actions, after it has made its final award? For a traditional view, see *United Mine Workers of Am. v. Island Creek Coal Co.*, 630 F.Supp. 1278 (W.D. Va. 1986) ("Once an arbitrator has issued his final ... award, [it] then becomes *functus officio* and lacks power to reconsider or amend.").

   More recently, courts in the United States have held that the *functus officio* doctrine is subject to exceptions for: (a) correcting obvious mistakes; (b) deciding issues deliberately left open by an interim or partial final award; and (c) clarifying ambiguities. In addition to *La Vale Plaza*, *see Martel v. Ensco Offshore Co.*, 449 F.Appx. 351, 356 (5th Cir. 2011) (three recognized exceptions to the functus officio doctrine: "An arbitrator can (1) correct a mistake which is apparent on the face of his award; (2) decide an issue which has been submitted but which has not been completely adjudicated by the original award; or (3) clarify or construe an arbitration award that seems complete but proves to be ambiguous in its scope and implementation."); *Glass, Molders, etc.*, 56 F.3d 844 (applying, generously, exception to *functus officio* rule permitting arbitrator to clarify or complete award within reasonable period after award); *Saxis S.S. Co. v. Multifacs Int'l Traders, Inc.*, 375 F.2d 577, 581 n.4 (2d Cir. 1967). *Compare Danella Const. Corp. v. MCI Telecomm. Corp.*, 1992 U.S. Dist. LEXIS 4952 (E.D. Pa.) (where institutional rules contain no authorization for arbitrator to modify awards, FAA does not permit such modifications).

   Is *La Vale Plaza* well-reasoned? What is the basis for the conclusion that arbitrators had the power to correct or interpret an award? Is that what the parties intended? Is it the result of an inherent adjudicative authority?

4. *National arbitration legislation granting arbitrators competence to correct awards.* Consider Article 33 of the UNCITRAL Model Law, excerpted at pp. 93-94 of the Documentary Supplement. What does the provision permit? See also Article 40(3) of the Japanese Arbitration law.

    Suppose an arbitral tribunal makes an obvious error of fact, incorrectly concluding that a party delivered goods of a particular quality (which satisfied the parties' contractual specifications), when it in fact delivered goods of a different quality (which clearly did not satisfy the specifications). If this error is pointed out under Article 33, does the tribunal have the authority to "correct" its award, holding that the seller breached its delivery obligations (instead of holding that the seller satisfactorily performed its obligations)? Is the tribunal's mistake an error in "computation" or a "clerical or typographical error"?

    Why are there such narrow limits under Article 33 on the circumstances in which an award may be corrected? Would a broader power to "correct" awards be consistent with the parties' objective of obtaining a speedy, final resolution of the parties' disputes, without the costs and delays of litigation? Is this objective sufficient to override the parties' (and society's) interest in correcting a patently "incorrect" result?

    Compare Article 83 of the 1907 Hague Convention, excerpted at p. 49 of the Documentary Supplement. In what circumstances may a tribunal correct an award under the Convention? Compare Articles 50 and 51 of the ICSID Convention, excerpted at pp. 23-24 of the Documentary Supplement. How do these provisions compare to Article 33 of the Model Law?

5. *National arbitration legislation granting arbitrators competence to interpret or supplement awards.* Consider Article 33(1)(a), 33(1)(b) and 33(3) of the UNCITRAL Model Law, excerpted at pp. 93-94 of the Documentary Supplement. Why are there differences between how these three types of post-award functions are treated? What do Articles 33(1)(b) and 33(3) mean when they provide that an award may be interpreted or supplemented "if so agreed by the parties" and "unless otherwise agreed by the parties"? Are these differences appropriate?

    Suppose an arbitral tribunal fails to decide one of the parties' claims. What consequences can this have for the award? Can the award be annulled (for example, under Article 34)?

6. *Institutional arbitration rules granting arbitrators competence to correct, interpret, or supplement awards.* Consider Articles 37-39 of the UNCITRAL Rules, excerpted at pp. 174-75 of the Documentary Supplement. How do they compare to Articles 33-35 of the ICC Rules and Article 27 of the LCIA Rules? Which approach to the subject is preferable? Would it be wiser for parties not to make any agreement regarding corrections, interpretations, or supplementations?

7. *Authority of national courts to correct, interpret, or supplement award.* Does anything in the UNCITRAL Model Law permit a national court—including a court in the arbitral seat—to correct, interpret, or supplement an international arbitral award? Compare the Swiss Law on Private International Law and the Japanese Arbitration Law. Would it be desirable for courts to have this power? Even if this power were limited in the manner that Article 33 of the Model Law limits the authority of arbitrators? Are there respects in which a court might be better suited than the arbitrators that made the award? Are there respects in which a court would be less well-suited?

8. *Authority of U.S. courts to correct, interpret, or supplement award under FAA*. Consider §11 of the FAA, excerpted at p. 106 of the Documentary Supplement. What power does it give to arbitrators to correct or interpret their awards? What power does the FAA give to U.S. courts? Is this wise? Why or why not?

9. *Character of corrections, supplementations and interpretations*. Suppose an arbitral tribunal issues a correction, supplementation, or interpretation of an award. What is the character of that instrument? Is it a new award, that can be challenged (*i.e.*, in an annulment action) in the same way as other awards? Does the new instrument supersede the initial award? Consider the issues addressed in *Judgment of 12 January 2005*. Note the concerns with narrowly limiting the departure from principles of *res judicata* and finality in dealing with corrections and interpretations.

What grounds may be raised to annul or deny recognition of a correction or interpretation? For example, suppose a party claims it was denied an opportunity to present its case: must that denial have occurred in the proceedings relating to the correction or may it have arisen in proceedings leading to the original award?

Note the magnitude of the arbitrators' error that was "corrected" by the tribunal in *Judgment of 12 January 2005*. Is it not unsettling that arbitrators could make a mistake of this magnitude? Does this affect the question whether the arbitrators should be permitted to correct their own award? Whether the initial arbitration was conducted fairly and regularly?

C. GROUNDS FOR ANNULMENT OF INTERNATIONAL ARBITRAL AWARDS

Award-debtors frequently comply voluntarily with arbitral awards against them. Nonetheless, there are cases where a party concludes, either for tactical reasons or because of a genuinely-held sense of injustice, that an award against it is fundamentally wrong. In these instances, where a correction or interpretation does not address their real complaints, parties may seek to annul or set aside the awards against them.

In the context of international commercial arbitrations, if an annulment action can be properly brought in a particular forum, then the New York Convention imposes no express international limits on the grounds available for annulment: these grounds are almost exclusively matters of local law.[11] Nonetheless, as discussed below, many national arbitration regimes have adopted broadly similar approaches to the available grounds for annulment of international awards—generally, but not always, limiting such review to bases roughly paralleling those applicable to non-recognition of awards in Article V of the Convention.

Most national arbitration legislation permits the annulment of international commercial arbitration awards if: (a) there was no valid arbitration agreement; (b) the award-debtor was denied an adequate opportunity to present its case; (c) the arbitration was not conducted in accordance with the parties' agreement or, failing such agreement, the law of the arbitral seat; (d) the award dealt with matters not submitted by the parties to arbitration; (e) the award dealt with a dispute that is not capable of settlement by arbitration; or (f) the award is contrary to public policy. In addition, many arbitration statutes also provide for the annulment of awards if: (g) the tribunal lacked independence or impartiality; (h) the

---

11. *See supra* pp. 623, 1071-72 & *infra* pp. 1155-58, 1194-95. As discussed below, however, the New York Convention is best interpreted as imposing limited implied restrictions on the grounds that may be invoked to annul an award. *See infra* pp. 1157-58.

award was procured by fraud; or (i) in some states, the arbitrator's substantive decision was seriously wrong on the merits.

Outside the context of commercial arbitration, the grounds for annulling or setting aside awards are equally limited. In investment arbitrations, Article 52 of the ICSID Convention enumerates limited grounds (broadly paralleling the New York Convention) for annulment of an ICSID award; at the same time, as described above, annulment applications are decided exclusively by annulment committees, also appointed by ICSID.[12] In inter-state arbitration, although no universal instrument comparable to the New York and ICSID Conventions exists,[13] the available grounds for annulment of an award are also very limited.

BELGIAN JUDICIAL CODE
Article 1717(4) (pre-1999 amendments)

Courts of Belgium may hear a request for annulment only if at least one of the parties to the dispute decided by the award is either a physical person having Belgian nationality or residence, or a legal entity created in Belgium or having a Belgian branch or other seat of operation.

BELGIAN JUDICIAL CODE
Article 1717(4) (pre-2013 amendments)

The parties may, through an express declaration in the arbitration agreement or through a later agreement, exclude any action for the annulment of an arbitrator's award when neither of them is either a natural person with a Belgian citizenship or a residence in Belgium, or a legal person having its main establishment or having a branch there.

BELGIAN JUDICIAL CODE
Article 1718 (as amended in 2013)

By an explicit declaration in the arbitration agreement or by a later agreement, the parties may exclude any application for the setting aside of an arbitral award, where none of them is a natural person of Belgian nationality or a natural person having his domicile or normal residence in Belgium or a legal person having its registered office, its main place of business or a branch office in Belgium.

CHINESE ARBITRATION LAW
Article 58

A party may apply for setting aside an arbitration award to the Intermediate People's Court in the place where the arbitration commission is located if he can produce evidence which

---

12. *See supra* p. 42; C. Schreuer *et al.*, *The ICSID Convention: A Commentary* Art. 52 ¶¶451-455 (2d ed. 2009)

13. *See infra* p. 1173; G. Born, *International Commercial Arbitration* 3168-73 (2d ed. 2014).

proves that the arbitration award involves one of the following circumstances: (1) There is no arbitration agreement; (2) The matters decided in the award exceed the scope of the arbitration agreement or are beyond the arbitral authority of the arbitration commission; (3) The formation of the arbitration tribunal or the arbitration procedure was not in conformity with the statutory procedure; (4) The evidence on which the award is based is forged; (5) The other party has withheld the evidence which is sufficient to affect the impartiality of the arbitration; or (6) The arbitrators have committed embezzlement, accepted bribes or done malpractice for personal benefits or perverted the law in the arbitration of the case. The Peoples Court shall rule to set aside the arbitration award if a collegial panel formed by the Peoples Court verifies upon examination that the award involves one of the circumstances set forth in the preceding paragraph. If the Peoples Court determines that the arbitration award violates the public interest, it shall rule to set aside the award.

ARGENTINE CODE OF CIVIL AND COMMERCIAL PROCEDURE
Article 758

All means of recourse available against court decisions can be raised against an arbitral award, if not waived in the arbitration agreement.

FIRST OPTIONS OF CHICAGO, INC. v. KAPLAN
514 U.S. 938 (1995)

[excerpted above at pp. 230-33]

BG GROUP PLC v. REPUBLIC OF ARGENTINA
134 S.Ct. 1198 (2014)

[excerpted above at pp. 233-47]

JUDGMENT OF 17 FEBRUARY 2011, GOV'T OF PAKISTAN, MIN. OF RELIGIOUS AFFAIRS v. DALLAH REAL ESTATE & TOURISM HLDG CO.
XXXVI Y.B. Comm. Arb. 590 (Paris Cour d'appel)

[excerpted above at pp. 570-73]

LAMINOIRS-TREFILERIES-CABLERIES DE LENS, SA v. SOUTHWIRE CO.
484 F.Supp. 1063 (N.D. Ga. 1980)

TIDWELL, District Judge.... Southwire, a Georgia corporation which manufactures cable products, and [Laminoirs-Trefileries-Cableries de Lens ("LTCL")], a French *société anonyme* which manufactures steel wire and rope, entered into a purchase agreement in 1974, whereby LTCL agreed to manufacture and sell, and Southwire agreed to buy, galvanized steel wire.... The price to be paid by Southwire was to be determined and adjusted according to a formula based on the world market price of steel wire.... [The] purchase agreement contained an arbitration clause, and also contained a governing law clause, stating that the agreement would be governed by the laws of Georgia insofar as these laws are in accordance with French laws.

Disputes arose…. Pursuant to the arbitration clause in the contract, LTCL demanded arbitration before an international tribunal in accordance with [ICC Rules]…. On February 8, 1979, the arbitrators made a partial arbitral award [in New York], which accepted LTCL's [claims]; ordered Southwire to pay LTCL the aggregate amount of underpayments caused by [Southwire's breach] (plus interest at the French legal rate); found in favor of Southwire [on certain counterclaims]; [and] reserved judgment on [other counterclaims] and the costs of the arbitration. The parties thereafter settled the [remaining counterclaim], and … the tribunal entered a further arbitral award, confirming settlement of [the remaining counterclaim and allocating costs.] Southwire filed a state court action in Georgia, seeking vacation of the awards, which was removed to this court by LTCL. LTCL also filed a separate suit seeking confirmation of the awards….

The arbitral award of interest [was attacked by Southwire] on several grounds. The arbitrators concluded, in response to LTCL's argument, that the French legal rate of interest (on judgments) should apply. The French statute relied upon by the tribunal was not specifically pleaded nor formally introduced into evidence, however. In their award, the tribunal merely states what the French law is and applies it. LTCL argues that the arbitrators took judicial notice of the French statute; Southwire argues that absent notice to it that French law would be relied upon, judicial notice was inappropriate.

The Court disagrees with Southwire's assertions. First of all, the contract's governing law clause contained a provision that the contract would be governed by Georgia law to the extent that it was in accordance with French law. The fact that this clause was cited by the Terms of Reference for arbitration should have, in and of itself, put Southwire on notice that French law had a potential bearing on the outcome of the case, thus precluding any issue of "unfair surprise." While Southwire now contends that the tribunal misconstrued the governing law clause as applicable to interest rate determination, Southwire argued before the arbitrators that interest "should be assessed in accordance with Georgia law," and in support of such contention itself referred the arbitrators to its pleadings, "concerning the application of Georgia law to the entire interpretation of the contract."

It was provided in the Terms of Reference for arbitration that the "arbitrators shall proceed and decide on the record." However, it has been held that arbitrators may draw on their own personal knowledge in making an award. *Bernhardt v. Polygraphic Co.*, 350 U.S. 198 n.4 (1955), citing *Am. Almond Products Co. v. Consolidated Pecan Sales*, 144 F.2d 448 (2d Cir. 1944)…. The Court … concludes that the manner in which the amount of interest payable was determined by the arbitrators is not grounds for vacation under 9 U.S.C. §§10(c) or (d).

[Southwire also contends] that the award of interest should not be enforced as being usurious and against public policy. In making their award, the arbitrators determined that under the French law, the applicable annual rate for the time periods in question should be 10.5% and 9.5% (depending upon the date of maturity of the underpaid invoice), "increasing to fifteen and a half percent and fourteen and a half percent respectively after two months from the date of notification of the award."

Article V(2)(b) of the [New York] Convention provides that enforcement of an award may be refused if such enforcement would be contrary to the public policy of the country where enforcement is sought. However, enforcement of foreign arbitral awards may be denied on this basis only where enforcement would violate the forum country's most basic notions of morality and justice. *Parsons & Whittemore Overseas Co. v. Societe Generale de l'Industrie du Papier (RAKTA)*, 508 F.2d 969, 974 (2d Cir. 1974).

While the exaction of usury ("… [taking] a greater sum for the use of money than the lawful interest." Ga. Code Ann. §57-102) has been characterized by the Georgia Supreme Court as "odious, illegal, and immoral," *First Federal Savings & Loan Assoc. of Atlanta v. Norwood Realty Co.*, 93 S.E.2d 763 (1956), the arbitrators concluded that the Georgia legal rate (7% per annum where the rate is not named in the contract, *see* Ga. Code Ann. §57-101 (1979)) was not applicable under the governing law clause. In Georgia, rates of interest of 9.5% and 10.5% are not prohibited per se—the legal rate may be as high as 10.5% per annum where the parties agree to such in writing, Ga. Code Ann. §57-101 (1979); the rate of interest on a principal sum exceeding $3,000 loaned to a profit corporation may be set without limit by the parties in writing, Ga. Code Ann. §57-118 (1979); interest rates on loans of $100,000 or more are limited only by the agreement of the parties in writing, Ga. Code Ann. §57-119. The existence of these statutes sufficiently convinces the Court that the exaction of interest rates of 9.5% and 10.5% per annum are not such as would violate this country's or this state's most basic notions of morality and justice. *See Parsons*, 508 F.2d at 974. We cannot have trade and commerce in world markets and international waters exclusively on our terms, governed by our laws, and resolved in our courts. *Scherk*, 417 U.S. at 519.

In applying the French law, however, the arbitrators held that the interest rates assessed should rise 5% per annum after two months from the date of the award, to rates of 14.5% and 15.5% per annum, respectively. (The French statute relied upon provides: "In the case of a judgment, the rate of legal interest shall be increased by 5 points upon the expiration of a period of two months from the day on which the court decision has become enforceable, even if only provisionally." [pre-2011] French Law No. 75-619, July 11, 1975.)

An award of interest is made so that a person wrongfully deprived of the use of his money should be made whole for his loss. A penalty, on the other hand, is a sum of money which the law exacts by way of punishment for doing something that is prohibited or omitting to do something that is required to be done. The law does not lightly impose penalties. A foreign law will not be enforced if it is penal only and relates to the punishing of public wrongs as contradistinguished from the redressing of private injuries. *Southern Ry Co. v. Decker*, 62 S.E. 678 (1908); *Sherman & Sons Co. v. Bitting*, 105 S.E. 848 (1921). Agreements to pay fixed sums as damages plainly without reasonable relation to any probable damage which may follow will not be enforced.

The Court concludes that the imposition of an additional 5% interest by the arbitrators in accordance with the French statute is penal rather than compensatory, and bears no reasonable relation to any damage resulting from delay in recovery of the sums awarded. Therefore, that portion of the award which purports to assess the rates of interest at 14.5% and 15.5% will not be enforced or recognized by this Court. Article V(2)(b), [New York Convention]. The rates of 9.5% and 10.5%, as imposed by the arbitrators, will continue to accrue until the date of Judgment….

JUDGMENT OF 21 NOVEMBER 2003
DFT 130 III 66 (Swiss Fed. Trib.)

[excerpted above at pp. 342-45]

CARD v. STRATTON OAKMONT, INC.
933 F.Supp. 806 (D. Minn. 1996)

[excerpted above at pp. 782-84]

I/S STAVBORG v. NATIONAL METAL CONVERTERS, INC.
500 F.2d 424 (2d Cir. 1974)

OAKES, Circuit Judge. National Metal Converters, Inc., appeals from an order entered August 2, 1973, by the district court granting I/S Stavborg's motion to confirm a 2-1 arbitration award made May 3, 1973, in New York City. Appellant [claims that] the decision of the majority of the arbitrators should be reversed on grounds of its being either "clearly erroneous" or "manifestly in disregard" of the applicable law…. [N]ot without some doubt, [we] affirm the award.

On August 8, 1972, appellant, as charterer, agreed to charter a vessel owned by appellee to transport bulk scrap steel from Bath, Maine, to Bilbao, Spain. Clause 37 of the contract of charter party entered into by the parties, governing the arbitration of disputes, reads as follows: "Any and all differences and disputes of whatsoever nature arising out of this Charter, shall be put to arbitration in the City of NEW YORK pursuant to the Laws relating to arbitration there in force, before a board of three persons consisting of one arbitrator to be appointed by the Owners [appellee], one by the Charterers [appellant], and one by the two so chosen. The decision of any two of the three on any point or points shall be final." …

[A] dispute arose concerning the payment of freight due under the charter party agreement; this dispute was submitted to arbitration in New York City. Both parties apparently agreed to submit the dispute to arbitration under clause 37…. Both parties appointed one arbitrator. Both parties agreed … to the appointment of a third arbitrator by the district court below and accepted that court's appointee. Both parties participated fully in the arbitration itself, including the submission of briefs, calling of witnesses and presenting of argument to the arbitrators. After an award for appellee had been handed down, appellant petitioned the district court to modify or vacate that award pursuant to 9 U.S.C. §9…. Appellant's … claims may be stated variously that the arbitrators' decision was "clearly erroneous," or was "in manifest disregard of the applicable law," or amounted to a "reformation" of the charter party agreement …

The facts surrounding the voyage itself were not in dispute…. The vessel, owned by appellee, left Bath, Maine, on or about August 17, 1972, carrying 4,091.95 long tons of bulk scrap steel. The steel was consigned to one Rosal, "F.O.B. stowed vessel." Under the charter party, freight was due to be paid by August 24, 1972, with Rosal having the initial obligation to pay the freight.[14] Rosal did not pay the freight by that date, nor had it been paid at the time of arbitration. The parties agree that the balance of the unpaid freight is $32,742.61. The vessel arrived at Bilbao, Spain, on or about August 27, 1972. Discharge of the cargo commenced on August 28, 1972. Under date of August 30, 1972, some hours

---

14. A bill of lading designating Rosal as the consignee and containing the clause "Freight prepaid as per charter party" was issued prior to sailing but both parties here conceded at arbitration that the freight had not in fact been prepaid.

prior to the completion of the discharge of the cargo, the president of appellant charterer wrote its broker a letter and enclosed a check to cover freight "as good faith of our guarantee in the event freight payment is not received from Rosal...." At some point prior to completion of the cargo discharge on August 31, 1972, the charterer requested that the discharge be discontinued because of Rosal's failure to pay the freight. Rosal's failure to pay was a fact known or that should have been known to the owner appellee because a typewritten addition to the charter party stated "Freight to be paid to Den Norske Creditbank, Stavanger, Norway, account O. H. Meling [appellee]."

In dispute below, then, was the responsibility for the payment of freight in a situation where the consignee, Rosal, had failed to make it. Appellant contended that it was the intent of the parties that the charterer was obligated to pay only to the extent the owner was unable to obtain payment by exercise of its lien. Appellant relies on clause 8 of the charter party...: "Owners [appellee] shall have a lien on the cargo for freight.... Charterers [appellant] also remain responsible for freight ... , but only to such extent as the Owners have been unable to obtain payment thereof by exercising the lien on the cargo." The clear import of this clause, taken alone, is that appellant remained responsible for payment of freight only to the extent that the appellee was unable to recoup freight by means of execution of the lien it held on the cargo. As a practical matter, this clause would cast the burden of taking affirmative action to secure payment of the freight due upon the only party to the agreement guaranteed to have a representative at the scene where the cargo is discharged (the owner's ship's captain). Despite this clause, the owner, aware of the fact that the freight was not prepaid and that the consignee was "initially obligated to pay the freight," did not seek to obtain payment by exercise of its lien on the cargo.

Appellee argues, and the majority of the arbitrators apparently found, that clause 1 of the charter party contradicts clause 8 and therefore the true intent of the parties must be otherwise ascertained. Clause 1 [reads]: "Freight to be telegraphically remitted to Owners by Messrs. Rosal E. Madrid, the Receivers. Charterers to remain fully responsible for fulfilment of charter party."

The arbitral majority speaks of "contradictions" in the charter party (presumably between clauses 1 and 8) and goes on to point out that "under Spanish law the master may not delay unloading the cargo because the freight has not been paid. He must complete discharge and then, if he desires, he can petition the Court to put the cargo under lien."[15] But Spanish law, which would permit a lien to arise after discharge apparently even in the absence of a charter party agreement to that effect, is not at all inconsistent with clause 8.

The arbitral majority then went on to inquire whether the master, after discharge, should have complied with clause 8 (by instituting lien proceedings in the Spanish courts) "in the face of a bill of lading which stated the freight had been paid?" In light of their previous finding that both parties were quite aware that the freight had not been prepaid, *see* note [14] *supra*, we fail to see any relevance the bill of lading might have to the obligation of

---

15. The majority opinion followed this statement with the sentence "In this case, Rosal held a bill of lading which stated the freight had been prepaid." The majority already having stated that this bill of lading was known by all parties to be incorrect in this respect, its treatment of the bill of lading is difficult to comprehend.

appellee under clause 8.[16] As we view it, the majority, in effect, read clause 8 out of the charter party.

It seems rather anomalous, but had the arbitral majority failed to render a written opinion in this case, our ability—ignoring the question of our power—to review that decision would be greatly limited. *See Sobel v. Hertz, Warner & Co.*, 469 F.2d 1211, 1214-15 (2d Cir. 1972). Indeed, the AAA apparently discourages the practice of written arbitral opinions in order to insulate the arbitral process from any judicial review. Faced, however, with a reasoned opinion that is, in our view, clearly erroneous both in logic and result, we are confronted with the question whether it is nevertheless our obligation under the [FAA] to affirm the award.

As was stated in *Sobel*, "the extent of an arbitrator's obligation to explain his award is necessarily related to the scope of judicial review of it." 469 F.2d at 1214. The *Sobel* court did not go so far as to say that where arbitrators voluntarily submit written opinions, they subject themselves to more thorough review by the courts; review in the federal courts is still governed by the provisions of the [FAA], 9 U.S.C. §§10 & 11. Appellant's briefs before this court significantly contain not so much as a passing reference to 9 U.S.C. §10, which is the only provision of the Act which is relevant to our scope of review. That section … exhausts the grounds upon which the district court, or this court on appeal, may disturb the arbitral award. Appellants do not advance any colorable claim under subsections (a), (b) or (c); we are left to consider whether their claim falls under subsection (d).

Appellant argues that an arbitral award may be modified if that award either "manifestly disregards the law," citing *Wilko v. Swan*, 346 U.S. 427 (1953), or is "irrational," citing … *Marcy Lee Mfg Co. v. Cortley Fabrics Co.*, 354 F.2d 42 (2d Cir. 1965).… [T]his court, citing simultaneously both the *Wilko* majority and dissenting opinions on the point, embraced the "manifest disregard" test, saying, however, that it is an "exception" that must be "severely limited." *See Trafalgar Shipping Co. v. Int'l Milling Co.*, 401 F.2d 568, 573 (2d Cir. 1968); *Saxis SS Co. v. Multifacs Int'l Traders, Inc.*, 375 F.2d 577, 582 (2d Cir. 1967).

Illustrative of the difficulty inferior courts are having in "attempts to define manifest disregard'" is our own *Sobel*. The *Sobel* court noted that it "is a truism that an arbitration award will not be vacated for a mistaken interpretation of law …," citing *Wilko* to that effect. The court then said, "But if the arbitrators simply ignore the applicable law, the literal application of a manifest disregard' standard should presumably compel vacation of the award." But perhaps the rubric "manifest disregard" is after all not to be given independent significance; rather it is to be interpreted only in the context of the specific narrow provisions of 9 U.S.C. §§10 & 11, as … this court indicated in *Amicizia Societa Navegazione v. Chilean Nitrate & Iodine Sales Corp.*, 274 F.2d 805, 808 (2d Cir. 1960). Judge Clark there said that "the misapplication … of … rules of contract interpretation does not rise to the statute of a 'manifest disregard' of law." …

[The court did not decide whether or not a non-statutory "manifest disregard" basis for annulment existed under the FAA, but instead assumed arguendo that the FAA permitted annulment on this ground. The court then reasoned that, if annulment on "manifest disregard" grounds were possible, it would provide (as under New York law) that "as long as

16. The dissenting arbitrator took the view that the bill of lading should not be read as indicating that the freight had been prepaid because it reads "Freight Prepaid as per Charter Party," and the charter party itself clearly indicated that the freight had not been prepaid.

arbitrators remain within their jurisdiction and do not reach an irrational result, they may fashion the law to fit the facts before them' and their award will not be set aside because they erred in the determination or application of the law...."] Even under this test, ... the result here remains the same, for even though erroneous the arbitral majority here was not irrationally so.

All of appellant's claims here reduce to the proposition that the arbitrators misconstrued the contract. The arbitral majority justified reading clause 8 out of the charter party by considering clause 1 to conflict with it and then by placing heavy reliance on the August 30 letter from appellant's president, which seemed to acknowledge that appellant was responsible for the freight given Rosal's failure to pay. In a court of law, this evidence would probably not have been properly admitted if, as we feel to be the case, the intent of the parties were made abundantly clear from within the four corners of the charter party. Even if admitted it should have been entitled to little or no weight since the letter was delivered when the discharge was almost complete and the check accompanying the letter was to be held in escrow pending effort by the owner to secure payment from the consignee. We see no basis, however, to reverse the award even though it is based on a clearly erroneous interpretation of the contract. Whatever arbitrators' mistakes of law may be corrected, simple misinterpretations of contracts do not appear one of them.

MANSFIELD, Circuit Judge, Dissenting. I must respectfully dissent. I agree with Judge Oakes' statement that a majority of the arbitrators have "read Clause 8 out of the charter party." However, I cannot agree with his conclusion that appellant's claims here "reduce to the proposition that the arbitrators misconstrued the contract" and that the arbitrators' decision, which he concedes to be "clearly erroneous," was based upon a "misinterpretation of the contract." As I see it, we are not confronted here with a mere error of law or misconstruction of an agreement, which would be insufficient to justify judicial intervention, but with a decision which manifestly disregards the clear and unambiguous terms of the controlling contract from which the arbitrators' powers are drawn, and which finds no basis in the provisions of that contract or elsewhere. Such conditions mandate our intervention.

The pertinent provisions of the charter party contract are crystal clear and there is no conflict between them. Clause 8 plainly and unambiguously provides that "Charterers shall also remain responsible for freight ... but only to such extent as the Owners have been unable to obtain payment thereof by exercising the lien on the cargo." There is not the slightest conflict between this specific obligation and the Charterer's general duty, as set forth in Clause 1 of the contract, "to remain fully responsible for fulfilment of charter party." The charter party obviously obligated the charterer to perform various obligations, including payment of freight according to the terms and conditions of Clause 8, and other specific duties according to the terms of other paragraphs of the agreement (*e.g.*, stowage of cargo, payment of demurrage, ... lay days, etc.).

The Charterer here assumed full responsibility for fulfilment of the charter party, including the obligation to pay the freight upon the owner's compliance with Clause 8, and the Owner obligated itself first to seek payment "by exercising the lien on the cargo." The Owner clearly failed to perform this latter obligation, which was a condition precedent to its exacting payment from the Charterer. The Owner should either have obtained payment of the freight from the consignee prior to or at the time of discharge or, upon completing discharge, have petitioned the court for an order placing the cargo under lien. It did neither....

Although we are obligated to avoid frustrating the purpose of arbitration, which is to resolve disputes quickly and inexpensively by minimizing judicial review or interference, we may not go so far as to countenance a wholly baseless and irrational award. To do so would be to deny due process. Our guideline was well stated by the Supreme Court in *United Steelworkers v. Am. Mfg. Co.*, 363 U.S. 564 (1960), where it said: "Nevertheless, an arbitrator is confined to interpretation and application of the collective bargaining agreement; he does not sit to dispense his own brand of industrial justice. He may of course look for guidance from many sources, yet his award is legitimate only so long as it draws its essence from the collective bargaining agreement. When the arbitrator's words manifest an infidelity to this obligation, courts have no choice but to refuse enforcement of the award." 363 U.S. at 597. Since the arbitrators' award fails to draw its essence from the charter party contract and is wholly baseless and irrational, I would reverse the decision of the district court and direct the entry of judgment vacating the award.

JUDGMENT OF 30 DECEMBER 1994
13 ASA Bull. 217 (Swiss Fed. Trib.) (1995)

[W is a Panamanian company controlled by A and B, two nationals of State K. W entered into a contract ("Fee Agreement") with two companies, F and U, incorporated in State Y, to assist F and U in obtaining orders from State K, particularly for deliveries of M-84 tanks, to the weapons industry of State Y. In the Fee Agreement, F committed to pay for W's services, which was guaranteed by U. F and the Minister of Defense of State K later entered into an agreement for the delivery of 215 M-84 tanks for a price of US$500,546,004 and 11,440,326.29 UK Sterling ("M-84 Agreement"). Subsequently, F terminated the Fee Agreement, claiming it was contrary to the mandatory laws of State K and State Y.

F and the Minister of Defense of State K then entered into a new agreement regarding construction of training facilities for M-84 tanks ("Building Agreement"), for a price of US$39,109,528. Pursuant to the M-84 Agreement, F delivered the tanks, ammunition and spare parts to State K. Although the extent to which F performed its part of the Building Agreement is unclear, F received a down payment of US$6,000,000. On the basis of the M-84 Agreement and Building Agreement, W claimed payment of its fees from F, amounting to 15% of the M-84 Agreement and 10% of the Building Agreement. F refused to pay. Pursuant to an arbitration clause in the Fee Agreement, W commenced an arbitration. The tribunal, seated in Geneva under ICC Rules, ordered F and U to pay to W US$46,099,140.36 and 1,029,629.37 UK Sterling. One member of the tribunal (Professor Mitrovic) dissented. F and U challenged the award under Article 190 of the SLPIL.]...

U grounded its [annulment action on Art. 190(2)(c) and (e)]. It argues that the tribunal accepted a modification of [W's] claim in breach of the principle which forbid it to decide *ultra petita* or at least in breach of the [ICC Rules].

[1.a] [Under Art. 190(2)(c)], an award can be challenged when the tribunal ruled on matters beyond the claim submitted to it or failed to rule on one of the claims. The award granting for something other than what was claimed (*ultra* or *extra petita*) falls within the ambit of this provision.... The rule "*ne eat judex ultra petita partium*" guarantees an aspect of the right to be heard, insofar as it prevents the tribunal from making an award on claims which the parties did not have an opportunity to express themselves on during the proceedings. However, as soon as [the parties' pleadings are] sufficiently developed, the jurisdiction—state court or arbitral tribunal, with the reservation for the latter of any contrary choice made by the parties—must apply on its own motion the law, without being bound by the grounds put forth by the parties. Therefore, if the tribunal applies legal grounds that were not raised by the parties, it does not decide *ultra petita* or *extra petita*, but merely undertakes a new legal characterization of the facts....

By its request for arbitration, W sought joint payment from F and U of the fees allegedly due under the Fee Agreement. In its final briefs, the respondent sought payment only by F, while seeking compensatory damages from U, claiming that the bank was a guarantor.... The tribunal accepted the modification of the claim, because W did not combine claims which were then undivided, but merely sought recovery from the guarantor on other legal grounds. In fact, W, which always based its claims against U on its status as a guarantor, partially withdrew its claim against U (which is always permitting). The tribunal ordered F and U to pay jointly the fees it considered owed under the Fee Agreement, without going beyond the sums claimed by W in its final briefs. In these circumstances, the tribunal did not rule *ultra petita*. W did not make any change nor did it extend its factual allegations underlying its claim in the course of the proceedings; instead, it did characterize in a new legal manner its claim against U. The latter did not suffer any breach of its right to be heard by this change of legal point of view. The factual circumstances underlying the claim remained unchanged and the right to be heard, in Swiss law, does not give to the parties the right to express their opinion regarding the legal characterization of the facts....

1(b). U claims that W could not modify the arguments supporting its claim in its final submission without seriously violating the ICC procedure, and procedural public policy under [Art. 190(2)(e)]. The argument is groundless. The Swiss Federal Tribunal, and a majority of scholars, considers that an award may annulled only if a breach of procedural rules ... triggered in turn a violation of public policy. It must be stressed that *procedural public policy is merely a reservation clause*, that is to say that it only has *protective role and no prescriptive effect*, because the legislator did not want that this principle would be construed in an expansive way....

[A procedural irregularity] would amount to a breach of procedural public policy only insofar as it related to fundamental principles of procedure that are generally recognized, where the failure to comply with such principles would conflict in an unbearable way with the sense of justice in Switzerland. Procedural public policy is also not violated if the result achieved in the award complies with a rule of procedure in force in Switzerland. Here, most Swiss procedural rules allow parties to change their claims if the factual allegations remain unchanged. Thus, the arbitral tribunal did not violate any fundamental legal principle when it permitted the modifications of claims. Pursuant to [Art. 190(2)(e)], whether the tribunal incorrectly or even arbitrarily applied its own procedural rules is not relevant, since the award rendered in the case of an international arbitration cannot be set aside on the only ground that it would amount to an incorrect legal result, because an obvious breach of the law would not necessarily be considered as being incompatible with public policy. It follows that U's claim that the modification of W's claim violated the ICC Rules, is not the basis for a violation of the procedural public policy under [Art. 190(2)(e)].

2. F and U claim that the award conflicts with substantive public policy. They claim that the Fee Agreement violated or evaded the mandatory laws of State K and that the agreement was a promise to pay bribes which was contrary to morals and therefore null and void.

2.a. The claim by F and U is an appellate criticism of the award, because their arguments are grounded to a large extent on factual claims which have no basis in the award. By doing so, F and U mistake the nature of the challenge provided by [Art. 190(2)]. The legislator intentionally limited the grounds that can be raised under Art. 190(2)—compared with those that can be used in domestic arbitration—to reduce the possibilities to obstruct the arbitral process and thus to increase arbitral efficiency. This objective would definitely be compromised if the Federal Tribunal could review freely the factual findings of the arbitral tribunal. The Federal [Legislative] Council originally proposed the possibility of challenging an award for "a manifest and arbitrary denial of justice," but this ground was deliberately removed at the stage of parliamentary debates, so as to restrain to a minimum the possibilities to challenge a decision.... Therefore the factual findings of an international arbitral tribunal cannot be criticized before the Federal Court unless they have been found in contempt of procedural safeguards or breach procedural public policy. F and U do not claim violation of such procedural safeguards. As for the reservation on public policy, the appellants did not specified the essential procedural principles and unanimously recognized that the violation of which would infringe in an unbearable way the sense of justice in Switzerland. When F alleges that the tribunal was mistaken about its own procedure, that it ascertained the facts in an approximate way without respecting the principle of "*instruction d'office*" (investigation on its own motion), ... or that it mistakenly assessed pieces of evidence. The appellant is claiming at the most, an incorrect application of the law, or even arbitrariness, but not any breach of procedural public policy. Therefore, the Federal Tribunal will use as a basis for its decision the factual findings of the arbitral tribunal.

2.b. [An award] breaches public policy only if it conflicts with fundamental legal principles to the extent to become incompatible with the legal order and the system of fundamental values. Among these principles are to be found notably the respect of contractual commitments, the prohibition of "*abus de droit*" and of discriminatory measures, as well as protection of people who lack legal capacity. Public policy, within the meaning of [Art. 190(2)(e),] is only an incompatibility clause, so that it would not have any positive or normative effect on the disputed legal relationships.... [W]hen the tribunal must apply a substantive law other than Swiss law, nothing justifies correcting its award ... by referring to Swiss public order. The uniform application of [Art. 190(2)(e)] therefore requires having regard to a universal notion of public policy, which considers whether the award is contrary to legal or moral fundamental principles recognized by the civilized States.

2.c. F and U claim that the Fee Agreement does not comply with the mandatory provisions of the law of State K., particularly Decree No. 4A/88 and Rules issued by the Ministry of Defence, which prohibit middle-men or agents in weapons trade. F and U reason that, pursuant to [Art. 19 of the SLPIL[17]], the tribunal should have had taken into account these provisions.

---

17. Article 19 provides:

"If, pursuant to Swiss legal concepts, the legitimate and manifestly preponderant interests of a party so require, a mandatory provision of a law other than that designated by this Code may be taken into account if the circumstances of the case are closely connected with that law. In deciding whether such a provision must be taken into account, its purpose is to be considered as well as whether its application would result in an adequate decision under Swiss concepts of law."

[Art. 19] empowers the judge to take into account foreign law regarding the status of an agreement, if the foreign law is mandatory. Most scholars do not regard this provision as compelling an international arbitral tribunal, particularly in the case of a choice of law, to apply foreign law to the contractual status. At the least—and on this point the scholars are unanimous—the disrespect of this law is not itself contrary to public policy in the meaning given by [Art. 190(2)(e)]. This opinion is all the more convincing given that [Art. 187 of the SLPIL] made express reservations, in the field of international arbitration, regarding the parties' autonomy to choose the applicable law and that [Art. 19] is a discretionary authority. However, there is no need to consider this issue here, as the tribunal found that the rules of the law of State K, to which the appellants are making references, are not mandatory. Because F and U did not demonstrate that these findings were reached in violation of public policy, they are binding on the Federal Tribunal. Hence, there is no basis for F and U's arguments....

2.d. F and U claimed that the Fee Agreement, according to its genuine content, obligates F to pay bribes to W so that the agreement is null and void under Swiss law ... and incompatible with substantive public policy. The promises as to payment of bribes, according to the Swiss legal conception, are contrary to morals and therefore null and void. These promises also conflict with public policy [citing Swiss authority]. The arbitral tribunal followed this reasoning. However, the tribunal concluded that it had not been shown that the parties to the agreement had jointly shared unlawful goals (such as bribery), and that it was not demonstrated that W, at the time of entering into the Fee Agreement, had the intention, without F and U knowing, to allocate a part of its fees to the payment of bribes to civil servants of State K. Thus, F and U's argument is not in accordance with the factual findings of the arbitral tribunal. In fact, as we previously said, the argument is a futile critic of the findings of the arbitral tribunal, which is irrelevant if the tribunal did not violate procedural public policy.... The challenges are therefore without basis ...

NORTHCORP CORP. v. TRIAD INTERNATIONAL MARKETING SA
811 F.2d 1265 (9th Cir. 1987)

BROWNING, JUDGE. In October 1970 Northrop and Triad entered into a 'Marketing Agreement,' under which Triad became Northrop's exclusive marketing representative [for certain armaments] in return for commissions on sales. Northrop made substantial sales to Saudi Arabia and paid Triad a substantial part of the commissions due under the Marketing Agreement. On September 17, 1975, the Council of Ministers of Saudi Arabia issued Decree No. 1275, prohibiting the payment of commissions in connection with armaments contracts. Northrop ceased paying commissions to Triad [which protested and then sought arbitration under AAA rules.]

[The Marketing Agreement contained a choice-of-law clause, which provided "The validity and construction of this Agreement shall be governed by the laws of the State of California." The arbitrators relied on the choice-of-law clause and rejected Northrop's argument that Saudi Decree No. 1275 rendered the Marketing Agreement unenforceable. The arbitrators also rejected Northrup's argument that the Marketing Agreement was invalid under California Civil Code §1511, which provides "performance of an obligation ... is excused ... [when] such performance ... is prevented ... by operation of law." The arbitrators held that the Saudi decree did not prevent Northrop's payment of the commissions, but instead only exposed it to possible liability under Saudi law, adopting reasoning from a Ninth Circuit decision: "It may be that Boeing has gotten itself into some trouble with the government of Kuwait by setting up and terminating a selling agency in a manner allegedly violative of Kuwait law. But as between Boeing and Alghanim, we think the contract provision must govern." *Alghanim v. Boeing Co.*, 477 F.2d 143, 150 (9th Cir. 1973).

Northrup refused to comply with the award and sought to annul it in the United States. In challenging the award, Northrup argued that the arbitrators had violated U.S. public policy.]

The district court examined the language and history of Saudi Arabia Decree No. 1275 in some detail and concluded that it prohibited the payment of the commissions involved in this case. But ... the question was whether payment was prohibited under California law, not Saudi law, and the answer to that question turned not upon whether Decree No. 1275 stated a rule of Saudi law under which the payment would be illegal, but rather upon whether the existence of such a rule in Saudi law excused performance under California Civil Code §1511.

Northrup also argues that if the Saudi Decree did not excuse performance of the Marketing Agreement under California [law], the choice-of-law clause in the Agreement should be set aside and the Saudi Decree should be applied directly to invalidate the Marketing Agreement under the principle announced in *Restatement (Second) Conflict of Laws* §187(2)(b) (1971). However, choice-of-law and choice-of-forum provisions in international commercial contracts ... should be enforced absent strong reasons to set them aside.... We agree with the arbitrators that the general principle of conflicts Northrup cites is not sufficient standing alone to overcome the strong policy consideration announced in *Scherk* and *Bremen*....

Northrup argues "that California law, as a matter of public policy, prohibits enforcement of a contract where performance of the contract would be illegal under the law of a foreign state. This rule is codified in California Civil Code §1511...." ... We do not regard §1511 as a declaration that it is the public policy of the state of California that contracts unenforceable under the laws of any other jurisdiction shall not be enforced in California. Section 1511 is a codification of a rule of purely private law embodying a common-law defense in an action between contracting parties for breach. If the statutory codification of such rules of contract law were regarded as converting them into principles of public policy cognizable only in courts, the capacity of arbitrators to resolve contract disputes would be seriously diminished.

Northrup's argument that the courts should decline to enforce the Marketing Agreement because it conflicts with the public policy Saudi Arabia announced in Decree No. 1275 flies in the face of the parties' agreement that the law of California, and not Saudi Arabia, would determine the validity and construction of the contract. Northrop has cited no California regulation, statute, or court decision demonstrating that enforcement of a contract to pay commissions to a marketing representative is contrary to the public policy of California, whether such commissions are illegal under the law of a foreign state or are not. Northrop's most substantial argument is that the public policy reflected in Decree No. 1275 was also the policy of the United States Department of Defense. In its opinion the district court said "it is clear [the Department of Defense] wished to conform its policy precisely to that announced by Saudi Arabia." ... To justify refusal to enforce an arbitration award on grounds of public policy, the policy "must be well defined and dominant." The Saudi

Arabian policy the Department of Defense arguably adopted was neither. It is clear the Department wished to accommodate Saudi Arabian interests and sensibilities. It is also clear, however, that the Department was interested in encouraging sales to Saudi Arabia of American manufactured military equipment, and considered the efforts of Triad critical to that end.... [The district court concluded that commissions on weapons were flatly prohibited,] but even if we were to agree, we could not say on this record the policy the Department adopted was "well-defined and dominant." The district court's refusal to enforce the arbitrators' decision on the ground that it conflicted with the policy of the Department of Defense was, therefore, unwarranted....

DESPUTEAUX v. EDITIONS CHOUETTE
[2001] J.Q. No. 1510 (Québec Ct. App.)

JUSTICE ROUSSEAU-HOULE. The picture of Caillou is known by children throughout the world. The appellant Hélène Desputeaux is the creator of this picture. Her first drawings of Caillou illustrated children books, the text of which was written by Christine l'Heureux, principal shareholder and principal director/administrator of the Editions Chouette (1987) Inc....

[The parties entered into a variety of agreements regarding Caillou.] On 1 September 1993, the parties entered into a license agreement for the use of the fictional character Caillou. In this agreement, Desputeaux and L'Heureux are described as co-authors of the work consisting of a fictional character with the name of Caillou. They sell to Editions Chouette, with the exception of the rights granted in the [parties' earlier] publishing agreements, the following rights for the entire world without specifying the contract term: (a) to reproduce in any form and on any media or merchandise; (b) to adapt Caillou for the purpose of realisation and production of recording work and/or audiovisual work, public performance and/or communication to the public; [and] (c) to adapt Caillou for the purpose of realisation and production of recording work and/or audiovisual work, public performance and/or communication to the public every resulting work.... The co-authors renounce any claim they might have in respect of their moral rights to Caillou and grant to Editions Chouette the right to grant any sub-license to third-parties without the co-author's approval.... Article 37 of the License Agreement provides: "37. Save express renunciation, all disputes on the interpretation of this contract is submitted, following the request of a party, to an arbitrator." ... [Disputes arose between the parties, which (following litigation in the Québec courts) were submitted to arbitration. The arbitrator made an award in favor of Editions Chouette. This application to annul the award followed.]

Determination of the arbitrators' mandate is not easy. It seems that the parties agreed that it encompasses interpretation of the License Agreement and [the parties' other agreements], with the view to determine the way in which the license should be commercially operated. In addition, the arbitrator was informed that the appellant had the intention to claim the termination of these agreements before the superior Court....

Before the [arbitrator], no witness testified and no document was disputed except as for its legal meaning. First, the arbitrator reviewed the [parties'] agreements. Stressing that these ones are bearing Christine L'Heureux' signature as "Publisher" and Hélène Desputeaux' as author, it was submitted that this was not the reality. Pursuant to the Copyright Act both could have claimed the status of author towards Caillou. This work was the result of a collaboration under article 2 of the Copyright Act.

According to the arbitrator, the [License Agreement] should be thought within its context. It was signed after lengthy negotiations among the parties assisted by their counsels. In this agreement, Desputeaux and L'Heureux recognize themselves as co-authors of the character Caillou. Some letters exchanged after the agreement was concluded ... confirmed this recognition so that the arbitrator did not hesitate to reject the argument that this agreement was a simulation. According to the arbitrator, by this contract the co-authors sold to the Editions Chouette the rights to commercialize Caillou in the entire world.... Without making any reference to the public policy provisions of the Law of Québec on the artists' professional status ..., [the arbitrator] considered that since the parties did not specify any term to the contract, the latter benefited from the protection provided by Art. 9 of the Copyright Act, that is 50 years after the last co-author's death.

[The Québec court referred to the Québec arbitration statute and its annulment provisions (964 C.p.c), which parallel those of Article 34 of the UNCITRAL Model Law. The court noted that annulment of the award is the only recourse against it.] ... To my opinion, the award exceeds the parties' intentions as it went further than the mere interpretation of the contractual documents. By deciding of the legal status of Desputeaux and L'Heureux with respect to the Caillou's character[,] a work protected by the law, the arbitrator went beyond its competence. Indeed, pursuant to article 946.5 C.p.c [paralleling Article 34(2)(b)(ii)] ... a dispute regarding the status and legal capacity of natural person or other questions involving public policy may not be resolved by arbitration. [The court also referred to article 2639 C.c.Q,] which provides:

"2639. Cannot be submitted to arbitration, a dispute regarding status and legal capacity of natural person], family matters or other questions involving public policy. However, the arbitration agreement should not be barred from application because the applicable rules to decide on the dispute have a public policy character." ...

It is not necessary to decide whether the consideration of this moral aspect of the copyright could be sufficient, to exclude the competence of the arbitrator since the present arbitral award should, to my opinion, be declared null and void pursuant to Article 37 of the Act that grants the Federal Court, in conjunction with provincial courts, an exclusive competence to decide on any procedure pertaining to the application of the Act. [Article 37 of the Copyright Act provides: "The Federal Court, in conjunction with the provincial courts, is competent of all proceedings regarding application of the present statute...."] The authorship of the copyright as well as disputes concerning the scope and validity of this right must be submitted exclusively to state courts since the decisions rendered are, as a matter of principle, binding on third parties and thus form the essence of judicial decisions.

In this case, the arbitrator ruled that Desputeaux and L'Heureux were co-authors of a work created in collaboration and that they had assigned all their property rights ... in the publishing contracts.... After observing that the parties describe themselves as co-authors, he found nothing in article 18.1 of the publishing contracts to change this conclusion. By deciding on the monopoly granted by the Act to an author, the arbitrator rendered a decision that not only impacts the authorship of the work, but that bound third parties....

[T]he arbitrator, in this cause, thought that he could determine whether the illustrator and the narrator qualifies themselves as co-authors pursuant to the *Act*. The fact that the two parties recognized themselves as such entitled the arbitrator to consider this fact but did not entitle him, without exceeding its competence, to determine that they definitely were co-authors of a work under the Act. It is not for the authors of a work to decide its qualification; this is determined by the Act and the facts.... In every case, the court will expect to see the work in dispute, to examine the topic and to hear testimony before deciding on the existence of the monopoly granted by the legislator.

If one assumed that the arbitrator only applied the Act's rules of public policy, he would then have misapplied them and his award would be no less invalid. No testimonial or documentary evidence was presented to the arbitrator with respect to the work or the involvement of the parties in its development. [Therefore, the arbitrator] was not able, with fairness, to [decide] the question of the qualification of the work....

I would add that the arbitrator, after having recognized that Desputeaux and L'Heureux were professional artists and that their agreements were subjected to the *Statute on the professional status of artists* ..., had to ensure that the mandatory formalities stipulated for by article 31 and 34 of this Act had been respected when concluding the contract. The Copyright Act states that concession of an interest within the copyright is valid only if made in written form and signed by the owner of the right or by its duly authorized agent.... In the fields it applies, the Law of Québec specifies provisions that must be included in any agreement between an artist and a publisher....[18] The arbitrator failed to recognize that some of these provisions imposed by the legislator did not appear on the license agreement and in the endorsement.... When an arbitrator has, pursuant to his mandate, to apply public policy rules, he must apply them correctly, that is to say in the same manner that the courts. The award could therefore be set aside because the arbitrator did not apply or misapply the provisions of articles 31 and 34.... I therefore propose to reverse the Superior Court's decision, ... and to set aside the award.

HALL STREET ASSOCIATES, LLC v. MATTEL, INC.
128 S.Ct. 1396 (2008)

JUSTICE SOUTER delivered the opinion of the Court. The [FAA] provides for expedited judicial review to confirm, vacate, or modify arbitration awards. The question here is

---

18. [Article 31 provides:

"The agreement has to be made in writing in two exemplary and clearly identifies: (1) the nature of the contract; (2) the work or the group of works that are its subject; (3) Any assignment of rights and any licensing agreed by the artist, the aims, the term or the way of determining the term and the territorial extension for which the right is assigned and the license given, as well as any assignment of property rights or of use of the work; (4) the possibility or the impossibility of transferring to third parties the license granted to the broadcaster; (5) the monetary compensation owed to the artists as well as terms and payments modalities; (6) the periodicity according to which the broadcaster has to inform the artist of the operations regarding works specified by the contract and regarding to which a monetary compensation remains owed after the signature of the contract."

Article 34 provides:

"Every understanding between a broadcaster and an artist reserving to the broadcaster the exclusivity of a future work of the artist or recognising to him the right to decide of its diffusing, must, in addition to comply with requirements of article 31: (1) concern a work determined at least regarding its nature; (2) be terminable at the request of the artist at the end of period of time agreed between the parties or after the creation of a determined number by this ones; (3) stipulate that the exclusivity ends to apply with respect to a reserved work when, after the termination of cooling-off period, the broadcaster, despite having been formally noticed, did not broadcast it; (4) specify the cooling-off period agreed among the parties for application of paragraph 30."—ED.]

whether statutory grounds for prompt vacatur and modification may be supplemented by contract. We hold that the statutory grounds are exclusive.

This case began as a lease dispute between landlord, petitioner Hall Street Associates, LLC, and tenant, respondent Mattel, Inc. The ... leases provided that the tenant would indemnify the landlord for any costs resulting from the failure of the tenant or its predecessor lessees to follow environmental laws while using the premises. Tests of the property's well water in 1998 showed high levels of trichloroethylene ("TCE")…. After the Oregon Department of Environmental Quality ("DEQ") discovered even more pollutants, Mattel stopped drawing from the well and ... signed a consent order with the DEQ providing for cleanup of the site.

After Mattel gave notice of intent to terminate the lease in 2001, Hall Street filed this suit, contesting Mattel's right to vacate on the date it gave, and claiming that the lease obliged Mattel to indemnify Hall Street for costs of cleaning up the TCE, among other things. Following a bench trial ..., Mattel won on the termination issue, and after an unsuccessful try at mediating the indemnification claim, the parties proposed to submit to arbitration. The ... parties drew up an arbitration agreement, which the court approved and entered as an order. One paragraph of the agreement provided that

> "[t]he U.S. District Court for the District of Oregon may enter judgment upon any award, either by confirming the award or by vacating, modifying or correcting the award. The Court shall vacate, modify or correct any award: (i) where the arbitrator's findings of facts are not supported by substantial evidence, or (ii) where the arbitrator's conclusions of law are erroneous."

Arbitration took place, and the arbitrator decided for Mattel. In particular, he held that no indemnification was due, because the lease obligation to follow all applicable federal, state, and local environmental laws did not require compliance with the testing requirements of the Oregon Drinking Water Quality Act ("Oregon Act"); that Act the arbitrator characterized as dealing with human health as distinct from environmental contamination.

Hall Street then filed a ... Motion for Order Vacating Modifying And/Or Correcting Arbitration Accord, on the ground that failing to treat the Oregon Act as an applicable environmental law under the terms of the lease was legal error. The District Court agreed, vacated the award, and remanded for further consideration by the arbitrator. The court expressly invoked the standard of review chosen by the parties in the arbitration agreement, which included review for legal error, and cited *LaPine Tech. Corp. v. Kyocera Corp.*, 130 F.3d 884, 889 (C.A.9 1997), for the proposition that the FAA leaves the parties "free ... to draft a contract that sets rules for arbitration and dictates an alternative standard of review." [After appellate proceedings, the Ninth Circuit relied on its subsequent decision, in *Kyocera Corp. v. Prudential-Bache Trade Servs., Inc.*, 341 F.3d 987, 1000 (2003), overruling *LaPine*, to hold that, "[u]nder *Kyocera* the terms of the arbitration agreement controlling the mode of judicial review are unenforceable and severable." 113 Fed.Appx. 272, 272-273 (2004).] ... [W]e granted certiorari to decide whether the grounds for vacatur and modification provided by §§10 and 11 of the FAA are exclusive. We agree with the Ninth Circuit that they are, but vacate and remand for consideration of independent issues.

Congress enacted the FAA to replace judicial indisposition to arbitration with a "national policy favoring [it] and plac[ing] arbitration agreements on equal footing with all other contracts." *Buckeye*, 546 U.S. at 443…. [I]n cases falling within a court's jurisdiction, the Act makes contracts to arbitrate "valid, irrevocable, and enforceable," so long as their subject involves "commerce." §2.... The Act also supplies mechanisms for enforcing arbitration awards: a judicial decree confirming an award, an order vacating it, or an order modifying or correcting it. §§9-11. An application for any of these orders will get stream-lined treatment as a motion, obviating the separate contract action that would usually be necessary to enforce or tinker with an arbitral award in court. §6. Under the terms of §9, a court "must" confirm an arbitration award "unless" it is vacated, modified, or corrected "as prescribed" in §§10 and 11. Section 10 lists grounds for vacating an award, while §11 names those for modifying or correcting one.

The Courts of Appeals have split over the exclusiveness of these statutory grounds when parties take the FAA shortcut to confirm, vacate, or modify an award, with some saying the recitations are exclusive, and others regarding them as mere threshold provisions open to expansion by agreement. As mentioned already, when this litigation started, the Ninth Circuit was on the threshold side of the split, *see LaPine*, from which it later departed en banc in favor of the exclusivity view, *see Kyocera*, which it followed in this case. We now hold that §§10 and 11 respectively provide the FAA's exclusive grounds for expedited vacatur and modification.

Hall Street makes two main efforts to show that the grounds set out for vacating or modifying an award are not exclusive, taking the position, first, that expandable judicial review authority has been accepted as the law since *Wilko v. Swan*. This, however, was not what *Wilko* decided, which was that §14 of the Securities Act of 1933 voided any agreement to arbitrate claims of violations of that Act, a holding since overruled by *Rodriguez de Quijas v. Shearson/American Express, Inc.*, 490 U.S. 477, 484 (1989). Although it is true that the Court's discussion includes some language arguably favoring Hall Street's position, arguable is as far as it goes.

The *Wilko* Court was explaining that arbitration would undercut the Securities Act's buyer protections when it remarked (citing FAA §10) that "[p]ower to vacate an [arbitration] award is limited," and went on to say that "the interpretations of the law by the arbitrators in contrast to manifest disregard [of the law] are not subject, in the federal courts, to judicial review for error in interpretation." Hall Street reads this statement as recognizing "manifest disregard of the law" as a further ground for vacatur on top of those listed in §10, and some Circuits have read it the same way. Hall Street sees this supposed addition to §10 as the camel's nose: if judges can add grounds to vacate (or modify), so can contracting parties.

But this is too much for *Wilko* to bear. Quite apart from its leap from a supposed judicial expansion by interpretation to a private expansion by contract, Hall Street overlooks the fact that the statement it relies on expressly rejects just what Hall Street asks for here, general review for an arbitrator's legal errors. Then there is the vagueness of *Wilko*'s phrasing. Maybe the term "manifest disregard" was meant to name a new ground for review, but maybe it merely referred to the §10 grounds collectively, rather than adding to them. *See, e.g., Mitsubishi*, 473 U.S. at 656 (Stevens, J., dissenting) ("Arbitration awards are only reviewable for manifest disregard of the law, 9 U.S.C. §§10, 207"). Or, as some courts have thought, "manifest disregard" may have been shorthand for §10(a)(3) or §10(a)(4), the paragraphs authorizing vacatur when the arbitrators were "guilty of misconduct" or "exceeded their powers." *See, e.g., Kyocera*, [341 F.3d] at 997. We, when speaking as a Court, have merely taken the *Wilko* language as we found it, without embellishment, *see First Options*, 514 U.S. at 942, and now that its meaning is implicated, we see no reason to accord it the significance that Hall Street urges.

Second, Hall Street says that the agreement to review for legal error ought to prevail simply because arbitration is a creature of contract, and the FAA is "motivated, first and foremost, by a congressional desire to enforce agreements into which parties ha[ve] entered." *Dean Witter Reynolds Inc. v. Byrd*, 470 U.S. 213, 220 (1985). But, again, we think the argument comes up short. Hall Street is certainly right that the FAA lets parties tailor some, even many features of arbitration by contract, including the way arbitrators are chosen, what their qualifications should be, which issues are arbitrable, along with procedure and choice of substantive law. But to rest this case on the general policy of treating arbitration agreements as enforceable as such would be to beg the question, which is whether the FAA has textual features at odds with enforcing a contract to expand judicial review following the arbitration.

To that particular question we think the answer is yes, that the text compels a reading of the §§10 and 11 categories as exclusive. To begin with, even if we assumed §§10 and 11 could be supplemented to some extent, it would stretch basic interpretive principles to expand the stated grounds to the point of evidentiary and legal review generally. Sections 10 and 11, after all, address egregious departures from the parties' agreed-upon arbitration: "corruption," "fraud," "evident partiality," "misconduct," "misbehavior," "exceed[ing] ... powers," "evident material miscalculation," "evident material mistake," "award[s] upon a matter not submitted;" the only ground with any softer focus is "imperfect[ions]," and a court may correct those only if they go to "[a] matter of form not affecting the merits." Given this emphasis on extreme arbitral conduct, the old rule of *ejusdem generis* has an implicit lesson to teach here. Under that rule, when a statute sets out a series of specific items ending with a general term, that general term is confined to covering subjects comparable to the specifics it follows. Since a general term included in the text is normally so limited, then surely a statute with no textual hook for expansion cannot authorize contracting parties to supplement review for specific instances of outrageous conduct with review for just any legal error. "Fraud" and a mistake of law are not cut from the same cloth.

That aside, expanding the detailed categories would rub too much against the grain of the §9 language, where provision for judicial confirmation carries no hint of flexibility. On application for an order confirming the arbitration award, the court "must grant" the order "unless the award is vacated, modified, or corrected as prescribed in §§10 and 11 of this title." There is nothing malleable about "must grant," which unequivocally tells courts to grant confirmation in all cases, except when one of the "prescribed" exceptions applies. This does not sound remotely like a provision meant to tell a court what to do just in case the parties say nothing else.[19] ...

---

19. Hall Street claims that §9 supports its position, because it allows a court to confirm an award only "[i]f the parties in their agreement have agreed that a judgment of the court shall be entered upon the award made pursuant to the arbitration." Hall Street argues that this language "expresses Congress's intent that a court must enforce the agreement of the parties as to whether, and under what circumstances, a judgment shall be entered." It is a peculiar argument, converting agreement as a necessary condition for judicial enforcement into a sufficient condition for a court to bar enforcement. And the text is otherwise problematical for Hall Street: §9 says that if the parties have agreed to judicial enforcement, the court "must grant" confirmation unless grounds for vacatur or modification exist under §10 or §11. The sentence nowhere predicates the

[A]nyone who thinks Congress might have understood §9 as a default provision should turn back to §5 for an example of what Congress thought a default provision would look like: "[i]f in the agreement provision be made for a method of naming or appointing an arbitrator ... such method shall be followed; but if no method be provided therein, or if a method be provided and any party thereto shall fail to avail himself of such method, ... then upon the application of either party to the controversy the court shall designate and appoint an arbitrator...." "[I]f no method be provided" is a far cry from "must grant ... unless" in §9.

Instead of fighting the text, it makes more sense to see the three provisions, §§9-11, as substantiating a national policy favoring arbitration with just the limited review needed to maintain arbitration's essential virtue of resolving disputes straightaway. Any other reading opens the door to the full-bore legal and evidentiary appeals that can "rende[r] informal arbitration merely a prelude to a more cumbersome and time-consuming judicial review process," *Kyocera*, 341 F.3d at 998, and bring arbitration theory to grief in post-arbitration process....

In holding that §§10 and 11 provide exclusive regimes for the review provided by the statute, we do not purport to say that they exclude more searching review based on authority outside the statute as well. The FAA is not the only way into court for parties wanting review of arbitration awards: they may contemplate enforcement under state statutory or common law, for example, where judicial review of different scope is arguable. But here we speak only to the scope of the expeditious judicial review under §§9, 10, and 11, deciding nothing about other possible avenues for judicial enforcement of arbitration awards....

JUSTICE STEVENS, with whom JUSTICE KENNEDY joins, dissenting. May parties to an ongoing lawsuit agree to submit their dispute to arbitration subject to the caveat that the trial judge should refuse to enforce an award that rests on an erroneous conclusion of law? Prior to Congress' enactment of the [FAA] in 1925, the answer to that question would surely have been "Yes."[20] Today, however, the Court holds that the FAA does not merely authorize the vacation or enforcement of awards on specified grounds, but also forbids enforcement of perfectly reasonable judicial review provisions in arbitration agreements fairly negotiated by the parties and approved by the district court. Because this result conflicts with the primary purpose of the FAA and ignores the historical context in which the Act was passed, I respectfully dissent.

Prior to the passage of the FAA, American courts were generally hostile to arbitration. They refused, with rare exceptions, to order specific enforcement of executory agreements to arbitrate. Section 2 of the FAA responded to this hostility by making written arbitration agreements "valid, irrevocable, and enforceable." This section, which is the centerpiece of the FAA, reflects Congress' main goal in passing the legislation: "to abrogate the general

court's judicial action on the parties' having agreed to specific standards; if anything, it suggests that, so long as the parties contemplated judicial enforcement, the court must undertake such enforcement under the statutory criteria. In any case, the arbitration agreement here did not specifically predicate entry of judgment on adherence to its judicial review standard....

20. *See Klein v. Catara*, 14 F.Cas. 732, 735 (C.C.D. Mass. 1814) ("If the parties wish to reserve the law for the decision of the court, they may stipulate to that effect in the submission; they may restrain or enlarge its operation as they please") (Story, J.).

common-law rule against specific enforcement of arbitration agreements," *Southland Corp. v. Keating*, 465 U.S. 1, 18 (1984) (Stevens, J., concurring in part and dissenting in part), and to "ensur[e] that private arbitration agreements are enforced according to their terms," *Volt Info. Sciences,* 489 U.S. at 478. Given this settled understanding of the core purpose of the FAA, the interests favoring enforceability of parties' arbitration agreements are stronger today than before the FAA was enacted. As such, there is more—and certainly not less—reason to give effect to parties' fairly negotiated decisions to provide for judicial review of arbitration awards for errors of law....

It is true that a wooden application of "the old rule of *ejusdem generis*," might support an inference that the categories listed in §§10 and 11 are exclusive, but the literal text does not compel that reading—a reading that is flatly inconsistent with the overriding interest in effectuating the clearly expressed intent of the contracting parties. A listing of grounds that must always be available to contracting parties simply does not speak to the question whether they may agree to additional grounds for judicial review. Moreover, in light of the historical context and the broader purpose of the FAA, §§10 and 11 are best understood as a shield meant to protect parties from hostile courts, not a sword with which to cut down parties' "valid, irrevocable and enforceable" agreements to arbitrate their disputes subject to judicial review for errors of law.[21] §2....

NOTES

1. *Substantive bases for annulling awards under national arbitration legislation*. Different national arbitration statutes provide different bases for annulling arbitral awards. Consider the general terms of the UNCITRAL Model Law, the SLPIL, the English Arbitration Act, the FAA and the Chinese Arbitration Law. In general terms, how are the various statutes similar and how do they differ? How significant are the similarities? The differences?

2. *National arbitration legislation providing exclusive grounds for annulling awards*. Consider the substantive grounds for annulling awards which are available under the arbitration statutes excerpted above. Are the bases set forth in Article 34 of the Model Law exclusive (that is, can an award be annulled based on grounds *other than* those in Article 34)? Compare Article 190 of the SLPIL, §10 of the FAA, §§67-69 of the English Arbitration Act and Article 58 of the Chinese Arbitration Law. Does each statute set forth an exclusive and exhaustive list of annulment grounds? What purposes does this serve?

   Consider the U.S. Supreme Court's analysis of §§9-11 of the FAA in *Hall Street*. What is the basis for the Court's decision that §10 of the FAA sets forth the exclusive basis for annulment of awards made in the United States? Note that the Court reaches its conclusion regarding the exclusivity of the statutory annulment grounds even in the (somewhat unusual) context of a post-dispute arbitration agreement executed to resolve an ongoing litigation, which received judicial approval. (Note however, that the Court remanded the case to the lower courts to consider whether the Federal Rules of

---

21. In the years before the passage of the FAA, arbitration awards were subject to thorough and broad judicial review.... In §§10 and 11 of the FAA, Congress significantly limited the grounds for judicial vacatur or modification of such awards in order to protect arbitration awards from hostile and meddlesome courts.

Civil Procedure would have permitted the parties' agreement to heightened judicial review.)

Consider the grounds for annulment set forth in §10 of the FAA. Under *Hall Street*, what is the status of annulment actions based on (a) public policy, and (b) nonarbitrability? Did the Court really mean to exclude annulment of awards on these grounds?

What is the rationale for narrowly limited grounds of annulment? Consider:

> "it is in the interest of efficient arbitration proceedings that review of arbitration awards should be limited in scope and that annulment of or refusal to recognize an award should be possible only in exceptional circumstances." *Eco Swiss China Time Ltd v. Benetton Int'l NV*, Case No. C-126/97, [1999] E.C.R. I-3055 (E.C.J.).

Is that persuasive? What are the countervailing policy considerations? What motivates the Argentine legislation excerpted above at p. 1136?

3. *Burden of proof in annulment action under national arbitration legislation*. What party bears the burden of proof in an annulment action? How explicit is this in each arbitration statute excerpted above? As discussed below, a central achievement of the New York Convention was to place the burden of proving grounds for non-recognition of an award on the party resisting recognition. *See infra* pp. 1191, 1195-96. Should the burden of proof required for annulment of an award differ from that required for non-recognition of an award? Recall that, under the Geneva Convention, the award creditor bore the burden of proving the award's validity. *See supra* pp. 30-33, 35-36.

4. *Annulment is discretionary, not mandatory, under leading arbitration statutes*. Suppose one of the grounds for annulment, specified in an arbitration statute, is fulfilled. In these circumstances, is annulment of the award required, or is it merely permitted, but not mandatory? Consider Article 34(2) of the Model Law, which provides that an "award *may* be set aside by the court ... only if" specified grounds are present. Is that text not discretionary? Compare the text of Article 190 of the SLPIL, §10 of the FAA, §§67-69 of the English Arbitration Act and Article 58 of the Chinese Arbitration Law. Which statutes make annulment mandatory? Which approach is appropriate? Why might annulment not be ordered even if one of the stated grounds permitted it?

5. *Timing for annulment actions under national arbitration legislation*. To what extent do arbitration statutes impose time limits for annulment actions? What are these time limits? What is the rationale for such limits?

6. *National arbitration statutes providing limited grounds for annulment of awards*. Compare the statutory grounds for annulment under Article 34 of the UNCITRAL Model Law to those available for non-recognition of an award (under Article V of the New York Convention and Article 36 of the Model Law). Are there any differences in the available grounds? Compare the statutory grounds for annulment under Article 190 of the SLPIL. Are these grounds broader or narrower than under the Model Law? Which statutory provisions provide for the narrowest grounds for annulment? Which statutory provisions provide for the broadest grounds for annulment?

7. *National arbitration legislation permitting more extensive grounds for annulling awards*. Some arbitration legislation continues to permit far-reaching judicial review of awards in actions to annul awards made locally. For example, Argentine's arbitration statute permits annulment on any ground available for review of a trial court judgment. Note also the extensive judicial review available in Egyptian courts (as reflected in *Chromalloy*, *infra* pp. 1174-77). Is this extensive judicial review of awards

appropriate? Why should awards be subject to any more limited grounds of judicial review than first instance court decisions?

Consider Article 58 of the Chinese Arbitration Law. What bases does it permit for annulling an award made in China? *See also* Belgian Judicial Code, Art. 1717(3).

8. *Appropriate bases for actions to annul an award.* What bases *should* be available for an action to annul an international arbitral award? Compare the Argentine legislation with the FAA and UNCITRAL Model Law. Is it appropriate to provide no judicial review? To provide *de novo* judicial review? What sort of review will best serve the international arbitration process?

9. *Possible limits imposed by New York Convention on bases for annulment of awards.* Does the New York Convention impose any limits on the grounds a Contracting State may rely on to annul awards made within its territory? Recall that Article V of the Convention imposes significant limits on the grounds that may be invoked to deny recognition of a foreign award. *See supra* pp. 35-36, 1070-72 & *infra* pp. 1194-95. Does anything in the literal text of the Convention impose comparable limits on the annulment of awards in the arbitral seat?

A decision of a U.S. appellate court in *Toys "R" Us*, excerpted above at pp. 1081-84, is representative of most authorities addressing this issue:

> "We read Article V(1)(e) ... to allow a court in the country under whose law the arbitration was conducted to apply domestic arbitral law, in this case the FAA, to a motion to set aside or vacate that arbitral award.... There is no indication in the Convention of any intention to deprive the rendering state of its supervisory authority over an arbitral award, including its authority to set aside that award under domestic law." *Yusuf Ahmed Alghanim & Sons, WLL v. Toys "R" Us, Inc.*, 126 F.3d 15, 22 (2d ed. 1997).

The *Toys "R" Us* court concluded:

> "the Convention mandates very different regimes for the review of arbitral awards (1) in the state in which, or under the law of which, the award was made, and (2) in other states where recognition and enforcement are sought. The Convention specifically contemplates that the state in which, or under the law of which, the award is made, will be free to set aside or modify an award in accordance with its domestic arbitral law and its full panoply of express and implied grounds for relief." *Id.* at 23.

Many commentators have, without detailed analysis, reached similar conclusions. For example:

> "What the Convention did not do ... was provide any international mechanism to insure the validity of the award where rendered. This was left to the provisions of local law. The Convention provides no restraint whatsoever on the control functions of local courts at the seat of arbitration." Craig, *Some Trends and Developments in the Laws and Practice of International Commercial Arbitration*, 30 Tex. Int'l L.J. 1, 11 (1995).

Is this persuasive? Can it in fact be correct that the Convention imposes no limits at all ("no restraint whatsoever") on the grounds for annulment of awards in the arbitral seat? Suppose a Contracting State provides (a) that all awards made against local nationals will be subject to review in local courts; or (b) that all awards will be subject to *de novo* review in local courts, with both parties having a full opportunity to present evidence. Would these grounds for annulment be consistent with the Convention? What provision(s) of the Convention might they contradict? Are such grounds for annulment consistent with the parties' agreement to arbitrate, given effect under Articles II of the Convention? Why not?

10. *National arbitration legislation providing option of no recourse against awards.*
Consider the Belgian Code excerpted above and the SLPIL, excerpted at pp. 157-60 of the Documentary Supplement. Suppose a Russian and an Argentine company arbitrate under ICC Rules in Belgium or Switzerland, and the Russian company is denied either notice of the proceedings or an opportunity to present its case; or suppose the Argentine company bribes the arbitrator. If the award is made in Belgium, would Article 1717 have permitted Belgian courts, prior to 1999, to entertain an action to annul the award? What effect do the 1999 and 2013 amendments to the Belgian Judicial Code have on this result?

If the award in the foregoing hypothetical is made in Switzerland, under what circumstances would Swiss courts entertain an action to annul the award? Under the Swiss statute, what grounds for annulling an award may be waived?

What were the legislative motivations for enacting the Belgian and Swiss arbitration statutes which forbid local judicial review of substantial categories of international arbitral awards made in Belgium and Switzerland? In part, the objective is reflected in national court decisions, discussed above, limiting the grounds for annulling arbitral awards under the FAA and New York Convention: the parties bargained for arbitration and should be bound by the tribunal's decision except in exceptional cases.

On the other hand, consider: "There has been a scramble among Western European nations to accommodate their arbitration laws to what they perceive to be the consumers' tastes, thereby attracting a greater share of the fees that go to lawyers and arbitrators at the place of the proceeding." Park, *Judicial Controls in the Arbitral Process*, 5 Arb. Int'l 230, 232-33, 256 (1989). The same authority reports that England's 1979 enactment of a revised arbitration act was accompanied by an estimate in Parliament that the reform would bring England approximately $1 billion in lawyers' and arbitrators' fees. 392 Parl. Deb., HL (5th series) 99 (1978). Less cynically, do not the Belgian and Swiss statutes do good (in addition to well)? Do they not further enhance the ability of international arbitration to resolve commercial disputes efficiently and definitively?

11. *Desirability of access to judicial review in arbitral seat.* As the statutes excerpted above illustrate, virtually all national laws provide for judicial review, through an action to annul, of awards made within national borders. The Belgian and Swiss statutes are atypical in their insulation of awards from judicial review. Is it wise to forbid essentially all access to local courts to annul awards made locally? Is it wise for the parties to agree upon this?

Consider: "[Judicial review of arbitral awards is a necessary] bulwark against corruption, arbitrariness, bias, … and … sheer incompetence, in relation to acts and decisions with binding legal effect for others. No one having the power to make legally binding decisions in this country should be altogether outside and immune from this system." Kerr, *Arbitration and the Courts: The UNCITRAL Model Law*, 34 Int'l & Comp. L.Q. 1, 15 (1985). *See also* Craig, *Uses and Abuses of Appeal from Awards*, 4 Arb. Int'l 174, 198-202 (1988) ("the concept of a non-reviewable award attracts the kind of contempt that was felt some years ago for divorces from Las Vegas or Chihuahua"). Are these comments fair? If sophisticated companies decide that they wish to forego any appellate review, why should that wish be frustrated? Is the limited judicial review available under most national arbitration legislation likely to prevent "wrong" decisions?

12. *Grounds for annulment under UNCITRAL Model Law and other national arbitration legislation.* Consider the grounds for annulment provided for by Article 34 of the UNCITRAL Model Law (and by other national arbitration statutes). Paraphrase what each one of the grounds for annulment set forth in Article 34(2)(a) and (b) contemplates.

    (a) *No valid arbitration agreement.* Article 34(2)(a)(i) of the Model Law provides that an award may be annulled if one of the parties was "under some incapacity" or if the arbitration agreement "is not valid under the law to which the parties have subjected it or, failing any indication thereon, under the law of [the State where the action to annul is brought]." These grounds for annulling an award parallel those set forth, in the context of non-recognition of an award, in Article V(1)(a) of the New York Convention. *See infra* pp. 1199-218. They are also recognized under other arbitration statutes. French Code of Civil Procedure, Art. 1520(1) (allowing appeal of recognition where "the arbitral tribunal wrongly upheld or declined jurisdiction"); SLPIL, Art. 190(2)(b) (allowing annulment "if the Arbitral Tribunal wrongly accepted or declined jurisdiction").

    The formation and validity of arbitration agreements is discussed in detail above. How is analysis in the context of an annulment action different from analysis before an award has been made (for example, under Articles 8 or 16 of the UNCITRAL Model Law)? Compare the burden of proof in the two scenarios. What other differences exist between consideration of the validity of an arbitration agreement in proceedings challenging the agreement and proceedings challenging the award?

    To what extent are the jurisdictional decisions of an arbitral tribunal binding on a court in an annulment action? Is judicial review of jurisdictional rulings *de novo*? Consider again the decisions in *First Options*, *BG Group* and the Swiss Federal Tribunal's *Judgment of 21 November 2003*. Recall the differing standards of deference applicable under *First Options* to the arbitrators' jurisdictional decision, depending on whether the parties have agreed to arbitrate jurisdictional issues. *See also supra* pp. 274, 281. Consider how those standards were applied in *BG Group*. Compare the approach in the *Judgment of 21 November 2003* and the Paris Cour d'appel in *Dallah*.

    To what extent are the factual findings and legal conclusions of the arbitral tribunal, in its consideration of jurisdictional issues, relevant in subsequent annulment proceedings? At all? Preclusive?

    (b) *Denial of opportunity to be heard.* A tribunal's failure to afford the losing party an equal and adequate opportunity to present its case during the arbitration can provide grounds for annulling an award. Article 34(2)(a)(ii) of the Model Law is again representative. The provision is closely-modeled on Article V(1)(b) of the New York Convention and is directed towards serious procedural unfairness. *See infra* pp. 1218-41.

Consider §68 of the English Arbitration Act, 1996, excerpted at pp. 131-32 of the Documentary Supplement. How does it compare with Article 34(1)(a)(ii) of the Model Law? Is it preferable? Why or why not? Compare Article 190(2)(d) of the SLPIL, excerpted at p. 160 of the Documentary Supplement. To what extent does Article 34(2)(a)(ii) of the Model Law extend to violations of Article 18 of the Model Law?

What law applies to determine the existence of a procedural defect under Article 34(1)(a)(ii) of the Model Law and similar statutory provisions? The law of the arbitral seat and annulment forum? Even in an international arbitration? What about international standards comparable to those under Article 52(1)(d) of the ICSID Convention? Consider the decisions in *Corporacion Transnacional*, *Judgment of 30 December 1994* and *Card*. What law did the court apply in each case in defining applicable standards of procedural fairness?

Consider the decision in *Judgment of 30 December 1994.* How do the Swiss Federal Tribunal's standards of procedural fairness compare to those in common law jurisdictions? Compare the analysis of the award-debtor's procedural objections in *Southwire*. How does the court treat *Southwire*'s claim that interest was awarded on the basis of a statute that was neither (a) submitted in evidence; or (b) relied upon by the claimant. How was Southwire afforded an opportunity to be heard in response to the claimant's interest claim? What if this had occurred with regard to a substantive claim, rather than an interest claim? Why, if at all, should interest be different?

What sorts of procedural defects will provide grounds for annulling an award? Consider again the decisions in *Card* and *Corporacion Transnacional*. Do the courts defer excessively to the arbitrators' procedural judgments?

(c) *Excess of jurisdiction.* An award may be set aside in most developed legal systems if the arbitral tribunal has "exceeded its authority." Article 34(2)(a)(iii) of the Model Law is again representative, providing that an award may be annulled if it "deals with a dispute not contemplated by or not falling within the terms of the submission to arbitration, or contains decisions on matters beyond the scope of the submission to arbitration." This provision is modeled on the grounds for non-recognition in Article V(1)(c) of the New York Convention. *See infra* pp. 1217-18.

The interpretation of arbitration agreements, particularly their scope, is discussed in detail above. *See supra* pp. 517-34. To what extent should an annulment court defer to the arbitrator's interpretation of the scope of the arbitration agreement? Recall the discussion of *First Options* and institutional rules granting the arbitrators' competence to resolve jurisdictional disputes. *See supra* pp. 534-41.

See also Rule 24n of the 2013 SIAC Rules: "the Tribunal shall have the power to … decide, where appropriate, any issue not expressly or impliedly raised in the submissions filed under Rule 17 provided such issue has been clearly brought to the notice of the other party and that the other party has been given adequate opportunity to respond." Will such an agreement work to exclude annulment for excess of jurisdiction? Is this a desirable provision?

(d) *Non-compliance with parties' agreed arbitral procedures.* A tribunal's failure to conduct the arbitral proceedings in accordance with the parties' arbitration agreement or agreed procedural rules can provide grounds for annulling an award in most developed jurisdictions. The first limb of Article 34(2)(a)(iv) of the Model Law is representative, providing for the setting aside of awards where "the arbitral procedure was not in accordance with the agreement of the parties." This basis for annulment parallels Article V(1)(d) of the New York Convention. *See infra* pp. 1231, 1238-41.

How serious a departure from the parties' agreed arbitral procedures is required before an award may be annulled? Consider *Karaha Bodas Co. v. Perusahaan Pertambangan Minyak Dan Gas Bumi Negara*, 190 F.Supp.2d 936, 945 (S.D. Tex. 2001) ("it is appropriate to set aside an award based on a procedural violation only if such violation worked substantial prejudice to the complaining party").

Consider the Swiss Federal Tribunal's decision in *Judgment of 30 December 1994*. Will a tribunal's breach of its own procedural rules (or applicable institutional arbitration rules) provide grounds to annul its award under Swiss law? Should it?

(e) *Non-compliance with procedures required by law of arbitral seat.* The failure of an arbitral tribunal to comply with procedural requirements imposed by the laws of the arbitral seat may, in the absence of contrary agreement by the parties, provide grounds for annulment of the arbitral award. Article 34(2)(a)(iv) of the Model Law is again representative, with its second limb providing for the annulment of an award where "the arbitral procedure ... failing ... agreement [between the parties], was not in accordance with this Law." This basis for annulment mirrors the second prong of Article V(1)(d) of the New York Convention. *See infra* pp. 1239-40.

What types of violations of the law of the arbitral seat are likely to arise under Article 34(2)(a)(iv)? Suppose local law requires an odd number of arbitrators, but the parties agree upon two arbitrations; suppose local law requires arbitrators who are of local religious faith or nationality, but the parties agree upon a foreigner; suppose local law requires impartial co-arbitrators and the parties to agree on partial ones?

(f) *Public policy.* Article 34(2)(b)(ii) of the Model Law provides that an award may be annulled if the court finds that "the award is in conflict with the public policy of this State." This exception is modeled on Article V(2)(b) of the New York Convention. *See infra* pp. 1250-60. Recall the role of public policy in the selection of the applicable substantive law. *See supra* pp. 979-81, 992-1005.

Consider Article 58 of the Chinese Arbitration Law. How does it differ from the Model Law? *Compare* French Code of Civil Procedure, Art. 1520(5) (providing for annulment where "recognition or enforcement of the award is contrary to international public policy"). Which approach is preferable?

Even in jurisdictions (such as the United States) where no statutory public policy basis for annulment exists, courts have recognized the doctrine as "a specific application of the more general doctrine, rooted in the common law, that a court may refuse to enforce contracts that violate law or public policy." *United Paperworkers Int'l Union v. Misco, Inc.*, 484 U.S. 29, 42 (1987). Consider the following explanation for application of the public policy doctrine in annulment actions:

> "it is in our view inconceivable that an English court would enforce an award made on a joint venture agreement between bank robbers, any more than it would enforce

an agreement between highwaymen…. Where public policy is involved, the interposition of an arbitration award does not insulate the successful party's claim from the illegality which gave rise to it…. The reason, in our judgment, is plain enough. The court declines to enforce an illegal contract, … not for the sake of the defendant, nor (if it comes to the point) for the sake of the plaintiff. The court is in our view concerned to preserve the integrity of its process, and to see that it is not abused. The parties cannot override that concern by private agreement. They cannot by procuring an arbitration conceal that they, or rather one of them, is seeking to enforce an illegal contract. Public policy will not allow it." *Soleimany v. Soleimany* [1999] QB 785, 800 (English Ct. App.).

Is that persuasive?

Compare the approaches to public policy in annulment actions in *Desputeaux* and *Judgment of 30 December 1994*. What is the standard of public policy in an action to annul an international arbitral award under Article 190 of the SLPIL? What if an arbitral tribunal makes a significant error in identifying and applying Swiss law; is that a public policy violation? Suppose the tribunal applies non-Swiss law, which it incorrectly interprets. Paraphrase the public policy standards articulated by *Judgment of 30 December 1994* in cases governed by (i) Swiss and (ii) non-Swiss law. What is the source for these standards?

Did the *Judgment of 30 December 1994* reach an acceptable conclusion? Isn't it obvious that the contract at issue involved bribery? Compare the decision in *Northrup Corp.* What standard does the *Northrup Corp.* court apply to review of the arbitral tribunal's decisions regarding foreign mandatory law? Is this the appropriate standard where issues of mandatory law and public policy are involved?

Recall the *Mitsubishi* and *Eco Swiss* decisions, *supra* pp. 486-92 & 492-93, where the U.S. and EU courts held that national courts would be permitted to take a "second look" at the decisions of arbitrators on matters of U.S. and EU competition/antitrust law. In an annulment context, what should be the nature of this "second look"? Should any deference be afforded the arbitrators' substantive decision on competition/antitrust matters? Consider *Baxter Int'l, Inc. v. Abbott Labs.*, 315 F.3d 829 (7th Cir. 2003) ("*Mitsubishi* did not contemplate that, once arbitration was over, the federal courts would throw the result in the waste basket and litigate the antitrust issues anew. That would just be another way of saying that antitrust matters are not arbitrable…. Starting from scratch in court, as Baxter proposes, would subvert the promises the United States made in acceding to the Convention."). Is that persuasive?

What are the standards of public policy applied in *Desputeaux*? Under *Desputeaux*, is it a public policy violation whenever an arbitral tribunal makes a significant error in applying Québec law? Is that appropriate? Would the court in *Judgment of 30 December 1994* have reached a similar conclusion?

Does *Southwire* reach a persuasive conclusion? Did the French rule concerning the legal rate of interest payable on certain obligations really violate "basic notions of morality and justice"? Note that French law imposes rates of interest in excess of market rates on post-award amounts in order to encourage payment of amounts found owing. Other countries do the same. Is that such a peculiar and offensive idea? Note that the parties' choice-of-law clause included specific reference to French law, which the arbitral tribunal applied.

What standards of public policy are applied in *Southwire*? Are they the same as in *Desputeaux*? Would the court in *Judgment of 30 December 1994* have reached a similar conclusion to that in *Southwire*? How would the Swiss Federal Tribunal approach the subject of public policy in a case where Swiss law was not applicable?

Should a court accord any deference to the arbitrators' consideration of public policy issues? What approaches did the courts take in the decisions excerpted above? Note that, in *W.R. Grace & Co. v. Local Union 749*, 461 U.S. at 766, the U.S. Supreme Court said that "the question of public policy is ultimately one for resolution by the courts." *See also Transmarine Seaways Corp. v. Marc Rich & Co.*, 480 F.Supp. 352 (S.D.N.Y. 1979) (rejecting "argument that the question of [a public policy violation] is foreclosed from judicial review by the conclusion of a majority of the arbitrators that ... the contract was enforceable. When public policy is asserted as the basis for vacating an arbitration award, the court is required to make its own, independent evaluation.").

Is that appropriate? The dividing line between public policy and other legal issues is a blurred one. Is it sensible to grant arbitrators virtually unfettered discretion on, for example, the merits of a billion dollar fraud claim, while affording no deference at all on the percentage rate of post-award interest? *See supra* p. 1016.

(g) *Nonarbitrability*. The nonarbitrability doctrine provides an exceptional basis for the annulment of arbitral awards. Article 34(2)(b)(i) of the Model Law provides that an award may be annulled if the court finds that "the subject-matter of the dispute is not capable of settlement by arbitration" under the law of the judicial annulment forum. This provision is modeled on Article V(2)(a) of the New York Convention, amended only slightly to confirm that the nonarbitrability standards of the annulment forum apply. *See infra* pp. 1260-66. Consider the treatment of nonarbitrability in *Desputeaux*. Why did the court conclude that Copyright Act disputes were arbitrable? Compare the analysis in *Mitsubishi Motors*, *supra* pp. 449.

13. *Grounds for annulment not contained in UNCITRAL Model Law*. Consider the English Arbitration Act, FAA, Chinese Arbitration Law and Belgian Judicial Code. What grounds for annulment of arbitral awards do these arbitration statutes provide which do not exist in the Model Law? Do these additional grounds correspond to any of the grounds for annulment in the Model Law? Other national arbitration statutes also provide a variety of grounds for annulment that do not exist under the Model Law.

(a) *Formal defects in award*. Under some national arbitration regimes, formal defects in an arbitral award are grounds for annulment. These defects can include:

(1) failure to sign an award—English Arbitration Act, 1996, §68(2)(h) ("failure to comply with the requirements as to the form of the awards"); Netherlands Code of Civil Procedure, Art. 1065(1)(d) ("award may be set aside ... [if it] has not been signed"); 1966 European Uniform Law on Arbitration, Art. 25(2)(h) ("if the formalities prescribed in paragraph 4 of Article 22 [requiring written, signed award] have not been fulfilled"). Is this a sufficient basis for annulling an award?

(2) failure to provide reasons—Netherlands Code of Civil Procedure, Art. 1065(1)(d) ("award may be set aside ... [if it] does not contain reasons"); 1966

European Uniform Law on Arbitration, Art. 25(2)(i) ("if the reasons for the award have not been stated"); Belgian Judicial Code, Art. 1717(3)(a)(iv) ("if the award is not reasoned"). Should a lack of reasons be sufficient grounds for annulling an award? Why is it not included in the UNCITRAL Model Law? *Compare* ICSID Convention, Art. 52(1)(e).

(3) failure to comply with other requirements for an award (*e.g.*, inclusion of date and place of award)—English Arbitration Act, 1996, §68(2)(h); Belgian Judicial Code, 1999, Art. 1704(2)(h) (repealed).

(4) failure to deposit award with local court—Netherlands Code of Civil Procedure, Art. 1058(1)(b) (award deposited with court if parties so agree), 1065 (failure to deposit award not listed as grounds for annulment); Belgian Judicial Code, Arts. 1713(8), 1717(3) (same).

In other jurisdictions, violations of form requirements may not constitute grounds for annulment or may be waivable. *See, e.g.*, UNCITRAL Model Law, Art. 34(2); Japanese Arbitration Law, Art. 44; 1966 European Uniform Law on Arbitration, Art. 25(2)(h), (3) (no annulment for absence on award of date, place of arbitration). Which of these various approaches is wisest?

(b) *Internally-contradictory awards.* Some national legal regimes provide for annulment of awards that are contradictory. For example, Article 1704(2)(j) of the Belgian Judicial Code, as amended in 1998, provided that an award could be annulled if it contained "conflicting provisions" (after the 2013 amendments this is no longer a ground for annulment). *See also* 1966 European Uniform Law on Arbitration, Art. 25(2)(j) ("the award contains conflicting provisions."); Finnish Arbitration Act, §40(1)(3) ("An award shall be null and void ... if the arbitral award is so obscure or incomplete if it does not appear in it how the dispute has been decided"); Argentine Code of Civil and Commercial Procedure, Art. 761(1) ("An award containing contradictory decisions shall be null and void."); Colombian Decree No. 1818 of 7 September 1998, Art. 163(7).

The basic rationale of such decisions is that an award that is contradictory is either not reasoned (since contradictory reasons are supposedly the equivalent of no reasons at all) or violates public policy (since it mandates inconsistent results). *Compare Judgment of 14 June 2000*, XXVI Y.B. Comm. Arb. 270 (2001) (French Cour de cassation) ("The ground for appeal based on contradictory reasons for the arbitral decision was thus inadmissible"). Is it appropriate to annul awards that are internally inconsistent? Is this not a means of reviewing the substance of the tribunal's decision?

14. *Judicial review of substance of arbitrators' decision under national arbitration legislation.* Consider whether the substantive correctness of the arbitrators' decision may be reviewed in an annulment proceeding.

(a) *No judicial review of arbitrators' substantive decision in action to annul award.* Consider Article 34 of the UNCITRAL Model Law and Article 190 of the SLPIL, excerpted at pp. 94-95 & 160 of the Documentary Supplement. What do they provide with respect to judicial review of the substantive merits of an arbitrator's ruling?

In Switzerland, historic practice and the Swiss Intercantonal Concordat provided for reasonably extensive judicial review of the merits of the arbitrators' decision. Swiss Intercantonal Concordat, 1969, Art. 36(f) (award may be annulled if "arbitrary," because of a "violation of law or equity"). The SLPIL deliberately abandoned that approach, instead providing for no review of the merits of arbitral awards in international matters. Consider the standard for annulment adopted in the *Judgment of 30 December 1994. See also Judgment of 8 April 2005*, DFT 4P.253/2004 (Swiss Fed. Trib.) ("it is not sufficient that the evidence be improperly weighed, that a factual finding be manifestly false, that a contractual clause not have been correctly interpreted or applied or that an applicable principle of law has been clearly breached"). What is the rationale for this approach?

(b) *Full judicial review of arbitrator's substantive decision in action to annul award.* Consider Article 758 of the Argentine Code of Civil and Commercial Procedure. Note that Article 758 contemplates review of arbitral awards on the same grounds as national court judgments. Compare Article 58 of the Chinese Arbitration Law.

(c) *Limited judicial review of arbitrators' substantive decision.* Arbitral awards made in the United States have generally been subject to actions to vacate if the arbitrators' decision was in "manifest disregard of law." *See infra* pp. 1165-68; Drahozal, *Codifying Manifest Disregard*, 8 Nev. L.J. 234 (2007); G. Born, *International Commercial Arbitration* 3341 (2d ed. 2014). Compare §69 of the English Arbitration Act, 1996. Contrast the standards and approach of §69 to the "manifest disregard" test.

15. *"Manifest disregard" as basis for annulment under FAA.* U.S. domestic law has historically permitted annulment of arbitral awards based on a very limited category of substantive errors in the arbitrators' decision on the merits of the parties' dispute—pursuant to the so-called "manifest disregard of law" doctrine. Both the meaning of the manifest disregard doctrine and the doctrine's continued viability are subject to substantial debate.

(a) *Basis for manifest disregard doctrine.* There is no provision of the FAA which permits annulment of an award based on a substantive review of the arbitrators' decision on the merits of the parties' dispute. Indeed, the rhetoric of U.S. judicial review emphatically rejects the notion of judicial review of the merits of arbitral awards:

> "The purpose of arbitration is to permit a relatively quick and inexpensive resolution of contractual disputes by avoiding the expense and delay of extended court proceedings. Accordingly, it is a well-settled proposition that judicial review of an arbitration award should be, and is, very narrowly limited." *Diapulse Corp. of Am. v. Carba, Ltd*, 626 F.2d 1108 (2d Cir. 1980).

U.S. courts routinely avow that even egregious mistakes of law and fact by the arbitrators are not a basis for refusing to enforce an award. As early as 1855, the U.S. Supreme Court held:

> "If the award is within the submission, and contains the honest decision of the arbitrators, after a full and fair hearing of the parties, a court of equity will not set it aside for error, either in law or fact. A contrary course would be a substitution of the judgment of the chancellor in place of the judges chosen by the parties, and would make an award the commencement, not the end, of litigation." *Burchell v. Marsh*, 58 U.S. 344 (1855).

Despite this, U.S. courts have fashioned a "manifest disregard" doctrine under the domestic FAA, which permits domestic awards to be vacated if they depart sufficiently from the clear dictates of applicable law. As the court's opinion in *Stavborg* describes, the "manifest disregard of law" formula derives from dicta in *Wilko*, where the U.S. Supreme Court remarked that "[i]n unrestricted submissions ... the interpretations of the law by the arbitrators, in contrast to manifest disregard are not subject, in the federal courts, to judicial review for error in interpretation." 346 U.S. at 436-37. Following *Wilko*'s dicta, a large body of U.S. lower court authority developed, considering whether awards should be annulled on "manifest disregard" grounds—and usually concluding that they should not.

(b) *"Manifest disregard of law" under FAA not established by proof of erroneous decision.* Under U.S. lower court decisions, "manifest disregard of law" is universally held to require more than an erroneous statement of applicable law or an erroneous interpretation of the parties' agreement. *See ARW Exploration Corp. v. Aguirre*, 45 F.3d 1455, 1462 (10th Cir. 1995) ("standard of review of arbitral awards is among the narrowest known to the law"); *San Martine Compania de Navegacion v. Saguenay Terminals, Ltd*, 293 F.2d 796, 801 (9th Cir. 1961) ("manifest disregard of the law must be something beyond and different from a mere error in the law or failure on the part of the arbitrators to understand or apply the law"); *Nat'l Oil Corp. v. Libyan Sun Oil Co.*, 733 F.Supp. 800 (D. Del. 1990) ("mere error of law would not ... be sufficient grounds to refuse recognition of the award.").

Although it is easy to say what "manifest disregard" is not, it is harder to say what it is. Different courts have given a range of divergent interpretations to the doctrine. As one court said, "[t]his standard of judicial review has taken on various hues and colorations in its formulations." *Advest, Inc. v. McCarthy*, 914 F.2d 6, 9 (1st Cir. 1990). In most U.S. jurisdictions, the manifest disregard standard requires a showing that the arbitrators were aware of the content of governing law, but refused to apply it. According to one leading formulation: "The two-prong test for ascertaining whether an arbitrator has manifestly disregarded the law has both an objective and a subjective component. We first consider whether the 'governing law alleged to have been ignored by the arbitrators [was] well defined, explicit, and clearly applicable.' [Second, we] then look to the knowledge actually possessed by the arbitrator. The arbitrator must '[appreciate] the existence of a clearly governing legal principle but [decide] to ignore or pay no attention to it.' Both of these prongs must be met before a court may find that there has been a manifest disregard of law." *Westerbeke Corp. v. Daihatsu Motor Co.*, 304 F.3d 200, 209 (2d Cir. 2002).

(c) *Rationale for manifest disregard rule.* Consider Judge Mansfield's dissent in *I/S Stavborg*. Is it persuasive? Where an arbitral tribunal clearly misinterprets the parties' agreement, or applicable law, should U.S. courts lend their coercive powers to enforcement of the tribunal's award? Do you think that the parties honestly felt justice was done in *Stavborg*?

Even if occasional injustice results, is either no, or an extremely narrow, manifest disregard rule nevertheless necessary to the effective functioning of the arbitral process? According to one court, "awards are subject to very limited review in order to avoid undermining the twin goals of arbitration, namely, settling disputes efficiently and avoiding long and expensive litigation." *Folkways Music Publishers v. Weiss*, 989 F.2d 108, 111 (2d Cir. 1993). Recall the objectives and benefits of arbitration in international commercial disputes. *See supra* pp. 108-12. How would those objectives and benefits be affected by national court review of the merits of arbitrators' decisions?

Compare the manifest disregard doctrine with the UNCITRAL Model Law and the Swiss decision in *Judgment of 30 December 1994*. Which approach is wiser? If an arbitral tribunal really reaches a result that contradicts applicable national law, by deliberately refusing to apply that law, should that decision be upheld? Does it not amount to an unauthorized decision *ex aequo et bono*? *See supra* pp. 1020-21. How is the arbitral process strengthened by giving effect to such awards? Or, do the costs of judicial review of arbitral awards exceed the benefits that come from occasionally identifying a grave error?

(d) *Lower U.S. court decisions holding that manifest disregard exists where award is irrational.* Some U.S. courts have suggested that an award that is irrational and without factual basis may be vacated. *Ainsworth v. Skurnick*, 960 F.2d 939 (11th Cir. 1992) (vacating award as arbitrary after concluding that there was no rational legal theory justifying conclusion); *Shearson Lehman Bros, Inc. v. Hedrich*, 639 N.E.2d 228 (Ill. App. 1994) (vacating award because "arbitrators impermissibly ignored the unambiguous contract language"). Other U.S. decisions have suggested that demonstrably wrong decisions need not be recognized. *Merrill Lynch, Pierce, Fenner & Smith v. Bobker*, 808 F.2d 930, 933 (2d Cir. 1986) (error on "well-defined, explicit, and clearly applicable" point of law that was "obvious and capable of being readily and instantly perceived by the average person qualified to serve as an arbitrator").

Do these decisions effectively involve appellate review of the arbitrator's decision on the merits? Is there not an inevitable slide towards such review under the manifest disregard doctrine? Is that undesirable?

(e) *No review of arbitrators' factual findings.* U.S. courts have generally declined to inquire at all into the correctness of the arbitrators' factual conclusions (as distinguished from conclusions of law). In *United Paperworkers*, 484 U.S. at 39, for example, the Court remarked: "No dishonesty is alleged; only improvident, even silly fact finding is claimed. This is hardly a sufficient basis for disregarding what the agent appointed by the parties determined to be the historical facts." *See also W. Elec. Co. v. Commc'n Equip. Workers, Inc.*, 554 F.2d 135, 138 (4th Cir. 1977) (because there were "some facts to support [the] arbitration award," the award was confirmed notwithstanding arbitrators' application of incorrect burden of proof). Compare the similar approach in *Judgment of 30 December 1994*. Why should factual findings be treated differently from legal conclusions? If such an approach is adopted, can't arbitrators use factual findings to sustain almost any result they wish?

(f) *Manifest disregard of foreign law.* Suppose the substantive law applied by the arbitrators is not the law of the arbitral seat. Should that affect the willingness of a national court either to apply the manifest disregard exception or their analysis thereunder? U.S. courts are much less likely to conclude that arbitrators have manifestly disregarded foreign than U.S. law. *See Brandeis Intsel Ltd v. Calabrian Chem. Corp.*, 656 F.Supp. 160 (S.D.N.Y. 1987). Note that *I/S Stavborg* involved a dispute governed by Spanish law. Does the "manifest disregard of law" doctrine even apply to non-U.S. law? Consider the approach under §69 of the English Arbitration Act. Compare the differences in public policy analysis in *Judgment of 30 December 1994*, depending on whether or not Swiss law was applicable. What reasons argue for greater judicial deference to decisions on foreign law than on domestic law?

(g) *Viability of "manifest disregard" doctrine after* Hall Street. Consider the U.S. Supreme Court's analysis of the FAA in *Hall Street*. Does the manifest disregard doctrine remain good law after *Hall Street*?

Although *Hall Street* did not concern, or expressly address, the status of the manifest disregard doctrine, the Court declared that "§§10 and 11 respectively provide the FAA's exclusive grounds for expedited vacatur and modification," and that "maybe" *Wilko* refers only to "§10 grounds collectively," rather than a "new ground for review" of an award. Consider the Court's rationale in holding that parties could not contractually expand the grounds for annulling an award under §10 of the FAA. Does the same rationale argue against the continued viability of the manifest disregard doctrine?

16. *Annulment of award for substantive errors under §69 of English Arbitration Act.* Consider §69 of the English Arbitration Act. When can an award be annulled under §69? Can an award be annulled because the tribunal made factual mistakes? Errors in evaluating the evidence? Errors in foreign (*i.e.*, non-English) law? Any error of English law? What do you think of the limitations on annulment under §69? Are these limitations wise? Or do they threaten the arbitral process and parties' commercial objectives? Compare the approach to annulment under §69 to the manifest disregard doctrine. Which is preferable?

17. *What standard of judicial review of arbitrators' substantive decisions in an award is appropriate in annulment actions?* Consider the various approaches of national legislation to judicial review of arbitrators' decisions in annulment actions. Which approach is preferable with respect to international awards? Why? Consider the following:

> "Among commercial men what are commonly called commercial arbitrations are undoubtedly and deservedly popular. That they will continue their present popularity I entertain no doubt, so long as the law retains sufficient hold over them to prevent and redress any injustice on the part of the arbitrator, and to secure that the law that is administered by an arbitrator is in substance the law of the land and not some home-made law of the particular arbitrator or the particular association. To release real and effective control over commercial arbitrations is to allow the arbitrator, or the Arbitration Tribunal, to be a law unto himself, or themselves, to give him or them a free hand to decide according to law or not according to law as he or they think fit, in other words to be outside the law ..." *Czarnikow v. Roth Schmidt & Co.* [1922] 2 KB 478, 484 (English Ct. App.).

Compare:

> "With the exception of the Sovereign and the Judicial Committees of the House of Lords and Privy Council, there is virtually no body, tribunal, authority or individual in

England whose acts or decisions give rise to binding legal consequences for others, but who are altogether immune from judicial review in the event of improper conduct, breaches of the principles of natural justice, or decisions which clearly transcend any standard of objective reasonableness. Such islands of immunity as remain are constantly shrinking.... This system is our bulwark against corruption, arbitrariness, bias, improper conduct and—where necessary—sheer incompetence, in relation to acts and decisions with binding legal effect for others. No one having the power to make legally binding decisions in this country should be altogether outside and immune from this system. No one below the highest tribunals should have unreviewable legal powers over others. Speaking from experience, I believe this to be as necessary in relation to arbitrations in England and abroad as in all other contexts." Kerr, *Arbitration and the Courts: The UNCITRAL Model Law*, 34 Int'l & Comp. L.Q. 1 (1985).

See also 2004 Cedric Barclay Lecture (Lord Mayor of London: "I shall encourage the view that there should be more appeals from arbitrations to the Courts not less."). Are these views persuasive? Are they consistent with the parties' objectives in agreeing to arbitrate? With the objectives of most legislatures in developed jurisdictions?

18. *Waiver of grounds for annulment.* Under virtually all national laws, some bases for annulment may be waived, either by inaction or inconsistent action or by statements.

   (a) *Waiver of claims of arbitrator bias.* Recall Articles 4 and 13 of the UNCITRAL Model Law. How do they deal with the timing for raising objections to an arbitrator's independence? Compare Article 180 of the SLPIL. Consider again the *Technostroyexport* case and the court's disposition of waiver claims. *See supra* pp. 766-67, 770-74. Note that at least some claims of arbitrator bias or lack of required qualifications may be waived by inaction.

   Are some types of defects in an arbitral tribunal non-waivable? *See supra* pp. 739-40, 770-71 & *infra* pp. 1247-48. Suppose a party accidentally learns of bribery by the other party, but does nothing at the time. Can it waive claims based on the corruption? Consider the alleged lack of independence that was waived in *Technostroyexport. See supra* pp. 770-74 for decisions suggesting that most such objections to arbitrators may be waived. Compare the IBA Guidelines on Conflicts of Interest. *See supra* p. 740 and pp. 363-78 of the Documentary Supplement.

   If an objection based on arbitrator bias can be waived by inaction, can't it also be waived by express agreement? What if the agreement is prospective, made as part of the parties' agreement to arbitrate? For example, some institutional rules provide for the waiver of rights to seek judicial review of an appointing authority's resolution of a challenge. *See* 2012 ICC Rules, Art. 11(4) (decisions "shall be final"); 2014 LCIA Rules, Art. 29(2) ("To the extent permitted by any applicable law, the parties shall be taken to have waived any right of appeal ...").

   Can an institutional challenge procedure wholly insulate an award from judicial review for arbitrator bias? Are there not limits on the extent to which parties may validly consent to biased arbitrators? *See supra* pp. 739-40, 770-74. Suppose, for example, that in *Veritas, supra* pp. 716-17, Dr. Wallersteiner survived an institutional challenge. Should this prevent his lack of impartiality from being raised in an annulment action? Consider also the English Court of Appeals' analysis in the *AT&T* case, *supra* p. 775.

   (b) *Waiver of claims based on procedural objections.* Most developed arbitration regimes require that a party have objected to the arbitrators' procedural rulings during the proceedings in order to preserve their rights to subsequently seek annulment of an award on the basis of those rulings. *See supra* pp. 1237, 1240-41. Many institutional rules contain provisions requiring the parties to promptly raise procedural objections, and deeming the failure to do so a waiver. *See, e.g.,* 2010 UNCITRAL Rules, Art. 32; 2012 ICC Rules, Art. 39; 2014 LCIA Rules, Art. 32(1). Even in the absence of such provisions, national law will produce the same result. As one court put it: "A party with an objection to an arbitration panel has an affirmative obligation to raise that objection with the arbitrators or else that objection shall be waived." *Avraham v. Shigur Express Ltd,* 1991 U.S. Dist. LEXIS 12267 (S.D.N.Y.). *See also Food Serv. of Am., Inc. v. Pan Pac. Specialties Ltd,* (1997) 32 B.C.L.R.(3d) 225, ¶¶38-43 (B.C. Sup. Ct.) ("failure to object at the time means that they are deemed to have waived the right to object"). This applies to annulment based on both denial of an opportunity to be heard (UNCITRAL Model Law, Art. 34(2)(a)(ii)) and non-compliance with the parties' arbitration agreement or the law of the arbitral seat (UNCITRAL Model Law, Art. 34(2)(a)(iv)).

      Is it appropriate to permit fundamental procedural protections to be the subject of waiver? Suppose the question is the adoption of utterly one-sided and unfair procedural rules? Should rights of this nature be subject to waiver? If so, what about advance waiver by express agreement? Recall the discussion of one-sided and unconscionable agreements to arbitrate. *See supra* pp. 404-12.

(c) *Waiver of jurisdictional objections.* Most arbitration regimes provide that the right to challenge the existence or validity of an agreement to arbitrate is subject to waiver. *See supra* pp. 391-92. To what extent is such a waiver relevant in the context of annulment actions (for example, under Articles 34(2)(a)(i) and (iii) of the UNCITRAL Model Law)? For example, suppose a party participates without any jurisdictional objection in an arbitration; may it subsequently seek annulment of an adverse award by claiming that there was no valid agreement to arbitrate? Suppose the arbitration agreement provides that the arbitrators may resolve all jurisdictional disputes; may a party subsequently seek annulment of an adverse award by claiming the tribunal exceeded the scope of the agreement to arbitrate? How would this issue be resolved under *First Options*? How should it be resolved?

(d) *Waiver of public policy or nonarbitrability objections.* Are public policy and nonarbitrability objections subject to waiver? Or are these matters of mandatory law that a private litigant cannot waive?

19. *Effect of agreement excluding annulment action.* Suppose an arbitration agreement provides: "Any award made pursuant to Article X shall not be subject to challenge or action to annul (or set aside), and each party expressly waives any rights to challenge or seek to annul (or set aside) such award." What effect does such an exclusion agreement have on a court's substantive review power?

(a) *National legislation permitting exclusion agreements.* Consider Article 192 of the SLPIL, excerpted at p. 160 of the Documentary Supplement. Note the grounds as to which an action to annul may be excluded. Is this wise? Is it appropriate to permit parties to delegate to a private decision-maker the power to resolve their dispute, and then to exclude *any* judicial review of the resulting decision? Note the limited circumstances, under Article 192(1), in which an exclusion agreement is enforceable. What is the reason for these limits? Are they appropriate? Compare the similar provisions which exist under Belgian law, *see infra* p. 1135. *See also* French Code of Civil Procedure, Art. 1522. Would an agreement to arbitrate under the ICC Rules be sufficient under French law to waive the opportunity to apply for setting aside an award?

(b) *National legislation not permitting exclusion agreements.* Some states do not permit exclusion agreements. *See, e.g.*, Egyptian Arbitration Law, Art. 54(1) ("The admissibility of the action for annulment of the arbitral award shall not be prevented by the applicant's renunciation of its right to request the annulment of the award prior to the making of the award."); Italian Code of Civil Procedure, Art. 829(1) (recourse available "notwithstanding any prior waiver"); Portuguese Law on Voluntary Arbitration, 2011, Art. 46(5) ("the right to apply for the setting aside of an arbitral award cannot be waived"). Is this approach appropriate? If the parties want to limit judicial review of the arbitrators' decision, should this not be permitted? Does it matter what the grounds for annulment are? Suppose they are gross fraud or corruption of the arbitrators or arbitral institution. Suppose they are violations of a fundamentally important national mandatory law (*i.e.*, prohibitions against trafficking in nuclear weapons; financing of terrorism)?

(c) *Exclusion agreements under UNCITRAL Model Law.* Consider Article 34 of the Model Law, excerpted at pp. 94-95 of the Documentary Supplement. Does it permit agreements to exclude annulment on some or all Article 34(2) grounds? Compare §69 of the English Arbitration Act. Can judicial review of the merits of the arbitrators' decision be excluded? What about other grounds for annulment, under §§67 and 68 of the Act? Why the difference?

(d) *Exclusion agreements under FAA.* U.S. courts have not addressed the issue with much care, but a number of lower court decisions have permitted parties to challenge an award on the grounds set forth in the FAA, despite their agreement that the arbitrators' award shall be "final." *See Hoeft v. MVL Group, Inc.*, 343 F.3d 57, 60, 66 (2d Cir. 2003) (agreement that award "shall not be subject to any type of review or appeal whatsoever" does not waive right to seek vacatur: "parties seeking to enforce arbitration awards through federal court confirmation judgments may not divest the courts of their statutory and common law authority to review both the substance of the awards and the arbitral process for compliance with §10(a) and the manifest disregard standard"). Other decisions have interpreted such waivers very narrowly, as not being intended to waive rights to seek vacatur. *See M & C Corp. v. Erwin Behr GmbH*, 87 F.3d 844, 947 (6th Cir. 1996) (interpreting waiver narrowly to bar only retrial on merits, not manifest disregard review); *Aerojet-Gen. Corp. v. Am. Arbitration Ass'n*, 478 F.2d 248, 251-52 (9th Cir. 1973) (provision that award is "final and binding" held not to preclude limited judicial review).

Consider the status of exclusion agreements after *Hall Street*. The U.S. Supreme Court's opinion did not expressly consider the validity of an agreement *excluding* judicial review in a vacatur action under §10, but instead an agreement *expanding* judicial review. Nonetheless, does the Court's view of the statutory annulment regime suggest how an exclusion agreement would be treated? Note the Court's emphasis on §10's character of a mandatory, exclusive enforcement regime. Can one distinguish between exclusion agreements, which limit judicial review, and agreements for expanded judicial review? Which would ordinarily raise greater enforceability concerns?

(e) *Should exclusion agreements be enforceable?* Should parties be permitted to waive rights to seek annulment? If arbitration is fundamentally a creature of contract, why shouldn't parties have the autonomy to waive any judicial review? Aren't parties permitted to settle disputes without any judicial scrutiny? Why can't they agree to arbitrate without any judicial scrutiny? Does the same conclusion apply to all possible grounds for annulment? Compare the Swiss and Belgian arbitration statutes with the English Arbitration Act. Should some grounds, but not others, be subject to advance exclusion of judicial review?

20. *Arbitration agreements providing for heightened judicial review of award.* Although it happens rarely, parties sometimes agree to more exacting judicial scrutiny of the arbitrators' award than that provided for by the law of the arbitral seat. *See* Smit, *Contractual Modification of the Scope of Judicial Review of Arbitral Awards*, 8 Am. Rev. Int'l Arb. 147 (1997); Ware, *"Opt-In" for Judicial Review of Errors of Law Under the Revised Uniform Arbitration Act*, 8 Am. Rev. Int'l Arb. 263 (1997). The agreement in *Hall Street* is an example of such an arrangement.

Historically, U.S. courts generally enforced provisions providing for heightened judicial review of awards. *See, e.g., Harris v. Parker College*, 286 F.3d 790 (5th Cir. 2002); *Syncor Int'l Corp. v. McLeland*, 120 F.3d 262 (4th Cir. 1997); *Gateway Tech., Inc. v. MCI Telecomm. Corp.*, 64 F.3d 993 (5th Cir. 1995) ("FAA does not prohibit parties who voluntarily agree to arbitration from providing contractually for more expansive judicial review of the award"). *Compare Kyocera Corp. v. Prudential Bache Trade Servs.*, 299 F.3d 769 (9th Cir. 2002), *vacating LaPine Tech. Corp. v. Kyocera Corp.*, 130 F.3d 884 (9th Cir. 1997); *Chicago Typo. Union v. Chicago Sun-Times, Inc.*, 935 F.2d 1501 (7th Cir. 1991).

Nonetheless, in *Hall Street*, the U.S. Supreme Court held that the grounds for vacatur under §10 of the FAA were exclusive and that the "statutory grounds for prompt vacatur and modification may [not] be supplemented by contract." The Court reached this conclusion notwithstanding its acknowledgement that the "FAA lets parties tailor some, even many features of arbitration by contract, including the way arbitrators are chosen, what their qualifications should be, which issues are arbitrable, along with procedure and choice of substantive law." How did the Court deal with the importance of party autonomy in holding that agreements on expanded judicial review were invalid? Is the Court's analysis of the statutory language persuasive? Does it take into account the underlying purposes of the FAA?

Is *Hall Street* wisely decided? If parties agreed to permit heightened judicial review of awards, what policies are offended by an agreement on such review?

21. *Fraud as basis for annulling award.* Suppose one party commits fraudulent actions during the arbitral proceedings. For example, suppose a party bribes several of the witnesses it produces to provide deliberately false and fraudulent testimony and submits forged documentary evidence. Does Article 34 of the UNCITRAL Model Law provide any basis for annulling the resulting award? *Compare* English Arbitration Act, 1996, §68(2)(g); Belgian Judicial Code, Art. 1717(3)(b)(iii). What provision of the Model Law might a party rely upon in seeking to annul an award for fraud?

Suppose a party's fraudulent conduct, in an arbitration, is only discovered after the time in which an annulment action may be brought under the law of the arbitral seat. Is there no possibility for the injured party to challenge the award? Does the Model Law provide any such basis? Does the Model Law forbid an action to challenge the award based upon fraud? Consider Article 5.

22. *Fraud under §10(a) of FAA.* Section 10(a) of the domestic FAA permits the non-enforcement of an award based on "fraud." A standard formulation of the showing that is required under the domestic FAA is:

> "First, the movant must establish the fraud by clear and convincing evidence. Second, the fraud must not have been discoverable upon the exercise of due diligence prior to or during the arbitration. Third, the person seeking to vacate the award must demonstrate that the fraud materially related to an issue in the arbitration." *Bonar v. Dean Witter Reynolds, Inc.*, 835 F.2d 1378, 1383 (11th Cir. 1988).

> Other courts have adopted similar formulae. *Dogherra v. Safeway Stores, Inc.*, 679 F.2d 1293, 1297 (9th Cir. 1982) ("The fraud must not have been discoverable upon the exercise of due diligence prior to the arbitration…. The fraud must materially relate to an issue in the arbitration … [and] must be established by clear and convincing evidence.").

> Fraud is most often invoked in cases involving perjured testimony or fabricated evidence. "Intentionally giving false testimony in an arbitration proceeding would constitute fraud." *Nat'l Oil Corp. v. Libyan Sun Oil Co.*, 733 F.Supp. 800, 814 (D. Del. 1990). For the type of extreme case that will satisfy the fraud exception, *see Bonar*, 835 F.2d 1378, where an "expert witness" was held to have "lied about all of his credentials—where he went to school, what degrees he had, and what jobs he had held."

23. *Grounds for annulment under ICSID Convention.* Consider Article 52 of the ICSID Convention, excerpted at p. 24 of the Documentary Supplement. How do the grounds for annulment in Article 52(1) compare to those in Article 34 of the UNCITRAL Model Law? What grounds exist in the Model Law but not in the ICSID Convention? Why not?

Consider the treatment of issues of public policy and nonarbitrability. May an award be annulled under Article 52 on either of these grounds? Why not? Consider the treatment of procedural defects. May an award be annulled under Article 52 for violations of the law of the arbitral seat? Why not? May an award be annulled for violation of the parties' agreed arbitral procedures? Why not? What does Article 52(1)(d) mean? May an award be annulled because an arbitrator was not independent? What does Article 52(1)(c) mean?

24. *Grounds for annulment in inter-state arbitration.* What are the grounds for annulment in an inter-state arbitration? Consider Article 83 of the 1907 Hague Convention, excerpted at p. 49 of the Documentary Supplement. What grounds for annulment (or "revision") of an award are permitted? In what circumstances may annulment be sought? Note that (a) absent agreement, no review of an award is possible, and (b) if the parties agree, review of an award is possible in limited cases of after-discovered evidence. What about excess of jurisdiction? Lack of impartiality of arbitrators? Gross procedural unfairness or failure to comply with the parties' agreement?

D. Consequences of Annulment of International Arbitral Awards

It is comparatively rare for international arbitral awards to be annulled, either in the courts of the arbitral seat or otherwise.[22] If an award is annulled, however, challenging questions arise as to the consequences of the judgment annulling the award and the continued legal effects of the award itself. In particular, *must* courts in foreign states recognize either the judgment annulling the award or the annulled award? Alternatively, *can* a foreign court recognize either the judgment or the award? The materials excerpted below consider these issues.

CHROMALLOY AEROSERVICES INC. v. ARAB REPUBLIC OF EGYPT
939 F.Supp. 907 (D.D.C. 1996)

June L. Green, District Judge. This matter is before the Court on the Petition of Chromalloy Aeroservices, Inc., ("CAS") to Confirm an Arbitral Award, and a Motion to Dismiss that Petition filed by the Arab Republic of Egypt ("Egypt"), the defendant in the arbitration.... The Court grants Chromalloy Aeroservices' Petition ... and denies Egypt's Motion to Dismiss....

On June 16, 1988, Egypt and CAS entered into a contract under which CAS agreed to provide parts, maintenance, and repair for helicopters belonging to the Egyptian Air Force. On December 2, 1991, Egypt terminated the contract by notifying CAS representatives in Egypt.... On December 15, 1991, CAS notified Egypt that it rejected the cancellation of the contract "and commenced arbitration proceedings on the basis of the arbitration clause contained in Article XII and Appendix E of the Contract." ...

On August 24, 1994, the arbitral panel ordered Egypt to pay to CAS the sums of $272,900... and $16,940,958 [plus interest].... On October 28, 1994, CAS applied to this Court for enforcement of the award.... On December 5, 1995, Egypt's Court of Appeal at Cairo issued an order nullifying the award.... Egypt argues that this Court should deny CAS' [petition to recognize the award] out of deference to its court....

A party seeking enforcement of a foreign arbitral award must apply for an order confirming the award within three years after the award is made. 9 U.S.C. §207. The award ... was made on August 14, 1994. CAS filed a petition to confirm the award ... on October 28, 1994.... CAS' Petition includes a "duly certified copy" of the original award as required by Article IV(1)(a) of the [New York] Convention, translated by a duly sworn translator, as required by Article IV(2) of the Convention, as well as a duly certified copy of the original contract and arbitration clause, as required by Article IV(1)(b) of the Convention. CAS' Petition is properly before this Court.

This Court must grant CAS' Petition to Recognize ... the arbitral "award unless it finds one of the grounds for refusal ... of recognition or enforcement of the award specified in the ... Convention." 9 U.S.C. §207. Under the Convention, "[r]ecognition and enforcement of the award *may* be refused" if Egypt furnishes to this Court "proof that ... [t]he award has ... been set aside ... by a competent authority of the country in which, or under the law of which, that award was made." Convention, Art. V(1) & V(1)(e) (emphasis added). In the

---

22. *See* G. Born, *International Commercial Arbitration* 3174 (2d ed. 2014).

present case, the award was made in Egypt, under the laws of Egypt, and has been nullified by the court designated by Egypt to review arbitral awards. Thus, [this] Court may, at its discretion, decline to enforce the award.[23]

While Article V provides a discretionary standard, Article VII of the Convention requires that, "[t]he provisions of the present Convention shall not ... deprive any interested party of any right he may have to avail himself of an arbitral award in the manner and *to the extent allowed by the law ... of the country where such award is sought to be relied upon.*" (Emphasis added.) In other words, under the Convention, CAS maintains all rights to the enforcement of this Arbitral Award that it would have in the absence of the Convention.... [T}he Court finds that, if the Convention did not exist, the [FAA] would provide CAS with a legitimate claim to enforcement of this arbitral award.

Under the laws of the United States, arbitration awards are presumed to be binding, and may only be vacated by a court under very limited circumstances [in 9 U.S.C. §10.] ... [Additionally, a]n arbitral award will also be set aside if the award was made in "'manifest disregard' of the law." "Manifest disregard of the law may be found if [the] arbitrator[s] understood and correctly stated the law but proceeded to ignore it." *Kanuth v. Prescott, Ball & Turben, Inc.*, 949 F.2d 1175, 1179 (D.C. Cir. 1991)....

In the present case, the language of the arbitral award that Egypt complains of reads: "The Arbitral Tribunal considers that it does not need to decide the legal nature of the contract. It appears that the Parties rely principally for their claims and defenses, on the interpretation of the contract itself and on the facts presented. Furthermore, the Arbitral Tribunal holds that the legal issues in dispute are not affected by the characterization of the contract." ... At worst, this decision constitutes a mistake of law, and thus is not subject to review by this Court.

In the United States, "[w]e are well past the time when judicial suspicion of the desirability of arbitration and of the competence of arbitral tribunals inhibited the development of arbitration as an alternative means of dispute resolution." *Mitsubishi,* 473 U.S. at 626-27. In Egypt, however, "[i]t is established that arbitration is an exceptional means for resolving disputes, requiring departure from the normal means of litigation before the courts, and the guarantees they afford." Egypt's complaint that, "[t]he Arbitral Award is null under Arbitration Law, ... because it is not properly 'grounded' under Egyptian law," reflects this suspicious view of arbitration, and is precisely the type of technical argument that U.S. courts are not to entertain when reviewing an arbitral award.

The Court's analysis thus far has addressed the arbitral award, and, as a matter of U.S. law, the award is proper. The Court now considers the question of whether the decision of the Egyptian court should be recognized as a valid foreign judgment.... [T]his is a case of first impression. There are no reported cases in which a court of the United States has faced a situation, under the Convention, in which the court of a foreign nation has nullified an otherwise valid arbitral award. This does not mean, however, that the Court is without guidance in this case. To the contrary, more than twenty years ago, in a case involving the enforcement of an arbitration clause under the FAA, the Supreme Court held that:

"An agreement to arbitrate before a specified tribunal is, in effect, a specialized kind of fo-

---

23. The French language version of the Convention, (which the Court notes is not the version codified by Congress), emphasizes the extraordinary nature of a refusal to recognize an award: "Recognition and enforcement of the award *will not be refused* ... unless ..." (emphasis in original).

rum-selection clause…. The invalidation of such an agreement … would not only allow the respondent to repudiate its solemn promise but would, as well, reflect a parochial concept that all disputes must be resolved under our laws and in our courts." *Scherk*, 417 U.S. at 519.

In *Scherk*, the Court forced a U.S. corporation to arbitrate a dispute arising under an international contract containing an arbitration clause…. [T]he Court … took the opportunity to comment upon the purposes of the newly acceded-to Convention:

> "The delegates to the Convention voiced frequent concern that courts of signatory countries in which an agreement to arbitrate is sought to be enforced should not be permitted to decline enforcement of such agreements on the basis of parochial views of their desirability or in a *manner* that would diminish the mutually binding nature of the agreements … [W]e think that this country's adoption and ratification of the Convention and the passage of Chapter 2 of the United States Arbitration Act provide strongly persuasive evidence of congressional policy consistent with the decision we reach today."

The Court finds this argument equally persuasive in the present case, where Egypt seeks to repudiate its solemn promise to abide by the results of the arbitration….

Appendix E to the contract … reads, in relevant part:

> "It is … understood that both parties have irrevocably agreed to apply Egypt (sic) Laws and to choose Cairo as seat of the court of arbitration. The decision of the said court shall be final and binding and cannot be made subject to any appeal or other recourse." …

Egypt argues that the first quoted sentence supersedes the second, and allows an appeal to an Egyptian court. Such an interpretation, however, would vitiate the second sentence, and would ignore the plain language on the face of the contract. The Court concludes that the first sentence defines choice of law and choice of forum for the hearings of the arbitral panel. The Court further concludes that the second quoted sentence indicates the clear intent of the parties that any arbitration of a dispute arising under the contract is not to be appealed to any court. This interpretation, unlike that offered by Egypt, preserves the meaning of both sentences in a manner that is consistent with the plain language of the contract…. In other words, the parties agreed to apply Egyptian Law to the arbitration, but, more important, they agreed that the arbitration ends with the decision of the arbitral panel.

The Court has already found that the arbitral award is proper as a matter of U.S. law, and that the arbitration agreement between Egypt and CAS precluded an appeal in Egyptian courts. The Egyptian court has acted, however, and Egypt asks this Court to grant *res judicata* effect to that action….

The U.S. public policy in favor of final and binding arbitration of commercial disputes is unmistakable, and supported by treaty, by statute, and by case law. The [FAA] "and the implementation of the Convention in the same year by amendment of the [FAA]," demonstrate that there is an "emphatic federal policy in favor of arbitral dispute resolution," particularly "in the field of international commerce." *Mitsubishi,* 473 U.S. at 631. A decision by this Court to recognize the decision of the Egyptian court would violate this clear U.S. public policy.

Egypt argues that by choosing Egyptian law, and by choosing Cairo as the situs of the arbitration, CAS has for all time signed away its rights under the Convention and U.S. law. This argument is specious. When CAS agreed to the choice of law and choice of forum provisions, it waived its right to sue Egypt for breach of contract in the courts of the United States in favor of final and binding arbitration of such a dispute under the Convention.

Having prevailed in the chosen forum, under the chosen law, CAS comes to this Court seeking recognition and enforcement of the award. The Convention was created for just this purpose. It is untenable to argue that by choosing arbitration under the Convention, CAS has waived rights specifically guaranteed by that same Convention.

As a final matter, Egypt argues that, "Chromalloy's use of [A]rticle VII [to invoke the FAA] contradicts the clear language of the Convention and would create an impermissible conflict under 9 U.S.C. §208," by eliminating all consideration of Article V of the Convention. As the Court has explained, however, Article V provides a permissive standard, under which this Court may refuse to enforce an award. Article VII, on the other hand, mandates that this Court must consider CAS' claims under applicable U.S. law.... Article VII does not eliminate all consideration of Article V; it merely requires that this Court protect any rights that CAS has under the domestic laws of the United States. There is no conflict between CAS' use of Article VII to invoke the FAA and the language of the Convention....

TERMORIO SA v. ELECTRANTA SP
487 F.3d 928 (D.C. Cir. 2007)

EDWARDS, Senior Circuit Judge. Appellant TermoRio SA ESP ("TermoRio") and appellee Electrificadora del Atlántico SA ESP ("Electranta"), a state-owned public utility, entered into a Power Purchase Agreement ("Agreement") pursuant to which TermoRio agreed to generate energy and Electranta agreed to buy it. When appellee allegedly failed to meet its obligations under the Agreement, the parties submitted their dispute to an arbitration Tribunal in Colombia in accordance with their Agreement. The Tribunal issued an award in excess of $60 million dollars in favor of TermoRio. Shortly after the Tribunal issued its award, Electranta filed an "extraordinary writ" in a Colombia court seeking to overturn the award. In due course, the Consejo de Estado ("Council of State"), Colombia's highest administrative court, nullified the arbitration award on the ground that the arbitration clause contained in the parties' Agreement violated Colombian law. Following the judgment by the Consejo de Estado, TermoRio and co-appellant LeaseCo Group, LLC ("LeaseCo"), an investor in TermoRio, filed suit in the District Court against Electranta and the Republic of Colombia seeking enforcement of the Tribunal's ... award. Appellants contended that enforcement of the award is required under the [FAA], which implements the [New York] Convention. The District Court ... dismissed appellants' enforcement action for failure to state a claim upon which relief could be granted....

We affirm the judgment of the District Court. The arbitration award was made in Colombia and the Consejo de Estado was a competent authority in that country to set aside the award as contrary to the law of Colombia. *See* New York Convention Art. V(1)(e). Because there is nothing in the record here indicating that the proceedings before the Consejo de Estado were tainted or that the judgment of that court is other than authentic, the District Court was, as it held, obliged to respect it. Accordingly, we hold that, because the arbitration award was lawfully nullified by the country in which the award was made, appellants have no cause of action in the United States to seek enforcement of the award under the FAA or the Convention.

The facts in this case are carefully set forth in the District Court's ... opinion[:]

"Defendant Republic of Colombia is a foreign state. Defendant [Electranta], incorporated in

1957 to provide electricity services ... was 87% owned and controlled by Colombia.... In the mid-1990s, Colombia's Atlantic coast experienced significant electricity shortages. In 1995 LeaseCo entered into discussions with Electranta to modernize Electranta's operations and build a new power plant in Colombia. [LeaseCo and Electranta formed a Colombian entity, TermoRio, which, after various transfers, was to be owned 99.9% by LeaseCo].

At the heart of this lawsuit is [the Agreement] between TermoRio and Electranta [executed] in June 1997. Under this Agreement, TermoRio agreed to generate energy and Electranta agreed to buy it. In reliance on this Agreement, TermoRio invested more than $7 million to construct a power plant. The Agreement also provided that any dispute between the parties would be resolved by binding arbitration in Colombia....

[O]n April 16, 1998, Colombia began to privatize [its electricity sector] by creating a new company, Electrocaribe, to receive and hold Electranta's assets and liabilities. However, at the behest of Colombia, Electranta did not transfer its duties under the Agreement to buy power from TermoRio. Electranta was left with obligations under the Agreement to buy power, but no resources to do so. As a result, Electranta failed to buy power from TermoRio and breached the Agreement.... The Agreement's arbitration clause provides (as translated):

> Any dispute or controversy arising between the Parties in connection to the execution, interpretation, performance or liquidation of the Contract shall be settled through mechanisms of conciliation, amiable composition or settlement, within a term no longer than three weeks. If no agreement is reached, either party may have recourse to an arbitral tribunal that *shall be governed in accordance with the Rules of Conciliation and Arbitration of the International Chamber of Commerce*. The tribunal shall be made up of three (3) members appointed by the Chamber, and shall be seated in the city of Barranquilla[, Colombia]. The award, which shall be binding on the parties, must be rendered within a maximum term of three months.

Pursuant to this provision, after defendants failed to meet their obligations under the Agreement, the parties entered into a long arbitration process. On December 21, 2000, a Tribunal of three arbitrators, applying ICC procedural rules, determined that Electranta breached the Agreement at the direction of Colombia. The Tribunal ordered Electranta to pay TermoRio an award of $60.3 million.... Neither the Republic of Colombia nor Electranta has complied with the $60 million arbitral award, and both have refused to pay any portion of it. Plaintiffs allege that Colombia and Electranta have also sought to undermine the award in several other respects....

[O]n December 23, 2000 (right after the Tribunal issued the award), Electranta filed an "extraordinary writ" with a court in Barranquilla, seeking to overturn the award. In response the Council of State vacated it. The Council of State reasoned that the arbitration had to be conducted in accordance with Colombian law, and Colombian law in effect as of the date of the Agreement did not expressly permit the use of ICC procedural rules in arbitration....

In the District Court, appellants TermoRio and LeaseCo [sought recognition of the ICC award].... Appellees filed a motion to dismiss in which they raised numerous defenses, including, *inter alia*, that the award was properly vacated by a Colombian court.... The District Court ... granted appellees' motion to dismiss. The trial court ruled as follows: "the ... arbitral award enforcement claim ... is dismissed for failure to state a claim; the Colombian courts have vacated the award." ...

The Supreme Court has recognized an "emphatic federal policy in favor of arbitral dispute resolution." *Mitsubishi* [*supra* p. 488]. "And at least since this Nation's accession in 1970 to the [New York] Convention, and the implementation of the Convention in the same year by amendment of the [FAA], that federal policy applies with special force in the field of international commerce." *Mitsubishi*, 473 U.S. at 631.... The Convention's purpose was to "encourage the recognition and enforcement of commercial arbitration agreements in international contracts and to unify the standards by which agreements to arbitrate are observed and arbitral awards are enforced in the signatory countries." *Scherk*, 417 U.S. at 520 n.15. And, as the Court has noted, "[t]he utility of the Convention in promoting the process of international commercial arbitration depends upon the willingness of national courts to let go of matters they normally would think of as their own." *Mitsubishi*, 473 U.S. at 639 n.21.

The basic understanding of the … Convention is that "[e]ach Contracting State shall recognize arbitral awards as binding and enforce them in accordance with the rules of procedure of the territory where the award is relied upon, under the conditions laid down in the … articles [of the Convention]." New York Convention, Art. III. Under the Convention, "the critical element is the place of the award: if that place is in the territory of a party to the Convention, all other Convention states are required to recognize and enforce the award, regardless of the citizenship or domicile of the parties to the arbitration." *Creighton Ltd v. Gov't of the State of Qatar*, 181 F.3d 118, 121 (D.C. Cir. 1999) (quoting *Restatement (Third) of Foreign Relations Law* §487 cmt. b (1987)).…

[T]he New York Convention enumerates specific grounds upon which a court may refuse recognition and enforcement of an arbitration award.… These provisions of [Article V of] the Convention have been implemented by the FAA. *See* 9 U.S.C. §207. The Convention provides a carefully crafted framework for the enforcement of international arbitral awards. Under the Convention, "[o]nly a court in a country with primary jurisdiction over an arbitral award may annul that award." *Karaha Bodas*, 364 F.3d at 287 ("*Karaha Bodas II*"). As the Second Circuit has noted:

> "the Convention mandates very different regimes for the review of arbitral awards (1) in the state in which, or under the law of which, the award was made, and (2) in other states where recognition and enforcement are sought. The Convention specifically contemplates that the state in which, or under the law of which, the award is made, will be free to set aside or modify an award in accordance with its domestic arbitral law and its full panoply of express and implied grounds for relief. *See* Convention Art. V(1)(e). However, the Convention is equally clear that when an action for enforcement is brought in a foreign state, the state may refuse to enforce the award only on the grounds explicitly set forth in Article V of the Convention." *Toys "R" Us,* 126 F.3d at 23.

In this case, appellees point out that, because the arbitration award was made by a Colombian Tribunal convened in that country, pursuant to an agreement between Colombian companies to buy and sell electrical power in that country, Colombia is the nation with primary jurisdiction over the dispute. Appellees argue further that, under the clear terms of the Convention, appellants' action to enforce the arbitration award fails to state a cause of action. On this latter point, appellees point to Article V(1)(e) of the Convention.… Pursuant to this provision of the Convention, a secondary contracting State normally may not enforce an arbitration award that has been lawfully set aside by a "competent authority" in the primary Contracting State. Because the Consejo de Estado is undisputedly a "competent authority" in Colombia (the primary State), and because there is nothing in the record here indicating that the proceedings before the Consejo de Estado were tainted or that the judgment of that court is other than authentic, appellees contend that appellants have no cause of action under the FAA or the New York Convention to enforce the award in a Contracting State outside of Colombia. On the record at hand, we agree.

In reaching this conclusion, we generally subscribe to the reasoning of the Second Circuit in *Baker Marine (Nig.) Ltd v. Chevron (Nig.) Ltd*, 191 F.3d 194 (2d Cir. 1999). In that case, Baker Marine, a barge company, executed a services contract with Danos, a shipping concern. The contract contained a clause requiring the parties to arbitrate disputes or controversies arising under their agreement. Following such a dispute, the parties "submitted to arbitration before panels of arbitrators in Lagos, Nigeria." The panels awarded Baker Marine nearly $3 million in damages, but the award was subsequently set aside by a Nigerian court. Baker Marine then sought enforcement of the award in the U.S. District Court. The trial court refused to recognize the award, citing Article V(1)(e) of the Convention, as well as principles of comity. On appeal, Baker Marine argued that the trial court erred in refusing to enforce the award, because it had been set aside by the Nigerian court on grounds that would have been invalid under U.S. law if presented in an American court. The appellate court rejected this argument and affirmed the trial court's decision not to recognize the award, noting that the parties "contracted in Nigeria that their disputes would be arbitrated under the laws of Nigeria." The court also remarked on the undesirable consequences that would likely follow from adoption of Baker Marine's argument:

> "[A]s a practical matter, mechanical application of domestic arbitral law to foreign awards under the Convention would seriously undermine finality and regularly produce conflicting judgments. If a party whose arbitration award has been vacated at the site of the award can automatically obtain enforcement of the awards under the domestic laws of other nations, a losing party will have every reason to pursue its adversary 'with enforcement actions from country to country until a court is found, if any, which grants the enforcement.'"

The same principles and concerns govern here, where appellants seek to enforce an arbitration award that has been vacated by Colombia's Consejo de Estado. For us to endorse what appellants seek would seriously undermine a principal precept of the New York Convention: an arbitration award does not exist to be enforced in other Contracting States if it has been lawfully "set aside" by a competent authority in the State in which the award was made....

Appellants argue that courts in the United States "have discretion under the Convention to enforce an award despite annulment in another country," *Karaha Bodas Co. v. Perusahaan Pertambangan Minyak Dan Gas*, 335 F.3d 357, 369 (5th Cir. 2003), because Article V(1)(e) merely says that "[r]ecognition and enforcement *may* be refused" if the award has been set aside by a competent authority in the primary state, New York Convention, Art. V(1)(e) (emphasis added). More particularly, appellants contend that "a state is not required to give effect to foreign judicial proceedings grounded on policies which do violence to its own fundamental interests." Appellants' characterizations of the applicable law are understated and thus misguided.

Appellants concede that *Baker Marine* is not incorrect in its holding that "it is insufficient to enforce an award solely because a foreign court's grounds for nullifying the award would not be recognized under domestic U.S. law." Rather, appellants allege that the District Court should have exercised its discretion to enforce the arbitration award in this case, because, *inter alia*, "the Council of State's decision was contrary to both domestic Colombian and international law; recognition of that decision would frustrate clearly expressed international and U.S. policy; and the process leading to the nullification decision demonstrated the Colombian government's determination to deny Plaintiff's fair process."

In advancing their claims, appellants rely heavily on *Chromalloy*. [That case involved an] express contractual agreement not to take any appeal from the arbitration award. We need not decide whether the holding in *Chromalloy* is correct, because, as appellees point out, "the present case is plainly distinguishable from *Chromalloy* where an express contract provision was violated by pursuing an appeal to vacate the award...."

Furthermore, appellants are simply mistaken in suggesting that the Convention policy in favor of enforcement of arbitration awards effectively swallows the command of Article V(1)(e). A judgment whether to recognize or enforce an award that has not been set aside in the State in which it was made is quite different from a judgment whether to disregard the action of a court of competent authority in another State. "The Convention specifically contemplates that the state in which, or under the law of which, the award is made, will be free to set aside or modify an award in accordance with its domestic arbitral law and its full panoply of express and implied grounds for relief." [*Yusuf Ahmed Alghanim & Sons, WLL v. Toys "R" Us, Inc.*, 126 F.3d 15, 23 (2d Cir. 1997).] This means that a primary State necessarily may set aside an award on grounds that are not consistent with the laws and policies of a secondary Contracting State. The Convention does not endorse a regime in which secondary States (in determining whether to enforce an award) routinely second-guess the judgment of a court in a primary State, when the court in the primary State has lawfully acted pursuant to "competent authority" to "set aside" an arbitration award made in its country. Appellants go much too far in suggesting that a court in a secondary State is free as it sees fit to ignore the judgment of a court of competent authority in a primary State vacating an arbitration award. It takes much more than a mere assertion that the judgment of the primary State "offends the public policy" of the secondary State to overcome a defense raised under Article V(1)(e).

The decision in *Baker Marine* notes that the "[r]ecognition of the [foreign court's] judgment in [that] case d[id] not conflict with U.S. public policy." 191 F.3d at 197 n. 3, thus at least implicitly endorsing a "public policy" gloss on Article V(1)(e). However, the decision does not say that a court in the United States has unfettered discretion to impose its own considerations of public policy in reviewing the judgment of a court in a primary State vacating an arbitration award based upon the foreign court's construction of the law of the primary State. Rather, as appellees argue, *Baker Marine* is consistent with the view that, "[w]hen a competent foreign court has nullified a foreign arbitration award, United States courts should not go behind that decision absent extraordinary circumstances not present in this case."

In applying Article V(1)(e) of the New York Convention, we must be very careful in weighing notions of "public policy" in determining whether to credit the judgment of a court in the primary State vacating an arbitration award. The test of public policy cannot be simply whether the courts of a secondary State would set aside an arbitration award if the award had been made and enforcement had been sought within its jurisdiction. As noted above, the Convention contemplates that different Contracting States may have different grounds for setting aside arbitration awards.... Article V(2)(b) of the Convention, unlike Article V(1)(e), incorporates an express public policy exception.... It is noteworthy that in construing this provision the courts have been very careful not to stretch the compass of "public policy." As one court has noted: "Under Article V(2)(b) of the New York Convention, a court may refuse to recognize or enforce an arbitral award if it would be contrary to the public policy of that country. The public policy defense is to be construed narrowly to be applied only where enforcement would violate the forum state's most basic notions of morality and justice." *Karaha Bodas II*, 364 F.3d at 305-06. Given that Article V(1)(e) contains no exception for public policy, it would be strange indeed to recognize such an implicit limitation in Article V(1)(e) that is broader than the express limitation in Article V(2)(b).

Accepting that there is a narrow public policy gloss on Article V(1)(e) of the Convention and that a foreign judgment is unenforceable as against public policy to the extent that it is "repugnant to fundamental notions of what is decent and just in the United States," *Tahan v. Hodgson*, 662 F.2d 862, 864 (D.C. Cir. 1981), appellants' claims still fail. Appellants have neither alleged nor provided any evidence to suggest that the parties' proceedings before Colombia's Consejo de Estado or the judgment of the court violated any basic notions of justice to which we subscribe.

Appellants contend that the Consejo de Estado's ruling conflicts with Colombia's obligation under the New York Convention, but that bare allegation surely provides no basis for us to ignore Article V(1)(e) on grounds of public policy. As the court noted in [*Toys "R" Us*]:

> "[U]nder the Convention, the power and authority of the local courts of the rendering state remain of paramount importance. What the Convention did not do ... was provide any international mechanism to insure the validity of the award where rendered. This was left to the provisions of local law. The Convention provides no restraint whatsoever on the control functions of local courts at the seat of arbitration.... From the plain language and history of the Convention, it is thus apparent that a party may seek to vacate or set aside an award in the state in which, or under the law of which, the award is rendered. Moreover, the language and history of the Convention make it clear that such a motion is to be governed by domestic law of the rendering state ..." 126 F.3d at 22-23.

The District Court correctly observed that "[t]his matter is a peculiarly Colombian affair," concerning, as it does, "a dispute involving Colombian parties over a contract to perform services in Colombia which led to a Colombian arbitration decision and Colombian litigation." To this, we would add that the parties also agreed to be bound by Colombian law. The Consejo de Estado, Colombia's highest administrative court, is the final expositor of Colombian law, and we are not in position to pronounce the decision of that court wrong....

NOTES

1. *Consequences of national court decisions annulling and refusing to recognize awards.* Significantly different consequences may flow from: (i) a court's refusal to enforce an arbitral award, and (ii) a court's decision setting aside or annulling the award. *See supra* pp. 1070-72.

    (a) *Consequences of decision refusing to recognize award.* If an award is denied recognition in a national court, it nonetheless remains a "binding" award. It can be taken to other jurisdictions, and efforts can be made to enforce it anew. No judicial act has purported to "set aside" or "annul" the award. For example, a court may deny recognition to an award on grounds of local public policy or nonarbitrability, *infra* pp. 1250-66. In neither case would the court's decision affect the underlying validity of the award or imply that it should not be recognized elsewhere. *See* H.

Gharavi, *The International Effectiveness of the Annulment of An Arbitral Award* 110 (2002); G. Born, *International Commercial Arbitration* 3608 (2d ed. 2014).

(b) *Consequences of decision in arbitral seat annulling award.* If an award is "annulled" in the arbitral seat, then it ceases to have legal effect (at least in the arbitral seat), just as an appellate court decision annuls or sets aside a trial court judgment. How does this differ from a refusal to recognize the award by a court outside the arbitral seat?

2. *National court decisions recognizing awards annulled in arbitral seat.* There is little judicial precedent on the question whether a nation may enforce an award that was annulled in the place where it was rendered. Consider the facts and procedural history in *Chromalloy.* The underlying award was made in Egypt and then annulled by an Egyptian court. Nonetheless, the prevailing party successfully enforced the annulled award in the United States. Other national courts have also recognized foreign awards that had been annulled in the arbitral seat. *See Judgment of 10 June 1997, Omnium de Traitement et de Valorisation v. Hilmarton*, XXII Y.B. Comm. Arb. 696 (1997) (French Cour de Cassation) (annulled award may be enforced); *Judgment of 14* January 1997, *Arab Repub. of Egypt v. Chromalloy Aeroservs., Inc.*, XXII Y.B. Comm. Arb. 691 (1997) (Paris Cour d'appel) (recognizing Egyptian award, despite Egyptian court decision annulling award); G. Born, *International Commercial Arbitration* 3625-28 (2d ed. 2014).

3. *National court decisions refusing to recognize awards annulled in arbitral seat.* A few courts have declined to enforce awards that were annulled in the arbitral seat. *Judgment of 20 June 1980, Berardi v. Clair*, VII Y.B. Comm. Arb. 319 (1982) (Paris Cour d'appel) (declining to enforce award made in Switzerland against French defendant after award was annulled as "arbitrary" by Swiss court); *Judgment of 13 August 1979, Götaverken v. GMTC*, VI Y.B. Comm. Arb. 237 (1981) (Swedish S.Ct.).

4. *Does New York Convention require recognition of award annulled in arbitral seat?* Was the court in *Chromalloy* required by the New York Convention to recognize the annulled Egyptian arbitral award? What did the *Chromalloy* court conclude? Consider Article V(1)(e) of the Convention. Does Article V(1)(e) not clearly apply to the Egyptian award and the action that annulled it, and thereby except the award from the Convention's recognition obligation?

When Article V(1)(e) refers to an award being set aside by a "competent authority," what does it mean? Is there any doubt that the Egyptian court was a "competent authority"? Does the fact that an Egyptian court apparently reviews awards on the merits mean that it is not a "competent authority"?

Suppose a court with no connection to the *Chromalloy* dispute (*e.g.*, Canada) had purported to annul the award made in Egypt. Would the Canadian court be a "competent authority"? *See supra* pp. 1099-112 & *infra* pp. 1183-87.

5. *Does an award annulled in arbitral seat still exist?* Consider the court's rationale in *TermoRio*, where it said recognition of an award annulled in the arbitral seat "would seriously undermine a principal precept of the New York Convention: an arbitration award does not exist to be enforced in other Contracting States if it has been lawfully 'set aside' by a competent authority in the State in which the award was made." What does the court mean when it suggests that an award "does not exist" if it has been annulled? Where does the Convention say that this is a "central precept" of the Con-

vention? Explain why *TermoRio* is wrong. Consider Article V(1)(e). What sense does it make to create an exception, in which the obligation to recognize awards does not apply if the award has been annulled, if there is no award in the first place?

6. *Does New York Convention forbid recognition of award annulled in the arbitral seat?* In *Chromalloy*, the Arab Republic of Egypt argued that the New York Convention *forbid* the U.S. court (or any other national court) from recognizing the annulled Egyptian award. How did *Chromalloy* dispose of this argument? Note the court's comment that it had "discretion" to recognize, or not to recognize, the award.

Compare *TermoRio*. Does the court hold that an award that has been annulled in the arbitral seat can never be recognized under the Convention? Or does it hold that an annulled award can only be recognized in more limited circumstances than those contemplated in *Chromalloy*? If the latter, how can an award that "doesn't exist" be recognized?

What is the argument that the Convention forbids recognition of an award which was annulled in the arbitral seat? Consider Article V(1), whose English version provides that "[r]ecognition and enforcement of the award *may* be refused" in certain circumstances. Does this not imply that recognition "may" also be granted, even if an exception applies?

Note, however, that there are differences between the English and French versions of Article V(1). *See supra* p. 1175 n. 23. The French version provides, in effect, that "[r]ecognition and enforcement of the award will not be refused ... unless." (Note that both the English and French versions of the Convention are equally authoritative. *See supra* p. 34.) Arguments that the Convention forbids recognition of an annulled award rely on the French text and its arguable suggestion that an award must be denied recognition if one of Article V(1)'s exceptions applies. For analysis of these linguistic issues, see Paulsson, *May or Must Under the New York Convention: An Exercise in Syntax and Linguistics*, 14 Arb. Int'l 227 (1998).

7. *How should New York Convention be interpreted with respect to annulled awards?* What interpretation of the New York Convention *should* be adopted with respect to the recognition of awards that have been annulled in the arbitral seat? *Compare* Smit, *A-National Arbitration*, 63 Tulane L. Rev. 629, 641 (1989) ("Convention does not ... impose an obligation to refuse enforcement [when an award has been set aside where it was made]; on the contrary, it leaves the court in the second state free to grant recognition"); Paulsson, *Arbitration Unbound: Award Detached From the Law of Its Country of Origin*, 30 Int'l & Comp. L.Q. 358, 373 (1981) ("one country might allow enforcement of an award even if it has been set aside in its country of origin"); van den Berg, *When Is An Arbitral Award Non-Domestic Under the New York Convention of 1958?*, 6 Pace L. Rev. 25, 41-42 (1985) ("if the arbitral award has been set aside in the country of origin, foreign courts are bound by that decision. In that case, they must refuse recognition and enforcement of the award").

Consider the following:

"Once a venue or a governing law is selected, the convention gives to it a primacy with regard to the validity of an award. If an award is rendered, let us say, in Switzerland and is nullified under Swiss law, nothing should be enforceable in any other jurisdiction. However, if the award is rendered in Switzerland but enforcement is refused in France where the award debtor has property, the French judgment should have no effect outside of France, even if it explicitly bases itself on a ground of nullity which would have nullified the award *erga omnes* had it been rendered in a primary jurisdiction. The award creditor may still seek enforcement simultaneously or sequentially in any other jurisdiction which is party to the convention. The critical difference, then, is radius of effects. As opposed to the nullification of the hypothetical award in Switzerland, a nullification in France has no effect beyond France.... For a control system like that established in the New York Convention to work, the primary and secondary assignments must be mandatory. Because of the language in the English text of the convention, the control system has appeared to some to be optional rather than imperative: "recognition and enforcement of the award *may* be refused" but may be refused "only" if there is proof of a defect, as detailed by the convention. The French text of the convention, which is equally authentic, suggests that the control system is mandatory. The Spanish text is even more clearly mandatory. This particular textual discrepancy between equally authentic languages is not uncommon in multilingual treaties, for the discretionary power intended and expressed in English by "may" is difficult to convey in French and Spanish, and the combination of "may ... only," which is, at once, permissive and restrictive, is not easily rendered in many other languages...." M. Reisman, *Systems of Control in International Adjudication and Arbitration* 115-16 (1992).

What policies would be served by forbidding recognition of an award that has been annulled in its country of origin? Consider the facts in *Chromalloy*. How would the international arbitral process be strengthened by forbidding national courts from recognizing the award made in Egypt? Consider the court's rationale in *Baker Marine*, quoted in *TermoRio*:

"[A]s a practical matter, mechanical application of domestic arbitral law to foreign awards under the Convention would seriously undermine finality and regularly produce conflicting judgments. If a party whose arbitration award has been vacated at the site of the award can automatically obtain enforcement of the awards under the domestic laws of other nations, a losing party will have every reason to pursue its adversary 'with enforcement actions from country to country until a court is found, if any, which grants the enforcement.'"

Note the court's assertion that "finality" would be undermined by recognizing an annulled award. Isn't finality one of the central objects of international arbitration? Does the annulment of an award advance or hinder policies of finality? *See supra* pp. 1113-25. Isn't it the court's decision in *TermoRio* (and *Baker Marine*) that frustrate policies of finality?

Is it helpful to consider generalized policies of finality? Doesn't the annulment of an award involve competing claims of finality—between the finality of the award and the finality of the national court judgment annulling the award? Isn't the real issue deciding which decision should be accorded finality? How should one go about resolving this issue?

8. *When should an annulled award be recognized under New York Convention?* Assume, as *Chromalloy* (and, apparently, *TermoRio*) held, that the New York Convention neither forbids nor requires recognition of an arbitral award that has been annulled in the arbitral seat. What standards then, if any, guide a national court in deciding whether or not to recognize the annulled award?

Note that the *Chromalloy* court held that it had "discretion" to recognize the Egyptian award. Does a court have unfettered "discretion" to recognize, or not to recognize, an annulled award? What sources of law might provide standards for recognizing annulled awards? The Convention? Local arbitration legislation (*e.g.*, the FAA)? In what circumstances is an annulled award subject to recognition under the *Chromalloy* analysis?

Consider the facts in *Chromalloy*. Suppose Egypt had won the arbitration, the U.S. investor had sought to annul the arbitral award in Egyptian courts, and the Egyptian courts had annulled the award. Should the U.S. court recognize the annulled award in these circumstances? Suppose that the grounds for annulling the award in Egyptian courts in *Chromalloy* were identical to those available under the FAA or UNCITRAL Model Law.

Suppose a Swiss court annuls an award made in a dispute between a Japanese and a Mexican company, on the grounds of serious procedural irregularity. Should a U.S. court recognize the award? Suppose the Egyptian court in *Chromalloy* had relied on procedural irregularities in annulling the award.

Consider the result in *TermoRio*. Note that the Colombian Council of State annulled an ICC award, against a Colombian state entity and in favor of a foreign-owned entity, based on the following rationale: "the arbitration had to be conducted in accordance with Colombian law, and Colombian law in effect as of the date of the Agreement did not expressly permit the use of ICC procedural rules in arbitration." Isn't this rationale a repudiation of (a) Colombia's obligations under Article II of the New York Convention, requiring Contracting States to recognize agreements to arbitrate; and (b) the parties' arbitration agreement? Is the U.S. court's refusal to recognize the ICC award, and its acquiescence in the Colombian court's repudiation of the Convention, a violation of the Convention itself? Explain why the court's decision in *TermoRio* on this issue is (again) wrong.

Note the *TermoRio* court's effort to distinguish *Chromalloy*, citing the exclusion of judicial review in the *Chromalloy* arbitration agreement. Consider Article 28(6) of the 1998 ICC Rules, which was part of the *TermoRio* arbitration agreement: "By submitting the dispute to arbitration under these Rules, the parties undertake to carry out any Award without delay, and shall be deemed to have waived their right to any form of recourse, insofar as such waiver can validly be made." Is that language any different from the agreement in *Chromalloy*? Is it clearer? *Compare* Drahozal, *Enforcing Vacated International Arbitration Awards: An Economic Approach*, 11 Am. Rev. Int'l Arb. 451 (2000).

Consider the court's discussion of public policy in *TermoRio*. When, under the court's analysis, would U.S. public policy ever provide a basis for recognition of an annulled award? Suppose the Colombian court had said what it was only thinking: "The award is annulled because it benefits a foreign entity at the expense of a Colombian state entity." Would the *TermoRio* court regard that as violating U.S. public policy?

Suppose the court that annuls an arbitral award is manifestly corrupt, biased, or arbitrary. In those circumstances, would *TermoRio* permit recognition of the annulled award? How difficult is it to prove that a foreign court was corrupt or arbitrary?

Suppose local law (as in *Chromalloy*) permits unfettered judicial review of the merits of arbitral awards. If a local court reviews the arbitrators' decision on the merits and simply reaches a different conclusion about the law and facts, should the award be recognized abroad? What would be the result under *TermoRio*? Under *Chromalloy*? Is it relevant that the parties agreed, expressly or impliedly, to arbitration in a place with broad judicial review? What if the enforcing court thought the court that annulled the award (not the arbitral tribunal) was right in its resolution of the dispute?

What if an award is annulled as contrary to the public policy of the enforcing court? Or as deciding a nonarbitrable dispute? If a court in the arbitral seat relies on local public policy or nonarbitrability rules to annul an award, should foreign courts give effect to those local policies? Or to the Convention's policies encouraging recognition of foreign awards? *See* Paulsson, *The Case for Disregarding LSAs (Local Standard Annulments) Under the New York Convention*, 7 Am. Rev. Int'l Arb. 99 (1996); Radicati di Brozolo, *The Control System of Arbitral Awards*, ICCA Congress Series No. 16, 102 (2011) ("Deference to foreign annulment decisions should be accorded only on a selective, reasoned and ad hoc basis, where the enforcing court considers it justified in the particular circumstances, and having regard to the commonality between the standards of review of awards of the enforcement forum and the concrete standards applied by the vacating court, as well as to the true expectations").

9. *Provisions of national legislation on enforcement of annulled awards.* Compare Articles 1520 and 1525 of the French Code of Civil Procedure and §103(2) of the English Arbitration Act, 1996, with the (official) Dutch and French versions of Article 1721 of the Belgian Judicial Code (Dutch: "(1) The court of first instance refuses recognition and enforcement of an arbitral award, regardless of the country where it was made, only in the following circumstances: ... (vi) the award has not yet become binding upon the parties or has been annulled or suspended by a court of the country in which, or under the law of which, it was made."; French: "... shall not refuse recognition and enforcement ... unless ...") and its (unofficial) English translation ("may only refuse ... in the following circumstances"). *Judicial Code Sixth Part: Arbitration*, in J. Paulsson (ed.), *International Handbook on Commercial Arbitration* 1-16 (Supp. No. 77 2013). How should such language as in the Belgian law be interpreted in light of the foregoing discussion of the New York Convention? Does a court have discretion to recognize annulled awards?

10. *Consequences of decision in arbitral seat refusing to annul award.* Suppose courts in the arbitral seat refuse, after entertaining an annulment action, to annul an award. What consequences should this refusal have in actions to enforce the award in other jurisdictions? For example, suppose that in *Chromalloy* a court in the arbitral seat (Egypt) had rejected arguments concerning arbitrator misconduct or excess of authority, and confirmed the award. What effect should this have in an action to enforce the award in the United States when the same arguments are raised as Article V exceptions? *See infra* pp. 1199-266.

11. *Consequences of annulment of arbitral award on arbitration agreement.* Suppose an award is annulled on the grounds that (a) the tribunal denied the respondent an opportunity to be heard; (b) the tribunal was biased; and (c) the tribunal acted in manifest disregard of mandatory law and public policy. Is the original agreement to arbitrate still applicable to future disputes? To the same dispute addressed by the first tribunal? Why shouldn't the arbitration agreement still be in full force and effect?

CHAPTER 16

RECOGNITION AND ENFORCEMENT OF INTERNATIONAL ARBITRAL AWARDS

This chapter addresses the recognition and enforcement of international arbitral awards. First, the chapter discusses the presumptive obligation of national courts, under the New York Convention and most other international instruments and national arbitration statutes, to recognize international arbitral awards. Second, the chapter discusses the various exceptions under international and national authorities to the presumptive enforceability of awards, which permit non-recognition of such awards. The chapter considers these issues in international commercial arbitration, as well as in investment and inter-state arbitrations.

A. PRESUMPTIVE OBLIGATION TO RECOGNIZE INTERNATIONAL ARBITRAL AWARDS

Most international arbitration regimes impose a presumptive obligation to recognize arbitral awards. That is true of the New York Convention and the Inter-American Convention, as well as of the ICSID Convention and other international arbitration instruments. Likewise, most national arbitration statutes presumptively require the recognition of international arbitral awards, subject only to a limited number of specifically-identified exceptions.[1]

1. Presumptive Obligations to Recognize International Commercial Arbitral Awards

As detailed above, the New York Convention was designed principally to facilitate the recognition and enforcement of foreign arbitral awards.[2] Article III of the Convention imposes a general obligation on Contracting States to recognize awards made in other countries, subject to procedural requirements no more onerous than those for domestic awards. Article III provides:

> Each contracting state shall recognize arbitral awards as binding and enforce them in accordance with the rules of procedure of the territory where the award is relied upon, under the conditions laid down in the following articles. There shall not be imposed substantially more onerous conditions or higher fees or charges on the recognition or enforcement of arbitral awards to which the Convention applies than are imposed on the recognition or enforcement of domestic arbitral awards.

Several aspects of the Convention give special force to the obligation imposed by Article III and underscore its drafters' goal of facilitating transnational enforcement of arbitral

---

1. *See* G. Born, *International Commercial Arbitration* 3410, 3418 (2d ed. 2014); Sanders, *A Twenty Years' Review of the Convention on the Recognition and Enforcement of Foreign Arbitral Awards*, 13 Int'l Law. 269 (1979).

2. *See supra* pp. 33-39; G. Born, *International Commercial Arbitration* 99-105, 3410-27 (2d ed. 2014); Pryles, *Foreign Awards and the New York Convention*, 9 Arb. Int'l 259 (1993).

awards.[3] Most importantly, the Convention presumes the validity of awards and places the burden of proving invalidity on the party opposing enforcement.[4] Moreover, as noted above, awards are not subject to "double *exequatur*" and need not be confirmed in the arbitral seat before recognition can be sought abroad.[5] In addition, as Article III provides, Contracting States may not impose procedural requirements that are more onerous than those applicable to domestic awards.[6]

The Inter-American Convention contains provisions that are substantially similar to the New York Convention.[7] Article 4 imposes a presumptive obligation to recognize arbitral awards that are subject to the Convention, while Article 5 sets forth an exclusive list of exceptions to this general requirement.

The ICSID Convention imposes even stricter requirements to recognize ICSID awards. Articles 53 and 54 of the Convention provide that ICSID awards are "binding" and require that "each Contracting State shall recognize an award rendered pursuant to this Convention as binding and enforce the pecuniary obligations imposed by the award within its territories as if it were a final judgment of a court of that State."[8] The Convention provides no grounds for denying recognition and enforcement of an ICSID award.

2. Presumptive Obligation to Recognize International Arbitral Awards Under National Arbitration Legislation

Most national arbitration statutes also treat international arbitral awards as presumptively valid. Articles 35 and 36 of the UNCITRAL Model Law provide that international awards shall be recognized, save where specified exceptions apply.[9] Articles 190 and 194 of the SLPIL adopt the same approach.[10] Other national arbitration statutes are similar.[11]

In the United States, §207 of the FAA restates the obligation imposed by Article III to enforce Convention awards, and then incorporates Article V's exceptions by reference: "The court *shall* confirm the award unless it finds one of the grounds for refusal or deferral of recognition or enforcement of the award specified in the said Convention."[12] Thus, where an award made outside the United States is covered by the Convention, U.S. courts have generally concluded that they must recognize the award, subject only to Article V's

---

3. *See* G. Born, *International Commercial Arbitration* 3414 (2d ed. 2014).

4. *See infra* pp. 1195-96; G. Born, *International Commercial Arbitration* 232, 749-62, 3410-27 (2d ed. 2014); Quigley, *Accession by the United States to the United Nations Convention on the Recognition and Enforcement of Foreign Arbitral Awards*, 70 Yale L.J. 1049, 1055 (1961); A. van den Berg, *The New York Arbitration Convention of 1958* (1981).

5. *See infra* pp. 1196-97; G. Born, *International Commercial Arbitration* 2905-07, 3424-25 (2d ed. 2014); Quigley, *Accession by the United States to the United Nations Convention on the Recognition and Enforcement of Foreign Arbitral Awards*, 70 Yale L.J. 1049, 1054 (1961); A. van den Berg, *The New York Arbitration Convention of 1958* 266-67 (1981).

6. The Convention thus does not require either expeditious or efficient procedural mechanisms for enforcing Convention awards; it merely requires signatory states to use procedures no more cumbersome than their domestic enforcement procedures. New York Convention, Art. III.

7. Inter-American Convention, Arts. 4, 5.

8. ICSID Convention, Art. 54(1).

9. UNCITRAL Model Law, Arts. 34, 35; *see infra* pp. 1195, 1198-99.

10. SLPIL, Arts. 190, 194; *see infra* pp. 1198-99.

11. English Arbitration Act, 1996, §§66-71, 99-104; French Code of Civil Procedure, Art. 1484.

12. 9 U.S.C. §207 (emphasis added). The second chapter of the FAA does not contain a separate list of exceptions to the general obligation to recognize arbitration awards subject to the Convention.

exceptions; other grounds for resisting awards, whether under §10 of the FAA or at common law, may not be relied upon.[13]

3. Proof of Foreign Awards

a. Proof of Award Under New York and Inter-American Conventions

The New York Convention sets forth, in Article IV, requirements of formal proof that must be satisfied in order to obtain the advantage of the Convention's provisions concerning recognition of awards. The party seeking enforcement must provide: (a) the original award or a certified copy; and (b) the original arbitration agreement or a certified copy. Additionally, if the award and/or agreement are not in the official language of the state where enforcement is sought, an official or sworn translation must be provided. These documents must be filed, together with an application for recognition of the award, with a "competent authority" in a Contracting State. If the foregoing materials are properly filed, and if it is shown that the award is subject to the Convention, then a *prima facie* case has been established for recognition of the award: the burden of proof then shifts to the party resisting enforcement to show that the award falls within one of Article V's exceptions.[14]

b. Proof of Award Under National Arbitration Legislation

Like the Convention, most national arbitration statutes contain provisions regarding proof of an award. Article 35(2) of the UNCITRAL Model Law requires parties seeking to enforce an award to provide the original award and arbitration agreement, or "duly certified" copies thereof.[15] Somewhat less simply, §13 of the FAA requires a party seeking to confirm an award to file (a) the arbitration agreement; (b) any selection or appointment of any "additional arbitrator"; (c) each "written extension of the time ... within which to make the award"; (d) the award; and (e) notices, affidavits, and other papers "used upon an application to confirm, modify, or correct the award," plus each court order upon such application.[16] Other national arbitration statutes adopt broadly similar approaches.[17]

4. Selected Materials on Presumptive Obligation to Recognize International Arbitral Awards

Excerpted below are materials on the presumptive obligation, imposed by most international arbitration instruments and national arbitration statutes, to recognize arbitral awards.

---

13. *See infra* p. 1195; G. Born, *International Commercial Arbitration* 2960-66 (2d ed. 2014). As discussed above, *see supra* pp. 1190-93, if a "nondomestic" award is made in the United States, authorities are divided on the question whether non-Article V exceptions may be relied on.

14. *See infra* pp. 1195-96; G. Born, *International Commercial Arbitration* 3402-05 (2d ed. 2014); A. van den Berg, *The New York Arbitration Convention of 1958* 13-15 (1981).

15. UNCITRAL Model Law, Art. 35(2).

16. U.S. FAA, 9 U.S.C. §13.

17. French Code of Civil Procedure, Art. 1515; SLPIL, Art. 193. *See* G. Born, *International Commercial Arbitration* 3406 (2d ed. 2014).

PARSONS & WHITTEMORE OVERSEAS CO. v. SOCIÉTÉ GÉNÉRALE DE L'INDUSTRIE DU PAPIER

508 F.2d 969 (2d Cir. 1974) (also excerpted below at pp. 1211, 1219-20 & 1251-52)

J. JOSEPH SMITH, Circuit Judge. Parsons & Whittemore Overseas Co., Inc., ("Overseas"), an American corporation, appeals from the entry of summary judgment ... on the counter-claim by Société Générale de l'Industrie du Papier ("RAKTA"), an Egyptian corporation, to confirm a foreign arbitral award holding Overseas liable to RAKTA for breach of contract.... We affirm the district court's confirmation of the foreign award.

In November 1962, Overseas consented by written agreement with RAKTA to construct, start up and ... supervise a paperboard mill in Alexandria, Egypt. The Agency for International Development ("AID"), a branch of the U.S. State Department, would finance the project by supplying RAKTA with funds.... Among the contract's terms was an arbitration clause which provided a means to settle differences arising in the course of performance, and a "force majeure" clause, which excused delay in performance due to causes beyond Overseas' reasonable capacity to control.

Work proceeded as planned until May 1967. Then, with the Arab-Israeli Six Day War on the horizon, recurrent expressions of Egyptian hostility to Americans—nationals of the principal ally of the Israeli enemy—caused the majority of the Overseas work crew to leave Egypt. On June 6, the Egyptian government broke diplomatic ties with the United States and ordered all Americans expelled from Egypt except those who would apply and qualify for a special visa. Having abandoned the project for the present with the construction phase near completion, Overseas notified RAKTA that it regarded this postponement as excused by the force majeure clause. RAKTA disagreed and sought damages for breach of contract. Overseas refused to settle and RAKTA, already at work on completing the performance promised by Overseas, invoked the arbitration clause. Overseas responded by calling into play the clause's option to bring a dispute directly to a three-man arbitral board governed by the [ICC Rules]. [The tribunal issued a preliminary award, which recognized Overseas' force majeure defense only during the period from May 28 to June 30, 1967, and a final award in March, 1973: Overseas was held liable to RAKTA for $312,507 in damages and $30,000 for RAKTA's costs.]

Subsequent to the final award, Overseas in the action here under review sought a declaratory judgment to prevent RAKTA from collecting the award out of a letter of credit issued in RAKTA's favor ... at Overseas' request.... RAKTA ... counter-claimed to confirm and enter judgment upon the foreign arbitral award. Overseas' defenses to this counterclaim, all rejected by the district court, form the principal issues for review on this appeal....

Both the legislative history of Article V, and the statute enacted to implement the United States' accession to the Convention are strong authority for treating as exclusive the bases set forth in the Convention for vacating an award. On the other hand, the [FAA], specifically 9 U.S.C. §10, has been read to include an implied defense to enforcement where the award is in "manifest disregard" of the law. *Wilko,* 346 U.S. at 436 (1953). This case does not require us to decide, however, whether this defense stemming from dictum in *Wilko* ... obtains in the international arbitration context. For even assuming that the "manifest disregard" defense applies under the Convention, we would have no difficulty rejecting the appellant's contention that such "manifest disregard" is in evidence here. Overseas in effect asks this court to read this defense as a license to review the record of arbitral proceedings for errors of fact or law—a role which we have emphatically declined to assume in the past and reject once again. "[E]xtensive judicial review frustrates the basic purpose of arbitration, which is to dispose of disputes quickly and avoid the expense and delay of extended court proceedings." *Saxis Steamship Co.* [*v. Multifacs Int'l Traders*, 375 F.2d 577, 582 (2d Cir. 1967).] Insofar as this defense to enforcement of awards in "manifest disregard" of law may be cognizable under the Convention, it, like the other defenses raised by the appellant, fails to provide a sound basis for vacating the foreign arbitral award....

DALLAH REAL ESTATE & TOURISM HOLDING CO. v. MINISTRY OF RELIGIOUS AFFAIRS, GOVERNMENT OF PAKISTAN
[2010] UKSC 46 (U.K. S.Ct.)

[excerpted above at pp. 247-70]

JUDGMENT OF 20 AUGUST 1984, NAVIGATION MARITIME BULGARE v. P.T. NIZWAR
XI Y.B. Comm. Arb. 508 (1986) (Indonesian S.Ct.)

[A sole arbitrator awarded Navigation Maritime Bulgare of Bulgaria ("NMB") $72,576.39 plus interest ... and arbitration costs in an arbitration seated in London against P.T. Nizwar of Indonesia. When Nizwar refused to pay the award, NMB applied to the Central Jakarta District Court to enforce the award. The District Court ordered Nizwar to pay the award. Nizwar appealed to the Indonesian Supreme Court.]

The Court began its analysis by stating that, as a general rule, foreign judgments and foreign arbitral awards cannot be enforced in Indonesia unless a treaty requires enforcement. It then took up the question of whether Indonesia was bound by the [1927 Geneva Convention], and concluded that it was not. The Court reasoned that although the Dutch Government acceded to the 1927 Convention on behalf of the Netherlands Indies in 1931, and although Art. 5 of the Agreement on Transitional Measures of 1949 (containing the terms upon which Indonesia obtained independence) provides that Indonesia will be bound by all international agreements entered into by the Dutch Government on behalf of the Netherlands Indies, nevertheless new principles of international law respecting State succession have emerged since World War II with the result that Indonesia is no longer bound by treaties acceded to during the colonial times.

The Court then addressed the question of whether Indonesia is bound by the New York Convention, and concluded that it was not. While acknowledging that Indonesia ratified the New York Convention in 1981, the Court stated that in accordance with Indonesian practice it is still necessary for the Government to promulgate implementing regulations concerning whether a request to enforce a foreign award should be made to a District Court (and if so, which District Court) or whether such request should be made directly to the Supreme Court for a determination as to whether the award is contrary to the Indonesian legal order. Pending promulgation of such implementing regulations, Indonesian courts cannot enforce foreign arbitral awards.

NOTES

1. *Basis under New York Convention for presumptive obligation to recognize Convention awards.* What is the textual basis under the New York Convention for concluding that foreign awards must presumptively be recognized? Consider Article III, excerpted at p. 1 of the Documentary Supplement. Does it require that awards must be recognized, subject to Article V exceptions? Or does Article III only impose a "national treatment" standard, requiring that foreign awards be treated no less favorably than domestic awards? What if domestic awards are subject to searching judicial review in a state? Does Article III permit similar judicial review of foreign awards?

   Consider Article V of the Convention. Does it impose a presumptive obligation to recognize foreign awards, subject to Article V's exceptions? Where exactly does the text of Article V impose such a requirement?

   Compare Article IX of the European Convention, excerpted at p. 33 of the Documentary Supplement. What approach does it take to the presumptive enforceability of foreign awards?

2. *Basis under Inter-American Convention for presumptive obligation to recognize Convention awards.* What is the textual basis for the presumptive obligation imposed by the Inter-American Convention to recognize awards? Consider the text of Articles 4 and 5, excerpted at pp. 9-10 of the Documentary Supplement. Does Article 5 require the recognition of Convention awards, subject only to its enumerated exceptions? Compare Article 5 with Article V of the New York Convention.

3. *Basis under ICSID Convention for presumptive obligation to recognize ICSID awards.* What is the textual basis for the presumptive obligation on Contracting States to recognize ICSID awards? Consider Article 54, excerpted at p. 25 of the Documentary Supplement. Does the ICSID Convention impose a presumptive obligation to recognize ICSID awards or a conclusive obligation? Are there any grounds on which a Contracting State may refuse to recognize an ICSID award? How are potential challenges to an ICSID award dealt with?

4. *Basis under national arbitration legislation for presumptive validity of foreign awards.* Consider how the UNCITRAL Model Law, the SLPIL, the English Arbitration Act and the FAA treat international arbitral awards in actions to recognize foreign awards. What do each of these statutes require with respect to the recognition of international arbitral awards? Are these statutory regimes all consistent with the Convention's requirements?

5. *National arbitration legislation denying foreign awards presumptive validity.* Not all arbitration legislation recognizes the presumptive validity of foreign awards, including awards governed by the New York Convention. Consider the possibilities for enforcing foreign awards in Indonesia, as detailed in *Navigation Maritime Bulgare v. P.T. Nizwar.* Note that, absent a treaty obligation, no foreign award was enforceable in Indonesia. Is Indonesia in breach of its treaty obligations under the Convention?

6. *Differing standards under some national arbitration statutes for actions to annul domestic awards and actions to enforce foreign awards.* Recall that the New York Convention imposes limits on the judicial forums in which actions to annul Convention awards may be bought. *See supra* pp. 1099-112. Specifically, an action to annul, on either Article V or non-Article V grounds, can be brought only in the country where

the award was "made" or "under the laws" of which the award was made. *See supra* pp. 1106-10.

As discussed above, some arbitration legislation provides differing standards of judicial review for actions to annul domestic awards and actions to recognize foreign or nondomestic awards. *See supra* pp. 1156-57, 1159-61. Compare, in this regard, Articles 34-36 of the UNCITRAL Model Law, excerpted at pp. 94-96 of the Documentary Supplement. Is there any difference in the grounds that are available under Article 34 and Article 36? Why are there two separate provisions in the Model Law?

Also compare §§69 and 103 of the English Arbitration Act, 1996, excerpted at pp. 132-33 & 140-41 of the Documentary Supplement. What are the differences in the treatment of foreign and domestic arbitral awards? Compare §§10 and 207 of the FAA. What are the differences in how domestic and Convention awards are treated?

Why, under these arbitration statutes, are foreign awards entitled to more favorable treatment in national courts than domestic awards? Wouldn't it be more logical that domestic awards be accorded more favorable, or at least equally favorable, treatment? Domestic awards are presumably made in accordance with more familiar and acceptable standards and subject to greater possibilities of local judicial intervention—given that, why grant foreign awards preferential treatment? What policies does this serve?

7. *Exclusivity of grounds for non-recognition enumerated in New York Convention.* The *Parsons* court raises, but does not decide, the question whether the Convention's enumerated defenses are the exclusive grounds for resisting recognition of a foreign award outside the arbitral seat. How should that question be resolved?

Consider the text of Article V(1) and its statement that recognition of an award may be refused "only" if certain showings are made. Compare Article III and its statement that "there shall not be imposed substantially more onerous conditions … on the recognition or enforcement of arbitral awards to which this Convention applies than are imposed on the recognition or enforcement of domestic arbitral awards." Does Article III mean that the Convention only requires Contracting States to accord Convention awards the same treatment that they afford to domestic awards? Does Article V more clearly provide that the Article V grounds for non-recognition are exclusive? Consider the U.K. Supreme Court's analysis in *Dallah*.

8. *Exclusivity of grounds for non-recognition under national arbitration legislation.* Are the grounds for non-recognition of an award enumerated in Article V of the Convention exclusive under the terms of leading national arbitration statutes? Consider Article 36 of the UNCITRAL Model Law, §207 of the FAA and §103 of the English Arbitration Act, 1996.

Should national courts recognize additional defenses to recognition under the Convention that are sometimes available in domestic annulment actions—such as substantive review of the arbitrators' decision, formal defects in the award, or an inconvenient arbitral forum? *See supra* pp. 1163-68. Could any of these defenses be fit within any of the Convention's enumerated exceptions?

9. *Burden of proof with respect to Convention's presumption of enforceability of award.* One of the central purposes of the New York Convention was to shift the burden of proof to parties resisting enforcement of an award:

"While the Geneva Convention [of 1927] placed the burden of proof on the party seeking enforcement of a foreign arbitral award and did not circumscribe the range of available defenses to those enumerated in the Convention, the 1958 Convention clearly shifted the burden of proof to the party defending against enforcement and limited his defenses to seven set forth in Article V." *Parsons*, 508 F.2d at 973.

Consider also the U.K. Supreme Court's analysis in *Dallah*. Is this shifting of the burden of proof appropriate? Why?

Consider Article V(1)(a) of the Convention, dealing with invalid arbitration agreements; is it appropriate that a party who denies it ever agreed to arbitrate be required to prove the nonexistence or invalidity of an arbitration agreement? Why? Consider the other exceptions under Article V(1). Are there any such provisions as to which the award creditor should bear the burden of proof?

10. *Non-recognition permitted, but not required, where an Article V exception applies.* Suppose one of Article V(1) or V(2)'s exceptions applies. Is non-recognition permitted or is it required? For example, suppose the court where recognition is sought holds that a party was denied its opportunity to present its case within the meaning of Article V(1)(b), or that the arbitral procedures did not comport with the parties' agreement within the meaning of Article V(1)(d)? Must the court then deny recognition of the resulting award? What might justify recognition of the award? *See also supra* p. 1156. Consider also the U.K. Supreme Court's analysis in *Dallah*.

Consider again the arbitration legislation excerpted above. Do any of these regimes go beyond the Convention (providing for recognition of foreign awards in circumstances where the Convention does not require such recognition)? Consider the French Code of Civil Procedure. Does the Convention permit Contracting States to recognize awards in circumstances where one of Article V's exceptions is applicable? *See supra* pp. 1174-87 & *infra* pp. 1212-13, 1238-40.

11. *No double exequatur requirement under New York Convention.* Under international arbitration conventions that preceded the New York Convention, enforcement of foreign awards was required only if those awards were "final." That was true, for example, under the Geneva Convention of 1927, which only mandated enforcement of "final" arbitral awards. Geneva Convention, Art. 1(2)(d); G. Born, *International Commercial Arbitration* 3424-25 (2d ed. 2014). Moreover, the burden of establishing "finality" was on the party seeking enforcement. As a consequence, parties seeking to enforce foreign awards were effectively required to follow a so-called "double *exequatur*" process. This entailed obtaining confirmation of the awards in the local courts in the arbitral seat (to prove their "finality"), and thereafter seeking judicial enforcement abroad. G. Born, *International Commercial Arbitration* 3410-11 (2d ed. 2014).

As discussed above, one of the principal (and deliberate) innovations of the New York Convention was abandonment of the "double *exequatur*" procedure, which was widely perceived as cumbersome and ineffective. To accomplish this, Article III of the Convention treated awards as presumptively valid and shifted the burden of proof of a basis for non-recognition under Article V to the award-debtor. In addition, the Convention abandoned the "finality" requirement. Instead, Article III of the Convention requires that "binding" awards be enforced, while Article V(1)(e) permits non-recognition of an award if it is not "binding" or if it has been set aside where it was made. Under these provisions, once an award becomes "binding," it must presumptively be recognized in every Contracting State—notwithstanding the fact that the award has not been confirmed in the courts of the state where it was made. *See supra* pp. 1120-23. Was it wise to abandon the double *exequatur* requirement? What purposes were served by requiring that an award be confirmed in the arbitral seat, before it could be recognized abroad? What costs were imposed by this system?

12. *No limits under New York Convention on permissible judicial forums for seeking recognition of foreign awards.* A fundamental objective of the New York Convention was ensuring the widest possible enforceability of international awards. *See supra* pp. 33-39, 1189-90. Consistent with this objective, nothing in Articles III, IV, or V of the Convention limits the places in which a party may seek to recognize an award in its favor. The same is true of the Inter-American Convention and the ICSID Convention. Is this appropriate? Should the Convention impose limits on the jurisdictions in which recognition may be sought? What limits could you imagine?

    Does anything in the Convention prevent an award-creditor from seeking recognition and enforcement of an award in multiple jurisdictions?

13. *Forum non conveniens defense to recognition of foreign award subject to New York Convention.* Some countries may impose jurisdictional, *forum non conveniens*, or other limits on actions to confirm foreign awards. For example, a U.S. appellate court dismissed on *forum non conveniens* grounds an action in the United States to enforce a Finnish award against a Finnish company. *Melton v. Oy Nautor AB*, 161 F.3d 13 (9th Cir. 1998). *See also Monegasque de Reassurances SAM v. Nak Naftogaz of Ukraine*, 158 F.Supp.2d 377, 383 (S.D.N.Y. 2001), *aff'd*, 311 F.3d 488, 499 (2d Cir. 2002); G. Born, *International Commercial Arbitration* 2984-87, 3409 (2d ed. 2014). Other nations can require significant jurisdictional contacts between the award-debtor and the enforcement forum, can impose time limits on actions to confirm, or otherwise restrict enforcement actions.

    Does the New York Convention permit a state to deny recognition of a Convention award based on the *forum non conveniens* doctrine? Is that one of the bases set forth in Article V of the Convention? Consider:

    > "The signatory nations simply are free to apply differing procedural rules consistent with the requirement that the rules in Convention cases not be more burdensome than those in domestic cases. If that requirement is met, whatever rules of procedure for enforcement are applied by the enforcing state must be considered acceptable, without reference to any other provision of the Convention. The doctrine of *forum non conveniens*, a procedural rule, may be applied in domestic arbitration cases brought under the provisions of the [FAA], and it therefore may be applied under the provisions of the Convention." *Monegasque de Reassurances SAM v. Nak Naftogaz of Ukraine*, 311 F.3d 488, 496 (2d Cir. 2002).

    Is that rationale persuasive? Does anything in the Convention allow non-recognition of awards because recognition in other forums might be more convenient? *See Restatement (Third) U.S. Law on International Commercial Arbitration* §4-29(a) (Tent. Draft No. 3 2013) ("An action to enforce a U.S. Convention award or enforce a foreign Convention award is not subject to a stay or dismissal in favor of a foreign court on *forum non conveniens* grounds.").

14. *Proof of foreign award under New York Convention.* What is required to prove the existence of an award under the New York Convention? Consider Article IV. What does Article IV mean when it refers to "the original agreement referred to in article

II"? Does this mean that the party seeking recognition of an award must prove the existence of a valid, written arbitration agreement under Article II? How would that requirement be reconciled with Article V(1)(a)? What does Article IV mean when it requires that the party seeking recognition of an award "supply" "the original agreement referred to in article II or a duly certified copy thereof"? *See infra* pp. 1211-12.

15. *Applicability of New York Convention's enforcement regime in national courts.* Consider again the Indonesian decision in *Navigation Maritime.* Why was the Convention's enforcement regime not applicable to the award? Why isn't the Convention automatically applicable (in U.S. terms, "self-executing")? Or is it? What result would have been reached in *Navigation Maritime* if the Convention were regarded as self-executing?

    Consider the practical importance of the question whether or not the New York Convention's enforcement regime was applicable in *Navigation Maritime.* What rules of enforceability applied to the award in question if the Convention was applicable? If it was not?

16. *No provision under New York Convention for non-recognition of foreign award based on judicial review of merits of arbitrator's decision.* Consider the bases for refusing to recognize foreign or nondomestic awards set forth in Article V of the New York Convention. Do any of the exceptions set forth in Article V expressly permit non-recognition of an award based on an error in an arbitrator's decision? For example, does the Article provide for non-recognition of an award because the arbitral tribunal misread the parties' contract, misjudged critical testimony, or misunderstood applicable law? Consider also Article 5 of the Inter-American Convention and Article IX of the European Convention, excerpted at pp. 9-10 & 33 of the Documentary Supplement. Do they permit non-recognition of an award based on a court's review of the arbitrator's substantive decisions?

17. *Judicial review of merits of arbitrator's decision in action to recognize foreign award under national arbitration legislation.* Consider Articles 34 and 36 of the UNCITRAL Model Law and Articles 190 and 194 of the SLPIL, excerpted at pp. 94-96 & 160 of the Documentary Supplement. Do they permit denying recognition based upon an erroneous decision by the arbitrators on the merits of the parties' dispute?

    Courts in most states have underscored that foreign awards are not subject to substantive review in recognition proceedings under the Convention. *See Judgment of 24 November 1993*, XXI Y.B. Comm. Arb. 617 (1996) (Luxembourg Cour Supérieure de Justice) ("The New York Convention does not provide for any control on the manner in which the arbitrators decide the merits, with as the only reservation, the respect of international public policy. Even if blatant, a mistake of fact or law, if made by the arbitral tribunal is not a ground for refusal of enforcement of the tribunal's award"); *Shenzhen Nan Da Indus. & Trade United Co. Ltd v. FM Int'l Ltd*, XVIII Y.B. Comm. Arb. 377 (1993) (H.K. Ct. First Inst. 1991) ("what Mr. Chan is effectively attempting to do is to appeal on the merits…. In my judgment, unless Mr. Chan can establish one of the New York Convention grounds … his ground of opposition must fail"). What is the rationale for this approach? Is it wise?

    What is the rationale for excluding substantive errors in an award as a potential basis for non-recognition of a Convention award? What are the costs and benefits of such an approach? If you were drafting the New York Convention, would you include errors in the arbitrators' decision as a ground for non-recognition? Why?

18. *Award does not "merge" into judgment confirming award in arbitral seat.* Suppose that the award creditor successfully resists an effort by the award-debtor to annul the award in the arbitral seat, and the award is then confirmed (or granted *exequatur*) in the arbitral seat. Alternatively, suppose that the award-creditor affirmatively seeks and obtains confirmation of the award in the arbitral seat. In either case, may recognition of the award still be sought? Or, alternatively, has the award disappeared, by being "merged" into the judgment confirming it? In the latter case, can the "award" only then be recognized and enforced by seeking recognition and enforcement of the resulting national court judgment?

What answers do the policies of the New York Convention and UNCITRAL Model Law suggest to the foregoing questions? *See also COSID, Inc. v. Steel Auth. of India, Ltd*, XI Y.B. Comm. Arb. 502 (1986) (Delhi High Ct. 1985) (rejecting argument that award made in England merged into English judgment confirming award); *Victrix SS Co. v. Salen Dry Cargo AB*, 825 F.2d 709, 713-14 (2d Cir. 1987) (award made and confirmed abroad can be enforced as either award or judgment); *Waterside Ocean Navigation Co. v. Int'l Navigation Ltd*, 737 F.2d 150, 154 (2d Cir. 1984) (same); *Oriental Commercial & Shipping Co. v. Rosseel, NV*, 769 F.Supp. 514, 517 (S.D.N.Y. 1991) ("even after an award had been confirmed in the foreign jurisdiction—making it enforceable as a foreign judgment—it was still enforceable as a foreign award under the Convention; the foreign confirmation had simply increased the options available to the enforcing party."). Is any other result conceivable? What if the law of the arbitral seat provides that the award merges into, and is no longer a separate instrument from the local court judgment when the award is confirmed? Does that affect Articles III and V of the New York Convention?

B. GROUNDS FOR REFUSAL TO RECOGNIZE INTERNATIONAL ARBITRAL AWARDS

Although the New York Convention and many national arbitration statutes establish a general presumption that international arbitral awards must be recognized, these sources also contemplate non-recognition of awards in specified circumstances. In general, the Convention and national arbitration statutes provide for non-recognition on the same, fairly-limited substantive grounds.[18] These grounds are: (a) no valid arbitration agreement;[19] (b) denial of an opportunity to be heard;[20] (c) excess of jurisdiction;[21] (d) violation of the parties' agreed procedures or the laws of the arbitral seat;[22] (e) the award is not

---

18. *See* New York Convention, Art. V; UNCITRAL Model Law, Arts. 35, 36; SLPIL, Art. 190, 194; FAA, 9 U.S.C. §207.

19. New York Convention, Art. V(1)(a); Inter-American Convention, Art. 5(1)(a); 1961 European Convention, Art. IX(1)(a).

20. New York Convention, Art. V(1)(b); Inter-American Convention, Art. 5(1)(b); 1961 European Convention, Art. IX(1)(b).

21. New York Convention, Art. V(1)(c); Inter-American Convention, Art. 5(1)(c); 1961 European Convention IX(1)(c).

22. New York Convention, Art. V(1)(d); Inter-American Convention, Art. 5(1)(d); 1961 European Convention, Art. IX(1)(d).

binding or has been annulled in the arbitral seat;[23] (f) violation of public policy;[24] or (g) nonarbitrability.[25] In addition, albeit improperly, some nations permit other grounds for resisting recognition of awards, including substantive errors by the arbitral tribunal. The materials excerpted below explore each of these various grounds for non-recognition.

1. No Valid Arbitration Agreement or Excess of Authority

International commercial arbitration is ordinarily consensual. As we have seen, a party cannot ordinarily be required to arbitrate unless an agreement to do so exists.[26] This principle is embodied in all leading national arbitration statutes and is universally accepted in commentary.[27] Unless the parties have agreed to arbitrate a dispute, the arbitrators lack authority to resolve it.

A corollary of the consensual nature of arbitration is the principle that awards which are not based on a valid arbitration agreement, applicable to the parties' dispute, may be subject to non-recognition. The New York Convention contains two provisions relating to the requirement for a valid agreement to arbitrate. First, Article V(1)(a) of the New York Convention (and Article 5(1)(a) of the Inter-American Convention) permits non-recognition of an award if:

> "the parties to the agreement referred to in Article II were, under the law applicable to them, under some incapacity, or the said agreement is not valid under the law to which the parties have subjected it or, failing any indication thereon, under the law of the country where the award was made."

Second, awards need not be recognized under the New York Convention if the award went beyond the scope of the parties' submissions to the arbitrators. Under Article V(1)(c) of the New York Convention (and Article 5(1)(c) of the Inter-American Convention), a party resisting recognition of an arbitral award may prevail by showing that: "The award deals with a difference not contemplated by or not falling within the terms of the submission to arbitration, or it contains decisions on matters beyond the scope of the submission to arbitration."

National arbitration legislation also permits an award to be denied recognition if it is not supported by a valid arbitration agreement. The UNCITRAL Model Law and the SLPIL are representative, containing exceptions applicable where there was no valid agreement to arbitrate or the arbitrators exceeded their authority under the arbitration agreement.[28] The materials below explore the application of these exceptions.

FIRST OPTIONS OF CHICAGO, INC. v. KAPLAN
514 U.S. 938 (1995)

[excerpted above at pp. 230-33]

---

23. New York Convention, Art. V(1)(e); Inter-American Convention, Art. 5(1)(e).

24. New York Convention, Art. V(2)(b); Inter-American Convention, Art. 5(2)(b).

25. New York Convention, Art. V(2)(a); Inter-American Convention, Art. 5(2)(a).

26. *See supra* pp. 116-37, 177; G. Born, *International Commercial Arbitration* 225 (2d ed. 2014).

27. *See supra* pp. 177-90, 375-474, 1159; G. Born, *International Commercial Arbitration* 225, 3448 (2d ed. 2014).

28. UNCITRAL Model Law, Art. 36(1)(a)(iii); SLPIL, Art. 190(2)(c).

CHINA MINMETALS MATERIALS IMP. & EXP. CO. v. CHI MEI CORP.
334 F.3d 274 (3d Cir. 2003)

GREENBERG, Circuit Judge. This matter comes on before this court on an appeal by the Chi Mei Corporation ("Chi Mei") from the district court's order entered June 11, 2002, granting the motion of China Minmetals Import & Export Co. ("Minmetals") to confirm and enforce a foreign arbitration award and from the judgment entered on August 26, 2002, in favor of Minmetals and against Chi Mei in the amount of $4,040,850.41.... [We] vacate the district court's order and judgment and ... remand the case for further proceedings.

Chi Mei is a New Jersey corporation and Minmetals is a corporation formed ... under the laws of the People's Republic of China ("PRC"). Production Goods and Materials Trading Corp. of Shantou S.E.Z. ("Shantou"), which also is implicated in this action, likewise is a corporation formed ... under the laws of the PRC.

This dispute arises out of a transaction involving Chi Mei, Minmetals, and Shantou. The parties dispute almost every detail of the transaction.... Chi Mei refers to it as a "currency conversation transaction"[29] while Minmetals calls it a contract for purchase by Minmetals of electrolytic nickel cathode.... Chi Mei argues that it never intended nor agreed to sell anything to Minmetals and alleges that the contracts on which Minmetals relies were forged. On the other hand, Minmetals argues that Chi Mei failed to deliver the goods it promised to sell after receiving payment by drawing on a line of credit of several million dollars.

According to Chi Mei, ... Shantou sought out Chi Mei to discount a certain sum of US dollars. Chi Mei orally agreed to provide discounting services for a 0.7% commission of the amount of US dollars before discount. Minmetals was to obtain the funds by way of a letter of credit obtained from the Bank of China, as the PRC apparently authorized Minmetals to engage in currency conversation transactions. Chi Mei asserts, however, that Shantou did not disclose its relationship with Minmetals to it and that it was unaware of Minmetals' role in the transaction until after the delivery of the proceeds of the letter of credit to Shantou. Chi Mei subsequently was to transfer the funds to accounts Shantou designated, and Chi Mei did so. By contrast, Minmetals asserts that the transaction involved an agreement to purchase electrolytic nickel cathode alloy, it issued letters of credit worth several million dollars to Chi Mei, and Chi Mei knowingly submitted to a New York bank numerous false documents evidencing the sale, including an invoice, weight packing list, quality certificate, and bill of lading, in order to collect funds under the letters of credit. Minmetals contends that Chi Mei did not deliver the goods described in the contracts.

Two contracts submitted to a bank in the PRC that purport to the contracts for the sale of nickel by Chi Mei to Minmetals for a sum equal to the amount of the letters of credit (the "Sale of Goods Contracts") are central to this dispute. Chi Mei alleges that the two contracts were entirely fraudulent, containing a forged signature of a nonexistent Chi Mei employee as well as a forged corporate stamp. Chi Mei further alleges that it was unaware of the existence of these contracts until it appeared at the arbitration that is the subject of this dispute. The contracts provide for binding arbitration of any disputes in connection

---

29. The PRC imposes strict restrictions on foreign currency transactions, allowing only authorized parties to convert PRC currency ("RMB") into United States dollars.

with the contracts before the China International Economic and Trade Arbitration Commission ("CIETAC").

According to Chi Mei, it performed its duties under the oral agreement governing the currency discounting transaction and delivered the funds to Shantou after collecting its 0.7% commission. Shantou then allegedly misappropriated the funds, refusing to remit any of them to Minmetals....

Minmetals initiated an arbitration proceeding before CIETAC against Chi Mei pursuant to the arbitration clauses contained in the Sale of Goods contracts. Chi Mei repeatedly objected to CIETAC's jurisdiction but, nevertheless, appeared before it, submitting evidence that the contracts which contained the arbitration clause on which Minmetals relied were forged. Chi Mei also argued that Minmetals' flouting of Chinese law should prevent its recovery in the arbitration. The arbitration tribunal held that Chi Mei failed to meet its burden of showing that the contracts at issue were forged, and that even if Chi Mei's signature and stamp had been forged, its actions, such as providing documents to the New York bank and drawing on the letters of credit, constituted "confirmation of the validity of the contracts." On August 30, 2000, the CIETAC panel awarded Minmetals an amount in excess of $4 million....

Minmetals moved in the district court for an order confirming and enforcing the arbitration award. Chi Mei opposed the motion ... submitting numerous documents and affidavits, including the affidavit of Jiaxiang Luo, the Chi Mei president. Minmetals did not submit any contrary affidavits. The district court heard oral argument on the motions and, without conducting an evidentiary hearing ... entered an order granting Minmetals' motion to confirm and enforce the award.... [T]he district court entered judgment in favor of Minmetals in the amount of $4,040,850.41. This appeal followed....

The primary issue in this case is whether the district court properly enforced the foreign arbitration panel's award where that panel, in finding that it had jurisdiction, rejected Chi Mei's argument that the documents providing for arbitration were forged so that there was no any valid writing exhibiting an intent to arbitrate. This issue actually involves two distinct questions. First, we must consider whether a foreign arbitration award might be enforceable regardless of the validity of the arbitration clause on which the foreign body rested its jurisdiction. In this regard, Minmetals points out that the [New York] Convention differs somewhat from the general provisions of the FAA, and particularly argues that Article V of the Convention requires enforcement of foreign awards in all but a handful of very limited circumstances, one of which is not the necessity for there to be a valid written agreement providing for arbitration. If we conclude, however, that only those awards based on a valid agreement to arbitrate are enforceable, we also must consider who makes the ultimate determination of the validity of the clause at issue....

[The Court quoted Articles II, IV and V of the Convention.] Minmetals argues that each article of the Convention governs a different aspect of arbitration procedure—Article II sets forth the grounds for compelling arbitration, Article IV describes the procedure required for seeking enforcement of an award, and Article V provides that once an award is made, the courts of a contracting state must enforce the award unless one of the narrow grounds for nonenforcement is proven. This case, according to Minmetals, therefore involves only Article V, under which in its view "the requirement of a valid written agreement is not necessary for enforcement." Chi Mei, on the other hand, argues that the Convention must be read as a whole and that Article V both explicitly and implicitly incorporates Article II's valid written agreement requirement. In addition, Minmetals argues that the arbitration panel's decision as to the validity of the arbitration agreement is conclusive unless an Article V exception applies, which, it argues, is not the case here. Chi Mei, for its part, argues that the district court had an obligation to determine independently the validity of the agreement.

Because the domestic FAA (chapter 1 of the FAA) is applicable to actions brought under the Convention (Chapter 2 of the FAA) to the extent they are not in conflict, 9 U.S.C. §208, Chi Mei relies heavily on the Supreme Court's decision in *First Options of Chicago, Inc. v. Kaplan*. *First Options* involved the domestic FAA, not the Convention, but involved facts similar to those in this case. In *First Options*, as here, the district court confirmed an arbitration award where the parties against whom the award was enforced had argued both in the arbitration proceedings and before the district court that they had not signed the document containing the arbitration clause. In that case, the Court held that the district court and not the arbitration panel must decide the question of arbitrability—that is, the question whether a certain dispute is subject to arbitration under the terms of a given agreement—unless the parties clearly and unmistakably have agreed that the arbitrator should decide arbitrability. In other words, the Court, relying on the principle that "a party can be forced to arbitrate only those issues it specifically has agreed to submit to arbitration," [514 U.S. at 945,] held that, unless the district court found that there was clear and unmistakable evidence that the parties agreed to arbitrate arbitrability, the district court independently must determine whether the parties agreed to arbitrate the merits of the dispute.

Chi Mei ... argues that, under *First Options*, the district court should have concluded that the parties did not agree to arbitrate arbitrability and ... that the dispute was not arbitrable because the contract had been forged.... [Chi Mei alternatively argued that the district court] at least should have conducted a hearing to resolve that issue. If this case had arisen under the domestic FAA, *First Options* clearly would have settled in Chi Mei's favor both the question of the need for a valid agreement to arbitrate and the question of the district court's role in reviewing an arbitrator's determination of arbitrability when an award is sought to be enforced. We, therefore, must determine whether *First Options* provides the rule of decision in a case involving enforcement of a foreign arbitration award under the Convention.

Our cases involving enforcement under the Convention largely have arisen under Article II, with one party seeking an order compelling another party to arbitrate a dispute. Under those cases, it is clear that if Minmetals had initiated proceedings in the district court to compel arbitration, the court would have been obligated to consider Chi Mei's allegations that the arbitration clause was void because the underlying contract was forged. *See Sandvik v. Advent Int'l Corp.*, 220 F.3d 99, 104-07 (3d Cir. 2000). It is, of course, true that the FAA, of which the Convention is a part, establishes a strong federal policy in favor of arbitration and that the presumption in favor of arbitration carries "'special force'" when international commerce is involved. *Id.* at 104 (quoting *Mitsubishi Motors*). Nonetheless, we have stated that the "'liberal federal policy favoring arbitration agreements ... is at bottom a policy guaranteeing the enforcement of private contractual arrangements,'" *id.* at 105 (quoting *Mitsubishi Motors*), and that because "arbitration is a matter of contract, ... no arbitration may be compelled in the absence of an agreement to arbitrate," *id.* at 107-08.

In *Sandvik*, we affirmed the district court's denial of a motion to compel arbitration where the district court had concluded that it had to determine whether the parties in fact had entered into a binding agreement to arbitrate before it could compel arbitration. In that case, there was a dispute as to whether the agreement containing the arbitration agreement was binding on the defendant corporation where it alleged that its attorney signed the contract without proper authorization. We relied on our decision on *Par-Knit Mills, Inc. v. Stockbridge Fabrics Co.*, 636 F.2d 51 (3d Cir. 1980), in which we stated:

> "Before a party to a lawsuit can be ordered to arbitrate and thus be deprived of a day in court, there should be an express, unequivocal agreement to that effect. If there is doubt as to whether such an agreement exists, the matter, upon a proper and timely demand, should be submitted to a jury. Only when there is no genuine issue of fact concerning the formation of the agreement should the court decide as a matter of law that the parties did or did not enter into such an agreement." *Id.* at 106 (quoting *Par-Knit Mills*, 636 F.2d at 54).

In *Sandvik*, we drew a distinction between contracts asserted to be void or nonexistent, as was the case there and is the case here, and contracts alleged to be voidable, in which case arbitration, including arbitration of the fraud question, may be appropriate under *Prima Paint Corp. v. Flood & Conklin Mfg. Co.* We concluded that "because under both the [Convention] and the FAA a court must decide whether an agreement to arbitrate exists before it may order arbitration, the District Court was correct in determining that it must decide whether [the attorney's] signature bound Advent before it could order arbitration." *Id.* at 107. Notably, although we supported our conclusion with reference to the "null and void" language in Article II of the Convention, we based our decision on straightforward notions of contract law rather than on any technical interpretation of the language of the treaty.

In this case, however, an arbitral tribunal already has rendered a decision, and has made explicit findings concerning the alleged forgery of the contract, including the arbitration clause. "The goal of the Convention, and the principal purpose underlying American adoption and implementation if it, was to encourage the recognition and enforcement of commercial arbitration agreements in international contracts and to unify the standards by which agreements to arbitrate are observed and arbitral awards are enforced in the signatory countries." *Scherk*, 417 U.S. at 520 n.15. In an oft-cited opinion concerning enforcement of a foreign arbitration award, the ... Second Circuit noted the "general pro-enforcement bias informing the Convention," explaining that the Convention's "basic thrust was to liberalize procedures for enforcing foreign arbitral awards." *Parsons & Whittemore*, 508 F.2d at 973. Consistently with the policy favoring enforcement of foreign arbitration awards, courts strictly have limited defenses to enforcement to the defenses set forth in Article V of the Convention, and generally have construed those exceptions narrowly. As the Court of Appeals for the Second Circuit has noted, "there is now considerable caselaw holding that, in an action to confirm an award rendered in, or under the law of, a foreign jurisdiction, the grounds for relief enumerated in Article V of the Convention are *the only* grounds available for setting aside an arbitral award." *Toys 'R' Us*, 126 F.3d at 20 (emphasis added).

This narrow interpretation of the Convention is in keeping with 9 U.S.C. §207 which unequivocally provides that a court in which enforcement of a foreign arbitration award is sought "*shall confirm* the award *unless it finds one of the grounds* for refusal or deferral of recognition or enforcement of the award *specified in the said Convention*." (Emphasis added.) The absence of a written agreement is not articulated specifically as a ground for refusal to enforce an award under Article V of the Convention. In fact, the Convention only refers to an "agreement in writing" in Article II, which requires a court of a contracting state to order arbitration when presented with an agreement in writing to arbitrate, unless it finds that agreement to be void, inoperative, or incapable of being performed. This distinction, according to Minmetals, is enough to differentiate this case from cases like *First Options*, which arose under the FAA,[30] as well as from cases like *Sandvik* ..., which arose under Article II. On the other hand, the crucial principles common to all of these decision—that arbitration is a matter of contract and that a party can be forced to arbitrate only those issues it specifically agrees to submit to arbitration—suggest that the district court here had an obligation to determine independently the existence of an agreement to arbitrate even though an arbitration panel in a foreign state already had rendered an award, unless Minmetals' argument concerning the exclusive nature of Article V or some other principle provides a meaningful reason to distinguish the cases we have cited....

We ... find that the absence of any reference to a valid written agreement to arbitrate in Article V does not foreclose a defense to enforcement on the grounds that there never was a valid agreement to arbitrate. Minmetals cannot point to any case interpreting Article V of the Convention so narrowly as to preclude that defense and we are aware of none. Nor do the text and structure of the Convention compel such an interpretation. Indeed, although only Article II contains an "agreement in writing" requirement, Article IV requires a party seeking to enforce an award under Article V to supply "the" original agreement referred to in Article II" along with its application for enforcement. Furthermore, Article V expressly provides that the party opposing enforcement may furnish "to the competent authority where the recognition and enforcement is sought proof that ... the said agreement is not valid...." Read as a whole, therefore, the Convention contemplates that a court should enforce only valid agreements to arbitrate and only awards based on those agreements. Thus, the concern we expressed in our decisions in Article II cases like *Sandvik* ...—that parties only be required to arbitrate those disputes they intended to arbitrate—is likewise present in this case. We therefore hold that a district court should refuse to enforce an arbitration award under the Convention where the parties did not reach a valid agreement to arbitrate, at least in the absence of a waiver of the objection to arbitration by the party opposing enforcement.[31]

We therefore are left with the question whether the international nature of this case distinguishes it from *First Options*. Stated more precisely, we must ask whether the international context of the arbitration at issue affects the principle that the district court should decide whether there was a valid agreement to arbitrate. As already noted, *First Options* held that, in a case arising under the domestic FAA, the district court independently should make that decision, even after the arbitrators have decided that they did have jurisdiction, absent clear and unmistakable evidence that the parties intended to leave that determination to the arbitrators....

---

30. As Minmetals notes, the grounds for refusal to enforce an award are broader under the FAA than under the Convention.

31. We do not, however, hold as Chi Mei urges, that Article V "incorporates" Article II's valid written agreement requirement. In this respect, there is indeed some distinction between Article II and Article V. The former explicitly requires an "agreement in writing" while the latter requires only that the parties have reached an agreement as to the arbitrability under ordinary contract principles.

[W]e previously had applied *First Options* in the international context, albeit in a case seeking to compel arbitration rather than to confirm an award. *See Deutz*, 270 F.3d at 155 ("We recognize that *First Options* is a domestic arbitration case, but the international nature of the present litigation does not affect the application of *First Options*' principles.").... There nonetheless may be reason to think that the international posture of this case removes it from the scope of *First Options*. For example, international arbitration rules tend to favor the rule of competence-competence (sometimes known as Kompetenz-kompetenz)—the principle that gives arbitrators the power to decide their own jurisdiction—more than American arbitration rules. The contracts in this case, for example, incorporate the rules of CIETAC. Those rules do indeed allow the arbitrators the power to determine their own jurisdiction. [2003] CIETAC Arbitration Rules Ch. I, §1. Art. 4 ("The Arbitration Commission has the power to decide on the existence and validity of an arbitration agreement and on Jurisdiction over an arbitration case."). Nonetheless, incorporation of this rule into the contract is relevant only if the parties actually agreed to its incorporation. After all, a contract cannot give an arbitral body any power, much less the power to determine its own jurisdiction, if the parties never entered in it.

Although incorporation of CIETAC rules in an allegedly forged contract is not enough in itself to require that Chi Mei be bound by the arbitration clause in this case, Minmetals nonetheless suggests that the international nature of this dispute is sufficient to distinguish this case from *First Options*. Thus, it could be argued that international norms favoring competence-competence, as well as American policy favoring arbitration particularly strongly in international cases, are sufficient to render *First Options* inapplicable in the international context. Competence-competence is applied in slightly different ways around the world. The one element common to all nations is the conferral of the power to decide jurisdiction on the arbitrators themselves. It is important to note, however, that this principle says nothing about the role of judicial review.

In its simplest form, competence-competence simply means that the arbitrators can examine their own jurisdiction without waiting for a court to do so; if one side says the arbitration clause is invalid, there is no need to adjourn arbitration proceedings to refer the matter to a judge. Under this brand of competence-competence, however, the arbitrators' jurisdictional decision is subject to judicial review at any time before, after, or during arbitration proceedings, as was traditionally the case under English law. The French form of competence-competence goes somewhat further. A court only can decide arbitrability before an arbitral panel has been constituted if the alleged arbitration agreement is clearly void; otherwise, courts must decline to hear the case until after an arbitral award is rendered. Finally, the strictest form of competence-competence is the traditional German kompetenz-kompetenz, under which an arbitral panel's jurisdictional decision in a case where the parties agreed to kompetenz-kompetenz clause essentially was insulated from any form of judicial review.

Despite these different formulations, however, and despite the principle's presumption in favor of allowing arbitrators to decide their own jurisdiction, it appears that every country adhering to the competence-competence principle allows some form of judicial review of the arbitrator's jurisdictional decision where the party seeking to avoid enforcement of an award argues that no valid arbitration agreement ever existed.... Furthermore, [the UNCITRAL Model Law] ... allows substantial opportunity for judicial review of that ruling. UNCITRAL Model Law Art. 16.... It therefore seems clear that international law overwhelmingly favors some form of judicial review of an arbitral tribunal's decision that it has jurisdiction over a dispute, at least where the challenging party claims that the contract on which the tribunal rested its jurisdiction was invalid. International norms of competence-competence are therefore not inconsistent with the Supreme Court's holding in *First Options*, at least insofar as the holding is applied in a case where, as here, the party resisting enforcement alleges that the contract on which arbitral jurisdiction was founded is and always has been void.

In sum, *First Options* holds that a court asked to enforce an arbitration award, at the request of a party opposing enforcement, may determine independently the arbitrability of the dispute. Although *First Options* arose under the FAA, the Court's reasoning in the case is based on the principle that "arbitration is simply a matter of contract between the parties; it is a way to resolve those disputes—but only those disputes—that the parties have agreed to submit to arbitration." *First Options*, 514 U.S. at 943. This rationale is not specific to the FAA. It is a crucial principle of arbitration generally, including in the international context. Indeed, even international laws and rules of arbitration that traditionally grant arbitrators more leeway to decide their own jurisdiction have allowed a party objecting to the validity of the agreement to arbitrate to seek judicial review of an arbitral panel's decision that it has jurisdiction under the alleged agreement. For these reasons, we hold that, under the rule of *First Options*, a party that opposes enforcement of a foreign arbitration award under the Convention on the grounds that the alleged agreement containing the arbitration clause on which the arbitral panel rested its jurisdiction was void *ab initio* is entitled to present evidence of such invalidity to the district court, which must make an independent determination of the agreement's validity and therefore of the arbitrability of the dispute, at least in the absence of a waiver precluding the defense.

In this case, the district court confirmed and enforced the arbitral award without opinion. Chi Mei asks us to reverse the district court's judgment and remand with instructions to enter judgment in its favor denying Minmetals' motion to confirm and enforce and granting its motion to dismiss. On this record, we cannot grant this relief. Although Chi Mei proffered evidence suggesting that the contracts providing for arbitration were forged, Minmetals presented the Sale of Goods contracts and other documents evidencing the existence of valid contracts to the district court. In the alternative, Chi Mei asks that we remand the case to the district court for further proceedings to ascertain the validity of the contracts. Given the apparent dispute of facts, we agree that a remand is appropriate....

Minmetals also argues that Chi Mei has waived the forgery/jurisdiction argument by participating voluntarily in the arbitration proceedings rather than seeking a stay of arbitration in the district court. Chi Mei counters by arguing that it did not participate on the merits of the arbitration, but rather appeared only to object to jurisdiction and that, regardless of its participation on the merits, it preserved its right to challenge jurisdiction by properly objecting to jurisdiction....

We repeatedly have held under the FAA, including in our opinion in *First Options* in which the Supreme Court affirmed our judgment, that a party does not waive its objection to arbitrability where it raises that objection in arbitration: "A party does not have to try to enjoin or stay an arbitration proceeding in order to preserve its objection to jurisdiction.... A jurisdictional objection, once stated, remains preserved for judicial review absent a clear and unequivocal waiver.... Therefore, where a party objects to arbitrability but nevertheless participates in the arbitration proceedings, waiver of the challenge to arbitral jurisdiction will not be inferred." *Kaplan v. First Options of Chicago, Inc.*, 19 F.3d 1503, 1510 (3d Cir. 1994), *aff'd*, 514 U.S. 938 [(1995)]....

The record in this case makes clear that Chi Mei's participation in the CIETAC proceedings largely was limited to arguing the forgery issue. Although it appears to have presented at least one alternative argument, it consistently objected to the arbitral panel's jurisdiction both in the arbitration proceedings and before the district court. Furthermore, its decision to proceed with the arbitration despite its jurisdictional objection was likely necessary to prevent an award being entered against it in its absence.... Thus, ... Chi Mei did not waive its objection to CIETAC's jurisdiction inasmuch as it participated in the arbitration primarily to argue the forgery/jurisdiction issue and consistently objected to CIETAC's jurisdiction throughout the proceedings.

For the foregoing reasons, we will vacate ... the judgment of the district court ... and remand ... for further proceedings....

ALITO, Circuit Judge, Concurring. I join the Court's opinion but write separately to elaborate on the importance of Article IV(1)(b) of the Convention in this case. As the Court notes, "the crucial principles ... that arbitration is a matter of contract and that a party can be forced to arbitrate only those issues it specifically agrees to submit to arbitration ... suggest that the district court held had an obligation to determine independently the existence of an agreement to arbitrate." These principles find expression in Article IV(1)(b), which provides that a party seeking to enforce an arbitral award must, "at the time of the application, supply ... the original agreement referred to in Article II or a duly certified copy thereof." Because a party seeking to enforce an arbitral award cannot satisfy this obligation by proffering a forged or fraudulent agreement, this provision required the District Court to hold a hearing and make factual findings on the genuineness of the agreement at issue here.

Article IV(1)(b), as noted, requires a party seeking enforcement to supply the court with "the" original agreement referred to in Article II," and it is apparent that this means that the party seeking enforcement must provide the court with either a duly signed written contract containing an arbitration clause or an agreement to arbitrate that is evidenced by an exchange of letters or telegrams.... Article II ... thus refers to an "agreement" on three occasions: (1) when discussing the obligation of each "Contracting State" to "recognize an agreement in writing"; (2) in defining an "agreement in writing"; and (3) in requiring the court in which enforcement is sought to compel arbitration when the parties "have made an agreement within the meaning of" Article II. Both the first and second references concern an "agreement in writing," and the third reference merely directs the reader to a definition of "agreement" set forth elsewhere in Article II. Since an "agreement in writing" is the only type of "agreement referred to in Article II" means an "agreement in writing" as defined in that Article. Thus, a party seeking enforcement of an arbitral award under Article IV must supply the court with an "agreement in writing" within the meaning of Article II.

An "agreement in writing," Article II tells us, means "an arbitral clause in a contract or an arbitration agreement, signed by the parties or contained in an exchange of letters or telegrams." [Convention,] Art. II(2). To enforce the award granted by the arbitral tribunal, Minmetals was therefore required to demonstrate to the District Court that it and Chi Mei had agreed to arbitrate any dispute arising out of the purported nickel contracts and that they had done some by means of either (1) a written contract signed by both parties or (2) an exchange of letters or telegrams between them. Since Minmetals does not contend that

Chi Mei agreed to arbitrate disputes relating to the purported nickel contracts by way of an exchange of letters or telegrams, it follows that Minmetals was required to prove to the District Court that Chi Mei signed a written agreement to arbitrate the dispute adjudicated by the arbitral tribunal. Chi Mei specifically disputes the issue, claiming that the signatures of its officers on the purported nickel contracts were forged. As a result, the Convention required the District Court to inquire into whether Chi Mei's officers signed the purported nickel contracts.

Minmetals contends, however, that where an arbitral tribunal has already determined that the parties entered into a written agreement to arbitrate their dispute, the Convention requires the District Court to assume that the tribunal's determination was correct. Minmetal's reading of the Convention, however, would render the prerequisites to enforcement of an award set forth in Article IV superfluous.... If Minmetal's reading were correct, there would be no purpose for Article IV(1)(b)'s requirement that a party "applying for recognition and enforcement" of an arbitral award supply the court with the parties' signed, written agreement or exchange of letters or telegrams. On Minmetal's view, the existence of a valid agreement would be conclusively established once the party seeking enforcement pointed out the portion of the arbitral tribunal's decision in which it found that the parties had entered into a written agreement to arbitrate, and therefore Minmetal's position would make the Convention's requirement that the party seeking enforcement submit the original agreement a meaningless formality.

The better reading of Article IV—which comports with fundamental principles of arbitration—requires that the party seeking enforcement both (1) supply a document purporting to be the agreement to arbitrate the parties' dispute and (2) prove to the court where enforcement is sought that such document is in fact an "agreement in writing" within the meaning of Article II(2). In the present case, accordingly, Minmetals was required to demonstrate to the District Court that an officer of Chi Mei signed the purported nickel contracts....

DALLAH REAL ESTATE & TOURISM HOLDING CO. v. MINISTRY OF RELIGIOUS AFFAIRS, GOVERNMENT OF PAKISTAN

[2010] UKSC 46 (U.K. S.Ct.)

[excerpted above at pp. 247-70]

JUDGMENT OF 19 JULY 2000

XXVI Y.B. Comm. Arb. 827 (2001) (Almelo Arrondissementsrechtbank)

[Société d'Etudes et de Commerce SA ("SEC") concluded a charter party with Weyl Beef Products BV ("Weyl"). The charter party was signed on Weyl's behalf by Husson Huijsman Reefer BV ("HHR"). The charter party contained a clause for arbitration in London. Following a dispute, a sole arbitrator rendered two awards in favour of SEC: a Final Award on October 19, 1999, and an Award of Costs on February 7, 2000, both made in London.]

SEC sought enforcement of the awards in the Netherlands. Weyl objected that the arbitrator lacked jurisdiction as HHR had no authority to enter into the charter party on behalf of Weyl and, therefore, there was no valid arbitration agreement between the parties. The President of the Court of First Instance in Almelo dismissed Weyl's objection and granted enforcement, holding that the enforcement court may not review whether there was a valid arbitration agreement between SEC and Weyl and that, under the applicable English law, "a party which has not exhausted all the possibilities at his disposal against an arbitrator's finding that he has jurisdiction may not … rely later on the arbitrator's lack of jurisdiction."

The request [for enforcement] is based on [the New York Convention]…. The grounds on which recognition and enforcement may be denied are limitatively listed in Art. V of the Convention and also in [the Netherlands' implementing legislation]. Although it applies in principle, the Convention allows SEC to rely on a law which is more favorable to it. SEC does rely on such law.

Recognition and enforcement of arbitral awards is denied *inter alia* if the arbitration agreement is not valid under the law to which the parties have subjected it or, failing any indication thereon, under the law of the country where the award was made. Since the voyage charter party, which contains the arbitral clause (clause 22), does not indicate the applicable law, and the arbitration took place in England, English law applies in the present case.

The [English] Arbitration Act 1996 provides in §67 that "a party to arbitral proceedings may apply to the court (a) challenging any award of the arbitral tribunal as to its substantive jurisdiction' on the conditions in §70…." [In addition,] §73(2) provides that:

> "(2) Where the arbitral tribunal rules that it has substantive jurisdiction and a party to arbitral proceedings who could have questioned that ruling—(a) by any available arbitral process of appeal or review, or (b) by challenging the award, does not do so, or does not do so within the time allowed by the arbitration agreement or any provision of this Part, he may not object later to the tribunal's substantive jurisdiction on any ground which was the subject of that ruling."

Weyl objected to the lack of jurisdiction of the arbitrator during the arbitration proceedings. It alleged that HHR was not authorized to enter into the voyage charter party containing the arbitral clause on Weyl's behalf, so that Weyl is a party neither to the voyage charter party not to the arbitration agreement. However, the arbitrator held that he had jurisdiction by an Order of 30 August 1999…:

> "I am satisfied from the evidence of Mr. Gerard Pors of Husson Huijsman Reefer BV that he was authorized to act on behalf of the Respondent when negotiating of the said Charter Party. Pursuant to that authority, I am satisfied that Mr. Pors agreed that clause 22 would be incorporated in the Charter. Having found that clause 22 was incorporated in the Charter Party, I am satisfied that the provisions of the Arbitration Act 1996 apply to the reference."

Weyl's main means of defence in the arbitration was its objection [to the arbitrators' jurisdiction]; it did not commence appellate arbitral proceedings or file an appeal with the arbitrator who rendered the award. A party which has not exhausted all the possibilities at his disposal against an arbitrator's finding that he has jurisdiction may not, according to §73(2) of the Arbitration Act 1996, rely later on the arbitrator's lack of jurisdiction.

The arbitration agreement is thus valid and has become final according to English law. The Dutch court may not, in the context of the present proceedings, review whether there was a valid arbitration agreement between SEC and Weyl. The English arbitrator already held that there was, and the law no longer allows Weyl to rely on the lack of jurisdiction of the arbitrator. The more so as the English arbitrator dealt explicitly with Weyl's objection that HHR was not authorized to enter into the charter party on behalf of Weyl.

PARSONS & WHITTEMORE OVERSEAS CO. v. SOCIÉTÉ GÉNÉRALE DE L'INDUSTRIE DU PAPIER
508 F.2d 969 (2d Cir. 1974)

J. JOSEPH SMITH, Circuit Judge. [The facts of the case are excerpted above at p. 1192.] … Both [Article V(1)(c) and FAA §10(d)] basically allow a party to attack an award predicated upon arbitration of a subject matter not within the agreement to submit to arbitration. This defense to enforcement of a foreign award, like the others already discussed, should be construed narrowly. [A] narrow construction would comport with the enforcement-facilitating thrust of the Convention. In addition, the case law under the similar provision of the [FAA] strongly supports a strict reading. *See, e.g., Coenen v. R.W. Pressprich & Co.*, 453 F.2d 1209 (2d Cir.).

In making this defense … Overseas must therefore overcome a powerful presumption that the arbitral body acted within its powers. Overseas principally directs its challenge at … $185,000 awarded for loss of production. Its jurisdictional claim focuses on the provision of the contract reciting that "[n]either party shall have any liability for loss of production." The tribunal cannot properly be charged, however, with simply ignoring this alleged limitation on the subject matter over which its decision-making powers extended. Rather, the arbitration court interpreted the provision not to preclude jurisdiction on this matter. As in *United Steelworkers of Am. v. Enterprise Wheel & Car Corp.*, 363 U.S. 593, 598 (1960), the court may be satisfied that the arbitrator premised the award on a construction of the contract and that it is "not apparent," that the scope of the submission to arbitration has been exceeded.

The appellant's attack on … $60,000 awarded for start-up expenses … cannot withstand the most cursory scrutiny. In characterizing the $60,000 as "consequential damages" (and thus proscribed by the arbitration agreement), Overseas is again attempting to secure a reconstruction in this court of the contract—an activity wholly inconsistent with the deference due arbitral decisions on law and fact…. Although the Convention recognizes that an award may not be enforced where predicated on a subject matter outside the arbitrator's jurisdiction, it does not sanction second-guessing the arbitrator's construction of the parties' agreement. The appellant's attempt to invoke this defense, however, calls upon the court to ignore this limitation on its decision-making powers and usurp the arbitrator's role….

NOTES

1. *Relationship between Article IV and Articles V(1)(a) and V(1)(c) of New York Convention.* What is the relationship between Article IV of the New York Convention and Articles V(1)(a) and V(1)(c) of the Convention? Consider Judge Alito's concurring opinion in *Minmetals*. What would Judge Alito require the award creditor to prove under Article IV of the Convention? Compare the majority opinion in *Minmetals* and the U.K. Supreme Court's decision in *Dallah*.

   Explain why Judge Alito's view of Articles IV and V(1) is wrong. How should Article IV(1)(b) be interpreted? *See Judgment of 28 November 2000*, XXXII Y.B. Comm. Arb. 540 (2007) (Spanish Tribunal Supremo) (refusing to consider formal validity of arbitration agreement under Article IV in recognition action: only issue is parties' "real intention" to arbitrate); *Dardana Ltd v. Yukos Oil Co.* [2002] EWCA Civ. 543, 327 (English Ct. App.) (Article IV merely requires proof of what appears to be an arbitration clause in document, not of substantive validity, which is dealt with by Article V(1)(a)); *Aloe Vera of Am., Inc. v. Asianic Food (S) Pte Ltd*, XXXII Y.B. Comm. Arb. 489 (2007) (Singapore High Ct. 2006) (no requirement for award-creditor to demonstrate existence of arbitration agreement concluded with award-debtor under Articles II, III and IV, where arbitration agreement was valid and award-debtor was found to be party to it based on alter ego theory and had signed it, albeit in different capacity). What does the word "supply" mean? If Judge Alito's view of Article IV were accepted, what would be the purpose of Article V(1)(a)? Why is it important to determine correctly whether Article IV or Article V(1)(a) applies to challenges to the existence of a valid arbitration agreement? Who has the burden of proof under Article IV? Under Article V(1)(a)?

2. *Choice of law governing validity of arbitration agreement under Article V(1)(a).* Article V(1)(a) of the Convention contains conflict of laws rules for selecting the law governing the validity of the arbitration agreement. Under Article V(1)(a), an award need not be enforced if the arbitration agreement "is not valid under the law to which the parties have subjected it or, failing any indication thereon, under the law of the country where the award was made." Some commentators have called this choice-of-law provision the crowning achievement of the Convention. *See* A. van den Berg, *The New York Arbitration Convention of 1958* (1981).

    What is the conflict of laws rule set forth in Article V(1)(a) with regard to the validity of the arbitration agreement? What law did the English court apply to the arbitration agreement in *Dallah*? Why?

    What law governed the arbitration agreement in *Minmetals*, for Article V(1)(a) purposes? Suppose the alleged contracts in *Minmetals* contained a choice-of-law clause providing that the contracts were governed by New York law. Applying Article V(1)(a), would the putative agreements to arbitrate be governed by New York law? Is that the law chosen by the parties to govern their arbitration agreement? If not, what law would apply to the agreements to arbitrate under Article V(1)(a)? What is the relevance of Chi Mei's claim that it had never concluded any agreement—whether an underlying contract, an arbitration agreement, or a choice-of-law agreement—with Minmetals? What law governed the arbitration agreement in the *Judgment of 19 July 2000* for Article V(1)(a) purposes?

    Suppose the agreement in *Minmetals* did not contain a choice-of-law clause. Under Article V(1)(a), Chinese law would then have been applicable to the validity of the agreement to arbitrate, right? Why? Suppose that, under Chinese law, the arbitration agreement would have been invalid. Suppose also that, under both the FAA and New Jersey law, the arbitration agreement would have been valid. In these circumstances, does Article V(1)(a) *require* non-recognition of the award? Why not? What might justify applying New Jersey law to uphold recognition of the award? Compare the application of French law in *Dallah*.

    Consider how the U.K. Supreme Court describes and applies French law in *Dallah*. Does it do so in the same manner a French court would? Recall the application of French law by the Paris Cour d'appel in *Dallah. See supra* pp. 570-73.

3. *Lack of capacity under Article V(1)(a).* Article V(1)(a) also permits non-recognition of an award because one of the parties lacked the capacity to enter into the arbitration agreement. Article V(1)(a) provides a specialized choice-of-law rule applicable to is-

sues of capacity, specifying the "law applicable to them." As discussed above, this appears to refer to the "personal law" of each of the parties, but does not define how that law is selected. *See supra* p. 470.

Suppose that, in the *Judgment of 19 July 2000*, the award had been made against a 19-year-old Dutch national, and that, under Dutch law, only adults (aged 21 or older) may validly conclude commercial agreements, but that, under English law (being the law of the arbitral seat), anyone older than 16 may validly conclude a contract. What law would apply, under Article V(1)(a), to the validity of the agreement to arbitrate?

4. *Applicability of Article II(2)'s writing requirement in actions to recognize award.* As discussed above, *see supra* pp. 375-92, and in *Minmetals*, Article II of the Convention requires that arbitration agreements be in "writing." Must Article II's "writing" requirement also be satisfied in recognition actions under Article V of the New York Convention? What answer does the *Minmetals* majority provide? Is there any reason that Article II's requirement for the written form should not apply in recognition actions? If Article II's uniform maximum form requirement was not applicable, would Contracting States be free to require more onerous formal requirements than those prescribed by Article II? Would any other provision of the Convention prevent this?

Suppose a Contracting State has adopted the 2006 Revisions to the UNCITRAL Model Law and wishes to apply the minimal (or nonexistent) form requirements of Article 7, *supra* p. 391, in a recognition action. Does the Convention prevent the Contracting State from doing so? Recall that Article V is permissive. Recall also Article VII.

How would Article II's form requirement have been satisfied in *Dallah*?

5. *Application of separability presumption under Article V(1)(a).* Consider Chi Mei's challenges to the putative arbitration agreements in *Minmetals* and Pakistan's challenge in *Dallah*. Are those challenges directed towards the agreements to arbitrate or the underlying contracts? Recall the discussion above of the separability presumption. *See supra* pp. 190-218.

Suppose Chi Mei's jurisdictional challenge in *Minmetals* was based on the fact that the underlying contracts, although not forgeries, were contrary to Chinese currency regulations and, therefore, invalid. Would that constitute a basis for challenging the validity of the agreements to arbitrate? Why not? Suppose the arbitrators had concluded that the underlying contracts were invalid under Chinese law, but nonetheless awarded Minmetals damages on a non-contractual basis. Would this provide Chi Mei a basis for challenging the award, on the basis that the arbitration agreements were void? Why not? What is the justification for treating claims that the underlying contracts were forged differently? *See supra* pp. 355-75, 415-20.

Suppose a party challenges the validity of the underlying contract, but does not specifically challenge the arbitration agreement—for example, as in *Fiona Trust, supra* pp. 205-11, where the underlying contracts were fraudulently induced. Assume that the challenge to the validity of the underlying contract is referred to the arbitrators (consistent with *Fiona Trust*, *Buckeye* and similar holdings, *supra* pp. 218-87), and that the arbitrators uphold the validity of the contract (and the contract's arbitration clause); in these circumstances, can a jurisdictional objection be raised in subsequent recognition proceedings, claiming that the arbitration clause was fraudulently induced?

6. *Judicial deference to arbitrators' jurisdictional ruling in recognition action.* Suppose an arbitral tribunal expressly or impliedly makes a jurisdictional ruling (that upholds its jurisdiction over disputed issues or claims). If an award is subsequently made dealing with the disputed issues, and the award is challenged under Article V(1)(a) (or Article V(1)(c)), what relevance (if any) does the tribunal's jurisdiction ruling have? Specifically, is the tribunal's jurisdictional ruling either binding or entitled to substantial deference in judicial enforcement proceedings?

    How did the Court in *Minmetals* decide the foregoing issue? What deference did it accord the CIETAC arbitrators' jurisdictional decision? What question is the U.S. trial court to decide upon remand? Is the Court's approach wise? Compare the approach taken in *Judgment of 19 July 2000.* What deference did the Dutch court accord to the arbitrators' award? Consider the final paragraph of the decision.

    Compare also the U.K. Supreme Court's deference to the arbitrators' jurisdictional ruling in *Dallah.* Is the Court's tennis analogy useful? Correct? What weight is given the two arbitrators' lack of certainty as to their jurisdictional ruling?

    What degree of deference *should* a recognition court accord to an arbitral tribunal's jurisdictional decision? Consider the alternatives: (a) never according any deference to the arbitrators' jurisdictional decisions; (b) always deferring to the arbitrators' jurisdictional decisions; or (c) affording limited deference to aspects of the arbitrators' jurisdictional decisions, for example, for factual findings. *Compare Judgment of 14 December 2006,* XXXII Y.B. Comm. Arb. 372 (2007) (Oberlandesgericht Celle) ("it is irrelevant that the English arbitrator discussed the issue of the coming into existence of an arbitration agreement.... When examining the requirements under the Convention, the German state court is bound neither by the legal judgment nor by the factual determinations of the arbitral tribunal") *with Rintin Corp., SA v. Domar Ltd,* 416 F.3d 1254, 1259 (11th Cir. 2007) ("Here the issue of validity was litigated before the Arbitrators, and they found that the Shareholders' Agreement was duly adopted and valid, contrary to Rintin's contentions, and also that the arbitration clause itself was valid and enforceable. We therefore have no authority to set aside the award on this basis") *and with Am. Constr. Mach. & Equip. Corp. v. Mechanised Constr. of Pakistan Ltd,* 659 F.Supp. 426 (S.D.N.Y. 1987) ("to accept [the award-debtor's] Article V(1)(a) defense would require this Court to reverse one of the Arbitrator's express finding of law. This can only be done if the findings were made in 'manifest disregard' of the law. The scope of the Court's review in this regard is extremely limited. An examination of the Arbitrator's findings shows he carefully considered the applicable Pakistani law in ruling that the Supplementary Agreement was invalid. Because his result is certainly a 'colorable justification for the outcome reached,'... [the] Article V(1)(a) defense is rejected."). What is wrong with each of these approaches? Is there a sensible alternative?

7. *Scope of U.S. judicial review of jurisdictional award in recognition action depends on arbitration agreement.* As we have seen, in *First Options,* the U.S. Supreme Court held that the standard of judicial review applicable to an arbitrator's jurisdictional award depended upon the parties' arbitration agreement. *See supra* pp. 278-83. According to *First Options,* where the parties agreed to submit questions of "arbitrability" to the arbitrators, the FAA's generally deferential standards of review would apply; where the parties had not agreed to arbitrate jurisdictional issues, however, ju-

dicial review of the arbitral award on these issues would be *de novo*. Recall the application of these rules in *BG Group*. *See supra* pp. 233-47. In the words of the *First Options* Court:

> "Just as the arbitrability of the merits of a dispute depends upon whether the parties agreed to arbitrate that dispute, so the question 'who has the primary power to decide arbitrability' turns upon what the parties agree about *that* matter. Did the parties agree to submit the arbitrability question itself to arbitration? If so, then the court's standard to reviewing the arbitrator's decision about *that* matter should not differ from the standard courts apply when they review any other matter that parties have agreed to arbitrate. That is to say, the court should give considerable leeway to the arbitrator, setting aside his or her decision only in certain narrow circumstances. *See, e.g.*, 9 U.S.C. §10. If, on the other hand, the parties did *not* agree to submit the arbitrability question itself to arbitration, then the court should decide that question just as it would decide any other question that the parties did not submit to arbitration, namely independently. These two answers flow inexorably from the fact that arbitration is simply a matter of contract between the parties; it is a way to resolve those disputes—but only those disputes—that the parties have agreed to submit to arbitration."

Minmetals holds that these standards are applicable to recognition proceedings under Article V(1)(a). Is this conclusion appropriate? Why should *First Options*, which dealt with actions to annul domestic awards under the FAA, apply to recognition proceedings under Article V(1)(a) of the Convention? What do you think of *Minmetals'* argument that international principles of competence-competence require complete deference to the arbitrators' jurisdictional decisions in all cases? What about an argument that, in international cases, *de novo* judicial review of the existence of an agreement to arbitrate should be exercised in all cases?

Note the U.K. Supreme Court's apparent endorsement of the *First Options* analysis in *Dallah*. Is that wise?

If *First Options* does apply in recognition proceedings, and assuming that the parties have not unmistakably agreed to arbitrate jurisdictional issues, should the arbitrators' jurisdictional ruling be entitled to no deference at all? Suppose that, as in *Minmetals*, the arbitrators' jurisdictional decision was based upon a ruling concerning the parties' underlying contract (*e.g.*, it never came into existence because one party's signature was forged; it never came into existence because it was never signed and the parties never agreed to it). Should the arbitrators' decision be entitled to no deference at all? What if the arbitral tribunal made choice-of-law determinations or determinations of foreign law, in which it was qualified (as in *Judgment of 19 July 2000*); should these decisions be afforded no deference at all?

Again assuming that *First Options* applies in recognition proceedings, what standard of review is applicable to arbitrators' jurisdictional rulings where the parties' arbitration agreement extends to questions of jurisdiction? What does *Minmetals* hold?

Identify cases where one could say that the parties had unmistakably agreed to arbitrate jurisdictional issues. Why wasn't that the case in *Minmetals*? Suppose that, in *Minmetals*, there was no dispute that the underlying contracts had been validly concluded, and that they contained valid arbitration clauses, but Chi Mei argued that the scope of the clauses did not extend to the parties' disputes in the arbitration.

8. *Institutional rules' provisions regarding arbitrators' jurisdictional rulings.* Recall the discussion above regarding provisions in institutional rules granting arbitrators competence to decide jurisdictional issues. *See supra* pp. 538-39; 2010 UNCITRAL Rules, Art. 23(1); 2012 ICC Rules, Art. 6(3). If the putative arbitration agreement incorporates such rules, does this satisfy *First Options'* requirement for a clear and unmistakable agreement submitting jurisdictional issues to the arbitrators' decision? Suppose the award-debtor denies concluding any arbitration agreement, including any agreement incorporating the allegedly-applicable institutional rules. Recall the comment in *Minmetals*: "After all, a contract cannot give an arbitral body any power, much less the power to determine its own jurisdiction, if the parties never entered into it." Conversely, suppose again there is no dispute that a valid arbitration agreement was concluded, and the award-debtor only challenges the scope of that agreement.

    Recall the treatment of these issues in *BG Group*, particularly in Chief Justice Roberts' dissent. *See supra* pp. 241-47. Note that the arbitration agreement in *Dallah* incorporated the ICC Rules.

9. *Practical context of arbitrators' jurisdictional ruling.* As discussed above, arbitrators are usually private lawyers who are compensated by the parties for their services. There can be vigorous business development efforts by arbitrators to develop their case-loads. *See supra* p. 285, *infra* pp. 1242-50. If an arbitrator holds that he or she lacks jurisdiction, the case will go away, and his or her fees may be substantially reduced. Does this affect the deference that courts should afford to an arbitrator's jurisdictional rulings, even where an arbitration agreement extends to issues of arbitrability? *Compare Ottley v. Sheepshead Nursing Home*, 688 F.2d 883, 898 (2d Cir. 1982) (Newman, J., dissenting) ("Our deference to arbitrators had gone beyond the bounds of common sense. I cannot understand the process of reasoning by which any court can leave to the unfettered discretion of an arbitrator the determination of whether there is any duty to arbitrate. I am even more mystified that a court could permit such unrestrained power to be exercised by the very person who will profit by deciding that an obligation to arbitrate survives, thus ensuring his own business. It is too much to expect even the most fair-minded arbitrator to be impartial when it comes to determining the extent of his own profit. We do not let judges make decisions which fix the extent of their fees, *see Tumey v. Ohio*, 273 U.S. 510, (1927). How, then, can we shut our eyes to the obvious self-interest of an arbitrator?"). *See supra* p. 285.

10. *Waiver of jurisdictional challenges by failure to seek to annul award in arbitral seat.* Consider the decision in *Judgment of 19 July 2000*. Does the *Almelo* court rely solely on the arbitrators' jurisdictional ruling? Suppose English law did not require an immediate challenge to the arbitrators' positive jurisdictional decision; would the *Almelo* court have still concluded that it did not need to address the merits of the award-debtor's jurisdictional objection?

    Is the *Almelo* court's reasoning in *Judgment of 19 July 2000* persuasive? Note that the award-debtor is denied any opportunity to argue in recognition proceedings that it never entered into any agreement to arbitrate. What justifies that conclusion? Suppose English law provided a possibility to challenge jurisdictional awards by arbitral tribunals, but did not provide that failure to do so waived jurisdictional objections? Could the award-debtor raise jurisdictional objections in a recognition action?

11. *Waiver of jurisdictional challenges by conduct in arbitration.* As discussed above, a party can waive its right to raise challenges to the validity of an asserted arbitration agreement, including by participating in the arbitral proceedings without objection. *See supra* pp. 367-68. As *Minmetals, Judgment of 19 July 2000* and *Dallah* illustrate, a party's waiver of jurisdictional objections can also be raised in subsequent recognition proceedings. Recall Article IV of the Convention. How does an award-creditor supply a copy of the parties' written arbitration agreement if the arbitral tribunal's jurisdiction was based upon the award-debtor's waiver?

    What conduct will constitute a waiver in a recognition action under Article V(1)(a) of the Convention? What law governs this issue? What law was applied in *Judgment of 19 July 2000*?

    In *First Options,* the Kaplans were argued to have waived by contesting the arbitrators' jurisdiction over them, without separately denying his power to render a jurisdictional award. That claim of waiver was rejected by the U.S. Supreme Court. Shouldn't a party's attempt to obtain a negative jurisdictional decision from the arbitrators constitute a waiver?

    Suppose that, in addition to seeking a negative jurisdictional award from the arbitrators, but being unsuccessful, a party then goes on to present arguments and evidence on the merits of the parties' dispute. Does that constitute a waiver of jurisdictional objections? How does *Minmetals* address this issue? What law applied? Compare the law applied in *Judgment of 19 July 2000.*

12. *Institutional arbitration rules' provisions concerning waiver of jurisdictional objections.* Many institutional rules contain provisions requiring that jurisdictional objections be raised promptly, failing which they are waived. 2010 UNCITRAL Rules, Art. 23(2); 2012 ICC Rules, Art. 39; 2014 LCIA Rules, Arts. 23(3), 32(1). What relevance do these rules have in recognition actions? Under the analysis in *Judgment of 19 July 2000*?

13. *Excess of authority under Article V(1)(c).* What is the relationship between Articles V(1)(a) and V(1)(c) of the Convention? What types of cases does Article V(1)(c) apply to? Is it clear that Article V(1)(c) applies to claims that the arbitrators exceeded the scope of the arbitration agreement? Or does Article V(1)(c) apply only to the scope of the specific dispute submitted during the arbitral proceedings to the arbitrators? What does the text of Article V(1)(c) suggest?

    Consider the "jurisdictional" challenge to the arbitrators' award of consequential damages in *Parsons & Whittemore.* Did the Court of Appeals regard this as a potential excess of authority under Article V(1)(c)? Or did the Court hold that the award-debtor was trying to relitigate its substantive defense in the arbitration? Suppose the arbitrators had awarded damages for breach of a different contract between the parties, which did not contain an arbitration clause and which was unrelated to the contract that did contain an arbitration clause. Would this provide the basis for resisting recognition under Article V(1)(c)?

    Why did *Minmetals* and *Dallah* involve Article V(1)(a), and not Article V(1)(c)?

    What degree of deference is appropriate to the arbitrators' interpretation of the scope of their authority under Article V(1)(c)? *Compare Mgt & Tech. Consultants v. Parsons-Jurden Int'l Corp.*, 820 F.2d 1531, 1534 (9th Cir. 1987) ("we construe arbitral authority broadly to comport with the enforcement facilitating thrust of the Convention") *and Fertilizer Corp. of India v. IDI Mgt*, 517 F.Supp. 948, 958-60 (S.D. Ohio 1981) (Article V(1)(c) not applicable to award of consequential damages even though "the contract between these parties clearly excluded consequential damages"; "this court, acting under the narrow judicial review of arbitral awards granted to American courts, may not substitute its judgment for that of the arbitrators") *with Judgment of 14 January 1981*, VIII Y.B. Comm. Arb. 386 (1983) (Trento Corte di Appello) ("an Italian judge deciding on the enforcement of a foreign award is not allowed to examine the merits of the decision. However, this principle does not apply to the examination as to whether the foreign arbitrator has exceeded the limits of the merits to be decided by him, and in particular not to the examination of questions pertaining to the arbitrator's competence which have to be examined by the Italian judge in an autonomous and independent manner."). Which approach is best?

14. *Excess of jurisdiction under ICSID Convention.* Consider Article 52(1)(b) of the ICSID Convention, excerpted at p. 24 of the Documentary Supplement. Note the standard formulated for an excess of jurisdiction: "the Tribunal has manifestly exceeded its powers." How does the standard compare to that under Article V(1)(c) of the New York Convention? What does Article 52(1)(b)'s standard encompass? Consider: *Amco Asia v. Indonesia, Judgment of the Ad Hoc Committee of 16 May 1986 on the Application for Annulment Submitted by the Republic of Indonesia Against the Arbitral Award in ICSID Case No. ARB/81/1 Rendered on 20 November 1984*, 1 ICSID Rep. 509, 515 (1993) ("The law applied by the Tribunal will be examined by the *Ad Hoc* Committee, not for the purpose of scrutinizing whether the Tribunal committed errors in the interpretation of the requirements of the applicable law or in the ascertainment or evaluation of the relevant facts to which such law has been applied. *Such scrutiny is properly the task of a court of appeals, which the ad hoc Committee is not.*") (emphasis added).

2. Denial of Opportunity to Present Party's Case and Irregular Procedural Conduct of Arbitration

Under all developed legal regimes, the recognition of international arbitral awards may be resisted on the grounds of procedural unfairness or irregularity.[32] This exception to the presumptive enforceability of an award includes the related topics of serious procedural irregularity or unfairness (*e.g.*, denial of an opportunity to present a party's case or a violation of due process) and of failure to comply with the procedural requirements of the parties' arbitration agreement or the procedural law governing the arbitration.

a. Denial of Opportunity to Present Party's Case

The New York Convention's grounds for refusal of recognition of a Convention award include cases where the "party against whom the award is invoked was not given proper notice of the appointment of the arbitrator or of the arbitration proceedings or was other-

---

32. *See* G. Born, *International Commercial Arbitration* 3255-57 (2d ed. 2014); Inoue, *The Due Process Defense to Recognition and Enforcement of Foreign Arbitral Awards in United States Federal Courts: A Proposal for A Standard*, 11 Am. Rev. Int'l Arb. 247 (2000); M. Kurkela, *Due Process in International Commercial Arbitration* (2005).

wise unable to present his case."[33] Most national arbitration legislation contains parallel grounds for resisting recognition of foreign awards.[34] Broadly speaking, this exception permits resisting recognition of awards based on grave procedural unfairness in the arbitral proceedings. This is variously termed a denial of procedural fairness, equality of treatment, natural justice, or due process.[35]

b. Irregular Procedural Conduct of Arbitration

The New York Convention and most national arbitration legislation also provide a related ground for challenging the procedural regularity of an arbitration. Under these instruments, a foreign award need not be recognized if the arbitral procedures deviated significantly from the parties' arbitration agreement or, in the absence of an agreement, the procedural law applicable to the arbitration. Thus, Article V(1)(d) of the Convention provides for non-enforcement of an award "where the composition of the arbitral authority or the arbitral procedure was not in accordance with the agreement of the parties, or, failing such agreement, was not in accordance with the law of the country where the arbitration took place."[36] This provision is given effect by Article 36(1)(a)(iv) of the UNCITRAL Model Law and comparable provisions of other national arbitration statutes.

The materials excerpted below explore these exceptions to the recognition of international awards. In considering these materials, distinguish between claims that the arbitrators acted in a fundamentally unfair manner and claims that the arbitrators failed to comply with the parties' agreed arbitral procedures or the law of the arbitral seat.

PARSONS & WHITTEMORE OVERSEAS CO. v. SOCIÉTÉ GÉNÉRALE DE L'INDUSTRIE DU PAPIER
508 F.2d 969 (2d Cir. 1974)

J. JOSEPH SMITH, Circuit Judge. [The facts of the case are excerpted above at p. 1192.] Under Article V(I)(b) of the Convention, enforcement of a foreign arbitral award may be denied if the defendant can prove that he was "not given proper notice ... or was otherwise unable to present his case." This provision essentially sanctions the application of the forum state's standards of due process.

Overseas seeks relief under this provision for the arbitration court's refusal to delay proceedings in order to accommodate the speaking schedule of one of Overseas' witnesses, David Nes, the United States Charge d'Affaires in Egypt at the time of the Six Day War.

---

33. New York Convention, Art. V(1)(b). The Inter-American Convention and the 1961 European Convention contain a similar (but not identical) exception. Inter-American Convention, Art. 5(1)(b); 1961 European Convention, Art. IX(1)(d).

34. *See, e.g.*, UNCITRAL Model Law, Art. 36(1)(a)(ii); SLPIL, Art. 190(2)(d).

35. Article 52(1)(d) of the ICSID Convention contains a similar provision in the annulment context. ICSID Convention, Art. 52(1)(d) ("there has been a serious departure from a fundamental rule of procedure").

36. New York Convention, Art. V(1)(d). The Inter-American Convention and the 1961 European Convention contain similar provisions. Article 5(1)(d) of the Inter-American Convention provides for non-recognition if "the arbitration procedure has not been carried out in accordance with the terms of the agreement signed by the parties or, in the absence of such agreement, that ... the arbitration procedure had not been carried out in accordance with the law of the State where the arbitration took place." *See also* 1961 European Convention, Art. IX(1)(d).

This attempt to state a due process claim fails for several reasons. First, inability to produce one's witnesses before an arbitral tribunal is a risk inherent in an agreement to submit to arbitration. By agreeing to submit disputes to arbitration, a party relinquishes his courtroom rights—including that to subpoena witnesses—in favor of arbitration "with all of its well known advantages and drawbacks." *Washington-Baltimore Newspaper Guild v. The Washington Post Co.*, 442 F.2d 1234, 1288 ([D.C. Cir.] 1971).

Secondly, the logistical problems of scheduling hearing dates convenient to parties, counsel and arbitrators scattered about the globe argues against deviating from an initially mutually agreeable time plan unless a scheduling change is truly unavoidable. In this instance, Overseas' allegedly key witness was kept from attending the hearing due to a prior commitment to lecture at an American university—hardly the type of obstacle to his presence which would require the arbitral tribunal to postpone the hearing as a matter of fundamental fairness to Overseas. Finally, Overseas cannot complain that the tribunal decided the case without considering evidence critical to its defense and within only Mr. Nes' ability to produce. In fact, the tribunal did have before it an affidavit by Mr. Nes in which he furnished, by his own account, "a good deal of the information to which I would have testified." … The arbitration tribunal acted within its discretion in declining to reschedule a hearing for the convenience of an Overseas witness. Overseas' due process rights under American law, rights entitled to full force under the Convention as a defense to enforcement, were in no way infringed by the tribunal's decision.…

JUDGMENT OF 3 APRIL 1987

XVII Y.B. Comm. Arb. 529 (1992) (Italian Corte di Cassazione)

[An award was made in Vienna in favor of Haupl and against Abati. Haupl sought recognition of the award against Abati in Italy. The Milan Court of Appeal granted recognition, and Abati appealed to the Italian Supreme Court.]

As to [the claim] that the [Milan] Court of Appeal violated Article V(1)(b) [of the New York Convention] …, we hold that [Abati] correctly contends that the reasons given by the [Milan Court of Appeal] were insufficient and illogical.… Abati was summoned on 11 August 1981 to appear before the Vienna arbitral tribunal. The date scheduled for Abati's appearance was 8 September 1981. The Court of Appeal held that this notice period was sufficient and reasoned inter alia that commercial activities cannot be unilaterally suspended because one of the two States involved habitually concentrates vacations in the month of August. The Supreme Court accepted the Court of Appeal's reasoning but noted that there are legal provisions concerning this issue. Particularly, the Supreme Court noted that the Italian legal notice period is ninety days and that all time limits for proceedings before Italian courts are suspended between 1 August and 15 September, with certain exceptions (Law No. 742 of 7 October 1969). The Supreme Court held that this provisions leads to a "thinning out" of all juridical activities, so that Abati's opportunity of defending itself may have been affected. Hence, the Supreme Court remanded the case to the [Milan] Court of Appeal, requesting that it determine whether Abati's opportunity of defending itself had been affected.

LAMINOIRS-TREFILERIES-CABLERIES DE LENS, SA v. SOUTHWIRE CO.

484 F.Supp. 1063 (N.D. Ga. 1980)

[excerpted above at pp. 1136-38]

JUDGMENT OF 23 APRIL 2004

XXX Y.B. Comm. Arb. 557 (2005) (Oberlandesgericht Köln)

By four contracts concluded in 2000, the German company bought viscose fibers from the Israeli trading company. The contracts contained an agreement for arbitration of disputes at the International Commercial Arbitration Court at the Chamber of Commerce and Industry of the Russian Federation ("ICAC"). A dispute arose between the parties when the German buyer failed to pay under the contracts. The Israeli company commenced proceedings before the justice of the peace in Tel Aviv. The German defendant relied on the arbitration clause in the contracts to object to the jurisdiction of the Israeli court, and the dispute was referred to arbitration. The parties filed a joint request for arbitration at ICAC, commencing three ... arbitral proceedings.... [T]he arbitrators rendered three awards in favor of the Israeli trading company. The Israeli company sought enforcement of one of these awards in Germany. The German defendant opposed enforcement.... [The German court granted enforcement in an opinion excerpted below.] ...

There is no violation of arbitral procedural law or procedural public policy. Pursuant to Art. V(1)(d) and (2)(b) [of the New York] Convention, enforcement can be refused when the decision so deviates from the basic principles of German procedural law that it cannot be deemed, according to the German legal system to have been rendered in proper legal proceedings. Not all procedural defects are relevant; rather, there must be a violation of minimum standards of procedural justice, and the award must be based on that violation. There are no such defects in the arbitration [in the present case].

Arbitral tribunals must essentially give [the parties] a fair hearing according to the same principles as state courts. Fair hearing is not merely giving the parties an opportunity to express themselves. Rather, the [arbitral] tribunal must also take note of and consider their respective statements. This was the case here. The arguments of the defendant, which was represented by counsel, were heard and evaluated by the arbitral tribunal. It does not appear that the arbitral proceedings were conducted in great haste in violation of the procedural rights and means of defense of the defendant. According to the arbitral award, the statement of claim was filed on 28 June 2001.... The defendant's reply is dated 5 September 2001. The defendant also took advantage of the opportunity to file a further statement. The oral hearing before the arbitral tribunal took place on 19 December 2001 and the arbitral award was rendered on 27 February 2002. It is not argued that the defendant's opportunity to express itself was restricted. It appears from the course of the events before the arbitral tribunal, as set out in the arbitral award, that the objections of the defendant were discussed. The arbitral tribunal stated the subject matter of the dispute in detail and considered the individual arguments of the parties in making its decision. There is no violation of the principle of due process even if the arbitral tribunal denies a request to supply evidence on formal or substantive law grounds. This is true even if this decision is erroneous, as long as it is not merely an excuse, for instance, to conceal the arbitral tribunal's failure to deal with that submission....

JUDGMENT OF 21 MAY 1976
III Y.B. Comm. Arb. 277 (1978) (Venice Corte di Appello)

In 1972 the Panamanian shipping company Pando concluded with the Italian company a charter-party [for] transportation of fertilizers from Tampa to Porto Marghera. The arbitration clause in the charter-party read...: "If any controversy may arise between the owners and the charterers, such a dispute must be referred to three persons in London, one to be appointed by each party, and the third by the two thus appointed. Their decision, or the decision of any of the two of them, shall be final, and for the purpose of rendering any decision enforceable, this agreement shall be made a rule of Court...."

When Filmo defaulted in its payments in 1973, Pando initiated arbitration. It informed Filmo that it had appointed an arbitrator and requested Filmo to do the same. Filmo did not comply with this request. Thereupon Pando appointed its arbitrator as sole arbitrator, relying on §7 of the English Arbitration Act 1950. The thus appointed sole arbitrator rendered an award in favor of Pando in London. Pando then sought enforcement of the award in Italy on the basis of the New York Convention. Filmo opposed the enforcement of the award on the grounds that the appointment of a party-appointed arbitrator as sole arbitrator was not in accordance with the agreement of the parties as provided for by Art. V(1)(d) of the New York Convention nor in accordance with the English Arbitration Act, and, moreover, violated the Italian public policy as the sole arbitrator could not be deemed to be impartial....

Referring to [Article V(1)(d)] of the Convention, the Court considered the appointment of the party-appointed arbitrator as sole arbitrator valid under English law. Although §7 of the English Arbitration Act only concerns a reference to two arbitrators, the Court interpreted by analogy with the other relevant sections of the Act (§§8 and 9) as permitting also in the case of a reference to three arbitrators the appointment by a party of his arbitrator as sole arbitrator where the other party fails to appoint his arbitrator.[37] Distinguishing between domestic public policy (according to which such an appointment would be invalid, Art. 829 Italian CCP) and international public policy, the Court did not regard the appointment as violation of fundamental principles of the Italian public order. Moreover, the English Arbitration Act safeguards the impartiality in several ways, as, for example, §7 declares at the end: "provided that the High Court or a judge thereof may set aside any appointment made in pursuance of this section." Consequently, there was no violation of Art. V of the Convention....

---

37. Section 7 of the English Arbitration Act of 1950 reads:

"Where an arbitration agreement provides that the reference shall be to two arbitrators, one to be appointed by each party, then, unless a contrary intention is expressed therein—(a) if either of the appointed arbitrators refuses to act, or is incapable of acting, or dies, the party who appointed him may appoint a new arbitrator in his place; (b) if, on such a reference, one party fails to appoint an arbitrator, either originally, or by way of substitution as aforesaid, for seven clear days after the other party, having appointed his arbitrator, has served the party making default with the notice to make the appointment, the party who has appointed an arbitrator may appoint that arbitrator to act as sole arbitrator in the reference and his award shall be binding on both parties as if he had been appointed by consent; Provided that the High Court of a judge thereof may set aside any appointment made in pursuance of this section."

ENCYCLOPAEDIA UNIVERSALIS SA v. ENCYCLOPAEDIA BRITANNICA, INC.
403 F.3d 85 (2d Cir. 2005)

B.D. PARKER, Circuit Judge. Encyclopaedia Universalis S.A. ("EUSA") appeals from a judgment of the U.S. District Court for the Southern District of New York denying its motion to confirm an arbitration award under the [New York] Convention. EUSA brought a suit against Encyclopaedia Britannica, Inc. ("EB") to enforce the award of an arbitral board in Luxembourg. For the reasons that follow, we affirm as to the District Court's holding under Article V of the New York Convention, reverse as to the ruling that the arbitrators "exceeded their powers," and vacate with respect to the District Court's order of a supplemental remedy.

The relevant facts are undisputed. EUSA is a *societe anonyme* (analogous to a corporation) organized under the laws of Luxembourg. EB is a Delaware corporation, with its principal place of business in Illinois.... In 1966, EUSA and EB entered into a Literary Property License Agreement ("License Agreement"), granting EB the right to translate, produce, distribute, and license in any language other than French the contents of a French reference work, Encyclopaedia Universalis. In exchange, EB agreed to pay royalties to EUSA based on sales of the non-French editions. On the same date, EB entered into a "Two Party Agreement" with Club Français du Livre ("CFL"), a French corporation. They agreed to form a new entity, Encyclopaedia Universalis France, which would have certain rights to the French-language version of the encyclopedia. The License Agreement required arbitration of all disputes between the parties and explicitly incorporated the arbitration procedures set out in the Two Party Agreement.[38] In October 1995, EB stopped making royalty payments to EUSA under the License Agreement. The parties disagreed about EB's obligation to continue such payments and were unable to resolve the matter. After an initial dispute over who would serve as EUSA's arbitrator, in May 1998, EUSA sent a letter to EB describing its claim and naming as its arbitrator Raymond Danziger, an accountant residing in Paris.

In July 1998, EB appointed Robert Layton, a New York attorney, to serve as its arbitrator. Layton and Danziger communicated by fax and telephone between September 1998 and December 1998. During this period, they discussed the scope of the arbitration and the

---

38. The Two Party Agreement provides that either party may demand that any dispute be referred to arbitration and that:

> "the Board of Arbitration shall be composed of two arbitrators of which one shall be chosen by EB and the other by CFL. In the event of disagreement between these two arbitrators, they shall choose a third arbitrator who will constitute with them the Board of Arbitration. Upon the failure of the two arbitrators to reach agreement upon the choice of a third arbitrator, the third arbitrator, who must be fluent in French and English, shall be appointed by the President of the Tribunal of Commerce of the Seine from a list of arbitrators maintained by the British Chamber of Commerce in London at the request of the arbitrator who is first to make such a request."

> Article 14 of the License Agreement provides, in part:

> "All disputes arising in connection with the present Agreement shall be finally settled by a Board of Arbitration established and governed by the procedures set forth in the [Two Party] Agreement entered into this day between EB and CFL; provided, however, that EUSA and not CFL shall select one of the arbitrators; and provided further, that the third arbitrator shall be selected by the President of the Tribunal de Commerce of Luxembourg from a list of arbitrators maintained by the British Chamber of Commerce in London at the request of the arbitrator who is first to make such a request."

arbitral procedures to be followed, but not the merits of the underlying claim or the identity of the third arbitrator. In March 1999, Danziger wrote to the President of the Tribunal of Commerce of Luxembourg ("Tribunal") asking the Tribunal to name a third arbitrator. He stated that he and Layton had been unable to agree on a third arbitrator and requested that the Tribunal appoint one pursuant to the License Agreement. Danziger also informed the Tribunal that the parties had agreed for the third arbitrator to be drawn from a list maintained by the British Chamber of Commerce ("Chamber"); he noted, however, that he had recently learned that the Chamber no longer maintained such a list.

Two weeks later, Danziger made Layton aware of his letter to the Tribunal, and Layton immediately had counsel in Luxembourg inform the Tribunal that he intended to object to Danziger's request for a third arbitrator. Before receiving Layton's letter of objection, however, Maryse Welter, the Presiding Judge of the Tribunal, appointed Nicolas Decker, a Luxembourg attorney, as the third arbitrator. Shortly thereafter, Layton wrote to the Tribunal, objecting that "a major step in the course to be followed under the applicable arbitration clause has been overlooked." According to Layton, he and Danziger "never had [an] opportunity to confer" regarding the choice of a third arbitrator, as required by the Two Party Agreement. The letter went on to suggest that, because the parties' agreement was to be interpreted under the laws of New York, it would be appropriate for the third arbitrator to be a New York lawyer or a London resident familiar with New York law. Layton recommended consulting the London Court of International Arbitration for a list of arbitrators.

In early May 1999, Judge Welter suspended all arbitration proceedings led by Decker. On May 27, 1999, Danziger responded to Layton's letter to the Tribunal, stating that he did not agree that the arbitrator should necessarily be a New York or London lawyer, and "therefore, there is no doubt that we failed to reach an agreement upon the choice of the third Arbitrator." In December 1999, Judge Welter held a hearing regarding Decker's appointment, which both EB and EUSA attended, and, in February 2000, issued an order that Decker proceed with the arbitration. Decker then scheduled a meeting between the arbitrators, which Layton refused to attend. In July 2000, Decker informed counsel for both parties that the Board of Arbitration, composed of Danziger and Decker, would commence proceedings. In January 2002, the Board of Arbitration, without the participation of EB or Layton, found that EUSA was entitled to terminate the License Agreement and ordered EB to pay EUSA 3.1 million Euros, plus interest and certain costs.

In June 2003, EUSA sued in the Southern District of New York seeking recognition and enforcement of the arbitration award pursuant to the New York Convention.... Plaintiff ... later moved for summary judgment and to confirm the arbitral award. The District Court denied enforcement on two grounds. First, the court concluded that Danziger's request to the Tribunal to appoint a third arbitrator was premature and thus the arbitral board was improperly composed under Article V(1)(d) of the Convention. The court reasoned that whereas the arbitration agreement required the parties to discuss the identity of a third arbitrator before asking the Tribunal to appoint one, there was no evidence that they had done so before Danziger petitioned the Tribunal. Second, the District Court found that the two-person Board of Arbitration exceeded its powers in issuing the award. The court reasoned that "because the arbitral tribunal was improperly composed, it had no power to bind the parties; any assertion of such power, by definition, exceeded its mandate." EUSA appeals both rulings....

When a party applies to confirm an arbitral award under the New York Convention, "the court shall confirm the award unless it finds one of the grounds for refusal or deferral of recognition or enforcement of the award specified in the said Convention." 9 U.S.C. §207. Article V of the Convention specifies seven exclusive grounds upon which courts may refuse to recognize an award. These grounds include when "the composition of the arbitral authority or the arbitral procedure was not in accordance with the agreement of the parties." ...

The party opposing enforcement of an arbitral award has the burden to prove that one of the seven defenses under the Convention applies. The burden is a heavy one, as "the showing required to avoid summary conformance is high." [*Toys "R" Us*], 126 F.3d 15, 23 (quoting *Ottley v. Schwartzberg*, 819 F.2d 373, 376 (2d Cir. 1987)). Given the strong public policy in favor of international arbitration, *Compagnie Noga d'Importation et d'Exp. SA v. Russian Fed'n*, 361 F.3d 676, 683 (2d Cir. 2004), review of arbitral awards under the Convention is "very limited ... in order to avoid undermining the twin goals of arbitration, namely, settling disputes efficiently and avoiding long and expensive litigation." [*Toys "R" Us*], 126 F.3d at 23. We find that EB has carried this substantial burden.

The License Agreement, which incorporates by reference the arbitration procedures set forth in the Two Party Agreement, provides that disputes between the parties are to be resolved by arbitration, and that the Board of Arbitration is initially to be composed of two arbitrators, one chosen by EUSA and one by EB. The Two Party Agreement further provides that "in the event of disagreement between these two arbitrators, they shall choose a third arbitrator.... Upon the failure of the two arbitrators to reach agreement upon the choice of a third arbitrator," the third arbitrator is to be selected by the President of the Tribunal from a list maintained by the British Chamber of Commerce. As previously noted, the Chamber ceased maintaining such a list prior to this dispute.

We agree with the District Court that the parties' agreement contains three requirements: (1) the arbitrators must "disagree" before appointing a third arbitrator; (2) the two party-appointed arbitrators must attempt to choose a third arbitrator; and (3) upon the failure of the two party-appointed arbitrators to agree on a third, the Tribunal must appoint one from the Chamber's list. Here, the first requirement was met because the arbitrators disagreed about the procedural rules to be applied to the proceedings. We reject EB's contention that Layton and Danziger were required to disagree as to the merits of the case. Nothing in the language of the Two Party Agreement limits the subject of qualifying disagreements.

Fatally for EUSA, the second requirement was not met. There is no evidence that the parties attempted to agree upon a third arbitrator before Danziger asked the Tribunal to appoint one. EUSA points to Danziger's May 27, 1999 letter to Layton, in which Danziger stated that he disagreed with Layton that the third arbitrator should be a New York or London lawyer. Layton had originally expressed this preference in his April 28, 1999 letter to the Tribunal. Danziger concluded in his May 27 letter to Layton that, "therefore, there is no doubt that we failed to reach an agreement upon the choice of the third Arbitrator." In relying on Danziger's letter, EUSA fails to appreciate that the arbitration clause required the two party-appointed arbitrators to disagree on a third arbitrator *before* asking the Tribunal to appoint one. However, Danziger's letter was written *after* Layton's letter, which was written *after* Danziger petitioned the Tribunal. Thus, it cannot serve as evidence that they disagreed *before* he approached the Tribunal. We agree with the District Court that the letter was merely an "ingenious but disingenuous" attempt to "construct a process of deliberation and deadlock after the fact."

That the Tribunal ultimately stayed Decker's appointment for approximately nine months did not remedy EUSA's failure to comply with the agreement. We agree, for the reasons expressed by the District Court, that "the Tribunal's premature appointment of Decker irremediably spoiled the arbitration process." Once it was clear that the Tribunal would likely reappoint Decker if Danziger and Layton failed to agree on a third arbitrator, there was no incentive for Danziger to negotiate in good faith. The nine-month hiatus had no remedial effect.

Furthermore, contrary to EUSA's assertion, the District Court did not improperly elevate "form over substance" in requiring that the two arbitrators disagree before Danziger petitioned the Tribunal. While we acknowledge that there is a strong public policy in favor of international arbitration, we have never held that courts must overlook agreed-upon arbitral procedures in deference to that policy. Indeed, as the Supreme Court has said in the related context of compelling arbitration under the FAA, "the federal policy is simply to ensure the enforceability, *according to their terms*, of private agreements to arbitrate." *Volt Info.*, 489 U.S. at 476 (emphasis added). Moreover, the issue of how the third arbitrator was to be appointed is more than a trivial matter of form. Article V(1)(d) ... itself suggests the importance of arbitral composition, as failure to comport with an agreement's requirements for how arbitrators are selected is one of only seven grounds for refusing to enforce an arbitral award. As to the complaint that this result exalts form over substance, ... we are left with the fact that the parties explicitly settled on a form and the Convention requires that their commitment be respected. We thus conclude that the District Court properly refused to confirm Plaintiff's arbitral award on the grounds that the appointment of a third arbitrator was premature, and, therefore, the composition of the arbitral authority was not in accordance with the parties' agreement.

The District Court also held that the award could not be enforced on the separate ground that the arbitrators "exceeded their powers." This conclusion was incorrect. The phrase "exceeded their powers" comes from the FAA, 9 U.S.C. §10(a)(4). Under the FAA, an award issued by arbitrators who are not appointed in accordance with agreed-upon procedures may be vacated because the arbitrators "exceeded their powers." That an arbitration panel exceeded its powers is not, however, one of the seven exclusive grounds for denying enforcement under the New York Convention. *See* Art. V.

While it is true that the FAA and the New York Convention provide "overlapping coverage" to the extent they do not conflict, we have held that a district court is strictly limited to the seven defenses under the New York Convention when considering whether to confirm a foreign award. [*Toys "R" Us*], 126 F.3d at 20 ("in an action to confirm an award rendered in, or under the law of, a foreign jurisdiction, the grounds for relief enumerated in Article V of the Convention are the only grounds available for setting aside an arbitral award"). Thus, we have explicitly declined to read into the Convention additional FAA defenses. For this reason, the District Court erred in refusing to confirm the arbitral award on the ground that the arbitrators "exceeded their powers."

After denying enforcement of the award, the District Court held that Decker and Danziger were disqualified from any future arbitration between EB and EUSA, that EB could reappoint Layton as its arbitrator, and that if the party-appointed arbitrators fail to agree on a third arbitrator, they should select one from a list maintained by the [LCIA].... [T]he

District Court erred in specifying these procedures. "The confirmation of an arbitration award is a summary proceeding," [*Toys "R" Us*], 126 F.3d at 23, and the role of a district court in reviewing an award under the New York Convention is "strictly limited,"[39] *Compagnie Noga*, 361 F.3d at 683. Here, the District Court lacked authority to go beyond refusing confirmation of the award by dictating how the parties should proceed after enforcement was denied. Consequently, we vacate the portion of the District Court's judgment that purports to regulate a subsequent arbitration....

FOOD SERVICES OF AMERICA INC. v. PAN PACIFIC SPECIALTIES LTD
(1997) 32 B.C.L.R.(3d) 225 (B.C. Sup. Ct.)

DROSSOS J. The petitioner ("Amerifresh") seeks an order pursuant to the International Commercial Arbitration Act, S.B.C. 1986, c. 14, s. 35 [("the Act"), which is based upon the UNCITRAL Model Law] and the Foreign Arbitral Awards Act, S.B.C. 1985, c. 74, s. 4 to enforce [an] Arbitration Award (the "Award") ... of the [AAA]. The Award required the respondent, ("Pan Pacific"), to pay to the petitioner the sum of U.S. $126,438.75 plus interest....

The petitioner is a Delaware corporation with offices in Seattle, Washington. The respondent has its registered office in Vancouver, B.C. The arbitration was a result of an Agreement to Arbitrate signed March 12, 1996 by the parties. The agreement stated, in part, as follows: "The parties agree that all controversies and claims ... shall be determined by arbitration in accordance with the International Arbitration Rules of the [AAA] and judgment on the award rendered by the Arbitrators may be entered in any Court having jurisdiction thereof."

[The first issue addressed by the court was whether the respondent waived its right to oppose enforcement of the award.] Under §36 of the Act, a number of grounds are set out upon which a party may rely to oppose enforcement of an award.

In the Agreement to Arbitrate, the parties waived the benefit of §36 in the following words:

> "11. Waiver of §36 of the International Commercial Arbitration Act of British Columbia. The parties intend that any award entered by the arbitrators in this case be final and binding, subject to enforcement either in Canada and/or the United States. In this regard, both parties hereby expressly waive any entitlement they have or may have to rely upon the provisions of §36 of the International Commercial Arbitration Act of British Columbia (SBC 1986) c. 14) and any similar provision in any comparable legislation in any other jurisdiction, to seek to avoid recognition or enforcement of an arbitration award made pursuant to this Agreement."

On the basis of this waiver, the petitioner argues that the respondent waived its right to oppose enforcement under §36.

The respondent argues the waiver only applies to an arbitration award made "pursuant to this agreement" and that the award in question was not made pursuant to the agreement. The respondent argues the agreement incorporated the [AAA] International Rules and

---

39. We distinguish this situation, which involves a motion to confirm an arbitral award under 9 U.S.C. §207, from the situation where a district court does have authority to appoint arbitrators after granting a motion to compel arbitration under 9 U.S.C. §206. We also do not address the situation where a district court that grants a motion to confirm makes necessary technical modifications to the award.

those Rules make a number of requirements that were not met in this case. Those are: that the arbitrators provide written reasons; that the arbitrators apply the applicable law to the dispute; and that the protocol for challenging arbitrators be followed during this arbitration.

Essentially, the respondent submits the waiver only applies where the arbitration was conducted in strict accord with the Rules. If that were the case, there would be no need to make use of §36 and the waiver would be meaningless. Section 36 allows for opposition to enforcement where there has been some jurisdictional or procedural breach by the arbitrators. If a waiver of §36 only applied where there were no jurisdictional or procedural breaches, it would be meaningless. That could not have been the intention of the parties or the meaning of the waiver under their agreement.

The Court of Appeal of British Columbia set out the standard with respect to the degree of deference to be accorded the decision of international arbitrators in *Quintette Coal Ltd. v. Nippon Steel Corp.*, [1991] 1 W.W.R. 219, 229 (B.C. C.A.):

> "It is meet therefore, as a matter of policy, to adopt a standard which seeks to preserve the autonomy of the forum selected by the parties and to minimize judicial intervention when reviewing international commercial arbitral awards in British Columbia. That is the standard to be followed in this case."

This narrow scope of court intervention with respect to international arbitral awards can equally be applied to an agreement between the parties with respect to such an arbitration. It would not be appropriate for a court to go beyond the clear meaning of the words in an arbitration agreement and interpret them in such a way as to render the clause meaningless. Accordingly, the only possible conclusion is that the parties waived their right to oppose enforcement of the award under §36 and the respondent's grounds for opposing enforcement cannot be supported as they clearly fall under that waiver. In any event, I will go on to address those further arguments of the respondent [contending that the Award should not be recognized].

The respondent argues that the arbitrators made 3 separate errors with respect to the arbitration and that on the basis of those errors the enforcement should be denied as they render the arbitral procedure "not in accordance with the agreement of the parties" (§36(1)(a)(v) of the Act). The agreement of the parties incorporated the [AAA International Rules] and the respondent submits these errors violate those Rules and, therefore, the agreement of the parties. The errors in question are: a) the arbitrators failed to deliver reasons for their award; b) the arbitrators failed to decide the dispute in accordance with the law; c) the arbitrators failed to follow the correct procedure following a challenge to their impartiality....

Article 28(2) of the [AAA International Rules] requires the arbitrators to state the reasons upon which the award is based. In this matter, written reasons were not issued. The respondent alleges this to be an error which renders the arbitral procedure not in accordance with the agreement of the parties and, therefore, a reason to refuse enforcement of the award under §36.

The award was made on December 6, 1996, and was to be paid no later than December 31, 1996. This petition was filed on January 27, 1997.... The respondent wrote to request reasons for the arbitral award on February 12, 1997. The petitioner submits that the respondent should have requested reasons within 30 days under Article 31 and by not doing so, waived the right to object to the failure to give reasons. Alternatively, the petitioner argues that the failure to give reasons is an irregularity only and does not render the award defective such as to preclude enforcement.

Article 31 [of the AAA Rules] states that: "1. Within 30 days after receipt of an award, any party, with notice to the other parties, may request the tribunal to interpret the award …" The petitioner submits that since the respondent, Pan Pacific, failed to request, within 30 days, written reasons under this Article as an interpretation of the award, the respondent cannot now raise the lack of written reasons as an issue. Whether this Article would apply to such a request is for the tribunal or the administrator of the AAA to determine under the provisions of Article 37 which read: "The tribunal shall interpret and apply these rules insofar as they relate to its powers and duties. All other rules shall be interpreted and applied by the administrator."

Although it may have been open to the respondent to so request under Article 31, it is not clear that a failure to make such a request bars the respondent from objecting after the 30 day period. The issue then is whether the failure to give reasons is sufficiently serious to render the arbitral procedure to have not been in accordance with the agreement of the parties such as a warrant denying enforcement of the award. In *Schreter v. Gasmac Inc.* (1992) 7 O.R.(3d) 608 (Gen. Div.), the court held that the failure of international arbitrators to give reasons did not amount to a ground upon which the court should exercise its discretion to refuse enforcement of the award and the respondent did not satisfy the onus to rely on §36. In coming to this conclusion, the court assessed the issues before the arbitrators and the extent to which the basis of the award could be unclear in the absence of reasons. It was found that only a small portion of the award was based on an issue upon which, in the absence of reasons, it was unclear whether the arbitrators took jurisdiction over that issue….

The respondent asserts the failure to give reasons falls under §36(1)(a)(v) as the "arbitral procedure was not in accordance with the agreement of the parties" as that agreement stipulated that the claims were to be "determined by arbitration in accordance with the [AAA Rules]." A large degree of deference is required by this court in exercising its discretion to refuse enforcement of an award: *Quintette Coal*. On that basis, a strict interpretation should be taken of §36.

The respondent['s Article §36(1)(a)(v) argument] relies on the agreement of the parties to have their claims determined by an arbitration which is in accordance with the [parties' agreement and the AAA Rules]. The plain meaning of this is that the arbitration itself, that is the hearing and the process of deciding the matter, be in accord with the Rules. The issuing of reasons after the fact is not part of the arbitration itself…. Even if the failure to give reasons were considered part of the arbitral procedure, the failure does not bring into question the fairness of the hearing or of the decision making process and is, therefore, not sufficiently serious to violate the parties' agreement to have an arbitration in accord with the Rules. The respondent has failed to bring itself under §36 to warrant the court existing its discretion to refuse enforcement on this basis.

The agreement of the parties required the arbitrators to apply the applicable law to the dispute. The respondent submits the arbitrators failed to do this and, rather, decided the dispute in accordance with "equity and good conscience." The respondent submits that in the absence of reasons from the arbitrators, there is no evidence before the court to indicate that their decision was based on law…. Following … *Quintette Coal*, this court should defer to the award of international arbitrators unless there is a clear reason their award should not be enforced. The respondent wishes the court to draw an inference that the arbitrators decided this matter on the basis of their conscience rather than based on the applicable law. To do that, the arbitrators would have been in direct contravention of their instructions. The respondent has offered no evidence to support this serious allegation. In the absence of any evidence, it is not open to this court to suggest that the arbitrators decided the matter in an improper manner....

During the arbitration hearing, the petitioner put on record that it was giving notice of its intention to challenge the impartiality of the arbitrators under Article 8. Article 8 of the [AAA International Rules] requires a written challenge to be submitted within 15 days of the circumstances giving rise to the challenge. After discussion, the arbitration proceeded on the basis that the petitioner had preserved its right to challenge the arbitrators. The respondent argues this was an error by the arbitrators in allowing the arbitration to proceed under the threat of a challenge to their impartiality.

The petitioner never did comply with Article 8 as there was never any written complaint filed. A concern was raised, discussed and the petitioner apparently chose not to pursue it. In the absence of a formal written complaint, there was no obligation on the arbitrators to withdraw or take any other action. While it could be said that they continued to act under the threat of a challenge, this is no different from the situation as it would have been absent the oral notice by the petitioner. Arbitrators can be challenged under Article 8 within 15 days of the circumstances which give rise to that challenge. For that reason, an arbitrator is always acting under the threat of a challenge and could be making special efforts to be impartial as the respondent alleges in this situation. As no formal complaint was ever made, there was no onus on the arbitrators to act in any different manner....

It is also significant that the respondent did not take issue with this alleged error during the arbitration. Article 26 of the Rules provides as follows:

> "A party who knows that any provision of the rules or requirement under the rules has not been complied with, but proceeds with the arbitration without promptly stating an objection in writing thereto, shall be deemed to have waived the right to object."

On the basis of Article 26, even if the arbitrators had committed an error in the handling of this issue, the respondent's failure to object at the time means that they are deemed to have waived the right to object and cannot properly bring an objection at this time....

KARAHA BODAS CO., LLC v. PERUSAHAAN PERTAMBANGAN MINYAK DAN GAS BUMI NEGARA

364 F.3d 274 (5th Cir. 2004)

[excerpted above at pp. 605-19]

JUDGMENT OF 24 FEBRUARY 1994

XXII Y.B. Comm. Arb. 682 (1997) (Paris Cour d'appel)

[excerpted above at pp. 682-83]

AAOT FOREIGN ECONOMIC ASS'N (VO) TECHNOSTROYEXPORT v. INT'L DEVELOPMENT & TRADE SERVICES, INC.
139 F.3d 980 (2d Cir. 1999)

[excerpted above at pp. 766-67]

NOTES

1. *Relationship between Articles V(1)(b) and V(1)(d) of New York Convention.* Consider Articles V(1)(b) and V(1)(d) of the Convention, excerpted at p. 2 of the Documentary Supplement, and their counterparts under national arbitration legislation. What is the difference between the exceptions set forth in Article V(1)(b) and Article V(1)(d)? Construct hypotheticals where one exception, but not the other, would apply.

   Suppose an arbitral tribunal grants one party ten days to present evidence, but the other party only one day to do so. Would this arguably violate Article V(1)(b)? Article V(1)(d)? Suppose the parties' agreement provides that one party may have ten days to present its evidence, and the other party only one day. If the arbitrators complied with this agreement, would their award be subject to challenge under Article V(1)(b)? If the arbitrators refused to comply with this agreement, would their award be subject to challenge under Article V(1)(d)?

2. *Desirability of judicial review of fairness of arbitral procedures under Article V(1)(b).* Is it appropriate for recognition courts to review the fairness of arbitral procedures under Article V(1)(b)? If the parties agree to arbitrate, why should there be *any* after-the-fact judicial scrutiny of the fairness of arbitral procedures?

   Note that claims of procedural unfairness can arise in two basic settings: (a) where the parties' arbitration agreement prescribes particular procedures; or (b) where the arbitration agreement does not prescribe particular procedures, and the arbitrators instead exercised their procedural discretion to order such procedures. How does the judicial role differ in these two cases? *See also supra* pp. 785-96.

3. *Law applicable to standards of procedural fairness under Article V(1)(b).* The New York Convention does not specify what nation's laws, or what international standards, apply in determining whether Article V(1)(b)'s exception for procedural unfairness is met. What law should be applied to determine whether an arbitral procedure was unfair and, if so, how serious that unfairness was? Possible choices include: (a) the national law of the recognition forum; (b) the national law of the arbitral seat; (c) a uniform international standard derived directly from Article V(1)(b). Which of these choices best serves the Convention's purposes? Which approach does the UNCITRAL Model Law appear to adopt in Article 36(1)(a)(ii), excerpted at p. 95 of the Documentary Supplement?

   If the national law of either the recognition forum or the arbitral seat is applied under Article V(1)(b), what rules of that national law are relevant? Is it the generally-applicable rules of procedural fairness applicable in local court proceedings (*e.g.*, rules of civil procedure)? More general standards of procedural fairness applicable in any domestic adjudicatory proceeding (*e.g.*, the U.S. Due Process Clause or Article 6 of the European Convention on Human Rights)? Rules of procedural fairness applicable specifically in arbitral (or international arbitral) proceedings?

Consider the opinion in *Parsons*. The court held that the law of the forum where recognition is sought—there, the United States—should be applied to determine whether a party was given "proper" notice or was "unable" to present his case. Compare the *Judgment of 23 April 2004*, where the court applied "the basic principles of German procedural law."

Compare also the *Judgment of 3 April 1987*. Did the Italian Supreme Court apply the provisions of domestic Italian law regarding notice periods in Italian litigation (*e.g.*, 90 days, plus a moratorium between August and mid-September)? Should the Court have applied these provisions? Wouldn't they be easily ascertainable to any tribunal fixing dates for an Italian party?

Why should Article V(1)(b) be read as requiring (or permitting) application of national law? Would this not contradict the Convention's goal of uniformity, while permitting individual Contracting States undesirable latitude in denying recognition of foreign awards? Suppose the courts of State X held that Article V(1)(b) permitted non-recognition of any award involving a State X party where the proceedings were not conducted in the official language of State X? Or where the arbitrators were not qualified to practice the law of State X?

If national law is applicable under Article V(1)(b) to establish standards of procedural fairness, are these the same standards that would apply in an action to annul an award made locally? For example, is the standard of procedural fairness applicable in a non-recognition action under Article 36(1)(a)(ii) of the UNCITRAL Model Law the same as that under Article 34(2)(a)(ii) of the Model Law? Why might the standards differ?

If Article V(1)(b) is read as establishing a uniform international standard of procedural fairness, what sources would this standard be derived from? Recall the fundamentally differing approaches to judicial and arbitral procedure in many parts of the world. *See supra* pp. 786-88, 818-23. Is it nonetheless possible to derive generally-applicable principles of procedural fairness? What about principles of procedural fairness common to the legal systems of the two parties to the arbitration?

4. *Application under Article V(1)(b) of due process standards under U.S. Constitution by U.S. courts.* As *Karaha Bodas* and *Parsons* illustrate, lower U.S. courts have generally concluded that awards falling under the Convention are subject to scrutiny under the "due process" standards of the U.S. Constitution. Is it appropriate to apply U.S. constitutional standards in the context of arbitral proceedings under Article V(1)(b)? Note that U.S. due process standards are developed for application to decisions by domestic courts, administrative agencies and similar governmental organs. Is it appropriate to apply these standards to arbitral tribunals? How are arbitral tribunals different from national courts and agencies? Does this justify different standards of procedural fairness?

Does it make sense to apply domestic U.S. constitutional standards to arbitrations seated abroad, governed by foreign procedural law, between parties from foreign jurisdictions? Suppose, for example, Swiss and French parties arbitrate in Tunisia. Should U.S. domestic constitutional standards really be used to evaluate the fairness of the arbitral procedures?

As *Karaha Bodas* and *Parsons* illustrate, some U.S. courts have referred to domestic FAA standards, in annulment contexts, in discussing the standards of procedural fairness under Article V(1)(b). *See Nat'l Oil Corp. v. Libyan Sun Oil Co.*, 733 F.Supp. 800, 817 (D. Del. 1990); *Biotronik Mess- und Therapiegeräte GmbH & Co. v. Medford Med. Instrument Co.*, 415 F.Supp. 133, 137-38 (D.N.J. 1976). Are standards of procedural fairness used in annulment contexts relevant to recognition under Article V(1)(b)? Are they more or less relevant than domestic constitutional standards?

Would it be possible to develop international standards of procedural fairness? Note that, as discussed above, Article 52(1)(d) of the ICSID Convention provides for annulment of an ICSID award where "there has been a serious departure from a fundamental rule of procedure." *See supra* pp. 796-97, 1173. This reference to "fundamental rules of procedure" must have meaning, right? Wouldn't the same standards also be capable of application under Article V(1)(b) of the New York Convention?

5. *Recognition of parties' procedural autonomy under Article V(1)(b)*. Should national courts ever deny recognition of an award based upon a conclusion that the parties' agreed procedures, as distinguished from the arbitrators' exercise of their procedural discretion, were fundamentally unfair? Does this not interfere with the parties' procedural autonomy? One court described this issue in stark terms, as follows:

> "short of authorizing trial by battle or ordeal or, more doubtfully, by a panel of three monkeys, parties can stipulate to whatever procedures they want to govern the arbitration of their disputes; parties are as free to specify idiosyncratic terms of arbitration as they are to specify any other terms in their contract." *Baravati v. Josephthal, Lyon & Ross*, 28 F.3d 704, 709 (7th Cir. 1994).

Although colorful, is this reasoning persuasive? Suppose the parties' agreement contains grossly one-sided terms (*e.g.*, one party may be represented by legal counsel, but the other party may not; one party may present witness testimony, but the other may not; one party may select the sole arbitrator, who may be one of its executives). *See supra* pp. 408-10, 683-85. Is there any reason that awards rendered pursuant to such procedures should not be subject to non-recognition under Article V(1)(b)? Suppose these were negotiated terms, which one party accepted in return for other commercial and contractual concessions?

6. *Recognition of arbitrators' procedural discretion under Article V(1)(b)*. Consider the opinions in *Judgment of 23 April 2004, Karaha Bodas* and *Parsons*. Do these decisions suggest a degree of deference to the arbitrators' procedural decisions? How much deference? What is the appropriate rule?

Consider the decision in *Judgment of 23 April 2004*, where the German court said: "There is no violation of the principle of due process even if the arbitral tribunal denies a request to supply evidence on formal or substantive law grounds"; the court goes on to say that this conclusion applies even if the denial was wrong. Should that be correct? *Compare Iran Aircraft Indus. v. Avco Corp.*, 980 F.2d 141 (2d Cir. 1992) (recognition refused because tribunal told party that it did not want to be presented with certain evidence (detailed invoices) by claimant, but later rejected claimant's claims on grounds that this evidence was necessary to prove those claims).

Compare the decision in *Judgment of 3 April 1987*. Did the Italian Supreme Court demonstrate any deference to the arbitral tribunal's choice of a one-month deadline? Or, is that a task that the Milan Court of Appeal can undertake? What deference should be afforded the tribunal in this case?

7. *Serious violation of fundamental legal protection required to warrant non-recognition under Article V(1)(b)*. Consider again the decisions in *Judgment of 3 April 1987*, *Judgment of 23 April 2004*, *Karaha Bodas* and *Parsons*. Is *every* denial of procedural fairness a basis for non-recognition of an award? What standard is adopted in each case? *Compare Judgment of 8 February 1978*, XI Y.B. Comm. Arb. 538 (1986) (Swiss Fed. Trib.) ("insofar as the procedure is concerned, not every irregularity will automatically entail refusal of enforcement of a foreign award, even if such irregularity would entail the annulment of an award rendered in Switzerland. It should rather involve a violation of fundamental principles of the Swiss legal order which hurts in an intolerable manner the notion of justice"). Are these standards appropriate? What would an arbitrator have to do in order to justify non-recognition under these standards?

8. *Material prejudice generally required to warrant non-recognition under Article V(1)(b)*. Suppose the arbitrators unfairly deny one party a procedural right (*e.g.*, refuse to permit the party to question a particular witness or grant the party a disproportionately short period of time to respond to an argument). Is any such procedural unfairness grounds for denying recognition of the award under Article V(1)(b)? Suppose the witness testified on matters that were irrelevant or incidental to the dispositive issues; suppose the party, despite having a disproportionately short period of time, submitted a persuasive response, which the arbitrators accepted. *Compare Judgment of 23 September 2004*, XXX Y.B. Comm. Arb. 568 (2005) (Bavarian Oberstes Landesgericht) ("A procedural defect is deemed essential to the arbitral award when it is causal to it … or when the arbitral tribunal would have decided differently had it not been for the procedural violation") *with Judgment of 28 April 1998*, XXIII Y.B. Comm. Arb. 731 (1998) (Hague Gerechtshof) (in case involving "violation of [award-debtor's] fundamental right to comment on … new documents, which can have played a role in the arbitrator's decision," there is no need to demonstrate whether "arbitral tribunal would have come to a different decision").

9. *Equality of treatment and opportunity to present case (revisited)*. Recall that Article 18 of the Model Law requires that "[t]he parties shall be treated with equality and each party shall be given a full opportunity of presenting his case." Similarly, Article 182(3) of the SLPIL provides, again in mandatory terms, that: "Whatever procedure is chosen [by the parties and/or tribunal], the arbitral tribunal shall assure equal treatment of the parties and the right of the parties to be heard in an adversarial procedure." Other arbitration regimes are similar in their approaches to mandatory procedural protections. *See supra* pp. 793-94.

   How are these principles—equality of treatment and the opportunity to be heard—applicable under Article V(1)(b)? Are they? Should they not provide the foundation for any standard of procedural fairness under Article V(1)(b)? Note that these principles are part of a uniform international instrument—the UNCITRAL Model Law—as to which growing body of interpretive authority exists.

10. *Representatives cases involving claims of a denial of an opportunity to be heard*. Consider the following examples of arguable denials of an opportunity to be heard, within the meaning of Article V(1)(b).

    (a) *Right to be heard in oral proceedings*. Suppose the arbitrators conclude that there is no need for an oral hearing, either for witness testimony or argument by counsel.

Does this constitute a denial of an opportunity to be heard under Article V(1)(b)? Are there any circumstances where such action would be justified? Suppose the parties' arbitration agreement provided either (a) there would be no oral hearing; or (b) the arbitrators had discretion whether or not to conduct an oral hearing. *See Judgment of 30 July 1998*, XXV Y.B. Comm. Arb. 714 (2000) (Hanseatisches Oberlandesgericht Hamburg) ("The rules of arbitration of the agreed arbitral tribunal provide that a decision may be rendered without an oral hearing"); *Dadras Int'l v. Islamic Repub. of Iran*, 31 Iran-US C.T.R. 127, 135-36, 143 (1995) ("even where no hearing has been held, Article 15, paragraph 2 does not oblige the Tribunal to accede to any request by a party for a hearing").

(b) *Opportunity to comment on evidence or arguments.* Suppose an arbitral tribunal permits one party to submit new documentary evidence late in the case (*e.g.*, after the hearing; shortly before the hearing), but denies the other party an opportunity either to submit evidence in response or to comment on the new evidence. Does this constitute a denial of an opportunity to be heard under Article V(1)(b)? Suppose the new evidence is merely responsive to an issue raised in the other party's last submission. Suppose the tribunal permits a written response to the new documentary evidence but refuses to hold a new witness hearing on issues raised by the evidence.

Recall the discussion of the Swiss Federal Tribunal in *Judgment of 30 December 1994*, in the annulment context, *supra* pp. 1143-46; what did the Federal Tribunal indicate with regard to an opportunity to comment on new factual allegations? Recall also that the Federal Tribunal held that a party is not guaranteed the right to respond to legal arguments (as distinguished from facts), on the theory that the arbitral tribunal knows, and is responsible for identifying and applying, the law. Is this an appropriate standard in an international context?

(c) *Opportunity to reply.* Suppose an arbitrator permits the claimant to have the last word in oral argument, despite the respondent's insistence that it should be permitted the final word. Suppose the reverse. Does either action constitute a denial of an opportunity to be heard under Article V(1)(b)? Could either action ever do so?

(d) *Decisions based on facts or arguments not presented by or discussed with parties ("surprise decisions").* Suppose the arbitrator makes her decision based on legal arguments (*e.g.*, interpretations of a contract or legislation) or factual assessments that neither party argued. Is this permitted? Consider the arguments advanced by the award-debtor in *Karaha Bodas*. Did the tribunal make a surprise decision?

Recall the principle that the tribunal knows the law and is responsible for applying it. *See supra* pp. 1143-46, 1235. What if the tribunal does not give the parties an opportunity to comment on the legal argument or factual assessment? *Compare Judgment of 6 December 2001*, XXIX Y.B. Comm. Arb. 742 (2004) (Oberlandesgericht Stuttgart) ("A decision is a surprise decision when the [tribunal] bases its decision on a point of view that was not mentioned by either party, discussed or drawn attention to.") *with Judgment of 8 February 1978*, XI Y.B. Comm. Arb. 538 (1986) (Swiss Fed. Trib.) ("the arbitrator, like a judge of a State court, is not obliged to submit to the discussion by the parties the legal principles on which he will base his decision. However, according to doctrinal opinion, the arbitrator who is specialized and who has access to sources of knowledge which are not always at the disposal of the parties, has the obligation to bring in advance to the attention of the parties the fundamental technical elements on which his decision will be based").

Recall the decision, in an annulment context, in *Southwire, supra* pp. 1136-38. Suppose the case had arisen in a recognition context (*i.e.*, the award had been made outside the United States). Would the tribunal's treatment of the claimant's interest claim have constituted a surprise decision? Would it be easier, or more difficult, to obtain non-recognition of an award than annulment?

(e) *Unequal treatment.* Suppose the arbitrator permits one party ten days to present testimony from its witnesses and the other party only one day. Does it matter if the first party has ten witnesses and the second party only one witness? What if the witnesses' testimony covers the same subjects? Suppose that the tribunal permits the claimant 90 days to prepare its statement of claims, but allows the respondent only 45 days to reply? 15 days?

(f) *Disclosure and discovery.* Consider the court's treatment of the award-debtor's complaints about the lack of disclosure in *Karaha Bodas.* If you were on the tribunal, would you have ordered disclosure? Is that the relevant question? Suppose the arbitrator refuses to order any disclosure. Is that necessarily a basis for non-recognition under Article V(1)(b)? Could it ever be? When? What if the parties' arbitration agreement provides that disclosure will be available? Does that raise issues under Article V(1)(b), or under Article V(1)(d)?

(g) *Examination or cross-examination.* Suppose the arbitrator refuses to permit either party to examine or cross-examine any witnesses, with the arbitrator instead conducting all questioning. Does this deny the parties an opportunity to be heard? Suppose this is the customary practice of domestic courts in the arbitral seat. *See Generica Ltd v. Pharm. Basics, Inc.*, 1996 U.S. Dist. LEXIS 13716 (N.D. Ill.) ("The right to cross-examine witnesses is not absolute"), *aff'd*, 125 F.3d 1123 (7th Cir. 1997). Consider the treatment of this issue in *Karaha Bodas.*

(h) *Ex parte contacts.* Suppose one of the co-arbitrators has *ex parte* contacts with the party that nominated him or her about the substance of the case. Suppose the contacts include comments on issues that are troubling the presiding arbitrator.

(i) *Inability of party to attend hearings.* Suppose one party (or its responsible officer) is unable to attend an important evidentiary hearing (*e.g.*, because of illness or travel restrictions). *See Consorcio Rive, SA de CV (Mexico) v. Briggs of Cancun., Inc.*, 82 F.Appx. 359 (5th Cir. 2003) (award-debtor's inability to physically attend hearings, because of fear of criminal prosecution, did not violate opportunity to be heard: "[award-debtor] could have simply sent an attorney or other corporate representative to represent it at the arbitration [or] participated by telephone"); *Grow Biz Int'l Inc. v. D.L.T. Holdings, Inc.*, XXX Y.B. Comm. Arb. 450 (2005) (Prince Edward Island S.Ct. 2001) (rejecting claim that party "was unable to attend the arbitration hearing because she could not afford to go," because no evidence supported claim). Consider again the decision in *Judgment of 3 April 1987.* Is it appropriate for an arbitral tribunal to set such a short deadline in a period customarily used for vacations? If the deadline was too short, what could the objecting party do? Suppose that the time period in question had fallen during religious holidays.

(j) *Biased arbitral tribunal*. Suppose the tribunal is alleged to have been partial to the award creditor. Recall various of the one-sided arbitration provisions, discussed above, permitting one party disproportionate influence over selection of the arbitrators. *See supra* pp. 408-09, 683-85. Do these sorts of arrangements provide grounds for non-recognition of an award under Article V(1)(b)? Consider the *Judgment of 3 June 1982*, where an award made by a sole arbitrator, appointed by one party, was upheld under Article V(1)(b). Is that appropriate? What is the relevance of the failure by the award-debtor to have participated in constituting the arbitral tribunal?

11. *Waiver of procedural objections under Article V(1)(b)*. Most national laws and institutional rules require that parties object to procedural or evidentiary rulings during the arbitral proceedings in order to preserve their right to annul an award. *See supra* pp. 1169-70. Will the failure to make a timely objection similarly prevent a party from relying on the disputed procedure in opposing recognition under Article V(1)(b)?

As the decision in *Technostroyexport* illustrates, most courts have held that procedural defects may be waived for purposes of Article V(1)(b). *See also Qinhuangdao Tongda Enter. Dev. Co. v. Million Basic Co.*, XIX Y.B. Comm. Arb. 675 (1994) (H.K. Ct. First Inst. 1993) (rejecting Article V(1)(b) defense to recognition: "defendant knew that the tribunal had fixed a deadline for the submission of evidence [which passed] without any application for an extension being made [and] it was not until after the proceedings had been formally declared closed that any attempt was made to have new evidence admitted"); *Minmetals Germany GmbH v. Ferco Steel Ltd*, [1999] 1 All ER 315 (Comm) (English High Ct.) (party "had been given every opportunity [to present its case]. What had gone wrong was that its counsel had simply failed to take that opportunity").

Suppose a party is alleged to have waived a fundamental procedural protection (*e.g.*, issues of corruption of arbitrator(s)). Is such a waiver effective in preventing reliance on the procedural defect? *Compare Marino v. Writers Guild of Am.*, 992 F.2d 1480, 1484 (9th Cir. 1993) (waiver "extends even to questions, such as arbitrator bias, that go to the very heart of arbitral fairness") *with Judgment of 10 June 1976*, IV Y.B. Comm. Arb. 258 (1979) (Oberlandesgericht Köln) (refusing to enforce award because of refusal of Copenhagen Arbitration Committee for Grain and Feed Stuff Trade (under institutional rules agreed to by award-debtor) to reveal arbitrators' names to parties).

12. *Consequences of failure to seek annulment of award for procedural unfairness*. Suppose a party does not seek to annul the award in the arbitral seat on grounds of procedural unfairness, but later seeks to resist recognition on those grounds. Does the absence of any annulment action waive the right to oppose recognition? *Compare IPOC Int'l Growth Fund Ltd v. LV Fin. Group Ltd*, Civ. App. No. 30 of 2006 (B.V.I. Ct. App. 2007) (procedural issues not raised in annulment action can be raised in recognition proceeding only in "[e]xceptional cases [which] are those cases in which the powers of the supervisory court are so limited that the court cannot intervene even where there has been serious disregard for basic principles of justice by the arbitrators or where for unjust reasons, such as corruption, they disregard such principles.") *with Judgment of 26 April 1990*, XXI Y.B. Comm. Arb. 532 (1996) (German Bundesgerichtshof) (requirement that party raise objections to award in arbitral seat ap-

plies "only to irregularities in the arbitral procedure which violate the law of the State where arbitration takes place"; this obligation "does not concern a violation of due process" under Article V(1)(b)).

13. *Non-compliance with agreed procedural rules as grounds for non-recognition under Article V(1)(d)*. Consider the text of Article V(1)(d) of the New York Convention. Compare Article 36(1)(a)(iv) of the UNCITRAL Model Law, excerpted at p. 95 of the Documentary Supplement. Note that Article V(1)(d) has two separate bases for non-recognition of an award: (i) non-compliance with the parties' agreed arbitral procedures; and (ii) absent any agreed procedures, non-compliance with the law of the arbitral seat. What sorts of procedural complaints are likely to arise under Article V(1)(d)'s first prong?

(a) *Agreements on constitution of tribunal*. One of the most common bases for challenges under Article V(1)(d) concerns the constitution of the arbitral tribunal. Consider the result in *Judgment of 3 June 1982*. Note that the parties' arbitration agreement provided for three arbitrators, but that the award was rendered by a sole arbitrator. Is this not a case where Article V(1)(d) could apply? Why didn't it? Is it relevant that the parties' agreement did not provide what would occur if one party failed to nominate a co-arbitrator?

Consider *Karaha Bodas*. Should the parties' agreements have been interpreted as authorizing consolidation and a single arbitral tribunal? Was the U.S. court correct in refusing to deny recognition under Article V(1)(d)? Suppose the tribunal had adopted the opposite interpretation (that consolidation was not permitted); would its award have been subject to non-recognition under Article V(1)(d)? How much deference to the tribunal's interpretation of the parties' arbitration agreements was given—and should have been given—by the recognition court?

Consider *Encyclopaedia Universalis*. Was the court correct in holding that the parties' agreed arbitral procedures had not been followed? Reread the parties' agreement to arbitrate, quoted *supra* p. 1223 n. 38. Was the U.S. court correct in holding that a third arbitrator was only to be appointed after the two arbitrators had failed to agree on selecting a chairman, rather than agreeing on the substantive resolution of the parties' dispute? Note that, historically, arbitration clauses provided for arbitration by two arbitrators with an umpire being appointed only if the two arbitrators fail to agree. *See, e.g.,* 1907 Hague Convention, Arts. 45, 54, 55.

Was *Encyclopaedia Universalis* correct in holding that the third arbitrator was not selected in accordance with the parties' agreement? Did the parties' agreement require a mutually-recognized deadlock? Or simply a failure to agree after a reasonable period of time? What about the fact that the co-arbitrators had very different views about the identity of an appropriate presiding arbitrator; did this not provide grounds for concluding that the co-arbitrators could not agree? Was any deference given by the U.S. court to the two arbitrators' views of the meaning of the arbitration agreement? Should any deference have been given?

What deference, if any, should be afforded in a recognition action to the decision of the courts of the arbitral seat interpreting the procedural terms of the parties' arbitration agreement? Consider the Luxembourg court's decisions in *Encyclopaedia Universalis*. Should the U.S. court have deferred to the Luxembourg court's conclusion that the co-arbitrators had failed to agree upon a presiding arbitrator and that it was appropriate for the local court to do so?

(b) *Other procedural agreements*. Consider *Food Services*. What is required in order to demonstrate that the parties' agreed arbitral procedures were not complied with? Note the court's deference to the arbitral tribunal and institution.

(c) *Conflicts between agreed arbitral procedures and law of arbitral seat*. Consider the decision in *Judgment of 24 February 1994*. Recall that the parties agreed to arbitrate before two arbitrators, but the two co-arbitrators selected a presiding arbitrator in order to comply with the law of the arbitral seat (Tunisia). Was the arbitral tribunal constituted in accordance with the parties' agreement? Why wasn't the award denied recognition under Article V(1)(d)? Should it have been? Recall that non-recognition under Article V(1) is not mandatory. *See supra* p. 1196. Is this a case where, even if Article V(1)(b) were potentially applicable, it was appropriate not to deny recognition?

Suppose the parties' agreed arbitral procedure violates mandatory provisions of the arbitral seat. Should an award issued in compliance with those mandatory provisions always be granted recognition, notwithstanding Article V(1)(d)? What if the law of the arbitral seat forbade arbitrating pursuant to the rules of any foreign arbitral institution (including the ICC, LCIA, SIAC, UNCITRAL/PCA, or ICDR)? What if the law of the arbitral seat required that all arbitrators be local nationals? If an arbitration is conducted—contrary to the parties' agreement—in accordance with these rules, should the resulting award be denied recognition under Article V(1)(d)?

Consider again §17 of the English Arbitration Act, 1996, excerpted at pp. 115-16 of the Documentary Supplement, which provides that if a party fails to nominate a co-arbitrator within the agreed time limits, then (absent contrary agreement) its counter-party may elect to treat its nominated co-arbitrator as a sole arbitrator. If an award is made pursuant to this authority, in circumstances where the parties' arbitration agreement provides for a tribunal of three arbitrators, is that award subject to non-recognition under Article V(1)(d) of the New York Convention? What is the argument that the award may be denied recognition? *See Judgment of 21 May 1976*, III Y.B. Comm. Arb. 277 (1978) (Venice Corte di Appello) (recognizing award made in England by sole arbitrator, where parties' agreement provided for three arbitrators, but one party failed to nominate co-arbitrator); *Judgment of 3 June 1982*, XI Y.B. Comm. Arb. 527 (1986) (Spanish Tribunal Supremo) (same). Are these results persuasive? What about the parties' agreement on three arbitrators? Is that agreement waived by the award-debtor's failure to nominate its co-arbitrator?

Consider the following statement: "The Convention allows recognition of an award which, although not in accord with the parties' agreement, complied with the laws of the country where the arbitration occurred. Convention, Art. V(1)(d)." *Al Haddad Bros. Enter. Inc. v. MS Agapi*, 635 F.Supp. 205, 206 (D. Del. 1986) (same), *aff'd*, 813 F.2d 396 (3d Cir. 1987). Doesn't the Convention "allow" recognition of any award? Isn't the real question whether the Convention would allow *non*-recognition of an award made by one arbitrator, when the parties had agreed upon a tribunal of three arbitrators? Would Article V(1)(d) permit non-recognition of an award in these circumstances? Even where the award-debtor failed to appoint its co-arbitrator?

Is there another basis for challenging an award made by a sole arbitrator, appointed by one party pursuant to §17 of the 1996 English Arbitration Act? For example, Article V(1)(b) or V(2)(b)? *See Judgment of 18 October 1999*, XXIX Y.B. Comm. Arb. 700 (2004) (Oberlandesgericht Stuttgart) ("the fact that the arbitral award was eventually rendered by the arbitrator appointed by the claimant is at odds with the requirement of impartiality and neutrality of foreign arbitrators, a requirement that also applies to international arbitrations governed by foreign substantive and procedural law"). Again, should Articles V(1)(b) and V(2)(b) apply where the award-debtor failed to take part in constitution of the tribunal?

14. *Non-compliance with law of arbitral seat as grounds for non-recognition under Article V(1)(d).* Consider the second prong of Article V(1)(d). In what circumstances is this basis for non-recognition applicable?

Suppose the law of the arbitral seat requires that all arbitral awards be rendered within six months of the commencement of the arbitration, *see supra* p. 796 and the award is not. Would Article V(1)(d) permit non-recognition? Suppose the parties' arbitration agreement permitted awards to be made within 12 months of the commencement of the arbitration. Again, would Article V(1)(d) permit non-recognition?

Suppose the law of the arbitral seat requires that all arbitrators be of a particular nationality or religious faith, but the arbitral institute appoints a presiding arbitrator of a different nationality or faith. Would Article V(1)(d) permit non-recognition?

Suppose the parties' arbitration agreement provides that the language of the arbitration shall be English and the law of the arbitral seat (State X) mandatorily requires that the arbitration be conducted in State X's official language. Would an award made after proceedings in English be subject to non-recognition under Article V(1)(d)? What about an award made after proceedings in State X's language?

Consider the decision in *Judgment of 24 February 1994*. What if the award had only been rendered by two arbitrators (rather than three, as required by the law of the arbitral seat)? Assuming the award was not annulled in the arbitral seat, would Article V(1)(d) have permitted the French courts to deny recognition? On what theory?

15. *Serious and prejudicial procedural disobedience required under Article V(1)(d).* Technical departures from the parties' agreed arbitration procedures will often not be grounds for non-recognition under Article V(1)(d). Consider the *Encyclopaedia Universalis* decision. Did the case involve a serious enough procedural defect to justify non-recognition? Compare the decision in *Food Services*. Was the failure to issue a reasoned award really a minor departure from the AAA International Rules? Compare *Indus. Risk Insurers v. M.A.N. Gutehoffnungshütte GmbH*, 141 F.3d 1434, 1444 (11th Cir. 1998) ("Arbitration rules, such as those of the AAA, are intentionally written loosely, in order to allow arbitrators to resolve disputes without the many procedural requirements of litigation"; rejecting defense under Article V(1)(d) on grounds that arbitral tribunal did not violate AAA rules in admitting evidence shortly before hearing).

16. *Waiver of objections to procedural defects under Article V(1)(d).* Suppose a party does not object to violations of the parties' agreed arbitral procedures during the arbitration. Does Article V(1)(d) nonetheless provide a basis for non-recognition of the award?

Note the conclusion in *Food Services*. Compare the result in *Technostroyexport*. Is there any reason that violations of agreed arbitral procedures should not be waivable? Is this true of all violations?

Suppose a party does not object to violations of the law of the arbitral seat. Again, does Article V(1)(d) provide a basis for non-recognition of the award?

17. *Prospective waiver of procedural objections*. Consider the court's analysis in *Food Services*. Note the first basis that the court identifies for its conclusion—namely, that the parties' arbitration agreement waived procedural objections. Is such an advance waiver permitted by the terms of the UNCITRAL Model Law? Should it be? Is *Food Services* wisely decided?

Would an advance waiver of procedural objections be valid under the FAA in the United States? Recall the *Hall Street* decision. Note that *Hall Street* is based on the supposedly exclusive, mandatory character of Chapter 1 of the FAA (particularly, §10). *See supra* pp. 1171-72. Is there anything equivalent in Article V of the New York Convention and §207 of the FAA?

18. *Failure to seek annulment in arbitral seat under Article V(1)(d)*. Suppose the award-debtor does not seek to annul the arbitral award in the arbitral seat on grounds that the arbitrators violated the procedural law of the arbitral seat, but later resists recognition on those grounds under Article V(1)(d). Does the absence of any annulment action waive the right to oppose recognition? *See Judgment of 26 April 1990*, XXI Y.B. Comm. Arb. 532 (1996) (German Bundesgerichtshof) (requirement that party raise objections to award in arbitral seat applies "to irregularities in the arbitral procedure which violate the law of the State where arbitration takes place"); *Judgment of 30 May 2006*, XXXII Y.B. Comm. Arb. 406 (2007) (Italian Corte di Cassazione) (failure of arbitrator to declare proceedings closed, as required by Hungarian Rules of Arbitration, is not a ground to refuse recognition, but instead, "only a defect in the arbitral proceedings which may be relied on, if at all, in the foreign legal system [*i.e.*, in the country of origin] through the means of recourse available therein"). Are these decisions persuasive? Do they read Article V(1)(d)'s second limb out of the Convention?

Suppose a party does raise alleged violations of the procedural law of the arbitral seat in an annulment action but is unsuccessful. What weight should the decision of the courts in the arbitral seat be accorded? Consider *Judgment of 23 November 2004*, XXXI Y.B. Comm. Arb. 786 (2006) (Jerusalem Dist. Ct.) ("It would not be reasonable to determine that this court is better able to examine the proper conduct of a foreign arbitral proceeding which was discussed and determined according to Swiss ZCC rules and Swiss procedure, than the Swiss courts. The judicial system of a civilized country and its ability to correctly assess the proper conduct of arbitration proceedings with which it is familiar and which were determined by the rules of its own legal system, must not be questioned").

19. *Limitations on authority of recognition court*. Consider the orders issued by the U.S. district court in *Encyclopaedia Universalis*. Were those orders permitted by the New York Convention? What if other Contracting States, where recognition was sought, issued comparable orders? Don't such orders conflict with the supervisory jurisdiction of the courts of the arbitral seat? *See supra* pp. 619-21, 622-24.

3. *Lack of Independence, Bias, Misconduct of Arbitrators and Fraud*

Virtually every jurisdiction insists on the observance of the basic principles of impartiality and independence by the arbitrators.[40] Despite this, international arbitration conventions (including the New York Convention) and arbitration statutes generally do not contain specific provisions concerning the lack of independence or impartiality of the arbitral tribunal, or the related ground of misconduct by the arbitrators, as a basis for non-recognition of an award. It is nonetheless clear that an arbitrator's lack of independence and/or impartiality can be a basis for denying recognition of an award under the New York Convention, as well as under national arbitration legislation. Different provisions of these instruments have been relied on to support such results.

As described above, Article V(1)(b) of the New York Convention permits non-recognition where a party was "unable to present his case," which can encompass at least some forms of arbitrator misconduct.[41] Similarly, Article V(1)(d) permits non-recognition where the "composition of the arbitral authority" was not "in accordance with the law of the country where the arbitration took place," which can incorporate standards relating to arbitrator bias and misconduct.[42] Beyond that, claims of fraud, bias and arbitrator misconduct have been considered under Article V(2)(b)'s public policy exception.[43]

Many national arbitration statutes also lack specific provisions for fraud and arbitrator bias or misconduct. That is true, for example, under the UNCITRAL Model Law and the SLPIL. Nonetheless, claims of arbitrator bias have been recognized under provisions parallel to those in the New York Convention. The materials excerpted below examine defenses to recognition of awards based on arbitrator bias and misconduct.

JUDGMENT OF 21 MAY 1976
III Y.B. Comm. Arb. 277 (1978) (Venice Corte di Appello)

[excerpted above at p. 1222]

JUDGMENT OF 24 FEBRUARY 1994
XXII Y.B. Comm. Arb. 682 (1997) (Paris Cour d'appel)

[excerpted above at pp. 682-83]

---

40. *See supra* pp. 716-58; G. Born, *International Commercial Arbitration* 3276 (2d ed. 2014).

41. *See supra* pp. 1218-19, 1231-34; G. Born, *International Commercial Arbitration* 3535-39; 3588 (2d ed. 2014).

42. *See supra* pp. 1218-19, 1238-40; G. Born, *International Commercial Arbitration* 1549-50, 2131, 2158-59 (2d ed. 2014).

43. *See, e.g., Nat'l Oil Corp. v. Libyan Sun Oil Co.*, 733 F.Supp. 800, 813 n.19 (D. Del. 1990); *Fertilizer Corp. of India v. IDI Mgt, Inc.*, 517 F.Supp. 948 (S.D. Ohio 1981); *Biotronik Mess- und Therapiegeräte GmbH & Co. v. Medford Med. Instrument Co.*, 415 F.Supp. 133, 137 (D.N.J. 1976); *Judgment of 12 January 1989*, XV Y.B. Comm. Arb. 509 (Swiss Fed. Trib.) (1990) (claim that arbitrator was partial falls within Article V(2)(b)); *Judgment of 15 May 1986*, XII Y.B. Comm. Arb. 489 (1987) (German Bundesgerichtshof) (same).

COMMONWEALTH COATINGS CORP. v. CONTINENTAL CASUALTY CO.
393 U.S. 145 (1968)

[excerpted above at pp. 717-21]

FERTILIZER CORP. OF INDIA v. IDI MANAGEMENT, INC.
517 F.Supp. 948 (S.D. Ohio 1981)

SPIEGEL, District Judge. [The facts are excerpted above at p. 1094.] ... IDI asserts that enforcement of the [Award] would violate the public policy of the United States, in violation of Article V(2)(b) of the Convention. They allege that Mr. B. Sen, the arbitrator nominated by FCI for the case (as well as for [a related arbitration] case) had served as counsel for FCI in at least two other legal or arbitral proceedings and that these facts were not disclosed to IDI. Respondent cites *Commonwealth Coatings* [*supra* pp. 717-21], to support the claim that American public policy demands that arbitrators be not only unbiased but free from even the appearance of bias. Further, they argue, since Mr. B. Sen was remunerated financially by FCI, the nondisclosure of the relationship is fatal to enforcement, despite the fact that the arbitration was unanimous and even though actual fraud or bias may be incapable of proof. IDI also claims that it had no constructive or other notice of Mr. Sen's relationship with FCI, although Indian counsel retained by IDI may have been aware of the arrangement. IDI has submitted affidavits of its responsible officers and past and present counsel to support this contention. FCI responds that Mr. Sen was chosen properly under the ICC rules as well as under the Convention.

Article V(1)(b) permits a refusal to enforce an award if the losing party was not given proper notice of the arbitrator's appointment or was otherwise unable to present his case; [Article V(1)(d)] covers the case where the composition of the arbitral panel was not in accord with the parties' agreement. IDI had proper notice and participated extensively in all sessions, presenting its case thoroughly. The contract between the parties calls for arbitration under the ICC rules by one or more arbitrators appointed in accordance with those rules. The ICC rules applicable at the time made no mention of neutrality, and not until the 1975 ICC rules became effective was an "independent" arbitrator required. FCI contends that even today it is not clear whether an "independent" arbitrator need be neutral. Moreover, they argue, Mr. Sen is a Senior Advocate and, as such, his relationship with FCI was not that of attorney and client. Rather, Senior Advocates in India are hired by the client's advocate (similar to the retention of a barrister by a solicitor under the British system), are paid by the advocate (who is normally reimbursed by the client), and the Senior Advocate is thus insulated from the client. He is an officer of the Court, like a British Queen's Counsel, and may argue for and against the same client at different times.

FCI answers further that, although not required by the ICC rules, a biographical data sheet on Mr. Sen was furnished to IDI; this indicated that he had a connection with the Indian Government, of which FCI is a wholly-owned entity. FCI also claims that IDI had actual or constructive notice of Mr. Sen's relationship with FCI. They argue that IDI's Indian counsel, ... was well-acquainted with the facts and that his knowledge should be imputed to IDI. They also claim that an IDI vice-president was given a copy of another arbitration award which clearly revealed that Mr. Sen appeared on FCI's behalf. IDI vigorously denies any such knowledge on its part and strongly protests the propriety of imputing to IDI [its Indian counsel's] knowledge.

FCI has submitted the affidavit of Colin Ross-Munro, Q.C. which states that there is no impropriety in an Indian Senior Advocate appearing in an arbitration on behalf of a party without disclosing that he had represented that party in another context. IDI has submitted the affidavit of George Mark Waller, Q.C. which asserts exactly the opposite.

The Court does not take lightly IDI's charge. In view of the unanimity of the [Award], there is nothing to suggest actual bias or prejudice on Mr. Sen's part, yet we strongly believe that full disclosure of any possible interest or bias is the better rule whenever one is in a position to determine the rights of others. However, we do not find that nondisclosure of Mr. Sen's relationship with FCI has so tainted the proceedings as to nullify the award.

FCI relies upon *Commonwealth Coating,* as the statement of American public policy with respect to neutrality of arbitrators. It is true that in this case a plurality of the Supreme Court found that "any tribunal permitted by law to try cases and controversies not only must be unbiased but also must avoid even the appearance of bias," and stated that "we should, if anything, be even more scrupulous to safeguard the impartiality of arbitrators than judges." Two justices concurred but emphasized that arbitrators are not to be held to the standards of Article III judges, or of any judges, and three Justices dissented, insisting that, in the absence of a showing of unfairness or partiality, there was no reason to set aside an award for failure to disclose a prior business relationship.

Moreover, *Commonwealth Coatings* is distinguishable on the facts. That case dealt with a so-called tri-partite arbitration where one party chose one arbitrator, the other party chose a second, and those two arbitrators selected the third. The controversy centered on the third arbitrator, "the supposedly neutral member of the panel." In the present case, we are dealing, not with the third member of the panel, but with the member appointed by the party, FCI, with whom the alleged undisclosed relationship existed. The third member of the panel was Lord Devlin. Although IDI claims that Lord Devlin was appointed at Mr. Sen's suggestion, while FCI claims that he was appointed at Mr. Rand's (IDI's former counsel's) suggestion, and each supplies a letter purporting to uphold its claim, there is nothing at all to suggest that Lord Devlin was other than totally impartial. In fact, it is undisputed that the identical panel of arbitrators found for IDI in the [a related] arbitration, with Mr. Sen dissenting, but with Lord Devlin and Mr. Wilson favoring IDI.

The ... Second Circuit has concluded that the Convention's public policy defense should be narrowly construed. "Enforcement of foreign arbitral awards may be denied on this basis only where enforcement would violate the forum state's most basic notions of morality and justice." *Parsons,* [*infra* pp. 1257-58]. Even in domestic arbitrations, that Court has "viewed the teachings of *Commonwealth Coatings* pragmatically, employing a case-by-case approach in preference to dogmatic rigidity." *Andros Compania Maritima v. Marc Rich & Co.,* 579 F.2d 691, 700 (2d Cir. 1978). And, in a very recent case, the Second Circuit decided specifically that awards should not be vacated because of an appearance of bias. *Int'l Produce, Inc. v. A/S Rosshavet,* 638 F.2d 548 (2d Cir. 1981). We believe, also, that the Court has given wise advice in counselling courts "to invoke the public policy defense with caution lest foreign courts frequently accept it as a defense to enforcement of arbitral awards rendered in the United States." *Parsons,* [*infra* pp. 1257-58]. We therefore find that recognition or enforcement of the [Award] would not be contrary to the public policy of the United States, and enforcement may not be denied on this basis. The stronger public policy, we believe, is that which favors arbitration, both international and domestic, as exemplified in *Scherk v. Alberto-Culver Co....*

SEVERE SENTENCES FOR A BOGUS "ARBITRATION"

Le Monde 18 (July 5, 1988)

Strasburg—On 1 July a criminal court of Strasburg sentenced Mr. Maurice Vignals, 63, President of the Centre national d'arbitrage (CNA), to three years imprisonment and a 200,000 francs fine for attempted fraud against a Canadian company, Bel Tronics, which owns a plant in Cernay in Haut-Rhin. The case began in 1986 in the aftermath of a commercial dispute between the Canadian company, which specialized in alarm systems and satellite TV antennas, and a Strasburg company, Portex, which one year earlier had signed a contract to become the exclusive distributor of Bel Tronics' products in Europe. The contract provided that in the event of a commercial dispute the two companies would refer the matter to an organization called the Centre national d'arbitrage (CNA), which had an office in Vendenheim in Bas-Rhin.

In May 1986, the conflict between the two companies became so acute that Portex invoked the arbitration clause and filed a request with the CNA that Bel Tronics be ordered to pay nearly 5 million francs in damages. There followed a brief procedural battle at the end of which the CNA tribunal, which had its seat in Bordeaux, decided that Bel Tronics should be ordered to pay 91 million francs to Portex and to pay the latter's fees and costs in an amount of nearly 2 million francs. This caused the Canadian company to worry; to pay such an amount would mean that it would have to shut down the factory it had built in Cernay with the help of various Alsatian municipal authorities. It therefore commenced an action before the Court of Appeal of Bordeaux to have the award set aside, but on 14 October 1987 that Court rejected the application. Thus in theory the CNA award took on executory force.

At this point, executives of the Canadian company asked for a more in-depth investigation of CNA. It was this investigation that led to the indictment of three men, on the grounds of fraud and attempted fraud and an appearance on 24 June before the criminal court of Strasburg. Mr. Maurice Vignals, President of the CNA, his Alsatian correspondent, Mr. Bernard Ardouin, and the general manager of Portex, Mr. Michel Viandier, were accused of having organized a fictitious arbitration to the detriment of the Canadian company. The investigation revealed that CNA barely existed except on paper and that the supposed members of the "arbitral tribunal" in fact never met to render the decisions that were served on Bel Tronics. The minutes of the meetings were forgeries. The arbitral tribunal was comprised of Mr. Maurice Vignals alone; Mr. Vignals had also succeeded in misleading the judges of the Bordeaux Court of Appeal.

Apart from the sentence against the President of the CNA, the criminal court of Strasburg severely punished the CNA's Alsatian representative, Mr. Bernard Ardouin, by sentencing him to two years imprisonment and a 100,000 franc fine, and the chief executive of Portex, Mr. Michael Viandier, 36, was found to be an accomplice and give a two year suspended sentence and a 100,000 franc fine.

KARAHA BODAS CO., LLC v. PERUSAHAAN PERTAMBANGAN MINYAK DAN GAS BUMI NEGARA
---
364 F.3d 274 (5th Cir. 2004)

[excerpted above at pp. 605-19]

AAOT FOREIGN ECONOMIC ASS'N (VO) TECHNOSTROYEXPORT v. INT'L DEVELOPMENT & TRADE SERVICES, INC.

139 F.3d 980 (2d Cir. 1999)

[excerpted above at pp. 766-67]

NOTES

1. *No specific provision under New York Convention for arbitrator bias.* Note that there is no provision in Article V of the New York Convention (or Article 36 of the UNCITRAL Model Law) directed specifically towards arbitrator bias or lack of impartiality. *Compare* ICSID Convention, Art. 52(1)(c) ("there was corruption on the part of a member of the Tribunal"); FAA, §10(b). Consider the exceptions set forth in Article V (and Article 36). Which exceptions are potentially applicable in cases involving claims of arbitrator bias? Note that each of these exception focuses on different concerns. Compare the concerns addressed by Articles V(1)(b) and V(2)(b) with those addressed by the first limb of Article V(1)(d); compare the concerns addressed by the second limb of Article V(1)(d).

2. *Arbitrator bias under Article V(1)(b).* How might an arbitrator's bias deny a party the opportunity to present its case under Article V(1)(b)? If a co-arbitrator has prejudged the parties' dispute, or is unacceptably predisposed towards one party, does the other party have a real opportunity to present its case to that arbitrator? What if the other co-arbitrator is similarly predisposed? The presiding arbitrator?

   What law applies to claims of arbitrator bias under Article V(1)(b)? Is it the law of the arbitral seat? The recognition forum? The place where the arbitrator in question is qualified? Uniform international standards? *See also supra* pp. 1231-32. What should the answer be? If the answer is international standards, how should the recognition forum define these? What is the relevance of the IBA Guidelines on Conflicts of Interest? Decisions under Article 52(1)(c) or (d) of the ICSID Convention?

3. *Arbitrator bias under Article V(1)(d).* How might an arbitrator's bias provide the basis for non-recognition under Article V(1)(d)? Consider both prongs of Article V(1)(d).

   (a) *Arbitrator bias violated parties' agreement.* If the parties' arbitration agreement expressly or implicitly requires that the arbitrators be impartial, an arbitrator's bias could provide grounds for an Article V(1)(d) challenge. Express agreements requiring impartial arbitrators are rare; the most common instance of such agreements involves institutional rules (such as the AAA and UNCITRAL Rules). *See supra* p. 741. In that case, however, won't institutional challenge procedures generally provide the (only) remedy? Do international arbitration agreements implicitly require that the arbitrators be independent and impartial? Consider the IBA Guidelines and customary practice. *See supra* pp. 742-48. Does an arbitrator's bias violate the parties' implied agreement, such that Article V(1)(d)'s first limb will apply? What law applies to define standards of arbitrator impartiality under Article V(1)(d)'s first limb?

   (b) *Arbitrator bias violated law of arbitral seat.* Alternatively, assuming the parties' agreement is silent, the law of the arbitral seat may require that the arbitrators be independent and impartial. *See supra* pp. 732-35; UNCITRAL Model Law, Art. 12. Suppose the law of the arbitral seat (*e.g.*, England) mandatorily requires that the co-arbitrators be impartial, but the parties proceed with partial co-arbitrators; if the award is sought to be recognized abroad, does Article V(1)(d)'s second limb provide a basis for non-recognition? What if the recognition is sought in the United States?

Suppose State A forbids an arbitrator (or his or her law firm) from ever having served as a lawyer for a party, and an arbitrator in an arbitration conducted in State A violates this requirement. Should a court in another state (*e.g.*, State B) recognize the award that the arbitrator makes? What if the complaining party does not challenge the award in State A?

4. *Arbitrator bias under Article V(2)(b)*. Consider the decisions in *Fertilizer Corp.* and *Judgment of 21 May 1976*. Note that both courts treated claims of arbitrator bias under Article V(2)(b)'s public policy exception. Is that appropriate? Why or why not?

What law applies to claims of arbitrator bias under Article V(2)(b)? *See infra* pp. 1254-56. Is this the same law as that applicable under Article V(1)(d)? Under Article V(1)(b)? What sources should a recognition court consider in defining public policy under Article V(2)(b)? *See infra* pp. 1254-60 for a more detailed discussion.

In considering challenges to recognition under Article V(2)(b) based on arbitrator bias, U.S. courts have often applied U.S. standards of arbitrator independence, principally derived from §10(b) of the FAA and *Commonwealth Coatings*. In addition to *Fertilizer Corp., see Andros Compania Maritima v. Marc Rich & Co.*, 579 F.2d 691 (2d Cir. 1978); *Nat'l Oil Corp. v. Libyan Sun Oil Co.*, 733 F.Supp. 800 (D. Del. 1990); *Transmarine Seaways Corp. v. Marc Rich & Co.*, 480 F.Supp. 352, 357 (S.D.N.Y. 1979) ("The Supreme Court's elucidation of arbitral propriety in *Commonwealth Coatings* is a declaration of public policy."). What exactly is U.S. public policy with regard to the impartiality of arbitrators in international arbitrations that are seated abroad and conducted under a foreign procedural law? Is it the same public policy with regard to the impartiality of arbitrators that applies in a domestic U.S. arbitration? Note the various sources that the *Fertilizer Corp.* court took into account.

When a national court recognizes a foreign court judgment, does it inquire into the impartiality of the foreign judge? Should it? If a national court does not inquire into the impartiality of foreign judges, why should it inquire into the impartiality of arbitrators in a recognition proceeding?

5. *Reliability of evidence of foreign standards of impartiality*. How readily can a recognition court determine the standards of impartiality applicable in the arbitral seat or the arbitrator's home jurisdiction? Consider the conflicting expert evidence in *Fertilizer Corp.* Is a foreign court able to reliably ascertain the content of another state's standards of professional responsibility and impartiality for purposes of Article V(1)(d)? Does this affect analysis under Articles V(1)(b) and V(2)(b)?

6. *Effect of challenge procedure under institutional rules on recognition of award*. Consider Articles 11-13 of the UNCITRAL Rules and Rules 12-20 of the AAA Rules, excerpted at pp. 166-67 & 235-38 of the Documentary Supplement. As these provisions illustrate, many institutional rules impose standards of impartiality on, and establish procedures for challenging, arbitrators. *See supra* pp. 741-42, 770-75. Most of these rules specifically provide that the institution's decisions on challenges are final. *See* 2010 UNCITRAL Rules, Arts. 11-13; 2012 ICC Rules, Arts. 13-15); 2014 ICDR

Rules, Arts 13-15. What effect do these standards and challenge procedures have on the recognition of awards, where arbitrator bias is the basis for the award?

Suppose an arbitrator complies with the applicable institutional rules concerning disclosure and a party unsuccessfully makes an institutional challenge; suppose also that the arbitral tribunal later makes an award against the party who made the unsuccessful challenge. Does the failure of such a challenge preclude a later argument under Article V that the award should be denied recognition because of the arbitrator's bias?

How would the foregoing hypothetical be addressed under Article V(1)(d) of the Convention? How would it be addressed under Article V(1)(b) or Article V(2)(b)? Suppose the institutional challenge process refused to remove a demonstrably corrupt presiding arbitrator. *Compare Judgment of 24 June 1999*, XXIX Y.B. Comm. Arb. 687 (2004) (Oberlandesgericht Schleswig) ("The defendant made use in the arbitration of its right to challenge [the arbitrator] for bias. The [ICC] deemed the defendant's request unfounded. This is the end of the matter, because this decision does not appear to be clearly defective, *e.g.*, for evident bias.") *and Judgment of 11 July 1992*, XXII Y.B. Comm. Arb. 715, 722 (1997) (Italian Corte di Cassazione) (rejecting challenge to award based on alleged partiality of arbitrators; relying on party's acceptance of rules of arbitral institution) with *Judgment of 27 August 2002*, XXVIII Y.B. Comm. Arb. 814 (2003) (Amsterdam Rechtbank) (refusing to recognize award on public policy grounds, where presiding arbitrator engaged in partial *ex parte* contacts and where arbitral institution's challenge decision "was not in accordance with the arbitration rules agreed upon by the parties" and the "arbitral procedure did not comply with the principles of due process accepted in the Netherlands").

Suppose that, although an institutional challenge procedure was available, a party did not make use of this process (despite having knowledge of grounds to question the arbitrator's independence). Does this constitute a waiver of the party's right to resist recognition of the award on grounds of arbitrator bias? How does the *Technostroyexport* decision deal with this issue? Do you agree? Suppose again that the presiding arbitrator was demonstrably corrupt and biased.

7. *Effect of action to annul award on grounds of arbitrator bias.* Suppose a party seeks to annul an award in the arbitral seat on grounds of arbitrator bias, but is unsuccessful. What is the relevance of the unsuccessful annulment proceedings in a subsequent action to recognize the award, when arbitrator bias is raised as a defense? Is the annulment decision preclusive in the recognition proceedings? Does it depend on whether recognition is resisted under Article V(1)(d) or Articles V(1)(b) and V(2)(b)? Recall the discussion above of the difficulties in establishing foreign standards of impartiality. *See supra* pp. 1246-47.

What if a party could, but does not, raise claims of arbitrator bias in an annulment action in the arbitral seat; what effect does this have in subsequent recognition proceedings? Consider *Judgment of 1 February 2001*, XXIX Y.B. Comm. Arb. 700, 713 (2004) (German Bundesgerichtshof) ("The notion of bias and its effects depend primarily on the procedural law according to which the arbitral award was rendered. Consequently, bias must be raised first in the country of origin. Only if this was impossible or unsuccessful may it be examined on the ground whether the recognition of the arbitral award would be obviously at odds with the fundamental principles of German law"). Do you agree with this analysis? What grounds are available for resisting recognition of an award? Are they limited to violation of the law of the arbitral seat?

8. *Relevance of tribunal's unanimity to arbitrator bias.* The court in *Fertilizer Corp.* and the dissent in *Commonwealth Coatings* relied on the fact that the arbitral award was unanimous. The implicit or explicit point is that the party-appointed arbitrator of the party resisting enforcement agreed with the award's result and, therefore, any bias was either harmless error or of trivial importance. Is it material to a charge of bias that the award was unanimous? Note that dissenting opinions are foreign to some legal systems and not particularly favored in international arbitration. *See supra* pp. 1067-68. In any case, how can one know what effect the biased arbitrator had on the arbitrator's deliberations? Could a unanimous vote overcome a clear showing of real bias (*e.g.*, a direct financial stake or bribe)?

9. *Relevance of arbitrator's rules of professional responsibility to issues of impartiality.* Note that in *Fertilizer Corp.*, the U.S. recognition court considered the rules of professional responsibility applicable to the challenged arbitrator. Why are these rules relevant, if at all? Suppose these rules permitted an arbitrator to simultaneously act as arbitrator and represent his or her appointing party in related proceedings? In advising on the arbitrating itself? How would this be relevant to analysis under Article V(1)(b)? To analysis under Article V(2)(b)? To analysis under Article V(1)(d)?

10. *Fraud under New York Convention.* It is not clear whether or not fraud is a defense to recognition under the New York Convention. Nothing in Article V(1) expressly refers to non-recognition based on fraud or comparable misconduct. *Compare* ICSID Convention, Art. 52(1)(c); FAA, §10(a)(1) ("corruption, fraud or undue means"). On the other hand, where there is fraud on a tribunal, is it conceivable that its award should be given effect? How does the *Karaha Bodas* court deal with this issue?

Consider the *Le Monde* article concerning the CAN. If the resulting "award" were taken to Canada, what grounds would there be for resisting recognition? Would the Convention really require recognition of an award obtained in this manner? Which of Article V's express exceptions might provide grounds for non-recognition? *See Nat'l Oil Corp. v. Libyan Sun Oil Co.*, 733 F.Supp. at 813 n.19; *Biotronik Mess- und Therapiegeräte GmbH & Co. v. Medford Med. Instrument Co.*, 415 F.Supp. 133, 137 (D.N.J. 1976). Suppose one party submits forged documents and perjured testimony which is central to the tribunal's decision. Consider the *Karaha Bodas* court's resolution of the award-debtor's fraud claims. What standard did the U.S. court apply? Did it reach the correct result?

For an English decision addressing the issue, see *Westacre Inv. Inc. v. Jugoimp.-SDPR Holdings Co.*, 4 All ER 570 [1998] ("Where a party to a foreign New York Convention arbitration award alleges at the enforcement stage that it has been obtained by perjured evidence that party will not normally be permitted to adduce in the English courts additional evidence to make good that allegation unless it is established that: (i) the evidence sought to be adduced is of sufficient cogency and weight to be likely to have materially influenced the arbitrators' conclusion had it been advanced at the hearing; and (ii) the evidence was not available or reasonably obtainable either (a) at the time of the hearing of the arbitration; or (b) at such time as would have enabled the party concerned to have adduced it in the court of supervisory jurisdiction to support an application to reverse the arbitrators' award if such procedure were available.").

4. Non-Recognition Based on Award Not Being "Binding"

As discussed above, Article V(1)(e) permits non-recognition of an award that has not become "binding." These issues raised by Article V(1)(e)'s requirement for a binding award are addressed above.[44]

5. Awards Annulled in Arbitral Seat

As also discussed above, Article V(1)(e) permits non-recognition of an award where "the award has ... been set aside or suspended by a competent authority of the country in which, or under the law of which, that award was made."[45] The UNCITRAL Model Law and other national legislation contain similar provisions.[46] The extent to which national courts have relied upon these provisions to deny recognition of awards annulled in the arbitral seat is discussed above.[47]

6. Awards Contrary to Public Policy

One of the most significant and controversial bases for refusing to recognize a foreign award is "public policy." A public policy exception is set forth in Article V(2)(b) of the New York Convention, which provides that recognition and enforcement of an award "may" be refused if it would "be contrary to the public policy of that country"—*i.e.*, the country "where recognition and enforcement [of the award] is sought."[48] National arbitration legislation also permits the non-recognition of awards because they violate public policy.[49] Article 36(1) of the UNCITRAL Model Law is representative, providing that an award may be denied recognition if enforcement of the award "would be contrary to the public policy of this State." The materials excerpted below illustrate the application of the public policy exception in the context of recognition of awards.

JUDGMENT OF 14 FEBRUARY 1995
XXI Y.B. Comm. Arb. 612 (1996) (Korean S.Ct.)

[Following a dispute between Adviso NV and Korea Overseas Construction Corp., an arbitral award was rendered in Zürich awarding damages to Adviso. XVII Y.B. Comm.

---

44. *See supra* pp. 1120-23.

45. New York Convention, Art. V(1)(e). *See* G. Born, *International Commercial Arbitration* 3621-23 (2d ed. 2014).

46. UNCITRAL Model Law, Art. 36(1)(a)(v); English Arbitration Act, 1996, 103(2)(f).

47. *See supra* pp. 1174-87.

48. New York Convention, Art. V(2)(b). *See* Bermann, *Public Law in the Conflict of Laws,* 34 Am. J. Comp. L. 157 (Supp. 1986); G. Born, *International Commercial Arbitration* 3595-96, 3606 (2d ed. 2014); Hwang & Lai, *Do Egregious Errors Amount to A Breach of Public Policy?*, 71 Arb. 1 (2005). The Inter-American Convention contains a substantially similar provision in Article 5(2)(b). Inter-American Convention, Art. 5(2)(b) ("recognition or execution of the decision would be contrary to the public policy ('ordre public') of that State.").

49. UNCITRAL Model Law, Art. 36(1)(b)(ii); SLPIL, Art. 190(2)(e); Netherlands Code of Civil Procedure, Art. 1065(1)(e). *See* G. Born, *International Commercial Arbitration* 3649-50.

Arb. 186 (1992). Adviso sought enforcement of the award in Korea. In a judgment of September 14, 1993, the Seoul Court of Appeals granted leave to enforce the award. On appeal, the Supreme Court affirmed.]

Art. V(2)(b) of the New York Convention provides that the competent court in the country where recognition and enforcement of an arbitral award is sought may refuse such recognition and enforcement if such court finds that the recognition or enforcement of the award would be contrary to the public policy of that country. The basic tenet of this provision is to protect the fundamental moral beliefs and social order of the country where recognition and enforcement of the award is sought from being harmed by such recognition and enforcement. As due regard should be paid to the stability of international commercial order, as well as domestic concerns, this provision should be interpreted narrowly. When foreign legal rules applied in an arbitral award are in violation of mandatory provisions of Korean law, such a violation does not necessarily constitute a reason for refusal. Only when the concrete outcome of recognizing such an award is contrary to the good morality and other social order of Korea, will its recognition and enforcement be refused.

The Court below held firstly, that the fact that the period of statute of limitations under the law of the Netherlands Antilles applied in this arbitral award was thirty years and this period was longer than that under the mandatory provisions of the Korean law, did not necessarily render the enforcement of this award in violation of the public order of Korea; secondly, that the determination of the arbitral tribunal that it had jurisdiction because the right of the plaintiff to the defendant on the know-how contract made on 8 November 1978 was not assigned to SECRC, was not in violation of the principle of estoppel or the public order of Korea; thirdly, that the allegation that the plaintiff blackmailed and exercised undue influence on the defendant was not supported by evidence. Also the Court below added that the contract was not unfair even if the contract was biased against the defendant and that the plaintiff's delay in asserting its right did not amount to an abuse. Thereby, the Court below rejected all the arguments claiming violations of the public order.

On review of the records, we conclude that these findings and holdings of the Court below are reasonable and do not agree that the Court below erred in applying Art. V(2)(b) of the New York Convention. We reject this argument....

PARSONS & WHITTEMORE OVERSEAS CO. v. SOCIÉTÉ GÉNÉRALE DE L'INDUSTRIE DU PAPIER
508 F.2d 969 (2d Cir. 1974)

J. JOSEPH SMITH, Circuit Judge. [The facts of the case are excerpted above at pp. 1192.] Article V(2)(b) of the Convention allows the court in which enforcement of a foreign arbitral award is sought to refuse enforcement, on the defendant's motion or *sua sponte*, if "enforcement of the award would be contrary to the public policy of [the forum] country." The legislative history of the provision offers no certain guidelines to its construction. Its precursors in the Geneva Convention and the 1958 Convention's ad hoc committee draft extended the public policy exception to, respectively, awards contrary to "principles of the law" and awards violative of "fundamental principles of the law." In one commentator's view, the Convention's failure to include similar language signifies a narrowing of the defense. Contini, *[International Commercial Arbitration,]* 8 Am. J. Comp. L. 283, 304. On the other hand, another noted authority in the field has seized upon this omission as indicative of an intention to broaden the defense. Quigley, *Accession by the United States to the United Nations Convention on the Recognition and Enforcement of Foreign Arbitral Awards,* 70 Yale L.J. 1049, 1070-71 (1961).

Perhaps more probative, however, are the inferences to be drawn from the history of the Convention as a whole. The general pro-enforcement bias informing the Convention and explaining its supersession of the Geneva Convention points toward a narrow reading of the public policy defense. An expansive construction of this defense would vitiate the Convention's basic effort to remove preexisting obstacles to enforcement.... Additionally, considerations of reciprocity—considerations given express recognition in the Convention itself—counsel courts to invoke the public policy defense with caution lest foreign courts frequently accept it as a defense to enforcement of arbitral awards rendered in the United States. We conclude, therefore, that the Convention's public policy defense should be construed narrowly. Enforcement of foreign arbitral awards may be denied on this basis only where enforcement would violate the forum state's most basic notions of morality and justice. *Cf.* 1 *Restatement (Second) Conflict of Laws* §117 comment c, at 340 (1971); *Loucks v. Standard Oil Co.*, 224 N.Y. 99, 111 (1918)....

Overseas argues that various actions by United States officials subsequent to the severance of American-Egyptian relations—most particularly, AID's withdrawal of financial support for the Overseas-RAKTA contract—required Overseas, as a loyal American citizen, to abandon the project. Enforcement of an award predicated on the feasibility of Overseas' returning to work in defiance of these expressions of national policy would therefore allegedly contravene U.S. public policy. In equating "national" policy with U.S. "public" policy, the appellant quite plainly misses the mark. To read the public policy defense as a parochial device protective of national political interests would seriously undermine the Convention's utility. This provision was not meant to enshrine the vagaries of international politics under the rubric of "public policy." Rather, a circumscribed public policy doctrine was contemplated by the Convention's framers and every indication is that the United States, in acceding to the Convention, meant to subscribe to this *supra*national emphasis. *Cf. Scherk v. Alberto-Culver Co.* [*supra* pp. 483-86]. To deny enforcement of this award largely because of the United States' falling out with Egypt in recent years would mean converting a defense intended to be of narrow scope into a major loophole in the Convention's mechanism for enforcement. We have little hesitation ... in disallowing Overseas' proposed public policy defense.

KARAHA BODAS CO., LLC v. PERUSAHAAN PERTAMBANGAN MINYAK DAN GAS BUMI NEGARA
364 F.3d 274 (5th Cir. 2004)

ROSENTHAL, District Judge. [The facts and procedural background of the case are excerpted above at pp. 605-19.] ... Pertamina [also] asserts that the Award violated public policy because it violated the international law doctrine of abuse of rights. Pertamina contends that the Award imposes punishment for obeying a government decree. Pertamina also asserts that KBC's failure to disclose the political risk insurance policy during the arbitration makes enforcement of the Award a violation of public policy.

Under Article V(2)(b) of the Convention, a court may refuse to recognize or enforce an arbitral award if it "would be contrary to the public policy of that country." The public policy defense is to be "construed narrowly to be applied only where enforcement would violate the forum state's most basic notions of morality and justice."[50] "The general pro-enforcement bias informing the Convention ... points to a narrow reading of the public policy defense."[51] Erroneous legal reasoning or misapplication of law is generally not a violation of public policy within the meaning of the Convention.

An action violates the abuse of rights doctrine if one of the following three factors is present: (1) the predominant motive for the action is to cause harm; (2) the action is totally unreasonable given the lack of any legitimate interest in the exercise of the right and its exercise harms another; and (3) the right is exercised for a purpose other than that for which it exists. The abuse of rights doctrine is not established in American law and KBC's actions do not meet the factors required to trigger its application.

The evidence in the record is that KBC pursued the arbitration to recover its costs, expenses, and lost profits from the non-performance of the JOC and ESC. The record does not support Pertamina's argument that enforcing the Award penalizes obedience to a governmental decree. The Tribunal explained in the Final Award that the JOC and ESC shifted the risk of loss resulting from a government-ordered suspension onto Pertamina and PLN. Pertamina is challenging the substance of the Tribunal's interpretation of the JOC and ESC. An arbitration tribunal's contract interpretation does not violate public policy unless it "violates the most basic notions of morality and justice." The Tribunal's interpretation of the JOC and ESC does not approach this steep threshold.

KBC's failure to disclose the political risk insurance policy does not provide a basis for refusing to enforce the Award. Enforcement of an arbitration award may be refused if the prevailing party furnished perjured evidence to the tribunal or if the award was procured by fraud.[52] Courts apply a three-prong test to determine whether an arbitration award is so affected by fraud: (1) the movant must establish the fraud by clear and convincing evidence; (2) the fraud must not have been discoverable upon the exercise of due diligence before or during the arbitration; and (3) the person challenging the award must show that the fraud materially related to an issue in the arbitration. It is not necessary to establish that the result of the arbitration would have been different if the fraud had not occurred. Courts, however, have held that an arbitration award is not fraudulently obtained when the protesting party had an opportunity to rebut his opponent's claims at the hearing.

In *Biotronik Mess- und Therapiegeräte GmbH & Co. v. Medford Med. Instrument Co.*, [415 F.Supp. 133 (D.N.J. 1976)], the party opposing enforcement of the award argued that the prevailing party knowingly withheld evidence of an agreement that undermined its case. The court stated that while the party opposing enforcement urged fraud, the real complaint was that the party prevailing in the arbitration should have presented evidence favorable to its opponent's case. The court rejected this argument, stating that "a party cannot complain about the non-production of evidence when it failed to offer such evidence itself." In *Catz Am. Co. v. Pearl Grange Fruit Exchange Inc.*, [292 F.Supp. 549 (S.D.N.Y. 1968)], the party opposing enforcement did not ask the arbitrators to bring cer-

---

50. *M & C Corp. v. Erwin Behr GmbH & Co., KG*, 87 F.3d 844, 851 n.2 (6th Cir. 1996) (quoting *Fotochrome, Inc. v. Copal Co., Ltd*, 517 F.2d 512, 516 (2d Cir. 1975)); *Parsons*, 508 F.2d at 974; *Slaney v. Int'l Amateur Athletic Fed'n*, 244 F.3d 580, 593 (7th Cir. 2001).

51. *Parsons*, 508 F.2d at 973.

52. *Karppinen v. Karl Kiefer Mach. Co.*, 187 F.2d 32, 34 (2d Cir. 1951).

tain witnesses before the panel, although the prevailing party offered to make the witnesses available. The panel never called for the witnesses' testimony. The party opposing enforcement of the award argued that the prevailing party should nonetheless have produced the witnesses. The court rejected this argument, stating that "arbitrators must be given discretion to determine whether additional evidence is necessary or would simply prolong the proceedings." Because the witnesses were not solely within the prevailing party's control and there was other evidence in the record supporting the other party's position, the court rejected the challenge....

Pertamina argues that KBC's failure to reveal its political risk insurance policy amounts to misconduct warranting a refusal to enforce the Award. There is no evidence in the record that KBC deliberately misled the Tribunal. When the question of political risk insurance arose and was not clearly resolved, Pertamina had the opportunity to ask additional questions, which it chose not to pursue. The Tribunal gave Pertamina an opportunity to pursue discovery requests, which it declined. KBC's failure to produce evidence of political risk insurance, given Pertamina's decisions not to pursue the subject, does not violate public policy. The district court did not err in refusing to deny enforcement of the Award on the basis of a public policy violation....

LAMINOIRS-TREFILERIES-CABLERIES DE LENS, SA v. SOUTHWIRE CO.

484 F.Supp. 1063 (N.D. Ga. 1980)

[excerpted above at pp. 1136-38]

NOTES

1. *Public policy exception under New York Convention.* One of the most commonly invoked defenses to the New York Convention's requirements for enforcement of arbitral awards involves the exception for cases where "the recognition or enforcement of the award would be contrary to the public policy of [the country asked to enforce the award]."

The Convention's public policy exception derives in part from historic common law treatment of foreign judgments. *See* G. Born, *International Commercial Arbitration* 3647-48 (2d ed. 2014). The public policy exception in Article V(2)(b) of the New York Convention derives more directly from Article 1 of the 1927 Geneva Convention, which provided for enforcement only if the award was "not contrary to the public policy or to the principles of law of the country in which it is sought to be relied upon." Similarly, as the *Parsons* court observes, early drafts of the New York Convention allowed enforcement of an award to be denied if the award violated "fundamental principles of the law." That basis for non-recognition was eventually omitted, however, confining Article V(2)(b) of the New York Convention to "public policy." In modifying the Geneva Convention's exception, the New York Convention's drafters sought to limit "the scope of the public policy clause as far as possible." A. van den Berg, *The New York Arbitration Convention of 1958* 361-68 (1981).

What is the rationale for the public policy exception to the enforceability of foreign awards? Is a public policy exception necessary; could the Convention be imagined without a public policy exception? Compare Article 52 of the ICSID Convention. What are the costs of a public policy exception?

2. *Public policy exception under national arbitration legislation.* Consider Article 36(1)(b)(ii) of the UNCITRAL Model Law and Article 190(2) of the SLPIL, excerpted at pp. 95 & 160 of the Documentary Supplement. How does each statute deal with the public policy exception to the recognition of awards? What differences are there between the two provisions? What is the source of public policy standards under Article 36(1)(b)(ii) of the Model Law?

    Other national arbitration statutes provide for application of "principles of international public policy" or "international public policy. *See, e.g.,* French Code of Civil Procedure, Art. 1520(5); Portuguese Voluntary Arbitration Law, 2011, Art. 56(1)(b)(ii); Algerian Code of Civil Procedure, Art. 458 bis 23(h); Lebanese New Code of Civil Procedure, Art. 817(5). Different formulations exist elsewhere. *See, e.g.,* Japanese Arbitration Law, Art. 45(2)(ix) ("public policy or good morals of Japan"); Libyan Code of Civil and Commercial Procedure, Arts. 407(4), 408; Omani Arbitration Law, Art. 53 ("contrary to public order"); Qatari Code of Civil and Commercial Procedure, Art. 380(4) ("does not breach the rules of public order and good morals"). What are the differences between these various formulations? Which is preferable?

3. *Source of public policy standards under Article V(2)(b)—domestic or international?* From what legal sources are standards of public policy derived in cases under Article V(2)(b)? Consider the text of Article V(2)(b) (and its counterpart in Article 36(1)(b)(2) of the UNCITRAL Model Law). To which state's public policy do these provisions refer? How should this reference be interpreted?

4. *"International" public policy.* A few national courts appear to have looked at least in part to what they have called "international" public policy, as distinguished from "domestic" public policy. *See Parsons*, 508 F.2d at 974 (requiring "*supra*national emphasis" rather than reliance on "national political interests"); *Judgment of 24 November 1993*, XXI Y.B. Comm. Arb. 617 (1996) (Luxembourg Cour Supérieure de Justice) ("the public policy of the State where the arbitral award is invoked is thus not the internal public policy of that country, but its international public policy, which is defined as being all that affects the essential principles of the administration of justice or the performance of contractual obligations"). In some cases (*e.g.,* the French Code of Civil Procedure), national arbitration legislation provides for the application of "international public policy." French Code of Civil Procedure, Art. 1520(5); Portuguese Voluntary Arbitration Law, 2011, Art. 56(1)(b)(ii) ("international public policy of the Portuguese State"); *Judgment of 12 March 1985, Intrafor Cofor v. Gagnant*, 1985 Rev. arb. 299 (Paris Cour d'appel) ("a breach of domestic public policy—assuming that it has been established—does not provide the grounds on which to appeal against a ruling granting enforcement in France of a foreign arbitral award, because Article 1502(5) only refers to cases in which the recognition and enforcement of an award would be contrary to international public policy").

    Note the court's consideration in *Karaha Bodas* of the "international law doctrine of abuse of rights." This is not a U.S. (or Indonesian) law concept, is it? Where does the doctrine come from?

    How are national courts to ascertain "*supra*national" or "international" public policy? Are courts intended to find international conventions or rules of customary international law articulating basic legal rules? Are they supposed to ascertain principles common to diverse legal systems? If so, which legal systems? Is there in fact any such thing as "international public policy"? Do you think that, for example, the courts of Saudi Arabia, Singapore, China, Nigeria, Sweden, the United States and Brazil will arrive at the same (or similar) views as to the content of such public policy?

Alternatively, "international" public policy might refer to local national public policies that are intended by national legislatures (or courts) to apply to international transactions and conduct. *See infra* pp. 1256-57.

5.   *Authorities adopting "national" public policy.* Notwithstanding the references to "international" public policy in decisions like *Parsons*, other national courts have invoked "national" public policy under Article V(2)(b). *See Waterside Ocean Nav. Co. v. Int'l Nav.*, 737 F.2d 150, 151 (2d Cir. 1984) ("public policy of the United States"); *Judgment of 30 September 1999*, XXXI Y.B. Comm. Arb. 640 (2006) (Hanseatisches Oberlandesgericht Bremen) ("an arbitral award may also be examined from the point of view of the correct application of substantive law when the decision whether its recognition violates German substantive public policy depends thereon"); *Judgment of 26 January 2005*, XXX Y.B. Comm. Arb. 421 (2005) (Austrian Oberster Gerichtshof) ("The relevant standard for the autonomous public policy review of the foreign arbitral award by the court of the enforcement state, Austria, is whether the arbitral award is irreconcilable with the fundamental principles of the Austrian legal system because it is based on a foreign legal principle that is totally irreconcilable with the domestic legal system"); *Hebei Imp. & Exp. Co. v. Polytek Eng'g Co.*, [1998] 1 HKLRD 287 (H.K. Ct. App.) ("The test we would therefore adopt [for the Convention's public policy exception] is: whether, in all the circumstances of the case, it would violate the most basic notions of morality and justice of the Hong Kong system if the foreign award in question is to be enforced.... We would be slow to condemn what happened before an arbitration tribunal in a foreign jurisdiction as having violated the most basic notions of morality and justice of our system unless it is quite clearly the case."), *aff'd*, [1999] 2 HCK 205 (H.K. Ct. Fin. App.); *Judgment of 14 February 1995*, XXI Y.B. Comm. Arb. 612 (1996) (Korean S.Ct.).

6.   *National public policies subject to international standards.* Alternatively, does "international" public policy mean that a court may consider local public policy, but only if it is consistent with international principles recognized in various nations as constituting vital public policies. For example, the United States, the European Union (and its member states), Japan and other developed nations have competition laws that are broadly similar. Do the U.S. antitrust laws reflect international public policy? What about the fact that, let us assume, countries with well over 50% of the world's population do not enforce such laws?

7.   *National public policies intended to have international application.* Alternatively, courts might look to local public policies but consider whether a particular public policy was intended, as a matter of local law, to have international application. That is arguably the approach taken in *Parsons. See, e.g., Belship Nav., Inc. v. Sealift, Inc.*, 1995 WL 447656, at *6 (S.D.N.Y.) (observing that "'public policy' is best served by promoting the '*supra*-national' goal of the Convention, promoting the enforcement of international arbitration agreements"); *Kashani v. Tsann Kuen China Enter. Co.*, 118 Cal.App.4th 531, 555 (Cal. Ct. App. 2004) (distinguishing between "public policy as

contemplated by Article V of the New York Convention," defined as "international public policy," and "national public policy that might cause a domestic court to consider a contract illegal"); *Judgment of 18 January 1990*, XVII Y.B. Comm. Arb. 503 (1992) (German Bundesgerichtshof) (public policy violation under Article V(2)(b) requires showing that "award is manifestly irreconcilable with a fundamental principle of German law. Such irreconcilability is not necessarily the result of a foreign arbitral procedure deviating from mandatory domestic procedural rules. What is required is rather an infringement of international public policy (*ordre public*)").

What does it mean to require that a public policy be intended to have international application? One possibility is that certain local public policies might be deemed not to apply in international disputes, because of countervailing systemic interests in permitting consensually arranged certainty in such disputes. *See Mitsubishi Motors Corp. v. Soler Chrysler-Plymouth Inc.*, 473 U.S. 614 (1985) (U.S. antitrust claims are arbitrable in international disputes, even if not in domestic disputes); *supra* pp. 495-96.

Alternatively (or additionally), the requirement that a policy be intended to have international application might contemplate a "conflict of policies" analysis, in which the appropriate scope of each policy is determined and any true conflicts resolved in an "interest analysis" derived from conflict of laws contexts. That is arguably the approach taken in U.S. cases dealing with forum selection clauses. *Bremen v. Zapata Off-Shore Co.*, 407 U.S. 1 (1972) (U.S. public policy against exculpation for negligence not applicable to conduct outside the United States); G. Born & P. Rutledge, *International Civil Litigation in United States Courts* 514 (5th ed. 2011).

Which approach, if either, is appropriate? How do these approaches compare to other possible sources of public policy under Article V(2)(b)? Recall again the text of Article V(2)(b). What standard for public policy does it appear to contemplate?

8. *Conflicts between national and international public policy.* What if international public policy permits actions that violate basic national policies and laws? For example, suppose a court were to conclude that international public policy permitted actions that contravened domestic policies regarding racial or religious discrimination or freedom of speech? *Compare Antco Shipping Co. v. & Sidermar, SpA*, 417 F.Supp. 207, 215-17 (S.D.N.Y. 1976) (rejecting public policy defense to stay pending arbitration where parties' agreement contained provisions requiring boycott of Israel). Which authority should prevail? Recall again Article V(2)(b)'s language regarding the source of public policy.

9. *Effect of foreign public policies on enforceability of awards in national courts.* To what extent should a national court give effect to the public policies of foreign states in applying the Convention? Suppose, for example, that an award orders European companies operating in Europe to take actions that violate EU competition laws? Or requires or rewards conduct in a foreign state that is unlawful there? Should a U.S. court (or other non-EU court) enforce the award? Would a U.S. court enforce a contract calling for such conduct? *See also Omnium de Traitement et de Valorisation SA v. Hilmarton Ltd* [1999] 2 All ER (Comm) (English High Ct.) ("there is nothing which offends English public policy if an Arbitral Tribunal enforces a contract which does not offend the domestic public policy under either the proper law of the contract or its curial law, even if English domestic public policy might have taken a different view"),

quoting *Westacre Invs. Inc. v. Jugoimp.-SDR Holding Co.* [1999] 1 All ER (Comm) 865 (English Ct. App.).

(a) *Basis for arbitrator to apply foreign public policy.* Recall that Articles 3(3) and 9(1) of the Rome I Regulation (and Articles 3(3) and 7(1) of the Rome Convention), excerpted and discussed above at pp. 984, 999-1004, provide for the application of public policies other than those of the forum in cases where the foreign state has a close connection to the underlying transactions. Recall also that §187 of the *Restatement (Second) Conflict of Laws* (1971), excerpted above at p. 507, provides that a parties' choice-of-law agreement will not be effective if it would "be contrary to a fundamental policy of a state which has a materially greater interest than the chosen state in the determination of the particular issue and which … would be the state of the applicable law in the absence of an effective choice of law by the parties." Is the same analysis applicable in the recognition context, to permit application of public policies other than those of the recognition forum? Consider again the text of Article V(2)(b).

(b) *National courts' reluctance to rely on foreign public policies.* Even if foreign public policy were demonstrably in conflict with an award, and even if the concerned foreign jurisdiction has a reasonably close relationship to the parties' dispute, courts have been reluctant to vacate the award. *Am. Constr. Mach. & Equip. Corp. v. Mechanised Constr. of Pakistan, Ltd*, 659 F.Supp. 426, 429 (S.D.N.Y. 1987) (rejecting argument that U.S. "public policy would be offended by confirming an arbitral award in the face of a Pakistani judgment that the arbitration clause and proceeding were void," at least where Pakistan was not arbitral seat). *Compare* Mayer, *Mandatory Rules of Law in International Arbitration*, 2 Arb. Int'l 274, 290 (1986) ("One is … hard put to understand why a judge would refuse to recognize an award dealing with, for example, foreign competition law on the grounds that under his own law such a dispute is not arbitrable. Obversely, the fact that the dispute may be arbitrable under his law should not lead him automatically to enforce an award which paid no heed to the fact that the dispute was not arbitrable under foreign laws whose applicability appears legitimate.").

An example of a court's refusal to enforce a foreign award based on a foreign public policy was *Victrix S.S. Co. v. Salen Dry Cargo AB*, 825 F.2d 709 (2d Cir. 1987). There, the court refused to enforce an English award against the assets of a company that had been declared bankrupt under Swedish law, because doing so would conflict with what was termed a U.S. public policy of giving effect to foreign bankruptcy proceedings and policies (Swedish, in this case) for the equitable distribution of bankrupt's assets. Is the U.S. court's decision permitted under Article V(2)(b)?

10. *Exceptional character of public policy exception.* As the opinions in *Judgment of 14 February 1995, Parsons* and *Karaha Bodas* indicate, most national court decisions have refused to invoke Article V(2)(b)'s public policy exception to deny recognition. Rather, decisions have referred to the exceptional character of the public policy exception. For examples of this analysis, see:

"Considerations of public policy can never be exhaustively defined, but they should be approached with extreme caution…. It has to be shown that there is some element of illegality or that the enforcement of the award would be clearly injurious to the public good or, possibly, that enforcement would be wholly offensive to the ordinary reasonable and fully informed member of the public on whose behalf the powers of the state are exercised." *Deutsche Schachtbau- und Tiefbohrgesellschaft mbH v. Ras Al Khaimah Nat'l Oil Co.* [1987] 2 Lloyd's Rep. 246, 254 (English Ct. App.).

"A violation of essential principles of German law (*ordre public*) exists only if the arbitral award contravenes a rule which regulates the bases of the public or commercial sphere, or if it contradicts the German ideas of justice in an unacceptable manner. A mere violation of the substantive or procedural law applied by the arbitral tribunal is not sufficient to constitute such violation." *Judgment of 12 July 1990*, 1990 NJW 3210, 3211 (German Bundesgerichtshof).

"[The contents] of the concept of public policy of the Russian Federation do not coincide with the contents of the national legislation of the Russian Federation.... The 'public policy of the Russian Federation' should be understood as basics of a social policy of the Russian state. The public policy rule can be applied only in those individual cases when application of the foreign law might cause a result inadmissible from the point of view of the Russian legal conscience." *Resolution of 25 September 1998*, 1999(3) Bull. S.Ct. Russian Fed. No. 3 (Russian S.Ct. Judicial Bd Civil Matters) (quoted in Tapola, *Enforcement of Foreign Arbitral Awards: Application of the Public Policy Rule in Russia*, 22 Arb. Int'l 151, 153-54 (2006)).

"The Commercial court applies the public policy exception as a ground to refuse recognition and enforcement of foreign arbitral awards in exceptional cases"; "[t]he recognition and enforcement of a foreign arbitral award cannot violate Russian public policy solely on the basis that Russian law does not contain legal rules analogous to the rules of the applied foreign law"; "[t]his ground is of extraordinary nature and is aimed at protecting the fundamental bases of the Russian legal order"; "the public policy of the Russian Federation is based on fundamental legal principles which have the highest imperativity, universality, special social and public importance." *Resolution of the Russian Supreme Commercial Court No.156 of 26 February 2013.*

Is this approach to public policy under Article V(2)(b) appropriate? Should national courts be more forceful in protecting national interests and public policies under the Convention? Does the resolution of important commercial disputes, and matters of public law, by private arbitrators require greater judicial supervision? Would the public policy exception provide a means for ensuring that the arbitral process respects the public interest?

11. *National court decisions holding that award violates applicable public policy under Article V(2)(b).* Only a few national court decisions have invoked Article V(2)(b)'s public policy exception to deny recognition to a foreign award. *See, e.g., Judgment of 26 May 1994*, XXIII Y.B. Comm. Arb. 754, 759 (1998) (Affoltern am Albis Bezirksgericht) (arbitration clause selecting one party's lawyer (who also drafted contract) as arbitrator is contrary to Swiss public policy and arbitrator's award will not be recognized); *Judgment of 10 June 1976*, IV Y.B. Comm. Arb. 258 (1979) (Oberlandesgericht Köln) (refusing to enforce award because of refusal of Copenhagen Arbitration Committee for Grain and Feed Stuff Trade (under institutional rules) to reveal arbitrators' names to parties); *Judgment of 3 April 1975*, II Y.B. Comm. Arb. 241 (1977) (Hanseatisches Oberlandesgericht Hamburg) (refusing to enforce award be-

cause of AAA's failure to forward letter from claimant to respondent); *Judgment of 27 August 2002*, XXVIII Y.B. Comm. Arb. 814 (2003) (Amsterdam Rechtbank).

Note that there are very few decisions involving denials of recognition based upon substantive public policies. Why is that? What does it suggest about the need for a provision such as Article V(2)(b)? *Compare* ICSID Convention, Art. 52(1).

12. *Procedural public policy under Article V(2)(b)*. Note that many of the cases in which public policy has been invoked to deny recognition of an award involved procedural issues. Some authorities refer to these decisions as involving the application of so-called "procedural public policy." Is it appropriate to apply Article V(2)(b) to procedural matters? Is that not what Articles V(1)(b) and V(1)(d) are designed to do? What benefits are served by permitting procedural complaints under Article V(2)(b)? What are the costs of such an approach? Would it not be wiser to consider complaints about procedural fairness under Article V(1)(b)? Why?

13. *Does Article V(2)(b)'s public policy exception focus on enforcement of award or underlying substantive dispute?* Suppose two parties conclude a contract that is unlawful, or in violation of applicable public policy. Suppose further that an arbitrator makes an award of money damages after a dispute arises under the contract. Does mere enforcement of the money damages award implicate issues of public policy? How?

Should Article V(2)(b)'s public policy exception require proof that enforcement of the arbitral award itself would violate applicable public policy or compel conduct that would violate a public policy? Or should it consider whether the claims or defenses asserted in the arbitration, and applied in the award, themselves violate applicable public policies?

7. Disputes Not "Capable of Settlement" by Arbitration

The New York Convention and most national arbitration legislation also provide for non-recognition of arbitral awards dealing with "nonarbitrable" matters.[53] Article V(2)(a) of the Convention permits national courts to deny recognition to arbitral awards that concern a subject-matter that is not capable of settlement by arbitration. Article 36(1)(b)(i) of the UNCITRAL Model Law is similar, implementing the Convention's nonarbitrability exception.

The nonarbitrability doctrine is discussed in detail in Chapter 4 above, as a defense to the enforceability of arbitration agreements.[54] That discussion is generally relevant in actions to enforce awards: an award dealing with nonarbitrable claims can usually be resisted on the same grounds that would have been available in a defense to an arbitration agreement. The materials excerpted below examine application of the nonarbitrability doctrine in the context of recognition of foreign awards.

ECO SWISS CHINA TIME LTD v. BENETTON INTERNATIONAL NV
Case No. C-126/97, [1999] E.C.R. I-3055 (E.C.J.)

[excerpted above at pp. 492-93]

---

53. G. Born, *International Commercial Arbitration* 944-47, 3695-704 (2d ed. 2014).
54. *See supra* pp. 475-510.

MITSUBISHI MOTORS CORP. v. SOLER CHRYSLER-PLYMOUTH, INC.
473 U.S. 614 (1985)

[excerpted above at pp. 486-92 & 522-25]

BAXTER INTERNATIONAL, INC. v. ABBOTT LABORATORIES
315 F.3d 829 (7th Cir. 2003)

EASTERBROOK, Circuit Judge. [Baxter International ("Baxter") invented sevoflurane, an anesthetic, and a process to produce it; it patented the process. Baxter later granted Maruishi Pharmaceutical Company ("Maruishi"), an exclusive worldwide license to use the process patents. Maruishi sublicensed Abbott Laboratories ("Abbott") to use those patents in the United States. Abbott spent substantial sums to obtain regulatory approval for sevoflurane in the United States. Sevoflurane is the best-selling anesthesia in the United States, with approximately 58% of sales. In 1999, Ohio Medical Associates ("Ohmeda") obtained a patent for a new way of making sevoflurane, distinct from Baxter's process but equivalently effective. Before Ohmeda could bring sevoflurane to market, it was acquired (in 1998) by Baxter—which decided to proceed with Ohmeda's plans and compete with the sevoflurane made by Maruishi and sold in the United States by Abbott.

Abbott, which contended that it had spent more than $1 billion to commercialize sevoflurane, initiated arbitration under the Baxter-Maruishi agreement (to which it had become a party in 1992). An arbitral tribunal, which consisted of a U.S. attorney, a Spanish attorney, and a Japanese law professor, was constituted. Abbott contended that Baxter's sale of Ohmeda-process sevoflurane before the Baxter patents expired would violate the exclusivity term of the license. Baxter replied, first, that the license does not explicitly forbid Baxter itself from competing with Maruishi (in other words, that exclusivity means only that Baxter can not issue any other licenses), and second, that if the license does forbid Baxter from competing, then it violates U.S. antitrust law, particularly § 1 of the Sherman Act, and is unenforceable.

The arbitrators ruled against Baxter on both issues. The tribunal held that the license is exclusive and that any reduction in competition is attributable to Baxter's decision to purchase the competing Ohmeda process while bound by this promise not to compete with its licensee. The district judge recognized the award, rejecting Abbott's contention that the license, as construed by the tribunal, violates the Sherman Act or the public policy of the United States. Baxter appealed, seeking to deny recognition of the award.]

Baxter argues at length in this court that the Baxter-Maruishi license, construed to keep Ohmeda-process sevoflurane off the U.S. market until 2006, is a territorial allocation unlawful *per se* under § 1 of the Sherman Act. But the initial question is whether Baxter is entitled to reargue an issue that was resolved by the arbitral tribunal. We think not; a mistake of law is not a ground on which to set aside an award. Section 207 [of the FAA] says that "[t]he court shall confirm the award unless it finds one of the grounds for refusal or deferral of recognition or enforcement of the award specified in the said Convention." Legal errors are not among the grounds that the Convention gives for refusing to enforce international awards. Under domestic law, as well as under the Convention, arbitrators "have completely free rein to decide the law as well as the facts and are not subject to appellate review." *Commonwealth Coatings*, 393 U.S. at 149. "Courts thus do not sit to hear claims of factual or legal error by an arbitrator." *United Paperworkers*, 484 U.S. at 38.

Arbitrators regularly handle claims under federal statutes. We do not see any reason why things should be otherwise for antitrust issues—nor, more importantly, does the Supreme Court, which held in *Mitsubishi*, that international arbitration of antitrust disputes is appropriate. *Mitsubishi* did not contemplate that, once arbitration was over, the federal courts would throw the result in the waste basket and litigate the antitrust issues anew. That would just be another way of saying that anti-trust matters are not arbitrable. Yet this is Baxter's position. It wants us to disregard the panel's award and make our own decision. The Supreme Court's approach in *Mitsubishi* was different. It observed:

> "The utility of the Convention in promoting the process of international commercial arbitration depends upon the willingness of national courts to let go of matters they normally would think of as their own.... [W]e decline to subvert the spirit of the United States' accession to the Convention by recognizing subject-matter exceptions where Congress has not expressly directed the courts to do so."

Starting from scratch in court, as Baxter proposes, would subvert the promises the United States made by acceding to the Convention.

According to Baxter, there is a difference between arbitrating an antitrust issue (the subject of *Mitsubishi*) and creating one—which it accuses these arbitrators of doing. If the tribunal had construed the Baxter-Maruishi agreement differently, there would have been no antitrust problem. Baxter [argues] that arbitrators are not allowed to command the parties to violate rules of positive law. That's true enough, but whether the tribunal's construction of the Baxter-Maruishi agreement has that effect was a question put to, and resolved by, the arbitrators. They answered no, and as between Baxter and Abbott their answer is conclusive. This is a point anticipated in *Mitsubishi*, which observed: "While the efficacy of the arbitral process requires that substantive review at the award-enforcement stage remain minimal, it would not require intrusive inquiry to ascertain that the tribunal took cognizance of the antitrust claims and actually decided them." The arbitral tribunal in this case "took cognizance of the antitrust claims and actually decided them." Ensuring this is as far as our review legitimately goes.

Treating Baxter as bound (*vis-à-vis* Abbott) by the tribunal's conclusion that the license (as construed to provide strong exclusivity) is lawful does not condemn the public to tolerate a monopoly. If the three-corner arrangement among Baxter, Maruishi, and Abbott really does offend the Sherman Act, then the United States, the FTC, or any purchaser of sevoflurane is free to sue and obtain relief. None of them would be bound by the award. As far as we can see, however, only Baxter is distressed by the award—and Baxter, as a producer, is a poor champion of consumers.

What relief the Antitrust Division, the FTC, or a consumer would obtain, if there is an antitrust problem, is an interesting question. Baxter thinks that the solution should be an order allowing it to sell Ohmeda-process sevoflurane.... [An alternative] remedy would be divestiture of the Ohmeda process patent.... But it is unnecessary to pursue this line of argument. All that matters today is that the arbitrators have concluded that the antitrust laws (and Baxter's related arguments, which we need not address) do not diminish Abbott's contractual rights—and that decision is conclusive between these parties.

CUDAHY, Circuit Judge, Dissenting. The majority upholds the arbitration award here by declaring that, once the arbitrators have spoken to the antitrust issues and in effect commanded the parties to violate the Sherman Act, the courts have no business intervening. Of course, the doctrine that requires extreme deference by the courts to arbitration awards is based on the theory that the parties to a contract may cede broad, almost unlimited, power to an arbitration panel to interpret their agreement. In fact, the arbitrators function almost as agents of the parties to extend their deal to cover unforeseen circumstances. All this rests on the proposition that the parties are free to adjust rights and liabilities among themselves as they see fit and through the instrumentality of arbitration to follow wherever the situation may demand. In this bilateral context a commitment to deference cannot be questioned. But other considerations enter the mix when the issue becomes a matter of the arbitrators, in interpreting a statute, commanding the parties to break the law or to violate clearly established norms of public policy. In the case before us, the arbitrators have instructed Abbott and Baxter (by imposing on Baxter a broad covenant not to compete with respect to sales of sevoflurane itself) to effect a horizontal allocation of markets, a clear violation of the Sherman Act. Under the arbitral decision, Abbott is granted a monopoly in the sale of sevoflurane in the United States....

The present case is a good example of the extent to which arbitration has come to pervade the legal culture. First, the parties here constructed an elaborate, predispute arbitration agreement that not only served to regulate the licensing agreement itself, but also, in an extraordinary spasm of creativity during the arbitration, generated a new and seemingly boundless cause of action, entirely separate from the license itself, under which the parties could presumably proceed. Then, during the arbitral process, Baxter submitted to the arbitrators the supplemental argument that, if the arbitrators pursued what eventually did become their line of decision, they would be commanding unlawful conduct under the Sherman Act. And finally, neither Baxter nor Abbott contend that arbitration was inappropriate for resolution of the antitrust claim.

Now, the majority has taken the process one giant step further and has found that *Mitsubishi* not only allows submission of statutory and antitrust claims to arbitration, but denies our prerogative to refuse to enforce awards that command unlawful conduct. The deciding circumstance, according to the majority, is that the question was put to, and decided by, the arbitrators themselves. Therefore, under the majority's analysis, the rule that unlawful conduct cannot be commanded by arbitrators is consumed by the exception that, if the arbitrators themselves say that what they have commanded is not unlawful, then "their answer is conclusive."

This cannot be correct. While *Mitsubishi* and its progeny make clear that the choice of the arbitral forum is to be respected, they do not confer on the arbitrators a prerogative to preemptively review their own decisions and receive deference on that review in subsequent judicial evaluations. The majority is way off-base when it says that Baxter seeks merely to have us disregard the panel's decision and "throw the result in the waste basket." Instead, we are performing exactly the traditional function of judicial review properly assigned only to us. Therefore, I do not think we can simply note the arbitration panel's resolution of the antitrust issue and consider our work done. Instead, we must fulfill our judicial responsibilities and examine the effect of the outcome commanded by the arbitral award. This means that we have to determine whether, going forward, the horizontal restraint on Baxter's competing with Abbott in the sevoflurane market violates the Sherman Act....

So while I agree with the majority that antitrust claims are arbitrable, and I also agree that the grounds for refusing to enforce an arbitration award are limited, I do not agree that there is support in the law for the majority's excision of antitrust arbitration from the general framework of judicial review that prohibits an arbitration panel's award from commanding illegal conduct. And in the case before us, the arbitration panel's ruling granting Abbott a monopoly in the United States sevoflurane market commands illegal conduct on the part both of Baxter and Abbott and is unenforceable....

NOTES

1. *Nonarbitrability under Article II(1) and Article V(2)(a) of New York Convention.* Article V(2)(b)'s public policy exception is closely related to the "nonarbitrability" exception in Article V(2)(a) of the New York Convention. Article V(2)(a) of the Convention excuses countries from the obligation to recognize Convention awards if "the subject matter of the difference is not capable of settlement by arbitration" under the law of the enforcing country. As we have seen, Article II(1) of the Convention is similarly worded (with respect to arbitration agreements). These provisions are examined in detail above at pp. 475, 482-83, 494.

    Most authorities have concluded that "question[s] of arbitrability" under Article II(1) and Article V(2)(a) are the "same." A. van den Berg, *The New York Arbitration Convention of 1958* 359 (1981). That is, if arbitration of a claim cannot be compelled under Article II(1), because it is nonarbitrable, then an arbitral award dealing with that claim is unenforceable under Article V(2)(a), subject to possible waiver arguments. *See Judgment of 12 May 1977,* IV Y.B. Comm. Arb. 254 (1979) (Liege Cour d'appel) (disputes over termination of exclusive distribution agreements are nonarbitrable under Belgian law and awards resolving such disputes will not be recognized). Is this approach correct? What differences are there between enforcement of an agreement to arbitrate and recognition of an award?

2. *Possible waiver of nonarbitrability objections.* If a party arbitrates a claim that is otherwise nonarbitrable under Article II(1), participation in the arbitration may render Article V(2)(a) inapplicable, because that participation may constitute an agreement to arbitrate an existing dispute. As we have seen in some jurisdictions, claims that would be nonarbitrable pursuant to agreements to arbitrate *future* disputes may be validly subjected to arbitration pursuant to an agreement to arbitrate an *existing* dispute. *See supra* pp. 481-82, 497; *Schattner v. Girard, Inc.,* 668 F.2d 1366, 1369 (D.C. Cir. 1981) ("Although a party is not required to arbitrate facts underlying a securities law claim, once the facts underlying those claims are in fact arbitrated the decision of the arbitrators is binding"); *Judgment of 21 July 2004,* XXXII Y.B. Comm. Arb. 315 (2007) (Oberlandesgericht Düsseldorf) (reasoning that nonarbitrability of competition law claims could not be raised in recognition proceeding because award-debtor contested substance of issues before arbitral tribunal without reservation). On the other hand, at least in some jurisdictions, nonarbitrability rules may not be waivable by private parties (even with respect to claims and disputes that are already in existence). *See supra* pp. 480-81, 508.

3. *Law applicable to nonarbitrability in recognition proceeding.* If a party resists recognition of an award under Article V(2)(a), what law applies to determine whether the award deals with a nonarbitrable matter? What does the language of Article V(2)(a) provide? Compare the conflict of laws discussions in the context of nonarbitrability and arbitration agreements, *supra* pp. 499-502, 502-10.

Like the public policy exception, nonarbitrability under Article V(2)(a) has the character of an exceptional escape mechanism where the local forum is permitted to deviate from the Convention's otherwise applicable international standards and apply local mandatory rules. Consistent with this, most courts in recognition proceedings have applied the nonarbitrability rules of the judicial recognition forum. *See, e.g., Judgment of 5 October 1994*, XXII Y.B. Comm. Arb. 637 (1997) (Brussels Tribunal de Commerce) (1997) ("Article V(2)(a) of the New York Convention expressly refers to the *lex fori* for the evaluation of the dispute in the phase of the recognition of the award"); *Judgment of 7 June 1995*, XXII Y.B. Comm. Arb. 727 (1997) (Italian Corte di Cassazione) ("non-arbitrability of the dispute according to Italian law, as it is the *lex fori* which determines the arbitrability of the subject matter"); *Judgment of 30 June 1976*, IV Y.B. Comm. Arb. 277 (1979) (Naples Corte di Appello) ("The Court also considered that the award was not contrary to Art. V(2) of the Convention. As regards Art. V(2)(a), the subject matter of the arbitral decision (claim for damages because of non-fulfilment of a contract for maritime transport) is, according to Italian law, capable of being referred to arbitration, in particular by virtue of Art. 806 CCP. As regards Art. V(2)(b), the enforcement of the award was not contrary to the Italian public order.").

Is this approach appropriate? What if the nonarbitrability rules of the recognition forum have no connection at all to the parties' dispute or the matters addressed in the award? For example, suppose that parties from States A and B arbitrate in State C; both parties assert claims under mandatory laws of States A and B, concerning allegedly wrongful conduct carried out in States A and B. Suppose that the prevailing party seeks recognition of the award in State D, which has no connection at all with the conduct or the legal claims: what relevance, if any, do State D's nonarbitrability rules have to non-recognition of the award? *See Judgment of 24 November 1994*, XXI Y.B. Comm. Arb. 635 (1996) (Rotterdam Rechtbank) (rejecting argument that award resolving inheritance dispute under Jewish law should be denied recognition under Article V(2)(a)'s nonarbitrability exception: "the present case concerns proceedings held in Israel before arbitrators according to the Israeli arbitration law and ... it is possible in Israel to arbitrate Jewish religious issues").

In the foregoing hypothetical, what if the legislation of both State A and State B made it very clear that the mandatory law claims at issue in the arbitration were nonarbitrable? Can a court in State D deny recognition under Article V(2)(a)?

4. *Judicial review of awards involving mandatory law claims.* As discussed previously, *supra* pp. 498-99, 509-10, antitrust, securities, and other "public law" claims are arbitrable in some states, but only subject to certain safeguards. After an arbitral tribunal has disposed of such claims, what level of judicial scrutiny of such awards is applicable under national law? As discussed above, *Eco Swiss* and *Mitsubishi Motors* appear to hold that EU and U.S. courts will have the opportunity to take a "second look" at arbitral dispositions of EU and U.S. antitrust/competition claims. In *Mitsubishi*'s words:

> "Having permitted the arbitration to go forward, the national courts of the United States will have the opportunity at the award enforcement stage to ensure that the legitimate interest in the enforcement of the antitrust laws has been addressed.... While the efficacy of the arbitral process requires that substantive review at the award-enforcement

stage remain minimal, it would not require intrusive inquiry to ascertain that the tribunal took cognizance of the antitrust claims and actually decided them."

What does this mean? What sort of review can a national court perform in a recognition proceeding? In a recognition proceeding, would Article V of the New York Convention permit a U.S. court to review the substantive antitrust conclusions of an arbitral tribunal? If the United States could declare antitrust claims nonarbitrable under Article V(2)(a), why can't it take the lesser step of subjecting awards dealing with antitrust claims to substantive review? What risks does that analysis pose?

5. *Limited judicial review of arbitrators' application of mandatory law.* Consider the analysis in *Baxter*. What degree of judicial review was applied to the arbitrators' decision regarding the U.S. antitrust laws? Did the court apply any scrutiny at all to the tribunal's antitrust analysis? Suppose the tribunal had been flatly and demonstrably wrong. Would there be any room in the majority's analysis in *Baxter* for reviewing that decision?

Who were the arbitrators in *Baxter*? Is there any indication that they had any antitrust expertise? Any U.S. antitrust expertise? Is that relevant? How would Judge Cudahy (in dissent) have approached the tribunal's antitrust analysis? Would he have afforded the arbitrators' conclusions any deference?

What if the arbitral award effectively ordered unlawful conduct, in violation of the U.S. antitrust laws? Is the *Baxter* majority really saying that this is not relevant to recognition of the arbitral award? Would that be unusual? What if the arbitrators had required payment of a bribe pursuant to a corrupt contract, in violation of the U.S. Foreign Corrupt Practices Act and other U.S. mandatory laws; would that award be recognizable, with no review of the arbitrators' statutory conclusions, in the United States?

If you had to choose, which opinion—Judge Easterbrook's or Judge Cudahy's—would you support? Suppose you could draft an alternative. What would it say?

TABLE OF CASES

Excerpted cases are indicated in bold.

ARBITRAL AWARDS

1267

COURT DECISIONS

TABLE OF CONVENTIONS AND STATUTES

Excerpted materials are indicated in bold.

CONVENTIONS

STATUTES

TABLE OF RULES, CODES AND GUIDELINES

Excerpted materials are indicated in bold.

INDEX